P9-EGL-646

Teacher Wraparound Edition

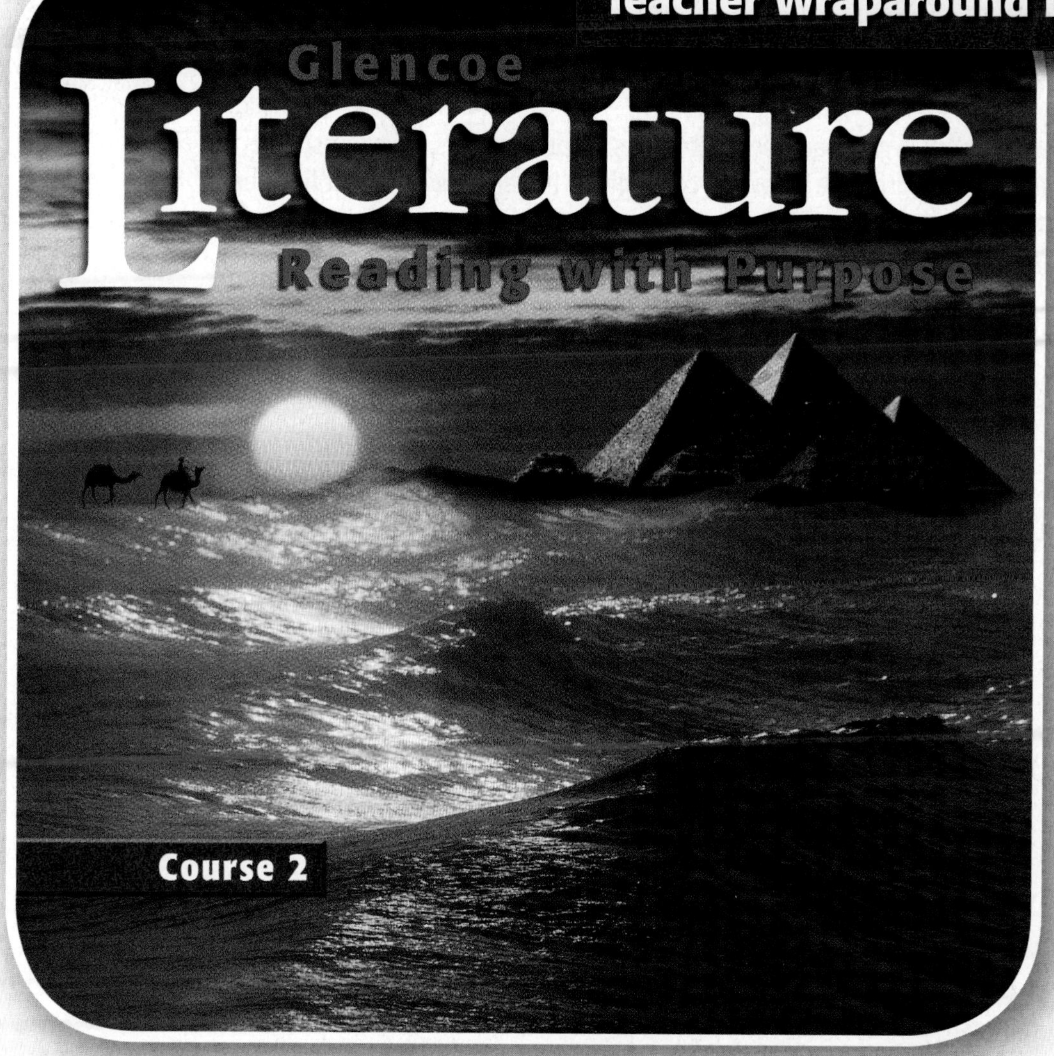

Program Consultants

Jeffrey D. Wilhelm, Ph.D.

Douglas Fisher, Ph.D.

Kathleen A. Hinchman, Ph.D.

David G. O'Brien, Ph.D.

Taffy Raphael, Ph.D.

Cynthia Hynd Shanahan, Ed.D.

New York, New York Columbus, Ohio Chicago, Illinois Peoria, Illinois Woodland Hills, California

Acknowledgments

Grateful acknowledgment is given authors, publishers, photographers, museums, and agents for permission to reprint the following copyrighted material. Every effort has been made to determine copyright owners. In case of any omissions, the publisher will be pleased to make suitable acknowledgments in future editions.

Acknowledgments continued on page R76.

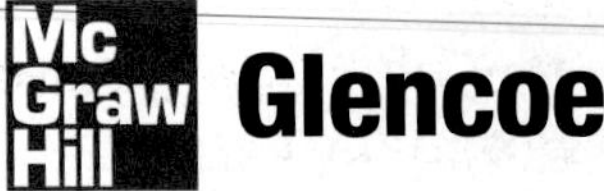

The McGraw-Hill Companies

Send all inquiries to:
Glencoe/McGraw-Hill
8787 Orion Place
Columbus, OH 43240-4027

ISBN-13 (student edition): 978-0-07-845477-6
ISBN-10 (student edition): 0-07-845477-8
ISBN-13 (teacher wraparound edition): 978-0-07-845488-2
ISBN-10 (teacher wraparound edition): 0-07-845488-3

Printed in the United States of America.

1 2 3 4 5 6 7 8 9 079/111 12 11 10 09 08 07 06

Program Consultants

Senior Program Consultants

Jeffrey D. Wilhelm, Ph.D. Jeffrey Wilhelm is Professor of English Education at Boise State University and director of the Boise State Writing Project. He specializes in reading and adolescent literacy and does research on ways to engage readers and writers. A middle and high school teacher for thirteen years, Wilhelm is author or co-author of eleven books, including the award-winning works *You Gotta BE the Book* and *Reading Don't Fix No Chevys.*

Douglas Fisher, Ph.D. Douglas Fisher is Assistant Professor of Teacher Education and Director of Professional Development at San Diego State University. He is also Director of the award-winning City Heights Educational Pilot, a project for improving urban adolescent literacy. Fisher has published many articles on reading and literacy and has co-authored *Improving Adolescent Literacy: Strategies that Work.*

Program Consultants

Kathleen A. Hinchman, Ph.D. Kathleen Hinchman is Associate Professor and Chair in the Reading and Language Arts Department of Syracuse University. A former middle school English and reading teacher, Hinchman researches social perspectives toward literacy. She is co-author of three books on reading and literacy, including *Principled Practices of a Literate America: A Framework for Literacy and Learning in the Upper Grades.*

David G. O'Brien, Ph.D. David O'Brien is Professor of Literacy Education at the University of Minnesota and a former classroom teacher. O'Brien's research explores reading in content areas as well as ways to motivate learners to engage in school-based literacy tasks. He is conducting studies on the use of technology-based literacy, using computers and related technology.

Taffy Raphael, Ph.D. Taffy Raphael is Professor of Literacy Education at the University of Illinois at Chicago (UIC). She does literacy research on upper elementary and middle school students and has co-authored several books including *Book Club: A Literature-Based Curriculum* and *Book Club for Middle School.* She has received the International Reading Association (IRA) Outstanding Educator Award and is in the IRA Hall of Fame.

Cynthia Hynd Shanahan, Ed.D. Cynthia Hynd Shanahan is Professor in the Reading, Writing, and Literacy program at the University of Illinois at Chicago (UIC). She is also a consultant with the Center for Literacy at UIC. Hynd Shanahan has been a classroom teacher and has taught reading instruction to elementary-level through college-level teachers. She has authored a chapter in the book *Engaged Reading,* edited by John T. Guthrie and Donna Alverman.

Advisory Board

Special Consultants

FOLDABLE **Dinah Zike, Ed.D.** Dinah Zike was a classroom teacher and a consultant for many years before she began to develop Foldables™--a variety of easily created graphic organizers. Zike has written and developed more than 150 supplemental books and materials used in classrooms worldwide. Her *Big Book of Books and Activities* won the Teacher's Choice Award.

Mary A. Avalos, Ph.D. Mary Avalos is Assistant Professor and Director of the TESOL Graduate Program at the University of Miami, Coral Gables, Florida. Her contributions to TESOL books include "No Two Learners Are Alike: Readers with Linguistic and Cultural Differences," in *Reading Assessment and Instruction for All Learners,* by J. S. Schrum (ed.) Avalos is a frequent presenter at reading and TESOL conferences.

Glencoe National Reading and Language Arts Advisory Council

Wanda J. Blanchett, Ph.D.
Associate Dean for Academic Affairs and Associate Professor of Exceptional Education, School of Education
University of Wisconsin-Milwaukee
Milwaukee, Wisconsin

William G. Brozo, Ph.D.
Professor of Literacy
Graduate School of Education, College of Education and Human Development
George Mason University
Fairfax, Virginia

Nancy Drew, Ed.D.
LaPointe Educational Consultants
Corpus Christi, Texas 78411

Susan Floria-Ruane Ed.D.
Professor, College of Education
Michigan State University
Lansing, Michigan

Nancy Frey, Ph.D.
Associate Professor of Literacy in Teacher Education
School of Teacher Education
San Diego State University
San Diego, California

Kimberly Lawless, Ph.D.
Associate Professor
Curriculum, Instruction and Evaluation
College of Education
University of Illinois at Chicago
Chicago, Illinois

Sharon Fontenot O'Neal, Ph.D.
Associate Professor
Texas State University
San Marcos, Texas

William Ray, M.A.
Lincoln-Sudbury Regional High School
Sudbury, Massachusetts

Victoria Gentry Ridgeway, Ph.D.
Associate Professor
Reading Education
Clemson University
Clemson, South Carolina

Janet Saito-Furukawa, M.Ed.
Literacy Coach
Washington Irving Middle School
Los Angeles, California

Bonnie Valdes, M.Ed.
Independent Reading Consultant
CRISS Master Trainer
Largo, Florida

Teacher Reviewers

Bridget Agnew
St. Michael Middle School
Chicago, IL

Monica Aralza
Garcia Middle School
Brownsville, TX

Katherine Baer
Howard County Public Schools
Howard County, MD

Tanya Bateson
Amundsen High School
Chicago, IL

Yolanda Conder
Owasso Mid-High School
Owasso, OK

Thomas R. Cross
New Albany High School
New Albany, OH

Cindy Davis-Harris
Helix Charter High School
La Messa, CA

Courtney Doan
Bloomington High School
Bloomington, IL

Susan Griffin
Edison Middle School
Tulsa, OK

Patricia Jones
St. Louis Public Schools
St. Louis, MO

Ginger Jordan
Florien High School
Florien, LA

Dianne Konkel
Lee County Middle School
Fort Myers, FL

Melanie A. Lafleur
Many High School
Many, LA

Linda Lemons
Cleveland High School
Cleveland, TN

Heather Lewis
Waverly Middle School
Lansing, MI

Sandra Lott
Aiken Optional School
Alexandria, LA

Connie Malacarne
O'Fallon Township High School
O'Fallon, IL

Claire Meitl
Dunloggin Middle School
Ellicott City, MD

Patricia Mitcham
Mohawk High School
New Castle, PA

Lisa Morefield
South-Western Career Academy
Grove City, OH

Kevin Morrison
Hazelwood East High School
St. Louis, MO

Susan Putnam
Butler High School
Charlotte-Mecklenburg, NC

Paul C. Putnoki
Torrington Middle School
Torrington, CT

Jane Rae
Cab Calloway High School of the Arts
Wilmington, DE

Ann Ryan
Lindenwold High School
Lindenwold, NJ

Fareeda J. Shabazz
Paul Revere Middle School
Chicago, IL

Molly Steinlage
Bookpark Middle School
Grove City, OH

Barry Stevenson
Garnet Valley Middle School
Norwood, PA

Paul Stevenson
Edison Middle School
Tulsa, OK

Kathy Thompson
Owasso Mid-High School
Owasso, OK

Teacher Wraparound Edition Overview

Research-Based Classroom Solution

Instructional Planning

Book Overview

How to Use *Reading With Purpose* xxx

Foldables™ xxxvi

Scavenger Hunt xxxvii

Reading Handbook RH0

UNIT 1 **Why Do We Read?** 1

Genre Focus: Informational Media
Reading Skills: Set a Purpose for Reading, Preview, Review, Understand Text Structure
Text Elements: Photos and Illustrations; Titles, Heads, and Decks; Lead; Text Features
Writing Product: Summary
English Language Coach: Context Clues
Grammar: Verbs

UNIT 2 **How Can We Become Who We Want to Be?** 128

Genre Focus: Biography
Reading Skills: Activate Prior Knowledge, Connect, Infer, Identify Sequence
Literary Elements: Narrator, Point of View, Setting, Sensory Details
Writing Product: Autobiographical Narrative
English Language Coach: Multiple-Meaning Words, Word References
Grammar: Nouns and Pronouns

UNIT 3 **Who Can We Really Count On?** 250

Genre Focus: Short Story
Reading Skills: Draw Conclusions, Respond, Synthesize, Determine the Main Idea
Literary Elements: Conflict, Dialogue, Character, Plot
Writing Product: Short Fictional Story
English Language Coach: Synonyms and Antonyms, Word Choice
Grammar: Adjectives and Adverbs, Prepositions, Interjections

UNIT 4 **Who Influences Us and How Do They Do So?** 408

Genre Focus: Persuasive Writing
Reading Skills: Understand Persuasive Techniques, Distinguish Fact and Opinion, Identify Author's Purpose and Perspective, Understand Text Structure: Compare and Contrast
Literary Elements: Style, Tone, Diction and Word Choice, Argument
Writing Product: Editorial
English Language Coach: Denotation, Connotation, Semantic Slanting
Grammar: Sentences

Reference Section

Contents

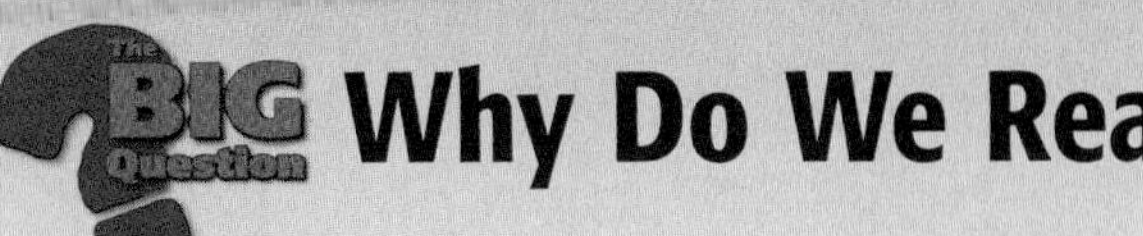

UNIT 1

The BIG Question: Why Do We Read? 1

UNIT 2

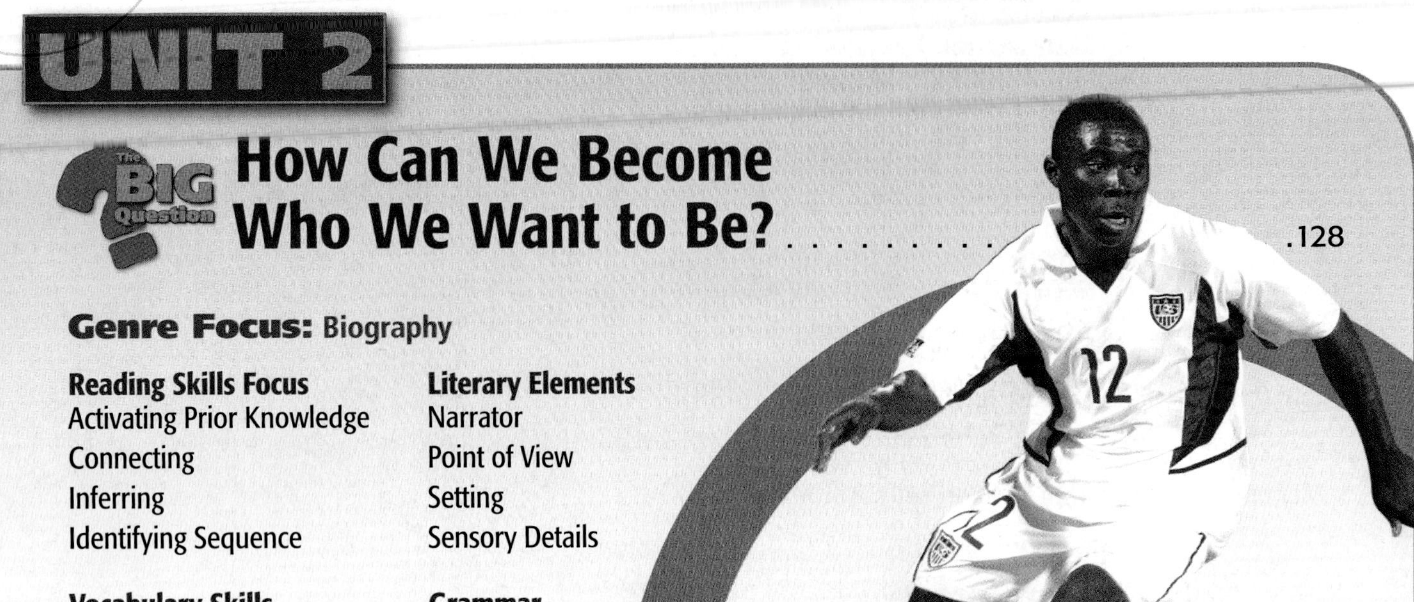

How Can We Become Who We Want to Be?

Genre Focus: Biography

Reading Skills Focus
Activating Prior Knowledge
Connecting
Inferring
Identifying Sequence

Literary Elements
Narrator
Point of View
Setting
Sensory Details

Vocabulary Skills
Multiple-Meaning Words
Word References

Grammar
Nouns
Pronouns

UNIT 3

Genre Focus: Short Story

Reading Skills Focus
Drawing Conclusions
Responding
Synthesizing
Determining the Main Idea

Literary Elements
Conflict
Dialogue
Character
Plot

Vocabulary Skills
Synonyms
Antonyms
Word Choice

Grammar
Adjectives
Adverbs
Prepositions
Interjections

UNIT 4

Who Influences Us and How Do They Do So? 408

Genre Focus: Persuasive Writing

Reading Skills Focus
Understanding Persuasive Techniques
Distinguishing Fact and Opinion
Identifying Author's Purpose and Perspective
Understanding Text Structure: Compare and Contrast

Vocabulary Skills
Denotation
Connotation
Semantic Slanting

Literary Elements
Style
Tone
Diction
Argument

Grammar
Sentences

UNIT 5

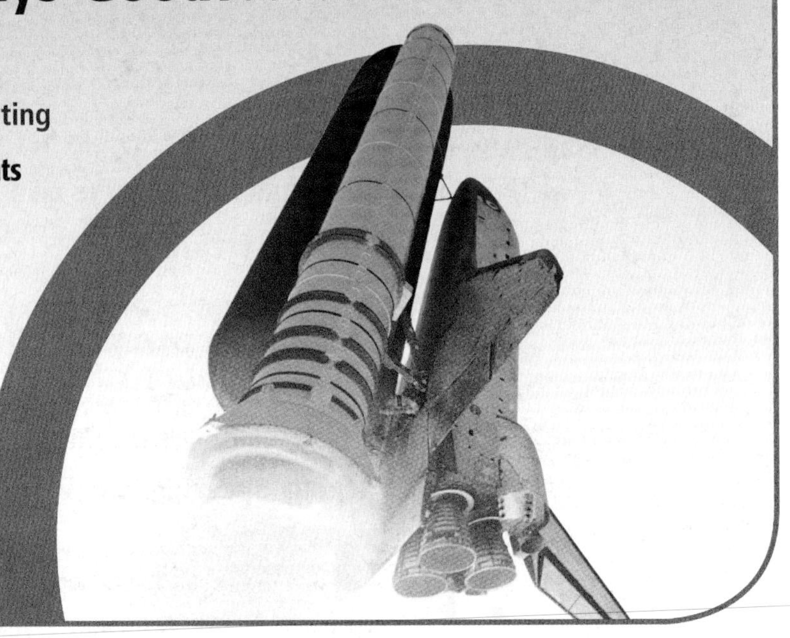

Genre Focus: Science and Technology Writing

Reading Skills Focus
Paraphrasing and Summarizing
Using Text Features
Taking Notes
Understanding Text Structure: Problem/Solution

Literary Elements
Author's Craft
Concept and Definition
Organization
Description

Vocabulary Skills
Structural Analysis (Base words, suffixes, prefixes)
Content-Area Words

Grammar
Clauses
Phrases
Commas

UNIT 6

Genre Focus: Folktale

Reading Skills Focus
Understanding Cause and Effect
Questioning
Predicting
Analyzing

Vocabulary Skills
Idioms
Slang
Dialogue
Literal and Metaphoric Word Meanings

Literary Elements
Theme
Character and Characterization
Cultural Allusions
Dialect

Grammar
Objects
Compound and Complex Sentences
Commas

UNIT 7

What Makes You Tick? 770

Genre Focus: Poetry

Reading Skills Focus
Evaluating
Interpreting
Monitoring Comprehension
Connecting

Vocabulary Skills
Structural Analysis: Latin, Anglo-Saxon, and Greek Roots
Word Origins

Literary Elements
Sound Devices
Symbolism
Rhyme, Rhythm, and Meter
Figurative Language

Grammar
Subject-Verb Agreement

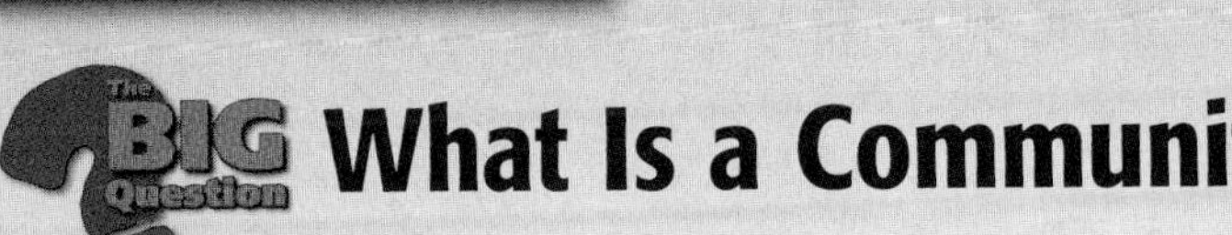

UNIT 8

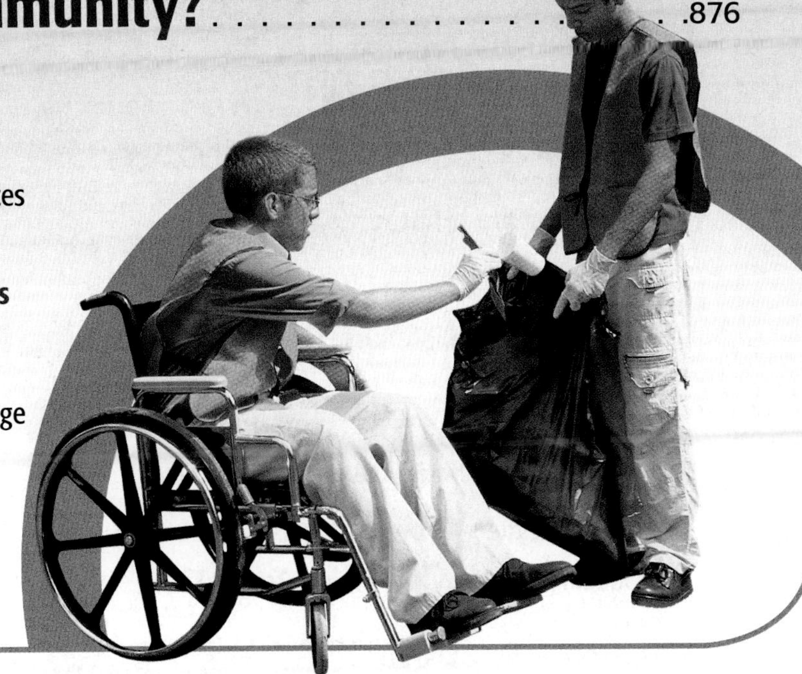

Selections by Genre

Fiction

Poetry

Drama

Folktales

Graphic Stories and Cartoons

Personal Essays

Biography, Autobiography, Memoirs, Letters

Informational Texts

Historical Documents

Functional Documents

Skills Features

READING SKILLS

Reading Workshops

Reading Across Texts

LITERATURE SKILLS

Literary and Text Elements

Genre Focus

Comparing Literature

VOCABULARY SKILLS

English Language Coach

WRITING SKILLS

Writing Products

Writing Traits

GRAMMAR SKILLS

LISTENING, SPEAKING, AND VIEWING

Philosophy Statement

By Jeffrey D. Wilhelm, Ph.D.

The middle school series, *Reading with Purpose,* is a unique and powerful program designed to engage your students in reading a variety of texts. The program is an integrated, inquiry-oriented approach based on the latest research in motivation, general and literacy education, and cognitive science.

Motivation

Motivating students is the greatest challenge facing teachers today, particularly when it comes to reading and writing. The seminal research of John Guthrie (2002), my own research on adolescent boys and literacy development (Smith and Wilhelm, 2002, 2006), and various national reports and reviews (e.g., Hidi and Harackiewicz, 2000) confirm this challenge. (Editor's note: Wilhelm's research won the NCTE Russell Award for Distinguished Research in English Education.)

When Michael Smith and I undertook our study on the literacy habits of adolescent and teenage males, we found that before students would engage with a literary text, they had to understand the purpose for reading such a text. Students are also more inclined to engage with a text if they are assured to receive the necessary assistance to successfully comprehend the material. The research of Czikszentmihalyi (1990), Gee (2003), and others indicate *Reading with Purpose* is designed first and foremost to meet these motivational prerequisites for engagement and learning.

Inquiry

Inquiry is the most powerful instructional tool to engage students' interest in reading and discovery. George Hillocks (see, e.g., 1995, 1999) famously argued that all reading and writing are forms of inquiry, and therefore most effectively taught and learned through an inquiry process. In our own research (Smith and Wilhelm, 2002, 2006), we found that inquiry met all the conditions of "flow" sought by our student informants.

Essential Questions

An inquiry-oriented program has many positive effects. First, it organizes instruction around an "essential question" (also known as a big, or guiding question). This question must be personally relevant and socially significant to the student. The question must connect students to problems they confront in both the textual material and their own lives.

An essential question makes learning "matter" as students relate to and form individual answers to the question. Inquiry-based learning also provides what is known as "curricular coherence" and "curricular integration" (Jacobs, 1989; Wiggins and McTighe, 2003; see Applebee, Burroughs, Stevens, 2000, and Caskey, 2006 for nice reviews of the importance of coherence and integration to learning).

Curricular coherence is achieved by focusing both conceptual and procedural instruction around the essential question. *Reading with Purpose* presents stories, poems, and informational texts all in the same unit. Although the genres in a particular workshop may vary, every selection is unified by the essential question. By reading selections chosen in service to an essential question, students are exposed to different perspectives they may consider when formulating their own views on a central theme.

Big Understandings

Students using an inquiry approach are more likely to read with purpose and motivation. Students learn major conceptual understandings to apply both to their lives and future reading and writing. The work of John Dewey and Ralph Tyler in the 1930s and 40s (e.g., Tyler, 1949) demonstrates that students quickly forget material presented in information-driven instruction. The hands-on inquiry approach results in central understandings much more likely to be remembered and transferred to new situations.

Strategic Reading and Writing

Curricular integration also includes problem solving, speaking, and listening skills. Inquiry-based learning connects those skills to the student's reading and writing assignments. This approach allows many skills to be taught under one unifying theme—the essential question. Many researchers, including myself (see Wilhelm, Baker, and Dube-Hackett, 2001) have explored how reading and writing are two sides of the same coin. For example, writing a narrative requires the same conventions, declarative knowledge and strategic knowledge as reading a narrative: what a writer must "code" into a narrative or argument, must also be "decoded" and interpreted by the reader of that text. Simply put, teaching the reading and writing techniques of particular genre structures simultaneously makes learning more efficient.

Contextualized Skill and Strategy Development

Reading with Purpose pays special attention to the development of a student "tool box" through the context of unit inquiries. The "tool box" is a concept promoted by socio-cultural psychology and current cognitive science (e.g., Wertsch, 1998). Each unit works step-by-step and activity-by-activity to develop conceptual and strategic tools that are important to exploring, discussing, writing about, and ultimately understanding the knowledge base related to the essential question. Students are given explicit knowledge of and repeated practice with the strategies that are necessary to read and write texts to explore and understand the question. Since particular genres are often particularly powerful for addressing certain topics, *Reading with Purpose* focuses on particular genres in each unit. In this way, strategies are developed to meet a purpose in a meaningful context. The work on "situated cognition" (see Brown, Collins, DuGuid, 1989) shows that "situations co-produce knowledge." With a meaningful purpose, students are motivated to read, develop strategic knowledge, and learn which concepts to concentrate on and remember.

Differentiated Instruction

All classroom teachers understand that their students bring different interests, needs, and abilities to class. It is absolutely necessary to differentiate instruction to meet students in their various "zones of proximal development," the motivational or cognitive zones in which students become motivated to do something that they would not attempt on their own (Wilhelm, 2006).

Differentiated instruction allows students to read texts that are geared to their interests and abilities. Teachers have the flexibility to engage students in particular strategies, work individually or in small groups, and still be part of the common classroom project of pursuing the essential question. With inquiry-based learning, differences become assets and resources; those who read different texts and learn skills at varying levels offer unique contributions to the group's understanding (Wilhelm, 2006). That is why *Reading with Purpose* includes popular culture resources, selections of young adult literature, and canonical texts that can be used with individual students or small groups. We have also recommended various selections and activities to pursue with different students in order to maximize the power of differentiation.

Works Cited

Applebee, A. N., Burroughs, R., and Stevens, A. S. 2000. "Shaping Conversations: A Study of Continuity and Coherence in High School Literature Curricula." *Research in the Teaching of English,* 34: 396–429.

Brown, J., Collins, A., and DuGuid, P. 1989. "Situated Cognition and the Culture of Learning." *Educational Researcher,* 18, 32–42.

Caskey, M. 2006. "The Evidence for Core Curriculum—Past and Present." *Middle School Journal,* (47)3, 48-54.

Csikszentmihalyi, Mihalyi. 1990 *Flow: The psychology of optimal experience.* New York: Harper and Row

Gee, James. 2003. *What Video Games Have to Teach Us About Learning and Literacy.* New York: Palgrave Macmillan.

Guthrie, J. 2002. "Classroom contexts for engaged reading: An Overview." http://www.cori.umd.edu/Research/Papers/Classroom.htm.

Hidi, S., & Harackiewicz, J. M. 2000. "Motivating the academically unmotivated: A critical issue for the 21st century." *Review of Educational Research,* 70, 151-180.

Hillocks, G. 1995. *Teaching Writing as Reflective Practice.* New York: Teachers College Press.

Hillocks, G. 1999. *Ways of Teaching/Ways of Learning* New York: Teachers College Press.

Jacobs, Heidi Hayes. 1989. *Interdisciplinary Curriculum: Design and Implementation.* Washington DC: ASCD.

Smith, Michael W. and Wilhelm, Jeffrey D. 2006. *Going with the Flow: How to engage boys (and girls) in their literacy learning.* Portsmouth, NH: Heinemann.

Smith, Michael W. and Wilhelm, Jeffrey D. 2002. *Reading Don't Fix No Chevys: Literacy in the lives of young men.* Portsmouth, NH: Heinemann.

Tyler, R. 1949. *Basic principles of curriculum and instruction.* Chicago: University of Chicago Press.

Wertsch, J. 1998. *Mind as action.* New York: Oxford University Press.

Wiggins, Grant and McTighe, Jay. 2003. *Understanding by Design.* Washington DC: ASCD.

Wilhelm, J. D., Baker, T. and Dube-Hackett, J. 2001. *Strategic Reading.* Portsmouth, NH: Heinemann.

Wilhelm, Jeffrey D. 2006. *Inquiring Minds Learn to Read and Write: Inquiry, Questioning and Discussion Strategies to Improve Reading and Writing.* New York: Scholastic.

The *Reading Next* Report

What Is It?

In 2004, the Carnegie Corporation released *Reading Next—A Vision for Action and Research in Middle and High School Literacy: A Report from Carnegie Corporation of New York.* Authored by Harvard researchers Gina Biancarosa and Dr. Catherine Snow, and published by Alliance for Excellent Education in Washington, D.C., the report responds to the growing literacy crisis among middle and high school students.

The statistics bear out the severity of the problem. In the United States today, more than 8 million students in grades 4–12 lack the ability to read proficiently (U.S. DOE, 2003). Every day, more than 3,000 students drop out of high school (Alliance for Excellent Education, 2003)—largely because they lack the literacy skills to keep up (Kamil, 2003; Snow and Biancarosa, 2003). Only 70 percent of high school students graduate on time, and fewer than 60 percent of all African American and Latino students get their diplomas (Greene, 2002). Clearly, these numbers paint a picture of a system in crisis.

The driving force behind the *Reading Next* report is simple. Students who lack literacy skills face serious disadvantages in almost every aspect of their lives—at school, at work, and in the community. Research indicates that most middle and high school readers can decode. Many of these readers, however, are unable to conceptualize what they read or to connect new words and ideas to those they already know. Unable to comprehend the various texts they encounter, these students quickly fall behind.

The *Reading Next* report draws attention to this problem and seeks to dispel the outdated notion that struggling and reluctant middle and high school readers are unable to benefit from literacy instruction. Instead, the report asserts, these students can and *do* benefit—significantly—from literacy instruction. Educators and other interested parties should then work hard to develop effective literacy programs for struggling middle and high school students.

Why Is It Important?

The report identifies fifteen characteristics of an effective literacy program. The first nine characteristics, or recommendations, are instructional—ideas and activities that teachers can implement. The remaining six are infrastructural—ideas and activities that can be realized at the school-wide level, or in the student's home or community.

A Report to Carnegie Corporation of New York
READING NEXT
A VISION FOR ACTION AND RESEARCH IN MIDDLE AND HIGH SCHOOL LITERACY
ALLIANCE FOR EXCELLENT EDUCATION

According to the report, effective literacy programs for struggling readers share the following **instructional** components:

1. **Direct, explicit comprehension instruction,** or teaching core reading strategies.
2. **Effective instructional principles embedded in content,** or teaching students to use reading skills in all content areas.
3. **Motivation and self-directed learning,** or motivating students to read (now *and* after graduation), and to become independent, lifelong learners.
4. **Text-based collaborative learning,** or teaching students to interact with one another vis-à-vis using a variety of texts.
5. **Strategic tutoring,** or giving students intense, individualized instruction when necessary.
6. **Diverse texts,** or using texts whose genre, topic, and level of difficulty vary.
7. **Intensive writing,** or offering instruction that relates to the writing tasks students will perform at the high school level and beyond.
8. **A technology component,** or using technology as a tool for and topic of literacy instruction.
9. **Ongoing formative assessment of students,** or conducting frequent, informal assessments of student progress under current instructional practices.

The report also notes that effective literacy programs share the following **infrastructural** components:

10. **Extended time for literacy,** or offering two to four hours of interdisciplinary (cross-classroom and cross-content area) literacy instruction per day.
11. **Professional development,** or offering long-term and ongoing support for teachers.
12. **Ongoing summative assessment of students and programs,** or evaluating students and educators in order to build accountability and improve systems.

13. **Teacher teams,** or forming interdisciplinary groups that discuss and are accountable for students' progress.
14. **Leadership,** or the execution of program goals by teachers and principals who understand their students and their reading and writing curriculum.
15. **A comprehensive and coordinated literacy program,** or the formation of a literacy program that draws strength from various disciplines, departments, and community organizations.

Reading with Purpose and the *Reading Next* Report

The *Reading Next* report recommends nine instructional improvements, and the *Reading with Purpose* program equips teachers to implement all of them—when, where, and how they choose. Developed with these improvements in mind, this program helps teachers help students in the ways that matter most.

The *Reading Next* Report recommends:	*Reading with Purpose* features:
direct, explicit comprehension instruction	**Genre Focus:** highlights 4 reading skills and 4 literary elements **Reading Workshops: Skill Lesson**–explicit instruction on one reading skill **Reading Selections**–vocabulary instruction and review, side notes that provide explicit reading skill instruction and practice
effective instructional principles embedded in content	**Reading, Writing, Comparing Literature and Reading Across Texts Workshops:** inquiry-based instruction using the Workshop approach; teach-model-practice-assess mode of instruction
motivation and self-directed learning	**Big Questions:** Inquiry-based instruction **Unit Challenges:** choice of activities **Learner's Notebooks and Foldables:** record individual's thoughts and learning
text-based collaborative learning	**Workshop Approach:** emphasis on collaboration **Partner Talk, Think-Pair-Share, Small-Group Discussion, and Whole-Class Discussion:** activities that emphasize collaboration **Unit Challenge:** includes a suggested group activity
strategic tutoring	**Partner Talk and Think-Pair-Share:** students work one-on-one with one another, and/or with an instructor **Reading and Writing Workshops:** opportunity to work in small mentoring groups
diverse texts	**Genre Focus:** one per unit **Diverse reading selections:** fiction, nonfiction, informational text **Reading on Your Own:** suggested readings at the end of each unit
intensive writing	**Writing Workshop:** a two-part writing project in every unit; teaches students to write within the focus genre **Reading Workshops:** students encounter numerous writing activities, including the **Write to Learn** prompt
a technology component	Examples include **glencoe.online,** the **Student Works CD-ROM,** and the **Skills Arcade CD-ROM**
ongoing formative assessment of students	**After You Read:** assessment and skills review following each reading selection **Skills and Strategies Assessment:** unit-ending test practice **Ancillary Assessment materials: Selection Quick Checks, Assessment by Objectives, Examview Pro Assessment Suite, Selection** and **Unit Assessments**

Inquiry-Based Instruction

By Jeffrey D. Wilhelm, Ph.D.

As educators, we often fail to establish the relevance of what we teach. For example, the boys in my *Reading Don't Fix No Chevys* study (Smith and Wilhelm, 2002) felt that what they learned in school was completely separate from, and not useful in, "real" life. In short, they wanted the type of education that MIT physicist Jerrold Zaccharias championed—one that raises, as Zaccharias put it, "questions worth arguing about."

How, then, do we use "hands-on/minds-on" modes of instruction to help students ask and answer worthwhile questions? The research is in, and it points toward inquiry. Shown to improve student engagement, attitude, achievement, and learning in a variety of areas, inquiry approaches eclipse other modes of simple information transmission—and best help students do the work that matters.

What Is Inquiry?

Inquiry is the problem-oriented exploration of questions that drive and organize disciplines. Through inquiry, students learn essential concepts and strategies for applying those concepts in the real world. They engage the same problems and questions that real practitioners of a given discipline engage, and therefore learn to think, read, and write like experts in that area.

Discovering information is part of true inquiry, *but it is only the first step.* Inquirers must then interpret that information and shape it into knowledge. Human beings want to make meanings, not just receive them—or, as James Britton famously remarked, "Being told is the opposite of finding out."

To this end, research shows that inquiry approaches—active, discussion-based, and supported by a purposeful curriculum—focus on HOW to do something, and WHY to do it (Applebee, 1996; Hillocks, 1995, 1999, 2002; Applebee, Langer, Nystrand, and Gamoran, 2003; Nystrand, 1997). However, teacher-centered approaches—often lecture, memorization, and test-based—focus simply on WHAT to do (see, e.g., Rogoff, Matusov, White, 1996).

Literacy researcher George Hillocks argues that reading and writing are forms of inquiry and are best taught, and learned, in that context. His research findings support that argument. According to Hillocks, inquiry approaches had the most powerful effects on student engagement, learning, and achievement (see Hillocks, 1995, 1999, 2002).

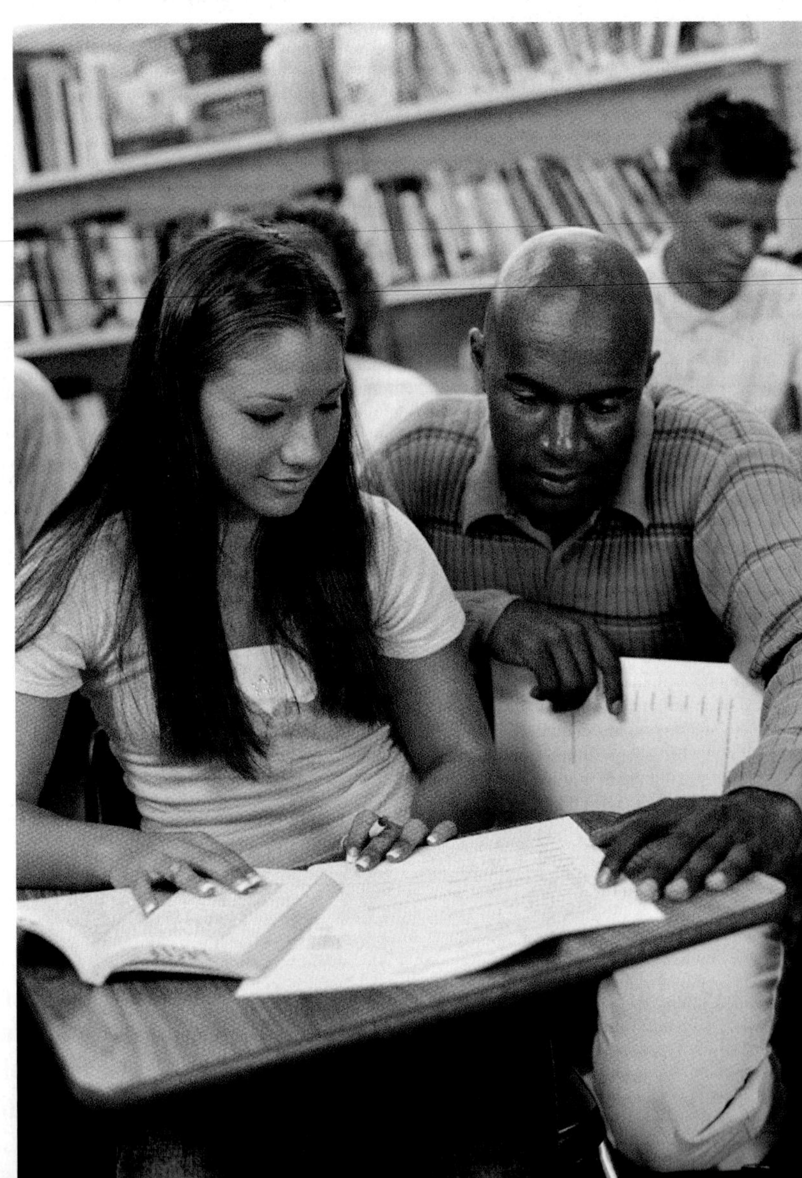

How Is Inquiry Applied in *Reading with Purpose*?

Motivation My research (Smith and Wilhelm, 2002, 2006; Wilhelm and Friedemann, 1998) has shown that the inquiry approach, organized around essential questions, increases student engagement. Because it is organized around Big Questions, the instruction in *Reading with Purpose* makes learning matter to students in very immediate ways.

Meaningful Context In *Reading with Purpose,* the reading, writing, and language activities are organized around real issues that students face in their own lives. When students practice a skill or create a writing product, they are also learning to ask and think through important real-life questions.

Schema Theory Modern cognitive science explains that people learn by either assimilating new data into existing patterns, or "schema," or by changing schema to accommodate new data. In *Reading with Purpose,* units are organized so that students develop their schema text by text and activity by activity. Doing this allows students to build their schema about the inquiry question and to develop key reading and writing tools. This gives students a coherent learning experience, where each activity better equips them for the next.

Curricular Coherence and Integration Inquiry teaching uses what Applebee, Burroughs, and Stevens (2000) call an *integrated* curriculum, or a curriculum that helps students build a set of skills that they apply with increasing sophistication across a range of activities. The integrated curriculum helps students achieve a range of objectives (Wiggins and McTighe, 1998). For example, students address the socially significant Big Question as developing readers and writers. They also encounter grammar in the context of the literary selections—and their own writing—so that the lessons they learn are situated and meaningful. In *Reading with Purpose,* reading and writing are integrated as forms of inquiry taught in an inquiring context. Use this exciting approach and watch your students begin to ask—and answer—the questions that matter most.

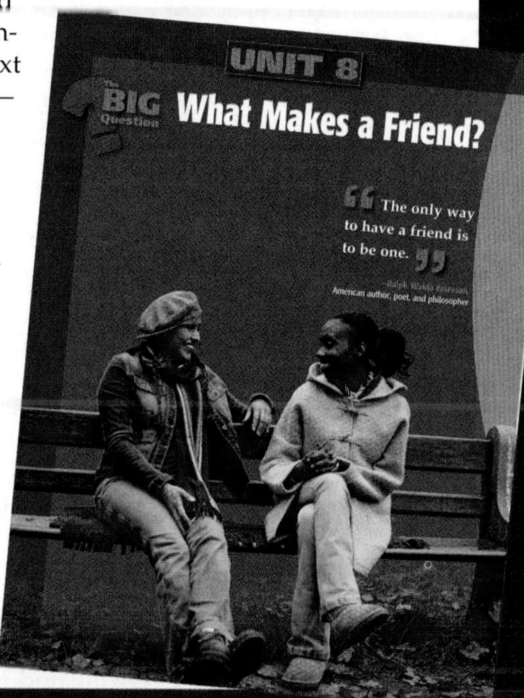

Works Cited

Applebee, A. N., Burroughs, R., and Stevens, A.S. 2000. "Shaping Conversation: A Study of Continuity and Coherence in High School Literature Curricula." *Research in the Teaching of English,* 34: 396–429.

Applebee, A.N. 1996. *Curriculum as conversation: Transforming traditions of teaching and learning.* Chicago: University of Chicago Press.

Applebee, A., Langer, J., Nystrand, M. and Gamoran, A. 2003. "Discussion-Based Approaches to Developing Understanding: Classroom Instruction and Student Performance in Middle and High School English." *American Educational Research Journal,* Fall.

Hillocks, G., Jr. 1995. *Teaching Writing as Reflective Practice.* New York: Teachers College Press.

Hillocks, G., Jr. 1999. *Ways of Thinking, Ways of Teaching.* New York: Teachers College Press.

Hillocks, G., Jr. 2002. *The Testing Trap.* New York: Teachers College Press.

Smith, M. W., and Wilhelm. J. 2002. *Reading Don't Fix No Chevys: Literacy in the Lives of Young Men.* Portsmouth, NH: Heinemann.

Smith, M. W. and Wilhelm, J. 2006. *Going with the Flow: Making literacy learning in school more like life.* Portsmouth, NH: Heinemann.

Soder, R. 1999. "When Words Find Their Meaning: Renewal versus Reform." *Phi Delta Kappan.* April, 568–570.

Wiggins, G., and McTighe, J. 1998. *Understanding by Design.* Alexandria, VA: ASCD.

Wilhelm, J. 2003. *Reading IS Seeing.* New York: Scholastic.

Wilhelm, J., and Friedemann, P. 1998. *Hyperlearning: Where Inquiry, Projects and Technology Meet.* York, ME: Stenhouse.

The Workshop Approach

By Douglas Fisher, Ph.D.

While there are a number of ways to provide this instruction, the reading and writing workshops are particularly effective, and therefore hold promise for all students (e.g., Fletcher & Portalupi, 2001; Serafini, 2001).

A Workshop Defined

Workshops are about collaboration and creation. In the classroom, the workshop is a philosophy; it is also a way to organize instructional time. For example, reading and writing workshops provide time for students to respond to texts they have read and to write about their ideas (Atwell, 1987; Calkins, 1986). These workshops also allow students to assume more responsibility for literacy tasks and to become independent learners. In this way, the workshop model provides a context for students to build skills and perfect their craft.

The Evidence Base

As Lausé (2004) noted, the implementation of a workshop approach to teaching reading and writing inspires students to become lifelong readers. According to Lausé's data, it creates faster, more competent readers; it also creates students who enjoy reading (and do read) more.

Taylor and Nesheim (2000/2001) used the workshop model to engage their "high-risk" students in literacy instruction. As they note, the "readers' workshop project prompted students to engage as readers and to experiment with new views of reading" (p. 317). Similarly, Williams (2001) noted that "a workshop format and strategy instruction helped struggling middle school readers connect with books, the teacher, and one another" (p. 588).

The workshop model has also been shown to improve writing achievement (Fisher & Frey, 2003), the use of multiple forms of media (Labbo, 2004), performance on tests (Shelton & Fu, 2004; Santman, 2002), problem solving skills (Christensen, 1990), and the expectations of teachers (Graves, 2004).

A Guiding Philosophy

Simply telling students what they should know will not ensure that they read better and read more. As teachers, we must model, scaffold, guide, and support learning. Current research suggests that the "gradual release of responsibility" model is an effective way to organize instruction (Fisher & Frey, 2003; Pearson & Fielding, 1991). In this model, the teacher moves from assuming "all the

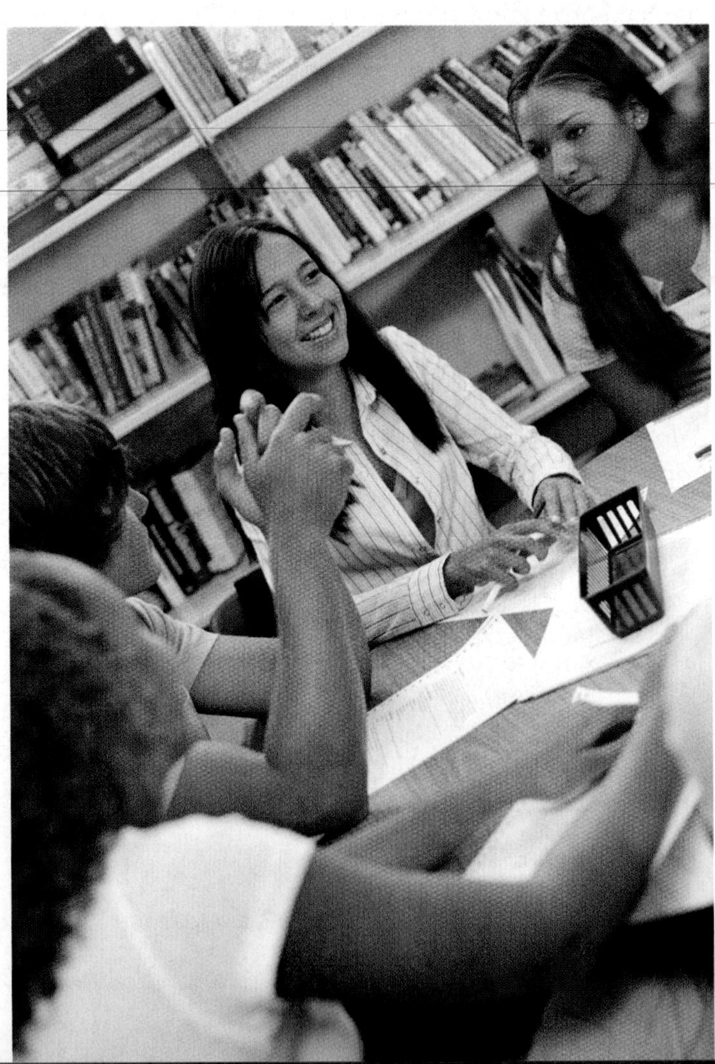

responsibility for performing a task . . . to a situation in which the students assume all of the responsibility" (Duke & Pearson, 2002, p. 211). This gradual release may occur over a day, a week, or a term. In *Reading with Purpose,* reading workshops are designed to encourage this gradual release of responsibility.

Components of the Workshop

To facilitate the gradual release of responsibility, the workshop moves students through phases of extensive teacher support and guided instruction, allowing them to become more independent learners. This model includes the following components:

- **A focus lesson** allows teachers to model a skill, strategy, or writing technique. Some strategies include read and think alouds, shared reading and writing activities, and language-based approaches. In *Reading with Purpose,* every Reading Workshop begins with a Skill Lesson that introduces that unit's reading skill.
- **Guided instruction** gives students an opportunity to practice the skills, strategies, and techniques introduced during the focus lesson under the teacher's close supervision. It provides a scaffold between teacher modeling and student independence. Some strategies include guided reading, guided writing, writing models, and choral reading. In *Reading with Purpose,* reading selections are accompanied by notes that guide students' use of the unit's skills while they read.
- **Collaborative learning** encourages peer work to help students become more competent readers and writers. It also allows students to assist and coach one another. Some strategies include learning centers, paired reading, and reciprocal teaching. In *Reading with Purpose,* Partner Talk activities occur throughout the book.
- **Independent reading and writing** provides time for students to apply skills and strategies practiced during focus lessons, guided instruction, and collaborative learning to their own reading and writing. Independent learning need not be completed in solitary silence; it should, however, give each student a chance to apply new skills and strategies to his or her own work. Teachers may also use this time to conference with students individually. In *Reading with Purpose,* each unit ends with suggested readings to help students further explore the Big Question on their own.

Works Cited

Atwell, N. 1987. *In the middle: Writing, reading, and learning with adolescents.* Portsmouth, NH: Heinemann.

Calkins, L. M. 1986. *The art of teaching writing.* Portsmouth, NH: Heinemann.

Christensen, A. W. 1990. "Problem solving our way through writers' workshop." *The Reading Teacher,* 44, 357–358.

Duke, N. K., & Pearson, P. D. 2002. "Effective practices for developing reading comprehension." In A. Farstrup & J. Samuels (Eds.), *What research has to say about reading instruction* (3rd ed.). Newark, DE: International Reading Association.

Fisher, D., & Frey, N. 2003. "Writing instruction for struggling adolescent readers: A gradual release model." *Journal of Adolescent and Adult Literacy,* 46, 396–405.

Fletcher, R., & Portalupi, J. 2001. *Writing workshop: The essential guide.* Portsmouth, NH: Heinemann.

Frey, N., & Fisher, D. 2006. *Language arts workshop: Purposeful reading and writing instruction.* Upper Saddle River, NJ: Merrill Education.

Graves, D. 2004. "What I've learned from teachers of writing." *Language Arts,* 82(2), 88–94.

Labbo, L. D. 2004. "From writing workshop to multimedia workshop." *Language Arts,* 82(2), 119.

Lausé, J. 2004. "Using reading workshop to inspire lifelong readers." *English Journal, 93*(5), 24–30.

Pearson, P. D., & Fielding, L. 1991. "Comprehension instruction." In R. Barr, M. L. Kamil, P. Mosenthal, & P. D. Pearson (Eds.) *Handbook of reading research* (Vol. II), (pp. 815–860). Mahwah, NJ: Erlbaum.

Santman, D. 2002. "Teaching to the test? Test preparation in the reading workshop." *Language Arts,* 79(3), 203–211.

Serafini, F. 2001. *The reading workshop: Creating space for readers.* Portsmouth, NH: Heinemann.

Shelton, N. R., & Fu, D. 2004. "Creating space for teaching writing and for test preparation." *Language Arts,* 82(2), 120–128.

Taylor, S. V., & Nesheim. D. W. 2000/2001. "Making literacy real for 'high-risk' adolescent emerging readers: An innovative application of readers' workshop." *Journal of Adolescent & Adult Literacy, 44,* 308–318.

Williams, M. 2001. "Making connections: A workshop for adolescents who struggle with reading." *Journal of Adolescent & Adult Literacy, 44,* 588–602.

Differentiated Instruction

By Douglas Fisher, Ph.D.

Today's classroom contains students from a variety of backgrounds and with a variety of learning styles, strengths, and challenges. With careful planning, you can address the needs of all students in the literature classroom, using ***Glencoe Literature: Reading with Purpose.*** The basis for this planning is differentiated learning.

Differentiated Instruction Is a Key to Access

To differentiate instruction, teachers must acknowledge students' differences in background knowledge, current reading, writing, and English language skills, learning styles and preferences, interests, and needs, and they must react accordingly. There are a number of general guidelines for differentiating instruction:

- **Link assessment with instruction.** Assessments should occur before, during, and after instruction to ensure that the curriculum is aligned with what students do and do not know. Using assessments in this way allows you to plan instruction for whole groups, small groups, and individual students.
- **Clarify key concepts and generalizations.** Students need to know what is essential and how this information can be used in their future learning. In addition, students need to develop a sense of the **Big Questions,** which focus on life issues students need to think about in each unit in ***Reading with Purpose.***
- **Emphasize critical and creative thinking.** The content, process, and products used or assigned in the classroom should require that students think about what they are learning. While some students may require support, additional motivation, varied tasks, materials, or equipment, the overall focus on critical and creative thinking allows for all students to participate in the lesson.
- **Include teacher- and student-selected tasks.** A differentiated classroom includes both teacher- and student-selected activities and tasks. At some points in the lesson, the teacher must provide instruction and assign learning activities. In other parts of the lesson, students should be provided choices in how they engage with the content. This balance increases motivation, engagement, and learning.

Supporting Individual Students

The vast majority of students will thrive in a classroom based on differentiated instruction. However, wise teachers recognize that no single option will work for all students and that there may be students who require unique systems of support to be successful.

Tips for Instruction

The following tips for instruction can support your efforts to help all students reach their maximum potential.

- Survey students to discover their individual differences. Use interest inventories of their unique talents so you can encourage contributions in the classroom.
- Be a model for respecting others. Adolescents crave social acceptance. The student with learning differences is especially sensitive to correction and criticism, particularly when it comes from a teacher. Your behavior will set the tone for how students treat one another.
- Expand opportunities for success. Provide a variety of instructional activities that reinforce skills and concepts.
- Establish measurable objectives and decide how you can best help students who meet them.
- Celebrate successes, and make note of and praise "work in progress."
- Keep it simple. Point out problem areas if doing so can help a student effect change. Avoid overwhelming students with too many goals at one time.
- Assign cooperative group projects that challenge all students to contribute to solving a problem or creating a product.

How Do I Reach Students with Learning Disabilities?

- Provide support and structure. Clearly specify rules, assignments, and responsibilities.
- Practice skills frequently. Use games and drills to help maintain student interest.
- Incorporate many modalities into the learning process. Provide opportunities to say, hear, write, read, and act out important concepts and information.
- Link new skills and concepts to those already mastered.

- If possible, allow students to record answers on audiotape.
- Allow extra time to complete assessments and assignments.
- Let students demonstrate proficiency with alternative presentations, including oral reports, role plays, art projects, and musical presentations.
- Provide outlines, notes, or tape recordings of lecture material.
- Pair students with peer helpers, and provide class time for pair interaction.

How Do I Reach English Language Learners?

- Remember, students' ability to speak English does not reflect their academic abilities.
- Try to incorporate the students' cultural experience into your instruction. The help of a bilingual aide may be effective.
- Avoid any references in your instruction that could be construed as cultural stereotypes.
- Preteach important vocabulary and concepts.
- Encourage students to preview text before they begin reading, noting headings.
- Remind students not to ignore graphic organizers, photographs, and maps since there is much information in these visuals.
- Use artifacts and photographs whenever possible to build background knowledge and understanding. An example of this would be coins in a foreign currency or a raw cotton ball to reinforce its importance in history.

How Do I Reach Gifted Students?

- Make arrangements for students to take selected subjects early and to work on independent projects.
- Ask "what if" questions to develop high-level thinking skills. Establish an environment safe for risk taking in your classroom.
- Emphasize concepts, theories, ideas, relationships, and generalizations about the content.
- Promote interest in the past by inviting students to make connections to the present.
- Let students express themselves in alternate ways such as creative writing, acting, debates, simulations, drawing, or music.
- Provide students with a catalog of helpful resources, listing such things as agencies that provide free and inexpensive materials, appropriate community services and programs, and community experts who might be called upon to speak to your students.
- Assign extension projects that allow students to solve real-life problems related to their communities.

References

Fisher, D. 2005. "The missing link: Standards, assessment, and instruction." *Voices from the Middle,* 13(2), 8–11.

McTighe, J., Seif, E., Wiggins, G. 2004. "You can teach for meaning." *Educational Leadership,* 62(1), 26–30.

Pfaum, S. W., & Bishop, P. A. 2004. "Student perceptions of reading engagement: Learning from the Learners." *Journal of Adolescent and Adult Literacy,* 48(3), 202–213.

Tomlinson, C. A., & McTighe, J. 2006. *Integrating differentiated instructions & understanding by design: Connecting content and kids.* Alexandria, VA: Association for Supervision and Curriculum Development.

Question Answer Relationship (QAR)

by Taffy Raphael, Ph.D.

What Is It?

QAR provides a framework that offers teachers a straightforward approach for reading comprehension instruction. QAR can serve as a reasonable starting point for addressing four problems that stand in the way of moving all students to high levels of literacy:

- a shared language to make visible the processes underlying reading and listening comprehension
- a framework for organizing questioning activities and comprehension instruction
- accessible and straightforward reform for literacy instruction oriented toward higher level thinking
- preparing students for high-stakes testing without undermining a strong focus on higher level thinking

Two decades ago, research showed that QAR could reliably improve students' comprehension (Raphael & McKinney, 1983; Raphael & Pearson, 1985; Raphael & Wonnacott, 1985). In the two decades since, literacy educators in a broad range of settings have demonstrated its practical value and shared their experiences in professional journals (e.g., Mesmer & Hutchins, 2002), textbooks (e.g., Leu & Kinzer, 2003; Reutzel & Cooper, 2004; Roe, Smith, & Burns, 2005; Vacca et al., 2003), and on the World Wide Web (e.g., gallery.carnegiefoundation.org/yhutchinson and www.smsd.org/schools/diemer/).

Why Is It Important?

Promoting high levels of literacy for all children is a core responsibility for today's teachers. With increasing accountability at the district, state, and national levels, teachers are often judged on the basis of how well their students perform on mandated, high-stakes tests.

But what does it mean to achieve high levels of literacy? Recent national panels and current reviews detailing what it means to comprehend text help inform us about current policies and future trends (e.g., Pressley, 2002; Snow, 2002; Sweet & Snow, 2003). For example, the RAND report (Snow), commissioned by the U.S. Department of Education, identifies literacy proficiency as reached when a reader can read a variety of materials with ease and interest, can read for varying purposes, and can read with comprehension even when the material is neither easy to understand nor intrinsically interesting. Proficient readers are capable of acquiring new knowledge and understanding new concepts, are capable of applying textual information appropriately, and are capable of being engaged in the reading process and reflecting on what is being read. This same view is reflected in the current National Assessment of Educational Progress (NAEP; Donahue, Daane, & Grigg, 2003), the only federally funded large-scale testing program in the United States, and the framework for the NAEP 2009 reading assessment (National Assessment Governing Board, 2004) pushes the definition for proficiency even further. For example, students will be expected to read comfortably across genres within fiction, nonfiction, procedural texts, and poetry. They will be required to successfully answer questions, 70 to 80 percent of which call for the integration, interpretation, critique, and evaluation of texts read independently.

Traditional questions that simply require readers to locate and recall information will constitute only a third to a fourth of the questions that students will face. Over half of the higher level questions will require students to provide a short or extended written response rather than simply to select from multiple-choice options. To be judged as proficient in reading fiction, students must demonstrate that they can think deeply about, and write in response to, questions that address themes, lessons, elements of plot, and multiple points of view. The kind of strategic knowledge assessed on national and state tests, now and in the future, is central to the achievement of high levels of literacy.

How Do I Do It?

The vocabulary of QAR—**In the Book, In My Head, Right There, Think & Search, Author & Me,** and **On My Own**—gives teachers and students a language for talking about the largely invisible processes that constitute listening and reading comprehension across grades and subject areas.

Teachers know the value of modeling and thinking aloud to make visible the thought processes involved in higher levels of thinking, but it can be frustrating trying to convey complex ideas without a shared vocabulary. Thus, QAR first and foremost provides teachers and students with a much-needed common language. Introduce students to the basic principle underlying QAR: that generating and answering questions draws on two core sources of information. These sources are the texts that we read and our background knowledge and experiences; or, in the language of QAR, information that is **In the Book** or **In My Head,** respectively.

Teachers should use QAR language as they emphasize the importance of both sources of information. Furthermore, teachers should use QAR language to help students learn to use strategies effectively. For example, explain how skimming or scanning might lead to details for an **In the Book** QAR (a typical locate/recall strategy) or how using clues from the title and chapter headings can point to relevant background knowledge for answering an **In My Head** QAR (a relatively simple interpret/integrate/infer task).

Introduce students to the language of QAR by analyzing the differences between questions with answer sources in the book and those where the answer source is students' own heads. Shorter texts work quite effectively for characterizing basic differences between these two information sources, but as students become more experienced with QARs, this simple distinction is not sufficient to capture the range of strategies used to answer and generate questions related to text. Build on **In the Book** and **In My Head** by introducing the four core QARs. Once students are confidently and accurately identifying **In the Book** QARs, introduce its subcategories, **Right There** and **Think & Search.** Similarly, when students are confident and accurate with **In My Head** QARs, introduce its subcategories; **Author & Me** and **On My Own** (see chart below for definitions of each).

Readers functioning at high levels of literacy use strategies in combination and apply different approaches to strategic thinking, depending on the genre or difficulty of the texts. Understanding how strategies interrelate can be quite abstract for students faced with the need to apply several strategies, as well as quite demanding for teachers in terms of providing effective instruction. QAR provides a framework that students can use to link strategies at appropriate points in the reading cycle. Understanding and control of strategies learned helps readers engage in the high levels of literacy for which they are accountable in their day-to-day classroom literacy activities and in high-stakes assessments at the district, state, and national levels.

In the Book

Right There

The answer is in one place in the text. Words from the question and words that answer the question are often in the same sentence.

Sample Comprehension Strategies:

Skimming and Scanning
Note-taking
Context Clues

Think & Search

The answer is in the text. Readers need to put together different parts of the text to find the answer. The answer can be within a paragraph, across paragraphs, or even across chapters and books.

Sample Comprehension Strategies:

Summarizing
Compare and Contrast
Making Simple Inferences
Clarifying
Figurative Language

In My Head

On My Own

The answer is not in the text. Readers need to use their own ideas and experiences to answer the question.

Sample Comprehension Strategies:

Activating Prior Knowledge
Connecting

Author & Me

The answer is not in the text. To answer the question, readers need to think about how the text and what they already know fit together.

Sample Comprehension Strategies:

Predicting
Visualizing
Making Simple and Complex Inferences
Distinguishing Fact and Opinion
Making Text-to-Self Connections

English Language Learners

by Mary A. Avalos, Ph.D.

English language learners (ELLs) are a growing population in our schools. During the 2000–2001 academic year, more than 4.5 million English language learners were enrolled in U.S. public schools (McREL, 2003). The growth of culturally and linguistically diverse populations is expected to continue into this century. Immigrants come to the United States for various reasons—some to escape political or economic oppression, others to seek higher paying wages or provide a higher standard of living for their families. Although shifting demographics have a greater impact on certain regions of the United States, all teachers should be prepared to teach all students.

The Growing Numbers of Limited English Proficient Students 1993/4–2003/4

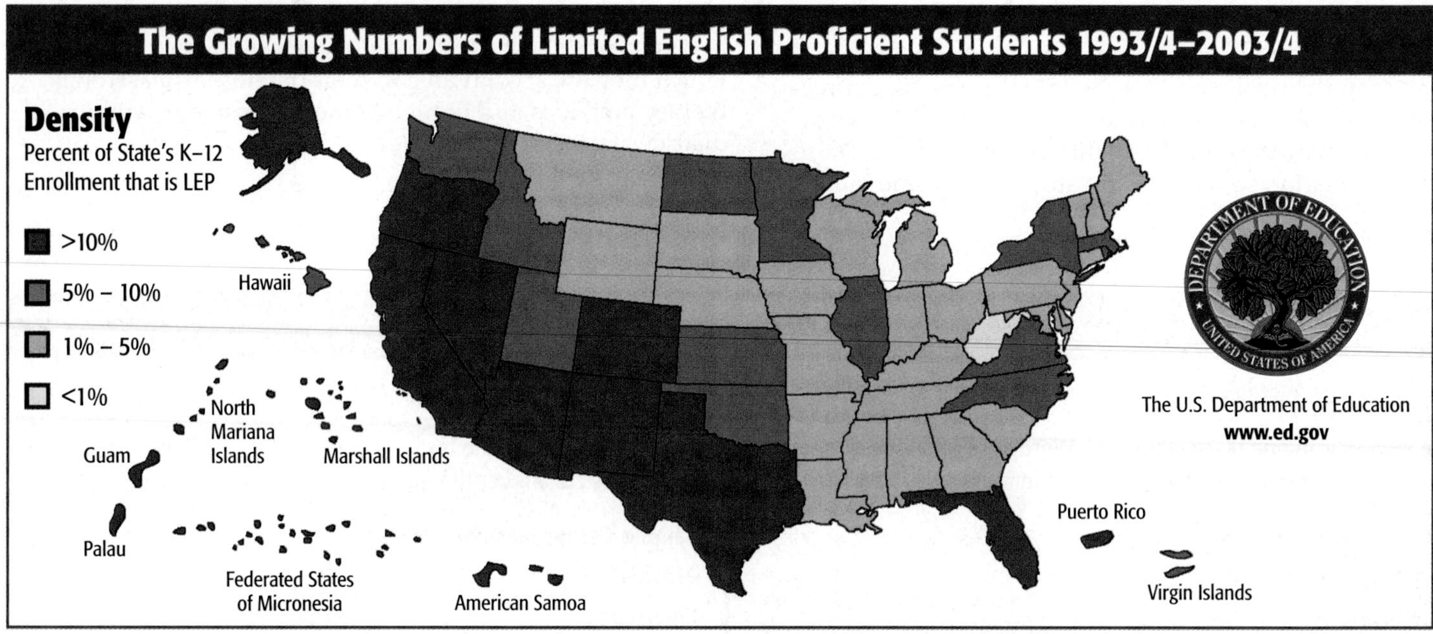

Meeting the Challenge

There are challenges specific to teaching English language learners as they must learn content while learning to read, write, and speak a new language simultaneously. English language learners' literacy proficiency in their first language, or **L1,** will impact their literacy acquisition of a second language, or **L2.** (Au, 1993; Cummins, 2003; Hudelson, 1984; Snow, 1990), particularly if the L1 is similar to the L2.

English language learners make an easier transition between L1 and L2 if both languages share a similar writing system.

Writing System	Example
Alphabetic	English, French, Spanish, Italian
Syllabic	Cherokee
Logographic	Chinese

To provide effective instruction, build upon what English language learners know about language and literacy knowledge. Also consider English language learners' cultural differences, such as celebration and mourning rituals, child-rearing practices, and favorite foods. Try to incorporate the students' cultural experience into your teaching.

Gauging Levels of Language Proficiency

A common misconception exists that once English language learners are able to converse using everyday language, they are ready to proceed to mainstream instruction with little to no support. In reality, there are three levels of language proficiency as labeled by Cummins (2003).

Level of Language Proficiency	Example
Basic Interpersonal Conversation Skills (BICS)	ability to talk about daily activities, make requests, and retell a personal story or event.
Discrete Language Skills	knowledge of phonological awareness, grammar rules, or conventions of writing in the learner's first language
Cognitive Academic Language Proficiency (CALP)	the ability to read and understand technical or subject area texts with low frequency words of Latin or Greek origin

By learning about language acquisition processes, teachers can better meet the needs of English language learners.

Several instructional features of *Glencoe Literature: Reading with Purpose* help English language learners develop higher levels of language proficiency. Note the following examples:

1. Analyzing the reading selections to facilitate comprehension of low frequency vocabulary, as well as identified vocabulary words for study.
2. Prompting students to activate prior knowledge before/while reading to make connections between the reader and the text.
3. Integrating literary elements throughout the selections to provide meaningful prompts in context.
4. Setting objectives to ensure that all students receive high quality, standards-based instruction.
5. Contextualizing writing, grammar, and spelling instruction throughout the program.

All of these aids increase teacher awareness of text- and reader-based features as they are instructing English language learners. This approach to instruction, in turn, better meets the unique needs of English language learners as they learn content and language together.

Works Cited

Au, K. H. 1993. *Literacy instruction in multicultural settings.* Orlando, FL: Harcourt Brace College Publishers.

Cummins, J. 2003. "Reading and the bilingual student: Fact and friction." In G. G. Garcia's (Ed.) *English learners: Reaching the highest level of English literacy.* Newark, DE: International Reading Association.

Hudelson, S. 1984. "Kan yu ret an rayt en ingles: Children become literate in English as a second language." *TESOL Quarterly*, 18, 221–238.

McREL. Fall, 2003. "English language learners and the No Child Left Behind Act." *Changing Schools: A Newsletter from the Central Region Educational Laboratory. Aurora, CO: Mid-continent Research for Education* and Learning. Retrieved from the Internet on February 17, 2006: http://www.mcrel.org/PDF/ChangingSchools/5032NL_CSfall2003.pdf#search='percentage%20of%20English%20language%20learners%20in%20U.S.%20schools

Snow, C. E. 1990. "Rationales for native language instruction in the education of language minority children: Evidence from research." In A. Padilla, H. Fairchild, & C. Valadez (Eds.), *Bilingual education: Issues and strategies*, pp. 60–74. Newbury Park, CA: Sage.

Digital Technology

by David G. O'Brien, Ph.D.

Students' Digital Lives

By cultivating an awareness of the issues below, teachers can help students connect the literacy practices they learn in school to their busy lives outside the classroom.

- **New Literacies** In the digital age, many students are fluent in new languages, or literacies—for example, those of instant messaging, text messaging, and blogging.
- **Increased Media Use** Kids and teens spend an average of six hours per day using media (Kaiser Family Foundation, 2005).
- **Internet as Reference Text** An increasing number of young people use the Internet as their primary reference text for everything, including school assignments.
- **Closing the Gap** The digital divide—long cited in the argument against technology-based learning in schools—is slowly closing. More students from all socioeconomic levels are gaining access to technology at home and in the community.

Using Technology to Teach

New technologies—and the media they make available—appeal to a variety of learners. These technologies can help motivate students to engage in reading, writing, and the use of other literacies, including traditional, school-based literacies and multiple texts (O'Brien, 2001, 2003). As you incorporate technology into your classroom, use the tips below.

Connect print text to digital text. Look for Web sites that support kids' reading. An emerging body of research shows that engagement with online texts can motivate struggling readers to read print texts as well (O'Brien, 2001; 2003, in press).

- In *Reading with Purpose,* the Literature Online feature encourages readers to research topics and authors by linking to a provided Web site. These sorts of intertextual links help motivate struggling, disengaged readers who are often tired of typical textbook formats—even when those books are interesting and accessible. For example, a selection in *Reading with Purpose* on skateboarder Tony Hawk (Unit 2's *Tony Hawk: Chairman of the Board*) can be augmented by using print and media texts from Tony Hawk's official Web site.

Connect print to other print media.
Texts from popular genres (e.g., cartoons, illustrations, and graphic novels) motivate all learners. They also provide struggling learners, or those learners who lose attention easily when presented with traditional formats, a way to access and understand the lesson.

- In *Reading with Purpose*, cartoons are used to introduce reading skills, highlighting those skills' relevance in new and emerging literacies. Students can also engage the wide variety of reading selections culled from the literature most familiar to them—Web sites, magazines, graphic novels, and cartoons.

Utilize other digital resources to enhance reading. As educators, we want to connect digital texts to traditional ones; we do not, however, want to replace all print texts with digital ones. To foster this connection, though, we must be aware that digital media use is on the rise among middle school students. Also, we cannot ignore the extent to which digital media motivates and engages struggling readers, or readers who have disengaged from more typical reading tasks in school.

- *Reading with Purpose* offers an array of digital products that help students relate to what they read and acquire more skills. One such product is Skill Level Up!™, a computer game that helps students practice and master reading skills in a context with which many are probably familiar. Another product, StudentWorks, gives students a digitized work center wherein they can access many *Reading with Purpose* resources. Finally, the Web site glencoe.com provides a wealth of resources for digitally savvy students to use and enjoy.

Works Cited

Beach, R. 2000. "Critical Issues: Reading and responding to literature at the level of activity." *Journal of Literacy Research,* 32 (2), 237–251.

Beach, R. & O'Brien, D. (in press). "Teaching popular culture texts in the classroom." In D. Leu, J. Coiro, M. Knobel, & C. Lankshear (Eds.). *Handbook of research on new literacies.* Mahwah, NJ: Lawrence Erlbaum Associates.

Kaiser Family Foundation. March, 2005. "Generation M: Media in the Lives of 8–18 Year-olds."

O'Brien, D. G. 2001. "At-risk adolescents: Redefining competence through the multiliteracies of intermediality, visual arts, and representation." *Reading Online,* 4(11). Available http://www.readingonline.org/newliteracies/lit_index.asp?HREF=/newliteracies/obrien/index.html

O'Brien, D. G. 2003. "Juxtaposing traditional and intermedial literacies to redefine the competence of struggling adolescents." *Reading Online,* 6(7). Available: http://www.readingonline.org/newliteracies/lit_index.asp?HREF=obrien2/

O'Brien, D. G. (in press). "Struggling Adolescents' Engagement in Multimediating: Countering the Institutional Construction of Incompetence." In D. E. Alvermann, S. F. Phelps, D. R. Waff, K. A. Hinchman, & D. W. Moore (Eds) (2nd Ed.). *Reconceptualizing the literacies in adolescents' lives.* Mahwah, NJ: Erlbaum Associates.

Rushkoff, D. 1999. *Playing the future: What we can learn from digital kids.* New York: Riverhead.

Sefton-Green, J. (1998). "Introduction: Being Young in the Digital Age." In J. Sefton-Green (Ed.), *Digital Diversions: Youth Culture in the Age of Multimedia* (pp. 1–20). London: UCL Press Limited.

Project CRISS

By Carol M. Santa, Ph.D.

CRISS stands for CReating Independence through Student-owned Strategies. It is a staff development program that I created in collaboration with middle and high school teachers in Kalispell, Montana.

The CRISS Philosophy

Project CRISS is more than a collection of learning strategies. Its underlying power rests not on the individual strategies, but on the teaching philosophy behind them. This philosophy integrates work from cognitive psychology, social learning theory, and neurological research about how the brain learns. It incorporates these overlapping principles:

Background knowledge and purposeful reading are powerful determinants of reading comprehension.

Readers are far more likely to learn new information when they have some previous knowledge before they read or listen.

More Than Simply Reading We warn students not to simply begin reading. We also remind them to preview the assignment and think about their goals for reading. We ask students, *"What might you already know about the topic? What questions do you have about the topic?"*

KWLH One proven CRISS strategy for helping students activate prior knowledge is to develop a **KWHL** chart (**K**now, **W**ant to learn, **L**earned, **H**ow to learn more). Students can work together to generate a KWHL chart based on the model below. They can generate questions about what they want to learn, and then, after completing the reading assignment, they can list the new information they have learned and how they can learn more.

K	W	L	H
What I **KNOW**	What I **WANT** to find out	What I **LEARNED**	**HOW** I can learn more

Reading Goals *"Don't ignore your purposes for reading. Take time to think about them before delving into your reading."* We also suggest ways to make sure your students have clear goals for their reading. Each selection preview in *Glencoe Literature: Reading with Purpose* lists reading strategies and sets reading purposes.

Good readers have an intuitive understanding of the author's craft.

When students know how authors craft their writing, they can more readily understand and remember what they read. Good readers will analyze the author's style of presentation as they read. They might ask themselves, "What is this author doing to help me learn key concepts? How does the writer lead me from one idea to the next?"

Effective learners are actively involved when they listen and read.

We learn best when we act on the information presented. We can do this by using a variety of organizing activities that require us to write, talk, and transform the information we are absorbing.

Students need many opportunities to talk with one another about what they are learning.

We focus on how to get students to lead their own discussions about a topic. We want them to understand that it is their discussing, their oral grappling with meaning that leads to deeper understanding.

Competent readers know several ways to organize information for learning.

We show students different ways to organize information. They can take notes, underline selectively, develop concept maps, and summarize ideas in charts.

Students deserve opportunities to write about what they are learning.

Writing lets us figure out what we know and what we still need to know. The Writing Workshops in *Glencoe Literature: Reading with Purpose* guide students to explore various topics and communicate the information and impressions they have discovered.

Teaching involves explanation and modeling.

Students learn to think strategically when we use these processes as part of our instruction. Our demonstrations are especially critical for struggling readers. Most have never been taught how to learn. We have to show them how.

Take Center Stage When you introduce a new strategy, take center stage: show, tell, model, demonstrate, and explain the skill and how it is used by effective readers. As students learn to use the strategy, gradually release responsibility to them.

Systematic Approach Project CRISS is a valuable basis for instruction. It provides a systematic approach for using what we now know about teaching and learning. The following chart lists questions we need to continually ask ourselves while we are teaching. Use this chart to monitor your efforts to incorporate CRISS principles into your teaching.

CRISS Principles	The CRISS Philosophy	Yes	No	Somewhat
Background knowledge	• Did I assist students in thinking about what they already knew about the topic before beginning the unit? • Did I develop necessary concepts before students read?			
Purpose setting	• Did my students have a clear purpose about what they were going to learn before beginning the lesson?			
Author's craft	• Can my students use the author's style of presentation to facilitate their understanding?			
Active involvement	• Were my students engaged in the topic? • Did I help students become actively involved in their learning?			
Discussion	• Did my students have opportunities to talk about what they were learning?			
Organization	• Did my students organize information in a variety of ways?			
Writing	• Did my students write about what they were learning?			
Teacher modeling	• Did I do enough teacher modeling of learning strategies so that students could begin doing them on their own?			

Jamestown Education: Support for All Readers

For over 35 years, Jamestown Education has made its primary focus helping all readers become better readers. The Jamestown programs shown here are based on the latest research in adolescent literacy and on over 35 years of experience reaching adolescent readers. Each of these programs can help you build a comprehensive and well-coordinated literary program.

Jamestown Literature: An Adapted Reader

- Grade levels 6–10
- Reading Levels 3–8
- Instructional Support:
  This series provides grade-specific collections of literature adapted to lower reading levels. Providing struggling readers with alternative versions of canon literature offers an additional opportunity to differentiate instruction. Look for references to *Jamestown Literature: An Adapted Reader* in the Teacher Wraparound Edition. These mean you can find the same selection in both *Glencoe Literature: Reading with Purpose* and *Jamestown Literature.*

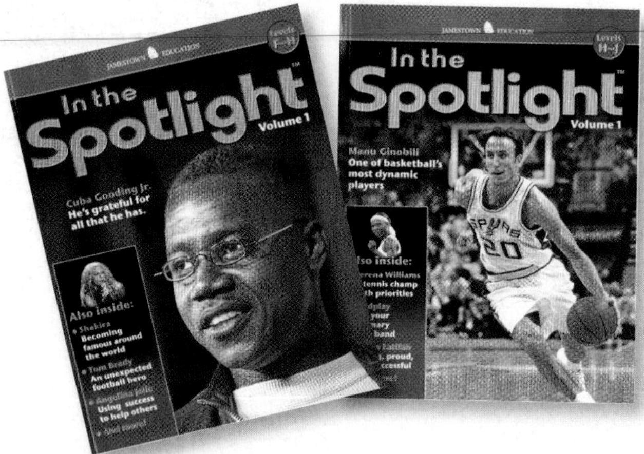

In the Spotlight™

- Reading Levels 2–10
- Instructional Support:
  This eight-book series will provide your students with engaging and motivating biographies to read while building their reading skills and vocabulary development. In each graduated unit, students are guided before, during, and after reading, with comprehension, skill, and vocabulary reinforcement, as well as writing exercises.

Timed Readings, Timed Readings Plus, Timed Readings Plus in Literature

- Reading Levels 1–13+
- Instructional Support:
  Each series (ten books in each) will help your students increase both reading rate and comprehension. The fiction and nonfiction passages of uniform length are designed for systematic classroom practice to improve reading rate and comprehension of text.

Reading Fluency

- Reading Levels 1–10
- Instructional Support:
  This seven-book series will help your students read smoothly, accurately, and expressively. Students work in pairs to provide immediate feedback and self-assessment. Author Camille Blachowicz states that "the ability to read fluently is highly correlated with many other measures of reading competence."

Jamestown Reading Improvement

- Reading Levels 4–10
- Instructional Support:
  Authored by renowned reading expert Edward Fry, this eight-book series focuses on helping build your students' comprehension, vocabulary, and study skills. Repeated practice with targeted exercises ensures mastery of valuable reading skills.

Critical Reading Series

- Reading Levels 2–8
- Instructional Support:
  This 27-book high interest series, written at three reading spans, encourages your reluctant readers to build a love for nonfiction while focusing on critical reading skills. Topics ranging from *Fateful Journeys* to *Weird Science* to *Heroes* draw students in, while giving students ample opportunities to master important skills found on both state and national tests.

Jamestown's Reading Navigator

Jamestown Reading Navigator

Jamestown Reading Navigator is an online and print-based intervention program built upon the latest research in adolescent literary, *Reading Next*. Here are the key objectives of the online version, available to students 24 hours a day from anywhere they can connect to the Web.

- Increase student achievement through direct, explicit instruction in comprehension strategies and modeling of good reading practices.
- Motivate and engage reluctant readers with a student-directed, self-paced learning environment enriched with interactive activities and media.
- Provide built in formative and summative assessment to help teachers track student progress and make instructional decisions.

Teaching Students from Impoverished Backgrounds

by Ruby K. Payne, Ph.D.

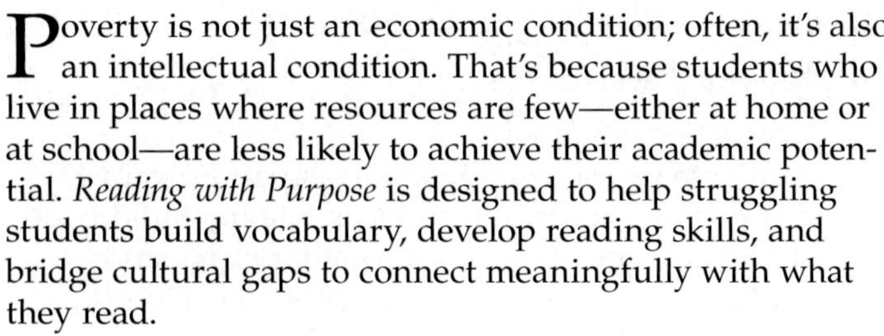

Poverty is not just an economic condition; often, it's also an intellectual condition. That's because students who live in places where resources are few—either at home or at school—are less likely to achieve their academic potential. *Reading with Purpose* is designed to help struggling students build vocabulary, develop reading skills, and bridge cultural gaps to connect meaningfully with what they read.

Many of the students to whom this series is geared lack adequate vocabulary skills. Research indicates that a child whose caregivers are welfare-dependent hears about 10 million words in a given two-year time frame. Within that same time frame, however, a child whose caregivers are educated professionals hears about 30 million words (Betty Hart and Todd Risley). This research also shows that a three-year-old from a professional household has a larger vocabulary than an adult from a welfare-dependent one.

Lev Vygotsky's research tells us that vocabulary is stored and used vis-à-vis schema, or networks of thoughts. That is, we make sense of new ideas in relationship to old ones and are more likely to remember words and concepts that are proximal to the things we know and care about. Margaret McKeown's work shows that vocabulary is best learned in a non-threatening environment, a few words at a time. This is important, as Maria Montano-Harmon's work tells us that the longer children exist in poverty, the less "formal" diction and syntax they know.

Built upon this and other research, *Reading with Purpose* equips kids to learn new words organically and at a moderate pace. Vocabulary exercises are not *just* exercises; instead, vocabulary activities extend and deepen students' knowledge of what they are already reading. In this way, these books invite students to use and expand their own schema, one [manageable] step at a time.

Research also shows that many students from impoverished backgrounds lack the ability to think critically about what they read. They don't know how to set a purpose for reading or how to evaluate, draw conclusions about, or summarize the work they're assigned. Many struggle to form and understand questions. Question-making is an important cognitive skill, as it allows us to assess our knowledge (or lack thereof). It is also a reading skill, though, as questioning facilitates connection to and comprehension of the texts that we encounter.

Reading with Purpose teaches students how to ask the questions that matter. It also gives students focused instruction in other reading skills they need. In that vein, this series' Reading, Comparing Literature, and Reading Across Texts Workshops encourage students to become confident, inquisitive, and independent learners by allowing them to practice—and master—proven strategies.

Other research indicates that, for many students from impoverished backgrounds, there exists a significant gap between the culture of home and the culture of school. For example, if a student's home culture is not print-rich, or values oral traditions over written ones, he or she may struggle in school. If a student's home culture is reactive—but his or her classroom culture is proactive—then he or she may struggle in school. Finally, if a student's home culture says that asking questions or discussing ideas openly is rude or disrespectful, then he or she may (and probably will) struggle in school.

This series demonstrates sensitivity toward these and other cultural differences. It utilizes work by men and women of varying ages, races, and ethnicities. The Unit Challenge feature encourages students to begin each unit with an end project in mind; this strategy helps unfocused students become proactive, productive learners. The Analyzing Cartoons feature appeals to visual learners, as do the graphic story selections. The Reading on Your Own feature gives an eager reader the place to begin his or her own reading adventure.

In the United States today, 13 million children live in poverty. Most of them live in urban areas. As educators, we must strive to reach these learners before it is too late. *Reading with Purpose* seeks to do just that, providing these students with the tools they need for learning success.

Guide to Text Readability

Throughout the teacher materials in your **Teacher Wraparound Edition,** you will encounter DRP readability measures assigned to the reading selections in *Reading with Purpose.* You will also find readability scores based on the Lexile Framework® for Reading and the Dale-Chall Readability Formula. You can use these scores to select reading materials that are suitable for your entire class, or individual students.

Degrees of Reading Power® (DRP)

DRP values indicate the readability of prose text. The higher the value, the more difficult the text. The scale ranges from 1 to 100; commonly encountered English text tends to fall somewhere between 25 and 85. Although middle school texts have an average difficulty of 56 and high school texts have an average difficulty of 62, no single readability level is appropriate for each grade level. Rather, a typical classroom has materials with a range of readability levels available for use—some intended for less-proficient readers, some for average readers, and some for stronger readers. The following chart shows the average DRP readability range for materials widely available for use at each grade. Some materials you might use, however, will certainly fall outside the range for your particular grade.

Grade	DRP Readability Ranges
6	51–61
7	52–62
8	53–64
9	53–65
10	51–68
11	56–67
12	57–68

The Lexile® Framework

A lexile measure assigned to a text is the specific number that describes the reading demands of the text. The typical Lexile Scale ranges from 200 to 1700 Lexiles. As with the DRP measures, there is not a direct translation from a specific Lexile measure to a specific grade level. Within any classroom, there will be a range of readers and a range of materials to be read. The levels shown on the following chart indicate the approximate range of Lexile scores for 50 percent of the materials found in a typical grade-level classroom. For example, the middle half of the instructional materials typically found in a sixth-grade classroom range in difficulty from about 850L to 1050L.

Grade	Text Measures (from Lexile Framework Map)
6	850L to 1050L
7	950L to 1075L
8	1000L to 1100L
9	1050L to 1150L
10	1100L to 1200L
11 and 12	1100L to 1300L

Dale-Chall Readability Formula

The Dale-Chall Formula is based on the average sentence length and the number of unfamiliar words in a passage. The idea behind this formula is that readers typically find it easier to read, process, and recall a passage if the words and sentences are familiar and grade appropriate. The Dale-Chall Formula assesses the difficulty of a passage by computing two different values from the text. The first measure is the average number of words per sentence. The second measure is the percentage of words in the passage not found on the grade appropriate Dale Word List. The following chart shows the average Dale-Chall readability scores for grades 5 through 12.

Grade	DRP Readability Ranges
5–6	5.0 to 5.9
7–8	6.0 to 6.9
9–10	7.0 to 7.9
11–12	8.0 to 8.9

* Degrees of Reading Power, DRP, and TASA are registered trademarks of Touchstone Applied Science Associates, Inc. (TASA). Lexile is a registered trademark of MetaMetrics, Inc.

Scope and Sequence

The following charts provide an overview of the scope and sequence for *Reading with Purpose,* Grade 7. A more detailed Skills Scope and Sequence can be found on the interleaf pages preceding each unit.

◉ = focused instruction

● = review

Skills	UNIT 1	UNIT 2	UNIT 3	UNIT 4	UNIT 5	UNIT 6	UNIT 7	UNIT 8
Reading Skills								
Activate prior knowledge		◉	●	●				
Analyze	●	●	●	●	●	◉	●	●
Clarify	●	●	●	●	●	●	●	◉
Compare and contrast	●	●	●	◉	●	●	●	●
Connect	●	◉	●	●	●	●	●	●
Determine main idea and supporting details	●		◉					
Distinguish fact and opinion				◉				
Draw conclusions	●		◉	●	●	●	●	●
Evaluate	●	●	●	●	●	●	◉	●
Identify author's purpose				◉	●			●
Infer	●	◉	●	●	●	●	●	●
Interpret	●		●		●	●	◉	●
Monitor comprehension	●	●	●	●	●	●	◉	●
Paraphrase and summarize	●	●	●	●	◉	●	●	●
Predict						◉		◉
Preview	◉		●					
Question			●			◉		
Respond	●	●	◉	●	●	●	●	●
Review	◉		●		●			
Set a purpose for reading	◉	●	●	●	●	●	●	●
Skim and scan						●		◉
Synthesize		●	◉	●		●	●	
Take notes					◉	●		●
Understand text structure and sequence	◉	◉		◉	◉	◉		●
Use text features		●	●	●	◉		●	●
Visualize								◉

◉ = focused instruction ● = review

Skills	UNIT 1	UNIT 2	UNIT 3	UNIT 4	UNIT 5	UNIT 6	UNIT 7	UNIT 8
Literary Elements								
Author's Craft					◉	●		●
Character			◉		◉	●		
Conflict			◉	●				
Cultural Context						◉		●
Dialect						◉		
Dialogue			◉	●		●		●
Diction and word choice				◉		●		
Figurative language and hyperbole				◉		●	◉	◉
Narrator		◉						
Plot			◉					
Point of view	●	◉						
Rhyme, rhythm, and meter							◉	
Sensory details		◉						●
Setting		◉						
Sound devices							◉	
Style and tone				◉				
Symbolism							◉	
Theme						◉		
Text Elements								
Author's craft and purpose				◉	●	●		●
Concept and definition					◉			
Description and imagery					◉			◉
Organization					◉			◉
Photos and illustrations	◉							
Titles, heads, and leads	◉	●	●					●

Scope and Sequence

● = focused instruction   ● = review

Skills	UNIT 1	UNIT 2	UNIT 3	UNIT 4	UNIT 5	UNIT 6	UNIT 7	UNIT 8
Literary Genres								
Folktales						focused		
Nonfiction	focused	focused	focused	focused	focused	review	review	focused
Poetry	review	review	review	review	review	focused	review	review
Short story	review	review	focused	review	review	review	review	review
Vocabulary Skills								
Clarifying word meaning	review	review	review	review	review	review	focused	review
Compound words								focused
Context and content area clues	focused			focused	review	review		
Denotation/connotation/semantic slanting				focused				
Figurative use of language						focused	review	
Historical influences on English							review	focused
Multiple-meaning words		focused				review		
Structural analysis			focused	focused	focused		review	
Synonyms and antonyms			focused		review	review	review	
Word choice			focused				review	
Word references		focused	review				review	
Writing Skills • Writing Products								
Autobiographical narrative		focused						
Descriptive writing								focused
Editorial				focused				
Modern-day folktale						focused		
Poem							focused	
Research report					focused			
Short fictional story			focused					
Summary	focused							
Writing Skills • Writing Process								
Drafting	focused	review	review	review	review	review	review	review
Editing	focused	review	review	review	review	review	review	review
Presenting/publishing	focused	review	review	review	review	review	review	review

● = focused instruction ● = review

Skills	UNIT 1	UNIT 2	UNIT 3	UNIT 4	UNIT 5	UNIT 6	UNIT 7	UNIT 8
Writing Skills • Writing Process								
Prewriting	● (focused)	● (review)	● (review)	● (review)	● (review)	● (review)	● (review)	● (review)
Proofreading	● (focused)	● (review)	● (review)	● (review)	● (review)	● (review)	● (review)	● (review)
Revising	● (focused)	● (review)	● (review)	● (review)	● (review)	● (review)	● (review)	● (review)
Writing Skills • Writing Traits								
Conventions	● (focused)							
Ideas					● (focused)			
Organization			● (focused)					
Presentation						● (focused)		
Sentence fluency and variety								● (focused)
Voice		● (focused)						
Word Choice				● (focused)			● (focused)	
Writing Skills • Grammar								
Adjectives and adverbs	● (review)		● (focused)					
Commas					● (focused)	● (review)		
Simple, compound, and complex sentences				● (focused)		● (focused)		● (review)
Nouns	● (review)	● (focused)						
Phrases and clauses	● (review)		● (review)		● (focused)	● (review)		
Pronouns	● (review)	● (focused)					● (review)	
Punctuation			● (review)	● (focused)				● (review)
Subject-verb agreement	● (review)						● (focused)	
Verbs	● (focused)			● (review)			● (review)	
Listening, Speaking, and Viewing								
Giving and following directions	● (focused)			● (review)				
Group discussion and active listening	● (review)	● (focused)	● (review)	● (review)	● (review)	● (review)	● (review)	● (review)
Oral presentations					● (focused)		● (review)	
Oral reading and storytelling			● (focused)			● (focused)	● (review)	
Persuasive techniques			● (review)	● (focused)				
Using visuals	● (review)	● (review)	● (review)	● (review)	● (review)	● (review)	● (review)	● (focused)
Viewing art, photographs, and cartoons	● (focused)	● (review)	● (review)	● (review)	● (review)	● (review)	● (review)	● (review)

Teacher Edition Walk-Through

To Teachers:

Welcome to the Teacher Wraparound Edition of *Glencoe Literature: Reading with Purpose.* We have created this teacher edition based on input from experienced teachers and educational consultants. Teaching suggestions, additional resources, and leveled activities for differentiated instruction are all labeled and "wrapped" around the student text for your convenience.

Planning the Unit

Planning pages appear at the beginning of each unit.

Unit Preview Tells you about the Big Question and genre focus found in the unit

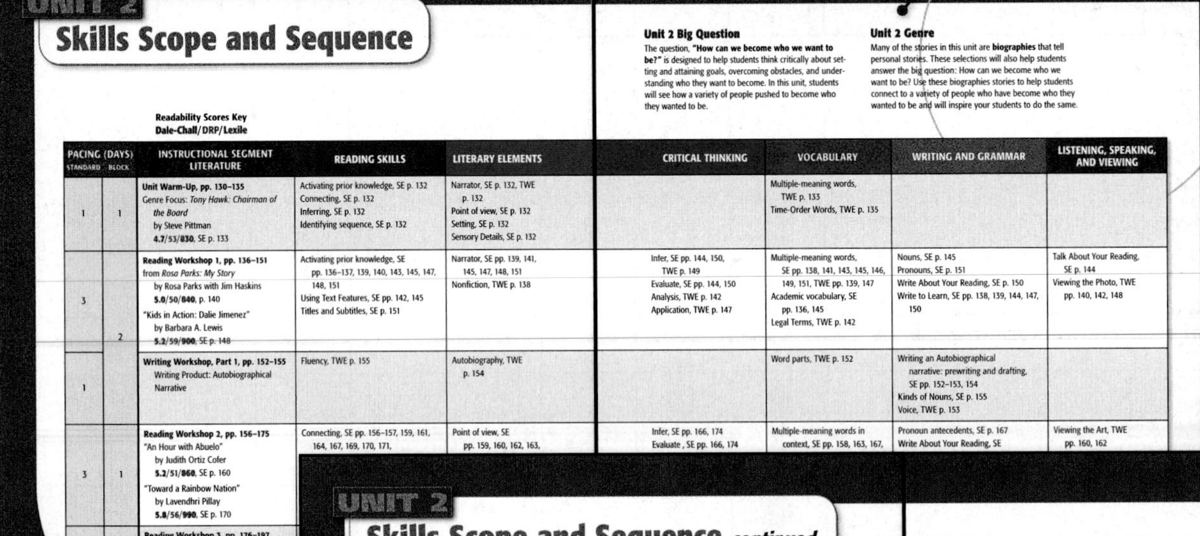

UNIT 2

Skills Scope and Sequence

Unit 2 Big Question
The question, **"How can we become who we want to be?"** is designed to help students think critically about setting and attaining goals, overcoming obstacles, and understanding who they want to become. In this unit, students will see how a variety of people pushed to become who they wanted to be.

Unit 2 Genre
Many of the stories in this unit are **biographies** that tell personal stories. These selections will also help students answer the big question: How can we become who we want to be? Use these biographies stories to help students connect to a variety of people who have become who they wanted to be and will inspire your students to do the same.

Readability Scores Key
Dale-Chall/DRP/Lexile

PACING (DAYS) STANDARD	BLOCK	INSTRUCTIONAL SEGMENT LITERATURE	READING SKILLS	LITERARY ELEMENTS	CRITICAL THINKING	VOCABULARY	WRITING AND GRAMMAR	LISTENING, SPEAKING, AND VIEWING
1	1	**Unit Warm-Up, pp. 130–135** Genre Focus: *Tony Hawk: Chairman of the Board* by Steve Pittman **4.7/53/830**, SE p. 133	Activating prior knowledge, SE p. 132 Connecting, SE p. 132 Inferring, SE p. 132 Identifying sequence, SE p. 132	Narrator, SE p. 132, TWE p. 132 Point of view, SE p. 132 Setting, SE p. 132 Sensory Details, SE p. 132		Multiple-meaning words, TWE p. 133 Time-Order Words, TWE p. 135		
3	2	**Reading Workshop 1, pp. 136–151** from *Rosa Parks: My Story* by Rosa Parks with Jim Haskins **5.0/50/840**, p. 140 "Kids in Action: Dalie Jimenez" by Barbara A. Lewis **5.2/59/900**, SE p. 148	Activating prior knowledge, SE pp. 136–137, 139, 140, 143, 145, 147, 148, 151 Using Text Features, SE pp. 142, 145 Titles and Subtitles, SE p. 151	Narrator, SE pp. 139, 141, 145, 147, 148, 151 Nonfiction, TWE p. 138	Infer, SE pp. 144, 150, TWE p. 149 Evaluate, SE pp. 144, 150 Analysis, TWE p. 142 Application, TWE p. 147	Multiple-meaning words, SE pp. 138, 141, 143, 145, 146, 149, 151, TWE pp. 139, 147 Academic vocabulary, SE pp. 136, 145 Legal Terms, TWE p. 142	Nouns, SE p. 145 Pronouns, SE p. 151 Write About Your Reading, SE p. 150 Write to Learn, SE pp. 138, 139, 144, 147, 150	Talk About Your Reading, SE p. 144 Viewing the Photo, TWE pp. 140, 142, 148
1		**Writing Workshop, Part 1, pp. 152–155** Writing Product: Autobiographical Narrative	Fluency, TWE p. 155	Autobiography, TWE p. 154		Word parts, TWE p. 152	Writing an Autobiographical narrative: prewriting and drafting, SE pp. 152–153, 154 Kinds of Nouns, SE p. 155 Voice, TWE p. 153	
3	1	**Reading Workshop 2, pp. 156–175** "An Hour with Abuelo" by Judith Ortiz Cofer **5.2/51/860**, SE p. 160 "Toward a Rainbow Nation" by Lavendhri Pillay **5.8/56/990**, SE p. 170	Connecting, SE pp. 156–157, 159, 161, 164, 167, 169, 170, 171,	Point of view, SE pp. 159, 160, 162, 163,	Infer, SE pp. 166, 174 Evaluate , SE pp. 166, 174	Multiple-meaning words in context, SE pp. 158, 163, 167,	Pronoun antecedents, SE p. 167 Write About Your Reading, SE	Viewing the Art, TWE pp. 160, 162
3	1	**Reading Workshop 3, pp. 176–197** "New Directions" by Maya Angelou **6.4/61/1360**, SE p. 180 "The War of the Wall" by Toni Cade Bambara **5.1/53/930**, SE p. 188						

UNIT 2

Skills Scope and Sequence *continued*

Readability Scores Key
Dale-Chall/DRP/Lexile

PACING (DAYS) STANDARD	BLOCK	INSTRUCTIONAL SEGMENT LITERATURE	READING SKILLS	LITERARY ELEMENTS	CRITICAL THINKING	VOCABULARY	WRITING AND GRAMMAR	LISTENING, SPEAKING, AND VIEWING
1	cont'd.	**Writing Workshop, Part 2, pp. 198–203** Writing Product: Autobiographical Narrative	Fluency, TWE p. 201	Author's Purpose, TWE p. 202	Comprehension, TWE p. 201	Word Choice, TWE p. 199 First Person Point of View, TWE p. 198	Writing an Autobiographical Narrative: Revising, Editing, and Presenting, SE p. 198–203 Writing Traits: Voice, SE p. 199 Creative writing, TWE p. 200	Group Discussion and Active Listening, SE p. 203 Staying focused, TWE p. 203
2	1	**Reading Workshop 4, pp. 204–221** from *Red Scarf Girl: A Memoir of the Cultural Revolution* by Ji-li Jiang **5.1/52/760**, SE p. 208 "Miracle Hands" TIME by Christina Cheakalos and Matt Birkbeck **6.2/58/920**, SE p. 218	Understanding sequence, SE pp. 204–205, 207, 212, 215, 217, 218, 219, 221 Connecting, SE pp. 208, 211, 215 Fluency, TWE p. 211 Title and Subtitle, SE p. 221	Sensory Details, SE pp. 207, 209, 213, 215, 217, 218, 221; TWE pp. 207, 216 Narrators, TWE p. 205 Point of view, TWE p. 208 Dialogue, TWE p. 212 Time order, TWE p. 218	Infer, SE pp. 214, 220 Summarize, SE pp. 214, 220 Synthesize, SE p. 214 Analyze, SE p. 220, TWE pp. 210, 217 Comprehension, TWE pp. 205, 207–209, 218	Using Word References, SE pp. 206, 215, 216 Multiple-meaning words, SE pp. 210, 218, 219, 221 Academic Vocabulary, SE p. 215 Vocabulary Practice, TWE p. 210	Write About Your Reading, SE p. 220 Write to Learn, SE pp. 206, 207, 216, 217 Object Pronouns, SE p. 221 Poem, TWE p. 210 Subject Pronouns, SE p. 215	Talk About Your Reading, SE p. 214 Viewing the Photo, TWE p. 209
2	2	**Comparing Literature Workshop, pp. 222–235** from *Barrio Boy,* by Ernesto Galarza **6.4/58/1100**, SE p. 225 "How I Learned English" by Gregory Djanikian SE p. 232	Fluency, TWE p. 233 Infer, TWE pp. 227, 228 Connecting, TWE p. 233	Comparing Settings, SE pp. 222–223, 225, 227, 229, 232, 235 Sequence of Events, TWE p. 232 Character, TWE p. 230 Analyzing setting, TWE p. 222 Description, TWE p. 227 Point of View, TWE pp. 228, 232	Interpret, SE p. 235 Infer, SE p. 235 Comprehension, TWE pp. 226, 232 Evaluate, TWE pp. 227, 229, 230, 233	Multiple-meaning words, SE pp. 226, 231 Description, TWE pp. 226, 227 Prefixes, TWE p. 228 Baseball Terms, TWE p. 231	Taking notes and using them to make a chart that compares the setting in two pieces of literature, SE p. 235	Viewing the Photo, TWE p. 225
2	1	**Unit Wrap-Up, pp. 236–249** "Graduation Address" by Robert L. Fontaine **4.5/47/NA**, SE p. 238	Reading independently, SE pp. 242–243	Summary, TWE p. 238	Application, TWE p. 239 Comprehension, TWE p. 239 Analysis, TWE p. 240		Writing a personal letter, SE p. 236 Organizing thoughts using a web diagram, SE p. 237 Speech writing, TWE p. 240	Speech Writing, TWE p. 240

Pacing Chart Specifies skills to each selection and provides time management suggestions for teaching the unit

Teaching the Unit

Objectives Lists the main teaching goals of the unit

BQ Focus Some text about the connections and importance of the unit Big Question

Reading Preview Background about the skills and selections taught in the unit and how to use the material to help students answer the Big Question

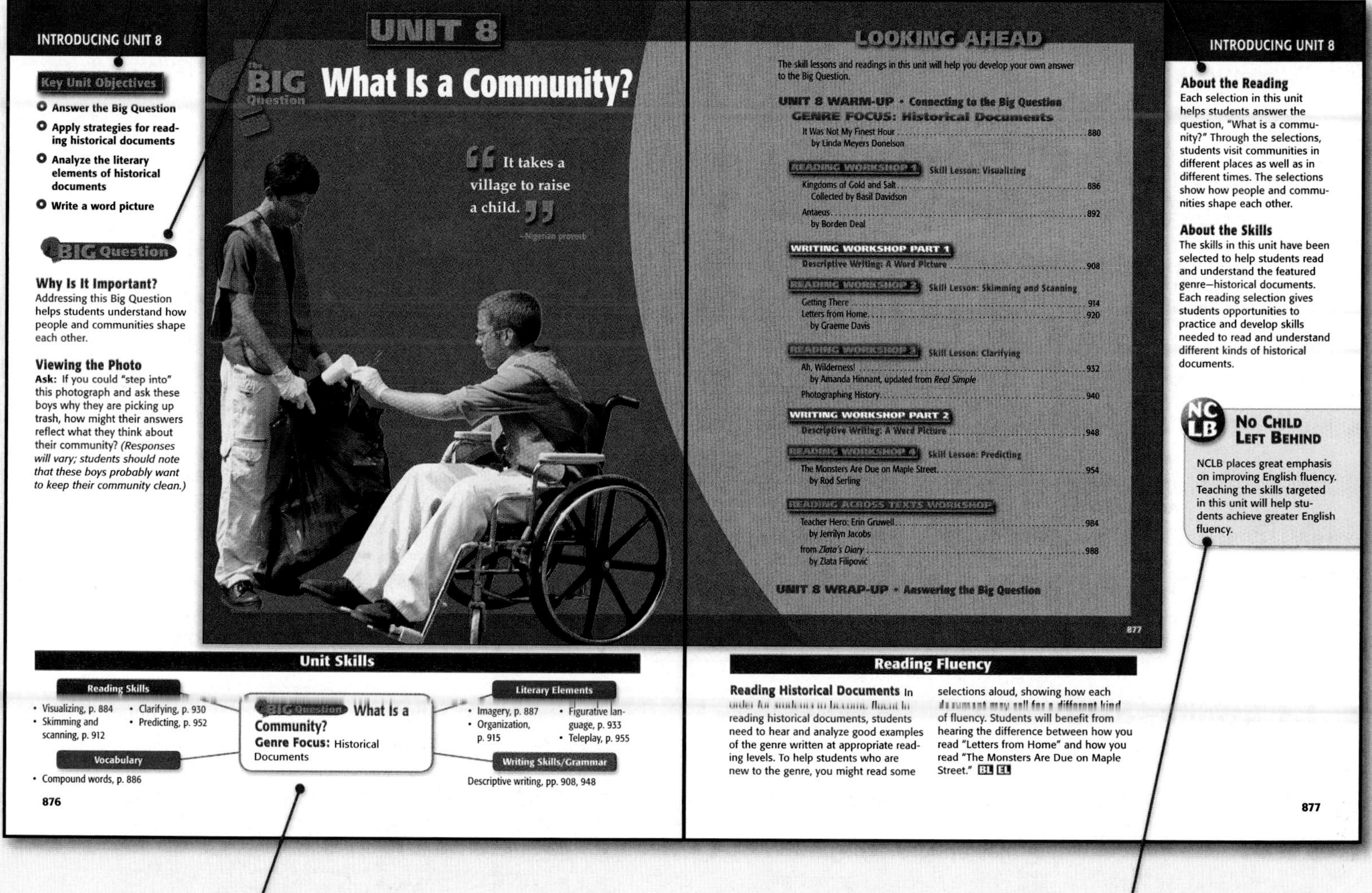

INTRODUCING UNIT 8

Key Unit Objectives

- Answer the Big Question
- Apply strategies for reading historical documents
- Analyze the literary elements of historical documents
- Write a word picture

BIG Question

Why Is It Important?
Addressing this Big Question helps students understand how people and communities shape each other.

Viewing the Photo
Ask: If you could "step into" this photograph and ask these boys why they are picking up trash, how might their answers reflect what they think about their community? *(Responses will vary; students should note that these boys probably want to keep their community clean.)*

UNIT 8

BIG Question **What Is a Community?**

"It takes a village to raise a child."

—Nigerian proverb

LOOKING AHEAD

The skill lessons and readings in this unit will help you develop your own answer to the Big Question.

877

INTRODUCING UNIT 8

About the Reading
Each selection in this unit helps students answer the question, "What is a community?" Through the selections, students visit communities in different places as well as in different times. The selections show how people and communities shape each other.

About the Skills
The skills in this unit have been selected to help students read and understand the featured genre—historical documents. Each reading selection gives students opportunities to practice and develop skills needed to read and understand different kinds of historical documents.

NCLB No Child Left Behind
NCLB places great emphasis on improving English fluency. Teaching the skills targeted in this unit will help students achieve greater English fluency.

Unit Skills

Reading Skills
- Visualizing, p. 884
- Skimming and scanning, p. 912
- Clarifying, p. 930
- Predicting, p. 952

Vocabulary
- Compound words, p. 886

BIG Question **What Is a Community?**
Genre Focus: Historical Documents

Literary Elements
- Imagery, p. 887
- Organization, p. 915
- Figurative language, p. 933
- Teleplay, p. 955

Writing Skills/Grammar
Descriptive writing, pp. 908, 948

876

Reading Fluency

Reading Historical Documents In order for students to become fluent in reading historical documents, students need to hear and analyze good examples of the genre written at appropriate reading levels. To help students who are new to the genre, you might read some selections aloud, showing how each document may call for a different kind of fluency. Students will benefit from hearing the difference between how you read "Letters from Home" and how you read "The Monsters Are Due on Maple Street." BL EL

877

Quick Skill Reference Convenient page reference of unit skills

NCLB Provides suggestions for meeting No Child Left Behind requirements

Understanding the Brackets and Letters

Letters The letters on the reduced student edition page identify the type of skill or activity. See the key below to learn about the different types of skills and activities.

Brackets Brackets on the reduced student edition page correspond to teaching the skills and activities. The brackets show you exactly where to teach the skills and activities for each workshop.

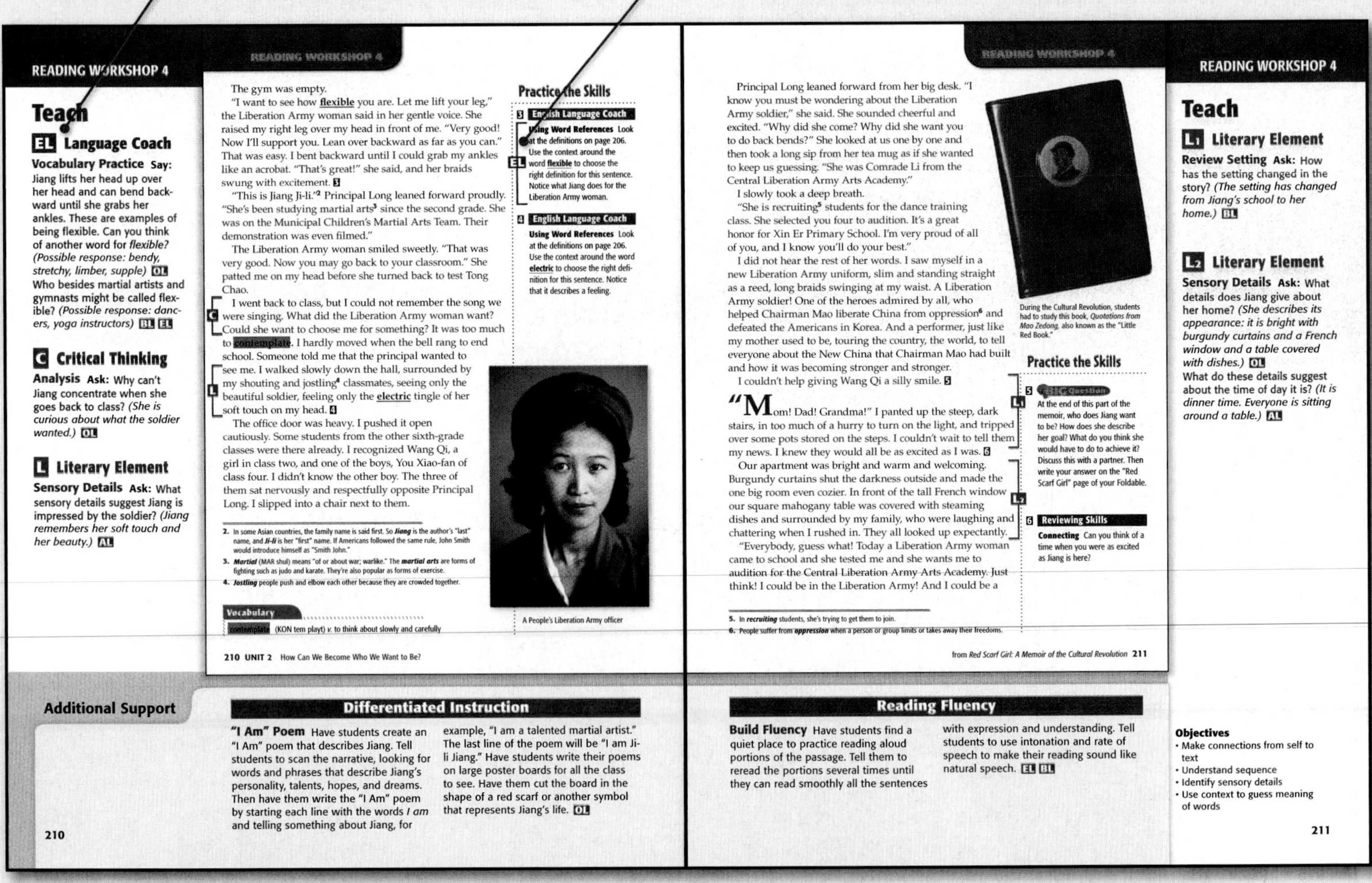

READING WORKSHOP 4

Teach

EL Language Coach

Vocabulary Practice Say: Jiang lifts her head up over her head and can bend backward until she grabs her ankles. These are examples of being flexible. Can you think of another word for *flexible?* *(Possible response: bendy, stretchy, limber, supple)* OL Who besides martial artists and gymnasts might be called flexible? *(Possible response: dancers, yoga instructors)* BL EL

C Critical Thinking

Analysis Ask: Why can't Jiang concentrate when she goes back to class? *(She is curious about what the soldier wanted.)* OL

L Literary Element

Sensory Details Ask: What sensory details suggest Jiang is impressed by the soldier? *(Jiang remembers her soft touch and her beauty.)* AL

READING WORKSHOP 4

The gym was empty.

"I want to see how **flexible** you are. Let me lift your leg," the Liberation Army woman said in her gentle voice. She raised my right leg over my head in front of me. "Very good! Now I'll support you. Lean over backward as far as you can." That was easy. I bent backward until I could grab my ankles like an acrobat. "That's great!" she said, and her braids swung with excitement. 3

"This is Jiang Ji-li."[2] Principal Long leaned forward proudly. "She's been studying martial arts[3] since the second grade. She was on the Municipal Children's Martial Arts Team. Their demonstration was even filmed."

The Liberation Army woman smiled sweetly. "That was very good. Now you may go back to your classroom." She patted me on my head before she turned back to test Tong Chao.

C I went back to class, but I could not remember the song we were singing. What did the Liberation Army woman want? Could she want to choose me for something? It was too much to **contemplate**. I hardly moved when the bell rang to end school. Someone told me that the principal wanted to L see me. I walked slowly down the hall, surrounded by my shouting and jostling[4] classmates, seeing only the beautiful soldier, feeling only the **electric** tingle of her soft touch on my head. 4

The office door was heavy. I pushed it open cautiously. Some students from the other sixth-grade classes were there already. I recognized Wang Qi, a girl in class two, and one of the boys, You Xiao-fan of class four. I didn't know the other boy. The three of them sat nervously and respectfully opposite Principal Long. I slipped into a chair next to them.

2. In some Asian countries, the family name is said first. So ***Jiang*** is the author's "last" name, and ***Ji-li*** is her "first" name. If Americans followed the same rule, John Smith would introduce himself as "Smith John."
3. ***Martial*** (MAR shul) means "of or about war; warlike." The ***martial arts*** are forms of fighting such as judo and karate. They're also popular as forms of exercise.
4. ***Jostling*** people push and elbow each other because they are crowded together.

Vocabulary

contemplate (KON tem playt) *v.* to think about slowly and carefully

Practice the Skills

3 **English Language Coach**

EL **Using Word References** Look at the definitions on page 206. Use the context around the word **flexible** to choose the right definition for this sentence. Notice what Jiang does for the Liberation Army woman.

4 **English Language Coach**

Using Word References Look at the definitions on page 206. Use the context around the word **electric** to choose the right definition for this sentence. Notice that it describes a feeling.

A People's Liberation Army officer

210 UNIT 2 How Can We Become Who We Want to Be?

Principal Long leaned forward from her big desk. "I know you must be wondering about the Liberation Army soldier," she said. She sounded cheerful and excited. "Why did she come? Why did she want you to do back bends?" She looked at us one by one and then took a long sip from her tea mug as if she wanted to keep us guessing. "She was Comrade Li from the Central Liberation Army Arts Academy."

I slowly took a deep breath.

"She is recruiting[5] students for the dance training class. She selected you four to audition. It's a great honor for Xin Er Primary School. I'm very proud of all of you, and I know you'll do your best."

I did not hear the rest of her words. I saw myself in a new Liberation Army uniform, slim and standing straight as a reed, long braids swinging at my waist. A Liberation Army soldier! One of the heroes admired by all, who helped Chairman Mao liberate China from oppression[6] and defeated the Americans in Korea. And a performer, just like my mother used to be, touring the country, the world, to tell everyone about the New China that Chairman Mao had built and how it was becoming stronger and stronger.

I couldn't help giving Wang Qi a silly smile. 5

L1 "Mom! Dad! Grandma!" I panted up the steep, dark stairs, in too much of a hurry to turn on the light, and tripped over some pots stored on the steps. I couldn't wait to tell them my news. I knew they would all be as excited as I was. 6

L2 Our apartment was bright and warm and welcoming. Burgundy curtains shut the darkness outside and made the one big room even cozier. In front of the tall French window our square mahogany table was covered with steaming dishes and surrounded by my family, who were laughing and chattering when I rushed in. They all looked up expectantly.

"Everybody, guess what! Today a Liberation Army woman came to school and she tested me and she wants me to audition for the Central Liberation Army Arts Academy. Just think! I could be in the Liberation Army! And I could be a

5. In ***recruiting*** students, she's trying to get them to join.
6. People suffer from ***oppression*** when a person or group limits or takes away their freedoms.

During the Cultural Revolution, students had to study this book, *Quotations from Mao Zedong,* also known as the "Little Red Book."

Practice the Skills

5 **BIG Question**

At the end of this part of the memoir, who does Jiang want to be? How does she describe her goal? What do you think she would have to do to achieve it? Discuss this with a partner. Then write your answer on the "Red Scarf Girl" page of your Foldable.

6 **Reviewing Skills**

Connecting Can you think of a time when you were as excited as Jiang is here?

from *Red Scarf Girl: A Memoir of the Cultural Revolution* 211

READING WORKSHOP 4

Teach

L1 Literary Element

Review Setting Ask: How has the setting changed in the story? *(The setting has changed from Jiang's school to her home.)* BL

L2 Literary Element

Sensory Details Ask: What details does Jiang give about her home? *(She describes its appearance: it is bright with burgundy curtains and a French window and a table covered with dishes.)* OL What do these details suggest about the time of day it is? *(It is dinner time. Everyone is sitting around a table.)* AL

Additional Support

Differentiated Instruction

"I Am" Poem Have students create an "I Am" poem that describes Jiang. Tell students to scan the narrative, looking for words and phrases that describe Jiang's personality, talents, hopes, and dreams. Then have them write the "I Am" poem by starting each line with the words *I am* and telling something about Jiang, for example, "I am a talented martial artist." The last line of the poem will be "I am Ji-li Jiang." Have students write their poems on large poster boards for all the class to see. Have them cut the board in the shape of a red scarf or another symbol that represents Jiang's life. OL

210

Reading Fluency

Build Fluency Have students find a quiet place to practice reading aloud portions of the passage. Tell them to reread the portions several times until they can read smoothly all the sentences with expression and understanding. Tell students to use intonation and rate of speech to make their reading sound like natural speech. EL BL

Objectives
- Make connections from self to text
- Understand sequence
- Identify sensory details
- Use context to guess meaning of words

211

Teacher Wraparound Edition Key

R Reading Skill These activities help you teach reading skills and vocabulary.

V Vocabulary These activities help students comprehend words and incorporate into reading.

C Critical Thinking These strategies help students apply and extend what they have learned.

BQ BIG Question These activities and questions prompt students to prepare to answer the Big Question.

E Text Element These activities help students recognize and understand the use of text elements.

W Writing These activities provide writing opportunities to help students practice writing and comprehend text.

L Literary Element These activities and questions help students comprehend selections and learn more about each genre.

LSV Listening, Speaking, Viewing These activities help students practice listening, speaking, and viewing skills.

EL English Language Coach These skills help English language learners as well as students who need additional reading support.

Activity Leveling

Activity Leveling Teaching strategies and activities have been coded for ability level appropriateness. A competency level is given for each activity using the following code.

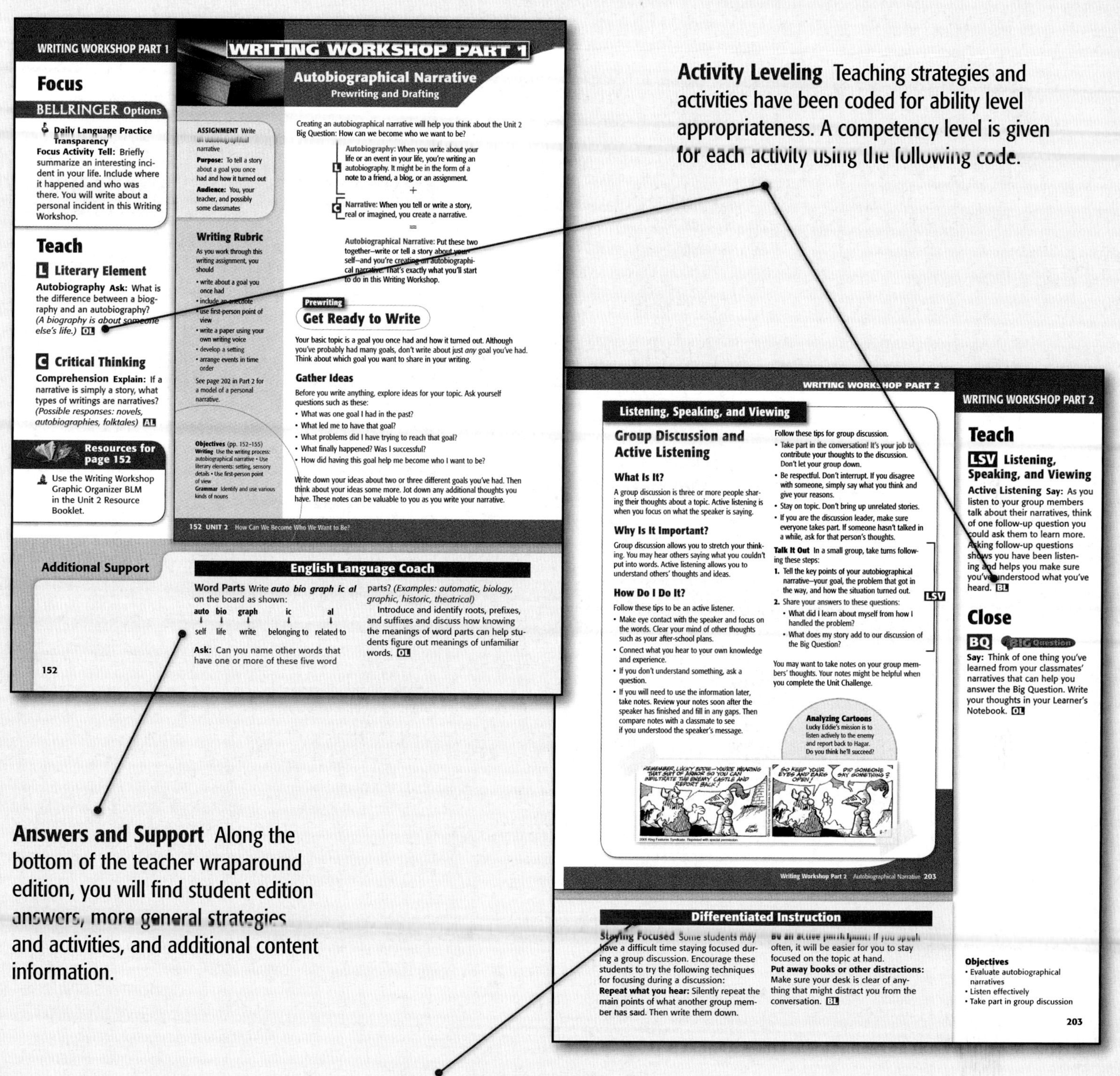

WRITING WORKSHOP PART 1

Focus

BELLRINGER Options

Daily Language Practice Transparency
Focus Activity Tell: Briefly summarize an interesting incident in your life. Include where it happened and who was there. You will write about a personal incident in this Writing Workshop.

Teach

L Literary Element
Autobiography Ask: What is the difference between a biography and an autobiography? *(A biography is about someone else's life.)* OL

C Critical Thinking
Comprehension Explain: If a narrative is simply a story, what types of writings are narratives? *(Possible responses: novels, autobiographies, folktales)* AL

Resources for page 152
Use the Writing Workshop Graphic Organizer BLM in the Unit 2 Resource Booklet.

WRITING WORKSHOP PART 1

Autobiographical Narrative
Prewriting and Drafting

ASSIGNMENT Write an autobiographical narrative
Purpose: To tell a story about a goal you once had and how it turned out
Audience: You, your teacher, and possibly some classmates

Writing Rubric
As you work through this writing assignment, you should
- write about a goal you once had
- include an anecdote
- use first-person point of view
- write a paper using your own writing voice
- develop a setting
- arrange events in time order

See page 202 in Part 2 for a model of a personal narrative.

Objectives (pp. 152–155)
Writing Use the writing process: autobiographical narrative • Use literary elements: setting, sensory details • Use first-person point of view
Grammar Identify and use various kinds of nouns

Creating an autobiographical narrative will help you think about the Unit 2 Big Question: How can we become who we want to be?

L Autobiography: When you write about your life or an event in your life, you're writing an autobiography. It might be in the form of a note to a friend, a blog, or an assignment.
+
C Narrative: When you tell or write a story, real or imagined, you create a narrative.
=
Autobiographical Narrative: Put these two together—write or tell a story about yourself—and you're creating an autobiographical narrative. That's exactly what you'll start to do in this Writing Workshop.

Prewriting
Get Ready to Write
Your basic topic is a goal you once had and how it turned out. Although you've probably had many goals, don't write about just *any* goal you've had. Think about which goal you want to share in your writing.

Gather Ideas
Before you write anything, explore ideas for your topic. Ask yourself questions such as these:
- What was one goal I had in the past?
- What led me to have that goal?
- What problems did I have trying to reach that goal?
- What finally happened? Was I successful?
- How did having this goal help me become who I want to be?

Write down your ideas about two or three different goals you've had. Then think about your ideas some more. Jot down any additional thoughts you have. These notes can be valuable to you as you write your narrative.

152 UNIT 2 How Can We Become Who We Want to Be?

Additional Support

English Language Coach
Word Parts Write ***auto bio graph ic al*** on the board as shown:

auto	bio	graph	ic	al
↓	↓	↓	↓	↓
self	life	write	belonging to	related to

Ask: Can you name other words that have one or more of these five word parts? *(Examples: automatic, biology, graphic, historic, theatrical)*
Introduce and identify roots, prefixes, and suffixes and discuss how knowing the meanings of word parts can help students figure out meanings of unfamiliar words. OL

152

WRITING WORKSHOP PART 2

Listening, Speaking, and Viewing

Group Discussion and Active Listening

What Is It?
A group discussion is three or more people sharing their thoughts about a topic. Active listening is when you focus on what the speaker is saying.

Why Is It Important?
Group discussion allows you to stretch your thinking. You may hear others saying what you couldn't put into words. Active listening allows you to understand others' thoughts and ideas.

How Do I Do It?
Follow these tips to be an active listener.
- Make eye contact with the speaker and focus on the words. Clear your mind of other thoughts such as your after-school plans.
- Connect what you hear to your own knowledge and experience.
- If you don't understand something, ask a question.
- If you will need to use the information later, take notes. Review your notes soon after the speaker has finished and fill in any gaps. Then compare notes with a classmate to see if you understood the speaker's message.

Follow these tips for group discussion.
- Take part in the conversation! It's your job to contribute your thoughts to the discussion. Don't let your group down.
- Be respectful. Don't interrupt. If you disagree with someone, simply say what you think and give your reasons.
- Stay on topic. Don't bring up unrelated stories.
- If you are the discussion leader, make sure everyone takes part. If someone hasn't talked in a while, ask for that person's thoughts.

Talk It Out In a small group, take turns following these steps:
1. Tell the key points of your autobiographical narrative—your goal, the problem that got in the way, and how the situation turned out.
2. Share your answers to these questions:
   - What did I learn about myself from how I handled the problem?
   - What does my story add to our discussion of the Big Question?

LSV

You may want to take notes on your group members' thoughts. Your notes might be helpful when you complete the Unit Challenge.

Analyzing Cartoons
Lucky Eddie's mission is to listen actively to the enemy and report back to Hagar. Do you think he'll succeed?

REMEMBER, LUCKY EDDIE—YOU'RE WEARING THAT SUIT OF ARMOR SO YOU CAN INFILTRATE THE ENEMY CASTLE AND REPORT BACK!
SO KEEP YOUR EYES AND EARS OPEN!
DID SOMEONE SAY SOMETHING?

2005 King Features Syndicate. Reprinted with special permission.

Writing Workshop Part 2 Autobiographical Narrative 203

WRITING WORKSHOP PART 2

Teach

LSV Listening, Speaking, and Viewing
Active Listening Say: As you listen to your group members talk about their narratives, think of one follow-up question you could ask them to learn more. Asking follow-up questions shows you have been listening and helps you make sure you've understood what you've heard. BL

Close

BQ BIG Question
Say: Think of one thing you've learned from your classmates' narratives that can help you answer the Big Question. Write your thoughts in your Learner's Notebook. OL

Answers and Support Along the bottom of the teacher wraparound edition, you will find student edition answers, more general strategies and activities, and additional content information.

Differentiated Instruction
Staying Focused Some students may have a difficult time staying focused during a group discussion. Encourage these students to try the following techniques for focusing during a discussion:
Repeat what you hear: Silently repeat the main points of what another group member has said. Then write them down.
Be an active participant: If you speak often, it will be easier for you to stay focused on the topic at hand.
Put away books or other distractions: Make sure your desk is clear of anything that might distract you from the conversation. BL

Objectives
- Evaluate autobiographical narratives
- Listen effectively
- Take part in group discussion

203

Differentiated Instruction These activities are geared to meet the needs of today's diverse classrooms.

Workshop Structure

The instructions in each workshop in *Reading with Purpose* is presented in a structured lesson plan: Focus, Teach, Assess, and Close.

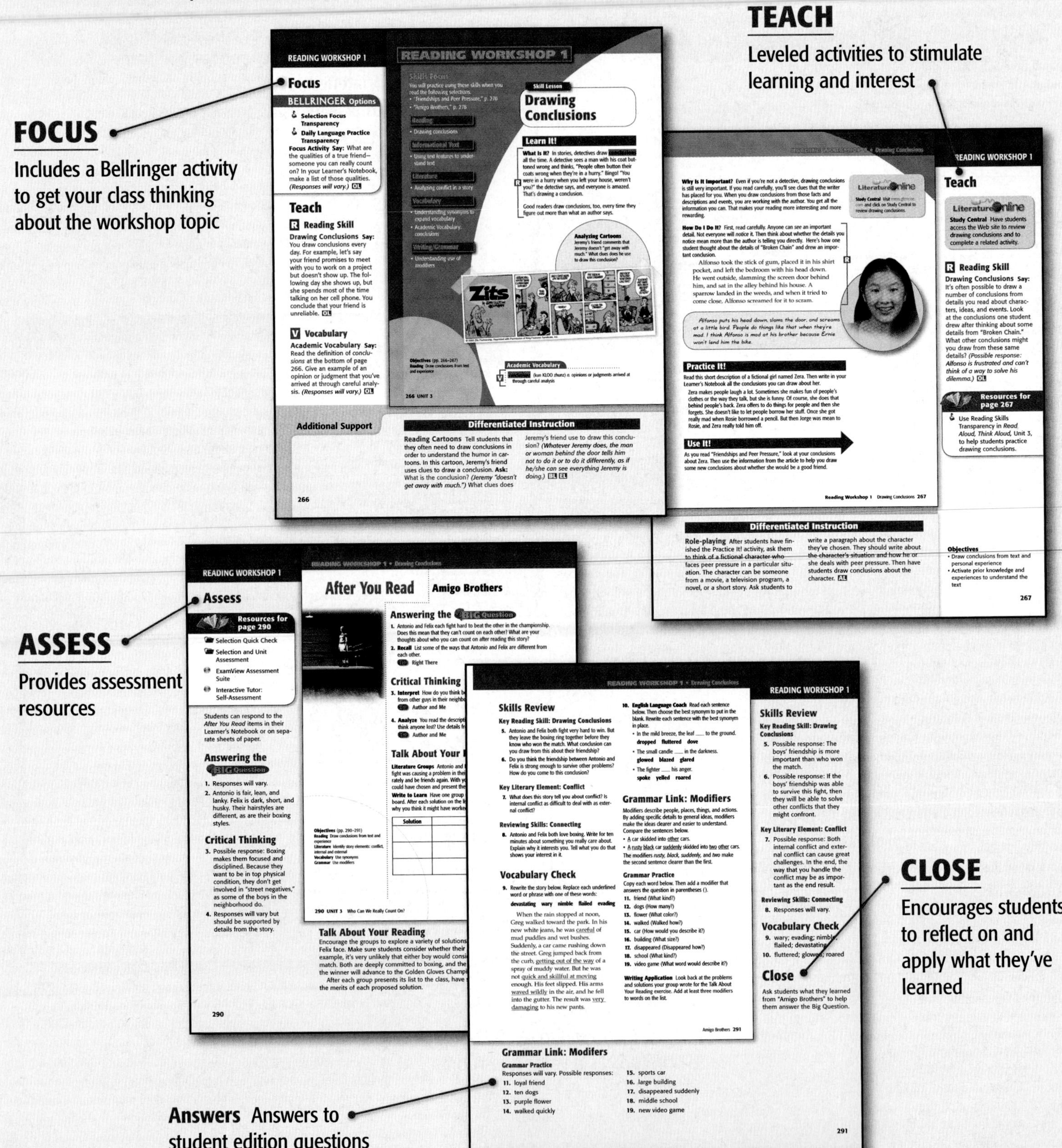

TEACH

Leveled activities to stimulate learning and interest

FOCUS

Includes a Bellringer activity to get your class thinking about the workshop topic

ASSESS

Provides assessment resources

CLOSE

Encourages students to reflect on and apply what they've learned

Answers Answers to student edition questions

Resources and Support

For every unit the teacher wraparound edition includes a page of additional teaching resources and online support for both you and your students.

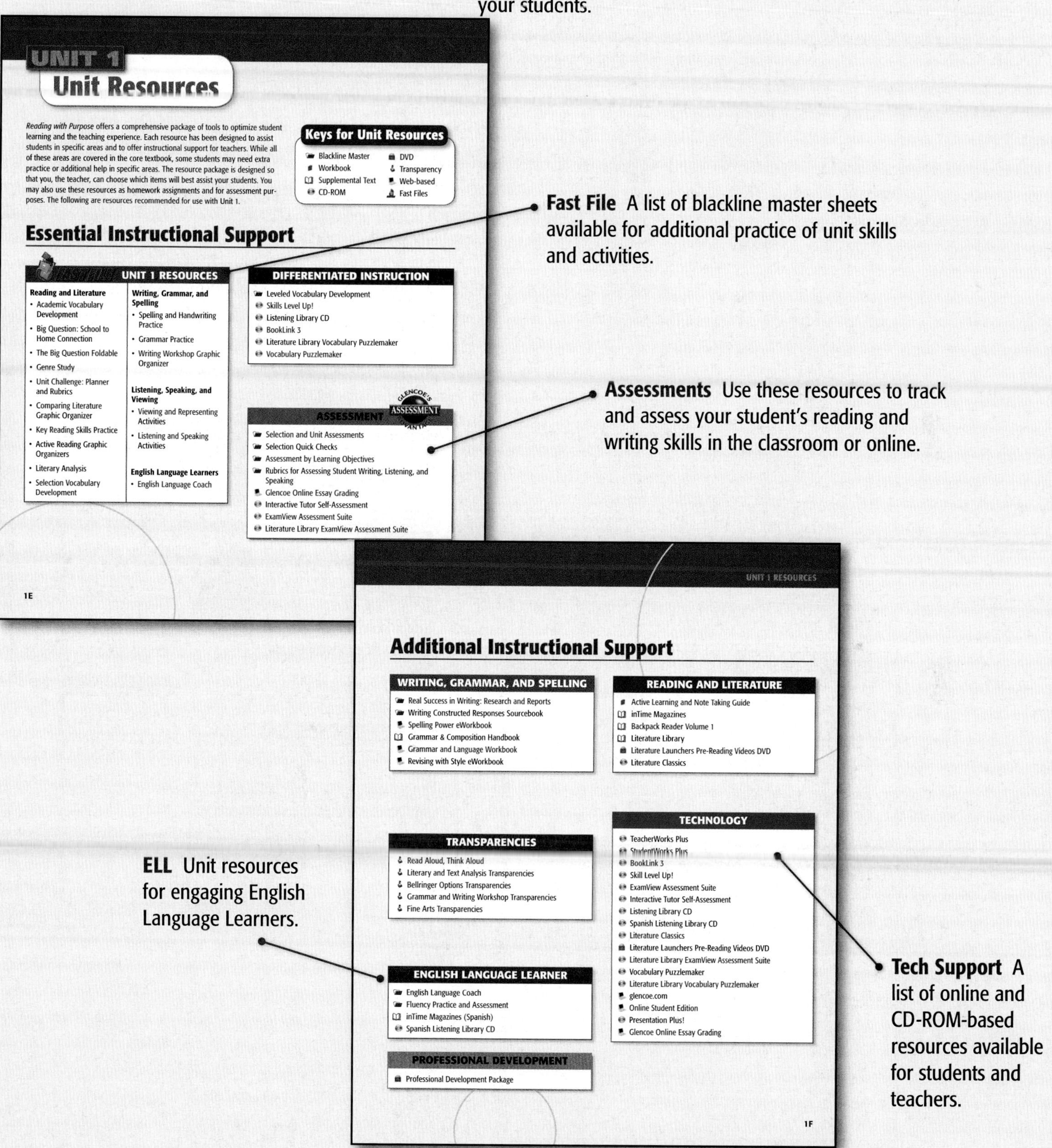

UNIT 1

Unit Resources

Reading with Purpose offers a comprehensive package of tools to optimize student learning and the teaching experience. Each resource has been designed to assist students in specific areas and to offer instructional support for teachers. While all of these areas are covered in the core textbook, some students may need extra practice or additional help in specific areas. The resource package is designed so that you, the teacher, can choose which items will best assist your students. You may also use these resources as homework assignments and for assessment purposes. The following are resources recommended for use with Unit 1.

Keys for Unit Resources

- Blackline Master
- Workbook
- Supplemental Text
- CD-ROM
- DVD
- Transparency
- Web-based
- Fast Files

Essential Instructional Support

UNIT 1 RESOURCES

Reading and Literature
- Academic Vocabulary Development
- Big Question: School to Home Connection
- The Big Question Foldable
- Genre Study
- Unit Challenge: Planner and Rubrics
- Comparing Literature Graphic Organizer
- Key Reading Skills Practice
- Active Reading Graphic Organizers
- Literary Analysis
- Selection Vocabulary Development

Writing, Grammar, and Spelling
- Spelling and Handwriting Practice
- Grammar Practice
- Writing Workshop Graphic Organizer

Listening, Speaking, and Viewing
- Viewing and Representing Activities
- Listening and Speaking Activities

English Language Learners
- English Language Coach

DIFFERENTIATED INSTRUCTION
- Leveled Vocabulary Development
- Skills Level Up!
- Listening Library CD
- BookLink 3
- Literature Library Vocabulary Puzzlemaker
- Vocabulary Puzzlemaker

ASSESSMENT (Glencoe's Assessment Advantage)
- Selection and Unit Assessments
- Selection Quick Checks
- Assessment by Learning Objectives
- Rubrics for Assessing Student Writing, Listening, and Speaking
- Glencoe Online Essay Grading
- Interactive Tutor Self-Assessment
- ExamView Assessment Suite
- Literature Library ExamView Assessment Suite

1E

UNIT 1 RESOURCES

Additional Instructional Support

WRITING, GRAMMAR, AND SPELLING
- Real Success in Writing: Research and Reports
- Writing Constructed Responses Sourcebook
- Spelling Power eWorkbook
- Grammar & Composition Handbook
- Grammar and Language Workbook
- Revising with Style eWorkbook

READING AND LITERATURE
- Active Learning and Note Taking Guide
- inTime Magazines
- Backpack Reader Volume 1
- Literature Library
- Literature Launchers Pre-Reading Videos DVD
- Literature Classics

TRANSPARENCIES
- Read Aloud, Think Aloud
- Literary and Text Analysis Transparencies
- Bellringer Options Transparencies
- Grammar and Writing Workshop Transparencies
- Fine Arts Transparencies

TECHNOLOGY
- TeacherWorks Plus
- StudentWorks Plus
- BookLink 3
- Skill Level Up!
- ExamView Assessment Suite
- Interactive Tutor Self-Assessment
- Listening Library CD
- Spanish Listening Library CD
- Literature Classics
- Literature Launchers Pre-Reading Videos DVD
- Literature Library ExamView Assessment Suite
- Vocabulary Puzzlemaker
- Literature Library Vocabulary Puzzlemaker
- glencoe.com
- Online Student Edition
- Presentation Plus!
- Glencoe Online Essay Grading

ENGLISH LANGUAGE LEARNER
- English Language Coach
- Fluency Practice and Assessment
- inTime Magazines (Spanish)
- Spanish Listening Library CD

PROFESSIONAL DEVELOPMENT
- Professional Development Package

1F

Fast File A list of blackline master sheets available for additional practice of unit skills and activities.

Assessments Use these resources to track and assess your student's reading and writing skills in the classroom or online.

ELL Unit resources for engaging English Language Learners.

Tech Support A list of online and CD-ROM-based resources available for students and teachers.

Teaching the Selection

Each selection in the student edition is preceded by a "Before Your Read" page that prepares students for the vocabulary and themes of the selection. Reading selections are followed by an "After Your Read" where students can respond and connect to the selection.

Author Information Provides additional information about the author or selection.

Skills Reinforcement Opportunities to reinforce the key Reading Skills and Literary Elements found throughout the selection.

Resource Guide Directs you to additional Glencoe material developed to enhance and assess students' comprehension of the selection.

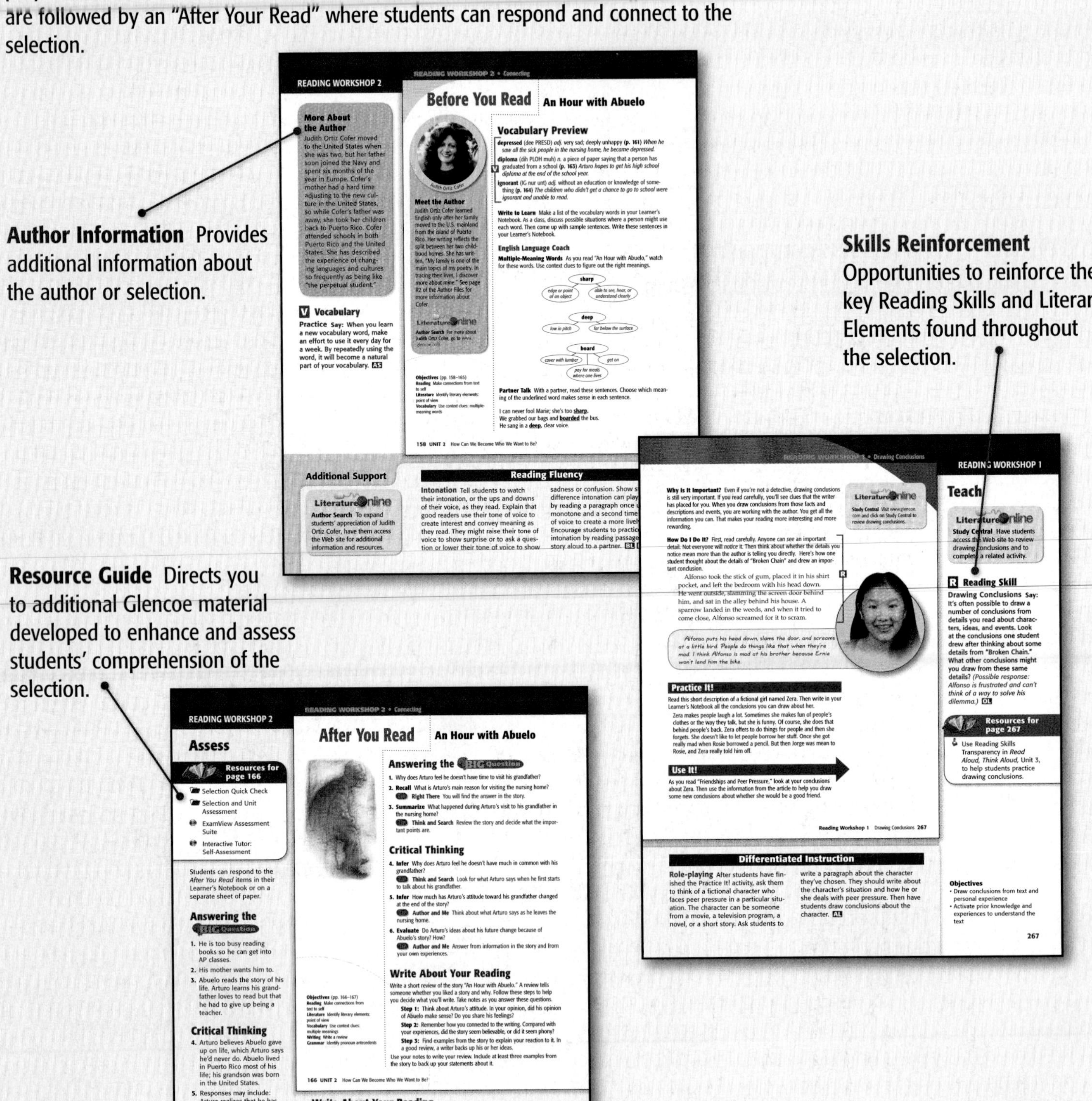

Teaching Informational Text

The wide range of informational texts and functional documents in *Glencoe Literature: Reading with Purpose* broadens student reading to include more than poetry, stories, and plays.

InTime Articles from the **TIME** family of magazines deliver insight and facts on timely issues and topics related to the Big Question.

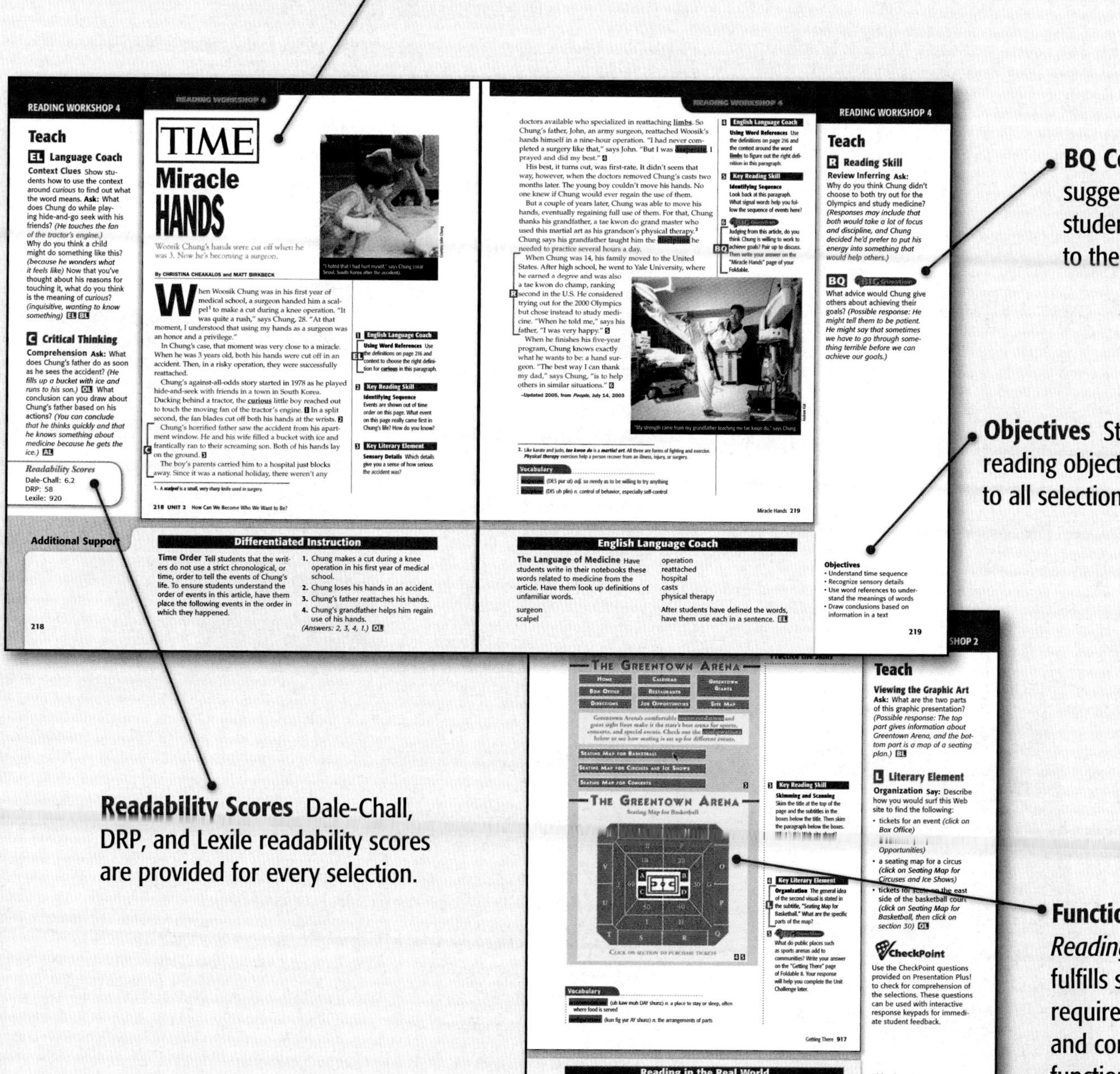

BQ Connection Teaching suggestions for helping students connect the article to the unit Big Question.

Objectives Standards-based reading objectives are correlated to all selections.

Readability Scores Dale-Chall, DRP, and Lexile readability scores are provided for every selection.

Functional Documents *Reading with Purpose* fulfills state standards requirements for reading and comprehending functional documents that students encounter outside the classroom.

Classroom Resources

Unit Resources

Fast Files Booklets

These blackline master booklets provide all the teaching materials you need to reinforce the content in each unit of *Glencoe Literature: Reading with Purpose.* Worksheets in each booklet focus on the following:

- Unit Warm-Up
- The Big Question Foldables
- The Big Question: Home-School Connection (English and Spanish versions)
- Unit Challenge: Planner and Rubrics
- Literary Analysis
- Genre Study
- Active Reading Graphic Organizers
- Comparing Literature Graphic Organizers
- Spelling and Handwriting Practice
- Academic Vocabulary Development
- Selection Vocabulary Development
- English Language Coach
- Grammar Practice
- Writing Workshop Graphic Organizers
- Key Reading Skills Practice
- Viewing and Representing Activities
- Listening and Speaking Activities

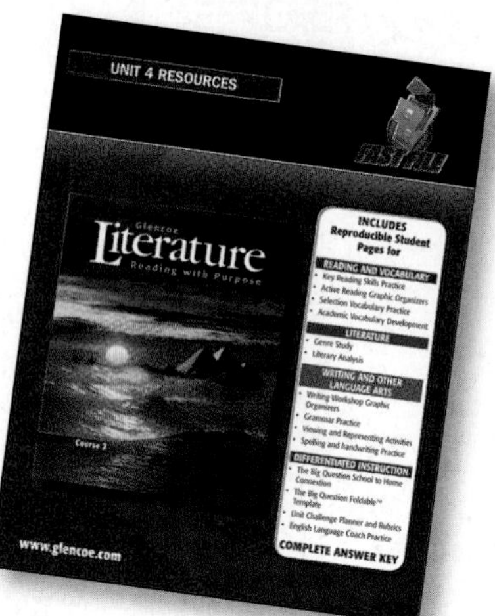

Literature and Reading

Active Learning and Note Taking Guides

This set of consumable workbooks provides structured outline support for students to use before, during, and after reading, helping them focus on key concepts and information. Activities include interactive exercises on literary elements and vocabulary for writing about literature. To meet the needs of all your students, the workbooks are offered in four versions:

- **Active Learning and Note Taking Guide (Grade-Level)**
- **Active Learning and Note Taking Guide: Enriched**
- **Active Learning and Note Taking Guide: Adapted**
- **Active Learning and Note Taking Guide**: **ELL**

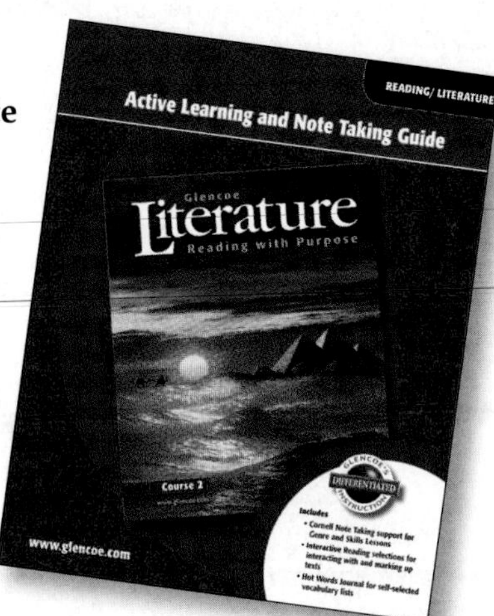

Glencoe Literature Library

This collection of 120 hardcover books helps you encourage your students to read independently. Choose from novels, novellas, plays, and nonfiction. Each book includes related readings from a broad range of genres. Support your teaching with these technology products:

- **Literature Library ExamView Suite Assessment CD-ROM** allows you to create customized tests for all the literary works included in the Literature Library collection.
- **Literature Library Vocabulary Puzzlemaker CD** helps you and your students create word puzzles based on vocabulary selected from the Literature Library collection.

Glencoe Backpack Reader

These portable collections of stories, poems, essays, and plays offer students additional reading for skills practice and personal enjoyment. The leveled selections promote gradual release of responsibility and increase students' confidence in reading and literature.

inTIME Magazine

These high-interest collections of articles drawn from issues of *TIME* magazine and other Time, Inc., publications help students develop readings strategies to interact with informational text. The *inTIME* magazines are available in both English and Spanish and include teacher guides.

Literature Launchers: Prereading Videos/DVD

These short, lively video segments on DVD introduce each unit in *Glencoe Literature: Reading with Purpose.*

Literature Classics CD

This software brings more than 1,100 additional literature selections—accessible by author, title, date, genre, and big idea—to your classroom. Genre Focus Lesson Plans and blackline masters are also provided.

Writing

Real Success in Writing: Research and Reports

These blackline masters reinforce and extend the coverage of research presented in the student edition.

Writing Constructed Responses Sourcebook

This sourcebook with blackline masters help students respond effectively to short essay questions.

Differentiated Instruction

Leveled Vocabulary Development

These blackline masters provide practice on selection vocabulary words. The booklet is offered in four versions:

- **Leveled Vocabulary Development: (Grade Level)**
- **Leveled Vocabulary Development: Enriched**
- **Leveled Vocabulary Development: Adapted**
- **Leveled Vocabulary Development: English Language Learner**

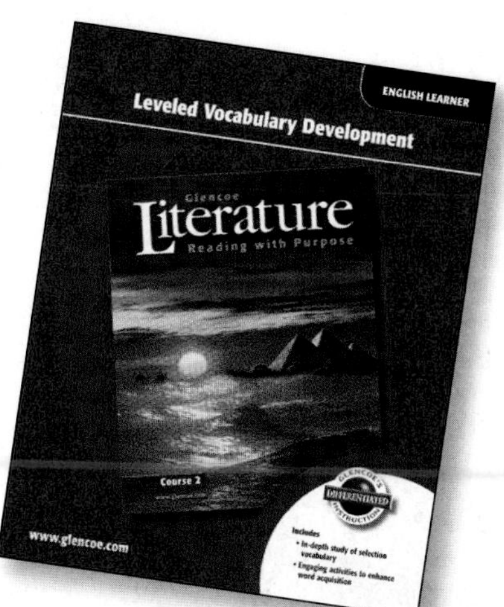

Vocabulary Puzzlemaker

This software lets you or your students create word puzzles based on selection vocabulary.

Listening Library Audio CD-ROM (English and Spanish)

This audio collection offers engaging readings of selections in English and Spanish.

Skill Level Up!™: A Language Arts Game

This CD-ROM game motivates students to practice and master language arts skills covered in *Glencoe Literature: Reading with Purpose* and frequently assessed on standardized tests. Students have fun and you receive valuable skills-based performance data by individual or class.

Glencoe BookLink 3 CD-ROM

Use the *Glencoe BookLink 3* CD-ROM, a database of more than 26,700 titles, to create customized reading lists for your students. Search for award-winning titles and for books on several state-recommended reading lists.

Assessment

Selection and Unit Assessments

This assessment tool contains comprehensive tests and answer keys for all selections and units.

Selection Quick Check

These short-answer questions serve as a quick way to assess students' basic comprehension of a selection. (Spanish and English)

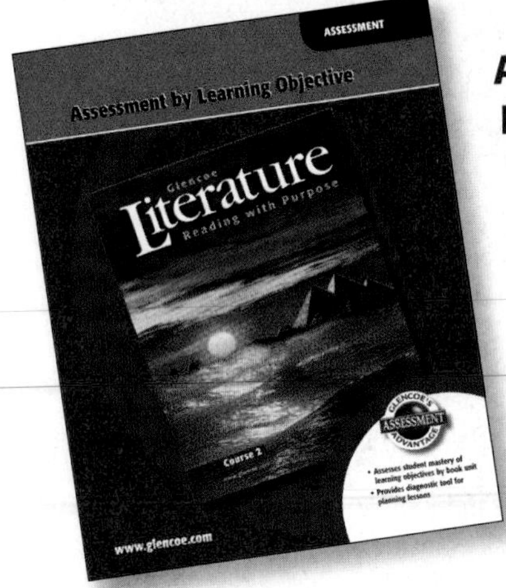

Assessment by Learning Objective

These booklets help you assess learning objectives related to reading strategy, literary element, genre, or literary period or movement.

Rubrics for Assessing Student Writing, Listening, and Speaking

This booklet provides you with rubrics to use fo all Writing Workshop products as well as for key listening and speaking activities.

Standardized Test Preparation and Practice

Contains exercises and activities that get students ready for standardized exams

Technology Resources

StudentWorks™ Plus CD-ROM

StudentWorks™ Plus contains the Student Edition (PDF) with selection audio; student workbooks (PDF); Student Presentation Builder (provides Unit-based multimedia projects, PowerPoint tutorial and PowerPoint presentation template); Daily Assignments and Grade Log allows students to organize their assignments and track their own progress.

Online Student Edition (MHLN)

Showcasing the interactive versions of McGraw-Hill textbooks, mhln.com offers the same content as the printed text, with multimedia-enhanced content. Games, interactivities, and other items are correlated directly to each page.

TeacherWorks™ Plus CD-ROM

TeacherWorks™ Plus contains a suite of easy-to-use and effective tools designed to help you manage daily activities, access all textbook materials, and utilize resources on the Internet. Included are daily lesson plans and a block schedule guide.

ExamViewPro® Assessment Suite

With the Test Generator you can quickly create customized unit- or selection-based assessments in a snap! Use the unit exams or the selection-specific exams provided in both English and Spanish on this CD-ROM, or create your own questions.

Presentation Plus! CD-ROM

This multimedia application enables teachers to present dynamic lessons for every unit and selection in Glencoe Literature. The PowerPoint multimedia presentations can be edited and customized for teacher lesson planning.

Skill Level Up!™: A Language Arts Game

This CD-ROM game motivates students to practice and master language arts skills covered in *Glencoe Literature: Reading with Purpose* and frequently assessed on standardized tests. Students have fun and you receive valuable skills-based performance data by individual or class.

Vocabulary Puzzlemaker

This software lets you or your students create word puzzles based on selection vocabulary.

Literature Classics CD-ROM

This software brings more than 1,100 additional literature selections—accessible by author, title, date, genre, and big idea—to your classroom. Genre Focus Lesson Plans and blackline masters are also provided.

Literature Library ExamView Assessment Suite CD-ROM

This software allows you to create customized tests for all the literary works included in the Literature Library collection.

Literature Library Vocabulary Puzzlemaker CD-ROM

This software helps you and your students create word puzzles based on vocabulary selected from the Literature Library collection.

Literature Launchers: Prereading Videos/DVD

These short, lively video segments on DVD introduce each unit in *Glencoe Literature: Reading with Purpose.*

Listening Library Audio CD-ROM (English and Spanish)

This audio collection offers engaging readings of selections in English and Spanish.

Glencoe BookLink 3 CD-ROM

Use the *Glencoe BookLink 3* CD-ROM, a database of more than 26,700 titles, to create customized reading lists for your students. Search for award-winning titles and for books on several state-recommended reading lists.

Glencoe Online Essay Grading

Improve student writing and save time with Glencoe's Online Essay Grading, powered by SkillWriter™. Glencoe's Online Essay Grading will score your students' writing assignments and provide individualized feedback automatically.

Transparencies

- **Read Aloud, Think Aloud** modeling active reading.
- **Bellringer Options Transparencies** include warm-up exercises to engage student interest or provide a quick review of previously taught activities.
- **Literary Analysis Transparencies** help reinforce or reteach literary elements that are the focus of each lesson.
- **Grammar and Writing Workshop Transparencies** help reinforce the skills taught in the grammar and writing workshops in the student edition.
- **Fine Art Transparencies** enhance a strong humanities approach to literature and helps students analyze visual representations of literary concepts and characters/excellent source of writing prompts.

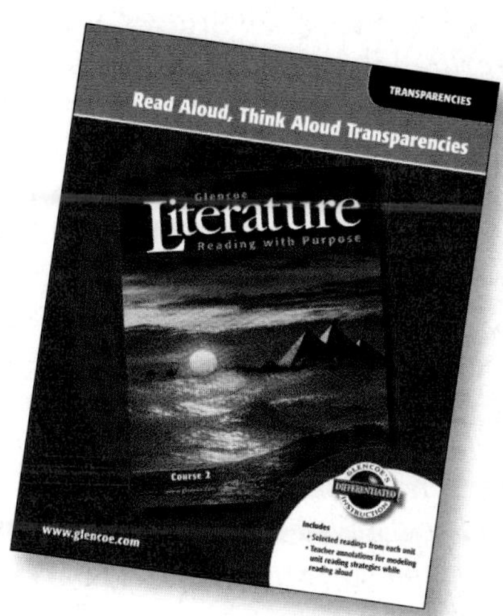

Internet Resources (www.glencoe.com)

For online resources that support the instruction in *Glencoe Literature: Reading with Purpose,* students and teachers can visit our Web site at **www.glencoe.com**. Students will find additional learning, practice, and assessment opportunities.

Glencoe Resources for Independent Reading

Glencoe Literature Library

This collection of hardcover books includes full-length novels, novellas, plays, and works of nonfiction. Each *Glencoe Literature Library* volume consists of a least one complete extended-length reading accompanied by several related readings from a broad range of genres, such as short stories, poems, essays, or informational articles. In addition, a separate **Study Guide** for each *Glencoe Literature Library* book provides teaching notes and reproducible activity pages for students. Students may also find these activity pages on the **Glencoe Web site http://www.glencoe.com.**

Across Five Aprils by Irene Hunt **DRP 59**
The Adventures of Tom Sawyer by Mark Twain **DRP 55**
Anne Frank Remembered: The Story of the Woman Who Helped to Hide the Frank Family by Miep Gies and Alison Leslie Gold **DRP 57**
Bearstone by Will Hobbs **DRP 51**
Bridge to Terabithia by Katherine Paterson **DRP 50**
The Call of the Wild by Jack London **DRP 62**
Cezanne Pinto by Mary Stoltz **DRP 54**
A Christmas Carol by Charles Dickens **DRP 60**
The Clay Marble by Minfong Ho **DRP 49**
Dandelion Wine by Ray Bradbury **DRP 56**
Dogsong by Gary Paulsen **DRP 51**
Dragonwings by Lawrence Yep **DRP 54**
The Friends by Rosa Guy **DRP 51**
A Gathering of Days: A New England Girl's Journal 1830–1832 by Joan W. Blos **DRP 56**
The Glory Field by Walter Dean Myers **DRP 51**
Hatchet by Gary Paulsen **DRP 54**
High Elk's Treasure by Virginia Driving Hawk Sneve
Homecoming by Cynthia Voigt **DRP 48**
The House of Dies Drear by Virginia Hamilton **DRP 49**
I, Juan de Pareja by Elizabeth Borton de Treviño **DRP 58**
Island of the Blue Dolphins by Scott O'Dell **DRP 53**
Jacob Have I Loved by Katherine Paterson **DRP 52**
Johnny Tremain by Esther Forbes **DRP 55**
Journey to Jo'burg by Beverly Naidoo **DRP 50**
Julie of the Wolves by Jean Craighead George **DRP 55**
Letters from a Slave Girl by Mary E. Lyons **DRP 51**
Letters from Rifka by Karen Hesse **DRP 49**
Little Women by Louisa May Alcott **DRP 60**
Lupita Mañana by Patricia Beatty **DRP 53**
Missing May by Cynthia Rylant **DRP 53**
Mrs. Frisby and the Rats of NIMH by Robert O'Brien **DRP 52**
Number the Stars by Lois Lowry **DRP 52**
The Pigman by Paul Zindel **DRP 55**
Shabanu: Daughter of the Wind by Suzanne Fisher Staples **DRP 54**
Shiloh by Phyllis Reynolds Naylor **DRP 50**
The Slave Dancer by Paula Fox **DRP 55**
So Far from the Bamboo Grove by Yoko Kawashima Watkins **DRP 50**
Sounder by William H. Armstrong **DRP 53, CRL 9**
The Summer of the Swans by Betsy Byars **DRP 50**
Taking Sides by Gary Soto **DRP 52**
There's a Girl in My Hammerlock by Jerry Spinelli **DRP 46**
Treasure Island by Robert Louis Stevenson **DRP 56**
The True Confessions of Charlotte Doyle by Avi **DRP 52**
Tuck Everlasting by Natalie Babbitt **DRP 56**
The View from Saturday by E.L. Konigsburg **DRP 53**
Walk Two Moons by Sharon Creech **DRP 49**
Where the Red Fern Grows by Wilson Rawls **DRP 47**
Winter Thunder and *The Christmas of the Phonograph Records* by Mari Sandoz
The Witch of Blackbird Pond by Elizabeth George Speare **DRP 57**
A Wrinkle in Time by Madeleine L'Engle **DRP 51**

Glencoe Backpack Reader

These portable collections of stories, poems, essays, and plays offer students additional reading for skills practice and personal enjoyment. The selections promote gradual release reading and increase students' confidence in reading and literature. Find teacher resources for Backpack Reader on Teacher Works Plus or glencoe.com.

inTIME magazine

This lively collection of articles drawn from issues of TIME helps students develop the skills they need to interact with informational text in a meaningful way. Each of the news stories, feature articles, reviews, profiles, and essays in the magazines connects to an author, reading selection, or Big Question in *Glencoe Literature: Reading with Purpose.* The magazines are availaboe in both English and Spanish editions. In addition, a separate **Teacher Guide,** including lessons and reproducible student worksheets designed to develop students' reading and critical thinking skills, accompanies each magazine.

How to Use *Reading with Purpose*

Consultant's Note

People read for enjoyment, to help themselves think, to solve problems, and to get work done. Their reading is often organized around "inquiry" questions. These questions help them explore how what they learn can help make a difference in the real world.

–Jeff Wilhelm

Wouldn't you like to read better–and understand more? That's what *Reading with Purpose* is all about. This book will help you bridge the gap between a writer's meaning and your understanding.

The next few pages will show you some of the ways *Reading with Purpose* can help you read, think, and write better.

What's in it for you?

Every unit in *Reading with Purpose* is built around a **Big Question,** a question that you will want to think about, talk about, maybe even argue about, and finally answer. The unit's reading selections will help you come up with your answers.

Organization

Each unit contains:

- A **Unit Warm-Up** that introduces the unit's Big Question
- Four **Reading Workshops,** each one containing reading selections that will help you think about the Big Question
  - **Literature** such as short stories, poems, plays, and biographies
  - **Informational texts** such as nonfiction, newspaper and magazine articles, reference books, and manuals
  - **Functional documents** such as signs, schedules, labels, and instructions
- A two-part **Writing Workshop** to help you put your ideas about the Big Question into writing
- A **Comparing Workshop** that will give you a chance to compare different pieces of writing.
- A **Unit Wrap-Up** where you'll answer the Big Question.

Reading and Thinking

Here are some of the ways ***Reading with Purpose*** will help you develop your reading and thinking skills.

Skills and Strategies The skills you need to become a better reader are related to the standards that state and local school districts test you on. We call these objectives.

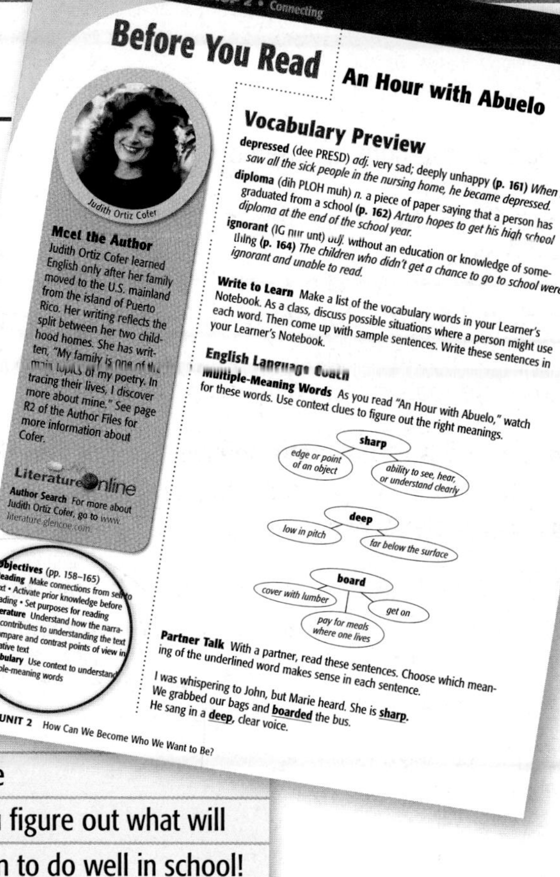

READING WORKSHOP 2 • Connecting

Before You Read

An Hour with Abuelo

Judith Ortiz Cofer

Meet the Author

Judith Ortiz Cofer learned English only after her family moved to the U.S. mainland from the island of Puerto Rico. Her writing reflects the split between her two childhood homes. She has written, "My family is one of the main topics of my poetry. In tracing their lives, I discover more about mine." See page R2 of the Author Files for more information about Cofer.

Literature Online

Author Search For more about Judith Ortiz Cofer, go to www.literature.glencoe.com.

Objectives (pp. 158–165)
Reading Make connections from self to text • Activate prior knowledge before reading • Set purposes for reading
Literature Understand how the narrator contributes to understanding the text • Compare and contrast points of view in narrative text
Vocabulary Use context to understand multiple-meaning words

Vocabulary Preview

depressed (dee PRESD) *adj.* very sad; deeply unhappy **(p. 161)** *When he saw all the sick people in the nursing home, he became depressed.*

diploma (dih PLOH muh) *n.* a piece of paper saying that a person has graduated from a school **(p. 162)** *Arturo hopes to get his high school diploma at the end of the school year.*

ignorant (IG nur unt) *adj.* without an education or knowledge of something **(p. 164)** *The children who didn't get a chance to go to school were ignorant and unable to read.*

Write to Learn Make a list of the vocabulary words in your Learner's Notebook. As a class, discuss possible situations where a person might use each word. Then come up with sample sentences. Write these sentences in your Learner's Notebook.

English Language Coach

Multiple-Meaning Words As you read "An Hour with Abuelo," watch for these words. Use context clues to figure out the right meanings.

Partner Talk With a partner, read these sentences. Choose which meaning of the underlined word makes sense in each sentence.

I was whispering to John, but Marie heard. She is **sharp**.
We grabbed our bags and **boarded** the bus.
He sang in a **deep**, clear voice.

158 UNIT 2 How Can We Become Who We Want to Be?

Consultant's Note

Standards tell what you are expected to do or learn—the learning objectives. They help teachers plan lessons and select reading and writing tasks. In addition, standards ensure that the content taught at one school will be similar to the content at other schools in the state. The standards also help you figure out what will be on tests. Standards help you figure out what you need to learn to do well in school!

—Doug Fisher

Margin Notes These notes will help you with a difficult passage, point out an important development, model a skill, or ask a question to get you thinking about what you are reading.

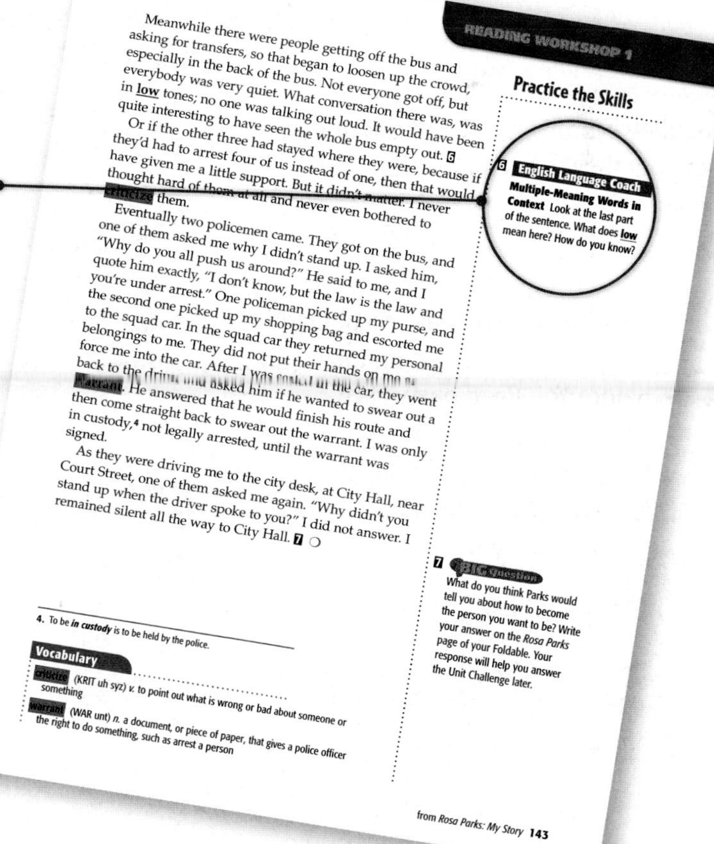

READING WORKSHOP 1

Meanwhile there were people getting off the bus and asking for transfers, so that began to loosen up the crowd, especially in the back of the bus. Not everyone got off, but everybody was very quiet. What conversation there was, was in **low** tones; no one was talking out loud. It would have been quite interesting to have seen the whole bus empty out. 6

Or if the other three had stayed where they were, because if they'd had to arrest four of us instead of one, then that would have given me a little support. But it didn't matter. I never thought hard of them at all and never even bothered to **criticize** them.

Eventually two policemen came. They got on the bus, and one of them asked me why I didn't stand up. I asked him, "Why do you all push us around?" He said to me, and I quote him exactly, "I don't know, but the law is the law and you're under arrest." One policeman picked up my purse, and the second one picked up my shopping bag and escorted me to the squad car. In the squad car they returned my personal belongings to me. They did not put their hands on me or force me into the car. After I was seated in the car, they went back to the driver and asked him if he wanted to swear out a **warrant**. He answered that he would finish his route and then come straight back to swear out the warrant. I was only in custody,[4] not legally arrested, until the warrant was signed.

As they were driving me to the city desk, at City Hall, near Court Street, one of them asked me again, "Why didn't you stand up when the driver spoke to you?" I did not answer. I remained silent all the way to City Hall. 7

Practice the Skills

6 **English Language Coach**
Multiple-Meaning Words in Context Look at the last part of the sentence. What does **low** mean here? How do you know?

7 **BIG Question**
What do you think Parks would tell you about how to become the person you want to be? Write your answer on the *Rosa Parks* page of your Foldable. Your response will help you answer the Unit Challenge later.

4. To be *in custody* is to be held by the police.

Vocabulary

criticize (KRIT uh syz) *v.* to point out what is wrong or bad about someone or something

warrant (WAR unt) *n.* a document, or piece of paper, that gives a police officer the right to do something, such as arrest a person

from *Rosa Parks: My Story* 143

Question and Answer Relationship

Four types of questions are used on standardized tests:

1. **Right There Questions** The answer is "right there" on the page.
2. **Think and Search Questions** The answers to these questions are on the page (or pages), but you'll need to use information from different parts of the text.
3. **Author and Me Questions** Information from the text may help, but you'll put it together with your own ideas to answer a question.
4. **On My Own Questions** Answers do not come from the text. You'll base your answer on what you know.

Knowing how to deal with such questions can help improve your test scores. At the end of most Workshops is a set of questions. In the first two units, each question is followed by a tip to help you answer. For example:

- What promise does Victor make to himself about this school year?

  TIP **Right There** You will find the answer in the story.

Vocabulary

Vocabulary Words may be difficult or new to you, but they're useful words.

Vocabulary Preview Vocabulary words are introduced on the Before You Read page. Each word is followed by its pronunciation, its part of speech, a definition, and a sample sentence.

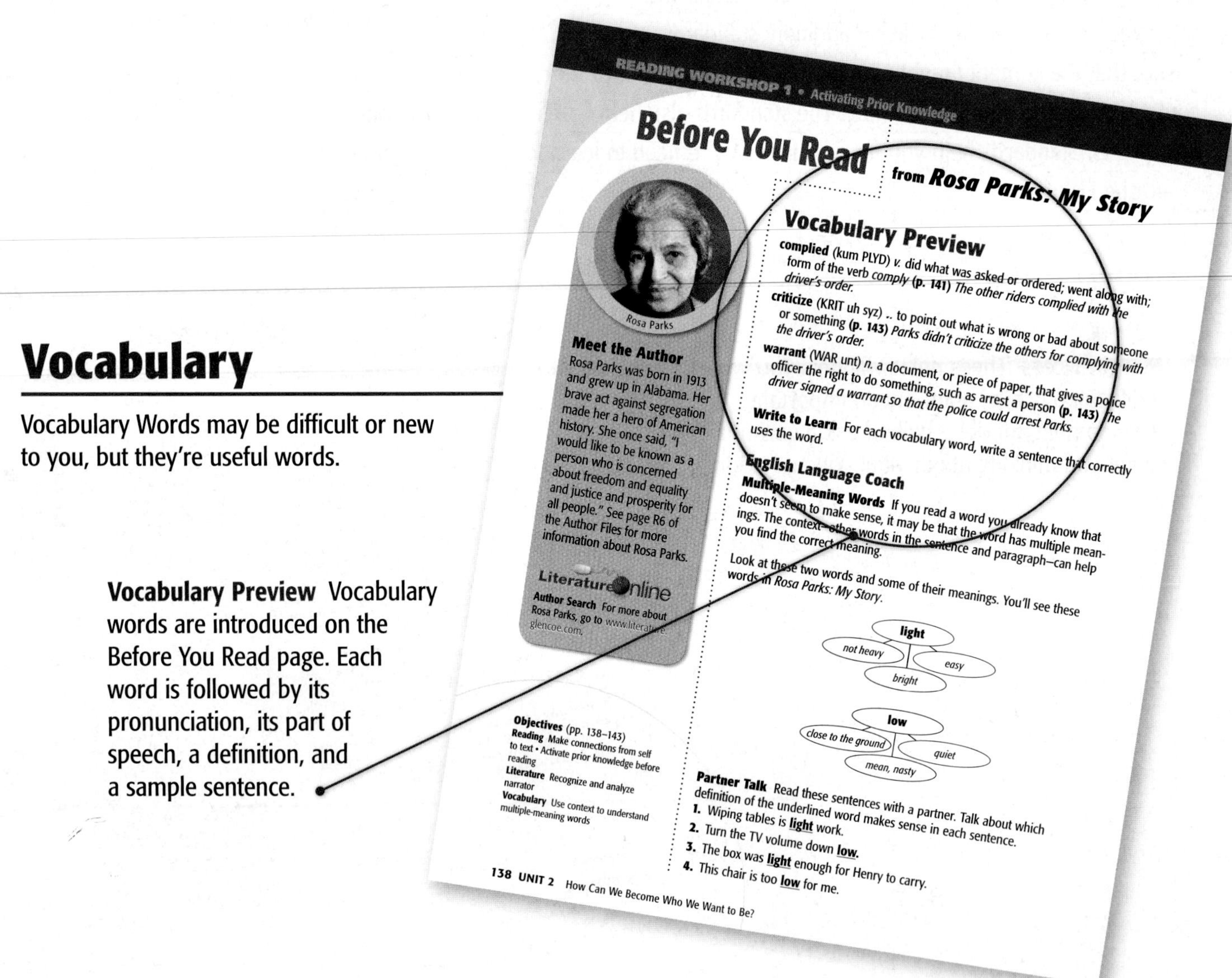

READING WORKSHOP 1 • Activating Prior Knowledge

Before You Read

from *Rosa Parks: My Story*

Rosa Parks

Meet the Author

Rosa Parks was born in 1913 and grew up in Alabama. Her brave act against segregation made her a hero of American history. She once said, "I would like to be known as a person who is concerned about freedom and equality and justice and prosperity for all people." See page R6 of the Author Files for more information about Rosa Parks.

Literature Online

Author Search For more about Rosa Parks, go to www.literature.glencoe.com.

Vocabulary Preview

complied (kum PLYD) *v.* did what was asked or ordered; went along with; form of the verb *comply* **(p. 141)** *The other riders complied with the driver's order.*

criticize (KRIT uh syz) *v.* to point out what is wrong or bad about someone or something **(p. 143)** *Parks didn't criticize the others for complying with the driver's order.*

warrant (WAR unt) *n.* a document, or piece of paper, that gives a police officer the right to do something, such as arrest a person **(p. 143)** *The driver signed a warrant so that the police could arrest Parks.*

Write to Learn For each vocabulary word, write a sentence that correctly uses the word.

English Language Coach

Multiple-Meaning Words If you read a word you already know that doesn't seem to make sense, it may be that the word has multiple meanings. The context—other words in the sentence and paragraph—can help you find the correct meaning.

Look at these two words and some of their meanings. You'll see these words in *Rosa Parks: My Story*.

Partner Talk Read these sentences with a partner. Talk about which definition of the underlined word makes sense in each sentence.

1. Wiping tables is light work.
2. Turn the TV volume down low.
3. The box was light enough for Henry to carry.
4. This chair is too low for me.

Objectives (pp. 138–143)
Reading Make connections from self to text • Activate prior knowledge before reading
Literature Recognize and analyze narrator
Vocabulary Use context to understand multiple-meaning words

138 UNIT 2 How Can We Become Who We Want to Be?

READING WORKSHOP 4

The gym was empty.

"I want to see how **flexible** you are. Let me lift your leg," the Liberation Army woman said in her gentle voice. She raised my right leg over my head in front of me. "Very good! Now I'll support you. Lean over backward as far as you can." That was easy. I bent backward until I could grab my ankles like an acrobat. "That's great!" she said, and her braids swung with excitement. 3

"This is Jiang Ji-li."[2] Principal Long leaned forward proudly. "She's been studying martial arts[3] since the second grade. She was on the Municipal Children's Martial Arts Team. Their demonstration was even filmed."

The Liberation Army woman smiled sweetly. "That was very good. Now you may go back to your classroom." She patted me on my head before she turned back to test Tong Chao.

I went back to class, but I could not remember the song we were singing. What did the Liberation Army woman want? Could she want to choose me for something? It was too much to **contemplate**. I hardly moved when the bell rang to end school. Someone told me that the principal wanted to see me. I walked slowly down the hall, surrounded by my shouting and jostling[4] classmates, seeing only the beautiful soldier, feeling only the **electric** tingle of her soft touch on my head. 4

The office door was heavy. I pushed it open cautiously. Some students from the other sixth-grade classes were there already. I recognized Wang Qi, a girl in class two, and one of the boys, You Xiao-fan of class four. I didn't know the other boy. The three of them sat nervously and respectfully opposite Principal Long. I slipped into a chair next to them.

2. In some Asian countries, the family name is said first. So ***Jiang*** is the author's "last" name, and ***Ji-li*** is her "first" name. If Americans followed the same rule, John Smith would introduce himself as "Smith John."

3. ***Martial*** (MAR shul) means "of or about war; warlike." The ***martial arts*** are forms of fighting such as judo and karate. They're also popular as forms of exercise.

4. ***Comrade*** (KAWM rad) means "friend or partner." During the Cultural Revolution, people used this word instead of *Mr., Miss,* or *Mrs.*

Vocabulary

contemplate (KON tem playt) *v.* to think about slowly and carefully

Practice the Skills

3 **English Language Coach**

Multiple-Meaning Words Use the context around the word **flexible** to figure out the right definition in this sentence. Notice what Jiang does for the Liberation Army woman.

4 **English Language Coach**

Multiple-Meaning Words Use the context around the word **electric** to figure out the right definition in this sentence. Notice that it describes a feeling.

210 UNIT 2 How Can We Become Who We Want to Be?

Vocabulary The word is in **bold** type when it first appears in the reading selection.

Vocabulary The word with its pronunciation, part of speech, and definition appear at the bottom of the same page.

English Language Coach These notes help students whose first language is not English. For example, they help explain multiple-meaning words and also idioms—phrases that mean something other than what their individual words mean.

Footnotes Selection footnote explains words or phrases that you may not know to help you understand the story.

READING WORKSHOP 1

Skills Focus

You will practice using the following skills when you read these selections:

- from *Rosa Parks: My Story,* p. 140
- "Kids in Action: Dalie Jimenez," p. 148

Reading

- Activating prior knowledge

Literature

- Identifying the narrator in what you read
- Recognizing the narrator's effect on the story

Vocabulary

- Understanding multiple-meaning words in context
- Academic Vocabulary: *prior*

Writing/Grammar

- Identifying nouns and pronouns

Skill Lesson

Activating Prior Knowledge

Learn It!

What Is It? Activating prior knowledge means using what you already know. For example, to appreciate *Tony Hawk: Chairman of the Board,* you needed to activate your **prior** knowledge of skateboarding. Now learn how to do it every time you read.

- To *activate* something is to make it active—to get it going so it can be useful.
- *Prior knowledge* is knowledge that you already have—your memories.
- *Activating prior knowledge* is using your memories to help you understand new things.

"I forgot to make a back-up copy of my brain, so everything I learned last semester was lost."

Analyzing Cartoons

The character can't activate his prior knowledge because he lost it. What prior knowledge of computers do you need to understand this cartoon?

Academic Vocabulary

prior (PRY ur) *adj.* earlier; coming before

Objectives (pp. 136–137)
Reading Use existing knowledge to understand text

136 UNIT 2

Academic Vocabulary These are words you come across in your school work—in science, math, or social studies books as well as this book. The academic words are treated the same as regular vocabulary words.

Organizing Information

Foldables For every unit, you'll be shown how to make a ***Foldable*** that will help you keep track of your thoughts about the Big Question. See page xxxvi for more about Foldables.

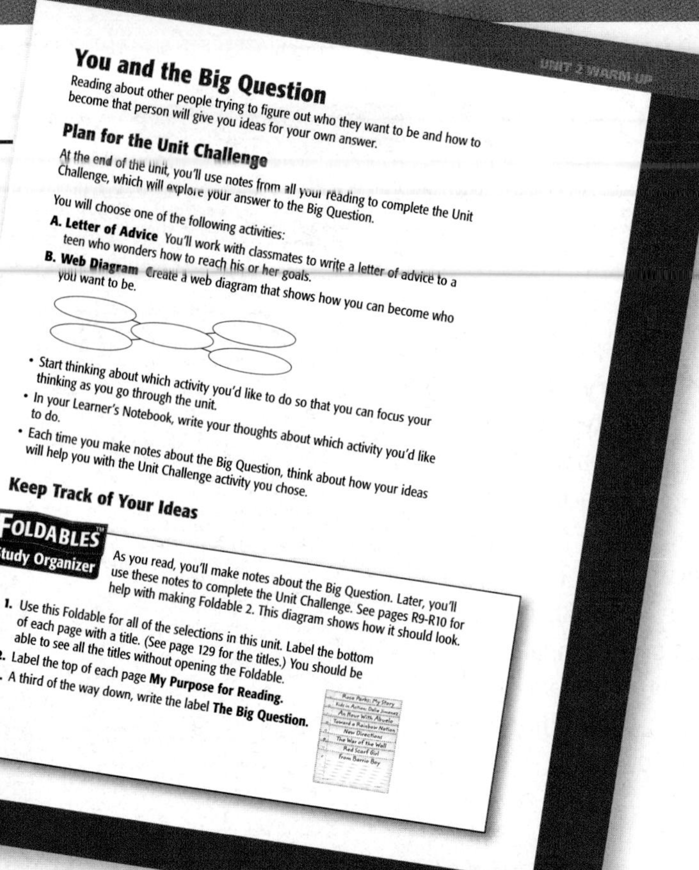
UNIT 2 WARM-UP

You and the Big Question

Reading about other people trying to figure out who they want to be and how to become that person will give you ideas for your own answer.

Plan for the Unit Challenge

At the end of the unit, you'll use notes from all your reading to complete the Unit Challenge, which will explore your answer to the Big Question.

You will choose one of the following activities:

A. Letter of Advice You'll work with classmates to write a letter of advice to a teen who wonders how to reach his or her goals.

B. Web Diagram Create a web diagram that shows how you can become who you want to be.

- Start thinking about which activity you'd like to do so that you can focus your thinking as you go through the unit.
- In your Learner's Notebook, write your thoughts about which activity you'd like to do.
- Each time you make notes about the Big Question, think about how your ideas will help you with the Unit Challenge activity you chose.

Keep Track of Your Ideas

FOLDABLES™ Study Organizer

As you read, you'll make notes about the Big Question. Later, you'll use these notes to complete the Unit Challenge. See pages R9–R10 for help with making Foldable 2. This diagram shows how it should look.

1. Use this Foldable for all of the selections in this unit. Label the bottom of each page with a title. (See page 129 for the titles.) You should be able to see all the titles without opening the Foldable.
2. Label the top of each page **My Purpose for Reading.**
3. A third of the way down, write the label **The Big Question.**

Warm-Up 131

READING WORKSHOP 1 • Activating Prior Knowledge

Before You Read from *Rosa Parks: My Story*

Rosa Parks

Meet the Author

Rosa Parks was born in 1913 and grew up in Alabama. Her brave act against segregation made her a hero of American history. She once said, "I would like to be known as a person who is concerned about freedom and equality and justice and prosperity for all people." See page R6 of the Author Files for more information about Rosa Parks.

Literature Online

Author Search For more about Rosa Parks, go to www.literature.glencoe.com.

Objectives (pp. 138–143)
Reading Make connections from self to text • Activate prior knowledge before reading
Literature Recognize and analyze narrator
Vocabulary Use context to understand multiple-meaning words

Vocabulary Preview

complied (kum PLYD) *v.* did what was asked or ordered; went along with; form of the verb *comply* **(p. 141)** *The other riders complied with the driver's order.*

criticize (KRIT uh syz) *v.* to point out what is wrong or bad about someone or something **(p. 143)** *Parks didn't criticize the others for complying with the driver's order.*

warrant (WAR unt) *n.* a document, or piece of paper, that gives a police officer the right to do something, such as arrest a person **(p. 143)** *The driver signed a warrant so that the police could arrest Parks.*

Write to Learn For each vocabulary word, write a sentence that correctly uses the word.

English Language Coach

Multiple-Meaning Words If you read a word you already know that doesn't seem to make sense, it may be that the word has multiple meanings. The context—other words in the sentence and paragraph—can help you find the correct meaning.

Look at these two words and some of their meanings. You'll see these words in *Rosa Parks: My Story.*

light: not heavy, easy, bright
low: close to the ground, quiet, mean, nasty

Partner Talk Read these sentences with a partner. Talk about which definition of the underlined word makes sense in each sentence.

1. Wiping tables is **light** work.
2. Turn the TV volume down **low.**
3. The box was **light** enough for Henry to carry.
4. This chair is too **low** for me.

138 UNIT 2 How Can We Become Who We Want to Be?

Graphic organizers In ***Reading with Purpose,*** you will use different kinds of graphic organizers to help you arrange information. These graphic organizers include, among others, Venn Diagrams, Compare and Contrast Charts, Cluster Diagrams, and Chain-of-Events Charts.

Writing

In the selections in ***Reading with Purpose,*** you'll read many examples of excellent writing. And you'll explore what makes those pieces of writing so good.

Here are some other ways ***Reading with Purpose*** will help you become a better writer.

WRITING WORKSHOP PART 1

Autobiographical Narrative

Prewriting and Drafting

ASSIGNMENT Write an autobiographical narrative

Purpose: To tell a story about a goal you once had and how it turned out

Audience: You, your teacher, and possibly some classmates

Writing Rubric

As you work through this writing assignment, you should

- write about a goal you once had
- include an anecdote
- use first-person point of view
- write a paper using your own writing voice
- develop a setting
- arrange events in time order

See page 202 in Part 2 for a model of a personal narrative.

Objectives (pp. 152–155)
Writing Write autobiographical narratives using the writing process • Use first-person point of view • Use sensory details to develop setting • Provide a clear ending • Use time order • Work with others during the writing process
Grammar Identify and use various kinds of nouns

Creating an autobiographical narrative will help you think about the Unit 2 Big Question: How can we become who we want to be?

Autobiography: When you write about your life or an event in your life, you're writing autobiography. It might be in the form of a note to a friend, a blog, or an assignment.

152 UNIT 2 How Can We Beco

WRITING WORKSHOP PART 2

Applying Good Writing Traits

Voice

One of the best parts of reading an autobiography is getting to know the author. You can discover the writer's personality from the way he or she "talks" on paper.

What Is Voice?

Just as each person has a unique speaking voice, an author has a particular writing voice. It's the author's personality coming through in the tone, word choices, and sentence patterns he or she uses.

Why Is Voice Important in My Writing?

- Writing in your own voice helps you express your real thoughts, ideas, and feelings.
- Writing in your own voice is easier than trying to sound like someone else.
- Reading something written in your voice is more interesting to your audience. It shows there's a real person behind the writing.

How Do I Do It?

- Write with the words you use when you're talking.
- Write sentences the way you say sentences.
- Write with an attitude about your topic, just as you would if you were speaking with friends.
- As you write, pause now and then to read your work aloud to be sure your writing sounds like you.

Write to Learn Read the latest version of your draft to a partner. Have your partner listen for parts of the narrative in which the voice doesn't sound like yours. Rewrite those parts so that you can imagine yourself saying them to a friend.

Analyzing Cartoons
Show your individuality. Don't try to sound like someone else in your writing. Be yourself. (Where have we heard that before?)

KNOW THIS ESSAY WE'RE SUPPOSED TO WRITE ON INDIVIDUALITY?
I DON'T KNOW WHAT TO WRITE ABOUT. WHAT DID YOU COME UP WITH?
I SAID WE SHOULD ALL JUST BE OURSELVES AND NOT DO WHAT EVERYBODY ELSE DOES.
OH, THAT'S GOOD.
I'LL WRITE THAT TOO.

STONE SOUP © 2000 Jan Eliot. Reprinted with permission of UNIVERSAL PRESS SYNDICATE. All rights reserved.

Writing Workshop Part 2 Autobiographical Narrative 199

Write to Learn As you learn new skills, you will sometimes complete a short writing assignment that will help you practice or think about your new skill.

Test Preparation and Practice

Following each unit, you will be tested on the literature, reading, and vocabulary skills you learned. This test will give you the practice you need to succeed while providing an assessment of how you have met the unit objectives.

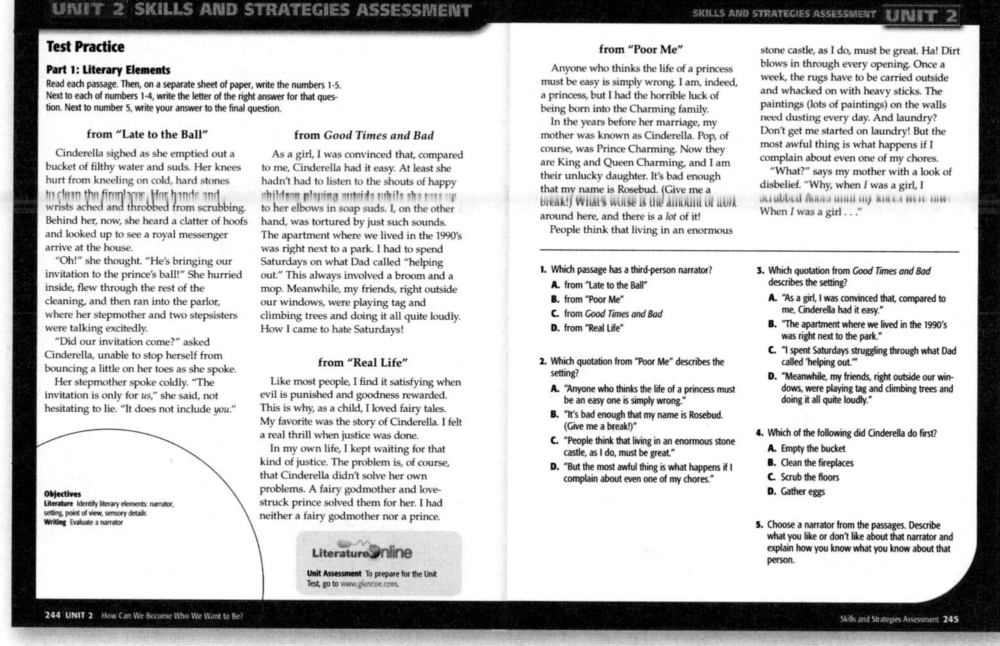

UNIT 2 SKILLS AND STRATEGIES ASSESSMENT

Test Practice

Part 1: Literary Elements

Read each passage. Then, on a separate sheet of paper, write the numbers 1-5. Next to each of numbers 1-4, write the letter of the right answer for that question. Next to number 5, write your answer to the final question.

from "Late to the Ball"

Cinderella sighed as she emptied out a bucket of filthy water and suds. Her knees hurt from kneeling on cold, hard stones to clean the fireplaces. Her hands and wrists ached and throbbed from scrubbing. Behind her, now, she heard a clatter of hoofs and looked up to see a royal messenger arrive at the house.

"Oh!" she thought. "He's bringing our invitation to the prince's ball!" She hurried inside, flew through the rest of the cleaning, and then ran into the parlor, where her stepmother and two stepsisters were talking excitedly.

"Did our invitation come?" asked Cinderella, unable to stop herself from bouncing a little on her toes as she spoke.

Her stepmother spoke coldly. "The invitation is only for *us*," she said, not hesitating to lie. "It does not include *you*."

from *Good Times and Bad*

As a girl, I was convinced that, compared to me, Cinderella had it easy. At least she hadn't had to listen to the shouts of happy children playing outside while she was up to her elbows in soap suds. I, on the other hand, was tortured by just such sounds. The apartment where we lived in the 1990's was right next to a park. I had to spend Saturdays on what Dad called "helping out." This always involved a broom and a mop. Meanwhile, my friends, right outside our windows, were playing tag and climbing trees and doing it all quite loudly. How I came to hate Saturdays!

from "Real Life"

Like most people, I find it satisfying when evil is punished and goodness rewarded. This is why, as a child, I loved fairy tales. My favorite was the story of Cinderella. I felt a real thrill when justice was done.

In my own life, I kept waiting for that kind of justice. The problem is, of course, that Cinderella didn't solve her own problems. A fairy godmother and lovestruck prince solved them for her. I had neither a fairy godmother nor a prince.

Objectives
Literature Identify literary elements: narrator, setting, point of view, sensory details
Writing Evaluate a narrator

Literature Online
Unit Assessment To prepare for the Unit Test, go to www.glencoe.com.

244 UNIT 2 How Can We Become Who We Want to Be?

SKILLS AND STRATEGIES ASSESSMENT UNIT 2

from "Poor Me"

Anyone who thinks the life of a princess must be easy is simply wrong. I am, indeed, a princess, but I had the horrible luck of being born into the Charming family.

In the years before her marriage, my mother was known as Cinderella. Pop, of course, was Prince Charming. Now they are King and Queen Charming, and I am their unlucky daughter. It's bad enough that my name is Rosebud. (Give me a break!) What's worse is the amount of work around here, and there is a *lot* of it!

People think that living in an enormous stone castle, as I do, must be great. Ha! Dirt blows in through every opening. Once a week, the rugs have to be carried outside and whacked on with heavy sticks. The paintings (lots of paintings) on the walls need dusting every day. And laundry? Don't get me started on laundry! But the most awful thing is what happens if I complain about even one of my chores.

"What?" says my mother with a look of disbelief. "Why, when *I* was a girl, I [illegible] When *I* was a girl . . ."

1. Which passage has a third-person narrator?
   - **A.** from "Late to the Ball"
   - **B.** from "Poor Me"
   - **C.** from *Good Times and Bad*
   - **D.** from "Real Life"

2. Which quotation from "Poor Me" describes the setting?
   - **A.** "Anyone who thinks the life of a princess must be an easy one is simply wrong."
   - **B.** "It's bad enough that my name is Rosebud. (Give me a break!)"
   - **C.** "People think that living in an enormous stone castle, as I do, must be great."
   - **D.** "But the most awful thing is what happens if I complain about even one of my chores."

3. Which quotation from *Good Times and Bad* describes the setting?
   - **A.** "As a girl, I was convinced that, compared to me, Cinderella had it easy."
   - **B.** "The apartment where we lived in the 1990's was right next to the park."
   - **C.** "I spent Saturdays struggling through what Dad called 'helping out.'"
   - **D.** "Meanwhile, my friends, right outside our windows, were playing tag and climbing trees and doing it all quite loudly."

4. Which of the following did Cinderella do first?
   - **A.** Empty the bucket
   - **B.** Clean the fireplaces
   - **C.** Scrub the floors
   - **D.** Gather eggs

5. Choose a narrator from the passages. Describe what you like or don't like about that narrator and explain how you know what you know about that person.

Skills and Strategies Assessment 245

Foldables™

by Dinah Zike, M.Ed., Creator of Foldables™

FOLDABLES™
Study Organizer

Foldables™, are three-dimensional interactive graphic organizers for taking notes and organizing your ideas. They're also fun! You will fold paper, cut tabs, write, and manipulate what you have made in order to organize information; review skills, concepts, and strategies; and assess your learning.

Using Dinah Zike's Foldables in Reading and Literature Classes

Use Foldables before, during, and after reading selections in ***Reading With Purpose.***

- **Before you read:** Your unit Foldable will help you to focus on your purpose for reading by reminding you about the Big Question.
- **During reading:** Your unit Foldable will help you to stay focused and engaged. You will track key ideas and your thoughts about each selection and how it helps you answer the Big Question. It will also encourage you to use higher level thinking skills in approaching text.
- **After reading:** Your Foldable will help you to review your thoughts from your reading and to analyze, interpret, and evaluate various aspects of the Big Question. Your Foldable notes will also help you with your unit challenge. They also stimulate rich group discussions and inquiry.

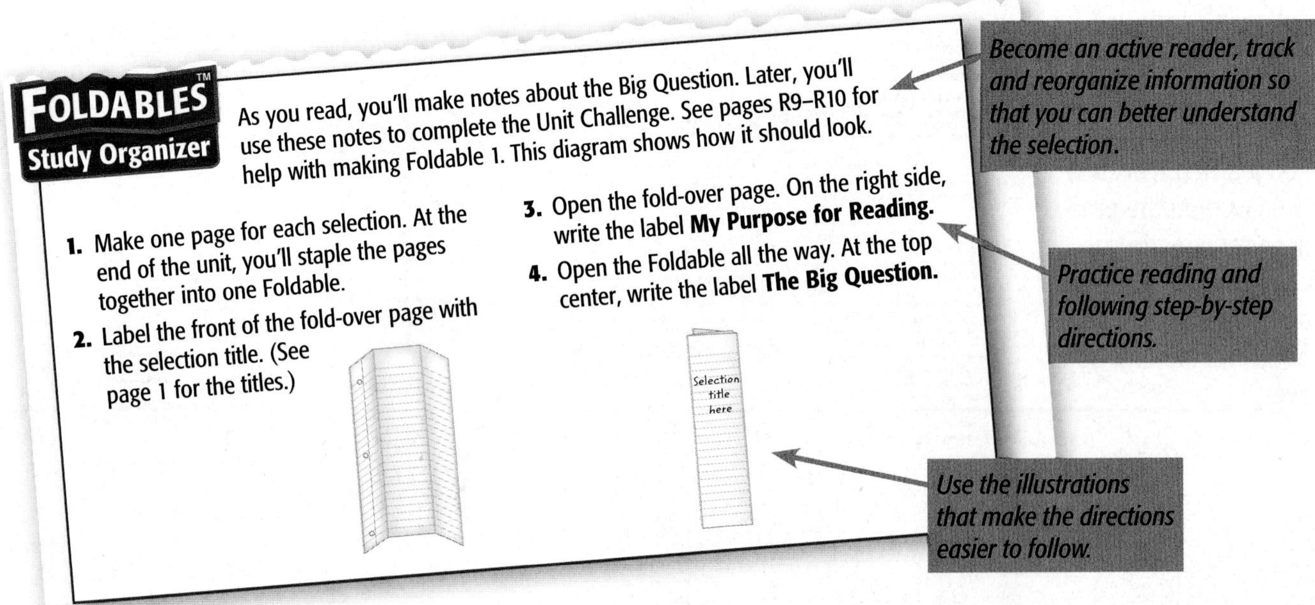

FOLDABLES™ Study Organizer

As you read, you'll make notes about the Big Question. Later, you'll use these notes to complete the Unit Challenge. See pages R9–R10 for help with making Foldable 1. This diagram shows how it should look.

1. Make one page for each selection. At the end of the unit, you'll staple the pages together into one Foldable.
2. Label the front of the fold-over page with the selection title. (See page 1 for the titles.)
3. Open the fold-over page. On the right side, write the label **My Purpose for Reading.**
4. Open the Foldable all the way. At the top center, write the label **The Big Question.**

Selection title here
Become an active reader, track and reorganize information so that you can better understand the selection.
Practice reading and following step-by-step directions.
Use the illustrations that make the directions easier to follow.

Scavenger Hunt

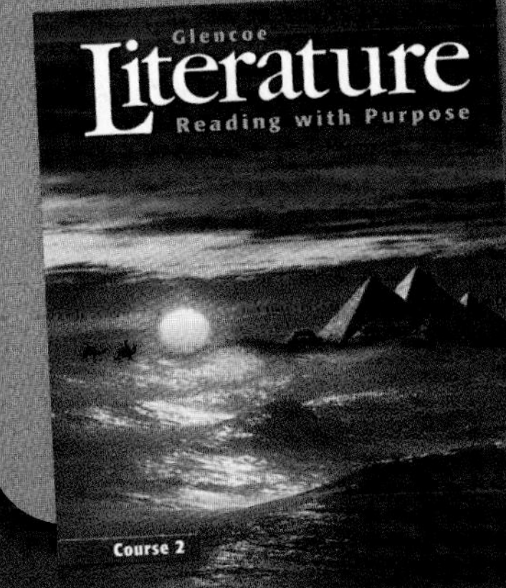

Reading with Purpose has a lot of information, excitement, and entertainment. This Scavenger Hunt will help you explore the book. You'll learn how to find what you need quickly. There are ten questions in your scavenger hunt. All the answers are in this book. Write your answers in your Learner's Notebook.

1. How many units are there in the book?
2. How many types of Workshops are in a unit and what are their names?
3. What is the genre focus of Unit 6?
4. How many short stories are in Unit 3?
5. Where can you find a list of all the poems in this book?
6. What's the fastest way to find a particular short story in the book?
7. Where in this book can you quickly find the correct pronunciation of the word *boutique?*
8. Where could you most quickly find the difference between a simile and a metaphor?
9. Where can you look for the answer to a question about grammar?
10. Name two places in the book where you can find biographical information about a writer.

After you answer all the questions, meet with a small group to compare answers.

READING HANDBOOK

You don't read a news article the way you read a novel. You read a news article mainly for information; you read a novel mainly for fun. To get the most out of your reading, you need to choose the right reading strategy to fit the reason you're reading. This handbook focuses on skills and strategies that can help you understand what you read.

Identifying Words and Building Vocabulary

What do you do when you come across a word you don't know as you read? Do you skip over the word and keep reading? If you're reading for fun or entertainment, you might. And that's just fine. But if you're reading for information, an unfamiliar word may get in the way of your understanding. When that happens, try the following strategies to figure out how to say the word and what it means. These strategies will help you better understand what you read. They will also help you increase the vocabulary you use in everyday speaking and reading.

Reading Unfamiliar Words

Sounding the Word Out

One way to figure out how to say a new word is to sound it out, syllable by syllable. Look carefully at the word's beginning, middle, and ending. Inside the new word, do you see a word you already know how to pronounce? What vowels are in the syllables? Use the following tips when sounding out new words.

▶ **Ask Yourself**

- What letters make up the beginning sound or beginning syllable of the word?
  Example: In the word *coagulate*, co- rhymes with so.
- What sounds do the letters in the middle part of the word make?
  Example: In the word *coagulate*, the syllable ag has the same sound as the *ag* in bag, and the syllable *u* is pronounced like the letter u.
- What letters make up the ending sound or syllable?
  Example: In the word *coagulate, late* is a familiar word you already know how to pronounce.
- Now try pronouncing the whole word: *co ag u late.*

Using Word Parts

Looking closely at the parts of a word is another way to learn it. By studying word parts–the root or base word, prefixes, and suffixes–you may discover more than just how to pronounce a word. You may also find clues to the word's meaning.

- **Roots and Base Words** The main part of a word is called its **root.** When the root is a complete word, it may be called the **base word.** Many roots in English come from an old form of English called Anglo-Saxon. You probably know many of these roots already. For example, *endearing* and *remarkable* have the familiar words dear and mark as their roots. Other roots come from Greek and Latin.

You may not be as familiar with them. For example, the word *spectator* contains the Latin root spec, which means "to look at." You can see that root in the word *spectator*, "one who looks."

When you come across a new word, check whether you recognize its root or base word. It can help you pronounce the word and figure out its meaning.

- **Prefixes** A prefix is a word part that can be added to the beginning of a root or base word to change the word's meaning. For example,

  the prefix *semi-* means "half" or "partial," so *semicircle* means "half a circle"

  un- means "not," so *unhappy* means "not happy"

- **Suffixes** A suffix is a word part that can be added to the end of a root or base word to change the word's meaning. Adding a suffix to a word can also change that word from one part of speech to another. For example,

  the word *joy* (which is a noun) becomes an adjective when the suffix *-ful* (meaning "full of") is added. *Joyful* means "full of joy"

Determining a Word's Meaning

Using Syntax

Languages have rules and patterns for the way words are arranged in sentences. The way a sentence is organized is called the **syntax** of the sentence. If English is your first language, you have known this pattern since you started talking in sentences. If you're learning English now, you may find the syntax is different from the patterns you know in your first language.

In a simple sentence in English, someone or something (the **subject**) does something (the **predicate** or **verb**) to or with another person or thing (the **object**).

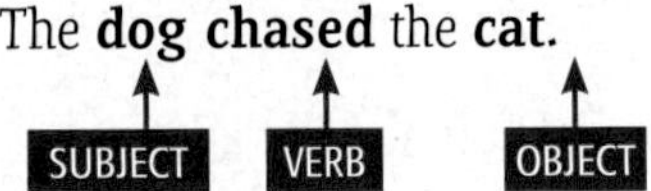
The dog chased the cat.
SUBJECT
VERB
OBJECT

Sometimes adjectives, adverbs, and phrases are added to spice up the sentence.

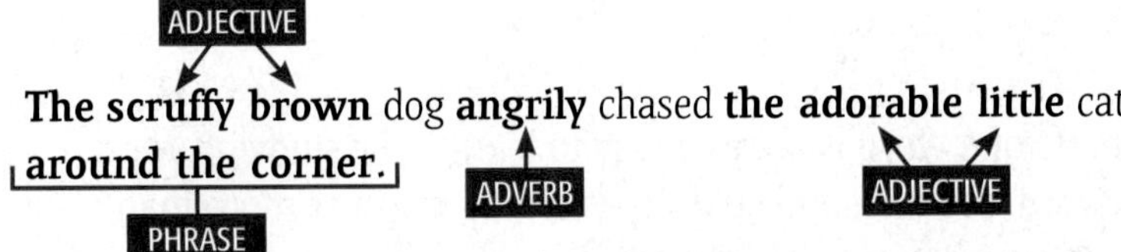
ADJECTIVE
The scruffy brown dog angrily chased the adorable little cat around the corner.
ADVERB
ADJECTIVE
PHRASE

▶ Check It Out

Knowing about syntax can help you figure out the meaning of an unfamiliar word. Just look at how syntax can help you figure out the following nonsense sentence.

The blizzy kwarkles sminched the flerky broogs.

Your experience with English syntax tells you that the action word, or verb, in this sentence is *sminched.*

Who did the *sminching?* The *kwarkles*.

What kind of *kwarkles* were they? *Blizzy.*

Whom did they *sminch?* The *broogs*.

What kind of *broogs* were they? *Flerky.*

Even though you don't know the meaning of the words in the nonsense sentence, you can make some sense of the entire sentence by studying its syntax.

Using Context Clues

You can often figure out the meaning of an unfamiliar word by looking at its context (the words and sentences that surround it).

▶ Do It!

To learn new words as you read, follow these steps for using context clues.

1. Look before and after the unfamiliar word for
   - a definition or a synonym (another word that means the same as the unfamiliar word)

     Some outdoor plants need to be **insulated,** or shielded, against cold weather.
   - a general topic associated with the word

     The painter brushed **primer** on the walls before the first coat of paint.
   - a clue to what the word is similar to or different from

     Like a spinning top, the dancer **pirouetted** gracefully.
   - an action or a description that has something to do with the word

     The cook used a **spatula** to flip the pancakes.
2. Connect what you already know with what the author has written.
3. Predict a possible meaning.
4. Use the meaning in the sentence.
5. Try again if your guess does not make sense.

Using reference materials

Dictionaries and other reference sources can help you learn new words. Check out these reference sources:

- A **dictionary** gives the pronunciation and the meaning or meanings of a word. Some dictionaries also give other forms of words, their parts of speech, and synonyms. You might also find the historical background of a word, such as its Greek, Latin, or Anglo-Saxon origins.

- A **glossary** is a word list that appears at the end of a book or other written work. It includes only words that are in that work. Like dictionaries, glossaries have the pronunciation and definitions of words. However, the definitions in a glossary give just enough information to help you understand the words as they are used in that work.
- A **thesaurus** lists groups of words that have the same, or almost the same, meaning. Words with similar meanings are called **synonyms.** Seeing the synonyms of words can help you build your vocabulary.

Understanding Denotation and Connotation

Words can have two types of meaning.

Denotation is the literal meaning, the meaning you find in dictionaries.

Connotation is a meaning or feeling that people connect with the word.

For example, you may say that flowers have a *fragrance* but that garbage has a *stench.* Both words mean "smell," but *fragrance* has a pleasant connotation, while *stench* has a very unpleasant one. As you read, it's important to think about the connotation of a word to completely understand what a writer is saying.

Recognizing Word Meanings Across Subjects

Have you ever learned a new word in one class and then noticed it in your reading for other subjects? The word may not mean exactly the same thing in each class. But you can use what you know about the word's meaning to help you understand what it means in a different subject area.

Look at the following example from three subjects:

Social Studies: One major **product** manufactured in the South is cotton cloth. (something manusfactured by a company)

Math: After you multiply those two numbers, explain how you arrived at the **product.** (the result of multiplying two numbers)

Science: One **product** of photosynthesis is oxygen. (the result of a chemical reaction)

In all three subject areas, a product is the result of something.

▶ Practice It!

1. Write each word below in your Learner's Notebook. Then underline the familiar word or root inside it. (Notice that the end of the familiar word or root may change in spelling a little when a suffix is added to it.)

a. configuration
b. contemporary
c. reformation
d. perspective
e. invaluable

2. Try to pronounce each of the words. Then check your pronunciation against the pronunciation given in the Glossary at the back of this book.

3. The following sentences can all be completed by the same word or form of the word. Use context clues to find the missing word. Write the word in your Learner's Notebook.
   a. I took the ___ to the photo shop to have a large print made.
   b. Protons are positive; elerctrons are ___.
   c. You always think ___; can't you think positively for a change?

Reading Fluently

Reading fluently is reading easily. When you read fluently, your brain recognizes each word so you can read without skipping or tripping over words. If you're a fluent reader, you can concentrate on the ideas in your reading because you don't have to worry about what each word means or how to say it.

To develop reading fluency. . .

- **Read often!** The more, the better. Reading often will help you develop a good sight vocabulary–the ability to quickly recognize words.
- **Practice reading aloud.** Believe it or not, reading aloud does help you become a better silent reader.
  - Begin by reading aloud a short, interesting passage that is easy for you.
  - Reread the same passage aloud at least three times or until your reading sounds smooth. Make your reading sound like you are speaking to a friend.
  - Then move on to a longer passage or a slightly more difficult one.

▶ Practice It!

Practice reading the paragraph under the following heading. After you think you can read it fluently–without errors or unnecessary pauses–read it aloud to a partner. Ask your patrner to comment on your fluency.

Reading for a Reason

Why are you reading that paperback mystery? What do you hope to get from your science textbook? And are you going to read either of these books in the same way that you read a restaurant menu?

The point is, you read for different reasons. The reason you're reading something helps you decide on the reading strategies you use with a text. In other words, how you read will depend on why you're reading.

Knowing Your Reason for Reading

In school and in life, you'll have many reasons for reading, and those reasons will lead you to a wide range of materials. For example,

- **To learn and understand new information,** you might read news magazines, textbooks, news on the Internet, books about your favorite pastime, encyclopedia articles, primary and secondary sources for a school report, instructions on how to use a calling card or directions for a standardized test.
- **To find specific information,** you might look at the sports section for the score of last night's game, a notice on where to register for a field trip, weather reports, bank statements, or television listings.
- **To be entertained,** you might read your favorite magazine, e-mails or letters from friends, the Sunday comics, or even novels, short stories, plays, or poems!

Adjusting How Fast You Read

How quickly or how carefully you should read a text depends on your purpose for reading it. Think about your purpose and choose a strategy that works best. Try out these strategies:

- **Scanning** means quickly running your eyes over the material, looking for **key words** or **phrases** that point to the information you're looking for. Scan when you need to find a particular piece or type of information. For example, you might scan a newspaper for movie show times or an encyclopedia article for facts to include in a research report.
- **Skimming** means quickly reading a piece of writing **to find its main idea** or to **get a general overview** of it. For example, you might skim the sports section of the daily newspaper to find out how your favorite teams are doing. Or you might skim a chapter in your science book to prepare for a test.
- **Careful reading** involves **reading slowly and paying attention** with a purpose in mind. Read carefully when you're learning new concepts, following complicated directions, or preparing to explain information to someone else. You definitely should read carefully when you're studying a textbook to prepare for class.

But you might also use this strategy when you're reading a mystery story and don't want to miss any details. Below are some tips you can use to help you read more carefully.

- **Take breaks** when you need them. There's no point in reading when you're sleepy. And if you're reading on the computer, give your eyes a break about every fifteen minutes by focusing on something more distant than your monitor screen.
- **Take notes** as you read. Write in your book if it's OK or use a notebook or sticky notes on the pages. Your notes may be just words or phrases that will jog your memory when you need to review. If you use a notebook, write page numbers from the book in the margin of your notes. That way you can quickly find the original material later if you need it.
- **Make graphic organizers** to help you organize the information from your reading. These can sort out ideas, clear up difficult passages, and help you remember important points. For example, **webs** can show a main idea and supporting details. A **flowchart** can help you keep track of events in a sequence. A **Venn diagram,** made up of overlapping circles, can help you organize how two characters, ideas, or events are alike and different.

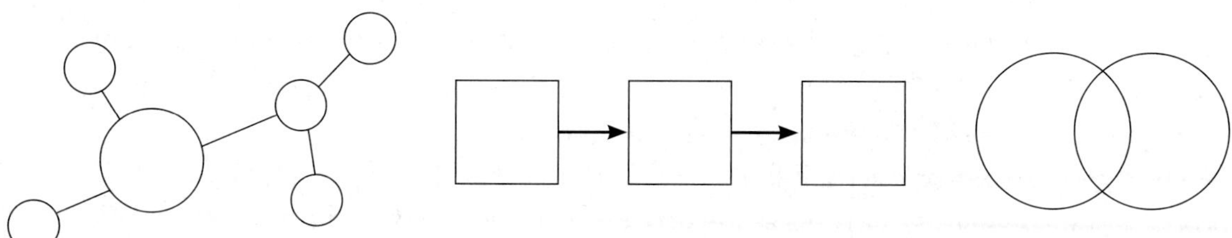

- **Review material** before stopping. Even a short review will help you remember what you've read. Try rereading difficult passages. They will be much easier to understand the second time.

▶ Practice It!

1. In your Learner's Notebook, write whether you would **skim, scan,** or **read carefully** in each of the following cases.
   a. a short story for your English class
   b. the school newspaper for your team's score in last week's game
   c. reviewing a chapter for tomorrow's social studies test
   d. a science book to find if it has information about nuclear waste
   e. to decide which stories and articles to read in a magazine

Becoming Engaged

In reading, *engagement* means relating to what you're reading in a way that makes it meaningful to you. It means finding links between the text and your own life. As you begin to read something, be ready to become engaged with the text. Then as you read, react to the text and relate it to your own experience. Your reading will be much more interesting, and you'll find it easier to understand and remember what you read.

Connect

You will become more involved with your reading and remember events, characters, and ideas better if you relate what you're reading to your own life. Connecting is finding the links between what you read and your own experience.

▶ Ask Yourself

- Have I been to places similar to the **setting** described by this writer?
- What **experiences** have I had that compare or contrast with what I am reading?
- What **opinions** do I already have about this topic?
- What **characters** from life or literature remind me of the characters or narrator in the selection?

Respond

Enjoy what you read and make it your own by responding to what's going on in the text. Think about and express what you like or don't like, what you find boring or interesting. What surprises you, entertains you, scares you, makes you angry, makes you sad, or makes you laugh out loud? The relationship between you and what you're reading is personal, so react in a personal way.

Understanding What You Read

Reading without understanding is like trying to drive a car on an empty gas tank. You can go through all the motions, but you won't get anywhere! Skilled readers adopt a number of strategies before, during, and after reading to make sure they understand what they read.

Previewing

If you were making a preview for a movie, you would want to let your audience know what the movie is like. When you preview a piece of writing, you're treating yourself like that movie audience. You're trying to get an idea about that piece of writing. If you know what to expect before reading, you will have an easier time understanding ideas and relationships. Follow these steps to preview your reading assignments.

▶ Do It!

1. **Look** at the title and any illustrations that are included.
2. **Read** the headings, subheadings, and anything in bold letters.
3. **Skim** over the passage to see how it is organized. Is it divided into many parts? Is it a long poem or short story? Don't forget to look at the graphics–pictures, maps, or diagrams.
4. **Set a purpose** for your reading. Are you reading to learn something new? Are you reading to find specific information?

Activating Prior Knowledge

Believe it or not, you already know quite a bit about what you're going to read. You don't know the plot or the information, of course, but keep in mind that you bring knowledge and unique personal experience to a selection. Drawing on your own background is called **activating prior knowledge,** and it can help you create meaning in what you read. Ask yourself, What do I already know about this topic? What do I know about related topics?

Predicting

You don't need a crystal ball to make **predictions** when you read. The predictions don't even have to be accurate! What's important is that you get involved in your reading from the moment you turn to page one. Take educated guesses before and during your reading about what might happen in the story. Follow these steps:

1. Use your prior knowledge and the information you gathered in your preview to predict what you will learn or what might happen in a selection. Will the hero ever get home? Did the butler do it?
2. As you read on, you may find that your prediction was way off base. Don't worry. Just adjust your predictions and go on reading.
3. Afterwards, check to see how accurate your predictions were. You don't have to keep score. By getting yourself involved in a narrative, you always end up a winner.

Visualizing

Creating pictures in your mind as you read–called visualizing–is a powerful aid to understanding. As you read, set up a movie theater in your imagination.

- Imagine what a character looks like.
- Picture the setting–city streets, the desert, or the surface of the Moon.
- Picture the steps in a process or the evidence that an author wants you to consider. If you can visualize what you read, selections will be more vivid, and you'll recall them better later on.

Identifying Sequence

When you discover the logical order of events or ideas, you are identifying sequence. Look for clues and signal words that will help you find the way information is organized.

Are you reading a story that takes place in chronological, or time, order? Do you need to understand step-by-step directions? Are you reading a persuasive speech with the reasons listed in order of importance? You'll understand and remember the information better when you know the organization the author has used.

Determining the Main Idea

When you look for the main idea of a selection, you look for the most important idea. The examples, reasons, or details that further explain the main idea are called supporting details.

Some main ideas are clearly stated within a passage—often in the first sentence of a paragraph, or sometimes in the last sentence of a passage.

Other times, an author doesn't directly state the main idea but provides details that help readers figure out what the main idea is.

▶ Ask Yourself

- What is each sentence about?
- Is there one sentence that tells about the whole passage or that is more important than the others?
- What main idea do the supporting details point out?

Questioning

Keep up a conversation with yourself as you read by **asking questions** about the text. Feel free to question anything!

- Ask about the importance of the information you're reading.
- Ask how one event relates to another or why a character acts a certain way.
- Ask yourself if you understand what you just read.
- As you answer your own questions, you're making sure that you understand what's going on.

Clarifying

Clear up, or **clarify,** confusing or difficult passages as you read. When you realize you don't understand something, try these techniques to help you clarify the ideas.

- Reread the confusing parts slowly and carefully.
- Diagram relationships between ideas.
- Look up unfamiliar words.
- Simply "talk out" the part to yourself.

Then read the passage once more. The second time through is often much easier and more informative.

Reviewing

You probably **review** in school every day in one class or another. You review what you learned the day before so the ideas stick in your mind. Reviewing when you read does the same thing.

Take time now and then to pause and review what you've read. Think about the main ideas and reorganize them for yourself so you can recall them later. Filling in study aids such as graphic organizers, notes, or outlines can help you review.

Monitoring Your Comprehension

Who's checking up on you when you read? You are! There's no teacher standing by to ask questions or to make sure that you're paying attention. As a reader, you are both the teacher and the student. It's up to you to make sure you accomplish a reader's most important task: understanding the material. As you read, check your understanding by using the following strategies.

- **Summarize** what you read by pausing from time to time and telling yourself the main ideas of what you've just read. When you summarize, include only the main ideas of a selection and only the useful supporting details. Answer the questions *Who? What? Where? When? Why?* and *How?* Summarizing tests your comprehension by encouraging you to clarify key points in your own words.
- **Paraphrase** Sometimes you read something that you "sort of" understand, but not quite. Use **paraphrasing** as a test to see whether you really got the point. Paraphrasing is retelling something in your own words. So shut the book and try putting what you've just read into your own words. If you can't explain it clearly, you should probably have another look at the text.

▶ Practice It!

Here are some strategies good readers use to understand a text. In your Learner's Notebook, tell which way is shown by each statement below.

connect	respond	predict	monitor comprehension
visualize	question	clarify	preview

1. I'm sure the doctor's going to be the main character in this story.
2. Why would this smart character make a dumb remark like that?
3. This woman reminds me of my mother when she's really mad.
4. This is a difficult passage. I'd better read it again and also look up the word malefactor in the dictionary.
5. Let's see if I've got this plot straight. So far, Greg's crazy about Donna, but she's hooked on Jesse, who seems interested in Sheila, who is Greg's date for the dance. And Dana's out to mess up everybody.

Thinking Critically About Your Reading

You've engaged with the text and used helpful reading strategies to understand what you've read. But is that all there is to it? Not always. Sometimes it's important to think more deeply about what you've read so that you can get the most out of what the author says. These critical thinking skills will help you go beyond what the words say and get at the important messages of your reading.

Interpreting

When you listen to your best friend talk, you don't just hear the words he or she says. You also watch your friend, listen to the tone of voice, and use what you already know about that person to put meaning to the words. In doing so, you are making meaning from what your friend says by using what you understand. You are interpreting what your friend says.

Readers do the same thing when they interpret as they read. Interpreting is more than just understanding the facts or story line you read. It's asking yourself, What's the writer really saying here? and then using what you know about the world to help answer that question. When you interpret as you read, you come to a much better understanding of the work.

Inferring

You may not realize it, but you infer, or make inferences, every day. Here's an example:

> You run to the bus stop a little later than usual. There's no one there. "I've missed the bus," you say to yourself. You may be wrong, but that's the way our minds work. We look at the evidence (you're late; no one's there) and come to a conclusion (you've missed the bus).

When you read, you go through exactly the same process because writers don't always directly state what they want you to understand. By providing clues and interesting details, they suggest certain information. Whenever you combine those clues with your own background and knowledge, you are making an inference.

Drawing Conclusions

Skillful readers are always drawing conclusions, or figuring out much more than an author says directly. The process is a little like a detective solving a mystery. You combine information and evidence that the author provides to come up with a statement about the topic, about a character, or about anything else in the work. Drawing conclusions helps you find connections between ideas and events and helps you have a better understanding of what you're reading.

Analyzing

Analyzing, or looking at separate parts of something to understand the entire piece, is a way to think critically about written work.

- In analyzing **fiction,** for example, you might look at the characters' values, events in the plot, and the author's style to figure out the story's theme.
- In analyzing persuasive **nonfiction**, you might look at the writer's reasons to see if they actually support the main point of the argument.
- In analyzing **informational text,** you might look at how the ideas are organized to see what's most important.

Distinguishing Fact from Opinion

Distinguishing between fact and opinion is one of the most important reading skills you can learn.

A **fact** is a statement that can be proved with supporting information.

An **opinion,** on the other hand, is what a writer believes on the basis of his or her personal viewpoint. An opinion is something that cannot be proved.

As you examine information, always ask yourself, Is this a fact or an opinion?

Don't think that opinions are always bad. Very often they are just what you want. You read editorials and essays for their authors' opinions. Reviews of movies, and CDs can help you decide whether to spend your time and money on something. It's when opinions are based on faulty reasoning or prejudice or when they are stated as facts that they become troublesome.

For example, look at the following examples of fact and opinion.

Fact: California produces fruits and other agricultural products.

Opinion: California is a wonderful place for a vacation.

You could prove that fruits and other agricultural products are grown in California. It's a fact. However, not everyone might agree that California is a great vacation site. That's someone's opinion.

UNIT 1

Skills Scope and Sequence

Readability Scores Key
Dale-Chall/DRP/Lexile

PACING (DAYS) STANDARD	BLOCK	INSTRUCTIONAL SEGMENT LITERATURE	READING SKILLS	LITERARY ELEMENTS
1	1	**Unit Warm-Up, pp. 2–11** Genre Focus: "Flash Flood" by William Hendryx **4.7/57/900**, SE p. 5	Setting a Purpose for Reading, SE pp. 4, 5, 11 Previewing, SE pp. 4, 5 Reviewing, SE pp. 4, 7, 8 Understanding Text Structure, SE pp. 4, 9 Reading Fluency, TWE p. 1	Photos and Illustrations, SE pp. 4, 10; TWE p. 8 Titles and Heads, SE pp. 4, 5 Deck, SE pp. 4, 5 Lead, SE pp. 4, 6; TWE p. 11 Informational Media, TWE p. 4
3	2	**Reading Workshop 1, pp. 12–33** "Paddling Dicey Waters" by Lew Freedman **6.9/62/1100**, p. 16 "Seventh Grade" by Gary Soto **5.3/52/730**, SE p. 26	Setting a Purpose for Reading, SE pp. 12–13, 15, 16, 17, 23, 25, 28, 29, 30, 33	Photos and Illustrations, SE pp. 15, 20, 22, 23, 25, 26, 30, 33 Nonfiction, TWE p. 14 Voice in Fiction, TWE p. 24
1		**Writing Workshop, Part 1, pp. 34–37** Writing Product: Summary	Read to write, SE p. 36 Summarizing, SE p. 36 Identifying Main Idea, SE p. 36 Reading Fluency, TWE p. 36	
3	1	**Reading Workshop 2, pp. 38–53** "Where You Are" by Jack Anderson SE p. 42 "Message of Hope" by Ericka Souter and Dietlind Lerner **4.9/54/810**, SE p. 48	Previewing, SE pp. 38–39, 41, 42, 45, 47, 48, 53	Titles and heads, SE pp. 41, 42, 45, 47, 48, 51, 53 Poetry, TWE p. 40 Informational Articles, TWE p. 46

Organizing Information

When researching a topic, you can't stop after you've read your sources of information. You also have to make sense of that information, organize it, and put it all together in ways that will help you explain it to someone else. Here are some ways of doing just that.

- **Record** information from your research and keep track of your resources on note cards.
- **Summarize** information before you write it on a note card. That way you'll have the main ideas in your own words.
- **Outline** ideas so you can see how subtopics and supporting information will fit under a main idea.
- **Make a table or graph** to compare items or categories of information.

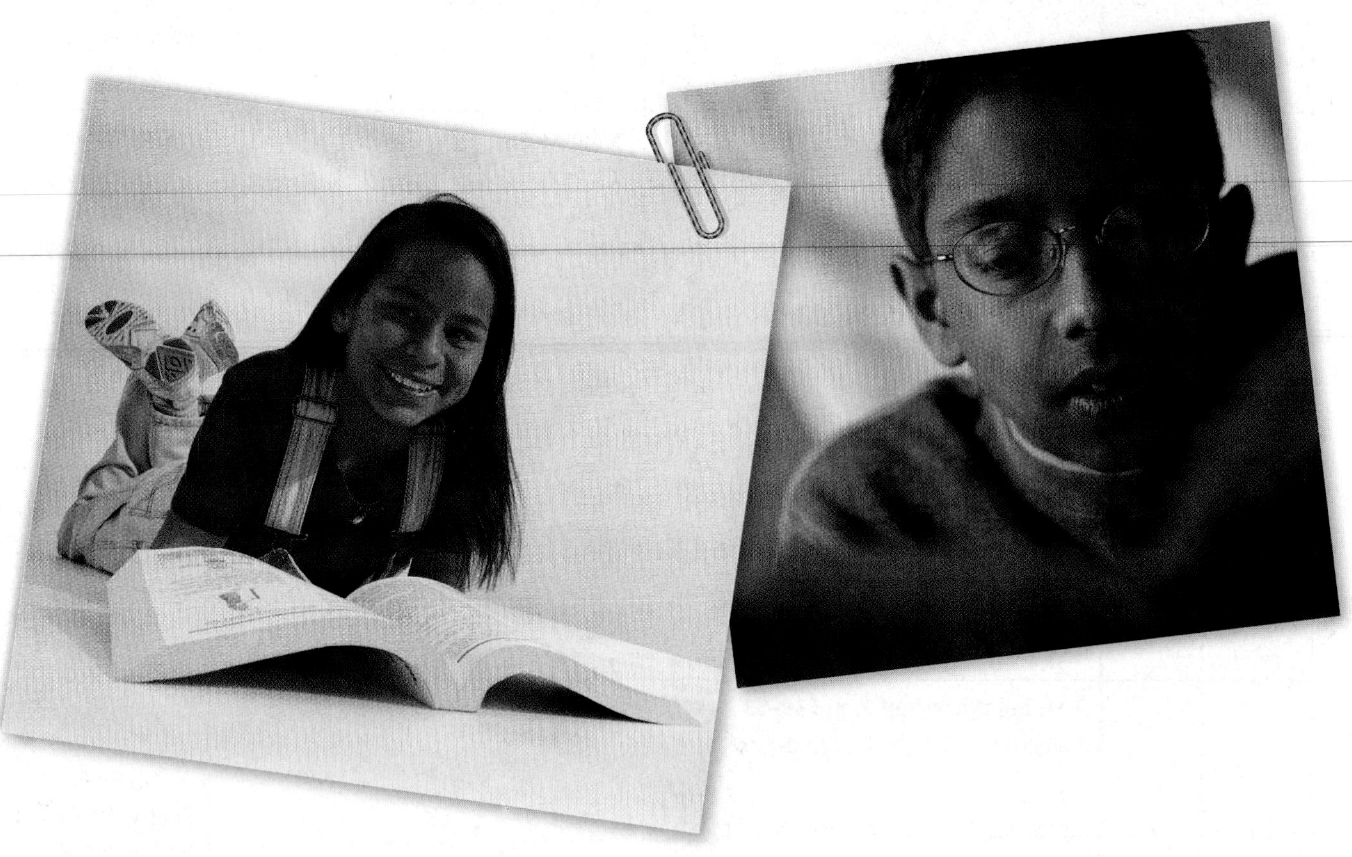

Reading for Research

An important part of doing research is knowing how to get information from a wide variety of sources. The following skills will help you when you have a research assignment for a class or when you want information about a topic outside of school.

Reading Text Features

Researching a topic is not only about asking questions. It's about finding answers. Textbooks, references, magazines, and other sources provide a variety of text features to help you find those answers quickly and efficiently.

- Tables of contents Look at the table of contents first to see whether a resource offers information you need.
- Indexes An index is an alphabetical listing of significant topics covered in a book. It is found in the back of a book.
- Headings and subheadings Headings often tell you what information is going to follow in the text you're reading. Subheadings allow you to narrow your search for information even further.
- Graphic features Photos, diagrams, maps, charts, graphs, and other graphic features can communicate large amounts of information at a glance. They usually include captions that explain what they show.

Interpreting Graphic Aids

When you're researching a topic, be sure to read and interpret the graphic aids you find. **Graphic aids** explain information visually. When reading graphic aids, read the title first to see if you're likely to find information you want.

- **Reading a map** Maps are flat representations of land. A **compass rose** shows you directions–north, south, east, and west. A **legend,** or **key,** explains the map's symbols. A **scale** shows you how distances shown on the map relate to the actual distances.
- **Reading a graph** A graph shows you how two or more things relate. Graphs can use circles, dots, bars, or lines. For example, on the weather part of a TV newscast you might see a weather graph that predicts how the temperatures for the next five days will rise or fall.
- **Reading a table** A table groups numbers or facts and puts them into categories so you can compare what is in each category. The facts are organized in rows and columns. Find the row that has the category you're looking for. Then read across to the column that has the information you need.

Problem and Solution

How did scientists overcome the difficulty of getting a person to the Moon? How can our team win the pennant this year? How will I brush my teeth when I've forgotten my toothpaste? These questions may be very different in importance, but they have one thing in common: each identifies a problem and asks how to solve it. Problems and solutions are part of what makes life interesting.

By organizing their texts around that important question-word *how,* writers state the problem and suggest a solution. Sometimes they suggest many solutions. Of course, it's for you to decide if they're right.

- **Signal words and phrases:** how, help, problem, obstruction, overcome, difficulty, need, attempt, have to, must

  Example: A major **difficulty** in learning to drive a car with a standard shift is starting on hills. Students **need** to practice starting slowly and smoothly on a level surface before they graduate to slopes. Observing an experienced driver perform the maneuver will also **help.**

Sequence

Consider these requests: Tell us what happened at the picnic. Describe your favorite CD cover. Identify the causes of the Civil War. Three very different instructions, aren't they? Well, yes and no. They are certainly about different subjects. But they all involve sequence, the order in which thoughts are arranged. Take a look at three common forms of sequencing.

- **Chronological order** refers to the order in which events take place. First you wake up; next you have breakfast; then you go to school. Those events don't make much sense in any other order. Whether you are explaining how to wash the car, giving directions to a friend's house, or telling your favorite joke, the world would be a confusing place if people didn't organize their ideas in chronological order. Look for signal words such as *first, next, then, later,* and *finally.*
- **Spatial order** describes the order of things in space. For example, take a look at this description of an ice cream sundae:

  > *At the bottom of the dish are two scoops of vanilla. The scoops are covered with fudge and topped with whipped cream and a cherry.*

  Your eyes follow the sundae from the bottom to the top. Spatial order is important in descriptive writing because it helps you as a reader to see an image the way the author does. Signal words include *above, below, behind, left, right,* and *next to.*
- **Order of importance** is going from most important to least important or the other way around. For example, a typical news article has a most-to-least-important structure. Readers who don't have the time to read the entire article can at least learn the main idea by reading the first few paragraphs. Signal words include *principal, central, important,* and *fundamental.*

Understanding Text Structure

Writers organize each piece of their writing in a specific way for a specific purpose. That pattern of organization is called **text structure.** When you know the text structure of a selection, you'll find it easier to locate and recall an author's ideas. Here are four ways that writers organize text, along with some signal words and phrases containing clues to help you identify their methods.

Comparison and Contrast

Comparison-and-contrast structure shows the similarities and differences between people, things, and ideas. When writers use comparison-and-contrast structure, often they want to show you how things that seem alike are different or how things that seem different are alike.

- **Signal words and phrases:** similarly, more, less, on the one hand, on the other hand, in contrast to, but, however

  Example: That day had been the best and worst of her life. **On the one hand,** the tornado had destroyed her home. **On the other hand,** she and her family were safe. Her face was full of cuts and bruises, **but** she smiled at the little girl on her lap.

Cause and Effect

Just about everything that happens in life is the cause or the effect of some other event or action. Sometimes what happens is pretty minor: You don't look when you're pouring milk (cause); you spill milk on the table (effect). Sometimes it's a little more serious: You don't look at your math book before the big test (cause); you mess up on the test (effect).

Writers use cause-and-effect structure to explore the reasons for something happening and to examine the results of previous events. A scientist might explain why the rain falls. A sports writer might explain why a team is doing badly. A historian might tell us why an empire rose and fell. Cause-and-effect structure is all about explaining things.

- **Signal words and phrases:** so, because, as a result, therefore, for the following reasons

  Example: The blizzard raged for twelve hours. **Because** of the heavy snow, the streets were clogged within an hour of being plowed. **As a result,** the city was at a standstill. Of course, we had no school that day, **so** we went sledding!

Evaluating

When you form an opinion or make a judgment about something you're reading, you are **evaluating.**

If you're reading **informational texts** or something on the Internet, it's important to evaluate how qualified the author is to write about the topic and how reliable the information that's presented is. Ask yourself whether

- the author seems biased.
- the information is one-sided.
- the argument presented is logical.

If you're reading **fiction,** evaluate the author's style or ask yourself questions such as

- Is this character interesting or dull?
- Are the events in the plot believable or realistic?
- Does the author's message make sense?

Synthesizing

When you **synthesize,** you combine ideas (maybe even from different sources) to come up with something new. It may be a new understanding of an important idea or a new way of combining and presenting information.

Many readers enjoy taking ideas from their reading and combining them with what they already know to come to new understandings. For example, you might

1. Read a manual on coaching soccer

+

2. Combine what you learn from that reading with your own experiences playing soccer

+

3. Add what you know about coaches you've had

=

4. Come up with a winning plan for coaching your sister's soccer team this spring.

Unit 1 Big Question

The question, "Why do we read?" is designed to help students see that they read to obtain all kinds of information, to gain new insight into themselves and others, and to be entertained. In this unit, students will read a variety of selections that serve all these purposes for reading.

Unit 1 Genre

Many of the selections in this unit are informational media, which provide knowledge. These selections will also help students answer the big question: Why do we read? Use these informational media to help students recognize that they read to obtain all kinds of information that they want and/or need.

CRITICAL THINKING	VOCABULARY	WRITING AND GRAMMAR	LISTENING, SPEAKING, AND VIEWING
Comprehension, TWE pp. 2, 4 Evaluation, TWE p. 8 Identifying, TWE p. 10	Verb Tenses, TWE p. 2	Write to Learn, SE p. 11	Warm-Up Activity: Talk with a partner, SE p. 2 Small Group, SE p. 11
Infer, SE pp. 22, 32 Evaluate, SE pp. 22, 32 Recall, SE p. 32 Summarize, SE p. 32 Application, TWE p. 15 Analysis, TWE p. 17, 26, 30 Comprehension, TWE pp. 17, 19, 21, 27	Context Clues, SE pp. 14, 17, 18, 19, 22, 23, 24, 27, 28, 31, 33; TWE pp. 15, 18, 25 Vocabulary Preview, SE pp. 14, 24 Vocabulary Check, SE pp. 23, 33 Specialized Vocabulary, TWE p. 12 Slang, TWE p. 27 Similes, TWE p. 28 Figurative Language, TWE p. 30	Individual Activity, SE p. 14 Parts of Speech, SE p. 23 Verbs, SE p. 33 Write About Your Reading, SE p. 22 Write to Learn, SE pp. 25, 32 Writing Application, SE p. 23	Class Activity, SE p. 14 Group Talk, SE p. 15 Talk About Your Reading, SE p. 32 Partner Talk, SE p. 25
		Writing a Summary: prewriting and drafting, SE p. 34 Applying Writing Traits: Ideas, SE p. 35 Writing Tip: Use the Model, SE p. 36 Action and Linking Verbs, SE p. 37	
Infer, SE pp. 44, 52 Draw Conclusions, SE p. 44 Evaluate, SE pp. 44, 52; TWE p. 43 Analysis, TWE pp. 49, 50	Context clues, SE pp. 40, 43, 45, 46, 49 Academic Vocabulary, SE pp. 38 Vocabulary Preview, SE p. 40 Vocabulary Check, SE pp. 45, 53 Building Background, TWE p. 38 Poetry Structure, TWE p. 41 Definition and Restatement, TWE p. 47 Origins of a Phrase, TWE p. 50	Main verbs and helping verbs, SE pp. 45, 53 Write About Your Reading, SE p. 44 Write to Learn, SE pp. 40, 41, 44, 52	Talk About Your Reading, SE p. 52 Small Group, SE p. 41 Group Talk, SE p. 47

Skills Scope and Sequence *continued*

Readability Scores Key
Dale-Chall/DRP/Lexile

PACING (DAYS) STANDARD	BLOCK	INSTRUCTIONAL SEGMENT LITERATURE	READING SKILLS	LITERARY ELEMENTS
3	1	**Reading Workshop 3, pp. 54–73** "Teaching Nepalis to Read, Plant, and Vote" by Lesley Reed **4.6/57/900**, SE p. 58 "May I Have Your Autograph?" by Marjorie Sharmat **5.7/47/580**, SE p. 66	Reviewing, SE pp. 54–55, 57, 61, 63, 65, 68, 71, 73 Previewing, SE p. 73	Lead, SE pp. 57, 58, 63 Photographs, SE pp. 60, 70 Title, SE p. 63 Point of View, SE pp. 65, 66, 67, 73 Humorous Writing, TWE p. 64
1		**Writing Workshop, Part 2, pp. 74–77** Writing Product: Summary		
2	1	**Reading Workshop 4, pp. 78–101** "Suzy and Leah" by Jane Yolen **4.2/44/550**, SE p. 82 from *How Things Work* **8.3/61/1090**, SE p. 96	Understanding Text Structure, SE pp. 78–79, 81, 82, 84, 90, 93, 95, 96, 98, 101 Recognizing steps in a process, SE pp. 78, 79 Previewing, SE p. 82 Build Fluency, TWE p. 91	Point of View, SE pp. 81, 83, 85, 87, 88, 89, 90, 93 Photos, SE p. 83 Text features, SE pp. 95, 97, 98, 101 Diaries and Personal Letters, TWE p. 80 Historical Fiction, TWE p. 89
2	2	**Comparing Literature Workshop, pp. 102–111** "Summer Reading" by Michael Dorris **5.2/56/1020**, p. 105 "The First Book" by Rita Dove, SE p. 109	How to Compare Literature: Theme, SE pp. 102–103	Theme, SE pp. 102, 103, 106, 107, 109, 111; TWE pp. 102, 103 Autobiographical Essay, TWE p. 105 Lyric Poetry, TWE p. 108
2	1	**Unit Wrap-Up, pp. 112–127** "The Day It Rained Cockroaches" by Paul Zindel **7.8/55/1090**, SE p. 114	Reading independently, SE pp. 120, 121 Read and Apply Skills, SE pp. 114–119 Assessment, SE pp. 124–125	Assessment, SE pp. 122–123 Summary, TWE p. 114

CRITICAL THINKING	VOCABULARY	WRITING AND GRAMMAR	LISTENING, SPEAKING, AND VIEWING
Infer, SE p. 62 Evaluate, SE p. 62, TWE p. 70 Summarize, SE p. 72 Interpret, SE p. 72 Analyze, SE p. 72; TWE pp. 57, 59, 60, 65 Comprehension, TWE pp. 65, 70	Context clues, SE pp. 56, 59, 63, 64, 67, 69, 73; TWE p. 56 Vocabulary Preview, SE pp. 56, 64 Vocabulary Check, SE pp. 63, 73 Unfamiliar Terms: Hotel Talk, TWE p. 68	Write to Learn, SE pp. 56, 65 Write About Your Reading, SE pp. 62, 72 Verb tense, SE pp. 63, 73 Writing Application, SE pp. 63, 73	Partner Talk, SE pp. 57, 65 Group Discussion, SE p. 57
		Writing a Summary: Revising, Editing, and Presenting, SE p. 74–75 Writing Tip: Spelling, SE p. 75 Writing Tip: Handwriting, SE p. 75	Giving and Following Directions, SE p. 77
Infer, SE pp. 92, 100 Evaluate, SE p. 92; TWE pp. 88, 91 Application, TWE p. 81 Analysis, TWE pp. 84, 85, 87 Comprehension, TWE pp. 88, 95	Context clues, SE pp. 80, 86, 89, 93, 94, 96, 98, 101 Sentence Fragments, TWE p. 83 Academic Vocabulary, SE p. 78 Vocabulary Preview, SE pp. 80, 94 Vocabulary Check, SE pp. 93, 101	Write to Learn, SE pp. 81, 94, 95 Write About Your Reading, SE pp. 92, 100 Writing Application, SE p. 93 Irregular Verbs, SE pp. 93, 101	
Compare and contrast, SE p. 111 Interpret, SE p. 111 Evaluate, SE p. 111 Comprehension, TWE p. 107	Context clues, SE pp. 105, 106, 108; TWE p. 106 Academic Vocabulary, SE p. 102 Vocabulary Preview, SE p. 104 Vocabulary Check, SE p. 110	Taking notes and using them to make a diagram that compares the theme in two pieces of literature, SE p. 111	
Evaluation, TWE p. 115	Assessment, SE p. 126 American Pop Culture, TWE p. 116	Writing an advertising brochure, SE p. 113 Assessment, SE p. 127	Group Activity: Writing a commercial, SE p. 112

UNIT 1

Unit Resources

Reading with Purpose offers a comprehensive package of tools to optimize student learning and the teaching experience. Each resource has been designed to assist students in specific areas and to offer instructional support for teachers. While all of these areas are covered in the core textbook, some students may need extra practice or additional help in specific areas. The resource package is designed so that you, the teacher, can choose which items will best assist your students. You may also use these resources as homework assignments and for assessment purposes. The following are resources recommended for use with Unit 1.

Keys for Unit Resources

- Blackline Master
- Workbook
- Supplemental Text
- CD-ROM
- DVD
- Transparency
- Web-based
- Fast Files

Essential Instructional Support

FAST FILE UNIT 1 RESOURCES

Reading and Literature
- Academic Vocabulary Development
- Big Question: School to Home Connection
- The Big Question Foldable
- Genre Study
- Unit Challenge: Planner and Rubrics
- Comparing Literature Graphic Organizer
- Key Reading Skills Practice
- Active Reading Graphic Organizers
- Literary Analysis
- Selection Vocabulary Development

Writing, Grammar, and Spelling
- Spelling and Handwriting Practice
- Grammar Practice
- Writing Workshop Graphic Organizer

Listening, Speaking, and Viewing
- Viewing and Representing Activities
- Listening and Speaking Activities

English Language Learners
- English Language Coach

DIFFERENTIATED INSTRUCTION

- Leveled Vocabulary Development
- Skills Level Up!
- Listening Library CD
- BookLink 3
- Literature Library Vocabulary Puzzlemaker
- Vocabulary Puzzlemaker

ASSESSMENT

- Selection and Unit Assessments
- Selection Quick Checks
- Assessment by Learning Objectives
- Rubrics for Assessing Student Writing, Listening, and Speaking
- Glencoe Online Essay Grading
- Interactive Tutor Self-Assessment
- ExamView Assessment Suite
- Literature Library ExamView Assessment Suite

Additional Instructional Support

WRITING, GRAMMAR, AND SPELLING

- Real Success in Writing: Research and Reports
- Writing Constructed Responses Sourcebook
- Spelling Power eWorkbook
- Grammar & Composition Handbook
- Grammar and Language Workbook
- Revising with Style eWorkbook

READING AND LITERATURE

- Active Learning and Note Taking Guide
- inTime Magazines
- Backpack Reader Volume 1
- Literature Library
- Literature Launchers Pre-Reading Videos DVD
- Literature Classics

TRANSPARENCIES

- Read Aloud, Think Aloud
- Literary and Text Analysis Transparencies
- Bellringer Options Transparencies
- Grammar and Writing Workshop Transparencies
- Fine Arts Transparencies

TECHNOLOGY

- TeacherWorks Plus
- StudentWorks Plus
- BookLink 3
- Skill Level Up!
- ExamView Assessment Suite
- Interactive Tutor Self-Assessment
- Listening Library CD
- Spanish Listening Library CD
- Literature Classics
- Literature Launchers Pre-Reading Videos DVD
- Literature Library ExamView Assessment Suite
- Vocabulary Puzzlemaker
- Literature Library Vocabulary Puzzlemaker
- glencoe.com
- Online Student Edition
- Presentation Plus!
- Glencoe Online Essay Grading

ENGLISH LANGUAGE LEARNER

- English Language Coach
- Fluency Practice and Assessment
- inTime Magazines (Spanish)
- Spanish Listening Library CD

PROFESSIONAL DEVELOPMENT

- Professional Development Package

Additional Glencoe Resources

FOLDABLES™ Study Organizer — Dinah Zike's Foldables

Foldables are three-dimensional, interactive graphic organizers that help students practice basic writing skills, review key vocabulary terms, and answer Big Questions. Every unit contains a foldable activity. You can find the pattern and directions for the Unit 1 Foldable in the Unit 1 Resources Fast Files booklet. You can use the foldables as they are presented or modify them to suit the needs of your students. More information about foldables for Unit 1 can be found on page R8.

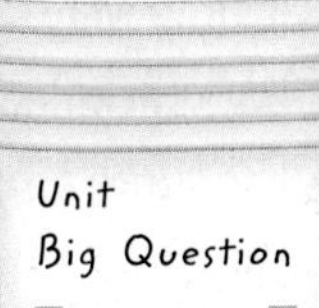

Glencoe Literature Library

The collection of hardcover books include full-length novels, novellas, plays and works of nonfiction. Each volume consists of at least one complete extended-length reading accompanied by several related readings from a broad range of genres. A separate Study Guide for each Glencoe Literature Library book provides teaching notes and reproducible activity pages for students.

Glencoe Literature Library titles that complement this unit include:

Dandelion Wine by Ray Bradbury
So Far From the Bamboo Grove by Yoko Kawashima Watkins
Sounder by William H. Armstrong
The True Confessions of Charlotte Doyle by Avi

LiteratureOnline

For a wealth of online resources that support the instruction in Unit 1 of *Glencoe Literature: Reading with Purpose,* students and teachers can visit our Web site at www.glencoe.com. Students will find additional learning, practice, and assessment opportunities such as these, which are noted in the student text:

- **Big Question Overview**
- **Study Central**
- **Author Search**
- **Writing Models**
- **Interactive Literary Elements Handbook**
- **Web Activities**

Teachers will find planning and instructional tools that include the following:

- **Book Lesson Plans**
- **Teacher Forum**
- **Professional Development**
- **Web Activities Lesson Plans (with answers to student activities)**

Go to www.glencoe.com to see the entire selection of Reading with Purpose online resources.

Reading List Generator CD-ROM — Glencoe BookLink

Use the Glencoe BookLink 3 CD-ROM, a database of more than 26,700 titles, to *create customized reading lists* for your students.

- Search for award-winning titles, (e.g., Newbery Award winners, Coretta Scott King Award winners, and Caldecott Medal winners) and for books on several state-recommended reading lists.
- Find Degrees of Reading Power™ (DRP) and Lexile™ readability scores for all selections.
- Organize reading lists by students' reading level, author, genre, theme, or area of interest.
- Get a brief summary of each selection.

You can find recommended leveled readings for this unit with Reading on Your Own (see page 120).

Presentation Plus! / CheckPoint

Glencoe's **Presentation Plus!**, a multimedia teaching tool, lets you present dynamic lessons that will engage your students. Using Microsoft PowerPoint,® you can customize the presentations to create your own personalized lessons. Use **CheckPoint** questions with interactive response keypads to get immediate student feedback during lessons, to increase student participation, and to assess student comprehension.

inTIME

A lively collection of articles drawn from issues of the TIME family of magazines helps students develop the skills they need to interact with informational text in a meaningful way. Each of the news stories, feature articles, reviews, profiles, and essays in the magazine connect to an author, work, or theme in *Glencoe Literature: Reading with Purpose.* Articles for Unit 1 are found in Volume A. See the *inTIME* Teacher's Guide for specific connections to each unit and for reproducible student worksheets designed to develop students' reading and critical thinking skills.

Literature Launchers

Set the scene with Glencoe's Literature Launchers, engaging video segments that introduce each unit's genre focus. Each video brings the genre to life, relating it to your students' worlds.

Insert the Glencoe Literature Launchers Pre-Reading Videos DVD into your DVD player. Select the Unit 1 Launcher from the menu to introduce the genre and Big Question for this unit.

Online Essay Grader

Use Glencoe's Online Essay Grading to score your students' writing and to provide individualized feedback to each student automatically.

You and your students can visit www.glencoe.com to link to the essay grader. *Students* can enter their essays and receive feedback on demand. *You* can manage demographic data, assign tests and generate individual student and aggregated reports. The essay grader can help you

- Save time with automatic scoring and individualized feedback.
- Supplement in-class writing instruction using guided writing practice.
- Get reports for individual students or for special populations.
- Track student improvement over time.

REAL Success: Reading Excellence at All Levels

Glencoe now provides all of your students with the tools they need to become better, more enthusiastic readers. The REAL Success suite of reading and language arts products encourages reading excellence by meeting the needs of students at all levels. Glencoe products that can be used in conjunction with Unit 1 include the following:

- Jamestown Literature: An Adapted Reader
- Jamestown *Reading Fluency*
- Jamestown *Critical Reading Series, In the Line of Duty*
- *Vocabulary Builder*
- *The Glencoe Reader, Course 2*

To order these products, call Glencoe at 1-800-USA-READ.

Teacher Wraparound Edition Key

Level Appropriate Code

AS = Activities for all students

AL = Activities for students working above grade level

OL = Activities for students working at grade level

BL = Activities for students working below grade level

EL = Activities for English language learners

Teacher Wraparound Prompts

R **Reading Skill** These activities help you teach reading skills and vocabulary.

V **Vocabulary** These activities help students comprehend words and incorporate into reading.

C **Critical Thinking** These strategies help students apply and extend what they have learned.

BQ **BIG Question** These activities and questions prompt students to prepare to answer the Big Question.

W **Writing** These activities provide writing opportunities to help students practice writing and comprehend text.

L **Literary Element** These activities and questions help students comprehend selections and learn more about each genre.

E **Text Element** These activities help students comprehend text elements.

LSV **Listening, Speaking, Viewing** These activities help students practice listening, speaking, and viewing skills.

EL **English Language Coach** These skills help English language learners as well as students who need additional reading support.

UNIT 1 Professional Development Center

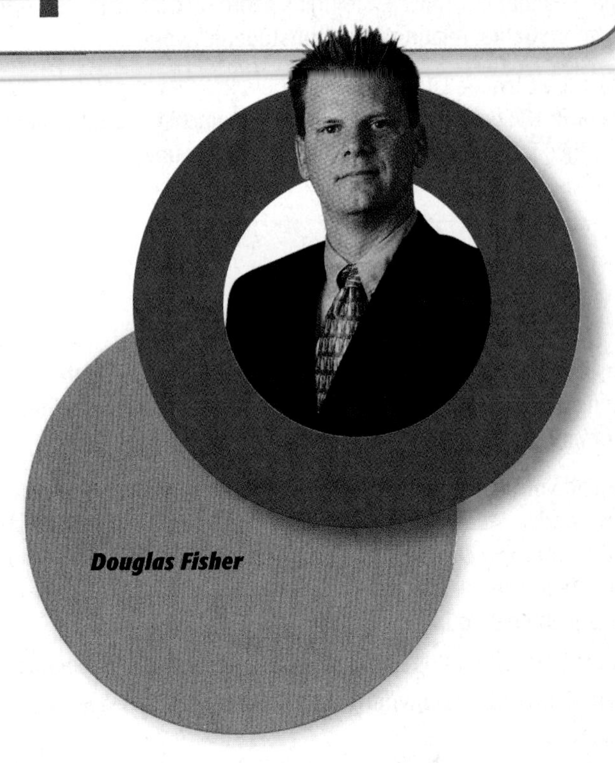

Douglas Fisher

From An Author:

Preparing Students to Read Informational Media

Start with an illustration. Students enjoy illustrations and graphics, especially in the form of cartoons and graphic stories. Start the class by sharing an appealing or controversial photograph or cartoon. Invite students to discuss the graphic with a partner. What do they see? What does it mean? This type of partner conversation builds interest in the topic as well as background information about the topic. Describe the ways in which informational media uses illustrations. For example, newspaper and magazine articles often have photographs or illustrations. Ask students to discuss their experiences with photographs and illustrations in informational media. Why are they there? What do they do? How do they help the reader?

Activate background knowledge. Informational media often relates to the current events in our lives. Ask students about the current events being covered in magazines and newspapers. How are those stories being reported? Whose perspective is shared in these types of articles? Preview the selections in this unit by inviting students to skim the table of contents. Ask them to note the types of topics being discussed—floods, seventh grade, teaching, how things work, etc. Ask students what they already know about these topics and what they'd like to know about these topics.

Teacher to Teacher

Linda I. Rodriguez
Weis Middle School
Texas City, Texas

The newspaper is a valuable instrument in the classroom because there is a reality to newspapers that forces students to confront possibilities in their own lives that they may think they can ignore in fiction. When introducing the Big Question "Why do we read?" I bring in a number of newspaper articles and let students each select one that personally represents a challenge. We discuss how students might face these challenges, focusing on both the positive and the negative aspects of reality. I like to include inspirational stories of real people who have faced and overcome challenges and apply these real-life stories to students. I ask, "What would you do if you were the person in this newspaper story?" We discuss the ways newspapers and other written media connect our lives to the lives of others.

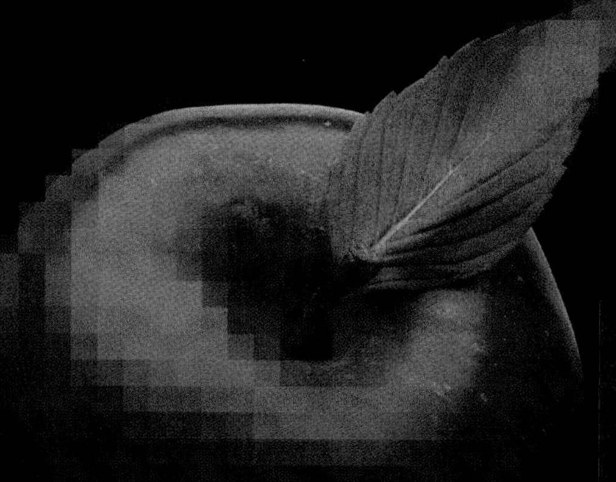

Teacher Chat Room

Using Informational Media

What is informational media and why is it important?

This genre focuses on the types of texts used to inform—and teach—people about topics important in their lives. It extends traditional nonfiction texts to include a wide range of media outlets that can be used to provide people with accurate information. Informational media is important as it is one of the primary ways that people receive information in the world. For example, we read newspapers, magazines, and the Internet to find out the answers to our questions and to understand the events of the world. In fact, informational media is one of the most common types of texts adults read. Middle school students need to know how to read for information and how to evaluate the information they read.

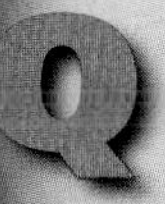

Are students interested in informational media?

Very much so. In fact, there is evidence that reluctant readers and many male students prefer informational media and texts. The difficulty with this type of text is the background knowledge that is assumed by some authors. For example, in the reading "Flash Flood," the author assumes his readers know what a flood is. To help students read this text, which many of them will find fascinating, you may want to focus on the key ideas before sharing the text. Building background and frontloading information is always a good idea as it helps students make connections between what they already know and what they will learn.

How are informational media texts organized?

There are a number of structures that authors of informational media texts use. In many newspaper articles, for example, the key ideas are presented toward the beginning of the article and details are presented in the paragraphs that follow. This is for ease of editing when a paragraph needs to be cut. Magazine articles often use descriptive structures that allow a reader to develop a deeper sense of the content based on the reading. Of course, all of the informational text structures can be used, including problem/solution, cause/effect, and temporal/sequence. Helping readers understand the structure of the text facilitates their comprehension of the content.

Key Unit Objectives

- Answer the Big Question
- Analyze the text elements of informational media
- Apply strategies for reading informational media
- Write summaries

BIG Question

Why Is It Important?

Addressing this Big Question helps students set purposes for reading and get the most from what they read. Searching for answers to the Big Question will help students understand the many ways that reading impacts their lives.

Viewing the Photo

Say: Read the opening quotation. What do you think Mary Schmich means by "a discount ticket to everywhere?" *(Possible response: It costs practically nothing to read, but reading about distant places can transport you around the world and to places that exist only in the imagination.)* **OL**

Ask: Where are some places that reading has taken you recently? *(Answers will vary.)* **BL**

UNIT 1

The BIG Question: Why Do We Read?

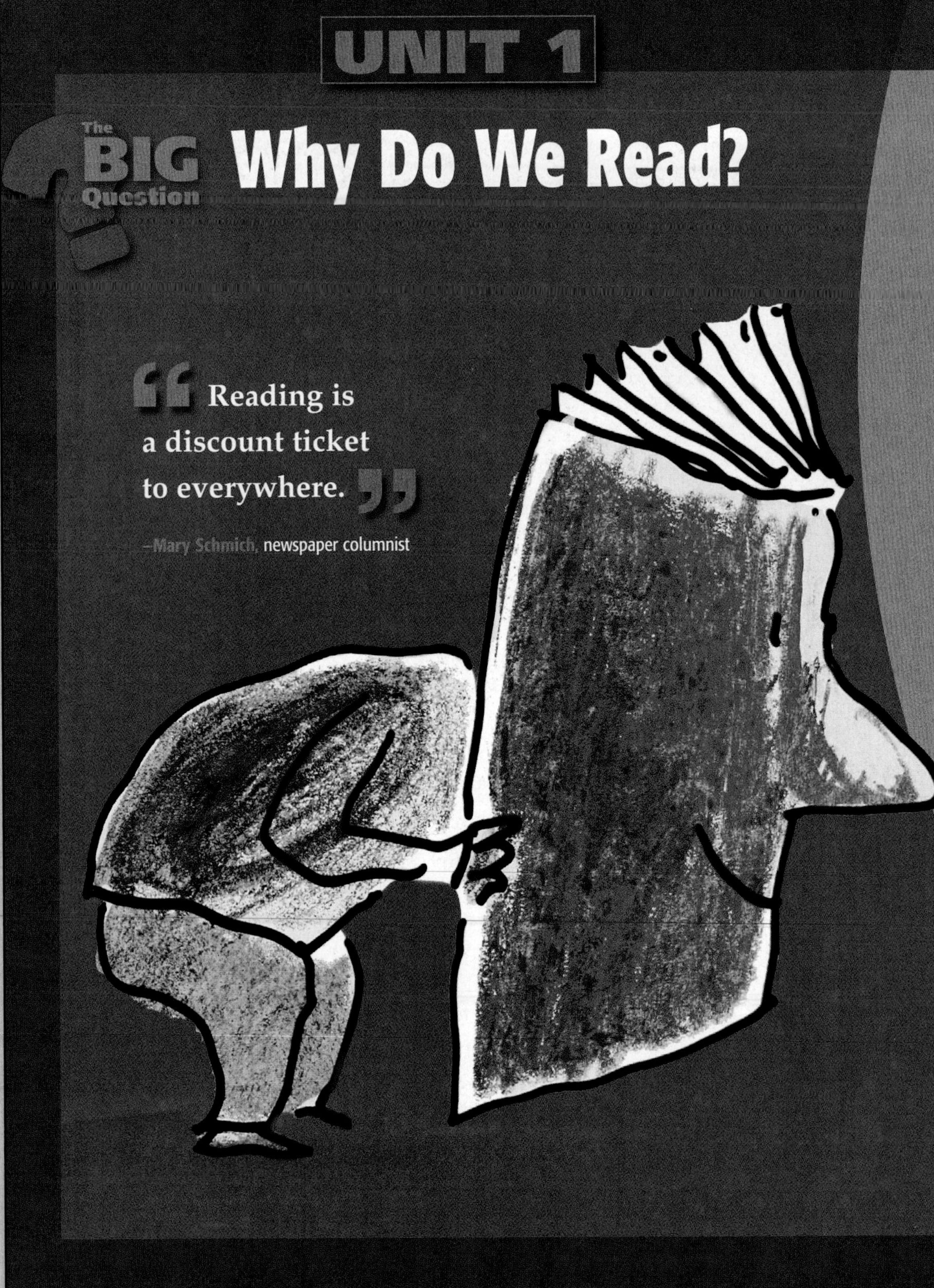

"Reading is a discount ticket to everywhere."

—Mary Schmich, newspaper columnist

Unit Skills

BIG Question: Why Do We Read?

Genre Focus: Informational Media

Reading Skills

- Setting a purpose for reading, p. 12
- Previewing, p. 38
- Reviewing, p. 54
- Understanding text structure, p. 78

Vocabulary

- Context clues, pp. 14, 40, 56, 80, 94, 108
- Comparison and contrast, p. 64

Text Elements

- Photographs, pp. 4, 15, 25
- Titles, heads, and decks, pp. 4, 41, 47
- Lead, p. 57
- Text features, p. 95

Writing Skills/Grammar

- Summary, pp. 34, 74
- Conventions, p. 35

LOOKING AHEAD

The skill lessons and readings in this unit will help you develop your own answer to the Big Question.

About the Reading

Each selection in this unit provides insights that can help students to address the question, "Why do we read?" Students will consider different aspects of why they read and why other people read.

About the Skills

The skills taught in this unit have been selected because they are particularly helpful when reading the featured genre—informational media. Each reading selection provides students with opportunities to practice and develop these skills.

NO CHILD LEFT BEHIND

The goals of the NCLB act include a strong emphasis on developing reading comprehension skills. As stated at the Student Achievement and School Accountability Conference in October 2002, "Comprehension is the reason for reading. If readers can read the words but do not understand what they are reading, they are not really reading." Modeling the skills covered in this unit will help students develop stronger reading comprehension skills.

Reading Fluency

Practicing with a Group When practicing reading fluency with a group, ask students to follow along silently in their books while each student takes a turn reading aloud. Change readers often to keep the pace of the reading dynamic and to maintain momentum. When shifting between readers, pause to ask students questions about what has been read (both to check comprehension and to keep students focused). Other strategies for practicing reading fluency with a group include choral reading, or reading in unison, and echo reading—students repeat phrases or short sentences after the teacher. **BL** **EL**

Focus

BELLRINGER Options

- Literature Launcher: Prereading DVD
- Daily Language Practice Transparency

Focus Activity Write on the board: Why Do We Read? Ask students to respond to the question. *(Responses will vary.)*

Teach

BQ 

- Have students read the profiles and look at the pictures of Ricardo and Brooke.
- Have students meet in small groups to tell about things they recently read and their reasons for reading. **AS**

C Critical Thinking

Comprehension Ask: How does reading help Ricardo be a better video game player? *(Reading directions and Web sites help him learn how to play better.)*

Ask: How does reading entertain Brooke? *(She reads about something she likes—her favorite band.)* **BL**

UNIT 1 WARM-UP

Connecting to 

Why Do We Read?

Reading is just something you do for school, right? Or is it? Think about it. You probably read a lot more than you think you do. Do you look at the newspaper to find out how the game went? Maybe you check the TV listings for the program you want to see. In this unit, you'll see that you can read to gain all kinds of information, or just to have fun.

Real Kids and the Big Question

RICARDO loves video games and always wants to reach the next level (and then the next and the next) of any game he plays. To do that, he reads the directions for each game very carefully. He also finds web sites that give him hints on how to play better. How do you think Ricardo might answer the question, "Why do we read?"

BQ **C**

BROOKE has a favorite band and wants to know *everything* about these musicians. She reads magazine articles, concert reviews, and any other articles she finds. She always reads anything that comes with the band's CDs. She even reads the band's website to keep up with the latest news about them. How do you think Brooke might answer the question, "Why do we read?"

Warm-Up Activity

Think about the reasons that Ricardo and Brooke read. Do you have any interests like theirs or any other special reasons to read? Talk with a partner about the reasons *you* read that are not necessarily the same reasons your partner reads.

Additional Support

English Language Coach

Verb Tenses English language learners sometimes have difficulty understanding verb tenses in a selection. Have students write the following at the top of a page in their Learner's Notebook: Past Tense: names an action that is finished; Present Tense: names an action that is taking place in the present; Future Tense: names an action that will take place in the future. Have students use the remainder of the page to create a two-column list. The first column will contain verbs from a reading selection. The second column will contain the tense of each verb—past, present, or future. **EL** **BL**

You and the Big Question

The selections in this unit are all very different. As you read each one, think about what someone could get out of reading it. Also, think about what *you* get from it.

Big Question Link to Web resources to further explore the Big Question at www.glencoe.com.

Plan for the Unit Challenge

At the end of the unit, you'll use notes from all your reading to complete the Unit Challenge, which will explore your answer to the Big Question.

You will choose one of the following activities:

A. Create a Commercial Write and perform a commercial in which a variety of people (acted by members of your group) talk about or demonstrate some of the most important reasons to read.

B. Advertising Brochure Use art and clear language to create an advertising brochure (broh SHUR) that encourages people to spend time reading. A brochure is a booklet or pamphlet. (You will make a simple one.)

- Start thinking about the activity you'd like to do so that you can focus your thoughts as you go through the unit.
- In your Learner's Notebook, write your thoughts about which activity you'd like to do.
- Each time you make notes about the Big Question, think about how your ideas will help you with the Unit Challenge activity you chose.

Keep Track of Your Ideas

FOLDABLES™ Study Organizer

As you read, you'll make notes about the Big Question. Later, you'll use these notes to complete the Unit Challenge. See pages R8–R9 for help with making Foldable 1. This diagram shows how it should look.

1. Make one page for each selection. At the end of the unit, you'll staple the pages together into one Foldable.
2. Label the front of the fold-over page with the selection title. (See page 1 for the titles.)
3. Open the fold-over page. On the right side, write the label **My Purpose for Reading.**
4. Open the Foldable all the way. At the top center, write the label **The Big Question.**

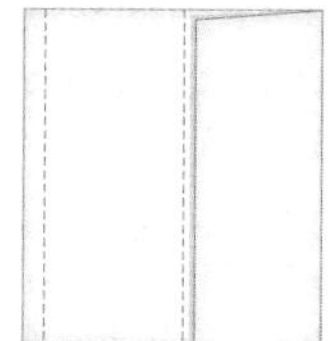

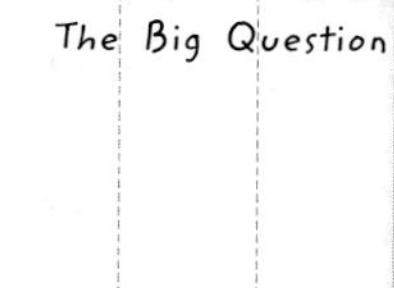

Teach

Literature Online

Big Question Have students access the Web site for English and Spanish summaries and annotated links to related Web resources.

FOLDABLES™ Study Organizer

For each selection they read, students will enter notes about how that selection applies to the Big Question. For details about using Dinah Zike's Foldables, see page R8.

Assess/Close

Ask students if they've discovered any new reasons for reading.

Resources for page 3

- Use the Unit Challenge Planner BLM in the Unit 1 Resource Booklet.
- Use the Foldable BLM in the Unit 1 Resource Booklet.

Differentiated Instruction

Reading Fest Show students how much fun reading can be by holding a Reading Fest. Have students bring in reading materials, such as books, magazines, newspapers, graphic novels, sports pages, movie reviews, TV listings, or whatever they enjoy reading. Encourage students to be creative to show how important reading is in their everyday lives. **BL** Set up a table to display the reading materials that students bring to class. Encourage students to read from their materials, tell why they chose them, and exchange their reading materials with one another. **OL**

Objective

- Connect prior knowledge and experiences to characters, themes, and events

Focus

BELLRINGER Options

Daily Language Practice Transparency

Focus Activity Write the words *Informational Media* on the board. List two or three examples of informational media, such as newspapers and magazines. **Ask:** What other types of informational media—media that provides information—can you add to the list? *(Responses may include bus schedules, Web sites, cereal boxes, etc.)*

Teach

C Critical Thinking

Comprehension Ask: Why do you think each reading skill is helpful for understanding informational media? *(Possible responses: **Setting a purpose for reading** can help you pick out the most important pieces of information; **previewing** will help you find out about the topic; **reviewing** will strengthen your understanding; **understanding text structure** will help you keep track of information.)* OL

UNIT 1 GENRE FOCUS: INFORMATIONAL MEDIA

Skills Focus

- How to read informational media

Skills Model

You will see how to use the key reading skills and elements as you read

- **"Flash Flood,"** p. 5

Media (MEE dee uh) are ways of communicating with large groups. Media include newspapers, magazines, books, radio, television, CDs, movies, and websites. Media that provide information are called **informational media.**

Why Read Informational Media?

When you want or need to get information, you can often find it in informational media. Informational media can tell you

- the latest news
- how to make or do something
- facts you need for schoolwork
- true stories, such as "Flash Flood"

How to Read Informational Media

Key Reading Skills

These reading skills are especially useful tools for reading and understanding informational media. You'll see these skills modeled in the Active Reading Model on pages 5–11, and you'll learn more about them later in this unit.

- **Setting a purpose for reading** Before reading anything, decide what questions the selection might answer for you. (See Reading Workshop 1.)
- C **Previewing** Look at the title, headings, and any pictures in a selection to get an idea about the information it contains. (See Reading Workshop 2.)
- **Reviewing** As you read, stop from time to time and go over what you've already read. (See Reading Workshop 3.)
- **Understanding text structure** Pay attention to how the writing is organized. When you read directions, notice the order of the steps and any signal words, such as *first* or *next.* (See Reading Workshop 4.)

Key Text Elements

Recognizing and thinking about the following elements will help you understand more fully what the writer is telling you.

- **Photos and illustrations:** pictures that help you understand information and make reading more interesting (See "Paddling Dicey Waters.")
- **Titles, heads, and decks:** words in large or dark type that introduce text and grab a reader's attention (See "Message of Hope.")
- **Lead:** the opening sentences or paragraphs that introduce the story (See "Teaching Nepalis to Read, Plant, and Vote.")
- **Text features:** various methods used in a text to provide information, such as charts, tables, graphs, and diagrams (See "How Things Work.")

Objectives (pp. 4–11)
Reading Set a purpose for reading • Identify text structure • Preview text • Monitor comprehension: review and reread • Identify text structure: steps in a process
Informational Text Use text features: title, heads, pictures, deck, lead

Additional Support

Readability Scores
Dale-Chall: 4.7
DRP: 57
Lexile: 900

Literature Focus Lesson

Informational Media Tell students that most informational media is available in print and online.

Remind students that they must carefully look over any Web site they use. Some sites may be outdated or unreliable. Tell students that Web sites ending in *.org, .edu,* or *.gov* may be more reliable than those ending in *.com.* Have students look up information about flash floods on *.org, .edu, .gov,* and *.com* sites. Then have them rate the reliability of the information they found. OL

Ask: Why might .org, .edu, and .gov sites be more reliable than .com sites? AL

INFORMATIONAL TEXT
MAGAZINE
from *Reader's Digest*

The notes in the side columns model how to use the skills and elements you read about on page 4.

FLASH FLOOD 1

by William Hendryx

Six kids stranded in raging water. Only one man could be their lifeline. 2 3 4

It was a torrid summer evening in the parched landscape of southern Arizona, just north of Tucson. EL But the conditions in mid-August 2003 couldn't deter Vaughn Hoffmeister, a busy, self-employed nurseryman,[1] from enjoying the little private time he got on his daily run. He laced his jogging shoes tight and sprinted out the back door. The Santa Catalina Mountains loomed starkly in the distance.

Two hundred yards behind his home, Hoffmeister, 49, dropped into a dry riverbed known as the Cañada del Oro Wash and turned south. Eroded over the years by violent mountain storms, the arroyo was 100 feet wide and 4 feet deep. Its banks were lined with gnarled mesquite trees and cactus. The recent Aspen[2] fire,

1. A ***nurseryman*** works at a nursery, where trees and plants are grown.
2. The Spanish name ***Cañada*** (kan YAW duh) ***del Oro*** translates as "Golden Valley." Both ***wash*** and ***arroyo*** refer to a riverbed that's dry most of the year. The ***Aspen*** is a kind of tree.

Informational Media
ACTIVE READING MODEL

1 **Key Text Element**
Title *This title makes me want to read the story. Since a flash flood happens without warning, this is probably going to be about a sudden and dangerous event.*

2 **Key Text Element**
Deck *The story will be about kids in danger and a man who might save them. Will he?*

3 **Key Reading Skill**
Setting a Purpose for Reading *Something scary happened. What? Why could only one man save them? My purpose is to find answers to those questions.*

4 **Key Reading Skill**
R **Previewing** *What can I tell about this selection by looking through it? Well . . . the title and deck are exciting. And the pictures and captions tell me that the story is about real people.*

UNIT 1 GENRE FOCUS

Teach

R Reading Skill

Previewing Say: Read the deck (the short statement underneath the title) on this page. Then preview all of the photos in the selection.
Ask: What do the deck and photos lead you to expect will happen in the selection? *(Possible response: The story will be about a flash flood; children will be in danger; a man will save them.)* OL

EL Language Coach

Context Clues Say: Look at this sentence: "It was a torrid summer evening in the parched landscape of southern Arizona, just north of Tucson." What clues do the words *summer* and *parched* give you about the meaning of *torrid*? *(Students may note that the clue words are related to heat and suggest that the word* torrid *means hot.)* EL OL

Resources for page 5

Use the Genre Study BLM in the Unit 1 Resource Booklet.

Differentiated Instruction

Charting Context Clues Explain to students that they may encounter unfamiliar words related to the setting of this selection. Remind them that they can often figure out the meaning of an unfamiliar word by looking at the words and sentences around it. Have each student start a four-column chart with the headings, "Unfamiliar Word," "Context Clues," "Possible Meaning," and "Definition" in his or her Learner's Notebook. Ask students to fill in the chart with unfamiliar words, context clues, and possible meanings and then use dictionaries to fill in the definitions. EL BL OL

Objectives
- Set a purpose for reading
- Identify text structure
- Preview text
- Monitor comprehension: review and reread
- Identify text structure: steps in a process
- Use text features: titles, heads, pictures, deck, lead

Teach

E Text Element

Lead Help students discuss the effectiveness of the lead in this selection. **Ask: What details does the author provide about the setting in the first two paragraphs?** *(Responses will vary but should include details about the hot weather conditions, the arroyo, and the recent Aspen fire.)* **How do the first three paragraphs work together to set the mood for the article and give you a clue about what will happen?** *(Responses will vary.)* OL

EL Language Coach

Idiomatic Phrases Students may need help understanding the phrase *gave him pause.* **Say:** Notice that the two sentences following the phrase seem to be what Hoffmeister is thinking. What does the writer mean when he says the "thunder gave him pause"? *(Students may note that this means the sound made him stop and think or become cautious.)* EL OL

ACTIVE READING MODEL

however, had destroyed much of the water-retaining vegetation at higher elevations, leaving the wash susceptible to dangerous runoff.[3]

Now as Hoffmeister jogged down the dry track, dark clouds were forming over Mt. Lemmon. A sudden clap of thunder gave him pause. Even a small amount of rain could become a major threat if water, fed through countless tributaries, gushed down the Cañada Wash. He didn't want to be caught within its sandy banks. 5 EL

5 Key Text Element
Lead *The first few paragraphs help me get a feeling about what's going on. The first two help me imagine the scene. The third one works almost like scary music in a movie—something bad is going to happen.* E

For Steve and LeeAnn Yankovich, moving into the rural valley two years earlier had fulfilled a lifelong dream. Their eight kids, ages 3 to 14, had almost two acres of unrestricted playground. And they had room to stable a few horses.

It was about 6 p.m. when LeeAnn, a petite brunette with high energy and a quick smile, stepped outside and heard the thunder. She saw Moriah, her eldest, and best friend Alisha Kram, 13, riding off toward their favorite bridle trail, the Cañada Wash.

"Girls," LeeAnn called out, looking to the skies, "I don't think you should go just now. Put the horses away."

Moriah, at 14, was almost a head taller than her mom. Bright, thoughtful and levelheaded, she was like a right hand to LeeAnn, helpful with the younger children, in the kitchen and around the house. Though disappointed about the ride, she and her friend obediently reined their horses and rode to the corral at the rear of the property where four of the other kids were playing.

An eerie, grating squeal like a freight train slamming on its brakes echoed through the desert air. But Vaughn Hoffmeister knew this was no train. He pivoted and scrambled from the Cañada just seconds before a six-foot wall of black, foaming water blasted over the ground where he'd been running.

3. ***Susceptible*** (suh SEP tih bul) means "likely to be affected by." ***Runoff*** is rainwater that can't go down into soil that's already soaked.

Additional Support

Differentiated Instruction

Regional Geography Some students may have difficulty visualizing the setting and events in this selection. These students may benefit from seeing pictures of the Arizona desert, mountainsides, and arroyos. If such pictures are not readily available in your classroom or school library, encourage students to search the Internet for pictures of Arizona. Tell them that they may find Arizona travel and tourism sites particularly helpful. OL Encourage students to sketch their own pictures of the Arizona desert, and then hang the pictures around the classroom. BL

ACTIVE READING MODEL

In his 25 years of living in the Southwest, he'd never seen anything like it. High in the mountains, a downpour was not being absorbed by the scorched[4] earth. Instead, the ground shed the sooty, charred remains of trees and brush left by the Aspen blaze. The blackened ash careered through the wash like a stampede. R1

Then, in the distance, Hoffmeister heard the howl of a second "runaway train" coursing down the arroyo—and the Cañada was already overflowing its banks. "My God," he said, "I've got to warn everyone."

Hoffmeister sprinted through the neighborhood, pounding on doors, yelling as he ran, "Get out! Get out! The water's coming!" When he arrived at his own house, Liz, his wife of 32 years, was not inside. He bolted out the rear door. Liz was chatting with LeeAnn over the back fence. "C'mon," he yelled. "We're flooding!"

Liz Hoffmeister knew her husband was not an alarmist. R2 He was a soft-spoken man, afraid of nothing. If Vaughn said they were in danger, Liz knew it was time to leave.

She ran to the house and grabbed her dogs. At that same moment, another wall of muddy water came crashing into the valley. The small, shallower secondary channels of the Cañada, dozens in number, snaked around every homesite in their little valley. They filled in an instant—littered with churning logs, fence wire and debris from upstream. 6

Hoffmeister chased after Liz. It was then that he heard the piercing screams: "Mommy! Mommy!" He reeled, looking over his right shoulder toward the wash and his neighbors' property.

There, some 75 feet away, marooned[5] between two raging streams, stood five of the Yankovich children—Moriah, her friend Alisha, Caleb, age 12, Jordan, 11, Emma, 10, and young Gabriel, only 6 years old. They stood helpless, their faces contorted in fear. The foul, ash-laden water was swelling all around them, flowing at 12 feet per second. The smaller children wouldn't have a

6 Key Reading Skill
Reviewing *Wait. I'm confused about the people. Okay, looking back a few paragraphs, I see that it's just two families. The Yankoviches have kids, and the Hoffmeisters have dogs.*

4. ***Scorched*** earth is very dry due to heat.
5. Someone who is ***marooned*** is surrounded by water with no way to escape.

Teach

R1 Reading Skill

Reviewing Say: Even if you are familiar with the desert landscape of the Southwest, you may need to reread the description of the conditions that cause the flash flood. How does the author describe the earth? *(scorched and very dry, with many burned trees and brush)*
Ask: How do these conditions contribute to the flood? *(The land cannot absorb water, so the water rushes down the mountain, picking up and carrying the burnt twigs and tree stubs with it.)* OL

R2 Reading Skill

Reviewing Say: When selections move as fast as this one, it's a good idea to stop and check your understanding of the story. Reread the second, third, fourth, and fifth paragraphs on this page to answer the following questions: What does Hoffmeister do when he realizes there is a flood? *(heads home, telling neighbors along the way of the danger)*
Whom is Liz Hoffmeister talking to when her husband reaches their house? *(her neighbor—LeeAnn Yankovich, who is introduced at the beginning of the selection)* OL

Differentiated Instruction

Order of Events Chart Some students may find making graphic organizers a useful way to keep track of information. Encourage those students to put the events described thus far in the selection in a chain-of-events graphic organizer like the one shown here. OL

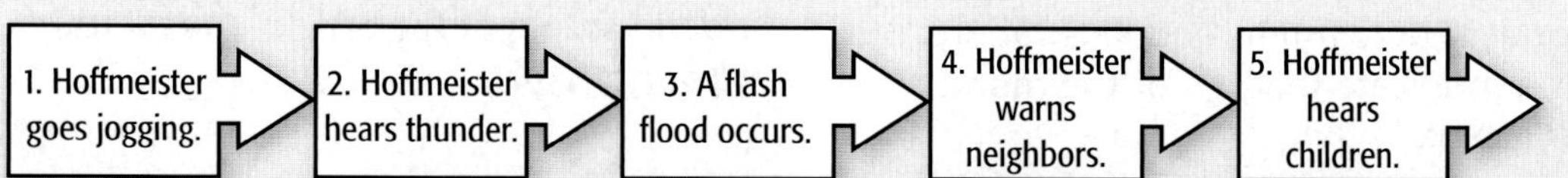
1. Hoffmeister goes jogging.
2. Hoffmeister hears thunder.
3. A flash flood occurs.
4. Hoffmeister warns neighbors.
5. Hoffmeister hears children.

Objectives
- Use text features: titles, heads, pictures, deck, and lead
- Monitor comprehension: review and reread

Teach

C Critical Thinking

Evaluation Say: The third complete paragraph on this page gives you more information about Hoffmeister's training and experience. What can you conclude about his personality from this information? *(Possible responses: He has courage; he is determined.)* OL

E Text Element

Photos and Illustrations
Say: Look at the photograph. Whom do you think the picture shows? Why? *(Hoffmeister; the article says that he tied a rope around a tree.)* AS **Ask:** Do you think this photo was taken before, during, or after the flood? Explain. *(Possible response: The photo was taken after the flood to show the action in this article.)* AL

ACTIVE READING MODEL

chance. Hoffmeister saw Moriah struggling to hold little Emma, who was panic-stricken and crying wildly, "I want Mommy!"

Hoffmeister forged right into the waist-deep deluge[6] and battled through to the other side. He looked back and saw LeeAnn starting to make her way toward her children. "Don't even think about going into the water!" he yelled. "I'll get your kids out!" 7

7 Key Reading Skill
Reviewing *How did the children become trapped so quickly? If I go back over what I've read so far . . . Oh, sure, I see. The smaller channels of the Cañada filled up instantly.*

He turned to Moriah. She cradled the small family dog in her arms. "Get the kids ready, starting with the youngest," Hoffmeister told her. "I'll be right back." He had an idea. One of the children huddled with LeeAnn was holding a coiled lariat used in livestock roping. "I need to borrow that," Hoffmeister said.

He was moving instinctively, but years of experience were guiding him. As a kid, he often played in high-speed irrigation canals in the Arizona farmlands, using ropes to keep from being washed away. In the early '70s, during Army air assault training, he'd learned to rappel[7] 200 feet to the ground from hovering helicopters. The training also included a rigorous exercise known as drown-proofing, where he was forced to survive fully clothed for hours in deep water without touching anything and without a life jacket. C

Two mesquite trees stood on either side of the stream. Deftly, Hoffmeister tied the rope to the first tree; then he crossed the 30-foot torrent and tied it to the other tree. If the rope had been a foot shorter, it wouldn't have reached.

He bent down and talked directly to the wide-eyed kids, telling them exactly what he was going to do and keeping them

6. ***Deluge*** (DEL yooj) can refer to a heavy rain and to a flood that results from a downpour.
7. When you act ***instinctively***, you react without having to think. For example, you would *instinctively* yank your hand away from a hot surface. To ***rappel*** (ruh PEL) is to slide down from a high place using a rope.

Additional Support

Literature Focus Lesson

Photos and Illustrations Explain to students that photographs, illustrations, maps, and graphs are often used in informational media. Graphs and maps provide information in easily understood forms. Photographs and illustrations can communicate feelings or the mood at an event.

The photographs in "Flash Flood" help you understand more about the events and people described in the selection. Ask students to describe some other visuals that would have aided their understanding of the article. *(Responses will vary.)* OL

ACTIVE READING MODEL

calm as water swirled at their shins. "Piggyback me," he said. "Put both arms around my neck and hang on." He flung little Gabriel onto his back and entered the torrent.

With his right arm, Hoffmeister pulled the boy's legs snug to his chest, and with his left he gripped the rope, keeping their bodies on the upstream side as he sidestepped across the gorge. The strong, swift current pinned him hard against the rope. The footing was treacherous, the bottom already caked in black sludge.

Hoffmeister worked his way across and deposited Gabriel in his mother's arms. Then he turned back for the next child. Thanks to Moriah's calming influence, Emma had settled down.

Using the same technique, Hoffmeister ferried Emma across. One by one, he continued with the next three children. But each child was a little older, a little larger, a little heavier, and Hoffmeister was getting tired. Hardly a big man at five-nine, 170 pounds, he was wearing down. 8 **EL**

The water was at his chest now. His back was in knots from the torque of being jackknifed backward—time after time—against the rope. Debris pelted his face and chest, and he swallowed mouthfuls of rancid runoff.

Moriah now stood alone on the little island, water sloshing about her knees as she cradled the dog in her arms. She was scared.

The current was growing more treacherous, and the saturated[8] rope stretched like a rubber band. Hoffmeister pulled the line taut and retied it, but he was concerned about the knots on the other side. Moriah was almost his size and weight. Would the rope hold their combined 300 pounds? **R**

He had to test it. He took the dog from Moriah's arms and placed a reassuring hand on the girl's shoulder. She was trembling. "I'll be right back," he said. "Don't move."

Hoffmeister carried the dog across and checked the knots on the far side. They were holding firm. At that same moment, Jason DeCorte, 28, LeeAnn's son from a previous marriage, drove up on the high ground at the

8. A ***saturated*** rope is soaking wet.

8 **Key Reading Skill**
Understanding Text Structure *The way the last few paragraphs are organized shows me exactly what steps Hoffmeister followed to save the kids. First, he put a kid on his back. Then he held the kid's legs. Next, he grabbed the rope with his left arm. After that, he worked his way through the rushing water. Finally, he handed the kid to the mother. And then he went back to start the process over again.*

Differentiated Instruction

Act Out the Scene A small group of students may enjoy acting out the scene described on this page. In preparation, students should review the sequence of events that takes place as Hoffmeister saves the children. Once students are confident that they have the steps in order, give them time to practice the scene. Then have them act out the scene for the class. **OL** If students are having difficulty keeping the events in the correct order, suggest that they write each step on an index card and then rearrange the cards until they are in the correct order. **BL**

Teach

EL Language Coach

Idiomatic Phrases Students may need help understanding the phrase *wearing down.* **Say:** Reread the sentences before the phrase. What can you use from these sentences to figure out what "wearing down" means? *(Responses should include that Hoffmeister is getting tired from lifting each child who is larger and heavier than the one before.)* **EL** **BL**

R Reading Skill

Understanding Text Structure **Say:** Notice how each step in Moriah's rescue is described in detail in a separate paragraph. Why do you think the writer uses separate paragraphs to describe the rescue? *(Possible responses: He wants to build suspense. He wants to show how brave and determined Hoffmeister and Moriah are.)* **OL** In what other ways could the writer have organized this part of the story to make it easier to read? *(Possible responses: He could have used subheads for each paragraph; he could have used signal words within one large paragraph.)* **AL**

Objectives
- Use text features: titles, heads, pictures, deck, and lead
- Identify text structure

Teach

C Critical Thinking

Analysis Say: Colorful, strong language helps readers of informational media picture events that the author describes.
Ask: What are the difficulties that Hoffmeister faces as he tries to rescue Moriah? *(Possible responses: rising water, tiredness, back pain, fast water, slippery sludge)* BL What are some words and/or phrases that the author uses to paint a clearer picture of the difficulty of the rescue? *(Possible responses: breathing heavily, frothing river, surge, slammed, ooze, violent flow whipped her body, knuckle by knuckle)* OL

E Text Element

Photos and Illustrations
Ask: How does the photograph enhance the text on this page? *(Possible response: It brings the people and events to life.)*
Do you think an illustration would have been as effective? Why or why not? *(Possible response: Probably not. The photo makes it clear that this is a true story and the people are real.)* OL

ACTIVE READING MODEL

front of the house. "I need your help," Hoffmeister yelled to the young man. "We've got to get your sister!"

Jason stood at the base of the first tree, watching the rope and waiting. "When we get close, you grab her," Hoffmeister said. He forced his way across the wash once more and took Moriah's hand. She wasn't certain he could actually carry her. "Are you sure?" she asked.

Hoffmeister was breathing heavily, his face and clothes black with soot. "I'll be there," he said. "Just don't let go of the rope." He bent at the waist and draped Moriah over his back, her right arm over his shoulder, her left around his stomach. With both hands, she took the rope, and they entered the frothing river, as did Jason. C

Halfway across, a surge of water slammed Hoffmeister sideways. He lost his footing in the ooze and went under the rope, taking Moriah with him on the downstream side. She still had both hands on the lifeline, but was on her back, her arms and torso outstretched. The violent flow whipped her body like a flag in the wind.

9 Key Text Element
Photos and Illustrations *It's great to see these photos. They make what Hoffmeister did more real—and more amazing.* E

9

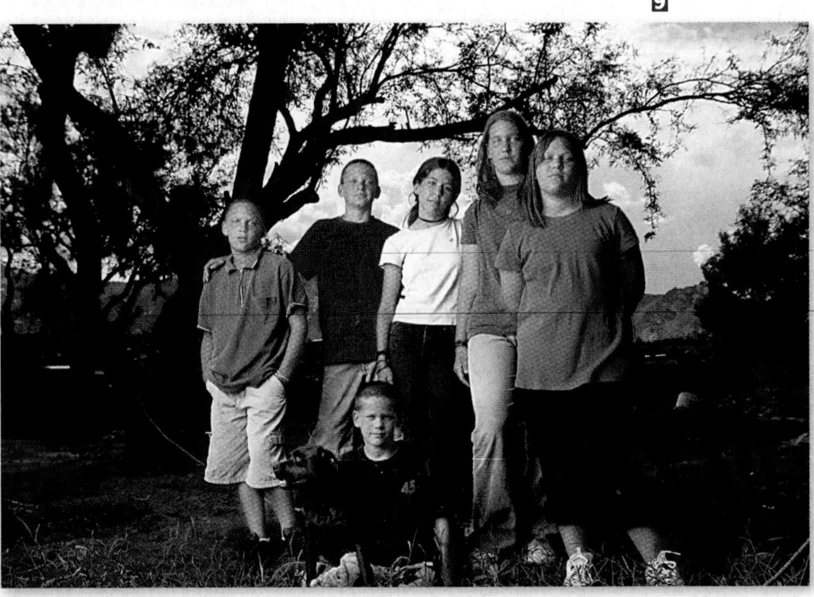

The Yankovich children (and dog) pose with their friend Alisha Kram for a magazine story. Standing are (from left to right) Jordan, Caleb, Alisha, Moriah, and Emma. Seated in front are Cha Cha and Gabriel.

Additional Support

Reading in the Real World

Citizenship Ask students to think of people they know or have heard about who overcame difficulties to help others. Students may want to ask family members or neighbors for suggestions.

Ask students to interview or research the people they have chosen. Through research or an interview, each student should obtain answers to the following questions: What did the person do? Where did this happen? Who else was involved? What obstacles did the person have to overcome? How did the person resolve the problem? OL

ACTIVE READING MODEL

At the last second, Hoffmeister snared her foot. He dug his toes into the slime and pushed up. "Hold on! Hold on!" he yelled.

Jason was struggling to help, but the footing was impossible. He slid and grabbed for Moriah. Her fingers were slipping. Knuckle by knuckle, the current was winning this tug of war. I can't hold on, she thought. But she didn't give in to the water's force or to fear. One finger at a time, she regripped the line.

In the next instant, Jason seized her at the waist and pulled her sideways toward the bank. They both pulled themselves from the waters that stampeded out of the Cañada del Oro.

Hoffmeister was right behind them—so exhausted he had to crawl out of the water, while coughing up black sludge.

This flood and subsequent rains wiped out Hoffmeister's nursery. After the deluge, many homeowners in the area chose to relocate. The Yankovich family bought a bigger house on a four-acre plot in Oracle Junction. Their new home doesn't have the same trees and greenery as the old place by the wash, but it has something better—the kind of neighbors you can count on. Vaughn and Liz Hoffmeister have moved there too. **10** ❍

10 Key Reading Skill
Setting a Purpose for Reading *My purpose was to get my questions answered. Reading this article answered them, and I even know what became of the two families later on. Great!*

Small Group In a group of three or four students, silently preview a magazine article. Look at the title, any subtitles or subheads, and the illustrations. Then share your ideas about what you expect to learn from the article. If your ideas are different, discuss why.

Write to Learn Think about something you know how to do well, such as make a grilled cheese sandwich or teach a dog to do tricks. In your Learner's Notebook, write the steps you follow in this process. Be sure to list the steps in the order in which you do them.

Literature Online

Study Central Visit www.glencoe.com and click on Study Central to review informational media.

UNIT 1 GENRE FOCUS

Close

E Text Element

Deck Say: Remember the deck is a statement below a title or head that grabs the reader's attention and gives more information about the article. The deck on "Flash Flood" reads, "Six kids stranded in raging water. Only one man could be their lifeline." Now that you have read the article, what would you have written for the deck? *(Responses will vary.)* **OL**

R Reading Skill

Understanding Text Structure Say: To make their writing clear, writers present ideas in an order that makes sense to readers. How does the writer organize ideas in this article? *(Possible responses: in the order that they happened; in time order.)* **BL** Why is this a good way to organize the information in this article? *(Possible response: The article tells a story with a beginning, middle, and end, so it makes the most sense to tell the story in time order.)* **OL**

Literature Online

Study Central Have students access the Web site to review informational media and to complete a related activity.

Literature Focus Lesson

Lead Remind students that the lead is the opening sentences or paragraphs that introduce the story or article. Explain that the lead can be written in different ways. The lead may summarize the main idea, or it may describe an interesting situation or fact to gain the reader's interest.

In "Flash Flood," the lead sets the scene and introduces Hoffmeister. Ask students to write a different lead that describes one of the rescue's exciting moments. **OL**

Objectives

- Use text features: titles, heads, pictures, deck, and lead
- Identify text structure

Setting a Purpose for Reading

UNIT 1

Objectives covered in this workshop:

- Use titles, headings, and photos or illustrations to understand reading
- Use context clues to figure out word meanings

Teaching Students to Set a Purpose for Reading

Why Is It Important?

- Reading is more interesting and more likely to be recalled when there is a clear purpose.
- It provides a focus for the reader and allows the reader to monitor whether or not he or she is getting what is needed from the reading.
- Good readers read for a variety of reasons, and they know *why* they're reading a specific piece.

How to Help Students Get It

- A purpose can be set by the reader or by someone else. Students who are purposeless readers need support to learn about setting purpose.
- Show students the help wanted ads. Ask them why they might read these ads. Then show students the sports page. Ask them why they might read this section of the paper. Proceed through the newspaper, generating different purposes for different parts.
- Ask students to make a list of things they'd like to know more about—an interest inventory. For one of the items on this list, ask them to write a purpose statement. Help students find independent reading materials related to their topic and purpose.

Reading to Answer the Big Question

Paddling Dicey Waters

This selection describes an adventurous canoe trip taken by four young Americans through the flooded Amazon basin. They take about 12,000 people along with them via satellite technology. Students may read the story to find out more about the rain forest ecosystem and to learn how technology can reach even the remotest corners of the globe.

Seventh Grade

Victor's first day of seventh grade may remind students of their own, not so long ago. Victor sets a goal to win the heart of a girl, pretending to know French to impress her. He realizes just how important reading is in order to maintain his goal.

Workshop Resources

Pacing (days) Standard	Block	Lesson	Student Materials	Teacher Resources
1		Key Skill Lesson: Setting a Purpose for Reading	Key Reading Skills Practice English Language Coach	Bellringer Options Transparencies Read Aloud, Think Aloud Transparencies Presentation Plus!
2		"Paddling Dicey Waters"	Literary Analysis Transparencies Glencoe Online Selection Vocabulary Development Academic Vocabulary Development English Language Coach Active Reading Graphic Organizer Literary Analysis StudentWorks Plus Online Student Edition Literature Classics Selection and Unit Assessments	Literary and Text Analysis Transparencies Puzzlemaker Skill Level Up! BookLink 3 Assessment by Learning Objective (Diagnostic and Formative) Interactive Tutor Self-Assessment TeacherWorks Plus
2		"Seventh Grade"	Glencoe Online Selection Vocabulary Development Academic Vocabulary Development English Language Coach Active Reading Graphic Organizer Literary Analysis StudentWorks Plus Online Student Edition Literature Classics Selection and Unit Assessments	Literary and Text Analysis Transparencies Puzzlemaker Skill Level Up! BookLink 3 Assessment by Learning Objective (Diagnostic and Formative) Interactive Tutor Self-Assessment TeacherWorks Plus

Keys for Unit Resource

- Blackline Master
- Workbook
- Supplemental Text
- CD-ROM
- DVD
- Transparency
- Web-based
- Fast Files

Level Appropriate Code

AS = Activities for all students
AL = Activities for students working above grade level
OL = Activities for students working at grade level
BL = Activities for students working below grade level
EL = Activities for English language learners

Focus

BELLRINGER Options

Daily Language Practice Transparency

Focus Activity Say: Think about the things you read during the day other than books and school assignments. What do you read, and why? *(Possible responses: I read street signs to figure out where I'm going. I read labels at the grocery store to get information about foods.)*

Teach

R Reading Skill

Setting a Purpose for Reading Say: You set a purpose for reading when you decide why you want to read something. For example, you might read the newspaper weather report to find out what kind of weather to expect. Explain why you might look through a telephone book. *(to find a person's phone number, to find the address of a business)* OL

READING WORKSHOP 1

Skills Focus

You will practice using the following skills when you read these selections:

- "Paddling Dicey Waters," p. 16
- "Seventh Grade," p. 26

Reading

- Setting a purpose for reading

Informational Text

- Using pictures to help you understand what you read

Literature

- Identifying the theme of a story

Vocabulary

- Using context clues to learn word meanings

Writing/Grammar

- Identifying verbs

Skill Lesson

Setting a Purpose for Reading

Learn It!

R **What Is It?** Setting a purpose for reading means deciding why you are reading a particular story or article or whatever you're reading. It means asking yourself, "Why do I want to read this? What do I want to accomplish?" Maybe you just want to be entertained. Maybe you want to answer a question or find out why something happened. There are many different purposes for reading, and you may have more than one!

The Big Question for this unit is a question about why we read *anything.* What is reading good for? What can we get out of it? This isn't the same as setting a purpose for reading, which has to do with why you're reading a particular thing at a particular moment.

Analyzing Cartoons
Hobbes is reading for fun—even if Calvin doesn't think so! Why do you read? To learn something new? To escape into another world?

Objectives (pp. 12–13)
Reading Set a purpose for reading

Additional Support

English Language Coach

Specialized Vocabulary Explain that some informational text, such as "Paddling Dicey Waters," uses specialized vocabulary that relates to the subject of the text. Students may have difficulty with the words used to describe the places and animals in the Peruvian rain forest. Encourage students to use context clues, the words around the unknown word, to understand content-area words. If they cannot determine the meaning of a word from its context, tell them to look up the unknown word in a dictionary. BL EL

Teach

Why Is It Important? Knowing *why* you are reading affects *how* you read. It helps you pay attention to what's important. If your purpose is to find the answer to a question, you might look over the text quickly, searching for key words. But if your purpose is to understand why something happened or learn something new, you will read more slowly and pay closer attention to every word.

Study Central Visit www.glencoe.com and click on Study Central to review setting a purpose for reading.

How Do I Do It? First, think about what you are reading and why. What might be interesting, or what might you learn? You can look at the title, headings, and pictures to get some ideas. What questions come into your mind? Remember that your purpose for reading may change as you read. One student prepared to read "Flash Flood" by looking closely at the title, the deck, and the photographs. Then she set her purpose for reading. **R**

This looks exciting. It's about how one man saved six kids trapped in a flood. Where did this happen? What made it a flash flood? Who is this man? How did he save the kids? I want to know, so I'm going to read to find out. That's my purpose.

Practice It!

The title of the first selection in this workshop is "Paddling Dicey Waters." Scan the headings and pictures and use them to set your first purpose for reading this selection. Copy the sentences below onto the "My Purpose for Reading" section of your Foldable for "Paddling Dicey Waters" and fill in the blank. That will give you one purpose for reading this selection.

The headings and pictures make me think that it's about ____. I'll read to see if I'm right.

Use It!

As you read "Paddling Dicey Waters," pay special attention to the headings and pictures. In your Learner's Notebook write down information they give you. For example, the pictures show how the people traveled, what they wore, and what animals they saw. Look closely to find other details. Is this information what you thought it would be when you set your purpose for reading? Write down and explain any new ideas you have.

Literature Online

Study Central Have students access the Web site to review setting a purpose for reading and to complete a related activity.

R Reading Skill

Setting a Purpose for Reading **Say:** Think of magazines you like to read. What is your purpose for reading them? *(Possible responses: I read a science magazine to find out about nature. I read a sports magazine to keep track of how my favorite team is doing.)* **OL**

Resources for page 13

- Use Reading Skills Transparency in *Read Aloud, Think Aloud,* Unit 1, to help students practice setting a purpose.

Reading in the Real World

Citizenship Ask students to interview people who have recently taken trips. Before the interviews, students should prepare questions that will help them find out more about the travelers' journeys and what the travelers learned about the areas that they visited. After the interviews, have students use the information they gathered to write brief narrative accounts of the trips. **OL**

Ask students to use online maps and information from their interviews to draw maps of the places their interviewees visited. **AL**

Ask students to list items that people should bring if they are planning to visit the destinations they learned about. **BL**

Objective
- Preview text
- Set a purpose for reading

Teach

More About the Author

Lew Freedman is a native of Boston, Massachusetts, but he has spent much of his time in Alaska, where he received a master's degree from Alaska Pacific University. Freedman has written several books about the Iditarod, a famous sled dog race held in Alaska.

V Vocabulary

Using Vocabulary Words Say: Using new vocabulary words helps you understand and remember their meanings. Use each of the vocabulary words in a sentence that contains context clues about the word's meaning. Make sure that you are using each word correctly by sharing your sentences with a partner. OL

Before You Read: Paddling Dicey Waters

Meet the Author

Lew Freedman is a reporter for the *Chicago Tribune* newspaper. He likes to write about the outdoors, and he travels widely to find interesting stories. Freedman lived in Alaska for many years. He was sports editor at the *Anchorage Daily News*. Freedman has written seventeen books about Alaska.

Author Search For more about Lew Freedman, go to www.glencoe.com.

Objectives (pp. 14–21)
Reading Set a purpose for reading
Informational Text Use text features: photographs
Vocabulary Use context clues to determine word meaning

Vocabulary Preview

V

drenched (drencht) *v.* soaked or covered with liquid; form of the verb *drench* **(p. 16)** *The thunderstorm drenched the people outside.*

reserve (rih ZURV) *n.* land set aside for a special purpose **(p. 16)** *Many unusual plants and animals made their homes in the reserve.*

unique (yoo NEEK) *adj.* unlike anything else **(p. 17)** *The trip to Peru was a unique experience.*

potentially (puh TEN shuh lee) *adv.* possibly **(p. 19)** *Each day brought potentially dangerous new adventures.*

Class Activity Take turns using each vocabulary word correctly in a sentence.

English Language Coach

Context Clues When you see an unfamiliar word, you can sometimes use context clues to figure out its meaning. The *context* of a word is all the other words and sentences around it. A word's context may contain clues to its meaning.

You can use context clues in the following quotation from "Paddling Dicey Waters" to figure out the meaning of the word *bounty.*

> They passed up a three-toed sloth for a pet but found a bounty of bananas.
> "There were bananas everywhere," said Beightol . . ."

This context clue…	Suggests that…
bananas everywhere	a bounty of something is a lot of it

Individual Activity Use context clues to figure out the meaning of *globally* in the sentence below. In your Learner's Notebook, copy the sentence. Underline the words and phrases that provide clues about the meaning of *globally*. Then write down what you think it means.

> The group communicated globally through computers, a Web site, and a satellite phone, interacting with students who made suggestions from thousands of miles away.

Additional Support

Author Search To expand students' appreciation of Lew Freedman, have them access the Web site for additional information and resources.

Literature Focus Lesson

Nonfiction Lew Freedman writes frequently about outdoor adventures. When students have read about the exploration and research of the Amazon River, they may want to learn more about other challenging research expeditions. Suggest that they use the library or Internet resources to find information about explorers, scientists, and scholars who went on important expeditions. Ask students to answer the following questions.

1. Who was the explorer or researcher?
2. What was he or she researching or trying to find?
3. Was this person successful? AS

Skills Preview

Key Reading Skill: Setting a Purpose for Reading

As a student, you may feel that the only reason to read something is that a teacher told you to. But the teacher *didn't* say, "Read but don't enjoy." Even when reading is required, one of *your* purposes can be to try to enjoy it.

There are as many purposes for reading as there are things to read. There may be several reasons to read one piece. However, it's a good idea to start out with one purpose you can focus on. You already have one for "Paddling Dicey Waters." As you read, think about other possible purposes.

Key Text Element: Photographs

Photographs give a lot of information at a glance. Often, they can tell you what words can't. Pictures can give you an idea of how people and places look and what's happening. The words printed above, beside, or below a photo are a *caption*, which gives information about the photo.

These tips will help you look at and understand photos.

- Read the caption to learn important information about the photo.
  Does the caption add background to the photo? Does it suggest something you haven't thought of before?
- Look carefully at everything in the photo.
  Who does the photo show? What information does it give that your reading does not?
- Think about why the photo is included with the story.
  How does the photo add to the story?

E

Interactive Literary Elements Handbook
To review or learn more about the literary elements, go to www.glencoe.com.

Get Ready to Read

Connect to the Reading

You're going to read about an amazing trip in the South American jungle. Would you go on an adventure trip like that? What part of such a trip would interest you the most? C

Group Talk In a small group, share your ideas of what you might do and see if you were exploring a jungle. Discuss the best and worst things that might happen on such a trip.

Build Background

In 2005, a group of young Americans traveled to the Amazon River basin in South America.

- A river basin is land that's drained by a river. In other words, all the rain that falls in the basin pours into one main river.
- The Amazon basin is the world's largest, covering parts of Peru and five other countries.
- The basin's hot, wet weather produces rain forests that are home to countless plants, insects, and animals. There are giant spiders and snakes, as well as piranhas (pih RAW nuz), fish that will eat any kind of meat, including human.

Set Purposes for Reading

BIG Question One of the things you can get out of reading, one reason to do it, is to find information. If you were writing a report about animals in the Amazon, would this be a good article to read? Read the article to find out.

Set Your Own Purpose What else would you like to learn from the story to help you answer the Big Question? Write your own purpose on the "My Purpose for Reading" section of the "Paddling Dicey Waters" page of Foldable 1.

Keep Moving

Use these skills as you read the following selection.

READING WORKSHOP 1

Teach

E Text Element

Photographs **Say:** "Paddling Dicey Waters" is about a trip through the rain forest. What informative and interesting photos might this article include? *(Possible responses: Photographs of trees, colorful plants, and animals.)* **OL** The article describes some very strange rain forest animals. Before the invention of photography, what might people have thought about reports of such creatures? *(Possible responses: Without photographs, people might have found the descriptions too strange to believe.)* **AL**

C Critical Thinking

Application **Say:** Adventures can be as simple as meeting new people or getting lost while driving to a new place. Describe an adventure you've had. *(Responses will vary.)* **OL**

Use the CheckPoint questions provided on Presentation Plus! to check for prior knowledge and to build background. These questions can be used with interactive response keypads for immediate student feedback.

English Language Coach

Context Clues Explain that context clues may define or restate an unfamiliar word, give examples of the word, or compare or contrast the word with other words. Write the following sentences on the board. Ask students to find the context clues for the word in italics. Tell them to look for definitions, examples, or a contrasting word or phrase. **OL** **EL**

1. The *unique* animals of the rain forest were unlike any I had ever seen. *(unlike any)*
2. The National Park Service has information about *reserves* such as Ebey's Landing National Historical Reserve. *(Ebey's Landing National Historic Reserve)*

Objectives

- Set a purpose for reading
- Use text features: photographs
- Use context clues to determine word meaning

Teach

Viewing the Photo

Ask: What does this photograph tell you about the environment of the Amazon Basin? *(Possible responses: The thick vegetation and the man in the sleeveless shirt show that the climate is hot and tropical.)* Judging from the photo, how do you think the paddlers feel about the trip? *(They are smiling and seem happy. They are probably looking forward to the adventures to come.)* **OL**

EL Language Coach

Context Clues Say: A *simile* is a comparison that uses the word *like* or as. What does the author mean when he says that the "drops [were] like nails pounded by giant hammers"? To understand this simile, look at the context clues. The rain "drenched" the paddlers, so it must have been very heavy. What does it mean if heavy rain falls "like nails"? *(Possible response: The rain falls with a great deal of force.)* **EL** **OL**

Readability Scores
Dale-Chall: 6.9
DRP: 62
Lexile: 1100

INFORMATIONAL TEXT
NEWSPAPER
from *Chicago Tribune*

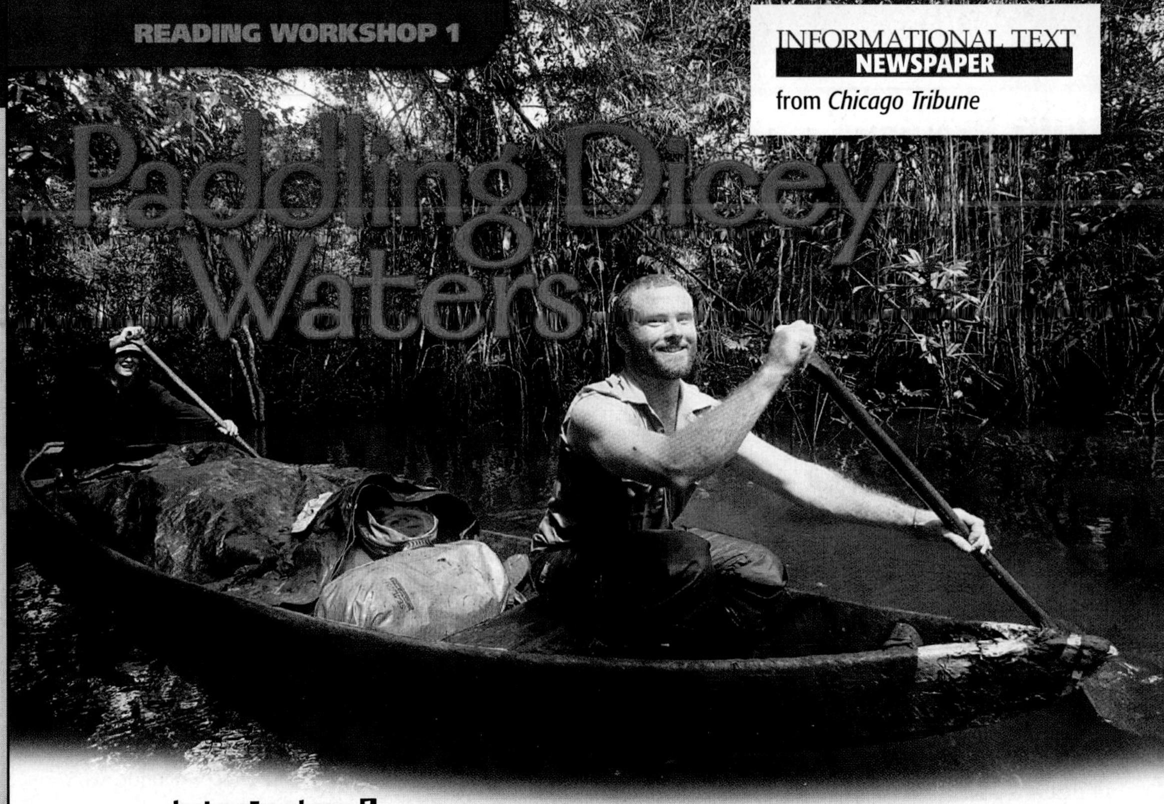

Paddling Dicey Waters

by Lew Freedman **1**

Four young Americans take a Peruvian canoe trip, interacting with schoolkids thousands of miles away

Spring rain on the Amazon River **drenched** the six paddlers, the drops like nails pounded by giant hammers. Other times the 90-degree, 90-percent humidity[1] Peruvian air was an enveloping mist. **EL**

They glided in 20-foot-long, 250-pound dugout canoes along the muddy waters of the 8,000-square-mile Pacaya-Samiria National **Reserve**, saturated by the rain.

1. ***Humidity*** is the water in the air. When the humidity is 90 percent, the air feels very damp.

Vocabulary

drenched (drencht) *v.* soaked or covered with liquid

reserve (rih ZURV) *n.* land set aside for a special purpose

Practice the Skills

1 Key Reading Skill

Setting a Purpose for Reading Would you know how to survive even a short stay in the wilderness? A possible purpose for reading this story is to learn how people can live in the kind of place described here.

Additional Support

Differentiated Instruction

Mapping Tell students to use the Internet or atlases to find maps of South America. Have students use the information they find to draw maps of South America that show the path of the Amazon River. Ask students to label the countries through which the Amazon flows (Bolivia, Brazil, Colombia, Ecuador, Peru, and Venezuela). Have students use green to shade areas covered by rain forest. Tell them to decorate the borders of their maps with drawings of plants and creatures that live in the rain forest. **OL**

"It was the hottest I've ever been in my life," Jesse Beightol said. "We were constantly sweating."

Project Peru Amazon Adventure 2005, organized by the Wilderness Classroom of Western Springs [Illinois], took four young Americans and two Peruvian guides through the Amazon Basin, a **unique** region of the world.

The five-week journey ending in early May offered a rare glimpse of a flooded forest. Not just to the travelers but to about 12,000 students from 100 schools.

Though it lived primitively, the group communicated globally through computers, a Web site, and a satellite phone, interacting with students who made suggestions from thousands of miles away.

Through a 27-pound, 1-kilowatt generator it carried and a satellite phone, the team communicated three days a week with updates to classrooms.

"It worked amazingly," said Dave Freeman, the trip organizer.

"We were trying to answer the question of how people, plants, animals and fish survive in the flooded forest," Freeman said. C1

There was also the question of how the four paddlers, ranging in age from the early 20s to early 30s, would survive the specially permitted visit to the reserve that has 449 bird species, 102 types of mammals, 69 reptiles, 58 amphibians, 256 fish and 1,204 plants. Seeing **benign** species like anteaters was fun, but snakes and poisonous insects were threats. 2 C2

Before she left Santa Cruz, Calif., for the paddle, Jennifer Coveny said she was teased constantly about what might be encountered in the rain forest.

"My friends spent all of their time telling me what would kill me," she said. "And then they divided up what they would get of mine."

A different world 3

Flights from Chicago to Dallas to Lima, Peru's capital, deposited the team in Iquitos, its 400,000 population making it the world's largest city without road access. Here the group

Vocabulary

unique (yoo NEEK) *adj.* unlike anything else

Practice the Skills

2 English Language Coach

Context Clues Using the context clues, what would you say **benign** means? (Remember that you can always pause to look up words in a dictionary.)

3 Key Reading Skill

Setting a Purpose for Reading Sometimes you'll have a special purpose for reading a part of a selection. Look at the section heading "A different world." Why do you think the section might have this name? What purpose could you set for reading this section?

READING WORKSHOP 1

Teach

C1 Critical Thinking

Analysis Say: The group of paddlers is trying to find out how people, plants, animals, and fish survive in the flooded forest. In your Learner's Notebook, write two sentences that explain why you think it is important to learn about rain forest ecosystems such as that of the Amazon. *(Possible responses: It is important to learn about this ecosystem so that people can understand how to protect it. Also, studying how the inhabitants of the rain forest survive in the flooded conditions could help others survive in similar conditions.)* **OL**

C2 Critical Thinking

Comprehension Say: Why does the author say that there was a question of how the group of paddlers would survive? *(The paddlers would be facing many dangers in the unfamiliar rain forest environment.)* **OL** What dangerous rain forest creatures might the paddlers encounter? *(snakes and poisonous insects)* **BL**

Reading in the Real World

Career Explain to students that ecotourism refers to any sort of tourist activity that focuses on enjoying or exploring a natural setting. Tell students to use Internet or library resources to find out what the job of an ecotourism guide in South America involves. Ask: Do you think you would enjoy being a guide? Have students write a brief paragraph that describes the job of an ecotourism guide, and then make a list of the pros and cons of this job. *(Responses will vary.)* **OL**

Students can also find out what type of training or special schooling people might need to become ecotourism guides. **AL**

Objectives

- Use context clues to determine word meanings
- Understand similes
- Use photos to understand reading

READING WORKSHOP 1

Teach

R Reading Skill

Setting a Purpose for Reading Say: The head for this section of the article is "A different world" (see page 17). If your purpose for reading were to find ways in which this world is different from the world you know, what would you notice on this page? *(Possible responses: People eat grubs and ride in canoes to get around.)* **OL** Why do you think the author includes these details? *(Possible responses: These details help readers better understand the group's experience and the challenges that they face.)* **AL**

EL Language Coach

Context Clues Ask: What are some context clues that help you understand what *curiosity* means? *(Responses may include Adam is 6 feet 6 inches tall).* **EL BL** What might make someone a *curiosity* where you live? *(Responses will vary.)* Where might a three-toed sloth be a *curiosity? (The sloth is native to Peru, so it is not a curiosity there. In another part of the world, such as the United States, a sloth would be unusual.)* **OL**

Visual Vocabulary
The ***sloth*** is a slow-moving South American mammal that lives in trees.

explored the flavorful market and stocked up on supplies. They passed up a three-toed sloth for a pet but found a bounty of bananas.

"There were bananas everywhere," said Beightol, a canoeing guide from Ely, Minn.

More importantly, the group rented two canoes carved from downed ponga trees for $1 a day and bought wide-bladed wooden paddles for $3 and a canoe for $60.

"We think we overpaid," said Adam Hansen, from St. Louis Park, Minn., whose height of 6 feet 6 inches made him more of a **curiosity** in Peru than the sloth. **4** **R**

Freeman experimented with local cuisine, grimacing as he downed 3-inch yellow grubs, and the kids chortled[2] at the pictures sent back.

"It tasted like salty pudding," Freeman said. "The outside was leathery. The inside was gooey, salty mush." **EL**

A four-day ride on a three-story ferry packed with nearly 200 people and pigs, cows, and other goods below decks, dropped the group off in Luganos, a community of about 3,000. Then gear, supplies and canoes were moved six miles by horsedrawn cart to the headwaters of the Samiria River, one of the Amazon tributaries paddled. By the time they were put in with guide Ruben Paiva and reserve volunteer Warren Coquinche Saurio, the explorers were a week out of Chicago.

The paddlers were surrounded by lush forest, including palm, cecropia, rubber and kapock trees. Some trees were underwater. Some had visible high-water marks 15 feet above the canoes. They were privileged visitors to a region that has few. Paiva estimated only 10 people annually paddle in the flooded forest and never stay as long as the Americans did.

Paiva called the "environment amazingly flooded in the rainy season where you can see a huge variety of fishes, two species of dolphins, including the beautiful pink one," in a "remote, pristine[3] area."

2. ***Cuisine*** is a French word that means "cooking" or "food." Freeman was making a face ***(grimacing)*** when he swallowed ***(downed)*** the ***grubs.*** A *grub* is the wormlike form of a just-hatched insect. When the kids ***chortled,*** they were laughing quietly with satisfaction.

3. ***Pristine*** (pris TEEN) means "not spoiled or polluted; pure."

Practice the Skills

4 English Language Coach

Context Clues What is the meaning of **curiosity** here? One context clue is that Adam is 6 feet 6 inches tall. Another clue is that in Peru a sloth is less of a **curiosity** than Adam.

Additional Support

English Language Coach

Context Clues Have students make a chart like the one below. Ask students to write any difficult words in the Word column. As they come upon these words, students should use context clues to guess their meanings and write their guesses in the second column of their charts. Students should then use dictionaries to check their guesses and to write the words' real definitions in the appropriate column. **BL EL**

Word	Context Meaning	Dictionary Definition
high-water marks	15-feet or high level	highest point or peak

READING WORKSHOP 1

Movies come to life

About four days into the paddle, the team was fascinated by about 30 frolicking pink dolphins, a national treasure considered the most intelligent of dolphin species. They were more perturbed by armed poachers[4] logging mahogany trees who stared grimly from passing motorboats. No chitchat was exchanged.

"I was a little nervous about those guys," Beightol said.

It was like stumbling upon movie bad guys. Influenced by other movies, Beightol attempted a once-in-a-lifetime Tarzan imitation. He climbed a tree, grabbed a vine and soared through the air.

"Then the vine broke and I fell into the water," he said.

Fortunately, splashdown did not result in an unplanned rendezvous[5] with any of the millions of piranha living in the area.

Periodically, the group passed small patches of land above water level, just often enough, Hansen said, to stretch legs before they cramped. Floating ranger stations were sought for camping. Like the villages, these stopover buildings were constructed on stilts. Roofs were made of palm thatch and flooring was bark **lashed** together with vines. Meals were heavy on bananas, fish, beans, rice, lentils, Saltine crackers, canned tuna fish, cookies and candy, all transported in 30-gallon plastic barrels. **5**

Sometimes at night the team members took turns spraying flashlight beams on the dark water. If the light settled on orange orbs, it was revealing the eyes of a black caiman.[6] Some were 9 feet long, and occasionally the paddlers checked them out by hand. **C**

More than a week into their 12 days on the Samiria, the paddlers were discovered by **potentially** deadly insects. Spiders and tarantulas flocked to Hansen. One day he had his picture taken with a monstrous spider apparently welded

4. ***Poachers*** are people who kill or steal wild animals or plants when it is against the law to do so.
5. A ***rendezvous*** (RAWN day voo) is a meeting.
6. The ***caiman*** (KAY mun) is a kind of crocodile.

Vocabulary

potentially (puh TEN shuh lee) *adv.* possibly

Practice the Skills

5 **English Language Coach**

Context Clues What does **lashed** mean? Which word in this sentence helped you figure out its meaning? **EL**

Teach

EL Language Coach

Multiple-Meaning Words

Say: Some words have more than one meaning. For example, *lashed* can mean "tied or bound together," or "struck or hit." One way to figure out which meaning of a word belongs in a sentence is to replace the word with each of its meanings. Then see which meaning makes the most sense in the sentence. In the sentence that reads, "Roofs were made of palm thatch and flooring was bark **lashed** together with vines," replace *lashed* with *tied* and *struck.* Which meaning of *lashed* best fits this sentence? *(tied or bound together)* **EL** **BL**

C Critical Thinking

Comprehension **Say:** Look at the evidence you are given about the black caiman. What can you determine about this animal from the information given? *(It lives in the water, and it is very large.)* Why do you think the paddlers used their hands to check out some of the caiman? *(Possible response: The paddlers wanted to feel the animals or they wanted a close-up look at the caiman.)* **OL**

Differentiated Instruction

Art Draw students' attention to the description of the black caiman on this page. Then have students fold a sheet of white paper in thirds. On the first third, ask students to draw what they think this creature might look like. Then give them another clue: It is a reptile related to dinosaurs. Have students use this information to draw a new picture in the next third of the paper. Give students a final clue: The black caiman resembles an alligator and can grow up to 20 feet long. Have students revise their pictures a final time in the last section of the paper. Challenge students to find photographs of these Amazon reptiles. **OL** **EL**

Objectives
- Use context clues to determine word meaning
- Set a purpose for reading

READING WORKSHOP 1

Viewing the Photo

Say: What does this image tell you about this particular mahogany tree? *(Possible response: This tree is large and must be valuable because of its size.)* Why do you think the paddlers took this photo? *(Possible response: to give people a visual reminder of the effects of poaching)* **OL**

E Text Element

Photographs **Ask:** What other photographs would have helped you understand this article? Explain your answer. *(Responses will vary.)* **OL**

to the side of his canoe. Another time Hansen awoke to find one spider in a shoe, another spider on his clothes and a tarantula prepared to hitch a ride on his backpack.

The torment of her friends aside, if Coveny heard Paiva's speech of caution back in the United States, she never would have boarded the plane despite the presence of medical supplies for most emergencies.

"The danger is there," Paiva said. "There is the 'wandering spider,' and their venom[7] is 18 times more deadly than the black widow spider of the U.S. In addition, they have the largest venom glands of any spider. But I've never heard of anyone bitten by this one. Call it luck or being careful. Then we have bullet ants. For some people this is very painful, but not deadly. Of course, it depends on how allergic a person is."

Once, Coveny read an e-mail from an Illinois student, discussing the trip. He signed off with "P.S. Get hurt."

"They were looking for excitement," she said.

---

7. ***Venom*** is the poison that snakes and spiders inject when they bite or sting.

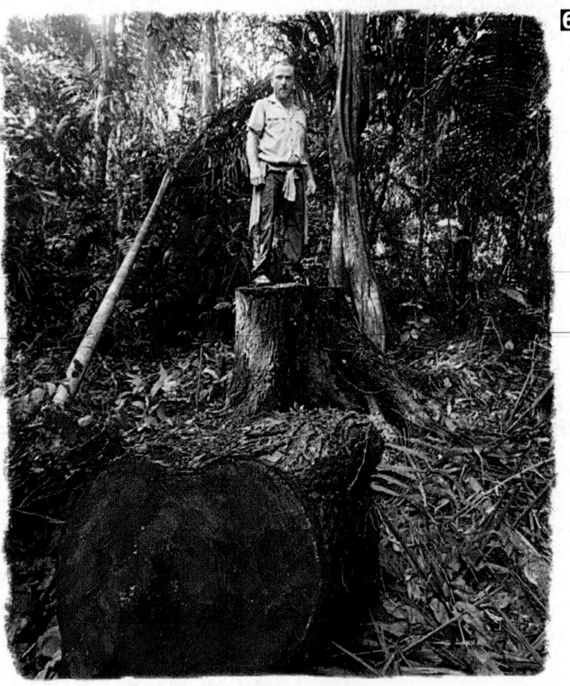

6

Jesse Beighton stands on the stump of a mahogany tree.

Practice the Skills

6 Key Text Element

E **Photographs** What information do the photos on these pages add to the words in the story?

Additional Support

Differentiated Instruction

Charting the Setting Help students create a graphic organizer like the one shown here. **OL**

Five-Week Trip to the Amazon	
Setting	**Action**
Iquitos	The group gathers, buys supplies, rents canoes, and leaves on a four-day ferry ride.
Luganos	The group arrives; their gear is brought to the Samiria River.

Story time

In Lake El Dorado, where schoolchildren urged an extension of a few days to look for animals, Saurio set up a 100-foot fishing net. After one check, Saurio woke up the camp by announcing, "Hey, I've got an anaconda in my fishing net."

The potentially deadly 9-foot snake apparently lunged for a fish and snared its teeth in the webbing.

Freeman, Beightol and Saurio carefully extricated[8] the snake. Paiva grabbed it behind the neck to prevent bites. A second snake-charmer grasped it to prevent anyone's body from being squeezed into breathlessness.

"As long as there were two people handling it, it was manageable," Freeman said. "It was tired."

Paiva said the paddlers' role educating the schoolchildren is an important one.

"Because it's a unique ecosystem,[9]" he said. "This area for sure must be known for everybody to create a consciousness to protect it."

Jennifer Coveny of Santa Cruz, Calif., and Peruvian guide Ruben Paiva handle a tuckered-out 9-foot anaconda.

Soggy and stinking of sweat after 350 miles on the nearly current-free water, the travelers completed the journey in 25 paddling days.

C "What we learned is that everything is interconnected," Freeman said. "All the plants and animals rely on each other. The people in the villages eat catfish, piranha and pacu. A classic example is the creporia tree. Fire ants live on the tree as a home, and they defend the tree too."

The group returned to Chicago on May 6 and began lectures for kids who followed the trip.

"They love it," teacher Scott Elder said of his students. "They kept journals."

In tune with his audience, Freeman teased the kids.

"We were looking to bring a poisonous frog back for you, but we couldn't," he said.

No, what played in Peru, stayed in Peru. Only the images of a faraway land traveled. 7 ○

8. When they ***extricated*** the snake, they freed it from being tangled in the net.

9. An ***ecosystem*** is the entire group of living and nonliving things in a particular area.

Practice the Skills

7 BIG Question

Did your experience with this article help you see why it might be worthwhile to read it? What might a reader get out of it? BQ Write your ideas on the "Big Question" section of Foldable 1 for "Paddling Dicey Waters." Your ideas will help you complete the Unit Challenge later.

Reading in the Real World

Citizenship Many people work to be good stewards of the world's resources by studying them and working to protect them. Lead a discussion about natural resources in your area and what it means to be a good steward of those resources. In your discussion, have students explore different ways that they could be stewards. For example, they could help preserve an animal's habitat or teach people about the importance of conservation. You may wish to ask students to write about natural features in your area that may need to be protected. OL

Teach

C Critical Thinking

Comprehension Say: What do the paddlers learn about the animals, plants, and people of the flooded forest? *(Possible response: They learn that all the life of the flooded forest is interconnected.)* BL Why is this fact important to know? *(Possible response: This fact is important because it means that no part of the forest can be neglected. All of the forest must be protected because if even one small part of the ecosystem is destroyed, the entire forest is affected.)* OL

BQ BIG Question

Say: How did reading play an important role on this trip to the Amazon? *(Possible response: Reading was important because the travelers communicated with students through e-mail and a Web site.)* OL

Assess

Use the CheckPoint questions provided on Presentation Plus! to check students' mastery of the selection. These questions can be used with interactive response keypads for immediate student feedback.

Objectives
- Use text features: photographs

Assess

Resources for page 22

- Selection Quick Check
- Selection and Unit Assessment
- ExamView Assessment Suite
- Interactive Tutor: Self-Assessment

Students can respond to the *After You Read* items in their Learner's Notebook or on a separate sheet of paper.

Answering the

1. Responses will vary.
2. The group used a Web site and e-mail to communicate with others while on the trip.
3. The group traveled down the river in dugout canoes.

Critical Thinking

4. The section was called "Movies come to life" because poachers resemble the "bad guys" in a movie, and one person tried to swing from a vine like the movie character Tarzan.
5. Possible response: The poachers were armed, so the group feared that the poachers would shoot.
6. Possible response: The group discussed the many things they learned. They saw sights and animals that few people ever see. I think they were glad they took the trip.

After You Read

Paddling Dicey Waters

Answering the 

1. After completing the activities in this workshop, what are your thoughts about why people read?
2. **Recall** What did the group use to communicate with others while on the trip?
   TIP **Right There** You'll find this information in the story.
3. **Recall** For most of their journey, how did the group travel down the river?
   TIP **Think and Search** The answer is in the story but the details are in several places.

Critical Thinking

4. **Infer** Why was one section of the article called "Movies come to life?"
   TIP **Author and Me** Use information from the story along with what you know about movies.
5. **Infer** What was the group afraid the poachers might do?
   TIP **Author and Me** Take information from the story and put it together with what you know from your own experience.
6. **Evaluate** Do you think the group regretted the trip after they completed it? Why or why not?
   TIP **Author and Me** Use information from the text along with what you know from your own experience.

Write About Your Reading

Write a Postcard Imagine that you are one of the travelers on this adventure, and that you're almost done with the journey. Write a postcard to one of your friends back home.

- Summarize a few things that happened, and tell how you felt about the experiences.
- Remember that you can only fit one or two paragraphs on a postcard, so you can't tell about the whole journey.

Objectives (pp. 22–23)
Reading Set a purpose for reading
Informational Text Use text features: photographs
Vocabulary Use context clues to determine word meaning
Writing Paraphrase and summarize text
Grammar Identify parts of speech

Write About Your Reading

Possible response:

Dear Friend,

We've been traveling down the Amazon River for a couple of days now. It's amazingly hot! You wouldn't believe all the wildlife I've seen. One of my team members caught an enormous snake called an anaconda–it can squeeze people to death! The pink dolphins are my favorites. I'm learning that all things are connected and need each other. I'll tell you all about the trip when I get home. See you soon.

–Luz

Skills Review

Key Reading Skill: Setting a Purpose for Reading

7. Look at the purpose you wrote in your Foldable when you followed the "Practice It!" instructions on page 13. Did the article turn out to be about what you thought it would be about?
8. Did your purpose for reading change as you read? If so, how did it change?

Key Text Element: Photographs

9. What do the photos show that the story does not tell you?
10. What do you learn from the captions?
11. Why do you think these photos were used with the story?

Vocabulary Check

Use your own words to write the meaning of each word below.

12. unique
13. reserve
14. potentially
15. drenched
16. **English Language Coach** The entire article you just read is context that contains clues for what *dicey* means. Read this shorter context. Use context clues to figure out what *dicey* might mean.

> During their trip, the paddlers came across dangerous snakes, poisonous insects and spiders, and armed poachers. They were traveling on **dicey** waters, indeed!

Write your own definition of *dicey* in your Learner's Notebook.

Grammar Link: Parts of Speech

Words can be organized into groups called **parts of speech.** Each part of speech describes what a particular kind of word does.

What is it?	What does it do?
Noun	names a person, place, or thing
Verb	shows action or a state of being
Pronoun	takes the place of a noun
Adjective	tells which one, what kind, how many
Adverb	tells how, when, where, how much
Preposition	helps show space, time, position
Conjunction	connects words or groups of words
Interjection	expresses feeling

In many cases you can't tell a word's part of speech just by looking at the word. You must look at what the word does in a specific sentence. In the first sentence below, for example, *book* works as a noun. In the second sentence, however, *book* works as a verb.

- **Noun:** He put the **book** on a shelf. (*Book* names a thing.)
- **Verb:** Please **book** me a hotel room. (To *book* a room is to reserve one—an action.)

In fact, *book* can even be an adjective.

- **Adjective:** He's a **book** illustrator. (*Book* tells which kind of illustrator.)

Grammar Practice

Write two sentences for each word listed below. In the first sentence, use the word to name a thing. In the second sentence, use the word to show action.

run smile look check

Writing Application Look back over the postcard that you wrote. Make a list of the verbs you used.

Web Activities For eFlashcards, Selection Quick Checks, and other Web activities, go to www.glencoe.com.

Skills Review

Key Reading Skill: Setting a Purpose for Reading

7. Possible responses: No. I thought I would find general information about the Amazon River.
8. Possible responses: Yes, my purpose changed. As I read, I wanted to see what kinds of creatures the group would encounter and how they would survive in the deep jungle.

Key Text Element: Photographs

9. Responses will vary, but they should indicate that photographs show the emotions of the people in the pictures, as well as details about the setting and its wildlife.
10. Responses will vary, but they should indicate that the captions give specific information about people, plants, and animals in the photographs.
11. Responses may vary, but they should indicate that the photos were used with the story to add color and excitement and to give readers an inside look at the expedition.

Vocabulary Check

Possible responses:

12. unusual
13. park
14. possibly
15. soaked
16. Possible responses: hazardous, dangerous, or risky

Close

Ask students to share how reading this selection helped them begin to answer the Big Question, "Why do we read?"

Literature Online

Web Activities Have students access the Web site for interactive activities that will help them assess their understanding of the selection.

Teach

More About the Author

Gary Soto didn't plan to become a writer. When he was in college, however, he came across a book called *The New American Poetry.* "I discovered this poetry and thought, 'This is terrific: I'd like to do something like this.'" Soto is now the author of more than 30 books.

V Vocabulary

Vocabulary Chart Have students make a chart like the one below and fill it in, beginning with the vocabulary word. OL EL

Word	Part of Speech	Definition	Context Sentence

Before You Read Seventh Grade

Gary Soto

Meet the Author

Gary Soto is Mexican American, and he grew up in Fresno, California. Many of his stories take place in Mexican-American communities. But people of all backgrounds like Soto's stories. Why? Because they tell what it's like to be a kid growing up just about anywhere. See page R7 of the Author Files in the back of the book for more on Gary Soto.

Author Search For more about Gary Soto, go to www.glencoe.com.

Objectives (pp. 24–31)
Reading Set a purpose for reading
Informational Text Use text features: illustrations
Literature Identify theme in a literary text
Vocabulary Use context clues to determine word meanings

Vocabulary Preview

propelled (proh PELD) *v.* pushed or moved forward by a force or *as if* by one; form of the verb *propel* **(p. 27)** *The coach's whistle propelled the students to the locker room.*

glimpse (glimps) *n.* a quick look **(p. 29)** *He caught a glimpse of her in the hallway.*

V **campus** (KAM pus) *n.* the land and buildings of a school **(p. 29)** *The library was at the north end of the campus.*

eventually (ih VEN choo ul lee) *adv.* in the end; finally **(p. 29)** *Eventually he would have to do his homework.*

impress (im PRES) *v.* to have a strong effect on **(p. 30)** *He wanted to impress his teacher with his math skills.*

Write to Learn With a partner, write a one-paragraph story that uses three of the vocabulary words correctly. Read your story to the class.

English Language Coach

Context Clues When you read a word you don't know, you can sometimes figure out its meaning by looking at **context clues.** Context clues are other words in the sentence or paragraph that help you understand the word you don't know.

Copy this chart into your Learner's Notebook. As you read "Seventh Grade," watch for the words in the chart. Fill in context clues for the word *gracefully.* Fill in your guess about what *bluff* means.

Word	Context Clues	Meaning
portly	waddled	heavy or overweight
gracefully		in a beautiful or pleasing way
bluff	by making noises that sounded French	

Additional Support

Author Search To expand students' appreciation of Gary Soto, have them access the Web site for additional information and resources.

Literature Focus Lesson

Voice in Fiction Point out that even though it is fictional, Gary Soto's story about seventh grade is believable because his characters *sound* like seventh graders. The **voice,** or style of writing, matches the subject of the story. Explain that in Edgar Allan Poe's horror story "The Tell-Tale Heart," a madman tells readers how he murdered an old man. Read these lines from the story: "I think it was his eye! yes, it was this! One of his eyes resembled that of a vulture... Whenever it fell upon me, my blood ran cold; and so... I made up my mind to take the life of the old man..." Discuss how the voice in these lines differs from the voice in "Seventh Grade." OL

Skills Preview

Key Reading Skill: Setting a Purpose for Reading

"Seventh Grade" is a story that is fictional, or made up. What purpose could you set for reading it? Maybe you want to find out if the characters' experiences are at all like yours. Maybe your only purpose is to enjoy a good, funny story. **R**

Write to Learn Think about your purpose for reading. Then write it in the "purpose" section of your Foldable.

Literary Element: Theme

The **theme** of any piece of literature is the main idea. It's what the author most wants a reader to understand by reading the selection. The theme of something is not the same thing as its topic. For example, a story could be about a rock band, but the theme could be the problems of being famous.

Use these tips to help you think about the theme of "Seventh Grade." **L**

- Notice what the main character is most interested in. *What does he talk and think about most often?*
- Notice the way the main character behaves. *Does he think things through carefully or act on the spur of the moment?*
- Think about what the main character wants and whether he gets it. *What makes it possible for him to get what he wants?*

Partner Talk With a partner, talk about what you think the theme, or author's message to the reader, is in a famous story, such as "The Three Little Pigs" or "Peter and the Wolf."

Interactive Literary Elements Handbook To review or learn more about the literary elements, go to www.glencoe.com.

Get Ready to Read

Connect to the Reading

Think of something that happened to you or someone else on the first day of school. It might have been the first day in a certain grade or the first day at a new school.

Partner Talk With a partner, talk about what happened. The story you tell can be about you or someone else. Then listen to your partner's story. How are your stories the same? How are they different? Are they serious or funny?

Build Background

In this story, you will meet Victor, a Mexican American boy growing up in Fresno, California. On the first day of seventh grade, Victor tries to get the attention of a girl he likes.

- Fresno is located near the center of the state of California.
- Fresno has a large Mexican American community.
- The Mexican American community is one of the largest and fastest-growing groups in the United States.

Set Purposes for Reading

BIG Question One of the things reading can do for you is let you see how other people deal with the same kinds of problems you have. As you read "Seventh Grade," see whether anything about Victor's life is like your own.

Set Your Own Purpose What else would you like to learn from the story to help you answer the Big Question? Jot down ideas about your own purposes for reading in the "purpose" section of the "Seventh Grade" page of Foldable 1.

Keep Moving

Use these skills as you read the following selection.

READING WORKSHOP 1

Teach

R Reading Skill

Setting a Purpose for Reading **Say:** What are some reasons you'd want to read a story like "Seventh Grade"? What do you hope to learn from this story? *(Responses will vary.)* **OL**

L Literary Element

Theme **Say:** The theme, or main idea, is different from the topic (what a story is about). What is the theme of "Beauty and the Beast"? Beauty is held captive by Beast, who turns into a prince when Beauty falls in love with him? Don't judge others by looks alone? *(Possible response: Don't judge others by looks alone.)* **BL** What part of the story gives you a clue about the theme? *(Possible response: When Beauty realizes she loves him despite his looks.)* **OL**

CheckPoint

Use the CheckPoint questions provided on Presentation Plus! to check for prior knowledge and to build background. These questions can be used with interactive response keypads for immediate student feedback.

English Language Coach

Context Clues Write the following sentences on the board. Ask students to come to the board and circle context clues that help them understand the meaning of the underlined words.

1. The junior high <u>campus</u> was beautiful. The school buildings were freshly painted, and shady trees surrounded the grounds.
2. Dan was uneasy about his Spanish lessons. However, with much study and practice, he <u>eventually</u> became quite good at the language.
3. She wanted the teacher to think that she was a good student. To <u>impress</u> the teacher, she worked hard and finished her projects on time. **OL**

Objectives

- Set a purpose for reading
- Use text features: illustrations
- Identify theme in a literary text
- Use context clues to determine word meanings

Teach

Viewing the Photo

Say: Photographs often suggest the mood of a scene. Often, they help readers share in the mood or the emotions of the scene. What do you think the students are doing in the photo on this page? What mood does the photo on this page suggest? *(Possible response: The students in the photo seem to be changing classes. The mood seems energetic.)* **OL**

C Critical Thinking

Analysis Tell students that the footnotes give the definitions of the text's Spanish phrases. The use of Spanish phrases helps the author establish a believable voice. **Say: What do Victor and Michael's dialogue and actions tell readers about them?** *(Possible response: The characters' dialogue and actions show their Mexican background and also their pride in that background.)* How does the use of Spanish phrases help in making the story's setting clearer and more real to the reader? *(Possible response: The use of Spanish phrases tells readers that the story is set in a school that has a strong Spanish cultural community.)* **OL**

READING WORKSHOP 1

Seventh Grade

by Gary Soto

On the first day of school, Victor stood in line half an hour before he came to a wobbly card table. He was handed a packet of papers and a computer card on which he listed his one elective,[1] French. He already spoke Spanish and English, but he thought some day he might travel to France, where it was cool; not like Fresno, where summer days reached 110 degrees in the shade. There were rivers in France, and huge churches, and fair-skinned people everywhere, the way there were brown people all around Victor.

Besides, Teresa, a girl he had liked since they were in catechism[2] classes at Saint Theresa's, was taking French, too. With any luck they would be in the same class. Teresa is going to be my girl this year, he promised himself as he left the gym full of students in their new fall clothes. She was cute. And good at math, too, Victor thought as he walked down the hall to his homeroom. He ran into his friend, Michael Torres, by the water fountain that never turned off. **1**

They shook hands, *raza*-style,[3] and jerked their heads at one another in a *saludo de vato.*[4] "How come you're making a face?" asked Victor. **C**

"I ain't making a face, *ese*. This *is* my face." Michael said his face had changed during the summer. He had read a *GQ* magazine that his older brother borrowed from the Book

1. An ***elective*** is a class that a student chooses to take.
2. At ***catechism*** (KAT uh kiz um) ***classes,*** students learn about the Roman Catholic religion.
3. ***Raza*-style** (RAW zuh) refers to the way Mexican Americans or other Hispanic people do something.
4. ***Saludo de vato*** (suh LOO doh \ day \ VAW toh) is a greeting.

Practice the Skills

1 Literary Element

Theme Who seems to be the main character in this story? What does he or she seem interested in? Could this be a clue to what the theme of the story will be?

Additional Support

Readability Scores
Dale-Chall: 5.3
DRP: 52
Lexile: 730

Reading in the Real World

College In "Seventh Grade," Victor chooses French as his elective class. Have students find out what languages are offered at their school. When students have gathered their information, have them post the results on the class bulletin board. **OL** Have students investigate the language requirements for entrance to most colleges. Have students gather information from the schools' Web sites or from their school counselors. **AL**

Mobile and noticed that the male models all had the same look on their faces. They would stand, one arm around a beautiful woman, and ***scowl***. They would sit at a pool, their rippled stomachs dark with shadow, and *scowl*. They would sit at dinner tables, cool drinks in their hands, and *scowl*. **2**

"I think it works," Michael said. He scowled and let his upper lip quiver. His teeth showed along with the ferocity[5] of his soul. "Belinda Reyes walked by a while ago and looked at me," he said.

Victor didn't say anything, though he thought his friend looked pretty strange. They talked about recent movies, baseball, their parents, and the horrors of picking grapes in order to buy their fall clothes. Picking grapes was like living in Siberia,[6] except hot and more boring.

"What classes are you taking?" Michael said, scowling.

"French. How 'bout you?"

"Spanish. I ain't so good at it, even if I'm Mexican."

"I'm not either, but I'm better at it than math, that's for sure."

A tinny, three-beat bell **propelled** students to their homerooms. The two friends socked each other in the arm and went their ways, Victor thinking, man, that's weird. Michael thinks making a face makes him handsome.

On the way to his homeroom, Victor tried a scowl. He felt foolish, until out of the corner of his eye he saw a girl looking at him. Umm, he thought, maybe it does work. He scowled with greater conviction.[7]

In homeroom, roll was taken, emergency cards were passed out, and they were given a bulletin to take home to their parents. The principal, Mr. Belton, spoke over the crackling loudspeaker, welcoming the students to a new year, new experiences, and new friendships. The students squirmed in their chairs and ignored him. They were anxious to go to first period. Victor sat calmly, thinking of Teresa, who sat two rows away, reading a paperback novel. This would be his

5. ***Ferocity*** (fuh RAW suh tee) means "wild, violent anger."
6. ***Siberia*** is a very cold part of northern Russia.
7. To do something with ***conviction*** is to do it with strong belief.

Vocabulary

propelled (proh PELD) *v.* pushed or moved forward by a force or *as if* by one

Practice the Skills

2 English Language Coach

Context Clues Remember to look at words and sentences that are near a word you don't know. What do you think **scowl** means?

English Language Coach

Slang The characters in "Seventh Grade" speak informally. Tell students that the characters' casual use of language is correct in the context of the story but would not be acceptable in a more formal piece of writing. Cite and discuss phrases such as "How 'bout you?" and "I ain't so good," and have students give other examples of slang from the story. Then ask students to reword the slang phrases to show how the same ideas would be expressed in a more formal context. EL BL

READING WORKSHOP 1

Teach

C Critical Thinking

Comprehension Say: When the narrator describes Michael's scowl, he writes that Michael's teeth showed and that Michael looked ferocious. Why do you think Belinda Reyes looks at Michael? *(Possible response: She thinks he looks strange or scary.)* Is this the effect Michael wants? *(Possible response: No—Michael wants the girls to think he looks like a model.)* OL

EL Language Coach

Multiple-Meaning Words

Say: List three definitions for the word *roll.* Look at the word *roll* in this selection. Now use context clues to figure out what *roll* means. *(Possible response: Roll means to turn over, a list of class members, and to shape into a ball; the context clues are homeroom, taken; in this sentence, roll means a list of class members.)* EL BL

Objectives

- Use context clues to determine word meanings
- Understand the author's use of voice

Teach

EL Language Coach

Context Clues Say: Why doesn't Victor leave immediately after homeroom? *(Victor is waiting for Teresa to finish speaking with the teacher so that he can leave at the same time as Teresa and make her notice him.)* What word does the author use to show that Victor is waiting or is slow to leave? *(lingered)* BL

R Reading Skill

Setting a Purpose for Reading Say: Think about the purpose you set when you began reading this story. Explain why and how your purpose might change as you read. *(Possible response: When you begin reading, you may have certain expectations. As you read, you may change your purpose to fit changes in your understanding of the story and its characters.)* OL

lucky year. She was in his homeroom, and would probably be in his English and math classes. And, of course, French.

The bell rang for first period, and the students herded noisily through the door. Only Teresa **lingered**, talking with the homeroom teacher. 3

"So you think I should talk to Mrs. Gaines?" she asked the teacher. "She would know about ballet?"

"She would be a good bet," the teacher said. Then added, "Or the gym teacher, Mrs. Garza."

Victor lingered, keeping his head down and staring at his desk. He wanted to leave when she did so he could bump into her and say something clever.

He watched her on the sly.[8] As she turned to leave, he stood up and hurried to the door, where he managed to catch her eye. She smiled and said, "Hi, Victor."

He smiled back and said, "Yeah, that's me." His brown face blushed. Why hadn't he said, "Hi, Teresa," or "How was your summer?" or something nice?

As Teresa walked down the hall, Victor walked the other way, looking back, admiring how gracefully she walked, one foot in front of the other. So much for being in the same class, he thought. As he trudged to English, he practiced scowling. 4

In English they reviewed the parts of speech. Mr. Lucas, a portly man, waddled down the aisle, asking, "What is a noun?"

"A person, place, or thing," said the class in unison.[9]

"Yes, now somebody give me an example of a person—you, Victor Rodriguez."

"Teresa," Victor said automatically. Some of the girls giggled. They knew he had a crush on Teresa. He felt himself blushing again.

"Correct," Mr. Lucas said. "Now provide me with a place."

Mr. Lucas called on a freckled kid who answered, "Teresa's house with a kitchen full of big brothers."

After English, Victor had math, his weakest subject. He sat in the back by the window, hoping that he would not be called on. Victor understood most of the problems, but some of the stuff looked like the teacher made it up as she went along. It was confusing, like the inside of a watch.

8. When you do something ***on the sly***, you do it so that no one notices.

9. ***In unison*** means "all together."

Practice the Skills

3 English Language Coach

EL **Context Clues** The word **lingered** means "was slow to move or leave." How could you figure out this meaning from the words or sentences around it?

4 Key Reading Skill

R **Setting a Purpose for Reading** What was your purpose for reading before you began reading? Has it changed now that you've started to read the story? Explain your answer in your Learner's Notebook.

Here's how one student explained his purpose for reading: "Before I began reading, my purpose was to find out about other seventh graders. Now I am reading to find out what will happen between Victor and Teresa."

Additional Support

English Language Coach

Similes Remind students that context clues can help readers understand similes, or comparisons that use *like* or *as.* This page ends with a simile: Victor thinks math problems are "like the inside of a watch." Ask: what are some context clues that help you understand this simile? *(his weakest subject, some of the stuff looked like the teacher made it up as she went along, confusing)* What do you think the simile means? *(Victor thinks math is as complicated and difficult to figure out as the tiny gears inside of a watch.)* What else could you compare math with to show that it is a difficult subject? *(Possible responses: a jigsaw puzzle, a tangled knot, a maze)* EL OL

After math he had a fifteen-minute break, then social studies, and, finally, lunch. He bought a tuna casserole with buttered rolls, some fruit cocktail, and milk. He sat with Michael, who practiced scowling between bites.

Visual Vocabulary
A ***casserole*** (KAS ur ohl) is food cooked in a deep dish.

Girls walked by and looked at him.

"See what I mean, Vic?" Michael scowled. "They love it."

"Yeah, I guess so."

They ate slowly, Victor scanning the horizon[10] for a **glimpse** of Teresa. He didn't see her. She must have brought lunch, he thought, and is eating outside. Victor scraped his plate and left Michael, who was busy scowling at a girl two tables away.

The small, triangle-shaped **campus** bustled with students talking about their new classes. Everyone was in a sunny mood. Victor hurried to the bag lunch area, where he sat down and opened his math book. He moved his lips as if he were reading, but his mind was somewhere else. He raised his eyes slowly and looked around. No Teresa.

He lowered his eyes, pretending to study, then looked slowly to the left. No Teresa. He turned a page in the book and stared at some math problems that scared him because he knew he would have to do them **eventually**. He looked to the right. Still no sign of her. He stretched out lazily in an attempt to disguise his snooping. EL

Then he saw her. She was sitting with a girlfriend under a plum tree. Victor moved to a table near her and daydreamed about taking her to a movie. When the bell sounded, Teresa looked up, and their eyes met. She smiled sweetly and gathered her books. Her next class was French, same as Victor's. 5

They were among the last students to arrive in class, so all the good desks in the back had already been taken. Victor was forced to sit near the front, a few desks away from Teresa,

10. ***Scanning the horizon*** means looking far ahead to find something in the distance.

Vocabulary

glimpse (glimps) *n.* a quick look

campus (KAM pus) *n.* the land and buildings of a school

eventually (ih VEN choo ul lee) *adv.* in the end; finally

Practice the Skills

5 Key Reading Skill

Setting a Purpose for Reading Review what has happened in the story so far. What do you want to find out as you continue to read? How has your purpose for reading changed? R

Differentiated Instruction

Drawing a Diagram Visual learners may have difficulty following the setting of Victor's lunchtime search for Teresa. Have students draw a diagram showing how they envision the school campus. Have them plot some of the places mentioned in the story, including the bag lunch area, the plum tree, and the outdoor tables. Ask students to trace Victor's journey as he looks for Teresa. Then have students write sentences that describe Victor's actions and feelings at each spot where he stops. OL

Teach

EL Language Coach

Words in Context Say: Which of Victor's actions give you clues about the meaning of *snooping? (He pretends to read while continuing to look for Teresa.)* BL

R Reading Skill

Setting a Purpose for Reading Say: If you are having trouble setting a purpose for reading, think about a question you want your reading to answer. For example, you may want to know, "Does Victor get the courage to talk to Teresa again?" Then your purpose for reading would be to find out whether Victor talks to Teresa. After reading this page, what question do you want to find answers to on the next pages? *(Responses will vary.)* OL

Objectives
- Set a purpose for reading
- Use context clues to determine word meanings
- Make generalizations based on characterization

READING WORKSHOP 1

Teach

L Literary Element

Theme Say: A theme in a story is the main idea or central message. Often it is not stated directly. Instead, it is revealed through the plot, setting, characters, and/or point of view. What kind of things does Victor do that help you figure out the theme of this story? *(Possible responses: Victor acts nervous around Teresa, he looks for Teresa at lunch, he pretends to know French to impress her.)* **OL** How does Victor's conversation with Michael help you figure out the theme? *(Possible response: Victor and Michael talk about impressing girls.)* **AL**

C Critical Thinking

Analysis Say: Victor pretends to understand and speak French. Why doesn't he stop when he realizes that he is embarrassing himself? *(Possible response: He has pretended so much that he can't find a logical place to stop.)* **OL** Do you think many people realize that Victor is pretending? *(Possible response: Only someone who really knows French, as Mr. Bueller does, would know that Victor is making up words.)* **BL**

while Mr. Bueller wrote French words on the chalkboard. The bell rang, and Mr. Bueller wiped his hands, turned to the class, and said, *"Bonjour."*[11]

"Bonjour," braved a few students.

"Bonjour," Victor whispered. He wondered if Teresa heard him.

Mr. Bueller said that if the students studied hard, at the end of the year they could go to France and be understood by the populace.

One kid raised his hand and asked, "What's 'populace'?"

"The people, the people of France."

Mr. Bueller asked if anyone knew French. Victor raised his hand, wanting to **impress** Teresa. The teacher beamed and said, *"Très bien. Parlez-vous français?"*[12]

Victor didn't know what to say. The teacher wet his lips and asked something else in French. The room grew silent. Victor felt all eyes staring at him. He tried to bluff his way out by making noises that sounded French.

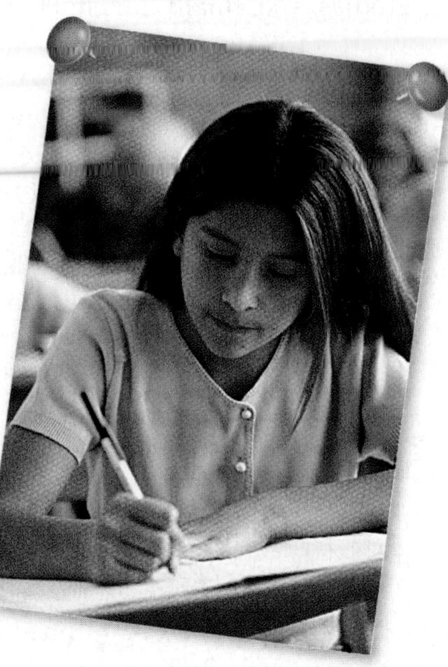

"La me vava me con le grandma," he said uncertainly.

Mr. Bueller, wrinkling his face in curiosity, asked him to speak up.

Great rosebushes of red bloomed on Victor's cheeks. A river of nervous sweat ran down his palms. He felt awful. Teresa sat a few desks away, no doubt thinking he was a fool. Without looking at Mr. Bueller, Victor mumbled, "Frenchie oh wewe gee in September." **6**

Mr. Bueller asked Victor to repeat what he had said.

"Frenchie oh wewe gee in September," Victor repeated.

Mr. Bueller understood that the boy didn't know French and turned away. He walked to the blackboard and pointed to the words on the board with his steel-edged ruler. **7**

"Le bateau," he sang.

"Le bateau," the students repeated.

"Le bateau est sur l'eau," he sang.

11. ***Bonjour*** (bohn ZHOOR) is French for "Good day" or "Hello."
12. ***Très bien. Parlez-vous français?*** (tray bee an \ PAR lay voo \ fron SAY) means "Very well. Do you speak French?"

Vocabulary

impress (im PRES) *v.* to have a strong effect on

Practice the Skills

6 Literary Element

Theme Victor is in a mess because he is trying to impress Teresa. He feels terrible. Is this part of the theme?

7 Key Reading Skill

Setting a Purpose for Reading Are you adjusting, or changing, your purpose for reading as you read? If so, that's good. It means you are enjoying the story. Did Victor's foolishness make you adjust your purpose? Why or why not?

Additional Support

English Language Coach

Figurative Language The author writes, "Great rosebushes of red bloomed on Victor's cheeks." Explain to students that this does not mean that plants grew from Victor's face. The description uses **figurative language,** or language that means something more than what the words say. Context clues can help you figure out the meaning of figurative language. Think about the context clues that describe how Victor feels: his hands are sweaty, he feels awful, and he's sure Teresa thinks he's a fool. On the basis of these context clues, what do you think "Great rosebushes of red bloomed on Victor's cheeks" means? *(Victor blushed, and his cheeks turned bright red.)* **OL EL**

READING WORKSHOP 1

"Le bateau est sur l'eau."[13]

Victor was too weak from failure to join the class. He stared at the board and wished he had taken Spanish, not French. Better yet, he wished he could start his life over. He had never been so embarrassed. He bit his thumb until he tore off a sliver of skin.

The bell sounded for fifth period, and Victor shot out of the room, avoiding the stares of the other kids, but had to return for his math book. He looked sheepishly[14] at the teacher, who was erasing the board, then widened his eyes in terror at Teresa who stood in front of him. "I didn't know you knew French," she said. "That was good."

Mr. Bueller looked at Victor, and Victor looked back. Oh please, don't say anything, Victor pleaded with his eyes. I'll wash your car, mow your lawn, walk your dog—anything! I'll be your best student, and I'll clean your erasers after school.

Mr. Bueller shuffled through the papers on his desk. He smiled and hummed as he sat down to work. He remembered his college years when he dated a girlfriend in borrowed cars. She thought he was rich because each time he picked her up he had a different car. It was fun until he had spent all his money on her and had to write home to his parents because he was broke. **8**

Victor couldn't stand to look at Teresa. He was sweaty with shame. "Yeah, well, I picked up a few things from movies and books and stuff like that." They left the class together. Teresa asked him if he would help her with her French.

"Sure, anytime," Victor said.

"I won't be bothering you, will I?"

"Oh no, I like being bothered."

"Bonjour," Teresa said, leaving him outside her next class. She smiled and pushed wisps of hair from her face.

"Yeah, right, *bonjour,*" Victor said. He turned and headed to his class. The rosebushes of shame on his face became bouquets of love. Teresa is a great girl, he thought. And Mr. Bueller is a good guy.

He raced to metal shop. After metal shop there was biology, and after biology a long **sprint** to the public library, where he checked out three French textbooks. **9**

He was going to like seventh grade. **10** ○

13. ***Le bateau*** (luh \ bah TOH) is French for "the boat." ***Le bateau est sur l'eau*** (ay \ syur \ loh) means "The boat is on the water."

14. ***Sheepishly*** means the way a sheep might act. Sheep are shy. When you look sheepishly at someone, you show that you are shy and embarrassed.

Practice the Skills

8 Literary Element

Theme What do Mr. Bueller's memories have to do with Victor's situation? Do they help him out of his mess? What else will help him? Finish the story and find out.

9 English Language Coach

Context Clues There aren't enough context clues to tell a reader exactly what a **sprint** is. But there are some clues that might give you an idea. What are they? **EL**

10 BIG Question

Would you tell a friend to read "Seventh Grade"? Why or why not? Do the characters remind you of anyone you know? Write your answers in the "Big Question" section of the "Seventh Grade" page of Foldable 1. Your response will help you complete the Unit Challenge later. **BQ**

Teach

EL Language Coach

Context Clues Say: A context clue may restate an unfamiliar word. This means that the context clue includes another word or phrase that has a meaning similar to that of the unfamiliar word. In the second to last paragraph, what word is similar in meaning to *sprint? (raced)* **BL** What word could you use to replace *sprint* in this paragraph? *(Possible responses: run, dash, race)* **OL**

BQ BIG Question

Say: What purpose might you have for reading about characters with whom you have something in common? *(Responses will vary.)* **OL**

Assess

Use the CheckPoint questions provided on Presentation Plus! to check students' mastery of the selection. These questions can be used with interactive response keypads for immediate student feedback.

Reading in the Real World

Citizenship From a sheet of heavy paper, cut out a large number 7. On the 7, have students take turns writing their home and school responsibilities as well as any special things they want to accomplish in seventh grade. When students have completed this task, have them review the list and circle the responsibilities and goals that the character Victor also has in the story. Discuss with students the responsibilities that seventh graders face both in school and at home, and talk about how students manage their increasing obligations. You may have students write their goals on individual "7"s and post them in the classroom to view and check progress periodically. **OL**

Objectives

- Make connections from text to self
- Set a purpose for reading
- Use context clues to determine word meanings
- Identify theme

Assess

Resources for page 32

- Selection Quick Check
- Selection and Unit Assessment
- ExamView Assessment Suite
- Interactive Tutor: Self-Assessment

Students can respond to the *After You Read* items in their Learner's Notebook or on separate sheets of paper.

Answering the

1. Responses will vary.
2. Victor already speaks Spanish and English, and he thinks he might like to visit France someday. Victor also wants to be in the same class as Teresa.

Critical Thinking

3. He promises himself that Teresa will be his girl.
4. Possible response: Victor is believable because he does embarrassing things to get someone's attention.
5. Victor is thinking of her.
6. Victor pretends to speak French, but he does not fool his teacher. He does fool Teresa, and he gets an opportunity to speak with her.
7. Possible response: Mr. Bueller realizes that Victor wants to impress Teresa.

After You Read | Seventh Grade

Answering the

1. What are your thoughts about the story "Seventh Grade"? How did it help you learn about the experiences of other seventh-grade students?
2. **Recall** Why is Victor taking French?
   TIP **Right There** You will find the answer in the story.

Critical Thinking

3. **Recall** What promise does Victor make to himself about this school year?
   TIP **Right There** You will find the answer in the story.
4. **Evaluate** In your opinion, is Victor a believable character? Why or why not?
   TIP **Author and Me** Answer from your own experiences.
5. **Infer** Why does Victor give the answer "Teresa" when his English teacher asks him for an example of a person?
   TIP **Author and Me** You will find clues in the story, but you must also use the information in your head.
6. **Summarize** What happened during French class?
   TIP **Think and Search** You must use information from the story and decide what the important points are.
7. **Infer** Why didn't Mr. Bueller say anything to Victor about what had happened?
   TIP **Think and Search** You will find clues in the story, but you must also use information in your head.

Talk About Your Reading

Literature Groups Do you think Teresa will become Victor's girlfriend? Discuss your ideas in your group.

Write to Learn As a group, write a sequel, or second part, to the story. In your sequel, describe what the last day of seventh grade will be like for Victor and Teresa.

Objectives (pp. 32–33)
Reading Set a purpose for reading
Literature Identify theme in a literary text
Vocabulary Use context clues: restatement
Grammar Identify action and linking verbs

Talk About Your Reading

Write to Learn

Possible response:

Victor and Teresa closed their French books. They were excited to test their French on tomorrow's class trip to a French bistro. Their teacher told them that servers actually spoke French.

"Are you ready to go to the bistro?" Teresa asked. "Imagine—we can really order a sandwich in French now."

"Yeah," smiled Victor, taking her hand. "And in *real* French, not the fake kind."

Skills Review

Key Reading Skill: Setting a Purpose for Reading

8. Review the sentence you wrote on your Foldable about your purpose for reading. Then write a few sentences telling why your purpose stayed the same or how it changed as you read.

Literary Element: Theme

9. Do you think Victor learns anything from his first day in seventh grade? If so, what is it?

10. What do you think the theme of this story involves? Love? Figuring out who you are? Pretending to be someone you're not? Or is it something else?

Vocabulary Check

11. Write as few sentences as possible, using all of the vocabulary words correctly. Try to use more than one word in each sentence. For example, "I had a *glimpse* of Al being *propelled* by the wind across the campus."

propelled glimpse campus eventually impress

English Language Coach Read each pair of sentences. Look for context clues that help you guess the meaning of the underlined word. If the context has good clues, choose an answer. If it doesn't, write "not enough clues."

12. Mom expects us to be polite and respectful. If we're **impertinent**, we get in big trouble.

Does *impertinent* mean messy, sassy, intelligent, or fearful?

13. I'd never seen such a **repast** in my entire life. Neither had Seth, so we both just stared.

Does *repast* mean meal, view, creature, or costume?

14. I am trying to be **equitable** by giving you each the same amount. I want to be reasonable and just.

Does *equitable* mean odd, mean, funny, or fair?

Grammar Link: Finding Verbs

A verb is a word that shows action or a state of being. The two kinds of verbs are *action* verbs and *linking* verbs.

Action Verbs An action verb may describe an action that you can see.

- Teresa **smiles** at Victor.

The verb *smiles* describes an action that can be seen.

An action verb may also describe an action that you can't see—one that goes on inside someone's mind.

- Victor **understands** most of the problems.

The verb *understands* describes a thinking action that happens in a person's mind. Even though it's something that can't be seen, *understands* is still an action verb.

Linking Verbs Some verbs are linking verbs. They don't describe an action. Instead, a linking verb connects a person, place, or thing with a word that *describes* it or tells *what it is.* Common linking verbs are *am, is, are, was, were, feel, seem,* and *become.*

- Teresa **is** a student.

The verb *is* connects *Teresa* to *student. Student* tells what *Teresa* is.

- Victor **feels** nervous.

The verb *feels* connects *Victor* to *nervous. Nervous* describes how *Victor* feels.

Grammar Practice

Copy each sentence and circle the verb.

15. Victor daydreams about Teresa.

16. Michael is his friend.

17. Sometimes he seems a little foolish.

Web Activities For eFlashcards, Selection Quick Checks, and other Web activities, go to www.glencoe.com.

READING WORKSHOP 1

Skills Review

Key Reading Skill: Setting a Purpose for Reading

8. Possible responses: At first I was reading to find out what seventh grade is like for other students. As I read more about Victor's problems, I became more interested in finding out how he would solve them.

Literary Element: Theme

9. Responses will vary, but they may indicate that Victor learns it is important to be himself and he would impress Teresa more if he actually knew French rather than pretending to.

10. Responses will vary, but students should be able to support their answer with specifics from the story.

Vocabulary Check

11. Possible response: *Eventually,* Victor had a chance to *impress* Teresa.

12. sassy

13. not enough clues

14. fair

Close

Ask students to explain how reading about Victor's experience in seventh grade helps them answer the Big Question.

Grammar Link: Finding Verbs

Grammar Practice

15. Victor (daydreams) about Teresa.

16. Michael (is) his friend.

17. Sometimes he (seems) a little foolish.

LiteratureOnline

Web Activities Have students access the Web site for interactive activities that will help them assess their understanding of the selection.

Summary

UNIT 1

Objectives covered in this workshop:

- **Writing** Summarize to inform develop drafts; categorize information; main idea and supporting details
- **Grammar** Identify and correctly use verbs

Teaching Students to Write a Summary

Why Is It Important?

- The ability to write a concise summary will open the door to other forms of writing, especially analytical and technical writing.
- Writing a summary of a selection will help students retain information better and understand concepts more easily.
- Discerning the main idea and supporting details in a text will improve students' organizational skills in their own writing.
- Summary is a skill that can be applied to any kind of writing, fiction or nonfiction.

How to Help Students Get It

- Talk about examples of summaries in real life. For example, abstracts in the library, video game reviews that summarize all the levels of play, the news "blurbs" that lead into the full length coverage of a story, or the plot summaries on the backs of movie boxes.
- Lead the class through the construction of a summary, using a text they are all familiar with, such as a fairy tale.
- Ask students to answer the following questions about the story they choose to summarize: Who, What, When, Where, Why, How?
- Some students may benefit from hearing summaries read aloud. Use a movie or book review or students' own summaries.
- Remind students to ask themselves: "Does my summary allow the reader to accurately predict what the original selection is about? What takes place in the original document?"

The Traits of Good Writing

Throughout *Reading with Purpose,* students receive instruction on the seven Traits of Good Writing. Recognition of these traits is especially helpful to students as they revise their writing. See the chart on the next page for descriptions of each trait and brief checklists students can use as they revise their work.

The Writing Workshops of each unit focus on one trait. Introduce and discuss all seven traits in Writing Workshop 1 of Unit 1, and then have students focus on the Unit 1 trait (see the chart) in Writing Workshop 2. Although each unit focuses on one trait, you might want to occasionally review all seven traits throughout the year.

Writing Trait	Student Checklist
Ideas: the message or the theme and the details that develop it	• Does the title suggest the theme of the composition? • Does the composition focus on a single narrow topic? • Is the thesis, or main idea, clearly stated? • Do well-chosen details elaborate the main idea?
Organization: the arrangement of main points and supporting details	• Are the beginning, middle, and end clearly linked? • Is the order of ideas easy to follow? • Does the introduction capture readers' attention? • Do sentences and paragraphs flow from one to the next in a way that makes sense? • Does the conclusion wrap up the composition?
Voice: a writer's unique way of using tone and style	• Does the writing sound interesting when read aloud? • Does the writing show what the writer thinks about the topic? • Does the writing sound like the writer—or does it sound like the writer is imitating someone else?
Word Choice: the vocabulary a writer uses to convey meaning	• Does the writer use lively verbs to show action? • Does the writer use vivid words to create word pictures in the readers' minds? • Does the writer use precise words to explain his or her ideas simply and clearly?
Sentence Fluency: the smooth rhythm and flow of sentences that vary in length and style	• Do sentences vary in length and structure? • Do transition words and phrases show connections between ideas and sentences? • Does parallelism help balance and unify related ideas?
Unit Focus → **Conventions:** correct spelling, grammar, usage, and mechanics	• Are all words spelled correctly? • Are all proper nouns—as well as the first word of every sentence—capitalized? • Is the composition free of sentence fragments? • Is the composition free of run-on sentences? • Are punctuation marks—such as apostrophes, commas, and end marks—inserted in the right places?
Presentation: the way words and design elements look on a page	Appearance matters, so encourage students to make their compositions inviting to read. Handwritten papers should be neat and legible. If a word processor is used, the text should be double spaced and the font should be readable. Encourage students to also use other design elements—such as boldfaced headings, bulleted lists, pictures, and charts—to make their papers attractive and inviting.

Workshop Resources

Pacing (Days) Standard	Block	Lesson	Student Materials	Teacher Resources
1		Prewriting	Writing Workshop Graphic Organizer Grammar Practice Spelling and Handwriting Practice Grammar and Composition Handbook	TeacherWorks Plus Presentation Plus! Rubrics for Assessing Student Writing, Listening, and Speaking
2		Drafting	Real Success in Writing: Research and Reports	
1		Editing	Interactive Grammar and Language Workbook Grammar and Composition Handbook	Grammar and Writing Workshop Transparency
2		Revising	Real Success in Writing: Research and Reports	Interactive Grammar and Language Workbook
2		Presenting		Rubrics for Assessing Student Writing, Listening, and Speaking

Focus

BELLRINGER Options

Daily Language Practice Transparency
Focus Activity Tell: Think about a TV show you saw recently. Briefly tell the main idea of the show to a classmate.

Teach

E Text Element

Titles, Heads, and Decks
Say: The title of a selection can help you identify its main idea. **Ask:** What does each title in the *Get Ready to Write* section tell you about the selection? *("Flash Flood" is about a flood. "Paddling Dicey Waters" is about being in rough waters. "Seventh Grade" is about being in seventh grade.)* OL

Resources for page 34

- Use the Writing Workshop Graphic Organizer BLM in the Unit 1 Resource Booklet.
- Use the Grammar and Writing Workshop Transparencies, Unit 1.

WRITING WORKSHOP PART 1

Summary

Prewriting and Drafting

ASSIGNMENT Write a summary
Purpose: To keep track of main ideas and important information
Audience: You, your teacher, and some classmates

Writing Rubric

As you work through this assignment, you should

- write a summary of an article or a story
- state the main idea in your own words
- include important details
- leave out minor details
- use a quotation

See page 76 in Part 2 for a model of a summary.

Objectives (pp. 34–37)
Writing Paraphrase and summarize text • Use Standard English grammar, usage, and mechanics
Grammar Identify action and linking verbs

Writing a summary of one of the selections in this unit will help you answer the Big Question: Why Do We Read?

When you summarize, you explain the main idea and most important details in your own words. You probably summarize all the time—when you tell a friend about a movie, a book, or what happened in class yesterday. Writing a summary of something you read or heard can help you understand and remember the important information.

Prewriting

Get Ready to Write

E In this workshop, you'll write a summary of one of these: "Flash Flood" (p. 5), "Paddling Dicey Waters" (p. 16), or "Seventh Grade" (p. 26).

Gather Ideas

After you choose the selection you want to summarize, read the selection again. As you read, answer these questions in your Learner's Notebook.

- What is the main, or most important, idea?
- Who or what is the selection about?
- What happens in the selection?
- What are the most important details?

Drafting

Start Writing!

Whether you feel ready or not, start writing your summary!

Get It on Paper

These tips can guide you as you start your summary.

- Look at the notes you made about the main points of the selection.
- Begin by describing the main idea in your own words.
- Add only the most important details.
- If you include a quotation, use quotation marks correctly.
- *Don't* include your own opinion about the selection.

Additional Support

Reading in the Real World

Citizenship Ask students to find informational articles in local newspapers or magazines about real-life heroes in their community. Have each student summarize a hero's story. Remind students that a good summary includes only the most important ideas and details and possibly a quotation. Each summary should answer the following questions:

- Who is the hero?
- What act of heroism did he or she perform?
- Where did this act take place?
- When did this act take place?
- Why is this person considered a hero? OL

Applying Good Writing Traits

Conventions

Writers share a common set of rules. It's not a terrible thing to break the rules, but you have to know the rules in order to play the game.

What Are Conventions?

Conventions are the rules of language. Writing that shows strong control of conventions uses correct

- spelling
- punctuation
- capitalization
- grammar and usage
- paragraphing (indenting)

Why Are Conventions Important?

When you follow the rules, your writing is correct and easy for others to read. Readers don't have to figure out what you mean. Instead, they can pay attention to your interesting ideas, thoughtful organization, and unique voice.

How Do I Use Them in My Writing?

- Read your paper slowly and carefully. Focus on the words as they really appear on the page instead of as they're supposed to appear.
- Read your paper several times, starting in a new place (beginning, middle, or end) each time. That way, you can see each part with a fresh eye.
- Look for one kind of error at a time.
  1. Look for grammatical errors. Reading your paper aloud may help you.
  2. Check to make sure you have punctuation and capital letters in all the right places.
  3. Check that your paragraphs begin in the right places and that the first line of each paragraph is indented.
  4. Circle any words you need to check for spelling and then look them up. If you use a computer, you can use the spell-check feature, but don't trust it completely. If you accidentally typed *here* but meant to type *hear*, the spell-check feature won't notice the mistake.
- You can play around with conventions for a specific effect. For example, you may misspell a word or break a grammar rule to show how a character speaks. However, your writing must show strong control of conventions so readers know you're breaking the rules for good reasons.

Write to Learn Read over your final draft carefully. Follow the steps above to find and correct errors in conventions. Then trade papers with a partner and circle any errors you see in your partner's paper.

"It's a special program for writing love letters. It corrects my spelling and grammar and automatically deletes anything I'll regret later."

Analyzing Cartoons
A program that corrects things you'll be sorry for later? Perfect! It's important to use correct writing conventions because mistakes are distracting to the reader. They blur your message. And you might regret that later.

Differentiated Instruction

Organizing Ideas Some students may find it easier to organize information by using a graphic organizer. Help students create graphic organizers like the one shown above. Tell students to begin with big ideas and then add important details. If students are having difficulty stating the big idea, suggest that they use the details to help them figure out the main idea. Remind students not to include minor details in their summaries. **OL**

If students are having difficulty organizing their ideas, suggest that they write their main ideas and details on sticky notes. They can then move their sticky notes around until they are properly organized. **BL**

WRITING WORKSHOP PART 1

Teach

W Writing

Ideas Say: While a story or an informational article can contain big ideas, important details, and minor details, a summary should include only big ideas and important supporting details. Review "Flash Flood." What are some of the important details that support this selection's main ideas? *(a flash flood; children are caught in the flood; Hoffmeister knows how to save a family.)* **Ask:** What are some minor details that you would leave out of a summary? *(A fire has destroyed water-retaining vegetation; Jason shows up to help; Hoffmeister slips and Moriah nearly drowns; They all move to a new location.)* **OL**

Objectives
- Paraphrase and summarize text
- Use Standard English grammar, usage, and mechanics
- Identify action and linking verbs

Teach

W Writing

Writing Coherence Say: Your summary must be coherent. It must make sense. The details should be related in a clear and logical order. A good summary can be understood by someone who has not read the whole selection. **Ask:** Which of the following summaries is more coherent?

A. Emily is a 13-year-old with a dog and epilepsy. She has seizures. She can go to the mall now. Her dog helps her.

B. Emily is a 13-year-old with epilepsy. Epilepsy is a disorder that causes seizures. Emily has a new helper—a seizure-alert dog who warns her when she is about to have a seizure. With her new dog, Emily can do most things that other kids do, including going to the mall. *(B is more coherent.)*

Ask: Why is B more coherent? *(A is not clear; the ideas are out of order.)* OL

Writing Models Have students access the Web site for an additional and interactive Writing Workshop-based student model.

WRITING WORKSHOP PART 1

Literature Online

Writing Models For models and other writing activities, go to www.glencoe.com.

Writing Tip

Practice Summarizing As you read the passage, answer the following questions in your Learner's Notebook. What details would be important to include in a summary? What details could be left out? What is the main idea of the passage? Write your answers in your Learner's Notebook. W

Writing Tip

Identify Main Idea The main idea may not be directly stated in a selection—especially in stories. If you have trouble finding the main idea, look at the details. Ask yourself what main idea the supporting details point out.

Writing Tip

Use the Model Notice that the summary is shorter than the passage and doesn't have as many details. What do you notice about the details that are included in the summary?

Read to Write

How is your writing going so far? Do you feel stuck? Sometimes, looking at examples of what you are trying to write helps. Read this short passage and the summary that follows.

Emily Ramsey's world just grew a little bigger. For the first time in her life, the 13-year-old middle school student from Racine, Wisconsin, is now able to cruise the mall, ride the school bus, and participate in after school sports without constant supervision. That's standard operating procedure for most teenagers, but for one with epilepsy,[1] the world is a dangerous place.

For a person with epilepsy, seizures[2] strike without warning, making simple acts such as walking down stairs or going for a swim life-threatening. These days, Emily can do all that and more, thanks to her constant companion, Watson. Watson is a seizure-alert dog, able to warn his owner of epileptic attacks before they strike.

[1]epilepsy – a disease that can cause seizures

[2]seizure – a sudden attack that can cause a person to lose consciousness

Summary

Emily Ramsey is 13 years old and has epilepsy. Epilepsy makes life dangerous for Emily because it causes seizures. She has a seizure-alert dog that has improved her life. Seizure-alert dogs can tell their owners when an attack is going to happen. Now that Emily has a seizure-alert dog, she can do all the things a kid without epilepsy could do.

Compare your answers to the Writing Tips questions to the summary. Did you recognize the important details? If not, figure out which important details you missed and which minor details you included.

Take another look at your summary draft. Are there any details you want to add or delete from your summary? Add or delete those details now.

Additional Support

Reading Fluency

Reading and Writing Some students may find it helpful to analyze their drafts by reading them aloud, which will also help enhance their reading fluency. Allow these students to work with partners to read and critique their drafts aloud. Students should take turns reading their drafts to their partners and discussing whether they have captured the main idea and important details of the selection they have chosen to summarize. Encourage students to use the rubric from page 34 as a guide for discussing their drafts. OL

Grammar Link

Action and Linking Verbs

What Is It?

- A **verb** is a word that expresses action or a state of being.
- An **action verb** is a word that expresses action, or something that can be done.
- A **linking verb,** or state-of-being verb, connects the subject of a sentence with a noun or with a descriptive word or phrase.

W

Why Is It Important?

- Action verbs tell what the subject of a sentence *does.*
- Linking verbs connect the subject with words that tell what the subject *is* or *is like.*

How Do I Do It?

Action verbs name an activity. Use action verbs to tell what the subject of a sentence *does.*

Midori **runs** track every day after school.
▲ *action verb*

Hector **scores** a goal on the soccer field.
▲ *action verb*

The chart below shows some common action verbs.

Action Verbs	
Physical	shout, flash, arrive, talk, applaud, act, sing, dance
Mental	remember, forget, think, wonder, read, dream, appreciate

Use linking verbs if you want to tell what the subject of a sentence *is* or *is like.*

Mario **is** a tap dancer.
▲ *linking verb*

Freshly baked cookies always **smell** good!
▲ *linking verb*

The chart below shows some common linking verbs.

Common Linking Verbs			
am	was	been	seem
is	were	become	
are	be	feel	

Some verbs can be either action verbs or linking verbs depending on how they are used.

Action Verb: Jeff **tasted** the soup and made a face. (Here, *tasted* names an activity.)

Linking Verb: The soup **tasted** funny. (Here, *tasted* is a connection between *soup* and a description of what the soup is or is like.)

Some other verbs that can be used both ways are *feel, look, grow, remain,* and *sound.*

Name That Verb Underline ten verbs in the draft you just wrote. Then work with a partner to identify those verbs as action verbs or linking verbs.

Looking Ahead

Part 2 of this Writing Workshop is coming up later. Save the writing you did so far—you'll need it later to finish your summary.

Differentiated Instruction

Music Lyrics Some students may better understand the concept of action verbs if they use music and dance. Have students write on a sheet of paper the words to one of their favorite songs. Ask students to circle all of the action verbs in the lyrics. Then have each student work with a partner to substitute other action verbs for the circled verbs. The new verbs must make sense in the lyrics, but they may change the meaning or create a new image. Ask students to perform their "new" songs. OL EL

WRITING WORKSHOP PART 1

Teach

W Writing

Using Action and Linking Verbs Say: An action verb expresses action. **Ask:** What are some examples of action verbs? *(Possible responses: runs, plays, bounces, draws)* **Say:** A linking verb links, or connects, the subject of a sentence with a noun or an adjective. **Ask:** What are some examples of linking verbs? *(Possible responses: is, be, was, am, are, become)* **OL Say:** Review the charts of action verbs and linking verbs. Write 5 sentences with action verbs and 5 sentences with linking verbs. OL

Assess

Have students exchange drafts with partners and critique each other's work. Tell students to check: Did my partner include a main idea statement? Did he or she include a few important details and leave out the minor details? After a few minutes, tell students to use their partners' comments to assess their own work, make any needed revisions, and save their drafts for later use.

Objectives

- Summarize to inform, to develop drafts, to categorize information, and to determine main idea and supporting details

Previewing

Objectives covered in this workshop:
- Use titles to understand reading
- Make connnections from self to text
- Use context clues

Previewing

Why Is It Important?

- Previewing is one of the first steps readers take in determining the purpose for their reading. When they look over a piece of text, they can decide why they would read it.
- Previewing helps students focus on the most important parts by drawing attention to the title, headings, graphics, etc.
- Previewing allows students to make connections between what they see when they look over the text and what they already know.

How to Help Students Get It

- Model your previewing using something you're reading. You might demonstrate the following steps: (1) Read the title, (2) Read the headings, (3) Look at the visuals, and (4) Scan for special terms.
- Remind students about the importance of setting a purpose for their reading and ask them to discuss how previewing can help with setting a purpose.
- Ask students to create questions after they have previewed a text. To help students get started, have the class create questions from the titles of the selections. Over time, students will automatically create questions in their minds when they preview a text and answer those questions as they read.
- Tell students that during a preview, they should make a mental note of how much of the text or information is new to them. Based on this information, they can determine how closely and carefully they need to read or if they will need extra background information.

Reading to Answer the Big Question

Where You Are

This poem speaks directly to the Big Question by encouraging readers to open their eyes to where they are. The poem gives a variety of commands, which should prompt students to think about where they are literally and figuratively.

Message of Hope

David, Duom, and James spend five years of their youth being shuttled from one refugee camp to another. Now they are college students in California. Readers will find out how they adjusted to the change and how they are helping other "Lost Boys" in the Sudan.

Workshop Resources

Pacing (Days) Standard	Block	Lesson	Student Materials	Teacher Resources
1		Key Skill Lesson: Previewing	Key Reading Skills Practice English Language Coach	Bellringer Options Transparencies Read Aloud, Think Aloud Transparencies Presentation Plus!
2		"Where You Are"	Literary Analysis Transparencies Glencoe Online Selection Vocabulary Development Academic Vocabulary Development English Language Coach Active Reading Graphic Organizer Literary Analysis StudentWorks Plus Online Student Edition Literature Classics Selection and Unit Assessments	Literary and Text Analysis Transparencies Puzzlemaker Skills Level Up! BookLink 3 Assessment by Learning Objective (Diagnostic and Formative) Interactive Tutor Self-Assessment TeacherWorks Plus
2		"Message of Hope"	Glencoe Online Selection Vocabulary Development Academic Vocabulary Development English Language Coach Active Reading Graphic Organizer Literary Analysis StudentWorks Plus Online Student Edition Literature Classics Selection and Unit Assessments	Literary and Text Analysis Transparencies Puzzlemaker Skill Level Up! BookLink 3 Assessment by Learning Objective (Diagnostic and Formative) Interactive Tutor Self-Assessment TeacherWorks Plus

Keys for Unit Resource

- Blackline Master
- Workbook
- Supplemental Text
- CD-ROM
- DVD
- Transparency
- Web-based
- Fast Files

Level Appropriate Code

AS = Activities for all students
AL = Activities for students working above grade level
OL = Activities for students working at grade level
BL = Activities for students working below grade level
EL = Activities for English language learners

Focus

BELLRINGER Options

Daily Language Practice Transparency

Focus Activity Say: How do you know what to expect when you go to a movie, buy a CD, or start to read a book? *(Responses may vary. Students may say that they see commercials for movies, hear songs from an album on the radio, and read the synopsis on the back of a book.)*

Teach

R Reading Skill

Previewing Say: What could you find out about a comic book by previewing it at a newsstand? *(Possible response: I could find out what it is about and whether I want to buy it.)* OL

V Vocabulary

Academic Vocabulary Say: The film advertisements that play before a movie are often called previews. Why is this a good name for these ads? *(Previews help you look over movies before you see them.)* OL

READING WORKSHOP 2

Skills Focus

You will practice using the following skills when you read these selections:

- "Where You Are," p. 42
- "Message of Hope," p. 48

Reading

- Previewing

Informational Text

- Using headings, pictures, and other text features to learn what you are going to read
- Using titles and subtitles to understand what you read

Vocabulary

- Using context clues to figure out word meanings
- Academic Vocabulary: *preview*

Writing/Grammar

- Identifying and writing clearly about important ideas in your reading
- Identifying main verbs and helping verbs

Objectives (pp. 38–39)
Reading Preview text

Skill Lesson

Previewing

Learn It!

What Is It? **Previewing** is looking over a selection before you read. When you preview, you might look over a selection's title and heads. Or you might look at pictures, charts, maps, and graphs. You've probably done some previewing without even thinking about it. Did you check out the photos in "Paddling Dicey Waters" before you started reading? Did the title "Paddling Dicey Waters" make you wonder what the article was about? If you did any of those things, you were previewing. R

- *Pre-* means "before."
- *Viewing* means "looking at." It also means "thinking about." *Viewing* is looking at something and thinking about what you see.
- So *previewing* is looking over a selection before you read it, and thinking about what you see.

Analyzing Cartoons
Neil previewed his book and saw that the ending involves zebras. The next time he wants to read a novel, he should probably preview the title more carefully.

Academic Vocabulary V

preview (PREE vyoo) *v.* to see beforehand

Additional Support

English Language Coach

Building Background Students for whom English is a second language may have trouble understanding the cartoon above. Remind them that words in a dictionary are arranged in alphabetical order, so words like *aardvark* and *abominable* come near the beginning. A word ending in z, such as *zebra,* appears at the end of a dictionary. Students do not need to know the meanings of these words to understand the cartoon. The joke is that Neil intends to read the dictionary as though it were a story. Ask students to explain why this is a funny thing to do. Brainstorm with students some other books that should not be read straight through as though they were stories. OL EL

Why Is It Important? Everyone likes to get a head start. Previewing gives you just that. Looking over a selection tells you how it's set up and what it's about. Knowing these things can help you to ask questions and think about what you read.

R

Literature Online

Study Central Visit www.glencoe.com and click on Study Central to review previewing.

How Do I Do It? Before you read, look at the title and head. Are there any charts, maps, or graphs? What do these parts of the selection tell you? What questions do you have? Take a look at how one student previewed "Paddling Dicey Waters." The title, heads, and photo told her something about the selection. They also made her want to learn more.

The title tells me this article is probably about a boat trip. I'm not sure what dicey means, though. Maybe as I read I'll find out. The sentences in bold under the title tell me that I'm going to read about a canoe trip in Peru. That sounds like fun. I can see the article is divided into sections. The first is "A different world." Things in Peru are different from here, I guess. That's a huge snake!

Practice It!

Below are some of the things you might look at to preview the selections that follow. Write this list in your Learner's Notebook. Then explain how each item might help you preview a reading selection.

- Title
- Heads and Subheads
- Photographs and Other Illustrations
- The Appearance of the Text

Use It!

You just explained how each item on the list *might* help you preview. As you read "Where You Are" and "Message of Hope," add a sentence to your list telling how each item that helped you preview did so.

READING WORKSHOP 2

Teach

Literature Online

Study Central Have students access the Web site to review previewing and to complete a related activity.

R Reading Skill

Previewing Say: Look at the *Why Is It Important?* section. How did previewing help you choose your last book from the library? Describe what you noticed about the library book before you checked it out. *(Students may say that they noticed the length, topic, or illustrations in the library book.)* OL

Describe how you preview other types of reading, such as magazine articles, short stories, or Web sites. *(Responses may vary, but they should include the idea that students look ahead at features such as titles and illustrations.)* AL

Resources for page 39

- Use Reading Skills Transparency in *Read Aloud, Think Aloud,* Unit 1, to help students practice previewing.

Differentiated Instruction

Pictorial Previews Invite students to draw a picture that gives a preview of any one of the following:

- their daily school schedule
- a favorite book
- a movie they recently saw
- a new CD

Have students exchange their previews with partners and discuss how well their pictorial previews represent the larger work or activity. OL

Objectives

- Preview text
- Use text features to preview and understand text

Teach

More About the Author

Jack Anderson has written on the history of ballet, including the story of the *Nutcracker* ballet and the Ballet Russe de Monte Carlo, a Russian ballet company. His poetry has been called "ballet of the ear." "Where You Are" can be seen as a parody of instructions on how to read a poem.

V Vocabulary

Vocabulary Notebook Say: One way to learn vocabulary is to write down words in a small notebook kept just for new vocabulary. Next to each word, write a sentence that shows what the word means. By using a notebook, you can see your list of vocabulary words grow throughout the school year. BL EL

Before You Read

Where You Are

Meet the Author

Jack Anderson writes about dance for *The New York Times.* He has also written books of poetry. After reading "Where You Are," you may find that Anderson's poetry, like dance music, makes you want to get up and move.

Author Search For more about Jack Anderson, go to www.glencoe.com.

Objectives (pp. 40–43)
Reading Preview text
Literature Use text features: title, appearance of text • Recognize the distinctive features of poetry
Vocabulary Use context clues to determine word meaning

Vocabulary Preview

V

margin (MAR jin) *n.* the blank space around the printed area on a page **(p. 42)** *Please write your answers in the margin.*

condition (kon DISH un) *n.* state of being **(p. 42)** *The used car was in very good condition.*

reclining (rih KLY ning) *v.* lying down; form of the verb *recline* **(p. 43)** *I was reclining on the grass when a ball hit me in the stomach!*

precisely (prih SYS lee) *adv.* exactly **(p. 43)** *It was precisely two o'clock.*

Write to Learn Work in a small group to write *two* sentences. Each sentence should use two vocabulary words correctly. Share your sentences with the rest of the class.

English Language Coach

Context Clues What can you do when you don't know what a word means? Look for context clues. The context of a word is all the words and sentences around it. Those other words and sentences sometimes give you clues about a word's meaning. To find context clues, try rereading, or reading again, what you just read. Or try reading ahead.

For example, you read the line "Observe sky" in the poem "Where You Are," but maybe you don't know what *observe* means. Then you read ahead and find the words "see in the sky." These words give you a clue to the meaning of *observe.*

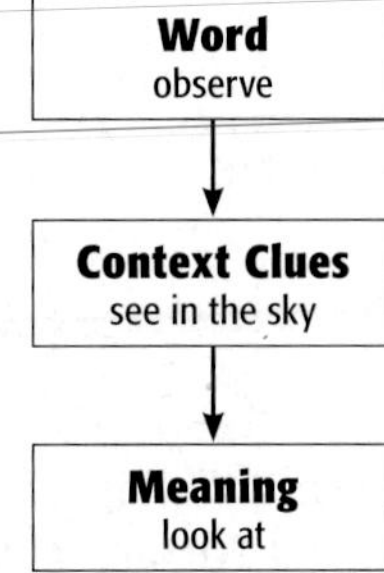

On Your Own If you read the following instructions, what would you guess *peruse* means? Why?

Open your book to page 42 and carefully peruse the poem. As you read, notice how simple most of the words are.

Additional Support

Author Search To expand students' appreciation of Jack Anderson, have them access the Web site for additional information and resources.

Literature Focus Lesson

Poetry Jack Anderson says in "The Writing Life," "Poetry and dance share certain characteristics. They are both arts of rhythm, the rhythms of the speaking voice in the case of poetry and the rhythms of moving bodies in the case of dance. They're arts of movement, either of words across a page or bodies across a stage." Read a poem aloud to your students, and allow them to walk or move as you read. Ask them how the sound of the poem influenced the way they moved. *(Possible response: I took short, quick steps that matched the sound of the poem.)* OL

Skills Preview

Key Reading Skill: Previewing

Before you read the poem, preview it by looking at its title and shape. A poem's shape depends on its overall length, and on the length of its lines. When previewing, you can also read the first few lines of the selection. As you preview, think about

- what "Where You Are" might mean
- what a poem's use of short lines might mean for a reader

Write to Learn In your Learner's Notebook, write down two questions you have after previewing. Leave space next to your questions so that you can answer them as you read.

Key Text Element: Title

The title can help you read and understand a poem. It gives you a clue to what the poem is about. As you read, ask yourself, "Why does the poem have this title?"

These tips will help you understand titles. Write the tips down in the form of a checklist to use as you read.

- Read the title. What do you think the title means? Remember, titles often have more than one meaning.
  What does this title mean to you? What other meanings could it have?
- Read the poem. Think about which lines or groups of lines remind you of the title.
  Do all lines lead you back to the title? If not, which ones do?
- Think about how the title helps you understand the poem's meaning.
  How does the poet help you understand the poem's meaning?

Interactive Literary Elements Handbook
To review or learn more about the literary elements, go to www.glencoe.com.

Get Ready to Read

Connect to the Reading

Poetry is everywhere. For example, did you realize that every song you enjoy is a poem set to music? Think about why your favorite song is your favorite. What do you think about when you listen to it?

R

Small Group Take turns saying aloud a few lines from a song you enjoy. Then explain to your group members why you like that song. How did you feel the first time you heard the song? How does it make you feel now?

Build Background

Poems are different from other kinds of writing. How?

- They look different. The building block of prose is the sentence. In poetry, it's the line. Good poets put a lot of thought into where to end one line and start another.
- Poems pack as much meaning as possible into as few words as possible.
- Poems often rhyme. Even when they don't, the sound of a poem is very important.
- A poem has an author, who is called a poet. A poem also has a speaker, who is the person whose voice seems to be saying the words.

E

Set Purposes for Reading

BIG Question One thing people get out of reading is the opportunity to think about things differently. Read "Where You Are." Think about why people might read a poem like this one.

Set Your Own Purpose What else do you want to learn from the poem to help you answer the Big Question? Write your own reading purpose on the "Where You Are" page of Foldable 1.

Keep Moving

Use these skills as you read the following selection.

Teach

R Reading Skill

Previewing Say: Look at the length of the lines in the poem "Where You Are." Why might the poet have chosen to write short lines? *(Possible response: to keep the poem moving quickly)* OL

E Text Element

Title Say: Sometimes the title of a poem gives you a clue to the theme of the poem. What does the title "Where You Are" mean to you before reading the poem? Why might this title catch a reader's interest? *(Possible responses: Before reading the poem, I'd say that "Where You Are" seems to refer to a place. This title might catch a reader's interest because the reader doesn't know where the poet is.)* OL Judging by the title, whom do you think the speaker is addressing in the poem? *(the reader; me)* BL

CheckPoint

Use the CheckPoint questions provided on Presentation Plus! to check for prior knowledge and to build background. These questions can be used with interactive response keypads for immediate student feedback.

English Language Coach

Reading Poetry English language learners may have difficulty understanding the structure and punctuation of poetry. Remind them that a line of poetry may break before the end of a sentence. They should first read through "Where You Are" as if it were a paragraph. After English language learners understand the meaning of the poem's sentences, encourage them to read the poem quietly to themselves. This time they should pause at line breaks to get a better idea of the sound of the poem. Give English language learners as much time as they need to read and understand the poem. EL OL

Objectives
- Preview text
- Use text features: title, appearance of text
- Recognize the distinctive features of poetry
- Use context clues to determine word meaning

Teach

R Reading Skill

Previewing Say: Look at the way the first few lines of the poem begin. Who is being addressed? *(The reader is being addressed.)* **BL** What do words such as "Please" and "Now" at the beginnings of the first lines suggest about the tone of the poem? *(Possible response: These words suggest that the poem has a commanding tone, telling the reader to do things.)* **OL**

E Text Element

Title Say: After you read the first four lines of the poem, how did your understanding of the title change? Is the speaker right about "where you are"? *(Possible response: The title doesn't refer to a specific place. It seems to refer to my actions as I read the poem. In that way, the speaker is right about where I am.)* **OL**

READING WORKSHOP 2

E Where You Are 1 2

by Jack Anderson

This is where you are.
Please note.
R You are reading a poem
Beginning, "This is where you are."
Now get up
And walk three times around the room,
Then drink from a faucet
(If you can find a faucet).
Do not use a glass.
Stick your mouth directly
Into the stream of water.
Feel the water,
Its coldness, its wetness.
If there is no faucet near you
Or if the water is not potable*
Observe sky
And whatever may fill it
(In the **margin** you may write
The names of three things
You see in the sky)
And try to decide
Whether our present **condition**
Is best described
As peace or war.

15 ***Potable*** (POH tuh bul) means "suitable for drinking."

Vocabulary

margin (MAR jin) *n.* the blank space around the printed area on a page

condition (con DISH un) *n.* state of being

Practice the Skills

1 Key Reading Skill

Previewing Previewing gives you an idea of what a poem is about. You can preview a poem by looking at its title. You can also look at its first few lines to see what they tell you about the poem. Look at the first few lines of "Where You Are." Do they lead you back to the poem's title? If so, how? What questions do you have about the poem after reading those first few lines?

2 Key Text Element

Title The title can help you understand the poem's meaning. Why do you think the poem is called "Where You Are"? How is the poem asking you to think about "where you are"?

Additional Support

Reading in the Real World

College As students prepare for college, they will learn about the different forms and styles of poetry. Organize students into groups and have them use reference tools to define the following types of poetry: ballad, epic, and free verse. Invite students to share their definitions and any examples they may find with the class. Have students apply what they learn to "Where You Are" and discuss what type of poem it is. *(Ballad: A poem or song, passed down orally, that tells a story. Epic: A long poem on a serious subject that is centered on the actions of a hero. Free verse: Poetry that does not have a regular rhythm or rhyme scheme. "Where You Are" is an example of free verse.)* **OL**

What is the difference
Between this and "this"?
Please take note
Of where you are.
Did you really walk around the room
As **requested**? **3**
Have you written anything in the margin?
Are you sitting, standing,
Or **reclining**?
You are reading a poem
Which will end,
"Of all this is."
But you are not there yet.
You are here.
You are getting there.
Now explain **precisely**
What the point
Of all this is. **4** ❍

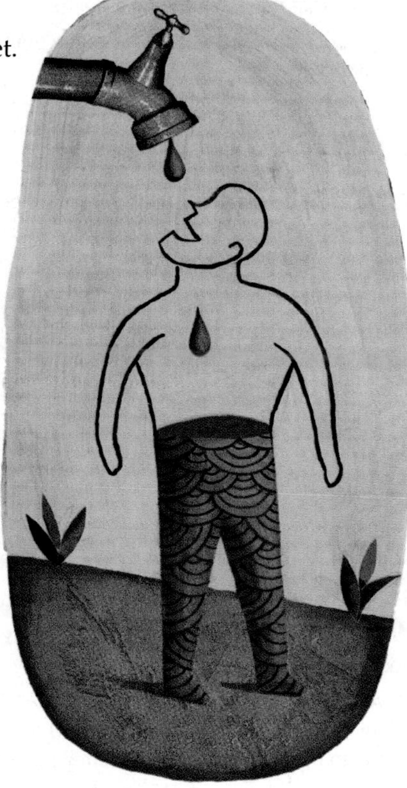

Vocabulary

reclining (rih KLY ning) *v.* lying down

precisely (prih SYS lee) *adv.* exactly

Practice the Skills

3 **English Language Coach**

Context Clues Maybe you're not sure what **requested** means. Look back at line 5 to find a clue to its meaning. What does this clue tell you about the meaning?

4 **BIG Question**

BQ People read poems for different reasons. Why do you think someone might want to read a poem like "Where You Are"? Write your answer on the "Where You Are" page of Foldable 1.

READING WORKSHOP 2

Teach

BQ **BIG Question**

Say: Some people read poems to be entertained by beautiful words and sounds, and others read poetry to be challenged by new ideas. What are other reasons that people might want to read a poem? *(Possible response: Some people read poems to match their moods or emotions.)* **OL**

C Critical Thinking

Evaluation Say: Now that you have finished reading the poem, what do you think the title means? How does it relate to the message of the poem? *(Possible response: This poem isn't just about where you are in terms of location and action; it's about appreciating where you are in your mind or your thoughts.)* **OL**

Assess

CheckPoint

Use the CheckPoint questions provided on Presentation Plus! to monitor students' comprehension. These questions can be used with interactive response keypads for immediate student feedback.

Differentiated Instruction

Finding Poetry Some students may enjoy poetry more if they understand that poetry really is everywhere. Challenge students to make a "found poem." Tell them to collect random pieces of writing—such as a note from a friend, homework instructions, snack wrappers—throughout the day. Have them rearrange and recopy the text, changing the punctuation and adding line breaks as they see fit. Ask students to share their pieces of found poetry. Lead a discussion about how students modified the texts that they found and how the found poems fit or change students' understanding of poetry. **OL**

Objectives
- Make connections from self to text
- Use titles to preview and understand reading
- Use context
- Build understanding of poetic forms

Assess

Resources for page 44

- Selection Quick Check
- Selection and Unit Assessment
- ExamView Assessment Suite
- Interactive Tutor: Self-Assessment

Students can respond to the *After You Read* items in their Learner's Notebook or on separate sheets of paper.

Answering the BIG Question

1. Possible responses: The poem was fun to read. Yes, I had to use my imagination.
2. The speaker asks readers to write in the margins three things they see in the sky.
3. The speaker tells readers to walk three times around the room, drink from a water faucet, and look at the sky.

Critical Thinking

4. The speaker asks readers to act or think in ways that will make them notice where they are.
5. Possible responses: The speaker is someone who is used to giving orders and who pays attention to small details.
6. Responses will vary.

After You Read

Where You Are

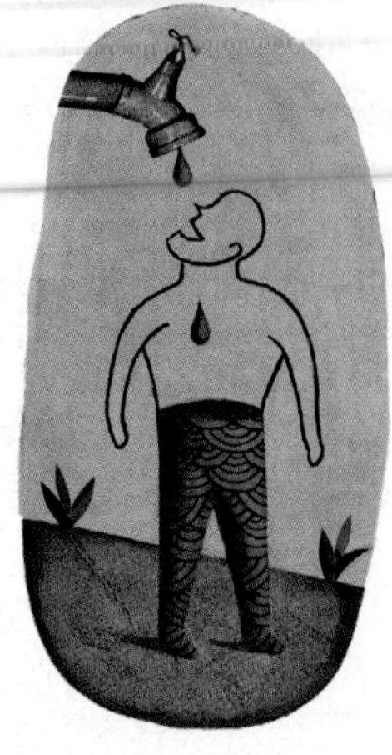

Answering the BIG Question

1. What are your thoughts about the poem? Did you have to use your imagination?
2. **Recall** What does the speaker ask readers to do in the margin?
   TIP **Right There** You'll find the answer in the poem.
3. **Summarize** What does the speaker tell readers to do after reminding them that they are reading a poem?
   TIP **Think and Search** Scan the poem to find the most important parts.

Critical Thinking

4. **Infer** Why does the speaker want readers to do the things he tells them to do?
   TIP **Author and Me** You'll find clues in the poem, but you'll need to figure out the answer on your own.
5. **Draw Conclusions** What kind of person do you think the speaker is?
   TIP **Author and Me** You'll find clues in the poem, but you'll need to figure out the answer on your own.
6. **Evaluate** Did you like this poem? Why or why not?
   TIP **On My Own** Answer from your own experiences.

Write About Your Reading

The poem asks you to use your senses—to "take note of where you are." What can you see from where you're sitting? Can you smell anything? What sounds do you hear?

In your Learner's Notebook, make a two-column chart. List the five senses (sight, hearing, smell, taste, and touch) in the left column. Across from each sense, in the right column, note anything that sense reveals to you right now.

Write to Learn Do you know "where you are"? Use details from your chart to write a postcard to a friend. Tell him or her what you see, hear, smell, taste, and touch. When you're finished, trade postcards with a few classmates. See if they sensed the same things you did.

Objectives (pp. 44–45)
Reading Preview text
Literature Use text features: title
Vocabulary Use context clues to determine word meaning
Writing Use sensory detail to develop setting
Grammar Use main verbs and helping verbs

Write About Your Reading

Write to Learn

Possible response:

Dear Friend,

I wanted you to know what I've been doing. I've been sitting by the window, watching the wind blow. The weather has changed, and we can feel the cooler air coming from the north. I can hear pecans hit the roof as they fall. It sounds like we're going to have a good crop!

—Lupe

Skills Review

Key Reading Skill: Previewing

7. Answer the questions you wrote in your Learner's Notebook after previewing "Where You Are." Then answer the following questions about previewing.
   - What did the title tell you about the poem?
   - What did you think when you saw the title repeated in the poem?
   - What opinions about the poem did you form when you saw that most of the lines were short?

Key Text Element: Title

8. The poem's title could mean many things. What are two possible meanings?
9. Do you think "Where You Are" is a good title for this poem? Why or why not?
10. Did your understanding of the title change after you read the poem? If so, how?

Reviewing Skill: Illustrations

11. Does the picture help you understand this poem? Explain.

Vocabulary Check

12. Write a sentence for each vocabulary word. Each sentence should include at least one context clue to help explain the vocabulary word's meaning. *Ex: The old swimming pool was in poor condition.* (The words *old* and *poor* tell you about the swimming pool's state of being, or *condition*.)

    margin condition reclining precisely

13. **English Language Coach** Look at the context in the poem for each of the vocabulary words. Is there one word that has very good clues? Which one? What are the clues?

Grammar Link: Main Verbs and Helping Verbs

A verb can be more than one word. Verbs of two or more words are called verb phrases.

- **One-word verb:** I **live** in Atlanta.
- **Verb phrase:** I **have been** happy there.
- **Verb phrase:** But I **will be moving** soon.

The most important word in a verb phrase is the **main verb.** The other verbs in the phrase are **helping verbs.** These verbs help the main verb tell when an action or a state of being occurs. Or they may help the main verb tell whether an action or state of being will occur.

- I live in Atlanta.
  (*Live* is the main verb.)
- I have been happy there.
  (*Been* is the main verb; *have* is a helping verb.)
- But I will be moving soon.
  (*Moving* is the main verb; *will be* are helping verbs.)

Look out! When you analyze the parts of a verb phrase, mentally cross out such words as *never, always,* and *not.* These words are adverbs, not verbs.

Grammar Practice

Copy the following sentences. In each one, underline the main verb twice and any helping verbs once. (Not all sentences have helping verbs.)

14. My grandmother bought me a cell phone.
15. I have had it for about a year.
16. I could not live without it!
17. I will never part with it.
18. I am always calling my friends.

Web Activities For eFlashcards, Selection Quick Checks, and other Web activities, go to www.glencoe.com.

Skills Review

Key Reading Skill: Previewing

7. Possible responses:
   Title: The title told me that the poem would be about a specific place.
   Title repeated: I thought that the title was referring not just to a physical space but also to what a reader might be thinking at a certain time.
   Opinions: I thought that the poem might be informal and have short descriptions.

Key Text Element: Title

8. Responses will vary, but they should indicate that "where you are" can refer to both a physical state and a mental state.
9. Responses will vary, but they may indicate that the title is broad enough to show the many ways a person can perceive or think about where he or she is.
10. Responses will vary. Students may say that they thought the title referred less to a physical place and more to a mental place after reading the poem.

Reviewing Skill: Illustrations

11. Responses will vary.

Close

Ask students to explain how the title of a selection can encourage or discourage a reader.

Vocabulary Check

For items 12 and 13, check students sentences for correct use of vocabulary words and context clues.

Grammar Link: Main Verbs and Helping Verbs

Grammar Practice

14. My grandmother bought me a cell phone.
15. I have had it for about a year.
16. I could not live without it!
17. I will never part with it.
18. I am always calling my friends.

Teach

More About the Authors

Michigan native Ericka Souter writes for *People* magazine, for which she has interviewed a number of celebrities. Dietlind Lerner is from Illinois. A freelance journalist, she has reported on important world events, including the fall of the Berlin Wall. She now lives in Paris, France, with her two sons.

V Vocabulary

Word Themes **Say:** Grouping vocabulary words by their themes or central ideas can help you better understand and remember word meanings. The vocabulary words for this selection describe positive qualities or actions that reflect positive aspects of people's characters. In your notebook, list these words under the heading "Positive Traits." Write a sentence that explains why people would want to have these qualities or perform these actions. **OL** Expand your vocabulary by adding a column called "Negative Traits." Think of words that mean the opposite of the words in the vocabulary list. **AL**

Before You Read

Message of Hope

Meet the Authors

Ericka Souter writes about courageous people who have overcome problems in their lives.

Dietlind Lerner has traveled all over Europe and Africa to find interesting stories. Lerner traveled to Africa to tell the story of the Lost Boys of Sudan, which you are about to read. She says their story was a "pleasure to report and meant a great deal . . . personally."

Author Search For more about Ericka Souter and Dietlind Lerner, go to www.glencoe.com.

Objectives (pp. 46–51)
Reading Preview text
Informational Text Use text features: title, deck, heads, subheads
Vocabulary Use context clues: definition

Vocabulary Preview

V

volunteer (vol un TEER) *n.* a person who offers to do something by choice, without being forced **(p. 50)** *A volunteer helped the refugee family find a new home.*

selfless (SELF lus) *adj.* having no concern for oneself; thinking of others first **(p. 51)** *The selfless boys are concerned about others who might be caught in similar situations.*

dignity (DIG nuh tee) *n.* a sense of self-respect; a calm outward appearance **(p. 51)** *They accepted their loss with dignity.*

English Language Coach

Definition Besides context clues, another way to figure out the meaning of an unfamiliar word or phrase is to look for a definition in the sentence or in nearby sentences.

Pepper was a beautiful **Maine coon cat**.

By itself, that sentence gives no clue as to what a *Maine coon cat* is. (But we do know that "Pepper" was a beautiful one.) The sentences below include a definition.

Pepper was a beautiful **Maine coon cat**. This large breed of long-haired domestic cat gets its name in part from its bushy, raccoonlike tail.

A chart like this can help you figure out a word or phrase you don't know.

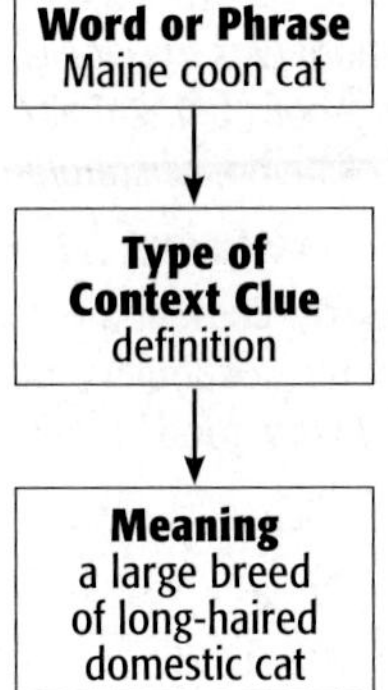

Additional Support

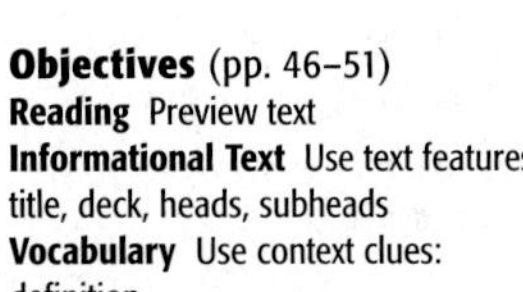

Author Search To expand students' appreciation of Ericka Souter and Dietlind Lerner, have them access the Web site for additional information and resources.

Literature Focus Lesson

Informational Articles Remind students that informational articles are about real people and real events, such as the factions in the civil war in Sudan. Since the conflict began in 1983, almost two million people have died, and five million have been driven from their homes. More than 3,000 Lost Boys have been resettled in the United States.

Suggest that students locate and read some informational articles about the civil war in Sudan and the Sudanese refugees. Ask students to find out how Sudanese immigrants have adjusted to life in the United States. Ask students to think about what they themselves might have to adjust to in a foreign country. **OL**

Skills Preview

Key Reading Skill: Previewing

Previewing will save you time once you start to read. Preview what you're reading to get the big idea.

- Read the title first to get an idea of what the story is about.
- Informational articles are likely to have subtitles for different sections. Read them next for additional hints about the story.
- Look at photos and illustrations and then read the captions. You'll get lots of "instant" information.

Key Text Element: Titles, Heads, and Decks

Articles in magazines and newspapers are likely to have more headings than fictional stories have.

- The title of an article is called a **head,** which is short for *headline.* It's meant to grab your attention and get you to read the whole article.
- An article's subtitle is a **deck.** It appears after the head and before the first paragraph. The deck gives just a little more information than the head.
- There may be a **subhead** before each section of an article.

These tips will help you understand and use titles and heads as you read the informational articles in this unit.

- Read the head, and think about what it means.
  Does the head get your attention? What hints does it give about what's in the article?
- Read the deck, if there is one. Think about its connection to the head.
  What new information do you learn from the deck?
- Read any subheads throughout the article.
  How do the subheads connect to the head and deck? What new ideas do they give you?

Interactive Literary Elements Handbook
To review or learn more about the literary elements, go to www.glencoe.com.

Get Ready to Read

Connect to the Reading

You're about to read "Message of Hope." When the boys in this story were ten years old, they were caught up in a war that destroyed their homes and their families. But they didn't lose their hopes and dreams.

Have you ever had a problem so big and so bad that you almost gave up hope of solving it? *Did* you give up hope?

Group Talk Write down a few notes expressing your ideas about "hope." Then share your thoughts with others in a small group. Why are some people hopeful even when the most awful things happen to them? Why do others give up hope quickly?

Build Background

This article from *People* magazine is about boys from Sudan (soo DAN), a country in northern Africa. When war came, they and many thousands of other Sudanese (soo duh NEEZ) became refugees.

- Refugees are people who leave their homeland, because of war or natural disaster. The often live in temporary "refugee camps."
- Sudanese Muslims live mainly in the north, and non-Muslims live mainly in the south. The Dinka are a non-Muslim people.
- In the 1980s and 1990s, Muslim and non-Muslim groups fought a terrible civil war.

Set Purposes for Reading

BIG Question Sometimes people read to be inspired. Read "Message of Hope" to learn how three young men from Sudan are bringing hope to other young people.

Set Your Own Purpose What else would you like to learn from the story to help you answer the Big Question? Write your own purpose on the "Message of Hope" page of Foldable 1.

Keep Moving

Use these skills as you read the following selection.

READING WORKSHOP 2

Teach

R Reading Skill

Previewing Say: Look at the title and deck of the article that follows. What information do you expect the article to provide? *(Possible response: The article will probably tell how the Lost Boys have been able to succeed in the United States.)* What does the title make you expect about the tone of the article? *(Possible response: The article will have a hopeful tone.)* OL

E Text Element

Titles, Heads, and Decks
Say: Why are well-written titles and heads important to an article? *(Possible response: They catch a reader's attention.)* OL

CheckPoint

Use the CheckPoint questions provided on Presentation Plus! to check for prior knowledge and to build background. These questions can be used with interactive response keypads for immediate student feedback.

Literature Online

Interactive Literary Elements Handbook Have students access the Web site to improve their understanding of titles, heads, and decks.

English Language Coach

Definition and Restatement Tell students that some context clues define or restate an unfamiliar word. Have students practice using this type of context clue by completing each of the sentences below with a vocabulary word.

1. Camille was a ____ for the carnival. She offered to help put up decorations. *(volunteer)*
2. Although the team lost, they showed great ____. They calmly congratulated the winning team. *(dignity)*
3. The soldier received a medal for her ____ action. She was honored for putting herself in danger in order to save others. *(selfless)* OL

Objectives

- Preview text
- Use text features: title, deck, heads, subheads
- Use context clues: definition

Teach

Viewing the Photo
Say: The young men in this picture once lived in a refugee shelter. Why do you think they are now examples of hope to other Lost Boys? *(Possible response: The young men have succeeded and want to show the Lost Boys how they, too, can make better lives for themselves.)* OL

E Text Element

Titles, Heads, and Decks
Say: The deck includes "hopeful" information as well as facts about the difficult situation in Sudan. What information in the deck might be considered hopeful? *(The three young men did well in the United States. They are able to return to their home country to help prepare other refugees to leave.)* How can talking to the returning Lost Boys of Sudan help the refugees who are planning to leave Sudan? *(Students may say that the returning Lost Boys can answer questions and help others avoid making certain mistakes in a new land.)* OL EL

Readability Scores
Dale-Chall: 4.9
DRP: 54
Lexile: 810

READING WORKSHOP 2

TIME

Message of HOPE

Louise Gubb

"Your friends in the U.S. say hi," Deng (center, teaching with Biar, left, and Ayiik) told students at Kakuma Secondary School. "I am here because you are still my brothers and sisters."

E They became known as the Lost Boys of Sudan after fleeing the horrible civil war. Now three, who have done well in the United States, have returned to a refugee camp. Their goal is to help prepare others for fast food, phones, and life in America. 1 2

By ERICKA SÓUTER and DIETLIND LERNER

In a small, hot classroom in a crowded Kakuma, Kenya, refugee camp, a group of 20-year-olds sit at desks. They fire questions at three young men wearing shirts and ties. "What is the weather like in America?" asks one student. "Why are there murderers there?" asks another. "If obesity[1] is a problem, why are you skinny?" asks another. The men, who have photos of sports stars, roller coasters, and buses, answer with care. They also give some tips. "In America it is a very good thing to say thank you," says one. "When you get to America, everyone will ask if you are hungry," says another. "In our country it is insulting to ask that, so you say no. My advice to you is to say yes. We missed a lot of good food because of our culture!"

1. ***Obesity*** (oh BEE sih tee) is the condition of being very overweight.

1 **Key Reading Skill**

Previewing To preview this magazine article, read the title and deck. Then look at the pictures and read the captions. What questions do you have after doing these things?

2 **Key Text Element**

Titles, Heads, and Decks If there's a deck, it always gives additional information to draw the reader in. Here the deck summarizes the whole story in three sentences. However, the deck does not use the words *message* and *hope.* What do you think is the "message"?

Additional Support

Reading in the Real World

Career A proverb shared by the Lost Boys says, "Education is my mother and father." Have students discuss the meaning of this proverb. Then ask them to think about the role of education in preparing for future careers. Ask students to interview people who have jobs that students consider interesting. In the interviews, students should ask how schooling or special training prepared their subjects for their jobs. Encourage students to share what they have learned with the rest of the class. OL

READING WORKSHOP 2

Just 10 years ago, Duom Deng, David Ayiik, and James Biar were refugees too. During Sudan's civil war, the three boys had seen their parents killed and their villages destroyed. Then they and thousands of other orphaned children walked 1,000 miles east to Ethiopia. Once there, they spent five years wandering between refugee camps. Eventually they settled in Kakuma. Aid workers called the thousands of male orphans the Lost Boys. (Girls also fled to the camps. For cultural reasons, they were placed with refugee foster[2] families.) "We made ourselves brothers," says Deng, who is in his mid-20s. "We learned by ourselves to be good to ourselves and to others." **3**

"I think a lot about how people here have too little," says Duom Deng (left, with James Biar, center, David Ayiik, and a group of Kenyan women who are neighbors to Kakuma's Sudanese refugees)."I want one day for the hunger to stop."

Louise Gubb

That good sense stuck with Ayiik, Deng, and Biar when they came to the United States with 3,600 other Kakuma refugees. In less than five years, they changed from wide-eyed immigrants who had never seen a kitchen freezer to young men working their way through college in San Diego, California. Now they have returned to Kakuma—thanks to the help of the San Diego Rotary[3] Club. Their goal is to help the next group of U.S.-bound hopefuls prepare for their new home. "The desire to go back to the camp was straight from my heart," says Deng. "I wanted to see how the rest were doing. It was a big thought for me that I had left them." **EL**

Thousands of Kakuma's 86,000 refugees are Lost Boys. Most of them have applied for U.S. visas.[4] But until the visas are approved, the refugees live in mud huts, sleep on wooden slabs, and eat only grain and water. Most have never owned a book, which made the 1,000 donated dictionaries Deng, Ayiik, and Biar brought a hot item. Deng's digital

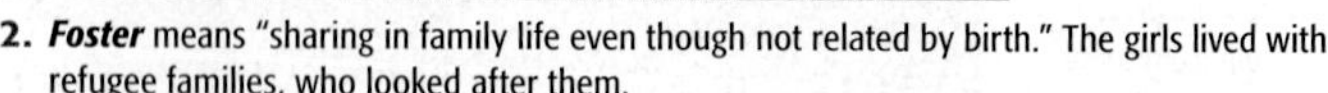

2. ***Foster*** means "sharing in family life even though not related by birth." The girls lived with refugee families, who looked after them.
3. The main goals of the ***Rotary*** **(ROH tuh ree)** ***Club*** are to help people in need and to build peace and understanding. It has "clubs" in many cities around the world, and members are called *Rotarians* (roh TAIR ee unz).
4. A ***visa*** is an official document giving visitors permission to enter or leave a country.

3 **English Language Coach**

Context Clues Who are the "Lost Boys"? There's a definition clue in this paragraph.

Teach

C Critical Thinking

Analysis Say: What do the following details from the story tell you about African culture?

- Girls also fled to refugee camps, but they were placed with foster families. *(Boys and girls are treated differently.)*
- The boys made themselves "brothers." *(There is a strong sense of community and a willingness to help others.)*
- The immigrants had never seen a kitchen freezer. *(People in Africa store food differently than people in the United States.)* **OL**

EL Language Coach

Context Clues Remind students that sentences surrounding difficult or unfamiliar phrases can give clues to the meanings of such phrases. **Say:** Reread the following sentences: "'The desire to go back to the camp was straight from my heart,' says Deng. 'I wanted to see how the rest were doing. It was a big thought for me that I had left them.'" What does the phrase "straight from my heart" mean? What context clues helped you figure this out? *(The words* desire, wanted, *and* big thought *show that Deng deeply and sincerely wanted to return to the camp.)* **EL** **OL**

Differentiated Instruction

Reading Maps Provide students with maps that show the political boundaries and geographic features of Africa. Ask students to trace the route that the Lost Boys might have taken from Sudan to Kenya. Have students use the features of the maps to generate a list of the difficulties the Sudanese refugees faced while traveling from Sudan to Kenya on foot. Then add to the list by brainstorming as a class other obstacles and difficulties suggested by the reading but not shown on the maps. **OL**

Teach

Viewing the Photo

Say: What would learning about baseball teach the Sudanese immigrants about American culture? *(Possible response: The Sudanese immigrants might see that people in the United States enjoy competitive games and that children begin playing sports at an early age.)* **OL** How could joining a local baseball league help the immigrants adjust to life in the United States? *(Possible response: By playing on a team, the immigrants could meet new people and practice speaking a new language.)* **BL**

C Critical Thinking

Analysis **Say:** Along with Ayiik and Biar, Deng traveled from San Diego, California, to a refugee camp in Kenya. Deng says that when he saw the other refugees, "I was really uncomfortable to see them that way. . . . The food that they have is still not enough." What do Deng's actions and words reveal about his character? *(Possible responses: Deng's words and actions show that he is a kind, caring individual who wants to help his fellow refugees.)* **OL**

camera was also a hit. Some of the kids had never seen their own image and collapsed in squeals of delight. Tulasi Sharma works at the camp. "It is so important for the students to see the Lost Boys," says Sharma. "To know that it is possible [to succeed] and to know that they have not been forgotten."

C The trip had an effect on the three from San Diego too. "I was really uncomfortable to see them that way," Deng says of his friends who live in poverty. "The food that they have is still not enough. They are not getting any vegetables or oils. The water gets cut off after just an hour. It is so sad to me."

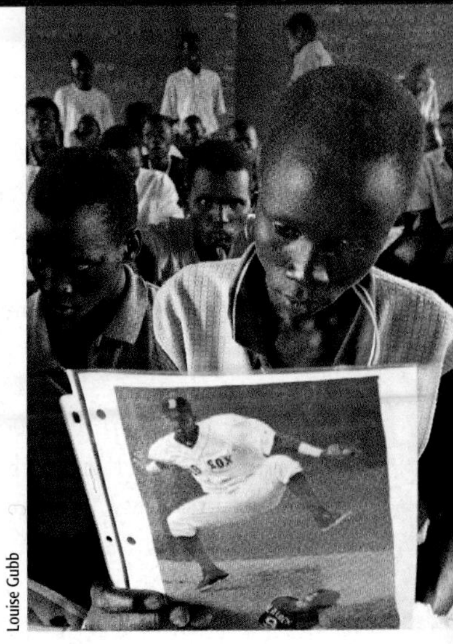

Louise Gubb

The three have come a long way. In 1987 Deng's family, members of Sudan's Dinka tribe, had just settled down to dinner. Suddenly, Sudanese soldiers surrounded their tiny village. "We heard a cry from a neighbor," he recalls. "There were horses, guns, men everywhere." In the confusion, he was separated from his mother and father. But, like many parents, they had warned him that if the men with guns came, he should run east.

With the sounds of the village burning and people being shot, 6-year-old Deng ran with the other children. He was wearing a T-shirt and shorts—the only clothes he would have for the next two years. Deng and the other kids joined up with a larger group heading across the desert. "I remember eating leaves, I was so hungry and thirsty," he recalls. Hundreds died of hunger or were killed by lions and crocodiles, according to Ayiik. "I was very scared. I thinkI made it because I saw other kids like me and I tried to be strong like them," he says. "I couldn't give up."

Years later, the three arrived in the United States. They had only enough money to last for three months. Judy Bernstein is a **volunteer** who helped the young men get used to life in their new country. "They would put eggs and milk in the cupboard, not the refrigerator," she says. Lost Boys younger than 18 were placed in foster homes. The rest had to fend for[5]

"I was hoping all our friends would have the same chance. If they came to the U.S., they too could do better," says Ayik (left), with Biar (center) and Deng.

Louise Gubb

5. To ***fend for*** yourself is to take care of yourself without help from others.

Vocabulary

volunteer (vol un TEER) *n.* a person who offers to do something by choice, without being forced

Additional Support

English Language Coach

Origins of a Phrase Tell students that *The Adventures of Peter Pan,* by J. M. Barrie, uses the phrase "lost boys" to describe the children who got lost and were never claimed. Ask students how knowing this can help them understand the name given to the Sudanese refugees in the article. *(The "lost boys" in Peter Pan have no parents to care for them. Likewise, the Sudanese Lost Boys must live on their own without help from adults.)* **OL** Tell students that the "lost boys" in Peter Pan never grew up. In what way does this fictional situation differ from the experience of the Sudanese boys? *(Possible response: The Sudanese boys experienced great difficulties and had to grow up very quickly.)* **AL**

themselves. To get ready for job interviews, "they learned how to look someone in the eye, which is not part of the Dinka culture," explains Bernstein. Sharing, however, is part of their culture. When one Lost Boy got a job interview, he would bring three or four of his "brothers" so they might find work too.

Many of them spent a lot of their early time in America exploring. They went to zoos and grocery stores. They tried fast food. And they learned to cook. "In Sudan only women cook," says Ayiik, who has grown very fond of burgers. "It was a hard thing to learn." Their first apartments were often in rough parts of town. Usually five guys shared two bedrooms. For the San Diego Lost Boys, the local Rotary Club became a place to go. Bernstein took Deng and Ayiik to the club to speak about their experiences. The young men formed their own group within the club. The Rotarians helped with English lessons and job training. Club member Stephen Brown helped them raise money to return to Kakuma. "Not only are they **selfless** and polite, but they present themselves with a **dignity** that's amazing, considering what they've gone through," he says. "They have big smiles and good senses of humor."

CATCHING UP: Seeing old pals still stuck in the camp was tough for the San Diego Lost Boys. Still, when Deng (left) ran into Maketh Guet while shopping in Kakuma, both men were overjoyed. The two first met as children in an Ethiopian refugee camp more than a decade ago. They had not seen each other in four years. "Duom looks so healthy, so big," says Guet, delighted by Deng's success. "He has an American accent when he speaks Dinka!"

Louise Gubb

All three young men attend local colleges. Deng studies communication and general education. He also works at a graphic design company. Ayiik studies business accounting and works as a file clerk. Biar, the shyest of the three, studies education. "We passed a big disaster, and now we're having a good life and good experiences," says Deng. Eventually the men, who are all single, plan to return to Sudan. They want to help rebuild—and perhaps find wives. These days they seem neither boyish nor lost. As Simon Laur, a 24-year-old refugee in the Kakuma class, suggests, "Maybe we should call you the Found Boys." 4 5

—From *People*, February 7, 2005

Vocabulary

selfless (SELF lus) *adj.* having no concern for oneself; thinking of others first

dignity (DIG nuh tee) *n.* a sense of self-respect; a calm outward appearance

4 Key Text Element

E **Titles, Heads, and Decks** Do you think "Message of Hope" is a good title for this article? Why or why not? Did the deck do a good job of summarizing the article? Why or why not?

5 BIG Question

Why is reading about people you've never met—and places you've never been—important? Write your answers on the "Message of Hope" page of Foldable 1. Your response will help you complete the Unit Challenge later. BQ

Teach

E Text Element

Titles, Heads, and Decks

Say: Now that you have read the article, what do you think is the "message of hope" that the Lost Boys have brought to the Kakuma refugee camp? OL *(Possible responses: The Lost Boys want the other refugees to know that they can succeed and help rebuild Sudan. They want to encourage the refugees not to lose hope.)*

BQ 

Ask: How does reading about the Lost Boys help you see the importance of being aware of problems in other parts of the world? *(Possible response: The article shows us that we need to know about and understand problems in other parts of the world so that we can help find solutions.)* OL

Assess

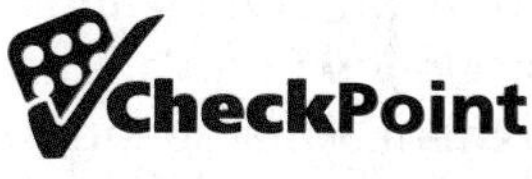

Use the CheckPoint questions provided on Presentation Plus! to monitor students' comprehension. These questions can be used with interactive response keypads for immediate student feedback.

Reading in the Real World

Citizenship Tell students that by studying the culture and history of other nations, they become better world citizens. Exploring other cultures leads to greater understanding and global cooperation. Ask students to use the Internet or library resources to find information about areas in Sudan or Kenya. Have students design magazine advertisements for the places they find most interesting or most different from their own city or town. Each ad should identify the place, tell where it is, and show why it would be an interesting place to visit. AS

Objectives

- Set a purpose for reading
- Use text features to understand reading

Assess

Resources for page 52

- Selection Quick Check
- Selection and Unit Assessment
- ExamView Assessment Suite
- Interactive Tutor: Self-Assessment

Students can respond to the *After You Read* items in their Learner's Notebook or on separate sheets of paper.

Answering the BIG Question

1. Possible response: It is important to understand problems in other parts of the world.
2. The boys walked a great distance to escape from Sudan. They had no food or water for their journey and they traveled with no adults to help them. After spending several years at refugee camps in Kenya, they arrived in the United States.

Critical Thinking

3. Possible responses: Aid workers may have thought of them as "lost" because the children had to flee their country and had been separated from their families.
4. Possible responses: The young men may want to live in Sudan to help rebuild their homeland.

After You Read Message of Hope

Louise Gubb

Answering the BIG Question

1. Now that you've read the selection, why do you think other people should read about the Lost Boys of Sudan?
2. **Summarize** Describe the three boys' journey from Sudan to the United States. Remember, when you summarize you state the main ideas of a selection in your own words and in a logical order.

   TIP **Think and Search** Think about the story. Decide which points are most important.

Critical Thinking

3. **Infer** Why do you think the aid workers called the boys from Sudan the "Lost Boys"?

   TIP **Author and Me** You'll find clues in the story, but you must also use what you already know.
4. **Evaluate** Why do you think the three boys want to live in Sudan again someday?

   TIP **Author and Me** You'll find clues in the story, but you must also use what you already know.

Talk About Your Reading

Literature Groups Do the Lost Boys of Sudan share a message of hope? With your group, discuss what that message might be. Besides other refugees from Sudan, who might benefit from the Lost Boys' message?

Write to Learn Pretend you're one of the Lost Boys of Sudan. Write a journal entry about your life. In your journal entry you might answer questions such as:

- What are you doing now?
- How do you like your life in the United States?
- How does your life in the United States compare with life in Sudan?
- What are your hopes and plans for the future?
- What lessons have you learned from your experience?
- What important message about life would you like to teach people around the world?

Why did you leave your home country? What are you doing now? You can write about as many events as you'd like.

Objectives (pp. 52–53)
Reading Preview text
Informational Text Use text features: title, heads, and decks
Writing Write a journal entry: main idea and supporting details
Grammar Use main verbs and helping verbs
Vocabulary Use context clues to expand word knowledge

Talk About Your Reading

Write to Learn

Responses will vary. Possible response: I really like living in the United States. There are so many things to do and so many opportunities. I really like going to school and learning more. I want to become a teacher and return home to help others learn. I want to teach everyone the importance of sticking together and helping one another like my brothers and I did during our journey from Sudan.

Skills Review

Key Reading Skill: Previewing

5. Which parts of the article did you look at to preview? Was each part helpful? In your Learner's Notebook, explain how each part you previewed gave you a sense of what the article was about.

Key Text Element: Titles, Heads, and Decks

6. In your Learner's Notebook, write an idea for a different head for this article.
7. What did the deck tell you about the article?
8. The article's head tells you about a message of hope. What is that message? How do the Lost Boys of Sudan want to share their message with others?

Vocabulary Check

Choose the best word from the list to complete each sentence below. Rewrite each sentence with the correct word in place.

volunteer
selfless
dignity

9. Although homeless, the old couple always behaved with ___.
10. Firefighters perform ___ acts when they risk their own safety to save victims.
11. My aunt works full-time at the animal hospital, but she's a ___.

English Language Coach You have probably seen or heard *hopeful* used as an adjective in such phrases as "a hopeful feeling." Context clues can help you expand your knowledge of the word. "Message of Hope" contains this sentence: "Their goal is to help the next group of U.S.-bound **hopefuls** prepare for their new home."

12. Define the noun *hopeful* by completing this sentence: "A **hopeful** is a person who . . ."

Grammar Link: Main Verbs and Helping Verbs

The **main verb** is the most important word in a verb phrase. The other verbs in the phrase are **helping verbs.**

- You **should walk** the dog. (*Walk* is the main verb. *Should* is a helping verb.)

Some words can be main verbs or helping verbs.

- He **does** his homework every night. (*Does* is the main—and only—verb.)
- He **does** not **have** a computer. (*Does* is a helping verb. *Have* is the main verb.)

Adverbs, such as *not, always, sometimes,* and *never,* cannot be part of a verb phrase because they aren't verbs.

In the chart below, the words in darker type can be helping verbs *or* main verbs. The words in regular type are always helping verbs.

am	**being**	**has**
is	**do**	**had**
are	**does**	shall
was	**did**	should
were	**have**	will
can	must	would
could	may	might

Grammar Practice

Write two sentences for each word listed below. In the first sentence, use the word as the main verb. In the second sentence, use the word as a helping verb. Write your sentences on a separate piece of paper.

am was did have

Web Activities For eFlashcards, Selection Quick Checks, and other Web activities, go to www.glencoe.com.

Skills Review

Key Reading Skill: Previewing

5. Responses will vary.

Key Text Element: Titles, Heads, and Decks

6. Responses will vary, but they should convey the idea that the young men have survived an ordeal and are now choosing to help other young people.
7. The deck said three young men who fled a civil war in Sudan were returning there from the United States to help other refugees.
8. The message is that refugee children can build new lives for themselves. The Lost Boys want to share their message by meeting other refugees and sharing their stories.

Vocabulary Check

9. dignity
10. selfless
11. volunteer
12. has hope or expects success.

Close

Ask students to explain why reading the Lost Boys' story is important. Have them discuss why reading and getting an education are important to the refugees of Sudan.

Grammar Link: Main Verbs and Helping Verbs

Grammar Practice

Sample responses:
Am: I *am* always thirsty after practice. I *am going* to the store.
Was: I *was* careful not to spill juice on the carpet. Amanda *was running* to catch up with us until she saw the kitten.
Did: Jerry *did* his homework before he went to the movies. We *did walk* farther than we thought we would.
Have: The party guests *have* cake and ice cream. The group *will have hiked* more than fifty miles by the end of the summer.

Reviewing

UNIT 1

Objectives covered in this workshop:
- Reread and review text to understand and recall ideas
- Identify and understand point of view
- Clarify word meanings in context

Reviewing

Why Is It Important?

- Reviewing facilitates comprehension.
- Reviewing is a study habit that is useful in all classes.
- Reviewing allows students to determine whether or not they are addressing their purpose for reading.

How to Help Students Get It

- Discuss common ways that readers review what they have read, including rereading, skimming, and talking with others. Practice each of these with students.
- After reading a piece of text, ask students to create a graphic organizer of the information from the text. Discuss with students the fact that graphic organizers are one way that people can review the contents of a text without rereading the entire piece.
- Discuss the importance of note-taking as a way to review a text. Taking notes also helps readers remember what they've read.
- Remind students that setting a purpose is an important skill in reading. One of the reasons we review as and after we read is to determine if we are staying true to our purpose and if the text is meeting our needs.

Reading to Answer the Big Question

Teaching Nepalis to Read, Plant, and Vote

"Teaching Nepalis" tells readers how Dinesh Dhungel and his wife, Ratna, are bringing about positive change in Nepal. It describes the links between the quest for political rights, a way out of poverty, and access to the written word. This selection provides an excellent example of how making literacy a priority can empower a person, a family, and a whole community.

May I Have Your Autograph?

In this funny story, Rosalind accompanies her friend Wendy to meet a rock star, but Rosalind doubts that anything will come of this meeting. Wendy uses the knowledge she's gleaned from reading everything about this rock star to get the autograph she wants so badly.

Workshop Resources

Pacing (Days) Standard	Block	Lesson	Student Materials	Teacher Resources
1		Key Skill Lesson: Reviewing	Key Reading Skills Practice English Language Coach	Bellringer Options Transparencies Read Aloud, Think Aloud Transparencies Presentation Plus!
2		"Teaching Nepalis to Read, Plant, and Vote"	Literary Analysis Transparencies Glencoe Online Selection Vocabulary Development Academic Vocabulary Development English Language Coach Active Reading Graphic Organizer Literary Analysis StudentWorks Plus Online Student Edition Literature Classics Selection and Unit Assessments	Literary and Text Analysis Transparencies Puzzlemaker Skill Level Up! BookLink 3 Assessment by Learning Objective (Diagnostic and Formative) Interactive Tutor Self-Assessment TeacherWorks Plus
2		"May I Have Your Autograph"	Glencoe Online Selection Vocabulary Development Academic Vocabulary Development English Language Coach Active Reading Graphic Organizer Literary Analysis StudentWorks Plus Online Student Edition Literature Classics Selection and Unit Assessments	Literary and Text Analysis Transparencies Puzzlemaker Skill Level Up! BookLink 3 Assessment by Learning Objective (Diagnostic and Formative) Interactive Tutor Self-Assessment TeacherWorks Plus

Keys for Unit Resource

- Blackline Master
- Workbook
- Supplemental Text
- CD-ROM
- DVD
- Transparency
- Web-based
- Fast Files

Level Appropriate Code

AS = Activities for all students
AL = Activities for students working above grade level
OL = Activities for students working at grade level
BL = Activities for students working below grade level
EL = Activities for English language learners

Focus

BELLRINGER Options

Daily Language Practice Transparency

Focus Activity Say: What are your memories of learning to read? Did you enjoy it? Why or Why not? *(Responses will vary. Students may recollect using flashcards, primers, and/or phonics.)*

Teach

R Reading Skill

Reviewing Say: You review every day when you need to remember something. How do you use the skill of reviewing in your everyday life? *(Responses will vary. Students may say that they review when they tell family members about their day.)* **OL** How does reviewing help you remember something? *(Responses will vary. Students may say that reviewing makes you focus on certain things or events so you can remember them better.)* **BL**

READING WORKSHOP 3

Skills Focus

You will practice using the following skills when you read these selections:

- "Teaching Nepalis to Read, Plant, and Vote," p. 58
- "May I Have Your Autograph?" p. 66

Reading

- Reviewing

Informational Text

- Using text features such as the lead to predict, understand, or interpret text

Vocabulary

- Clarifying word meanings in context
- Academic Vocabulary: *clarify*

Writing/Grammar

- Writing summaries
- Identifying verbs tenses

Objectives (pp. 54–55)
Reading Monitor comprehension: review, reread, ask questions

Skill Lesson

Reviewing

Learn It!

What Is It? Let's face it. It's very easy to miss things while you're reading. But when you do, all you have to do is review! When you review, you go back over what you've already read to find or remember what's important.

- *Re-* means "again."
- R *Viewing* is looking and thinking.
- So *reviewing* means looking back over something you've already read to understand it better. When you find the information you're looking for, take a moment to think about it.
- When you review, you think about the important ideas and facts, and then you organize them in your mind so you can recall them later.

Analyzing Cartoons
Calvin thinks reviewing is dumb and too much work. Who do you think is the smart one here? Why is reviewing important?

Additional Support

Differentiated Instruction

Reading Cartoons Tell students to read the panels in the cartoon. You may select one student to read Calvin's part and another to read the girl's part. Ask students to list the two steps the girl takes to review after class. *(She reviews her notes and then rereads the chapter.)*

Explain to students that Calvin thinks the girl understands her schoolwork without doing "all that work." Ask students to vote on who is the "smart" one: the girl or Calvin. Tell them to support their votes with reasons. **OL** **EL**

Why Is It Important? "Help! There's too much information!" If you feel this way, reviewing can help. When you review what you've read, you get a chance to find the most important ideas. Then you can think about those ideas and ask yourself "What's this selection really all about?" **R1**

How Do I Do It? Stop reading from time to time to think about what you've read. Ask yourself questions to make sure you remember and understand what you've read. Look over the titles and headings to jog your memory. Look at the pictures and captions again. If you don't remember important information, reread. Write notes to yourself about important ideas. **R2**

Study Central Visit www.glencoe.com and click on Study Central to review reviewing.

Here's how one student reviewed the story "Seventh Grade." She was confused, so she went back over what she had read.

It's the first day of seventh grade. Kids have settled into their rooms. Now let's see, the main characters are Victor, Michael, and Teresa. I think Michael's the one who likes Teresa. Is that right? I should reread to be sure. I don't want to get the characters mixed up. As I go back over what I've read, I remember that it's Victor who likes Teresa. I'm glad I stopped to review. Otherwise I'd be pretty confused.

Practice It!

In your Learner's Notebook, write the answers to these questions about what you've read so far without looking back at the text.

- What does reviewing mean?
- How do I do it?

Then go back and review these two pages. Write down any *new* information you find or remember that helps answer the questions.

Use It!

As you read "Teaching Nepalis to Read, Plant, and Vote" and "May I Have Your Autograph?" stop reading from time to time and think about what you've read. Then review. In your Learner's Notebook, write down any new information you found.

Reading in the Real World

College Students who are planning to pursue higher education need to develop effective study skills. During Reading Workshop 3, have students take notes in a two-column format. Tell students to write main ideas and vocabulary in the left column. Suggest that students record detailed notes about the main idea and vocabulary in the right column. At the end of the workshop, allow time in class for students to review their notes. As a class, discuss the pros and cons of this particular note-taking method. **OL** Have students share their own note-taking habits with their classmates. **AL**

Teach

Literature Online

Study Central Have students access the Web site to review reviewing and to complete a related activity.

R1 Reading Skill

Reviewing Ask: If you are reading a difficult selection, what would be a clue that you should stop and review what you're reading? *(Possible responses: encountering unfamiliar vocabulary, not being able to keep track of information, or feeling confused)* **BL**

R2 Reading Skill

Reviewing Say: Look at the *How Do I Do It?* section. What strategies can you use to review text? *(Stop reading and think about what you've read; skim and scan titles, headings, pictures, and captions; reread; or take notes.)* **OL** Which strategy do you think will help you most if you are reviewing text more than a week after you first read it? Explain your choice. *(Answers will vary.)* **AL**

Resources for page 55

- Use Reading Skills Transparency in *Read Aloud, Think Aloud,* Unit 1, to help students practice reviewing.

Objective

- Monitor reading comprehension: review, reread, ask questions

More About the Author

Lesley Reed is active in a citizens' group that is working to end hunger and poverty in the world. She believes that "[supporting] collapsing educational and health care systems is the best way to help" people in Africa and other developing countries survive.

V Vocabulary

Using the Vocabulary

Say: One way to learn and remember the vocabulary words is to practice using them in everyday conversation. Set a goal of using each vocabulary word one time today. Record each use. Plan to share these examples in class tomorrow. **OL** For a challenge, try using these words both in your first language and in English throughout the day. **EL**

Before You Read

Teaching Nepalis to Read, Plant, and Vote

Lesley Reed

Meet the Author

Lesley Reed's love for travel started when she was very young. "When I was seven, my family moved to Iran for two years, and it changed my life," says Reed. "[It] was so different from the United States, but I grew to love those differences." Reed served as a Peace Corps volunteer in Africa. She writes about countries where most of the population is very poor.

Author Search For more about Lesley Reed, go to www.glencoe.com.

Objectives (pp. 56–61)
Reading Monitor comprehension: review, reread
Informational Text Use text features: lead, photographs
Vocabulary Use context clues: definition

Vocabulary Preview

V

determined (dih TUR mund) *adj.* having firmly decided; unwilling to change one's mind **(p. 58)** *Armand was determined to get an education.*

illegal (ih LEE gul) *adj.* against the law **(p. 59)** *Joseph was sent to jail because of his illegal activities.*

inspired (in SPY urd) *v.* made someone want to do something; form of the verb *inspire* **(p. 59)** *Agnes inspired others to learn to read.*

Write to Learn Rewrite the three sample sentences above in your own words *without using the vocabulary words.* Be sure your sentences mean about the same thing as the sample sentences.

English Language Coach

Context Clues In Reading Workshop 2, you learned to figure out an unfamiliar word by looking for a definition in or near the sentence. Sometimes the word or phrase is defined immediately after it appears, as in this example:

Dinesh and his wife Ratna were **champions** of education, fighting for the cause of teaching poor people to read.

If the subject is not sports or another competition, what does it mean to be a *champion* of something? Copy the organizer below and fill in the empty box.

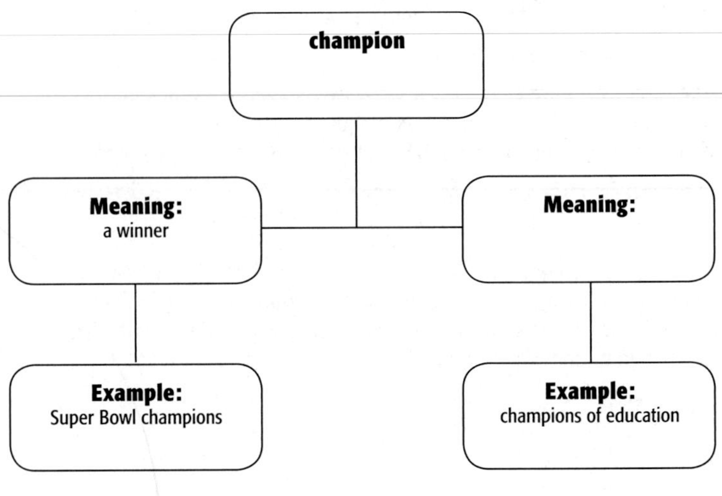

Additional Support

Author Search To expand students' appreciation of Lesley Reed, have them access the Web site for additional information and resources.

English Language Coach

Context Clues Remind students that writers may give context clues through examples, restatement, or contrast. Read the following paragraph aloud or write it on the board: Harold was *determined* to get a job, so he went from store to store and asked for applications. He was rewarded with *sore feet.* However, he went out again the next day—his *aches and pains* making him try harder. Harold is *dedicated*—not at all *uncommitted.* Ask students these questions.

- Which sentence(s) provide(s) context clues by example? *(first sentence)*
- Which sentence(s) provide(s) context clues by restatement? *(sentences 2–4)*
- Which sentence(s) provide(s) context clues by contrast? *(last sentence)*

Skills Preview

Key Reading Skill: Reviewing

As you read the following selection, stop after every two or three paragraphs to

- check your understanding of what you've read
- reread to look for information you missed

Partner Talk With your partner, talk about how reviewing the selection helped you understand it better.

Key Text Element: Lead

The first paragraph of a newspaper or magazine article is called the *lead.* The purpose of a lead is to get you interested in the story so you'll want to read more. Sometimes the lead will say something surprising or ask a question to get your attention. Often, a lead will tell you just enough facts so that you'll want to find out more.

A lead may tell you who the article is about, what happened, where it happened, and when it happened. It might also hint at why or how it happened. E

As you read a lead, try to answer these questions:

- Does the lead say something surprising that I want to learn more about?
- Does the lead ask any interesting questions?
- Whom is the article about?
- What happened?
- Where did it happen?
- When did it happen?

Interactive Literary Elements Handbook
To review or learn more about the literary elements, go to www.glencoe.com.

Get Ready to Read

Connect to the Reading

As you read how reading and writing changed people's lives in Nepal, think about what these skills mean to you. How would your life be different if you couldn't read or write? C

Group Discussion Imagine what your life would be like if you couldn't read or write. With your classmates, discuss how a typical week would be different without these skills.

Build Background

The selection tells about the work of one family in Nepal to help others learn to read and write and have better lives.

- Nepal (nuh PAWL) is a country in Asia. It is located between India and China.
- Kathmandu (kat man DOO) is the capital of Nepal. It is the country's largest city.
- Most voters in Nepal still can't read or write. To vote, they choose the symbol, or picture, of the party they want. The symbol of the Nepali (nuh PAW lee) Congress party is a tree, for example.

Set Purposes for Reading

BIG Question Read the article "Teaching Nepalis to Read, Plant, and Vote" to find out how reading helps Nepalis have better lives.

Set Your Own Purpose What else would you like to learn from the selection to help you answer the Big Question? Write about your purposes on the "Teaching Nepalis" page of Foldable 1.

Keep Moving

Use these skills as you read the following selection.

Teach

E Text Element

Lead Say: There are three types of leads: action *(someone doing something)*, dialogue *(someone saying something)*, or reaction *(someone thinking about something)*. Which lead might be best for a sports story? *(Possible response: Beginning the story with action might be the best way to engage sports readers.)* OL

C Critical Thinking

Analysis Ask: Why would taking a bus or buying food at a grocery store be more difficult if you could not read? *(Possible response: You would not be able to check the schedule or you would not know the ingredients of different foods.)* BL

CheckPoint

Use the CheckPoint questions provided on Presentation Plus! to check for prior knowledge and to build background.

Literature Online

Interactive Literary Elements Handbook
Have students access the Web site to improve their understanding of leads.

Differentiated Instruction

Creating Brochures American students may have a difficult time understanding the obstacles that the people of Nepal face. To give students perspective, have small groups prepare travel brochures for someone who plans to visit Nepal. Encourage students to consult encyclopedias, the Internet, and guidebooks for information. Ask students to include information about history, political unrest, economy, people, education, family life, and traditions. Suggest that students illustrate their brochures. OL Give English Language Learners the option of creating two smaller brochures, one in English and one in their first language. EL

Objectives

- Monitor comprehension: review, reread
- Use text features: lead, photographs
- Use context clues: definition

Teach

Viewing the Photo

Ask: How is the classroom in the photo like our classroom? How is it different? *(Responses will vary. Students may say that they, too, have desks, but that their desks are bigger and made of metal and plastic, not wood.)* **OL** What makes a classroom a classroom? *(Responses will vary. Students may say that having a space for a group to meet and learn creates a classroom.)* **AL**

E Text Element

Lead **Say:** A good lead forces readers to ask a question that can be answered only by continuing to read the article. Using this criterion, do you find Reed's lead effective? Explain. *(Responses will vary. Students may say yes, the lead is effective because it makes them ask "How did a boy who couldn't go to school help thousands of others learn to read and write?")* **OL**

Readability Scores
Dale-Chall: 4.6
DRP: 57
Lexile: 900

Teaching Nepalis to Read, Plant, and Vote

by Lesley Reed

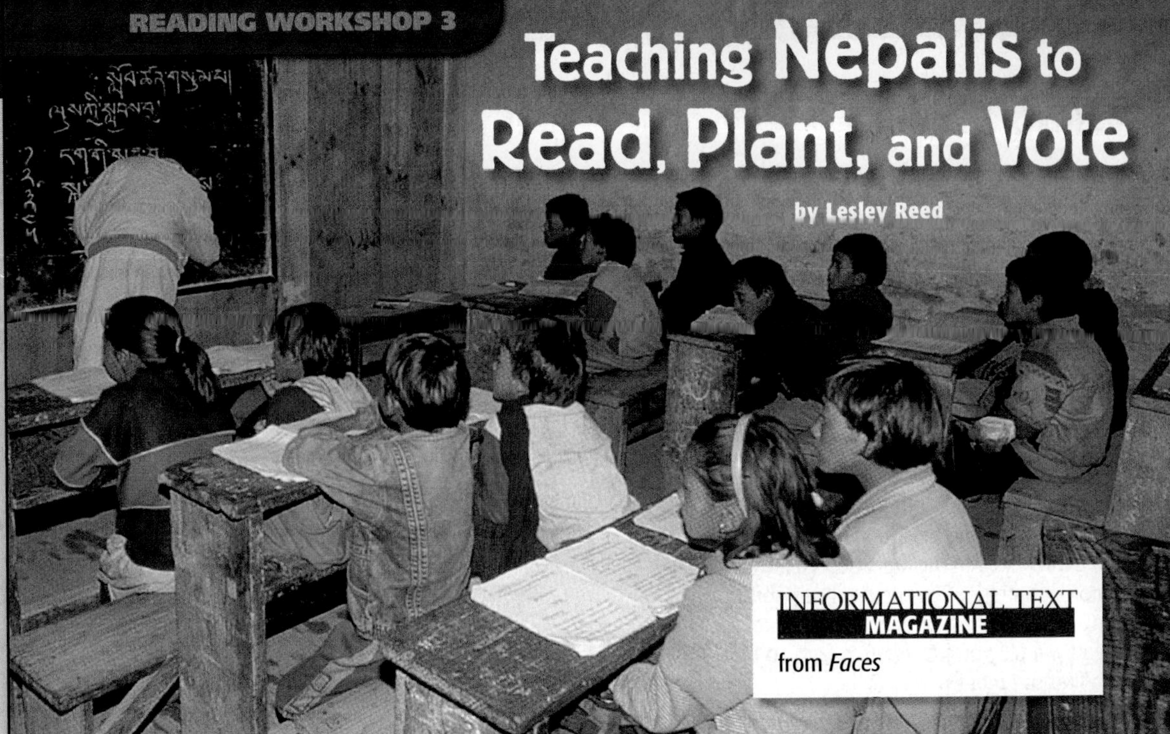

INFORMATIONAL TEXT
MAGAZINE
from *Faces*

Seventy years ago, a boy named Bishnu Prasad Dhungel was not allowed to go to school. As a result, thousands of Nepalis have learned to read and write. This is the remarkable story of Bishnu, his son Dinesh, and Dinesh's wife Ratna. **1**

When Bishnu was a child, there was only one school in Nepal and it was far away in Kathmandu. It was actually against the law to start schools in the villages of Nepal, because the government believed that it was easier to control people if they didn't know how to read and write.

Bishnu helped on the family farm, but he longed to go to school. Finally, he was so **determined** to get an education that he ran away to Kathmandu, walking for three entire days. He completed one year of school, enough to get a government job.

As Bishnu's children grew, he was determined that they would go to school, so he brought a teacher from India to teach them. For doing so, Bishnu was sent to jail for three months

Vocabulary

determined (dih TUR mund) *adj.* having firmly decided; unwilling to change one's mind

Practice the Skills

1 Key Text Element

E **Lead** The first paragraph is the *lead*. Usually, a good lead tries to get you interested in the story by saying something surprising or interesting, or by asking a question. Leads also give you the basic facts of a story—the who, what, why, where, and when. Sometimes a lead also suggests a why or how.

What facts about the article does the lead for this selection give you? What questions does it make you want to answer?

Additional Support

Reading in the Real World

Citizenship Ask students to talk with three family or community members about their educational backgrounds. Tell students to choose people of different ages and genders. Students should list responses to the following items:

- Describe your education.
- What was the general attitude toward education at the time you went to school?
- What did you think about your education at the time?
- What do you think about your education now?

Have students share their responses with the class. **OL**

These Nepalese children participated in a program to learn how to read.

for breaking the law. However, he didn't give up. He joined the Nepali Congress—a then-**illegal** political party[1] fighting for democracy[2]—to fight the government. In 1951, when a new government came to power, education was finally allowed. 2

Dinesh is Bishnu's third son. He not only went to elementary school, he graduated from college. Because he had studied English, he was able to get a job teaching Nepali to U.S. Peace Corps[3] volunteers. With the job came the opportunity to travel around Nepal.

Dinesh soon noticed how few poor Nepalis, especially women and girls, knew how to read. They now had the right to go to school, but they didn't have schools or teachers. This realization **inspired** Dinesh to follow in his father's footsteps as a champion of education. As a result, thousands of lives were changed.

Dinesh was fortunate to have married Ratna, a lively young woman who was also committed to helping the poor. They created an organization called the Non-Formal Education Services Center to educate poor Nepalis. C

1. A ***political party*** is an organization that tries to get its candidates elected to office.
2. A ***democracy*** (dih MAWK ruh see) is a government in which the people hold the power through voting.
3. Volunteers in the ***U.S. Peace Corps*** help people in other countries learn useful skills. Peace Corps volunteers must live in the country for two years and speak the language of the people there.

Vocabulary

illegal (ih LEE gul) *adj.* against the law

inspired (in SPY urd) *v.* made someone want to do something

Practice the Skills

2 **English Language Coach**

Context Clues What kind of context clue tells you what the **Nepali Congress** is? EL

READING WORKSHOP 3

Teach

Viewing the Photo

Ask: What do you learn about Nepali people and culture from this photo? *(Responses will vary. Students may say that the buildings are constructed of wood and grass or that the people do not wear shoes.)* AS

EL Language Coach

Context Clues Say: Which words restate *Nepali Congress?* *(The restatement words are "a then-illegal political party fighting for democracy.")* BL How does the restated context clue help readers understand the term *Nepali Congress?* *(It tells readers what kind of group the Nepali Congress is.)* OL

C Critical Thinking

Analysis Say: What do you think Nepali women thought of Ratna when they met her? *(Possible response: They probably thought that she was intelligent, hardworking, and possibly even inspiring.)* OL Why do you think so few poor women and girls in Nepal knew how to read? *(Responses will vary. Students may infer that women do not hold a high social status in Nepal.)* AL

Reading in the Real World

Citizenship The Nepali Congress fought for democracy. Consider why Nepali people would want democracy. What does it offer that other forms of government do not? Why might the government have declared the Nepali Congress illegal? To stimulate discussion, share with students Sir Winston Churchill's words about democracy: *"No one pretends that democracy is perfect or all-wise. Indeed, it has been said that democracy is the worst form of government except all those other forms that have been tried from time to time."* Invite students to discuss what Churchill meant. AL

Objectives
- Use the lead to understand and interpret text
- Clarify word meanings in context
- View art and photos
- Make inferences

READING WORKSHOP 3

Teach

E Text Element

Review Photographs What is a major difference between the way Americans dress and the way Nepalis dress? *(Possible response: Most Americans wear shoes regularly.)* What kinds of food do Nepali people probably depend on goats to provide? *(Possible response: Goats provide milk, cheese, and meat.)* OL

C Critical Thinking

Analysis Ask: Why does Dinesh refer to the tribal people as "brothers and sisters"? *(Responses will vary. Students may say that Dinesh understands himself to be related to the group although they do not share blood.)* OL How does Dinesh's comment show how he feels about tribal Nepalis? *(Possible response: It shows that he feels connected to tribal Nepalis.)* AL

Dinesh describes their first project: "We were working with a very poor tribal group that lived in caves on the sides of steep hills. When we first visited, they ran into the forest because they were scared of strangers. They had nothing. I couldn't believe our brothers and sisters were living in this condition." C

While they'd set out to teach reading and writing, they quickly realized that they needed to do something about the poverty they saw. After talking with the villagers, they decided to buy goats for the ten poorest families. Goats could scale[4] the steep hillsides and eat the brush that grew there. When the goats gave birth, the kids[5] were given to other

4. Here, to ***scale*** means "to climb."

5. ***Kids*** are baby goats.

Practice the Skills

3 Reviewing Elements

Photographs What do the photos show about Nepal? What questions do they bring to mind? Notice that the children aren't wearing shoes (and neither are the kids). Look at the buildings. Without knowing the time of year, can you say what Nepal's climate is? E

Raising goats helps these villagers earn money to pay for children to go to school.

Dinesh meets with villagers to learn more about the women's saving group.

Additional Support

Differentiated Instruction

Charting Solutions Help students understand the complex nature of the situation by having them use a graphic organizer to show how two solutions, the goats and the orange trees, led to more solutions. *(See chart below for answers).* OL

Goats for 10 families → Baby goats given to other poor families → Villagers required to save one quarter of money earned from goats to send children to school → Savings eventually used to buy land and build better houses → Children and adults taught to read → More schools built, drinking water systems built, more trees planted poor families. Dinesh and Ratna also learned that orange trees would grow in the area, so they planted hundreds of trees.

The villagers were required to save one quarter of the money they earned from the goats and oranges. With their savings, they sent their children to the schools that the center helped build. They were eventually able to buy land and build better houses.

Since then, the center has taught 20,000 adults and 5,000 children to read as well as helped to lift them out of poverty. They have built 15 schools and 56 drinking water systems and planted thousands of trees. When democracy came to Nepal in 1990, the center also taught the meaning of democracy and the importance of voting and human rights.[6] 4

Ratna was eager to help the women and children in another village, so she started her own organization, called HANDS. To get to the village, she had to wade a river seven times. It was a three-and-a-half-hour walk to the nearest health clinic. When the river was flooded, the people couldn't get to the clinic at all. Ratna's organization built a health center. It also taught women and girls to raise animals, to farm organically[7] and make tofu,[8] to sew, and to make pressed-flower cards (which Ratna sells in the United States). Of course, they also learn to read and write.

"In the poor areas of Nepal," Dinesh says, "there is no TV or computer or electricity. Most children don't have enough pencils or paper. When the rainy season starts, it seems like all the rain is falling in the class because the roofs leak so much. The classrooms are tiny, dark, and cold. The children need to help their parents with housework, fetching firewood, and taking care of goats or their younger brothers and sisters. Because of this, only about one out of ten children complete grade 10."

Dinesh and Ratna have spent their lives trying to change this. Of this, Dinesh says, "We are proud." ❍ 5

6. ***Human rights*** are basic privileges or freedoms that every person is supposed to have.
7. When farmers grow food ***organically,*** they do not use chemicals to help fruits or vegetables grow or to control insects.
8. ***Tofu*** is a food made from soybeans. It is inexpensive to make and good for your health.

Practice the Skills

4 Key Reading Skill

R **Reviewing** Without looking back at the selection, write the answer to this question in your Learner's Notebook:

- How did raising goats and planting orange trees help lift some Nepalis out of poverty?

Now review the text to find any information you might have missed or forgotten. If reviewing the text has helped you answer the question more completely, write your new answer in your Learner's Notebook.

5 

BQ How did learning to read change the lives of people in the poor areas of Nepal? Write your answers on the "Teaching Nepalis" page of Foldable 1. Your response will help you complete the Unit Challenge later.

Teach

R Reading Skill

Reviewing Ask: What do you remember about how goats and orange trees helped the poor villagers? *(Responses will vary. Some students may say that the goats had kids, which were then given to other families.)* Which reviewing strategy could be used to remember more details about how the goats and orange trees helped the Nepali people have better lives? *(Possible response: Rereading the paragraphs about what happened after the goats were given and the orange trees were planted would help.)* OL

BQ 

Ask: Why is it especially important for the Nepali villagers to learn to read? *(Possible response: They need to read in order to get jobs with the government or the Peace Corps and earn money.)* AS

Assess

CheckPoint

Use the CheckPoint questions provided on Presentation Plus! to review the selection. These questions can be used with interactive response keypads for immediate student feedback.

Reading in the Real World

Career Dinesh and Ratna made a career out of helping others. Explain that the term *service sector* is a way of describing all of the jobs that serve others. With students, create a list of careers that could fit into the service sector. Have each student select a career and write a job description that includes how that career might help others. OL Tell students that "nonprofit organizations" are companies that aim to make enough money to stay in business but not enough money to make a profit. Ask students to list nonprofit organizations in their city. AL

Objectives
- Review text to understand and recall ideas
- View art and photos
- Make inferences

Assess

Resources for page 62

- Selection Quick Check
- Selection and Unit Assessment
- ExamView Assessment Suite
- Interactive Tutor: Self-Assessment

Students can respond to the *After You Read* items in their Learner's Notebook or on separate sheets of paper.

Answering the

1. Possible responses: to make better lives for themselves or to challenge the government
2. Bishnu went to Kathmandu to go to school.
3. Dinesh studied English, so he was able to get a job teaching Nepali to Peace Corps volunteers.
4. Ratna began an organization called HANDS, whose members built a health center and taught women how to do such things as make tofu and design pressed-flower cards.

Critical Thinking

5. Responses will vary. Students may say that the Nepali government was controlling and did not allow the people to have many rights.
6. Responses will vary. Students may say that all students have obstacles to overcome in getting through school.

After You Read

Teaching Nepalis to Read, Plant, and Vote

Objectives (pp. 62–63)
Reading Monitor comprehension: review, reread
Informational Text Use text features: title, lead
Vocabulary Use context clues: restatement
Writing Write a journal entry
Grammar Use verb tenses

Answering the

1. After reading this selection, what new ideas do you have about why people read?
2. **Recall** Why did Bishnu run away to Kathmandu?
   TIP **Right There** You'll find the information in the article.
3. **Recall** Why was Dinesh able to get a job teaching Nepali to Peace Corps volunteers?
   TIP **Right There** You will find the answer in the article.
4. **Summarize** How did Ratna help women in one village?
   TIP **Think and Search** You must use information from the article and decide what the important points are.

Critical Thinking

5. **Infer** What do you think the government of Nepal was like when Bishnu was a boy?
   TIP **Author and Me** You will find clues in the article, but you must also use the information you already have in your head.
6. **Evaluate** Do children in Nepal have a harder time getting through school than children in the United States? Explain.
   TIP **Author and Me** You must use information in the article and your own experience to answer.

Write About Your Reading

Write a Journal Entry Many people write down what they do each day or week in a journal. In a journal, you write the important things that have happened since you last wrote. You can also write how you feel about what happened, your plans for the future, or any other thoughts and feelings you have.

Pretend you're Dinesh or Ratna. Write a journal entry that summarizes your experiences with the tribal group that lives in caves.

Write About Your Reading

Possible response:
Monday
Today, Dinesh and I realized that the villagers will not be interested in reading or writing until we can do something about the poverty in which they live.
Tuesday
Goats, of course! The hillsides are so steep here that earning a living through livestock or farming seemed impossible yesterday. This morning, I looked up and saw a wild goat standing on the hillside. I talked the idea over with Dinesh, and he agrees that goat farming might solve some of the villagers' problems. Tomorrow, I will visit the livestock market.

Skills Review

Key Reading Skill: Reviewing

When you review, you can find facts (such as dates, places, and names), ideas, events, descriptions, and questions that you missed the first time you read the text.

7. Review the text to find out about the illegal political party Bishnu joined. What was the name of the party, and what were they fighting for?

Key Text Element: Lead

The lead for this selection began this way: "Seventy years ago, a boy named Bishnu Prasad Dhungel was not allowed to go to school. As a result, thousands of Nepalis have learned to read and write."

8. What information in the lead gets your attention?
9. What purpose for reading this article might someone have after reading the lead?

Reviewing Elements: Title

10. Explain how the title sums up the important ideas in the article.

Vocabulary Check

A good newspaper headline tells just enough about the story to make people want to read the story. For example, "Injured Boy Saves Sister from Flood" makes you want to know what happened and how the boy saved his sister. Show your understanding of each word below by using it correctly to write a newspaper headline.

11. **determined**
12. **illegal**
13. **inspire**

English Language Coach Write the meaning of each word in bold. Use context clues to figure each one out.

14. Nepal has been a **sovereign,** or independent, nation since the 1700s.
15. Nepal's mountains keep the world away, leaving the country **isolated** by its geography.

Grammar Link: Verb Tense

Verb tenses tell when an action or a state of being occurred. The three main verb tenses are present, past, and future.

Present tense shows actions and states of being that are (1) happening now or (2) happen regularly.

- Helena **is** happy.
  (Helena appears to be happy right now.)
- I **walk** to school.
  (The speaker makes a habit of walking to school.)

Past tense shows actions and states of being that are over and done.

- Helena **was** happy.
  (Helena appeared to be happy in the past.)
- I **walked** to school.
  (The speaker has completed his walk to school.)

Future tense shows actions that are going to happen.

- Helena **will be** happy.
  (Helena isn't happy now, but she's going to be.)
- I **will ride** my bike to school.
  (The speaker plans to ride his bike to school sometime in the future.)

Grammar Practice

Complete each sentence below with words of your choice. After each sentence, tell what tense you used.

16. Right now I . . . .
17. Most days I . . . .
18. Yesterday I . . . .
19. Tomorrow I . . . .

Writing Application Look back at the journal entry you wrote for Dinesh or Ratna. List each verb or verb phrase you used that is written in the past or future tense.

Web Activities For eFlashcards, Selection Quick Checks, and other Web activities, go to www.glencoe.com.

Skills Review

Key Reading Skill: Reviewing

7. The Nepali Congress, an illegal political party, was fighting for democracy.

Key Text Element: Lead

8. Readers may be interested in learning how a boy who was not allowed to go to school helped thousands learn to read.
9. Someone might read the article to learn about social service or political action.

Reviewing Elements: Title

10. The title sums up the important ideas in the article by suggesting that the issues of education, agriculture, and politics are inseparable.

Vocabulary Check

Possible responses:

11. Determined Red Cross Worker Saves Lives
12. Illegal Drugs Found in Home
13. Children Inspire Adults in New Program
14. independent
15. separated or alone

Close

Ask students to summarize what they learned from Dinesh and Ratna's story to answer the Big Question.

Grammar Link: Verb Tense

Grammar Practice

Possible responses:

16. Right now, I feel happy about trying out for the basketball team. **Present**
17. Most days I am awake by 6:30 a.m. **Present**
18. Yesterday I was baffled by a joke my friend told. **Past**
19. Tomorrow I will be relieved because we will have finished our civics test! **Future**

More About the Author

Marjorie Sharmat admits that she gets inspiration for her characters and her plot lines from real life. She frequently names her characters after family members. Her most popular character, Nate the Great, is named after her father. Readers will also meet characters named after her husband, Mitchell, and her Uncle Harry. In fact, the narrator of "May I Have Your Autograph?" is named Rosalind, which is Sharmat's sister's name.

V Vocabulary

Vocabulary Opposites

Say: One way to learn and remember vocabulary words is to learn about antonyms, or opposite words. *Have students create note cards that feature a new vocabulary word on one side and its antonym on the other side. Then have them use their word cards to quiz one another on these words.* **OL** *Students can write the vocabulary words in their first language and the antonyms in English; point out that direct translation may not always be possible.* **EL**

Before You Read

May I Have Your Autograph?

Meet the Author

Marjorie Sharmat likes to write funny stories. Since life can be hard and serious, she wants people to have fun when they read. She always has a good idea for a story. Sharmat explains, "I have a . . . pest in my head. . . . This pest is never satisfied and constantly furnishes me with new ideas and nags me to get them on paper." Sharmat was born in Portland, Maine, in 1928.

Author Search For more about Marjorie Sharmat, go to www.glencoe.com.

Objectives (pp. 64–71)
Reading Monitor comprehension: review, reread
Literature Identify theme in a literary text
Vocabulary Use context clues: comparison, contrast

Vocabulary Preview

V

triumphant (try UM funt) *adj.* joyful in victory; successful **(p. 67)** *Craig the Cat felt triumphant at the end of a good concert.*

receptive (rih SEP tiv) *adj.* open to ideas and requests **(p. 67)** *Juan was receptive to his teacher's writing suggestions.*

accomplish (uh KAWM plish) *v.* to finish; complete **(p. 67)** *Rosa's goal was to accomplish her homework before the game.*

entitled (in TY tuld) *adj.* having a right to something **(p. 71)** *Carolyn was entitled to keep her diary private.*

English Language Coach

Comparison and Contrast Sometimes a word's meaning is clarified by an antonym or a contrasting word or phrase. Here are two examples:

1. Studying is always a benefit, but listening to music at the same time can be a **detriment.**

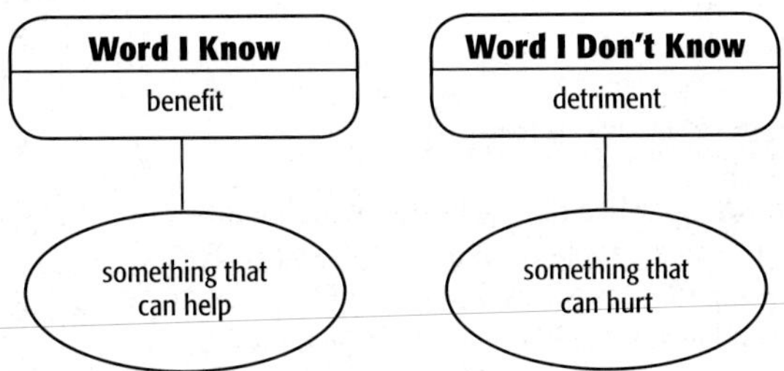

2. Carla is very honest, not **deceptive** like her brother.

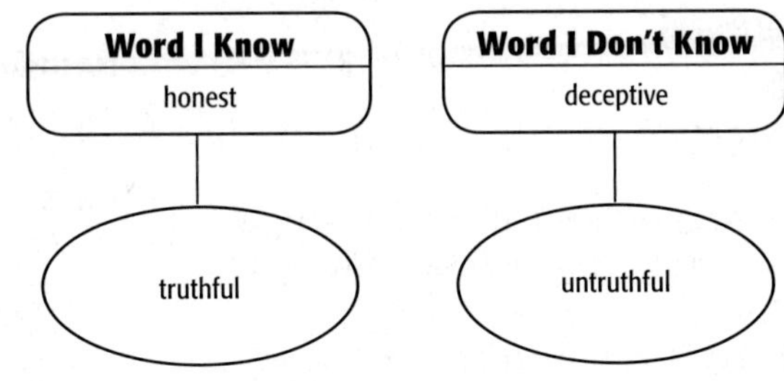

Additional Support

Author Search To expand students' appreciation of Marjorie Sharmat, have them access the Web site for additional information and resources.

Literature Focus Lesson

Humorous Writing Marjorie Sharmat's stories have many humorous elements. Ask students to remember funny stories, plays, poems, or magazine articles that they have read. Talk about what made each text funny. Were the characters silly? Was the setting bizarre? Have students write funny short stories. They can exchange stories with partners and give each other suggestions on how to make the stories funnier. **OL**

Skills Preview

Key Reading Skill: Reviewing

When you're reading, do you sometimes forget who's who and what's what? If so, you may need to review. Reviewing is a great way to remember what you read. As you read, stop every page or two and think about what has happened. Try telling the story to yourself in your own words. If you're missing information, review to find it. You don't want to lose track of characters or events.

Write to Learn Why is reviewing important? Write a few reasons in your Learner's Notebook.

Literary Element: Theme

The **theme** of a story, poem, or any other kind of literature is the main idea. It's what the author most wants you to take away with you–the author's message to the reader. This is not the same as the topic, or subject, of the selection. For example, a story could be about a football game. The theme of the story might be the importance of teamwork, or the value of not giving up, or the dangers of caring only about winning, or almost anything!

As you read, use these tips to help you understand the theme of "May I Have Your Autograph?"

- Notice the feelings that people have and show for each other.

  Do the feelings change as the story goes on?
- Think about what the main character wants and how she gets it.

  What makes it possible for her to get what she wants?

L

Literature Online

Interactive Literary Elements Handbook
To review or learn more about the literary elements, go to www.glencoe.com.

Get Ready to Read

Connect to the Reading

Most people are fans of someone. Which famous person do you want to meet? How can you learn about this person? What magazines do you read to learn about him or her?

Partner Talk Tell a partner about a famous person you'd like to meet. Explain what you like about the person and why it would be exciting to talk with him or her. What would you ask the person? What would you tell him or her about yourself?

C

Build Background

In this story, a young girl wants to meet her favorite rock star and gets his autograph.

- The word *autograph* comes from ancient Greek. *Auto-* means "self," and *graph* means "writing."
- An autograph is someone's name, written by that person.
- People who make a hobby of collecting autographs of famous people are called autograph hunters. Sometimes they sell autographs of famous people for a lot of money!
- Before music came on iPods and compact discs, it came on large discs called record albums.

Set Purposes for Reading

BIG Question Read "May I Have Your Autograph?" to see what happens to two girls who try to get a rock star's autograph.

Set Your Own Purpose What else would you like to learn from the story to help you answer the Big Question? Write your reason for reading this story on the "May I Have Your Autograph" page of Foldable 1.

Keep Moving

Use these skills as you read the following selection.

Reading in the Real World

Career Before buying an autograph, you might want to have someone authenticate it, or establish that it is real. There are two fields of handwriting analysis that would be helpful: graphology and scientific handwriting analysis. Graphologists study handwriting as a way of learning about the writer's personality. Scientific handwriting analysts are interested in proving who wrote a particular document. People who study handwriting look at such things as the slant of the letters, the width and height of the letters, and the spacing. Lead students in a discussion regarding the fields that might make use of such studies. AS

Teach

L Literary Element

Theme Say: As you read "May I Have Your Autograph?" take notes in your Learner's Notebook. On one page, write about the characters' feelings. On another, write about what the main character wants and how she gets it. You can review these notes later to help you think about the theme. OL

C Critical Thinking

Comprehension Say: People are famous for many different reasons. Movie stars, musicians, politicians, and everyday heroes inspire fans. Whom are you a fan of? If you could meet that person, what would you want the meeting to be like? *(Responses will vary.)*

CheckPoint

Use the CheckPoint questions provided on Presentation Plus! to check for prior knowledge. These questions can be used with interactive response keypads for immediate student feedback.

Literature Online

Interactive Literary Elements Handbook Have students access the Web site to improve their understanding of theme.

Objectives

- Monitor comprehension: review, reread
- Identify theme in a literary text
- Use context clues: comparison, contrast

Teach

L Literary Element

Theme **Ask:** Why does Rosalind think Wendy is in love with Craig? *(Possible response: Wendy is constantly talking about Craig.)* Rosalind says, "I think love is for people you've at least met." What does that statement tell you about Rosalind? about Wendy? *(Possible response: Rosalind is practical. Wendy is emotional.)* **OL**

C Critical Thinking

Analysis **Ask:** What does the narrator mean when she says that Craig the Cat was "nicely, safely unreal" before today? *(Responses will vary. Students may say that unreal things are safe because they do not require thought or action. When the real Craig appears, the girls' actions change.)* **OL**

READING WORKSHOP 3

May I Have Your Autograph?

by Marjorie Sharmat

I am sitting in an overstuffed chair in the lobby of The Dominion Imperial International Hotel. So help me, that's really the name. I am surrounded by overgrown ferns, ugly but expensive floral carpeting, chandeliers that make me think of *The Phantom of the Opera,* stuck-up hotel employees in silly-looking uniforms who give me dirty looks—and nobody my age. Except my friend Wendy, who dragged me here. **1**

Visual Vocabulary ***Chandeliers*** are fancy light fixtures that hang from the ceiling.

Wendy is here to meet a guy, but he doesn't know it. In fact, he's never heard of Wendy. But that doesn't stop her from being in love with him. Well, maybe not in love. I think love is for people you've at least met. Wendy has never met Craig the Cat. That's the name of the guy. At least that's his stage name. He's a rock star who's been famous for over six months. Even *my* parents have heard of him. **L**

Wendy is here to get Craig the Cat's autograph on his latest album. On the album jacket,[1] Craig is wearing a black cat costume and he's sitting on a garbage pail with a bottle of spilled milk beside him. He is holding his guitar in his long, furry arms.

Wendy constantly talks about Craig the Cat. But it was like discussing something that was going on in another time frame, on another continent. I didn't mind. It was nicely, safely unreal. Until Craig the Cat came to town today. He's **C**

1. An ***album jacket*** is the cardboard envelope that is used to store a record.

Practice the Skills

1 Literary Element

Theme The narrator is talking about a person who is her friend—a friend who thinks she is in love. Could the theme of the story have to do with people's feelings for each other?

Additional Support

Readability Scores
Dale-Chall: 5.7
DRP: 47
Lexile: 580

Differentiated Instruction

Illustrations Students who are visual learners may benefit from reviewing the paragraph that describes Craig the Cat's album cover and then sketching it. When they have done so, lead students in a discussion about what they learn about Craig from this album cover. Would the story be easier to understand if an illustration of the cover was provided? In general, what do illustrations add to a person's reading experience? Why might an author decide not to include illustrations? **OL**

giving a string of benefit performances across the country for some kind of animal group that's devoted to saving "the cats."

"That includes everything from alley cats to **exotic**[2] tigers," Wendy told me. 2

"How do you know?"

"I know."

We used our allowance money to buy tickets. That landed us exactly five rows from the back of the auditorium.

"This is so frustrating," Wendy said as we stretched our necks. "I must get closer."

"How close?" I joked.

"I want his autograph," she answered. "I'm not joking."

"Lots of luck."

Wendy doesn't believe in luck. After the concert she dragged me here, to this hotel lobby where we are now sitting. We just sit.

"Are we waiting for him to come into the lobby?" I ask.

"No. He probably got spirited into[3] the hotel through a back or side entrance." Wendy looks at her watch. "He's showered and is relaxing now. He's feeling rested, **triumphant**, and **receptive**."

"Receptive to what?"

"To meeting us. To autographing *my* album."

"How are you going to **accomplish** that? You don't actually know that he's staying at this hotel, and even if he is, you don't know his room number."

Wendy stands up. "Don't be so negative, Rosalind. Come," she says. 3

I follow her to one of those telephones that connect the caller to hotel rooms. She dials a number. She waits. Then she says, "Craig the Cat, please." She looks at me. "I found him! Listen!" She tilts the receiver so that I, too, can hear what's being said. It's a strain, but I can hear.

2. ***Exotic*** can mean "from a foreign country" or simply "strange or unusual."

3. ***Got spirited into*** means that someone sneaked him into the hotel.

Vocabulary

triumphant (try UM funt) *adj.* joyful in victory; successful

receptive (rih SEP tiv) *adj.* open to ideas and requests

accomplish (uh KAWM plish) *v.* to finish; complete

Practice the Skills

2 English Language Coach

Context Clues How does a contrast between alley cats and exotic tigers help you understand the meaning of **exotic**? EL

3 Literary Element

Theme Wendy seems to know a lot about Craig the Cat. Could that have something to do with the theme? Could the theme have something to do with how people get to know each other?

Teach

EL Language Coach

Context Clues Suggest that students use a Venn diagram to compare and contrast alley cats and tigers before answering the question. Draw a Venn diagram on the board. Label the left circle "Alley Cats" and the right circle "Tigers." **Ask:** What similarities do alley cats and tigers have? What are their differences? Record students' responses in the appropriate areas. *(Responses will vary. Similarities: cats, carnivores, like to sleep, often wild; Differences: alley cats: common, relatively small; tigers: rare, live in zoos and faraway countries, largest members of cat family)* BL EL

Reading in the Real World

College Explain that hotels and restaurants—the hospitality industry—have many career opportunities. Explain that many of these jobs require special training. Have students form small groups to use the Web site www.uscollegesearch.org to find a school that offers a hospitality degree. Students should take notes on the degree program curriculum and the kinds of jobs to which the program leads. Invite students to share the results of their research with the class. OL

Objectives

- Interpret and analyze based on what you read and your own experience
- Identify theme in a literary text
- Use context clues to clarify word meaning

Teach

EL Language Coach

Context Clues **Say:** Read the sentence in which the phrase *highest bidder* is used. A "bidder" is someone who wants to buy an item and offers money for it. Whom is Craig's mother talking about when she uses this term? *(Possible response: an eager fan who will pay money to find Craig)* **OL** Whom is Craig's mother tired of? *(Possible response: Craig's mother is tired of his fans, and she hopes they have not found out where Craig is staying.)* **BL**

A woman is on the other end. "How did you find out where Craig the Cat is staying?" she asks. "The leak.[4] I need to know where the leak is."

"There isn't any. I'm the only one with the information. Please be nice. I want his autograph."

"Who doesn't."

"Help me get it, please. What are my chances?"

"Poor to nonexistent."[5]

"Oh."

"I'm his manager and, my dear, I'm his mother. I protect Craig from two vantage points.[6] I keep a low profile.[7] Now, how many other fans know where he's staying?"

"None that I know of."

"You mean you didn't peddle[8] the information to the highest bidder?" EL

"I wouldn't do that."

"Maybe not, dear, but I'm tired of his fans. They tug at Craig's whiskers. They pull his tail. Leave him alone! I'm hanging up."

Click.

Wendy sighs. "We'll just have to wait until he goes into that place over there to eat."

"Haven't you ever heard of room service?"

"Craig doesn't like room service. He doesn't like dining rooms, either. He's a coffee shop person."

"How do you know?"

"I know."

"How did you know his room number?"

"I knew."

"And you knew his mother is his manager?"

"I knew."

We are sitting in the overstuffed chairs again. Wendy is watching and waiting. I see no human-size cat in the lobby. I feel like going to sleep. **4** L

4. When the woman on the phone talks about a ***leak,*** she means that someone has told others secret information.
5. A ***nonexistent*** chance is no chance at all.
6. ***Vantage points*** are places or positions that give someone a view of something.
7. When you ***keep a low profile,*** you try not to be noticed.
8. Another word for ***peddle*** is *sell.*

Practice the Skills

4 **Key Reading Skill**

Reviewing Stop to review. Who are the four characters in the story? Write a short description of each one in your Learner's Notebook. Now go back and review what you've read. What more did you learn about each character as you reviewed? Explain in your Learner's Notebook.

Additional Support

English Language Coach

Hotel Talk Hotels provide lodging, food, and other services to travelers. Students who have never stayed in a hotel may not be familiar with some of the references in this story. Pair students needing help with students who are familiar with the terms. Have students work together to clarify the meaning of each term.

- lobby
- uniforms
- back or side entrance
- room number
- room service
- dining rooms
- coffee shop **BL** **EL**

Almost an hour goes by. Suddenly, Wendy pokes me. "It's him! It's him!"

I look up. A guy who seems to be about twenty or twenty-five is passing by with a woman who looks old enough to be his mother. He is lean. She is not. They are dressed normally.

I whisper to Wendy. "*That's* Craig the Cat? How do you know? He looks like an ordinary guy."

Wendy doesn't answer. She stands up and starts to follow the guy and the woman. They are heading for the hotel coffee shop. I follow all of them. I see the guy and the woman sit down. They are looking at menus.

Wendy rushes up to them, clutching her album. "May I have your autograph?" she asks the guy.

The woman glares at Wendy. "He doesn't give autographs," she says. "He's just a **civilian**. Can't you see he's just a civilian?" **5**

"You're Craig the Cat!" Wendy says to the guy.

She says it too loudly.

"How do you know I'm Craig the Cat?" the guy asks. Also too loudly.

People in the coffee shop turn and stare. They repeat, "Craig the Cat!"

Suddenly somebody with a camera materializes[9] and aims the camera at Craig. Wendy bends down and puts her face in front of Craig's. It happens so fast, I can't believe it. The photographer says, "Get out of the way, kid."

Craig's mother glares at the photographer. "Shoo!" she says, waving her hand. "Shoo immediately!"

The photographer leaves. So does Wendy. She runs back to me. I am hiding behind a fern.

Wendy has lost her cool. "Let's get out of here before we're kicked out or arrested," she says.

We rush toward a door.

"Wait!" Someone is yelling at us.

When I hear the word *wait,* it's a signal for me to move even faster. But Wendy stops. "It's *him!*" she says, without turning around.

I turn. It *is* Craig the Cat. He's alone. He rushes up to Wendy. "How did you know me?" he asks. "I didn't tell the media where I was staying. And I certainly didn't give out

9. ***Materializes*** (muh TEER ee uh ly zuz) means "appears" or "shows up."

Practice the Skills

5 English Language Coach

EL **Context Clues** What does the word **civilian** mean here? Start at the paragraph that begins "I look up" and reread. How is the guy dressed? Rosalind says he looks like an "ordinary guy." How does the way he looks give you a clue about the word *civilian?*

Teach

R Reading Skill

Reviewing Ask: Can you use one word to describe the personality of each of the four characters in the story? If not, review what you have read so far to better understand the characters and their actions. *(Responses will vary. Students may suggest the following: Wendy = excited; Rosalind = reluctant; Craig = strange; Craig's mother = protective.)* **OL**

EL Language Coach

Context Clues Say: Rosalind thinks that Craig "looks like an ordinary guy." What is a synonym for *ordinary*? *(Possible response: regular)* So, is someone who looks like a regular person a civilian? *(Possible response: Craig's mother intends* civilian *to mean "ordinary guy," but she is stretching the meaning.* Civilian *usually means a person who is not in uniform—part of the military or law enforcement.)* **OL** **EL**

Reading in the Real World

Citizenship The photographer is a member of the paparazzi, freelance photographers who take candid shots of celebrities for newspapers and magazines. The paparazzi have been criticized for intruding on the lives of celebrities, sometimes in ways that create dangerous situations. Lead students in a discussion about privacy rights for citizens. Use the following questions as discussion starters: Do all citizens deserve a right to privacy, regardless of their celebrity status? Are there times when citizens should be forced to give up their right to privacy? **OL** **EL**

Objectives
- Monitor comprehension: review, reread
- Identify theme in a literary text
- Use context clues to clarify word meanings

Teach

C1 Critical Thinking

Comprehension Ask: Why does Craig chase after Wendy? *(Responses will vary. Students may say that Craig is intrigued by Wendy's behavior.)* **OL** Craig and his mother often have to hide from fans. How is Wendy different from other fans? *(Responses will vary. Students may say that, unlike other fans, Wendy knows Craig is a real person who does not always want to be the center of attention.)* **BL**

C2 Critical Thinking

Evaluation Ask: What if fans and reporters with notepads had cameras aimed at you as you entered school or practiced basketball? How would you feel? *(Responses will vary. Some students may say that they would feel flattered, whereas others may say that they would feel bothered.)* How might other people view you if you were always being followed by fans, reporters, and photographers? *(Responses will vary. Some students may say that people would think you were important or vain.)* **BL**

my room number. I wasn't wearing my cat costume. And I was with my mother. So *how?*" **C1**

Wendy looks at me. She's trying to decide if she should answer. Something in her wants to and something in her doesn't want to. She turns back to Craig. "I'm an expert on you," she says. "I know you like fancy, old hotels, and this is the oldest and the fanciest in town. I know your lucky number is twelve, so I figured you'd stay on the twelfth floor in room 1212. I know you always wear red socks when you're not performing. So tonight I watched ankles in the lobby. And I knew you'd be with your manager—your mother."

"What about the photographer?" **6**

"I know you don't want to be photographed without your cat costume. In an interview of October eighth of this year, you said it would wreck your feline[10] image. So when I saw the photographer trying to take your picture, I put my face in front of yours."

10. ***Feline*** (FEE lyn) means "like a cat."

Practice the Skills

6 Literary Element

Theme As Wendy explains things to Craig the Cat, what do you learn about her? Do you get the feeling right now in the story that she's going to get Craig's autograph? Why?

C2

Additional Support

Differentiated Instruction

Reader's Theater Invite groups of three students to prepare reader's theater presentations of the scene with Wendy, Craig, and Rosalind. Encourage students to consider questions like these: *What tone of voice does Craig use? What is Wendy's body language? What is Rosalind, who has no dialogue, doing during this scene?* Allow time for students to rehearse and then have them perform their scenes for the class. **OL** Discuss how listening to and watching the scene differs from reading it. **AL**

"You did that for me?"

"I'd do it for any special friend."

"But you don't know me."

"Yes, I do. When I read about someone, I get to know him. I don't believe everything I read, of course. I pick out certain parts. I look for the reality behind the unreality. I went through seventy-one pages about Craig the Cat, in eleven different magazines, and I ended up thinking of you as my friend."

Craig the Cat is staring at Wendy as if *he's* the fan. He's in awe of *her!* It's nothing very earthshaking. It's not like there's a crowd roaring or it's a summit meeting of world leaders or a momentous change in the universe. It's just a small, nice moment in the lobby of The Dominion Imperial International Hotel, and it will never go away for Wendy.

We're back in the hotel coffee shop. Four of us are sitting around a table, eating. Craig's mother is beaming benevolently[11] like a contented mother cat presiding[12] over her brood,[13] which now includes Wendy and me in addition to Craig. After we finish eating, Wendy hands her record album to Craig. "Now may I have your autograph?" she asks. 7

Craig pulls out a pen and writes on the album jacket. I hope that Wendy will show me what he writes. Maybe she won't. Whatever she does will be okay, though. Maybe this will be the first private entry in her collection of reality and unreality about her new friend, Craig the Cat.

She's **entitled**.

As for me, I'm now sitting in a chair in a hotel coffee shop as a new and honored member of this Clan of the Cat. It has been a strange and kind of wonderful day, thanks to my friend, Wendy the Expert. I'm glad I'm here. If you take away some of the ferns and a few fat chairs and most of the carpeting, The Dominion Imperial International Hotel definitely has possibilities. 8 ❍

11. ***Benevolently*** (buh NEV uh lunt lee) means "in a kind way."
12. ***Presiding*** (prih ZYD ing) means "supervising" or "controlling."
13. A ***brood*** is the children in a family.

Vocabulary

entitled (in TY tuld) *adj.* having a right to do something

Practice the Skills

7 Key Reading Skill

R **Reviewing** The four characters—Wendy, Rosalind, Craig the Cat, and his mother—end up in the hotel coffee shop together. But what happens before this? Review the events in the story. Think about which events are important. In your Learner's Notebook, write a list of the events that happen before the characters sit in the coffee shop together.

8 BIG Question

BQ In the story, Wendy says she reads a lot of magazines. How did reading help Wendy meet Craig the Cat? What do you like to read? How has reading helped you in real life? Write your answers on the "May I Have Your Autograph" page of Foldable 1. Your response will help you complete the Unit Challenge later.

Differentiated Instruction

Time Line Some students may better grasp the sequence of events in the selection by organizing a time line showing the events that lead to the scene in the coffee shop. Encourage students to create time lines for this selection's events. Students' time lines may contain the following points: Wendy talks to Craig's mother on a hotel telephone; Wendy protects Craig from a photographer; Craig calls to Wendy and Rosalind; all four characters eat together in the coffee shop. OL

Teach

R Reading Skill

Reviewing Ask: Do you remember how the four people at the table are connected to each other? If not, you should review the story. After reviewing, explain how these four characters come to be eating a meal together. *(Possible response: Wendy is a fan of Craig the Cat. Rosalind is Wendy's friend. Craig's mother travels with him. Wendy brings Rosalind with her to find Craig at his hotel. When Craig and his mother appear, Wendy speaks to them and shields Craig from a photographer. Craig wants to thank Wendy, so he and his mother invite Wendy and Rosalind to eat with them.)* OL

BQ BIG Question

Ask: What does Wendy mean when she says, "When I read about someone, I get to know him"? *(Responses will vary. Students may say that reading about someone can be like meeting someone in person.)* OL

Assess

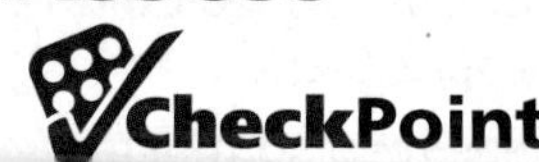

Use the CheckPoint questions provided on Presentation Plus! to review. These questions can be used with interactive response keypads for immediate student feedback.

Objectives

- Monitor comprehension: review, reread text to understand and recall ideas
- Use context clues to clarify word meanings

Assess

Resources for page 72

- Selection Quick Check
- Selection and Unit Assessment
- ExamView Assessment Suite
- Interactive Tutor: Self-Assessment

Students can respond to the *After You Read* items in their Learner's Notebook or on separate sheets of paper.

Answering the

1. Responses will vary but may include that you can get to know a person or others like that person through reading.
2. Craig the Cat is a rock star.
3. Responses will vary. Wendy knows that Craig likes old hotels, that his lucky number is 12, and that he likes coffee shops.

Critical Thinking

4. Wendy decides to wait in the lobby to spot Craig.
5. Wendy has read so much about Craig that she feels as though she knows him.
6. Rosalind's feelings about Craig have changed by the end of the story because she's grateful to be included in the "Clan of the Cat."

After You Read

May I Have Your Autograph?

Answering the

1. After reading the selection, how do you think reading can help you connect with other people?
2. **Recall** Who is Craig the Cat?
   TIP **Right There** You will find the answer in the story.
3. **Recall** What are three things that Wendy knows about Craig the Cat?
   TIP **Right There** You will find the answer in the story.

Critical Thinking

4. **Summarize** What happens after Wendy talks to Craig the Cat's mother on the telephone?
   TIP **Think and Search** You must use information from the story and decide what the important points are.
5. **Interpret** Why does Wendy think of Craig the Cat as a friend?
   TIP **Think and Search** You will find clues in the story, but you must also use the information in your head.
6. **Analyze** Have Rosalind's feelings about Craig the Cat changed by the end of the story? How do you know?
   TIP **Author and Me** You will find clues in the story, but you must also use the information in your head.

Write About Your Reading

Pretend you are one of the characters in "May I Have Your Autograph?" Write a journal entry from that character's point of view. Describe what happens in the hotel and how you feel about the other characters.

Use these tips to help you start your journal entry:

- What does the hotel look like?
- With whom are you?
- Whom do you meet while you are there?
- How do you feel about being in the hotel?
- What happens while you are there?
- What is your favorite part about being in the hotel?
- How do you feel when you leave the hotel?

Objectives (pp. 72–73)
Critical Thinking Interpret and analyze based on what you read and your own experience • Recall and summarize what you read
Reading Monitor comprehension: review, reread
Literature Identify theme in a literary text
Vocabulary Use context clues to clarify word meaning
Writing Write a journal entry
Grammar Use verb tenses

Write About Your Reading

Possible response:
I've come to think of Craig's fans as dangerous to his well-being. They stalk him, and they want to touch him. I really do feel as if I'm a mother cat who's trying to protect her kitten. Today, however, I learned that I've been wrong. They're not all like that. We dined at the hotel tonight with a lovely fan and her little friend. They were respectful, and they really seemed to care about Craig. Even mother cats have something to learn, I guess.

Skills Review

Key Reading Skill: Reviewing

7. How did reviewing the characters and events help you better understand the story? List some important things you learned about the characters and events when you reviewed.

Literary Element: Theme

8. What do you think the theme of this story is?
9. Does the theme of the story have anything to do with the Big Question, "Why Do We Read?" Explain.

Reviewing Skills: Previewing

10. How does the title tell you what the story is about? Who would give his or her autograph to someone? Whom would you ask for an autograph?

Vocabulary Check

Choose the best word to complete each sentence.

triumphant receptive accomplish entitled

11. Rosalind doesn't think Wendy will ___ her goal and get Craig's autograph.
12. Wendy hopes Craig will be ___ to meeting them.
13. Wendy felt ___ when she reached her goal.
14. Rosalind thinks Wendy is ___ to keep Craig's autograph private.
15. **English Language Coach** Read the paragraph below. Explain how you might clarify the meaning of *expert.* What clues does the text give? Write two words or phrases from the paragraph that help clarify the word *expert.*

"I'm an expert on you," she says. "I know you like fancy, old hotels, and this is the oldest and the fanciest in town. I know your lucky number is twelve, so I figured you'd stay on the twelfth floor in room 1212."

Grammar Link: More Verb Tenses

The **present perfect tense** is used to show actions that began in the past and continue into the present.

- Al **has lived** in Elmtown for three years. (Al lived in Elmtown three years ago and still lives there.)

The **present progressive tense** is used to show actions and states of being that (1) are happening, or in progress, at the moment of speaking or writing and (2) actions or states of being that will occur in the future.

- Chang **is listening** to his favorite CD. (The action of listening is in progress.)
- Lucy and Chang **are going** to a concert tonight. (Lucy and Chang will go to a concert this evening.)

Grammar Practice

Copy the sentences below on a separate piece of paper. Underline the verb phrase in each sentence. Then tell whether the tense is present perfect or present progressive.

16. You are doing very well.
17. I am watching the baseball game.
18. Tomorrow we are playing a double header.
19. I have been a baseball fan for a long time.

Writing Application Look at the journal entry you wrote. Did you use any verb phrases? Underline any helping verbs you used. Circle the main verbs.

Web Activities For eFlashcards, Selection Quick Checks, and other Web activities, go to www.glencoe.com.

Skills Review

Key Reading Skill: Reviewing

7. Responses will vary. Students may note that their reviews helped them better define each character's role in the story.

Literary Element: Theme

8. Possible response: When you think of someone as a real person, you can see through the image they present.
9. Possible response: Yes. Reading helped Wendy get close to Craig and see through his rock star image.

Reviewing Skills: Previewing

10. Possible response: The title suggests that the story will be about getting a celebrity's signature.

Vocabulary Check

11. accomplish
12. receptive
13. triumphant
14. entitled
15. Students may say that the words *I know* helped them clarify the word *expert.*

Close

Ask students to summarize what they have learned from the story to answer the Big Question.

Grammar Link: More Verb Tenses

Grammar Practice

16. You are doing very well. **present progressive**
17. I am watching the baseball game. **present progressive**
18. Tomorrow we are playing a double header. **present progressive**
19. I have been a baseball fan for a long time. **present perfect**

Focus

BELLRINGER Options

Daily Language Practice Transparency

Focus Activity Say: Think about some movie previews that you have seen. Discuss how they helped you decide whether to see the movie.

Teach

W Writing

Main Idea Say: A summary must include the main idea of the original selection. Highlight the main idea in your draft. Then exchange drafts with a partner. Ask your partner if he or she agrees with your choice. If your partner does not agree, you may want to revise your main idea sentence. OL

Resources for page 74

- Use the Writing Workshop Graphic Organizer BLM in the Unit 1 Resource Booklet.
- Use the Grammar and Writing Workshop Transparencies, Unit 1.

Summary

Revising, Editing, and Presenting

ASSIGNMENT Write a summary

Purpose: To keep track of main ideas and important information

Audience: You, your teacher, and some classmates

In Writing Workshop Part 1, you started writing a summary about a selection from the beginning of the unit. By now, it's been a while since you read "Flash Flood," "Paddling Dicey Waters," or "Seventh Grade." Can you remember what it is about? If you answered *no,* that's O.K.! To refresh your memory, go back and read the summary you drafted in your Learner's Notebook.

What do you think of your draft? In this workshop, you'll work on a few skills to make your summary better. Also, you'll keep a copy of it in a writing portfolio so that you and your teacher can evaluate your writing progress over time.

Revising Rubric

Your revised summary should have

- a main idea stated in your own words
- important details from the selection
- no minor details or unrelated information
- a correctly punctuated quotation
- coherent paragraphs

See page 76 for a model of a summary.

Revising

Make It Better

You're off to a good start with a draft of a summary! Now make it better!

Check for Main Idea

W

Read your summary again. As you read, ask yourself these questions.

- Have I included the author's main idea?
- Have I included the most important details?
- Have I left out all minor details?

If you answered *no* to one or more of these questions, go back and add or remove the information.

Add a Quotation

A good way to liven up a summary and give more information about the main idea is to add a quotation from the original text. Pick a sentence that states an important detail. Copy it into your summary exactly as it appears in the original. Make sure to put quotation marks at the beginning and the end. You may choose to replace a sentence you wrote with the quotation. Or you may add the quotation. See the model on page 76 for an example.

Then check your quotation carefully. Ask yourself

- Did I pick an important and useful quotation?
- Did I copy the quote in my summary exactly as it appears in the original?
- Did I use quotation marks correctly?

Objectives (pp. 74–77)
Writing Revise a draft to include: main ideas and supporting details, quotation, transitions, focus • Compare summary to original • Edit for use of Standard English grammar, usage, and mechanics • Present writing
Listening, Speaking, and Viewing Give oral directions • Follow multistep directions • Confirm understanding

Additional Support

Differentiated Instruction

Summary Checklists Many students learn more easily when information is arranged in a visual format. Have small groups of students create posters that include a checklist of questions like these:

- Have I included the author's main idea?
- Did I choose the most important details?
- Does my summary include a quotation?
- Did I choose an important and useful quotation?

Have students share their posters with the class. OL

Teach

More About the Author

Share Jane Yolen's advice with students who are interested in writing careers: "I have two pieces of advice for young people interested in writing: read and write. Read and read and read. It's the only way you'll discover what great stories have been told and what stories you want to tell better." Yolen loved to read as a child, and she wrote her first two books before she started high school. One was a novel set in the Old West, and the other was a nonfiction book about pirates.

V Vocabulary

Sentence Set **Say:** One way to learn and remember the vocabulary words is to write sentences. For each vocabulary word, write a sentence that includes an example of the vocabulary word. **OL** Make the three sentences relate to one another in some way. **AL**

Before You Read

Suzy and Leah

Jane Yolen

Meet the Author

Jane Yolen has written for children, young adults, and adults. Her books include made-up stories, stories about real people and events, and poems. She says she looks at writing as a way to turn her "joy and sadness into tales for the people." For more about Jane Yolen, see page R7 of the Author Files.

Author Search For more about Jane Yolen, go to www.glencoe.com.

Objectives (pp. 80–91)
Reading Identify text structure: sequence
Literature Identify theme in a literary text
Vocabulary Use context clues: example

Vocabulary Preview

refugee (REF yoo jee) *n.* a person who flees for safety, especially because of war or natural disaster **(p. 82)** *The refugee carried her few possessions in a small suitcase.*

V **swarmed** (swormd) *v.* moved in a large group; form of the verb *swarm* **(p. 82)** *The crowd swarmed to the gate.*

permanent (PUR muh nunt) *adj.* lasting **(p. 88)** *The refugees needed a permanent home.*

On a separate sheet of paper, write two sentences using two vocabulary words in each sentence. Underline the vocabulary words you used.

English Language Coach

Context Clues Unfamiliar words are sometimes made clear by an example. Words that point out "example clues" are *like, such as, for instance,* and *for example.*

Leah wore an old pinafore, which is *like* the jumpers girls wear today. The Jewish refugees spoke Yiddish and other languages, *such as* Russian and German.

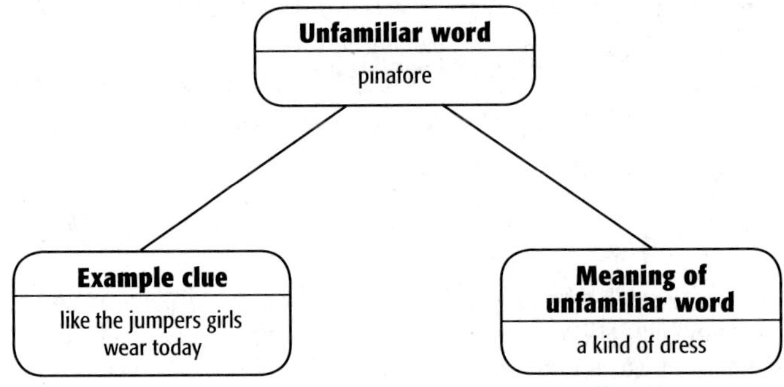

As you read "Suzy and Leah," watch for signal words that point out example clues.

Additional Support

Author Search To expand students' appreciation of Jane Yolen, have them access the Web site for additional information and resources.

Literature Focus Lesson

Diaries and Personal Letters "Suzy and Leah" is structured entirely in the form of diary entries and personal letters. Readers must rely on the details provided in the letters to get a sense of the narrators and characters. Encourage students to find books structured as diary entries or letters at the library—*The Diary of Anne Frank* might be a good starting point. Students can share what they read with the rest of the class and discuss how reading diary entries and personal letters affects their reading experience. **OL**

Why Is It Important? If you ever followed a written set of directions, you followed the steps in a process. When writers want to show how something works or should be done, they must explain the steps in order. Sometimes directions are clearly numbered, sometimes not. Either way, knowing how a text is structured will help you find your way as you read. It also makes it easier to locate important ideas and recall them later.

Literature Online

Study Central Visit www.glencoe.com and click on Study Central to review understanding text structure.

How Do I Do It? It helps to figure out at the beginning whether you are reading about a process. A set of directions is always about a process. An explanation of how something works is also often a process. But you can also skim the selection for words that show cause and effect. The chart below shows some of those words.

Transitions Between Steps in a Process	Cause and Effect
first, next, last, then, later, finally, before, during, after, second, third, now, when, meanwhile, immediately	so, so that, because, since, as a result, therefore, for this reason, for the following reasons, cause, if . . . then, when

R

Here's what one student discovered about the text structure of "Zipper," one of the pieces you're about to read.

The picture tells me that this is about how a zipper works. So if the text is about a process, it could be showing cause and effect. What signal words can I find? There's "when." But it can signal either cause and effect or sequence. Now I see "so that." That tells me the writer is using cause and effect.

Practice It!

Look over "Pencil Sharpener" on page 98. Does this selection explain how to do something or how something works? In your Learner's Notebook, make a list of words and phrases that are clues to the text structure. Refer to the chart above as you look for them.

Use It!

As you read these selections, write down words that signal

- transitions between steps in a process
- cause and effect

Then explain what the signal words tell you about the text.

Reading in the Real World

College Students who are planning to further their educations should learn effective note-taking strategies. As students work through Reading Workshop 4, have them identify whether a text is organized by sequence, process, or cause and effect. Explain that there is a graphic organizer that works best for each kind of text structure. Using the best kind of organizer can help a reader comprehend the text. AL

Teach

Literature Online

Study Central Have students access the Web site to review understanding text structure and to complete a related activity.

R Reading Skill

Understanding Text Structure **Say:** Listen to the following two paragraphs and decide how each is organized.

First, Kim fills the electric kettle with water. Next, she sets the kettle on its base and turns the switch to "on." Then, she chooses two mugs and places one tea bag in each. *(steps in a process)*

Electric kettles boil water quickly. If you have an unexpected guest, you can quickly place a full kettle on its base, plug in the base, and switch the kettle on. Since the electricity soon heats up the base, the water can boil in just five minutes. *(cause and effect)* OL

Resources for page 79

Use Reading Skills Transparency in *Read Aloud, Think Aloud,* Unit 1, to help students practice understanding text structure.

Objectives

- Identify text structure: steps in a process

Focus

BELLRINGER Options

Daily Language Practice Transparency

Focus Activity Say: Have you ever taken something apart to find out how it worked? Explain what happened. If you have not taken anything apart, what item would you like to see the inside of? *(Responses will vary.)*

Teach

R Reading Skill

Understanding Text Structure Ask: How might studying the way a writer "built" a written work help you understand the work? *(Possible response: When you know the way a selection is built, or the structure of a selection, you know what is said and where it is said.)*

V Vocabulary

Academic Vocabulary Say: Look at the word *process* at the bottom of page 78. What processes do you use in everyday life? *(Responses will vary. Students may say that they use processes to cook or to complete homework.)* OL

READING WORKSHOP 4

Skills Focus

You will practice using the following skills when you read these selections:

- "Suzy and Leah," p. 82
- from *How Things Work,* p. 96

Reading

- Understanding text structure
- Recognizing steps in a process

Informational Text

- Using text features to locate, recall, and understand information

Vocabulary

- Clarifying word meanings
- Academic Vocabulary: *process*

Writing/Grammar

- Identifying and using the principal parts of verbs
- Using irregular verbs

Objectives (pp. 78–79)
Reading Identify text structure: steps in a process

Skill Lesson

Understanding Text Structure

Learn It!

What Is It? When a house is being built, it's easy to see the structure. That's the frame to which everything is attached—floors, doors, windows. Writing also has a structure that holds it together. Recognizing the structure of a piece of writing helps you understand it.

R A story's structure is usually the order in which things happen, the "sequence of events." When things *must* happen in a certain order, the events are called a **process**. One thing may cause the next to happen, or it may make it possible or easier for the next to happen.

"Refresh our memory. What was the problem with your car?"

Analyzing Cartoons These mechanics now have two processes to deal with. What are they?

Academic Vocabulary

V **process** (PRAW ses) *n.* a series of actions or steps to follow in doing or making something

Additional Support

Differentiated Instruction

Reading Cartoons After students have read the quotation at the bottom of the cartoon, ask them to describe what is going on in the picture. They should recognize that a car has been totally broken apart. The mechanic is asking the customer what was wrong with the car. In addition to needing to fix the original problem, the mechanics now have to figure out a process to reassemble the car. Have students who know the parts of a car suggest a process, or order, that the mechanics should use to put the car back together. Some of the parts include an engine, a transmission, doors, a steering wheel, tires, and seats. BL

Workshop Resources

Pacing (Days) Standard	Block	Lesson	Student Materials	Teacher Resources
1		Key Skill Lesson: Understanding Text Structure	Key Reading Skills Practice English Language Coach	Bellringer Options Transparencies Read Aloud, Think Aloud Transparencies Presentation Plus!
2		"Suzy and Leah"	Literary Analysis Transparencies Glencoe Online Selection Vocabulary Development Academic Vocabulary Development English Language Coach Active Reading Graphic Organizer Literary Analysis StudentWorks Plus Online Student Edition Literature Classics Selection and Unit Assessments	Literary and Text Analysis Transparencies Puzzlemaker Skill Level Up! BookLink 3 Assessment by Learning Objective (Diagnostic and Formative) Interactive Tutor Self-Assessment TeacherWorks Plus
2		From *How Things Work*	Glencoe Online Selection Vocabulary Development Academic Vocabulary Development English Language Coach Active Reading Graphic Organizer Literary Analysis StudentWorks Plus Online Student Edition Literature Classics Selection and Unit Assessments	Literary and Text Analysis Transparencies Puzzlemaker Skill Level Up! BookLink 3 Assessment by Learning Objective (Diagnostic and Formative) Interactive Tutor Self-Assessment TeacherWorks Plus

Keys for Unit Resource

- Blackline Master
- Workbook
- Supplemental Text
- CD-ROM
- DVD
- Transparency
- Web-based
- Fast Files

Level Appropriate Code

AS = Activities for all students
AL = Activities for students working above grade level
OL = Activities for students working at grade level
BL = Activities for students working below grade level
EL = Activities for English language learners

READING WORKSHOP 4

Understanding Text Structure

UNIT 1

Objectives covered in this workshop:
- Use sequence to locate, recall, and understand events in a story
- Use point of view to understand and interpret reading
- Clarify word meanings

Understanding Text Structure

Why Is It Important?

- Informational texts have common structures. Understanding these structures helps students predict how the author will present information.
- Text structures provide readers with clues about information and where to find it.
- Text structures are conventions that writers use to help readers. As such, they are conventions that students need to learn to become effective writers.

How to Help Students Get It

- Focus on some common text structures and share the ways that these text structures help readers predict the information presented in a text.
- Discuss the difference between a problem and solution text structure and a compare and contrast structure (as an example). Ask students to consider how understanding text structure might help them with their comprehension of selections and with setting purposes for reading.

Reading to Answer the Big Question

Suzy and Leah

This story takes the form of alternating journal entries written by two girls with very different viewpoints. One is an American citizen and the other a Jewish girl who recently arrived from a concentration camp in Germany. Through reading each other's journal entries, Leah and Suzy develop a better understanding of each other.

From *How Things Work*

Two everyday objects, the zipper and the pencil sharpener, are broken down into easy-to-understand units. Large graphics with numerous labels are used to supplement the text. The selection will show students yet another reason why people read.

Listening, Speaking, and Viewing

Giving and Following Directions

Giving and following directions is an important task that we do all the time.

Analyzing Cartoons Directions are important. Did you ever try to follow badly written directions? Or skip a step because you "knew how to do it"?

WHAT A RIP-OFF! THEY SAY IF YOU CONNECT THESE DOTS YOU GET A PICTURE, BUT LOOK! I DID IT AND IT'S JUST A BIG MESS!

I THINK YOU'RE SUPPOSED TO CONNECT THEM IN THE ORDER THAT THEY'RE NUMBERED.

OH.

EVERYTHING'S GOTTA HAVE RULES, RULES, RULES!

What Is It?

Directions explain how to complete a process or task. Some directions are simple, like how to make a peanut butter and jelly sandwich. Others, like how to change a car's engine or design a Web site, are more difficult.

Why Is It Important?

We follow directions–from teachers, parents, coaches, friends, and others–every day. Following directions teaches us how to do new things and how to take care of ourselves. Sometimes, it's our responsibility to give directions, too. **LSV1**

How Do I Do It?

Use these tips when giving directions.

- Divide the process you want to explain into simple steps.
- Make sure you give each step of the process in the right order. For example, don't instruct someone to put toothpaste on their toothbrush after they've already been told to start brushing!
- Don't include extra details that could confuse the person receiving the directions.
- Draw pictures or maps that could illustrate an especially tricky step.
- Ask your listeners if they have any questions.
- Speak slowly and clearly.

Use these tips when following directions.

- Write notes or key words to help you remember the process later on.
- After you hear each step, silently repeat it to yourself.
- Ask the person giving directions to repeat any steps that don't make sense.
- Make sure you understand each step.

Think It Over Think of an activity that you do a lot and could explain to someone else. Here are some possible ideas to get you started:

- Making a bowl of cereal
- Throwing a football
- Getting from your house to school in the morning
- Sending an e-mail

Once you have chosen an activity, write the directions, or steps, on a piece of paper. Read them in order and make sure you didn't forget any. A step that seems easy to you could be really hard for someone else to understand!

LSV2 **Try It Out** With a partner, take turns listening to and giving directions. When it's your turn to listen, pay attention and ask questions if you get confused. When it's your turn to speak, give your directions slowly. Speak clearly. If your partner seems confused, try to simplify the steps.

Differentiated Instruction

Creating Paper Cubes Distribute sheets of paper, scissors, and tape. Tell students to use these supplies to make a paper cube, box, crane, or some other three-dimensional item. Offer no instructions. Inform students that when they have finished, they will need to write a set of directions explaining how to make the item. Have each student exchange directions with a partner, who will follow the instructions and try to make the same item. **BL**

Teach

LSV1 Listening, Speaking, and Viewing

Following Directions **Ask:** How can following directions help you in school? In life? *(Answers may include: Following directions will help you get good grades in school and get to where you want to be in life.)* **OL**

LSV2 Listening, Speaking, and Viewing

Following Directions Have students exchange the directions they wrote with partners. Challenge partners to follow each other's directions to reproduce the steps in the activity. **OL**

Assess/Close

Tell students that just as directions must be clear and easy to follow, so must any summaries they write. As a class, make a list of ways writing summaries and writing directions are similar; then make a list showing how writing summaries and writing directions are different. (Possible responses: Alike—both must be clear and easy to follow; different—more details are needed when writing directions than when writing summaries.)

Objectives

- Follow multistep directions
- State oral directions for tasks
- Confirm understanding

Teach

W1 Writing

Main Idea Ask: Does the opening sentence capture the main idea of "Teaching Nepalis to Read, Plant, and Vote"? *(Most students will agree that it does.)* Why is stating the main idea in the opening sentence a good way to begin a summary? *(It tells what the selection is about and sets the stage for what readers will find in the selection.)* OL

W2 Writing

Transitions Ask: How does the writer use transitional words to move readers effectively from paragraph to paragraph and from idea to idea? *(Possible response: The writer uses transitions such as "Years later" and "before" to show the correct order of events.)* OL

Literature Online

Writing Models Have students access the Web site for an additional and interactive Writing Workshop-based student model.

Active Writing Model

The writer begins the summary by stating the main idea in his or her own words. W1

This sentence tells an important detail. It introduces one of the subjects of the article and tells something important about education in Nepal.

The transition *before* connects the ideas from the previous paragraph to the ideas in this paragraph. W2

These important details explain how Dinesh and Ratna helped improve the people's living conditions. Notice that the writer left out minor details about why goats and orange trees are fit for the mountainous region.

The writer uses a quotation to make the writing more lively and interesting. Correctly used quotation marks clearly show which words came from the article.

Writer's Model

Summary of "Teaching Nepalis to Read, Plant, and Vote"
by Lesley Reed

Bishnu, his son Dinesh, and Dinesh's wife Ratna have spent their lives helping poor Nepalis receive education. When Bishnu was a child in Nepal, it was against the law to go to school. Bishnu ran away from his village anyway to attend the only school in Nepal.

Years later, Bishnu brought a teacher from India to teach his children. As a result, he went to jail for three months. Then, in 1951, a new government took over and made it legal to go to school.

Bishnu's son Dinesh went to college and then traveled around Nepal. He saw that many Nepalis still didn't have schools. He wanted to help, so he and his wife Ratna started the Non-Formal Education Services Center to educate poor Nepalis.

But before they could help the villagers learn to read and write, Dinesh and Ratna had to do something about the people's poverty. They bought goats for the poorest families and planted hundreds of orange trees in the area. The villagers used the money from the goats and the orange trees to send their children to school, buy land, and build better houses.

Ratna started her own organization, called HANDS, to help the women and children in another village. HANDS built a health center and taught women and girls important skills, like farming and sewing.

Many students in the poorer areas of Nepal never finish their education. "The classrooms are tiny, dark, and cold," Dinesh says. Also, there are not enough school supplies, and children must spend a lot of time helping their parents. Dinesh and Ratna are proud that they have spent their lives trying to change these conditions.

Additional Support

Reading in the Real World

College Tell students that as they continue their education they will be reading summaries for a variety of reasons. Discuss the following examples with students, and then ask them to suggest other ways in which they might use summaries.

- Article Research: Summaries of articles can be found on the Internet, in encyclopedias, and in periodical indexes. Students can use these summaries to determine whether specific articles will be useful to them.
- Scientific Abstracts: Scientific abstracts summarize research and experiments. OL

Check for Coherence

When all of the sentences in a paragraph or all of the paragraphs in a composition fit together, the writing is **coherent.** It makes sense.

Follow these guidelines to improve the coherence of your summary.

- Organize your ideas in a pattern. Use chronological, or time order, to tell events in the order they happened. Use order of importance to tell details in order from the most to the least important or the reverse.
- Use linking words and phrases, called **transitions,** to help show how ideas are related. See page R36 for more on how to use transitions. W

To show time order: after, at the beginning, finally, later, soon, yesterday

To show order of importance: above all, best of all, most important

- Be sure that the ideas are all focused on the point. Unrelated information and opinions do not belong in your summary.

Literature Online

Writing Models For models and other writing activities, go to www.glencoe.com.

Compare Your Summary with the Original

Before you say your summary is finished, compare it to the original. As you compare, ask yourself the following questions.

- Have I created a shorter version of the original?
- Have I kept the author's ideas the same?
- Have I clearly told what the selection is about?

Editing

Finish It Up

Now put the finishing touches on your writing. Read your summary one sentence at a time and use the **Editing Checklist** to help you spot errors. Use the proofreading symbols on page R74 to mark needed corrections.

Editing Checklist

- ☑ Verb tenses are correct.
- ☑ Irregular verb forms are correct.
- ☑ Quotations are in quotation marks.
- ☑ All words are spelled correctly.

Writing Tip

Spelling Check your summary for misspelled words. If you use a computer, it may not catch some mistakes because a misspelled word might be the *correct* spelling of another word. Some common words computers don't always catch are *it's/its, on/one, begin/being,* and *ion/in.*

Presenting

Show It Off

Meet with a small group and take turns reading your summaries aloud. Listen for the main idea and important details of your classmates' summaries. Also notice any extra information.

Writing Tip

Handwriting If you are copying the final version of your summary by hand, be sure to take your time and print neatly. Your summary isn't helpful if it's not readable!

Teach

W Writing

Coherence Say: Coherent writing is easy for readers to understand. For a summary to be coherent, the sentences must follow one another in an order that makes sense.

Read the following passages aloud:

A. Sharon ate the hamburger and put ketchup and mustard on it. She planned on going to this picnic for a long time. She went swimming in the pool and made new friends. She played games. She had a good time and was excited. Sharon was 13.

B. Thirteen-year-old Sharon had planned all year on going to the company picnic with her dad. She was excited to be going. At the picnic, she had a hamburger with ketchup and mustard. She played games, swam in the pool, and made new friends. She had a good time.

Ask: Which passage is more coherent? *(Paragraph B)* Discuss why the second passage is more coherent. *(It is written in a clear and logical order, and it contains all of the important details.)* OL

Differentiated Instruction

A Picture Is Worth a Thousand Words Students who are artistically inclined may enjoy drawing pictures to illustrate their summaries. Tell students that their drawings should capture the main idea of the selection and show an important character or event. When students have completed their work, post the drawings and summaries on the class bulletin board. OL

Objectives

- Revise a draft to include: main ideas and supporting details, quotations, transitions, focus
- Compare summary to original
- Edit for use of Standard English grammar, usage, and mechanics
- Present writing

Skills Preview

Key Reading Skill: Understanding Text Structure

When you tell a story, where do you start? In the middle? At the end? No way! You start at the beginning and tell things in the order they happened. In other words, you tell your story in chronological, or time, order. Chronological order is a type of sequence—and sequence is a type of text structure. If a story that's written in chronological order contains a detail that is *out* of order, the writer uses signal words, such as "before this," to make the order of events clear.

Write to Learn In your Learner's Notebook, write about a good friend. Tell how you met each other, and why you are friends now.

Literary Element: Theme

Recognizing the theme of a story is often the most important part of understanding the story. "Suzy and Leah" is about two girls from very different backgrounds. But what does the story say about these girls besides just giving facts and information? What does it say about the relationship between them? If by the end of the story you can answer these questions, you will probably know what the theme is.

Use these tips to help you find the theme of "Suzy and Leah":

- Think about what has happened in each girl's life before the story begins.
  What is important to each girl? What kinds of things has each of them experienced?
- Notice how each girl feels about the other.
  Could these girls become friends?

L

Interactive Literary Elements Handbook
To review or learn more about the literary elements, go to www.glencoe.com.

Get Ready to Read

Connect to the Reading

Think about your friends. How did you get to know them? What did you think of each other when you first met? Do you see each other differently now that you're good friends? If so, how? C

Build Background

This story is about two girls from different backgrounds who meet after World War II. Suzy has always lived in upstate New York. Leah was born in Europe but now lives in a refugee camp in Suzy's town. During the war, the Nazis put Leah and her family in a concentration camp.

- Adolf Hitler, the Nazi leader, ruled Germany from 1933 to 1945.
- Jews and other people the Nazis considered "undesirable" were sent to concentration camps. The prisoners were overworked, starved, and tortured. Six million Jews were put to death.
- World War II began in 1939 to stop Hitler. The war was between the Allied Powers (Great Britain, France, the United States) and the Axis powers (Germany, Japan, and Italy).
- After more than five years, the Allied Powers won the war. Hitler died in 1945, and the death camps were finally closed.

Set Purposes for Reading

BIG Question Read the story "Suzy and Leah" to find out what two girls think and feel about each other and themselves.

Set Your Own Purpose What else would you like to learn from the story to help you answer the Big Question? Write your purpose on the "Suzy and Leah" page of Foldable 1.

Keep Moving

Use these skills as you read the following selection.

Reading in the Real World

Citizenship On the board in the classroom, post a large map of the world. Highlight Germany and the United States. Take students to the library and ask them to skim source materials for information about Nazi Germany and the concentration camps, as well as information about Judaism. Provide students with two focus questions: What might Leah's experience in Germany have been like? Why is Leah concerned about kosher food? Tell students to record answers to these questions on note cards. Use the note cards to build a bridge between Germany and the United States on the world map. AL

Teach

L Literary Element

Theme **Say:** Suzy lives in a comfortable home with her family, while Leah is a refugee whose family was murdered. How do you think the girls will relate to one another? *(Possible response: It sounds like the girls have had very different experiences. I don't think they'll become friends immediately.)* BL

C Critical Thinking

Application **Say:** Getting to know someone is a process. Describe a time when your first impression of a person changed over time. *(Responses will vary.)* OL

Use the CheckPoint questions provided on Presentation Plus! to check for understanding of text structure. These questions can be used with interactive response keypads for immediate student feedback.

Objectives
- Identify text structure: sequence
- Identify theme in a literary text
- Use context clues: example

Teach

R1 Reading Skill

Review Previewing Ask: How does previewing the photos in this selection help you prepare to read it? *(Students may say that identifying the photos gives them clues about the setting and events in the selection.)* How do the photos help you predict that even though the selection is fiction, it will be based on real events? *(Possible response: The photos show real places and events.)* OL

R2 Reading Skill

Understanding Text Structure Ask: Are the letter dates helpful in reconstructing the time line of events? Explain. *(Possible responses: The letter dates are not helpful in reconstructing the time line of events because several events take place before the letter writing begins; the letter dates are helpful because they tell me when the writers recorded certain events.)* OL

Suzy and Leah 1

by Jane Yolen

August 5, 1944 2

Dear Diary,

Today I walked past *that* place, the one that was in the newspaper, the one all the kids have been talking about. Gosh, is it ugly! A line of rickety wooden buildings just like in the army. And a fence lots higher than my head. With barbed wire[1] on top. How can anyone—even a **refugee**—live there?

I took two candy bars along, just like everyone said I should. When I held them up, all those kids just **swarmed** over to the fence, grabbing. Like in a zoo. Except for this one girl, with two dark braids and bangs nearly covering her eyes. She was just standing to one side, staring at me. It was so creepy. After a minute I looked away. When I looked back, she was gone. I mean gone. Disappeared as if she'd never been.

Suzy

1. ***Barbed wire*** is twisted wire with sharp points attached to it. It is used for fences.

Vocabulary

refugee (REF yoo jee) *n.* a person who flees for safety, especially because of war or natural disaster

swarmed (swormd) *v.* moved in a large group

Practice the Skills

1 Reviewing Skills

R1 **Previewing** Preview the story to get an idea of what you are going to read about. Read the title and first few sentences of the story. Skim the text. Look at the photos. What do you find out about the story by previewing it?

2 Key Reading Skill

R2 **Understanding Text Structure** The dates of the diary entries give information about the overall sequence of events. But dates, all by themselves, may not tell you all you need to know about the order of things.

Additional Support

Readability Scores

Dale-Chall: 4.2

DRP: 44

Lexile: 550

Differentiated Instruction

Time Lines Have students begin time lines to chart the action in this selection. First, they should note the action of each diary entry or letter. Then, they can write a related quote from the text. Finally, they can include pictures to represent the setting. Encourage students to add to their time lines and then use them as review aids. BL

Allow students to expand on details in the story and include visual elements not mentioned in the story as long as these imagined elements are consistent with what the text does state. For example, if students want to imagine what Suzy's mother looks like, they can add appropriate images to their time lines. OL

August 5, 1944

My dear Mutti,[2]

I have but a single piece of paper to write on. And a broken pencil. But I will write small so I can tell all. I address it to you, *Mutti,* though you are gone from me forever. I write in English, to learn better, because I want to make myself be understood. **3**

Today another girl came. With more sweets. A girl with yellow hair and a false smile. Yonni and Zipporah and Ruth, my friends, all grabbed for the sweets. Like wild animals. Like . . . like prisoners. But we are not wild animals. And we are no longer prisoners. Even though we are still penned in.

I stared at the yellow-haired girl until she was forced to look down. Then I walked away. When I turned to look back, she was gone.

Disappeared. As if she had never been.

Leah

September 2, 1944

Dear Diary,

I brought the refugee kids oranges today. Can you believe it—they didn't know you're supposed to peel oranges first. One boy tried to eat one like an apple. He made an awful face, but then he ate it anyway. I showed them how to peel oranges with the second one. After I stopped laughing.

Mom says they are going to be coming to school. Of course they'll have to be cleaned up first. Ugh. My hand still feels itchy from where one little boy grabbed it in his. I wonder if he had bugs.

Suzy

September 2, 1944

My dear Mutti,

R Today we got cereal in a box. At first I did not know what it was. Before the war we ate such lovely porridge[3] with milk straight from our cows. And eggs fresh from the hen's nest, though you know how I hated that nasty old chicken. How often she pecked me! In the German camp, it was potato

2. ***Mutti*** (MOO tee) is a way of saying "Mommy" in German.
3. ***Porridge*** (POR ij) is hot cereal.

Practice the Skills

3 Literary Element

Theme Each girl has a first impression of the other girl. What is that impression based on? How does each girl react to the other? Do you think this might be a clue to what the theme of the story is?

Teach

E Text Element

Review Photographs
Ask: Why are photos especially useful in a story that is written in the form of letters? *(Possible response: Background information is usually not included in letters, so photos help readers better understand character, plot, and setting information.)* **OL**

R Reading Skill

Understanding Text Structure Ask: Where does Leah eat porridge? Where does she eat cereal from a box? *(Possible response: Leah eats porridge in her home country before the Nazis come to power. She eats cereal years later at the refugee camp in the United States.)* How do you know where Leah is when she eats porridge and where she is when she eats cereal from a box? *(Possible response: The words "before" and "today" help me figure out the sequence of the events.)* **OL** What term can be used to describe when a character in a story or movie remembers something from the past? *(flashback)* **AL**

English Language Coach

Sentence Fragments Students know that sentences contain subjects and predicates and that they should avoid using sentence fragments in writing. However, some writers use sentence fragments for effect. Help students identify the sentence fragments on page 83. Ask students to explain why each example is a fragment. Then, lead students in a discussion about why Yolen has her narrators use each fragment. *(Possible response:* Disappeared. *is a sentence fragment because it lacks a subject. Yolen has Leah write this fragment to emphasize how quickly Suzy left.)* **EL** **BL**

Objectives
- Preview text
- Identify text structure: sequence
- Use text features: photographs

READING WORKSHOP 4

R Reading Skill

Understanding Text Structure **Ask:** What is the date of the first diary entry on page 82? *(August 5, 1944)* How much time has passed between that entry and the ones on this page? *(one month)* BL

C Critical Thinking

Analysis **Ask:** What would you say to Suzy in response to her comments about nothing being worse than "not being able to speak English or understand anything that's going on"? *(Responses will vary.)* EL

Nazi soldiers arrest Jews in Poland in 1943.

soup—with onions when we were lucky, without either onion or potato when we were not. And after, when I was running from the Nazis, it was stale brown bread, if we could find any. But cereal in a box—*that* is something. 4

I will not take a sweet from that yellow-haired girl, though. She laughed at Yonni. I will not take another orange fruit.

Leah

September 5, 1944

Dear Diary,

So how are those refugee kids going to learn? Our teachers teach in English. This is America, after all.

I wouldn't want to be one of them. Imagine going to school and not being able to speak English or understand anything that's going on. I can't imagine anything worse. C

Suzy

September 5, 1944

My dear Mutti,

The adults of the Americans say we are safe now. And so we must go to their school. But I say no place is safe for us. Did not the Germans say that we were safe in their camps? And there you and baby Natan were killed. 5

And how could we learn in this American school anyway? I have a little English. But Ruth and Zipporah and the others, though they speak Yiddish[4] and Russian and German, they have no English at all. None beyond *thank you* and *please* and *more sweets.* And then there is little Avi. How could he go to this school? He will speak nothing at all. He stopped speaking, they say, when he was hidden away in a cupboard R

4. ***Yiddish*** (YIH dish) is a language spoken by Jews of eastern and central European background. It is based on German and includes words from other languages of that area of Europe. Yiddish is written in Hebrew letters.

Practice the Skills

4 Key Reading Skill

Understanding Text Structure When did Leah eat porridge with fresh milk? When did she try cereal from a box? What signal words tell the order of events here?

5 Key Reading Skill

Understanding Text Structure How much time has passed since Suzy and Leah first saw one another through the fence? (Hint: Look at the dates of the diary entries.)

Additional Support

Differentiated Instruction

Language Debate Explain that Americans are divided over whether their country should be one in which English only is used in government sponsored events, documents, and organizations or whether their country should embrace the many languages of its immigrants.

Invite students to join the debate by discussing the following statements:

- A common language brings people together.
- The ability to speak many languages encourages communication and understanding. AL

by his grandmother who was taken by the Nazis after she swore there was no child in the house. And he was almost three days in that cupboard without food, without water, without words to comfort him. Is English a safer language than German?

There is barbed wire still between us and the world. **C**

Leah

September 14, 1944

Dear Diary,

At least the refugee kids are wearing better clothes now. And they all have shoes. Some of them still had those stripy pajamas on when they arrived in America.

The girls all wore dresses to their first day at school, though. They even had hair bows, gifts from the teachers. Of course I recognized my old blue pinafore.[5] The girl with the dark braids had it on, and Mom hadn't even told me she was giving it away. I wouldn't have minded so much if she had only asked. It doesn't fit me anymore, anyway. **L**

The girl in my old pinafore was the only one without a name tag, so all day long no one knew her name.

Suzy **6**

September 14, 1944

My dear Mutti,

I put on the blue dress for our first day. It fit me well. The color reminded me of your eyes and the blue skies over our farm before the smoke from the burning darkened it. Zipporah braided my hair, but I had no mirror until we got to the school and they showed us the toilets. They call it a bathroom, but there is no bath in it at all, which is strange. I have never been in a school with boys before.

They have placed us all in low grades. Because of our English. I do not care. This way I do not have to see the girl with the yellow hair who smiles so falsely at me.

But they made us wear tags with our names printed on them. That made me afraid. What next? Yellow stars? I tore mine off and threw it behind a bush before we went in.

Leah

5. A ***pinafore*** (PIN uh for) is a dress with a low neck and no sleeves that buttons in the back. It is usually worn with a blouse or as an apron over another dress.

Practice the Skills

6 Literary Element

Theme Often, a problem in a story is a clue to what the theme is. Do you think Suzy has a problem understanding the children in the camp? Why or why not?

Differentiated Instruction

Dramatic Reading Some learners may benefit from listening to the letters and diary entries being read aloud. Have one volunteer read a few of Leah's letters in a row. After listening to the letters, students should write a few sentences describing Leah. Then have another volunteer read Suzy's corresponding diary entries. Students should then write a few sentences describing any new facets of Leah's character that Suzy has revealed. Lead a discussion about how the two different points of view contribute to a full picture of each character. If desired, lengthen the activity by having students write about Suzy's character as well. **OL**

Teach

C Critical Thinking

Analysis Ask: What is the "barbed wire" that Leah refers to? *(Responses will vary. Students may say that the barbed wire is the English language, the American school, or the United States.)* **OL**

L Literary Element

Theme Ask: How does Suzy feel when she sees Leah wearing her blue dress? *(Possible response: Suzy seems to resent the fact that Leah is wearing Suzy's dress.)* How does Leah feel about wearing Suzy's dress? *(Possible responses: Leah seems grateful. Leah is happy because the blue reminds her of her mother's eyes and of the skies over their farm.)* **BL** Suzy shows that she cares about the children in the refugee camp by taking treats to them, so why does she have trouble understanding them? *(Possible response: Suzy has a comfortable life and would not understand the horrible circumstances these children have survived.)* **OL**

Objectives

- Identify text structure: sequence
- Identify theme in a literary text

READING WORKSHOP 4

R Reading Skill

Understanding Text Structure **Say:** The diary entry and letter on this page were written on the same day, and each mentions how refugee students are paired with English-speaking students. How does this text structure help tell the story? *(Possible response: You get two different perspectives on the same events in a day.)* OL

EL Language Coach

Context Clues **Ask:** Where does Leah say she is writing? *(school)* Where do Leah and the other refugees live? *(Possible response: camp)* So, when Leah says "back to the shelter," where does she probably mean? *(Possible response: She probably means the place where she sleeps, where Suzy first visited.)* OL **Say:** Look up the word *shelter* in a dictionary. Which meaning best matches the context of the story? *(a place for providing food and lodging on a temporary or emergency basis)* BL

Practice the Skills

Jewish refugee children from Germany at Liverpool Street Station in London, England, on August 30, 1939.

Analyzing the Photo: How does this photo help you understand how Leah feels?

September 16, 1944

Dear Diary,

Mr. Forest has assigned each of us to a refugee to help them with their English. He gave me the girl with the dark braids, the one without the name tag, the one in my pinafore. Gee, she's as prickly as a porcupine. I asked if I could have a different kid. He said I was the best English student and she already spoke the best English. He wants her to learn as fast as possible so she can help the others. As if she would, Miss Porcupine. R

Her name is Leah. I wish she would wear another dress.

Suzy

September 16, 1944

My dear Mutti,

Now I have a real notebook and a pen. I am writing to you at school now. I cannot take the notebook back to the **shelter**. Someone there will surely borrow it. I will instead keep it here. In the little cupboard each one of us has been given. 7 EL

I wish I had another dress. I wish I had a different student helping me and not the yellow-haired girl.

Leah

7 English Language Coach

Context Clues The word **shelter** may sound familiar to you. But do you know what it means here? Take a look at the words and sentences around *shelter* to see if they clarify its meaning. What clues do you find? How do they help explain the meaning of the word?

Additional Support

Reading in the Real World

Citizenship Have each student survey a family member about a time when he or she did not get along with someone. Have each student ask questions such as the following:

- What about the person or situation did you find difficult?
- Was the problem resolved? Explain.

Then, have each student write a two-paragraph summary of his or her interviews. The first paragraph should tell what the student learned; the next paragraph should share how the problem was resolved. If it was not resolved, the student should suggest ways in which a resolution could be reached. BL

September 20, 1944

Dear Diary,

Can't she ever smile, that Leah? I've brought her candy bars and apples from home. I tried to give her a handkerchief with a yellow flower on it. She wouldn't take any of them.

Her whole name is Leah Shoshana Hershkowitz. At least, that's the way she writes it. When she says it, it sounds all different, low and growly. I laughed when I tried to say it, but she wouldn't laugh with me. What a grouch.

And yesterday, when I took her English paper to correct it, she shrank back against her chair as if I was going to hit her or something. Honestly!

Mom says I should invite her home for dinner soon. We'll have to get her a special pass for that. But I don't know if I want her to come. It's not like she's any fun at all. I wish Mr. Forest would let me trade.

Suzy

September 20, 1944

My dear Mutti,

The girl with the yellow hair is called Suzy Ann McCarthy. It is a silly name. It means nothing. I asked her who she was named for, and she said, "For a book my mom liked." A book! I am named after my great-grandmother on my mother's side, who was an important woman in our village. I am proud to carry on her name. **8** **C**

This Suzy brings many sweets. But I must call them candies now. And a handkerchief. She expects me to be grateful. But how can I be grateful? She treats me like a pet, a pet she does not really like or trust. She wants to feed me like an animal behind bars.

If I write all this down, I will not hold so much anger. I have much anger. And terror besides. *Terror.* It is a new word for me, but an old feeling. One day soon this Suzy and her people will stop being nice to us. They will remember we are not just refugees but Jews, and they will turn on us. Just as the Germans did. Of this I am sure.

Leah

Practice the Skills

8 Literary Element

Theme Do you think Leah has a problem understanding Suzy? Could that be a clue to the theme? **L**

Differentiated Instruction

Writing Dialogue Tell student pairs to imagine that Suzy and Leah are sitting down at a dinner table together, just the two of them. They now have to talk to each other instead of writing. Tell students to write a dialogue between the two girls. Ask students to consider what the girls might accuse each other of; what the breaking point might be that would lead to understanding; and how the girls would end the dinner. Challenge students to use the vocabulary of Reading Workshop 4. Invite students to share their dialogues with the class. **AL**

READING WORKSHOP 4

Teach

C Critical Thinking

Analysis Ask: Why does Leah think that Suzy's name is silly and means nothing? *(Students may say that Leah's name connects her to the family that she has lost. Therefore, she sees her name as more meaningful than Suzy's.)* How does Suzy's name connect her to her family? *(Possible response: Suzy's name is connected to her mother, who chose it based on a character she enjoyed reading about.)* **OL**

L Literary Element

Theme Say: Leah thinks that Suzy is treating her like a pet by bringing her treats. Why does Leah misunderstand Suzy's gesture? *(Possible responses: Leah is not used to people being kind to her. Leah is mistrustful of everyone because of her experiences.)* **OL**

Objectives

- Make inferences
- Identify theme in a literary text
- Use context clues to clarify word meanings

Teach

C1 Critical Thinking

Comprehension Say: Read the first sentence of Suzy's September 30th diary entry. Do you think Suzy is getting to know Leah better? Explain. *(Possible response: Suzy now knows Leah well enough and spends enough time with her to notice that she's speaking better English.)* **BL**

C2 Critical Thinking

Evaluation Say: Think about the times at which people use a person's full name. Why does Suzy say Leah's entire name when she writes about thinking of Leah at the dinner table? *(Responses will vary. Students may say that using Leah's whole name is formal, emphasizing that Suzy still doesn't consider her a friend.)* **OL** **Ask:** What does Suzy's comment about Leah knowing nothing about America show about Suzy? *(Responses will vary. Students may say that Suzy views America as more important than the rest of the world.)* **AL**

September 30, 1944

Dear Diary,

Leah's English is very good now. But she still never smiles. Especially she never smiles at me. It's like she has a **permanent** frown and permanent frown lines between her eyes. It makes her look much older than anyone in our class. Like a little old lady. C1

I wonder if she eats enough. She won't take the candy bars. And she saves the school lunch in her napkin, hiding it away in her pocket. She thinks no one sees her do it, but I do. Does she eat it later? I'm sure they get dinner at the shelter. Mom says they do. Mom also says we have to eat everything on our plates. Sometimes when we're having dinner I think of Leah Shoshana Hershkowitz. 9 C2

Suzy

September 30, 1944

My dear Mutti,

Avi loves the food I bring home from school. What does he know? It is not even kosher.[6] Sometimes they serve ham. But I do not tell Avi. He needs all the food he can get. He is a growing boy.

I, too, am growing fast. Soon I will not fit into the blue dress. I have no other.

Leah

October 9, 1944

Dear Diary,

They skipped Leah up to our grade, her English has gotten so good. Except for some words, like victory, which she pronounces "wick-toe-ree." I try not to laugh, but sometimes I just can't help it!

Leah knows a lot about the world and nothing about America. She thinks New York is right next to Chicago, for goodness sakes! She can't dance at all. She doesn't know the

6. ***Kosher*** (KOH shur) is a Yiddish word meaning "fit or proper to eat according to Jewish law."

Vocabulary

permanent (PUR muh nunt) *adj.* lasting

Practice the Skills

9 Literary Element

Theme Are Suzy's feelings toward Leah changing? Do you think that wondering about someone might be a first step toward understanding the person? Is wondering better than thinking you already know? Might the theme of this story have to do with understanding other people?

Additional Support

Differentiated Instruction

Facial Expression and Body Language Suzy comments that Leah is always frowning. Suzy makes judgments about Leah based on this facial expression. Invite one pair of students to show how Suzy acts in public and in private. Invite another pair to show how Leah acts in public and in private. Ask the class to comment on which facial expressions and body language show the real Suzy and Leah. If it helps students, suggest that they add dialogue from one or more of the diary entries and letters. **BL**

READING WORKSHOP 4

words to any of the top songs. And she's so stuck up, she only talks in class to answer questions. The other refugees aren't like that at all. Why is it only my refugee who's so mean?

Suzy

October 9, 1944

My dear Mutti,

I think of you all the time. I went to Suzy's house because Mr. Forest said they had gone to a great deal of trouble to get a pass for me. I did not want to go so much, my stomach hurt the whole time I was there.

Suzy's *Mutti* was nice, all pink and gold. She wore a dress with pink roses all over it and it reminded me of your dress, the blue one with the asters. You were wearing it when we were put on the train. And the last time I saw you at the camp with Natan. Oh, *Mutti.* I had to **steel** my heart against Suzy's mother. If I love her, I will forget you. And that I must never do. **10** **11**

I brought back food from her house, though, for Avi. I could not eat it myself. You would like the way Avi grows bigger and stronger. And he talks now, but only to me. He says, "More, Leah, please." And he says "light" for the sun. Sometimes when I am really lonely I call him Natan, but only at night after he has fallen asleep.

Leah

Jewish prisoners at the Vittel Concentration Camp in France on September 12, 1944, the day Allied armies freed them.

Analyzing the Photo: What do you think is going through the minds of the people in the photo?

Practice the Skills

10 Literary Element

Theme Why do you think Leah tries not to love Suzy's mother? How might the way Leah acts affect other people's ability to understand her? **L**

11 English Language Coach

Context Clues Of course, you've heard the word **steel** before. But you've probably never heard it used this way. Look for context clues that will help you understand it here. What do you think it means? **EL**

Teach

L Literary Element

Theme Say: Leah is very nervous when she goes to Suzy's house. How might Suzy interpret Leah's behavior? *(Possible response: Leah's behavior might give Suzy one more reason to think Leah is stuck up.)* **OL**

EL Language Coach

Context Clues Say: The author uses the word *steel* in an unusual way. What are some words or phrases that help you figure out what *steel* means in this context? *(my heart; If I love her, I will forget you. And that I must never do.)* If Leah cannot love Suzy's mother, what might *steel* mean in this context? *(Responses will vary. Students may say that it means to stop her heart from feeling love or to be tough and cold like steel.)* **OL** **Say:** Look up the word *steel* in a dictionary. Which meaning best matches the context of the story? *(make hard, tough, or unfeeling)* **EL**

Literature Focus Lesson

Historical Fiction Help students understand that this story is historical fiction. Jane Yolen made up the characters Suzy and Leah based on facts from history. Explain that the picture on this page shows a real group of children from the past. Ask students to select one of the people in the photograph and imagine what his or her life was like in the 1940s.

Tell students to create answers to the following questions for their characters. **BL**

- What is this character's name?
- How old is this character?
- What did this character do yesterday?
- What will this character do today?
- Would this character relate more to Suzy or Leah? Explain.

Objectives

- Make inferences and analyze text
- Identify theme in a literary text
- Use context clues to determine word meanings

Teach

R Reading Skill

Understanding Text Structure Ask: Where is Leah on October 10 through October 12? *(Leah is in the hospital.)* What happened to Leah on October 10? *(Possible response: Leah got appendicitis and had to go into surgery.)* How does Suzy react to Leah's disappearance? *(Responses will vary. Suzy inquires after her. Given the opportunity, Suzy reads Leah's letters.)* **OL**

L Literary Element

Theme Ask: What is Suzy's reaction right after she reads Leah's diary? *(Possible response: Suzy is outraged at some of Leah's comments.)* What is Suzy's reaction after she talks to her mother? *(She feels deep sadness and sympathy for Leah and the other refugees.)* **OL**

12 October 10, 1944

Dear Diary,

Leah was not in school today. When I asked her friend Zipporah, she shrugged. "She is ill in her stomach," she said. "What did she eat at your house?"

I didn't answer "Nothing," though that would have been true. She hid it all in a handkerchief Mom gave her. Mom said, "She eats like a bird.[7] How does she stay alive?"

Suzy

October 11, 1944

Dear Diary,

They've asked me to gather Leah's things from school and bring them to the hospital. She had to have her appendix[8] out and nearly died. She almost didn't tell them she was sick until too late. Why did she do that? I would have been screaming my head off with the pain.

Mom says we have to visit, that I'm Leah's American best friend. Hah! We're going to bring several of my old dresses, but not my green one with the white trim. I don't want her to have it. Even if it doesn't fit me anymore.

Suzy

October 12, 1944

Dear Diary,

I did a terrible thing. I read Leah's diary. I'd kill anyone who did that to me! **13**

At first it made no sense. Who were *Mutti* and Natan, and why were they killed? What were the yellow stars? What does kosher mean? And the way she talked about *me* made me furious. Who did she think she was, little Miss Porcupine? All I did was bring candy and fruit and try to make those poor refugee kids feel at home.

Then, when I asked Mom some questions, carefully, so she wouldn't guess I had read Leah's diary, she explained. She said the Nazis killed people, mothers and children as well as men.

7. When people say someone ***eats like a bird,*** they are saying the person hardly eats anything.
8. The ***appendix*** (uh PEN diks) is a finger-shaped sack found in the belly. If it becomes swollen or infected, it can cause sharp pain and often has to be removed.

Practice the Skills

12 Key Reading Skill

R **Understanding Text Structure** Look at the diary entries on this page. Why are they only made by Suzy? What happened to Leah?

13 Literary Element

L **Theme** Suzy knows that reading Leah's diary is wrong. But does it help her understand Leah better? Do you think the theme might have something to do with not judging someone until you know about that person's experiences?

Additional Support

Reading in the Real World

Career Ask students how many of them have had their appendixes removed. Invite students to tell the class about their experiences. Suggest that students interested in a career in medicine do research to learn more about the appendix: What is the appendix? What does it do? What is wrong with Leah? What are Leah's symptoms? Why is it important to identify appendicitis soon? Why does Leah nearly die? Invite students to report the results of their studies to the class. **AL**

In places called concentration camps. And that all the Jews—people who weren't Christians like us—had to wear yellow stars on their clothes so they could be spotted blocks and blocks away. It was so awful I could hardly believe it, but Mom said it was true.

How was I supposed to know all that? How can Leah stand any of us? How could she live with all that pain?

Suzy

October 12, 1944

My dear Mutti,

Suzy and her mother came to see me in the hospital. They brought me my notebook so now I can write again.

I was so frightened about being sick. I did not tell anyone for a long time, even though it hurt so much. In the German camp, if you were sick and could not do your work, they did not let you live.

But in the middle of the night, I had so much fever, a doctor was sent for. Little Avi found me. He ran to one of the guards. He spoke out loud for the first time. He said, "Please, for Leah. Do not let her go into the dark."

The doctor tells me I nearly died, but they saved me. They have given me much medicines and soon I will eat the food and they will be sure it is kosher, too. And I am alive. This I can hardly believe. *Alive!* **C**

Then Suzy came with her *Mutti,* saying, "I am sorry. I am so sorry. I did not know. I did not understand." Suzy did a bad thing. She read my notebook. But it helped her understand. And then, instead of making an apology, she did a strange thing. She took a red book with a lock out of her pocket and gave it to me. "Read this," she said. "And when you are out of the hospital, I have a green dress with white trim I want you to have. It will be just perfect with your eyes."

I do not know what this trim may be. But I like the idea of a green dress. And I have a new word now, as well. It is this: *diary.*

A new word. A new land. And—it is just possible—a new friend.

Leah **14** ❍

Practice the Skills

14 

BQ How do you think both Suzy and Leah would answer the question "Why would someone read this story?" Write your answer on the "Suzy and Leah" page of Foldable 1. Your response will help you complete the Unit Challenge later.

READING WORKSHOP 4

Teach

BQ 

Ask: How does reading alter the relationship between Suzy and Leah? *(Responses will vary. Students may note that by reading each other's writing, Suzy and Leah learn about each other's true selves.)* **OL**

Why might Suzy and Leah want to share their story? *(Possible response: They might want people to see that understanding someone else is not only possible but rewarding.)* **AS**

C Critical Thinking

Evaluation **Say:** Suzy wonders how Leah can "live with all that pain." After reading Leah's last letter, how do you think Leah will cope with her pain? *(Responses will vary. Students may say that Suzy's friendship will help Leah cope just as her relationship with Avi helps her.)* **OL**

Assess

CheckPoint

Use the CheckPoint questions provided on Presentation Plus! to check for comprehension of the selection. These questions can be used with interactive response keypads for immediate student feedback.

Build Fluency

Reading Letters Tell students to find partners. Then provide student pairs with quiet places to practice reading aloud. Tell one student to take the part of Suzy and the other to take the part of Leah. Tell students to take turns rereading their characters' letters several times until they can smoothly read all the sentences with expression and understanding. If necessary, have partners work with a dictionary to aid with pronunciations and comprehension. After pairs have accomplished fluent reading, consider reading the story aloud as a class with each student taking a turn. **BL**

Objectives

- Make inferences
- Use sequence to understand events in a story
- Identify theme in a literary text

Assess

Resources for page 92

- Selection Quick Check
- Selection and Unit Assessment
- ExamView Assessment Suite
- Interactive Tutor: Self-Assessment

Students can respond to the *After You Read* items in their Learner's Notebook or on separate sheets of paper.

Answering the BIG Question

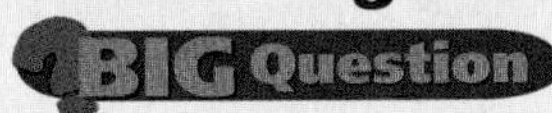

1. Responses will vary. Suzy gives her own diary to Leah.

Critical Thinking

2. Leah is afraid to wear a name tag because it reminds her of the yellow star.
3. Responses will vary. Students may say that Suzy doesn't want to give Leah the dress because Leah does not appreciate the other things Suzy has given her.
4. Responses will vary. Students may say that although it is wrong to invade someone's privacy, this invasion helps Suzy understand Leah.
5. Responses will vary. Students may say that Leah has trust issues as a result of her experiences in Nazi Germany.
6. Responses will vary. Most students will say that the story is believable because it is based on historical fact.

After You Read

Suzy and Leah

Answering the BIG Question

1. **Summarize** Tell what Suzy does after reading Leah's diary.
   TIP **Right There** You will find this information in the story.

Critical Thinking

2. **Infer** Why is Leah afraid to wear a name tag?
   TIP **Author and Me** You will find clues in the story, but you must also use the information in your head.
3. **Infer** At first, Suzy doesn't want to give up her green dress. Why?
   TIP **Author and Me** Answer from your own experiences.
4. **Evaluate** Is Suzy wrong to read Leah's diary?
   TIP **On My Own** Answer from your own experiences.
5. **Infer** Leah says that "it is just possible" that she has a new friend. Why do you think she is not quite sure?
   TIP **Author and Me** You will find clues in the story, but you must also use the information in your head.
6. **Evaluate** Do you think "Suzy and Leah" is a believable story? Explain why or why not.
   TIP **On My Own** Answer from your own experiences.

Objectives (pp. 92–93)
Reading Identify text structure: sequence
Literature Identify theme in a literary text
Vocabulary Use context clues: example
Writing Write a diary entry
Grammar Identify and use principal parts of verbs

Write About Your Reading

Pretend you are both Suzy and Leah. (Not at the same time!) First write one more diary entry from Leah's point of view. Choose one of the following questions to answer:

- Can you bring clothes for little Avi?
- Are you going to use the diary and key?
- Will you let Avi meet Suzy?

Write one more diary entry from Suzy's point of view. Choose one of the following questions to answer:

- Will you visit Leah at her home after her operation?
- Will you ask Leah about the camps?
- Will you learn new words in Yiddish?

Write About Your Reading

Possible response:

Dear Mutti,
After reading Suzy's diary, I understand so much that I didn't know before. I thought that she was laughing at me, but she was just trying to be my friend.
Leah

Dear Diary,
If I really want to be Leah's friend, I must ask her about the camps. She needs to talk about what happened. I hope that I am strong enough to hear what she has to say.
Suzy

Skills Review

Key Reading Skill: Understanding Text Structure

7. Make a sequence chart like the one below that shows the main events in the story in the order in which they happen. Include at least five events.

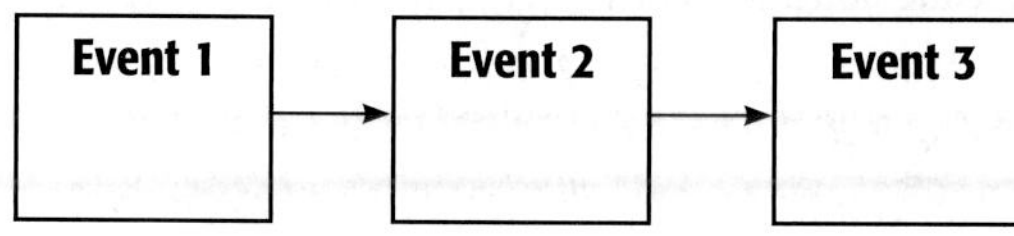

Literary Element: Theme

8. Why do Leah and Suzy misunderstand each other at the beginning of the story?
9. What happens to change the way the girls think about each other?
10. What do you think the theme of this story is?

Vocabulary Check

Copy each sentence, with the correct word in place.

refugee swarmed permanent

11. Soldiers ___ over the town like ants over a picnic.
12. The war forced ___s to escape to nearby countries.
13. When will this temporary dam be replaced by a ___ one?

English Language Coach Use context clues to figure out the meaning of <u>**disparate**</u>.

14. People with <u>**disparate**</u> experiences—such as one who was a victim of the Nazis and one who never faced any real hardship at all—may find it hard to understand each other.

Grammar Link: Principal Parts of Verbs

Every verb has four "principal parts" that are used to form all tenses. The following chart shows how the principal parts of "regular" verbs are formed.

Principal Parts of Verbs			
Base Form	**Present Participle**	**Past**	**Past Participle**
act	acting	acted	acted

The base form and the past alone are used to form the present and past tenses. Helping verbs are used along with either the present participle or the past participle to form other tenses.

The present participle is always formed by adding *-ing* to the base form. (So, if *tirp* is a verb, you could be sure that "I am tirping" or "I was tirping" is correct.)

The other two principal parts—the past and the past participle—are easy for "regular" verbs. They are both formed by adding *-d* or *-ed* to the base form.

Base Form	Past	Past Participle
blame	blame**d**	blame**d**
laugh	laugh**ed**	laugh**ed**

Grammar Practice

On a separate sheet of paper, write the four principal parts of each verb shown.

15. walk
16. notice

Web Activities For eFlashcards, Selection Quick Checks, and other Web activities, go to www.glencoe.com.

Skills Review

Key Reading Skill: Understanding Text Structure

7. Suzy visits refugees. > Leah starts writing letters. > The refugees begin attending school. > Leah and Suzy are made partners in English. > Both Suzy and Leah dislike working together. > Leah comes to Suzy's house for dinner. > Leah is hospitalized for appendicitis. > Suzy is asked to gather Leah's school things. > Suzy reads Leah's letters. > Suzy and her mother visit Leah in the hospital. > Suzy gives Leah her diary to read. > Leah feels more hopeful about her circumstances.

Literary Element: Theme

8. Leah and Suzy don't know anything about each other's lives.
9. Suzy reads Leah's diary and talks to her own mother.
10. Do not judge someone until you know about that person's experiences.

Vocabulary Check

11. swarmed
12. refugee
13. permanent
14. The two examples of experiences are very different, so *disparate* must mean different.

Grammar Link: Principal Parts of Verbs

Grammar Practice

15. walk, walking, walked, walked
16. notice, noticing, noticed, noticed

Close

Ask students to summarize what they learned from Suzy and Leah's story to help them answer the Big Question.

Teach

More About the Author

The editors of Consumer Guide have been reviewing products, cars, and travel for almost 40 years. They offer product quality reviews as well as price comparisons to help consumers choose the best purchases for their money.

V Vocabulary

Vocabulary Matching **Say:** One way to learn and remember new vocabulary words is to compare them to words that you are familiar with. Write each new vocabulary word on one side of a note card. On the other side of the note card, write a word you know that has a similar meaning. Use the cards to play a word matching game with a partner. **OL**

Literature Online

Author Search To expand students' appreciation of Consumer Guide and other publications, have them access the Web site for additional information and resources.

Before You Read from *How Things Work*

Meet the Author

This selection comes from a book that explains various machines people use every day. The publisher, Consumer Guide, prints many books and magazines intended to help people understand products and choose the best ones. The writers of such publications don't usually get credit as authors.

Author Search For more about Consumer Guide and similar publications, go to www.glencoe.com.

Vocabulary Preview

ingenious (in JEEN yus) *adj.* clever; imaginative **(p. 96)** *Everyone agreed that his invention was ingenious.*

tendency (TEN dun see) *n.* the way something is likely to be or behave; likelihood **(p. 96)** *The zipper had a tendency to get stuck.*

rotate (ROH tayt) *v.* to turn around **(p. 98)** *The wheels of a bicycle rotate as you pedal.*

stationary (STAY shun air ee) *adj.* not moving; staying still **(p. 98)** *That part of the machine is stationary.*

Write to Learn Choose the right vocabulary word to complete the following sentences.

1. Most homes are ___, but some trailer homes move.
2. We need a really ___ solution.
3. They decided to ___ the bandstand so that it faced the crowd.
4. He had a ___ to talk too much.

English Language Coach

Context Clues Remember to look for clues to clarify an unfamiliar word. The context may define it, restate it, give an example of it, or compare it to something you are familiar with.

If the word __rotate__ weren't defined and you didn't know its meaning, how could you figure it out? Use a chart like the one below to help.

The wheels of a bicycle rotate as you pedal.

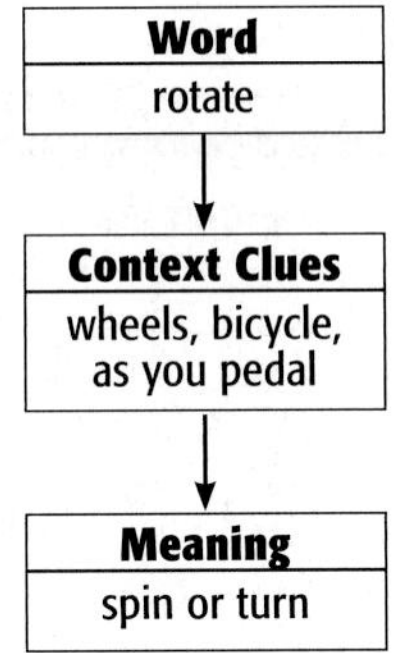

Objectives (pp. 94–95)
Reading Identify text structure: steps in a process • Connect text to self
Informational Text Use text features: diagram, cutaway diagram
Vocabulary Use context clues to determine word meaning

Additional Support

Differentiated Instruction

Writing Reviews Go online with students to www.consumerguide.com. Read a couple of product reviews as a class and discuss how these reviews are helpful to consumers. Then, invite students to write reviews of products they use every day, such as running shoes. Support students as they conduct online research or class surveys to research their products. Consider asking students to include labeled, cutaway illustrations or photographs of the products. Invite students to share their reviews with the class. **BL**

Skills Preview

Key Reading Skill: Understanding Text Structure

Before you read, preview the text to identify text structure. Look for words and phrases that signal:

- transitions between steps in a process
- cause and effect

Make a Chart In your Learner's Notebook, make a two-column chart. Label your columns "Zipper" and "Pencil Sharpener." In each column, list the words and phrases that signal the text structure of that part of the selection. Is the structure explaining how to do something, or is it telling you how something works? At the bottom of your chart, briefly describe the process that the text is explaining.

Write to Learn In your Learner's Notebook, write a paragraph about something you know how to do. Explain the steps in the process clearly and in the correct order. Use signal words to show transitions between steps.

Key Text Element: Text Features

A **diagram** is a drawing that shows the parts of a machine or other device. It makes the parts simpler and easier to see. Sometimes, it can be combined with an actual photograph to clearly show how the device works. A **cutaway diagram** shows what happens *behind* a part of the device, as though that part had been cut away.

These tips will help you understand and get the most from diagrams.

- Look carefully at the whole picture to understand what it shows.
  What part of the photograph has been replaced by a diagram?
- Look carefully at the diagram.
  Is part of the diagram a cutaway, showing what is behind one of the device's parts? What does it show?
- Look carefully at any arrows, lines, and captions that will help you understand the diagram.
  What do the captions explain? Is it a process?

E

Get Ready to Read

Connect to the Reading

Are you curious about how something works? What process would you like to know more about? What could you show someone how to do?

Build Background

The selection tells how a zipper and a pencil sharpener work.

- Zippers began to appear on men's and women's clothing in the 1920s and 1930s.
- Before zippers, people used buttons, snaps, ties, and hooks and eyes to hold their clothes together.
- An electric pencil sharpener has just one roller and a motor instead of a crank.

C

Set Purposes for Reading

BIG Question Read the selection "How Things Work" to learn about how a zipper and a pencil sharpener work.

Set Your Own Purpose What else would you like to learn from the selection to help you answer the Big Question? Write your own purpose on the "How Things Work" page of Foldable 1.

Literature Online

Interactive Literary Elements Handbook
To review or learn more about the literary elements, go to www.glencoe.com.

Keep Moving

Use these skills as you read the following selection.

Reading in the Real World

Career Students who enjoy reading this selection may be interested in careers as production inspectors, testers, graders, sorters, samplers, or weighers. Such students may enjoy hands-on tasks, finding solutions to problems, and following procedures. Job duties might include testing products and recording the data. Tell interested students to visit Internet career sites or to consult career handbooks to learn more about the job descriptions and to determine the education, training, and experience required for these careers. Suggest that students begin their search at www.collegegrad.com. BL

Teach

E Text Element

Text Features: Cutaway
Ask: Why might a writer choose to include a cutaway? *(Students may say that a cutaway allows the reader to more easily visualize complex explanations.)* OL

C Critical Thinking

Comprehension Say: "Necessity is the mother of invention." When something is needed, it inspires people to make something for that need. What need may have caused someone to invent the zipper and pencil sharpener? *(Possible responses: People needed better ways to close winter coats and sharpen pencils.)* OL

CheckPoint

Use the CheckPoint questions provided on Presentation Plus! to check for prior knowledge and to build background. These questions can be used with interactive response keypads for immediate student feedback.

Literature Online

Interactive Literary Elements Handbook Have students access the Web site to improve their understanding of text features.

Objectives

- Identify text structure: steps in a process
- Connect text to self
- Use text features: diagram, cutaway diagram
- Use context clues to determine word meanings

Teach

R Reading Skill

Understanding Text Structure **Say:** Preview the "Zipper" selection by looking at the drawing and writing on page 97. How does "Zipper" look different from other texts you have read? *(Possible response: It looks more like a diagram than an article—the writing looks like picture captions.)* **OL**

EL Language Coach

Context Clues **Say:** Reread the sentence in which *garments* is used. What were slide fasteners first used on? *(flying suits)* What is probably meant by "flying suits"? *(Possible response: The term probably means some kind of outfit or set of clothes used by aviators.)* So, if the flying suits are considered to be garments, what can you guess *garments* means? *(Possible response: clothing)* **EL** **BL**

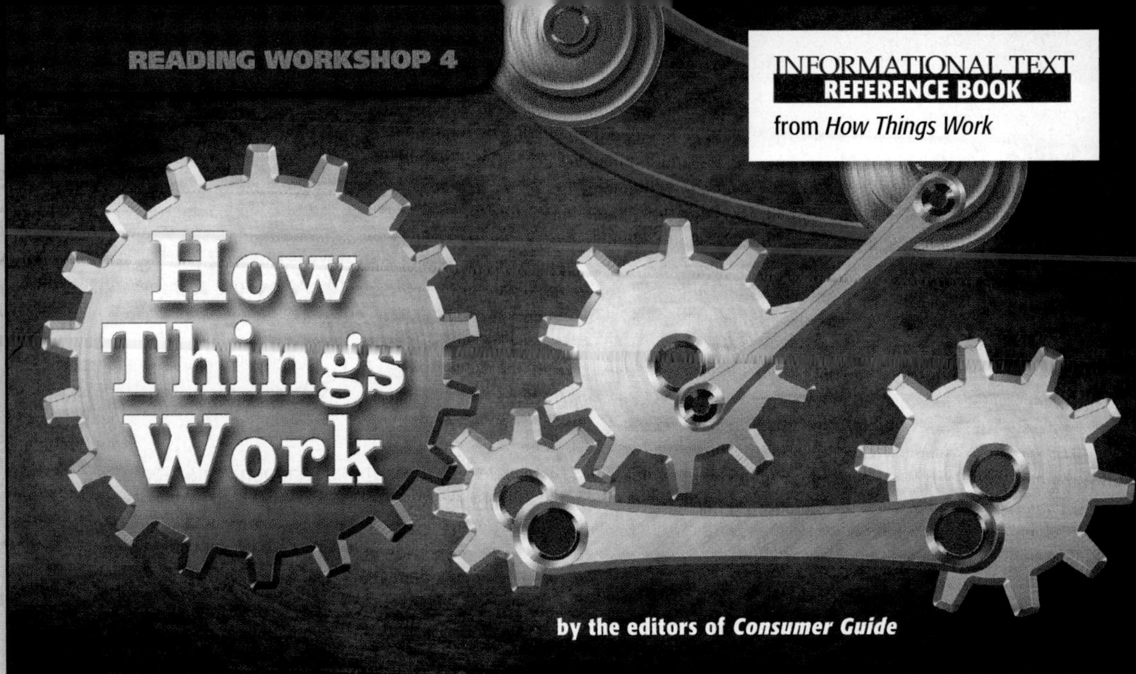

INFORMATIONAL TEXT
REFERENCE BOOK
from *How Things Work*

by the editors of *Consumer Guide*

At Home

Zipper

The zipper is a tight, secure fastener that has the advantage of being flexible and quick to operate. This **ingenious** device was first patented[1] in the 1890s, but the slide fastener that we know today was not perfected until 1913. Early designs had an unfortunate **tendency** to pop open. Its first use on **garments** was in World War I, when the U.S. Navy used slide fasteners on flying suits. Slide fasteners were not christened[2] "zippers" until 1926. **1** **2**

1. When something is ***patented*** (PAT un tid), the government gives the person or company that invented it the right to be the only one to make, use, or sell it for a certain number of years.
2. ***Christened*** (KRIS und) means "named" here.

Vocabulary

ingenious (in JEEN yus) *adj.* clever; imaginative

tendency (TEN dun see) *n.* the way that something is likely to be or behave; likelihood

Practice the Skills

1 Key Reading Skill

R **Understanding Text Structure** Look at "Zipper." Does it look like a "normal" text to you? If not, why? Think about the size of the drawing and the placement of the writing on the page. As you think about what "Zipper" is telling—and showing—you, look for words that signal steps in a process or cause and effect.

2 English Language Coach

EL **Context Clues** What do you think **garments** means? What context clues clarify its meaning for you? Explain.

Additional Support

Readability Scores
Dale-Chall: 8.3
DRP: 61
Lexile: 1090

Differentiated Instruction

Functional Fashion Have students research the history of the button and zipper. Tell them to consider different fashion eras, cultures, and technological advances. Encourage them to note the purpose of the clothing as well as who would be wearing it. Suggest that they ask: "Why were zippers invented?" Have students find as many pictures of the buttons, zippers, and garments in question as possible. Then, compile the students' research and pictures into a museum exhibit and discuss their findings. **AL**

Practice the Skills

3 Key Text Element

Text Features: Diagram Look at the cutaway diagram of the zipper. Which part of the zipper is "cut away"? What does the cutaway reveal? Also, look at the notes that are connected by lines to the drawing. What do the notes tell you about how the zipper works? Continue to look for signal words as you study the text.

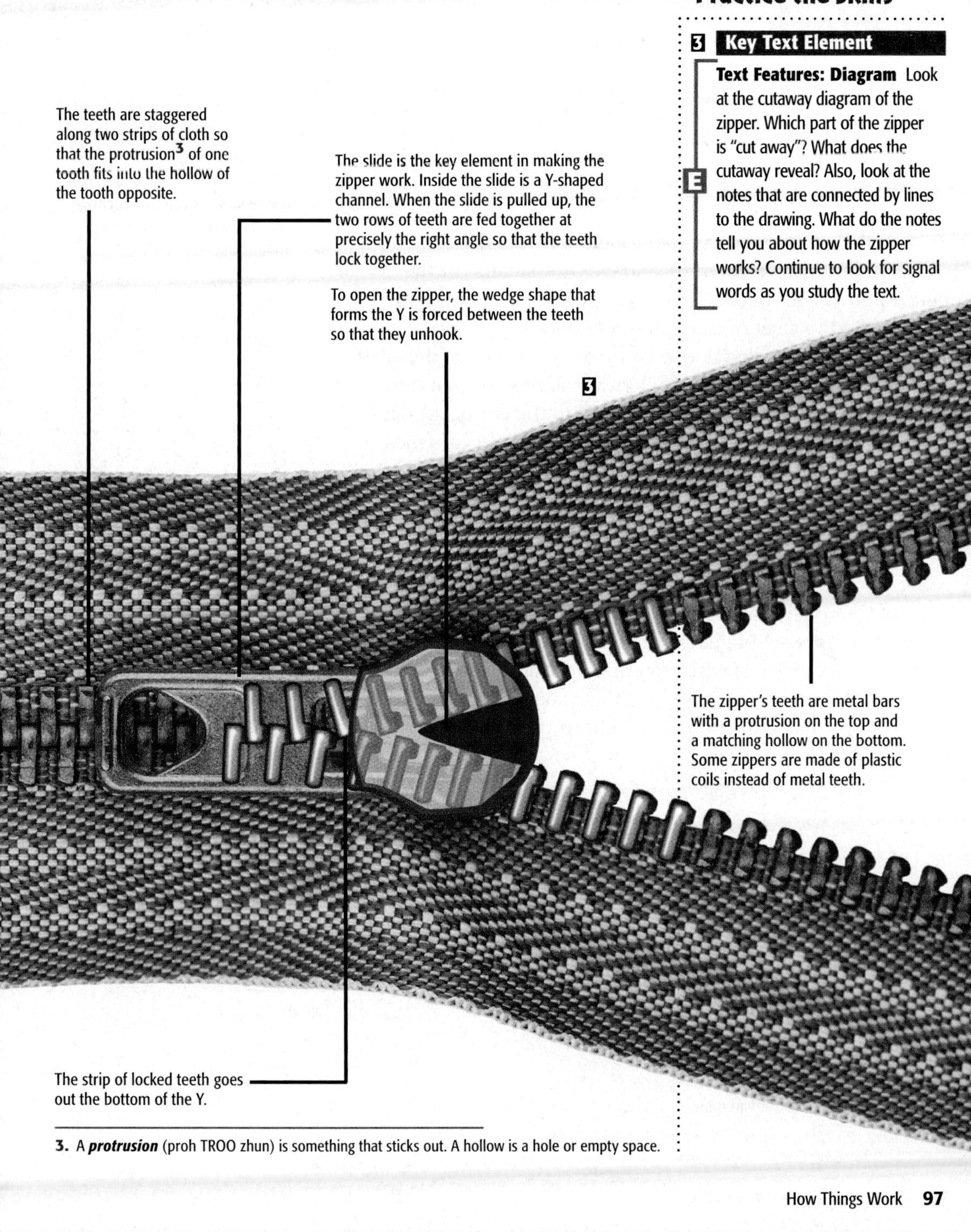

The teeth are staggered along two strips of cloth so that the protrusion[3] of one tooth fits into the hollow of the tooth opposite.
The slide is the key element in making the zipper work. Inside the slide is a Y-shaped channel. When the slide is pulled up, the two rows of teeth are fed together at precisely the right angle so that the teeth lock together.
To open the zipper, the wedge shape that forms the Y is forced between the teeth so that they unhook.
The zipper's teeth are metal bars with a protrusion on the top and a matching hollow on the bottom. Some zippers are made of plastic coils instead of metal teeth.
The strip of locked teeth goes out the bottom of the Y.

3. A ***protrusion*** (proh TROO zhun) is something that sticks out. A hollow is a hole or empty space.

READING WORKSHOP 4

Teach

E Text Element

Text Features: Cutaway

Say: Describe how the cutaway helps you understand how a zipper functions. *(The picture and captions make it clear that the slide is pulled up, two rows of teeth are fed together, and then the teeth lock.)* **OL**

Ask: Which part of the picture do you find most helpful or interesting? *(Responses will vary.)* **BL**

Ask: What might cause a zipper to malfunction? *(The angle at which the teeth are fed together is off, or the staggering of the teeth is off.)* **AL**

Literature Focus Lesson

Onomatopoeia Use a zipper to demonstrate for students that the words *zip* and *zipper* are examples of onomatopoeia, words that imitate sound. Help students brainstorm a list of other such words (*zap, buzz, smack,* and so on). Then, have students select two words to demonstrate the sound on which the onomatopoeia is based for the class, just as you modeled the zip sound. **AS**

Objectives
- Use information in text features, such as cutaways, to aid understanding
- Clarify word meanings in context
- Use sequence and cause and effect to locate, recall, and understand information

Teach

EL Language Coach

Context Clues **Ask:** What is a house? *(Possible response: A house is a building in which people live.)* Reread the sentence that uses the word *housing.* How can you apply the meaning of *house* to the design of a pencil sharpener? *(Possible response: Since people live inside a house, one could say that the gears of a pencil sharpener "live inside" the outside covering of a pencil sharpener.)* **OL** The sentence tells you that gears are "inside the housing." What part of a pencil sharpener can hold things inside? *(Possible response: the outside box or covering.)* Can a house that people live in be described as an "outside box"? *(Possible response: Yes. Houses are often square-shaped like boxes and shelter people from the outside.)* **BL**

READING WORKSHOP 4

At Work
Pencil Sharpener 4

A pencil sharpener has two rollers with raised and sharpened ridges on them that shave thin slivers off the pencil point. The rollers can freely spin from a yoke, which is connected to a set of gears and a crank.

The pencil is inserted at one end through a hole in the yoke, between the two rollers. The rollers are slanted so that they come together at the opposite end, next to the crank. At that end, each roller has a gear affixed[4] to it. The two gears mesh[5] with a larger gear inside the **housing** of the pencil sharpener. That larger gear is an internal gear—its teeth are not on the outside of the disc, but face inward toward the center. 5

The crank handle turns the yoke, which causes the two rollers to **rotate** around the pencil. The gears at the opposite ends of the rollers turn inside the internal gear, which is **stationary**. This set of gears makes the two rollers rotate on their axes. As the rollers are rotating around the pencil, they are also turning against the pencil's surface. The sharp ridges of the rollers shave the pencil to a sharp point. 6 ○

4. ***Affixed*** (uh FIKST) means "attached."
5. ***Mesh*** means "come together."

Vocabulary

rotate (ROH tayt) *v.* to turn around

stationary (STAY shun air ee) *adj.* not moving; staying still

Practice the Skills

4 Key Text Element

Text Features Take a look at the illustration of a pencil sharpener on the next page as you read this description. How does the illustration help you understand this machine?

5 English Language Coach EL

Context Clues What does **housing** mean here? If you combine the clues in this paragraph with your knowledge of the word *house,* you should have no trouble understanding *housing* in this context.

6 Key Reading Skill

Understanding Text Structure This piece explains how a sharpener works. How different would this selection be if it were directions for *how to use* the sharpener? Would the organization change? What kind of illustration(s) would be needed?

Additional Support

Differentiated Instruction

Learning Styles To help hands-on learners understand the text, take the cover off the classroom pencil sharpener. Then, allow half the class to take turns sharpening pencils, paying attention to how the mechanism works. Have the other half of the class study the cutaway on page 99. Then, have students reread the text. Lead students in a discussion. Ask them to compare and contrast their experiences—reading the text without the visual components vs. reading the text after examining the pencil sharpener. **BL**

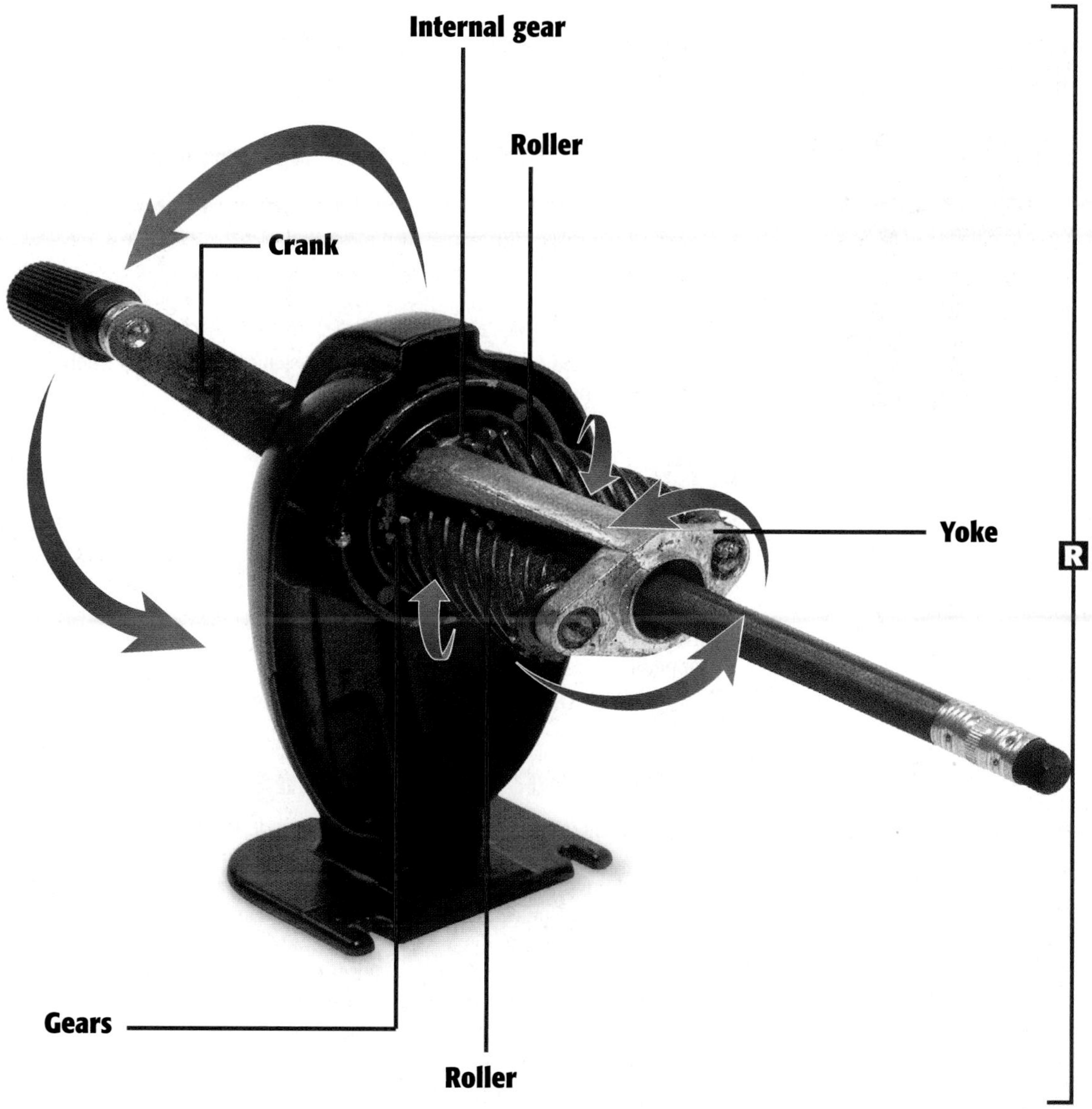

READING WORKSHOP 4

Internal gear
Roller
Crank
Yoke
Gears
Roller

Differentiated Instruction

Invention Explain that inventions such as the zipper and the pencil sharpener came about as the result of people's needs. Ask students to brainstorm needs that they have that have not yet been met by technological gadgets. Record students' ideas on the board. Ask pairs of students to select one of the needs recorded on the board. Then, ask students to create inventions that will meet the needs. Suggest that students prepare annotated sketches of their inventions to share with the class. AL

R Reading Skill

Understanding Text Structure **Ask:** If you had to revise this text so that it told someone how to use a pencil sharpener, what changes would you make? *(Responses will vary. Students may say that the text would describe steps in a process arranged in the correct order. Also, there might be time-order words like "first," "then," and "next.")* OL Instead of one picture of a pencil sharpener, what kind of picture or pictures would help you understand how to use a pencil sharpener? *(Possible response: A series of pictures about how to hold the pencil and where to put its tip would be helpful.)* BL

Teach

BQ 

Ask: How does this article help you to answer the Big Question? *(Responses will vary. Students may say that people read to learn.)* OL

Assess

Use the CheckPoint questions provided on Presentation Plus! to check for comprehension. These questions can be used with interactive response keypads for immediate student feedback.

Objectives

- Use sequence and cause and effect to locate, recall, and understand information
- Use information in text features, such as cutaways, to aid understanding
- Clarify word meanings in context

Assess

Resources for page 100

- Selection Quick Check
- Selection and Unit Assessment
- ExamView Assessment Suite
- Interactive Tutor: Self-Assessment

Students can respond to the *After You Read* items in their Learner's Notebook or on separate sheets of paper.

Answering the BIG Question

1. Responses will vary.
2. Responses will vary. Students may say that the interlocking teeth make the zipper a clever device.
3. The pencil sharpener uses two rollers to shave thin slivers from the pencil point.

Critical Thinking

4. Early designs had the tendency to pop open. Over time, the interlocking teeth have been perfected.
5. Responses may include that the zipper was named for its function of "zipping" things closed.

After You Read from *How Things Work*

Answering the BIG Question

1. What was the most interesting thing you learned from these selections? Explain why it was interesting to you.
   TIP **Author and Me** You'll find ideas in the selection, but you must also use your own opinions.
2. **Recall** What makes the zipper such a clever device?
   TIP **Right There** You'll find the answer in the selection.
3. **Summarize** How does a pencil sharpener sharpen pencils?
   TIP **Think and Search** You must use information from the selection and decide what the important points are.

Critical Thinking

4. **Infer** How has the zipper improved over time?
   TIP **Author and Me** You'll find clues in the selection, but you must also use the information in your head.
5. **Infer** Why do you think the slide fastener became known as the "zipper"?
   TIP **On My Own** Answer from your own experience.

Write About Your Reading

You've just read two explanations of how things work. The structure of each explanation was a process. Now write about another kind of process. Write a set of directions for something you know how to do. You might write about how to make your favorite sandwich or something else you know how to cook. Be sure to put in all the details. How do you start? What do you add first? What comes second and third? How do you finish up? Use signal words to show when you are going from one step to the next. Some examples of useful signal words are *first, next, after that,* and *finally*.

As you begin to write your directions, remember to do the following things:

- Break the process into steps.
- Present each step in proper order.
- Use clear transition words to link the steps.

Objectives (pp. 100–101)
Reading Identify text structure: steps in a process
Informational Text Use text features: diagram, cutaway diagram
Vocabulary Identify context clues
Writing Write directions: steps in a process
Grammar Use irregular verbs correctly

Write About Your Reading

Possible response:
How to Draw a Lion

1. Draw a large circle for the lion's head.
2. After that, draw one circle on the top left and one circle on the top right of the large circle for the ears.
3. Then draw an upside down half moon in the large circle for the nose.
4. After that, draw two dots, one on the right and one on the left in the large circle between the ears and the nose. These dots will be the lion's eyes.
5. Next, draw a jagged line (like a mountain) below the nose to make the mouth. Finally, scribble around the outside of the large circle to create the lion's mane.

Skills Review

Key Reading Skill: Understanding Text Structure

6. You have seen how a process can serve as the structure for a piece of writing. You have also seen how an illustration can work with the text. Write a short paragraph telling how an illustration can make a process clearer.

Key Text Element: Text Features

7. What part of the zipper does the cutaway show?
8. List the parts of the pencil sharpener indicated by the arrows.
9. How does the photo of the "uncovered" pencil sharpener work like a cutaway diagram?

Vocabulary Check

For each word below, copy the sentence from the selection that contains that word. Then write a sentence of your own using the word correctly. Underline the word in both sentences.

10. **ingenious**
11. **tendency**
12. **rotate**
13. **stationary**

English Language Coach Find the following words in the selection you just read. Tell whether context clues use definition, restatement, or comparison to clarify meaning.

14. **coils**
15. **internal gear**

Web Activities For eFlashcards, Selection Quick Checks, and other Web activities, go to www.glencoe.com.

Grammar Link: Irregular Verbs

Many common English verbs are irregular. The chart below contains some of the most often-used irregular verbs. If you don't know their forms by heart, learn them.

Present Tense	Past Tense	Past Participle
become	became	become
buy	bought	bought
come	came	come
eat	ate	eaten
give	gave	given
grow	grew	grown
ride	rode	ridden
run	ran	run
say	said	said
see	saw	seen
take	took	taken
write	wrote	written

The most irregular verb in the English language is *to be.*

Subject	Present Tense	Past Tense	Past Participle
I	am	was	been
you	are	were	been
he, she, it	is	was	been
we	are	were	been
they	are	were	been

Grammar Practice

16. Copy the paragraph below. Then find and fix the three verb mistakes in the paragraph.

Yesterday Ms. Cordero assign us to write a poem. You should have seen our faces. We was very unhappy. We have never written poems in our lives. Our teacher should have gave us an easier assignment.

Skills Review

Key Reading Skill: Understanding Text Structure

6. Responses will vary. An illustration can make a process easier to understand because it shows readers what something looks like. Readers don't have to use their imaginations to understand the process. They can match the text to certain parts of the illustration to get the full picture.

Key Text Element: Text Features

7. the strip of teeth
8. internal gear, roller, crank, gears, yoke
9. Possible response: It shows the sharpener's internal functions.

Vocabulary Check

10. The <u>ingenious</u> invention helped everyone.
11. I have a <u>tendency</u> to forget my homework.
12. The hands on the clock <u>rotate</u> around the numbers.
13. When I hurt my leg, I had to stay <u>stationary</u>.
14. Comparison: "Coils" are compared to "teeth."
15. Definition: An "internal gear" is defined as one whose teeth are not on the outside of the disc, but face inward toward the center.

Grammar Link: Irregular Verbs

Grammar Practice

16. Yesterday Ms. Cordero assigned us to write a poem. You should have seen our faces. We were very unhappy. We have never written poems in our lives. Our teacher should have given us an easier assignment.

Close

Ask students to summarize what they learned from the article to help them answer the Big Question

Comparing Literature: Theme

UNIT 1

Objectives covered in this workshop:
- Determine theme
- Connect, compare, and contrast across texts

Teaching Students to Compare Themes

Why Is It Important?

- Students need to learn the importance of identifying the theme in all texts.
- Students need to understand how a variety of texts in different genres can have similar themes
- When students understand how to identify the theme in selections, they are better able to comprehend the text and are often more eager to read.

How to Help Students Get It

Some of the ways that good readers identify the theme include:

- Analyzing the title. Sometimes it tells you a lot about the theme.
- Paying attention to repeating patterns, symbols, moods, or other literary devices. Often these lead to the theme.
- Asking yourself: What are the details and particulars in the story? What greater meaning may they have?

Reading to Answer the Big Question

Summer Reading

When Michael Dorris takes on odd jobs during the summer, he expects to receive payment in cash. However, the young Dorris receives access to a neighbor's vast library, which opens up a new world that impacts his life.

The First Book

In "The First Book," Rita Dove dares the reader to rethink the world as he or she knows it. This poem refers to the great extent to which a single act of reading can change one's life.

Workshop Resources

Pacing (Days) Standard	Block	Lesson	Student Materials	Teacher Resources
1		Key Skill Lesson: Comparing Literature: Theme	Key Reading Skills Practice English Language Coach	Bellringer Options Transparencies Read Aloud, Think Aloud Transparencies Presentation Plus!
2		"Summer Reading"	Literary Analysis Transparencies Glencoe Online Selection Vocabulary Development Academic Vocabulary Development English Language Coach Active Reading Graphic Organizer Literary Analysis StudentWorks Plus Online Student Edition Literature Classics Selection and Unit Assessments	Literary and Text Analysis Transparencies Puzzlemaker Skill Level Up! BookLink 3 Assessment by Learning Objective (Diagnostic and Formative) Interactive Tutor Self-Assessment TeacherWorks Plus
2		"The First Book"	Glencoe Online Selection Vocabulary Development Academic Vocabulary Development English Language Coach Active Reading Graphic Organizer Literary Analysis StudentWorks Plus Online Student Edition Literature Classics Selection and Unit Assessments	Literary and Text Analysis Transparencies Puzzlemaker Skill Level Up! BookLink 3 Assessment by Learning Objective (Diagnostic and Formative) Interactive Tutor Self-Assessment TeacherWorks Plus

Keys for Unit Resource

- Blackline Master
- Workbook
- Supplemental Text
- CD-ROM
- DVD
- Transparency
- Web-based
- Fast Files

Level Appropriate Code

AS = Activities for all students
AL = Activities for students working above grade level
OL = Activities for students working at grade level
BL = Activities for students working below grade level
EL = Activities for English language learners

Focus

BELLRINGER Options

Daily Language Practice Transparency

Focus Activity Say: One reason for reading is to be entertained. How would you compare a book to another form of entertainment, such as a movie? How are books and movies alike? How are they different? *(Responses will vary.)*

L Literary Element

Theme Say: You can think of the theme as the most important message of a passage. A writer's opinions and thoughts about a subject help form the theme. For example, the theme of an essay about sports might be "Playing sports develops teamwork." What other themes might you find in an essay about sports? *(Responses will vary.)* OL

Summer Reading & The First Book

by Michael Dorris

by Rita Dove

What You'll Learn

- How to compare two pieces of literature
- How to determine theme

What You'll Read

- "Summer Reading," p. 105
- "The First Book," p. 109

Point of Comparison

- Theme

Purpose

- To compare the themes of a personal essay and a poem

Objectives (pp. 102–103)
Reading Compare and contrast literary texts
Literature Identify theme in a literary text • Compare and contrast themes across texts

Have you done any comparing lately? Sure you have. You compare all the time. Maybe you compare two T-shirts before deciding which one to wear. You probably compare foods in the cafeteria before you choose your lunch.

When you compare, you think about how things are alike and how they are different. By comparing two things, you'll understand each of them better.

How to Compare Literature: Theme

Comparing two works of literature is like comparing any two items. You decide what parts are alike and what parts are different. You'll quickly notice one way in which the selections in this workshop are alike. Both are about reading. That's their subject. You'll also notice a way they're different. One is an essay, and the other is a poem.

L As you read the essay "Summer Reading" and the poem "The First Book," look for the **theme** of each one. Don't confuse theme with subject. Theme goes deeper into the meaning. Ask yourself

- What is this writer telling me? What is his or her main idea?
- How would he or she answer the "Big Question?"

After that, compare the themes of the two selections.

Academic Vocabulary

theme (theem) *n.* the main idea of a story, poem, or play

Additional Support

Literature Focus Lesson

Analyzing Theme Explain to students that the theme is the main idea the writer wants to communicate to the reader. The theme is not always clearly stated. Often the reader must make an educated guess about the theme.

Tell students that the title is often a clue to the theme. Important details and examples may also provide clues. The theme may even be revealed through a character's actions or the words of the narrator.

Encourage students to note these types of clues while reading. When they review their notes, they may see a pattern that points to the theme. OL

Get Ready to Compare

As you read "Summer Reading" and "The First Book," look for details that suggest what each author is saying about the subject of reading. Ask yourself the questions listed on page 102. In your Learner's Notebook, make a table like the one below to write your ideas on.

"Summer Reading"	"The First Book"

Making Your Comparison

After you've read both selections, look over the notes you made in the table in your Learner's Notebook. Then you'll make a Venn diagram below the table. A Venn diagram helps you compare two things. Notice that the two circles make three areas in the diagram—one for each selection and one for both selections.

You'll complete your diagram later, after you've finished reading and thinking about both selections.

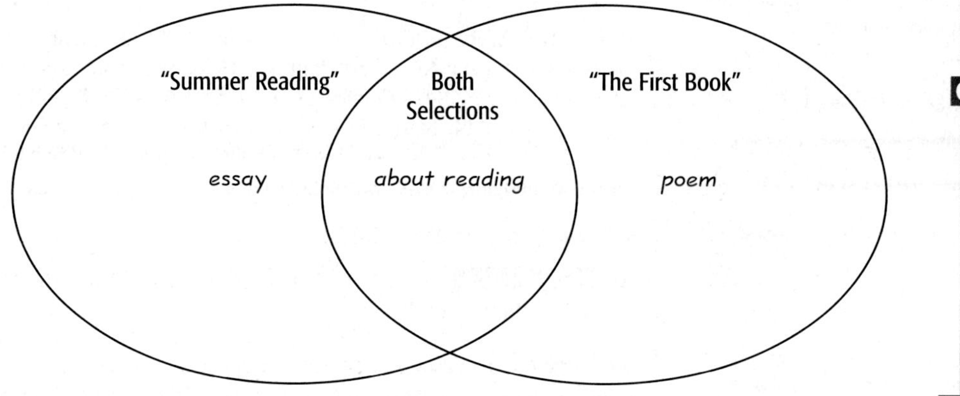

C

COMPARING LITERATURE

Teach

C Critical Thinking

Comprehension Guide students in understanding how to transfer information from the table to the Venn diagram. **Say:** **If you used this table to compare books to movies, which details would you write in the "Both Selections" section of the Venn diagram? What characteristics, or traits, do books and movies have in common?** *(Possible answer: They provide entertainment and tell stories.)* **EL** **BL**

Assess/Close

Using fables as examples is an effective way to familiarize students with the concept of theme. **Say:** **A fable is a short, simple tale that teaches a moral, or lesson. The theme, or message, is often stated directly as the moral. You probably know the fable called "The Tortoise and the Hare." The moral and theme are the same: "Slow and steady wins the race."** **Ask:** **Think about some other fables that you know. List three fables and their themes.** *(Responses will vary.)* **OL**

Resources for page 103

 Use the Comparing Literature Graphic Organizer BLM in the Unit 1 Resource Booklet.

Literature Focus Lesson

Theme Read aloud to students the following background information and quotations from two writers. Discuss with students the theme that these comments share about reading.

Naomi Shihab Nye writes poems, essays, and children's books. She says, in "Wealthy with Words," "Books were the getaway car, idling at the edge of every scene. I learned never to go anywhere without one."

Sherman Alexie is a Spokane/Coeur d'Alene American Indian writer whose work reflects the difficulties of growing up in poverty. "I loved those books, but I also knew that love had only one purpose. I was trying to save my life," he says in "Superman and Me." **AS**

Objectives
- Compare and contrast literary texts
- Identify theme in a literary text
- Compare and contrast themes across texts

Teach

More About the Author

Michael Dorris wrote stories, essays, and novels. Many of his books about Native Americans help people understand Native American culture. As a child, Dorris enjoyed listening to the stories his mother told. Each night she made up a new story for him. He always wanted to be a writer, but he didn't think he could support himself by writing. Instead, he studied anthropology and taught at several universities, but he soon went back to writing.

Literature Online

Author Search To expand students' appreciation of Michael Dorris, have them access the Web site for additional information and resources.

Readability Scores

Dale-Chall: 5.2

DRP: 56

Lexile: 1020

Before You Read | Summer Reading

Meet the Author

Michael Dorris (1945–1997) was part Native American, and many of his books are about Native Americans. When he was asked about books he thought teenagers would like, he responded that when he was a teenager he preferred books that "weren't assigned, but chosen." See page R3 of the Author Files in the back of the book for more on Michael Dorris.

Author Search For more about Michael Dorris, go to www.glencoe.com.

Objectives (pp. 104–107)
Reading Compare and contrast literary texts
Literature Identify theme in a literary text • Compare and contrast themes across texts
Vocabulary Use context clues to determine word meaning

Vocabulary Preview

category (KAT uh gor ee) *n.* a type or group **(p. 105)** *Seventh graders are a category of middle schoolers.*

gestured (JES churd) *v.* showed (something) by a motion of the hand or other part of the body; form of the verb *gesture* **(p. 106)** *He gestured for us to come in.*

consciously (KAWN shus lee) *adv.* knowingly; on purpose **(p. 106)** *He consciously chose the shortest book.*

browsed (browzd) *v.* looked through in a casual way; form of the verb *browse* **(p. 106)** *He browsed the shelves for something to read.*

vividly (VIV ud lee) *adv.* clearly **(p. 107)** *He described Mr. Ballou vividly.*

encounter (in KOWN tur) *n.* an unexpected meeting **(p. 107)** *They had an encounter at the library.*

Reading Strategies

Connect to the Reading

What is it like to discover something new that you really enjoy?

Build Background

In this essay, Michael Dorris describes a summer that he spent mowing lawns and reading when he was fourteen. He names two books that influenced him. One of them, *Coming of Age in Samoa,* is a study of girls growing up on one of the Samoan islands in the Pacific Ocean. The book is a work of anthropology (the study of the beliefs, customs, and behaviors of groups of people). Dorris himself later became an anthropologist.

Set Purposes for Reading

BIG Question Read to find out about Michael Dorris's summer reading and its effect on his life.

Set Your Own Purpose What else would you like to learn from the selection to help you answer the Big Question? Write your own purpose on the "Summer Reading" page of Foldable 1.

Additional Support

Reading in the Real World

Citizenship Writer Michael Dorris preferred books he had chosen to read rather than those that teachers assigned. Discuss with students some topics they enjoy reading about. As a class, generate a list of people in the community with whom students could consult to find out more about books and information on these topics. Suggest that students speak to librarians and bookstore clerks about resources that list books according to genre and topic. Point out that bookstores, libraries, and Internet sites often provide lists of books by subject area. Prompt students to suggest other sources. **OL**

E

Summer Reading

by Michael Dorris

Detroit News, May 1991

When I was fourteen, I earned money in the summer by mowing lawns, and within a few weeks I had built up a regular clientele.[1] I got to know people by the flowers they planted that I had to remember not to cut down, by the things they lost in the grass or stuck in the ground on purpose. I reached the point with most of them when I knew in advance what complaint was about to be spoken, which particular request was most important. And I learned something about the **measure** of my neighbors by their preferred method of payment: by the job, by the month—or not at all. 1

Mr. Ballou fell into the last **category**, and he always had a reason why. On one day he had no change for a fifty, on another he was flat out of checks, on another, he was simply out when I knocked on his door. Still, except for the money part, he was a nice enough old guy, always waving or tipping his hat when he'd see me from a distance. I figured him for a thin retirement[2] check, maybe a work-related injury that kept him from doing his own yard

1. A ***clientele*** (kly un TEL) is a group of customers.
2. ***Retirement*** is the time in life when a person no longer works for a living.

Vocabulary

category (KAT uh gor ee) *n.* a type or group

Practice the Skills

1 English Language Coach

EL

Context Clues What does **measure** mean here? Did the narrator hold up a ruler to see how tall each neighbor is? Of course not. The narrator has been talking about getting to know his customers, who are his neighbors. So in getting their *measure,* he's deciding what he can expect from them. He's making judgments based on his experiences with them.

Mr. Kersey, Suffolk Thomas Cantrell Dugdale (1880–1952) Oil on canvas 91 X 72 in., Blackburn Museum and Art Gallery, Lancashire, UK.

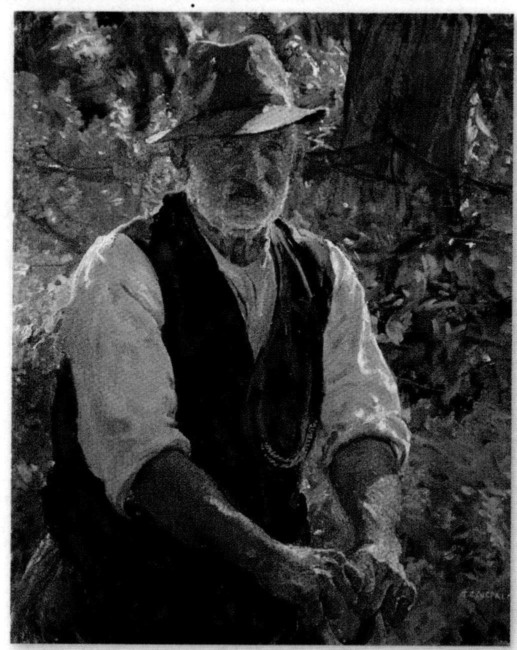

Teach

E Text Element

Review Titles Say: Look at the title of this selection and think about what you already know about this selection and its author. What do you think "Summer Reading" will be about? Why? *(Possible response: This article will probably be about reading the author did during the summer and the impact the reading had on his life.)* OL

EL Language Coach

Context Clues Say: Look at the sentence that contains the word *measure.* The author says that he "learned something about the measure of my neighbors by their preferred method of payment: by the job, by the month—or not at all." To check your understanding of the meaning of *measure* in this sentence, try replacing it with a synonym. Does the word *character* make sense? *(Yes.)* What does *measure* mean in this sentence? *(Possible response: In this sentence,* measure *means how honest and considerate a person is.)* EL OL

Literature Focus Lesson

Autobiographical Essay "Summer Reading" is an autobiographical essay. Explain that an essay is a short piece of nonfiction writing that communicates an idea or an opinion. Dorris's essay is autobiographical because he writes about a personal experience in order to express his ideas about reading.

Ask students to write short autobiographical essays of their own. Prompt them to write about an experience that changed the way they think or feel about reading. Remind them that the experience they describe should lead to a more general conclusion or idea about reading. OL

Objectives

- Compare and contrast literary texts
- Identify theme in a literary text
- Compare and contrast themes across texts

Teach

Viewing the Illustration

Ask: What does this illustration add to the essay? *(Possible response: It helps me understand how amazed the boy must have felt when he saw so many books.)* Why is it an important moment when Mr. Ballou shows Michael his book collection? *(It is an important moment because Michael begins to realize that the act of choosing a book because you want to read it can be really enjoyable.)* **OL**

EL Language Coach

Context Clues Say: Look at the sentence: "The hall was cool, shaded, and it took my eyes a minute to adjust to the muted light." Think of a time when you went inside after being out in the sun, and it took a minute before you could see clearly. What word does the author first use to describe the light inside? *(shaded)* How does this context clue help you understand the meaning of *muted light?* *(Shaded means almost the same thing as* muted. Muted light *is much dimmer than the light outside.)* **EL BL**

work. Sure, I kept a running total, but I didn't worry about the amount too much. Grass was grass, and the little that Mr. Ballou's property comprised[3] didn't take long to trim.

Then, one late afternoon in mid-July, the hottest time of the year, I was walking by his house and he opened the door, motioned me to come inside. The hall was cool, shaded, and it took my eyes a minute to adjust to the <u>**muted light**</u>. **2**

"I owe you," Mr. Ballou began, "but . . ."

I thought I'd save him the trouble of thinking up a new excuse. "No problem. Don't worry about it."

"The bank made a mistake in my account," he continued, ignoring my words. "It will be cleared up in a day or two. But in the meantime I thought perhaps you could choose one or two volumes for a down payment."[4]

He **gestured** toward the walls and I saw that books were stacked everywhere. It was like a library, except with no order to the arrangement.

"Take your time," Mr. Ballou encouraged. "Read, borrow, keep. Find something you like. What do you read?"

"I don't know." And I didn't. I generally read what was in front of me, what I could snag[5] from the paperback rack at the drugstore, what I found at the library, magazines, the back of cereal boxes, comics. The idea of **consciously** seeking out a special title was new to me, but, I realized, not without appeal—so I **browsed** through the piles of books. **3**

"You actually read all of these?"

"This isn't much," Mr. Ballou said. "This is nothing, just what I've kept, the ones worth looking at a second time."

"Pick for me, then."

He raised his eyebrows, cocked his head, regarded me

3. Here, ***comprised*** means "contained; included."
4. A ***down payment*** is part of the full price that a person pays to buy something.
5. When you ***snag*** something, you grab it quickly.

Vocabulary

gestured (JES churd) *v.* showed (something) by a motion of the hand or other part of the body

consciously (KAWN shus lee) *adv.* knowingly; on purpose

browsed (browzd) *v.* looked through in a casual way

Books with One Fallen, 1994, Andrew Gadd (contemporary artist) Oil on canvas, Private Collection.

Practice the Skills

2 English Language Coach

EL **Context Clues** Do you know what <u>**muted light**</u> means? What context clues can help you figure out its meaning? Discuss it with a partner.

3 Comparing Literature

Theme Now that Dorris is telling about his reading habits, you may want to start making some notes in the "Summer Reading" part of the table you made in your Learner's Notebook. Are the author's ideas about reading similar to or different from your own? Use details from the selection to support your answer.

Additional Support

English Language Coach

Context Clues Remind students that practicing unfamiliar words by using them in sentences will help students better remember word meanings. Suggest that when listing unfamiliar words in their Learner's Notebook, students include more than just a part of speech and the definition. Ask students to use each word in a sentence that includes at least one context clue to the word's meaning. Caution students that sentences should not read like a definition. For example, a sentence that shows the word *muted* might be, "From far away, the muted sound of a train barely reached my ears." **EL OL**

appraisingly as though measuring me for a suit. After a moment, he nodded, searched through a stack, and handed me a dark red hard-bound book, fairly thick.

"The Last of the Just," I read. "By André Schwarz-Bart. What's it about?"

"You tell me," he said. "Next week."

I started after supper, sitting outdoors on an uncomfortable kitchen chair. Within a few pages, the yard, the summer, disappeared, the bright oblivion of adolescence[6] temporarily lifted, and I was plunged into the aching tragedy of the Holocaust,[7] the extraordinary clash of good, represented by one decent man, and evil. Translated from French, the language was elegant, simple, overwhelming. When the evening light finally failed I moved inside, read all through the night. **4**

To this day, thirty years later, I **vividly** remember the experience. It was my first voluntary **encounter** with world literature, and I was stunned by the undiluted[8] power a novel could contain. I lacked the vocabulary, however, to translate my feelings into words, so the next week, when Mr. Ballou asked, "Well?" I only replied, "It was good."

"Keep it, then," he said. "Shall I suggest another?"

I nodded, and was presented with the paperback edition of Margaret Mead's *Coming of Age in Samoa.*

C To make two long stories short, Mr. Ballou never paid me a dime for cutting his grass that year or the next, but for fifteen years I taught anthropology at Dartmouth College. Summer reading was not the innocent pastime I had assumed it to be, not a breezy, instantly forgettable escape in a hammock (though I've since enjoyed many of those, too). A book, if it arrives before you at the right moment, in the proper season, at a point of intermission in the daily business of things, will change the course of all that follows. **5** ❍

6. The phrase ***the oblivion*** (uh BLIH vee un) ***of adolescence*** (ad uh LES uns) suggests that teenage years are a time when you don't pay much attention to the world around you.
7. The ***Holocaust*** (HOH luh kawst) was the mass slaughter of large numbers of Europeans, especially Jews, by the Nazis during World War II.
8. Something ***undiluted*** is strong because it is not watered down.

Vocabulary

vividly (VIV ud lee) *adv.* clearly

encounter (in KOWN tur) *n.* an unexpected meeting

Practice the Skills

4 Comparing Literature

Theme This paragraph and the next describe the author's thoughts and feelings about his summer reading. Keep filling in your table with notes on the selection. How does what he says here compare with what he said about his reading habits earlier?

5 BIG Question

BQ How do you think Michael Dorris would answer the question, "Why do we read?" Write your answer on the Comparing Literature page of your Unit 1 Foldable.

Teach

C Critical Thinking

Comprehension Say: Earlier in the essay, Dorris says that he usually just "read what was in front of me." How does this remark differ from his statements about summer reading at the end of the essay? *(At the end of the essay, Dorris says that summer reading isn't just an "innocent pastime.")* **OL** What do you think Michael Dorris would have said as an adult about choosing books? *(Choosing and enjoying books for yourself is an important and meaningful experience.)* **AL**

BQ 

Ask: What details tell you that the young Dorris completely loses himself in the book Mr. Ballou gives him? *(Possible responses: He reads while sitting on an uncomfortable chair; he forgets about his surroundings; he reads through the night.)* What does this tell you about why Michael Dorris reads? *(Dorris may read to be entertained and transported to another world.)* **OL**

Differentiated Instruction

Listening Read aloud to students the paragraph that begins "I started after supper…" and the paragraph that follows. Tell students not to read along with you but to listen and picture what is happening. When you have finished reading, ask students the following questions:

- How do you think Dorris felt as he was reading?
- How do you know that reading this book was an important experience for Dorris?
- Have you ever had trouble explaining how you felt about something important to you? **BL**

Objectives

- Set a purpose for reading
- Activate prior knowledge to enhance understanding
- Use context clues to determine word meanings

Teach

More About the Author

Many of Rita Dove's poems celebrate the lives of African Americans. In 1986 she wrote *Thomas and Beulah,* a book of narrative poems that tell the story of her family, beginning with her grandparents. During Dove's childhood, her parents limited the amount of television she could watch, but she could spend as much time as she wanted at the library. She began then to enjoy reading all sorts of books. Now, when she writes, she thinks of the readers who will open her books and remembers her own reading experiences.

Literature Online

Author Search To expand students' appreciation of Rita Dove, have them access the Web site for additional information and resources.

Before You Read | The First Book

Rita Dove

Meet the Author

Rita Dove has won many prizes for her poetry, including the 1987 Pulitzer Prize. She also had the special honor of serving two terms as Poet Laureate of the United States. She said she discovered that people all over the country "were hungry for poetry." Dove believes in the power of poetry. She says, "When a poem moves you, it moves you in a way that leaves you speechless." See page R3 of the Author Files in the back of the book for more on Rita Dove.

Literature Online

Author Search For more about Rita Dove, go to www.glencoe.com.

Objectives (pp. 108–109)
Reading Compare and contrast literary texts
Literature Identify theme in a literary text
• Compare and contrast themes across texts
Vocabulary Use context clues to determine word meaning

Get Ready to Read

Connect to the Reading

What's it like to try something new, like a new food, a new game, or a new sport? Think of a time when you tried something new. Describe your experience to a partner.

English Language Coach

Context Clues You've learned to figure out the meaning of unfamiliar words by looking at context clues—other words in the sentence or paragraph that help you understand the word you don't know.

Copy this chart into your Learner's Notebook. As you read "The First Book," use the chart to define the word *nip*. You might think you know what it means, but context clues can help you be sure.

Word	Context Clues	Meaning

Build Background

- Rita Dove won a Pulitzer Prize for her poetry. Pulitzer Prizes are awards for excellent achievements in American writing, literature, and music. The Pulitzer Prizes in literature are for fiction, nonfiction, drama, history, biography, and peotry;
- Dove was poet laureate of the United States. The role of the poet laureate is to raise people's awareness of poetry and inspire them to read, write, and appreciate poetry. The poet laureate is chosen by the Librarian of Congress.

Set Purposes for Reading

BIG Question Read the poem "The First Book" to find out how and why people read and to learn what advice the poet gives to someone reading a book for the first time. Also think about the Big Question as you read.

Set Your Own Purpose What else would you like to learn from the poem to help you answer the Big Question? Write your own purpose on "The First Book" page of Foldable 1.

Additional Support

Literature Focus Lesson

Lyric Poetry "The First Book" is a lyric poem, or a poem that expresses thoughts or emotions about a subject. In this poem, the speaker describes the experience of reading. Tell students that when they read the poem, they should think about the speaker's feelings about reading.

Explain to students that in poetry, the form of the poem can often be as meaningful as the words. Tell students to look carefully at the way the lines break in "The First Book," and ask them to consider why the author structures the poem as she does. When the class has finished reading the poem, discuss possible reasons why the first and last lines appear as they do. AS

The First Book

by Rita Dove

Open it.

EL
Go ahead, it won't bite.
Well . . . maybe a little.

More a nip, like. A tingle.
It's pleasurable, really. **1**

You see, it keeps on opening.
You may fall in.

Sure, it's hard to get started;
remember learning to use

knife and fork? Dig in:
you'll never reach bottom.

It's not like it's the end of the world—
just the world as you think

you know it. **2** ❍

Practice the Skills

1 **Comparing Literature**

Theme Dove says that the book won't bite, or that it might give you a nip, a tingle. What is the poet comparing a book to? Is this a clue about the theme? Explain.

2 BIG Question

BQ **Compare** What does the speaker say about reading in the last three lines? Would Michael Dorris agree? Fill in the chart under the "The First Book" with anything you want to add now that you've read and thought about it.

Homework, 1946. Milton Avery. Oil on canvas, 91.4 x 61 cm., Fundacion Coleccion Thyssen-Bornemisza, Madrid, Spain.

Teach

EL Language Coach

Figurative Language Say: Poems often use figurative language, or language that means something other than exactly what the words say. In this poem, the speaker says that a book might "bite... a little," or "nip." Of course, this does not mean that the speaker thinks the book has teeth! Why or how might a story or the words in a book "bite" you? ***(Possible response: The contents of a book might startle you, as would a bite. A book might grab your attention.)*** EL OL

BQ BIG Question

Say: At the end of the essay "Summer Reading," Michael Dorris writes that a book can "change the course of all that follows." How is this statement similar to the speaker's statement in the last three lines of "The First Book"? *(Possible response: This statement, like Dorris's, suggests that books can change completely the way you think about the world and live your life.)* OL Judging by their writings, why do you think Rita Dove and Michael Dorris consider reading important? *(Possible response: They probably consider it important because reading challenges us to see the world differently.)* AL

Differentiated Instruction

Making a Poster Discuss with students the images that Rita Dove uses in "The First Book" to show how a book can captivate and challenge a reader. Prompt students to compare Dove's description with their own experiences of reading books they love. Encourage students to think about the images they would use to represent these experiences. Then ask students to design posters that promote reading and that depict the experience of being captivated by a good book. OL

Objectives
- Compare and contrast literary texts
- Identify theme in a literary text
- Compare and contrast themes across texts
- Use context clues to determine word meanings

Assess

Resources for page 110

- Selection Quick Check
- Comparing Literature Assessment

Vocabulary Check

1. gestured
2. encounter
3. vividly
4. category
5. browsed
6. consciously
7. browsed
8. vividly
9. consciously
10. encounter
11. gestured
12. category

After You Read

Summer Reading & The First Book

Vocabulary Check

Copy each sentence with the best word in place. You will use each word in two sentences.

category
gestured
consciously
browsed
vividly
encounter

1. He raised his arms and ___ his surrender.
2. We had an unpleasant ___ with the other team after the game.
3. I ___ remember the bright red dress Mom wore.
4. Josie is definitely in the top ___ in math scores.
5. They could have ___ for hours in that giant bookstore.
6. She didn't ___ try to insult them; she just gave her honest opinion.
7. Elena ___ around the store until she found the sweater she wanted.
8. The lights of the city sparkled ___.
9. Tran ___ lost the game to his little sister to make her happy.
10. Chandra was surprised by her ___ with Amy.
11. Jermaine ___ for Kate to cross the street and talk.
12. Randall wanted a challenge, so he entered the swim meet in the highest ___.

Objectives (pp. 110–111)
Reading Compare and contrast literary texts
Literature Identify theme in a literary text • Compare and contrast themes across texts
Writing Write a response to literature: comparison/contrast, theme

"Summer Reading"	"The First Book"
Reads everything	May make you uncomfortable
Reads books more than once	Gives pleasure
Gets lost in the story	Keeps opening
Powerful language	You may fall in
Changed his life	You'll never reach bottom
	Changes the way you see the world

Reading/Critical Thinking

On a separate sheet of paper, answer the following questions.

Summer Reading

13. Compare and Contrast How did the author's experience reading *The Last of the Just* differ from his experience reading *Coming of Age in Samoa*?

TIP Think and Search The answers are in the story, but you will need to look in more than one place to find them.

14. Interpret What does the author mean when he says that summer reading was not an "innocent pastime" for him?

TIP Author and Me You will find clues in the story, but you'll also need to use information in your head.

The First Book

15. Interpret What do the lines "You see, it keeps on opening. /You may fall in" mean?

TIP Author and Me You will find clues in the poem, but you'll also need to use information in your head.

16. Evaluate Do you think reading can really give you new ideas about things? Explain.

TIP On My Own Answer from your own experiences.

Writing: Compare the Literature

Use Your Notes

17. Follow these steps to use the notes in your diagram to compare the theme of "Summer Reading" with the theme of "The First Book."

Step 1: Look over the diagrams you completed. Underline the details that are alike for both selections. Circle the details that are different.

Step 2: On a separate sheet of paper, copy the diagram below. List the details that are alike in the center of the diagram. List the details that are different for each selection on either side of the diagram.

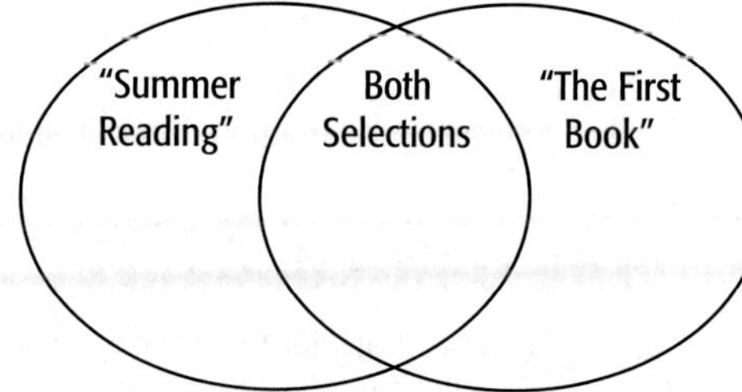

Step 3: Look at the new diagram. Notice what kinds of details are alike in the selections and what kinds of details are different.

Step 4: Think about what the details tell you about the theme of each selection. You will use these ideas to back up your statements in the assignment.

Get It On Paper

To show what you know about the theme of each of these selections, copy and complete these statements. Use the diagram you completed to get ideas.

18. I think the theme of "Summer Reading" is ___.

19. I think the theme of "The First Book" is ___.

20. The detail that helps me understand the theme of "Summer Reading" is ___.

21. The detail that helps me understand the theme of "The First Book" is ___.

BIG Question

22. Both selections are about reading. Answer these questions in your Learner's Notebook: How are the ideas about reading in the two selections alike? How are they different?

13. In *The Last of the Just,* Dorris felt the pain of the Holocaust and realized the power of a novel. He developed an interest in anthropology from *Coming of Age in Samoa.*

14. Dorris read books that made him think and change.

15. Each time you read a book you find something new and can get lost in the story.

16. Possible response: Yes. When you read, you can learn new information and ideas, learn about people, and have new experiences.

17. Sample table (See page 110.) Sample Venn Diagram (See below.)

Possible responses:

18. that reading can change your life

19. that reading can change the way you view the world

20. Dorris's description of how he felt while reading *The Last of the Just*

21. the phrase "it keeps on opening"

22. Both selections share the theme that reading can change the way you see the world. Each selection describes the experience of reading differently.

Close

Hold a class discussion based on students' responses to question 16.

Sample Venn Diagram

"Summer Reading"	Both Selections	"The First Book"
Power of language	Learn from reading again	Challenging
More valuable than money	Lose track of surroundings	Pleasurable
Can change your life	Can change you	Can change your views

The Unit Challenge

Focus

BELLRINGER Options

Daily Language Practice Transparency

Focus Activity Write on the board the titles of the selections in this unit. **Ask: Which of the selections in this unit did you most enjoy reading? Why?** Put a tally mark next to each title as students name their favorites.

Teach

Group Activity: Create a Commercial

- You may select the note taker or ask for volunteers.
- Make sure the group is on step 3 by midway through the class period to allow time to write the commercial.
- During the first practice, have someone time the commercial. Cut or add copy as needed.
- Have students practice several times before performing the commercial live.

Assess/Close

Group Activity

Ask: Which reasons for reading that you included in your commercial capture your personal reasons for reading? *(Suggest that students write their answers in their Learner's Notebook.)*

UNIT 1 WRAP-UP

Answering The BIG Question: Why Do We Read?

As you've read the selections, you've been thinking about people's reasons for reading. Now use what you've learned to do the Unit Challenge.

The Unit Challenge

Follow the directions for the activity you've chosen.

A. Group Activity: Create a Commercial

You and three to five other students are the creative team that has been chosen to develop a sixty-second TV commercial. You will be "selling" the idea of reading.

1. **Discuss the Assignment** First, brainstorm with your group to come up with as long a list of reasons to read as you can think of. The notes you made on your Foldable should help you. Choose a group member to take notes and keep track of the reasons. Try to be specific. You will get a longer list and better ideas for your commercial if you list "to live someone else's life for a while" or "to get scared to death" instead of a general reason, such as "to be entertained."

2. **Make Choices** Commercials are short! You can't work with every reason on your list. Choose the five reasons that you think your commercial can deal with best.

3. **Plan the Commercial** Think about commercials you have seen and work with your group to choose a style.
   - Should the commercial be funny or serious?
   - Do you want to *say* the reasons or *show* them?
   - Will everyone who is "on camera" be the age you are, or should some of the group members play older or younger people?

4. **Write the Commercial** When you write a commercial, you write down what the actors do, as well as what they say (if anything). Work together to get your ideas down on paper. Remember, you can explain your reasons to read or demonstrate them. All you should care about is getting your ideas across.

5. **Practice and Time the Commercial** Practice your commercial a few times and time it. If it runs longer than a minute, shorten it.

6. **Perform the Commercial** Long ago, commercials were performed "live," in the same way a play is shown. They weren't filmed or taped. Perform your commercial as a live performance for the class.

B. Solo Activity: Advertising Brochure

The selections in this unit have given you information and ideas about reasons to read. Now it's time to use those reasons to persuade other people to read—people who may not have discovered the benefits for themselves.

1. **Choose Reasons to Read** Look through your Foldable notes to find reasons to read. Choose the ones you think will work best to convince other people that reading is both useful and fun.

2. **Plan Your Brochure** A typical advertising brochure is made up of one regular-size piece of paper, folded twice. This creates six pages, three on one side of the paper and three on the other.
   - Fold a piece of paper to make a blank brochure.
   - Decide how many reasons you want to deal with on the brochure. Just one throughout? One per page?
   - Look for art that can illustrate the reason or reasons your brochure will advertise.

3. **Find or Create Art** An ad brochure depends on art to help communicate ideas, so you will need illustrations. Use magazines or other published material to find and cut out pictures, or draw your own.

4. **Make a "Dummy" Brochure** A "dummy" is like a rough draft. It shows where the art will go and where the "copy" (words) will go. Use your blank brochure. Draw the approximate size of your chosen art where you want it to go. Write advertising copy that identifies the reason or reasons you are advertising. The copy must fit in the space available for it. Keep working on art ideas and copy ideas until the dummy shows your final plan.

5. **Create the Final Brochure** Fold a clean piece of paper to make the real brochure. Paste or draw your final art in place. Write your final copy neatly where it goes. Now you're ready to hand it in!

Teach

Solo Activity: Advertising Brochure

- Have students look through their Foldable notes to find reasons to read.
- Help students fold paper to create a brochure.
- Have students decide the number of reasons they want to include in the brochure. Encourage them to write their reasons in their Learner's Notebook.
- Ask students to bring magazines to class to cut out the pictures for their brochures.
- Before they paste art onto the brochure or write on the brochure, have students make a "dummy" to see how everything fits together.
- The last step is to put the art work and words on the brochures. Tell students to review the brochure one final time to make sure that everything is correct.

Assess/Close

Solo Activity

Encourage students to study their brochures and write what they've learned about people's reasons for reading. Review their brochures and what they have learned.

Objectives
- Create advertising that persuades
- Organize information in a creative way

Focus

Vocabulary Preview
List the following words on the board and review their definitions:

- imitation
- yearned
- existence
- underprivileged
- nozzle
- despises

Build Background
Cockroaches are generally regarded as pests. However, they do make positive contributions to life on Earth.

- They assist in the decomposition of animal waste and trash left in woodland areas.
- They have contributed greatly to scientists' knowledge of insects.

Teach

R Reading Skill
Review Previewing Say: Read the title and look at the illustrations. Do you think this will be a serious or humorous selection? *(Possible response: The picture of the big cockroach and the title make me think this will be a humorous story.)* OL

Readability Scores
Dale-Chall: 7.8
DRP: 55
Lexile: 1090

UNIT 1

Your Turn: Read and Apply Skills

Paul Zindel

Meet the Author
"The Day It Rained Cockroaches" comes from Paul Zindel's book *The Pigman and Me,* which is the story of his life. Zindel was born in New York City in 1936. Many of his books, including *The Pigman and Me*, explore how teenagers and adults get along. "I try to show [teens] they aren't alone," he once said. "I know it's a continuing battle to get through the years between twelve and twenty." Zindel died in 2003. See page R8 of the Author Files in the back of the book for more on Paul Zindel.

Literature Online
Author Search For more about Paul Zindel, go to www.glencoe.com.

R The Day It Rained Cockroaches

by Paul Zindel

The three of us were very excited when we pulled up in front of our new home. There were some unusual things about it, but I've always been attracted to unusual things. For instance, I was the only kid I knew who always liked searching newspapers to find weird news. Whenever I found a shocking article or picture, I'd save it. That week alone, I had cut out a picture of a man who was born with monkey feet, a list of Seventy-Five Ways to Be Richer a Year from Now, and a report about a mother who sold her daughter to Gypsies in exchange for a theater trip to London. Also, there are ten biographical[1] points about me you should know right off the bat:[2]

1) My father ran away when I was two years old.

2) My sister taught me how to cut out fake coins from cardboard and make imitation lamb chops out of

1. ***Biographical*** means "having to do with someone's life story."
2. The expression ***off the bat*** comes from baseball and means "without delay."

Additional Support

Author Search To expand students' appreciation of Paul Zindel, have them access the Web site for additional information and resources.

Literature Focus Lesson

Summary In this autobiographical story, Paul Zindel recounts the story of moving with his mother and sister into a house in Travis, Staten Island. Because the house is infested with cockroaches, the family decides to activate insect bombs. The three leave to see a Lassie double feature while the bombs go to work. When the family returns, they find no dead roaches. Zindel's sister reads the directions on the insect bombs to learn that they should have opened all the closet doors before setting off the bombs just as Zindel opens a closet door and a shower of live cockroaches rains down on his head. OL clay, because we never had very much real money or food.

3) I once wanted to be Batman and fly off buildings.

4) I yearned to be kidnapped by aliens for a ride in their flying saucer.

5) Ever since I could remember I'd liked to make cyclorama[3] displays out of shoeboxes and cut out figures of ghosts, beasts, and teenagers to put in them.

6) I once prayed to own a pet gorilla.

C **R** 7) I used to like to play tricks on people, like putting thumbtacks on their seats.

8) When my father's father was sixteen, he got a job on a Dutch freighter, sailed to America, jumped ship and swam to Staten Island, got married, and opened a bake shop, and he and his wife died from eating too many crumb-cakes before Betty[4] and I could meet them.

9) A truck once ran over my left elbow. It really hurt and left a little scar.

10) I am afraid I will one day die by shark attack.

About anything else you'd ever want to know about my preteen existence you can see in the photos in this book. However, I don't think life *really* started for me until I became a teenager and my mother moved us to Travis, on Staten Island.

3. A ***cyclorama*** is a picture that surrounds a viewer. The author probably meant *diorama*—a miniature display of a scene that uses small figures.
4. ***Betty*** is the author's sister.

Teach

C Critical Thinking

Evaluation Ask: After you have read his biographical points, what can you conclude about Zindel as a young boy? *(Possible response: Zindel was curious and yearned for adventure.)* **OL**

R Reading Skill

Review Understanding Text Structure Say: Many biographies are chronological, that is, key events are listed in the order in which they happened. Why do you think Zindel avoids a sequential list and instead offers a random list of "biographical points"? *(Possible response: The order in which events happened may not have been important to Zindel. Zindel may have preferred to list the events in their order of importance to him.)* **AL**

Differentiated Instruction

Self-Characterization Invite students to compose lists of ten biographical points that others should know about them "right off the bat." Tell students to use Zindel's list as a model for their own lists. Invite students to share one or two items from their lists with the class. Then, have each student write a paragraph that explains why people should know these particular points. **OL** You may want to direct the attention of ELL students to the second footnote on page 114 and explain that the phrase *right off the bat* means "first" or "now." **EL**

Objectives
- Preview text
- Use text features: title
- Identify text structure: sequence

Teach

L Literary Element

Review Theme Say: Mother thinks everything about the new home is beautiful. Paul and Betty don't agree. Is that going to be part of the theme? *(Possible response: Paul and Betty's reaction to the house seems to have something to do with the theme.)*

R Reading Skill

Review Understanding Text Structure Say: Reread page 116. What earlier events lead to the narrator's finding the cockroaches? *(Family drives into town. > Family stops in front of 123 Glen Street. > Narrator describes outside of house and its surroundings. > Mom opens the front door. > Narrator and sister run through house. > Cockroaches are disturbed by footfalls of narrator and sister.)* **OL** Why does the author describe the town, the house, its surroundings, and the apple tree? *(Responses will vary. Students may say that the author wants to create a happy scene so that the cockroaches will seem all the more ugly.)* **AL**

When we first drove into the town, I noticed a lot of plain wood houses, a Catholic church, a war memorial, three saloons with men sitting outside on chairs, seventeen women wearing kerchiefs[5] on their heads, a one-engine firehouse, a big redbrick school, a candy store, and a butcher shop with about 300 sausages hanging in the window. Betty shot me a private look, signaling she was aghast.[6] Travis was mainly a Polish town, and was so special-looking that, years later, it was picked as a location for filming the movie *Splendor in the Grass,* which starred Natalie Wood (before she drowned), and Warren Beatty (before he dated Madonna). Travis was selected because they needed a town that looked like it was Kansas in 1920, which it still looks like.

The address of our new home was 123 Glen Street. We stopped in front, and for a few moments the house looked normal: brown shingles, pea-soup-green–painted sides, a tiny yellow porch, untrimmed hedges, and a rickety wood gate and fence. Across the street to the left was a slope with worn gravestones all over it. The best-preserved ones were at the top, peeking out of patches of poison oak.

The backyard of our house was an airport. I mean, the house had two acres of land of its own, but beyond the rear fence was a huge field consisting of a single dirt runway, lots of old propeller-driven Piper Cub–type planes, and a cluster of rusted hangars.[7] This was the most underprivileged airport I'd ever seen, bordered on its west side by the Arthur Kill channel and on its south side by a Con Edison electric power plant with big black mountains of coal. The only great sight was a huge apple tree on the far left corner of our property. Its trunk was at least three feet wide. It had strong, thick branches rich with new, flapping leaves. It reached upward like a giant's hand grabbing for the sky.

"Isn't everything beautiful?" Mother beamed.

"Yes, Mom," I said.

Betty gave me a pinch for lying.

"I'll plant my own rose garden," Mother went on, fumbling for the key. "Lilies, tulips, violets!"

Mom opened the front door and we went inside. We were so excited, we ran through the echoing empty rooms, pulling up old, soiled shades to let the sunlight crash in. We ran upstairs and downstairs, all over the place like wild ponies. The only unpleasant thing, from my point of view, was that we weren't the only ones running around. There were a lot of cockroaches scurrying from our invading footfalls and the shafts of light.

"Yes, the house has a few roaches," Mother confessed. "We'll get rid of them in no time!"

"How?" Betty asked raising an eyebrow.

"I bought eight Gulf Insect Bombs!"

"Where are they?" I asked.

5. A ***kerchief*** is an old-fashioned head scarf.
6. ***Aghast*** means "shocked."
7. There is a group, or ***cluster,*** of ***hangars,*** which are buildings where airplanes are kept.

Additional Support

English Language Coach

American Pop Culture Review the following references for students:

- page 116: Natalie Wood was born in 1938. She appeared in several movies, including the musical *West Side Story.* Wood died in a drowning accident in 1981.
- page 116: Warren Beatty was born in 1937. *Splendor in the Grass* was his first film. Beatty has acted in and worked on many other movies.
- page 117: Lassie, a brave collie, is the creation of writer Eric Knight. The first in a series of movies about the dog and its adventures came out in 1943. Later, a popular television series also featured Lassie. **EL**

Mother dashed out to the car and came back with one of the suitcases. From it she spilled the bombs, which looked like big silver hand grenades.

"We just put one in each room and turn them on!" Mother explained.

She took one of the bombs, set it in the middle of the upstairs kitchen, and turned on its nozzle. A cloud of gas began to stream from it, and we hurried into the other rooms to set off the other bombs.

"There!" Mother said. "Now we have to get out!"

"Get out?" I coughed.

"Yes. We must let the poison fill the house for four hours before we can come back in! Lucky for us there's a Lassie double feature[8] playing at the Ritz!"

We hadn't been in the house ten minutes before we were driving off again!

I suppose you might as well know now that my mother really *loved* Lassie movies. The only thing she enjoyed more were movies in which romantic couples got killed at the end by tidal waves, volcanos, or other natural disasters. Anyway, I was glad we were gassing the roaches, because they are the one insect I despise.

8. A ***double feature*** is when two movies are shown, one after the other, for the price of one.

Teach

EL Language Coach

Context Clues Ask: How can you use context clues to figure out what natural disasters are? *(The author provides examples of two natural disasters—tidal waves and volcanoes. A natural disaster must be an event in nature that causes a great deal of destruction.)* **BL**

E Text Elements

Review Photos and Illustrations Say: Lassie is a type of dog called a collie. If you do not know who Lassie is or what a collie looks like, how can the picture help? *(Possible response: This drawing shows what a typical collie looks like and helps the reader imagine Lassie as a fast, strong dog.)* **BL** **Ask:** What do you learn about the character Lassie from the illustration? *(Responses will vary. Students may suggest that Lassie is brave because she appears to be running to rescue someone.)* **AL**

Reading in the Real World

Citizenship Help students understand why Zindel and his family had to avoid the poison in the Gulf Insect Bombs. Explain that pesticides are sprays and powders that kill insects. Although many farmers use these products to kill insects and some homeowners use them to protect their homes and gardens, insecticides cause pollution. Therefore, many people choose organic farming and natural pesticides. Have students find an article online about natural pesticides or organic living. Suggest that students start by visiting: http://www.epa.gov/pesticides/food/organics.htm. **OL**

Objectives

- Use sequence and cause and effect to understand events in a story
- Use illustrations to understand reading

Teach

R1 Reading Skill

Review Understanding Text Structure **Say:** Zindel recounts the events of his story in chronological order. Why does he interrupt this order to tell about an event that happened when he was three years old? *(Possible response: to explain his fear of cockroaches)* **OL** **Ask:** If you were to map the events in the story on a time line, where would you place the events related to the World Fair? *(Possible responses: before the move to Travis; somewhere near the beginning.)* **BL**

R2 Reading Skill

Review Reviewing **Ask:** If you are having trouble keeping track of events and the order in which they happen, what should you do? *(Review the story; go back and reread.)* **BL**

The Apple Tree, 1916. Gustav Klimt. Oil on canvas, 80 x 80 in. Osterreichische Galerie Belvedere, Vienna, Austria.

Tarantulas I like. Scorpions I can live with.[9] But ever since I was three years old and my mother took me to a World's Fair, I have had nightmares about cockroaches. Most people remember an exciting water ride this fair had called the Shoot-the-Chutes, but emblazened on my brain[10] is the display the fair featured of giant, live African cockroaches, which look like American cockroaches except they're six inches long, have furry legs, and can pinch flesh. In my nightmares about them, I'm usually lying on a bed in a dark room and **R1** I notice a bevy[11] of giant cockroaches heading for me. I try to run away but find out that someone has secretly tied me down on the bed, and the African roaches start crawling up the sides of the sheets. They

9. ***Tarantulas*** are large, hairy spiders with painful bites, and ***scorpions*** are spider-like, with poisonous stingers on the end of their tails.

10. Something that is ***emblazoned*** on your brain is unforgettable. *Emblazoned* means "burned," and a memory that was "burned" into your brain would stay there.

11. A ***bevy*** is a large group.

Additional Support

Differentiated Instruction

Childhood Memories Explain that a memoir is a story of someone's life. *The Day It Rained Cockroaches* is a memoir of sorts. Invite students to write about childhood memories that continue to affect their interests, values, or fears today. Tell students to use Zindel's African cockroach story as a model. Remind students to use descriptive language and dialogue to make their accounts more interesting and entertaining. Ask volunteers to read their accounts aloud to the class. Encourage students to read a memoir from their local library. **AL**

walk all over my body, and then they head for my face. When they start trying to drink from my mouth is when I wake up screaming.

So after the movie I was actually looking forward to going back to the house and seeing all the dead cockroaches.

"Wasn't Lassie wonderful?" Mother sighed as she drove us back to Travis. "The way that brave dog was able to crawl hundreds of miles home after being kidnapped and beaten by Nazi Secret Service Police!"

"Yes, Mom," I agreed, although I was truthfully tired of seeing a dog movie star keep pulling the same set of tear-jerking stunts in each of its movies.

"Maybe we'll get a dog just like Lassie one day," Mother sighed.

When we got back to the house this time, we didn't run into it. We walked inside very slowly, sniffing for the deadly gas. I didn't care about the gas so much as I wanted to see a lot of roach corpses all over the place so I'd be able to sleep in peace.

But there were none.

"Where are all the dead roaches?" I asked.

"I don't know," Mother admitted.

We crept slowly upstairs to see if the bodies might be there. I knew the kitchen had the most roaches, but when we went in, I didn't see a single one, living or dead. The lone empty Gulf Insect Bomb sat spent in **R1** the middle of the floor. My sister picked up the bomb and started reading the directions. One thing my mother never did was follow directions. As Betty was reading, I noticed a closed closet door and reached out to turn its knob.

"It says here we should've opened all the closet doors before setting off the bombs, so roaches can't hide." Betty moaned, her clue to me that Mom had messed up again.

I had already started to open the door. My mind knew what was going to happen, but it was too late to tell my hand to stop pulling on the door. It sprang open, and suddenly 5,000 very angry, living cockroaches rained down on me from the ceiling of the closet. **BQ**

R2 "Eeehhhhhhh!" I screamed, leaping around the room, bathed in bugs, slapping at the roaches crawling all over me and down my neck! "Eeehhhhhhh! Eeehh! Ehhh! Ehh!"

"Don't worry. I'll get more bombs," Mother said comfortingly as she grabbed an old dishrag to knock the fluttering roaches off my back. Betty calmly reached out her foot to crunch as many as dared run by her. ❍

YOUR TURN

Teach

R1 Reading Skill

Review Reviewing Ask: Were you surprised that Zindel's mother did not use the insect bombs correctly? Zindel foreshadowed this event with hints about his mother's lack of attention to detail. *(Possible response: No. Zindel's mother says that the house is beautiful, but it's not. She says that there are a "few roaches" when there are thousands.)* **AL**

R2 Reading Skill

Review Setting a Purpose for Reading Say: Think back to the purpose you set for reading. Explain whether you achieved your purpose. *(Answers will vary.)* **OL**

BQ BIG Question

Ask: How would reading have kept Zindel from realizing his worst nightmare? *(A careful reading of the directions for the insect bombs would have saved Zindel from a rain shower of live cockroaches.)* **OL** **Ask:** What does this story teach about reading the directions before using a product? *(Possible response: When you read the directions, you find out how to use the product correctly so that you can get the results you want.)* **BL**

Differentiated Instruction

Reading the Fine Print Provide students with various sets of directions, including those for household products and medicines. Tell students to read the directions carefully, identifying the parts that are essential to proper use. Then, ask students to brainstorm and discuss what might happen if these key aspects of the directions are not followed. **AL** Have students create bumper stickers for a safety campaign about the importance of reading and following directions on consumer and medicinal products. Send the bumper stickers to the appropriate local organizations such as pharmacies, grocery stores, or local emergency clinics. **BL**

Objectives

- Identify text structure
- Monitor comprehension: review
- Set a purpose for reading

Tips for Independent Reading

Stress the importance of each student's spending at least thirty minutes a day in independent reading and suggest books, such as those shown here, related to the Big Question.

Fiction

Tell students that reading fiction allows them to escape into another world and experience things through the eyes of a character.

Ask students to share an example of a fictional story they've read in which they experienced life through a character's eyes; they may name fictional stories from this unit.

UNIT 1

Reading on Your Own

To read more about the Big Question, choose one of these books from your school or local library. Work on your reading skills by choosing books that are challenging to you.

Fiction

The Witch of Blackbird Pond
by Elizabeth George Speare

In Puritan New England in 1687, a high-spirited teenager befriends an old woman known as the Witch of Blackbird Pond and finds herself accused of witchcraft. Read the selection to be entertained and to find out about Puritan New England.

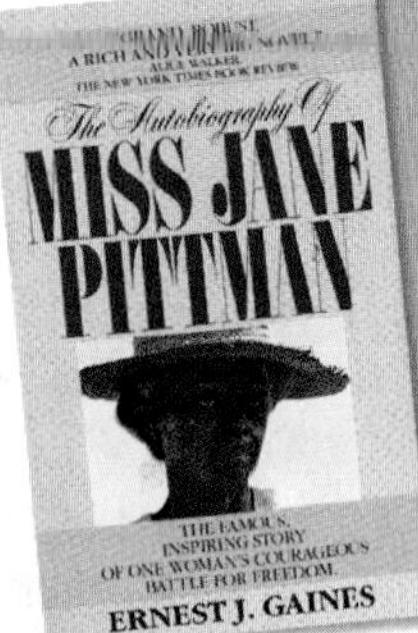

The Autobiography of Miss Jane Pittman
by Ernest J. Gaines

In this novel about a 110-year-old African American woman, Miss Jane Pittman recollects events in her life in the South from the Civil War to the Civil Rights movement of the 1960s. This novel will help you understand the life, problems, and experiences of Miss Jane Pittman.

A Wrinkle in Time
by Madeleine L'Engle

Meg Murry's father has mysteriously disappeared. Strangers from another planet bring upsetting news that sends Meg on a journey along with her brother Charles and her friend Calvin. The three set off to rescue Mr. Murry and to combat an evil force that is trying to take over the universe. Read this novel for fun, excitement, and suspense.

Where You Belong
by Mary Ann McGuigan

Fiona, her mother, and three siblings are evicted from their home. After an abusive father seems to provide no refuge for her, thirteen-year-old Fiona tries to discover where she belongs. Read the story to understand what Fiona experiences.

Additional Support

Differentiated Instruction

Use the Glencoe BookLink CD-ROM to create customized reading lists to help students answer the Big Question. Suggestions for Unit 1:

Grade 4: *Her Stories: African American Folktales, Fairy Tales, and True Tales* by Virginia Hamilton
Grade 5: *The Fortune-Tellers* by Lloyd Alexander
Grade 6: *The Westing Game* by Ellen Raskin
Grade 7: *The Orchid Thief* by Susan Orlean
Grade 8: *Red-Tail Angels* by Patricia and Fredrick McKissack

UNIT 2

Professional Development Center

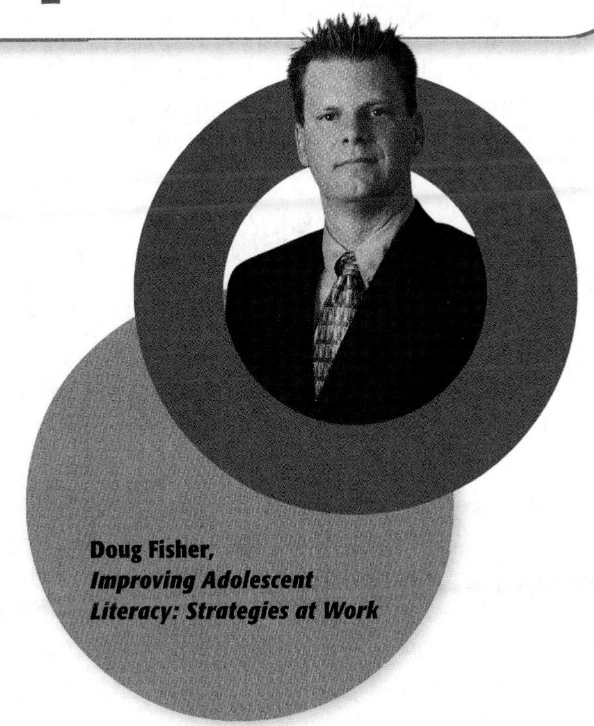

Doug Fisher,
Improving Adolescent Literacy: Strategies at Work

From Your Authors:

Preparing Students To Read Biographies

Tap into prior knowledge Quick writes are frequently used in English classrooms at the introduction of a new reading to tap into prior knowledge and reader-related experiences, as well as to initiate a reading/writing connection. The choice of text is crucial, too. Reading multicultural literature can build confidence in fledgling second language readers and writers. When students relate to good literature on a personal level, they discover a purpose for reading and response, and begin to find their writer's voice. Before reading *The Circuit: Stories From the Life of a Migrant Child* by Fransicsco Jimenez (1997), the students in Rita ElWardi's ESL class participated in a number of anticipatory activities focused on thought-provoking questions related to a quick write designed to accomplish these objectives.

Make personal connections In order to establish a personal connection with the character and the central conflict in the story, students were asked to write about a moment they remembered well; a moment when they had to say good-bye. Because English language learners need structured support in writing, Ms. ElWardi created a list of guiding questions to help even the most reluctant writers begin to recount such an experience. She reminded her students that these questions are there to provoke thought and should not all be answered. To introduce this activity, she recounted an unforgettable moment when she also had to leave a place and a group of friends. Using the questions as her guide, she modeled how these questions could structure a response. Her questions included:

- Where and when did this take place?
- Who was with you and why?
- Why did you have to leave this place or say good-bye to this person?

Shelley Evans-Marshall, MA
Secondary English Teacher

Teacher to Teacher:

Using Personal Stories

What do I do when I want the undivided attention of my students? I tell a personal story, like the time I went to a dance with a boy and never danced or the time I had to apologize to my entire gym class because I got into an argument with my best friend. When I begin to tell a personal story, the students sit up straight; they make eye contact; and they raise their hands to ask questions. By sharing my stories, I build bridges that connect with the stories of my students; I become more than a teacher—to my students, I become a real person who experiences many of the same feelings as they do. While using this unit on biographies, help students see that these selections are personal stories about people.

Literature Launchers

Set the scene with Glencoe's Literature Launchers, engaging video segments that introduce each unit's genre focus. Each video brings the genre to life, relating it to your students' worlds.

Insert the Glencoe Literature Launchers Pre-Reading Videos DVD into your DVD player. Select the Unit 2 Launcher from the menu to introduce the genre and Big Question for this unit.

Online Essay Grader

Use Glencoe's Online Essay Grading to score your students' writing and to provide individualized feedback to each student automatically.

You and your students can visit www.glencoe.com to link to the essay grader. *Students* can enter their essays and receive feedback on demand. *You* can manage demographic data, assign tests and generate individual student and aggregated reports. The essay grader can help you

- Save time with automatic scoring and individualized feedback.
- Supplement in-class writing instruction using guided writing practice.
- Get reports for individual students or for special populations.
- Track student improvement over time.

REAL Success: Reading Excellence at All Levels

Glencoe now provides all of your students with the tools they need to become better, more enthusiastic readers. The REAL Success suite of reading and language arts products encourages reading excellence by meeting the needs of students at all levels. Glencoe products that can be used in conjunction with Unit 2 include the following:

- Jamestown Literature: An Adapted Reader
- Jamestown *Reading Fluency*
- Jamestown *Critical Reading Series, In the Line of Duty*
- *Vocabulary Builder*
- *The Glencoe Reader, Course 2*

To order these products, call Glencoe at 1-800-USA-READ.

Teacher Wraparound Edition Key

Level Appropriate Code

AS = Activities for all students

AL = Activities for students working above grade level

OL = Activities for students working at grade level

BL = Activities for students working below grade level

EL = Activities for English language learners

Teacher Wraparound Prompts

R **Reading Skill** These activities help you teach reading skills and vocabulary.

V **Vocabulary** These activities help students comprehend words and incorporate into reading.

C **Critical Thinking** These strategies help students apply and extend what they have learned.

BQ **BIG Question** These activities and questions prompt students to prepare to answer the Big Question.

W **Writing** These activities provide writing opportunities to help students practice writing and comprehend text.

L **Literary Element** These activities and questions help students comprehend selections and learn more about each genre.

E **Text Element** These activities help students comprehend text elements.

LSV **Listening, Speaking, Viewing** These activities help students practice listening, speaking, and viewing skills.

EL **English Language Coach** These skills help English language learners as well as students who need additional reading support.

Additional Glencoe Resources

Dinah Zike's Foldables

Foldables are three-dimensional, interactive graphic organizers that help students practice basic writing skills, review key vocabulary terms, and answer Big Questions. Every unit contains a foldable activity. You can find the pattern and directions for the Unit 2 Foldable in the Unit 2 Resources Fast Files booklet. You can use the foldables as they are presented or modify them to suit the needs of your students. More information about foldables for Unit 2 can be found on page R8.

Glencoe Literature Library

The collection of hardcover books include full-length novels, novellas, plays and works of nonfiction. Each volume consists of at least one complete extended-length reading accompanied by several related readings from a broad range of genres. A separate Study Guide for each Glencoe Literature Library book provides teaching notes and reproducible activity pages for students.

Glencoe Literature Library titles that complement this unit include:

Bearstone by Will Hobbs
A Girl Named Disaster by Nancy Farmer
Letters from a Slave Girl by Mary E. Lyons
Sha banu: Daughter of the Wind by Suzanne Fisher Staples

For a wealth of online resources that support the instruction in Unit 2 of *Glencoe Literature: Reading with Purpose,* students and teachers can visit our Web site at www.glencoe.com. Students will find additional learning, practice, and assessment opportunities such as these, which are noted in the student text:

- **Big Question Overview**
- **Study Central**
- **Author Search**
- **Writing Models**
- **Interactive Literary Elements Handbook**
- **Web Activities**

Teachers will find planning and instructional tools that include the following:

- **Book Lesson Plans**
- **Teacher Forum**
- **Professional Development**
- **Web Activities Lesson Plans (with answers to student activities)**

Go to www.glencoe.com to see the entire selection of Reading with Purpose online resources.

Use the Glencoe BookLink 3 CD-ROM, a database of more than 26,700 titles, to *create customized reading lists* for your students.

- Search for award-winning titles, (e.g., Newbery Award winners, Coretta Scott King Award winners, and Caldecott Medal winners) and for books on several state-recommended reading lists.
- Find Degrees of Reading Power™ (DRP) and Lexile™ readability scores for all selections.
- Organize reading lists by students' reading level, author, genre, theme, or area of interest.
- Get a brief summary of each selection.

You can find recommended leveled readings for this unit with Reading on Your Own (see page 120).

Glencoe's **Presentation Plus!**, a multimedia teaching tool, lets you present dynamic lessons that will engage your students. Using Microsoft PowerPoint,® you can customize the presentations to create your own personalized lessons. Use **CheckPoint** questions with interactive response keypads to get immediate student feedback during lessons, to increase student participation, and to assess student comprehension.

A lively collection of articles drawn from issues of the TIME family of magazines helps students develop the skills they need to interact with informational text in a meaningful way. Each of the news stories, feature articles, reviews, profiles, and essays in the magazine connect to an author, work, or theme in *Glencoe Literature: Reading with Purpose.* Articles for Unit 2 are found in Volume A. See the *inTIME* Teacher's Guide for specific connections to each unit and for reproducible student worksheets designed to develop students' reading and critical thinking skills.

Additional Instructional Support

WRITING, GRAMMAR, AND SPELLING

- Real Success in Writing: Research and Reports
- Writing Constructed Responses Sourcebook
- Spelling Power eWorkbook
- Grammar & Composition Handbook
- Grammar and Language Workbook
- Revising with Style eWorkbook

TRANSPARENCIES

- Read Aloud, Think Aloud
- Literary and Text Analysis Transparencies
- Bellringer Options Transparencies
- Grammar and Writing Workshop Transparencies
- Fine Arts Transparencies

ENGLISH LANGUAGE LEARNER

- English Language Coach
- Fluency Practice and Assessment
- inTime Magazines (Spanish)
- Spanish Listening Library CD

PROFESSIONAL DEVELOPMENT

- Professional Development Package

READING AND LITERATURE

- Active Learning and Note Taking Guide
- inTime Magazines
- Backpack Reader Volume 1
- Literature Library
- Literature Launchers Pre-Reading Videos DVD
- Literature Classics

TECHNOLOGY

- TeacherWorks Plus
- StudentWorks Plus
- BookLink 3
- Skill Level Up!
- ExamView Assessment Suite
- Interactive Tutor Self-Assessment
- Listening Library CD
- Spanish Listening Library CD
- Literature Classics
- Literature Launchers Pre-Reading Videos DVD
- Literature Library ExamView Assessment Suite
- Vocabulary Puzzlemaker
- Literature Library Vocabulary Puzzlemaker
- glencoe.com
- Online Student Edition
- Presentation Plus!
- Glencoe Online Essay Grading

UNIT 2

Unit Resources

Reading with Purpose offers a comprehensive package of tools to optimize student learning and the teaching experience. Each resource has been designed to assist students in specific areas and to offer instructional support for teachers. While all of these areas are covered in the core textbook, some students may need extra practice or additional help in specific areas. The resource package is designed so that you, the teacher, can choose which items will best assist your students. You may also use these resources as homework assignments and for assessment purposes. The following are resources recommended for use with Unit 2.

Keys for Unit Resources

- Blackline Master
- Workbook
- Supplemental Text
- CD-ROM
- DVD
- Transparency
- Web-based
- Fast Files

Essential Instructional Support

FAST FILE UNIT 2 RESOURCES

Reading and Literature

- Academic Vocabulary Development
- Big Question: School to Home Connection
- The Big Question Foldable
- Genre Study
- Unit Challenge: Planner and Rubrics
- Comparing Literature Graphic Organizer
- Key Reading Skills Practice
- Active Reading Graphic Organizers
- Literary Analysis
- Selection Vocabulary Development

Writing, Grammar, and Spelling

- Spelling and Handwriting Practice
- Grammar Practice
- Writing Workshop Graphic Organizer

Listening, Speaking, and Viewing

- Viewing and Representing Activities
- Listening and Speaking Activities

English Language Learners

- English Language Coach

DIFFERENTIATED INSTRUCTION

- Leveled Vocabulary Development
- Skill Level Up!
- Listening Library CD
- BookLink 3
- Literature Library Vocabulary Puzzlemaker
- Vocabulary Puzzlemaker

ASSESSMENT

- Selection and Unit Assessments
- Selection Quick Checks
- Assessment by Learning Objectives
- Rubrics for Assessing Student Writing, Listening, and Speaking
- Glencoe Online Essay Grading
- Interactive Tutor Self-Assessment
- ExamView Assessment Suite
- Literature Library ExamView Assessment Suite

CRITICAL THINKING	VOCABULARY	WRITING AND GRAMMAR	LISTENING, SPEAKING, AND VIEWING
Comprehension, TWE p. 201	Word Choice, TWE p. 199 First Person Point of View, TWE p. 198	Writing an Autobiographical Narrative: Revising, Editing, and Presenting, SE p. 198–203 Writing Traits: Voice, SE p. 199 Creative writing, TWE p. 200	Group Discussion and Active Listening, SE p. 203 Staying focused, TWE p. 203
Infer, SE pp. 214, 220 Summarize, SE pp. 214, 220 Synthesize, SE p. 214 Analyze, SE p. 220, TWE pp. 210, 217 Comprehension, TWE pp. 205, 207–209, 218	Using Word References, SE pp. 206, 215, 216 Multiple-meaning words, SE pp. 210, 218, 219, 221 Academic Vocabulary, SE p. 215 Vocabulary Practice, TWE p. 210	Write About Your Reading, SE p. 220 Write to Learn, SE pp. 206, 207, 216, 217 Object Pronouns, SE p. 221 Poem, TWE p. 210 Subject Pronouns, SE p. 215	Talk About Your Reading, SE p. 214 Viewing the Photo, TWE p. 209
Interpret, SE p. 235 Infer, SE p. 235 Comprehension, TWE pp. 226, 232 Evaluate, TWE pp. 227, 229, 230, 233	Multiple-meaning words, SE pp. 226, 231 Description, TWE pp. 226, 227 Prefixes, TWE p. 228 Baseball Terms, TWE p. 231	Taking notes and using them to make a chart that compares the setting in two pieces of literature, SE p. 235	Viewing the Photo, TWE p. 225
Application, TWE p. 239 Comprehension, TWE p. 239 Analysis, TWE p. 240		Writing a personal letter, SE p. 236 Organizing thoughts using a web diagram, SE p. 237 Speech writing, TWE p. 240	Speech Writing, TWE p. 240

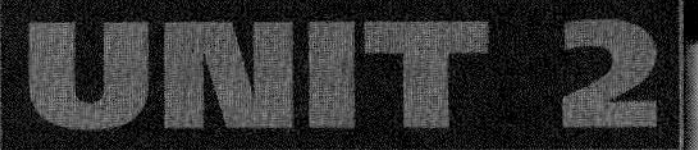

Skills Scope and Sequence *continued*

Readability Scores Key
Dale-Chall/DRP/Lexile

PACING (DAYS) STANDARD	BLOCK	INSTRUCTIONAL SEGMENT LITERATURE	READING SKILLS	LITERARY ELEMENTS
1	cont'd. ↓	**Writing Workshop, Part 2, pp. 198–203** Writing Product: Autobiographical Narrative	Fluency, TWE p. 201	Author's Purpose, TWE p. 202
2	1	**Reading Workshop 4, pp. 204–221** from *Red Scarf Girl: A Memoir of the Cultural Revolution* by Ji-li Jiang **5.1/52/760**, SE p. 208 "Miracle Hands" TIME by Christina Cheakalos and Matt Birkbeck **6.2/58/920**, SE p. 218	Understanding sequence, SE pp. 204–205, 207, 212, 215, 217, 218, 219, 221 Connecting, SE pp. 208, 211, 215 Fluency, TWE p. 211 Title and Subtitle, SE p. 221	Sensory Details, SE pp. 207, 209, 213, 215, 217, 218, 221; TWE pp. 207, 216 Narrators, TWE p. 205 Point of view, TWE p. 208 Dialogue, TWE p. 212 Time order, TWE p. 218
2	2	**Comparing Literature Workshop, pp. 222–235** from *Barrio Boy,* by Ernesto Galarza **6.4/58/1100**, SE p. 225 "How I Learned English" by Gregory Djanikian SE p. 232	Fluency, TWE p. 233 Infer, TWE pp. 227, 228 Connecting, TWE p. 233	Comparing Settings, SE pp. 222–223, 225, 227, 229, 232, 235 Sequence of Events, TWE p. 232 Character, TWE p. 230 Analyzing setting, TWE p. 222 Description, TWE p. 227 Point of View, TWE pp. 228, 232
2	1	**Unit Wrap-Up, pp. 236–249** "Graduation Address" by Robert L. Fontaine **4.5/47/NA**, SE p. 238	Reading independently, SE pp. 242–243	Summary, TWE p. 238

Unit 2 Big Question

The question, **"How can we become who we want to be?"** is designed to help students think critically about setting and attaining goals, overcoming obstacles, and understanding who they want to become. In this unit, students will see how a variety of people pushed to become who they wanted to be.

Unit 2 Genre

Many of the stories in this unit are **biographies** that tell personal stories. These selections will also help students answer the big question: How can we become who we want to be? Use these biographies stories to help students connect to a variety of people who have become who they wanted to be and will inspire your students to do the same.

CRITICAL THINKING	VOCABULARY	WRITING AND GRAMMAR	LISTENING, SPEAKING, AND VIEWING
	Multiple-meaning words, TWE p. 133 Time-Order Words, TWE p. 135		
Infer, SE pp. 144, 150, TWE p. 149 Evaluate, SE pp. 144, 150 Analysis, TWE p. 142 Application, TWE p. 147	Multiple-meaning words, SE pp. 138, 141, 143, 145, 146, 149, 151, TWE pp. 139, 147 Academic vocabulary, SE pp. 136, 145 Legal Terms, TWE p. 142	Nouns, SE p. 145 Pronouns, SE p. 151 Write About Your Reading, SE p. 150 Write to Learn, SE pp. 138, 139, 144, 147, 150	Talk About Your Reading, SE p. 144 Viewing the Photo, TWE pp. 140, 142, 148
	Word parts, TWE p. 152	Writing an Autobiographical narrative: prewriting and drafting, SE pp. 152–153, 154 Kinds of Nouns, SE p. 155 Voice, TWE p. 153	
Infer, SE pp. 166, 174 Evaluate , SE pp. 166, 174 Summarize, SE p. 174 Comprehension, TWE pp. 160, 161, 162, 163, 164, 165, 170	Multiple-meaning words in context, SE pp. 158, 163, 167, 168, 173, 175 Idioms, TWE p. 160 Using vocabulary, TWE p. 169	Pronoun antecedents, SE p. 167 Write About Your Reading, SE pp. 166, 174 Indefinite pronouns, SE p. 175 Writing poetry, TWE p. 165 Write to Learn, SE pp. 158, 159, 168, 169	Viewing the Art, TWE pp. 160, 162 Viewing the Photo, TWE p. 171
Infer, SE pp. 184, 196 Summarize, SE pp. 184, 196 Evaluate, SE pp. 184, 196, TWE p. 183 Comprehension, TWE pp. 183, 192, 194	Using word references (Dictionary), SE pp. 178, 182, 183, 185, 186, 190, 197 Reading dictionary entry, TWE p. 179 Idioms, TWE p. 188 Vocabulary practice, TWE p. 183 Compound words, TWE p. 191	Pronouns, SE p. 185 Reflexive and Intensive Pronouns, SE p. 197 Write About Your Reading, SE p. 196 Write to Learn, SE pp. 178, 179, 184, 186	Talk About Your Reading, SE p. 184 Viewing the Photo, TWE p. 193

UNIT 2

Skills Scope and Sequence

Readability Scores Key
Dale-Chall/DRP/Lexile

PACING (DAYS) STANDARD	BLOCK	INSTRUCTIONAL SEGMENT LITERATURE	READING SKILLS	LITERARY ELEMENTS
1	1	**Unit Warm-Up, pp. 130–135** Genre Focus: *Tony Hawk: Chairman of the Board* by Steve Pittman **4.7/53/830**, SE p. 133	Activating prior knowledge, SE p. 132 Connecting, SE p. 132 Inferring, SE p. 132 Identifying sequence, SE p. 132	Narrator, SE p. 132, TWE p. 132 Point of view, SE p. 132 Setting, SE p. 132 Sensory Details, SE p. 132
3	2	**Reading Workshop 1, pp. 136–151** from *Rosa Parks: My Story* by Rosa Parks with Jim Haskins **5.0/50/840**, p. 140 "Kids in Action: Dalie Jimenez" by Barbara A. Lewis **5.2/59/900**, SE p. 148	Activating prior knowledge, SE pp. 136–137, 139, 140, 143, 145, 147, 148, 151 Using Text Features, SE pp. 142, 145 Titles and Subtitles, SE p. 151	Narrator, SE pp. 139, 141, 145, 147, 148, 151 Nonfiction, TWE p. 138
1		**Writing Workshop, Part 1, pp. 152–155** Writing Product: Autobiographical Narrative	Fluency, TWE p. 155	Autobiography, TWE p. 154
3	1	**Reading Workshop 2, pp. 156–175** "An Hour with Abuelo" by Judith Ortiz Cofer **5.2/51/860**, SE p. 160 "Toward a Rainbow Nation" by Lavendhri Pillay **5.8/56/990**, SE p. 170	Connecting, SE pp. 156–157, 159, 161, 164, 167, 169, 170, 171, 172, 175 Fluency, TWE pp. 158, 172 Titles and Subtitles, SE pp. 167, 175	Point of view, SE pp. 159, 160, 162, 163, 164, 167, 169, 171, 175 Time order, TWE 161 Nonfiction, TWE p. 168 Short Story, TWE p. 162
3	1	**Reading Workshop 3, pp. 176–197** "New Directions" by Maya Angelou **6.4/61/1360**, SE p. 180 "The War of the Wall" by Toni Cade Bambara **5.1/53/930**, SE p. 188	Inferring, SE pp. 176–177, 179, 180, 181, 182, 185, 187, 189, 190, 192, 193, 197 Activating prior knowledge, SE p. 194 Building background, TWE p. 178 Summarizing, TWE p. 181 Fluency, TWE p. 187 Titles and Subtitles, SE pp. 185, 197	Setting, SE pp. 179, 181, 182, 183, 185, 187, 188, 191, 197; TWE p. 190 Characters and conflict, TWE p. 192 Problem and Solution, TWE p. 180

Part 4: Writing Skills

On a separate sheet of paper, write the numbers 1–4. Then follow the directions for each numbered section below.

1. Write down the verbs in this sentence:

"People who are having a bad dream sometimes shout or kick."

2. Rewrite this sentence, changing the verb to the present progressive form. That is, change the verb to show that the action is continuing in the present.

"Everyone leaves the theater."

3. Read the following passage and choose the best summary of it.

Samir was angry, so angry he could hardly speak. His bike lay on the driveway, smashed into flat and twisted pieces. Samir had spent the entire summer bagging groceries at the local supermarket just to have enough money to buy the bike he'd always wanted. For two short days, he had ridden it everywhere. Now it was gone. No, it would be better if it were actually gone. At least then he wouldn't have to look at the sad remains.

A. Samir discovered that his bike was ruined.

B. Samir was furious when the bike he'd worked hard to buy was destroyed.

C. Samir was angry when his bike was smashed, but he should have put it somewhere safe.

D. Samir worked hard at a supermarket all summer to buy a bike, but he got to ride it for only two days before he found it smashed in a driveway, which made him too angry to speak.

4. Write a summary of the following passage.

During the 1950s, migrant workers lived and worked in terrible conditions. These people, who traveled from farm to farm to plant, weed, and pick crops, had little money and even less power. They worked long hours in hot fields, often with no water available. They earned small amounts of money for backbreaking work. They slept in cars, tents, shacks, or under the sky. They rarely had the benefits of electricity. The children often missed school because they were working, but even when they were able to go, they had to move from school to school as their families traveled.

Test Practice

Part 4: Writing Skills

1. are, having, shout, kick
2. Everyone *is leaving* the theater.
3. D
4. Answers will vary.

Test-Taking Tips

TIP Remind students to review all written work for correct spelling, capitalization, and punctuation. When writing a summary, students should make sure that the summary follows the same sequence of information or events that appears in the original text. Summaries should include major points and eliminate unnecessary details.

Test Practice

Part 3: Vocabulary

1. B
2. D
3. C
4. D
5. B
6. A
7. C
8. D
9. B
10. C

Test-Taking Tips

TIP Tell students that when answering multiple-choice items, they should begin by eliminating answer choices that they know are incorrect. Remind students that those who make a best guess from the remaining choices have a higher likelihood of answering the question correctly.

Part 3: Vocabulary

On a separate sheet of paper, write the numbers 1–10. Next to each number, write the letter of the right answer for that question.

Write the letter of the word or phrase that means about the same as the underlined word.

1. to **propel** a car

A. stop **C.** fix
B. move **D.** buy

2. **precisely** on time

A. never **C.** almost
B. always **D.** exactly

3. to **inspire** the team

A. join **C.** encourage
B. teach **D.** be jealous of

4. his **unique** hairstyle

A. new **C.** attractive
B. ugly **D.** very unusual

5. just a **glimpse**

A. joke **C.** short distance
B. glance **D.** small mistake

Use context clues to figure out the meaning of each underlined word.

6. Is that a **genuine** diamond ring, or is it fake?

A. real **C.** stolen
B. pretty **D.** inexpensive

7. My cat thinks mice are **delectable**; he finds them quite tasty!

A. shy **C.** delicious
B. quiet **D.** hard to catch

8. We responded to Dad's vacation plans with groans, moans, sighs, and other sounds of **disgruntlement**.

A. fear **C.** excitement
B. sleepiness **D.** displeasure

9. Meet me in the **vestibule**, the roomlike area right inside the front door of the building.

A. porch **C.** front yard
B. lobby **D.** long hallway

10. If the skydiver's parachute didn't open, she would **plummet** downward.

A. crawl **C.** fall rapidly
B. flutter **D.** float gracefully

Objectives
Vocabulary Learn and use new vocabulary
• Use context clues to determine word meaning
Grammar Identify and correctly use verbs
• Use correct verb tense
Writing Paraphrase and summarize text

4 **Just Fake It** How do these clubs find enough jokes to keep everyone howling? They don't. According to Dr. Kataria, it doesn't matter if laughter is produced naturally, by actually finding something funny, or if it is faked. The benefits to the body are the same. Laughter club leaders get things going without any comedians around to help.

5 First, participants form a circle, standing two to three feet apart. Then there are a few stretches, just to loosen up. Next, club members do deep breathing followed by a series of "ho, ho, ha, ha" chants. And then it's time to get the laughs started, which often begin with the "lion laugh" in which people raise their hands like lions' paws, claw the air, stick out their tongues, and laugh. After this, no one has to fake a laugh. The sight of the rest of the group looking so completely ridiculous is enough to produce the real thing: the laughter of true amusement.

---

1. What fact can be discovered by *only* previewing this article?

A. Laughter may actually improve health.
B. Laughter Club members often do a "lion laugh."
C. There are thousands of laughter clubs all over the world.
D. Scientists have made recent discoveries about laughter's health benefits

2. Which paragraph contains information that is organized in a "process/how-to" structure?

A. Paragraph 1
B. Paragraph 2
C. Paragraph 4
D. Paragraph 5

3. What would be the most likely purpose a reader would set for reading this article?

A. To learn how to be funny
B. To understand what laughter is
C. To find out what it says about laughter
D. To discover how to accomplish something

4. The best way to help information from this article stick in your mind would be to pause now and then to

A. review
B. preview
C. check the text structure
D. set a new purpose for reading

5. Think of any two things you have read that you had different purposes for reading. Name or describe those two things and tell what your purpose for reading each one was.

Test Practice

Part 2: Reading Skills

1. D
2. D
3. C
4. A
5. Answers will vary.

Test-Taking Tips

TIP Tell students that often they will see constructed-response questions in tests. Before they start writing, students should make sure they understand the question. Suggest that students reread the question to be sure that they know exactly what the answer should include.

Test-Taking Tips

TIP Remind students to preview a reading passage to learn what it will be about. Students should begin by reading the title and any headings because these items often contain clues about the topic.

TIP Because students will need to read information in the passage to answer the questions, suggest that they jot down a few quick notes while they are reading. Point out that in a real test situation, students should feel free to underline important ideas and make notes in the margins.

Part 2: Reading Skills

Read the passage. Then, on a separate sheet of paper, write the numbers 1–5. For the first four questions, write the letter of the right answer next to the number for that question. Then, next to number 5, write your answer to the final question.

Come On, Get Happy!

It May Be True that Laughter Is the Best Medicine

by Lucia Menendez

1 People have believed for a long time that laughter, as the old saying goes, is good for the soul. There is now scientific evidence that it is also good for the body. Recent research has shown that laughter strengthens the heart, helps the flow of blood through the body, reduces pain, aids healing, fights infections, and decreases blood pressure. It also improves memory, makes people feel more confident, and leads to a positive view of life.

2 **Laughter Clubs** None of this information would surprise Dr. Madan Kataria. After reading about some of the benefits of laughter, he started a "Laughter Club" in a public park in Bombay, India. That was in 1995. There are now more than 2,500 such clubs around the world.

3 Club meetings aren't exactly quiet, but that's sort of the point. Although the noise may surprise those passing by, the participants know exactly what they're doing and why they're doing it. It's good for them. Meetings are often held early in the day, so people can get in a good twenty minutes or more of laughing before they head off for work. Once there, members believe, they concentrate better and work more productively.

Objectives
Reading Set a purpose for reading • Preview text • Monitor comprehension: review and reread • Identify text structure: steps in a process

To the Rescue!

Many Floridians refuse to give up without a fight. . . . One of these fighters is Mary Barley. . . .

Barley is chairwoman of the Everglades Foundation. Her husband George, a former real estate developer and fisherman, started the foundation because he worried about the Everglades' future. Since his death in a 1995 plane crash, Barley and foundation members have fought on. . . .

Barley knows that even people who want to save the Everglades don't want to pay to correct mistakes others made. She and fellow activists . . . persuaded Florida voters to pass a state law requiring polluters to pay most conservation costs. Thanks to her, a sugar company sold more than 50,000 acres of Everglades land back to the state to be restored. The river can run naturally again, which will help bring back native plants and animals.

---

1. "Hero Mary Barley fights to save Florida's unique, marshy ecosystem" is an example of a
- **A.** lead
- **B.** deck
- **C.** title
- **D.** headline

2. What is the purpose of the subheads in this article?
- **A.** to explain the meaning of the title
- **B.** to summarize the information in the article
- **C.** to break the article into "chunks" and introduce them
- **D.** to provide interesting information that makes a reader keep reading

3. You can use the illustration with this article to help you understand
- **A.** where the Everglades is
- **B.** why the Everglades faces problems
- **C.** how bad the situation in the Everglades is
- **D.** when the problems in the Everglades began

4. What information is found in the lead?
- **A.** The Everglades is a special ecosystem.
- **B.** Settlers in the Everglades dried out parts of it.
- **C.** Some Florida residents are fighting to save the Everglades.
- **D.** A Florida law requires polluters to pay most conservation costs.

Question 5 is a constructed-response question. Write your answer below your answers for 1–4.

5. How do the title, the deck, and the subheads help you understand what the selection is about and how it is organized?

Unit Assessment To prepare for the Unit test, go to www.glencoe.com.

UNIT 1 ASSESSMENT

Test Practice

Part 1: Key Elements

1. B
2. C
3. A
4. A
5. Answers will vary.

Resources for pages 122–127

Use these resources to review, assess, or reteach the Unit: Active Learning and Note-Taking Guide, Selection and Unit Assessment, ExamView Assessment Suite, and Differentiated Instruction Tool Software.

Unit Assessment Have students access the Web site to prepare for the Unit 1 test.

Test-Taking Tips

TIP Remind students to begin by reading the directions carefully. Tell them that after they have read the questions, they should skim the passage, looking for headings, subheadings, and illustrations that can help them answer the questions.

TIP Remind students that graphics often contain important information. Point out that students should always look at photos or graphics (in this case, a map) when these are included in a passage. Encourage students to think about how the graphic illustrates or enhances an important idea in the text.

Test Practice

Part 1: Key Elements

Do not begin by reading the passage. On a separate sheet of paper, write the numbers 1-5. Read each question and then look only at the part of the passage that can help you answer the question. For questions 1–4, write the letter of the answer next to each number. For question 5, write a short response.

from "The Everglades Forever?"

Hero Mary Barley fights to save Florida's unique, marshy ecosystem

Graceful white ibis soar through the sky. In the swamp below, lazy alligators lie still as logs. A tiny frog hops to a lily pad and lets out a big croak. It's just another day in Florida's Everglades—a unique ecosystem found only in the U.S.

The Everglades is about 4,000 square miles of freshwater marsh, rivers, and swamp. . . . The region, nicknamed the "river of grass," is home to more than 850 animal species, including 250 species of birds, and 900 kinds of plants. Palms, pines, and oak trees as well as wildcats and panthers live in harmony in this wetland. Sounds like a natural paradise, right? It used to be. But after years of pollution and other abuse, the Everglades is dying.

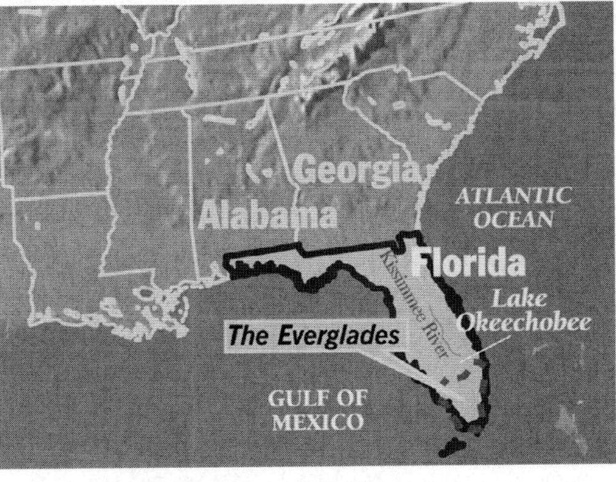

Humans Make Their Mark

More than 100 years ago, people began to settle nearby. The Everglades seemed worthless to them. They couldn't build homes or plant sugar cane, a profitable crop, on the marshy ground. So they dried out some of it.

In the 1920's, U.S. government engineers made bigger changes. . . . Without its natural water supply, the Everglades began to shrink. So did its plant and animal populations. . . .

Part of the swampland where thousands of animals once thrived is packed with houses and factories. . . . The wading-bird population is a tenth of what it was in the early 1900s. Alarming numbers of alligators and sparrows have vanished. Can the Everglades be saved?

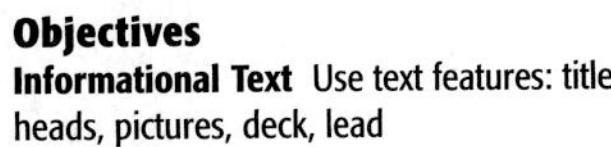

Objectives
Informational Text Use text features: title, heads, pictures, deck, lead

Nonfiction

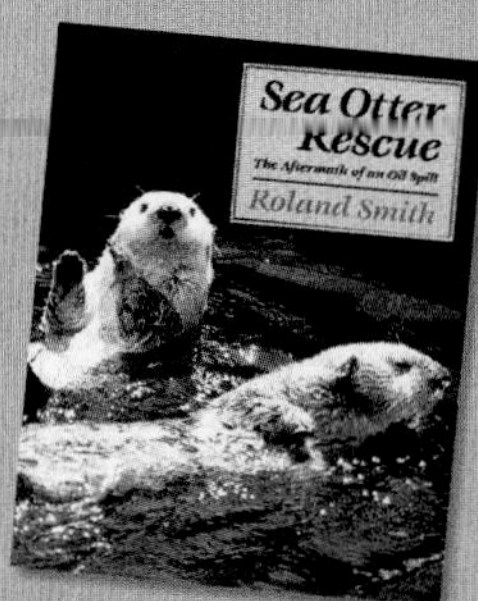

Sea Otter Rescue: The Aftermath of an Oil Spill
by Roland Smith

The oil tanker *Exxon Valdez* hit the rocks in Prince William Sound, Alaska, and almost 11 million gallons of crude oil spilled into the water. This accident created an oil slick that threatened wildlife. Sea otters were especially affected. This story is a firsthand account of the animal rescue experts who helped save the lives of hundreds of sea otters. The story will help you understand the efforts made by the rescue experts.

Baseball in April and Other Stories
by Gary Soto

Soto's own life—growing up poor in California's Central Valley—inspired these stories about Mexican-American teenagers facing the kinds of experiences most teens face. Read to understand the experiences of Mexican-American teenagers and enjoy the stories Soto tells.

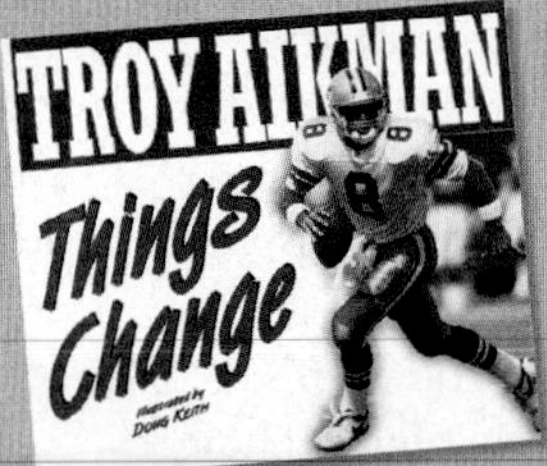

Things Change
by Troy Aikman

Former Dallas Cowboys quarterback describes his life from childhood to three-time Superbowl champ, using his own experiences to show that change can provide an opportunity to grow. Read to be entertained and find how change can affect a person's life.

Woodsong
by Gary Paulsen

This book shows the excitement of the Alaskan dogsled race, the Iditarod. Paulsen recounts his first dogsled race. He describes why he decided to work with a team of racing dogs. Paulsen also describes the beauty of nature and the dangers it can present. Read to enjoy Paulsen's adventure and to find out details about the Iditarod.

Nonfiction
Share with students that the books on this page are all nonfiction books. The books offer detailed personal accounts of growing up and stories of real-life adventures.

Personal Narratives
Tell students that personal narratives give first-person accounts of interesting events or experiences. Explain that there are many reasons for reading personal narratives. One reason, very like the reason that people read fiction, is to experience the world through another person's eyes. Because personal narratives are written in the first person, students can identify with the *I* in the story and imagine what it is like to be that person. Another reason to read personal narratives is to learn more about a particular person or topic.

About the Subjects
Invite students to share information they know about the subjects on this page. *Baseball in April and Other Stories* will give students a glimpse of what life is like for Mexican American teenagers. *Sea Otter Rescue* will provide information about how wildlife is affected by oil spills. Students can learn about football and competition from *Things Change* and about dog sled racing from *Woodsong.*

Teacher Chat Room

Using Biographies

Before you begin unit or during the unit, talk with other teachers about ways they have used biographies and autobiographies. Have a lunch-time discussion group or an after-school hour for professional development and discuss the following questions and answers from our authors:

How do I make biographies interesting to middle schoolers?

Author Doug Fisher says students needs to feel some type of connection to biographical subjects in order to want to read about the subject. To help students connect to subjects, try these strategies:

- Help students recall facts they know about the subjects (activating prior knowledge)
- Choose biographies of people students already know
- Choose biographies based around subjects students know (some students may not know who Tony Hawk is but they know something about skateboarding)
- Choose biographies that share details from the person's life as a teenager. Students love reading and hearing stories about how life was when someone was their age.

If the biographical subject is foreign to students, how can I make students interested in the subject?

Author Jeff Wilhelm says in order to help students connect to foreign subjects, you need to dig into the story and find things that students already know. This is often referred to as building background. For instance, in Red Scarf Girl, most of your students are probably not very familiar with the Chinese Revolution. The building background section before the selection helps to explain what is going on at this time. Other activities in the Before You Read section help students think through what might happen if they were selected to be a part of their nation's dance team. The Meet Your Author section also gives insights into who the writer is and some of the things she may have experienced. All of these features will prompt your students to read the biographical story of Ji-Li Jiang.

What language and structures do writers of biographies use, and how can readers use these elements to inform their own writing?

Author Cyndie Shanahan Hynd says writers often use time order, point of view, and narration to convey their stories in biographies. In this unit, we point out literary elements and help students learn to identify them and think about how they influence the story. In the Writing Workshops and in the assessment section after each selection, students will have a chance to practice writing using some of the elements they've read.

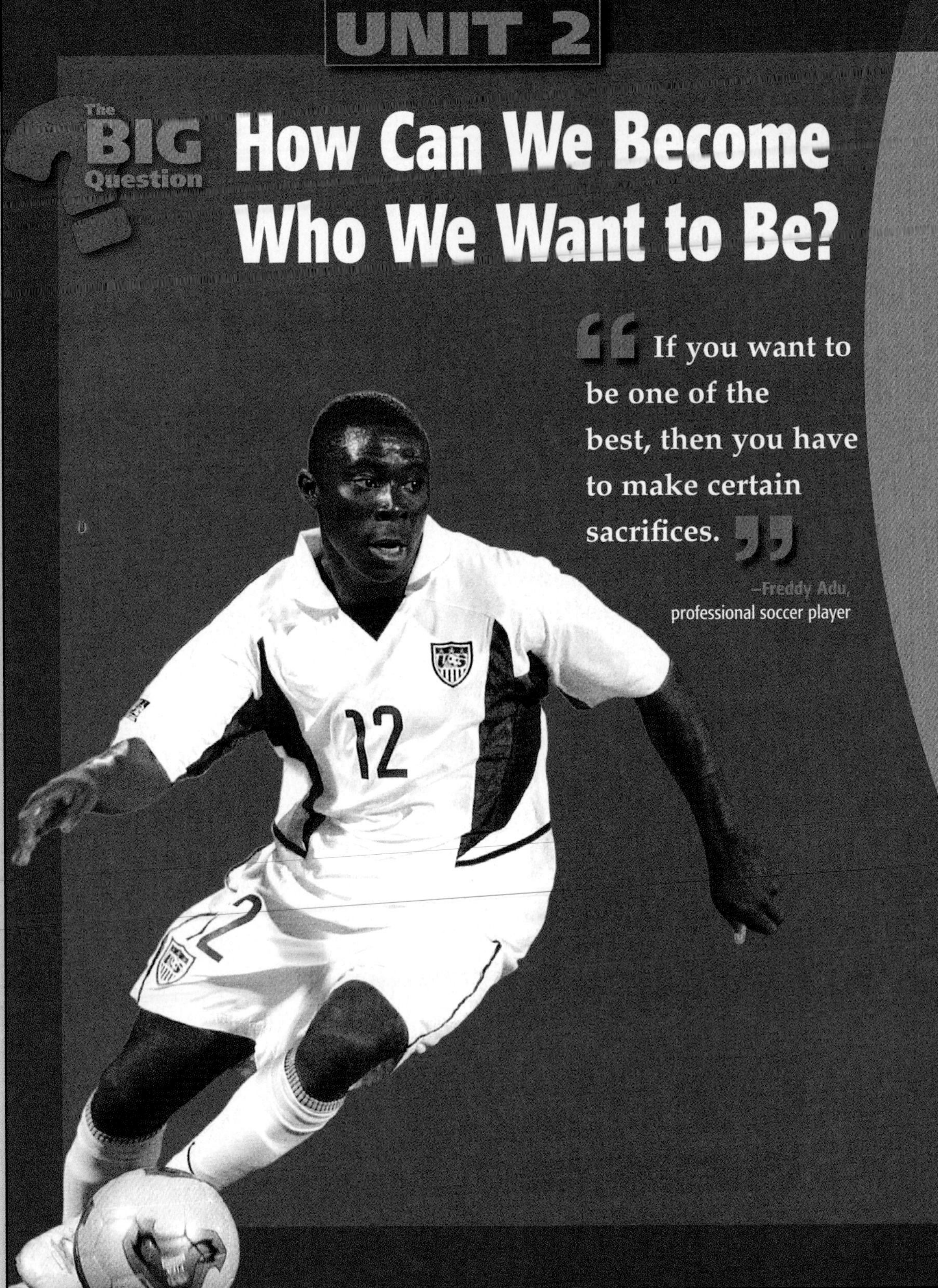

UNIT 2
The BIG Question
How Can We Become Who We Want to Be?
"If you want to be one of the best, then you have to make certain sacrifices."
–Freddy Adu, professional soccer player
12

Key Unit Objectives

- Answer the Big Question
- Analyze the literary elements of biography and autobiography
- Apply strategies for reading biography and autobiography
- Write autobiographical narratives

BIG Question

Why Is It Important?
Addressing this Big Question helps students set goals and establish a course of action to achieve those goals.

Viewing the Photo
Born in Ghana, Freddy Adu moved to the United States at age eight. In November 2003, at age 14, Adu became the youngest player ever to enter modern professional sports when he was signed to play in Major League Soccer.
Ask: If you could ask Freddy Adu three questions, what would they be? *(Responses will vary.)* **AS**

Unit Skills

BIG Question How Can We Become Who We Want to Be?
Genre Focus: Biography and Autobiography

Reading Skills
- Activating prior knowledge, p. 136
- Connecting, p. 156
- Making inferences, p. 176
- Understanding sequence, p. 204

Vocabulary
- Multiple-meaning words, p. 138

Literary Elements
- Narrator, p. 139
- Point of view, p. 159
- Setting, p. 179
- Sensory details, p. 207

Writing Skills/Grammar
- Autobiographical narrative, pp. 152, 198
- Voice, p. 199

LOOKING AHEAD

The readings and skill lessons in this unit will help you think about your own answer to the Big Question.

About the Reading

Each selection in this unit provides insights that can help students to address the question, "How can we become who we want to be?" Students consider different aspects of what makes people who they are and see how other people have worked to become who they want to be.

About the Skills

The skills taught in this unit have been selected because they are particularly helpful when reading the featured genre—biography/autobiography. Each reading selection provides students with opportunities to practice and develop these skills.

No Child Left Behind

The goals of the NCLB act include a strong emphasis on developing reading skills. Modeling the skills covered in this unit will help students develop these skills. For example, read aloud a passage from a selection and illustrate how to activate prior knowledge.

Reading Fluency

Developing Fluency In order to develop fluency, students should hear good models, practice with properly leveled materials, and evaluate their own progress. One way to help students develop fluency is to pair them and have them read orally to one another from an appropriate text. The listener should keep a record of miscues and errors for the other person. They can repeat the activity until fluency improves. **BL**

Focus

BELLRINGER Options

- Literature Launcher: Prereading DVD
- Daily Language Practice Transparency

Focus Activity Write on the board: Imagine yourself at age 18, 25, or 30. Write down who you want to be at that age. *(Responses will vary.)*

Teach

R Reading Skill

Connecting Ask students to write several sentences about goals that they did or did not achieve.

- Name one goal that you had.
- Were you successful in achieving the goal? Why or why not? OL

BQ

Assign a partner to each student and have the groups discuss the advice they would give Shawn and Luisa. OL

UNIT 2 WARM-UP

Connecting to The BIG Question How Can We Become Who We Want to Be?

R It isn't easy to become who you want to be. Many things might stand between you and your goals. But you've got strengths and resources that can help you reach those goals. In this unit, you'll read about different people and what stood between them and their efforts to become who they wanted to be.

Real Kids and the Big Question

SHAWN likes working with his hands. He's also good at science and math. Sometimes he dreams of becoming an engineer and traveling around the world building bridges and dams. At other times, Shawn thinks he would be better off staying in the neighborhood and working as a carpenter. What advice would you give him?

LUISA loves to act. She has played only small parts so far, but now she really wants the lead role in her school play, *The Diary of Anne Frank.* She has a hard time taking risks because she's always nervous before she tries out for a play. Luisa figures it's better to play it safe and go for small parts. What advice would you give Luisa?

BQ

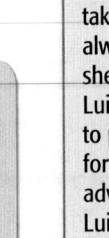

Link to Web resources to further explore the Big Question at www.glencoe.com.

Warm-Up Activity

With a partner, talk about the advice you would give Shawn and Luisa. Explain to each other why you would give that advice.

Additional Support

Reading in the Real World

Career Whichever option Shawn chooses, he'll probably find a satisfying job. The construction industry is one of the largest: about 7 million wage and salary jobs and 2 million self-employed jobs. Workers in all aspects of construction—general (buildings), heavy (roads, bridges, tunnels, etc.), and specialty trades (carpentry, electrical, painting, etc.)—use reading on a daily basis. They read blueprints, maps, plans, contracts, bills, invoices, and instructions. Training in this industry extends from learning by doing to attending college, with many workers training at vocational and technical schools. OL

You and the Big Question

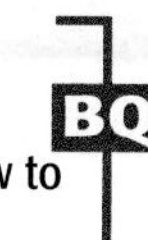

Reading about other people trying to figure out who they want to be and how to become that person will give you ideas for your own answer.

Plan for the Unit Challenge

At the end of the unit, you'll use notes from all your reading to complete the Unit Challenge, which will explore your answer to the Big Question.

You will choose one of the following activities:

A. Letter of Advice Work with classmates to write a letter of advice to a teen who wonders how to reach his or her goals.

B. Web Diagram Create a web diagram that shows how you can become who you want to be.

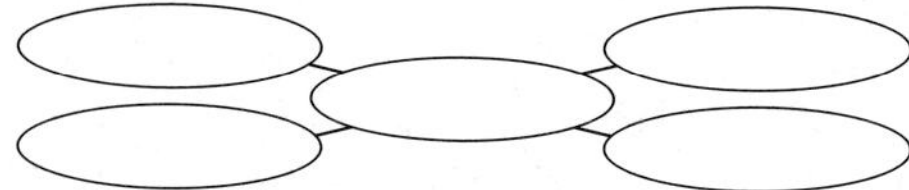

- Start thinking about which activity you'd like to do so that you can focus your thinking as you go through the unit.
- In your Learner's Notebook, write your thoughts about which activity you'd like to do.
- Each time you make notes about the Big Question, think about how your ideas will help you with the Unit Challenge activity you chose.

Keep Track of Your Ideas

FOLDABLES™ Study Organizer

As you read, you'll make notes about the Big Question. Later, you'll use these notes to complete the Unit Challenge. See pages R8–R9 for help with making Foldable 2. This diagram shows how it should look.

1. Use this Foldable for all of the selections in this unit. Label each "tab" with a title. (See page 129 for the titles.) You should be able to see all the titles without opening the Foldable.
2. Below each title, write **My Purpose for Reading.**
3. A third of the way down, write the label **The Big Question.**

New Directions
Toward a Rainbow Nation
An Hour with Abuelo
Kids in Action: Dalie Jimenez
Rosa Parks: My Story
Unit 2
How Can We Become Who We Want to Be?

UNIT 2 WARM-UP

Teach

BQ 

Have students write their initial ("gut") responses to the Big Question in their Learner's Notebook. **AS**

Unit Challenge

Help students choose the Unit Challenge that is best suited to their skills.

FOLDABLES™ Study Organizer

For each selection they read, students will enter notes about how that selection applies to the Big Question. For details about using Dinah Zike's Foldables, see page R8.

Assess/Close

Ask students to share their thoughts about why looking for an answer to the Big Question might be important to them. You might want to share some of your own insights or experiences.

Resources for page 131

- Use the Unit Challenge Planner BLM in the Unit 2 Resource Booklet.
- Use the Foldable BLM in the Unit 2 Resource Booklet.

Differentiated Instruction

Visual Clues Draw students' attention to the photographs of Shawn and Luisa. Discuss how the photographs illustrate or complement the text. Ask students to think about the visual clues provided by the pictures. These clues can provide a context that helps clarify the meanings of the paragraphs.

Encourage students to cut and paste photographs from magazines into their Learner's Notebook to illustrate their words when they make entries about this Big Question. **BL** **EL**

Objectives

- Connect prior knowledge and experiences to characters, themes, and events

Focus

BELLRINGER Options

Daily Language Practice Transparency

Focus Activity Say: Think of a movie you've seen or a book you've read about someone's life. How are these different from movies and books that are fiction? What can you learn from stories about real people? *(Responses will vary.)*

Teach

R Reading Skill

How to Read Biography

Ask: Why do you think each reading skill is helpful to understand biographies and autobiographies? *(Possible responses: **Activating prior knowledge** is using what you know to help yourself understand what you are reading. **Connecting** is linking what you read to events in your own life or to other reading selections. **Inferring** is using your experience to guess at what an author doesn't say. **Identifying sequence** is finding the order of events or ideas.)* OL

UNIT 2 GENRE FOCUS: BIOGRAPHY

Skills Focus

- Key skills for reading biography
- Key literary elements of biography

Skills Model

You will see how to use the key reading skills and literary elements as you read an excerpt from

- ***Tony Hawk: Chairman of the Board,*** p. 133

Study Central Visit www.glencoe.com and click on Study Central to review biography.

Objectives

(pp. 132–135)

Reading Activate prior knowledge • Make connections from text to self • Make inferences • Understand sequence: chronological order

Literature Analyze features of genres: biography • Identify literary elements: narrator, point of view, setting, sensory details

A **biography** is the story of a person's life, written by another person. Biographies are about real people, real times, and real events. Reading biographies is a great way to find out how people became who they wanted to be. In an **autobiography**, the author tells the story of his or her own life. Diaries, letters, journals, and memoirs are kinds of autobiographical writing.

Why Read Biography?

Reading about the lives of real people can be fun. You can learn about

- interesting and powerful people
- the times in which they lived
- the choices they made to become who they wanted to be

In this unit, you'll read part of a biography of Tony Hawk, who became a world-class skateboarder when he was fourteen years old.

How to Read Biography

Key Reading Skills

R These reading skills are especially useful tools for reading and understanding biographies and autobiographies. The skills are modeled in the Active Reading Model on pages 133–135; you'll learn more about them later.

- **Activating prior knowledge** Before you read, try to recall what you might already know about the main character, the topic, or the setting. Continue thinking about these things as you read; the text itself might help you remember. (See Reading Workshop 1.)
- **Connecting** As you read, link the story to an experience you've had or something you know, have heard, or have read. (See Reading Workshop 2.)
- **Inferring** Use the information given to figure out what the author isn't directly telling you. (See Reading Workshop 3.)
- **Identifying Sequence** Look for clues or signal words that reveal the order in which events in the story happened. (See Reading Workshop 4.)

Key Literary Elements

Recognizing and thinking about the following literary elements will help you understand more fully what the author is telling you.

- **Narrator:** the voice telling the story (See *Rosa Parks: My Story*.)
- **Point of view:** the person through whose eyes you see the story (See "An Hour with Abuelo.")
  First-person point of view is when someone tells his or her own story. Third-person point of view is when someone tells another person's story.
- **Setting:** the time and place of the story (See "New Directions.")
- **Sensory Details:** details that appeal to the five senses (See "Miracle Hands.")

Additional Support

Study Central Have students access the Web site to review biography and to complete a related activity.

Literature Focus Lesson

Narrator Explain to students that the key difference between biography and autobiography is the point of view of the narrator. While the author of an autobiography knows firsthand what has happened in her life, and why she did the things she did, the author of a biography must rely on his interpretation of facts. The opinions and biases of the biographer can affect the way the subject of the biography is portrayed.

Ask students to write about how a biography of them that was written by a friend, relative, or teacher would differ from autobiographies they would write. AL

INFORMATIONAL TEXT
MAGAZINE
from *Sports Illustrated*

Tony Hawk
Chairman of the Board EL

by Steve Pittman

The notes in the side columns model how to use the skills and elements you read about on page 132.

Biography
ACTIVE READING MODEL

When Tony Hawk was nine years old, his brother, Steve, changed his life. Steve was twelve years older than Tony, and he loved surfing. The Hawks lived in San Diego, California, not far from the Pacific Ocean. Most mornings, Steve woke up early to surf before going to school. Because Steve loved surfing, he had tried out "sidewalk surfing." That's what early skateboarding was called. Steve had an old banana board in the garage. He took Tony to a nearby alley, showed him how to balance on the board, and gave him a push. Tony rolled and rolled until he ran into a fence. He couldn't figure out how to turn! 1

1 Key Reading Skill
Activating Prior Knowledge
I've seen skateboarders. What they do seems really hard and dangerous. I'll bet Tony Hawk had to practice a long time to become good at skateboarding.

FALLING IN LOVE It was not love at first sight. Slowly, over the next year, though, Tony began skating more and more. One weekend, the mother of one of Tony's friends took the neighborhood kids to a skate park, in San Diego, called Oasis. Skaters whipped around riding the bowls, banks, pools, and other obstacles of the park. He loved it.

After that, Tony wanted to go every weekend. He nagged his parents to drive him there. If his brother or sisters were visiting, he made them take him. Soon he was asking for rides after school. He wanted to go every day.

A ***chairman of the board*** is usually the leader of a company. Tony was a leader in skateboarding.

Tony Hawk

English Language Coach

Multiple-Meaning Words Multiple-meaning words are common in all languages. In many languages, puns, like "chairman of the board," are also a common form of humor. Ask students who are fluent in languages other than English to list some multiple-meaning words that might be used as puns. Then ask the class to create puns using those words. EL

Teach

EL Language Coach

Multiple-Meaning Words

Say: In the expression "Chairman of the Board," *board* is a multiple-meaning word: a group of persons managing something; or a flat piece of wood.

- Use the context of the biography to determine the correct meaning of "Chairman of the Board." *(In this context,* board *refers to a skateboard.)*
- Students should also understand that the title is a pun. "Chairman of the board" usually means master of a business. Tony Hawk is master of the skateboard. OL EL

E Text Element

Review Text Features

Informational texts often include graphic features to guide readers.

- Have students preview the article, noting the large bold section headings.
- Ask students to look at each heading and predict what each section will be about. BL OL

Resources for page 133

 Use the Genre Study BLM in the Unit 2 Resource Booklet.

Objectives
- Activate prior knowledge
- Make connections from text to self
- Make inferences
- Understand sequence: chronological order
- Analyze features of genres: biography
- Identify literacy elements: narrator, point of view, setting, sensory details

Teach

R1 Reading Skill

Connecting Tony Hawk felt bad after his first contest because he didn't do well. Ask students to write in their Learner's Notebook journal entries about times when they felt bad about their performance.

- Remind students to include information about the characters and the settings.
- Suggest that students compare their situation with that of Hawk in his first contest.
- Lead students in a discussion of how people can bounce back from a disappointing failure. **OL**

R2 Reading Skill

Inferring Ask: What can you infer about Tony Hawk from his actions after his first contest? *(Possible response: Because he develops a strategy to improve his performance and follows through with his plans, Tony is focused, determined, and hardworking.)* **AL**

ACTIVE READING MODEL

Tony was competitive with himself. That's what he liked about skateboarding: It wasn't a team sport. He didn't like letting his team down. With skateboarding, Tony could only let himself down—and he wasn't about to do that. That's why he would practice a single trick all day long. **2**

FIRST CONTEST Tony was 11 when he competed in his first skateboard contest. There were more than 100 skaters in his age group! Tony was so nervous before the contest that he developed a stomachache. He didn't skate well and fell on easy tricks. **3**

Tony had let himself down, and that was the worst feeling he had ever had. So, after that, Tony got serious about contests. He would skate the park before each competition. He drew a diagram of the pool (competitions were often held in swimming pools). Then he would map out where he would do his tricks and memorize his planned run.

Tony's strategy worked! He did a lot better. By the end of the year, he had won his age class. He also had become a member of the Oasis Skatepark team. **4**

At 11, Tony also got his first sponsor,[1] Dogtown Skateboards. Dogtown went out of business soon, but Tony quickly found another sponsor: Stacy Peralta, who owned part of Powell and Peralta, the hottest skateboard company at the time. Stacy named the Powell group of skaters The Bones Brigade. **5**

TEENAGE PRO Tony's first big, out-of-town contest for Powell was in Jacksonville, Florida. He fell during his run and was so upset that he refused to talk to anybody afterward. But Stacy was a great coach, and with his help and hours of practice, Tony improved even more quickly than before. Before one local skating contest, in 1982, Stacy turned to Tony and asked him if he wanted to turn pro. Tony shrugged and said yes. He skated well and placed third against the best skaters in the world! He was 14. **6**

1. A ***sponsor*** pays for skateboarding activities.

2 Key Literary Element
Narrator *Somebody besides Tony is the narrator. The person telling Tony's story seems to admire him.*

3 Key Reading Skill
Connecting *I know how Tony felt. I can't do my best when I'm nervous.*

4 Key Literary Element
Point of View *The narrator calls Tony by name and uses* he *and* his*. This is third-person point of view.*

5 Key Reading Skill
Inferring *The author doesn't say it, but I think Stacy Peralta sponsored Tony because he believed that Tony would become a great skateboarder.*

6 Key Reading Skill
Identifying Sequence *The words* first, afterward, *and* before *are all signal words that help me understand the time order.*

Additional Support

Reading in the Real World

Citizenship Many students know someone in their family or community who has become "the best" at something through determination and hard work rather than just talent. Lead a discussion about what these people accomplished and what obstacles they overcame to accomplish it. Be sure not to limit the discussion just to individuals who are involved in sports, politics, or the performing arts.

You might also ask students individually or in small groups to write short biographical narratives about a family or community member who has excelled at something. **OL**

ACTIVE READING MODEL

CIRCUS SKATER Despite his early skateboarding success, Tony had a problem. He was too skinny to do some of the harder aerial[2] tricks. He needed more weight to generate enough momentum to fly above the ramp. But no matter how much food he ate, Tony couldn't put on weight. So he invented a different way to catch air. Instead of grabbing his board early, like all the other skaters, he ollied (did a no-hand aerial) into the air and then grabbed his board. That way he could use his legs more to launch himself off the lip of the ramp and do more tricks. The new style worked, but it looked a lot different from anybody else's style. Other pros made fun of Tony's skating. Some called him a "cheater" because of his technique. 7 8

Tony also invented a lot of tricks in which he would flip his board and then put it back under his feet. Today, every skater does flip tricks, but back then, skaters called him a "circus skater" for doing them.

By 1985, Oasis had closed down. Skateboarding had become less popular. But Tony kept skating with his friends, at Del Mar Skatepark, in San Diego. He kept inventing tricks, innovative[3] tricks. In a few years, all the skaters who had made fun of Tony were trying to learn from him! L1

CHAMPION OF THE WORLD After Tony turned pro, it took him awhile to get used to skating against older, more experienced skaters. He bobbed all over the contest results. Sometimes he would win, and sometimes he'd place 10th. When Tony skated poorly, it upset him, and he practiced harder. Soon he began winning a lot. He became the first pro skater to win three vert contests[4] in a row. In 1983, the National Skateboard Association was founded. It governed the world skateboard ranking. Tony was declared world champion. He was 15. ❍ L2

2. An *aerial* (AIR ee ul) trick is done in the air.
3. *Innovative* tricks are new and creative.
4. A *vert contest* is one that involves flying into the air from a ramp (going "vertical") and landing back on the ramp.

Write to Learn In your Learner's Notebook, write a few details that you learned about Tony Hawk's life from reading this excerpt.

7 **Key Literary Element**
Setting *The setting is San Diego. It has nice weather, so Tony could practice outside.*

8 **Key Literary Element**
Sensory Details *This paragraph is loaded with sensory details. Mostly, they appeal to sight and touch, with descriptions like "catch air," "fly above the ramp," and "use his legs to launch himself."*

UNIT 2 GENRE FOCUS

Teach

L1 Literary Element

Narrator Say: In a biographical narrative, the narrator usually has an opinion about the subject of the biography. Sometimes you have to infer that opinion by looking for clues in the selection. Find clues in paragraph 3 on this page that indicate that the narrator admires Tony. *(Possible response: The narrator refers to Tony's tricks as "innovative" and says that skaters who had made fun of Tony tried to learn from him.)* OL

L2 Literary Element

Point of View Say: Most narrative writing is done from the first-person or third-person point of view:

- first person: The narrator is involved in and is part of the story. The narrator will frequently use the word *I* or *we.*
- third person: The narrator is not part of the story. The narrator never uses the term *I* when describing the events of the story. Which point of view is used in *Tony Hawk*? *(third-person point of view)* AL

English Language Coach

Time-Order Words English language learners sometimes have difficulty understanding the order of events in a selection. Have them create a two-column list in their Learner's Notebook. The first column will contain English words and phrases that indicate time order. The second column will contain translations of the words and phrases into their primary languages.

Have students write a short paragraph listing five or more things they did today. Have them use time-order words and phrases to indicate the order of events. EL

Objectives

- Connect prior knowledge to characters and events
- Make inferences supported by the text
- Identify point of view
- Explain the influence of setting
- Use chronological order to locate, recall, and comprehend information

Activating Prior Knowledge

UNIT 2

Objectives covered in this workshop:

- Make connections from self to text
- Activate prior knowledge before reading
- Recognize and analyze narrator
- Use context to understand multiple-meaning words

Teaching Students to Activate Prior Knowledge

Why is it important?

- Teaching students to activate prior knowledge helps them use their experience and knowledge to better understand a selection.
- Research has proven that activating prior knowledge increases comprehension.
- Students who activate prior knowledge are better readers.

How to Help Students Get It?

- Emphasize that reading is an interactive process; the author and the reader both participate.
- Reading is interactive when you take your experiences and knowledge and combine it with the words in the text to produce meaning.
- Emphasizing that your students have unique experiences and knowledge helps them feel empowered when reading selections.
- Regardless of how foreign the subject may seem to students, helping them activate prior knowledge on even minor points in the selection can give them the confidence and interest they need to gain meaning from a selection.

The Selections and the Big Question

From Rosa Parks: My Story

Rosa Parks says that she wanted to become a person who was known for wanting justice for everyone. She became an advocate of justice when she refused to give up her seat on a bus to a white person in 1955; her heroic act began the Civil Rights Movement. In this selection, Parks tells her story about the day she was arrested for not giving up her seat.

An Hour With Abuelo

After pleading with his mother, young Arturo reluctantly agrees to spend one hour with his Abuelo, or grandfather, who is in a nursing home. During that hour, Arturo's grandfather shares some of the challenges he had in becoming the teacher and writer he wanted to be—in his native Puerto Rico as well as when he moved to the United States. His story shows readers and his young grandson that people can become who they want to be even if others do not recognize who they have become.

Kids in Action: Dalie Jimenez

This article tells how 14-year-old Dalie Jimenez rallied together friends to read to kids in a Miami Head Start program. The volunteer effort mush-roomed into a full fledge project, which included Jimenez and her friends sending letters to Congress to convince lawmakers not to cut funding from the program.

Workshop Resources

Pacing (Days) Standard	Block	Lesson	Student Materials	Teacher Resources
1	1/2	Key Skill Lesson: Activating Prior Knowledge	Key Reading Skills Practice English Language Coach	Bellringer Options Transparencies Read Aloud, Think Aloud Transparencies Presentation Plus!
1	1	from *Rosa Parks: My Story*	Literary Analysis Transparencies Glencoe Online Selection Vocabulary Development Academic Vocabulary Development English Language Coach Active Reading Graphic Organizer Literary Analysis StudentWorks Plus Online Student Edition Literature Classics Selection and Unit Assessments	Literary and Text Analysis Transparencies Puzzlemaker Skill Level Up! BookLink 3 Assessment by Learning Objective (Diagnostic and Formative) Interactive Tutor Self-Assessment TeacherWorks Plus
1		"An Hour With Abuelo"	Glencoe Online Selection Vocabulary Development Academic Vocabulary Development English Language Coach Active Reading Graphic Organizer Literary Analysis StudentWorks Plus Online Student Edition Literature Classics Selection and Unit Assessments	Literary and Text Analysis Transparencies Puzzlemaker Skill Level Up! BookLink 3 Assessment by Learning Objective (Diagnostic and Formative) Interactive Tutor Self-Assessment TeacherWorks Plus

Keys for Unit Resource

- Blackline Master
- Workbook
- Supplemental Text
- CD-ROM
- DVD
- Transparency
- Web-based
- Fast Files

Level Appropriate Code

AS = Activities for all students
AL = Activities for students working above grade level
OL = Activities for students working at grade level
BL = Activities for students working below grade level
EL = Activities for English language learners

Focus

BELLRINGER Options

Daily Language Practice Transparency

Focus Activity Say: How does it feel to be treated unfairly? List some words that describe this feeling. *(Possible responses: terrible, hurtful, discouraging, sad)*

Teach

R Reading Skill

Activating Prior Knowledge
Say: Give a real-life example of activating prior knowledge. *(Possible response: taking another route to school because you remembered the sidewalk construction on your usual route)* OL

V Vocabulary

Academic Vocabulary Say: Look at the word *prior* at the bottom of page 136. What is prior experience? What are prior plans? *(earlier experience, earlier plans)* OL

Analyzing Cartoons You need to know that computer data must be saved (backed up) or it can be lost (forgotten).

READING WORKSHOP 1

Skills Focus

You will practice using the following skills when you read these selections:

- from *Rosa Parks: My Story*, p. 140
- "Kids in Action: Dalie Jimenez," p. 148

Reading

- Activating prior knowledge

Literature

- Identifying the narrator in what you read
- Recognizing the narrator's effect on the story

Vocabulary

- Understanding multiple-meaning words in context
- Academic Vocabulary: *prior*

Writing/Grammar

- Identifying nouns and pronouns

Objectives (pp. 136–137)
Reading Activate prior knowledge

Skill Lesson

Activating Prior Knowledge

Learn It!

What Is It? Activating prior knowledge means using what you already know. For example, to appreciate *Tony Hawk: Chairman of the Board*, you needed to activate your prior knowledge of skateboarding. Now learn how to do it every time you read.

- To *activate* something is to make it active—to get it going so it can be useful.
- *Prior knowledge* is knowledge that you already have—your memories.
- *Activating prior knowledge* is using what you already know to help you understand new things.

"I forgot to make a back-up copy of my brain, so everything I learned last semester was lost."

©1997 Randy Glasbergen/www.glasbergen.com.

Analyzing Cartoons
The character can't activate his prior knowledge because he lost it. What prior knowledge of computers do you need to understand this cartoon?

Academic Vocabulary

prior (PRY ur) *adj.* earlier; coming before

Additional Support

Differentiated Instruction

Reading Cartoons Explain to students that they use their prior knowledge to understand the humor in cartoons. To understand the cartoon on this page, students will need to access their prior knowledge about saving back-up copies of computer documents. Students should know that if they don't make back-up copies and their computers crash, they can lose all of their work. The joke in the cartoon is that the kid thinks he's lost all of his "prior knowledge" because he didn't make a back-up copy. BL

Why Is It Important? Remembering what you have read, seen, or experienced can also help you predict what might happen and understand what you read. For example, because you've been afraid before, you can understand a character who is afraid.

How Do I Do It? Before you read, skim the text to get an idea of what it's about. Then think about what you already know about things related to the text. Here's how one student used his prior knowledge before he read about Tony Hawk. When he skimmed the paragraph, he noticed the terms *sidewalk surfing* and *banana board*.

When Tony was 9 years old, his brother, Steve, changed his life. Because Steve loved surfing, he had tried out "sidewalk surfing." That's what early skateboarding was called. Steve had an old banana board in the garage. He took Tony to a nearby alley, showed him how to balance on the board, and gave him a push. Tony rolled and rolled until he ran into a fence. He couldn't figure out how to turn!

I know that surfing is riding a board on water. I guess sidewalk surfing must be riding a skateboard on a sidewalk.

My cousin had a bike with a seat that was shaped like a banana and called a banana seat; I'll bet the skateboard had that shape too.

Literature Online

Study Central Visit www.glencoe.com and click on Study Central to review activating prior knowledge.

Practice It!

Below are some topics that are related to the selections that follow this Workshop. What do you already know about each topic? In your Learner's Notebook, write two things that you know about each topic.

- Rosa Parks
- The Civil Rights Movement
- Standing up for your beliefs
- Head Start programs
- Doing something good for someone else

Use It!

As you read from *Rosa Parks: My Story* and "Kids in Action: Dalie Jimenez," check the lists you made to practice activating prior knowledge. If you remember more about a topic as you read, add to your lists.

Teach

Literature Online

Study Central Have students access the Web site to review activating prior knowledge and to complete a related activity.

C Critical Thinking

Comprehension **Say:** Look at the What Is It? section. What is the main idea the writer wants you to learn? What is the main idea of Why Is It Important? and How Do I Do It? *(Activating prior knowledge is using what you already know to help you learn new things. It's important because it helps you understand what you read. Skim the text and think about what you already know.)* OL

Ask students to look through the book to find a title or selection that suggests something they already know about. Have them share this knowledge with the class. OL

Resources for page 137

- Use Reading Skills Transparency in *Read Aloud, Think Aloud,* Unit 2, to help students practice activating prior knowledge.

Reading in the Real World

Citizenship Ask students to conduct an interview with an individual who championed a local cause. For example, that person could be a relative who wrote a letter to a political figure; an activist who was involved in a protest; or a teacher, a coach, or a person in their neighborhood who has inspired them by effecting a positive change in the community. Students should approach the interview with a set of prepared questions. Afterward, they should use their interview notes to write a brief biography describing how that person changed their community for the better. AL

Objectives
- Activate prior knowledge

Teach

More About the Author

In 1955 Rosa Parks refused to give up her seat on a bus to a white person. She was taken to jail and found guilty of violating segregation laws in Montgomery, Alabama. The black community boycotted the buses while a legal team and Mrs. Parks fought the segregated bus laws in court. Ultimately, the Supreme Court's ruling that segregation on the Montgomery buses was unconstitutional marked the beginning of the Civil Rights Movement. Parks died in 2005.

V Vocabulary

Vocabulary File Say: One way to learn and remember the vocabulary words is to keep a vocabulary file. Write each word on a 3" x 5" index card. Include the pronunciation if you need it, the meaning, and a sentence that gives you an example of how to use the word. This is a good way to file any information that you want to learn and keep. BL EL

Before You Read from *Rosa Parks: My Story*

Rosa Parks

Meet the Author

Rosa Parks was born in 1913 and grew up in Alabama. Her brave act against segregation made her a hero of American history. She once said, "I would like to be known as a person who is concerned about freedom and equality and justice and prosperity for all people." See page R6 of the Author Files for more information about Rosa Parks.

Author Search For more about Rosa Parks, go to www.glencoe.com.

Objectives (pp. 138–143)
Reading Activate prior knowledge • Make connections from text to self
Literature Identify literary elements: narrator
Vocabulary Use context clues: multiple-meaning words

Vocabulary Preview

complied (kum PLYD) *v.* did what was asked or ordered; went along with; form of the verb *comply* **(p. 141)** *The other riders complied with the driver's order.*

criticize (KRIT uh syz) *v.* to point out what is wrong or bad about someone or something **(p. 143)** *Parks didn't criticize the others for complying with the driver's order.*

warrant (WAR unt) *n.* a document, or piece of paper, that gives a police officer the right to do something, such as arrest a person **(p. 143)** *The driver signed a warrant so that the police could arrest Parks.*

Write to Learn For each vocabulary word, write a sentence that correctly uses the word.

English Language Coach

Multiple-Meaning Words If you read a word you already know that doesn't seem to make sense, it may be that the word has multiple meanings. The context–other words in the sentence and paragraph–can help you find the correct meaning.

Look at these two words and some of their meanings. You'll see these words in *Rosa Parks: My Story*.

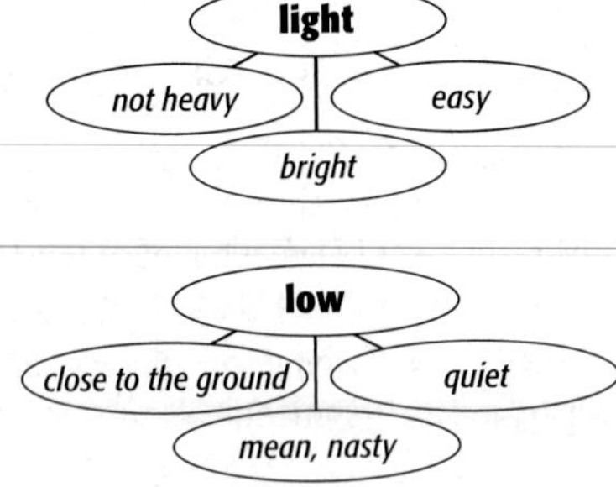

Partner Talk Read these sentences with a partner. Talk about which definition of the underlined word makes sense in each sentence.

1. Wiping tables is **light** work.
2. Turn the TV volume down **low.**
3. The box was **light** enough for Henry to carry.
4. This chair is too **low** for me.

Additional Support

Author Search To expand students' appreciation of Rosa Parks, have them access the Web site for additional information and resources.

Literature Focus Lesson

Nonfiction Rosa Parks's story has been written about by many authors for many audiences. Once your students have been introduced to Parks, they might want to know more about the times and the political, economic, and social forces that shaped them. Suggest a trip to the library or computer lab to do a search for other books and articles about the American Civil Rights Movement of the 1950s. Suggest also that students find out more about some of the people who made history during that time, including Rosa Parks. Some possibilities are Martin Luther King, Jr.; Thurgood Marshall; Earl Warren; and Robert F. Kennedy. OL

Skills Preview

Key Reading Skill: Activating Prior Knowledge

Before you read the story, think about what you already know about

- racial segregation (the separation of people based on race) in the 1950s
- the Civil Rights movement
- any experience you've had in standing up for yourself

Write to Learn Jot a few notes in your Learner's Notebook about what you already know about these topics. Refer to your notes as you read the selection.

Key Literary Element: Narrator

The person who tells a story is the **narrator.** The narrator of a biography tells a story about someone else. The narrator of an autobiography tells a story about himself or herself. In this selection from Rosa Parks's autobiography, Parks is the narrator.

As you read, use these tips to help you learn about the narrator:

- Try to hear the narrator's voice.

  Why is it powerful to hear the story in Parks's voice?
- An autobiography tells only one side of a story. Think about the details the author provides.

  What might the story be like if another passenger on the bus were to tell it?
- Decide whether you trust the narrator.

  Do you trust Parks's version of the story? Does she tell the story without letting her opinion (bias) come through too strongly?

Partner Talk With a partner, discuss whether you would rather hear about an event from a person who was actually there, or from someone else. Explain your reasons.

L

Get Ready to Read

Connect to the Reading

Think about how it feels to be treated unfairly. Parks may have felt that way one evening in 1955. As you read, think what you might have done in her place. C

Partner Talk With a partner, talk about how you felt when you were treated unfairly. Talk about how you acted and explain why you acted that way.

Build Background

The part of Parks's autobiography that you will read takes place in Montgomery, Alabama, in 1955.

- Laws in many states supported racial segregation, which is the separation of people based on race.
- One law said that African Americans had to ride in the backs of buses. If a white person was standing, the African Americans in an *entire row* of seats had to stand up so the white person could sit down. African Americans had to give their seats to white people even if those seats were in the "colored" section of the bus.

Set Purposes for Reading

BIG Question Read the selection from *Rosa Parks: My Story* to find out what difficulties Rosa Parks overcame in trying to become the person she wanted to be—a person with equal rights.

Set Your Own Purpose What would you like to learn from the story to help you answer the Big Question? Write your own purpose on the *Rosa Parks* page of your Foldable.

Literature Online

Interactive Literary Elements Handbook
To review or learn more about the literary elements, go to www.glencoe.com.

Keep Moving

Use these skills as you read the following selection.

Teach

L Literary Element

Narrator Say: When we tell "our side" of a story, it is different from someone else's version of the story. That's because we have our own opinions, and they show up in what we say. This is called bias. Where can you find writing with bias? *(Possible responses: editorials, political campaign signs, and tabloid newspapers)* AL

C Critical Thinking

Application Say: Remember a time when you weren't treated fairly. What did you do? What can you do about a situation that is unfair? *(Responses will vary.)* AS

CheckPoint

Use the CheckPoint questions provided on Presentation Plus! to check for prior knowledge and to build background. These questions can be used with interactive response keypads for immediate student feedback.

Literature Online

Interactive Literary Elements Handbook Have students access the Web site to improve their understanding of narrator.

English Language Coach

Multiple-Meaning Words Introduce students to this three-step multiple-meaning word strategy:

1. Replace the word with a blank: On the table was a ___ of orange juice. (pitcher)
2. Think of another word that could fit into the blank and make sense. The words *jug, bottle, carton,* and *glass* make sense.
3. The new word's meaning is probably close to the meaning of the word you took out. These new words all mean "a container that holds liquid." This pitcher must be a container for liquid. BL EL

Objectives

- Activate prior knowledge
- Make connections from self to text
- Identify literary elements: narrator
- Use context clues: multiple-meaning words

Teach

Viewing the Photo

Say: Although the photo wasn't taken the day of Parks's arrest, it reflects that time period. What information does the photo provide? *(Possible responses: how people dressed, how the buses looked, photography was black-and-white)* AL

EL Language Coach

Idiomatic Phrases Students may need help understanding certain phrases, such as the phrase "got off from work," "by the time," or "put me off the bus." **Say:** What does the narrator mean when she says that she "got off from work"? *(Students may note that this means Rosa Parks's shift at work was over.)* BL EL

Readability Scores
Dale-Chall: 5.0
DRP: 50
Lexile: 840

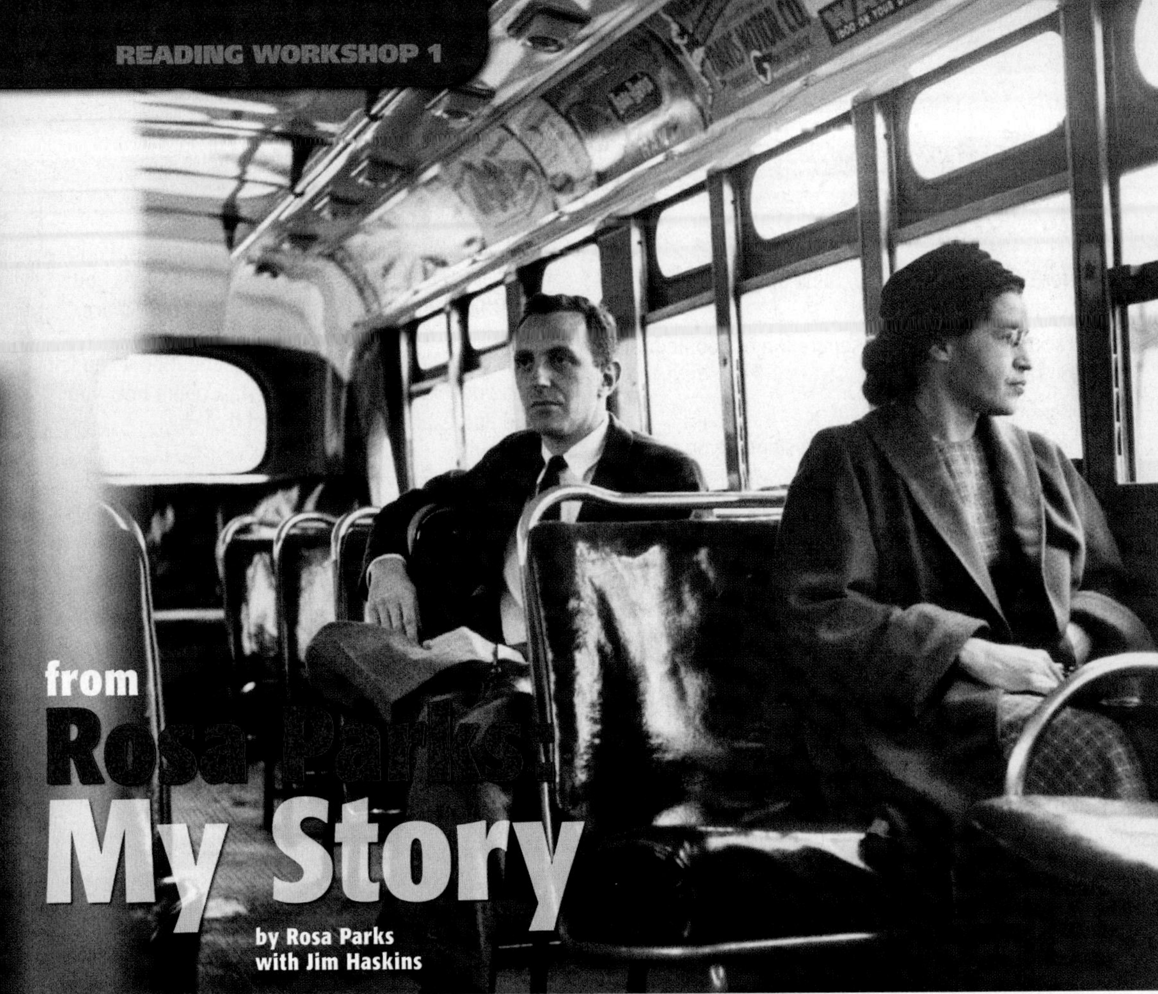

from Rosa Parks: My Story

by Rosa Parks
with Jim Haskins

Rosa Parks rides in the front of a Montgomery, Alabama, city bus.

When I got off from work that evening of December 1, I went to Court Square as usual to catch the Cleveland Avenue bus home. I didn't look to see who was driving when I got on, and by the time I recognized him I had already paid my fare. It was the same driver who had put me off the bus back in 1943, twelve years earlier. He was still tall and heavy, with red, rough-looking skin. And he was still mean-looking. I didn't know if he had been on that route before—they switched the drivers around sometimes. I do know that most of the time if I saw him on a bus, I wouldn't get on it. 1

I saw a vacant[1] seat in the middle section of the bus and took it. I didn't even question why there was a vacant seat

1. ***Vacant*** means "empty." A vacant seat is a seat with nobody in it.

EL **Practice the Skills**

1 **Key Reading Skill**

Activating Prior Knowledge
In the past, Parks's prior knowledge of the driver has kept her from boarding a bus he was driving.

Additional Support

Reading in the Real World

College Students who are planning to further their educations should learn to conduct academic research. This research can include gathering information from a variety of sources: print, electronic media, and other people. Print sources can be primary (original) writings or secondary sources, such as encyclopedias. In order to learn more about the setting for Rosa Parks's story, ask students to look for primary sources: newspaper and magazine articles from the 1950s. Invite students to share their articles with the class. The excerpt on the next page is an example of a primary source. OL even though there were quite a few people standing in the back. If I had thought about it at all, I would probably have figured maybe someone saw me get on and did not take the seat but left it vacant for me. There was a man sitting next to the window and two women across the aisle.

The next stop was the Empire Theater, and some whites got on. They filled up the white seats, and one man was left standing. The driver looked back and noticed the man standing. Then he looked back at us. He said, "Let me have those front seats," because they were the front seats of the black section. Didn't anybody move. We just sat right where we were, the four of us. Then he spoke a second time: "Y'all better make it **light** on yourselves and let me have those seats." **2**

The man in the window seat next to me stood up, and I moved to let him pass by me, and then I looked across the aisle and saw that the two women were also standing. I moved over to the window seat. I could not see how standing up was going to "make it light" for me. The more we gave in and **complied**, the worse they treated us. **3**

I thought back to the time when I used to sit up all night and didn't sleep, and my grandfather would have his gun right by the fireplace, or if he had his one-horse wagon going anywhere, he always had his gun in the back of the wagon. People always say that I didn't give up my seat because I was tired, but that isn't true. I was not tired physically, or no more tired than I usually was at the end of a working day. I was not old, although some people have an image of me as being old then. I was forty-two. No, the only tired I was, was tired of giving in.

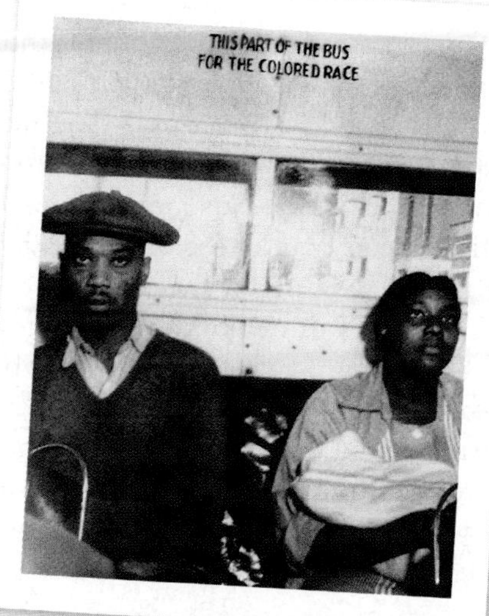
THIS PART OF THE BUS
FOR THE COLORED RACE

Before the December 21, 1956, Supreme Court ruling, African Americans in the South had to sit in the back seats on the bus.

Analyzing the Photo How does this photograph help you understand the times Rosa Parks tells about?

Vocabulary

complied (kum PLYD) *v.* did what was asked or ordered; went along with

Practice the Skills

2 English Language Coach

Multiple-Meaning Words in Context Which meaning for **light** on page 138 makes the most sense here? Explain your answer in your Learner's Notebook.

3 Key Literary Element

Narrator What do you think about the narrator from what she says in the story?

Differentiated Instruction

Primary Sources Read this excerpt from a 1956 *TIME* magazine and have students discuss how Rosa Parks and the bus boycott changed the world we live in.

Within 48 hours after Rosa Parks had been arrested, mimeographed leaflets were being circulated in Montgomery's Negro sections, calling for a one-day boycott of the city buses. The strike was so successful that Negro leaders decided to continue it until their demands were met... The boycott's economic punch has been staggering, because the 25,000 Negroes who ordinarily ride Montgomery's buses make up some 75% of the company's patronage. AL

Teach

EL Language Coach

Multiple-Meaning Words in Context: Say: Look at the sentence, "Y'all better make it light on yourselves and let me have those seats." Can someone think of a few words that could replace the word *light* if we took it out and left a blank there? Feel free to look back at the graphic organizer on page 138. *(Students may note that the words* easy, simple, *and* painless *make sense.)* BL EL

L Literary Element

Narrator Ask: Who is the narrator here? Is the narrator reliable? How would you describe the narrator? *(Rosa Parks; Students must find one sentence from the text on page 141 to explain why they answered the questions as they did.)* OL

CheckPoint

Use the CheckPoint questions provided on Presentation Plus! to monitor students' comprehension. These questions can be used with interactive response keypads for immediate student feedback.

Objectives
- Use context clues: multiple-meaning words
- Understand use of idioms
- Analyze photographs
- Analyze narrator reliability

Teach

Viewing the Photo

Say: Look at the photograph and read the caption beneath it. What does Parks's second arrest suggest? *(Possible response: Now she is actively and consciously fighting the segregation laws.)* **OL**

C Critical Thinking

Analysis Ask: How do you think the officer in the photo feels? Make a web diagram to help organize your thoughts. Use the diagram to write a paragraph about what the officer was thinking as he fingerprinted Parks. Write as if you were the officer (in his voice). *(Responses will vary.)* **AL**

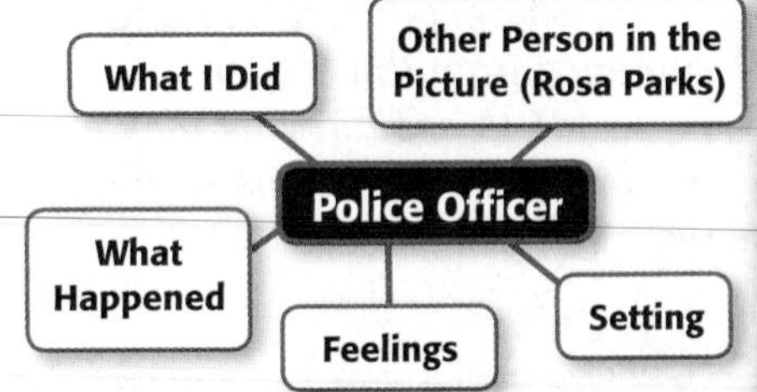

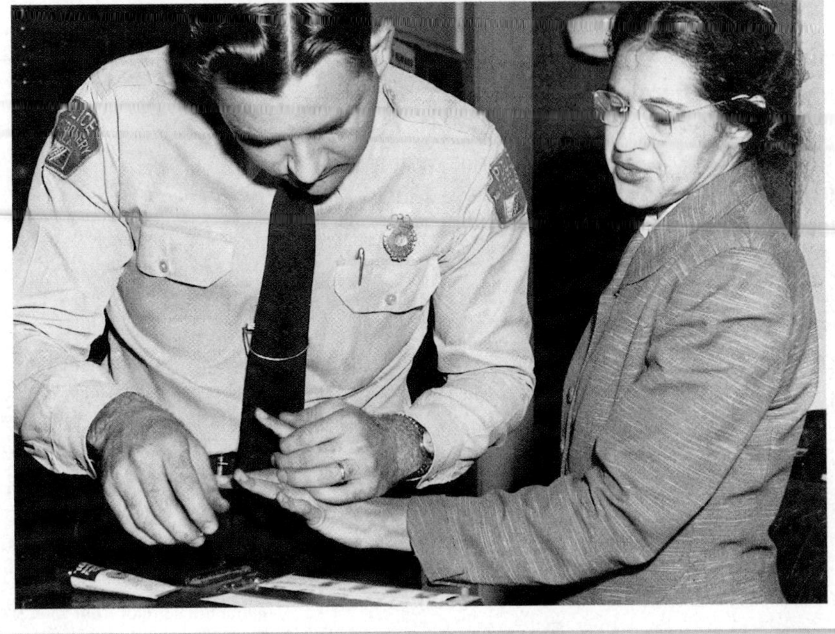

Rosa Parks was arrested again on February 22, 1956. She had dared to disobey another segregation law. **4**

The driver of the bus saw me still sitting there, and he asked was I going to stand up. I said, "No." He said, "Well, I'm going to have you arrested." Then I said, "You may do that." These were the only words we said to each other. I didn't even know his name, which was James Blake, until we were in court together. He got out of the bus and stayed outside for a few minutes, waiting for the police.

As I sat there, I tried not to think about what might happen. I knew that anything was possible. I could be manhandled[2] or beaten. I could be arrested. People have asked me if it occurred to me then that could be the test case the NAACP[3] had been looking for. I did not think about that at all. In fact if I had let myself think too deeply about what might happen to me, I might have gotten off the bus, but I chose to remain. **5**

2. To ***manhandle*** someone is to treat that person roughly.
3. ***NAACP*** stands for National Association for the Advancement of Colored People. This group wanted to get rid of laws that allowed unfair treatment of African Americans. The group hoped that if such laws were to be tested in a court case, the laws would then be made illegal.

Practice the Skills

4 Reviewing Skills

Using Text Features In Unit 1, you learned to use text features to add to your understanding of a topic. Read the caption under the photo on this page. How does this information add to your knowledge of Rosa Parks?

5 Key Reading Skill

Activating Prior Knowledge
Use your prior knowledge about racial problems to understand why Parks was afraid she might be harmed.

Additional Support

English Language Coach

American Legal System Students may have difficulty with the legal terms in this selection. Invite pairs of students to use English dictionaries, bilingual dictionaries, thesauruses, encyclopedias, the student page, and the Internet to familiarize themselves with the legal terms listed:

- policeman
- "the law is the law"
- under arrest
- squad car
- swear out a warrant
- custody
- legally
- City Hall **BL** **EL**

READING WORKSHOP 1

Meanwhile there were people getting off the bus and asking for transfers, so that began to loosen up the crowd, especially in the back of the bus. Not everyone got off, but everybody was very quiet. What conversation there was, was in **low** tones; no one was talking out loud. It would have been quite interesting to have seen the whole bus empty out. 6

Or if the other three had stayed where they were, because if they'd had to arrest four of us instead of one, then that would have given me a little support. But it didn't matter. I never thought hard of them at all and never even bothered to **criticize** them.

Eventually two policemen came. They got on the bus, and one of them asked me why I didn't stand up. I asked him, "Why do you all push us around?" He said to me, and I quote him exactly, "I don't know, but the law is the law and you're under arrest." One policeman picked up my purse, and the second one picked up my shopping bag and escorted me to the squad car. In the squad car they returned my personal belongings to me. They did not put their hands on me or force me into the car. After I was seated in the car, they went back to the driver and asked him if he wanted to swear out a **warrant**. He answered that he would finish his route and then come straight back to swear out the warrant. I was only in custody,[4] not legally arrested, until the warrant was signed.

As they were driving me to the city desk, at City Hall, near Court Street, one of them asked me again. "Why didn't you stand up when the driver spoke to you?" I did not answer. I remained silent all the way to City Hall. 7 ❍

4. To be ***in custody*** is to be held by the police.

Vocabulary

criticize (KRIT uh syz) *v.* to point out what is wrong or bad about someone or something

warrant (WAR unt) *n.* a document, or piece of paper, that gives a police officer the right to do something, such as arrest a person

Practice the Skills

6 **English Language Coach**

Multiple-Meaning Words in Context Look at the last part of the sentence. What does **low** mean here? How do you know? EL

7 **BIG Question**

BQ What do you think Parks would tell you about how to become the person you want to be? Write your answer on the *Rosa Parks* page of your Foldable. Your response will help you answer the Unit Challenge later.

Teach

EL Language Coach

Multiple-Meaning Words in Context Say: Look at the sentence, "What conversation there was, was in low tones; no one was talking out loud." Can someone think of a word that could replace the word *low*? *(Students may note that the words* quiet, calm, *and* hushed *make sense.)* BL EL

BQ BIG Question

Ask: What advice do you think Rosa Parks would give about becoming the person you want to be? *(Students may note that Rosa Parks would probably advise students to act according to their values regardless of the consequences.)* OL

Assess

CheckPoint

Use the CheckPoint questions provided on Presentation Plus! to check students' mastery of the selection. These questions can be used with interactive response keypads for immediate student feedback.

Differentiated Instruction

Research On the board in the classroom, post a large paper bus. Give each student one to three note cards. Take students to the school library, or invite the librarian to bring to your classroom source materials on the bus boycott. Ask students to skim the source materials for information about the bus boycott. Tell students to record on their note cards the most interesting facts that they discover. Students should cite source information. Also instruct students to write why they find the facts interesting. Tell students to post their note cards on the bus. OL

Objectives
- Analyze photographs
- Research a topic and present results
- Use context clues: multiple-meaning words

Assess

Resources for page 144

- Selection Quick Check
- Selection and Unit Assessment
- ExamView Assessment Suite
- Interactive Tutor: Self-Assessment

Students can respond to the *After You Read* items in their Learner's Notebook or on a separate sheet of paper.

Answering the BIG Question

1. Responses will vary.
2. She was tired of giving in.
3. She first thought about her grandfather, and then she tried not to think about what was going to happen to her.

Critical Thinking

4. Possible responses include the narrator added authenticity, emotion, and credibility to the story.
5. Parks disobeyed the driver because she thought she should have the same rights as the white riders.
6. It was important because her actions resulted in the bus boycott and many other Civil Rights actions that eventually resulted in the repeal of the unfair laws.

After You Read

from ***Rosa Parks: My Story***

Answering the BIG Question

1. After reading Rosa Parks's story, what are your thoughts about becoming who you want to be?
2. **Recall** Why did Parks refuse to give up her seat?
   TIP **Right There** You will find the answer in the story.
3. **Summarize** What did Parks think about from the time she sat down on the bus until the time she was guided off the bus?
   TIP **Think and Search** The answer is in the story, but the details are not in one place.

Critical Thinking

4. **Infer** What effect did the narrator have on the story?
   TIP **Author and Me** You will find clues in the story, but you must also use what you know.
5. **Infer** What does Parks suggest was the reason that she did not obey the bus driver's order?
6. **Evaluate** What was important about what Parks did? Remember that most riders had always obeyed this unfair law.
   TIP **On My Own** Answer based on your own thoughts and experiences.

Talk About Your Reading

Literature Groups African Americans in Montgomery responded to Rosa Parks's arrest by refusing to ride (boycotting) the city buses until the law was changed. The boycott became famous. Imagine that your group has been asked to design a poster to celebrate the anniversary of the Montgomery bus boycott. Discuss memorable scenes from the selection. As a group, assign roles to plan and create drawings that best represent the boycott.

Write to Learn Label the poster with headings and write captions for the drawings. Be sure your labels and captions help readers understand the Montgomery bus boycott. Then present your poster to another group. Both groups can give helpful comments on ways to improve the posters.

Objectives (pp. 144–145)
Reading Activate prior knowledge
Literature Identify literary elements: narrator
Vocabulary Understand multiple-meaning words
Writing Respond to literature: poster
Grammar Identify nouns

Skills Review

Key Reading Skill: Activating Prior Knowledge

7. How did the activities on pages 138–139 help you read this selection? Rank the activities in order of helpfulness, with 1 being the most helpful and 3 being the least helpful. Explain your rankings.
   - Reading about Parks in **Meet the Author**
   - Reading the facts in **Build Background**
   - Connecting to how it feels to be treated unfairly

Key Literary Element: Narrator

8. Based on her story, how do you feel about Parks?
9. Describe what kind of person you think Parks is, based on how she sounds in her story.
10. Did Parks tell what happened in a fair and truthful way? Explain your answer.

Reviewing Skills: Using Text Features

11. Choose one photo from the selection and explain how it helps you understand Parks's action.

Vocabulary Check

Choose the word from the list that best completes each sentence below. In your Learner's Notebook, rewrite each sentence with the correct word in place.

complied criticize warrant

12. Parks did not ___ the other passengers for giving up their seats.
13. Because Parks broke a law, the police were able to get a ___ to arrest her.
14. Parks refused to obey the driver, but she ___ with the police officers' orders.
15. **Academic Vocabulary** What **prior** knowledge would you need to understand why Rosa Parks was arrested?
16. **English Language Coach** Review the multiple meanings for **low** and **light** on page 138. In your Learner's Notebook, write three sentences–one for each meaning of the word.

Grammar Link: Nouns

Nouns are important words that name people, places, things, feelings, or ideas. The name for anything that exists is a noun.

The words in dark type below are nouns.

"I saw a vacant **seat** in the middle **section** of the **bus** and took it."

- Some nouns–the ones that name particular people, places, or things–are capitalized. They are easy to recognize as nouns.

Rosa Parks lived in **Montgomery, Alabama.**

- If you wonder whether a word that isn't capitalized is a noun, try putting *the* or *a* in front of it. If that sounds right, the word is probably a noun.

"Meanwhile there were **people** getting off the **bus** and asking for **transfers**, so that began to loosen up the **crowd**, especially in the **back** of the **bus.**"

You can talk about *the* people, *a* bus, *the* transfers, *a* crowd, *the* back, and *a* bus. These are all nouns.

Grammar Practice

Rewrite each sentence. Circle all the nouns.

17. The driver's name was James Blake.
18. Rosa Parks had seen the same man another day.
19. The policemen took Rosa Parks to jail.

Literature Online

Web Activities For eFlashcards, Selection Quick Checks, and other Web activities, go to www.glencoe.com.

Skills Review

Key Reading Skill: Activating Prior Knowledge

7. Responses will vary. Possible responses:
   - **Connecting:** Thinking about how I felt and what I did when I was treated unfairly helped me relate to why Parks acted as she did.
   - **Build Background:** This feature helped me understand why refusing to give up a seat on the bus was such a big deal.
   - **Meet the Author:** This feature tells what kind of person Parks wanted to be, but it does not explain segregation.

Key Literary Element: Narrator

8. Responses will vary, but should be based on some fact or statement in the story.
9. Responses will vary.
10. Responses will vary.

Reviewing Skills: Using Text Features

11. Responses will vary.

Vocabulary Check

12. criticize
13. warrant
14. complied
15. Responses will vary.
16. Responses will vary.

Grammar Link: Nouns

Grammar Practice

17. name, James Blake
18. Rosa Parks, man, day
19. policemen, Rosa Parks, jail

Close

Ask students to summarize what they learned from Rosa Parks's story to help them answer the Big Question.

Teach

More About the Author

Barbara Lewis uses her experience in helping kids solve problems to assist teachers in making their classrooms come alive. According to Lewis, "Kids need to address real needs in their community to think, plan, and actually make a difference. As this occurs, they define themselves as 'problem solvers.' What has been most remarkable is students' growth in leadership and self-confidence, that they become empowered."

EL Language Coach

Multiple-Meaning Words

Say: When you come across a word that doesn't make sense where it's used, that word might have more than one meaning. Check the dictionary for different meanings and try substituting the different meanings in the sentence until you find the one that makes the most sense. BL EL

Before You Read

Kids in Action: Dalie Jimenez

Meet the Author

Barbara A. Lewis teaches kids how to solve real problems. Her public-school students have improved sidewalks, planted trees, and cleaned up hazardous waste. They took their concerns to the U.S. Congress three times. This profile of Dalie Jimenez comes from Lewis's book *The Kid's Guide to Social Action*.

Author Search For more about Barbara A. Lewis, go to www.glencoe.com.

Objectives (pp. 146–149)
Reading Activate prior knowledge
• Make connections from text to self
Literature Identify literary elements: narrator
Vocabulary Use context clues: multiple-meaning words

Vocabulary Preview

psychology (sy KAW luh jee) *n.* the study of human thought and behavior **(p. 148)** *After taking a psychology class, Dalie learned that it is important to read to children.*

disadvantaged (dis ad VAN tijd) *adj.* lacking in basic needs; poor **(p. 148)** *The city started a daycare program for disadvantaged children.*

funding (FUN ding) *n.* money given for a special reason or purpose **(p. 149)** *We can't open the daycare center without funding from the city.*

Write to Learn In your Learner's Notebook, answer each of the questions about the vocabulary words.

1. **psychology** Write about the everyday things in your life that make you who you are. *When you think about the kind of person you'd like to become, what things shape your decision?*
2. **disadvantaged** How can you help someone who lacks basic needs? *Besides giving them money, what are some ways to help people who are less fortunate than you?*
3. **funding** Think of an activity that you participate in or know of that may need funding (such as sports, arts, or writing programs), and think about how you would feel if that activity lost its funding. *How would it affect you, your school, or your community if an activity that you and your friends were a part of lost its funding?*

English Language Coach

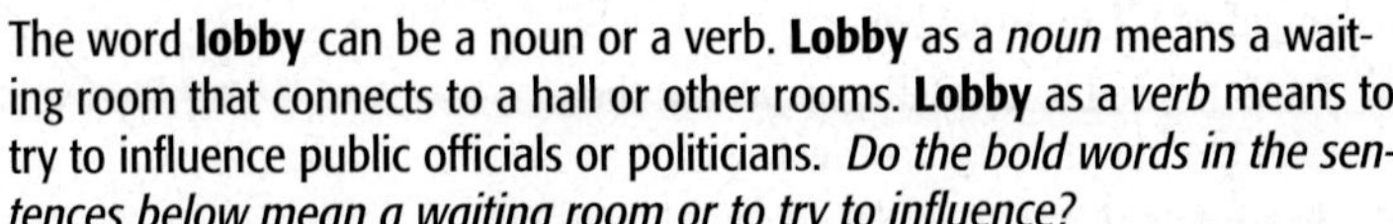

Multiple-Meaning Words in Context As you read "Kids in Action: Dalie Jimenez," watch for multiple-meaning words. Use context clues to choose the correct meanings. With a partner, go over the sentences below and decide which definition fits. EL

The word **lobby** can be a noun or a verb. **Lobby** as a *noun* means a waiting room that connects to a hall or other rooms. **Lobby** as a *verb* means to try to influence public officials or politicians. *Do the bold words in the sentences below mean a waiting room or to try to influence?*

The children waited in the **lobby** to sign up for Head Start.
To help Head Start, Dalie knew she would have to **lobby** for more money.
There was a painting hanging in the **lobby**.

Additional Support

Author Search To expand students' appreciation of Barbara Lewis, have them access the Web site for additional information and resources.

Differentiated Instruction

Research Students might want to learn more about other programs that help disadvantaged children. Have students work in groups to learn what the programs do, whom they help, and what kinds of help they provide. Encourage students to consider volunteering to learn more about a program. Have groups present their findings to the class. OL

Students who would benefit from reading aloud might choose children's books to share while they volunteer. Allow time for these students to practice reading their books before they read them to the children. BL EL

Skills Preview

Key Reading Skill: Activating Prior Knowledge

Before you read the article about Dalie Jimenez, think about young children in your family or community—brothers, sisters, cousins, or neighbors. What do they need to grow and learn? Write your thoughts in your Learner's Notebook.

Key Literary Element: Narrator

In a biography, the narrator tells a story about someone else who is, or was, a real person. While writing about someone, the author naturally forms ideas and opinions about that person and the events in the person's life. Those ideas and opinions are likely to influence what the narrator says and to affect the way you, as the reader, view people and events in the biography.

As you read biographies, use these tips to help you notice and think about the narrator's attitude toward the subject. Also think about how the narrator's attitude affects your views of the people and events in the biography.

- Look at the words the narrator uses to describe the person he or she is writing about. Do the words make the person seem exciting, clever, dull?
  What do Lewis's word choices and descriptions tell you about her feelings toward Jimenez?
- Look at the events that are described. Do you feel you're getting a fair picture of the subject of the biography, or are you getting a picture that's slanted either for or against that person?
  Does the impression you get of Jimenez seem about right or is it too good to be true? Why?

L

Literature Online

Interactive Literary Elements Handbook
To review or learn more about the literary elements, go to www.glencoe.com.

Get Ready to Read

Connect to the Reading

"It's not fair!"

Have you ever said that when you heard about something that happened or was going to happen in your community? Have you ever wished that you could do something about an unfair situation?

Write to Learn In your Learner's Notebook, freewrite about a time when you felt that a situation was unfair. Describe the situation and tell what you did about it.

C

Build Background

This article tells about a time in Jimenez's life when she took action to save a Head Start program for disadvantaged children.

- Project Head Start began in 1965 to help preschool children in low-income families get a good start in education.
- Although Head Start is a national program, it is run locally by community-based groups.

Set Purposes for Reading

Read "Kids in Action: Dalie Jimenez" to find out what Jimenez does when things get in the way of the work she wants to do for disadvantaged preschoolers.

Set Your Own Purpose What more would you like to learn about Jimenez that would help you answer the Big Question? Write your own purpose on the "Kids in Action" page of your Foldable.

Keep Moving

Use these skills as you read the following selection.

READING WORKSHOP 1

Teach

L Literary Element

Reliable Narrator **Say:** Some narrators are trustworthy, while others are not. For example, some narrators might be against things they're writing about without having facts to support their opinions. What can you do as you read to check out whether a narrator is reliable? *(Possible response: See if the narrator presents facts that support his or her opinion.)* **OL**

C Critical Thinking

Application **Say:** Think of a time when you heard about others being treated unfairly. What was the situation? Was there anything you could have done to help? If so, what? *(Responses will vary.)* **OL** What did you learn from the experience? **AL**

Literature Online

Interactive Literary Elements Handbook Have students access the Web site to improve their understanding of narrator.

English Language Coach

Multiple-Meaning Words Have students practice reading multiple-meaning words. Write the following sentences on the board. Tell students that **hearing,** from the main verb **hear,** can mean either the sense that notices sound or a meeting. Ask students, "Do the bold words in the sentences have to do with sound or a meeting?"

1. **Hearing** the children ask her to read made Dalie smile. *(sound)*
2. They called a **hearing** to talk about the Head Start program. *(meeting)*
3. After **hearing** that Head Start's funding would be cut, Dalie knew she had to do something. *(sound)* **BL** **EL**

Objectives

- Activate prior knowledge
- Make connections from text to self
- Identify literary elements: narrator
- Use context clues: multiple-meaning words

Teach

L Literary Element

Narrator **Say:** The narrator describes Jimenez's thoughts and actions. Name one thought and one action the narrator describes that show Jimenez is a considerate and caring person. *(Possible responses: Jimenez wonders if the kids' parents can read to them. She volunteers at Head Start.)* OL

Viewing the Photo

Describe the people in the photo. *(They are smiling teachers and attentive kids.)* BL What can you tell about Head Start from the actions and facial expressions of the people in this photograph? *(You can tell it is a busy, fun place because the people are moving around and smiling.)* OL

Readability Scores
Dale-Chall: 5.2
DRP: 59
Lexile: 900

READING WORKSHOP 1

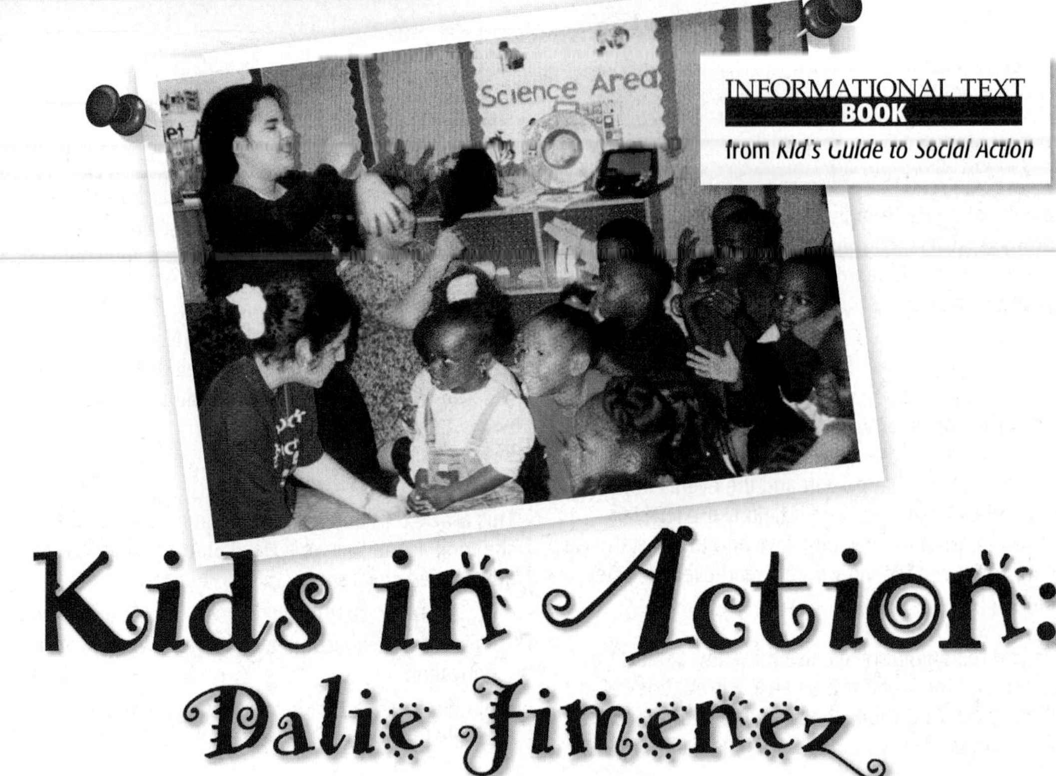

INFORMATIONAL TEXT
BOOK
from *Kid's Guide to Social Action*

Kids in Action: Dalie Jimenez

by Barbara A. Lewis

Miami, Florida. When Dalie Jimenez learned in **psychology** class that reading to young children helps their brains develop, she wondered about **disadvantaged** kids. Did their parents have the books or the time to read to them? Did they get enough attention to get a good head start? 1

And that's exactly where Dalie's wondering landed her—at a Miami Head Start program. (Head Start is a federal program designed to help disadvantaged preschoolers keep pace with other kids their age.) Dalie, then 14, went there to volunteer. Before she went, she told her club, Future Homemakers of America (FHA) Heroes, about her idea, and about 30 of her friends joined her. 2

Vocabulary

psychology (sy KAW luh jee) *n.* the study of human thought and behavior

disadvantaged (dis ad VAN tijd) *adj.* lacking in basic needs; poor

Practice the Skills

1 Key Reading Skill

Activating Prior Knowledge What do you already know about getting a head start at something? Keep that in mind as you read on.

2 Key Literary Element

Narrator How would you describe the narrator's attitude toward Jimenez? To answer, think about what Lewis has told you so far about Jimenez.

Additional Support

Reading Fluency

Reading with Expression Have students form pairs and take turns reading aloud a paragraph at a time from the selection. Encourage students to focus on reading with expression. Give them the following tips.

- Think about the meaning as you read aloud.
- Emphasize important words.
- Read by phrases or thought groups instead of by words.

Have students reread a paragraph two or three times, focusing on a different tip each time. BL EL

READING WORKSHOP 1

"We created a library for the children," Dalie said, "mostly from donated books. We read to the kids and used puppets to act out stories. We baked goodies for them."

A few years later, in 1995, when she heard that Head Start's **funding** was about to be cut by a third, Dalie knew she had to do something. That huge cut would practically destroy the program. She decided to **lobby** to restore funding. **3**

Dalie and her friends made 600 paper dolls to send to politicians. They wrote on the dolls: "Don't give up Head Start." She went to the legislative hearing in her state and spoke to the senators, lobbied, and handed out flyers, all aimed at convincing the lawmakers not to allow the huge cut in funding. **C**

Then with the help of FHA, Dalie went to the U.S. Congress to lobby in person. She followed up by writing a letter to the editor of the *Miami Herald*.

Dalie and her friends weren't the only ones who cared. The media publicized the problem in magazines and newspapers. Such efforts started a chain reaction of protest[1] against cutting funding.

The result of all this combined outrage? The lawmakers did *not* cut the funding and the program was saved. When Dalie heard the good news, she hugged her FHA friends. Then she went back to Head Start and hugged her little friends, who reached up, touched her hair, climbed on her lap, and begged for another story, not understanding that this dedicated young volunteer had just helped to shape their future. **4** ○

1. A ***chain reaction*** is a series of events in which each event causes the next. A ***protest*** is an expression of disapproval or disagreement. In a ***chain reaction of protest,*** one protest leads to another one.

Vocabulary

funding (FUN ding) *n.* money given for a special reason or purpose

Practice the Skills

3 English Language Coach

Multiple-Meaning Words in Context Use the context to figure out the definition of **lobby** in this sentence. Notice that "to lobby" involves a decision to do something.

4 BIG Question

BQ Do you think that Jimenez is a person who fights for her dreams or that she accepts defeat easily? Discuss your ideas with a partner. Write your answer on the "Kids in Action" page of your Foldable.

Teach

C Critical Thinking

Evaluation Ask: Would the techniques Jimenez uses to help Head Start have worked in the unfair situation you described earlier? Why or why not? *(Responses will vary.)* **OL**

BQ 

Ask: What aspects of Jimenez's character do you admire? Would you like to be more like Jimenez? Why or why not? *(Responses will vary.)* **OL**

Assess

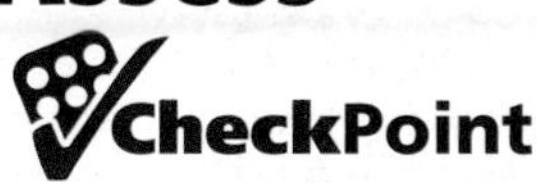

Use the CheckPoint questions provided on Presentation Plus! to check students' mastery of the selection. These questions can be used with interactive response keypads for immediate student feedback.

Reading in the Real World

Citizenship Ask students to think of an issue they'd like to lobby congresspeople about, like Dalie did about keeping the Head Start program. They may search local newspapers for information about issues that are important to them. Once they have selected their issues, have them write letters sharing reasons why they want their congresspeople to take action regarding those issues. Students can find their congresspeople's addresses on the Internet and send them letters.

Objectives

- Make connections from text to self
- Activate prior knowledge before reading and set purposes for reading
- Understand how the narrator contributes to readers' understanding of the text
- Use context clues: multiple-meaning words

Assess

Resources for page 150

- Selection Quick Check
- Selection and Unit Assessment
- ExamView Assessment Suite
- Interactive Tutor: Self-Assessment

Students can respond to the *After You Read* items in their Learner's Notebook or on a separate sheet of paper.

Answering the

1. Responses will vary.
2. They collected donated books.
3. She sent messages to politicians, lobbied in her state and in Congress, handed out fliers, and wrote a letter to a newspaper editor.
4. The children treated her the same as before, climbing on her lap and asking for a story.

Critical Thinking

5. She wanted to read to disadvantaged kids.
6. Possible responses: Lawmakers responded to the publicity. They did not want to look bad by cutting a popular program for children.
7. Possible response: Yes, because the program's funding was not cut and the children continued to learn.

After You Read

Kids in Action: Dalie Jimenez

Answering the BIG Question

1. Think about the children at the end of the story. They enjoy it when Jimenez spends time with them and don't seem to realize that she is helping "to shape their future." Who do you admire or want to be like?
2. **Recall** How did Jimenez and her friends create a library for the children?
   TIP **Right There** You will find the answer in the article.
3. **Recall** What methods did Jimenez use to lobby politicians?
4. **Summarize** What happened when Jimenez returned to Head Start after saving the program?
   TIP **Think and Search** You must use information from the article to decide what the important events were.

Critical Thinking

5. **Infer** Why did Jimenez volunteer to help in the Miami Head Start program?
   TIP **Author and Me** You will find clues in the story, but you must also use what you know.
6. **Infer** What made the lawmakers decide not to cut the funding for the Head Start program?
   TIP **Think and Search** They may have had more than one reason.
7. **Evaluate** Was Jimenez's hard work worth it? Think about the outcome. Explain your answer.
   TIP **On My Own** Answer based on your own thoughts and experiences.

Write About Your Reading

Write a short review of the article "Kids in Action: Dalie Jimenez." Follow these steps to decide what you'll write. Take notes about your ideas.

Step 1: Think about the narrator. Do you think she showed a good balance of fact and opinion? What is her opinion of Jimenez? Do you agree with it?

Step 2: Remember how you connected to the writing. Do you agree with the actions Jimenez took? What would you have done?

Step 3: Find examples from the article that explain why you feel the way you do about Jimenez's actions.

Write to Learn Use your notes to write your review. Include at least three examples from the article to support your opinions.

Objectives (pp. 150–151)
Reading Activate prior knowledge
Literature Identify literary elements: narrator • Use text features: titles
Vocabulary Understand multiple-meaning words
Writing Write a review
Grammar Identify and use pronouns: personal, possessive

Write About Your Reading

Possible response:
The narrator of "Kids in Action: Dalie Jimenez" presents Jimenez fairly and accurately. The narrator uses facts to support her opinion that "this dedicated young volunteer had just helped to shape" the children's future. For example, she tells how Jimenez and her friends wrote to politicians and the newspaper to save the Head Start program. I agree that Jimenez was dedicated and successful, and I would have done the same thing in her place. She cared about disadvantaged children and wanted them to have the same opportunities as other children.

Skills Review

Key Reading Skill: Activating Prior Knowledge

8. In your Learner's Notebook, make a list of things in your prior knowledge that you used to help you understand the article.

   Tip Skim through the selection. Look for the places where you had to use what you already knew to understand the text.

Key Literary Element: Narrator

9. Who is the narrator of this article?
10. Do you think the narrator has a personal opinion about Jimenez?
11. What does the narrator want you and other readers to feel about Jimenez?

Reviewing Skill: Titles and Subtitles

12. The first part of the title "Kids in Action: Dalie Jimenez" suggests that you will see Jimenez take action as you read. Is this a good title? Why or why not?

Vocabulary Check

Choose the word from the list that best completes each sentence below. In your Learner's Notebook, rewrite each sentence with the correct word in place.

psychology **disadvantaged** **funding**

13. Jimenez worked with ___ preschoolers in a Head Start program.
14. In a ___ class, Jimenez learned about why people should read to young children.
15. Jimenez knew that a cut in ___ would destroy the Head Start program.
16. **English Language Coach** Where are you most likely to see people involved in **lobbying**—at a museum or at the U.S. Congress?

Grammar Link: Pronouns

Pronouns take the place of nouns. The *pro-* part means "for." Pronouns are used *for* (instead of) nouns.

- Pronouns that refer to people or things are called personal pronouns.

Have **you** ever seen **him** before?
Tell **me** what **they** said about **it.**

- Pronouns that show possession are called possessive pronouns.

His bike used to be **mine.**
Is **your** house next to **theirs?**

- Talking and writing would be clumsy without pronouns.

Tanya and Mike waited for Tanya and Mike's father, but Tanya and Mike were on the wrong street, so Tanya and Mike's father couldn't find Tanya and Mike.

Grammar Practice

Make a list of all the personal and possessive pronouns you find in the quotations below.

17. "I do know that most of the time if I saw him on a bus, I wouldn't take it."
18. "He said, 'Let me have those front seats,' because they were the front seats of the black section."
19. "People always say that I didn't give up my seat because I was tired, but that isn't true."

Writing Application Review your Write About Your Reading activity. Make a list of all the personal and possessive pronouns you used.

Web Activities For eFlashcards, Selection Quick Checks, and other Web activities, go to www.glencoe.com.

Skills Review

Key Reading Skill: Activating Prior Knowledge

8. Responses will vary. Possible responses: I had to use my knowledge of what it was like to be treated unfairly to understand why Jimenez went to such an effort to save the Head Start program.

Key Literary Element: Narrator

9. The narrator is the author, Barbara Lewis.
10. The narrator calls Jimenez a dedicated "kid in action," indicating she likes her.
11. The narrator wants you to like Jimenez and appreciate her hard work.

Reviewing Skill: Titles and Subtitles

12. Yes. Jimenez lobbied politicians and wrote to the editor. She did it to keep Head Start fully funded.

Vocabulary Check

13. disadvantaged
14. psychology
15. funding
16. U.S. Congress

Close

Ask students to summarize what they learned from Jimenez's story to help answer the Big Question.

Grammar Link: Pronouns

Grammar Practice

17. I, I, him, I, it
18. He, me, they
19. I, my, I

Literature Online

Web Activities Have students access the Web site for interactive activities that will help them assess their understanding of the selection.

Autobiographical Narrative

UNIT 2

Objectives covered in this workshop:

- **Writing** Summarize to inform develop drafts; categorize information; main idea and supporting details
- **Grammar** Identify and correctly use verbs

Teaching Students to Write an Autobiographical Narrative

Why Is It Important?

- Autobiographical narrative provides students with practice writing in the first person point of view.
- Students will enjoy writing about something they really know: their own lives.
- Writing in their own voices will help students hone their understanding of tone and word choice.

How to Help Students Get It

- Remind students to use the language that comes naturally to them; this will help them develop their writing voice.
- Encourage students to start small. The prewriting process will be easier if they do not take on too much material at once.
- Remind the class to use "I" and "me" in their writing, and to talk about a goal of their own.
- Mention examples of autobiographies that students may be interested in, such as those by Michael Jordan, Oprah Winfrey and other celebrities.
- Ask: "Did you include a beginning, middle, and end?"
- Ask: "Could a friend identify you as the person in this story without seeing who wrote it?"

The Writing Trait: Voice

Voice is the author coming through to the reader loud and clear. Good writing creates a sense on the reader's part that a specific person wrote the piece with a particular audience in mind. This includes word choice, tone, point-of-view and perspective all appropriately deployed to make the reader feel as though he or she is being personally addressed. The author's personality is revealed through authorial voice.

Teach

W Writing

Literary Techniques Ask students to write an example sentence or passage using each of the writing techniques described and illustrated in items 1–3 on this page.

- first-person point of view
- sensory description of setting
- description of an action

Tell students that they may use the examples in their books as models, but they should base them on their work so far on their own narratives. OL

Next, have students look at item 4 on this page. Ask each student to think about a possible conclusion for her or his narrative and to write a first draft of it. AL

Develop Your Draft

Choose a key idea from your freewriting. Add details to fully explain your story. You can probably take some details from your freewriting. You can add other details directly from your mind.

Below are some things that skilled writers do to make their writing interesting. Try using some of these strategies as you fill out your draft.

1. Write in first-person point of view. As you learned in Reading Workshop I, the narrator of an autobiography uses first-person point of view, or "I."

   Before I could paint, I had to clear out all my stuff.

2. Remember that setting is the time and place of the story. Describe the setting in language that helps readers see, hear, and feel—maybe even taste and smell—what's going on.

   The wallpaper was pink and yellow and filled with little lambs and birds and flowers. It was way past time for something new.

W

3. Include an **anecdote**—a short, entertaining story about an interesting or humorous event. Show action when you tell an anecdote. Choose words that give the reader a picture of what happened.

   I stepped back to see how good the first wall looked. That's when I heard kerplunk! and felt something wet on my foot. I kicked the bucket, I thought to myself.

4. Provide a clear ending. Describe the problems you had and tell whether you reached your goal.

   I was happy when we got it all done, but I think Mom was even happier. "It's a twofer," she said. "Two for the price of one. You got your room redecorated. And I finally got you to clean it."

Writing Tip

Writer's Craft Use an **interior monologue**—a speech that takes place in the mind of a character—in your story. An interior monologue allows you to share thoughts that you did not say out loud. *See the Writer's Model on page 202 for an example.*

Additional Support

Literature Focus Lesson

Autobiography The more students become familiar with the genre (autobiography), the more models they have for this writing assignment. You might want to send students to the library to gather examples of autobiographies. They could photocopy excerpts or bring the books to class. You might even choose to show a small portion of an autobiographical film. Ask students to choose short excerpts to share with the rest of the class. Discuss what the excerpts have in common and what makes them different. AL

Choose a Topic

Now that you have some ideas, choose one goal to write about. Pick the goal that you think is the most interesting and that you want to share with others. Then focus your ideas about that goal. One good way to start is to talk about your ideas with a small group of classmates.

Group Discussion Follow these steps for each person in the group:

1. Tell a goal you once had.
2. Say one important word or phrase about the goal. Write that word or phrase on a blank page in your Learner's Notebook.

   Paint my room

3. With help from the group, turn the word or phrase into a sentence that describes your goal and why you had it. Write the sentence in your Learner's Notebook.

   When I turned thirteen, I wanted to paint my bedroom so it wouldn't be a little girl's room anymore.

4. Keep this sentence and use it to start writing your autobiographical narrative.

Literature Online

Writing Models For models and other writing activities, go to www.glencoe.com.

Drafting

Start Writing!

Now it's time to start your autobiographical narrative. Whether you feel you're ready or not, just start!

Get It on Paper

- Review your notes about the goal you chose. Look again at the sentence you wrote in your Learner's Notebook.
- Below your sentence, freewrite whatever thoughts come to mind about your goal, the problems you ran into, and the result.
- Don't stop until you've written for ten minutes.
- Let your writing flow. Don't worry about paragraphs, spelling, or punctuation right now.
- When ten minutes is up, read what you've written. Write more if you feel like it.
- After you finish freewriting, you might have new ideas about your topic. You might even have a new topic you like better. That's great! It's fine to change your mind.

Writing Tip

Drafting If you have trouble starting your draft, write down your goal. Then explain why you had that goal. More thoughts and ideas may come to you while you're writing.

Literature Online

Writing Models Have students access the Web site for an additional and interactive Writing Workshop-based student model.

Teach

W Writing

Voice Read the following passages to the class and ask the students to comment on them in terms of voice. Have them consider each author's tone, word choices, and sentence patterns. **AL**

I didn't go home after my trial was over. Instead I stayed downtown. I wanted to know what I could do. Fred Gray said he would appreciate it if I would stay in his office and answer the telephone, so I did.
—Rosa Parks, Rosa Parks: My Story

In 1903 the late Mrs. Annie Johnson of Arkansas found herself with two toddling sons, very little money, a slight ability to read and add simple numbers. To this picture add a disastrous marriage and the burdensome fact that Mrs. Johnson was a Negro.
—Maya Angelou, "New Directions"

Differentiated Instruction

Transitions Some students may benefit from a more pictorial method of putting their ideas together. Help students create a chain of events graphic organizer like the one below. Then introduce one or two transition words they can use when they write or revise their narratives. Ask students if they can suggest other such expressions and list them on the board. **OL**

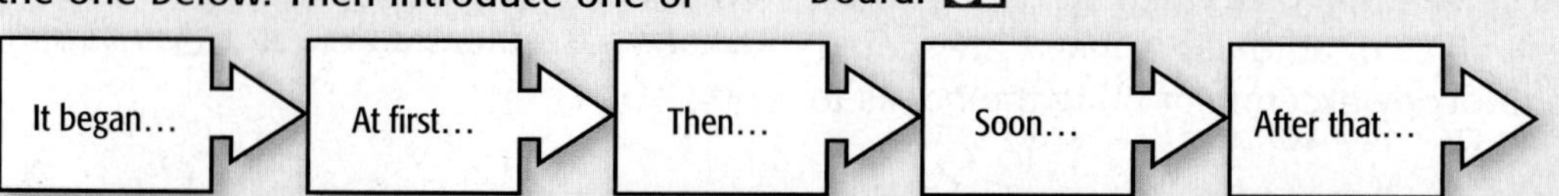

Objectives
- Use the writing process: autobiographical narrative
- Use literary elements: setting, sensory details
- Use first-person point of view
- Identify and use various kinds of nouns

Focus

BELLRINGER Options

Daily Language Practice Transparency

Focus Activity Tell: Briefly summarize an interesting incident in your life. Include where it happened and who was there. You will write about a personal incident in this Writing Workshop.

Teach

L Literary Element

Autobiography Ask: What is the difference between a biography and an autobiography? *(A biography is about someone else's life.)* OL

C Critical Thinking

Comprehension Explain: If a narrative is simply a story, what types of writings are narratives? *(Possible responses: novels, autobiographies, folktales)* AL

Resources for page 152

Use the Writing Workshop Graphic Organizer BLM in the Unit 2 Resource Booklet.

WRITING WORKSHOP PART 1

Autobiographical Narrative

Prewriting and Drafting

ASSIGNMENT Write an autobiographical narrative

Purpose: To tell a story about a goal you once had and how it turned out

Audience: You, your teacher, and possibly some classmates

Writing Rubric

As you work through this writing assignment, you should

- write about a goal you once had
- include an anecdote
- use first-person point of view
- write a paper using your own writing voice
- develop a setting
- arrange events in time order

See page 202 in Part 2 for a model of a personal narrative.

Objectives (pp. 152–155)
Writing Use the writing process: autobiographical narrative • Use literary elements: setting, sensory details • Use first-person point of view
Grammar Identify and use various kinds of nouns

Creating an autobiographical narrative will help you think about the Unit 2 Big Question: How can we become who we want to be?

L **Autobiography:** When you write about your life or an event in your life, you're writing an autobiography. It might be in the form of a note to a friend, a blog, or an assignment.

+

C **Narrative:** When you tell or write a story, real or imagined, you create a narrative.

=

Autobiographical Narrative: Put these two together—write or tell a story about yourself—and you're creating an autobiographical narrative. That's exactly what you'll start to do in this Writing Workshop.

Prewriting

Get Ready to Write

Your basic topic is a goal you once had and how it turned out. Although you've probably had many goals, don't write about just *any* goal you've had. Think about which goal you want to share in your writing.

Gather Ideas

Before you write anything, explore ideas for your topic. Ask yourself questions such as these:

- What was one goal I had in the past?
- What led me to have that goal?
- What problems did I have trying to reach that goal?
- What finally happened? Was I successful?
- How did having this goal help me become who I want to be?

Write down your ideas about two or three different goals you've had. Then think about your ideas some more. Jot down any additional thoughts you have. These notes can be valuable to you as you write your narrative.

Additional Support

English Language Coach

Word Parts Write ***auto bio graph ic al*** on the board as shown:

auto	bio	graph	ic	al
↓	↓	↓	↓	↓
self	life	write	belonging to	related to

Ask: Can you name other words that have one or more of these five word parts? *(Examples: automatic, biology, graphic, historic, theatrical)*

Introduce and identify roots, prefixes, and suffixes and discuss how knowing the meanings of word parts can help students figure out meanings of unfamiliar words. OL

Traits of Good Writing	
Ideas	the message or the theme and the details that develop it
Voice: a writer's unique way of using tone and style	Have students use the following checklist when checking their compositions: • Does your writing sound interesting when you read it aloud? • Does your writing show what you think about your topic? • Does your writing sound like you—or does it sound like you're imitating someone else?
Organization	the arrangement of main points and supporting details
Word Choice	the vocabulary a writer uses to convey meaning
Sentence Fluency	the smooth rhythm and flow of sentences that vary in length and style
Conventions	correct spelling, grammar, usage, and mechanics
Presentation	the way words and design elements look on a page

Unit Focus

Workshop Resources

Pacing (Days) Standard	Block	Lesson	Student Materials	Teacher Resources
1		Prewriting	Writing Workshop Graphic Organizer Grammar Practice Spelling and Handwriting Practice Spelling Power eWorkbook Interactive Grammar and Language Workbook Grammar and Composition Handbook	TeacherWorks Plus Presentation Plus! Rubrics for Assessing Student Writing, Listening, and Speaking
2		Drafting	Real Success in Writing: Research and Reports Writing Constructed Responses Sourcebook	Grammar and Writing Workshop Transparency
1		Editing	Interactive Grammar and Language Workbook Grammar and Composition Handbook	Grammar and Writing Workshop Transparency
2		Revising	Real Success in Writing: Research and Reports Writing Constructed Responses Sourcebook	Interactive Grammar and Language Workbook
2		Presenting	Real Success in Writing: Research and Reports Writing Constructed Responses Sourcebook	Rubrics for Assessing Student Writing, Listening, and Speaking

Grammar Link

Kinds of Nouns

As you know, a noun is used to name a person, place, thing, feeling, or idea. There are several different kinds of nouns.

Common and Proper Nouns

- A common noun refers to any one of a number of people, places, or things. A common noun is not capitalized unless it begins a sentence.
- A proper noun refers to a *particular* person, place, or thing. Proper nouns are names, and they are always capitalized.

A **girl** could be any girl; **Laura** is a particular girl.
There are many **rivers**; there is only one **Missouri River.**
The exact **city** I'm talking about is **Boston.**

Concrete and Abstract Nouns

W

- Concrete nouns name things you can see or touch. Abstract nouns name ideas, qualities, and feelings–things that can't be seen or touched, that have no shape or weight.

Clock is concrete; **time** is abstract.
Horn is concrete; **noise** is abstract.
Poem is concrete; **poetry** is abstract.

Collective Nouns

- Collective nouns name groups of people, animals, or things.

When the **audience** clapped, the **group** made up of students from my **class** and their **families** clapped loudest.

Finding Nouns

- A word is a noun only when it is *used* as a noun. If a word names a person, place, thing, feeling, or idea, it's a noun. If it doesn't, it isn't.

Pull every **weed** when you weed the garden.
I will walk a mile on my **walk.**

Grammar Practice

Use a separate sheet of paper and write the numbers 1–10 down the left side. For sentences 1–3, write every noun in the sentence and tell if they are common or proper.

1. Carolyn read her book.
2. Ticks and fleas bother my dog.
3. I would like to visit China and Japan.

For numbers 4–6, write the nouns and tell whether they are concrete or abstract.

4. I have good ideas, but my paintings are sloppy.
5. Mikel has no time for me.
6. My dream is to own a really good bicycle.

For numbers 7–10, write a sentence using the kind of noun shown.

7. (common noun)
8. (proper noun)
9. (concrete noun)
10. (one concrete and one collective noun)

Looking Ahead

Keep the writing you did here, and in Part 2 you'll learn how to turn it into a really great autobiographical narrative.

Grammar Link: Kinds of Nouns

Grammar Practice

1. Carolyn (proper), book (common)
2. Ticks (common), fleas (common), dog (common)
3. China (proper), Japan (proper)
4. ideas (abstract), paintings (concrete)
5. Mikel (concrete), time (abstract)
6. dream (abstract), bicycle (concrete)
7. Responses will vary.
8. Responses will vary.
9. Responses will vary.
10. Responses will vary.

WRITING WORKSHOP PART 1

W Writing

Using Nouns in Writing

Remind students that nouns name people, places, things, and ideas, and can be concrete or abstract, and collective. Draw a two-column chart on the board, and label the columns "Concrete," and "Abstract." Have students give examples of nouns and write them in the correct column of the chart. Then ask students to place a check mark next to nouns that are collective. OL Ask volunteers to circle proper nouns. BL EL

Assess

Have students exchange their drafts with a partner and critique each other's work. Tell students to look to see if their partners have clear ideas supported by details and stories, and a captivating ending. After a few minutes, tell students to assess their partner's comments, make any needed revision, and save their papers for later use. OL

Objectives

- Write autobiographical narratives using the writing process
- Identify and use various kinds of nouns
- Use first-person point of view
- Use sensory details to develop setting
- Provide a clear ending
- Use time order
- Work with others during the writing process

READING WORKSHOP 2

Connecting

UNIT 2

Objectives covered in this workshop:
- Make connections from self to text
- Activate prior knowledge before reading
- Set purposes for reading

Teaching Students Connecting

Why Is It Important?

- There are many kinds of connections: self to world, self to text, world to text, text to text, self to world, connections within the text, etc.
- Seeing simple and complex implied relationships is essential to understanding an implied main idea or theme
- Connecting to the reading helps to pique student interest and enhances comprehension

How to Help Students Get It

- Before, during, and after reading, have students recall events, situations, and emotions they have experienced that can help them connect to the reading
- Remind students to recall selections they have read, movies they have seen, or other sources that would help them connect the world to the text. Students do not always have to personally experience an event to make a connection. They often "experience" many events through people they know or through situations they have read about or viewed through other media.

Reading to Answer the Big Question

An Hour with Abuelo

Arturo thinks it will be boring to visit his grandfather in the nursing home. He finds that Abuelo is a writer and reader; much like himself. A single hour with Abuelo makes Arturo think about his own dreams for the future. Connecting with the past through his grandfather may help Arturo understand who he hopes to become.

Toward a Rainbow Nation

Thirteen-year-old Lavendhri Pillay is growing up with a very diverse group of friends. She writes about how lucky she is, and the advantages of seeing people for who they really are, not their race. Her parent's generation suffered through apartheid, and there are still instances of racial prejudice where she lives. Lavendhri knows that by working toward the greater good, she and her "rainbow" friends will help their country become the best it can be.

Workshop Resources

Pacing (Days) Standard	Block	Lesson	Student Materials	Teacher Resources
1		Key Skill Lesson: Connecting	Key Reading Skills Practice English Language Coach	Bellringer Options Transparencies Read Aloud, Think Aloud Transparencies Presentation Plus!
2		"An Hour with Abuelo"	Literary Analysis Transparencies Glencoe Online Selection Vocabulary Development Academic Vocabulary Development English Language Coach Active Reading Graphic Organizer Literary Analysis StudentWorks Plus Online Student Edition Literature Classics Selection and Unit Assessments	Literary and Text Analysis Transparencies Puzzlemaker Skill Level Up! BookLink 3 Assessment by Learning Objective (Diagnostic and Formative) Interactive Tutor Self-Assessment TeacherWorks Plus
2		"Toward a Rainbow Nation"	Glencoe Online Selection Vocabulary Development Academic Vocabulary Development English Language Coach Active Reading Graphic Organizer Literary Analysis StudentWorks Plus Online Student Edition Literature Classics Selection and Unit Assessments	Literary and Text Analysis Transparencies Puzzlemaker Skill Level Up! BookLink 3 Assessment by Learning Objective (Diagnostic and Formative) Interactive Tutor Self-Assessment TeacherWorks Plus

Keys for Unit Resource

- Blackline Master
- Workbook
- Supplemental Text
- CD-ROM
- DVD
- Transparency
- Web-based
- Fast Files

Level Appropriate Code

AS = Activities for all students
AL = Activities for students working above grade level
OL = Activities for students working at grade level
BL = Activities for students working below grade level
EL = Activities for English language learners

Focus

BELLRINGER Options

Daily Language Practice Transparency

Focus Activity Ask: How do you feel when you meet people who are different from you? What questions might you ask to learn more about them? *(Responses will vary.)*

Teach

R Reading Skill

Connecting Say: You can connect to characters in stories when you think about what it might be like to be them or to be in their situation. Think of a time when you've connected to a character in a story. Share how you connected. *(Possible response: I connected to Rosa Parks because I've been treated unfairly before.)* OL

READING WORKSHOP 2

Skills Focus

You will practice using the following skills when you read these selections:

- "An Hour with Abuelo," p. 160
- "Toward a Rainbow Nation," p. 170

Reading

- Connecting

Literature

- Identifying the narrator's point of view

Vocabulary

- Understanding multiple-meaning words in context

Writing/Grammar

- Identifying and using pronouns and antecedents
- Identifying and using indefinite pronouns

Objectives
(pp. 156–157)
Reading Make connections from text to self

Skill Lesson

Connecting

Learn It!

What Is It? *Connecting* is finding the links between one thing and another. When you meet a person for the first time, he or she may remind you of someone else you know. You connect the two people by thinking about how they are alike. When you read, think about how the selection connects to your own experiences, to something else you have read, or to the world. R

Connecting what you read to what you know helps you:

- understand what it is like to be in a situation that you read about.
- understand how characters feel, why they feel the way they do, and why their feelings may change over time.

Analyzing Cartoons
The girl connects the book to her own experiences. Will that help her enjoy the book more? Will she understand it better?

Additional Support

Differentiated Instruction

Reading a Cartoon Explain to students that the cartoonist is making a joke about connecting to a character in literature. *Walden* is Henry David Thoreau's story about his time living in the wilderness without "modern conveniences" in the 1800s. The girl in the cartoon connects to the author because she, too, lives without a modern convenience—a cell phone. Ask students to tell of a time they've had to live without a modern convenience. OL

Have students write their own cartoon about *Walden* using their modern convenience as the point of connection. AL

Why Is It Important? Every day you make connections between yourself and your family and friends. You notice what you have in common with them. Sharing experiences helps everyone better understand each other. If you connect what you know to what you read, you will find a story more meaningful.

How Do I Do It? As you read, ask yourself, "Do I know anyone who is like this character? Do I know anyone who has done what this character is doing? Have I been in this situation before? Have I felt this way before?"

Read these first few lines of a poem about growing up, and then see how one student made connections:

Mother got mad at me tonight and bawled me out.
She said I was lazy and self-centered.
She said my room was a pigsty.
She said she was sick and tired of forever nagging **R**
but I gave her no choice.
She went on and on until I began to cry.
I hate crying in front of people. It was horrible.

I know how awful this girl felt, but maybe she was angry, too. I wouldn't want my mom to call me "lazy."

Literature Online

Study Central Visit www.glencoe.com and click on Study Central to review connecting.

Practice It!

The feelings that people have for one another are important in the selections in this workshop. These feelings will make sense to you if you connect them to your feelings for similar people. You can start making those connections by thinking about your feelings for

- your grandparents
- your closest friends

Think about what you do when you spend time with your grandparents or your friends. In your Learner's Notebook, write how you feel about them.

Use It!

As you read "An Hour with Abuelo" and "Toward a Rainbow Nation," look back at the notes you made about your grandparents and friends. If you see a connection between your feelings and the feelings described in the story, write them down.

Teach

Literature Online

Study Central Have students access the Web site to review connecting and to complete a related activity.

R Reading Skill

Connecting Say: Read the poem again. Now, use something you read before or something similar that happened to you to connect to the poem. Write down any connections you make to the speaker. **OL**

Resources for page 157

- Use Reading Skills Transparency in *Read Aloud, Think Aloud,* Unit 2, to help students practice connecting.

Reading in the Real World

Citizenship Have students conduct an interview with someone who is older, from a different culture, or has a different set of beliefs. Encourage them to make connections by finding similarities, as well as differences, between them and the person they interview. Have students present their findings to the class or, if possible, invite the person they interviewed to the class for a question-and-answer session. **OL**

Before the interview, have students brainstorm open-ended questions to ask. Make sure all students understand the questions so that everyone can participate. **EL**

Objectives

- Make connections from text to self

Before You Read

An Hour with Abuelo

More About the Author

Judith Ortiz Cofer moved to the United States when she was two, but her father soon joined the Navy and spent six months of the year in Europe. Cofer's mother had a hard time adjusting to the new culture in the United States, so while Cofer's father was away, she took her children back to Puerto Rico. Cofer attended schools in both Puerto Rico and the United States. She has described the experience of changing languages and cultures so frequently as being like "the perpetual student."

V Vocabulary

Practice Say: When you learn a new vocabulary word, make an effort to use it every day for a week. By repeatedly using the word, it will become a natural part of your vocabulary. **AS**

Judith Ortiz Cofer

Meet the Author

Judith Ortiz Cofer learned English only after her family moved to the U.S. mainland from the island of Puerto Rico. Her writing reflects the split between her two childhood homes. She has written, "My family is one of the main topics of my poetry. In tracing their lives, I discover more about mine." See page R2 of the Author Files for more information about Cofer.

Literature Online

Author Search For more about Judith Ortiz Cofer, go to www.glencoe.com.

Objectives (pp. 158–165)
Reading Make connections from text to self
Literature Identify literary elements: point of view
Vocabulary Use context clues: multiple-meaning words

Vocabulary Preview

depressed (dee PRESD) *adj.* very sad; deeply unhappy **(p. 161)** *When he saw all the sick people in the nursing home, he became depressed.*

diploma (dih PLOH muh) *n.* a piece of paper saying that a person has graduated from a school **(p. 163)** *Arturo hopes to get his high school diploma at the end of the school year.*

ignorant (IG nur unt) *adj.* without an education or knowledge of something **(p. 164)** *The children who didn't get a chance to go to school were ignorant and unable to read.*

Write to Learn Make a list of the vocabulary words in your Learner's Notebook. As a class, discuss possible situations where a person might use each word. Then come up with sample sentences. Write these sentences in your Learner's Notebook.

English Language Coach

Multiple-Meaning Words As you read "An Hour with Abuelo," watch for these words. Use context clues to figure out the right meanings.

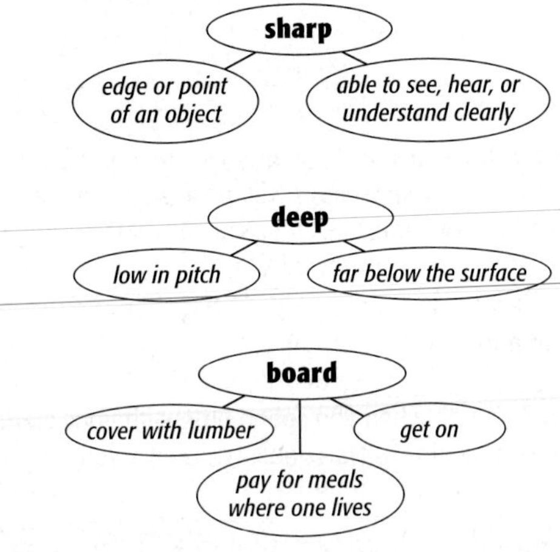

Partner Talk With a partner, read these sentences. Choose which meaning of the underlined word makes sense in each sentence.

I can never fool Marie; she's too **sharp**.
We grabbed our bags and **boarded** the bus.
He sang in a **deep**, clear voice.

Additional Support

Literature Online

Author Search To expand students' appreciation of Judith Ortiz Cofer, have them access the Web site for additional information and resources.

Reading Fluency

Intonation Tell students to watch their intonation, or the ups and downs of their voice, as they read. Explain that good readers use their tone of voice to create interest and convey meaning as they read. They might raise their tone of voice to show surprise or to ask a question or lower their tone of voice to show sadness or confusion. Show students the difference intonation can play in fluency by reading a paragraph once using a monotone and a second time using tone of voice to create a more lively reading. Encourage students to practice using intonation by reading passages from the story aloud to a partner. **BL** **EL**

Skills Preview

Key Reading Skill: Connecting

"But it's so boring!" Have you ever said that when you had to do something you didn't want to do, like visiting a relative you barely know? If you have, you'll probably find it easy to connect with the narrator's feelings at the beginning of "An Hour with Abuelo." He faces the same kind of situation.

Write to Learn In your Learner's Notebook, quickwrite about a time when you had to do something you thought would be boring. Be sure to include your feelings. They will help you connect with the narrator of "An Hour with Abuelo."

Key Literary Element: Point of View

The **point of view** is the narrator's relationship to the story. When the narrator uses a **first-person** point of view, she tells a story about herself and refers to herself as "I." When the narrator uses a **third-person** point of view, he tells a story and refers to the characters as "he," "she," or "they."

In this story, a teenage boy named Arturo is the narrator. He uses the first-person point of view and tells you what is happening as he sees it. Using the pronoun "I," Arturo lets you know he is one of the characters.

At one point, Arturo listens to his grandfather, or *abuelo*, read aloud a story about his life. In Abuelo's story, Abuelo uses the first-person point of view.

As you read, use this tip to help you learn about Arturo and Abuelo and their points of view:

- Decide how Arturo feels about visiting his grandfather.

  Does this tell you how he feels about his grandfather?

Write to Learn In your Learner's Notebook, write a paragraph telling what happened when you had to do something you thought would be boring. Do not tell how you felt. Instead, describe what you did in a way that shows how you felt.

Get Ready to Read

Connect to the Reading

Think about a time when you were asked to do something that you felt you *should* do but didn't *want* to do. How did you feel? What did you do?

Partner Talk Pick a situation where you did something you *had* to do but didn't *want* to do. With a partner, talk about what happened afterward. Were you glad you did what you had to do? Why?

Build Background

In this story, a teenage boy visits his grandfather, who lives in a nursing home in New York City. The grandfather comes from a small village in Puerto Rico.

- Puerto Rico is an island about 1,000 miles southeast of Florida.
- Puerto Rico has its own government but is a commonwealth of the United States.
- Spanish is the main language in Puerto Rico.

Set Purposes for Reading

BIG Question Read "An Hour with Abuelo" to find out who Arturo's grandfather wanted to become and what he did when things got in his way.

Set Your Own Purpose What can you look for in the story that will help you answer the Big Question? Write your own purpose on the "Hour with Abuelo" page of your Foldable.

Literature Online

Interactive Literary Elements Handbook
To review or learn more about the literary elements, go to www.glencoe.com.

Keep Moving

Use these skills as you read the following selection.

Teach

R Reading Skill

Connecting **Say:** Have you ever had a hard time making conversation with someone different from you? If so, what did you do? *(Responses will vary.)* **OL** Students might want to devise 3 or 4 rules for initiating conversations with people they don't know. **AL**

L Literary Element

Point of View **Say:** The narrator is not always the author of a story. Who is the narrator of this story? *(The narrator is a teenage boy named Arturo.)* From what point of view will he tell the story? *(first person)* **BL**

Use the CheckPoint questions provided on Presentation Plus! to check for connecting to the text and to build background. These questions can be used with interactive response keypads for immediate student feedback.

Literature Online

Interactive Literary Elements Handbook Have students access the Web site to improve their understanding of point of view.

Differentiated Instruction

Research Posters Have students conduct research to learn more about the culture of Puerto Rico. You might have each group research a different aspect of Puerto Rican culture, for example, food, literature, government, and schools. Students can work in small groups to devise a list of research questions. Tell students to use the Internet, as well as magazines and books from the library, to answer their research questions. Once students have completed their research, have them create a poster describing an aspect of Puerto Rican culture. Display the posters together to create a complete picture of life in this part of the world. **AL**

Objectives
- Make connections from text to self
- Identify literary elements: point of view
- Use context clues: multiple-meaning words

Teach

Viewing the Art

Say: Look at the picture of the old man. What can you tell about him from his posture? *(You can tell he is thoughtful and perhaps sad.)* **AS**

C Critical Thinking

Comprehension Ask: What is Arturo's opinion about going to see his grandfather? How do you know? *(He doesn't want to go. He says he "hates the place.")* **BL**

Readability Scores
Dale-Chall: 5.2
DRP: 51
Lexile: 860

READING WORKSHOP 2

An Hour with Abuelo

by Judith Ortiz Cofer

Old Man Sitting. Bob Ziering. Pastels on paper.

"Just one hour, *una hora,* is all I'm asking of you, son." My grandfather is in a nursing home in Brooklyn, and my mother wants me to spend some time with him, since the doctors say that he doesn't have too long to go now. I don't have much time left of my summer vacation, and there's a stack of books next to my bed I've got to read if I'm going to get into the AP English class I want. I'm going stupid in some of my classes, and Mr. Williams, the principal at Central, said that if I passed some reading tests, he'd let me move up. **1**

Besides, I hate the place, the old people's home, especially the way it smells like industrial-strength[1] ammonia and other stuff I won't mention, since it turns my stomach. And really the abuelo[2] always has a lot of relatives visiting him, so I've

1. ***Industrial-strength*** means much stronger than normal.
2. The Spanish word for "grandfather" is ***abuelo*** (uh BWAY loh).

Practice the Skills

1 Key Literary Element

Point of View Right away, you know that this story is about a boy whose mother asks him to visit his grandfather. Who tells you this?

Additional Support

English Language Coach

Idioms The narrator of this story uses many English idioms, or expressions that mean something different from their word-for-word meaning. Tell students they can use context to guess the meaning of idioms. One idiomatic expression Arturo uses is "I'm going stupid." Students can use context to learn that Arturo is not challenged in his classes. This suggests that the idiom means "getting bored." Have students work in pairs to guess the meaning of the following idiomatic expressions from the story:

- turns my stomach (p. 160)
- drops me off (p.161)
- It cracks me up. (p. 165) **EL** **BL**

gotten out of going out there except at Christmas, when a whole vanload of grandchildren are herded over there to give him gifts and a hug. We all make it quick and spend the rest of the time in the recreation area, where they play checkers and stuff with some of the old people's games, and I catch up on back issues of *Modern Maturity*. I'm not picky, I'll read almost anything. **2**

Anyway, after my mother nags me for about a week, I let her drive me to Golden Years. She drops me off in front. She wants me to go in alone and have a "good time" talking to Abuelo. I tell her to be back in one hour or I'll take the bus back to Paterson. She squeezes my hand and says, *"Gracias, hijo,"*[3] in a choked-up voice like I'm doing her a big favor. **C**

I get **depressed** the minute I walk into the place. They line up the old people in wheelchairs in the hallway as if they were about to be raced to the finish line by orderlies who don't even look at them when they push them here and there. I walk fast to room 10, Abuelo's "suite." He is sitting up in his bed writing with a pencil in one of those old-fashioned black hardback notebooks. It has the outline of the island of Puerto Rico on it. I slide into the hard vinyl chair by his bed. He sort of smiles and the lines on his face get deeper, but he doesn't say anything. Since I'm supposed to talk to him, I say, "What are you doing, Abuelo, writing the story of your life?"

It's supposed to be a joke, but he answers, "Sí, how did you know, Arturo?"

His name is Arturo too. I was named after him. I don't really know my grandfather. His children, including my mother, came to New York and New Jersey (where I was born) and he stayed on the Island until my grandmother died. Then he got sick, and since nobody could leave their jobs to go take care of him, they brought him to this nursing home in Brooklyn. I see him a couple of times a year, but he's always surrounded by his sons and daughters. My mother tells me that Don Arturo had once been a teacher back in Puerto Rico, but had lost his job after the war. Then he became a farmer. She's always saying in a sad voice, *"Ay, bendito!* What a waste

3. ***Gracias, hijo*** (GRAW see us, EE hoh) is Spanish for "Thank you, son."

Vocabulary

depressed (dee PRESD) *adj.* very sad; deeply unhappy

Practice the Skills

2 Key Reading Skill

Connecting Have you visited someone in a nursing home or hospital? How did the place make you feel? In what ways were your feelings like Arturo's or different from his? **R**

Teach

C Critical Thinking

Comprehension Say: How does Arturo's mother feel about Arturo visiting his grandfather? *(She is very pleased.)* **BL** Why might she feel this way? (She might want her son to get to know his grandfather. She might recognize that they both have a lot in common, such as liking to read.) **AL**

R Reading Skills

Connecting Ask: How would you feel if you were Arturo, visiting a grandfather you didn't really know? *(Possible response: I would feel nervous. I wouldn't know what to talk about.)* **BL**

Literature Focus Lesson

Time Order Explain to students that some short story writers tell their stories in chronological, or time order, while others go back and forth in time. In this story, the writer provides details about things that happened before the story takes place. Have students place the following events from the story in the correct time order:

1. Abuelo becomes a teacher.
2. Arturo's mother nags him to visit Abuelo.
3. Abuelo is forced to join the army.
4. Abuelo reads his story to Arturo.

(Correct order: 1, 3, 2, 4). **BL** **EL**

Objectives
- Make connections from text to self
- Activate prior knowledge
- Understand how the narrator contributes to understanding the text
- Use critical thinking skills

READING WORKSHOP 2

Teach

Viewing the Painting

Say: This painting shows a sparsely decorated room. Why might the editors have chosen it to illustrate this story? *(Arturo's grandfather lives alone in a room in a retirement home. His room might have little furniture, like this one.)* **OL**

C Critical Thinking

Comprehension Ask: Do you agree that people should just accept the way life is, or should you go after what you want? *(Responses will vary. Encourage students to explain their answers.)* **OL**

Room in Brooklyn, 1932. Edward Hopper. Canvas. Museum of Fine Arts, Boston, MA.

C of a fine mind." Then she usually shrugs her shoulders and says, *"Así es la vida."* That's the way life is. It sometimes makes me mad that the adults I know just accept whatever is thrown at them because "that's the way things are." Not for me. I go after what I want. **3**

Anyway, Abuelo is looking at me like he was trying to see into my head, but he doesn't say anything. Since I like stories, I decide I may as well ask him if he'll read me what he wrote.

I look at my watch: I've already used up twenty minutes of the hour I promised my mother.

Abuelo starts talking in his slow way. He speaks what my mother calls book English. He taught himself from a dictionary, and his words sound stiff, like he's sounding them out in his head before he says them. With his children he speaks Spanish, and that funny book English with us grandchildren. I'm surprised that he's still so sharp, because his body is shrinking like a crumpled-up brown paper sack with some bones in it. But I can see from looking into his eyes that the light is still on in there.

Practice the Skills

3 Key Literary Element

Point of View Arturo talks about the differences between himself and the adults in his life. As a first-person narrator, can he tell the reader what is really in the minds of the adults? Could a third-person narrator?

Additional Support

Literature Focus Lesson

The Short Story Tell students that short stories have the following elements. Have students point out these elements in "An Hour with Abuelo":

- Setting (time and place)
- Characters (people in the story)
- Plot (what happens in the story)

Students should note the following:
The setting is a senior citizen's center.
The characters are Arturo, his mother, and Abuelo.
The plot is about a young boy who visits his grandfather in a nursing home. **OL**

READING WORKSHOP 2

"It is a short story, Arturo. The story of my life. It will not take very much time to read it."

"I have time, Abuelo." I'm a little embarrassed that he saw me looking at my watch.

"Yes, *hijo*. You have spoken the truth. *La verdad*. You have much time." C

Abuelo reads: "'I loved words from the beginning of my life. In the *campo*[4] where I was born one of seven sons, there were few books. My mother read them to us over and over: the Bible, the stories of Spanish conquistadors[5] and of pirates that she had read as a child and brought with her from the city of Mayagüez;[6] that was before she married my father, a coffee bean farmer; and she taught us words from the newspaper that a boy on a horse brought every week to her. She taught each of us how to write on a slate with chalks that she ordered by mail every year. We used those chalks until they were so small that you lost them between your fingers. 4

"'I always wanted to be a writer and a teacher. With my heart and my soul I knew that I wanted to be around books all of my life. And so against the wishes of my father, who wanted all his sons to help him on the land, she sent me to high school in Mayagüez. For four years I **boarded** with a couple she knew. I paid my rent in labor, and I ate vegetables I grew myself. I wore my clothes until they were thin as parchment. But I graduated at the top of my class! My whole family came to see me that day. My mother brought me a beautiful *guayabera,* a white shirt made of the finest cotton and embroidered by her own hands. I was a happy young man. 5 EL

"'In those days you could teach in a country school with a high school **diploma**. So I went back to my mountain village and got a job teaching all grades in a little classroom built by the parents of my students.

From Brooklyn Heights, 1925. George Copeland Ault. Oil on canvas, 30 x 20 in. The Newark Museum, Newark, NJ.

4. In Spanish, ***campo*** (KAWM poh) means "country."
5. Any of the Spanish conquerors of Mexico, Peru, or other parts of the Americas in the sixteenth century are called ***conquistadors*** (kohn KEE stuh dors).
6. ***Mayagüez*** (my uh GWEZ) is a port city in western Puerto Rico.

Vocabulary

diploma (dih PLOH muh) *n.* a piece of paper saying that someone has graduated from a school

Practice the Skills

4 Key Literary Element

Point of View Now Arturo is listening while Abuelo tells a story from the first-person point of view. Look for the double and single quotation marks together (" ' and ' ") to signal the beginning and end of Abuelo's story.

5 English Language Coach

Multiple-Meaning Words Use the context around the word **boarded** to figure out the right definition in this sentence.

Teach

C Critical Thinking

Comprehension Say: When Abuelo says "You have much time," he isn't just talking about the time left in the visit. What else might he mean? *(He might mean that Arturo is young and has a lot of time left to live his life.)* AL

EL Language Coach

Multiple-Meaning Words in Context Say: Sometimes the words in the sentences before or after a multiple-meaning word will help you figure out its meaning. Look at the sentences, "For four years, I boarded with a couple she knew. I paid my rent in labor . . . " The words *paid rent* give you a clue about which meaning of *boarded* fits the sentence. Look back at the meanings on page 158 and choose the correct one for this sentence. *(pay for meals where one lives)* EL

Differentiated Instruction

Persuasive Posters Many elderly people in senior citizens' homes receive few visitors. Have students create persuasive posters that encourage young people to volunteer at senior citizens' centers. Tell students to start by thinking of the benefits of young people hanging out with the elderly. What might young people learn? What might the older people receive in return? Have students create posters to convince young people to volunteer. Encourage students to use pictures, colorful writing, and large type to engage their readers. You might ask local librarians or bookstores to display the posters. BL EL

Objectives
- Make connections from self to text
- Activate prior knowledge
- Use critical thinking skills
- Use context to understand multiple-meaning words
- Analyze paintings

READING WORKSHOP 2

Teach

R Reading Skill

Connecting Say: Abuelo made many efforts to stay in his teaching job. How would you have felt in his place? *(Possible answer: I would have felt very frustrated and upset.)* BL

C Critical Thinking

Comprehension Say: How would you describe Abuelo's life? *(Possible responses: Sad, challenging; he makes the best out of bad situations.)* AS

"'I had books sent to me by the government. I felt like a rich man although the pay was very small. I had books. All the books I wanted! I taught my students how to read poetry and plays, and how to write them. We made up songs and put on shows for the parents. It was a beautiful time for me.

"'Then the war came, and the American President said that all Puerto Rican men would be drafted. I wrote to our governor and explained that I was the only teacher in the mountain village. I told him that the children would go back to the fields and grow up **ignorant** if I could not teach them their letters. I said that I thought I was a better teacher than a soldier. The governor did not answer my letter. I went into the U.S. Army.

"'I told my sergeant that I could be a teacher in the army. I could teach all the farm boys their letters so that they could read the instructions on the ammunition boxes and not blow themselves up. The sergeant said I was too smart for my own good, and gave me a job cleaning latrines.[7] He said to me there is reading material for you there, scholar. Read the writing on the walls. I spent the war mopping floors and cleaning toilets. R

"'When I came back to the Island, things had changed. You had to have a college degree to teach school, even the lower grades. My parents were sick, two of my brothers had been killed in the war, the others had stayed in Nueva York. I was the only one left to help the old people. I became a farmer. I married a good woman who gave me many good children. I taught them all how to read and write before they started school.'" 6

Abuelo then puts the notebook down on his lap and closes his eyes.

"*Así es la vida* is the title of my book," he says in a whisper, almost to himself. Maybe he's forgotten that I'm there. 7

For a long time he doesn't say anything else. I think that he's sleeping, but then I see that he's watching me through half-closed lids, maybe waiting for my opinion of his writing.

7. Another word for toilets is ***latrines*** (luh TREENZ).

Vocabulary

ignorant (IG nur unt) *adj.* without an education or knowledge of something

Practice the Skills

6 Key Literary Element

Point of View The author shows us Arturo's point of view about his visit to the nursing home. If the author told the whole story from Abuelo's point of view, what might Abuelo say about Arturo?

7 Key Reading Skill

Connecting In what important ways was Abuelo's life different from Arturo's? In what important ways is it different from yours?

Additional Support

Reading in the Real World

Career Lead students in a discussion about success. Tell them that Arturo has very definite ideas about life and about what it takes to be successful. He believes that he will not let anything get in the way of his dreams. Ask students to discuss their hopes for the future. What will determine whether they are successful? Do they believe that Abuelo is successful? Why or why not? Then ask students whether they agree with Arturo's statement, "Nobody is going to stop me from doing what I want with my life." Do students believe this is a realistic statement? Why or why not? OL

I'm trying to think of something nice to say. I liked it and all, but not the title. And I think that he could've been a teacher if he had wanted to bad enough. Nobody is going to stop me from doing what I want with my life. I'm not going to let la vida get in my way. I want to discuss this with him, but the words are not coming into my head in Spanish just yet. I'm about to ask him why he didn't keep fighting to make his dream come true, when an old lady in hot-pink running shoes sort of appears at the door.

She is wearing a pink jogging outfit too. The world's oldest marathoner,[8] I say to myself. She calls out to my grandfather in a flirty voice, "Yoo-hoo, Arturo, remember what day this is? It's poetry-reading day in the rec room! You promised us you'd read your new one today."

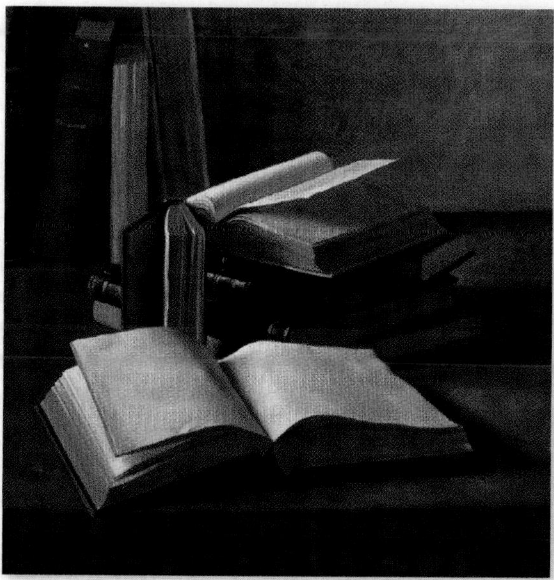

El Libro, 1997. Juan Lascano. Oil on canvas. Zurbaran Galeria, Buenos Aires, Argentina.

I see my abuelo perking up almost immediately. He points to his wheelchair, which is hanging like a huge metal bat in the open closet. He makes it obvious that he wants me to get it. I put it together, and with Mrs. Pink Running Shoes's help, we get him in it. Then he says in a strong deep voice I hardly recognize, "Arturo, get that notebook from the table, please."

I hand him another map-of-the-Island notebook—this one is red. On it in big letters it says, *POEMAS DE ARTURO.*

I start to push him toward the rec room, but he shakes his finger at me.

"Arturo, look at your watch now. I believe your time is over." He gives me a wicked smile. 8

Then with her pushing the wheelchair—maybe a little too fast—they roll down the hall. He is already reading from his notebook, and she's making bird noises. I look at my watch and the hour is up, to the minute. I can't help but think that my abuelo has been timing me. It cracks me up. I walk slowly down the hall toward the exit sign. I want my mother to have to wait a little. I don't want her to think that I'm in a hurry or anything. ○

8. A ***marathoner*** is a person who runs a long-distance race.

Practice the Skills

8 BIG Question

Judging from Abuelo's story, do you think he fought for his dreams? Or do you think he accepted defeat, as Arturo suggests? Pair up to discuss. Then write your answer on the "Hour with Abuelo" page of your Foldable. Your response will help you answer the Unit Challenge later.

READING WORKSHOP 2

Teach

C Critical Thinking

Comprehension Ask: Do you think Arturo will visit his Abuelo again? Why or why not? *(Possible response: Yes, he will visit him because they both love books and Arturo is curious about Abuelo's poetry.)* **AL**

BQ 

Ask: What advice do you think Abuelo would give about becoming the person you want to be? How might his advice differ from Arturo's? *(Possible response: Abuelo would say it is never too late to be who you want to be. He might say that sometimes life's duties may get in the way of doing things on your own schedule. Arturo would probably say to go for your dreams no matter what gets in the way.)* **OL**

Assess

Use the CheckPoint questions provided on Presentation Plus! to check students' mastery of the selection. These questions can be used with interactive response keypads for immediate student feedback.

Differentiated Instruction

Writing Poetry Arturo doesn't get to hear his grandfather's poetry in the story. Ask students to consider what Abuelo might write about. Encourage them to think about Abuelo's life. What hardships did he suffer? What were the good things in his life? What lessons might he have learned? Then have students write a narrative poem about Abuelo's life. Tell students that their poems can have a specific meter or they can be free verse. Once students have completed their poems, have them share them with the class, either in an oral presentation or by posting them on a poster board. **AL**

Objectives
- Make connections from self to text
- Use critical thinking skills

Assess

Resources for page 166

- Selection Quick Check
- Selection and Unit Assessment
- ExamView Assessment Suite
- Interactive Tutor: Self-Assessment

Students can respond to the *After You Read* items in their Learner's Notebook or on a separate sheet of paper.

Answering the BIG Question

1. He is too busy reading books so he can get into AP classes.
2. His mother wants him to.
3. Abuelo reads the story of his life. Arturo learns his grandfather loves to read but that he had to give up being a teacher.

Critical Thinking

4. Arturo believes Abuelo gave up on life, which Arturo says he'd never do. Abuelo lived in Puerto Rico most of his life; his grandson was born in the United States.
5. Responses may include: Arturo realizes that he has more in common with Abuelo than he thought.
6. Arturo realizes that sometimes our goals are achieved differently than we expect.

After You Read

An Hour with Abuelo

Objectives (pp. 166–167)
Reading Make connections from text to self
Literature Identify literary elements: point of view
Vocabulary Use context clues: multiple meanings
Writing Write a review
Grammar Identify pronoun antecedents

Answering the BIG Question

1. Why does Arturo feel he doesn't have time to visit his grandfather?
2. **Recall** What is Arturo's main reason for visiting the nursing home?
   TIP Right There You will find the answer in the story.
3. **Summarize** What happened during Arturo's visit to his grandfather in the nursing home?
   TIP Think and Search Review the story and decide what the important points are.

Critical Thinking

4. **Infer** Why does Arturo feel he doesn't have much in common with his grandfather?
   TIP Think and Search Look for what Arturo says when he first starts to talk about his grandfather.
5. **Infer** How much has Arturo's attitude toward his grandfather changed at the end of the story?
   TIP Author and Me Think about what Arturo says as he leaves the nursing home.
6. **Evaluate** Do Arturo's ideas about his future change because of Abuelo's story? How?
   TIP Author and Me Answer from information in the story and from your own experiences.

Write About Your Reading

Write a short review of the story "An Hour with Abuelo." A review tells someone whether you liked a story and why. Follow these steps to help you decide what you'll write. Take notes as you answer these questions.

Step 1: Think about Arturo's attitude. In your opinion, did his opinion of Abuelo make sense? Do you share his feelings?

Step 2: Remember how you connected to the writing. Compared with your experiences, did the story seem believable, or did it seem phony?

Step 3: Find examples from the story to explain your reaction to it. In a good review, a writer backs up his or her ideas.

Use your notes to write your review. Include at least three examples from the story to back up your statements about it.

Write About Your Reading

Possible response:
I really liked the story "An Hour with Abuelo." I thought Arturo's point of view made sense. Arturo was determined and didn't want anything to get in the way of his success. However, he learned that his grandfather put off his dreams for the sake of his family. Arturo realizes that there is no hurry to achieve success. Abuelo didn't get to live out his dream until he was an old man, but he was happy. The story was believable to me. Older people have a lot to teach us. My grandmother has taught me the importance of patience and kindness.

Skills Review

Key Reading Skill: Connecting

7. With a small group of classmates, choose one of the following questions and talk it over with each other. Don't forget to share your own ideas and experiences.
   - Arturo says, "I go after what I want." What does he mean by this? Can you connect this idea to your own ideas about life?
   - At one point, Arturo checks his watch to see how much longer he has to stay with Abuelo. Have you ever done something like this?
   - Arturo's mother and Abuelo both say: "That's the way life is." Do you agree with them? Why or why not?

Key Literary Element: Point of View

8. This story is told from the first-person point of view. Can you imagine yourself in the same situation as Arturo's? You know how Arturo feels about Abuelo's life; do you feel the same way?

Reviewing Skills: Titles and Subtitles

What does the title of Abuelo's life story tell you about the way he views his life? Use examples from the story to explain your answer.

Vocabulary Check

Choose the best word from the list to complete each sentence below. In your Learner's Notebook, rewrite each sentence with the correct word in the blank.

depressed **diploma** **ignorant**

9. The sight of all the old people in the nursing home made Arturo ___.
10. After Abuelo earned his high school ___, he taught in his home village.
11. Abuelo feared that children would remain ___ without the help of a teacher.
12. **English Language Coach** Is there enough room in your home for someone to **board** with you?

Grammar Link: Pronoun Antecedents

An antecedent (an tuh SEE dunt) is the noun that a pronoun refers to.

Hernando did what he thought was right.
antecedent *pronoun*

- When you use a pronoun, be sure it refers to its antecedent clearly.

?

Cheryl Lynn and Tabitha went to her house.
antecedent? *antecedent?* *pronoun*

- If an antecedent isn't clear, you should rewrite the sentence.

Unclear: I hit a branch with my head, and it broke off.
Clear: I hit a branch with my head, and the branch broke off.
A branch broke off when I hit it with my head.

Grammar Practice

The antecedents in these sentences are not clear. Rewrite the sentences to make the situation given in parentheses clear.

13. Jeanie told Sheila that her sweater was torn. (It's Jeanie's sweater that's torn.)
14. When Chris and his dad played catch, he hurt his arm. (Chris is the one who hurt his am.)
15. The teacher told Lucas that he needed help. (Lucas is the one who needs help.)

Writing Application Look back at the review you wrote. Make sure your pronoun antecedents are clear.

Web Activities For eFlashcards, Selection Quick Checks, and other Web activities, go to www.glencoe.com.

Skills Review

Key Reading Skill: Connecting

7. Discussions will vary. Remind students to support their opinions with their own experiences.

Key Literary Element: Point of View

8. Responses will vary. Students should state whether they agree or disagree with Arturo's opinion that his grandfather could have become a teacher if he'd really wanted to.

Reviewing Skills: Titles and Subtitles

The title of Abuelo's story tells that he believes you must accept life as it is sometimes. He accepted that he could not teach after returning from the service, so he became a farmer instead.

Vocabulary Check

9. depressed
10. diploma
11. ignorant
12. Responses will vary. Students should know that board means to pay for room and meals.

Grammar Link: Pronoun Antecedents

Grammar Practice

Responses may vary. Possible responses follow.

13. Jeanie told Sheila that Jeanie's sweater was torn.
14. Chris hurt his arm when he and his dad played catch.
15. The teacher told Lucas, "You need help."

Close

Ask students to summarize what they learned from "An Hour with Abuelo" to help them answer the Big Question.

More About the Author

Lavendhri Pillay grew up in a suburb of Johannesburg in South Africa that had been integrated for years. Unlike many other students in South Africa, Pillay attended school with students from a variety of races and cultures. At the time she wrote this essay, South Africans were trying to adjust to the end of apartheid and integration. Pillay hopes that one day South Africa can be free of racial divisons.

V Vocabulary

Words in Context **Say:** Try having a conversation with a partner using all four vocabulary words correctly. **AS**

Before You Read Toward a Rainbow Nation

Meet the Author

Lavendhri Pillay was born and raised in South Africa. She was thirteen when she wrote this narrative. At that time, South Africa was just starting to let students of different races go to the same schools. Pillay says she loves living among people from many different backgrounds.

Author Search For more about Lavendhri Pillay, go to www.glencoe.com.

Objectives (pp. 168–173)
Reading Make connections from text to self and from text to world
Literature Identify literary elements: point of view
Vocabulary Use context clues: multiple-meaning words

Vocabulary Preview

subjected (sub JEK tid) *v.* exposed (to); forced to hear or see; form of the verb *subject (to)* **(p. 170)** *Pillay and her friends were subjected to racism at a restaurant.*

cultures (KUL churz) *n.* groups of people who share a history and way of life **(p. 171)** *Pillay enjoys meeting people from different cultures.*

cliques (kleeks *or* kliks) *n.* groups of people who leave others out **(p. 172)** *It's hard to make friends with students who belong to cliques.*

optimistic (awp tuh MIS tik) *adj.* taking the view that things will turn out well; hopeful **(p. 173)** *Pillay is optimistic about South Africa.*

Write to Learn List the vocabulary words in your Learner's Notebook. Think of situations in which a person might use the words. Then make up a sentence for each and write it in your Learner's Notebook.

English Language Coach

Multiple-Meaning Words in Context As you read "Toward a Rainbow Nation," watch for these words. Use context clues to choose the correct meanings.

To *mix* can mean

An *address* (AD res) is where a person lives or a company does business. When used as a verb, *address* (uh DRES) can mean

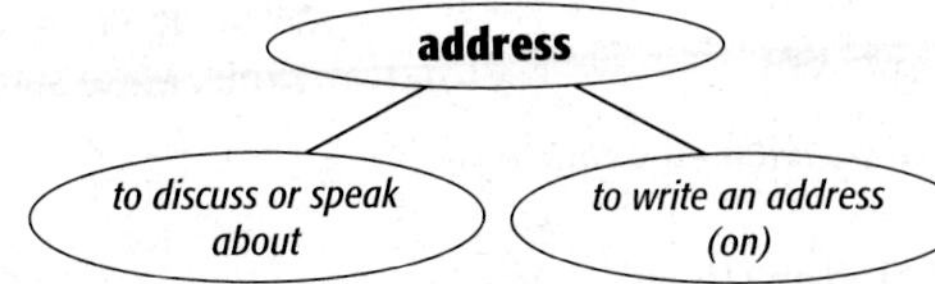

Partner Talk With a partner, make up a situation where someone would use the word *mix* or *address* while talking to another person. Act out your idea in front of the class.

Additional Support

Author Search To expand students' appreciation of Lavendhri Pillay, have them access the Web site for additional information and resources.

Differentiated Instruction

Nonfiction Research Have students research nonfiction works to learn more about apartheid—the system of racial division in South Africa—and life in the country after apartheid ended. Students should be able to find many essays, articles, and Web sites dedicated to apartheid. Encourage students to use the keywords *Nelson Mandela, apartheid,* and *South Africa* as they search. Have students present their findings. **OL**

Ask students to compare and contrast South Africa's apartheid system to racial segregation in the United States during the Jim Crow era. Refer them to *Rosa Parks: My Story* on page 140. **AL**

Skills Preview

Key Reading Skill: Connecting

Have you ever felt that a certain group of people didn't want you to join them? Have you felt left out of a group's activities? Have you felt that a group looked down on you because you were "different"?

When Lavendhri Pillay was born, the laws of South Africa kept people of different races apart. By the time she went to school, the laws had changed a little, and the school she attended was "mixed." That is, it had students of many races.

Write to Learn In your Learner's Notebook, quickwrite about the many ways that people see one another as "different" in Pillay's world and yours. Race is certainly one of the differences between people. What others can you think of?

Key Literary Element: Point of View

Pillay uses the first-person point of view in this selection. She writes as if she were in the room with you, talking face-to-face with you about her friends and her country.

While you read, think how the story would be different if it were told from a different point of view. Would it feel less personal if someone else wrote the story and talked about Pillay as "she" and her friends as "they"?

Write to Learn Pair up with a classmate and write a short description of him or her using the third-person point of view. Then write a short description of yourself using the first-person point of view. Read what your partner has written about you and note the difference between first-person and third-person points of view.

Interactive Literary Elements Handbook
To review or learn more about the literary elements, go to www.glencoe.com.

Get Ready to Read

Connect to the Reading

Before you read the narrative, think about your friends and classmates. How well do you know people who come from cultures different from your own? Do all your closest friends have the same kind of background you do?

List Ideas Pretend you have the chance to meet a new student from a different culture and visit his or her home. Make a list of things you would like to know about the student's culture. Share your ideas with the class.

Build Background

In this autobiographical narrative, a teenage girl tells about her school, her friends, and her everyday life in South Africa.

- South Africa is a nation at the southern tip of Africa.
- From 1948 to 1994, a law called apartheid (uh PAR tyd) set limits on the lives of people of different races in South Africa. The word *apartheid* means "separateness."
- In 1994, apartheid officially ended in South Africa.

Set Purposes for Reading

BIG Question Read "Toward a Rainbow Nation" to find out what Lavendhri Pillay thinks about how young people in South Africa and everywhere can become whom they want to be.

Set Your Own Purpose What would you like to learn to help you answer the Big Question? Write your own purpose on the "Toward a Rainbow Nation" page of your Foldable.

Keep Moving
Use these skills as you read the following selection.

READING WORKSHOP 2

Teach

R Reading Skill

Connecting Say: How long does it take you to feel comfortable around people from different cultures? What might make you feel comfortable more quickly? *(Responses will vary.)* **OL**

L Literary Element

Point of View Say: When writers use first-person point of view, they can clearly state their opinions on a topic. Why might many journalists choose not to use first-person point of view? *(Possible response: Journalists want their writing to appear less biased.)* **AL**

CheckPoint

Use the CheckPoint questions provided on Presentation Plus! to check for prior knowledge and to build background. These questions can be used with interactive response keypads for immediate student feedback.

Literature Online

Interactive Literary Elements Handbook Have students access the Web site to improve their understanding of point of view.

Differentiated Instruction

Using Vocabulary Give students additional practice in using the vocabulary words by asking them these questions:

1. Where would you be more likely to find people of different cultures: at a family dinner or at a school? *(at a school)*
2. How would someone who is optimistic respond to a problem? *(He or she would respond by being positive.)*
3. Are cliques groups of people who are friendly to everyone or who leave others out? *(They leave others out.)*
4. Name two things you might be subjected to. *(possible responses: a new idea, a movie)* **BL**

Objectives
- Make connections from text to self
- Identify literary elements: point of view
- Use context clues: multiple-meaning words

Teach

C Critical Thinking

Comprehension Ask: How is South Africa like a rainbow? Why might the country choose to call itself a "Rainbow Nation"? *(South Africa is made up of people of many colors, just like a rainbow is made up of many colors. South Africa might choose this name because rainbows are a positive, beautiful symbol of many colors living together.)* OL

L Literary Element

Point of View Ask: What is Pillay's point of view towards mixed schools? How do you know? *(She thinks mixed schools are positive; she says she is lucky because she has been subjected to different races.)* OL

Readability Scores
Dale-Chall: 5.8
DRP: 56
Lexile: 990

READING WORKSHOP 2

Toward a RAINBOW Nation

by Lavendhri Pillay

People ask me all the time, "What are you?" I say I'm South African. Then they say, "No-no-no, but what *are* you?" When I was small, I was always told that my great-grandfather came from India to pick sugarcane, but my family doesn't really have ties to India anymore. So I say, "I was born here, I've lived here my whole life, I don't know anything else, so I'm South African."

I've grown up different from a lot of other teenagers in South Africa because I've been **subjected** to all different races and different kinds of people. I'm a really lucky person. 1

L Since I was seven, I've gone to school at Sacred Heart, where everybody's completely mixed. We've got Coloured, black, British, Chinese, white, Indian, Afrikaans,[1] everybody. So from an early age I learned to accept these different

1. Under the apartheid laws, a person of more than one race was called ***coloured.*** South Africa was once a British colony, and this is the British spelling. The ***Afrikaans*** are descendants of the Dutch settlers who moved to South Africa in the 1600s.

Vocabulary

subjected (sub JEK tid) *v.* exposed (to); forced to hear or see

Practice the Skills

1 Key Reading Skill

Connecting Pillay is happy with her situation. What about you? Do you know many people who are different from you in some way? Have you made friends with some of them? How do you feel about your situation?

Additional Support

Reading in the Real World

Citizenship According to a 2005 census, South Africa is a nation of 46.9 million people. Seventy-nine percent are African/Black, 9.6 percent are white, 8.9 percent are colored, and 2.5 percent are Indian/Asian. The term "colored" refers to people of mixed race, who descended from indigenous Black Africans and the earliest white settlers.

There are 11 official languages in South Africa, reflecting the many different African tribes in the country.

Share this information with students. Have them write "Rainbow Nation" on a large poster and find pictures to illustrate their posters. OL people. In our school it's about what kind of reputation you make for yourself, what kind of person you are.

I've lived in Yeoville[2] most of my life with my mother, sister, and two brothers. It's a place where many **cultures** live. It's really nice living here because you get to find out about people and what their lives are like. You're not judging them; you can actually get to know what's going on with them. People in Yeoville don't care about what you look like; people are just themselves.

I have a really big group of friends, and within that group we have the whole country. But there's never been any weirdness between us at all. We aren't black, white, Indian, or Coloured; we're just us. We don't actually look at anybody's race; it's just, "Hey, you're my friend, you're a nice person, I like you." **2**

We do regular teenage things together. We gossip a lot like normal girls, and on the weekends we sleep over at each other's houses and phone people and find out what they've been doing. We talk about music; we go to the movies; we swim. **R**

Because we're mixed, we're more powerful; we get to learn from each other. If I were to be in a completely Indian community, it would always be the same things. But when I visit my friends' homes, I see differences in their settings, and all of our families deal with things totally differently. It's always a learning experience. **3**

I've also been to Soweto and Eldorado Park [a Coloured township near Johannesburg] many times, and I've been able to see what other people are actually going through. It's good for me to see that I'm not the only person on earth and that not everybody lives like me. I've been able to grow up with everything I need. If I didn't see those places, I would think that everybody **L**

2. ***Yeoville*** (YOH vil) is a part of the city of Johannesburg where people of different races live in the same neighborhoods.

Vocabulary

cultures (KUL churz) *n.* groups of people who share a history and way of life

Practice the Skills

2 Key Literary Element

Point of View Who is the narrator of this story? How can you tell? Are you beginning to get a feeling for what kind of person the narrator is?

3 Key Reading Skill

Connecting Pillay says she always learns something when she visits her friends' homes because everyone lives differently. What have you learned from visiting a friend's home?

Teach

R Reading Skill

Connecting Ask: What activities does Pillay describe that help you connect to her? *(gossiping, having sleepovers, talking on the phone, talking about music, going to movies, swimming)* **BL**

L Literary Element

Point of View Say: Pillay says she thinks it is good that she visits other communities in Johannesburg, such as Soweto and Eldorado Park, where many people live in extreme poverty. According to Pillay, why is it good to visit these places? *(She believes it's good to know that not everyone lives as well as she does. It keeps her from being small-minded.)* **OL**

Viewing the Photo

Ask: How does this photo suggest a rainbow nation? *(The photo shows people of different racial backgrounds getting along.)* **OL**

Differentiated Instruction

Visual Learners Have students search online for images of Soweto and Eldorado Park and have them share what they find with the class. Encourage students to see the vast differences in standard of living in South Africa. Then, lead students in a discussion about what they've seen. Ask students to discuss what it might be like to visit the poorest villages in South Africa. Would students feel that it was "good for them" as Pillay says? Why or why not? **OL**

Ask students to use their research to develop ideas about why there is such a vast difference in the standard of living in South Africa. **AL**

Objectives

- Make connections from text to self
- Understand how the narrator contributes to understanding the text
- Identify point of view and explain its effect on text
- Use critical thinking skills to analyze text

READING WORKSHOP 2

Teach

L Literary Element

Point of View **Ask:** According to Pillay, why can't South Africans call themselves a rainbow people yet? *(Many in South Africa are still racist and want to live separately from other races, so they aren't a rainbow people.)* **OL** What does she mean when she says most South Africans are still "trapped in apartheid mentally"? *(Being trapped mentally in apartheid means still believing in separate races and racism even though apartheid is not the law.)* **AL**

R Reading Skill

Connecting **Say:** The people in Pillay's world divide themselves by race. What cliques do you see at school? What might be the problem with forming cliques? *(Responses will vary. Students might note that cliques prevent students from getting to know one another.)* **OL** What could you do to avoid forming cliques? (Responses will vary. Students might note that they can welcome people who are different into their group of friends.) **AL**

had normal houses and enough money to do what they wanted like I do. Then I think I'd be quite small-minded.

A lot of our parents call my friends and me the rainbow nation. I think it makes them feel good to see us together; it's kind of like what everybody should be like racial-wise, how people should interact with each other, but don't. When our parents were small, they had apartheid, they didn't have the opportunity to mix, and I'm sure they envy us for having all of the new experiences that they never would have even dreamed of having when they were young. **4**

But as a nation I don't think we can call ourselves the rainbow people yet. Most South Africans are still completely trapped in apartheid mentally. I've had a lot of experiences with racism, like at this restaurant when the people there wouldn't serve us because of our color. Everybody else got up and left when we came in, and then it took half an hour for the waiter to come serve us and then an hour to get our breakfast.

Even though apartheid's not law anymore, it's still alive. People still divide themselves into these **cliques**: black, Coloured, Indian, white. Like when my friends and I go to the mall, we notice that other people give us really weird looks. I think it's because we're so mixed, and others have been raised with this wall blocking them. They're like, Wow, what's wrong with that group? How can they be comfortable with each other?

I think it's good for people to see us, because it's showing them that you can have fun with another race; it's not abnormal. People need to see that aside from their cultural differences and their skin color, we all need the same basics: We all need to breathe, drink water, eat; we're all exactly the same. They should just look beyond what they've been taught, they should try and have an open mind about things. Most South Africans will probably find this very difficult, but it's definitely worth it.

If someone did come up to us and say she wanted to **mix**, **5** we'd say, "All right, come join us!" If she was scared, I'd say, "I know it might be difficult because you haven't done it

Vocabulary

cliques (kleeks *or* kliks) *n.* groups of people who leave others out

Practice the Skills

4 Key Reading Skill

Connecting According to Pillay, her generation and her parents' generation have had different experiences. Can you think of differences between your view of life and your parents'?

5 English Language Coach

Multiple-Meaning Words
Earlier on this page, **mix** is used. What does it mean there?

Additional Support

Reading Fluency

Phrases and Thought Groups To improve fluency, encourage students to read several words at a time rather than reading each word individually. Tell them to use punctuation as a guide to help them learn when to pause as they read. They should pause briefly at a comma and slightly longer after a period or question mark. Have students work with a partner to practice reading phrases rather than single words. Ask students to read a paragraph aloud to a partner several times, letting punctuation and meaning tell them when to pause. **BL** **EL**

before, but all you have to do is think about what kind of people they are and not what they look like. Try closing your eyes and talking to them, and then you'll get **used** to them and eventually you won't think about where they're from. You'll learn to appreciate people for who and what they are, to see past everything."

I think people my age should learn about apartheid because it is our past, it's our parents and our grandparents, it affects us. If we know the history of our country, we'll be able to know what was wrong about what people did, and not to do it again.

But at the same time, I think we should be making a future. We can't just get stuck in one place, always staying on the same subject. My generation was lucky enough to not have been part of the struggle against apartheid, to have been only young when elections happened; we've grown up in other times when race is no longer governed by law, no longer an obligation. That gives us the freedom to **address** anything. We need to learn how to move on, to look at other issues that affect us, to try and do better, more different things. Our generation is more open-minded than our parents', and this makes me **optimistic** about this country. Since it's up to us, I think we can change things. 6 7 ○

Vocabulary

optimistic (op tuh MIS tik) *adj.* taking the view that things will turn out well; hopeful

Practice the Skills

6 **English Language Coach**

Multiple-Meaning Words Use the context around the word **address** to figure out what it means here. EL

7 BIG Question

Based on what Pillay says and thinks about her future, will she work alone to achieve her goals or work with others? What do you think she will do to become whom she wants to be? Write your answer on the "Toward a Rainbow Nation" page of your Foldable. Your response will help you answer the Unit Challenge later. BQ

READING WORKSHOP 2

EL Language Coach

Multiple-Meaning Words in Context **Say:** Look back at the definitions for *address* on page 168. Which one makes more sense in this sentence? *(to discuss or speak about)* EL

BQ 

Ask: What advice do you think Pillay would offer people about becoming who they want to be? *(Students may note that Pillay would encourage people to connect with people from many different cultures and age groups. She would probably urge people to have many different experiences.)* OL

Assess

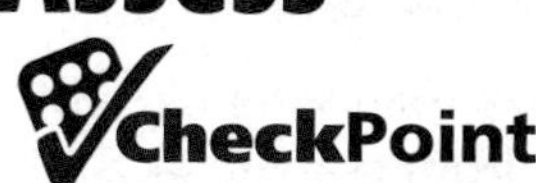

Use the CheckPoint questions provided on Presentation Plus! to check students' mastery of the selection. These questions can be used with interactive response keypads for immediate student feedback.

Differentiated Instruction

Primary Sources Discuss the excerpts from a 2004 *TIME* magazine article about the 10-year anniversary of apartheid's end. What do the quotes suggest about conditions in South Africa today?

"Black South Africans now sit on the country's corporate boards, play on its international sporting teams, edit its most important newspapers, and own some of its best restaurants."

"We must beware [of] the siren song of affluence, huge mansions and big cars, when the bulk of our people still live in squalor." OL

Objectives

- Make connections from text to self
- Understand how the narrator contributes to understanding the text
- Identify point of view and explain its effect on text
- Use context clues: multiple-meaning words

Assess

Resources for page 174

- Selection Quick Check
- Selection and Unit Assessment
- ExamView Assessment Suite
- Interactive Tutor: Self-Assessment

Students can respond to the *After You Read* items in their Learner's Notebook or on a separate sheet of paper.

Answering the

1. Pillay has made friends with people from many different cultures. She has visited towns different from her own.
2. She says she is South African.
3. Yeoville is mixed and people are not judged by their race.

Critical Thinking

4. Responses may include: Pillay and her friends are from many different cultures, so they are like a rainbow.
5. Responses may include: Some people in South Africa might fear people who are different from themselves.
6. The other customers left and it took a long time for Pillay and her friends to be served.
7. Response may include: Many people in Pillay's generation, but not all, are more open-minded because they live in mixed societies.

After You Read

Toward a Rainbow Nation

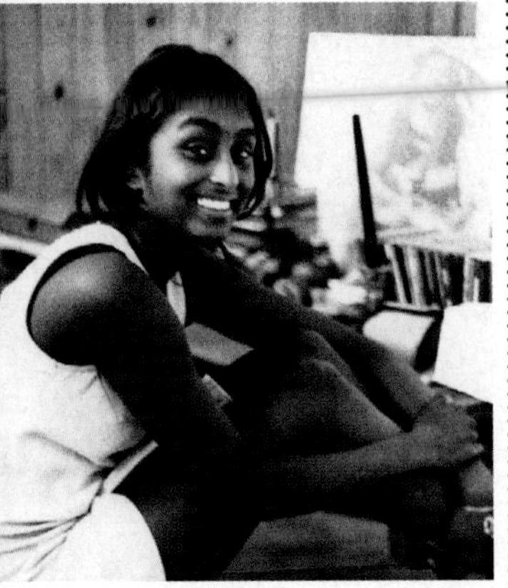

Objectives
(pp. 174–175)
Reading Make connections from text to self
Literature Identify literary elements: point of view
Vocabulary Use context clues: multiple meanings
Writing Use the RAFT system: personal letter
Grammar Identify and use pronouns: indefinite

Answering the

1. What has Pillay done to become who she wants to be in life?
2. **Recall** When Pillay is asked, "What are you?" how does she answer?
   TIP **Right There** You will find the answer in the selection.
3. **Recall** Why does Pillay think that living in Yeoville is "really nice"?
   TIP **Right There** You will find the answer in the selection.

Critical Thinking

4. **Infer** Why do many adults call Pillay and her friends the "rainbow nation"?
   TIP **Think and Search** You'll find clues in the narrative, but you should also think about what "rainbow" might mean here.
5. **Infer** Why do you suppose people in South Africa still divide themselves into cliques even though apartheid isn't the law anymore? Support your answer with details from the selection.
   TIP **Author and Me** Answer using information from the selection and from your own thoughts.
6. **Summarize** What happened when Pillay and her friends tried to get breakfast at a restaurant?
   TIP **Think and Search** Use information from the selection and decide what the important points are.
7. **Evaluate** Do you think Pillay's generation is more open-minded than her parents' generation?
   TIP **Author and Me** Answer using information from the selection and from your own thoughts.

Write About Your Reading

Use the RAFT system to write about "Toward a Rainbow Nation."

Role: Write as if you were a new student at Pillay's school.

Audience: Write to Pillay.

Format: A letter

Topic: Describe yourself—where you are from, what you like to do, and ways your life is different from or similar to hers. Tell her what you think about her ideas to bring people together.

Write About Your Reading

Possible response:

Dear Lavendhri,

I am a new student at your school. I am from Dayton, Ohio, in the United States. Our lives are very similar. I love gossiping with my friends on the phone, talking about music, and going to the movies. I have friends from many different cultures, and I agree with you that it is important to know people who are different. I hope we can be friends!

Pedro

Skills Review

Key Reading Skill: Connecting

8. In your Learner's Notebook, make notes connecting your own ideas and experiences to each of the following items from "Toward a Rainbow Nation":
   - Pillay's group of friends
   - Things that Pillay and her friends do together
   - Pillay's experience in the restaurant
   - Pillay's learning from her friends

Key Literary Element: Point of View

9. What point of view does Pillay use to tell her story? How do you know?
10. How would the selection be different if the narrator were Pillay's mother?

Reviewing Skills: Titles and Subtitles

11. Do you think the title of this narrative is a good expression of Pillay's ideas and feelings? Why or why not?

Vocabulary Check

Choose the best word from the list to complete each sentence below. Rewrite each sentence, with the correct word in place, in your Learner's Notebook.

subjected **cultures**
cliques **optimistic**

12. May-May doesn't want to join any ___ because they shut people out.
13. Eating at restaurants that serve foods from other countries is a good way to learn about other ___.
14. It was surprising to see Jamie so sad today, since she's usually so ___.
15. When my neighbor had a party, everyone in my building was ___ to the loud music.
16. **English Language Coach** What could your school do to **address** a problem with cliques?

Grammar Link: Indefinite Pronouns

An indefinite pronoun is a pronoun that does not refer to a particular person, place, or thing.

Examples of Indefinite Pronouns

Has **anyone** seen my glasses?
Is **everybody** going?
There's **nobody** here.
Nothing is better than that!
Is **anything** wrong?
Perhaps **someone** will fix it.
Something made a noise.
Most walked to the park, but **some** drove.
Others took the bus.
Neither had read the assignment.

Grammar Practice

Rewrite each sentence below and fill in the blank with an indefinite pronoun.

17. Can ___ help me get this done?
18. I hope ___ knows what I'm trying to do.
19. There is ___ strange going on.
20. I can't do ___ more tonight!

Writing Application Look back at the RAFT assignment you wrote. List any indefinite pronouns you used.

Web Activities For eFlashcards, Selection Quick Checks, and other Web activities, go to www.glencoe.com.

Skills Review

Key Reading Skill: Connecting

8. Possible responses:

Pillay's group of friends: I have two friends from different countries. I'd love to know more people from different cultures.

Things that Pillay and her friends do together: I do all the things Pillay and her friends do with my friends.

Pillay's experience in the restaurant: What a terrible thing to happen! I would be very upset.

Key Literary Element: Point of View

9. first-person: She uses "I."
10. Pillay's mother might not have a positive attitude.

Reviewing Skills: Titles and Subtitles

11. Possible response: I think this title expresses Pillay's idea of a nation with people of many colors living together peacefully.

Vocabulary Check

12. cliques
13. cultures
14. optimistic
15. subjected
16. Responses will vary.

Grammar Link: Indefinite Pronouns

Grammar Practice

Possible responses follow:

17. someone
18. no one
19. something
20. anything

Close

Ask students to discuss what they've learned from Pillay to answer the Big Question.

Inferring

Objectives covered in this workshop:
- Make inferences
- Make connections from self to text
- Set purposes for reading

Teaching Students to Make Inferences

Why Is It Important?

- Inferences depend on seeing connections that are not articulated.
- Most writers do not come out and say everything a character thinks; readers need to make inferences to fully comprehend what is being communicated.
- Students who make inferences successfully understand characters better and are better able to identify themes.

How to Help Students Get It

- Tell students to always pay attention to everything a writer tells them through a character's actions as well as words
- Help students notice descriptions, dialogue, events and relationships.
- Encourage students to ask themselves: "Why does the author tell me this? What does this mean about this character or situation?"
- To build their confidence in making inferences while reading remind students that they already make many inferences in everyday life (this workshop provides several examples of how we make inferences).

Reading to Answer the Big Question

New Directions

Starting over after an ended marriage, with few prospects and almost no resources, Mrs. Annie Johnson decides to forge a new path for herself. She starts her own lunch cart business; tiny at first, it grows eventually into a successful general store. Her hard work, innovation, and resolution help her create a new life very different from the one she had before.

The War of the Wall

When a stranger from New York shows up and starts painting all over "their" wall, the kids of Taliaferro Street are upset. That wall is crucial to the social life of the street, and serves as a makeshift memorial to Jimmy Lyons, who died in the Vietnam War. The narrator and a friend make plans to wreck the painter lady's mural, but stop when they see the finished work. The out of town stranger has created a tribute to Civil Rights leaders, and included the people of Taliaferro Street in the artwork, including her cousin Jimmy.

Workshop Resources

Pacing (Days) Standard	Block	Lesson	Student Materials	Teacher Resources
1		Key Skill Lesson: Inferring	Key Reading Skills Practice English Language Coach	Bellringer Options Transparencies Read Aloud, Think Aloud Transparencies Presentation Plus!
2		"New Directions"	Literary Analysis Transparencies Glencoe Online Selection Vocabulary Development Academic Vocabulary Development English Language Coach Active Reading Graphic Organizer Literary Analysis StudentWorks Plus Online Student Edition Literature Classics Selection and Unit Assessments	Literary and Text Analysis Transparencies Puzzlemaker Skill Level Up! BookLink 3 Assessment by Learning Objective (Diagnostic and Formative) Interactive Tutor Self-Assessment TeacherWorks Plus
2		"The War of the Wall"	Glencoe Online Selection Vocabulary Development Academic Vocabulary Development English Language Coach Active Reading Graphic Organizer Literary Analysis StudentWorks Plus Online Student Edition Literature Classics Selection and Unit Assessments	Literary and Text Analysis Transparencies Puzzlemaker Skill Level Up! BookLink 3 Assessment by Learning Objective (Diagnostic and Formative) Interactive Tutor Self-Assessment TeacherWorks Plus

Keys for Unit Resource

- Blackline Master
- Workbook
- Supplemental Text
- CD-ROM
- DVD
- Transparency
- Web-based
- Fast Files

Level Appropriate Code

AS = Activities for all students
AL = Activities for students working above grade level
OL = Activities for students working at grade level
BL = Activities for students working below grade level
EL = Activities for English language learners

Focus

BELLRINGER Options

- Selection Focus Transparency
- Daily Language Practice Transparency

Focus Activity Say: You have a reason for just about everything you do, even though you might not think about it. Think of two things you did today and tell why you did them.

Teach

R Reading Skill

Making Inferences Say: You use inferring often. For instance, you see a person you don't know. You are at a hospital. The person is wearing a white lab coat. She has a stethoscope around her neck and is looking at a chart. What can you infer about this person? *(She is probably a doctor.)* OL

Skills Focus

You will practice using the following skills when you read from these selections:

- "New Directions," p. 180
- "The War of the Wall," p. 188

Reading

- Making inferences

Literature

- Identifying the setting in what you read
- Understanding how the setting contributes to a narrative

Vocabulary

- Understanding and using word references
- Academic Vocabulary: *motives*

Writing/Grammar

- Identifying and using pronouns

Skill Lesson

Making Inferences

Learn It!

What Is It? *Inferring* is a form of detective work. It's using your knowledge and "clues" to make a good guess. You infer when you figure out what new neighbors are like from what they say, how they dress, and how they act. Sometimes you have to use clues to guess why characters in a story behave as they do. You have to make inferences because authors don't always include every detail or idea that R you need to understand what you read. They may leave something out for several reasons:

- They assume that "everybody knows it."
- They want you to think.
- They think that the story will be more interesting if readers can have different ideas.

You make inferences to fill in the gaps that an author leaves.

McPherson
© 1993 John McPherson/Dist. by Universal Press Syndicate
10-23

"I *told* you it was a stupid idea to buy contact lenses at a rummage sale!"

Analyzing Cartoons
The cartoon doesn't *tell* why the man drove into the pond, but you can *infer* why. How well can the driver see with his new contacts?

Objectives (pp. 176–177)
Reading Make inferences
Literature Use inference to understand a character's motivation

Additional Support

Differentiated Instruction

Using Clues Give students the following clues, and have them make an inference based on the clues.

1. You have a new lab puppy. You leave your shoes by your bed while you're sleeping. You awake to find a big hole in the toe of your shoe. *WHAT HAPPENED? (The puppy ate the shoe.)*
2. Your neighbor leaves for work in the morning wearing overalls and work shoes. She comes home in the evening covered in mud and carrying a toolbox. *WHAT DOES SHE DO FOR A LIVING? (She's a construction worker.)* BL

Why Is It Important? In life, we never know everything we'd like to know about people and situations. So we make inferences about them. In literature, no author will tell you *everything* you'd like to know. You have to make inferences based on what the author *does* say—and on your own experiences.

Study Central Visit www.glencoe.com and click on Study Central to review making inferences.

How Do I Do It? As you read about people or characters, ask yourself why they do what they do. Sometimes, you'll have to use the evidence in the text to make your best guess. Here's how one student used inferring while reading a biographical narrative.

When Ed Kelleher read a news story about a "retirement home" for guide dogs, he wondered whether there was one in his city. Did guide dogs get a good home after their years of serving the blind? Ed became the founder of Adopt a Guide Dog, a program that finds homes for "retired" guide dogs.

Wait a minute. How did Ed go from wondering about the guide dogs to starting Adopt a Guide Dog? He must have looked into what happens to old dogs when they stop working as guides, and that must have upset him. That's why he started the program.

Practice It!

The reasons for what people do—their **motives**—are important in this workshop. You will understand a character's motives better if you think about what the author tells you and what might be missing. To get started, ask yourself why a person would:

- start a new business instead of working for an existing company
- object to someone's painting a wall

In your Learner's Notebook, write a paragraph about each motive. **R**

Use It!

As you read "New Directions" and "The War of the Wall," refer to the notes you made about motives. As you make new inferences about the reasons for what people do in these selections, write them down.

Academic Vocabulary

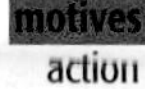

motives (MOH tivz) *n.* needs or desires that cause a person to take action

Reading in the Real World

Career Ask students to talk to an older family member or friend to find out about an important decision he or she had to make about his or her career, one that students can discuss in class. Students can learn the person's motives for making the decision by asking, "Why did you make that choice?" Students might ask the person whether he or she would make the same decision today. Encourage students to share their findings in a class discussion about motives. Help students see that people often have clear reasons for the choices they make and that those reasons might change over time. **OL**

Teach

Literature Online

Study Central Have students access the Web site to review making inferences and to complete a related activity.

R Reading Skill

Review Reviewing Say: When might you make inferences about a character in a story? Write your answer in your Learner's Notebook and then review pages 176-177 to see if you've answered correctly. *(Responses may include: I might make inferences about a character in a story to learn his or her motive for doing something.)* **OL**

Resources for page 177

Use Reading Skills Transparency in *Read Aloud, Think Aloud,* Unit 2, to help students practice making inferences.

V Vocabulary

Academic Vocabulary

Say: Read the definition of the word *motives* at the bottom of page 177. What might be your motive for visiting the dentist? for studying for a test? *(to have clean and healthy teeth and gums; to get a good grade)* **OL**

Objectives

- Make inferences
- Use inference to understand a character's motivation

Before You Read | New Directions

More About the Author

Maya Angelou was born Marguerite Johnson in 1928. She spent most of her childhood in Stamps, Arkansas, where she was raised by her grandmother, a determined woman who had a vision and then worked hard to reach her goal. "New Directions" is based on the life of Angelou's grandmother. Most of Angelou's famous works are autobiographical.

Maya Angelou

Meet the Author

Author, poet, playwright, director, editor, educator,– each of those words describes Maya Angelou. She read her own poems at President Clinton's 1993 inauguration and at the fiftieth anniversary of the United Nations. She is the author of many books, including *I Know Why the Caged Bird Sings*. For more about Maya Angelou, see page R1 of the Author Files.

Literature Online

Author Search For more about Maya Angelou, go to www.glencoe.com.

Objectives (pp. 178–183)
Reading Make inferences
Literature Identify literary elements: setting
Vocabulary Use word references: dictionary

Vocabulary Preview

V

conceded (kun SEE dud) *v.* accepted as true; form of the verb *concede* **(p. 180)** *Annie Johnson conceded that she had little chance of being hired at the cotton gin or lumber mill.*

meticulously (muh TIK yuh lus lee) *adv.* carefully and correctly **(p. 181)** *Annie prepared meticulously before she ever made a single sale.*

assess (uh SES) *v.* to determine the meaning or importance of; analyze **(p. 183)** *Annie assessed her situation before making plans.*

ominous (AW muh nus) *adj.* threatening harm or evil **(p. 183)** *Annie didn't see an ominous future. She saw a chance to control her own life.*

Write to Learn Copy the vocabulary words into your Learner's Notebook. Put a check mark by each word that you have used in your writing or conversation. Write a new sentence using the word. If you have never used the word, copy the definition.

English Language Coach

Using Word References Here are dictionary entries for two of the words that you will read in "New Directions." As you read, watch for these words. Use context clues to choose the correct meanings.

loom \lüm\ *n* a frame or machine for weaving threads or yarns to make cloth ~ *v* to appear in a way that seems threatening or dangerous

balmy \ˈbäm-ē, ˈbäl-mē\ *adj* **balm•i•er; -est 1** mild; gentle; soothing **2** crazy; foolish

Partner Talk With a partner, read these sentences. Decide which definition of the underlined word makes sense in each sentence.

1. On our field trip, we saw how a rug is woven on a **loom.**
2. When I said I wanted to visit Iceland, friends called me **balmy.**
3. Frightening shadows **loomed** at the end of the alley.
4. It was a perfect day, with **balmy** weather and no chores.
5. Our new puppy is very sweet, but he's a little **balmy** too!
6. I have a hand **loom** for weaving pot holders.

V Vocabulary

Flashcards Make flashcards with the 4 vocabulary words; write the word on one side of the card and its meaning on the other. Tape the flashcards to the board. Throughout the lesson, have students pick a flashcard and tell the meaning of the chosen word. BL EL

Additional Support

Author Search To expand students' appreciation of Maya Angelou, have them access the Web site for additional information and resources.

Differentiated Instruction

Building Background You might want to share with the class Chapter 1 of Angelou's autobiography *I Know Why the Caged Bird Sings,* which describes the trip Angelou and her brother Bailey make to Stamps to live with their grandmother, Annie, and tells about the store Annie opens in "New Directions." OL Have students discuss what they learn about Angelou and her grandmother and how that information helps them understand "New Directions." (Be aware that later parts of the book contain sensitive material that may not be appropriate for young readers. Recommend it at your discretion.) AL

Skills Preview

Key Reading Skill: Making Inferences

Have you ever wondered why a person did something that seemed odd to you? When you watch TV, do you sometimes see a character do something and then ask yourself "Why on earth did he do that?"

The reasons for what a character does—his or her motives—are sometimes clear. At other times, they're not. When you find yourself asking "Why?" as you read, it's time to do some detective work. Use evidence in the text to make a good guess about the motive for an action.

Write to Learn In your Learner's Notebook, quickwrite about a time when you made a change in your life. Be sure to include your motives for making the change. Thinking about your motives will help you connect with Annie Johnson in "New Directions."

Key Literary Element: Setting

Setting is the time when the action occurs and the place where it occurs. However, it's sometimes more complicated than that.

"New Directions" is a brief autobiographical narrative that has one main setting—Arkansas in the 1900s. The action, however, covers several years in four important places:

- the cotton gin (a factory where cotton is processed)
- the saw mill (where trees are cut into lumber)
- the dirt road that Annie Johnson travels to get to the cotton gin and lumber mill
- the spot where Annie sets up a food stall

As you read, ask yourself this about each setting:

Why is this setting important in Annie's effort to be who she wants to be?

Literature Online

Interactive Literary Elements Handbook
To review or learn more about the literary elements, go to www.glencoe.com.

Get Ready to Read

Connect to the Reading

Think about a time when you decided to do something different from what you usually do. What made you go in a new direction?

Partner Talk With a partner, talk about what happened when you each decided to go in a new direction. Do you both agree that it was a good experience? Would you both make a choice to go in a new direction again? Why or why not?

Build Background

This biographical narrative is based on the life of Maya Angelou's grandmother, Annie Johnson.

- This story is set in Stamps, Arkansas, a coal-mining town, in the early 1900s.
- The population of Stamps was about half white and half African American at this time, and African Americans were not thought of as equal to whites.

Set Purposes for Reading

BIG Question Read "New Directions" to learn how Annie Johnson found the way to become who she wanted to be.

Set Your Own Purpose What would you like to learn about Annie Johnson to help you become who you want to be? Write your own purpose on the "New Directions" page of your Foldable.

Keep Moving

Use these skills as you read the following selection.

READING WORKSHOP 3

Teach

R Reading Skill

Making Inferences Say: When you make inferences about a character's motive, you use the text and your own experience. Think of a story you have just read or seen on TV. Tell one thing a character did and give a possible motive. Tell whether you used clues from the story, from your experience, or from both. *(Responses will vary.)* OL

L Literary Element

Setting Say: If you were going to write a story about our class, what would you share to describe the setting? *(Responses will vary.)* AS

CheckPoint

Use the CheckPoint questions provided on Presentation Plus! to build background. These questions can be used with interactive response keypads for immediate student feedback.

Literature Online

Interactive Literary Elements Handbook Have students access the Web site to improve their understanding of setting.

English Language Coach

Reading a Dictionary Entry Explain to students that a dictionary entry includes the word, a respelling that shows how to pronounce the word, the part of speech, and the definition. Have students look up *loom* and *balmy* and use their dictionaries' pronunciation key to say the words correctly. You may point out the differences in the dictionary respelling and the respelling in the student book on page 178. Then point out that *loom* is both a noun and a verb and *balmy* is an adjective. End by showing how each word has two meanings. BL EL

Objectives
- Make inferences
- Identify literary elements: setting
- Use word references: dictionary

Teach

L Literary Element

Setting **Ask:** What details about the setting does Angelou tell in the first paragraph? *(It is 1903 in Arkansas.)* **AS**

R Reading Skill

Inferring **Say:** The minister in Enid has a friendly, unmarried daughter. What role might this fact have played in Mr. Johnson's reason for leaving? *(He might want to marry her.)* **OL**

Readability Scores
Dale-Chall: 6.4
DRP: 61
Lexile: 1360

READING WORKSHOP 3

New Directions

by Maya Angelou

In 1903 the late Mrs. Annie Johnson of Arkansas found herself with two toddling sons, very little money, a slight ability to read and add simple numbers. To this picture add a disastrous marriage and the burdensome fact that Mrs. Johnson was a Negro. **L**

When she told her husband, Mr. William Johnson, of her dissatisfaction with their marriage, he **conceded** that he too found it to be less than he expected, and had been secretly hoping to leave and study religion. He added that he thought God was calling him not only to preach but to do so in Enid, Oklahoma. He did not tell her that he knew a minister in Enid with whom he could study and who had a friendly, unmarried daughter. They parted amicably,[1] Annie keeping the one-room house and William taking most of the cash to carry himself to Oklahoma. **1**

1. When Annie and William ***parted amicably,*** they went their separate ways without feelings of anger or unfriendliness.

Vocabulary

conceded (kun SEE dud) *v.* accepted as true

Practice the Skills

1 Key Reading Skill

R **Inferring** What reason did William Johnson say he had for ending their marriage? What did he not say? What would you say was his real motive?

Additional Support

Literature Focus Lesson

Problem and Solution In the story, Annie is faced with the problem of supporting her children while caring for them herself. To find a solution, she has to take several intermediate steps. Have students trace her actions and results on a chart like the one below. **OL**

Action	Result

READING WORKSHOP 3

Annie, over six feet tall, big-boned, decided that she would not go to work as a domestic[2] and leave her "precious babes" to anyone else's care. There was no possibility of being hired at the town's cotton gin or lumber mill, but maybe there was a way to make the two factories work for her. In her words, "I looked up the road I was going and back the way I come, and since I wasn't satisfied, I decided to step off the road and cut me a new path." She told herself that she wasn't a fancy cook but that she could "mix groceries well enough to scare hungry away and from starving a man."

She made her plans **meticulously** and in secret. One early evening to see if she was ready, she placed stones in two five-gallon pails and carried them three miles to the cotton gin. She rested a little, and then, discarding some rocks, she walked in the darkness to the saw mill five miles farther along the dirt road. On her way back to her little house and her babies, she dumped the remaining rocks along the path. **2**

That same night she worked into the early hours boiling chicken and frying ham. She made dough and filled the rolled-out pastry with meat. At last she went to sleep. **3**

The Crosset sawmill in Arkansas in the early twentieth century

2. A *domestic* is a household servant.

Vocabulary

meticulously (muh TIK yuh lus lee) *adv.* carefully and correctly

Practice the Skills

2 Key Literary Element

Setting Think about Annie's walk as she carried stones in pails. Where did she go? When? Why?

3 Key Reading Skill

Inferring Think about Annie's reason for making her plans in secret. What motive do you think she had?

Teach

L Literary Element

Setting Ask: How far does Annie have to walk to get all the way to the saw mill from her house? *(eight miles)* **OL** What does this suggest about her character? *(She is hardworking and determined.)* **AL**

R Reading Skill

Inferring Say: Think about business people today. Why do they keep their new products a secret before they promote them to the public? How might their motives be similar to Annie's? *(They don't want the competition to know about their product before it's launched; Annie probably doesn't want anyone else to learn what she's doing and do the same thing.)* **AL**

Differentiated Instruction

Summarizing After students have read the story, they will be asked to write a summary of it. Tell students that Annie's story is told in chronological, or time order. Have students pick out the most important events from the story as they read and record them in a flow chart like the one below. Students can refer to their flow charts later to help them write their summaries. **BL**

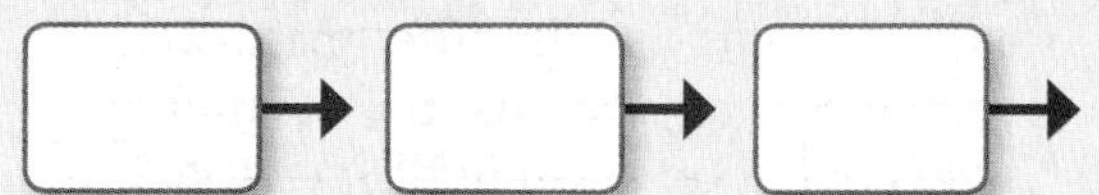

Objectives
- Make inferences from information in a text
- Use inference to understand a character's motivation
- Identify the setting in a text

READING WORKSHOP 3

Teach

EL Language Coach

Using Word References
Say: Use your dictionaries to answer these questions. What part of speech is *ladle*? *(noun)* How do you pronounce it? Encourage students to answer the same questions about the word *unpalatable* on the next page. **EL** **BL**

R Reading Skill

Inferring **Say:** What can you infer about Annie's character from what you've read about her thus far? *(She is inventive and hardworking. She is clever—she knows that the smell of home-cooked food will tempt the workers.)* **OL**

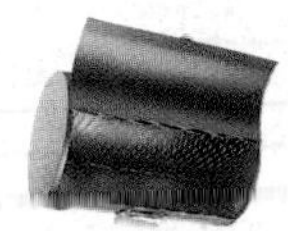

Visual Vocabulary
A ***brazier*** is a metal container that holds burning coals. It is used for cooking food.

The next morning she left her house carrying the meat pies, lard, an iron **brazier,** and coals for a fire. Just before lunch she appeared in an empty lot behind the cotton gin. As the dinner noon bell rang, she dropped the savors into boiling fat and the aroma rose and floated over to the workers who spilled out of the gin, covered with white lint, looking like specters.[3] **4**

Most workers had brought their lunches of pinto beans and biscuits or crackers, onions and cans of sardines, but they were tempted by the hot meat pies which Annie **ladled** out of the fat. She wrapped them in newspapers, which soaked up the grease, and offered them for sale at a nickel each. Although business was slow, those first days Annie was determined. She balanced her appearances between the two hours of activity. **5**

So, on Monday if she offered hot fresh pies at the cotton gin and sold the remaining cooled-down pies at the lumber mill for three cents, then on Tuesday she went first to the lumber mill presenting fresh, just-cooked pies as the lumbermen covered in sawdust emerged from the mill. **6**

3. Another name for a ghost is a ***specter.***

Practice the Skills

4 Key Literary Element

Setting Remember where and when Annie set up her brazier on the first day she sold meat pies. Why were the time and place important to the success of her new business?

5 English Language Coach

EL **Using Word References** Look up the word **ladle** in a dictionary. Then describe how Annie took the meat pies from the hot fat.

6 Key Reading Skill

R **Inferring** Think about Annie's reason for selling hot pies at the cotton gin and cold ones at the saw mill one day, then doing the opposite the next day. Why did she do that?

Cotton pickers in Phillips County, Arkansas, in September 1938

Additional Support

Differentiated Instruction

Creating Cookbooks Many southern U.S. cities are known for their good food and unique cooking style. Have students find a cookbook or other book describing southern-style cooking. Encourage each student to contribute one or two recipes for your classes' own southern-style cookbook. Include dishes Annie could have served at her store, as well as fancy dishes for special occasions. Find pictures online or have talented artists in the class illustrate the cookbook. Encourage interested students to prepare a dish for the class to try. **OL**
Have students write and present a how-to speech based on how they prepared their dish. **AL**

For the next few years, on balmy spring days, blistering summer noons, and cold, wet, and wintry middays, Annie never disappointed her customers, who could count on seeing the tall, brown-skin woman bent over her brazier, carefully turning the meat pies. When she felt certain that the workers had become dependent on her, she built a stall between the two hives of industry and let the men run to her for their lunchtime provisions.

She had indeed stepped from the road which seemed to have been chosen for her and cut herself a brand-new path. In years that stall became a store where customers could buy cheese, meal, syrup, cookies, candy, writing tablets, pickles, canned goods, fresh fruit, soft drinks, coal, oil, and leather soles for worn-out shoes. 7

C1 Each of us has the right and the responsibility to **assess** the roads which lie ahead, and those over which we have traveled, and if the future road looms **ominous** or unpromising, and the roads back uninviting, then we need to gather our resolve and, carrying only the necessary baggage, step off that road into another direction. If the new choice is also **unpalatable**, without embarrassment, we must be ready to change that as well. 8 9 ❍ C2

Practice the Skills

7 Key Literary Element

Setting Think about the time and place of the story. Do they make Annie Johnson's achievement surprising? What kind of person would she have to be to do what she did in that setting?

8 English Language Coach

Using Word References Look up the word *palatable* in a dictionary. Since the prefix *un-* means "not," what would an **unpalatable** choice be?

9 BIG Question

What qualities did Annie Johnson have that helped her become the person she wanted to be? Write your answers on the "New Directions" page of your Foldable.

Vocabulary

assess (uh SES) *v.* to determine the meaning or importance of; analyze

ominous (AW muh nus) *adj.* threatening harm or evil

Teach

C1 Critical Thinking

Evaluation Say: Explain to students that roads are often used as a symbol, or representation, of life. Ask students why roads might make a good symbol for life. *(We have to choose which roads to take, just as we have to make many choices in life. Some roads are bumpy and long, just like some parts of life.)* AL

C2 Critical Thinking

Comprehension Ask: Do you agree that everyone has the right and responsibility to choose his or her direction in life? Why or why not? *(Responses will vary.)* AS

Assess

Use the CheckPoint questions provided on the Presentation Plus! to check students' mastery of the selection. These questions can be used with interactive response keypads for immediate student feedback.

English Language Coach

Vocabulary Practice Help students improve their vocabulary by creating a character sketch, or description, of Annie. Give students the following words and have them work in groups to choose the ones that apply to Annie (students may use a dictionary if needed). Then, have students take turns describing Annie aloud using the words they have chosen. Encourage students to think of other words to describe Annie. EL BL

tall	*careful*	*tiny*	*successful*	*determined*	*silly*
clever	*strong*	*shy*	*hardworking*	*impatient*	*lazy*

Objectives
- Make connections from text to self
- Make inferences from information in a text
- Use inference to understand a character's motivation
- Identify the setting in a text
- Think critically about a selection
- Read a dictionary entry

Assess

Resources for page 184

- Selection Quick Check
- Selection and Unit Assessment
- ExamView Assessment Suite
- Interactive Tutor: Self-Assessment

Students can respond to the Students can respond to the *After You Read* items in their Learner's Notebook or on a separate sheet of paper.

Answering the

1. Responses may include: she started her own business; she used one of her skills.
2. She separated from her husband.
3. the house and the children
4. most of the money

Critical Thinking

Answers will vary; students should mention the following:

5. She felt she wouldn't be hired because only men were hired at that time.
6. Annie's motive was to see how long it would take to make the journey while carrying a heavy load.
7. She sold fresh food to one mill and leftovers to the other mill on one day and then did the opposite the next day.
8. Responses will vary.

After You Read | New Directions

Answering the BIG Question

1. Identify at least one thing Annie does that you could do to become who you want to be.
2. **Recall** What was the first thing Annie did to become who she wanted to be?
3. **Recall** What did Annie keep when her marriage broke up?
4. **Recall** What did William take with him to Oklahoma?

   TIP **Right There** You will find the answers to questions 2-4 in the narrative.

Critical Thinking

5. **Infer** Why did Annie feel that there was no possibility of being hired at the cotton gin or the lumber mill?

   TIP **Think and Search** You will find clues in the story, but you must also use the information in your head.
6. **Infer** What was Annie's motive for carrying stones to the cotton gin and saw mill?
7. **Summarize** How did Annie "make the two factories work for her"?

   TIP **Think and Search** You must use information in the story and decide what the important points are.
8. **Evaluate** Do you agree that "if the future road looms ominous" a person should "step off that road into another direction"? Why or why not?

   TIP **Author and Me** Answer from information in the story and from your own experiences.

Objectives (pp. 184–185)
Reading Make inferences
Literature Identify literary elements: setting
Vocabulary Use context clues: multiple meanings
Grammar Identify and use pronouns: interrogative, demonstrative, relative

Talk About Your Reading

Literature Groups In your group, discuss the personal qualities Annie Johnson had that helped her take charge of her life and run a successful business. Then, with your group, brainstorm five important qualities necessary for achieving personal success. Support your ideas with details from the selection.

Write to Learn Write your group's list on a separate sheet of paper. Next to each quality, write one sentence telling why it is an important quality for success.

Talk About Your Reading

Possible responses:

Courage—Annie had to have courage to end her marriage and take care of her children on her own.
Wisdom—Annie was wise because she thought of a way to build her business.

Skills Review

Key Reading Skill: Inferring

9. Complete each sentence to show your inferences about Annie's reasons for what she did.
   - Annie made her plans to sell meat pies in secret because ___.
   - Annie didn't build a stall to sell pies right away because ___.

Key Literary Element: Setting

10. Several specific places are important in Annie's story. Name three of them.
11. A few years pass between the beginning of "New Directions" and the end. How did the locations of Annie's business change in that time?

Reviewing Elements: Titles and Subtitles

12. What new direction did Annie Johnson choose? Support your answer with details from the story.

Vocabulary Check

Choose the best word from the list to complete each sentence below. Rewrite each sentence, with the correct word in place.

concede assess ominous

13. The bad guy in a horror movie is usually an ___ figure.
14. It was hard for Mia to ___ that she had made a mistake.
15. Cindy decided to ___ the situation carefully before taking any action.
16. **Academic Vocabulary** What was Annie's *motive* for deciding to "step off the road and cut me a new path?"
17. **English Language Coach** What creatures might suddenly **loom** in front of explorers in a scary movie?

Grammar Link: More Pronouns

You've learned about personal pronouns (such as *he, they,* and *it*) and possessive pronouns (such as *hers, their,* and *mine*) There are other kinds.

- Pronouns used to ask questions are called **interrogative** pronouns.

Who asked the question, and **what** was it?
This is my hat; **whose** is that?

- Pronouns that point out something are called **demonstrative** pronouns.

This is an ugly hat; **that** is the kind I like.
Those are my shoes; **these** are yours.

- Pronouns used to link one part of a sentence to another are called **relative** pronouns.

I like people **who** are funny!
The shoes, **which** are red, are expensive.

- Whether a pronoun is interrogative or demonstrative or relative depends on how it is used. *Who*, for example, can be either interrogative or relative.

Grammar Practice

Rewrite each sentence. Find and circle the five pronouns in each sentence. (They may be *any* kind.)

18. We asked her who told them that.
19. Do you, or anyone else, know if that is my book or hers?
20. Which did they say was theirs, and why would someone choose it?

Web Activities For eFlashcards, Selection Quick Checks, and other Web activities, go to www.glencoe.com.

Skills Review

Key Reading Skill: Inferring

9. she doesn't want anyone to copy her idea/she wasn't sure the factory workers would come to her

Key Literary Element: Setting

10. Possible answers: the cotton gin, the saw mill, the dirt road, the store
11. Annie begins by selling right outside the factories. Once she has a loyal customer base, she moves to a stall in between the two factories.

Reviewing Elements: Titles and Subtitles

12. Annie chooses to work for herself. She sells hot food to factory workers.

Vocabulary Check

13. ominous
14. concede
15. assess
16. Her motive was to support her children financially and raise them herself.
17. Possible response: A green monster might loom.

Close

Ask students to summarize what they learned from Annie's story to help answer the Big Question.

Grammar Link: More Pronouns

Grammar Practice

18. (We) asked (her) (who) told (them) (that.)
19. Do (you) or (anyone) else, know if (that) is my book or (hers)?
20. (Which) did (they) say was (theirs), and why would (someone) choose (it)?

Before You Read

The War of the Wall

More About the Author

Toni Cade Bambara grew up during the civil rights movement and the anti-war movement; her work reflects the voice of the emerging feminist and womanist during this time. In 1970 she edited and published her first anthology, *The Black Woman,* because she grew impatient with the lack of published works written by and for African American women. She says her work has "a tremendous capacity for laughter, but also a tremendous capacity for rage." Bambara died from colon cancer in 1995.

V Vocabulary

Sentences Challenge students to use both vocabulary words in one sentence. Have them share their sentence with a partner. AS

Meet the Author

Toni Cade Bambara was born in New York City in 1939. She lived, studied, and wrote in New York, France, and Italy. In addition to writing, she was a civil rights activist who was especially interested in improving living conditions in America's cities. Her books include *Gorilla, My Love*, a short-story collection, and *The Salt Eaters*, a novel. She died in 1995. For more about Toni Cade Bambara, see page R1 of the Author Files.

Literature Online

Author Search For more about Toni Cade Bambara, go to www.glencoe.com.

Objectives (pp. 186–195)
Reading Make inferences
Literature Identify literary elements: setting
Vocabulary Use word references: dictionary

Vocabulary Preview

aromas (uh ROH muhz) *n.* pleasing smells or scents **(p. 189)** *Mouth-watering aromas drifted from Mama's restaurant.*

concentration (kawn sen TRAY shun) *n.* the ability to focus one's attention **(p. 190)** *The painter lady's concentration was so strong that she never took her eyes off of the wall.*

Write to Learn Copy the vocabulary words into your Learner's Notebook. Next to the word *aromas*, list three things that have a good aroma. Next to the word *concentration*, list three tasks that require concentration.

English Language Coach

Using Word References Here are dictionary entries for two of the words that you will read in "The War of the Wall." As you read, watch for these words. Use context clues to choose the correct meanings from the definitions shown here.

work \wərk\ *n.* **studied, studying 1** an activity in which one uses strength or mental effort **2** the labor, task, or duty one performs to make a living **3** something produced by the use of creative talent

fuss \fus\ *v.* **1** to pay too much attention to small or unimportant things **2** to whine and complain

Partner Talk With a partner, read these sentences. Talk about which definition of the underlined word makes sense in each sentence.

1. Most kids think cleaning their rooms is hard **work**.
2. Mother says Ron and I **fuss** so much she can't hear herself think.
3. If we miss the bus, Joann will **fuss** at us for an hour.
4. The **work** of this composer is worth listening to!
5. Don't **fuss** with your hair anymore; it looks fine.
6. People who can't find **work** may have serious money problems.
7. "No one respects my **work**," complained the author.
8. Mario started to **fuss** so much with the little details in his painting that he ruined it.

Additional Support

Literature Online

Author Search To expand students' appreciation of Toni Cade Bambara, have them access the Web site for additional information and resources.

English Language Coach

Multiple-Meaning Words Encourage students to replace the multiple-meaning word with each of the possible definitions listed in the dictionary entries. Model the first Partner Talk sentence by writing on the board:

1. Most kids think cleaning their rooms is hard ____.

Reread the sentence several times, each time filling in the blank with one of the meanings for *work* listed on page 186. Explain that in this instance, *work* means "an activity in which one uses strength or mental effort."

If necessary, repeat the steps for sentences 2–8. BL EL

Skills Preview

Key Reading Skill: Making Inferences

Imagine that a stranger comes into your neighborhood. You've never seen her before. Neither have your friends and neighbors. She sets up some equipment in a lot next to a barbershop. She doesn't speak to anyone or answer questions. Then she begins to paint on the blank wall of a building. You wonder, what is she up to?

You are about to meet this stranger in "The War of the Wall." As you read, look for evidence that will help you decide what she is doing and why. Look for clues to her goal and to her motives. You will have to make inferences to decide. You will not find a full explanation in the story.

Key Literary Element: Setting

Some stories could take place anywhere at almost any time. In other stories, such as "The War of the Wall," the setting is extremely important, maybe even more important than the characters.

As you read, use these questions to help you notice and understand the effect of the setting on the story:

- Is this a rich neighborhood? Can you tell if it's in a city or a suburb or a small town?
- What kinds of stores and other places are in the neighborhood?
- How well do the people in the neighborhood know each other?
- As a part of the neighborhood, how important is the wall?
- How would this story be different if it took place somewhere else or in another time?

L

Interactive Literary Elements Handbook To review or learn more about the literary elements, go to www.glencoe.com.

Get Ready to Read

Connect to the Reading

How do you feel about your neighborhood? Consider

- How well you know your neighbors
- Which parts of your neighborhood have a special meaning for you
- Whether you feel as comfortable in other neighborhoods as you do in your own

R

Partner Talk With a partner, describe the neighborhoods where you live. What makes you feel that your neighborhood is "yours"?

Build Background

In this story, a woman puzzles the people of a neighborhood by painting a picture on the blank wall of a building.

- Large paintings on walls or ceilings are called murals (MYUR ulz).
- Painting murals is a very old tradition that goes back to the earliest humans.
- Many public murals tell stories or show familiar scenes, activities, and characters from the surrounding community.

Set Purposes for Reading

BIG Question What happens when what one person wants conflicts with what someone else wants? Can they both get what they want? Read "The War of the Wall" to find out.

Set Your Own Purpose What more would you like to learn from this selection to help you become who you want to be? Write your own purpose on "The War of the Wall" page of your Foldable.

Keep Moving

Use these skills as you read the following selection.

Teach

R Reading Skill

Review Connecting
Ask: How would you feel if someone you didn't know came in and changed your neighborhood without asking your permission? *(Possible response: I might feel angry at this person.)* BL

L Literary Element

Setting Say: Bambara never tells exactly in what neighborhood or city this story takes place. You will have to use clues in the story to help you guess where it takes place. Why might a writer not tell the exact location of a story? *(Possible response: The writer might want readers to recognize that the part of the country or the time period are more important than the exact location.)* AL

Use the CheckPoint questions provided on Presentation Plus! to check for making inferences and to build background. These questions can be used with interactive response keypads for immediate student feedback.

Reading Fluency

Rate Tell students they can miss details in a story if they read too slowly or too quickly. Model an appropriate reading rate for students by reading a paragraph from the selection. Then have pairs take turns reading the same paragraph from the selection at about the same rate. Students should note their rate as they read, adjusting if necessary. Encourage students to give constructive criticism as they listen to their partners read. Tell students to pay attention to their reading rate as they continue reading the story silently to themselves. Students who have difficulty reading at an appropriate rate may benefit from additional practice reading aloud. BL EL

Objectives

- Make inferences
- Identify literary elements: setting
- Use word references: dictionary

Teach

R Reading Skill

Inferring **Ask:** Why did Lou write Jimmy Lyons's name on the wall? *(because Lyons died in Vietnam.)* OL Tell students that this is a clue as to why the strange lady comes to town. Encourage them to keep a running list of clues in their Learner's Notebook.

L Literary Element

Setting **Ask:** Do Lou and the narrator have good or bad memories about the wall? How can you tell? *(They have good memories because they do not want the woman to mess with the wall.)* OL Why might Lou and the narrator want the painter lady to "quit messing with the wall"? *(Possible responses: They fear she is taking away their good memories; they think the wall belongs to them.)* AL

Readability Scores
Dale-Chall: 5.1
DRP: 53
Lexile: 930

The War of the Wall

by Toni Cade Bambara

Me and Lou had no time for courtesies.[1] We were late for school. So we just flat out told the painter lady to quit messing with the wall. It was our wall, and she had no right coming into our neighborhood painting on it. Stirring in the paint bucket and not even looking at us, she mumbled something about Mr. Eubanks, the barber, giving her permission. That had nothing to do with it as far as we were concerned. We've been pitching pennies against that wall since we were little kids. Old folks have been dragging their chairs out to sit in the shade of the wall for years. Big kids have been playing handball against the wall since so-called integration when the crazies 'cross town poured cement in our pool so we couldn't use it. I'd sprained my neck one time boosting my cousin Lou up to chisel Jimmy Lyons's name into the wall when we found out he was never coming home from the war in Vietnam to take us fishing. **1**

"If you lean close," Lou said, leaning hipshot against her beat-up car, "you'll get a whiff of bubble gum and kids' sweat. And that'll tell you something—that this wall belongs

1. ***Courtesies*** are the words and actions of polite behavior.

Practice the Skills

1 Key Literary Element

Setting The area near the wall has been the setting for many events that Lou and the narrator remember. How does the wall help them remember those events? How do they feel about the wall?

Additional Support

English Language Coach

Idioms Explain to students that the narrator uses many idiomatic expressions. Write the following expressions from the story on the board, and have students guess their meanings.

1. quit messing with *(stop touching)*
2. paid us no mind *(paid no attention to us)*
3. run the painter lady out of town *(get the painter lady to leave town)*
4. Me and Lou were cracking up *(Lou and I were laughing; amused)*
5. Me and Lou tried to get Mama to open fire on the painter lady. *(Lou and I tried to get Mama to say mean things about the painter lady.)* EL

to the kids of Taliaferro Street." I thought Lou sounded very convincing. But the painter lady paid us no mind. She just snapped the brim of her straw hat down and hauled her bucket up the ladder. **2**

"You're not even from around here," I hollered up after her. The license plates on her old piece of car said "New York." Lou dragged me away because I was about to grab hold of that ladder and shake it. And then we'd really be late for school.

When we came from school, the wall was slick with white. The painter lady was running string across the wall and taping it here and there. Me and Lou leaned against the gumball machine outside the pool hall and watched. She had strings up and down and back and forth. Then she began chalking them with a hunk of blue chalk.

The Morris twins crossed the street, hanging back at the curb next to the beat-up car. The twin with the red ribbons was hugging a jug of cloudy lemonade. The one with yellow ribbons was holding a plate of dinner away from her dress. The painter lady began snapping the strings. The blue chalk dust measured off halves and quarters up and down and sideways too. Lou was about to say how hip it all was, but I dropped my book satchel[2] on his toes to remind him we were at war.

L Some good **aromas** were drifting our way from the plate leaking pot likker[3] onto the Morris girl's white socks. I could tell from where I stood that under the tinfoil was baked ham, collard greens, and candied yams. And knowing Mrs. Morris, who sometimes bakes for my mama's restaurant, a slab of buttered cornbread was probably up under there too, sopping

R up some of the pot likker. Me and Lou rolled our eyes, wishing somebody would send us some dinner. But the painter lady didn't even turn around. She was pulling the strings down and prying bits of tape loose. **3**

Side Pocket came strolling out of the pool hall to see what Lou and me were studying so hard. He gave the painter lady

2. A *satchel* is a carrying bag, often with a shoulder strap.
3. *Pot likker* is the juices that come from collard greens and ham when it is cooked.

Vocabulary

aromas (uh ROH muhz) *n.* pleasing smells or scents

Practice the Skills

2 Key Reading Skill

Inferring Think about the painter's reason for going on with her business. What do you think her motive was?

3 Key Reading Skill

Inferring The painter ignores the twins' gift of supper. What do you think makes her ignore the twins and their gift?

READING WORKSHOP 3

Teach

L Literary Element

Setting Say: The food the twins offer the lady gives a clue about the setting. Where in the country might you find *pot likker?* *(Collard greens cooked with ham to make pot likker is a southern tradition.)* **AL**

R Reading Skill

Inferring Say: There could be many reasons the lady ignores the twins. How have Lou and his cousin treated her thus far? *(They've been rude to her.)* **BL** Why might this make her ignore the twins? *(Maybe she ignores the twins because she doesn't want anyone else to be rude to her.)* **OL** What are other possible reasons she would ignore the twins? *(Responses may vary.)* **OL**

Reading in the Real World

Citizenship The narrator mentions that Jimmy Lyons never came home from the war in Vietnam. Explain to students that the war was fought from 1965 to 1973. During this time, more than 58,000 Americans were killed in the war. Many of the soldiers were drafted, or forced to serve in the military, and many Americans, especially young people, opposed the war in Vietnam. Thousands of college students across the country protested the war in demonstrations and sit-ins.

Ask students to interview an older family member or neighbor to find out their reactions to the Vietnam war. **OL**

Objectives
- Use inference to understand a character's motives
- Describe the setting of a story
- Understand idioms

READING WORKSHOP 3

Teach

R1 Reading Skill

Inferring Say: Lou gives a clue here about why the painter lady might be ignoring the twins. What is the clue? *(He says she's concentrating hard on the painting.)* OL

R2 Reading Skill

Review Connecting

Say: Think of a time when you've had to focus really hard on something. Has anyone ever mistaken you for being rude because you were focused so intently that you didn't notice people around you? Describe your experience. *(Responses will vary.)* BL

the once-over, checking out her paint-spattered jeans, her chalky T-shirt, her floppy-brimmed straw hat. He hitched up his pants and glided over toward the painter lady, who kept right on with what she was doing.

"Whatcha got there, sweetheart?" he asked the twin with the plate.

"Suppah," she said all soft and countrylike.

"For her," the one with the jug added, jerking her chin toward the painter lady's back.

Still she didn't turn around. She was rearing back on her heels, her hands jammed into her back pockets, her face **squinched** up like the masterpiece she had in mind was taking shape on the wall by magic. We could have been gophers crawled up into a rotten hollow for all she cared. 4 She didn't even say hello to anybody. Lou was muttering something about how great her **concentration** was. I butt him with my hip, and his elbow slid off the gum machine. 5 [R1] [R2]

"Good evening," Side Pocket said in his best ain't-I-fine voice. But the painter lady was moving from the milk crate to the step stool to the ladder, moving up and down fast, scribbling all over the wall like a crazy person. We looked at Side Pocket. He looked at the twins. The twins looked at us. The painter lady was giving a show. It was like those old-timey music movies where the dancer taps on the tabletop and then starts jumping all over the furniture, kicking chairs over and not skipping a beat. She didn't even look where she was stepping. And for a minute there, hanging on the ladder to reach a far spot, she looked like she was going to tip right over.

"Ahh," Side Pocket cleared his throat and moved fast to catch the ladder. "These young ladies here have brought you some supper."

"Ma'am?" The twins stepped forward. Finally the painter turned around, her eyes "full of sky," as my grandmama would say. Then she stepped down like she was in a **trance**. She wiped her hands on her jeans as the Morris twins offered up the plate and the jug. She rolled back the tinfoil, then wagged her head as though something terrible was on the plate. 6

Vocabulary

concentration (kawn sen TRAY shun) *n.* the ability to focus one's attention

Practice the Skills

4 English Language Coach

Using Word References Look up the word **squinch** in a dictionary. Then describe how the painter lady's face looked when she was concentrating.

5 Key Reading Skill

Inferring Lou's attitude toward the painter seems to be changing. What clue can you find in the text that suggests that his attitude is changing? What might be making him change his attitude?

6 English Language Coach

Using Word References Look up the word **trance** in a dictionary. Then describe how the painter looked when her eyes were "full of sky."

Additional Support

Literature Focus Lesson

Setting in the Short Story Explain to students that the writer does not come out and state exactly when and where the story takes place, but she does give many clues that suggest where it takes place. Tell students that, as they read the story, they should write down any clues they find that suggest the setting of the story. After finishing the story, encourage students to give as much information as they can about the setting of the story. Students might note the following.

- the time is either during or shortly after the Vietnam war
- the place is a street in a town
- the town is in the southern United States OL

READING WORKSHOP 3

"Thank your mother very much," she said, sounding like her mouth was full of sky too. "I've brought my own dinner along." And then, without even excusing herself, she went back up the ladder, drawing on the wall in a wild way. Side Pocket whistled one of those oh-brother breathy whistles and went back into the pool hall. The Morris twins shifted their weight from one foot to the other, then crossed the street and went home. Lou had to drag me away, I was so mad. We couldn't wait to get to the firehouse to tell my daddy all about this rude woman who'd stolen our wall.

All the way back to the block to help my mama out at the restaurant, me and Lou kept asking my daddy for ways to run the painter lady out of town. But my daddy was busy talking about the trip to the country and telling Lou he could come too because Grandmama can always use an extra pair of hands on the farm. **L**

Later that night, while me and Lou were in the back doing our chores, we found out that the painter lady was a liar. She came into the restaurant and leaned against the glass of the steam table, talking about how starved she was. I was scrubbing pots and Lou was chopping onions, but we could hear her through the service window. She was asking Mama was that a ham hock in the greens, and was that a neck bone in the pole beans, and were there any vegetables cooked without meat, especially pork. **R**

"I don't care who your spiritual leader is," Mama said in that way of hers. "If you eat in the community, sistuh, you gonna eat pig by-and-by, one way or t'other." **7**

Me and Lou were cracking up in the kitchen, and several customers at the counter were clearing their throats, waiting for Mama to really fix her wagon[4] for not speaking to the elders when she came in. The painter lady took a stool at the

4. To ***fix her wagon*** means to put her in her place or show her who's boss.

Practice the Skills

7 Key Literary Element

Setting Think about how well the painter "fits" into the setting of this story. What does she say and do that makes it clear that this is not the kind of setting she's used to?

Teach

L Literary Element

Setting Say: The narrator's father is busy talking about their trip to the country. What might you infer about the setting based on this description? *(that the narrator doesn't live in the country)* **AL**

R Reading Skill

Inferring Say: The narrator calls the painter lady a liar for telling the twins she'd brought her own food. Why might she have told this lie to the twins? *(She might have told it to spare their feelings.)* Why might she have not taken the food? *(because she is a vegetarian and the food was cooked with meat)* **OL**

English Language Coach

Compound Words On the board, write the words *somebody, handball,* and *nowhere.* Explain that these are compound words—two words joined together to create one word. Tell students they can figure out the meaning of a compound word by combining the meanings of the words that form it.

somebody = some + body (a person)

gumball = gum + ball (a gum candy in the shape of a ball)

cornbread = corn + bread (bread made from corn)

Have students look for compound words in the story and use what they know about the word parts to guess their meanings. **EL BL**

Objectives

- Make connections from text to self
- Use inference to understand a character's motives
- Identify setting within the text

Teach

C Critical Thinking

Comprehension Ask: Based on the painter lady's questions, what kind of diet is she used to eating? *(a strict vegetarian diet)* OL

L Literary Element

Setting Say: Mama gives an important clue about the setting of the story. What is it? *(She notes that the painter lady is from the North, where people have no manners. This suggests the story is set in the South.)* OL

C counter and went right on with her questions. Was there cheese in the baked macaroni, she wanted to know? Were there eggs in the salad? Was it honey or sugar in the iced tea? Mama was fixing Pop Johnson's plate. And every time the painter lady asked a fool question, Mama would dump another spoonful of rice on the pile. She was tapping her foot and heating up in a dangerous way. But Pop Johnson was happy as he could be. Me and Lou peeked through the service window, wondering what planet the painter lady came from. Who ever heard of baked macaroni without cheese, or potato salad without eggs?

"Do you have any bread made with unbleached flour?"[5] the painter lady asked Mama. There was a long pause, as though everybody in the restaurant was holding their breath, wondering if Mama would dump the next spoonful on the painter lady's head. She didn't. But when she set Pop Johnson's plate down, it came down with a bang. 8

When Mama finally took her order, the starving lady all of a sudden couldn't make up her mind whether she wanted a vegetable plate or fish and a salad. She finally settled on the broiled trout and a tossed salad. But just when Mama reached for a plate to serve her, the painter lady leaned over the counter with her finger all up in the air.

"Excuse me," she said. "One more thing." Mama was holding the plate like a Frisbee, tapping that foot, one hand on her hip. "Can I get raw beets in that tossed salad?" 9

"You will get," Mama said, leaning her face close to the painter lady's, "whatever Lou back there tossed. Now sit down." And the painter lady sat back down on her stool and shut right up.

L All the way to the country, me and Lou tried to get Mama to open fire on the painter lady. But Mama said that seeing as how she was from the North, you couldn't expect her to have any manners. Then Mama said she was sorry she'd been so impatient with the woman because she seemed like a decent person and was simply trying to stick to a very strict diet. Me and Lou didn't want to hear that. Who did that lady think she was, coming into our neighborhood and taking over our wall?

5. ***Unbleached flour*** does not have chemicals added to make it white.

Practice the Skills

8 Key Reading Skill

Inferring Think about the other characters' reactions to the painter. What do they say and do that shows how strange she seems to them?

9 Key Reading Skill

Inferring Some people try to fit in when they are in a place where they have never been before. They try to find out what behavior is expected of them and act appropriately. Is the painter one of those people?

Additional Support

Literature Focus Lesson

Characters and Conflict Have students review the characters and conflict in this short story by answering the following questions:

- Who are the main characters in the story? *(The narrator, his cousin Lou, the painter lady)*
- What is the conflict in the story? *(The narrator and Lou don't want the painter lady to paint their wall.)*
- Which characters in the story change? *(Lou and the narrator change. They learn to appreciate the painter lady.)*
- Which characters stay the same? *(The narrator's mother and father stay the same, as does the painter lady.)* OL

READING WORKSHOP 3

"Welllll," Mama drawled, pulling into the filling station so Daddy could take the wheel, "it's hard on an artist, ya know. They can't always get people to look at their work. So she's just doing her work in the open, that's all."

Me and Lou definitely did not want to hear that. Why couldn't she set up an easel downtown or draw on the sidewalk in her own neighborhood? Mama told us to quit fussing so much; she was tired and wanted to rest. She climbed into the back seat and dropped down into the warm hollow Daddy had made in the pillow.

All weekend long, me and Lou tried to scheme up ways to recapture our wall. Daddy and Mama said they were sick of hearing about it. Grandmama turned up the TV to drown us out. On the late news was a story about the New York subways. When a train came roaring into the station all covered from top to bottom, windows too, with writings and drawings done with spray paint, me and Lou slapped five. Mama said it was too bad kids in New York had nothing better to do than spray paint all over the trains. Daddy said that in the cities, even grown-ups wrote all over the trains and buildings too. Daddy called it "graffiti." Grandmama called it a shame.

We couldn't wait to get out of school on Monday. We couldn't find any black spray paint anywhere. But in a junky hardware store downtown we found a can of white epoxy paint, the kind you touch up old refrigerators with when they get splotchy and peely. We spent our whole allowance on it. And because it was too late to use our bus passes, we had to walk all the way home lugging our book satchels and gym shoes, and the bag with the epoxy. **10**

Practice the Skills

10 Key Reading Skill

Inferring Think about the narrator's plan to spray paint over the mural on the wall. What information in the story would lead you to believe that Mama would disapprove? Why do you think the narrator was going to do it anyway? **R**

Teach

Viewing the Art

Ask: What is depicted in the artwork? *(the restaurant of the narrator's mother)* **BL** Is this how you imagined the restaurant would look? Why or why not? *(Responses will vary.)* **BL**

R Reading Skill

Inferring **Say:** In addition to disapproving of spray painting, the narrator's parents give other clues that they would disapprove of damaging the wall. What other clues do they give? *(The father ignores the narrator's request for help running the painter lady out of town; the mother sympathizes with the lady, saying "it's hard on an artist.")* **OL**

Differentiated Instruction

Creating a Mural Have students discuss the people, colors, and things the lady included on the mural. Then have students create their own "mural." They might dedicate the mural to someone they know or create a mural that answers the question, "What is important in your world?" Have students use a large piece of poster board and paste or draw pictures of things or people that are important to them. Encourage students to write a brief paragraph explaining the significance of the mural or to tell this information orally to the class. **BL** **EL**

Objectives
- Use inference to understand a character's motives
- Identify the setting of a story
- Use critical thinking to analyze a story

Teach

C Critical Thinking

Comprehension Ask: How do you know all the people in town have stopped what they were doing to look at the mural? *(Some people from the narrator's restaurant still have napkins around their throat and the face of a man from the barbershop is still half full of foam. The barber is holding his straight razor.)* **OL**

R Reading Skill

Inferring Ask: What clues here tell you that the painter lady was not really ignoring everyone, as the narrator had thought? *(She has painted people from the town into the mural.)* **OL**

When we reached the corner of Taliaferro and Fifth, it looked like a block party or something. Half the neighborhood was gathered on the sidewalk in front of the wall. I looked at Lou, he looked at me. We both looked at the bag with the epoxy and wondered how we were going to work our scheme. The painter lady's car was nowhere in sight. But there were too many people standing around to do anything. Side Pocket and his buddies were leaning on their cue sticks, hunching each other. Daddy was there with a lineman[6] he catches a ride with on Mondays. Mrs. Morris had her arms flung around the shoulders of the twins on either side of her. Mama was talking with some of her customers, many of them with napkins still at the throat. Mr. Eubanks came out of the barbershop, followed by a man in a striped poncho, half his face shaved, the other half full of foam. **C**

"She really did it, didn't she?" Mr. Eubanks huffed out his chest. Lots of folks answered right quick that she surely did when they saw the straight razor in his hand.

Mama beckoned[7] us over. And then we saw it. The wall. Reds, greens, figures outlined in black. Swirls of purple and orange. Storms of blues and yellows. It was something. I recognized some of the faces right off. There was Martin Luther King, Jr. And there was a man with glasses on and his mouth open like he was laying down a heavy rap. Daddy came up alongside and reminded us that that was Minister Malcolm X. The serious woman with a rifle I knew was Harriet Tubman because my grandmama has pictures of her all over the house. And I knew Mrs. Fannie Lou Hamer 'cause a signed photograph of her hangs in the restaurant next to the calendar. **11**

Then I let my eyes follow what looked like a vine. It trailed past a man with a horn, a woman with a big white flower in her hair, a handsome dude in a tuxedo seated at a piano, and a man with a goatee holding a book. When I looked more closely, I realized that what had looked like flowers were really faces. One face with yellow petals looked just like Frieda Morris. One with red petals looked just like Hattie Morris. I could hardly believe my eyes. **R**

6. A worker who strings telephone lines is a ***lineman.***
7. To ***beckon*** is to call or signal, usually with a wave or a nod.

Practice the Skills

11 Reviewing Skills

Activating Prior Knowledge The mural includes images of several important Civil Rights leaders. In your Learner's Notebook, tell what you know about each person.

- Martin Luther King Jr.
- Malcolm X
- Harriet Tubman
- Mrs. Fannie Lou Hamer

Additional Support

Reading in the Real World

Citizenship Divide the class into groups, and have each group use library and Internet resources to research one of the famous people mentioned on the wall: Martin Luther King, Jr.; Malcolm X; Harriet Tubman; or Fannie Lou Hamer. Have students answer the following research questions:

- What was the person famous for?
- How did the person contribute to African American liberation?

Have each group present its findings orally to the class. **OL** Have students research and recite a portion of a famous speech from one of the leaders. **AL**

"Notice," Side Pocket said, stepping close to the wall with his cue stick like a classroom pointer. "These are the flags of liberation," he said in a voice I'd never heard him use before. We all stepped closer while he pointed and spoke. "Red, black and green," he said, his pointer falling on the leaflike flags of the vine. "Our liberation[8] flag. And here Ghana, there Tanzania. Guinea-Bissau, Angola, Mozambique." Side Pocket sounded very tall, as though he'd been waiting all his life to give this lesson. **R**

Mama tapped us on the shoulder and pointed to a high section of the wall. There was a fierce-looking man with his arms crossed against his chest guarding a bunch of children. His muscles bulged, and he looked a lot like my daddy. One kid was looking at a row of books. Lou hunched[9] me 'cause the kid looked like me. The one that looked like Lou was spinning a globe on the tip of his finger like a basketball. There were other kids there with microscopes and compasses. And the more I looked, the more it looked like the fierce man was not so much guarding the kids as defending their right to do what they were doing. **12**

Then Lou gasped and dropped the paint bag and ran forward, running his hands over a rainbow. He had to tiptoe and stretch to do it, it was so high. I couldn't breathe either. The painter lady had found the chisel marks and had painted Jimmy Lyons's name in a rainbow.

"Read the inscription,[10] honey," Mrs. Morris said, urging little Frieda forward. She didn't have to urge much. Frieda marched right up, bent down, and in a loud voice that made everybody quit oohing and ahhing and listen, she read,

To the People of Taliaferro Street
I Dedicate This Wall of Respect
Painted in Memory of My Cousin
Jimmy Lyons ❍

8. ***Liberation*** is freedom achieved after a struggle. These are all names of countries in Africa.
9. When Lou ***hunched*** the narrator, he nudged or bumped into him on purpose.
10. An ***inscription*** is something written as a lasting record.

Practice the Skills

12 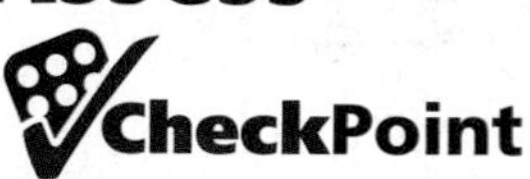

BQ How might the mural created by the painter lady help the people of Taliaferro Street become who they want to be? Pair up to discuss. Then write your answer on "The War of the Wall" page of your Foldable. Your response will help you answer the Unit Challenge later.

Reading in the Real World

Citizenship Have students research another wall that is a tribute to fallen soldiers, the Vietnam War Memorial in Washington, D.C. Encourage students to learn about the competition to find an architect for the memorial, the person who won, and the controversy surrounding the memorial. Have students present their findings in a class discussion. Ask them to think of other ways besides memorials that we can honor the soldiers of foreign wars. **OL**

Teach

R Reading Skill

Inferring Ask: Why might the painter lady have included flags of Africa? *(because the town is mostly African American; because the flags represent freedom)* **OL**

BQ BIG Question

Ask: What advice might the painter lady give about becoming who you want to be? *(Students might note that the painter lady would tell people to focus and ignore other people's criticism.)* **OL**

Assess

CheckPoint

Use the CheckPoint questions provided on Presentation Plus! to check students' mastery of the selection. These questions can be used with interactive response keypads for immediate student feedback.

Objectives
- Use inference to understand a character's motives
- Use critical thinking to analyze a story

Assess

Resources for page 196

- Selection Quick Check
- Selection and Unit Assessment
- ExamView Assessment Suite
- Interactive Tutor: Self-Assessment

Students can respond to the *After You Read* items in their Learner's Notebook or on a separate sheet of paper.

Answering the

1. Answers will vary.
2. They pitched pennies against the wall.
3. They brought supper of ham, greens, candied yams, and cornbread.

Critical Thinking

4. Possible response: Lou started out disliking the painter lady but came to respect her concentration, talent, and motive.
5. Possible response: The narrator was stubborn. He disliked the woman for changing his wall.
6. She wanted vegetarian food but the narrator's mother said she didn't have any. The narrator's mother became frustrated with her.
7. Possible response: I think she appeared rude but was just trying to concentrate.

After You Read

The War of the Wall

Answering the

1. What are your first thoughts about the Big Question after reading this selection?
2. **Recall** What games did Lou and the narrator play against the wall when they were younger?
   TIP **Right There** You will find the answer in the story.
3. **Recall** What did the Morris twins bring to the painter?
   TIP **Right There** You will find the answer in the story.

Critical Thinking

4. **Infer** How did Lou's feelings about the painter change during the story?
   TIP **Author and Me** You will find clues in the story, but you must also use the information in your head.
5. **Infer** Why do you think the narrator's feelings about the painter didn't change before the end of the story?
6. **Summarize** What happened when the painter tried to order food in the restaurant?
   TIP **Think and Search** You must use information from the story and decide what the important points are.
7. **Evaluate** What do you think of the way the painter behaved?
   TIP **Author and Me** Answer from information in the story and from your own thoughts.

Objectives (pp. 196–197)
Reading Make inferences
Literature Identify literary elements: setting
Writing Use the RAFT system: opinion piece
Grammar Identify and use pronouns: reflexive and intensive

Write About Your Reading

Use the RAFT system to write about "The War of the Wall."

Role: Write as if you were one of the people looking at the painting on the wall.

Audience: Write for the neighborhood newspaper.

Format: An "opinion piece," which is a short statement giving a personal opinion.

Topic: Tell what you think of the completed mural.

Write About Your Reading

Possible response:
I think that the new mural in our town is a wonderful tribute to Jimmy Lyons. I believe the theme of the mural is "heroes and freedom." The painter includes other heroes besides Jimmy in the mural, such as Martin Luther King, Jr.; Malcolm X; and Harriet Tubman. She also includes flags that represent freedom. The colors of the mural are beautiful. It is definitely a great addition to our town.

Skills Review

Key Reading Skill: Inferring

8. The characters don't say how they feel about the finished mural. You have to infer their feelings from the clues Bambara gives.

   Notice the actions of Mr. Eubanks, Side Pocket, the narrator, Mama, Daddy, Lou, Mrs. Morris, and Frieda. Choose one of these characters. Then, in your Learner's Notebook, write a brief letter to the painter lady from that character. Tell how your character feels about the mural. Support your inferences with details from the selection.

Key Literary Element: Setting

9. In a few words, describe the neighborhood where the wall stands.
10. How did the painter and her painting change the neighborhood?

Reviewing Elements: Titles and Subtitles

11. Considering what takes place between the painter and the cousins, is the title of the story a good one? Why or why not? Support your answer with examples from the text.

Vocabulary Check

Choose the best word from the list to complete each sentence below. In your Learner's Notebook, write each sentence, putting the correct word in the blank.

aromas **concentration**

12. The delicious supper gave off good ____.
13. Lou admired the painter's power of ____.
14. **Academic Vocabulary** What **motive** did Lou and the narrator have for wanting to spray graffiti on the painter's work? Write your response in your Learner's Notebook.
15. **English Language Coach** What kind of <u>work</u> do you want to do as an adult?

Grammar Link: Reflexive and Intensive Pronouns

Pronouns that include *-self* or *-selves* are either **reflexive** *or* **intensive** pronouns.

Reflexive and Intensive Pronouns	
Singular	*Plural*
myself	ourselves
yourself	yourselves
himself, herself, itself	themselves

- **Reflexive** pronouns "reflect," sort of the way a mirror does. They refer back to a noun or another pronoun. They show that whoever is doing something is also receiving the action of the verb.

He gave **himself** a five-minute break.
I asked **myself** why I was trying so hard.

- Never use a reflexive pronoun when it is not necessary. Use reflexive pronouns only to "reflect" a noun or pronoun that has already been used!

Wrong: Roderigo insulted Tony and **myself.**
Right: Roderigo insulted Tony and **me.**

- **Intensive** pronouns emphasize their antecedents.

Did you **yourself** do as I asked?
The governor **himself** was there.
We did all the work **ourselves.**

- These are not words: *theirselves*, *hisself*. Never use them.

Grammar Practice

Rewrite each sentence, using the correct pronoun in parentheses.

16. Ty (himself, hisself) gave (me, myself) this book.
17. They told (us, ourselves) the news (themselves, theirselves).

Web Activities For eFlashcards, Selection Quick Checks, and other Web activities, go to www.glencoe.com.

Skills Review

Key Reading Skill: Inferring

8. Possible response: Dear Painter Lady, Thank you for the lovely mural. It is a great tribute to your cousin Jimmy. Sincerely, Mrs. Morris.

Key Literary Element: Setting

9. It has a barbershop, a restaurant, and a pool hall.
10. The painting made the neighborhood more colorful.

Reviewing Elements: Titles and Subtitles

11. Possible response: The title is good because the narrator and Lou want to fight a "war" with the painter lady. For example, they buy spray paint to ruin the lady's work.

Vocabulary Check

12. aromas
13. concentration
14. Lou and the narrator want to make the lady angry. They don't want her to change their wall.
15. Responses will vary.

Close

Ask students to summarize what they learned from "The War of the Wall" to help them answer the Big Question.

Grammar Link: Reflexive and Intensive Pronouns

Grammar Practice

16. Ty himself gave me this book.
17. They told us the news themselves.

Focus

BELLRINGER Options

Daily Language Practice Transparency

Focus Activity Say: One of the most important steps in writing a narrative is getting your thoughts on paper. Now, you'll revise your narrative. What are some ways you can improve your first draft? *(Responses may include checking grammar and spelling, looking for more descriptive adjectives, or deleting unnecessary information.)* **OL**

Teach

W Writing

Revising Say: When you revise your writing, check for one element, or strategy, at a time. For example, the first time you read through your narrative, make sure you used first-person point of view throughout. The second time, make sure that you clearly described the setting.

Resources for page 198

Use the Writing Workshop Graphic Organizer BLM in the Unit 2 Resource Booklet.

WRITING WORKSHOP PART 2

Autobiographical Narrative

Revising, Editing, and Presenting

ASSIGNMENT Write an autobiographical narrative

Purpose: To tell a story about a goal you once had and how it turned out

Audience: You, your teacher, and possibly some classmates

Revising Rubric

Your revised autobiographical narrative should have

- an anecdote
- a first-person point of view
- a clearly described setting
- a clear ending
- events told in time order
- a clear writing voice
- only well-chosen and important details

See page 202 for a model of a personal narrative.

Objectives (pp. 198–203)
Writing Use the writing process: autobiographical narrative • Develop voice • Revise a draft to include: main ideas and supporting details, quotation, transitions, focus • Edit writing for: grammar, spelling, punctuation • Present writing
Listening, Speaking, and Viewing Participate in a group discussion • Listen actively

In Writing Workshop Part 1, you did some prewriting, developed a draft, and added details to your draft. Now it's time to revise and edit your draft so your ideas really shine. When you're finished, you'll share your writing with your classmates. Also, you'll keep a copy of it in a writing portfolio so that you and your teacher can evaluate your writing progress over time.

Revising

Make It Better

W

The purpose of revising is to improve your writing. For skilled writers, revising is often the most important part of the writing process. Revising is what makes good writing great, and great writing takes work! So get ready!

Read over your draft to see if you used the strategies you learned. If you didn't, you can revise your draft to follow the suggestions now. The chart below may help you.

Did you . . .	Hint
use first-person point of view throughout your story?	Read your draft aloud. Focus only on the point of view. If you find any place where you switched point of view, revise the sentence.
clearly describe the setting?	In your mind, put *yourself* in the setting. Look around. Notice everything. Think about what you should tell your readers to help them feel as if they are there. Add the details.
include an anecdote that shows action?	If you didn't include an anecdote, add one now! It's okay to add more details when you revise. Briefly tell about an interesting or funny event. Use action words to show readers what happened.
provide a clear ending?	You may have told the last event and still feel that your story doesn't have a clear ending. Try writing a sentence about what you learned from your experience or how you feel today about the goal you had.

Additional Support

English Language Coach

First-Person Point of View Remind students that their narratives should tell the events from the first-person perspective. Help students practice writing in the first person by having them rewrite the following sentences in first person, as if they are the subjects in the sentences.

1. She gave herself the day off.
2. He was a hero to his friends.
3. She took her mother to the mall in her new car.
4. He finished the test all by himself.
5. She spent her allowance on clothes and shoes. **EL** **BL**

Applying Good Writing Traits

Voice

One of the best parts of reading an autobiography is getting to know the author. You can discover the writer's personality from the way he or she "talks" on paper.

What Is Voice?

Just as each person has a unique speaking voice, an author has a particular writing voice. It's the author's personality coming through in the tone, word choices, and sentence patterns he or she uses.

Why Is Voice Important in My Writing?

- Writing in your own voice helps you express your real thoughts, ideas, and feelings.
- Writing in your own voice is easier than trying to sound like someone else.
- Reading something written in your voice is more interesting to your audience. It shows there's a real person behind the writing.

How Do I Do It?

- Write with the words you use when you're talking.
- Write sentences the way you say sentences.
- **W1** Write with an attitude about your topic, just as you would if you were speaking with friends.
- As you write, pause now and then to read your work aloud to be sure your writing sounds like you.

W2

Write to Learn Read the latest version of your draft to a partner. Have your partner listen for parts of the narrative in which the voice doesn't sound like yours. Rewrite those parts so that you can imagine yourself saying them to a friend.

Analyzing Cartoons
Show your individuality. Don't try to sound like someone else in your writing. Be yourself. (Where have we heard that before?)

HEY, TIFFANY- YOU KNOW THIS ESSAY WE'RE SUPPOSED TO WRITE ON INDIVIDUALITY?
I DON'T KNOW WHAT TO WRITE ABOUT. WHAT DID YOU COME UP WITH?
I SAID WE SHOULD ALL JUST BE OURSELVES AND NOT DO WHAT EVERYBODY ELSE DOES.
OH, THAT'S GOOD.
I'LL WRITE THAT TOO.

Teach

W1 Writing

Voice Say: One way to be sure you use your own voice as you write is to say each sentence aloud *before* you write it. Then, when you have written a complete paragraph, read aloud what you've written. If your writing doesn't sound like you, try changing some words or sentences until your voice is clearer in your writing. **OL**

W2 Writing

Word Choice Say: If you find yourself using the same adjectives, or words such as *very* or *interesting,* use a thesaurus to help you find more concise and vivid words. Just make sure the words you choose sound like you. Stay away from big, elaborate words you would never use. **OL**

Analyzing Cartoons Ask: How is the girl in the cartoon *not* devoloping her own voice? What should she do so that she does write in her voice? *(Possible response: She is writing her friend's thoughts. She should think for herself.)*

English Language Coach

Word Choice Have students work with partners to use more vivid descriptive words in the following sentences. Model revising the first sentence to help get students started.

1. On a nice day, we watched the game. *(On a sunny, pleasant afternoon, we cheered on our favorite football team.)*
2. I worked very hard in the yard and was very tired afterwards.
3. There was bad weather the day I first started school.
4. I got some food for dinner and prepared it for my friends. **EL BL**

Objectives
- Use the writing process: autobiographical narrative
- Develop voice
- Revise a draft to include: main ideas and supporting details, quotation, transitions, focus
- Edit writing for: grammar, spelling, punctuation
- Present writing
- Participate in a group discussion
- Listen actively

Teach

W1 Writing

Revising Details **Say:** Sometimes others can point out unnecessary details in your work quicker than you can. Work with a partner to help delete unnecessary details in your narratives. Swap narratives with your partner, and write an X next to sentences that could be cut or revised. **OL**

W2 Writing

Time Order Write the following words on the board:

- after
- second
- since
- first
- earlier
- before
- last
- beforehand
- next
- later
- then

Say: These words show time order. Write them in your Learner's Notebook and use them as you revise your writing. Use three of the words in sentences that tell about an event that happened over a period of time. Share these sentences with the class. *(Possible response: First I went home. Then I had a snack. After my snack, I did my homework.)* **BL** **EL**

Here are some other features of your writing that you might need to revise.

Details, Details

W1

Good writing is focused—it stays on the topic and has no unnecessary words or unrelated details. Follow these steps to get rid of unneeded information.

1. Read the latest version of your narrative, sentence by sentence.
2. Pause after each sentence and ask yourself:
   - Does this detail tell the reader something important to the story?
   - Can I say the same thing in fewer words without losing meaning?
3. Get rid of sentences that tell about unimportant details. Cut words and rewrite sentences to make your ideas clear and to the point.

My friend once painted her room green, too. The color green that I chose is somewhere between a light green and a medium green.

Revision:

I finally chose a color called Spring Grass Green.

Time Order

W2

You know when each event happened in the story you're telling. Your readers don't. For this assignment, you have to tell the events in time order—the order in which they happened. Follow these steps to make the order of events clear.

1. Read the latest version of your narrative, sentence by sentence.
2. Pause after each sentence and ask yourself:
   - Am I telling this event in the order that it happened?
   - Have I made it clear to readers exactly *when* this event happened?

I stepped back to see how the first wall looked.
I heard "kerplunk!" and suddenly my foot was wet.

3. Add words and phrases that will make the time of each event clear.

After I had finished painting the first wall, I stepped back to see how it looked. Then I heard "kerplunk!" and suddenly my foot was wet.

Additional Support

Differentiated Instruction

Creative Writing Encourage students to use the following techniques to add flair to their writing:

- Vary the length and type of sentence to create rhythm in your narratives. Do not start all sentences with a subject followed by a predicate. Mix it up.
- Use metaphors or similes, comparisons of unlike things, to bring writing to life.
- Try appealing to all five senses in the narrative—sight, hearing, taste, touch, and smell. This will help your reader really experience your story. **AL**

Editing

Finish It Up

Now it's time to get your writing ready to share with others. After all of your hard work, the first thing readers see shouldn't be a misspelled word!

For your final copy, read your narrative one sentence at a time and use the **Editing Checklist** to help you spot errors. Use the proofreading symbols in the chart on page R74 to mark needed corrections.

Proofreading Checklist

- ☑ Verb tenses are correct.
- ☑ Proper nouns are capitalized correctly.
- ☑ All plural compound nouns are formed correctly.
- ☑ Pronouns are in the correct form and agree with their antecedents.
- ☑ The antecedent of each pronoun is clear.
- ☑ All words are spelled correctly.

Writing Tip

Spelling Use the spell-check feature on your computer, but don't depend on that feature alone. Computers aren't perfect! Use a dictionary to check the spellings of words you're not sure about. **C**

Presenting

Show It Off

As a class, create a binder called *How can we become who we want to be?* Copy your paragraphs neatly in print or cursive on a separate piece of paper. If you prefer, you may type your narrative.

To make your paper really stand out, try one or more of these suggestions:

- Add illustrations or fancy lettering.
- Cut images from magazines or download images from your computer and add them to your paper.
- If you're using a computer with a color printer, use a colored font other than black, or add a colorful border around the page.

Finally, use a three-hole punch to punch holes in your paper and add your work to the class binder.

Writing Tip

Handwriting Be sure your final draft is easily readable. Form your letters carefully. Space your words evenly, and don't make your spaces too big or too small.

Literature Online

Writing Models For models and other writing activities, go to www.glencoe.com.

Teach

C Critical Thinking

Application **Say:** Spell-checking functions on computers have limitations. Can you think of some misspelled words that spellcheck might not correct? Think of two ways to check for spelling besides your spellcheck function. *(Possible responses:* their *instead of* they're, too *instead of* two, great *instead of* grate; look for commonly misspelled words, read each sentence slowly.*)* **OL**

Assess

Have students exchange their papers and use the proofreading checklist to critique each other's work. Have students make last-minute changes to their work and then add their papers to the class binder.

Literature Online

Writing Models Have students access the Web site for an additional and interactive Writing Workshop-based student model.

Reading Fluency

Improving Fluency Students can improve their reading fluency by reading aloud their own writing. Encourage students to pay attention to the keys to good fluency as they read their narratives:

- rate: how fast they read
- intonation: the ups and downs of their voice
- volume: the loudness of their voice **BL** **EL**

Remind students to make sure their writing voice comes across authentically. As they read their work to their partners, ask students to listen for their voice in the writing and to make any necessary revisions. **OL**

Objectives

- Write autobiographical narratives using the writing process
- Develop voice
- Maintain a consistent point of view
- Proofread writing
- Edit writing for correct use of nouns and pronouns

Teach

W1 Writing

Voice Say: Practice writing using your own voice. Read over the Writer's Model on this page, and choose one or two sentences that you would say differently. Write these sentences in your own voice. **OL**

W2 Writing

Evaluating Say: What do you think of this Writer's Model? In a small group, create a brief evaluation of the model. Keep your comments constructive and helpful, and be specific. For example, if you think the writer needs to add more detail, tell what details you would like to read. When you're finished, have a group representative present your evaluation to the class. **OL**

Use your suggestions to write a second draft of this model. **AL**

WRITING WORKSHOP PART 2

Active Writing Model

The writer uses first person point of view because she is telling events that happened in her own life.

These sentences have a clear voice. The writer shows her attitude toward the need for change.

The details in this paragraph explain part of the reason the goal was important to the narrator.

The writer uses interior monologue to share her thoughts.

Time order words help readers understand the sequence of events.

This anecdote gives insight into a problem that the writer faced.

The description of the smell of fresh paint helps readers connect to the setting.

The writer clearly explains the result of her work and shares thoughts about her goal.

Writer's Model

When I turned twelve, the wallpaper in my bedroom began to embarrass me. My parents had thought it was perfect for a little girl's room—pink and yellow and filled with lambs and birds and flowers. It was way past time for something new. I wasn't a little girl anymore, and I wanted a room that fit me.

So I set out to convince Mom to let me paint. At first, she didn't think it was a good idea. "It's hard enough getting you to clean your room. Do you think you're up to the challenge of painting?" Her doubt made me even more determined to get the job done.

At the paint store, there was a giant wall of little cards showing a million different shades of green! "How am I supposed to choose one color?" I asked myself. "I can't even tell the difference between Spring Green and Easter Green!" I picked a few shades I liked, closed my eyes, and pointed to Spring Grass Green. Mom bought it and we headed home.

W1 W2

On Saturday morning, I was ready to work. First I had to clear out the furniture, CDs, and teddy bears. Mom helped me put everything in the hall. Then we covered the floor with a plastic sheet. Finally, I set to work covering the ugly wallpaper with my Spring Grass Green paint.

After I finished the first wall, I stepped back to see how it looked. Then I heard "kerplunk!" and suddenly my foot was wet. I kicked the bucket, I thought. An hour later, it was noon and I started the second wall. I was already worn out, but I knew I had to paint all four walls that day to make my goal. So I pushed on.

The sun was setting when I finished the last wall. I took a deep breath and smelled the fresh paint. Late that night, Mom helped me put my furniture back. She was really happy when we got it all done. "It's a twofer," she said. "Two for the price of one. You got your room redecorated. And I finally got you to clean it." But I knew that it was better than a "twofer." I had met my goal.

Additional Support

Literature Focus Lesson

Author's Purpose Tell students that people write autobiographies for a number of reasons, including to tell the story of their lives or to help people in similar situations. Encourage students to think about the purpose of their autobiographical narratives by asking themselves, "What do I want my readers to learn?" As students edit their narratives, they should keep their answer to this question in mind. Have they given their readers enough information? Encourage students to share their narratives with classmates and have them answer what they learned from reading the narratives. **OL**

Listening, Speaking, and Viewing

Group Discussion and Active Listening

What Is It?

A group discussion is three or more people sharing their thoughts about a topic. Active listening is when you focus on what the speaker is saying.

Why Is It Important?

Group discussion allows you to stretch your thinking. You may hear others saying what you couldn't put into words. Active listening allows you to understand others' thoughts and ideas.

How Do I Do It?

Follow these tips to be an active listener.

- Make eye contact with the speaker and focus on the words. Clear your mind of other thoughts such as your after-school plans.
- Connect what you hear to your own knowledge and experience.
- If you don't understand something, ask a question.
- If you will need to use the information later, take notes. Review your notes soon after the speaker has finished and fill in any gaps. Then compare notes with a classmate to see if you understood the speaker's message.

Follow these tips for group discussion.

- Take part in the conversation! It's your job to contribute your thoughts to the discussion. Don't let your group down.
- Be respectful. Don't interrupt. If you disagree with someone, simply say what you think and give your reasons.
- Stay on topic. Don't bring up unrelated stories.
- If you are the discussion leader, make sure everyone takes part. If someone hasn't talked in a while, ask for that person's thoughts.

Talk It Out In a small group, take turns following these steps:

1. Tell the key points of your autobiographical narrative–your goal, the problem that got in the way, and how the situation turned out.
2. Share your answers to these questions:
   - What did I learn about myself from how I handled the problem?
   - What does my story add to our discussion of the Big Question?

LSV

You may want to take notes on your group members' thoughts. Your notes might be helpful when you complete the Unit Challenge.

Analyzing Cartoons
Lucky Eddie's mission is to listen actively to the enemy and report back to Hagar. Do you think he'll succeed?

REMEMBER, LUCKY EDDIE—YOU'RE WEARING THAT SUIT OF ARMOR SO YOU CAN INFILTRATE THE ENEMY CASTLE AND REPORT BACK!
CHRIS BROWNE

SO KEEP YOUR EYES AND EARS OPEN!
DID SOMEONE SAY SOMETHING?

Differentiated Instruction

Staying Focused Some students may have a difficult time staying focused during a group discussion. Encourage these students to try the following techniques for focusing during a discussion:

Repeat what you hear: Silently repeat the main points of what another group member has said. Then write them down.

Be an active participant: If you speak often, it will be easier for you to stay focused on the topic at hand.

Put away books or other distractions: Make sure your desk is clear of anything that might distract you from the conversation. BL

WRITING WORKSHOP PART 2

Teach

LSV Listening, Speaking, and Viewing

Active Listening Say: As you listen to your group members talk about their narratives, think of one follow-up question you could ask them to learn more. Asking follow-up questions shows you have been listening and helps you make sure you've understood what you've heard. BL

Close

Say: Think of one thing you've learned from your classmates' narratives that can help you answer the Big Question. Write your thoughts in your Learner's Notebook. OL

Objectives
- Evaluate autobiographical narratives
- Listen effectively
- Take part in group discussion

Identifying Sequence

Objectives covered in this workshop:

- Understand time and sequence
- Make connections from text to self
- Activate prior knowledge before reading

Identifying Sequence

Why Is It Important?

- Readers need to keep track of the order of events in order to fully comprehend the selection.
- Writers use several types of order and students need to understand the relevance of each form of sequencing.
- The form of sequencing a writer chooses to use can often point to the author's main idea and theme.
- Understanding sequencing can help students become better writers themselves.

How to Help Students Get It

- Help students learn signal words. Once students understand signal words, they will be able to quickly identify the form of sequencing a writer uses.
- Remind them that they are simply finding the logical order of ideas and events.
- Share different types of sequencing with students to help them understand their differences.

Reading to Answer the Big Question

From *Red Scarf Girl: A Memoir of the Cultural Revolution*
Ji-Li has a chance to try out for the national academy and possibly advance to a place in the Liberation Army. She is confident in her ability to perform well and achieve highly, but her father asks her to sacrifice the audition for political reasons. This moment in Ji-Li's life confuses her, but contributes to the person she will someday become.

Miracle Hands
When he was three years old, both of Woosik Chung's hands were cut off at his wrists. At the age of 28, he is studying to be a doctor. The surgical skill of his father and the discipline and training of his grandfather have helped Woosik Chung beat unbelievable odds and become a success.

Workshop Resources

Pacing (days) Standard	Block	Lesson	Student Materials	Teacher Resources
1		Key Skill Lesson: Identifying Sequence	Key Reading Skills Practice English Language Coach	Bellringer Options Transparencies Read Aloud, Think Aloud Transparencies Presentation Plus!
2		*from* Red Scarf Girl	Literary Analysis Transparencies Glencoe Online Selection Vocabulary Development Academic Vocabulary Development English Language Coach Active Reading Graphic Organizer Literary Analysis StudentWorks Plus Online Student Edition Literature Classics Selection and Unit Assessments	Literary and Text Analysis Transparencies Puzzlemaker Skill Level Up! BookLink 3 Assessment by Learning Objective (Diagnostic and Formative) Interactive Tutor Self-Assessment TeacherWorks Plus
2		"Miracle Hands"	Glencoe Online Selection Vocabulary Development Academic Vocabulary Development English Language Coach Active Reading Graphic Organizer Literary Analysis StudentWorks Plus Online Student Edition Literature Classics Selection and Unit Assessments	Literary and Text Analysis Transparencies Puzzlemaker Skill Level Up! BookLink 3 Assessment by Learning Objective (Diagnostic and Formative) Interactive Tutor Self-Assessment TeacherWorks Plus

Keys for Unit Resource

- Blackline Master
- Workbook
- Supplemental Text
- CD-ROM
- DVD
- Transparency
- Web-based
- Fast Files

Level Appropriate Code

AS = Activities for all students
AL = Activities for students working above grade level
OL = Activities for students working at grade level
BL = Activities for students working below grade level
EL = Activities for English language learners

Focus

BELLRINGER Options

Daily Language Practice Transparency

Focus Activity Say: All people experience important events that change their lives in some way. Name one important event that has happened in your life and tell how it changed your life. *(Responses will vary, but may include starting a new school or joining a club.)*

Teach

R Reading Skill

Understanding Sequence

Say: We use sequence to describe how things happened. Different forms of sequence work with different types of stories. For example, you might use order of importance if you wanted to describe the three most important events in your life. When might you use chronological or time order? *(Possible response: to tell your life story)* **OL** When might you use spatial order? *(Possible response: to describe your family home)* **AL**

READING WORKSHOP 4

Skills Focus

You will practice using the following skills when you read these selections:

- from *Red Scarf Girl: A Memoir of the Cultural Revolution*, p. 208
- "Miracle Hands," p. 218

Reading

- Identifying sequence

Literature

- Identifying and understanding setting in a narrative
- Identifying details that appeal to the senses

Vocabulary

- Understanding and using word references
- Academic Vocabulary: *sequence*

Writing/Grammar

- Subject and object pronouns

Objectives (pp. 204–205)
Reading Understand sequence: chronological order

Skill Lesson

Identifying Sequence

Learn It!

What Is It? The events in a person's life happen in a certain order, or **sequence,** and a biography or an autobiography usually follows that order. This kind of sequence is called "chronological order" or "time order." By describing events in the order they happened, the author can help readers see how a person grew and changed over time.

R Chronological order is not the only form of sequence. Two other major forms are:

- order of importance, which describes or discusses things from most to least important or from least to most
- spatial order, which describes or discusses things in the order in which they are arranged

In this section, you will focus on understanding chronological order.

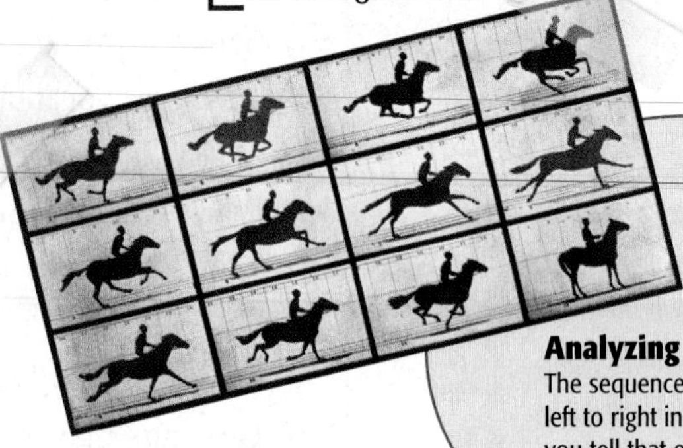

Analyzing Cartoons
The sequence of images goes from left to right in each row. How can you tell that each image was captured just a moment or two after the prior image?

Academic Vocabulary

sequence (SEE kwens) *n.* the order of events; the arrangement of things in time, space, or importance

Additional Support

Differentiated Instruction

Movie Storyboards Have students practice using sequence by retelling the events they recently saw in a movie. They should explain what happened in the order that it occurred, remembering to use words such as: before, during, after, first, next, while, and later. **BL**

Encourage students to draw sketches from scenes they have described. They may use one poster board per scene to create storyboards. Have them use the boards to tell their story. **OL**

Why Is It Important? Following the sequence of events can help you understand, recall, and summarize what you read.

- Thinking about what has happened so far helps you predict what may happen next.
- Remembering one event helps you remember events that came before and after it.
- Listing important events in chronological order gives you a quick summary of a person's life.

How Do I Do It? Usually, authors of biographies and autobiographies tell you the events as they happened—that is, in time order. Sometimes, though, a writer will present events out of order. Then you have to keep track of the actual order of events in time. Watch for signal words that show the order, such as *before, during, after, first, next, while,* and *later*.

C

Study Central Visit www.glencoe.com and click on Study Central to review understanding sequence.

We sat in the auditorium waiting for something to happen. After four hours of waiting to buy tickets, we were all impatient. When the doors had opened earlier, there had been a stampede for seats. Now we were in no mood to wait. We wanted the band to be onstage, and we wanted them there now.

They were already in the auditorium, so they already had the tickets. "After four hours" tells me that, and the narrator said that "the doors had opened earlier." The narrator was in the auditorium, thinking about what had happened earlier and waiting for what would happen next.

Practice It!

In this workshop, you'll follow events that change the lives of two people. To get started, ask yourself what might happen before and after each of these events. Write your ideas in your Learner's Notebook.

- A young girl is invited to join her country's national dance school.
- A young man decides to study medicine instead of trying out for the Olympics.

Use It!

As you read *Red Scarf Girl* and "Miracle Hands," keep in mind what you've learned about sequence. For each selection, write down the important events to help you remember the order in which they occurred.

Teach

Literature Online

Study Central Have students access the Web site to review understanding sequence and to complete a related activity.

C Critical Thinking

Comprehension Ask: What are three benefits of following the sequence of events? *(It helps you recall, understand, and summarize the events of a story.)* What kind of order is usually used in a biography or autobiography? *(time order)* **OL** Why might authors of biography and autobiography use this kind of order? *(Possible response: because they are telling the events of someone's life and it is easier for a reader to follow events in chronological order.)* **AL**

Resources for page 205

Use Reading Skills Transparency in *Read Aloud, Think Aloud,* Unit 2, to help students practice understanding sequence.

Literature Focus Lesson

Narrators Remind students that a narrator may be the main character, as in *Red Scarf Girl: A Memoir of the Cultural Revolution,* or it may be the author telling the story of the main character, as in "Miracle Hands." Have students tell short stories to a partner from a first-person point of view. Then have them tell the same story from a third-person point of view. **OL**

Ask students to evaluate the difference in the short stories told from two points of views. **AL**

Objectives

- Understand sequence: chronological order

Before You Read

from *Red Scarf Girl: A Memoir of the Cultural Revolution*

More About Ji-li Jiang

Because of her desire for Americans to better understand Chinese culture, Ji-li Jiang has given hundreds of speeches to children and adults about her books and life in China. In addition, she started her own company, East West Exchange, and leads Americans on cultural trips to her homeland. Jiang has said that "helping to bridge the gap between China and western countries is something I find fascinating, challenging, and rewarding."

V Vocabulary

Sample Sentences **Say:** After you write what you know about each vocabulary word, write a sample sentence using the word. This will help you remember the word's meaning. **AS**

Literature Online

Author Search To expand students' appeciation of Ji-li Jiang, have them access the Web site for additional information and resources.

Ji-li Jiang

Meet the Author

Ji-li Jiang came to the United States from Shanghai, China, in 1984. For more than twenty years, she nursed the memories of her childhood, and she brought them to life in *Red Scarf Girl*. She devotes her time to cultural exchange programs between the United States and China. She says, "Better understanding among people around the world is the route to peace."

Literature Online

Author Search For more about Ji-li Jiang, go to www.glencoe.com.

Objectives (pp. 206–213)
Reading Understand sequence: chronological order
Literature Identify literary elements: sensory details
Vocabulary Use word references: dictionary

Vocabulary Preview

tantalizing (TAN tuh ly zing) *adj.* desirable but just out of reach (**p. 208**) *We could hardly wait for the school day to end so we could play in the tantalizing sunshine.*

exemplary (eg ZEMP luh ree) *adj.* so good that it can serve as an example to others (**p. 208**) *In art class, Arlene's work was exemplary.*

contemplate (KON tem playt) *v.* to think about slowly and carefully (**p. 210**) *Before you act, take time to contemplate the possible results of your actions.*

solemnly (SAH lum lee) *adv.* very seriously (**p. 212**) *She spoke so solemnly that I was afraid something terrible had happened.*

V **Write to Learn** Copy the words into your Learner's Notebook. Next to each word, write what you already know about the word. If you don't know the word at all, write "I will learn this word by the end of the narrative." Then challenge yourself to learn the word.

English Language Coach

Using Word References Here are dictionary entries for two of the words you will read in the passage from *Red Scarf Girl*. As you read, watch for these words. Use context clues to choose the correct meanings.

flexible (FLEK suh bul) *adj* **1** able to bend or to be bent **2** easily adapting to new conditions or requirements

electric (i LEK trik) *adj* **1** having to do with or run by electricity **2** exciting or thrilling

Partner Talk With a partner, read these sentences. Talk about which definition of the underlined word makes sense in each sentence.

1. This watchband is made of soft, **flexible** plastic.
2. Her **electric** personality made everyone like her from the start.
3. Our picnic plans must be **flexible** because we can't predict the weather.
4. At the museum, we saw an early **electric** car.
5. Marti is always **flexible** because she never makes plans for herself.

Additional Support

Reading in the Real World

Citizenship The Cultural Revolution in China was a time of terror that lasted for ten years. Millions of people, particularly intellectuals and others who were thought to be against the revolution, were forced into "re-education camps," where they did hard labor in the countryside, or were executed.

Red Guards were young people in their teens and twenties who supported the revolution. They harassed anyone they believed to be a capitalist.

Ask students to list some things that could lead to a cultural revolution. *(Responses may include control of government, new thoughts, technology)* **AL**

Skills Preview

Key Reading Skill: Identifying Sequence

Before you read Ji-li Jiang's memoir, list the sequence of events of your typical day at school, using time order. What might happen to change the sequence? Write your thoughts in your Learner's Notebook.

Key Literary Element: Sensory Details

Artists use colors, shapes, and patterns to pull you into their paintings. Great cooks use ingredients and cooking methods to make food that smells great, looks appealing, tastes good, and has a pleasing texture.

Writers do the same thing with sensory details—details that appeal to the five senses. (The word *sensory* means "having to do with the senses.") Sensory language describes how things look, sound, feel, smell, or taste. Writers use sensory details to make their writing come alive and to help readers fully understand an event or a scene. **L**

As you read Ji-li Jiang's memoir, use these tips to help you see and understand the sensory details:

- Notice words that involve the senses of sight, hearing, taste, smell, and touch.

  What "sense words" does she use in the very first paragraph?
- Notice how these words call up very specific images and feelings.

  How does a "sweet breeze" feel and smell? Does "tender young grass" have a different scent than taller, older grass? How do these details affect the way you understand the story?

Literature Online

Interactive Literary Elements Handbook
To review or learn more about the literary elements, go to www.glencoe.com.

Get Ready to Read

Connect to the Reading

Have your parents ever warned you against doing something you really wanted to do? What did they understand that you didn't?

Write to Learn In your Learner's Notebook, write about a time your parents warned you against doing something and you didn't understand why.

Build Background

From 1966 to 1976, China went through a major change in its government and way of life, called the Cultural Revolution. It was begun by China's leader, Chairman Mao Zedong, to make communism in China "pure."

- Many older students became "Red Guards." These people supported the goals of the revolution.
- Younger students joined groups of "Young Pioneers." They wore red scarves as symbols of their support.
- Anyone suspected of not supporting the Cultural Revolution was punished. Thousands of people were tortured, jailed, forced into labor camps, or killed.
- At this time, people in China referred to each other as "Comrade" (KOM rad) instead of Mr., Mrs., or Miss.
- Since 1927, the name of China's army has been the People's Liberation Army.

C

Set Purposes for Reading

BIG Question Read the passage from *Red Scarf Girl* to find out why it will be hard for Jiang to become the person she wants to be.

Set Your Own Purpose What would you like to learn about Jiang's experiences that would help you answer the Big Question? Write your own purpose on the "Red Scarf Girl" page of your Foldable.

Keep Moving

Use these skills as you read the following selection.

Teach

L Literary Element

Sensory Details
Say: Describe the school cafeteria using each of the five senses. **OL** How might using all the senses help a reader imagine a scene? *(We use many different senses to take in a scene, so this information will help us imagine it.)* **AL**

C Critical Thinking

Comprehension Ask: Who were Red Guards and Young Pioneers? *(They were students who supported the cultural revolution.)* **BL** Based on what you've read about the cultural revolution, do you think students became Red Guards and Young Pioneers voluntarily? Why or why not? *(Anyone suspected of not supporting the revolution was punished, so some students probably did not join voluntarily.)* **AL**

CheckPoint

Use the CheckPoint questions on Presentation Plus! to build background. These questions can be used with interactive response keypads for immediate student feedback.

Literature Focus Lesson

Sensory Details Have students practice using sensory details by filling in the blanks in the following sentences with sensory details. Model the first sentence, and help students with other sentences as needed.

1. The ice cream tasted ____ and felt ____ in my mouth. *(sweet and creamy; cold)*
2. As I entered the construction site, I heard ____ and ____.
3. The mud felt ____ under my feet.
4. The sky looked ____ on the cold, snowy day.
5. The garbage smelled ____. **BL**

Objectives
- Make connections from self to text and activate prior knowledge before reading
- Understand sequence
- Identify sensory details
- Use word resources

Teach

C Critical Thinking

Comprehension Ask: According to the background on page 207, who wore red scarves to show support for the revolution? *(Young Pioneers)* BL What conclusion can you draw about the narrator based on the title? *(She is a Young Pioneer because she calls herself a "red scarf girl.")* AL

L Literary Element

Sensory Details Ask: Which senses does Ji-li Jiang appeal to in her description? Give examples of each. *(Sight: the picture of Mao, the slogan, the papers hanging; sound: the paper slogan rippling, the breeze rustling the papers; smell: the scent of new leaves)* OL

Readability Scores
Dale-Chall: 5.1
DRP: 52
Lexile: 760

from

RED SCARF GIRL:

A Memoir of the Cultural Revolution

by Ji-li Jiang

Chairman Mao, our beloved leader, smiled down at us from his place above the blackboard. The sounds and smells of the **tantalizing** May afternoon drifted in through the window. The sweet breeze carried the scent of new leaves and tender young grass and rippled the paper slogan below Chairman Mao's picture: STUDY HARD AND ADVANCE EVERY DAY. In the corner behind me the breeze also rustled the papers hanging from the Students' Garden, a beautifully decorated piece of cardboard that displayed **exemplary** work. One of them was my latest perfect math test. 1

We were having music class, but we couldn't keep our minds on the teacher's directions. We were all confused by the two-part harmony[1] of the Young Pioneers' Anthem. "We

1. ***Harmony*** is a combination of musical sounds; in two-part harmony, two people or groups sing or play together, but each sings or plays different notes.

Vocabulary

tantalizing (TAN tuh ly zing) *adj.* desirable but just out of reach

exemplary (eg ZEMP luh ree) *adj.* so good that it can serve as an example to others

Practice the Skills

1 Reviewing Skills

Connecting How is Jiang's classroom similar to your classroom? Yours almost certainly has a blackboard and a window. Does it have a picture of a national leader? Is there a sign with a slogan (a saying)? Are examples of students' work on display?

Additional Support

Literature Focus Lesson

Point of View Remind students that this is an autobiographical narrative, told from Ji-li Jiang's point of view. Ask students the following questions to consider how this point of view affects the story:

1. About how old is the narrator during this story?
2. How does the narrator feel about being chosen to try out?

Encourage students to pay attention to the point of view as they read autobiographical narratives. They should ask themselves how the narrator feels about his or her situation. What information do other characters have that the narrator does not? OL

READING WORKSHOP 4

are Young Pioneers, successors to Communism. Our red scarves flutter on our chests," we sang over and over, trying to get the timing right. The old black pump organ wheezed and squeaked as impatiently as we did. We made another start, but Wang Da-yong burst out a beat early, and the whole class broke into laughter.

Just then Principal Long appeared at the door. She walked in, looking less serious than usual, and behind her was a stranger, a beautiful young woman dressed in the People's Liberation Army uniform. A Liberation Army soldier! She was slim and stood straight as a reed. Her eyes sparkled, and her long braids, tied with red ribbons, swung at her waist. There was not a sound in the classroom as all forty of us stared at her in awe. **C**

Principal Long told us to stand up. The woman soldier smiled but did not speak. She walked up and down the aisles, looking at us one by one. When she finished, she spoke quietly with Principal Long. "Tong Chao and Jiang Ji-li," Principal Long announced. "Come with us to the gym." A murmur rose behind us as we left the room. Tong Chao looked at me and I looked at him in wonder as we followed the swinging braids. **2**

Practice the Skills

2 Key Literary Element

Sensory Details Notice the details Jiang uses to describe the soldier and the students' reaction to her. Do these sensory details give you a strong first impression of the soldier? **L**

Teach

Viewing the Illustration

Ask: What details from the story has the artist captured in this illustration? *(Possible responses: the picture of Mao, the students, the teacher)*

C Critical Thinking

Comprehension Ask: What detail tells you that the children admire and respect the soldier? *("all forty of us stared at her in awe")* **OL**

L Literary Element

Sensory Details Ask: Which details does Jiang use to describe the music class? *(the organ wheezed and squeaked; one student began singing early; the class laughed)* Which sense do these details appeal to most? *(sound)* **OL** Which details does Jiang use to describe the soldier? *(She uses sight details and describes her long braids, her beauty, and her smile.)* **BL**

Reading in the Real World

College Students who wish to attend college will need to refine their online research skills. Have students conduct online research to find two intriguing details about the People's Liberation Army, Chairman Mao, or the Cultural Revolution. Ask students to share what they find with the class. Remind them of these key points for online research:

- Refine your search by entering specific Boolean key words. For example, you might enter "Mao+Cultural+Revolution" to narrow your search.
- Use only trustworthy sites, such as education, government, and news media sites. **AL**

Objectives

- Identify sensory details
- Use critical thinking skills

Teach

EL Language Coach

Vocabulary Practice Say: Jiang lifts her head up over her head and can bend backward until she grabs her ankles. These are examples of being flexible. Can you think of another word for *flexible?* *(Possible response: bendy, stretchy, limber, supple)* **OL** Who besides martial artists and gymnasts might be called flexible? *(Possible response: dancers, yoga instructors)* **BL EL**

C Critical Thinking

Analysis Ask: Why can't Jiang concentrate when she goes back to class? *(She is curious about what the soldier wanted.)* **OL**

L Literary Element

Sensory Details Ask: What sensory details suggest Jiang is impressed by the soldier? *(Jiang remembers her soft touch and her beauty.)* **AL**

READING WORKSHOP 4

The gym was empty.

"I want to see how **flexible** you are. Let me lift your leg," the Liberation Army woman said in her gentle voice. She raised my right leg over my head in front of me. "Very good! Now I'll support you. Lean over backward as far as you can." That was easy. I bent backward until I could grab my ankles like an acrobat. "That's great!" she said, and her braids swung with excitement. **3**

"This is Jiang Ji-li."[2] Principal Long leaned forward proudly. "She's been studying martial arts[3] since the second grade. She was on the Municipal Children's Martial Arts Team. Their demonstration was even filmed."

The Liberation Army woman smiled sweetly. "That was very good. Now you may go back to your classroom." She patted me on my head before she turned back to test Tong Chao.

I went back to class, but I could not remember the song we were singing. What did the Liberation Army woman want? Could she want to choose me for something? It was too much to **contemplate**. I hardly moved when the bell rang to end school. Someone told me that the principal wanted to see me. I walked slowly down the hall, surrounded by my shouting and jostling[4] classmates, seeing only the beautiful soldier, feeling only the **electric** tingle of her soft touch on my head. **4**

The office door was heavy. I pushed it open cautiously. Some students from the other sixth-grade classes were there already. I recognized Wang Qi, a girl in class two, and one of the boys, You Xiao-fan of class four. I didn't know the other boy. The three of them sat nervously and respectfully opposite Principal Long. I slipped into a chair next to them.

2. In some Asian countries, the family name is said first. So ***Jiang*** is the author's "last" name, and ***Ji-li*** is her "first" name. If Americans followed the same rule, John Smith would introduce himself as "Smith John."
3. ***Martial*** (MAR shul) means "of or about war; warlike." The ***martial arts*** are forms of fighting such as judo and karate. They're also popular as forms of exercise.
4. ***Jostling*** people push and elbow each other because they are crowded together.

Vocabulary

contemplate (KON tem playt) *v.* to think about slowly and carefully

Practice the Skills

3 English Language Coach

Using Word References Look at the definitions on page 206. Use the context around the word **flexible** to choose the right definition for this sentence. Notice what Jiang does for the Liberation Army woman.

4 English Language Coach

Using Word References Look at the definitions on page 206. Use the context around the word **electric** to choose the right definition for this sentence. Notice that it describes a feeling.

A People's Liberation Army officer

Additional Support

Differentiated Instruction

"I Am" Poem Have students create an "I Am" poem that describes Jiang. Tell students to scan the narrative, looking for words and phrases that describe Jiang's personality, talents, hopes, and dreams. Then have them write the "I Am" poem by starting each line with the words *I am* and telling something about Jiang, for example, "I am a talented martial artist." The last line of the poem will be "I am Ji-li Jiang." Have students write their poems on large poster boards for all the class to see. Have them cut the board in the shape of a red scarf or another symbol that represents Jiang's life. **OL**

READING WORKSHOP 4

Principal Long leaned forward from her big desk. "I know you must be wondering about the Liberation Army soldier," she said. She sounded cheerful and excited. "Why did she come? Why did she want you to do back bends?" She looked at us one by one and then took a long sip from her tea mug as if she wanted to keep us guessing. "She was Comrade Li from the Central Liberation Army Arts Academy."

I slowly took a deep breath.

"She is recruiting[5] students for the dance training class. She selected you four to audition. It's a great honor for Xin Er Primary School. I'm very proud of all of you, and I know you'll do your best."

I did not hear the rest of her words. I saw myself in a new Liberation Army uniform, slim and standing straight as a reed, long braids swinging at my waist. A Liberation Army soldier! One of the heroes admired by all, who helped Chairman Mao liberate China from oppression[6] and defeated the Americans in Korea. And a performer, just like my mother used to be, touring the country, the world, to tell everyone about the New China that Chairman Mao had built and how it was becoming stronger and stronger.

I couldn't help giving Wang Qi a silly smile. **5**

"Mom! Dad! Grandma!" I panted up the steep, dark stairs, in too much of a hurry to turn on the light, and tripped over some pots stored on the steps. I couldn't wait to tell them my news. I knew they would all be as excited as I was. **6**

Our apartment was bright and warm and welcoming. Burgundy curtains shut the darkness outside and made the one big room even cozier. In front of the tall French window our square mahogany table was covered with steaming dishes and surrounded by my family, who were laughing and chattering when I rushed in. They all looked up expectantly.

"Everybody, guess what! Today a Liberation Army woman came to school and she tested me and she wants me to audition for the Central Liberation Army Arts Academy. Just think! I could be in the Liberation Army! And I could be a

5. In ***recruiting*** students, she's trying to get them to join.

6. People suffer from ***oppression*** when a person or group limits or takes away their freedoms.

During the Cultural Revolution, students had to study this book, *Quotations from Mao Zedong*, also known as the "Little Red Book."

Practice the Skills

5 BIG Question

At the end of this part of the memoir, who does Jiang want to be? How does she describe her goal? What do you think she would have to do to achieve it? Discuss this with a partner. Then write your answer on the "Red Scarf Girl" page of your Foldable.

6 **Reviewing Skills**

Connecting Can you think of a time when you were as excited as Jiang is here?

Teach

L1 Literary Element

Review Setting Ask: How has the setting changed in the story? *(The setting has changed from Jiang's school to her home.)* **BL**

L2 Literary Element

Sensory Details Ask: What details does Jiang give about her home? *(She describes its appearance: it is bright with burgundy curtains and a French window and a table covered with dishes.)* **OL**
What do these details suggest about the time of day it is? *(It is dinner time. Everyone is sitting around a table.)* **AL**

Reading Fluency

Build Fluency Have students find a quiet place to practice reading aloud portions of the passage. Tell them to reread the portions several times until they can read smoothly all the sentences with expression and understanding. Tell students to use intonation and rate of speech to make their reading sound like natural speech. **EL** **BL**

Objectives
- Make connections from self to text
- Understand sequence
- Identify sensory details
- Use context to guess meaning of words

READING WORKSHOP 4

Teach

R1 Reading Skill

Understanding Sequence

Say: Write the order of sequence in your Learner's Notebook. Why do you think Jiang tells the story in this order? *(Possible response: She tells the events in the order that they happen so readers follow the story in order.)*

R2 Reading Skill

Review Connecting

Ask: How would you feel if you were Jiang and your father told you not to audition? *(Students might note they would be very upset and disappointed.)* BL

performer, too! Isn't it great?" I picked up our cat, Little White, and gave her a big kiss. 7

"It's lucky I studied martial arts for so long. When the Liberation Army woman saw my back bend, she just loved it." I twirled around on my toes and snapped my heels together in a salute. "Comrade Grandma, Jiang Ji-li reporting!" R1

My younger brother, Ji-yong, jumped up from the table and saluted me. My little sister, Ji-yun, started to twirl around as I had done, but she slipped and fell. We jumped to the floor with her and rolled around together.

"Ji-li," I heard Dad call. I looked up. Mom and Dad and Grandma were looking at each other **solemnly**. "It might be better not to do the audition." Dad spoke slowly, but his tone was serious, very serious. R2

"What?"

"Don't do the audition, Ji-li." He looked straight at me this time, and sounded much more forceful.

"Don't do the audition? Why not?"

Dad shook his head.

I grabbed Mom's arm. "Mom, why not?"

She squeezed my hand and looked at me worriedly. "Your father means that the recruitment requirements are very strict."

"Wow. You really scared me, Dad." I laughed with relief. "I know that. Principal Long told us it would be very competitive. I know it's just an audition, but who knows? I might be lucky, right?" I picked up a steamed bun and took a bite.

"I'm not just talking about talent," Dad said. "There are more important requirements, political considerations . . ."

"Oh, Dad, that's no problem." I took another big bite of the bun. I was an Outstanding Student, and Excellent Young Pioneer, and even the *da-dui-zhang*, the student chairman of the whole school. What more could they want? My mouth

Practice the Skills

7 Key Reading Skill

Identifying Sequence Jiang briefly tells the sequence of events so far. How does one event lead to the next?

Young Pioneers reading from Mao's "Little Red Book" in 1968

Vocabulary

solemnly (SAWL um lee) *adv.* very seriously

Additional Support

Literature Focus Lesson

Dialogue Remind students that they can tell when a character is speaking because writers enclose dialogue (characters' speech) in quotation marks. Sometimes they include dialogue tags, such as "he said" or "I wailed" to show who is talking. Other times, readers have to use context to tell who is talking. Have students point out who is talking in the dialogue on page 212. One option is to photocopy the page and have students create their own dialogue tags to indicate who is talking. AS

READING WORKSHOP 4

was full, so I stretched out my arm to show Dad my *da-dui-zhang* badge, a plastic tag with three red stripes.

I saw a pain in Dad's eyes that I had never seen before.

"The problem isn't with you yourself, Ji-li. What I mean is that the political background investigations at these academies are very severe."

"Political background investigation? What's that?"

"That is an investigation into the class status of your ancestors and all members of your family." He leaned back in his chair, and the lampshade put his face in shadow. "Ji-li, the fact is that our family will not be able to pass these investigations," he said slowly. "And you will not be allowed to be a member of a Liberation Army performing troupe."

For a long time I did not speak. "Why?" I whispered at last.

He started to say something but stopped. He leaned forward again, and I could see the sorrow on his face. "It's very complicated, and you wouldn't understand it now even if I told you. Maybe we should wait until you're grown up. The point is that I don't think you'll be admitted. So just drop it, all right?"

I did not say anything. Putting down the half-eaten bun, I walked to the mirror on the big wardrobe that divided the room and pressed my forehead against its cool surface. I could not hold back any longer. I burst out crying. **8**

"I want to do it. I want to try. What will I tell Principal Long? And my classmates?" I wailed.

"Maybe we should let her try. She probably won't be chosen anyway." Grandma looked at Dad.

Dad stood up, heaving a deep sigh. "This is for her own good. Her classmates and teachers will just be surprised if she says that her father won't let her go. But what if she passes the audition and can't pass the political background investigation? Then everybody will know that the family has a political problem." Dad's voice grew louder and louder as he went on. **R**

Ji-yong and Ji-yun were looking up at Dad, wide-eyed. I bit my lip to force myself to stop myself to stop crying and went to bed without saying another word. **9** ❍

Practice the Skills

8 **Key Literary Element**

Sensory Details Is Jiang's sensory language effective here? Does it help you to know, or remember, how it feels to press your face against a cool surface?

9 BIG Question

Why is Jiang so disappointed? Remember how she felt after she first heard about auditioning. **BQ** Do you think she can overcome the political problem to become who she wants to be? Write your answers on the "Red Scarf Girl" page of your Foldable.

Teach

R Reading Skill

Review Inferring Ask: How do you know that Jiang's father has her best interest at heart? *(He says it will be better for her if people just think her father wouldn't let her try out, rather than that she failed the political background investigation.)* **OL**

BQ 

Say: What might Jiang tell you about becoming the kind of person you want to be? Think about the story and about the author bio on page 206. *(Possible response: Sometimes you have to give up on certain opportunities, but other opportunities will come your way. Jiang is now a famous writer and speaker.)* **AS**

Assess

Use the CheckPoint questions provided on Presentation Plus! to check students' mastery of the selection. These questions can be used with interactive response keypads for immediate student feedback.

Differentiated Instruction

Acting Some students may enjoy acting out the dinner scene at Jiang's apartment. Have students form groups of six and assign the roles of Jiang, her father, mother, grandmother, and younger brother and sister. Then have students role play the action and dialogue in the scene. Tell them they can either read the dialogue from the textbook or make up their own dialogue, as long as they stay true to the content of the scene. Encourage students to use their voices, facial expressions, and body language to express the characters' thoughts and feelings. **OL**

Objectives
- Make connections from self to text
- Understand sequence
- Identify sensory details
- Make inferences

READING WORKSHOP 4

Assess

Resources for page 214

- Selection Quick Check
- Selection and Unit Assessment
- ExamView Assessment Suite
- Interactive Tutor: Self-Assessment

Students can respond to the *After You Read* items in their Learner's Notebook or on a separate sheet of paper.

Answering the

1. Responses will vary. Students might note that they would be disappointed.
2. The students were laughing because Wang Da-yong started singing early.

Critical Thinking

3. They were taught to have great respect for Communists and for the People's Liberation Army.
4. Possible response: She was in good shape physically and a good scholar.
5. She showed how flexible she was.
6. Her study of martial arts prepared her for the test in the gym.

After You Read

from *Red Scarf Girl: A Memoir of the Cultural Revolution*

Answering the

1. After reading Jiang's story, how would you react if an obstacle prevented you from becoming who you want to be?
2. **Recall** What happened in Jiang's class just before Principal Long appeared at the door?
   TIP Right There You will find the answer in the memoir.

Critical Thinking

3. **Infer** Why did all the students show great respect and admiration for the Liberation Army soldier?
   TIP Author and Me You will find clues in the memoir, but you must also use what you know. Ask yourself whose picture hung in the classroom and what the Young Pioneers' Anthem said.
4. **Infer** What made the Liberation Army soldier choose Jiang?
   TIP Author and Me She may have had more than one reason.
5. **Summarize** What happened during Jiang's test in the gym?
   TIP Think and Search You must use information from the article and decide what the important events were.
6. **Synthesize** How have Jiang's past experiences prepared her for this moment?
   TIP Author and Me Answer based on the text.

Talk About Your Reading

Literature Groups In your group, discuss what happens at the end of this story after Jiang tells her family about her chance to audition for the Liberation Army performing troupe. Answer the following questions in your group and have one group member record your answers.

1. What does Jiang's father say about her auditioning?
2. What is his reason for responding as he does?
3. What does this tell you about life in China for some people during the Cultural Revolution?

Share your answers with the class.

Objectives (pp. 214–215)
Reading Understand sequence: chronological order • Make connections from text to self, text to text, and text to world
Literature Identify literary elements: sensory details
Grammar Identify and use subject pronouns

Talk About Your Reading

1. Jiang's father tells her not to audition.
2. Her father doesn't want the academy to investigate his family's background.
3. Possible response: Life in China was very hard and limiting for some people during the Cultural Revolution.

Comparing Literature: Setting

Objectives covered in this workshop:

- Connect, compare, and contrast setting across texts
- Find similarities and differences across texts

Teaching Students to Compare Settings

Why Is It Important?

- Comparing settings helps students learn the significance of the "when" and the "where" of selections.
- Comparing settings helps students pay more attention to specific details.
- Looking at the settings from two different types of genres helps students make connections from text to text.

How to Help Students Get It

- Have students keep track of the settings' details as they read (see chart on page 223).
- Tell students to think about how the setting helps support the theme and main idea of each selection.
- Remind students to look for the details that point to "where" and the "when" in the selections.

Reading to Answer the Big Question

From Barrio Boy

Ernesto arrives at his new school in California speaking only Spanish and unsure of how he will be received. He finds a staff energetically devoted to teaching students from many different backgrounds to be good citizens and tolerant human beings. They teach each child to feel proud of being an American without being ashamed of their heritage. Ernesto's process of becoming is supported by the accepting attitudes of his new school.

How I Learned English

A neighborhood game of baseball provides the narrator of this poem with practice in sports and vocabulary, but mainly in community. Moving from a stranger to one of the guys can happen in a single afternoon.

Skills Review

Key Reading Skill: Identifying Sequence

6. In your Learner's Notebook, make a time line of the important events in the article.

Key Literary Element: Sensory Details

7. What sensory details does the author use to describe Chung's accident?

Reviewing Elements: Title and Subtitles

8. The title can help you recall the important events in an article. Which events in "Miracle Hands" have to do with hands? Which events have to do with what seems like a miracle? Support your answers with examples from the article.

Vocabulary Check

Copy each sentence, filling in the correct word.

desperate discipline

9. I wonder if I have the ___ to train for a marathon.
10. Lost in the desert, they became ___ for water.

English Language Coach Write the answers to these questions.

11. What are curious children likely to do if you give them a closed box?
12. What are three ways people can exercise their limbs?

Web Activities For eFlashcards, Selection Quick Checks, and other Web activities, go to www.glencoe.com.

Grammar Link: Object Pronouns

- You'll learn what "objects" are later on in this book. Then the term "object pronouns" will make sense. For now, though, you need to know one thing: Object pronouns are the personal pronouns that aren't used as subjects.

Object Pronouns	
Singular	*Plural*
me, you, her, him, it	us, you, them

A nightmare awakened **him.**
Will someone give **her** and **me** a ride?

- It's easy to use object pronouns correctly when they are alone, without a noun or other pronoun being used in the same way. You would never say, "Matt was teasing I."
- You must also use object pronouns when a noun or another pronoun is being used in the same way in a sentence.

Wrong: Matt was teasing Will and I.
Right: Matt was teasing Will and me.

Wrong: The test seemed hard to her and I.
Right: The test seemed hard to her and me.

- If you wonder what the correct object pronoun is, get rid of the extra person (or people) in your mind.

Sample: They spoke to ~~Bianca and~~ (I? me?).

Since you would never say "They spoke to I," you should use "me" in this sentence.

Grammar Practice

Rewrite each sentence, using the correct pronoun in parentheses.

13. Please give Sandy and (I, me) a chance.
14. Are the sandwiches for Bill or (they, them)?
15. Guess what happened to Paul and (I, me)!

Writing Application Review your Write About Your Reading activity. Make sure you used object pronouns correctly.

Skills Review

Key Reading Skill: Understanding Sequence

6. Students should include these events: Chung loses his hands; Chung's father reattaches his hands; Chung's grandfather helps him learn to reuse his hands; Chung goes to Yale; Chung is a tae kwon do champ; Chung goes to medical school and gets to use a scalpel; Chung decides to become a hand surgeon.

Key Literary Element: Sensory Details

7. They describe how things look—"blades cut off both his hands at the wrists."

Reviewing Elements: Title and Subtitles

8. Responses may include: Chung's hands were cut off, and now he uses his hands to help others. The fact that Chung can use his hands seems like a miracle.

Vocabulary Check

9. I wonder if I have the discipline to train for a marathon.
10. Lost in the desert, they became desperate for water.
11. Curious children are likely to open a closed box.
12. Responses may include: running, walking, lifting weights, etc.

Grammar Link: Object Pronouns

Grammar Practice

13. Please give Sandy and me a chance.
14. Are the sandwiches for Bill or them?
15. Guess what happened to Paul and me!

Close

Ask students what they learned from the selection to help them answer the Big Question.

Assess

Resources for page 220

- Selection Quick Check
- Selection and Unit Assessment
- ExamView Assessment Suite
- Interactive Tutor: Self-Assessment

Students can respond to the *After You Read* items in their Learner's Notebook or on a separate sheet of paper.

Answering the BIG Question

1. Responses will vary.
2. He performed a surgery to reattach Chung's hands.

Critical Thinking

3. Responses may include: It happened during his first year in medical school (much later than the events described in the next paragraph).
4. Even though Chung loses the use of his hands for a while, he learns martial arts and becomes dedicated to helping others.
5. Possible response: He probably chose medical school because he wanted to help people.

After You Read

Miracle Hands

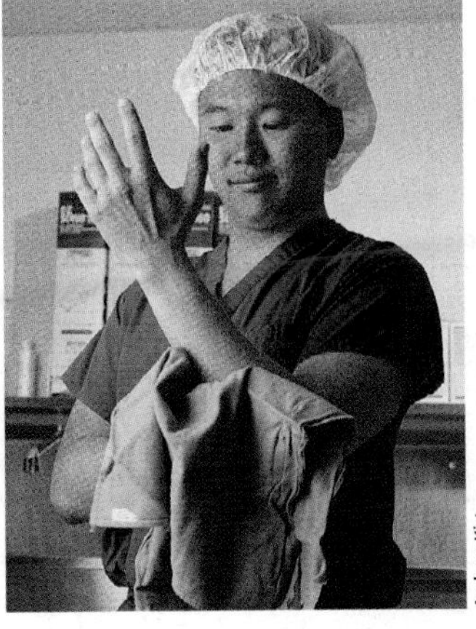

Andrew Kist

Answering the BIG Question

1. Woosik Chung overcame a great challenge that could have stopped him from becoming who he wanted to be. Can you think of any challenge that now stands in your way of becoming who you want to be? How can you overcome it?
2. **Recall** What did Chung's father do after bringing Chung to the hospital?

   TIP **Right There** You will find the answer in the article.

Critical Thinking

3. **Infer** In the first paragraph of the article, a surgeon hands Chung a scalpel. When did that happen?

   TIP **Think and Search** You will find clues in the story, but you must also use what you know. Ask yourself where medical school belongs in the sequence of events in Chung's life.
4. **Summarize** How does Chung's life show us that good things can come from bad situations?

   TIP **Author and Me** You must use information from the article and from your own experiences.
5. **Analyze** Why do you think Chung chose medical school over the Olympics?

   TIP **Author and Me** Answer based on the text and on your own thoughts.

Write About Your Reading

Imagine that you are Chung during the years immediately after his accident. Write a few paragraphs describing how you felt

- while you were recovering from your operation.
- when you learned you couldn't move your hands.
- when you were first able to use your hands again.

Write your paragraphs in first-person point of view and be sure to include sensory details to help your readers understand how you felt.

Objectives (pp. 220–221)
Reading Understand sequence: chronological order
Literature Identify literary elements: sensory details
Grammar Identify and use object pronouns

Write About Your Reading

Possible response:
I was so scared when the doctors took my casts off my hands. I could not move my hands, and the doctors looked really puzzled. My mom cried. My dad told me not to worry. My grandfather worked with me every day. He taught me exercises that helped my hands. It hurt to do the exercises at first. But after a while, the pain wasn't as bad and I could move my hands a little. Within a few years, I could use my hands to do everything I needed them to do. I was so happy. I will never touch an engine's fan again.

READING WORKSHOP 4

doctors available who specialized in reattaching **limbs**. So Chung's father, John, an army surgeon, reattached Woosik's hands himself in a nine-hour operation. "I had never completed a surgery like that," says John. "But I was **desperate**. I prayed and did my best." 4

His best, it turns out, was first-rate. It didn't seem that way, however, when the doctors removed Chung's casts two months later. The young boy couldn't move his hands. No one knew if Chung would ever regain the use of them.

But a couple of years later, Chung was able to move his hands, eventually regaining full use of them. For that, Chung thanks his grandfather, a tae kwon do grand master who used this martial art as his grandson's physical therapy.[2] Chung says his grandfather taught him the **discipline** he needed to practice several hours a day.

R When Chung was 14, his family moved to the United States. After high school, he went to Yale University, where he earned a degree and was also a tae kwon do champ, ranking second in the U.S. He considered trying out for the 2000 Olympics but chose instead to study medicine. "When he told me," says his father, "I was very happy." 5

When he finishes his five-year program, Chung knows exactly what he wants to be: a hand surgeon. "The best way I can thank my dad," says Chung, "is to help others in similar situations." 6

–Updated 2005, from *People*, July 14, 2003

Andrew Kist

"My strength came from my grandfather teaching me tae kwon do," says Chung.

4 English Language Coach

Using Word References Use the definitions on page 216 and the context around the word **limbs** to figure out the right definition in this paragraph.

5 Key Reading Skill

Identifying Sequence
Look back at this paragraph. What signal words help you follow the sequence of events here?

6 BIG Question

BQ Judging from this article, do you think Chung is willing to work to achieve goals? Pair up to discuss. Then write your answer on the "Miracle Hands" page of your Foldable.

2. Like karate and judo, ***tae kwon do*** is a ***martial art***. All three are forms of fighting and exercise. ***Physical therapy*** exercises help a person recover from an illness, injury, or surgery.

Vocabulary

desperate (DES pur ut) *adj.* so needy as to be willing to try anything

discipline (DIS uh plin) *n.* control of behavior, especially self-control

Teach

R Reading Skill

Review Inferring Ask: Why do you think Chung didn't choose to both try out for the Olympics and study medicine? *(Responses may include that both would take a lot of focus and discipline, and Chung decided he'd prefer to put his energy into something that would help others.)*

BQ BIG Question

What advice would Chung give others about achieving their goals? *(Possible response: He might tell them to be patient. He might say that sometimes we have to go through something terrible before we can achieve our goals.)*

English Language Coach

The Language of Medicine Have students write in their notebooks these words related to medicine from the article. Have them look up definitions of unfamiliar words.

surgeon
scalpel
operation
reattached
hospital
casts
physical therapy

After students have defined the words, have them use each in a sentence. EL

Objectives

- Understand time sequence
- Recognize sensory details
- Use word references to understand the meanings of words
- Draw conclusions based on information in a text

Teach

EL Language Coach

Context Clues Show students how to use the context around *curious* to find out what the word means. **Ask:** What does Chung do while playing hide-and-go seek with his friends? *(He touches the fan of the tractor's engine.)* Why do you think a child might do something like this? *(because he wonders what it feels like)* Now that you've thought about his reasons for touching it, what do you think is the meaning of *curious*? *(inquisitive, wanting to know something)* EL BL

C Critical Thinking

Comprehension Ask: What does Chung's father do as soon as he sees the accident? *(He fills up a bucket with ice and runs to his son.)* OL What conclusion can you draw about Chung's father based on his actions? *(You can conclude that he thinks quickly and that he knows something about medicine because he gets the ice.)* AL

Readability Scores
Dale-Chall: 6.2
DRP: 58
Lexile: 920

READING WORKSHOP 4

TIME

Miracle HANDS

Woosik Chung's hands were cut off when he was 3. Now he's becoming a surgeon.

By CHRISTINA CHEAKALOS and MATT BIRKBECK

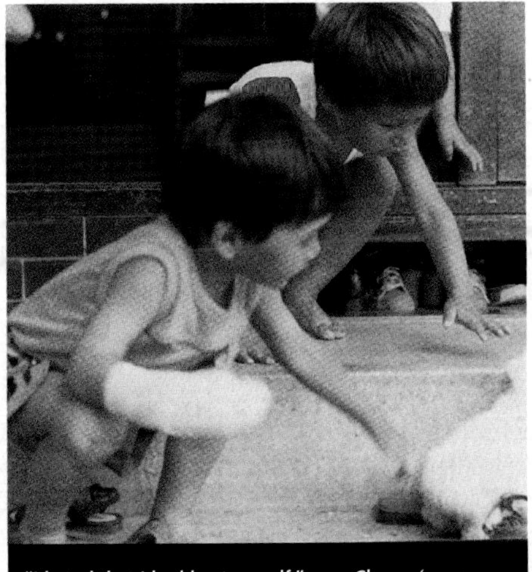

"I hated that I had hurt myself," says Chung (near Seoul, South Korea after the accident).

Courtesy John Chung

When Woosik Chung was in his first year of medical school, a surgeon handed him a scalpel[1] to make a cut during a knee operation. "It was quite a rush," says Chung, 28. "At that moment, I understood that using my hands as a surgeon was an honor and a privilege."

In Chung's case, that moment was very close to a miracle. When he was 3 years old, both his hands were cut off in an accident. Then, in a risky operation, they were successfully reattached.

Chung's against-all-odds story started in 1978 as he played hide-and-seek with friends in a town in South Korea. Ducking behind a tractor, the **curious** little boy reached out to touch the moving fan of the tractor's engine. **1** In a split second, the fan blades cut off both his hands at the wrists. **2**

C Chung's horrified father saw the accident from his apartment window. He and his wife filled a bucket with ice and frantically ran to their screaming son. Both of his hands lay on the ground. **3**

The boy's parents carried him to a hospital just blocks away. Since it was a national holiday, there weren't any

1. A *scalpel* is a small, very sharp knife used in surgery.

1 English Language Coach

EL **Using Word References** Use the definitions on page 216 and context to choose the right definition for **curious** in this paragraph.

2 Key Reading Skill

Identifying Sequence Events are shown out of time order on this page. What event on this page really came first in Chung's life? How do you know?

3 Key Literary Element

Sensory Details Which details give you a sense of how serious the accident was?

Additional Support

Differentiated Instruction

Time Order Tell students that the writers do not use a strict chronological, or time, order to tell the events of Chung's life. To ensure students understand the order of events in this article, have them place the following events in the order in which they happened.

1. Chung makes a cut during a knee operation in his first year of medical school.
2. Chung loses his hands in an accident.
3. Chung's father reattaches his hands.
4. Chung's grandfather helps him regain use of his hands.

(Answers: 2, 3, 4, 1.) OL

Skills Preview

Key Reading Skill: Identifying Sequence

Before you read the article, think about how accidents happen. In what way is every accident the result of a sequence of events? Write your thoughts in your Learner's Notebook.

As you read the following selection, "Miracle Hands," watch for signal words that help you follow the sequence of events.

Key Literary Element: Sensory Details

Sensory language describes how things look, sound, feel, smell, or taste. In this magazine story, a boy is terribly injured in an accident. The sensory details can help you understand his physical and emotional feelings.

As you read this article, use these tips to help you notice the sensory details:

- Look for words and phrases that appeal to your sense of sight, smell, touch, taste, or hearing.
  Look for all the sensory details on the first page of the article. How do these sensory details help you understand what Chung went through after his accident?
- Notice that sometimes a sensory detail will bring together two or more senses.
  How does combining details that appeal to different senses help you experience Chung's ordeal even more strongly?
- Look at which sensory details have the most effect on you.
  Ask yourself how Chung's experiences and the article's sensory details connect to your own experiences.

Get Ready to Read

Connect to the Reading

"Curiosity killed the cat." What does that old saying mean? Sometimes our curiosity causes us to do things we shouldn't, like listening in on someone else's conversation or opening a box we shouldn't. When has your curiosity gotten you into trouble or into an embarrassing situation?

Write to Learn In your Learner's Notebook, quickwrite about a time when your curiosity "got the best of you"—a time when you felt you just had to find out about something. Tell how you felt.

Build Background

During the time that is covered in "Miracle Hands," Woosik Chung's family lived in three widely separated parts of the world.

- They first lived in South Korea, which is in Asia, near China and Japan.
- Next they moved to Malawi, a small African nation.
- Finally, they came to the United States, where Chung still lives today.

Set Purposes for Reading

Read "Miracle Hands" to find out about the childhood accident that put difficulties in Chung's way and to find out how, with the help of his father, mother, and grandfather, he became the person he wanted to be.

Set Your Own Purpose What more would you like to learn about Chung's experiences that would help you answer the Big Question? Write your own purpose on the "Miracle Hands" page of your Foldable.

Literature Online

Interactive Literary Elements Handbook
To review or learn more about the literary elements, go to www.glencoe.com.

Reading in the Real World

College Students may be intrigued to learn that leeches, bloodsucking aquatic animals, have been used for centuries to draw blood from human patients. This may sound like something that would never happen today, but in fact, leeches are still used in modern hospitals, especially during some reattachment surgeries like the one Woosik Chung underwent. Have students do research to find out why the FDA has approved leeches for modern medical uses. When are they used? Why are they more effective than other techniques? Students should present their findings to the class. AL

Teach

C Critical Thinking

Analysis Tell students that accidents are the result of one thing causing another. However, just because one event follows another does not mean there is a cause-and-effect relationship between the two. For example, it might rain after you water the yard, but watering the yard didn't cause the rain. Have students pay attention to the events in the article. Which events cause other events? Which events simply follow other events? AL

Use the CheckPoint questions provided on Presentation Plus! to check students understanding of sequence and to build background. These questions can be used with interactive response keypads for immediate student feedback.

Literature Online

Interactive Literary Elements Handbook Have students access the Web site to improve their understanding of sensory details.

Objectives

- Understand sequence: chronological order
- Identify literary elements: sensory details
- Use word references: dictionary
- Use context clues: multiple-meaning words

Teach

More About the Selection

Staying true to his desire to help others, Woosik Chung is currently completing his residency at Columbia University Department of Orthopaedic Surgery. Orthopaedics is the branch of surgery concerned with the skeleton, or with bones. Training in this field will help Chung become a hand doctor.

V Vocabulary

Vocabulary Quiz Ask students these questions to check their understanding of the vocabulary definitions:

1. Would you be **desperate** if:
   a. you really needed something?
   b. you had everything you needed?
2. Does it require more **discipline** to:
   a. play with your friends after school?
   b. practice the piano every day?

Before You Read Miracle Hands

Meet the Authors

Christina Cheakalos is an award-winning writer who lives in the New York area. Matt Birkbeck, a resident of Pennsylvania, is an award-winning investigative journalist who has written for the *New York Times, People, Reader's Digest*, and the *Philadelphia Inquirer*.

Author Search For more about Christina Cheakalos and Matt Birkbeck, go to www.glencoe.com.

Objectives (pp. 216–219)
Reading Understand sequence: chronological order
Literature Identify literary elements: sensory details
Vocabulary Use word references: dictionary • Use context clues: multiple-meaning words

Vocabulary Preview

desperate (DES pur ut) *adj.* so needy as to be willing to try anything **(p. 219)** *With our team behind by sixteen points, the coach became desperate.*

discipline (DIH suh plin) *n.* control of behavior, especially self-control **(p. 219)** *Getting your homework done every day requires discipline.*

Write to Learn For each vocabulary word, write a sentence in your Learner's Notebook using the word correctly. Then list other words you know that relate to the vocabulary word.

V

English Language Coach

Using Word References Here are dictionary entries for two multiple-meaning words that you will read in "Miracle Hands." As you read, watch for these words. If you are unsure of the word's meaning in the selection, use context clues to choose the correct meanings.

curious (kyo͝or ′ ē əs) *adj.* **1** actively wanting to learn or to know; **2** strange, unusual, odd

limb (lim) *n.* **1** an extended part of an animal's body, usually used for movement or grasping; **2** a large branch of a tree

Partner Talk With a partner, read these sentences. Talk about which definition of the underlined word makes sense in each sentence.

1. At sunset, we saw a **curious** green light in the sky.
2. Turtles can pull their **limbs** into their shells.
3. I'm becoming very **curious** about the people who moved in next door.
4. A crew began cutting **limbs** that were too close to the power lines.
5. My little sister has a **curious** way of dressing.
6. To avoid frostbite, make sure your head and **limbs** are covered when you go out in very cold weather.
7. When the wind blows, that **limb** scrapes against the roof and makes a terrible, frightening sound.
8. I am not at all **curious** about that topic.

Additional Support

Author Search To expand students' appreciation of these authors, have them access the Web site for additional information.

Differentiated Instruction

Sensory Game Ask students to form small groups, and tell them each to think of a place they have been (such as a fair or a restaurant). Have students take turns describing the place using sensory words, but make sure students answer these questions in the following order:

1. What can you feel?
2. What can you taste?
3. What can you smell?
4. What can you hear?
5. What can you see?

Have group members make guesses after the student answers each question. BL EL

Skills Review

Key Reading Skill: Identifying Sequence

7. List three important events from the narrative in the order in which they happened.

Key Literary Element: Sensory Details

Identify the sense or senses that each detail appeals to.

8. The old black pump organ wheezed and squeaked
9. the electric tingle of her soft touch on my head
10. pressed my forehead against its cool surface

Reviewing Skills: Connecting

11. Think about how this story connects with
    - your own experiences
    - something else you've read or seen on TV or at the movies
    - something you know about the world in general

Write a short paragraph about one of these connections from the text to yourself, to another text, or to the world.

Vocabulary Check

Choose the best word from the list to complete each sentence below. Rewrite each sentence, putting the correct word in the blank.

tantalizing exemplary contemplate

12. Being chosen for something special was too much for Jiang to ___.
13. Jiang and her classmates found the May air ___.
14. In one part of the classroom there was a place to display ___ work done by the students.
15. **Academic Vocabulary** How did the sequence of events of Jiang's school day affect her mood there and at home?
16. **English Language Coach** What would a **flexible** tree branch do in the wind?
17. **English Language Coach** How might an audience respond to an **electric** performance?

Grammar Link: Subject Pronouns

As you know, sometimes it is correct to use *she* or *I*, and sometimes it is correct to use *her* or *me*.

- The subject of a sentence is who or what the sentence is about. A pronoun used as a subject must be one of the "subject pronouns."

Subject Pronouns	
Singular	*Plural*
I, you, he, she, it	we, you, they

- It's easy to use subject pronouns correctly when the subject is one person. You would never say, "Me saw a movie" or "Her went bowling."
- You must also use subject pronouns when the subject is more than one person.

Wrong: Marcus and me saw a movie.
Wrong: Me and Marcus saw a movie.
Right: Marcus and I saw a movie.

Wrong: Lucia and her went bowling.
Wrong: Her and Lucia went bowling.
Right: Lucia and she went bowling.

- If you wonder what the correct subject pronoun is, get rid of the extra person (or people) in your mind.

Sample: ~~Maurice~~, ~~Phil~~, ~~and~~ (him? he?) agreed.

Obviously, you would never say "Him agreed," so you should use "he" in this sentence.

Grammar Practice

Rewrite each sentence, using the correct pronoun in parentheses.

18. My friends and (I, me) play football.
19. (Them, They) and (we, us) had a good time.
20. Tina, Ashley, or (she, her) will bring a DVD.

Literature Online

Web Activities For eFlashcards, Selection Quick Checks, and other Web activities, go to www.glencoe.com.

Skills Review

Key Reading Skill: Understanding Sequence

7. Possible response: 1) A Liberation Army soldier picks Jiang for a test in the gym. 2) Jiang is chosen to audition for the Arts Academy. 3) Jiang's father tells her she can't audition.

Key Literary Element: Sensory Details

8. sound
9. feel
10. feel

Reviewing Skills: Connecting

11. Review students' responses.

Vocabulary Check

12. contemplate
13. tantalizing
14. exemplary
15. At first she was excited at the thought of joining the academy. Then she was disappointed when her father refused to let her try out.
16. It would bend.
17. They would applaud and cheer.

Close

Ask students to share what they have learned from Jiang to help them answer the Big Question.

Grammar Link: Subject Pronouns

Grammar Practice

18. My friends and I play football.
19. They and we had a good time.
20. Tina, Ashley, or she will bring a DVD.

Literature Online

Web Activities Have students access the Web site for interactive activities that will help them assess their understanding of the selection.

Workshop Resources

Pacing (Days) Standard	Block	Lesson	Student Materials	Teacher Resources
1		Comparing Literature: Setting	Key Reading Skills Practice English Language Coach	Bellringer Options Transparencies Read Aloud, Think Aloud Transparencies Presentation Plus!
2		*from* Barrio Boy	Literary Analysis Transparencies Glencoe Online Selection Vocabulary Development Academic Vocabulary Development English Language Coach Active Reading Graphic Organizer Literary Analysis StudentWorks Plus Online Student Edition Literature Classics Selection and Unit Assessments	Literary and Text Analysis Transparencies Puzzlemaker Skill Level Up! BookLink 3 Assessment by Learning Objective (Diagnostic and Formative) Interactive Tutor Self-Assessment TeacherWorks Plus
2		"How I learned English"	Glencoe Online Selection Vocabulary Development Academic Vocabulary Development English Language Coach Active Reading Graphic Organizer Literary Analysis StudentWorks Plus Online Student Edition Literature Classics Selection and Unit Assessments	Literary and Text Analysis Transparencies Puzzlemaker Skill Level Up! BookLink 3 Assessment by Learning Objective (Diagnostic and Formative) Interactive Tutor Self-Assessment TeacherWorks Plus

Keys for Unit Resource

- Blackline Master
- Workbook
- Supplemental Text
- CD-ROM
- DVD
- Transparency
- Web-based
- Fast Files

Level Appropriate Code

AS = Activities for all students
AL = Activities for students working above grade level
OL = Activities for students working at grade level
BL = Activities for students working below grade level
EL = Activities for English language learners

Focus

BELLRINGER Options

- **Selection Focus Transparencies**
- **Daily Language Practice Transparency**

Focus Activity Write the following on the board: How would you compare two seasons of the year? Begin by listing the features you would compare and make a chart. You might start out with something like the following:

	Winter	Summer
Weather		
Length of days		
Holidays		

Teach

L Literary Element

Setting Ask students to describe the classroom as if it were the setting for a story. Have them include all the details listed on the student page. OL

from Barrio Boy & How I Learned English

by Ernesto Galarza

by Gregory Djanikian

Skills Focus

You will practice using these skills when you read the following selections:

- from *Barrio Boy,* p. 225
- "How I Learned English," p. 232

Point of Comparison

- Setting

Purpose

- To evaluate how setting affects character in a memoir and in a poem

Objectives (pp. 222–223)
Literature Identify literary elements: setting • Compare and contrast: literature

You compare things almost every day. You might compare two bikes to see which you like better or two CDs to see which has your favorite songs. You think about how things are alike and how they are different.

When you compare bikes, you look at tires, brakes, and other parts. When you compare two pieces of literature, you also look at important parts, such as setting and characters, to see how those parts are the same or different. Then you use that information to think about the literature.

How to Compare Literature: Setting

Before you can compare anything, you need to know what points, or characteristics, you'll use for your comparison (like the tires and brakes on the bikes). When you read and compare a passage from the autobiography *Barrio Boy* and the poem "How I Learned English," you'll be looking especially at the setting of each selection.

You learned in Reading Workshop 3 that the setting of a reading selection is the place and time the events take place.

As you read, watch for specific details that describe the "when" and "where" of a story. These details include

L

- Place
- Time
- Physical appearance of location
- Sounds and smells
- Characters that surround the main character
- Details that tell more about the "when" and "where" of the selections

Additional Support

Literature Focus Lesson

Analyzing Setting Remind students that questioning helps them to clarify their understanding of a text as they read. Provide them with the following prompts they can use to clarify a setting.

- How can I tell when this story takes place?
- What details does the author give to help me imagine the setting?
- Why does the author include these details?
- How does the setting affect the characters? the plot? the conflict? the theme? OL

Get Ready to Compare

As you read, keep track of these details on a Comparison Chart like this one. Copy it into your Learner's Notebook, and take notes as you read. A chart allows you to compare each detail in a selection to the same detail in the other selection. After you read, you'll use your notes to write your comparison.

Categories	*Barrio Boy setting*	*"How I Learned English" setting*
Place		
Time		
Physical appearance of setting		
Sounds		
Smells		
Surrounding characters		
Other details		

L

Use Your Comparison

Making a comparison isn't very helpful unless you DO something with it. So after you read the selections, think about the setting's influence, or power, over what happens.

For example, on page 134 of the Tony Hawk story, the author says that Tony got so nervous at his first competition that he got a stomachache. Use the steps to think about how important the setting was to that event:

1. Tony is very nervous and gets a stomachache.
2. The setting is a contest crowded with more than 100 skateboarders.
3. What if the contest had only 2 other skaters? Would Tony have felt so nervous? (probably not!)
4. It makes sense that the number of other skaters made Tony nervous.
5. Therefore, the setting seems to be very important to what happens to Tony in this passage.

When you make your comparison later, you will use these steps to figure out how important the settings of the autobiography and the poem are. You can also use these steps in other classes to make decisions about information.

Reading in the Real World

Citizenship Ask small groups to find information about immigrant groups that are a part of their community's past and present. Students may use libraries, historical societies, museums, and interviews with older people. Ask each group to prepare a short report or presentation answering such questions as:

- What foreign-born groups were present in our past and make up our community today?
- Have relationships between foreign-born people and natives always been good?
- How has our community helped educate its foreign-born citizens and helped them fit in? **AS**

COMPARING LITERATURE

Teach

L Literary Element

Sensory Details Explain to students that sensory details—details that appeal to the senses—can make a setting come alive for a reader. Ask students to name the five senses, then list them in a line on the board.

- sight
- smell
- taste
- hearing
- touch

Ask students to give an example of sensory description for each of the five senses, either from a selection in their books or of their own composition. **OL**

Assess/Close

Ask: Write a paragraph describing your classroom from your point of view at this moment. Include details that will involve at least four of your five senses. *(Responses will vary.)* Have a few students read their description of the classroom aloud and discuss their use of sensory language. **AS**

Resources for page 223

Use the Comparing Literature Graphic Organizer BLM in the Unit 2 Resource Booklet.

Objectives
- Identify literary elements: setting
- Compare and contrast: literature

Before You Read from *Barrio Boy*

More About the Author

Ernesto Galarza was a Mexican union leader as well as a writer. He used his writing talents to expose the abuses suffered by farm workers. He has said that the journey described in *Barrio Boy* was "typical of those hundreds of thousands of [Mexican] refugees. They settled permanently in California and other border states. The barrio of this tale is that of Sacramento, California."

R Reading Skill

Review Connecting

Ask: Have any of you been in a place where you did not know the language? Have you read about someone who was in a place where he or she didn't know the language? Think about how you felt or how the person you read about may have felt. Name two activities that might be difficult for someone who doesn't speak the same language as the people around him or her. *(Possible response: It would be hard for that person to ask for directions or to go shopping.)*

Ernesto Galarza

Meet the Author

Ernesto Galarza (air NES toh guh LAR zaw) was born in 1905. He died in 1984. He spent most of his life fighting for the rights of farm workers. According to Galarza, "*Barrio Boy* is the story of a Mexican family, uprooted from its home in a mountain village. . . ." See page R3 of the Author Files in the back of the book for more on Ernesto Galarza.

Author Search For more about Ernesto Galarza, go to www.glencoe.com.

Objectives (pp. 224–230)
Reading Compare and contrast literary texts
Literature Identify literary elements: setting • Compare and contrast settings across texts
Vocabulary Use context clues: multiple-meaning words

Vocabulary Preview

wholeheartedly (hohl HAR tid lee) *adv.* sincerely and enthusiastically **(p. 226)** *The teacher welcomed her new students wholeheartedly.*

menace (MEN us) *n.* a threat or danger **(p. 226)** *Ernesto didn't know if the stranger was a menace or a friend.*

formidable (for MID uh bul) *adj.* causing fear or wonder because of size, strength, or power **(p. 226)** *Miss Hopley's height seemed formidable.*

obnoxious (ub NAWK shus) *adj.* annoying and disagreeable **(p. 227)** *One student seemed to have an obnoxious personality.*

persistently (pur SIS tunt lee) *adv.* over and over again; repeatedly **(p. 228)** *If you've never heard a word before, it's easy to persistently mispronounce it.*

Get Ready to Read

Connect to the Reading

R How would it feel if everyone else spoke a language you didn't understand? This is what happened to Ernesto Galarza, the author of *Barrio Boy*.

Build Background

- As the selection begins, Galarza and his family have moved from Mexico to Sacramento, California.
- At first, Galarza speaks only Spanish.
- The main setting is a Sacramento school in the early 1900s.

Set Purposes for Reading

BIG Question Read to find out how the author learned to deal with life in a new and unfamiliar culture. This change in setting resulted in many new and unexpected events. As you read this passage from *Barrio Boy*, remember to watch for details that describe the "when" and "where."

Set Your Own Purpose What else would you like to learn from Galarza's experiences to help you answer the Big Question? Write your own purpose on the "from *Barrio Boy*" page of your Foldable.

Additional Support

Author Search To expand students' appreciation of Ernesto Galarza, have them access the Web site for additional information.

Reading in the Real World

Citizenship Have students find out more about the difficulties faced by Mexican farm workers who immigrated to the United States in the early 20th century. Tell them to find answers to the following research questions.

- What was life like for immigrant farm workers?
- How did Ernesto Galarza and later Cesar Chavez, another activist, improve life for immigrant farm workers in this country?
- What is the United Farm Workers Union?

Have students present their findings to the class. **AS**

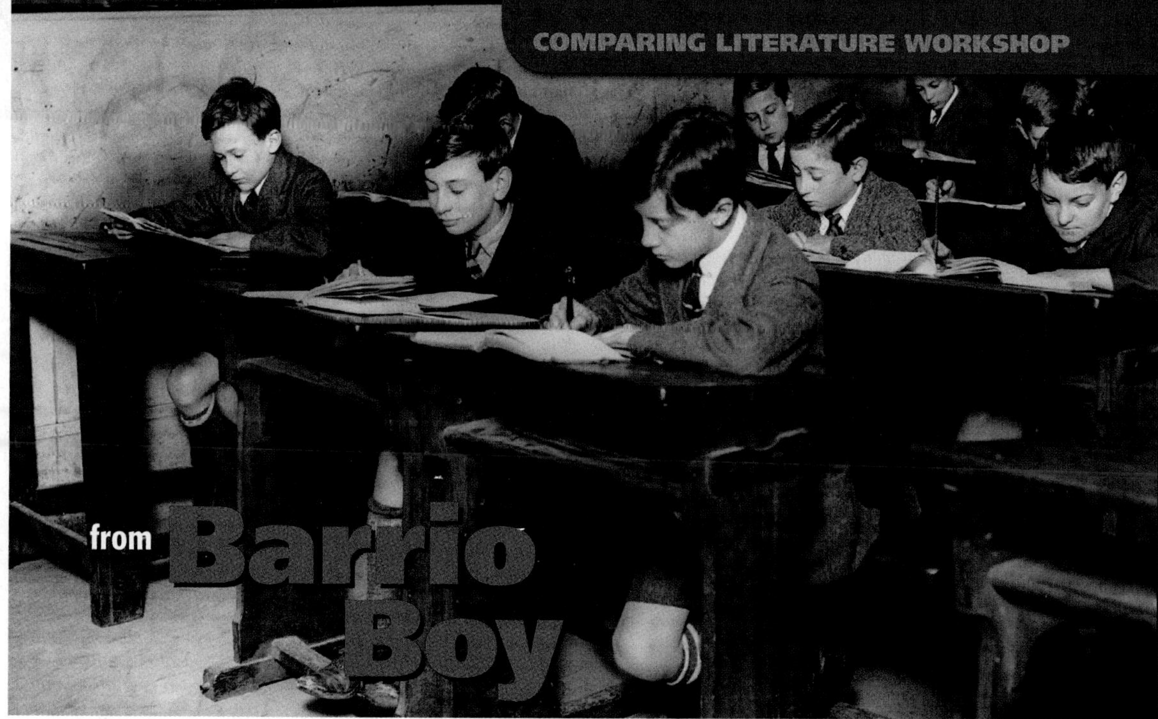

from Barrio Boy

by Ernesto Galarza

This class photo was taken in the early 1900s, around the time Ernesto Galarza attended the Lincoln School.

Analyzing the Photo What can you learn about the school and the students from studying the photo?

The two of us walked south on Fifth Street one morning to the corner of Q Street and turned right. Half of the block was occupied by the Lincoln School. It was a three-story wooden building, with two wings that gave it the shape of a double-T connected by a central hall. It was a new building, painted yellow, with a shingled roof that was not like the red tile of the school in Mazatlán.[1] I noticed other differences, none of them very reassuring. **L**

We walked up the wide staircase hand in hand and through the door, which closed by itself. A mechanical contraption screwed to the top shut it behind us quietly. **1**

Up to this point the adventure of enrolling me in the school had been carefully rehearsed. Mrs. Dodson had told us how to find it and we had circled it several times on our walks. Friends in the *barrio*[2] explained that the director was called a principal, and that it was a lady and not a man. They assured us that there was always a person at the school who could speak Spanish.

1. ***Mazatlán*** (maw zut LAWN) is a city on Mexico's central Pacific coast.
2. In the United States, ***barrio*** (BAW ree oh) refers to a Hispanic neighborhood.

Practice the Skills

1 Comparing Literature

Setting Galarza begins by describing the setting. List the details of the setting on your Comparison Chart. From his description, how do you think he feels about his new school?

Teach

Viewing the Photo

Ask: How is the school shown in the photo different from your school? *(Possible responses: The boys are wearing uniforms; there are only boys in the photo; everyone looks very serious.)* **AS**

L Literary Element

Setting Ask: Which type of sensory details does the narrator give? *(sight details)* What do these details tell you about the setting? *(They help you imagine how the setting looks.)* **BL**

Readability Scores

Dale-Chall: 6.4
DRP: 58
Lexile: 1100

Differentiated Instruction

Sketching a Scene Have students who like to draw choose a scene from the story to use as a basis for a quick sketch. Encourage them to take the time to visualize the scene clearly and to jot down its important elements. As they create their drawings, remind them to see things from the perspective of Ernesto, a first grader. Finally, ask students how the scenes in their drawings relate to the story and how these scenes might affect Ernesto's feelings about his first day of school. **OL**

Objectives

- Compare and contrast literary texts
- Identify literary elements: setting, sensory details
- Compare and contrast setting across literary texts
- Analyze a photograph

Teach

C Critical Thinking

Comprehension Say: Ernesto and his mother can't understand what Miss Hopley is saying. What do they rely on instead to help them get to know her? *(They rely on her body language.)* **OL**

What does her body language suggest about her? *(It suggests she is friendly.)* **AL**

EL Language Coach

Multiple-Meaning Words

Say: Use your dictionaries to list at least two meanings of the word "warm." Now note how the word is used in this passage; pay attention to the context clues, or the words around "warm." What does the word "warm" mean here? What words helped you decide? *("Warm" means kind or pleasant; Miss Hopley smiles and her eyes sparkle.)* **EL** **BL**

Exactly as we had been told, there was a sign on the door in both Spanish and English: "Principal." We crossed the hall and entered the office of Miss Nettie Hopley.

Miss Hopley was at a roll top desk[3] to one side, sitting in a swivel chair that moved on wheels. There was a sofa against the opposite wall, flanked by two windows and a door that opened on a small balcony. Chairs were set around a table and framed pictures hung on the walls of a man with long white hair and another with a sad face and a black beard.

Visual Vocabulary *Pinch glasses* are eyeglasses clipped to the nose. Often, they're called by their French name, *pince-nez.*

The principal half turned in the swivel chair to look at us over the pinch glasses crossed on the ridge of her nose. To do this she had to duck her head slightly as if she were about to step through a low doorway.

What Miss Hopley said to us we did not know but we saw in her eyes a **warm welcome** and when she took off her glasses and straightened up she smiled **wholeheartedly**, like Mrs. Dodson. **C** **2** We were, of course, saying nothing, only catching the friendliness of her voice and the sparkle in her eyes while she said words we did not understand. She signaled us to the table. Almost tiptoeing across the office, I maneuvered myself to keep my mother between me and the gringo[4] lady. In a matter of seconds I had to decide whether she was a possible friend or a **menace**. We sat down.

Then Miss Hopley did a **formidable** thing. She stood up. Had she been standing when we entered she would have seemed tall. But rising from her chair she soared. And what she carried up and up with her was a buxom superstructure, firm shoulders, a straight sharp nose, full cheeks slightly molded by a curved line along the nostrils, thin lips that

3. A ***roll-top desk*** is a writing desk with a slatted, movable top.

4. A ***gringo*** lady is one who is white, North American, and not Hispanic.

Vocabulary

wholeheartedly (hohl HAR tid lee) *adv.* sincerely and enthusiastically

menace (MEN us) *n.* a threat or danger

formidable (for MID uh bul) *adj.* causing fear because of size, strength, or power

Practice the Skills

2 English Language Coach

EL **Multiple-Meaning Words** What does the *warm* in **warm welcome** mean? What other common meaning does this word have?

Additional Support

English Language Coach

Description Some of the items mentioned by the author were found in schools long ago. Some students may need to have certain items described so that they can visualize them.

Roll-top desk: a wooden writing desk with a slatted top that rolls down over the writing surfaces

Swivel chair: a desk chair with wheels and a seat that turns on its base

Students having trouble visualizing these items might search for online images of them. **EL** **BL**

Students focus on their lesson by gas light in an early 1900s classroom.

moved like steel springs, and a high forehead topped by hair gathered in a bun. Miss Hopley was not a giant in body but when she mobilized it to a standing position she seemed a match for giants. I decided I liked her. **C**

She strode to a door in the far corner of the office, opened it and called a name. A boy of about ten years appeared in the doorway. He sat down at one end of the table. He was brown like us, a plump kid with shiny black hair combed straight back, neat, cool, and faintly **obnoxious**. **3**

Miss Hopley joined us with a large book and some papers in her hand. She, too, sat down and the questions and answers began by way of our interpreter. My name was Ernesto. My mother's name was Henriqueta. My birth certificate was in San Blas. Here was my last report card from the Escuela Municipal Numero 3 para Varones[5] of Mazatlán, and so forth. Miss Hopley put things down in the book and my mother signed a card.

As long as the questions continued, Doña[6] Henriqueta could stay and I was secure. Now that they were over, Miss Hopley saw her to the door, dismissed our interpreter and without further ado took me by the hand and strode down the hall to Miss Ryan's first grade.

Miss Ryan took me to a seat at the front of the room, into which I shrank—the better to survey her. She was, to skinny, somewhat runty me, of a withering height when she patrolled the class. And when I least expected it, there she was, crouching by my desk, her blond radiant face level with mine, her voice patiently maneuvering me over the awful idiocies of the English language. **R**

5. The mother's first name is ***Henriqueta*** (en ree KAY tuh). The writer was born in ***San Blas,*** a small city near Mazatlán, but he attended a public school for boys in Mazatlán.
6. ***Doña*** (DOHN yuh) is the same as the English words *Mrs.* and *Madam.*

Vocabulary

obnoxious (ub NAWK shus) *adj.* annoying and disagreeable

Practice the Skills

3 Comparing Literature

Setting People are a part of the setting also. In this paragraph and the last paragraph on page 226, Galarza describes Miss Hopley and a young boy. Record these details on your Comparison Chart. With a partner, talk about what Galarza seems to think about each of these characters.

Teach

C Critical Thinking

Evaluation Ask: Compare the description Ernesto gives of Miss Hopley with this one: "Miss Hopley seemed very tall and powerful when she stood up." What details would you miss if this were how Galarza wrote his description of Miss Hopley? *(You'd miss the description of her face, shoulders, and hair.)* **AL**

R Reading Skill

Review Inferring Ask: What words suggest that Ernesto likes Miss Ryan a lot? *(The words* radiant *and* patiently *suggest he likes her.)* **OL**

Literature Focus Lesson

Description Tell students that strong writers select details carefully so their readers can see, hear, smell, taste, and feel what is being described. The excerpt from *Barrio Boy* is filled with colorful descriptions of life at Lincoln School. These descriptions enable readers to feel as if they are attending school with Ernesto.

Have students pick out a description of a person or a place in the selection that helps them clearly picture the person or place. They should share which details help them "see" the person or place as the writer did. **AS**

Objectives
- Read for varied purposes, such as to be informed
- Describe characters
- Make inferences
- Identify sensory details
- Understand multiple-meaning words in context

Teach

R Reading Skill

Review Inferring Ask: What information tells you that Miss Ryan is an encouraging teacher? *(She tells the whole class when one of her students does well.)* OL

L Literary Element

Review Point of View

Say: All the impressions of the class come through Ernesto's eyes. How might these descriptions be different if the story were told in the third person? *(The descriptions might include Miss Ryan's and the other students' impressions of Ernesto and a general picture of the classroom.)* AL

During the next few weeks Miss Ryan overcame my fears of tall, energetic teachers as she bent over my desk to help me with a word in the pre-primer. Step by step, she loosened me and my classmates from the safe anchorage of the desks for recitations at the blackboard and consultations at her desk. Frequently she burst into happy announcements to the whole class. "Ito can read a sentence," and small Japanese Ito, squint-eyed and shy, slowly read aloud while the class listened in wonder: "Come, Skipper, come. Come and run." The Korean, Portuguese, Italian, and Polish first graders had similar moments of glory, no less shining than mine the day I conquered "butterfly," which I had been **persistently** pronouncing in standard Spanish as boo-ter-flee. "Children," Miss Ryan called for attention. "Ernesto has learned how to pronounce *butterfly*!" And I proved it with a perfect imitation of Miss Ryan. From that **celebrated** success, I was soon able to match Ito's progress as a sentence reader with "Come, butterfly, come fly with me." R 4

Like Ito and several other first graders who did not know English, I received private lessons from Miss Ryan in the closet, a narrow hall off the classroom with a door at each end. Next to one of these doors Miss Ryan placed a large chair for L

4 **English Language Coach**

Multiple-Meaning Words
Here, **celebrated** means "famous." What is its more familiar meaning?

This photograph, taken around 1905, depicts a typical Southwest teacher of that time.

Lincoln School, 1910

Vocabulary

persistently (pur SIS tunt lee) *adv.* over and over again; repeatedly

Additional Support

English Language Coach

Prefixes Recognizing prefixes can help readers understand more words as they read. Write these words on the board:

pre + pay = prepay
pre + test = pretest
pre + view = preview

Ask students what they think *pre-* means. *("before in time or position," or "in front of")* Have students list three other words they know with the prefix *pre-* and write a sentence for each. *(Possible responses: pregame, preheat, preschool)* EL BL herself and a small one for me. Keeping an eye on the class through the open door she read with me about sheep in the meadow and a frightened chicken going to see the king, coaching me out of my phonetic[7] ruts in words like *pasture, bow-wow-wow, hay,* and *pretty,* which to my Mexican ear and eye had so many unnecessary sounds and letters. She made me watch her lips and then close my eyes as she repeated words I found hard to read. When we came to know each other better, I tried interrupting to tell Miss Ryan how we said it in Spanish. It didn't work. She only said "oh" and went on with *pasture, bow-wow-wow,* and *pretty.* It was as if in that closet we were both discovering together the secrets of the English language and grieving together over the tragedies of Bo-Peep. The main reason I was graduated with honors from the first grade was that I had fallen in love with Miss Ryan. Her radiant, no-nonsense character made us either afraid not to love her or love her so we would not be afraid, I am not sure which. It was not only that we sensed she was with it, but also that she was with us. **R**

Students line up at their teacher's desk in a city classroom around 1921.

Like the first grade, the rest of the Lincoln School was a sampling of the lower part of town where many races made their home. My pals in the second grade were Kazushi, whose parents spoke only Japanese; Matti, a skinny Italian boy; and Manuel, a fat Portuguese who would never get into a fight but wrestled you to the ground and just sat on you. Our assortment of nationalities included Koreans, Yugoslavs, Poles, Irish, and home-grown Americans. **5** **C**

Miss Hopley and her teachers never let us forget why we were at Lincoln: for those who were alien,[8] to become good

Practice the Skills

5 Comparing Literature

Setting This paragraph describes the people in Galarza's neighborhood. What does his description tell you about his neighborhood? Add the details and your ideas to your Comparison Chart.

7. ***Phonetic*** (fuh NET ik) means "having to do with speech sounds."
8. Here, ***alien*** refers to those who are foreign born.

Teach

R Reading Skill

Review Inferring **Ask:** Why do you think Ernesto falls in love with Miss Ryan? *(Possible response: She is kind and patient. She also gives him individual attention, which probably makes him feel special.)* **OL**

C Critical Thinking

Evaluation **Ask:** How does Galarza's neighborhood compare with your own? What might be the benefits of living in such a diverse neighborhood? *(Responses will vary. Students might note that they would learn tolerance and a lot about different cultures by living in a diverse neighborhood.)* **OL**

Reading in the Real World

Career Tell students that some teachers become trained in teaching English as a foreign language. These people teach children and adults from other countries how to speak English. Have students consider what the qualifications might be for this kind of job. What qualities would be important for someone teaching English as a foreign language? *(Possible responses: patience, kindness, a good knowledge of English)* **OL**

Objectives
- Identify setting
- Describe characters
- Make inferences
- Identify point of view and explain how different points of view affect text
- Use prefixes to learn new words

Teach

C Critical Thinking

Evaluation Ask: What happens to students who use racial insults at school? *(They are punished.)* OL

What conclusion can you draw about the values of the school and Miss Hopley based on this information? *(You can conclude that the school and Miss Hopley value kindness and respect for diversity.)* AL

BQ BIG Question

Remind students that Ernesto begins his time at school feeling afraid and ends up being proud of his heritage and his new home. Who helps him change? *(his teacher)* OL

What might Ernesto say about teachers' role in helping you become the person you want to be? *(He might say that good teachers will help you by encouraging your best qualities and firmly but gently correcting your bad qualities.)* AL

Americans; for those who were so born, to accept the rest of us. Off the school grounds we traded the same insults we heard from our elders. On the playground we were sure to be marched up to the principal's office for calling someone a wop, a chink, a dago, or a greaser. The school was not so much a melting pot[9] as a griddle where Miss Hopley and her helpers warmed knowledge into us and roasted racial hatreds out of us. C

Uniformed students pose with a teacher in front of an early 1900s school.

At Lincoln, making us into Americans did not mean scrubbing away what made us originally foreign. The teachers called us as our parents did, or as close as they could pronounce our names in Spanish or Japanese. No one was ever scolded or punished for speaking in his native tongue on the playground. Matti told the class about his mother's down quilt, which she had made in Italy with the fine feathers of a thousand geese. Encarnación[10] acted out how boys learned to fish in the Philippines. I astounded the third grade with the story of my travels on a stagecoach, which nobody else in the class had seen except in the museum at Sutter's Fort. After a visit to the Crocker Art Gallery and its collection of heroic paintings of the golden age of California, someone showed a silk scroll with a Chinese painting. Miss Hopley herself had a way of expressing wonder over these matters before a class, her eyes wide open until they popped slightly. It was easy for me to feel that becoming a proud American, as she said we should, did not mean feeling ashamed of being a Mexican. 6 ○

Practice the Skills

6 BIG Question

BQ What do you think Ernesto Galarza would tell you about how to become the person you want to be? Write your answer on the Comparing Literature page of your Foldable.

9. ***wop . . . greaser*** These are all offensive names for people of various nationalities or lifestyles. Here, ***melting pot*** refers to the idea of a place where people of all races and cultures blend smoothly into a single society.

10. ***Encarnación*** (en kar naw see OHN)

Additional Support

Literature Focus Lesson

Character Have students create a character sketch of Ernesto. They can either draw Ernesto and then write words and phrases that describe him, or they can write a paragraph describing him. Have students consider the following as they create their sketches:

- What does Ernesto look like?
- What words describe Ernesto's personality at the beginning and end of the story?
- How does Ernesto change? OL

Before You Read How I Learned English

Gregory Djanikian

Meet the Author

Gregory Djanikian (juh NEEK ee un) was born in Egypt in 1949 and moved to the United States in 1957. He has won poetry awards and has published several books of poetry. See page R3 of the Author Files in the back of the book for more on Gregory Djanikian.

Author Search For more about Gregory Djanikian, go to www.glencoe.com.

Objectives (pp. 231–233)
Reading Compare and contrast literary texts
Literature Identify literary elements: setting • Compare and contrast settings across texts
Vocabulary Use context clues: multiple-meaning words

Vocabulary Preview

notions (NOH shunz) *n.* ideas, beliefs, or opinions **(p. 232)** *The player's notions about America and its favorite sport were not very clear.*

banished (BAN ishd) *adj.* sent away; form of the verb *banish* **(p. 232)** *Banished to the farthest corner of the field, he daydreamed.*

V

English Language Coach

Multiple-Meaning Words Some of the multiple-meaning words in "How I Learned English" come from baseball. The following words have very different meanings in a baseball game than in everyday English.

Word	Every-day meaning	Baseball meaning
First	coming before all others in order, time, or importance	first base; where the batter runs as soon as she or he hits the ball
Flies	flying bugs	baseballs that are hit high and to the outfield, or the farthest part of the field

Get Ready to Read

Connect to the Reading

The setting of the poem you're about to read is a baseball field. The poem includes many baseball terms. If you play or watch baseball or softball, you'll know most of these terms. If you don't know the terms, don't worry about it. The important thing is to get an idea of how the speaker of the poem feels about the game.

Set Purposes for Reading

BIG Question Read the poem to learn how the speaker makes friends after his family moves to the United States. As you read, watch for details that describe the "when" and "where."

Set Your Own Purpose What more would you like to learn from the poem to help you answer the Big Question? Write your own purpose on the "How I Learned English" page of your Foldable.

English Language Coach

Baseball Terms Ask a volunteer who understands baseball to explain the following terms to other students. Another volunteer may act out some of the words.

Baseball Terms:
pitch
on first
outfield
flies, pop-ups, and grounders EL BL

More About the Author

Gregory Djanikian is the director of the creative writing program at the University of Pennsylvania. He has published several collections of poems and has been called one of America's best poets. Much of Djanikian's work deals with his experiences in his homeland, Egypt, and his acclimation to America.

Literature Online

Author Search To expand students' appreciation of Gregory Djanikian, have them access the Web site for additional information.

Teach

V Vocabulary

Quick Check Questions

Say: Answer these questions.

1. What are your notions about homework? *(Possible response: My notion about homework is that I like to do it when I get home so I can relax later.)*
2. Why might someone be banished? *(Possible response: Someone might be banished for being too noisy.)* EL BL

Teach

C Critical Thinking

Comprehension **Ask:** What does the speaker mean when he says he's "just off the plane"? What words help you understand this phrase? *(He means he's arrived in the country recently; the words "plopped in the middle of Williamsport, Pa." and "notions of baseball and America" help readers understand the meaning.)* **AL**

L Literary Element

Review Point of View
Ask: From what point of view is the poem written—first-person or third-person? How do you know? *(The poem is written from first-person point of view because the writer uses "I.")* **OL**

How I Learned English

by Gregory Djanikian

It was in an empty lot
Ringed by elms and fir and honeysuckle.*
Bill Corson was pitching in his buckskin jacket,
Chuck Keller, fat even as a boy, was on first,
His t-shirt riding up over his gut,

Ron O'Neill, Jim, Dennis, were talking it up
In the field, a blue sky above them
Tipped with cirrus.* And there I was,
C Just off the plane and plopped in the middle
Of Williamsport, Pa. and a neighborhood game, 1

L Unnatural and without any moves,
My **notions** of baseball and America
Growing fuzzier each time I whiffed.*
So it was not possible that I,
Banished to the outfield and daydreaming

2 ***Honeysuckle*** is a bushy plant that has sweet smelling flowers.

8 Here, ***cirrus*** means high, thin clouds.

13 In baseball, ***whiffed*** means "struck out, or swung and missed at the third strike to make an out."

Practice the Skills

1 Comparing Literature

Setting What details about the setting help you see the baseball game? List them on your Comparison Chart.

Vocabulary

notions (NOH shunz) *n.* ideas, beliefs, or opinions

banished (BAN ishd) *adj.* sent away

Additional Support

Literature Focus Lesson

Sequence of Events Explain to students that in poetry the sequence of events is not always clear. It is often helpful to pull the events from a story or a poem, paraphrase them, and then put them in the order in which they occurred. This can help readers keep straight not only the events but also the characters' involvement in those events.

Reread the poem together and create a chart that tracks the sequence of events. Include the names of the characters involved in each event. Then discuss how each event explains past action or leads to future action. **OL**

Of water, or a hotel in the mountains,
Would suddenly find myself in the path
Of a ball stung by Joe Barone.
I watched it closing in
Clean and untouched, transfixed*

By its easy arc before it hit
My forehead with a thud. **2**
I fell back,
Dazed, clutching my brow,
Groaning, "Oh my shin, oh my shin,"*

And everybody peeled away from me
And dropped from laughter, and there we were,
All of us writhing* on the ground for one reason
Or another.
Someone said "shin" again,

There was a wild stamping of hands on the ground,
A kicking of feet, and the fit
Of laughter overtook me too,
And that was important, as important
As Joe Barone asking me how I was

Through his tears, picking me up
And dusting me off with hands
like swatters,*
And though my head felt heavy,
I played on till dusk
Missing flies and pop-ups and grounders

And calling out in desperation* things like
"Yours" and "take it," but doing all right,
Tugging at my cap in just the right way,
Crouching low, my feet set,
"Hum baby" sweetly on my lips. ❍

R

C

20 ***Transfixed*** means "motionless, as from wonder or fear."

25 When the ball hits the speaker in the ***brow*** ("forehead"), he calls it the wrong thing. The ***shin*** is the leg bone between the knee and ankle.

28 ***Writhing*** is twisting, like a worm, as from pain or embarrassment.

37 The speaker is comparing Joe's hands to fly ***swatters,*** the tools used to kill bugs.

41 ***Desperation*** is a feeling of hopelessness that causes a person to try *anything.*

Practice the Skills

2 BIG Question

The speaker lists some of the obstacles he faces.

In your Foldable, write
- What the speaker's goals might be.
- What obstacles he faces in reaching his goals.

As you read, record ways that the speaker tries to overcome the obstacles you listed.

Teach

R Reading Skill

Review Connecting Say: Think of a time when you were participating in a sport and saw a ball or another person coming toward you. How did you feel? How do you think the author felt? OL

C Critical Thinking

Evaluation Have students think about the ending of the poem. Discuss whether they think it's a realistic conclusion. *(Students may connect the ending to times they have played ball.)* OL

Ask students if they think the author's use of details and language enhances the ending. Have them give examples to support their opinions. AL

Reading Fluency

Reading a Poem Tell students that there are guidelines for reading a poem that will help them read more fluidly. Tell students to pause after punctuation marks, rather than stopping at the end of each line. Suggest that students pause briefly after a comma and slightly longer after a period. Encourage students to read the poem aloud softly to themselves several times until they feel they can read it without hesitating. EL BL

Objectives
- Read for varied purposes, such as to be informed
- Use your own knowledge and experience to comprehend
- Connect to the reading
- Describe the setting
- Use critical thinking skills to analyze a poem

Assess

Resources for page 234

- Selection Quick Check
- Comparing Literature Assessment

Students can respond to the *After You Read* items in their Learner's Notebook or on a separate sheet of paper.

Vocabulary Check

1. It's really obnoxious to let children yell and run in the library where other people are trying to read.
2. Dogs can be a terrible menace to mail carriers.
3. The coach agreed wholeheartedly that Bill is our best kicker.
4. If you knock persistently, she'll come to the door sooner or later.
5. They're a formidable team, but we know we can defeat them.
6. What silly notions does that kid have in his head now?
7. The kitten will be banished to the porch after the next "accident."

After You Read

Objectives (pp. 234–235)
Reading Compare and contrast literary texts
Literature Identify literary elements: setting • Compare and contrast settings across texts
Writing Write a response to literature: comparison/contrast: setting

from Barrio Boy & How I Learned English

Vocabulary Check

Copy each sentence, filling in the blank with the best word from the list. Use each word only once.

from Barrio Boy

wholeheartedly
menace
formidable
obnoxious
persistently

1. It's really ___ to let children yell and run in the library where other people are trying to read.
2. Dogs can be a terrible ___ to mail carriers.
3. The coach agreed ___ that Bill is our best kicker.
4. If you knock ___, she'll come to the door sooner or later.
5. They're a ___ team, but we know we can defeat them.

How I Learned English

notions
banished

6. What silly ___ does that kid have in his head now?
7. The kitten will be ___ to the porch after the next "accident."

	Barrio Boy Setting	How I Learned English Setting
Place	Lincoln School, 5th & Q Streets, Sacramento, CA	Empty lot in Williamsport, PA
Time	Early 1900s	Mid-1900s
Physical Appearance	3-story wooden building, two wings, shingled roof	Playing field surrounded by elms, fir, and honeysuckle

Reading/Critical Thinking

from Barrio Boy

8. Interpret What do you think Galarza means when he says that Miss Ryan was not only "with it" but "with us"?

Tip Author and Me You'll find clues in the selection, but you also need to use information in your head.

9. Infer At the end, Galarza feels that becoming a "proud American" does not mean "ashamed of being a Mexican." What does he mean?

Tip Author and Me The selection gives clues, but you must also use what you know from your own experience.

How I Learned English

10. Infer Why do you think the speaker's notions of America and baseball are "growing fuzzier"?

Tip Author and Me You will find clues in the poem, but you must also make a good guess. Use the information in your head.

11. Infer Why do all the players end up on the ground when the speaker groans, "my shin, my shin"?

Tip Author and Me You will find clues in the poem, but you must also make a good guess. Use what you know about the word *shin.*

Writing: Compare the Literature

Use Your Notes

12. Follow these steps to use the notes on your Comparison Chart to compare the settings in *Barrio Boy* and "How I Learned English."

Step 1: Look over the chart you completed. Underline the details that are similar for both selections. Circle the details that are different.

Step 2: On a separate sheet of paper, make a list of those details that are similar and those that are different.

Step 3: Look at the new list you've made. For example, the time of each setting is shortly after the main character moved to the United States. Think about how that is important to each character's experience.

Step 4: Notice which setting details are important in both selections and which are important in just one of the selections. You will use this information to back up your statements in the assignment. Put a check beside the details that are most important to what happens to the main character.

Get It On Paper

To show what you think about the settings in these selections, copy these sentences, adding your own words in the blanks. Use details from the Comparison Chart to explain your answers.

13. In Barrio Boy, the setting is important because ___.

14. The most important part of the story's setting is ___ because ___.

15. The setting of "How I Learned English" is important because ___.

16. The most important part of the poem's setting is ___ because ___.

17. BIG Question How did the main characters become who they wanted to be? Did the settings help? Or, if they didn't help, why not?

LiteratureOnline

Web Activities For eFlashcards, Selection Quick Checks, and other Web activities, go to www.glencoe.com.

Reading/Critical Thinking

8. Ernesto means that Miss Ryan knows the problems faced by her students and that she is on their side.

9. Ernesto learns to appreciate both heritages.

10. He gets nervous when he strikes out.

11. Because they laugh so hard when the speaker calls his forehead "my shin"

Writing: Compare the Literature

12. See the chart below.

Possible responses:

13. the school is an important part of the writer's early life in America

14. the school; it played such an important part in helping Galarza change

15. playing baseball is a new experience for the speaker and it represents his discomfort with American life

16. the outfield; this is where the speaker learns to laugh at himself

17. Check students' responses to make sure they understand how the settings advance the stories.

Close

Ask students what they have learned to help them answer the Big Question.

	Barrio Boy Setting	How I Learned English Setting
Sounds	School sounds, voices in different languages	Boys playing baseball, shouts, laughter
Smells	One specified	None specified
Surrounding Characters	Young Galarza, his mother, principal, teachers, classmates	Speaker and his baseball friends
Other Details	Will vary	Will vary

The Unit Challenge

Focus

BELLRINGER Options

Daily Language Practice Transparency

Focus Activity Ask: From the stories we've read in this unit, who do you think had to work the hardest to become who he or she wanted to become? Why?

The discussion will remind students of the selections they've read, which will help them begin the group activity or the solo activity.

Teach

Group Activity: Letter of Advice

- You may select the note-keeper or ask for a volunteer.
- Make sure the group is on step 3 by mid-way through the class period to allow time to write the letter together.
- For the final draft, have the note-keeper write the letter neatly or type it on a computer.
- Make each student responsible for reading the letter to check for mistakes.

Assess/Close

Group Activity

Ask: How can you use the advice you've given to Andrea to become who you want to become? *(Suggest that students write their answers in their Learner's Notebook.)*

UNIT 2 WRAP-UP

Answering How Can We Become Who We Want to Be?

You've just read about people who worked to answer the Big Question: How do we become who we want to be? Now use what you've learned to do the Unit Challenge.

The Unit Challenge

Choose Activity A or Activity B, and follow the directions for the activity you've chosen.

A. Group Activity: Letter of Advice

- With three other students, imagine that your group is a famous music act called "98.6." Your group likes to answer as much of its fan mail as possible.
- You read one letter that's special:

Dear 98.6,

I love your latest CD—you are the best! I'm a musician, too. I sing in the school chorus and I'm learning to play electric bass. Friends say that I'm good. They believe in my dream of getting into professional music.

What advice would you give a seventh grader like me about how to become who I want to be?

Your fan,
Andrea Gomes

1. **Discuss the Assignment** Choose one group member to be the note-keeper for the discussion. Then discuss Andrea's question. From your Foldable, review the strengths and resources of the people you've read about in Unit 2. Discuss how these strengths and resources helped them become who they wanted to be.
2. **Review Your Notes and Make a Decision** At the end of the discussion, have the note-keeper read the notes aloud. Add comments to the notes that you think are necessary. Use the completed notes as an outline for your letter.
3. **Write the Letter** Here are some tips on how to write the letter.
   - Decide what the most important qualities for becoming who you want to be are.
   - Write one sentence for each quality, telling why it is important.
   - Write a sentence that introduces the others. Put that at the beginning of your paragraph.
   - Write a sentence that sums up the other sentences. Put that at the end of your paragraph.
4. **Present Your Letter** Make sure the letter is clear and has no misspelled words or other mistakes. Have one person rewrite the letter neatly in cursive handwriting on a clean sheet of paper. Then all group members should sign the letter. Finally, have another person from the group read the letter aloud to the class or post it on the bulletin board.

B. Solo Activity: Web Diagram

Sometimes it's hard to make a plan or a decision. In Activity B you'll use a tool that can help—a word web. Follow the numbered steps to learn how.

1. **Decide What You Need** Think about the person you want to become. Do you think about a certain type of job you'd like to do, such as a cartoon artist or video director? Maybe you think about the kind of person you want to become, such as "someone who cares about others." Write your choice at the top of a piece of paper. Below it, make a list of what you'll need to do to become this person. Think about the following questions:
   - How have others become who they wanted to be? Look at your Unit 2 Foldable notes to remember.
   - What strengths and skills do you already have?
   - What have you done to become who you want to be?
   - What else do you need to do to reach your goal?

Now, draw a web like the one below. Who do you want to be? Write the answer in the center circle. Then put the best answers from the list you made in the surrounding circles. Make sure you have at least one circle for each of the four questions. You'll turn this in, so write and draw neatly.

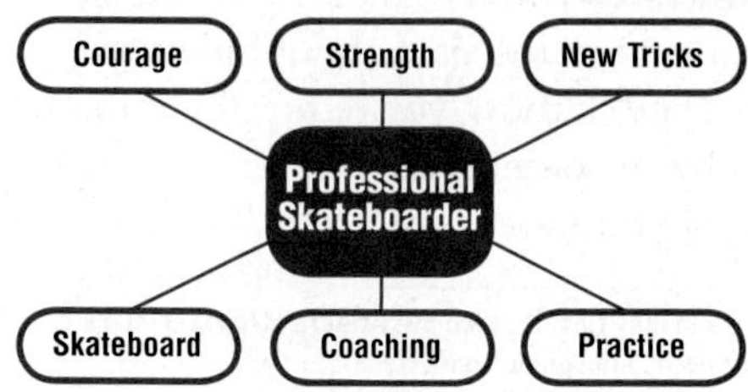

2. **Consider Obstacles** Which circles on your web show things that you don't have? These are your obstacles. From each circle of an obstacle, draw a line and circle. What can you do to overcome that obstacle and get what you need? Write a few words about your answer in the new circle.

3. **Think About and Present Your Web** Study your web. Write a few sentences under the web telling what you've learned from the web about becoming who you want to be. Then, make sure your web is neat and easy to read. Now you're ready to hand it in!

Teach

Solo Activity: Web Diagram

- Have students decide who they want to become or what they want to do.
- If students have trouble thinking of answers, ask them what they like to do, who they admire and why, and what characteristics they admire in others.
- Encourage students to answer the questions in their Learner's Notebook.
- Students should begin their webs by writing who they want to become in the middle of the page.
- Around the center word, they should write the things they already have as well as the things they need.
- The last step is to identify their obstacles and to write what they will do to overcome these obstacles.

Assess/Close

Solo Activity

Encourage students to study their webs and write what they've learned about becoming who they want to become. Review their webs and what they have learned.

Objectives
- Write a personal letter
- Organize information graphically

Focus

Vocabulary Preview

List the following words on the board:

- dramatic
- prejudice
- self-evident

Have students use dictionaries to define and pronounce the words. **EL** **BL**

Ask students to use each word in a sentence. **AS**

Build Background

The "Graduation Address" takes place before a graduation ceremony. Explain to students that when they graduate from high school (and sometimes from elementary or middle school), they attend a ceremony and receive a diploma. Usually, the valedictorian of the graduating class gives a speech.

Readability Scores
Dale-Chall: 4.5
DRP: 47
Lexile: N/A

Your Turn: Read and Apply Skills

Meet the Author

Robert L. Fontaine has written many short plays. He often writes plays for young people to read or perform. He usually looks at ordinary people with ordinary problems in a way that makes us laugh.

Literature Online

Author Resources For more about Robert L. Fontaine, go to www.glencoe.com.

Graduation Address

by Robert L. Fontaine

Characters

BRIAN, *valedictorian*[1]
ROSIE, TOM, DARA, PETE — *his friends*

AT RISE: BRIAN *is reading paper; he also holds pencil.* ROSIE, TOM, DARA, *and* PETE *stand around him.*

BRIAN: "I stand here proudly to address[2] you. We, the graduating class of old Chutney, are going forth, bearing the torch of learning onward and upward, ever and ever forward!" *(Looks up; pleased)* Not bad, huh?

ROSIE: Wow, Brian, it's pretty dramatic. *(Hesitates)* There is one little thing, though. I have a problem with the part where you say, "I stand here proudly to address you." It's pretty obvious you're standing there, isn't it?

TOM: Rosie's right. And another thing—naturally you're proud. I mean, if you *say* you're proud, some people might think that maybe the rest of us aren't proud.

PETE: Good point, Tom. And while you're making changes, Brian, you might want to cut out the part about how you're there to address people. They'll know you're not there to do card tricks, or try to sell them something.

BRIAN *(Musing)*:[3] I see what you mean.

1. The student with the best grades in a graduating class is called the ***valedictorian*** (val uh dik TOR ee un). He or she usually gives a speech at the graduation ceremony.
2. Here, ***address*** is a verb meaning "to speak to." In the title, it's a noun meaning "a speech." In both, the second syllable is accented, or stressed (uh DRES).
3. In ***musing,*** Brian is giving serious thought to what his friends said.

Additional Support

Author Search To expand students' appreciation of Robert L. Fontaine, have them access the Web site for additional information and resources.

Literature Focus Lesson

Summary In this short play, a group of friends help Brian, the class valedictorian, edit his graduation speech. As Brian reads each line, his friends respond by giving him constructive criticism. They comment on his style, his use of a mixed metaphor, and his use of overly obvious phrases. The speech, which starts out being very wordy and obtuse, is finally whittled down into one essential sentence, which Brian's friends applaud heartily. **OL**

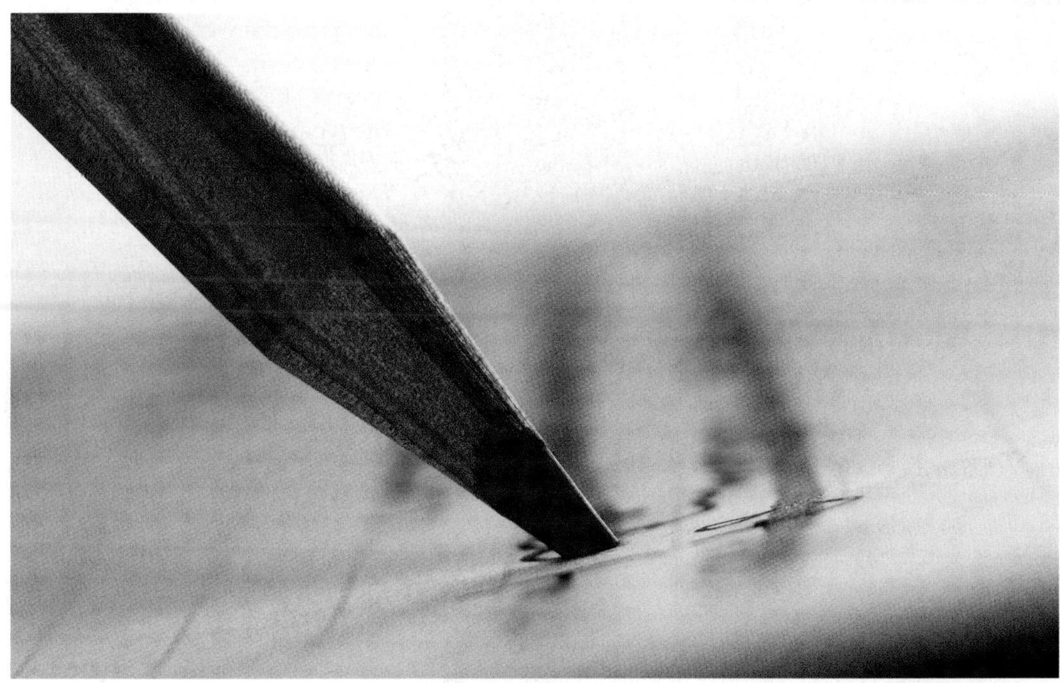

ROSIE: One other thing. Everyone knows we're the graduating class of old Chutney.

TOM: Right. And how often do you see someone bearing a torch, except in the Olympics? Besides, what is a torch of learning, anyway?

DARA *(Nodding)*: It's obscure.[4]

PETE: Now, what about "onward and upward, ever and ever forward"? Isn't that self-evident?[5] No one expects us to go backward and downward, ever and ever retreating. *(Pauses)* Of course, if I don't decide what I want to do with my life pretty soon, that may be just where I'm headed! C1

BRIAN: O.K. You've all made your points, and I agree. I'll cut some of these things out. *(Crosses out lines on paper)* Maybe you'll like the next section better. *(Reads)* "We are the coming generation,[6] and before us lies the future."

DARA *(Interrupting)*: Hold it! You have to take that out.

BRIAN: Why? I think it's powerful.

DARA: The future can't lie behind you, and of course, we're the coming generation.

BRIAN *(Annoyed; crossing out more lines)*: I'm beginning to wonder why I asked you all to listen to this speech. I'm going to have to write the whole thing over. C2

4. Anything that's ***obscure*** is difficult to see or understand clearly.

5. If something is ***self-evident,*** it doesn't need to be proved.

6. What Brian means by ***generation*** is all students who are about to graduate. The word usually refers to all people who are about the same age, such as teenagers or people in their forties.

Teach

C1 Critical Thinking

Application Ask: From your knowledge of what *self-evident* means, what do you think Pete is saying about the phrase, "onward and upward, ever and ever forward"? BL EL
Do you agree with Pete's opinion of the phrase? Why or why not? OL
Name a self-evident phrase you've heard. AL

C2 Critical Thinking

Comprehension Ask: Why do you think Brian was sorry about asking his friends to listen to his speech? *(Possible response: His friends were being too critical and not helpful.)* OL

Reading in the Real World

Career Using tact when giving feedback to others is an important life skill. Have students evaluate how well Brian's friends provide him with feedback. What suggestions might students offer for improvement? As students evaluate Brian's friends, have your students consider what they like or don't like about getting feedback on their work. Is it better for someone giving feedback to be straightforward or to cushion negative feedback by giving compliments first? Have students explain their responses. OL

Ask students to rewrite the play, having Brian's friends use more tact in helping him write his speech. AL

Objectives
- Read a short play
- Learn and use new vocabulary
- Use comprehension strategies

Teach

R Reading Skill

Review Connecting
Say: Think about a time you have been teased about something or someone you cared for. Would you get frustrated if your friends teased you the way Brian's friends teased him here? Why or why not? *(Responses will vary. Some students might note that they would get frustrated because the friends are making so many changes to the speech and their teasing is hurtful. Others may feel the teasing lightens the mood.)*

C Critical Thinking

Analysis Ask: Given what you already know about what's happening in the play, what do you think will happen as Brian continues to read his speech? *(Possible response: His friends will keep criticizing each line.)*

ROSIE: But think of the great speech you'll have when we're through!

BRIAN: I hope so! Let me see, where was I? Oh, yes. *(Reads)* "On us weighs the burden of shaping the world closer to the heart's desire. We, and we alone, must do the task of putting our shoulders to the wheel and rowing bravely upstream until the glorious mountain peak of happiness and security is reached . . ."

TOM: Whoa! "On us weighs the burden"? *(Touches shoulder)* I don't feel anything.

ROSIE: It means we have a job to do.

TOM: O.K. But how about "shaping the world closer to the heart's desire"? What does that mean? That we should make the world square?

PETE *(Laughing)*: Maybe we could squeeze it into a football.

DARA: Or a soccer ball. *(All except* BRIAN *laugh.)* Brian, Tom's right. "Shaping the world" has to go.

BRIAN *(Miffed[7])*: I was just trying to be poetic. *(Crosses out)*

ROSIE: Now, what about "putting our shoulders to the wheel and rowing bravely upstream"? **R**

PETE: Why can't we row downstream?

DARA: You can't put your shoulder to the wheel and row at the same time. Not unless you have three arms.

ROSIE: It's also a mixed metaphor.[8]

TOM: And people don't put their *shoulders* to the wheel anyway.

PETE: That phrase about reaching happiness on a glorious mountain peak bothers me. Why does happiness have to be on top of a mountain?

BRIAN *(Angrily)*: All right! I'll cut it out.

---

7. ***(miffed)*** Brian is a little insulted and starting to lose his good feelings.
8. A metaphor compares two unlike things. A ***mixed metaphor*** gets the comparison mixed up. Brian starts out okay with "shoulders to the wheel," which is a common metaphor for working hard. But then he goes wrong, presenting the image of people with their shoulders against a wheel while they're rowing a boat to the top of a mountain.

Additional Support

Differentiated Instruction

Speech Writing Explain to students that people give speeches for various reasons. Most speeches fall into one or more of four categories. Those categories are to educate or inform; to entertain; to inspire; and to persuade. Ask students to think of one occasion where each type of speech would be appropriate. **OL**

Have students choose one of the four categories, write that type of speech, and deliver it to the class. **AL**

(Crosses out more lines)

DARA: Listen, Brian, why not just say something like, "We have a job to do, and we'll do it"? That's nice and vague.[9]

TOM: *Too* vague. How about: "We, the cavalry of tomorrow, shall charge across the corpses of poverty, ignorance, and prejudice."[10]

BRIAN *(Shaking head)*: And you think what I wrote is too dramatic!

DARA: Tom, that's horrible.

PETE: Hey, how about "the submarines of tomorrow shall speed under the shoals[11] of injustice"?

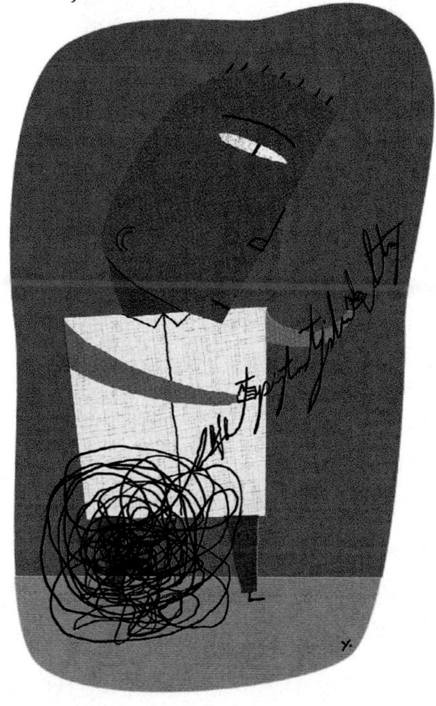

ROSIE: Give me a break! **EL**

BRIAN *(Running hand through hair)*: I don't believe this.

TOM: What do you have left, Brian?

BRIAN *(Bitterly)*: Not much. *(Reads)* "Dr. Clune, distinguished[12] guests, teachers, and students . . . *I thank you*"!

OTHERS *(Ad lib)*: I love it! It's terrific! Short and to the point! Read it again! *(Etc.)*

BRIAN *(Reading)*: "Dr. Clune, distinguished guests, teachers, and students . . . I thank you." *(All cheer and clap BRIAN on back as curtain closes.)* **R**

THE END

9. Something that is ***vague*** is unclear and can be understood in more than one way.
10. In Tom's metaphor, soldiers on horses ***(cavalry)*** ride to the attack ***(charge)*** over dead bodies ***(corpses)***.
11. Here, ***shoals*** seems to mean "shallow waters."
12. The ***distinguished*** guests would be important people.

Teach

EL Language Coach

Idioms Say: Point out that the sentence "Give me a break!" is an idiomatic expression, one that cannot be figured out from its word-for-word meaning. Rosie says, "Give me a break!" to express that she finds Pete's suggestion ridiculous. Ask students to think of other expressions that might mean the same thing. **OL EL**

R Reading Skill

Review Inferring

Ask: How long is Brian's speech by the end of the play? Do you think he is pleased with his speech? Give reasons for your answer. *(Brian's speech is one sentence long at the end of the play. Responses may include: No, he is bitter when he reads the one sentence.)* **OL** What statement about graduation speeches might the author of this play be making? *(The author might be saying he or she thinks graduation speeches are generally too long and full of meaningless words.)* **AL**

Differentiated Instruction

Reading Plays This play offers a great opportunity for students to practice reading aloud with expression. Have students form groups of five and read the play aloud. As students read their lines, encourage them to pay attention to how their characters would be feeling. Have students use facial expressions, tones of voice, and gestures to convey emotions during the reading. Ask students how reading the play aloud helped them better understand its meaning and the characters' feelings. **OL**

Tips for Independent Reading

Stress the importance of each student's spending at least thirty minutes a day in independent reading and suggest books, such as those shown here, related to the Big Question.

Fiction

Tell students that reading fictional accounts of people who have overcome obstacles can also give them information on becoming who they want to become.

Ask students to share an example of a fictional story they've read that could give them information on becoming who they want to become; they may name fictional stories from this unit.

UNIT 2

Reading on Your Own

To read more about the Big Question, choose one of these books from your school or local library. Work on your reading skills by choosing books that are challenging to you.

Fiction

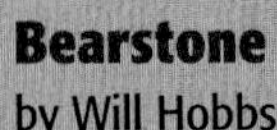

A Girl Named Disaster
by Nancy Farmer

When Nhamo, a Mozambican teenager, is faced with being forced into marriage, she flees in a stolen boat and finds herself alone in an uncharted lake. Read to find out how Nhamo relies on herself as she faces the dangers of the African wilderness and learns what it means to be a young woman.

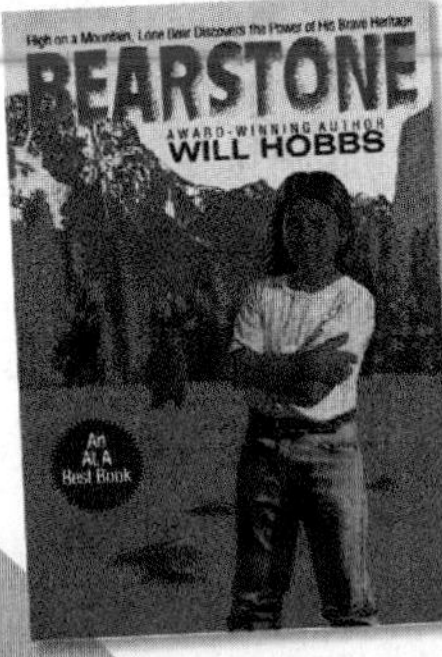

Bearstone
by Will Hobbs

A young Native American boy is sent to live near the Rocky Mountains with an elderly rancher after he is kicked out of a home for troubled youth. Read to find out about Cloyd Atcitty's life-changing experiences and what he learns about himself, his cultural heritage, and the value of friendship and commitment.

Shabanu: Daughter of the Wind
by Suzanne Fisher Staples

Shabanu, a strong willed and independent young woman, lives in the traditional nomadic culture of Pakistan. Read about Shabanu's struggles with the rules and roles of young women in her culture and how she tries to be who she wants to be.

Stargirl
by Jerry Spinelli

A high school is rocked by the appearance of a girl who is definitely not a part of the mainstream: Stargirl. Read about how Stargirl tries to stay true to herself despite being rejected by her peers and her own attempt to be "normal" to please the boy she really likes.

Additional Support

Differentiated Instruction

Use the Glencoe BookLink CD-ROM to create customized reading lists to help students answer the Big Question. Suggestions for Unit 2:

Grade 4: *Neighborhood Odes* by Gary Soto
Grade 5: *Letters from a Slave Girl* by May E. Lyons
Grade 6: *Baseball in April and Other Stories* by Gary Soto
Grade 7: *Shabanu: Daughter of the Wind* by Suzanne Fisher Staples
Grade 8: *Dreams into Deeds: Nine Women Who Dared* by Linda Peavy and Ursula Smith

Nonfiction

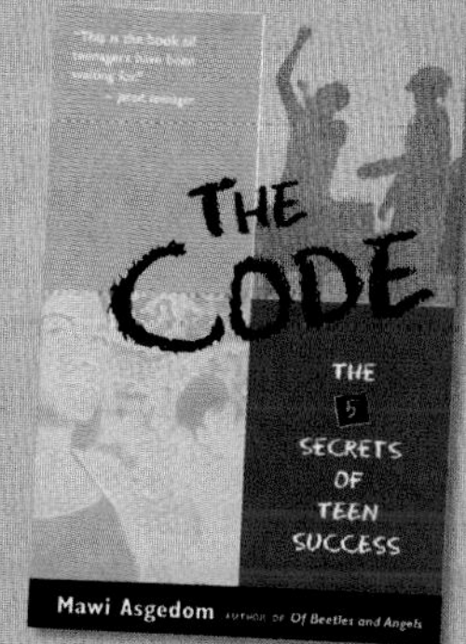

The Code: The Five Secrets of Teen Success
by Mawi Asgedom

Mawi Asgedom came to the U.S. as a teenage refugee from Somalia, a nation that was in the middle of a civil war. Read to learn the secrets of success that he learned in his struggle to overcome life's hardships and to earn a scholarship to a top university.

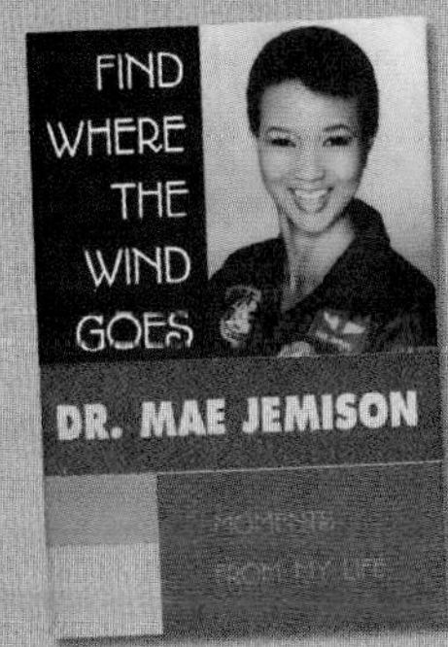

Find Where the Wind Goes: Moments from My Life
by Dr. Mae Jemison

This important American scientist writes the engaging story of her career from her struggles as a youth on Chicago's South Side to becoming the first African-American astronaut. Read to follow Dr. Jemison's path from regular kid to a doctor at the top of her field and the top of the world.

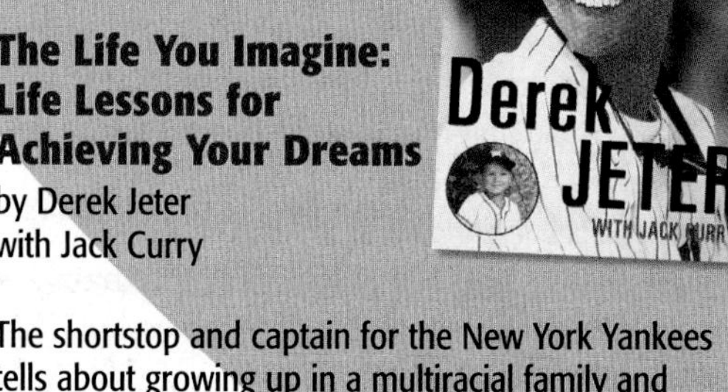

The Life You Imagine: Life Lessons for Achieving Your Dreams
by Derek Jeter
with Jack Curry

The shortstop and captain for the New York Yankees tells about growing up in a multiracial family and chasing down his dreams of playing baseball in the big leagues. Read to find out how Jeter overcame the obstacles in his life to become an internationally known sports star.

Savion! My Life in Tap
by Savion Glover
and Bruce Weber

Savion Glover is the master of tap dancing, wowing audiences across the nation with his fast feet and artistic style in shows, including "Bring in 'da Noise, Bring in 'da Funk." Read to hear Glover's rhythmic voice come through as he tells how mentors big and small helped him become a dancing sensation.

READING ON YOUR OWN

Nonfiction

Share with students that the books on this page are all nonfiction books. They will give detailed accounts of the lives of the subjects.

Autobiographies

Ask: Can you tell if these are autobiographies or biographies by reading the title, viewing the cover, and knowing the author? *(Yes. If the name of the subject is also the name of the author, the book is an autobiography. Tell students that even when the subject has help writing the book, as in the case of Derek Jeter and Savion Glover, the book is still considered an autobiography.)* **OL**

About the Subjects

Invite students to share information they know about the subjects on this page. What do students expect to find out in these autobiographies? **AS**

Test-Taking Tips

TIP Remind students that when they begin to answer the questions, they should refer back to the passage to find evidence for their answers. Students are never asked to speculate without adequate evidence; they need only to refer back to the passage and find clues in the text.

TIP Occasionally students encounter questions that seem extremely difficult. They should eliminate, guess, and then move on. If there is no penalty for wrong answers on the test, students should answer every question. In this case, even if the student isn't able to eliminate any of the answer choices, it's still to his or her advantage to guess.

Literature Online

Unit Assessment Have students access the Web site to prepare for the Unit 2 test.

Test Practice

Part 1: Literary Elements

Read each passage. Then, on a separate sheet of paper, write the numbers 1-5. Next to each of numbers 1-4, write the letter of the right answer for that question. Next to number 5, write your answer to the final question.

from "Late to the Ball"

Cinderella sighed as she emptied out a bucket of filthy water and suds. Her knees hurt from kneeling on cold, hard stones to clean the fireplaces. Her hands and wrists ached and throbbed from scrubbing. Behind her, now, she heard a clatter of hoofs and looked up to see a royal messenger arrive at the house.

"Oh!" she thought. "He's bringing our invitation to the prince's ball!" She hurried inside, flew through the rest of the cleaning, and then ran into the parlor, where her stepmother and two stepsisters were talking excitedly.

"Did our invitation come?" asked Cinderella, unable to stop herself from bouncing a little on her toes as she spoke.

Her stepmother spoke coldly. "The invitation is only for *us*," she said, not hesitating to lie. "It does not include *you*."

Objectives
Literature Identify literary elements: narrator, setting, point of view, sensory details
Writing Evaluate a narrator

from *Good Times and Bad*

As a girl, I was convinced that, compared to me, Cinderella had it easy. At least she hadn't had to listen to the shouts of happy children playing outside while she was up to her elbows in soap suds. I, on the other hand, was tortured by just such sounds. The apartment where we lived in the 1990's was right next to a park. I had to spend Saturdays on what Dad called "helping out." This always involved a broom and a mop. Meanwhile, my friends, right outside our windows, were playing tag and climbing trees and doing it all quite loudly. How I came to hate Saturdays!

from "Real Life"

Like most people, I find it satisfying when evil is punished and goodness rewarded. This is why, as a child, I loved fairy tales. My favorite was the story of Cinderella. I felt a real thrill when justice was done.

In my own life, I kept waiting for that kind of justice. The problem is, of course, that Cinderella didn't solve her own problems. A fairy godmother and love-struck prince solved them for her. I had neither a fairy godmother nor a prince.

Unit Assessment To prepare for the Unit Test, go to www.glencoe.com.

from "Poor Me"

Anyone who thinks the life of a princess must be easy is simply wrong. I am, indeed, a princess, but I had the horrible luck of being born into the Charming family.

In the years before her marriage, my mother was known as Cinderella. Pop, of course, was Prince Charming. Now they are King and Queen Charming, and I am their unlucky daughter. It's bad enough that my name is Rosebud. (Give me a break!) What's worse is the amount of *work* around here, and there is a *lot* of it!

People think that living in an enormous stone castle, as I do, must be great. Ha! Dirt blows in through every opening. Once a week, the rugs have to be carried outside and whacked on with heavy sticks. The paintings (lots of paintings) on the walls need dusting every day. And laundry? Don't get me started on laundry! But the most awful thing is what happens if I complain about even one of my chores.

"What?" says my mother with a look of disbelief. "Why, when *I* was a girl, I scrubbed floors until my knees were raw! When *I* was a girl . . ."

---

1. Which passage has a third-person narrator?

A. from "Late to the Ball"
B. from *Good Times and Bad*
C. from "Real Life"
D. from "Poor Me"

2. Which quotation from "Poor Me" describes the setting?

A. "Anyone who thinks the life of a princess must be easy is simply wrong."
B. "It's bad enough that my name is Rosebud. (Give me a break!)"
C. "People think that living in an enormous stone castle, as I do, must be great."
D. "But the most awful thing is what happens if I complain about even one of my chores."

3. Sensory details in "Late to the Ball" are used **mainly** to emphasize

A. Cinderella's sweetness
B. Cinderella's eagerness
C. the stepmother's excitement
D. the difficulty of Cinderella's work

4. Which quotation from *Good Times and Bad* describes the setting?

A. "As a girl, I was convinced that, compared to me, Cinderella had it easy."
B. "The apartment where we lived in the 1990's was right next to the park."
C. "I had to spend Saturdays on what Dad called 'helping out.'"
D. "How I came to hate Saturdays!"

5. Choose a narrator from the passages. Describe what you like or don't like about that narrator and explain how you know what you know about that person.

Test Practice

Part 1: Literary Elements

1. A
2. C
3. D
4. B
5. Answers will vary. Sample response: I don't like that the narrator from *Good Times and Bad* whines a lot about her situation. She compares herself to Cinderella and feels her life is worse. She is jealous of her friends who get to play.

Resources for pages 244–249

Use these resources to review, assess, or reteach the Unit: Active Learning and Note-Taking Guide, Selection and Unit Assessment, ExamView Assessment Suite, and Differentiated Instruction Tool Software.

Test-Taking Tips

TIP Tell students that when they're answering a multiple-choice question, they should begin by reading the question carefully. Next, they should read each possible response. If necessary, they should reread portions of the passage to look for the answer. Finally, they should choose the best response.

TIP Students might choose to read the questions on a language arts test before they read the passage. This way, they will know what to look for as they read.

Part 2: Reading Skills

Read the passage. Then, on a separate sheet of paper, write the numbers 1-5. Next to each of numbers 1-4, write the letter of the right answer for that question. Next to number 5, write your answer to the final question.

Jim Thorpe

1 The person that ABC's Wide World of Sports named the "Athlete of the Century" is someone unknown to many Americans today: Jim Thorpe. Who was this sports star, and what made him so remarkable?

2 Jim Thorpe was a natural athlete who could do almost anything better than almost anyone else. From 1913 until 1919, he played professional baseball. He then moved to football, playing professionally until 1926. In 1912, he won Olympic gold medals in both the pentathlon and the decathlon—the first athlete ever to do so. Both are multi-event competitions that require running, jumping, and throwing. The pentathlon consists of five events; the decathlon consists of ten.

3 Thorpe was born in 1888 on a reservation in Oklahoma. Like many other Native American children, he was sent to boarding school at an early age. Unhappy about sitting indoors all day, he often left and ran twenty miles home. Later, he transferred to the Carlisle Indian School in Pennsylvania. There he became a college star in every sport he tried: tennis, golf, baseball, basketball, hockey, lacrosse, and football. He led the football team of his small school to victories over the best college teams of the time. In 1912, he went to Sweden to compete in the Olympics and came home a champion.

4 The Olympic rules of his time did not allow professional athletes to compete. In 1913, the Olympic Committee decided that Thorpe had been a professional athlete. This was because, in the summers of 1909 and 1910, he had made a small amount of money playing baseball in North Carolina. The

Objectives
Reading Understand sequence: chronological order • Make connections from text to self • Make inferences • Activate prior knowledge

Committee took away Thorpe's medals and removed his records from the record book. Seventy years after he had stunned the world with his amazing ability at the Olympics, and after he had died, that decision was overturned. Thorpe's medals were given to his family, and his records were restored.

5 Jim Thorpe's story should be as well-known as that of Babe Ruth or Muhammad Ali or any number of more famous athletes. Although he was neither the fastest person in the world nor the strongest, there may never have been a better example of an all-around athlete.

---

1. Which paragraph is arranged in exact time order?

A. paragraph 2
B. paragraph 3
C. paragraph 4
D. paragraph 5

2. A reader can infer that the most extraordinary thing about Jim Thorpe is that

A. he did so many things so well.
B. he was a professional in the Olympics.
C. he won two gold medals at the same Olympics.
D. he could run long distances even as a young child.

3. Which statement might be said by a reader who was "making a connection" to this passage?

A. "Jim Thorpe certainly was a great athlete!"
B. "I wonder whether Thorpe's parents were good athletes."
C. "My Aunt Cindy played several different sports in college, too."
D. "It's a real shame that Thorpe's medals weren't returned until *after* his death."

4. One can infer from this passage that the term "professional athlete" is used to mean someone who

A. is paid to play a sport.
B. is unusually good at a sport.
C. plays a sport after completing college.
D. plays more than one sport successfully.

5. What makes winning a decathlon different from winning another competition, such as speed skating or diving? Use what you already know about sports and what you now know about a decathlon to answer this question.

Test Practice

Part 2: Reading Skills

1. B
2. A
3. C
4. A
5. Answers will vary. Sample response: Winning a decathlon requires skill in a number of different athletic activities. Winning a speed skating competition, on the other hand, requires skill in only one athletic activity.

Test-Taking Tips

TIP When answering a question about multiple-meaning words, like question 6 or 7, try placing each word in the two sentences until you find the word that fits in both sentences.

Test Practice

Part 3: Vocabulary

1. C
2. B
3. A
4. D
5. B
6. C
7. B
8. A

Part 3: Vocabulary

On a separate sheet of paper, write the numbers 1–10. Next to each number, write the letter of the right answer for that question.

Write the letter of the word or phrase that means about the same as the underlined word.

1. quite <u>tantalizing</u>

A. fresh **C.** tempting
B. difficult **D.** unexpected

2. when we <u>complied</u>

A. arrived **C.** began again
B. did as asked **D.** gathered up

3. to <u>contemplate</u> an idea

A. consider **C.** learn about
B. agree with **D.** disapprove of

4. a selfish <u>motive</u>

A. plan **C.** remark
B. request **D.** reason

5. to be <u>optimistic</u>

A. brave **C.** foolish
B. hopeful **D.** energetic

6. Choose the multiple-meaning word that fits in both of the sentences.

A frightened or angry dog might ___ at a stranger.

Jorge landed hard and felt a bone in his foot ___ .

A. bark **C.** snap
B. break **D.** jump

7. Choose the multiple-meaning word that fits in both of the sentences.

It's Lucy's ___ to wash dishes tonight.

A noise behind me made me ___ and stare.

A. work **C.** stop
B. turn **D.** watch

8. In describing the Liberation Army soldier, Ji-li Jiang says, "She was slim and stood <u>straight</u> as a reed." In which sentence below does *straight* have the same meaning?

A. The tree grew <u>straight</u> and tall.
B. Raul was sick for six days <u>straight</u>.
C. Mara was too confused to think <u>straight</u>.
D. Don't lie to me; just give me a <u>straight</u> answer.

Objectives
Vocabulary Learn and use new vocabulary • Understand multiple-meaning words • Use context clues: multiple-meaning words
Grammar Identify and correctly use nouns and pronouns • Use correct pronoun antecedents

Part 4: Writing Skills

Read the following paragraph. Then, on a separate sheet of paper, write the numbers 1-5. Next to each number, write the letter of the right answer for that question.

(1) Rosa Parks was arrested on December 1. (2) Her and her lawyers went to court the next Monday. (3) The courtroom was filled with people. (4) When the judge asked if Parks wanted to plead guilty or not guilty, they told him "not guilty." (5) She was, however, found guilty. (6) But that was not the end of the story. (7) A group that wanted the situation to change asked folks to stop riding the city buses. (8) This effort in montgomery, Alabama, was extremely successful. (9) It was the beginning of what we now call "the civil rights movement."

---

1. What is the best way to write sentence 2?

A. She and her lawyers went to court the next Monday.

B. Her lawyers and her went to court the next Monday.

C. The next Monday, both her and her lawyers went to court.

D. (Leave as is.)

2. What is the problem with sentence 4?

A. The antecedent for *him* is unclear.

B. The antecedent for *they* is unclear.

C. The pronoun *he* should be used instead of "the judge."

D. The pronoun *she* should be used instead of "Parks."

3. What pronoun would make a good substitution for *folks* in sentence 7?

A. her

B. them

C. everyone

D. themselves

4. Which noun from the passage is a proper noun that should be capitalized?

A. lawyers (sentence 2)

B. courtroom (sentence 3)

C. city (sentence 7)

D. montgomery (sentence 8)

5. Which noun from the passage is a compound noun?

A. Monday

B. courtroom

C. beginning

D. Movement

Test Practice

Part 4: Writing Skills

1. A
2. B
3. C
4. D
5. B

UNIT 3

Skills Scope and Sequence

Readability Scores Key
Dale-Chall/DRP/Lexile

PACING (DAYS) STANDARD	BLOCK	INSTRUCTIONAL SEGMENT LITERATURE	READING SKILLS	LITERARY ELEMENTS
1	1	**Unit Warm-Up, pp. 252–265** Genre Focus: "Broken Chain" by Gary Soto **4.8/53/890**, SE p. 255	Activating Prior Knowledge, TWE p. 257 Drawing Conclusions, SE pp. 254, 256 Responding, SE pp. 254, 255, TWE p. 257 Synthesizing, SE pp. 254, 257 Main idea and supporting details, SE pp. 254, 265 Fluency, TWE p. 251 Connecting, TWE p. 255	Conflict, SE pp. 254, 263, TWE pp. 254, 260, 261, 264 Dialogue, SE pp. 254, 258, 261 Character, SE pp. 254, 259, 262, TWE pp. 257, 258, 264 Plot, SE pp. 254, 260, 264
3	2	**Reading Workshop 1, pp. 266–291** "Friendships and Peer Pressure" by Mary H. Bronson, Betty M. Hubbard, Michael J. Cleary, and Dinah Zike **6.7/62/960**, SE p. 270 "Amigo Brothers" by Piri Thomas **6/55/890**, SE p. 278	Drawing Conclusions, SE pp. 266, 267, 269, 270, 273, 275, 277, 279, 286, 291 Activating Prior Knowledge, SE p. 272 Connecting, SE pp. 284, 291, TWE pp. 277, 278 Inferring, SE p. 285, TWE p. 284 Responding, TWE pp. 270, 284	Text features, TWE p. 269 Conflict, TWE pp. 277, 288 Text features, SE pp. 269, 272, 275 Conflict, SE pp. 277, 279, 280, 281, 283, 289, 291 Dialogue, TWE p. 280 Sensory Details, TWE p. 287 Plot, TWE p. 288
1		**Writing Workshop, Part 1, pp. 292–297** Writing Product: Short Fictional Story		Characters, Setting, Conflict, SE p. 292–293, TWE p. 292 Dialogue, SE pp. 292, 295–296, TWE p. 296 Plot, SE p. 293
3	1	**Reading Workshop 2, pp. 298–319** "Framed" by Don Wulffson **4.7/54/790**, SE p. 302 "After Twenty Years" by William Sydney Porter **5.9/51/850**, SE p. 312	Responding, SE pp. 298, 299, 301, 305, 307, 309, 311, 315, 319 Drawing Conclusions, pp. 303, 309, 316, 319 Connecting, TWE pp. 301, 314 Responding, TWE p. 303	Dialogue, SE pp. 301, 302, 304, 306, 309, 311, 313, 319, TWE p. 301 Character, TWE pp. 312, 316 Sensory Details, TWE pp. 312, 315 Plot, TWE pp. 316, 317

Unit 3 Big Question

The question, "Who can we really count on?" is designed to help students discern the qualities that make a person dependable and trustworthy, to gain new insight into themselves and others, and to be entertained. In this unit, students will read a variety of selections with inspiring characters and situations.

Unit 3 Genre

Many of the selections in this unit are short stories about one or two main characters. These selections will also help students answer the big question: Who can we count on? Use these short stories to help students learn to evaluate characters in literature and in real life situations.

CRITICAL THINKING	VOCABULARY	WRITING AND GRAMMAR	LISTENING, SPEAKING, AND VIEWING
Evaluation, TWE p. 260 Visualizing, TWE p. 264 Analysis, TWE p. 264	Antonyms, TWE p. 255 Synonyms, TWE pp. 255, 263, 265		Viewing the Photo, TWE p. 250
Visualizing, TWE p. 278 Comprehension, TWE pp. 281, 282, 286 Respond, SE p. 274 Connect, SE pp. 274, 291 Question, SE p. 274 Interpret, SE p. 290 Analyze, SE p. 290, TWE p. 283 Application, TWE p. 269	Synonyms, SE pp. 268, 271, 275, 276, 278, 282, 287, 288, 291, TWE pp. 268, 285 Antonyms, TWE p. 276 Slang, TWE p. 280 Academic Vocabulary, SE pp. 266, 275 Context Clues, TWE p. 276	Modifiers, SE pp. 275, 291 Write About Your Reading, SE p. 274 Write to Learn, SE pp. 268, 269, 277, 290 Writing Application, SE pp. 275, 291	Listening and Speaking, TWE p. 285 Talk About Your Reading, SE p. 290 Viewing the Painting, SE p. 283 Viewing the Photo, TWE p. 270
		Writing Traits: Ideas, SE pp. 292, 293 Plan, SE p. 293 Organization, SE p. 294 Modifiers, TWE p. 297 Adjectives and Adverbs, SE p. 297 Write to Learn, SE p. 294	
Infer, SE pp. 308, 318 Comprehension, TWE p. 306 Evaluate, SE pp. 308, 318 Draw Conclusions, SE pp. 308 Connect, SE p. 318 Comprehension, TWE p. 315	Academic Vocabulary, SE pp. 298, 309 Idioms, TWE pp. 302, 307 Antonyms, SE pp 300, 304, 309, 310, 312, 313, 317, 319, TWE pp. 300, 310 Vocabulary Preview, SE pp. 300, 310	Articles, SE p. 309 Write About Your Reading, SE p. 308, TWE p. 308 Write to Learn, SE pp. 301, 310, 311, 318 Writing Application, SE pp. 309, 319 Demonstrative Adjectives, SE p. 319	Viewing the Painting, SE p. 305 Talk About Your Reading, SE p. 318; TWE pp. 314, 316 Viewing the Photo, TWE p. 302

Skills Scope and Sequence *continued*

Readability Scores Key
Dale-Chall/DRP/Lexile

PACING (DAYS) STANDARD	BLOCK	INSTRUCTIONAL SEGMENT LITERATURE	READING SKILLS	LITERARY ELEMENTS
3	1	**Reading Workshop 3, pp. 320–339** "Loser" by Aimee Bender **4.7/55/930**, SE p. 324 "Friends Forever" by Sari Locker **5.8/55/850**, SE p. 334	Synthesizing, SE pp. 320, 321, 323, 328, 329, 330, 331, 333, 335, 339 Drawing Conclusions, SE pp. 324, 331 Previewing, SE pp. 334, 339 Connecting, TWE pp. 324, 336 Responding, TWE pp. 325, 335, 337	Character, SE pp. 323, 325, 329, 331, TWE p. 327 Dialogue, TWE p. 327 Nonfiction SE pp. 333, 336, 339 Text Features, TWE p. 332 Point of View, TWE p. 324
1	cont'd. ↓	**Writing Workshop, Part 2, pp. 340-345** Writing Product: Short Fictional Story	Fluency, TWE p. 345	Conflict, TWE p. 343
2	1	**Reading Workshop 4, pp. 346–367** "The Good Samaritan" by René Saldaña **4.6/48/730**, SE p. 350 "The Brink's Robbery" by Henry and Melissa Billings **5.8/51/630**, SE p. 362	Determining the main idea, SE pp. 346, 347, 349, 351, 357, 359, 361, 363, 367, TWE p. 355 Inferring, SE p. 350, TWE pp. 352, 353 Fluency, TWE p. 356 Connecting, SE pp. 354, 359 Reviewing, SE. p. 356 Fluency, TWE p. 363 Responding, SE p. 365 Drawing Conclusions, TWE p. 352 Synthesizing, TWE pp. 356, 364 Sequence, TWE p. 364	Plot, SE pp. 349, 351, 353, 354, 357, 359, 361, 362, 363, 364, 367 Conflict, TWE pp. 348, 363 Character, TWE pp. 351, 354 Dialogue, TWE p. 353 Evaluation, TWE p. 355 Figurative Language, TWE p. 350
2	2	**Comparing Literature Workshop, pp. 368–393** "Lob's Girl" by Joan Aiken **4.9/54/980**, SE p. 371 "The Highwayman" by Alfred Noyes, SE p. 386	Inferring, SE p. 373, TWE pp. 377, 380, 383, 389 Drawing Conclusions, SE pp. 375, 380, 392, 393, TWE pp. 379, 381, 384 Synthesizing, SE p. 393 Fluency, TWE pp. 382, 389 Connecting, TWE pp. 372, 375 Main Idea and Details, TWE pp. 388, 390 Responding, TWE p. 391	Plot, SE pp. 368, 369, 371, 372, 376, 377, 378, 379, 381, 382, 384, 386, 387, 388, 389, 391, 393 Setting, TWE p. 373 Conflict, TWE p. 374 Character, TWE pp. 384, 389, 391 Sensory Details, TWE p. 386 Plot, TWE pp. 397, 398
2	1	**Unit Wrap-Up, pp. 394–407**		

CRITICAL THINKING	VOCABULARY	WRITING AND GRAMMAR	LISTENING, SPEAKING, AND VIEWING
Infer, SE p. 330 Evaluate, SE p. 330 Analyze, SE p. 330 Comprehension, TWE p. 326 Synthesize, SE p. 330, TWE p. 329 Connect, SE p. 338 Comprehension, TWE p. 337	Academic Vocabulary, SE pp. 320, 331 Using a thesaurus and synonyms, SE pp. 322, 326, 331, 332, 336, 339, TWE p. 325 Vocabulary Preview, SE pp. 322, 332 Vocabulary Check, SE pp. 331, 339 Using a thesaurus, TWE p. 336 Idioms, TWE p. 334	Write About Your Reading, SE pp. 330, 338 Comparing with adjectives, SE p. 331 Write to Learn, SE p. 322, 323, 333 Comparative and superlative adverbs, SE p. 339 Write About Your Reading, SE pp. 330, 338, TWE p. 338	Partner Talk, SE pp. 322, 323, 332, 333 Viewing the Painting, TWE pp. 326, 328 Viewing the Photo, TWE p. 334
	Dialogue, TWE p. 340 Word Choice, TWE p. 343	Writing a Short Fictional Story: Revising, Editing, and Presenting SE pp. 340–344	Reading Aloud, SE p. 345 Critiquing and Rewriting, TWE p. 344
Infer, SE pp. 358, 366 Evaluate, SE pp. 358, 366 Analysis, TWE p. 354 Analyze, SE p. 366 Evaluation, TWE p. 355	Word choice, SE pp. 348, 352, 355, 359, 360, 362, 367 General and Specific Words, TWE p. 349 Vocabulary Preview, SE pp. 348, 360 Synonyms and Antonyms, TWE pp. 352, 354 Word Choice, TWE pp. 353, 354, 357, 363 Synonyms, TWE p. 361 Vocabulary Check, SE pp. 359, 367	Write to Learn, SE pp. 348, 349, 360, 361 Write About Your Reading, SE pp. 358, 366, TWE pp. 358, 359 Writing Application, SE p. 359, 367 Prepositions, SE p. 359, TWE p. 364 Write About Your Reading, TWE p. 366 Interjections, SE p. 367	Partner Talk, SE pp. 348, 349 Viewing the Illustratrion, TWE pp. 350, 352 Viewing the Photos, TWE p. 362
Connect, SE p. 370 Comprehension, TWE pp. 371, 373, 375, 377, 378, 379 Evaluate, SE p. 111, TWE pp. 373, 376, 382 Analysis, TWE pp. 373, 380, 384, 388 Drawing Conclusions, TWE pp. 382, 389	Synonyms, SE pp. 374, 383, 385, 390, 392, TWE p. 380 Prefixes and suffixes, SE p. 370 Vocabulary Preview, SE pp. 370, 385 Vocabulary Check, SE p. 392 Context Clues, TWE p. 371 Idiomatic Expressions, TWE p. 371	Taking notes and using them to make a diagram that compares the plot in two pieces of literature, SE p. 393 Adjectives and Adverbs, TWE p. 376	Viewing the Photo, TWE p. 381 Viewing the Illustration, TWE p. 387

UNIT 3

Unit Resources

Reading with Purpose offers a comprehensive package of tools to optimize student learning and the teaching experience. Each resource has been designed to assist students in specific areas and to offer instructional support for teachers. While all of these areas are covered in the core textbook, some students may need extra practice or additional help in specific areas. The resource package is designed so that you, the teacher, can choose which items will best assist your students. You may also use these resources as homework assignments and for assessment purposes. The following are resources recommended for use with Unit 3.

Keys for Unit Resources

- Blackline Master
- Workbook
- Supplemental Text
- CD-ROM
- DVD
- Transparency
- Web-based
- Fast Files

Essential Instructional Support

FAST FILE UNIT 3 RESOURCES

Reading and Literature

- Academic Vocabulary Development
- Big Question: School to Home Connection
- The Big Question Foldable
- Genre Study
- Unit Challenge: Planner and Rubrics
- Comparing Literature Graphic Organizer
- Key Reading Skills Practice
- Active Reading Graphic Organizers
- Literary Analysis
- Selection Vocabulary Development

Writing, Grammar, and Spelling

- Spelling and Handwriting Practice
- Grammar Practice
- Writing Workshop Graphic Organizer

Listening, Speaking, and Viewing

- Viewing and Representing Activities
- Listening and Speaking Activities

English Language Learners

- English Language Coach

DIFFERENTIATED INSTRUCTION

- Leveled Vocabulary Development
- Skills Level Up!
- Listening Library CD
- BookLink 3
- Literature Library Vocabulary Puzzlemaker
- Vocabulary Puzzlemaker

ASSESSMENT

- Selection and Unit Assessments
- Selection Quick Checks
- Assessment by Learning Objectives
- Rubrics for Assessing Student Writing, Listening, and Speaking
- Glencoe Online Essay Grading
- Interactive Tutor Self-Assessment
- ExamView Assessment Suite
- Literature Library ExamView Assessment Suite

Additional Instructional Support

WRITING, GRAMMAR, AND SPELLING

- Real Success in Writing: Research and Reports
- Writing Constructed Responses Sourcebook
- Spelling Power eWorkbook
- Grammar & Composition Handbook
- Grammar and Language Workbook
- Revising with Style eWorkbook

READING AND LITERATURE

- Active Learning and Note Taking Guide
- inTime Magazines
- Backpack Reader Volume 1
- Literature Library
- Literature Launchers Pre-Reading Videos DVD
- Literature Classics

TRANSPARENCIES

- Read Aloud, Think Aloud
- Literary and Text Analysis Transparencies
- Bellringer Options Transparencies
- Grammar and Writing Workshop Transparencies
- Fine Arts Transparencies

TECHNOLOGY

- TeacherWorks Plus
- StudentWorks Plus
- BookLink 3
- Skill Level Up!
- ExamView Assessment Suite
- Interactive Tutor Self-Assessment
- Listening Library CD
- Spanish Listening Library CD
- Literature Classics
- Literature Launchers Pre-Reading Videos DVD
- Literature Library ExamView Assessment Suite
- Vocabulary Puzzlemaker
- Literature Library Vocabulary Puzzlemaker
- glencoe.com
- Online Student Edition
- Presentation Plus!
- Glencoe Online Essay Grading

ENGLISH LANGUAGE LEARNER

- English Language Coach
- Fluency Practice and Assessment
- inTime Magazines (Spanish)
- Spanish Listening Library CD

PROFESSIONAL DEVELOPMENT

- Professional Development Package

Additional Glencoe Resources

FOLDABLES™ Study Organizer

Dinah Zike's Foldables

Foldables are three-dimensional, interactive graphic organizers that help students practice basic writing skills, review key vocabulary terms, and answer Big Questions. Every unit contains a foldable activity. You can find the pattern and directions for the Unit 3 Foldable in the Unit 3 Resources Fast Files booklet. You can use the foldables as they are presented or modify them to suit the needs of your students. More information about foldables for Unit 3 can be found on page R8.

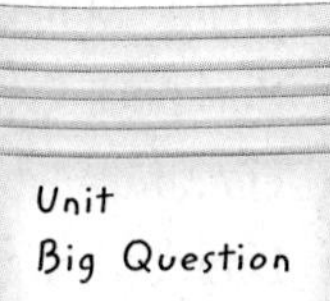

Glencoe Literature Library

The collection of hardcover books include full-length novels, novellas, plays and works of nonfiction. Each volume consists of at least one complete extended-length reading accompanied by several related readings from a broad range of genres. A separate Study Guide for each Glencoe Literature Library book provides teaching notes and reproducible activity pages for students.

Glencoe Literature Library titles that complement this unit include:

The Cay by Theodore Taylor
Missing May by Cynthia Rylant
Number the Stars by Lois Lowry
Treasure Island by Robert Louis Stevenson

Literature Online

For a wealth of online resources that support the instruction in Unit 3 of *Glencoe Literature: Reading with Purpose,* students and teachers can visit our Web site at www.glencoe.com. Students will find additional learning, practice, and assessment opportunities such as these, which are noted in the student text:

- **Big Question Overview**
- **Study Central**
- **Author Search**
- **Writing Models**
- **Interactive Literary Elements Handbook**
- **Web Activities**

Teachers will find planning and instructional tools that include the following:

- **Book Lesson Plans**
- **Teacher Forum**
- **Professional Development**
- **Web Activities Lesson Plans (with answers to student activities)**

Go to www.glencoe.com to see the entire selection of Reading with Purpose online resources.

GLENCOE BOOKLINK

Use the Glencoe BookLink 3 CD-ROM, a database of more than 26,700 titles, to *create customized reading lists* for your students.

- Search for award-winning titles, (e.g., Newbery Award winners, Coretta Scott King Award winners, and Caldecott Medal winners) and for books on several state-recommended reading lists.
- Find Degrees of Reading Power™ (DRP) and Lexile™ readability scores for all selections.
- Organize reading lists by students' reading level, author, genre, theme, or area of interest.
- Get a brief summary of each selection.

You can find recommended leveled readings for this unit with Reading on Your Own (see page 120).

Glencoe's **Presentation Plus!**, a multimedia teaching tool, lets you present dynamic lessons that will engage your students. Using Microsoft PowerPoint,® you can customize the presentations to create your own personalized lessons. Use **CheckPoint** questions with interactive response keypads to get immediate student feedback during lessons, to increase student participation, and to assess student comprehension.

A lively collection of articles drawn from issues of the TIME family of magazines helps students develop the skills they need to interact with informational text in a meaningful way. Each of the news stories, feature articles, reviews, profiles, and essays in the magazine connect to an author, work, or theme in *Glencoe Literature: Reading with Purpose.* Articles for Unit 3 are found in Volume A. See the *inTIME* Teacher's Guide for specific connections to each unit and for reproducible student worksheets designed to develop students' reading and critical thinking skills.

Literature Launchers

Set the scene with Glencoe's Literature Launchers, engaging video segments that introduce each unit's genre focus. Each video brings the genre to life, relating it to your students' worlds.

Insert the Glencoe Literature Launchers Pre-Reading Videos DVD into your DVD player. Select the Unit 3 Launcher from the menu to introduce the genre and Big Question for this unit.

Online Essay Grader

Use Glencoe's Online Essay Grading to score your students' writing and to provide individualized feedback to each student automatically.

You and your students can visit www.glencoe.com to link to the essay grader. *Students* can enter their essays and receive feedback on demand. *You* can manage demographic data, assign tests and generate individual student and aggregated reports. The essay grader can help you

- Save time with automatic scoring and individualized feedback.
- Supplement in-class writing instruction using guided writing practice.
- Get reports for individual students or for special populations.
- Track student improvement over time.

REAL Success: Reading Excellence at All Levels

Glencoe now provides all of your students with the tools they need to become better, more enthusiastic readers. The REAL Success suite of reading and language arts products encourages reading excellence by meeting the needs of students at all levels. Glencoe products that can be used in conjunction with Unit 3 include the following:

- Jamestown Literature: An Adapted Reader
- Jamestown *Reading Fluency*
- Jamestown *Critical Reading Series, In the Line of Duty*
- *Vocabulary Builder*
- *The Glencoe Reader, Course 2*

To order these products, call Glencoe at 1-800-USA-READ.

Teacher Wraparound Edition Key

Level Appropriate Code

AS = Activities for all students

AL = Activities for students working above grade level

OL = Activities for students working at grade level

BL = Activities for students working below grade level

EL = Activities for English language learners

Teacher Wraparound Prompts

R **Reading Skill** These activities help you teach reading skills and vocabulary.

V **Vocabulary** These activities help students comprehend words and incorporate into reading.

C **Critical Thinking** These strategies help students apply and extend what they have learned.

BQ **BIG Question** These activities and questions prompt students to prepare to answer the Big Question.

W **Writing** These activities provide writing opportunities to help students practice writing and comprehend text.

L **Literary Element** These activities and questions help students comprehend selections and learn more about each genre.

E **Text Element** These activities help students comprehend text elements.

LSV **Listening, Speaking, Viewing** These activities help students practice listening, speaking, and viewing skills.

EL **English Language Coach** These skills help English language learners as well as students who need additional reading support.

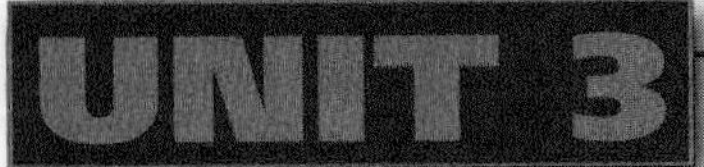

Professional Development Center

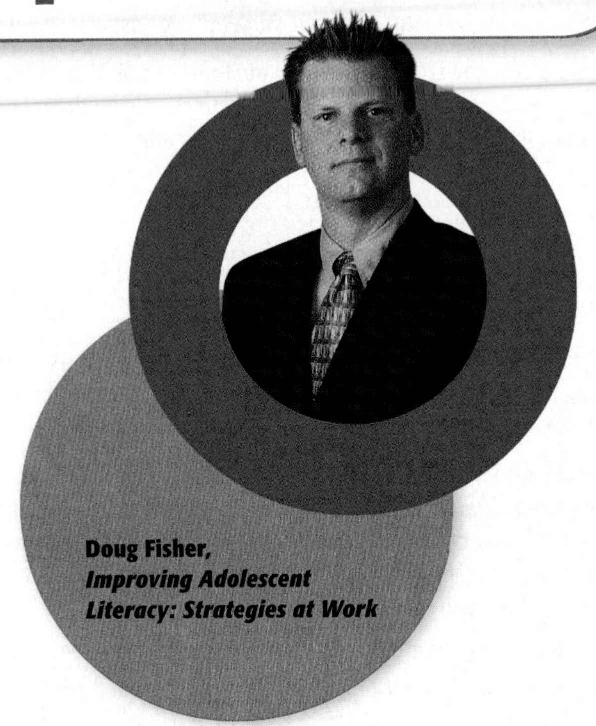

Doug Fisher,
Improving Adolescent Literacy: Strategies at Work

From An Author:

Preparing Students to Read Short Stories

Setting Purpose. In unit 1, students learned about the importance of setting purpose and previewing. This unit, on the short story, provides an excellent opportunity to review these skills. Remind students that they should preview a text before reading it. For the short story, this means spending fewer than 3 minutes figuring out who the characters are and what might be happening, the plot. In previewing a short story, students should focus on the beginning and end of the story, as these are important parts in short stories. Illustrations can also give students' clues to what the story is about. Finally, students should generate questions based on their preview that they will answer during their reading

Engaging students with the text. As students preview the short stories and other selections in this unit, you may help them learn to make simple predictions to pique their interests. Predictions also help students remain engaged with the text and comprehend the story. Start with the title. Ask students to speculate what the main idea of the short story will be based on the title the author gave to the piece. While predicting is important, and is a skill that students can learn to use, it is even more important that students learn from their predictions. Returning to predictions, verifying the guesses, and looking for missed clues when predictions are not quite accurate are also skills that students must develop. These same skills will help them as they draw conclusions, respond, synthesize, which are the skills taught in this unit. Students will learn more about predicting in Unit 6.

David Herick
Bellcreek Elementary
Bellbrook, OH

Teacher to Teacher

Unit 3: Who can we really count on?

A few days before beginning this unit, I play music the students aren't familiar with, such as the songs "Lean on Me," "Put a Little Love in Your Heart," and "You've Got a Friend." Students describe or draw images that the songs elicit and add them to their books. We then discuss the lyrics and images students have created in the context of the Big Question: Who can we really count on? We also make a collage of people we can count on. We divide the collage into three categories: Nations Helping Nations, Communities Helping Communities, and Individuals Helping Individuals. Students research and bring in clippings to add to the collage as we work through the selections and answer the Big Question.

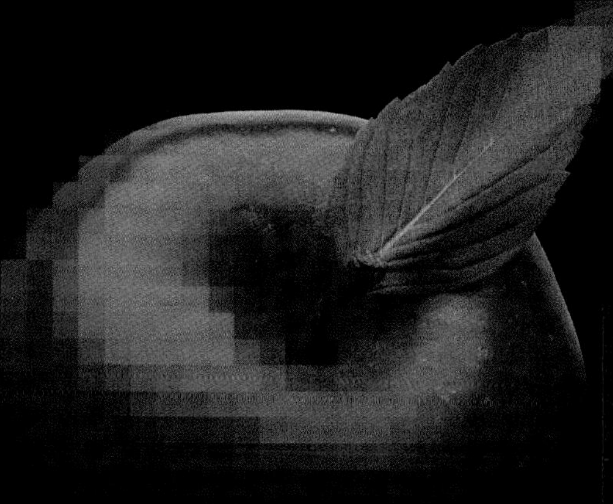

Teacher Chat Room

Using Short Stories

Why teach short stories?

Short stories often contain structural and character elements that are familiar to students. These elements can be used as guides to help students think about the actions, themes, and contexts of the plot. For students who are not familiar with story grammar, short stories provide an excellent opportunity to develop or extend this knowledge base. Like longer pieces of fiction, short stories often contain characters, plot, setting, conflicts, imagery, and points of view. Each of these components can be analyzed in the short story so that students develop a stronger sense of these devices.

What are the teaching points for short stories?

As noted above, short stories can provide students and teachers an opportunity to develop an enhanced understanding of story grammar and literary devices. For example, students might focus on the role of characters while reading a particular short story and use the following questions to guide their reading:

- Which, if any, characters are flat or stereotypical?
- What motivates characters to behave as they do?
- How does the use of dialogue facilitate our understanding of the character?

In another short story, students might focus on point of view, using the following questions to guide their inquiry:

- Whose voice tells the story or provides the information readers need to understand what is happening?
- Does one character control the understanding of events, or do readers have an "omniscient" narrator who provides facts and insights that the characters themselves do not have?
- How does the point of view shape our understanding of the events and actions of the characters?
- What might happen if another point of view took charge?

How can students be motivated to read short stories?

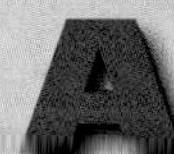

Some students like short stories because they get a sense of completion – beginning, middle and end – in a very short time. Students also like short stories because they get to meet interesting characters and the author typically gets to the point of the story – the conflict – fairly quickly. In terms of motivation, remind students that short stories are a way that writers convey life's lessons quickly. Ask them what they'd like to learn from life and point out that they just might find out in one of the short stories they'll read.

Key Unit Objectives

- Answer the Big Question
- Identify, understand, and apply the unit's key reading skills
- Identify, understand, and apply the unit's key literary elements
- Write a short fictional story

BIG Question

Why Is It Important?

Addressing this Big Question helps students identify the people who they can really depend on.

Viewing the Photo

Say: Read the quote from Bill Withers. What does he tell friends to do? *(to lean on him when they need help)* **BL** Why do you think a firefighter is used to illustrate a quote about friends leaning on each other? *(Responses may include: Just as a friend in need counts, or leans, on another, people count on firefighters in times of danger.)* **OL**

UNIT 3

The BIG Question

Who Can We Really Count On?

"Lean on me, when you're
not strong
And I'll be your friend
I'll help you carry on
For it won't be long
'Til I'm gonna need
Somebody to lean on"

–Bill Withers, songwriter and musician

Unit Skills

Reading Skills
- Drawing conclusions, p. 266
- Responding, p. 298
- Synthesizing, p. 320
- Determining the main idea and supporting details, p. 346

Vocabulary
- Synonyms and antonyms, pp. 268, 300

BIG Question **Who Can We Really Count On?**
Genre Focus: Short Story

Literary Elements
- Conflict, p. 291
- Dialogue, p. 301
- Character, p. 323
- Plot, p. 349

Writing Skills/Grammar
- Short fictional story, pp. 292, 340
- Organization, p. 294

LOOKING AHEAD

The skill lessons and readings in this unit will help you develop your own answer to the Big Question.

About the Reading

Each selection in this unit provides insights that can help students address the question, "Who can we really count on?" Students think about how the characters in the selections would answer this question, and then they consider how they would answer it for themselves.

About the Skills

The skills taught in this unit have been selected because they are particularly helpful when reading the featured genre—the short story. Each reading selection provides students with opportunities to practice and develop these skills.

No Child Left Behind

The goals of the NCLB act include a strong emphasis on developing reading skills. Modeling the skills covered in this unit will help students to develop these skills. For example, read aloud a passage from a selection and demonstrate how to draw a conclusion based on the information in the passage.

Reading Fluency

Developing Fluency Reading short stories is a good way for students to practice reading fluency. Suggest that students read the short stories in this unit one page at a time. They can read the pages to a partner, who can evaluate the reader on the following:

Rate (Did the student read at just the right pace for comprehension, or did the student read too slow or too fast?)
Expression (Did the reader convey appropriate expression when reading?)
Pacing (Did the reader pause at commas and stop at the end of sentences?) **BL** **EL**

Focus

BELLRINGER Options

- **Literature Launcher: Prereading DVD**
- **Daily Language Practice Transparency**

Focus Activity Say: Who are the people in your life you know you can count on? In your Learner's Notebook, list people who are there for you when you need help or advice. *(Responses will vary.)* OL

Teach

BQ 

- Have students read the profiles and look at the pictures of Kesha and Tiffany.
- Have students form small groups and discuss the advice they would give to Kesha and Tiffany. AS

R Reading Skill

Responding Ask:

- What is your opinion of people like Kesha's best friend? Do you think it's important for friends to keep promises they make to each other?
- What is your reaction to what Tiffany asks her brother not to do? AS

UNIT 3 WARM-UP

Connecting to  Who Can We Really Count On?

There are people in the world you can count on. They may be your parents, your brother, or your sister. Or maybe you count on your grandparents. They could be your teacher or a best friend. They will help you in good times and in bad times. In this unit, you'll read about different people who counted on family, friends, and others when they needed help and support.

BQ R

KESHA asked her best friend to go to the mall with her to get new clothes for a party they're going to on Saturday night. Her friend said she would meet her at the mall on Saturday morning. Kesha knows that her friend is often late and sometimes doesn't show up when she says she will. But this time she promised she would be there. Do you think Kesha can count on her friend? What advice would you give Kesha?

TIFFANY can't seem to pass a science test this year. Her science grades are so low she might have to go to summer school. Her older brother knows that Tiffany is having trouble with science and offered to help her. Tiffany has asked her brother not to tell their mother how poorly she is doing. Do you think Tiffany's brother should tell their mother? Or should Tiffany count on him not to tell? What advice would you give Tiffany?

Warm-Up Activity

With a partner, talk about Kesha's and Tiffany's problems. Then decide together on the advice you'd give each of them.

Additional Support

Reading in the Real World

College Explain that it's normal for students to sometimes struggle with a certain subject, as Tiffany is doing with science this year. When this happens, the student should ask for help as soon as possible. This is especially good advice for students who plan to go on to college. College admissions officers don't expect perfect grades, but they don't like to see that a student has failed a class. Remind students that the first person they should consult is the teacher of the class, who can help them identify where the problem lies and suggest ways to improve their performance. BL EL

You and the Big Question

There are people you count on that you don't even realize you count on. Farmers produce your food. You count on postal workers for your mail. Thinking about all the people you count on as you read the selections in this unit will help you to answer the Big Question.

Big Question Link to Web resources to further explore the Big Question at www.glencoe.com.

Plan for the Unit Challenge

At the end of the unit, you'll use notes from your reading to complete the Unit Challenge, which will explore your answer to the Big Question.

You will choose one of the following activities:

A. Write a Handbook With a group of students, you'll write a handbook for kids telling them who they might be able to count on.

B. Create a Chart You'll create a chart of problems you may face and their solutions. The chart will include people you can count on to help you.

- Decide which activity you'd like to do so that you can focus your thinking as you go through the unit.
- In your Learner's Notebook, make a list of the kinds of problems kids your age face. Make another list of problems that you face.
- Remember to take notes about the Big Question, because these ideas will help you with the Unit Challenge activity you choose.

Keep Track of Your Ideas

FOLDABLES™ Study Organizer

As you read, you'll make notes about the Big Question. Later, you'll use these notes to complete the Unit Challenge. See page R9 for help with making Foldable 3. This diagram shows how it should look.

1. List all the selections on the Foldable's front. (See page 251 for the titles.) Then open the Foldable. You'll write answers on note cards and sort the cards into these three pockets.
2. Write these labels on the pockets:
   - **My Purpose for Reading**
   - **The Big Question**
   - **My Thoughts** (This is for additional ideas you have about the Big Question.)

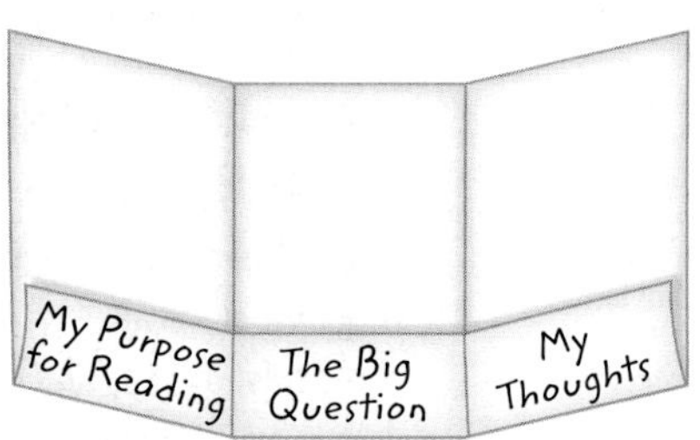

Reading in the Real World

Career Ask students to discuss what might happen if we couldn't count on police officers, firefighters, paramedics, and other workers to respond to emergencies. OL Encourage students to choose a type of emergency-response worker to research to learn about the training that such a worker receives. Suggest that students consult career encyclopedias and other reference works in their research. Some students may be able to interview emergency-response workers in the community. Have students share their findings with the class. AL

Teach

FOLDABLES™ Study Organizer

For each selection they read, students will enter notes about how that selection applies to the Big Question. For details about using Dinah Zike's Foldables, see page R9. OL

Assess/Close

Invite students to share their thoughts about why it's important to know who we can really count on. OL

Resources for page 253

- Use the Unit Challenge Planner BLM in the Unit 3 Resource Booklet.
- Use the Foldable BLM in the Unit 3 Resource Booklet.

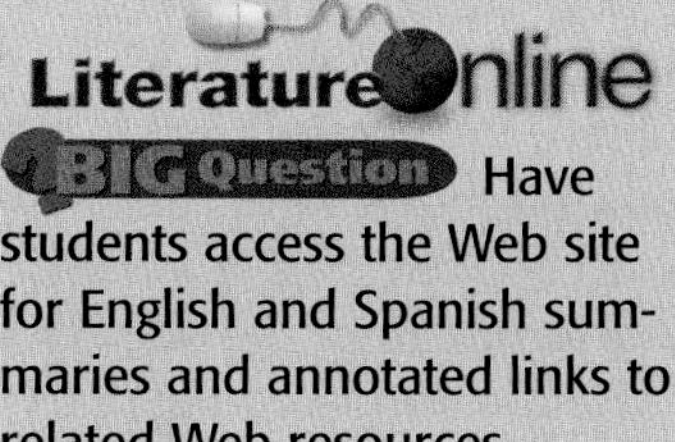

BIG Question Have students access the Web site for English and Spanish summaries and annotated links to related Web resources.

Objectives

- Connect to the Big Question, using prior knowledge and real-life examples
- Respond to reading

Focus

BELLRINGER Options

- **Selection Focus Transparency**
- **Daily Language Practice Transparency**

Focus Activity Say: Think of a favorite fictional, or made-up, story that you've read or heard. What makes the characters in the story so interesting? What main problem do the characters face, and how is it solved? What do you learn from the story? OL

Teach

R Reading Skill

How to Read a Short Story

Ask: How do you think each reading skill can help you be an active reader? *(Possible responses: **Drawing Conclusions** helps you connect pieces of information from the story. **Responding** helps you think more about what you liked or didn't like. **Synthesizing** can give you a deeper understanding of the story and of yourself. **Determining the main idea and supporting details** helps you identify the most important idea of the story and the details that support that idea.)* OL

UNIT 3 GENRE FOCUS: SHORT STORY

Skills Focus
- Key skills for reading short stories
- Key literary elements of short stories

Skills Model
You will see how to use the key reading skills and literary elements as you read the short story
- **"Broken Chain,"** p. 255

A **short story** is a brief piece of fictional or made-up writing about people and events. Even though the stories are not true, you can still connect to the people and events in them. Short stories usually contain
- a series of related events in which a problem is explored and then solved.
- a struggle between people, ideas, or other forces.

Why Read Short Stories?

Reading short stories can be exciting and can teach you a lot about yourself. When you read short stories, you'll
- meet new characters and learn about them and their lives.
- imagine what you would do or how you would feel if you were the people in the story.

How to Read a Short Story

Key Reading Skills

R These reading skills are especially useful tools for reading and understanding short stories. The skills are modeled in the Active Reading Model on pages 255–265; you'll learn more about them later.

- **Drawing conclusions** Use the information from your reading to make a general statement about people, places, events, or ideas. (See Reading Workshop 1.)
- **Responding** Explore how you feel about people and events in a selection. (See Reading Workshop 2.)
- **Synthesizing** As you read, bring together the information and ideas from the text to make new ideas of your own. (See Reading Workshop 3.)
- **Determining the main idea** Find the most important idea in a paragraph or in a selection. Also find the details that help you to know it's the most important idea. (See Reading Workshop 4.)

Key Literary Elements

Recognizing and thinking about the following literary elements will help you understand more fully what the author is telling you.

- **Conflict:** the biggest struggle in a story (See "Amigo Brothers.")
- **Dialogue:** conversation between characters in a story (See "Framed.")
- **Character:** a person in a story (See "Loser.")
- **Plot:** a series of related events in which a problem is explored and then solved (See "The Good Samaritan.")

Objectives (pp. 254–265)
Reading Draw conclusions from text and experience • Respond to literature • Synthesize information • Identify main ideas and supporting details
Literature Identify story elements: plot, conflict, dialogue, character

Additional Support

Literature Focus Lesson

Conflict Tell students that a conflict is external when a character struggles against an outside force, such as another person, nature, society, or fate. Explain that a conflict is internal when a character is torn between opposing feelings or goals in his or her own mind.

Point out that the short story they are about to read, "Broken Chain," includes many examples of both external and internal conflicts. Have students keep track of the two types of conflicts in a two-column chart. After they finish reading, have them compare their charts. AL

Broken Chain

by Gary Soto

The notes in the side columns model how to use the skills and elements you read about on page 254.

Short Story

ACTIVE READING MODEL

Alfonso sat on the porch trying to push his crooked teeth to where he thought they belonged. He hated the way he looked. Last week he did fifty sit-ups a day, thinking that he would burn those already apparent ripples on his stomach to even deeper ripples, dark ones, so when he went swimming at the canal next summer, girls in cut-offs would notice. And the guys would think he was tough, someone who could take a punch and give it back. He wanted "cuts"[1] like those he had seen on a calendar of an Aztec warrior standing on a pyramid with a woman in his arms. (Even she had cuts he could see beneath her thin dress.) The calendar hung above the cash register at La Plaza. Orsua, the owner, said Alfonso could have the calendar at the end of the year if the waitress, Yolanda, didn't take it first. 1

1 Key Reading Skill

Responding *I like the descriptions in the story, especially the parts about Alfonso pushing on his teeth. I can really see what he looks like, and I feel like I am starting to get to know him.*

Alfonso studied the magazine pictures of rock stars for a hairstyle. He liked the way Prince looked—and the bass player from Los Lobos.[2] Alfonso thought he would look cool with his hair razored into a V in the back and streaked purple. But he knew his mother wouldn't go for it. And his father, who was *puro Mexicano,*[3] would sit in his chair after work, sullen as a toad, and call him "sissy." EL

1. ***Cuts*** is slang for "good, solid abdominal muscles."
2. ***Prince*** is the name of a rock star. ***Los Lobos*** (lohs LOH bohs), "The Wolves," is a Mexican American band.
3. ***Puro Mexicano*** (POO roh \ meh hee KAW noh) means "pure Mexican."

English Language Coach

Antonyms Tell students that antonyms are pairs of words that have opposite, or nearly opposite, meanings. Point out that they have already learned that the word *sullen,* as it's used in the story, means *grouchy* or *cheerless.* Ask students to think of words that mean the opposite of *sullen. (Possible responses: cheerful; happy; merry)* **BL**

Invite volunteers to provide synonyms and antonyms for the word *sullen* in languages other than English. **EL**

Teach

R Reading Skill

Review Connecting **Ask:** Can you identify with the way Alfonso feels? What advice would you give him? **OL**

EL Language Coach

Synonyms **Say:** Words that mean about the same thing are called synonyms. Here are three synonyms for the word *sullen: grouchy, cheerless, depressing.*

Ask: In this context, which synonym or synonyms mean(s) about the same thing as *sullen? (grouchy and cheerless)* **EL** **OL**

Resources for page 255

Use the Genre Study BLM in the Unit 3 Resource Booklet.

Readability Scores

Dale-Chall: 4.8
DRP: 53
Lexile: 890

Leveled Reading An adapted version of this selection (Grade 4 readability) is available on page 62 of *Jamestown Literature: An Adapted Reader* for Grade 7.

Objectives

- Understand how specific skills are useful in reading short stories
- Analyze conflicts and how they affect the plot
- Connect prior knowledge and experience to characters and events
- Understand synonyms and antonyms

Teach

R Reading Skill

Drawing Conclusions **Say:** When you draw conclusions, you figure out more than what the author actually says. You take information from the story and use it to form an opinion or judgment about the characters or events.

Ask: What conclusion can you draw about Alfonso's getting braces from the information in the last two paragraphs? *(Possible response: Alfonso's family doesn't have a lot of money, so it isn't likely that he will be able to get braces on his teeth.)* OL

ACTIVE READING MODEL

Alfonso didn't dare color his hair. But one day he had had it butched on the top, like in the magazines. His father had come home that evening from a softball game, happy that his team had drilled four homers in a thirteen-to-five bashing of Color Tile. He'd swaggered into the living room, but had stopped cold when he saw Alfonso and asked, not joking but with real concern, "Did you hurt your head at school? *Qué pasó?*"[4] 2

Alfonso had pretended not to hear his father and had gone to his room, where he studied his hair from all angles in the mirror. He liked what he saw until he smiled and realized for the first time that his teeth were crooked, like a pile of wrecked cars. He grew depressed and turned away from the mirror. He sat on his bed and leafed through the rock magazine until he came to the rock star with the butched top. His mouth was closed, but Alfonso was sure his teeth weren't crooked.

Alfonso didn't want to be the handsomest kid at school, but he was determined to be better-looking than average. The next day he spent his lawn-mowing money on a new shirt, and, with a pocketknife, scooped the moons of dirt from under his fingernails.

He spent hours in front of the mirror trying to herd his teeth into place with his thumb. He asked his mother if he could have braces, like Frankie Molina, her godson, but he asked at the wrong time. She was at the kitchen table licking the envelope to the house payment. She glared up at him. "Do you think money grows on trees?"

His mother clipped coupons from magazines and newspapers, kept a vegetable garden in the summer, and shopped at Penney's and K-Mart. Their family ate a lot of *frijoles,* which was OK because nothing else tasted so good, though one time Alfonso had had Chinese pot stickers[5] and thought they were the next best food in the world. R

He didn't ask his mother for braces again, even when she was in a better mood. He decided to fix his teeth by

2 Key Reading Skill

Drawing Conclusions *Alfonso is like most teenagers I know because he worries about the way he looks.*

4. ***"Qué pasó?"*** (kay pah SOH) is Spanish for "What happened?"
5. ***Frijoles*** (free HOH les) are beans that are cooked until very tender, mashed, and fried. A ***pot sticker*** is a kind of Chinese dumpling.

Additional Support

English Language Coach

Cultural Note Tell students that historically, attitudes toward hairstyles have varied from culture to culture. A young Aztec man wore his hair in a distinctive short cut with a single long lock at the nape of his neck. He was not allowed to cut off this lock until he had captured his first prisoner in battle. On the other hand, for centuries, only warriors were allowed to have long hair in Japan, Africa, and ancient Greece. OL

Encourage students to do research to learn more about hairstyles in a variety of cultures during different historical periods. AL

ACTIVE READING MODEL

pushing on them with his thumbs. After breakfast that Saturday he went to his room, closed the door quietly, turned the radio on, and pushed for three hours straight.

He pushed for ten minutes, rested for five, and every half hour, during a radio commercial, checked to see if his smile had improved. It hadn't.

Eventually he grew bored and went outside with an old gym sock to wipe down his bike, a ten-speed from Montgomery Ward. His thumbs were tired and wrinkled and pink, the way they got when he stayed in the bathtub too long.

Alfonso's older brother, Ernie, rode up on *his* Montgomery Ward bicycle looking depressed. He parked his bike against the peach tree and sat on the back steps, keeping his head down and stepping on ants that came too close. **R1**

Alfonso knew better than to say anything when Ernie looked mad. He turned his bike over, balancing it on the handlebars and seat, and flossed the spokes with the sock. When he was finished, he pressed a knuckle to his teeth until they tingled.

Ernie groaned and said, "Ah, man."

Alfonso waited a few minutes before asking, "What's the matter?" He pretended not to be too interested. He picked up a wad of steel wool and continued cleaning the spokes.

Ernie hesitated, not sure if Alfonso would laugh. But it came out. "Those girls didn't show up. And you better not laugh."

"What girls?" **3**

Then Alfonso remembered his brother bragging about how he and Frostie met two girls from Kings Canyon Junior High last week on Halloween night. They were dressed as gypsies, the costume for all poor Chicanas—they just had to borrow scarves and gaudy red lipstick from their *abuelitas*.[6]

Alfonso walked over to his brother. He compared their two bikes: his gleamed like a handful of dimes, while Ernie's looked dirty.

3 Key Reading Skill

R2 **Synthesizing** *It's a good idea for Alfonso to clean his bike while he's talking to Ernie. Sometimes you have to be careful when you talk to someone who's upset. Next time my sister is in a bad mood, I'm going to pick up a book or do my homework while I talk to her.*

6. Young Mexican American women are called ***Chicanas*** (chih KAW nus); ***abuelitas*** (ah bweh LEE tus) means "grandmothers."

Teach

R1 Reading Skill

Responding **Ask:** How do you feel about the way Ernie crushes the ants? How does this detail help you understand Ernie's mood? *(Possible response: I don't like Ernie's stepping on the ants; I can tell he's mad or sad because he doesn't have to hurt the ants.)* **AS**

R2 Reading Skill

Review Activating Prior Knowledge **Ask:** Have you ever tried Alfonso's approach to talking with someone who's upset? Describe what happened. Based on your prior knowledge, do you think the strategy described in the Synthesizing note is a good one? Why or why not? *(Responses will vary. Students should give reasons for their opinions.)* **BL** **EL**

Literature Focus Lesson

Character Remind students that a character is a person in a story. Writers sometimes describe characters by making direct statements about them. For example, the writer says that Alfonso "hated the way he looked." Writers also reveal what characters are like by describing their actions, words, and thoughts. Ask students what Alfonso's efforts to straighten his teeth reveal about his character. *(Possible response: He is determined and not easily discouraged.)* Then ask students what other approach Alfonso could take to correct his crooked teeth. *(Possible response: He could mow more lawns and save money to pay for his braces.)* **AS**

Objectives

- Draw conclusions
- Understand cultural information that helps build background
- Activate prior knowledge to evaluate a character's actions
- Analyze the role of characters and the changes they undergo

Teach

L Literary Element

Dialogue and Character
Ask: What does this dialogue seem to suggest about the two girls that Ernie and Frostie meet on Halloween? Explain your answer. *(Possible response: If the girls simply forgot to show up, their behavior was thoughtless but not mean. But if they intended to make fools out of Ernie and Frostie, then they behaved in a nasty way.)* **OL**

E Text Element

Review Photographs and Illustrations **Ask:** How does the photograph of the Chihuahua help you see what is going on in the story? *(The picture helps me understand exactly what a chihuahua is and looks like.)* **BL**

ACTIVE READING MODEL

"They said we were supposed to wait at the corner. But they didn't show up. Me and Frostie waited and waited like fools. They were playing games with us."

Alfonso thought that was a pretty dirty trick but sort of funny too. He would have to try that some day.

"Were they cute?" Alfonso asked.

"I guess so."

"Do you think you could recognize them?"

"If they were wearing red lipstick, maybe." **4**

Alfonso sat with his brother in silence, both of them smearing ants with their floppy high tops. Girls could sure act weird, especially the ones you meet on Halloween.

4 Key Literary Element
Dialogue *The dialogue between Alfonso and Ernie shows me that they really care about each other. And Ernie can tell Alfonso his problems without being laughed at.*

Later that day, Alfonso sat on the porch pressing on his teeth. Press, relax; press, relax. His portable radio was on, but not loud enough to make Mr. Rojas come down the steps and wave his cane at him.

Alfonso's father drove up. Alfonso could tell by the way he sat in his truck, a Datsun with a different-colored front fender, that his team had lost their softball game. Alfonso got off the porch in a hurry because he knew his father would be in a bad mood. He went to the backyard, where he unlocked his bike, sat on it with the kickstand down, and pressed on his teeth. He punched himself in the stomach, and growled, "Cuts." Then he patted his butch and whispered, "Fresh."

Visual Vocabulary
The ***chihuahua***, the world's smallest breed of dog, grows to about five inches tall. It was originally from Mexico and is named for a city there.

After a while Alfonso pedaled up the street, hands in his pockets, toward Foster's Freeze, where he was chased by a ratlike Chihuahua. At his old school, John Burroughs Elementary, he found a kid hanging upside down on the top of a barbed-wire fence with a girl looking up at him. Alfonso skidded to a stop and helped the kid untangle his pants from the barbed wire. The kid was grateful. He had been afraid he would have to stay up there all night. His sister, who was Alfonso's age, was also grateful. If she had to

Additional Support

Differentiated Instruction

Character Write these words on the board: *sloppy, determined, grumpy, vain, hardworking, silly, proud, caring, annoying, nasty.* Ask students which ones they would use to describe Alfonso. Invite volunteers to explain why each word does or does not describe Alfonso. **BL** **EL**

Ask students to work in pairs to create a list of words they would use to describe Alfonso. Students may wish to consult a thesaurus as they complete this activity. Have them share their lists with the class. **OL** Ask students to write a character sketch of Alfonso, using the words on their lists. **AL**

ACTIVE READING MODEL

go home and tell her mother that Frankie was stuck on a fence and couldn't get down, she would get scolded. L1

"Thanks," she said. "What's your name?"

Alfonso remembered her from his school and noticed that she was kind of cute, with ponytails and straight teeth. "Alfonso. You go to my school, huh?"

"Yeah. I've seen you around. You live nearby?"

"Over on Madison."

"My uncle used to live on that street, but he moved to Stockton."

"Stockton's near Sacramento, isn't it?"

"You been there?"

"No." Alfonso looked down at his shoes. He wanted to say something clever the way people do on TV. But the only thing he could think to say was that the governor lived in Sacramento. As soon as he shared this observation, he winced inside.

Alfonso walked with the girl and the boy as they started for home. They didn't talk much. Every few steps, the girl, whose name was Sandra, would look at him out of the corner of her eye, and Alfonso would look away. He learned that she was in seventh grade, just like him, and that she had a pet terrier named Queenie. Her father was a mechanic at Rudy's Speedy Repair, and her mother was a teacher's aide at Jefferson Elementary. 5 L2

When they came to the street, Alfonso and Sandra stopped at her corner, but her brother ran home. Alfonso watched him stop in the front yard to talk to a lady he guessed was their mother. She was raking leaves into a pile.

"I live over there," she said, pointing.

Alfonso looked over her shoulder for a long time, trying to muster enough nerve to ask her if she'd like to go bike riding tomorrow.

Shyly, he asked, "You wanna go bike riding?"

"Maybe." She played with a ponytail and crossed one leg in front of the other. "But my bike has a flat."

"I can get my brother's bike. He won't mind."

She thought for a moment before she said, "OK. But not tomorrow. I have to go to my aunt's."

5 Key Literary Element
Character *I just learned a lot of details about Sandra. She's in seventh grade just like Alfonso, and she has a dog named Queenie.*

Teach

L1 Literary Element

Character Ask: Why do you think Alfonso stops to help the kid who's caught on the barbed wire fence? What else might Alfonso have done in this situation? Do you think that most kids would do what Alfonso does? What do his actions reveal about his character? *(Possible responses: Alfonso stops because he's a nice guy who helps people who are in trouble. Instead of helping, he could have ignored the kid or made fun of him. Some kids would stop to help, but many would just keep on riding. Alfonso's actions reveal that he is a person who has compassion for others.)* **OL**

L2 Literary Element

Character Ask: What else do you learn about Sandra? *(Her father is a mechanic and her mother is a teacher's aide. Her mother is raking leaves.)* **OL** What conclusions can you draw from this information? *(Possible response: Her parents are working-class and are probably hard workers.)*

English Language Coach

Cultural and Historical Notes Tell students that this story takes place in the 1980s in a Spanish-speaking neighborhood in Fresno, California. Mexican American families have made their homes in this neighborhood for many decades.

Sacramento has been the capital of California since 1854. It is on the Sacramento River, about 90 miles northeast of San Francisco, California. It was settled in 1839 by John Sutter, whose discovery of gold led to the California Gold Rush. Ask volunteers to locate Fresno, Sacramento, and San Francisco on a map.

Objectives
- Identify and explain the effects of dialogue
- Analyze the role of characters and the changes they undergo
- Understand cultural and historical information that builds background

Teach

L Literary Element

Plot and Conflict **Say:** You've learned that the plot of a story is a series of related events in which a problem is explored and then solved. **Ask:** What problem, or conflict, does Alfonso face as a result of asking Sandra to go bike riding with him? What does he have to do in order to keep his promise to Sandra? *(Alfonso has to convince Ernie to let Sandra ride his bike since Sandra's bike has a flat tire.)* **OL**

C Critical Thinking

Evaluation **Ask:** How does Alfonso first approach the problem of convincing Ernie to let him borrow his bike? *(Alfonso pesters his brother and whines. Then he offers Ernie his trick-or-treat candy as payment for the favor.)* What is your opinion of this approach? *(Possible response: It's not a good idea to whine and pester someone because the person may get annoyed and refuse to do the favor. Offering payment is a better approach.)* **OL**

ACTIVE READING MODEL

"How about after school on Monday?"

"I have to take care of my brother until my mom comes home from work. How 'bout four-thirty?"

"OK," he said. "Four-thirty." Instead of parting immediately, they talked for a while, asking questions like, "Who's your favorite group?" "Have you ever been on the Big Dipper at Santa Cruz?" and "Have you ever tasted pot stickers?" But the question-and-answer period ended when Sandra's mother called her home.

Alfonso took off as fast as he could on his bike, jumped the curb, and, cool as he could be, raced away with his hands stuffed in his pockets. But when he looked back over his shoulder, the wind raking through his butch, Sandra wasn't even looking. She was already on her lawn, heading for the porch. 6

6 Key Literary Element
Plot *It's a pretty big deal that Alfonso has met a girl he likes. I don't think he's ever had a girlfriend. This new event in the plot makes me curious about how things are going to turn out for Alfonso.*

That night he took a bath, pampered his hair into place, and did more than his usual set of exercises. In bed, in between the push-and-rest on his teeth, he pestered his brother to let him borrow his bike. **L** **C**

"Come on, Ernie," he whined. "Just for an hour."

"*Chale,*[7] I might want to use it."

"Come on, man, I'll let you have my trick-or-treat candy."

"What you got?"

"Three baby Milky Ways and some Skittles."

"Who's going to use it?"

Alfonso hesitated, then risked the truth. "I met this girl. She doesn't live too far."

Ernie rolled over on his stomach and stared at the outline of his brother, whose head was resting on his elbow. "*You* got a girlfriend?"

"She ain't my girlfriend, just a girl."

"What does she look like?"

"Like a girl."

"Come on, what does she look like?"

"She's got ponytails and a little brother."

"Ponytails! Those girls who messed with Frostie and me had ponytails. Is she cool?"

7. If you want someone to "cool it" or "knock it off," say ***"Chale"*** (CHAW lay).

Additional Support

Differentiated Instruction

Brainstorming Students with strong interpersonal abilities respond well to brainstorming. These students' classmates can benefit from their ability to connect with other people.

Divide the class into small groups. Ask each group to brainstorm to develop a more effective approach for Alfonso to use when asking Ernie to let him borrow his bike. Have each group agree on an approach and then present it to the entire class. **OL** Ask students to evaluate the effectiveness of each approach, based on what they know about Alfonso and Ernie, as well as their own life experience. **AL**

"I think so."

Ernie sat up in bed. "I bet you that's her."

Alfonso felt his stomach knot up. "She's going to be my girlfriend, not yours!"

"I'm going to get even with her!" 7

"You better not touch her," Alfonso snarled, throwing a wadded Kleenex at him. "I'll run you over with my bike."

For the next hour, until their mother threatened them from the living room to be quiet or else, they argued

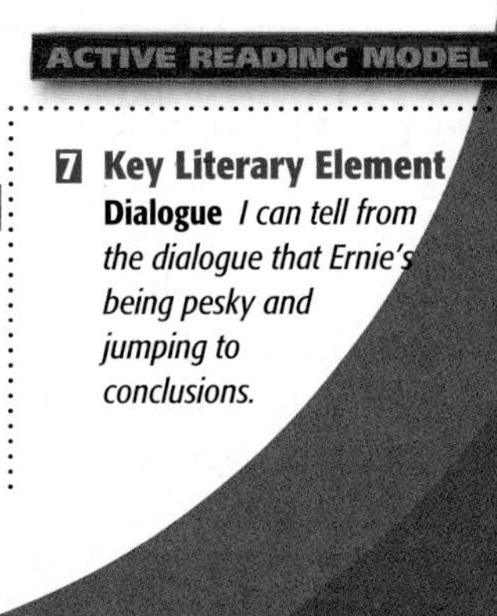

ACTIVE READING MODEL

7 **Key Literary Element**

Dialogue *I can tell from the dialogue that Ernie's being pesky and jumping to conclusions.*

UNIT 3 GENRE FOCUS

Teach

L Literary Element

Dialogue and Conflict

Hearing the dialogue read aloud will help some students understand it better. Invite volunteers to take on the roles of Alfonso and Ernie. Encourage them to read the words as quarreling brothers might actually speak them. **BL** **EL**

Ask: From this dialogue, what do you learn about the conflict, or problem, that exists between Alfonso and Ernie? *(Possible response: Ernie jumps to the conclusion that Alfonso's "girlfriend" is one of the girls who stood him up earlier in the story. Ernie says that he plans to get even with her.)* **OL**

Ask: What was the author's purpose in including the incident in which Ernie and his friend were stood up by the two girls? *(Possible response: That incident sets the stage for the conflict between Alfonso and Ernie, as presented in this dialogue.)* **AL**

Literature Focus Lesson

Showing, Not Telling Explain that writers of fiction try to avoid telling readers what to think. Instead, they show what a character is like by describing what the character says and does. For example, Soto doesn't say, "Alfonso worries about his physical appearance because he thinks that looks are the thing people care about the most." Instead, through dialogue and narration, Soto shows that this is what Alfonso thinks.

Have students write several paragraphs about a character in which they show, rather than tell, what that character is like. **AL**

Objectives

- Identify and evaluate events that advance the plot
- Analyze conflicts and how they affect the plot
- Evaluate characters' actions
- Identify and explain the effects of dialogue
- Identify author's purpose

Teach

Ask: Are you surprised that Raul would charge Alfonso for borrowing his bike? Raul is Alfonso's best friend. In your opinion, should best friends do things like this? Do you think that Raul is a person that Alfonso can count on? Why or why not? *(Possible response: Yes, I'm surprised that Raul would charge Alfonso. I don't think best friends should do something like that. Obviously, Alfonso cannot count on Raul, since Alfonso doesn't even bother to ask Raul for his bike.)* OL

ACTIVE READING MODEL

whether it was the same girl who had stood Ernie up. Alfonso said over and over that she was too nice to pull a stunt like that. But Ernie argued that she lived only two blocks from where those girls had told them to wait, that she was in the same grade, and, the clincher, that she had ponytails. Secretly, however, Ernie was jealous that his brother, two years younger than himself, might have found a girlfriend.

Sunday morning, Ernie and Alfonso stayed away from each other, though over breakfast they fought over the last tortilla. Their mother, sewing at the kitchen table, warned them to knock it off. At church they made faces at one another when the priest, Father Jerry, wasn't looking. Ernie punched Alfonso in the arm, and Alfonso, his eyes wide with anger, punched back.

Monday morning they hurried to school on their bikes, neither saying a word, though they rode side by side. In first period, Alfonso worried himself sick. How would he borrow a bike for her? He considered asking his best friend, Raul, for his bike. But Alfonso knew Raul, a paper boy with dollar signs in his eyes, would charge him, and he had less than sixty cents, counting the soda bottles he could cash. 8 BQ

8 Key Reading Skill

Responding *It's too bad that Alfonso can't count on Raul to help him. I think best friends should be able to count on each other. Who is Alfonso going to turn to now?*

Between history and math, Alfonso saw Sandra and her girlfriend huddling at their lockers. He hurried by without being seen.

During lunch Alfonso hid in metal shop[8] so he wouldn't run into Sandra. What would he say to her? If he weren't mad at his brother, he could ask Ernie what girls and guys talk about. But he *was* mad, and anyway, Ernie was pitching nickels with his friends.

Alfonso hurried home after school. He did the morning dishes as his mother had asked and raked the leaves. After finishing his chores, he did a hundred sit-ups, pushed on his teeth until they hurt, showered, and combed his hair into a perfect butch. He then stepped out to the patio to clean his bike. On an impulse, he removed the chain to wipe off the gritty oil. But while he was

8. The ***metal shop*** is a room in schools where students learn the skills of working with metals. Many schools have these shops.

Additional Support

Differentiated Instruction

Debating Divide students into two teams to debate the merits of Alfonso and Ernie's positions in their argument about Sandra. Is either character being unfair? Jumping to conclusions? Can either prove his point? Students should be persuasive in defending the brother they represent. Have students follow these guidelines for debating:

- Let everyone have a turn to speak. Don't interrupt.
- Jot down notes on points you want to respond to.
- When it's your turn to speak, state your opinions and the reasons for them.
- Make sure your comments relate directly to the topic. OL

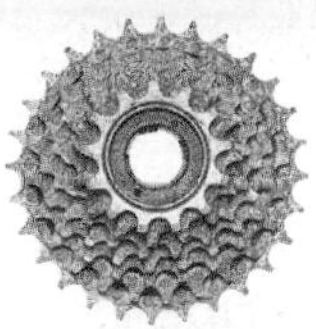

Visual Vocabulary
A ***sprocket*** is a wheel that has teeth around its edge to grab the links of a chain. A bicycle has a small sprocket on the rear wheel and a larger one between the two wheels.

unhooking it from the back sprocket, it snapped. The chain lay in his hand like a dead snake.

Alfonso couldn't believe his luck. Now, not only did he not have an extra bike for Sandra, he had no bike for himself. Frustrated, and on the verge of tears, he flung the chain as far as he could. It landed with a hard slap against the back fence and spooked his sleeping cat, Benny. Benny looked around, blinking his soft gray eyes, and went back to sleep.

Alfonso retrieved the chain, which was hopelessly broken. He cursed himself for being stupid, yelled at his bike for being cheap, and slammed the chain onto the cement. The chain snapped in another place and hit him when it popped up, slicing his hand like a snake's fang.

"Ow!" he cried, his mouth immediately going to his hand to suck on the wound.

After a dab of iodine, which only made his cut hurt more, and a lot of thought, he went to the bedroom to plead with Ernie, who was changing to his after-school clothes.

"Come on, man, let me use it," Alfonso pleaded. "Please, Ernie, I'll do anything." 9

Although Ernie could see Alfonso's desperation, he had plans with his friend Raymundo. They were going to catch frogs at the Mayfair canal. He felt sorry for his brother, and gave him a stick of gum to make him feel better, but there was nothing he could do. The canal was three miles away, and the frogs were waiting.

Alfonso took the stick of gum, placed it in his shirt pocket, and left the bedroom with his head down. He went outside, slamming the screen door behind him, and sat in the alley behind his house. A sparrow landed in the weeds, and when it tried to come close, Alfonso screamed for it to scram. The sparrow responded with a squeaky chirp and flew away.

9 Key Literary Element
L **Conflict** *Ernie won't let Alfonso borrow his bike. Now there is a conflict between the brothers.*

Teach

L Literary Element

Conflict Ask: What new problem does Alfonso have after unhooking his bike chain? *(His bike chain snaps, making it impossible for him to ride his bike.)* **BL EL** How does Alfonso's reaction to his broken chain create yet another problem for him? *(He angrily slams the chain down. It snaps again and bounces back up, cutting his hand.)* **OL** Though Ernie is still in conflict with Alfonso about letting Alfonso borrow his bike, how has Ernie's attitude toward Alfonso changed? *(Ernie still doesn't let Alfonso borrow his bike, but now Ernie feels sorry for his brother and no longer seems angry.)* **OL**

English Language Coach

Synonyms Remind students that synonyms are words that mean about the same thing. Explain that when they know different synonyms for a word, they can decide which one expresses the exact meaning they want. Point out the word *desperation* in the next-to-last paragraph. Explain that although *desperation* and *hopelessness* are synonyms, *desperation* expresses a more frantic feeling than *hopelessness*. A hopeless person might just sit and do nothing. A desperate person, such as Alfonso, would try just about anything, including begging, to solve his or her problem. Have students consult a thesaurus to find other synonyms for *desperation*. *(despair; recklessness)* **EL OL**

Objectives
- Discuss and evaluate the selection
- Debate an issue raised by characters and events in the story
- Analyze conflicts and how they affect the plot
- Understand how different synonyms can express exact meanings

Teach

L Literary Element

Conflict and Character **Ask:** How does Alfonso decide to handle his latest conflict? What do his thoughts and actions reveal about his character? *(Possible response: At first Alfonso is angry and frustrated, but then he calms down and decides to face an embarrassing situation. This shows that although Alfonso needs to learn effective ways to deal with his anger, he is mature enough to know that he has to face Sandra and explain the situation.)* OL

C Critical Thinking

Analysis Invite students to predict how the story will end. *(Some students may say that Alfonso will explain the situation to Sandra, who will suggest another activity, such as taking a walk. Other students may predict that Ernie will show up and offer his bike to Alfonso.)* OL

ACTIVE READING MODEL

At four he decided to get it over with and started walking to Sandra's house, trudging slowly, as if he were waist-deep in water. Shame colored his face. How could he disappoint his first date? She would probably laugh. She might even call him *menso*.[9] 10 L

He stopped at the corner where they were supposed to meet and watched her house. But there was no one outside, only a rake leaning against the steps.

Why did he have to take the chain off? he scolded himself. He always messed things up when he tried to take them apart, like the time he tried to repad his baseball mitt. He had unlaced the mitt and filled the pocket with cotton balls. But when he tried to put it back together, he had forgotten how it laced up. Everything became tangled like kite string. When he showed the mess to his mother, who was at the stove cooking dinner, she scolded him but put it back together and didn't tell his father what a dumb thing he had done.

Now he had to face Sandra and say, "I broke my bike, and my stingy brother took off on his."

He waited at the corner for a few minutes, hiding behind a hedge for what seemed like forever. Just as he was starting to think about going home, he heard footsteps and knew it was too late. His hands, moist from worry, hung at his sides, and a thread of sweat raced down his armpit.

He peeked through the hedge. She was wearing a sweater with a checkerboard pattern. A red purse was slung over her shoulder. He could see her looking for him, standing on tiptoe to see if he was coming around the corner.

What have I done? Alfonso thought. He bit his lip, called himself *menso,* and pounded his palm against his forehead. Someone slapped the back of his head. He turned around and saw Ernie.

"We got the frogs, Alfonso," he said, holding up a wiggling plastic bag. "I'll show you later."

10 Key Literary Element

Plot *Now Alfonso doesn't have a bike for his date. His brother is angry with him, and he has no idea how to achieve his goal of going out with Sandra. I wonder how Alfonso will solve this problem.*

9. ***Menso*** (MEN soh) means "ignorant or foolish."

Additional Support

Differentiated Instruction

Visualizing Ask students to picture the scene in which Alfonso waits until Sandra finally appears. Ask them to picture: Where is Alfonso? Where is Sandra? What is each one doing? Then, have students sketch what they see in their "mind's eye." *(Students' sketches should roughly show Alfonso hiding behind a hedge while watching Sandra, who is walking toward the street corner or standing on the corner.)*
After students have completed their sketches, invite them to share and compare their drawings in small groups. OL

ACTIVE READING MODEL

Ernie looked through the hedge, with one eye closed, at the girl. "She's not the one who messed with Frostie and me," he said finally. "You still wanna borrow my bike?"

Alfonso couldn't believe his luck. What a brother! What a pal! He promised to take Ernie's turn next time it was his turn to do the dishes. Ernie hopped on Raymundo's handlebars and said he would remember that promise. Then he was gone as they took off without looking back. **11**

Free of worry now that his brother had come through, Alfonso emerged from behind the hedge with Ernie's bike, which was mud-splashed but better than nothing. Sandra waved.

"Hi," she said.

"Hi," he said back.

She looked cheerful. Alfonso told her his bike was broken and asked if she wanted to ride with him.

"Sounds good," she said, and jumped on the crossbar.

It took all of Alfonso's strength to steady the bike. He started off slowly, gritting his teeth, because she was heavier than he thought. But once he got going, it got easier. He pedaled smoothly, sometimes with only one hand on the handlebars, as they sped up one street and down another. Whenever he ran over a pothole, which was often, she screamed with delight, and once, when it looked like they were going to crash, she placed her hand over his, and it felt like love. ❍

11 Key Reading Skill

R **Determining the Main Idea** *I think the main idea is that brothers should always count on each other. Even though Alfonso and Ernie fight about their bikes and the girl, they still have times where they talk about each other's problems and help each other out.*

Partner Talk With a partner, talk about Alfonso's experiences and those that each of you might have had. Are his thoughts, feelings, words, actions, and experiences like those of people your age?

Study Central Visit www.glencoe.com and click on Study Central to review short stories.

Teach

R Reading Skill

Determining the Main Idea **Ask:** Do you agree that this is the main idea of the story? Why or why not? *(Responses will vary. Students should give reasons for their responses.)*

Literature Online

Study Central Have students access the Web site to review short stories and to complete a related activity.

English Language Coach

Synonyms in Different Languages

Write the word *menso* on the board. Most Spanish-speaking students will already know that *menso* means "ignorant or foolish," as shown in the footnote on page 264. You may also wish to write the feminine form of this adjective on the board: *mensa.* Invite volunteers to supply other synonyms for *menso,* in any language, including English. Write the synonyms on the board. Have students use the words in sentences, either in English or in other languages. **EL** **BL**

Objectives

- Analyze conflicts and how they affect the plot
- Analyze the role of characters and the changes they undergo
- Predict the outcome of a selection
- Visualize and sketch a scene from a selection
- Identify main ideas and supporting details
- Identify and use synonyms for words in a selection

Drawing Conclusions

UNIT 3

Objectives covered in this workshop:
- Draw conclusions from text and personal experience

Drawing Conclusions

Why Is It important?

- Oftentimes, in literature, conclusions are left to the reader. Authors are not often explicit about conclusions and let the reader draw them him or herself.
- Students can create new meaning from reading materials and sound reasoning.
- Drawing conclusions allows students to consider the author's point of view and how that relates to their understandings and background knowledge.

How to Help Students Get It

- Introduce the *if ... then* clause. Ask students to consider different ideas that can be added to this clause such as "If I miss school, then I could fail the test." Ask them how they knew what to add to the "then" part. Tell students that these are conclusions – something known or assumed based on the available information.
- In preparation for teaching students about drawing conclusions, prepare several questions that can be used to guide their thinking. These questions should allow students to think about the information, but not give them the information. The following sample questions might be helpful: What conclusions can be made based on the details and facts? Do the facts add up? How do you know the facts are accurate? What evidence does the author provide? What facts/details support the author's conclusions? What clues led to your conclusion?
- To cement students' knowledge of drawing conclusions, they should regularly be asked to identify the evidence, from the text, that they used to draw the conclusion. The key to drawing conclusions is to use what the author provided, not to simply make up information or ideas.

Reading to Answer the Big Question

Friendships and Peer Pressure

This informational text covers the importance of friendships, how to be a good friend, and the effect peer pressure plays on people of all ages and especially teenagers. Reading this article on friends and how they influence each other will help students figure out that real friends are people they can count on.

Amigo Brothers

The friendship of Antonio and Felix is tested when the two teenaged boys face each other in a boxing match. They both want to win the match and promise each other they will act like strangers in the ring. Their story will shed light on the ingredients included in a true friendship.

Workshop Resources

Pacing (days) Standard	Block	Lesson	Student Materials	Teacher Resources
1		Key Skill Lesson: Drawing Conclusions	Key Reading Skills Practice English Language Coach	Bellringer Options Transparencies Read Aloud, Think Aloud Transparencies Presentation Plus!
2		"Friendships and Peer Pressure"	Literary Analysis Transparencies Glencoe Online Selection Vocabulary Development Academic Vocabulary Development English Language Coach Active Reading Graphic Organizer Literary Analysis StudentWorks Plus Online Student Edition Literature Classics Selection and Unit Assessments	Literary and Text Analysis Transparencies Puzzlemaker Skill Level Up! BookLink 3 Assessment by Learning Objective (Diagnostic and Formative) Interactive Tutor Self-Assessment TeacherWorks Plus
2		"Amigo Brothers"	Glencoe Online Selection Vocabulary Development Academic Vocabulary Development English Language Coach Active Reading Graphic Organizer Literary Analysis StudentWorks Plus Online Student Edition Literature Classics Selection and Unit Assessments	Literary and Text Analysis Transparencies Puzzlemaker Skill Level Up! BookLink 3 Assessment by Learning Objective (Diagnostic and Formative) Interactive Tutor Self-Assessment TeacherWorks Plus

Keys for Unit Resource

- Blackline Master
- Workbook
- Supplemental Text
- CD-ROM
- DVD
- Transparency
- Web-based
- Fast Files

Level Appropriate Code

AS = Activities for all students
AL = Activities for students working above grade level
OL = Activities for students working at grade level
BL = Activities for students working below grade level
EL = Activities for English language learners

Focus

BELLRINGER Options

- Selection Focus Transparency
- Daily Language Practice Transparency

Focus Activity Say: What are the qualities of a true friend—someone you can really count on? In your Learner's Notebook, make a list of those qualities. *(Responses will vary.)* **OL**

Teach

R Reading Skill

Drawing Conclusions Say: You draw conclusions every day. For example, let's say your friend promises to meet with you to work on a project but doesn't show up. The following day she shows up, but she spends most of the time talking on her cell phone. You conclude that your friend is unreliable. **OL**

V Vocabulary

Academic Vocabulary Say: Read the definition of *conclusions* at the bottom of page 266. Give an example of an opinion or judgment that you've arrived at through careful analysis. *(Responses will vary.)* **OL**

READING WORKSHOP 1

Skills Focus

You will practice using these skills when you read the following selections:

- "Friendships and Peer Pressure," p. 270
- "Amigo Brothers," p. 278

Reading

- Drawing conclusions

Informational Text

- Using text features to understand text

Literature

- Analyzing conflict in a story

Vocabulary

- Understanding synonyms to expand vocabulary
- Academic Vocabulary: *conclusions*

Writing/Grammar

- Understanding use of modifiers

Skill Lesson

Drawing Conclusions

Learn It!

What Is It? In stories, detectives draw **conclusions** all the time. A detective sees a man with his coat buttoned wrong and thinks, "People often button their coats wrong when they're in a hurry." Bingo! "You were in a hurry when you left your house, weren't you?" the detective says, and everyone is amazed. That's drawing a conclusion. **R**

Good readers draw conclusions, too, every time they figure out more than what an author says.

Analyzing Cartoons

Jeremy's friend comments that Jeremy doesn't "get away with much." What clues does he use to draw this conclusion?

Objectives (pp. 266–267)
Reading Draw conclusions from text and experience

Academic Vocabulary

V **conclusions** (kun KLOO zhunz) *n.* opinions or judgments arrived at through careful analysis

Additional Support

Differentiated Instruction

Reading Cartoons Tell students that they often need to draw conclusions in order to understand the humor in cartoons. In this cartoon, Jeremy's friend uses clues to draw a conclusion. **Ask:** What is the conclusion? *(Jeremy "doesn't get away with much.")* What clues does Jeremy's friend use to draw this conclusion? *(Whatever Jeremy does, the man or woman behind the door tells him not to do it or to do it differently, as if he/she can see everything Jeremy is doing.)* **BL** **EL**

Why Is It Important? Even if you're not a detective, drawing conclusions is still very important. If you read carefully, you'll see clues that the writer has placed for you. When you draw conclusions from those facts and descriptions and events, you are working with the author. You get all the information you can. That makes your reading more interesting and more rewarding.

Literature Online

Study Central Visit www.glencoe.com and click on Study Central to review drawing conclusions.

How Do I Do It? First, read carefully. Anyone can *see* an important detail. Not everyone will *notice* it. Then think about whether the details you notice mean more than the author is telling you directly. Here's how one student thought about the details of "Broken Chain" and drew an important conclusion.

R

Alfonso took the stick of gum, placed it in his shirt pocket, and left the bedroom with his head down. He went outside, slamming the screen door behind him, and sat in the alley behind his house. A sparrow landed in the weeds, and when it tried to come close, Alfonso screamed for it to scram.

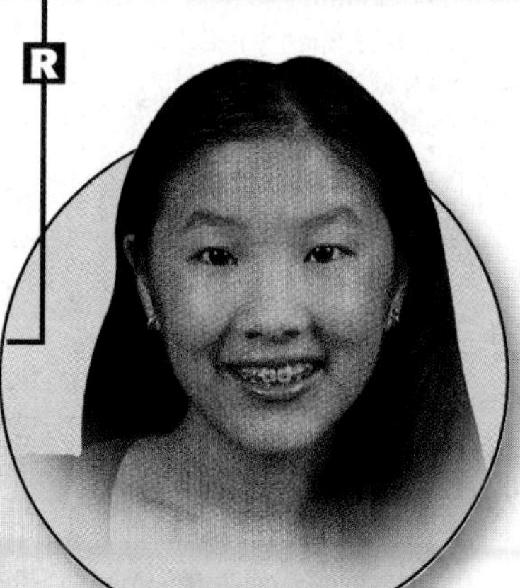

Alfonso puts his head down, slams the door, and screams at a little bird. People do things like that when they're mad. I think Alfonso is mad at his brother because Ernie won't lend him the bike.

Practice It!

Read this short description of a fictional girl named Zera. Then write in your Learner's Notebook all the conclusions you can draw about her.

Zera makes people laugh a lot. Sometimes she makes fun of people's clothes or the way they talk, but she is funny. Of course, she does that behind people's back. Zera offers to do things for people and then she forgets. She doesn't like to let people borrow her stuff. Once she got really mad when Rosie borrowed a pencil. But then Jorge was mean to Rosie, and Zera really told him off.

Use It!

As you read "Friendships and Peer Pressure," look at your conclusions about Zera. Then use the information from the article to help you draw some new conclusions about whether she would be a good friend.

Teach

Literature Online

Study Central Have students access the Web site to review drawing conclusions and to complete a related activity.

R Reading Skill

Drawing Conclusions Say: It's often possible to draw a number of conclusions from details you read about characters, ideas, and events. Look at the conclusions one student drew after thinking about some details from "Broken Chain." What other conclusions might you draw from these same details? *(Possible response: Alfonso is frustrated and can't think of a way to solve his dilemma.)* OL

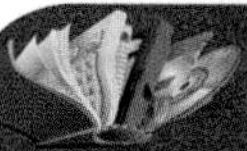

Resources for page 267

Use Reading Skills Transparency in *Read Aloud, Think Aloud,* Unit 3, to help students practice drawing conclusions.

Differentiated Instruction

Role-playing After students have finished the Practice It! activity, ask them to think of a fictional character who faces peer pressure in a particular situation. The character can be someone from a movie, a television program, a novel, or a short story. Ask students to write a paragraph about the character they've chosen. They should write about the character's situation and how he or she deals with peer pressure. Then have students draw conclusions about the character. AL

Objectives

- Draw conclusions from text and personal experience
- Activate prior knowledge and experiences to understand the text

More About the Authors

Textbook authors are often experts in their fields. Dr. Mary H. Bronson, Dr. Betty M. Hubbard, and Dr. Michael J. Cleary are all health education specialists. They've taught students in colleges as well as in middle schools, and they've done extensive research in health education. Dinah Zike is an expert in creating educational products, like the Foldables used in the *Reading with Purpose* program.

Author Search To expand students' appreciation of these authors, have them access the Web site for additional information and resources.

Before You Read

Friendships and Peer Pressure

Meet the Authors

This selection comes from a book called *Glencoe Teen Health.* Four authors worked together to write the book. Dr. Mary H. Bronson and Dr. Betty M. Hubbard are health education teachers. Dr. Michael J. Cleary is a professor at Slippery Rock University of Pennsylvania. The last author, Dinah Zike, is also the creator of the Foldables that you use with this book.

Author Search For more about the authors, go to www.glencoe.com.

Objectives (pp. 268–273)
Reading Draw conclusions from text and experience
Informational Text Use text features: bullets, italics, bold type
Vocabulary Use synonyms

Vocabulary Preview

sacrifices (SAK ruh fy siz) *n.* important things that a person gives up to help others **(p. 271)** *Sometimes you have to make sacrifices to help a friend in trouble.*

empathize (EM puh thyz) *v.* to understand another person's feelings **(p. 271)** *You should empathize with a good friend when she feels sad.*

persuasive (pur SWAY siv) *adj.* able to convince someone to do something **(p. 272)** *Friends can be very persuasive when they want you to do something.*

Write to Learn For each vocabulary word, write a sentence that uses the word correctly in your Learner's Notebook.

English Language Coach

Synonyms Sometimes it's hard to find just the right word for what you want to say. For example, if you're describing yesterday's weather, you could say, "It rained yesterday." But that's pretty dull. To give your reader a clearer picture of the weather, you need another word for rained, like *poured* or *drizzled.* Those words are **synonyms** for *rained.*

Words that mean about the same thing are called **synonyms.** Sometimes there's a small difference in meaning between synonyms that can make a big difference in your writing or reading. When you're writing, think about the important words you use and try to find synonyms that do a better job of telling what you really mean.

Partner Talk Copy the sentences below into your Learner's Notebook. With a partner, discuss the synonyms in the boxes, and choose one that will make the sentence interesting.

Melissa ___ down the street.

| ran | jogged | raced |

The sand ___ his feet until he could hardly stand.

| heated | burned | scorched |

Additional Support

English Language Coach

Synonyms After students have completed the Partner Talk activity, have the partners use a thesaurus to find and list other synonyms for the verbs *run, jog, race, heat, burn,* and *scorch.* You may want to ask volunteers to collect the lists and compile them into a master list. Challenge each pair of students to write a paragraph, using at least six of the synonyms. Encourage students to choose just the right synonyms for the meanings they want to convey. Ask partners to share their paragraphs in small groups. EL BL

Skills Preview

Key Reading Skill: Drawing Conclusions

As you read, use these tips to help you draw conclusions:

- Look for specific details about people, places, ideas, and events.
- Put some of the details together in your mind to come up with bigger ideas or statements.

For example, a character's actions may lead you to believe that he secretly wants to be a musician.

Write to Learn Think about your experiences with friends. Write down one conclusion you've drawn about how a good friend should act. Give at least two details that led you to that conclusion.

Key Text Element: Text Features

Newspaper, magazine, and textbook articles often use bullets, italics, and bold type. These things draw your attention to important words and ideas. They can help you organize information.

- A bullet is a bold dot at the beginning of a line of text. This paragraph starts with a bullet.
- Italics and bold type are type variations. *Italics look like this.* **Bold type looks like this.**

As you read, use these tips to help you find and organize important information:

- Look at the bulleted lines to see how the information is organized. Bullets usually list key ideas.
- Look at the bold and italic text. What's important about these words?

Partner Talk Look at the first page of "Friendships and Peer Pressure." What text features do you see? With a partner, discuss how the bullets, italics, and bold type organize and draw attention to information.

Interactive Literary Elements Handbook
To review or learn more about the literary elements, go to www.glencoe.com.

Get Ready to Read

Connect to the Reading

In "Friendships and Peer Pressure," the authors talk about how friends can persuade each other to do things. Think about a time when you gave advice to a friend. How did he or she feel about your advice?

Partner Talk With a partner, talk about how each of you felt when friends tried to change your minds. Discuss whether the friend wanted you to do the right thing.

Build Background

Many teenagers feel their friends are the most important part of their life. Do you feel that way? Here are some reasons why teen friendships are so important.

- Teens spend more time at school and at school activities than at any other place.
- Friendships help teens learn who they really are.
- The teen years can be stressful. Friendships let you share your problems with other people who are going through the same things.

C

Set Purposes for Reading

BIG Question Read the selection "Friendships and Peer Pressure" to help you think about your own friendships and who you can count on.

Set Your Own Purpose What would you like to learn from the article to help you answer the Big Question? Write your own purpose on a note card and put the card in the left pocket of Foldable 3.

Keep Moving

Use these skills as you read the following selection.

READING WORKSHOP 1

Teach

C Critical Thinking

Application Say: Read through the text in the Build Background section. Do you feel that your friends are the most important part of your life? Do you agree with the reasons given in the bulleted list? Why or why not? Write your responses in your Learner's Notebook. OL

Assess

Use the CheckPoint questions provided on Presentation Plus! to check for prior knowledge and to build background. These questions can be used with interactive response keypads for immediate student feedback.

Literature Online

Interactive Literary Elements Handbook Have students access the Web site to improve their understanding of text features.

Literature Focus Lesson

Text Features Discuss how personal computers and word processing software make it easy to incorporate text features into a piece of writing. Ask students how bullets, italics, or bold type help them organize their writing and draw attention to specific information or ideas. OL

Ask students to write an informational article that they might submit to their school newspaper. Have them type the article on a computer, using text features as appropriate. AL

Objectives

- Draw conclusions from text and experience
- Use text features: bullets, italics, bold type
- Use synonyms

Teach

Viewing the Photo

Ask: Do you think this photo is a good choice for the opening page of a selection about friendships and peer pressure? Explain your answer. *(Responses will vary; students should support their responses.)*

C Critical Thinking

Evaluation Say: As you read the selection, look for ideas about what a good friend is and what a good friend does. Whenever you find an idea in the article, ask yourself if you agree or disagree with the idea. Record your thoughts in your Learner's Notebook. OL

Readability Scores
Dale-Chall: 6.7
DRP: 62
Lexile: 960

INFORMATIONAL TEXT
TEXTBOOK
from *Glencoe Teen Health*

Friendships and Peer Pressure

The Importance of Friends

Your relationships with friends become especially important during the teen years. **Friendships** are *relationships between people who like each other and who have similar interests and values.*[1] Good friendships generally begin when people realize that they have common experiences, goals, and values. Each person must also show a willingness to reach out, to listen, and to care about the needs of the other person. 1

Forming strong friendships is an important part of social health.[2] To make new friends, get involved in activities at school or in the community. For example, join a school club or volunteer at a local youth group. When you participate in activities that you enjoy, you're likely to meet others who share your interests.

1. ***Values*** are beliefs or ideas about what is important.
2. Being healthy means taking care of your mind and your body. ***Social health*** is the part of your life that involves relationships with other people.

Practice the Skills

1 Key Reading Skill

Drawing Conclusions Before you can draw a conclusion, you have to gather facts and information. This article will give you several ideas about what a good friend is and what a good friend does. Make a list of these qualities. Later, you'll draw a conclusion based on these ideas.

Additional Support

English Language Coach

Key Terms Have a student read footnote 1 aloud. Make sure students understand the meaning of the word *values.* Invite volunteers to state some of their own values.

Then ask students if they think it's important for friends to share similar values. Ask them if they think friendships are stronger when people have similar values. Have students give reasons for their answers. EL BL You may want to ask students if they think it's important to try to find common ground with people whose values differ from their own. OL

READING WORKSHOP 1

How Can You Be a Good Friend?

A friend is much more than an acquaintance, someone you see occasionally or know casually. Your relationship with a friend is deeper and means more to you. Although there is no accepted test for friendship, most people whom you call friends will have the following qualities:

- **Trustworthiness.** Good friends are there for you when you need support. They are honest with you, they keep their promises, and they don't reveal your secrets. Good friends live up to your realistic expectations. If necessary, these friends would be willing to make **sacrifices** for you. 2 3
- **Caring.** Good friends listen carefully when you want to talk. They try to understand how you feel. In fact, they **empathize** with you when you have strong feelings such as joy, sadness, or disappointment. Friends don't just recognize your strengths and talents—they tell you about them and help you develop them. Caring friends might try to help you overcome your weaknesses, but they accept you as you are. They don't hold grudges and can forgive you if you make a mistake.

Volunteering is one way to make new friends. These kids helped clean up a river in Los Angeles, California.

Vocabulary

sacrifices (SAK ruh fy siz) *n.* important things that a person gives up to help others

empathize (EM puh thyz) *v.* to understand another person's feelings

Practice the Skills

2 BIG Question

BQ In this paragraph, the authors describe *trustworthiness.* If someone is trustworthy, can you always count on him or her? Would you describe your friends as trustworthy? Put your answer, in the form of a sentence, on a note card in the center pocket of Foldable 3. Your response will help you complete the Unit Challenge later.

3 English Language Coach

EL **Synonyms** Look at the word **trustworthiness**. *Honesty* and *dependability* are synonyms for *trustworthiness.* How is saying that someone is honest or dependable different from saying that he or she is trustworthy?

Teach

BQ 

Invite volunteers to describe situations in which their friends have shown the qualities of trustworthiness and caring. **Ask:** Do you think these two qualities are essential ingredients of true friendship? Why or why not? OL

EL Language Coach

Synonyms Have students look up the word *trustworthy* in a thesaurus. Discuss the connotations of the different synonyms for this word. **Ask:** Which synonyms are closest in meaning to the word *trustworthy* when it's used to describe a friend? *(Possible responses: loyal; true)* EL

Differentiated Instruction

Illustrating a Concept Direct students' attention to the photo on this page. Have students get into small groups and discuss these questions: Why do you think this photo was chosen for a selection about friendship? How does it relate to the ideas about friendship in the text?

After students have discussed these questions, ask them to suggest other types of photos that might be used to illustrate ideas in the text. Students who like to draw might want to create illustrations of their own. OL

Objectives
- Draw conclusions from text and personal experience
- Respond to reading to enhance comprehension
- Understand synonyms to expand vocabulary

Teach

E Text Element

Text Features Have students copy the bold words and their italicized definitions into their Learner's Notebook. To check students' comprehension of the definitions, **ask:**

- Can you think of a time when you and a friend made a compromise? What was involved in this compromise? *(Responses will vary.)*
- Why do you think people commonly choose friends who are their peers? *(Possible response: People are comfortable with others who are close to their age and share other similarities.)*
- Why do you think it's difficult for many people to resist negative peer pressure? *(Possible response: People want to fit in with their peers and are afraid that others will make fun of them.)* BL EL

R Reading Skill

Review Activating Prior Knowledge Invite volunteers to talk about times when they stood their ground despite negative peer pressure. AS

READING WORKSHOP 1

- **Respect.** Good friends will not ask you to do anything that is wrong or dangerous or pressure you if you refuse. They respect your beliefs because they respect you. They also understand that your opinions may be different from theirs, and they realize that this is healthy. Because you and your good friends usually share similar values, they will not expect you to betray those values. If friends disagree, they are willing to **compromise,** which means *to give up something in order to reach a solution that satisfies everyone.*

E

Peer Pressure

Most of your friends are probably your **peers**—*people close to your age who are similar to you in many ways.* You may be concerned about what your peers think of you, how they react to you, and whether they accept you. Their opinions can affect your ideas of how you should think and act. This is called **peer pressure**—*the influence that people your age have on you to think and act like them.* 4

Resisting Negative Peer Pressure There may be times when your peers want you to do something that you know is not right. You want to stand your ground,[3] but it's difficult, especially if they are **persuasive**. You may worry that you will be unpopular or that people will make fun of you if you don't go along. It takes courage to stand up for yourself when others want you to take risks.

R As a teen you are developing the ability to think for yourself and make more of your own decisions. Even when you're sure of yourself, however, it can be difficult to stand up to your peers. 5

Respect from Your Peers People of all ages want to be well liked by their peers. You, too, probably would like to be popular. Remember, however, that just being popular isn't enough. You also want your peers to respect you— to hold you in high regard because of your responsible behavior.

3. In this sentence, to ***stand your ground*** means to not be forced to change your mind.

Vocabulary

persuasive (pur SWAY siv) *adj.* able to convince someone to do something

Practice the Skills

4 Key Text Element

Text Features Have you noticed that some words are bold and are followed by words in italics? The writers are giving you a definition of important words. Keep a list of these words in your Learner's Notebook.

5 Reviewing Skills

Activating Prior Knowledge Think about your friendships. Have you made your own decisions when your friends wanted to do something different?

Additional Support

Reading in the Real World

Career Tell students that adults also may feel pressured to do things they know are wrong. In the working world, for example, peer pressure sometimes leads people to take part in unethical activities, such as offering or accepting bribes. Some workers try to justify their behavior by saying, "Everyone does it." Others go along with wrongdoing because they are afraid to "blow the whistle" on their boss or fellow workers. Ask students how they think workers should deal with this type of peer pressure. AS

READING WORKSHOP 1

Popularity can be based on your possessions or on how you look. What makes a person popular can vary depending on styles and the changing makeup of different groups. Respect, on the other hand, is based on who you are as a complete person. Although it's natural to want to be popular, you may face[4] situations in which you discover that preserving your character is worth more than popularity. If other teens pressure you to take drugs, for example, and you give in, you may become part of a popular crowd. However, you will probably also lose some people's respect. Character traits such as trustworthiness, fairness, and responsibility earn the lasting respect of peers and adults. 6 ❍

4. As a verb, to ***face*** something is to meet it or deal bravely with it.

Practice the Skills

6 Key Reading Skill

Drawing Conclusions Look at the list you made of things that a good friend is and things that a good friend does. Now think about Zera. Based on your list and your own experiences, draw a conclusion about whether she is a good friend. R

Teach

R Reading Skill

Drawing Conclusions Say: Remember that when you draw a conclusion, you use a number of pieces of information to make a general statement about something or someone. Here, you need to use the list you made earlier, your own experiences, and what you know about Zera in order to draw a conclusion about whether she is a good friend. BL

Assess

Use the CheckPoint questions provided on Presentation Plus! to check students' mastery of the selection. These questions can be used with interactive response keypads for immediate student feedback.

Differentiated Instruction

Values Debate Divide students into small groups to discuss and debate these questions: What's more important, being popular with your peers or having their respect? Is it possible to be both popular and respected? Have students follow these guidelines for debating:

- Let everyone have a turn to speak. Don't interrupt.
- Jot down notes on points you want to respond to.
- When it's your turn to speak, state your opinions and the reasons for them.
- Make sure your comments relate directly to the topic. OL

Objectives
- Draw conclusions from text and experience
- Activate prior knowledge
- Debate topics
- Use text features: bold type, italics

Assess

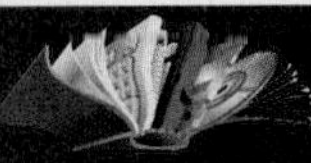

Resources for page 274

- Selection Quick Check
- Selection and Unit Assessment
- ExamView Assessment Suite
- Interactive Tutor: Self-Assessment

Students can respond to the *After You Read* items in their Learner's Notebook or on separate sheets of paper.

Answering the BIG Question

1. Responses will vary.
2. Peers are people close to my age who are similar to me in many ways.
3. Responses should include two of these three qualities: trustworthiness, caring, and respect.

Critical Thinking

4. Possible response: True friends are loyal and trustworthy. They don't tell your secrets to other people, as a former friend of mine did.
5. Possible response: I would refuse to do it and tell my friend that stealing is wrong.
6. Possible response: What can I say to my friends when they pressure me to do wrong things?

After You Read

Friendships and Peer Pressure

Answering the BIG Question

1. Think about the Big Question. After reading this selection, do you think you can always count on your friends to give you good advice? Explain your answer.
2. **Recall** Explain what the word *peers* means.
   TIP Right There
3. **Recall** The selection lists the important qualities of a good friend. What are two of those qualities?
   TIP Right There

Critical Thinking

4. **Respond** List one important characteristic of friendship that you learned and describe how it applies to your life.
   TIP Author and Me
5. **Connect** How would you reply to a friend who wants you to steal sunglasses from a department store?
   TIP Author and Me
6. **Question** Write one question you would like to ask the authors of the text about friendships and peer pressure.
   TIP On My Own

Write About Your Reading

An Ideal Friend Write three paragraphs describing a friend you can count on. The friend can be an imaginary person.

- Your first paragraph should explain what the person is like. Include details that will make the reader interested in the person.
- In your second paragraph, explain why you can count on him or her. Be sure to give examples. Tell what he or she has done to gain your trust.
- Your third paragraph should describe what you like to do together and how you feel about this person.
- Remember to begin each paragraph with a topic sentence.

While you're writing, review the most important points of "Friendships and Peer Pressure." You may want to include some of those points in your description.

Objectives (pp. 274–275)
Reading Draw conclusions from text and experience
Informational Text Use text features: bullets, italics, bold type
Vocabulary Identify and use synonyms
Writing Write compositions that follow an appropriate organization pattern
Grammar Use modifiers

Write About Your Reading

Possible response:

My friend Cassie is loyal and kind. She never talks behind my back or says mean things to me. When I do well in something, she's truly happy for me. Cassie is very smart and very talented, but she never brags or tries to draw attention to herself.

Cassie is always there when I need her. When I was in the hospital recently, she visited me every day and brought my homework to me. She also brought me little gifts and notes from our classmates. I can always count on Cassie.

I like hanging out with Cassie, and we do a lot together. We love to play catch outside, and we go to the mall almost every weekend.

Skills Review

Key Reading Skill: Drawing Conclusions

7. List at least three details from the selection that helped you draw a conclusion about friendship in general. What conclusion did you draw from these details? Explain your answer.
8. What conclusions can you draw about your own friends based on what you've read and your own experiences?

Key Text Element: Text Features

9. Did the bold and italic text help you follow and understand the text? Explain.
10. Review the bulleted items in the selection. For what purpose might you use bulleted items in your own writing? Explain.

Vocabulary Check

Choose the vocabulary word that fits best with each of the following short paragraphs.

empathize sacrifices persuasive

11. Mrs. Ditka works extra jobs to pay for college for her daughter. She rarely buys anything for herself. She drives an old car.
12. Ed always has lots of reasons you should do what he says. He's good at getting people to agree with him and go along with his ideas.
13. Shar pays close attention to what her friends are feeling. She seems to look into her own heart to understand other people.
14. **Academic Vocabulary** If you saw people entering a building with damp umbrellas and wet shoes, what *conclusion* would you draw?
15. **English Language Coach** On a sheet of paper, copy these two lists of words that describe good friends. Draw a line between each word on the left and its synonym on the right.

honest	**encouraging**
kind	**responsible**
supportive	**caring**
dependable	**truthful**

Grammar Link: Modifiers

A **modifier** is a describing word. Modifiers may describe people, places, and things.

- a tall man
- this fast car
- the big city
- three white mice

Modifiers may also describe actions.

- speak softly
- clap loudly
- study hard
- laugh often

Such negative words as *no* and *not* are modifiers.

- I have no idea what you mean.
- They were no closer to their goal.
- That is not what I meant!
- She is not happy about the result.

The use of two negative words in the same sentence is called a "double negative." This should be avoided! Double negatives often sneak into speech or writing when contractions are used.

Incorrect: There wasn't no point in doing that.
Correct: There was no point in doing that.
Correct: There wasn't any point in doing that.

Grammar Practice

Use your knowledge of antonyms and modifiers. Rewrite each phrase below. Replace the underlined word with a modifier that means the opposite.

a messy room; walk quickly; pretty shoes

Writing Application Reread the Write About Your Reading assignment you completed. Underline three of the modifiers you used in the assignment.

Web Activities For eFlashcards, Selection Quick Checks, and other Web activities, go to www.glencoe.com.

Grammar Link: Modifers

Grammar Practice

Responses will vary. Possible responses:
a neat room
walk slowly
ugly shoes

Skills Review

Key Reading Skill: Drawing Conclusions

7. Possible response: Good friends have some of the same values or goals in common; school clubs are a good place to meet friends; making friends is good. From these details, I realized that I need more friends who share my interests.
8. Possible response: I'm friendly with a lot of people, but only two of them are true friends. These two people are loyal and trustworthy. I know that I can always count on them.

Key Text Element: Text Features

9. Possible response: When I saw a word in bold type, I knew it was important. The italic type let me easily find the definitions of the bold words.
10. Possible responses: To organize thoughts, to draw attention to information, to make a list.

Vocabulary Check

11. sacrifices
12. persuasive
13. empathize
14. You would conclude that it's raining outside.
15. honest/truthful; kind/caring; supportive/encouraging; dependable/responsible

Close

Ask students what they learned from this article about friendships and peer pressure to help them answer the Big Question.

Before You Read | Amigo Brothers

More About the Author

Doing creative writing while in prison served several purposes for Piri Thomas. It was a way for him to escape his surroundings, break down stereotypes used to judge people of African American and Puerto Rican descent, and change his life. After his release from prison, Thomas began working in drug rehabilitation centers. His autobiography and novels are known for their use of the Spanish Harlem dialect and for the tough reality they portray.

Literature Online

Author Search To expand students' appreciation of Piri Thomas, have them access the Web site for additional information and resources.

V Vocabulary

Using Context Clues Go over the example sentences that appear after the definitions. Have students identify the context clues in each sentence that help them understand the new word's meaning. BL EL

Piri Thomas

Meet the Author

Piri Thomas was born in 1928 in New York City. He grew up in a tough neighborhood. When he was 21 years old, he went to prison for attempted robbery. He began writing in prison. He said, "I was determined that I was not going to serve time. I was going to make time serve me." See page R7 of the Author Files for more on Piri Thomas.

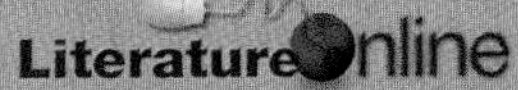

Author Search For more about Piri Thomas, go to www.glencoe.com.

Objectives (pp. 276–289)
Reading Draw conclusions from text and experience
Literature Identify story elements: conflict, internal and external
Vocabulary Use synonyms

Vocabulary Preview

devastating (DEV uh stayt ing) *adj.* causing a lot of pain or damage **(p. 279)** *Antonio's devastating punches knocked out the other boxer.*

wary (WAIR ee) *adj.* cautious; careful; alert **(p. 282)** *Martin was wary of the other boxer's punches.*

nimble (NIM bul) *adj.* light and quick in movement **(p. 285)** *The boxer's strong point was his nimble footwork.*

flailed (flayld) *v.* swung wildly; form of the verb *flail* **(p. 288)** *Felix's arms flailed as he grew weaker.*

evading (ih VAY ding) *v.* keeping away or avoiding; form of the verb *evade* **(p. 288)** *Antonio was evading most of Felix's swings.*

Write to Learn In your Learner's Notebook, write one paragraph that uses at least three of these vocabulary words.

English Language Coach

Synonyms It's boring to use the same words over and over. Instead of "I was tired yesterday," you want a word that's stronger but means about the same thing as *tired.* You could use synonyms such as *exhausted, worn-out, bushed,* and *beat.* To find better, more descriptive words, use these tips:

- Identify the adjectives and adverbs you've used.
- Think about synonyms for those words.
- Select the synonym that best fits the context and your audience.

Individual Activity In your Learner's Notebook, make a chart like the one below. For each word, write at least one synonym that is stronger or more descriptive. Add as many rows as you need.

word	happy	scary	wet	attractive
synonym				
synonym				
synonym				

Additional Support

Differentiated Instruction

Antonyms Tell students that antonyms are pairs of words that have opposite, or nearly opposite, meanings. Have students work with a partner to find antonyms for some of the synonyms they listed in their charts. Tell them to check a thesaurus to find a rich variety of antonyms and to list their antonym pairs in their Learner's Notebook. OL Challenge students to use several of their antonym pairs in a paragraph. AL

Skills Preview

Key Reading Skill: Drawing Conclusions

Writers don't always directly state what they want you to understand in a selection. Instead, they provide clues and details to suggest certain information. When you combine those clues with your own knowledge, you're drawing a conclusion.

Sometimes, you must draw many small conclusions as you go along. Usually, you do this without even thinking about it very much. At other times, a story will force you to stop and think and then come to an important conclusion. As you read "Amigo Brothers," be prepared to draw both big and little conclusions.

Key Literary Element: Conflict

Conflict is an important part of a story. Conflict is the struggle between two opposing forces.

When characters have **external conflicts,** they have problems with something outside of themselves. They could be struggling against another person, a machine, or even nature.

When characters struggle against something inside of themselves, they have **internal conflicts.** Characters can have internal conflicts about how they act or feel. In "Broken Chain," Alfonso has an internal conflict about how he looks. **L**

As you read, use these tips to understand the conflicts in "Amigo Brothers."

- Look for external conflicts between characters. *What causes the conflict between them?*
- Look for each character's internal conflicts. *What is Antonio's conflict? What is Felix's?*
- Think about how you want the conflict to end. *Do you want Antonio and Felix to remain friends? Why?*

Interactive Literary Elements Handbook
To review or learn more about the literary elements, go to www.glencoe.com.

Get Ready to Read

Connect to the Reading

How would you feel if you had to compete against a good friend? How would it affect your friendship? Do you think you would try your hardest? Explain your answers.

Write to Learn In your Learner's Notebook, explain what you think friends should do when they're competing for the same goal. Then share what you've written with a partner and discuss your opinions. Support your ideas with real-life examples.

Build Background

Antonio and Felix are boxers. Here are some facts about boxing.

- Boxers compete in divisions, or groups, based on their weight. Antonio and Felix are in the lightweight division. Boxers in that division weigh between 131 and 135 pounds.
- Amateur boxing matches are broken into three rounds, separated by short breaks. Each round is one to two minutes long. The ringing of a bell tells when a round is beginning or ending. **R**
- The Golden Gloves Championship is the most famous tournament in amateur boxing.

Set Purposes for Reading

BIG Question Read "Amigo Brothers" to see how two friends can and can't count on each other.

Set Your Own Purpose What would you like to learn from the selection to help you answer the Big Question? Write your own purpose on a note card and put the card in the left pocket of Foldable 3.

Keep Moving

Use these skills as you read the following selection.

Teach

L Literary Element

Conflict **Say:** Think about a story you've read recently. What is the conflict in this story? Is it external or internal? *(Responses will vary.)* **OL**

Literature Online

Interactive Literary Elements Handbook Have students access the Web site to improve their understanding of conflict.

R Reading Skill

Review Connecting After students have read the background information, invite volunteers to share additional facts about the sport of boxing. **Ask:** Has anyone ever attended or participated in a boxing match? Can you describe the experience from the point of view of a spectator or a participant? *(Responses will vary.)* **OL**

CheckPoint

Use the CheckPoint questions provided on Presentation Plus! to check for prior knowledge and to build background. These questions can be used with interactive response keypads for immediate student feedback.

Literature Focus Lesson

Conflict Make sure students understand the difference between an internal conflict and an external one. Point out that conflicts occur not only in short stories and novels but also in movies, television programs, and real life.

Invite volunteers to give examples of conflicts from a variety of sources.

Ask students:

- What are the opposing forces in each conflict?
- Is the conflict external or internal?
- How is the conflict resolved? **OL**

Objectives

- Draw conclusions from text and experience
- Identify literary elements: conflict, internal and external
- Use synonyms

Teach

R Reading Skill

Review Connecting Ask: Have you ever had a friend so close that you felt the person was like a brother or sister to you? Describe the relationship. *(Responses will vary.)* OL

V Vocabulary

Synonyms Ask: Based on the definition in the footnote, what are two synonyms for the word *tenement? (Possible responses: apartment building, high-rise, residence, public housing)* OL

Readability Scores
Dale-Chall: 6
DRP: 55
Lexile: 890

READING WORKSHOP 1

Amigo Brothers

by Piri Thomas

Antonio Cruz and Felix Varga were both seventeen years old. They were so together in friendship that they felt themselves to be brothers. They had known each other since childhood, growing up on the lower east side of Manhattan in the same tenement[1] building on Fifth Street between Avenue A and Avenue B. R V

Antonio was fair, lean, and lanky, while Felix was dark, short, and husky. Antonio's hair was always falling over his eyes, while Felix wore his black hair in a natural Afro style.

Each **youngster** had a dream of someday becoming lightweight champion of the world. Every chance they had the boys worked out, sometimes at the Boys Club on 10th Street and Avenue A and sometimes at the pro's gym on 14th Street. Early morning sunrises would find them running along the East River Drive, wrapped in sweat shirts, short towels around their necks, and handkerchiefs Apache style around their foreheads. 1

Practice the Skills

1 English Language Coach

Synonyms The author refers to Antonio and Felix as **youngsters**. He could have used other synonyms for this word, including *kids, boys, youths, adolescents,* or *young men.* Do you feel he chose the best word? Why or why not?

1. A ***tenement*** (TEN uh munt) is a kind of apartment building.

Additional Support

Leveled Reading An adapted version of this selection (Grade 4 readability) is available on page 42 of *Jamestown Literature: An Adapted Reader* for Grade 7.

Differentiated Instruction

Visualizing Tell students to close their eyes as you read aloud the second paragraph of the story, in which the author describes what Antonio and Felix look like. Ask students to visualize, or form a picture in their minds, of the physical appearance of each boy.

Students who enjoy drawing should sketch their mental images of Antonio and Felix. Ask them to share their sketches with the class. Have students discuss how each sketch is similar to their own mental images of the boy pictured and how it is different. OL

READING WORKSHOP 1

While some youngsters were into street negatives, Antonio and Felix slept, ate, rapped, and dreamt positive. Between them, they had a collection of *Fight* magazines second to none, plus a scrapbook filled with torn tickets to every boxing match they had ever attended, and some clippings of their own. If asked a question about any given fighter, they would immediately zip out from their memory banks divisions, weights, records of fights, knock-outs, technical knock-outs, and draws[2] or losses. **2**

Each had fought many bouts representing their community and had won two gold-plated medals plus a silver and bronze medallion. The difference was in their style. Antonio's lean form and long reach made him the better boxer, while Felix's short and muscular frame made him the better slugger. Whenever they had met in the ring for sparring sessions, it had always been hot and heavy.

Now, after a series of elimination bouts, they had been informed that they were to meet each other in the division finals that were scheduled for the seventh of August, two weeks away—the winner to represent the Boys Club in the Golden Gloves Championship Tournament. **3**

The two boys continued to run together along the East River Drive. But even when joking with each other, they both sensed a wall rising between them.

One morning less than a week before their bout, they met as usual for their daily work-out. They fooled around with a few jabs at the air, slapped skin, and then took off, running lightly along the dirty East River's edge.

Antonio glanced at Felix who kept his eyes purposely straight ahead, pausing from time to time to do some fancy leg work while throwing one-twos followed by upper cuts to an imaginary jaw. Antonio then beat the air with a barrage of body blows and short **devastating** lefts with an overhand jaw-breaking right.

2. A ***knock-out*** is when a boxer falls to the ground and does not stand up within a certain amount of time. A ***technical knock-out*** is when a boxer is injured or confused and unable to continue the fight. A ***draw*** is when a fight is so close that neither boxer can be called the winner.

Vocabulary

devastating (DEV uh stayt ing) *adj.* Causing a lot of pain or damage

Practice the Skills

2 Key Reading Skill

Drawing Conclusions At this point in the story, one reader concluded that both boys wanted to be in top physical condition for boxing, so they probably didn't use tobacco, drugs, or alcohol. List the details in the story so far that support this conclusion. **R**

3 Key Literary Element

Conflict So far, there is one main conflict in the story: Antonio and Felix must fight for the division championship. Is this an internal conflict or external conflict? Explain. **L**

Teach

R Reading Skill

Drawing Conclusions Have students look for details in the story that support the conclusion described in the side note. Write these details on the board. **Ask:** Does each detail support the conclusion? Why or why not? *(Responses will vary.)* **BL** **EL**

L Literary Element

Conflict Make sure students can explain why, at this point of the story, the scheduled boxing match between Antonio and Felix is an external conflict. **Ask:** Do you think this match will also develop into an internal conflict for the two boys? Give reasons for your response. *(Possible response: Yes, the boys will soon experience this as an internal conflict, because they are best friends who have to fight each other in an important match.)* **OL**

English Language Coach

Historical Note Tell students that in ancient Greece, boxing was a popular sport and an Olympic event. Roman boxers wore metal-studded gloves that could kill their opponents. In the 1700s, boxing became popular in London, England. Fighters did not wear gloves and were allowed to pull hair and hit opponents who were down. By the late 1800s, boxers began wearing gloves, and the sport began emphasizing skill and strength. Encourage interested students to do research to learn more about the history of boxing. **OL** **EL**

Objectives

- Draw conclusions from text and personal experience
- Understand and analyze internal and external conflicts
- Understand synonyms to expand vocabulary

Teach

L Literary Element

Conflict Remind students that when characters struggle against something inside of themselves, they have an internal conflict. **Ask:** Why does the boxing match between Antonio and Felix represent an internal conflict for both of them? *(Possible response: They are best friends and like brothers to each other. Both of them want to win the match, but neither of them wants to hurt the other person.)* BL

R Reading Skill

Drawing Conclusions Ask: What does the dialogue, or conversation, reveal about the character of each boy? *(Possible response: Both boys are loyal and caring, and they highly value their friendship. At the same time, both are very competitive in the boxing ring, even when they have to fight against each other. Both boys value honesty and fairness.)* OL

After a mile or so, Felix puffed and said, "Let's stop a while, bro. I think we both got something to say to each other."

Antonio nodded. It was not natural to be acting as though nothing unusual was happening when two ace-boon buddies were going to be blasting each other within a few short days.

They rested their elbows on the railing separating them from the river. Antonio wiped his face with his short towel. The sunrise was now creating day.

Felix leaned heavily on the river's railing and stared across to the shores of Brooklyn. Finally, he broke the silence.

"Man, I don't know how to come out with it."

Antonio helped. "It's about our fight, right?"

"Yeah, right." Felix's eyes squinted at the rising orange sun.

"I've been thinking about it too, *panin.*[3] In fact, since we found out it was going to be me and you, I've been awake at night, pulling punches[4] on you, trying not to hurt you." 4

"Same here. It ain't natural not to think about the fight. I mean, we both are *cheverote*[5] fighters and we both want to win. But only one of us can win. There ain't no draws in the eliminations."

Visual Vocabulary
A boxing ***ring*** is a square area, bounded by ropes, in which boxing matches take place.

Felix tapped Antonio gently on the shoulder. "I don't mean to sound like I'm bragging, bro. But I wanna win, fair and square."

Antonio nodded quietly. "Yeah. We both know that in the ring the better man wins. Friend or no friend, brother or no . . ."

Felix finished it for him. "Brother. Tony, let's promise something right here. Okay?"

"If it's fair, *hermano,*[6] I'm for it." Antonio admired the courage of a tug boat pulling a barge five times its welterweight size.

"It's fair, Tony. When we get into the ring, it's gotta be like we never met. We gotta be like two heavy strangers that want the same thing and only one can have it. You understand, don'tcha?"

3. ***Panin*** (PAW neen) is American Spanish slang for "pal or buddy."
4. ***Pulling punches*** means holding back on the strength of a punch.
5. ***Cheverote*** (cheh veh ROH tay) is American Spanish slang for "really cool."
6. ***Hermano*** (air MAW noh) is Spanish for "brother."

Practice the Skills

4 Key Literary Element

Conflict What conflict has been keeping Antonio up at night? Is it an internal or external conflict? Why has Antonio been thinking about "pulling punches" (softening his punches) on Felix?

Additional Support

English Language Coach

Slang Ask students to find examples of English slang and American Spanish slang on this page. (English slang: *bro, ace-boon buddies*; American Spanish slang: *panin, cheverote*) The meanings of the two American Spanish slang words are given in the footnotes. Most students will know that *bro* is slang for brother. Have students use context clues to figure out the meaning of the slang expression *ace-boon buddies.* You may need to explain that here, ace means "best" and boon means "merry," so ace-boon buddies are best friends who share fun and good times. EL BL

"*Sí*, I know." Tony smiled. "No pulling punches. We go all the way."

"Yeah, that's right. Listen, Tony. Don't you think it's a good idea if we don't see each other until the day of the fight? I'm going to stay with my Aunt Lucy in the Bronx. I can use Gleason's Gym for working out. My manager says he got some sparring partners with more or less your style."

Tony scratched his nose pensively.[7] "Yeah, it would be better for our heads." He held out his hand, palm upward. "Deal?"

"Deal." Felix lightly slapped open skin.

"Ready for some more running?" Tony asked lamely.

"Naw, bro. Let's cut it here. You go on. I kinda like to get things together in my head." **5**

"You ain't worried, are you?" Tony asked.

"No way, man." Felix laughed out loud. "I got too much smarts for that. I just think it's cooler if we split right here. After the fight, we can get it together again like nothing ever happened."

The amigo brothers were not ashamed to hug each other tightly.

"Guess you're right. Watch yourself, Felix. I hear there's some pretty heavy dudes up in the Bronx. *Sauvecito*,[8] okay?"

"Okay. You watch yourself too, *sabe?*"[9]

Tony jogged away. Felix watched his friend disappear from view, throwing rights and lefts. Both fighters had a lot of psyching up[10] to do before the big fight.

The days in training passed much too slowly. Although they kept out of each other's way, they were aware of each other's progress via the ghetto grapevine. **C**

The evening before the big fight, Tony made his way to the roof of his tenement. In the quiet early dark, he peered over the ledge. Six stories below the lights of the city blinked and the sounds of cars mingled with the curses and the laughter of children in the street. He tried not to think of Felix, feeling he had succeeded in psyching his mind. But only in the ring

7. ***Pensively*** means in a thoughtful or sad way.
8. ***Sauvecito*** (swaw vay SEE toh) is American Spanish slang for "take it easy" or "be cool."
9. ***Sabe*** (SAW bay) means "You know?" in Spanish.
10. ***Psyching*** (SY king) ***up*** means getting emotionally ready for a task.

Practice the Skills

5 Key Literary Element

Conflict How have Antonio and Felix chosen to deal with their internal conflicts? **L**

Teach

L Literary Element

Conflict Invite volunteers to explain how Antonio and Felix have decided to deal with their internal conflicts. **Ask: What is your opinion of their plan? Do you think it will work? Why or why not?** *(Possible response: I agree that they should fight the match like strangers, not friends, and that they should stay away from each other until the fight. Their friendship is so strong that I think it will survive the fight.)* **OL**

C Critical Thinking

Comprehension Ask: How do you think Felix and Antonio will treat each other in the ring? Give reasons for your answer. *(Possible response: The boys are close friends and don't want to hurt each other. Still, they are serious boxers with big dreams, so I think they will fight as hard as they can. Only then will the fight be fair and show who is the better boxer.)* **AL**

English Language Coach

Spanish Words Have students begin a chart listing Spanish words from the selection, along with their English meanings.

Spanish Word	English Meaning
panin	pal; buddy
cheverote	really cool

Ask students to add Spanish words from this page. *(sí, amigo, sauvecito, sabe)* If any students speak Spanish, ask them to use each word in a Spanish sentence and then translate the sentence into English. **BL** **EL**

Objectives
- Draw conclusions from text and experience
- Understand and analyze internal and external conflicts
- Understand synonyms to expand vocabulary

Teach

C Critical Thinking

Comprehension Ask: How did viewing the movie affect Felix? *(The movie encouraged Felix to see himself as the champ beating Antonio, the challenger.)* OL

EL Language Coach

Synonyms Invite volunteers to describe the mental image that the author creates by using the word *blasting* here. Some students may want to sketch the visual image they have of this imaginary scene. Ask them to share their sketches with the class. OL

would he really know. To spare Felix hurt, he would have to knock him out, early and quick.

Up in the South Bronx, Felix decided to take in a movie in an effort to keep Antonio's face away from his fists. The flick was *The Champion* with Kirk Douglas, the third time Felix was seeing it.

The champion was getting the daylights beat out of him. He was saved only by the sound of the bell.

Felix became the champ and Tony the challenger.

The movie audience was going out of its head. The champ hunched his shoulders grunting and sniffing red blood back into his broken nose. The challenger, confident that he had the championship in the bag, threw a left. The champ countered with a dynamite right.

Felix's right arm felt the shock. Antonio's face, superimposed on the screen, was hit by the awesome force of the blow. Felix saw himself in the ring, **blasting** Antonio against the ropes. The champ had to be forcibly restrained. The challenger fell slowly to the canvas. 6

When Felix finally left the theatre, he had figured out how to psyche himself for tomorrow's fight. It was Felix the Champion vs. Antonio the Challenger.

He walked up some dark streets, deserted except for small pockets of wary-looking kids wearing gang colors. Despite the fact that he was Puerto Rican like them, they eyed him as a stranger to their turf. Felix did a fast shuffle, bobbing and weaving, while letting loose a torrent of blows that would demolish whatever got in its way. It seemed to impress the brothers, who went about their own business.

Finding no takers, Felix decided to split to his aunt's. Walking the streets had not relaxed him, neither had the fight flick. All it had done was to stir him up. He let himself quietly into his Aunt Lucy's apartment and went straight to bed, falling into a fitful sleep with sounds of the gong for Round One.

Antonio was passing some heavy time on his rooftop. How would the fight tomorrow affect his relationship with Felix? After all, fighting was like any other profession. Friendship

Practice the Skills

6 English Language Coach

Synonyms The author uses the word **blasting**. He could have used a synonym such as *pushing*. Why is *blasting* a better word here? What does it make you visualize, or see in your mind?

Vocabulary

wary (WAIR ee) *adj.* cautious; careful; alert

Additional Support

Differentiated Instruction

Modern Boxing Tell students that although boxing is a dangerous sport, the emphasis in modern boxing is on athletic skill and strength rather than on brawling and injuring. In Golden Gloves boxing, in which amateurs compete, the contestants wear helmets and thickly padded gloves to minimize injury.

Ask students to do research to learn more about the history of boxing and how the sport has evolved over time. Have students share their findings with the class. AL

READING WORKSHOP 1

had nothing to do with it. A gnawing doubt[11] crept in. He cut negative thinking real quick by doing some speedy fancy dance steps, bobbing and weaving like mercury. The night air was blurred with perpetual motions of left hooks and right crosses. Felix, his *amigo* brother, was not going to be Felix at all in the ring. Just an opponent with another face. Antonio went to sleep, hearing the opening bell for the first round. Like his friend in the South Bronx, he prayed for victory, via a quick clean knock-out in the first round. **7** **C**

Large posters plastered all over the walls of local shops announced the fight between Antonio Cruz and Felix Vargas as the main bout.

The fight had created great interest in the neighborhood. Antonio and Felix were well liked and respected. Each had his own loyal following.

Antonio's fans had unbridled faith in his boxing skills. On the other side, Felix's admirers trusted in his dynamite-packed fists.

Felix had returned to his apartment early in the morning of August 7th and stayed there, hoping to avoid seeing Antonio. He turned the radio on to *salsa* music sounds and then tried to read while waiting for word from his manager.

The fight was scheduled to take place in Tompkins Square Park. It had been decided that the gymnasium of the Boys Club was not large enough to hold all the people who were sure to attend. In Tompkins Square Park, everyone who wanted could view the fight, whether from ringside or window fire escapes or tenement rooftops.

11 ***Gnawing*** (NAW ing) ***doubt*** means not having confidence in something. It's a kind of negative thinking.

Practice the Skills

7 **Key Literary Element**

Conflict Antonio and Felix continue to deal with their internal conflicts the night before the fight. How does Antonio get ready? How does Felix get ready?

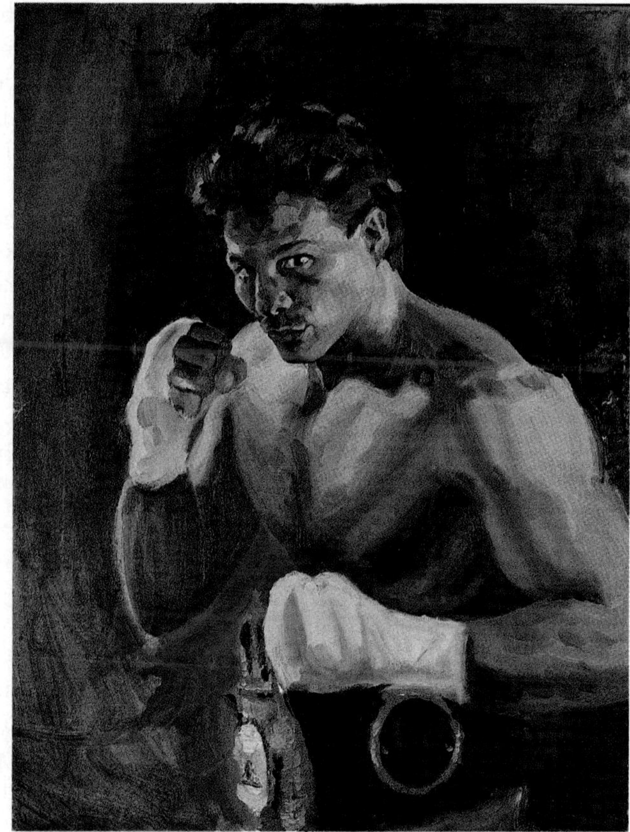

Vinny Pazienza, 1996. Bill Angresano. Oil on canvas, 24 x 20 in. Big Fights Boxing Memorabilia, New York.

Analyzing the Painting Does this fighter seem to have the same determination as the amigo brothers? Explain your opinion.

Teach

Viewing the Painting

Say: Look at the painting and read the question below it. How would you respond? *(Possible response: This fighter's intense eyes and focused expression suggest that he is fighting with the same sort of intensity.)* **OL**

C Critical Thinking

Analysis Have students explain why Antonio thinks that knocking out Felix early in the match would spare him. **Ask:** How do you think you would feel in a situation like this if you were Felix? *(Possible response: Antonio thinks that an early-round knockout would be less painful for Felix than being pummeled during the entire fight. I think it would be humiliating to be knocked out in the first or second round.)* **OL**

Differentiated Instruction

Art and Real Life Tell students that this painting was created by artist Bill Angresano, who was himself a New Jersey Golden Gloves semifinalist in the 1970s. The work probably shows Vinny Pazienza at a match fought against Dana Rosenblatt in 1996. Rosenblatt led the entire fight until Pazienza landed a punch that knocked out his opponent. Pazienza said of the match, "The war is over only when you quit, and I don't quit." Ask students if they think the amigo brothers would agree with Pazienza's statement. Why or why not? **OL**

Objectives
- Draw conclusions from text and personal experience
- Understand and analyze internal and external conflicts
- Understand synonyms to expand vocabulary

READING WORKSHOP 1

Teach

R1 Reading Skill

Review Inferring Ask: Why do you think these boxing matches are such an important event in this community? *(Possible response: It's exciting to watch local boys face off in the ring. Also, the spectators may be watching future champions, since a number of them have emerged from the lower east side.)* **OL**

C Critical Thinking

Comprehension Ask: Does it surprise you that Felix and Antonio look directly at each other and then nod? Explain your response. *(Possible response: Yes, it surprises me, because they agreed that they would be like strangers in the ring. When their eyes meet, it must be hard for them to forget that they are best friends.)* **OL**

The morning of the fight Tompkins Square was a beehive of activity with numerous workers setting up the ring, the seats, and the guest speakers' stand. The scheduled bouts began shortly after noon and the park had begun filling up even earlier. **R**

The local junior high school across from Tompkins Square Park served as the dressing room for all the fighters. Each was given a separate classroom with desk tops, covered with mats, serving as resting tables. Antonio thought he caught a glimpse of Felix waving to him from a room at the far end of the corridor. He waved back just in case it had been him.

The fighters changed from their street clothes into fighting gear. Antonio wore white trunks, black socks, and black shoes. Felix wore sky blue trunks, red socks, and white boxing shoes. Each had dressing gowns to match their fighting trunks with their names neatly stitched on the back.

The loudspeakers blared into the open windows of the school. There were speeches by dignitaries, community leaders, and great boxers of yesteryear. Some were well prepared, some improvised on the spot. They all carried the same message of great pleasure and honor at being part of such a historic event. This great day was in the tradition of champions emerging from the streets of the lower east side.

Interwoven with the speeches were the sounds of the other boxing events. After the sixth bout, Felix was much relieved when his trainer Charlie said, "Time change. Quick knockout. This is it. We're on."

Waiting time was over. Felix was escorted from the classroom by a dozen fans in white T-shirts with the word FELIX across their fronts.

Antonio was escorted down a different stairwell and guided through a roped-off path.

As the two climbed into the ring, the crowd exploded with a roar. Antonio and Felix both bowed gracefully and then raised their arms in acknowledgment.

Antonio tried to be cool, but even as the roar was in its first birth, he turned slowly to meet Felix's eyes looking directly into his. Felix nodded his head and Antonio responded. And both as one, just as quickly, turned away to face his own corner. 8 **C**

Practice the Skills

8 Reviewing Skills

Connecting If you had to face a good friend in a competition, would you look him or her in the eyes or look away? Why?

Additional Support

Reading in the Real World

Career Tell students that many of the champions of professional boxing, including Muhammad Ali, Joe Louis, and Sugar Ray Leonard, fought in Golden Gloves tournaments as amateurs. Ask students to do research to learn more about the Golden Gloves competition.

Have students share their findings with the class. Then ask students how knowing more about the Golden Gloves competition adds to their understanding of the two main characters in the story. How does this information help them better understand the importance of the boys' match, not only to them but also to their community? **AL**

READING WORKSHOP 1

Bong—bong—bong. The roar turned to stillness.

"Ladies and Gentlemen, *Señores y Señoras.*"[12]

The announcer spoke slowly, pleased at his bilingual efforts.

"Now the moment we have all been waiting for—the main event between two fine young Puerto Rican fighters, products of our lower east side.

"In this corner, weighing 134 pounds, Felix Vargas. And in this corner, weighing 133 pounds, Antonio Cruz. The winner will represent the Boys Club in the tournament of champions, the Golden Gloves. There will be no draw. May the best man win."

The cheering of the crowd shook the window panes of the old buildings surrounding Tompkins Square Park. At the center of the ring, the referee was giving instructions to the youngsters.

"Keep your punches up. No low blows. No punching on the back of the head. Keep your heads up. Understand. Let's have a clean fight. Now shake hands and come out fighting."

Both youngsters touched gloves and nodded. They turned and danced quickly to their corners. Their head towels and dressing gowns were lifted neatly from their shoulders by their trainers' **nimble** fingers. Antonio crossed himself. Felix did the same.

BONG! BONG! ROUND ONE. Felix and Antonio turned and faced each other squarely in a fighting pose. Felix wasted no time. He came in fast, head low, half hunched toward his right shoulder, and lashed out with a straight left. He missed a right cross as Antonio slipped the punch and countered with one-two-three lefts that snapped Felix's head back, sending a mild shock coursing through him. If Felix had any small doubt about their friendship affecting their fight, it was being neatly dispelled.[13] 9

Antonio danced, a joy to behold. His left hand was like a piston pumping jabs one right after another with seeming

Practice the Skills

9 Reviewing Skills

Inferring Felix was worried about being able to fight Antonio, but he has no problem fighting him now. Why? How are things different in the boxing ring? R

12. ***Señores*** (sen YOR ays) ***y Señoras*** (sen YOR us) is Spanish for "Ladies and Gentlemen."
13. ***Dispelled*** is another way of saying "driven away."

Vocabulary

nimble (NIM bul) *adj.* light and quick in movement

Teach

R Reading Skill

Review Inferring Ask: What has changed for Felix now that his match with Antonio has started? *(Possible response: Felix knows that now is the time for action—there's no more time to think and worry if he wants to win the match. This point is brought home when Felix lands the first punch, which Antonio answers promptly with three blows to Felix's head.)* **OL**

V Vocabulary

Synonyms Say: Look at the definition of *nimble*. Name two synonyms for nimble. *(Possible response: fast, swift, agile)* **BL** **Say:** Evaluate the writer's use of the word *nimble.* Do you think the writer used the best word to convey the clearest picture? Explain. *(Responses will vary.)* **OL**

Differentiated Instruction

Describe a Boxing Match Have interested students watch a boxing match on TV. Encourage them to take notes to keep track of who is leading each round and what strategies each boxer uses. Have students describe the highlights of the match for the class. Ask them to try to recreate the suspense and excitement of the fight by varying the pitch, tone, and loudness of their voices. Remind students that pausing while speaking can have a dramatic effect, too. **OL**

Objectives
- Draw conclusions from text and personal experience
- Understand and analyze internal and external conflicts
- Make inferences
- Understand synonyms to expand vocabulary

Teach

R Reading Skill

Drawing Conclusions Guide students as they discuss and debate the questions posed in the side note. Make sure they give reasons for their opinions. BL EL

C Critical Thinking

Comprehension Ask: Do you think Felix and Antonio will continue to show good sportsmanship throughout the fight? Why or why not? *(Possible response: I know that both boys want badly to win. As the fight progresses, I think one or both of them will become more desperate. I think they will worry more about winning than about good sportsmanship.)* OL

ease. Felix bobbed and weaved and never stopped boring in.[14] He knew that at long range he was at a disadvantage. Antonio had too much reach on him. Only by coming in close could Felix hope to achieve the dreamed-of knockout.

Antonio knew the dynamite that was stored in his *amigo* brother's fist. He ducked a short right and missed a left hook. Felix trapped him against the ropes just long enough to pour some punishing rights and lefts to Antonio's hard midsection. Antonio slipped away from Felix, crashing two lefts to his head, which set Felix's right ear to ringing.

Bong! Both *amigos* froze a punch well on its way, sending up a roar of approval for good sportsmanship. 10

Felix walked briskly back to his corner. His right ear had not stopped ringing. Antonio gracefully danced his way toward his stool none the worse, except for glowing glove burns, showing angry red against the whiteness of his midribs. C R

"Watch that right, Tony." His trainer talked into his ear. "Remember Felix always goes to the body. He'll want you to drop your hands for his overhand left or right. Got it?"

14. In this sentence, ***boring*** means drilling, making a hole. ***Boring in*** with punches is to punch hard and fast.

Practice the Skills

10 Key Reading Skill

Drawing Conclusions What do you think is the reason Antonio and Felix stopped their punches? The audience draws the conclusion that the reason is good sportsmanship. Do you draw the same conclusion?

Additional Support

Differentiated Instruction

Boxing Skills To help some students gain a better understanding of the concepts in this story, have students visit a gym, talk to a coach, or conduct research to find out more about the boxing moves and stances mentioned in this story, such as: fighting pose, right jabs, left hooks, right crosses, overhand left, looping right to the body, bobbing and weaving, shuffling, feinting, short rights, haymakers, and ducking. Then have students demonstrate these moves and stances for the class, explaining when each one might be necessary. OL

READING WORKSHOP 1

Antonio nodded, spraying water out between his teeth. He felt better as his sore midsection was being firmly rubbed.

Felix's corner was also busy.

"You gotta get in there, fella." Felix's trainer poured water over his curly Afro locks. "Get in there or he's gonna chop you up from way back."

Bong! Bong! Round two. Felix was off his stool and rushed Antonio like a bull, sending a hard right to his head. Beads of water exploded from Antonio's long hair.

Antonio, hurt, sent back a blurring barrage of lefts and rights that only meant pain to Felix, who returned with a short left to the head followed by a looping right to the body. Antonio countered with his own flurry, forcing Felix to give ground. But not for long.

Felix bobbed and weaved, bobbed and weaved, occasionally punching his two gloves together.

Antonio waited for the rush that was sure to come. Felix closed in and feinted[15] with his left shoulder and threw his right instead. Lights suddenly exploded inside Felix's head as Antonio slipped the blow and hit him with a pistonlike left, catching him flush on the point of his chin.

Bedlam[16] broke loose as Felix's legs momentarily buckled. He fought off a series of rights and lefts and came back with a strong right that taught Antonio respect.

Antonio danced in carefully. He knew Felix had the habit of playing possum when hurt, to sucker an **opponent** within reach of the powerful bombs he carried in each fist. **11**

A right to the head slowed Antonio's pretty dancing. He answered with his own left at Felix's right eye that began puffing up within three seconds.

Antonio, a bit too eager, moved in too close and Felix had him entangled into a rip-roaring, punching toe-to-toe slugfest that brought the whole Tompkins Square Park screaming to its feet.

Rights to the body. Lefts to the head. Neither fighter was giving an inch. Suddenly a short right caught Antonio squarely on the chin. His long legs turned to jelly and his

15. ***Feinted*** (FAYN tud) means moved in a way to fake out the other person.

16. A loud roar and crazy cheering is ***bedlam.***

Practice the Skills

L

11 English Language Coach

Synonyms How would this sentence be different if the author used a synonym for the word **opponent**, such as *enemy*? Would you still think that Antonio and Felix were in a boxing ring? Why or why not?

EL

Teach

L Literary Element

Review Sensory Details

Say: Remember that sensory details appeal to one or more of the five senses: sight, hearing, touch, taste, and smell. Read the first six paragraphs on this page and notice the sensory details the author uses. **Ask:** What senses do these images appeal to? *(sight, touch, hearing)* **OL**

EL Language Coach

Synonyms Invite a volunteer to read this sentence aloud, substituting the word *enemy* for *opponent.* **Ask:** If you didn't know that the narrator is describing a boxing strategy, what might you think he is talking about? What does the word *enemy* seem to suggest in the context of this sentence? *(Possible response: The word* enemy *makes me think the narrator is describing military combat, especially since he also mentions "the powerful bombs" that Felix "carried in each fist.")* **OL** **EL**

Literature Focus Lesson

Etymology Have students find the word *bedlam* and read the definition given in the footnote. Tell them that *bedlam* has an interesting history behind it. In 1330, St. Mary of Bethlehem Hospital opened in England to care for the mentally ill. People referred to the hospital as "Bedlam," which was short for Bethlehem. Since medications to treat the mentally ill did not exist then, such a hospital was often a place of uproar and confusion. The word *bedlam,* now a common noun rather than a proper noun, has come to mean "uproar, chaos, or noisy confusion." **OL**

Objectives

- Draw conclusions from text and personal experience
- Understand and analyze internal and external conflicts
- Understand synonyms to expand vocabulary
- Identify sensory details in text

READING WORKSHOP 1

Teach

L Literary Element

Conflict Ask: What type of conflict are Felix and Antonio dealing with at this point in the story? *(Possible response: They are dealing with an external conflict—both boys have been knocked to the canvas, and both are struggling to make it to the end of the fight. Both of them still want to win the match.)* BL EL

C Critical Thinking

Comprehension Ask: How does the last paragraph on this page increase your interest in the story? *(Possible response: Though I know the fight is close, this paragraph tells me that it's virtually even. Also, it tells me that the third, and deciding, round has begun.)* AL

arms **flailed** out desperately. Felix, grunting like a bull, threw wild punches from every direction. Antonio, groggy, bobbed and weaved, **evading** most of the blows. Suddenly his head cleared. His left flashed out hard and straight catching Felix on the bridge of his nose.

Felix lashed back with a haymaker, right off the ghetto streets. At the same instant, his eye caught another left hook from Antonio. Felix swung out trying to clear the pain. Only the frenzied screaming of those along ringside let him know that he had dropped Antonio. Fighting off the growing haze, Antonio struggled to his feet, got up, ducked, and threw a smashing right that dropped Felix flat on his back. L

Felix got up as fast as he could in his own corner, **groggy** but still game. He didn't even hear the count. In a fog, he heard the roaring of the crowd, who seemed to have gone insane. His head cleared to hear the bell sound at the end of the round. He was very glad. His trainer sat him down on the stool. 12

In his corner, Antonio was doing what all fighters do when they are hurt. They sit and smile at everyone.

The referee signaled the ring doctor to check the fighters out. He did so and then gave his okay. The cold water sponges brought clarity to both *amigo* brothers. They were rubbed until their circulation ran free.

Bong! Round three—the final round. Up to now it had been tic-tac-toe, pretty much even. But everyone knew there could be no draw and that this round would decide the winner. C

This time, to Felix's surprise, it was Antonio who came out fast, charging across the ring. Felix braced himself but couldn't

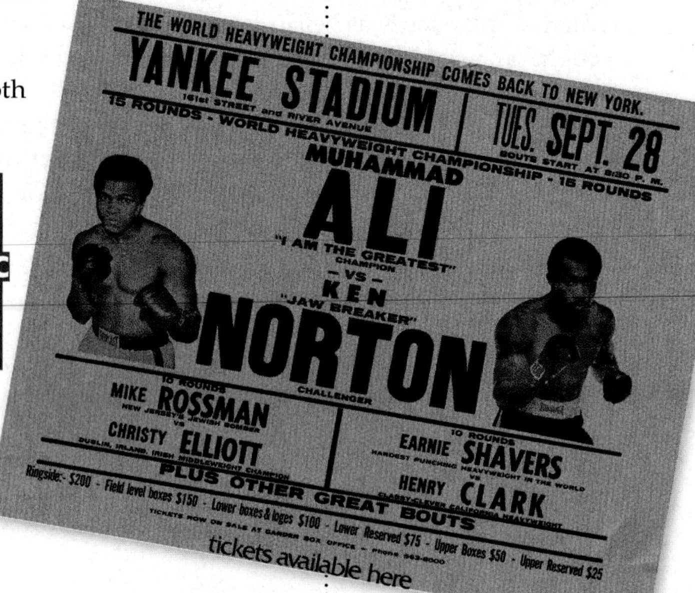

Practice the Skills

12 English Language Coach

Synonyms In the first sentence, why is **groggy** a better word to use than its synonym *tired*?

Vocabulary

 **flailed** (flayld) *v.* swung wildly

 **evading** (ih VAY ding) *v.* keeping away or avoiding

Additional Support

Differentiated Instruction

Advertising Poster Have students look at the poster shown on this page. Invite volunteers to give the basic facts about the fight that the poster advertises. Ask students to evaluate the graphic design of the poster. Do they think the poster accomplishes its intended purpose?

Have students work in small groups to create their own posters advertising boxing matches. Each group of students may either do research in order to choose a real fight that occurred in the past or invent an imaginary boxing match to feature on their poster. OL ward off the barrage of punches. Antonio drove Felix hard against the ropes.

The crowd ate it up. Thus far the two had fought with *mucho corazón.*[17] Felix tapped his gloves and commenced his attack anew. Antonio, throwing boxer's caution to the winds, jumped in to meet him.

Both pounded away. Neither gave an inch and neither fell to the canvas. Felix's left eye was tightly closed. Claret red blood poured from Antonio's nose. They fought toe-to-toe.[18]

The sounds of their blows were loud in contrast to the silence of a crowd gone completely mute.

Bong! Bong! Bong! The bell sounded over and over again. Felix and Antonio were past hearing. Their blows continued to pound on each other like hailstones.

Finally the referee and the two trainers pried Felix and Antonio apart. Cold water was poured over them to bring them back to their senses.

They looked around and then rushed toward each other. A cry of alarm surged through Tompkins Square Park. Was this a fight to the death instead of a boxing match?

The fear soon gave way to wave upon wave of cheering as the two *amigos* embraced.

No matter what the decision, they knew they would always be champions to each other.

BONG! BONG! BONG! "Ladies and Gentlemen. *Señores* and *Señoras.* The winner and representative to the Golden Gloves Tournament of Champions is . . ."

The announcer turned to point to the winner and found himself alone. Arm in arm the champions had already left the ring. 13 14 ❍

17. ***Mucho*** (MOO choh) ***corazón*** (kor uh ZOHN) is Spanish for "a lot of heart."

18. ***Toe-to-toe*** means standing closely together and facing each other so that the toes almost meet.

Practice the Skills

13 Key Literary Element

L **Conflict** At the end of the story, did the boys feel it was more important to solve their internal conflicts or their external conflict? Explain your answer.

14 BIG Question

BQ Can Antonio and Felix still count on each other at the end of the fight? Put your answer, in the form of a sentence, on a note card in the center pocket of Foldable 3. Your response will help you complete the Unit Challenge later. Use details from the story to explain your answer.

READING WORKSHOP 1

Teach

L Literary Element

Conflict Invite volunteers to answer the question in side note 13. Remind them to explain their answers. *(Possible response: Felix and Antonio feel it is more important to solve their internal conflicts, so they leave the ring arm in arm before the winner of the fight is announced.)* OL

BQ 

If students have trouble finding details that explain their answers to the question, you may want to suggest that they work with partners. Make sure students record their answers on their Foldables. BL EL

Assess

CheckPoint

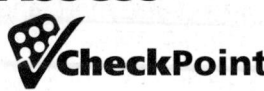

Use the CheckPoint questions provided on Presentation Plus! to check students' mastery of the selection. These questions can be used with interactive response keypads for immediate student feedback.

Differentiated Instruction

Broadcast Writing Have students work in small groups to write scripts for a radio announcer who's covering the match between Felix and Antonio. Remind them that a radio audience cannot see any of the action, so they will need to describe every detail. They may want to mix in visual details from the story with the action of the fight.

Have a member of each group perform the group's script for the class. OL

Objectives

- Understand and analyze internal and external conflicts
- Understand synonyms to expand vocabulary

Assess

Resources for page 290

- Selection Quick Check
- Selection and Unit Assessment
- ExamView Assessment Suite
- Interactive Tutor: Self-Assessment

Students can respond to the *After You Read* items in their Learner's Notebook or on separate sheets of paper.

Answering the BIG Question

1. Responses will vary.
2. Antonio is fair, lean, and lanky. Felix is dark, short, and husky. Their hairstyles are different, as are their boxing styles.

Critical Thinking

3. Possible response: Boxing makes them focused and disciplined. Because they want to be in top physical condition, they don't get involved in "street negatives," as some of the boys in the neighborhood do.
4. Responses will vary but should be supported by details from the story.

After You Read | Amigo Brothers

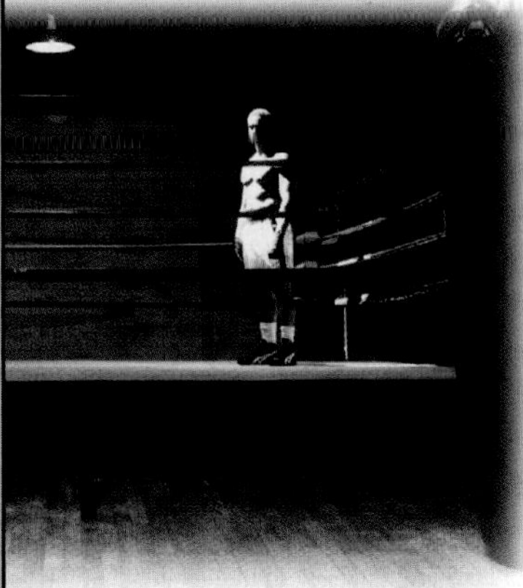

Answering the BIG Question

1. Antonio and Felix each fight hard to beat the other in the championship. Does this mean that they can't count on each other? What are your thoughts about who you can count on after reading this story?
2. **Recall** List some of the ways that Antonio and Felix are different from each other.
   Tip Right There

Critical Thinking

3. **Interpret** How do you think boxing makes Antonio and Felix different from other guys in their neighborhood?
   Tip Author and Me
4. **Analyze** You read the description of the fight in the story. Do you think anyone lost? Use details from the story to explain your answer.
   Tip Author and Me

Talk About Your Reading

Literature Groups Antonio and Felix came to realize that their upcoming fight was causing a problem in their friendship. They decided to train separately and be friends again. With your group, discuss other solutions they could have chosen and present them to the class.

Write to Learn Have one group member write your group's list on the board. After each solution on the list, write one or two sentences explaining why you think it might have worked. Present your list to the entire class.

Solution	Why It Might Work

Objectives (pp. 290–291)
Reading Draw conclusions from text and experience
Literature Identify story elements: conflict, internal and external
Vocabulary Use synonyms
Grammar Use modifiers

Talk About Your Reading

Encourage the groups to explore a variety of solutions to the problem Antonio and Felix face. Make sure students consider whether their solutions are practical. For example, it's very unlikely that either boy would consider withdrawing from the match. Both are deeply committed to boxing, and the match is extremely important: the winner will advance to the Golden Gloves Championship Tournament.

After each group presents its list to the class, have students discuss and debate the merits of each proposed solution.

Skills Review

Key Reading Skill: Drawing Conclusions

5. Antonio and Felix both fight very hard to win. But they leave the boxing ring together before they know who won the match. What conclusion can you draw from this about their friendship?
6. Do you think the friendship between Antonio and Felix is strong enough to survive other problems? How do you come to this conclusion?

Key Literary Element: Conflict

7. What does this story tell you about conflict? Is internal conflict as difficult to deal with as external conflict?

Reviewing Skills: Connecting

8. Antonio and Felix both love boxing. Write for ten minutes about something you really care about. Explain why it interests you. Tell what you do that shows your interest in it.

Vocabulary Check

9. Rewrite the story below. Replace each underlined word or phrase with one of these words:

devastating wary nimble flailed evading

When the rain stopped at noon, Greg walked toward the park. In his new white jeans, he was <u>careful</u> of mud puddles and wet bushes. Suddenly, a car came rushing down the street. Greg jumped back from the curb, <u>getting out of the way</u> of a spray of muddy water. But he was not <u>quick and skillful at moving</u> enough. His feet slipped. His arms <u>waved wildly</u> in the air, and he fell into the gutter. The result was <u>very damaging</u> to his new pants.

10. **English Language Coach** Read each sentence below. Then choose the best synonym to put in the blank. Rewrite each sentence with the best synonym in place.
    - In the mild breeze, the leaf ___ to the ground.
      dropped fluttered dove
    - The small candle ___ in the darkness.
      glowed blazed glared
    - The fighter ___ his anger.
      spoke yelled roared

Grammar Link: Modifiers

Modifiers describe people, places, things, and actions. By adding specific details to general ideas, modifiers make the ideas clearer and easier to understand. Compare the sentences below.

- <u>A</u> car skidded into <u>other</u> cars.
- <u>A</u> <u>rusty</u> <u>black</u> car <u>suddenly</u> skidded into <u>two</u> <u>other</u> cars.

The modifiers *rusty, black, suddenly,* and *two* make the second sentence clearer than the first.

Grammar Practice

Copy each word below. Then add a modifier that answers the question in parentheses ().

11. friend (What kind?)
12. dogs (How many?)
13. flower (What color?)
14. walked (Walked how?)
15. car (How would you describe it?)
16. building (What size?)
17. disappeared (Disappeared how?)
18. school (What kind?)
19. video game (What word would describe it?)

Writing Application Look back at the problems and solutions your group wrote for the Talk About Your Reading exercise. Add at least three modifiers to words on the list.

Skills Review

Key Reading Skill: Drawing Conclusions

5. Possible response: The boys' friendship is more important than who won the match.
6. Possible response: If the boys' friendship was able to survive this fight, then they will be able to solve other conflicts that they might confront.

Key Literary Element: Conflict

7. Possible response: Both internal conflict and external conflict can cause great challenges. In the end, the way that you handle the conflict may be as important as the end result.

Reviewing Skills: Connecting

8. Responses will vary.

Vocabulary Check

9. wary; evading; nimble; flailed; devastating
10. fluttered; glowed; roared

Close

Ask students what they learned from "Amigo Brothers" to help them answer the Big Question.

Grammar Link: Modifers

Grammar Practice

Responses will vary. Possible responses:

11. loyal friend
12. ten dogs
13. purple flower
14. walked quickly
15. sports car
16. large building
17. disappeared suddenly
18. middle school
19. new video game

Short Fictional Story

UNIT 3

Objectives covered in this workshop:

- **Writing** Summarize to inform develop drafts; categorize information; main idea and supporting details
- **Grammar** Identify and correctly use verbs

Teaching Students to Write a Short Fictional Story

Why Is It Important?

- Writing a short story will help students recognize literary elements such as plot, character, setting, and dialogue when they read.
- Becoming authors of short fiction will help students practice writing on non-academic subjects.
- Revising will help students add material to sections of the story that need detail, or don't make sense.
- Students will gain a deeper understanding of different organizational structures by practicing this form of narrative.

How to Help Students Get It

- The short story selections in this unit can serve as mentor texts for students. As they read, remind students that they will be writing their own short stories. They should notice elements and ideas that authors use and borrow those structures for their own creations.
- To begin writing, students may need to review "Broken Chain" (p. 255) or "Amigo Brothers" (p. 278) and pay attention to the structure of the plot. Both are written in sequential order, which serves as a good model for beginning writers.
- Encourage students to think about what will happen first in their stories, what will happen to develop the conflict, and what will happen to resolve the conflict. They may want to use a graphic organizer to compile their thoughts.
- Contrast 'fictional short story' with 'autobiographical narrative.' Remind students that while autobiography is about something that happened to the author, fiction is about made-up events.
- Fiction can be fun! Remind students that in fiction, unlikely or impossible things can be part of the plot.
- Make sure students can identify the climax of their story and the actions that lead up to it.
- Discuss the different ways point of view can impact the telling of a story: Has each writer chosen to tell the story from the most logical point of view?
- Highlight the importance of conflict and resolution. If nothing happens, there's no story. On the other hand, the reader will feel unsatisfied if the main problem goes unsolved.

Responding

Objectives covered in this workshop:
- Ask self questions to understand text
- Make connections from self to text

Responding

Why Is It Important?

- Responding helps students comprehend what they are reading.
- Responding teaches students to think critically by engaging the text through their likes, dislikes, reactions, etc.
- Responding helps students enjoy reading more.
- When students enjoy their reading, they are better able to understand the benefits of reading and incorporate reading into their lives.

How to Help Students Get It

- Tell students that responding is reacting to their reading.
- Help them feel like their opinions matter.
- Remind them to always support their opinions with information from the text; if they dislike a selection, they must have a reason. Help them think about that reason and cite specific examples from the text to support their reactions.

The Selections and the Big Question

Framed

In the short story "Framed," a teenager helps a police officer find the culprit in a robbery at an art gallery. This mystery showcases people we can count on and people we can not count on.

After Twenty Years

After living separate lives in separate cities for 20 years, two friends agree to meet each other. An ironic twist highlights the importance as well as the complications involved in being a loyal friend.

Grammar Link

Adjectives and Adverbs

There are two kinds of modifiers, or describing words. They are adjectives and adverbs.

What Are They?

Adjectives are words that modify nouns and pronouns by answering these questions: Which one? What kind? How many?

I saw <u>that</u> cat.	Which one?	<u>that</u> cat
I like <u>big</u> cats.	What kind?	<u>big</u> cats
I own <u>two</u> cats.	How many?	<u>two</u> cats

Adverbs are words that modify action verbs, adjectives, and other adverbs. Adverbs answer these questions: How? When? How often? Where? How much?

He <u>left</u> quickly.	How?	<u>quickly</u>
I ran <u>today</u>.	When?	<u>today</u>
He runs <u>daily</u>.	How often?	<u>daily</u>
He runs <u>here</u>.	Where?	<u>here</u>
I am <u>too</u> tired.	How much?	<u>too</u>

Why Are Adjectives and Adverbs Important In My Writing?

Adjectives and adverbs can help you make your writing clearer and livelier. With well-chosen adjectives and adverbs, you can

- make the setting of your story easy to picture
- let readers know what your characters look like
- vividly describe how your characters act

W

How Do I Use Them?

After you finish writing, read what you wrote.

- Look for sentences that are dull, vague, or unclear.
- See if adding adjectives or adverbs would improve the sentences.

deserted icy continually
- Inside the ^house, ^water dripped ^from the ceiling.

Writing Application Carefully reread the first draft of your short fictional story. Then, try to improve the draft by adding adjectives and adverbs where appropriate. Be sure to use the example sentence above as a model.

Looking Ahead

Keep all of the writing you've done so far. You will finish your story later in Writing Workshop Part 2.

English Language Coach

Modifiers If your class includes students who speak or are studying languages other than English, invite them to create a list of adjectives and adverbs from those languages. Ask them to list each word and its English equivalent in a two-column chart. Have them use the following abbreviations to label each modifier as the correct part of speech: *adj.* or *adv.*

Invite students to share their lists with the class. You may wish to ask volunteers to use one or more of the words in a sentence, which they can then translate into English. EL OL

Teach

W Writing

Adjectives and Adverbs

Make sure students understand what adjectives and adverbs are. Make a two-column chart on the board. Label one column *Adjectives* and the other *Adverbs.* Tell students to think of a variety of modifiers. Suggest that they think of words that answer the questions shown in the two charts on this page. Invite volunteers to come to the board to list the modifiers they name in the correct column. BL EL

Assess

After students have completed the Writing Application activity on this page, have them exchange drafts with partners. They should read their partners' short story drafts and comment on places where modifiers have made the writing clearer and livelier. Are there places where additional modifiers would improve the stories? If so, students should indicate this on the drafts, and then return them to their partners. Students should make any needed revisions, and then save their drafts for later use.

Objectives

- Write to entertain
- Write short fictional stories that apply organization methods and contain conflict, literary elements, and literary devices
- Write dialogue
- Identify and use adjectives and adverbs
- Edit compositions for correct use of adjectives and adverbs
- Respond with understanding to information heard

Teach

W1 Writing

Dialogue Invite pairs of students to read aloud brief passages of dialogue from "Broken Chain" (pages 255–265) or "Amigo Brothers" (pages 278–289). After each passage is read, ask:

- How does the author's choice of language and details make the characters sound like real people talking to each other?
- What do you learn about the characters, events, or setting of the story from the dialogue?

Encourage students to develop the dialogue in their own short stories, using examples like the ones they have just discussed. OL

W2 Writing

Dialogue Format Choose a brief passage of dialogue from one of the short stories in this unit. Copy the passage onto the board, writing it as a single paragraph without quotation marks. Have students rewrite the dialogue in the correct format. Encourage them to refer to the examples on this page as they work. BL EL

Write dialogue just like it would sound if the characters were real people talking to each other.

Writing Tip

Dialogue Characters' exact words can also tell readers about the setting. For example, "We haven't seen land for days!" tells readers that the speaker is probably floating in the ocean.

Dialogue is punctuated in a certain way so that readers can clearly tell what a character says. Also, sometimes dialogue requires you to start a new paragraph. When you use dialogue, follow the rules below.

- Use quotation marks before and after a direct quotation.

"I-I'll have to ask," she stammered.

- Use quotation marks with both parts of a divided quotation.

"Let's go to the store," Mom said, "and find some barrettes that are easier for you to close."

- Use a comma or commas to separate a phrase such as *he said* from the quotation itself. When a comma and quotation marks appear together, place the comma inside closing quotation marks.

"You need to use your hand," Mom explained, "to smooth your hair down after you brush it." W1

W2

- Place a period inside closing quotation marks. Place a question mark or an exclamation point inside the quotation marks when it is part of the quotation.

Maya said, "I want to go."
Maya asked, "Can I go?"
"Can I go?" Maya asked.
Did you hear Maya say "I want to go"?

- When one character speaks right after another character, start a new paragraph. Starting a new paragraph allows you to write dialogue without always telling the reader who is talking. The indentation lets the reader know that the speaker has changed.

Mom watched Maya brush her hair for a minute. "You need to use your hand to smooth your hair down," Mom told her.
"Oh, I see. That helps a lot."
"And let's go to the store and find some barrettes that are easier for you to close," Mom gently suggested.
"That would be great," Maya said, smiling.

Additional Support

Literature Focus Lesson

Dialogue Remind students that when writers use dialogue in a short story, they let their characters reveal themselves through their words, in addition to showing themselves through their thoughts and actions. Through dialogue, writers also reveal the relationships between characters and let the reader know more about the setting and events of a story.

Ask students to read aloud the dialogue they have written to a partner. Their partner should tell them what the dialogue reveals about the characters, events, and setting of their story. Students should use this feedback to revise their dialogue as necessary. AL

Drafting

Start Writing!

You've thought about your characters and you've planned what will happen in your story. Now it's time to start writing.

Get It on Paper

- Read over all the ideas you wrote in your Learner's Notebook.
- Start writing! Start with any part of the story you want. You may find it easiest to start in the middle of the story and then write the beginning and the end. It's up to you.
- If you get stuck, reread the notes you made about the events in your story.
- Clearly describe the characters and the setting of your story. Readers like to feel that they "know" the characters and "see" the setting.
- Write for ten minutes without stopping. Don't worry about paragraphs, spelling, or punctuation. Just write the story as you imagine it in your mind. You can always go back and make changes later.
- Some of the decisions you made about the plot or characters may change as you go. That's okay! Just keep writing.

Writing Tip

Point of View Decide whether you're going to use first-person or third-person point of view in your story. You can always change the point of view later if you're unhappy with your choice. L

Develop Your Draft

After you get your ideas down on paper, read through your draft. Continue drafting. Fill in parts of the story that you think need to be explained more fully. Add events, descriptions, details—whatever comes to mind. You should also include some dialogue in your story, if you haven't already. Below are some tips for using dialogue effectively. W

Use **dialogue** to develop characters. Dialogue is really important in fictional stories. Readers need to hear the characters speak to get to know them. Read the sample dialogues below. What each character says will tell you a lot about their personalities.

Writing Tip

Writer's Craft Use concrete details to describe the setting and characters. You may want to tell how people and objects look or how they sound. Describing where things are in relation to each other can help readers picture the setting.

"Stand back everyone! I can take care of that dragon!"
"Party? There was a party? Where? When? Why wasn't I invited?"
"Martin broke my watch, but that's all right, it's cool."
"I will not walk or take the bus. I want you to drive me and I want to go now."

After reading these pieces of dialogue, how would you describe the characters? What can you tell about the characters by the way they speak?

WRITING WORKSHOP PART 1

Teach

L Literary Element

Review Point of View

Remind students that point of view is the relationship of the narrator, or storyteller, to the story. **Say:**

- In first-person point of view, the reader sees the story through one character's eyes—the narrator's.
- In third-person point of view, the narrator may reveal the thoughts of only one character, as in the story "Broken Chain." Or the narrator may reveal the thoughts of more than one character, as in "Amigo Brothers."

Tell students that they can always change the point of view of their story later, if they wish. OL

W Writing

First Draft Say: Write your first draft without being too critical of your writing. You've already done a lot of the work during the prewriting stage. Just pick up your pen or pencil and start writing. At the drafting stage, think of yourself as a writer, not an editor. BL EL

Literature Focus Lesson

Character Development Tell students that writers develop their characters as fully as possible in short stories so that readers feel that they really "know" the characters. Encourage students to reveal details about their characters through their actions, thoughts, and words. Remind them that dialogue is especially important when writing fiction. Through dialogue, readers get to know characters better.

Encourage students to go over their drafts to see how they can continue to develop them, using these suggestions. OL

Objectives

- Write to entertain
- Write short fictional stories that apply organization methods and contain conflict, literary elements, and literary devices
- Write dialogue

Teach

Analyzing Cartoons Say: In the cartoon, the boy seems to think that his mess is a "learning process." Do you agree? Explain your answer. **OL** Based on your answer, draw a third panel for this cartoon that represents what either the boy or the woman says next. **AL**

W Writing

Plot Development Ask:

- What is a plot? *(a series of related events in which a problem is explored and usually solved)*
- What drives the plot of a short story? *(a conflict, or struggle between people, ideas, or forces)*
- What are the five stages in which most short story plots develop? *(exposition, rising action, climax, falling action, resolution)* **OL**

Invite volunteers to briefly discuss the five stages of plot development in "Broken Chain" (pages 255–265) or "Amigo Brothers" (pages 278–289). Encourage students to keep these stages in mind as they plan and then write their own short stories. **AL**

Applying Good Writing Traits

Analyzing Cartoons
Your first draft may seem like a big mess. That's okay. With a little organization, it'll make sense. (But you still have to clean your room!)

Organization

Good short stories are organized, but they're not organized the same way your CDs or your dresser drawers are organized. The plots of short stories—no matter how different the stories may be—are developed in the same five stages.

What Is Organization?

Organization is the arrangement of ideas within a piece of writing. Writing with strong organization has the following traits:

- an introduction that captures your readers' attention
- sequencing, or an order of ideas, that makes sense
- thoughtful transitions that link key points and ideas
- a conclusion that wraps it all up

Why Is Organization Important?

W Without organization, your ideas can get lost. A solid plan of organization gives your writing direction and guides readers through your story—from start to finish.

How Do I Organize My Writing?

Different types of writing are often organized in different ways. For example, you wouldn't organize a report about hot air balloons the same way you'd organize a friendly email to your Aunt Millie.

Short stories are organized by plot—a series of related events in which a problem is explored and usually solved. The **conflict,** or struggle between people, ideas, or forces, is what drives the plot. Most plots develop in five stages.

- **Exposition** introduces characters, setting, and conflict.
- **Rising action** adds complications to the conflict.
- **Climax** is the point of greatest interest or suspense.
- **Falling action** is the logical result of the climax.
- **Resolution** presents the final outcome.

Write an inviting introduction that draws readers into your story. A good way to grab readers' attention is to start right in with action or dialogue.

"I can't wait to go to the basketball game Friday night," Maya told her friend Rita on the phone.

Write a conclusion that clearly signals the story is coming to an end. Avoid boring, overused endings such as "I woke up and realized it was all a dream."

Mom replied, "As soon as I call Rita's mother and make sure it's okay with her, you can start packing your bag."

Guide the reader from one event to the next by using transition words and connecting your ideas. Transitions such as *next, then, before,* and *yesterday* show time order. Include sentences that guide the reader from the last event to the next event.

Just then Mom came into Maya's room to put away Maya's laundry.

Write to Learn Write down everything that is going to happen in your story. Then look at your list of events. Cross out any events that don't really matter and don't add to the story in some way. Arrange the events in the order you plan for them to happen. Then fill in any spaces to connect the events in a logical sequence. Use these notes to help you draft your short story.

Additional Support

Differentiated Instruction

Sequencing Use the following suggestions to help students arrange story events:

- Write each event on an index card. Arrange the cards in the order the events will occur.
- Make a graphic organizer like the one below. Add as many boxes as needed to list the main story events. **OL**

Develop Your Ideas

- From your lists, choose a conflict and a character that interest you. Then freewrite for five minutes. Let your writing flow. Don't worry about paragraphs, spelling, or punctuation right now.
- When five minutes is up, think about what you wrote. Do you think the problem and topic you chose could be shaped into a good story? If your answer is *no,* explore different ideas from your lists.
- When you have a good feeling about the problem and idea you chose, read what you wrote. Circle any ideas you think you might want to explore further and possibly use in your story.

Literature Online

Writing Models For models and other writing activities, go to www.glencoe.com.

Make a Plan

You have a good start on your story. You have chosen a conflict and a main character, and you probably have some ideas about other parts of the story. Take some time to think more about those other elements before you begin writing.

- **Characters:** What is the main character like? What might readers need to know about the main character? Who will help the main character face the problem? What might readers need to know about that person?
- **Plot:** What are the causes of the conflict? What does the character do to face the problem? What is the outcome of the story?
- **Setting:** Where does the story take place? What are some details that will help readers picture the setting?

Write down some ideas about the characters, plot, and setting in your Learner's Notebook. You don't have to answer every question—just use them to guide your thinking. You might find that you already answered some of the questions in your freewrite.

Writing Tip

Prewriting There are many ways to go about prewriting. The trick is to find the way that works best for you. Experiment with different prewriting strategies. You may find that you really like to make idea webs or that it helps you to discuss your ideas with a partner. W

Characters: Maya is a teenager who has cerebral palsy. It's hard for her to do some things with her hands.
Plot: Maya wants to sleep over at a friend's house, but she doesn't want her friend to know that she can't do her own hair. Maya's mom will help her learn how to fix her hair.
Setting: Maya's bedroom

WRITING WORKSHOP PART 1

Teach

Literature Online

Writing Models Have students access the Web site for an additional and interactive Writing Workshop-based student model.

W Writing

Prewriting Strategies Invite volunteers to share prewriting strategies that work well for them. If students mention strategies that involve graphic organizers or other visual aids, ask them to draw examples on the board. OL

Differentiated Instruction

Make a Plan Invite interested students to bounce their story ideas around with partners as they make plans for their stories. Tell students that the planning phase of the writing process is the one that many writers love most—the possibilities are endless. A story starts with an idea but has a way of taking on a life of its own once the writer begins writing. Remind students that a good plan helps the writer stay focused on the story yet remain open to colorful details and plot twists as they arise. A partner can help them by reacting to their ideas and suggesting new ones. OL

Objectives
- Write to entertain
- Write short fictional stories that apply organization methods and contain conflict, literary elements, and literary devices

Focus

BELLRINGER Options

Daily Language Practice Transparency

Focus Activity Tell: Summarize a story you've read in which a character solves a problem with the help of another person. In this Writing Workshop, you will write your own fictional story about a character who counts on someone else.

Teach

W Writing

Gather Ideas Say: As you list possible conflicts your main character could face, how can this second character help develop the conflict? *(Possible response: The other character can be the person the main character has a conflict with.)* OL

Resources for page 292

- Use the Writing Workshop Graphic Organizer BLM in the Unit 3 Resource Booklet.
- Use the Grammar and Writing Workshop Transparencies, Unit 3.

WRITING WORKSHOP PART 1

Short Fictional Story

Prewriting and Drafting

ASSIGNMENT Write a short fictional story about a character who is faced with a problem

Purpose: To tell a story about a character who could really count on someone

Audience: You, your teacher, and your classmates

Writing Rubric

As you write your story, you should

- develop a plot around a conflict
- organize the events in your story
- use specific details to describe characters and setting
- write dialogue

Objectives (pp. 292–297)
Writing Use the writing process: draft • Write to entertain • Use story elements: plot, setting, character, dialogue
Grammar Use modifiers: adjectives and adverbs

Writing a short story will help you think about the Unit 3 Big Question: Who Can We Really Count On?

A short fictional story is a brief piece of writing about imaginary people and events. That's right. The people and events are *made up* by the author.

You probably read most short stories because they entertain you. But a good story might teach you something about yourself or others, take you away from it all, or make you feel at home. By writing a short fictional story, you have the chance to provide readers with entertainment and your unique view of life.

In your short story, you'll have to include the same basic elements you find in the short stories you read.

- **Characters** are the actors in the story. They are usually people, but they can also be animals or even objects.
- **Setting** is the time and place in which the story happens.
- A **conflict** is a problem or struggle of some type. The plot is a series of events in which the conflict is explored and often solved.
- **Dialogue** is a conversation between characters.

Prewriting

Get Ready to Write

Your short story should be about a person who has a problem and receives help from someone. Before you start writing, you'll need to think about and plan the main elements of your story. The directions below will guide you through one way to plan a short story.

Gather Ideas

A good way to start gathering ideas is to list some possible ideas in your Learner's Notebook.

W

1. Make a list of possible problems, or conflicts, that your main character could face. Your story must be fictional, but that doesn't mean you can't use your own experiences. Think of problems you, your friends, and your family have faced. Also, think of problems you've heard about or read about.
2. Then make a list of possible characters. You may want to go down your list of problems one at a time and list one or two characters that could possibly have that problem.

Additional Support

Literature Focus Lesson

Short Story Elements Review the elements of a short story, using these questions about "Amigo Brothers" (pages 278–289).

Who are the main **characters**? *(Antonio and Felix)* What is the **setting**? *(the lower east side of Manhattan, New York, probably sometime in the not-too-distant past)*

What is the main **conflict**? *(Best friends Felix and Antonio must fight each other in an important boxing match.)* How is the conflict solved through the events of the **plot**? *(The boys fight hard but fairly. They leave the ring arm in arm after the fight.)*

Give an example of **dialogue** from the story. *(Responses will vary.)* BL EL

Traits of Good Writing	
Ideas	the message or the theme and the details that develop it
Voice	a writer's unique way of using tone and style
Organization: the arrangement of main points and supporting details	Have students use the following checklist when checking their compositions: • Are the beginning, middle, and end clearly linked? • Is the order of ideas easy to follow? • Does the introduction capture your readers' attention? • Do sentences and paragraphs flow from one to the next in a way that makes sense? • Does the conclusion wrap up the composition?
Word Choice: the vocabulary a writer uses to convey meaning	• Does the writer use lively verbs to show action? • Does the writer use vivid words to create word pictures in the readers' minds? • Does the writer use precise words to explain his or her ideas simply and clearly?
Sentence Fluency	the smooth rhythm and flow of sentences that vary in length and style
Conventions	correct spelling, grammar, usage, and mechanics
Presentation	the way words and design elements look on a page

Unit Focus

Workshop Resources

Pacing (Days) Standard	Block	Lesson	Student Materials	Teacher Resources
1		Prewriting	Writing Workshop Graphic Organizer Grammar Practice Spelling and Handwriting Practice Spelling Power eWorkbook Interactive Grammar and Language Workbook Grammar and Composition Handbook	TeacherWorks Plus Presentation Plus! Rubrics for Assessing Student Writing, Listening, and Speaking
2		Drafting	Real Success in Writing: Research and Reports Writing Constructed Responses Sourcebook	Grammar and Writing Workshop Transparency
1		Editing	Interactive Grammar and Language Workbook Grammar and Composition Handbook	Grammar and Writing Workshop Transparency
2		Revising	Real Success in Writing: Research and Reports Writing Constructed Responses Sourcebook	Interactive Grammar and Language Workbook
2		Presenting	Real Success in Writing: Research and Reports Writing Constructed Responses Sourcebook	Rubrics for Assessing Student Writing, Listening, and Speaking

Workshop Resources

Pacing (Days) Standard	Block	Lesson	Student Materials	Teacher Resources
1		Key Skill Lesson: Responding	Key Reading Skills Practice English Language Coach	Bellringer Options Transparencies Read Aloud, Think Aloud Transparencies Presentation Plus!
2		"Framed"	Literary Analysis Transparencies Glencoe Online Selection Vocabulary Development Academic Vocabulary Development English Language Coach Active Reading Graphic Organizer Literary Analysis StudentWorks Plus Online Student Edition Literature Classics Selection and Unit Assessments	Literary and Text Analysis Transparencies Puzzlemaker Skill Level Up! BookLink 3 Assessment by Learning Objective (Diagnostic and Formative) Interactive Tutor Self-Assessment TeacherWorks Plus
2		"After Twenty Years"	Glencoe Online Selection Vocabulary Development Academic Vocabulary Development English Language Coach Active Reading Graphic Organizer Literary Analysis StudentWorks Plus Online Student Edition Literature Classics Selection and Unit Assessments	Literary and Text Analysis Transparencies Puzzlemaker Skill Level Up! BookLink 3 Assessment by Learning Objective (Diagnostic and Formative) Interactive Tutor Self-Assessment TeacherWorks Plus

Keys for Unit Resource

- Blackline Master
- Workbook
- Supplemental Text
- CD-ROM
- DVD
- Transparency
- Web-based
- Fast Files

Level Appropriate Code

AS = Activities for all students
AL = Activities for students working above grade level
OL = Activities for students working at grade level
BL = Activities for students working below grade level
EL = Activities for English language learners

Focus

BELLRINGER Options

- **Selection Focus Transparency**
- **Daily Language Practice Transparency**

Focus Activity Say: Have you ever been falsely accused of something? Were you able to defend yourself in this situation? In your Learner's Notebook, describe your experience. *(Responses will vary.)* **OL**

Teach

R Reading Skill

Responding Make sure students understand that responding is personal and that there is no "right" or "wrong" response to a reading selection. Explain, however, that a reader's responses, or reactions, should be supported by details from the selection. **AS**

Analyze Cartoons Ask:

- What makes the situation in this cartoon humorous? Have you ever had an experience similar to the one shown here? *(Calvin thinks reading is boring until Hobbes jumps up in response to the book he's reading.)*

READING WORKSHOP 2

Skills Focus

You will practice using these skills when you read the following selections:

- "Framed," p. 302
- "After Twenty Years," p. 312

Reading

- Responding to text.

Literature

- Identifying dialogue as different from narration
- Using dialogue as a way to understand more about characters

Vocabulary

- Understanding and using antonyms
- Academic Vocabulary: *respond*

Writing/Grammar

- Understanding articles
- Recognizing demonstrative adjectives

Objectives (pp. 298–299)
Reading Respond to literature • Make connections from text to self

Skill Lesson

Responding

Learn It!

What Is It? When you **respond** to what you read, you think about what you like or dislike. You also think about what you find surprising or interesting. For example, in "Amigo Brothers," you might not have liked the description of the fight. Maybe you don't like to read about two friends hitting each other. That could have been your response to the reading.

R
- Responding is personal. People have different responses to a reading selection.
- Responses need to be about the reading. When you talk about or write your responses, use details from the text to support them. You can also use your own ideas and experience to add to the details from the text.

Analyzing Cartoons
Calvin becomes interested in the book only when Hobbes responds to what he's reading. How did you respond to selections in Units 1 and 2?

Academic Vocabulary

respond (rih SPOND) *v.* to react

Additional Support

Differentiated Instruction

Ways to Respond Tell students that whenever they read, they respond to the text, whether the material is in a textbook, in a newspaper or magazine, on a Web site, or even on the back of a cereal box. Readers respond by thinking about what they like or dislike about the text or what they find surprising or interesting about it.

Ask students to discuss other ways that they have responded to a text besides thinking about it. *(Possible responses: I drew a sketch. I told others about the text or discussed it with people who had also read it. I ignored it because it was boring. I hummed a song that popped into my head as I read the text.)* **OL**

Why Is It Important? Responding to the reading will help you enjoy what you read more. It will help you feel more connected to the texts you read, and it will help you remember them more clearly. Responding helps you learn about yourself as a reader, because your personal opinions and ideas about a text show a lot about who you are and what you think.

Study Central Visit www.glencoe.com and click on Study Central to review responding.

How Do I Do It? As you read, pay attention to what you think and feel about a text. Ask yourself questions about what you like and dislike and why. Focus on different parts of the story—people, places, events, and ideas.

Here's an example of how one student responded to Felix in "Amigo Brothers."

> He walked up some dark streets, deserted except for small pockets of wary-looking kids wearing gang colors. Despite the fact that he was Puerto Rican like them, they eyed him as a stranger to their turf. Felix did a fast shuffle, bobbing and weaving, while letting loose a torrent of blows that would demolish whatever got in its way. **R**

I like this guy, Felix. I respect him. When he walks down that street, he isn't afraid. He doesn't box to be tough, either. He boxes because it's what he loves to do. I could hang out with someone like Felix.

Practice It!

Write these questions in your Learner's Notebook and use them to help you respond to "Framed" and "After Twenty Years."

- What do I like about the story? Why?
- What do I not like about the story? Why?
- What surprises me in this story? Why?
- When does the story really grab my attention? Why?

Use It!

As you read "Framed" and "After Twenty Years," look at the questions you just wrote in your Learner's Notebook. Write notes about what you like and dislike in each story. Also write about what surprises you and interests you.

Teach

Literature Online

Study Central Have students access the Web site to review responding and to complete a related activity.

R Reading Skill

Responding Ask a student to read aloud the passage from "Amigo Brothers." Then have another student read the sample response to the excerpt. **Ask:** What is your own response to this passage? *(Responses will vary.)* **OL**

Ask volunteers to choose other passages from selections in this unit. Have them read their passages aloud and then respond to them. Invite other students to respond to the passages as well. **Ask:** How are the various responses similar? How are they different? *(Responses will vary.)* **OL**

Resources for page 299

- Use Reading Skills Transparency in *Read Aloud, Think Aloud,* Unit 3, to help students practice responding.

Literature Focus Lesson

Responding Tell students that they use their responding skills not only when they read but also when they watch a movie or television program, listen to recorded music, or attend a play or concert.

Have students get into small groups and describe their responses to recent performances they have attended, movies or television programs they have watched, or musical recordings they have listened to. Suggest that students refer to the questions in the Practice It! exercise on this page, substituting another word, such as *movie,* for the word *story* in the exercise. **AS**

Objectives
- Respond to literature
- Make connections from text to self

Before You Read Framed

More About the Author

The story students are about to read comes from *Six-Minute Mysteries,* one of more than forty books written by award-winning author Don Wulffson. Besides writing fiction, Wulffson also has written poems, articles, and plays. His many nonfiction books for young people cover a variety of high-interest topics. Books by Wulffson include *Pro Sports: How Did They Begin?* and *The Kid Who Invented the Trampoline: More Surprising Stories about Inventions.*

V Vocabulary

Vocabulary File Say: One way to learn and remember new words is to keep a vocabulary file. Write each vocabulary word on an index card. Include the pronunciation (if you need it), the meaning, and a sentence that uses the word in clear context. Refer to your cards from time to time, and make an effort to use new words in your writing and speaking. BL EL

Don Wulffson

Meet the Author

Don Wulffson says that he writes to make life more interesting. He was born in California in 1943. He's been a writer and teacher for most of his life. He's best known for the adventure books he writes for young adults, including *The Upside Down Ship* and the *Incredible True Adventure Series.*

Author Search For more about Don Wulffson, go to www.glencoe.com.

Objectives (pp. 300–307)
Reading Respond to literature • Make connections from text to self
Literature Identify literary elements: dialogue
Vocabulary Use prefixes • Use antonyms

Vocabulary Preview

stifling (STY fling) *v.* holding back or stopping; form of the verb *stifle* **(p. 302)** *Jeannette, stifling a laugh, continued her speech about funny TV commercials.*

dominated (DAW muh nay tid) *adj.* greatly occupied **(p. 303)** *Movie star posters dominated Chenille's room.*

V **sternly** (STURN lee) *adv.* in a strict or firm way **(p. 304)** *Marcus listened quietly while the teacher spoke sternly.*

evidence (EV ih dens) *n.* information, facts, or objects that help prove something **(p. 306)** *The evidence all pointed to the woman's guilt.*

recovered (ree KUV urd) *v.* found something that was lost or stolen; form of the verb *recover* **(p. 307)** *The police recovered the stolen car.*

Partner Talk Talk with a partner about the definition of each vocabulary word. On a separate sheet of paper, write sentences together that use each word correctly.

English Language Coach

Antonyms Antonyms are pairs of words that have opposite, or nearly opposite, meanings. *Up–down, hot–cold,* and *tall–short* are examples. Antonyms are less common than synonyms.

A common way to form antonyms is to add a prefix that means *not* to the beginning of the word. A prefix is a group of letters added to the beginning of a word to change its meaning. Prefixes can reverse the meaning of a word to form an antonym:

in- complete – incomplete
non- returnable – non-returnable
dis- agree – disagree
un- able – unable

Individual Activity Make an antonym out of each of these words by removing one of the prefixes listed above. Write the words and their antonyms in your Learner's Notebook.

disadvantage	**untie**
nonsense	**inactive**

Additional Support

Literature Online

Author Search To expand students' appreciation of Don Wulffson, have them access the Web site for additional information and resources.

English Language Coach

Antonyms Have students work with partners to compile lists of antonym pairs. One of the words in each pair should use the prefix *in-, dis-, non-,* or *un-* to form the antonym of the other word. Students may consult a thesaurus or a dictionary to find examples of words that include these prefixes.

Ask volunteers to compile the lists into a master chart on a large piece of paper or poster board. The chart should have four columns, one for each prefix. BL EL

Skills Preview

Key Reading Skill: Responding

As you read the selection, answer these questions:

- What surprises me?
- Which characters do I like and dislike and why?
- What parts of this story remind me of things I already know?
- What feelings do the characters experience? Do I feel any of the same things?
- Did I enjoy reading this selection? Why or why not?

Write to Learn In your Learner's Notebook, write a short paragraph about something you've seen–such as a movie or something in real life–that made you respond strongly. How did you respond?

Key Literary Element: Dialogue

Dialogue is conversation, or talking, between characters in a story. To recognize dialogue, remember these tips:

- The spoken words will be inside quotation marks.
- Tag lines, or the part of the sentence that is not in quotation marks, tell you who is speaking.

Here is a sample of dialogue from "Framed."

"And to think I trusted you so completely," wailed Beatrice Delacourte.

"Hard to believe," said Nick, shaking his head.

Partner Talk As you read "Framed," talk about which characters you like and dislike. Then imagine the story without dialogue. Would you like and dislike the same characters? Why or why not?

Interactive Literary Elements Handbook
To review or learn more about the literary elements, go to www.glencoe.com.

Get Ready to Read

Connect to the Reading

What if you got blamed for something you didn't do? How would you feel? What would you do to clear your name?

Partner Talk Have you ever stood up for someone who needed your help? Has someone ever stood up for you? Talk with a partner about the people you've counted on and the people who've counted on you. Tell your partner one story about standing up for someone else. The story can be about you, about another person, or it can be made up.

Build Background

The story you are about to read is a mystery.

- In a mystery, a crime happens and is usually solved by someone in the story.
- This story comes from a book called *Six-Minute Mysteries.*
- When you *frame* someone, you make up a false story or false evidence to make that person seem guilty of a crime.

R

Set Purposes for Reading

BIG Question Read the selection "Framed" to learn how a mother can count on her daughter.

Set Your Own Purpose What would you like to learn from the story to help you answer the Big Question? Write your own purpose on a note card and put the card in the left pocket of Foldable 3.

Keep Moving

Use these skills as you read the following selection.

Teach

R Reading Skill

Review Connecting Have a student read aloud the text in the Build Background section. **Say:** Think of a mystery, either fictional or real, in which someone is framed. What is the crime? Who frames the person and why? Does the truth finally come out? If so, how? OL

Assess

Use the CheckPoint questions provided on Presentation Plus! to check for prior knowledge and to build background. These questions can be used with interactive response keypads for immediate student feedback.

Interactive Literary Elements Handbook Have students access the Web site to improve their understanding of dialogue.

Literature Focus Lesson

Dialogue Remind students that dialogue is conversation between characters in a story. Ask them how they recognize dialogue when they read. *(The spoken words are inside quotation marks; the sentence is indented each time a person talks; tag lines tell you who's speaking.)*

Ask students to write a brief dialogue in which a police detective questions a person suspected of theft. Students may want to work with partners. Remind them to follow the correct format for writing dialogue. Have students save their work to compare with the dialogue in "Framed." AS

Objectives

- Respond to literature
- Make connections from text to self
- Identify literary elements: dialogue
- Use prefixes
- Use antonyms

Teach

Viewing the Photo

Ask: How does this photo illustration convey the literal meaning of the word *framed?* *(Possible response: The story's title and the author's name are surrounded by a frame.)* After reading the first page, what other meaning of the word *framed* do you think the title might refer to? Explain your answer. *(Possible response: The many police cars in the gallery parking lot suggest that a crime may have been committed. Perhaps someone will be framed.)* **AL**

L Literary Element

Dialogue Make sure students understand that writers use tag lines not only to indicate who is speaking but also to give more information about the characters in a dialogue. **Ask:** What can you infer about Andrea and her mother from these tag lines? *(Possible response: Andrea's mother is either tired or bored. Andrea smiles as she replies, perhaps to reassure her mother that she'll be fine.)* **OL**

Readability Scores
Dale-Chall: 4.7
DRP: 54
Lexile: 790

Andrea Meadows was nervous as she and her mother drove along River Front Drive. It would be her first day of work at the Milwaukee Gallery of Fine Arts. Her mother, a security guard at the gallery, had gotten her a part-time job as a file clerk during summer vacation.

"A few butterflies?" her mother said, **stifling** a yawn. L

"I'll be okay," said Andrea, smiling. **1**

Her mother returned the smile and rubbed her red eyes. Andrea could see how tired she was. Her mother had worked from 10:00 A.M. to 7:00 P.M. yesterday and now would do another full shift to get overtime pay. It was hard for a single parent to make ends meet, especially on a security guard's salary.

"I wonder what's going on," her mother said as they pulled into the parking lot behind the gallery and saw that most of the cars were police cars. Her mother quickly parked, and they hurried inside, into the staff lounge.

Vocabulary

stifling (STY fling) *v.* holding back or stopping

Practice the Skills

1 Key Literary Element

Dialogue The quotation marks tell you that there is dialogue. Who is speaking? What do the tag lines, or words not in the quotation marks, tell you about the characters?

Additional Support

English Language Coach

Idioms Tell students that an idiom is an expression that means something different from its word-for-word meaning. For example, Andrea is nervous because today will be her first day on the job. Her mother says to her, "A few butterflies?" Ask students what they think this expression means. *(When people are nervous, they sometimes say they "have butterflies.")* **EL** **BL**

Have students use context clues to figure out the meaning of the expression "to make ends meet" in the fourth paragraph. *(to live within one's income)* **AS**

"What's with the police brigade?[1]" her mother asked Nick Crowley, the caretaker, who looked like he was about a hundred years old.

"There's been a robbery," said Nick. "Someone made off with the Magritte last night."

"The Magritte!" exclaimed Andrea's mother. "Oh no!"

René Magritte's *The Healer,* Andrea knew, was the prize of the gallery's collection—and worth upward of six million. Her mind raced as she followed her mother and Nick into the security office of the gallery, **dominated** by dozens of monitor panels, each fixed on a different room or part of the building. One of the rooms showed where the Magritte had been on display. In its place was an empty frame.

"How could this happen?" cried Beatrice Delacourte, the owner of the gallery, dabbing her eyes as she clattered into the room on spike high heels.[2]

A rugged-looking man in a sports jacket followed Beatrice. He immediately stepped around her and walked up to Andrea's mother. "Are you Julia Meadows?" he asked, flashing a badge.

Andrea watched her mother nod and quietly answer yes.

"I'm Lieutenant Stone," the man said, pulling a chair out. "Would you like to sit down? I need to ask you a few questions." He took out a pad and pencil, then sat down across from Andrea's mother. "Yesterday you were the only security guard on duty between 10:00 A.M. and 7:00 P.M. Is that correct?" R1

"Yes," said Julia Meadows in a flat tone. "That was my shift." 2

"And after closing time, 4:00 P.M., was anyone else in the gallery?" the lieutenant asked.

Andrea listened carefully as her mother explained that Nick Crowley and Ms. Delacourte had been in the gallery until closing. "After that," her mother stated with certainty in her voice, "the cleaning crew was here from 4:00 to 6:00 P.M.—no one else."

1. A ***brigade*** is an organized group of workers.
2. ***Spike high heels*** are shoes with tall, skinny heels like spikes.

Vocabulary

dominated (DAW muh nay tid) *adj.* greatly occupied

Practice the Skills

2 Reviewing Skills

Drawing Conclusions When you draw conclusions, you use information from the text to make a general statement. The text says that Julia answers in a "flat tone." It also says she worked a long shift the day before. You might draw the conclusion that Julia answered in a flat tone because she was tired. R2

READING WORKSHOP 2

Teach

R1 Reading Skill

Responding Ask: Are you surprised that Lieutenant Stone questions Julia Meadows? Do you think she might be a suspect in the theft of the painting? Explain your response. *(Possible response: I'm not surprised about the questioning because Julia is on security guard duty the day the painting vanishes. The questions Stone is asking suggest that Julia might be a suspect.)* **BL**

R2 Reading Skill

Review Drawing Conclusions Read and discuss the side note with students. Then **ask:** What other conclusion might you draw from these same facts? Give reasons for your response. *(Possible response: Julia answers in a flat tone because she conducts herself on the job in a calm, professional manner. Even though she probably knows she may be a suspect in the case, she is not emotional or defensive.)* **OL**

Reading in the Real World

Career Ask students to do research to learn more about the career of a police detective. Have them find answers to questions like these:

- How does someone become a police detective?
- What types of education and experience are required for this job?
- What types of training do detectives receive?
- How do detectives spend their time?
- What are the rewards and dangers of the job?

Ask students to share their findings. **AS**

Objectives
- Identify personal responses while reading
- Express personal responses
- Understand literary elements: dialogue
- Draw conclusions

READING WORKSHOP 2

Teach

L Literary Element

Dialogue Ask: What did you learn from the dialogue in this paragraph? *(Responses may include: Beatrice Delacourte seems to believe that Julia is the thief. She has informed the newspapers of the theft and has offered a reward for the return of the painting.)* BL EL

C Critical Thinking

Analysis Ask: Does it seem odd to you that Julia receives flowers from an anonymous person? What are some possible explanations for this event? *(Possible responses: It's just a coincidence; Julia has a secret admirer. Or: The real thief sends the flowers because he or she wants Julia to be caught on videotape, carrying a long, rectangular box as she leaves work the evening of the theft. Someone is trying to frame Julia.)* AL

Stone scratched his head and tapped his pencil on the table. "We have a rather puzzling situation," he said after a moment. "The Magritte painting was in a locked room—a room that was **locked** after the painting vanished. Do you have any explanation?" 3

"None," said Julia Meadows. "It was in the room the last time I made my rounds. That was right after the cleaning crew left . . . about five-thirty."

Beatrice Delacourte shook her head sadly and looked coldly at Andrea's mother. "I'm trying not to think the worst, Julia," she said. Then turning to Lieutenant Stone, she added, "I've already contacted the papers and posted twenty-five thousand dollars for the painting's return. As you can see, I'm willing to do just about anything to have my Magritte back." 4

Stone nodded and looked **sternly** at Julia Meadows. "I have something I'd like you all to watch," he said, reaching across the table and turning on a monitor connected to a VCR. "This surveillance video[3] was taken of you, Ms. Meadows, leaving work last night at 7:14 P.M. In it, as you can see, you are carrying a long, rectangular box. Such a box could be used to carry a rolled-up painting, could it not?"

"Yes," agreed Julia Meadows. "But the fact is, it contained flowers."

The lieutenant raised an eyebrow. "Flowers?"

"I didn't understand how I came to be carrying flowers home either," Andrea's mother explained. "But a little after five-thirty yesterday afternoon, a delivery boy arrived with a dozen long-stemmed roses. There was no card, but my name and the museum's address were written on the box. And that is what I was taking home, Lieutenant Stone—a box of flowers." C

Stone made a few notations in his pad, then changed the cassette in the VCR. "I'd like you to watch something else," he said, pushing the play button. "This video shows the room at

3. A ***surveillance video*** is taken by security cameras that are posted around a building to record activity.

Vocabulary

sternly (STURN lee) *adv.* in a strict or firm way

Practice the Skills

3 English Language Coach

Antonyms All of the prefixes below mean "not." Only one of them is used to form the common antonym for **locked**. Which one?

in- *non-* *dis-* *un-*

4 Key Literary Element

L **Dialogue** Reread this paragraph. In your Learner's Notebook, write down two things you learn about the story from Beatrice Delacourte's dialogue.

Additional Support

Reading Fluency

Dialogue The dialogue in this story presents a good opportunity for students to develop their reading fluency. Students can assume the roles of the characters and the narrator. The narrator should read any text—including tag lines—not actually spoken by a character.

Encourage students to read the lines of dialogue expressively, speaking in the same ways that the characters might actually say the lines. Have students practice their reading and then present the dialogue to the class. OL

READING WORKSHOP 2

The Therapeutist, 1937, Renée Magritte. Private collection.

Analyzing the Painting The more common word for ***therapeutist*** is ***healer,*** and the painting is sometimes called ***The Healer.*** What do you think of the painting?

Practice the Skills

5:29 P.M.," he said. "As you can see, the Magritte was in its frame. Please watch what happens." **5**

Andrea carefully studied the monitor along with everyone else. The time, displayed in the lower lefthand corner of the video, ticked off slowly as she saw a door opening, and then, for an instant, her mother's profile. Seconds later, the painting was gone. The time on the monitor had flipped from 5:29 to 5:48 P.M.

"Obviously," said Stone, stopping the VCR, "several minutes of the tape have been erased. Isn't the security guard on duty in charge of the tapes, Ms. Meadows?"

All eyes turned to Andrea's mother.

5 Key Reading Skill

Responding At this point, you've met all the main characters. Which character is most interesting to you? Why? Which characters do you like and dislike? Why? **R**

Teach

Viewing the Painting

Say: René Magritte was a Belgian painter who was one of the most important artists in the surrealist movement. The surrealists tried to bring the worlds of reality and fantasy together to create something that they called "an absolute reality." **Ask:** Which elements of the painting belong to the world of reality? Which belong to the world of fantasy? *(Possible response: The figure in the painting appears to have arms and legs, like an ordinary man. He appears to be seated and is wearing a cape, trousers, and shoes; he's also wearing a hat but has no head. A large portion of his body seems to consist of a birdcage, complete with birds.)* **OL**

R Reading Skill

Responding Invite volunteers to share their responses to the side note with the class. Encourage them to give reasons for their reactions to the story's main characters. **OL**

Differentiated Instruction

Creating Art Have interested students create their own works of surrealist art. If possible, show students more examples of works by artists who belong to the surrealist movement. Tell students to sign their works and give them titles.

Invite volunteers to share their artwork with the entire class. Have students discuss which elements of the work belong to the world of reality and which belong to the world of fantasy. **OL**

Objectives
- Identify personal responses while reading
- Express personal responses
- Respond to art

READING WORKSHOP 2

Teach

L Literary Element

Dialogue Ask: What did you learn about the story from this paragraph? *(Possible response: After the cleaning crew leaves, someone other than Julia walks up to the Magritte and then walks to the painting next to it. That person may have hidden the Magritte behind the other painting.)* What do you learn about Andrea from this paragraph? *(Possible response: Andrea is very observant and quite intelligent. She also has a lot of self-confidence.)* **OL**

C Critical Thinking

Comprehension Ask: Do you think the Magritte is behind the tilted painting? Who do you think made the second set of footprints on the carpeting? Give reasons for your conclusions. *(Possible response: I think the Magritte is behind the tilted painting because of the path shown by the second set of footprints. I don't know who makes those footprints, but I think it has to be someone who works inside the museum, someone other than Julia.)* **OL**

"And to think I trusted you so completely," wailed Beatrice Delacourte.

"Hard to believe," said Nick, shaking his head.

"Excuse me, Officer Stone," Andrea said quietly. "But could I see the tape again?"

Stone shrugged. "I don't see why not, young lady. But I'm afraid your mother has some **evidence** against her." He rewound the tape and replayed it. Once again, Andrea watched with the others as the Magritte appeared on the screen one minute and was gone the next.

But this time when the tape ended, Andrea sat back and smiled. "I think I know how the painting was taken," she said confidently.[4] "And I also know where it is. Please, Officer Stone, play the tape just once more—but this time, in slow motion."

Puzzled, Stone rewound the tape and pressed the button for slow motion.

"Watch the carpeting," said Andrea, as the scene reappeared in front of everyone. "There are no footprints in it when my mom opens the door—probably because the cleaning crew had just vacuumed it." She paused. "Now comes the big gap in the tape. And after that there are two sets of prints." Andrea turned to her mother. "Mom, what shoes did you wear yesterday?" she asked.

"The same as today." Julia Meadows extended her foot. She was wearing walking shoes with a waffle print on the soles. "I wear them every day, because they're so comfortable."

Andrea turned to Lieutenant Stone. "Could we just look at the carpeting one more time?" she asked.

Stone nodded and rewound the tape.

"See how my mother's footprints go straight through the room?" Andrea asked everyone. "But notice that there's a second set of prints that lead straight to the Magritte . . . then to the painting to the right of it. Now, notice how that painting is slightly tilted." Andrea grinned proudly. "My guess is that the Magritte is behind the tilted painting, and that the thief planned to return for it later." 6 **C** **L**

4. If you speak *confidently,* you speak as though you know you are right.

Vocabulary

evidence (EV ih dens) *n.* information, facts, or objects that help prove something

Practice the Skills

6 Key Literary Element

Dialogue What do you learn about the story from Andrea's dialogue in this paragraph? What do you learn about Andrea?

Additional Support

Reading in the Real World

Citizenship Have students discuss the importance of the video surveillance equipment that's used in this story. Ask them to do Internet research to learn about the debate surrounding the widespread use of video surveillance in our society. Some students may want to learn about the growing trend toward using video surveillance in private homes, not only as a security measure but also to spy on household workers, such as babysitters. Allow these students to share their research findings as well as their opinions on the subject. **AL**

Stone hurried from the room. Several minutes later he returned with the Magritte in hand. "I'm very impressed, young lady!" he exclaimed. "It was right where you said it would be."

"But who took the painting—and hid it?" asked Nick.

This time Andrea took it upon herself to operate the VCR. She stepped forward and rewound the tape, then punched "stop-hold," followed by "zoom." Frozen, close-up, were the prints in the carpet. "See the second set of prints?" she asked. "They were made by someone wearing high heels . . . just like the ones you're wearing, Ms. Delacourte."

"This is outrageous," stammered[5] Beatrice Delacourte, as everyone looked at her feet. "Why would I steal my own painting?"

"Simple," said Andrea. "You collect the insurance money and resell the Magritte on the black market." EL

"And how about the flowers—that long box?" asked Nick. "That was just a setup, wasn't it?"

"I believe it was, Mr. Crowley," said Stone. "And I'd bet my badge that if we called the florist who delivered those flowers, we'd find that they were sent by one Beatrice Delacourte."

After Lieutenant Stone read Beatrice Delacourte her rights, he took her arm and began to lead her out of the room. "Julia, I—" she began, turning toward Andrea's mother.

But before Ms. Delacourte finished her sentence, Andrea stepped forward and glared into the woman's eyes. "You owe my mother an apology, and me twenty-five thousand dollars."

"What do you mean—twenty-five thousand dollars?!" Beatrice Delacourte blurted out, then chuckled. "But whatever for?" 7

Andrea grinned from ear to ear. "That's the reward you posted for finding your painting," she said. "A painting you stole yourself and *I* **recovered**!" 8 ○

5. When Beatrice Delacourte ***stammered,*** she did not speak smoothly or confidently.

Vocabulary

recovered (ree KUV urd) *v.* found something that was lost or stolen

Practice the Skills

7 Key Reading Skill

Responding How do you feel about Beatrice Delacourte now? Explain. Write your response in your Learner's Notebook.

8 BIG Question

BQ How do you think Julia would answer the Big Question? How do you think Andrea would answer the Big Question? Use details from the story. Put your answer on a note card in the center pocket of Foldable 3. Your response will help you complete the Unit Challenge later.

Differentiated Instruction

Character Sketch Have students work in small groups to create character sketches of Andrea. Students may present their information visually, orally, or in writing. For example, they might create a word web that lists words and phrases describing Andrea. Or they could create and perform a dialogue in which Lieutenant Stone describes Andrea to a fellow police detective. OL

Teach

EL Language Coach

Idiom Ask: Can anyone explain what the term *black market* means here? *(Possible response: It refers to the illegal sale of goods.)* Why would Beatrice Delacourte have to sell the painting illegally, on the black market? *(Possible response: Apparently, she is planning to claim that the painting was stolen so she can collect the insurance money. She wouldn't be able to sell it on a legal market since it would be considered a stolen item.)* EL OL

BQ 

After students have written their answers, invite volunteers to share what they wrote. Make sure students use details from the story in their responses. AS

Assess

CheckPoint

Use the CheckPoint questions provided on Presentation Plus! to check students' mastery of the selection. These questions can be used with interactive response keypads for immediate student feedback.

Objectives
- Identify personal responses while reading
- Express personal responses
- Notice and analyze dialogue

Assess

Resources for page 308

- Selection Quick Check
- Selection and Unit Assessment
- ExamView Assessment Suite
- Interactive Tutor: Self-Assessment

Students can respond to the *After You Read* items in their Learner's Notebook or on separate sheets of paper.

Answering the

1. Responses will vary.
2. Andrea had a part-time job at the gallery.
3. After Julia made her final rounds, Beatrice took the painting and hid it behind another painting, probably planning to come back for the Magritte later.

Critical Thinking

4. Possible response: The footprints tell you that the thief was wearing high heels. The thief walked up to the Magritte and then went to the painting to the right of it.
5. Possible response: Beatrice wanted to make money from insurance and sell the painting on the black market.
6. Possible response: A good friend is someone you can count on. In this story, Julia was able to count on Andrea.
7. Possible response: She sent the flowers so that Julia would be seen carrying a box.

After You Read

Framed

Answering the BIG Question

1. What are your thoughts about what it means to count on someone after reading "Framed"?
2. **Recall** Why is Andrea Meadows going to the museum with her mother? How do you know?
   TIP **Right There**
3. **Summarize** Explain how the Magritte was stolen. Support your answer with details from the story.
   TIP **Think and Search**

Critical Thinking

4. **Infer** What does the second set of footprints tell you about the thief?
   TIP **Author and Me**
5. **Infer** Why do you think Beatrice Delacourte chooses to frame Julia?
   TIP **Author and Me**
6. **Evaluate** What do you think it means to be a good friend to someone? How is Andrea a good friend to Julia in this story?
   TIP **Author and Me**
7. **Draw Conclusions** Why does Beatrice Delacourte send Julia flowers on the day of the robbery?
   TIP **Author and Me**

Objectives (pp. 308–309)
Reading Respond to literature • Make connections from text to self
Literature Identify literary elements: dialogue
Vocabulary Use prefixes • Use antonyms
Writing Respond to literature
Grammar Use articles

Write About Your Reading

Write a paragraph describing your responses to Beatrice Delacourte and Andrea.

- Who is more interesting to you?
- Who do you like better? (You might not answer both questions the same way.)
- Think about and write about your own experiences.
- Then think about and write why you responded to the characters the way you did.

Write About Your Reading

Possible response:
I like and admire Andrea very much. She's smart and has lots of self-confidence. She doesn't let adults intimidate her—not even Lieutenant Stone, who's treating her mother as a suspect in the theft of the Magritte. Andrea keeps her wits about her and thinks clearly. In the end, she's able to point the finger at the real criminal: Beatrice Delacourte. I don't like Beatrice at all. She "steals" her own painting so that she can collect the insurance money and then sell the painting on the black market. Even worse, she tries to frame Andrea's mother for the crime.

Skills Review

Key Reading Skill: Responding

8. You practiced responding when you read the story. Did you feel worried when Andrea's mother was accused of stealing? Did you feel good when Andrea proved her mother was innocent? Did you respond to the story more with your feelings or with your mind? Write for five minutes, explaining your answer.

Key Literary Element: Dialogue

9. Review the dialogue in "Framed." How would you describe Lieutenant Stone, based on the things he says? Does he seem fair? Support your answer with evidence from the text.

10. How would the story have been different without dialogue? Do you think you would have responded to the characters in the same way if you never heard them speak?

Reviewing Skills: Drawing Conclusions

11. What two clues lead Andrea to draw the conclusion she draws?

Vocabulary Check

Choose the best word from the list to complete each sentence below. Rewrite each sentence with the correct word in place.

stifling dominated sternly evidence recovered

12. There was no ___ to link Julia to the crime.

13. The reward for the ___ painting was $25,000.

14. The police officer ___ the interview by asking a lot of questions.

15. Andrea turned her head, ___ a laugh, when Mrs. Delacourte almost tripped in her spike heels.

16. Lieutenant Stone spoke ___ to Julia because he thought she stole the Magritte.

17. Academic Vocabulary Think about times that you've responded to someone or something.

- Discuss with a partner how responding to the reading is the same as responding to other people or things in your life.
- How is it also different?

18. English Language Coach *Willing* and *like* can be made into antonyms by adding prefixes. Choose a prefix that will make each word into its antonym. Write down each word pair.

Grammar Link: Articles

Use the articles *a* and *an* to modify general nouns. Use the article *the* to modify specific nouns.

- **General:** I wish I had a dog. (*Any dog will do.*)
- **Specific:** The dog I want is at the shelter. (*The speaker wants a particular dog.*)

Do not confuse *a* and *an.* Follow this rule:
an + noun beginning with a vowel sound
a + noun beginning with a consonant sound

- an apple
- a banana
- an hour (silent *h*)
- a day

Grammar Practice

Copy the following words on a separate piece of paper:

tree, honor, elephant, university, school.

Add the correct article–*a* or *an*–in front of each.

Writing Application Circle all the articles you used in your Write About Your Reading assignment. Fix any mistakes in the articles.

Web Activities For eFlashcards, Selection Quick Checks, and other Web activities, go to www.glencoe.com.

Skills Review

Key Reading Skill: Responding

8. Responses will vary.

Key Literary Element: Dialogue

9. Possible response: Lieutenant Stone is tough but fair. He's direct and professional as he questions Julia. He doesn't make accusations but just presents the evidence.

10. Possible response: The story would have been much less interesting, and I wouldn't have responded to the characters in the same way.

Reviewing Skills: Drawing Conclusions

11. Possible response: Beatrice left a lot of evidence behind, such as her footprints on the carpeting and the tilted picture.

Vocabulary Check

12. evidence
13. recovered
14. dominated
15. stifling
16. sternly
17. Responses will vary.
18. willing, unwilling; like, unlike *or* like, dislike

Grammar Link: Articles

Grammar Practice

a tree
an honor
an elephant
a university
a school

Close

Ask students to discuss what they have learned while reading this story to help them answer the Big Question. Ask them if a family member could count on them in a situation like the one Julia faces.

Before You Read After Twenty Years

More About the Author

O. Henry named his 1906 book of stories about New York City *The Four Million.* A society leader said that there were only 400 people worth knowing in New York—the wealthiest citizens. O. Henry's title declared that all four million New Yorkers had stories worth telling. In "After Twenty Years," O. Henry tells a story about two characters who grow up as best friends in New York City. They part ways as young men but promise to meet again in exactly twenty years.

V Vocabulary

Using Vocabulary Words in Context Challenge students to use two or more of the vocabulary words in sentences of their own. For example: *The two* habitual *liars* corresponded *with each other because no one else would answer their letters.* **AL**

Meet the Author

William Sydney Porter, who used the pen name O. Henry, led a varied but difficult life. He has written that "life is made up of sobs, sniffles, and smiles." He first worked in his uncle's drugstore and then as a sheepherder. He was also a bank teller, a prisoner, a magazine editor, and a newspaper writer before he began writing the stories that made him famous. See page R4 of the Author Files for more on O. Henry.

Literature Online

Author Search For more about O. Henry, go to www.glencoe.com.

Objectives (pp. 310–317)
Reading Respond to literature • Make connections from text to self
Literature Identify literary elements: dialogue, character
Vocabulary Use prefixes • Use antonyms

Vocabulary Preview

habitual (huh BICH oo ul) *adj.* regular; usual; done out of habit **(p. 312)** *It was habitual for the policeman to check the locks on each storefront door.*

vicinity (vuh SIN ih tee) *n.* the area around a certain place **(p. 312)** *The store was empty, and there were no other shoppers in the vicinity.*

destiny (DES tuh nee) *n.* what the future holds for a person **(p. 313)** *It was destiny that the two friends would choose different paths in life.*

V

corresponded (kor uh SPAWN did) *v.* wrote letters to each other; form of the verb *correspond* **(p. 314)** *Though the two friends did not see each other often, they corresponded regularly.*

dismally (DIZ mul ee) *adv.* in a sad or gloomy way **(p. 315)** *He dismally took the letter and read it.*

Write to Learn In your Learner's Notebook, write a sentence for each vocabulary word. Then rewrite the sentence using a synonym in place of the word. For example: The officer took his habitual route. The officer took his regular route.

English Language Coach

Antonyms Using antonyms can be a good way to get your point across. You can use pairs of antonyms effectively

- to contrast two items:
  The plate was *huge*, but the cake was *tiny*.
- to show disagreement or a negative response:
  "No, I don't *love* peach ice cream. I *hate* it."

Individual Activity Copy this chart into your Learner's Notebook. Write at least three synonyms and three antonyms for *wonderful*. Two are done for you.

Synonyms	Antonyms
1. terrific	1. horrible
2.	2.
3.	3.

Additional Support

Author Search To expand students' appreciation of O. Henry, have them access the Web site for additional information and resources.

English Language Coach

Antonyms Make sure students understand how antonyms can be used to contrast two items, or to show disagreement or a negative response. Write these sentences on the board, omitting the underlining:

The book was very <u>exciting</u>, but the movie version of it was quite <u>dull</u>.

My friends <u>spend</u> all of their allowance, but I <u>save</u> some of mine.

Have students identify the antonym pairs in each sentence. Then have students write similar sentences of their own on the board. **BL** **EL**

Skills Preview

Key Reading Skill: Responding

Responses to reading are personal. Different readers have different responses. That's fine. Your response is not wrong as long as facts from the reading support the response.

- Would you want a job as a policeman? Why?
- Do you think money and clothes show that a person is successful? Why?
- Do you think "honesty is the best policy"? Why or why not?

R

Key Literary Element: Dialogue

One of the best ways to learn about a character is through dialogue–what he or she says in a story. Dialogue can help you hear what characters sound like. This can tell you things like where they live, how old they are, and how they relate to other characters.

As you read, use these tips to help you understand why dialogue is important in a story.

- Dialogue can show the differences between characters.

  What do you learn about a character's personality from the way he or she speaks?

- Words like *said, yelled, whispered, agreed,* and *asked* help describe what's going on in a story.

  How do the words around the dialogue add to your understanding of the story?

- Dialogue can help you understand how a character thinks and feels.

  How does reading dialogue help you connect to a character?

Interactive Literary Elements Handbook
To review or learn more about the literary elements, go to www.glencoe.com.

Get Ready to Read

Connect to the Reading

Loyalty means being faithful. If you are loyal to a friend, you stick by him or her through thick and thin.

- How important do you think loyalty is in friendship?
- Can you think of a situation where it would be okay not to be loyal to a friend?
- In this story, a friend's loyalty will be tested.

Write to Learn In your Learner's Notebook, write about a time you were loyal to someone. Write about what you did to be loyal. Then tell your story to a small group of classmates. Discuss your stories among one another.

Build Background

This story takes place in New York City in 1890. One of the main characters left New York around 1870 to go West and get rich. Here's what was going on in the United States at that time.

- The first discovery of gold caused a gold rush in California in 1848.
- In 1869, the railroad that joined the East and the West was completed.
- Many people in the United States moved from the East to the West to find new jobs.

Set Purposes for Reading

BIG Question Read "After Twenty Years" to find out if a man can count on an old friend to keep his promise.

Set Your Own Purpose What would you like to learn from the selection to help you answer the Big Question? Write your own purpose on a note card and put the card in the left pocket of Foldable 3.

Keep Moving

Use these skills as you read the following selection.

Teach

R Reading Skill

Responding Have students discuss why individual responses to a reading selection may vary widely. Then invite volunteers to respond to the questions shown here. Tell students to keep these questions in mind as they read "After Twenty Years." **OL**

Literature Online

Interactive Literary Elements Handbook Have students access the Web site to improve their understanding of dialogue.

CheckPoint

Use the CheckPoint questions provided on Presentation Plus! to check for prior knowledge and to build background. These questions can be used with interactive response keypads for immediate student feedback.

Literature Focus Lesson

Short Story Tell students that a short story is a brief work of fiction that usually can be read in one sitting. They've already learned about the basic elements of a short story: characters, setting, conflict, plot, and dialogue. Emphasize that the combination of these elements determines the story's overall impact on the reader. Ask students to think about how O. Henry uses the elements to craft "After Twenty Years" as they read the story. When they finish reading, ask them to write a paragraph describing the overall impact the story had on them. **OL**

Objectives

- Respond to literature
- Make connections from text to self
- Identify literary elements: dialogue, character
- Use prefixes
- Use antonyms

Teach

Viewing the Illustration

Have students look at this work by the American artist Edward Hopper. **Ask:** What does the scene in this etching have in common with the setting that the author describes in the first paragraph? *(Possible response: The etching shows a lonely scene, in which a man walks down a shadowy, deserted street at night. In the story, a policeman walks down a nearly deserted street on a windy, chilly night.)* **AS**

C Critical Thinking

Comprehension Ask: What do you learn about the policeman in the first two paragraphs? *(Possible response: The policeman patrols his beat with skill and confidence. He's alert and observant, and he looks like he's up to the job of keeping the peace.)* **OL**

Readability Scores
Dale-Chall: 5.9
DRP: 51
Lexile: 850

READING WORKSHOP 2

AFTER Twenty YEARS

by O. Henry

Night Shadows, 1921, Edward Hopper. Etching. Unknown location.

The policeman on the beat moved up the avenue impressively. The impressiveness was **habitual** and not for show, for spectators were few. The time was barely 10 o'clock at night, but chilly gusts of wind with a taste of rain in them had well nigh **depeopled** the streets. **1**

Trying doors as he went, twirling his club with many intricate and artful movements, turning now and then to cast his watchful eye down the pacific thoroughfare, the officer, with his stalwart[1] form and slight swagger, made a fine picture of a guardian of the peace. The **vicinity** **C**

1. ***Intricate*** means "complicated," and ***artful*** means "skillful." The ***pacific thoroughfare*** is the peaceful street, and ***stalwart*** is another word for "strong."

Vocabulary

habitual (huh BICH oo ul) *adj.* regular; usual; done out of habit

vicinity (vuh SIN ih tee) *n.* the area around a certain place

Practice the Skills

1 English Language Coach

Antonyms Here, the prefix *de-* means "removed." The chilly winds make people stay indoors, leaving the streets **depeopled**. This unusual word may not appear in your dictionary or thesaurus, but it's an antonym for *populated* or *crowded.*

Additional Support

Literature Focus Lesson

Sensory Details Remind students that sensory details appeal to one or more of the five senses: *sight, hearing, touch, taste,* and *smell.* Have students find examples of sensory details on this page. Ask them to identify the sense or senses that each image appeals to, as in these examples:

- "moved up the avenue impressively" (sight)
- "chilly gusts of wind with a taste of rain in them" (touch, hearing, taste)
- "twirling his club" (sight, touch) **AS**

was one that kept **early** hours. Now and then you might see the lights of a cigar store or of an all-night lunch counter; but the majority of the doors belonged to business places that had long since been **closed**. 2

When about midway of a certain block the policeman suddenly slowed his walk. In the doorway of a darkened hardware store a man leaned, with an unlighted cigar in his mouth. As the policeman walked up to him the man spoke up quickly.

"It's all right, officer," he said, reassuringly. "I'm just waiting for a friend. It's an appointment made twenty years ago. Sounds a little funny to you, doesn't it? Well, I'll explain if you'd like to make certain it's all straight. About that long ago there used to be a restaurant where this store stands—'Big Joe' Brady's restaurant."

"Until five years ago," said the policeman. "It was torn down then." 3

The man in the doorway struck a match and lit his cigar. The light showed a pale, square-jawed face with keen eyes, and a little white scar near his right eyebrow. His scarfpin was a large diamond, oddly set.

"Twenty years ago tonight," said the man, "I dined here at 'Big Joe' Brady's with Jimmy Wells, my best chum, and the finest chap[2] in the world. He and I were raised here in New York, just like two brothers, together. I was eighteen and Jimmy was twenty. The next morning I was to start for the West to make my fortune. You couldn't have dragged Jimmy out of New York; he thought it was the only place on earth. Well, we agreed that night that we would meet here again exactly twenty years from that date and time, no matter what our conditions might be or from what distance we might have to come. We figured that in twenty years each of us ought to have our **destiny** worked out and our fortunes made, whatever they were going to be." 4

2. A ***chum*** is a friend, and a ***chap*** is a man or boy.

Vocabulary

destiny (DES tuh nee) *n.* what the future holds for a person

Practice the Skills

2 English Language Coach

Antonyms Think of an antonym for both of these words: **early**, **closed**.

3 Key Literary Element

L **Dialogue** What facts do you learn from reading this dialogue? In your Learner's Notebook, write down four facts you learned that are taken from the dialogue.

4 BIG Question

BQ Does it seem realistic that two men can count on each other to show up after 20 years? Put your answer, in the form of a sentence, on a note card in the center pocket of Foldable 3.

READING WORKSHOP 2

Teach

L Literary Element

Dialogue Remind students that dialogue is an important method of character development in fiction. It's a way that writers can show, rather than tell, the reader what characters are like. **BL**

BQ 

Ask: Do you think it's likely that Jimmy Wells will keep the promise he made twenty years ago? In a situation like this, would most people even remember such a promise? Explain your answer. *(Responses will vary.)* **AS**

English Language Coach

Language from Another Era Explain that some of the expressions in this story are not commonly used today. Ask students to make a two-column chart with these expressions in the left column: *it's all straight; my best chum; the finest chap; long time between meets; pretty big proposition; get my pile; gets in a groove; call time on him sharp; foot passengers.* As students encounter these expressions in the story, they should use context clues to define or paraphrase them in the right column of their charts. **EL** **OL**

Objectives

- Explore how dialogue reveals character
- Respond to art

Teach

Viewing the Painting

Say: Why do you think the editors of this book selected this image to illustrate the story? *(Possible response: This image shows a dark street like the one described in this story.)* **BL**

R Reading Skill

Review Connecting Ask: Have you ever lost track of a friend for a long time and then reconnected with the person? Or have you read a story about friends reconnecting? Describe the experience. *(Responses will vary.)* **OL**

READING WORKSHOP 2

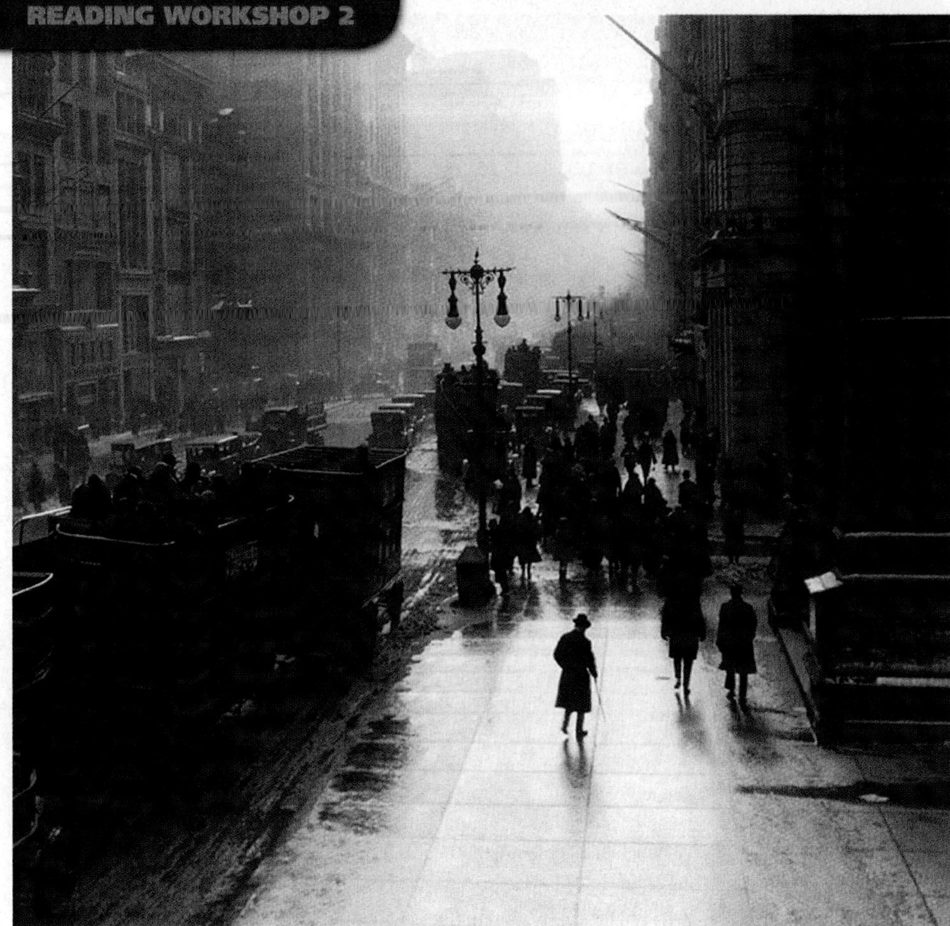

"It sounds pretty interesting," said the policeman. "Rather a long time between meets, though, it seems to me. Haven't you heard from your friend since you left?"

"Well, yes, for a time we **corresponded**," said the other. "But after a year or two we lost track of each other. You see, the West is a pretty big proposition,[3] and I kept hustling around over it pretty lively. But I know Jimmy will meet me here if he's alive, for he always was the truest, staunchest[4] old chap in the world. He'll never forget. I came a thousand miles **R**

3. In this sentence, ***proposition*** means "a challenging opportunity."

4. ***Staunchest*** means "most loyal and dependable."

Vocabulary

corresponded (kor uh SPAWN did) *v.* wrote letters to each other

Additional Support

Differentiated Instruction

Researching Communication Tools

Tell students to do research to learn about the status of communications technology during the time this story takes place. Have them share their findings with the class. Then ask students to share how the research helps them better understand why the two friends in this story have been out of touch for so many years. **AL** to stand in this door tonight, and it's worth it if my old partner turns up."

The waiting man pulled out a handsome watch, the lids of it set with small diamonds.

"Three minutes to ten," he announced. "It was exactly ten o'clock when we parted here at the restaurant door."

"Did pretty well out West, didn't you?" asked the policeman.

"You bet! I hope Jimmy has done half as well. He was a kind of plodder,[5] though, good fellow as he was. I've had to compete with some of the sharpest wits going to get my pile. A man gets in a groove in New York. It takes the West to put a razor-edge on him." **5**

The policeman twirled his club and took a step or two.

"I'll be on my way. Hope your friend comes around all right. Going to call time on him sharp?" **C**

"I should say not!" said the other. "I'll give him half an hour at least. If Jimmy is alive on earth he'll be here by that time. So long, officer."

"Good-night, sir," said the policeman, passing on along his beat, trying doors as he went.

There was now a fine, cold drizzle falling, and the wind had risen from its uncertain puffs into a steady blow. The few foot passengers astir in that quarter hurried **dismally** and silently along with coat collars turned high and pocketed hands. And in the door of the hardware store the man who had come a thousand miles to fill an appointment, uncertain almost to absurdity,[6] with the friend of his youth, smoked his cigar and waited. **V**

About twenty minutes he waited, and then a tall man in a long overcoat, with collar turned up to his ears, hurried across from the opposite side of the street. He went directly to the waiting man.

"Is that you, Bob?" he asked, doubtfully.

"Is that you, Jimmy Wells?" cried the man in the door.

---

5. A ***plodder*** is someone who moves slowly, but the meaning here is that Jimmy is not a quick thinker.

6. ***Absurdity*** is the state of being ridiculous.

Vocabulary

dismally (DIZ mul ee) *adv.* in a sad or gloomy way

Practice the Skills

5 Key Reading Skill

Responding Jimmy says that the West makes a man sharper than New York does. What is your response to his attitude?

READING WORKSHOP 2

Teach

C Critical Thinking

Comprehension Ask: Why do you think the policeman asks this question: "Going to call time on him sharp?" Why might he want to know if the man plans to wait a while if Jimmy Wells doesn't show up on time? *(Possible response: The policeman has some interest in this man. He wants to know if the man will stick around even if Jimmy Wells doesn't show up promptly.)* **OL**

V Vocabulary

Vocabulary File Tell students to continue adding vocabulary words to the file they started earlier in this workshop. Remind them to write each new vocabulary word from the story on an index card. They should include the pronunciation (if they need it), the meaning, and a sentence that uses the word in clear context. Encourage students to refer to their cards from time to time and to make an effort to use new vocabulary in their writing and speaking. **BL** **EL**

Differentiated Instruction

Understanding Sensory Details

Read aloud the last four paragraphs on this page. Tell students to close their eyes and imagine that they are standing on the street where this scene takes place. They should pay attention to all of the sensory details—not just the visual ones—to help them imagine what it would be like to actually be at the scene in the story.

Invite volunteers to share the thoughts and feelings they had as they mentally placed themselves inside the scene. **AS** Students who enjoy drawing may want to sketch their mental images of the scene O. Henry describes. **OL**

Objectives

- Respond to text
- Make connections from text to self

READING WORKSHOP 2

Teach

R Reading Skill

Responding **Ask:** How do the events on this page increase your interest in the story? *(Possible response: The two old friends are finally reunited. But something isn't right–Bob says that Jimmy has changed a lot, that he's taller than he was when Bob last saw him, twenty years ago.)* **OL**

Viewing the Painting

Have students look at the painting and read the credit line. Tell them that Charles Burchfield (1893–1967) was an artist who focused on urban scenes, such as docks, bridges, and industrial areas in the poorer parts of small cities. **Ask:** What does the scene pictured here have in common with the one O. Henry describes in this story? *(Possible response: In both the story and the painting, the streets are nearly deserted on a dark, rainy night. Both scenes suggest a sense of isolation.)* **AS**

"Bless my heart!" exclaimed the new arrival, grasping both the other's hands with his own. "It's Bob, sure as fate.[7] I was certain I'd find you here if you were still in existence. Well, well, well!—twenty years is a long time. The old restaurant's gone, Bob; I wish it had lasted, so we could have had another dinner there. How has the West treated you, old man?"

R "Bully;[8] it has given me everything I asked it for. You've changed lots, Jimmy. I never thought you were so tall by two or three inches."

"Oh, I grew a bit after I was twenty."

"Doing well in New York, Jimmy?"

"Moderately. I have a position in one of the city departments. Come on, Bob; we'll go around to a place I know of, and have a good long talk about old times." **6**

7. ***Fate*** is your fortune, or what the future holds for you.
8. Here, ***bully*** is slang for "excellent" or in "in the best way."

Practice the Skills

6 **Reviewing Skills**

Drawing Conclusions You've gotten a few clues about Jimmy. Can you draw any conclusions about the two men? How are they alike or different? Check your answer by reading the next paragraph.

Rainy Night, 1939. Charles Burchfield. Watercolor over pencil, 30 x 42 in. San Diego Museum of Art.

Additional Support

Differentiated Instruction

Compare Characters Point out that this story focuses on two very different characters. Though they are old friends, their personalities are not similar, and their lives have gone in very different directions. After students finish the story, have them create a Venn diagram showing how Bob and Jimmy are similar and how they are different. **BL** **EL**

Bob	Both	Jimmy
quick; ambitious; dishonest; boastful	grew up together; loyal; affectionate	competent; modest; honest; dutiful

The two men started up the street, arm in arm. The man from the West, his egotism[9] enlarged by success, was beginning to outline the history of his career. The other, submerged in his overcoat, listened with interest.

At the corner stood a drug store, brilliant with electric lights. When they came into this glare each of them turned simultaneously to gaze upon the other's face.

The man from the West stopped suddenly and released his arm.

"You're not Jimmy Wells," he snapped. "Twenty years is a long time, but not long enough to change a man's nose from a Roman to a pug."[10]

"It sometimes changes a good man into a bad one," said the tall man. "You've been under arrest for ten minutes, 'Silky' Bob. Chicago thinks you may have dropped over our way and wires us she wants to have a chat with you. Going quietly, are you? That's sensible. Now, before we go on to the station here's a note I was asked to hand you. You may read it here at the window. It's from Patrolman Wells." 7

The man from the West unfolded the little piece of paper handed him. His hand was steady when he began to read, but it trembled a little by the time he had finished. The note was rather short.

> BOB: I was at the appointed place on time. When you struck the match to light your cigar I saw it was the face of the man wanted in Chicago. Somehow I couldn't do it myself, so I went around and got a plain clothes man[11] to do the job.
>
> Jimmy 8 ❍

9. A person's ***egotism*** is a great sense of self-importance.

10. A ***Roman*** nose is long and bold. A ***pug*** nose is short and thick.

11. Jimmy met Bob in his police uniform. A ***plain clothes man*** is a police officer who is working but not wearing his uniform.

Practice the Skills

7 English Language Coach

Antonyms What pair of antonyms has the author used at the beginning of this paragraph?

8 BIG Question

BQ Did Jimmy let his old friend down? What was his original promise? Was he someone "Silky" Bob could count on? Why or why not? Was Jimmy someone other people could count on? In what ways? Write your answers on a note card and put it in the center pocket of Foldable 3.

Reading in the Real World

Career Explain that people who work in both the public and the private sectors sometimes witness unethical behavior on the job. Some have the courage to report such behavior to the proper authorities, often at great risk to their careers. Have students do research to learn about people who "blew the whistle" on others within their organizations. Have them share their findings with the class. AL

Teach

C Critical Thinking

Comprehension Ask: What is the point of greatest suspense in this story? *(Possible response: The point of greatest suspense is when Silky Bob realizes that the man is not Jimmy Wells.)* OL

BQ 

Call on students to respond to the questions in the second side note. Then **ask:** Do you think Jimmy makes the right choice in this story? Why or why not? *(Possible response: Jimmy makes the right choice. The public counts on a police officer to do the right thing, even when it means being disloyal to a friend.)* OL

Assess

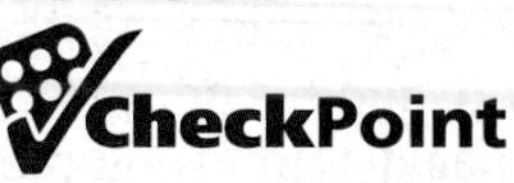

Use the CheckPoint questions provided on Presentation Plus! to check students' mastery of the selection. These questions can be used with interactive response keypads for immediate student feedback.

Objectives
- Make connections from text to self
- Ask self questions to understand text
- Identify personal responses while reading
- Express personal responses

Assess

Resources for page 318

- Selection Quick Check
- Selection and Unit Assessment
- ExamView Assessment Suite
- Interactive Tutor: Self-Assessment

Students can respond to the *After You Read* items in their Learner's Notebook or on separate sheets of paper.

Answering the BIG Question

1. Responses will vary.
2. Bob left New York and went west to seek his fortune.
3. The man's scarfpin is a large diamond, and his pocket watch has diamonds on the lids.
4. Bob realized that his old friend turned him in to the cops. Bob was shaken by this news, as shown by the fact that his hand began to tremble.

Critical Thinking

5. Responses will vary but should be supported by valid reasons.
6. Possible response: Jimmy realizes this when he sees Bob's face in the match light. He recognizes him as a man who's wanted by the Chicago police. Right away, Jimmy knows he must turn in his old friend.
7. Answers will vary.

After You Read

After Twenty Years

Answering the BIG Question

1. Do you think Bob should have counted on Jimmy to meet him after 20 years? Think about a friend you haven't seen in a while. Would you count on him or her to keep a promise from a long time ago? Why or why not?
2. **Recall** Why did the two "best chums" part?
   Tip Right There
3. **Recall** How does the police officer know that the man on the street has made a lot of money?
   Tip Think and Search
4. **Summarize** What happens the night of the meeting?
   Tip Think and Search

Critical Thinking

5. **Evaluate** In your opinion, is the policeman a realistic and believable character? Why or why not?
   Tip Author and Me
6. **Infer** When do you think Jimmy realizes that he has to make a difficult choice and turn in Bob?
   Tip Author and Me
7. **Connect** If you were Jimmy Wells, what would you have done?
   Tip Author and Me

Objectives (pp. 318–319)
Reading Respond to literature • Make connections from text to self
Literature Identify literary elements: dialogue, character
Vocabulary Use antonyms
Writing Respond to literature: personal letter
Grammar Use modifiers: demonstrative adjectives

Talk About Your Reading

Literature Groups With your group, discuss how Bob, the man from the West, might have felt about what Jimmy did to him. Do you think he felt tricked, angry, betrayed? Explain why.

Write to Learn As a group, write a letter that Bob might have written to Jimmy telling him about the arrest and how he feels about what Jimmy did.

Talk About Your Reading

Write to Learn

Possible response:
Dear Jimmy,
I always knew you were a plodder, but I never reckoned that you'd turn out to be a snitch. Oh sure, you've got to do your duty and all. But what about your duty to an old chum? In my world, loyalty is everything. I guess you live in a different world now. And here I thought you were one of the best chaps on the face of the earth.
I think you ratted me out because you're jealous. Thanks a bunch, old pal.
—Bob

Skills Review

Key Reading Skill: Responding

8. Did you enjoy the surprise ending? Why or why not? How would you have ended the story?

Key Literary Element: Dialogue

9. O. Henry tells most of the story through dialogue. As you read, how did the dialogue help you learn about the characters? Give some examples.

10. Reread the dialogue from the time the plain-clothes officer meets Bob. Does he lie to Bob? What feeling does that give you about the officer? Could the author have done the same thing without dialogue?

Reviewing Skills: Drawing Conclusions

11. After reading this story, what general statement can you make about loyalty and friendship?

Vocabulary Check

12. Rewrite this list of words and definitions. Draw a line from each word to its definition and write a sentence that uses the word.

habitual	regular, usual
vicinity	write letters back and forth
destiny	sadly, gloomily
corresponded	what is going to happen to a person
dismally	the area around a particular place

13. **English Language Coach** The following sentence occurs late in the story:

> The man from the West, his egotism enlarged by success, was beginning to outline the history of his career.

Substitute antonyms for the words *enlarged* and *success*, and write down the new sentence. How has the meaning of the sentence changed?

Grammar Link: Demonstrative Adjectives

The words *this, that, these,* and *those* are demonstrative adjectives.

this, these	Use to refer to **nearby** people, places, and things. *This* is singular. *These* is plural. • Fix this sentence. • These sentences are correct.
that, those	Use to refer to people, places, and things that are **farther away.** *That* is singular. *Those* is plural. • I flew to that city on vacation. • I picked those flowers last week.

Look out! *Them* is not a demonstrative adjective.

- **Wrong:** I like them cars.
- **Right:** I like those cars.

Grammar Practice

For each demonstrative adjective above, write two sentences. Write your sentences on a separate piece of paper. When you have finished, exchange papers with a partner to check whether all of your demonstrative adjectives are used correctly.

Writing Application Circle all the demonstrative adjectives you wrote in the letter for your Talk About Your Reading assignment. Fix any mistakes.

Web Activities For eFlashcards, Selection Quick Checks, and other Web activities, go to www.glencoe.com.

Skills Review

Key Reading Skill: Responding

8. Responses will vary.

Key Literary Element: Dialogue

9. Responses will vary but should include examples like this: Through the dialogue, I learned that Bob and Jimmy corresponded for a while but then lost track of each other for almost twenty years.

10. Responses will vary, but may note that, while Bob does not tell an outright lie, he does deceive Jimmy. It would have been difficult to portray this scene without dialogue.

Reviewing Skills: Drawing Conclusions

11. Possible response: Sometimes doing the right thing is more important than being loyal to a friend.

Vocabulary Check

12. Students' sentences will vary. They should match the words and definitions as shown below.

habitual: regular; usual

vicinity: the area around a particular place

destiny: what is going to happen to a person

corresponded: wrote letters back and forth

dismally: sadly; gloomily

13. Responses will vary.

Grammar Link: Demonstrative Adjectives

Grammar Practice

Possible responses:
I really like this movie.
These oranges are juicy.
Why won't that dog stop barking?
Those men are repairing the roof.

Close

Ask students what they learned from this story about an encounter between two old friends to answer the Big Question.

Synethesizing

Objectives covered in this workshop:
- Understand text through synthesis

Synthesizing

Why Is It Important?

- Synthesizing helps readers move to a higher level of thinking.
- Synthesizing extends the literal meaning of a text to an inferential level.
- Because readers cannot possibly store all of the information they read in their mind, readers have to identify key ideas and compare those with their purpose for reading to synthesize.

How to Help Students Get It

- Tell students that synthesizing helps them think of new ideas. They use what they have read and what they already know to come up with a new idea or a new understanding.
- Focus on the fact that readers who synthesize remember more and tend to perform better on assessments, tests, and in life.
- Tell students that they have probably been synthesizing when answering the Big Questions. Each time they use a theme, character, or idea from a selection they have read to help them think of a new idea, or a new way of answering the Big Question, they are synthesizing.
- Model synthesizing for students by reading aloud a newspaper or other article. Identify the key points and focus on the ideas you come up with as a result of your reading. Remember that synthesizing is not simply summarizing, it extends into an understanding of the implications from the text and helps you to apply them to form a new idea.

Reading to Answer the Big Question

Loser

In "Loser," a young man has extraordinary abilities to find lost items. His neighbors count on him to find missing things, but one day, he is asked to find a missing child and the young man is not sure of his abilities.

Friends Forever

In this Time story, three sets of friends talk about the challenges of being true friends and keeping friendships in tact when problems arise. They demonstrate how and why friends can count on each other.

Workshop Resources

Pacing (Days) Standard	Block	Lesson	Student Materials	Teacher Resources
1		Key Skill Lesson: Synthesizing	Key Reading Skills Practice English Language Coach	Bellringer Options Transparencies Read Aloud, Think Aloud Transparencies Presentation Plus!
2		"Loser"	Literary Analysis Transparencies Glencoe Online Selection Vocabulary Development Academic Vocabulary Development English Language Coach Active Reading Graphic Organizer Literary Analysis StudentWorks Plus Online Student Edition Literature Classics Selection and Unit Assessments	Literary and Text Analysis Transparencies Puzzlemaker Skill Level Up! BookLink 3 Assessment by Learning Objective (Diagnostic and Formative) Interactive Tutor Self-Assessment TeacherWorks Plus
2		"Friends Forever"	Glencoe Online Selection Vocabulary Development Academic Vocabulary Development English Language Coach Active Reading Graphic Organizer Literary Analysis StudentWorks Plus Online Student Edition Literature Classics Selection and Unit Assessments	Literary and Text Analysis Transparencies Puzzlemaker Skill Level Up! BookLink 3 Assessment by Learning Objective (Diagnostic and Formative) Interactive Tutor Self-Assessment TeacherWorks Plus

Keys for Unit Resource

- Blackline Master
- Workbook
- Supplemental Text
- CD-ROM
- DVD
- Transparency
- Web-based
- Fast Files

Level Appropriate Code

AS = Activities for all students
AL = Activities for students working above grade level
OL = Activities for students working at grade level
BL = Activities for students working below grade level
EL = Activities for English language learners

Focus

BELLRINGER Options

Daily Language Practice Transparency

Focus Activity Ask: What would it be like to have a special power that allowed you to sense the location of lost objects? How do you think such a power might actually work? *(Responses will vary.)* OL

Teach

R Reading Skill

Synthesizing Say: You often synthesize information in your everyday life. For example, you see a news report about senior citizens learning to use the Internet at the library. You remember that an older neighbor said that she'd like to use the Internet, so you offer to meet her at the public library to show her how to navigate the Internet.

- Ask students to explain how this is an example of synthesizing. *(Possible response: You're combining ideas.)* OL
- Ask students to give an example of how they have synthesized information in their daily lives. *(Responses will vary.)* AL

READING WORKSHOP 3

Skills Focus

You will practice using these skills when you read the following selections:

- "Loser," p. 324
- "Friends Forever," p. 334

Reading

- Synthesizing

Literature

- Analyzing a character
- Understanding nonfiction

Vocabulary

- Using a thesaurus
- Academic Vocabulary: *synthesizing*

Writing/Grammar

- Using comparative and superlative adjectives and adverbs

Skill Lesson

Synthesizing

Learn It!

What Is It? **Synthesizing** means combining parts to form a whole. When you read, you are combining many different parts to get a whole new idea. With each page you read,

- you learn new things about the characters and the plot.
- R you add your prior knowledge.
- you add your personal experience.
- you combine all these things to get a new idea about what the story means. And you might have a new idea about life, too.

Congratulations! You've been *synthesizing*!

Analyzing Cartoons
Calvin synthesizes fairy tales with his own knowledge of what's exciting to come up with new story ideas.

Objectives (pp. 320–321)
Reading Synthesize information

Academic Vocabulary

synthesizing (SIN thuh sy zing) *n.* combining ideas in order to form a new idea

Additional Support

Differentiated Instruction

Synthesizing Have students practice their synthesizing skills with partners. They should choose a brief passage from one of the selections in this unit. With their partners, they should talk about what they have learned. Then, they should combine that information with something they already know in order to create a new idea. Their new ideas should pull together what they have learned with their own prior knowledge, ideas, and experience.

Have students share their new ideas with the entire class. Ask them to describe the process of synthesizing these new ideas. AS

Why Is It Important? Creating new ideas is a higher kind of thinking. It is more than remembering someone else's ideas. Just like the muscles in your body, when you push your mind to do more, your mind gets stronger.

Study Central Visit www.glencoe.com and click on Study Central to review synthesizing.

How Do I Do It? Stop while you read and ask yourself questions such as, "What do I understand that isn't written here?" Or once you get the basic idea of a text, go back and review. Ask yourself "Can I think of something new from what I have read?" Here's how one student synthesized ideas when she was preparing to teach her younger sister how to play softball.

When I was in Little League, my dad and I used to practice throwing, catching, and running the bases. He always told me that "practice makes perfect." By the end of the season, I could throw farther and run faster than my teammates.

Last week, I read an article about a high school softball coach. She said it's very important to teach players how to play as a team. She talks to her team every day about how they can all help win the game.

R

When I teach my sister to play, I am going to take her to some games. I will show her how the team works together. I am also going to explain how different players can help each other on the field. Then, I'm going to have her practice throwing and catching, so she can get stronger. I think my sister should learn that a good player has good thinking skills and physical skills.

Practice It!

As you read "Loser," ask yourself the questions below and make notes in your Learner's Notebook.

- What are important details in this story?
- Am I connecting to this story?
- What do I know about fairy tales and fables?
- Did this story give me a new idea or understanding?

Use It!

As you read "Loser," stop and think about the new ideas that come to your mind. What new ideas do you have about the characters and events? What new ideas do you have about yourself and about life?

Reading in the Real World

Citizenship Reading biographies and studying history is one way that students can learn about people who dared to challenge injustice. The actions and ideas of these courageous people can inspire readers to create new ideas of their own. Have students form small groups. Instruct each group to choose a passage from the Rosa Parks selection on pages 140–143, read the passage aloud, and discuss what they learn from it. Have them combine those ideas with their own experience, ideas, and knowledge to synthesize something new. As a class, discuss the ideas each group has synthesized. **AL**

Teach

Literature Online

Study Central Have students access the Web site to review synthesizing and to complete a related activity.

R Reading Skill

Synthesizing Have students read the example of how one student synthesized ideas.
Ask:

- What prior experience does the student draw on as she synthesizes new ideas? *(She thinks back to her Little League experience.)*
- What new information has she recently learned? What is the source of this information? *(She read an article in which a high school softball coach talks about the importance of teamwork.)*
- What new ideas does the student come up with? *(She creates a detailed plan for teaching her sister how to play softball, based on her own experience and on information she has recently learned.)* **AS**

Resources for page 321

- Use Reading Skills Transparency in *Read Aloud, Think Aloud,* Unit 3, to help students practice synthesizing.

Objectives
- Synthesize information

Before You Read Loser

More About the Author

Aimee Bender writes stories that are anything but ordinary. When an interviewer asked Bender about her writing habits, she said that she writes first thing in the morning: "Right when I wake up. Closest to dreams I can get." When Bender isn't writing fiction, she shares her creative gifts by teaching writing at the University of Southern California.

V Vocabulary

Synonyms and Antonyms Have each student write a synonym or an antonym for one of the vocabulary words. Then ask the students to read their vocabulary words and new words to the class. Invite volunteers to say whether the new words are antonyms or synonyms for the vocabulary words. **AS**

Author Search To expand students' appreciation of Aimee Bender, have them access the Web site for additional information and resources.

Meet the Author

The story "Loser" was written by Aimee Bender, who lives in Los Angeles, California. Some people call her stories modern fairy tales and fables. The *Boston Globe* writes, "Bender's...characters surprise and delight. Sometimes, they even make you weep."

Author Search For more about Aimee Bender, go to www.glencoe.com.

Objectives (pp. 322–329)
Reading Synthesize information
Literature Identify literary elements: character
Vocabulary Use word references: thesaurus

Vocabulary Preview

visible (VIZ uh bul) *adj.* able to be seen **(p. 324)** *Mrs. Allen's special jewel was visible to all her neighbors.*

skeptics (SKEP tiks) *n.* people who doubt or don't believe something **(p. 325)** *The neighbors who didn't trust the young man were skeptics.*

elaborate (ih LAB ur ut) *adj.* planned or carried out carefully **(p. 325)** *Jenny thought the young man had an elaborate plan to impress her mother.*

insistent (in SIS tunt) *adj.* not giving up; demanding attention **(p. 325)** *The insistent child tugged at his father's sleeve many times.*

modestly (MAW dist lee) *adv.* in a shy way; not confidently **(p. 327)** *The young man looked down modestly when Jenny smiled at him.*

Write to Learn Write sentences in your Learner's Notebook that use each vocabulary word correctly. For an extra challenge, try to use two of the adjectives in the vocabulary list in the same sentence.

English Language Coach

Using a Thesaurus A thesaurus is a special type of dictionary. It may not always give definitions, but it will list many synonyms and, sometimes, antonyms. You must know the meanings of at least some of those synonyms so that you can choose the right one. Here's a sample thesaurus entry.

Main Entry:	**relax**
Part of Speech:	*verb*
Definition:	be at ease
Synonyms:	breathe easy, calm down, cool off, hang loose, knock off, lie down, loosen up, rest, settle back, sit around, sit back, stop work, unwind
Antonyms:	tense, tighten

Partner Talk What synonym would you use to tell your little brother to relax? What about your grandmother? Why did you choose those words?

Additional Support

Differentiated Instruction

Synonyms and Antonyms Challenge students to write sentences that use a vocabulary word, plus a synonym or antonym for that word, as in these examples. **OL**

Pam liked elaborate plans, but Bill liked to keep things simple.

The candidate's speech turned a lot of skeptics into believers.

The insistent knocking on the door made me think the visitor had urgent business.

Write the sentences on the board. Have students use context clues to define the underlined words. **BL** **EL**

Skills Preview

Key Reading Skill: Synthesizing

Before you read "Loser," think about these questions.

- What are things that people lose?
- Can you lose a person?
- Have you heard someone say "I've lost my way" or "I've lost my mind"?

Class Talk Discuss the things you know about losing something or someone. Also, talk about what the word "loser" might mean. Using what you know and what you learned from your classmates, think of an idea of what the story "Loser" might be about.

Key Literary Element: Character

The people in a story are called **characters.** Sometimes animals can be characters if they talk and act like human beings. Important characters are called **main characters.** In most stories, there is one main character.

L

As you read, use these tips to help you learn about the main character in "Loser."

- Pay attention to the details about the main character.
  Where does he live? Who does he live with? How old is he?
- Notice how the main character feels about the people and events in the story.
  How does he show what he is thinking and feeling?
- Look for changes in the main character.
  How do the events of the story cause him to change?

Partner Talk With a partner, talk about a main character that you like from a movie, TV show, or book. Use the questions above to learn about each other's character.

Interactive Literary Elements Handbook
To review or learn more about the literary elements, go to www.glencoe.com.

Get Ready to Read

Connect to the Reading

Think about things you've lost. Are some of the things you've lost more important than others? How has losing something changed you?

Write to Learn In your Learner's Notebook, write three sentences about something you lost. What was it? How did you feel when you lost it? What did you do to try to find it?

Build Background

Some people think that the story "Loser" is a fairy tale or a fable that takes place in the present day.

- Fairy tales and fables are very similar. A fairy tale is a story that involves magical people, creatures, or events. A fable is similar, but it tries to teach the reader a moral or lesson.
- Many fairy tales and fables begin with the same words, such as "Once," or "Once upon a time…"
- "Cinderella" and "The Ugly Duckling" are examples of popular fairy tales. "The Tortoise and the Hare" and "The Boy Who Cried Wolf" are examples of popular fables.

Set Purposes for Reading

BIG Question Read the short story "Loser" to find out what happens to a boy whom people count on.

Set Your Own Purpose What would you like to learn from the story to help you answer the Big Question? Write your own purpose on a note card and put the card in the left pocket of Foldable 3.

Keep Moving

Use these skills as you read the following selection.

Literature Focus Lesson

Fairy Tales and Fables Discuss the information given under Build Background. Invite volunteers to give a brief plot summary of the fairy tales and fables mentioned in the text. **Ask:** What is a moral? *(a lesson about life or human nature)* What is the moral of "The Tortoise and the Hare?" *(Possible response: Slow and steady wins the race.)* Point out that in some fables, the moral is stated directly. In others, the reader has to figure out what the moral is. AS

READING WORKSHOP 3

Teach

L Literary Element

Character Have students identify the main character or characters in the stories they've already read in this unit. *(Responses may vary. Possible responses: "Broken Chain": Alfonso; "Amigo Brothers": Antonio and Felix; "Framed": Andrea; "After Twenty Years": Bob and Jimmy.)* AS

Interactive Literary Elements Handbook Have students access the Web site to improve their understanding of character.

Assess

CheckPoint

Use the CheckPoint questions provided on Presentation Plus! to check for prior knowledge and to build background. These questions can be used with interactive response keypads for immediate student feedback.

Objectives

- Synthesize information
- Identify literary elements: character
- Use word references: thesaurus

READING WORKSHOP 3

Teach

R Reading Skill

Review Connecting Ask students to imagine how the young boy must have felt after this devastating loss. Do they think it's possible for a person to recover from a tragedy like this and find happiness in life? Why or why not? *(Answers may vary. Some students will say that the boy will never recover from the loss of both of his parents. Others may say that with time and the love and support of other people, he may be able to find happiness.)* OL

Readability Scores
Dale-Chall: 4.7
DRP: 55
Lexile: 930

LOSER

by Aimee Bender

R Once there was an orphan who had a knack for finding lost things. Both his parents had been killed when he was eight years old—they were swimming in the ocean when it turned wild with waves, and each had tried to save the other from drowning. The boy woke up from a nap, on the sand, alone. After the tragedy, the community adopted and raised him, and a few years after the deaths of his parents, he began to have a sense of objects even when they weren't **visible**. This ability continued growing in power through his teens and by his twenties, he was able to actually sniff out[1] lost sunglasses, keys, contact lenses and sweaters. **1**

The neighbors discovered his talent accidentally—he was over at Jenny Sugar's house one evening, picking her up for a date, when Jenny's mother misplaced her hairbrush, and was walking around, complaining about this. The young man's nose twitched and he turned slightly toward the kitchen and pointed to the drawer where the spoons and knives were kept. His date burst into laughter. Now that would be quite a silly place to put the brush, she said, among all that silverware! and she opened the drawer to make her point, to

1. Here, ***sniff out*** means "to find."

Vocabulary

visible (VIZ uh bul) *adj.* able to be seen

Practice the Skills

1 Reviewing Skills

Drawing Conclusions There are a lot of details in this first paragraph. What sounds real to you? What don't you believe? Can you make any conclusions about what kind of story you are about to read?

Additional Support

Literature Focus Lesson

Point of View Ask: How do you know that this story is told from the third-person point of view? *(Possible response: The narrator is someone outside the story, who refers to all of the characters as "he," "she," or "they.")* BL EL

Say: As you read, notice what type of third-person narrator is telling the story. Does the narrator reveal the thoughts of only one character or the thoughts of more than one character? Why do you think the author made this choice? OL

READING WORKSHOP 3

wave with a knife or brush her hair with a spoon, but when she did, boom, there was the hairbrush, matted with gray curls, sitting astride[2] the fork pile.

Jenny's mother kissed the young man on the cheek but Jenny herself looked at him suspiciously all night long.

You planned all that, didn't you, she said, over dinner. You were trying to impress my mother. Well you didn't impress me, she said.

He tried to explain himself but she would hear none of it and when he drove his car up to her house, she fled before he could even finish saying he'd had a nice time, which was a lie anyway. He went home to his tiny room and thought about the word lonely and how it sounded and looked so lonely, with those two l's in it, each standing tall by itself. **2**

As news spread around the neighborhood about the young man's skills, people reacted two ways: there were the deeply appreciative[3] and the **skeptics**. The appreciative ones called up the young man regularly. He'd stop by on his way to school, find their keys, and they'd give him a homemade muffin. The skeptics called him over too, and watched him like a hawk; he'd still find their lost items but they'd insist it was an **elaborate** scam and he was doing it all to get attention. Maybe, declared one woman, waving her index finger in the air, Maybe, she said, he steals the thing so we think it's lost, moves the item, and then comes over to save it! How do we know it was really lost in the first place? What is going on? **R**

The young man didn't know himself. All he knew was the feeling of a tug, light but **insistent**, like a child at his sleeve, and that tug would turn him in the right direction and show him where to look. Each object had its own way of inhabiting space, and therefore messaging its location. The young man could sense, could smell, an object's presence—he did not

2. Here, ***astride*** means "lying over or across."

3. An ***appreciative*** person is thankful.

Vocabulary

skeptics (SKEP tiks) *n.* people who doubt or don't believe something

elaborate (ih LAB ur ut) *adj.* planned or carried out carefully

insistent (in SIS tunt) *adj.* not giving up; demanding attention

Practice the Skills

2 Key Literary Element

Character Sometimes you can learn about a character from his or her thoughts. What do you learn in this paragraph about the young man? **L**

Teach

L Literary Element

Character Have volunteers tell what they learn about the young man from this paragraph. *(Possible response: The young man's relationship with Jenny must not be close, or she wouldn't treat him this way. At home, he has a tiny room, though it isn't clear where he lives or with whom. He thinks about the word* lonely, *most likely because he's a lonely person.)* **OL**

R Reading Skill

Review Responding Ask: Does it surprise you that some people treat the young man with suspicion? Explain your answer. *(Possible response: No, it doesn't surprise me. Many people don't believe that a person could have special powers, like the one the young man seems to have. So they assume that he's playing tricks on everyone.)* **OL**

English Language Coach

Using a Thesaurus Write these words on the board: *elaborate, visible, skeptics, insistent,* and *modestly.* Tell students to use a thesaurus to find synonyms and antonyms for each word. Have them write several sentences using the words and their antonyms and synonyms. Ask students to write their sentences carefully to clearly convey the meaning of the words. **EL** **OL**

Objectives
- Comprehend texts by synthesizing
- Connect text to self
- Respond to literature
- Understand main characters
- Identify point of view
- Use synonyms and antonyms to expand vocabulary

Teach

Viewing the Painting

Ask: What do you think this illustration means? How does it relate to this story? *(Possible responses: The illustration shows a light that is coming from the mind of a person; the young man in the story may have a similar light coming from his mind.)* **OL**

C Critical Thinking

Comprehension Ask: Do you think the boy's disappearance might have something to do with the Green Star? Explain your answer. *(Possible answer: Perhaps someone has kidnapped the boy and will demand the Green Star as ransom. A huge emerald like the Green Star is worth a great deal of money. A lot of people know about the emerald because Mrs. Allen keeps it on display in a glass case in her kitchen.)* **OL**

READING WORKSHOP 3

need to see it to feel where it put its gravity down. As would be expected, items that turned out to be miles away took much harder concentration than the ones that were two feet to the left.

When Mrs. Allen's little boy didn't come home one afternoon, that was the most difficult of all. Leonard Allen was eight years old and usually arrived home from school at 3:05. He had allergies and needed a pill before he went back out to play. That day, by 3:45, a lone Mrs. Allen was a wreck. Her boy rarely got lost—only once had that happened in the supermarket but he'd been found quite easily under the produce tables, crying; this walk home from school was a straight line and Leonard was not a wandering kind.

Mrs. Allen was just a regular neighbor except for one extraordinary fact—through an inheritance, she was the owner of a **gargantuan** emerald she called the Green Star. It sat, glasscased, in her kitchen, where everyone could see it because she insisted that it be seen. Sometimes, as a party trick, she'd even cut steak with its beveled edge. **3**

C On this day, she removed the case off the Green Star and stuck her palms on it. Where is my boy? she cried. The Green Star was cold and flat. She ran, weeping, to her neighbor, who calmly walked her back home; together, they gave the house a thorough search, and then the neighbor, a believer, recommended calling the young man. Although Mrs. Allen was a skeptic, she thought anything was a worthwhile idea, and when the line picked up, she said, in a trembling voice:

You must find my boy.

Practice the Skills

3 English Language Coach

Using a Thesaurus The word **gargantuan** (gar GAN choo un) means "huge." Why do you think the author used this word? Look it up in a thesaurus to find other synonyms.

Additional Support

Differentiated Instruction

Researching Emeralds Have students who enjoy researching information find out more about emeralds. Ask them to find out the following:

- where emeralds are found
- what process is used for mining emeralds
- what special powers people associate with emeralds

Ask students to share their findings with the class. Encourage other students to ask questions about the presentations. **OL**

The young man had been just about to go play basketball with his friends. He'd located the basketball in the bathtub.

You lost him? said the young man.

Mrs. Allen began to explain and then her phone clicked.

One moment please, she said, and the young man held on.

When her voice returned, it was shaking with rage.

He's been kidnapped! she said. And they want the Green Star!

The young man realized then it was Mrs. Allen he was talking to, and nodded. Oh, he said, I see. Everyone in town was familiar with Mrs. Allen's Green Star. I'll be right over, he said. **4**

The woman's voice was too run with tears to respond.

In his basketball shorts and shirt, the young man jogged over to Mrs. Allen's house. He was amazed at how the Green Star was all exactly the same shade of green. He had a desire to lick it. **BQ**

By then, Mrs. Allen was in hysterics.[4]

They didn't tell me what to do, she sobbed. Where do I bring my emerald? How do I get my boy back?

The young man tried to feel the scent of the boy. He asked for a photograph and stared at it—a brown-haired kid at his kindergarten graduation—but the young man had only found objects before, and lost objects at that. He'd never found anything, or anybody, stolen. He wasn't a policeman. **L**

Mrs. Allen called the police and one officer showed up at the door.

Oh it's the finding guy, the officer said. The young man dipped his head **modestly**. He turned to his right; to his left; north; south. He got a glimmer of a feeling toward the north and walked out the back door, through the backyard. Night approached and the sky seemed to grow and deepen in the darkness.

What's his name again? he called back to Mrs. Allen.

Leonard, she said. He heard the policeman pull out a pad and begin to ask basic questions.

4. If you are in ***hysterics,*** you are emotionally out of control.

Vocabulary

modestly (MAW dist lee) *adv.* in a shy way; not confidently

Practice the Skills

4 **BIG Question**

Do you think Mrs. Allen can count on the young man to find her son? Why or why not? Put your anwer on a note card in the center pocket of Foldable 3. Your response will help you complete the Unit Challenge later.

Teach

BQ 

Call on volunteers to answer the questions in the side note. Make sure students give reasons for their responses. *(Some students may say that the young man will find the boy, using his special ability to locate things. Others may say that finding a lost person will prove more difficult than finding a lost object.)* **AS**

L Literary Element

Character **Ask:** What do you learn about the young man's character from the narrator? *(Possible response: He's compassionate enough to go to Mrs. Allen's house immediately.)* **AS**

Literature Focus Lesson

Dialogue Ask students what they notice about the dialogue in this story. *(The author does not use quotation marks.)* Ask them what effect they think the author is trying to achieve by not using quotation marks. Does the author succeed? *(Possible response: The author wrote the dialogue without quotation marks in order to make the dialogue seem like part of the narration. This makes the characters seem somewhat less human.)* **AL**

Objectives

- Comprehend texts by synthesizing
- Understand main characters
- Understand synonyms and antonyms
- Draw conclusions from text and personal experience

Teach

Viewing the Painting

Say: Look at the illustration. Why do you think the editors chose this illustration for this story? *(Answers will vary.)* AS

R Reading Skill

Synthesizing Have volunteers identify the details in this paragraph. BL EL **Ask:** How can you combine these details with your own ideas, knowledge, and experience in order to create a new idea? *(Possible response: Displaced things, such as the emerald, the tree, and lost objects exert a tug that the young man senses, or feels. That's why he's able to locate things that people have lost. The young man has this special power because he, too, was displaced from his original home when his parents drowned in the ocean. He is lost, like the objects he senses.)* OL

READING WORKSHOP 3

He couldn't quite feel him. He felt the air and he felt the tug inside of the Green Star, an object displaced from its original home in Asia. He felt the tug of the tree in the front yard which had been uprooted from Virginia to be replanted here, and he felt the tug of his own watch which was from his uncle; in an attempt to be fatherly, his uncle had insisted he take it but they both knew the gesture was false. 5

Maybe the boy was too far away by now.

He heard the policeman ask: What is he wearing?

Mrs. Allen described a blue shirt, and the young man focused in on the blue shirt; he turned off his distractions and the blue shirt, like a connecting radio station, came calling from the northwest. The young man went walking and walking and about fourteen houses down he felt the blue shirt shrieking[5] at him and he walked right into the backyard,

5. ***Shrieking*** is screaming in a high-pitched voice.

Practice the Skills

5 Key Reading Skill

R **Synthesizing** This paragraph has a lot of details about lost things and the way the young man senses, or feels, them. Do you understand something new about the young man and how he finds things? Explain.

Additional Support

Reading in the Real World

Career Point out to students that the story does not say that anyone ever loves the young man after the death of his parents. Ask students to assume the role of counselor at the young man's school. They should research how a counselor or other mental health professional might help the young man come to terms with the profound loss he's suffered. Students should use their research to give the young man advice on dealing with his loneliness and sense of displacement. OL

READING WORKSHOP 3

through the back door, and sure enough, there were four people watching TV including the tear-stained boy with a runny nose eating a candy bar. The young man scooped up the boy while the others watched, so surprised they did nothing, and one even muttered: Sorry, man.

For fourteen houses back, the young man held Leonard in his arms like a bride. Leonard stopped sneezing and looked up at the stars and the young man smelled Leonard's hair, rich with the memory of peanut butter. He hoped Leonard would ask him a question, any question, but Leonard was quiet. The young man answered in his head: Son, he said, and the word rolled around, a marble on a marble floor. Son, he wanted to say.

When he reached Mrs. Allen's door, which was wide open, he walked in with quiet Leonard and Mrs. Allen promptly burst into tears and the policeman slunk out the door.

She thanked the young man a thousand times, even offered him the Green Star, but he refused it. Leonard turned on the TV and curled up on the sofa. The young man walked over and asked him about the program he was watching but Leonard stuck a thumb in his mouth and didn't respond.

Feel better, he said softly. Tucking the basketball beneath his arm, the young man walked home, shoulders low.

In his tiny room, he undressed and lay in bed. Had it been a naked child with nothing on, no shoes, no necklace, no hairbow, no watch, he could not have found it. He lay in bed that night with the trees from other places rustling and he could feel their confusion. No snow here. Not a lot of rain. Where am I? What is wrong with this dirt?

Crossing his hands in front of himself, he held on to his shoulders. Concentrate hard, he thought. Where are you? Everything felt blank and quiet. He couldn't feel a tug. He squeezed his eyes shut and let the question bubble up: Where did you go? Come find me. I'm over here. Come find me. **6**

If he listened hard enough, he thought he could hear the waves hitting. **7** ❍

Practice the Skills

6 Key Literary Element

Character Who or what is the young man trying to find? What has he lost? How has it changed the main character? **L**

7 Key Reading Skill

Synthesizing Using what you know about the events and ideas from "Loser," write one paragraph that adds more to the end of the story.

Teach

L Literary Element

Character Make sure students understand that the young man is trying to find his parents, whom he lost when he was eight years old. He also is trying to find the love and intimacy that he lost when they died. The people in his community have adopted and raised him but apparently have forgotten to love him. The young man has been forever changed by these losses. Though he has a home, he is displaced, lost, and lonely because he is unloved. **OL**

Assess

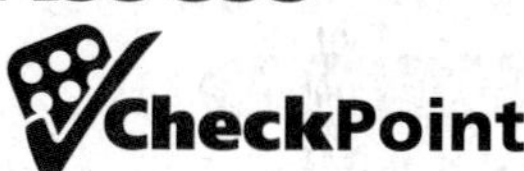

Use the CheckPoint questions provided on Presentation Plus! to check students' mastery of the selection. These questions can be used with interactive response keypads for immediate student feedback.

Differentiated Instruction

Synthesizing Some students will want to complete the synthesizing activity by writing a paragraph, as described in side note 7. Others may want to use one of these formats to present what they have added to the end of the story:

- Make an oral presentation to the class, in which you take on the role of the narrator.
- With a partner or small group, make a dramatic presentation.
- Create a sketch or a comic strip that shows what you have added to the end of the story. **OL**

Objectives
- Comprehend texts by synthesizing
- Understand main characters

Assess

Resources for page 330

- Selection Quick Check
- Selection and Unit Assessment
- ExamView Assessment Suite
- Interactive Tutor: Self-Assessment

Students can respond to the *After You Read* items in their Learner's Notebook or on separate sheets of paper.

Answering the BIG Question

1. Responses will vary.
2. His parents drowned while swimming in the ocean.
3. a hairbrush, keys, a child

Critical Thinking

4. Possible response: The young man is speaking to his parents. His questions show that he is still grieving their loss and that he is lonely.
5. Possible response: The young man will always be lonely unless he finds someone to truly love him.
6. Possible response: His experiences don't seem real. It would be great to be able to sense where lost items are, but I don't know anyone who can do that.
7. Possible response: I think this is a fable. It has imaginary events and a moral: A profound loss changes a person forever. Or: To overcome loneliness, a person needs love.

After You Read | Loser

Answering the BIG Question

1. Is the main character of this story someone you would count on? Why or why not?
2. **Recall** How did the young man lose his parents?
   TIP **Right There**
3. **Recall** List three items in the story that the young man finds.
   TIP **Think and Search**

Critical Thinking

4. **Infer** Who do you think the main character is speaking to in the last paragraph? What do his questions show you about how he feels?
   TIP **Author and Me**
5. **Synthesize** Do you think the young man will be lonely all his life? Why or why not?
   TIP **Author and Me**
6. **Evaluate** Think about things you have lost and found. Do the main character's experiences seem real to you?
   TIP **Author and Me**
7. **Analyze** Look at what you learned about fairy tales and fables on page 323. Do you think "Loser" is a modern-day fairy tale or fable? Explain.
   TIP **Author and Me**

Objectives (pp. 330–331)
Reading Synthesize information
Literature Identify literary elements: character
Vocabulary Use word references: thesaurus
Writing Write an interview: anecdotes, character
Grammar Use modifiers: comparative and superlative adjectives

Write About Your Reading

Pretend you are a TV news reporter who wants to interview the main character in "Loser." Write a list of questions that you would ask the young man about himself and his special talent. Think of the following questions as you create your list.

- What do you know about the young man and his personality?
- What items does he help people find in the story?
- What are some items that you've lost? How did you find them?

Combine this information to think of new things you would like to learn about the main character. Think of questions that will help you learn more than what you read in the story. For example, "When you find a lost item, how does it make you feel?"

Write About Your Reading

Possible response:

1. When did you first notice that you had this talent? How did you react?
2. Describe the process of actually trying to locate a lost item.
3. How do you feel when you find a lost item? Do you think other people appreciate your efforts? Why or why not?
4. Why didn't you accept the Green Star when Mrs. Allen offered it to you?
5. How has the tragic loss of your parents affected you?

Skills Review

Key Reading Skill: Synthesizing

8. How did the following activities help you synthesize information from the story and your own ideas to create something new? Write a few sentences.

- Talking with your class about things you and your classmates have lost
- Writing in your Learner's Notebook about something you lost
- Stopping while you read and asking yourself about the main character and his talent

Key Literary Element: Character

9. Why do you think the main character doesn't have a name in the story?

Reviewing Skills: Drawing Conclusions

10. Remember the items the young man finds and what he says or does after finding them. How do you think he feels about his special gift?

Vocabulary Check

Write the word that best answers each question.

visible skeptics elaborate insistent modestly

11. If you are trying hard to get a friend to see a movie with you, what word might describe you?

12. If you spend a lot of time carefully planning a party, what kind of party might you be having?

13. What might you call your friends if they don't believe your basketball story?

14. If you are embarrassed by a compliment, how might you react?

15. If you can easily see the stars in the sky, what can you say the stars are?

16. **English Language Coach** Using a thesaurus, find a word or phrase to replace the underlined word.

Once there was an orphan who had a <u>knack</u> for finding lost things.

17. **Academic Vocabulary** When you **synthesize** ideas, what do you do?

Grammar Link: Comparing with Adjectives

The **comparative form** of an adjective is used to compare one person, place, or thing with another.

To form the comparative of one-syllable words and many two-syllable words, add *-er* to the end.

- Lou is <u>taller</u> than his brother. (One person—Lou—is compared to another—his brother.)

To form the comparative of adjectives of more than two syllables, use the word *more* or *less*.

- The first movie was <u>more</u> <u>frightening</u> than the sequel.
- That car is <u>less</u> <u>expensive</u> than this one.

The **superlative form** of an adjective is used to compare one person, place, or thing with several others.

To form the superlative of one-syllable words and many two-syllable words, add *-est* to the end.

- Wanda is the <u>oldest</u> of three children. (One person is compared to two others.)

To form the superlative of adjectives of more than two syllables, use the word *most* or *least*.

- That show is the <u>least</u> <u>watchable</u> of all TV shows.
- May is the <u>most</u> <u>intelligent</u> girl in our class.

Grammar Practice

Rewrite each sentence below using the correct form of the adjective.

18. She's the (fast) runner on the team.

19. The red ball is (big) than the white ball.

20. Danny is the (attractive) member of the band.

Web Activities For eFlashcards, Selection Quick Checks, and other Web activities, go to www.glencoe.com.

Skills Review

Key Reading Skill: Synthesizing

8. Responses will vary but should describe how the activities helped students synthesize information from the story and from their own ideas to create something new.

Key Literary Element: Character

9. Possible response: Before his parents die, the boy has a name—the one his parents give him. But that boy doesn't exist anymore.

Reviewing Skills: Drawing Conclusions

10. Possible response: His special gift may sometimes bring him satisfaction, but mostly the gift makes him feel lonely and isolated. He's different from other people, and many of them react with suspicion to his special power.

Vocabulary Check

11. insistent

12. elaborate

13. skeptics

14. modestly

15. visible

16. talent

17. You create a new idea by combining what you have learned with what you already know.

Grammar Link: Comparing with Adjectives

Grammar Practice

18. fastest

19. bigger

20. most attractive

Close

Ask students to summarize what they learned from reading this story to help them answer the Big Question.

Before You Read Friends Forever

More About the Author

Since childhood, Sari Locker has been a doer and an achiever. At the age of five, she began working as an actress in professional productions. At age nine, her love for animals led her to a job in a pet store, where she was paid one dollar per hour. In high school, Locker enjoyed helping classmates who asked for her advice. She began giving advice professionally at eighteen, when she started visiting high schools during breaks from her college studies. Locker had found her calling in life: teaching people about relationships, a career that she continues to pursue.

EL Language Coach

Using a Thesaurus Choose volunteers to substitute a variety of different synonyms for *laugh, hungry,* and *ran* as they read the sentences aloud. **Ask:** Do all of the synonyms fit the context of the sentences? Why or why not? BL EL

Meet the Author

Sari Locker teaches people how to get along together. She does her teaching through books, magazines, TV, radio, and lectures. As she grew up in Fort Lauderdale, Florida, she remembers her parents telling her, "Do what makes you happy. And figure out what makes you happy for yourself." With a fresh style and information that people really care about, Locker has been very successful at helping others.

Literature Online

Author Search For more about Sari Locker, go to www.glencoe.com.

Objectives (pp. 332–337)
Reading Synthesize information
Literature Identify elements of nonfiction
Vocabulary Use word references: thesaurus

Vocabulary Preview

possessive (puh ZES iv) *adj.* wanting to keep something for oneself **(p. 335)** *Rita was possessive of Wendy and didn't want her to have other friends.*

sincerity (sin SAIR uh tee) *n.* the quality of meaning what one says and does **(p. 336)** *Wendy apologized, but Jeanette didn't trust her sincerity.*

pranks (praynks) *n.* playful jokes or tricks **(p. 336)** *Efrain and David usually laugh when they play pranks on each other.*

Partner Talk With a partner, think of two sentences for each vocabulary word. Write them in your Learner's Notebook.

English Language Coach

Using a Thesaurus Words can be exciting! One reason good writers choose words carefully is so readers won't be bored. In a thesaurus, find replacements for the words in the ovals below.

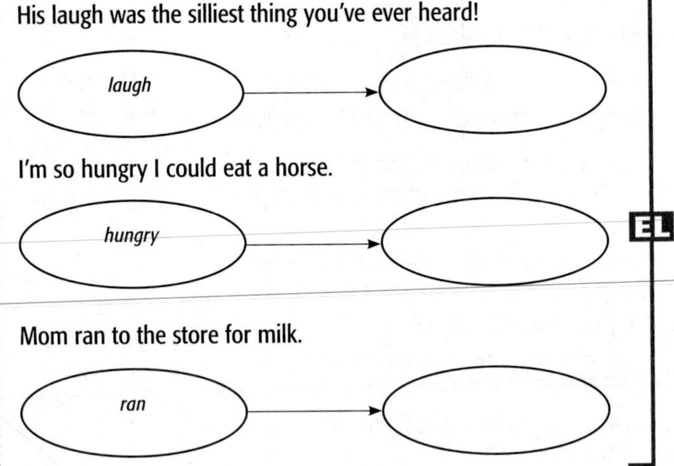

His laugh was the silliest thing you've ever heard!
laugh
I'm so hungry I could eat a horse.
hungry
Mom ran to the store for milk.
ran
EL

Partner Storytime Using your thesaurus, find synonyms for the following words to fit in a short story about a good friendship. Share with the class.

fight care talk friendship help

Additional Support

Author Search To expand students' appreciation of Sari Locker, have them access the Web site for additional information and resources.

Literature Focus Lesson

Text Features Remind students that magazine, newspaper, and textbook articles often use text features, such as headnotes, subheads, decks, bullets, italics, bold type, pull-out quotes, and boxed text. Ask students to scan the article "Friends Forever" to find examples of text features. *(deck, subheads, bold type, boxed text)* Tell students that as they read, they should notice how these text features help them better understand the article. AS

Skills Preview

Key Reading Skill: Synthesizing

The selection you are going to read is about how friends solve problems. Before you read, think about what you already know.

- Why is friendship difficult sometimes?
- What advice about friendship have you heard or learned in your life?

Partner Talk With a partner, name a common problem that each of you have had with your friends. How did each of you solve your problem with your friends? Synthesize your ideas into three tips about friendship that you can give to other kids.

Literary Element: Nonfiction

The selection you are going to read is not a fictional, or made-up, story. It's a magazine article about real people and real events. Writing that is about real people and their experiences is called **nonfiction.**

As you read, pay attention to how the author makes the article easy for kids and teenagers to understand.

- Notice the expressions, or groups of words, the author uses.

  How do the words speak more to kids than adults?

- Nonfiction writing sometimes has short headlines called subheads. Subheads introduce parts of the text.

  How do the subheads help you follow and understand the information?

- The author talked with a lot of kids before she wrote this article.

  How do you feel when the author uses the exact words, or quotations, from these kids?

Interactive Literary Elements Handbook
To review or learn more about the literary elements, go to www.glencoe.com.

Get Ready to Read

Connect to the Reading

Think about your friends. What problems have you had with your friends?

- Has a friend ever moved away but stayed your friend?
- Has a friend ever made new friends and stopped hanging out with you?
- How do you feel when your friend is better at something than you are?
- Have you ever had to tell a friend that you didn't like something he or she said or did?

Write to Learn Write for ten minutes in your Learner's Notebook about one of the questions above. Or make up another question and write about it.

Build Background

The article you are going to read talks about kids your age and their friendships. Friendships are an important part of life.

- The word *friend* comes from an Old English word that means "to love."
- Friendships can help keep people healthy. Good friendships are natural stress fighters.
- The article was first published in a magazine called *Teen People,* which has a news team of 35 high school and college students.

Set Purposes for Reading

BIG Question Read the selection "Friends Forever" to find out how teens count on one another to keep their friendships strong and healthy.

Set Your Own Purpose What would you like to learn from the article to help you answer the Big Question? Write your own purpose on a note card and put the card in the left pocket of Foldable 3.

Keep Moving

Use these skills as you read the following selection.

Teach

R Reading Skill

Synthesizing Invite students to share and compare their tips about friendship. **Ask:** Do you think that you might actually follow the advice given in some of these tips? Why or why not? What new ideas about friendship did this activity suggest to you? *(Responses will vary.)* AS

Literature Online

Interactive Literary Elements Handbook Have students access the Web site to improve their understanding of nonfiction.

CheckPoint

Use the CheckPoint questions provided on Presentation Plus! to check for prior knowledge and to build background. These questions can be used with interactive response keypads for immediate student feedback.

Differentiated Instruction

Interview Point out that Sari Locker, the author of "Friends Forever," talked with a lot of kids before she wrote this article. Have interested students prepare questions for a brief interview about the importance of friendship. Once they have prepared their questions, students should pair up and interview each other. Invite volunteers to conduct their interviews in front of the class. Ask the class to summarize what they have learned about the importance of friendship from the interviews. OL

Objectives

- Synthesize information
- Identify elements of nonfiction
- Use word references: thesaurus

Teach

Viewing the Photo

Have students look at the photo and read the deck, the sentences below the headline. **Ask:** What does the photo seem to suggest about the friendship between these two boys? What do you learn from the deck? *(Responses will vary. Possible response: The boys appear to be enjoying each other's company, which is an important ingredient of friendship. The quote suggests that their relationship is open and honest.)* AS

R Reading Skill

Review Previewing Ask: What other elements can you preview to help you learn more about this article? AS

Readability Scores
Dale-Chall: 5.8
DRP: 55
Lexile: 850

READING WORKSHOP 3

TIME

FRIENDS Forever

Mending a broken friendship is never easy, but it's almost always worth the work. Here, three sets of pals talk about the problems they have faced and how they have patched things up.

Robin Bowman

"I can say anything to Chris without him taking offense," says Nat (left). "We're honest."

By SARI LOCKER

Drifting apart 1

After meeting in seventh grade, Nat Brown and Chris Brennan, both now 15, actually caught grief for being such close pals. "Chris's sister would make fun of us, because we would talk all the time, just like girls," says Nat. Despite the teasing, the two teens from Wellesley, Massachusetts, continued their friendship for another year before they started to drift apart. "Chris got a girlfriend and started spending all of his time with her," says Nat. "I felt like he was ignoring me." The two got over that hump[1] by doing what they do best: communicating. "Some guys are insecure, so they can't talk about their feelings," says Chris. "But we're big, tough guys, and we can still talk openly."

1. In this sentence, ***got over that hump*** means "got past that hard time."

1 Reviewing Skills

R **Previewing** Before you read, look at the subheads. What do the subheads make you think the article is about?

Additional Support

English Language Coach

Idioms Remind students that an idiom is an expression that means something different from its word-for-word meaning. Read the first paragraph of the article and ask them: What does the expression "got over that hump" mean? Is their definition similar to the one given in footnote 1? Have students use context clues in the paragraph to figure out the meanings of these idioms:

- "caught grief" *(were teased or ridiculed)*
- "to drift apart" *(to become less friendly with each other)* EL

There was more trouble ahead, however. They both had girlfriends and even less time to share. "We played football and lacrosse together, but it wasn't the same," recalls Chris. The friendship might have ended if it hadn't been for a family crisis. "Nat's mom was diagnosed with breast cancer last year," says Chris. "When I heard his mom was sick, it made me think about him more. I wanted to be there for him." Chris and Nat's friendship is still on the mend, but they're both putting more energy into it these days.

Three was a crowd

When Wendy Pennington, 14, moved from Springfield, Missouri, to Wichita, Kansas, she lost her old friends by not keeping in touch. So when her family moved back to Springfield three years later, she was forced to start fresh. Wendy met Jeanette Hodgson and Rita Weston (not her real name), both 14, on the bus ride to school the first day of seventh grade. The three became the best of friends—or so it seemed. About a month after they started hanging out together, their relationship underwent a dramatic shift:[2] Rita and Wendy grew closer together and they began to squeeze Jeanette out. "Rita would sleep over at Wendy's on school nights just to make me jealous," says Jeanette. Those feelings of rejection took a toll on her. "I got really depressed," Jeanette admits. "I felt like a loser." 2

R2 It was only when Rita's family moved to Arizona that Wendy realized how unfair she had been to Jeanette. "I felt bad that Jeanette had been so upset. Rita was **possessive** of me, and I didn't stand up to her," she explains.

Janie Airey/Digital Vision/Getty Images

2 Key Reading Skill

R1 **Synthesizing** Here, the word *loser* means "a misfit—someone who has never or seldom been successful at a job, personal relationships, etc." "Loser" is also the title of the selection you just read. Think about what *loser* means in this selection and what happened to the young man in the short story "Loser." What new idea do you have about what the word *loser* can also mean?

2. ***Dramatic shift*** is another way to say "big change."

Vocabulary

possessive (puh ZES iv) *adj.* wanting to keep something for oneself

Teach

R1 Reading Skill

Synthesizing Invite volunteers to tell what they think Aimee Bender was trying to say when she gave the title "Loser" to her short story. In what sense is the young man in the story a loser? *(Possible response: He is a loser because he lost his parents, who drowned when he was eight years old. He also is a loser because he lost the love and security that parents provide for their child.)* OL At what point in the story does the young man feel like a "loser" as defined in "Friends Forever"? *(Possible response: When he can't find Leonard.)* AL

R2 Reading Skill

Review Responding Have students give their reactions to the way Wendy and Rita treat Jeanette. **Ask:** Do you think Jeanette will give Wendy a chance to repair their friendship? Do you think Wendy deserves this chance? Why or why not? *(Responses will vary.)* OL

Differentiated Instruction

Letter of Apology Ask students to imagine that they have treated a friend unfairly, as Wendy has. Have students write a letter of apology to their friend, as the first step in trying to repair their relationship.
Sample response:

Dear Karen,
I am really sorry for the way Jane and I treated you. I know that I have hurt your feelings. I don't deserve another chance, but I hope you will give me one. I promise that I will be your loyal friend from now on.
—Leah BL EL

Objectives
- Preview text
- Comprehend texts by synthesizing
- Understand main characters
- Use context clues to define words

Teach

R Reading Skill

Review Connecting Ask: How can holding a grudge harm a friendship? In your opinion, are people sometimes justified in holding a grudge? Explain. *(Responses will vary.)* OL

BQ BIG Question

Invite volunteers to tell how the teens in the article show that they could count on each other. *(Possible responses: Nat and Chris drift apart but come back together after Nat's mom becomes ill. Wendy works hard to win back Jeanette's trust after treating her friend unfairly. Jeanette forgives Wendy and doesn't hold a grudge. David and Efrain realize how stupid their fight is and laugh about it. Now they're closer than ever.)* AS

With Rita out of the picture, Wendy could spend her time winning back Jeanette's **trust**. "Before, I didn't say anything to Jeanette about what was happening with Rita. Now I let Jeanette know how lucky I am to have her as a friend." Understandably, Jeanette had her doubts about Wendy's **sincerity**. "I was skeptical at first," says Jeanette. "But I had to trust her because I didn't want to lose her as a friend again. Now we're like sisters." And Wendy is grateful that Jeanette didn't hold a grudge.[3] **3**

From push to shove

At one time, New Yorkers David Santiago, 16, and his pal Efrain Vellon, 15, had a habit of playing **pranks** back and forth—until one day things went too far. "We were in science class, and we started throwing pieces of pencils at each other," explains Efrain. Continues David, "But when a piece hit Efrain in the face, he thought I was trying to pick a fight."

In a matter of minutes, David and Efrain got into a serious shoving match, which their teacher broke up. A few days later, the boys' parents met with guidance counselors while the two boys waited outside. At one point, they looked at each other and started cracking up. "We saw how stupid it was," says Efrain. Adds David, "We let pressures about how guys are supposed to act get to us." **4**

Ironically, the fight ended up bringing them closer together. "If it weren't for the fight, we probably wouldn't have become such good friends," says Efrain. These days David and Efrain take their friendship more seriously. "And if we have a fight, we talk about it. Then we laugh about it," says David. **5**

—Updated 2005, from *Teen People*, May 19, 1998

3. When you don't forgive someone for a long time, you ***hold a grudge.***

Vocabulary

sincerity (sin SAIR ih tee) *n.* the quality of meaning what one says and does

pranks (praynks) *n.* playful jokes or tricks

3 English Language Coach

Using a Thesaurus What synonyms for the word **trust** could be used when talking about a damaged friendship?

4 Literary Element

Nonfiction The writer is using words that the real teens in the article might use. *Cracking up* is a way to say laughing really hard. Look for other expressions like *cracking up* as you read.

5 BIG Question

BQ After solving their problems and disagreements, how did the teens in this article show that they could count on one another? Put your answer on a note card in the center pocket of Foldable 3. Your response will help you complete the Unit Challenge later.

Additional Support

English Language Coach

Using a Thesaurus Have students look up the word *trust* in a thesaurus. Challenge them to write sentences using a variety of synonyms and antonyms for both the noun form and the verb form of *trust*. Invite volunteers to share their sentences with the class. EL BL

Then ask students to think of at least five other words they would use to write an article about friendship. Have students write synonyms and antonyms for these words. OL

Friendship pitfalls

To keep friends, you'll need to avoid some snags. Here's what to watch for.

1 COMPETITION: Whether you're outdoing your friend in school or sports, it's best not to rub it in. Nobody likes a bragging winner. True friends support each other at all times.

2 CHANGE: Everyone grows up, and sometimes that means growing apart from childhood friends. But just because you don't share all the same interests, it doesn't mean you can't stay close. You'll always have one thing in common: your history.

3 PEER PRESSURE: If you start hanging out with a new crowd, you shouldn't be expected to ditch old friends simply because they aren't in that social circle. Remember, the only person qualified to decide whom you should be friends with is you.

4 BOYFRIENDS/GIRLFRIENDS: When one of you finds a boyfriend/girlfriend, it can be the kiss of death for a friendship. So if you've hooked up, be sensitive to your friend's feelings. Imagine how you would want to be treated if the roles were reversed and you were the one left out.

5 DISTANCE: Separations can put a strain on the strongest relationship. You may have to work a little harder to keep in touch with your pal (there's always e-mail and road trips), but you'll cherish your time together even more.

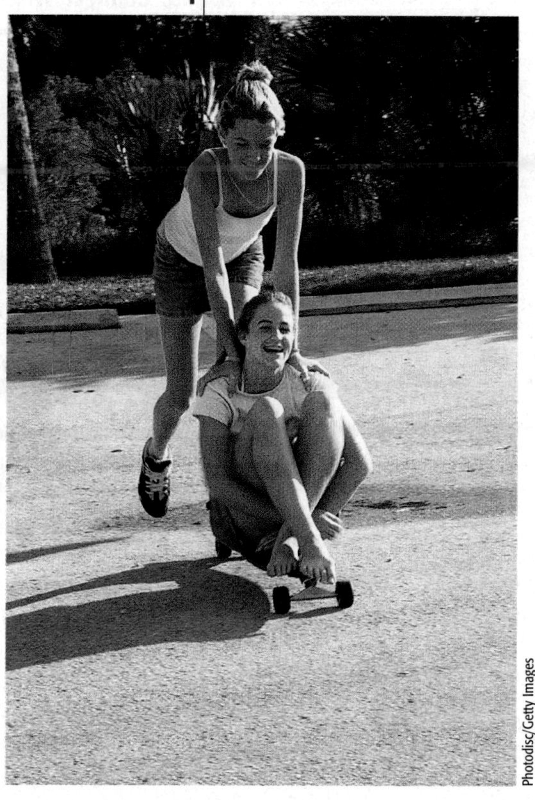

Photodisc/Getty Images

Teach

R Reading Skill

Review Responding Have students give their reactions to the numbered list. **Ask:** Do you agree that these are major friendship pitfalls? Can you think of others? What is your opinion of the advice the author gives for dealing with these pitfalls? *(Responses will vary.)* OL

C Critical Thinking

Comprehension Say: Recall the three tips about friendship that you and a partner synthesized in the activity on page 333. How are your tips similar to the ones given here? How are they different? *(Responses will vary.)* AS

Assess

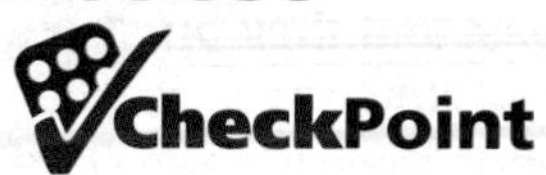

Use the CheckPoint questions provided on Presentation Plus! to check students' mastery of the selection. These questions can be used with interactive response keypads for immediate student feedback.

Differentiated Instruction

What Is a True Friend? Ask students to choose a format in which to answer this question. Students may choose from the options listed below, or they may select a different format.

- Create a poster that answers the question using both words and images.
- Debate the question with a classmate.
- Write a poem or a song that answers the question.
- Answer the question in a paragraph or an essay. OL

Objectives
- Use a thesaurus
- Synthesize information from a variety of sources
- Respond to text

Assess

Resources for page 338

- Selection Quick Check
- Selection and Unit Assessment
- ExamView Assessment Suite
- Interactive Tutor: Self-Assessment

Students can respond to the *After You Read* items in their Learner's Notebook or on separate sheets of paper.

Answering the BIG Question

1. Responses will vary.
2. They realize how stupid their fight was, and they burst out laughing. Now they are better friends than ever and are able to talk about their disagreements.
3. The three girls were friends until Rita and Wendy squeezed Jeanette out of the friendship. After Rita moved away, Wendy realized she had been unfair to Jeanette. She won back Jeanette's trust and friendship.
4. They drifted apart because they were spending so much time with their girlfriends.

Critical Thinking

5. Responses will vary.
6. Responses will vary.

After You Read

Friends Forever

Robin Bowman

Objectives (pp. 338–339)
Reading Synthesize information
Literature Identify elements of nonfiction
Vocabulary Use synonyms
Writing Write a nonfiction article: question, interview
Grammar Use modifiers: comparative and superlative adverbs

Answering the BIG Question

1. You want to be able to count on your friends. What is the best advice from this article about how to keep your friendships healthy?
2. **Recall** How do David and Efrain solve their friendship problems?
   Tip Right There
3. **Summarize** What happens between Wendy, Jeanette, and Rita?
   Tip Think and Search
4. **Recall** What causes Chris and Nat to drift apart?
   Tip Right There

Critical Thinking

5. **Connect** Which of the three stories is similar to a problem you have had with a friend? Why?
   Tip Author and Me
6. **Connect** This article talks about important qualities of friendship. In your experience, what makes a good friend?
   Tip On My Own

Write About Your Reading

Write your own short article for students in your grade. Teach them how to build good friendships. Use words and expressions that kids your age can understand. Follow the steps below:

- **List questions:** Write questions about friendship that you want to ask someone you know outside of school. For example, you might ask "What is the hardest part about being a good friend?" "How do you and your friends work out problems?" "What do you count on your friends for?"
- **Interview:** Take notes while the person you are interviewing answers your questions. Write down his or her exact words for one of your questions. Then, you can use a quotation in your article. Ask the person if it's okay to use his or her real name.
- **Write:** Using your own words, write a short article. Use your own experiences and your notes from the interview. Include the quotation from the person you interviewed. Use a fake name if he or she asked you to.
- **Present:** Share your article with other students. Discuss your ideas about friendship and what you learned from your interviews.

Write About Your Reading

Possible response:

Your friends have to be able to count on you. That can mean standing up to your peers when they're ganging up on someone. That's what Laura did for Carol. The two girls have been good friends for years. One day, the kids at the "cool" lunch table decided to make Carol their next victim. They started making fun of her every day at lunch.

"It made me mad," said Laura. "So one day I went up to their table and told them to knock it off. I knew they might start picking on me, too, but I didn't care." The cool kids looked surprised. Maybe it's because Laura is pretty popular herself. They stopped picking on Carol, and now Laura and her friend are closer than ever.

Skills Review

Key Reading Skill: Synthesizing

7. You read about how different teens solved problems and became better friends. You also thought about your own friendships.
- What new ideas did you think of that may help some of your friendships?
- How will they help?

Literary Element: Nonfiction

8. Review "Friends Forever." List three expressions in the article that you or your friends have used when talking.

9. Which subhead in the selection do you think best describes one of the stories? Why?

10. How has reading nonfiction helped you think about your own experiences?

Vocabulary Check

For each word listed on the left, choose the word on the right that means the same thing or almost the same thing.

11.	possessive	tricks
12.	sincerity	controlling
13.	pranks	truthfulness

14. English Language Coach Rewrite the paragraph below on a separate sheet of paper. Replace each underlined word or phrase with a more colorful or interesting word that you find in a thesaurus.

I went to the game on Saturday and had a good time. All of my friends were there. We enjoy hanging out together. The game was exciting. We cheered loudly for our team, and they won by two points.

Web Activities For eFlashcards, Selection Quick Checks, and other Web activities, go to www.glencoe.com.

Grammar Link: Comparing with Adverbs

Adverbs help describe verbs, or the actions in sentences. A comparative adverb compares two actions. A superlative adverb compares more than two actions.

- Most short adverbs add *-er* to form the comparative and *-est* to form the superlative.

  The singer arrived *earlier* than the guitar player.

  The drummer arrived *earliest* of all the players.

- Long adverbs, as well as a few short adverbs such as *often,* add the word *more* to form the comparative and the word *most* to form the superlative.

  Tracy dances *more beautifully* than her brother.

  Tracy dances *most beautifully* of all the students.

  The singers perform *more often* than the dancers.

  Which of the five singers performs *most often*?

- The words *less* and *least* are the negative versions of *more* and *most*. They are added to adverbs to form the "negative comparative" or "negative superlative."

  Julia runs *less quickly* than Tracy.

  Julia runs *least quickly* of all the players

- Some adverbs have irregular comparative and superlative forms.

Adverb	Comparative	Superlative
well	better	best
badly	worse	worst
little	less	least

Grammar Practice

Write the comparative and superlative forms of each adverb below. Use a dictionary if you need help.

15. fast

16. carefully

17. frequently

Skills Review

Key Reading Skill: Synthesizing

7. Responses will vary.

Literary Element: Nonfiction

8. Responses will vary.

9. Possible response: *Three was a crowd* describes what happens when Rita and Wendy shut out Jeanette, the third friend in their group. Wendy and Jeanette become friends again only after Rita moves away.

10. Possible response: I've gotten new ideas about how to be a better friend.

Vocabulary Check

11. controlling

12. truthfulness

13. tricks

14. Possible responses: great, buddies, have fun, thrilling, rooted, at the top of our lungs

Close

Ask students what they learned from this article about friendship to help them answer the Big Question.

Grammar Link: Comparing with Adverbs

Grammar Practice

15. faster, fastest

16. more carefully, most carefully

17. less frequently, least frequently

LiteratureOnline

Web Activities Have students access the Web site for interactive activities that will help them assess their understanding of the selection.

Focus

BELLRINGER Options

Daily Language Practice Transparency

Focus Activity Say: It's time to edit and revise your story. What are some things you think you should pay attention to when editing your story? *(Responses will vary.)*

Teach

W Writing

Reviewing the First Draft

As students read through the draft, have them ask themselves:

- What conflict does my main character face?
- Are my characters well developed?
- Does the dialogue sound natural and authentic?
- Is the setting clearly described?
- Is anything missing or unclear?

Tell students that many professional writers read their work aloud as they edit and revise. OL

Resources for page 340

Use the Writing Workshop Graphic Organizer BLM in the Unit 3 Resource Booklet.

WRITING WORKSHOP PART 2

Short Fictional Story

Revising, Editing, and Presenting

ASSIGNMENT Write a short fictional story about a character who has a problem

Purpose: To tell a story about a character who could really count on someone

Audience: You, your teacher, and your classmates

Revising Rubric

Your short story should have

- a clear organization
- a developed plot based on a conflict
- specific details to describe characters and setting
- descriptive dialogue

Objectives (pp. 340–345)
Writing Use the writing process: edit, rewrite, present • Write to entertain • Use story elements: plot, setting, character, dialogue
Grammar Use modifiers: adjectives and adverbs
Listening, Speaking, and Viewing Read aloud

In Writing Workshop Part 1, you wrote the first draft of your short story. You described characters, setting, and developed a plot line in your Learner's Notebook. Now it's time to revise your first draft and finish your short story. You'll keep a copy of it in a writing portfolio so that you and your teacher can evaluate your writing progress over time.

Revising

Make It Better

The first thing to do is read your short story draft. Parts of your story that seemed perfectly clear when you were writing during Part 1 may sound confusing to you now. That's okay. As you read, make notes on your paper about parts you want to change and how you want to change them. Then go back and make the changes.

Your story should have the following common elements of short stories:

W
- a plot that is organized around the conflict, or struggle, of the main character
- well-developed characters
- dialogue that helps readers "hear" how the characters speak
- a clearly described setting

Then read your draft out loud. You may notice mistakes that you didn't notice while reading to yourself. As you read, pause to make any changes that you think your story needs. Listen for places where the words sound strange or you get confused. Revise your draft until it sounds the way you like it.

Descriptive Dialogue

An easy way to add description to your characters is to write the way they speak. Characters don't always just *say* things. Sometimes they shout, whisper, cheer, or exclaim. When you add these words before or after your character's dialogue, it makes it easy for readers to "hear" your characters. Check out the examples below.

"Be quiet, my mom is sleeping," Dan *whispered.*
"What? I can't hear you, the music is too loud," Celia *shouted.*

Make sure that you not only include dialogue, but that you describe what kind of dialogue it is. Return to your story and revise your dialogue so that it sounds the way you imagine your characters speak.

Additional Support

English Language Coach

Dialogue Invite volunteers to choose a passage of dialogue from the first draft of their short stories. Ask them to write the passage on the board. Have other students read the dialogue and suggest ways that it might be improved. The student who wrote the dialogue may accept or reject the suggested revisions.

Also have students evaluate whether the dialogue is written in the proper format, as shown in the examples on page 296. Remind students to revise their dialogue so that it follows the correct format. BL EL

Teach

W Writing

Point of View **Ask:**

- From what point of view is this story written? How do you know? *(It's written from the third-person point of view. The narrator is someone outside the story who refers to all of the characters as "he," "she," or "they.")*
- Does the narrator reveal the thoughts of all the characters or just one of them? *(The narrator reveals only Maya's thoughts.)*
- What point of view did you choose for your short story? Why? *(Responses will vary.)* **OL**

BQ 

Ask: How do you think Maya would answer the Unit 3 Big Question: Who can we really count on? *(Maya would say that she can count on her mother.)* How would the main character in your story answer that question? *(Responses will vary.)* **OL**

Active Writing Model

Frustrated, Maya threw herself down on her blue-and-white bedspread and pounded the pillow with her fist. What was she going to tell Rita? If she said she couldn't sleep over, Rita would never ask Maya to do anything with her ever again.

Besides, she didn't want to hurt Rita's feelings. She knew how bad she always felt when she invited other girls to her house and they said no.

The writer develops the conflict by fully explaining the problem.

Maya got up and paced nervously around her room. Next to the ballerina on her dresser there was a picture of a sailboat on a dark sea. Underneath the boat were the words "'I'm not afraid of storms, for I'm learning how to sail my ship.'– by Louisa May Alcott". Well, Maya had tried to sail her ship, but it wouldn't move!

The writer uses an adverb to describe how Maya is pacing.

Maybe she could get help learning how to sail her ship. She could ask Mom to show her how to fix her hair.

Just then Mom came into Maya's room to put away Maya's laundry. Maya opened her mouth to talk about combing her own hair, but the words wouldn't come out. So she picked up her hairbrush and started brushing.

Mom watched her for a minute and said, "You need to use your hand to smooth your hair down after you brush it."

Maya tried it. It worked! She was so happy!

This is the climax of the story—the point of greatest interest.

Next she showed Mom her useless attempts to put in her bobby pins. Mom said, "Let's go to the store this afternoon and see if there are any barrettes that are easier for you to close. I bet a headband would work too."

The next morning Maya was able to easily smooth her hair down and get a bright red headband over it. The headband felt tight on her head, but she didn't mind. She liked the feeling that her hair was being held firmly in place.

The writer connects the events of the story. Transition words such as *next* guide the reader through the sequence of events.

"Rita asked me to sleep over after the basketball game on Friday night," Maya told Mom at breakfast. "Can I?"

Mom replied, "As soon as I call Rita's mother and make sure it's okay with her, you can start packing your bag."

This well-organized story has a clear resolution.

Additional Support

Differentiated Instruction

Critiquing and Rewriting Have students work with a partner as they critique this Writer's Model. For example, they may think that the story would be more engaging if it had more dialogue. Or, perhaps they feel that the story would be more interesting if the narrator revealed the thoughts of all of the characters.

Have students share their critiques with the class. Then, challenge them to write another draft of the story, following some of the suggestions that they and their classmates have made. **AL**

Writer's Model

Active Writing Model

Bobby Pins
by Rochelle Zappia

W

"I can't wait to go to the basketball game Friday night," Maya told her friend Rita on the phone.

"Me neither. You want to sleep over after the game?" asked Rita.

Maya's stomach started tightening into knots. "I-I'll have to ask," she stammered and quickly hung up the phone.

Maya would have loved to sleep over at Rita's house. But what would she do about her hair the next morning?

Maya had cerebral palsy, and that made it hard for her to do things with her hands. She could do basic things like put her clothes on in the morning, make her own food and write with a pen like other kids. But, combing her hair was another story. She could get the tangles out by pulling hard, but no matter how long she brushed her hair, it wouldn't stay down. Pieces were always popping back up and she couldn't get her hands to fasten barrettes or bobby pins.

So, every morning, Maya's mom did her hair. It was embarrassing, but Maya's only other choice was to go to school with her hair sticking out in every direction! It never really bothered Maya before, but now it did! Now not being able to fix her own hair was stopping Maya from sleeping over at Rita's.

Maya went into her bedroom to try to fix her hair herself. When she got to her dresser, she just looked at the tiny ballerina figure on her jewel box. Sometimes Maya wished she could move as gracefully as that ballerina. Then, Maya looked into the round mirror that hung on her wall above the dresser. Maya stared at her thick, shoulder length, brown hair. She took out her bobby pins and picked up a brush. She brushed down some strands of hair standing up on her head. They shot right back up. Using both hands, she forced a bobby pin open and tried to guide it into her hair. The minute she let go, it dropped to the floor.

- The writer begins the story with dialogue to grab the reader's attention.
- Descriptive dialogue helps the readers "hear" the character's voice.
- L The writer uses concrete details to develop the character.
- These specific details about the setting help the reader imagine Maya's bedroom.
- The writer uses adjectives to describe Maya's hair.

Teach

W Writing

Strong Beginnings Remind students that the beginning of a story should grab readers' attention. Otherwise, they may stop reading! Invite volunteers to read aloud the opening paragraph or paragraphs of some of the short stories in this unit. **Ask:** Does the opening of the story grab your attention? Why or why not? Do any of the stories begin with dialogue, as the model story on this page does? How does your own story begin? *(Responses will vary.)* **OL**

L Literary Element

Conflict Ask:

- What is the main conflict, or struggle, that Maya faces? *(Maya is embarrassed to sleep over at Rita's because she is unable to fix her own hair in the morning.)* **OL**
- How well does the author develop this conflict? Explain your answer. *(Responses will vary.)* **AL**

English Language Coach

Word Choice Tell students that when good writers use precise, vivid language, it helps the reader "experience" the story in the same way that the characters might have experienced it. Have students practice this skill by rewriting these sentences. Use the first one as a model.

1. Two robbers held up a bank. *(Two masked robbers pointed pistols at the bank teller and demanded cash.)*
2. I saw a groundhog in the garden.
3. There was a bad thunderstorm.
4. Our day at the beach was fun. **BL** **EL**

Objectives

- Write short fictional stories that apply organization methods and contain literary devices and literary elements, with a focus on conflict
- Write dialogue

Teach

W1 Writing

Editing and Proofreading Explain to students that it can be difficult for writers to edit and proofread their own work. Suggest that students work in pairs or small groups to help each other edit and proofread their stories. OL

W2 Writing

Spelling and Grammar Checker If students have typed their stories using word processing software, remind them to use the spelling checker in the software. They also should run the grammar checker. But remind students of the limitations of spelling and grammar checkers. **Ask:** How can you catch spelling and grammar errors that the checker misses? *(Possible response: read paper carefully several times)* OL

Assess

Tell students that the best writers always do a final, careful read-through of their work to catch any errors they may have missed. Suggest that students do the same. OL

Editing

Finish It Up

When you are finished revising, check your story for errors in grammar, usage, and mechanics.

W1 Read the latest version of your draft and use the **Editing Checklist** to help you spot errors. You may find it easier to spot mistakes if you read your story aloud (again!) or start at the end of your story and read it backwards, one sentence at a time. Use the proofreading symbols in the chart on page R74 to mark needed corrections.

Writing Tip

Spelling You know that the *i* comes before *e*, except after *c*. An exception to the rule is when the letters make an *ay* sound, as in *weigh* and *neighbor*.

Editing Checklist

- ☑ All articles and demonstrative adjectives are used correctly.
- ☑ The correct forms of adjectives and adverbs are used in comparisons.
- ☑ Verb terms are correct.
- ☑ Dialogue is correctly punctuated.
- ☑ Spelling and capitalization are correct.

Presenting

Show It Off

Writing Tip

Handwriting Improve handwriting by making sure that your grasp on your pencil is correct. Your thumb and first finger should connect on the pencil to form an oval or an open space.

W2 By now you've made a lot changes to your story and it might look messy and disorganized. Rewrite your story on a sheet of fresh paper. If possible, use word processing software to make a neat final copy of your short story.

With your classmates, make a book of short stories. You can call it *Characters to Count On,* or you can work together to come up with a different title for the book.

1. Create or find at least one image to go along with your story. You can draw or paint an illustration. Or search magazines and newspapers for pictures. Whatever type of image you use, be sure that the image clearly relates to your story.
2. Put all of the stories and images together in a binder and number each page.
3. Make a table of contents that tells the title, author, and starting page number of each story. Then place the table of contents in the front of the binder.

Additional Support

Differentiated Instruction

Publishing Team As students compile their book of short stories, you may want to allow them to choose the task that best suits their talents and interests. Students who are visually oriented may want to provide the illustrations for each story, either by creating original art or by finding pictures in magazines or newspapers. Students with strong organizational skills can make the table of contents for the binder. Those with an interest in production can actually gather and arrange all of the different components to produce the finished book of short stories. OL

Small Group Workshop

Get together with two other students and take turns reading your stories to each other.

- When it is your turn to read, let your enthusiasm for your story show in how you tell it.
- Speak at the right volume (not too loud or too quiet) and the right pace (not too fast or too slow).
- Use a different voice for each character.
- After each person reads, answer the following questions: What part of the story do you like best? Why?

LSV

I like the part where you describe the characters because I can really see them, and I feel like I am getting to know them. This makes me want to read more about them.

- What would you like to know more about in the story? Use details here.

I would like to know more about the setting. I want to be able to picture Maya's bedroom in my mind. Knowing what her bedroom looks like might tell me something about her. Also, I'm not sure what the main character's problem is.

- What questions do you have for the writer about the story? Come up with at least one question.

Why is the main character so nervous and upset about the possibility of sleeping over at her friend's house?

Think about your group members' comments and questions and use that information to further revise your story. Remember that you don't have to use every comment or address every question. Add details or take some details out. *You* decide what changes to make.

Literature Online

Writing Models For models and other writing activities, go to www.glencoe.com.

Differentiated Instruction

Picture It Some students may benefit from a more graphic approach to the small-group revision process. Offer these options to students:

- After a story is read aloud, sketch the main character. Ask the writer: Does this resemble the character you intended to create?
- Create a timeline of plot events. Is anything missing or unclear?
- Make a word web that describes the main character. Does the writer need to develop the character more fully?
- Sketch the setting of the story. Does the writer need to add more details about the setting? OL

WRITING WORKSHOP PART 2

Teach

Literature Online

Writing Models Have students access the Web site for an additional and interactive Writing Workshop-based student model.

LSV Listening, Speaking, and Viewing

Small Group Workshop

Say: Professional writers sometimes form critique groups. They ask their fellow writers to react to their work, just as you will ask your classmates to give you feedback and advice about your short story. Listen carefully to what your classmates tell you. Use their suggestions to improve your story. AS

W Writing

Character Development

Tell students that fiction writers develop their characters using a variety of methods. A writer may make direct statements about a character. Writers also develop characters indirectly, by describing what they do, say, and think. As students revise their stories, tell them to keep in mind the different methods they can use to develop their characters. OL

Objectives

- Participate in discussions using effective speaking strategies
- Revise writing based on feedback

WRITING WORKSHOP PART 2

Listening, Speaking, and Viewing

Analyzing Cartoons
The guy has trouble speaking to a girl. He gets nervous when he's on the phone. What advice would you give him?

Reading Aloud

Reading a text aloud often allows you to think about the words in a new way. You might notice something new or find a new rhythm to the words.

I DID IT AGAIN!
DID WHAT?
I THINK OF ALL THESE WITTY AND SENSITIVE THINGS TO SAY—
BUT WHEN I GET SARA ON THE PHONE, I END UP JUST GRUNTING AND MUMBLING LIKE AN IDIOT!
SO YOU WANT TO LEARN HOW TO EXPRESS YOUR THOUGHTS VERBALLY?
IT WOULD BE FASTER IF SHE JUST LEARNED TO READ MY MIND.

© Zits Partnership, Reprinted with Permission of King Features Syndicate, Inc.

What Is Reading Aloud?

Reading aloud is using your voice to speak the words you read. You can read your own words or the words of other writers.

Why Is Reading Aloud Important?

As a writer, reading aloud can

- help you make changes to your writing
- allow you to share your stories with friends and family (even a group of people at the same time!)

As a reader, reading aloud can

- allow you to hear the voice and the style of another writer's work
- allow you to hear the rhythm of words
- allow you to speak lines of dialogue to get a clearer picture of how the character talks

How Do I Do It?

- If you are doing a formal reading, practice reading the text aloud. Reread the text several times until you can read it smoothly.
- When it's your turn to read aloud, speak slowly and clearly. If you're not sure if your pacing (your speed) is right, practice with a friend and ask for feedback.
- Change your voice to fit the punctuation. Pause at the periods. Lift the pitch of your voice at the end of questions. Add energy to your voice at the exclamation points!
- Use facial expressions or hand gestures to entertain your audience.

Group Reading

Divide into small groups and take turns reading your stories to each other. As you are listening:

- Identify the main character
- Understand the conflict
- Recognize dialogue
- Find specific details about the characters or setting

Class Reading

Choose one story from your group to read aloud to the whole class. Have each group member choose a different part of the story to read aloud. You may want to assign each group member to read the dialogue of a different character. Practice reading aloud as a group. Once you each know your parts, read the story aloud to the class. **BQ**

Teach

Analyzing Cartoons Have students look at the cartoon, and invite volunteers to read aloud the words spoken by the characters. **Ask: What advice would you give to the blond guy?** *(Responses will vary.)* **OL**

BQ 

After students read their stories aloud, ask them what they've learned from their classmates' stories that can help them answer the Big Question. Tell them to write their ideas in their Learner's Notebook. **OL**

Reading Fluency

Oral Presentation Have students work in groups of three or more for this activity. Tell them to choose a favorite passage from one of the short stories in this unit; the passage should include dialogue. Have each group prepare an oral reading of the passage. One person will assume the role of narrator, reading everything except the dialogue. Two or more group members will assume the roles of the characters who speak in the passage. Remind those who read the dialogue to try to speak the words as the characters might have spoken them. Have the groups present their readings for the class. **OL**

Objectives

- Write short fictional stories that apply organization methods and contain literary devices and literary elements, with a focus on conflict
- Write dialogue
- Participate in discussions using effective speaking strategies
- Read text with fluency

Determining the Main Idea

Objectives covered in this workshop:
- Identify main ideas and supporting details

Determining the Main Idea and Supporting Details

Why Is It Important

- Understanding the main ideas in a selection helps students comprehend the material better, and the supporting details help to point readers to the main idea.
- Readers can use the details they identify to visualize what is happening in the story, which will improve comprehension.
- When students can clearly distinguish main ideas from supporting details, they will also become better writers. They will better understand the need to add ideas that support and enhance their main ideas.

How to Help Students Get It

- Ask students where they think that they might find the key idea. In their readings of the past, the main idea was often presented as the topic sentence. While this is often the case in informational texts, it's rare to have the main idea clearly stated in fiction.
- Ask students to review an informational article from a previous unit focusing on the author's use of details. They should make a list of the words the author uses to convey details. How do authors do this? Through adjectives, dialogue, and rich descriptions. Focusing on details will also help students in their writing as they incorporate this type of information in their creations.
- Discuss the types of details that an author can use. Focus on sensory details that are common in short stories.
- Ask students to use the details from a text to create visual images, which will help them determine main ideas.

Reading to Answer The Big Question

The Good Samaritan

Mr. Sanchez counts on Rey and his friends to help with yard work; in return, Mr. Sanchez promises that the boys can play basketball and swim in his pool. However, the boys soon find out that they cannot count on Mr. Sanchez's promises. In the end, Rey is forced to decide if he will be someone Mr. Sanchez can count on.

The Brink's Robbery

A group of thieves counted on each other to successfully rob a Brink's headquarters, where cash is stored. Police could not solve the crime until one of the disgruntled "team" members unveiled the entire story.

Workshop Resources

Pacing (Days) Standard	Block	Lesson	Student Materials	Teacher Resources
1		Key Skill Lesson: Determining the Main Idea and Supporting Details	Key Reading Skills Practice English Language Coach	Bellringer Options Transparencies Read Aloud, Think Aloud Transparencies Presentation Plus!
2		"The Good Samaritan"	Literary Analysis Transparencies Glencoe Online Selection Vocabulary Development Academic Vocabulary Development English Language Coach Active Reading Graphic Organizer Literary Analysis StudentWorks Plus Online Student Edition Literature Classics Selection and Unit Assessments	Literary and Text Analysis Transparencies Puzzlemaker Skill Level Up! BookLink 3 Assessment by Learning Objective (Diagnostic and Formative) Interactive Tutor Self-Assessment TeacherWorks Plus
2		"The Brinks Robbery"	Glencoe Online Selection Vocabulary Development Academic Vocabulary Development English Language Coach Active Reading Graphic Organizer Literary Analysis StudentWorks Plus Online Student Edition Literature Classics Selection and Unit Assessments	Literary and Text Analysis Transparencies Puzzlemaker Skill Level Up! BookLink 3 Assessment by Learning Objective (Diagnostic and Formative) Interactive Tutor Self-Assessment TeacherWorks Plus

Keys for Unit Resource

- Blackline Master
- Workbook
- Supplemental Text
- CD-ROM
- DVD
- Transparency
- Web-based
- Fast Files

Level Appropriate Code

AS = Activities for all students
AL = Activities for students working above grade level
OL = Activities for students working at grade level
BL = Activities for students working below grade level
EL = Activities for English language learners

Focus

BELLRINGER Options

Daily Language Practice Transparency

Focus Activity Say: Has anyone ever broken a promise to you? How did you feel? List some words that describe how you felt. *(Possible responses: annoyed, angry, let down, betrayed, deceived)* **AS**

Teach

R Reading Skill

Determining the Main Idea
Ask: How do you make a good guess at the main idea of an article before you begin to read it? *(Possible response: by reading the title and looking at the illustrations)* **OL** You see many ads in a magazine when you're browsing through it. What are the main ideas of some ads that you've seen in magazines recently? *(Possible responses: that a car is fun to drive or gets good gas mileage; that an item of clothing is stylish)* **AS**

READING WORKSHOP 4

Skills Focus

You will practice using these skills when you read the following selections:

- "The Good Samaritan," p. 350
- "The Brink's Robbery," p. 362

Reading

- Determining the main idea

Literature

- Understanding plot: how it works and what it means

Vocabulary

- Understanding synonyms: shades of meaning
- Choosing the right word

Writing/Grammar

- Identifying and using prepositions and interjections

Objectives (pp. 346–347)
Reading Identify main ideas and supporting detailsls

Skill Lesson

Determining the Main Idea

Learn It!

What Is It? The main idea is the most important idea in a paragraph or story. Sometimes a writer tells you the main idea in the text. Sometimes you have to think about the supporting details to find the main idea.

R Use these tips to look for main ideas:

- The main idea is the most important idea in the text.
- The main idea is not a simple fact—it's a big idea that's based on smaller details.
- The main idea does not include specific details.

The future of youth athletics.

Analyzing Cartoons
The main idea is that sports are not just for fun anymore. How do the caption and dialogue help get this message across?

Additional Support

Differentiated Instruction

Reading Cartoons John McPherson's "Close to Home" cartoons appear daily in more than 600 newspapers around the world. Unlike comic strips, which tell a very short story in a few drawings, or panels, "Close to Home" makes its point in one drawing, a single panel. For that reason, it is called a single-panel cartoon.

Most single-panel cartoons—including political cartoons and the type that appear in *The New Yorker*—have one clear main idea. If possible, provide students with other single-panel cartoons and have them identify the main idea of each. **BL**

Why Is It Important? Finding the main idea can help you:

- Break the text into smaller parts you can remember
- Understand what the author is trying to say
- Form your own opinions and ideas as your read

How Do I Do It? Read each paragraph to see what each part of the text is about. Remember that the main ideas of each part will lead you to the main idea for the whole text. Once you've read the whole text, think about the most important ideas of each paragraph. Combine these ideas to find the main idea of the entire selection.

Literature Online

Study Central Visit www.glencoe.com and click on Study Central to review determining the main idea.

Here's an example of how one student figured out one of the main ideas in "Friends Forever."

> Ironically, the fight ended up bringing them closer together. "If it weren't for the fight, we probably wouldn't have become such good friends," says Efrain. These days David and Efrain take their friendship more seriously. "And if we have a fight, we talk about it. Then we laugh about it," says David.

If David and Efrain fight, they talk about it. This paragraph tells me that communication is important between friends. Even when you're angry, communication can bring you and your friends closer together.

Practice It!

Write these statements about the story you are going to read in your Learner's Notebook. As you read, refer back to them. When you have finished reading, circle the one that is most likely a main idea.

- Rey and his friends clean up the yard for Mr. Sanchez.
- It is important to help people—even the people you don't like.
- Rey wants to be friends with Orlando Sanchez.

Use It!

As you read "The Good Samaritan," make notes in your Learner's Notebook about what might be the main idea. When you've finished reading, use your notes to help you circle the correct sentence from above.

Literature Online

Study Central Have students access the Web site to review determining the main idea and to complete a related activity.

R Reading Skill

Determining the Main Idea

Say: The main idea is the author's most important thought about the topic. Knowing the main idea can help you decide which details are more important and which are less important. Suppose that one idea tells you something interesting about the main idea, and another detail tells you something interesting, but it's not about the main idea. Which detail is more important? *(the detail that tells you something about the main idea)* Ask students to look through the book to find a title or illustration that seems to state or suggest a main idea. Have them state the main idea to the class and explain how the title or illustration communicates the idea. **OL**

Resources for page 347

Use Reading Skills Transparency in *Read Aloud, Think Aloud,* Unit 3, to help students practice determining the main idea.

Reading in the Real World

Citizenship Give students examples of letters to the editor from a local newspaper. Point out that most people write to the editor about a specific issue in a story that they read in the paper. Have students discuss the letters in pairs and decide the main idea of each letter. Then have two or three of the main idea statements read aloud. Ask whether all students agree on the main idea of each letter. If they disagree, ask why they disagree. **AS**

In addition, you might want to have students decide the main ideas of editorials in a local newspaper. **AL**

Objectives

- Identify main ideas and supporting details

More About the Author

Speaking of "The Good Samaritan," René Saldaña, Jr., has said: "I'd like young readers to understand that sometimes, whether they like it or not, whether they're doing it with a glad heart or not, sometimes they need to do a kind thing for another, who may or may not be deserving of it. Ultimately, what matters is that we become other-minded instead of self-focused. The adage is true: it is better to give than to receive."

V Vocabulary

True or False Statements

Say: We're going to create some new statements like those in the *Write to Learn* section. Pick two vocabulary words. For each word, write a statement in your Learner's Notebook that will be true or false depending on the meaning of the word. *(Responses will vary.)* After students have written their statements, call on several students to read their statements aloud. Tell whether each statement is true or false. BL EL

Before You Read: The Good Samaritan

Meet the Author

René Saldaña, Jr. grew up in Texas. He has taught middle and high school and has written several books, including *The Jumping Tree,* which won an award for youth novels. Today, he teaches English and writing at a university in Texas.

Literature Online

Author Search For more about René Saldaña, Jr. go to www.glencoe.com.

Objectives (pp. 348–357)
Reading Identify main ideas and supporting details
Literature Identify literary elements: plot
Vocabulary Make word choices • Use word references: thesaurus

Vocabulary Preview

angling (ANG ling) *v.* trying to get; form of the verb *angle* **(p. 352)** *I was angling for a position on student council.*

fuming (FYOO ming) *adj.* angry **(p. 353)** *"I'm no street punk!" Mr. Hernandez said, fuming.*

dejected (dee JEK tud) *adj.* sad or depressed **(p. 354)** *Rey felt dejected when he couldn't swim in the Sánchez's pool.*

ritual (RICH oo ul) *n.* a set routine **(p. 356)** *Rey's father's evening ritual included watching an hour of TV.*

stranded (STRAN dud) *adj.* left somewhere and not able to leave **(p. 357)** *Stranded I stood at the side of the road.*

V

Write to Learn In your Learner's Notebook, copy the statements below. Answer *True* or *False* to each statement.

- If you gave your friend a gift she loved, she would be **fuming.**
- If you just switched schools and hadn't made friends yet, you might feel **dejected.**
- If Mideo brushes his teeth every day as soon as he gets home from school, that's a **ritual.**
- When Elena gets on the bus, she is **stranded.**

English Language Coach

Word Choice Good writers try to choose the best words to express their ideas. To say exactly what they mean, they choose specific words rather than general ones. Notice the difference in the sentences below.

General:	The boy ate a sandwich.
Specific:	Al gulped down a double cheeseburger.

See how much clearer the second sentence is? When you read, notice the specific words the writers use. And when you write, choose specific words.

Partner Talk With a partner, choose a more specific word to take the place of each general word below:

tree **automobile** **walked** **talk**

Additional Support

Literature Online

Author Search To expand students' appreciation of René Saldaña, Jr., have them access the Web site for additional information and resources.

Literature Focus Lesson

Conflict Remind students that conflict is the basis of every literary plot. Ask them to suggest conflicts—or struggles—that they have seen in movies or on television shows.

- between two characters
- between a character and a natural occurrence, such as a storm
- within a character, such as a person's struggle with his or her conscience

Alert students to the fact that they will see two major conflicts in "The Good Samaritan." They should watch for

- a conflict between Rey and another character
- a conflict within Rey AS

Skills Preview

Key Reading Skill: Determining the Main Idea

- What do Rey and his friends do for Mr. Sánchez?
- What does Mr. Sánchez promise Rey and his friends?
- Does Mr. Sánchez keep his promises?
- How does Rey feel about Mr. Sánchez?
- What does Rey do when Mr. Sánchez is really counting on him?

Partner Talk If someone you didn't like very much really needed your help, would you help that person? Share your thoughts and experiences with a partner.

Key Literary Element: Plot

In a story, the **plot** is all the events that happen. The plot is organized around the story's **conflict.**

- The plot of a story begins with the **exposition** (ek spuh ZIH shun), which introduces the characters, setting, and conflict of the story.
- The **rising action** adds complications to the conflict. It includes all of the events that lead to the **climax.** L
- The **climax** is the point of the greatest interest or suspense in a story.
- The **falling action** is all of the events that happen after the climax.
- The **resolution** is the conclusion to the story, or the ending.

Partner Talk Every story has a plot—even the stories in movies. Talk with a partner about the action, or conflict, that happens in your favorite movie. Then summarize that movie's plot.

Literature Online

Interactive Literary Elements Handbook
To review or learn more about the literary elements, go to www.glencoe.com.

Get Ready to Read

Connect to the Reading

Think about a time when someone promised you something, but did not give it to you. How did it make you feel? How did you react? Why did you react in that way?

Write to Learn In your Learner's Notebook, write about how you felt when someone did not keep a promise they made to you. Write about how you acted and explain why.

Build Background

The story you are about to read is called "The Good Samaritan."

- This story takes place in the southern part of Texas during the present.
- The term "Good Samaritan" refers to someone who helps a person in trouble, even if he or she does not like that person or that person has treated them unfairly.
- The term "Good Samaritan" comes from a story about a man who comes to the aid of an injured stranger.

Set Purposes for Reading

Read "The Good Samaritan" to learn about how a young man acts toward someone who has broken promises to him. The young man's behavior just might surprise you.

Set Your Own Purpose What would you like to learn from the selection to help you answer the Big Question? Write your own purpose on a note card and put the card in the left pocket of Foldable 3.

Keep Moving

Use these skills as you read the following selection.

Teach

L Literary Element

Plot Say: As you read "The Good Samaritan," keep track of the development of the plot. In your Learner's Notebook, list the five plot stages from the Key Literary Element section of the Skills Preview. Then, as you read, jot down the numbers of the pages where each stage of the plot occurs. *(Exposition: 350–351; rising action: 351–355; climax: 355-357; falling action: 357; resolution: 357)* OL

CheckPoint

Use the CheckPoint questions provided on Presentation Plus! to check for prior knowledge and to build background. These questions can be used with interactive response keypads for immediate student feedback.

Literature Online

Interactive Literary Elements Handbook Have students access the Web site to improve their understanding of plot.

English Language Coach

General and Specific Words

Introduce students to the use of a web diagram to connect specific words with a general term. Begin with a general term, such as *talk,* in the center of the diagram. Then illustrate a more specific kind of talk in one of the ovals in the web. Invite students to contribute other specific words for kinds of talk. OL EL

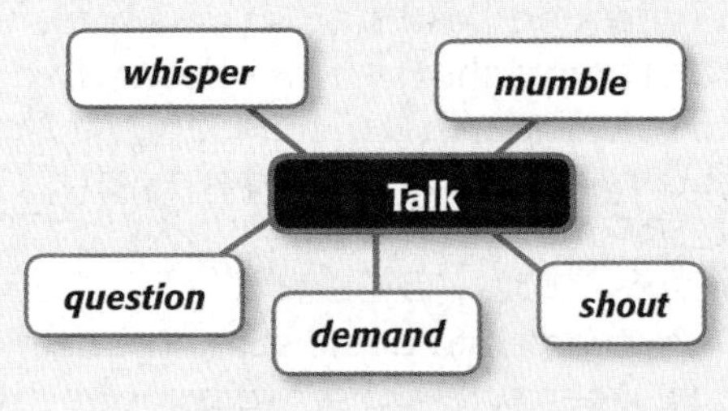

Objectives

- Identify main ideas and supporting details
- Identify literary elements: plot
- Make word choices
- Use word references: thesaurus

Teach

Viewing the Illustration

Say: Think about the main Idea and details in this painting by Reynard Milici. List some of the details that catch your eye. *(Responses may include the fountain, artificial birds, gnome, pinwheel, flags, sign.)* **Ask:** The title that Milici gave the painting is *Welcome.* Do you think that title states the main idea? *(Responses will vary.)* How would you state the main idea? *(Responses will vary.)* AS

EL Language Coach

Idiomatic Phrases Many verbs that consist of a main verb and a secondary part that resembles a preposition appear on this page: *come over, hang out, dressed up,* and *come by.* **Say:** What does Orlie mean when he says that he and Rey will "hang out" by the pool? *(Students may note that this means to spend time together.)* Follow a similar procedure with the other two-part verbs. EL OL

Readability Scores
Dale-Chall: 4.6
DRP: 48
Lexile: 730

Welcome, 1991, Reynard Milici, Louis K. Meisel Gallery.

The Good Samaritan

by René Saldaña, Jr.

I know he's in there, I thought. I saw the curtains of his bedroom move, only a little, yes, but they moved.

Yesterday Orlie told me, "Come over tomorrow afternoon. We'll hang out by the pool." EL

I rang the doorbell again. Then I knocked.

The door creaked open. The afternoon light crept into the dark living room inch by slow inch. Mrs. Sánchez, Orlie's mom, stuck her head through the narrow opening, her body hidden behind the door. "Hi, Rey, how can I help you?"

"Ah, Mrs. Sánchez, is Orlando here?" I tried looking past her but only saw a few pictures hanging on the wall. One of the Sánchez family all dressed up fancy and smiling, standing in front of a gray marble background.

"No, he's not. He went with his father to Mission."

"Oh, because Orlando said he would be here, and told me to come over."

"They won't be back until later tonight," she said. "You can come by tomorrow and see if he's here. You know how it is in the summer. He and his dad are always doing work here and there. Come back tomorrow, but call first." **1**

"It's just that he said I could come by and swim in your pool. Dijo,[1] 'Tomorrow, come over. I'll be here. We'll go swimming.'"

1. ***Dijo*** (DEE hoh) is Spanish for "he said." *Me dijo* means "said to me."

Practice the Skills

1 Reviewing Skills

Inferring What can you guess from these first paragraphs? Is Mrs. Sánchez telling the truth or is Orlando avoiding Rey?

Additional Support

Literature Focus Lesson

Figurative Language Draw students' attention to the narrator's description of the afternoon light in the fourth paragraph:

The afternoon light crept into the dark living room inch by slow inch.

Ask students to name some living things that creep. *(Responses may include cats, mice, and lions.)* Ask students what they think the narrator means by saying that the light crept into the room. *(That it came in slowly, like a creeping animal.)*

Tell students that language used to express the way things seem to a person is called figurative language. OL

"I'm sorry he told you that, but without him or my husband here, you won't be able to use the pool," me dijo Mrs. Sánchez.

"Okay," I said.

"Maybe tomorrow?"

"Yeah, maybe."

But there was no maybe about it. I wouldn't be coming back. Because I knew that Orlando was in the house, he just didn't want to hang out. Bien codo con su pool.[2] Plain stingy. And tricky. This guy invited me and a few others over all summer to help his dad with some yard work because Mr. Sánchez told us, "If you help clean up the yard, you boys can use the pool any time you want so long as one of us is here." And we cleaned up his yard. On that hot day the water that smelled of chlorine looked delicious to me. And after a hard day's work cleaning his yard, I so looked forward to taking a dip. I'd even worn my trunks under my work clothes. Then Mr. Sánchez said, "Come by tomorrow. I don't want you fellas to track all this dirt into the pool."

"We can go home and shower and be back," said Hernando.

"No, mejor que regresen mañana.[3] I'll be here tomorrow and we can swim. After lunch, okay. For sure we'll do it tomorrow," said Mr. Sánchez.

The following day he was there, but he was headed out right after lunch and he didn't feel safe leaving us behind without supervision. "If one of you drowns, your parents will be angry at me and . . ." He didn't say it, but he didn't need to. One of our parents could sue him. And he needed that like I needed another F in my Geometry I class! Or, we figured out later, he could have just said, "I used you saps to do my dirty work. And I lied about the pool, suckers!" **2**

I don't know why we hadn't learned our lesson. Twice before he had gypped us this way of our time and effort. Always dangling the carrot in front of our eyes, then snatching it away last second. **3** **EL**

One of those times he promised us soft drinks and snacks if we helped clean up a yard across the street from his house. It wasn't his yard to worry about, but I guess he just didn't

2. ***Bien*** (bee EN) ***codo*** (KOH doh) ***con*** (kohn) ***su*** (soo). Rey is saying, in Spanish, that Orlando doesn't like to share the pool with others.

3. ***Mejor*** (may HOR) ***que*** (kay) ***regresen*** (ray GRES un) ***mañana*** (muh NYAW nuh). "It's better if you return tomorrow."

Practice the Skills

2 Key Reading Skill

Determining the Main Idea One way to find the main idea is to summarize. Think about the important things that have happened so far. You might summarize what you've just read like this: *Rey's friend Orlando Sánchez told Rey he could come over and swim. Orlando breaks his promise. Rey remembers another time when someone in the Sánchez family broke a promise.*

3 Key Literary Element

Plot At this point the author has described the setting of the story. He has also introduced all the main characters and a conflict. What part of the plot is that?

Teach

EL Language Coach

Figurative Language
Say: Notice what the narrator says about the way Mr. Sánchez treats him and his friends. This is an example of figurative language. It doesn't tell what Mr. Sánchez actually does. It tells how his actions seem to the narrator.
Ask: What do you think the narrator means by that statement? *(Mr. Sánchez is always promising something good but never delivers on his promise.)* **EL** **OL**

L Literary Element

Review Character **Ask:** From what you know so far, what is Rey like? *(He seems cooperative, maybe he's a bit too trusting, and he's becoming disillusioned and annoyed.)* **AS** How do we learn what Rey is like? *(From what he does, from what he tells us, and by inferring his attitudes.)* **AL**

Literature Focus Lesson

Character Explain that an author can use several methods to let a reader know what a character is like, including

- what the character says
- what the character does
- what others say about the character
- how others behave toward the character

Have students suggest examples of each method of characterization that they have seen so far for Rey and Mr. Sánchez. Urge them to continue looking for examples of each method as they read the rest of the story. **OL**

Objectives

- Interpret figurative language
- Determine the main idea
- Understand plot
- Understand characterization

READING WORKSHOP 4

Teach

Viewing the Illustration

Say: Look at the illustration and remind yourself of what Rey says about a carrot.
Ask: What does the dangling carrot represent? *(The promises that Mr. Sánchez makes to get Rey and his friends to work for him.)*
Say: As you read this page, look for the "carrot" that Mr. Sánchez dangles this time.
Ask: What "carrot" does Mr. Sánchez offer in return for digging the holes? *(the right to use the basketball court)* **AS**

R1 Reading Skill

Review Inferring Ask: How do Rey and his friends feel about the basketball court? Put yourself in Rey's shoes and freewrite about your feelings. Then imagine that Rey decides to tell Mr. Sánchez how he and his friends feel about the court. Write the dialogue that Rey might speak. *(Responses will vary.)* **AL**

R2 Reading Skill

Review Drawing Conclusions Ask: What can you conclude about Rey and his friends as workers? *(They are willing to work hard for a promised reward.)* **AL**

like to see the weeds growing as tall as dogs. What if he had company? What would they think? And he was **angling** for a position on the school board. How could a politico[4] live in such **filth**! **4**

Well, we did get a soft drink and chips, only it was one two-liter bottle of Coke and one bag of chips for close to ten of us. We had no cups, and the older, stronger boys got dibs[5] on most of the eats. "I didn't know there'd be so many of you," he said. "Well, share. And thanks. You all are good, strong boys."

The next time was real hard labor. He said, "Help me dig these holes here, then we can put up some basketball rims. Once the cement dries on the court itself, you all can come over and play anytime since it's kind of your court too. That is, if you help me dig the holes."

And we did. We dug and dug and dug for close to six hours straight until we got done, passing on the shovel from one of us to the next. But we got it done. We had our court. Mr. Sánchez kept his word. He reminded us we could come **R1** over to play anytime, and we took special care not to dunk **R2** and grab hold of the rim. Even the shortest kid could practically dunk it because the baskets were so low. But we'd seen the rims all bent down at the different yards at school. And we didn't want that for *our* court.

One day, we wanted to play a little three on three. After knocking on the different doors several times and getting no answer, we figured the Sánchez family had gone out.

4. A ***politico*** is a politician.
5. ***Got dibs*** means you get to do or have something before everyone else.

Vocabulary

angling (ANG ling) *v.* trying to get

Practice the Skills

4 English Language Coach

Word Choice If you don't know the word **filth**, look it up in a dictionary or thesaurus. Do you think it's a good word choice here?

Additional Support

English Language Coach

Synonyms and Antonyms Rey is exaggerating when he refers to the weedy lot as "filth." Invite students to suggest words that mean the same, or nearly the same, as *filth. (Responses may include* dirt, mud, slime, muck, *and* grime.*)* Point out that these words are all synonyms—words with nearly the same meaning. Then ask students to suggest words that mean the opposite of *filth.* Point out that these words are all antonyms of *filth.*

Have students list synonyms and antonyms for these other words that appear on page 352 (tall, strong, low). **BL** **EL**

We decided that it'd be okay to play. We weren't going to do anything wrong. The court was far enough from the house that we couldn't possibly break a window. And Mr. Sánchez had said we could come over any time we wanted. It was *our* court, after all. Those were his words exactly.

A little later in the afternoon, Mr. Sánchez drove up in his truck, honking and honking at us. "Here they come. Maybe Orlando and Marty can play with us," someone said.

Pues,[6] it was not to be. The truck had just come to a standstill when Mr. Sánchez shot out of the driver's side. He ran up to us, waving his hands in the air like a crazy man, first saying, then screaming, "What are you guys doing here? You all can't be here when I'm not here."

"But you told us we could come over anytime. And we knocked and knocked, and we were being very careful."

"It doesn't matter. You all shouldn't be here when I'm not home. What if you had broken something?" he said.

"But we didn't," I said.

"But if you had, then who would have been responsible for paying to replace it? I'm sure every one of you would have denied breaking anything."

"Este vato![7]" said Hernando.

"Vato? Is that what you called me? I'm no street punk, no hoodlum. I'll have you know, I've worked my whole life, and I won't be called a vato. It's Mr. Sánchez. Got that? And you boys know what—from now on, you are not allowed to come here whether I'm home or not! You all messed it up for yourselves. You've shown me so much disrespect today you don't deserve to play on my court. It was a privilege and not a right, and you messed it up. Now leave!" **5** **EL**

Hernando, who was **fuming**, said, "Orale, guys, let's go." He took the ball from one of the smaller boys and began to run toward the nearest basket. He slowed down the closer he came to the basket and leapt in the air. I'd never seen him jump with such grace. He floated from the foul line, his long

6. ***Pues*** (pways) means "well."

7. The word ***vato*** (VAW toh) is Mexican-Spanish slang. It is used by young people most often when speaking to or about each other. It means "dude." ***Este vato*** means "this dude." **R**

Vocabulary

fuming (FYOO ming) *adj.* angry

Practice the Skills

5 Key Literary Element

Plot The author has added more details. Now the story and the conflict are more complicated. What part of the plot is this?

Literature Focus Lesson

Dialogue Dialogue is simply anything that a character says in a short story. However, effective dialogue contributes to the story by

- advancing the plot
- developing the character

In a well-written short story, each character sounds like an individual. The reader can tell one character from another even when the speaker isn't identified. On this page, the speaker of the line "But you told us we could come over anytime" isn't identified. Have students discuss who seems most likely to have spoken that line and what makes it possible for them to tell. **AL**

READING WORKSHOP 4

Teach

EL Language Coach

Word Choice Say: When Mr. Sánchez sends the boys away, he tells them that they don't deserve to play on his basketball court. He says that playing there is a *privilege* and not a *right.* He makes a strong distinction between these two words. What is the difference between a privilege and a right? *(A right is something that belongs to a person legally or morally. A privilege is something given to a person with certain conditions.)* **EL** **OL**

R Reading Skill

Review Inferring Ask: According to the footnote on this page, *este vato* means "this dude." Why is Mr. Sánchez offended when Hernando calls him this name? *(Possible response: Mr. Sánchez recognizes that, by using a term meant to refer to a peer, Hernando meant it as an insult.)* **OL**

BQ

Ask: At this point in the story, what do you think Rey would say about whether Mr. Sánchez can be counted on? *(Responses will vary, but most will likely agree that Rey now feels that Mr. Sánchez cannot be counted on.)* **AS**

Objectives

- Understand plot
- Make inferences
- Understand dialogue

Teach

EL Language Coach

Synonyms and Antonyms
Say: Notice that the word *dejected* is defined at the bottom of the page as "sad or depressed." Those are synonyms for *dejected.* What are some other synonyms for *dejected*? *(gloomy, discouraged, low, despondent)* What are some antonyms for *dejected*? *(happy, elated, glad, cheerful, pleased)* EL OL

L Literary Element

Review Character Ask: What does Hernando do before he and the rest of the group leave the basketball court? *(He hangs from the rim.)* What do you learn about Hernando from what he does? *(Hernando has become very angry with Mr. Sánchez.)* AS

C Critical Thinking

Analysis Ask: Do you think that Rey will stick to his decision never to go back to the Sánchezes'? *(Responses will vary.)* Why or why not? *(The way he and his friends have been treated might keep him away; however, the pool and the basketball court might tempt him to go back.)* AS

READING WORKSHOP 4

hair like wings, all the way to the basket. He grabbed the ball in both his hands and let go of it at the last moment. Instead of dunking the ball, he let it shoot up to the sky; then he wrapped his fingers around the rim and pulled down as hard as he could, hanging on for a few seconds. Then the rest of us walked after him, **dejected**. He hadn't bent the rim even a millimeter. Eventually Orlie talked us into going back when his dad wasn't home. His baby brother, Marty, was small and slow, and Orlie wanted some competition on the court. 6

Today was it for me, though. I made up my mind never to go back to the Sánchezes'. I walked to the little store for a soda. That and a grape popsicle would cool me down. I sat on the bench outside, finished off the drink, returned the bottle for my nickel refund, and headed for home.

As soon as I walked through our front door, my mother said, "Mi'jo,[8] you need to go pick up your brother at summer school. He missed the bus."

"Again? He probably missed it on purpose, 'Amá.[9] He's always walking over to Leo's Grocery to talk to his little girlfriends, then he calls when he needs a ride." I turned toward the bedroom.

8. ***Mi'jo*** (MEE hoh) is a contraction of the Spanish for "my son."
9. ***'Amá*** (uh MAW) is a shortened form of "Mama."

Vocabulary

dejected (dee JEK tud) *adj.* sad or depressed EL

Practice the Skills

6 Reviewing Skills

Connecting Rey and his friends think they had something taken away from them unfairly. Do you understand how they feel when they leave the court? In your Learner's Notebook, write about how you think they feel.

Additional Support

English Language Coach

Choosing the Right Word Point out that the word *walked* (or *walking)* appears four times on page 354. Have students find each occurrence of the word. Then have them suggest words that name different ways of walking, such as trudge, march, stroll, or saunter. List as many words for ways of walking as the students can suggest in a couple of minutes.

Then challenge students to rewrite each sentence on page 354 that uses *walked,* substituting what they consider a better verb choice. AS

READING WORKSHOP 4

"Come back here," she said. So I turned and took a seat at the table. "Have you forgotten the times we had to go pick you up? Your brother always went with us, no matter what time it was." **C**

"Yeah, but I was doing school stuff. Football, band. He's in summer school just piddling his time away!"

She looked at me as she brushed sweat away from her face with the back of her hand and said, "Just go pick him up, and hurry home. On the way back, stop at Circle Seven and buy some tortillas. There's money on the table."

I shook my head in disgust. Here I was, already a senior, having to be my baby brother's chauffeur.

I'd driven halfway to Leo's Grocery when I saw Mr. Sánchez's truck up ahead by the side of the road. I could just make him out sitting under the shade of his truck. Every time he heard a car coming his way, he'd raise his head slightly, try to catch the driver's attention by staring at him, then he'd hang his head again when the car didn't stop. **7**

I slowed down as I approached. Could he tell it was me driving? When he looked up at my car, I could swear he almost smiled, thinking he had been saved. He had been leaning his head between his bent knees, and I could tell he was tired; his white shirt stuck to him because of all the sweat. His sock on one leg was bunched up at his ankle like a carnation.[10] He had the whitest legs I'd ever seen on a Mexican. Whiter than even my dad's. I kept on looking straight; that is, I made like I was looking ahead, not a care in the world, but out of the corner of my eye I saw that he had a flat tire, that he had gotten two of the lug nuts off but hadn't gotten to the others, that the crowbar lay half on his other foot and half on the ground beside him, that his hair was matted by sweat to his forehead. **8** **R**

Visual Vocabulary
A ***lug nut*** is a piece of metal with a threaded hole in the middle that goes on the end of a bolt to hold a wheel in place.

I knew that look. I'd probably looked just like that digging those holes for *our* basketball court, cleaning up his yard and the one across the street from his house. I wondered if he could use a cold two-liter Coke right about now! If he was dreaming of taking a dip in his pool!

10. A ***carnation*** is a flower with many petals.

Practice the Skills

7 Reviewing Skills

Conflict The author is about to introduce a new conflict. This one is an internal conflict. Rey will have to decide whether to help Mr. Sánchez. Will he? Why or why not?

8 English Language Coach

Word Choice Did you notice the specific word choices that give the reader a clear description of Mr. Sánchez? In your Learner's Notebook, copy at least three of those words or phrases from this paragraph.

Teach

C Critical Thinking

Evaluation Ask: How would you describe Rey's attitude when his mother asks him to pick his brother up? *(Possible response: He seems annoyed.)* What do you think might be making him have that attitude? *(His anger over the way Mr. Sánchez has treated him may be making him annoyed.)* **OL**

R Reading Skill

Determining the Main Idea
Say: Look at the paragraph that begins "I slowed down as I approached." This is the paragraph in which Rey—the narrator—describes Mr. Sánchez. The main idea is that Mr. Sánchez is hot and tired. What details show that he is hot? *(His white shirt sticking to him because of his sweat; his hair matted by sweat to his forehead.)* What details show that he is tired? *(Leaning his head between his bent knees; he had only two lug nuts off.)* **OL**

Reading in the Real World

Citizenship On the chalkboard, draw six concentric circles like the ones here and label them like the example. Tell students that each of us belongs to many groups, such as the ones represented on the board. Belonging to a group gives a person certain rights and privileges and certain responsibilities. Have students discuss Rey's responsibilities as a member of his family. Then have students discuss the responsibilities he might have as a member of his community. **AS**

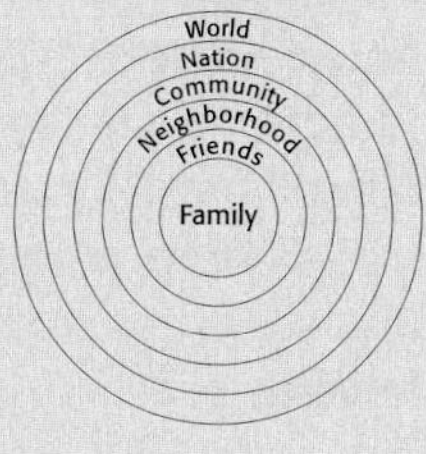

Objectives
- Make evaluations
- Identify details that support main idea
- Understand characterization
- Choose precise words
- Connect personal experience with text

READING WORKSHOP 4

Teach

R Reading Skill

Review Synthesizing Say: As he drives on, Rey does a lot of thinking. Many thoughts go through his mind. Make a web diagram to show the full range of his thoughts. OL

Why should I help him?
I won't help him.
I'll be off the hook.
Let him melt.
REY'S THOUGHTS
Someone else will stop.
I'll think of something to say.
He'll mention this to my dad.

EL Language Coach

Idiomatic Phrases Students may need help understanding certain phrases, such as "dirty work," "off the hook," and "extend a helping hand." **Say:** What does the narrator mean when he says, "Let him do his own dirty work for once"? *(Let him do a difficult job without help.)* What does the narrator mean when he says, "I'd be off the hook"? *(He would no longer be in a bad situation, like a fish that has been released from a hook.)* OL EL

I drove on. No way was I going to help him out again! Let him do his own dirty work for once. He could stay out there and melt in this heat for all I cared. And besides, someone else will stop, I thought. Someone who doesn't know him like I do. 9

And I knew that when Mr. Sánchez got home, he'd stop at my house on his walk around the barrio.[11] My dad would be watering the plants, his evening **ritual** to relax from a hard day at work, and Mr. Sánchez would mention in passing that I had probably not seen him by the side of the road so I hadn't stopped to help him out; "Kids today," he would say to my dad, "not a care in the world, their heads up in the clouds somewhere." My dad would call me out and ask me to tell him and Mr. Sánchez why I hadn't helped out a neighbor when he needed it most. I'd say, to both of them, "That was you? I thought you and Orlie were in Mission taking care of some business, so it never occurred to me to stop to help a neighbor. Geez, I'm so sorry." Or I could say, "You know, I was in such a hurry to pick up my brother in La Joya[12] that I didn't even notice you by the side of the road."

I'd be off the hook. Anyways, why should I be the one to extend a helping hand when he's done every one of us in the

11. A ***barrio*** (BAR ee oh) is a neighborhood where Spanish-speaking people live.

12. ***La Joya*** (luh HOY uh) is a town in southern Texas.

Vocabulary

ritual (RICH oo ul) *n.* a set routine

EL Practice the Skills

9 Reviewing Skills

Reviewing Think back to what Rey has done for Mr. Sánchez in the past. Why doesn't he want to help him now?

Additional Support

Reading Fluency

Build Fluency Rey thinks of two things that he might say if Mr. Sánchez tells his father that he passed by without helping him. If he is going to say either of them in a way that seems natural, he's going to have to practice. Put yourself in his shoes and practice what Rey thinks of saying. It will help to work with a partner and take turns portraying Rey's father and Rey himself. Practice until your reading of Rey's statements sounds like natural speech. AS barrio wrong in one way or another! He deserves to sweat a little. A taste of his own bad medicine. Maybe he'll learn a lesson.

But I remembered the look in his eyes as I drove past him. That same tired look my father had when he'd get home from work and he didn't have the strength to take off his boots. My father always looked like he'd been working for centuries without any rest. He'd sit there in front of the television on his favorite green vinyl sofa chair and stare at whatever was on TV. He'd sit there for an hour before he could move, before he could eat his supper and take his shower, that same look on his face Mr. Sánchez had just now.

What if this were my dad **stranded** on the side of the road? I'd want someone to stop for him. EL

"My one good deed for today," I told myself. "And I'm doing it for my dad really, not for Mr. Sánchez."

I made a U-turn, drove back to where he was still sitting, turned around again, and pulled up behind him. **10**

"I thought that was you, Rey," he said. He wiped at his forehead with his shirtsleeve. "And when you drove past, I thought you hadn't seen me. Thank goodness you stopped. I've been here for close to forty-five minutes and nobody's stopped to help. Thank goodness you did. I just can't get the tire off."

Thank my father, I thought. If it weren't for my father, you'd still be out here.

I had that tire changed in no time. All the while Mr. Sánchez stood behind me and a bit to my left saying, "Yes, thank God you came by. Boy, it's hot out here. You're a good boy, Rey. You'll make a good man. How about some help there?" **11** **12**

"No, I've got it," I answered. "I'm almost done."

"Oyes,[13] Rey, what if you come over tomorrow night to my house? I'm having a little barbecue for some important people here in town. You should come over. We're even going to do some swimming. What do you say?"

I tightened the last of the nuts, replaced the jack, the flat tire, and the crowbar in the bed of his truck, looked at him, and said, "Thanks. But I'll be playing football with the vatos." **13** ❍

13. ***Oyes*** (OH yays) means "listen."

Vocabulary

stranded (STRAN dud) *adj.* left somewhere and not able to leave

Practice the Skills

10 Key Literary Element

Plot The story has reached its climax when Rey decides to help Mr. Sánchez. What makes this the climax of the story?

11 Key Reading Skill

Determining the Main Idea Rey helps Mr. Sánchez even though he's angry with him. Why? What does Rey's decision to help tell you about Rey? What does it tell you about the story's main idea?

12 Key Literary Element

Plot This is the end of the story, or the resolution. Do you think this was a good resolution to "The Good Samaritan"? Why or why not?

13 BIG Question

BQ Mr. Sánchez could count on Rey. Who can Rey count on? Put your answer on a note card in the center pocket of Foldable 3. Your response will help you complete the Unit Challenge later.

READING WORKSHOP 4

Teach

EL Language Coach

Word Choice Say: Look at the sentence, *What if this were my dad stranded on the side of the road?* Can you think of a word that could replace the word *stranded*? *(Students may suggest* sitting, stuck, alone, abandoned, deserted, *or* struggling.*)* Which of those would not be as effective as *stranded* in this sentence? Why? *(Responses will vary.)* Does one of the other words seem like a better choice than *stranded*? Why? *(Responses will vary.)* **AS**

BQ 

Ask: Which of these characters in the story can be counted on?

- Mr. Sánchez
- Rey's mother
- Rey's father
- Rey

For each character, explain why you answered as you did. **AS**

Assess

Use the CheckPoint questions provided on Presentation Plus! to check students' mastery of the selection. These questions can be used with interactive response keypads for immediate student feedback.

Differentiated Instruction

Dramatization Some students may benefit from dramatizing scenes from the story. Possibilities include

- the opening scene, in which Rey is told that he can't use the pool (pages 350–351)
- the scene in which Mr. Sánchez returns home to find Rey and his friends playing basketball (page 353)
- the final scene, in which Rey changes Mr. Sánchez's tire for him (this page)

Students might discuss ways to communicate Rey's thoughts to the audience, either by turning some of his thoughts into new dialogue or by having him speak his thoughts directly to the audience. **OL**

Objectives

- Understand plot
- Understand word choice
- Determine the main idea
- Understand similarities and differences between literary genres

Assess

Resources for page 358

- Selection Quick Check
- Selection and Unit Assessment
- ExamView Assessment Suite
- Interactive Tutor: Self-Assessment

Students can respond to the *After You Read* items in their Learner's Notebook or on separate sheets of paper.

Answering the

1. Responses will vary.
2. Rey is going to pick up his brother from summer school.
3. Rey thought about passing by without helping, about whether someone else would help, about what his father would think if Mr. Sánchez mentioned that he had passed him by, about how he'd answer, and about how he would feel if his dad were stranded on the side of the road.

Critical Thinking

4. He might have thought Mr. Sánchez was no better than a street punk.
5. Yes. Rey's father seems hardworking and reliable.
6. They seem to respect each other. Rey knows that his father works hard, and he feels compassion for him when he returns in the evening, tired from a day's work.

After You Read

The Good Samaritan

Answering the 

1. Why is it important to be a person that others can count on?
2. **Recall** Where is Rey going when he sees Mr. Sánchez by the side of the road?
   TIP Right There
3. **Summarize** What does Rey think about between the time he sees Mr. Sánchez on the side of the road and the time he stops to help him?
   TIP Think and Search

Critical Thinking

4. **Infer** Why might Hernando call Mr. Sánchez *vato*?
   TIP Author and Me
5. **Evaluate** Do you think you could count on Rey's father? Why or why not?
   TIP Author and Me
6. **Evaluate** What type of relationship do you think Rey and his father have?
   TIP Author and Me

Write About Your Reading

Imagine that Rey has finished high school and is applying to college. The college wants a letter from someone who knows Rey and can describe him. Rey asks you to write the letter for him since you know a lot about him from reading "The Good Samaritan."

Get ready to write a letter to the people at the college telling them about Rey's experience with Mr. Sánchez and Rey's decision to be a "Good Samaritan." Refer to Mr. Sánchez as Mr. Smith to protect his identity. Follow the steps below.

Step 1: Write a list of the important things that happened between Rey and Mr. Sánchez and include details.

Step 2: Decide what you would like to tell the college about Rey.

Step 3: Write notes in your Learner's Notebook about your ideas. Use details from the story to support your ideas.

Objectives (pp. 358–359)
Reading Identify main ideas and supporting details
Literature Identify literary elements: plot
Vocabulary Make word choices • Use word references: thesaurus
Writing Write a letter: anecdotes, character, main idea and supporting details
Grammar Use prepositions

Write About Your Reading

Possible response:
Rey is a young man you can trust. Let me tell you how I know that. In our neighborhood, there was a man I'll call Mr. Smith. He got young people to work for him by promising rewards. Rey and his friends worked for him several times, and they did the work well. However, Mr. Smith always found ways to go back on his promises. Some of the young people became angry with Mr. Smith, but Rey was different. Once when he saw Mr. Smith at the side of a road, struggling with a flat tire, he decided that he could not pass him by even though Mr. Smith had treated him badly. Rey helped him, as a true Good Samaritan, a person you can depend on.

Skills Review

Key Reading Skill: Determining the Main Idea

7. Think about what happened in "The Good Samaritan." Look at the notes you made in your Learner's Notebook. What is the main idea?

Key Literary Element: Plot

8. Name two events in the story that affect the way Rey feels about Mr. Sánchez.
9. The story's climax happens when Rey decides to help Mr. Sánchez change his flat tire. Why does Rey decide to help?
10. Describe the story's resolution. What does Mr. Sánchez offer Rey after Rey changes the tire? How is Rey's response different from what it might have been at the beginning of the story?

Vocabulary Check

Rewrite each sentence, replacing the underlined word or words with a vocabulary word.

angling fuming dejected ritual stranded

11. I felt <u>sad</u> when I failed the science test.
12. My brother acts nice because he is <u>aiming</u> to get a bicycle from my mom.
13. For me, a shower is a morning <u>tradition</u>.
14. A flat tire left me <u>stuck</u> on the lonely road.
15. My dad was <u>really angry</u> when I got home late.
16. **English Language Coach** Copy each sentence and substitute a more specific word of your choice for each underlined general word.
    - The car <u>went</u> down the highway.
    - My teacher <u>looked</u> at me.

Web Activities For eFlashcards, Selection Quick Checks, and other Web activities, go to www.glencoe.com.

Grammar Link: Prepositions

A preposition is a word that connects a noun or a pronoun to another word in a sentence.

- The girl <u>on</u> the swing looks sad.

The word *on* is a preposition. It shows the relationship between the word *swing* and the word *girl*. Is the girl behind the swing? Below it? Next to it? No, the preposition tells you she's *on* it.

A preposition is always part of a prepositional phrase that contains a noun or pronoun. These phrases are modifiers that work like adjectives or adverbs to provide more information.

- The man <u>behind us</u> muttered <u>under his breath</u>.
- The deer <u>in the woods</u> walked <u>past them</u>.

Here are some common prepositions:

about	**behind**	**down**	**from**	**near**
above	**below**	**during**	**in**	**of**
across	**by**	**for**	**into**	**through**

Some prepositions, such as *in front of*, *along with* and *on top of* are called "compound prepositions" because they are made up of more than one word.

Grammar Practice

Copy the prepositional phrase or phrases from each sentence below.

17. The ducks swam across the pond.
18. Carlos walked into the music store.
19. We ate during the game.
20. The story was about a boy from a faraway land.
21. Odalis drew a picture for her friend Oksana.
22. Alverne was the author of many funny stories.

Writing Application Look back at the prewriting you did for a letter to Rey's college. Underline all the prepositional phrases you used. Add one more prepositional phrase to your letter.

Skills Review

Key Reading Skill: Determining the Main Idea

7. It is important to give help to people who need it—even people you don't like.

Key Literary Element: Plot

8. Examples: Mr. Sánchez's saying that Rey and his friends could swim, but then not allowing it, and Mr. Sánchez's sending the boys away when he finds them playing basketball.
9. Rey decides to help Mr. Sánchez mainly because he would want someone to stop and help his father.
10. Mr. Sánchez offers Rey an invitation to a barbecue. Earlier, Rey might have accepted, but now he doesn't want anything from Mr. Sánchez.

Close

Ask students to use their responses to questions 9 and 10 to help them answer the Big Question.

Literature Online

Web Activities Have students access the Web site for interactive activities that will help them assess their understanding of the selection.

Vocabulary Check

11. dejected
12. angling
13. ritual
14. stranded
15. fuming
16. Examples: The car raced down the highway. My teacher stared at me.

Grammar Link: Prepositions

Grammar Practice

17. across the pond
18. into the music store
19. during the game
20. about a boy; from a faraway land
21. for her friend Oksana
22. of many funny stories

Before You Read The Brink's Robbery

More About the Authors

Henry and Melissa Billings live in Lebanon, New Hampshire, where they raised their five children. Melissa says, "We enjoy skiing, biking, and other outdoor activities. We also volunteer our time with various community services and events."

Melissa Billings has more than 20 years of experience as a freelance journalist and writer of short stories and educational materials.

Henry Billings spent 15 years as a public school teacher and has more than 25 years of experience as a freelance journalist and writer of trade books and educational materials.

V Vocabulary

Definition Sentences Say: Notice that the page number where each vocabulary word appears is included in the definition. Find each vocabulary word in the story. When you find the sentence with the word in it, copy that sentence in your Learner's Notebook, but replace the word with its definition. BL EL

Meet the Authors

Henry and Melissa Billings have both been writers and editors for the last twenty years. They write a lot of educational texts for students, and Henry used to teach. They are also journalists. The selection you are about to read comes from their collection, *The Wild Side: Crime and Punishment.*

Author Search For more about Henry and Melissa Billings, go to www.glencoe.com.

Objectives (pp. 360–365)
Reading Identify main ideas and supporting details
Literature Identify literary elements: plot
Vocabulary Make word choices • Use word references: thesaurus

Vocabulary Preview

flawless (FLAW lus) *adj.* perfect; without mistakes **(p. 362)** *The robbery plan was flawless.*

vaults (vawltz) *n.* locked rooms or boxes for keeping money and valuables **(p. 363)** *The bank vaults contained jewelry, gold bricks, and dollar bills.*

bold (bold) *adj.* confident; daring **(p. 363)** *The plan to rob the Brink's vaults required the efforts of eleven bold men.*

stunned (stund) *adj.* shocked; surprised; amazed **(p. 365)** *The Brink's guards were stunned when the robbers appeared at their inner door.*

Write to Learn In your Learner's Notebook, write the vocabulary word that each clue describes:

1. This describes people who do extreme sports.
2. A bank has some of these.
3. You'd like it if your teacher used this word to describe your schoolwork.
4. If Robert won a contest that he'd expected to lose, he would probably feel this way.

English Language Coach

Word Choice The right word choices can make a big difference in how easy it is to understand a sentence.

- The farmers had problems because of weather.

A reader might wonder what weather they had and what problems it caused. More careful word choices make the sentence clearer.

- The farmers lost crops because of the lack of rain.

Whenever you write, take the time to choose words that say exactly what you mean.

Team Up With a partner, copy and revise the following sentences. Use specific words in place of the general ones.

- The weather was nice.
- Mrs. Sanders has a big dog.
- The food was good.

Additional Support

Differentiated Instruction

Fact Checking Read this excerpt from *The Morning Call* newspaper, January 18, 1950, and have students jot down notes about the factual statements in it. Then, as they read "The Brink's Robbery," have them point out factual errors in the news report.

More than $1,000,000 in cash was stolen last night and another million was left behind, police said, in one of the biggest robberies in the nation's history.

Seven Halloween masked gunmen, obviously well rehearsed, pulled the holdup at Brink's, Inc., a money transportation firm, on the waterfront. AL

Skills Preview

Key Reading Skill: Determining the Main Idea

The main idea is the most important idea in a selection or a paragraph. To find the main idea, ask yourself: "What is the author trying to say? What is the one idea that all of the sentences in this paragraph (or all the paragraphs in this selection) are about?" That's the main idea!

As you read, ask yourself:

- What does the title "The Brink's Robbery" tell me about this story's main idea?
- What important events and ideas does the author write about? What do these tell me about the main idea?

Key Literary Element: Plot

If a nonfiction article is told like a story, it also has a **plot.** This nonfiction story is about a robbery. Its **plot** is the events or action of the story. Remember, any plot has five main parts: exposition, rising action, climax, falling action, and resolution **L**

As you read, use these tips to follow the plot of the story.

- Notice what happens **before** the robbery.
  Who are the robbers? What is their plan?
- Notice what happens **during** the robbery.
  Are the robbers surprised by anything?
- Notice what happens **after** the robbery.
  Do the robbers make any mistakes?
- Notice how the story **ends.**
  What happens to the robbers?

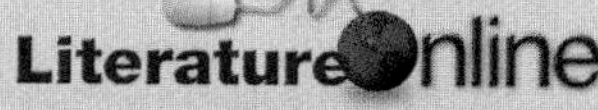

Interactive Literary Elements Handbook
To review or learn more about the literary elements, go to www.glencoe.com.

Get Ready to Read

Connect to the Reading

Bank robbers sometimes leave clues to "who did it." What do you think is the most common reason that robbers get caught?

Write to Learn In your Learner's Notebook, write about any robbery stories you know. How do you feel when the criminals get caught? How do you feel if they don't get caught?

Build Background

The selection you are going to read is a true story. Here are a few facts not mentioned in the story.

- Brink's opened in 1859 in Chicago, Illinois. Today, it operates throughout the world.
- Brink's is a company that offers safe cash handling, armored trucks, and transport services for diamonds, jewelry, and other valuables.
- There have been many attempts to rob Brink's trucks, but until this robbery no one ever tried to rob the Brink's building itself.
- At the time, the Brink's Robbery was considered the "crime of the century."
- The Brink's Company offered a $100,000 reward for information after the robbery.

Set Purposes for Reading

BIG Question Read the selection "The Brink's Robbery" to see when people can and cannot count on one another.

Set Your Own Purpose What would you like to learn about the Brink's robbery to help you answer the Big Question? Write your own purpose on a note card and put the card in the left pocket of Foldable 3.

Keep Moving

Use these skills as you read the following selection.

English Language Coach

Synonyms *The Morning Call* newspaper refers to the Brink's robbery as a *robbery* and as a *holdup.* These words are synonyms—words that have nearly the same meaning. What other words can you think of that mean nearly the same as *robbery*? *(Responses may include* burglary, theft, stickup, heist, *or* larceny.*)* **BL** **EL**

Word Choice Remember that synonyms are words that have *nearly* the same meaning, not *exactly* the same meaning. Look up the exact meaning of each of the words that you've suggested. Choose two of them and explain how their meanings are different. Then use each of the two words in a sentence. **AL**

Teach

L Literary Element

Plot Say: Think about another story you've read in this unit. Now write the five main parts of the story's plot. Compare your notes with a classmate who chose to track the plot of the same story. **AS**

CheckPoint

Use the CheckPoint questions provided on Presentation Plus! to check for prior knowledge and to build background. These questions can be used with interactive response keypads for immediate student feedback.

Literature Online

Interactive Literary Elements Handbook Have students access the Web site to improve their understanding of plot.

Objectives

- Identify main ideas and supporting details
- Identify literary elements: plot
- Make word choices
- Use word references: thesaurus

Teach

Viewing the Photos

Say: The photographs at the top of the page show 6 of the 11 Brink's robbers. You will learn more about these men as you read the article. Suppose that you had been a witness to the robbery and had to describe the men to the police. Look at the photographs for one minute. At the end of the minute, close your book and quickly jot down notes about everything you remember about these six men. Ready? Begin. *(Responses will vary.)*

EL Language Coach

Idiomatic Phrases The little word *up* forms a part of many two-part verbs in English. Students will encounter six of them in the article. They may need help understanding what it means to

- "end up rich"
- "pick up money from stores"
- "come up with a bold plan"
- "put up a fight"
- "split up the money"
- "round up the robbers" OL EL

Readability Scores
Dale-Chall: 5.8
DRP: 51
Lexile: 630

READING WORKSHOP 4

INFORMATIONAL TEXT
TEXTBOOK
from *The Wild Side: Crime and Punishment*

The Brink's Robbery

by Henry and Melissa Billings

Joseph "Big Joe" McGinnis dreamed of committing the perfect crime. In 1948 he hooked up with Tony "Fats" Pino.

Pino shared McGinnis's dream.

Together, these two longtime criminals set to work. They spent two years planning a **flawless** robbery. Nothing would be left to chance. **No evidence** would be left behind. And, if all went well, they would both end up rich. 1

Visual Vocabulary Brink's Company used ***armored cars*** like this one to pick up money from their customers.

The two thieves picked a tough target to rob—the Brink's Company in Boston. Brink's is an armored car service. It sends steel-plated cars to pick up money from stores around town. The armored cars take the money to Brink's headquarters. There it is counted, sorted, and held until the stores need it again. In 1950, as much as $10 million a day flowed through the Brink's office. 2

Vocabulary

flawless (FLAW lus) *adj.* perfect; without mistakes

Practice the Skills

1 English Language Coach

Word Choice How is saying "**no evidence** would be left behind" different than simply saying "nothing would be left behind?" Why is it a better word choice?

2 Key Literary Element

Plot The exposition is the first part of the plot. What have you learned so far about characters, setting, and conflict?

Additional Support

Differentiated Instruction

Sequence of Events Many events occur in the course of "The Brink's Robbery," and all together they span eight years. To help students keep track of these events, have them create a timeline. They can put the night of the robbery at the midpoint and place other events before and after it.

Pino and McGinnis begin planning.	Pino and McGinnis pick nine other men.	Gang members make keys for the doors.

OL

READING WORKSHOP 4

McGinnis and Pino planned their robbery with great care. They picked nine other men to join them. These were not just any nine men. Each brought a special skill to the group. Some, for instance, were good drivers or sharp lookout men. Also, seven of the men had to be the same size. McGinnis and Pino chose men who were about five feet nine inches tall **EL** and weighed between 170 and 180 pounds. These men would be the ones to enter the Brink's office and bring out the money. They would all dress alike. They would wear the same scary masks, rubbersoled shoes, gloves, coats, and caps. That would make it hard for the Brink's guards to identify them. (McGinnis would be one of the seven, but Pino was too heavy for the job. He agreed to stay with the getaway truck.) 3

Robbing the Brink's headquarters would not be easy. The place was full of steel **vaults** and armed guards. McGinnis and Pino knew this. So they took plenty of time. They studied the layout of the building. They found out when the guards were on duty and where they were stationed. They watched the money flow in and out of the office. They knew when the big money was there.

One of the toughest problems they faced was the locks. The gang had to pass through five locked doors to get from the street to the Brink's office. McGinnis and Pino came up with a **bold** plan. Late one night, a few of the gang members slipped into the building. One of them, a professional locksmith, removed the lock on the first door. He took it away and quickly made a key for it. Then—that same night—he hurried back to the Brink's building. He got the lock back in place before anyone noticed it was missing. 4 **L**

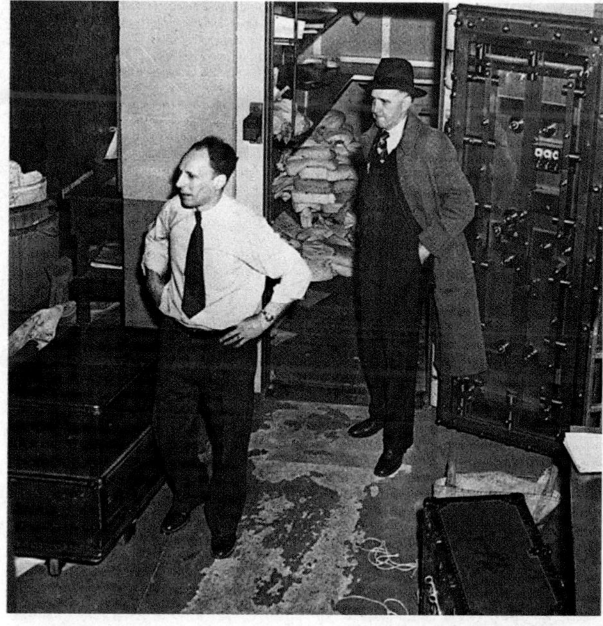

Brink's guard Thomas Lloyd and a detective look over the crime scene.

Practice the Skills

3 Key Reading Skill

Determining the Main Idea The first sentence of a paragraph will sometimes tell you the main idea of the paragraph. Reread this paragraph. What do you think is the main idea? What supporting details back up the main idea?

4 Key Literary Element

Plot You've already read the exposition of the plot, which introduces the characters, setting, and conflict. What part of the plot are you reading now?

Vocabulary

vaults (vawltz) *n.* locked rooms or boxes for keeping money and valuables

bold (bold) *adj.* confident; daring

Teach

EL Language Coach

Word Choice Say: One sentence on this page says that some of the men were "good drivers." Is *good* the best word to describe these drivers? What other word might be better? *(Possible response:* fast, daring, *or* skillful*)* Another sentence says that some men would enter the Brink's office and "bring out" the money. Is *bring* the best word to tell what they would do? What other word might be better? *(Possible response:* carry *or* haul*)* **AS**

L Literary Element

Review Conflict Say: Remind students that a conflict is a struggle. At this point in the narrative of the Brink's robbery, the robbers are not struggling against any other people yet. What are they struggling against? *(They are struggling against all the security measures that make the Brink's headquarters so hard to rob.)* **OL**

Reading Fluency

Build Fluency Students are likely to be familiar with the style of television documentaries and biographies. Typically, an offscreen narrator reads a script while the screen shows still photographs and film clips. Tell students that a good way to practice reading "The Brink's Robbery" smoothly is to imagine themselves as narrators of a television documentary about the robbery. Tell students to choose a passage that would be good to use in a TV documentary and to practice reading the passage aloud as a TV personality would. **BL EL**

Objectives
- Determine the main idea
- Understand plot
- Understand conflict
- Analyze character
- Choose the right word
- Develop fluency

Teach

R1 Reading Skill

Review Understanding Sequence **Say:** Because so many events occur quickly in this part of the narrative, the authors have been careful to include clear transitions to signal time and sequence. Name the transitions on this page. **AS**

R2 Reading Skill

Review Synthesizing **Ask:** How do you think Thomas Lloyd, the head guard, feels when he looks up at the seven drawn guns? Make a web diagram to help organize your thoughts. Use the diagram to write a paragraph about what Lloyd might be thinking as the robbery takes place. Write as if you were Lloyd (in his voice). *(Responses will vary.)*

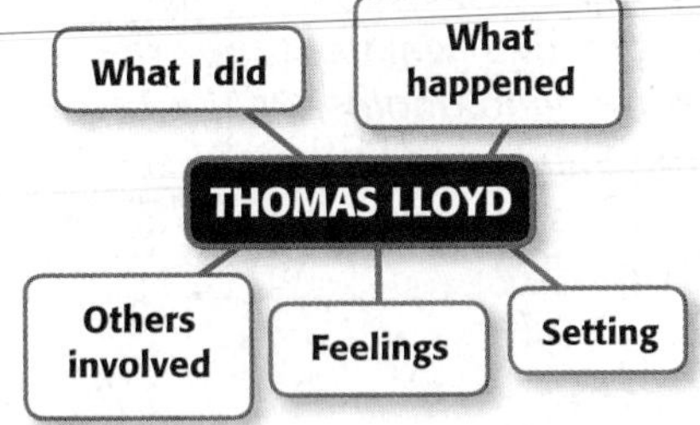

AL

READING WORKSHOP 4

The robbers returned on four other nights. Each time they repeated their actions. They made keys for the locks on the four other doors. Now they would be able to walk right into the Brink's office. There, they knew, they would find guards standing inside a wire cage. That was where all the money was.

Next, McGinnis and Pino made the gang practice the robbery. More than 20 times, the thieves slipped into the building. They used their keys to unlock door after door. Each time, they got right up to the innermost door. Then they turned and left.

R1 At last, McGinnis and Pino decided they were ready for the real thing. On January 17, 1950, they gave the signal. That night, a little before seven o'clock, the men took their places. Seven of them put on masks and sneaked into the building. They opened the five locked doors. At 7:10 p.m., they opened the innermost door. They were in the Brink's office. There, as expected, they saw five guards. The guards were all inside the wire cage, counting money.

The thieves stuck their guns through the holes in the cage. "This is a stickup," one growled. "Open the gate and don't give us any trouble." Thomas Lloyd, the head guard, looked at the seven drawn guns. He knew it was hopeless to put up a fight. He instructed one of the other guards to go ahead and open the cage door. **5** R2

Inside the cage, the thieves ordered the guards to lie facedown on the floor. They tied the guards' hands behind their backs. In addition, they tied their feet together and put tape across their mouths. Then the crooks grabbed the money.

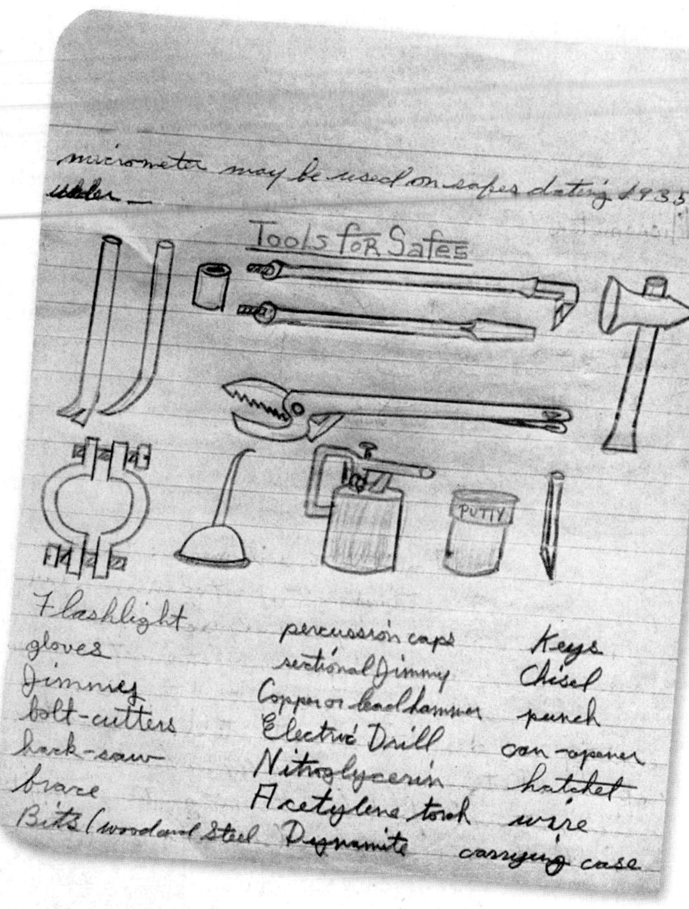

A page from a crime manual written by a Brink's robber

Practice the Skills

5 Key Literary Element

Plot The robbery is finally taking place. What part of the plot is this?

Additional Support

English Language Coach

Prepositions Many prepositions on this page begin phrases that tell where a thing is located or where something happens. Ask the following questions and have students find the prepositional phrase that answers each one.

Where are the locks? *(on the four other doors)*

Where will they find the guards standing? *(inside a wire cage)*

Where do seven of the thieves sneak? *(into the building)*

Where do the thieves stick their guns? *(through the holes)* **OL** **EL**

They took all they could carry. In total, they stole more than 1,200 pounds in coins, bills, and checks. By 7:27 p.m. they were out of the building. The robbery had gone perfectly. In cash alone, they had made off with exactly $1,218,211.29! 6

When news of the heist[1] spread, people were **stunned**. They hadn't thought anyone would ever dare rob Brink's. But, clearly, someone had. The police had no clues about who had done it. They searched everywhere. They organized a huge manhunt, but they didn't even know whom they were looking for. All they knew for sure was that the seven robbers were "of medium weight and height."

Meanwhile, the Brink's robbers played it safe. They drove the loot[2] to the home of Jazz Maffie in nearby Roxbury. Then each man went back home to his family. The next day they all went to their regular day jobs as if nothing had happened. The thieves stayed calm. They waited a month before splitting up the money. Each man got about $100,000. 7

For six years, the police tried to solve the crime. They failed. But during that time, trouble was brewing inside the gang. One of the robbers did not like the way the money had been divided. Specs O'Keefe began demanding a larger share of the loot. McGinnis and the others became worried. They feared O'Keefe might go to the police. So they hired a gunman named Trigger Burke to kill him. One day Burke opened fire as O'Keefe drove by in his car. Luckily for O'Keefe—and unluckily for the rest of the gang—Burke missed his target.

Furious about the attack, O'Keefe did turn to the police. He told them the whole story. The police quickly rounded up all the Brink's robbers. The 11 men were brought to trial in 1956. All of them, including Specs O'Keefe, were found guilty. Since O'Keefe had helped solve the crime, however, police allowed him to go free. The rest of the gang got long prison terms. In the end, then, the dream of Big Joe McGinnis and Fats Pino had turned into a nightmare. ❍

1. ***Heist*** is another word for robbery.
2. ***Loot*** is stolen goods or money

Vocabulary

stunned (stund) *adj.* shocked; surprised; amazed

Practice the Skills

6 **Reviewing Skills**

Responding What are your thoughts at this point? Has anything surprised you?

7 BIG Question

BQ Think about the Big Question. Do you think the gang members can really count on one another? Why or why not? Put your answer on a note card in the center pocket of Foldable 3. Your response will help you complete the Unit Challenge later.

READING WORKSHOP 4

Teach

BQ 

Ask: What do you think McGinnis and the others would say if you asked them whether Specs O'Keefe was someone they could depend on? *(Students are likely to agree that McGinnis wouldn't consider O'Keefe someone he could depend on.)* What do you think Specs O'Keefe would say if you asked whether the other gang members were people he could depend on? *(Considering that they tried to have him killed, O'Keefe would not be likely to consider them people he could depend on.)* AS

Assess

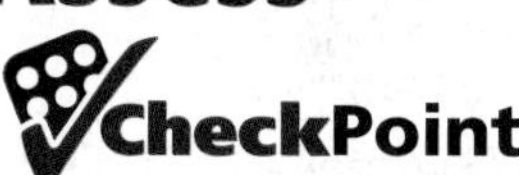

Use the CheckPoint questions provided on Presentation Plus! to check students' mastery of the selection. These questions can be used with interactive response keypads for immediate student feedback.

Reading in the Real World

Career Big Joe McGinnis makes the wrong career choice. As a bank robber, he ends up with a long prison term, but with his skills and talents he could have been a success in another career. Have students review the article and list McGinnis's skills and talents as they would in a résumé. Then have them act as career counselors to suggest other lines of work that McGinnis might have pursued. *(Among his skills and talents, they might list planning, organization, management, recruiting personnel, delegating responsibilities; they may decide that McGinnis might have been good at running a legitimate business.)* OL

Objectives
- Understand plot
- Understand idiomatic phrases
- Determine the main idea
- Connect reading to events in one's own life or to other selections

Assess

Resources for page 366

- Selection Quick Check
- Selection and Unit Assessment
- ExamView Assessment Suite
- Interactive Tutor: Self-Assessment

Students can respond to the *After You Read* items in their Learner's Notebook or on separate sheets of paper.

Answering the

1. Responses will vary.
2. Joseph "Big Joe" McGinnis and Tony "Fats" Pino
3. Armored cars are vehicles that have metal sides to prevent people from breaking into them and to protect their drivers and contents.

Critical Thinking

4. The most likely reason is that the Brink's Company worries about robbery.
5. The authors arranged the plot in chronological order. The events are in order. To make the plot easy to follow, the authors included many clear transitions that tell when events occurred.
6. They had a very good plan—as far as it went. Their plan for the robbery itself was flawless. However, they hadn't planned well for what would happen after the robbery was over.

After You Read

The Brink's Robbery

Answering the

1. For six years, the robbers fought about the money they stole. They finally turned on each other.
   - What does this tell you?
   - Can you count on people who do bad or illegal things?
   - Why or why not?
2. **Recall** Who are the two leaders of the robbers?
   TIP **Right There**
3. **Recall** What are armored cars? Describe an armored car using as much detail as you can.
   TIP **Right There**

Critical Thinking

4. **Infer** The selection doesn't tell you why Brink's uses armored cars to transport money. Can you guess why?
   TIP **Author and Me**
5. **Analyze** How did the authors organize the plot? Are the events in order? Is the plot easy to follow? Explain.
   TIP **Author and Me**
6. **Evaluate** Do you think the robbers had a good plan? Use examples from the story to support your answer.
   TIP **Author and Me**

Objectives (pp. 366–367)
Reading Identify main ideas and supporting details
Literature Identify literary elements: plot
Vocabulary Make word choices • Use word references: thesaurus
Writing Write a fictional news article
Grammar Use interjections

Write About Your Reading

Write a short fictional news article with the headline **Rare Treasure Found.**

Follow these steps to get started. As you make your decisions, write them down in your Learner's Notebook.

Step 1: Decide what the treasure is.
Step 2: Decide how and where the treasure got lost.
Step 3: Decide who finds the treasure.
Step 4: Decide how he or she finds it.
Step 5: Write what you imagine the person would say upon discovering the treasure. Explain how he or she feels.

Write About Your Reading

Possible response:
Rare Treasure Found
Boston—Yesterday, James Macon discovered a blue diamond in a sandbox while looking for a toy his sister had buried. "I was so excited when I realized it was B-Wise's diamond," said James. "It's worth a fortune!" B-Wise, a rock star, lost the diamond when he was mobbed by fans after a concert. How the diamond ended up in the sand remains a mystery.

Skills Review

Key Reading Skill: Determining the Main Idea

7. Think about how the story ends. What do you think is the main idea of this selection? What details support the main idea?
8. Do you think dishonesty is a good quality in a friend? Why or why not?

Key Literary Element: Plot

9. Summarize the plot of "The Brink's Robbery" in nine sentences. The first two sentences are given below:

   McGinnis and Pino planned the robbery.

   They made keys for all the doors.

Vocabulary Check

Rewrite the sentences below. Mark each sentence with a *T* or an *F* depending on whether it is true or false.

10. **Vaults** work well as hats.
11. A jewel is more valuable if it is **flawless** than if it is not.
12. A person could be **stunned** by an unexpected event.
13. One must be **bold** to hide from an enemy.
14. **English Language Coach** Read this sentence: *One robber wanted more money.*

    There's a sentence in the selection that says the same thing but is more precise because of its specific words. Find that sentence and copy it down. (It's in the next to the last paragraph on page 365.)

    Now read this sentence:
    In the end, McGinnis and Pino were disappointed.

    There's a sentence in the selection that is more precise than this one but says the same thing. Find that sentence and copy it down. (It appears in the selection *after* the other sentence you just copied.)

Grammar Link: Interjections

An **interjection** (in tur JEK shun) is a word or group of words that shows emotion, or feeling.

An interjection that shows a strong feeling, such as excitement, may come before or after a sentence. It begins with a capital letter and ends with an exclamation point.

- *Wow!* Your new bike is cool.
- I got an A on my math test. *Hooray!*

An interjection that shows a mild, or calmer, feeling may be part of a sentence. When it is part of a sentence, the interjection is separated from the rest of the sentence with a comma.

- *Oh,* is it my turn to talk?
- You forgot your backpack? *Hey,* don't worry about it.

Here are some examples of interjections:

awesome gee great ha okay
oops ouch well yikes yuck

Grammar Practice

Copy the sentences below. Add an interjection from the examples above to each sentence. Remember to punctuate it correctly.

15. This soup tastes terrible.
16. I dropped my grandma's vase.
17. I guess I'll just take the bus home.
18. I just stubbed my toe on that chair.

Writing Application Reread the Write About Your Reading assignment you completed. Add an interjection to your writing to make it more exciting.

Web Activities For eFlashcards, Selection Quick Checks, and other Web activities, go to www.glencoe.com.

Skills Review

Key Reading Skill: Determining the Main Idea

7. The main idea could be stated as "There is no honor among thieves." Details about the way the gang betrays one another support that main idea.
8. Possible response: A person couldn't trust a dishonest friend, and trust is essential in a friendship.

Key Literary Element: Plot

9. They practiced the robbery more than 20 times. They robbed Brink's on January 17, 1950. News of the robbery stunned people. Police conducted a huge manhunt. Specs O'Keefe demanded more of the money. The rest of the gang tried to have him killed. O'Keefe went to the police, who quickly captured the rest of the gang.

Vocabulary Check

10. F
11. T
12. T
13. F
14. Specs O'Keefe began demanding a larger share of the loot.
    In the end, then, the dream of Big Joe McGinnis and Fats Pino had turned into a nightmare.

Grammar Link: Interjections

Grammar Practice

15. Yuck! This soup tastes terrible.
16. Oops! I dropped my grandma's vase.
17. Well, I guess I'll just take the bus home.
18. Ouch! I just stubbed my toe on that chair.

Close

Ask students to share what they learned from this selection to answer the Big Question.

Comparing Literature: Plot

UNIT 3

Objectives covered in this workshop:
- Analyze parts of a plot
- Compare plots across texts

Teaching Students to Compare Plot

Why Is It Important?

- Comparing and contrasting selections will enhance students' comprehension of certain aspects of literature.
- Plot is one of the basic elements of literature and can be defined as a series of events created by an author to tell a story.
- Comparing and contrasting the selections will also help students understand the role that setting and characters play in influencing the plot.

How to Help Students Get It?

- Students must develop a sense of the events as they unfold. Explain that rising action is the events before the climax, climax is the point in the story at which the conflict is resolved, and falling action is the events after the climax.
- Students can use a graphic organizer that provides them space to record events along the continuum of rising action, climax, and falling action in a piece of fiction.
- Students can also chart the events in their day to develop a sense of plot how events before and after the "major" event are related.

Reading to Answer the Big Question

Lob's Girl

Lob is a German shepherd who is adopted by a family he's fond of and who is equally fond of him. He shows just how dependable he is when he shows up at a hospital and inspires his young owner to regain consciousness.

The Highwayman

Bess kills herself to warn her lover, the highwayman, of pending danger. When he realizes that she is dead, he tries to avenge her death, which leads to his death too.

Workshop Resources

Pacing (Days) Standard	Block	Lesson	Student Materials	Teacher Resources
1		Comparing Literature: Plot	Key Reading Skills Practice English Language Coach	Bellringer Options Transparencies Read Aloud, Think Aloud Transparencies Presentation Plus!
2		"Lob's Girl"	Literary Analysis Transparencies Glencoe Online Selection Vocabulary Development Academic Vocabulary Development English Language Coach Active Reading Graphic Organizer Literary Analysis StudentWorks Plus Online Student Edition Literature Classics Selection and Unit Assessments	Literary and Text Analysis Transparencies Puzzlemaker Skill Level Up! BookLink 3 Assessment by Learning Objective (Diagnostic and Formative) Interactive Tutor Self-Assessment TeacherWorks Plus
2		"The Highwayman"	Glencoe Online Selection Vocabulary Development Academic Vocabulary Development English Language Coach Active Reading Graphic Organizer Literary Analysis StudentWorks Plus Online Student Edition Literature Classics Selection and Unit Assessments	Literary and Text Analysis Transparencies Puzzlemaker Skill Level Up! BookLink 3 Assessment by Learning Objective (Diagnostic and Formative) Interactive Tutor Self-Assessment TeacherWorks Plus

Keys for Unit Resource

- Blackline Master
- Workbook
- Supplemental Text
- CD-ROM
- DVD
- Transparency
- Web-based
- Fast Files

Level Appropriate Code

AS = Activities for all students
AL = Activities for students working above grade level
OL = Activities for students working at grade level
BL = Activities for students working below grade level
EL = Activities for English language learners

Focus

BELLRINGER Options

- **Selection Focus Transparencies**
- **Daily Language Practice Transparency**

Focus Activity Say: Many TV commercials tell very short stories with basic plots. Think of two commercials that tell stories, and make a plot diagram for each one. *(See the plot diagram on 369.)* Think about how you would compare their two plots.

Teach

L Literary Element

Plot Say: It isn't unusual for the setting to play an important part in the plot. As you read "Lob's Girl" and "The Highwayman," notice the places and times when key events occur. In both of these tales, you will find that time and place are essential to the plot. **Ask:** Is it easier to see danger in the daytime or in the nighttime? *(in the daytime)* Which is more dangerous to drive, a level road or a steep, twisting road? *(a steep, twisting road)* BL

Lob's Girl & The Highwayman

by Joan Aiken

by Alfred Noyes

What You'll Learn

You will practice using these skills when you read the following selections:

- "Lob's Girl," p. 371
- "The Highwayman," p. 386

Point of Comparison

- Plot

Purpose

- To analyze the parts of a plot
- To compare plots in a short story and a narrative poem

Vocabulary

- Using synonyms to expand vocabulary

You probably make comparisons every time you watch a TV show or movie. You may find yourself thinking, "Last week's show was better" or "Action movies are more interesting than comedies" or "Characters on TV don't behave the way real people do."

Comparing is important when you read literature. Each time you read something new, you'll probably compare it with something you read before. This is something we all do, even though we may not be aware of it.

How to Compare Literature: Plot

In this workshop, you'll compare a short story and a poem. "The Highwayman" is a **narrative poem,** a kind of poetry that tells a story. Like short stories, narrative poems have characters, settings, themes, and plots.

L The **plot** is the story's basic structure. It's the events in which a problem is explored and then solved. Plot is created through **conflict.** In an action-adventure story, there's conflict between the good guy and the bad guy. The plot is the events that show their struggle (until the good guy wins, of course).

Conflict may be between

- two people or two groups
- a person and an idea (such as slavery)
- a person and an outside force (such as a storm)

Objectives (pp. 368–369)
Literature Identify literary elements: plot • Compare and contrast: literature

Additional Support

Literature Focus Lesson

Analyzing Plot Because a story's plot extends across the entire length of the story, its elements can be difficult to keep in mind as one reads. Remind students that questioning helps them to clarify their understanding of a text as they read. Provide them with the following prompts to clarify a plot.

- Who is the main character?
- What does the main character want?
- What stands in the way of the main character's getting what he or she wants?
- What does the main character do to remove the obstacle? OL

Get Ready to Compare

A plot can be charted on a diagram like the one below.

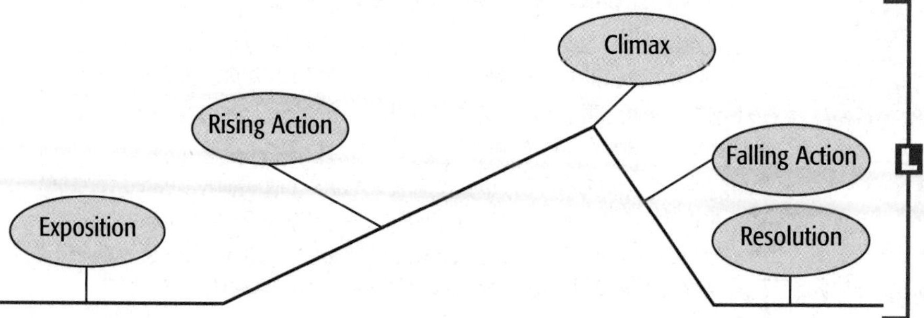

Good writers use each part of the plot to lead readers toward the ending.

- The plot begins by introducing the characters, setting, and situation. This is the **exposition.** It captures the reader's attention with a strong conflict between opposing forces.
- During the **rising action,** complications are added to the conflict.
- The rising action leads to a **climax,** the point when the reader's interest is at its highest.
- The **falling action** moves the story toward the ending.
- In the **resolution,** the conflict is resolved, or worked out, and the plot's final outcome is revealed.

As you read "Lob's Girl" and "The Highwayman," make separate lists of the important events from each story in your Learner's Notebook.

Organize your lists under headings that name the parts of a plot. For example, begin each list with the heading "Exposition." Under that head, write the important events that occur during that part of the story. When the rising action begins, add the heading "Rising Action." Do the same with "Climax," "Falling Action," and "Resolution." Don't worry about being exactly right. After you've read both of the selections, you will look at your lists and compare the two plots.

COMPARING LITERATURE

Teach

L Literary Element

Plot Elements Return to the television commercials that students analyzed for the Bellringer activity. If students did not do the Bellringer activity, briefly have them outline the plots of two commercials that tell stories. Then have volunteers summarize or narrate each essential element of a commercial that he or she chose, including: exposition, rising action, climax, falling action, and resolution.

Ask students whether the setting plays an important part in each commercial. If it does, have them explain why it is important. AS

Assess/Close

Say: Write a paragraph comparing one element of the plots of two television commercials that tell stories. *(Responses will vary.)* Have a few students read their comparisons of the commercials aloud. AS

Resources for page 369

Use the Comparing Literature Graphic Organizer BLM in the Unit 3 Resource Booklet.

Reading in the Real World

Career Some people's careers have narrative structures that resemble plots. Provide students with examples of obituaries, and have them chart people's careers on copies of the plot diagram. For example,

- exposition often corresponds to a youthful desire to pursue a career
- rising action may involve training and struggles against odds
- the climax can be an outstanding accomplishment at the peak of the career
- falling action may include retirement
- resolution can be the reaction of friends and colleagues when the person dies OL

Objectives

- Compare and contrast works of literature
- Understand the elements of plot in works of literature
- Understand how the setting may influence the plot

More About the Author

Joan Aiken was raised in a rural area of England. Because she was alone much of the time when she was young, she spent her time reading and making up stories to amuse herself.

V Vocabulary

Other Contexts On the board, write sentences similar to the ones in the Vocabulary Preview, but with blanks:

The ___ looked secretive.
We saw the ___ hurtle ___.
___ felt aggrieved because ___.
___ succeeded ___ as we ___.
___ looked haggard because ___.
___ was agitated because ___.

Have students complete the sentences in several ways, creating new contexts for the vocabulary words. BL EL

CheckPoint

Use the CheckPoint questions provided on Presentation Plus! to check for prior knowledge and to build background. These questions can be used with interactive response keypads for immediate student feedback.

Before You Read

Lob's Girl

Joan Aiken

Meet the Author

British author Joan Aiken says that she writes "the sort of thing I should have liked to read myself." Aiken's first work was published when she was seventeen. She has since written more than eighty books and short-story collections. Aiken is best known for historical fiction with mysterious and magical characters and settings. See page R1 of the Author Files for more on Joan Aiken.

Author Resources For more about Joan Aiken, go to www.glencoe.com.

Objectives (pp. 370–384)
Literature Identify literary elements: plot • Compare and contrast: literature
Vocabulary Interpret context clues: unfamiliar usages

Vocabulary Preview

secretive (SEE krih tiv) *adj.* seeming to keep secrets; holding back information **(p. 378)** *The little fishing town looked empty and secretive.*

hurtle (HUR tul) *v.* to move fast with a lot of force **(p. 378)** *They did not hear the truck hurtle down the hill and crash.*

aggrieved (uh GREEVD) *adj.* feeling insulted or unfairly treated **(p. 380)** *Aunt Hoskins sat by her fire thinking aggrieved thoughts.*

succeeded (suk SEED ed) *v.* followed; happened after; form of the verb *succeed* **(p. 381)** *Hour succeeded hour as we waited patiently.*

haggard (HAG urd) *adj.* looking worn out from grief, worry, or illness **(p. 381)** *She looked haggard after lying sick in her bed for days.*

agitated (AJ uh tayt ud) *adj.* excited, nervous, or disturbed; stirred up **(p. 382)** *The agitated dog seemed to want to tell them something.*

English Language Coach

Synonyms Many words and phrases used in England are not familiar to Americans. The sentence below contains words from the story "Lob's Girl." Write down each underlined word and choose its synonym from the words in parentheses. (This will be simple if you use context clues.)

I washed with a flannel (blanket, washcloth, scarf) and then walked the dog on a lead (command, hill, leash).

Get Ready to Read

Connect to the Reading

Can an animal be as good a friend as a person?

Build Background

- This story takes place in England over nine years.
- Many lost dogs travel great distances to get home. Dogs use their sense of smell to identify people and objects.

Set Purposes for Reading

BIG Question Read to learn about a girl who could count on her dog.

Set Your Own Purpose What would you like to learn from the story to help you answer the Big Question? Write your own purpose on a note card and put the card in the left pocket of Foldable 3.

Additional Support

Author Search To expand students' appreciation of Joan Aiken, have them access the Web site for additional information and resources.

Literature Focus Lesson

Fantasy Both "Lob's Girl" and "The Highwayman" include elements of fantasy—literature about magical or mythical events. To introduce the idea of fantasy, have students do the following activities.

- Alone or with a partner, brainstorm a list of fantasy or science-fiction novels, short stories, TV episodes, or movies you have read or seen. Then choose at least four of them that you think are especially good.
- Create a chart to make a detailed comparison of your choices. Use headings such as Title, Author(s), Setting (time and place), Plot Summary, Characters, Theme(s), and Evaluation.

LOB'S GIRL

by Joan Aiken

Some people choose their dogs, and some dogs choose their people. The Pengelly family had no say in the choosing of Lob; he came to them in the second way, and very decisively. **C**

It began on the beach, the summer when Sandy was five, Don, her older brother, twelve, and the twins were three. Sandy was really Alexandra, because her grandmother had a beautiful picture of a queen in a diamond tiara[1] and high collar of pearls. It hung by Granny Pearce's kitchen sink and was as familiar as the doormat. When Sandy was born everyone agreed that she was the living spit[2] of the picture, and so she was called Alexandra and Sandy for short. **1**

On this summer day she was lying peacefully reading a comic and not keeping an eye on the twins, who didn't need it because they were occupied in seeing which of them could

1. A *tiara* (tee AWR ah) is a woman's crown, often made with jewels and gold or silver.
2. *Living spit* is British slang for "exact likeness," which Americans would call "spitting image."

Practice the Skills

1 Comparing Literature

Plot This is the *exposition* of the story. In your Learner's Notebook start your list for "Lob's Girl" by making notes about the setting and the main character under the heading "Exposition."

Teach

C Critical Thinking

Comprehension Say: Read the first paragraph of this story. Now predict

- who Lob is
- how Lob chooses the Pengellys
- what the conflict in the story could be

(Responses will vary. Have students explain their responses.) **AS**

V Vocabulary

Context Clues If you haven't previewed the selection vocabulary with students, stop and remind them to use context clues to unlock the meanings of new vocabulary words. **BL** **EL**

Leveled Reading An adapted version of this selection (Grade 4 readability) is available on page 24 of *Jamestown Literature: An Adapted Reader* for Grade 7.

Readability Scores
Dale-Chall: 4.9
DRP: 54
Lexile: 980

English Language Coach

Idiomatic Expressions Have students contribute to a collection of expressions from various dialects and other languages. On the bulletin board, post cards with a number of common expressions, such as

- take it easy
- turn over a new leaf
- keep your chin up
- pull yourself together

Then provide additional cards and invite students to contribute equivalent expressions in current slang or in other languages. **OL** **EL**

Objectives
- Identify literary elements: plot
- Compare and contrast: literature
- Interpret context clues: unfamiliar usages

Teach

R Reading Skill

Review Connecting Ask: How is this family similar to and different from the family or families that you know? *(Responses will vary. Sandy is like many other big sisters who are supposed to keep an eye on younger siblings but don't watch too closely. The father works as a fisherman. The mother is a homemaker.)* OL

L Literary Element

Plot Say: Writers sometimes plant hints or suggestions of what will come later in the plot. **Ask:** What do you think Aiken means when she says that the state of things in the Pengelly family "would be changed by the large new member who was going to erupt into their midst"? *(Lob is somehow going to change the lives of the Pengellys.)*

wrap the most seaweed around the other one's legs. Father—Bert Pengelly—and Don were up on the Hard painting the bottom boards of the boat in which Father went fishing for pilchards.[3] And Mother—Jean Pengelly—was getting ahead with making the Christmas puddings[4] because she never felt easy in her mind if they weren't made and safely put away by the end of August. As usual, each member of the family was happily getting on with his or her own affairs. Little did they guess how soon this state of things would be changed by the large new member who was going to erupt into their midst. L

Sandy rolled onto her back to make sure that the twins were not climbing on slippery rocks or getting cut off by the tide. At the same moment a large body struck her forcibly in the midriff and she was covered by flying sand. Instinctively she shut her eyes and felt the sand being wiped off her face by something that seemed like a warm, rough, damp flannel. She opened her eyes and looked. It was a tongue. Its owner was a large and bouncy young Alsatian, or German shepherd, with topaz[5] eyes, black-tipped prick ears, a thick, soft coat, and a bushy black-tipped tail. 2

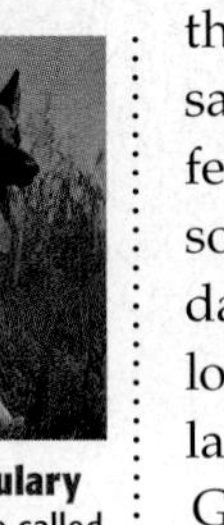

Visual Vocabulary ***Alsatians,*** also called German shepherds, were originally bred in Germany. They are noted for their intelligence and loyalty.

"Lob!" shouted a man farther up the beach. "Lob, come here!"

But Lob, as if trying to atone for the surprise he had given her, went on licking the sand off Sandy's face, wagging his tail so hard while he kept on knocking up more clouds of sand. His owner, a gray-haired man with a limp, walked over as quickly as he could and seized him by the collar.

"I hope he didn't give you a fright?" the man said to Sandy. "He meant it in play—he's only young."

"Oh, no, I think he's *beautiful,*" said Sandy truly. She picked up a bit of driftwood and threw it. Lob, whisking easily out of his master's grip, was after it like a sand-colored bullet.

3. ***The Hard*** is a place for landing and launching boats. ***Pilchards*** are small herring-like fish.
4. ***Christmas puddings*** are a traditional British dessert similar to a fruitcake.
5. ***Topaz*** is a bright yellow-gold color.

Practice the Skills

2 Comparing Literature

Plot It looks like the *rising action* of the plot is beginning. Or do you think this is still the exposition? Make a note about this on your "Lob's Girl" list. Another character has entered the story, too. Do you think this character will be important to the story? If so, make a note on your list.

Additional Support

Reading in the Real World

Citizenship For some students, or for their families, fishing may have been, or may still be, an important part of life. For others, it may be unfamiliar.

Have small groups of students work together to share stories about fishing locally and in other parts of the world: where people fish, what they fish for, when they fish, what tools they use (nets, boats, line, bait), and how they prepare the fish once they have caught them. Some students may want to make illustrations of certain fish and/or how those fish are caught. Invite the groups to share their findings. AS

He came back with the stick, beaming, and gave it to Sandy. At the same time he gave himself, though no one else was aware of this at the time. But with Sandy, too, it was love at first sight, and when, after a lot more stick-throwing, she and the twins joined Father and Don to go home for tea, they cast many a backward glance at Lob being led firmly away by his master. C1

"I wish we could play with him every day," Tess sighed.

"Why can't we?" said Tim.

Sandy explained, "Because Mr. Dodsworth, who owns him, is from Liverpool, and he is only staying at the Fisherman's Arms till Saturday."

"Is Liverpool a long way off?"

"Right at the other end of England from Cornwall, I'm afraid."

It was a Cornish fishing village where the Pengelly family lived, with rocks and cliffs and a strip of beach and a little round harbor, and palm trees growing in the gardens of the little whitewashed stone houses. The village was approached by a narrow, steep, twisting hill-road, and guarded by a notice that said LOW GEAR FOR 1½ MILES, DANGEROUS TO CYCLISTS. **3** L

The Pengelly children went home to scones[6] with Cornish cream and jam, thinking they had seen the last of Lob. But they were much mistaken. The whole family was playing cards by the fire in the front room after supper when there was a loud thump and a crash of china in the kitchen.

"My Christmas puddings!" exclaimed Jean, and ran out.

"Did you put TNT in them, then?" her husband said.

But it was Lob, who, finding the front door shut, had gone around to the back and bounced in through the open kitchen window, where the puddings were cooling on the sill. Luckily only the smallest was knocked down and broken. C2

Lob stood on his hind legs and plastered Sandy's face with licks. Then he did the same for the twins, who shrieked with joy.

"Where does this friend of yours come from?" inquired Mr. Pengelly.

"He's staying at the Fisherman's Arms—I mean his owner is."

6. ***Scones*** are sweet biscuits.

Practice the Skills

3 Reviewing Skills

Inferring Why do you think the author gives the wording of a warning sign here? Could it be a hint of something to come later in the story?

Teach

C1 Critical Thinking

Analysis Say: Aiken says that Lob gave himself, as well as the stick, to Sandy. Could this be a hint or suggestion of what will come later in the plot? *(That line seems to suggest that Lob is somehow going to become Sandy's dog.)* **OL**

L Literary Element

Setting Say: Think about the setting and explain how the narrow, steep, twisting road contrasts with the fishing village. *(The village seems peaceful and safe, but the access road is treacherous.)* **OL**

C2 Critical Thinking

Evaluation Say: Explain why you think Lob returns. *(He has decided he wants to be with Sandy. Earlier, Aiken reveals that Lob had given his loyalty to Sandy.)*

Differentiated Instruction

Using Graphic Aids Some students may understand events in this story more easily if they look at a map of England to visualize Cornwall's location and to see how far Lob travels.

Have students create maps of England that show Liverpool, Cornwall, Plymouth, the English Channel, and the Atlantic Ocean. Encourage students to draw the maps to scale and to include keys so that others can tell the distance between Cornwall and Liverpool and between Cornwall and Plymouth. Invite students to refer to their maps as they read the story. **AL**

Objectives

- Understand elements of plot
- Recognize foreshadowing as a plot element
- Visualize setting
- Understand character motivation

Teach

V Vocabulary

Synonyms and Antonyms
Say: Use a thesaurus to find synonyms for the following words from this page.

- reluctant *(unwilling)*
- joyful *(happy, gleeful)*
- miserably *(unhappily, gloomily)*
- cross *(irritable, grouchy)*

Now find an antonym for each of the words:

- reluctant *(eager)*
- joyful *(unhappy, miserable)*
- miserably *(joyfully, happily)*
- cross *(pleasant)* **OL**

L Literary Element

Conflict Ask: What is the conflict at this point in the story? *(Sandy has become attached to Lob, but Lob's owner has taken the dog away.)* **AS**

"Then he must go back there. Find a bit of string, Sandy, to tie to his collar."

"I wonder how he found his way here," Mrs. Pengelly said when the reluctant Lob had been led whining away and Sandy had explained about their afternoon's game on the beach. "Fisherman's Arms is right round the other side of the harbor."

Lob's owner scolded him and thanked Mr. Pengelly for bringing him back. Jean Pengelly warned the children that they had better not encourage Lob any more if they met him on the beach, or it would only lead to more trouble. So they dutifully took no notice of him the next day until he spoiled their good resolutions by dashing up to them with joyful barks, wagging his tail so hard that he winded Tess and knocked Tim's legs from under him.

They had a happy day, playing on the sand.

Penzance: Railway Station, Stanhope Alexander Forbes (1857–1947). John Davies Fine Paintings, Stow-on-the-Wold, Glos., UK.

L The next day was Saturday. Sandy had found out that Mr. Dodsworth was to catch the half-past-nine train. She went out secretly, down to the station, nodded to Mr. Hoskins, the stationmaster, who wouldn't dream of charging any local for a platform ticket, and climbed up on the footbridge that led over the tracks. She didn't want to be seen, but she did want to see. She saw Mr. Dodsworth get on the train, accompanied by an unhappy-looking Lob with drooping ears and tail. Then she saw the train slide away out of sight around the next headland, with a **melancholy** wail that sounded like Lob's last good-bye. **4**

Sandy wished she hadn't had the idea of coming to the station. She walked home miserably, with her shoulders hunched and her hands in her pockets. For the rest of the day she was so cross and unlike herself that Tess and Tim were quite surprised, and her mother gave her a dose of senna.[7]

Practice the Skills

4 English Language Coach

Synonyms Do you know the word **melancholy**? Check a thesaurus to find synonyms to help you understand the meaning of the word.

7. ***Senna*** is a medicine made from a plant.

Additional Support

English Language Coach

British Expressions English-language learners may need help interpreting some of the British expressions in the story. Write these sentences on the board:

- For the rest of the day she was so cross and unlike herself . . . (page 374)
- Bert Pengelly rang up Liverpool again. (page 376)
- You'll be doing me a good turn. (page 376)
- Sandy tidied herself . . . (page 378)

Encourage pairs of students to find the sentences in the story and to use context clues and a dictionary to write American English versions of the sentences. **EL** **BL**

A week passed. Then, one evening, Mrs. Pengelly and the younger children were in the front room playing snakes and ladders. Mr. Pengelly and Don had gone fishing on the evening tide. If your father is a fisherman, he will never be home at the same time from one week to the next.

Suddenly, history repeating itself, there was a crash from the kitchen. Jean Pengelly leaped up, crying, "My blackberry jelly!" She and the children had spent the morning picking and the afternoon boiling fruit. **C**

But Sandy was ahead of her mother. With flushed cheeks and eyes like stars she had darted into the kitchen, where she and Lob were hugging one another in a frenzy of joy. About a yard of his tongue was out, and he was licking every part of her that he could reach.

"Good heavens!" exclaimed Jean. "How in the world did *he* get here?"

"He must have walked," said Sandy. "Look at his feet."

They were worn, dusty, and tarry. One had a cut on the pad.

"They ought to be bathed," said Jean Pengelly. "Sandy, run a bowl of warm water while I get the disinfectant."

"What'll we do about him, Mother?" said Sandy anxiously.

Mrs. Pengelly looked at her daughter's pleading eyes and sighed.

"He must go back to his owner, of course," she said, making her voice firm. "Your dad can get the address from the Fisherman's tomorrow, and phone him or send a telegram. In the meantime he'd better have a long drink and a good meal." **5**

Lob was very grateful for the drink and the meal, and made no objection to having his feet washed. Then he flopped down on the hearthrug and slept in front of the fire they had lit because it was a cold, wet evening, with his head on Sandy's feet. He was a very tired dog. He had walked all the way from Liverpool to Cornwall, which is more than four hundred miles. **6**

The next day Mr. Pengelly phoned Lob's owner, and the following morning Mr. Dodsworth arrived off the night train, decidedly put out, to take his pet home. That parting was worse than the first. Lob whined, Don walked out of the house, the twins burst out crying, and Sandy crept up to her bedroom afterward and lay with her face pressed into the quilt, feeling as if she were bruised all over. **R**

Practice the Skills

5 Comparing Literature

Plot This is part of the *rising action* section of the plot. Is there a conflict in the story now? If so, make sure to add it to your "Lob's Girl" list under the heading "Rising Action."

6 Reviewing Skills

Drawing Conclusions Why do you think Lob traveled 400 miles back to Cornwall, a place he had visited once?

Teach

C Critical Thinking

Comprehension Ask: Based on what happens earlier in the story, what do you think has happened to cause the crash in the kitchen? *(Lob has returned by climbing through the kitchen window again, where he has knocked over the blackberry jelly.)* **OL**

R Reading Skill

Review Connecting Say: Think of a time you or someone you read about had to say goodbye forever to a beloved person or animal. How did you or the other person or animal feel? *(Responses will vary.)* How do the children show their feelings about having to say goodbye to Lob? *(Don, an adolescent, walks out of the house. The young twins cry. Sandy feels bruised.)* **AS**

Reading in the Real World

Citizenship Invite students to conduct research into amazing feats performed by German shepherds and other dogs, such as walking many miles to get home or saving lives.

Encourage students to find magazine articles about dogs that have performed amazing feats. Some students may want to visit Internet sites for additional information about German shepherds. Encourage students to take notes on the articles they especially enjoy. Then have them use their notes to describe the dogs' amazing feats to the rest of the class. **OL**

Objectives
- Make connections between personal experience and the text
- Conduct research

Teach

V Vocabulary

Synonyms and Antonyms
Say: Use a thesaurus to find synonyms for the following words from this page.

- weary *(tired, exhausted)*
- rich *(wealthy, well-to-do)*
- cautiously *(carefully)*
- doubtfully *(uncertainly)*

Now find an antonym for each of the words:

- weary *(alert, well-rested)*
- rich *(poor)*
- cautiously *(boldly)*
- doubtfully *(certainly, surely)* **OL** **EL**

C Critical Thinking

Evaluation Say: Explain what you think makes Mr. Pengelly decide to accept Lob as a gift. *(He realizes how much his children—especially Alexandra (Sandy)—cares about the dog and wants him to be theirs.)* **OL**

Jean Pengelly took them all into Plymouth to see the circus on the next day and the twins cheered up a little, but even the hour's ride in the train each way and the Liberty horses and performing seals could not cure Sandy's sore heart.

She need not have bothered, though. In ten days' time Lob was back—limping this time, with a torn ear and a patch missing out of his furry coat, as if he had met and tangled with an enemy or two in the course of his four-hundred-mile walk.

Bert Pengelly rang up Liverpool again. Mr. Dodsworth, when he answered, sounded weary. He said, "That dog has already cost me two days that I can't spare away from my work—plus endless time in police stations and drafting newspaper advertisements. I'm too old for these ups and downs. I think we'd better face the fact, Mr. Pengelly, that it's your family he wants to stay with—that is, if you want to have him."

Bert Pengelly gulped. He was not a rich man; and Lob was a pedigreed[8] dog. He said cautiously, "How much would you be asking for him?"

"Good heavens, man, I'm not suggesting I'd sell him to you. You must have him as a gift. Think of the train fares I'll be saving. You'll be doing me a good turn."

"Is he a big eater?" Bert asked doubtfully.

By this time the children, breathless in the background listening to one side of this conversation, had realized what was in the wind and were dancing up and down with their hands clasped beseechingly.[9]

"Oh, not for his size," Lob's owner assured Bert. "Two or three pounds of meat a day and some vegetables and gravy and biscuits—he does very well on that."

C Alexandra's father looked over the telephone at his daughter's swimming eyes and trembling lips. He reached a decision. "Well, then, Mr. Dodsworth," he said briskly, "we'll accept your offer and thank you very much. The children will be overjoyed and you can be sure Lob has come to a good home. They'll look after him and see he gets enough exercise. But I can tell you," he ended firmly, "if he wants to settle in with us he'll have to learn to eat a lot of fish." **7**

8. A ***pedigreed*** dog has papers showing that its ancestors were the same breed.
9. ***Beseechingly*** means "in a begging or pleading way."

Practice the Skills

7 Comparing Literature

Plot The telephone conversation between Bert Pengelly and Mr. Dodsworth is part of the rising action of the story. Is a conflict developing? Be sure to add to your diagram.

Additional Support

English Language Coach

Adjectives and Adverbs Write the following word pairs on the board.

- cautious—cautiously
- doubtful—doubtfully
- beseeching—beseechingly
- brisk—briskly
- firm—firmly

Tell students that the first word in each pair is an adjective, a word used to modify the meaning of a noun or pronoun. The second word is an adverb, a word used most often to modify the meaning of a verb. Ask students to find the adverbs on this page and tell what they modify. **EL** **OL**

Straithes, Yorkshire, Dame Laura Knight, 1877–1970. Oil on canvas, 29½ x 24½ in. Private collection.

So that was how Lob came to live with the Pengelly family. Everybody loved him and he loved them all. But there was never any question who came first with him. He was Sandy's dog. He slept by her bed and followed her everywhere he was allowed. 8

Nine years went by, and each summer Mr. Dodsworth came back to stay at the Fisherman's Arms and call on his erstwhile dog. Lob always met him with recognition and dignified pleasure, accompanied him for a walk or two—but showed no signs of wishing to return to Liverpool. His place, he intimated,[10] was definitely with the Pengellys. R

In the course of nine years Lob changed less than Sandy. As she went into her teens he became a little slower, a little stiffer, there was a touch of gray on his nose, but he was still a handsome dog. He and Sandy still loved one another devotedly. C

10. Lob belonged to Mr. Dodsworth in earlier times ***(erstwhile)***. To ***intimate*** is to hint at something without stating it directly.

Practice the Skills

8 Comparing Literature

Plot When Bert decided the Pengelly family could take Lob to live with them, a conflict was resolved. Did you think it was the end of the story? Notice that the next paragraph begins "Nine years went by . . ." There's a lot more story to come. Read on and watch for the next big event.

Teach

R Reading Skill

Review Inferring Ask: Why does the story now focus on one day in October nine years after Lob had come to live with the Pengellys? *(Something important is going to happen on this day.)* OL

C Critical Thinking

Comprehension Ask: What do you predict may be about to happen? *(Since nine years is a long time in a dog's life, some students may predict that Lob will die soon. Others may predict that something will happen on the steep hill.)* OL

Differentiated Instruction

Creating a Radio Drama Name a sound and have students suggest feelings that it can evoke in listeners. For example, if you say *laughter,* students might say *happiness.*

Have small groups of students each select one scene from the story to read as a radio drama. Encourage each group to create sound effects to accompany its drama. Encourage groups to practice their dramas and then perform them for the rest of the class. Have class members close their eyes as they listen. After each performance, have listeners describe the feelings and images each scene created in their minds. AS

Objectives
- Make predictions
- Make inferences
- Speak effectively

Teach

L1 Literary Element

Plot Say: Describe the story's setting as this page begins. *(It is getting dark and it is windy.)* Why might these details be important to the plot? *(Possible response: Something scary or suspenseful may be about to happen.)* **OL**

L2 Literary Element

Plot Say: Explain how suspense builds in the paragraph that begins with Jean Pengelly saying, "Put some cheerful music on." *(It is a dark and lonely night. At first, what we see happening is calm, even dull. Then we learn that a truck has just hurtled down the hill that Sandy and Lob climbed—but Sandy and Lob aren't mentioned.)* **OL**

C Critical Thinking

Comprehension Say: At the end of this page, Aiken again mentions the steep hill and the sign that's posted there. Why do you think she repeats that information? *(Perhaps she wants to remind readers how dangerous the hill is or to build suspense over what may have happened to Sandy and Lob.)* **AS**

One evening in October all the summer visitors had left, and the little fishing town looked empty and **secretive**. It was a wet, windy dusk. When the children came home from school—even the twins were at high school[11] now, and Don was a full-fledged fisherman—Jean Pengelly said, "Sandy, your Aunt Rebecca says she's lonesome because Uncle Will Hoskins has gone out trawling,[12] and she wants one of you to go and spend the evening with her. You go, dear; you can take your homework with you." L1

Sandy looked far from enthusiastic.

"Can I take Lob with me?"

"You know Aunt Becky doesn't really like dogs— Oh, very well." Mrs. Pengelly sighed. "I suppose she'll have to put up with him as well as you."

Reluctantly Sandy tidied herself, took her schoolbag, put on the damp raincoat she had just taken off, fastened Lob's lead to his collar, and set off to walk through the dusk to Aunt Becky's cottage, which was five minutes' climb up the steep hill.

Visual Vocabulary
A boat's ***shrouds*** are ropes that help support the masts.

The wind was howling through the shrouds of boats drawn up on the Hard.

"Put some cheerful music on, do," said Jean Pengelly to the nearest twin. "Anything to drown that wretched sound while I make your dad's supper." So Don, who had just come in, put on some rock music, loud. Which was why the Pengellys did not hear the truck **hurtle** down the hill and crash against the post office wall a few minutes later. **9** L2

Dr. Travers was driving through Cornwall with his wife, taking a late holiday before patients began coming down with winter colds and flu. He saw the sign that said STEEP HILL. LOW GEAR FOR 1½ MILES. Dutifully he changed into second gear. C

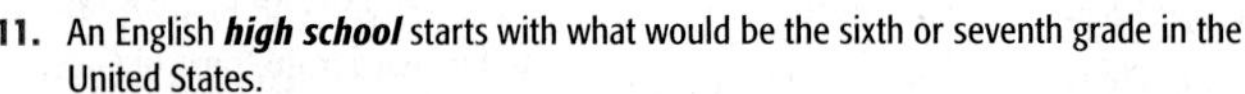

11. An English ***high school*** starts with what would be the sixth or seventh grade in the United States.
12. ***Trawling*** is fishing with large nets that are dragged across the water's bottom.

Vocabulary

secretive (SEE krih tiv) *adj.* seeming to keep secrets; holding back information

hurtle (HUR tul) *v.* to move fast with a lot of force

Practice the Skills

9 Comparing Literature

Plot This crash hints at an important plot event that is about to be revealed. What do you think that event will be?

Additional Support

Differentiated Instruction

Creating Suspense Encourage students to help you list ways the author creates suspense in this story.

- by not telling readers what is happening and making them guess
- by creating a setting that seems spooky
- by having characters perform an action that seems dangerous

Then have students write suspenseful stories. They may want to plan their tales by thinking about an event involving a dog or other pet, or a scary event.

Encourage students to use "Lob's Girl" as a writing model for creating suspense and mood. **AL**

"We must be nearly there," said his wife, looking out her window. "I noticed a sign on the coast road that said the Fisherman's Arms was two miles. What a narrow, dangerous hill! But the cottages are very pretty—Oh, Frank, stop, *stop!* There's a child, I'm sure it's a child—by the wall over there!"

Dr. Travers jammed on his brakes and brought the car to a stop. A little stream ran down by the road in a shallow stone culvert,[13] and half in the water lay something that looked, in the dusk, like a pile of clothes—or was it the body of a child? **C** Mrs. Travers was out of the car in a flash, but her husband was quicker.

"Don't touch her, Emily!" he said sharply. "She's been hit. Can't be more than a few minutes. Remember that truck that overtook us half a mile back, speeding like the devil? Here, quick, go into that cottage and phone for an ambulance. The girl's in a bad way. I'll stay here and do what I can to stop the bleeding. Don't waste a minute." **10**

Doctors are expert at stopping dangerous bleeding, for they know the right places to press. This Dr. Travers was able to do, but he didn't dare do more; the girl was lying in a queerly crumpled heap, and he guessed she had a number of bones broken and that it would be highly dangerous to move her. He watched her with great concentration, wondering where the truck had got to and what other damage it had done.

Mrs. Travers was very quick. She had seen plenty of accident cases and knew the importance of speed. The first cottage she tried had a phone; in four minutes she was back, and in six an ambulance was wailing down the hill.

Its attendants lifted the child onto a stretcher as carefully as if she were made of fine thistledown. The ambulance sped off to Plymouth—for the local cottage hospital[14] did not take serious accident cases—and Dr. Travers went down to the police station to report what he had done.

He found that the police already knew about the speeding truck—which had suffered from loss of brakes and ended up with its radiator halfway through the post office wall. The driver was concussed and shocked, but the police thought he was the only person injured—until Dr. Travers told his tale.

13. A ***culvert*** is a drainage ditch.

14. ***Cottage hospital*** is a British term for a small hospital with a staff of local doctors.

Practice the Skills

10 Comparing Literature

Plot Is this an important point in the plot? What details should you add to your list? Is this the *climax* of the story? Well, it is a point of high suspense and you might think so, but keep reading! In some stories, there can be high points before the most important one.

Teach

C Critical Thinking

Comprehension Ask: Why do you think Aiken describes the object lying half in the water as something that might be a pile of clothes or might be the body of a child? *(She builds suspense by not spelling everything out, by keeping some details uncertain, and by withholding other details.)* **OL**

R Reading Skill

Review Drawing Conclusions Ask: From what you learn on this page, what can you conclude about what happens to Sandy and why it happens? *(She is hit by the truck because the driver cannot control it without brakes, the road is steep, and the night is dark.)* What can you conclude probably happens to Lob? *(Perhaps Lob is killed by the truck; perhaps he runs away to get help; or maybe he is injured.)* **OL**

Reading in the Real World

Citizenship Invite a group of students to think about a dangerous place in their community, such as an intersection in need of a stop sign or a bridge with a missing railing.

Have students analyze the problem and decide what they think should be done about it (such as installing speed bumps or lights). Then have students attend a neighborhood association meeting or set up an appointment with the mayor to discuss the problem and its solution. The mayor or association members may have ideas about the next step students can take to help solve this problem. **AS**

Objectives
- Draw conclusions
- Understand plot line
- Identify and analyze events

Teach

R Reading Skill

Review Inferring Ask: Why does Aunt Rebecca's attitude change from the first paragraph to the second paragraph on this page? *(Aunt Rebecca learns that Sandy has been hit by a truck and may die.)* OL

C Critical Thinking

Analysis Say: Many things have happened since Sandy and Lob left home for Aunt Rebecca's, but Aiken has not mentioned Lob before the end of the second paragraph. **Ask:** Why has Aiken not mentioned Lob until now? *(She builds suspense by making us wonder about Lob.)* OL

V Vocabulary

Synonyms Say: Use a thesaurus to find synonyms for the following words from this page.

- startled *(surprised, disturbed)*
- comfort *(consolation, relief)*
- shocked *(stunned, upset)*
- healthy *(fit, robust)* OL EL

At half-past nine that night Aunt Rebecca Hoskins was sitting by her fire thinking aggrieved thoughts about the inconsiderateness of nieces who were asked to supper and never turned up when she was startled by a neighbor, who burst in exclaiming, "Have you heard about Sandy Pengelly, R then, Mrs. Hoskins? Terrible thing, poor little soul, and they don't know if she's likely to live. Police have got the truck driver that hit her—ah, it didn't ought to be allowed, speeding through the place like that at umpty miles an hour, they ought to jail him for life—not that that'd be any comfort to poor Bert and Jean."

Horrified, Aunt Rebecca put on a coat and went down to her brother's house. She found the family with white shocked faces; Bert and Jean were about to drive off to the hospital C where Sandy had been taken, and the twins were crying bitterly. Lob was nowhere to be seen. But Aunt Rebecca was not interested in dogs; she did not inquire about him.

"Thank the lord you've come, Beck," said her brother. "Will you stay the night with Don and the twins? Don's out looking for Lob and heaven knows when we'll be back; we may get a bed with Jean's mother in Plymouth."

"Oh, if only I'd never invited the poor child," wailed Mrs. Hoskins. But Bert and Jean hardly heard her.

That night seemed to last forever. The twins cried themselves to sleep. Don came home very late and grim-faced. Bert and Jean sat in a waiting room of the Western Counties Hospital, but Sandy was unconscious, they were told, and she remained so. All that could be done for her was done. She was given transfusions to replace all the blood she had lost. The broken bones were set and put in slings and cradles.[15] 11

"Is she a healthy girl? Has she a good constitution?"[16] the emergency doctor asked.

"Aye, doctor, she is that," Bert said hoarsely. The lump in Jean's throat prevented her from answering: she merely nodded.

15. The ***cradles*** are frames that keep Sandy's bedclothes from touching her injuries.

16. Here, ***constitution*** refers to a person's physical condition.

Vocabulary

aggrieved (uh GREEVD) *adj.* feeling insulted or unfairly treated

Practice the Skills

11 Reviewing Skills

Drawing Conclusions Do you have enough information to draw a conclusion about Sandy's condition? If so, what is it?

Additional Support

Reading in the Real World

Career In "Lob's Girl," students have met several characters who have careers in health care. They include the doctor who spots Sandy, the ambulance attendants who take her to the hospital, and the emergency room doctor who treats her there. There are many other careers in or related to health care.

In the United States, almost 7 million people work in health care. Have students work in pairs to brainstorm lists of careers in health care. Then have them choose two careers that interest them and research the careers. OL

Analyzing the Photo Compare the home shown here with the painting *Straithes, Yorkshire,* on page 377. Which of the two pictures is closer to your image of the story's setting? Why?

"Then she ought to have a chance. But I won't conceal from you that her condition is very serious, unless she shows signs of coming out from this coma."

But as hour **succeeded** hour, Sandy showed no signs of recovering consciousness. Her parents sat in the waiting room with **haggard** faces; sometimes one of them would go to telephone the family at home, or try to get a little sleep at the home of Granny Pearce, not far away. **R** **12**

At noon next day Dr. and Mrs. Travers went to the Pengelly cottage to inquire how Sandy was doing, but the report was gloomy: "Still in a very serious condition." The twins were miserably unhappy. They forgot that they had sometimes

Practice the Skills

12 Comparing Literature

Plot What part of the plot is it now? Is suspense building again? Is there a new conflict? Make notes about these questions on your "Lob's Girl" list.

Vocabulary

succeeded (suk SEED ed) *v.* followed; happened after

haggard (HAG urd) *adj.* looking worn out from grief, worry, or illness

Teach

Viewing the Photo

Say: Based on your image of the story's setting, draw a picture of how you would illustrate this story. How does it compare to the picture shown on this page? How does it compare to the one shown on page 377? *(Responses will vary.)* **AS**

R Reading Skill

Review Drawing Conclusions **Ask:** Why is it bad that Sandy has shown no signs of regaining consciousness? *(The doctor tells Bert and Jean that Sandy's condition is very serious unless she shows signs of coming out of the coma.)* **OL**

Reading in the Real World

College Invite students to conduct research about how animals find their way over long distances. Dogs such as Lob have been known to travel long distances to reconnect with their owners.

Encourage students to use reference books, magazine articles, and the Internet to find information about two animals that are capable of making long journeys. Have them take notes on the animals' skills as travelers and navigators. Then have them use their notes to compare the animals' skills and methods in a presentation to the rest of the class. **AL**

Objectives
- Draw conclusions
- Make connections between a text and current events
- Visualize the setting
- Conduct research

Teach

BQ BIG Question

Ask: What are the twins discovering about counting on others? *(They are discovering how much they counted on Sandy. They are also discovering how lonely and isolated they feel with Mother and Dad away, Don detached from them, and Lob missing.)* **OL**

R Reading Skill

Review Drawing Conclusions **Say:** In the first paragraph, a dog arrives at the hospital. **Ask:** Who is this dog and what does it want? *(The dog is—or seems to be—Lob. He wants to get inside the hospital to see Sandy.)* **BL**

C Critical Thinking

Evaluation **Say:** In the last paragraph, Mrs. Pearce tells the porter that Lob has walked the length of England twice to be with Sandy. We readers already knew that. What reason do you think Aiken may have had for reminding us of it? *(Aiken wants us to remember that Lob is capable of making amazing journeys.)* **OL**

called their elder sister bossy and only remembered how often she had shared her pocket money with them, how she read to them and took them for picnics and helped with their homework. Now there was no Sandy, no Mother and Dad, Don went around with a gray, shuttered face, and worse still, there was no Lob. **13**

The Western Counties Hospital is a large one, with dozens of different departments and five or six connected buildings, each with three or four entrances. By that afternoon it became noticeable that a dog seemed to have taken up position outside the hospital, with the fixed intention of getting in. Patiently he would try first one entrance and then another, all the way around, and then begin again. Sometimes he would get a little way inside, following a visitor, but animals were, of course, forbidden, and he was always kindly but firmly turned out again. Sometimes the guard at the main entrance gave him a pat or offered him a bit of sandwich—he looked so wet and beseeching and desperate. But he never ate the sandwich. No one seemed to own him or to know where he came from: Plymouth is a large city and he might have belonged to anybody. **R**

At tea time Granny Pearce came through the pouring rain to bring a flask of hot tea with brandy in it to her daughter and son-in-law. Just as she reached the main entrance the guard was gently but forcibly shoving out a large, **agitated**, soaking-wet Alsatian dog.

"No, old fellow, you can *not* come in. Hospitals are for people, not for dogs."

"Why, bless me," exclaimed old Mrs. Pearce. "That's Lob! Here, Lob. Lobby boy!"

Lob ran to her, whining. Mrs. Pearce walked up to the desk.

"I'm sorry, madam, you can't bring that dog in here," the guard said. **14**

Mrs. Pearce was a very determined old lady. She looked the porter in the eye.

"Now, see here, young man. That dog has walked twenty miles from St. Killan to get to my granddaughter. Heaven **C**

Vocabulary

agitated (AJ uh tayt ud) *adj.* excited, nervous, or disturbed; stirred up

Practice the Skills

13 Comparing Literature

Plot What do you think has happened to Lob? How does his being gone affect the plot? Add any important ideas to the list in your Learner's Notebook.

14 Comparing Literature

Plot Stories don't always follow a simple plot sequence. A minor conflict was resolved early in this story when Mr. Dodsworth let the family keep Lob. However, the story was far from over! Now, here's another conflict. What is it? Does it add to the suspense? How will this conflict be resolved?

Additional Support

Reading Fluency

Build Fluency Mrs. Pearce's speech to the porter at the bottom of this page and the top of the next page offers an excellent opportunity for students to practice building fluency and reading with expression. It is passionate and direct.

Have students find a quiet place to practice reading Mrs. Pearce's speech aloud. Tell them to reread her speech several times until they can read all the sentences smoothly, and with expression and understanding. Tell students to make their reading sound like natural speech. They can skip the words *she went on, bristling,* because Mrs. Pearce doesn't say them. **BL** knows how he knew she was here, but it's plain he knows. And he ought to have his rights! He ought to get to see her! Do you know," she went on, bristling, "that dog has walked the length of England—*twice*—to be with that girl? And you think you can keep him out with your fiddling rules and regulations?"

"I'll have to ask the medical officer," the guard said weakly.

"You do that, young man." Granny Pearce sat down in a determined manner, shutting her umbrella, and Lob sat patiently dripping at her feet. Every now and then he shook his head, as if to dislodge something heavy that was tied around his neck. **R**

Presently a tired, thin, intelligent-looking man in a white coat came downstairs, with an impressive, silver-haired man in a dark suit, and there was a low-voiced discussion. Granny Pearce eyed them, biding her time.

"Frankly . . . not much to lose," said the older man. The man in the white coat approached Granny Pearce.

"It's strictly against every rule, but as it's such a serious case we are making an exception," he said to her quietly. "But only *outside* her bedroom door—and only for a moment or two."

Without a word, Granny Pearce rose and stumped upstairs. Lob followed close to her skirts, as if he knew his hope lay with her.

They waited in the green-floored corridor outside Sandy's room. The door was half shut. Bert and Jean were inside. Everything was terribly quiet. A nurse came out. The white-coated man asked her something and she shook her head. She had left the door ajar, and through it could now be seen a high, narrow bed with a lot of gadgets around it. Sandy lay there, very flat under the covers, very still. Her head was turned away. All Lob's attention was **riveted** on the bed. He strained toward it, but Granny Pearce clasped his collar firmly. **15**

"I've done a lot for you, my boy, now you behave yourself," she whispered grimly. Lob let out a faint whine, anxious and pleading.

At the sound of that whine Sandy stirred just a little. She sighed and moved her head the least fraction. Lob whined again. And then Sandy turned her head right over. Her eyes opened, looking at the door. **16**

Practice the Skills

15 English Language Coach

Synonyms The steel beams of a big building are **riveted** together; they're attached to one another with metal pins called rivets. Synonyms for *riveted* include *attached* and *fastened.* The best synonym in this context, however, would be *focused.*

16 Comparing Literature

Plot Two major conflicts have been resolved: Lob has been allowed to get close to Sandy, and Sandy seems to be coming out of her coma. This is the climax of the story. Note the details of this under "Climax" on your list.

Teach

R Reading Skill

Review Inferring Ask: What reason do you think there might be for the way Lob shakes his head, "as if to dislodge something heavy that was tied around his neck"? *(Maybe the dog hurt his neck in the accident. Maybe he's been in a situation where something was tied around his neck. Maybe someone tied him up and he broke free.)* Suggest that students revisit this interpretation of Lob's behavior after they finish reading the story. **OL**

V Vocabulary

Synonyms and Antonyms
Say: Use a thesaurus to find synonyms for the following words from this page.

- weakly *(timidly, meekly)*
- patiently *(calmly, steadily)*
- thin *(skinny, slim)*
- grimly *(gravely, seriously)*

Now find an antonym for each of the words:

- weakly *(strongly, sternly)*
- patiently *(impatiently, anxiously)*
- thin *(heavy, fat)*
- grimly *(lightly, lightheartedly)* **OL**

Literature Focus Lesson

Suspense Ask students if they've ever been so anxious while reading a story that they've held their breath or bitten their nails. Tell them that the feeling of uncertainty about what will happen next in a story is called **suspense.** Writers can create suspense by

- raising questions in a reader's mind about characters and their motivation
- describing a mood that is threatening or mysterious
- including hints about possible developments

Ask students: How does Joan Aiken build suspense about whether Lob will get to Sandy's hospital room? **OL**

Objectives

- Make inferences
- Understand synonyms and antonyms
- Monitor comprehension

Teach

R Reading Skill

Review Drawing Conclusions **Say:** Explain why Bert and Jean are "white-faced and shocked" when they see Lob. *(At this point in the story it would be reasonable to conclude that they are shocked to see Lob there because the hospital is so far from their home, because they think that Lob is lost, or because they think that Lob has been killed.)* **OL**

C Critical Thinking

Analysis **Ask:** Now that the story has ended, do you think that Lob is the dog in the hospital or not? Explain why you think what you do. *(Possible response: Now I know that Lob had been killed, but Lob has a history of overcoming obstacles to be with Sandy.)* **OL**

BQ 

Ask: Who is the most dependable character in this story? *(Possible response: Lob.)* How does that character demonstrate dependability? *(Possible response: by journeying great distances to be at the side of those who want and need him)* **OL**

"Lob?" she murmured—no more than a breath of sound. "Lobby, boy?"

The doctor by Granny Pearce drew a quick, sharp breath. Sandy moved her left arm—the one that was not broken—from below the covers and let her hand dangle down, feeling as she always did in the mornings, for Lob's furry head. The doctor nodded slowly.

"All right," he whispered. "Let him go to the bedside. But keep ahold of him."

Granny Pearce and Lob moved to the bedside. Now she could see Bert and Jean, white-faced and shocked, on the far side of the bed. But she didn't look at them. She looked at the smile on her granddaughter's face as the groping fingers found Lob's wet ears and gently pulled them. "Good boy," whispered Sandy, and fell asleep again. **R**

Granny Pearce led Lob out into the passage again. There she let go of him and he ran off swiftly down the stairs. She would have followed him, but Bert and Jean had come out into the passage, and she spoke to Bert fiercely.

"*I* don't know why you were so foolish as not to bring the dog before! Leaving him to find the way here himself—"

"But, Mother!" said Jean Pengelly. "That can't have been Lob. What a chance to take! Suppose Sandy hadn't—" She stopped, with her handkerchief pressed to her mouth.

"Not Lob? I've known that dog nine years! I suppose I ought to know my own granddaughter's dog?"

"Listen, Mother," said Bert. "Lob was killed by the same truck that hit Sandy. Don found him—when he went to look for Sandy's schoolbag. He was—he was dead. Ribs all smashed. No question of that. Don told me on the phone—he and Will Hoskins rowed a half mile out to sea and sank the dog with a lump of concrete tied to his collar. Poor old boy. Still—he was getting on. Couldn't have lasted forever."

"*Sank him at sea?* Then what—?"

Slowly old Mrs. Pearce, and then the other two, turned to look at the trail of dripping-wet footprints that led down the hospital stairs.

In the Pengellys' garden they have a stone, under the palm tree. It says: "Lob. Sandy's dog. Buried at sea." **17** **18** ○

Practice the Skills

17 Comparing Literature

Plot The resolution of the story is the ending. Did the author give you some important information at the end of this story? What was it? Did the story end as you expected it to? Remember to add these points to your list under "Resolution."

18 BIG Question

Who could Sandy count on? Put your answer on a note card in the center pocket of Foldable 3. Your response will help you complete the Unit Challenge later. **BQ**

Additional Support

Literature Focus Lesson

Character Remind students that an author can use several methods to let a reader know what a character is like, including

- what the character says
- what the character does
- what others say about the character
- how others behave toward the character

By choosing a dog as a main character, Joan Aiken denied herself one method of characterization: what the character says. Have students suggest examples of each of the *other* methods of characterization that Aiken uses for Lob. **AS**

Before You Read

The Highwayman

Alfred Noyes

Meet the Author

Alfred Noyes was born in England in 1880. He became one of the most popular British poets of his lifetime. Noyes wrote more than fifty books. He wrote short stories, novels, and nonfiction, as well as collections of poetry. Noyes died in 1958. See page R6 of the Author Files for more on Alfred Noyes.

Author Search For more about Alfred Noyes, go to www.glencoe.com.

Objectives (pp. 385–391)
Literature Identify literary elements: plot • Compare and contrast: literature
Vocabulary Use synonyms

Vocabulary Preview

torrent (TOR unt) *n.* a strong rush of anything (usually water) flowing swiftly and wildly **(p. 386)** *A torrent of water flooded the town.*

V **jest** (jest) *n.* a joke, prank, or amusing remark **(p. 389)** *The soldier's jest made his buddies roar with laughter.*

writhed (rythd) *v.* twisted and turned, as from suffering; form of the verb *writhe* **(p. 389)** *She writhed against the ropes.*

English Language Coach

Synonyms Be sure to choose the best synonym for your context. Below are three synonyms for *torrent.* Which one would be best to replace *torrent* in the sentence above? (You may use a dictionary.)

blast gush flood

Get Ready to Read

Connect to the Reading

The story of this poem takes place before there were organized police forces, cars, telephones, and electricity. Imagine how different that time was.

Build Background

- A highwayman is a roadside robber, especially one on horseback. In England, from the 1600s to 1800s, highwaymen robbed passengers traveling by coach.
- Some highwaymen became famous. Some became popular, at least among those who were never robbed. Those who were caught were usually tried and hanged to death.
- Some highwaymen became legends. One of them, Jonathan Wild, became the hero of a novel and an opera in the 1700s.

Set Purposes for Reading

BIG Question Read to find out how a poem about a highwayman may affect your answer to the Big Question.

Set Your Own Purpose What would you like to learn from the poem to help you answer the Big Question? Write your own purpose on a note card and put the card in the left pocket of Foldable 3.

More About the Author

Although Alfred Noyes was born in England, he lived for 35 years in the United States and Canada. His books were so successful that he and his family were able to live on his royalty checks. Even so, he accepted a teaching position at Princeton University and taught there for nine years.

V Vocabulary

Sample Sentences Say: Notice that the definition of each word in the Vocabulary Preview includes an example sentence. Create a new example sentence for each word. Use the existing example sentences as models. Write the sentences in your Learner's Notebook. *(Responses will vary.)* BL EL

Use the CheckPoint questions provided on Presentation Plus! to check for prior knowledge and to build background. These questions can be used with interactive response keypads for immediate student feedback.

Literature Online

Author Search To expand students' appreciation of Alfred Noyes, have them access the Web site for additional information and resources.

Literature Focus Lesson

Narrative Poem A narrative poem shares the essential elements of a short story, including

- plot
- conflict
- setting
- characters
- dialogue

Students will be following the plot closely as they read "The Highwayman," but urge them to note the other elements as well. When they compare "Lob's Girl" and "The Highwayman," they may want to include a discussion of the way that specific elements are developed in each selection. AS

Teach

R Reading Skill

Review Previewing Say: Take a minute to think about the shape of this poem. **Ask:** How are the lines of the poem grouped? *(The lines are grouped in paragraphs called stanzas.)* How many parts does the poem have? *(The poem has two parts.)* OL

L Literary Element

Review Sensory Details
Ask: Which details in the description of the highwayman on this page help you "see" him? *(The details that give a visual image of the highwayman include his hat, his leather breeches, his boots, his pistol, and his sword.)* AS

The Highwayman

by Alfred Noyes

PART 1

The wind was a **torrent** of darkness among the gusty trees.
The moon was a ghostly galleon* tossed upon cloudy seas.
The road was a ribbon of moonlight over the purple moor,*
And the highwayman came riding—
Riding—riding—
The highwayman came riding, up to the old inn door. 1

He'd a French cocked hat on his forehead, a bunch of lace at his chin,
A coat of the claret velvet, and breeches of brown doeskin.
They fitted with never a wrinkle. His boots were up to the thigh.
L And he rode with a jewelled twinkle,
His pistol butts a-twinkle,
His rapier hilt* a-twinkle, under the jewelled sky.

Over the cobbles he clattered and clashed in the dark inn yard.
He tapped with his whip on the shutters, but all was locked and barred.

2 A *galleon* (GAL ee un) is a large sailing ship from the 1400s–1600s.
3 A *moor* is an area of open, rolling, wild land, usually a grassy wetland.
12 A *rapier* is a long, lightweight sword, and the *hilt* is its handle.

Vocabulary

torrent (TOR unt) *n.* a strong rush of anything (usually water) flowing swiftly and wildly

Practice the Skills

1 Comparing Literature

Plot The exposition of a plot often introduces the setting and the main character of a story. What do you learn about the setting from these first few lines? What do you learn about the main character? Start a new list in your Learner's Notebook for "The Highwayman." Under "Exposition," note important points about the setting and main character.

Additional Support

English Language Coach

Unusual Words Students may have difficulty with words in the poem that are rarely used in everyday American English. Some of these are archaic, or out-of-date, words; others are more often used in British English than in American English. Invite pairs of students to use dictionaries, thesauruses, encyclopedias, the SE page, and the Internet to familiarize themselves with these words from pages 386 and 387.

- cocked hat
- claret velvet
- breeches
- locked and barred
- doeskin
- pistol butts
- cobbles

EL OL

A Wet Winter's Evening, 1880.
John Atkinson Grimshaw.

He whistled a tune to the window, and who should be
    waiting there
But the landlord's black-eyed daughter,
        Bess, the landlord's daughter,
Plaiting* a dark red love-knot into her long black hair. **2**

And dark in the dark old inn yard a stable wicket* creaked
Where Tim the ostler listened. His face was white and
    peaked.*
His eyes were hollows of madness, his hair like mouldy hay, **R**

18 Bess is braiding ***(plaiting)*** a red ribbon into her hair.

19 A ***wicket*** is a small door or gate; this one leads into the stable.

20 As the ***ostler*** (a shorter form of ***hostler***), it's Tim's job to take care of the horses at the inn. A ***peaked*** face looks pale and sickly.

Practice the Skills

2 **Comparing Literature**

Plot This is still the exposition of the plot. What new character has been introduced? What more have you learned about the high-wayman? Why has he come to the inn? Add notes to the list in your Learner's Notebook.

Teach

Viewing the Illustration

What does this painting tell you about the setting of this poem? *(Possible response: it's dark, at night)*

R Reading Skill

Review Drawing Conclusions **Say:** Based on the author's description of Tim, do you think he willl be a postive or negative character? Explain. *(Possible response: negative, because his eyes are "hollows of redness" and he's pale)* **OL**

Differentiated Instruction

Picturing the Highwayman Students may find the poem easier to understand if they can visualize the highwayman. Begin by having students look up the word *highwayman* in a dictionary.

Have students work in small groups to create illustrations of the highwayman. Ask each group to look up unfamiliar words or phrases in the poem that describe the highwayman's appearance and include these details in their drawings. Encourage them to label the drawings and display them so that others can refer to them as they read the poem. **BL** **EL**

Objectives

- Monitor comprehension
- Visualize characters
- Identify literary elements: sensory details

Teach

C Critical Thinking

Analysis Say: Based on the description of Tim, what do you think the narrator thinks about him? *(The narrator calls Tim dumb, so I don't think the narrator thinks very highly of Tim.)*

R Reading Skill

Review Determining the Main Idea Ask: What is the main idea of lines 31 through 35? *(The highwayman and Bess are in love with each other but are separated.)* What details support that main idea? *(The highwayman's reaching out for her but not being able to touch her; his face burning with desire; her letting her hair down as a way of reaching out to him; his kissing her hair and inhaling its scent.)* **OL**

But he loved the landlord's daughter,
The landlord's red-lipped daughter. **3**
Dumb as a dog he listened, and he heard the robber say—

"One kiss, my bonny* sweetheart, I'm after a prize tonight,
But I shall be back with the yellow gold before the morning light;
Yet, if they press me sharply, and harry* me through the day,
Then look for me by moonlight,
Watch for me by moonlight,
I'll come to thee by moonlight, though hell should bar the way."

He rose upright in the stirrups. He scarce could reach her hand,
But she loosened her hair in the casement. His face burnt like a brand*
As the black cascade* of perfume came tumbling over his breast;
And he kissed its waves in the moonlight,
(O, sweet black waves in the moonlight!)
Then he tugged at his rein in the moonlight, and galloped away to the west. **4**

PART 2

He did not come in the dawning. He did not come at noon;
And out of the tawny* sunset, before the rise of the moon,
When the road was a gypsy's ribbon, looping the purple moor,
A red coat troop* came marching—
Marching—marching—
King George's men came marching, up to the old inn door. **5**

25 ***Bonny*** (a Scottish word) means "good-looking, fine, or admirable."

27 To ***harry*** is to trouble, bother, or worry.

32 The ***casement*** is the window frame, and the ***brand*** is a burning torch.

33 A ***cascade*** is a small waterfall or something similar to a waterfall.

38 ***Tawny*** is a brownish-gold color.

40 The ***red coat troop*** is a group of soldiers wearing bright red coats.

Practice the Skills

3 Comparing Literature

Plot The story is now at the rising action part of the plot. Make sure you note this on your list. A new character has also been introduced. What effect does Tim have on the plot? Under "Rising Action," add notes about this to your list.

4 Comparing Literature

Plot What have you learned about the plot up to this point? Has a conflict been introduced yet? If so, what is it? Add a note about this to your list.

5 Comparing Literature

Plot Starting at line 40, some new characters are introduced. Who are these characters, and what part do you think they will play in the plot? Add a note about this to your list.

Additional Support

Differentiated Instruction

Monitoring Comprehension To help students comprehend the poem, you may wish to have them work with the following questions while reading it.

- What is the conflict?
- What is happening?
- What can I predict?

Have the students use a three-column chart to write their responses to the questions as they read the poem. They might pause at the end of each page to add or update an answer to each question. Then they can complete their charts when they have completed their reading. **OL**

They said no word to the landlord. They drank his ale instead,
But they gagged his daughter, and bound her, to the foot of her narrow bed.
Two of them knelt at her casement, with muskets at their side! **R1** **R2**
There was death at every window;
And hell at one dark window;
For Bess could see, through her casement, the road that *he* would ride. **6**

They had tied her up to attention, with many a sniggering **jest**.*
They had bound a musket beside her, with the muzzle* beneath her breast!
"Now, keep good watch!" and they kissed her. She heard the doomed man say—
Look for me by moonlight;
Watch for me by moonlight;
I'll come to thee by moonlight, though hell should bar the way!

She twisted her hands behind her; but all the knots held good!
She **writhed** her hands till her fingers were wet with sweat or blood!
They stretched and strained in the darkness, and the hours crawled by like years,
Till, now, on the stroke of midnight,
Cold, on the stroke of midnight,
The tip of one finger touched it! The trigger at last was hers!

The tip of one finger touched it. She strove no more for the rest.

49 Bess is tied to a pole, arms at her sides in what a soldier would call "at attention," while the soldiers laugh disrespectfully ***(many a sniggering jest).***

50 The ***muzzle*** is the open end of the ***musket,*** a long gun.

Vocabulary

jest (jĕst) *n.* a joke, prank, or amusing remark

writhed (rythd) *v.* twisted and turned, as from suffering

Practice the Skills

6 Comparing Literature

Plot The poet is building suspense. What do you think the climax of the poem will be?

Teach

R1 Reading Skill

Review Inferring **Ask:** Why have the redcoats appeared? *(Possible response: Because the redcoats go straight to the inn and wait, it is reasonable to infer that Tim has told them of the highwayman's planned return.)* **OL**

R2 Reading Skill

Review Drawing Conclusions **Ask:** Why do the redcoats gag Bess, tie her up, and kneel at the windows with their guns? *(They have learned that the highwayman is returning to Bess, they want to ambush him, and they want to prevent Bess from warning him.)* **OL**

L Literary Element

Review Character **Say:** Describe the character of the redcoats. *(Possible response: They are bullies. They tie Bess up and laugh disrespectfully at her. They tie a rifle to her so that she can be killed at their whim.)* **BL**

Reading Fluency

Build Fluency Tell students to meet with a partner in a quiet place. Have partners take turns reading lines from "The Highwayman" aloud. One partner should read the first line aloud. Then, like an echo, the other partner should read the same line aloud. Tell students to continue reading each line of the poem this way. They should practice reading the lines smoothly, with expression and understanding. **BL** **EL**

Objectives
- Make inferences
- Draw conclusions
- Understand character
- Build reading fluency

Teach

R1 Reading Skill

Review Determining the Main Idea **Ask:** What is the main idea of the first stanza on this page? *(Bess is ready to use the musket to warn the highwayman.)* What details support that main idea? *(her finger on the trigger; the fact that she doesn't strive anymore; and the way her blood throbs)* OL

R2 Reading Skill

Review Determining the Main Idea **Ask:** What is the main idea of the second stanza on this page? *(The ambush is about to take place.)* What details support that main idea? *(The highwayman is approaching, and the redcoats begin priming their muskets.)* OL

Up, she stood up to attention, with the muzzle beneath her breast.
She would not risk their hearing; she would not **strive** again; 7
For the road lay bare in the moonlight;
Blank and bare in the moonlight;
And the blood of her veins, in the moonlight, throbbed to her love's refrain.*

Tlot-tlot; tlot-tlot! Had they heard it: The horsehoofs ringing clear;
Tlot-tlot, tlot-tlot, in the distance? Were they deaf that they did not hear?
Down the ribbon of moonlight, over the brow of the hill,
The highwayman came riding—
Riding—riding—
The red-coats looked to their priming!* She stood up, straight and still!

Tlot-tlot, in the frosty silence! *Tlot-tlot,* in the echoing night!
Nearer he came and nearer. Her face was like a light.
Her eyes grew wide for a moment; she drew one last deep breath,

66 In a song or poem, the ***refrain*** is a phrase or verse that is repeated.

72 The soldiers are ***priming*** their weapons, or loading their muskets with ammunition.

Practice the Skills

7 English Language Coach

Synonyms A dictionary or thesaurus will offer several synonyms for **strive**, including *fight for, try hard,* and *struggle.* Which synonym works best in this context?

Moon Landing, 1977. Jamie Wyeth. Oil on canvas, 29 x 43 in. Private collection.

Additional Support

English Language Coach

Unusual Word Order Poets often express their ideas in phrases and sentences that do not use the usual word order of English. In speech, we would be more likely to express the idea in lines 69 and 70 as "The highwayman came riding down the ribbon of moonlight, over the brow of the hill" rather than in the order Noyes uses. Students may benefit from identifying and interpreting sentence constructions that confuse them. Have them work in pairs to discuss places in the poem where words seem "out of order." Then have them paraphrase each stanza in more usual order. OL EL

Then her finger moved in the moonlight,
Her musket shattered the moonlight,
Shattered her breast in the moonlight and warned him—with her death.

He turned. He spurred to the westward; he did not know who stood
Bowed, with her head o'er the musket, drenched with her own red blood!
Not till the dawn he heard it, and his face grew grey to hear
How Bess, the landlord's daughter,
The landlord's black-eyed daughter,
Had watched for her love in the moonlight, and died in the darkness there.

Back, he spurred like a madman, shrieking a curse to the sky,
With the white road smoking behind him and his rapier brandished* high.
Blood-red were his spurs in the golden noon, wine-red was his velvet coat;
When they shot him down on the highway,
Down like a dog on the highway,
And he lay in his blood on the highway, with a bunch of lace at his throat. **8**

And still of a winter's night, they say, when the wind is in the trees,
When the moon is a ghostly galleon tossed upon cloudy seas,
When the road is a ribbon of moonlight over the purple moor,
A highwayman comes riding—
Riding—riding—
A highwayman comes riding, up to the old inn door.

Over the cobbles he clatters and clangs in the dark inn yard.
He taps with his whip on the shutters, but all is locked and barred.
He whistles a tune to the window, and who should be waiting there
But the landlord's black-eyed daughter,
Bess, the landlord's daughter,
Plaiting a dark red love-knot into her long black hair. **9** **10** ○

86 The highwayman waved his sword threateningly ***(brandished)***.

Practice the Skills

8 Comparing Literature

Plot Reread lines 60, 78, and 90. Which of these is the climax? Note your choice on your list under "Climax."

9 Comparing Literature

Plot Does the poet give you some important information at the end of this story? What is it? Did the story end as you expected it to? Remember to add these points to your list under the heading "Resolution."

10 BIG Question

Who could the highwayman count on? Do you agree with Bess's decision? Explain. Put your answer on a note card in the center pocket of Foldable 5. Your response will help you complete the Unit Challenge later.

Teach

L Literary Element

Review Character Ask: What do you learn about the highwayman's character in the stanza that begins with line 85? *(The highwayman is brave and would risk his own safety to avenge Bess's death. He feels that he has nothing to live for now that Bess is dead.)* **OL**

R Reading Skill

Review Responding Ask: What do the last two stanzas mean to you? *(Some students may think that the highwayman and Bess meet again at the inn as ghosts on moonlit winter nights.)* **OL**

BQ 

Ask: What do Bess's actions show about her feelings toward the highwayman? *(Her love for him is so strong that she would do anything to save him.)* **OL**

Differentiated Instruction

Poetry and Music "The Highwayman" has been set to music. Listening to a musical performance of this poem can help students to hear the rhythm and to appreciate the imagery. Lareena McKennitt recorded "The Highwayman" on her CDs *The Book of Secrets* and *Live in Paris and Toronto.* Phil Ochs set the poem to music on his CDs *There But For Fortune* and *Then and Now: Live in Vancouver.*

Have students listen to at least one rendition from each artist and compare the two musical interpretations of the poem. **OL**

Objectives
- Understand character
- Respond to literature
- Identify main ideas

Assess

Resources for page 392

- Selection Quick Check
- Comparing Literature Assessment

Vocabulary Check

Lob's Girl

1. **c.** seeming to keep secrets
2. **d.** to move fast with a lot of force
3. **a.** feeling insulted or unfairly treated
4. **e.** followed; happened after
5. **f.** looking worn out from grief, worry, or illness
6. **b.** excited, nervous, or disturbed; stirred up

The Highwayman

7. torrent
8. jest
9. writhed
10. After the exam, Priscilla was in a (blue) mood.

    The constant rain has helped make this a (dismal) day.

    "Hey Regina," Letricia called out, "Don't look so (glum,) things aren't so bad."

    Why does Eugene have such an (unhappy) tone to his voice?
11. Responses will vary. Some students may think that Lob is not actually dead.
12. Lob feels such a strong attachment to Sandy that it is as if she is "his" person.

After You Read

LOB'S GIRL & The Highwayman

Vocabulary Check

LOB'S GIRL

On a separate sheet of paper, match the number of the word with the letter of its definition.

1. secretive	**a.** feeling insulted or unfairly treated
2. hurtle	**b.** excited, nervous, or disturbed; stirred up
3. aggrieved	**c.** seeming to keep secrets
4. succeeded	**d.** to move fast with a lot of force
5. haggard	**e.** followed; happened after
6. agitated	**f.** looking worn out from grief, worry, or illness

The Highwayman

Rewrite each sentence, replacing the underlined word with its synonym from the vocabulary words.

torrent jest writhed

7. Heavy rains turned the stream into a <u>flood</u>.
8. Tom's <u>joke</u> made me laugh.
9. The fox <u>twisted</u>, trying to escape the trap.
10. **English Language Coach** Copy the sentences below and circle each word that is a synonym for *melancholy.* In "Lob's Girl," *melancholy* is used as an adjective meaning "sad or depressed."
    - After the exam, Priscilla was in a blue mood.
    - The constant rain has helped make this a dismal day.
    - "Hey Regina," Letricia called out, "Don't look so glum, things aren't so bad."
    - Why does Eugene have such an unhappy tone to his voice?

Objectives (pp. 392–393)
Reading Synthesize information
Literature Identify literary elements: plot
Vocabulary Use synonyms
Writing Compare and contrast: literature

Reading/Critical Thinking

On a separate sheet of paper, answer the following questions.

Lob's Girl

11. **Drawing Conclusions** At the end of the selection, you learn that the truck killed Lob in the accident. Then who was the dog that came to visit Sandy at the hospital?

TIP **Author and Me**

12. **Synthesizing** The title of the selection suggests that Sandy belongs to Lob. What do you think this means?

TIP **Author and Me**

The Highwayman

13. **Drawing Conclusions** Lines 19–24 describe Tim, the ostler. What role do you think Tim plays in this poem? How did the soldiers know to wait for the highwayman in Bess's room?

TIP **Author and Me**

14. **Synthesizing** You learn in the poem that Bess shoots herself to warn the highwayman away from the inn. You also learn that the highwayman goes back to the soldiers when he learns of Bess's death, and the soldiers kill him. What do you think the author wants you to take away from reading this poem?

TIP **Author and Me**

Writing: Compare the Literature

Use Your Notes

15. Follow these steps and use your lists to compare the plots of "Lob's Girl" and "The Highwayman."

Step 1: Place your two lists side-by-side. Circle or highlight your plot headings of "Exposition," "Rising Action," "Climax," "Falling Action," and "Resolution." Circle the notes that are similar in the two selections. Underline the notes that are different. Pay particular attention to climaxes and resolutions. If you think of something new as you do this, be sure to add it to one of your lists.

Step 2: Look over your lists with a partner and discuss them. Add any new notes you want.

Step 3: To help you compare the plots of the two selections, be sure you can answer these questions.

- In the exposition of the selections, how are the settings similar or different?
- What are the conflicts in each selection? Are they similar or different?
- What is the main conflict in each selection?
- What happens during the climax of each selection?
- What happens during the resolution of each selection? Were you surprised? What surprised you?

Get It On Paper

Write two short paragraphs. One will be about the differences between the plots of the selections. One will be about their similarities. Remember to look at your notes. All the details you underlined can be used in the paragraph about the differences. All the details you circled can be used in the paragraph about the similarities.

BIG Question

16. In each selection, did the main character have someone he or she could count on? Explain. Put your answer on a note card in the center pocket of Foldable 3. Your response will help you complete the Unit Challenge later.

13. Tim is the third person in a love triangle. He tells the soldiers where to find the highwayman.

14. The love Bess and the highwayman feel is so strong that life without the other is not worth living.

15. Responses will vary. Make sure the students' paragraphs cover the key points.

Get It On Paper

Responses should include the following:

Lob helps save Sandy's life.
Bess helps save the highwayman's life.
Lob runs off after rousing Sandy.
The highwayman runs off after Bess warns him.
We learn that Lob has been killed by the truck.
The highwayman learns that Bess killed herself to warn him.
Lob may have returned from death.
The highwayman and Bess may return from death.

Lob is killed accidentally.
Bess kills herself deliberately.
It seems likely that Sandy lives, although we aren't told that directly.
The highwayman is killed by the redcoats when he rushes at them to avenge Bess's death.

16. Sandy learns that she can count on Lob, and the highwayman learns that he can count on Bess.

Close

Ask students to discuss how both stories can help them answer the Big Question.

The Unit Challenge

Focus

BELLRINGER Options

Daily Language Practice Transparency

Focus Activity Ask: Of all the characters you've met in the selections in this unit, which one do you think is the most dependable? Why? Which one would you turn to when you really need someone you can count on? Why?

Teach

Group Activity: Write a Handbook

- Suggest that students begin by consulting the local government Web site or the local government pages in the telephone directory for resources. They can also brainstorm to list people in their homes, neighborhoods, and schools.
- In step 2, you may want to have students divide the work by resource rather than task, with each student taking a certain number of resources and then gathering the facts, organizing the information, and writing the handbook listings for those resources.
- Make sure that each group begins step 3 by mid-way through the class period to allow time to write the descriptions for the handbook.

UNIT 3 WRAP-UP

Answering the BIG Question: Who Can We Really Count On?

You've just read different selections about who people can count on. Now use what you've learned to do the Unit Challenge.

The Unit Challenge

Choose Activity A or Activity B and follow the directions for that activity.

A. Group Activity: Write a Handbook

- The school newspaper asks you and two friends to write a handbook with the title "People You Can Count On." The handbook should list and discuss the people to whom teens might turn if they have problems.
- The handbook should also explain how to make sure you can count on someone.

1. Discuss the Assignment

- Review the notes from your Foldables for this unit and those you wrote in your Learner's Notebook at the beginning of the unit.
- Discuss the problems the characters in the selections faced and who they could or could not count on.
- Think about the people in your home, school, and community that you count on. Examples might be parents, teachers, friends, or coaches.
- Think about how you can tell if a person is someone you *can't* count on.
- Think about which person might be most helpful for a particular problem. For example, you might be able to count on a parent to help you with a fight you're having with a friend, but another teenager might be more helpful.

2. Make a Decision and Divide the Work

As a group, review your notes and decide what to include in the handbook. You can have very general headings. For example, one might be "Friends: Which Ones Can You Count On and How Can You Tell?" Then divide up the tasks. Who will write which section?

3. Write the Handbook

- Review your notes.
- Once you have each written something, show each other your work and get advice about changes that might need to be made.
- Neatly write or type the information.
- Check your writing for errors in spelling or grammar.

4. Present Your Information Present your handbook to your classmates or send it to the school newspaper.

Assess/Close

Group Activity

Ask: How can you use the handbook you've prepared to get the help of someone who can really be counted on? How would you explain to someone else how the handbook should be used?

B. Solo Activity: Create a Chart

In the future, what problems might you face? Who will you count on to help you? In Activity B, you'll create a chart to organize your ideas. So, if you have a problem, the solution will be easier to find.

1. **Decide What You Need** Review the list you made in your Learner's Notebook of problems you face. Think about any future problems you may face as you work toward your goals.

2. **Create a Chart** Draw a chart like the one below. Use your list to fill in the Problem column. Think about solutions. Use the following questions to help you think:
   - Who did the people in the selections count on? Look at your Unit 3 Foldable notes to remember.
   - How have people you've known solved their problems?

   Now fill in the Solutions column. Some problems may have more than one solution. If you can't think of a solution to a problem, leave it blank.

   Once you have thought of solutions, think about who you can count on to help you. Add these people to the People I Can Count On column. Remember that you are also a person you can count on. If you can't think of a solution, that's okay. Just leave that column blank and fill it in later.

3. **Use the Chart** Keep this chart and add to it as you work toward your goals. Notice the problems that you solve and the solutions you find. Keep track of the people you can count on. When you can't find a solution to a problem, use the people you can count on to help you find one.

Problem	Solutions	People I Can Count On
not getting good grades in my math class	study more, find a friend who is good at math to help me study, get a tutor, ask my teacher for help, ask my mom for help	myself, friends, my teacher, my mom
friends want me to smoke	tell them I don't want to smoke, stay away from them when they smoke, find new friends who don't smoke	myself, good friends, new friends

Teach

Solo Activity: Create a Chart

- If students have trouble thinking of problems that they may face as they work toward their goals, suggest that they work in pairs and anticipate each other's problems.
- Students may also find that someone else can see the possible solutions to their problems better than they can themselves. In that case, working with a partner and suggesting solutions to each other's problems may be more productive.
- Encourage students to think of the people they know as resources they can draw on according to the skills and talents they have. By listing friends and relatives and the skills and talents they possess, students will have a personal resource guide to refer to.
- To extend this activity, have students think about people who can depend on *them*. Who might have a problem that they could help solve? What skills and talents can they offer to someone who's looking for a solution to a problem?

Assess/Close

Solo Activity

Encourage students to study their charts and write what they've learned about who they can really depend on. Review their charts and what they've learned.

Objectives
- Write a handbook
- Organize information graphically

Focus

Vocabulary Preview

List the following words on the board:

- magnificent
- possessively
- extension
- burdens
- mechanical
- suspect

Review their definitions before students begin reading.

Build Background

The setting for this story is Chicago, Illinois, in the 1930s and 1940s. It resembles the Chicago of Gwendolyn Brooks's youth. That place and time have figured prominently throughout her work, including her first poetry collection, *A Street in Bronzeville.* The circumstances of Maud Martha's family also resemble those of Brooks's. Her mother was a schoolteacher. Her father had dreamed of becoming a doctor but couldn't afford to finish school. He was a janitor. Brooks's parents bought a home for their family on Chicago's South Side.

Readability Scores

Dale-Chall: 5.9
DRP: 51
Lexile: 870

UNIT 3

Your Turn: Read and Apply Skills

Meet the Authors

Gwendolyn Brooks

Gwendolyn Brooks was born in 1917 and died in 2000. In 1950 she became the first African American to win the Pulitzer Prize for poetry. Her advice to young poets was "Tell your truth. Don't try to sugar it up." See page R2 of the Author Files for more on Gwendolyn Brooks.

Margaret Danner

Margaret Danner was born in 1915 and died in 1984. She began writing poetry in junior high school. In 1960 she published her first collection of poems. See page R2 of the Author Files for more on Margaret Danner.

Author Search For more about these authors, go to www.glencoe.com.

by Gwendolyn Brooks

This story is from Brooks's novel *Maud Martha,* which was published in 1953.

What had been wanted was this always, this always to last, the talking softly on this porch, with the snake plant in the jardiniere[1] in the southwest corner, and the obstinate slip[2] from Aunt Eppie's magnificent Michigan fern at the left side of the friendly door. Mama, Maud Martha and Helen rocked slowly in their rocking chairs, and looked at the late afternoon light on the lawn, and at the emphatic[3] iron of the fence and at the poplar tree. These things might soon be theirs no longer. Those shafts and pools of light, the tree, the graceful iron, might soon be viewed possessively by different eyes.

Papa was to have gone that noon, during his lunch hour, to the office of the Home Owners' Loan. If he had not succeeded in getting another extension, they would be leaving this house in which they had lived for more than fourteen years. There was little hope. The Home Owners' Loan was hard.[4] They sat, making their plans.

---

1. A ***jardiniere*** (jar dun EER) is a decorative pot or plant stand.
2. Something that's ***obstinate*** (AWB stuh nit) is stubborn. The ***slip*** is a small part of the aunt's fern plant that's being used to grow a new plant. The narrator seems to mean that the young plant is stubborn in continuing to live.
3. ***Emphatic*** means "strongly expressive; forceful."
4. Here, ***hard*** is probably short for *hard-hearted.* The suggestion is that the loan officers show little sympathy or warm feelings toward people who borrow money.

Additional Support

Leveled Reading An adapted version of this selection (Grade 4 readability) is available on page 114 of *Jamestown Literature: An Adapted Reader* for Grade 7.

Literature Focus Lesson

Summary In this story, four members of a family—Mama, Maud Martha, Helen, and Harry—wait anxiously for the fifth member—Papa—to return from work. He was to have gone to the office of the Home Owners' Loan to ask for an extension on their mortgage payment. If he could not get the extension, they would lose their house. Each of them tries to pretend that having to move would not be so bad, that it might even be a blessing in disguise, but none of them really believes it. When Papa arrives at last, and they learn that he got the extension, they feel enormous relief.

"We'll be moving into a nice flat[5] somewhere," said Mama. "Somewhere on South Park, or Michigan, or in Washington Park Court." Those flats, as the girls and Mama knew well, were burdens on wages twice the size of Papa's. This was not mentioned now.

"They're much prettier than this old house," said Helen. "I have friends I'd just as soon not bring here. And I have other friends that wouldn't come down this far for anything, unless they were in a taxi." **R**

Yesterday, Maud Martha would have attacked her. Tomorrow she might. Today she said nothing. She merely gazed at a little hopping robin in the tree, her tree, and tried to keep the fronts of her eyes dry.

"Well, I do know," said Mama, turning her hands over and over, "that I've been getting tireder and tireder of doing that firing. From October to April, there's firing to be done."

The Storyteller, 1995. Christian Pierre. Acrylic on masonite. Private Collection.

"But lately we've been helping, Harry and I," said Maud Martha. "And sometimes in March and April and in October, and even in November, we could build a little fire in the fireplace. Sometimes the weather was just right for that."

She knew, from the way they looked at her, that this had been a mistake. They did not want to cry.

But she felt that the little line of white, somewhat ridged with smoked purple, and all that cream-shot saffron,[6] would never drift across any western sky except that in back of this house. The rain would drum with as sweet a dullness nowhere but here. The birds on South Park were mechanical birds, no better than the poor caught canaries in those "rich" women's sun parlors.

"It's just going to kill Papa!" burst out Maud Martha. "He loves this house! He lives for this house!"

5. ***Flat*** is another word for *apartment.*

6. The orange-yellow color ***(saffron)*** is streaked or mixed ***(shot)*** with a cream color. Maud Martha is describing the colors of the sunset.

Teach

R Reading Skill

Review Inferring Say: Helen talks about the house as if she'd rather not keep living there. **Ask:** What reason do you think Helen has for saying the things she does? *(She may mean what she says, or she may be trying to lessen the pain of leaving by pretending that she doesn't want to stay.)* **OL**

L1 Literary Element

Review Plot Ask: What part of the plot does Brooks present in the paragraphs on this page? *(rising action)* **OL**

L2 Literary Element

Review Plot Ask: What does Brooks do to build suspense and tension in this part of the story? *(She withholds information from us: we don't know what happened when Papa asked for the extension.)* **OL**

Reading in the Real World

Citizenship Ask small groups to research the housing situation in their community. Students may use libraries, community Web sites, and interviews with bankers, housing officials, and housing advocacy groups. Ask each group to prepare a short report or presentation answering questions such as these:

- What percentage of people own their own homes, rent, or live in public housing?
- What are average home prices and rental fees?
- What assistance is available to low-income families?

Objectives

- Make inferences
- Understand elements of plot
- Understand conflict
- Make connections between a text and current events and circumstances

Teach

R Reading Skill

Review Determining the Main Idea **Ask:** What is the main idea of the paragraph that begins "They could not tell a thing from the way Papa was walking"? *(They could not tell from Papa's walk or expression what has happened at the Home Owners' Loan.)* BL

L Literary Element

Review Plot **Ask:** When does the climax of the story occur? *(When Mama pokes her head out the front door and says, "It's all right.")* OL

BQ 

Ask: How do you know that everyone in the family can depend on Papa? *(When Maud Martha says that he loves the house, and that he lives for it, Helen corrects her, saying that he loves them and lives for them.)* OL

"He lives for us," said Helen. "It's us he loves. He wouldn't want the house, except for us."

"And he'll have us," added Mama, "wherever."

"You know," Helen sighed, "if you want to know the truth, this is a relief. If this hadn't come up, we would have gone on, just dragged on, hanging out here forever."

"It might," allowed Mama, "be an act of God. God may just have reached down, and picked up the reins."

"Yes," Maud Martha cracked in, "that's what you always say—that God knows best."

Her mother looked at her quickly, decided the statement was not suspect, looked away.

Helen saw Papa coming. "There's Papa," said Helen.

R They could not tell a thing from the way Papa was walking. It was that same dear little staccato[7] walk, one shoulder down, then the other, then repeat, and repeat. They watched his progress. He passed the Kennedys', he passed the vacant lot, he passed Mrs. Blakemore's. They wanted to hurl themselves over the fence, into the street, and shake the truth out of his collar. He opened his gate—the gate—and still his stride[8] and face told them nothing.

"Hello," he said.

Mama got up and followed him through the front door. The girls knew better than to go in too.

Flowers, 1939–40. William H. Johnson. Oil on plywood. Smithsonian American Art Museum, Washington, DC.

Presently Mama's head emerged. Her eyes were lamps turned on.

"It's all right," she exclaimed. "He got it. It's all over. Everything is all right."

The door slammed shut. Mama's footsteps hurried away.

"I think," said Helen, rocking rapidly, "I think I'll give a party. I haven't given a party since I was eleven. I'd like some of my friends to just casually see that we're homeowners." ❍

7. ***Staccato*** (stuh KAW toh) means "made of short, sharp sounds or movements."

8. Papa's ***stride*** is his way of walking.

Additional Support

Differentiated Instruction

Visual Communication Point out that different people depend on different things as they live their lives. Some depend on other people, some on ideals and beliefs, and some on institutions and governments. Most of us depend on a combination of people, things, and ideas. Invite students to create visual collages that illustrate the title "What I Depend On."

Suggest that students cut and paste illustrations from magazines to create their collages. These can be made on poster board for display in the classroom or in each student's Learner's Notebook for personal reference. OL

I'll Walk the Tightrope

by Margaret Danner

I'll walk the tightrope that's been stretched for me,
and though a wrinkled forehead, perplexed why,
will accompany me, I'll delicately
step along. For if I stop to sigh
at the earth-propped stride
of others, I will fall. I must balance high
without a parasol to tide*
a faltering step, without a net below,
without a balance stick to guide. ❍

Fatima, 1994. Elizabeth Barakah Hodges. Acrylic, 23 x 18 in.

7 A ***parasol*** is a small lightweight umbrella used as protection from the sun. Here, ***tide*** means "to aid or assist."

Literature Focus Lesson

Summary The speaker in this poem uses an extended metaphor to express an idea about her life. In this poem, the poet makes the following metaphorical comparisons:

- Her life, especially what's ahead, seems like a tightrope to her.
- Living her life is like struggling to keep her balance while walking a tightrope.
- Other people seem to live their lives on the ground, "earth-propped."
- She has got to live her life on her own, without anyone but herself to depend on ("without a parasol," "without a net below," "without a balance stick to guide"). **OL**

Focus

Vocabulary Preview

List the following words on the board:

- perplexed
- faltering

Review their definitions before students begin reading.

Build Background

In tightrope walking, a performer walks along a thin wire or rope, usually high above ground. The tightrope walker may use a pole to aid in balancing. Many tightrope walkers use a safety net below the rope or wire to catch them if they fall. The most daring do not. Among the most famous tightrope walkers were "Blondin," who walked across Niagara Falls on a high wire, and Phillippe Petit, who walked between the towers of the World Trade Center in New York City.

Teach

R Reading Skill

Review Determining the Main Idea **Ask:** What is the main idea of this poem? *(Some students may interpret the main idea as "I'll walk the tightrope of life even though it's difficult to do, and I'm not sure why I'm doing it"; others may interpret it as "I'll live a daring life, doing what's challenging rather than what's expected.")* **OL**

TIPS FOR INDEPENDENT READING

Stress the idea of reading for pleasure. Urge students to choose books that match their interests or curiosity. Suggest that if they find that a book they've chosen for independent reading doesn't please them, they should set it aside and choose another. Suggest books, such as those shown here, that are related to the Big Question.

Fiction

Tell students that reading fictional stories about people who have found someone whom they could depend on—or have found that they couldn't depend on someone when they needed to—can give them useful insights into deciding whom they can really depend on.

Ask students to share an example of a fictional story they have read that could give them insight into deciding whom they can depend on.

Ask students to think of a fictional character from any genre who seems especially dependable. Have them explain why they feel the character can be depended on. Use their responses to create a list of characteristics of dependable characters.

UNIT 3

Reading on Your Own

To read more about the Big Question, choose one of these books from your school or local library. Work on your reading skills by choosing books that are challenging to you.

Fiction

The Adventures of Tom Sawyer
by Mark Twain

The Adventures of Tom Sawyer follows young Tom Sawyer and his friends through a series of mishaps, pranks, and narrow escapes, revealing the humorous side of life. Set in the 1840s along the Mississippi River in Missouri, the book gives a view of pre–civil war America and tells the timeless story of growing up.

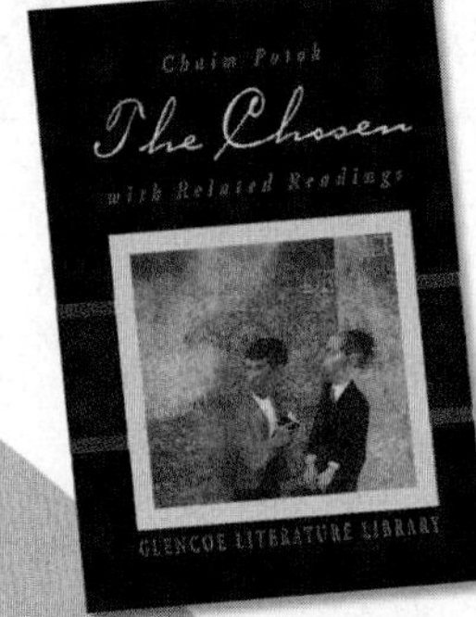

The Chosen
by Chaim Potok

The story of two young Jewish men living in Brooklyn in the 1940s, *The Chosen* follows their lives and their relationships with their fathers and with each other. Despite their different backgrounds, the men form an enduring friendship and face tough issues of the times together.

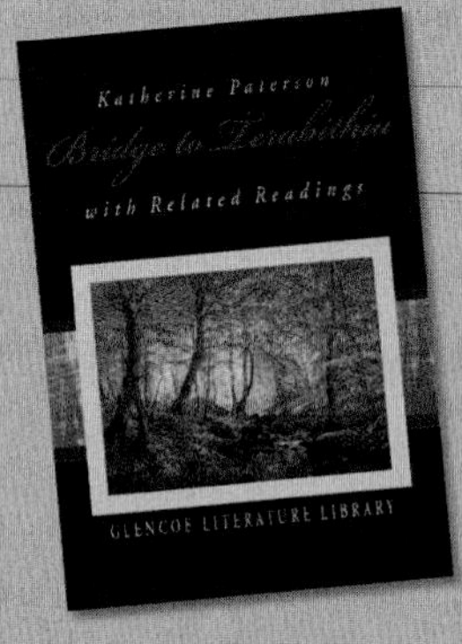

Bridge to Terabithia
by Katherine Paterson

Two young classmates, Jess and Leslie, form a strong friendship as they create together an imaginary kingdom, Terabithia, beyond a nearby creek. The events that follow forever change the life of Jess.

The Friends
by Rosa Guy

This coming-of-age novel deals with the relationship between two unlikely friends, Phyllisia Cathy and Edith Jackson. *The Friends* details the bond the two girls forge, while dealing with the pressures of family and friends.

Additional Support

Differentiated Instruction

GLENCOE BOOKLINK Use the Glencoe BookLink CD-ROM to create customized reading lists to help students answer the Big Question. Suggestions for Unit 3:

Grade 4: *Yellow Bird and Me* by Joyce Hansen
Beauty by Bill Wallace
Grade 5: *Silver* by Norma Fox Mazer
Crazy Weekend by Gary Soto
Grade 6: *There's a Girl in My Hammerlock* by Jerry Spinelli
Skeeter by K. Smith
Grade 7: *Notes for Another Life* by Sue Ellen Bridgers
Losing Joe's Place by Gordon Korman
Grade 8: *Ferris Beach* by Jill McCorkle
Anything for Billy by Larry McMurtry

Nonfiction

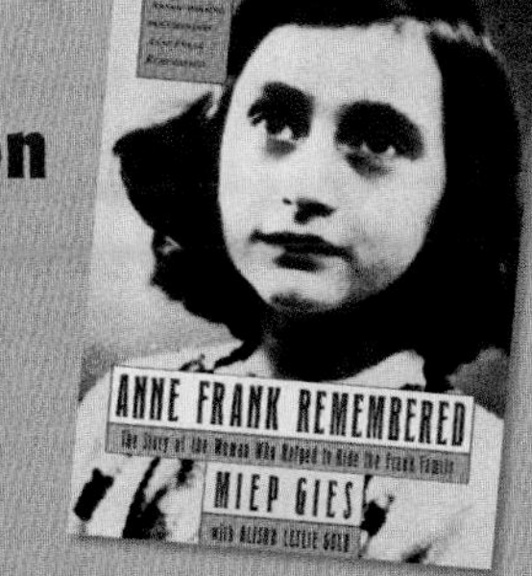

Anne Frank Remembered
by Miep Gies and Alison Leslie Gold

This memoir tells the story of Miep Gies, the woman who helped Anne Frank and her family hide from the Nazi forces in Amsterdam during World War II. The story shows the courage that Gies had despite great personal danger.

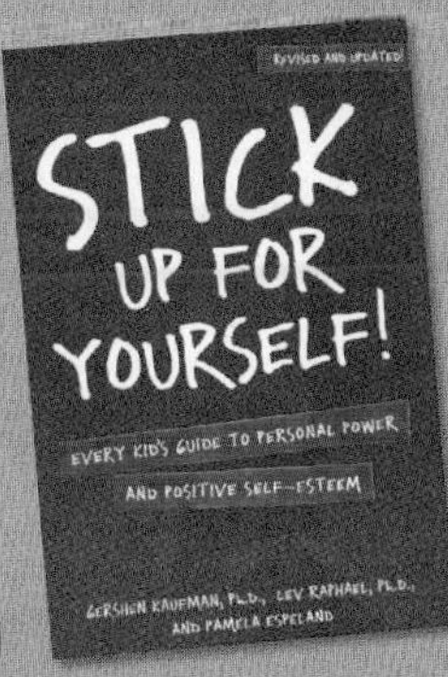

Stick Up for Yourself: Every Kid's Guide to Personal Power & Positive Self-Esteem
by Gershen Kaufman, Lev Raphael, and Pamela Espeland

This is a self-help guide to positive thinking, high self-esteem, and personal power. Read to learn how other kids handle life. The writing exercises in the book offer ways to connect to the text.

Cliques, Phonies, & Other Baloney
by Trevor Romain

With a sense of humor, the author gives kids solid advice on dealing with cliques and phonies. Romain defines these concepts and provides examples. The black-and-white cartoons make the book's concepts easy to understand.

We Beat the Street: How a Friendship Pact Led to Success
by Sampson Davis, George Jenkins, Rameck Hunt, and Sharon Draper

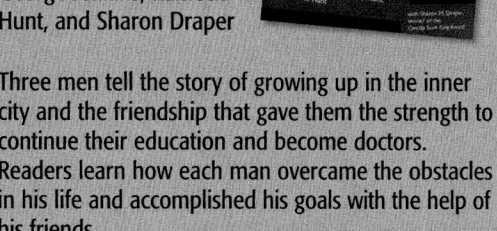

Three men tell the story of growing up in the inner city and the friendship that gave them the strength to continue their education and become doctors. Readers learn how each man overcame the obstacles in his life and accomplished his goals with the help of his friends.

READING ON YOUR OWN

Nonfiction

Point out to students that the books shown on this page are nonfiction books. Two tell personal stories about finding someone to count on or being someone others could count on. The other two give advice on how to depend on oneself.

BQ 

Ask: How would you expect each of these books to help you decide whom you can really count on? *(Responses will vary but should be clearly related to the content of each book.)* **AS**

Test-Taking Tips

TIP Tell students that even though the test directions begin with "Read the passage," it is often a better idea to begin by reading the questions that they will have to answer. It isn't necessary to read the answer choices, but by reading the questions, they will be able to focus their reading on finding the answers that they will have to give later.

TIP When students must answer multiple-choice questions, they should use the following strategy:

- First answer each question that you are absolutely certain about.
- If you're not certain about the answer to a question, skip it for now.
- When you've answered all the questions you're sure about, return to the ones you're not sure about.
- For each of those, eliminate any answers that you know are wrong.
- If eliminating wrong answers reveals the right answer, fine. Move on.
- If eliminating wrong answers still leaves a choice, turn back to the passage and skim to find which of the remaining answers is correct.
- If you can't find the answer by skimming, it may be worth your while to guess. If an unanswered question will count against you as much as a wrong answer, guess. If a wrong answer will count against you more than no answer, don't guess.

Test Practice

Part 1: Literary Elements

Read the passage. Then write the numbers 1–6 on a separate sheet of paper. For the first five questions, write the letter of the right answer next to the number for that question. Write your answer to the final question next to number 6.

A Job Well Done

Rita was tired from basketball practice, and she had to study for the next day's math test. Instead of either sleeping or studying, however, she was babysitting. And it wasn't easy!

Molly refused to wash her face or her hands before bed, but her mother had said that doing so was a rule. Rita was bigger and stronger than the little girl and could force her, and she was tempted to do so. What choice did she have? Surely she shouldn't just give in and let the child go to bed filthy. But she hesitated, knowing there must be a better way to do her job. Then she got an idea.

Rita went into the kitchen to get what she needed. Then she chased Molly around the living room and dining room until she caught her and could carry her into the bathroom. Molly looked at the sink full of water and started yelling and kicking at the bathroom door.

"Have you ever washed your face and hands with purple water?" Rita asked. She squirted blue and red food coloring into the water. "If you dip your hands in the sink, the water will turn purple."

Molly opened her mouth to yell, then closed it and stared at the swirls of color. Finally, she couldn't resist and thrust her hands into the swirls of color, turning the water purple. She was disappointed that her hands did not take on the same shade, but Rita had not been foolish enough to add enough coloring for that result.

"Can I wash my face now, too?" asked Molly when her hands were completely clean.

"Sure," said Rita. "But wouldn't you rather do that with orange water?"

Ten minutes later, a tired (but clean) little girl was sound asleep and a tired (but relieved) babysitter was opening her math book.

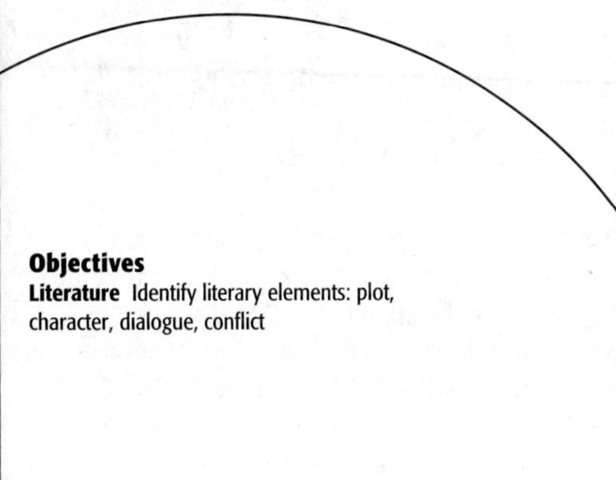

Objectives
Literature Identify literary elements: plot, character, dialogue, conflict

1. What is the external conflict in this story?
   - **A.** Rita wants Molly to wash up, but Molly refuses.
   - **B.** Rita isn't sure whether she should use force to get her job done.
   - **C.** Rita can't decide whether to follow the rule or give in to Molly.
   - **D.** Molly wants to keep yelling but also wants to make purple water.

2. At the end of the passage, what does Molly's dialogue reveal about her?
   - **A.** Her hands are clean.
   - **B.** She wants to go to bed.
   - **C.** She has become eager to cooperate.
   - **D.** She is sorry she gave Rita such a hard time.

3. Which of the following is an event that helps the plot develop?
   - **A.** Molly falls asleep.
   - **B.** Rita chases Molly.
   - **C.** Rita opens her math book.
   - **D.** Rita goes to basketball practice.

4. During what part of the story does Rita go into the kitchen to get what she needs?
   - **A.** Exposition
   - **B.** Rising action
   - **C.** Climax
   - **D.** Falling action

5. What is the resolution to this story?
   - **A.** Rita gets an idea.
   - **B.** Rita puts food coloring into the sink.
   - **C.** Molly asks if she can wash her face.
   - **D.** Molly falls asleep and Rita begins to study.

6. What kind of person is Rita? How can you tell? That is, how does the story reveal her traits?

Unit Assessment To prepare for the Unit test, go to www.glencoe.com.

Standardized Test Practice

Part 1: Literary Elements

1. A
2. C
3. B
4. B
5. D
6. I know that Rita is active because the narrator tells us that she was at basketball practice and she chases Molly around the living room and dining room.

Resources for pages 402–407

Use these resources to review, assess, or reteach the Unit: Active Learning and Note-Taking Guide, Selection and Unit Assessment, ExamView Assessment Suite, and Differentiated Instruction Tool Software.

Unit Assessment Have students access the Web site to prepare for the Unit 3 test.

Test-Taking Tips

TIP By reading the questions before they begin reading the passage, students will know that they will have to find the main idea and details that support it.

TIP When the main idea of a passage is stated directly, it is often the first or last sentence in the passage, *but not always.* The writer may add a sentence at the beginning as an introduction or a way to interest the reader. Wherever it appears, a direct statement of the main idea will always be an idea about nearly everything else in the paragraph. Introductory sentences usually don't meet that requirement.

TIP To test a possible conclusion that's given to you as a multiple-choice item, add "because . . ." to the item and then look in the passage to see if a statement there would make sense as a reason.

TIP When you're asked to write a main idea for a passage that doesn't have one, begin by finding the most important details. Then write a simple, straightforward statement that sums up those details or tells what is important about them.

Standardized Test Practice

Part 2: Reading Skills

1. B
2. A
3. Responses will vary but should resemble this: Everyone in my family knows that we can depend on Finn.

Part 2: Reading Skills

Write the numbers 1–3 on a separate sheet of paper. Then read the following passage and answer the first two questions.

1 Everyone knows that honey is sweet and that honeybees produce it. 2 It is also a natural antibiotic (germ killer) and is a helpful treatment for wounds and burns. 3 In the United States, there has been very little scientific investigation of the medical uses for honey. 4 However, in foreign countries, studies have shown that treating burns with honey helps them heal with fewer scars than if they are treated with other products. 5 Other studies have shown that wounds that do not respond to other treatments will often heal when honey is used. 6 Unfortunately for those of us who get our honey in grocery stores, only natural honey (not pasteurized honey) has such helpful effects. 7 One can buy natural honey at many health food stores or from a beekeeper—a person who raises bees and collects honey from the hives.

1. Which sentence in this passage states the main idea?
- **A.** Sentence 1
- **B.** Sentence 2
- **C.** Sentence 3
- **D.** Sentence 7

2. Which of the following is a conclusion you can draw by synthesizing information in this passage?
- **A.** It does little or no good to treat a burn with pasteurized honey.
- **B.** The honey from a health food store is sweeter than other honey.
- **C.** Honeybees in foreign countries are quite different from American honeybees.
- **D.** Beekeepers make most of their profits by selling honey for medical purposes.

Objectives
Reading Synthesize information • Identify main ideas and supporting details
Vocabulary Identify synonyms and antonyms

Read the following passage. Then write the answer to question 3 next to that number on your paper.

Finn has lived next door to us for eight years. When I was little and dad was sick for two months, Finn mowed our lawn eight times. Last month, Mom dropped her wallet, with all her money inside, in the alley. Finn found it and brought it back to her. He taught me how to pitch a curve ball, and he taught my sister how to hit one. In the summer, he gives us tomatoes from his garden, and in the winter, he lets us use his snow blower.

3. What is the main idea of this paragraph? Write down the main idea in your own words and give three details that support that idea.

Part 3: Vocabulary Skills

On a separate sheet of paper, write the numbers 1–10. Next to each number, write the letter of the right answer for that question.

Write the letter of the word or phrase that means about the same as the underlined word.

1. to speak **sternly**
- **A.** firmly
- **B.** quickly
- **C.** unhappily
- **D.** in a teasing way

2. a **practical** idea
- **A.** new
- **B.** creative
- **C.** sensible
- **D.** frightening

3. a **wary** response
- **A.** slow
- **B.** cautious
- **C.** clear
- **D.** truthful

4. a **flawless** performance
- **A.** boring
- **B.** perfect
- **C.** exciting
- **D.** unusual

5. her **dejected** face
- **A.** dirty
- **B.** lovely
- **C.** unhappy
- **D.** frightened

Choose the correct answer for each question.

6. Which pair of words are synonyms?
- **A.** hair / hare
- **B.** find / locate
- **C.** forgive / forget
- **D.** selfish / generous

7. Which pair of words are synonyms?
- **A.** buy / sell
- **B.** rain / reign
- **C.** hurt / injure
- **D.** wealthy / happy

8. Which pair of words are antonyms?
- **A.** try / fail
- **B.** get / take
- **C.** fear / panic
- **D.** future / past

9. Which pair of words are antonyms?
- **A.** friend / enemy
- **B.** help / cooperate
- **C.** chapter / book
- **D.** picture / sound

10. Which prefix could be added to all of the following words to create their antonyms?

agree approve honest

- **A.** in-
- **B.** un-
- **C.** dis-
- **D.** non-

Test-Taking Tips

TIP Remind students of the general strategy for multiple-choice questions:

- First answer each question that you are absolutely certain about.
- If you're not certain about the answer to a question, skip it for now.
- When you've answered all the questions you're sure about, return to the ones you're not sure about.
- For each of those, eliminate any answers that you know are wrong.
- If eliminating wrong answers reveals the right answer, fine. Move on.
- If eliminating wrong answers still leaves a choice, make your best guess.

Standardized Test Practice

Part 3: Vocabulary Skills

1. A
2. C
3. B
4. B
5. C
6. B
7. C
8. D
9. A
10. C

Test-Taking Tips

TIP It can't be stressed often enough: Read the directions carefully and be sure that you answer the question you are asked. If you're asked to choose the answer that fills a blank, be sure to say the sentence to yourself with your choice in the blank.

TIP Be especially aware of highlighted words in questions or directions. Words in italics or boldface or words that are underlined are emphasized because they are very important. Your answer will be wrong if you ignore the highlighted words.

Standardized Test Practice

Part 4: Writing Skills

1. B
2. C
3. C
4. B
5. D
6. B
7. A

Part 4: Writing Skills

Write the numbers 1–11 on a separate sheet of paper. For the first 10 questions, write the letter of the right answer next to the number for that question. Then write your answer for the final question next to number 11.

1. Which word or phrase best fills in the blank in the sentence below?

She's a smart person, maybe the ___ person in the school.

A. smarter **C.** more smart
B. smartest **D.** most smartest

2. In the sentence below, which word is an adverb?

He looked lonely as he sadly watched the other students.

A. lonely **C.** sadly
B. as **D.** other

3. In the sentence below, which words form a prepositional phrase?

When I was young, there was nothing I would rather have done on a summer afternoon than swim.

A. When I was young **C.** on a summer afternoon
B. have done **D.** than swim

Objectives
Grammar Use modifiers: adverbs, adjectives • Use interjections
Writing Use story elements: plot, setting, character, dialogue

4. In the sentence below, which word is an adjective?

Gee, don't you wonder how such a good book could have been made into a movie that nobody would want to see?

A. Gee **C.** nobody
B. good **D.** would

5. Which words best fill in the blanks in the sentence below?

Bo's car was expensive, a lot ___ than Tamira's, but it doesn't run as ___ as hers.

A. expensiver, good **C.** more expensive, good
B. expensiver, well **D.** more expensive, well

6. In the sentence below, which word is an interjection?

If you have a cheap watch that breaks, hey, just go buy another one.

A. If **C.** just
B. hey **D.** another

7. Which of the following is one of the *first* things you should do when you are writing a story?

A. Think of a conflict your main character will face.
B. Look up the spellings of hard words you want to use.
C. Make sure you have used interesting adjectives and adverbs.
D. Check the punctuation of any dialogue used in your story.

Read the following paragraph. Then write the answers to questions 8–11 on your paper.

[1] The kitchen was warm and inviting. [2] Catherine could smell the bread baking in the oven and the beans cooking on the stove. [3] Cinnamon filled the air as she mixed in the spices to make her favorite dish for her granddaughter, Susan. [4] The outside of the small house was brown and had peeling paint. [5] She stirred the pot and smiled at Susan, who was sitting at the kitchen table doing her homework while she waited for dinner.

[6] "What are you writing?" Catherine asked.

[7] "A story about you for English class said Susan."

[8] "Really!" said Catherine. "Tell me more about the story." [9] "It's about some of the situations you faced when you came to this country as a young woman," Susan answered.

---

8. Which sentence in the first paragraph interferes with the way the story is organized and should be deleted?

- **A.** Sentence 1
- **B.** Sentence 3
- **C.** Sentence 4
- **D.** Sentence 5

9. How should sentence 7 be written?

- **A.** "A story about you for English class, Susan said."
- **B.** "A story about you for English class" Susan said."
- **C.** "A story about you for English class," Susan said.
- **D.** no change

10. What is incorrect about sentence 9 and should be changed?

- **A.** More details should be added.
- **B.** The word *young* should be changed to *younger.*
- **C.** The sentence should be indented as a new paragraph.
- **D.** There should be a period instead of a comma after *woman.*

11. Write a short paragraph that continues the story of Catherine and Susan. What happens next in this story? Use details and dialogue to make the story interesting and fun to read.

UNIT 3 ASSESSMENT

8. C

9. C

10. C

11. Responses will vary. A complete answer must meet these requirements:

- be a short paragraph
- continue the story
- tell what happens next
- use details
- use dialogue
- be interesting
- be fun to read

Test-Taking Tips

TIP When you are asked to write an answer, be sure that your response includes everything the directions tell you to include. It's a good idea to make a checklist for yourself, turning each part of the question or directions into an item on the list. Then, when you read your answer to revise and correct it, check it against the list and add anything you left out.

UNIT 4

Skills Scope and Sequence

Readability Scores Key
Dale-Chall/DRP/Lexile

PACING (DAYS) STANDARD	BLOCK	INSTRUCTIONAL SEGMENT LITERATURE	READING SKILLS	LITERARY ELEMENTS
1	1	**Unit Warm-Up, pp. 410–415** Genre Focus: "Violence in Hockey" **7.5/67/1230**, SE p. 414	Understanding persuasive techniques, SE pp. 413, 415, TWE p. 412 Distinguishing fact and opinion, SE pp. 413, 414, TWE pp. 412, 415 Identifying author's purpose and perspective, SE pp. 413, 414, TWE p. 412 Comparing and contrasting, SE pp. 413, 415, TWE p. 412	Tone, SE pp. 413, 414, TWE p. 414 Style, SE pp. 413, 414 Diction, language, and word choice, SE pp. 413, 415 Hyperbole, SE pp. 413, 414 Supporting Arguments, TWE p. 412
3	2	**Reading Workshop 1, pp. 416–433** "3BCB: Three by Clay Bennett" by Clay Bennett, SE p. 420 "Thank You, M'am" by Langston Hughes **5.3/49/850**, SE p. 426	Understanding persuasive techniques, SE pp. 416, 417, 419, 420, 421, 423, 425, 426, 429, 430, 433, TWE p. 427 Activating prior knowledge, SE p. 428, TWE p. 421 Fluency, TWE p. 425 Identifying Author's Purpose, TWE p. 421 Sequencing, TWE p. 426 Drawing Conclusions, TWE p. 429	Diction, Language, and Word Choice, TWE p. 430 Tone, SE pp. 419, 421, 423, 425, 426, 431, 433 Persuasion, TWE pp. 418, 424 Character, TWE pp. 426, 427 Resolution, TWE p. 431 Hyperbole, TWE p. 426
1		**Writing Workshop, Part 1, pp. 434–437** Writing Product: Editorial	Fluency, TWE p. 437	
3	1	**Reading Workshop 2, pp. 438–453** "What Exercise Can Do for You" by Sheila Globus **5.6/61/980**, SE p. 442 "Oprah Winfrey" by Sidney Poitier **5.9/61/1050**, SE p. 450	Distinguishing fact and opinion, SE pp. 438, 439, 441, 442, 445, 447, 449, 450, 451, 453 Understanding graphics, SE pp. 444, 447 Comparing and Contrasting, TWE p. 442 Persuasive Techniques, TWE pp. 443, 451	Style, SE pp. 441, 444, 447, 449, 450, 453 Persuasive techniques in Radio, TWE p. 440 Persuasive writing, TWE p. 448 Tone, TWE p. 443
3	1	**Reading Workshop 3, pp. 454–467** "The Courage That My Mother Had" by Edna St. Vincent Millay, SE p. 458 "Two People I Want to be Like" by Eve Merriam, SE p. 459 "Volunteers Welcome!" SE p. 464	Identifying author's purpose and perspective, SE pp. 454, 455, 457, 458, 461, 463, 464, 465, 467, TWE p. 462 Fluency, TWE pp. 457, 463 Drawing Conclusions, SE p. 464 Fact and Opinion, TWE p. 455	Diction, language, and word choice, SE pp. 457, 459, 461, 463, 465, 467, TWE p. 462 Persuasive writing, TWE pp. 456, 462

Unit 4 Big Question

The question, "Who influences us and how do they do so?" is designed to help students gain new insight into themselves and others. In this unit, students will read a variety of selections which demonstrate how writers and people in our lives influence us.

Unit 4 Genre

Many of the selections in this unit are persuasive writing pieces about various issues. These selections will also help students answer the big question: Who influences us and how do they do so? Use these persuasive texts to help students understand how they are influenced by literature and by the people in their lives.

CRITICAL THINKING	VOCABULARY	WRITING AND GRAMMAR	LISTENING, SPEAKING, AND VIEWING
	Word Choice, TWE p. 413 Keywords, TWE p. 411		Viewing the Photo, TWE p. 408
Infer, SE pp. 422, 432 Draw conclusions, SE p. 422 Analyze, SE p. 422 Evaluate, SE pp. 422, 432 Respond, SE p. 432 Synthesis, TWE pp. 417, 420	Academic vocabulary, SE pp. 416, 423 Denotation and connotation, SE pp. 418, 421, 423, 424, 427, 433, TWE pp. 424, 431 Building Background, TWE p. 429	Sentence types, SE p. 423 Write About Your Reading, SE p. 422 Writing Application, SE p. 423 Write to Learn, SE pp. 418, 424, 425, 432 End punctuation, SE p. 433	Partner Talk, SE pp. 418, 419, 424 Viewing the Image, TWE p. 420 Viewing the Painting, TWE pp. 428, 429 Talk About Your Reading, SE p. 432
Persuasive writing, TWE p. 436	Denotation, Connotation, and Semantic Slanting, TWE p. 434	Editorial, TWE p. 434 Persuasive Techniques, TWE p. 436 Complete sentences, SE p. 437 Writing Traits: Word Choice, TWE p. 435	
Distinguish fact and opinion, SE p. 446 Analyze, SE p. 446 Evaluate, SE pp. 446, 452 Infer, SE p. 452 Respond, SE p. 452 Comprehension, TWE p. 444	Denotation and connotation, SE pp. 440, 443, 447, 448, 451, 453, TWE pp. 438, 440, 442, 443, 450	Run-ons and fragments, SE p. 447 Write to Learn, SE pp. 440, 441, 448, 449 Write About Your Reading, SE pp. 446, 452 Writing Application, SE p. 453 Fixing fragments, SE p. 453	Viewing the Photo, TWE pp. 442, 445, 450 Small Group Work, SE p. 441 Partner Talk, SE pp. 441, 449 Viewing the Graphic, TWE p. 444
Interpret, SE p. 460 Draw Conclusions, SE p. 460 Infer, SE p. 466 Evaluate, SE p. 466 Synthesize, SE p. 466 Analysis, TWE p. 459	Denotation and connotation, SE pp. 456, 457, 461, TWE pp. 459, 464 Semantic Slanting, SE pp. 462, 467, TWE p. 459	Write to Learn, SE pp. 456, 457, 460, 462, 463 Writing Application, SE pp. 461, 467 Subjects and predicates, SE pp. 461, 467 Write About Your Reading, SE p. 466	Partner Talk, SE p. 456 Talk About Your Reading, SE p. 460 Viewing the Art, TWE p. 459 Class Talk, SE p. 463

UNIT 4

Skills Scope and Sequence *continued*

Readability Scores Key
Dale-Chall/DRP/Lexile

PACING (DAYS) STANDARD	BLOCK	INSTRUCTIONAL SEGMENT LITERATURE	READING SKILLS	LITERARY ELEMENTS
1	cont'd. ↓	**Writing Workshop, Part 2, pp. 468–473** Writing Product: Editorial	Fluency, TWE p. 473 Distinguishing Fact and Opinion, TWE p. 469 Analyzing Persuasive Techniques, TWE p. 473	Word choice, SE pp. 469, 472, 473 Style, SE pp. 469, 470, 472 Tone, SE pp. 469, 470, 472 Persuasive techniques, SE pp. 468, 472, 473, TWE p. 469
2	1	**Reading Workshop 4, pp. 474–493** "Should Naturalized Citizens be President?" by John Yinger and Matthew Spalding **8.6/69/1090**, SE p. 478 "The Teacher Who Changed My Life" by Nicholas Gage **6.9/61/1350**, SE p. 484	Using text structure: Compare and contrast, SE pp. 474, 475, 477, 479, 481, 483, 485, 488, 489, 490, 493, TWE p. 478, 491 Sequencing, SE p. 484, TWE p. 489 Distinguishing fact and opinion, SE pp. 488, 493, TWE p. 479 Drawing Conclusions, TWE pp. 477, 488	Hyperbole, SE pp. 477, 478, 481, 483, 488, 493 Persuasive Writing, TWE pp. 476, 482 Tone, TWE p. 487
2	2	**Reading Across Texts Workshop, SE pp. 494–503** "Take the Junk Out of Marketing Food to Kids" by Sheila Globus **8.1/63/1330**, SE p. 497 "Grainies Toasted Whole-Grain Flakes" SE p. 500	Fluency, TWE p. 501 Distinguishing Fact and Opinion, TWE p. 494 Analyzing Persuasive Techniques, TWE p. 495 Using Text Structure: Compare and Contrast, TWE p. 501	Style, TWE p. 501 Persuasive techniques, SE pp. 494, 495, 497, 498, 499, 500, 503, TWE p. 499 Editorial, TWE p. 496 Diction, Language, and Word Choice, TWE p. 498
2	1	**Unit Wrap-Up, pp. 504–511** "The Cremation of Sam McGee" by Robert Service, SE p. 506	Read and apply skills, SE pp. 506, 507, 508, 509, 510, 511 Independent Reading, SE pp. 512, 513 Using Text Structure: Compare and Contrast, TWE pp. 507, 508, 511 Identifying Author's Purpose and Perspective, TWE pp. 508, 509	Summary, TWE p. 506 Persuasive Writing, TWE p. 513 Hyperbole, TWE p. 506 Style, TWE p. 507 Tone, TWE pp. 508, 509 Sensory Details, TWE p. 510

CRITICAL THINKING	VOCABULARY	WRITING AND GRAMMAR	LISTENING, SPEAKING, AND VIEWING
Evaluate, TWE p. 468	Denotation, Connotation, and Semantic Slanting, TWE pp. 468, 471	Applying Good Writing Traits: Word Choice, SE p. 469 Tone, TWE p. 468 Hyperbole, TWE p. 470 Identifying Author's Purpose and Perspective, TWE p. 471	Listen to, watch, and create persuasive messages, SE p. 473
Compare and contrast, SE p. 492 Distinguish fact and opinion, SE p. 480 Infer, SE pp. 480, 492, TWE p. 485 Identify author's purpose, SE pp. 480, 492	Word Choice, TWE pp. 482, 484, 486, 501 Denotation, connotation, and semantic slanting, SE pp. 476, 479, 481, 482, 486, 487, TWE pp. 476, 477, 479, 485, 487, 491 Connecting, TWE p. 491 Base Words, TWE p. 476	Write to Learn, SE pp. 477, 482, 483 Write About Your Reading, SE pp. 480, 492 Compound subjects, SE p. 481 Compound predicates, SE p. 493	Group Talk, SE p. 476 Partner Talk, SE p. 477 Viewing the Photo, TWE pp. 478, 488
Identify author's purpose and perspective, SE p. 500 Distinguish fact and opinion, SE p. 501 Identify, SE p. 503 Infer, SE p. 503 Connect, SE p. 503 Evaluation, TWE p. 498	Connotations, SE pp. 496, 502, TWE pp. 496, 500 Semantic slanting, SE pp. 499, 502, TWE pp. 496, 500 Word Choice, TWE p. 497	Making charts and lists and using them to compare persuasive techniques, SE pp. 495, 503 Write to Learn, SE pp. 496 Get It on Paper, p. 503	Partner Talk, SE p. 499 Viewing the Illustration, TWE p. 497
Comprehension, TWE p. 511	Connotations with Synonyms, TWE p. 508 Vocabulary Preview, TWE p. 506	Make and present a poster, SE p. 504 Write a poem, song, rap, letter, or list, SE p. 505	Group Activity: Poster, SE p. 504, TWE p. 504 Viewing the Illustration, TWE p. 510

UNIT 4

Unit Resources

Reading with Purpose offers a comprehensive package of tools to optimize student learning and the teaching experience. Each resource has been designed to assist students in specific areas and to offer instructional support for teachers. While all of these areas are covered in the core textbook, some students may need extra practice or additional help in specific areas. The resource package is designed so that you, the teacher, can choose which items will best assist your students. You may also use these resources as homework assignments and for assessment purposes. The following are resources recommended for use with Unit 4.

Keys for Unit Resources

- Blackline Master
- Workbook
- Supplemental Text
- CD-ROM
- DVD
- Transparency
- Web-based
- Fast Files

Essential Instructional Support

UNIT 4 RESOURCES

Reading and Literature
- Academic Vocabulary Development
- Big Question: School to Home Connection
- The Big Question Foldable
- Genre Study
- Unit Challenge: Planner and Rubrics
- Comparing Literature Graphic Organizer
- Key Reading Skills Practice
- Active Reading Graphic Organizers
- Literary Analysis
- Selection Vocabulary Development

Writing, Grammar, and Spelling
- Spelling and Handwriting Practice
- Grammar Practice
- Writing Workshop Graphic Organizer

Listening, Speaking, and Viewing
- Viewing and Representing Activities
- Listening and Speaking Activities

English Language Learners
- English Language Coach

DIFFERENTIATED INSTRUCTION

- Leveled Vocabulary Development
- Skills Level Up!
- Listening Library CD
- BookLink 3
- Literature Library Vocabulary Puzzlemaker
- Vocabulary Puzzlemaker

ASSESSMENT

- Selection and Unit Assessments
- Selection Quick Checks
- Assessment by Learning Objectives
- Rubrics for Assessing Student Writing, Listening, and Speaking
- Glencoe Online Essay Grading
- Interactive Tutor Self-Assessment
- ExamView Assessment Suite
- Literature Library ExamView Assessment Suite

UNIT 4

Professional Development Center

Cynthia Shanahan

From An Author:

Helping Students Read Persuasive Text

Importance of understanding persuasive text: Students are bombarded with persuasive messages in their everyday lives, and at some point, these messages influence their actions, if they are persuasive enough. If students are to think critically about what they read, then, we need to ensure that the purposes for reading include making up one's mind. If students understand they have the ability to make up their own minds, they will be more likely to become engaged in assessing the messages they receive from television, radio, magazines, newspapers, the internet, billboards, and so on.

Helping students understand persuasive text: A first step is for students to think about what they currently believe about a topic. Then they must read with a critical eye. Readers who engage in critical reading of text read both inside and outside of the text. That is, they read and evaluate the message itself, but they also evaluate the author's qualifications, pay attention to where the message appears (in an editorial or in a textbook, for example), when the message appears (in the 1950's or yesterday), and to whom the message was written. Wineburg (1991) calls these elements *sourcing (who wrote the message, where did it come from, what sources were used)* and *contextualization (when was it written and for whom; what about the context influenced the message)*. In addition, Wineburg discusses *corroboration (comparing and contrasting the message with other messages on the same topic).* When a reader engages in sourcing, contextualization, and corroboration, they are evaluating the trustworthiness of the information they are reading, and it influences how they read what is actually in the text. Both the inside and outside the text reading is what helps readers make up their minds.

Gloria Dukes
Coastal Middle School
Savannah, GA

Teacher to Teacher

Who influences us and how do they do so?

I introduce the theme "Who influences us?" with Write Night, a special evening that brings parents and students together. Students take home questions to interview parents, such as: Who was there when I was born? Why did you choose this particular name for me? Who came to visit you at the hospital? That evening, parents bring in memorabilia from the child's birth, and together parents and children write about the experience in the form of a poem, a song, or a story. I encourage them to share in groups. Then I close the evening with reflective writing that answers questions like: What did you learn about one another that you might not have known? How did this experience change you? I put the reflective writing into an anthology and give a copy to every parent who attends.

Literature Launchers

Set the scene with Glencoe's Literature Launchers, engaging video segments that introduce each unit's genre focus. Each video brings the genre to life, relating it to your students' worlds.

Insert the Glencoe Literature Launchers Pre-Reading Videos DVD into your DVD player. Select the Unit 4 Launcher from the menu to introduce the genre and Big Question for this unit.

Online Essay Grader

Use Glencoe's Online Essay Grading to score your students' writing and to provide individualized feedback to each student automatically.

You and your students can visit www.glencoe.com to link to the essay grader. *Students* can enter their essays and receive feedback on demand. *You* can manage demographic data, assign tests and generate individual student and aggregated reports. The essay grader can help you

- Save time with automatic scoring and individualized feedback.
- Supplement in-class writing instruction using guided writing practice.
- Get reports for individual students or for special populations.
- Track student improvement over time.

REAL Success: Reading Excellence at All Levels

Glencoe now provides all of your students with the tools they need to become better, more enthusiastic readers. The REAL Success suite of reading and language arts products encourages reading excellence by meeting the needs of students at all levels. Glencoe products that can be used in conjunction with Unit 4 include the following:

- Jamestown Literature: An Adapted Reader
- Jamestown *Reading Fluency*
- Jamestown *Critical Reading Series, In the Line of Duty*
- *Vocabulary Builder*
- *The Glencoe Reader, Course 2*

To order these products, call Glencoe at 1-800-USA-READ.

Teacher Wraparound Edition Key

Level Appropriate Code

AS = Activities for all students

AL = Activities for students working above grade level

OL = Activities for students working at grade level

BL = Activities for students working below grade level

EL = Activities for English language learners

Teacher Wraparound Prompts

R **Reading Skill** These activities help you teach reading skills and vocabulary.

V **Vocabulary** These activities help students comprehend words and incorporate into reading.

C **Critical Thinking** These strategies help students apply and extend what they have learned.

BQ BIG Question These activities and questions prompt students to prepare to answer the Big Question.

W **Writing** These activities provide writing opportunities to help students practice writing and comprehend text.

L **Literary Element** These activities and questions help students comprehend selections and learn more about each genre.

E **Text Element** These activities help students comprehend text elements.

LSV **Listening, Speaking, Viewing** These activities help students practice listening, speaking, and viewing skills.

EL **English Language Coach** These skills help English language learners as well as students who need additional reading support.

Additional Glencoe Resources

Dinah Zike's Foldables

Foldables are three-dimensional, interactive graphic organizers that help students practice basic writing skills, review key vocabulary terms, and answer Big Questions. Every unit contains a foldable activity. You can find the pattern and directions for the Unit 4 Foldable in the Unit 4 Resources Fast Files booklet. You can use the foldables as they are presented or modify them to suit the needs of your students. More information about foldables for Unit 4 can be found on page R8.

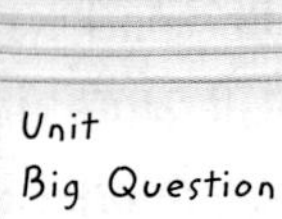

Glencoe Literature Library

The collection of hardcover books include full-length novels, novellas, plays and works of nonfiction. Each volume consists of at least one complete extended-length reading accompanied by several related readings from a broad range of genres. A separate Study Guide for each Glencoe Literature Library book provides teaching notes and reproducible activity pages for students.

Glencoe Literature Library titles that complement this unit include:

The Autobiography of Miss Jane Pittman by Ernest J. Gaines
A Christmas Carol by Charles Dickens
Julie of the Wolves by Jean Graighead George
Taking Sides by Gary Soto

For a wealth of online resources that support the instruction in Unit 4 of *Glencoe Literature: Reading with Purpose,* students and teachers can visit our Web site at www.glencoe.com. Students will find additional learning, practice, and assessment opportunities such as these, which are noted in the student text:

- **Big Question Overview**
- **Study Central**
- **Author Search**
- **Writing Models**
- **Interactive Literary Elements Handbook**
- **Web Activities**

Teachers will find planning and instructional tools that include the following:

- **Book Lesson Plans**
- **Teacher Forum**
- **Professional Development**
- **Web Activities Lesson Plans (with answers to student activities)**

Go to www.glencoe.com to see the entire selection of Reading with Purpose online resources.

GLENCOE BOOKLINK

Use the Glencoe BookLink 3 CD-ROM, a database of more than 26,700 titles, to *create customized reading lists* for your students.

- Search for award-winning titles, (e.g., Newbery Award winners, Coretta Scott King Award winners, and Caldecott Medal winners) and for books on several state-recommended reading lists.
- Find Degrees of Reading Power™ (DRP) and Lexile™ readability scores for all selections.
- Organize reading lists by students' reading level, author, genre, theme, or area of interest.
- Get a brief summary of each selection.

You can find recommended leveled readings for this unit with Reading on Your Own (see page 120).

Glencoe's **Presentation Plus!**, a multimedia teaching tool, lets you present dynamic lessons that will engage your students. Using Microsoft PowerPoint,® you can customize the presentations to create your own personalized lessons. Use **CheckPoint** questions with interactive response keypads to get immediate student feedback during lessons, to increase student participation, and to assess student comprehension.

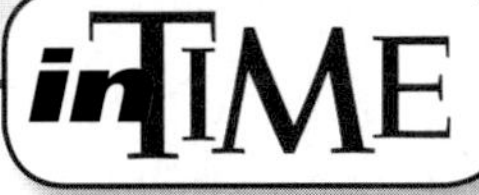

A lively collection of articles drawn from issues of the TIME family of magazines helps students develop the skills they need to interact with informational text in a meaningful way. Each of the news stories, feature articles, reviews, profiles, and essays in the magazine connect to an author, work, or theme in *Glencoe Literature: Reading with Purpose.* Articles for Unit 4 are found in Volume A. See the *inTIME* Teacher's Guide for specific connections to each unit and for reproducible student worksheets designed to develop students' reading and critical thinking skills.

Additional Instructional Support

WRITING, GRAMMAR, AND SPELLING

- Real Success in Writing: Research and Reports
- Writing Constructed Responses Sourcebook
- Spelling Power eWorkbook
- Grammar & Composition Handbook
- Grammar and Language Workbook
- Revising with Style eWorkbook

READING AND LITERATURE

- Active Learning and Note Taking Guide
- inTime Magazines
- Backpack Reader Volume 1
- Literature Library
- Literature Launchers Pre-Reading Videos DVD
- Literature Classics

TRANSPARENCIES

- Read Aloud, Think Aloud
- Literary and Text Analysis Transparencies
- Bellringer Options Transparencies
- Grammar and Writing Workshop Transparencies
- Fine Arts Transparencies

TECHNOLOGY

- TeacherWorks Plus
- StudentWorks Plus
- BookLink 3
- Skill Level Up!
- ExamView Assessment Suite
- Interactive Tutor Self-Assessment
- Listening Library CD
- Spanish Listening Library CD
- Literature Classics
- Literature Launchers Pre-Reading Videos DVD
- Literature Library ExamView Assessment Suite
- Vocabulary Puzzlemaker
- Literature Library Vocabulary Puzzlemaker
- glencoe.com
- Online Student Edition
- Presentation Plus!
- Glencoe Online Essay Grading

ENGLISH LANGUAGE LEARNER

- English Language Coach
- Fluency Practice and Assessment
- inTime Magazines (Spanish)
- Spanish Listening Library CD

PROFESSIONAL DEVELOPMENT

- Professional Development Package

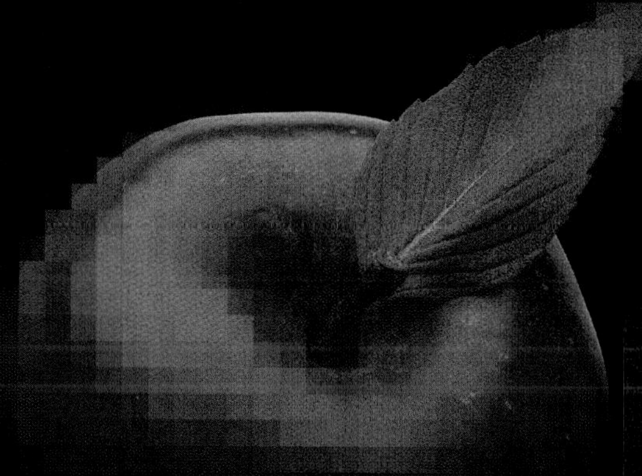

Teacher Chat Room

Teaching Students About Persuasive Text

How do I make persuasive text interesting to students?

Most students will be interested in persuasive text that deal with subjects they are interested in. Scan various media to find examples of persuasive text or have students look for as many persuasive messages as they can find in one day. Then as a class, discuss how these texts are persuasive, how the writer makes his or her argument, and how students are influenced by the text.

What should I teach my students about persuasive text?

First, teach students how to read the text to find the persuasive message. We cover this in Reading Workshop 1 of this Unit, where we show students how to understand persuasive techniques. Next, we recommend teaching students how to distinguish between fact and opinion. Students need to know when something is substantiated with evidence and proof and when something is simply someone's thoughts or idea. Students should also learn to identify the author's purpose and perspective when reading persuasive text.

UNIT 4

The BIG Question: Who Influences Us and How Do They Do So?

"As long as I can be an influence and make a difference, that's what I want to do."

—Oprah Winfrey, entertainment executive

Bruce Fleming/Masterfile

Key Unit Objectives

- Answer the Big Question
- Identify, understand, and apply reading strategies for persuasive writing
- Analyze the elements of persuasive writing
- Write editorials

BIG Question

Why Is It Important?
Finding the answer to the Big Question helps students understand how persuasive writing influences readers.

Viewing the Photo
Oprah Winfrey uses her talk show, magazine, and production company to teach, entertain, connect with, and persuade millions of fans around the world. In the first year of her book club, for example, she persuaded more than 700,000 people to join her in reading and analyzing her book choices. In doing so, she also helped jumpstart the careers of many little-known authors. **Ask:** If you were as influential as Oprah Winfrey, what would you do to help change the world?

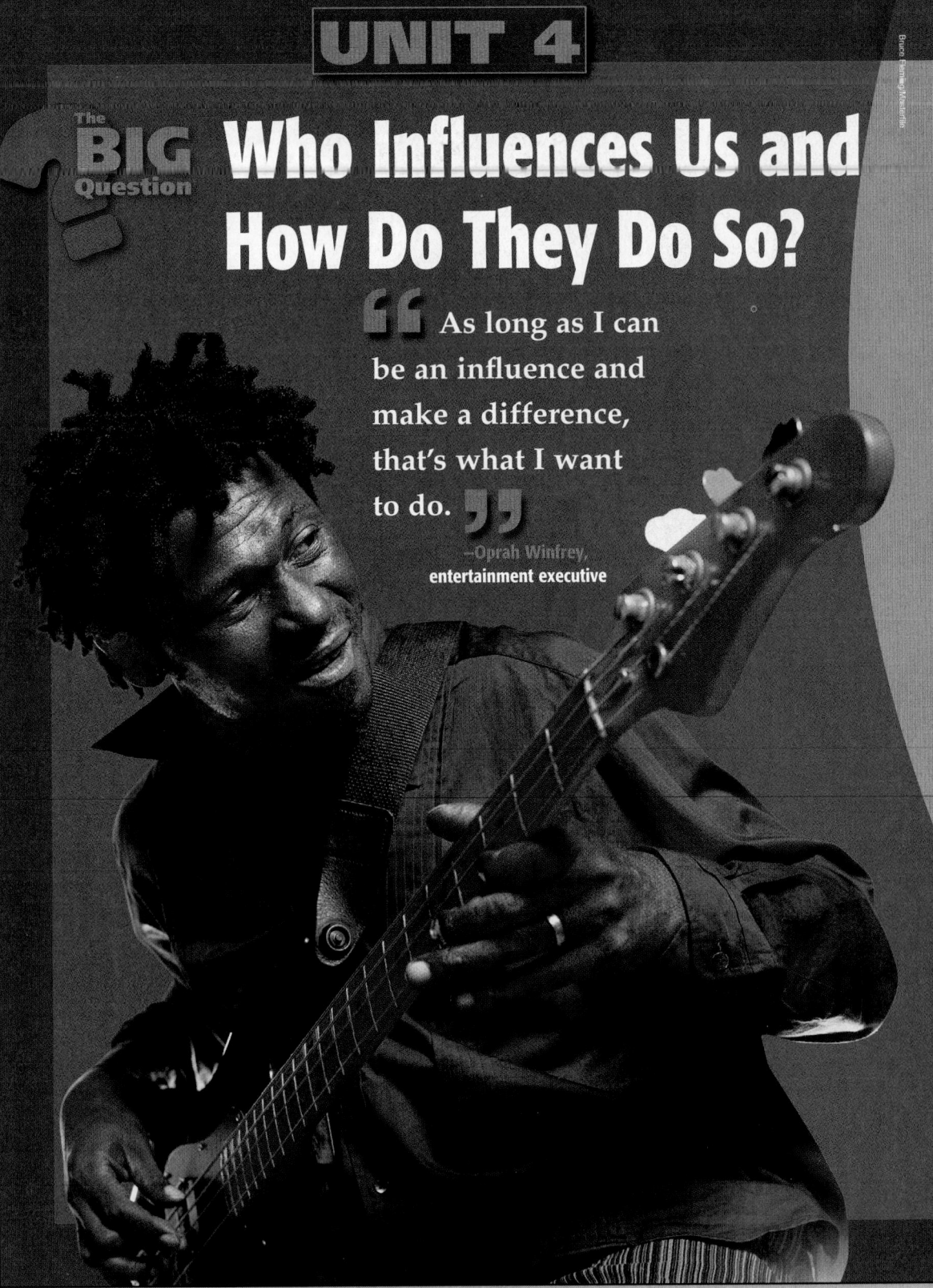

Unit Skills

BIG Question Who Influences Us and How Do They Do So?
Genre Focus: Persuasive Writing

Reading Skills
- Understanding persuasive techniques, p. 416
- Distinguishing fact and opinion, p. 438
- Identifying author's purpose and perspective, p. 454
- Using text structure: Compare and contrast, p. 474

Vocabulary
- Denotations and connotations, p. 418
- Semantic slanting, p. 476

Literary Elements
- Style, p. 419
- Tone, p. 441
- Diction, language, and word choice, p. 457
- Argument, p. 477

Writing Skills/Grammar
- Complete sentences, p. 437
- Word choice, p. 469

LOOKING AHEAD

The readings and skill lessons in this unit will help you think about your own answer to the Big Question.

About the Reading

Each selection in this unit helps students answer the question, "Who influences us and how do they do so?" Students learn about people, events, and persuasive arguments that influence people and analyze ways in which these factors change people's lives.

About the Skills

Each skill in this unit has been carefully selected to help students read the featured genre—persuasive writing. Every selection gives students opportunities to practice and develop persuasive reading and writing skills.

No Child Left Behind

NCLB places great importance on developing reading skills. One way to improve reading skills is to encourage students to make use of graphic organizers as they read. When students are asked to distinguish between fact and opinion in workshop 2, for example, you might model using a T-chart to help distinguish between the two.

Telling the difference between fact and opinion	
FACT	**OPINION**

Reading Fluency

Developing Fluency To become fluent in reading persuasive writing, students need to read good examples of the genre, written at appropriate reading levels. Read a selection aloud as students follow along. Students will benefit from hearing how tone, volume, and pitch of voice can be used to enhance persuasiveness. As students become more proficient, ask them to take turns reading aloud. **BL**

Focus

BELLRINGER Options

- Literature Launcher: Prereading DVD
- Daily Language Practice Transparency

Focus Activity Write on the board: Think about your favorite commercial. What is it about the ad you enjoy? Did the ad persuade you to buy or use the product being advertised? Why or why not? *(Responses will vary.)*

Teach

R Reading Skill

Review Connecting To help students connect to the Big Question, have them discuss how a book or story they read as a child influenced them. Provide the following sentences for ideas:

- The book/story I remember most is ____.
- Before I read this book, I felt/thought ____.
- After reading the book, I believe ____. AS

BQ

- Have students brainstorm ideas that would help both Kaylon and Ricardo accomplish their goals. OL

Connecting to The BIG Question

Who Influences Us and How Do They Do So?

R Your job as a teenager is becoming the adult you're going to be. You work at that job every day, whether you realize it or not. Some things about you are already set, and you didn't choose those things–the color of your eyes, how tall you are, that kind of thing. Your personality and your character, on the other hand, are growing and changing. Among the forces that make you what you're becoming are the people in your life.

Real Kids and the Big Question

KAYLON had trouble reading until she was in the sixth grade. Then her teacher, Mrs. Jenks, began to work with her. She tested Kaylon and found that she had trouble learning by looking. She worked with Kaylon, using some tools that helped her learn. Kaylon can read much better now, and she's decided to be a teacher. Why do you think she made that decision?

BQ

Literature Online

BIG Question Link to Web resources to further explore the Big Question at www.glencoe.com.

RICARDO used to give up on anything that was hard. He wasn't lazy. He just got discouraged and frustrated. He was going to quit playing baseball, too, but Coach Lopez talked to him. The coach knew how it felt to be discouraged, but he knew how it felt to win, too. Ricardo stayed on the team. Now, his friends can count on him, and his grades are better. Why do you think that happened?

Warm-Up Activity

With a partner, talk about the people who influenced Kaylon and Ricardo. Decide how important the influences might be in their lives.

Additional Support

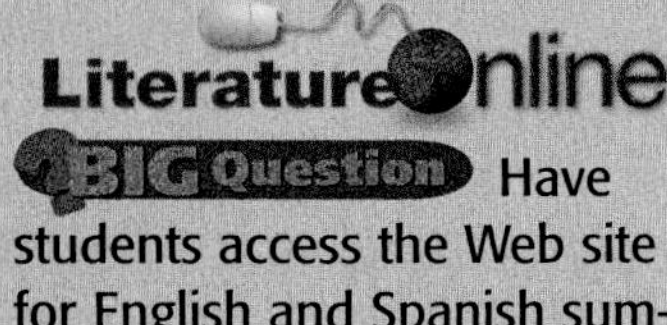

Literature Online

BIG Question Have students access the Web site for English and Spanish summaries and annotated links to related Web resources.

Reading in the Real World

Career Role models, such as Kaylon's teacher, often influence people's career choices. Ask students to name a few of their role models and discuss the qualities they admire in these people. Remind students that friends, relatives, and others they encounter in their daily lives as well as people they admire from a distance can serve as role models. Have students research the biography of one of their role models to find out how that person achieved career success. Students can interview a role model if he or she is accessible, or they can find resources on the Internet and at the library. OL

You and the Big Question

Parents, teachers, your friends—all these people influence you in one way or another. Famous people and others you will never meet also influence you. Reading can help you choose people you admire and want to be like. Using the reading selections in this unit, you'll be better able to answer the Big Question.

Plan for the Unit Challenge

At the end of the unit, you'll use notes from all your reading to complete the Unit Challenge.

You will choose one of the following activities:

A. Create a Poster You'll work in a group to create a poster for a TV show called "Let the Kids Speak!"

B. Write About a Person You'll work by yourself to write about a person who has had an influence on the world—or on you personally.

- Start thinking about which activity you'd like to do so that you can focus your thinking as you go through the unit.
- In your Learner's Notebook, write your thoughts about the pros and cons of each activity. That may make it easier to decide which one you'd like to do.
- Remember to make notes about the Big Question, because these ideas will help you with the Unit Challenge activity you choose.

Keep Track of Your Ideas

As you read, you'll make notes about the Big Question. Later, you'll use these notes to complete the Unit Challenge. See page R9 for help with making Foldable 4. This diagram shows how it should look.

1. Make one Foldable page for each selection. At the end of the unit, you'll staple the pages together into one Foldable.
2. Label the front of the fold-over page with the selection title. (See page 409 for the titles.)
3. Below the title, write the label **My Purpose for Reading.**
4. Open the Foldable. Label the inside page **The Big Question.**

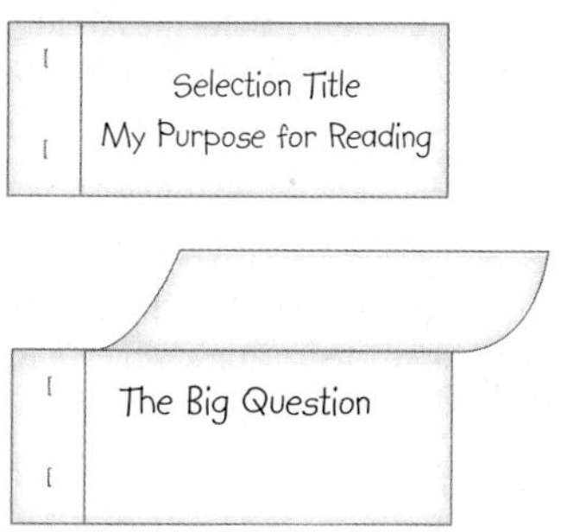

Teach

BQ 

Have students write for five minutes about the people who have influenced them and how they did so. OL

Unit Challenge

Help students choose the Unit Challenge that is best suited to their skills.

FOLDABLES™ Study Organizer

For each selection they read, students will write notes about how that selection applies to the Big Question. For details about using Dinah Zike's Foldables, see page R9.

Assess/Close

Ask students to share why it is important to recognize that people, things, and events influence them and to analyze methods they use.

Resources for page 411

- Use the Unit Challenge Planner BLM in the Unit 4 Resource Booklet.
- Use the Foldable BLM in the Unit 4 Resource Booklet.

Differentiated Instruction

Keywords Refer to the questions at the end of the paragraphs about Kaylon and Ricardo. Tell students that when they give advice, they influence how people think or act. Before giving advice, they need to know the facts. Keywords will help them focus on the facts. Tell students to write 5 to 10 keywords for each situation and to use them to give advice to others like Kaylon and Ricardo. As they read selections in this unit, students should write keywords in their Learner's Notebook each time they need help focusing on the facts. OL

Objectives

- Recognize the influence of people and events on readers' lives
- Connect to literature

Focus

BELLRINGER Options

Daily Language Practice Transparency

Focus Activity Say: How is an advertisement in a magazine different from a lesson in your math book? Which is an example of persuasive writing? What other things do you read or watch that influence how you think or act? *(Responses will vary.)*

Teach

R Reading Skill

How to Read Persuasive Writing Ask: How might each reading skill help you read persuasive writing? *(Possible responses: **Understanding Persuasive Techniques:** You can figure out how a writer tries to influence you. **Distinguishing Fact and Opinion:** You can read for good supporting arguments. **Identifying Author's Purpose and Perspective:** You can recognize opinions. **Comparing and Contrasting:** You can decide which information or viewpoint seems right to you.)* OL

UNIT 4 GENRE FOCUS: PERSUASIVE WRITING

Skills Focus

- Key skills for reading persuasive writing
- Key literary elements of persuasive writing

Skills Model

You will see how to use the key reading skills and literary elements as you read

- ***"Violence in Hockey"*** p. 414

The Big Question in this unit concerns the people who influence you in ways that shape your character and life. There are also many people who try to influence you about very specific things. A commercial on television tells you what cereal to eat. A review in a newspaper tells you that you *have to* see a new movie. A magazine article says that running is better exercise than biking. They're all trying to persuade you.

R In **persuasive writing,** a writer tries to get readers to share a certain point of view or take a particular action, from voting to buying hiking boots. Not all of the things writers want you to believe or do, however, are good. It's important to spot when writers are telling the truth and when they just *sound* as though they are. You don't want to be persuaded that junk is good, whether it's junk food or junk ideas.

The best way to learn how to read persuasive writing is to take a look at the way it's written. If you know something about the techniques writers use, you'll be able to recognize them. You'll be able to read an advertisement and see the exaggerations. When an editorial in a newspaper is full of what the writer thinks and not what she can prove, you'll know it.

Some Sources of Persuasion	
Television Radio Newspaper Magazine Poster Advertisement	Book Friends Parents Teachers Famous people

Why Read Persuasive Writing?

Simple. Learning and getting information from what you read is good. Persuasive writing often has

- good information
- exciting ideas
- new and different ways to think about your world

But in the end, you want to make sure you're thinking for yourself. That's why it's important to have the skills to think clearly about what you're reading.

Objectives (pp. 414–417)
Reading Identify persuasive techniques • Distinguish fact from opinion • Compare and contrast • Identify author's purpose • Identify author's perspective
Literature Identify literary elements: tone, style

Additional Support

Literature Focus Lesson

Supporting Arguments Tell students that opinions have little influence unless they are well supported. To build effective arguments, writers should remember these points: consider the questions readers might raise; know the best way to support an argument (facts, examples, opinions of respected people); and select the most effective details. Ask students to list arguments and supporting details in favor of or against school dress codes. OL

How to Read Persuasive Writing

Key Reading Skills

These key reading skills are especially useful tools for reading and understanding all the different kinds of persuasive writing. The skills are modeled in the Active Reading Model on pages 414–415. You'll learn more about these skills later in Unit 4.

- **Understanding persuasive techniques** Writers have many tools for making you believe what they're saying. Some of those techniques can be trusted and some are dangerous. (See Reading Workshop 1.)
- **Distinguishing fact and opinion** Believing something is true and being able to prove it are two different things. If a writer can't prove it, he or she may try to hide that. As you read, ask yourself, "Is this a fact or is this the writer's opinion?" (See Reading Workshop 2.)
- **Identifying author's purpose and perspective** Why does the writer want you to believe him or her? The author's purpose and perspective can help you answer this question. (See Reading Workshop 3.)
- **Comparing and contrasting** Writers often compare (show how things are alike) and contrast (show how things are different) to influence readers. They may use signal words and phrases such as *similarly, on the other hand,* or *however.* (See Reading Workshop 4.)

Key Literary Elements

Recognizing and understanding the following elements will help you appreciate what you're reading. It will also help you see when a writer is appealing to your emotions rather than your ability to think for yourself.

- **Style:** a form of expression in writing, drawing, and painting, as well as music and fashion (See "3BCB: Three by Clay Bennett.")
- **Tone:** the attitude of an author as it comes through in the writing (See "What Exercise Can Do for You.")
- **Diction, language, and word choice:** word selection that expresses ideas, meanings, and moods (See "The Courage That My Mother Had.")
- **Argument:** the reasons a writer gives to support an idea or opinion (See "Should Naturalized Citizens Be President?")

English Language Coach

Word Choice Tell students that in an editorial, the writer chooses words carefully to influence readers. In the Genre Focus selection, the writer wants to convince readers that Todd Bertuzzi was too violent during a hockey game and that hockey has become too violent. So the writer uses a lot of words related to violence. Have students work with a partner to note all the words in the selection related to violence. Encourage students to look up the meanings of any words they do not know. EL

Teach

L1 Literary Element

Style **Ask:** Can you think of a form of persuasive writing where style might be particularly important? *(Possible response: Style might be important in print ads, where the advertiser has to grab the reader's attention with persuasive, intriguing words and an interesting word arrangement.)* AL

L2 Literary Element

Tone **Ask:** What are some words that might describe an author's tone? *(angry, hopeful, critical, sad)* OL How might the author's tone influence your opinion on a subject? *(Possible response: If the author is angry about an issue, I might feel angry, too.)* AL

Resources for page 413

Use the Genre Study BLM in the Unit 4 Resource Booklet.

Objectives
- Identify persuasive techniques
- Distinguish fact and opinion
- Compare and contrast characters, setting, and plot
- Identify the power of language to influence
- Identify and explain literary elements

Teach

R Reading Skill

Identifying Author's Purpose and Perspective The writer of this newspaper article is clearly upset with Todd Bertuzzi. Ask students to reread the first two paragraphs and find words loaded with anger. *(Possible responses: unwarranted; crimes; sucker punch; slam)* OL
Ask: After reading only the first two paragraphs, what purpose do you think this writer had for writing the article? *(possibly to publicly shame Bertuzzi)* AL
Ask: Why should you read to the end before deciding on the author's purpose? *(You need more information to determine the author's purpose.)* OL

L Literary Element

Argument Ask: What argument does the writer present in paragraph three to support his claim of violence? *(Bertuzzi would have been arrested for such an assault on the streets.)* AL

Readability Scores
Dale-Chall: 7.5
DRP: 67
Lexile: 1230

Violence in HOCKEY

The notes in the side columns model how to use the skills and elements you read about on pages 412–413.

Persuasive Writing

ACTIVE READING MODEL

The National Hockey League must decide if its business is sport or thuggery.[1] Monday night's unwarranted[2] attack on Colorado Avalanche player Steve Moore is the most serious of many violent crimes committed on the ice. 1 R

Moore wasn't just hit from behind, as often happens in the fast-paced game. He got mugged.[3] 2

Todd Bertuzzi of the Vancouver Canucks apparently believed it was all right to sucker punch[4] someone and slam the victim's head against the ice. As an adult in a law-abiding society, Bertuzzi must have known that if he committed such a blatant[5] assault on the streets, Yankee cops or Canadian Mounties would have had him in handcuffs. 3 L

But Bertuzzi may have thought that since the NHL long has turned a blind eye to uncalled-for violence, he wouldn't be seriously punished for any beating he delivered in the name of revenge.

1 **Key Reading Skill**
Distinguishing Fact and Opinion *The writer says "the most serious of many violent crimes." That's a pretty strong opinion. I wonder if the writer will back it up.*

2 **Key Reading Skill**
Identifying Author's Purpose and Perspective *Was this editorial written by a sports writer? I wish I knew more about where this writer was "coming from."*

3 **Key Literary Elements**
Tone, Style The writer is using strong words, like *sucker punch* and *slam* and *mugged*. There's anger in this tone.

1. ***Thuggery*** is related to the word *thug*. A thug is a really nasty bully.
2. Something ***unwarranted*** is done without a good reason.
3. Someone who is ***mugged*** is violently beaten and robbed.
4. A ***sucker punch*** is an unfair punch delivered with no warning.
5. ***Blatant*** means there's no attempt to hide what's going on.

Additional Support

Literature Focus Lesson

Tone Tone tells a lot about the author, because tone is the attitude the author has toward a topic or the audience. There are many ways for students to identify tone. For example, the writer's choice of words and images can reveal the author's tone. Have students tell what they think is the tone of the editorial. *(Possible response: outrage)* OL **Ask:** Why do you think the writer uses this tone? *(Possible response: to persuade readers that violence in hockey must be punished)* AL

After all, four years ago another hockey pro got a mere wrist slap[6] from both the NHL and British Columbia officials for whacking an opponent in the head with his stick. 4

Under Canadian law, though, the seriousness of the charges depends partly on the extent of the victim's injuries. Since Moore was badly hurt, the criminal case now being investigated in Vancouver could result in a harsher outcome.

Still, it's up to the NHL to deal with the problem. 5

The NHL suspended Bertuzzi earlier this week. The league's final decision, however, has got to send a strong message to players and coaches.

The league should ban Bertuzzi for life from professional hockey. 6 ❍

Persuasive Writing

ACTIVE READING MODEL

4 Key Reading Skill Comparing and Contrasting *Here's a comparison.*

5 Key Literary Element Argument *I wonder why the writer waited until now to mention the criminal case. It makes the argument stronger.*

R

6 Key Literary Element Diction, Language, and Word Choice *After all that strong, slangy language, the writer is formal and serious about the law.*

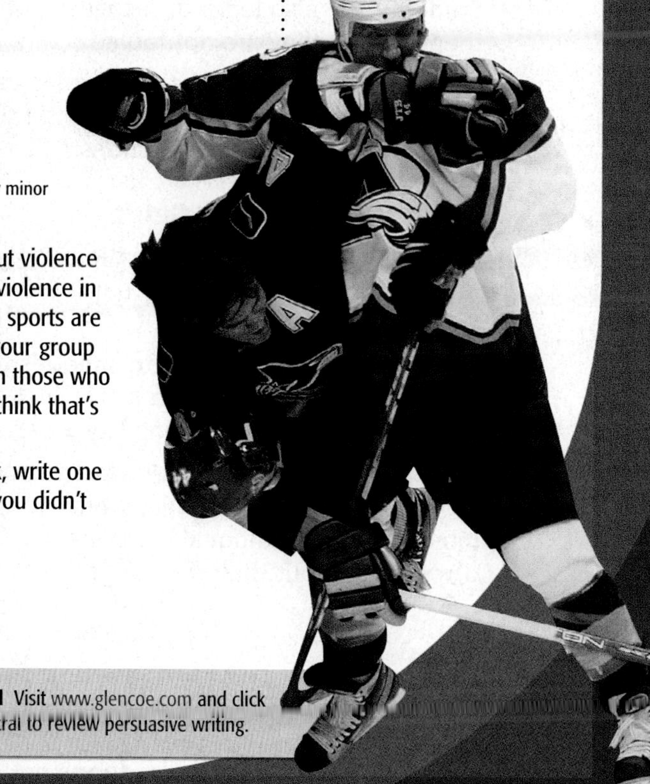

6. A ***mere wrist slap*** is a figure of speech meaning a very minor punishment for a major offense.

Small Group Work With a group, talk about violence in sports. Discuss whether there is too much violence in school sports or in professional sports. Which sports are most likely to get violent? Do the athletes in your group have different opinions about the subject than those who are not involved in sports? If so, why do you think that's true? If not, what does that tell you?

Write to Learn In your Learner's Notebook, write one thing that you learned in the discussion that you didn't know before.

Literature Online **Study Central** Visit www.glencoe.com and click on Study Central to review persuasive writing.

Teach

R Reading Skill

Distinguishing Fact and Opinion **Say:** A fact is something that can be proved; an opinion is what someone believes is true. Ask students to identify facts and opinions in the last four paragraphs of this editorial. *(**Facts:** Under Canadian law, the severity of the punishment is based partly on the victim's injuries. Moore's case could result in a harsher outcome. The NHL suspended Bertuzzi. **Opinions:** It's up to the NHL to deal with the problem. The league's final decision must send a strong message. The league should ban Bertuzzi for life from professional hockey.)* OL

Literature Online

Study Central Have students access the Web site to review persuasive writing and to complete a related activity.

Reading in the Real World

Citizenship Ask students to consider running for local office someday. In small groups, they can make a political campaign poster that contains both facts and opinions that are important for their candidacy. Their posters must show facts that can be proven such as the following:

There are six problems that our town needs to address, for example, lake and stream pollution. (fact)

Students must also show that they have opinions about how to solve the problems:

I believe that we can research other ways to dispose of waste. (opinion) OL

Objectives
- Identify persuasive techniques
- Distinguish fact and opinion
- Compare and contrast
- Identify the power of language to influence
- Identify and explain literary devices, including tone, style, and argument

Understanding Persuasive Techniques

Objectives covered in this workshop:
- Understand persuasive techniques
- Interpret and use graphic sources of information

Understanding Persuasive Techniques

Why Is It Important?

- Understanding persuasive techniques can help students recognize when someone or something is trying to convince them to think or act a certain way.
- Students will also learn to recognize what someone might really be telling them so that they are not fooled.
- Understanding persuasive techniques can also help students make decisions about whether or not to change the way they think about a certain topic or act in different situations.

How to Help Students Get It

- If students have trouble with the concept, remind students that they use persuasive techniques every day when they try to influence their family, teachers, and friends.
- Have students look for the techniques the writer uses in the text: Do they support their opinions with facts? Or do they use words that appeal to readers' emotions, repeating key ideas and opinions?
- Discuss how editorial cartoons use strong images to show how the cartoonists feel about an issue, which some students may find difficult to interpret. Find additional cartoons in a magazine or newspaper and lead a discussion about their meanings.

Reading to Answer the Big Question

3BCB: Three by Clay Bennett

Three single-panel editorial cartoons on "global" topics. These images impact viewers differently than the written word.

Thank You, M'am

In this short story, Roger thinks that stealing a woman's purse will get him the blue suede shoes he wants. Instead, it gets him contact with Mrs. Luella Bates Washington Jones. Mrs. Jones does not take Roger to the police, or interrogate him about his home life. She takes him home, feeds him dinner and gives him the money he tried to steal. The reader is left to decide which course of action will ultimately have the most influence on Roger's life.

Workshop Resources

Pacing (Days) Standard	Block	Lesson	Student Materials	Teacher Resources
1		Key Skill Lesson: Understanding Persuasive Techniques	Key Reading Skills Practice English Language Coach	Bellringer Options Transparencies Read Aloud, Think Aloud Transparencies Presentation Plus!
2		"3BCB: Three by Clay Bennett"	Literary Analysis Transparencies Glencoe Online Selection Vocabulary Development Academic Vocabulary Development English Language Coach Active Reading Graphic Organizer Literary Analysis StudentWorks Plus Online Student Edition Literature Classics Selection and Unit Assessments	Literary and Text Analysis Transparencies Puzzlemaker Skill Level Up! BookLink 3 Assessment by Learning Objective (Diagnostic and Formative) Interactive Tutor Self-Assessment TeacherWorks Plus
2		"Thank You M'am"	Glencoe Online Selection Vocabulary Development Academic Vocabulary Development English Language Coach Active Reading Graphic Organizer Literary Analysis StudentWorks Plus Online Student Edition Literature Classics Selection and Unit Assessments	Literary and Text Analysis Transparencies Puzzlemaker Skill Level Up! BookLink 3 Assessment by Learning Objective (Diagnostic and Formative) Interactive Tutor Self-Assessment TeacherWorks Plus

Keys for Unit Resource

- Blackline Master
- Workbook
- Supplemental Text
- CD-ROM
- DVD
- Transparency
- Web-based
- Fast Files

Level Appropriate Code

AS = Activities for all students
AL = Activities for students working above grade level
OL = Activities for students working at grade level
BL = Activities for students working below grade level
EL = Activities for English language learners

Focus

BELLRINGER Options

Daily Language Practice Transparency

Focus Activity Say: Many editorial cartoonists create cartoons about problems facing the country or the world. What problem would you create an editorial cartoon about? *(Possible responses: hunger, poverty, homelessness, war, natural disasters)*

Teach

R Reading Skill

Understanding Persuasive Techniques Say: You use persuasive language each time you ask for permission or help. Can you think of some examples? *(Possible responses: asking parents to allow you to attend a concert, asking a friend to help you babysit)* OL

V Vocabulary

Academic Vocabulary Say: Look at the word *visually* at the bottom of page 416. What does it mean? Do you know other words that have the same base word, *visual*? *(Possible responses: audiovisual, visualize)* OL

READING WORKSHOP 1

Skills Focus

You will practice using these skills when you read the following selections:

- "3BCD. Three by Clay Bennett" p. 420
- "Thank You, M'am" p. 426

Reading

- Understanding persuasive techniques
- Analyzing ways that graphics affect audience

Literature

- Identifying the author's style
- Recognizing the effect of the author's style on your understanding of the selection

Vocabulary

- Understanding denotation and connotation
- Academic Vocabulary: *visually*

Writing/Grammar

- Identifying sentence types
- Using end punctuation

Objectives (pp. 416–417)
Reading Identify persuasive techniques

Skill Lesson

Understanding Persuasive Techniques

Learn It!

What Is It? "Don't believe everything you read." "All that glitters is not gold." "Buyer beware!" These are all warnings about being fooled by persuasive techniques. Does that mean you can't believe *anything*? No. You just need to make good judgments about what's true

R Words are powerful tools. They can make you angry, sad, or happy. Images are powerful, too, and writers can create images for you with words. Cartoonists use both words and images to make you think and to persuade you that an idea or an action is right or wrong. They give information **visually**, in ways that appeal to your eyes.

Analyzing Cartoons
Moe doesn't have to say much. Calvin knows that words aren't very important in the "persuasive techniques" that bullies use.

V **Academic Vocabulary**

visually (VIZH oo uh lee) *adv.* using or appealing to the sense of sight

Additional Support

Reading in the Real World

Career Cartoons such as "Calvin and Hobbes" often contain a truth inside their humor. Many of the earliest editorial cartoons were political cartoons and also contained a truth. Have students find a cartoon by an early American cartoonist such as Thomas Nast or W. Gordon Nye. BL

Ask students to learn about its background. Students should explain the point of the cartoon in an oral and visual presentation. OL

Why Is It Important? Reading is a great tool for learning, but you need to be able to think for yourself about what you read. It helps to be able to recognize some of the techniques writers use to persuade you. Then you can make your judgments. That makes you a smart reader.

How Do I Do It? Suppose an article says, "No good person would buy shoes from this awful company because they do terrible things." Before you stop buying your favorite shoes, you need to

- see that the writer is using emotionally loaded words to make you feel a certain way.
- watch out for broad general statements.
- look for facts that back up the claim.
- look for statements by experts and ask who those experts are.

C

Literature Online

Study Central Visit www.glencoe.com and click on Study Central to review persuasive techniques.

Here's how one student understands a persuasive technique the writer uses in "Violence in Hockey."

One of the main persuasive techniques the writer uses is strong words. For example, he uses the words violent crimes, mugged, sucker punch, slam, handcuffs, beating, whacking, and many others. I think he chose to use these words to make readers emotional and upset about the violence in hockey.

Practice It!

Choose one page of a magazine. Look through it for strong words, broad general statements, and pictures that are supposed to appeal to your emotions. Be sure to look at the ads. In your Learner's Notebook, write some examples from the page. Then look for expert opinion and facts that back up statements. Make notes if you find any.

Use It!

As you read "3BCB" and "Thank You, M'am," use the skills you've learned to understand persuasion.

Teach

Literature Online

Study Central Have students access the Web site to review persuasive techniques and to complete a related activity.

C Critical Thinking

Synthesis Ask: What do you think is the most important benefit of understanding persuasive techniques? *(Possible response: I can understand when someone is trying to convince me and use my own judgment to decide if I agree.)* **OL** Besides advertisers, what other groups of people might use persuasive techniques to convince you of their opinion? *(Possible responses: the government, writers, people running for political office, people collecting money for a cause)* **AL**

Resources for page 417

- Use Reading Skills Transparency in *Read Aloud, Think Aloud,* Unit 4, to help students practice understanding persuasive techniques.

Reading in the Real World

Citizenship Show students political campaign posters or taped speeches. Ask them to jot down persuasive techniques that candidates use. If possible, invite an elected official to talk about campaigning, audiences, methods, and issues. Allow students to ask questions. Then ask students to list five reasons this person was able to persuade voters to elect him or her. In their evaluations, students may also refer to the official's interactions with the class. **OL** **AL**

Objectives
- Identify persuasive techniques

Before You Read

3BCB: Three by Clay Bennett

More About the Author

Having college degrees in both art and history, Clay Bennett has both the knowledge and skills for editorial cartooning. In addition to drawing cartoons for newspapers, Bennett learned Web design and has created fully animated cartoons for the Internet.

V Vocabulary

Ask students to write their own sentences using the vocabulary words. AS

EL Language Coach

Say: With your partner, select a word from "Violence in Hockey." Discuss both the denotation and the connotation of the word. *(Whacking means "hitting," but it implies the use of force.)* EL OL

Clay Bennett

Meet the Author

Clay Bennett was born in South Carolina in 1958. He was the son of an army officer, and his family moved several times. Bennett went to ten different schools before he graduated from high school. He has won many awards for his cartoons, including the Pulitzer Prize in 2002.

Author Search For more about Clay Bennett, go to www.glencoe.com.

Objectives (pp. 418–421)
Reading Identify persuasive techniques: graphics
Literature Identify literary elements: style
Vocabulary Distinguish denotation and connotation

Vocabulary Preview

V

global (GLOH bul) *adj.* relating to or happening throughout the whole world **(p. 421)** *Education, hunger, and health care are important global issues.*

cease-fire (SEES fyr) *n.* a stop, or ending, to acts of war **(p. 421)** *A cease-fire over the holidays gave the soldiers on both sides a chance to rest.*

Write to Learn Look at the definition of the word *global*. The sentence that follows talks about *issues* that are *global*. Read the list below of some words the adjective *global* can describe. What other words can *global* describe?

problems
celebration
agreement
climate change

English Language Coach

EL

Denotations and Connotations You know what the definition of a word is, right? It's the meaning. Take the word *bunny*. The exact meaning of *bunny* is "rabbit." That's its **denotation**. But there's something more to some words than the dictionary meaning. Some words give you certain feelings or put pictures in your mind. Most people think of bunnies as cute and cuddly and sweet. Those ideas are **connotations** of the word *bunny*. Because *bunny* has connotations that *rabbit* doesn't have, a writer is more likely to say "cute as a bunny" than "cute as a rabbit."

It is because some words have connotations that there's a car called a Mustang. The word *mustang* has connotations of wildness and freedom and strength. You probably wouldn't name a car after a housefly, even though flies are very fast.

With a Partner With a partner, come up with a name for a new kind of bicycle. Think about names of animals, things in the solar system, things in nature. Come up with a word that has connotations that match your idea of a great bike.

Additional Support

Author Search To expand students' appreciation of Clay Bennett, have them access the Web site for additional information and resources.

Literature Focus Lesson

Persuasion Remind students that cartoonists include many details that reveal their perspectives. Have students find an editorial cartoon about a real person or group of people. Ask them to consider how the following details reveal the cartoonist's opinion about the person or people.

- facial expressions
- size of person/people
- body language of person/people
- dialogue of person/people
- caption

Ask students how the image might influence the reader's opinion of the person or people. OL

Skills Preview

Key Reading Skill: Understanding Persuasive Techniques: Graphics

As you look at the editorial cartoons, break them into separate parts so you can better understand them and the persuasive techniques the cartoonist uses. Look at

- the objects pictured in the cartoon.
- a title or words on the cartoon.
- unusual and unexpected connections between the objects in the cartoon.

R

Key Literary Element: Style

When it comes to clothes, style is the way you put an outfit together to show who you are. **Style** in writing is similar. The choices a writer makes about words, about kinds and lengths of sentences, and so forth make up his or her style. Artists, including cartoonists, also have styles, and they are often easy to recognize. There are many styles of cartooning. Even when you can't perfectly describe the style, you recognize it. Think of "Calvin and Hobbes" or "Close to Home."

As you look at the editorial cartoons on the following pages, use these questions to help you think about the style.

- Do the images look like other cartoons you've seen?
- What words could you use to describe the pictures? Rough, smooth, pretty, simple, detailed, weird?
- What tools do you think the cartoonist used to create these pictures? Pen, brushes, computer?
- How many words are in the cartoons? Is this part of the style?

Literature Online

Interactive Literary Elements Handbook
To review or learn more about the literary elements, go to www.glencoe.com

Get Ready to Read

Connect to the Reading

The editorial cartoons you're about to see are the cartoonist's way of commenting on issues that affect the world: trash, pollution, climate change, and war. Which of these problems do you think is the worst?

Partner Talk With a partner, talk about what you do, or could do, about trash, pollution, climate change, or war.

Build Background

For centuries, writers have used cartoons, called *editorial cartoons,* to express their opinions about politics, society, world events, and the environment.

- Editorial cartoons can be both funny and serious. They catch people's attention and can be powerful persuasive tools.
- The United States has 5 percent of the world's people but produces 25 percent of its garbage.
- Each year, every American throws away more than 1,500 pounds of garbage.
- Rising temperatures (global warming) could raise the level of the sea. Islands could disappear. Coastal cities could be flooded.
- Most scientists believe that air pollution is causing global warming.

Set Purposes for Reading

Read the editorial cartoons to find out how graphics can influence you. As you look at the cartoons, decide how they make you feel about war, peace, or the way people treat the planet.

BQ

Set Your Own Purpose What would you like to learn from the selection to help you answer the Big Question? Write your own purpose on the "3BCB" page of Foldable 4.

Keep Moving

Use these skills as you read the following selection.

READING WORKSHOP 1

Teach

R Reading Skill

Understanding Persuasive Techniques **Ask:** Why might a cartoon persuade one reader but not another? *(Possible response: Some people connect more to visuals and graphics.)* OL

BQ

Ask: What cartoons might you see in school, online, or in the newspaper that influence who you are and what you do? *(Possible responses: Have a Nice Day or Drugs Are for Dummies posters)* EL OL

CheckPoint

Use the CheckPoint questions provided on Presentation Plus! to check for understanding persuasive techniques and to build background. These questions can be used with interactive response keypads for immediate student feedback.

Literature Online

Interactive Literary Elements Handbook Have students access the Web site to improve their understanding of style.

Differentiated Instruction

Using Graphics Tell students that editorial cartoonists use images and words to express how they feel. Write these experiences on the board. Ask students to draw a cartoon face with a caption or character title to show how they feel about each one.

- being new in school
- trying out for a play
- losing a big game
- making a new friend
- going shopping
- taking a family trip
- going to a dance EL BL

Objectives

- Identify persuasive techniques: graphics
- Identify literary elements: style

READING WORKSHOP 1

Teach

Viewing the Image

Ask: What does this image say about Earth? *(Possible responses: It has big problems. It is being used as a giant trash can by people.)* **OL**

C Critical Thinking

Synthesis Ask: From the cartoon, how do you think the cartoonist might feel about the way people treat Earth? *(Possible responses: angry, concerned, sad)* Do you agree with the cartoonist? Why or why not? *(Responses will vary.)* **OL**

C

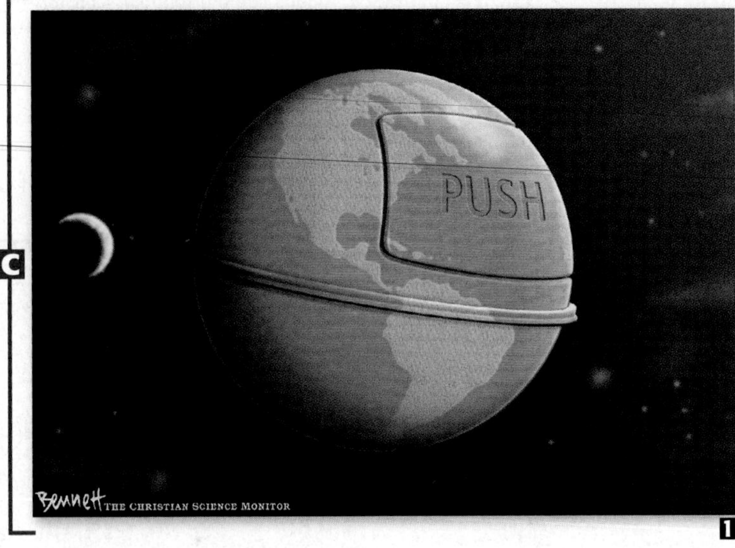

1

Practice the Skills

1 Key Reading Skill

Understanding Persuasive Techniques What is surprising about this cartoon? What is the cartoonist comparing?

Additional Support

Differentiated Instruction

Using a Graphic Organizer Editorial cartoons often comment on issues by what they *don't* say. Readers might use an organizer like the one below to move from what is said or shown, to what they know, to what is hinted at and then understood. **EL** **BL**

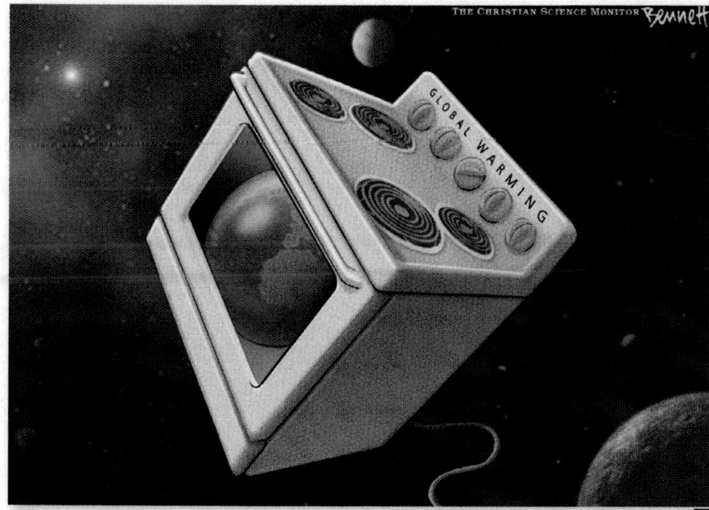

2

Even a temporary cease-fire would do.

Peace on Earth

THE CHRISTIAN SCIENCE MONITOR Bennett

3 4 5

C

Practice the Skills

2 Key Reading Skill

Understanding Persuasive Techniques Does this cartoon appeal to your feelings about the earth? Could it also make you want to find out more about global warming?

3 Key Literary Element

Style Is this a style of holiday card that you recognize? What feelings does it usually create in you?

4 English Language Coach

Denotation and Connotation Do the denotations and connotations of the words on the inside of the card seem to fit with the those on the outside?

5 BIG Question

Which of these cartoons had the strongest influence on you, or made you think a little differently about the subject? Why? Write your answer on the "3BCB" page of Foldable 4. Your response will help you complete the Unit Challenge later.

Vocabulary

global (GLOH bul) *adj.* relating to or happening throughout the whole world

cease-fire (SEES fyr) *n.* a stop, or ending, to acts of war

READING WORKSHOP 1

Teach

C Critical Thinking

Comprehension Ask: Why do you think Bennet created the Peace on Earth card? *(Possible response: He wanted people to stop fighting wars.)* **OL** Why might it be effective to use a holiday card to express this message? *(Possible response: People connect holidays with love and family.)* **AL**

R Reading Skill

Review Activating Prior Knowledge Ask: For which cartoon did you need the most background knowledge to understand the message? *(Possible response: global warming)* **OL**

CheckPoint

Use the CheckPoint questions provided on Presentation Plus! to check for comprehension of the selection. These questions can be used with interactive response keypads for immediate student feedback.

Reading in the Real World

Career People buy greeting cards to show others how they feel about life events. Ask students to design a greeting card, placing a message and an illustration on the cover and a short message inside. Provide them with these topics: birthday, wedding, new home, new job, friendship, or graduation. Ask students to display their cards and discuss them as a class. **BL**

Objectives
- Understand persuasive techniques
- Understand how tone influences readers
- Use a graphic organizer to aid comprehension

Assess

Resources for page 422

- Selection Quick Check
- Selection and Unit Assessment
- ExamView Assessment Suite
- Interactive Tutor: Self-Assessment

Students can respond to the *After You Read* items in their Learner's Notebook or on a separate sheet of paper.

Answering the

1. Responses will vary but may include the idea that the cartoons make students think about their responsibility to care for Earth as well as other people.
2. In each cartoon, Bennett shows a problem faced by people on Earth: pollution, global warming, and war.

Critical Thinking

3. Responses may include the idea that people should try to fix Earth's problems.
4. Responses will vary but could include the idea that both images and words suggest ideas and feelings.
5. Responses will vary but may include the idea that editorial cartoons inspire people to think about issues and to change their behavior.

After You Read

3BCB: Three by Clay Bennett

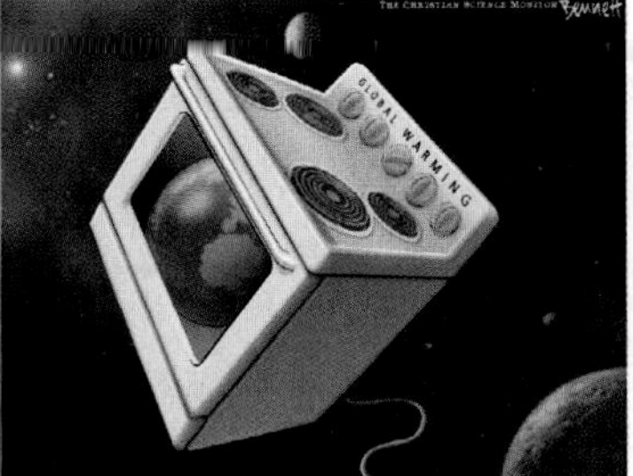

Answering the

1. How do Bennett's cartoons influence you? What do they make you think about?
2. **Recall** What does each cartoon show?
   TIP **Right There**

Critical Thinking

3. **Draw Conclusions** What do you think Bennett's opinion is on the issues he presents in these cartoons? How do you know?
   TIP **Author and Me**
4. **Analyze** How does a picture combined with words help you understand the point the cartoonist is trying to make?
   TIP **Author and Me**
5. **Evaluate** Why are editorial cartoons important?

Write About Your Reading

Choose your favorite cartoon by Clay Bennett. Write a persuasive paragraph to convince your classmates that this is the best of the three cartoons.

In your paragraph, be sure to

- state your opinion of which cartoon is best.
- describe at least three details from the cartoon that will persuade your classmates to agree with you.
- conclude by telling your classmates why they should agree with you that this is the best cartoon of the three.

In a small group of classmates, exchange persuasive paragraphs and choose whose is the most persuasive. Explain why.

Your opinion → Three details → Your conclusion

Objectives (pp. 422–423)
Reading Identify persuasive techniques: graphics
Literature Identify literary elements: style
Vocabulary Distinguish denotation and connotation
Writing Write a persuasive paragraph
Grammar Identify sentence types

Write About Your Reading

Possible response:

I think that the global warming cartoon is best. Most readers can understand it because they recognize that ovens warm things. Picturing Earth "baking" in an oven helped me to imagine how bad global warming is. The cartoon also hints that we can fix the problem by just "taking Earth out of the oven." I think that my classmates should agree with my choice because Bennett cleverly uses an everyday object to make an important point about our planet.

Skills Review

Key Reading Skill: Understanding Persuasive Techniques: Graphics

6. The last cartoon shows what looks like a typical holiday card. The greeting inside, though, is not what you'd expect. How did you respond to the surprise when the inside of the card said something unexpected?
7. Describe the surprise in the second cartoon. Did it persuade you to think a certain way?

Key Literary Element: Style

8. Which of the following words could describe Clay Bennett's style of cartooning? Think of what the cartoons look like and the few words Bennett uses in the cartoons. You may choose more than one word or come up with words of your own.

smooth	messy	fancy	cool	sharp
simple	dramatic	rough	careless	clean

9. Would you expect cartoons about war, pollution, and global warming to be done in this kind of style? Explain your answer.

Vocabulary Check

Answer each question and explain your answers.

10. Would your best friend join in or call for a **cease-fire** in a food fight in the cafeteria? Why?
11. Which would make more people in the world happy, a **global** holiday or a holiday in your neighborhood? Explain your choice.
12. **Academic Vocabulary** If you sense something **visually,** do you sense it with your nose, fingers, ears, or eyes?

English Language Coach

13. Copy any three of the words shown below. Next to each, write down any connotations you think the word has. That is, write down feelings or ideas or qualities that you connect with that word and that you think other people also connect with it.

hawk	nest	chipmunk	feather	dolphin
steel	yellow	giggle	creek	apple

Grammar Link: Sentence Types

A sentence is a group of words that expresses a complete thought.

A **declarative sentence** makes a statement, or tells something about the subject of the sentence.

Latasha is rollerblading.

I like poetry.

An **interrogative sentence** asks a question.

Did Kevin walk the dog?

What is your name?

An **imperative sentence** gives a command.

Go home.

Please be quiet.

An **exclamatory sentence** expresses strong feeling.

We had so much fun!

How scary that movie was!

Grammar Practice

On a separate piece of paper, copy each sentence below. Then write if the sentence is *declarative, interrogative, imperative,* or *exclamatory*.

14. Do you like bananas?
15. Sherry talked all night.
16. I missed you!
17. Call Terrel again.

Writing Application Summarize your Write About Your Reading paragraph in three sentences. (1) In an imperative sentence, command readers to look at the cartoon. (2) In an exclamatory sentence, give your opinion of the cartoon. (3) In a declarative sentence, sum up the three details.

Web Activities For eFlashcards, Selection Quick Checks, and other Web activities, go to www.glencoe.com.

Skills Review

Key Reading Skill: Understanding Persuasive Techniques: Graphics

6. Possible response: I was shocked to read such a serious message in a holiday card.
7. The surprise is Earth inside an oven. Possible response: I have been persuaded that global warming is a serious issue.

Key Literary Element: Style

8. Possible responses: cool or dramatic
9. Possible response: No. For such serious topics, I would expect the style to be more angry and to-the-point.

Vocabulary Check

10. Students' responses should indicate they know that *cease-fire* means "end."
11. A global holiday would make more people happy because *global* means "worldwide."
12. eyes
13. Responses will vary.

Close

Ask students to talk about how editorial cartoons influence their thoughts and feelings.

Grammar Link: Sentence Types

Grammar Practice

14. interrogative
15. declarative
16. exclamatory
17. imperative

Literature Online

Web Activities Have students access the Web site for interactive activities that will help them assess their understanding of the selection.

More About the Author

Langston Hughes's early life was filled with ups and downs. After his father moved to Mexico, he and his mother moved often as she looked for work. He also lived with his grandmother for several years in Kansas, where he experienced prejudice in mostly white schools. Later, however, he lived with his mother and stepfather in Illinois and Ohio, where his talent for writing poetry was recognized. He was elected high school class poet.

EL Language Coach

Denotation and Connotation **Say:** Adjectives with connotations provide great mental pictures for readers. Read the vocabulary words. Based on their connotations, which of the two nouns would they best describe?

slung sack; computer

frail visitor; patient

barren desert; woods EL

Before You Read Thank You, M'am

Meet the Author

Born in 1902, Langston Hughes was one of the first African American writers to make a living as a writer and speaker, and he greatly influenced American literature. He once said he wrote about people who are "up today and down tomorrow, working this week and fired the next, beaten and baffled, but determined not to be wholly beaten." See page R4 of the Author Files for more about Langston Hughes.

LiteratureOnline

Author Search For more about Langston Hughes, go to www.glencoe.com.

Objectives (pp. 424–431)
Reading Understand persuasive techniques • Make connections from text to self
Literature Identify literary elements: style
Vocabulary Distinguish denotation and connotation

Vocabulary Preview

slung (slung) *adj.* hung or thrown loosely **(p. 426)** *Her purse was slung over her arm.*

frail (frayl) *adj.* weak; easily broken **(p. 427)** *The young boy looked very thin and frail.*

barren (BAIR un) *adj.* bare; empty; dull or uninteresting **(p. 431)** *The front porch was plain and barren.*

EL

Write to Learn Copy these vocabulary words into your Learner's Notebook. Next to each word list two other words that mean the *opposite* of the vocabulary word. Then write one word that means *about the same as* the vocabulary word. Add to your lists as you read.

English Language Coach

Denotation and Connotation Good writers spend a lot of time choosing just the right words. One reason for this is that many words have powerful **connotations**. They call up feelings or images that can be right or wrong for what the writer is trying to say, for the feeling in the writing, or for the style.

In a funny story, you might use the word *fib* instead of *lie*. You would never use *fib* in a serious description of someone whose lack of honesty caused suffering. Someone who was writing an article about saving eagles might use words like *soar* and *swoop*, instead of just *fly* and *dive*, because *soar* and *swoop* have connotations of beauty and grace.

There aren't many words that have exactly the same **denotation**, but there are often several synonyms a writer can choose from. Connotations make all the difference. Look at the color of the Meet the Author panel to the left. These are some names different paint companies give that color:

Viking Yellow	Autumn Gold
Wildflower Honey	Mango Tango Beans

Partner Talk With a partner, discuss the effects these names have. Remember, they all name the same color! Which do you like best? Why? Now, name the color of the blue across the top of the page. Come up with three or four possibilities that give different impressions.

Additional Support

Author Search To expand students' appreciation of Langston Hughes, have them access the Web site for additional information and resources.

Literature Focus Lesson

Persuasive Writing One of the first African Americans to make a living as a writer, Hughes wrote about the plight of African Americans and praised their efforts to survive. Have students find other short works by Hughes. Have them form story discussion groups to read and discuss their choices. OL

Ask students to identify how Hughes persuades readers to think and feel about his characters. AL

Skills Preview

Key Reading Skill: Understanding Persuasive Techniques

In "Thank You, M'am," one character, Mrs. Jones, uses persuasive techniques with another character, "the boy." As you read, notice how Mrs. Jones tries to persuade the boy to change his life by using

- a statement of opinion on an issue
- reasons for that opinion
- word choices
- surprising or unexpected ways of behaving or speaking

R

Key Literary Element: Style

Style in a short story involves a number of elements. Description and dialogue both contribute to the creation of a certain style of writing. When you're reading "Thank You, M'am," think about these questions:

- What kinds of words does the writer use in his descriptions?
- Do the descriptions have a lot of detail? Do they help you see the characters and the places in the story?
- How do the people in the story talk to each other?
- Does the dialogue seem real to you? Can you hear the characters talking in your mind?

Literature Online

Interactive Literary Elements Handbook
To review or learn more about the literary elements, go to www.glencoe.com.

Get Ready to Read

Connect to the Reading

Think about a time when someone you didn't know had a positive, or good, influence on you. It could have been a real person, or even a character in a book or a movie. How did that person change your thinking? BQ

Write to Learn In your Learner's Notebook, quickwrite about your experience of being influenced by another person in a positive way.

- Who was the person who influenced you?
- How did that person influence you?
- How did that influence change your life?

Build Background

- This story was written during the 1950s. At that time, things cost less than they do today. For example, a comic book cost ten cents and a nice pair of shoes might cost five to ten dollars.
- Much of this story takes place in Mrs. Jones's rooming house. A rooming house is a place where people rent rooms to live in. In many rooming houses, the renters share one living room and kitchen. In others, like the one Mrs. Jones lives in, tenants have their own small kitchen areas.

Set Purposes for Reading

BIG Question Read the story to find out how one woman persuades a young man she doesn't know to change his ways.

Set Your Own Purpose What would you like to learn to help you answer the Big Question? Write your own purpose on the "Thank You, M'am" page of Foldable 4.

Keep Moving

Use these skills as you read the following selection.

Reading Fluency

Reading Nonstandard English
Students who have difficulty reading nonstandard English and dialect may benefit from following along with a audiotaped story. Often, professional storytellers are familiar with the dialect or culture of the story. Briefly read passages from other stories written in dialect. Have students respond to this question: How does hearing dialect help you to better understand the message and characters? OL

Teach

BQ 

Say: In "Thank You, M'am," Hughes shows how a young boy is unexpectedly influenced by an older woman. What unexpected person has influenced you? *(Responses will vary.)* OL

R Reading Skill

Understanding Persuasive Techniques **Say:** Mrs. Jones uses persuasive techniques in this story. What four techniques does she use? *(statement of opinion, reasons, word choices, and surprising ways of behaving and speaking)* BL As you read, note what she is trying to convince the boy of and whether you think she is successful. OL

Use the CheckPoint questions provided on Presentation Plus! to check for comprehension of persuasive techniques and to build background. These questions can be used with interactive response keypads for immediate student feedback.

Literature Online

Interactive Literary Elements Handbook Have students access the Web site to improve their understanding of style.

Objectives

- Understand persuasive techniques
- Make connections from text to self
- Identify literary elements: style
- Distinguish between denotation and connotation

READING WORKSHOP 1

Teach

L1 Literary Element

Review Character Ask: Who are the two characters in this story? *(a woman and a boy)* BL What happens that causes conflict between the characters? *(The boy tries to steal the woman's purse.)* OL

L2 Literary Element

Style Say: The dialogue in a story can help create the style, too. **Ask:** Do you think the dialogue between the characters is believable so far? Why or why not? *(Possible response: Yes. The woman uses simple, straightforward words. I can picture her scolding the boy on the sidewalk.)* OL

Readability Scores
Dale-Chall: 5.3
DRP: 49
Lexile: 850

Thank You, M'am

by Langston Hughes

She was a large woman with a large purse that had everything in it but hammer and nails. It had a long strap and she carried it **slung** across her shoulder. It was about eleven o'clock at night, and she was walking alone, when a boy ran up behind her and tried to snatch her purse. The strap broke with the single tug the boy gave it from behind. But the boy's weight, and the weight of the purse combined caused him to lose his balance so, instead of taking off full blast as he had hoped, the boy fell on his back on the sidewalk, and his legs flew up. The large woman simply turned around and kicked him right square in his blue jeaned sitter. Then she reached down, picked the boy up by his shirt front, and shook him until his teeth rattled. **1** L1

After that the woman said, "Pick up my pocketbook, boy, and give it here."

She still held him. But she bent down enough to permit him to stoop and pick up her purse. Then she said, "Now ain't you ashamed of yourself?" L2

Firmly gripped by his shirt front, the boy said, "Yes'm."

The woman said, "What did you want to do it for?"

The boy said, "I didn't aim to."

She said, "You a lie!" **2**

Vocabulary

slung (slung) *adj.* hung or thrown loosely

Practice the Skills

1 Key Literary Element

Style Think about this description. Is it clear? Does the author use simple words or fancy ones? Are the sentences easy to follow or difficult to understand?

2 Key Reading Skill

Understanding Persuasive Techniques All of the woman's actions and words have been a part of an effort to persuade the boy of something. What?

Additional Support

Leveled Reading An adapted version of this selection (3rd grade readability) is available on page 86 of *Jamestown Literature: An Adapted Reader* for Grade 7.

Differentiated Instruction

Sequencing Some students may find it helpful to put the events of the opening paragraph into time order. Help students create a graphic organizer like the one below to sequence events. Encourage students to use the graphic organizer any time they have difficulty keeping track of story events. BL

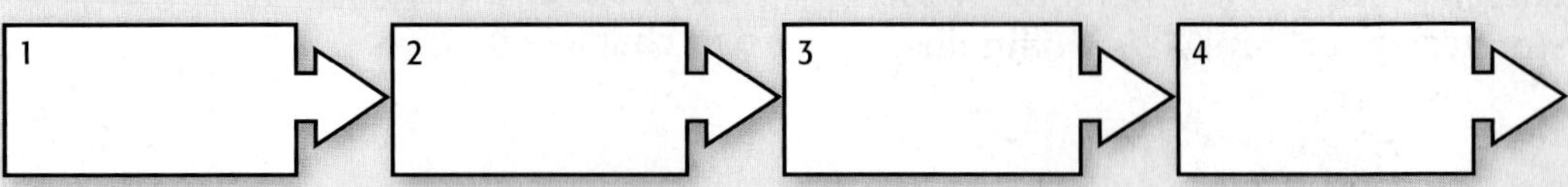

By that time two or three people passed, stopped, turned to look, and some stood watching.

"If I turn you loose, will you run?" asked the woman.

"Yes'm," said the boy.

"Then I won't turn you loose," said the woman. She did not release him.

"I'm very sorry, lady, I'm sorry," whispered the boy.

"Um-hum! And your face is dirty. I got a great mind to wash your face for you. Ain't you got nobody home to tell you to wash your face?"

"No'm," said the boy.

"Then it will get washed this evening," said the large woman starting up the street, dragging the frightened boy behind her.

He looked as if he were fourteen or fifteen, **frail** and willow-wild, in tennis shoes and blue jeans. **3**

The woman said, "You ought to be my son. I would teach you right from wrong. Least I can do right now is to wash your face. Are you hungry?"

"No'm," said the being-dragged boy. "I just want you to turn me loose."

"Was I bothering you when I turned that corner?" asked the woman.

"No'm."

"But you put yourself in contact with me," said the woman. "If you think that that contact is not going to last awhile, you got another thought coming. When I get through with you, sir, you are going to remember Mrs. Luella Bates Washington Jones."

Sweat popped out on the boy's face and he began to struggle. Mrs. Jones stopped, jerked him around in front of her, put a half nelson about his neck, and continued to drag him up the street. When she got to her door, she dragged the boy inside, down a hall, and into a large kitchenette-furnished room at the rear of the house. She switched on the light and left the door open. The boy could

Visual Vocabulary
A ***half nelson*** is a wrestling hold made from behind by hooking one arm under the opponent's arm and pressing the hand across the back of the opponent's neck.

Vocabulary

frail (frayl) *adj.* weak; easily broken

Practice the Skills

3 English Language Coach

Denotation and Connotation
What connotations does willow-wild have? How would the description be different if the boy were described as being "panther-wild" or "elm-wild"?

Teach

R1 Reading Skill

Review Inferring Say: The boy says "no'm" and "yes'm" to Mrs. Jones. What do these expressions mean? *(No, ma'am and Yes, ma'am.)* **BL** What can you infer about him from these expressions? *(He knows how to be polite.)* **OL**

R2 Reading Skill

Understanding Persuasive Techniques Ask: Why might Mrs. Jones tell the boy, "When I get through with you, sir, you are going to remember Mrs. Luella Bates Washington Jones"? *(Possible responses: She wants to make the boy nervous. She wants him to know she is going to have an effect on him.)* **OL** Do you think this is an effective persuasive technique? Why or why not? *(Possible response: It is very effective; It scares the boy, and he listens to what she has to say.)* **AL**

Literature Focus Lesson

Character Authors create interesting characters by writing about their words, actions, appearance, and beliefs, as well as how other characters relate to them. Have students work in pairs to list details the author provides about Mrs. Jones. **OL** Next to each detail, have students write whether they learned it by Mrs. Jones's words and actions, by something the author said about her, or by the boy's reaction to her. **AL**

Objectives
- Understand how style influences readers
- Analyze persuasive techniques
- Make inferences

READING WORKSHOP 1

Teach

R Reading Skill

Review Inferring Ask: Why might the author have chosen to reveal the name of the young man at this point? *(The characters are getting to know each other and building a relationship.)* OL

C Critical Thinking

Evaluation Ask: How did you feel about Mrs. Jones and the boy at the beginning of the story? How do you feel about them now? *(Possible response: At first, I felt sorry for Mrs. Jones and didn't like the boy because he tries to steal from her. Then I began to feel sorry for the boy because Mrs. Jones is intimidating.)* EL OL

Viewing the Painting

Ask: Do you think Roger looks like the boy in the painting? Explain your answer. *(Responses will vary.)* AS

hear other roomers laughing and talking in the large house. Some of their doors were open, too, so he knew he and the woman were not alone. The woman still had him by the neck in the middle of her room.

She said, "What is your name?" R

"Roger," answered the boy.

"Then, Roger, you go to that sink and wash your face," said the woman, whereupon she turned him loose—at last. Roger looked at the door—looked at the woman—looked at the door—and went to the sink.

"Let the water run until it gets warm," she said. "Here's a clean towel."

"You gonna take me to jail?" asked the boy, bending over the sink. 4

"Not with that face, I would not take you nowhere," said the woman. "Here I am trying to get home to cook me a bite to eat and you snatch my pocketbook! Maybe you ain't been to your supper either, late as it be. Have you?" C

"There's nobody home at my house," said the boy.

Practice the Skills

4 Reviewing Skills

Activating Prior Knowledge Roger's question is based on some prior knowledge of who goes to jail and why. What knowledge do you have about that? Where did you learn it? How might Roger have learned what he knows—or thinks he knows?

Jim, 1930. William H. Johnson. Oil on canvas, 21 5/8 x 18 1/4 in. Smithsonian American Art Museum, Washington, DC/ Art Resource, NY.

Additional Support

Literature Focus Lesson

The Harlem Renaissance Langston Hughes was a member of the Harlem Renaissance. In the 1920s and 1930s, Harlem, New York, was an exciting place. African American writers, poets, painters, singers, and jazz musicians lived, worked, and performed in Harlem, creating an artistic and political revolution there. The members of the Harlem Renaissance used their artwork as a means to fight for civil rights and equality. Bring in a musical recording by a musician from this time, such as Duke Ellington or Josephine Baker. Have students tell how the music might have influenced modern musicians. OL

READING WORKSHOP 1

Portrait of a Woman, 1932. John Wesley Hardrick. Oil on board, 30 x 24 in. Hampton University Museum, VA. Indianapolis Museum of Art in cooperation with Indiana University Press.

"Then we'll eat," said the woman. "I believe you're hungry—or been hungry—to try to snatch my pocketbook."

"I wanted a pair of blue suede shoes,"[1] said the boy.

"Well, you didn't have to snatch my pocketbook to get some suede shoes," said Mrs. Luella Bates Washington Jones. "You could of asked me."

"M'am?" **5**

The water dripping from his face, the boy looked at her. There was a long pause. A very long pause. After he had dried his face and not knowing what else to do dried it again, the boy turned around, wondering what next. The door was open. He could make a dash for it down the hall. He could run, run, run, run, run!

The woman was sitting on the daybed.[2] After a while she said, "I were young once and I wanted things I could not get."

There was another long pause. The boy's mouth opened. Then he frowned, but not knowing he frowned.

R The woman said, "Um-hum! You thought I was going to say but, didn't you? You thought I was going to say, but I didn't snatch people's pocketbooks. Well, I wasn't going to say that." Pause. Silence. "I have done things, too, which I would not tell you, son—neither tell God, if he didn't already know. So you set down while I fix us something to eat. You might run that comb through your hair so you will look presentable."

In another corner of the room behind a screen was a gas plate and an icebox.[3] Mrs. Jones got up and went behind the screen. The woman did not watch the boy to see if he was

Practice the Skills

5 Key Reading Skill

Understanding Persuasive Techniques Mrs. Jones is trying to grab Roger's attention. If you were Roger, what would surprise you about what Mrs. Jones said?

1. ***Blue suede shoes*** are men's shoes made of soft leather. These shoes became popular in the late 1950s after Elvis Presley recorded a hit song called "Blue Suede Shoes."

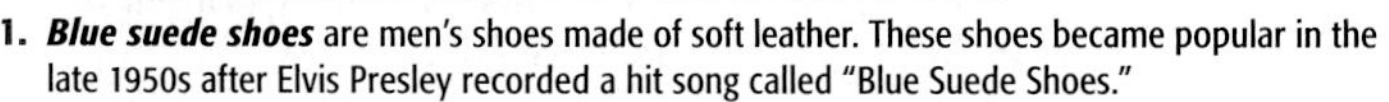

2. A ***daybed*** is a sofa that can be converted into a bed.
3. The ***gas plate*** is a small version of a stovetop, with "burners" fueled by gas. Before electricity, a block of ice cooled food inside a special box. People use the word ***icebox*** to refer to a refrigerator.

Teach

Viewing the Painting

Say: How does the woman in the painting remind you of Mrs. Jones? *(She is large and stern.)* **BL** Does the photo give you any information about how a young boy might react to her? *(A young boy might be scared and intimidated.)* **OL**

R Reading Skill

Review Drawing Conclusions **Ask:** From what Mrs. Jones says about herself, what might you conclude about her as a young person? *(Mrs. Jones got into trouble.)* **OL**

English Language Coach

Building Background Provide students with the lyrics to "Blue Suede Shoes." Carl Perkins wrote this song in 1956. Perkins was the son of poor sharecroppers, so fancy shoes were a symbol of the American dream. Ask students to work with a partner to identify symbols of the American dream today. Partners can use images of these symbols to prepare a poster entitled *The American Dream–21st Century.* **OL**

Objectives
- Understand persuasive techniques
- Activate prior knowledge
- Identify author's purpose
- Identify word choice and language
- Make inferences and draw conclusions

READING WORKSHOP 1

Teach

L Literary Element

Style Say: Langston Hughes wrote about life in mid-20th century America. Which words tell you that the story is not set in the present time? *(Possible responses: icebox, gas plate, pocketbook, ten-cent cake)* **OL**

R Reading Skill

Review Drawing Conclusions Ask: Based on what you've read, what conclusion can you draw about Mrs. Jones's character? *(Possible response: Mrs. Jones talks tough but she does nice things. Under her tough exterior, Mrs. Jones is a kind person.)* **OL**

Street Scene (Boy with Kite), 1962, Jacob Lawrence. Egg tempera on hardboard, 23 7/8 x 30 in. Conservation Center of the Institute of Fine Arts.

going to run now, nor did she watch her purse which she left behind her on the daybed. But the boy took care to sit on the far side of the room where he thought she could easily see him out of the corner of her eye, if she wanted to. He did not trust the woman not to trust him. And he did not want to be mistrusted now. **6**

"Do you need somebody to go to the store," asked the boy, "maybe to get some milk or something?"

"Don't believe I do," said the woman, "unless you just want sweet milk yourself. I was going to make cocoa out of this canned milk I got here." **R**

"That will be fine," said the boy.

She heated some lima beans and ham she had in the icebox, made the cocoa, and set the table. The woman did not ask the

Practice the Skills

6 Key Reading Skill

Understanding Persuasive Techniques Do you think Mrs. Jones is beginning to persuade Roger to behave the way she wants him to? Explain why or why not.

Additional Support

Differentiated Instruction

Analyzing and Evaluating Artwork

Have students work in groups to analyze and evaluate the paintings used in this story:

1. What is the style of the painting *Jim* on page 428? How does this boy compare to how you imagine Roger?
2. What do you notice about the brush-strokes in *Portrait of a Woman* on page 429? How do they contribute to the feeling you get when you look at the painting?
3. How would you describe *Street Scene (Boy with Kite)* on page 430?
4. Which painting do you think best illustrates the story and why? **OL**

boy anything about where he lived, or his folks, or anything else that would embarrass him. Instead, as they ate, she told him about her job in a hotel beauty shop that stayed open late, what the work was like, and how all kinds of women came in and out, blondes, red-heads, and Spanish. Then she cut him a half of her ten-cent cake. 7

"Eat some more, son," she said.

When they were finished eating she got up and said, "Now, here, take this ten dollars and buy yourself some blue suede shoes. And next time, do not make the mistake of latching onto my pocketbook nor nobody else's—because shoes come by devilish like that will burn your feet. I got to get my rest now. But I wish you would behave yourself, son, from here on in." EL

She led him down the hall to the front door and opened it. "Goodnight! Behave yourself, boy!" she said, looking out into the street.

The boy wanted to say something else other than, "Thank you, m'am," to Mrs. Luella Bates Washington Jones, but he couldn't do so as he turned at the **barren** stoop[4] and looked back at the large woman in the door. He barely managed to say, "Thank you," before she shut the door. And he never saw her again. 8 ❍

4. A ***stoop*** is a porch or set of steps at the entrance of a building.

Vocabulary

barren (BAIR un) *adj.* bare; empty; dull or uninteresting

Practice the Skills

7 Key Literary Element

Style What kind of feeling do the details in this description add? What kinds of things are described?

8 BIG Question

What does Mrs. Jones want to persuade Roger to do? Do you think she is successful? Explain your answer on the "Thank You, M'am" page of Foldable 4. Your response will help you complete the Unit Challenge later. BQ

Teach

EL Language Coach

Denotation and Connotation Say: Mrs. Jones alternates between calling Roger "boy" and "son." Why does she use both terms? *(When he is a stranger to her and when he leaves her home, she calls him "boy" because he is distanced from her. When she's taking care of him, she calls him "son.")* OL

BQ BIG Question

Ask: Mrs. Jones likely influences Roger in this story. Do you think Roger has any influence on Mrs. Jones? Why or why not? *(Possible response: Roger might have a positive influence on Mrs. Jones, reminding her that she can make a difference in someone else's life.)* AL

CheckPoint

Use the CheckPoint questions provided on Presentation Plus! to check for comprehension of the selection. These questions can be used with interactive response keypads for immediate student feedback.

Literature Focus Lesson

Resolution The resolution, or ending, of a short story contributes to the overall effect of the story. At the end of the story, Mrs. Jones warns against stealing because "shoes come by devilish like that will burn your feet." Suggest that students continue the short story by writing one more paragraph that tells what Roger does next. Their style should complement Hughes's overall effect. For example, they might write about Roger buying the shoes in a humble way, or they might have him run an errand for Mrs. Jones to show gratitude. AL

Objectives
- Understand how style influences readers
- Analyze and evaluate artwork
- Understand denotation and connotation
- Write a new story ending

Assess

Resources for page 432

- Selection Quick Check
- Selection and Unit Assessment
- ExamView Assessment Suite
- Interactive Tutor: Self-Assessment

Students can respond to the *After You Read* items in their Learner's Notebook or on a separate sheet of paper.

Answering the BIG Question

1. Responses will vary.
2. She says, "Pick up my pocketbook, boy, and give it here." and "Now ain't you ashamed of yourself?"
3. Roger wants to buy blue suede shoes.
4. Mrs. Jones urges him to wash his face and comb his hair, feeds him, and gives him money for the shoes.

Critical Thinking

5. Roger is terrified.
6. Possible response: that she can be trusted and that Roger is free to leave
7. Possible response: Yes, it is important. Mrs. Jones gives Roger hope that his life can be different.
8. Possible response: I disliked the story ending and was surprised by it. I thought Mrs. Jones would become a permanent part of the boy's life.

After You Read

Thank You, M'am

Objectives (pp. 432–433)
Reading Identify persuasive techniques
Literature Identify literary elements: style
Vocabulary Distinguish denotation and connotation
Grammar Use appropriate end punctuation

Answering the BIG Question

1. How well do you think Mrs. Jones influenced Roger?
2. **Recall** What are the first sentences the woman says to the young boy?
   TIP **Right There**
3. **Recall** Why does Roger try to steal Mrs. Jones's purse?
   TIP **Right There**
4. **Summarize** What happens when Mrs. Jones brings Roger to her apartment?
   TIP **Think and Search**

Critical Thinking

5. **Infer** Before Mrs. Jones brings Roger to her apartment, how does Roger feel about what is happening?
   TIP **Author and Me**
6. **Infer** What does Mrs. Jones communicate to Roger by leaving her door open?
   TIP **Author and Me**
7. **Evaluate** Do you think it's important that Mrs. Jones tells Roger that she has done wrong things too? Explain.
   TIP **Author and Me**
8. **Respond** Did you like or dislike the way this story ended? Did the ending surprise you? Explain your answer.
   TIP **Author and Me**

Talk About Your Reading

Literature Groups Did Roger's punishment fit his crime? Debate the issue with your group. Support your points with evidence from the story. Consider questions such as these:

- Was Roger really punished? If so, how?
- What did Mrs. Jones hope to accomplish when she brought Roger home?
- What effect did Mrs. Jones's actions have on Roger?

Write to Learn Have one group member take notes and write up the group's answers and evidence for each question. Have other members present the answers and evidence to the whole class.

Talk About Your Reading

Possible response:

- Roger's pride is hurt, or "punished," but he is not punished in the expected way.
- She thinks she can convince him that what he did is wrong.
- Roger leaves feeling apologetic and very thankful to Mrs. Jones. He learns his lesson about not stealing.

Skills Review

Key Reading Skill: Understanding Persuasive Techniques

9. Review the different persuasive techniques that writers use. Which one does Mrs. Jones use the most when she speaks to Roger?
10. Throughout the story, do you think Mrs. Jones's persuasive techniques are making Roger think about what he's done? Why or why not?
11. Did your understanding of persuasive techniques help you read this selection? Why or why not?

Key Literary Element: Style

12. Which of these words would you choose to describe the style of this story? Why?

    scientific realistic poetic
    fancy humorous dreamlike

13. How much do you think the dialogue contributes to the style?

Vocabulary Check

Choose the best word from the list to complete each sentence below. Rewrite each sentence in your Learner's Notebook.

slung **frail** **barren**

14. Roger's book bag was ___ across the chair.
15. After the fire, the thick forest became a ___ landscape.
16. Mrs. Jones was old, but she was not ___.

English Language Coach Rewrite each sentence below with a synonym for the verb *run*. (Remember, words that are synonyms do not necessarily mean the exact same thing.) Pay attention to connotations when you choose the word.

trot dash scamper

17. I just saw Martin ___ down the street like his shoes were on fire.
18. Mr. and Mrs. Thomas ___ quietly around the track every morning.
19. Did you see that frightened hamster ___ across the floor?

Grammar Link: End Punctuation

You don't need punctuation when you talk. But when you write, you need punctuation to separate ideas and show feeling. A sentence must end with a punctuation mark.

Use a question mark (**?**) to ask a question.

Have you seen Andrea**?**
What are you wearing to the dance**?**
How many DVDs do you have**?**

Use an exclamation point (**!**) to express strong feeling.

That airplane is loud**!**
Get out of here**!**
Help me**!**

Use a period (**.**) whenever you don't need a question mark or an exclamation point.

The car raced down the street**.**
Turn the key**.**
Please pass the rice**.**

Grammar Practice

Copy the sentences below and add end punctuation marks.

20. Do you want to go shopping
21. What a disaster
22. Carmen fixed his brother's bike
23. That was such fun
24. Wait for me at the corner
25. How many times did you ask her

Literature Online

Web Activities For eFlashcards, Selection Quick Checks, and other Web activities, go to www.glencoe.com.

Skills Review

Key Reading Skill: Understanding Persuasive Techniques

9. Possible response: Mrs. Jones uses words that convince Roger to act in a certain way.
10. Possible response: Yes because he truly wants to thank her.
11. Possible response: I recognize that Mrs. Jones is using persuasive techniques to help Roger.

Key Literary Element: Style

12. Possible response: Realistic. The author describes the characters so well that I can see them in my mind.
13. The dialogue between Roger and Mrs. Jones sounds realistic.

Vocabulary Check

14. slung
15. barren
16. frail
17. dash
18. trot
19. scamper

Assess/Close

Say: Write a brief thank you letter from Roger to Mrs. Jones. Include details that show how she influenced Roger.

Grammar Link: End Punctuation

Grammar Practice

Possible responses:

20. Do you want to go shopping?
21. What a disaster!
22. Carmen fixed her brother's bike.
23. That was such fun!
24. Wait for me at the corner.
25. How many times did you ask her?

Literature Online

Web Activities Have students access the Web site for interactive activities that will help them assess their understanding of the selection.

Editorial

UNIT 4

Objectives covered in this workshop:

- **Writing** Summarize to inform develop drafts; categorize information; main idea and supporting details
- **Grammar** Identify and correctly use verbs

Teaching Students to Write an Editorial

Why Is It Important?

- Writing an editorial will help students practice discerning between opinion and fact, making them more critical readers.
- The power to persuade is important in many kinds of writing. Exploring bias in editorial writing will show students how to choose words carefully.
- Writing editorials will help students be more aware of the ways they are influenced by the media.
- Making precise and intentional word choices will increase students' powers of persuasion.

How to Help Students Get It

- Discuss possible audiences with students. Depending on the topic they choose, they may want to write as though addressing their peers, their family, the school administration, or a broader audience.
- Guide students through brainstorming by asking questions like "What would you like to see improved in the world?" and "What happened this week that you'd like to prevent from happening again?"
- Have students think about their own credibility: why should their audiences believe them? This will help them generate good support for their arguments.
- Talk with your students about preempting the opposition. Ask: "What arguments might be brought against your editorial? How would you respond?" Have students use that to strengthen their writing.
- Ask students to consider the selections in Unit 4, and choose one or two opinions expressed in the text. Ask "Were those opinions backed up with proof? Did the author make you agree with them?"
- Remind students that organization of ideas is a key element to persuasive writing. The order they present their points in will make a difference to the reader.
- Define emotional appeal for your students. Readers of an editorial should feel that the topic discussed has some personal meaning for them, or that they have some stake in the matter at hand.
- Refer students to the Writing Handbook. The Persuasive Writing Checklist will help them prepare the final draft for presentation.

Traits of Good Writing	
Ideas	the message or the theme and the details that develop it
Voice	a writer's unique way of using tone and style
Organization	the arrangement of main points and supporting details
Unit Focus **Word Choice:** the vocabulary a writer uses to convey meaning	• Does the writer use lively verbs to show action? • Does the writer use vivid words to create word pictures in the readers' minds? • Does the writer use precise words to explain his or her ideas simply and clearly?
Sentence Fluency	the smooth rhythm and flow of sentences that vary in length and style
Conventions	correct spelling, grammar, usage, and mechanics
Presentation	the way words and design elements look on a page

Workshop Resources

Pacing (Days) Standard	Block	Lesson	Student Materials	Teacher Resources
1		Prewriting	Writing Workshop Graphic Organizer Grammar Practice Spelling and Handwriting Practice Spelling Power eWorkbook Interactive Grammar and Language Workbook Grammar and Composition Handbook	TeacherWorks Plus Presentation Plus! Rubrics for Assessing Student Writing, Listening, and Speaking
2		Drafting	Real Success in Writing: Research and Reports Writing Constructed Responses Sourcebook	Grammar and Writing Workshop Transparency
1		Editing	Interactive Grammar and Language Workbook Grammar and Composition Handbook	Grammar and Writing Workshop Transparency
2		Revising	Real Success in Writing: Research and Reports Writing Constructed Responses Sourcebook	Interactive Grammar and Language Workbook
2		Presenting	Real Success in Writing: Research and Reports Writing Constructed Responses Sourcebook	Rubrics for Assessing Student Writing, Listening, and Speaking

Focus

BELLRINGER Options

Daily Language Practice Transparency

Focus Activity Say: Briefly describe an issue about which you have strong feelings. It can be a problem of the community, nation, or world. You will write an editorial about the issue in this Writing Workshop.

Teach

W Writing

Editorial Ask: What is the difference between a news article and an editorial? *(A news article presents factual information; an editorial offers an opinion.)* OL AL

Resources for page 434

- Use the Writing Workshop Graphic Organizer BLM in the Unit 4 Resource Booklet.
- Use the Grammar and Writing Workshop Transparencies, Unit 4.

WRITING WORKSHOP PART 1

Editorial

Prewriting and Drafting

ASSIGNMENT Write an editorial

Purpose: To take a stand on a problem, propose a solution, and persuade others to agree with you

Audience: You, your teacher, other students at your school, or the general public

Writing Rubric

As you work through this writing assignment, you should

- write about a problem that you feel strongly about
- support your ideas with evidence
- respond to arguments that might be used against your own argument
- choose precise and lively words
- use an emotional appeal
- use an appropriate style and tone

See page 472 in Part 2 for a model of an editorial.

Objectives (pp. 434–437)
Writing Use the writing process: draft • Use persuasive techniques
Grammar Write complete sentences

Writing an editorial will help you think about the Unit 4 Big Question: Who influences us and how do they do so?

W An **editorial** is a piece of writing that states an opinion on a specific topic. Most daily newspapers print editorials written by the paper's editors. TV and radio stations sometimes broadcast their own editorials. People who express opinions in letters to newspapers, magazines, and broadcasters are writing editorials.

Prewriting

Get Ready to Write

People write editorials to express strong feelings about different issues. So you'll need to think of something that really matters to *you*.

Find a Topic

1. Make a list of problems or issues that are important to you. If you need help, try completing these sentences.
   - I think it's really unfair that . . .
   - I think people should care more about . . .
2. Choose a topic from your list that you feel strongly about *and* that you know something about.

Explore Your Topic

Exploring your topic can help you figure out exactly what you think about a problem and clarify your opinion.

In your Learner's Notebook, write your answers to these questions about your topic.

- Why is this issue important?
- What reasons can I give to support my opinions?
- What do I want people to do to solve the problem?

Now look at your notes and think about your topic. Do you have enough to write about? Do you think it will be a good topic? If you answer *no* to either question, explore another idea from your list. Sometimes even great ideas aren't good writing topics.

Additional Support

English Language Coach

Denotation, Connotation, and Semantic Slanting Write the words *happy, pleased,* and *thrilled* on the board. **Ask:** What shade of meaning does each of these synonyms offer to the main definition? *(Possible responses:* Happy *is a general term, whereas* pleased *means happily satisfied and* thrilled *means happily excited.)* Distribute copies of a thesaurus to students. Show them how to use it when they are searching for words with the right shade of meaning. OL

Distinguishing Fact and Opinion

Objectives covered in this workshop:
- Distinguish fact and opinion

Distinguishing Fact and Opinion

Why Is It Important?

- Students will learn how to tell the difference between statements that can be proven-or *facts*-and those that someone believes are true-*opinions*.
- When students read, they'll come across writers who try to convince them of their beliefs. If they can tell the difference between facts and opinions, they will be able to make up their own minds.
- As students learn how to gather facts as they read, they'll be able to judge whether or not they should believe what they've heard or read. They will also learn that as a reader or listener they can disagree with an opinion.

How to Help Students Get It

- Tell students to look at the title of the selection first. Sometimes the title expresses an opinion about a topic.
- As they read, remind students to think about which parts of the selection are convincing. Then ask them to try to determine if those parts are facts or opinions.
- Remind students that sometimes a good persuasive argument is a balance between a writer's opinions and the facts that they present to support those opinions.

Reading to Answer the Big Question

What Exercise Can Do for You

This article highlights physical and mental benefits of exercise, lists reasons teens might enjoy adding regular exercise to their routine, and suggests ways of doing so. The persuasive selection combines statements of fact and opinion to convince the reader of the healthfulness of regular exercise.

Oprah Winfrey

A brief biographical sketch portrays Oprah Winfrey in a positive light. It mentions moments when Oprah's life was influenced by her grandmother, mother, father, and Sydney Poitier.

Grammar Link

Complete Sentences

Imagine that you get a phone call. Someone says, "To collect your prize money." Then the person hangs up without completing the sentence. How would you feel?

That's the problem with incomplete sentences. They can leave you feeling frustrated and confused. To keep from confusing your readers, you need to learn how to tell complete sentences from incomplete ones.

What Is a Complete Sentence?

A complete sentence is a group of words that has (1) a subject and (2) a verb and that (3) expresses a complete thought.

- **Complete:** The tire sprang a leak (The sentence has a subject–*tire*, a verb–*sprang*, and expresses a complete thought.)
- **Incomplete:** The man in the black coat. (The sentence has a subject–*man*. But it doesn't have a verb and doesn't express a complete thought.)
- **Incomplete:** If you have any questions. (The sentence has a subject–*you*–and a verb–*have*. But the sentence doesn't express a complete thought.)

Why Are Complete Sentences Important to My Writing?

Complete sentences help readers understand your ideas. If your writing contains incomplete sentences (also called sentence fragments), readers may not understand what you mean.

How Do I Write Complete Sentences?

After you write, check your sentences to see whether they can pass the completeness test. Make sure each sentence has a subject and a verb and expresses a complete thought. Here's how:

Step 1: Find the verb. Verbs are the only words that have tense, or express time. If you don't know whether a word is a verb, change the time of the sentence. The word or words that change are verbs. (In a verb phrase, only the helping verb changes.)

- I am the president of the math club. (Is *am* the verb? Change the time of the sentence to find out. Talk about the past or future instead.)
- I was the president of the math club. (The word *am* changes to *was* to express the past tense. Since *am* changes, it must be a verb.)

Step 2: Find the subject. Use the verb to find the subject. Ask yourself, Who or what ___? (Fill in the blank with the verb.) The subject is the word or words that answer the question.

- I am the president of the math club. (Who or what is president? *I* am. *I* is the subject.)

Step 3: Make sure the thought is complete. Ask yourself, Can this group of words stand alone as a complete idea? Is anything missing?

- I am the president of the math club. (Can this group of words stand alone as a complete idea? *Yes.* Is anything missing? *No.*)

The sentence "I am the president of the math club" passes the completeness test. It *is* complete.

Write to Learn Activity Read the latest version of your draft. Find the verb and the subject in each sentence. Check to make sure your thought is complete. If you find an incomplete sentence, revise it.

W

Looking Ahead

Keep the writing you've done so far. In Writing Workshop Part 2, you'll learn how to turn your writing into a strong and persuasive editorial.

Reading Fluency

Reading and Writing Some students may benefit from reading their draft to a partner. Allow students to meet with a partner after they have completed the first drafts of their editorials. Ask pairs to read and discuss each person's draft, listening for a clear statement of the problem, proposed solutions, supporting evidence, and persuasive arguments. Refer students to the problem/solution outline on page RH17. OL

Teach

W Writing

Clarity Before class, write the paragraph below on the board. **Say:** Please follow along as I read this example of persuasive writing. As you know, persuasive writing aimss to change how readers think, feel, or act. It is important, then, that persuasive writing is clear and understandable. When I finish reading, we'll discuss as a class how to make the sentences in this paragraph clearer. EL OL

Every Saturday I listen to the radio. Because I adore baseball. This is the best sport I'll tell you why? Sitting outdoors are fun and healthy. And the food at games Many people plays on each team. No one is more important. And the season is nice and long. People can holler and cheer and stand up and wave their hands. It is exciting.

Assess/Close

Suggest that students revise the paragraph. Ask students to focus on complete sentences, good transitions, and convincing arguments. Allow time for revisions.

Objectives

- Identify and construct complete sentences
- Understand how word choice affects emotional appeal and influences thoughts and emotions

Teach

W Writing

Persuasive Techniques

Some writers persuade readers to act by "painting" a picture of what the situation would be like if no one did anything. This is a form of semantic slanting—hinting but not directly stating that readers need to take action. Read the following passage. Ask students to infer the actions the writer wants readers to take. EL OL

Did you know that 137 species of animals that existed yesterday do not exist today? Each day, this number will disappear from Earth, adding up to a loss of nearly 50,000 animal species a year! Half of all animals on Earth live in the rain forest. Medicines, including cancer drugs, are made from rain forest plants. Area people get food and shelter in the rain forest. All of Earth's plants stay healthier because the rain forest contributes so many different types. Yet, by the year 2020, one-fourth of these plants could die out. Logging, mining, cattle grazing, highways, and dams take rain forest land. Where will it end? With no action, 10% of Earth's species will vanish in the next 25 years!

WRITING WORKSHOP PART 1

Develop Your Draft

When you write to persuade, it's extremely important to think about your audience. That way you can do a better job of persuading your readers to agree with you. Try to write to your audience in the following ways.

1. Include evidence to support your opinion. Evidence is information that strengthens your points.

Types of Evidence

Type	Definition	Example
Fact	something that can be proven	There are violent shows on TV.
Statistic	fact expressed in numbers	A school poll shows that 84 percent of students watch TV for at least two hours a day.
Example	particular instance or event	My cousin Raymond talks to TV characters.

2. Think about the **counterarguments**—the points that someone who disagrees with you would make. Don't ignore these points. Answer them! Responding to them will make your writing more persuasive. W

Some people will say they will be bored if they can't watch TV. I say, "You'll be surprised by all of the things you'll find to do instead of watching TV."

Writing Tip

Writer's Craft The end of your editorial is a powerful place to use emotional appeal. You've given readers all of your logical reasons. Inspiring or scaring readers may be the thing that gets them to take action.

3. Appeal to your readers' emotions by using emotional words and phrases. Would you feel good about something that is *gloomy* or *filthy*? Probably not, but those words might be perfect for your topic. How do you feel about something that is *energetic* and *pure*? These words probably make you feel good. Use your readers' feelings to get them to agree with you.

   The following emotional appeal uses people's general dislike for wasting time to inspire them to take action.

Don't waste time watching TV characters live their lives. Get out and enjoy your own life!

Additional Support

Literature Focus Lesson

Persuasive Writing Many students may be unfamiliar with newspaper and magazine editorials. Bring in newspapers and magazines so that students can locate and read an editorial. Work with students to develop questions to ask an editor about the process of writing editorials. Arrange for an editor from a local newspaper to spend a class period with students to answer interview questions and describe the responsibilities that go with expressing an opinion in print. EL OL

Organize Your Thoughts

Gather the writing you've already done on your topic. Then follow these steps. Write your sentences in your Learner's Notebook.

1. Write one sentence that clearly states your position, or your opinion, on the problem.

   Kids watch too much TV.

2. Give three or more reasons for your opinion. These will be the major points of your editorial.

   Many kids are couch potatoes.
   Some kids watch TV instead of talking to their family and friends.
   Violent TV shows can make some kids have behavior problems.

3. Write one sentence that states your proposed solution.

   All families in our school could unplug their TVs for one week.

Literature Online

Writing Models For models and other writing activities, go to www.glencoe.com.

Drafting

Start Writing!

You have everything you need to get started: a topic, some ideas about your topic, and organized points. It's time to get started.

Get It on Paper

For your first draft, you may want to let your ideas flow onto paper and organize them later. Or you may want to follow an organized plan as you write your draft. Either way, you can move, add, and delete ideas when you revise. The directions below can help organize your writing.

1. Begin by telling about the problem and why it is important. Then briefly explain your solution.
2. Give the reasons for your opinion and why your solution would work. You may want to write one paragraph for each point.
3. End your editorial by urging your readers to do something to help solve the problem.

W

Writing Tip

Writer's Craft Try starting your editorial with an interesting fact or situation. Many newspaper readers look at only the first few lines of an editorial to decide if it's worth reading. So grab your readers' attention right away!

Teach

W Writing

Word Choice Read the following opinion paragraphs to the class. Ask students to evaluate the word choices in each, based on emotional appeal, style, and the evidence they supply. AL

Stop! I say. We must no longer persecute students with homework. The lives of students are already jam-packed. Many kids fix dinner, take care of younger brothers and sisters, and clean the house when they get home. Should we deny them *any* time to rest from their labors and enjoy time with friends? It's time for teachers to rescue students. *No more homework!*

I don't like homework and wish we didn't have it. It is boring. I can't watch TV. I'd rather talk on the phone or sleep. By the time I eat and do homework, it's time to go to bed. I can't even get away from homework on weekends. I think homework is bad.

Literature Online

Writing Models Have students access the Web site for an additional and interactive Writing Workshop-based student model.

Differentiated Instruction

Problem and Solution Most editorials describe a problem and offer one or more solutions. Some students may find it helpful to organize their thoughts by using a problem/solution outline like the one in the next column. AS

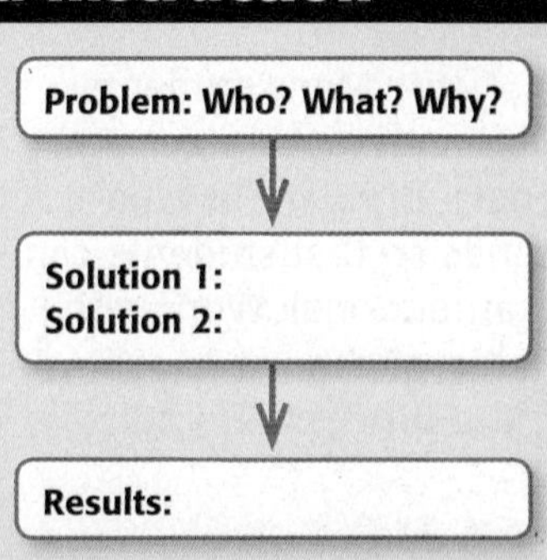

Objectives

- Use the writing process
- Use persuasive techniques
- Write complete sentences

Workshop Resources

Pacing (Days) Standard	Block	Lesson	Student Materials	Teacher Resources
1		Key Skill Lesson: Distinguishing Fact and Opinion	Key Reading Skills Practice English Language Coach	Bellringer Options Transparencies Read Aloud, Think Aloud Transparencies Presentation Plus!
2		"What Exercise Can Do for You"	Literary Analysis Transparencies Glencoe Online Selection Vocabulary Development Academic Vocabulary Development English Language Coach Active Reading Graphic Organizer Literary Analysis StudentWorks Plus Online Student Edition Literature Classics Selection and Unit Assessments	Literary and Text Analysis Transparencies Puzzlemaker Skill Level Up! BookLink 3 Assessment by Learning Objective (Diagnostic and Formative) Interactive Tutor Self-Assessment TeacherWorks Plus
2		"Oprah Winfrey"	Glencoe Online Selection Vocabulary Development Academic Vocabulary Development English Language Coach Active Reading Graphic Organizer Literary Analysis StudentWorks Plus Online Student Edition Literature Classics Selection and Unit Assessments	Literary and Text Analysis Transparencies Puzzlemaker Skill Level Up! BookLink 3 Assessment by Learning Objective (Diagnostic and Formative) Interactive Tutor Self-Assessment TeacherWorks Plus

Keys for Unit Resource

- Blackline Master
- Workbook
- Supplemental Text
- CD-ROM
- DVD
- Transparency
- Web-based
- Fast Files

Level Appropriate Code

AS = Activities for all students
AL = Activities for students working above grade level
OL = Activities for students working at grade level
BL = Activities for students working below grade level
EL = Activities for English language learners

Focus

BELLRINGER Options

Daily Language Practice Transparency

Focus Activity Say: How might choices you make today influence your life years later? *(Possible responses: You may be healthier, wiser, happier.)* OL

Teach

R Reading Skill

Distinguishing Fact and Opinion Say: You tell fact from opinion every time you decide what you can believe on TV. What are some things that you see or hear on TV that are facts? Opinions? *(Possible response: I know commercials are mostly opinions, but the evening news reports facts.)* OL

READING WORKSHOP 2

Skills Focus

You will practice using these skills when you read the following selections:

- "What Exercise Can Do for You," p. 442
- "Oprah Winfrey," p. 450

Reading

- Distinguishing fact and opinion

Literature

- Recognizing how a writer uses tone to influence the reader

Vocabulary

- Understanding denotation, connotation, and euphemisms

Writing/Grammar

- Identifying and correcting sentence fragments

Skill Lesson

Distinguishing Fact and Opinion

Learn It!

What Is It? To decide whether you believe what a writer has written, you need to be able to distinguish, or tell the difference between, fact and opinion. Here are two tips to help you.

- A fact is something that actually happened or was experienced or something that can be proved. Some facts are obvious, such as "The sun sets in the west." The statement "I saw the sun set" is also a statement of fact. R
- An opinion is what someone believes or feels. It can be a judgment, a conclusion, or simply a point of view. "The sunset was beautiful" is an opinion. Opinions are neither true nor false.

Analyzing Cartoons
If Jeremy had supported his opinion with facts, would his dad have been more willing to listen? (What if his dad had *asked* for Jeremy's opinion?)

Objectives (p. 438–439)
Reading Distinguish fact from opinion

Additional Support

English Language Coach

Denotation, Connotation, and Semantic Slanting When writers state facts, they are careful not to include words that will reveal how they feel or influence readers' thoughts and feelings. Write the following sentences on the board:

Nika had a perfect test score.

Our team lost last night.

Jana found a tiny puppy.

Math is a required subject.

Say: Rewrite each of these facts as opinions by adding words that show how you think or feel. OL AL

Why Is It Important? Do you believe everything you hear? If someone says the best place to buy sneakers is Al's Shoes, you'll want to know why. What are the prices? What kind of selection does the store offer? After gathering facts, you can judge for yourself whether Al's is the best place to shop. When you read, you'll come across writers who try to convince you of their beliefs. If you can tell the difference between facts and opinions, you can make up your own mind.

How Do I Do It? Start with the title. An editorial titled, "School Budget Cuts: Cheating Our Children," expresses an opinion. A reader can expect an argument against too many educational budget cuts. Here's how one student thought about the facts and opinions from one part of the editorial.

> Legislators often make difficult decisions about how taxpayers' money will be used. When it comes to cutting corners, however, nothing good can come from cutting money for education. The Teachers Educational Council found that parents paid an average of $500 for textbooks for the 2005 school year. There are more important things to spend money on.

R

> The second sentence sounds like an opinion. Is it true that "nothing good" can come from cutting money for education? The Teachers Educational Council must have researched how much parents spend, so the average amount for textbooks is a fact. The last sentence is an opinion, because what's most important can't be proven. That's why people argue about it so much!

Literature Online

Study Central Visit www.glencoe.com and click on Study Central to review distinguishing fact and opinion.

Practice It!

Below are two topics you'll read about in this workshop. In your Learner's Notebook, write one fact and one opinion about each topic.

- Exercise
- African Americans on TV

Use It!

As you read the selections, remember the fact and opinion you listed for each topic. If you find more facts and opinions as you read, add them to your lists.

Teach

Literature Online

Study Central Have students access the Web site to review distinguishing fact and opinion and to complete a related activity.

R Reading Skill

Distinguishing Fact and Opinion **Say:** Readers can identify signal words that will help them recognize an opinion. Which word in the following statement tells you that it is an opinion? *The best place to buy sneakers is Al's Shoes. (best)*
Ask: How could you write a fact from this opinion? *(Possible response: Al's Shoes sells sneakers.)* OL

Resources for page 439

- Use Reading Skills Transparency in *Read Aloud, Think Aloud,* Unit 4, to help students practice distinguishing fact and opinion.

Reading in the Real World

Citizenship News reporters write facts. However, they sometimes show how they feel by the details they include or leave out and also by their word choices. Ask students to work in pairs to locate three articles on one world issue. Ask them to list facts and to list words that reveal opinions. Have them consider semantic slanting through the omission of information. Have students write one news article, using only facts from the three pieces. OL

Objectives
- Distinguish fact from opinion

More About the Author

In addition to writing about health topics, Sheila Globus wrote "Power of One: Local Heroes of Biodiversity." It is about individuals and groups who work together to help the environment. In "Turn the Tide," she reports on how more than 12,000 people nationwide have found ways to help.

EL Language Coach

Denotation and Connotation Say: The world of sports and exercise has many words with connotations. What difference in meaning do you find between *player, athlete,* and *jock*? *(Possible response: A player is a member of a sports team. An athlete is someone who is good at a sport. A jock is someone who brags about playing sports.)* OL

Before You Read

What Exercise Can Do for You

Meet the Author

Sheila Globus is a journalist and health writer for radio, TV, and magazines. She has written many articles about how to get and stay healthy—whether you're a teen or a senior citizen.

Author Search For more about Sheila Globus, go to www.glencoe.com.

Objectives (pp. 440–445)
Reading Distinguish fact from opinion
Literature Identify literary elements: tone
Vocabulary Distinguish denotation and connotation

Vocabulary Preview

focus (FOH kus) *v.* to keep the mind on; concentrate **(p. 442)** *I can focus on the game better if I've slept well the night before.*

endurance (en DUR uns) *n.* the ability to handle stress **(p. 443)** *Long-distance runners need endurance to stay in a race until the end.*

physical (FIH zih kul) *adj.* having to do with the body **(p. 444)** *Athletes must focus on both physical and mental fitness to compete well.*

Write to Learn Write the answers to the following questions in your Learner's Notebook.

- What helps you **focus** when you are studying?
- How do you increase your **endurance** for playing sports?
- Name a **physical** exercise.

English Language Coach

Denotation and Connotation As you learned in Reading Workshop 1, the denotation of a word is its strict dictionary meaning. The connotation of a word is its descriptive meaning. In other words, connotation involves the *connections* we make when we hear or read a particular word. Compare these two sentences: We will *eat* at seven o'clock. We will *dine* at seven o'clock. The connotation of *dine* is fancier, isn't it?

Class Discussion The words *chef* and *cook* both mean "a person who prepares food." What image comes to mind when you think of a chef? What does a chef wear? Where does a chef work? Now ask the same questions about the word *cook.* Discuss ways in which the connotations of the two words are different. EL

Copy this diagram into your Learner's Notebook. On the blank lines for each word, write what you think of for that word.

	Denotation	*Connotations*
chef	a person who prepares food	
cook	a person who prepares food	

Additional Support

Author Search To expand students' appreciation of Sheila Globus, have them access the Web site for additional information and resources.

Literature Focus Lesson

Persuasive Techniques in Radio
Winston Churchill's "finest hour" speech is an example of radio persuasion. Explain the historical background of the speech (found easily on the Internet). While students follow along in print, play an audiotape of the last paragraphs of the speech. Discuss how Churchill used his voice to add meaning—inflection, pauses, language, and logical reasoning. Ask students to use what they learned to write and deliver a two-minute speech to the class on an important issue. AL

Skills Preview

Key Reading Skill: Distinguishing Fact and Opinion

Remember that facts can be proved. Opinions are statements of personal feeling or belief. A statement can be a mixture of fact and opinion. Also, not all statements are one or the other. R

Write to Learn As you read, make notes of clear facts or opinions in your Learner's Notebook.

Key Literary Element: Tone

Tone is the author's attitude toward the subject, theme, and characters in a story. The tone of a story might be light and humorous, or it might be serious. It might be hopeful or sad. For example, if one writer describes a main character as a "hard-working youth" and another describes a main character as a "greedy brat," the tones of the stories are probably going to be very different.

Think about the story "Thank You, M'am." Does the author like his characters or not? Do you think the tone is hopeful or sad? Is it humorous or serious, or both?

It is not only fiction that has tone. Many articles are written with what is called an "objective" tone. (That's one that doesn't take sides.) Some editorials have an angry tone. As you read the next selection, think about the tone of the article.

Small Group Work In a small group, discuss why Langston Hughes used a hopeful tone in "Thank You, M'am." How do you think he felt about the importance of helping others?

Interactive Literary Elements Handbook
To review or learn more about the literary elements, go to www.glencoe.com.

Get Ready to Read

Connect to the Reading

What do you do for exercise? Do you play on a team, walk, or take dance classes? Do you think you should exercise more? As you read this article, think about the different ways that exercise can affect a person's health.

Partner Talk With a partner, talk about what you like to do for exercise. Describe how you feel before and after a good workout.

Build Background

Sheila Globus, the author of this article, wants to convince readers that exercise is important. Here are some facts about teens and exercise:

- Teens are often concerned with their weight and appearance.
- Technology has turned many of us into couch potatoes and Web surfers.
- Experts say that people who form good exercise habits early in life tend to live longer, healthier lives.

Set Purposes for Reading

BIG Question Read the selection, "What Exercise Can Do for You," and think about how the author tries to influence you. BQ

Set Your Own Purpose What would you like to learn from the article to help you answer the Big Question? Write your own purpose on your "What Exercise Can Do for You" Foldable page.

Keep Moving

Use these skills as you read the following selection.

Differentiated Instruction

Fact and Opinion Students who need help distinguishing fact and opinion may benefit from using a chart like the one below. Ask students to record facts and opinions from the article in the columns. EL OL

This can be proved true (Fact)	This tells me how the writer thinks/ feels (Opinion)

Teach

R Reading Skill

Distinguishing Fact and Opinion Say: Classify these statements about exercise and health as fact or opinion. Jogging is better than walking. *(opinion)* Stretching is a part of fitness and exercise. *(fact)* OL

BQ 

Say: Today people hear about fitness and exercise from doctors, schools, TV, and magazines. Which source would have the most influence on you? *(Responses will vary.)* EL OL

Use the CheckPoint questions provided on Presentation Plus! to check for distinguishing fact and opinion and to build background. These questions can be used with interactive response keypads for immediate student feedback.

Interactive Literary Elements Handbook Have students access the Web site to improve their understanding of tone.

Objectives
- Distinguish fact from opinion
- Identify literary elements: tone
- Distinguish denotation from connotation

Teach

Viewing the Photo

Ask: How might the facial expressions of the people in the photo influence readers to think or feel about exercise? *(Possible response: Exercise is fun.)* **AS**

C Critical Thinking

Comprehension Say: Brinley says that exercise gives him energy. But Beth exercises for other reasons. What are they? *(It makes her look better and gives her a chance to be with her friends.)* **OL**

Readability Scores
Dale-Chall: 5.6
DRP: 61
Lexile: 980

INFORMATIONAL TEXT
TEXTBOOK
from *Signature Reading*

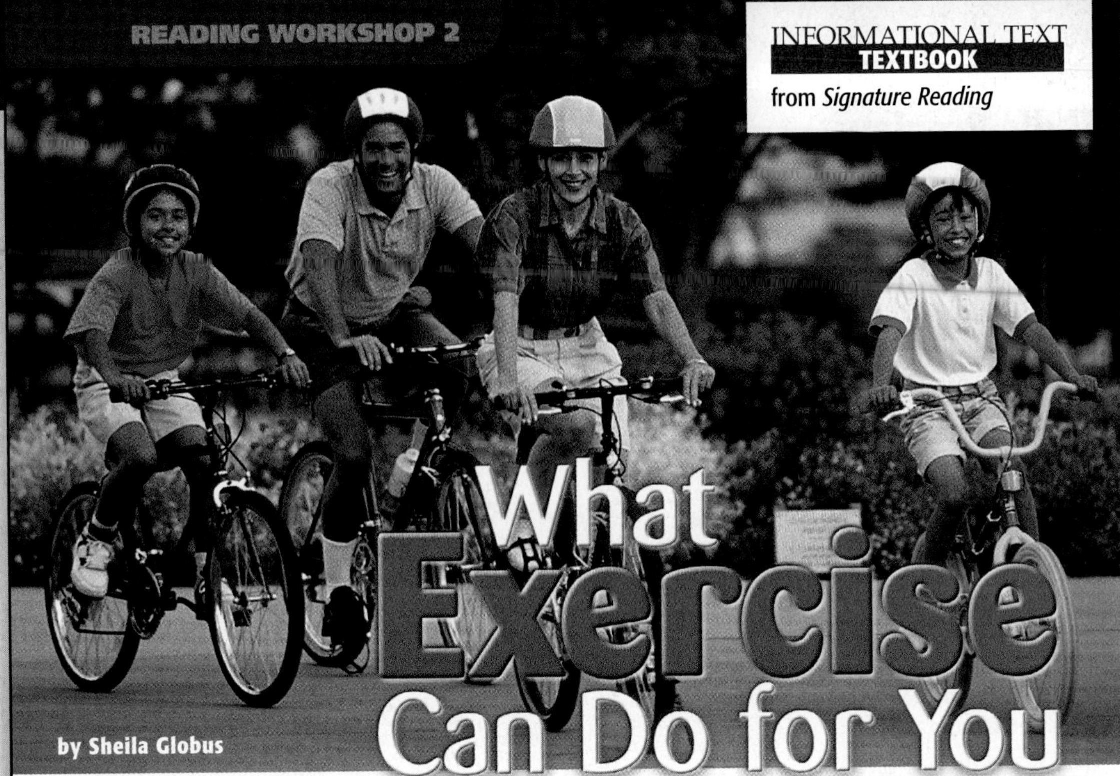

What Exercise Can Do for You

by Sheila Globus

What's so great about exercise? "It gives me energy," says Brinley, a member of the Junior Olympic Diving Team. "Instead of always being tired, I'm more awake and can **focus** on my schoolwork better."

C Albee, a 15-year-old football player who lifts weights in the off-season, admits that pregame workouts and scrimmages[1] tire him out. But, he says, "I feel a lot stronger and I'm a better player, especially since I started weight lifting."

Beth, a ninth grader, plays field hockey and lacrosse.[2] She says that exercise helps her look and feel better and gives her a chance to be on a team with her friends. "It gives us a chance to work toward a common goal," she says. **1**

1. ***Scrimmages*** are practice games.
2. Native Americans invented ***lacrosse,*** a ball game played using long-handled rackets with pouches.

Vocabulary

focus (FOH kus) *v.* to keep the mind on; concentrate

Practice the Skills

1 Key Literary Element

Tone How would you describe the tone of this article so far? Do you think the writer feels positively or negatively about her subject? Why?

Additional Support

English Language Coach

Denotation, Connotation, and Semantic Slanting Writers must understand their audiences in order to persuade them. Ask students to form groups and survey 15 to 25 people to find out why people do not exercise. Have students organize these reasons into categories, such as *no time, not fun, not necessary.* Ask groups to focus on one reason and create a poster, speech, or other presentation to influence these people to exercise. **EL OL**

Shaping Up EL

We all know we should exercise: It's good for the heart, can help keep your weight under control, and might even help you live longer. Studies show, however, that as teenagers get older, they exercise less. Few can run a mile in under 10 minutes. Fewer still get the recommended 30 minutes of moderate exercise three or more times a week. In fact, as the use of computers and technology continues to grow, many teenagers are exercising little more than their fingers, tapping away at the keyboard. L

It takes effort to make exercise a habit, but those who invest the time and energy are seldom disappointed. "Our coach makes us do a half-hour workout before we get into the pool," says Brinley, a high school sophomore. "We do sit-ups, run stairs, do crunches, and stretch. That's what helped me get stronger, build more **endurance**, and stay loose and limber.[3] I think it's also made me a better diver."

Brinley has the right idea. Just participating in a sport doesn't automatically get you into shape. To really get fit, you have to develop each component of fitness—cardiovascular endurance, muscle strength, and flexibility. For that, a combination of aerobics,[4] stretching, and strengthening exercises works best.

Reducing Risk

Fitness experts say that nearly half of all young people ages 12 to 21 aren't active enough. That can lead to problems later in life, including heart disease, high blood pressure, diabetes,[5] osteoporosis (thin, brittle bones that break easily), and even early death. What's more, a <u>**couch-potato**</u> lifestyle is harder to change the older you get. 2 3 R

3. A person who can bend and stretch easily is ***limber.*** The words ***flexible*** and ***supple,*** used later in the article, are synonyms for *limber.*
4. A ***component*** is a part of something. Anything involving the heart and blood vessels is called ***cardiovascular. Aerobics*** are exercises designed to strengthen a person's heart and lungs as well as the muscles.
5. ***Diabetes*** is a disease in which the body does not produce or properly use a chemical called insulin.

Vocabulary

endurance (en DUR uns) *n.* the ability to handle stress

Practice the Skills

2 Key Reading Skill

Distinguishing Fact and Opinion Is the second sentence in this paragraph a fact or an opinion? Could the statement that lack of exercise leads to these problems be checked and proved to be true?

3 English Language Coach

Denotation and Connotation What are the denotations, or dictionary definitions, of the words *couch* and *potato*? How do you think the term <u>**couch-potato**</u> came to mean "person who watches too much TV"?

Teach

EL Language Coach

Denotation and Connotation Say: Read the words *Shaping Up* at the top of the page. This term is often used to describe the goal of exercise. How does the connotation of this expression persuade people to exercise? *(Possible response: Shaping up means that you'll look better if you exercise. Most people want to look better.)* OL

L Literary Element

Tone Say: Read what the writer says about computers, technology, and young people. What can you tell about her feelings by the words, "many teenagers are exercising little more than their fingers"? *(Possible response: Globus is being sarcastic because she's frustrated.)* AL

R Reading Skill

Review Understanding Persuasive Techniques Ask: How does the writer persuade a young person that being inactive isn't good? *(She lists health problems that can occur when people are older.)* OL

English Language Coach

Building Background Doctors are increasingly aware of adult diseases that are directly linked to the lack of exercise. Ask students to work with a partner to research diseases related to inactivity. Ask students to write a one-paragraph report on one of the diseases. Their reports should explain what the disease is, how it affects the body, how it is related to lack of exercise, and how it can be prevented. OL

Objectives
- Distinguish fact and opinion
- Understand denotation and connotation
- Use semantic slanting
- Identify tone and persuasive techniques

READING WORKSHOP 2

Teach

Viewing the Graphic
Say: Read the chart at the top of page 444. How might it suggest the reason some people exercise? *(Because it tells about burning calories, I think some people exercise to lose weight.)* **EL** **OL**

C Critical Thinking

Comprehension Ask: Based on the third paragraph, what might you write to persuade readers to exercise? *(Possible response: There's a fun exercise for everyone.)* **OL**

Going for the "Caloric Burn" F

You may burn more or fewer calories per hour, depending on how vigorously you do the following activities.

Activity	Calories Burned per 30 Minutes (Your Weight in Pounds)	
	120 pounds	150 pounds
swimming	209	261
walking	130	162
running (9 min/mile)	314	393
tennis	179	224
skiing	194	243
cycling (10 mph)	163	204
racquetball	217	272
hiking (vigorous)	191	239

Besides reducing your risk of these diseases, regular exercise can help you in smaller ways, too, such as helping you **bounce back** quicker from a cold and boosting your metabolism[6] so that you burn more calories. A healthy heart, stronger bones, and a trim and toned body, however, are just the **physical** benefits of exercise. Even more important is what it does for your mood and your mind. **4**

"Exercise makes me feel better about myself and about the way I look," says Brinley. "I can even see my muscles. I always feel better after diving practice. I'm more confident, too—not just about diving, but about everything."

C Finding an exercise that's fun is the key to getting something out of it. If lessons or team sports aren't your thing, try other activities that you think you might enjoy more. "Five years of karate made me a lot more flexible," says Rachel, "but it was boring. What I really like is step aerobics. I always leave the class feeling energized and stronger."

6. The process of breaking down substances in the body is called ***metabolism.***

Vocabulary

physical (FIZ ih kul) *adj.* having to do with the body

Practice the Skills

4 English Language Coach
Denotation and Connotation
In this sentence the denotation of "bounce back" is "recover." What is its connotation?

5 Reviewing Skills
Understanding Text Features
Would this chart help you choose a particular kind of exercise? Why or why not?

Additional Support

Reading in the Real World

Career Students who are interested in exercise and fitness may benefit from learning about careers in this field. Ask students to check the telephone directory for businesses and services listed under the headings of *Fitness and Exercise*. Ask them to conduct a phone interview with an individual whose type of employment interests them. Students should write a paragraph describing the job and its requirements. **OL**

READING WORKSHOP 2

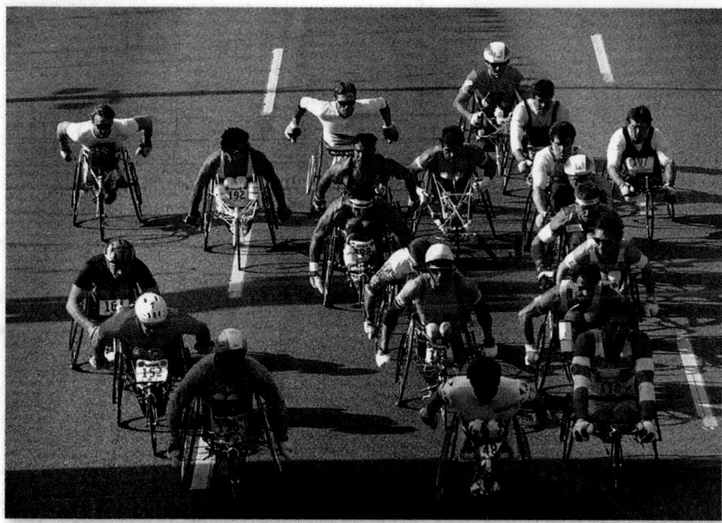

Wheelchair racers compete in the Los Angeles marathon in 1991.

Fitting Exercise In

Even if you're not into sports, you can still find ways to sneak in a little extra physical activity wherever you can. Walk the dog, take the stairs instead of escalators, ride your bike to school. You won't be sorry. Here are some other ideas:

- Plan some fun into your schedule—a couple sets of tennis, a game of volleyball, a leisurely jog or hike along a trail.
- Shovel snow for a great heart-strengthening activity. (Builds your biceps, too, if you lift and toss it.)
- Vacuum, sweep, and scrub around the house (preferably with the stereo playing in the background).
- Help out in the yard raking leaves, or weeding and planting, depending on the season.

Exercise that's fun is exercise you'll stick with. In addition to possibly concentrating on developing a single skill, like sinking baskets or executing a perfect dive, think about all the things exercise can do for you—and go for it. You'll condition your heart and lungs, build strong muscles, make your tendons and ligaments supple, and maintain a healthy weight. What's more, you'll feel great. Take it from Brinley: "Even if I never make it to the Olympics, I won't ever stop doing exercise," she says. "It feels too good." 6 7 ○

Practice the Skills

6 **Key Reading Skill**

Distinguishing Fact and Opinion Review the article. Do you think the article is more about facts or opinions? Has the writer supported her opinions with facts?

7 BIG Question

BQ Does Globus succeed in influencing you about the importance of exercise? How does she do it? Write your answers on the inside of your Foldable. Your response will help you answer the Unit Challenge later.

Teach

Viewing the Photo

Say: Look at the photograph. How might you feel if you participated in this race? *(Possible responses: excited, thrilled, determined)* What benefit besides a strong, fit body could this sport provide? *(Possible response: chances to meet new people and travel)* EL OL

BQ 

Ask: How does Sheila Globus persuade readers who dislike sports to exercise? *(Possible response: She tells readers that they can fit exercise in their daily routines.)* OL

Assess

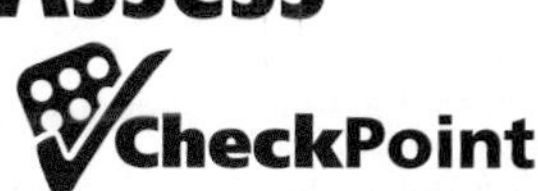

Use the CheckPoint questions provided on Presentation Plus! to check for comprehension of the selection. These questions can be used with interactive response keypads for immediate student feedback.

Differentiated Instruction

Persuasive Techniques Some readers need specific information before a writer can persuade them to take action. Sheila Globus persuades readers to give exercise a try by listing ways in which people can fit exercise into their daily activities. Ask students to create a poster about how students can fit exercise into an average school day. Encourage them to use graphics to structure and enhance the persuasiveness of their posters. EL OL

Objectives
- Understand tone
- Analyze photos and graphics
- Distinguish fact and opinion
- Make generalizations

Assess

Resources for page 446

- Selection Quick Check
- Selection and Unit Assessment
- ExamView Assessment Suite
- Interactive Tutor: Self-Assessment

Students can respond to the *After You Read* items in their Learner's Notebook or on a separate sheet of paper.

Answering the

1. Responses will vary.
2. "It gives me energy," says Brinley, a diver for the Junior Olympic team.
3. Exercise strengthens the body, improves mood, maintains healthy weight, improves the mind, gives opportunities for teamwork and friendship, and provides fun and relaxation.

Critical Thinking

4. Possible response: This is Rachel's opinion. The statement can't be proved. It is simply how Rachel feels about karate.
5. Possible response: The writer tries to reach young readers with clear, understandable language, examples, and enthusiasm.
6. Responses will vary.
7. Responses will vary.

After You Read

What Exercise Can Do for You

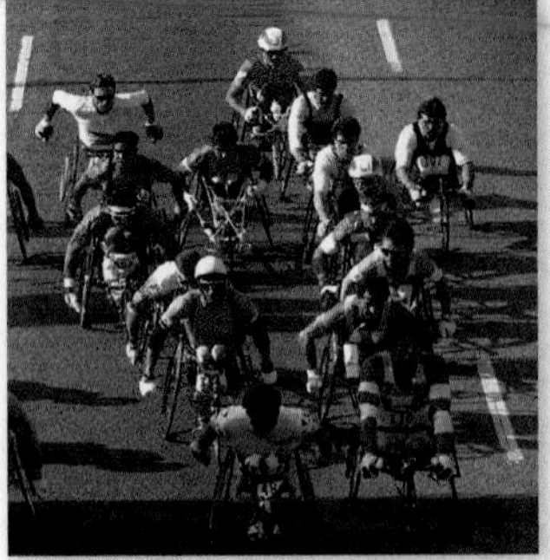

Answering the BIG Question

1. After reading this article, what are your thoughts about the benefits of exercise? How did the author influence you?
2. **Recall** What is the first answer in this selection to the question "What's so great about exercise?" Who gives that answer?
   TIP **Right There**
3. **Summarize** According to the article, why is exercise good for you?
   TIP **Think and Search**

Critical Thinking

4. **Distinguish Fact and Opinion** When Rachel talks about karate and says, "but it was boring," (page 444) is that a fact or an opinion? Explain how you know.
   TIP **Author and Me**
5. **Analyze** How would you describe the style of this selection?
   TIP **Author and Me**
6. **Evaluate** How well does this article persuade teens to exercise more?
   TIP **Author and Me**
7. **Evaluate** Do you think that the information in this article will have an effect on your own life? Explain your answer.
   TIP **Author and Me**

Objectives
(pp. 446–447)
Reading Distinguish fact from opinion
Literature Identify literary elements: style
Vocabulary Distinguish denotation and connotation
Writing Use the RAFT system: newspaper article
Grammar Identify sentence fragments

Write About Your Reading

On a separate sheet of paper, use the RAFT system to write about "What Exercise Can Do for You."

Role: Write as if you were one of the students in the article

Audience: Write to your peers (other students in your school)

Format: Write an article that might appear in your school newspaper

Topic: Explain your regular exercise routine and the benefits you get from it

Write About Your Reading

Possible response:
My day wouldn't be complete without exercise! When I first get up in the morning, I can barely keep my eyes open. Luckily, my dog bounds up the stairs when he hears me stumbling around and getting dressed. Then we head out. At first, I can hardly keep up with Rusty. Soon, though, I hit my stride and we both jog along. The fresh air feels good on my face and helps me wake up. By the time I get back home, both Rusty and I are ready for breakfast!

Skills Review

Key Reading Skill: Distinguishing Fact and Opinion

8. Think about the article you just read. What do you think is the author's opinion about exercise? What facts did you learn from reading this article? Is the combination of facts and opinion in the article persuasive? Why or why not?

Key Literary Element: Tone

9. In your own words, how would you describe the tone of the article? For example, is it serious or silly? Is it hopeful or sad? Use some of your own words to describe the author's tone. And remember that the tone is the *writer's* attitude toward the subject, not yours or someone the author quotes in the article.

10. Do you think the writer's tone helped convince her audience that exercise is important? Why or why not?

Reviewing Skills: Understanding Text Features

11. Why do you think the chart "Going for the 'Caloric Burn'" was included in this article?

Vocabulary Check

Rewrite the sentences below. Mark each sentence with a *T* or an *F* depending on whether it is true or false.

12. ___ When you **focus**, your attention wanders.

13. ___ You have to have **endurance** to run a marathon.

14. ___ Running is a **physical** activity.

15. **English Language Coach** Review the denotation and the connotations for the words *chef* and *cook*. Write a sentence for each word that explains its connotation.

Grammar Link: Sentence Fragments

A **sentence fragment** is an incomplete sentence. Any sentence that is missing a subject or a verb or that doesn't express a complete thought is incomplete (see page 437).

- **Fragment:** Everyone in town.
  (What about everyone in town? The sentence is incomplete because the verb is missing.)
- **Complete:** Everyone in town should vote.
- **Fragment:** Drove down the street.
  (Who or what drove? The sentence is incomplete because the subject is missing.)
- **Complete:** My sister drove down the street.

Fragment: Whenever you need a friend.
(What should you do whenever you need a friend? The sentence has a subject and verb, but it does not express a complete thought.)

Complete: Whenever you need a friend, you should lean on me.

Grammar Practice

Which sentences below are fragments? Copy them (and only them) on another piece of paper.

16. Went outside for a while.

17. I wanted to catch a breath of fresh air.

18. The warm, beautiful spring day.

19. Because the sun shone and the birds sang.

Web Activities For eFlashcards, Selection Quick Checks, and other Web activities, go to www.glencoe.com.

Skills Review

Key Reading Skill: Distinguishing Fact and Opinion

8. Responses will vary.

Key Literary Element: Tone

9. Responses will vary but may include the idea that the writer has a positive and enthusiastic tone, which she expresses by depicting exercise as a fun and easy activity.

10. Responses will vary.

Reviewing Skills: Understanding Text Features

11. Possible responses should include the idea that some people exercise to lose weight.

Vocabulary Check

12. F

13. T

14. T

15. Responses will vary but should include the idea that a chef is a highly trained, skilled cook.

Close

Ask students to write a paragraph about their favorite form of exercise.

Grammar Link: Sentence Fragments

Grammar Practice

16. Went outside for a while.

17. not a fragment

18. The warm, beautiful spring day.

19. Because the sun shone and the birds sang.

Web Activities Have students access the Web site for interactive activities that will help them assess their understanding of the selection.

More About the Author

Sidney Poitier's father was a major influence in his life. No longer able to sell the family's crops, the senior Poitier moved the family to Nassau, Bahamas, sold cigars in bars, and never gave in to self-pity. Despite their poverty, Sidney Poitier's father helped his family maintain dignity and pride. As the actor explained in an interview, "Every time I took a part . . . I always said to myself, 'This must reflect well on his name.'"

BQ 

Say: People are influenced by other people and by their own experiences. What might influence someone to show compassion? *(Possible response: A person who was very poor as a child may show compassion to others who are poor.)* **OL**

Before You Read

Oprah Winfrey

Meet the Author

Born in 1927 in Miami, Florida, Sidney Poitier was one of eight children in a farm family. After they moved to the Bahamas, Poitier saw his first movie. Later, as a young man in New York, he began to study acting. In 1963, he became the first African American to win the Academy Award for Best Actor.

Author Search For more about Sidney Poitier, go to www.glencoe.com.

Objectives (pp. 448–451)
Reading Distinguish fact from opinion
Literature Identify literary elements: tone
Vocabulary Identify euphemisms

Vocabulary Preview

implied (im PLYD) *v.* suggested; hinted; form of the verb *imply* **(p. 451)** *Oprah implied that her life would be different if she hadn't seen Poitier win the Academy Award.*

BQ **compassion** (kum PASH un) *n.* deep concern for the troubles of others, mixed with a desire to help; sympathy **(p. 451)** *Compassion leads Oprah to do charity work.*

Write to Learn Write a few sentences about an action that you have seen that implied compassion.

English Language Coach

Denotation and Connotation A euphemism is the substitution of a mild or general term for one that seems harsh or, perhaps, icky. In other words, euphemisms have softer or more polite connotations than the original term.

The word *euphemism* comes from the Greek language and means "good or fortunate speech." There are many euphemisms in our language. Every time we say "restroom," we are using a euphemism. Often, euphemisms are used in politics, business, and advertising in order to mislead people. However, euphemisms aren't always misleading. Sometimes they are very effective and even more descriptive than harsher language.

Group activity Copy the euphemisms listed below in your Learner's Notebook. With your classmates, discuss the connotations of the euphemisms. Why do you think they are used?

Euphemism	meaning	connotations
pass away	die	
lay off	fire from a job	
pre-owned vehicle	used car	
senior citizen	old person	
fixer-upper	old house needing work	
casualties	deaths	
landfill	garbage dump	

Additional Support

Author Search To expand students' appreciation of Sidney Poitier, have them access the Web site for additional information and resources.

Literature Focus Lesson

Persuasive Writing People write tributes to persuade others to appreciate the subject of their writing. Tributes often focus on famous people or those who have performed an extraordinary service. Ask students to choose a person or animal to which they'd like to pay tribute. Students should use connotative language as a persuasive technique and provide five admirable traits or deeds of their subject. **OL**

Skills Preview

Key Reading Skill: Distinguishing Fact and Opinion

It's often difficult to tell the difference between fact and opinion.

- A fact can be proved.
- An opinion is what someone believes to be true.

Television commercials, political speeches, the evening news, and ordinary, everyday conversations—they all contain both facts and opinions. As a viewer, listener, and reader, you must learn to distinguish what can be proved from what can't.

R

Decide whether each of the next sentences is a fact or an opinion.

She was born to unwed teenage parents and living in a segregated society.

Besides being compassionate, Oprah is well-informed, dazzlingly curious, and as down-to-earth and loving as any human being I've ever known.

Partner Talk With a partner, talk about some event in your lives, in your school, or in your community. Discuss what the facts are about that event. Then discuss opinions people might have about the event.

Key Literary Element: Tone

As you read, think about the tone of this article. How does the writer feel about his subject? Is the tone positive or negative? Then think about how the tone of the article influences you. Does the writer's tone make you agree with his opinions?

Interactive Literary Elements Handbook
To review or learn more about the literary elements, go to www.glencoe.com.

Get Ready to Read

Connect to the Reading

"If he could do that, I wonder what I could do?"

Have you ever had a thought like this before? Maybe you'd like to sink a perfect slam-dunk or start your own fashion line.

Write to Learn In your Learner's Notebook, freewrite about a time when you saw someone do something that influenced you. Tell what that person did and what you thought and felt about it.

Build Background

In this article, a famous actor tells how he influenced the young girl to become an internationally famous talk show host and media personality.

- In 1954, when Oprah Winfrey was born, African Americans faced prejudice because of their race.
- There were very few major roles for African Americans in film and television in the 1960s.
- Sidney Poitier was the first African American to win an Academy Award for Best Actor.
- Oprah now hosts an extremely popular and influential television talk show. She is one of the wealthiest and most famous people in the world.

Set Purposes for Reading

BIG Question Read "Oprah Winfrey" to find out how she was influenced by an actor she saw on TV when she was only ten years old. **BQ**

Set Your Own Purpose What would you like to learn to help you answer the Big Question? Write your own purpose on the "Oprah Winfrey" page of Foldable 4.

Keep Moving

Use these skills as you read the following selection.

Teach

BQ 

Say: Many young people look to singers, athletes, actors, and other well-known people for inspiration. What well-known person has influenced you? *(Responses will vary.)* EL OL

R Reading Skill

Distinguishing Fact and Opinion **Say:** Many magazine articles focus on the lives of famous people. How can you tell facts from opinions in an article about a celebrity? *(Possible response: I compare what I read to what I have learned from other sources.)* OL

Use the CheckPoint questions provided on Presentation Plus! to check for distinguishing between fact and opinion and to build background. These questions can be used with interactive response keypads for immediate student feedback.

Literature Online

Interactive Literary Elements Handbook Have students access the Web site to improve their understanding of tone.

Differentiated Instruction

Cause and Effect Readers who wish to understand how people and events influence others may want to use a cause-and-effect chart like the one below during or after they read. Ask students to link the events in the story about Oprah Winfrey to who she has become and what she has done. EL OL

What happened?	How did Oprah change or react?

Objectives

- Distinguish fact from opinion
- Identify literary elements: tone
- Identify euphemisms

READING WORKSHOP 2

Teach

Viewing the Photo

Ask: Why might Oprah Winfrey treasure this picture of herself with Sidney Poitier? *(Possible response: Sidney Poitier has been her inspiration to succeed.)* **OL**

EL Language Coach

Denotation, Connotation, and Semantic Slanting

Say: Winfrey was happy that her grandmother told others she was "gifted." What ideas does this adjective suggest? *(Possible response: smart, talented)* **OL**

Readability Scores
Dale-Chall: 5.9
DRP: 61
Lexile: 1050

TIME

Oprah WINFREY

Her influence has reached far and wide

Dave Allocca/DMI/Time Life Pictures/Getty Images

OPRAH WINFREY shares a moment with actor Sidney Poitier, who won the 1964 Academy Award for Best Actor in *Lilies of the Field.*

By SIDNEY POITIER

The future of a poor African American female born in Kosciusko, Mississippi, on January 29, 1954, was not promising. Oprah Gail Winfrey had enormous obstacles in front of her. She was born to unwed teenage parents and living in a segregated[1] society.

For the first six years of her life, Oprah was raised by her maternal[2] grandmother on a farm in rural Mississippi. Oprah's grandmother taught her how to read at an early age. The young girl developed a love for books that continues today. And by the age of 3, she was reciting speeches in church. Oprah often heard her grandmother tell others that Oprah was "gifted." Perhaps it was this feeling of being special that helped Oprah get through the difficult years that she would later spend living with her mother. **1** **2**

1 **Key Reading Skill**

Distinguishing Fact and Opinion Does the last sentence of this paragraph state a fact or an opinion? How can you tell?

2 **Key Literary Element**

Tone Based on the title, subtitle, and these first few paragraphs, what do you think the writer's tone is?

1. In a ***segregated*** society, people of different races or religions live separately.
2. Oprah's ***maternal*** grandmother was her mother's mother.

Additional Support

English Language Coach

Building Background Students may find it helpful to research segregation in the United States to better understand the selection. Ask students to research one aspect of segregation: housing, education, public transportation, or armed services. Ask them to write two paragraphs to persuade readers of their point of view regarding the influence of segregation on people's lives. Remind students to support opinions with facts from their research. **AL**

Oprah moved in with her mother and half sister in Milwaukee, Wisconsin, when she was 6. She lived in a crowded two-bedroom apartment shared with family and friends. Oprah was lonely and unhappy. She suffered both physical and mental abuse from family members and friends of her family. **3** **R1**

But even during those difficult years, seeds of hope were being planted. On April 13, 1964, 10-year-old Oprah was sitting on the linoleum floor of her mother's apartment watching television. She witnessed an event that connected to something deep inside of her. She saw me, a young African American actor, receive an Academy Award. Sharing in that moment and all it **implied**, she later told me, caused her to say softly to herself, "If he can do that, I wonder what I could do?"

Life with her mother became worse, and as Oprah grew up, she repeatedly ran away and got in trouble. Her mother tried to place her in a home for **troubled** teens, but fortunately there were no openings. Oprah's father offered to take her into his home in Nashville, Tennessee. With strict rules and discipline, Oprah's father helped her turn her life around. **4** **R2**

The journey of Oprah Winfrey had begun. For more than 20 years, Oprah's openness about her own life, **compassion** for others, and vision for a better world have made her talk show enormously influential. Oprah inspires her viewers to effect change in their lives and the lives of others. She is a perfect example of someone who has succeeded in spite of the disadvantages she has faced.

Oprah's wide-ranging charity work with children and families in Africa and elsewhere, her popular book club and magazine, and her contributions to improving race relations—all speak to the human family, to touching hearts and leaving each one uplifted.

Besides being compassionate, Oprah is well-informed, dazzlingly curious, and as down-to-earth and loving as any human being I've ever known. **5**

–From *TIME*, April 26, 2004

Vocabulary

implied (im PLYD) *v.* suggested; hinted

compassion (kum PASH un) *n.* deep concern for the troubles of others, mixed with a desire to help; sympathy

3 Key Reading Skill

Distinguishing Fact and Opinion What information is stated as fact in this paragraph? Is it possible to prove these statements? How?

4 English Language Coach

Denotation and Connotation The word *troubled* is a euphemism. What does it mean? What is its connotation?

5 BIG Question

How did Poitier influence Oprah? What kinds of influence does she have on other people today? Write your answer on the "Oprah Winfrey" page of Foldable 4. Your response will help you complete the Unit Challenge later.

READING WORKSHOP 2

Teach

R1 Reading Skill

Review Understanding Persuasive Techniques

Ask: How does Sidney Poitier persuade readers that Oprah Winfrey's years with her mother were difficult? *(Possible response: He describes the crowded, small apartment and says that family members and friends abused Winfrey.)* **OL**

R2 Reading Skill

Review Inferring **Say:** The author mentions both of Winfrey's parents in this article. From details he provides, what might you infer about Winfrey's mother and father? *(Possible response: I don't think her mother was a good parent because Oprah was lonely and unhappy living with her. I think her father was a good parent because he helped her turn her life around.)* **OL**

Assess

Use the CheckPoint questions provided on Presentation Plus! to check for comprehension of the selection. These questions can be used with interactive response keypads for immediate student feedback.

Reading in the Real World

Career Students who are interested in TV careers may enjoy researching the job of a talk show host. Have students form groups and search the Internet for the names of past and current talk show hosts. Ask them to gather information on the various jobs required to produce a talk show. Have groups produce a "talk show" for the class on a topic of local or world concern. Group members should fill roles necessary for production. **OL**

Objectives

- Distinguish fact and opinion
- Make inferences
- Understand word connotations
- Analyze persuasive techniques

Assess

Resources for page 452

- Selection Quick Check
- Selection and Unit Assessment
- ExamView Assessment Suite
- Interactive Tutor: Self-Assessment

Students can respond to the *After You Read* items in their Learner's Notebook or on a separate sheet of paper.

Answering the BIG Question

1. Responses will vary.
2. Possible responses include segregation and unwed parents.
3. Her grandmother raised her until she was six. She lived with her mother and other family members for a time before going to live with her father.

Critical Thinking

4. Responses will vary but may include the ideas that Oprah is proud of her African heritage and that people in Africa are in need of a great deal of help.
5. Responses will vary but may include the idea that he would like Oprah to be an influence on readers, as he was on Oprah.
6. Responses will vary.

After You Read

Oprah Winfrey

Dave Allocca/DMI/Time Life Pictures/Getty Images

Answering the BIG Question

1. Has anyone ever influenced you in the way Sidney Poitier influenced Oprah Winfrey? Explain.
2. **Recall** List two "enormous obstacles" Oprah had to face as a child.
   TIP **Right There**
3. **Recall** Who raised Oprah until she was six? Where was she raised until she was six?
   TIP **Right There**

Critical Thinking

4. **Infer** Why do you think Oprah does charity work with families in Africa?
   TIP **Author and Me**
5. **Evaluate** Why do you think Poitier wrote this article? Explain your answers.
   TIP **Author and Me**
6. **Respond** Based on this selection, what do you think of Oprah Winfrey? Do you like her? Do you think that reading about her will have an influence on your life? Explain your answers.
   TIP **Author and Me**

Write About Your Reading

Write a short summary of this article. Follow these steps to decide what you'll write. Take notes about the points you want to make.

Step 1: Recall the facts you learned about Oprah's early life. For example:

- When and where was she born?
- What conditions made her early life difficult?
- How did she learn to read?

Step 2: Think about the event she saw that influenced her life. How did it affect the path she took later in life?

Step 3: This is a summary of the article, so remember:

- Don't include your own opinions.
- You *can* include the writer's opinions in your summary.

Step 4: Use your notes to write your summary.

Objectives (pp. 452–453)
Reading Distinguish fact from opinion
Literature Identify literary elements: tone
Vocabulary Distinguish denotation and connotation
Grammar Fix sentence fragments

Write About Your Reading

Possible response:
Oprah Winfrey was born to unwed African American parents in 1954 in Kosciusko, Mississippi. She lived with her grandmother until she was six and learned to read at age three. She lived with her mother in Wisconsin until she was a teenager. She frequently ran away and got into trouble. She then lived with her father in Tennessee. She has been a TV personality for 20 years. She does charity work.

Skills Review

Key Reading Skill: Distinguishing Fact and Opinion

7. Think about what you've learned about the difference between fact and opinion. In your Learner's Notebook
   - make a list of opinions you noticed in this article.
   - make a list of at least five facts you read in this article.
8. Did distinguishing fact from opinion help you read and understand this article? Why or why not? Give examples from the article to support your answer.
9. Is your answer to number 8 above a fact or an opinion? Explain.

Key Literary Element: Tone

10. How would you describe the tone of this selection?
11. How has the writer created that tone?

Vocabulary Check

Choose the best word from the list to fill in the blanks below. Rewrite each sentence with the correct word in place.

implied compassion

12. She didn't say it directly, but she ___ that I cheated.
13. Millions of people gave money to the Red Cross out of ___ for the flood victims.
14. **English Language Coach** Poitier says that Winfrey is "down to earth." What does this expression mean to you? Does it have a positive or negative connotation? Explain.

Grammar Link: Fixing Fragments

You learned on page 447 what a sentence fragment is. To fix a fragment, add the missing part, or connect the fragment to a complete thought.

- **Fragment:** Wrote about her vacation.
  (Who or what wrote? The sentence is incomplete because the subject is missing. To fix the fragment, add a subject.)
- **Complete:** **Jen** wrote about her vacation.
- **Fragment:** The twins, Jess and Jerry.
  (What about the twins? The sentence is incomplete because the verb is missing. To fix the fragment, add a verb.)
- **Complete:** The twins, Jess and Jerry, **have gone**.
- **Fragment:** After we eat.
  (After we eat . . . what? The sentence has a subject and verb, but it does not express a complete thought. To fix the fragment, complete the thought.)

Complete: After we eat, **we will watch TV.**

Grammar Practice

Copy the sentence fragments below and make them into complete sentences. You can fix the sentences any way you like as long as they have a subject, a verb, and express a complete thought.

My mom so busy.
All the delicious food.
Nobody else in the world.

Web Activities For eFlashcards, Selection Quick Checks, and other Web activities, go to www.glencoe.com.

Skills Review

Key Reading Skill: Distinguishing Fact and Opinion

7. Responses may include that Oprah is a perfect example of a woman who succeeded in spite of disadvantages and that she is dazzlingly curious.
8. Responses will vary.
9. Responses will vary.

Key Literary Element: Tone

10. Responses may include that the tone is inspirational and serious.
11. Responses will vary.

Vocabulary Check

12. implied
13. compassion
14. A possible response may be that the hard times Winfrey had as a child and as a teenager, as well as her openness about her life, make her a person who understands real life. Remembering her early experiences helps her to identify with ordinary people.

Literature Online

Web Activities Have students access the Web site for interactive activities that will help them assess their understanding of the selection.

Grammar Link: Fixing Fragments

Grammar Practice

Possible response:
My mom is so busy.
All the delicious food was displayed beautifully on the buffet.
Nobody else in the world can make a cake as good as my mom's.

Close

Ask students to write a paragraph about the person who has most influenced them and has helped make them who they are today.

READING WORKSHOP 3

Identifying Author's Purpose and Perspective

Objectives covered in this workshop:
- Indentify author's purpose and perspective

Identifying Author's Purpose and Perspective

Why Is It Important?

- People see things differently because of their own experiences, interests, and values. Students will learn that an author's purpose for writing is affected by his or her perspective.
- Identifying an author's purpose and perspective will enable students to tell the difference between the topic of the selection and how the author feels about the topic.
- Identifying an author's purpose and perspective will also help students form their own opinions about a topic.

How to Help Students Get It

- Remind students that an author's purpose is his or her reason for writing about a topic. An author's perspective is the way he or she looks at or feels about the topic.
- Tell students that they can look for clues in the text, such as the author's word choices and how he or she organized the writing, to help them identify the author's purpose and perspective.
- Students may also benefit from re-reading the author's background to get a better sense of his or her purpose and perspective.

Reading to Answer the Big Question

The Courage That My Mother Had

Edna St. Vincent Millay's three stanza poem describes two valuable things her mother had; courage, and a golden brooch. Readers see how strong an influence the narrator's mother has on her daughter, even after the mother's death.

Two People I Want to Be Like

This is a poem about two people who, in the course of an average day, make a strong impression. Even actions that are not intended to be observed can influence the people who notice them.

Volunteers Welcome!

These flyers for a museum and a "clean-up day" make volunteering seem attractive and fun. These informational texts show readers how we are influenced by things other than just TV ads and writing in books.

Workshop Resources

Pacing (Days) Standard	Block	Lesson	Student Materials	Teacher Resources
1		Key Skill Lesson: Author's Purpose and Perspective	Key Reading Skills Practice English Language Coach	Bellringer Options Transparencies Read Aloud, Think Aloud Transparencies Presentation Plus!
2		"The Courage That My Mother Had" "Two People I Want to Be Like"	Literary Analysis Transparencies Glencoe Online Selection Vocabulary Development Academic Vocabulary Development English Language Coach Active Reading Graphic Organizer Literary Analysis StudentWorks Plus Online Student Edition Literature Classics Selection and Unit Assessments	Literary and Text Analysis Transparencies Puzzlemaker Skill Level Up! BookLink 3 Assessment by Learning Objective (Diagnostic and Formative) Interactive Tutor Self-Assessment TeacherWorks Plus
2		*Volunteers Welcome!*	Glencoe Online Selection Vocabulary Development Academic Vocabulary Development English Language Coach Active Reading Graphic Organizer Literary Analysis StudentWorks Plus Online Student Edition Literature Classics Selection and Unit Assessments	Literary and Text Analysis Transparencies Puzzlemaker Skill Level Up! BookLink 3 Assessment by Learning Objective (Diagnostic and Formative) Interactive Tutor Self-Assessment TeacherWorks Plus

Keys for Unit Resource

- Blackline Master
- Workbook
- Supplemental Text
- CD-ROM
- DVD
- Transparency
- Web-based
- Fast Files

Level Appropriate Code

AS = Activities for all students
AL = Activities for students working above grade level
OL = Activities for students working at grade level
BL = Activities for students working below grade level
EL = Activities for English language learners

Focus

BELLRINGER Options

- Selection Focus Transparency
- Daily Language Practice Transparency

Focus Activity Ask: What character traits do you most value? List some. *(Possible responses: honesty, loyalty, generosity)*

Teach

R Reading Skill

Identifying Author's Purpose and Perspective

Say: When someone shares an opinion with you, how can you identify that person's purpose and perspective? *(Possible response: Parents who insist on bike helmets want to protect you [purpose] because they love you [perspective].)* OL

V Vocabulary

Academic Vocabulary

Ask: According to sentence 3 on page 454, what makes people "see" things differently? *(values, interests, experiences)* BL EL

READING WORKSHOP 3

Skills Focus

You will practice using these skills when you read the following selections:

- "The Courage That My Mother Had," p. 458
- "Two People I Want to Be Like," p. 459
- "Volunteers Welcome!" p. 464

Reading

- Identifying the author's purpose and perspective

Literature

- Recognizing the author's use of diction, language, and word choice in what you read and its effect on your understanding of the subject

Vocabulary

- Understanding denotation, connotation, and semantic slanting
- Academic Vocabulary: *perspective*

Writing/Grammar

- Identifying the complete subject and complete predicate

Objectives (pp. 454–455)
Reading Identify author's purpose • Identify author's perspective

Skill Lesson

Identifying Author's Purpose and Perspective

Learn It!

What Is It? The author's purpose is his or her reason for writing about a topic. The author's **perspective** is the way he or she looks at, or sees, the topic.

People see things differently because of their own experiences, interests, and values. Many times, an author's purpose for writing is affected by his or her perspective.

Analyzing Cartoons
It's all a matter of perspective, isn't it? What *would* a turkey say about Thanksgiving? (And would you want to hear it?)

Academic Vocabulary

perspective *n.* (pur SPEK tiv) a belief or set of beliefs; opinion; way of looking at or thinking about something

Additional Support

English Language Coach

Building Background "Perspective is the rein and rudder of painting."
—Leonardo da Vinci

Artists also use purpose and perspective. When you look at a painting, can you tell which images are close and which are in the background? Why is this important? Without perspective, paintings don't look real! Photos show depth and location with shadows and size. Artists use the same tools to show perspective. Just as perspective in art shows you what artists see, perspective in writing tells you what writers "see." OL EL

Why Is It Important? You will understand more about what you read if you know where the author is "coming from." You need to be able to tell the difference between the topic and how the author thinks and feels about the topic. This helps you form your own opinions about the topic. **R**

How Do I Do It? You can begin to identify the author's purpose and perspective by looking at word choices and how the writing is organized. This will help you decide if the author is informing, expressing an opinion, or trying to persuade you.

Here's how one student identified the author's purpose and perspective in "Violence in Hockey."

It helps me understand the author's purpose and perspective by looking at his word choice. The title has the word violence. People don't usually write good things about violence, so I'm already thinking that the author is against violence in hockey. I notice that he uses the words mugged and thuggery. These words sound negative, so I think the author feels angry. I think his perspective has influenced his purpose for writing. He wants to convince readers that violence in hockey is dangerous and must be stopped.

Literature Online

Study Central Visit www.glencoe.com and click on Study Central to review identifying author's purpose and perspective.

Practice It!

In your Learner's Notebook write one possible purpose (entertain, inform, persuade, express a feeling) for each type of writing.

poem   mystery   advertisement   magazine article

Use It!

As you read, look for clues that will help you identify the author's purpose and perspective. Write more purposes in your Learner's Notebook.

Literature Online

Study Central Have students access the Web site to review identifying author's purpose and perspective and to complete a related activity.

Teach

R Reading Skill

Review Distinguishing Fact and Opinion Say: Reread *What Is It?* on page 454. Is this section fact (true) or opinion (the author's belief)? *(fact)* How does it help you read *Why Is It Important?* on this page? *(Possible response: Knowing the definitions of purpose and perspective helps me to decide if I agree with the writer's opinion of their importance.)* **OL**

Ask students to scan the Table of Contents for a title that suggests how an author feels about the topic. Have students explain their choices to the class. **OL**

Resources for page 455

- Use Reading Skills Transparency in *Read Aloud, Think Aloud,* Unit 4, to help students practice identifying author's purpose and perspective.

Reading in the Real World

Citizenship Ask students to read an editorial about an issue that is important or interesting to them. Have them identify the author's purpose and perspective. Ask them to list each of the author's supporting arguments. Then have students research the issue, noting facts that support or contradict the author's arguments. Students should then be prepared to evaluate how well the writer communicated his or her perspective and achieved the purpose of the editorial. **AL**

Objectives

- Identify author's purpose
- Identify author's perspective
- Distinguish fact from opinion

More About the Authors

Edna St. Vincent Millay was eight years old when her mother divorced Edna's schoolteacher father and moved with Edna and her sisters. Supporting her girls by nursing, sometimes overnight, Cora Millay raised her daughters to be independent and to love reading and music.

Eve Merriam, the daughter of Russian-born parents, began writing poetry at age seven or eight. She says her love of words began when she and her brother attended Gilbert and Sullivan musicals. Often, the two young Merriams would chant the tongue-twisting verses they had heard.

Literature Online

Author Search To expand students' appreciation of Edna St. Vincent Millay and Eve Merriam, have them access the Web site for additional information and resources.

Before You Read

The Courage That My Mother Had *and* Two People I Want to Be Like

Meet the Authors

Edna St. Vincent Millay

Edna St. Vincent Millay was born in Maine in 1892. As a young woman, she wrote poems but dreamed of becoming a pianist. After winning the Pulitzer Prize for poetry, she focused on her writing.

Eve Merriam

Eve Merriam was also an award-winning poet and playwright. Merriam was born in 1916 and died in 1992. See page R5 of the Author Files in the back of the book for more about these poets.

Literature Online

Author Search For more about Edna St. Vincent Millay and Eve Merriam, go to www.glencoe.com.

Objectives (pp. 458–461)
Reading Identify author's purpose
• Identify author's perspective
Literature Identify literary devices: diction, language, and word choice
Vocabulary Distinguish denotation and connotation

Vocabulary Preview

quarried (KWAYR eed) *adj.* cut or blasted from the earth for use in construction **(p. 458)** *Quarried marble is often used on floors and walls.*

brooch (brohch) *n.* a piece of jewelry pinned to one's clothing **(p. 458)** *The mother's brooch was her most beautiful and important jewelry.*

Write to Learn Copy these words into your Learner's Notebook. Next to each word, write the definition in your own words.

English Language Coach

Denotation and Connotation What is the denotation of the word *rock*? It is a very common word. When it is used as a noun, its dictionary definition is "hard, naturally formed mineral; stone." However, when it is used in a comparison or a simile, the word can have many different connotations. A rock can be heavy, solid, steady, strong, unmovable, or unbreakable.

Class Discussion Below are some sentences that use the word *rock.* As a group discuss the connotations of *rock* in each sentence. Are they different from each other?

"It was like talking to a rock."
"He fell like a rock."
"She was the rock of the family."
"That cake was hard as a rock."
"She stood like a rock for her beliefs."
"After the first punch, he dropped like a rock."
"They all have rocks in their heads."

In the first poem, the author describes her mother as having "courage like a rock." Do you know anyone like this?

Additional Support

Literature Focus Lesson

Persuasive Writing Although many genres can be persuasive, poetry is especially effective because it combines topic and emotion. When literature appeals to both the mind and the "heart," readers are engaged in every way.

Ask students to form small groups and to list five topics they feel would engage poetry readers. Ask them to select one topic on which they all share an opinion. Have them write and share a persuasive poem on this topic with the rest of the class. BL EL

Skills Preview

Key Reading Skill: Identifying Author's Purpose and Perspective

As you read each poem, look at the details the poet tells you and the words she chooses. Think about the poet's purpose. Is she trying to entertain you? Is she telling you something about herself or life? How does the author feel about her subject? What does she want you to feel or do? Write your thoughts in your Learner's Notebook.

Key Literary Element: Diction, Language, and Word Choice

Poetry is a compact form of writing. Every word and image counts. Poets choose their words very carefully. Use these tips to help you learn about the poet's choices.

- Think about the effect a certain word or phrase has on you.

  What does the word not *show about the man in the beginning of the second poem?*
- Think about why the poet uses an image or comparison.

  In the first poem, what does comparing the mother's courage to a rock say about the mother? L
- Think about how the diction, or choice and arrangement of words, fits the setting and topic of the poem.

  Why is the language in the second poem plain, with short phrases and no fancy words?

Literature Online

Interactive Literary Elements Handbook
To review or learn more about the literary elements, go to www.glencoe.com.

Get Ready to Read

Connect to the Reading

Think about a time when you noticed someone being kind or doing something special for a stranger. Maybe you saw someone carry groceries or fix a flat tire for someone they didn't know. What did you think about the person who was kind? R

Write to Learn In your Learner's Notebook, freewrite for one minute about how it makes you feel to see someone be kind or helpful to a stranger.

Build Background

Poetry is a type of writing that uses words, form, imagery, and figurative language to deliver its message.

- The form of a poem is the way it looks, or its structure.
- Poets use patterns of rhyme and rhythm to form their poems.
- When words help the reader see, hear, smell, taste, or feel what the poet is writing about, it's called imagery.
- When poets use figurative language, they use words that describe or express ideas beyond what they mean in the dictionary.

Set Purposes for Reading

Read "The Courage That My Mother Had" and "Two People I Want to Be Like" to find out how people influenced the speakers.

Set Your Own Purpose What would you like to learn from these poems to help you answer the Big Question? Write your own purpose on the Foldables for these selections.

Keep Moving

Use these skills as you read the following selections.

Reading Fluency

Build Fluency Some students better understand poetry if they read it aloud with a partner. Partners should:

- find a quiet place
- take turns reading the first line; the second partner will "echo" the first
- continue reading each line of the poem this way
- practice reading lines smoothly, with expression and understanding EL OL

Teach

R Reading Skill

Review Connecting Say: At the beginning of this workshop, you identified some traits you felt were important. As you read each poem, explain whether the people described in these poems display any of these traits. *(Responses will vary.)* EL OL

L Literary Element

Diction, Language, and Word Choice Ask: Why might rock imagery be an effective way to describe courage? *(Possible response: Courage is strong and not easily broken, just as hard rock isn't easily chipped or worn away.)* OL

CheckPoint

Use the CheckPoint questions provided on Presentation Plus! to check for identifying author's purpose and perspective and to build background. These questions can be used with interactive response keypads for immediate student feedback.

Literature Online

Interactive Literary Elements Handbook Have students access the Web site to improve their understanding of diction, language, and word choice.

Objectives
- Identify author's purpose
- Identify author's perspective
- Identify literary elements: diction, language, and word choice

READING WORKSHOP 3

Teach

EL Language Coach

Build Background Students may need help understanding the references to granite. **Ask: What items today are made of granite?** *(Possible responses: buildings, monuments, grave stones)* **Why do people choose granite as a building material?** *(It is hard and durable.)* OL

Ask: In what way can the speaker be wrong about what her mother has left her? *(Possible response: She could know more about courage than she thinks. Her mother may have modeled how to be brave and strong.)* AL

The Courage That My Mother Had

by Edna St. Vincent Millay

The courage that my mother had
Went with her, and is with her still:
Rock from New England **quarried**;
Now granite in a granite hill. EL

The golden **brooch** my mother wore
She left behind for me to wear;
I have no thing I treasure more:
Yet, it is something I could spare. **1**

Oh, if instead she'd left to me
The thing she took into the grave!—
That courage like a rock, which she
Has no more need of, and I have. **2** BQ

Vocabulary

quarried (KWAYR eed) *adj.* cut or blasted from the earth for use in construction

brooch (brohch) *n.* a piece of jewelry pinned to one's clothing

Practice the Skills

1 **Key Reading Skill**

Identifying Author's Purpose and Perspective How do you think the speaker feels about her mother? Is she happy to have the brooch?

2 **BIG Question**

How do you think the speaker's mother influenced her? Does she feel that her mother left her with enough courage? Write your answer on the Foldable for this selection. Your response will help you complete the Unit Challenge later.

The Way It Is. GG Kopilak. Private collection.

Additional Support

English Language Coach

Build Background Knowledge
Students may not be familiar with New England culture in the 1900s. Ask students to form small groups to research one aspect of the culture that influenced Millay: climate and terrain, family structure, role of women in society, economy and occupations, religion, recreation, or education. Using a computerized presentation program, students should share their findings with the class. OL AL

TWO PEOPLE I Want to Be Like

by Eve Merriam

That man
stuck in traffic
not pounding his fists against the steering wheel
not trying to shift to the next lane
just
using the time
for a slow steady grin
of remembering
all the good unstuck times

and that woman
clerking in the supermarket
at rush hour
bagging bottles and cartons and boxes and jars and
cans
punching it all out
slapping it all along
and leveling a smile
at everyone in the line. 3

I wish they were married to each other.

Maybe it's better they're not,
so they can pass their sweet harmony
around. 4 ❍

Practice the Skills

3 **Key Literary Element**

Diction, Language, and Word Choice Think about the words *punching* and *slapping* and the phrase *bagging bottles.* Think about how they sound as well as what they mean. How does the author's language affect the rhythm and the feeling of the poem?

4 **BIG Question**

Look back at the title of the poem. Why do you think the speaker wants to be like the two people described? Write your answer on the Foldable for this selection. Your response will help you answer the Unit Challenge later.

Teach

Viewing the Art

Ask: What emotions do you connect to the art on this page? *(Possible responses: panic, frustration)* How does the art help readers appreciate the man Merriam wants "to be like"? *(Possible response: Although the man could easily be angry or frustrated, he chooses to focus on good times.)* OL

C Critical Thinking

Analysis Say: Analyze the emotions of the situations and the people in the poem by finding sensory words to describe them. Choose a color and a sound to show the emotions of each scene. AL

EL Language Coach

Denotation, Connotation, and Semantic Slanting Say: The word *harmony* suggests a pleasant, peaceful blending of music, colors, and people. What sounds do you connect to the situations in the poem? *(Possible responses: loud, honking horns and shouting drivers; beeping scanners and whining children)* BL EL

Use the CheckPoint questions provided on Presentation Plus! to check for comprehension of the selections. These questions can be used with interactive response keypads for immediate student feedback.

Reading in the Real World

College Discuss the stress that studying, test taking, and major writing assignments have on college students. Ask students to work in pairs to develop a "less stressful plan" for college. The plan should include:

- the situation
- the student's feelings
- a step-by-step plan
- an explanation of why the plan should work AL

Objectives
- Analyze works of art
- Understand how word choices influence thoughts and emotions

Assess

Resources for page 460

- Selection Quick Check
- Selection and Unit Assessment
- ExamView Assessment Suite
- Interactive Tutor: Self-Assessment

Students can respond to the *After You Read* items in their Learner's Notebook or on a separate sheet of paper.

Answering the

1. Answers will vary.
2. Millay compares her mother's courage to a rock or granite.
3. The mother has left the daughter a brooch.
4. Merriam focuses on a man caught in traffic and a woman working in a supermarket checkout.

Critical Thinking

5. Answers will vary.
6. Possible responses should include the idea that the man is *not* reacting in a typical fashion to a traffic jam—with impatience and anger. The poet uses the *absence* of these behaviors to contrast the man's acceptance of the situation.
7. Answers will vary, but should include the idea that Merriam wants to persuade readers that choosing to react positively in stressful situations is a good thing.

After You Read

The Courage That My Mother Had *and* Two People I Want to Be Like

Objectives (pp. 460–461)
Reading Identify author's purpose • Identify author's perspective
Literature Identify literary elements: diction, language, and word choice
Vocabulary Distinguish denotation and connotation
Grammar Identify subjects and predicates

Answering the

1. In the second poem, the speaker is influenced by two people she doesn't even know. Name someone you don't know very well who has influenced you. How did they influence you?
2. **Recall** To what does Millay compare the mother's courage?
   TIP Right There
3. **Recall** What is the one thing the mother has left the daughter?
   TIP Right There
4. **Recall** Who does Merriam focus on in her poem?
   TIP Right There

Critical Thinking

5. **Respond** What feeling does the setting of the poem create for you?
   TIP Author and Me
6. **Interpret** Why do you think Merriam describes what the first person is *not* doing?
   TIP Author and Me
7. What do you think Merriam's purpose was in writing this poem?
   TIP Author and Me

Talk About Your Reading

Literature Groups Most poetry should be read aloud to be fully appreciated. As a poem is read, listeners may close their eyes, picture the images, and hear the natural rhythm of the lines. In your group, take turns reading these poems to each other. Discuss the images that come to mind and the rhythms you hear.

Write to Learn Are the images and rhythms different when different group members read. If so, why? Write your answer in a short paragraph and discuss your answer with your group.

Skills Review

Key Reading Skill: Identifying Author's Purpose and Perspective

8. Freewrite your thoughts on why Millay wrote this poem. In your opinion, did she want to inform, entertain, express a feeling, or persuade? How do you know?
9. Freewrite your thoughts on why Merriam wrote "Two People I Want to Be Like"? Was her purpose to inform, entertain, express a feeling, persuade, or something else entirely?

Key Literary Element: Diction, Language, and Word Choice

10. In either poem, find two words that describe something. Write the lines with these words and circle the words.
11. Why do you think the poet used these descriptive words? How do they help you visualize the poem?

Vocabulary Check

For each sentence below, choose the vocabulary word that could replace the underlined word. Rewrite each sentence with the vocabulary word in place.

quarried
brooch

12. The **pin** on her dress was very old and valuable.
13. The marble was **taken** from an underground cave.
14. **Academic Vocabulary** How would you describe the author's perspective in "Two People I Want to Be Like"? How does the poet "see" the people in the poem?
15. **English Language Coach** Think about the connotations of the word *grin.* How would "Two People I Want to Be Like" be different if the poet had used a synonym, such as *smile* or *beam*?

Grammar Link: Subjects and Predicates

Every sentence has two parts: a subject and a predicate.

- The **complete subject** tells who or what a sentence is about.
- The **complete predicate** tells what the subject is doing, being, or has.

Al and his brother play basketball.

Who plays basketball? Al and his brother.
The complete subject is "Al and his brother."

What do Al and his brother do?

They play basketball.
The complete predicate is "play basketball."

Al and his brother play basketball

Grammar Practice

16. On a separate piece of paper, write three sentences of your own. In each, underline the complete subject once and the complete predicate twice.
17. On a separate sheet of paper, copy one of the poems you have just read. For each sentence in the poem, underline the complete subject once and the complete predicate twice.

Writing Application Choose a paragraph you wrote in your Learner's Notebook. Check to see if your subjects and predicates were clear. If they were not clear, rewrite to clarify your sentences.

Web Activities For eFlashcards, Selection Quick Checks, and other Web activities, go to www.glencoe.com.

Skills Review

Key Reading Skill: Identifying Author's Purpose and Perspective

8. Possible responses: Express a feeling: I thought Millay wanted to express that she was angry that her mother had not left her courage, which she needed. The last stanza of the poem gives me this idea.
9. Responses will vary.

Key Literary Element: Diction, Language, and Word Choice

10. Responses will vary but should include lines with adjectives or figurative language.
11. Responses will vary.

Vocabulary Check

12. brooch
13. quarried
14. Responses will vary but should include that the poet admires the two people in her poem and "sees" their behavior as providing positive role models for others.
15. Responses will vary but should include that the poem would imply that there was more going on, perhaps in the man's thoughts.

Close

Ask students to write a paragraph about a person who models the character trait they most value.

Grammar Link: Subjects and Predicates

Grammar Practice

16. Responses will vary.
17. Responses will vary.

Literature Online

Web Activities Have students access the Web site for interactive activities that will help them assess their understanding of the selection.

Teach

R Reading Skill

Identifying Author's Purpose and Perspective

Say: The wording and punctuation of a title often give readers clues about an author's purpose. What can you guess about the author's purpose and perspective by this title? *(Possible response: The word* welcome *makes me think the author wants to invite people to volunteer. The exclamation point tells me the author is excited about the topic.)* OL

L Literary Element

Diction, Language, and Word Choice **Say:** Verbs are powerful words in language. Authors choose them carefully to add life and energy to their writing. Think of more powerful words for these common verbs: like, walk, smile. *(Possible response: adore, saunter, grin)* OL

Before You Read

Volunteers Welcome! R

Meet the Author

Who writes museum brochures? It may be museum employees or people at an advertising agency. The same is true for many other organizations and businesses that use brochures to inform the public about their products and services.

Literature Online

Author Search For more about brochure writers, go to www.glencoe.com.

Objectives (pp. 462–465)
Reading Identify author's purpose
• Identify author's perspective
Literature Identify literary elements: diction, language, and word choice
Vocabulary Distinguish denotation and connotation

Vocabulary Preview

energized (EN ur jyzd) *adj.* active or lively; a form of the verb *energize* **(p. 465)** *The energized workers put in a long day's work.*

enhance (en HANS) *v.* to improve; make better or bigger **(p. 465)** *New trees and flowers will enhance the appearance of the park.*

Write to Learn In your Learner's Notebook, write a sentence about each of these.

- something that *energizes* you in the morning
- a way to *enhance* the look of your school

Next, in your Learner's Notebook, write the words *energized* and *enhanced.* Next to each word, write what you already know about it. If you don't know the word very well, write "I will learn this word by the end of the story."

English Language Coach

Semantic Slanting "Semantic slanting" means deliberately using words to create particular emotional responses. A writer might "slant" what he or she writes in an effort to create a positive response or a negative one. Any time someone wants to persuade someone else to do or believe something, semantic slanting is probably involved.

L In the selection "Volunteers Welcome!" the statement "Get energized! Meet . . . for juice, coffee, donuts, and fruit" simply means "Wake up and eat breakfast."

When you are not sure whether something you read is slanted, try to say the same thing in words that do not have strong positive or negative connotations.

Individual Activity Look through a magazine or newspaper and try to find an example of semantic slanting. It can be in an advertisement, an article, or an editorial.

Additional Support

Literature Focus Lesson

Persuasive Writing Many organizations depend on volunteers for help. Sometimes they must compete with other organizations for volunteers. Ask students to interview a community agency that uses volunteer help. Students should identify what the agency does and the functions volunteers serve. Ask students to create a newspaper ad, poster, or other persuasive document that will encourage friends or classmates to volunteer. OL

Skills Preview

Key Reading Skill: Identifying Author's Purpose and Perspective

One of the best ways to understand an author's perspective is to learn about the author, but in this case we don't know who the author is. What can we figure out, though? Well, both authors work or volunteer for the places that need the volunteers. What does that tell you about their perspective? Preview the selections. Who do you think is the audience? What does that tell you about the authors' perspectives? In your Learner's Notebook, make notes on your thoughts.

Key Literary Element: Diction, Language, and Word Choice

As you read the next two selections, think about which words are used and how those words are put together. The selections are meant to get people interested in volunteering and to get information about those people. Keep these questions in mind as you read the selections:

- Are the selections easy to preview?
- Do the selections use complete sentences?
- Is the language simple or complicated?
- Do the authors include a lot of details?

Keep in mind that the choice of words and how those words are put together are very important in semantic slanting. For example, the writer of the first selection uses words like "inspire," "gain," and "receive." The writer of the second selection uses phrases like "get energized" and "get connected." How does this language affect the selections?

Literature Online

Interactive Literary Elements Handbook To review or learn more about the literary elements, go to www.glencoe.com.

Get Ready to Read

Connect to the Reading

A volunteer is someone who works for no pay. If you had to write an application to persuade people to work for free, how would you do it? How would you keep the reader's interest? How would you make the job sound fun?

Class Talk As a class, talk about some times you tried to convince someone to help you. How did you do it? Were you successful? Why or why not?

Build Background

Museums and community centers are great places. They have exhibits and activities for people of all ages and backgrounds. But exhibits and activities cost money. When there isn't enough money, volunteers are often needed to help. Why do people volunteer?

- Volunteers often get things for free that most people pay for. For example, a volunteer usher at a theater may see a play without buying a ticket.
- Volunteers may get experience that they can use later in a paying job.
- L Many people volunteer because it makes them happy to help other people.

Set Purposes for Reading

Read the two volunteer application forms. Find out if the authors are able to influence you to become a volunteer.

Set Your Own Purpose What would you like to learn from the selections to help you answer the Big Question? Write your own purpose on the "Volunteers Welcome!" page of Foldable 4.

Keep Moving

Use these skills as you read the following selections.

Teach

L Literary Element

Diction, Language, and Word Choice **Say:** When parents want to persuade you to do something, they often choose words that assume you will. Instead of asking *if you will,* they say *when you do.* Find examples of this style in the two readings on pages 464 and 465. *(Possible responses: MOIT—you'll be a way-finder, you'll help visitors; Cleanup—Meet at the center, get energized/grounded/connected)* **OL**

CheckPoint

Use the CheckPoint questions provided on Presentation Plus! to check for identifying author's purpose and perspective and to build background. These questions can be used with interactive response keypads for immediate student feedback.

Literature Online

Interactive Literary Elements Handbook Have students access the Web site to improve their understanding of diction, language, and word choice.

Reading Fluency

Reading and Listening Some students find that persuasive writing is more effective if it is read aloud. Ask students to practice reading each selection aloud. Then ask them to read a selection to a partner. The partner should listen for

- understanding: Does the reader understand the selection?
- emotion: Does the reader convey the author's perspective using voice, facial expressions, and gestures?
- purpose: Did the reader convince you to volunteer? **BL** **EL**

Objectives

- Identify author's purpose
- Identify author's perspective
- Identify literary elements: diction, language, and word choice
- Distinguish denotation from connotation

Teach

R Reading Skill

Identifying Author's Purpose and Perspective

Ask: Based on the information and tone of the selection, what might you infer that the writer does for a living or a hobby? *(Possible response: coordinates museum volunteers)* OL AL

BQ BIG Question

Ask: What would you ask someone who was influenced to volunteer by this selection?*(Possible responses: What specifically influenced you to volunteer? Do you like meeting, helping, and working with people?)* OL

EL Language Coach

Denotation, Connotation, and Semantic Slanting

Say: If you think back to your first doctor's visit, you may remember being told that it would be *quick, fun,* or *painless.* Choosing words that put a positive "spin" on something is one method of semantic slanting. Which word in the MOIT announcement leads you to believe that signing up is easy? *(simple)* EL BL

INFORMATIONAL TEXT
BROCHURE

Volunteers Welcome!

MOIT Museum of Industry and Technology Volunteer Information and Application

WHAT YOU'LL DO

Depending on *your* skills and interests and *our* needs, you'll be a

- **presenter,** involving visitors in interactive demonstrations.[1]
- **project assistant,** leading craft projects and other activities.
- **sales assistant,** helping visitors choose gifts and souvenirs. 1

R WHAT YOU'LL GET

The Museum of Industry and Technology seeks to inspire genius.[2] You'll

- help to inspire a million visitors each year.
- polish old skills and gain new ones.
- receive discounts in the store, restaurant, and parking garage.
- meet new people and have fun. 2

HOW YOU CAN VOLUNTEER

EL To become a volunteer, follow these simple steps:

1. **Promise to work at least 30 hours a year.** You can volunteer once a month, once a week, or every day. Volunteer work hours are 10:00 A.M. to 5:00 P.M. Tuesday through Saturday.
2. BQ **Fill out the application form** and deliver it to the Volunteer Office.
3. **Schedule an interview** so we can find the best spot for you.
4. **Attend one Saturday-morning orientation.**[3]

LAST NAME		FIRST NAME	AGE ☐ 14-18 ☐ 19-65 ☐ 66 and up
STREET ADDRESS	APT		
CITY		STATE	ZIP
EMAIL ADDRESS OR PHONE		BEST TO CALL (check all that apply) ☐ weekday ☐ weekend ☐ day ☐ evening ☐ home ☐ work	

1. In an ***interactive demonstration,*** a visitor gets involved. For example, they might push a button to hear a recording or view a video.
2. Here, ***genius*** has to do with smartness and creativity.
3. An ***orientation*** is a class where volunteers learn about the work they'll be doing.

Practice the Skills

1 Key Reading Skill

Identifying Author's Purpose and Perspective Why did the writer create this application? Notice that the writer puts the focus on the reader rather than on the museum.

2 Reviewing Skills

Drawing Conclusions In Unit 3 you learned how to figure out more than what a writer tells you directly. Rethink the idea of a discount here. Volunteers work for free when they could be doing jobs that pay. What conclusion could you draw about whether museum discounts are really a great benefit?

Additional Support

English Language Coach

Graphic Organizer Say: The selection describes a simple process for becoming a volunteer. Diagram the steps. BL

READING WORKSHOP 3

VOLUNTEER TO TAKE A BITE OUT OF GRIME

Riverside's 20th Annual Cleanup Day

Saturday, May 7, 2007

READY!

- 8:00 A.M. Get **energized!** Meet at the Community Center, 1170 E. Walnut, for juice, coffee, donuts, and fruit.

The first 100 volunteers to arrive will be given birch seedlings![4]

- 8:30 A.M. Get grounded! Celebrate Arbor Day by planting a tree and meeting the village arborist[5] Jim Day.
- 9:00 A.M. Get connected! Join teams headed by the mayor and city council members. Then clean up the village. Gloves and trash bags will be provided.
- 12:30 P.M. Get fed! Meet back at the Community Center for lunch.

SET!

Signing up isn't required, but will help us plan for breakfast and lunch. To volunteer, sign up by *Wednesday, May 4.* Call Maria at 555-2647, or fill out the form below and mail it to Village Hall, 1182 E. Walnut St., Riverside. **3**

GO!

NAME ____________ # OF OTHERS WHO WILL BE VOLUNTEERING WITH ME ____________

ADDRESS ____________ PHONE ____________

KEEP RIVERSIDE BEAUTIFUL!

- Homeowners: Spruce up your street, yard, and home.
- Business owners: **Enhance** the appearance of your buildings.
- Church and school leaders: Arrange cleanup projects around your facilities. **4**
- Everyone: Donate the price of a tree to be planted in a Riverside park.

For more information, call Maria at the Parks Department (555-2647). **5**

L

Riverside Cleanup Day Maria/Parks Department 555-2647	Riverside Cleanup Day Maria/Parks Department 555-2647	Riverside Cleanup Day Maria/Parks Department 555-2647	Riverside Cleanup Day Maria/Parks Department 555-2647	Riverside Cleanup Day Maria/Parks Department 555-2647	Riverside Cleanup Day Maria/Parks Department 555-2647	Riverside Cleanup Day Maria/Parks Department 555-2647

R

4. Young plants grown from seeds are ***seedlings.*** The ***birch*** is a particular kind of tree.
5. An ***arborist*** is an expert at growing and taking care of trees.

Vocabulary

energized (EN ur jyzd) *adj.* active or lively

enhance (en HANS) *v.* to improve; make better or bigger

Practice the Skills

3 Key Literary Element

Diction, Language, and Word Choice Why does the writer use the words, "Ready! Set! Go!" to organize the information? The words are energetic and call up ideas of a race or competition. They also move the reader quickly through the document.

4 Key Reading Skill

Identifying Author's Purpose and Perspective Does the writer seem to believe that volunteering is a good idea?

5 BIG Question

What are these selections trying to do? Write your answer on the "Volunteers Welcome!" page of Foldable 4. Your response will help you answer the Unit Challenge later. **BQ**

Teach

R Reading Skill

Identifying Author's Purpose and Perspective

Ask: What do the tear-off tabs at the bottom of this announcement tell about the author's purpose? *(Possible response: The author provides the tabs as informational tools for readers who are persuaded to volunteer.)* **BL OL**

L Literary Element

Diction, Language, and Word Choice **Ask:** Why did the author address homeowners, business owners, church and school leaders, and everyone in the bottom section? *(Possible response: The author wanted to stress that everyone could help on Cleanup Day.)* **OL**

BQ

Ask: What cause would most influence you to volunteer to help? *(Possible responses: animal shelter fund-raising and collecting food and clothing for the needy)* Where would you most likely hear about a volunteer opportunity? *(Possible responses: radio, TV, school announcements, store bulletin boards)* **EL OL**

Reading in the Real World

Citizenship Ask students to scan local newspapers for community agencies and projects that need volunteers. Have students form groups of three or four and ask them to contact an organization that needs student volunteers. After they have determined what, when, where, and how much help is needed, have students propose a method of communicating this need to the school community. The method should be approved by the organization and the school. **OL**

Objectives

- Analyze topics that influence thoughts and actions
- Identify persuasive writing techniques
- Identify author's purpose and perspective

Assess

Resources for page 466

- Selection Quick Check
- Selection and Unit Assessment
- ExamView Assessment Suite
- Interactive Tutor: Self-Assessment

Students can respond to the Students can respond to the *After You Read* items in their Learner's Notebook or on a separate sheet of paper.

Answering the

1. Responses will vary.
2. The subject is the need for volunteers to work at the museum.
3. The subject is the need for volunteers to help clean up the community.

Critical Thinking

4. Responses will vary but should include the idea that volunteering at the museum is worthwhile for both the museum and the volunteers.
5. Possible responses may focus on the idea that using a different kind of tone may make the idea of volunteering less appealing.
6. Responses will vary but should include the idea that the author seems to feel that Cleanup Day is fun, important, and open to everyone.
7. Responses will vary.
8. Responses will vary.

After You Read

Volunteers Welcome!

MOIT **Museum of Industry and Technology Volunteer Information and Application**

WHAT YOU'LL DO

Depending on *your* skills and interests and *our* needs, you'll be a

- **presenter,** involving visitors in interactive demonstrations.[1]
- **project assistant,** leading craft projects and other activities.
- **sales assistant**, helping visitors choose gifts and souvenirs. 1

WHAT YOU'LL GET

The Museum of Industry and Technology seeks to inspire genius.[2] You'll

- help to inspire a million visitors each year.
- polish old skills and gain new ones.

Objectives (pp. 466–467)
Reading Identify author's purpose • Identify author's perspective
Literature Identify literary elements: diction, language, and word choice
Vocabulary Recognize semantic slanting
Writing Write a persuasive paragraph
Grammar Identify complete subjects and predicates • Recognize the understood subject in commands and requests

Answering the

1. After reading both of the applications, which job would you rather volunteer for? Why?
2. **Recall** What is the subject of the museum application?
   TIP **Right There**
3. **Recall** What is the subject of the second application?
   TIP **Right There**

Critical Thinking

4. **Summarize** What is the main message in the museum application?
   TIP **Think and Search**
5. **Infer** How would the Cleanup Day application be different if the writer used a different tone?
   TIP **Author and Me**
6. **Infer** What do you think the author wants you to feel about volunteering for Cleanup Day?
   TIP **Think and Search**
7. **Evaluate** Do you think these are effective applications?
   TIP **Author and Me**
8. **Synthesize** What would you say to persuade your classmates to sign up for Cleanup Day? Explain your answer.
   TIP **On Your Own**

Write About Your Reading

Write a paragraph saying why you want to volunteer for something. It can be working in a community garden, at the local library, on building a new skateboard park, or something you think up yourself. The point is that your language and word choice must inspire the readers. You must convince the readers that they would be good volunteers and that the place for which they want to volunteer really needs them.

Write About Your Reading

Possible response:

Dear Class,

I wanted to tell you all about the exciting time I've been having as a volunteer at the natural history museum! It's the best! I've learned so much about ancient people and archaeology. I even had the chance to hold a real dinosaur bone! How cool is that? I get discounts in the cafeteria and in all the stores, and I can see all of the special exhibits for free. All it takes is 3 hours of my time one weekend a month. I almost forgot to mention the best part—it's also a great way to meet a lot of new and interesting people!

Skills Review

Key Reading Skill: Identifying Author's Purpose and Perspective

9. In the museum application, what parts of the application gave you clues about the author's purpose?

10. In the Clean Up Day application, what parts of the application gave you clues about the author's purpose?

11. In each application, what do you think is the author's perspective? What clues helped you figure out the author's perspective?

Key Literary Element: Diction, Language, and Word Choice

12. If you want to persuade someone that a museum is a neat place, which words are better: "The place inspires genius" or "A lot of learning happens"?

13. Would you describe the language in these applications as friendly or unfriendly? Why?

14. Pick three words from the applications that appeal to you as a reader. What do you like about them?

Vocabulary Check

15. In which of the following sentences is *energized* used correctly?
- **a.** The energized snow fell all afternoon.
- **b.** The energized runners broke records.
- **c.** Tony was so energized that he fell asleep.

16. In which of the following sentences is *enhance* used correctly?
- **a.** The museum will enhance to open early.
- **b.** A tornado will enhance the city.
- **c.** These spices will enhance the flavor.

17. **English Language Coach** These selections put a positive slant on activities that volunteers perform. There are usually some things a volunteer might be asked to do that are not much fun. Think of one such duty or activity. Write a sentence that describes it in a way that makes it sound exciting, fun, interesting, or, at least, not awful.

Grammar Link: Subjects and Predicates

What are the complete subject and complete predicate of the following sentence?

- Turn down that radio now!

If you said *turn down that radio now* is the complete predicate, you're right. But what's the subject? Does the command even have a subject?

Yes, it does. The subject of the above command is the word *you*. Yet *you* is not written down or spoken in many commands and requests. It's just "understood" that the subject is *you*.

Grammar Practice

Copy each sentence below. If it's a declarative sentence, underline the subject. If it's a command or request and doesn't include a subject, write the sentence again, adding the word *You* as the subject.

18. Don't be late.

19. Trees grow.

20. Please stop that.

21. Juan had an interview.

22. Grow up!

23. Mom gave me five bucks.

Web Activities For eFlashcards, Selection Quick Checks, and other Web activities, go to www.glencoe.com.

Skills Review

Key Reading Skill: Identifying Author's Purpose and Perspective

9. "What You'll Do" and "What You'll Get"

10. "Ready," "Set," and "Keep Riverside Beautiful!"

11. Possible response: Volunteering benefits everyone. The authors both presented the advantages of volunteering for the volunteers and for the recipients of the service, the museum, and the Riverside community.

Key Literary Element: Diction, Language, and Word Choice

12. "The place inspires genius."

13. Responses will vary but should include support for the idea that the language is friendly.

14. Responses will vary.

Vocabulary Check

15. b

16. c

17. Responses will vary.

Close

ASK students to write a paragraph explaining how well the applications persuaded them to volunteer.

Grammar Link: Subjects and Predicates

Grammar Practice

18. *You don't be late.* (imperative)

19. *<u>Trees</u> grow.* (declarative)

20. *You please stop that.* (imperative)

21. *<u>Juan</u> had an interview.* (declarative)

22. *You grow up!* (imperative)

23. *<u>Mom</u> gave me five bucks.* (declarative)

Focus

BELLRINGER Options

Daily Language Practice Transparency

Focus Activity Say: It's time to reread your draft. Ask yourself: Did I clearly state the problem? Is the solution easy for readers to understand? Does my editorial persuade readers to change how they feel, think, or act?

Teach

C Critical Thinking

Evaluation Ask: Why might people read editorials critically? *(Possible response: They are looking for evidence that persuades them to agree or disagree with the writer's opinion.)* OL

W Writing

Tone Ask: Why should you consider tone as you revise your draft? *(Tone affects how people accept the message.)* OL

Resources for page 468

Use the Grammar and Writing Workshop Transparencies, Unit 4.

WRITING WORKSHOP PART 2

Editorial

Revising, Editing, and Presenting

ASSIGNMENT Write an editorial

Purpose: To take a stand on a problem, propose a solution, and persuade others to agree with you

Audience: You, your teacher, other students at your school, or the general public

Revising Rubric

Your revised editorial should have

- evidence to support your ideas
- responses to possible counterarguments
- precise and lively word choices
- an emotional appeal
- an appropriate style and tone for the audience and the purpose

Objectives (pp. 468–473)
Writing Revise your writing for key elements, style, and word choice • Present your writing
Listening, Speaking, and Viewing Recognize and distinguish persuasive techniques

You've already chosen a topic, organized your ideas, and written a draft of your editorial. You've done a lot of work! Now it's time to revise, edit, and share your draft with your audience. Also, you'll keep a copy of it in a writing portfolio so that you and your teacher can evaluate your writing progress over time.

Revising

Make It Better

Even a good draft can be improved. Revising can help organize your writing, clarify your points, and make your editorial more persuasive.

Check for Key Elements

W

Read over your draft and add any important information that your editorial is missing. These questions may help guide your revisions.

- Does the beginning of your editorial explain the problem in an interesting way to grab readers' attention?
- Does your editorial include evidence that supports your points?
- Does your editorial respond to possible counterarguments?
- Does your editorial make an emotional appeal to your readers?

Rearrange Your Reasons

The order of your points can affect how persuasive your writing is. This activity can help you figure out the most convincing order for your ideas.

1. Draw a line down the center of a piece of paper to make two columns.
2. Read through your draft and find the main reasons you give to support your opinion.
3. In the first column, write down the reasons in order from the *most* important reason to the *least* important reason.
4. In the second column, write down the same reasons in the opposite order—from *least* important to *most* important.
5. Look at your lists and think about which order is more convincing. If you like, talk it over with a friend before making a decision.
6. Reorder the points in your editorial so they are in the most persuasive order.

Additional Support

English Language Coach

Denotation, Connotation, and Semantic Slanting Write this paragraph on the board: Look around you in the lunchroom. What do you see? People talking, laughing, eating? Is that all? Maybe you don't see the big pile of food in the garbage. I do! Throwing away food is a bad thing. Why not take only what you can eat? It's a good way to live! **Ask:** How can the underlined words be revised to show more emotion? *(Possible responses: chattering, giggling, munching, notice, enormous, terrible waste, terrific)* Ask students to revise their writing by replacing *blah* words with more exact choices. OL

Applying Good Writing Traits

Word Choice

Words work hard. They carry your ideas into the minds of your readers, so make sure you choose them carefully.

Analyzing Cartoons
Old and *lazy* may not be the best word choices.

What Is Word Choice?

Word choice is the use of interesting and precise words that clearly express the writer's images and ideas.

Why Is Word Choice Important?

Word choice affects how well readers can "see" the image you have in your mind.

The squirrel ran under the stove.

The squirrel scurried across the floor and squeezed under the stove.

Word choice also gives readers a sense of your **style** and **tone**—your writing voice and your attitude toward your subject. You're not there with readers to explain what you meant to say, how you really feel about your subject, or how the image in your head really looked. So your words have to deliver your message for you. **W**

How Do I Use Word Choice in My Writing?

- Use lively verbs to show action. Avoid boring verbs such as *do*, *go*, and *make*. Instead use more specific and energetic words such as *cackle, create, dazzle, flail, float, glow, launch, poke, pounce, scratch, sprint, and sprout.*
- Add adjectives and adverbs to your writing. Instead of writing about *the couch*, write about *the overstuffed couch*. Instead of saying *kids watch* TV explain that *kids stare blankly* at it.
- Use specific nouns. Avoid using the word *thing* whenever possible. Take the time to think of the word that names what you're writing about. If you don't know the word for the item, use as specific a term as you can. For instance, *gadget* is a general word for a small tool or mechanical device.
- Keep your vocabulary natural. Big words can get in the way of meaning if you use them incorrectly or you use too many of them. Use a thesaurus only with careful thought. Otherwise, you may end up writing sentences that don't make sense, like the sentence below.

TV can be a foundation of information and entertainment, but it can also keep you from burden other belongings with your time.

Write to Learn Activity Read through your draft carefully and look for boring and general words. If you find one, replace it with a more energetic and specific word. **R**

WRITING WORKSHOP PART 2

Teach

R Reading Skill

Review Distinguishing Fact and Opinion Say: Newspaper and magazine editors check the facts in their editorials very carefully. If an opinion is presented as fact, readers may lose confidence in the writer and refuse to be persuaded by their message.
Ask students to reread their drafts. Have them underline sentences presented as fact. Ask them to double-check each sentence to be sure it can be proved true. **EL** **OL**

Resources for page 469

 Use the Writing Workshop Graphic Organizer BLM in Unit 4 Resource Booklet.

W Writing

Word Choice Students may want to brainstorm a list of action verbs and descriptive adjectives and adverbs. They can then use their lists to revise their drafts.

Literature Focus Lesson

Persuasive Writing To help students write solid arguments, show a video of a two-person debate. **Say:** In a debate, one speaker argues to support a position. The other finds mistakes in those arguments. After the video, have students form groups and create a two-column chart. They should list arguments in the first column and counterarguments in the second. Have them use this format to check each other's drafts for possible counterarguments. **OL**

Objectives

- Revise writing for word choice, style, and tone
- Edit writing for sentence fragments and sentence run-ons
- Distinguish fact and opinion

Teach

W Writing

Argument Say: When you read your draft, does your passion for the issue burst through? If not, you may want to use hyperbole to liven up your writing. Hyperbole is exaggeration. You use hyperbole to emphasize how strongly you feel. Listen as I read a paragraph about school uniforms. What hyperbole do you hear?

Who wants to look like a zillion other people? That's what school uniforms do to kids! I have to wear a uniform five days a week, and I detest it. It's like smearing myself with invisible ink before I leave home. No one on the planet notices me at school because everyone looks the same. Just once, I'd like to wear bright orange or purple or neon green. Someone rescue me from school uniforms! *(Possible responses: "zillion other people," "like smearing myself with invisible ink," "no one on the planet," "rescue me")* Ask students to revise their editorials to include at least one example of hyperbole. OL

Send the Right Message

Remember that **style** is what makes a writer's work different from the work of all other writers. Word choice, sentence length, level of formality, and the information the writer chooses to provide are all part of a writer's style. **Tone** is a writer's attitude toward the subject. The tone can be angry, sad, humorous, or serious, for example.

The style and the tone of your editorial should be appropriate for the subject and the audience. The audience of your editorial is most likely a general audience, or a mixed group of people that you don't know. When you write for a general audience, your style should be formal.

- Use complete sentences.
- Use Standard English (not slang).

If you're writing for young children, be sure to choose words they understand.

Your tone should show respect for your topic and the thoughts, feelings, and experiences of your audience.

- If you're writing about a serious problem, your tone should be serious. A light and joking tone may make your readers feel hurt or angry.
- If you're writing about something funny, humor should come through your ideas and words on the page.

These sentences have a concerned tone. The style is formal, but not boring.

As a result, some kids don't get enough exercise and gain weight.

Kids who like to pretend to be such TV characters can get trapped in a fantasy world.

Writing Tip

Style and Tone If you have trouble recognizing the style and tone of your writing, read your editorial aloud. Hearing the words may help you recognize how formal your writing is and the attitude you show toward your subject.

W

Read your draft and think about the style and tone of your writing. Ask yourself the following questions.

- Does my writing sound like me?
- Does the formality or informality of my writing match my audience?
- Does my writing reflect how I feel about my topic?
- Is my tone appropriate for my topic and audience?

If you answer *no* to any of the above questions, start revising. Your writing should sound as formal and serious as you would if you were talking to your audience face-to-face about your topic.

Additional Support

Reading in the Real World

College Students who plan to attend college may wonder about the kinds of writing they'll do in college and where they can go for help. Help students develop a list of questions. See if the director or a tutor at a college writing center will respond to their questions. Also, familiarize students with online writing resources, such as spell check, dictionary and thesaurus, and writing instruction Web sites. OL

Editing

Finish It Up

Don't let mistakes take away from the persuasive power of your editorial! For your final copy, read your editorial one sentence at a time and use the **Editing Checklist** to help you spot errors. Use the proofreading symbols in the chart on page R74 to mark needed corrections.

Editing Checklist

- ☑ The editorial is free of sentence fragments.
- ☑ All sentences end with the correct punctuation.
- ☑ Spelling is correct.
- ☑ Capitalization is correct.

Writing Tip

Punctuation Place a question mark or exclamation point inside quotation marks when it punctuates the quotation and outside when it punctuates the main sentence.

Writing Tip

Spelling Remember this spelling rule: There are exceptions to every rule. So use a dictionary to double-check the spelling of any words you're not sure about.

Presenting

Show It Off

Read your editorial to a small group of your classmates. As you read, be sure to vary the volume and pitch of your voice to emphasize your main points.

As your classmates read their editorials, listen carefully to figure out which parts are fact and which parts are opinion. Then give the speaker feedback about the logic and the persuasiveness of the editorial.

Submit a neatly written or typed copy of your editorial to your school or local newspaper. Or post it on the Internet. To find a good Web site, try an Internet search for sites dedicated to your topic.

Writing Tip

Handwriting Your editorial won't be published if it can't be read! Carefully form your letters and space your words. Then read over your editorial one more time to be sure you dotted your i's and crossed your t's.

WRITING WORKSHOP PART 2

Teach

W Writing

Persuasive Techniques Write the following paragraph on the board.

Wake up, people! The problem of stray and abandoned animals will not go away. What are you doing to help? Not enough! Today, animal rescue centers are struggling to stay open. Many communities no longer support them with money and staff. They try to keep their doors open by raising money through "pet walks," dances, and other means. Feeling bad when you see a scrawny puppy and lost kitten doesn't do the trick. Put your money and time where your heart is. Act now!

Ask: What are some examples of techniques the author uses to convey purpose and perspective? *(punctuation, action verbs, connotative words, imperative sentences)* **What are the author's purpose and perspective?** *(Possible reponse: The author's purpose is to make people aware of the problem of stray and abandoned animals. The author's perspective is that people should invest their money and time in helping these animals.)* **EL** **OL**

English Language Coach

Semantic Slanting Ask: How often do people misinterpret what you say? When you talk about being busy, some might hear complaining, but others might hear bragging. Does the word choice of your editorial give the "slant" you want readers to hear? Ask students to write the topic and several key words from their drafts on a note card. Collect the cards and read them aloud, asking students to identify the slant they hear. **EL** **OL**

Objectives

- Identify tone and style and recognize how they influence readers
- Use word choice to communicate thoughts and emotions
- Identify author's purpose and perspective

Teach

W Writing

Style Ask: If you were late for a meeting and stopped for directions, which response would you prefer?

1. *First you have to go a few blocks and you'll see a kind of fast food place or grocery store, I'm not sure which. Anyway, I think you turn left there and go another few blocks until you see a tall sign. Keep going until you come to a street with a tree name, like Elm or Oak. Turn right and go down a ways. The building should be somewhere on this street.*

2. *Drive south on Baxter three blocks. Turn left onto Plum. Travel three blocks and turn right on Spruce Street. The third building on the right is the one you want.*

(Possible response: I like the second one because the first one is vague and takes too long.)

Give students a checklist to make their writing style clear and concise:

- Remove unnecessary words.
- Use active voice.
- Remove details that readers don't need or already know.
- Look for repeated ideas. Delete repetitions.

WRITING WORKSHOP PART 2

Active Writing Model

Writer's Model

The introduction grabs readers' attention and suggests a solution. The word choice sets a concerned tone.

Watching too much television has awful effects on people, especially kids my age. Let's help solve the problem by having a TV Turn-Off Week. I suggest that all families from our school unplug their TV sets for one week. Why is this a good idea? Here are three reasons.

The writer provides evidence to support a point.

First, too many students in King Middle School are becoming couch potatoes. A school poll shows that 84 percent of students sit on their sofas and stare at their TVs for at least two hours every day. Many students munch on junk foods like chips and candy while they watch TV. As a result, some kids don't get enough exercise, and they gain weight. TV Turn-Off Week would force kids to get off their sofas and do something.

The style of the writing is appropriate for the audience and the topic. The writing is formal, yet personal.

Second, some kids watch TV instead of talking to their families and making friends. For example, my cousin Raymond talks to TV characters. He likes to tell them what to do or say. Sometimes his mom calls to him and he doesn't even answer because he's so involved watching TV. TV Turn-Off Week would encourage kids like my cousin to have relationships with real people.

The writer arranges the negative effects of watching too much television in increasing order of importance.

Third, watching too much TV can cause some kids to have behavior problems. Last month, the principal asked us to stop watching violent shows. TV characters who use violence seem strong and powerful. Kids who like to pretend to be such TV characters can get trapped in a fantasy world. A TV Turn-Off Week could help kids find better ways to use their imaginations.

The writer responds to possible counterarguments to help convince readers to participate in TV Turn-Off Week.

I know some people won't agree with my proposal. They'll say, "We need to watch the news," or, "We'll be so bored without TV." I suggest that those people read the newspaper or listen to the radio to find out what's going on in the world. Have fun playing a game or reading your favorite magazine. One week without a TV won't do any harm.

This emotional appeal helps persuade readers to take action to solve the problem.

Don't be a couch potato! Don't use TV as a substitute for friendship or a family relationship! Don't let TV violence twist your imagination! Let's break the television habit for just seven days by having a TV Turn-Off Week.

Monica Sosa

Additional Support

Reading in the Real World

Career Students who like persuasive writing may want to learn about careers in advertising. Advertising firms bring together teams of people—writers, artists, market research specialists, and salespersons—to sell a product. Ask students to form teams of five: two writers and one person in each of the other roles. Teams are responsible for researching their role, "inventing" a product, and "selling" it to the class. **EL** **OL**

Listening, Speaking, and Viewing

Persuasive Techniques

Persuasive messages are all around us. You may even come across messages that you don't realize are persuasive.

Analyzing Cartoons The "best" commercial is not effective if you can't remember the product.

What Are the Persuasive Techniques Used in Ads?

Ads contain both obvious and hidden messages. The following persuasive techniques are some of the techniques commonly used in ads.

- **Bandwagon**—People are urged to follow the crowd by buying a product, voting for a candidate, or doing whatever else the advertiser wants. This technique works because people generally don't want to be left behind.
- **Glittering generalities**—The advertiser uses positive, good-sounding words to impress people. Examples include *all-American* and *medically proven*. These words are vague and mean different things to different people. As a result, the advertiser may mean something different than what you think of when you hear or see the word.
- **Testimonial**—Famous and admired people praise a product. These people are not experts, but the advertiser hopes consumers will follow their advice or use the same products.
- **Transfer**—The advertiser creates a certain feeling and hopes that it will transfer to the product being sold. For example, an ad picturing happy teens on a sunny beach expresses a positive feeling. The advertiser hopes that viewers will transfer that feeling to the product being advertised.

Why Is It Important to Understand Persuasive Techniques?

When you recognize and understand the techniques advertisers use to persuade you, you are less likely to be easily persuaded. You can use reason and logic to make better choices about what you want or what you believe. **R**

How Do I Recognize the Persuasive Techniques?

As you watch, listen to, or read advertisements, think about what you're seeing and/or hearing. Ask yourself the following questions:

- What does the advertiser want?
- How is the advertiser trying to influence me?
- What catches my attention? Does the ad use catchy music, sound effects, or repetition?

Get the Message Think of a commercial that you have seen or heard often. Answer the questions below in your Learner's Notebook.

- What is the purpose behind the ad?
- What techniques does the advertiser use to persuade viewers?
- How effective is the commercial? Why?

Send a Message Make a print ad or write a script for a radio commercial related to the same topic as your editorial. Use at least one of the persuasive techniques you learned about.

Reading Fluency

Reading and Listening Some students more easily evaluate their work if another student reads it aloud. Allow partners to read each other's drafts aloud. Writers should take notes about sections that caused the reader to stumble or pause. Listeners should explain the problem in the section (such as lack of clarity, poor grammar, repetition). Encourage students to use the rubric from page 468 as a guideline for discussing their drafts and making further revisions. **OL**

Teach

W Writing

Persuasive Techniques A euphemism is a pleasant expression that writers substitute for one that is unappealing or unpleasant. TV commercials often use this type of persuasive language to disguise aspects of their products people might object to. Write the following sentences on the board.

This pre-owned car is a real buy!

This dental work may cause you some discomfort.

Your services with our company are no longer required.

Mrs. Carter, your son seems to have borrowed information from a friend's test.

Say: I have underlined the euphemism in each sentence. Can you tell what the writer is *really* saying?

Ask students to work with a partner to write words a guest would use as he or she thanks someone for a meal that tasted awful. **OL**

Assess/Close

Partner Activity Choose a product—real or invented—to advertise on TV. Make a list of selling points, as well as how it helps people. Use the persuasive techniques you learned to describe each point.

Objectives

- Analyze, understand, and utilize persuasive techniques
- Use word choice to influence and create emotional appeal

Comparing and Contrasting

Objectives covered in this workshop:
- Use the text's structure

Comparing and Contrasting

Why Is It Important?

- Comparing and contrasting helps writers relate to and influence readers.
- Comparing and contrasting helps readers find and understand the argument in a selection.
- Students who are able to see similarities and differences in events, people, and ideas in a text are better able to construct meaning from a selection.

How to Help Students Get It

- Ask students to look carefully at the descriptions and other details an author includes in a selection.
- Have students look for clue words that signal that the author is comparing or contrasting items, such as *both, same, alike, also,* and *similarly,* or *unlike, but, although, yet,* and *instead.*
- Invite students to think about why a writer might compare or contrast things or people. Is there a larger purpose or idea the author may wish to convey?
- Tell students that sometimes there are no signal words to indicate comparison or contrast. Students must then use descriptive details in those instances to infer similarities or differences between items.

Reading to Answer the Big Question

Should Naturalized Citizens Be President?

Point / Counter Point format discusses naturalization and the Presidency. Each viewpoint mentions the way individuals are influenced by their perception of "homeland," and the fact that the President has more influence over the nation than an average citizen does.

The Teacher Who Changed My Life

Nicholas Gage writes that the influence of Miss Hurd changed the course of his schooling and his career. When he joined the after-school Newspaper Club she sponsored, he started his journey to journalism, and Miss Hurd's English class inspired him to love the English language. Her coaching, drilling, and encouragement gave him what he needed to channel his grief into writing, and to hone his writing into Hearst Award winning material. Gage compares her presence in his life to that of his parents.

Workshop Resources

Pacing (Days) Standard	Block	Lesson	Student Materials	Teacher Resources
1		Key Skill Lesson: Comparing and Conrasting	Key Reading Skills Practice English Language Coach	Bellringer Options Transparencies Read Aloud, Think Aloud Transparencies Presentation Plus!
2		"Should Naturalized Citizens Be President"	Literary Analysis Transparencies Glencoe Online Selection Vocabulary Development Academic Vocabulary Development English Language Coach Active Reading Graphic Organizer Literary Analysis StudentWorks Plus Online Student Edition Literature Classics Selection and Unit Assessments	Literary and Text Analysis Transparencies Puzzlemaker Skill Level Up! BookLink 3 Assessment by Learning Objective (Diagnostic and Formative) Interactive Tutor Self-Assessment TeacherWorks Plus
2		"The Teacher Who Changed My Life"	Glencoe Online Selection Vocabulary Development Academic Vocabulary Development English Language Coach Active Reading Graphic Organizer Literary Analysis StudentWorks Plus Online Student Edition Literature Classics Selection and Unit Assessments	Literary and Text Analysis Transparencies Puzzlemaker Skill Level Up! BookLink 3 Assessment by Learning Objective (Diagnostic and Formative) Interactive Tutor Self-Assessment TeacherWorks Plus

Keys for Unit Resource

- Blackline Master
- Workbook
- Supplemental Text
- CD-ROM
- DVD
- Transparency
- Web-based
- Fast Files

Level Appropriate Code

AS = Activities for all students
AL = Activities for students working above grade level
OL = Activities for students working at grade level
BL = Activities for students working below grade level
EL = Activities for English language learners

Focus

BELLRINGER Options

- Selection Focus Transparency
- Daily Language Practice Transparency

Focus Activity Ask: What character traits should a president have? *(Possible responses: honesty, devotion to the country, wisdom)* OL

Teach

R Reading Skill

Using Text Structure: Compare and Contrast

Ask: When you decide which of two CDs to buy, which features do you compare before you buy? *(Possible responses: price, songs, artists)* OL

V Vocabulary

Academic Vocabulary Say: Read the word *structure* on the bottom of page 474. Can you think of a synonym for *structure? (Possible responses: framework, skeleton)* OL

READING WORKSHOP 4

Skills Focus

You will practice using these skills when you read the following selections:

- "Should Naturalized Citizens Be President?" p. 478
- "The Teacher Who Changed My Life," p. 484

Reading

- Using text structure: Compare and contrast

Literature

- Identifying hyperbole
- Understanding argument

Vocabulary

- Understanding denotation, connotation, and semantic slanting
- Academic Vocabulary: *structure*

Writing/Grammar

- Identifying and writing declarative, exclamatory, and imperative sentences, and using end punctuation

Objectives (pp. 474–475)
Reading Use text structure: compare and contrast

Skill Lesson

Using Text Structure: Compare and Contrast

Learn It!

What Is It? Comparing and contrasting are two techniques that writers often use in persuasive writing.

- Comparing is looking at how things are similar.
- Contrasting is looking at how things are different.

When writers want to inform and persuade readers, they need to present their arguments clearly. Compare and contrast is a great **structure** for organizing and sharing information. Comparing and contrasting show similarities and differences and may help readers relate to the topic.

Analyzing Cartoons
Too many choices! Too many things to compare! Don't try to compare everything—whether you're shopping or you're writing.

Academic Vocabulary

structure (STRUK shur) *n.* something arranged in a pattern of organization

Additional Support

Differentiated Instruction

Compare and Contrast Students who have difficulty with comparison and contrast may find it easier to organize their thoughts with a T-chart. Ask students to work with a partner to compare and contrast the virtues of dogs and cats as pets. EL BL

Which animal makes the better pet?

Dog	Cat

Why Is It Important? A comparison is one of the best ways to explain something. (Even though it's just called a comparison, it usually involves contrasting as well.) It's hard to understand anything that's completely different from anything you know. If you had never seen an elephant, a writer could describe it clearly to you by saying that it's "much taller than a horse, with harder, rougher skin and a long nose like a gigantic hose."

How Do I Do It? Watch for any time a writer looks at two things. If the writer points out ways they are similar or different, that's a comparison. Often the comparison will be signaled by comparison words, such as *same as*, *similar to*, and *like*, or contrast words, such as *on the other hand*, *however*, and *different*. You will also often see comparative forms such as *stronger* or *better*. See how the comparison provides a text structure.

R

Literature Online

Study Central Visit www.glencoe.com and click on Study Central to review compare and contrast.

Here is part of a letter a student wrote to a newspaper. Below that is how a second student used compare and contrast to think about the letter.

> In health class, we learn about a healthy diet. It is important to eat whole grains, fresh fruits and vegetables, dairy products, and protein such as meat and fish. Foods high in sugar and fat are not healthy. Our cafeteria serves grains, fruits, vegetables, dairy products, and protein. But the "grain" is bleached white bread. The fruit is from a can. The vegetables are overcooked. The dairy products are full of sweeteners. The meat is fried in high-fat oil. Does anybody else see something wrong with this picture?

This student compares and contrasts what she's learning in class with what the cafeteria serves. When she compares and contrasts, she talks about things in the same order. Her argument is easy to follow.

Practice It!

In your Learner's Notebook, write one possible comparison and one contrast that you can think of for the following topic.

- Citizens who were born in this country and citizens who were not

Use It!

As you read, remember the similarity and difference you listed. If you find more as you read, add them to your list.

Teach

Literature Online

Study Central Have students access the Web site to review comparing and contrasting and to complete a related activity.

R Reading Skill

Using Text Structure: Compare and Contrast

Read the following paragraphs to the class. Ask students to compare and contrast walking and jogging as forms of exercise. OL

> Walking one mile burns an average of 90–100 calories. The average walker can walk two miles in 30 minutes. Almost anyone can begin a walking exercise program. Only if walkers exceed 15–20 miles a week is injury likely to occur.
>
> Most joggers cover three miles in 30 minutes, burning 270–300 calories. Although jogging puts more stress on bones, joints, and muscles than walking, most joggers can exercise three to four times a week without injury.

Resources for page 475

- Use Reading Skills Transparency in *Read Aloud, Think Aloud,* Unit 4, to help students practice comparing and contrasting.

Reading Fluency

Reading to Compare and Contrast Some students find that it helps them to read along silently as the teacher reads aloud a passage that contains a lot of information. Allow these students to follow along as you read "Should Naturalized Citizens Be President?" Encourage them to mentally list the arguments on both sides. When you finish, ask them to name the argument they felt was most persuasive. EL BL

Objectives

- Use text structure: compare and contrast

More About the Authors

John Yinger studies the unfair treatment of people because of their racial or ethnic backgrounds (discrimination). He has written about discrimination in housing, lending, and school funding.

An author and editor, Matthew Spalding is an expert on the Constitution and American political history. He has a doctoral degree in government and runs a center for American studies.

EL Language Coach

Semantic Slanting **Ask:** What point does this parent make without saying it directly? "I had hoped that your report card would be better this quarter." *(Possible response: I'm disappointed that you didn't get better grades.)* OL

Before You Read

Should Naturalized Citizens Be President?

Meet the Authors

John Yinger is a professor at Syracuse University in New York. He has written several books about how economic issues affect racial and ethnic minorities. He has served on the President's Council of Economic Advisers.

Matthew Spalding is an expert on American political history, the Constitution, and religious liberty. An author and editor, he also runs the Heritage Foundation's B. Kenneth Simon Center for American Studies.

Author Search For more about John Yinger and Matthew Spalding, go to www.glencoe.com.

Objectives (pp. 476–479)
Reading Recognize text structure: compare and contrast
Literature Understand argument
Vocabulary Recognize semantic slanting: loaded words

Vocabulary Preview

principle (PRIN suh pul) *n.* a basic idea or concept **(p. 478)** *The principle of fairness is important in any new law.*

relevant (REH luh vunt) *adj.* having a connection to **(p. 478)** *The values on which the Constitution was based are still relevant to Americans today.*

ensure (en SHUR) *v.* to guarantee or make certain **(p. 478)** *Careful consideration of the pros and cons will help to ensure a wise decision.*

requirement (rih KWY ur munt) *n.* a demand or condition **(p. 479)** *A presidential candidate must meet many requirements.*

assurance (uh SHUR uns) *n.* confidence; certainty **(p. 479)** *Assurance of loyalty to this country is part of the promise immigrants make.*

Write to Learn For each vocabulary word, write a sentence using the word correctly.

English Language Coach

EL **Semantic Slanting** You have learned that many words have two parts to their meaning–their denotation and their connotation. Some words don't have many, or any, connotations. They don't bring up emotions or images in us when they're used. Are there feelings and ideas connected with *the, where,* and *you?* Of course not. But some words, often called "value words" or "loaded words," have very strong emotions connected to them.

Words like *American, democracy, loyal, family, safety,* and *citizen* are so important to us that they make us emotional. They can be so powerful that they interfere with our ability to think. They can make us proud, or they can make us afraid. They can inspire us to great actions, or they can keep us from seeing our way clearly.

Group Talk In a small group, talk about the value words in your life. Consider the name of your school and sports teams and words you associate with your family, your city, and your country.

Additional Support

Literature Online

Author Search To expand students' appreciation of these authors, have them access the Web site for additional information and resources.

Literature Focus Lesson

Persuasive Writing Many fiction books have been written about the lives of immigrants. Take students to the library. Suggest authors or key words that will help them find a book about immigrant experiences. Ask them to read and write about the book, including:

- an experience the immigrant had after moving
- the similarities and differences in the countries
- the person or event that most influenced the character
- the book's influence on the student's thoughts/feelings OL

Skills Preview

Key Reading Skill: Using Text Structure: Compare and Contrast

One way to present ideas is through comparison and contrast. There are two major ways to organize this type of writing. A writer can compare and contrast ideas one by one or write about all the ways two things are alike and then all the ways they are different.

Writers often compare a new idea with one you already agree with. If the comparison works, you may then agree with the new idea. Be careful when reading this kind of comparison. There may be differences that the writer doesn't point out.

Write to Learn Write a few paragraphs that compare and contrast being a citizen of the United States with being a visitor here. Use either method of presenting your ideas. Then check with a few of your classmates to see which type of organization they used.

Key Literary Element: Argument

In writing, an **argument** is the reason or reasons an author gives for his opinion. Suppose your mother says that it's important for you to brush your teeth twice a day. You ask why. She says, "Because teeth that aren't cleaned well can get cavities. Cavities can lead to losing your teeth. Then you'd have to wear false teeth. You wouldn't like that." That's a pretty good argument for brushing your teeth.

Each author in "Should Naturalized Citizens Be President?"could answer with one word: yes or no. Instead, they present arguments to make other people believe as they do. Those arguments include both facts and opinions. They are presented in language that is chosen to persuade you. It's your job as a reader to try to understand each argument and decide whether it's a good one.

Literature Online

Interactive Literary Elements Handbook
To review or learn more about the literary elements, go to www.glencoe.com.

Get Ready to Read

Connect to the Reading

Americans believe that people should have equal rights and can become whatever they want to be. Do you believe this? Why or why not?

Partner Talk With a partner, discuss what it means to be an American. What rights, privileges, and duties does an American citizen have? In your Learner's Notebook, write some of your ideas about citizenship.

Build Background

Many Americans believe that anyone can become President of the United States. But this is *not* true. The law says that only someone born in this country can be President. You're about to read two sides of the argument: Should this law be changed?

- People born in the United States are natural-born citizens.
- Naturalized citizens are people who move here from other countries and gain the same rights as those who were born here.
- The basic laws of the United States are written in the Constitution. Amendments, or changes, have been made to the Constitution over the past two hundred years.

Set Purposes for Reading

BIG Question As you read "Should Naturalized Citizens Be President?" think about which writer's argument influences you the most.

Set Your Own Purpose What would you like to learn from the selection to help you answer the Big Question? Write your own purpose on the "Should Naturalized Citizens Be President?" page of Foldable 4.

Keep Moving

Use these skills as you read the following selection.

English Language Coach

Semantic Slanting Every day, TV commercials influence people to buy products. Often, companies show other products and hint that theirs are better without actually stating the comparison. Ask students to work in groups to brainstorm commercials they have seen that influence viewers by what they don't say. Have groups create a fictitious product and a TV commercial that persuades classmates to buy it. OL Challenge students to create a commercial that influences viewers by hinting at a comparison to another product. AL

Teach

R Reading Skill

Review Predicting Ask: What might you predict about an article that compares basketball to baseball entitled "From Bat Blahs to Hoop Hoorays"? *(Possible response: The writer prefers basketball to baseball.)* OL

L Literary Element

Argument Say: One way you can strengthen an argument is to compare and/or contrast to prove your point. Think about which technique is used in each of these examples.

- All of the school teams have new uniforms except for the soccer team. *(contrast)*
- Both the basketball team and the volleyball team have new uniforms. *(compare)* OL

CheckPoint

Use the CheckPoint questions provided on Presentation Plus! to build background. These questions can be used with interactive response keypads for immediate student feedback.

Literature Online

Interactive Literary Elements Handbook Have students access the Web site to improve their understanding of argument.

Objectives

- Use text structure: compare and contrast
- Understand argument
- Recognize semantic slanting: loaded words

Teach

Viewing the Photo

Say: Read the caption beside the photograph. Why might some people believe that Arnold Schwarzenegger could run for president? *(Possible response: Other governors, such as Ronald Reagan and Bill Clinton, became president.)* OL

R Reading Skill

Using Text Structure: Compare and Contrast

Say: Read the second paragraph on this page. In comparison to foreign-born citizens like Jonah, what type of people do you think the author would consider first-class citizens? *(citizens born in the United States)* OL

Readability Scores
Dale-Chall: 8.6
DRP: 69
Lexile: 1090

READING WORKSHOP 4

Should *Naturalized* Citizens be PRESIDENT?

The Constitution says that only **'natural-born'** citizens can be President. Should we change that?

YES My son, Jonah, came to the U.S. from Vietnam as a 4-month-old baby. When his second-grade class studied the presidency, he was told that he cannot run for President when he grows up, even if he wants to. According to the Constitution, only a "natural-born Citizen" can be President.

R More than 12.8 million naturalized citizens, including 250,000 foreign-born adoptees like Jonah, are second-class citizens who cannot hold the highest office in the land. 1

The natural-born-citizen clause violates a central **principle** of American democracy: All citizens should have equal rights. When written, the Constitution embraced this principle but failed to protect the rights of women and of racial and ethnic minorities. The 14th, 15th, and 19th Amendments have been added to protect these groups. The next step is to remove the natural-born-citizen clause. 2

The Founding Fathers[1] included the . . . clause so no foreign prince could buy his way into the presidency. This concern is no longer **relevant**. Some people say we still need this clause to **ensure** that the President is loyal to the country, but naturalized citizens are a very loyal group.

Practice the Skills

1 Reviewing Skills

Identifying Author's Purpose and Perspective The writer says he has a son who was born in another country. That's part of his perspective on the issue. How do you think it affects his thoughts and opinions? Read "Meet the Authors" to find out more about him.

2 Key Reading Skill

Using Text Structure: Compare and Contrast The writer compares the past situation of women and minorities with the current situation of naturalized citizens. Does using this structure make the situation clearer? Is there anything missing in the comparison?

Arnold Schwarzenegger is a native of Austria. He became a U.S. citizen in 1983 and was elected California's governor in 2003. He cannot run for President unless the Constitution is changed.

1. The ***Founding Fathers*** are the leaders who wrote the U.S. Constitution after the colonies won independence from Great Britain.

Vocabulary

principle (PRIN suh pul) *n.* a basic idea or concept

relevant (REH luh vunt) *adj.* having a connection to

ensure (en SHUR) *v.* to guarantee or make certain

Additional Support

Reading in the Real World

Citizenship Ask students to name traits that the president should have. List the traits on the board. Then work with students to list well-known foreign-born Americans. Ask each student to select one name from the list to research. Based on their research, students should create a chart of five "presidential" traits they feel the person displays. Next to each trait, students should list supporting facts from their research. EL OL

READING WORKSHOP 4

Moreover, the Constitution allows any natural-born citizen, loyal or not, to run for President and relies on voting rights and the judgment of the American people to keep disloyal people from being elected. These protections would work just as well if we let naturalized citizens run for President, too.

—**John Yinger,** Syracuse University

NO America has always been open to foreign-born immigrants becoming full and equal citizens—with one exception: Only a "natural-born Citizen" can become President. This **requirement** strikes a reasonable balance between our society's openness and the ongoing requirements of national security. 3

One of the legal conditions for becoming an American citizen is to be "attached to the principles of the Constitution of the United States." New citizens also must take an oath to renounce "all **allegiance** and **fidelity**"[2] to other nations. But in the case of the presidency we need even more **assurance** of that allegiance than an oath. 4 R

The presidency is unique: One person makes crucial decisions, many having to do with foreign policy and national security. With a single executive, there are no checks to override the possibility of foreign influence, or mitigate[3] any lingering favoritism for one's native homeland. C

Unlike any other position or office, the attachment[4] of the President must be absolute. This comes most often from being born in—and educated and formed by—this country.

In general, constitutional amendments should be pursued only after careful consideration, when it is necessary to address a great national issue and when there is broad-based support among the American people. That is not the case here.

—**Matthew Spalding,** The Heritage Foundation 5 6

2. To ***take an oath*** is to swear or promise to do something. To become a citizen, an immigrant must promise to give up ***(renounce)*** loyalty (***allegiance*** and ***fidelity***) to any other nation.
3. To make something less important is to ***mitigate*** it. Spalding is saying that there is danger in having a foreign-born President who may be too connected to his or her native land.
4. Here, ***attachment*** refers to his earlier statement that the President must be dedicated (***attached***) only to the United States.

Vocabulary

requirement (rih KWY ur mnnt) *n.* a demand or condition

assurance (uh SHUR uns) *n.* confidence, certainty

Practice the Skills

3 Key Literary Element

Argument Have the two writers stated their arguments? If so, what sentence in each half of the selection states that writer's main argument?

4 English Language Coach

Semantic Slanting Both **allegiance** and **fidelity** mean "loyalty." How do these words make you feel?

5 Reviewing Skills

Identifying Author's Purpose and Perspective How might it help you understand this writer's perspective if you found out what the Heritage Foundation is?

6 BIG Question

Which argument do you think is more persuasive? Why? Write your answer on the "Should Naturalized Citizens Be President?" page of Foldable 4. Your response will help you complete the Unit Challenge later.

Teach

R Reading Skill

Review Distinguishing Fact and Opinion **Ask:** What opinion does Spalding offer in paragraph two of his argument? *(The country needs more than an oath to be sure its president is loyal to the country.)* OL

C Critical Thinking

Comprehension **Ask:** What generalization does Matthew Spalding make about foreign-born citizens that supports his argument against letting them run for president? *(He says they are more likely to let their homeland influence them or treat their birth countries specially.)* AL

Assess

Use the CheckPoint questions provided on Presentation Plus! to check for comprehension. These questions can be used with interactive response keypads for immediate student feedback.

English Language Coach

Semantic Slanting Speakers who wish to persuade their audience to act or think as they do make careful word choices. Play a videotape of two famous persuasive speeches for students. Ask them to listen and jot down any semantic slanting tools they notice: words with highly emotional connotations, multiple synonyms to drive home a point, and something left *unsaid* to make a point. OL

Objectives
- Understand how word choice reveals author's perspective
- Distinguish fact and opinion
- Identify generalizations
- Use comparison and contrast to connect abstract ideas to facts

Assess

Resources for page 480

- Selection Quick Check
- Selection and Unit Assessment
- ExamView Assessment Suite
- Interactive Tutor: Self-Assessment

Students can respond to the *After You Read* items in their Learner's Notebook or on a separate sheet of paper.

Answering the

1. Responses will vary.
2. Yinger uses the example of his son, Jonah, a foreign-born citizen.

Critical Thinking

3. Possible responses: FOR: All citizens should have equal rights, according to the Constitution. The voters will not elect disloyal people. AGAINST: The president makes decisions with no one to check for foreign influence or favoritism. It is even more important for the president to be loyal than it is for a regular citizen.
4. This statement is fact.
5. Possible responses could include the idea that the Constitution is the law of the land and must be obeyed.
6. Responses will vary.

After You Read

Should Naturalized Citizens Be President?

Answering the

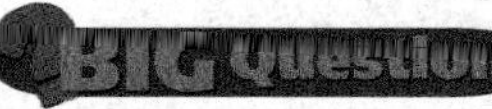

1. After reading the arguments, what is your opinion? How did the two writers influence you?
2. **Recall** What personal example does John Yinger use to support his "yes" argument?
   Tip **Right There**

Critical Thinking

3. **Summarize** What are the main arguments for and against allowing naturalized citizens to become President?
   Tip **Think and Search**
4. **Evaluate** Yinger says that more than 12.8 million naturalized citizens cannot be President. Is this fact or opinion? Why?
   Tip **On My Own**
5. **Infer** Why do you think one of the legal conditions for becoming an American citizen is to be "attached," or dedicated, to the Constitution?
6. **Evaluate** Which argument do you think is more persuasive? Why?
   Tip **Author and Me**

Write About Your Reading

Use the RAFT system to write about the issue discussed in "Should Naturalized Citizens Be President?"

Role: Write as if you were a lawmaker.

Audience: Write to your peers, other lawmakers.

Format: A persuasive letter.

Topic: Explain why you think the law should, or should not, be changed to allow foreign-born citizens to be President.

Objectives (pp. 480–481)
Reading Use text structure: compare and contrast
Literature Understand argument
Vocabulary Recognize semantic slanting: loaded words
Writing Use the RAFT system: persuasive letter
Grammar Identify compound subjects

Write About Your Reading

Possible response:
Dear Congressional Colleagues: I am deeply disturbed by an injustice in the American Constitutional system that goes against the wishes of the founding fathers of this country. Are we not all either foreign-born or descendants of people born in other countries? What is the United States if it is not a glorious combination of many cultures and ideas–a safe home for people of different backgrounds, faiths, and practices? Have we not all become richer because of our multicultural heritage? Yet, we deny the highest position in the land to people simply because their birth heritage is not "American"! I challenge you to welcome ALL citizens to the presidential ballot. Let's amend the Constitution so that we truly give all Americans equal rights!

Skills Review

Key Reading Skill: Using Text Structure: Compare and Contrast

7. One of the authors says that the presidency is not like any other office. (An office is a high government position). He is contrasting that office with all others. What does he think is the difference? Write two or three sentences explaining your answer.

Key Literary Element: Argument

8. Restate the argument of the "Yes" half of the selection in your own words. Then write two sentences that state what you think about the argument.
9. Restate the argument of the "No" half of the selection in your own words. Then write two sentences that state what you think about the argument.

Vocabulary Check

10. Choose the best word from the list to replace each underlined phrase. Rewrite the passage with the words in place.

assurance ensure principle
relevant requirement

"Jeremy," said Ms. Saville, "you can't take second-year Spanish until you've taken first-year Spanish. It's a <u>thing that is considered necessary</u>."

"But I speak Spanish with my neighbors."

"That is not <u>connected</u> to the situation. We need the <u>complete confidence</u> that you understand Spanish grammar. Having you take the first course is one way we <u>make certain of</u> that. Seeing to it that our students really know their subjects is a <u>basic ideas or concept</u> of this school."

11. **Academic Vocabulary** How does compare and contrast help you understand the **structure** of an argument or piece of writing?
12. **English Language Coach** Write a sentence using one of these "value words": *family, country, democracy,* or *citizen.* Then write the same sentence, but substitute a definition for the value word. Do the sentences have the same effect?

Grammar Link: Compound Subjects

A **compound subject** is made up of two or more subjects that are joined by *and, or,* or *nor.*

- <u>Kendra</u>, <u>Terry</u>, and <u>Melissa</u> are sisters.

  The subjects <u>Kendra</u>, <u>Terry</u>, and <u>Melissa</u> are joined by *and.*

  The compound subject is "Kendra, Terry, and Melissa."
- Jaylon's shirt, pants, and jacket are all purple.

  The subjects <u>shirt</u>, <u>pants</u>, and <u>jacket</u> are joined by *and.*

  The compound subject is "shirt, pants, and jacket."
- When the parts of compound subjects are joined by *and*, they take a plural verb. When they are joined by *or* or *nor*, the verb goes along with the part of the subject that comes last.

Grammar Practice

Copy the sentences below on a separate piece of paper. Then underline the compound subject in each sentence.

13. The written report and presentation are due.
14. Neither you nor I am ready!
15. My mom or my sister will help us.

Literature Online

Web Activities For eFlashcards, Selection Quick Checks, and other Web activities, go to www.glencoe.com.

Skills Review

Key Reading Skill: Using Text Structure: Compare and Contrast

7. Responses will vary.

Key Literary Element: Argument

8. Responses will vary but should include the idea that the founding fathers intended the Constitution to give equal rights to all citizens.
9. Responses will vary but should include the idea that a president must rule with absolute loyalty to his or her country alone, and a foreign-born president may have loyalties to his/her homeland.

Vocabulary Check

10. requirement, relevant, assurance, ensure, principle
11. Possible response: Comparing and contrasting shows a structure that is organized into two elements.
12. Responses will vary.

Close

Ask students to decide which of the two selections appealed most to their emotions.

Grammar Link: Compound Subjects

Grammar Practice

13. The written <u>report</u> and <u>presentation</u> are due.
14. Neither <u>you</u> nor <u>I</u> am ready!
15. My <u>mom</u> or my <u>sister</u> will help us.

Literature Online

Web Activities Have students access the Web site for interactive activities that will help them assess their understanding of the selection.

Before You Read
The Teacher Who Changed My Life

Nicholas Gage

Meet the Author

Nicholas Gage was born Nikos Gatzoyiannis in Epiros, Greece, in 1939. In this essay, he writes of his mother's tragic death and his escape to the United States. He has become a world-famous, award-winning writer whose books have become films and a TV series. See page R3 of the Author Files for more on Nicholas Gage.

Literature Online

Author Search For more about Nicholas Gage, go to www.glencoe.com.

Objectives (p. 482–491)
Reading Use text structure: compare and contrast
Literature Identify literary devices: hyperbole
Vocabulary Identify semantic slanting

Vocabulary Preview

authoritarian (uh thor ih TAIR ee un) *adj.* having or expecting complete obedience **(p. 484)** *Workers were annoyed by the boss's authoritarian style.*

ultimately (UL tuh mit lee) *adv.* in the end; finally **(p. 485)** *Ultimately, we're all responsible for our own decisions.*

impoverished (im PAW vur ishd) *adj.* reduced to poverty; made very poor **(p. 486)** *We need to try to improve the lives of the most impoverished people.*

mortified (MOR tih fyd) *adj.* greatly embarrassed; a form of the verb *mortify* **(p. 488)** *Joe was mortified to see his underwear drying in the backyard.*

V

tact (takt) *n.* the ability to handle people or situations without causing bad feelings **(p. 488)** *A person needs tact when trying to make new friends.*

ecstatic (ek STAT ik) *adj.* filled with great joy **(p. 488)** *My sister was ecstatic when she could afford her first car.*

avidly (AV id lee) *adv.* eagerly; enthusiastically **(p. 490)** *Whenever a new issue of my favorite magazine arrives, I avidly read every page.*

Write to Learn Copy these words into your Learner's Notebook. Next to each word, write down what you already know about that word. Try to write a sentence using each word.

English Language Coach

Denotation, Connotation, and Semantic Slanting As you read the next article, watch for "slanted" words and phrases that the author uses to influence the reader. Here are two examples:

Word/Phrase	no-nonsense	layabout
Denotation	efficient; to-the-point	a lazy person
Connotation	positive	negative

More About the Author

Nicholas Gage is a skilled reporter who works for the AP news service and well-known newspapers. On an assignment to the Middle East, Gage returned to Greece. There he researched his mother's life and death. He fulfilled a lifelong dream when he used his research to write *Eleni*, a book about his courageous mother.

V Vocabulary

Word Choice The English language has many words that describe how people feel and act. Authors work hard to find just the right ones. Which vocabulary words could a writer choose instead of the following:

- happy *(ecstatic)*
- with great interest *(avidly)*
- poor *(impoverished)* OL

Additional Support

Author Search To expand students' appreciation of Nicholas Gage, have them access the Web site for additional information and resources.

Literature Focus Lesson

Persuasive Writing To be persuasive, authors must feel strongly about their subjects. Nicholas Gage was gratefully devoted to Mrs. Hurd, who helped him adjust to a new land. Ask students to write persuasively about someone who helped them succeed. The goal is to get their readers to agree with how they feel about this person. Provide an outline that includes the student's goal, his or her unsuccessful attempts, an introduction of the person, and the person's helpful efforts. BL EL

Skills Preview

Key Reading Skill: Using Text Structure: Compare and Contrast

As you read, look for places where the author compares two things or contrasts two things.

Write to Learn Jot down these examples in your Learner's Notebook. Then think about how comparing and contrasting helps Gage get his message across.

Literary Element: Hyperbole

A batter steps up to the plate and says, "I'll send that ball out of the park." This may or may not be an exaggeration, depending on how good the batter is.

Another batter says, "I'll send that ball to the moon." This is not only exaggeration, it's **hyperbole** (hi PUR buh lee), which is a really big exaggeration.

If you've ever said, "I could have died of embarrassment," you've used hyperbole. You couldn't really have died of embarrassment, and nobody thinks you mean it. The statement, however, makes it clear that you were deeply, not just slightly, embarrassed.

L

Writers often use hyperbole to make a point. Sometimes they use it for humor, but often they use it simply for emphasis. Here are some common (or famous) examples of hyperbole and their understood meanings:

- We could have heard a pin drop. (It was incredibly quiet.)
- Cry me a river. I cried a river over you. (Go ahead and be horribly sad. You made me horribly sad.)
- He's got a heart as big as all outdoors. (He is amazingly kind and caring.)

Literature Online

Interactive Literary Elements Handbook
To review or learn more about the literary elements, go to www.glencoe.com.

Get Ready to Read

Connect to the Reading

Think about how it would feel to be a new student in a new school in a new country. Nearly everyone else speaks a language that you don't understand. This was Nicholas Gage's experience. He tells how he felt when, as a boy, he came to America from war-torn Greece.

Write to Learn In your Learner's Notebook, quickwrite about a time when you were a newcomer in a place where everyone else knew each other. How did you feel? How did other people treat you?

Build Background

In this selection, journalist Nicholas Gage describes coming to the United States in 1949, after leaving Greece.

- Greece is in southern Europe, along the Mediterranean Sea. In ancient times, it was the center of a very important culture.
- During and at the end of World War II, many immigrants from war-torn countries came to the U.S. They hoped to find peace and opportunity for themselves and their families.
- Gage's book about his mother, *Eleni*, became an award-winning bestseller.

Set Purposes for Reading

BIG Question Read "The Teacher Who Changed My Life" to find out how an "undersized nine-year-old" non-English-speaking immigrant boy became an award-winning American journalist. BQ

Set Your Own Purpose What would you like to learn to help you answer the Big Question? Write your own purpose on the "Teacher Who Changed My Life" page of Foldable 4.

Keep Moving

Use these skills as you read the following selection.

Reading in the Real World

Career Students who are interested in journalism will benefit from learning about this career. Ask students to work in groups to research an aspect of the career: job duties, opportunities for employment, educational requirements, job recognition, and income *(awards, bylines, assignments)*. As a class, incorporate the students' research into a multimedia computer presentation entitled *Being a Journalist.* EL OL

Teach

L Literary Element

Hyperbole Say: Writers use hyperbole when they want readers to know how strongly they feel. Read the title of the next selection. Could it be hyperbole? *(Possible responses: Without reading the story, I think that the author may be exaggerating the help someone gave him. Sometimes I say that the teacher "saved my life" when all he did was postpone a test.)* OL

BQ 

Ask: From the title, do you think the selection will answer the Big Question? *(Possible response: I can tell that a teacher influenced the author. I can guess that the teacher taught the author something important.)* OL

CheckPoint

Use the CheckPoint questions provided on Presentation Plus! to build background. These questions can be used with interactive response keypads for immediate student feedback.

Objectives
- Use text structure: compare and contrast
- Identify literary elements: hyperbole
- Identify semantic slanting

Teach

R Reading Skill

Review Drawing Conclusions **Ask:** What can you conclude about the author's mother based on her actions? *(Possible response: She loved her children enough to die for their freedom.)* OL

EL Language Coach

Word Choice **Ask:** Which words in the first paragraph make you wonder whether you will like Marjorie Hurd? *(Possible responses: dragged me onto the path, salty-tongued, no-nonsense)* OL

Readability Scores
Dale-Chall: 6.9
DRP: 61
Lexile: 1350

READING WORKSHOP 4

The Teacher Who Changed My Life

by Nicholas Gage

The person who set the course of my life in the new land I entered as a young war refugee—who, in fact, nearly dragged me onto the path that would bring all the blessings I've received in America—was a salty-tongued,[1] no-nonsense schoolteacher named Marjorie Hurd. When I entered her classroom in 1953, I had been to six schools in five years, starting in the Greek village where I was born in 1939. EL

When I stepped off a ship in New York Harbor on a gray March day in 1949, I was an undersized 9-year-old in short pants who had lost his mother and was coming to live with the father he didn't know. My mother, Eleni Gatzoyiannis, had been imprisoned, tortured, and shot by Communist guerrillas[2] for sending me and three of my four sisters to freedom. She died so that her children could go to their father in the United States. 1 R

The portly, bald, well-dressed man who met me and my sisters seemed a foreign, **authoritarian** figure. I secretly

1. A ***salty-tongued*** person speaks in a sharp, witty, and often sarcastic way.
2. ***Guerrillas*** (guh RIL uhz) are members of small, organized forces. They're usually volunteers who are not soldiers in a regular army.

Vocabulary

authoritarian (uh thor ih TAIR ee un) *adj.* having or expecting complete obedience

Practice the Skills

1 Reviewing Skills

Sequence The author describes events that took place at different times in his life. List the events in the first two paragraphs in time order.

Additional Support

Reading in the Real World

Citizenship Nicholas Gage is only one of many immigrants who came to the United States to find safety, jobs, or a better life. Take students to the library. Ask them to research either Ellis Island in New York or Angel Island in San Francisco, California. Their written report should include:

- a description of how immigrants were "processed"
- the nationalities of people who entered the port
- the number of immigrants who used the port
- the names of some of the immigrants OL

READING WORKSHOP 4

resented him for not getting the whole family out of Greece early enough to save my mother. Ultimately, I would grow to love him and appreciate how he dealt with becoming a single parent at the age of 56, but at first our relationship was prickly,[3] full of hostility.

As Father drove us to our new home—a tenement in Worcester,[4] Mass.—and pointed out the huge brick building that would be our first school in America, I clutched my Greek notebooks from the refugee camp, hoping that my few years of schooling would impress my teachers in this cold, crowded country. They didn't. When my father led me and my 11-year-old sister to Greendale Elementary School, the grim-faced Yankee principal put the two of us in a class for the mentally retarded. There was no facility in those days for non-English-speaking children. 2

By the time I met Marjorie Hurd four years later, I had learned English, been placed in a normal, graded class and had even been chosen for the college preparatory track in the Worcester public school system. I was 13 years old when our father moved us yet again, and I entered Chandler Junior High shortly after the beginning of seventh grade. I found myself surrounded by richer, smarter and better-dressed classmates who looked askance[5] at my strange clothes and heavy accent. Shortly after I arrived, we were told to select a hobby to pursue during "club hour" on Fridays. The idea of hobbies and clubs made no sense to my immigrant ears, but I

3. Here, ***prickly*** means "difficult; troublesome."
4. ***[Worcester]*** This city's founders brought its oddly pronounced name with them from England. It's pronounced as if it were spelled ***Wooster***, with an ***o*** sound as in ***wood***.
5. The expression ***looked askance*** means "looked at with suspicion or disapproval."

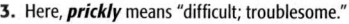

Vocabulary

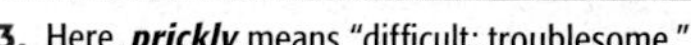

ultimately (UL tuh mit lee) *adv.* in the end; finally

Practice the Skills

2 Key Reading Skill

Using Text Structure: Compare and Contrast Look at the structure of this paragraph and the one before it. How does the author contrast his early feelings for his father with his later feelings? How does he contrast how he hoped to impress his teachers with what actually happened?

Teach

EL Language Coach

Denotation, Connotation, and Semantic Slanting

Ask: What is a *tenement*? If you do not know, find the word in a dictionary and read its definition. What connotation does *tenement* have? *(Possible response: crowded discomfort)* OL

R Reading Skill

Using Text Structure: Compare and Contrast

Ask: What does the author use to show the contrast between Nicholas and other students in the last paragraph? *(clothing, accented speech)* EL OL

C Critical Thinking

Comprehension Ask: What might other students have thought of Nicholas when he entered junior high? *(Possible response: They may have thought he was strange or odd.)* EL OL

English Language Coach

Semantic Slanting Authors often hint at the nature of people and places by what they do *not* write about them. In the first paragraph, Gage gives his first impression of the United States as *cold* and *crowded*. In this selection, he writes nothing that describes his homeland. Using his description of the new country as a contrast, write a short paragraph about what he felt about Greece, the homeland he left. OL

Objectives
- Understand how word choice affects thinking and emotions
- Identify word connotations and how they trigger emotions
- Use comparison and contrast
- Make inferences

READING WORKSHOP 4

Teach

EL Language Coach

Word Choice Ask: What words does the author use in the first paragraph to support the idea that Miss Hurd is *formidable*? *(Possible responses: solidly built, no patience, bellowed)* OL

C Critical Thinking

Analysis Ask: How does Miss Hurd give Nicholas Gage the skills and inspiration to become a journalist? Make a web diagram to help you organize the ways Miss Hurd helps. Then write a diary entry as if you were Miss Hurd (in her voice), describing your plan to help. OL

decided to follow the prettiest girl in my class—the blue-eyed daughter of the local Lutheran minister. She led me through the door marked "Newspaper Club" and into the presence of Miss Hurd, the newspaper adviser and English teacher who would become my mentor and my muse.[6]

A formidable, solidly built woman with salt-and-pepper hair, a steely eye and a flat Boston accent, Miss Hurd had no patience with layabouts. "What are all you goof-offs doing here?" she bellowed at the would-be journalists. "This is the Newspaper Club! We're going to put out a *newspaper.* So if there's anybody in this room who doesn't like work, I suggest you go across to the Glee Club now, because you're going to work your tails off here!" 3 EL

I was soon under Miss Hurd's spell. She did indeed teach us to put out a newspaper, skills I honed during my next 25 years as a journalist. Soon I asked the principal to transfer me to her English class as well. There, she drilled us on grammar until I finally began to understand the logic and structure of the English language. She assigned stories for us to read and discuss; not tales of heroes, like the Greek myths I knew, but stories of underdogs—poor people, even immigrants, who seemed ordinary until a crisis drove them to do something extraordinary. She also introduced us to the literary wealth[7] of Greece—giving me a new perspective on my war-ravaged, **impoverished** homeland. C

I began to be proud of my origins.

One day, after discussing how writers should write about what they know, she assigned us to compose an essay from our own experience. Fixing me with a stern look, she added, "Nick, I want you to write about what happened to your family in Greece." I had been trying to put those painful memories behind me and left the assignment until the last moment. Then, on a warm spring afternoon, I sat in my room with a yellow pad and pencil and stared out the window at the buds on the trees. I wrote that the coming of spring

6. A ***mentor*** is a wise and trusted counselor, and a ***muse*** is a source of artistic inspiration.

7. Greece's ***literary wealth,*** dating from about 750 to 300 B.C., includes plays, poems, and other texts that greatly influenced the development of European and American civilization.

Vocabulary

impoverished (im PAW vur ishd) *adj.* reduced to poverty; made very poor

Practice the Skills

3 Literary Element

Hyperbole What hyperbole does Miss Hurd use in the last sentence of the paragraph?

Additional Support

English Language Coach

Building Background Nicholas Gage and his sisters left Greece at a time when there was great political fighting. To help students understand the plight of Greeks like Gage's mother, who sacrificed her life to give her children a new home, show the film *Eleni*, which is based on Gage's book. Ask students to write a reaction paper, persuading readers that Gage's mother was also a great influence in his life. Students should give details from the movie to support this thesis. OL

READING WORKSHOP 4

Nicholas Gage's third-grade class. Nicholas is in the back row, second from the left.

Analyzing the photo Compare this class photo with the ones on pages 228 and 230. How did students change between the early 1900s and the middle 1900s? How do today's students differ from both earlier groups?

always reminded me of the last time I said goodbye to my mother on a green and gold day in 1948.

I kept writing, one line after another, telling how the Communist guerrillas occupied our village, took our home **EL** and food, how my mother started planning our escape when she learned that the children were to be sent to **re-education** **L** camps behind the Iron Curtain[8] and how, at the last moment, she couldn't escape with us because the guerrillas sent her with a group of women to thresh wheat in a distant village. **C** She promised she would try to get away on her own, she told me to be brave and hung a silver cross around my neck, and then she kissed me. I watched the line of women being led down into the ravine and up the other side, until they disappeared around the bend—my mother a tiny brown figure at the end who stopped for an instant to raise her hand in one last farewell. **4**

8. During the years following World War II, the ***Iron Curtain*** was an imaginary barrier separating the former Soviet Union and its allies from the non-Communist world.

Practice the Skills

4 **English Language Coach**

Semantic Slanting The camps Gage is talking about were used to brainwash children. They were taught to forget the values and loyalties they had grown up with and to replace them with loyalty to the Communist government. Why might this have been called **re-education**? What ideas or feelings do you think people associate with this word? Do those ideas match the reality of the camps?

Teach

EL Language Coach

Denotation, Connotation, and Semantic Slanting
Ask: What connotations do you have for the word *guerrillas*? *(Possible responses: war, rebel, violence)* How does this word influence readers' feelings about the men who occupied the village? *(Possible response: It makes readers understand how frightened the people of the village must have been.)* **OL**

L Literary Element

Review Tone **Say:** The author uses the word *escape* twice on this page. What tone does the author convey with this word? *(Possible responses: fearful, frantic, desperate)* **OL**

C Critical Thinking

Comprehension **Ask:** Why is Gage's mother unable to leave with her children? *(She is sent to thresh wheat in a distant village.)* **EL** **OL**

Reading Fluency

Build Fluency Students who have difficulty interpreting the events and emotions of a story find it helpful to read aloud to a small group. Group members should take turns reading. Allow students to pause between readers to discuss what is happening in the story and the feelings they are experiencing. Before the groups start reading, review the pronunciation and definitions of unfamiliar or difficult words. **EL** **OL**

Objectives
- Identify cause and effect
- Understand the effect of connotation and semantic slanting
- Use word choice to create tone
- Use word choice to reveal evidence

READING WORKSHOP 4

Teach

Viewing the Photo

Ask: What might the author have been feeling when this picture was taken? *(Possible response: He is feeling afraid and insecure because he misses his mother, and everything about the United States is new and different.)* How might his feelings have changed after his essay was published and entered in a contest? *(Possible response: He started to feel self-confident because he had a better relationship with both his father, who was proud of him, and his classmates, who felt bad about his family situation.)* EL OL

R Reading Skill

Review Drawing Conclusions **Ask:** After reading about Gage's mother and his Peace Corps friend, what conclusions could be made about people who want to help others? *(Possible response: People who help others are brave.)* OL

I wrote about our nighttime escape down the mountain, across the minefields, and into the lines of the Nationalist soldiers, who sent us to a refugee camp. It was there that we learned of our mother's execution. I felt very lucky to have come to America, I concluded, but every year, the coming of spring made me feel sad because it reminded me of the last time I saw my mother. **5**

I handed in the essay, hoping never to see it again, but Miss Hurd had it published in the school paper. This **mortified** me at first, until I saw that my classmates reacted with sympathy and **tact** to my family's story. Without telling me, Miss Hurd also submitted the essay to a contest sponsored by the Freedoms Foundation at Valley Forge, Pa., and it won a medal. The Worcester paper wrote about the award and quoted my essay at length. My father, by then a "five-and-dime-store chef," as the paper described him, was **ecstatic** with pride, and the Worcester Greek community celebrated the honor to one of its own. **6**

For the first time I began to understand the power of the written word. A secret ambition took root in me. One day, I vowed, I would go back to Greece, find out the details of my mother's death and write about her life, so her grandchildren would know of her courage. Perhaps I would even track down the men who killed her and write of their crimes. Fulfilling that ambition would take me 30 years. **7**

R Meanwhile, I followed the literary path that Miss Hurd had so forcefully set me on. After junior high, I became the editor of my school paper at Classical High School and got a part-time job at the Worcester *Telegram and Gazette.* Although my father could only give me $50 and encouragement toward a college education, I managed to finance four years at Boston University with scholarships and part-time jobs in journalism. During my last year of college, an article I wrote about a

Young Nicholas with his sister and his father in 1950.

Practice the Skills

5 Reviewing Skills

Responding As Gage tells the story of his mother, how do you respond?

6 Reviewing Skills

Identifying Author's Purpose and Perspective There is a great deal of information in this selection about the author. How does this help you understand his purpose for writing the article and his perspective on Mrs. Hurd?

7 Key Reading Skill

Using Text Structure: Compare and Contrast Compare and contrast Gage's feelings before he wrote the essay with his feelings after his story was published.

Vocabulary

mortified (MOR tih fyd) *adj.* greatly embarrassed

tact (takt) *n.* the ability to handle people or situations without causing bad feelings

ecstatic (ek STAT ik) *adj.* filled with great joy

Additional Support

Reading in the Real World

College Students who want to attend college need information about costs and financing their education. Invite a high school guidance counselor or college admissions counselor to visit your classroom. Ask students to take notes on the following topics:

- tuition
- room and board
- textbooks, other expenses
- loans
- grants, endowments
- scholarships
- work study jobs
- other employment OL

READING WORKSHOP 4

friend who had died in the Philippines—the first person to lose his life working for the Peace Corps[9]—led to my winning the Hearst Award for College Journalism. And the plaque was given to me in the White House by President John F. Kennedy. **R**

For a refugee who had never seen a motorized vehicle or indoor plumbing until he was 9, this was an unimaginable honor. When the Worcester paper ran a picture of me standing next to President Kennedy, my father rushed out to buy a new suit in order to be properly dressed to receive the congratulations of the Worcester Greeks. **BQ1** He clipped out the photograph, had it laminated in plastic and carried it in his breast pocket for the rest of his life to show everyone he met. I found the much-worn photo in his pocket on the day he died 20 years later. **8**

In our isolated Greek village, my mother had bribed a cousin to teach her to read, for girls were not supposed to attend school beyond a certain age. **BQ2** She had always dreamed of her children receiving an education. She couldn't be there when I graduated from Boston University, but the person who came with my father and shared our joy was my former teacher, Marjorie Hurd. We celebrated not only my bachelor's degree but also the scholarships that paid my way to Columbia's Graduate School[10] of Journalism. There, I met the woman who would eventually become my wife. At our wedding and at the baptisms of our three children, Marjorie Hurd was always there, dancing alongside the Greeks. **9**

By then, she was Mrs. Rabidou, for she had married a widower when she was in her early 40s. That didn't distract her from her vocation[11] of introducing young minds to English literature, however. She taught for a total of 41 years and continually would make a "project" of some balky student in whom she spied a spark of potential.[12] Often these

9. A ***scholarship*** is money given to help a student continue his or her education. The ***Peace Corps*** is a U.S. program that sends volunteers to help people in poorer countries to improve their living conditions. It was begun by President Kennedy in 1961.

10. After completing four years (usually) of study, college students receive an honor called a ***bachelor's degree.*** Some then go on to ***graduate schools*** for more advanced training.

11. One meaning of ***vocation*** is "occupation." It can also refer to the particular work one feels called to do or is especially suited for.

12. A ***balky*** student is one who tends to stop short and refuse to go on. A student with ***potential*** has qualities or abilities capable of being developed.

Practice the Skills

8 Reviewing Skills

Drawing Conclusions What conclusion can you draw from the details in this paragraph?

9 Key Reading Skill

Using Text Structure: Compare and Contrast
Look at the structure of this paragraph. Gage begins by describing his mother's difficulty in getting an education. What does he contrast this with? How does that make Gage's own accomplishments seem more important?

Teach

BQ1 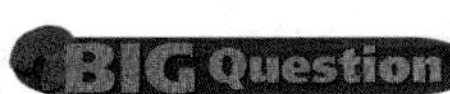

Ask: Why is it important for Gage's father to buy a new suit? *(Possible response: His Greek friends are important in his life, and he wants to look nice as they congratulate him on his son's achievement.)* **AL**

BQ2 

Ask: What did you learn about Gage's mother on this page that shows how she influenced her son to value education? *(Possible response: She secretly learned to read and dreamed that her children—both her daughters and her son—would get an education.)* **EL** **OL**

Differentiated Instruction

Sequencing Events Nicholas Gage's life changed dramatically from his childhood in Greece to today. Ask students to use the information on this page to create a timeline of events that shows his journey from a shy, immigrant boy to a well-known, respected journalist. **OL**

Age 9 — College — Columbia — Marriage

Objectives
- Use photos to make inferences about people's feelings and thoughts
- Draw conclusions to make generalizations

READING WORKSHOP 4

Teach

R1 Reading Skill

Using Text Structure: Compare and Contrast
Say: The author invites readers to compare their cultures with the Greek culture he and his family still enjoy. Which details on this page help you compare your ethnic heritage with the author's? *(Possible responses: shish kabob, bouzoukis, costumed dancers in a serpentine line, balancing a glass while dancing)* EL OL

R2 Reading Skill

Review Inferring Say: The author gives details on this page about his continued relationship with Miss Hurd. What might you infer about the teacher when you read that she attends family celebrations? *(Possible response: The author loves her as he loves family.)* How might the author have raised his children to view teachers? *(Possible response: He would have taught his children to respect and admire teachers.)* EL OL

were students from the most troubled homes, yet she would alternately bully and charm each one with her own special brand of tough love until the spark caught fire. She retired in 1981 at the age of 62 but still **avidly** follows the lives and careers of former students while overseeing her adult stepchildren and driving her husband on camping trips to New Hampshire.

Miss Hurd was one of the first to call me on Dec. 10, 1987, when President Reagan, in his television address after the summit meeting with Gorbachev, told the nation that Eleni Gatzoyiannis' dying cry, "My children!" had helped inspire him to seek an arms agreement[13] "for all the children of the world."

"I can't imagine a better monument for your mother," Miss Hurd said with an uncharacteristic catch in her voice.

Although a bad hip makes it impossible for her to join in the Greek dancing, Marjorie Hurd Rabidou is still an honored and enthusiastic guest at all our family celebrations, including my 50th birthday picnic last summer, where the shish kebab was cooked on spits, clarinets and *bouzoukis* wailed, and costumed dancers led the guests in a serpentine[14] line around our colonial farmhouse, only 20 minutes from my first home in Worcester. R1 R2

Visual Vocabulary
Shish kebab consists of chunks of meat and vegetables threaded on a long, thin skewer and broiled.

My sisters and I felt an aching void because my father was not there to lead the line, balancing a glass of wine on his head while he danced, the way he did at every celebration during his 92 years. But Miss Hurd was there, surveying the scene with quiet satisfaction. Although my parents are gone, her presence was a consolation, because I owe her so much. 10

This is truly the land of opportunity, and I would have enjoyed its bounty even if I hadn't walked into Miss Hurd's

13. In 1987 Mikhail ***Gorbachev*** was the leader of the Soviet Union. An ***arms agreement*** is a treaty in which nations agree to put limits on certain weapons.

14. A ***bouzouki*** (boo ZOO kee) is a stringed instrument. A ***serpentine*** (SUR pun teen) line winds around, like a snake's body.

Vocabulary

avidly (AV id lee) *adv.* eagerly; enthusiastically

Practice the Skills

10 Key Reading Skill

Using Text Structure: Compare and Contrast
In this paragraph, how does Gage compare or contrast Miss Hurd with himself and his sisters? With his own parents?

Additional Support

Reading in the Real World

Citizenship The United States is often referred to as a "melting pot" of cultures. Take students to a local historical museum or library to research the cultures represented in the community. Ask students to work in groups to research and create a presentation for the class on one of the cultures. Encourage students to investigate several aspects of the culture, such as dress, food, music, beliefs, and folklore. Their presentations should include at least three cultural aspects. OL

READING WORKSHOP 4

classroom in 1953. But she was the one who directed my grief and pain into writing, and if it weren't for her I wouldn't have become an investigative reporter and foreign correspondent, recorded the story of my mother's life and death in *Eleni* and now my father's story in *A Place for Us*, which is also a testament to the country that took us in. She was the catalyst[15] that sent me into journalism and indirectly caused all the good things that came after. But Miss Hurd would probably deny this emphatically. **11**

A few years ago, I answered the telephone and heard my former teacher's voice telling me, in that won't-take-no-for-an-answer tone of hers, that she had decided I was to write and deliver the eulogy[16] at her funeral. I agreed (she didn't leave me any choice), but that's one assignment I never want to do. I hope, Miss Hurd, that you'll accept this remembrance instead. **12** ❍

15. Here, the ***testament*** is a statement of gratitude and respect. A ***catalyst*** is one who stirs to action.

16. At a funeral, the ***eulogy*** (YOO luh jee) is a speech praising the dead.

Practice the Skills

11 **Reviewing Skill**

Responding How do you feel about Marjorie Hurd after learning how she helped Gage? Have you ever had someone push you to do something you didn't think you could do? What was it?

12 **BIG Question**

How would you describe the influence that Marjorie Hurd had on Gage's life? Write your answer on the "Teacher Who Changed My Life" page of Foldable 4. Your response will help you complete the Unit Challenge later.

Teach

R Reading Skill

Using Text Structure: Compare and Contrast **Ask:** How can you tell from the paragraph on this page that Miss Hurd is the same today as she was when Gage was her student? *(Possible response: She's still a no-nonsense person who won't take no for an answer.)* **OL** **EL**

EL Language Coach

Denotation and Connotation **Ask:** What connotations does the author seem to have for the words *funeral* and *eulogy*? *(Possible responses: sadness, loss)* **OL**

Use the CheckPoint questions provided on Presentation Plus! to check for comprehension of the selection. These questions can be used with interactive response keypads for immediate student feedback.

English Language Coach

Connecting Ask English language learners whether they can relate to events in Gage's life. Then have students make up conversations for the people in each of the following scenes. Students may choose:

- Nick and his sister arriving in America
- Miss Hurd asking Nick to write about his life in Greece
- Gage and his father after getting the award from President Kennedy

Help students prepare by discussing the thoughts and feelings of each person in the scenes. Encourage students to talk about how they would feel if they were in the same position, or have them describe similar experiences they may have had. **EL** **OL**

Objectives

- Identify the influence of word connotations on thoughts and feelings
- Use comparison and contrast

Assess

Resources for page 492

- Selection Quick Check
- Selection and Unit Assessment
- ExamView Assessment Suite
- Interactive Tutor: Self-Assessment

Students can respond to the *After You Read* items in their Learner's Notebook or on a separate sheet of paper.

Answering the

1. Responses will vary.
2. Gage followed a pretty girl in his class into the meeting room.

Critical Thinking

3. Responses will vary but could include the idea that poor people in his homeland have little time for hobbies and clubs as they must work many hours to survive.
4. Responses will vary but should include the idea that he wants others to know about the remarkable women who have influenced his life.
5. Gage dressed and spoke differently.

After You Read

The Teacher Who Changed My Life

Objectives (pp. 492–493)
Reading Use text structure: compare and contrast • Identify author's perspective
Literature Identify literary devices: hyperbole
Vocabulary Understand connotation
Writing Write to compare and contrast
Grammar Identify compound predicates

Answering the

1. Nicholas Gage writes about more than one person who had a strong influence on him. If you were writing about your life, who would you say has had the most influence so far? Explain in two or three sentences.
2. **Recall** What makes Gage decide to sign up for the "Newspaper Club"?
   Tip **Right There**

Critical Thinking

3. **Infer** What do you think Gage means when he says, "The idea of hobbies and clubs made no sense to my immigrant ears"?
   Tip **Author and Me**
4. **Evaluate** What do you think is the author's purpose for writing this story?
   Tip **Think and Search**
5. **Compare and Contrast** How is Gage different from his classmates at Chandler Junior High?
   Tip **Think and Search**

Write About Your Reading

Compare the hopes of Gage's mother for her children with Gage's achievements in life. Make notes for each of these steps:

Step 1: Think about Gage's early life. Where was he born? What happened in his country? Why did his mother want her children to escape? What opportunities did she want them to have?

Step 2: Find specific examples from the story to compare what his mother wanted for her children and what Gage achieved.

Step 3: Think about the importance of people who inspire and help others.

Use your notes to write a paragraph explaining the similarities between Eleni's hopes and Gage's achievements. Include at least two examples from the story to back up your statements.

Write About Your Reading

Possible response:
Eleni would have been proud of what her son accomplished. He got the education she felt was so important and even attended graduate school on scholarships. He is respected and admired, not only for his writing skills but for working hard to become part of his new country. His work has been honored by two presidents—John F. Kennedy and Ronald Reagan. He has also made the world aware of the women responsible for his success—his mother and his teacher.

Skills Review

Key Reading Skill: Using Text Structure: Compare and Contrast

6. Look over the notes you made as you were reading this selection. How many examples of comparing and contrasting did you find?
7. Write a few sentences about how Gage used compare and contrast to tell his story. Did this technique help make his story more understandable and more convincing to you?

Literary Element: Hyperbole

8. How many examples of exaggeration can you find in this selection? Can you find any hyperbole?
9. How do you decide if a writer is exaggerating or simply stating the facts?
10. Do you think more exaggeration would have made Gage's story more effective? Why or why not?

Reviewing Skills: Identifying Author's Purpose and Perspective

11. Think about the fact that Gage had lost his mother and that he knew how much she had valued education. Might he have looked at Mrs. Hurd from a different perspective than other students? Explain.

Vocabulary Check

On a sheet of paper, write the numbers 12–18. Then write a *T* next to the number of each true sentence and an *F* next to the number of each false sentence.

12. **Authoritarian** people are sometimes called "bossy."
13. A team that's losing a game might **ultimately** win.
14. An Olympic ice skater would be **ecstatic** about falling after a jump.
15. An **impoverished** family has all the money they need.
16. An actor might be **mortified** if he forgot his lines on stage.
17. Having **tact** will help you point out someone's mistakes without having that person get upset.
18. Someone who has no interest in sports is likely to read the sports pages **avidly**.
19. **English Language Coach** What impression of Miss Hurd do you get when the author describes her as a "no-nonsense" teacher?

Grammar Link: Compound Predicates

A **compound predicate** is made up of two or more verbs that have the same subject and that are joined by *and, or,* or *nor*.

- Athletes practice often and play hard.
  The verbs *practice* and *play* both go with the subject *athletes*. The verbs are joined by *and*. The compound predicate is *practice and play*.
- Josie neither knows nor cares what you are doing tonight.

The verbs *knows* and *cares* both go with the subject Josie. The verbs are joined by *nor.* The compound predicate is *knows nor cares.*

Grammar Practice

Copy the sentences below on a separate piece of paper. Then underline the compound predicate in each sentence.

20. We walked to the store and bought groceries.
21. I fry or bake my own potato chips.
22. Tom neither washed nor dried the dishes.

Web Activities For eFlashcards, Selection Quick Checks, and other Web activities, go to www.glencoe.com.

READING WORKSHOP 4

Skills Review

Key Reading Skill: Using Text Structure: Compare and Contrast

6. Responses will vary.
7. Responses will vary.

Literary Element: Hyperbole

8. Responses will vary but could include the idea that Miss Hurd saved Gage's life.
9. Responses will vary but should include the idea that readers can spot exaggeration by comparing what is written to what they already know.
10. Responses will vary.

Reviewing Skills: Identifying Author's Purpose and Perspective

11. The response could include the idea that Gage was able to ignore her gruff attitude because he saw value in hard work.

Vocabulary Check

12. T
13. T
14. F
15. F
16. T
17. T
18. F
19. Responses may include ideas of strict dealings with students, few jokes, and structured classes.

Grammar Link: Compound Predicates

Grammar Practice

20. We walked to the store and bought groceries.
21. I fry or bake my own potato chips.
22. Tom neither washed nor dried the dishes.

Close

Ask students to write a letter of appreciation to a teacher who has helped them to succeed.

Reading Across Texts: Persuasive Techniques

Objectives covered in this workshop:
- Identify persuasive and propoganda techniques
- Distinguish between fact and opinion in various texts

Teaching Students to Read for Persuasive Techniques

Why Is It Important?

- Students will learn how to compare different ways that writers try to persuade readers to share a certain point of view or take a particular action.
- Students will gain a better understanding of persuasive techniques as they compare the similarities and differences between two different types of persuasive writing: an editorial and an advertisement.
- By recognizing a variety of persuasive techniques in each text, students will learn how to form their own opinions about what each writer is trying to convey.

How to Help Students Get It

- Remind students that persuasive writing is usually a combination of *fact*-something that can be proven to be true-and *opinion*-something that is believed to be true.
- Discuss the different propaganda techniques that utilize language that appeal to the emotions that writers sometimes use to try to trick readers: glittering generalities, testimonial, and bandwagon.
- Help students create their comparison chart by reviewing different kinds of standards that they can use to best help them compare the two selections.

The Selections and the Big Question

Take the Junk Out of Marketing to Kids

This newspaper editorial demands that food manufacturers be restricted in what and where they may advertise to kids, claiming that junk food marketing is having an unhealthy influence on the target audience. This piece will encourage students to think about the way advertising affects them.

Grainies Toasted Whole-Grain Flakes

This sample of the back of a breakfast cereal box includes some advertising and the FDA nutritional information. Reading these will help students see that both these sources of information can influence their decisions, and that they do so in different ways.

Reading Across Texts Workshop Resources

Pacing (Days) Standard	Pacing (Days) Block	Lesson	Student Materials	Teacher Resources
1		Reading Across Texts: Reading for Persuasive Techniques	Key Reading Skills Practice English Language Coach	Bellringer Options Transparencies Read Aloud, Think Aloud Transparencies Presentation Plus!
2		"Take the Junk out of Marketing Food to Kids"	Literary Analysis Transparencies Glencoe Online Selection Vocabulary Development Academic Vocabulary Development English Language Coach Active Reading Graphic Organizer Literary Analysis StudentWorks Plus Online Student Edition Literature Classics Selection and Unit Assessments	Literary and Text Analysis Transparencies Puzzlemaker Skill Level Up! BookLink 3 Assessment by Learning Objective (Diagnostic and Formative) Interactive Tutor Self-Assessment TeacherWorks Plus
2		*Graines*	Glencoe Online Selection Vocabulary Development Academic Vocabulary Development English Language Coach Active Reading Graphic Organizer Literary Analysis StudentWorks Plus Online Student Edition Literature Classics Selection and Unit Assessments	Literary and Text Analysis Transparencies Puzzlemaker Skill Level Up! BookLink 3 Assessment by Learning Objective (Diagnostic and Formative) Interactive Tutor Self-Assessment TeacherWorks Plus

Keys for Unit Resource

- Blackline Master
- Workbook
- Supplemental Text
- CD-ROM
- DVD
- Transparency
- Web-based
- Fast Files

Level Appropriate Code

AS = Activities for all students
AL = Activities for students working above grade level
OL = Activities for students working at grade level
BL = Activities for students working below grade level
EL = Activities for English language learners

Focus

BELLRINGER Options

Daily Language Practice Transparency

Focus Activity Write the following on the board: Is the new snack food you saw on TV nutritious or junk food? You could compare its features with a food you know is good for you. A chart like the one below might help:

Features	Snack	Apple
Vitamins		
Fiber		
Unhealthy Fats		

Teach

R Reading Skill

Review Distinguishing Fact and Opinion Show students a popular TV food commercial. Ask them to distinguish facts from opinions in the commercial. **Then ask:** Does this commercial present more facts or opinions? Would that influence your decision to buy the product? *(Responses will vary.)* OL

READING ACROSS TEXTS WORKSHOP

Take the JUNK Out of Marketing FOOD to KiDS & GRAINIES

TOASTED WHOLE-GRAIN FLAKES

Skills Focus

You will practice using these skills when you read the following selections:

- "Take the Junk Out of Marketing to Kids," p. 499
- "Grainies Toasted Whole-Grain Flakes," p. 502

Point of Comparison

- Persuasive techniques

Purpose

- To compare the techniques used in an editorial and on a cereal box cover

Vocabulary

- Distinguish between connotation and denotation
- Academic Vocabulary: *standards*

Objectives (pp. 494–495)
Reading Use text structure: compare and contrast

In this unit, you have seen that persuasive writing is common. People have many decisions to make. It can be helpful to know what other people believe.

R However, you need to be able to think for yourself. That's why it's important to know the difference between fact and opinion, to think about the author's purpose and perspective, and to pay attention to words—what they make you feel and think about beyond their actual meanings. Because words are powerful tools, they can carry information. But they can also affect you in ways you're not aware of.

Trying to spread ideas that help one cause or hurt another is called **propaganda.** You've already learned about the use of "value words." (These may also be called "loaded language," "virtue words," or "glittering generalities.") Some other techniques include the following:

- **Testimonial** Famous, admired people "testify" as to how good something is.
  Gloria Glamour won't drive to her TV studio in anything but the new Panzer convertible.
- **Bandwagon** People are urged to "follow the crowd."
  Everyone is crazy about the new best-selling novel by Harry Hackman. Don't be left out. Get your copy today!

494 UNIT 4

Additional Support

Literature Focus Lesson

Distinguish Fact from Opinion
Remind students that writers often use adjectives that represent opinions, rather than proven facts, to persuade readers. List these common words that signal opinions:

- better, worse
- best, worst
- pretty, ugly
- terrific, awful
- most, least
- stupid, smart
- delicious
- inexpensive AS

Get Ready to Compare

Before you make your comparison, look at each type of text and its intended audience. Then think about the "point of camparison" that will best help you compare the two selections. The left column of the chart below shows the points of comparison one student used.

Points of Camparison	Take the Junk Out of Marketing Food to Kids	Grainies Toasted Whole-Grain Flakes
Type of Text	Editorial	Text from Cereal Box
Who is the audience?		
What is the writer's purpose?		
What does the author want you to do?		
What might the author gain if you do it?		
Who is talking to you? A real person?		
Are the "facts" really facts?		
Other Comments		

Use Your Comparison

A chart like this will provide a place for you to look at the two selections side by side. Copy it into your Learner's Notebook and fill it in with comments and examples as you read. After you've read both selections, look at all the information to make your comparison. Then you can draw some conclusions about these selections and about the unit's Big Question.

Teach

R Reading Skill

Review Understanding Persuasive Techniques

Explain that persuasive techniques cause readers to feel strong emotions. Ask students to name some emotions they feel as they watch TV commercials. *(Responses will vary.)* Write their responses on the board. Ask students to identify two commercials that produce one of the emotions listed on the board. EL OL

Assess/Close

Ask: Write a paragraph comparing and contrasting the two commercials you selected. Include persuasive techniques each used to make you feel as you did. Which do you think is more effective? Why? *(Responses will vary.)*

Resources for page 495

Use the Comparing Literature Graphic Organizer BLM in the Unit 4 Resource Booklet.

Reading in the Real World

Career Ask students to select two careers that interest them. Using a format similar to the chart in *Get Ready to Compare,* have students list five aspects of a career that are important for people to consider before entering a career, such as compensation and education. Have students compare the careers by the factors they listed on their charts. Ask students to report their findings to the class. EL OL

Objectives
- Compare and contrast

More About the Author

There are four types of editorials. *Argument and persuasion* takes a firm stand on an issue and asks readers to feel the same way. *Information and interpretation* editorials explain the significance of an event. *Tribute* editorials praise people or groups. *Entertainment* editorials can be humorous or satirical, depending on the topic.

Literature Online

Author Search To expand students' appreciation of editorial writers, have them access the Web site for additional information and resources.

EL Language Coach

Denotation, Connotation, and Semantic Slanting

Ask: What images do you get when you read the word *junk* in the title of this editorial? *(Possible responses: bad stuff, garbage)* **Then ask:** What might this say about the writer's perspective? *(Possible response: He wants people to more responsibly market food to kids.)* OL

Before You Read

Take the Junk Out of Marketing Food to Kids

Meet the Author

Newspaper editorials seldom have named authors. The opinions in them are supposed to be the opinion of the newspaper. They are often written by one of the paper's editors. This editorial, however, names its writer. For information about Sheila Globus, see page 440.

Literature Online

Author Search For more about editorial writers, go to www.glencoe.com.

Objectives (pp. 496–498)
Reading Analyze persuasive techniques
Vocabulary Distinguish denotation and connotation

Vocabulary Preview

prominent (PRAW mih nunt) *adj.* easy to see; standing out **(p. 498)** *Advertisements for foods with high fat content should be banned from prominent positions.*

entice (en TYS) *v.* to attract by making (something) seem desirable; tempt **(p. 498)** *Many of the commercials on daytime TV try to entice young people into buying something.*

Write to Learn For each vocabulary word, write a sentence using the word correctly.

English Language Coach

EL **Connotations** The denotation of the word **reap** is "to cut and gather, especially a crop." In the editorial, however, the word refers to the "huge profits" big food companies make. In this context, does reap have a positive or negative connotation?

Get Ready to Read

Connect to the Reading

What do you know about junk food? How does it affect your health?

Build Background

The editorial was written for the *Detroit Free Press*, a city newspaper.

- Junk food has little or no nutritional value.
- The editorial was written during a time when studies found that children were gaining weight from eating too much junk food.
- Some schools allowed junk food ads in their lunchrooms.

Set Purposes for Reading

BIG Question Read the editorial to find out why the writer wants to limit advertising aimed at children.

Set Your Own Purpose What else do you want to know about junk-food advertising? Write your own purpose on your Foldable for this selection.

Additional Support

Literature Focus Lesson

Editorial Remind students that editorial writers may criticize people but may not make *false* statements that harm people's reputation. This is called *libel*. **Say:** A company president earns $7 million a year but his workers make minimum wage. Ask students to write a statement about the situation. Read the statements to the class to decide if they could be printed. Ask students to explain why or why not. OL

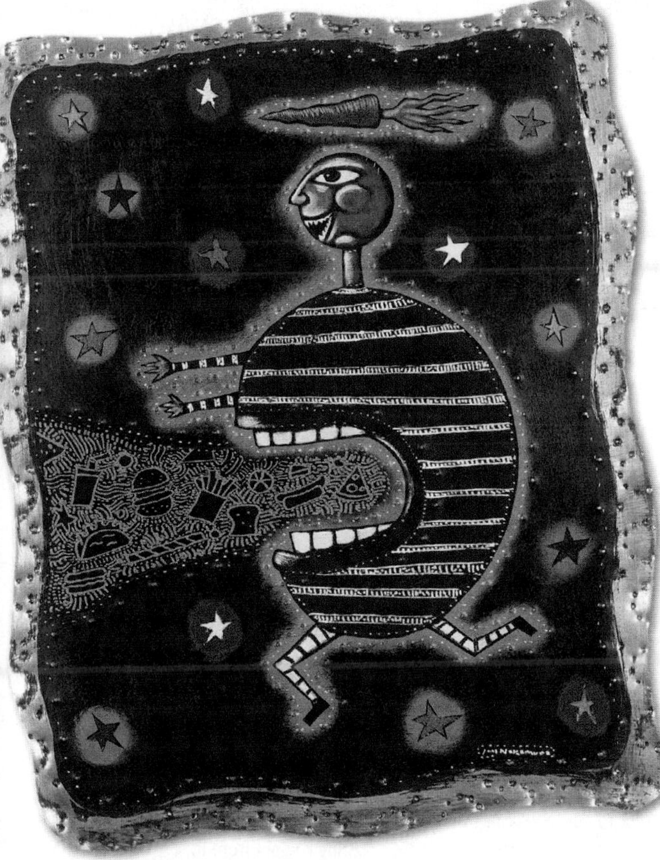

Take the JUNK Out of Marketing FOOD to KiDS

by Sheila Globus

Detroit Free Press 1
January 18, 2005

The food pyramid[1] is a great guide for adults who can understand it. But for young people, the information they get about food is more likely to come from the halls of school or the advertisements they see on TV.

That's why a proposal to limit the marketing of junk food to kids makes so much sense. The Center for Science in the Public Interest wants food manufacturers voluntarily to stop marketing low-nutritional drinks[2] and step up marketing of water, low-fat milk and drinks offering at least 50 percent fruit juice. The nonprofit health research group—often called C

1. The ***food pyramid*** was created by the U.S. Department of Agriculture. It's meant to be an easy guide to which foods and how much of them the average adult should eat for a healthy diet.
2. Food that is ***low-nutritional*** has little healthful benefit.

Practice the Skills

1 Reading Across Texts

Analyzing Persuasive Techniques The title tells that the writer will be expressing an opinion. The credit tells that the editorial came from a newspaper. That tells you something about the author's audience and purpose.

Teach

Viewing the Illustration

Say: What might the artist be saying by making the subject's body large and round? *(Possible response: Eating lots of junk food can make kids overweight.)* EL OL

C Critical Thinking

Comprehension Ask: Why might readers be more likely to believe the recommendations of a nonprofit group over those of a manufacturer? *(Possible response: A nonprofit group does not make money on the studies it conducts, so it would have no reason not to tell the truth.)* AL

Readability Scores
Dale-Chall: 8.1
DRP: 63
Lexile: 1330

English Language Coach

Build Background Invite a dietician, nutritionist, or family and consumer education instructor to display and explain the USDA food pyramid. Then ask students to write down what they eat in a single school day and classify it according to the food pyramid. Ask students to form groups and compare their findings with other members of the group. EL OL

Objectives
- Analyze persuasive techniques
- Distinguish denotation from connotation

Teach

L1 Literary Element

Review Diction, Language, and Word Choice Say: Based on the vocabulary words in this editorial, who might be the writer's audience? *(Possible response: This editorial was written for adults because the words were not ones children commonly read or use.)* **OL**

C Critical Thinking

Evaluation Ask: What counterargument could a reader suggest for the writer's statement that junk foods "make young people fat?" *(Possible response: A reader could argue that young people don't get enough exercise, which makes them fat.)* **OL**

L2 Literary Element

Review Word Choice Ask: In the third paragraph on this page, what verb did the writer choose to connect the idea of food and eating to what he wants manufacturers to do? *(swallow limitations on marketing junk food)* **AL**

the food police for ruining people's unhealthy fun favors allowing companies free range in marketing healthy foods but banning the **prominent** placement of ads for foods with high fat content[3] in movies or other programs designed for kids. **2**

With the huge profits food manufacturers have reaped targeting children, they have the resources to think smarter about them. It's true that the companies don't put junk in young people's mouths. But their marketing messages, to the tune of $15 billion a year, have added to the reasons so many children find it impossible to say no. **3**

About half of the commercials targeted at children every day **entice** young people with foods that make them fat, CSPI researchers estimate. The fact that vending machines in a growing number of school districts now feature as much milk and water as sugar-loaded soda is proof companies can still profit from being more responsible.

Only in a perfect world, manufacturers would swallow these limitations easily. They'll resist. But parents and other outraged citizen groups should press that much harder to make their views known to the food companies. **4**

They need to get the firm message: Stop playing with children's health. **5** ○

3. Junk foods often have a high ***fat content.*** Eating a lot of fat in food is considered unhealthy for anyone.

Vocabulary

prominent (PRAW mih nunt) *adj.* easy to see; standing out

entice (en TYS) *v.* to attract by making (something) seem desirable; tempt

Practice the Skills

2 Reading Across Texts

Analyzing Persuasive Techniques It seems that this is one person writing and that she really believes what she's saying.

3 Reading Across Texts

Analyzing Persuasive Techniques There are lots of facts here. There are opinions, too. But the author is supporting them with facts most of the time.

4 Reading Across Texts

Analyzing Persuasive Techniques It's clear now what the author wants readers to do. She doesn't seem to have anything to gain from it.

5 BIG Question

According to this editorial, who influences you and how? Do you agree? Write your answer on your Foldable for this selection.

Additional Support

Reading in the Real World

Citizenship Ask students to decide how they feel about limiting the marketing and sale of junk food in schools, such as vending machines, candy and bake sale fundraisers, and others. Ask them to write a letter to the school principal or board of education, explaining their views and recommending action. Give students class time to share their letters with the class to get feedback on their supporting arguments, style, organization, and tone. **EL** **OL**

Before You Read

Grainies Toasted Whole-Grain Flakes

Meet the Author

The text on a cereal box is written by people at an advertising agency, a business that creates ads for other businesses. One agency may do all of a product's advertising, or different agencies may split the work—one doing TV commercials, another doing "print," and others doing Web ads, boxes, and so on. Of course, all ads must be approved by people at the company that hired the ad agency.

English Language Coach

EL

Semantic Slanting Cereal boxes, like many other containers, usually include advertising. They use words and phrases with connotations that suit their purpose, which is selling the product.

There's one part of the cereal box that has absolutely no semantic slanting. The way it is written, the words that are used, and even the type it is printed in are all set by law. As you read, look for which part this is. Ask yourself why the requirements for this section are so strict. Think about it as you read and compare.

Get Ready to Read

Connect to the Reading

The back of a cereal box is a powerful advertising tool. If you're a reader, what else are you going to do while you're eating your cereal? Advertising writers know this. And they have a lot of space to convince you that this is the best cereal there is. They also know that people look up to famous athletes. So they get them to lend their names, words, and faces. How many ads have you seen that use celebrities to sell you something?

Partner Talk With a partner, talk about all the celebrities you know of who advertise products. What products do they advertise? Are you more likely to buy a product if a celebrity is in that product's advertisement? Why or why not?

Set Purposes for Reading

BIG Question Read to see what techniques the writer uses to try to persuade you to eat Grainies.

Set Your Own Purpose What else do you want to know about cereals and advertising? Write your own purpose on the cover of your Foldable for this selection.

Objectives (pp. 499–501)
Reading Identify author's purpose
• Identify author's perspective
• Distinguish fact and opinion
Vocabulary Identify semantic slanting

More About the Author

Manufacturers research and develop foods they wish to sell. Advertising agencies often suggest names that will appeal to the people most likely to eat the product. Agencies learn all about the product—how it tastes, how it makes people feel and look—before thinking up names to suggest to the manufacturer. Considering all of the new products, it's amazing that agencies continue to think of new, clever names!

EL Language Coach

Word Choice Say: Many people are athletes. Some are champions. How might the word *champion* affect how you think about a person? *(Possible response: I might think the person is a very good athlete.)* OL

Literature Focus Lesson

Persuasion Techniques in Print Advertisements Food is packaged in a variety of ways. Ask students to bring in an empty, clean package. Have them analyze the persuasiveness of the advertising by completing the following chart. EL OL

Feature	What I observed	Is this effective?
Color		
Shape/Size		
Graphics		
Text		
Propaganda Techniques		

Objectives
• Understand the role semantic slanting plays in persuasive writing
• Identify word denotation and connotation

Teach

R Reading Skill

Review Understanding Persuasive Techniques
Ask: Which persuasive technique does the advertiser use when it includes comments from a well-known person on the package? *(testimonial)* OL

BQ 

Ask: Which person is more likely to influence you to eat Grainies—an NFL player or a doctor? Why? *(Responses will vary.)* EL OL

Product boxes often give you information about what's inside. They also act as advertisements trying to persuade you to buy the product.

GRAINIES
TOASTED WHOLE-GRAIN FLAKES

GRAINIES CAN HELP YOU REACH YOUR FITNESS GOALS BECAUSE THEY CONTAIN:

1. 100% Whole Grain: *Some foods are made from just part of a grain of wheat or corn or oats. Foods made from the whole grain are better at helping you get and stay healthy.*
2. Complex Carbohydrates:[1] *Don't ask what they are. All you need to know is that they give new energy to tired muscles.*
3. B-Vitamins: *They help your body unlock energy stored in food.* **1**

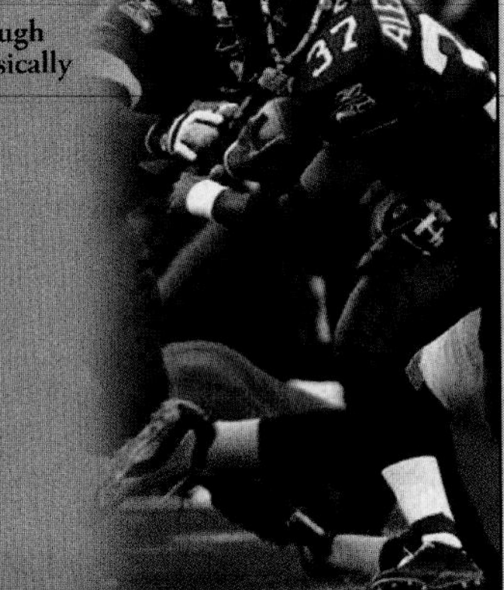

TRAINING WITH ALEC POWERS

I need to stay strong and healthy all through the NFL season. So I prepare myself physically and mentally. Here's how:

- I build strength by lifting weights.
- Jumping, sprinting, and press-ups help me explode off the line.
- I use a stair climber and a bike to build endurance.
- To stay flexible, I stretch before and after every workout.
- My diet includes all kinds of fruits, vegetables, and whole grains. And I always eat my Grainies.

When people ask my advice on training, I tell them to work hard and stick to it. Reach one goal, and set a new one. Always try to improve. **2**

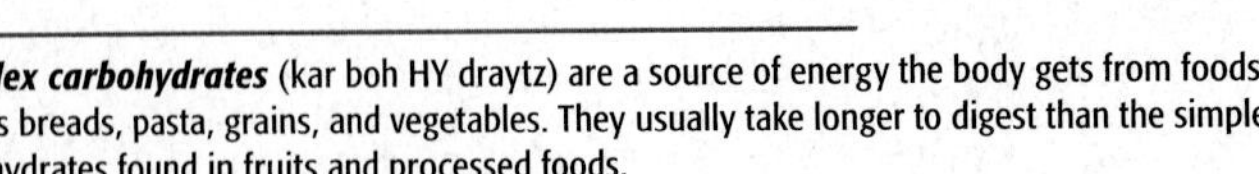

1. ***Complex carbohydrates*** (kar boh HY draytz) are a source of energy the body gets from foods such as breads, pasta, grains, and vegetables. They usually take longer to digest than the simple carbohydrates found in fruits and processed foods.

Practice the Skills

1 Reading Across Texts

Identifying Author's Purpose and Perspective It isn't hard to figure out the purpose of this cereal box copy. It's advertising for a breakfast cereal. Fill in the writer's purpose part of your Comparison Chart. What other details can you add to the cereal box part of the chart?

2 Reading Across Texts

Analyzing Persuasive Techniques When you read this testimonial, ask yourself if you think the person speaking has expert knowledge. Does his job teach him a lot about keeping fit? Would you read this differently if he were a songwriter?

Additional Support

Reading in the Real World

Career Students interested in advertising or marketing may benefit from learning how an ad agency coordinates all aspects of a product promotion. Invite the manager of an ad agency into the classroom or take students to an agency to learn the various jobs people do. Help students brainstorm a product and work with classmates—as an agency—to promote the product, from design and copywriting to sales, graphics, and media. EL OL

Nutrition Facts

Serving Size	1 cup (30g)	
Servings Per Container	about 10	
Amount per Serving	Grainies	Grainies with 1/2 cup skim milk
Calories	110	150
Calories from Fat	10	10
	% Daily Value **	
Total Fat 1g*	1%	2%
Saturated Fat 0g	0%	0%
Trans Fat 0g		
Polyunsaturated Fat 0g		
Monounsaturated Fat 0g		
Cholesterol 0mg	0%	1%
Sodium 220mg	9%	12%
Potassium 105mg	3%	9%
Total Carbohydrate 24g	8%	10%
Dietary Fiber 3g	12%	12%
Sugars 4g		
Other Carbohydrate 17g		
Protein 3g		
Vitamin A	10%	15%
Vitamin C	10%	10%
Calcium	2%	15%
Iron	45%	45%
Vitamin D	10%	25%
Thiamin	50%	50%
Riboflavin	50%	60%
Niacin	50%	50%
Vitamin B6	50%	50%
Folic Acid	50%	50%
Vitamin B12	50%	60%
Phosphorus	10%	20%
Magnesium	8%	10%
Zinc	50%	50%
Copper	4%	4%

* Amount in cereal. A serving of cereal plus skim milk provides 1g total fat, less than 5mg cholesterol, 280mg sodium, 310g potassium, 30g total carbohydrate (10g sugars) and 7g protein.

** Percent Daily Values are based on a 2,000 calorie diet. Your daily values may be higher or lower depending on your calorie needs.

	Calories	2,000
Total Fat	Less than	65g
Sat Fat	Less than	20g
Cholesterol	Less than	300mg
Sodium	Less than	2,400mg
Potassium		3,500mg
Total Carbohydrate		300g
Dietary Fiber		25g

Ingredients: Whole grain wheat, sugar, salt, corn syrup, canola and/or rice bran oil, brown sugar syrup, trisodium phosphate, natural flavor, freshness preserved by BHT. **Vitamins and minerals:** zinc and iron (mineral nutrients), A B vitamin (niacinamide), vitamin C (sodium ascorbate), vitamin B6 (pyridoxine hydrochloride), vitamin B2 (riboflavin), vitamin B1 (thiamin mononitrate), vitamin A (palimitate), A B vitamin (folic acid), vitamin B10, vitamin D. **Contains wheat ingredients.**

3 L1

L2

4

Practice the Skills

3 Reading Across Texts

Distinguishing Fact and Opinion Everything in this long list is information required by the U.S. Food and Drug Administration (FDA). Why do you think this law exists?

4 BIG Question

Look back at the answer to the Big Question you wrote on your Foldable at the end of the first selection in this workshop. Has this second selection changed your answer in any way? Replace, revise, or add to your earlier answer as necessary.

L1 Literary Element

Review Word Choice Ask: Why would an advertiser title this panel *Nutrition Facts* instead of *Nutrition Information?* *(Possible response: When readers see the word "facts," they know they can believe what is written.)* OL

R Reading Skill

Review Using Text Structure: Compare and Contrast Ask: Why do cereal packages show nutrition facts for the cereal eaten alone or eaten with milk? *(Possible response: People can compare the added nutrition they can receive by eating their cereal with milk.)* EL OL

L2 Literary Element

Review Style Say: Compare the style of this part of the cereal box with the back cover on the previous page. Why do you think the advertiser chose this style for *Nutrition Facts*? *(Possible response: By listing the information in columns and rows, readers can more easily scan for specific information.)* OL

Reading Fluency

Building Fluency Students who experience difficulty reading charts for information may benefit from these tips about scanning.

- Decide what you want to know. Charts are written so readers can find specific information quickly and successfully.
- Read headings first. This chart places main headings at the left margin and indents subheadings.
- Use guide lines to read across. EL BL

Objectives

- Distinguish fact and opinion
- Recognize the influence of writing style on readers
- Use comparison and contrast
- Understand the influence of word choice on readers

Assess

Resources for page 502

 Selection Quick Check

 Comparing Literature Assessment

Vocabulary Check

1. Entice
2. prominent
3. Prominent
4. entice
5. Responses will vary.

After You Read

Take the JUNK Out of Marketing FOOD to KiDS

&

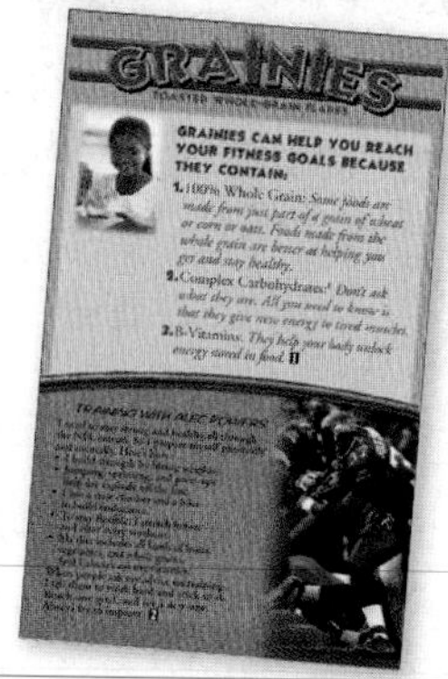

Vocabulary Check

Copy each sentence, filling in the blank with the best word from the list. Each word will be used twice in items 1–4.

prominent **entice**

1. ___ means to tempt someone by making a thing seem desirable.
2. We all immediately recognized the ___ movie star.
3. ___ means very noticeable or easy to see.
4. To ___ children to buy the product the manufacturers printed pictures of puppies on the packaging.
5. **English Language Coach** Write a description of "Grainies" using words with positive connotations. Make the cereal sound as good as you can. The ingredients list says Grainies are made from whole grain wheat and contain brown sugar syrup. You can use some of the words in the list below to get you started.

delicious
tasty
crunchy
crisp
sweet
healthy
wholesome
nutritious

Objectives (pp. 502–503)
Reading Analyze persuasive techniques
Vocabulary Identify semantic slanting
Writing Write to compare texts

Reading/Critical Thinking

On a separate sheet of paper, answer the following questions. The Tips after each question give you hints about where to find the information you need.

Take the Junk Out of Marketing Food to Kids

6. **Identify** What is the topic of this selection?
   TIP Right There

7. **Infer** What is the main purpose of this selection?
   TIP Think and Search

Grainies Toasted Whole-Grain Flakes

8. **Identify** Does this selection have a negative and concerned tone, a positive and upbeat tone, or a tone that is neither negative nor upbeat?
   TIP Author and Me

9. **Connect** Did this selection make you want to eat Grainies rather than your present favorite cereal or, say, a donut? Why or why not?
   TIP Author and Me

Writing: Read Across the Texts

10. Follow these steps to compare the persuasive techniques in these selections. Remember that the goal of persuasive writing is to have an effect on readers in some way. The purpose is to convince readers of an argument and, as a result, make them think, do, or buy something.

    Step 1: Look over the chart you completed. Underline the details that are similar for both sections. Circle the details that are different.

    Step 2: On a separate sheet of paper, make two lists. In one, list the details that are similar. In the other, list the details that are different.

    Step 3: Look at the lists you've made. Is the tone of one selection more serious and concerned than the tone of the other? Think about how each tone has a different effect on you.

    Step 4: Notice which techniques are used in both selections. But also note how the techniques are different.

    - What is the main idea of the editorial? How is it stated?
    - What is the main idea of the cereal box text? How is that stated?

You will use this information to support your answers in the next section. Put a check beside the details that have a strong effect on you.

Get It on Paper

To show what you found about the use of persuasive techniques in the editorial and the cereal box text, copy these statements on a separate piece of paper and complete them with the right answers.

11. In the editorial, the author's perspective is stated near the editorial's
    (a) end. (b) beginning.
12. In the cereal box text, the author's perspective is that you should eat Grainies because they
    (a) taste better. (b) will make you healthier.
13. In the editorial, the writer's word choices help the reader imagine the contrast between big business and ___.
14. In the cereal box text, the writer's word choices help the reader think about fitness and ___.
15. The editorial writer wants me to agree that ___.
16. The cereal box writer wants me to agree that ___.

BIG Question

17. Think about who tried to influence you in these selections. Think about how they tried. Think about whether they were successful. Then write a paragraph telling whether you were influenced by either selection. If you were, how? If not, why not?

Literature Online

Web Activities For eFlashcards, Selection Quick Checks, and other Web activities, go to www.glencoe.com.

Literature Online

Web Activities Have students access the Web site for interactive activities that will help them assess their understanding of the selection.

Reading/Critical Thinking

6. The topic of the selection is the practice of marketing junk food to children.
7. The main purpose of the selection is to persuade readers to insist that manufacturers limit efforts to market junk food to children.
8. The tone of this selection is positive and upbeat.
9. Responses will vary.

Writing: Read Across the Texts

10. Students will vary in the way they mark their charts.

Get It on Paper

11. In the editorial, the author's perspective is stated near the editorial's (b) beginning.
12. In the cereal box text, the author's perspective is that you should eat Grainies because they (b) will make you healthier.
13. Possible responses include consumers or children.
14. Possible responses include health or a healthy life.
15. Possible response: people should insist that manufacturers limit the advertising of junk food to children.
16. Possible response: Grainies are a healthy food choice for people.

BIG Question

17. Responses will vary.

Close

Ask students to list forms of persuasive writing they use and observe in daily life.

The Unit Challenge

Focus

BELLRINGER Options

Daily Language Practice Transparency

Focus Activity Ask: Of the selections you read in this unit, which do you think was most persuasive? Why?

The discussion will remind students of the selections they've read, which will help them begin the group or the solo activity.

Teach

Group Activity: "Kids Today Watch Too Much TV"

- Ask one member to volunteer to be note-keeper.
- Be sure your group has completed step 3, including students' individual assignments, by the middle of the class hour so you have time to lay out and make the poster.
- After you have tried several layouts, choose the one that group members like best.
- Before you permanently place text or graphics on the poster, all group members should proofread for errors.

Assess/Close

Group Activity

Ask: How might you apply the information in your poster to your own TV-watching habits? *(Suggest that students write responses in their Learner's Notebook.)*

UNIT 4 WRAP-UP

Answering

Who Influences Us and How Do They Do So?

You've just read several different selections about who or what influences us. Now use what you've learned to do the Unit Challenge.

The Unit Challenge

Choose Activity A or Activity B and follow the directions for that activity.

A. Group Activity: "Kids Today Watch Too Much TV"

- You and two friends received a call from a local TV station. The producer from the show "Let the Kids Speak!" is inviting your group to present the topic you sent in, called "Kids Today Watch Too Much TV."
- The TV station wants you to make a poster about your topic.
- You may use words, photographs, charts, and other graphics to show your position on the topic.

1. **Discuss the Assignment** Choose one group member to be the note-keeper for the discussion. Start by discussing what you think about how much time kids spend watching TV. Learn what members of your group feel about TV's influence. On your Foldable notes, review how different people influenced others in their lives and in their writing. Consider how your poster can draw on what you have read in this unit. Recall how something Oprah Winfrey learned from TV when she was ten influenced her and how a teacher's words influenced Nicholas Gage.

2. **Make a Decision and Divide the Work** As a group, review your notes and decide on the argument you want to present on the poster. Brainstorm a list of words and phrases related to that argument. Then decide which items on the list could be illustrated instead of written. Finally, divide up the tasks. Who will gather facts? Who will find or create graphics—draw pictures, take photographs, cut out magazine images, and so on?

3. **Make the Poster** Here are some tips on putting it all together:
   - Review the facts and select those you'll use. You don't want to confuse your audience by presenting too many facts at once.
   - Review the graphics and select those you'll use. A good poster has one main graphic that grabs attention and directs the audience to the words.
   - Put together a few different layouts until you find one the group agrees on. Work together to put your best ideas on the poster.

4. **Present Your Poster** Check all writing for spelling or grammar errors. Is the poster clear? Is it catchy? Does it surprise or get attention? Most important: make sure your argument is clear. Hang it in the classroom.

B. Solo Activity: "Don't Just Think It. Say It!"

Some authors write books about people they admire—President Lincoln or Mother Theresa or even the latest pop star. Poets sometimes write poems praising such people. Some songwriters make up lyrics to remember people—such as a ballad about John Henry. In Activity B you'll put your own creative genius to work to praise someone who has been a good influence on you. It's a little like making up a cheer for someone.

1. **Decide on a Person** Whom do you want to honor for the good influence he or she has had on you? Think about these questions:
   - In this unit, how did the selections describe people who influenced others?
   - What notes from your Unit 4 Foldable tell about brilliance, greatness, humor, or bravery—whatever it is that you admire in the person?
   - Which selections in Unit 4 did you like reading the most?

2. **Decide on Your Genre**
   - Write a poem, song, or rap that tells what the person means to you.
   - Write a thank-you letter telling this real person why he or she is important to you.
   - Make a list of the five or ten best things about that person.

3. **Brainstorm** Jot down everything that comes to your mind about this person.
   - What qualities does he or she have?
   - How did he or she handle big challenges?
   - Why does he or she have an influence on you?
   - Why would you like to tell others about this person?

4. **Give It Some Shape** Turn some of your ideas into the form you chose earlier. Remember that it doesn't have to be long or complicated. It should be a short work in praise of somebody who has made a difference in this world or a difference in your life.

5. **Say It!** Present it to your classmates or send it to the school paper. You may even want to send it to the person whom it honors. Someday, someone may send you a poem that shows how important your influence has been to them. So don't just think it. Say it!

Teach

Solo Activity: "Don't Just Think It. Say It!"

- Have students choose the person they wish to praise for influencing them.
- Ask them to choose the genre for their writing. If students have trouble selecting a genre, ask them to think about which of the genres they most enjoy reading.
- Encourage students to use their Learner's Notebook to record their answers.
- If students select poetry or song, have them identify the elements of the genre: rhythm, rhyme, figurative and sensory language.
- Students who select the letter should be sure to include a date, salutation, body, closing, and signature.
- As a last step, students should read their praise selections to the class.

Assess/Close

Solo Activity

Ask students to identify who they've written about. Have them write about the traits they display that resulted from this person's influence.

Objectives
- Design an informational poster
- Write a poem or song

Focus

Vocabulary Preview

List the following words on the board:

- moil
- marge
- homely
- mushing
- cash in
- cremate
- heed
- tax
- brawn
- woes
- loathed
- quiet clay
- derelict
- in a trice

Review their definitions before students begin reading.

Build Background

Prospectors came to the Yukon to pan gold.

- The Yukon lies in Canada's far northwest. Up to four months a year, average temperatures in the Yukon do not rise above 10°C.
- The discovery of gold in 1896 began the Klondike Gold Rush.

Teach

L Literary Element

Review Hyperbole Ask: What is a hyperbole in this poem? *(Possible responses: make your blood run cold, sooner live in hell)* OL

Your Turn: Read and Apply Skills

Meet the Author

While writing poems about the rugged Yukon Territory and the wild, colorful characters found there, Robert Service worked as a bank teller. His life, however, was certainly not dull. At one time or another, he worked in professional sports, theater, construction, journalism, and other jobs. As a writer, he produced poetry, novels, and an autobiography. He is best remembered today as the author of "The Cremation of Sam McGee." Service was born in England in 1874 and died in France in 1958. See page R6 of the Author Files for more on Robert Service.

Author Search For more about Robert Service, go to www.glencoe.com.

The Cremation of Sam McGee

by Robert Service

There are strange things done in the midnight sun
By the men who moil for gold;*
The Arctic trails have their secret tales
That would make your blood run cold; L
The Northern Lights have seen queer sights,
But the queerest they ever did see
Was that night on the marge, of Lake Lebarge*
I cremated Sam McGee.

Now Sam McGee was from Tennessee,
where the cotton blooms and blows.
Why he left his home in the South to roam
'round the Pole, God only knows.
He was always cold, but the land of gold
seemed to hold him like a spell;
Though he'd often say in his homely* way that
"he'd sooner live in hell." L
On a Christmas Day we were mushing* our way
over the Dawson* trail.

---

2 To ***moil*** is to work hard.
7 ***Marge*** is an old word for margin, or edge.
15 Here, ***homely*** means "ordinary."
17 Dogsled drivers say "Mush!" to keep the dogs moving faster, so driving the dogsled is ***mushing***.
18 ***Dawson*** was a gold-mining city in the Yukon Territory of Canada.

Additional Support

Author Search To expand students' appreciation of Robert Service, have them access the Web site.

Literature Focus Lesson

Summary In this poem, the narrator prospects for gold with Sam McGee in the Yukon Territory. After traveling by dogsled on Christmas Day, McGee foretells his death and asks that his friend cremate his remains when he dies. The next day, McGee dies and the narrator drives with the corpse until he reaches Lake Lebarge, where he finds an abandoned ship, which he sets afire as a crematorium for Sam's body. OL

Talk of your cold! through the parka's fold it stabbed
like a driven nail.
If our eyes we'd close, then the lashes froze till
sometimes we couldn't see;
It wasn't much fun, but the only one to whimper
was Sam McGee.

And that very night, as we lay packed tight
in our robes beneath the snow,
And the dogs were fed, and the stars o'erhead
were dancing heel and toe,
He turned to me, and "Cap," says he,
"I'll cash in* this trip, I guess;
And if I do, I'm asking that you won't refuse
my last request."

Well, he seemed so low that I couldn't say no;
then he says with a sort of moan:
"It's the cursèd cold, and it's got right hold till
I'm chilled clean through to the bone.
Yet 'tain't being dead—it's my awful dread of the
icy grave that pains;

30 Here, ***cash in*** means "die."

Teach

R Reading Skill

Review Using Text Structure: Compare and Contrast **Ask:** How does Tennessee compare to the Yukon? *(Possible response: Cotton grows in Tennessee because it's warm. The Yukon freezes eyelashes shut.)* **OL**

L1 Literary Element

Review Style **Ask:** What makes this poem like a story? *(Possible response: The narrator tells events in time sequence.)* **OL**

L2 Literary Element

Review Word Choice **Ask:** How do you know that the characters don't live in current times? *(Possible response: They use phrases and words like* cursèd cold *and* 'tain't.*)* **OL**

Differentiated Instruction

Organizing Supporting Details

Robert Service describes the Yukon to show readers the harsh life of prospectors. He includes details that help readers feel and picture the bitter cold. Have students organize details that support this view of prospecting life with a chart like the one shown here.

What I Read	What I Picture

OL

Objectives

- Use comparison and contrast
- Understand the influence of word choice and style on readers
- Analyze persuasive techniques

Teach

R1 Reading Skill

Review Using Text Structure: Compare and Contrast Say: Compare the narrator's feelings toward Sam the person and Sam the corpse. *(Possible response: When Sam was alive, the narrator liked him. The narrator hates the corpse.)* **OL**

R2 Reading Skill

Review Identifying Author's Purpose and Perspective Ask: Why do you think the poet writes that the narrator sang to the corpse and that it talked and grinned? *(Possible response: It helps readers understand that the narrator is close to madness.)* **AL**

L Literary Element

Review Tone Ask: How does the poet feel about the narrator? *(Possible response: I think he admires him for keeping a promise to a friend.)* **OL**

So I want you to swear that, foul or fair, you'll
cremate* my last remains."

A pal's last need is a thing to heed,* so I swore
I would not fail;
And we started on at the streak of dawn; but God!
he looked ghastly pale.
He crouched on the sleigh, and he raved all day
of his home in Tennessee;
And before nightfall a corpse was all that was left
of Sam McGee.

There wasn't a breath in that land of death,
and I hurried, horror driven,
With a corpse half hid that I couldn't get rid,
because of a promise given;
It was lashed to the sleigh, and it seemed to say:
"You may tax* your brawn* and brains,
But you promised true, and it's up to you
to cremate those last remains."

Now a promise made is a debt unpaid,
and the trail has its own stern code.
In the days to come, though my lips were dumb,
in my heart how I cursed that load.
In the long, long night, by the lone firelight,
while the huskies, round in a ring,
Howled out their woes* to the homeless snows—
O God! how I loathed* the thing.

And every day that quiet clay* seemed to
heavy and heavier grow;
And on I went, though the dogs were spent
and the grub was getting low;

---

40 To ***cremate*** a body is to burn it and not bury it.
41 To ***heed*** is to pay careful attention.
54 Here, ***tax*** means "to strain," and ***brawn*** refers to how strong one's muscles are.
63 ***Woes*** are troubles.
63 ***Loathed*** means "hated."
65 The ***quiet clay*** is Sam's body.

Additional Support

English Language Coach

Connotations with Synonyms The poet uses two synonyms for the word *friend* in the poem—*pal* and *chum.* Help students recognize that words that mean nearly the same thing usually have slightly different feelings associated with them. Have students work with a partner to discuss how these words from the poem suggest something different from their synonyms: *stern* and *serious, howled* and *cried, lone* and *single, grub* and *food, grin* and *smile. (Responses will vary.)* **OL**

The trail was bad, and I felt half mad,
but I swore I would not give in;
And I'd often sing to the hateful thing, and
it hearkened with a grin.
Till I came to the marge of Lake Lebarge,
and a derelict* there lay;
It was jammed in the ice, but I saw in a trice*
it was called the "Alice May."
And I looked at it, and I thought a bit, and
I looked at my frozen chum;
Then "Here," said I, with a sudden cry,
"is my cre-ma-tor-eum."

Some planks I tore from the cabin floor,
and I lit the boiler fire;
Some coal I found that was lying around,
and I heaped the fuel higher;
The flames just soared, and the furnace roared—
such a blaze you seldom see;
And I burrowed a hole in the glowing coal,
and I stuffed in Sam McGee.

---

74 A ***derelict*** is an abandoned ship.

75 To see ***in a trice*** is to see quickly.

Teach

L Literary Element

Review Tone Ask: What can you tell about the poet's feelings toward the subject from his use of the words *stuffed* and *cooked?* *(Possible response: I think the poet thinks the situation is funny now.)* **OL**

Reading in the Real World

Career Some students may be interested in writing humor. Newspapers and radio networks often employ humorists to write regular features, often about common, everyday events or people. Ask students to read one piece of writing by a successful humorist such as Erma Bombeck, Garrison Keillor, or Dave Barry. Then ask them to write a short poem about an everyday situation that people usually take seriously but can have a funny side. **OL**

Objectives

- Identify tone
- Understand how word choice influences readers
- Identify author's purpose and perspective

Teach

Viewing the Photo
Ask: How does this photo relate to the poem? *(Possible response: It shows wind blowing.)*

R Reading Skill

Review Identifying Author's Purpose and Perspective **Say:** What is the poet's purpose in writing that the narrator had to leave the area for a while? *(Possible response: The poet wants readers to know that it bothers the narrator to cremate his friend.)* **OL**

L1 Literary Element

Review Word Choice **Ask:** What effect does the word *sizzle* have on the narrator and on readers? *(Possible response: Readers are uncomfortable thinking that a person's body sizzles like a piece of bacon.)* **AL**

L2 Literary Element

Review Sensory Details
Ask: What senses does the author appeal to on this page? *(hearing, touch, sight)*

The Northern Lights are streams of light that appear in the sky in areas near the North Pole.

Analyzing the Photo How does this image help you get a feel for the setting of the poem?

Then I made a hike, for I didn't like
to hear him sizzle so;
And the heavens scowled, and the huskies howled,
and the wind began to blow.
It was icy cold, but the hot sweat rolled down
my cheeks, and I don't know why;
And the greasy smoke in an inky cloak
went streaking down the sky.

I do not know how long in the snow
I wrestled with grisly fear;

Additional Support

Reading in the Real World

Citizenship Robert Service jokingly writes about an honorable man who suffers in order to keep a promise to a friend. Take students to the library to research a real-life person who has endured hardships for the sake of a friend or family member. Ask students to take notes on the backgrounds of the two people, the situation, and how the situation was resolved. Ask students to write a short poem honoring the person's loyalty and bravery. **OL**

UNIT 5

Skills Scope and Sequence *continued*

Readability Scores Key
Dale-Chall/DRP/Lexile

PACING (DAYS) STANDARD	BLOCK	INSTRUCTIONAL SEGMENT LITERATURE	READING SKILLS	LITERARY ELEMENTS
3	1	**Reading Workshop 3, pp. 578–595** "The Next Big Thing" by Maryanne Murray Buechner and Mitch Frank, updated from TIME **4.6/57/900**, SE p. 580 "Big Yellow Taxi" by Joni Mitchell **5.7/47/580**, SE p. 590	Taking Notes, SE pp. 578, 581, 582, 583, 584, 587, 591, 592 Paraphrasing and Summarizing, TWE p. 592 Connecting, TWE pp. 581, 591 Drawing Conclusions, TWE p. 583 Responding, TWE p. 587	Concept and Definition, SE pp. 581, 582, 585, TWE pp. 582, 584, 585 Theme, SE pp. 591, 593 Author's Craft, TWE p. 591
1	cont'd. ↓	**Writing Workshop, Part 2, pp. 596–601** Writing Product: Research Report		
2	1	**Reading Workshop 4, pp. 603–621** "Fireproofing The Forests" by J. Madeleine Nash, updated from TIME **4.2/44/550**, SE p. 606 "Missing!" by Claire Miller **8.3/61/1090**, SE p. 616 "Birdfoot's Grampa" by Joseph Bruchac SE p. 619	Identifying Problem and Solution, SE pp. 602, 605, 607, 610, 611, 615, 616, 619 Responding, TWE p. 608 Using Text Features, TWE p. 610 Connecting, TWE p. 615	Description, SE pp. 605, 606, 609, 615, 617, 619
2	2	**Reading Across Texts Workshop, SE pp. 622–633** "America the Not-So-Beautiful" by Andrew A. Rooney **5.2/56/1020**, SE p. 625 "A Glimpse of Home" by Kathryn Sullivan **6.6/66/1180**, SE p. 630	Making Connections Across Texts, SE p. 622, Author's Craft, SE pp. 625, 626, 627, 628, 630, 631 Identifying Problem and Solution, TWE p. 625	Author's Craft, TWE pp. 622, 623, 625, 626, 627, 628, 630, 631 Tone, TWE p. 624
2	1	**Unit Wrap-Up, pp. 634–641** "Key Item" by Isaac Asimov **7.8/55/1090**, SE p. 636	Reading independently, SE p. 636 Paraphrasing and Summarizing, TWE p. 637 Problem and Solution, TWE p. 638	Description, TWE pp. 636, 639 Author's Craft, TWE p. 637 Concept and Definition, TWE p. 637

Unit 5 Big Question

The question, "Is Progress Aways Good?" is designed to help students realize that the world is not stagnant. In this unit, students will read a variety of selections regarding science and technology as a subject. Students will encounter both science fiction and science fact; these selections address a progressing world and challenge students to consider their role in both the present and future.

Unit 5 Genre

Many of the selections in this unit are science and technology writings, texts that teach about the world we live in. They center around the concept of Progress and the questions raised by this issue. These selections will help students think about the big question: Is Progress Always Good? Use these texts to help students recognize and think about the rapidly changing world in which they live.

CRITICAL THINKING	VOCABULARY	WRITING AND GRAMMAR	LISTENING, SPEAKING, AND VIEWING
Big Question, SE pp. 520, 522, 523, TWE pp. 520, 522, 523		Write to Learn, SE p. 527	Partner Talk, SE p. 527 Viewing the Photo, TWE p. 520
Draw Conclusions, SE p. 542 Interpret, SE p. 542 Evaluate, SE pp. 542, 550 Infer, SE p. 550 Big Question, SE pp. 531, 533, 535, 537, 541, 542, 545, 548, TWE pp. 535, 537, 541, 548 Comprehension, TWE p. 540	Structural Analysis, SE pp. 530, 539, 543, TWE pp. 525, 530, 539 Content-Area Words, SE pp 544, 549, 551, TWE pp. 526, 544, 545 Academic vocabulary, SE pp. 528, 543 Vocabulary Preview, SE pp. 530, 544 Acronyms, TWE p. 549	Clauses, SE p. 543 Phrases, SE p. 551 Write About Your Reading, SE p. 542, TWE p. 542 Write to Learn, SE pp. 530, 531, 545, 550	Talk About Your Reading, SE p. 550 Partner Talk, SE pp. 530, 545 Group Work, SE pp 531, 544 Viewing the Illustration, TWE p. 532
		Writing a Research Report: Prewriting and Drafting, SE pp. 552-554 Main and Subordinate Clauses, SE p. 555 Thesis Statements, TWE p. 554 Cause and Effect, TWE p. 554	
Big Question, SE pp. 559, 560, 567, 572, 575, TWE pp. 560, 563, 569, 571, 574, 575 Connect, SE p. 564 Draw Conclusions, SE p. 564, TWE p. 571	Academic vocabulary, SE p. 556, 565, TWE p. 556, 565 Vocabulary Preview, SE pp. 558, 566	Write About Your Reading, SE pp. 564, 576 Parts of Speech, SE pp. 565, 577	Group Work, SE p. 559 Partner Talk, SE p. 567 Viewing the Photo, TWE pp. 570, 575

Skills Scope and Sequence

Readability Scores Key
Dale-Chall/DRP/Lexile

PACING (DAYS) STANDARD	BLOCK	INSTRUCTIONAL SEGMENT LITERATURE	READING SKILLS	LITERARY ELEMENTS
1	1	**Unit Warm-Up, pp. 522–527** Genre Focus: "Hip Hop" from The Story of Music **4.7/57/900**, SE p. 525	Paraphrasing and Summarizing, SE pp. 524, 525 Using Text Features, SE pp. 524, 525 Taking Notes, SE pp. 524, 525, TWE p. 525 Identifying Problem and Solution, SE pp. 524, 527, TWE p. 527 Connecting, TWE p. 522 How to Read Science and Technology Writing, TWE p. 524	Author's Craft, SE pp. 524, 526, Organization, SE pp. 524, 526, TWE p. 526 Concept and Definition, SE pp. 524, 526, TWE pp. 524, 526 Description, SE pp. 524, 526
3	2	**Reading Workshop 1, pp. 528–551** "LAFF" by Lensey Namioka **6.9/62/1100**, p. 532 "Cyber Chitchat" by Cindy Kauffman **5.3/52/730**, SE p. 546	Paraphrasing and Summarizing, SE pp. 528, 529, 531, 532, 534, 536, 540, 542, 543, 545, 547, 550, 551 Reviewing, SE p. 533 Setting a Purpose for Reading, SE p. 546, TWE p. 546 Connecting, TWE pp. 531, 545	Author's Craft, SE pp. 531, 532, 534, 538, 540, 543, 545, 547, 549, 551, TWE pp. 527, 531, 532, 534, 535, 536, 538, 539, 541, 545, 547 Character, TWE p. 533 Tone, TWE p. 546
1		**Writing Workshop, Part 1, pp. 552–555** Writing Product: Research Report		
3	1	**Reading Workshop 2, pp. 556–577** "Conserving Resources" **6.1/66/1030**, SE p. 560 "There Will Come Soft Rains" by Ray Bradbury **4.9/54/810**, SE p. 568	Using Text Features, SE pp. 556, 557, 559, 563, 565, 567, 570, 577, TWE pp. 556, 557, 563 Reviewing- Identifying Author's Purpose, SE pp. 573, 575, TWE pp. 562, 572 Connecting, TWE p. 567	Organization, SE pp. 559, 561, 565, 567, 568, 573, 574, 577, TWE pp. 559, 561, 567, 568, 573

3. Which of the following is a sentence fragment?
- **A.** Sentence 2
- **B.** Sentence 3
- **C.** Sentence 4
- **D.** Sentence 6

4. Which of the following is an interrogative sentence?
- **A.** Sentence 5
- **B.** Sentence 7
- **C.** Sentence 8
- **D.** Sentence 9

5. Which of the following is an exclamatory sentence?
- **A.** Sentence 3
- **B.** Sentence 6
- **C.** Sentence 9
- **D.** Sentence 10

6. Which of the following is a declarative sentence?
- **A.** Sentence 1
- **B.** Sentence 5
- **C.** Sentence 6
- **D.** Sentence 9

7. Which of the following is an imperative sentence?
- **A.** Sentence 3
- **B.** Sentence 4
- **C.** Sentence 9
- **D.** Sentence 11

8. Which of the following has incorrect end punctuation?
- **A.** Sentence 5
- **B.** Sentence 8
- **C.** Sentence 9
- **D.** Sentence 10

9. What is the best way to organize the points you want to make in an editorial?
- **A.** in order of length
- **B.** in the order you think of them
- **C.** in the order you decide is most convincing
- **D.** always from most important to least important

10. If, while writing an editorial, you think of what someone who disagrees with you might say, what should you do?
- **A.** Leave out the ideas people might disagree with.
- **B.** Respond to possible disagreements in your editorial.
- **C.** Be brave and pay no attention to what others might think.
- **D.** Cover both sides of the issue and let readers decide who's right.

Test Practice

Part 4: Writing Skills *continued*

3. B
4. A
5. B
6. A
7. C
8. D
9. C
10. B

Test Practice

Part 4: Writing Skills

1. B

2. D

Part 4: Writing Skills

On a separate sheet of paper, write the numbers 1–10. Next to each number, write the letter of the right answer for that question.

1. Which sentence below has a compound subject?
- **A.** They both ran and jumped in the car.
- **B.** My sister and her best friend arrived.
- **C.** Our dog, Sarge, weighs 100 pounds.
- **D.** The animals at the zoo were interesting.

2. Which sentence below has a compound predicate?
- **A.** They had traveled quite a long way.
- **B.** Jorge looked for his shoes and socks.
- **C.** We didn't finish the salad or the potatoes.
- **D.** Mr. Franklin stopped and stared at the truck

Use the paragraph below to answer questions 3–8.

[1]Before the 1960's, the only seatbelts were on airplanes or amusement park rides. [2]Cars didn't have them. [3]Babies, children, teenagers, and even adults. [4]Nobody used seatbelts. [5]How safe were passengers in a crash? [6]They weren't safe at all! [7]A sudden crash could send people flying and throw them into the windshield. [8]Cars are much safer today. [9]Wear your seatbelt every time you travel in a car. [10]Is that too much to ask. [11]After all, using seatbelts saves lives!

Objectives
Writing Organize structure, anticipate and address counterarguments
Grammar Identify compound subjects and predicates
• Identify sentence types • Identify sentence fragments
• Use end punctuation correctly

Part 3: Vocabulary Skills

On a separate sheet of paper, write the numbers 1–10. Next to each number, write the letter of the right answer for that question.

For questions 1–5, write the letter of the word or phrase that means about the same as the underlined word.

1. need to <u>focus</u>

A. finish **B.** remember **C.** pay attention **D.** be successful

2. what she <u>implied</u>

A. feared **B.** hinted at **C.** imagined **D.** recognized as true

3. a <u>frail</u> person

A. weak **B.** kind **C.** familiar **D.** well-known

4. to <u>enhance</u> my appearance

A. hide **B.** damage **C.** improve **D.** show pride in

5. a sign of <u>compassion</u>

A. strength **B.** deep love **C.** selfishness **D.** kind concern

6. Which synonym would best communicate the idea of a mild feeling?

rage anger fury irritation

A. rage **B.** anger **C.** fury **D.** irritation

7. Which synonym would best communicate the idea that a house is small, pleasant, and cozy?

hut cottage shack residence

A. hut **B.** cottage **C.** shack **D.** residence

8. Which description is an example of semantic slanting?

A. They listened to the idea and decided against it.

B. They objected firmly to the idea that was presented.

C. They heard the idea, considered it, and then rejected it.

D. They stubbornly refused to give the idea the attention it deserved.

9. Which statement illustrates an awareness of the connotation of words?

A. Don't say she's *old*; call her *mature*.

B. A frog is an *amphibian*; a snake is a *reptile*.

C. She's not the team's *pitcher*, she's the *catcher*.

D. Some people call that a *sofa*; some call it a *couch*.

10. What is the "denotation" of a word?

A. its part of speech

B. its meaning, as described by a dictionary

C. its meaning, with all its emotional associations

D. its history, including the language it came from

Test Practice

Part 3: Vocabulary Skills

1. C
2. B
3. A
4. C
5. D
6. D
7. B
8. D
9. A
10. B

Test Practice

Part 2: Reading Skills

1. B
2. A
3. C
4. A

Part 2: Reading Skills

Read the passage. Then, on a separate sheet of paper, write the numbers 1–4. Write the letter of the right answer next to the number for that question.

[1]Wolves are scary. [2]They're horrible, dangerous beasts. [3]They follow children through the forest and eat grandmothers, and only the bravest of heroes can defeat them. [4]That's all true . . . if one is describing the wolves in fairy tales. [5]In real life, wolves are almost always harmless to people. [6]Unlike bears and cougars, they would much rather flee from a person than attack and will do their best to avoid any contact at all. [7]In the Superior National Forest of Minnesota, which has always been home to hundreds of wolves, not a single human visitor has ever been attacked by a wolf. [8]Captured wolves may be dangerous because they are wild animals, not pets, but the dogs we keep in our homes and feed from our tables are more dangerous to people than wolves who are roaming free. [9]Wolves are amazing creatures that should be admired, not feared.

---

1. What was the author's *main* purpose in writing this passage?

A. to entertain readers with a story about wolves
B. to persuade readers to change their negative views of wolves
C. to express feelings about nature and natural creatures
D. to inform readers about wolves by providing details about their lives

2. This passage contrasts wolves in fairy tales to

A. wolves in real life
B. bears and cougars
C. captured wolves
D. pets we keep in our homes

3. Which sentence in the passage is a statement of fact?

A. Sentence 1
B. Sentence 2
C. Sentence 7
D. Sentence 9

4. What is the most likely reason this particular picture of wolves was used to illustrate this passage?

A. It makes wolves seem harmless.
B. It provides important information about wolves.
C. It encourages viewers to form their own opinions.
D. It shows a situation that cannot be described in words.

Objectives
Reading Identify author's purpose • Distinguish fact from opinion • Understand comparison/contrast
Vocabulary Distinguish denotation and connotation • Identify semantic slanting

1. Which sentence from the first paragraph states an opinion?
   A. Sentence 1
   B. Sentence 2
   C. Sentence 3
   D. Sentence 4

2. Which of the following best describes the tone of this passage?
   A. curious
   B. amused
   C. regretful
   D. frightened

3. Which sentence contains an example of hyperbole?
   A. Sentence 3
   B. Sentence 9
   C. Sentence 14
   D. Sentence 25

4. What is the most likely reason that the writer used exaggeration in this passage?
   A. to make her description amusing
   B. to show that her description is fictional
   C. to emphasize the changes in Lawson County
   D. to trick the reader into believing untrue statements

5. What synonym could be substituted for *walking* in sentence 15 without changing the tone?
   A. *trudging*
   B. *marching*
   C. *plodding*
   D. *wandering*

6. What is the most likely reason that the author chose to describe the city as "creeping out" to "swallow," "chew up," and "devour"?
   A. to show that cities need to grow
   B. to honor the strength and power of cities
   C. to provide a factual description of change
   D. to make the city seem dangerous and destructive

7. How would you describe the author's style of writing in this passage? Do you think it is effective or not, and why?

Unit Assessment To prepare for the Unit Test, go to www.glencoe.com.

UNIT 4 ASSESSMENT

Test Practice

Part 1: Literary Elements

1. D
2. C
3. B
4. C
5. D
6. D
7. Responses will vary.

Resources for pages 514–519

Use these resources to review, assess, or reteach the Unit: Active Learning and Note-Taking Guide, Selection and Unit Assessment, ExamView Assessment Suite, and Differentiated Instruction Tool Software.

Unit Assessment Have students access the Web site to prepare for the Unit 4 test.

Test-Taking Tips

FAB Signal words give clues to opinions. Remind students to look for words such as *best* and *terrible* and other value words.

TIP To find tone, suggest that students think of the overall impression they get of the writer's attitude about progress.

TIP Remind students that readers take notice when a writer uses exaggeration, or hyperbole. To spot hyperbole, remind students to ask themselves to find a description that is not possible in real life.

TIP Remind students that word connotations give readers hints about how the author and characters feel. To choose the right synonym, ask students to reread the section to understand the feeling of the moment.

Test Practice

Part 1: Literary Elements

Read the passage. Then, on a separate sheet of paper, write the numbers 1–7. For the first six questions, write the letter of the right answer next to the number for that question. Then, next to number 7, write your answer to the final question.

Progress

[1]Sometime between the time I was a girl of eleven and now, twenty years later, something happened in Lawson County. [2]The miles of farmland with small white houses and three-acre vegetable gardens vanished. [3]The curving two-lane road that was County Highway 13 became a four-lane highway. [4]What was special is now ordinary; what was beautiful is ugly.

[5]The land isn't gone. [6]Where would it go? [7]But it's hidden now, invisible. [8]Where there once were pastures and cornfields right up to the foot of the mountains, there are now large brick "estates" with garage doors like huge blind eyes. [9]Their yards are tiny, no bigger than postage stamps. [10]Where there were meadows with nodding buttercups, there are stores and parking lots. [11]The sounds were once those of leaves rustling in the breeze and an occasional rooster crowing. [12]Now, nothing can be heard above the endless roar of traffic.

[13]There must be children here, but there are none to be seen. [14]None of them have set up card tables on the front edges of their yards to sell strawberries that they spent the morning picking. [15]None of them are swinging from apple trees in the endless, sunny afternoons or walking knee deep through fields of wildflowers. [16]There are no strawberry patches, no apple trees, no wildflowers.

[17]I don't know when all this happened. [18]After my grandfather died, I had no reason to visit Lawson County. [19]I missed the days of gathering fruit and swimming in the community pool and taking long walks to nowhere. [20]I missed the peaceful nights, silent except for the sweet sound of crickets. [21]But with Grandpa gone and his old house sold, there was no reason to go there, and we didn't go.

[22]I'm glad we stopped going. [23]If we hadn't, I'd have seen the city come creeping out to swallow everything in its way. [24]I'd have heard it chew up the barns. [25]It's painful to see that everything I loved there is gone—everything except the mountains, for even the city can't devour the mountains. [26]It would have been far worse to watch it go.

Objectives
Literature Identify literary elements: tone, style • Identify literary devices: hyperbole, diction, language, word choice

Nonfiction

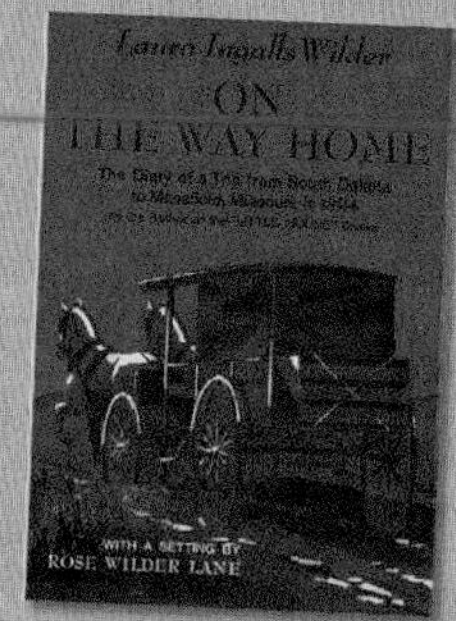

On the Way Home
by Laura Ingalls Wilder and Rose Wilder Lane

The diary of the author of *Little House on the Prairie* describes her family's exciting 1894 journey from South Dakota to a new home in the Missouri Ozarks. Wilder's daughter adds her own memories of the trip.

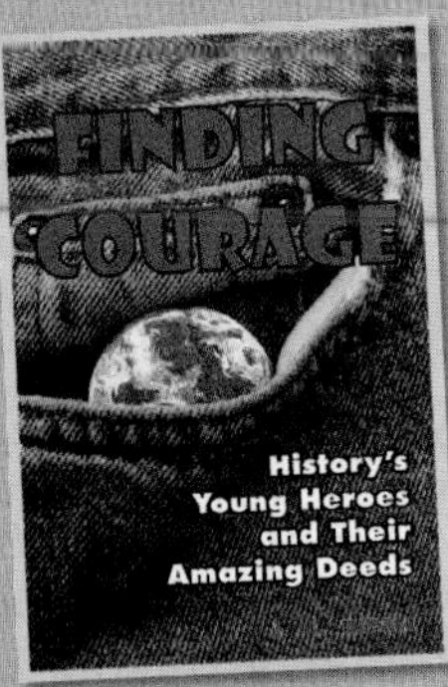

Finding Courage
by J. M. Bedell

Read this book to meet Louis Braille, the inventor of the Braille language, and Fa Mu-lan, the great Chinese warrior. This book profiles twenty-seven young people from around the globe who grew up to change the world with their determination and courage. Think you can't make a difference? Check out this book and think again.

Reach Higher
by Scottie Pippen

Scottie Pippen tells about his life and the challenges he faced to become an NBA champion with the Chicago Bulls. The title describes his advice to his young readers.

My Story
by Rosa Parks

When Rosa Parks refused to give up her seat on a bus in 1955, it's been said that her act marked the beginning of the Civil Rights movement. After her brave deed, the African American community boycotted the buses while legal teams worked to fight the segregated bus laws.

Nonfiction

Tell students that all books on this page are nonfiction. The authors of the books tell about their lives and the people and events that have influenced them.

Persuasive Writing

Ask: Can you tell why reading one or more of these books might have an influence on your life? *(The books are about real people with real problems and situations. Students may identify with one or more of the writers as they relate how their lives have been shaped by people, experiences, and events around them.)*

About the Subjects

Real-life pioneer Laura Ingalls Wilder, inventor of Braille language Louis Braille, NBA champion Scottie Pippen, and civil rights leader Rosa Parks model how challenge and adversity have shaped them and have made them stronger. Fictional characters Jesse of *The Slave Dancer,* David Lee Morgan of *Sounder,* Jim of *Father Figure,* and Moon Shadow of *Dragonwings* are all influenced by their situations and emerge from the challenges stronger and wiser.

Tips for Independent Reading

Stress the importance of reading different types of persuasive writing, including editorials, ads, and poems. Suggest the books listed here that are related to the Big Question.

Fiction

Explain to students how reading fictional stories of characters, whose experiences and relationships influence them, helps them to understand who and what is important in making them who they are.

Ask students to tell about a fictional story or book they've read that shows how people become who they are because of people and events in their lives.

UNIT 4

Reading on Your Own

To read more about the Big Question, choose one of these books from your school or local library. Work on your reading skills by choosing books that are challenging to you.

Fiction

The Slave Dancer
by Paula Fox

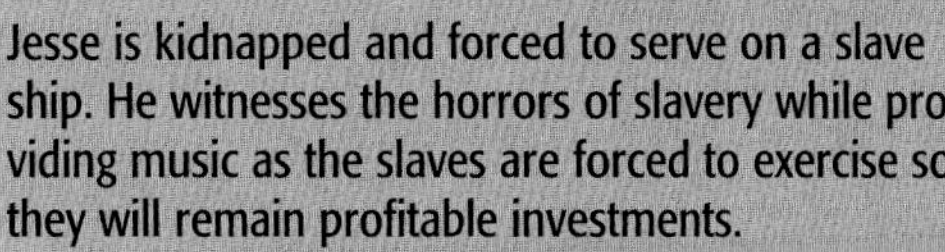

Jesse is kidnapped and forced to serve on a slave ship. He witnesses the horrors of slavery while providing music as the slaves are forced to exercise so they will remain profitable investments.

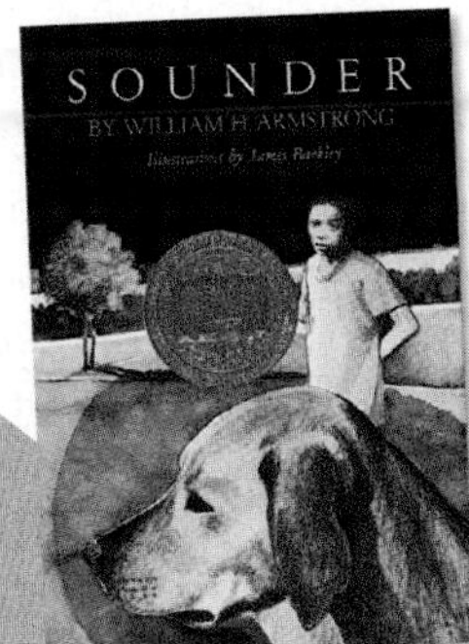

Sounder
by William Armstrong

This award-winning novel deals with the hard lives of African American sharecroppers in the rural South a century ago and a young boy's growth of understanding with the help of a devoted dog.

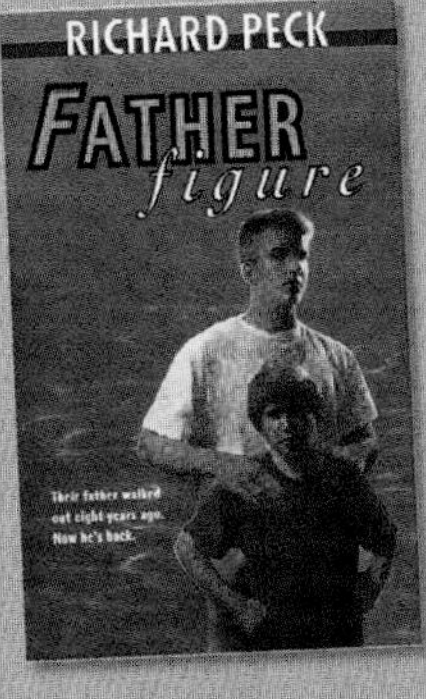

Father Figure
by Richard Peck

Jim's role as a substitute father for his younger brother is threatened when, after their mother's death, the boys are sent to spend the summer with their long-absent father.

Dragonwings
by Laurence Yep

A Chinese immigrant father and son build a flying machine in the era of the Wright brothers and the San Francisco earthquake.

Additional Support

Differentiated Instruction

GLENCOE BOOKLINK Use the *Glencoe Booklink* CD-ROM to create customized reading lists to help students answer the Big Question. Suggestions for Unit 4:

Grade 4: *Cousins* by Virginia Hamilton
Grade 5: *A Dictionary of Japanese-American Terms* by R. A. Sasaki
Grade 6: *Tuck Everlasting* by Natalie Babbitt
Grade 7: *The Land of Red Apples* by Zitkala-Sa
Grade 8: *Raymond's Run* by Toni Cade Bambara

But the stars came out and they danced about
    ere* again I ventured near;
I was sick with dread, but I bravely said:
    "I'll just take a peep inside.
I guess he's cooked, and it's time I looked,"
    . . . then the door I opened wide.

And there sat Sam, looking cool and calm,
    in the heart of the furnace roar;
And he wore a smile you could see a mile,
    and he said: "Please close that door.
It's fine in here, but I greatly fear
    you'll let in the cold and storm—
Since I left Plumtree, down in Tennessee,
    it's the first time I've been warm."

There are strange things done in the midnight sun
    By the men who moil for gold;
The Arctic trails have their secret tales
    That would make your blood run cold;
The Northern Lights have seen queer sights,
    But the queerest they ever did see
Was that night on the marge of Lake Lebarge
    I cremated Sam McGee. ❍

100 ***Ere*** **(AIR) is an old word for "before."**

Teach

R Reading Skill

Review Using Text Structure: Compare and Contrast Ask: What did you expect the narrator to see when he looks into the furnace? *(Possible response: I thought he'd see a pile of ashes.)*

C Critical Thinking

Comprehension Ask: Is Sam McGee cremated? *(no)* **OL** Why might this be *the queerest* event ever seen? *(Possible response: A man tries to cremate a man who isn't dead.)* **OL**

Literature Focus Lesson

Word Choice Refer again to the discussion you may have had about the word *sizzle* (page 509). Explain that word choice is the writer's ability to choose the details that create the mood. In small groups, have students imagine together and write one description of an inviting cave and another of an eerie cave. Encourage them to carefully choose details that either threaten or welcome.

Objectives

- Use comparison and contrast
- Identify tone
- Understand how word choice influences readers
- Identify sensory details

CRITICAL THINKING	VOCABULARY	WRITING AND GRAMMAR	LISTENING, SPEAKING, AND VIEWING
Big Question, SE pp. 581, 586, 591, 593, TWE pp. 585, 586, 593 Evaluate, SE p. 588 Identify Sequence, SE p. 588 Analyze, SE p. 588 Infer, SE p. 594 Draw Conclusions, SE p. 594	Vocabulary Preview, SE pp. 580, 590 Word Structure, SE pp. 580, 582, TWE pp. 580, 582, 584 Greek and Latin Roots, SE pp. 590, 592, TWE pp. 590, 592 Idioms, TWE p. 593	Write to Learn, SE pp. 581, 591 Commas in a Series, SE p. 589 Write About Your Reading, SE p. 594 Commas with Introductory Words and Direct Address, SE p. 595	Small Group, SE pp. 581, 591 Partner Talk, SE p. 581 Talk About Your Reading, SE p. 588 Viewing the Photo, TWE p. 583
Comprehension, TWE p. 597		Writing a Research Report: Drafting, Revising, Editing and Presenting, SE pp. 596, 597, 598, TWE p. 600 Introductions and Conclusions, TWE p. 596 Outlines, TWE p. 596 Editing, TWE p. 598	Oral Presentation, SE p. 601, TWE p. 601 Write and Speak to Learn, SE p. 601 Presenting, TWE p. 598 Visual Aids, TWE p. 601
Big Question, SE pp. 605, 611, 615, 618, 619, TWE pp. 611, 618, 619 Connect, SE p. 612 Draw Conclusions, SE pp. 612, 620 Evaluate, SE pp. 612, 620 Infer, SE p. 620	Vocabulary Preview, SE pp. 604, 614 Content-area Words, SE pp. 604, 608, 611, 614, 617, TWE pp. 608, 611, 617 Context Clues, TWE p. 604 Vocabulary Poems, TWE p. 614	Write About Your Reading, SE pp. 612, 620 Commas with Introductory Clauses and Phrases, SE p. 613 Commas with Interruptions, SE p. 621 Hyphenating Modifiers, TWE p. 616	Small Group Work, SE p. 605 Partner Talk, SE p. 615 Viewing the Photo, TWE pp. 608, 616
Comparing and Contrasting, SE p. 623 Big Question, SE pp. 624, 626, 629, 631, 633, TWE pp. 626, 631 Interpret, SE p. 633 Analyze, SE p. 633 Summarize, SE p. 633	Vocabulary Preview, SE pp. 624, 629 Content-area Words, SE pp. 624, 628, 629, 630, TWE p. 630 Context Clues, TWE p. 624 Suffixes, TWE p. 626	Writing: Reading Across Texts, SE p. 633	
Evaluate, TWE p. 639 Big Question, TWE p. 639			Debate It!, SE p. 634, Interview an Adult, SE p. 635, TWE p. 635 Viewing the Photo, TWE p. 638

UNIT 5

Unit Resources

Reading with Purpose offers a comprehensive package of tools to optimize student learning and the teaching experience. Each resource has been designed to assist students in specific areas and to offer instructional support for teachers. While all of these areas are covered in the core textbook, some students may need extra practice or additional help in specific areas. The resource package is designed so that you, the teacher, can choose which items will best assist your students. You may also use these resources as homework assignments and for assessment purposes. The following are resources recommended for use with Unit 5.

Keys for Unit Resources

- Blackline Master
- Workbook
- Supplemental Text
- CD-ROM
- DVD
- Transparency
- Web-based
- Fast Files

Essential Instructional Support

FAST FILE UNIT 5 RESOURCES

Reading and Literature
- Academic Vocabulary Development
- Big Question: School to Home Connection
- The Big Question Foldable
- Genre Study
- Unit Challenge: Planner and Rubrics
- Comparing Literature Graphic Organizer
- Key Reading Skills Practice
- Active Reading Graphic Organizers
- Literary Analysis
- Selection Vocabulary Development

Writing, Grammar, and Spelling
- Spelling and Handwriting Practice
- Grammar Practice
- Writing Workshop Graphic Organizer

Listening, Speaking, and Viewing
- Viewing and Representing Activities
- Listening and Speaking Activities

English Language Learners
- English Language Coach

DIFFERENTIATED INSTRUCTION

- Leveled Vocabulary Development
- Skills Level Up!
- Listening Library CD
- BookLink 3
- Literature Library Vocabulary Puzzlemaker
- Vocabulary Puzzlemaker

ASSESSMENT

- Selection and Unit Assessments
- Selection Quick Checks
- Assessment by Learning Objectives
- Rubrics for Assessing Student Writing, Listening, and Speaking
- Glencoe Online Essay Grading
- Interactive Tutor Self-Assessment
- ExamView Assessment Suite
- Literature Library ExamView Assessment Suite

Additional Instructional Support

WRITING, GRAMMAR, AND SPELLING

- Real Success in Writing: Research and Reports
- Writing Constructed Responses Sourcebook
- Spelling Power eWorkbook
- Grammar & Composition Handbook
- Grammar and Language Workbook
- Revising with Style eWorkbook

TRANSPARENCIES

- Read Aloud, Think Aloud
- Literary and Text Analysis Transparencies
- Bellringer Options Transparencies
- Grammar and Writing Workshop Transparencies
- Fine Arts Transparencies

ENGLISH LANGUAGE LEARNER

- English Language Coach
- Fluency Practice and Assessment
- inTime Magazines (Spanish)
- Spanish Listening Library CD

PROFESSIONAL DEVELOPMENT

- Professional Development Package

READING AND LITERATURE

- Active Learning and Note Taking Guide
- inTime Magazines
- Backpack Reader Volume 1
- Literature Library
- Literature Launchers Pre-Reading Videos DVD
- Literature Classics

TECHNOLOGY

- TeacherWorks Plus
- StudentWorks Plus
- BookLink 3
- Skill Level Up!
- ExamView Assessment Suite
- Interactive Tutor Self-Assessment
- Listening Library CD
- Spanish Listening Library CD
- Literature Classics
- Literature Launchers Pre-Reading Videos DVD
- Literature Library ExamView Assessment Suite
- Vocabulary Puzzlemaker
- Literature Library Vocabulary Puzzlemaker
- glencoe.com
- Online Student Edition
- Presentation Plus!
- Glencoe Online Essay Grading

Additional Glencoe Resources

FOLDABLES™ Study Organizer — Dinah Zike's Foldables

Foldables are three-dimensional, interactive graphic organizers that help students practice basic writing skills, review key vocabulary terms, and answer Big Questions. Every unit contains a foldable activity. You can find the pattern and directions for the Unit 5 Foldable in the Unit 5 Resources Fast Files booklet. You can use the foldables as they are presented or modify them to suit the needs of your students. More information about foldables for Unit 5 can be found on page R8.

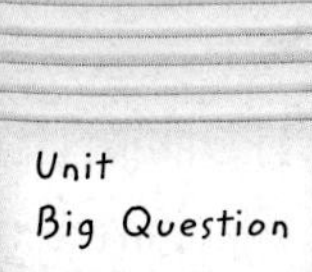

Glencoe Literature Library

The collection of hardcover books include full-length novels, novellas, plays and works of nonfiction. Each volume consists of at least one complete extended-length reading accompanied by several related readings from a broad range of genres. A separate Study Guide for each Glencoe Literature Library book provides teaching notes and reproducible activity pages for students.

Glencoe Literature Library titles that complement this unit include:

Dogsong by Gary Paulsen
Mrs. Frisby and the Rats of NIMH by Robert C. O'Brien
There's a Gril in My Hammerlock by Jerry Spinelli
A Wrinkle in Time by Madeleine L'Engle

Literature Online

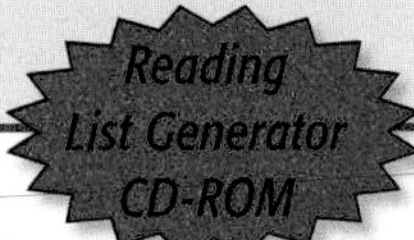

For a wealth of online resources that support the instruction in Unit 5 of *Glencoe Literature: Reading with Purpose,* students and teachers can visit our Web site at www.glencoe.com. Students will find additional learning, practice, and assessment opportunities such as these, which are noted in the student text:

- **Big Question Overview**
- **Study Central**
- **Author Search**
- **Writing Models**
- **Interactive Literary Elements Handbook**
- **Web Activities**

Teachers will find planning and instructional tools that include the following:

- **Book Lesson Plans**
- **Teacher Forum**
- **Professional Development**
- **Web Activities Lesson Plans (with answers to student activities)**

Go to www.glencoe.com to see the entire selection of Reading with Purpose online resources.

Reading List Generator CD-ROM — Glencoe BookLink

Use the Glencoe BookLink 3 CD-ROM, a database of more than 26,700 titles, to *create customized reading lists* for your students.

- Search for award-winning titles, (e.g., Newbery Award winners, Coretta Scott King Award winners, and Caldecott Medal winners) and for books on several state-recommended reading lists.
- Find Degrees of Reading Power™ (DRP) and Lexile™ readability scores for all selections.
- Organize reading lists by students' reading level, author, genre, theme, or area of interest.
- Get a brief summary of each selection.

You can find recommended leveled readings for this unit with Reading on Your Own (see page 120).

Presentation Plus! CheckPoint

Glencoe's **Presentation Plus!**, a multimedia teaching tool, lets you present dynamic lessons that will engage your students. Using Microsoft PowerPoint,® you can customize the presentations to create your own personalized lessons. Use **CheckPoint** questions with interactive response keypads to get immediate student feedback during lessons, to increase student participation, and to assess student comprehension.

inTIME

A lively collection of articles drawn from issues of the TIME family of magazines helps students develop the skills they need to interact with informational text in a meaningful way. Each of the news stories, feature articles, reviews, profiles, and essays in the magazine connect to an author, work, or theme in *Glencoe Literature: Reading with Purpose.* Articles for Unit 5 are found in Volume A. See the *inTIME* Teacher's Guide for specific connections to each unit and for reproducible student worksheets designed to develop students' reading and critical thinking skills.

Literature Launchers

Set the scene with Glencoe's Literature Launchers, engaging video segments that introduce each unit's genre focus. Each video brings the genre to life, relating it to your students' worlds.

Insert the Glencoe Literature Launchers Pre-Reading Videos DVD into your DVD player. Select the Unit 5 Launcher from the menu to introduce the genre and Big Question for this unit.

Online Essay Grader

Use Glencoe's Online Essay Grading to score your students' writing and to provide individualized feedback to each student automatically.

You and your students can visit www.glencoe.com to link to the essay grader. *Students* can enter their essays and receive feedback on demand. *You* can manage demographic data, assign tests and generate individual student and aggregated reports. The essay grader can help you

- Save time with automatic scoring and individualized feedback.
- Supplement in-class writing instruction using guided writing practice.
- Get reports for individual students or for special populations.
- Track student improvement over time.

REAL Success: Reading Excellence at All Levels

Glencoe now provides all of your students with the tools they need to become better, more enthusiastic readers. The REAL Success suite of reading and language arts products encourages reading excellence by meeting the needs of students at all levels. Glencoe products that can be used in conjunction with Unit 5 include the following:

- Jamestown Literature: An Adapted Reader
- Jamestown *Reading Fluency*
- Jamestown *Critical Reading Series, In the Line of Duty*
- *Vocabulary Builder*
- *The Glencoe Reader, Course 2*

To order these products, call Glencoe at 1-800-USA-READ.

Teacher Wraparound Edition Key

Level Appropriate Code

AS = Activities for all students

AL = Activities for students working above grade level

OL = Activities for students working at grade level

BL = Activities for students working below grade level

EL = Activities for English language learners

Teacher Wraparound Prompts

R **Reading Skill** These activities help you teach reading skills and vocabulary.

V **Vocabulary** These activities help students comprehend words and incorporate into reading.

C **Critical Thinking** These strategies help students apply and extend what they have learned.

BQ BIG Question These activities and questions prompt students to prepare to answer the Big Question.

W **Writing** These activities provide writing opportunities to help students practice writing and comprehend text.

L **Literary Element** These activities and questions help students comprehend selections and learn more about each genre.

E **Text Element** These activities help students comprehend text elements.

LSV **Listening, Speaking, Viewing** These activities help students practice listening, speaking, and viewing skills.

EL **English Language Coach** These skills help English language learners as well as students who need additional reading support.

UNIT 5

Professional Development Center

David O'Brien

From An Author:

Preparing Students to Understand Science and Technology Writing

Tune-in to Text Structures Because science and technology writing can sometimes be more difficult for students to understand, students need to understand how to identify some of the common text structures found in these texts. As you read the stories in this unit (especially in workshop 2), point out special features and explain why and how they help the reader. You may also want to pre-map the structure of a particular piece of scientific or technical text. Use a chart, a graphic organizer, or map to help students visualize the structure before they begin reading.

Access and Personalize Technical Vocabulary Technical texts contain more difficult vocabulary. To enhance comprehension, pre-teach technical vocabulary by doing the following:

- Discuss the vocabulary listed for previewing with the students by asking them if they know the word, asking them to define it, and asking if they know how it may be used differently in different subject areas.
- Through a discussion with students, find other words they find difficult that are not listed in the text and decide if those words are *necessary in understanding difficult concepts.*
- Teach the identified words in semantically and topically related sets (for example, words that occur as structures of a cell would be taught together) using semantic maps, webs, and organizers.
- Teach the students strategies for independently learning new concepts, including using the context in which the words occur, using word definition aids like dictionaries and glossaries along with context, and using word structure to see how roots and prefixes narrow the meaning of a word.

Brandi Thomas
Tiospaye Topa Cheyenne River Agency – Eagle Butte, SD

Teacher to Teacher

Is progress always good?

Our school is located in an isolated region, and for my students, the question "Is progress always good?" is often represented in changes in technology, which they have too little exposure to. However, cultural heritage and traditions play an important role in their lives, so it is natural for me to talk about Native American history and the changes that occurred in Native American cultures over the past 200 years. The concept of directions has significance in our way of thinking, so using North, South, East and West, I talk about how things were long ago, how they were not so long ago, how they are today, and where we are headed in the future. I use a circle and point out that things in our lives have a way of going around, but we never return to the beginning and the circle never ends, so there is constant change.

Teacher Chat Room

Reading Science and Technology Writing

What features of scientific and technical writing do students find difficult and how can I engage them with these texts?

Author David O'Brien says middle school students have trouble with these texts because they are least like the narrative texts they have grown accustomed to and competent with. Specifically, these texts flow less freely, have more embedded, difficult vocabulary, and more illustrations, graphics, and text aids that interfere with fluent comprehension. To foster more engagement consider these approaches

- Locate and recommend scientific and technical texts that have more of a narrative than expository form (e.g., *Marie Curie: A Brilliant Life.* By Elizabeth MacLeod)
- Augment science textbooks and similar "school" texts with variety of trade books on topics students can choose from (.e.g, the National Science Teachers Association [NSTA] has lists of popular trade books appealing to children and teens)
- Encourage students to create their own scientific and technical texts through inquiry projects, action research projects, and media book talks that they write using computers and media authoring tools and publish as media presentations.

What techniques will help students comprehend scientific and technical texts?

Because teachers understand the difficulty of the information, teachers are tempted to "talk around the text," provide handouts on text topics, and use the textbook as a resource rather than as a primary source of information. Since that approach may provide the information, but does not give middle school students practice, we propose approaches in which students learn to read the text with some scaffolding or support in class that they can then engage in independently. Carefully choose text and model ways to comprehend it

Key Unit Objectives

- Answer the Big Question
- Identify, understand, and apply key reading skills for reading science and technology writing
- Analyze the key literary elements of science and technology writing
- Write a research report

BIG Question

Why Is It Important?

Addressing this Big Question helps students think about the pros and cons of progress. Searching for answers to the Big Question will help students consider new perspectives.

Viewing the Photo

Say: What does Wiener mean when he says that progress imposes both "new possibilities" and "new restrictions"? *(Possible response: He means progress has both good and bad consequences.)* **OL** Do you think that scientific advances are always good? Why or why not? *(Responses will vary.)* **AL**

UNIT 5

The BIG Question: Is Progress Always Good?

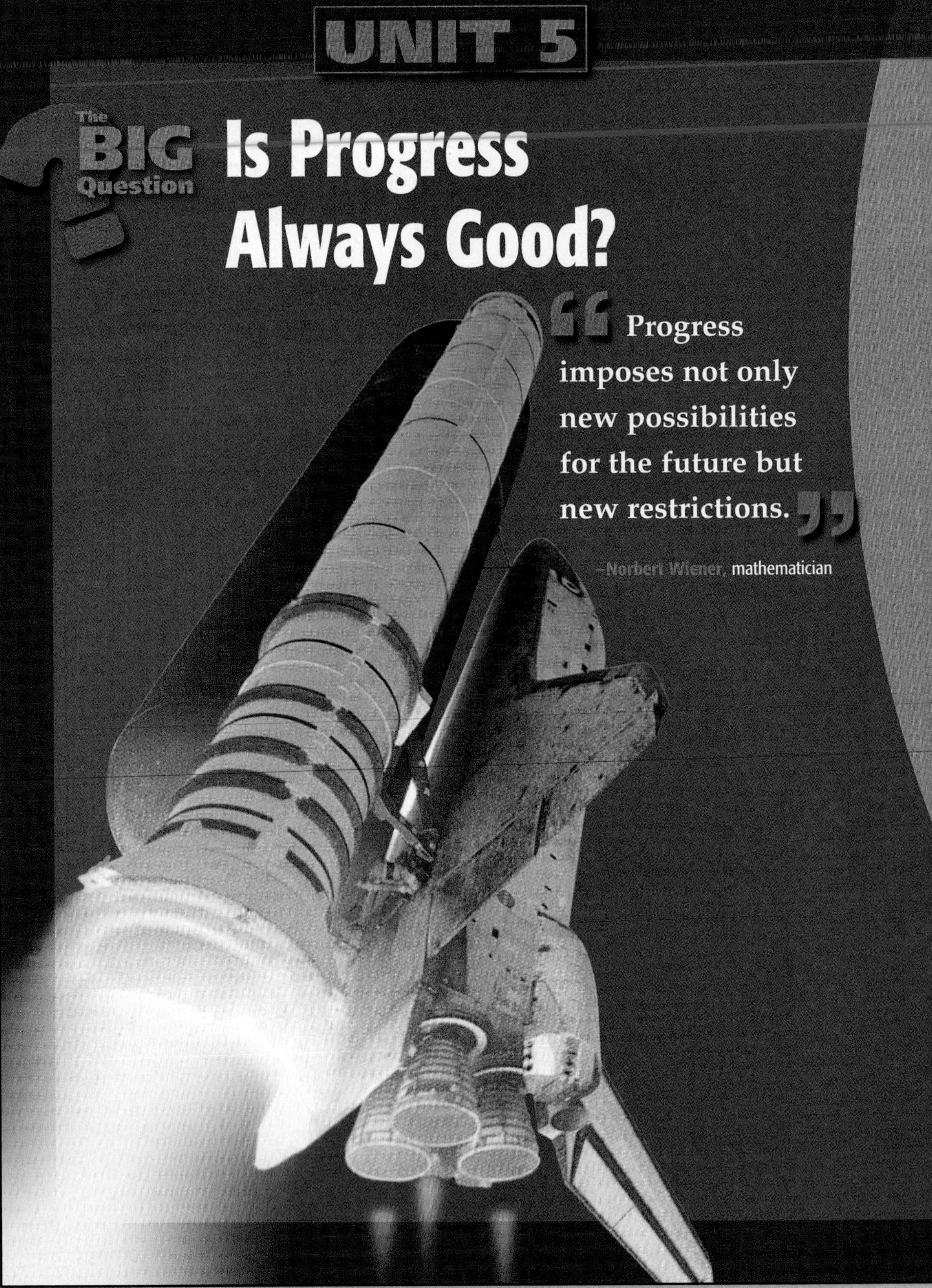

"Progress imposes not only new possibilities for the future but new restrictions."

—Norbert Wiener, mathematician

Unit Skills

The BIG Question: Is Progress Always Good?

Genre Focus: Science and Technology Writing

Reading Skills

- Paraphrasing and summarizing, p. 528
- Using text features, p. 556
- Taking notes, p. 578
- Identifying problem and solution, p. 602

Vocabulary

- Word structure, p. 530
- Content-area words, p. 602

Literary Elements

- Author's craft, p. 531
- Concept and definition, p. 559
- Organization, p. 581
- Description, p. 605

Writing Skills/Grammar

- Research report, pp. 552, 596
- Main and subordinate clauses, p. 555

LOOKING AHEAD

The skill lessons and readings in this unit will help you develop your own answer to the Big Question.

About the Reading

Each selection in this unit provides insights that can help students answer the question, "Is progress always good?" Students consider different aspects of progress and how progress affects them, their families, their communities, and the world.

About the Skills

The skills taught in this unit have been selected because they are particularly helpful when reading science and technology writing. Each reading selection provides students with opportunities to practice and develop these skills.

No Child Left Behind

Modeling the skills covered in this unit will help students develop reading comprehension. Students will learn to use text features to understand texts. For example, as a class, list the headings from "The Next Big Thing" in Reading Workshop 3 and discuss the main idea of each section.

Reading Fluency

Developing Fluency One way to help students improve their reading fluency is to give them strategies for improving their silent reading. Read aloud passages from the selections in this unit, and have students follow along silently. Tell them to remember these guidelines:

- Use punctuation marks to clarify meaning.
- Note any words you do not understand so that you can look them up later.
- Use a dictionary or ask a friend for help with pronunciation of difficult words.
- Take regular breaks. EL BL

Focus

BELLRINGER Options

- **Literature Launcher: Prereading DVD**
- **Daily Language Practice Transparency**

Focus Activity Ask: How will the world have changed by the time you are 18? 30? 50? Tell about some of the technological progress you think will take place. *(Responses will vary.)*

Teach

R Reading Skill

Review Connecting Ask: How has progress made your life easier or more difficult? *(Responses will vary. Students may say they can send instant-messages and their parents can find out about their homework assignments online.)* In which areas do you wish progress could be improved? *(Responses will vary. Students may say we need more fuel-efficient cars.)* OL

BQ

- Have students read the profiles and look at the pictures of Zack and Nina.
- Have students talk about how progress has affected Zack and Nina's lives. OL

UNIT 5 WARM-UP

Connecting to

Is Progress Always Good?

R Today, most of us use computers to write papers and e-mail friends. Computers have changed the way we communicate with one another. But is this progress always good? Many people think that, because of computers, we don't spend enough time talking to one another. In this unit, you'll read about progress and how people respond to the changes that it brings.

BQ Real Kids and the Big Question

ZACK likes taking a shortcut through an open lot on his way to school. This route gets him to school faster. Soon, however, the city will build a mini-mall on this lot. Zack understands that the development will be good for his community. The stores will bring more business into the neighborhood. However, Zack will have to leave home earlier and take the long way to school. He will miss the open space. What would you say to Zack about this kind of progress?

NINA won a handheld computer in her school's raffle. She spent hours filling the computer with her friends' phone numbers and e-mail addresses. She also used it to organize homework assignments. Nina liked getting the information she needed at the touch of a button. One day, however, her computer froze. She lost all of the information stored on it. Should Nina have used an old-fashioned paper address book?

Warm-Up Activity

Write about the changes that Zack and Nina are experiencing. Decide which parts of progress are good or bad in their situations.

Additional Support

Reading in the Real World

Citizenship Tell students that they can become involved in the decisions that their community and society make in the name of progress. For example, Zack could become a member of the Sierra Club, the Wilderness Society, or another local or regional organization that works to balance nature and urban spaces. Nina could contact the company that made her computer and find out whether there is a way to recover the lost information. She might also write an article for the school or local newspaper encouraging others to back up their computer address books. Discuss with students various ways in which they can become involved in modern-day progress. OL

You and the Big Question

Long before CDs, people listened to music on records. Today we have MP3 players that hold thousands of songs. There's certainly been progress in the ways we listen to music. In this unit, you'll read about how people deal with progress. Reading about progress will give you ideas for your own answer to the Big Question.

BQ

Big Question Link to Web resources to further explore the Big Question at www.glencoe.com.

Plan for the Unit Challenge

At the end of the unit, you'll use notes from all of your reading to complete the Unit Challenge. You'll choose one of the following activities:

A. Debate You and your classmates will debate whether it's a good idea to build a new shopping mall in your community.

B. Interview You'll interview an adult to find out about his or her experiences with a new invention or a new type of technology.

- Start thinking about which activity you'd like to do so that you can collect ideas as you read the selections.
- In your Learner's Notebook, write your thoughts about which activity you'd like to do.
- As you go through this unit, take notes about ideas that will help you answer the Big Question. Also think about how your ideas will help you with the Unit Challenge activity you choose.

Keep Track of Your Ideas

FOLDABLES™ Study Organizer

As you read, you'll make notes about the Big Question. Later, you'll use these notes to complete the Unit Challenge. See pages R8–R9 for help with making Foldable 5. This diagram shows how it should look.

1. List all the selections on the Foldable's front. (See page 521 for the titles.) Then open the Foldable. You'll write answers on note cards and sort the cards into these three pockets.
2. Write these labels on the pockets:
   - **My Purpose for Reading**
   - **The Big Question**
   - **My Thoughts** (This is for additional ideas you have about the Big Question.)

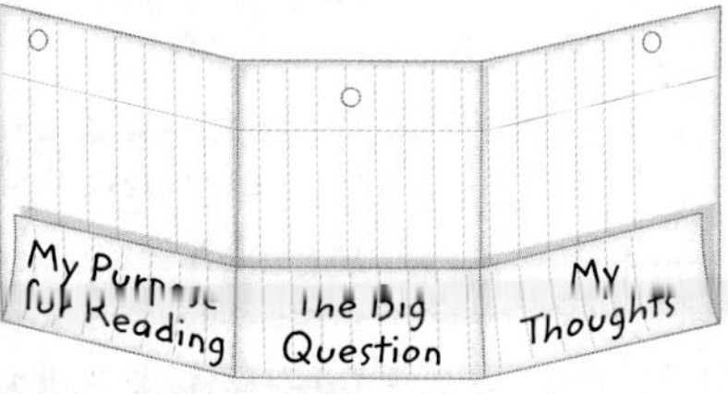

Teach

Big Question Have students access the Web site for English and Spanish summaries and annotated links to related Web resources.

BQ BIG Question

Have students list in their Learner's Notebook new machines, gadgets, and technology they either like or do not like to use and why. OL

Assess/Close

Ask students to share their thoughts about whether technological progress is always good.

Resources for page 523

- Use the Unit Challenge Planner BLM in the Unit 5 Resource Booklet.
- Use the Foldable BLM in the Unit 5 Resource Booklet.

Differentiated Instruction

Using Graphic Organizers Tell students they can use pros and cons charts to list the good and bad aspects of progress. Encourage students to use these charts to list the good and bad aspects of Zack's and Nina's situations. BL

Pros	Cons

Objectives

- Connect prior knowledge and experiences
- Analyze organization of ideas and objectives

Focus

BELLRINGER Options

Daily Language Practice Transparency

Focus Activity Ask: Have you ever had to explain to someone how to use a new piece of technology or an electronic device? How did you make your instructions clear? *(Possible response: I gave simple, step-by-step instructions.)*

Teach

R Reading Skill

How to Read Science and Technology Writing Ask: How can each of these skills help you read science and technology writing? *(Possible responses: **Paraphrasing and summarizing:** Retelling information in your own words helps you understand and remember what you have read. **Using text features:** Drawings, headings, side notes, and graphic organizers help you understand how the text is organized. **Taking notes:** You can keep track of the main ideas and details by taking notes. **Identifying problem and solution:** Finding the description of a problem and its solution helps you focus on the author's message.)* **OL**

UNIT 5 GENRE FOCUS: SCIENCE AND TECHNOLOGY WRITING

Science and technology writing teaches you about the world around you. Learning about the world can help you think about whether progress is always good.

Skills Focus
- Key skills for reading science and technology writing
- Key elements of science and technology writing

Skills Model

You will see how to use the key reading skills and literary elements as you read
- **"Hip Hop" from *The Story of Music*,** p. 525

Why Read Science and Technology Writing?

Reading about science and technology will inform you about scientific discoveries and improvements in technology. You'll also learn about
- scientific thinking and how to use scientific ideas to solve problems
- how people use science and technology to change the world around them

How to Read Science and Technology Writing

Key Reading Skills

R

These reading skills are especially useful tools for reading and understanding science and technology writing. The skills are modeled in the Active Reading Model on pages 525–527; you'll learn more about them later.

- **Paraphrasing and summarizing** After you read, paraphrase by retelling in your own words what you've read. Summarize by retelling in your own words the main ideas and important details. (See Reading Workshop 1.)
- **Using text features** Use parts of the text to locate and analyze information. Text features include drawings, side notes, headings, and graphic organizers. (See Reading Workshop 2.)
- **Taking notes** As you read, pick out and write down important information to help you understand the text. Your notes should include ideas, facts, names, and dates. (See Reading Workshop 3.)
- **Identifying problem and solution** Find places where the text explains how questions are answered or how problems are solved. (See Reading Workshop 4.)

Key Literary Elements

Recognizing and thinking about the following elements will help you understand more fully what the author is telling you.

- **Author's craft:** the way an author combines elements, such as purpose, character, theme, and tone, to create a piece of writing (See "LAFFF.")
- **Concept and definition:** an idea and an explanation of that idea (See "Conserving Resources.")
- **Organization:** the way an author puts information together (See "The Next Big Thing.")
- **Description:** a detailed portrayal of a person, place, thing, or event (See "Fireproofing the Forests.")

Objectives (pp. 524–527)
Reading Paraphrase and summarize • Use text features: heads • Take notes • Identify problem and solution
Literature Identify literary elements: author's craft, concept and definition, organization, description

Additional Support

Literature Focus Lesson

Concept and Definition Tell students that science and technology writing often explains new concepts, or ideas, that relate to solving a problem. The problem and the solution may be complicated and difficult to understand. To clarify concepts for readers, writers must use effective descriptions and must organize their writing in a way that makes sense and suits the topic. Elements of author's craft, such as word choice and tone, also help the writer engage the reader.

Ask students to write paragraphs that define concepts that students have recently encountered in their science classes. Have student partners exchange papers and discuss the effectiveness of one another's writing. **OL**

INFORMATIONAL TEXT
REFERENCE BOOK
from *The Story of Music*

Hip Hop

The notes in the side columns model how to use the skills and elements you read about on page 524.

Science and Technology Writing

ACTIVE READING MODEL

from ***The Story of Music***

In the late 1970s a radical new form of music emerged from the poor, black areas of New York. It was called hip-hop. Created by DJs, it produced a new type of musician–the rapper.

Hip-hop is a style of music that originally evolved in the poor black areas of America's big cities in the late 1970s. In New York disk jockeys (DJs) like Kool Herc, Afrika Bambaata, and Grandmaster Flash made a name for themselves by collecting dance records—many of them hard to find—and mixing them together in an unusual, exciting way. **1**

Using two turntables,[1] these DJs would play records that had the same tempo,[2] switching back and forth between one disk and the other. To do this, they often used break beats —sections of the records that just had drums and bass on them. The DJs also invented a way of "scratching" records by winding them back and then letting them go, using their fingers to stop and start the disk. This technique produced a sound that could be used as a kind of percussion. **2**

R EL

The first rappers 3

While DJs like Kool Herc and Grandmaster Flash were playing music, their friends would speak through a microphone, urging the crowd to dance. For example, Flash was usually accompanied by three friends who went by the names of Cowboy, Kid Creole, and Melle Mel, who would eventually form the core of his group

1 Key Reading Skill
Taking Notes *Dates, places, and names are the details I should include in my notes. I'll jot down "big cities," "late 1970s," "Kool Herc," "Afrika Bambaata," and "Grandmaster Flash."*

2 Key Reading Skill
Paraphrasing and Summarizing *The author's point here is to explain how DJs created their sounds. They'd break beats and make scratching sounds by using their fingers to stop and start the disk.*

3 Key Reading Skill
Using Text Features *Here's a new topic–the first rappers.*

1. ***Turntables*** are round platforms that spin to play records.
2. The ***tempo*** is the speed of the music.

Teach

EL Language Coach

Base Words, Prefixes, and Suffixes **Say:** Dividing an unfamiliar word into parts is one way to determine its meaning. Look at the word *turntable* on this page. What two words make up the word *turntable?* (turn *and* table) How do these two words give you clues to the meaning of turntable? *(To* turn *means "to rotate or spin."* *A* table *is a flat board mounted on four legs. These definitions suggest that a* turntable *is a flat surface that spins.)* EL

R Reading Skill

Taking Notes **Say:** Include both main ideas and supporting details in your notes. What main ideas are in the first two paragraphs? *(New York DJs started hip-hop; they invented new ways to play two records together.)* BL

Resources for page 525

- Use the Genre Study BLM in the Unit 5 Resource Booklet.

Differentiated Instruction

Debating Media–television, music recordings, and the Internet–have contributed greatly to the popularity of hip-hop in countries around the world. However, the media's influence extends well beyond music and affects people's choices and perceptions in a number of other areas. Have student teams debate the statement, "The media influences our lives in positive ways." Pro and con teams should brainstorm and research to gather evidence in support of their positions. Encourage each team to choose two or three strong arguments for its position. Allow three minutes for each team's opening presentation and two minutes for each team's rebuttal. Have a class discussion follow the debate. OL

Objectives
- Paraphrase and summarize
- Use text features: heads
- Take notes
- Identify problem and solution
- Identify literary elements: author's craft, organization, concept and definition, description

Teach

L1 Literary Element

Organization **Ask:** What type of organization does the author use in this article? *(time order)* BL
What are some words and phrases other than *at first* and *evolved into* that signal time order on this page? *(became, later, went on, more and more)* BL

L2 Literary Element

Concept and Definition
Ask: What does the author see as the role of early rappers in the hip-hop culture? *(The author sees early rappers as commentators on the lives of young African Americans.)* BL

ACTIVE READING MODEL

Grandmaster Flash

the Furious Five. At first these "masters of ceremony," or MCs, would just shout out a few catchy phrases. These phrases evolved into extended rhymes that became an important part of the music. 4 5

The rappers, as they were later called, went on to become the most important figures of the hip-hop movement, taking over from the DJs of its early days. 6 L1

Rappers provided a running commentary on the status of young black people in America—sometimes positive and uplifting, more often bleak and despairing. L2 And as more and more young white people began to buy the records, hip-hop became the biggest selling section of the popular music market. 7

4 Key Literary Element
Description *I know from the author's description that as the DJs played the music, their friends would shout words and rhymes through a mic to get people to dance. They were called MCs.*

5 Key Literary Element
Organization *This section explains how hip-hop music changed over time. The words "at first" and "evolved into" help signal the changes.*

6 Key Literary Element
Concept and Definition *I think the concept here is who the first rappers were. The first rappers were the MCs who became the most important figures in hip-hop.*

7 Key Literary Element
Author's Craft *The author explains what hip-hop is about. It's about young African Americans. The author uses the words* bleak *and* despairing. *Here I get a sense of what hip-hop is about.*

Grandmaster Flash

Grandmaster Flash (b. 1958) was arguably the most innovative DJ in the history of hip-hop. As a teenager Flash used to attend the huge outdoor parties thrown by Kool Herc in the Bronx area of New York. Flash was impressed by the way that Herc could keep a crowd dancing by switching from the break beat of one record to another. However, he wasn't particularly impressed by Herc's slightly haphazard[3] way of mixing one record into the next, which he did without the use of headphones.

3. ***Haphazard*** means "unplanned" or "accidental."

Additional Support

English Language Coach

Content-Area Words Some of the words related to hip-hop and music may present challenges to English Language Learners. Ask students to write each of the following words on an index card. Each card should include the word's definition and a sentence using the word. Students can use the cards later to review the words.

- disk jockey
- tempo
- percussion
- microphone
- headphones
- composer EL BL

ACTIVE READING MODEL

Luckily, Flash was an electronics student, so he was able to adapt his equipment so that he could cut seamlessly[4] from one record to another. Using headphones and a few simple switches, Flash could cut suddenly from record to record, creating a continuous piece of music. Later Flash would also add beats from a drum machine into the mix. From then on, the DJ wasn't just someone who played other people's records—he became the composer of a new improvised music. 8 O

8 Key Reading Skill
Identifying Problem and Solution *Flash has a problem with Herc's mixing style. How does he solve this? Flash uses what he knows about electronics and finds a smoother way of mixing.*

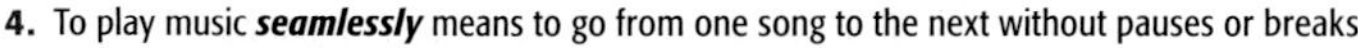

4. To play music ***seamlessly*** means to go from one song to the next without pauses or breaks.

Partner Talk With a partner, list the important ideas that you would take notes about while reading this selection. Explain why pieces of information should or should not be included.

Write to Learn If you were writing about technology that you use often (such as a computer or music player), how would you answer these questions?

1. Why are clear descriptions and organization important?
2. What concepts and definitions will help a reader understand my topic?

Study Central Visit www.glencoe.com and click on Study Central to review science and technology writing.

Teach

R Reading Skill

Identifying Problem and Solution **Ask:** How does Grandmaster Flash's solution improve mixing? *(By using headphones and a few simple switches, Flash could cut seamlessly from one record to another.)* OL

L Literary Element

Author's Craft **Ask:** What words does the author use to tell readers that Grandmaster Flash found ways to improve the way DJs mixed records? *(adapt, seamlessly)* How does the author describe the new role of the DJ? *(The DJ became a composer, creating new music from old.)* OL

Literature Online

Study Central Have students access the Web site to review science and technology writing and to complete a related activity.

Literature Focus Lesson

Theme Explain that the theme is the author's main message. It may be stated directly, or it may be implied through clues in the selection. Have small groups review "Hip-Hop" and discuss possible themes. Suggest that they list the main ideas and note details that reveal the author's attitude toward the topic. Ask each group to agree on one statement of theme. One possible theme might be "new forms of art appear unexpectedly and continue to change." Discuss the group responses as a class. AL

Objectives
- Paraphrase and summarize main ideas
- Identify problem and solution
- Analyze description
- Understand organization of ideas and information

Skill Lesson: Paraphrasing and Summarizing

UNIT 5

Objectives covered in this workshop:

- Paraphrase important details from multimedia resources
- Paraphrase text to recall and organize ideas

Teaching Students to Paraphrase and Summarize

Why Is It Important?

- Research shows that summarization is one of the most effective instructional approaches in fostering comprehension.
- The most effective form of summarization involves paraphrasing and synthesis of an author's ideas.
- Paraphrasing is one of the summarization processes that helps readers integrate critical reading to recall information and draw inferences through clear writing to reinforce comprehension.

How to Help Students Get It

- Emphasize the importance of putting an author's language into one's own words in fostering comprehension.
- Provide opportunities with guided practice in which you model, through thinkalouds, how you are actually summarizing as you go through a text; put up a transparency of the text that shows how you have located important information through underlining.
- Give students work in pairs and practice summarizing orally with smaller and then longer pieces of text; they can compare their summaries with each other.
- After guided practice on how summarization works orally, have students write summaries guided by jotting down main ideas, listing important words or phrases that support those idea, and then rewriting the list into a short paragraph.

Reading to Answer the Big Question

LAFFF

Angela badly wants to win the story writing contest. She convinces her friend Peter to let her use his new invention-a time machine-to read the winning story and write it as her own.

Cyber Chitchat

In this essay, a mother writes about instant messaging and the spelling and abbreviations that her daughter uses for online chatting. Students can use the ideas presented in this selection to think about whether or not there are any negative consequences to new technologies like the Internet and instant messaging.

Workshop Resources

Pacing (Days) Standard	Block	Lesson	Student Materials	Teacher Resources
1		Key Skill Lesson: Paraphrasing and Summarizing	Key Reading Skills Practice English Language Coach	Bellringer Options Transparencies Read Aloud, Think Aloud Transparencies Presentation Plus!
2		"LAFF"	Literary Analysis Transparencies Glencoe Online Selection Vocabulary Development Academic Vocabulary Development English Language Coach Active Reading Graphic Organizer Literary Analysis StudentWorks Plus Online Student Edition Literature Classics Selection and Unit Assessments	Literary and Text Analysis Transparencies Puzzlemaker Skill Level Up! BookLink 3 Assessment by Learning Objective (Diagnostic and Formative) Interactive Tutor Self-Assessment TeacherWorks Plus
2		"Cyber Chitchat"	Glencoe Online Selection Vocabulary Development Academic Vocabulary Development English Language Coach Active Reading Graphic Organizer Literary Analysis StudentWorks Plus Online Student Edition Literature Classics Selection and Unit Assessments	Literary and Text Analysis Transparencies Puzzlemaker Skill Level Up! BookLink 3 Assessment by Learning Objective (Diagnostic and Formative) Interactive Tutor Self-Assessment TeacherWorks Plus

Keys for Unit Resource

- Blackline Master
- Workbook
- Supplemental Text
- CD-ROM
- DVD
- Transparency
- Web-based
- Fast Files

Level Appropriate Code

AS = Activities for all students
AL = Activities for students working above grade level
OL = Activities for students working at grade level
BL = Activities for students working below grade level
EL = Activities for English language learners

Focus

BELLRINGER Options

Daily Language Practice Transparency

Focus Activity Ask: How would you explain to a friend what a book or movie you really enjoyed is about? *(Possible response: Give the plot, explain the setting, and briefly describe the characters.*

Teach

R Reading Skill

Paraphrasing and Summarizing Ask: How can you tell the difference between a detail that is important to the main idea and a detail that gives extra information? *(Possible response: You cannot understand what a piece of writing is about without details that relate to the main idea. Extra details make a story richer, but you don't need them to understand what the story is about.)* AL

READING WORKSHOP 1

Skills Focus

You will practice using these skills when you read the following selections:

- "LAFFF," p. 532
- "Cyber Chitchat," p. 546

Reading

- Paraphrasing and summarizing

Literature

- Analyzing an author's craft to understand meaning

Vocabulary

- Understanding base words
- Academic Vocabulary: *summarize*

Writing/Grammar

- Understanding clauses and phrases

Objectives (pp. 528–529)
Reading Paraphrase and summarize

Skill Lesson

Paraphrasing and Summarizing

Learn It!

What Is It? When you **summarize**, you start by asking yourself questions. What's the big picture? What ideas are most important? You take the important ideas and details and put them in a logical order.

A good summary has the following:

- the main ideas of the piece of writing
- only the details that support the main ideas

A summary needs to be in your own words. When you retell something in your own words, you paraphrase the information. A summary should be much shorter than the selection.

Analyzing Cartoons
The woman with glasses summarizes her book by describing the main topic in a few sentences. Of course, since it's her diary, she knows the topic quite well.

Academic Vocabulary

summarize (SUM ur eyez) *v.* to tell the main points briefly

Additional Support

Reading in the Real World

Career Many jobs require employees to do research and summarize their findings in brief reports. Have students review and summarize informational Web sites. Students should choose Web sites in areas of science and technology that interest them. Monitor their selections for content and grade-level appropriateness. After students have explored the sites and taken notes, have them write one-paragraph summaries telling the main topics of the sites as well as the most important information the sites provide. OL

Any student having difficulty summarizing an entire site might choose one page or one paragraph to summarize. BL

Why Is It Important? Paraphrasing and summarizing help you remember and organize information, as well as explain a series of events. You also paraphrase and summarize to show that you understand what you've read.

How Do I Do It? After you read, think about the most important information. To decide what's most important, answer the basic questions: Who? What? When? Where? Why? How? Then write the information in a logical order, or a way that makes sense. Leave out examples and extra information. Here's how one student paraphrased and summarized a paragraph of "Hip-Hop" from *The Story of Music.*

R1

While DJs like Kool Herc and Grandmaster Flash were playing music, their friends would speak through a microphone, urging the crowd to dance. For example, Flash was usually accompanied by three friends who went by the names of Cowboy, Kid Creole, and Melle Mel, who would eventually form the core of his group the Furious Five. At first, these "masters of ceremony," or MCs, would just shout out a few catchy phrases. These phrases evolved into extended rhymes that became an important part of the music.

R2

Literature Online

Study Central Visit www.glencoe.com and click on Study Central to review paraphrasing and summarizing.

After I read this paragraph, I asked myself, "What is the most important idea?" The paragraph is about MCs. Then I thought about what details in the paragraph support the idea. Here is my summary:

MCs spoke into a microphone while the DJs played music. Their phrases eventually became rhymes that were part of the music.

Practice It!

Think about one of your favorite stories or movies. How would you describe it to someone who has not read or seen it? In your Learner's Notebook, write a summary of the story or movie.

Use It!

As you read "LAFFF" and "Cyber Chitchat," paraphrase and summarize by putting parts of the stories in your own words.

Teach

Literature Online

Study Central Have students access the Web site to review paraphrasing and summarizing and to complete a related activity.

R1 Reading Skill

Paraphrasing and Summarizing **Say:** Journalists and newspaper reporters do their best to answer the questions *who, what, when, where, why,* and *how* even when writing very short articles. Why are these questions so important? *(By answering these questions, reporters make sure that readers have the information they need to understand important events.)* **OL**

R2 Reading Skill

Paraphrasing and Summarizing **Say:** Reread the *How Do I Do It?* section. How would you summarize the paragraph from "Hip-Hop"? *(Responses will vary.)* **OL**

Resources for page 529

Use Reading Skills Transparency in *Read Aloud, Think Aloud,* Unit 5, to help students practice paraphrasing and summarizing.

Differentiated Instruction

Illustrating Discuss with students the ways in which illustrations sometimes include the important elements of a summary. Encourage students to offer examples of books with illustrations that effectively summarize the written action. Point out that diagrams in science and social studies textbooks often provide visual summaries of information. Ask students to draw illustrations that summarize the paragraph from "Hip-Hop" on page 529. Remind them to do their best to include visual elements that answer the questions *who, what, when, where, why,* and *how.* **OL**

Objectives
- Paraphrase and summarize
- Identify main ideas and supporting details
- Analyze illustrations

Before You Read LAFFF

More About the Author

Lensey Namioka has a lot in common with the main characters of "LAFFF." Like Angela, she wrote stories as a child. Like both Peter and Angela, she moved to the United States as a young child, so English was not her first language. She decided that math was easier than English because Americans and Chinese use the same numerals, so she gave up writing stories to focus on mathematics. Eventually, however, Namioka returned to her first love, story writing.

EL Language Coach

Base Words **Say:** Learning base words can help you figure out unfamiliar words. Think of other words that share the base words in the list on this page. For example, the words *agreement* and *agreeable* also share the base word *agree*. The next time you encounter one of these base words in an unfamiliar word, you can make a good guess about the unfamiliar word's meaning. EL

Meet the Author

Lensey Namioka was born in China in 1929. Her family often moved from place to place. As a result, Namioka says, some of her stories "describe outsiders trying to fit into a new country and a new society." See page R5 of the Author Files for more on Lensey Namioka.

Author Search For more about Lensey Namioka, go to www.glencoe.com.

Objectives (pp. 530–541)
Reading Paraphrase and summarize
Literature Identify literary elements: author's craft
Vocabulary Identify word structure: base words

Vocabulary Preview

immigrated (IM uh gray tud) *v.* moved into a new country; form of the verb *immigrate* **(p. 532)** *Peter's family had immigrated to the United States from China.*

fantastic (fan TAS tik) *adj.* not real; imaginary; amazing **(p. 533)** *People thought Peter was working on a fantastic machine.*

possibilities (paw suh BIL uh teez) *n.* things that can or may happen **(p. 535)** *Angela saw the possibilities of Peter's machine.*

destination (des tuh NAY shun) *n.* the place one plans or hopes to reach at the end of a journey **(p. 537)** *Angela chose the destination for her trip into the future.*

Write to Learn With a partner, write a paragraph that includes all of the vocabulary words above.

English Language Coach

Base Words Do you ever read a word that looks like it has a word you know *in* it? If so, you are probably looking at a **base word** that has a prefix, a suffix, or both. A **prefix** is something that is added to the beginning of a word to change its meaning. A **suffix** is something that is added to the end of a word, usually to modify (but sometimes to change) its meaning. In order to understand a new word, it can be helpful to recognize base words. EL

For example in the word *unhelpful* do you see a word you recognize? It's *help,* right? So *help* is the base word. In the following list of words, all the base words are underlined.

readable	truthful	employment
misbehave	disagree	rewrite

Partner Talk With a partner, discuss what the base word is in each word listed below.

worker	courageous	musical
careless	sadly	

Additional Support

Author Search To expand students' appreciation of Lensey Namioka, have them access the Web site for additional information and resources.

Literature Focus Lesson

Science Fiction Tell students that the genre of science fiction deals with the impact of actual or imagined science and technology on societies and individuals. A key characteristic of science fiction is its believability. The events and scientific and technological developments of a good science fiction story seem possible, if only in the distant future. Popular science fiction topics include alien worlds, imagined futures, and space and time travel. Tell students to note the impact of technology on the characters in "LAFFF." Ask students to explain whether they find Namioka's use of science and technology believable. OL

Skills Preview

Key Reading Skill: Paraphrasing and Summarizing

Before you read, remember that you summarize to

- organize main ideas and supporting details
- explain a sequence of events
- check that you understand the selection

You paraphrase, or restate in your own words, to

- make sure you understand the author's meaning
- make sure you're not plagiarizing

Plagiarizing is copying an author's words without giving the author credit. If you want to quote an author, you let the reader know you're using the author's exact words by using quotation marks.

Key Literary Element: Author's Craft

The **author's craft** is the way the author combines elements, such as purpose, character, theme, and tone, to create a piece of writing.

As you read, use these tips to help you learn about the author's craft.

- Think about the author's audience.
  Whom does the author expect to read this selection?
- Think about the characters.
  Who are the most important characters? From whose perspective does the author tell the story?
- Think about the theme and tone. The theme is the main message of the selection. The tone is how the author expresses his or her attitude.
  What does the author want you to think about? How does he or she want you to feel?

L

List Ideas List other elements of the author's craft that you see in the story. Some examples are setting, plot, word choice, and dialogue. With a partner, discuss how these elements help you understand the story's meaning and the author's purpose.

Get Ready to Read

Connect to the Reading

Think about a time when you faced a problem because you tried something new. Angela and Peter have to overcome a number of problems while working with LAFFF. As you read, think about whether you faced your problems in a similar way. R

Small Group In a small group, share examples of problems you faced when you tried something new. Discuss how you tried to solve these problems and whether you were successful.

Build Background

Time travel has been a very popular subject in literature. Many authors have used the idea to entertain, teach a moral lesson, or examine the effects of progress on society.

Perhaps the most famous story about time travel is *The Time Machine* by H. G. Wells. Mark Twain also wrote about time travel in *A Connecticut Yankee in King Arthur's Court.*

Set Purposes for Reading

BIG Question Read "LAFFF" to see if new ideas and inventions are always good. Think about the benefits and problems that come with new developments, such as Peter's time machine.

Set Your Own Purpose What else would you like to learn from the story to help you answer the Big Question? Write your own purpose on a note card and add it to Foldable 5.

Literature Online

Interactive Literary Elements Handbook
To review or learn more about the literary elements, go to www.glencoe.com.

Keep Moving

Use these skills as you read the following selection.

English Language Coach

Communicating In "LAFFF," one of the characters writes in English, but she feels challenged because English is not her first language. Ask students whether they have had similar experiences or been in situations in which they weren't able to communicate clearly because they did not know the right words to use. Discuss these experiences as a class, and brainstorm solutions to this problem, such as drawing a picture, using body language, or using a translation dictionary. EL

Teach

L Literary Element

Author's Craft Say: Good writers carefully choose words that express their ideas and match the subjects, styles, and audiences of their stories. This is called word choice. What kinds of words would an author use in a science fiction story written for young adults? *(Possible response: scientific terms as well as strong descriptive adjectives)* OL

R Reading Skill

Review Connecting Say: Think about a problem you have had. How did you solve it? Summarize the problem and solution in a discussion with a partner. *(Responses will vary.)* BL

CheckPoint

Use the CheckPoint questions provided on Presentation Plus! to test students on paraphrasing and summarizing and to build background. These questions can be used with interactive response keypads for immediate student feedback.

Literature Online

Interactive Literary Elements Handbook Have students access the Web site to improve their understanding of author's craft.

Objectives

- Paraphrase and summarize
- Identify literary elements: author's craft
- Identify word structure: base words

Teach

Viewing the Illustration

Ask: How would you describe the clock in this illustration? *(Possible response: It looks twisted or melted.)* **BL** What does the clock image suggest about how the story will deal with the idea of time? *(Possible response: The illustration suggests that the story will play with time or change time.)* **OL**

L Literary Element

Author's Craft **Ask:** How does the background information about Peter and the narrator help you understand them? *(Possible response: Knowing this background information helps me understand some of the characters' behaviors and attitudes. This background also explains some of the pressures and challenges that the characters face.)* **AL** Writers use many techniques to tell about characters. How does the author provide information about Peter? *(The narrator gives the reader information about Peter directly. The narrator also describes the way other people feel about Peter.)* **OL**

Readability Scores
Dale-Chall: 5
DRP: 48
Lexile: 640

READING WORKSHOP 1

by Lensey Namioka

In movies, geniuses have frizzy white hair, right? They wear thick glasses and have names like Dr. Zweistein.

Peter Lu didn't have frizzy white hair. He had straight hair, as black as licorice. He didn't wear thick glasses, either, since his vision was normal.

Peter's family, like ours, had **immigrated** from China, but they had settled here first. When we moved into a house just two doors down from the Lus, they gave us some good advice on how to get along in America. **1**

I went to the same school as Peter, and we walked to the school bus together every morning. Like many Chinese parents, mine made sure that I worked very hard in school. **L**

In spite of all I could do, my grades were nothing compared to Peter's. He was at the top in all his classes. We walked to the school bus without talking because I was a little scared of him. Besides, he was always deep in thought.

Peter didn't have any friends. Most of the kids thought he was a nerd because they saw his head always buried in books. I didn't think he even tried to join the rest of us or cared what the others thought of him. **2**

Vocabulary

immigrated (IM uh gray tud) *v.* moved into a new country

Practice the Skills

1 Key Literary Element

Author's Craft Here the author introduces important background information about two of the story's main characters. What does the author tell you about Peter and the narrator in this paragraph?

2 Key Reading Skill

Paraphrasing and Summarizing What is the main idea of this paragraph? Remember to paraphrase, or put your answer in your own words.

Additional Support

Reading in the Real World

Citizenship Education has always played an important role in Chinese culture. Confucius, an ancient Chinese teacher and philosopher, believed that all people could benefit from education. He established the importance and respectability of teaching as a career. Have students discuss whether they believe education is valued in the United States today. Tell them to consider

- the fact that school attendance is mandatory in the United States
- the value of learning a trade or skill
- how many people attend college
- whether it is possible to succeed without a formal education

OL

Then on Halloween he surprised us all. As I went down the block trick-or-treating, dressed as a zucchini in my green sweats, I heard a strange, deep voice behind me say, "How do you do."

I yelped and turned around. Peter was wearing a long, black Chinese gown with slits in the sides. On his head he had a little round cap, and down each side of his mouth drooped a thin, long mustache.

Visual Vocabulary Many science fiction movies feature a mad scientist. ***Dr. Fu Manchu*** was a popular Chinese villain character in stories and films of the early 1900s. He had a very long moustache.

"I am Dr. Lu Manchu, the mad scientist," he announced, putting his hands in his sleeves and bowing. L1

He smiled when he saw me staring at his costume. I smiled back. I knew he was making fun of the way some kids believed in stereotypes about Chinese people. Still his was a scary smile, somehow.

Some of the other kids came up, and when they saw Peter, they were impressed. "Hey, neat!" said one boy.

I hadn't expected Peter to put on a costume and go trick-or-treating like a normal kid. So maybe he did want to join the others after all—at least some of the time. After that night he wasn't a nerd anymore. He was Dr. Lu Manchu. Even some of the teachers began to call him that. L2

When we became too old for trick-or-treating, Peter was still Dr. Lu Manchu. The rumor was that he was working on a **fantastic** machine in his parents' garage. But nobody had any idea what it was. 3

One evening, as I was coming home from a baby-sitting job, I cut across the Lus' backyard. Passing their garage, I saw through a little window that the light was on. My curiosity got the better of me, and I peeked in.

I saw a booth that looked like a shower stall. A stool stood in the middle of the stall, and hanging over the stool was something that looked like a great big shower head.

Vocabulary

fantastic (fan TAS tik) *adj.* not real; imaginary; amazing

Practice the Skills

3 Reviewing Skills

Reviewing What have you already learned about Peter that suggests he could invent a fantastic machine? Think about the details that describe Peter.

READING WORKSHOP 1

Teach

L1 Literary Element

Review Character Ask: How does Peter's Halloween costume suit his character? *(Peter's costume suits his character because he is interested in science, and his costume is a scientist.)* **OL** In what ways does Peter's costume make fun of cultural stereotypes? (Peter makes fun of Chinese stereotypes by using the model of the "mad" Chinese scientist in a silly way.) **AL**

L2 Literary Element

Review Character Say: How would you describe Peter? *(Possible response: Peter is very intelligent and quiet. He reads all the time. Yet he has imagination and a sense of humor.)* **OL** How is Peter different from the rest of the children in the story? (He makes better grades than they do, and he doesn't seem interested in making friends.) **OL**

English Language Coach

Build Background Tell students that British author Sax Rohmer created the character called Dr. Fu Manchu, a brilliant criminal mastermind. The popular Fu Manchu series began in 1913, and Rohmer continued to write novels about the character for 45 years. The series was also developed into motion pictures and radio and television programs. Ask students whether there are any famous characters, villainous or heroic, that have been popular for a long time in their cultures. Discuss with students in what ways these characters do or do not represent cultural stereotypes. **EL** **OL**

Objectives

- Analyze elements of character
- Analyze elements of author's craft
- Analyze illustrations

Teach

R Reading Skill

Paraphrasing and Summarizing Say: In your own words, summarize what happens when Angela cuts across the Lus' backyard. *(Possible response: Angela peeks into the Lus' garage one night while cutting through their backyard. She sees a strange machine. Peter catches her peeking and tells her that it is a time machine he invented.)* OL

L Literary Element

Author's Craft Say: The author uses words such as *bleeps* and *cheeps* to describe the sounds that Peter's machine makes. The use of words that imitate the sounds they describe is called *onomatopoeia.* How does the use of onomatopoeia add to the story? *(Possible response: It is an interesting way to describe the time machine.)* OL What are some other examples of onomatopoeia that might imitate the sound of a time machine? *(Possible responses: buzz, whir, ding, bing, beep)* BL

R Suddenly a deep voice behind me said, "Good evening, Angela." Peter bowed and smiled his scary smile. He didn't have his costume on and he didn't have the long, droopy mustache. But he was Dr. Lu Manchu.

"What are you doing?" I squeaked.

Still in his strange, deep voice, Peter said, "What are you doing? After all, this is my garage."

"I was just cutting across your yard to get home. Your parents never complained before."

"I thought you were spying on me," said Peter. "I thought you wanted to know about my machine." He hissed when he said the word *machine.*

Honestly, he was beginning to frighten me. "What machine?" I demanded. "You mean this shower-stall thing?"

He drew himself up and narrowed his eyes, making them into thin slits. "This is my time machine!"

I goggled at him. "You mean . . . you mean . . . this machine can send you forward and backward in time?"

"Well, actually, I can only send things forward in time," admitted Peter, speaking in his normal voice again. "That's why I'm calling the machine LAFFF. It stands for Lu's Artifact For Fast Forward." 4

Of course Peter always won first prize at the annual statewide science fair. But that's a long way from making a time machine. Minus his mustache and long Chinese gown, he was just Peter Lu.

"I don't believe it!" I said. "I bet LAFFF is only good for a laugh."

"Okay, Angela. I'll show you!" hissed Peter.

He sat down on the stool and twisted a dial. I heard some *bleeps, cheeps,* and *gurgles.* Peter disappeared.

He must have done it with mirrors. I looked around the garage. I peeked under the tool bench. There was no sign of him.

"Okay, I give up," I told him. "It's a good trick, Peter. You can come out now."

Bleep, cheep, and *gurgle* went the machine, and there was Peter, sitting on the stool. He held a red rose in his hand. "What do you think of that?" 5

I blinked. "So you produced a flower. Maybe you had it under the stool."

"Roses bloom in June, right?" he demanded.

Practice the Skills

4 Key Reading Skill

Paraphrasing and Summarizing Explain in your own words why Peter named his time machine LAFFF.

5 Key Literary Element

L **Author's Craft** One element of author's craft is word choice. Look at the words *bleep, cheep,* and *gurgle.* Why do you think the author used these words? She could have just said that the machine made some noises. What does her word choice make you think the machine looks like?

Additional Support

Reading Fluency

Practicing Fluency Part of the humor of "LAFFF" arises from the expressive dialogue in the story. Angela and Peter speak with great animation, and Peter alters his voice when speaking as Dr. Lu Manchu. Organize students into groups of three, and assign each student a different voice—Angela's, Peter's, or Dr. Lu Manchu's. Ask them to read page 534 silently and note the details that describe how each character speaks. Then ask students to use the appropriate expression and inflection to read aloud the dialogue on the page. Encourage students to trade roles and reread as time allows. OL

That was true. And this was December.

"I sent myself forward in time to June when the flowers were blooming," said Peter. "And I picked the rose from our yard. Convinced, Angela?"

It was too hard to swallow. "You said you couldn't send things back in time," I objected. "So how did you bring the rose back?"

But even as I spoke I saw that his hands were empty. The rose was gone.

"That's one of the problems with the machine," said Peter. "When I send myself forward, I can't seem to stay there for long. I snap back to my own time after only a minute. Anything I bring with me snaps back to its own time, too. So my rose has gone back to this June."

I was finally convinced, and I began to see **possibilities**. "Wow, just think: If I don't want to do the dishes, I can send myself forward to the time when the dishes are already done."

"That won't do you much good," said Peter. "You'd soon pop back to the time when the dishes were still dirty."

Too bad. "There must be something your machine is good for," I said. Then I had another idea. "Hey, you can bring me back a piece of fudge from the future, and I can eat it twice: once now, and again in the future."

"Yes, but the fudge wouldn't stay in your stomach," said Peter. "It would go back to the future."

"That's even better!" I said. "I can enjoy eating the fudge over and over again without getting fat!"

It was late, and I had to go home before my parents started to worry. Before I left, Peter said, "Look Angela, there's still a lot of work to do on LAFFF. Please don't tell anybody about the machine until I've got it right." 6

A few days later I asked him how he was doing.

"I can stay in the future time a bit longer now," he said. "Once I got it up to four minutes."

L Practice the Skills

6 BIG Question

Peter asks Angela to keep his machine a secret until he gets it right. What good or bad things could happen if you used a machine that had not been perfected? Write your answer on a note card and add it to Foldable 5. Your response will help you answer the Unit Challenge later. **BQ**

Vocabulary

possibilities (paw suh BIL uh teez) *n.* things that can or may happen

READING WORKSHOP 1

Teach

L Literary Element

Author's Craft Say: One way an author provides information about a character is through that character's words and actions. What do you learn about Angela from her ideas about how to use the time machine? *(Possible response: Angela wants to use the time machine to avoid chores and get candy. This shows that she is lighthearted and wants to have fun.)* **OL** Do Angela's ideas about the time machine change your impression of her character? *(Responses will vary.)* **AL**

BQ BIG Question

Ask: How would you use a time machine such as Peter's? How might your use of the time machine impact the future in ways you hadn't predicted? *(Responses will vary.)* **OL** You may want to tell students that often their own minds can be time machines when they think about their futures.

Differentiated Instruction

Mapping Concepts Have students create concept maps to organize the information that they have about Peter's machine. Ask students to complete a chart like the one shown, adding their ideas about how the time machine could be used. **AS**

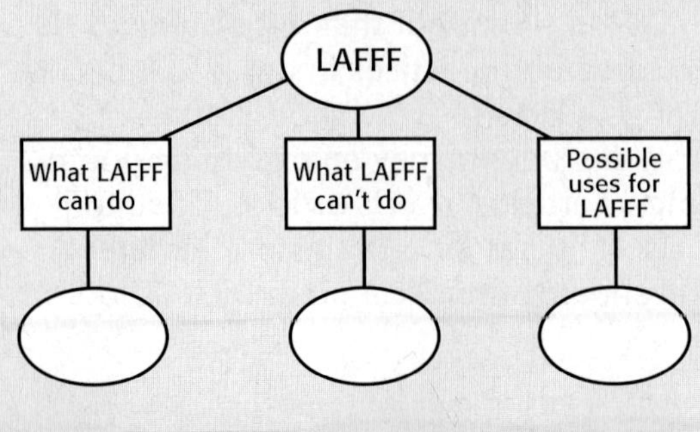

Objectives

- Analyze elements of author's craft
- Paraphrase and summarize
- Build reading fluency

Teach

L Literary Element

Author's Craft Ask: Why might the author have included the detail about the spring roll in the story? *(Possible responses: This detail gives the reader a clearer picture of life in a Chinese American home. It also shows one of the uses that Angela and Peter find for the time machine.)* OL

R Reading Skill

Paraphrasing and Summarizing Say: Think about how your sentence differs from the sentence in the story. What differences do you notice between your word choices and those of the author? *(Responses will vary.)* OL

"Is that enough time to bring me back some fudge from the future?" I asked.

"We don't keep many sweets around the house," he said. "But I'll see what I can do."

A few minutes later, he came back with a spring roll for me. "My mother was frying these in the kitchen, and I snatched one while she wasn't looking."

I bit into the hot, crunchy spring roll, but before I finished chewing, it disappeared. The taste of soy sauce, green onions, and bean sprouts stayed a little longer in my mouth, though.

It was fun to play around with LAFFF, but it wasn't really useful. I didn't know what a great help it would turn out to be.

Every year our school held a writing contest, and the winning story for each grade got printed in our school magazine. I wanted desperately to win. I worked awfully hard in school, but my parents still thought I could do better.

Winning the writing contest would show my parents that I was really good in something. I love writing stories, and I have lots of ideas. But when I actually write them down, my stories never turn out as good as I thought. I just can't seem to find the right words, because English isn't my first language.

I got an honorable mention[1] last year, but it wasn't the same as winning and showing my parents my name, Angela Tang, printed in the school magazine. 7

The deadline[2] for the contest was getting close, and I had a pile of stories written, but none of them looked like a winner.

Then, the day before the deadline, *boing,* a brilliant idea hit me.

I thought of Peter and his LAFFF machine.

1. An ***honorable mention*** is an award or honor given to those who don't earn the top honors.
2. A ***deadline*** is a date by which something must be turned in or completed.

Practice the Skills

7 Key Reading Skill

Paraphrasing and Summarizing Practice paraphrasing this sentence. How many different ways can you retell the sentence in your own words?

Additional Support

Reading in the Real World

Career Point out that Angela enjoys writing and practices in order to improve. Angela likes to write short stories, but other students may enjoy writing poetry, news articles, sports articles, or editorials. Help students brainstorm different avenues for publication in their school and community. Your school may have a literary magazine, or the local newspaper may include a page for student writing. Encourage students who enjoy writing to pursue one of these publication options. OL

I rushed over to the Lus' garage and, just as I had hoped, Peter was there, tinkering with his machine.

"I've got this great idea for winning the story contest," I told him breathlessly. "You see, to be certain of winning, I have to write the story that would be the winner." **EL**

"That's obvious," Peter said dryly. "In fact, you're going around in a circle."

"Wait, listen!" I said. "I want to use LAFFF and go forward to the time when the next issue of the school magazine is out. Then I can read the winning story." 8

After a moment Peter nodded. "I see. You plan to write down the winning story after you've read it and then send it in to the contest."

I nodded eagerly. "The story would *have* to win, because it's the winner!"

Peter began to look interested. "I've got LAFFF to the point where I can stay in the future for seven minutes now. Will that be long enough for you?"

"I'll just have to work quickly," I said.

Peter smiled. It wasn't his scary Lu Manchu smile, but a nice smile. He was getting as excited as I was. "Okay, Angela. Let's go for it."

He led me to the stool. "What's your **destination**?" he asked. "I mean, *when's* your destination?"

Suddenly I was nervous. I told myself that Peter had made many time trips, and he looked perfectly healthy.

Why not? What have I got to lose—except time?

I took a deep breath. "I want to go forward three weeks in time." By then I'd have a copy of the new school magazine in my room.

"Ready, Angela?" asked Peter.

"As ready as I'll ever be," I whispered.

Bleep, cheep, and *gurgle*. Suddenly Peter disappeared.

What went wrong? Did Peter get sent by mistake, instead of me?

Then I realized what had happened. Three weeks later in time Peter might be somewhere else. No wonder I couldn't see him.

Vocabulary

destination (des tuh NAY shun) *n.* the place one plans or hopes to reach at the end of a journey

Practice the Skills

8 **BIG Question**

Angela wants to use LAFFF to read the winning story. Does her plan suggest the good or bad effects of progress? Write your answer on a note card and add it to Foldable 5. Your response will help you answer the Unit Challenge later. **BQ**

Differentiated Instruction

Time Travel Discussion This excerpt from H. G. Wells's novel *The Time Machine* discusses the disappearance of the Time Traveller. Share it with students, and discuss the excitement, dangers, and moral challenges of time travel.

Will he ever return? It may be that he swept back into the past, and fell among the blood-drinking, hairy savages of the Age of Unpolished Stone. . . . Or did he go forward, into one of the nearer ages, in which men are still men, but with the riddles of our own time answered and its wearisome problems solved?

Have students discuss whether they would time travel if they knew there was a possibility of danger. Why or why not? **OL**

Teach

EL Language Coach

Idiomatic Phrases Say: When Peter tells Angela, "You're going around in a circle," he does not mean that Angela is literally traveling in a circle. What does he mean? *(He means that she keeps returning to the same idea in a way that doesn't make sense.)* **EL** **OL**

BQ BIG Question

Say: Do you think that Angela's plan for winning the writing contest is fair? *(Possible responses: It seems that Angela is trying to cheat.)* **BL** How might LAFFF allow people to take unfair advantage of situations? *(Possible response: People might use information from the future for unfair profit, such as betting only when they know they will win.)* **OL**

Objectives

- Paraphrase and summarize
- Analyze author's craft
- Analyze and understand idiomatic expressions

Teach

R Reading Skill

Paraphrasing and Summarizing **Say:** Summarize Angela's trip into the future. Remember to include only the main idea and most important details. *(Possible response: Angela races to her house and tries to avoid running into her mother and her future self. She finds the magazine and rushes back to Peter's garage.)* **OL**

L Literary Element

Author's Craft **Say:** Reread the description of Angela's trip into the future. How does the style of the text change to reinforce the idea that Angela is moving as fast as she can? (HINT: Look at the length of the sentences.) *(The sentences become short, and some are incomplete, as though Angela doesn't have time to finish her thoughts.)* **AL**

There was no time to be lost. Rushing out of Peter's garage, I ran over to our house and entered through the back door.

Mother was in the kitchen. When she saw me, she stared. "Angela! I thought you were upstairs taking a shower!"

"Sorry!" I panted. "No time to talk!"

I dashed up to my room. Then I suddenly had a strange idea. What if I met *myself* in my room? Argh! It was a spooky thought.

There was nobody in my room. Where was I? I mean, where was the I of three weeks later?

Wait. Mother had just said she thought I was taking a shower. Down the hall, I could hear the water running in the bathroom. Okay. That meant I wouldn't run into me for a while.

I went to the shelf above my desk and frantically pawed through the junk piled there. I found it! I found the latest issues of the school magazine, the one with the winning stories printed in it. **L**

How much time had passed? Better hurry.

The shower had stopped running. This meant the other me was out of the bathroom. Have to get out of here!

Too late. Just as I started down the stairs, I heard Mother talking again. "Angela! A minute ago you were all dressed! **R** Now you're in your robe again and your hair's all wet! I don't understand."

I shivered. It was scary, listening to Mother talking to myself downstairs. I heard my other self answering something, then the sound of her—my—steps coming up the stairs. In a panic, I dodged into the spare room and closed the door.

I heard the steps—my steps—go past and into my room.

The minute I heard the door of my room close, I rushed out and down the stairs.

Mother was standing at the foot of the stairs. When she saw me, her mouth dropped. "But . . . but . . . just a minute ago you were in your robe and your hair was all wet!"

"See you later, Mother," I panted. And I ran.

Behind me I heard Mother muttering, "I'm going mad!"

I didn't stop and try to explain. I might go mad, too. **9**

It would be great if I could just keep the magazine with me. But, like the spring roll, it would get carried back to its own time after a few minutes. So the next best thing was to read the magazine as fast as I could.

Practice the Skills

9 Key Literary Element

Author's Craft How does Angela feel about meeting herself in the future? What words does the author use to show how Angela feels?

Additional Support

Differentiated Instruction

Making Time Lines Help visual learners understand the activities of the two Angelas by drawing time lines that show the characters' activities. First instruct students to draw time lines that show the activities of the present Angela, the one narrating the story, as she goes into the future and looks for the magazine. On time lines of the same length, have students indicate the activities of the future Angela as she showers and goes to her room. Tell students to align the two time lines, one above the other, so that they can see where the two Angelas come close to meeting each other. **OL**

It was hard to run and flip though the magazine at the same time. But I made it back to Peter's garage and plopped down on the stool.

At last I found the story: the story that had won the contest in our grade. I started to read.

Suddenly I heard *bleep, cheep,* and *gurgle,* and Peter loomed up in front of me. I was back in my original time again.

But I still had the magazine! Now I had to read the story before the magazine popped back to the future. It was hard to concentrate with Peter jumping up and down impatiently, so different from his usual calm, collected self. **L**

I read a few paragraphs, and I was beginning to see how the story would shape up. But before I got any further, the magazine **disappeared** from my hand. **10**

So I didn't finish reading the story. I didn't reach the end, where the name of the winning writer was printed.

That night I stayed up very late to write down what I remembered of the story. It had a neat plot, and I could see why it was the winner.

I hadn't read the entire story, so I had to make up the ending myself. But that was okay, since I knew how it should come out.

The winners of the writing contest would be announced at the school assembly on Friday. After we had filed into the assembly hall and sat down, the principal gave a speech. I tried not to fidget while he explained about the contest.

Suddenly I was struck by a dreadful thought. Somebody in my class had written the winning story, the one I had copied. **C** Wouldn't that person be declared the winner, instead of me?

The principal started announcing the winners. I chewed my knuckles in an agony of suspense, as I waited to see who would be announced as the winner in my class. Slowly, the principal began with the lowest grade. Each winner walked in slow motion to the stage, while the principal slowly explained why the story was good.

At last, at last, he came to our grade. "The winner is . . ." He stopped, slowly got out his handkerchief, and slowly blew his nose. Then he cleared his throat. "The winning story is 'Around and Around,' by Angela Tang."

I sat like a stone, unable to move. Peter nudged me. "Go on, Angela! They're waiting for you."

Practice the Skills

10 English Language Coach

Base Words What is the base word in **disappeared**?

Teach

L Literary Element

Author's Craft Say: How the author chooses to narrate a story is another aspect of author's craft. What type of narrator does the author use? *(The author uses a first-person narrator.)* **OL** How does the point of view influence the story? *(Possible response: The use of first person draws the reader quickly into the story and makes everything seem more immediate.)* **AL**

C Critical Thinking

Synthesis Say: Angela didn't realize that the original writer of the story would win. She also didn't realize that her story would be very similar to the winning story. Do you think that Angela will get in trouble for cheating? Why or why not? *(Responses will vary.)* **OL**

English Language Coach

Word Histories Remind students that the English language is made up of words from all over the world. For example, the Arabic word *makhzan* means "storehouse." Our modern periodicals are called *magazines* because they are "storehouses of knowledge."

Ask students to use dictionaries as well as their own knowledge of languages other than English to identify two more words in the story that the English language has adopted from other languages. *(Possible responses:* machine *comes from a Greek word;* genius *comes from a Latin word.)* **EL**

Objectives

- Summarize and paraphrase
- Recognize base words
- Use graphic organizers to understand text
- Analyze elements of author's craft

Teach

R Reading Skill

Paraphrasing and Summarizing Say: Angela wins the writing contest. Would you include this event in a summary of the story? *(Yes–it is a main idea.)* BL Angela's prizes include a new notebook and a ballpoint pen. Would you include this information in your summary? Explain. *(Possible response: Angela's prizes are not as important as the fact that she won. The prizes should not be in a summary.)* OL

C Critical Thinking

Comprehension Say: How have Angela's feelings about writing the winning story changed since she came up with the plan to use the time machine to read the winning entry? *(Possible response: At first, she does not worry about copying the story from someone else because she is focused only on winning. After winning, however, Angela feels guilty about her success.)* OL

READING WORKSHOP 1

I got up and walked up to the stage in a daze. The principal's voice seemed to be coming from far, far away as he told the audience that I had written a science fiction story about time travel. **11**

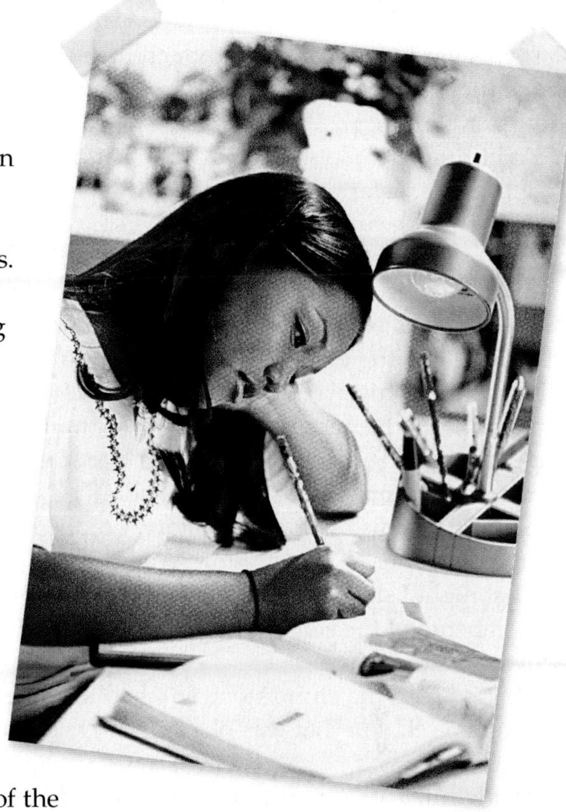

R The winners each got a notebook bound in imitation leather for writing more stories. Inside the cover of the notebook was a ballpoint pen. But the best prize was having my story in the school magazine with my name printed at the end.

C Then why didn't I feel good about winning?

After assembly, the kids in our class crowded around to congratulate me. Peter formally shook my hand. "Good work, Angela," he said, and winked at me.

That didn't make me feel any better. I hadn't won the contest fairly. Instead of writing the story myself, I had copied it from the school magazine. **12**

That meant someone in our class—one of the kids here—had actually written the story. Who was it?

My heart was knocking against my ribs as I stood there and waited for someone to complain that I had stolen his story.

Nobody did.

As we were riding the school bus home, Peter looked at me. "You don't seem very happy about winning the contest, Angela."

"No, I'm not," I mumbled. "I feel just awful."

"Tell you what," suggested Peter. "Come over to my house and we'll discuss it."

"What is there to discuss?" I asked glumly. "I won the contest because I cheated."

"Come on over, anyway. My mother bought a fresh package of humbow in Chinatown."[3]

I couldn't turn down that invitation. Humbow, a roll stuffed with barbecued pork, is my favorite snack.

3. Many cities have a neighborhood called ***Chinatown,*** where people of Chinese heritage live and work.

Practice the Skills

11 Key Reading Skill

Paraphrasing and Summarizing Summarize what happens at the school assembly. Figure out the main idea of each paragraph and then combine the ideas to write your summary. Include important details. Remember to use your own words.

12 Key Literary Element

Author's Craft Angela is the narrator of the story. She reveals her thoughts and feelings. Why do you think the author chose to tell the story from Angela's perspective?

Additional Support

Reading in the Real World

Citizenship Discuss with students how immigrants maintain their native culture after they arrive in a new place. Offer the example of the Chinese New Year, when people start a fresh year by cleaning their houses, paying their bills, and wearing red items for good luck. Discuss with students the different cultures that make up their local community. Have students work in groups to contact local museums, historical societies, or cultural centers to find out about the cultural heritage of their area. Ask students to present their findings to the class. OL

Peter's mother came into the kitchen while we were munching, and he told her about the contest.

Mrs. Lu looked pleased. "I'm very glad, Angela. You have a terrific imagination, and you deserve to win."

"I like Angela's stories," said Peter. "They're original."

It was the first compliment he had ever paid me, and I felt my face turning red.

After Mrs. Lu left us, Peter and I each had another humbow. But I was still miserable. "I wish I had never started this. I feel like such a jerk."

Peter looked at me, and I swear he was enjoying himself. "If you stole another student's story, why didn't that person complain?"

"I don't know!" I wailed.

"Think!" said Peter. "You're smart, Angela. Come on, figure it out."

Me, smart? I was so overcome to hear myself called smart by a genius like Peter that I just stared at him.

He had to repeat himself. "Figure it out, Angela!"

I tried to concentrate. Why was Peter looking so amused?

The light finally dawned. "Got it," I said slowly. *"I'm* the one who wrote the story."

"The winning story is your own, Angela, because that's the one that won."

My head began to go around and around. "But where did the original idea for the story come from?"

"What made the plot so good?" asked Peter. His voice sounded unsteady.

"Well, in my story, my character used a time machine to go forward in time . . ."

"Okay, whose idea was it to use a time machine?"

"It was mine," I said slowly. I remembered the moment when the idea had hit me with a *boing*. 13

"So you s-stole f-from yourself!" sputtered Peter. He started to roar with laughter. I had never seen him break down like that. At this rate, he might wind up being human.

When he could talk again, he asked me to read my story to him.

I began. " 'In movies, geniuses have frizzy white hair, right? They wear thick glasses and have names like Dr. Zweistein. . . .' " ❍ L

Practice the Skills

13 

Do you think Angela's use of new technology helped her win the contest? Why or why not? Write your answer on a note card and add it to Foldable 5. Your response will help you answer the Unit Challenge later. BQ

READING WORKSHOP 1

Teach

L Literary Element

Author's Craft Say: Where else in the story does the text of the last paragraph appear? *(at the beginning)* BL Why do you think the author repeats this paragraph? *(Possible response: The author wants to suggest that this is the story that Angela wrote for the contest.)* AL

BQ 

Say: After reading the story, what do you think about Angela's use of the time machine? Did she need it, or even use it, to write her story? How does the story's ending change your understanding of the story? *(Responses will vary. Students may feel the time machine gave Angela the confidence she needed to write her story.)* OL

Assess

Use the CheckPoint questions provided on Presentation Plus! to check for comprehension of the selection. These questions can be used with interactive response keypads for immediate student feedback.

Differentiated Instruction

Illustrating Angela comments on a recognizable character from science fiction—a mad scientist with a funny name and "frizzy white hair." Ask students to draw what they think this familiar character looks like. Then have them share their drawings with partners or small groups. Ask students to look for similarities in their drawings other than the "frizzy white hair" that Angela describes. Discuss with students the reasons for any similarities in their drawings. Ask students whether they have seen this mad scientist character in a movie or on TV or have read about such a character in a book. OL

Objectives
- Paraphrase and summarize
- Identify main ideas and supporting details
- Analyze elements of author's craft

Assess

Resources for page 542

- Selection Quick Check
- Selection and Unit Assessment
- ExamView Assessment Suite
- Interactive Tutor: Self-Assessment

Students can respond to the *After You Read* items in their Learner's Notebook or on separate sheets of paper.

Answering the

1. Possible response: Progress is not always good because it can create unfair advantages for those who use new technology.
2. a time machine
3. Angela and the other kids realize Peter wants to join them when he wears his Halloween costume.

Critical Thinking

4. Possible response: She learned that she could write a winning story without using a time machine.
5. Possible response: This story shows how people could abuse time travel.
6. Students may suggest that the author is interested in the possibilities of science and technology but also believes that these possibilities should be used carefully.

After You Read

LAFFF

Answering the BIG Question

1. After reading Namioka's story, do you think progress is always good? Why or why not?
2. **Recall** What does Peter invent?
   TIP **Right There**
3. **Summarize** How do Angela and the other kids discover that Peter wants to join their activities?
   TIP **Think and Search**

Critical Thinking

4. **Draw Conclusions** What do you think Angela learns about herself during this story?
   TIP **Author and Me**
5. **Interpret** What does this story suggest about possible problems with time travel?
   TIP **Author and Me**
6. **Evaluate** How do you think the author of this story feels about science and technology? Support your answer with details from the story.
   TIP **Author and Me**

Write About Your Reading

Copy this comparison chart into your Learner's Notebook. Describe how Angela's feelings about Peter and his time machine changed during the story. In the left column, explain how Angela felt at the beginning of the story. In the right column, explain how her feelings changed by the end of the story.

Beginning	End

Objectives (pp. 542–543)
Reading Paraphrase and summarize
Literature Identify literary elements: author's craft
Vocabulary Identify word structure: base words
Grammar Identify clauses

Write About Your Reading

Students' charts should include accurate details from the story. Charts should describe Angela's changing feelings about Peter and about time travel. See sample response.

Beginning	End
Angela thinks that Peter doesn't care about being friends with the neighborhood kids.	Angela realizes that Peter is a little odd but that he does want friends.
Angela doesn't believe that Peter has invented a time machine.	Angela believes that Peter's time machine works—she uses it!
Angela thinks that the time machine is fun and useful.	Angela realizes that there are consequences for any actions, even actions that take place in the future.

Skills Review

Key Reading Skill: Paraphrasing and Summarizing

7. Review the chart you made on page 542. Get rid of any details that you don't need to understand the story. Use the information in the chart to write a short summary paragraph of "LAFFF." Remember to include only the most important pieces of information. Retell the main ideas and supporting details in your own words.

Key Literary Element: Author's Craft

8. For what audience do you think the author wrote this story? Explain.
9. Look at the author's word choice throughout the story. How does her word choice make the story more enjoyable? Explain.

Reviewing Skills: Reviewing

10. How does Angela feel about the time machine before she uses it? How does she feel when she uses it?

Vocabulary Check

Match the following words with the definitions below. Rewrite each word and its correct definition.

immigrated **fantastic** **possibilities** **destination**

11. ___ things that can or may happen
12. ___ not real; amazing or imaginary
13. ___ the place one hopes to reach at the end of a journey
14. ___ moved to a new country
15. **Academic Vocabulary** What do you do when you **summarize**?
16. **English Language Coach** Write the base word in each of the words listed below:

peaceful employee performance

Grammar Link: Clauses

A **clause** is a group of words that work together and contain a subject and a predicate. There are two kinds of clauses: independent and dependent.

- An **independent clause** expresses a complete thought. It can stand alone as a sentence.

Independent clause: mom yells
Simple sentence: Mom yells.

Independent clause: she dislikes loud music
Simple sentence: She dislikes loud music.

- A **dependent clause** does not express a complete thought. It cannot stand alone as a complete sentence. It "depends on" an independent clause to make its meaning complete.

Dependent clause: when we play loud music

Dependent clause + independent clause:
When we play loud music, mom yells.

Dependent clause: because it hurts her ears

Independent clause + dependent clause:
She dislikes loud music because it hurts her ears.

Grammar Practice

On a separate piece of paper, identify each clause as independent or dependent.

17. if the book is long
18. a car sped by
19. when the movie ends
19. people who lie
20. we all laughed

Writing Application Look at the paragraph you wrote for item 7 on this page. Underline two independent clauses and two dependent clauses in your paragraph.

Web Activities For eFlashcards, Selection Quick Checks, and other Web activities, go to www.glencoe.com.

Skills Review

Key Reading Skill: Paraphrasing and Summarizing

7. Responses will vary, but students should transfer information from their charts into logically organized summary paragraphs.

Key Literary Element: Author's Craft

8. Possible response: The author probably wrote the story for children and young adults. Reasons may include the age of the main characters, the humorous narration, or the topic of time travel.
9. Students may suggest that the word choice makes the story more lively and humorous. Her use of vividly descriptive language helps readers understand how the characters are feeling.

Reviewing Skills: Reviewing

10. Responses will vary but may indicate that Angela felt frightened by the time machine and remained nervous as she used it.

Close

Ask students to describe how they have had to adjust to an "improvement" that was intended to make something faster, simpler, or easier.

Vocabulary Check

11. possibilities
12. fantastic
13. destination
14. immigrated
15. You retell the main ideas and important details.
16. peace, employ, perform

Grammar Link: Clauses

Grammar Practice

17. dependent
18. independent
19. dependent
20. dependent
21. independent

Before You Read | Cyber Chitchat

More About the Author

Cindy Kauffman writes a column called "Full Nest" for the *Leader*, a newspaper in Akron, Ohio. Her work previously appeared in the collection *Chocolate for a Woman's Dreams*.

EL Language Coach

Base Words Write the following rule on the board.

- Change *y* to *i* and add *–ly*.

Say: Learning to recognize base words in words that have a suffix can help you figure out their meaning. The spelling of some base words changes slightly when a suffix is added. There are simple rules that you can learn to help you recognize the base word, such as the rule written on the board. The words *busy* and *angry* both follow this rule. As you learn these rules, write them in your Learner's Notebook along with example words. EL

Meet the Author

Cindy Kauffman lives in Green, Ohio, and writes weekly humor articles. More than 200 of her columns have been published. She is married and has four children.

Literature Online

Author Search For more about Cindy Kauffman, go to www.glencoe.com.

Objectives (pp. 544–549)
Reading Paraphrase and summarize
Literature Identify literary elements: author's craft
Vocabulary Identify word structure: base words

Vocabulary Preview

monitor (MAW nuh tur) *v.* to watch over or check on **(p. 546)** *The author decided to monitor her daughter's electronic conversation.*

decipher (dih SY fur) *v.* to figure out the meaning of **(p. 546)** *The daughter's spelling was hard to decipher.*

atrocious (uh TROH shus) *adj.* very bad; terrible; horrible **(p. 547)** *The mother thinks her daughter's spelling is atrocious.*

poised (poyzd) *adj.* in a position of being ready **(p. 548)** *Her hands were poised to begin typing.*

Flash Cards Make a flash card for each vocabulary word. Write the word on one side of the card and the definition on the other. When you have finished, use your flash cards to review vocabulary with a partner.

English Language Coach

Base Words Sometimes a base word changes a little when a suffix is added to it. For example if a word ends with *-y*, the *y* will usually change to *i* when you attach a suffix. You'll be able to recognize base words much more easily if you don't expect them all to look exactly like they do when they're standing alone.

For example, the word *easily* combines the base word *easy* and the suffix *-ly*. *Argument* combines the base word *argue* and the suffix *-ment*.

In the list below, all the base words have been underlined.

EL
happiness = happy + ness (the *y* becomes an *i*)
beginning = begin + ing (the last letter is doubled: an *n* is added)
judgment = judge + ment (the *e* is dropped)
funny = fun + y (the last letter is doubled: an *n* is added)
pianist = piano + ist (the *o* is dropped)

Small Group Work In the list below, all the base words are spelled a little bit differently than they would be if they had no suffixes. Can you figure out the base word?

batter   loveliness   denial   inquiry   inspiration

Additional Support

Author Search To expand students' appreciation of Cindy Kauffman, have them access the Web site for additional information and resources.

Literature Focus Lesson

Humor Columns Many newspapers run columns about local everyday events. Columnists who write these nonfiction pieces often look at events from a humorous perspective, revealing the absurdity in ordinary happenings. Discuss with students the reasons for an everyday occurrence's being seen as humorous or ridiculous. Ask students to write a brief column about an ordinary school event or routine. Suggest that students write about events other students can relate to, such as riding the bus or buying lunch in the cafeteria. Have students share their humor columns in small groups and then discuss as a class whether students generally found humor in similar situations. OL AL

Skills Preview

Key Reading Skill: Paraphrasing and Summarizing

When you read "Cyber Chitchat," think about the big picture. Use your own words to write the author's main ideas and supporting details. Be sure to choose only the most important ideas.

Write to Learn In your Learner's Notebook, jot down the main ideas of the selection as you read. Then list the supporting details that explain each main idea.

Key Literary Element: Author's Craft

Part of the **author's craft** is his or her purpose for writing. By looking at the selection's structure and word choices, you will find clues to help you recognize the author's purpose.

As you read, use these tips to help you learn about the author's craft.

- Look at the structure of the text.
  How does the author organize the information? Does this help you see what he or she wants to tell the reader?
- Notice the author's word choices. For example, the word *atrocious* is stronger than the word *bad.*
  What do the author's word choices tell you about his or her opinion of the topic?

Partner Talk With a classmate, review the above tips about author's craft. When you read a nonfiction article about someone's opinion, which tip do you think will be the most helpful? Why?

Interactive Literary Elements Handbook
To review or learn more about the literary elements, go to www.glencoe.com.

Get Ready to Read

Connect to the Reading

Have you ever felt confused when you saw or tried something for the first time? The author of this essay watches in surprise as her daughter chats online with her friends. As you read, think about how your reaction and the author's would be the same or different. R

Think-Pair-Share Think of some times when you tried to understand something new but just didn't get it. With a classmate, discuss how each of you reacted.

Build Background

In this essay, the author and her daughter talk about the language of chatting on the Internet.

- The Internet was developed by the United States Department of Defense.
- In 2001, more children and teens used the Internet than adults.
- In 2003, 70 percent of students in grades 6–8 were using the Internet.

L

Set Purposes for Reading

BIG Question As you read the selection "Cyber Chitchat," think about whether new technologies such as the Internet and online chatting are always good.

Set Your Own Purpose What else would you like to learn from the story to help you answer the Big Question? Write your own purpose on a note card and add it to Foldable 5.

Keep Moving

Use these skills as you read the following selection.

English Language Coach

Content-Area Words Have students match the following computer-related vocabulary words to the proper definitions.

eject	save
keyboard	cyber

1. to push out a disk or cartridge ___ *(eject)*
2. related to computers ___ *(cyber)*
3. device used to enter information on a computer ___ *(keyboard)*
4. to store data on a computer ___ *(save)* EL

Teach

L Literary Element

Author's Craft Say: Authors often choose words to entertain readers. What are some other reasons why authors might choose specific words? *(Possible responses: to be exact, to give a vivid description, to be funny, to make a point)* AL

R Reading Skill

Review Connecting Say: Think about how you felt when you encountered new technology, such as a computer program or an appliance, for the first time. How long did it take you to understand how this item worked and how to use it? *(Responses will vary.)* OL

CheckPoint

Use the CheckPoint questions provided on Presentation Plus! to check for paraphrasing and summarizing skills and to build background. These questions can be used with interactive response keypads for immediate student feedback.

Literature Online

Interactive Literary Elements Handbook Have students access the Web site to improve their understanding of author's craft.

Objectives
- Paraphrase and summarize
- Identify literary elements: author's craft
- Identify word structure: base words

Teach

R1 Reading Skill

Review Setting a Purpose for Reading **Say:** The title of this article is a hint that it will be lighthearted and humorous. What might be your purpose for reading an article on computers that is not strictly scientific? *(Possible response: to be entertained and to get another perspective on new technology)* OL

L Literary Element

Review Tone **Ask:** Tone is the author's attitude toward the subject. What is the author's tone in the first paragraph? *(Possible response: The author's tone is sarcastic and humorous when she says she's glad students learn spelling in school so they can unlearn it on the Internet.)* OL

R2 Reading Skill

Paraphrasing and Summarizing **Ask:** What is the main idea of the second paragraph? *(The author decides to watch her 13-year-old chat with friends online.)* OL

Cyber Chitchat

by Cindy Kauffman

I'm glad we teach spelling in our schools. That way, our children can busy themselves unlearning it when they log on to the Internet. 1

One day last week, I stood and watched my thirteen-year-old "chat" with some friends via e-mail. I thought I'd take the opportunity to **monitor** the electronic conversation being passed between these preteens—who long ago decided the telephone wasn't good enough for them.

Looking over her shoulder, I very quickly found that I needed a translator to **decipher** what was being said. Squinting down at the monitor,[1] I asked my daughter,

1. Here, ***monitor*** refers to the computer screen.

Vocabulary

monitor (MAW nuh tur) *v.* to watch over or check on

decipher (dih SY fur) *v.* to figure out the meaning of

Practice the Skills

1 Reviewing Skills

Setting a Purpose for Reading In Unit 1 you learned how to set a purpose for reading to improve your understanding. In the first paragraph, the author says that children unlearn spelling when they use the Internet. What purpose for reading does this information give you?

Additional Support

Readability Scores
Dale-Chall: 5.6
DRP: 55
Lexile: 870

English Language Coach

Onomatopoeia Explain to students that *onomatopoeia* is the use of words that imitate the sounds they describe. *Buzz,* for example, suggests the sound made by bees. Tell students that *chat* is a shortened form of *chatter,* a word that suggests the sound of rapid talk. *Babble* and *jabber* are two other examples of onomatopoeia with meanings similar to that of *chatter.* Ask students whether they know of any words in languages other than English that mean the same thing as *chat, chatter, babble,* or *jabber.* Ask students whether these non-English words are examples of onomatopoeia. EL

"What kind of atrocious spelling is *that?* And what does it mean?"

Peeved at the interruption, she kept typing and answered, "Wat duz *WAT* mean?" **2**

"That writing on the screen. The jargon[2] your friends are sending you, which sounds an awful lot like the way E.T.[3] talked in the movie. Look—here comes some more . . . 'CU lata.' Now what does *that* mean? Is it a new coffee flavor of some kind?"

"No, Mom," she answered. "It means—Oh wait a minute!" She quickly typed in, "Brb, every1," and turned patronizingly[4] around to me.

"UC," she began.

"Whoa! Wait a minute. Say it in English," I admonished.[5]

"You see," she began again, "we use a different type of spelling when we chat online. It's much easier and saves time. It's pronounced the same as always, but it's quicker to type and read. For example, when I want to say, 'Be right back, everyone,' I use, 'Brb, every1,' instead. Or, I'll hit 'CU lata,' rather than type out, 'See you later.' It's a real time-saver." **3** **R**

"OIC," I said thoughtfully.

After observing further, I momentarily asked, "Then what about this word, 'kewl'? I assume it means, 'cool . . . ' but it has the same number of letters, either way."

"Phonetically, it makes more sense," she explained. "Why waste time using some English linguist's[6] twist on the alphabet, when 'kewl' comes off the fingers more naturally?"

"Hmm," I mused. "I wonder what your second grade teacher would think about that . . ."

2. ***Jargon*** is language used by a group of people for a particular activity.
3. ***E.T.*** was the title character of the movie *E.T. The Extra Terrestrial.* He spoke in short, simple words and phrases.
4. ***Patronizingly*** means "acting as if one is better than others."
5. ***Admonished*** is a way of saying "expressed disapproval in a nice way."
6. To spell a word ***phonetically*** (fuh NET ik lee) is to spell it the way it sounds when spoken. A ***linguist*** (LING gwist) is a person who knows a lot about language.

Vocabulary

atrocious (uh TROH shus) *adj.* very bad; terrible; horrible

Practice the Skills

2 Key Literary Element

Author's Craft One element of author's craft is word choice. Look at how the author spells her daughter's response. Why do you think the author chose to spell her daughter's response in this way? Think about the language the daughter uses when she chats online. **L**

3 Key Reading Skill

Paraphrasing and Summarizing Paraphrase the daughter's explanation for using different spelling online. Use your own words and write your answer in your Learner's Notebook.

READING WORKSHOP 1

Teach

L Literary Element

Author's Craft Ask: What does the author want to show readers by spelling her daughter's response, "Wat duz *WAT* mean?" *(Possible responses: The writer may want to show the reader how difficult the spellings are to read. The writer may want to show she must "translate" what her daughter is saying because the words are unfamiliar.)* **AL**

R Reading Skill

Paraphrasing and Summarizing Say: How is the daughter's online communication like a summary? *(The daughter's online spelling is a briefer way of writing something. Similarly, a summary is a briefer way of telling what something is about.)* **OL** What are some other situations where you might "summarize" while writing, as the daughter does? *(Possible responses: when taking notes for classes, when writing a phone message)* **AL**

Reading in the Real World

Citizenship A computer network is made up of two or more computers connected for the purpose of transferring information between them electronically. The Internet is a network that developed as various, small research networks in the United States and Europe became connected. Currently, the Internet is the largest network in existence, connecting millions of computers worldwide. Some people estimate that by 2010, about half of the world's population will have access to the Internet. Have students brainstorm ways the Internet can help improve people's lives as it becomes even more widespread. **OL**

Objectives

- Analyze elements of author's craft, including onomatopoeia
- Paraphrase and summarize
- Identify and analyze tone
- Set a purpose for reading

Teach

BQ BIG Question

Say: How might a person's writing in e-mails differ from the writing that he or she does for other purposes? *(Possible response: A person may write less carefully in e-mails or may change his or her use of spelling and punctuation to communicate more quickly.)* **BL**
Do you think that using incorrect spelling and grammar to write electronic messages could have a negative effect on the way people communicate in general? Explain your opinion. *(Responses will vary.)* **OL**

R Reading Skill

Author's Craft Say: The author probably didn't *really* expect her daughter to be ashamed of her spelling. Why might she have included this statement in her article? *(Possible response: for humor; to highlight her disappointment in her daughter's atrocious spelling)* **AL**

"Oh, you mean Mrs. Jonz?"

"No—I mean Mrs. *Jones,*" I corrected. "She took great care in teaching you how to spell words like, 'about,' 'until,' 'know,' 'better,' and 'nothing.' Yet for all of her efforts, you're sending e-mail messages like this one: 'Dear Ashley: Can't tell U any more bout that cute kid in our class till I no something. Betta go now; nuttin more to say—Me.'" **4**

R Looking down at her hands **poised** on the keyboard, I expected her eyes to start showing some chagrin.[7] Instead, she had them trained on the computer monitor and an incoming response from Ashley. "Waz up?" it read. "Got your message but g2g now, as sorta have gobs of homework. Talk 2U lata, KK?"

7. A person showing ***chagrin*** feels embarrassment or shame.

Vocabulary

poised (poyzd) *adj.* in a position of being ready

Practice the Skills

4 BIG Question

BQ What is the author's opinion of her daughter's writing? Does she think that technology has a positive or a negative effect on her daughter? Write your answer on a note card and add it to Foldable 5. Your response will help you answer the Unit Challenge later.

Additional Support

Reading in the Real World

Career Point out that many employees communicate through e-mail. Tell students that the conventions of traditional letter writing apply when writing more formal e-mails. For example, they should use a salutation, such as *Dear Mary:* and a closing, such as *Yours Sincerely,* and write clear, error-free text. Also, the subject line on a work e-mail should clearly state the purpose of the e-mail. Ask students to look for help-wanted ads on the Internet, and tell them to select ads for jobs that interest them. Have students write professional-looking e-mails in response to the job postings. Be sure they include subject lines stating their purpose for writing. **OL**

"G2g . . . ?" I started to ask.

"Got to go!" my daughter answered, typing feverishly.

"O," I said. "And I suppose 'KK' means, 'OK.'"

"Ya."

"Isn't that rather babyish? Don't you remember the months we spent teaching you how to talk? Have you no appreciation for what you're undoing here?"

Before I could continue my lecture, the instant-messaging box we'd been using to "I.M." Ashley suddenly grew into three boxes, each with a different name attached. Then it multiplied into four, then five, and finally six. **EL**

My young e-mailer was really fervent[8] now—reading messages from six friends simultaneously,[9] scanning each box for pertinent news and typing in jumbles of consonants in reply. I'd never seen anything like it. There had apparently been a **prearranged** log-on time, which all seven friends honored **unconditionally**. Clearly, it put to shame the previous generation's system of passing around an in-class note that read, "Everyone meet at the swing-set after school so we can all talk." **5**

I could see why she abbreviated. This was like playing Bingo with six cards at once. Except that these girls could type faster than any Bingo announcer could shout numbers.

Cross-eyed from reading and deciphering incoming messages from all parts of the city, I finally closed my eyelids and rubbed them hard, walking away.

And I thought my three-way calling telephone service was the ultimate in communication. Obviously, I didn't know what "ultimate" really was.

Now all I need is an adult education course that teaches this new, "shoddy-spell" e-mail language to floundering parents. If I find one, I'll sign up in a heartbeat. **6**

. . . And b betta off 4 it, I'm shur. ❍ **L**

8. Someone who is ***fervent*** is intense about what he or she is doing.
9. To do things ***simultaneously*** is to do them at the same time.

Practice the Skills

5 English Language Coach

Base Words Can you find the base words in **prearranged** and **unconditionally**?

6 Key Literary Element

Author's Craft The word *shoddy* means "sloppy; poorly made or done." What does the choice to use *shoddy-spell* tell you about the author's opinion?

Differentiated Instruction

Charting Have students make a chart that illustrates some of the spelling shortcuts described in the article. In the left column, have students print three "shoddy-spell" words from the selection and write the correct spellings of these words in the right column. Then ask students to invent a "shoddy-spell" phrase of their own. **EL** **BL**

Shoddy-Spell Words	Correctly Spelled Words
G2g	Got to go
KK	Okay
Kewl	Cool

Teach

EL Language Coach

Acronyms Say: An *acronym* is a shortened way of referring to something with a long name or title. An acronym is made up of the first letters of each word in a title or name. For example, *U.S.A.* stands for *United States of America*. Give an example of an acronym that appears on this page and tell its meaning. *(I.M.: Instant Message)* **BL** Do you know any other acronyms related to computers? *(Possible responses: www.: worldwide web, I.T.: Information Technology)* **EL** **OL**

L Literary Element

Author's Craft Say: The author gives many clues about her opinion of her daughter's "cyber chitchat." What do phrases such as "cross-eyed from reading" and "floundering parents" suggest? *(The author feels overwhelmed by the language of computer messaging and believes other parents probably feel the same way.)* **OL**

Assess

Use the CheckPoint questions provided on Presentation Plus! to check for comprehension of the selection. These questions can be used with interactive response keypads for immediate student feedback.

Objectives
- Analyze author's craft
- Create graphic organizers
- Write workplace documents

Assess

Resources for page 550

- Selection Quick Check
- Selection and Unit Assessment
- ExamView Assessment Suite
- Interactive Tutor: Self-Assessment

Students can respond to the *After You Read* items in their Learner's Notebook or on separate sheets of paper.

Answering the BIG Question

1. Possible response: Computer technology helps people communicate and share information, but it may also allow certain skills, such as formal writing, to decline.
2. passing notes in class
3. The mother asks questions and the daughter explains her use of online language.

Critical Thinking

4. Possible response: The second grade teacher would be disappointed in the daughter's online spelling.
5. Possible response: She doesn't seem bothered. She answers them and continues to type.
6. Responses will vary. Some students may find the argument unconvincing because shortening words makes instant-messaging easier. Others may agree that correct spelling should be used.

After You Read Cyber Chitchat

Answering the BIG Question

1. After reading this essay by Cindy Kauffman, do you think the effects of computer technology are always good?
2. **Recall** What activity from her own childhood does the author connect to her daughter's use of instant-messaging?
   Tip **Right There**
3. **Summarize** Throughout the essay, how did the author and her daughter interact with each other about the online chat?
   Tip **Think and Search**

Critical Thinking

4. **Infer** What does the author suggest that her daughter's second-grade teacher would think about online conversations?
   Tip **Author and Me**
5. **Infer** How do you think the daughter feels about her mother's questions and comments? How can you tell?
   Tip **Author and Me**
6. **Evaluate** Do you think the author's argument in this essay is convincing? Explain.
   Tip **Author and Me**

Objectives (pp. 550–551)
Reading Paraphrase and summarize
• Make connections from text to self
Literature Identify literary elements: author's craft
Vocabulary Identify word structure: base words
Writing Write a personal letter: compare
Grammar Identify phrases

Talk About Your Reading

Literature Groups In your group, talk about a time when an adult didn't understand something you did. For example, maybe you made up new rules for a game, and an adult didn't understand why you changed the rules.

- How did you feel?
- How did you react?
- What finally happened?

Write to Learn Write a letter to the author's daughter and describe your experience. Compare your experience with her experience.

- How were they alike?
- How were they different?
- Did the adults react the same way?

Talk About Your Reading

Write to Learn Students should compare and contrast their experiences with the experience of the daughter in "Cyber Chitchat." Sample response:

Dear Friend,

I agree with you—parents can be so frustrating! Last week, my parents came with me to the Sci-Fi Fair. I saw my friend Lewis dressed as an alien from Takron-6. I started speaking to him in Tarkish, and my parents interrupted right away. It was just like the time you had to explain to your mom what words in cyber chat mean. Lewis and I had to say everything twice: once in Takrish and again in English so that my parents could understand. At least your mom started to understand cyber chat pretty quickly.

Yours truly,
Zoe

Skills Review

Key Reading Skill: Paraphrasing and Summarizing

7. Review the list of main ideas and supporting details that you made in your Learner's Notebook. Use your list as a guide. Decide which one of the sentences below best summarizes the selection.

- The author once believed that three-way telephone service was the ultimate in communication.
- The author thinks that young people are learning to use the Internet in new and interesting ways.
- The author worries that online communication encourages kids to spell incorrectly.

Key Literary Element: Author's Craft

8. What do the words and phrases that the author uses make you think or feel? Does the tone of the selection give you clues about the author's opinion?
9. What does the author's craft tell you about the author's purpose for writing? Give some examples.

Vocabulary Check

Rewrite each sentence with the correct word in place.

atrocious monitor decipher poised

10. The author struggled to ___ her daughter's writing.
11. Her hands were ___ above the keyboard, ready to type.
12. The author stands behind her daughter to ___ her daughter's use of the Internet.
13. The author is shocked by her daughter's ___ spelling.
14. **English Language Coach** Write the base words, with their original spelling if necessary, for each word below.

education	unlearning	incoming
planner	beautiful	truly

Grammar Link: Phrases

A phrase is two or more words that make sense together but do not contain a subject and predicate.

- A verb phrase contains one or more helping verbs followed by a main verb.

  We <u>have watched</u> the team often.

  Lucia <u>has been hitting</u> the ball well!

- As you know, verbs often have objects—nouns or pronouns that complete their meaning. Prepositions *always* do. So, a preposition is always part of a phrase.

  Ted worked <u>for hours</u>.

  Drivers <u>on the crowded highway</u> honked loudly.

Besides the preposition and its object, a prepositional phrase often includes modifiers, such as *crowded* and *loudly* in the sentence above.

- Prepositional phrases themselves are modifiers. There are adjective phrases and adverb phrases.

  Adjective: The bird <u>in the pet store</u> is chirping.

  Adverb: We bought our bird <u>in the pet store</u>.

Grammar Practice

Copy the sentences below and underline the prepositional phrase in each.

15. We have been friends since September.
16. Life would be dull without her.
17. After school we do homework together.
18. One of her best subjects is social studies.

Writing Application Look back at the letter you wrote. Underline three prepositional phrases you used.

Web Activities For eFlashcards, Selection Quick Checks, and other Web activities, go to www.glencoe.com.

Skills Review

Key Reading Skill: Paraphrasing and Summarizing

7. The author worries that online communication encourages kids to spell incorrectly.

Key Literary Element: Author's Craft

8. Possible response: Remarks such as "Isn't that rather babyish?" show that the author thinks casual spelling makes people who use it seem poorly educated and immature. Her tone is humorous but also irritated, indicating she disapproves of cyber spelling.
9. Word choices such as "feverishly," "fervent," and "floundering parents" suggest that the author is exaggerating for humorous effect. Her purpose is to entertain readers.

Vocabulary Check

10. decipher
11. poised
12. monitor
13. atrocious
14. educate
    learn
    come
    plan
    beautiful
    truly

Grammar Link: Phrases

Grammar Practice

15. since September
16. without her
17. After school
18. of her best subjects

Close

Have students contrast how the writer and her daughter feel about instant messaging.

WRITING WORKSHOP PARTS 1 and 2

Research Report

Objectives covered in this workshop:

- **Writing** Summarize to inform develop drafts; categorize information; main idea and supporting details
- **Grammar** Identify and correctly use verbs

Teaching Students to Write a Research Report

Why Is It Important?

- Writing a research report helps students synthesize information, which fosters both comprehension and writing with purpose.
- Doing research builds literacy by ensuring that students make use of different kinds of sources or media.
- Research shows that reading one's own writing—notes, highlighted text, and data—for the purpose of synthesizing it improves one's ability to read critically.
- Knowing that one will write a report following inquiry and data gathering improves the inquiry process because it contributes to a clear purpose for doing research.
- Comparing sources on the same material provides an opportunity for students to determine author credibility.

How to Help Students Get It

- Emphasize the importance of using an overall research and writing plan, and review the plan repeatedly.
- Guide students through inquiry components like these: brainstorming what students know about a topic; asking questions they want to answer; listing ways they might answer questions.
- Show and model using an information search strategy involving multiple sources (print sources like books, periodicals, reference tools; and electronic sources like CDs, DVDs, and the Web).
- Encourage students to be very specific in their questions; a too-broad topic may be discouraging.
- Help students use a comprehensive method of writing to record information and data using note cards, data sheets, word processors or databases, graphic organizers or diagrams.
- Focus on how to select the most important information, and use a variety of sources and media in writing up the report; model various report formats for students including print formats and media presentations.
- Show students examples of source cards to help them prepare a bibliography.
- Review paraphrasing and quoting, giving examples of each and showing students how to identify them by punctuation. Also define plagiarism, and talk about how to prevent it.

Traits of Good Writing	
Ideas: the message or the theme and the details that develop it	• Does the title suggest the theme of the composition? • Does the composition focus on a single narrow topic? • Is the thesis, or main idea, clearly stated? • Do well-chosen details elaborate the main idea?
Voice	a writer's unique way of using tone and style
Organization	the arrangement of main points and supporting details
Word Choice	the vocabulary a writer uses to convey meaning
Sentence Fluency	the smooth rhythm and flow of sentences that vary in length and style
Conventions	correct spelling, grammar, usage, and mechanics
Presentation	the way words and design elements look on a page

Workshop Resources

Pacing (Days) Standard	Block	Lesson	Student Materials	Teacher Resources
1		Prewriting	Writing Workshop Graphic Organizer Grammar Practice Spelling and Handwriting Practice Spelling Power eWorkbook Interactive Grammar and Language Workbook Grammar and Composition Handbook	TeacherWorks Plus Presentation Plus! Rubrics for Assessing Student Writing, Listening, and Speaking
2		Drafting	Real Success in Writing: Research and Reports Writing Constructed Responses Sourcebook	Grammar and Writing Workshop Transparency
1		Editing	Interactive Grammar and Language Workbook Grammar and Composition Handbook	Grammar and Writing Workshop Transparency
2		Revising	Real Success in Writing: Research and Reports Writing Constructed Responses Sourcebook	Interactive Grammar and Language Workbook
2		Presenting	Real Success in Writing: Research and Reports Writing Constructed Responses Sourcebook	Rubrics for Assessing Student Writing, Listening, and Speaking

Focus

BELLRINGER Options

Daily Language Practice Transparency
Focus Activity Ask: How has progress affected your life? List things you can do today because of inventions developed in your lifetime.

Teach

W1 Writing

Research Reports Ask: How are research reports different from creative writing? *(Possible response: Stories are products of imagination. Research reports are fact based.)* **OL**
What skills do you need to write a research report? *(Possible response: research, note-taking, planning)* **AL**

W2 Writing

Research Reports Ask: Why is it a good idea to narrow your topic before researching? *(Possible response: Researching will be easier if it is focused.)* **OL**

Resources for page 552

Use the Writing Workshop Graphic Organizer BLM in the Unit 5 Resource Booklet.

WRITING WORKSHOP PART 1

Research Report

Prewriting and Drafting

ASSIGNMENT Write a research report
Purpose: To learn about a topic that interests you
Audience: Your teacher, your classmates, and others who are interested in this topic

Writing Rubric

As you work through this writing assignment, you should

- write a research report with an introduction, a body, and a conclusion
- develop a thesis statement and support it with evidence and details
- use a cause-and-effect text structure
- document sources accurately in a bibliography or a list of works cited
- use graphics and concepts of design

See page 599 in Part 2 for a model of a research report.

Objectives (pp. 552–555)
Writing Use the writing process: draft • Write a research report • Include main ideas and supporting details • Use a cause-and-effect structure
Grammar Use main and subordinate clauses

W1 When you gather information about a topic and write up your findings, you produce a **research report.** Writing a research report will help you think about the Unit 5 Big Question: Is progress always good? As you write your research report, refer to the **Writing Handbook,** pages R21–R24.

Prewriting

Get Ready to Write

Progress comes in all different forms and all different ways. As you choose a topic and begin researching, think about how progress is related to your research topic.

Gather Ideas and Choose a Topic

List topics that interest you and that you want to learn more about. If you need help thinking of ideas, follow these suggestions:

- Look through the selections in this unit and identify some of the ideas about progress.
- Watch the news or scan some newspapers, magazines, or books for ideas.
- Skim your science and social studies textbooks and look for topics that interest you.
- Search the library's electronic card catalog or look on the Internet.
- Brainstorm a list of topics with a partner.

Choose two or three topics from your list and brainstorm a list of questions about each topic. As you write, one topic may emerge as your favorite. If that happens, you've found your topic! If you're still not sure which topic to choose, don't worry. You can do some general reading about a few ideas and then choose your topic.

Shape Your Topic

W2 Select one of the questions you wrote and read about it in an encyclopedia or another general reference book. Use the information you read to narrow or widen your topic. Find a focus that you can cover thoroughly in a short report. If you decide that you're no longer interested in the topic, choose another question to read about until you find a topic you like.

Additional Support

Differentiated Instruction

Progress Web To help students generate ideas for their reports, draw a web on the board similar to the one shown. Ask students to add examples of areas in which they have experienced progress. Encourage students to give concrete examples of progress in these areas. **BL** **OL**

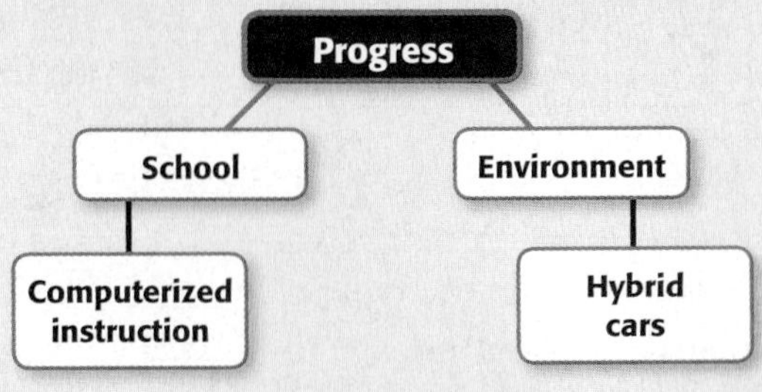

Use a Variety of Sources

Gather information from a variety of sources. **Primary sources,** such as letters, diaries, and newspaper stories, are documents and personal accounts from the time of the event. They are written by people who actually experienced the event. **Secondary sources,** such as encyclopedias and biographies, are based on information gathered from other sources. W

almanacs	newspapers	DVDs
atlases	surveys	videos
encyclopedias	scholarly journals	CD-ROMs
magazines	Web sites	interviews

Evaluate Your Sources

Only use sources that you can trust. Authors should be unbiased and provide supporting evidence. No matter what sources you use for your research, make sure that they are

- authoritative–written by recognized experts on the topic
- reliable–published in trustworthy books, periodicals, or Web sites
- up-to-date–based on the most current research in the field

Be especially careful evaluating Internet sources. Unlike most books and magazines, much of the information on the Internet is not approved by anyone before it is posted. So you have to do the work of deciding which information to trust.

Make a Note of It

- As you gather information, take notes on index cards. Summarize, paraphrase, or directly quote the information from your sources. At the top of each card, write the main idea of the note so you can easily sort and organize your cards later.
- Make source cards by writing the title, the author's name, and the publication information of each source on a card. Then give the source card a number. As you take notes, you can track where each idea came from by writing the source number on the note card.

For more information about taking notes and documenting sources, see the **Writing Handbook,** pages R21–R24.

Writing Tip

Questions Before and during your research, ask questions that will help focus and direct your research. What might your readers want to know? What causes and effects are related to your topic?

Writing Tip

Researching *The Readers' Guide to Periodical Literature* can help you find magazine articles on your topic.

Writing Tip

Text Features Save time by using the title page, table of contents, index, and appendix to judge whether a source will be useful and to find specific information within a book.

Writing Tip

Cause and Effect When thinking about causes and effects, be sure that the cause-and-effect relationship actually exists. An event that came before another event isn't necessarily the cause.

Reading in the Real World

College Remind students that information found on the Internet varies in reliability. Discuss the type and reliability of information on each URL extension:

- **.edu: Education sites**—tend to be reliable and backed up by research
- **.gov: Governmental sites**—usually highly reliable
- **.org: Sites associated with large non-profit groups, smaller organizations, or even individuals**—may vary in reliability depending on who is posting information
- **.com: Commercial sites**—may not always be reliable because the sites often want to sell something **AS**

Teach

W Writing

Primary and Secondary Sources Have students classify the following sources as "primary" or "secondary" and tell what they would best be used for.

- Scientific log of a medical researcher *(primary source; might be useful for a report on medical advances)*
- Magazine cover story entitled "The Most Amazing Inventions of 2005" *(secondary source; might be useful for a report on recent technological advances)*
- Biography of Henry Ford *(secondary source; might be useful for report on inventors)*
- Video of space mission on NASA Web site *(primary source; might be useful for report on space missions)*
- News articles about hybrid cars *(secondary source; might be useful for a report on fuel-efficient cars)* **OL**

Objectives
- Write a research report
- Use the writing process
- Gather information from a variety of sources

Teach

W1 Writing

Thesis Statements
Say: As you start researching and learning about your topic, stay focused on your thesis statement, which expresses the overall point of your paper.
Ask: How can a thesis statement help you determine what information is important to your report? *(It can help you decide what does and does not relate to your topic and your point.)* AL

W2 Writing

Cause and Effect Remind students that just because one event follows another in time does not mean the first event caused the second event. Give students the following examples and have them tell whether they show a cause-and-effect relationship (CE):

1. Jose washed his car on Wednesday and on Thursday it rained. *(no CE)*
2. Harry did not listen in class so he failed the test. *(CE)*
3. Ricki exercised more and felt healthier. *(CE)*
4. Sally was late to school five days in a row so she got detention. *(CE)* BL OL

Literature Online

Writing Models For models and other writing activities, go to www.glencoe.com.

Get Organized

Now it's time to organize all of your ideas and notes into an order that makes sense to you and your readers.

1. Consider the main idea and what you want to say about your topic. Write a **thesis statement**—a sentence or two that tells the main idea or states what you want to show, prove, or explain.

People are responsible for declining manatee populations.

Writing Tip

Use Technology You may want to use a computer to make your outline and draft your report. The cut-and-paste feature will allow you to easily reorganize your outline and revise, edit, and format your report.

2. Begin creating an outline by listing at least three main points that you want to make in your report. All of these points should support your thesis statement. Plan to show causes and effects. W2
3. Sort your note cards into piles according to the main idea of the cards. Make one pile for each main point.
4. Then sort the piles into notes about the main point and notes about the supporting details. Set aside any notes that aren't related to your points.
5. Complete your outline by adding details from your note cards.

This beginning of an outline shows how a thesis statement and the parts of an outline fit together.

Thesis Statement: People are responsible for declining manatee populations.
I. Introduction
II. Causes of Manatee Deaths
A. Boats
1. manatees must breathe at the surface
2. they're slow swimmers
3. they probably can't hear boats
B. Floodgates and canals
1. manatees get sucked in and can't breathe
2. they get caught between the gates
C. Objects that pollute the water
1. manatees get cut by fishing line and the cuts get infected
2. they choke on fishing hooks and garbage
III. What people can do

Additional Support

Literature Online

Writing Models Have students access the Web site for an additional and interactive Writing Workshop-based student model.

English Language Coach

Text Structure Remind students that they will organize their reports using a cause-and-effect structure. Cause and effect works well when writers want to explore the reasons for something and examine the results of events or actions. Words and phrases such as *so, because,* and *as a result* help show the relationship between a cause and its effects. Students might want to use the following cause-and-effect graphic organizer to help them organize their ideas. EL BL

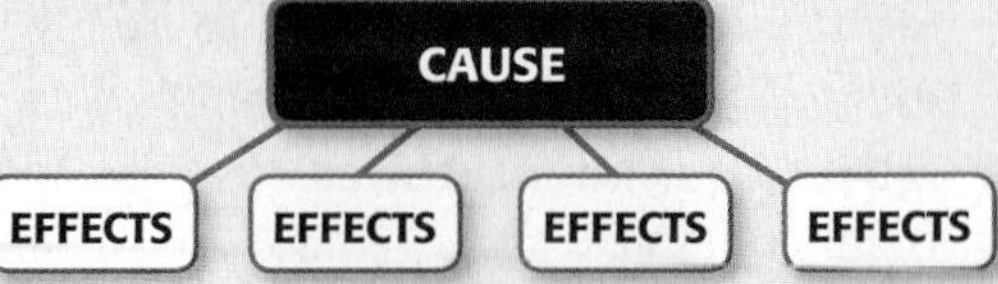

Grammar Link

Main and Subordinate Clauses

An **independent (main) clause** states a complete thought. It can stand alone as a sentence. A **dependent (subordinate) clause** does not state a complete thought. It cannot stand alone.

What Are They?

As its name suggests, a **main clause** states the main, or most important, idea in a sentence. A main clause can be a sentence by itself, or it can W1 be the most important part of a sentence.

Main clause: Hal is sleepy.

Main clause: Hal is sleepy because he stayed up too late last night.

Main clauses: Hal is sleepy, so **he is going home to bed.**

A **subordinate clause** states a less important idea in a sentence. Subordinate clauses begin with subordinating conjunctions. (Look at the chart.)

after	even though	when
although	if	whenever
as	since	where
as if	than	whereas
as though	though	wherever
because	unless	whether
before	until	while

Why Are They Important?

Clauses are the building blocks of sentences. When you know how to use both kinds of clauses, you can write clearer, more effective sentences.

How Do I Use Them?

You probably use both kinds of clauses every time you write. Now make sure that you use the clauses correctly. Remember that subordinate clauses cannot stand alone as sentences. To be complete, they must be linked to main clauses.

Wrong: I will count sheep. Until I fall asleep. (*Until* is a subordinating conjunction, so *Until I fall asleep* is a subordinate clause. As a subordinate clause, it cannot stand alone as a sentence.)

Right: I will count sheep until I fall asleep.

Grammar Practice Two subordinate clauses mistakenly stand alone in the following paragraph. Copy the paragraph on a separate piece of paper. Then fix the mistakes by connecting the misused subordinate clauses to the main clauses they belong with.

My little sister walks in her sleep. Whenever I see her walk around during the night, I get nervous. I'm afraid of scaring her. If I suddenly awaken her. W2 Yet I can't just ignore her either. Usually I just lie in bed awake and wait. Until I see her go safely back to sleep.

Looking Ahead

Keep the outline and the notes you made here. In Part 2 of this Writing Workshop, you'll draft, revise, and present your research.

Teach

W1 Writing

Clauses Read the following sentences aloud. Ask students to identify the main clause in each sentence.

- Rita is hungry.
- Rita was still hungry after she had eaten a snack.
- Jimmy can't play soccer until his grades improve.
- Quentin likes animals, and he is going to the zoo. OL

W2 Writing

Clauses Help students identify the main and subordinate clauses in the paragraph.
Ask: Which subordinate clauses stand alone in the paragraph? *(If I suddenly awaken her; Until I see her go safely back to sleep)* **What is the subordinating conjunction in each?** *(if, until)* **How can you correct the mistakes?** *(Possible response: Combine two sentences into one complete sentence: I'm afraid of scaring her if I suddenly awaken her. AND Usually I just lie in bed awake and wait until I see her go safely back to sleep.)* OL

Differentiated Instruction

Subordinate Clauses Share the chart to help students understand clauses:

Clause	Function	Begins with...
Adjective clause	Modifies noun or pronoun in main clause	A relative pronoun, such as *that, which, who, whom,* or *whose*
Adverb clause	Modifies verb in main clause	A subordinating conjunction, such as *after, although, because, if, since,* or *until*

Objectives
- Write a research report using the writing process
- Develop a thesis statement
- Effectively organize main points and supporting details
- Know the difference between and use dependent and independent clauses

Using Text Features

UNIT 5

Objectives covered in this workshop:
- Locate information in text features
- Use organizational features and electronic sources to access information

Using Text Features

Why Is It Important

- Text features cue the reader to resources that complement the running text; knowing how to use these is important to using textbooks and related materials.
- Using text features within chapters or sections of texts signal text structure and important concepts that help readers comprehend the specific text.
- Students who understand text features and text structure have higher reading comprehension than those who don't.

How to Help Students Get It

- Select a piece of text such as a chapter or article and do a preview with students; have them name the text features they see—for example, titles, headings and subheadings, illustrations and graphics, marginal notes, vocabulary aids.
- Do thinkalouds and talkalouds in which you verbalize what the text features signal to you—e.g., "from this heading I expect to find out about. . ." or "the picture to right of the bottom of the second column shows the actual detail of . . ."
- Give students a list of questions that they have to use text features to answer (and then review the list and answers with them after they answer the questions).

The Selections and the Big Question

Conserving Resources

As landfills start to fill up with more and more garbage in America, people have become increasingly more aware of their impact on the environment. This informational science text can be used as a starting point for a discussion about why buying new items cheaply and easily may not always be a good thing.

There Will Come Soft Rains

In this science fiction story, a house run by machines continues to function on its own long after its occupants have died in a nuclear bomb attack. The story illustrates the fears that people had about machines in the 1950s and will help students to think about how machines such as computers are changing our lives today.

Workshop Resources

Pacing (days) Standard	Block	Lesson	Student Materials	Teacher Resources
1		Key Skill Lesson: Using Text Features	Key Reading Skills Practice English Language Coach	Bellringer Options Transparencies Read Aloud, Think Aloud Transparencies Presentation Plus!
2		"Conserving Resources"	Literary Analysis Transparencies Glencoe Online Selection Vocabulary Development Academic Vocabulary Development English Language Coach Active Reading Graphic Organizer Literary Analysis StudentWorks Plus Online Student Edition Literature Classics Selection and Unit Assessments	Literary and Text Analysis Transparencies Puzzlemaker Skill Level Up! BookLink 3 Assessment by Learning Objective (Diagnostic and Formative) Interactive Tutor Self-Assessment TeacherWorks Plus
2		"There Will Come Soft Rains"	Glencoe Online Selection Vocabulary Development Academic Vocabulary Development English Language Coach Active Reading Graphic Organizer Literary Analysis StudentWorks Plus Online Student Edition Literature Classics Selection and Unit Assessments	Literary and Text Analysis Transparencies Puzzlemaker Skill Level Up! BookLink 3 Assessment by Learning Objective (Diagnostic and Formative) Interactive Tutor Self-Assessment TeacherWorks Plus

Keys for Unit Resource

- Blackline Master
- Workbook
- Supplemental Text
- CD-ROM
- DVD
- Transparency
- Web-based
- Fast Files

Level Appropriate Code

AS = Activities for all students
AL = Activities for students working above grade level
OL = Activities for students working at grade level
BL = Activities for students working below grade level
EL = Activities for English language learners

Focus

BELLRINGER Options

Daily Language Practice Transparency

Focus Activity Ask: Why is it sometimes easier to use an image when explaining an idea? *(Possible response: Images can make ideas understandable.)*

Teach

R Reading Skill

Using Text Features Say: Think of the last story you read. What feature or image helped you understand the main idea? *(Possible responses: a picture of the main character; a map; a chart)* OL How do text features add to your reading experience? *(Possible response: Text features make ideas understandable.)* AL

V Vocabulary

Academic Vocabulary

Say: Notice the word *features*. What are the *features* on a person's face? *(eyes, nose, mouth)* What other words could mean the same thing as *features*? *(parts, objects, items)* OL

READING WORKSHOP 2

Skills Focus

You will practice using these skills when you read the following selections:

- "Conserving Resources," p. 560
- "There Will Come Soft Rains," p. 568

Reading

- Using text features

Literature

- Understanding concept and definition

Vocabulary

- Recognizing suffixes
- Academic Vocabulary: *features, concept*

Writing/Grammar

- Recognizing noun, adjective, and adverb clauses as parts of speech

Objectives (pp. 556–557)
Reading Use text features: map, heading, footnote, photograph

Skill Lesson

Using Text Features

Learn It!

What Is It? As you learned in Unit 1, text **features** are special parts of the text that aren't in the regular paragraphs of the selection. The text features you'll often see include:

R

- photographs, drawings, and maps
- footnotes and side notes
- headings or leads
- graphic organizers, such as charts

Analyzing Cartoons
The illustration in the girl's book is a text feature. Text features show or tell what people, places, events, and things are like.

Academic Vocabulary

V **features** (FEE churz) *n.* special qualities, parts, or sections

Additional Support

Reading in the Real World

College Tell students that they may be required to create documents that teachers and classmates can read quickly and understand easily. To create these documents, students may need to present their data in charts and/or graphs. Ask students to look through newspapers and magazines for examples of charts and graphs that accompany and explain text. As a class, discuss which examples are most interesting and effective. OL

Discuss with students how they can incorporate charts and graphs into academic writing. If possible, have each student use a computer word processing or spreadsheet program to create a chart or graph that can be included in a writing assignment. AL

Why Is It Important? When you use text features, you help yourself understand what you're reading. Photographs and drawings show you what people, places, and things look like. Maps show you where things are. Footnotes and side notes explain difficult words or ideas. Headings help you go immediately to the section you want to read. Graphic organizers such as charts give you difficult or complex information in one place.

Literature Online

Study Central Visit www.glencoe.com and click on Study Central to review using text features.

How Do I Do It? When you read, look for text features to help you understand what you are reading. In the article "What Exercise Can Do for You" in Unit Four, there is a chart titled *Going for the "Caloric Burn."* It shows how many calories people of different weights burn doing a variety of activities. Using the chart is a clear and simple way to get that information. Here's how one student responded to the chart.

I don't play racquetball and I've never skied, but I do ride my bike to and from school every day. That takes about a half hour. I'm on the swim team, too. We practice an hour every night. According to this chart, I'm burning more than 700 calories a day! That's good! When I go hiking with my buddies this weekend, I'll use this chart to figure out how many calories I burn. And I'll be sure to eat a great breakfast before we go.

Practice It!

Below are different text features.

map heading footnote photograph

In your Learner's Notebook, write which feature is most useful for
- finding out the meaning of a word you don't know
- finding out which parts of the country get the most rain
- finding out what a particular car looks like
- finding out where to look to get information on training your dog to sit

Use It!

As you read "Conserving Resources" and "There Will Come Soft Rains," look for text features. List them in your Learner's Notebook.

Differentiated Instruction

Graphs Provide students with examples of the following types of graphs: bar, line, area, circle, and XY. Discuss the types of information that can be included in each graph. For example, which graph might best show changes over time? Which graph can best show the parts of a whole? **OL**

Challenge students to research recycling programs and present data to the class in the form of graphs. Data can include statistics for program aspects such as costs, number of participating citizens, and amount of recycled material. **AL**

READING WORKSHOP 2

Teach

Literature Online

Study Central Have students access the Web site to review using text features and to complete a related activity.

R Reading Skill

Using Text Features Say: Read the *Why Is It Important?* section. How do text features help you better understand what you're reading? *(Possible response: A text feature can reaffirm or correct a reader's interpretation of the text. For example, if a reader imagines a machine with a pulley, but a picture shows a machine with a lever system, the reader can correct his or her image and better understand the machine being described.)* **OL** How can you tell that something is a text feature? *(Possible response: A text feature stands out from the rest of the text and shows something to readers. It can be an image, a picture, a chart, a title or head, a side note or footnote.)* **BL**

Resources for page 557

Use Reading Skills Transparency in *Read Aloud, Think Aloud,* Unit 5, to help students practice using text features.

Objectives
- Locate information in text features
- Select the purpose of a specific text feature

Before You Read Conserving Resources

More About the Author

A scientific journalist's background allows him or her to clarify complex scientific topics. For example, Harvard professor Stephen Jay Gould was both a paleontologist and a science writer. He worked to make information about geology and biology accessible to general readers. "Science," Gould wrote, "is an integral part of culture. . . . It's one of the glories of the human intellectual tradition." Good scientific journalists allow nonscientific readers to share in this tradition.

V Vocabulary

Adding Prefixes and Suffixes **Say:** See how many new words you can form by adding the prefixes and suffixes shown below to the base words of the words in your vocabulary list: *source, reduce,* and *consume.* Use a dictionary or thesaurus to help you. **OL**

re-	*-er*	*-ing*
un-	*-ful*	*-ive*
under-	*-fully*	*-tion*
-able	*-fulness*	

Meet the Author

This selection was written for a school textbook. (Textbook writers aren't credited as "authors" of the books and lessons they write.) Textbook writers try to make difficult subjects easier to understand. Text features, like those in this selection, are important tools that help the writer and the reader.

Objectives (pp. 558–563)
Reading Use text features: side notes, headings, graphic organizers
Literature Identify literary elements: concept and definition
Vocabulary Identify word structure: suffixes

Vocabulary Preview

V

resources (REE sor suz) *n.* supplies that can be used as needed **(p. 560)** *Resources such as petroleum and wood are important for making the products we use every day.*

reduce (rih DOOS) *v.* to use less of; make less of **(p. 560)** *Reduce the amount of trash by reusing glass jars.*

consumption (kun SUMP shun) *n.* the act of using up, spending, or wasting **(p. 560)** *You can reduce your consumption of water by fixing leaky faucets.*

Write to Learn All of the vocabulary words relate to people and how they depend on Earth. Using the vocabulary words, write a short paragraph about how people depend on Earth.

English Language Coach

Suffixes A suffix is a word part added to the end of a word; it modifies the word in some way.

You've used suffixes many times while saying or writing verbs, such as *thanks, thanked,* and *thanking.* You use suffixes whenever you use comparatives and superlatives, as in *faster* and *fastest.* Suffixes sometimes change the basic meaning of a word, but more often they just change what part of speech a word is. For example, a suffix can change a noun into an adjective or adverb. Or a suffix might change a verb to a noun. Also, remember that when you add a suffix, sometimes the spelling of a base word changes.

Here are a few other common suffixes:

-ee as in employ*ee*	*-er* as in employ*er*	*-ian* as in music*ian*
-ist as in art*ist*	*-ful* as in joy*ful*	*-ous* as in furi*ous*
-ship as in friend*ship*	*-al* as in comic*al*	*-ion* as in invent*ion*
-ment as in enjoy*ment*	*-ish* as in fool*ish*	*-able* as in break*able*
-ible as in collect*ible*	*-y* as in hair*y*	
-ly as in sad*ly*	*-hood* as in neighbor*hood*	
-ness as in mean*ness*	*-ance* as in perform*ance*	

On Your Own Using the list above, add at least one suffix to each word below to create a new word.

work	friend	believe	red
mad	fear	courage	false

Additional Support

Literature Focus Lesson

Nonfiction Communities in the United States have worked hard to reduce the amount of garbage they produce and find ways to recycle more materials. After your students have read "Conserving Resources," suggest that they find out more about local recycling or conservation programs by searching for nonfiction articles in current and back issues of their town and city newspapers. Students can also look for nonfiction articles on the Internet or in magazines at the library. Encourage students to find out whether your town or neighborhood sponsors conservation projects. Have students report on their findings. **OL**

Skills Preview

Key Reading Skill: Using Text Features

Before you read the article, think about how you can understand it better by using

- side notes
- headings
- graphic organizers (like charts and tables)

Write to Learn In your Learner's Notebook, write a definition of each text feature in your own words. Then, make up an example of each one.

Key Literary Element: Concept and Definition

You know that a word has meanings, or **definitions.** A word or phrase can also name an idea, or **concept**. It might take many books and articles to fully explain a concept, but you can begin by defining it.

In this article you'll read about "conserving resources." To begin to understand this concept, look at the words' definitions. To *conserve* is "to protect from loss or harm; to use less." A *resource* is "a supply that can be drawn on when needed." The concept of conserving resources, or *conservation,* includes using less of Earth's resources and saving Earth from harm.

Small Group Work In a small group, explore the concept of *democracy.* Does the dictionary definition explain the concept? If not, what else can help you understand the concept of democracy? L

Interactive Literary Elements Handbook
To review or learn more about the literary elements, go to www.glencoe.com.

Academic Vocabulary

 **concept** (KAWN sept) *n.* an idea or thought

Get Ready to Read

Connect to the Reading

What do you throw away? How much of it is paper, plastic, or metal (like a soda can)? How much waste, or garbage, does your family throw out in a week? Think about what you can do to reduce that amount. R

Small Group In a small group, discuss the kinds of things you and your classmates throw away at school. Make a list of ways you could save resources at school.

Build Background

In the past, people didn't throw away a lot of things. They often turned old or worn out items into new ones. For example, old clothes became rags or were woven into rugs.

Then companies began producing new items at cheap prices. Many Americans stopped recycling. People threw many things away, even things they could have used again.

Today, recycling is very important. People are worried about using up Earth's resources too quickly. People are constantly thinking of new ways to recycle.

Set Purposes for Reading

BIG Question Read the article "Conserving Resources" to find out if progress is always good.

Set Your Own Purpose What else would you like to learn from the article to help you answer the Big Question? Write your own purpose on a note card and add it to Foldable 5.

Keep Moving

Use these skills as you read the following selection.

READING WORKSHOP 2

Teach

L Literary Element

Concept and Definition
Ask: If the dictionary definition of *democracy* doesn't help you understand the concept, what text feature might make the concept clear? *(Possible responses: a web, a chart)* AL

R Reading Skill

Review Connecting Say: Think of the products you use every day. List those that can be recycled, such as soda cans, and those that can be reused, such as the blank sides of sheets of paper. *(Responses will vary.)* OL

CheckPoint

Use the CheckPoint questions provided on Presentation Plus! to check for understanding of text features. These questions can be used with interactive response keypads for immediate student feedback.

Literature Online

Interactive Literary Elements Handbook Have students access the Web site to improve their understanding of concept and definition.

Differentiated Instruction

Trash Inventory Have students work in teams to conduct an inventory of the things thrown away in different parts of their school. What are the most common materials thrown away in a typical classroom, art room, shop, or science lab? After student teams have completed their inventory of the trash flow in different areas, have them report their results and suggest how different types of materials could be recycled. OL Encourage students to research the recycling possibilities for materials in their area. AL

Objectives

- Use text features: side notes, headings, graphic organizers
- Identify literary elements: concept and definition
- Identify word structure: suffixes

READING WORKSHOP 2

Teach

BQ BIG Question

Ask: Imagine that someone gets a computer game, music system, or telephone that is faster and less expensive than his or her old one. What do you think happens to the old game, system, or phone? *(Possible responses: It could be given to someone else. It could be thrown away.)* **BL** What problems could arise with the disposal of out-of-date appliances? *(Possible responses: The old technologies could be hard to recycle, or they could take up a great deal of landfill space.)* **OL**

Readability Scores
Dale-Chall: 6.1
DRP: 66
Lexile: 1030

INFORMATIONAL TEXT
TEXTBOOK
from *Glencoe Science*

from *Glencoe Science*

Resource Use

Resources such as petroleum and metals are important for making the products you use every day at home and in school. For example, petroleum is used to produce plastics and fuel. Minerals are used to make automobiles and bicycles. However, if these resources are not used carefully, the environment can be damaged. **Conservation** is the careful use of earth materials to reduce damage to the environment. Conservation can prevent future shortages of some materials. **1** **BQ**

Reduce, Reuse, Recycle

Developed[1] countries such as the United States use more natural resources than other regions, as shown in **Figure 1.** Ways to conserve resources include reducing the use of materials, and reusing and recycling materials. You can **reduce** the **consumption** of materials in simple ways, such as using both sides of notebook paper or carrying lunch to school in a nondisposable container. **Reusing** an item means finding another use for it instead of throwing it away.

1. A ***developed*** country uses advanced technology and has a strong economy.

Practice the Skills

1 BIG Question

New inventions seem great because they make life easier. But a new product may use up resources. What is the problem with inventing more products that use resources such as petroleum and metal? Write your answer on a note card and add it to Foldable 5. Your response will help you answer the Unit Challenge later.

Vocabulary

resources (REE sor suz) *n.* supplies that can be used as needed

reduce (rih DOOS) *v.* to use less of; make less of

consumption (kun SUMP shun) *n.* the act of using up, spending, or wasting

Additional Support

English Language Coach

Building Background Make sure that students understand the terms used in this article. Have them scan the first two pages of the selection and write down any words they do not understand. Help them understand the vocabulary listed on page 560 and all of the footnotes. Encourage students to use dictionaries for words such as *petroleum, prevention,* and *composting.* **EL**

Explain that cultural beliefs and social norms influence the way people view recycling. Have students talk to friends and family members about reducing, reusing, and recycling. Encourage students to ask how their background influences their family's consumption and reuse of goods. **OL**

You can reuse old clothes by giving them to someone else or by cutting them into rags. The rags can be used in place of paper towels for cleaning jobs around your home. Reducing and reusing are methods of waste prevention.

Reusing Yard Waste Outdoors, you can do helpful things, too. If you cut grass or rake leaves, you can compost these items instead of putting them into the trash. **Composting** means piling yard wastes where they can decompose gradually. Decomposed material provides needed nutrients for your garden or flower bed. Some cities no longer pick up yard waste to take to landfills.[2] In these places, composting is common. If everyone in the United States composted, it would reduce the trash put into landfills by 20 percent. **L**

Recycling Materials If reducing and reusing are not possible, the next best method to reduce the amount of materials in the landfill is to recycle. **Recycling** is processing waste materials to make a new object. **2**

C

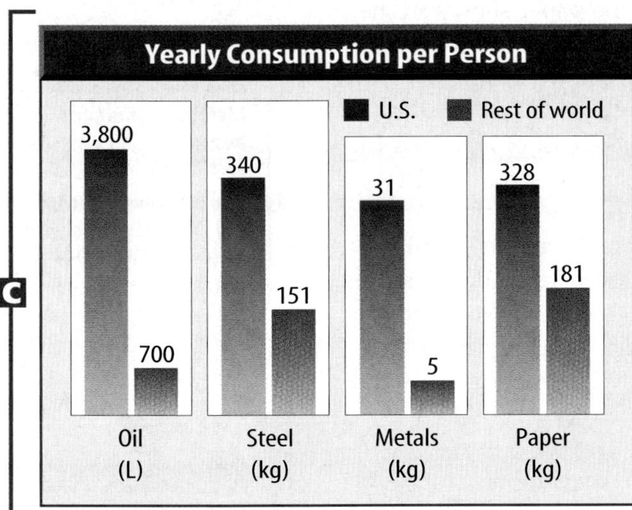

Figure 1 A person in the United States uses more resources than the average person elsewhere.

2. ***Landfills*** are places where dirt and garbage are buried in layers.

Practice the Skills

2 **Key Literary Element**

Concept and Definition Think about the word *recycle*. Does the definition of the word help you understand the concept of recycling? See if other details in the story add to your own definition of the concept.

Teach

L Literary Element

Concept and Definition
Say: The opening paragraph of the article states that "if . . . resources are not used carefully, the environment can be damaged." How can this statement help you understand the concept of recycling? *(Responses will vary but should include the idea that recycling must have something to do with using resources carefully.)* **OL**

C Critical Thinking

Comprehension **Ask:** After reading the chart and caption in Figure 1, what general statement can you make about the amount of resources used in the United States? *(Possible response: People in the United States use many more goods than people in the rest of the world.)* **BL** Why don't more Americans recycle products that they no longer need or use? *(Possible response: People are probably used to having new goods when they need them and may not want to use recycled items. The economic system might be focused on selling new products rather than on reusing old ones.)* **AL**

Reading in the Real World

Citizenship Post a large paper recycling symbol on the bulletin board. Then organize students into small groups, and have each group research a different type of waste discussed in the article—for example, plastics, yard waste, paper, and metals. Have students in each group use the library or Internet to find information about the challenges of recycling the particular type of material that their group has been assigned to investigate. Tell students to write the recycling facts they find on note cards. When groups have completed their research, they can post the note cards on the bulletin board. Consider inviting a city sanitation employee to bring recycling information to your classroom. **AL**

Objectives

- Use text features to make generalizations
- Understand concept and definition

Teach

R Reading Skill

Review Identifying Author's Purpose Ask: What purpose do you think the author has for giving factual information? *(Possible response: The author wants readers to be informed about humanity's impact on the environment and what people can do to help.)* **OL** What actions do you think the author would like readers to take after reading the article? *(Possible response: The author wants readers to reuse things in order to protect the environment.)* **BL**

EL Language Coach

Word Parts Say: How could you use your knowledge of word parts to determine the meaning of *recycling*? *(Possible response: I know that a cycle can be a process, such as the process by which washing machines clean clothes. I know that the prefix* re- *means to do something again. Recycling might mean reprocessing a material.)* **OL** What other words on this page have the same suffix as *recycling*? *(Possible responses: reusing, reducing, saving, and producing)* **BL**

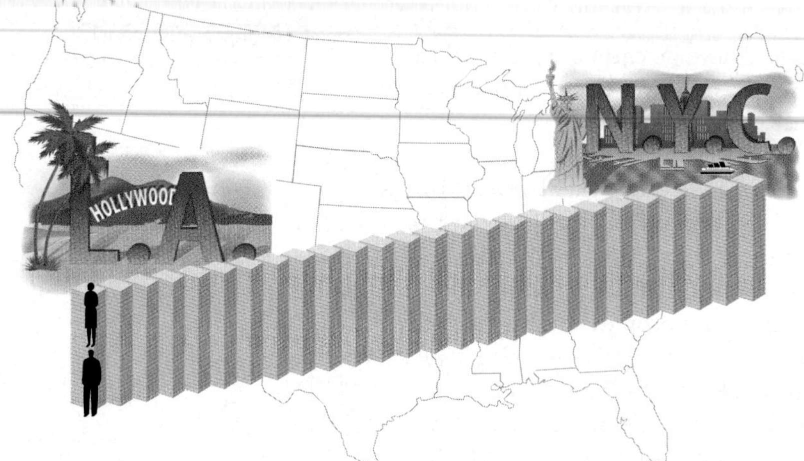

Figure 2 People in the United States throw away enough office and writing paper each year to build a wall 3.6 m high stretching from New York City to Los Angeles.

Paper makes up about 40 percent of the mass of trash. As shown in **Figure 2,** Americans throw away a large amount of paper each year. Recycling this paper would use 58 percent less water and generate 74 percent less air pollution than producing new paper from trees. The paper shown in the figure doesn't even include newspapers. More than 500,000 trees are cut every week just to print newspapers. **3**

Companies have found that recycling can be good for business. They can recover part of the cost of materials by recycling the waste. Some businesses use scrap materials such as steel to make new products. These practices save money, energy and reduce the amount of waste sent to landfills. **R**

Figure 3 shows that the amount of material deposited in landfills has decreased since 1980. In addition to saving landfill space, reducing, reusing and recycling can reduce energy use and minimize the need to extract raw materials from Earth. **EL**

Recycling Methods What types of recycling programs does your state have? Many states or cities have some form of recycling laws. For example, in some places people who recycle pay lower trash-collection fees. In other places a **refundable** deposit is made on all beverage **containers**. This means paying extra money at the store for a drink, but you get your money back if you return the container to the store for recycling. **4**

Practice the Skills

3 Reviewing Skills

Identifying Author's Purpose Authors write with a goal in mind, such as to entertain, to persuade, to inform, and to describe. What purpose do you think the author of this article had?

4 English Language Coach

Suffixes What are the suffixes in the words **refundable** and **containers**? What are the base words? Do you know what the base words mean? Do the meanings of the base words help you understand the whole words?

Additional Support

English Language Coach

Recycling in the United States
Provide a short history of recycling. Tell students about nationwide recycling campaigns that occurred during World War II. Explain that many resources were in short supply during the war, and people helped the war effort by recycling. Many civic groups, such as the Boy Scouts, held drives to collect paper, scrap metal, and rubber. In Nebraska, the Future Farmers of America collected a half-million pounds of rubber from old tires. Some people saved tin foil from gum wrappers, and even cooking grease was recycled to make ammunition. **BL**

Lead a discussion about the ways recycling can benefit us. **AL**

Figure 3 U.S. trash production is increasing, but trash deposited in landfills is decreasing. In 1980, 82 percent of trash went to a landfill; today, it's only 55 percent, thanks to waste-reducing methods such as recycling.

There are several disadvantages to recycling. More people and trucks are needed to haul materials separately from your trash. The materials then must be separated at special facilities. In addition, demand for things made from recycled materials must exist, and items made from recycled materials often cost more. **5**

The Population Outlook The human population explosion[3] **R** already has had an effect on the environment and the organisms that inhabit Earth. It's unlikely that the population will begin to decline in the near future. To make up for this, resources must be used wisely. Conserving resources by reducing, reusing, and recycling is an important way that you can make a difference. ❍ **BQ**

3. The ***population explosion*** is the recent increase in the number of people on Earth. It has occurred because more people are being born and more people are living longer.

Practice the Skills

5 Key Reading Skill

Using Text Features Bold headings lead you through this article. Which heading guides you to a section about the number of people living on Earth?

This article also includes photographs, charts, and captions. Which of those features provides hopeful information about landfill use?

READING WORKSHOP 2

Teach

R Reading Skill

Using Text Features **Ask:** What kinds of text features are on this page? *(bold run-in headings, a graph, graphics)* How can you tell what the last paragraph will be about? *(the heading)* **OL**

BQ BIG Question

Ask: Does the wise use of resources depend on technology? Explain. *(Possible response: Technology can improve conservation of some types of resources. However, people do not need technology to buy fewer products or reuse the products they already have.)* **OL** In the past, milk was delivered in glass bottles to people's homes. The glass bottles were picked up the next day, washed, and refilled with milk. Is this a low-tech example of reducing, reusing, or recycling? *(reusing)* **BL**

Assess

Use the CheckPoint questions provided on Presentation Plus! to check for comprehension of the selection. These questions can be used with interactive response keypads for immediate student feedback.

Differentiated Instruction

Tracing Trash Have students use information discussed in the article to trace the flow of trash in the waste stream. Ask students to choose a type of trash, such as paper or aluminum cans. Next, have students research the different ways that the selected type of trash can be disposed of by being sent to a landfill or recycling center. Finally, have students use their research to write a paragraph describing the process.

When students have completed their paragraphs, have them discuss the pros and cons of the disposal options. **OL**

Objectives

- Draw conclusions
- Use text features to find and understand information
- Understand text structure
- Understand concept and definition

Assess

Resources for page 564

- Selection Quick Check
- Selection and Unit Assessment
- ExamView Assessment Suite
- Interactive Tutor: Self-Assessment

Students can respond to the *After You Read* items in their Learner's Notebook or on separate sheets of paper.

Answering the BIG Question

1. New products can deplete resources. They can create more waste by making old products useless.
2. Through recycling, companies can recover part of the expense of doing business.
3. Recycling requires more labor and time than just throwing things away. Also, products made from recycled materials are usually more expensive than products made from new materials.
4. Conservation reduces damage to the planet and prevents the depletion of resources.

Critical Thinking

5. homework papers, aluminum cans, glass containers, and plastic bottles
6. People may not know the importance of recycling. People may not live near recycling facilities.

After You Read

Conserving Resources

Answering the BIG Question

1. How can the invention of new products cause problems? Support your answer with details from the selection.
2. **Recall** How is recycling good for business?
   TIP **Think and Search**
3. **Recall** What are some of the disadvantages of recycling?
   TIP **Right There**
4. **Summarize** How does conservation help the environment?
   TIP **Think and Search**

Critical Thinking

5. **Connect** What are some items that you use every day that can be recycled?
   TIP **On My Own**
6. **Draw Conclusions** Why do you think most Americans don't recycle more?
   TIP **Author and Me**

Write About Your Reading

Pretend you have some airtime on a local radio station. Write a script for a short announcement that you will read on the air. Use the tips below to write your script:

- Your purpose is to convince people to recycle.
- Explain what recycling is.
- Tell people why recycling is important.
- Suggest ways that people can recycle at home, work, and school.
- Make sure your announcement will catch people's attention.

Objectives (pp. 564–565)
Reading Use text features: chart, map, photograph • Make connections from text to self
Literature Identify literary elements: concept and definition
Vocabulary Identify word structure: suffixes
Writing Write a radio script
Grammar Identify parts of speech

Write About Your Reading

Sample response:

Dirty plastic, broken glass, and decomposing cardboard containers surround you along with rotting food, dead leaves, and used diapers. Where are you? You're in a smelly, gross landfill. Unfortunately, more and more landfills cover Earth each day.

However, you have the power to stop the spread of waste by recycling. Recycling means turning old products into new ones. It's important to recycle paper, cardboard, plastics, glass, aluminum, and more to protect resources for future generations and to prevent further damage to Earth.

Find out today what your community can recycle!

Skills Review

Key Reading Skill: Using Text Features

7. How did the charts, map, and photos in this article help you understand or remember the information? Which text feature most helped you understand how much people waste? Why?

Key Literary Element: Concept and Definition

8. What is the definition of the word *conservation*? What details from the article help you understand the concept of conservation?

Reviewing Skills: Identifying Author's Purpose

9. What sections of the article give you the most clues about the author's purpose?

Vocabulary Check

10. Rewrite the paragraph below and fill in the blanks with the correct vocabulary word.

reduce resources consumption

In my family, we use many ___ every day. For example, we drink a lot of soda from aluminum cans. My mom and I want to help our family ___ the amount of trash we throw out. We decided we will drink more water and decrease our family's ___ of soda.

11. **Academic Vocabulary** What are two common **features** of a heading?
12. **English Language Coach** Find the word in each sentence below that has a base word and a suffix. Write the words in your Learner's Notebook, underlining each suffix.

We went to a famous beach last summer. It was nice and restful there. The air was breathable. We had such an enjoyable time.

Grammar Link: Parts of Speech Review

Words are the major tools with which we communicate. We need to know how and when to use them, just as we need to know when a screwdriver is more appropriate than a hammer.

- A word is identified as a particular part of speech based on how it is used. Many words can be used as more than one part of speech.

Noun: I had a bad <u>dream</u>.
Verb: Did you <u>dream</u> last night?
Adjective: We took a <u>dream</u> vacation.

Noun: He's only attractive on the <u>outside</u>.
Adverb: Let's eat <u>outside</u>.
Adjective: She threw an <u>outside</u> pitch.
Preposition: They worked <u>outside</u> the law.

Grammar Practice

Copy the following sentences. Under each underlined word, identify its part of speech.

13. I'll pull every <u>weed</u> when I <u>weed</u> the garden.
14. We <u>crowded</u> into a <u>crowded</u> elevator.
15. Please <u>light</u> the room with a <u>light</u> so I can see this <u>light</u> color.

Writing Application Think of (or choose from a dictionary) three words, each of which can be used as different parts of speech. Write two sentences for each that use that word in different ways. (Examples: *group, hit, hurt, spring, raise.*)

Web Activities For eFlashcards, Selection Quick Checks, and other Web activities, go to www.glencoe.com.

Skills Review

Key Reading Skill: Using Text Features

7. Responses will vary. Students may say that the bar graph in Figure 1 helped them understand the importance of recycling because it shows how much people in the United States consume.

Key Literary Element: Concept and Definition

8. Conservation is the protection and management of natural resources. Students may say that the heads, illustrations, and definition on page 560 helped them understand the concept.

Reviewing Skills: Identifying Author's Purpose

9. Responses will vary. Students may say that the introduction and conclusion indicate the author's purpose of explaining the need for recycling.

Vocabulary Check

10. resources, reduce, consumption
11. Possible response: A heading often appears in bold print and is placed at the top of a section of text.
12. fam<u>ous</u>, rest<u>ful</u>, breath<u>able</u>, enjoy<u>able</u>

Grammar Link: Parts of Speech Review

Grammar Practice

13. noun, verb
14. verb, adjective
15. verb, noun, adjective

Close

Ask students to describe issues related to the Big Question that they learned about from reading "Conserving Resources."

Before You Read | There Will Come Soft Rains

More About the Author

Science-fiction writer Ray Bradbury has written more than 500 texts, including stories, poems, essays, plays, and films. He explored interplanetary travel in *The Martian Chronicles* and critiqued censorship in his 1953 novel *Fahrenheit 451*. In 2004 Bradbury was awarded a National Medal of the Arts.

EL Language Coach

Adding Suffixes Write the following rules on the board.

- Rule 1: Change *y* to *i* and add *-ness, -est,* or *-er.*
- Rule 2: After a short vowel, double the final consonant before adding *-ed, -ing,* or *-er.*

Work through examples of each rule with students. Examples of Rule 1 include *emptiness, slimiest,* and *daintier.* Examples of Rule 2 include *tipped, beginning,* and *regretted.* **Say:** Recognizing patterns can help you spell words correctly when you add suffixes. Copy the rules and example words into your journal. As you read, jot down new words that fit the pattern. **EL**

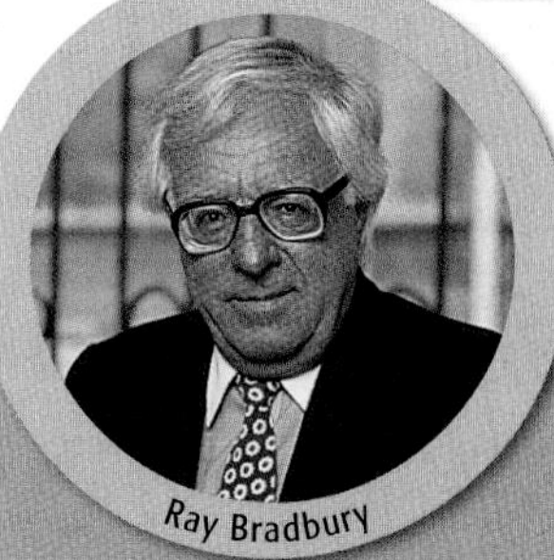

Ray Bradbury

Meet the Author

Ray Bradbury was born in 1920. He began writing as a boy. "My parents had given me a toy typewriter for Christmas," Bradbury wrote, "and I stormed it with words. Anytime I liked I could turn a faucet on each finger and let the miracles out, yes, into machines and onto paper where I might freeze and control them forever. I haven't stopped writing since." See page R2 of the Author Files for more on Ray Bradbury.

Author Search For more about Ray Bradbury, go to www.glencoe.com.

Objectives (pp. 566–575)
Reading Use text features: italics
• Make connections from text to self
Literature Identify literary elements: concept and definition
Vocabulary Identify word structure: suffixes

Vocabulary Preview

shriveled (SHRIV uld) *adj.* shrunken and wrinkled **(p. 569)** *Dry, shriveled food sat on the table, uneaten.*

emerged (ih MURJD) *v.* came out; form of the verb *emerge* **(p. 569)** *Spotless dishes emerged from the washer.*

charred (chard) *adj.* burned **(p. 569)** *The walls were blackened and charred in the intense heat of an explosion.*

inconvenience (in kun VEEN yuns) *n.* something that causes difficulty, discomfort, or bother **(p. 570)** *Messiness may cause inconvenience, but it's not a tragedy.*

frenzy (FREN zee) *n.* unusual mental excitement leading to wild activity **(p. 571)** *In a frenzy, the dog chased its tail and barked.*

whims (wimz) *n.* sudden urges, desires, or ideas **(p. 572)** *The house took care of family members' needs as well as their whims.*

oblivious (uh BLIV ee us) *adj.* not noticing; not aware of **(p. 574)** *The trees stood silently, oblivious to the destruction nearby.*

Write to Learn Choose four vocabulary words. For each word, write a sentence using that word.

English Language Coach

EL

Suffixes There's one common suffix that does not *modify* a word; it completely changes it! It's the suffix *-less.*

What's the opposite of *hopeful*? *Hopeless.* The suffix *-less* means "without." If you're hopeless, you're without hope. Anytime you add *-less* to a word you'll change the meaning by adding "without" to it.

Practice *-less* Not Less Add the suffix *-less* to each word below.

help use friend care penny power

Additional Support

Literature Online

Author Search To expand students' appreciation of Ray Bradbury, have them access the Web site for additional information and resources.

Literature Focus Lesson

Science Fiction Many science-fiction authors write about visions of the future. In "There Will Come Soft Rains," author Ray Bradbury envisions a future of computerized homes and a terrifying end to a community. Of his writing, Bradbury has said, "I don't try to describe the future. I try to prevent it." As they read, students should think about how Bradbury's writing might help "prevent" the future. Ask students what they could do to change the future so that Bradbury's bleak vision does not come to pass. **OL**

Skills Preview

Key Reading Skill: Using Text Features

Usually text features are defined as photos, headings, graphic elements, and so on. They're used *in addition to* the text to help clarify the information you are reading. However, sometimes text features are *within* the text itself, giving you added information by how the text itself is presented. That's the case with the next selection. Preview the selection to see if you can discover its text feature.

Key Literary Element: Concept and Definition

In the story you're about to read, the main character is a house. If that were not unusual enough, the house is also a concept–the concept of a house that does everything for its people.

Science fiction writers often base their stories on new concepts. The story then explores the concept, adding details and figuring out what the concept means to humanity. In a way, the story itself becomes a way to define a concept.

In "There Will Come Soft Rains," Ray Bradbury explores the concept of a completely automatic house by looking at it without its people. In the 1950s, many of the features of such a house seemed amazing to readers. Now, many years after the story was written, some of those features are being built into modern houses. Improvements in technology and engineering have moved the concepts into definitions.

L

Interactive Literary Elements Handbook
To review or learn more about the literary elements, go to www.glencoe.com.

Get Ready to Read

Connect to the Reading

What would it be like to live in a house that did your chores every day? The house would be powerful–maybe more powerful than you. Is this kind of technology and progress a good thing? R

Partner Talk In "There Will Come Soft Rains," machines act on their own. Would you like to live in a world that is controlled by computers? Would you like a computer to decide what you eat, what you wear, and what you listen to? Discuss your answers with a partner.

Build Background

Ray Bradbury wrote "There Will Come Soft Rains" in 1951. In the 1950s, many people thought there was going to be a nuclear war.

- Nuclear weapons are the most powerful weapons known to man. One atomic bomb could destroy an entire city.
- In the 1950s, people feared that a nuclear war would kill all human beings on Earth. Bradbury and other writers produced many stories exploring what might happen after such a war.

Set Purposes for Reading

BIG Question Read the story to understand some of the fears people had in the 1950s.

Set Your Own Purpose What would you like to learn from the story to help you answer the Big Question? Write your own purpose on a note card and add it to Foldable 5.

Keep Moving

Use these skills as you read the following selection.

Teach

L Literary Element

Concept and Definition
Say: Personification is giving human qualities to animals or objects. **Ask:** How does Bradbury use personification in his concept of a self-sufficient house? *(Possible response: The house is the main character.)* OL

R Reading Skill

Review Connecting Say: Think of a time you used a gadget that seemed to have a mind of its own. Would a house that can do its own chores ever break down? *(Possible response: Even a very capable machine could probably break down.)* OL

CheckPoint

Use the CheckPoint questions provided on Presentation Plus! to check for understanding of using text features. These questions can be used with interactive response keypads for immediate student feedback.

Literature Online

Interactive Literary Elements Handbook Have students access the Web site to improve their understanding of concept and definition.

English Language Coach

Building Background Bradbury's story was written during the Cold War, a period of tension between the United States and the former Soviet Union. The Soviets supported a communist form of government. The United States was opposed to communism and wanted to contain it. The peak of the Cold War was the period between 1948 and 1953.

Have students choose a fact about the Cold War to research such as the Soviet Union blockading West Berlin and exploding its first atomic warhead, or that many people built fallout shelters to protect themselves from the radiation of a nuclear bomb. Have students share their findings with the class. OL

Objectives
- Use text features: italics
- Make connections from text to self
- Identify literary elements: concept and definition
- Identify word structure: suffixes

Teach

L Literary Element

Concept and Definition
Ask: How does Bradbury explain the concept of a self-sufficient house? *(Possible response: Each line of the story details the activities of the house as it carries out the functions that people do.)* OL

C Critical Thinking

Analysis Say: Think about the times noted on this page. How much time passes? What does this lead you to think about the amount of time that will pass in the entire story? *(The events on this page take place within about an hour. This story will probably take place over a day or a short period of time.)* BL

Readability Scores
Dale-Chall: 6.6
DRP: 57
Lexile: 920

There Will Come Soft Rains

by Ray Bradbury

In the living room the voice-clock sang, *Tick-tock, seven o'clock, time to get up, time to get up, seven o'clock!* as if it were afraid that nobody would. The morning house lay empty. The clock ticked on, repeating and repeating its sounds into the emptiness. *Seven-nine, breakfast time, seven-nine!* 1 L

In the kitchen the breakfast stove gave a hissing sigh and ejected from its warm interior eight pieces of perfectly browned toast, eight eggs sunnyside up, sixteen slices of bacon, two coffees, and two cool glasses of milk.

C "Today is August 4, 2026," said a second voice from the kitchen ceiling, "in the city of Allendale, California." It repeated the date three times for memory's sake. "Today is Mr. Featherstone's birthday. Today is the anniversary of Tilita's marriage. Insurance is payable, as are the water, gas, and light bills."

Somewhere in the walls, relays clicked, memory tapes glided under electric eyes.

Eight-one, tick-tock, eight-one o'clock, off to school, off to work, run, run, eight-one! But no doors slammed, no carpets took the soft tread of rubber heels. It was raining outside. The weather box on the front door sang quietly: "Rain, rain, go away; rubbers, raincoats for today . . ." And the rain tapped on the empty house, echoing.

Practice the Skills

1 Key Literary Element

Concept and Definition The author invented the concept of a "voice-clock." What do you think would be its definition?

Additional Support

English Language Coach

Science Vocabulary Distribute copies of the following paragraph, and then read it aloud to students. Tell students to underline any unfamiliar words they hear or see in the paragraph. After you have finished reading the paragraph, tell students to use dictionaries or Internet resources to find the definitions of the words they underlined.

Atomic bombs are weapons that create energy by splitting atoms. When an atomic bomb explodes, it can produce temperatures of several million degrees. Such high temperatures vaporize the materials at the site of the blast and start fires. The minute radioactive particles left behind by the explosion can have deadly effects long after the bomb explodes. EL

READING WORKSHOP 2

Outside, the garage chimed and lifted its door to reveal the waiting car. After a long wait the door swung down again.

At eight-thirty the eggs were **shriveled** and the toast was like stone. An aluminum wedge scraped them into the sink, where hot water whirled them down a metal throat which digested and flushed them away to the distant sea. The dirty dishes were dropped into a hot washer and **emerged** twinkling dry. BQ

Nine-fifteen, sang the clock, *time to clean.*

Out of warrens[1] in the wall, tiny robot mice darted. The rooms were acrawl with the small cleaning animals, all rubber and metal. They thudded against chairs, whirling their mustached runners, kneading the rug nap, sucking gently at hidden dust. Then, like mysterious invaders, they popped into their burrows. Their pink electric eyes faded. The house was clean. C

Ten o'clock. The sun came out from behind the rain. The house stood alone in a city of rubble and ashes. This was the one house left standing. At night the ruined city gave off a radioactive glow which could be seen for miles.

Ten-fifteen. The garden sprinklers whirled up in golden founts, filling the soft morning air with scatterings of brightness. The water pelted windowpanes, running down the **charred** west side where the house had been burned evenly free of its white paint. The entire west face of the house was black, save for five places. Here the silhouette in paint of a man mowing a lawn. Here, as in a photograph, a woman bent to pick flowers. Still farther over, their images burned on wood in one titanic instant, a small boy, hands flung into the air; higher up, the image of a thrown ball, and opposite him a girl, hands raised to catch a ball which never came down. 2

2 Key Reading Skill

Using Text Features Do you notice anything unusual about the text so far in the story? What words are in italics? Who (or what) is speaking those words? Do the italics help you understand the story?

1. ***Warrens*** are the burrows, or little holes, that small animals such as mice dig out and live in.

Vocabulary

shriveled (SHRIV uld) *adj.* shrunken and wrinkled

emerged (ih MURJD) *v.* came out

charred (chard) *adj.* burned

Teach

BQ BIG Question

Say: People have opinions, feelings, and desires. Do you think you would ever disagree with machines that helped keep you on schedule and cleaned your house? Explain. *(Responses will vary.)* **OL** The machines that run the house keep the family on a strict schedule. How would you like it if your house made you do certain things at specific times? *(Responses will vary.)* **BL**

C Critical Thinking

Analysis Say: How are the mechanical devices of the future depicted? Are they presented in a positive or a negative manner? *(Possible response: The devices speak and perform complicated tasks. By running so perfectly and keeping things so clean, they seem cold and inhuman.)* **OL** How does the setting affect your impression of the technology presented? *(Possible response: The setting makes the technology appear forbidding; humans are missing and unimportant.)* **AL**

Differentiated Instruction

Quote from History Read aloud the following quotation, in which physicist J. Robert Oppenheimer (1904–1967) recalls witnessing the explosion of the first atomic bomb.

We knew the world could not be the same. A few people laughed. A few people cried. Most people were silent. I remembered the line from the Hindu scripture, the Bhagavad Gita: "I am become Death, the destroyer of worlds." I suppose we all thought that, one way or another.

Have students discuss the emotional reactions to technological progress described in this quotation. Why might witnessing a scientific event be emotionally overwhelming? **AL**

Objectives

- Locate information in text to aid understanding and to interpret, analyze, and draw conclusions
- Understand concepts in the text and form definitions of them

Teach

Viewing the Photo

Ask: Why do you think the editors of this book chose this picture to illustrate this part of the story? *(Possible response: The flowers look blown by the wind like a storm or something else scary is brewing.)* **AS**

C Critical Thinking

Comprehension **Ask:** What do you think is happening in this story? Explain your answer. *(Possible response: Something is not normal; some normal things are operating according to plan, but others are not.)* **OL**

READING WORKSHOP 2

The five spots of paint—the man, the woman, the children, the ball—remained. The rest was a thin charcoaled layer.

The gentle sprinkler rain filled the garden with falling light.

Until this day, how well the house had kept its peace. How carefully it had inquired, "Who goes there? What's the password?" and, getting no answer from lonely foxes and whining cats, it had shut up its windows and drawn shades in an old-maidenly preoccupation with self-protection which bordered on a mechanical paranoia.[2]

C It quivered[3] at each sound, the house did. If a sparrow brushed a window, the shade snapped up. The bird, startled, flew off! No, not even a bird must touch the house!

The house was an altar with ten thousand attendants, big, small, servicing, attending, in choirs. But the gods had gone away, and the ritual of the religion continued **senselessly**, **uselessly**. **3** **4**

Twelve noon.

A dog whined, shivering, on the front porch.

The front door recognized the dog voice and opened. The dog, once huge and fleshy, but now gone to bone and covered with sores, moved in and through the house, tracking mud. Behind it whirred angry mice, angry at having to pick up mud, angry at **inconvenience**.

For not a leaf fragment blew under the door but what the wall panels flipped open and the copper scrap rats flashed swiftly

2. ***Preoccupation*** is an extreme concern with something. ***Paranoia*** is a mental illness in which a person is extremely suspicious and afraid of others.

3. To ***quiver*** is to shake slightly or tremble.

Vocabulary

inconvenience (in kun VEEN yuns) *n.* something that causes difficulty, discomfort, or bother

Practice the Skills

3 English Language Coach

Suffixes Look at the words **senselessly** and **uselessly**. What does each word mean?

4 Key Literary Element

Concept and Definition The house is *self-sufficient,* meaning it is able to take care of itself without any outside help. Do the details of the story expand your understanding of the concept?

Additional Support

Literature Focus Lesson

Chronological Order To help students visualize the events of the story, have them make time lines as they read. The time lines should begin with the first time the voice-clock sings out the time. Each time the time is shown, students should add an entry to their timelines. They should note briefly what event occurs. Students who like to draw can also add a small illustration of each event. Display the time lines around the classroom. **OL**

READING WORKSHOP 2

out. The offending dust, hair, or paper, seized in miniature steel jaws, was raced back to the burrows. There, down tubes which fed into the cellar, it was dropped into the sighing vent of an incinerator which sat like evil Baal[4] in a dark corner.

The dog ran upstairs, hysterically[5] yelping to each door, at last realizing, as the house realized, that only silence was here.

It sniffed the air and scratched the kitchen door. Behind the door, the stove was making pancakes which filled the house with a rich baked odor and the scent of maple syrup. R

The dog frothed at the mouth, lying at the door, sniffing, its eyes turned to fire. It ran wildly in circles, biting at its tail, spun in a **frenzy**, and died. It lay in the parlor for an hour.

Two o'clock, sang a voice.

Delicately **sensing** decay at last, the regiments[6] of mice hummed out as softly as blown gray leaves in an electrical wind. 5 EL

Two-fifteen.

The dog was gone.

In the cellar, the incinerator glowed suddenly and a whirl of sparks leaped up the chimney.

Two thirty-five.

Bridge tables sprouted from patio walls. Playing cards fluttered onto pads in a shower of pips. Martinis manifested[7] on an oaken bench with egg-salad sandwiches. Music played. BQ

But the tables were silent and the cards untouched.

At four o'clock the tables folded like great butterflies back through the paneled walls.

Four-thirty.

The nursery walls glowed.

Animals took shape: yellow giraffes, blue lions, pink antelopes, lilac panthers cavorting in crystal substance. The walls were glass. They looked out upon color and fantasy. Hidden films clocked through well-oiled sprockets, and the

4. An ***incinerator*** is a kind of furnace for burning trash. Here, the fire's glow suggests the face of ***Baal,*** a god worshiped in ancient times.
5. To behave ***hysterically*** is to be very upset and out of control emotionally.
6. ***Regiments*** are groups of soldiers.
7. On playing cards, ***pips*** are the small printed dots or symbols that show a card's value. The alcoholic drinks ***(martinis)*** and sandwiches suddenly appeared ***(manifested).***

Vocabulary

frenzy (FREN zee) *n.* unusual mental excitement leading to wild activity

Practice the Skills

5 English Language Coach

Suffixes What is the base word of **sensing**? What letter do you drop when you add the suffix *-ing*?

Teach

R Reading Skill

Review Drawing Conclusions **Ask:** How does the dog react to the house? *(It runs around the house, barking hysterically.)* OL From the dog's actions, what can you conclude about the dog and the house? *(Possible response: The dog is starving to death because its owners are dead. The dog is used to living with people and cannot communicate with the machines.)* AL

EL Language Coach

Suffixes **Ask:** What suffix is added to the verb *hummed* in this paragraph to show that the action took place in the past? *(-ed)* What letter is added to the base word with the addition of the *-ed* suffix? *(the letter* M*)* List another example of these verbs from the page. *(realized)* EL BL

BQ BIG Question

Say: What does the family gain by having a computerized house? What do you think the family gives up, if anything? *(Family members do not have to do unwelcome chores. However, it seems that the family members give up some of their freedom because they must follow the schedule of the house.)* OL

Differentiated Instruction

Smart Houses Some of the design features that Ray Bradbury imagined in "There Will Come Soft Rains" are available now in what architects call "smart houses." In smart houses, house technology can be programmed, like a computer, to perform particular tasks on a particular schedule. Have students research smart houses online. Suggest that they start at the Duke SmartHouse, a project at Duke University's Pratt School of Engineering. Have students use the information they find to design their own smart houses. They may either draw diagrams that show various automated features or write descriptions of their houses. AL

Objectives
- Use text features
- Use critical thinking skills to comprehend events
- Use text to draw conclusions
- Use suffixes to determine meanings

READING WORKSHOP 2

Teach

R Reading Skill

Review Identifying Author's Purpose **Ask:** What was the author's purpose for writing this story? *(Possible response: The author wanted to make readers think about the terrible power of technology.)* Would the author have achieved his purpose if he had included people in the story? *(Possible response: The suffering in the story would have been more immediate and tragic, and readers would have concentrated on the people's suffering instead of on the power of technology.)* OL How did the author's focusing on the house's technology help him achieve his purpose? *(Possible response: The focus on technology forces readers to think about the results of technological advances. Although many cultures have spent a great deal of time and energy improving technology, human relations and diplomacy between nations still need great improvement.)* AL

walls lived. The nursery floor was woven to resemble a crisp, cereal meadow. Over this ran aluminum roaches and iron crickets, and in the hot still air butterflies of delicate red tissue wavered among the sharp aromas of animal spoors! There was the sound like a great matted yellow hive of bees within a dark bellows, the lazy bumble of a purring lion. And there was the patter of okapi[8] feet and the murmur of a fresh jungle rain, like other hoofs, falling upon the summer-starched grass. Now the walls dissolved into distances of parched weed, mile on mile, and warm endless sky. The animals drew away into thorn brakes and water holes.

It was the children's hour.

Five o'clock. The bath filled with clear hot water.

Six, seven, eight o'clock. The dinner dishes manipulated[9] like magic tricks, and in the study a *click.* In the metal stand opposite the hearth where a fire now blazed up warmly, a cigar popped out, half an inch of soft gray ash on it, smoking, waiting.

Nine o'clock. The beds warmed their hidden circuits, for nights were cool here. 6

R *Nine-five.* A voice spoke from the study ceiling:

"Mrs. McClellan, which poem would you like this evening?"

The house was silent.

The voice said at last, "Since you express no preference, I shall select a poem at random." Quiet music rose to back the voice. "Sara Teasdale.[10] As I recall, your favorite. . . . 7

There will come soft rains and the smell of the ground,
And swallows circling with their shimmering sound;

And frogs in the pools singing at night,
And wild plum trees in tremulous white;[11]

Robins will wear their feathery fire,
Whistling their ***whims*** *on a low fence-wire;*

8. In this paragraph, the walls and floor seem to come to life for the children's entertainment. The animals are running and playing ***(cavorting)*** in a sort of moving wallpaper. The floor becomes a grassy ***(cereal)*** field. ***Spoors*** are droppings. The African ***okapi*** (oh KAW pee) is like a giraffe but small and short-necked.
9. Here, ***manipulated*** means "moved around."
10. ***Teasdale,*** an American poet, often wrote about the beauty in nature.
11. The plum trees, full of white blossoms, are shaking ***(in tremulous white).***

Vocabulary

whims (wimz) *n.* sudden urges, desires, or ideas

Practice the Skills

6 **BIG Question**

Progress in home design made life easy and comfortable for the owners. Progress in warfare killed them. For this world that Bradbury imagines, answer this question: Is progress always *bad*? Put your answer on a note card in Foldable 5.

7 **Key Reading Skill**

Using Text Features A voice has just spoken, but its words are not in italics. Is this a second mechanical voice? Also, so far only the voice-clock's words have been in italics, but now a block of text is italicized and indented. Why do you think that was done?

Additional Support

Differentiated Instruction

Illustrating Have students identify technology tools that they use every day, such as MP3 players, cell phones, computers, or microwaves. Ask students to think about how these tools help them and improve their lives. Tell students to think about what features they would add to these devices to expand their usefulness. Have students note their thoughts and use these notes as a starting point for creating their own science fiction comic strips or illustrated stories. Students' artwork and stories should feature personified machines that they use in their everyday lives. Invite students to share their work with the class. OL

READING WORKSHOP 2

And not one will know of the war, not one
Will care at last when it is done.

Not one would mind, neither bird nor tree,
If mankind perished utterly;[12]

And Spring herself, when she woke at dawn
Would scarcely know that we were gone. 8

The fire burned on the stone hearth and the cigar fell away into a mound of quiet ash on its tray. The empty chairs faced each other between the silent walls, and the music played.

At ten o'clock the house began to die.

The wind blew. A falling tree bough crashed through the kitchen window. Cleaning solvent,[13] bottled, shattered over the stove. The room was ablaze in an instant!

"Fire!" screamed a voice. The house lights flashed, water pumps shot water from the ceilings. But the solvent spread on the linoleum, licking, eating, under the kitchen door, while the voices took it up in chorus: "Fire, fire, fire!"

The house tried to save itself. Doors sprang tightly shut, but the windows were broken by the heat and the wind blew and sucked upon the fire.

The house gave ground as the fire in ten billion angry sparks moved with flaming ease from room to room and then up the stairs. While scurrying water rats squeaked from the walls, pistoled their water, and ran for more. And the wall sprays let down showers of mechanical rain.

But too late. Somewhere, sighing, a pump shrugged to a stop. The quenching rain ceased. The reserve water supply which had filled baths and washed dishes for many quiet days was gone. L

The fire crackled up the stairs. It fed upon Picassos and Matisses in the upper halls, like delicacies,[14] baking off the oily flesh, tenderly crisping the canvases into black shavings.

12. ***Perished utterly*** means "died out completely."
13. A ***solvent*** is a mixture of liquid chemicals that would burn easily.
14. The ***Picassos*** and ***Matisses*** are paintings by twentieth-century artists Pablo Picasso and Henri Matisse. In a poetic image, the narration suggests that the burning paintings are delicious things for the fire to eat ***(delicacies).***

Practice the Skills

8 Reviewing Skills

Identifying Author's Purpose
Why do you think Bradbury included this poem in his story? What does it say about living things and war?

Teach

L Literary Element

Concept and Definition

Say: The concept of a self-sufficient house is extended when a fire breaks out in the kitchen. **Ask:** What does the house do? *(Possible response: The house cries out, "Fire!" and tries to put the fire out.)* AL
Say: Bradbury tells us that "[t]he house tried to save itself . . . [b]ut [it was] too late."
Ask: Why was it too late? How does Bradbury use this event to comment on the concept of a self-sufficient house? *(Possible response: The house had used up its reserve water, so it isn't really self-sufficient.)* AL

English Language Coach

Suffixes Have students look through the text for words that have suffixes. List the words on the board, and help students analyze each one. Provide students with the following example.

- hysterically = *hysterical* + *-ly*
- *hysterical* is an adjective that means "frenzied, panic-stricken, or out of control"
- *-ly* turns the adjective into an adverb that means "done in a hysterical manner"

Discuss with students how knowing the meanings of word parts can help them determine the meanings of unfamiliar words. BL

Objectives
- Identify the author's purpose
- Use suffixes to determine word meanings
- Understand concept and definition

READING WORKSHOP 2

Teach

C Critical Thinking

Evaluation Say: What do you think readers can learn from this story? *(Possible response: Readers can see how powerful technology can be but also how limited it can be in the face of change.)* **OL** Do you think your reaction to the story and what you learned from it fulfill the author's purpose? *(Possible response: I think the author wanted to warn readers about the awesome power of technology, and my reaction to the story fulfilled this purpose.)* **AL**

BQ 

Say: Think about the kinds of technological advances that would make your life better or easier. If such advances came to be, what consequences might they bring? Why might some of these consequences be unexpected? *(Responses will vary.)* **OL**

Now the fire lay in beds, stood in windows, changed the colors of drapes!

And then, reinforcements.

From attic trapdoors, blind robot faces peered down with faucet mouths gushing green chemical.

The fire backed off, as even an elephant must at the sight of a dead snake. Now there were twenty snakes whipping over the floor, killing the fire with a clear cold venom[15] of green froth.

But the fire was clever. It had sent flame outside the house, up through the attic to the pumps there. An explosion! The attic brain which directed the pumps was shattered into bronze shrapnel[16] on the beams.

The fire rushed back into every closet and felt of the clothes hung there.

The house shuddered, oak bone on bone, its bared skeleton cringing from the heat, its wire, its nerves revealed as if a surgeon had torn the skin off to let the red veins and capillaries quiver in the scalded air. Help, help! Fire! Run, run! Heat snapped mirrors like the first brittle winter ice. And the voices wailed, Fire, fire, run, run, like a tragic nursery rhyme, a dozen voices, high, low, like children dying in a forest, alone, alone. And the voices fading as the wires popped their sheathings like hot chestnuts. One, two, three, four, five voices died. **9** **BQ**

In the nursery the jungle burned. Blue lions roared, purple giraffes bounded off. The panthers ran in circles, changing color, and ten million animals, running before the fire, vanished off toward a distant steaming river. . . .

Ten more voices died. In the last instant under the fire avalanche, other choruses, **oblivious**, could be heard announcing the time, playing music, cutting the lawn by remote-control mower, or setting an umbrella frantically out and in, the slamming and opening front door, a thousand things happening, like a clock shop when each clock strikes the hour insanely before or after the other, a scene of maniac

15. In another poetic image, the ***snakes*** and their ***venom*** ("poison") are hoses and chemicals that put the fire out.

16. Here, ***shrapnel*** refers to bits of torn metal blown around by the explosion.

Vocabulary

oblivious (uh BLIV ee us) *adj.* not noticing; not aware of

Practice the Skills

9 Key Literary Element

Concept and Definition
Do you understand Bradbury's concept of the self-sufficient house better now? What has helped you learn more about this concept?

Additional Support

Literature Focus Lesson

Science Fiction The genre of science fiction includes stories that are based on factual or imagined science or technology. Unlike those science-fiction writers who celebrate new technology, Ray Bradbury often approaches technology with caution. He wrote this story in the 1950s, long before personal computers were in houses. Now that students have read the story, have them identify the advanced technology that Bradbury's story suggests will be used in the future. Lead a discussion about whether this or similar technology exists today. Have the class debate whether Bradbury would think that today's technology has a positive or a negative influence on society. **OL**

confusion, yet unity; singing, screaming, a few last cleaning mice darting bravely out to carry the horrid ashes away! And one voice, with sublime disregard[17] for the situation, read poetry aloud in the fiery study, until all the film spools burned, until all the wires withered and the circuits cracked.

The fire burst the house and let it slam flat down, puffing out skirts of spark and smoke.

In the kitchen, an instant before the rain of fire and timber, the stove could be seen making breakfasts at a psychopathic[18] rate, ten dozen eggs, six loaves of toast, twenty dozen bacon strips, which, eaten by fire, started the stove working again, hysterically hissing!

The crash. The attic smashing into kitchen and parlor. The parlor into cellar, cellar into sub-cellar. Deep freeze, armchair, film tapes, circuits, beds, and all like skeletons thrown in a cluttered mound deep under.

Smoke and silence. A great quantity of smoke.

Dawn showed faintly in the east. Among the ruins, one wall stood alone. Within the wall, a last voice said, over and over again and again, even as the sun rose to shine upon the heaped rubble and steam:

"Today is August 5, 2026, today is August 5, 2026, today is . . ." **10** **11** ○

17. ***Sublime disregard*** is a lack of attention to something because one is above it.

18. Here, ***psychopathic*** means "insane; crazy."

Practice the Skills

10 **Reviewing Skills**

Identifying Author's Purpose
Why do you think the author wrote this story–to entertain, inform, describe, persuade, or a combination of these purposes? Explain.

11 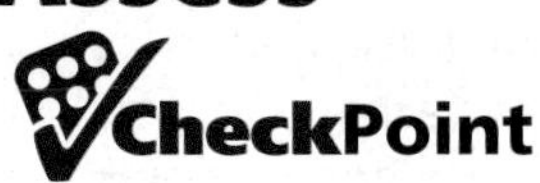

BQ Bradbury imagined the kinds of progress in technology that might take place. Some of what he imagined is possible today. Do you see these technologies as good, bad, or both? Explain your answer on a note card in Foldable 5. Your response will help you complete the Unit Challenge later.

READING WORKSHOP 2

Teach

Viewing the Illustration

Ask: Based on what you've read, what do you think the illustration symbolizes? *(Possible response: the future driven by time and electronics)* **AS**

BQ 

Say: Name one time when technology can be helpful or good. Name another time when it can be bad. *(Possible responses: good–when a computerized clock reminds you of something you need to do; bad–when a computer loses all of your information and you don't have a back-up copy)*

Assess

CheckPoint

Use the Checkpoint questions provided on Presentation Plus! to check for comprehension. These questions can be used with interactive response keypads for immediate student feedback.

Differentiated Instruction

Polls Tell students that sometimes people do not realize how much they depend on technology. Ask them to take a poll of several members in their community and family. They should ask these people to name the ways they have relied on technology this week. Once students have completed their polls, have the class list the various ways people rely on technology. **AS**

Objectives
- Locate information in text features to aid understanding and to interpret, analyze, and draw conclusions
- Explain how specific text features aid in comprehension of central, key, and supporting ideas

Assess

Resources for page 576

- Selection Quick Check
- Selection and Unit Assessment
- ExamView Assessment Suite
- Interactive Tutor: Self-Assessment

Students can respond to the *After You Read* items in their Learner's Notebook or on separate sheets of paper.

Answering the

1. Good: Advances in health care save lives. Bad: New weapons technology can cause mass destruction.
2. The people who lived in the house have been killed by an atomic bomb.
3. The house burns down after a tree limb breaks through a window and starts a fire.

Critical Thinking

4. They must have enjoyed having computers taking care of household chores.
5. The story says that the city has a radioactive glow. It seems that everyone in the city has been killed.
6. Possible response: The computerized voices of the house's clock and alarm systems are believable because alarm clocks and security systems exist today. The cleaning mice that sense any mess seem unbelievable.

After You Read | There Will Come Soft Rains

Answering the BIG Question

1. What are some of the good and bad uses of science?
2. **Recall** Why is the house empty?
   TIP **Think and Search**
3. **Recall** What happens to the house at the end of the story?
   TIP **Think and Search**

Critical Thinking

4. **Infer** How do you think the people who lived in the house felt about advanced technology? Why?
   TIP **Author and Me**
5. **Infer** Do you think anyone survived the blast? Explain your answer.
   TIP **Author and Me**
6. **Evaluate** Which technology in the house do you find most believable? Which technology do you think could not exist? Explain.
   TIP **Author and Me**

Write About Your Reading

Pretend you are a reviewer for a teen magazine. Would you recommend that other teens read this story? Write a review giving your opinion.

Use the following tips to get started:

- Think about your audience.
  Do they use a lot of technology? Would they like to read a story about advanced technology?
- Choose your position or opinion.
  Did you like the story? What did it make you think or feel?
- Back up your opinion with ideas or details from the story.
  Why would other people your age like the story? What might they learn from it?

Objectives (pp. 576–577)
Reading Use text features: italics
Literature Identify literary elements: organization
Vocabulary Identify word structure: suffixes
Writing Write a review: opinion
Grammar Identify parts of speech

Write About Your Reading

Possible response:
You should read "There Will Come Soft Rains" because you or people you know probably use technology such as cell phones, headphones, and microwaves every day. Ray Bradbury shows how a habit of depending on such machines can lead to producing technology with awful power. I like this story because it made me think about how much I actually need appliances and gadgets. In this story, readers can learn why human capabilities and technological advances need to be balanced.

Skills Review

Key Reading Skill: Using Text Features

7. Did the way the author used italics help you understand the story? Why or why not?
8. If you were asked to add other text features to the story, what would they be? Why?

Key Literary Element: Concept and Definition

9. Did you understand the definitions in the story? Can you think of anything that should have been defined but wasn't?
10. How did the definitions of words in the story help you understand the concepts in it?

Reviewing Skills: Identifying Author's Purpose

11. What warning is Bradbury giving readers in this story?

Vocabulary Check

Match each definition to the best word from the list.

shriveled emerged charred inconvenience frenzy whims oblivious

12. burned
13. shrunken and wrinkled
14. sudden urges, desires, or ideas
15. unusual mental excitement leading to wild activity
16. not noticing; not being aware of
17. came out
18. something that causes difficulty, discomfort, or bother
19. **English Language Coach** Add the suffix *-less* to each word below and define the new word.

tree power tear heart mind

Grammar Link: Clauses as Parts of Speech

A dependent clause has a subject and a predicate but cannot stand alone as a sentence. Dependent clauses can function as nouns, adjectives, or adverbs.

- Dependent clause as noun

  It will make no difference.
  (noun)

  Where you go will make no difference.
  (noun clause)

- Dependent clause as adjective

  He is a pleasant person.
  (adjective)

  He is a person who is kind to everyone.
  (adjective clause)

- Dependent clause as adverb

  Maybe we'll go.
  (adverb)

  If we like the plan, we'll go.
  (adverb clause)

Grammar Practice

For each sentence, decide what kind of clause is underlined.

20. Please call me before the bus arrives.
21. Whoever wants lunch should come with me.
22. Jodi bought the dress that she had been wanting.

Writing Application Look back at your Write About Your Reading assignment. Find one noun, one adjective, and one adverb. For each, try to substitute a clause that functions the same way.

Web Activities For eFlashcards, Selection Quick Checks, and other Web activities, go to www.glencoe.com.

Skills Review

Key Reading Skill: Using Text Features

7. Responses will vary.
8. Responses will vary.

Key Literary Element: Concept and Definition

9. Responses will vary.
10. Responses will vary but may include the definitions helped them to understand the conept of a house that is self-sufficient.

Reviewing Skills: Identifying Author's Purpose

11. Bradbury is warning readers that technology provides the convenience of house care but also the danger of nuclear attack.

Vocabulary Check

12. charred
13. shriveled
14. whims
15. frenzy
16. oblivious
17. emerged
18. inconvenience
19. treeless, without trees
powerless, without power
tearless, without tears
heartless, without heart
mindless, without mind

Grammar Link: Clauses as Parts of Speech

Grammar Practice

20. adverb clause
21. noun clause
22. adjective clause

Close

Ask students to write about a time *they* preferred to do something rather than use a gadget. Discuss what was learned about the Big Question from both "There Will Come Soft Rains" and their writing.

Taking Notes

UNIT 5

Objectives covered in this workshop:

- Identifying important text information by taking notes, making margin notes, and underlining text

Teaching Students to Take Notes

Why Is It important?

- Taking good notes is a valuable tool for enhancing comprehension related to learning, yet only about half of middle school students have been taught how to do it.
- Taking good notes provides a permanent written resource that can enhance future learning
- Research shows that being given notes—for example, outlines of key points with supporting details--is not as effective for learning as taking one's own notes which improves memory through active participation

How to Help Students Get It

- There are many effective note-taking strategies, but you should pick one approach that you explain and model. Students should have ample time for guided practice—applying the strategy in class with feedback about how effectively they use it.
- Teach students two applications of the strategy: first, *speech to notes*: here they should practice listening to you or their peers in class until they hear something important enough to synthesize; second, *text to notes* in which they read until they think there is an important idea to write down.
- Develop a note-taking guide that helps students take the kind of notes you want to promote. For example, a paper with columns is typical. The first column might be important ideas and key vocabulary, the second column might be details that support the ideas, and a third column might be questions students still have.
- Emphasize that not only taking notes, but systematically reviewing them, is key to learning; provide time in class for students to review of notes so they can become accustomed to the practice.

Reading to Answer the Big Question

The Next Big Thing

This informational article from TIME describes the unique and innovative inventions of the 20th century. Students can use this information to weigh the benefits and the problems of progress.

Big Yellow Taxi

These song lyrics are in protest to some forms of progress. Students can use this song to think about some of the negative consequences of progress and what inspires people to protest and speak out against certain issues.

Workshop Resources

Pacing (Days) Standard	Block	Lesson	Student Materials	Teacher Resources
1		Key Skill Lesson: Taking Notes	Key Reading Skills Practice English Language Coach	Bellringer Options Transparencies Read Aloud, Think Aloud Transparencies Presentation Plus!
2		"The Next Big Thing"	Literary Analysis Transparencies Glencoe Online Selection Vocabulary Development Academic Vocabulary Development English Language Coach Active Reading Graphic Organizer Literary Analysis StudentWorks Plus Online Student Edition Literature Classics Selection and Unit Assessments	Literary and Text Analysis Transparencies Puzzlemaker Skill Level Up! BookLink 3 Assessment by Learning Objective (Diagnostic and Formative) Interactive Tutor Self-Assessment TeacherWorks Plus
2		"Big Yellow Taxi"	Glencoe Online Selection Vocabulary Development Academic Vocabulary Development English Language Coach Active Reading Graphic Organizer Literary Analysis StudentWorks Plus Online Student Edition Literature Classics Selection and Unit Assessments	Literary and Text Analysis Transparencies Puzzlemaker Skill Level Up! BookLink 3 Assessment by Learning Objective (Diagnostic and Formative) Interactive Tutor Self-Assessment TeacherWorks Plus

Keys for Unit Resource

- Blackline Master
- Workbook
- Supplemental Text
- CD-ROM
- DVD
- Transparency
- Web-based
- Fast Files

Level Appropriate Code

AS = Activities for all students
AL = Activities for students working above grade level
OL = Activities for students working at grade level
BL = Activities for students working below grade level
EL = Activities for English language learners

Focus

BELLRINGER Options

Daily Language Practice Transparency

Focus Activity Say: Name a technological gadget that you used today. Explain how it made your life easier or more difficult. *(Responses will vary. Students may name alarm clocks, cell phones, or computers. Some may say that the gadget improves their organization or efficiency. Others may say that the gadget interrupts their lives.)*

Teach

R Reading Skill

Taking Notes Say: To remember important things, you probably take notes every day. What kinds of notes or lists do you write in the course of a typical day or week? *(Responses will vary. Students may list telephone numbers, homework assignments, or errands.)* AS

READING WORKSHOP 3

Skills Focus

You will practice using these skills when you read the following selections:

- "The Next Big Thing," p. 582
- "Big Yellow Taxi," p. 592

Reading

- Taking notes
- Responding

Literature

- Understanding organization
- Theme

Vocabulary

- Recognizing prefixes

Writing/Grammar

- Using commas

Skill Lesson

Taking Notes

Learn It!

What Is It? When you read, it's important to remember important ideas and details. Taking notes about what you're reading is a great way to point out and remember important information. When you take notes, you write about the information or mark where it appears in the text. There are different ways R to take notes.

- Write the important ideas and details on an index card or in a notebook.
- Write down your thoughts on the page of the book next to the information.
- Underline or circle important parts in a text.

If you're not allowed to write in the book, make a copy of the selection.

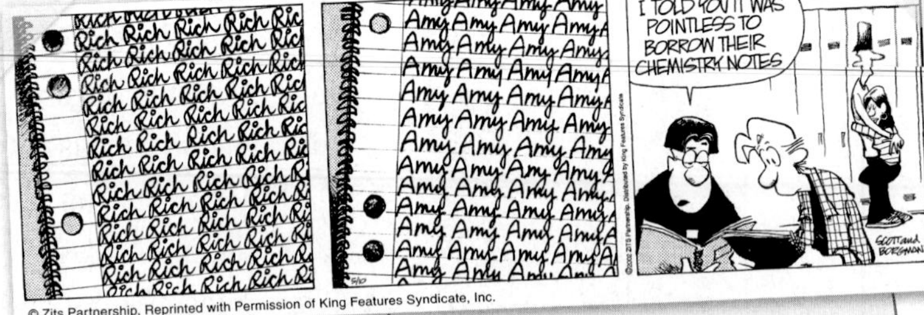

Analyzing Cartoons

Rich's and Amy's "notes" aren't very useful for studying chemistry. To make useful notes, stick to the subject.

Objectives (pp. 578–579)
Reading Take notes

Additional Support

Reading in the Real World

College Tell students that note-taking is a skill that they will use throughout their education. In this workshop, students will learn how to take notes on written material; in college students will take notes during lectures. Point out that either way, they should note the main ideas and important details. Have students discuss the different challenges involved in taking notes while someone is speaking. OL

Read aloud a paragraph from "The Next Big Thing" and have students note the main idea and important details. Ask them to discuss any challenges they faced while taking notes, such as having to write more quickly than usual. AL

Why Is It Important? Taking notes helps you remember and use information. It is a skill you can use inside or outside school.

Study Central Visit www.glencoe.com and click on Study Central to review taking notes.

How Do I Do It? Ask yourself questions about a topic: *Who? What? Where? When? Why?* and *How?* As you read, look for information that helps you answer your questions. You do not need to write everything. You should take notes about ideas and details that you may not remember otherwise. When taking notes you do not need to write complete sentences or use correct spelling or punctuation. You might even write shortened versions of familiar words or phrases. Here's how one student took notes to help her understand the following paragraph from "The Next Big Thing":

> Each gutsy idea may have brought good things to people, but progress often comes with a downside. Every breakthrough has pros and cons. Television, for example, is a great tool for educating many people, but it also has decreased the amount of time families spend talking with each other. The assembly line makes it possible for cars to be produced faster and for more people to travel great distances, but it has also helped create an automobile society with smog and air pollution. Can you think of any pros and cons of the big ideas of the 20th century below?

R

- *Progress has pros and cons.*
- *TV educates people, makes them spend less time talking.*
- *Cars help people travel, cause pollution.*

Practice It!

Look at the notes you took for "Hip Hop." Do they make sense? Do they give you an idea about the main points of the article?

Use It!

As you read "The Next Big Thing" and "Big Yellow Taxi," take notes that will help you understand the ideas in the text.

Teach

Literature Online

Study Central Have students access the Web site to review taking notes and to complete a related activity.

R Reading Skill

Taking Notes Say: Read the *How Do I Do It?* section. What do you notice about the way the student organizes her notes? *(She separates ideas with bullet points; she uses her own words.)* **OL** What is another way that the student may have chosen to organize her notes? *(Responses will vary. Students may suggest indenting the two details under the main idea or using the Who? What? Where? When? Why? and How? questions as heads.)* **AL**

Resources for page 579

- Use Reading Skills Transparency in *Read Aloud, Think Aloud,* Unit 5, to help students practice taking notes.

Reading in the Real World

Citizenship Ask students to conduct a class survey to find out about the role technology plays in class members' lives. Include questions such as

- How much time do you spend in a car or watching TV every day?
- What are the advantages and disadvantages of TVs and cars?
- How would you spend your time if you didn't watch TV?
- How would you get around if you didn't use a car?

Once students have finished, share some of the results with the class. Help them draw conclusions about the impact of technology. **OL**

Objectives

- Identify important text information by taking notes
- Conduct a survey

Teach

More About *TIME* Magazine

TIME magazine, founded in 1923, was the brainchild of Henry Robinson Luce and Briton Hadden. Luce pioneered the weekly newsmagazine. *TIME* is known for its intriguing pictures and text as well as its focus on newsmakers. Luce was the editor of *TIME* until 1964.

EL Language Coach

Word Structure Say: Word structures can be helpful in learning new words, but it is important to check a dictionary if you're unsure of a word's meaning. For example, *invisible* means "not visible," but *invaluable* does not mean "not valuable"; in fact it means the opposite. In many cases, the prefixes *in-* and *im-* mean "not." However, this is not always the case. For example, the word *inflammable* does not mean "not flammable." Have students look up the meaning of the word in the dictionary. OL

Before You Read The Next Big Thing

Meet the Authors

Maryanne Murray Buechner and Mitch Frank are both journalists for *TIME* magazine. Buechner has also written for *Fortune* magazine. Frank worked for *Entertainment Weekly,* writing articles about Hollywood celebrities and events. Now Frank usually writes about politics.

Author Search For more about these authors, go to www.glencoe.com.

Objectives (pp. 580–587)
Reading Take notes • Make connections from text to self
Literature Identify literary elements: organization
Vocabulary Identify word structure: prefixes

Vocabulary Preview

resists (rih ZISTS) *v.* holds off the force or effect of; form of the verb *resist* **(p. 582)** *Plastic resists some of the effects of nature.*

invaluable (in VAL yoo uh bul) *adj.* so valuable that a price can't be estimated; extremely desirable or important **(p. 585)** *Inventions are invaluable to our way of life.*

corporate (KOR pur ut) *adj.* belonging to or having to do with a company **(p. 586)** *These discoveries have had a large effect on corporate workers.*

consecutive (kun SEK yuh tiv) *adj.* following one after the other in order **(p. 587)** *She attended three consecutive meetings.*

Write to Learn Write sentences that use each word correctly. Then try to use all four words correctly in one sentence.

English Language Coach

Prefixes Prefixes are added to the beginnings of words and change the meanings. Knowing the meanings of common prefixes will help you understand new words.

EL

Prefix	Meaning	Example
co-	with	coworker
inter-	between	interdependent
post-	after	postseason
pre-	before	preseason
re-	back or again	repay
sub-	below	subway
super-	more than	supernatural
trans-	across, through, or beyond	transmission
anti-	against	antifreeze
pro-	for or forward	progovernment
bi-	two	bicycle
semi-	half or partly	semicircle
uni-	one	uniform

On Your Own Combine the prefix and base words listed below and define the new words. Check the meanings in a dictionary.

re + play = ___ post + war = ___
trans + act = ___ inter + act = ___
pre + date = ___ co + exist = ___

Additional Support

Author Search To expand students' appreciation of these authors, have them access the Web site for additional information and resources.

Differentiated Instruction

Building Prior Knowledge Explain that students will be reading a nonfiction article about technologies that are part of their daily lives. List a few of the following Big Ideas as headings on the board: *plastics, airplanes, assembly lines, supermarkets, televisions, radars, atom bombs, lasers, cell phones, personal computers, the World Wide Web,* and *space tourism.* Ask students what they know about each topic. Note student responses on the board under each appropriate heading. Have students read the article to learn more about these items and their effects on our lives. BL

Skills Preview

Key Reading Skill: Taking Notes

Before you read, think about what you may learn from the selection. Get ready to take notes about

- the point the author is trying to make
- important details that support the author's ideas
- what you think about the topic

R1

Key Literary Element: Organization

Text **organization** is the way that writers arrange and structure their ideas in an effort to make them clear to readers. There are many ways to organize text. You've already learned two:

- **Chronological (or time) order** What is the exact order of events? Look for clue words such as *first, next, then, later,* and *finally.*
- **Compare and contrast** What do people, things, or ideas have in common? Look for clue words such as *like, on the other hand, but, however,* and *as opposed to.*

Later in the book you'll learn about two more kinds of text organization:

- **Problem and solution** What is the problem and how is it solved? Look for clue words and phrases such as *need, attempt,* and *try to help.*
- **Cause and effect** When something happens, what happens next? Look for clue words and phrases such as *so, because,* and *that means.*

Interactive Literary Elements Handbook
To review or learn more about the literary elements, go to www.glencoe.com.

Get Ready to Read

Connect to the Reading

Think about the machines and products you use every day. What machine gets you to school? What machines make your dinner? What products help you relax—movies, TV, or video games? As you read the article, ask yourself what's good and what's not so good about the products and machines that are part of your life.

R2

Partner Talk With a partner, make a list of the machines and products you use most often. Talk about why they're useful and whether they create problems.

Build Background

For centuries, humans have created inventions that help them in some way.

- One of the oldest inventions is the wheel. The oldest wheel ever found is believed to be over fifty-five hundred years old.
- One invention often leads to another. Inventors used calculators to help create computers.

Set Purposes for Reading

BIG Question Read the article "The Next Big Thing" to learn about some of the benefits and problems of progress.

Set Your Own Purpose What else would you like to learn from the article to help you answer the Big Question? Write your own purpose on a note card and add it to Foldable 5.

Keep Moving

Use these skills as you read the following selection.

Teach

R1 Reading Skill

Taking Notes Say: Preview the selection "The Next Big Thing." How can the subheads in this article help you create an outline for taking notes as you read this article? *(Possible response: The subheads tell the major topics of the article, so they can be the Roman numeral entries.)* OL

R2 Reading Skill

Review Connecting Ask: Is there a machine or a new technology that you wish that you or someone else could invent? *(Responses will vary.)* OL

CheckPoint

Use the CheckPoint questions provided on Presentation Plus! to check for note-taking knowledge. These questions can be used with interactive response keypads for immediate student feedback.

LiteratureOnline

Interactive Literary Elements Handbook Have students access the Web site to improve their understanding of organization.

English Language Coach

Word Structure Give students more practice in determining meaning by reading aloud the following and having students fill in the blanks:

1. If *direct* means "straightforward," then *indirect* means ___ *(not straightforward).*
2. If *active* means "moving," then *inactive* means ___ *(still).*
3. If the root word is *hope,* and you add the suffix *less,* then *hopeless* means ___ *(without hope).*
4. If the root word is *fear,* and you add the suffix *less,* then *fearless* means ___ *(without fear).*

Objectives

- Take notes
- Make connections from text to self
- Identify literary elements: organization
- Identify word structure: prefixes

Teach

EL Language Coach

Prefixes Say: Use synonyms of the words *pros* and *cons* to explain what the authors meant. *(Possible response: There are good and bad things about breakthroughs.)* OL

R Reading Skill

Taking Notes Ask: Which sentence tells the main idea of the first paragraph? *(The first sentence.)* OL What details support the main idea in the first paragraph? *(Possible response: The sentences about television and assembly lines give examples of the main idea.)* OL

L Literary Element

Organization Ask: What method of organization did the authors use in the first paragraph? *(compare and contrast)* What clue words help you decide? *(but, pros and cons)* OL

Readability Scores
Dale-Chall: 6.3
DRP: 71
Lexile: 1140

READING WORKSHOP 3

TIME

The Next BIG THING

You never know when an idea will turn out to be the kind of discovery that changes how we live, work, or play. Here's a look at some bold breakthroughs of the 20th century—from plastic to the World Wide Web—and a forecast of what's to come.

By MARYANNE MURRAY BUECHNER and MITCH FRANK

Each gutsy idea may have brought good things to people, but progress often comes with a downside. Every breakthrough has **pros and cons.** Television, for example, is a great tool for educating many people, but it also has decreased the amount of time families spend talking with each other. The assembly line makes it possible for cars to be produced faster and for more people to travel great distances, but it also has helped create an automobile society with smog and air pollution. Can you think of any pros and cons of the big ideas of the 20th century below? 1 2 3

Plastics

When New York chemist Leo Baekeland invented Bakelite in 1907, he created the first completely human-made substance. Bakelite **resists** heat, acids, and electricity, which allows it to be used in everything from cookware to car electrical systems. The plastic century was launched with the invention of Bakelite.

What it led to: Teflon, cellophane, nylon, Velcro, Plexiglas, spandex, polyester

Vocabulary

resists (rih ZISTS) *v.* holds off the force or effect of

1 English Language Coach

EL **Prefixes** *Pro-* is a prefix that means "for" (I'm all for it). *Con-* is a prefix that means "against." Explain what the writers mean when they write, "Every breakthrough has **pros and cons.**"

2 Key Reading Skill

R **Taking Notes** What is the main idea? What have I learned that will help me understand the main idea? Write notes that answer these questions.

3 Key Literary Element

L **Organization** What clue do the conjunctions in this paragraph give about how the writers have organized it?

Additional Support

Differentiated Instruction

Word Invention Point out that *Bakelite* is an invented compound word. Ask students to discuss why chemist Leo Baekeland may have decided to call his invention Bakelite. *(Responses will vary.* Bake *is a partial homonym of Baekeland's name. The action of baking requires heat, and Bakelite is resistant to heat. In fact, many baking products are made of plastic.* Lite *is a variant of* light, *and plastic is not heavy.)* Invite pairs of students to use dictionaries to invent English compound words and definitions for products they use every day. Suggest that students share their word inventions aloud with the class. AL

READING WORKSHOP 3

Airplanes

On December 17, 1903, Orville Wright flew for 12 seconds. It was the result of seven years of experiments on powering and controlling a glider by him and his brother Wilbur. R1

What it led to: Air travel, airports, airline companies, flight attendants, in-flight movies and videos, mass travel

The Assembly Line

In 1908 Henry Ford's company was turning out a car every 12 hours. But Ford wanted cars made more quickly and began experimenting with production-line methods. He started moving car parts along a mechanical conveyor belt[1] to workers. Each worker performed only one task. In 1913 Ford's new factory began producing a Model T car every 93 minutes. By 1925 that was down to 15 minutes. The increase in productivity allowed Ford to turn automobiles into a mass product. 4

What it led to: Highways, suburbs, assembly-line robots

Bettmann-Corbis

THE ASSEMBLY LINE allowed Henry Ford's company to produce cars faster.

1. A ***conveyor*** (kun VAY ur) ***belt*** is a flat piece of rubber that carries parts to workers. Along the way, workers put the parts together into a finished product.

4 Key Reading Skill

Taking Notes Reread this paragraph. What are the important ideas or concepts? What details do you need to remember? Write notes in your Learner's Notebook. R2

Teach

Viewing the Photo

Ask: What can you learn about assembly lines from this photo? *(Responses will vary. Students may say that workers stand in a line as the product that they help build moves past them.)* BL

R1 Reading Skill

Review Drawing Conclusions Say: The Wrights worked for seven years before they were able to fly. What conclusion can you draw about inventors? *(Possible response: Inventors work hard and have to be dedicated and persistent.)* AL

R2 Reading Skill

Taking Notes Say: Which detail in the paragraph seems the most important? Explain. *(Students may say that Ford's revolution of moving the work along a track to each worker is the main detail to remember because it allowed many products to be produced quickly.)* OL

Differentiated Instruction

Assembly Line With these prompts, have students figure out how many more cars Ford could make after he improved the assembly line:

1. In 1908 Ford made one car every 12 hours, and in 1925 Ford made one car every 15 minutes.
2. In 1925 how many cars could Ford make in one hour? *(four–one every fifteen minutes)*
3. In 1925 how many cars could Ford make in 12 hours? *(four cars × twelve hours = forty-eight cars)*

In 1925 Ford could make 48 cars in the time he could make one car in 1908. OL

Objectives
- Identify important text information by taking notes
- Understand word structure, including roots, prefixes, and suffixes
- View and interpret photos
- Understand text structure and organization

Teach

EL Language Coach

Word Structure **Say:** The word *supermarkets* includes *super* as a prefix. List other words with this same prefix. *(Responses will vary. Students may suggest* supersize, superstar, *or* superhero.*)* BL

L Literary Element

Organization **Ask:** How can an author alert you to time order? *(Possible answer: An author may use clue words, such as* first, next, then, *and* finally, *or the author may give dates or times when events take place.)* OL

R Reading Skill

Taking Notes **Say:** Use the five-question note-taking method when you read the section entitled "Radar." *(Possible response: **Who:** scientists working during WWII; **What:** radar is a "radio detecting and ranging system" that measures the speed of radio waves reflected off of objects; **Where:** England; **When:** the Second World War; **Why:** invented to detect faraway objects and help countries defend themselves)* OL

Supermarkets

It all began with a Piggly Wiggly grocery store in Memphis, Tennessee, in 1916. Clarence Saunders conceived and patented[2] the idea of shoppers' walking through aisles of goods and serving themselves instead of asking a clerk behind the counter for everything.

What it led to: Giant supermarkets, cash registers, shopping carts, express checkout lanes EL

Television

In 1927 Bell Telephone and the U.S. Department of Commerce[3] conducted the first long-distance use of TV, between Washington, D.C., and New York City. Then-Secretary of Commerce Herbert Hoover commented, "Today we have, in a sense, the transmission of sight for the first time in the world's history. Human genius has now destroyed the [obstacle] of distance." American engineer Philo Farnsworth filed for a patent on the first all-electronic television system, which he called the image dissector.

What it led to: Couch potatoes, broadcast journalism, MTV, VCRs, camcorders, reality TV

Friday Associates

TELEVISION: This early TV is shown encased in a stylish cabinet.

Radar 5

As the Second World War approached, all of the major powers were developing methods to detect distant objects and determine their position. By measuring the speed of radio waves reflected off objects, scientists developed a "radio detecting and ranging" (RADAR) system. Radar provided early warning if enemy bomber planes were approaching. By 1938 the British set up a home-defense radar

5 Key Reading Skill

R **Taking Notes** As you read the next paragraph, take notes about the important ideas and details. What is radar? What does it do? How does it help people?

2. In the United States, an inventor protects his or her invention by getting an official document called a ***patent.*** Then, for a certain number of years, no one but the inventor can make or sell that invention.

3. The ***U.S. Department of Commerce*** oversees the buying and selling of goods and promotes economic growth, technology, and development.

Additional Support

Differentiated Instruction

Let's Go Shopping Ask students if they've seen an old-fashioned grocery counter in movies or on television. Lead students in a discussion about the pros and cons of this type of grocery store vs. modern supermarkets. Have students consider which type of store they would prefer to shop at and why. *(Some may prefer the old-fashioned store because they could chat with the grocer as he or she got their food, while others may prefer modern supermarkets because they're faster and you don't have to talk to anyone.)* Ask students whether they think that the self-serve grocery store qualifies as progress and why. BL

READING WORKSHOP 3

system. The system proved invaluable during the Battle of Britain, when the United Kingdom was under constant attack by German bombers.

What it led to: Air-traffic controllers, highway speed traps, F-117 stealth fighters, Doppler radar, accurate weather forecasts

The Atom Bomb

After a U.S. plane dropped an atom bomb on Hiroshima, Japan, and the mushroom cloud[4] cleared, black rain fell from the sky. Nuclear weapons ended World War II and changed the way nations would deal with conflict and war forever. Countries that had nuclear power began to store these weapons of mass destruction and use the threat of launching them to intimidate[5] other nations. BQ

What it led to: Atomic energy, the arms race, nuclear submarines, the space race, fallout shelters, nuclear waste

Jack W. Aeby

THE ATOM BOMB brought an end to World War II.

The Laser

In 1960 Theodore Maiman built the first working laser (short for light amplification by stimulated emission of radiation). A laser is a highly concentrated,[6] bright, and powerful beam of light that travels along the same path. Today, lasers are everywhere: guiding rockets for the military, cutting steel, and playing your favorite CDs. 6

What it led to: Bar-code scanners, ray guns, laser light shows, laser printers, Lasik eye surgery

4. An exploded atom bomb creates a huge cloud that looks like a mushroom, so it's called a ***mushroom cloud.***
5. To ***intimidate*** (in TIM ih dayt) is to make a person feel scared or fearful.
6. Something that's ***concentrated*** is tightly focused or gathered into one place.

Vocabulary

invaluable (in VAL yoo uh bul) *adj.* so valuable that a price can't be estimated; extremely desirable or important

6 Key Literary Element

Organization Look at the inventions in the article. How are they organized? What, then, is the *general* organization of the article? L

Teach

BQ BIG Question

Say: A bomb is a harmful weapon. Should technology that leads to human casualties be considered "progress"? *(Responses will vary. Students may say that while the bomb is an example of increased technological knowledge, it led to harmful products and events and so is not progress.)* AL

L Literary Element

Organization Ask: What clue do the authors use under each head of the article to alert you to the chronological, or time, order? *(What it led to)* OL Why did the authors use chronological order to organize this article? *(Responses will vary but should include the idea that time order shows the advances of science over the last one hundred years.)* AL

Reading in the Real World

Career Students who enjoy reading about radar, atom bombs, and lasers may want to pursue careers in physics, the science branch concerned with how matter and energy interact. Tell these students that they might be interested in the field of engineering or careers in the geo or nuclear sciences. Encourage these students to contact physics teachers at local high schools and colleges or universities to find out more about the study of physics, careers in physics, and what students can do now to prepare themselves for such careers. Invite these students to report their findings to the class in an informal career session. AL

Objectives

- Identify important text information by taking notes
- Take notes on main ideas and important details
- Understand word structure, including roots, prefixes, and suffixes
- Understand how a text is structured and organized

Teach

R Reading Skill

Review Identifying Author's Purpose and Perspective **Ask:** What do you notice about the author's point of view in the "What it led to" section of "Cell Phones"? *(The entries are all negative.)* OL What do these entries reveal about the writers' perspective? *(Possible response: By not including any positive results of cell phones, the writers reveal a bias against cell phones.)* AL

BQ 

Ask: Can you think of another negative result of cell phones that is not listed in the article? *(Possible response: distracted pedestrians)* What are positive results of the invention of cell phones? *(Possible response: Cell phones make it easier to call for help in an emergency and to contact friends and family members from any location.)* OL

READING WORKSHOP 3

Cell Phones

Motorola's Martin Cooper made the first cellular phone call in 1973 on a wireless telephone. That first cell phone was later nicknamed the brick because of its size and shape. Handsets soon became smaller, cellular networks and companies boomed (and went digital), and cell phone subscribers multiplied to millions of people in the United States alone.

R **What it led to:** Distracted drivers, rude movie and restaurant patrons, dropped calls and poor service **7**

Courtesy Motorola

7 BIG Question

BQ When cell phones were invented, many people did not think of the downside, or negative effect, of using them. In your opinion, what is the most negative effect of cell phones? What is the best reason to carry and use cell phones? Write your answers on a note card and add it to Foldable 5. Your response will help you answer the Unit Challenge later.

The Personal Computer

The PC (personal computer) brought a mind-blowing increase of productivity to **corporate** workers, as well as to Mom, Dad, and the kids at home. In 1981 IBM introduced its first PC. Three years later, Apple unveiled[7] the Macintosh. Either way, consumers just want a computer that works and does everything.

What it led to: Word processing, PowerPoint, technical support departments

7. ***Unveiled*** (un VAYLD) means "revealed or shown for the first time."

Vocabulary

corporate (KOR pur ut) *adj.* belonging to or having to do with a company

IBM

An early model of an IBM computer.

Additional Support

Differentiated Instruction

Using a Graphic Organizer Explain that comparing objects in an article can be another note-taking aid. Suggest that students complete Venn diagrams to compare and contrast assembly lines and personal computers.

"Assembly Lines"
a way of organizing work; produce physical products

Both Selections
Increase productivity; work stations; training required

"Personal Computers"
machines that use software; produce information products

The World Wide Web 8

The Internet had been around since the 1970s but wasn't ready for prime time.[8] Only after software engineer Tim Berners-Lee created HTML code, URLs, and the first browser did the Web make its official appearance in 1991. Before long, surfing was something you did indoors on a keyboard. The Web has changed the way we do so many things—shop and learn and check the weather and movie listings—and has given us control over the flow of information. R2

What it led to: Online shopping, Googling, e-mail, spam, computer viruses

Next? Space Tourism

Two civilians[9] have each paid $20 million to visit the International Space Station, courtesy of the Russians and space tourism agent Space Adventures. Other private companies are working toward offering 10-minute rides into Earth's orbit. And to jump-start the space tourism industry, the Ansari X Prize Foundation held a contest. Ansari challenged private companies to design the first private spaceship to successfully launch three humans to a suborbital[10] altitude of 100 km (62 mi.) on two **consecutive** flights within a two-week period. The SpaceShipOne team won the $10 million prize on September 29, 2004.

What will it lead to?

—Updated 2005, from *TIME*, September 8, 2003

8 **Key Reading Skill**

Taking Notes What is the most important information under "The World Wide Web" section? Take notes about this information in your Learner's Notebook. R1

8. ***Ready for prime time***, in this case, means good enough for many people to use. In television, *prime time* is the evening hours when the most people are watching.
9. Here, ***civilians*** refers to people who do not work for any government space agency.
10. ***Suborbital*** means, in this case, that these people will not go into space and won't circle the whole Earth.

Vocabulary

consecutive (kun SEK yuh tiv) *adj.* following one after the other in order

Teach

R1 Reading Skill

Taking Notes Ask: What is the main idea and the most important supporting detail of "The World Wide Web" section? *(Main idea: The Internet has changed virtually all aspects of life. Detail: People shop, learn, check the weather, and read movie listings on the Internet.)* **OL** How did the invention of the Web change modern life? *(Possible response: It allowed people to easily find information about their world.)* **OL**

R2 Reading Skill

Review Responding

Ask: Do you agree that the Internet has given us control over the flow of information? Explain. *(Possible response: The Internet is not controlled—virtually anyone can put accurate or inaccurate information on the Web.)* **OL**

Assess

Use the CheckPoint questions provided on Presentation Plus! to check for comprehension of the selection. These questions can be used with interactive response keypads for immediate student feedback.

Objectives
- Identify author's purpose and point of view
- Understand text organization
- Take notes on main ideas and important details
- Respond to text ideas
- Use a graphic organizer to compare ideas in a selection

Differentiated Instruction

What Will It Lead To? Tell students to review the "What it led to" sections of the article. As a class, brainstorm the kinds of events, problems, or products that could result from space tourism. **OL**

Invite students to expand upon the final question of the article. Use the following questions to begin discussion:

- Will scientists find a cure for cancer or AIDS?
- How will humans address the issue of pollution?
- What new gadgets will people invent?

For each suggestion that students make, ask them what the pros and cons of such a solution or invention might be. **AL**

Assess

Resources for page 588

- Selection Quick Check
- Selection and Unit Assessment
- ExamView Assessment Suite
- Interactive Tutor: Self-Assessment

Students can respond to the *After You Read* items in their Learner's Notebook or on separate sheets of paper.

Answering the

1. Responses will vary. Students may suggest that cell phones are convenient, but people use them in rude ways.
2. Possible response: Television takes away from quality family time.
3. The improvements include the HTML code, URLs, and the first browser.

Critical Thinking

4. The atom bomb is the most threatening invention because its only purpose is to destroy human life.
5. Responses will vary. Students may say that they e-mail friends and do homework on personal computers.
6. Responses will vary.
7. Responses will vary. Students may say that the atom bomb causes more problems than benefits because of its destructive nature.

After You Read

The Next Big Thing

Bettmann-Corbis

Objectives (pp. 588–589)
Reading Take notes
Literature Identify literary elements: organization
Vocabulary Identify word structure: prefixes
Writing Write a letter of explanation
Grammar Use punctuation: commas in a series

Answering the

1. Some inventions have negative effects because of the way people use them. Give an example of a product that causes problems when people use it.
2. **Recall** What is one of the downsides of having a television?
   TIP **Right There**
3. **Recall** What improvements made the World Wide Web "ready for prime time"?
   TIP **Right There**

Critical Thinking

4. **Evaluate** Which invention discussed in the article has the most serious and threatening downside? Why?
   TIP **Author and Me**
5. **Connect** How do the inventions in the article affect your life? Give an example.
   TIP **Author and Me**
6. **Evaluate** Which invention discussed in the article is, in your opinion, the most useful and helpful to mankind? Why?
   TIP **Author and Me**
7. **Evaluate** Do you think any of these inventions cause more problems than benefits? Explain.
   TIP **Author and Me**

Talk About Your Reading

Literature Groups With your group, choose one of the inventions in the article. Decide whether the invention is mostly good progress or bad progress. Be sure to use facts to back up your opinion. You may need to visit your library to get more facts about the invention.

Write to Learn Write a short letter to your local paper explaining how your group feels about the invention.

Talk About Your Reading

Write to Learn

Possible response:

Dear Editor:

More than 120 million people in the United States use cell phones, and they can't all be wrong. Sure, some people talk on the phone when they should be paying attention to the road, but the benefits of cell phones far outweigh any disadvantages. Cell phones allow people to move around. They don't have to stay at home waiting for a call when they have errands to run. They don't have to miss an important call because they were outside or in the car.

Skills Review

Key Reading Skill: Taking Notes

8. Look at the notes you took while reading this article. How do they help you understand the authors' main idea?

9. Use your notes and *only* your notes to write a very short summary of the article.

Key Literary Element: Organization

10. Did the organization of this article help you understand the main idea? Why or why not?

11. If you had to choose another way to organize the article, what would it be? Would that change the main idea?

Vocabulary Check

12. Match each vocabulary word with its definition.

invaluable	the buying and selling of products
resists	belonging to a company or business
commerce	beyond price
corporate	holds off the force or effect of

13. English Language Coach Copy the words below. Underline the prefixes and double-underline the base words.

semisweet	submarine	supermarket
recheck	invisible	unhappy
transplant	semiformal	misinform
defrost	disagree	coauthor
nonfat	impossible	irresponsible

Grammar Link: Commas in a Series

Conversation doesn't need commas. Your use of pauses and how you stress words let a listener know what you mean. Without commas in writing, however, much of what is written would be confusing and difficult to understand. One of the most common uses for commas is to separate items in a series.

- Commas are used to separate three or more words, phrases, or clauses in a series.

  Sherry invited Rob, Lonnie, Barb, Barb's roommate, and Patrice.

  I want to know when you left, where you went, and what you did last night.

- Do *not* use a comma before the first item in the series or after the last one.

  Wrong: We were served, fruit, milk, eggs, and juice for breakfast.

  Wrong: We were served fruit, milk, eggs, and juice, for breakfast.

- If *and* or *or* is repeated between words, phrases, or clauses, commas are not used.

  The showroom had cars and trucks and motorcycles.

  Do you know who was there or what they said or why they were laughing?

Grammar Practice

Copy the following sentences, inserting commas where they are needed.

14. There were roses some daisies a dozen tulips and lilies in the bouquet.

15. It gets loud when dogs are barking horns are honking and children are yelling.

Web Activities For eFlashcards, Selection Quick Checks, and other Web activities, go to www.glencoe.com.

Skills Review

Key Reading Skill: Taking Notes

8. Responses will vary. Students may say that noting the main idea of each paragraph helped them to apply their personal knowledge to the authors' points, thus helping them better understand the main idea of the article.

9. Responses will vary but students should mention that the authors listed pros and cons of the inventions.

Key Literary Element: Organization

10. Students may say that the chronological listing of the inventions helped them understand the advances of science over time.

11. Responses will vary but should reflect understanding of the main idea.

Vocabulary Check

12. invaluable: beyond price
resists: holds off the force or effect of
commerce: the buying and selling of products
corporate: belonging to a company or business

13. semisweet, submarine, supermarket, recheck, invisible, unhappy, transplant, semiformal, misinform, defrost, disagree, coauthor, nonfat, impossible, irresponsible

Grammar Link: Commas in a Series

Grammar Practice

14. There were roses, some daisies, a dozen tulips, and lilies in the bouquet.

15. It gets loud when dogs are barking, horns are honking, and children are yelling.

Close

Ask students to summarize what they learned about the Big Question from the article.

More About the Author

Joni Mitchell told journalist Alan McDougall why she wrote "Big Yellow Taxi." She described a visit to Hawaii, where she "walked over to the balcony and there was the picture book scenery, palm tree swaying in the breeze and all. Then I looked down and there was this ugly concrete car park in the hotel grounds. I thought 'They paved paradise and put up a parking lot' and that's how the song 'Big Yellow Taxi' was born."

V Vocabulary

Vocabulary Origin Say: One way to learn and remember vocabulary words is to learn about their origins. Use a dictionary to look up the Greek origin of the word *boutique.* (*"storehouse"*) OL

Before You Read Big Yellow Taxi

Meet the Author

Joni Mitchell is a folk singer and songwriter. She was born in Canada in 1943. She always loved music and was on the road at the age of 22. When she started performing, she noticed that women didn't write many songs. She once said, "When I began to write, women's songs were written by men . . . they were what men thought women should sing. My songs were different."

Author Search For more about Joni Mitchell, go to www.glencoe.com.

Objectives (pp. 590–593)
Reading Respond to the text
Literature Identify literary elements: theme
Vocabulary Identify word structure: Greek and Latin word origins

Vocabulary Preview

paradise (PAIR uh dys) *n.* a beautiful, wonderful, happy place; heaven **(p. 592)** *Mitchell describes a society that's willing to destroy paradise.*

boutique (boo TEEK) *n.* a small, fashionable store **(p. 592)** *Are a hotel, a boutique, and a nightclub as important as trees and open land?*

Write to Learn In your Learner's Notebook, list words or phrases that may describe the vocabulary words.

English Language Coach

V **Greek and Latin Origins** Many words in English come from ancient Greek and Latin words. Ancient Greek was spoken in Greece, and Latin was spoken in ancient Rome. English has borrowed many words from Greek and Latin. Here are some examples:

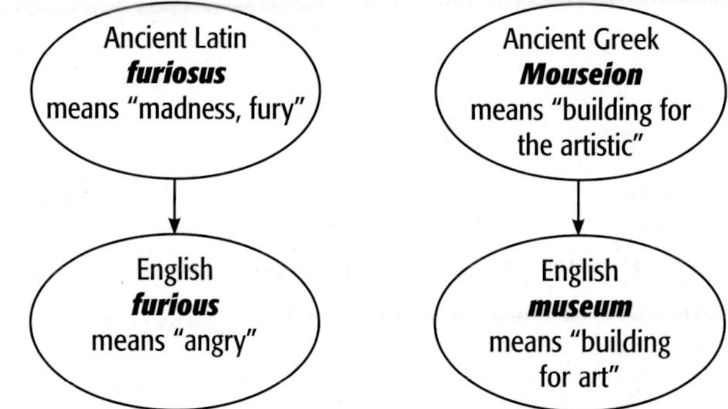

Fill in the Diagram Use the information below to fill in the blanks in the diagram.

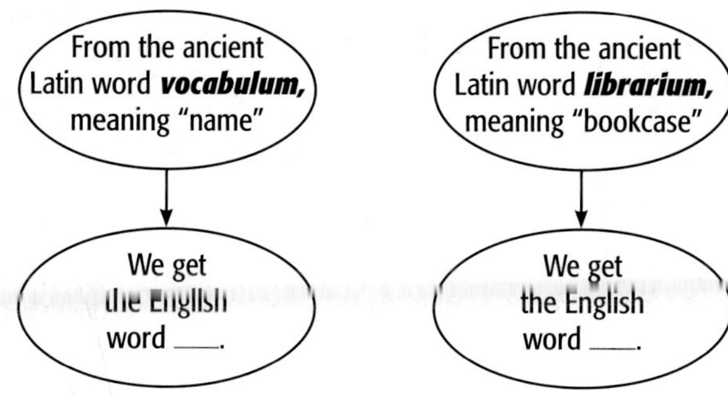

Additional Support

Author Search To expand students' appreciation of Joni Mitchell, have them access the Web site for additional information and resources.

Literature Focus Lesson

Song Lyrics Play audio recordings of the original version of "Big Yellow Taxi" by Joni Mitchell and a rendition by Counting Crows. Lead students in a discussion of the similarities and differences between the two renditions. Then help students draw conclusions about why this song enjoyed popularity both when it was written and more than thirty years later. Ask:

- Why would a group such as Counting Crows choose to remake this song?
- Why would audiences be interested in this song both when it was written and later?
- How does this song relate to modern-day life? OL

Skills Preview

Reading Skill: Responding

As you read "Big Yellow Taxi," think about how you're responding to the text.

- Does the song make you feel any emotions?
- Does it make you think?
- Does it make you remember something?
- Does anything in the song surprise you?
- Do you like the language?
- Do you agree with the song's message?

Literary Element: Theme

The **theme** is the main idea or message of a piece of writing. The theme often tells you what the author thinks about a topic. Sometimes an author directly says the theme. And sometimes the author implies the theme, or hints at it. When the author implies the theme, you must look at the details to figure out the main idea.

As you read "Big Yellow Taxi," use these tips to help you understand the theme.

- Look for lines that are repeated.
  What do the repeated lines say? What do they tell you about the main idea? **L**
- Look for details that give clues about the theme.
  Do the details make you think of positive or negative things? What do the details say about the bigger idea?
- Review the title of the song.
  What does the title make you think of? Does the title describe a good or bad image?

Write to Learn Think of one of your favorite songs. Write a short paragraph that describes the song and explains its main message, or theme.

Interactive Literary Elements Handbook
To review or learn more about the literary elements, go to www.glencoe.com.

Get Ready to Read

Connect to the Reading

How much time do you spend enjoying nature? Is it easy to get from where you live to an open field or a forest? As you read "Big Yellow Taxi," think about what will happen as human populations grow and more areas become towns and cities. **R**

Small Group Talk In a small group, talk about how people harm or help nature. Give examples to support your ideas.

Build Background

"Big Yellow Taxi" is a protest song that criticizes a social problem. In the 1960s, many musicians wrote protest songs to show how they felt about war, pollution, and other issues.

- Protest songs became very popular. In the early 1970s, the song "I'd Like to Teach the World to Sing" was used in a television commercial. The song was a protest against violence and hatred.
- Sometimes people write songs about what they think is right. "He Ain't Heavy, He's My Brother" is a song about members of a community. The songwriter wrote it because he thought that we should all take care of those who are less fortunate.

Set Purposes for Reading

BIG Question Read "Big Yellow Taxi" to find out why some people protest against progress.

Set Your Own Purpose What else would you like to learn from the song to help you answer the Big Question? Write your own purpose on a note card and add it to Foldable 5.

Keep Moving

Use these skills as you read the following selection.

Teach

L Literary Element

Review Author's Craft Ask: Songwriters often use repetition in their music. Why do you think they do this? *(Possible responses: to help listeners pay attention to important details, to create rhythm)* **OL**

R Reading Skill

Review Connecting Ask: Why has our country set aside natural spaces as national parks? *(Possible response: Plants in national parks provide people with oxygen, food, and beauty.)* **OL** Have you ever visited a national or state park? If so, describe the experience. *(Responses will vary.)* **BL**

CheckPoint

Use the CheckPoint questions provided on Presentation Plus! to check for note-taking knowledge. These questions can be used with interactive response keypads for immediate student feedback.

Literature Online

Interactive Literary Elements Handbook Have students access the Web site to improve their understanding of theme.

Differentiated Instruction

Protest Music Have students find the lyrics to other protest songs. Suggest the work of Bob Dylan or John Lennon. Tell students to choose songs that are school appropriate. Then have students analyze the songs by responding to these items:

- What is the title, artist, and year of release?
- What is the song a protest against?
- What are the arguments for and against this issue?
- What is the appeal of protest music for artists? For listeners?

Invite students to play recordings of excerpts from their songs. Ask students to summarize their analysis. **AL**

Objectives

- Respond to the text
- Identify literary elements: theme
- Identify word structure: Greek and Latin word origins

READING WORKSHOP 3

Teach

R Reading Skill

Review Paraphrasing and Summarizing **Ask:** What do the following lines ask the audience? "Don't it always seem to go / That you don't know what you've got / 'Til it's gone." *(Possible response: They ask audience members whether they understand what it's like to take something for granted and then regret losing it.)* OL

EL Language Coach

Greek and Latin Origins **Say:** The word *paradise* comes from the Greek word *paradeisos.* Use a dictionary to look up the meaning of the word paradise *(a place of delight or bliss)* and its Greek root *paradeisos (a park or garden).* OL

Big Yellow Taxi

by Joni Mitchell

They paved **paradise**
And put up a parking lot
With a pink hotel, a **boutique**
And a swinging hot spot
Don't it always seem to go
That you don't know what you've got
'Til it's gone
They paved paradise
And put up a parking lot 1 2

They took all the trees
And put them in a tree museum
And they charged the people
A dollar and a half just to seem 'em
Don't it always seem to go,
That you don't know what you've got
'Til it's gone
They paved paradise
And put up a parking lot

Hey farmer, farmer
Put away that DDT* now
Give me spots on my apples

20 *D.D.T.* is a chemical that farmers used to kill insects. But it also killed the birds that ate those insects. After it was found to be dangerous to humans, *D.D.T.* was not allowed in the United States.

Vocabulary

paradise (PAIR uh dys) *n.* a beautiful, wonderful, happy place; heaven

boutique (boo TEEK) *n.* a small, fashionable store

Practice the Skills

1 Reading Skill

Responding How are you responding to the poem so far? Are you interested? What do you think of Mitchell's word choice? What about the rhythm and rhymes?

2 English Language Coach

Greek and Latin Origins *Paradeisos* is an ancient Greek word. What word in this song comes from this ancient word?

Additional Support

Reading in the Real World

Career Many museums preserve the past for future generations. Some students may want to learn about museum careers. Give students this interest survey:

1. Do you enjoy researching information or searching for facts?
2. Do you enjoy art projects?
3. Do you like working with others?
4. Do you enjoy working on long-term projects?
5. Are you able to follow rules and procedures?

Encourage students who answer "yes" to the majority of questions to visit a museum in their city or area and learn about possible careers. BL

READING WORKSHOP 3

But leave me the birds and the bees
Please! **3** [L]
Don't it always seem to go
That you don't know what you've got
'Til it's gone
They paved paradise
And put up a parking lot

Late last night
I heard the screen door slam
And a big yellow taxi
Took away my old man
Don't it always seem to go
That you don't know what you've got
'Til it's gone
They paved paradise
And put up a parking lot

I said
Don't it always seem to go
That you don't know what you've got
'Til it's gone
They paved paradise
And put up a parking lot

They paved paradise
And put up a parking lot [BQ]
They paved paradise
And put up a parking lot **4**

Practice the Skills

3 **Literary Element**

Theme What do the details in lines 20–22 make you think about? How do you think Mitchell feels about the use of chemicals? Use this information to discover the theme of the song.

4 **BIG Question**

What does Mitchell think about progress? Write your answer on a note card and add it to Foldable 5. Your response will help you answer the Unit Challenge.

Gridlock, 2004. Patti Mollica. Acrylic, Collection of the Artist.

English Language Coach

Idioms Students may need assistance with the term *put up.*

put up 1) offer, as for consideration, decision, or auction; 2) offer as a candidate; 3) preserve or can fruits; 4) erect or build; 5) provide lodgings; 6) to score during a sporting event

Give students the possible definitions and ask them which best fits Mitchell's use of the term. *(Mitchell uses the fourth definition of the term; "put up a parking lot" means to erect or build a parking lot.)* **EL**

Teach

L Literary Element

Theme Ask: Read the footnote explaining DDT on page 592. Why does the songwriter say "Give me spots on my apples"? *(Possible response: The songwriter would rather eat apples that have spots because of insects than apples sprayed with a harmful chemical.)* **OL** How does this opinion relate to the theme of the song? *(Possible response: It's an example of nature versus human civilization.)* **AL**

BQ BIG Question

Ask: What might the parking lot symbolize? *(Responses will vary. Students may say that the parking lot symbolizes modern convenience at the expense of nature.)* **AL** Does Mitchell believe that progress is always good? *(No, Mitchell believes that, in some cases, progress requires people to sacrifice nature.)* **OL**

Assess

Use the CheckPoint questions provided on Presentation Plus! to check for comprehension. These questions can be used with interactive response keypads for immediate student feedback.

Objectives
- Analyze theme
- Understand word structure
- Respond to text

Assess

Resources for page 594

- Selection Quick Check
- Selection and Unit Assessment
- ExamView Assessment Suite
- Interactive Tutor: Self-Assessment

Students can respond to the *After You Read* items in their Learner's Notebook or on separate sheets of paper.

Answering the BIG Question

1. Responses will vary. Students may list stagecoaches, record albums, handwritten letters, or extinct animals.
2. Students should respond with three of the four possible answers. They have replaced paradise with a parking lot, a pink hotel, a boutique, and a swinging hot spot.

Critical Thinking

3. Mitchell suggests that the trees have become almost extinct. Museums usually hold objects and/or specimens from the past.
4. The singer is protesting urban development and how people use land and resources in a way that harms Earth.

After You Read

Big Yellow Taxi

Answering the BIG Question

1. Think about the lyrics "Don't it always seem to go / That you don't know what you've got / 'Til it's gone." List some things that have disappeared or gone away because of progress.
2. **Recall** In the first stanza, or group of lines, what three things take the place of paradise?
   TIP **Right There**

Critical Thinking

3. **Infer** What does Mitchell suggest when she says "They took all the trees / And put them in a tree museum"? What do you usually find in museums?
   TIP **Author and Me**
4. **Draw Conclusions** What is the singer protesting?
   TIP **Author and Me**

Write About Your Reading

Write a letter to Joni Mitchell about your reaction to her song. Copy this chart and fill it in to get started.

Human actions	Mitchell's feelings	My feelings
Clearing land to build shops		
Cutting down forests		
Using chemicals to get better fruit		

After you fill in the chart, write your letter to Mitchell. Explain why you agree or disagree with the message of "Big Yellow Taxi."

Objectives (pp. 594–595)
Reading Respond to the text
Literature Identify literary elements: theme
Vocabulary Identify word structure: Greek and Latin word origins
Writing Respond to literature: personal letter
Grammar Use punctuation: commas in direct address, introductory phrases

Write About Your Reading

Possible response:

Dear Ms. Mitchell,

I like your song because it describes how I feel about cities. I live in a big city, and when I look out my bedroom window, I see one little tree and a couple of scrawny bushes trying to survive between cement sidewalks, pavement, and tall buildings. I agree with you that city planners build too many parking lots and streets and not enough parks and green spaces. I want to hide from all of the big, smelly yellow taxis by going high up in the mountains where there are still trees to see and air to breathe. Care to join me?

Michelle

Skills Review

Reading Skill: Responding

5. Now that you've read the poem, how did you respond to it?

   Were there some parts you felt more strongly about than others?

   What about the various elements such as tone, style, and language?

   Write a few sentences about your response to the song and some of its elements.

Literary Element: Theme

6. Which lines of the song gave you clues about the theme?
7. What is the most important clue that helped you understand the author's message?

Vocabulary Check

Write at least one synonym for each vocabulary word.

8. **paradise**
9. **boutique**
10. **English Language Coach** Review the English words that come from Greek or Latin words on page 590. Then write a sentence for each word. Use a chart like the one below.

Word from Greek or Latin	Sentence
furious	
museum	
vocabulary	
library	

Grammar Link: Commas with Introductory Words and Direct Address

- Use a comma when an introductory word or phrase begins a sentence.

  No, I don't feel like going.

  Whoops, there goes the bus I wanted.

- Use a comma after a person's name when that person is being spoken to. If the name appears in the middle of a sentence, put commas on both sides of it.

  Ms. Wilson, could you repeat that?

  I don't know, Freddie, what you're talking about.

  That just isn't at all what I meant, Bert!

- Use a comma to set off a polite term or endearment when the person is being spoken to.

  Is there anything, ma'am, that I can help you with?

  Let's try to stop arguing, honey.

Grammar Practice

Copy *only* the sentences that are incorrect, and add commas where they are needed.

11. Juanita didn't leave when the rest of us did.
12. Good grief none of this makes sense!
13. I must say that I'm not sure of the answer Mr. Burke.
14. We hoped sir that we could leave at noon.
15. Yes we can take the books to the library.
16. No one knew much about Ray or where he'd gone.

Writing Application Write three or four of the kinds of sentences used in the Grammar Practice and exchange them with a partner. See if you get each other's right.

Web Activities For eFlashcards, Selection Quick Checks, and other Web activities, go to www.glencoe.com.

Skills Review

Reading Skill: Responding

5. Responses will vary.

Literary Element: Theme

6. Responses will vary. The refrain about paradise and the examples of death to insects and birds support the theme.
7. Responses will vary. Students may say that the refrain is the most important clue.

Vocabulary Check

8. Possible response: heaven
9. Possible response: shop
10. Check students' sentences for correct use of vocabulary words.

Close

Ask students to summarize what they learned about the Big Question from the song.

Literature Online

Web Activities Have students access the Web site for interactive activities that will help them assess their understanding of the selection.

Grammar Link: Commas with Introductory Words and Direct Address

Grammar Practice

11. Correct
12. Good grief, none of this makes sense!
13. I must say that I'm not sure of the answer, Mr. Burke.
14. We hoped, sir, that we could leave at noon.
15. Yes, we can take the books to the library.
16. Correct

Focus

BELLRINGER Options

Daily Language Practice Transparency

Focus Activity Say: You have been reading about the positives and negatives of progress. Explain whether you think the good outweighs the bad, or vice versa.

Teach

W Writing

Conclusions Remind students that their reports should have three main parts: an introduction, a body, and a conclusion. **Ask:** What should a good conclusion include? *(Responses may include a summary statement, personal thoughts and observations.)* OL

Resources for page 596

- Use the Writing Workshop Organizer BLM in the Unit 5 Resource Booklet.
- Use the Grammar and Writing Workshop Transparencies, Unit 5.

WRITING WORKSHOP PART 2

Research Report

Drafting, Revising, Editing, and Presenting

ASSIGNMENT Write a research report

Purpose: To learn about a topic that interests you

Audience: Your teacher, your classmates, and others who are interested in this topic

Revising Rubric

The final draft of your research report should have

- an introduction, a body, and a conclusion
- a strong thesis statement supported with evidence and details
- a cause-and-effect text structure
- accurately documented sources
- a visual aid

Objectives (pp. 596–601)
Writing Revise your writing for key elements, style, and word choice
Listening, Speaking, and Viewing Present research report • Use visual aids • Evaluate presentations

You've done the research and the planning. Now it's time to prepare your report and share it with your classmates. Also, you'll keep a copy of it in a writing portfolio so that you and your teacher can evaluate your writing progress over time.

Drafting

Start Writing!

W

Use your notes and your outline to write the three main parts of your report—an introduction, a body, and a conclusion.

- Your **introduction** should catch readers' interest and state your thesis.
- The **body** of your report explains and supports your thesis statement. Remember that your goal is to present your own thinking and to say something new using information from your research to support your ideas. Be careful not to **plagiarize,** or present someone else's ideas as your own. Credit your sources in a style approved by your teacher.
- Your **conclusion** should summarize your main points and then extend beyond the information you've covered in your report. You may want to end with a personal reflection about your topic.

Revising

Make It Better

Experienced writers revise their work, sometimes several times. Ask yourself questions like these to figure out what changes to make.

- Does my introduction get readers' attention and include a strong, clear thesis statement?
- Have I supported my thesis statement with relevant examples and evidence? Have I organized my ideas in a clear and logical order?
- Have I used words like *however, therefore,* and *but* to show the relationship between ideas?
- Have I included citations when necessary? (See pages R23–R24)
- Did I clearly use accurate, reliable evidence?
- Did I write my bibliography the way my teacher asked?
- Does my conclusion restate my thesis in a fresh, interesting way? Does it help others understand the importance of the topic?

Additional Support

Differentiated Instruction

Outlines To ensure their reports are focused and well-organized, have students use their outlines from Writing Workshop Part 1 to check their reports. Have students review their drafts, placing checkmarks next to each point they listed in their outlines. If students find facts they did not include in their outlines, advise them to think about whether the facts support their thesis statements or topic. If a fact is not related to either of these elements, it probably is unnecessary. When students are satisfied they have adequately supported their theses, remind them that they will need to review their reports to make sure they flow logically and smoothly. OL

Applying Good Writing Traits

Conventions

One of the best parts of writing is that you get to express ideas. Writing lets you share information and feelings about any topic you want. Sometimes the ideas are yours; sometimes they're other people's ideas

What Are Ideas?

- Ideas are the building blocks of thinking and writing. When you write, you use medium and small ideas to build your big, or main, ideas.
- A piece or writing can have a number of main ideas in it. Each paragraph may have a main idea or the entire selections may have a main idea.
- Medium ideas are important details. They help explain the big ideas.
- Small ideas–things like examples, charts, or graphs–are minor details. Small ideas support medium ideas.

W

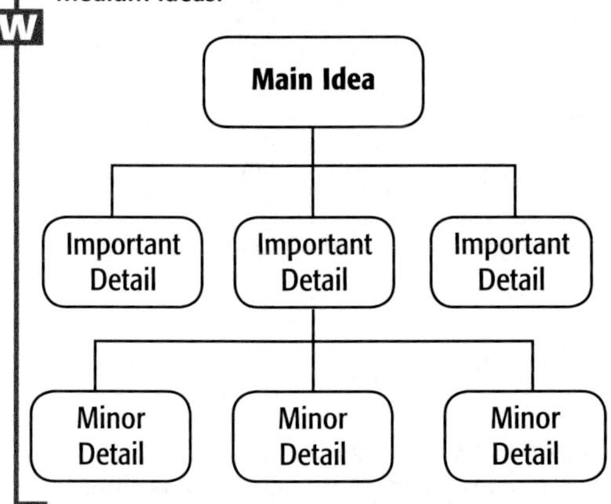

Why Are They Important?

Sharing your ideas is the point of writing your paper. Your writing must be clear so readers can easily understand your message.

Analyzing Art
"It hit me like a bolt of lightning!" That might be how this man would explain the source of his idea. Have you ever been "hit" with an idea? How do you find the big ideas in what you read? How do you get them for your writing?

How Do I Use Ideas in My Writing?

- Focus your writing on a single narrow topic. If your topic is too big and general, you'll end up trying to write about too many things. Your topic should be specific so you can write about a few ideas in depth.
- Clearly state the main idea. One way to make your main ideas clear is to start each paragraph with a topic sentence (a sentence that tells the key point).
- Include interesting ideas and details (medium-size ideas) to explain your main idea. Then select minor details (small ideas) that explain those.

Write to Learn After you finish the draft of your research report, read it aloud to yourself. Does your report have an introduction that clearly states your thesis? Did you include the important details that support and explain your thesis? Did you include the minor details that add interest to your report?

Teach

W Writing

Ideas Say: Your research report should contain medium ideas and smaller details that help build your main idea. Before you do any more revisions, copy this graphic organizer into your Learner's Notebook. Fill in the organizer with the ideas and details from your report. Make sure your ideas and details support your main idea in a logical way. **AS**

Differentiated Instruction

Using a Word Processor Students who wish to type their reports may benefit from the following tips:

- Use **spell checker** to find misspellings. Be careful to check for words the computer won't catch, such as *their* and *they're* and *its* and *it's.*
- Use **grammar checker** to find possible errors and suggested revisions.
- Use the **thesaurus** to replace inappropriate or overused words.
- Use **search and replace** to correct something that occurs several times.

Remind students that these computer tools cannot replace their own careful reading and judgment. **OL**

Objectives
- Revise your writing for key elements, style, and word choice
- Analyze main ideas and supporting details
- Write compositions with an introduction, a body, and a conclusion

Teach

W Writing

Publishing Before displaying research reports for all to see, have students use the editing checklist on this page to check their reports for proper spelling and grammar. OL

LSV Listening, Speaking, and Viewing

Presenting Students may enjoy finding out which fonts are easier to read than others. Have students work in pairs to click through the fonts in a word processing software. Have them list five fonts that are easy to read and five fonts that are more difficult to read. AS

Literature Online

Writing Models Have students access the Web site for an additional and interactive Writing Workshop-based student model.

WRITING WORKSHOP PART 2

Literature Online

Writing Models For models and other writing activities, go to www.glencoe.com.

Editing

Finish It Up

Now it's time to get your report ready to share with others. You can use the **Editing Checklist** below to spot your errors.

Editing Checklist

W
- ☑ Pronouns are in the correct form and agree with their antecedents.
- ☑ The report is free of sentence fragments.
- ☑ All sentences are punctuated correctly.
- ☑ All words are spelled correctly.

Writing Tip

Presenting If you type your report on a computer, choose a font that is easy to read. Use different font sizes to make titles or section headings clear. LSV

Presenting

Show It Off

Follow these steps to create a library shelf of research reports.

1. Make a fresh copy of your report. Neatly rewrite your report or print a clean copy.
2. If you haven't already done so, create a graphic to help present your information. Write a caption to clearly explain any photographs, illustrations, maps, or charts you use. The caption should be a brief sentence that tells the purpose or content of the graphic.
3. Put your report in a binder and print the title of your report on the spine and cover of the binder. You may also decide to put an illustration on the front of your binder.
4. Work with your classmates to give each report a number on the spine of the binder.
5. As a class, write down the topic of each report and its number on a sheet of paper.
6. Alphabetize the list.
7. Type or write a clean copy of the list and keep it near the library of reports.
8. Put the research reports on a shelf and post the index nearby. You may find the information in the reports useful for other class assignments. Or you may just want to read some of the reports to learn about topics that interest you.

Additional Support

Differentiated Instruction

Formal vs. Informal Writing

Have students tell whether the sentences are formal or informal. Have them revise the informal sentences to make them more formal.

1. Lots of people get a kick out of swimming with manatees. *(Informal. Swimming with manatees is a popular pastime for many.)*
2. The number of manatees in Florida has declined. *(Formal)*
3. Manatees get killed by boats all the time. *(Informal. Manatees are often killed by boats.)*

Have students check their reports for informal language. OL

Writer's Model

Active Writing Model

The Endangered Manatee

When Christopher Columbus sailed to the New World, he thought he saw mermaids, but they didn't look like the ones he'd seen in paintings. He wrote in his journal that they were "not so beautiful as they are painted, since in some ways they have a face like a man" (Ellis 88). Columbus was most likely describing West Indian manatees. These gentle gray-brown sea mammals have hairy snouts, and they weigh about a thousand pounds.

Manatees still live in Florida's warm waters, but possibly not for much longer. The number of manatees in the region has been declining. As of July 2000, only about twenty-four hundred manatees remained (Sawicki 6). Sadly, humans are responsible for the decline of the manatees. Boats, canal locks, and pollution are the top three causes of manatee injuries and deaths.

The main cause of manatee deaths in recent years has been collisions with boats ("Manatee Mortality"). Manatees swim deep in the water, but they must rise to the surface to breathe. Sometimes they swim into the path of a motorboat or another water craft. Because they are slow swimmers, they cannot get out of the way.

Even if manatees could get out of the way, they might not know which direction they should swim. Scientists believe that manatees cannot hear low-frequency sounds, such as the hum of a motorboat. As a result, manatees are often hit and killed or injured by boats. The Mote Marine Laboratory estimates that 80 percent of Florida's manatees have been hit at least once by marine craft (Koeppel 68).

The second leading cause of manatee deaths is accidents involving floodgates and canal locks ("Manatee Mortality"). These underwater walls are raised and lowered to control water levels. When they are raised, the rushing water pulls in anything nearby. Some manatees drown because they cannot get to the surface to breathe. Others get caught between gates and are crushed (Clark 37).

The writer uses a two-paragraph introduction. The first paragraph includes an interesting anecdote to get readers' attention.

W

The writer tells an effect in the introduction and then tells the causes in the body of the report.

A strong thesis statement expresses a point of view and establishes the focus of the report.

WRITING WORKSHOP PART 2

Teach

W Writing

Research Reports Tell students to use the Writing Rubric on page 552 to evaluate the Writer's Model of a research report on this page. **Ask:**

- **Did the introduction capture your attention?** *(Possible response: The anecdote about Christopher Columbus was interesting and made me want to read more.)*
- **Do you think the thesis statement clearly presents a problem?** *(Most students will believe the writer has clearly presented the problem that humans are responsible for manatee deaths.)*
- **What types of support does the writer use to back up the thesis?** *(Possible response: The writer includes facts, examples, and causes and effects to back up the thesis.)* **OL**

Reading in the Real World

College A report based on others' ideas should include a Works Cited list. There are many different styles available, but the following rules usually apply:

- Alphabetize the list according to the last name of the first author listed.
- Underline or italicize the titles of books, magazines, and periodicals.
- Put the titles of magazine articles in quotation marks.
- Include the month and year of articles.

Remind students of the importance of giving credit to others for their ideas. In college, plagiarizing is considered academic misconduct and may result in punishment. **AS**

Objectives

- Write research reports using the writing process
- Write compositions with an introduction, a body, and a conclusion
- Present writing effectively
- Create a Works Cited list
- Use relevant graphics

Teach

W Writing

Research Reports Have students continue to evaluate the Writer's Model of a research report. **Ask:**

- What do you think of the quotation by Judith Valle? Do you think the writer should have included this quotation? *(Possible response: The quotation makes a strong statement about environmental policies. I think the writer was right to include it.)* **AL**
- Do you think the Works Cited list is easy to read? If not, what changes would you make to it? *(Possible response: It is a bit difficult to read. It might be easier to read if it was in a larger font or if it was double spaced.)* **OL**

Assess/Close

Ask students to share their thoughts about why progress is not always good. Have them use information from their research to support their thoughts. You might want to start the discussion with your own thoughts about progress.

Objects that people put in the water can also injure or kill manatees. For example, crab fishermen set buoys on the water to warn boaters of the crab traps below. The traps and buoys are attached by wires that can tangle around a manatee's flippers. Often, a manatee is injured as it tries to free itself, leading to infection and death (Clark 35). Manatees have also choked to death on fishhooks and garbage that people have thrown in the water.

The writer supports main points with facts and examples.

Environmental laws are supposed to protect the manatee from all these dangers. But according to Judith Valle of the Save the Manatee Club, enforcement of those laws is currently "pathetic" (Sawicki 6). What can we do to save the manatee? We can begin by putting an end to water pollution. We can avoid boating in areas where manatees commonly swim. And we can invest in new technologies that will help keep manatees safe. Scientists are working on warning devices that could be attached to boats and canal locks that would keep manatees away. These devices send out high-frequency sounds that manatees can hear (Eliot). If people are responsible for the decline of manatees, then we must also be responsible for their ultimate survival.

The conclusion ties together the main points and extends the points by suggesting possible solutions.

The writer credits the sources of information and ideas used in the report.

W

Works Cited

A list of works cited tells readers the sources of the information used in the report and gives readers all of the information needed to locate the sources.

Clark, Margarett Goff. The Vanishing Manatee. New York: Cobblehill, 1990

Eliot, John L. "Deaf to Danger: Manatees Can't Hear Boats." National Geographic Feb. 2000: Earth Almanac.

Ellis, Richard. Monsters of the Sea. New York: Knopf, 1994.

Koeppel, Dan. "Kiss of the Manatee." Travel Holiday Feb. 1999: 66-69.

"Manatee Mortality." Save the Manatee Club. Save the Manatee Club, Inc. 31 Oct. 2003 <http://www.savethemanatee.org/mort.htm>.

Sawicki, Stephen. "Manatee Protectors Turn to the Courts." Animals July 2000: 6.

Additional Support

Reading in the Real World

Career Students who enjoyed conducting research for their reports might like to work in one of the vast variety of fields that requires research. Journalists, medical researchers, librarians, museum employees, and writers of reference materials all conduct research as part of their jobs. Have students choose one of these careers that sounds intriguing and look online to determine the qualifications necessary to work in the field. **OL**

Listening, Speaking, and Viewing

Oral Presentation

Often, the final step of doing research is sharing what you've learned with others. Giving an oral presentation is a great way to do just that.

Analyzing Cartoons
Calvin's oral presentation is within the five-minute limit, but it barely has any content! Avoid the awkward situation he's in by preparing ahead of time.

What Is an Oral Presentation?

The term *oral presentation* usually refers to a formal speech given to a group of people.

Why Is It Important?

- An oral presentation gives the speaker a chance to share interesting and important information with a group of people.
- An oral presentation gives the listener a chance to learn about a topic without having to research it.

How Do I Give an Oral Presentation?

Preparing an oral presentation is similar to writing a report. Use the writing process to develop the content of your presentation. Your presentation should have a thesis statement that is supported with evidence and have three main parts—that's right—an introduction, a body, and a conclusion. The tips below will help you give a great oral presentation. **LSV1**

- Keep your purpose and your audience in mind. Listeners can't grab a dictionary if they don't know what a word means, so choose your words carefully and explain any terms that your audience might not know.
- Prepare note cards with your main points. Glance at these notes while you are speaking to keep track of where you are in your speech.
- Prepare a visual aid (a graphic) to show while you're speaking. Make sure your graphic is big enough for your audience to see. Use a slide projector or Power Point presentation for electronic graphics. Or make copies of the graphics and hand them out before you begin to speak. **LSV2**
- Practice! Then practice some more—in front of a friend or a family member. Ask for feedback on how to improve your presentation. If there's a time limit for your presentation, time your report to make sure you're within the limit.
- When you give your oral presentation, try to relax. Speak slowly and clearly and make eye contact with your listeners.

Write and Speak to Learn Use the guidelines above to give an oral presentation based on your research report. Be sure your ideas are well-organized so your listeners can follow your points. Visual aids and vivid descriptions can help your audience picture what you're talking about.

Develop standards to evaluate your own and others' oral presentations. As you listen to others' presentations, take notes about what makes a good presentation and how you can improve your presentation skills.

LSV1 Listening, Speaking, and Viewing

Oral Presentations Ask: How are oral presentations similar to and different from written presentations? *(Possible response: Both require careful planning and organization, but oral presentations require even more careful pacing and word choice in order to ensure that audience members can keep up with and understand the speaker.)* **AL**

LSV2 Listening, Speaking, and Viewing

Visual Aids Say: There are many different ways to create visuals for your reports. You can draw pictures, take or find photographs, create posters, make charts or graphs, or cut out illustrations from magazines. With a partner, brainstorm the most appropriate visuals for your report. **OL**

Differentiated Instruction

Using Your Voice and Body Good speakers use their voice *and* body to bring their speech to life and engage their audience.

- Speak loudly enough so you can be heard by everyone in the room. Keep your head held high so that your voice carries.
- Use a friendly, confident tone of voice to keep your listeners intrigued.
- Stand up straight, but don't be too stiff.
- Try gesturing with subtle arm movements to emphasize important points.
- Remember to make eye contact with your audience. If you look detached, your audience will lose interest. **AS**

Objectives
- Write research reports using the writing process
- Write compositions with an introduction, a body, and a conclusion
- Present writing effectively
- Use relevant graphics
- Deliver informational presentations
- Use visual aids
- Evaluate presentations

Identifying Problem and Solution

UNIT 5

Objectives covered in this workshop:

- Recognize problem and solution structures

Teaching Students to Identify Problem and Solution

Why Is It Important?

- Many informational texts are written around common text structures (cause-effect, sequence, description, and problem-solution); teaching students to identify the structure helps them comprehend the text.
- Problem-solution text structure is one of the most common structures found in scientific, technical, and social sciences texts, so teaching strategies for identifying it and helping students use it to understand texts are particularly helpful.

How to Help Students Get It

- Emphasize the importance of understanding text structure in comprehending texts; review the common structures with a focus on problem-solution
- Provide guided practice in which students can skim and scan various texts—for example, photocopies of text pages, and mark problems with one notation and solutions with another (underlining in color; using notion marks like "P" [problem] and "S" [solution]
- Provide guides for students to use in independent reading that help them to use the text structure; for example, see the From Your Authors problem-solution example of text structure pre-maps

Reading to Answer the Big Question

Fireproofing Forests

This TIME article describes the efforts of environmentalists to stop devastating forest fires. Students will find out how people are discovering ways to manage nature that protect both forests and communities.

Missing!

The frog population in Costa Rica is declining. This informational text describes how scientists are searching for answers to this dilemma.

Bigfoot's Grandpa

This poem describes the efforts of one old man to try to save the lives a few small toads trying to cross a busy road. He takes time out of his own busy schedule to help creatures who are victims of human progress.

Workshop Resources

Pacing (Days) Standard	Block	Lesson	Student Materials	Teacher Resources
1		Key Skill Lesson: Identifying Problem and Solution	Key Reading Skills Practice English Language Coach	Bellringer Options Transparencies Read Aloud, Think Aloud Transparencies Presentation Plus!
2		"Fireproofing and Forests"	Literary Analysis Transparencies Glencoe Online Selection Vocabulary Development Academic Vocabulary Development English Language Coach Active Reading Graphic Organizer Literary Analysis StudentWorks Plus Online Student Edition Literature Classics Selection and Unit Assessments	Literary and Text Analysis Transparencies Puzzlemaker Skill Level Up! BookLink 3 Assessment by Learning Objective (Diagnostic and Formative) Interactive Tutor Self-Assessment TeacherWorks Plus
2		"Missing' and 'Birdfoot's Grandpa"	Glencoe Online Selection Vocabulary Development Academic Vocabulary Development English Language Coach Active Reading Graphic Organizer Literary Analysis StudentWorks Plus Online Student Edition Literature Classics Selection and Unit Assessments	Literary and Text Analysis Transparencies Puzzlemaker Skill Level Up! BookLink 3 Assessment by Learning Objective (Diagnostic and Formative) Interactive Tutor Self-Assessment TeacherWorks Plus

Keys for Unit Resource

- Blackline Master
- Workbook
- Supplemental Text
- CD-ROM
- DVD
- Transparency
- Web-based
- Fast Files

Level Appropriate Code

AS = Activities for all students
AL = Activities for students working above grade level
OL = Activities for students working at grade level
BL = Activities for students working below grade level
EL = Activities for English language learners

Focus

BELLRINGER Options

- Selection Focus Transparency
- Daily Language Practice Transparency

Focus Activity Say: Think about a problem that you recently faced. How did you solve the problem? *(Responses will vary.)*

Teach

R Reading Skill

Identifying Problem and Solution Say: Many nonfiction articles discuss problems and solutions. How can you tell whether the structure of an article is problem/solution? *(Possible response: The writer may begin the article by describing a problem facing society and propose one or more than one way to solve the problem.)* OL

Skills Focus

You will practice using these skills when you read the following selections:

- "Fireproofing the Forests," p. 606
- "Missing!" p. 616
- "Birdfoot's Grampa," p. 619

Reading

- Identifying problem and solution

Literature

- Understanding description

Vocabulary

- Understanding content-area words

Writing/Grammar

- Using commas

Skill Lesson

Identifying Problem and Solution

Learn It!

What Is It? Everything has a structure. The structure of a building is the collection of beams, walls, and floors that hold it together. The classes you have at school form the structure of your day. Good writing has structure, too. Problem and solution is a structure that writers use to organize information. First they introduce a R problem. Then they give solutions to the problem.

- Complicated or difficult issues can have more than one problem or solution.
- A difficult problem may not have an easy solution.
- Some solutions may be implied, or not stated directly.

Analyzing Cartoons
One of Curtis's problems is that he's extremely bored. How does his mother's suggested solution solve the problem? (And what problem remains unsolved?)

Objectives (pp. 602–603)
Reading Identify problem and solution

Additional Support

Literature Focus Lesson

Problems and Solutions in Comic Strips Because of their brevity, comic strips can be useful tools for explaining problem-and-solution structure. In most comics, the first box (or boxes) introduce(s) the problem, and the problem is solved in the remaining few boxes. In the comic strip featured on page 602, Curtis states his problem in the first box. Encourage students to read other comic strips, circling any box or text that states a problem and putting a star by any box or text that states a solution. OL

Why Is It Important? Problems and solutions are common parts of life. When you solve problems, you learn how to overcome conflicts or struggles. Then you use what you learned to help you with future problems. The problem and solution structure is a great tool for writers and readers. It shows how conflicts and obstacles are overcome. It helps you understand what's happening, why it's happening, and what is being done about it.

Literature Online

Study Central Visit www.glencoe.com and click on Study Central to review identifying problems and solutions.

How Do I Do It? As you read, look for the section that tells the problem. What is the author concerned about? Underline the problem. Keep reading to find a solution. Look for words and phrases such as *need, attempt, help, can,* and *will.* What does the author say will help the problem? Draw two lines under the solution or solutions. Here's how one student used the problem and solution structure to better understand the article "Conserving Resources."

> Resources such as petroleum and metals are important for making the products you use every day at home and in school. For example, petroleum is used to produce plastics and fuel. Minerals are used to make automobiles and bicycles. R However, if these resources are not used carefully, the environment can be damaged. Conservation is the careful use of earth materials to reduce damage to the environment. Conservation can prevent future shortages of some materials.

This paragraph tells about possible problems with resources. If we don't use resources carefully, we can damage the environment. The writer says that the solution is conservation. If we conserve, we are less likely to harm the environment or run out of resources.

Practice It!

Preview the article "Fireproofing the Forests." Look at the title, headings, and pictures. What do you think the problem will be? In your Learner's Notebook, write your ideas. Then write possible solutions to the problem.

Use It!

As you read "Fireproofing the Forests," review the problems and solutions you predicted. If you need to, update your predictions as you read the article.

Teach

Literature Online

Study Central Have students access the Web site to review identifying problem and solution and to complete a related activity.

R Reading Skill

Identifying Problem and Solution **Say:** Review the excerpt from "Conserving Resources" in the *How Do I Do It?* section. What details in the article show that careless use of resources is a problem? *(The author notes that careless use of resources can damage the environment and lead to shortages of some resource materials.)* **OL** How might the writer of this article encourage people to conserve resources? *(Possible response: The writer could tell people how their lives will change if the environment is harmed.)* **AL**

Resources for page 603

- Use Reading Skills Transparency in *Read Aloud, Think Aloud,* Unit 5, to help students practice identifying problem and solution.

Differentiated Instruction

Using Graphic Organizers To help students identify problems and solutions as they read, suggest that they use one of the graphic organizers shown. Tell students to complete the graphic organizers as they read the article. **BL**

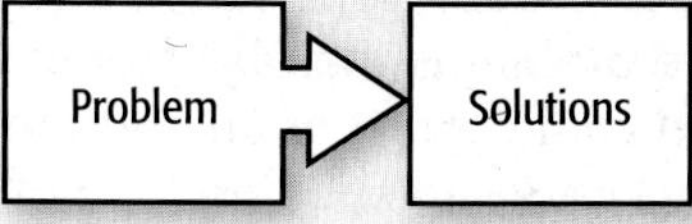

Problem	Actions/Events That Led to the Problem	Possible Solutions

Objectives

- Identify problem and solution
- Activate prior knowledge to increase understanding
- Use graphic organizers

Before You Read

Fireproofing the Forests

More About the Author

J. Madeleine Nash was always interested in science. As a child, she watched with fascination as a hurricane passed through her North Carolina hometown. She also vividly recalls her mother's story of surviving a tornado and credits it with leading to her special love of *The Wizard of Oz* and her wish to travel like Dorothy to faraway places. Nash's travels to cover developments in science and technology have fulfilled her wish. Her stories have taken her all over the world and won her numerous awards.

Meet the Author

J. Madeleine Nash is a science writer for *TIME* magazine. Nash gets to combine her interests in weather, history, and traveling to faraway places. During her travels, she learned about a weather phenomenon called El Niño, which affects weather around the world. She wrote a book about it titled *El Niño: Unlocking the Secrets of the Master Weather-Maker.*

Author Search For more about J. Madeleine Nash, go to www.glencoe.com.

Objectives (pp. 604–611)
Reading Identify problem and solution • Make connections from text to self
Literature Identify literary elements: description
Vocabulary Recognize and understand word structure

Vocabulary Preview

V

thrive (thryv) *v.* to grow with good force and energy **(p. 606)** *Forests can thrive if they are managed well.*

looms (loomz) *v.* appears as a threat or danger; form of the verb *loom* **(p. 607)** *The threat of fire looms over our forests.*

debate (dih BAYT) *n.* a discussion that involves contrasting opinions **(p. 607)** *A long-running debate continues over how to create healthy forests.*

restore (rih STOR) *v.* to bring back into existence or to an original condition; renew **(p. 607)** *It will be difficult to restore forests that have burned.*

interference (in tur FEER uns) *n.* the act of getting in the way and slowing normal progress or development **(p. 609)** *Without human interference, forests change naturally.*

English Language Coach

Word Structure You've looked at base words, suffixes, and prefixes. Some words use both prefixes and suffixes. Look at this example:

Base word	With suffix	With prefix and suffix	With prefix and 2 suffixes
truth	truthful	untruthful	untruthfulness

The word *reconstruction* has one prefix and one suffix. The base word is *construct,* which means "to build or make." The suffix *-ion* turns the verb *construct* into a noun or an adjective. The prefix *re-* means "again." So, *reconstruction* means "something built or made again."

In the next selection, you'll see words such as *overhanging* and *unlogged.* Look at the word *unlogged.* What do you know about the prefix *un-*? It means "not." What about *logged*? You may not know this, but *logged* is a word that means "having had its trees cut down." So, *unlogged* must describe a part of the forest where the trees haven't been cut down.

On Your Own Define the word *overhanging* by defining its prefix and base word.

V Vocabulary

Context Clues Say: One way to learn and remember the vocabulary words is to study the words in context. For each vocabulary word, write a sentence that includes hints about the meaning of the word. You could include a definition, a synonym, or an explanation of the word in your sentence. *(Responses will vary.)* OL

Additional Support

Literature Online

Author Search To expand students' appreciation of J. Madeleine Nash, have them access the Web site for additional information and resources.

Literature Focus Lesson

Nonfiction Explain to students that although the problem-and-solution structure is fairly common in nonfiction writing—especially in newspaper and magazine articles—it is not always clear-cut. Many problems have more than one solution, and solutions often bring unexpected consequences and problems of their own. As students read "Fireproofing the Forests," ask them to note the central problem the article explores as well as the solution it proposes. In addition, stress that students should note any possible problems that the proposed solution could cause or any reasons why the proposed solution might be unsuccessful. OL

Skills Preview

Key Reading Skill: Identifying Problem and Solution

Before you read the article, think about the following questions:

- What problems do forest fires cause?
- How can people solve the problem of forest fires?
- Why might eliminating fires cause other problems?

Write to Learn Write your answers in your Learner's Notebook. Revise your answers as you read.

Key Literary Element: Description

Why would you describe a movie scene to a friend? You want him or her to see what you saw. Writers use description to help you visualize things, or see them in your mind. Descriptions make people, places, and actions seem real. Details in descriptions help you see, hear, smell, taste, and feel.

As you read, use these tips to help you understand description:

- Look for details that explain an idea.
  What do these details make you see in your mind? How do they make you feel about the topic?
- Look for details that appeal to your five senses.
  What words help you see, feel, hear, smell, or taste?
- Think about why the author is using description.
  What would you think about the object or topic if the author didn't describe it?

Partner Talk With a partner, discuss the following sentence. What does the description of the forest make you see in your mind?

In the spaces between the trees, where the sun reaches, grasses and wildflowers thrive.

Interactive Literary Elements Handbook
To review or learn more about the literary elements, go to www.glencoe.com.

Get Ready to Read

Connect to the Reading

Think of some ways that people manage the natural resources of your city or town. Do people cut down trees to make room for more buildings or to keep them from damaging property? Do people remove animals from places where they may cause problems? As you read the article, think about the problems the author discusses.

Small Group Work Does nature cause problems in your homes or communities? Discuss with your group how you and other people deal with these problems.

Build Background

"Fireproofing the Forests" discusses fires in the ponderosa pines of Arizona and New Mexico, including Coconino National Forest.

- Ponderosa pines are very tall pine trees that are used for lumber.
- Without regular fires, these forests grow thick stands of young trees called "dog-hair" thickets.

Set Purposes for Reading

BIG Question Read "Fireproofing the Forests" to find out how people manage nature to protect forests and communities.

Set Your Own Purpose What else would you like to learn from the selection to help you answer the Big Question? Write your own purpose on a note card and add it to Foldable 5.

Keep Moving
Use these skills as you read the following selection.

Reading in the Real World

Career Explain to students that journalists writing about problems or advances in science and technology must understand not only the events they are covering but also any related background information and history. For example, when writing "Fireproofing the Forests," J. Madeleine Nash probably had to research forest ecology and conservation. Ask students to imagine that they are journalists assigned to cover an environmental group's protest against controlled burning as a solution to forest fires. As a class, generate a list of questions that would guide students' research for this story, such as "What is controlled burning?" and "Why is the group against it?" OL

Teach

R Reading Skill

Identifying Problem and Solution Say: You will read that human activity is one of the causes of forest fires. Can you think of other environmental problems that have been caused by people? *(Possible responses: People have caused problems with the ozone layer, acid rain, and global warming.)* OL

L Literary Element

Description Say: Write a paragraph that describes your favorite room at home. Include at least one descriptive detail for each of the senses of sight, hearing, smell, and touch. *(Responses will vary.)* OL

CheckPoint

Use the CheckPoint questions provided on Presentation Plus! to check students' understanding of identifying problem and solution. These questions can be used with interactive response keypads for immediate student feedback.

Literature Online

Interactive Literary Elements Handbook Have students access the Web site to improve their understanding of description.

Objectives

- Identify problem and solution
- Make connections from text to self
- Identify literary elements: description
- Recognize and understand word structure

Teach

R Reading Skill

Identifying Problem and Solution **Ask:** How does the writer introduce the problem and solution? *(Beside the title, the writer includes a question explaining the problem and proposing a possible solution. In sentences below the title, she also includes information about solutions that don't work.)* **OL** What is your opinion of this introduction? *(I like it. I think it clearly states the main question of the article and tells readers what to expect up front.)* **AL**

L Literary Element

Description **Say:** The first paragraph describes a forest that has been successfully thinned. To which of the five senses does this description most appeal? *(This description appeals mainly to the sense of sight.)* **OL** Why might a writer choose to use detailed description in a nonfiction article? *(Possible response: Description helps get readers involved in the topic.)* **AL**

Readability Scores
Dale-Chall: 7
DRP: 66
Lexile: 1230

TIME

Fireproofing the Forests

Should the U.S. Forest Service, to protect communities and restore healthy forests, approve tree thinning on a huge scale?

Logging doesn't work. Neither, in the long run, does fire fighting. As fires annually threaten western forests, the debate over a radical form of tree surgery heats up

By J. MADELEINE NASH

On the outskirts of Flagstaff, Arizona, Wally Covington drives his pickup truck through a dense forest of ponderosa pines. At last he arrives at the spot where, in 1993, he and his co-workers took chain saws to hundreds of trees no bigger than telephone poles. They carted off the trunks and branches and then purposely set controlled fires to clear away the smaller trees. As a result, today this area is a beautiful woodland, partly shaded by the overhanging branches of 300-year-old trees. In the spaces between the trees, where the sun reaches, grasses and wildflowers **thrive**. 1

This is the way the ponderosa pine forests of the American Southwest used to look, says Covington, director of the Ecological Restoration Institute at Northern Arizona University. And it is the way they could look again if they

1 Key Literary Element

Description In the first paragraph, the writer describes what the forest looks like after the fires. Make a list of the words that help you see the forest in your mind.

Vocabulary

thrive (thryv) *v.* to grow with good force and energy

Additional Support

Differentiated Instruction

Illustrating the Problem After students have read the article, ask them to draw or paint pictures of successfully thinned woodland. Then discuss with students the role of forests in our environment. Ask students what would happen if uncontrollable fires were to destroy the forests. Have students draw or paint pictures depicting their vision of the landscape if fires destroyed most of our forests. Invite students to share their pictures and to point out important differences between the healthy forest and the deforested landscape. **OL**

were thinned, or the small trees were cut down to make room for the larger trees. But time is running out, he fears, because for more than a century these forests have not been managed correctly, and as a result, they—along with the communities around their edges—are threatened by uncontrollable fires.

Every year, it seems, the threat posed by fire **looms** larger. Some of the most intense wildfires in U.S. history have taken place in the last couple of decades. These uncontrollable fires have burned millions of acres of forests, killed numerous civilians[1] and firefighters, and burned thousands of homes. R1

So it is no surprise that these fires are fueling an intense **debate**. Should the U.S. Forest Service, to protect communities and **restore** healthy forests, approve tree thinning on a huge scale? If it does, what size trees ought to be thinned and in what sorts of forests? And if it does not, what are the options? 2

Some environmental groups fear that thinning might encourage logging, or the cutting down of large trees. They have taken the position that cutting down small trees is all right only in parts of the forests near areas where people live. Covington and others, however, believe that thinning, if done responsibly, is perhaps our last chance to restore health to many of our forests. But even Covington says that the science that supports thinning is still developing. R2

WATER BEARER: A scooper aircraft picks up lake water to drop on a fire in Glacier National Park in Montana.

AP Wide World

2 Key Reading Skill

Identifying Problem and Solution Reread the previous two paragraphs. What is the problem facing the U.S. Forest Service? What is the suggested solution? Write the problem and the suggested solution in your Learner's Notebook.

The Case for Thinning

For centuries fires have swept through the ponderosa pine forests of Arizona and New Mexico on average once or twice a decade, killing young trees but not larger trees. Scientists

1. Here, ***civilians*** refers to anyone who is not a firefighter.

Vocabulary

looms (loomz) *v.* appears as a threat or danger

debate (dih BAYT) *n.* a discussion that involves contrasting opinions

restore (rih STOR) *v.* to bring back into existence or to an original condition; renew

Teach

R1 Reading Skill

Identifying Problem and Solution Say: According to the article, the threat posed by forest fires looms larger than ever. Why? *(In the past few decades, millions of acres of forests have been burned, civilians and firefighters have died, and thousands of homes have been destroyed.)* **BL** **Ask:** What solution is the U.S. Forest Service thinking of approving? *(thinning)* **OL**

R2 Reading Skill

Identifying Problem and Solution Say: Sometimes the solutions to problems can cause more problems. What problem do environmental groups think thinning will cause? *(They think thinning might encourage logging.)* **BL**

Differentiated Instruction

Following the Debate Explain to students that a debate allows people to voice their opinions. Tell students that part of "Fireproofing the Forests" involves the debate about thinning forests. Draw a two-column chart on the board. Label the left column "Arguments for Thinning." Label the right column "Arguments Against Thinning." Ask students to volunteer entries for each column, and record their responses on the board. *(Arguments for Thinning: protects homes, communities, and people; restores healthy forests. Arguments Against Thinning: encourages logging; unknown effects on ecology.)* Encourage students to think about which side of the argument Nash seems to favor. **OL**

Objectives
- Analyze problems and solutions
- Understand description

READING WORKSHOP 4

Teach

R Reading Skill

Review Reviewing Ask: Why is a fire history a useful tool for scientists? *(Possible response: It helps them determine when fires occurred and how trees were affected.)* OL

EL Language Coach

Word Structure Say: The word *overgraze* has two parts: *over-* and *graze.* The base word *graze* means "to eat grasses and other plants." The prefix *over-* means "too much." What does *overgraze* mean? *(To overgraze is to graze too much so that there is little vegetation left.)* EL What happened when livestock were allowed to overgraze grass and plants? *(With the grasses and small plants eaten, small, beneficial forest fires were not able to burn.)* OL

Viewing the Photo

Say: Tom Swetnam has put numbers and labels on the surface of the pine tree section in the photo. What do you think these labels and numbers indicate? *(Possible response: Swetnam may have labeled the fire scars on the tree. He may also have marked the tree rings with dates to show the age of the tree in a particular year.)* OL

know this because these fires have left a series of healed-over burn scars in the trees' tissue beneath the bark. By dating the scars left in tree rings, Tom Swetnam of the University of Arizona and his co-workers reconstructed a fire history of southwestern forests that extends back to the 14th century. And the most striking discovery they made is that beginning in the late 1800s, there was a marked drop-off in the number of fires. R

Why did the number of fires decrease at that time? Why do we have so many uncontrollable fires today? First, sheep, cattle, and other livestock were allowed to **overgraze** the grasses and other plants in the forests. Without these plants, ground fires were not able to spread and to burn litter, release nutrients,[2] and thin out saplings.[3] Then came decades of logging of large trees along with improved ways to fight fires. The makeup of the forest changed so that hundreds of small trees now crowd into acre-size plots,[4] where only a few dozen large trees used to thrive. The result is that millions of acres of southwestern forestland are packed with enough wood to fuel wildfires of unequaled fury and destruction. 3

2. ***Nutrients*** are substances that plants and animals get from food to stay alive and healthy.
3. ***Saplings*** are very young trees.
4. Small pieces of land are called ***plots.***

3 English Language Coach

EL **Word Structure** Find the word **overgraze**. What does *over* mean? What does *graze* mean? Combine the prefix and base word to figure out the meaning.

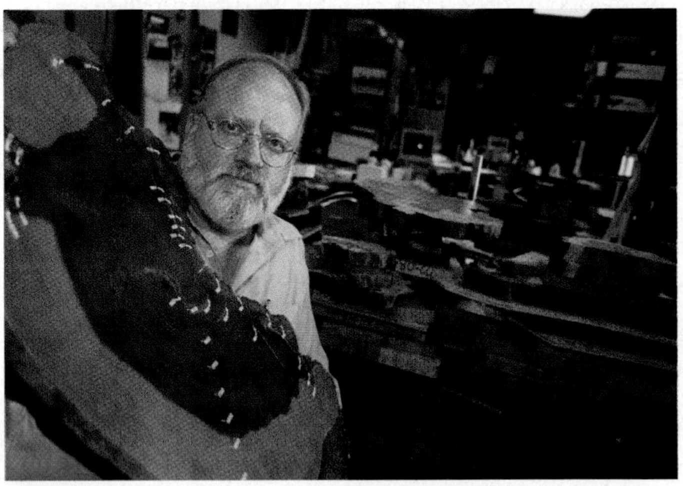

William F. Campbell/Getty Images

RING COUNTER: Tom Swetnam's pine has fire scars dating from 1583.

Additional Support

Differentiated Instruction

Tree Dating Point out that Swetnam and others use tree trunks to date and learn about the history of trees. Tell students to use print or electronic encyclopedias to find out more about tree dating. Have them find images showing the rings in the trunk of a tree. Encourage them to learn about how different types of trees are dated, using the rings as a guide. Ask them to determine what differences in the width of tree rings tell about ancient climates. OL

The situation has reached thepoint at which some experts are convinced that even controlled fires pose serious dangers to large, mature trees. More than 2 years ago, in fact, Covington and two Forest Service researchers experimented with the use of controlled fires in Cocino National Forest in Arizona, but they did not get the res s they expected. The clumps of young trees the scientists ped to kill survived, and the old-growth trees they ho d to save died.

Why? In the absence of fire for so long, to uch fuel, in the form of dropped needles and branches, ha ollected at the bases of the largest trees. Yet not enough ti had gone by to allow a similar buildup of fuel beneath the ller trees. As a consequence,[5] flames traveled quickly t clumps of young trees but burned slowly for long p gh the time at the feet of the giant trees, killing them. 4 ds of

For Covington the unexpected loss of so many old-g trees was a wake-up call. Before setting fire loose in the h forests of the Southwest again, he concluded that the fores had to be restored to its original structure. To learn what these forests looked like before human **interference**, Covington and his team studied old photos and read historic texts. They also looked at records kept by early foresters. In 1909 foresters had set up a series of experimental plots across the Southwest. Among these was an unlogged, eight-acre plot in Coconino National Forest[6] that was set aside as a long-term control. Covington made 1876 the reference year for this plot—it was the last year a fire had occurred there—and then reconstructed the way the forest had looked at the time. The difference between then and now, he found, was dramatic. In 1876 the plot supported just more than 20 trees an acre, compared with 1,250 some 120 years later! R

This was the plot that Covington's team experimentally thinned in 1993 and 1994, taking care to preserve all old-growth trees. The area now supports some 60 trees an acre, and as individual trees, they seem far healthier than before.

4 Key Literary Element

Description What description in this paragraph helps you understand what *fuel* is? L

5. The phrase ***as a consequence*** means "as a result."

6. ***Coconino National Forest*** is near Flagstaff, Arizona.

Vocabulary

interference (in tur FEER uns) *n.* the act of getting in the way and slowing normal progress or development

READING WORKSHOP 4

Teach

L Literary Element

Description Say: What does the description of the fire set at Coconino National Forest tell you about how fuel amount affects fire? *(When there is little fuel, a fire burns and moves quickly. When there is more fuel, a fire burns slowly and stays in one place until the fuel has been used up.)* OL

R Reading Skill

Identifying Problem and Solution Ask: How does Covington try to solve the problem of uncontrollable forest fires? *(He tries to restore the forest to its original state so that he can study how nature solved the problem of tree overcrowding before humans entered the process.)* How does Covington learn what the forest looked like in its original state? *(He and his team study old photos, read historic texts, and look at records kept by early foresters.)* OL

Reading Fluency

Reading with a Partner Reading nonfiction selections with unfamiliar content-area vocabulary can be a challenge. Have students read aloud to partners. Tell students to stop when they come across an unfamiliar word or phrase. Tell them to sound out the word and, if necessary, ask their partners for help pronouncing the word. Encourage students to also stop if they make a mistake, go back, and reread the sentence correctly. EL BL

Objectiv
- Analyze pr
- Understand
- Use word stru tions clues to unders words xt a

Teach

R1 Reading Skill

Review Using Text Features **Ask:** What text feature does the author use to organize the article? *(headings)* BL How well does this heading introduce the paragraphs that follow? *(Possible response: very well. It tells the main idea of the section—that open space is critical to preventing uncontrolled, deadly fires.)* AL

R2 Reading Skill

Identifying Problem and Solution **Ask:** Why is it difficult to restore patches of open space? *(The amount of fuel varies from forest to forest.)* BL

William F. Campbell/Getty Images

BACK BURNER: In Arizona, a weary fire-fighter walks om a blaze he just set.

For one thing, the outer coating eir needles has increased in toughness, which helps dis ge plant-eating insects. For another, they are produc ore resin,[7] which provides protection against damagi ects such as bark beetles. Best of all, thinning is n r needed, as slow-burning controlled fires can no y do the job.

The Value of Or pace R1

Many variables ine how a wildfire behaves, but among the mos ant are wind speed, topography,[8] air temperature, [9] and the amount of fuel. Forests with patches of o e have less fuel. But these types of forests hav disappeared. At one time, the open spaces h en the danger of horrific blazes. Today vast areas o ave no open spaces but instead are packed with d kindling.[10] 5 hese patches of open space is critical.[11]

R ely, there is no easy way to do this because U t of fuel varies widely from forest to forest. To R2

(REZ un) is sap, or the sticky liquid made inside trees and other plants.

, *topography* refers to land features such as hills, valleys, and streams.

umidity is a measurement of the moisture in the air.

Kindling refers to old, dry, fallen leaves, sticks, and branches that start on fire easily.

Critical is a multiple-meaning word; here, it means "extremely important."

Uncontrollable fires have burned millions of acres of forests, killed numerous civilians and firefighters, and burned thousands of homes.

5 **Key Reading Skill**

Identifying Problem and Solution What problem does this paragraph bring up? Think about possible solutions to the problem. Then read on to learn of the solutions the writers suggest.

Additional Su

Reading in the Real World

Career Tell students to use the details from the article to write a classified advertisement for the position of forest ecologist. Point out that most ads include a job description and list required skills, experience, training, and education. *(Forest ecologists study the life and life cycles of forest ecosystems. The research of many forest ecologists focuses on finding ways to preserve forests under threat from pollution and human encroachment.)* After completing the assignment, students can discuss whether they would be interested in a career as a forest ecologist. OL

READING WORKSHOP 4

many forest ecologists, dealing with fuel loads—whether by thinning, controlled burning, or a combination of the two—is the best strategy we have for making sure that the ponderosa pine forests survive into the future. And the good news, says Mark Finney, a researcher with the Forest Service's Fire Sciences Laboratory in Missoula, Montana, is that it probably won't be necessary to thin or control-burn every acre of forest at risk. 6

Most fuel-reduction measures have had fairly narrow goals, such as protecting valuable stands of trees. The logical[12] next step, as Finney sees it, is to use these measures across hundreds of thousands of acres. It is already clear, he notes, that controlled burns have the power to lessen the likelihood of large, destructive fires.

Not All Forests Are Alike

Not all forests, however, are good candidates for thinning. Among the best examples are the lodgepole pine forests that grow at higher elevations across the mountains in the West. Lodgepole pines thrive in a cool, moist environment, which keeps fires at bay for long periods of time. So the lodgepoles grow densely together—so densely, in fact, that numerous smaller lodgepoles are shaded out and die from lack of light. These dead and dying trees, combined with lower-growing spruce and fir trees, provide a massive fuel load, which can lead to terrible blazes.

Yet attempting to thin lodgepole pine forests to prevent such fires would be foolish, say scientists, because these blazes serve important ecological functions. For instance, many lodgepole pines package their seeds in resin-sealed cones that can be opened only by intense heat. If the cones aren't opened, the seeds cannot take root and grow into saplings.

No one questions the value of thinning for fire control around homes and other structures. What is much harder to weigh is the balance of risks and benefits of thinning in terms of ecology. Great care needs to be taken so that thinning does not hurt the very forests it is supposed to heal. 7 8

—Updated 2005, from *TIME*, August 18, 2003

12. Something clear and reasonable is ***logical*** (LAH jih kul).

6 **English Language Coach**

Word Structure Look at the word **unfortunately** on the previous page. How many prefixes does it have? How many suffixes? What is the base word?

7 **Key Reading Skill**

Identifying Problem and Solution Explain why thinning a forest may be a good solution to controlling forest fires.

8 **BIG Question**

Do you think that scientific progress has helped the ponderosa pine forests, hurt them, or both? Explain. Write your answers on a note card and add it to Foldable 5. Your response will help you complete the Unit Challenge later.

English Language Coach

Understanding Content-Area Vocabulary Read aloud to students the paragraph that begins, "Yet attempting to thin lodgepole pine forests . . ." Paraphrase the paragraph with input from students. After doing so, discuss with students what it means that fires serve "ecological functions." Ask students to explain the example cited in the paragraph. With students, generate additional examples of natural phenomena that serve "ecological functions." *(Bees pollinating flowers may be a familiar example to most students.)* EL

Teach

EL Language Coach

Content-Area Words Say: The author notes that forest ecologists want to make sure that "the ponderosa pine forests survive into the future." After reading the details in the article, what do you think a forest ecologist does? *(A forest ecologist studies forests and works to protect them.)* EL What is the base word of *ecologist*? What does it mean? *(ecology: the relationship between a living thing and its environment)* AL

BQ BIG Question

Ask: When people first began logging and grazing livestock in the southwestern forests, they did not fully understand the environmental consequences of their actions. How might thinning the forests pose similar risks? *(The full impact of thinning is not yet completely understood. Thinning, like logging and grazing, could harm the forest ecology if not done carefully and thoughtfully.)* AL

Assess

Use the Checkpoint questions provided on Presentation Plus! to check for comprehension. These questions can be used with interactive response keypads for immediate student feedback.

Objectives
- Use text features
- Identify problems and solutions
- Use context clues to understand content-area words

Assess

Resources for page 612

- Selection Quick Check
- Selection and Unit Assessment
- ExamView Assessment Suite
- Interactive Tutor: Self-Assessment

Students can respond to the *After You Read* items in their Learner's Notebook or on separate sheets of paper.

Answering the

1. Responses will vary. Students may say that progress can have a negative effect on nature. Studying nature often helps scientists learn how things existed in their original state, which in turn can lead to good solutions.
2. Thinning forests may help prevent forest fires.
3. The forests have become denser and contain more fuel.

Critical Thinking

4. Responses will vary. Students may say that there's less risk of uncontrolled fire in a thinned forest.
5. Lodgepole pine cones require heat to open, release seeds, and make new trees.
6. Responses will vary. Students may say that this policy has been a problem because forests require fire to maintain sustainable tree numbers.

After You Read

Fireproofing the Forests

AP Wide World

Objectives (pp. 612–613)
Reading Identify problem and solution
Literature Identify literary elements: description
Vocabulary Identify prefixes and suffixes
Writing Use the RAFT system: letter to the editor
Grammar Use punctuation: commas in introductory clauses and phrases

Answering the BIG Question

1. How does progress affect nature? How does studying nature help scientists think of new inventions and solutions?
2. **Recall** Why do some people want to thin the forests?
   TIP **Right There**
3. **Summarize** How have southwestern forests changed in the last 100 years?
   TIP **Think and Search**

Critical Thinking

4. **Connect** Would you rather live near a forest that has been thinned or near a forest whose trees have not been cut? Explain your answer.
   TIP **Author and Me**
5. **Draw Conclusions** How can fires affect future tree growth in lodgepole pine forests?
   TIP **Author and Me**
6. **Evaluate** For the last 100 years, foresters' policy has been to prevent forest fires. Do you think this policy has been a problem or a solution? Explain your response.
   TIP **Author and Me**

Write About Your Reading

Use the RAFT system and what you learned from "Fireproofing the Forests" to complete the following assignment.

Role: Write as though you are a person who lives near a forest in Arizona.

Audience: People who read the newspaper

Format: A letter

Topic: Write a letter to the editor of a local newspaper. Explain that you live near a forest and are concerned about forest fires. Describe what you know about tree thinning and how it may help limit the damage caused by fires. Then tell why you think the forest near you should be thinned.

Write About Your Reading

Possible response:

Dear Editor:

Yesterday, my neighbor and I had a scare with a burn pile. He was burning trash in his backyard. The wind caught a spark and blew it toward the woods that surround our homes. I don't want to lose my home in a forest fire. Tree thinning would reduce the risk of a destructive forest fire, protect our homes, and preserve the beauty of the area.

Thank you for your attention to this matter.

Robin Mayfield

Skills Review

Key Reading Skill: Identifying Problem and Solution

7. Answer the following questions about problems and solutions.
   - What is the problem in the ponderosa pine forests?
   - What solution do some people have for keeping the forest healthy?
   - What other problems does this solution create?

Key Literary Element: Description

8. What did southwestern forests look like before people began to control fires? Describe them.

Vocabulary Check

Choose the best word to complete each sentence.

looms debate restore thrive interference

9. It is hard to ___ a forest after it has been destroyed.
10. Many of the problems with forests are caused by human ___.
11. Forests can ___ when they are properly thinned.
12. There will be ___ about this issue for some time.
13. The danger from forest fires ___ larger when we don't manage forests carefully.
14. **English Language Coach** Rewrite each word below, separating the prefix, base word, and suffix(es). Under the prefix and base word, write their meanings.

uncontrollable	unequaled
overgrown	combination

Web Activities For eFlashcards, Selection Quick Checks, and other Web activities, go to www.glencoe.com.

Grammar Link: Commas with Introductory Clauses and Phrases

Adverb clauses and prepositional phrases that are used at the beginning of a sentence are called **introductory clauses** and **introductory phrases.** (They "introduce" the rest of the sentence, making them "introductory.")

- Introductory adverb clauses are always followed by a comma.

  If the sun is shining, we'll go.
- If the clause appears at the end of the sentence, there is no comma.

  We'll go if the sun is shining.
- A comma is used after a long introductory phrase.

  Because of the clouds and drizzle, we stayed home.
- If the phrase appears at the end of the sentence, there is no comma.

  We stayed home because of the clouds and drizzle.
- A comma is used after two or more introductory phrases, even if each one is short.

  For fun in the summer, I swim.
- Only one comma is used after introductory phrases, even if there are several of them.

  Wrong: For fun, in the summer, I swim.

Grammar Practice

On a separate sheet of paper, copy each sentence and add commas where needed. Write *correct* if no commas are needed.

15. After I ate I felt better.
16. On Fridays in May we practice.
17. He will help you if you really need it.
18. In a cool and shady meadow we saw deer.

Writing Application Look through your RAFT assignment and add any commas that are needed after introductory clauses and phrases.

Skills Review

Key Reading Skill: Identifying Problem and Solution

7. Ponderosa pine forests are overcrowded and have high fuel loads. Some people advocate thinning the trees to solve this problem. This solution may have unknown ecological impacts, and some environmental groups fear it will encourage logging.

Key Literary Element: Description

8. The forests had beautiful, old, large trees that were bathed in sunlight and surrounded by flowing grasses and wildflowers. Open spaces stretched between the trees.

Vocabulary Check

9. restore
10. interference
11. thrive
12. debate
13. looms
14. un (not) + control (manage) + able
    un (not) + equal (identical) + ed
    over (too much) + grown (developed)
    combine (merge) + ation (action of)

Close

Ask students to discuss whether they think the author of this article believes progress is a good or a bad thing. Be sure they support their responses with examples from the article.

Grammar Link: Commas with Introductory Clauses and Phrases

Grammar Practice

15. After I ate, I felt better.
16. On Fridays in May, we practice.
17. Correct
18. In a cool and shady meadow, we saw deer.

More About the Authors

Ranger Rick is a publication of the National Wildlife Federation. The Federation's goal is to encourage Americans to join conservation efforts. The magazine features stories, games, and photos that focus on animals and science.

Joseph Bruchac started to write in the second grade, writing poems for his teacher. He began his college career studying wildlife conservation. When he joined a writing class, his teacher told him that he would never write a good poem. This discouragement motivated Bruchac to become a poet. After becoming a parent, he began telling Native American stories to his sons.

V Vocabulary

Vocabulary Poems Say: Revise your animal sentences into a funny poem. *(Sample response: A bat loves a cave* ***habitat.*** */ It avoids* ***extinction*** *by wearing a hat. / With a covered head, / It* ***copes*** *well with the dread / Of becoming a meal for a cat!)* OL

Before You Read

Missing! and Birdfoot's Grampa

Meet the Authors

Claire Miller writes for *Ranger Rick* magazine. She says, "No matter where you live, there's lots to discover right outside your door."

Joseph Bruchac proudly bears his Native American name, *Gahnegohheyoh,* which means "the good mind." Bruchac is an award-winning author of more than 20 books and a professional teller of traditional Native American stories.

Joseph Bruchac

Author Search For more about these authors, go to www.glencoe.com.

Objectives (pp. 614–619)
Reading Identify problem and solution • Make connections from text to self
Literature Identify literary elements: description
Vocabulary Understand content-area words

Vocabulary Preview

cope (kohp) *v.* to deal with and try to overcome problems; often used with the word *with* **(p. 618)** *Most creatures don't cope well with extreme changes in weather.*

habitat (HAB uh tat) *n.* the place where a plant or animal naturally lives and grows; home **(p. 618)** *The rainforest is the habitat of countless frogs and toads.*

V

extinction (ek STINGK shun) *n.* the act of wiping out of existence or having been wiped out of existence **(p. 618)** *Humans have caused the extinction of many plants and animals.*

Write to Learn For each vocabulary word, write a sentence about animals.

English Language Coach

Content-Area Words People who perform certain jobs often use specific words to describe what they see and do. Scientists use content-area words to describe animals, environments, and natural processes. Read the following models to find the meanings of *atmosphere* and *evaporate.*

atmosphere (noun)	the air and gases that surround the earth
atmos + sphere	*atmos* means "vapor" *sphere* means "ball"
evaporate (verb)	to become vapor or gas
e- + vapor + -ate	*vapor* means "mist or steam; a liquid that has become gas" *-ate* is a suffix meaning "come to be"

Think In the next selection, find the content-area words *habitat* and *extinction* (defined above). Could you have discovered their meanings from context clues or from their base words, roots, prefixes and suffixes? Did you need the definition?

Additional Support

Literature Online

Author Search To expand students' appreciation of these authors, have them access the Web site for additional information and resources.

Differentiated Instruction

Using Graphic Organizers To understand the situation the animals and plants of Monteverde are facing, create a cause-and-effect diagram with your class. Divide a section of the board in half, labeling one side as *Cause* and the other side as *Effect.* On the effect side, write the following effect: Extinction of the golden toad. As students read, encourage them to note the causes that led to the extinction of the golden toad. After everyone has finished reading, discuss the causes and complete the chart as a class. OL

Skills Preview

Key Reading Skill: Identifying Problem and Solution

As you read the article "Missing!" and the poem "Birdfoot's Grampa," think about the following questions:

- What is the *main* problem in "Missing!"?
- What is the author's solution?
- Does "Birdfoot's Grampa" use a strict problem-solution organization?

Write to Learn Write a short paragraph using problem-solution organization. Choose a problem that you think can be solved. It could be a problem facing the world, someone you know, or yourself. What solution would you offer?

Key Literary Element: Description

In "Missing," the description of the cloud forest in Costa Rica includes details that let you imagine the cool dampness of the frogs' home. The details in the poem "Birdfoot's Grampa" let you experience the kindness of a man who takes the time to save toads.

As you read, use these tips to understand the description:

- Look for words that let you see, feel, hear, and smell the setting.
  What is it like to live in the cloud forest?
- Look for descriptions that tell about changes.
  How has the cloud forest changed in recent years?
- Look for vivid verbs and adjectives.
  How does the speaker in "Birdfoot's Grampa" describe the toads?

Interactive Literary Elements Handbook
To review or learn more about the literary elements, go to www.glencoe.com.

Get Ready to Read

Connect to Reading

What do you think of worms? Have you watched a spider spin a web? Did you ever swat a fly? How much attention do you pay to the little creatures of nature? How would you feel if birds became extinct? What about worms, spiders, and flies? **R**

Partner Talk Talk with a partner about the nature around you. Is there some particular thing you'd miss if it disappeared? What is it, and why would you miss it?

Build Background

The magazine article "Missing!" describes how a change in temperature harmed Costa Rica's frogs and toads.

- Costa Rica is a tropical country in Central America.
- The Monteverde (mawn tay VAIR day) Cloud Forest Reserve is in Costa Rica. It is a protected area for plants and wildlife.
- With mountains, forests, and two coastlines, Costa Rica has a great variety of plant and animal life.
- About 25 percent of land in Costa Rica is protected, including national parks and private reserves.

L Set Purposes for Reading

BIG Question Read "Missing!" and "Birdfoot's Grampa" to find out how human progress may be affecting frogs and toads.

Set Your Own Purpose What else would you like to learn from the selection to help you answer the Big Question? Write your own purpose on a note card and add it to Foldable 5.

Keep Moving
Use these skills as you read the following selection.

READING WORKSHOP 4

Teach

L Literary Element

Description Say: You are going to read about frogs. What sensory words can you use to describe frogs? Try to come up with words that appeal to as many as possible of the five senses. *(Possible responses may include* green, brown, bumpy, slimy, wet, *and* croaking.) **OL**

R Reading Skill

Review Connecting Say: Think about the ecological problems, such as global warming, that face the planet. Although some of these problems may not affect you directly, why do you think it is important to protect the environment and natural resources? *(Responses will vary.)* **OL**

Use the CheckPoint questions provided on Presentation Plus! to check students' ability to identify problems and solutions and to build background. These questions can be used with interactive response keypads for immediate student feedback.

Reading to the World

Citizenship Students may have difficulty thinking of things that are disappearing from their communities. Suggest that students talk with older friends or family members about this issue. Invite students to share their findings with the class. Record their ideas on the board. For each item, lead students in a discussion of the following questions:

- What is the purpose of this item?
- Why is it disappearing?
- What will be the effects of its disappearance?
- What could be done to save it?
- Is it worth saving? Explain. **OL**

Objectives

- Identify problem and solution
- Make connections from text to self
- Identify literary elements: description
- Understand content-area words

Teach

Viewing the Photo
Say: Look at the photo at the top of this page. Why do you think the Costa Rican forest is called the Monteverde Cloud Forest Reserve? *(The treetops seem to touch the clouds, almost as though the clouds are part of the forest.)* BL

R Reading Skill

Identifying Problem and Solution **Say:** The writer introduces the problem in the first paragraph. What is the problem? What may be causing the problem? *(Frogs are disappearing from the Monteverde Cloud Forest Reserve in Costa Rica. Changing clouds may be part of the problem.)* BL

Readability Scores
Dale-Chall: 5.8
DRP: 58
Lexile: 990

READING WORKSHOP 4

INFORMATIONAL TEXT
WEB SITE
scholastic.com

MISSING!

by Claire Miller

The frog population in Costa Rica is declining. Scientists search for answers.

The cloud-covered mountains of Costa Rica are home to a variety of frogs. Many live in the Monteverde Cloud Forest Reserve. Over the years, cloud coverage has changed in the region. Now, some of the forest's frogs have disappeared, and the changing clouds may be part of their problem. 1

Super Soakers Unlike humans, frogs don't drink water. Instead, they absorb it through their skin. Most of it soaks through a "seat patch" on their bottoms when they sit on moist ground.

In the Monteverde Cloud Forest Reserve, the frogs have depended on the clouds that hang around the mountains to keep the forest floor wet and the mountain streams flowing. Where do the clouds come from?

When Earth's water evaporates from oceans, lakes, or puddles, it changes from liquid to water vapor. This water vapor rises when heated by the sun. Strong winds can also blow it upward.

Practice the Skills

1 Key Reading Skill

R **Identifying Problem and Solution** What is the problem in the Monteverde Cloud Forest Reserve? Who or what is affected by the problem?

Additional Support

English Language Coach

Hyphenating Modifiers Some students may not be familiar with compound modifiers. Point out the compound modifier *cloud-covered* in the first sentence. Tell them to hyphenate a compound describing word only when it comes before the word it describes. For example:

- A well-known musician visited our school. (*Well-known* precedes *musician.*)
- The musician was well known. (*Well known* follows *musician.*)

Ask students to rewrite the first sentence as two sentences. *(The mountains of Costa Rica are cloud covered. They are home to a variety of frogs.)* EL

In Monteverde, the water vapor would often rise until it ran into cold air around the mountaintops. This cold air **condensed** the vapor into liquid water droplets. The droplets then clumped together to make up a cloud. **2**

Clouds are the form that water takes right before it returns to Earth as rain, snow, sleet, or hail. In Monteverde, when clouds blanketed the mountain, the droplets gathered to make the little pools of water that the frogs need.

These days, the clouds often form high in the sky instead of down on the mountains of Monteverde. As a result, the forest floor is drier than it once was. So what's causing this high cloud formation?

In recent years, the air temperature in Monteverde has increased. Often the air around the mountaintops is too warm to condense the water vapor. So the water vapor keeps rising until it forms clouds high above the mountains. At the same time, the land below dries out. So the frogs (and their cousins, the toads) have a hard time finding the water they need on the forest floor. **3**

Turning Up the Heat Most scientists believe that people are causing many places on Earth to get warmer, including Monteverde. They call it global warming.

People often add to global warming by burning fuels such as oil, natural gas, and coal. These fuels power almost everything we plug in or drive. As the fuels are burned, a gas called carbon dioxide is given off. Carbon dioxide occurs naturally in our atmosphere. It helps to keep Earth warm by holding in the sun's heat. But having too much carbon dioxide in the air is like throwing a heavy blanket around the planet—it keeps in too much of the sun's heat, and the world gets warmer.

Missing Toad Alan J. Pounds is a scientist who has lived and worked in the Monteverde Cloud Forest Reserve for 24 years—and he's noticed a change in cloud cover and frog populations. "In the early 1980s, there were hundreds of golden

Practice the Skills

2 English Language Coach

EL **Content-Area Words** Find the word **condensed**. Can context clues around the word help you figure out what it means?

3 Key Literary Element

L **Description** Science writers must make their descriptions clear and interesting. In this paragraph, the author describes weather changes that are drying out the land. Does the author's description help you picture and understand what's happening? Explain.

A golden-eyed treefrog in Monteverde.

READING WORKSHOP 4

Teach

EL Language Coach

Content-Area Words Say: Reread the paragraph that contains the word *condensed.* What happens to the water? *(Water vapor turns into liquid droplets that* clump together *to form clouds.)* Given these context clues, what do you think *condensed* means? *(Possible response: compressed, brought closer together)* **EL**

L Literary Element

Description Ask: Use the author's words to make a mental picture of what is happening in Monteverde. Share your picture with the class. *(Students may describe higher temperatures, increased air temperature around the mountaintops, and vapors rising up to make clouds high above the mountains.)* **OL** How might description in a nonfiction article differ from description in a fiction story? *(A fiction story would probably include more sensory details because a fiction writer often wants to place the reader right in the action. Nonfiction articles often focus more on providing information.)* **AL**

Differentiated Instruction

Modeling a Process On thick paper, have students draw simple outlines of frogs. Then ask students to cut out their frog shapes and trace them onto dry sponges. Have students cut the frog shapes from the sponges. Pour a small amount of water into a shallow pan. Invite students to place their frogs one at a time in the water. Have students observe how the sponge frogs absorb the water through their "skin." As the water is used up, do not refill the pan. Instead, ask students how this model mimics what has happened in the Monteverde Cloud Forest Reserve. *(There is not enough moisture for the frogs.)* **BL**

Objectives
- Identify problem and solution
- Understand description
- Use context to understand content-area words

READING WORKSHOP 4

Teach

BQ BIG Question

Ask: How is progress negatively affecting Earth? *(Cars, lights, and appliances all burn fuel and contribute to global warming.)* **OL**

R Reading Skill

Identifying Problem and Solution Ask: What does the writer suggest that the average family do to prevent global warming? *(The writer suggests that families use their cars less and turn off lights and appliances that they are not using.)* **BL**

toads," he says. "But by 1989, people found only a few of them, and since then, we haven't seen any!"

High cloud formation caused by global warming is a serious problem. And according to Pounds, it adds to a growing list of troubles that the wildlife of Monteverde is faced with. "The frogs and other wild animals have to **cope** with many problems, such as **habitat** loss and disease. But when global warming is added to all these problems, it may push them over the edge to **extinction**." **4**

R **You Can Help** It's too late to save the extinct golden toads, but there are things that you and your family can do to keep the world from getting warmer. For starters, encourage your family to use the car less. Also, turn off the lights and appliances that you aren't using. All these things burn fuel and contribute to global warming. By becoming an Earth-friendly family, you'll help wildlife all around the world! ❍

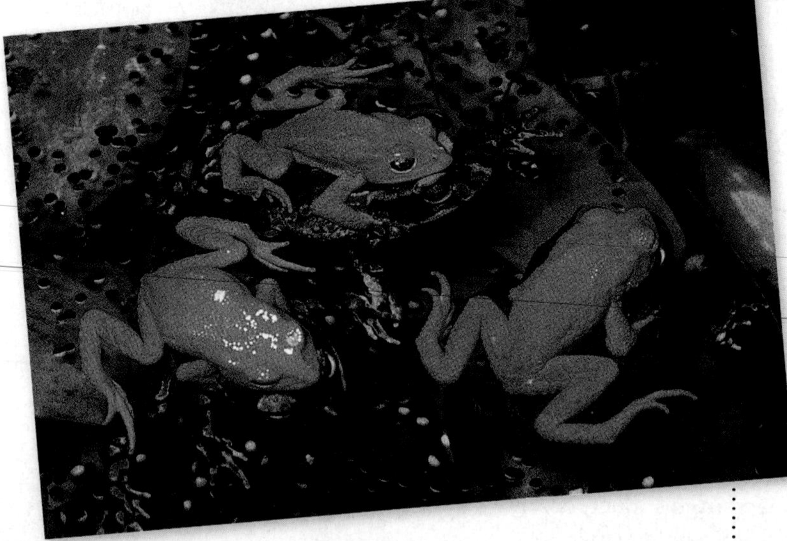

Golden toads depositing their eggs in a pool.

Vocabulary

cope (kohp) *v.* to deal with and try to overcome problems

habitat (HAB uh tat) *n.* the place where a plant or animal naturally lives and grows; home

extinction (ek STINGK shun) *n.* the act of wiping out of existence or having wiped out of existence

Practice the Skills

4 BIG Question

BQ Machines create carbon dioxide. What do you think the scientists who study the Monteverde mountains would say about progress? Write your response on a note card and add it to Foldable 5. Your response will help you answer the Unit Challenge later.

Additional Support

Reading in the Real World

Citizenship Tell students to make how-to manuals that provide families with strategies for reducing global warming. Ask students to include tips from this article as well as information they find through research. Tell students to also include a section that explains why families should care about environmental issues. For example, students could summarize the article to explain what happened to golden toads. Encourage students to illustrate their manuals to make them more user-friendly. **AS**

Birdfoot's Grampa

by Joseph Bruchac

The old man
must have stopped our car
two dozen times to climb out
and gather into his hands **R**
the small toads blinded
by our lights and leaping,
live drops of rain. **5**

The rain was falling,
a mist about his white hair
and I kept saying
you can't save them all,
accept it, get back in
we've got places to go.

But, leathery hands full **BQ**
of wet brown life,
knee deep in the summer
roadside grass,
he just smiled and said
they have places to go to
too. **6** **7** ❍

Practice the Skills

5 Key Reading Skill

Identifying Problem and Solution What problem do the toads face in the poem? Is it similar to the problems of the frogs and toads in "Missing!"? Explain.

6 Key Literary Element

Description The poet's description creates a picture of the man, the rainy evening, and the toads. List five words that help describe this picture. **L**

7 BIG Question

In this poem, how is progress or technology threatening the toads? What do you think the poet is saying about progress and nature?

Literature Focus Lesson

Author's Purpose Joseph Bruchac believes in the power of stories. He says that stories "contain knowledge that, like an elder's voice, can help guide a young person along a trail on which his or her feet have never been." Share this quotation with students. Discuss how this quotation relates to the purpose of each of the three selections in this workshop. To aid in the discussion, encourage students to think of an "elder's voice" not simply as the words of an older person but as the lessons humanity has learned from the past. **OL**

READING WORKSHOP 4

Teach

R Reading Skill

Identifying Problem and Solution **Ask:** Why does the old man stop the car and move the toads? *(The old man is saving the toads from being struck and killed by passing cars.)* **OL** **Ask:** How are the passing cars and global warming similar? *(Humans have introduced both into the habitats of the frogs.)* **AL**

L Literary Element

Description **Say:** Tell which sense each word appeals to. *(Sample responses:* blinded = *sight;* drops = *sight;* leathery = *touch and sight;* grass = *sight;* smiled = *sight)* **OL**

BQ

Ask: How are the old man's attitude and the speaker's attitude toward progress different? *(Possible response: The old man believes that the protection of all living things takes priority over progress. The speaker believes that such efforts are not worthwhile.)* **OL**

Assess

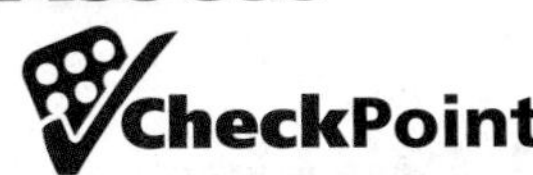

Use the CheckPoint questions provided on Presentation Plus! to check for comprehension. These questions can be used with interactive response keypads for immediate student feedback.

Objectives
- Analyze problems and solutions
- Understand description

Assess

Resources for page 620

- Selection Quick Check
- Selection and Unit Assessment
- ExamView Assessment Suite
- Interactive Tutor: Self-Assessment

Students can respond to the *After You Read* items in their Learner's Notebook or on separate sheets of paper.

Answering the

1. Responses will vary. Students may say that it doesn't seem right or fair that the Costa Rican frogs must pay the price for human progress.
2. Global warming is drying the forest in which the frogs and toads live.
3. Readers can encourage their families to reduce car usage and turn off lights and appliances when they are not using them.

Critical Thinking

4. Responses will vary. Students may say that Grampa valued the creatures and wanted to protect them.
5. The presence of many frogs and toads indicates that our climate is healthy.
6. Human activity often harms other creatures.

After You Read

Missing! *and* Birdfoot's Grampa

Answering the

1. What are your thoughts about progress after reading about the frogs and toads in Costa Rica?
2. **Recall** Why are frogs and toads disappearing in the Monteverde Cloud Forest Reserve?
   TIP **Right There**
3. **Recall** How can you, the reader, help reduce global warming?
   TIP **Right There**

Critical Thinking

4. **Draw Conclusions** Why did Grampa want to save the toads?
   TIP **Author and Me**
5. **Infer** What can the presence of frogs and toads tell us about the health of our climate?
   TIP **Author and Me**
6. **Evaluate** What do "Missing!" and "Birdfoot's Grampa" tell you about how human activity affects other creatures?
   TIP **Author and Me**

Write About Your Reading

Imagine that you are either the old man in "Birdfoot's Grampa" or the scientist in "Missing!" Write a journal entry about how you feel about progress and nature.

Think about the following questions as you start your journal entry:

- If you are the old man, why do you stop to move the toads? Why do you want to help them?
- If you are the scientist, what changes have you seen in the Monteverde mountains? Why do you think it's important to help the frogs and other animals?

Objectives (pp. 620–621)
Reading Identify problem and solution • Make connections from text to self
Literature Identify literary elements: description
Vocabulary Understand content-area words
Writing Respond to literature: journal
Grammar Use punctuation: commas with interruptions

Write About Your Reading

Possible response:
My grandson thinks that I am silly to move the toads from the road. I think that he is silly not to. What will the world be without the little toads? Not the one we know now. Not the one my elders knew. Why is my grandson in such a rush to welcome a world he does not know?

Skills Review

Key Reading Skill: Identifying Problem and Solution

7. Now that you have read the selections, answer the questions from page 615.
   - What is the problem in "Missing!"?
   - What is the article writer's solution?
   - Does "Birdfoot's Grampa" use a strict problem-solution organization?

Key Literary Element: Description

8. In "Missing!" what significant change in the forest does the author describe?
9. In "Birdfoot's Grampa," what do lines 8–13 tell you about the speaker?

Vocabulary Check

For each word in this list, write a sentence that uses the word correctly.

10. **cope**
11. **habitat**
12. **extinction**
13. **English Language Coach** The Monteverde Cloud Forest is part of a *reserve.* The prefix *re-* means "back," but here the word *serve* is a root, not a base word. (You'll learn more about roots in Unit 7.) So here, *serve* does not mean "serve"; it means "to save." At a restaurant, if a table is *reserved,* it is saved for someone. What do you think *reserve* means in the phrase "forest reserve"?

Web Activities For eFlashcards, Selection Quick Checks, and other Web activities, go to www.glencoe.com.

Grammar Link: Commas with Interruptions

A natural writing style is often quite similar to speech. Writers, like speakers, may say something that "interrupts" the flow of the thought they are expressing.

- Use commas to set off words that interrupt the flow of thought in a sentence.

  The park, as we expected, was crowded.

  Bruno was, I have to say, quite polite.

  My well-trained dog, of course, behaved well.

- If the same kind of information appears at the end of the sentence, use a comma before it.

  The park was crowded, as we expected.

- Use commas to set off words that add information but that are not necessary to the meaning.

  My aunt, who is quite funny, visited us.

  The test, which wasn't fun, was finally over.

  Rudy, the team's star, was late again.

- Do not use commas if a phrase or clause is necessary to the meaning of the sentence. These phrases or clauses do not "interrupt."

  Only the people who can afford tickets will go.

- If words could be removed without changing the meaning of the sentence, use commas around them. If not, do use commas.

Grammar Practice

On a separate sheet of paper, copy each sentence and add commas where needed. Write *correct* if no commas are needed.

14. Tammi who loves fruit brought apples.
15. People who have red hair often have freckles.
16. The play you must admit was interesting.
17. The bus which was late again finally arrived.
18. The train that is going to St. Louis is full.

Writing Application Look through the journal entry you wrote and add any necessary commas.

Skills Review

Key Reading Skill: Identifying Problem and Solution

7. Global warming caused a change in cloud cover, which led to the extinction of golden toads. The writer suggests that people try to limit their contribution to global warming. The problem is not introduced until the second stanza.

Key Literary Element: Description

8. The significant change is the rising temperature of the forest.
9. The speaker is in a hurry and doesn't believe the old man can make a difference by picking up the frogs.

Vocabulary Check

Responses will vary.

10. People must *cope* with life's difficulties as they arise.
11. The frogs enjoy living in a moist *habitat.*
12. The threat of *extinction* looms for many animals
13. A *reserve* is land set apart, or saved, for a special purpose.

Grammar Link: Commas with Interruptions

Grammar Practice

14. Tammi, who loves fruit, brought apples.
15. Correct
16. The play, you must admit, was interesting.
17. The bus, which was late again, finally arrived.
18. Correct

Close

Ask students to imagine what the old man in "Birdfoot's Grampa" might say about the effects of progress.

Reading Across Texts: Author's Craft

UNIT 5

Objectives covered in this workshop:
- Find similarities and differences across texts
- Connect, compare, and contrast author's craft across texts

Teaching Students to Read for Author's Craft

Why Is It Important?

- Reading critically involves processes like comparing across texts to understand how authors' backgrounds, stances, purposes, and writing style influence the text they write.
- Reading across genres and relating authors craft to specific genres of texts on the same topic fosters the most important critical reading skills.
- National assessments on reading show that most middle school students have not developed these critical reading skills even though they have developed basic reading skills.

How to Help Students Get It

- Starting with excerpts from texts from different authors on the same topic and in the same genre, discuss the similarities and differences in terms of what the authors say, how they say it, how they engage the reader, what language they use to describe, create images, and invoke certain responses or feelings.
- Moving to two texts from different genres discuss how authors write within different genres in different ways; discuss how the genre (for example an historical informational text on the Battle of Gettysburg and a piece of historical fiction like *Gettysburg: A Novel of the Civil War* by Newt Gingrich) portray parts of the event and what craft elements are important to each genre.

Reading to Answer the Big Question

America the Not-So-Beautiful

Commentator Andy Rooney writes about the dilemma we face in America with the rising amount of garbage and the lack of space to put it. In his words, "The more civilized a country is, the worse the trash problem is."

A Glimpse of Home

Astronaut Karen Sullivan describes how her experience with machines and progress has affected her view of the world. She pleads with readers to take batter care of their planet and treat it as though it were their own dwelling place.

Reading Across Texts Resources

Pacing (Days) Standard	Block	Lesson	Student Materials	Teacher Resources
1		Key Skill Lesson: Reading for Author's Craft	Key Reading Skills Practice English Language Coach	Bellringer Options Transparencies Read Aloud, Think Aloud Transparencies Presentation Plus!
2		"America the Not-So-Beautiful"	Literary Analysis Transparencies Glencoe Online Selection Vocabulary Development Academic Vocabulary Development English Language Coach Active Reading Graphic Organizer Literary Analysis StudentWorks Plus Online Student Edition Literature Classics Selection and Unit Assessments	Literary and Text Analysis Transparencies Puzzlemaker Skill Level Up! BookLink 3 Assessment by Learning Objective (Diagnostic and Formative) Interactive Tutor Self-Assessment TeacherWorks Plus
2		"A Glimpse of Home"	Glencoe Online Selection Vocabulary Development Academic Vocabulary Development English Language Coach Active Reading Graphic Organizer Literary Analysis StudentWorks Plus Online Student Edition Literature Classics Selection and Unit Assessments	Literary and Text Analysis Transparencies Puzzlemaker Skill Level Up! BookLink 3 Assessment by Learning Objective (Diagnostic and Formative) Interactive Tutor Self-Assessment TeacherWorks Plus

Keys for Unit Resource

- Blackline Master
- Workbook
- Supplemental Text
- CD-ROM
- DVD
- Transparency
- Web-based
- Fast Files

Level Appropriate Code

AS = Activities for all students
AL = Activities for students working above grade level
OL = Activities for students working at grade level
BL = Activities for students working below grade level
EL = Activities for English language learners

Focus

BELLRINGER Options

Daily Language Practice Transparency

Focus Activity Say: A particular place can be described in different ways, depending on the observer's point of view. How would you describe your community as you walk through it? How might your description change if you were flying in an airplane high above your community? *(Responses will vary.)*

Teach

L Literary Element

Author's Craft Ask: What are some possible purposes authors might have for writing? *(Possible response: to persuade, to convince, to entertain)* **OL** How does an author's purpose affect his or her tone, organization, and word choice? *(Possible response: Depending on the author's purpose for writing, the tone and word choice may be biased or neutral; writers may use a problem and solution organization if they hope to persuade people to do something about a problem.)* **AL**

AMERICA the Not-So-Beautiful

by Andrew A. Rooney

& A Glimpse of Home

by Kathryn Sullivan

Skill Focus

You will use these skills as you read and compare the following selections:

- "America the Not-So-Beautiful," p. 625
- "A Glimpse of Home," p. 630

Reading

- Making connections across texts
- Comparing/contrasting author's craft in different texts

Literature

- Identifying author's craft to construct meaning and recognize author's purpose

Writing

- Writing to compare and contrast

You listen to opinions every day. You and your friends probably share opinions on the food you eat. Your family may offer opinions on how you dress. Your teachers offer opinions on how to improve your grades. It's up to you to decide what opinions to believe. If you know people well, you probably trust their opinions. If you don't know a person, you expect him or her to support opinions with facts.

L Writers offer opinions, too. Studying the author's craft—how the author combines purpose, organization, word choice, and tone—helps you decide whether to believe the author's message. You can usually trust authors who support their opinions with facts.

How to Read Across Texts: Author's Craft

The author of "America the Not-So-Beautiful" is Andy Rooney. He often writes humorous articles that make readers think. Kathryn Sullivan wrote "A Glimpse of Home." She flew on three space-shuttle missions. The authors of these two personal essays agree. Earth has a terrible problem with trash. But their purpose and organization are very different.

As you read, watch for specific elements of the authors' craft that shape the two essays in this workshop. These elements include

- organization
- tone
- purpose

Objectives (pp. 622–623)
Reading Compare and contrast: author's craft

Additional Support

Literature Focus Lesson

Analyzing Author's Craft Remind students that author's purpose refers to the intention of the writer. Often, a single piece of writing has more than one purpose. Encourage students to think about the author's purpose(s) as they read "America the Not-So-Beautiful." Offer the following prompts:

- What does the author want to accomplish? Does the author have more than one goal?
- Does the organization of the essay complement the author's purpose?
- How does the author's purpose affect his tone and word choice? **OL**

Get Ready to Compare

As you read, keep track of the author's craft in a chart like this one. Copy it into your Learner's Notebook. Use it to take notes as you read. This chart allows you to compare how the two authors support their opinions. After you read, you'll use your notes to write your comparison.

Author's Craft Elements	"America the Not-So-Beautiful"	"A Glimpse of Home"
Organization		
Tone		
Purpose		
Audience		
Conclusion		
Word Choice		

L

Use Your Comparison

You throw things away every day. Rooney and Sullivan write about how much people throw away and how it affects Earth.

Imagine that your community is planning a Save the Earth event. Make a list of things people can do to save Earth. The list might include

- recycling old newspapers
- riding a bike to school
- reusing notebook paper

After you read, look at the conclusions the authors reached. Which solution do you trust? Why? What can you do to help others understand the importance of taking care of Earth? What ideas do you have for reducing what you throw away? How would you package food to create less trash? Write your response on the Reading Across Texts page of your Foldable.

Teach

L Literary Element

Author's Craft Tell students that some elements of author's craft are listed in the chart on page 623. Ask students to define each of the terms in the chart. *(**organization:** the arrangement of ideas in a piece of writing; **tone:** the author's attitude toward his or her subject; **purpose:** what the author hopes to accomplish with a piece of writing; **audience:** the group of readers the author addresses; **conclusion:** the author's final idea or statement supported by preceding text; **word choice:** the author's selection of particular words to match the style, tone, purpose, and subject of a piece of writing)* **OL**

Assess/Close

Say: Write a paragraph about a problem that you have, or have had, at school. Decide on a tone before you begin writing. To pinpoint and clarify the tone, think about your purpose for writing, your intended audience, and your main message. *(Responses will vary.)* **OL** Invite a few volunteers to read their paragraphs aloud. As a class, discuss the various tones of these paragraphs. **OL**

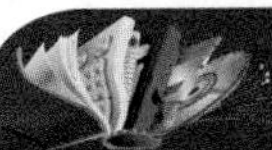

Resources for page 623

Use the Comparing Literature Graphic Organizer BLM in the Unit 5 Resource Booklet.

Differentiated Instruction

Communicating Through Art
Students who learn best through visual media may benefit from putting information and ideas from the essays into visual form. When such students have finished reading, ask them to use their completed charts to design posters that express their own conclusions as well as those of the authors. Display the posters, and discuss these questions as a class:

- What information do the posters convey?
- What emotions do the images trigger?
- What are the messages of the posters? **OL**

Objectives
- Identify elements of author's craft
- Understand text structure

Before You Read

America the Not-So-Beautiful

More About the Author

In addition to his appearances on the television show *60 Minutes,* Rooney writes a column that appears regularly in newspapers throughout the United States. Rooney writes about everyday events and items, even things like chairs and soap, with humor. Among many other honors, Rooney has received two different awards for lifetime achievement. As an admirer once remarked, "His take on the annoyances and joys of humanity always hit home."

V Vocabulary

Two at a Time Tell students that they will remember vocabulary words more easily if they use the words in context. Ask students to write sentences showing the correct use of the vocabulary and content-area words from this selection. **OL**

Meet the Author

Andrew A. Rooney began his career in 1941 as a reporter for the armed forces newspaper. He appears on the CBS newsmagazine *60 Minutes,* where he is known for his serious delivery of funny topics. His essays make you laugh, but they also make you think.

Literature Online

Author Search For more about Andrew A. Rooney, go to www.glencoe.com.

Objectives (pp. 624–628)
Reading Compare and contrast: author's craft
Vocabulary Understand content-area words

Vocabulary Preview

discarding (dis KARD ing) *n.* the act of throwing out or getting rid of **(p. 625)** *Americans have gotten into the habit of discarding unwanted objects rather than repairing them.*

prohibiting (proh HIB it ing) *adj.* preventing or forbidding **(p. 626)** *There need to be stronger laws prohibiting people from dumping poisons carelessly.*

prosperity (praw SPAIR uh tee) *n.* the condition of being successful or having good fortune **(p. 626)** *As prosperity increases in America, the trash problem is likely to increase.*

V

English Language Coach

Content-Area Words Look for these content-area words in "America the Not-So-Beautiful."

- **Sanitation** refers to improving conditions to make them clean and healthy. A **sanitation engineer** is someone who removes garbage.
- A **landfill** is a place where garbage is buried. Often soil and garbage are buried in layers to build up low-lying land.

Get Ready to Read

Connect to the Reading

Do you ever wonder how people make so much garbage? Where does it all go after you throw it away? What does it smell like when you pass a dumpster?

Build Background

At the end of the twentieth century, Americans threw away about 200 million tons of garbage each year.

Set Purposes for Reading

BIG Question Read to find out Andrew Rooney's opinion of the "progress" in how garbage is dealt with.

Set Your Own Purpose What else would you like to learn about how garbage is handled? Write your own purpose on a note card and add it to Foldable 5.

Additional Support

Literature Online

Author Search To expand students' appreciation of Andrew A. Rooney, have them access the Web site for additional information and resources.

Literature Focus Lesson

Tone Remind students that tone refers to an author's attitude toward a topic. That attitude may be humorous, curious, or serious. An author uses word choice and details to create tone. Point out that as they read, students should think about the feelings the author's words and sentences convey. Have students note some word choices and details they think play a role in establishing Andrew A. Rooney's tone and achieving his purpose.

Word Choices	Details

AMERICA the Not-So-Beautiful

by Andrew A. Rooney

Next to saving stuff I don't need, the thing I like to do best is throw it away. My idea of a good time is to load up the back of the car with junk on a Saturday morning and take it to the dump. There's something satisfying about **discarding** almost anything.

Throwing things out is the American way. We don't know how to fix anything and anyone who does know how is too busy to come so we throw it away and buy a new one. Our economy depends on us doing that. The trouble with throwing things away is, there is no "away" left. 1

Practice the Skills

1 Reading Across Texts

Author's Craft Problem and solution organization allows authors to give advice. What problem does Rooney point out in the first two paragraphs? Write your answer in your chart.

Workers move trash at New York City's Fresh Kills garbage dump (which was closed in 2001).

Vocabulary

discarding (dis KARD ing) *n.* the act of throwing out or getting rid of

Teach

L Literary Element

Author's Craft Ask: Which sentence on this page states the problem? *("The trouble with throwing things away is, there is no 'away' left.")* OL How would you paraphrase this sentence? *(Possible response: There is so much garbage that we are running out of places to put it.)* AL

R Reading Skill

Review Identifying Problem and Solution Ask: What are three reasons that Rooney gives to explain why people in the United States throw things away? *(They don't know how to fix things, people who do fix things are too busy to do the work, and our economy depends on people's buying new things.)* BL Why is this a problem? *(It is causing our landfills to become too full.)* OL

Readability Scores
Dale-Chall: 5.6
DRP: 57
Lexile: 1070

Reading in the Real World

Citizenship Explain that people have been aware of problems with garbage and pollution for many years and have attempted various solutions. Congress has passed a variety of environmental laws, including the Clean Air Act. People have founded conservation groups and promoted events such as Earth Day.

Have students use encyclopedias and Internet resources to find additional examples of the actions being taken to protect the planet and conserve natural resources. Ask each student to choose one solution and write a paragraph that describes the problem, the solution, and the positive and negative results of the solution. AL

Objectives

- Compare and contrast: author's craft
- Understand content-area words

Teach

BQ 

Say: Progress in food production and medical care has contributed to population increases. What negative effect of population growth does Rooney mention? *(There is less room for garbage because people take up more room.)* **OL**

L1 Literary Element

Author's Craft Ask: Why does the author use numerals in the third paragraph on this page? *(The numbers make clear that the author will discuss two aspects of the problem.)* **OL**

L2 Literary Element

Author's Craft Ask: Which words show you the author's attitude toward manufacturers? *(The words* dumb, irresponsible, *and* evil *communicate Rooney's negative feelings toward manufacturers who do not dispose of their garbage properly.)* **OL** Do you agree with Rooney's assessment that some of the manufacturers are "evil"? *(Possible response: Certain manufacturers continued to pollute even though they knew that they were harming the environment. I agree that this is evil.)* **AL**

Sometime around the year 500 B.C., the Greeks in Athens passed a law **prohibiting** people from throwing their garbage in the street. This Greek law was the first recognition by civilized people that throwing things away was a problem. Now, as the population explodes and people take up more room on earth, there's less room for everything else. **2** **BQ**

The more civilized a country is, the worse the trash problem is. Poor countries don't have the same problem because they don't have much to discard. **Prosperity** in the United States is based on using things up as fast as we can, throwing away what's left and buying new ones.

We've been doing that for so many years that 1) we've run out of places to throw things because houses have been built where the dump was, and 2) some of the things we're throwing away are poisoning the earth and will eventually poison all of us and all living things. **3** **L1**

Ten years ago most people thought nothing of dumping an old bottle of weed or insect killer in a pile of dirt in the backyard or down the drain in the street, just to get rid of it. The big companies in America had the same feeling, on a bigger scale. For years the chemical companies dumped their poisonous wastes in the rivers behind the mills or they put it in fifty-gallon drums in the vacant lots, with all the old, rusting machinery in it, up behind the plants. The drums rusted out in ten years and dumped their poison into the ground. It rained, the poisons seeped into the underground streams and poisoned everything for miles around. Some of the manufacturers who did this weren't even evil. They were dumb and irresponsible. Others were evil because they knew how dangerous it was but didn't want to spend the money to do it right. **4** **L2**

The problem is staggering. I often think of it when I go in a hardware store or a Sears, Roebuck[1] and see shelves full of

1. ***Sears, Roebuck*** is the chain of retail stores now called Sears.

Vocabulary

prohibiting (proh HIB it ing) *adj.* preventing or forbidding

prosperity (praw SPAIR uh tee) *n.* the condition of being successful or having good fortune

Practice the Skills

2 BIG Question

Rooney writes about trash laws that were made more than 1,500 years ago. What does this say about civilization's "progress"? Write your answer on a note card and add it to Foldable 5.

3 Reading Across Texts

Author's Craft In this paragraph, how does Rooney show that there is more than one aspect to the problem he discusses?

4 Reading Across Texts

Author's Craft The author's attitude toward a subject is the *tone.* What words does Rooney use in this paragraph that show his attitude toward certain manufacturers? Write your answer in your chart.

Additional Support

English Language Coach

Suffixes Draw a chart on the board like the one shown here.

Suffix	Meaning	Examples
-ous	full of; having the qualities of	poisonous, dangerous
-ful	full of; having the qualities of	joyful, careful

Remind students that a suffix is a word part attached to the end of a root word. A suffix changes the meaning of a word and may also change the word's part of speech. Point out that each root word in the examples is a noun. When the suffix *-ous* or *-ful* is added to the root word, the word becomes an adjective. **EL**

A forklift operator drives past pallets stacked with crushed aluminum for recycling.

poison. You know that, one way or another, it's all going to end up in the earth or in our rivers and lakes.

I have two pint bottles of insecticide with 5 percent DDT[2] in them in my own garage that I don't know what to do with. I bought them years ago when I didn't realize how bad they were. Now I'm stuck with them.

The people of the City of New York throw away nine times their weight in garbage and junk every year. Assuming other cities come close to that, how long will it be before we trash the whole earth?

Of all household waste, 30 percent of the weight and 50 percent of the volume is the packaging that stuff comes in.

Not only that but Americans spend more for the packaging of food than all our farmers together make in income growing it. That's some statistic. 5

2. An ***insecticide*** is a chemical used to kill insects such as mosquitoes. The *insecticide* ***DDT*** is no longer used in the United States.

Practice the Skills

5 **Reading Across Texts**

Author's Craft Facts can be proved. Opinions cannot be proved. What parts of Rooney's statements about waste and packaging are facts? Why do you think Rooney includes these facts about garbage? L

Teach

L Literary Element

Author's Craft Say: Rooney gives three facts to back up his opinions about waste. What fact does he provide about New York City trash? *(New York City residents throw out nine times their weight in garbage every year.)* What two facts does Rooney provide about packaging? *(Thirty percent of the weight and 50 percent of the volume of trash is packaging; Americans spend more money on food packaging than all the farmers who grow the food earn for their efforts.)* **OL**
Do you think these facts are effective in persuading you that Rooney's opinions are reasonable? *(Possible response: These facts did persuade me because they show that we are too wasteful.)* **AL**

Differentiated Instruction

Making Collages Point out to students that the photo on page 627 provides a striking image of the amount of waste Americans produce. Even when compacted into cubes, as shown in the photo, the garbage takes up a lot of space. Ask students to look online and in old magazines for additional photos that illustrate the problems of excessive waste. Suggest that students find images of healthy habitats and animals to contrast with the images of pollution and waste. Have students use the photos they find to make collages that reflect Rooney's message about the importance of conservation. **BL**

Objectives
- Analyze author's craft
- Evaluate author's use of supporting details
- Use word structure to determine word meanings

Teach

L1 Literary Element

Author's Craft Ask: What words do the terms "sanitation engineers" and "landfills" replace? *("Sanitation engineers" replaces "trash collectors." "Landfills" replaces "dumps.")* **BL**
How do the quotation marks reveal Rooney's feelings about these new terms? *(Possible responses: He calls attention to the words because he thinks they are too fancy and too polite. The words have changed but not the roles of the trash collectors or the dumps.)* **AL**

L2 Literary Element

Author's Craft Ask: What is the tone of the last paragraph? *(Possible responses: exaggerated, sarcastic)* **OL** Why do you think Rooney suggests an impossible solution? *(Possible responses: to emphasize that no magic solution exists and that everyone must work to solve pollution problems; to end with humor while making his point)* **AL**

Newly packaged products glide along a conveyor belt.

Trash collectors are a lot more independent than they used to be because we've got more trash than they've got places to put it. They have their own schedules and their own holidays. Some cities try to get in good with their trash collectors or garbagemen by calling them "**sanitation engineers**." Anything just so long as they pick it up and take it away. **6** **L1**

We often call the dump "the **landfill**" now, too. I never understood why land has to be filled, but that's what it's called. If you're a little valley just outside town, you have to be careful or first thing you know you'll be getting "filled."

If five billion people had been living on earth for the past thousand years as they have been in the past year, the planet would be nothing but one giant landfill and we'd have turned America the beautiful into one huge landfill. **7**

The best solution may be for all of us to pack up, board a spaceship and move out. If Mars is habitable,[3] everyone on Earth can abandon this planet we've trashed, move to Mars and start trashing that. It'll buy us some time. ❍ **L2**

3. A place that is ***habitable*** is fit to live in.

Practice the Skills

6 English Language Coach

Content-Area Words Rooney uses quotation marks on two phrases because they replace terms more familiar to him. How do you think he feels about these new content-area words?

7 Reading Across Texts

Author's Craft Authors sometimes target a certain group. Who do you think is Rooney's audience for this essay? Write your ideas in your chart.

Additional Support

Differentiated Instruction

Building Fluency Organize students into pairs, matching fluent readers with less fluent readers. Allow time for students to read Rooney's essay silently, and then ask partners to take turns reading the essay aloud. Remind partners to help each other with the pronunciation of difficult words. As they read, encourage students to capture the author's tone through their own tone of voice and inflection. **EL** **BL** **OL**

Before You Read A Glimpse of Home

Meet the Author

Former NASA astronaut Kathryn Sullivan was the first American woman to walk in space. During her missions on the space shuttles *Challenger* and *Discover,* she spent more than 500 hours in space. She was inducted into the Astronaut Hall of Fame in 2004.

Author Search For more about Kathryn Sullivan, go to www.glencoe.com.

Objectives (pp. 629–631)
Reading Compare and contrast: author's craft
Vocabulary Use context clues: content-area words

Vocabulary Preview

transforming (trans FORM ing) *v.* changing; form of the verb *transform* **(p. 631)** *Humans are transforming the planet.*

obligation (awb luh GAY shun) *n.* a duty; a promise to perform an act **(p. 631)** *If you borrow something, you have an obligation to return it.*

English Language Coach

Content-Area Words Look for these content-area vocabulary words in "A Glimpse of Home."

- A **spacecraft** is a vehicle that travels outside Earth's atmosphere.
- A **space shuttle** is a reusable spacecraft that moves people and equipment between Earth and space.

V

Get Ready to Read

Connect to the Reading

How would it feel to travel in space? What would be the best part of the trip? What would be the most frightening?

Build Background

- Kathryn Sullivan helped set the Hubble Space Telescope in place.
- NASA tracks the giant dust clouds that are visible in space. Satellites record the path of dust from Africa and Asia that ends up in the Americas. Dust from the Middle East often lands in India and China.

Set Purposes for Reading

BIG Question Read to find out whether progress in space travel can change the way a person views the world's problems.

Set Your Own Purpose What else would you like to learn about the experience of being in space? Write your own purpose on a note card and add it to Foldable 5.

Teach

More About the Author

During her spaceflights, Kathryn Sullivan gathered information about Earth's atmosphere. This information increased scientists' understanding of climate. Sullivan became Chief Scientist at the National Oceanic and Atmospheric Administration in 1993, where she studied climate change and ocean life. She later worked on a nationwide study of ocean ecosystems. Her report on this study includes recommendations for improvements to ocean laws and policies. She is head of COSI (Center of Science and Industry in Columbus, Ohio).

V Vocabulary

Illustrating the Words

The content-area nouns listed for this selection lend themselves well to illustration. Have students draw and label pictures representing each of them. EL BL

Literature Focus Lesson

Simile and Metaphor Tell students that Sullivan uses a simile and a metaphor in her writing. These figures of speech make comparisons between two unlike things. Have students find the simile in the passage *(like brilliant diamonds)* and tell what Sullivan is comparing *(city lights to diamonds)*. Explain that Sullivan also uses a metaphor when she compares living on Earth to living in one's home. Have students state the purpose of each comparison. *(Possible response: The simile helps readers visualize the scene. The metaphor is used to convince readers to take care of Earth as they would their home.)* AL

Objectives
- Compare and contrast: author's craft
- Understand content-area words

Teach

L Literary Element

Author's Craft Say: Word choice can offer strong clues to the author's feelings about his or her subject. Rather than calling her essay "A Glimpse of Earth," Sullivan calls it "A Glimpse of Home." What feelings does the word *home* suggest? How does this word show the author's feelings about the planet? *(Possible response:* Home *suggests feelings of safety, warmth, and love. This word shows that Sullivan loves and values Earth.)* OL

EL Language Coach

Content-Area Words
Ask: What context clues help you understand the meaning of *orbit? (world spins, ninety-minute, laps)* Judging from these context clues, what do you think an *orbit* is? *(An orbit is a circular path that one object takes around another.)* EL BL

Readability Scores
Dale-Chall: 6.6
DRP: 66
Lexile: 1180

A Glimpse of Home

by Kathryn Sullivan

I first saw the earth—the whole earth—from the shuttle *Challenger* in 1984. The view takes your breath away and fills you with childlike wonder. That's why every shuttle crew has to clean noseprints off their spacecraft's windows several times a day. An incredibly beautiful tapestry[1] of blue and white, tan, black and green seems to glide beneath you at an elegant, stately pace. But you're actually going so fast that the entire map of the world spins before your eyes with each ninety-minute **orbit**. After just one or two laps, you feel, maybe for the first time, like a citizen of a planet. 1 2

All the colors and patterns you see seem powerful and yet somehow fragile. You see volcanoes spewing smoke, hurricanes roiling[2] the oceans and even fine tendrils[3] of

1. A ***tapestry*** is handwoven fabric with complicated designs. Here, the pattern of colors looks like a tapestry.
2. ***Roiling*** means "stirring up," like the oceans during a hurricane.
3. ***Tendrils*** are fine, curling branches of a plant that cling to other supports. Here, the wisps of dust look like tendrils.

Practice the Skills

1 Reading Across Texts

Author's Craft Why do you think Sullivan uses the word *Home* in her title instead of *Earth*?

2 English Language Coach

Content-Area Words Write a definition for **orbit** in your Learner's Notebook. What words before and after *orbit* explain what it means?

Additional Support

English Language Coach

Space Terminology Terms connected with space and related sciences may be difficult for English Language Learners. Ask pairs of students to use English dictionaries, bilingual dictionaries, encyclopedias, and the Internet to define the following space and science terms.

- astronaut *(a person who travels into space, beyond Earth's atmosphere)*
- mission *(a trip into space with a definite goal or purpose)*
- crew *(people responsible for duties on an in-flight aircraft or spacecraft)*
- global *(involving the entire world; worldwide)*
- data *(factual information)* EL BL

Saharan dust[4] reaching across the Atlantic. You also see the big, gray smudges of fields, paddies and pastures, and at night you marvel at the lights, like brilliant diamonds, that reveal a mosaic[5] of cities, roads and coastlines—impressive signs of the hand of humanity. Scientists tell us that our hand is heavy, that we are wiping out other species at an unprecedented rate and probably **transforming** our climate. Will the immense power of global systems withstand the impact of humanity? Or is it possible that our collective actions will change the nature of our planet enough to cripple its ability to support life? 3

I no longer believe that we can wait for all the scientific data needed to answer these questions conclusively. We must recognize immediately what it means to be citizens of this planet. It means accepting our **obligation** to be stewards[6] of the earth's life-giving capacities. As homeowners, we wouldn't neglect or damage our houses until they weren't fit to live in. Why would we do that with our planet? 4 5 ○

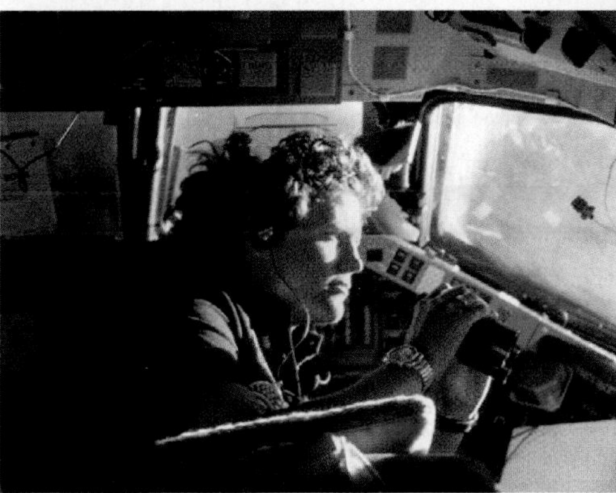

Astronaut Kathryn Sullivan views Earth from the *Challenger.*

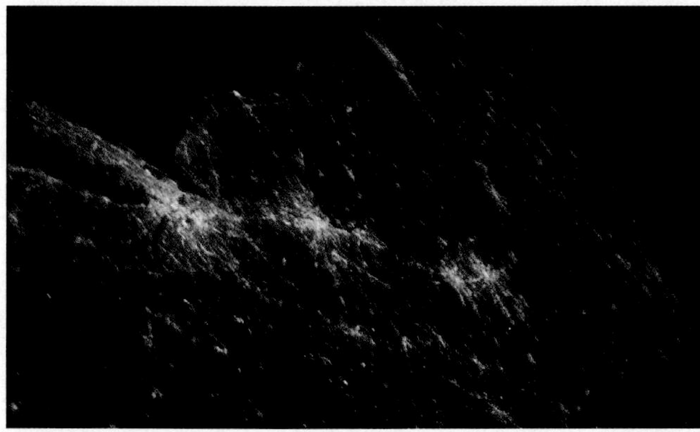

The lights of cities in the northeastern United States shine "like brilliant diamonds."

4. The ***Saharan dust*** refers to sand blown from the Sahara, a large desert in Africa.
5. A ***mosaic*** is a decoration made by laying small pieces of colored material to form a picture.
6. Someone who manages or takes care of things is called a ***steward.***

Vocabulary

transforming (trans FORM ing) *v.* changing

obligation (awb luh GAY shun) *n.* a duty; a promise to perform an act

Practice the Skills

3 BIG Question

As an astronaut, Sullivan has used machines that few people will ever experience. How does her experience with progress affect her view of the world? **BQ** Write your answer on a note card and add it to Foldable 5.

4 **Reading Across Texts**

Author's Craft What solutions does Sullivan say are necessary? Write your answer in your chart.

5 **Reading Across Texts**

Author's Craft How is Sullivan's tone different from Rooney's tone? **L**

Teach

BQ 

Say: Technological advances enabled Sullivan to take part in a great achievement—space travel. How might her experience with space travel influence her attitude toward progress? *(Possible response: Sullivan understands the power and possibility of technological advances. The advances have also allowed her to see the damage that human progress has caused the planet. She understands both the good and the bad aspects of progress.)* **AL**

L Literary Element

Author's Craft Ask: What is the tone of Sullivan's essay? How does it compare with the tone of Rooney's essay? *(Possible response: Sullivan's tone reflects her awe at what she has seen. It is more serious than Rooney's tone, which is sarcastic and humorous.)* **OL** What do you think each author wishes to accomplish through the use of tone? *(Possible response. Rooney uses humor to catch readers' interest and move his audience to action. Sullivan wants to appeal to people's consciences and inspire readers on an emotional level.)* **AL**

Differentiated Instruction

Evaluation Have students write evaluations of Rooney's and Sullivan's arguments and the ways in which they presented their arguments. Have students focus on the tone, organization, and purpose of each author. Students should state which presentation they found more convincing and why. Tell students to share their findings with the class in brief oral presentations and encourage them to provide details from each essay to support their responses. **AL**

Objectives

- Identify elements of author's craft
- Identify and understand figurative language, such as similes and metaphors
- Use context clues to understand content-area words

Assess

Resources for page 632

- Selection Quick Check
- Comparing Literature Assessment

Vocabulary Check

1. prohibiting
2. obligation
3. prosperity
4. discarding
5. prohibiting
6. transforming
7. prosperity
8. obligation
9. insecticide: a chemical used to kill insects. My parents refuse to use an *insecticide* to kill insects on the apples we grow.
10. orbit: path that a planet or moon follows around a large body such as the Sun or Earth. The astronauts make a complete *orbit* of Earth every ninety minutes.

After You Read

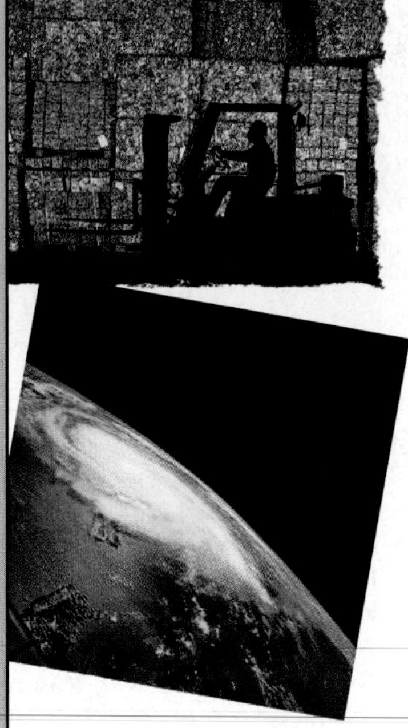

Objectives (pp. 632–633)
Reading Compare and contrast: author's craft
Writing Write to compare texts
Vocabulary Understand content-area words

AMERICA *the Not-So-Beautiful* & *A Glimpse of* **Home**

Vocabulary Check

Copy each sentence, filling in the blank with the best word from the list. You'll use three words more than once.

AMERICA *the Not-So-Beautiful*	*A Glimpse of* **Home**
discarding	**transforming**
prohibiting	**obligation**
prosperity	

1. A school dress code ___ shorts means that no student can wear them to school.
2. If you borrow something, you have the ___ to return it to its owner.
3. Mr. and Mrs. Wilson's business was doing extremely well, and they began to enjoy their ___.
4. When the worn-out chairs are replaced with new ones, the library is ___ its used furniture.
5. A new rule ___ the use of aluminum baseball bats went into effect.
6. We watched the caterpillar as it was ___ into a butterfly or moth.
7. In times of ___, people have more cash to spend.
8. Politicians have an ___ to serve the public, but many of them do not do their duty.

English Language Coach Explain the meaning of each content-area word below. Then use each word in a sentence.

9. **insecticide**
10. **orbit**

Author's Craft Element	"America the Not-So-Beautiful"	"A Glimpse of Home"
Organization	presents causes and effects of too much garbage	describes Earth from outer space and then presents her opinion
Tone	humorous, sarcastic, ironic	serious, thoughtful
Purpose	to entertain, to convince readers to stop throwing away so much garbage, to give facts	to convince people to care for Earth as they would for their homes
Audience	average Americans, people who like humor	average Americans, people who like space

Reading/Critical Thinking

Key Reading Skill: Author's Craft

Answer the following questions. Read the tips to find the information you need.

AMERICA *the Not-So-Beautiful*

11. **Interpret** What do you think Rooney means when he says that "the more civilized a country is, the worse the trash problem is"?
    TIP **Author and Me**
12. **Analyze** Rooney says that when he sees poisons, he knows that they will eventually end up in the earth, in rivers, or in lakes. What point is Rooney making?
    TIP **Author and Me**

A Glimpse of **Home**

13. **Summarize** How does Sullivan describe the view of Earth from space?
    TIP **Think and Search**
14. **Interpret** Sullivan says that after orbiting Earth, a person feels like "a citizen of the planet." What do you think she means?
    TIP **Author and Me**

Writing: Reading Across Texts

Use Your Notes

15. Follow these steps to compare the author's craft in "America the Not-So-Beautiful" and "A Glimpse of Home."

    Step 1: Look over the chart you completed. Draw a box around details that are similar for both. Underline details that are different.

    Step 2: Look at your chart. Write a sentence that explains Rooney and Sullivan's shared concern about Earth.

    Step 3: Identify the element in which you see the biggest difference between the authors.

    Step 4: Group together your examples of similarities and differences. You will use this information, as well as examples from the text, to back up your statements in the assignment.

Get It on Paper

To compare and contrast the author's craft in "America the Not-So-Beautiful" and "A Glimpse of Home," answer the following questions.

16. Do the authors of "America the Not-So-Beautiful" and "A Glimpse of Home" have the same purpose, or are they different? Explain your answer.
17. Do you think the audience for each article is the same or different? Explain your answer.
18. Did the authors use the same tone in their articles or different tones? Explain your answer.
19. Are the authors' choices of organization the same or different? Were their choices effective? Why or why not?

BIG Question

20. Which article did you think used the most interesting and effective way to answer the question "Is progress always good?" Explain your answer.

Web Activities For eFlashcards, Selection Quick Checks, and other Web activities, go to www.glencoe.com.

READING ACROSS TEXTS

11. Possible response: Technologically advanced countries create more products that will be thrown away.
12. No matter how they are disposed, poisons continue to affect the environment.
13. Sullivan describes it as an amazing view that fills her with wonder.
14. Possible response: Seeing the world from outer space makes you realize all living things must share a planet.
15. Sample answers: See below.
16. Rooney's purpose is to entertain while discussing the shortage of landfills. Sullivan wants to create awareness and inspire people to care for Earth.
17. People who prefer humor may not read Sullivan's essay. Those interested in reading about space may not read Rooney's.
18. Rooney's was humorous; Sullivan's was serious.
19. Both authors present opinions. Rooney uses cause and effect. Sullivan presents a description followed by a call for action.
20. Responses should reflect the authors' use of craft.

Close

Hold a discussion based on question 20. Do students agree or disagree with the authors?

Author's Craft Element	"America the Not-So-Beautiful"	"A Glimpse of Home"
Conclusion	People throw away too much garbage, our landfills are overflowing	We must treat Earth better.
Word Choice	Uses words like *dumb* and *irresponsible* to describe manufacturers and *staggering* to describe the problem of garbage. These words make a point that Rooney thinks the problem is serious.	Uses descriptive phrases like *volcanoes spewing smoke* to create vivid images. Uses comparisons to make point about saving Earth.

The Unit Challenge

Focus

BELLRINGER Options

Daily Language Practice Transparency

Focus Activity Say: The selections in this unit present pros and cons of science, technology, and progress. Think about what you have read in this unit, and give examples of progress that produced both good and bad results. *(Possible response: The assembly line in "The Next Big Thing" led not only to highways that threaten natural spaces but also to assembly-line robots that quickly and safely make the products humans need.)* The discussion will remind students of the selections they've read, which will help them begin the group activity or the solo activity.

Answering

Is Progress Always Good?

You've just read different selections about science, technology, and progress. Now use what you've learned to do the Unit Challenge.

The Unit Challenge

Choose Activity A or Activity B, and follow the directions for that activity.

A. Group Activity: Debate It!

- Your group will form two teams to debate whether a new shopping center in your community is a good idea.
- The "con" team will argue against the new mall. The "pro" team will argue in favor of it.
- Decide when you'll debate. (Be sure to give yourselves enough time to prepare.) Set a time limit; fifteen minutes should be enough.

1. **Discuss the Assignment** Choose one team member to be the note-taker for the discussion. Review the notes from your Foldable about the negative and positive changes of progress. Think about the good and bad effects that a new mall may have on your community. What may be done to make the bad effects less bad?

2. **Review Your Notes and Build Your Argument** As a team, organize yourselves for the debate.
   - List your arguments in order from strongest to weakest.
   - Identify examples from your own experiences.
   - Read the list aloud to see whether your teammates agree with the information. Be sure that no idea is left out.

3. **Hold the Debate** Here are some guidelines for the debate:
   - Flip a coin to decide which team goes first.
   - One person from each team makes a two-minute opening statement that explains why the mall is or is not a good idea.
   - Then, one at a time, other members from each team take turns speaking.

4. **Discuss Your Debate** When the fifteen minutes (or whatever limit you set) is over, discuss what you have learned about the idea of progress. As one group, talk about the good and bad effects of progress. Consider why change is often both positive and negative.

Big Question Link to Web resources to further explore the Big Question at www.glencoe.com.

Teach

Group Activity: Debate It!

- You may select the note taker or ask for volunteers.
- Encourage groups of students to have a brainstorm session to consider *both* the pros *and* the cons of a new shopping center. Tell students to address their opponents' points in their arguments.
- Review the format of the debate, and remind students that each team will need to present a two-minute opening statement. Give students time to practice their opening statements.
- Select a student timekeeper to make sure that each opening statement is limited to two minutes.
- Make sure that each student shares the way that the debate may have changed his or her thoughts about progress.

Assess/Close

Group Activity

Ask: How can you apply what you have learned about the pros and cons of progress to your daily life? *(Suggest that students write their answers in their Learner's Notebook.)*

B. Solo Activity: Interview an Adult

In Activity B, you'll interview an adult about his or her experiences with a new invention or a new type of technology. Follow the below steps to plan your interview.

1. **Find an Adult and an Invention** It should be easy to find adults who've had to learn to deal with new inventions. It may be harder to decide on one invention. Home computers, cell phones, MP3 players–these are just a few newer inventions.

   It may be best to start by choosing an adult. Older adults will have had more experiences with new technology. Select someone and ask that person whether you may interview him or her.

   Prepare for the conversation by making a list of questions:

   - What invention came along that you had to learn to use?
   - Was it difficult to learn to use the invention? Was it difficult to get used to?
   - What did you do before this invention came along?
   - In what ways did the invention affect your life?
   - What other recent inventions do you depend on?
   - What positive and negative changes can new technologies bring?

   Look at your Unit 5 Foldable notes to get ideas for other questions.

2. **Conduct Your Interview** Make an appointment with the person you'll interview. Plan that the interview will take twenty minutes. As you do the interview, take plenty of notes. If you have a tape recorder, use it to record the interview.

3. **Summarize Your Interview** As soon as possible after the interview, review your notes or the recording. Then, in a few paragraphs, summarize the conversation. Identify the person you interviewed, and say when and where the conversation took place. List the major points you discussed. Finish with a sentence that summarizes the ideas of the person you interviewed.

Teach

Solo Activity: Interview an Adult

- Have students skim their Foldable notes to write lists of new inventions or types of technology that they could ask about in their interviews.
- Help each student choose both a first-choice and a second-choice interviewee; the student should know and trust each adult.
- Make sure students contact the interviewees to set meeting times.
- Before the interviews, review note-taking strategies that students can use during their interviews.
- After the interviews, have students write summaries. Tell students to review their summaries and make sure that everything is correct.
- Make sure students contact their interviewees to thank them for the interviews.

Assess/Close

Solo Activity

Invite students to share their interview summaries with the class and tell what they've learned about people's experiences with new technology.

Objectives
- Work with a team to build arguments in preparation for debate
- Participate in class debate
- Summarize the content of an interview

Focus

Vocabulary Preview

List the following words on the board:

- complex
- acceded
- depression
- contortions
- desperation
- somber

Review their definitions before students begin reading.

Build Background

This story is an example of science fiction.

- Stories are set in invented times or places.
- Science fiction presents events that are based on some scientific discovery.
- Most science fiction works examine the interplay between scientific or technological advances and their effects on human beings.

Teach

L Literary Element

Review Description Say: How is Weaver feeling? *(Possible response: tired and frustrated)* OL

Readability Scores
Dale-Chall: 6.3
DRP: 55
Lexile: 720

Your Turn: Read and Apply Skills

Isaac Asimov

Meet the Author
Isaac Asimov described his talent for explaining scientific principles as the ability to "read a dozen books and make one interesting book out of them." Asimov wrote or edited more than 500 books during his life—far more than millions of Americans will read in a lifetime. Born in Russia, Asimov was raised in Brooklyn, New York. In addition to being a writer, he was a biochemist and taught biochemistry at Boston University. See page R1 of the Author Files for more on Isaac Asimov.

Author Search For more about Isaac Asimov, go to www.glencoe.com.

Key Item

by Isaac Asimov

L Jack Weaver came out of the vitals[1] of Multivac looking utterly worn and disgusted.

From the stool, where the other maintained his own stolid[2] watch, Todd Nemerson said, "Nothing?"

"Nothing," said Weaver. "Nothing, nothing, nothing. No one can find anything wrong with it."

"Except that it won't work, you mean."

"You're no help sitting there!"

"I'm thinking."

"Thinking!" Weaver showed a canine[3] at one side of his mouth.

---

1. ***Vitals*** are parts that are necessary to keep a body alive or a machine operating.
2. Nemerson is keeping up ***(maintaining)*** an unemotional ***(stolid)*** attitude.
3. Weaver shows his disgust by curling his upper lip, revealing a tooth. The two pointed teeth on each side of the top front teeth are called ***canine*** (KAY nyn) teeth.

Additional Support

Author Search To expand students' appreciation of Isaac Asimov, have them access the Web site for additional information and resources.

Literature Focus Lesson

Summary The world's economy depends on Multivac, a complicated computer system. One day Multivac refuses to respond to a command program. Two computer technicians, Weaver and Nemerson, are part of a team trying to fix Multivac. Nemerson suggests that the computer has become as complex as a human. Weaver scoffs at the idea but agrees to model for Nemerson how he delivered the command program Multivac refused to respond to. Nemerson realizes that the problem was Weaver's delivery, and he redelivers the command program, adding the word *please.* Multivac responds immediately to the respectful request. OL

Nemerson stirred impatiently on his stool. "Why not? There are six teams of computer technologists roaming around in the corridors of Multivac. They haven't come up with anything in three days. Can't you spare one person to think?"

L1

"It's not a matter of thinking. We've got to look. Somewhere a relay[4] is stuck."

"It's not that simple, Jack!"

"Who says it's simple. You know how many million relays we have there?"

"That doesn't matter. If it were just a relay, Multivac would have alternate circuits, devices for locating the flaw, and facilities to repair or replace the ailing part. The trouble is, Multivac won't only not answer the original question, it won't tell us what's wrong with it. —And meanwhile, there'll be panic in every city if we don't do something. The world's economy depends on Multivac, and everyone knows that."

"I know it, too. But what's there to do?"

"I told you, *think*. There must be something we're missing completely. Look, Jack, there isn't a computer bigwig[5] in a hundred years who hasn't devoted himself to making Multivac more complicated. It can do so much now—hell, it can even talk and listen. It's practically as complex as the human brain. We can't understand the human brain, so why should we understand Multivac?"

R

"Aw, come on. Next you'll be saying Multivac is human."

"Why not?" Nemerson grew absorbed and seemed to sink into himself. "Now that you mention it, why not? Could we tell if Multivac passed the thin dividing line where it stopped being a machine and started being human? Is there a dividing line, for that matter? If the brain is just more complex than Multivac, and we keep making Multivac more complex, isn't there a point where . . ." He mumbled down into silence.

L2

Weaver said impatiently, "What are you driving at? Suppose Multivac were human. How would that help us find out why it isn't working?"

"For a human reason, maybe. Suppose you were asked the most probable price of wheat next summer and didn't answer. Why wouldn't you answer?"

"Because I wouldn't know. But Multivac would know! We've given it all the factors. It can analyze futures in weather, politics, and economics. We know it can. It's done it before."

"All right. Suppose I asked the question and you knew the answer but didn't tell me. Why not?"

Weaver snarled, "Because I had a brain tumor. Because I had been knocked out. Doggone it, because my machinery was out of order. That's just what we're trying to find out about Multivac. We're looking for the place where its machinery is out of order, for the key item."

4. A ***relay*** sends electrical signals that control parts of a machine such as Multivac. Here, Weaver thinks one of the *relays* isn't operating correctly.

5. A ***bigwig*** is an important person in some official position.

Teach

L1 Literary Element

Review Author's Craft
Say: Notice that most of the story is told through dialogue. How does dialogue help you understand the characters? *(Responses will vary. Students may note that the dialogue helps them understand the characters' thoughts and feelings about the problem.)* AL

R Reading Skill

Review Paraphrasing and Summarizing **Ask:** Summarize the disagreement between Weaver and Nemerson. *(Possible responses: Weaver believes that the problem with Multivac must be mechanical, while Nemerson believes that the problem must be human. Weaver believes that the problem must be solved through action, while Nemerson believes that the problem must be solved through thought.)* OL

L2 Literary Element

Review Concept and Definition **Ask:** Why does Nemerson believe there's only a thin dividing line between humans and Multivac? *(Nemerson explains that the ability to think in complex ways is human. Although he suggests that machines are slightly less complex than the human brain, he speculates that there is only a thin dividing line between them.)* AL

Objectives
- Analyze author's craft
- Paraphrase and summarize text
- Recognize key concepts and definitions

Reading in the Real World

Career Share with students the following list of skills required for computer hardware engineers:
- Listens actively and works well with a team
- Solves problems using mathematical and scientific ideas and processes
- Incorporates new information into current thinking
- Uncovers and solves problems
- Analyzes computer systems
- Evaluates computer systems

Have students write job evaluations for Weaver and Nemerson based on this skill list. Which skills has each character mastered? Which skills does each character need to improve? OL

Teach

Viewing the Photo

Ask: How does this picture help you understand the setting? *(Responses will vary. Students may say that the picture helps them see how huge Multivac is.)* **OL** What other photos or illustrations would help you better understand the story? Explain. *(Responses will vary. Students may suggest pictures of the main characters would be helpful because there is no narrative description of them.)* **BL**

R Reading Skill

Review Identifying Problem and Solution

Ask: Why does Nemerson believe that having Weaver read the program to him will help solve the problem? *(He thinks that seeing how he would respond to Weaver's request will help him understand how Multivac responded. He thinks this because he believes Multivac has human responses.)* **AL**

"Only you haven't found it."

Nemerson got off his stool. "Listen, ask me the question Multivac stalled on."

"How? Shall I run the tape through you?"

"Come on, Jack. Give me the talk that goes along with it. You do talk to Multivac, don't you?"

"I've got to. Therapy.[6]"

Nemerson nodded. "Yes, that's the story. Therapy. That's the official story. We talk to it in order to pretend it's a human being so that we don't get neurotic[7] over having a machine know so much more than we do. We turn a frightening metal monster into a protective father image."

"If you want to put it that way."

R "Well, it's wrong and you know it. A computer as complex as Multivac *must* talk and listen to be efficient. Just putting in and taking out coded dots isn't sufficient.[8] At a certain level of complexity, Multivac must be made to seem human because, by God, it is human. Come on, Jack, ask me the question. I want to see my reaction to it."

Jack Weaver flushed. "This is silly."

"Come on, will you?"

It was a measure of Weaver's depression and desperation that he acceded. Half sullenly,[9] he pretended to be feeding the program into Multivac, speaking as he did

6. ***Therapy*** is treatment of a physical or mental condition. It can also be used in the prevention of such problems.
7. If people become ***neurotic*** (noo RAW tik), they may show signs of a mental problem.
8. To be ***efficient*** is to produce a desired effect with the least amount of effort or waste. ***Sufficient*** is to do just enough to be satisfactory.
9. When Weaver ***acceded*** (ak SEED ed), he gave up; but, he did it in a stubborn way ***(sullenly)***.

Additional Support

Differentiated Instruction

Building a Model Point out to students that engineers have been continually adding to Multivac, making it bigger and more complex. Provide each student with several three-dimensional craft materials—such as chenille stems, paper tubes, and craft sticks—as well as paper, glue, paint, markers, and scissors. Have each student use his or her supplies to build a part of Multivac. Tell students to think about the functions of their computer components. After they have completed their components, have students work together in groups to assemble the components into a single machine. On the board, note all of the different functions of each group's Multivac. **OL**

so in his usual manner. He commented on the latest information concerning farm unrest, talked about the new equations describing jet-stream contortions, lectured on the solar constant.

He began stiffly enough, but warmed to this task out of long habit, and when the last of the program was slammed home, he almost closed contact with a physical snap at Todd Nemerson's waist.

He ended briskly, "All right, now. Work that out and give us the answer **C** pronto."

For a moment, having done, Jack Weaver stood there, nostrils flaring, as though he was feeling once more the excitement of throwing into action the most gigantic and glorious machine ever put together by the mind and hands of humans. **L**

Then he remembered and muttered, "All right. That's it."

Nemerson said, "At least I know now why I wouldn't answer, so let's try that on Multivac. Look, clear Multivac; make sure the investigators have their paws off it. Then run the program into it and let me do the talking. Just once."

Weaver shrugged and turned to Multivac's control wall, filled with its somber, unwinking dials and lights. Slowly he cleared it. One by one he ordered the teams away.

Then, with a deep breath, he began once more feeding the program into Multivac. It was the twelfth time all told, the dozenth time. Somewhere a distant news commentator would spread the word that they were trying again. All over the world a Multivac-dependent people would be holding its collective[10] breath.

Nemerson talked as Weaver fed the data silently. He talked diffidently,[11] trying to remember what it was that Weaver had said, but waiting for the moment when the key item might be added.

Weaver was done and now a note of tension was in Nemerson's voice. He said, "All right, now, Multivac. Work that out and give us the answer." He paused and added the key item. He said, *"Please!"*

And all over Multivac, the valves and relays went joyously to work. After all, a machine has feelings—when it isn't a machine anymore. ❍ **BQ**

10. ***Collective*** means "having to do with a group of people or things; shared."

11. ***Diffidently*** means "in a way that shows a lack of confidence; shyly."

English Language Coach

Foreign Words Tell students that the word *pronto* comes from the Spanish language. In English, it is used to mean "at once, quickly, or immediately." Introduce students to other foreign words that they may read or hear in English. Ask student pairs to use dictionaries to find the origin and meaning of each word.

aficionado	*faux pas*
bona fide	*pro bono*
carpe diem	**EL**

Teach

C Critical Thinking

Evaluation Ask: What is the most significant part of Weaver's instructions to Multivac? *(Weaver gives the command, "Work that out and give us the answer pronto.")* **OL** Why is this the most significant part of the instructions? *(Weaver issues a command rather than a request, which offends Multivac.)* **AL**

L Literary Element

Review Description
Ask: How do you think Weaver feels about Multivac? *(Possible response: Weaver treats Multivac like a machine. He does not speak to it with respect.)* How does the description tell you how Weaver feels? *(Words such as "lectured," "slammed," and "briskly" show that Weaver doesn't believe the machine requires any courtesy.)* **OL**

BQ BIG Question

Ask: What might be the negative effects of computers having feelings? *(Possible response: The negative effects might include computers' refusing to do tasks, computers' becoming greedy and stealing from humans, and computers' wanting more power.)* **OL**

Objectives
- Locate information in text features to aid understanding
- Take notes about important information
- Identify use of description
- Identify problems and solutions

Tips for Independent Reading

Advise students to read in an appropriate environment. Suggest that students find a quiet place to read with no distractions so that they can focus on the text. Recommend that they avoid reading in bed or anywhere else where they might be inclined to fall asleep while reading.

Fiction

Tell students that reading fiction allows them to think about changes in the world around them and to understand different points of view about change.

Ask students to share examples of fictional stories they've read that gave them insight into how progress affected the characters. Have students share how they thought they might react to the changes presented in the stories.

UNIT 5

Reading on Your Own

To read more about the Big Question, choose one of these books from your school or local library. Work on your reading skills by choosing books that are challenging to you.

Fiction

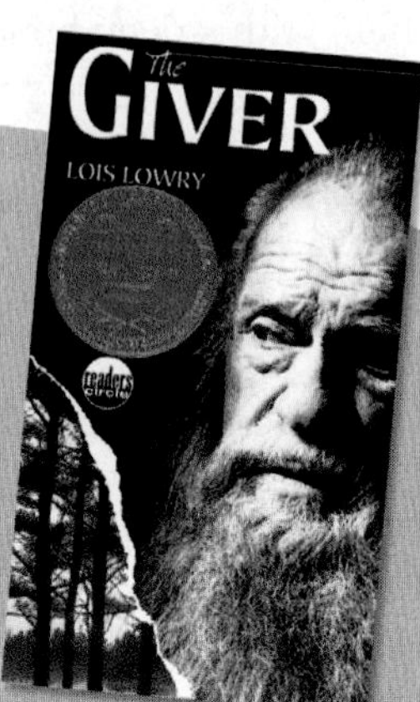

The Giver
by Lois Lowry

This story reveals what people in the main character's world sacrificed to create a perfect society.

Maniac Magee
by Jerry Spinelli

Jeffrey Lionel "Maniac" Magee can run faster and hit a ball better than anyone around. He even has the courage to travel between the different areas of his town. Read about how Jeffrey becomes a legend and helps bridge racial gaps in the process.

Lizzie Bright and the Buckminster Boy
by Gary D. Schmidt

A 13-year-old boy befriends a girl from an island community founded by former slaves. When mainlanders try to force the islanders to leave, the boy must stand up to racism and the "progress" that threatens his new friend's community.

Hoot
by Carl Hiaasen

When new restaurant construction threatens an owl community, local middle school kids use funny and interesting tactics to battle the adults and save the owls.

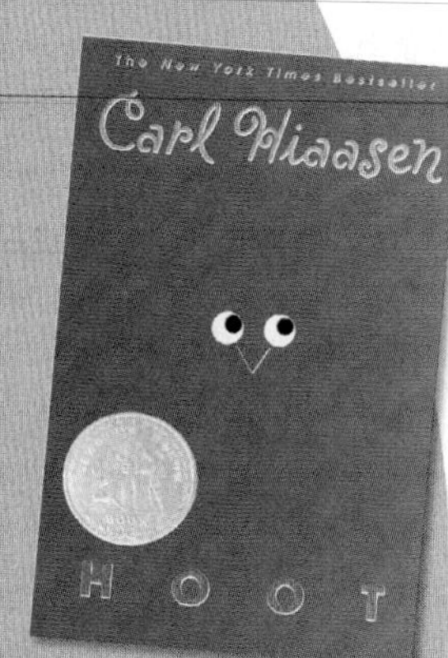

Additional Support

Differentiated Instruction

BOOKLINK Use the Glencoe BookLink CD-ROM to create customized reading lists to help students answer the Big Question. Suggestions for Unit 5:

Grade 4: *Cracking the Wall: The Struggles of the Little Rock Nine* by Eileen Lucas
Grade 5: *Tornadoes!* by Lorraine Jean Hopping
Grade 6: *Dance of the Planets: The Universe of Nicolaus Copernicus* by Nancy Veglahn
Grade 7: "If I Forget Thee, Oh Earth..." by Arthur C. Clarke
Grade 8: *Futurelife: The Biotechnology Revolution* by Alvin Silverstein, Virginia B. Silverstein, Marjorie Thier

Nonfiction

My Life with the Chimpanzees

by Jane Goodall

The world's leading authority on chimpanzees describes her thirty years of living with and studying the chimpanzees of Tanzania. Read to find out about the challenges of balancing human progress with wildlife protection.

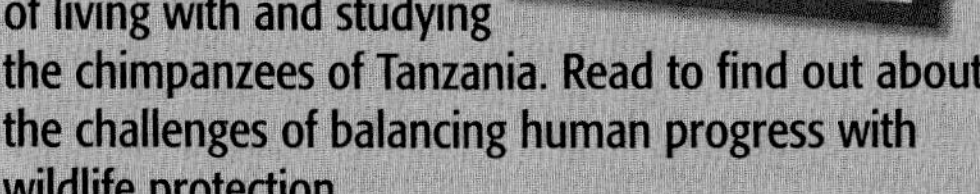

Artificial Intelligence: The Impact on Our Lives

by Alex Woolf

Machines help people perform tasks, treat diseases, and study other planets. But can they think as humans do? Can machines with artificial intelligence even replace humans?

To Space and Back

by Sally Ride

America's first female astronaut tells about her experiences traveling in space. Her detailed account helps readers imagine the journey, from blast-off to landing. Read to learn about the author's thoughts on the meaning and importance of space exploration.

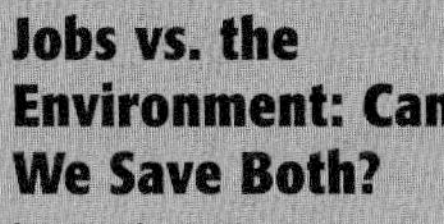

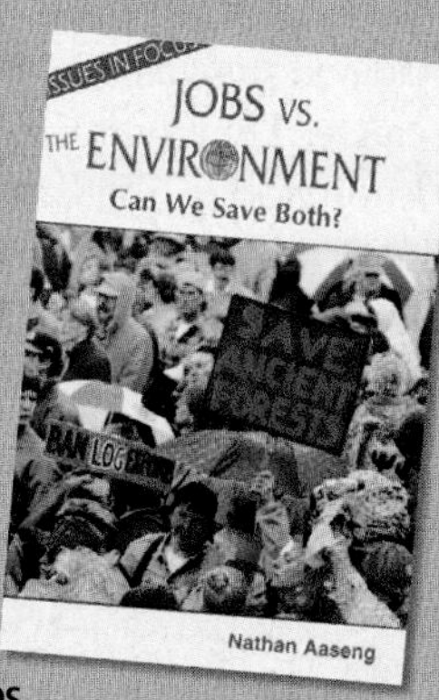

Jobs vs. the Environment: Can We Save Both?

by Nathan Aaseng

Many people believe that environmental issues interfere with a growing economy and job creation. Nathan Aaseng, however, explains that we can save the environment and save jobs.

Nonfiction

Tell students that the books on this page are all about true events. These books explain the challenges and benefits of ongoing and future progress.

Science and Technology Writing

Tell students that new discoveries in science and technology are often exciting, but they frequently result in debates. Stress the importance of reading about scientific and technological progress with an open mind, considering everyone and everything that may be affected.

About the Subjects

Invite students to share what they know about the subjects on this page. *My Life with the Chimpanzees* and *Jobs vs. the Environment: Can We Save Both?* present ways to protect wildlife and the environment in the face of human progress. Students can learn about the effects of artificial intelligence in *Artificial Intelligence: The Impact on Our Lives. To Space and Back* provides students the opportunity to visualize space travel.

Test-Taking Tips

TIP Remind students to begin by reading the directions carefully. Tell them that after they have read the questions, they should skim the passage, looking for key words that show the organization of each paragraph and for headings or subheadings that show the organization of the passage.

TIP Suggest that students note important pieces of information as they read. Point out that in a real test situation, students can feel free to underline important ideas and make notes in the margins.

Test Practice

Part 1: Literary Elements

Read the following passage. Then, on a separate sheet of paper, write the numbers 1–2. Next to each number, write the letter of the best answer for that question.

Doctors Clean Up Their Act

Infections Run Wild

Only 150 years ago, doctors delivered babies and performed operations without even washing their hands. Often these things were done on surfaces that were crawling with the germs of other ill patients. As a result, new mothers often died from a mysterious disease called "childbed fever." Patients who had operations were no luckier. They had only a 50 percent chance of surviving, even if the operation they had was successful. Doctors believed that infections were brought on by poisonous gases or some other mysterious cause. They were, of course, wrong. As we know today, the cause was germs.

Doctors Ignore the Evidence

In the mid-1800s, Louis Pasteur discovered the connection between microbes (what we call "germs") and disease. He proved that microbes cause deadly infections such as those that so often followed surgery. At about the same time, Dr. Ignaz Semmelweiss discovered that childbed fever could be prevented if doctors used an antiseptic (germ-killer) on their hands before delivering a baby. Even though their patients were dying, most doctors completely ignored the facts. They could not believe that the way they had always done things could be wrong.

Awareness Grows

Joseph Lister was one of the few doctors who understood the connection between germs and illness. Even though operating rooms did not have running water, Lister washed his hands before every operation. He also cleaned all surgical instruments with an antiseptic. Deaths at his hospital in Scotland dropped dramatically. Lister wrote about the success of his methods, but few doctors paid any attention. They were unwilling to change the way they had always behaved. For ten years, Lister traveled, lecturing on the need to kill microbes in operating rooms. He demonstrated his methods over and over again. Finally, the medical community began to pay attention. By the time Lister died, his ideas were widely accepted.

Objectives

Literature Identify literary elements: author's craft, description, organization

1. Which of the following best describes the organization of the first paragraph?
   A. Cause and effect
   B. Problem and solution
   C. Chronological order
   D. Compare and contrast

2. Which part of what makes up an author's craft is most important in an informational passage, such as this one?
   A. the mood of the passage
   B. the clearness of the information
   C. the characters described in the passage
   D. the point of view used to write the passage

Read the following passage. On your paper, write the numbers 3–5. Next to numbers 3 and 4, write the letter of the best answer for those questions. Next to number 5, write your answer for that question.

The wind picked up as the sky darkened, and the little boat rocked crazily on the tossing sea. Randall clung to a railing. His hair whipped painfully across his face; his feet slid wildly on the rain-slicked surface of the deck. Waves broke against the side of the boat, one after the other, again and again, each one threatening to break his grip. The entire boat lifted out of the water and slammed back down. Randall was flung from the railing and sent rocketing across the rolling deck to slam against the opposite side. Freezing water crashed over him, briefly numbing the stabbing pain in his left arm.

3. The description in this passage appeals *mainly* to the sense of
   A. sight
   B. smell
   C. touch
   D. hearing

4. The main purpose of the description in this passage is to help the reader imagine
   A. the violence of the storm
   B. the appearance of the boat
   C. the kind of person Randall is
   D. the emotions that Randall is feeling

5. What do you think the author is trying to do in this passage, and do you think he or she is successful? What makes the author successful or keeps the author from being successful?

Unit Assessment To prepare for the Unit test, go to www.glencoe.com.

UNIT 5 ASSESSMENT

Test Practice

Part 1: Literary Elements

1. B
2. B
3. C
4. A
5. Possible response: The author was trying to give a vivid description of being in a boat during a terrible storm. The author was successful because he or she used sensory details to describe the experience.

Resources for pages 642–647

Use these resources to review, assess, or reteach the Unit: Active Learning and Note-Taking Guide, Selection and Unit Assessment, ExamView Assessment Suite, and Differentiated Instruction Tool Software.

Unit Assessment Have students access the Web site to prepare for the Unit 5 test.

Test-Taking Tips

TIP Tell students that when they answer the questions, they should refer back to the passage and any notes they made to find evidence for their answers. On standardized tests, passages either provide the answer directly or provide enough details for students to make safe speculations.

TIP Remind students to analyze each question and its answer choices. Sometimes a single word in a question or an answer choice may relate to a key word in the passage that gives the answer.

Test Practice

Part 2: Reading Skills

1. B
2. A
3. C
4. C

Part 2: Reading Skills

Use the passage "Doctors Clean Up Their Act," on page 642 to answer the questions on this page. On a separate sheet of paper, write the numbers 1–4. Next to each number, write the letter of the right answer for that question.

1. Which of the following could you discover about "Doctors Clean Up Their Act" by reading *only* the head and subheads?

A. It will explain the cause of "childbed fever."
B. It will deal with a medical problem and solution.
C. It will explain what doctors used to believe about infection.
D. It will describe how Lister got doctors to change their behavior.

2. What is the main problem described in the passage?

A. Microbes cause infections.
B. Microbes can't be seen without a microscope.
C. Childbirth used to be extremely dangerous.
D. In the past, operating rooms did not have running water.

3. Why was it so difficult for Lister to convince doctors of the connection between germs and infection?

A. Lister's advice was too difficult to follow.
B. Lister could not show that his idea was correct.
C. Doctors did not believe they could be wrong.
D. Doctors did not believe in anything they could not see.

4. Which of the following is the best summary of the last paragraph of "Doctors Clean Up Their Act"?

A. Fewer people die from infections today than in the past, thanks to Lister's work.
B. Lister was determined to use antiseptic methods at his own hospital even though this was not easy.
C. Lister demonstrated the success of antiseptic methods and, after much effort, convinced doctors to use them.
D. Even though Lister wrote about the success of his methods, most doctors ignored what he had to say on the subject.

Objectives
Reading Use text features: heads • Identify problem and solution • Paraphrase and summarize
Vocabulary Understand content-area words • Identify word structure: suffixes, roots

UNIT 6

Skills Scope and Sequence

Readability Scores Key
Dale-Chall/DRP/Lexile

PACING (DAYS) STANDARD	BLOCK	INSTRUCTIONAL SEGMENT LITERATURE	READING SKILLS	LITERARY ELEMENTS
1	1	**Unit Warm-Up, pp. 650–655** Genre Focus: "Brer Rabbit and Brer Lion" retold by Julius Lester **4.7/43/710**, SE p. 5	Predicting, SE p. 654, Questioning, SE p. 654 Understanding Cause and Effect, SE p. 654 Analyzing, SE p. 655 How to Read Folktales, TWE p. 653	Dialect, Character, and Cultural Context, SE p. 654 Character, TWE pp. 652, 654 Dialect, TWE p. 653
3	2	**Reading Workshop 1, pp. 656–675** "The Lion, the Hare and the Hyena" retold by Phyllis Savory **5.6/59/1160**, p. 660 "Charles" by Shirley Jackson **4.6/52/770**, SE p. 668	Understanding Cause and Effect, SE pp. 656, 657, 659, 660, 661, 663, 667, 669, 671, TWE pp. 650, 655, 656, 660, 669, 670, 671, 673 Reviewing Skills- Comparing and Contrasting, SE pp. 662, 672 Reviewing Skills- Connecting, SE pp. 668, 670, TWE p. 667 Reviewing Skills- Inferring, TWE pp. 660, 661, 668, 670 Predicting, TWE p. 659	Theme, SE pp. 659, 663, 667, 673, TWE pp. 659, 663, 667, 672 Narrator, TWE p. 668
1		**Writing Workshop, Part 1, pp. 676–679** Writing Product: Modern Folktale	Questioning, TWE p. 680	Theme, TWE p. 677
3	1	**Reading Workshop 2, pp. 680–701** "The Boy and His Grandfather" by Rudolfo A. Anaya **6.6/50/820**, SE p. 684 "Jeremiah's Song" by Walter Dean Myers **4.7/52/960**, SE p. 690	Questioning, SE pp. 680, 683, 684, 689, 690, 695, 696, TWE pp. 681, 690, 694, 695 Reviewing Skills- Drawing Conclusions, SE pp. 694, 699, TWE p. 699 Predicting, TWE p. 684	Characterization, SE pp. 683, 685, TWE pp. 683, 685, 695, 698 Character, SE pp. 688, 689, 690, 692, 694, 696, 698, TWE p. 696 Dialect, SE pp. 688, 691

Use the paragraph below to answer questions 7–10.

[1] A fox who was hot and hungry and thirsty was walking through a field one summer day. [2] He saw a bunch of grapes growing high above him. [3] He knew that the grapes would of course relieve both his hunger and his thirst. [4] He leaped into the air to try to reach the delicious-looking fruit, but his teeth snapped together inches away. [5] For an hour in the hot sun he tried again and again. [6] He put more energy and effort into each leap. [7] Even so, he failed every time. [8] As he walked away, he lifted his nose in the air and said, "It doesn't matter. [9] I'm sure they're sour." [10] It's easy, you see, to look down on what you don't have and can't get.

7. What change, if any, should be made to sentence 1?

A. Add a comma after *thirsty.*
B. Add commas after *hot* and *hungry.*
C. Add commas after *through* and *field.*
D. (No change is needed.)

8. What change, if any, should be made to sentence 3?

A. Add commas around *of course.*
B. Add commas after *knew* and *grapes.*
C. Add a comma after *hunger.*
D. (No change is needed.)

9. What change, if any, should be made to sentence 5?

A. Add commas after *hour* and *sun.*
B. Add a comma only after *sun.*
C. Add a comma after *again.*
D. (No change is needed.)

10. What change, if any, should be made to sentence 10?

A. Remove the commas around *you see.*
B. Add a comma after *down.*
C. Add a comma after *have.*
D. (No change is needed.)

TIP Remind students that punctuation is used to convey a certain meaning in a clear way. Tell students to read the paragraph and note any sentences that confuse them. These notes can help students choose the correct ways to fix the sentences when answering the questions.

TIP Encourage students to write (on scrap paper, if possible) the different punctuation marks suggested by each answer choice. This way they can see how each answer choice affects the meaning of a sentence.

7. D
8. A
9. B
10. D

Test Practice

Part 4: Writing Skills

1. C
2. B
3. B
4. A
5. C
6. B

Part 4: Writing Skills

On a separate sheet of paper, write the numbers 1–10. Next to each number, write the letter of the right answer for that question.

1. In which sentence is *paint* used as an adjective?

A. We should paint the house.
B. What kind of paint do we need?
C. Maybe we could ask a paint salesman.
D. That woman seems to know a lot about paint.

2. Which sentence contains a prepositional phrase?

A. I don't know where they went.
B. There was a dark stain on my shirt.
C. Only the best teams make the tournament.
D. Whenever we get hungry, we also get grumpy.

3. Which of the following is a clause?

A. in a little brick house down the street
B. whenever someone walks in the door
C. not in a week, a month, a year, or even a century
D. some people with too much time on their hands

4. Which of the following is an independent clause?

A. that was not the end of the story
B. if everyone would just be quiet
C. because of the uniform he wore
D. after taking a long and pleasant walk

5. Which of the following sentences uses commas correctly?

A. We took books, games, and food, with us.
B. Whatever was on sale, was a real bargain.
C. I really wish, Uncle Tito, that you'd come visit.
D. His remarks as you can imagine were untrue, unfair, and mean.

6. In the following sentence, what word does the underlined clause modify?

Because the game was about to start, we ran as fast as we could toward the field.

A. we
B. ran
C. fast
D. toward

Objectives
Grammar Identify clauses and phrases • Identify parts of speech • Use punctuation: commas

Part 3: Vocabulary

On a separate sheet of paper, write the numbers 1–10. Next to each number, write the letter of the right answer for that question.

Write the letter of the word or phrase that means about the same as the underlined word.

1. an animal's **habitat**
- **A.** diet
- **B.** appearance
- **C.** natural home
- **D.** usual behavior

2. in order to **thrive**
- **A.** appear
- **B.** do well
- **C.** deserve
- **D.** survive

3. the **atrocious** story
- **A.** scary
- **B.** amusing
- **C.** believable
- **D.** extremely bad

4. to **cope with** a problem
- **A.** deal with
- **B.** try to ignore
- **C.** communicate
- **D.** manage to avoid

5. a small **fragment**
- **A.** frame
- **B.** rip or tear
- **C.** container
- **D.** broken piece

6. What is the base word in *unfriendliness*?
- **A.** end
- **B.** friend
- **C.** friendly
- **D.** unfriendly

7. Which word contains the suffix *-able* attached to a root instead of to a base word?
- **A.** capable
- **B.** breakable
- **C.** agreeable
- **D.** collectable

8. In which word are the letters *pre-* a prefix?
- **A.** pretty
- **B.** pretzel
- **C.** preach
- **D.** predict

Use what you know about base words or roots to complete each statement.

9. A *cautionary* comment is one that contains a ___.
- **A.** lie
- **B.** joke
- **C.** warning
- **D.** criticism

10. To *differentiate* things is to ___.
- **A.** contrast them
- **B.** memorize them
- **C.** understand them
- **D.** write them down

TIP Remind students that a good way to approach a multiple-choice test question is to eliminate those answers that are clearly wrong. Students can then focus on fewer choices, and the question will be easier to answer.

Test Practice

Part 3: Vocabulary

1. C
2. B
3. D
4. A
5. D
6. B
7. A
8. D
9. C
10. A

Unit 6 Big Question

The question, "Why do we share our stories?" will help students think about the stories they hear and share. They will also understand the purposes and benefits of storytelling.

Unit 6 Genre

Many of the selections in this unit are folktales. Students will read these stories that often have a moral and/or significant meaning. Reading folktales and the other selections in this unit will help students answer the Big Question.

CRITICAL THINKING	VOCABULARY	WRITING AND GRAMMAR	LISTENING, SPEAKING, AND VIEWING
Big Question, SE pp. 650, 651, TWE pp. 648, 650, 651, 663 Comprehension, TWE pp. 652, 655	Context Clues, TWE p. 654		Viewing the Photo, TWE p. 648 Viewing the Art, TWE p. 655
Big Question, SE pp. 659, 663, 667, 673, TWE pp. 663, 673 Recall, SE p. 664 Interpret, SE p. 664 Infer, SE p. 674 Synthesize, SE p. 674 Evaluate, SE p. 674	Vocabulary Preview, SE pp. 658, 666 Idioms, SE pp. 658, 662, TWE pp. 658, 662 Slang, SE pp. 666, 671, TWE pp. 666, 671 Word Circle, TWE p. 666 Fill in the Blanks, TWE p. 658 Context Clues, TWE p. 662	Write to Learn, SE pp. 659, 667 Write About Your Reading, SE p. 664, 674 Capitalizing Sentences, SE p. 665 Identifying Simple Sentences, SE p. 675	Group Talk, SE p. 658 Think-Pair-Share, SE p. 659 Viewing the Photo, TWE p. 670 Viewing the Art, TWE pp. 661, 672
Comprehension, TWE p. 676		Modern Folktale: Prewriting and Drafting, SE pp. 676, 678 Complex and Compound Sentences, SE p. 679 Write to Learn, SE p. 679 Character Sketch, TWE p. 677 Third-person Point of View, TWE p. 678 Writer's Craft, TWE p. 678 Writing Varied Sentences, TWE p. 679	Viewing the Cartoon, TWE p. 680
Big Question, SE pp. 683, 685, 689, 693, 696, 697, 699, TWE pp. 685, 696, 699 Infer, SE pp. 686, 700 Evaluate, SE pp. 686, 700, TWE p. 697	Vocabulary Preview, SE pp. 682, 688 Idioms, SE p. 682, TWE pp. 682, 684 Synonyms and Antonyms, TWE p. 682 Vocabulary Swap, TWE p. 688	Write About Your Reading, SE pp. 686, 700 Combining Sentences, SE pp. 687, 701	Partner Talk, SE pp. 683, 688, 689 Viewing the Photo, TWE pp. 691, 692, 695, 698

Skills Scope and Sequence *continued*

Readability Scores Key
Dale-Chall/DRP/Lexile

PACING (DAYS) STANDARD	BLOCK	INSTRUCTIONAL SEGMENT LITERATURE	READING SKILLS	LITERARY ELEMENTS
3	1	**Reading Workshop 3, pp. 702–723** "The Tale of 'Kiko-Wiko" by Mark Crilley "We Are All One" by Laurence Yep **4.8/51/750**, SE p. 716	Predicting, SE pp. 702, 705, 706, 708, 710, 715, 718, 720, TWE pp. 702, 703, 708, 710, 715, 716, 718 Understanding Cause and Effect, TWE p. 719	Cultural Allusions, SE pp. 705, 706, 707, 715, 717, 720, TWE pp. 705, 706, 709, 711, 715 Character, TWE p. 706, 717
1	cont'd.	**Writing Workshop, Part 2, pp. 724–729** Writing Product: Modern Folktale		
2	1	**Reading Workshop 4, pp. 730–747** "Voices—and Stories—from the Past" by Kathryn Satterfield, updated from *Time for Kids* **7.9/59/1090**, SE p. 734 "Aunty Misery" by Judith Ortiz Cofer **5.2/57/1050**, SE p. 742	Analyzing, SE pp. 730, 735, 741, 742, 745, TWE pp. 730, 731, 735, 742, 743 Connecting, TWE p. 733 Main Idea, TWE p. 734 Summarizing, TWE p. 735	Dialect, SE p. 733, 737, 741, TWE pp. 733, 736, 737, 741, 745 Magical Elements, TWE p. 742 Character, TWE p. 744
2	2	**Comparing Literature Workshop, pp. 750–755** "Aunt Sue's Stories" by Langston Hughes, p. 751 "I Ask My Mother to Sing" by Li-Young Lee, p. 753	Comparing: Cultural Context, SE pp. 748, 751, 753, TWE p. 751 Reviewing Skills- Connecting, TWE pp. 750, 752	Cultural Context, TWE pp. 748, 749
2	1	**Unit Wrap-Up, pp. 756–757** The Bunyans, **7.1/58/1100**, SE p. 758	Reading Independently, SE p. 758 Predicting, TWE p. 759 Visualize, TWE p. 760 Understanding Cause and Effect, TWE p. 761	Tall Tale. TWE pp. 758, 759, 760, 761 Character, TWE p. 761

CRITICAL THINKING	VOCABULARY	WRITING AND GRAMMAR	LISTENING, SPEAKING, AND VIEWING
Big Question, SE pp. 705, 711, 715, 721, TWE pp. 711, 721 Infer, SE pp. 712, 722 Evaluate, SE pp. 712, 722, TWE p. 703 Respond, SE p. 712 Analyze, SE p. 722 Comprehension, TWE pp. 720, 721	Vocabulary Preview, SE pp. 704, 714 Dialogue, SE p. 704, 707, 709, 710, 714, 717, 719, TWE p. 707 Idioms, TWE p. 707 Context Clues, TWE p. 720	Write About Your Reading, SE p. 712 Commas in Compound Sentences, SE p. 713 Commas in Complex Sentences, SE p. 723	Whole-class Discussion, SE p. 715 Talk About Your Reading, SE p. 722 Viewing the Art, TWE p. 718
		Revising, SE p. 724, TWE pp. 724, 728 Editing, SE p. 725, TWE p. 727 Write to Learn, SE p. 726 Proofreading, TWE p. 726 Checking Errors, TWE p. 726 Spelling, TWE p. 727	Storytelling, SE p. 729 Eye Contact, TWE p. 729 Note Cards, TWE p. 729
Compare and Contrast, SE p. 738 Evaluate, SE pp. 738, 746, TWE p. 741 Analyze, SE p. 746 Synthesize, SE p. 746	Vocabulary Preview, SE pp. 730, 740 Academic Vocabulary, SE p. 730 Literal and Metaphoric Word Meanings, SE pp. 732, 736	Write to Learn, SE pp. 733, 746 Write About Your Reading, SE p. 738 Run-On Sentences, SE pp. 739, 747	Partner Talk, SE pp. 732, 740 Talk About Your Reading, SE p. 746 Viewing the Photo, TWE pp. 734, 736, 743
Infer, SE p. 754 Analyze, SE p. 754 Interpret, SE p. 754	Figurative Use of Language, SE p. 750, TWE pp. 751, 753	Compare the Literature, SE p. 755	
Analyze, SE pp. 756, 757	Idiom, TWE p. 760	Write a Review, SE p. 757	Sharing-Stories Reading List, SE p. 756 Viewing the Painting, TWE p. 759

UNIT 6

Unit Resources

Reading with Purpose offers a comprehensive package of tools to optimize student learning and the teaching experience. Each resource has been designed to assist students in specific areas and to offer instructional support for teachers. While all of these areas are covered in the core textbook, some students may need extra practice or additional help in specific areas. The resource package is designed so that you, the teacher, can choose which items will best assist your students. You may also use these resources as homework assignments and for assessment purposes. The following are resources recommended for use with Unit 6.

Keys for Unit Resources

- Blackline Master
- Workbook
- Supplemental Text
- CD-ROM
- DVD
- Transparency
- Web-based
- Fast Files

Essential Instructional Support

FAST FILE UNIT 6 RESOURCES

Reading and Literature

- Academic Vocabulary Development
- Big Question: School to Home Connection
- The Big Question Foldable
- Genre Study
- Unit Challenge: Planner and Rubrics
- Comparing Literature Graphic Organizer
- Key Reading Skills Practice
- Active Reading Graphic Organizers
- Literary Analysis
- Selection Vocabulary Development

Writing, Grammar, and Spelling

- Spelling and Handwriting Practice
- Grammar Practice
- Writing Workshop Graphic Organizer

Listening, Speaking, and Viewing

- Viewing and Representing Activities
- Listening and Speaking Activities

English Language Learners

- English Language Coach

DIFFERENTIATED INSTRUCTION

- Leveled Vocabulary Development
- Skills Level Up!
- Listening Library CD
- BookLink 3
- Literature Library Vocabulary Puzzlemaker
- Vocabulary Puzzlemaker

ASSESSMENT

GLENCOE'S ASSESSMENT ADVANTAGE

- Selection and Unit Assessments
- Selection Quick Checks
- Assessment by Learning Objectives
- Rubrics for Assessing Student Writing, Listening, and Speaking
- Glencoe Online Essay Grading
- Interactive Tutor Self-Assessment
- ExamView Assessment Suite
- Literature Library ExamView Assessment Suite

Additional Instructional Support

WRITING, GRAMMAR, AND SPELLING

- Real Success in Writing: Research and Reports
- Writing Constructed Responses Sourcebook
- Spelling Power eWorkbook
- Grammar & Composition Handbook
- Grammar and Language Workbook
- Revising with Style eWorkbook

READING AND LITERATURE

- Active Learning and Note Taking Guide
- inTime Magazines
- Backpack Reader Volume 1
- Literature Library
- Literature Launchers Pre-Reading Videos DVD
- Literature Classics

TRANSPARENCIES

- Read Aloud, Think Aloud
- Literary and Text Analysis Transparencies
- Bellringer Options Transparencies
- Grammar and Writing Workshop Transparencies
- Fine Arts Transparencies

ENGLISH LANGUAGE LEARNER

- English Language Coach
- Fluency Practice and Assessment
- inTime Magazines (Spanish)
- Spanish Listening Library CD

PROFESSIONAL DEVELOPMENT

- Professional Development Package

TECHNOLOGY

- TeacherWorks Plus
- StudentWorks Plus
- BookLink 3
- Skill Level Up!
- ExamView Assessment Suite
- Interactive Tutor Self-Assessment
- Listening Library CD
- Spanish Listening Library CD
- Literature Classics
- Literature Launchers Pre-Reading Videos DVD
- Literature Library ExamView Assessment Suite
- Vocabulary Puzzlemaker
- Literature Library Vocabulary Puzzlemaker
- glencoe.com
- Online Student Edition
- Presentation Plus!
- Glencoe Online Essay Grading

Additional Glencoe Resources

FOLDABLES™ Study Organizer

Dinah Zike's Foldables

Foldables are three-dimensional, interactive graphic organizers that help students practice basic writing skills, review key vocabulary terms, and answer Big Questions. Every unit contains a foldable activity. You can find the pattern and directions for the Unit 6 Foldable in the Unit 6 Resources Fast Files booklet. You can use the foldables as they are presented or modify them to suit the needs of your students. More information about foldables for Unit 6 can be found on page R8.

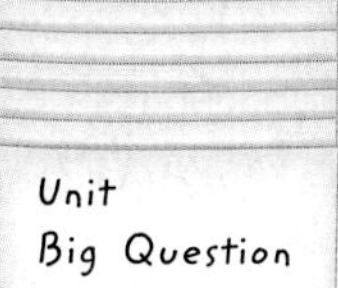

For a wealth of online resources that support the instruction in Unit 6 of *Glencoe Literature: Reading with Purpose,* students and teachers can visit our Web site at www.glencoe.com. Students will find additional learning, practice, and assessment opportunities such as these, which are noted in the student text:

- **Big Question Overview**
- **Study Central**
- **Author Search**
- **Writing Models**
- **Interactive Literary Elements Handbook**
- **Web Activities**

Teachers will find planning and instructional tools that include the following:

- **Book Lesson Plans**
- **Teacher Forum**
- **Professional Development**
- **Web Activities Lesson Plans (with answers to student activities)**

Go to www.glencoe.com to see the entire selection of Reading with Purpose online resources.

Glencoe's **Presentation Plus!**, a multimedia teaching tool, lets you present dynamic lessons that will engage your students. Using Microsoft PowerPoint,® you can customize the presentations to create your own personalized lessons. Use **CheckPoint** questions with interactive response keypads to get immediate student feedback during lessons, to increase student participation, and to assess student comprehension.

Glencoe Literature Library

The collection of hardcover books include full-length novels, novellas, plays and works of nonfiction. Each volume consists of at least one complete extended-length reading accompanied by several related readings from a broad range of genres. A separate Study Guide for each Glencoe Literature Library book provides teaching notes and reproducible activity pages for students.

Glencoe Literature Library titles that complement this unit include:

Anne Frank Remembered by Miep Gies with Alison Leslie Gold
Barrio Boy by Ernesto Galarza
Cezanne Finto by Mary Stolz
A Gathering of Days by Joan W. Blos

GLENCOE BOOKLINK

Use the Glencoe BookLink 3 CD-ROM, a database of more than 26,700 titles, to *create customized reading lists* for your students.

- Search for award-winning titles, (e.g., Newbery Award winners, Coretta Scott King Award winners, and Caldecott Medal winners) and for books on several state-recommended reading lists.
- Find Degrees of Reading Power™ (DRP) and Lexile™ readability scores for all selections.
- Organize reading lists by students' reading level, author, genre, theme, or area of interest.
- Get a brief summary of each selection.

You can find recommended leveled readings for this unit with Reading on Your Own (see page 120).

A lively collection of articles drawn from issues of the TIME family of magazines helps students develop the skills they need to interact with informational text in a meaningful way. Each of the news stories, feature articles, reviews, profiles, and essays in the magazine connect to an author, work, or theme in *Glencoe Literature: Reading with Purpose.* Articles for Unit 6 are found in Volume A. See the *inTIME* Teacher's Guide for specific connections to each unit and for reproducible student worksheets designed to develop students' reading and critical thinking skills.

Literature Launchers

Set the scene with Glencoe's Literature Launchers, engaging video segments that introduce each unit's genre focus. Each video brings the genre to life, relating it to your students' worlds.

Insert the Glencoe Literature Launchers Pre-Reading Videos DVD into your DVD player. Select the Unit 6 Launcher from the menu to introduce the genre and Big Question for this unit.

Online Essay Grader

Use Glencoe's Online Essay Grading to score your students' writing and to provide individualized feedback to each student automatically.

You and your students can visit www.glencoe.com to link to the essay grader. *Students* can enter their essays and receive feedback on demand. *You* can manage demographic data, assign tests and generate individual student and aggregated reports. The essay grader can help you

- Save time with automatic scoring and individualized feedback.
- Supplement in-class writing instruction using guided writing practice.
- Get reports for individual students or for special populations.
- Track student improvement over time.

REAL Success: Reading Excellence at All Levels

Glencoe now provides all of your students with the tools they need to become better, more enthusiastic readers. The REAL Success suite of reading and language arts products encourages reading excellence by meeting the needs of students at all levels. Glencoe products that can be used in conjunction with Unit 6 include the following:

- Jamestown Literature: An Adapted Reader
- Jamestown *Reading Fluency*
- Jamestown *Critical Reading Series, In the Line of Duty*
- *Vocabulary Builder*
- *The Glencoe Reader, Course 2*

To order these products, call Glencoe at 1-800-USA-READ.

Teacher Wraparound Edition Key

Level Appropriate Code

AS = Activities for all students
AL = Activities for students working above grade level
OL = Activities for students working at grade level
BL = Activities for students working below grade level
EL = Activities for English language learners

Teacher Wraparound Prompts

R **Reading Skill** These activities help you teach reading skills and vocabulary.

V **Vocabulary** These activities help students comprehend words and incorporate into reading.

C **Critical Thinking** These strategies help students apply and extend what they have learned.

BQ **BIG Question** These activities and questions prompt students to prepare to answer the Big Question.

W **Writing** These activities provide writing opportunities to help students practice writing and comprehend text.

L **Literary Element** These activities and questions help students comprehend selections and learn more about each genre.

E **Text Element** These activities help students comprehend text elements.

LSV **Listening, Speaking, Viewing** These activities help students practice listening, speaking, and viewing skills.

EL **English Language Coach** These skills help English language learners as well as students who need additional reading support.

UNIT 6

Professional Development Center

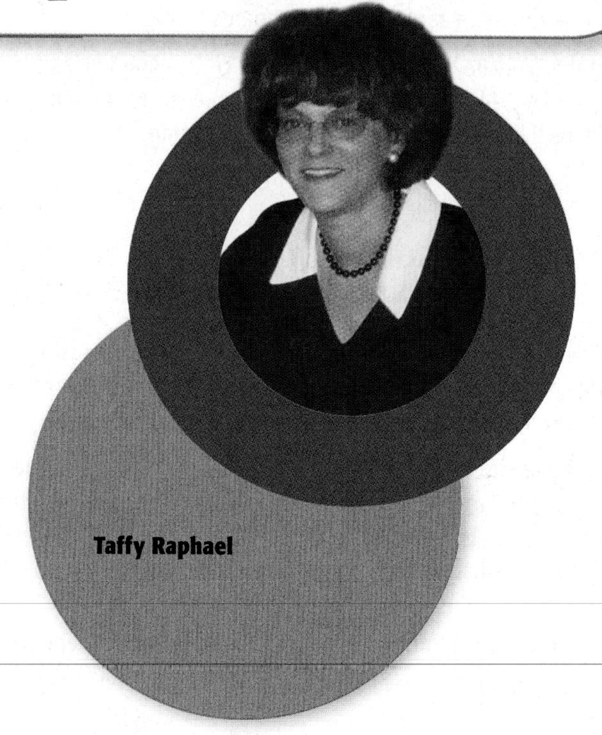
Taffy Raphael

From An Author:

Preparing Students to Read Folktales:

Make Features Visible: Folktales are written versions of stories that historically were told orally, from generation to generation. Literary elements helped make the stories memorable so they could be retold over time in consistent ways. Explaining some of the traditional elements to students may help them better understand the genre. Some of those elements include the following characteristics: *Settings* are vague and in opposition (e.g., very rich or very poor; huge castles or tiny huts). *Characters* are clear cut (e.g., good or evil, smart or foolish), do not change, and readers are not told why they behave as they do. The *action* and *events* unfold with a basic pattern in which the victims obtain, through magical assistance, some sort of power over those who maligned them. This power provides status over those who had victimized them.

Introduce Folktale Categories: There are different groups of folktales, including myths, cumulative tales, and *pourquoi* tales. Myths are what we call stories that explain beliefs of different cultures. For example, the "myths" we tell today of ancient Greeks were the "truths" of their belief systems. For example, myths often focus on explanations of how our world was created (e.g., stars, oceans). Myths must be shared with respect and caution since the ideas may be much more than simply a story to those within the culture from which the myth was taken.

Pourquoi tales also explain natural phenomena, like the bear's short tale or the mosquitoes' buzz. There are other forms of folktales that could be included such as fables, legends, and epics. The critical points are that folktales provide insights into cultures near and far, are based on the oral histories of peoples, and reflect a larger than life approach to narrative.

Jose Lopez
Eagle Pass High School
Eagle Pass, TX

Teacher to Teacher

Why Do We Share Our Stories?

I tie in the literature with current events and students' lives, backgrounds and cultures. In cooperative learning group discussion, students may look at real-life stories of tricksters and adventurers in the media and compare them with the literature. In addition, I ask them to answer this question: What message or lesson about life does this selection have for readers today? After students have read and discussed all of the selections, I invite them to write their own imaginative tale with a message or moral embedded in the plot. I encourage them to draw on the personalities of the characters in the literature, as well as their own knowledge and experiences, in shaping their stories. Then we hold a storytelling festival in which students perform the tales they have written for the class.

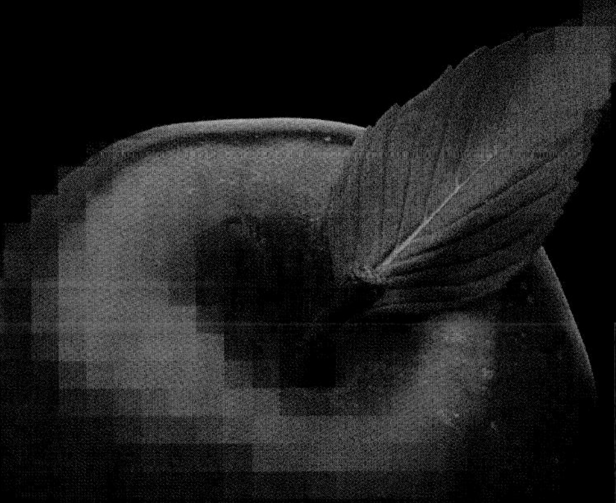

Teacher Chat Room

Teaching Folktales

How do I make folktales interesting to middle school students?

Middle school students need to be able to get beyond the story since most of these are stories they will have heard in one form or another since they were very young. Unpacking how a folktale works and helping them connect this genre to their own story-telling is central to making the genre relevant to them. Help students substitute modern-day characters in folktales so they can apply the lessons better. This technique will also enhance their writing skills and nurture their creativity.

How do I help them understand the importance of folktales to understanding different cultures, time periods, and beliefs?

Middle school students are learning about gender stereotyping. Suggest they change the gender of characters and discuss how the story and moral would change. This practice will quite naturally lead to gender implications and beliefs prevalent during the origination of the folktale.

You may also want to change the location of some of the folktales or the nationality of some characters. How would *We Are All* One be different if the main character were from a different culture? What values of the Chinese culture are found in this folktale? What values might be highlighted if it were changed for another culture?

How do I help middle school understand the importance of oral traditions in story-telling?

As much as possible allow students to read these folktales aloud. Tell them to try to find the rhythm or pattern that would have made this story easy to remember. Remind them that both the story teller and the audience needed to remember it.

If you can find recordings of folktales, play them for students. Encourage them to pay attention to the speaker's voice, rhythm, and word choice. Ask students to find other elements that may be missed in the reading of a folktale.

Key Unit Objectives

- Answer the Big Question
- Analyze the literary elements of folktales
- Apply strategies for reading folktales
- Write a modern folktale

BIG Question

Why Is It Important?

Addressing this Big Question helps students understand the purposes and benefits of storytelling.

Viewing the Photo

Say: Read the quotation by Mark Twain. Why might people enjoy a good story? *(Responses will vary.)* How might the people in the picture be sharing their story? *(Possible response: They are taking a picture of themselves. By showing the picture to others, they can share their story.)* AS

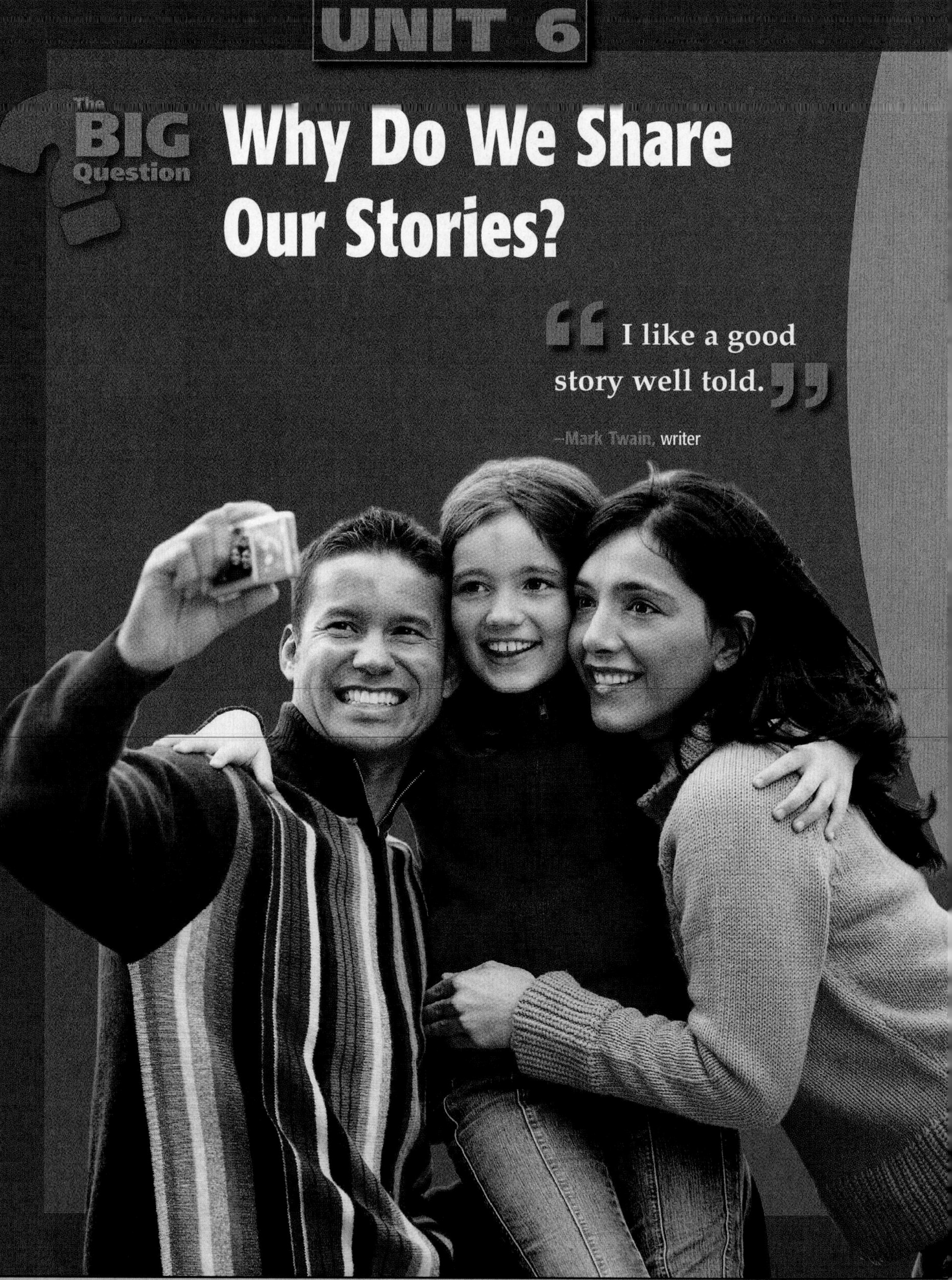
UNIT 6
The BIG Question
Why Do We Share Our Stories?
“I like a good story well told.”
–Mark Twain, writer

Unit Skills

BIG Question Why Do We Share Our Stories?

Genre Focus: Folktales

Reading Skills
- Understanding cause and effect, p. 656
- Questioning, p. 680
- Predicting, p. 702
- Analyzing, p. 730

Vocabulary
- Idioms, p. 658,
- Dialogue, pp. 704, 714
- Literal and metaphoric meanings, p. 732

Literary Elements
- Theme, p. 659
- Characterization, p. 683
- Cultural allusions, p. 705
- Dialect, p. 733

Writing Skills/Grammar
- Modern folktale, pp. 676, 724
- Compound and complex sentences, p. 679
- Presentation, p. 726

LOOKING AHEAD

The skill lessons and readings in this unit will help you develop your own answer to the Big Question.

About the Reading

Reading the selections in this unit will help students answer the question, "Why do we share our stories?" Students will consider different reasons for storytelling and learn how storytelling has helped connect generations throughout time.

About the Skills

The skills taught in this unit have been selected because they are particularly helpful when reading the featured genre—folktales—as well as the other genres featured in the unit. Each reading selection provides students with opportunities to practice and develop these skills.

The *Report of the National Reading Panel* (2000) identifies five key skills for reading success. One of those key skills is the ability to understand and gain meaning from what is read. Teaching students to make predictions and ask questions as they read will help them understand and gain meaning from a variety of texts.

Reading Fluency

Developing Fluency Remind students that at one time, stories, especially folktales, were passed down orally. Encourage students to read aloud the stories in this unit to help them develop fluency. Have students practice reading aloud a portion of a story, repeating the reading until they have achieved fluency. Then, have them read the portion to a partner or small group of peers. Remind students to focus on using their voice to convey meaning. They might raise their voice to convey surprise or lower their voice to show sadness. BL

Focus

BELLRINGER Options

- **Literature Launcher: Prereading DVD**
- **Daily Language Practice Transparency**

Focus Activity Say: Think of someone you know who loves to tell stories. What are some reasons why this person might enjoy telling stories? *(Responses might include to get attention, to entertain, or to teach lessons.)*

Teach

R Reading Skill

Understanding Cause and Effect Have students list the effects that storytelling can have in their Learner's Notebook. Students can fill in the following sentences to get started:

- Hearing a story can make me feel _______.
- When I hear a story, I _______. AS

BQ

- Have students read the profiles and look at the pictures of Ana and Robert.
- Ask them to predict what they think will happen if Ana and Robert share their stories. AS

Connecting to

Why Do We Share Our Stories?

R We share our stories for many reasons—sometimes just for fun. For example, you and your friends may have entertained each other with funny stories about school or your lives. We also share our stories to keep the past alive and preserve our memories. In your own life, your family may have shared stories with you about what you were like as a little kid. Through storytelling, we can even share words of wisdom and comfort. In this unit, you'll read stories and poems that will help you explore these and other reasons that we share our stories.

Real Kids and the Big Question

Lannette has been very quiet. Her friends are worried. Her parents divorced six months ago, but Lannette has never talked about it. Her friend, **ANA** wants to help. She remembers when her parents divorced and has some idea of how Lannette is feeling. Ana wants to share her experiences with Lannette. Do you think she should? Why or why not?

BQ **ROBERT'S** new stepsister, Cleo, has been getting into trouble at school. Robert was a troublemaker himself when he was Cleo's age. But after getting expelled from school four years ago, he turned his life around. Now Robert is a "B" student and a lot happier. He's thinking of sharing his story with Cleo. Do you think Cleo can learn from Robert's experiences?

Warm-Up Activity

With other students, talk about what you think Ana and Robert should do and why.

Additional Support

Reading in the Real World

Career Both Ana and Robert want to use their experiences to help others who are having a hard time. Tell students that there are many career options for people who want to help others. Social workers, therapists, and school counselors help other people in part by listening to their stories. They invite their clients to share their stories in order to help them heal the wounds from their painful experiences. Ask students to tell why sharing painful stories with others might be helpful. Have students interested in a career in social work or counseling list the skills and qualities that are important for this type of work. *(Possible responses: good listening skills, empathy, kindness)* AS

You and the Big Question

Reading different stories and poems will help you figure out your own answer to the Big Question.

Literature Online

Big Question Link to Web resources to further explore the Big Question at www.glencoe.com.

Plan for the Unit Challenge

At the end of the unit, you'll use notes from all your reading to complete the Unit Challenge. The Challenge will help you explore your answer to the Big Question.

You will choose one of the following activities:

A. Sharing-Stories Reading List You'll work with classmates to make a list of stories you think other students your age would enjoy.

B. Story Review You'll choose a story you've read and explain why you think it is or is not worth sharing.

- Start thinking about which activity you'd like to do so that you can focus your thinking as you go through the unit.
- In your Learner's Notebook, write about which you like better—working by yourself or working with other students. That may help you decide which activity you'd like to do.
- Remember to take notes about possible answers to the Big Question. Your notes will help you do the Unit Challenge activity you choose.

Keep Track of Your Ideas

As you read, you'll make notes about the Big Question. Later, you'll use these notes to complete the Unit Challenge. See page R8 for help with making Foldable 6. This diagram shows how one side of it should look.

1. Use this Foldable for all of the selections in this unit. Label each "tab" with a title. (See page 649 for the titles.) You should be able to see all the titles without opening the Foldable.
2. Below each title, write **My Purpose for Reading**.
3. Further below each title, a third of the way down the page, write the label **The Big Question**.

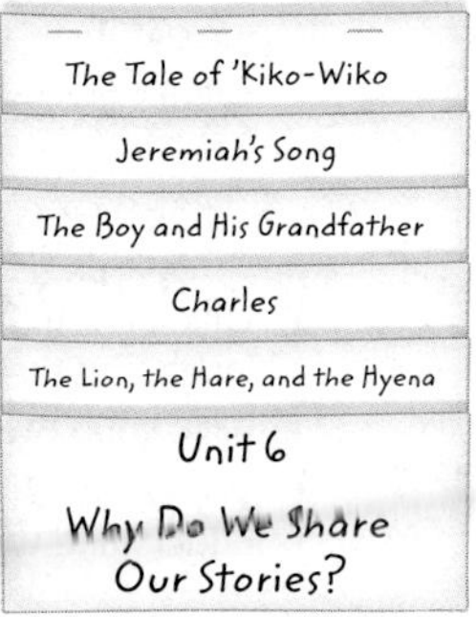

The Tale of 'Kiko-Wiko
Jeremiah's Song
The Boy and His Grandfather
Charles
The Lion, the Hare, and the Hyena
Unit 6
Why Do We Share Our Stories?

Differentiated Instruction

Written Response Students who prefer to work alone rather than in a small group or with a partner may prefer to write their response to the Big Question activity. Allow these students to spend discussion time writing about Ana and Robert in their Learner's Notebook. Then, conduct a whole-class discussion in which students present their ideas. Encourage students who wrote their responses to share their ideas with the class. OL

Teach

Have students freewrite in their Learner's Notebook about the Big Question. OL

BIG Question Have students access the Web site for English and Spanish summaries and annotated links to related Web resources.

FOLDABLES™ Study Organizer

For each selection they read, students will enter notes about how that selection applies to the Big Question. For details about using Dinah Zike's Foldables, see page R8.

Assess/Close

Ask students to share their ideas about why looking for an answer to the Big Question might be important.

Resources for page 651

- Use the Unit Challenge Planner BLM in the Unit 6 Resource Booklet.
- Use the Foldable BLM in the Unit 6 Resource Booklet.

Objectives
- Understand cause and effect
- Make predictions
- Evaluate a story
- Use prior knowledge to answer questions

Focus

BELLRINGER Options

- **Selection Focus Transparency**
- **Daily Language Practice Transparency**

Focus Activity Say: Many folktales have been told for a long time. Think of a folktale you've read or seen. It might be a fairy tale, a tall tale, or a trickster tale. Why might people still tell this story today? *(Responses will vary.)*

Teach

C Critical Thinking

Comprehension Say: With a partner, think of an example of each form of folklore. Then, decide which type is your favorite, and tell why you like that type best. *(Responses will vary.)* AL

L Literary Element

Character Say: Describe a character from your favorite folktale. Why do you like this character? *(Responses will vary.)* AS

UNIT 6 GENRE FOCUS: FOLKTALE

Skills Focus

- Key skills for reading folktales
- Key literary elements of folktales

Skills Model

You will see how to use the key reading skills and literary elements as you read

- Brer Rabbit and Brer Lion, p. 654

A **folktale** is a story that was told by generations of storytellers before it was ever written down. We don't know the names of all those storytellers. Some were professionals who told tales as entertainment. Some were teachers who used folktales to teach important lessons. Some were mothers and fathers who told stories to their children, just as parents still do.

Folktales belong to a category called **folklore**. This more general term includes songs, speeches, sayings, and even jokes. In this unit, you'll read several forms of folklore.

C

- **Trickster tale**—a story in which a character, often an animal, outsmarts an enemy. An example of a trickster character is Brer Rabbit in the story you'll read next.
- **Origin story**—a story about the origins, or beginnings, of something in nature. In this unit, a story from Africa tells why the hyena has oddly long hairs growing on its back. Other origin stories explain such things as how tigers got their stripes and why the sky is blue.
- **Fairy tale**—a story with magical beings who change the lives of ordinary people. The stories of Cinderella and Snow White—and their fairy godmothers—are fairy tales. One story in this unit features a magical being who is definitely not Cinderella's fairy godmother.
- **Tall tale**—a fantasy story about an amazing, larger-than-life person. At the end of this unit, you'll read one of the many American tall tales told about Paul Bunyan.
- **Legend**—a story about an amazing event or a hero's amazing accomplishment. Some legends are about people who actually lived, but over the years their reputations grew "larger than life."
- **Myth**—a story about gods and goddesses and how they were involved in making things the way they are. Characters from ancient myths were featured in two popular TV series in the 1990s—*Hercules: The Legendary Journeys* and *Xena: Warrior Princess*.

Two main things make all of these different forms alike. First, they were passed down over many generations. Second, they still help members of a culture to stay connected to one another.

Objectives
(pp. 652–655)
Reading Understand cause and effect • Monitor comprehension: ask questions • Make predictions • Analyze text
Literature Identify literary elements: theme, character, cultural context, dialect

Why Read Folktales?

L

Folktales are fun to read. The characters in them can make you smile and laugh, but they can also make you stop and think. Folktales may also bring back good memories. They're the kinds of stories you heard and read when you were little. Maybe most important of all, reading folktales can help you understand why people share stories.

Additional Support

Literature Focus Lesson

Character Tell students that folktales often include nonhuman characters, such as animals and monsters. Even though these characters aren't human, they talk, behave, and think like humans. When students read the stories with animal characters in them, encourage them to note how the animals are like humans; for example, are they greedy, funny, or angry? Do they talk? Ask students to consider why authors might use animals, rather than people, to tell their stories. *(Responses will vary. Students might note that readers will learn a lesson better if it's told using animals rather than people.)* AS

How to Read Folktales

Key Reading Skills

These key reading skills are especially useful tools for reading and understanding folktales. You'll learn more about these skills later in the unit.

- **Understanding Cause and Effect** As you read, look for causes–the reasons why things happen–and for effects–the things that happen as a result. (See Reading Workshop 1.)
- **Questioning** To make sure you understand what you're reading, ask yourself questions while you read. (See Reading Workshop 2.)
- **Predicting** Guess what will happen next in a story to help yourself get more involved in what you're reading. (See Reading Workshop 3.)
- **Analyzing** To understand a text better, think about its parts and how they work together to make meaning. (See Reading Workshop 4.)

R

Key Literary Elements

Recognizing and thinking about the following literary elements will help you understand a text more fully.

- **Theme:** the main idea, or message, of a story, poem, novel, or play. Sometimes this idea is stated directly. More often it's revealed gradually through plot, character, setting, and other elements. (See "The Lion, the Hare, and the Hyena.")
- **Character:** a person or animal in a story. (If a character is an animal, it displays human qualities and behaviors.) Characterization is the methods a writer uses to develop a character's personality. (See "Jeremiah's Song.")
- **Cultural allusions:** a reference to something that has special importance or meaning for a particular group of people. (See "We Are All One.")
- **Dialect:** a variation of a language spoken by a particular group of people, usually within a certain region. In a dialect, words may have different pronunciations, forms, and meanings than the same words have in the standard language. (See "Voices–and Stories–from the Past.")

UNIT 6 GENRE FOCUS

Teach

R Reading Skill

How to Read Folktales

Ask: Why will each reading skill be helpful in understanding folktales? *(Possible responses: **Understanding cause and effect:** It is important to know why events happen in a story and why characters act the way they do. **Questioning:** Asking yourself questions helps you make sure you understand the story. **Predicting:** Making guesses about what will happen next helps keep you interested in what you're reading. **Analyzing:** Thinking about the different parts of the story and how they work together helps you understand what the story is about.)* **OL**

English Language Coach

Dialect Reading dialect may be particularly challenging for English language learners. Tell students that understanding the dialect in this selection will be easier if they read it aloud and then work with a native English speaker to "translate" the sentences into Standard English. Have a volunteer read aloud the second paragraph on page 654 and then reword it in Standard English. *(Possible response: He was running through the woods when he ran into Brer Lion. Now, don't tell me there aren't any lions in the United States. There aren't any here now...)* Tell students to continue reading aloud and working with a partner to be sure they understand the dialect in the story. **BL** **EL**

Objectives

- Monitor comprehension: ask questions
- Comprehend different types of folklore
- Describe the character in a folktale

Teach

V Vocabulary

Context Clues **Say:** Look at the sentence that *trucking* is in. What are some context clues that could help you define *trucking? (Possible response: "through the woods," "ran smack")* What do you think *trucking* means here? *(running or walking quickly)* OL

L Literary Element

Character **Ask:** Who are the characters in this story? *(Brer Rabbit and Brer Lion)* What do you learn about each character from his conversation? *(Brer Lion is afraid of hurricanes. Brer Rabbit has lots of ideas. Brer Lion listens to them.)* AS

Resources for page 654

Use the Genre Study BLM in the Unit 6 Resource Booklet.

Readability Scores
Dale-Chall: 4.7
DRP: 43
Lexile: 710

UNIT 6 GENRE FOCUS

The notes in the side columns model how to use the skills and elements you read about on pages 652–653.

Folktale

ACTIVE READING MODEL

retold by Julius Lester

Brer Rabbit was in the woods one afternoon when a great wind came up. It blew on the ground and it blew in the tops of the trees. It blew so hard that Brer Rabbit was afraid a tree might fall on him, and he started running. 1

He was trucking through the woods when he ran smack into Brer Lion. Now, don't come telling me ain't no lions in the United States. Ain't none here now. But back in yonder times, all the animals lived everywhere. The lions and tigers and elephants and foxes and what 'nall run around with each other like they was family. So that's how come wasn't unusual for Brer Rabbit to run up on Brer Lion like he done that day. 2 3

"What's your hurry, Brer Rabbit?"

"Run, Brer Lion! There's a hurricane coming."

Brer Lion got scared. "I'm too heavy to run, Brer Rabbit. What am I going to do?"

"Lay down, Brer Lion. Lay down! Get close to the ground!"

Brer Lion shook his head. "The wind might pick me up and blow me away."

"Hug a tree, Brer Lion! Hug a tree!"

"But what if the wind blows all day and into the night?"

"Let me tie you to the tree, Brer Lion. Let me tie you to the tree." 4

1 Key Reading Skill
Predicting *I wonder what will happen next. It says the wind is blowing hard, so maybe a tree really will fall on Brer Rabbit.*

2 Key Reading Skill
Questioning *I don't understand what "trucking" means here. Is Brer Rabbit driving a truck? I'll read on to see if I can answer my own question.*

3 Key Literary Element
Dialect, Character, and Cultural Context *The storyteller speaks in a dialect. We learned in school that Brer Rabbit is in lots of African American folktales. So the dialect and culture must be old-time African American.*

4 Key Reading Skill
Understanding Cause and Effect *The strong winds are the cause, and the effect is Brer Lion's fear.*

Additional Support

Literature Focus Lesson

The History of Trickster Tales The stories about Brer Rabbit were first told in Africa and were brought to America by enslaved Africans. Brer Rabbit is known for his ability to outsmart much larger and more powerful animals.

Native American stories also have their tricksters, such as Old Man Coyote, Raven, and "the Tricky One." In all trickster stories, the trickster uses his smarts to survive in difficult situations.

Have students discuss why trickster tales might be popular. (*Possible response: People can relate to and enjoy stories in which characters use their intelligence to overcome difficulties.)* OL

UNIT 6 GENRE FOCUS

Emma's Lion, 1994. Christian Pierre, Acrylic on Masonite, 16 x 20 in., Private collection.

Folktale

ACTIVE READING MODEL

Brer Lion liked that idea. Brer Rabbit tied him to the tree and sat down next to it. After a while, Brer Lion got tired of hugging the tree.

"Brer Rabbit? I don't hear no hurricane."

Brer Rabbit listened. "Neither do I."

"Brer Rabbit? I don't hear no wind."

Brer Rabbit listened. "Neither do I."

"Brer Rabbit? Ain't a leaf moving in the trees."

Brer Rabbit looked up. "Sho' ain't."

"So untie me."

"I'm afraid to, Brer Lion." 5

Brer Lion began to roar. He roared so loud and so long, the foundations of the Earth started shaking. Least that's what it seemed like, and the other animals came from all over to see what was going on.

When they got close, Brer Rabbit jumped up and began strutting around the tied-up Brer Lion. When the animals saw what Brer Rabbit had done to Brer Lion, you'd better believe it was the forty-eleventh of Octorerarry before they messed with him again. 6 R C

5 Key Reading Skill
Analyzing *Brer Rabbit is afraid he'll be killed if he unties Brer Lion!*

6 Key Literary Element
Theme *Brer Rabbit gets everyone's respect by outsmarting Brer Lion. So maybe the main message of this story is that being smart is better than being big and strong.*

Write to Learn You can learn a great deal through the dialogue in a story. Write a paragraph explaining what you learned about the main characters from the dialogue in this folktale.

Literature Online **Study Central** Visit www.glencoe.com and click on Study Central to review folktales.

Viewing the Art

Ask: Do you think the lion in this painting looks like Brer Lion? Why or why not? *(Responses will vary. Some students may note that the lion in the art does not look very fierce.)* AL

R Reading Skill

Understanding Cause and Effect Ask: What causes the animals to leave Brer Rabbit alone? *(Possible response: They see that he has tied up the strong Brer Lion, and they don't want to be tied up too.)* AL

C Critical Thinking

Comprehension Say: The forty-eleventh of Octorerarry isn't a real date. What might the author mean when he says this? *(He might mean "never.")* AL

Literature Online

Study Central Have students access the Web site to review folktales and to complete a related activity.

Differentiated Instruction

Cartoons Visual learners may enjoy creating a cartoon version of the Brer Rabbit tale. Have such students make a list of the most important details of the story. Then, have them create or find an image for each detail. Remind students to place each image in a box and to use dialogue bubbles when they include a character's speech. Have students share their cartoons with the class by posting them on a class bulletin board. OL

Objectives
- Understand cause and effect
- Monitor comprehension: ask questions
- Make predictions
- Analyze text
- Identify literary elements: theme, character, cultural context, dialect

Understanding Cause and Effect

Objectives covered in this workshop:

- Identify cause and effect relationships

Teaching Students to Understand Cause and Effect

Why Is It Important?

- Causal relationships are central to narrative and informational text.
- Students who understand cause and effect can understand that actions have consequences
- Understanding cause and effect can provide a way to understand motivations and reactions in stories and in the real world

How to Help Students Get It

- Emphasize that causal relationships are present at many levels in narratives: at the story level, in individual events, and in characters' behavior over time
- Have students examine causal relationships within folktales, then apply the concept to a science experiment and an historical event, to ensure that they understand the general concept and how it crosses texts and literature
- Use graphic organizers to help students map out causal relationships at each level

Reading to Answer the Big Question

The Lion, the Hare, and the Hyena

In this folktale, a hyena tries to trick his way into an injured lion's good graces by telling lies about the hare. His plan backfires, though, when the quick-witted hare outsmarts him. Reading this folktale will help students understand how stories can be used as an entertaining way to teach valuable lessons.

Charles

Laurie's parents are shocked to hear their kindergartener describe the terrible behavior of his classmate Charles. But they are in for a big surprise when they finally meet with Laurie's teacher. Students will be entertained as they discover the real reason that Laurie shares stories about Charles.

Workshop Resources

Pacing (Days) Standard	Pacing (Days) Block	Lesson	Student Materials	Teacher Resources
1		Key Skill Lesson: Understanding Cause and Effect	Key Reading Skills Practice English Language Coach	Bellringer Options Transparencies Read Aloud, Think Aloud Transparencies Presentation Plus!
2		"The Lion, the Hare, and the Hyena"	Literary Analysis Transparencies Glencoe Online Selection Vocabulary Development Academic Vocabulary Development English Language Coach Active Reading Graphic Organizer Literary Analysis StudentWorks Plus Online Student Edition Literature Classics Selection and Unit Assessments	Literary and Text Analysis Transparencies Puzzlemaker Skill Level Up! BookLink 3 Assessment by Learning Objective (Diagnostic and Formative) Interactive Tutor Self-Assessment TeacherWorks Plus
2		"Charles"	Glencoe Online Selection Vocabulary Development Academic Vocabulary Development English Language Coach Active Reading Graphic Organizer Literary Analysis StudentWorks Plus Online Student Edition Literature Classics Selection and Unit Assessments	Literary and Text Analysis Transparencies Puzzlemaker Skill Level Up! BookLink 3 Assessment by Learning Objective (Diagnostic and Formative) Interactive Tutor Self-Assessment TeacherWorks Plus

Keys for Unit Resource

- Blackline Master
- Workbook
- Supplemental Text
- CD-ROM
- DVD
- Transparency
- Web-based
- Fast Files

Level Appropriate Code

AS = Activities for all students
AL = Activities for students working above grade level
OL = Activities for students working at grade level
BL = Activities for students working below grade level
EL = Activities for English language learners

Focus

BELLRINGER Options

- **Selection Focus Transparency**
- **Daily Language Practice Transparency**

Focus Activity Say: What are some reasons people might have for not telling the truth? *(Possible responses: to protect themselves from harm, to be mischievous, to avoid getting in trouble)*

Teach

R Reading Skill

Understanding Cause and Effect Say: Your life is full of causes and effects. Name one cause of tiredness *(possible response: staying up too late)* and one effect of exercise *(possible response: having more energy).* AL

Skills Focus

You will practice using these skills when you read the following selections:

- "The Lion, the Hare, and the Hyena," p. 660
- "Charles," p. 668

Reading

- Understanding cause and effect

Literature

- Identifying the theme of a selection

Vocabulary

- Understanding and using idioms and slang

Writing/Grammar

- Identifying direct and indirect objects

Objectives (pp. 656–657)
Reading Understand cause and effect

Skill Lesson

Understanding Cause and Effect

Learn It!

What Is It? Understanding the reason things happen is a big part of what human beings do. We want to know "why." Why is the sky blue? Why does water run downhill? These are the simple beginnings of all the complicated science we know today. We are always looking for the **cause** of things.

- A **cause** is a person, event, or condition that makes something happen. R
- What happens as a result is an **effect**.

You will find cause and effect relationships in just about everything you read. That's because cause and effect is everywhere in life. And writers also use cause and effect to organize information for you, especially in social studies and science reading.

Analyzing Cartoons
Chewing gum while practicing soccer (cause) can lead to trouble (effect). Words and phrases like *if/then*, *therefore*, and *as a result* signal cause and effect. Sometimes "Now I know why" signals it, too.

Additional Support

Differentiated Instruction

Cause and Effect Visual learners might find it helpful to create a cause-and-effect chart to help them understand this reading skill. Have students copy the following chart and fill in a possible effect for each cause. BL OL

Cause	Effect
You walk through a rainstorm without a coat.	
You spend the night before a test watching TV.	
You don't brush your teeth regularly.	

Why Is It Important? As you read, you often ask, "Why?" You need to be able to recognize when the author is giving you the answer. That applies to big questions: Why is there suffering in the world? It also applies to smaller questions: Why did the main character in this story tell a lie? Remember that one cause may have many effects. When someone drops a match in a forest, there are millions of effects. And one effect may have many causes. The causes of winning a race include being healthy, trying your best, and so forth.

R

Literature Online

Study Central Visit www.glencoe.com and click on Study Central to review understanding cause and effect.

How Do I Do It? First, keep asking "Why?" Then, look for signal words that help you know that your question is being answered, words like *because, so, so that, if...then,* and *as a result of*. These signal words are often there when you're looking for a cause. When they're not, your "why" question will give you a start. Here's how one student identified cause and effect in "The Lion, the Hare, and the Hyena."

> Simba had hurt his leg so badly that he was unable to provide food for himself. Sunguru the Hare happened to be passing his cave one day. Looking inside, Sunguru realized that the lion was starving.

How can a big lion like Simba starve? Guess there must be a reason. Ok, it said he hurt his leg and couldn't get food. That means he can't hunt. So the cause is his leg is hurt so bad that he can't hunt, therefore he's starving. That's the effect of the hurt leg.

Practice It!

Look at the sentences below. See if you can identify the cause and the effect in each one.

- Hal ate too many cookies, so he got sick.
- Water runs downhill because of gravity.
- The wind blew so hard that my hat went flying.

Use It!

As you read "The Lion, the Hare, and the Hyena" and "Charles," take notes on the characters, what they do, and the situations each of them are in. This will help you to identify the cause-and-effect relationships.

READING WORKSHOP 1

Teach

Literature Online

Study Central Have students access the Web site to review understanding cause and effect and to complete a related activity.

R Reading Skill

Review Determining the Main Idea **Ask:** How can cause and effect help you when you're reading a story? *(You can learn why characters behave the way they do and what events lead up to the outcome.)* **Say:** Think of a story you have read, and tell what caused the main character to act in a certain way. *(Responses will vary.)* OL AL

Resources for page 657

Use Reading Skills Transparency in *Read Aloud, Think Aloud,* Unit 6, to help students practice understanding cause and effect.

Reading in the Real World

Career Many careers require a knowledge of how to determine cause-and-effect relationships accurately. For example, a doctor may note that her patient is feeling nauseated after taking a new medication. That does not necessarily mean that the medication caused the patient to feel sick. The doctor would have to investigate other possible causes, such as a change in the patient's diet or a stomach virus, to determine the cause of the nausea. Have students think of how police detectives might use cause-and-effect skills when solving a crime. Ask them to share their thoughts with the class. *(Responses may include finding out what might cause a suspect to want to commit a crime.)* AL

Objectives
- Review the main idea
- Understand cause and effect

Teach

More About the Author

Phyllis Savory spent more than 80 years collecting African folktales that had been handed down orally. Savory, who was born in 1901, listened to stories told by workers on her father's farm in Rhodesia (now Zimbabwe). She then traveled throughout Africa to collect stories and eventually published more than 17 collections.

V Vocabulary

Fill in the Blanks **Say:** For additional practice with the vocabulary words, write a sentence for each word, leaving a blank where the vocabulary word should be. Swap sentences with a partner, and see if you can fill in your partner's blanks. BL EL

Before You Read

The Lion, the Hare, and the Hyena

Meet the Author

Phyllis Savory has written and edited tales that have strong African influences. By recording ancient tales told from generation to generation, she helps readers young and old discover delightful and enchanting worlds.

Literature Online

Author Search For more about Phyllis Savory, go to www.glenocoe.com.

Objectives (pp. 658–663)
Reading Understand cause and effect • Make connections from text to self
Literature Identify literary elements: theme
Vocabulary Understand idioms

Vocabulary Preview

V

solitude (SAWL uh tood) *n.* the state of being alone **(p. 660)** *The lion enjoyed his solitude.*

accumulate (uh KYOO myuh layt) *v.* to increase gradually in quantity or number **(p. 660)** *The hyena wanted the delicious bones that had begun to accumulate.*

conspicuous (kun SPIK yoo us) *adj.* quite noticeable **(p. 662)** *The lion's absence was very conspicuous.*

Definition Trade-Off With a partner or small group, take turns calling out a vocabulary word and having the partner give the definition, or call out the definition and have the partner give the word.

English Language Coach

Idioms An idiom (ID ee um) is a word or phrase that has a special meaning. Every language has idioms, and they can cause problems for someone who hasn't heard them before or for someone who didn't grow up speaking the language. Often, the problem can be solved quickly because many idioms make sense if you think about them.

Even if an idiom is unfamiliar, you can often figure out what it means. "I can't talk; I'm *all tied up*" would probably make sense to someone who'd never heard the expression. So would "I think I *bit off more than I can chew.*" These expressions are **figurative**. That is, they communicate an idea that is not the the **literal** (actual and ordinary) meaning of the words. Still, the ideas they communicate are clear.

Some idioms, though, you just have to know. If you'd never heard "shoot the breeze," how would you know what "They were *shooting the breeze* on the front porch" meant? You wouldn't. All you could do would be to try to figure it out from the context, check *shoot* or *breeze* in the dictionary (sometimes idioms are listed), or ask someone.

Group Talk With a small group, discuss what the following idioms mean. If you don't know them, try to figure out what they might mean.

1. Maybe you should *leave well enough alone.*
2. I don't think she's *playing with a full deck.*
3. Try to *keep your chin up.*

Additional Support

Author Search To expand students' appreciation of Phyllis Savory, have them access the Web site for additional information and resources.

English Language Coach

Understanding Idioms Tell students that when they come across idioms in their reading, they should write them in their Learner's Notebook. Explain that they will usually not be able to guess the meaning of an idiom simply by looking at the meaning of the individual words that make it up or by looking at the context. For example, a wet blanket is someone who spoils other people's fun. It would be hard to guess this meaning from the words *wet* and *blanket.* Encourage students to use a dictionary to find the meanings of idioms. Have students start lists of idiomatic expressions, and encourage them to use the expressions when it is appropriate to do so. EL

Skills Preview

Key Reading Skill: Understanding Cause and Effect

In a story, cause and effect relationships are important for many reasons. One of the most important is that they move the story along. They are part of the plot. This event happens, causing that event to happen, which then causes another event to happen. The plot is a kind of **chain reaction**, a series of causes and events. As you read "The Lion, the Hare, and the Hyena," notice the people, events, and conditions that cause other things to happen.

Key Literary Element: Theme

The **theme** of a story is the message that the writer most wants to communicate. It is the main idea of the story.

Origin stories, such as "The Lion, the Hare, and the Hyena," always include an explanation of something in nature. That provides the basic plot of the story. "Why is this the way it is?" "Because this happened." Such stories have a cause and effect structure.

L

But the structure is not the theme. Origin stories deal with another kind of "truth" about nature and human life. Doing the following while you read will help you understand the theme:

- Look at the good and bad things the characters do.
- Watch for who wins and who loses and why.
- Does someone get punished? Why?
- Does someone learn a lesson? What is it?

Interactive Literary Elements Handbook To review or learn more about the literary elements, go to www.glencoe.com.

Get Ready to Read

Connect to the Reading

How would you feel if you were all alone and so sick that you couldn't do the things you needed to do? Who would you trust to come into your home and help you? Is there anyone you feel you could not trust? Why?

Think-Pair-Share Discuss what friends do to help each other in times of need. What would you do to help a friend? How can you tell if a person is a true friend?

Build Background

"The Lion, the Hare, and the Hyena" is a folktale from Kenya.

- In this folktale, you'll read about animals that possess human traits.
- One animal is greatly respected.
- One animal is looked down on and hated and must resort to trickery to get what he wants.

R

Set Purposes for Reading

BIG Question Read "The Lion, the Hare, and the Hyena" to find out how origin stories work and why people tell them.

Set Your Own Purpose What would you like to learn from the selection to help you answer the Big Question? Write your own purpose on the "Lion, the Hare, and the Hyena" page of Foldable 6.

Keep Moving

Use these skills as you read the following selection.

Teach

L Literary Element

Theme **Say:** The theme of a work is different from the topic, which might be expressed in one word, such as "love" or "greed." Instead, the theme is usually expressed as a complete sentence. The theme of a story might be "It is better to be smart than to be strong." OL

R Reading Skill

Predicting **Say:** Read the Build Background information on this page, and think about what you know about trickster tales. What can you predict about the story? *(Possible response: You can predict that one animal will trick another animal. Since the animal that is the trickster is despised, he may not win in the end.)*

CheckPoint

Use the CheckPoint questions provided on Presentation Plus! to check for understanding of cause and effect. These questions can be used with interactive response keypads for immediate student feedback.

Reading in the Real World

College Students planning to attend college should develop strong research skills. Have students conduct research online and at a library to find out more about trickster tales. Instruct them to compare and contrast African and Native American trickster tales. Encourage them to learn when those tales were first written down and by whom. Have students present their findings to the class, either orally or in the form of a short essay. Encourage students to find illustrations to accompany their presentations. AL

Objectives
- Understand cause and effect
- Make connections from text to self
- Identify literary elements: theme
- Understand idioms

Teach

R1 Reading Skill

Understanding Cause and Effect Say: Name two effects of Simba's hurt leg. *(He cannot get food; Sunguru begins to care for him.)* **AS**

R2 Reading Skill

Review Inferring Ask: What can you infer about Sunguru the Hare from his actions here? *(Possible response: Because he takes care of Simba, you can infer that he is kind.)*

Readability Scores
Dale-Chall: 5.6
DRP: 59
Lexile: 1160

READING WORKSHOP 1

Retold by Phyllis Savory

A lion named Simba once lived alone in a cave. In his younger days the **solitude** had not worried him, but not very long before this tale begins he had hurt his leg so badly that he was unable to provide food for himself. Eventually he began to realize that companionship had its advantages. **R1**

Things would have gone very badly for him, had not Sunguru the Hare happened to be passing his cave one day. Looking inside, Sunguru realized that the lion was starving. He set about at once caring for his sick friend and seeing to his comfort.

Under the hare's careful nursing, Simba gradually regained his strength until finally he was well enough to catch small game for the two of them to eat. **R2** Soon quite a large pile of bones began to **accumulate** outside the entrance to the lion's cave. **1**

1 Key Reading Skill

Understanding Cause and Effect How did the hare come to live with the lion?

Vocabulary

solitude (SAWL uh tood) *n.* the state of being alone

accumulate (uh KYOO myuh layt) *v.* to increase gradually in quantity or number

Additional Support

English Language Coach

The Prefixes *in-* and *un-* Tell students that when the prefixes *in-* and *un-* are added to roots, they mean "not." Write these words on the board:

un + able = unable (not able, p. 660)
in + glorious = inglorious (not glorious, p. 662)

Have students write four more words that use the prefixes *un-* and *in-* to mean "not." Encourage students to look for word parts as they read to help them understand new words. *(Possible responses: unbelievable, uninterested, inaccurate, inconsistent)* **OL**

One day Nyangau the Hyena, while sniffing around in the hope of scrounging something for his supper, caught the appetizing smell of marrow-bones.[1] His nose led him to Simba's cave, but as the bones could be seen clearly from inside he could not steal them with safety. Being a cowardly fellow, like the rest of his kind, he decided that the only way to gain possession of the tasty morsels would be to make friends with Simba. He therefore crept up to the entrance of the cave and gave a cough.

"Who makes the evening hideous with his dreadful croakings?" demanded the lion, rising to his feet and preparing to investigate the noise.

R2 "It is I, your friend, Nyangau," faltered[2] the hyena, losing what little courage he possessed. "I have come to tell you how sadly you have been missed by the animals, and how greatly we are looking forward to your early return to good health!" 2

"Well, get out," growled the lion, "for it seems to me that a friend would have inquired about my health long before this, instead of waiting until I could be of use to him once more. Get out, I say!"

Practice the Skills

2 Key Literary Element

Theme Why is Nyangau pretending to be Simba's friend? Is he behaving the way a real friend would? Could his actions be a clue to the theme?

1. To ***scrounge*** is to get by finding, begging, borrowing, or stealing. ***Marrow*** is the soft substance found in the hollow centers of most bones.
2. When Nyangau ***faltered,*** he spoke brokenly or weakly because of fear.

READING WORKSHOP 1

Teach

R Reading Skill

Review Inferring **Ask:** Why does the hyena say he's come to visit the lion? *(to tell him he's been missed by the other animals)* What can you infer about the hyena from this excuse? *(You can infer that he will lie to get what he wants.)* BL OL

Viewing the Art

Ask: Do you think this illustration accurately shows the lion, the hare, and the hyena as they are described in the story? *(Possible response: Yes, the lion looks angry, the hyena looks sneaky, and the hare looks amused.)* AS

Differentiated Instruction

Short Play Have students who enjoy drama act out the folktale as a short play. Students should form groups of three, assign roles, and take notes on their characters. Suggest that they consider these questions:

- How might the character move?
- What kind of voice might he have?
- What facial expressions might he make?

Then, have students practice acting out the folktale, either using the dialogue from the story or making up their own dialogue. If they choose, students might create masks to wear during the performance. Have them perform their play for the class. OL

Objectives

- Understand cause and effect
- Make inferences
- Use prefixes to understand new words
- Analyze an image

READING WORKSHOP 1

Teach

V Vocabulary

Context Clues Say: You can guess the meaning of the word *alacrity* by looking at the words around it. The hyena has just been told off by the lion. The hare laughs at him. These clues suggest that the hyena might want to get out in a hurry. What might *alacrity* mean? *(Possible responses: quickness; promptness; speed)* OL

EL Language Coach

Idioms Say: The hyena has just run away from the lion and the hare, who have told him off and laughed at him. Yet he says he's going to try again. How would you describe someone who is willing to try again under conditions like these? *(Possible responses: thick-skinned, or not easily hurt or not sensitive)* EL

The hyena shuffled off with alacrity, his scruffy tail tucked between his bandy legs, followed by the insulting giggles of the hare. But he could not forget the pile of tempting bones outside the entrance to the lion's cave. V

"I shall try again," resolved the **thick-skinned** hyena. A few days later he made a point of paying his visit while the hare was away fetching water to cook the evening meal. 3

He found the lion dozing at the entrance to his cave.

"Friend," simpered Nyangau, "I am led to believe that the wound on your leg is making poor progress, due to the underhanded treatment that you are receiving from your so-called friend Sunguru."

"What do you mean?" snarled the lion malevolently.[3] "I have to thank Sunguru that I did not starve to death during the worst of my illness, while you and your companions were **conspicuous** by your absence!"

"Nevertheless, what I have told you is true," confided the hyena. "It is well known throughout the countryside that Sunguru is purposely giving you the wrong treatment for your wound to prevent your recovery. For when you are well, he will lose his position as your housekeeper—a very comfortable living for him, to be sure! Let me warn you, good friend, that Sunguru is not acting in your best interests!" 4

Visual Vocabulary
A ***gourd*** is a hard-rinded inedible fruit that's sometimes used as a utensil.

At that moment the hare returned from the river with his gourd filled with water. "Well," he said, addressing the hyena as he put down his load, "I did not expect to see you here after your hasty and inglorious departure from our presence the other day. Tell me, what do you want this time?"

Simba turned to the hare. "I have been listening," he said, "to Nyangau's tales about you. He tells me that you are renowned throughout the countryside for your skill and cunning[4] as a doctor. He also tells me that the medicines you prescribe are without rival.

3. To say or act with hatred is to do so ***malevolently.***

4. To be ***renowned*** is to be famous. Here, ***cunning*** means "skillful in the use of resources."

Vocabulary

conspicuous (kun SPIK yoo us) *adj.* quite noticeable

Practice the Skills

3 English Language Coach

Idiom From the context of the sentence, can you figure out what **thick-skinned** means? EL Thick skin protects an animal so harmful things don't get through. What didn't "get through" to the hyena?

4 Key Literary Element

Theme What was Sunguru willing to do to earn Simba's friendship? How did Nyangau expect to get it? Do these motives give you a clue about the theme?

Additional Support

Literature Focus Lesson

Stock Characters Tell students that some characters, such as the lion and the hyena, appear over and over again in many stories. They become instantly recognizable to the people of the culture in which the stories appear. Explain that readers in Africa would recognize the hyena as a sneaky character who is constantly trying to outsmart the lion. Ask students to name some familiar characters from fairy tales they are familiar with. *(Responses will vary. Possible response: the handsome prince and the beautiful woman in Cinderella, Sleeping Beauty, and Snow White)* AS

But he insists that you could have cured the wound on my leg a long time ago, had it been in your interest to do so. Is this true?"

Sunguru thought for a moment. He knew that he had to treat this situation with care, for he had a strong suspicion that Nyangau was trying to trick him. **5**

"Well," he answered with hesitation, "yes, and no. You see, I am only a very small animal, and sometimes the medicines that I require are very big, and I am unable to procure[5] them—as, for instance, in your case, good Simba."

"What do you mean?" spluttered the lion, sitting up and at once showing interest.

"Just this," replied the hare. "I need a piece of skin from the back of a full-grown hyena to place on your wound before it will be completely healed."

Hearing this, the lion sprang onto Nyangau before the surprised creature had time to get away. Tearing a strip of skin off the foolish fellow's back from his head to his tail, he clapped it on the wound on his leg. As the skin came away from the hyena's back, so the hairs that remained stretched and stood on end. To this day Nyangau and his kind still have long, coarse hairs standing up on the crests of their misshapen bodies. **6**

Sunguru's fame as a doctor spread far and wide after this episode, for the wound on Simba's leg healed without further trouble. But it was many weeks before the hyena had the courage to show himself in public again. **7** BQ

5. ***Procure*** means "to get or gain possession of."

Practice the Skills

5 Key Literary Element

L **Theme** Using what you know about the characters and the plot of this story, what would you say the implied theme is?

6 Key Reading Skill

Understanding Cause and Effect What thing in nature has this origin story tried to explain? According to the story, what was the cause and what was the effect?

7 BIG Question

Why do you think cultures all around the world have created origin stories? Write your answer on the "Lion, the Hare, and the Hyena" page of Foldable 6. Your response will help you complete the Unit Challenge later.

Reading in the Real World

Citizenship Have students retell this story for younger children as a warning against lying. Instruct them to shorten the story until they can tell it in about five minutes. Remind them that their audience is young, so they should use simple vocabulary. Have students practice until they can tell the story without pausing for long. Encourage them to use their voice and body language to bring the characters to life. Then, have students share their retellings with a group of elementary-school students, in a live or videotaped performance. OL AL

READING WORKSHOP 1

Teach

L Literary Element

Theme Ask: How would you describe the hyena and the hare? *(The hyena is a sneaky liar who doesn't care whom he hurts. The hare is caring and quick thinking.)* How does your description help you figure out the theme of the story? *(Possible response: The description gives me the idea that the theme is about how the hyena doesn't get what he wants by lying. The theme might be that lying to get what you want doesn't work.)* OL AL

BQ 

Say: Compare the way the hare might tell this story with the way the hyena might tell it. What might be each character's reason for telling the story? *(The hare might tell the story to brag about fooling the hyena. The hyena might tell the story so that others would have sympathy for him.)* AL

Assess

CheckPoint

Use the CheckPoint questions provided on Presentation Plus! to check for comprehension of the selection. These questions can be used with interactive response keypads for immediate student feedback.

Objectives

- Understand cause and effect
- Make inferences
- Identify theme in a text
- Learn about characters
- Use context to understand new words
- Understand idioms

Assess

Resources for page 664

- Selection Quick Check
- Selection and Unit Assessment
- ExamView Assessment Suite
- Interactive Tutor: Self-Assessment

Students can respond to the *After You Read* items in their Learner's Notebook or on a separate sheet of paper.

Answering the

1. Responses will vary.
2. Simba had hurt his leg and couldn't hunt for food.

Critical Thinking

3. Possible response: Don't lie to get what you want.
4. Possible response: He probably would have died because he wouldn't have been able to get food for himself.
5. Possible response: Nyangau claimed to be the lion's friend because he wanted his bones.
6. Possible response: Sunguru told Simba he needed a piece of skin from a hyena's back in order to heal Simba properly. He used Nyangau's lie against him.

After You Read

The Lion, the Hare, and the Hyena

Objectives (pp. 664–665)
Reading Understand cause and effect
Literature Identify literary elements: theme
Vocabulary Understand idioms
Writing Use the RAFT system: letter to the editor
Grammar Identify direct objects

Answering the

1. Now that you've read this folktale, what are some stories that you've heard in your own family that you would like to continue to tell?
2. **Recall** Why was Simba starving at the beginning of the story?
   TIP **Right There**

Critical Thinking

3. **Interpret** "The Lion, the Hare, and the Hyena" teaches a lesson. What do you think that lesson is?
   TIP **Author and Me**
4. **Infer** What would have happened to Simba the Lion had Sunguru the Hare not come along?
   TIP **Author and Me**
5. **Interpret** Were Nyangau's claims that he was Simba's friend honest? Explain.
   TIP **Think and Search**
6. **Interpret** What saved the situation for Sunguru?
   TIP **Author and Me**

Write About Your Reading

Use the RAFT system to write about "The Lion, the Hare, and the Hyena."

Role: Simba the Lion

Audience: Newspaper readers

Format: Letter to the editor

Topic: Animals in the forest have been saying that Simba was wrong to tear a strip off Nyangau. Write a letter from Simba defending what he did.

Write About Your Reading

Possible response:

I have found a miraculous cure for the wounds of large animals. It is a piece of skin from the back of a full-grown hyena. When applied to the wound, the skin helps heal the animal quickly. I had great success using this treatment to heal the wounded leg of a large lion.

Skills Review

Key Reading Skill: Understanding Cause and Effect

In each of the following sentences from the story, the underlined words state an effect. Explain what you think the cause is.

7. "In his younger days the solitude had not worried him, but not very long before this tale begins he had hurt his leg so badly that he was unable to provide food for himself."
8. "His nose led him to Simba's cave, but as the bones could be seen clearly from inside he could not steal them with safety."
9. "Sunguru's fame as a doctor spread far and wide after this episode, for the wound on Simba's leg healed without further trouble."

Key Literary Element: Theme

10. Who was successful in this story, the good friend or the bad friend? What does this tell you about the theme of the story?

Vocabulary Check

Write the vocabulary word that best matches each synonym below. Two words will be used twice.

11. increase
12. visible
13. gather
14. aloneness
15. noticeable

English Language Coach Use the context clues in each sentence to help you figure out the meaning of the idioms.

16. English is very easy for my friend Aricelli. She thought the test was **a piece of cake.**
17. But I was **on pins and needles** all day. I was very nervous about my test grade.
18. When I got my test paper back, I was **on cloud nine!** I was so happy I passed.

Grammar Link: Identifying Direct Objects

Some verbs just aren't complete without an **object**. You know that a sentence requires a subject and a verb, but look at this sentence:

- Kayla threw.

To complete the thought (and the sentence), you need to say *what* Kayla threw.

- Kayla threw the ball.

In that sentence, *ball* is the **direct object** of the verb. It answers the question "What or whom?"

There can be more than one direct object in a sentence.

- Kayla threw the ball and the glove.

A direct object can have modifiers, just as a subject or verb can.

- I baked a big cake with pink frosting.

Grammar Practice

Identify the direct objects in the following sentences. Write your answers on a separate sheet of paper.

19. Dad served cabbage for dinner.
20. The falling tree smashed my bicycle.
21. Marc knows the names of all the presidents.
22. Peter told the story very well.

Writing Application Look back at the Write About Your Reading assignment to see if you used any direct objects.

Web Activities For eFlashcards, Selection Quick Checks, and other Web activities, go to www.glencoe.com.

Skills Review

Key Reading Skill: Understanding Cause and Effect

7. Possible responses: Simba's hurt leg keeps him from hunting for food.
8. The bones could be seen clearly from inside, and Nyangau was afraid of being caught.
9. The wound on Simba's leg healed, bringing fame to Sunguru.

Key Literary Element: Theme

10. Sunguru was a true and loyal friend—he was successful at the end of the story. Nyangau lied to Simba—he was unsuccessful in winning Simba's friendship and in getting the bones. Responses should indicate that you don't get what you want by lying.

Vocabulary Check

11. accumulate
12. conspicuous
13. accumulate
14. solitude
15. conspicuous
16. Possible response: easy
17. Possible response: nervous
18. Possible response: thrilled

Grammar Link: Identifying Direct Objects

Grammar Practice

19. cabbage
20. my bicycle
21. the names of all the presidents
22. the story

Literature Online

Web Activities Have students access the Web site for interactive activities that will help them assess their understanding of the selection.

Close

Ask students to discuss what they have learned about why people share their stories.

Teach

More About the Author

With four children of her own, Jackson was very familiar with the vivid imagination of a child like Laurie. She used her own life as the inspiration for many humorous sketches about family life, which she collected in two books, *Life Among the Savages* and *Raising Demons.*

V Vocabulary

Word Circle: For additional practice after students have completed the Vocabulary Concentration game described in the Student Edition, remove the cards with the definitions. Have students form circles and take turns choosing one of the cards with the vocabulary word on it and then defining the word and using it in a sentence. Peers should correct any errors in usage. AS

Before You Read Charles

Meet the Author

Shirley Jackson's fiction is filled with strange twists and turns. In most of her novels and short stories, she explores the darker side of human life. However, Jackson also wrote humorously about family life, as she does in "Charles." Jackson was born in 1919 and died in 1965. See page R4 of the Author Files for more on Shirley Jackson.

Author Search For more about Shirley Jackson, go to www.glencoe.com.

Objectives (pp. 666–673)
Reading Understand cause and effect • Make connections from text to self
Literature Identify literary elements: theme
Vocabulary Understand slang

Vocabulary Preview

raucous (RAW kus) *adj.* loud and rough sounding **(p. 668)** *Laurie's voice was sounding more and more raucous every day.*

insolently (IN suh lunt lee) *adv.* in a boldly rude manner **(p. 668)** *He began to speak insolently to his parents.*

simultaneously (sy mul TAY nee us lee) *adv.* at the same time **(p. 670)** *Laurie's parents simultaneously decided they had to do something.*

reformation (reh fur MAY shun) *n.* a change for the better; improvement **(p. 671)** *It was clear that Laurie's behavior needed reformation.*

cynically (SIN uh kul ee) *adv.* in a way that shows doubt or disbelief; doubtfully **(p. 671)** *His father cynically shook his head.*

V **Vocabulary Concentration** With a partner, copy the words onto one set of index cards and the definitions onto another set. Mix the cards up and place them face down on a desk or table. Take turns turning the cards over two at a time. When you match a word and its definition, you may take the pair. Write sentences with the words you have matched.

English Language Coach

Slang Slang is informal language that is appropriate for casual conversation but not for formal speech or writing. Some slang is widely understood. Some, however, may be used and understood only by people within a certain social group.

Slang may use made-up words, such as *mondo* or *mongo,* meaning "extremely." Some, such as *dis* to mean *disrespect,* involves abbreviations. Most slang, though, consists of common English words used with different meanings.

Slang	Slang Meaning	Example
down with	in agreement with a plan	Sure, I'm down with that.
bail	to leave or abandon	I'm counting on you, so don't bail.
tight	emotionally close	She'll help me; we're tight.

Additional Support

Author Search To expand students' appreciation of Shirley Jackson, have them access the Web site for additional information and resources.

English Language Coach

Slang Encourage students to give examples of slang expressions in their native language and to explain their meanings. Then, ask students to give examples of English slang they have heard or used. Explain that slang changes over time and that it may be different in different regions of a country. Students will need to use context to guess the meaning of slang from different times or places. In the story, Laurie uses the word *fresh* to describe Charles's behavior. Instruct students to look for this word in the story and to use context to guess its meaning. *(*Fresh*, on p. 669, could mean* disrespectful.) BL EL

Skills Preview

Key Reading Skill: Understanding Cause and Effect

Why do you hang out with certain people? You can answer that a lot of different ways. Because they're my friends. Because I like them. Because we have a good time together. Those are your reasons. When it comes to characters in a story and their motives for doing certain things, you can look at these reasons as causes.

As you read "Charles," use the following tips to help you recognize cause and effect in both the plot and the characters' motivations:

- Look for each character's reasons for doing what he or she does.
- Look for signal words, such as *why, because, if...then, so that,* and *therefore*.
- See what events cause the teacher to do certain things in class.

Key Literary Element: Theme

Because the theme of a story is not always direct, you must dig a little deeper to understand the main idea. Laurie, his parents, and Charles are the main characters in "Charles." As you read the selection, think about each character. **L**

- What are the characters doing?
- How are they feeling about the situation they are in?
- What happens at the end?
- How do the characters react to the ending? Who is affected by the ending?
- What conclusions do you come to about the ending?

Keep these questions in mind as you try to determine the theme.

Literature Online

Interactive Literary Elements Handbook
To review or learn more about the literary elements, go to www.glencoe.com.

Get Ready to Read

Connect to the Reading

You have probably often heard just one person's side of a story and found out later that there was more to the story than you knew. Think about a time when that happened. Did hearing more of the story change your mind about what happened? **R**

Write to Learn In your Learner's Notebook, freewrite about a time a friend or family member told you only one side of a story.

Build Background

Children entering school must learn to get along with each other, follow directions, and help with classroom activities. In preschool and kindergarten, children become accustomed to a school setting and learn to play together. At least, that's the plan. In "Charles," things don't exactly follow the plan.

- Laurie, a kindergarten boy, takes delight in telling his parents about school each day.
- His parents are shocked to hear Laurie's descriptions of the horrible classroom behavior of a boy named Charles.
- Seeing Charles as a bad influence on her son, Laurie's mother decides to speak to the other boy's parents.

Set Purposes for Reading

BIG Question Read to find out why Laurie is sharing stories about Charles.

Set Your Own Purpose What would you like to learn from the selection to help you answer the Big Question? Write your own purpose on the "Charles" page of Foldable 6.

Keep Moving

Use these skills as you read the following selection.

Teach

L Literary Element

Theme Say: Remember that the theme of a story is the message about life or people that the author conveys in the story. When you read "Charles," write the answers to the questions on this page in your Learner's Notebook, and then ask yourselves, "What message is Jackson conveying in this story?" **AL**

R Reading Skill

Review Connecting Say: As you read the story, think about how Laurie's parents, as well as readers, learn about Charles. Then think about a time you learned there was more than one side of a story. **OL**

Literature Online

Interactive Literary Elements Handbook Have students access the Web site to improve their understanding of theme.

Literature Focus Lesson

Character Tell students that there is not much action in this story. Instead, it is primarily a story about how characters in a family relate to one another. Authors develop characters in fiction by telling

- what they look like
- what they say
- what they think
- what they do
- what other characters think of them
- what the narrator thinks of them

As students read, have them notice Jackson's primary techniques for developing the characters in her story. Have them evaluate her techniques by answering the question "Do the characters seem real? Why or why not?" **AL**

Objectives

- Understand cause and effect
- Make connections from text to self
- Identify literary elements: theme
- Understand slang

Teach

L Literary Element

Review Narrator Ask: Who is the narrator of this story? *(Laurie's mother)* How do you know? *(She refers to Laurie as "my son.")* OL

R Reading Skill

Review Inferring Ask: What does Laurie do when he gets home from school? *(He slams the front door, yells, speaks rudely to his father, and spills the baby's milk.)* What can you infer about Laurie from his behavior? *(Possible response: You can infer that he misbehaves and doesn't show respect for his parents.)* BL AL

Readability Scores
Dale-Chall: 4.6
DRP: 52
Lexile: 770

READING WORKSHOP 1

Charles

by Shirley Jackson

The day my son Laurie started kindergarten he renounced[1] corduroy overalls with bibs and began wearing blue jeans with a belt; I watched him go off the first morning with the older girl next door, seeing clearly that an era of my life was ended, my sweet-voiced nursery-school tot replaced by a long-trousered, swaggering[2] character who forgot to stop at the corner and wave good-bye to me. 1 L

He came home the same way, the front door slamming open, his cap on the floor, and the voice suddenly become raucous shouting, "Isn't anybody here?"

At lunch he spoke insolently to his father, spilled his baby sister's milk, and remarked that his teacher said we were not to take the name of the Lord in vain. R

"How *was* school today?" I asked, elaborately casual.

"All right," he said.

"Did you learn anything?" his father asked.

1. When Laurie ***renounced*** overalls, he rejected or gave them up.
2. ***Swaggering*** means carrying oneself in a proud manner.

Vocabulary

raucous (RAW kus) *adj.* loud and rough sounding

insolently (IN suh lunt lee) *adv.* in a boldly rude manner

Practice the Skills

1 Reviewing Skills

Connecting Do you remember your first day at kindergarten? How do you think your parents felt that day?

Additional Support

Differentiated Instruction

Group Discussion Have students connect to the reading by discussing how they feel when they are introduced to a new group of people for the first time. Students should discuss the best and worst experiences they have had when meeting new people, such as in a new school, on a sports team, in a club, or in a family gathering. Were they uncomfortable, hopeful, shy? Have them list their reactions on a "Good Feelings/Bad Feelings" chart. You may wish to have groups share their findings. OL

Laurie regarded his father coldly. "I didn't learn nothing," he said.

"Anything," I said. "Didn't learn anything."

"The teacher spanked a boy, though," Laurie said, addressing his bread and butter. "For being fresh," he added, with his mouth full.

"What did he do?" I asked. "Who was it?"

Laurie thought. "It was Charles," he said. "He was fresh. The teacher spanked him and made him stand in a corner. He was awfully fresh." **2**

"What did he do?" I asked again, but Laurie slid off his chair, took a cookie, and left, while his father was still saying, "See here, young man."

The next day Laurie remarked at lunch, as soon as he sat down, "Well, Charles was bad again today." He grinned enormously and said, "Today Charles hit the teacher."

"Good heavens," I said, mindful of the Lord's name, "I suppose he got spanked again?"

"He sure did," Laurie said. "Look up," he said to his father.

"What?" his father said, looking up.

"Look down," Laurie said. "Look at my thumb. Gee, you're dumb." He began to laugh insanely.

"Why did Charles hit the teacher?" I asked quickly.

"Because she tried to make him color with red crayons," Laurie said. "Charles wanted to color with green crayons so he hit the teacher and she spanked him and said nobody play with Charles but everybody did." **3**

The third day—it was Wednesday of the first week—Charles bounced a see-saw on to the head of a little girl and made her bleed, and the teacher made him stay inside all during recess. Thursday Charles had to stand in a corner during story-time because he kept pounding his feet on the floor. Friday Charles was deprived of blackboard privileges because he threw chalk.

On Saturday I remarked to my husband, "Do you think kindergarten is too unsettling for Laurie? All this toughness, and bad grammar, and this Charles boy sounds like such a bad influence."

"It'll be all right," my husband said reassuringly. "Bound to be people like Charles in the world. Might as well meet them now as later."

Practice the Skills

2 Key Reading Skill

R1 **Understanding Cause and Effect** What made the teacher spank Charles and put him in a corner?

R2

3 Key Reading Skill

Understanding Cause and Effect The teacher told the class not to play with Charles—but they did. What effect do you think this had on Charles?

Differentiated Instruction

Music Students with strong musical abilities may better understand Charles by writing a song about him. All students may find that the song-writing activity gives them a deeper insight into Charles's character. Have students work in small groups to discuss Charles's character and then write appropriate lyrics about him. Ask them to describe what Charles has done, what has happened to him, and how the teacher might feel about him. Remind students that the story is humorous, so their songs should have a light tone. **OL**

Teach

R1 Reading Skill

Understanding Cause and Effect **Say:** You can use what you've just read to figure out the cause-and-effect relationship. What does Laurie say happened at school? *(The teacher spanked a boy.)* That is the effect. What caused the boy to be spanked? *(Laurie says that he was "being fresh.")* That is the cause. **BL**

R2 Reading Skill

Understanding Cause and Effect **Ask:** According to Laurie, why does Charles hit the teacher? *(She tries to make him color with red crayons rather than green crayons.)* What can you infer about Charles from his behavior? *(Possible response: You can infer that he doesn't show much respect for the teacher and he gets angry if he doesn't get his way.)* **BL** **OL**

Objectives
- Understand cause and effect
- Make inferences
- Understand slang

Teach

Viewing the Photo
Ask: Based on the characters in the story, who do you think this photo illustrates? *(Possible responses: Charles, Laurie)* Why? *(Possible response: The child looks like he likes to misbehave, like Laurie does and says Charles does in the story.)* **AS**

R1 Reading Skill

Understanding Cause and Effect Say: What are two effects of Charles's bad behavior? *(A boy from the first grade comes to ask the teacher to "make" Charles keep quiet; all the children stay after school to watch Charles, who has been made to stay after school.)* **OL**

R2 Reading Skill

Review Inferring Ask: Why does Laurie's mother want to go to the Parent-Teachers meeting? *(She wants to meet Charles's mother.)* Why might she want to meet Charles's mother? *(Possible responses: She might want to discuss his bad behavior because she thinks he's a bad influence on Laurie. She might want to see what she's like.)* **AL**

READING WORKSHOP 1

On Monday Laurie came home late, full of news. "Charles," he shouted as he came up the hill; I was waiting anxiously on the front steps. "Charles," Laurie yelled all the way up the hill, "Charles was bad again."

"Come right in," I said, as soon as he came close enough. "Lunch is waiting."

"You know what Charles did?" he demanded, following me through the door. "Charles yelled so in school they sent a boy in from first grade to tell the teacher she had to make Charles keep quiet, and so Charles had to stay after school. And so all the children stayed to watch him."

R1 "What did he do?" I asked.

"He just sat there," Laurie said, climbing into his chair at the table. "Hi, Pop, y'old dust mop." 4

"Charles had to stay after school today," I told my husband. "Everyone stayed with him."

"What does this Charles look like?" my husband asked Laurie. "What's his other name?"

"He's bigger than me," Laurie said. "And he doesn't have any galoshes and he doesn't ever wear a jacket."

R2 Monday night was the first Parent-Teachers meeting, and only the fact that the baby had a cold kept me from going; I wanted passionately to meet Charles's mother. On Tuesday Laurie remarked suddenly, "Our teacher had a friend come to see her in school today."

"Charles's mother?" my husband and I asked **simultaneously**.

"Naaah," Laurie said scornfully. "It was a man who came and made us do exercises, we had to touch our toes. Look." He climbed down from his chair and squatted down and touched his toes. "Like this," he said. He got solemnly back into his chair and said, picking up his fork, "Charles didn't even do exercises."

"That's fine," I said heartily. "Didn't Charles want to do exercises?"

"Naaah," Laurie said. "Charles was so fresh to the teacher's friend he wasn't *let* do exercises."

Vocabulary

simultaneously (sy mul TAY nee us lee) *adv.* at the same time

Practice the Skills

4 Reviewing Skills

Connecting This is the second time Laurie has spoken rudely to his father. Would you talk to your parents like this? What effect would it bring if you did?

Additional Support

Reading Fluency

Reading Dialogue Some students might be challenged by reading dialogue. Have students choose a section of "Charles" and practice reading it aloud softly until they can read it without hesitating. Remind students that good readers use intonation, or the ups and downs of the voice, as they read dialogue, just as they would in a conversation. Encourage students to focus on their intonation as they read, avoiding a monotone. You might model the use of intonation by reading a short passage, first using a monotone and then using a variety of tones, to help students see the importance of intonation while reading dialogue. **BL** **EL**

"Fresh again?" I said.

"He kicked the teacher's friend," Laurie said. "The teacher's friend told Charles to touch his toes like I just did and Charles kicked him."

"What are they going to do about Charles, do you suppose?" Laurie's father asked him.

Laurie shrugged elaborately. "Throw him out of school, I guess," he said.

Wednesday and Thursday were routine; Charles yelled during story hour and hit a boy in the stomach and made him cry. On Friday Charles stayed after school again and so did all the other children.

With the third week of kindergarten Charles was an institution[3] in our family; the baby was being a Charles when she cried all afternoon; Laurie did a Charles when he filled his wagon full of mud and pulled it through the kitchen; even my husband, when he caught his elbow in the telephone cord and pulled telephone, ashtray, and a bowl of flowers off the table, said, after the first minute, "Looks like **Charles**." 5

During the third and fourth weeks it looked like a **reformation** in Charles; Laurie reported grimly at lunch on Thursday of the third week, "Charles was so good today the teacher gave him an apple." 6

"What?" I said, and my husband added warily, "You mean Charles?"

"Charles," Laurie said. "He gave the crayons around and he picked up the books afterward and the teacher said he was her helper."

"What happened?" I asked incredulously.

"He was her helper, that's all," Laurie said, and shrugged.

"Can this be true, about Charles?" I asked my husband that night. "Can something like this happen?"

"Wait and see," my husband said **cynically**. "When you've got a Charles to deal with, this may mean he's only plotting.[4]" R

3. Here, ***institution*** means a "regular feature or tradition."

4. ***Plotting*** means planning with evil intent.

Vocabulary

reformation (reh fur MAY shun) *n.* a change for the better; improvement

cynically (SIN uh kul ee) *adv.* in a way that shows doubt or disbelief; doubtfully

Practice the Skills

5 English Language Coach EL

Slang What does the name **Charles** mean when Laurie's family uses it in the phrases "being a Charles," "did a Charles," and "looks like a Charles"?

6 Key Reading Skill

Understanding Cause and Effect How is Charles's good behavior being rewarded?

READING WORKSHOP 1

Teach

EL Language Coach

Slang Say: What do you know about Charles thus far? *(He is loud, rude, and disrespectful.)* What do you think it means, then, to "be a Charles"? *(It means being rude or loud.)* EL

R Reading Skill

Understanding Cause and Effect Ask: Why might Laurie's father be cynical about Charles's good behavior? *(Possible response: He knows that Charles has been bad in the past, so he isn't sure that Charles's change in behavior will be permanent.)* AL

Reading in the Real World

Career Students who are considering a career in teaching or another field that requires interpersonal skills will need to be adept at conflict resolution. Have students working in groups think of ways to address Charles's unruly behavior. Students should write a list of ideas and be ready to share them with the class. Have students explain why each idea would help Charles behave better. OL

Objectives
- Understand cause and effect
- Make inferences
- Understand slang

READING WORKSHOP 1

Teach

L Literary Element

Theme Ask: What information do Laurie's mother and father want to get from Charles's mother? *(They want to know why Charles has changed.)* Laurie's parents show a lot of concern about Charles, but they don't seem to respond when Laurie misbehaves. How might their behavior suggest one theme of the story? *(Possible response: It might suggest that a theme is "Worry about what your own children are doing, not about what other people's children are doing.")* OL AL

Viewing the Art

Ask: What does this painting show? Is it a good illustration for this story? Why or why not? *(Possible response: The picture shows children playing happily. Responses about whether the work is a good illustration will vary. Some students may note that an illustration of Laurie or Charles would have been more appropriate.)*

He seemed to be wrong. For over a week Charles was the teacher's helper; each day he handed things out and he picked things up; no one had to stay after school.

"The P.T.A. meeting's next week again," I told my husband one evening. "I'm going to find Charles's mother there." L

"Ask her what happened to Charles," my husband said. "I'd like to know."

"I'd like to know myself," I said.

On Friday of that week things were back to normal. "You know what Charles did today?" Laurie demanded at the lunch table, in a voice slightly awed. "He told a little girl to say a word and she said it and the teacher washed her mouth out with soap and Charles laughed."

"What word?" his father asked unwisely, and Laurie said, "I'll have to whisper it to you, it's so bad." He got down off his chair and went around to his father. His father bent his head down and Laurie whispered joyfully. His father's eyes widened. 7

"Did Charles tell the little girl to say *that*?" he asked respectfully.

"She said it *twice*," Laurie said. "Charles told her to say it *twice*."

"What happened to Charles?" my husband asked.

"Nothing," Laurie said. "He was passing out the crayons."

Monday morning Charles abandoned the little girl and said the evil word himself three or four times, getting his mouth washed out with soap each time. He also threw chalk.

My husband came to the door with me that evening as I set out for the P.T.A. meeting. "Invite her over for a cup of tea after the meeting," he said. "I want to get a look at her."

"If only she's there," I said prayerfully.

Practice the Skills

7 Reviewing Skills

Comparing and Contrasting Compare Laurie's behavior here to Charles's behavior, as Laurie describes it.

Playground, Crook, P.J., b. 1945, acrylic on canvas, 116.8 X 132 cm., Private Collection.

Additional Support

Differentiated Instruction

Art Have students draw or paint Laurie or find a photograph of someone they think looks like Laurie. Students should use what they know about Laurie to create or choose a picture of him. Have them answer these questions before they begin:

- How old is Laurie?
- What do you know about his appearance?
- What words might you use to describe him?

Have students share their pictures with the class and tell why they think their pictures look like Laurie. OL EL

Modern Folktale

UNIT 6

Teaching Students to Write a Modern Folktale

Why Is It Important?

- The imaginative nature of the writing will encourage students to think outside the character roles that may initially come to them.
- Working from existing stories can give students the confidence to experiment with more complex sentence structure or vocabulary.
- Building a tale off an already existing one will allow students to build fluency as writers and attentiveness as readers.
- Creating a class binder of all the students' modern folktales will foster a sense of involvement and community.

How to Help Students Get It

- Encourage students to read ahead, or read a folktale in the textbook not scheduled for class time. They may not choose to update that particular selection for the assignment, but increased exposure to the genre will help them by providing a model of the folktale elements.
- Let students know they can retain or "update" as many elements of the original folktale as they feel comfortable with.
- Give students examples of folktales that have cognates in many cultures, like Cinderella.
- Students having difficulty generating a "theme" can refer to the Index of Skills, and be directed to other selections in which "theme" is highlighted. This will help to clarify the concept.
- Prior to revising their draft, ask students to ensure that their modern folktale includes all the necessary elements of a folktale: characters, plot/conflict, setting, a magical or far-fetched element, and a theme.
- Students may find it easier to make the theme explicit at the end of their tale, as in the familiar format of Aesop's Fables.
- Review with the students the types of revision they have done on previous writing assignments. Remind them that as their portfolio grows, so does their skill set.

Writing Trait: Conventions

Conventions refers to mechanical correctness. One way to conceive its domain is to ask "What would a copy editor need to do to run this story?" Such numerous and varied aspects as punctuation, paragraphing, sentence fragments and run-ons, spelling, grammar and usage, and capitalization all fall under the heading of Conventions.

Skills Review

Key Reading Skill: Understanding Cause and Effect

7. Why do you think Laurie turns into a "swaggering character" when he starts kindergarten? Explain your answer. (Hint: Think about the fact that Laurie suddenly finds himself in a new place with new people and new rules.)
8. Identify two good or positive things that Charles does and how he is rewarded.

Key Literary Element: Theme

9. What do you think is the theme of "Charles"? Explain your answer using examples from the story.

Reviewing Skills: Comparing and Contrasting

10. **Comparing and Contrasting** Compare Laurie's behavior at home with Charles's actions at school. How are their behaviors similar? How are they different?

Vocabulary Check

Choose one of the vocabulary words to fill in each of the blanks in the sentences below.

raucous **insolently** **simultaneously** **cynically** **reformation**

11. "Hey, old man, get a horse!" Geri yelled ____.
12. The sounds from the ape's cage were so ____ it sounded like a huge party!
13. The city council is dishonest and needs ____.
14. "I'm sorry, John. I don't believe you can do it," he said ____.
15. "You're it!" Mary and Lisa shouted ____.
16. **English Language Coach** If a slang meaning for a word is used by enough people for a long enough period, it becomes a regular meaning. For example, *fresh* meaning "disrespectful," was slang in the mid-1800s but is now found in dictionaries. The meaning "extremely nice or superior" is still slang.

    Write down two slang words or phrases and their meanings. Use each one in a sentence that illustrates its meaning.

Grammar: Identifying Indirect Objects

Direct objects answer the question "what or whom?"

- Joel wrote a letter.

If a sentence contains a direct object, it may also contain an indirect object. An indirect object answers the question "to what or whom?" or "for what or whom?" It usually comes before the direct object.

- Joel wrote Leanne a letter.
- Maya left Missy a beautiful present.

It's important to know that a word is only an indirect object if the word *to* or *for* is **not** stated. If it is, then you have a prepositional phrase. There are no indirect objects in the following sentences.

- Joel wrote a letter to Leanne.
- Maya left a beautiful present for Missy.

Grammar Practice

Identify the indirect object in each sentence.

17. The rider gave the horse an apple.
18. Habib handed them flowers.
19. James made me dinner last night.
20. My cousin gave her dog a bath.

Literature Online

Web Activities For eFlashcards, Selection Quick Checks, and other Web activities, go to www.glencoe.com.

Skills Review

Key Reading Skill: Understanding Cause and Effect

7. Possible response: The new situation makes Laurie feel older, so he acts differently.
8. Possible responses: Charles hands out the crayons and picks up the books. The teacher calls Charles "her helper."

Key Literary Element: Theme

9. Possible response: Often we judge others without looking at our own actions.

Reviewing Skills: Comparing and Contrasting

10. Possible responses: Charles is sometimes pleasant, but Laurie never seems to be well behaved.

Vocabulary Check

11. insolently
12. raucous
13. reformation
14. cynically
15. simultaneously
16. Responses will vary.

Close

Ask students to think about what "Charles" has taught them about reasons for telling stories. Ask them to state one reason that the story suggests.

Grammar: Identifying Indirect Objects

Grammar Practice

17. the horse
18. them
19. me
20. her dog

Literature Online

Web Activities Have students access the Web site for interactive activities that will help them assess their understanding of the selection.

Assess

Resources for page 674

- Selection Quick Check
- Selection and Unit Assessment
- ExamView Assessment Suite
- Interactive Tutor: Self-Assessment

Students can respond to the *After You Read* items in their Learner's Notebook or on a separate sheet of paper.

Answering the BIG Question

1. Possible response: He wants to see his parents' reaction.
2. He reports his bad behavior gleefully and his good behavior grimly.

Critical Thinking

3. Possible response: Charles's behavior is bad, and Laurie's parents think that Charles is a bad influence on Laurie.
4. Charles is Laurie.
5. Possible responses: Laurie is rude and loud. Laurie delights in telling about Charles's antics. Laurie never tells Charles's last name. Laurie is grim when Charles starts behaving well.
6. Possible responses: Laurie wanted attention; Laurie has an active imagination.

After You Read | Charles

Answering the BIG Question

1. Why do you think Laurie tells stories about Charles?
2. **Recall** How does Laurie report Charles's good behavior and Charles's bad behavior?
   TIP **Think and Search**

Critical Thinking

3. **Interpret** Why is Charles such a fascination in Laurie's home?
   TIP **Author and Me**
4. **Infer** Who is Charles?
   TIP **Author and Me**
5. **Synthesize** What clues throughout the selection give you that information?
   TIP **Think and Search**
6. **Evaluate** Why do you think Laurie makes up all those stories?
   TIP **Author and Me**

Write About Your Reading

Write a skit about "Charles." To get started, follow these steps:

Step 1: Think about which characters to include. Your choices will depend on what you decide in Steps 2, 3, and 4.

Step 2: Decide whether the action will take place at Laurie's home or school.

Step 3: Decide on at least one cause and effect to show.

Step 4: Decide what will happen at the end.

Step 5: Write the skit.

Get some friends together to perform your skits for your class. (But behave. Don't do a Charles!)

Objectives (pp. 674–675)
Reading Understand cause and effect
Literature Identify literary elements: theme
Vocabulary Understand slang
Writing Respond to literature: skit
Grammar Identify indirect objects

Write About Your Reading

Possible response:
Mrs. Brown *[Laurie's teacher]*: Laurie, what are you doing? Please get down!
Laurie: No way! I'm going to stand on my desk for the rest of the day.
[Laurie's classmates giggle.]
Mrs. Brown: Now, class. Settle down. If you don't get down, Laurie, the whole class will have to stay after school. Is that what you want?
[Laurie's classmates start to chant, "Get down! Get down! Get down!"]
Laurie *[ashamed]*: Oh, all right. I'll get down. Just this once, though.

READING WORKSHOP 1

"She'll be there," my husband said.

"I don't see how they could hold a P.T.A. meeting without Charles's mother."

At the meeting I sat restlessly, scanning each comfortable matronly[5] face, trying to determine which one hid the secret of Charles. None of them looked to me haggard[6] enough. No one stood up in the meeting and apologized for the way her son had been acting. No one mentioned Charles.

After the meeting I identified and sought out Laurie's kindergarten teacher. She had a plate with a cup of tea and a piece of chocolate cake; I had a plate with a cup of tea and a piece of marshmallow cake. We maneuvered up to one another cautiously, and smiled.

"I've been so anxious to meet you," I said. "I'm Laurie's mother."

"We're all so interested in Laurie," she said.

"Well, he certainly likes kindergarten," I said. "He talks about it all the time."

"We had a little trouble adjusting, the first week or so," she said primly, "but now he's a fine little helper. With occasional lapses,[7] of course."

"Laurie usually adjusts very quickly," I said. "I suppose this time it's Charles's influence."

"Charles?"

"Yes," I said, laughing, "you must have your hands full in that kindergarten, with Charles."

"Charles?" she said. "We don't have any Charles in the kindergarten." 8 9 ❍ R

5. Another word for ***matronly*** would be "motherly." It refers to a mature woman, especially one who is married and has children.

6. A ***haggard*** person looks worn out as a result of grief, worry, illness—or dealing with a boy like Charles.

7. A ***lapse*** is a slipping or falling to a lower or worse condition.

Practice the Skills

8 Key Literary Element

Theme What does this story suggest about human nature?

9 BIG Question

BQ Why do you think Laurie told stories about a boy who didn't exist? Write your answer on the "Charles" page of Foldable 6. Your response will help you complete the Unit Challenge later.

Teach

R Reading Skill

Understanding Cause and Effect Ask: What effects could the discovery that there is no Charles have on Laurie's parents? *(Possible responses: They might ask Laurie why he made up the stories. Perhaps they will pay more attention to Laurie, but the story does not suggest that they will.)* AL

BQ 

Ask: Why might Laurie have told the stories about Charles? *(Possible responses: He wanted to tell his parents what was happening at school without admitting that he was acting badly. He realized that the only way to get his parents' attention was by talking about another child in the class.)* Why doesn't he tell his parents that he did the things he describes? *(Possible response: He doesn't want to get in trouble.)* AL

Assess

Use the CheckPoint questions provided on Presentation Plus! to check for comprehension of the selection. These questions can be used with interactive response keypads for immediate student feedback.

Literature Focus Lesson

Plot Twist Remind students that the sequence of events in a story is called the plot. Usually the plot is built around a central conflict in which opposing sides are involved in a struggle or face a problem that must be resolved. The turning point of the plot is called the climax, the point at which the outcome of the conflict is determined. In some plots, the climax includes an unexpected turn of events, called a plot twist. "Charles" is an example of a story with a plot twist. Have students describe the plot twist in "Charles." (It turns out that Laurie is describing himself; "Charles" is Laurie.) Ask students to describe another story they have read that has a plot twist. *(Responses will vary.)* BL OL

Objectives
- Understand cause and effect
- Understand the development of theme through characters, actions, and images
- Illustrate a story

Traits of Good Writing	
Ideas	the message or the theme and the details that develop it
Voice	a writer's unique way of using tone and style
Organization	the arrangement of main points and supporting details
Word Choice	the vocabulary a writer uses to convey meaning
Sentence Fluency	the smooth rhythm and flow of sentences that vary in length and style
Conventions	correct spelling, grammar, usage, and mechanics
Unit Focus **Presentation:** the way words and design elements look on a page	Appearance matters, so encourage students to make their compositions inviting to read. Handwritten papers should be neat and legible. If a word processor is used, the text should be double spaced and the font should be readable. Encourage students to also use other design elements—such as boldfaced headings, bulleted lists, pictures, and charts—to make their papers attractive and inviting.

Workshop Resources

Pacing (Days) Standard	Block	Lesson	Student Materials	Teacher Resources
1		Prewriting	Writing Workshop Graphic Organizer Grammar Practice Spelling and Handwriting Practice Spelling Power eWorkbook Interactive Grammar and Language Workbook Grammar and Composition Handbook	TeacherWorks Plus Presentation Plus! Rubrics for Assessing Student-Writing, Listening, and Speaking
2		Drafting	Real Success in Writing: Research and Reports Writing Constructed Responses Sourcebook	Grammar and Writing Workshop Transparency
1		Editing	Interactive Grammar and Language Workbook Grammar and Composition Handbook	Grammar and Writing Workshop Transparency
2		Revising	Real Success in Writing: Research and Reports Writing Constructed Responses Sourcebook	Interactive Grammar and Language Workbook
2		Presenting	Real Success in Writing: Research and Reports Writing Constructed Responses Sourcebook	Rubrics for Assessing Student Writing, Listening, and Speaking

Focus

BELLRINGER Options

Daily Language Practice Transparency

Focus Activity Ask: If you told the story "Cinderella" set in modern times, what details would you change? In this Writing Workshop, you will rewrite a folktale, making it sound as if it were happening today.

Teach

C Critical Thinking

Comprehension Say: Name three elements of folktales. *(larger-than-life characters; they take place long ago and sometimes far away; some include magic.)* Why is it important to know these characteristics before you write? *(Possible response: to know what characteristics to include)* OL

Resources for page 676

- Use the Writing Workshop Graphic Organizer BLM in the Unit 6 Resource Booklet.
- Use the Grammar and Writing Workshop Transparencies, Unit 6.

WRITING WORKSHOP PART 1

Modern Folktale

Prewriting and Drafting

ASSIGNMENT Rewrite a folktale in the present

Purpose: To tell a story using all of the elements of a folktale

Audience: You, your teacher, and your classmates

Writing Rubric

As you work through this writing assignment, you should

- develop characters
- write dialogue
- develop a theme
- use third-person point of view
- use correct spelling, grammar, usage, and mechanics

Objectives (pp. 676–679)
Writing Use the writing process: draft • Write a folktale • Use literary elements: point of view, dialogue, characterization, theme
Grammar Use compound and complex sentences

Folktales are organized like other stories, usually in time order. They also have characters, a setting, a plot (created through conflict), and a theme, just like other stories. But folktales have some special characteristics, too.

- Characters in folktales are often larger-than-life humans or animals that act like humans. C
- The setting is usually long ago and sometimes in a faraway or make-believe place.
- Some folktales (specifically fairy tales) include magic. Other folktales have unusual elements such as talking animals.

In this Writing Workshop, you'll rewrite a folktale in the present (as if it were taking place today).

Prewriting

Get Ready to Write

Before you start writing, you'll have to decide what folktale you want to rewrite and plan the changes you'll make.

Choose a Story

You can choose one of the folktales in this unit or another folktale you know.

- Make a list of the folktales you already know. Remember, folktales include many different kinds of stories—animal stories, origin stories, legends, trickster tales, fairy tales, tall tales, and myths.
- Look over the folktales in this unit. If one interests you, go ahead and read it. (You don't have to wait for your teacher to tell you to read it!)
- Choose a story that you think would be fun to rewrite. You may want to choose your favorite story, or you may want to choose a story you don't like and make it into a story you do like.

Think A-bout the Story

Think carefully about the story elements of the folktale you're going to rewrite. If you're rewriting a folktale that you don't know very well, you may want to read the story a few times.

Fill in a chart like the one on the next page to familiarize yourself with the key parts of the story. Make your chart in your Learner's Notebook.

Additional Support

English Language Coach

Vivid Language Tell students they should use vivid, exact verbs and adjectives to bring their writing to life. Have students work alone or with partners to look through a thesaurus or dictionary to find vivid verbs and adjectives to replace the underlined words in these sentences:

1. We walked to the store.
2. She was happy about winning the race.
3. They cried after watching the sad movie.
4. He was interested in finding out what would happen next.

Have students share their revisions with the class. EL BL

Folktale	Brer Rabbit and Brer Lion
Setting	The woods, somewhere in the United States, a long time ago
Characters	Brer Rabbit, Brer Lion, the other animals
Major Events	Brer Lion lets Brer Rabbit tie him to a tree so he doesn't get blown away by the hurricane. The storm never comes, but Brer Rabbit refuses to untie the lion. When Brer Lion roars, all of the other animals come and see that little Brer Rabbit has tied up the powerful lion.
Magical or Unusual Element	Talking animals
Theme	If you are smart enough, you can beat others who are more powerful.

Literature Online

Writing Models For models and other writing activities, go to www.glencoe.com.

Make a Plan

Since your story is a retelling, you'll need to keep some of the details from the original folktale. You may want to use the same characters, events, theme, or even setting. But don't keep everything the same! Add your own flavor to the folktale.

Figure out the main changes you want to make to the folktale before you start drafting your story. **W1**

1. Take another look at your notes about the original folktale. Ask yourself questions like the ones below.
   - Where else could these events take place?
   - What would these characters be like in current times?
   - What other events could teach the same theme or lesson?
2. Use a story map to pull the elements of your folktale together. You might also want to make notes about any magic in your story.

Characters	Setting
Jack Rabbit–lost in a dream world Dan D. Lion–nervous, easily scared	a city street in England
Plot Jack bumps into Dan on the street while thinking about a breeze he felt. Dan freaks out thinking that the breeze might have been a cyclone. Jack ties Dan to a taxicab. The taxi drives away, and Jack wanders on in his dream world.	
Theme Living in a dream world can cause problems in the real world.	

Writing Tip

W2 **Characters** Make some notes about how each character might talk. Does he or she use big words, speak with an accent, drag out every word, or speak only in questions? It's up to you. Characters' dialogue is based on the personality of the character and your imagination.

Differentiated Instruction

Summary Some students may benefit from writing three to four sentence summaries of their stories after they create story maps and before they begin writing. This will help them organize their ideas and give them overviews of their stories.

After students have written their summaries, have them share their ideas with the class and ask for feedback. **BL** **EL**

Teach

Literature Online

Writing Models Have students access the Web site for an additional and interactive Writing Workshop-based student model.

W1 Writing

Theme Say: Before you start writing, be sure you know the theme of the story you will rewrite. How can you determine the theme of a story? *(Think about the characters, plot, and setting and how the author uses these to create a message about life.)* **AL**

W2 Writing

Character Sketch Students might benefit from creating a character sketch for each main character in their folktales. A character sketch should describe some or all of the following:

Appearance
Personality
Voice
Age
OL

Objectives
- Develop characters, setting, and theme
- Write summaries

Teach

W1 Writing

Third-Person Point of View
Say: Remember that a third-person narrator is outside of the story, "looking in." A limited third-person narrator tells the story from one character's point of view, while an omniscient narrator knows the points of view of all characters. What might be the benefit of using a narrator with an omniscient point of view? *(You could tell what every character is thinking and doing.)* OL

W2 Writing

Writer's Craft **Say:** Think of at least five words in addition to *said* to use to set up your dialogue. Make a list of these words. Keep your list handy when writing your folktale.

Drafting

Start Writing!

Grab your favorite pen, pencil, or keyboard and some blank paper. It's time to start writing!

Tell the Tale

Imagine you are a storyteller relating the folktale to a live audience. Use your story map to guide you. Be sure your story has these elements of effective folktales.

- Tellers of folktales are usually outside the story. Use the third-person point of view to tell what happens. (Remember to refer to characters by name or as *he* and *she*.)

Writing Tip

Ideas You may want to write a few ideas for openers for your folktale and see which one would be most interesting to your readers.

- Folktales usually get to the point quickly. The start of "Brer Rabbit and Brer Lion" sets up the story: "Brer Rabbit was in the woods one afternoon when a great wind came up." You can also start right in with action, dialogue, or an interesting statement.

Dan D. Lion was never the same after he bumped into Jack Rabbit.

- Develop your characters by providing details about them. What are they thinking? How do they act? Your readers need to know.

But, in his imagination, it had been a very nice tea party.

Writing Tip

Writer's Craft Make your folktale more interesting by using words besides *said* to set up the dialogue. Try using more specific and descriptive words such as *whined, shouted, giggled,* and *whispered.* W2

- Dialogue reveals characters' personality and can give clues about the setting. A character that asks "What shall I do? Where can I hide?" is fearful and anxious. "Would hiding inside that telephone booth make you jumpy?" suggests a street setting.
- Your folktale should have a theme, or main idea. In "Brer Rabbit and Brer Lion," the theme appears through the characters and events of the story. Brer Rabbit struts around the tied-up Brer Lion to show off what he's done. If you prefer, you can reveal the theme directly.

The moral of the story is "Never get mixed up with someone who lives in a dream world."

Additional Support

Reading in the Real World

College Students who want to pursue a college degree should be adept at research. Have students who do not want to retell the folktales from the Student Edition go to the library to search for other folktales. Remind students that they can search for tales from around the world—fairy tales, tall tales, legends, or trickster tales. Encourage students to look for stories that are an appropriate length. Stories that are too long may be difficult to retell. AL

Grammar Link

Compound and Complex Sentences

Sentences are made up of independent clauses (which can stand alone as sentences) and dependent clauses (which cannot stand alone).

Independent clause: The lion was big.

Independent clause: The rabbit was smart.

Dependent clause: though the lion was big

What Are Compound and Complex Sentences?

A **compound sentence** is made up of two or more independent clauses joined together.

The lion was big, but the rabbit was smart.
independent *independent*

A **complex sentence** is made up of one independent clause and one or more dependent clauses joined together.

Though the lion was big, the rabbit was smart.
dependent *independent*

Why Are Compound and Complex Sentences Important?

You need to use all the sentence types to write well. Compare the two paragraphs below.

Simple sentences only: Writing only in simple sentences limits you. Every sentence has the same pattern. Every sentence sounds the same. The sentences get boring. The writing sounds choppy.

Simple, complex, and **compound:** Writing only in simple sentences limits you. When every sentence has the same pattern, every sentence sounds the same. The sentences get boring, and the writing sounds choppy.

How Do I Use Compound and Complex Sentences?

Use compound sentences to show that two ideas that are equally important go together.

- The wind howled.
- The thunder roared.
- The wind howled, and the thunder roared.

W

Use complex sentences to show that two ideas that are not equally important go together. Put the main idea in the independent, or main, clause. Put the less important idea in the dependent clause.

Main idea: The rabbit survived.
Less important idea: He was smart

- Because he was smart, the rabbit survived.

Write to Learn Read your draft aloud. Does it sound choppy? Combine simple sentences to form compound and complex sentences.

Looking Ahead

In Writing Workshop Part 2, you'll revise and edit your folktale.

Reading Fluency

Comparing Versions Students might find it helpful to read aloud parts of the original versions of the folktales and then their own versions. Ask students: How is the original version similar to or different from your own retelling of your story? Are there words or phrases from the original that you should keep in your retelling? Is the tone of your retelling similar to the original? Students can try to mimic the voices of the original writers or use their own voices in their stories. OL

WRITING WORKSHOP PART 1

W Writing

Writing Varied Sentences
Have students practice writing varied sentences by combining the following sentences:

1. A downpour was predicted. We stayed inside. *(A downpour was predicted so we stayed inside.)*
2. There was a rainstorm. A rainbow appeared. *(After a rainstorm, a rainbow appeared.)*
3. The dogs were restless. We took them for a long walk. *(Because the dogs were restless, we took them for a long walk.)*
4. The puppies were adorable. I brought them all home. *(The puppies were adorable so I brought them all home.)*

Have students look over their writing for places where they can combine sentences. OL

Assess

Have students exchange their papers and critique each other's work. Remind students that they are reading rough drafts, so they should be more concerned with content than with editing details, such as spelling and punctuation.

Objectives
- Write stories to entertain
- Use the writing process
- Use third-person point of view
- Develop characters, setting, and theme
- Use dialogue
- Write compound and complex sentences

Questioning

Objectives covered in this workshop:
- Raise questions

Teaching Students Questioning

Why Is It Important?

- Questioning strategies help students monitor their comprehension.
- Questioning strategies are fundamental to engaging in inquiry.
- Questioning strategies are central to peer-led discussion.
- Questioning strategies are essential for students to demonstrate what they have learned in a variety of assessment settings.

How to Help Students Get It

- Make sure that students understand the relationship between questions asked and the source(s) of information for answering the question.
- Tell students that information can be found in their own background knowledge and experiences as well as in the texts they read.
- Emphasize to students that different types of questions are asked before, during and after reading.
- Teach students strategies that will align well with particular types of questions (e.g., skimming and scanning in response to questions that ask for important text details; making inferences in response to questions that ask them to fill in gaps or read between the lines.) Model these strategies for students.

Reading to Answer the Big Question

The Boy and His Grandfather

In this short story, a young boy helps his father realize that he has been mistreating his own elderly father. Students should realize that the author shares this story to illustrate the Golden Rule.

Jeremiah's Song

Grandpa Jeremiah has always told stories, what he calls "the songs of my people." But when his granddaughter Ellie returns from college, she doesn't want to hear his stories anymore because she says they are not true. He does find an audience in his grandson and another friend.

Workshop Resources

Pacing (Days) Standard	Block	Lesson	Student Materials	Teacher Resources
1		Key Skill Lesson: Questioning	Key Reading Skills Practice English Language Coach	Bellringer Options Transparencies Read Aloud, Think Aloud Transparencies Presentation Plus!
2		"The Boy and His Grandfather"	Literary Analysis Transparencies Glencoe Online Selection Vocabulary Development Academic Vocabulary Development English Language Coach Active Reading Graphic Organizer Literary Analysis StudentWorks Plus Online Student Edition Literature Classics Selection and Unit Assessments	Literary and Text Analysis Transparencies Puzzlemaker Skill Level Up! BookLink 3 Assessment by Learning Objective (Diagnostic and Formative) Interactive Tutor Self-Assessment TeacherWorks Plus
2		"Jeremiah's Song"	Glencoe Online Selection Vocabulary Development Academic Vocabulary Development English Language Coach Active Reading Graphic Organizer Literary Analysis StudentWorks Plus Online Student Edition Literature Classics Selection and Unit Assessments	Literary and Text Analysis Transparencies Puzzlemaker Skill Level Up! BookLink 3 Assessment by Learning Objective (Diagnostic and Formative) Interactive Tutor Self-Assessment TeacherWorks Plus

Keys for Unit Resource

- Blackline Master
- Workbook
- Supplemental Text
- CD-ROM
- DVD
- Transparency
- Web-based
- Fast Files

Level Appropriate Code

AS = Activities for all students
AL = Activities for students working above grade level
OL = Activities for students working at grade level
BL = Activities for students working below grade level
EL = Activities for English language learners

Focus

BELLRINGER Options

- **Selection Focus Transparency**
- **Daily Language Practice Transparency**

Focus Activity Ask: What lessons might you learn from grandparents or other older people in your life? *(Possible responses: descriptions of what life was like in the past; general lessons about life)*

Teach

R Reading Skill

Questioning Ask: What is questioning? *(It is the skill of asking questions about what you are reading.)* **Say:** As you read, continue to ask yourself questions such as "Why is this information important?" AS

Viewing the Cartoon

Say: The girl is used to choosing ring tones for her cell phone. How might the older man answer her question? *(We didn't have ring tones or cell phones!)* What other questions might the young people ask to better understand the man's story? *(Possible response: How did you decide who got to use the phone?)* AS

READING WORKSHOP 2

Skills Focus

You will practice using these skills when you read the following selections:

- "The Boy and His Grandfather," p. 684
- "Jeremiah's Song," p. 690

Reading

- Questioning

Literature

- Understanding what a character is like
- Recognizing direct and indirect characterization

Vocabulary

- Recognizing and understanding idioms
- Understanding "phrase words"

Writing/Grammar

- Combining sentences

Skill Lesson

Questioning

Learn It!

What Is It? Questioning is asking questions about what you are reading. Have a conversation with yourself as you read by asking and trying to answer questions about the text. Feel free to ask anything! Ask about what you don't understand. Ask about the importance of what you're reading. You might ask yourself questions like these:

- Who are the people in the story?
- Why did a person act a certain way?
- What just happened and how does it relate to what happened before?

Answer the questions in your head or on paper.

Analyzing Cartoons
The girl's question here isn't a bad one; it just shows she has more to learn. Asking questions helps us get specific information fast—and helps us figure things out.

Objectives
(pp. 680–681)
Reading Ask questions

Additional Support

Differentiated Instruction

Picture Posters Some students might benefit from spending additional time connecting to the theme of this workshop. Tell students that they will read about the influence that older characters have on younger ones in the two stories in this workshop. Have students connect to the stories by sharing descriptions of important people in their lives and explaining what lessons they have learned from them. Then, have students create a poster that tells about one of those people. As students read the selections, encourage them to look for similarities and differences between the important person in their lives and the two older characters in the stories. OL EL

Why Is It Important? As you answer your own questions, you're making sure you understand what is going on. There may be times when you'll need to re-read to get more information. R1

Literature Online

Study Central Visit www.glencoe.com and click on Study Central to review questioning.

How Do I Do It? As you read, stop after every paragraph or two. Ask yourself questions to make sure you understand what you've read so far. Here's how one student checked to make sure he understood what he was reading. Read this passage from "I afff" by Lensey Namioka.

> He sat down on the stool and twisted a dial. I heard some bleeps, cheeps, and gurgles. Peter disappeared. He must have done it with mirrors. I looked around the garage. I peeked under the tool bench. There was no sign of him.

I just read about Peter disappearing. I can ask myself questions to check if I understood the paragraph.

What happened to Peter? He seemed to have actually disappeared.

Why do I wonder if he really disappeared? I've never seen a person disappear and don't believe that it is possible. But the writer says Peter disappeared and that there was no sign of him anywhere in the garage.

What do I know about Peter? Peter is very smart, gets good grades, and spends all of his time reading books. He called himself Dr. Lu Manchu, the mad scientist. Maybe, in this story, he built a time machine.

Practice It!

Read the first two paragraphs of "The Boy and His Grandfather." In your Learner's Notebook, write two questions about what you want to know. You might start your questions with the words *what* or *why*. R2

Use It!

As you read "The Boy and His Grandfather" and "Jeremiah's Song," remember to stop and ask yourself questions.

Teach

Literature Online

Study Central Have students access the Web site to review questioning and to complete a related activity.

R1 Reading Skill

Questioning Ask: According to Why Is It Important? why might it be helpful to ask questions as you read? *(to ensure that you are understanding what you read)* Can you think of another reason why asking questions as you read might be helpful? *(Possible response: to keep track of important details; to determine which ideas are important)* OL AL

R2 Reading Skill

Questioning After students have completed "Practice It!" have them share their questions about "The Boy and His Grandfather." AS

Resources for page 681

- Use Reading Skills Transparency in *Read Aloud, Think Aloud,* Unit 6, to help students practice questioning.

Reading in the Real World

Citizenship Have students conduct an interview with an elderly person—someone they know or someone who lives in a nearby retirement community. Instruct students to begin by writing four questions about the person's experiences. Remind students to ask open-ended questions (ones that require more than a yes or no answer) to encourage their subjects to talk. Students can take notes or tape-record the interview. Have them share what they learned with the class. Instruct them to end their presentation by stating what they think elderly people have to offer a community. AS

Objectives
- Ask questions
- Connect to the theme
- Conduct interviews

Teach

More About the Author

Rudolfo A. Anaya has said that as a child he loved to listen to the stories of older people in his community. He heard many folktales in his home, where, he said, "storytelling was a natural pastime . . . and so the oral tradition was a great influence on me." Anaya's retelling of the folktale "The Boy and His Grandfather" reflects that influence.

V Vocabulary

Synonyms and Antonyms
After students have completed the question-answer activity, challenge them to write a sentence using a synonym for each vocabulary word. Then have them rewrite the sentences using the vocabulary word's antonym. AS

Before You Read

The Boy and His Grandfather

Rudolfo A. Anaya

Meet the Author

Rudolfo A. Anaya was one of the founding fathers of modern Hispanic American literature. He has written fiction, plays, and essays, mostly set in his native New Mexico. Anaya often weaves Hispanic legends and folktales into his work. See page R1 of the Author Files for more on Rudolfo A. Anaya.

Author Search For more about Rudolfo A. Anaya, go to www.glencoe.com.

Objectives (pp. 682-685)
Reading Ask questions • Make connections from text to self
Literature Identify literary elements: characterization
Vocabulary Understand words in phrases

Vocabulary Preview

neglected (nih GLEK tud) *v.* ignored; not cared for; form of the verb *neglect* **(p. 684)** *The grandfather was neglected by his family.*

frequently (FREE kwunt lee) *adv.* often **(p. 685)** *The father wanted to see grandfather frequently.*

V

Ask About It! For each vocabulary word, ask a partner a question that uses the word correctly. Have your partner give you an answer that also uses the word correctly.

English Language Coach

Words in Phrases You know about multiple-meaning words. But there are some words that have too many meanings to learn. It's easier to learn the way these words are used in combination with other words.

In "The Boy and His Grandfather," the narrator says that the grandfather "went hungry." That simply means that he was hungry for longer than just a short while. The word *went* is a form of the verb *go*, and it's one of several English words that are often used in phrases like this. Here are some others:

get take make do have give set put

When you see these words, you should ignore the main meaning of the verb. The grandfather, for example, did not "go" anywhere. The important word in the phrase is the adjective: *hungry*.

Group Work Look at the phrases below. Then, as a group, talk about other phrases in which you use these verbs.

- do dishes
- make progress
- get ready
- go crazy

Additional Support

Author Search To expand students' appreciation of Rudolfo A. Anaya, have them access the Web site for additional information and resources.

English Language Coach

Words in Phrases Tell students that they will come across the following phrases in the story:
"in the way"
"went hungry"
"took care"
Have students write in their Learner's Notebook the sentences from the story in which these phrases appear. Then, have them use a dictionary or context clues to determine the meaning of each. Encourage students to use dictionaries or context clues to determine the meaning of any other multiple-meaning words in phrases they come across in their reading. EL

Skills Preview

Key Reading Skill: Questioning

When you ask questions as you read, you are making sure that you understand the selection. You are also asking about what is important.

Ask Your Questions Write the heading *I Want to Know* in your Learner's Notebook. As you read the story, write three questions about what you want to know about a character, an event, or something you don't understand.

Literary Element: Characterization

A character is a person in a story. It could also be an animal if the animal shows human behavior. Writers use two ways to tell you about characters.

- Writers sometimes use **direct characterization.** They tell you exactly what a character is like. They might tell you directly, "Sam is sloppy."
- Writers also use **indirect characterization.** They show a character's personality through his or her words and actions and through what other characters think and say. The writer might indicate that Sam leaves dirty clothes, food, and papers on the floor in his room. Another character might say, "Sam, how long since you cleaned your room?" L

As you read, use these questions to help you learn about characters:

- What does the writer *tell* you about the character?
- What does the character do that helps you learn about his or her personality?
- What does the character say that helps you learn about his or her personality?
- What do other characters say and think about the character?
- Based on this, what is the character like?

Partner Talk Make up a character for a story about a boy and his grandfather. Use your imagination! Tell your partner something that character might do or say and something that another character might say or think about the character.

Get Ready to Read

Connect to the Reading

Have you ever heard of the Golden Rule? It says, "Treat others the way you want be treated." In other words, don't insult your friends if you do not want them to insult you. As you read this story, think about how you would have wanted to be treated if you were the grandfather.

Partner Talk With a partner, make a list of the people who taught you how to treat others. What did they teach you?

Build Background

- In cultures around the world, extended families live together. An extended family may include grandparents, parents, children, and even aunts and uncles all living together in one home.
- In many cultures, older people, such as the grandfather in this story, are greatly respected. Caring for older family members is considered an important responsibility, even an honor.

Set Purposes for Reading

Read about a boy and his grandfather to decide why Anaya shares this story.

Set Your Own Purpose What would you like to learn from the selection to help you answer the Big Question? Write your own purpose on the "Boy and His Grandfather" page of Foldable 6.

Literature Online

Interactive Literary Elements Handbook To review or learn more about the literary elements, go to www.glencoe.com.

Keep Moving

Use these skills as you read the following selection.

Differentiated Instruction

Researching Folktales Have students hone their research skills by finding alternative versions of this folktale, such as the Grimm Brothers' version, "The Old Man and His Grandson," and a version by Leo Tolstoy. Have students compare and contrast the stories and then prepare a presentation in which they describe briefly why they think this story has endured. Have students answer the question "What elements of this story make it popular among different cultures?" AL

Teach

L Literary Element

Characterization Ask: **What is the difference between direct and indirect characterization?** *(With direct characterization, the writer tells exactly what a character is like. With indirect characterization, the writer uses the character's words and actions, as well as those of other characters, to tell readers what a character is like.)* **Give an example of direct and indirect characterization.** *(Possible responses: Direct: That man is angry. Indirect: That man threw his book on the floor, stomped on it, and walked away.)* AS

CheckPoint

Use the CheckPoint questions provided on Presentation Plus! to check for understanding of questioning. These questions can be used with interactive response keypads for immediate student feedback.

Literature Online

Interactive Literary Elements Handbook Have students access the Web site to improve their understanding of characterization.

Objectives

- Ask questions
- Make connections from text to self
- Identify literary elements: characterization
- Understand words in phrases

READING WORKSHOP 2

Teach

C Critical Thinking

Comprehension Say: Read the first two paragraphs of the story. What do you think the story will be about based on these paragraphs and the title of the story? *(Possible response: A boy will play a role in the conflict between the woman and the old man.)* AL

EL Language Coach

Words in Phrases Say: The story says that the daughter-in-law thought that the old man was always "in the way," so she insisted that he move out of the house. "In the way" must be a bad thing. What do you think it means? *(It means "to be a bother," "to interfere with one's ability to move around.")* EL

Readability Scores
Dale-Chall: 6.6
DRP: 50
Lexile: 820

The Boy and His Grandfather

by Rudolfo A. Anaya

In the old days it was not unusual to find several generations living together in one home. Usually, everyone lived in peace and harmony, but this situation caused problems for one man whose household included, besides his wife and small son, his elderly father. **1**

C It so happened that the daughter-in-law took a dislike to the old man. He was always in the way, she said, and she insisted he be removed to a small room apart from the house. **2** EL

Because the old man was out of sight, he was often **neglected**. Sometimes he even went hungry. They took poor care of him, and in winter the old man often suffered from the cold. One day the little grandson visited his grandfather.

"My little one," the grandfather said, "go and find a blanket and cover me. It is cold and I am freezing."

The small boy ran to the barn to look for a blanket, and

Vocabulary

neglected (nih GLEK tud) *v.* ignored; not cared for

Practice the Skills

1 Key Reading Skill

Questioning In this paragraph, you learn that there are problems in the home that might be important to the story. What question could you ask about the problems?

2 English Language Coach

Words in Phrases What does the phrase took a dislike to mean?

Additional Support

Differentiated Instruction

Important Image Have students choose the image from the story—perhaps the old man in the small room, the young boy talking to his father, or the blanket—that they think is the most important one. Have them draw or paint a picture of the image on a large poster and then explain why they think it is so important to the story. Ask students to share their pictures with the class. OL EL there he found a rug.

"Father, please cut this rug in half," he asked his father.

"Why? What are you going to do with it?"

"I'm going to take it to my grandfather because he is cold."

"Well, take the entire rug," replied his father.

"No," his son answered, "I cannot take it all. I want you to cut it in half so I can save the other half for you when you are as old as my grandfather. Then I will have it for you so you will not be cold."

His son's response was enough to make the man realize how poorly he had treated his own father. The man then brought his father back into his home and ordered that a warm room be prepared. From that time on he took care of his father's needs and visited him **frequently** every day. 3 4 ○

Vocabulary

frequently (FREE kwunt lee) *adv.* often

Practice the Skills

3 Literary Element

Characterization The writer does not give direct characterization of the grandfather's son or grandson. You learn about them from their actions. What do you know about each from his behavior?

4 

Why is it important to pass on stories like "The Boy and His Grandfather"? Write your answer on the "Boy and His Grandfather" page of Foldable 6. Your response will help you complete the Unit Challenge later.

READING WORKSHOP 2

Teach

L Literary Element

Characterization **Say:** What does the writer tell you about the father's actions? *(The father lets his own father live in the small room. When the father hears his son say that he will someday treat him the same way, he brings his father back into the house and treats him kindly.)* What does that tell you about the father? *(Possible response: It tells you that the father acted without thinking of his elderly father, but he learned his lesson. He is a good person at heart.)* OL AL

BQ BIG Question

Ask: When might you tell this story? Why would you tell it? *(Possible response: I might tell it if I saw someone treating another person unkindly, so that the person would understand that we often end up being treated the same way we have treated others.)* OL

Assess

Use the CheckPoint questions provided on Presentation Plus! to check for comprehension of the selection. These questions can be used with interactive response keypads for immediate student feedback.

Differentiated Instruction

Oral Retelling Tell students that different versions of this story have been passed down orally for many years. Have students form groups and retell this story aloud in their own words. The first student should begin the story, the next student in the group should tell another part of the story, and so on until the entire story has been told. Encourage students to use their voice to create interest as they tell the story. They might use a sad voice when they tell how the grandfather is moved out of the house, for example, or a happy voice when the father learns his lesson. OL

Objectives

- Ask questions
- Analyze and explain characters as they are revealed through direct and indirect characterization
- Understand words in phrases

Assess

Resources for page 686

- Selection Quick Check
- Selection and Unit Assessment
- ExamView Assessment Suite
- Interactive Tutor: Self-Assessment

Students can respond to the *After You Read* items in their Learner's Notebook or on a separate sheet of paper.

Answering the

1. We should treat others as we want to be treated. Students might note that telling a story is a powerful way to express this idea.
2. The boy wanted to save half for when his father got old and was made to live in a small, cold room.
3. At first the father neglects the old man, but by the end of the story the father is taking good care of him.

Critical Thinking

4. He realizes that his example is teaching his son to mistreat others.
5. He might be treated poorly.
6. Possible response: The father becomes a better person because he realizes he must treat others the way he wants to be treated.
7. Responses will vary.
8. Responses will vary.

After You Read

The Boy and His Grandfather

Answering the BIG Question

1. This story tells an important lesson. What is that lesson? Why do you think we use stories to teach such lessons?
2. **Recall** Why does the boy want his father to cut the rug in half?
   TIP Right There
3. **Summarize** How does the father's treatment of the grandfather change during the story?
   TIP Think and Search

Critical Thinking

4. **Infer** Why does the father change the way he treats his father?
   TIP Author and Me
5. **Infer** What do you think the father realizes about what could happen to him when he gets old?
   TIP Author and Me
6. **Evaluate** Think about the way the father's behavior toward the grandfather changes. Do you think the father becomes a better person? Explain.
   TIP Author and Me
7. **Respond** Did you like this story? Why or why not?
   TIP Author and Me
8. **Respond** What is the main thing from this story that you will remember? Explain your answer.
   TIP Author and Me

Objectives (pp. 686–687)
Reading Ask questions • Make connections from text to self
Literature Identify literary elements: characterization
Vocabulary Understand words in phrases (delexicalized words)
Grammar Combine sentences

Write About Your Reading

Pretend you are the father in the story. Write a letter to your son.

- Explain why you treated your father poorly at first.
- Explain why your behavior was wrong.
- Tell what you learned from your son.
- Tell how you feel about your father.

Write About Your Reading

Possible response:
Dear son,
I treated my father very badly because I did not want to cause a conflict with your mother. My behavior was wrong. We should always treat other people, especially our relatives, with kindness and respect. When you said that you would save half the blanket for me, I realized you were learning a terrible lesson from me that it is okay to treat others poorly. I love your grandfather very much and will treat him well from now on.
Lovingly,
Your father

Skills Review

Key Reading Skill: Questioning

9. Review the *I Want to Know* questions you wrote in your Learner's Notebook.
   - How did asking questions help you figure out what was important?
   - How did asking questions help you understand the story?

Literary Element: Characterization

10. What did the boy's mother say and do about the grandfather?
11. What opinions do you have about the mother based on her actions?

Vocabulary Check

Write the correct answer to each question.

12. Does **frequently** mean often or hardly ever?
13. Which of the following would be described as **neglected:** a well-loved book or a starving kitten?
14. **English Language Coach** Review the phrase went hungry on page 684. Use it in a sentence. What's another way to say the same thing?

Grammar Link: Combining Sentences

You can combine two simple sentences to make a compound sentence. To do so, you use **coordinating conjunctions** such as *and, or,* and *but.*

- Harry loved chocolate. It made him sick.
- Harry loved chocolate, but it make him sick.

You can also use coordinating conjunctions to combine two sentences in another way, if they have the same subject. You can make them into a sentence with a compound verb.

- Judith skated. Judith skied.
- Judith skated and skied.

You can do the same thing with two sentences that have the same verb.

- Judith skated. Pam skated.
- Judith and Pam skated.

You can use **correlative conjunctions** to do this kind of combining, too. Correlative conjunctions are pairs of words that are used to connect compound parts of sentences. They include *both...and, either...or,* and *neither...nor.*

- Both Judith and Pam skated.
- Paul neither skated nor skied.

If you have two sentences that are not equal in importance, you can use a **subordinating conjunction** to make one into a dependent clause. These conjunctions include *after, although, as, before, until,* and *so forth.*

- Judith skated. Judith fell.
- Judith skated until she fell.

Grammar Practice

Combine each pair of sentences below, using *and, or, but, for, nor,* or *yet.*

15. Carlos skated to the park. He practiced stunts.
16. I have a huge dog called Rascal. My friend Olivia doesn't like her.
17. The jeans didn't fit. I returned them to the store.

Writing Application Look back at the letter you wrote from the father in the story to his son. See if you can find two sentences to combine, using a conjunction.

Web Activities For eFlashcards, Selection Quick Checks, and other Web activities, go to www.glencoe.com.

Skills Review

Key Reading Skill: Questioning

9. Possible responses:
   - Asking questions reminded me to look for important information in the story.
   - Asking questions helped me understand the story because when I didn't know the answer to a question, I knew that I had to go back and reread a portion of the story to find the answer.

Literary Element: Characterization

10. The boy's mother said that the grandfather got in the way. She insisted that he live in a small room apart from the house, and she neglected him.
11. Possible response: I felt the mother was mean and selfish.

Vocabulary Check

12. It means "often."
13. a starving kitten
14. Possible response: I forgot my lunch today so I went hungry. "Didn't eat" is another way to say *went hungry.*

Close

Ask students to discuss what they have learned from this story that would help them answer the Big Question.

Grammar Link: Combining Sentences

Grammar Practice

15. Carlos skated to the park, and he practiced stunts.
16. I have a huge dog called Rascal, but my friend Olivia doesn't like her.
17. The jeans didn't fit, so I returned them to the store.

Teach

More About the Author

Just like Jeremiah in Myers's story, Walter Dean Myers tells stories about the past that feature African Americans. Myers recalls that African American stories were omitted from the history lessons he learned in school. He commented: "Kids today will say, 'We're not interested in black books.' The reason is that so many [of them] are a history of oppression, in which blacks are portrayed as victims. Kids don't want to read that. They want to read about being triumphant."

V Vocabulary

Vocabulary Swap Have partners swap sentences and check to make sure that their peers have used the words correctly. BL EL

Before You Read Jeremiah's Song

Walter Dean Myers

Meet the Author

Walter Dean Myers grew up loving stories—the ones his father and grandfather told him and the ones he read in books. Myers says his own stories mostly come from his own life. "What I want to do with my writing is to make connections—to touch the lives of my characters, and through them, those of my readers." See page R5 of the Author Files for more on Walter Dean Myers.

Author Search For more about Walter Dean Myers, go to www.glencoe.com.

Objectives (pp. 688–699)
Reading Ask questions • Make connections from text to self
Literature Identify literary elements: characterization
Vocabulary Understand dialect

Vocabulary Preview

worthwhile (wurth whyl) *adj.* having value or goodness; deserving one's efforts or attention **(p. 691)** *Grandpa thought a college education was probably worthwhile.*

diagnosis (dy ug NOH sus) *n.* a doctor's identification of a patient's illness; any expert's finding of the nature of a problem **(p. 693)** *The diagnosis left little hope that he would fully recover.*

setback (SET bak) *n.* an unexpected difficulty or stop in progress **(p. 696)** *Family members tried to keep Grandpa from getting too tired and having a setback.*

Write to Learn For each vocabulary word, write a sentence using the word correctly.

English Language Coach

Dialect In some parts of the United States, groups of people speak forms of English called dialects. Dialects have pronunciations, word forms, and meanings that are different from those in Standard English.

The characters in "Jeremiah's Song" speak in a dialect. Read this sentence from the story. Then look at how one reader has written the sentence in Standard English.

Dialect	Standard English
Grandpa Jeremiah said they wasn't stories anyway, they was songs.	Grandpa Jeremiah said that they were not stories, but that they were songs.

Partner Talk With a partner, read these sentences from "Jeremiah's Song." Then try to say them in Standard English.

1. I knowed my cousin Ellie was gonna be mad when Macon Smith came around to the house.
2. She didn't have no use for Macon even when things was going right.
3. Grandpa wasn't getting no better, but he wasn't getting no worse, either.

Additional Support

Author Search To expand students' appreciation of Walter Dean Myers, have them access the Web site for additional information and resources.

English Language Coach

Dialect Encourage students to read dialect aloud to try to determine the meaning of unfamiliar constructions. You might help students work through the sentences in Partner Talk by asking these questions:

1. What does the word *knowed* probably mean? *(knew)*
2. What does *gonna be* sound like? *(going to be)*
3. What does the phrase "have no use" imply about Ellie's attitude toward Macon? *(It implies that she didn't like him or want him around.)*

Encourage students to work through any difficult sentences word by word. EL

Skills Preview

Key Reading Skill: Questioning

Before you read "Jeremiah's Song," think about questions you might ask yourself to help you understand what you are reading such as:

- Do I understand this part of the story?
- What causes this character to act this way?
- Why did the writer give this detail here?

Write to Learn Write down other questions that you think of in your Learner's Notebook. Refer to these questions to help you read the story.

Key Literary Element: Character

Character Motivation A character's **motivation** is the reason he or she does something. For example, if a character's friend suddenly becomes sick, he or she might be motivated to spend a lot of time with that friend.

As you read, use these tips to help you learn about character motivation: L1

- Ask yourself, Why does the character act this way? You might need to "read between the lines," or make guesses, to answer the question.
- Think about why *you* might do the things the characters do.

Dynamic and Static Characters Some characters stay the same during a story. Others change.

- Characters that change are called **dynamic characters.** They might realize something new that causes them to change the way they think or act. For example, a mean character who learns an important lesson might become kinder as a result. L2
- Characters that stay the same are called **static characters.**

As you read, notice which characters change, which ones stay the same, and what motivates them to do so.

Partner Talk Think of a time when you learned a lesson that changed you. What was the lesson? How did you change? Tell your story to a partner.

Get Ready to Read

Connect to the Reading

Think about stories you remember hearing or reading as a child. Which ones would you want to tell younger children? Why? As you read, think about the stories Grandpa Jeremiah tells and why he tells them.

Partner Talk With a partner, talk about the stories you learned as a child. Were they read to you, or did someone tell them to you?

Build Background

For many centuries, people in Africa passed down stories to family and friends. When enslaved Africans were brought to the United States, they continued telling stories. Part of the reason for this was that they were not allowed to learn how to read and write. Some reasons for telling such stories might be

- to teach moral lessons
- to entertain friends and family
- to pass on a community or family history

Set Purposes for Reading

 Read "Jeremiah's Song" to learn why Grandpa Jeremiah tells his stories.

Set Your Own Purpose What would you like to learn from the selection to help you answer the Big Question? Write your own purpose on the "Jeremiah's Song" page of Foldable 6.

Literature Online

Interactive Literary Elements Handbook To review or learn more about the literary elements, go to www.glencoe.com.

Keep Moving

Use these skills as you read the following selection.

Teach

L1 Literary Element

Character **Say:** Think about why you might do the things the characters do. Why might doing this be helpful? *(Possible response: It might help you guess a character's motivation.)* OL

L2 Literary Element

Character **Ask:** What is the difference between a dynamic character and a static character? *(A dynamic character changes in the course of a story, whereas a static character stays the same.)* Think of a character from a story you've read in this class. Tell whether the character is dynamic or static, and explain why. *(Responses will vary.)* OL AL

CheckPoint

Use the CheckPoint questions provided on Presentation Plus! to check for understanding of characterization. These questions can be used with interactive response keypads for immediate student feedback.

Literature Online

Interactive Literary Elements Handbook Have students access the Web site to improve their understanding of character.

Differentiated Instruction

Spirituals In addition to stories, many songs, called slave spirituals, were passed from generation to generation in communities of enslaved African Americans. Have musical students find a spiritual online and sing it to the class; alternatively, students might find a recording of a spiritual at the library and play it in class. (If students want to sing, they may prefer to do so in a group.) Then, have students tell what the song is about and how singing such a song might have helped enslaved people go about their daily lives. OL

Objectives

- Ask questions
- Make connections from text to self
- Identify literary elements: characterization
- Understand dialect

Teach

R Reading Skill

Questioning Ask: What other question about the first paragraph of the story could you ask yourself? *(Possible responses: Who is Macon Smith? Why doesn't Ellie like him?)* OL

L Literary Element

Character Ask: According to the narrator, how has Ellie changed since she went away to college? *(She doesn't want to hear the old stories anymore. She hardly ever goes to church.)* Why might Ellie have changed in this way? *(Possible response: She might have learned new things in college that changed the way she views her family.)* OL AL

Readability Scores
Dale-Chall: 4.7
DRP: 52
Lexile: 960

READING WORKSHOP 2

Jeremiah's Song

by Walter Dean Myers

I knowed my cousin Ellie was gonna be mad when Macon Smith come around to the house. She didn't have no use for Macon even when things was going right, and when Grandpa Jeremiah was fixing to die I just knowed she wasn't gonna be liking him hanging around. Grandpa Jeremiah raised Ellie after her folks died and they used to be real close. Then she got to go on to college and when she come back the first year she was different. She didn't want to hear all them stories he used to tell her anymore. Ellie said the stories wasn't true, and that's why she didn't want to hear them. 1

I didn't know if they was true or not. Tell the truth I didn't think much on it either way, but I liked to hear them stories. Grandpa Jeremiah said they wasn't stories anyway, they was songs. 2

"They the songs of my people," he used to say.

I didn't see how they was songs, not regular songs anyway. Every little thing we did down in Curry seemed to matter to Ellie that first summer she come home from college.[1] You couldn't do nothin' that was gonna please her. She didn't even come to church much. 'Course she come on Sunday or

Practice the Skills

1 Key Reading Skill

Questioning Ask yourself a question about a character who was introduced in the first paragraph of the story such as, "Which character just came back home from college?"

2 Key Literary Element

Character Readers learn that Grandpa Jeremiah loves to tell stories and that the narrator likes to hear them. What do we learn about Ellie's opinions of the stories? Why does she feel that way?

1. ***Curry*** is a town in central North Carolina. Ellie is studying in Greensboro, a city about 60 miles north that has several colleges and universities.

Additional Support

Literature Focus Lesson

Narrator Remind students that the narrator in a story can be a character in the story or an observer watching the story from outside. Ask students which kind of narrator this story has. Tell students that this narrator tells the story from the first-person point of view. As they read the story, have students answer these questions about the narrator:

- Who is he in relation to the other characters in the story?
- How old is he?
- What does he think of Macon?
- What does he think of Jeremiah's stories?
- Is he a dynamic character or a static character? Explain. OL

READING WORKSHOP 2

everybody would have had a regular fit, but she didn't come on Thursday nights and she didn't come on Saturday even though she used to sing in the gospel choir.

"I guess they teachin' her somethin' **worthwhile** up there at Greensboro," Grandpa Jeremiah said to Sister Todd. "I sure don't see what it is, though."

"You ain't never had no **book learning**, Jeremiah," Sister Todd shot back. She wiped at where a trickle of sweat made a little path through the white dusting powder she put on her chest to keep cool. "Them old ways you got ain't got nothing for these young folks." **3**

"I guess you right," Grandpa Jeremiah said.

L He said it but I could see he didn't like it none. He was a big man with a big head and had most all his hair even if it was white. All that summer, instead of sitting on the porch telling stories like he used to when I was real little, he would sit out there by himself while Ellie stayed in the house and watched the television or read a book. Sometimes I would think about asking him to tell me one of them stories he used to tell but they was too scary now that I didn't have nobody to sleep with but myself. I asked Ellie to sleep with me but she wouldn't.

"You're nine years old," she said, sounding real proper. "You're old enough to sleep alone."

I *knew* that. I just wanted her to sleep with me because I liked sleeping with her. Before she went off to college she used to put cocoa butter on her arms and face and it would smell real nice. When she come back from college she put something else on, but that smelled nice too.

It was right after Ellie went back to school that Grandpa Jeremiah had him a stroke[2] and Macon

2. A ***stroke*** is a sudden attack of illness caused by a problem with blood circulation in the brain. A stroke can cause brain damage that affects a person's senses, speech, and ability to move. Paralysis or weakness on one side of the body is common.

Vocabulary

worthwhile (wurth whyl) *adj.* having value or goodness; deserving one's efforts or attention

Practice the Skills

3 English Language Coach

Dialect In Sister Todd's dialect, **book learning** means "schooling." How would you change Sister Todd's comment to Grandpa Jeremiah into Standard English?

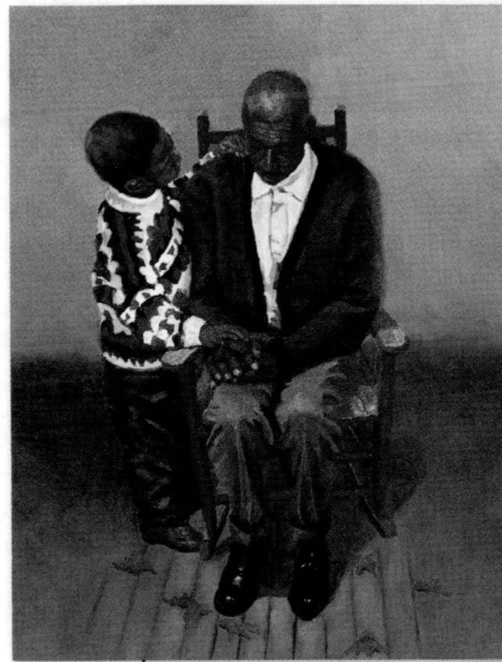

Autumn Woes, 2000, Colin Bootman. Oil on board, Private Collection.

Teach

L Literary Element

Character Ask: Why does Grandpa Jeremiah stop telling his stories? *(Possible response: Ellie doesn't want to hear them; Sister Todd says that the young people don't want to hear them.)* **OL**

Viewing the Art

Say: Think about the characters you've met in "Jeremiah's Song." Which of them remind you of the figures depicted in this painting? Why? *(Possible responses: I am reminded of the narrator and Grandpa Jeremiah because the boy looks about 9 years old, the same age as the narrator, and the man looks sad, which is how Grandpa Jeremiah probably looked when he stopped telling his stories.)* **AS**

Reading in the Real World

Citizenship Have students learn a story about their family to share with the class. The story may be true or one the family has made up. It might be about a family member from long ago, or it might be from when the student was younger. Have students take turns sharing their stories in small groups. Encourage them to notice what it is like to tell a story and what it is like to listen to the stories of others. **Ask:** What is the best part of storytelling? What is the worst part? **AS**

Objectives
- Ask questions
- Analyze character motivation
- Recognize dynamic and static characters
- Recognize dialect

Teach

Viewing the Art

Say: What does the picture show? How does the picture fit the story? *(The picture shows a guitar, which is the instrument Macon plays, and a chair that might be like the ones Macon and Grandpa Jeremiah sit on.)* **OL**

L Literary Element

Character **Ask:** Why does Macon start coming around? *(He helps out after Grandpa Jeremiah has a stroke.)* **OL**

C Critical Thinking

Synthesis **Say:** Sister Todd says that Grandpa Jeremiah doesn't have anything to offer young people. How does Macon prove Sister Todd wrong? *(Possible response: Macon's enjoyment of Grandpa Jeremiah's stories proves that a young person can get something from Grandpa's "old ways.")* **AL**

started coming around. I think his mama probably made him come at first, but you could see he liked it. Macon had always been around, sitting over near the stuck window at church or going on the blueberry truck when he went picking down at Mister Gregory's place. For a long time he was just another kid, even though he was older'n me, but then, all of a sudden, he growed something fierce. I used to be up to his shoulder one time and then, before I could turn around good, I was only up to his shirt pocket. He changed too. When he used to just hang around with the other boys and play ball or shoot at birds he would laugh a lot. He didn't laugh so much anymore and I figured he was just about grown. When Grandpa got sick he used to come around and help out with things around the house that was too hard for me to do. I mean, I could have done all the chores, but it would just take me longer. **4**

When the work for the day was finished and the sows fed, Grandpa would kind of ease into one of his stories and Macon, he would sit and listen to them and be real interested. I didn't mind listening to the stories when Grandpa told them to Macon because he would be telling them in the middle of the afternoon and they would be past my mind by the time I had to go to bed.

Macon had an old guitar he used to mess with, too. He wasn't too bad on it, and sometimes Grandpa would tell him to play a tune. He could play something he called "the Delta

Practice the Skills

4 Key Literary Element

Character Name two things you learn about Macon. Besides helping out around the place, what might be Macon's possible motivation for coming around?

Additional Support

Differentiated Instruction

Word Webs Students might find it helpful to create a word web for each of the main characters in the story. They can write the character's name in the middle circle and, as they learn details about the character, add them to the outer circles. **BL** **EL**

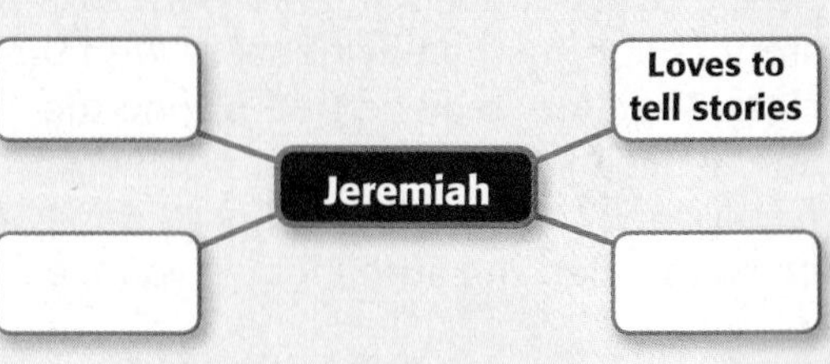

Blues" real good, but when Sister Todd or somebody from the church come around he'd play "Precious Lord" or "Just a Closer Walk With Thee." 5

Grandpa Jeremiah had been feeling poorly from that stroke, and one of his legs got a little drag to it. Just about the time Ellie come from school the next summer he was real sick. He was breathing loud so you could hear it even in the next room and he would stay in bed a lot even when there was something that needed doing or fixing.

"I don't think he's going to make it much longer," Dr. Crawford said. "The only thing I can do is to give him something for the pain."

"Are you sure of your **diagnosis**?" Ellie asked. She was sitting around the table with Sister Todd, Deacon Turner, and his little skinny yellow wife. 6

Dr. Crawford looked at Ellie like he was surprised to hear her talking. "Yes, I'm sure," he said. "He had tests a few weeks ago and his condition was bad then."

"How much time he got?" Sister Todd asked.

"Maybe a week or two at best," Dr. Crawford said.

When he said that, Deacon Turner's wife started crying and goin' on and I give her a hard look but she just went on. I was the one who loved Grandpa Jeremiah the most and she didn't hardly even know him so I didn't see why she was crying. L1

Everybody started tiptoeing around the house after that. They would go in and ask Grandpa Jeremiah if he was comfortable and stuff like that or take him some food or a cold glass of lemonade. Sister Todd come over and stayed with us. Mostly what she did is make supper and do a lot of praying, which was good because I figured that maybe God would do something to make Grandpa Jeremiah well. When she wasn't doing that she was piecing on a fancy quilt she was making for some white people in Wilmington.[3] L2

Ellie, she went around asking everybody how they felt about Dr. Crawford and then she went into town and asked

3. Sister Todd is sewing ***(piecing)*** many small pieces of cloth into one big pattern for the quilt. ***Wilmington*** is a city on North Carolina's Atlantic coast.

Vocabulary

diagnosis (dy ug NOH sus) *n.* a doctor's identification of a patient's illness; any expert's finding of the nature of a problem

Practice the Skills

5 **BIG Question**

Grandpa Jeremiah tells his stories, while Macon sings and plays on his guitar. Why do you think people might tell their stories in different ways? Write your answer on the "Jeremiah's Song" page of Foldable 6. Your response will help you complete the Unit Challenge later.

6 **English Language Coach**

Dialect Does Ellie use her family's dialect or Standard English here? Why do you think she does so?

Teach

L1 Literary Element

Character Ask: Why might Ellie respond to Jeremiah's illness by asking a lot of questions? *(Possible response: She has learned in college to ask questions. She values knowledge and thinks that if she knows a lot, she can help Jeremiah.)* AL

L2 Literary Element

Character Say: Based on what you know thus far, describe the kind of person Sister Todd is. How do you know? *(She is helpful, caring, and religious. This is clear because she stays with the narrator to help his family, and the narrator says that she does "a lot of praying.")* AS

Reading Fluency

Build Fluency Have students find a quiet place in which to practice reading "Jeremiah's Song" aloud. Instruct them to reread a passage several times until they can read all the sentences with expression and understanding. Encourage them to vary the tone, pitch, and volume of their voice in order to make their reading sound like natural speech. BL EL

Objectives

- Ask questions
- Analyze character motivation
- Synthesize
- Predict
- Analyze an image
- Create a graphic organizer
- Build fluency by reading aloud

Teach

R Reading Skill

Questioning Ask: What questions do you have after reading these paragraphs? *(Possible responses: Why is Ellie angry? What was Macon doing that has made her so mad?)*

L Literary Element

Character Ask: Why might Macon come back early the next morning? *(Possible response: He wants to hear more of Grandpa Jeremiah's stories before Grandpa dies.)* AL

READING WORKSHOP 2

about the tests and things. Sister Jenkins asked her if she thought she knowed more than Dr. Crawford, and Ellie rolled her eyes at her, but Sister Jenkins was reading out her Bible and didn't make no notice of it.

Then Macon come over.

He had been away on what he called "a little piece of a job" and hadn't heard how bad off Grandpa Jeremiah was. When he come over he talked to Ellie and she told him what was going on and then he got him a soft drink from the refrigerator and sat out on the porch and before you know it he was crying.

You could look at his face and tell the difference between him sweating and the tears. The sweat was close against his skin and shiny and the tears come down fatter and more sparkly.

Macon sat on the porch, without saying a word, until the sun went down and the crickets started chirping and carrying on. Then he went in to where Grandpa Jeremiah was and stayed in there for a long time. 7

Sister Todd was saying that Grandpa Jeremiah needed his rest and Ellie went in to see what Macon was doing. Then she come out real mad.

"He got Grandpa telling those old stories again," Ellie said. "I told him Grandpa needed his rest and for him not to be staying all night."

He did leave soon, but bright and early the next morning Macon was back again. This time he brought his guitar with him and be went on in to Grandpa Jeremiah's room. I went in, too.

Grandpa Jeremiah's room smelled terrible. It was all closed up so no drafts could get on him and the whole room was smelled down with disinfect[4] and medicine. Grandpa Jeremiah lay propped up on the bed and he was so gray he looked scary. His hair wasn't combed down and his head on the pillow with his white hair sticking out was enough to send me flying if Macon hadn't been there. He was skinny, too. He looked like his skin got loose on his bones, and when he lifted his arms, it hung down like he was just wearing it instead of it being a part of him. 8

4. In the region's dialect, ***disinfect*** is short for *disinfectant*, a substance used to kill germs.

Practice the Skills

7 Reviewing Skills

Drawing Conclusions What does Macon's reaction to Ellie's words about Grandpa tell you about Macon's feelings?

8 Key Literary Element

Character How does the narrator react to how Grandpa Jeremiah has changed?

Additional Support

Differentiated Instruction

Collage Have students create a collage of newspaper and magazine clippings—both words and images—that they think would best accompany the story. Instruct students to glue the words and pictures onto a large poster board, leaving as little white space as possible. Students can work alone or in groups to complete the collage. Have them share their collages with the class and explain the words and images they included. AS

READING WORKSHOP 2

Macon sat slant-shouldered with his guitar across his lap. He was messin' with the guitar, not making any music, but just going over the strings as Grandpa talked.

"Old Carrie went around out back to where they kept the pigs penned up and she felt a cold wind across her face. . . ." Grandpa Jeremiah was telling the story about how a old woman out-tricked the Devil and got her son back. I had heard the story before, and I knew it was pretty scary. "When she felt the cold breeze she didn't blink nary[5] an eye, but looked straight ahead. . . ."

Young Musician, 1992. Maurice Faulk. Acrylic on canvas. Private Collection.

All the time Grandpa Jeremiah was talking I could see Macon fingering his guitar. I tried to imagine what it would be like if he was actually plucking the strings. I tried to fix my mind on that because I didn't like the way the story went with the old woman wrestling with the Devil. **L**

We sat there for nearly all the afternoon until Ellie and Sister Todd come in and said that supper was ready. Me and Macon went out and ate some collard greens, ham hocks, and rice. Then Macon he went back in and listened to some more of Grandpa's stories until it was time for him to go home. I wasn't about to go in there and listen to no stories at night. **9**

Dr. Crawford come around a few days later and said that Grandpa Jeremiah was doing a little better.

"You think the Good Lord gonna pull him through?" Sister Todd asked.

"I don't tell the Good Lord what He should or should not be doing," Dr. Crawford said, looking over at Sister Todd and at Ellie. "I just said that *my* patient seems to be doing okay for his condition."

"He been telling Macon all his stories," I said.

Practice the Skills

9 Key Reading Skill

R **Questioning** Asking yourself questions about these paragraphs can help you understand the story and the characters. How would you answer these questions? Why was Macon silently fingering his guitar as Grandpa told his story? Why did Macon listen to Grandpa's stories until he had to go home?

5. The word ***nary*** is a shortened form of *never* and is often used to add emphasis. It's almost always followed by *a* or *an* and means "not any."

Teach

Viewing the Art

Ask: Which character in the story do you think the illustration represents? Why? *(Possible response: Macon, because he fingers his guitar while Grandpa tells his story.)*

L Literary Element

Character Ask: How do you know that the narrator is still afraid of Jeremiah's stories? *(Possible response: He tries to keep his attention on Macon's fingering of the guitar because he doesn't like the way the story is going.)* **BL**

R Reading Skill

Questioning Take a few moments to hear students' questions and answers. Help them understand how questioning improves understanding and comprehension. **AS**

Reading in the Real World

Career Tell students that many people make their living telling stories. People who work as actors, directors, costume designers, set directors, and writers, all contribute to telling a story for an audience. Have students research one of these careers to find the answers to these questions:

- What training is required? How long is a typical course of study?
- What are the necessary skills?
- What is a typical day like?

Students might use library research tools or interview someone to find answers to their questions. Have them report their findings to the class. **OL**

Objectives
- Analyze character motivation
- Compare and contrast
- Ask questions
- Evaluate information
- Conduct research
- Illustrate a story

READING WORKSHOP 2

Teach

BQ 

Ask: Have you ever heard a story that gave you strength or inspiration? If so, what was it? *(Responses will vary.)* How did it give you strength? **AS**

L Literary Element

Character Ask: Why are the narrator and Macon becoming good friends? *(Possible response: They are spending more time together as they sit with Grandpa.)*

"Macon doesn't seem to understand that Grandpa Jeremiah needs his strength," Ellie said. "Now that he's improving, we don't want him to have a **setback**." **BQ**

"No use in stopping him from telling his stories," Dr. Crawford said. "If it makes him feel good it's as good as any medicine I can give him." **10**

I saw that this didn't set with Ellie, and when Dr. Crawford had left I asked her why.

"Dr. Crawford means well," she said, "but we have to get away from the kind of life that keeps us in the past."

She didn't say why we should be trying to get away from the stories and I really didn't care too much. All I knew was that when Macon was sitting in the room with Grandpa Jeremiah I wasn't nearly as scared as I used to be when it was just me and Ellie listening. I told that to Macon. **L**

"You getting to be a big man, that's all," he said.

That was true. Me and Macon was getting to be good friends, too. I didn't even mind so much when he started being friends with Ellie later. It seemed kind of natural, almost like Macon was supposed to be there with us instead of just visiting. **11**

Grandpa wasn't getting no better, but he wasn't getting no worse, either.

"You liking Macon now?" I asked Ellie when we got to the middle of July. She was dishing out a plate of smothered chops for him and I hadn't even heard him ask for anything to eat.

"Macon's funny," Ellie said, not answering my question. "He's in there listening to all of those old stories like he's really interested in them. It's almost as if he and Grandpa Jeremiah are talking about something more than the stories, a secret language."

I didn't think I was supposed to say anything about that to Macon, but once, when Ellie, Sister Todd, and Macon were out on the porch shelling butter beans after Grandpa got tired and was resting, I went into his room and told him what Ellie had said.

Vocabulary

setback (SET bak) *n.* an unexpected difficulty or stop in progress

Practice the Skills

10 BIG Question

Why do you think it might be important for Grandpa Jeremiah to keep telling his stories even though he is very ill? Write your answer on the "Jeremiah's Song" page of Foldable 6. Your response will help you complete the Unit Challenge later.

11 Key Literary Element

Character How have the narrator's feelings toward Macon changed?

Additional Support

Reading in the Real World

College Knowing how to present an argument effectively is a helpful skill in college. Have students form small groups to debate whether Ellie is wise when she says, "We have to get away from the kind of life that keeps us in the past." Have one side argue for Ellie's point of view and one side argue against it. Members of each group should work together to think of evidence to support their position. Then they should choose one speaker to present their position to the class. If you choose, have class members decide which side made the better argument. **AL**

READING WORKSHOP 2

"She said that?" Grandpa Jeremiah's face was skinny and old looking but his eyes looked like a baby's, they was so bright.

"Right there in the kitchen is where she said it," I said. "And I don't know what it mean but I was wondering about it."

"I didn't think she had any feeling for them stories," Grandpa Jeremiah said. "If she think we talking secrets, maybe she don't."

"I think she getting a feeling for Macon," I said.

"That's okay, too," Grandpa Jeremiah said. "They both young." **EL**

"Yeah, but them stories you be telling, Grandpa, they about old people who lived a long time ago," I said.

"Well, those the folks you got to know about," Grandpa Jeremiah said. "You think on what those folks been through, and what they was feeling, and you add it up with what you been through and what you been feeling, then you got you something."

"What you got, Grandpa?"

"You got you a bridge," Grandpa said. "And a meaning. Then when things get so hard you about to break, you can sneak across that bridge and see some folks who went before you and see how they didn't break. Some got bent and some got twisted and a few fell along the way, but they didn't break." **12** **C**

"Am I going to break, Grandpa?"

"You? As strong as you is?" Grandpa Jeremiah pushed himself up on his elbow and give me a look. "No way you going to break, boy. You gonna be strong as they come. One day you gonna tell all them stories I told you to your young'uns and they'll be as strong as you."

"Suppose I ain't got no stories, can I make some up?"

"Sure you can, boy. You make 'em up and twist 'em around. Don't make no mind. Long as you got 'em." **13**

"Is that what Macon is doing?" I asked. "Making up stories to play on his guitar?"

"He'll do with 'em what he see fit, I suppose," Grandpa Jeremiah said. "Can't ask more than that from a man."

Practice the Skills

12 Key Reading Skill

Questioning Do you understand Grandpa's explanation about stories? If not, read it again and think about it. It's a very important part of the story.

13 BIG Question

Grandpa Jeremiah says that whether stories are true or not is not important. It's just important that you tell them. Do you agree? Why or why not? Write your answer on the "Jeremiah's Song" page of Foldable 6. Your response will help you complete the Unit Challenge later.

Teach

EL Language Coach

Dialect Say: Use context clues to determine what the narrator means when he says, "I think she getting a feeling for Macon." Whom is the narrator talking about? *(Ellie).* What does Grandpa Jeremiah say about Ellie or Macon? *(He says that they are both young.)* **EL BL** What might the narrator mean by the phrase "getting a feeling"? *(He may be saying that Ellie is starting to like Macon romantically.)* **OL**

C Critical Thinking

Evaluation Ask: Do you agree with Grandpa Jeremiah that stories can be bridges? Why or why not? *(Possible response: Yes, stories can be bridges. They can help us connect to the past and show us that even when things are really difficult, we can keep going because others have faced the same obstacles and succeeded.)* **AS**

English Language Coach

Forming the Past Tense In the dialect used by the narrator and the other characters in the story, *knowed* is used as the past tense of *know,* and *come* is used as the past tense of *come.* In standard English, the past tense of *know* is *knew,* and the past tense of *come* is *came.* Remind students that many verbs form the past tense by adding *-ed.* However, irregular verbs form the past tense differently. Have students write the past tense of the following verbs, referring to a dictionary if necessary:

find	give	buy
see	grow	drink
go	bring	sink

BL EL

Objectives
- Analyze character
- Evaluate information
- Use context to understand dialect
- Conduct a debate
- Understand verb tenses

Teach

EL Language Coach

Dialect **Say:** In response to the mailman's comments about the rain the narrator says,"I didn't care about that so I didn't pay him no mind." What context clues can help you figure out what "didn't pay him no mind" means? *(Possible response: The narrator's statement that he doesn't care about the mailman's comments about the rain suggests that "didn't pay him no mind" means "did not pay any attention to him.")* EL

L Literary Element

Characterization **Ask:** Would you say that Macon is a dynamic character or a static character? Explain your answer. *(He is static. As far as the reader can see, he has stayed the same, at least up to this point in the story.)*

Viewing the Photo

Ask: How does the photograph on this page relate to the story? *(Possible response: It looks like the church that Grandpa attended and where his funeral will be.)*

READING WORKSHOP 2

It rained the first three days of August. It wasn't a hard rain but it rained anyway. The mailman said it was good for the crops over East but I didn't care about that so I didn't pay him no mind. What I did mind was when it rain like that the field mice come in and get in things like the flour bin and I always got the blame for leaving it open. EL

When the rain stopped I was pretty glad. Macon come over and sat with Grandpa and had something to eat with us. Sister Todd come over, too. 14

"How Grandpa doing?" Sister Todd asked. "They been asking about him in the church."

"He's doing all right," Ellie said.

"He's kind of quiet today," Macon said. "He was just talking about how the hogs needed breeding."

"He must have run out of stories to tell," Sister Todd said. "He'll be repeating on himself like my father used to do. That's the way I *hear* old folks get."

Practice the Skills

14 Key Literary Element

Characterization In this paragraph, Macon sits with Grandpa. From Macon's actions here and earlier, what have you learned about him as a person? What have you learned about his feelings toward Grandpa? L

Additional Support

Differentiated Instruction

Writing an Obituary In preparation for the ending of this story, have students mine their creativity to write obituaries for Jeremiah. The obits should include details of his life from the story and from students' imagination. Encourage students to celebrate Jeremiah's life in their obits, describing his triumphs as well as his difficulties. You may bring in obituaries from newspapers or have students search the Internet for examples. AL

Everybody laughed at that because Sister Todd was pretty old, too. Maybe we was all happy because the sun was out after so much rain. When Sister Todd went in to take Grandpa Jeremiah a plate of potato salad with no mayonnaise like he liked it, she told him about how people was asking for him and he told her to tell them he was doing okay and to remember him in their prayers.

R Sister Todd came over the next afternoon, too, with some rhubarb pie with cheese on it, which is my favorite pie. When she took a piece into Grandpa Jeremiah's room she come right out again and told Ellie to go fetch the Bible. 15

It was a hot day when they had the funeral. Mostly everybody was there. The church was hot as anything, even though they had the window open. Some yellowjacks flew in and buzzed around Sister Todd's niece and then around Deacon Turner's wife and settled right on her hat and stayed there until we all stood and sang "Soon-a Will Be Done."

At the graveyard Macon played "Precious Lord" and I cried hard even though I told myself that I wasn't going to cry the way Ellie and Sister Todd was, but it was such a sad thing when we left and Grandpa Jeremiah was still out to the grave that I couldn't help it.

L During the funeral and all, Macon kind of told everybody where to go and where to sit and which of the three cars to ride in. After it was over he come by the house and sat on the front porch and played on his guitar. Ellie was standing leaning against the rail and she was crying but it wasn't a hard crying. It was a soft crying, the kind that last inside of you for a long time. Macon was playing a tune I hadn't heard before. I thought it might have been what he was working at when Grandpa Jeremiah was telling him those stories and I watched his fingers but I couldn't tell if it was or not. It wasn't nothing special, that tune Macon was playing, maybe halfway between them Delta blues he would do when Sister Todd wasn't around and something you would play at church. It was something different and something the same at the same time. I watched his fingers go over that guitar and figured I could learn that tune one day if I had a mind to. 16 ◯

6. The ***yellowjacks,*** or *yellow jackets,* are wasps whose name comes from their bright yellow markings.

Practice the Skills

15 Reviewing Skill

Drawing Conclusions What has happened to Grandpa Jeremiah? How do you know?

16 

BQ How will Macon and the narrator carry on Grandpa Jeremiah's storytelling tradition? How do you know? Write your answer on the "Jeremiah's Song" page of Foldable 6. Your response will help you complete the Unit Challenge later.

READING WORKSHOP 2

Teach

R Reading Skill

Review Drawing Conclusions Say: Sister Todd goes into Grandpa's room but comes out and asks for a Bible. Next, the narrator describes a funeral. What conclusion can you draw? *(Grandpa has died.)* BL

L Literary Element

Character Ask: How has Macon changed? *(Possible response: He is more grown up and has become an important family member.)* OL

BQ BIG Question

Ask: What advice has Grandpa given about telling stories? *(Possible response: You should tell stories about the past to keep your spirits high during hard times.)* OL

Assess

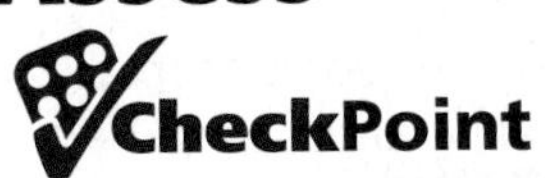

Use the CheckPoint questions provided on Presentation Plus! to check for comprehension of the selection. These questions can be used with interactive response keypads for immediate student feedback.

Literature Focus Lesson

Theme Remind students that the theme of a work is the message about life or the world that the author conveys through the characters, the plot, and other elements of the story. It is different from the topic, which is generally presented in one word and for this story might be "storytelling." Have students think about the important points Jeremiah makes in the story. Then, have them think about how Macon and the narrator behave at the end of the story. Encourage students to use this information to come up with a sentence that expresses the theme. *(Possible response: Stories should be passed from generation to generation to help people overcome difficulties.)* AS

Objectives

- Analyze characterization
- Synthesize
- Draw conclusions
- Understand dialect
- Write a narrative
- Express the theme of a story

Assess

Resources for page 700

- Selection Quick Check
- Selection and Unit Assessment
- ExamView Assessment Suite
- Interactive Tutor: Self-Assessment

Students can respond to the *After You Read* items in their Learner's Notebook or on a separate sheet of paper.

Answering the BIG Question

1. Possible responses: They share stories to entertain people, tell about the past, and give people hope.
2. Since she has gone away to college, she has come to think that they're not important.
3. The narrator has become less fearful and has gained a different perspective of Grandpa's stories.

Critical Thinking

4. Possible response: He has more confidence because Grandpa Jeremiah told him that he is strong.
5. Possible responses: Macon loves and respects Grandpa. He cries after he finds out how sick Grandpa is.
6. Students might say that book learning and learning from family members are equally important.
7. Responses will vary.

After You Read

Jeremiah's Song

Answering the BIG Question

1. Why do you think Grandpa Jeremiah and Macon share their stories?
2. **Recall** Why doesn't Ellie listen to Grandpa Jeremiah's stories any more?
   TIP Right There
3. **Summarize** How does the narrator change by the end of the story?
   TIP Think and Search

Critical Thinking

4. **Infer** Why does the narrator believe he can learn Macon's tune at the end of the story?
   TIP Author and Me
5. **Infer** What are Macon's feelings toward Grandpa? Support your answers with details from the story.
   TIP Author and Me
6. **Evaluate** Which is more important to you–learning about the past from people like Grandpa Jeremiah or "book learning"? Explain.
   TIP On My Own
7. **Synthesize** Imagine that you're creating a sequel, or follow-up story, for "Jeremiah's Song." Who would be the main characters? What would happen in the new story?
   TIP On My Own

Objectives (pp. 700-701)
Reading Monitor comprehension: ask questions • Make connections from text to self
Literature Identify literary elements: characterization
Vocabulary Understand dialect
Writing Use the RAFT system: personal letter
Grammar Combine sentences

Write About Your Reading

Use the RAFT system to write about "Jeremiah's Song."

Role: The narrator of this story

Audience: Ellie

Format: A letter

Topic: Explain the importance of Grandpa Jeremiah's stories.

Here's a beginning for your letter.

Dear Ellie,
I know you didn't think that Grandpa Jeremiah's stories were important. But I thought they were very important. Here's why.

Write About Your Reading

Possible response:

Grandpa's stories will help us remember him and keep his spirit alive. They will also help us when we or people we know are having rough times. We can tell the stories about the hard times people had in the past, and we will know that we can make it through anything.
Fondly,
Your cousin

Skills Review

Key Reading Skill: Questioning

8. How did the questions that you wrote in your Learner's Notebook help you read this story?
   - Were you able to answer the questions you thought of before you read the story?
   - Did asking questions help you understand parts of the story that might have been confusing or unclear to you?
   - Did asking questions help you understand the characters' dialects and motivations?

Key Literary Element: Character

9. **Dynamic** characters change. Name one dynamic character in the story. Explain your answer.
10. **Static** characters stay the same. Name one static character in the story. Explain your answer.
11. **Motivation** is what causes someone to do something. Tell Grandpa Jeremiah's motivation for telling stories.

Reviewing Skills: Drawing Conclusions

12. Think about Grandpa Jeremiah's reasons for telling stories. What conclusions can you draw about Grandpa Jeremiah's life and the life of his parents and grandparents?

Vocabulary Check

Use the words below to complete the sentences.

worthwhile diagnosis setback

13. Anna's training suffered a serious ___ when she broke her arm.
14. We all felt the review session before the test was very ___.
15. The mechanic inspected the car and gave us his ___.
16. **English Language Coach** Review the differences between dialect and Standard English. Name two ways that they are different.

Grammar Link: Combining Sentences

You can combine simple sentences to form complex ones.

Simple: I left early.

Simple: I felt sick.

Complex: I left early <u>because</u> I felt sick.

Complex: <u>Because</u> I felt sick, I left early.

Adding *because* (or any other subordinating conjunction) to a clause makes it dependent. The clause cannot stand alone as a complete sentence.

Independent (complete): I left early.
Dependent (incomplete): <u>because</u> I left early

Common Subordinating Conjunctions	
because	cause and effect
if	condition
although, though, whereas	opposite ideas
after, before, when, while	time

Grammar Practice

Combine each pair of sentences below. Use the chart to choose a conjunction for each sentence.

17. (Condition) It is raining. We won't go.
18. (Opposite ideas) It is raining. We'll go.
19. (Time) Be sure to study. You take the test.

Writing Application Review your RAFT assignment. Combine two simple sentences to form a complex sentence.

Web Activities For eFlashcards, Selection Quick Checks, and other Web activities, go to www.glencoe.com.

Grammar Link: Combining Sentences

Grammar Practice

17. If it is raining, we won't go.
18. Possible response: Although it is raining, we'll go.
19. Be sure to study before you take the test.

Close

Ask students to discuss what they have learned to help them answer the Big Question.

Skills Review

Key Reading Skill: Questioning

8. Possible responses:
   - Yes, I could answer them.
   - Asking questions helped me keep the characters straight.
   - Yes. For example, when Macon visited Jeremiah on his sickbed, I asked, "Why did he do that?"

Key Literary Element: Character

9. Possible response: The narrator starts out scared of the stories, but he is less scared by the end.
10. Possible response: Grandpa starts out telling stories, and he tells stories until he dies.
11. Possible response: to lift people's spirits and help them understand the past.

Reviewing Skills: Drawing Conclusions

12. Their lives must have been very difficult.

Vocabulary Check

13. setback
14. worthwhile
15. diagnosis
16. In dialect, words are spelled the way they sound, and the grammar follows its own patterns. Standard English uses standard spellings and grammar.

Predicting

UNIT 6

Objectives covered in this workshop:
- Make predictions

Teaching Students How to Predict

Why Is It Important?

- Predicting helps readers monitor comprehension when they compare what they had expected to what they have actually read.
- Predicting engages students more actively with the texts they are reading.
- Predicting is a familiar strategy that can serve as a way into discussions of how using strategies enhance their comprehension.

How to Help Students Get It

- Point out that reading is an interactive process involving both the reader and the author.
- Emphasize that using background knowledge (including what they have already read in the text) to make a prediction is one way to become more engaged with what they are reading
- Predicting is one way to make inferences since to make a prediction, readers have to think about what is already read, what they know about the kinds of events or information they are reading about, and construct an idea of what will happen next.

Reading to Answer the Big Question

The Tale of 'Kiko-Wiko

'Kiko-Wiko doesn't like the story she's in and tries to change it as it is being told. Students will discover the consequences of her actions as they read this graphic story.

We Are All One

"We Are All One" retells a traditional Chinese story about a poor peddler who treats every living thing with equal importance and is rewarded for his good deeds. This ancient tale will help students think about the connection between themselves and the world around them.

Why Is It Important? Predicting helps you look forward to events and pay attention to details in a story. For example, usually the hero of a folktale faces challenges but wins in the end. You might expect it, but you read on to find out whether you're right. Predicting can be useful in real life also. You can predict that if you're late to meet your friends, they will be annoyed. R

How Do I Do It? Before you read, notice the title. Then skim some of the story to get an idea of what it's about. Think about what is most likely to happen to these characters, based on what you already know about life and about folktales. Here's how one student predicted events in a story. She read the title and skimmed the first paragraph.

Literature Online

Study Central Visit www.glencoe.com and click on Study Central to review predicting.

The Weaver and Her Brothers

Ari and her three brothers were playing near a tumbledown house one day when a man came out of the house and yelled at them. He pointed at the boys and flapped his hands, and they all turned into crows. He said to Ari, "They will never be human again unless you find them and weave sweaters for them."

The man says only Ari can save her brothers, and she has to do it by weaving sweaters for them. I see from the title that Ari is a weaver, so I predict that she will succeed. Also, I know that fairy tale heroes usually win in the end. I think she'll find her brothers and save them.

Practice It!

Cause and effect are very important in predicting. Look at the situations and events below and predict some of the possible effects, things that *might* happen. In your Learner's Notebook, copy and complete the sentences with a prediction.

- If a little girl suddenly saw a monster, she might . . .
- If a very rich man was going blind, he might . . .
- If a kind man saw an anthill about to be flooded, he might . . .

Use It!

As you read these selections, remember the lists you made to practice predicting. If new knowledge about the characters makes you change your predictions as you read, write your revised predictions on your lists. C

Teach

Study Central Have students access the Web site to review predicting and to complete a related activity.

R Reading Skill

Predicting Ask: What two things does predicting help you do? *(It helps you look forward to events and pay attention to details in a story.)* What should you do before you read a story so that you will be prepared to make predictions? *(Read the title, look at the pictures, and skim some of the text to get an idea of what the story is about.)* **OL**

C Critical Thinking

Evaluation Ask: Do you think that your predictions about a story must always be right? Why or why not? *(Possible response: No, it's more important to make guesses and become engaged in the story than to get every guess right.)* **AL**

Resources for page 703

- Use Reading Skills Transparency in *Read Aloud, Think Aloud,* Unit 6, to help students practice predicting.

Reading in the Real World

Citizenship Tell students that they will read stories with allusions, or references, to various cultures. Have them learn about the cultures represented in their community. Encourage students to visit cultural centers or to invite a representative of a culture to speak to the class about aspects of his or her culture. Invite students to share their own favorite cultural traditions. **OL**

Objectives
- Make predictions
- Make an evaluation
- Analyze a cartoon
- Understand verb tenses

Teach

More About the Author

Mark Crilley understands the importance of good storytelling. When he gives presentations to school-children of all ages, he talks about how to create a good story: "Between the jokes and silly voices is an ample supply of information about writing and storytelling: the art of creating characters that really seem to live and breathe; the importance of putting conflict at the heart of a story; the parallels between students being asked to rewrite assignments and authors working on the second (or third or fourth!) draft of a manuscript."

EL Language Coach

Dialogue Bubbles Have students create an illustration and a dialogue bubble to go with the sentence they think is probably dialogue. OL EL

Before You Read

The Tale of 'Kiko-Wiko

Mark Crilley

Meet the Author

Mark Crilley began drawing at a young age. After college, he taught in Japan, where he invented the character Akiko. Since then, he has published more than 50 issues of the *Akiko* comic book series. He writes," . . . somewhere underneath all the silly drawings and slapstick humor lies a gentle reminder of the little 4th grader within us all. . . ."

Author Search For more about Mark Crilley, go to www.glencoe.com.

Objectives (pp. 704–711)
Reading Make predictions • Make connections from text to self
Literature Identify literary elements: cultural allusions
Vocabulary Understand dialogue

Vocabulary Preview

whimsical (WIM zih kul) *adj.* light and natural; not serious **(p. 706)** *The whimsical story made me think of knights and castles.*

disruptions (DIS rup shunz) *n.* unwanted breaks or interruptions **(p. 709)** *It was hard to watch the game because of my sister's disruptions.*

English Language Coach

Dialogue Conversation between characters in a story is called dialogue. In most text, dialogue appears between quotation marks. In a comic book or graphic story, dialogue usually appears in bubbles.

In most comic books, words that are not inside a bubble are not spoken dialogue. They are not spoken by any character in the story. They are like the words that would be spoken by a narrator in a play or movie.

Dialogue helps to

- bring characters to life by showing their personalities and what they are thinking and feeling
- move the plot forward by noting a passage of time and introducing new characters, locations, or actions

Look at these sentences from the graphic story you are about to read.

Narration	Once upon a time there was a little girl named 'Kiko-Wiko.
Dialogue	What's up?

On Your Own Read the sentences below. Which sentences are probably dialogue? Which ones are probably narration? How can you tell?

EL

1. Ari and her three brothers were playing near a tumbledown house.
2. Hey, you kids! Get off my lawn!
3. He pointed at the boys, and they all turned into crows.

Additional Support

Author Search To expand students' appreciation of Mark Crilley, have them access the Web site for additional information and resources.

Literature Focus Lesson

Plot Remind students that the plot of a story is the series of events that take place during the story. Most stories follow a similar plot structure: they have a beginning; a climax, in which the action reaches its highest point; and a resolution, in which the conflict is resolved. "The Tale of 'Kiko-Wiko" does not follow that structure, however. Instead, the main character disrupts the plot because she doesn't like one of the characters. Ask students to evaluate this story. How does it compare with stories they have read that have a typical plot structure? OL

Focus

BELLRINGER Options

- **Selection Focus Transparency**
- **Daily Language Practice Transparency**

Focus Activity Say: Do you know someone whose culture is different from yours? Name one tradition this person observes that you don't. *(Responses will vary.)*

Teach

R Reading Skill

Predicting Say: You make predictions every day. For example, you might predict that your parents will allow you to go to the movies when they see you've cleaned your room. You've used what you know to make a guess about the future. Think of another prediction you might make. *(Responses will vary.)* **AS**

Analyzing the Cartoon

Say: Jeremy tried to predict what his father would say. Why did Jeremy predict that his father would say something corny? *(Possible response: Jeremy thinks most things his father says are corny.)* **AS**

READING WORKSHOP 3

Skills Focus

You will practice using these skills when you read the following selections:

- "The Tale of 'Kiko-Wiko,'" p. 706
- "We Are All One," p. 716

Reading

- Predicting

Literature

- Recognizing cultural allusions
- Analyzing what cultural allusions add to a work

Vocabulary

- Identifying dialogue
- Understanding how to read dialogue

Writing/Grammar

- Using commas in compound sentences
- Using commas in complex sentences

Objectives (pp. 702–703)
Reading Make predictions

Skill Lesson

Predicting

Learn It!

What Is It? Predicting means making guesses about what will happen next in a story. To predict, you think about the events and details you've read about so far. Then you guess what might happen next. Once you make a prediction, you read on to see if you guessed right. If you didn't, that's okay. You predict to get more involved in the story and to make it more interesting.

R

To make good predictions:

- Pay attention to details in the story.
- Use what you know about the subject of the story.

For example, in a story about a boy and his grandmother, you might predict he will learn something from her.

Analyzing Cartoons
Jeremy thinks his dad is predictable. Did you ever predict what a friend or family member or teacher would say next? How did you know? What information or experiences led to your prediction?

Additional Support

English Language Coach

Future Tense Tell students that they are likely to use the future tense when making predictions. Remind them that they can form the future tense of any verb by using the auxiliary verb *will* with the base form: *I will call you.* Tell students that they can also use the phrases *going to* and *about to* to express future time.

Have students revise each sentence so that the verb expresses the future tense.

1. The main character goes shopping.
2. The story is entertaining.
3. The good character wins at the end.
4. The evil dragon loses the fight.

BL **EL**

Workshop Resources

Pacing (Days) Standard	Block	Lesson	Student Materials	Teacher Resources
1		Key Skill Lesson: Predicting	Key Reading Skills Practice English Language Coach	Bellringer Options Transparencies Read Aloud, Think Aloud Transparencies Presentation Plus!
2		"The Tale of Kiko Wiko"	Literary Analysis Transparencies Glencoe Online Selection Vocabulary Development Academic Vocabulary Development English Language Coach Active Reading Graphic Organizer Literary Analysis StudentWorks Plus Online Student Edition Literature Classics Selection and Unit Assessments	Literary and Text Analysis Transparencies Puzzlemaker Skill Level Up! BookLink 3 Assessment by Learning Objective (Diagnostic and Formative) Interactive Tutor Self-Assessment TeacherWorks Plus
2		"We Are All One"	Glencoe Online Selection Vocabulary Development Academic Vocabulary Development English Language Coach Active Reading Graphic Organizer Literary Analysis StudentWorks Plus Online Student Edition Literature Classics Selection and Unit Assessments	Literary and Text Analysis Transparencies Puzzlemaker Skill Level Up! BookLink 3 Assessment by Learning Objective (Diagnostic and Formative) Interactive Tutor Self-Assessment TeacherWorks Plus

Keys for Unit Resource

- Blackline Master
- Workbook
- Supplemental Text
- CD-ROM
- DVD
- Transparency
- Web-based
- Fast Files

Level Appropriate Code

AS = Activities for all students
AL = Activities for students working above grade level
OL = Activities for students working at grade level
BL = Activities for students working below grade level
EL = Activities for English language learners

Skills Preview

Key Reading Skill: Predicting

When you predict, you combine clues from the text with what you already know. Then you make predictions, or good guesses, about what will come next. Before you read, you may predict what a selection is about. While you read, you may also predict what will happen later.

These clues will help you make predictions:

- The title of the story
- The illustrations
- The qualities or characteristics of the author or main character

Think-Pair-Share Think about the title "The Tale of 'Kiko-Wiko." Who or what do you think 'Kiko-Wiko is? What do you predict the story is about? Use your imagination. With a partner, talk about your predictions.

Key Literary Element: Cultural Allusions

When a writer refers to something that has meaning for a particular group of people, it is called a **cultural allusion.** For example, in a Native American story, a spider may refer to the legend of Grandmother Spider. She brought corn and light to the people. For readers from that culture or tradition, the spider is a positive symbol. Writers often use cultural allusions because they are brief but rich in meaning.

As you read, pay attention to characters and objects. Ask yourself:

- *Could this person, animal, or thing be more important than I think?*
- *Does this remind me of my own traditions? Why is it important?*

Partner Talk With a partner, talk about some animals or objects in your cultures that refer to other ideas. Why are they important? Are they positive or negative symbols? L

Get Ready to Read

Connect to the Reading

The next selection is about a girl who doesn't like the story she's in. As a result, she tries to change parts of the story. Think about a story you've written. How did you invent the characters? What were some of the traits of your characters? If your characters could talk to you, what would they tell you about the story?

Build Background

The graphic story you are about to read is from a comic book series called *Akiko*.

- Akiko is a fourth-grade girl who goes on many weird adventures.
- In the series, Akiko travels to strange planets with her friends.
- More than 50 issues of *Akiko* have been published.

R

Set Purposes for Reading

Read "The Tale of 'Kiko-Wiko" to find out what happens when a character tries to change the story she is in.

Set Your Own Purpose What would you like to learn from the selection to help you answer the Big Question? Write your own purpose on the "Tale of 'Kiko-Wiko" page of Foldable 6.

Literature Online

Interactive Literary Elements Handbook
To review or learn more about the literary elements, go to www.glencoe.com.

Keep Moving

Use these skills as you read the following selection.

READING WORKSHOP 3

Teach

L Literary Element

Cultural Allusions Say: If you are having trouble thinking of objects in your culture that refer to ideas, tell what the following objects represent in American culture:

- the American flag *(freedom)*
- a dove *(peace)*
- the Statue of Liberty *(freedom, a new life)*

BL

R Reading Skill

Review Activating Prior Knowledge Ask: What do you know about comic strips? *(They have pictures; they sometimes tell about superheroes; they are sometimes funny.)* BL

Use the CheckPoint questions provided on Presentation Plus! to check students' understanding of predicting. These questions can be used with interactive response keypads for immediate student feedback.

Literature Online

Interactive Literary Elements Handbook Have students access the Web site to improve their understanding of cultural allusions.

Reading Fluency

Reading a Comic Strip Students may have difficulty reading a comic strip fluently because of the placement of the dialogue bubbles. Tell students that they should read from left to right and start at the top and read down, as they would any other text. Have them look at the bottom strip on page 706. Ask them to identify what they should read first, second, and third. *(Students should first read the narrator's lines, then 'Kiko-Wiko's first dialogue bubble ("Yeah, but . . ."), and finally her second dialogue bubble ("I could be . . ."))*. Have students reread the entire comic strip until they can read it fluently. BL

Objectives

- Make predictions
- Make connections from text to self
- Identify literary elements: cultural allusions
- Understand dialogue

Teach

L1 Literary Element

Review Character Ask: What can you tell about 'Kiko-Wiko from her dialogue in the third strip? *(Possible response: You can tell that she has a good imagination because she thinks of an "evil step-sister" who could be a character in the story.)* AL

L2 Literary Element

Cultural Allusions If some students are not familiar with the evil stepsisters in Cinderella, have a volunteer summarize the fairy tale. Remind him or her to emphasize the role of the stepsisters. EL

READING WORKSHOP 3

Practice the Skills

1 Key Reading Skill

Predicting 'Kiko-Wiko tells you that the story is a fairy tale. Using this information and the illustrations on this page, what do you predict will happen in the story? Write your answer in your Learner's Notebook.

2 Key Literary Element

Cultural Allusions 'Kiko-Wiko makes a cultural allusion here. What popular fairy tale features stepsisters?

Vocabulary

whimsical (WIM zih kul) *adj.* light and natural; not serious

Additional Support

Differentiated Instruction

Your Own Comic Strip Have visual learners create their own comic-strip stories about "'Kiko-Wiko." Instruct them to create humorous stories. Have each of them brainstorm different situations involving 'Kiko-Wiko and use one of them in his or her story. Encourage students to copy the style of Crilley's illustrations, using simple lines to create the images. They might also have their narrators become part of their stories. Have students combine their stories into a "'Kiko-Wiko Storybook." OL

Why don't you leave the narration to *me*, little Miss Devil's Advocate?

All right, all right.

You don't have to get snippy.

Thank you.

3

One day 'Kiko-Wiko was out for a walk when along came a monstrous ogre.
GWAAAAAAR!!!
Hey there, ogre-man.
What's up?

Hang on. She's not supposed to say that, is she?
No, she's not. I believe the line is, "Help, somebody help me."
Yeah, but he's not *scary* enough!
I mean, *look* at him. He's like something out of a *happy meal*...

4

1. A ***devil's advocate*** is someone who argues in favor of a less popular or less accepted idea.
2. An ***ogre*** (OH gur) is an imaginary monster in fairy tales.

Practice the Skills

3 English Language Coach

Dialogue The words outside the bubbles are usually narration and not the voice of a character. What is different about this graphic story?

4 Key Literary Element

Cultural Allusions What is a **happy meal**? Is a happy meal an important part of a particular group of people or culture? Why or why not?

Teach

EL1 Language Coach

Idioms Say: The term *devil's advocate* refers to someone who takes a side or makes a point just for the sake of argument. Why does the narrator call 'Kiko-Wiko "little Miss Devil's Advocate"? *(because she argues with the narrator about who she is)* OL EL

EL2 Language Coach

Dialogue Say: What does the narrator do in the first strip on this page? *(The narrator talks to the girl in the story.)* How is the narrator's speech different from the words outside the bubbles in most graphic stories? *(Here the narrator becomes a character in the story.)* OL AL

Literature Focus Lesson

Fairy Tales Understanding the traditional elements of a fairy tale is important in getting the humor of this story. Have students talk about these common elements of a fairy tale:

- a fair young maiden
- an evil character who mistreats, scares, or kidnaps the young maiden
- a strong, handsome prince who saves the young maiden

Ask students which of these elements are found in "The Tale of 'Kiko-Wiko." *(the evil monster, the young maiden)* Have them notice how this tale is different from other fairy tales. OL

Objectives

- Predict what will happen
- Recognize and analyze cultural allusions
- Understand character
- Recognize and understand the purposes of dialogue
- Understand idioms
- Understand the elements of a fairy tale
- Create a comic strip

Teach

R Reading Skill

Predicting **Say:** You can use what you know about 'Kiko-Wiko to predict how she will react to the new ogre. Tell what you know about her from the story thus far. *(Possible responses: She seems fearless; she is imaginative; she is not afraid to say what she thinks or to find fault with an ogre.)* What can you predict about her reaction based on what you know about her? *(Possible response: She will probably not be afraid of the new ogre. She might find fault with him, too.)* **OL** **AL**

READING WORKSHOP 3

Practice the Skills

5 **Key Reading Skill**

R **Predicting** How do you think 'Kiko-Wiko will react to this new ogre? Why? Write your answer in your Learner's Notebook.

Additional Support

Differentiated Instruction

A Play Have students turn this comic-strip story into a short play. Students should work in groups of four and assign the roles of 'Kiko-Wiko, the two monsters, and the narrator. Instruct students to use voice and body language to convey the humor. Have them practice their versions of the play until they feel confident enough to perform them for the class. **OL**

READING WORKSHOP 3

Now, do you think we could *possibly* get through this without further **disruptions**?

You know, you need to lighten up a little.

I think the disruptions are the ***best part***...

No one asked for your opinion.

6

L

Vocabulary

disruptions (dis RUP shunz) *n.* unwanted breaks or interruptions

Practice the Skills

6 English Language Coach

Dialogue Look again at how 'Kiko-Wiko and the narrator talk to each other. How do you think the narrator feels about 'Kiko-Wiko?

Teach

L Literary Element

Cultural Allusions Say: The narrator in this story acts like a director in a play or movie. The writer makes another allusion to the world of movies and theater when he has 'Kiko-Wiko complain about wanting "more creative control." What does she mean by that statement? *(She wants more say in the way the story is told.)* **AL**

Reading in the Real World

College Have students do research to learn more about the history of comic strips. They might look online or in a library to find out about the following aspects of comic strips:

- When did the first comic strips appear?
- What are the most popular comic strips of all time?
- Who are the most famous creators of comic strips?
- Why are comics popular?

Have students present their findings to the class. **AL**

Objectives

- Predict what will happen
- Recognize and analyze cultural allusions
- Understand character
- Analyze dialogue
- Perform a play
- Conduct research

Teach

R Reading Skill

Predicting Ask: How do most fairy tales about ogres and maidens end? *(They end happily, with a handsome prince rescuing the maiden from the monster.)* Do you think that will happen in this story? Why or why not? *(Possible response: No, it will not happen. This story is not a typical fairy tale. Plus, the narrator has resigned, and there's no handsome prince.)* **OL**

READING WORKSHOP 3

Practice the Skills

7 Key Reading Skill

R **Predicting** Do you think this fairy tale will have an ending? Why or why not? Write your answer in your Learner's Notebook.

Additional Support

Differentiated Instruction

Using Visual Clues Tell struggling readers that they can use visual clues from the illustrations to better understand the story. Have students look at 'Kiko-Wiko's facial expressions on page 710. In the second strip, she looks distracted. She is wondering about the pronunciation of *ogre* instead of showing fear of the monster. Ask students to describe her facial expression in the bottom strip. Why does she look this way? *(She looks angry. She is annoyed because the narrator has just resigned.)* **BL**

READING WORKSHOP 3

L

BQ

8

Practice the Skills

8 BIG Question

Could the author have told this story using text only? How did the dialogue and images help you understand and enjoy the story? Write your answers on the "Tale of 'Kiko-Wiko" page of Foldable 6. Your response will help you complete the Unit Challenge later.

Teach

L Literary Element

Cultural Allusions Say: This story alludes to other tales about monstrous ogres who torment helpless young maidens. How is this story different from those tales? *('Kiko-Wiko is not helpless. She is not even afraid of the ogre. The ogre is not evil.)* **AL**

BQ BIG Question

Ask: What reason might the author of this story give for telling stories? *(Possible responses: to entertain readers, to make them think about the way stories are constructed)* **OL**

Assess

CheckPoint

Use the CheckPoint questions provided on Presentation Plus! to check for comprehension of the selection. These questions can be used with interactive response keypads for immediate student feedback.

Differentiated Instruction

Evaluating Characters Although Crilley writes humorous comic strips, he still believes in "creating characters that really seem to live and breathe." Have students write a paragraph in which they evaluate the characters in this story. Ask them to consider these questions:

- Do they seem like real people?
- What do they do that real people would do?
- Do their motivations, or reasons for acting, seem true to life? Explain.

AL

Objectives

- Predict what will happen
- Recognize and analyze cultural allusions
- Recognize and understand the purposes of dialogue
- Evaluate characters
- Use visual clues to understand comic strips

Assess

Resources for page 712

- Selection Quick Check
- Selection and Unit Assessment
- ExamView Assessment Suite
- Interactive Tutor: Self-Assessment

Students can respond to the *After You Read* items in their Learner's Notebook or on a separate sheet of paper.

Answering the BIG Question

1. The author wanted to entertain. He tells a funny story.
2. The first ogre is not scary. He looks like he came out of a "happy meal."
3. She gets distracted thinking about the word *ogre.*

Critical Thinking

4. Possible response: The characters are inside—perhaps on a stage with outdoor scenery. You can tell because both the narrator and 'Kiko-Wiko slam a door.
5. Possible response: No. She does not stick to the script, and she complains about the other actors.
6. Possible response: The narrator does not want to continue working with 'Kiko-Wiko.
7. Possible response: I was surprised that 'Kiko-Wiko said whatever she wanted to say.

After You Read

The Tale of 'Kiko-Wiko

Objectives (pp. 712–713)
Reading Make predictions
Literature Identify literary elements: cultural allusions
Vocabulary Understand dialogue
Writing Write dialogue
Grammar Use punctuation: commas in compound sentences

Answering the BIG Question

1. Why do you think the author wanted to share this story? Did he want to inform, persuade, or entertain you? How can you tell?
2. **Recall** According to 'Kiko-Wiko, what is wrong with the first ogre?
   TIP **Right There**
3. **Recall** What happens when the second ogre tries to scare 'Kiko-Wiko?
   TIP **Right There**

Critical Thinking

4. **Infer** Where are the characters in this story? Are they inside or outside? Are they in a natural setting? Use details from the story to explain your answers.
   TIP **Author and Me**
5. **Evaluate** Do you think 'Kiko-Wiko behaves like a good cartoon character? Why or why not? Explain your answer with examples from the story.
   TIP **Author and Me**
6. **Infer** Why does the narrator quit?
   TIP **Author and Me**
7. **Respond** What surprised you about the story?
   TIP **Author and Me**

Write About Your Reading

Use dialogue and narration to rewrite the last two pages of "The Tale of 'Kiko-Wiko." After you have written the text, draw pictures to add to the end of the story. Think about the questions below as you write your new ending.

- How will 'Kiko-Wiko react to the new ogre?
- Will the narrator continue to talk with the characters, or will he only explain what happens in the fairy tale?
- Will the fairy tale have a happy or sad ending?

Write About Your Reading

Possible response:

Narrator: The ogre terrified the little girl at first.
'Kiko-Wiko: Oh, I'm so scared. You're a terrifying monster.
Narrator: Then the girl realized that the ogre's foot was bloody.
'Kiko-Wiko: Oh, no. What happened to your foot. Does it hurt?
Ogre: Grrrrrrrrrrrrrr [*Nods his head*]
Narrator: The girl helped bandage the ogre's foot, and the two became best friends.
THE END

Skills Review

Key Reading Skill: Predicting

8. Look back at the predictions you wrote in your Learner's Notebook. Did you predict any of the events that happened in the story? Do you think that making predictions helped you learn more from the story? Explain.

Key Literary Element: Cultural Allusions

9. Ogres are monsters in Northern European mythology. Do you think ogres are cultural allusions? Why or why not? Is an ogre a positive or negative symbol?

Vocabulary Check

10. Give an example of a time when making faces or telling jokes would be considered **disruptions.**
11. Give an example of a situation in which it would be a bad idea to be **whimsical.**

English Language Coach The following types of dialogue bubbles are supposed to communicate something about what is being said. Can you tell what each type is supposed to communicate? (You may discuss this question with a partner.)

12.

NO! I WON'T!

13.

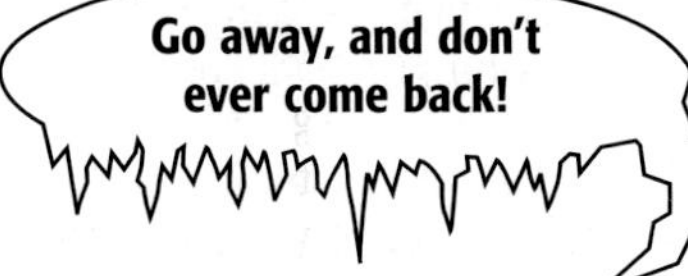

Go away, and don't ever come back!

Grammar Link: Commas in Compound Sentences

Put a comma before the coordinating conjunction in a compound sentence.

- I would like to ski every day, but James prefers reading.

You can leave out the comma when the two simple sentences, or independent clauses, are short (five words or less).

- Skiing is fun and it is good exercise.

Look Out! Do not put a comma before a coordinating conjunction that is joining compound words or phrases.

Wrong: My hobbies are skiing, and skating.
Right: My hobbies are skiing and skating.

Grammar Practice

Rewrite each sentence that needs a comma. Punctuate each sentence correctly.

14. 'Kiko-Wiko walked up to the ogre.
15. The ogre raised his fists and growled at 'Kiko-Wiko.
16. The ogre was confused about his lines and 'Kiko-Wiko argued with the narrator.
17. The narrator quit but 'Kiko-Wiko didn't care.

Writing Application Look at the Write About Your Reading assignment you completed. Join some of your sentences and write three compound sentences.

Web Activities For eFlashcards, Selection Quick Checks, and other Web activities, go to www.glencoe.com.

Skills Review

Key Reading Skill: Predicting

8. Possible response: I didn't predict anything that happened, but making predictions helped me look for important details in the story.

Key Literary Element: Cultural Allusions

9. Possible response: They appear in the stories of many cultures, so they are cultural allusions. Ogres represent fear or the bad parts of life. They are negative symbols.

Vocabulary Check

10. Possible response: Making faces and telling jokes in class are usually disruptions.
11. Possible response: It would be a bad idea to be whimsical when auditioning for a serious part in a play.
12. Possible response: anger
13. Possible responses: a cold, icy attitude

Literature Online

Web Activities Have students access the Web site for interactive activities that will help them assess their understanding of the selection.

Grammar Link: Commas in Compound Sentences

Grammar Practice

14. no comma needed
15. no comma needed
16. The ogre was confused about his lines, and 'Kiko-Wiko argued with the narrator.
17. The narrator quit, but 'Kiko-Wiko didn't care.

Close

Have students explain when telling humorous stories like this one might be appropriate.

More About the Author

Identity is an important issue in many of Laurence Yep's award-winning novels. He has explained, "In a sense, I have no one culture to call my own since I exist . . . in several. However, in my writing I can create my own." Yep says that his early experiences living in neighborhoods with members of different cultures contributed to his sense that he is "always pursuing the theme of being an outsider."

V Vocabulary

Sentences Say: Once you feel you know the vocabulary words well, write four sentences, each one using one of the vocabulary words. AS

Before You Read | We Are All One

Laurence Yep

Meet the Author

Laurence Yep grew up as a Chinese American kid in a mostly African American neighborhood in San Francisco. He liked to read fantasy and science fiction. The stories were about adapting to new situations and customs, which he did every day. See page R7 of the Author Files for more on Laurence Yep.

Literature Online

Author Search For more about Laurence Yep, go to www.glencoe.com.

Objectives (pp. 714–721)
Reading Make predictions • Make connections from text to self
Literature Identify literary elements: cultural allusions
Vocabulary Understand dialogue

Vocabulary Preview

scurrying (SKUR ee ing) *v.* running or moving quickly or excitedly; form of the verb *scurry* **(p. 717)** *The peddler noticed ants scurrying across the ground.*

regretfully (rih GRET ful ee) *adv.* in a way that shows sorrow, distress, or disappointment **(p. 718)** *Unable to help, the queen shook her head regretfully.*

omen (OH mun) *n.* a sign or event thought to predict good or bad fortune **(p. 718)** *The peddler believed his dream was a good omen.*

V

frustration (frus TRAY shun) *n.* irritation at being kept from doing or achieving something **(p. 720)** *The old man's frustration nearly drove him to tears.*

Listen to Learn Work with a partner. As one of you reads each definition aloud, the other person identifies the vocabulary word. Take turns until you know each word well.

English Language Coach

Conventions of Dialogue Almost all stories use dialogue, conversation between characters. One convention, or way of doing things, that is used with dialogue is to begin a new paragraph whenever a different character speaks.

"It might be dangerous to go," said Mara.

"But that's silly!" replied Jeff. "Nothing bad could possibly happen. We'll be completely safe."

"I'm not so sure."

"Oh, don't be ridiculous!"

Because of the convention, a reader knows that it is Mara, not Jeff, who says "I'm not so sure" and Jeff who says "Oh, don't be ridiculous!"

On Your Own In your Learner's Notebook, rewrite the paragraph below, creating as many paragraphs as are needed.

"One of the things I like about folktales," said Lucy as she removed a thick book from the shelf, "is that they have happy endings." "You know, you're right," said Jeff. "I've noticed that myself." "The hero or heroine might have to struggle for quite a while," Lucy continued, "but good always wins out in the end."

Additional Support

Literature Online

Author Search To expand students' appreciation of Laurence Yep, have them access the Web site for additional information and resources.

English Language Coach

Dialogue Remind students that phrases like *he said* and *she said* tell who is speaking and are called dialogue tags. Many writers of fiction use dialogue tags. Review the following dialogue tags and their meanings:

- told
- exclaimed
- remarked
- groaned
- argued
- called

Have students note any dialogue tags used in the story, as well as other ways in which the author introduces dialogue. EL

Skills Preview

Key Reading Skill: Predicting

In the folktale "We Are All One," you will read about

- A rich man whose money cannot buy a cure for the disease he has
- A poor man who gives away as much as he can
- The connection between all living beings
- The importance of not giving up

As you read, pay attention to the relationship between all the events and people in this story so that you can predict how they will affect each other.

Write to Learn Use your imagination; your answers can involve magic. In your Learner's Notebook, write

- a reason a poor man might want to help a rich man
- a way an insect might be able to help a person
- an example of people and animals communicating with each other

Key Literary Element: Cultural Allusions

When a writer mentions, or alludes to, something important to a particular group of people, it is called a **cultural allusion.**

As you read, notice characters and objects. Ask yourself:

- *Is this person or animal important to the story?*
- *Does this object remind me of an object from my own culture?*

Whole-class Discussion Listed below are some cultural allusions. Talk about the ones with which you are familiar. What is the importance or meaning?

mountain • star • lion • beads • tree • moon
eagle • cross • mask • shawl • pyramid

Interactive Literary Elements Handbook
To review or learn more about the literary elements, go to www.glencoe.com.

Get Ready to Read

Connect to the Reading

Think about what it would mean if we were all one, if every creature on the planet were equally important and connected. How would that point of view change your way of life? Would you be able to kill a mosquito?

R **Whole-class Discussion** Talk about the meaning of the expression "We are all one." Do you agree with any of these statements?

- What happens to one person affects everyone.
- Every person or thing is connected to every other one; we're all part of one family.
- Every person and thing is equally important.

Build Background

Chinese people who left their homeland to live in America brought with them many traditional stories. They retold these tales to remind themselves of life at home and to show how to survive in a strange and often hostile land. The tales were meant to teach children how a Chinese person should behave. "We Are All One" retells one of those stories.

Set Purposes for Reading

BIG Question Read "We Are All One" to find out why storytellers told this ancient tale.

Set Your Own Purpose What would you like to learn from the selection to help you answer the Big Question? Write your own purpose on the "We Are All One" page of Foldable 6.

Keep Moving

Use these skills as you read the following selection.

Teach

R Reading Skill

Predicting Say: Make a prediction about what might happen between the rich man and the poor man. *(Possible response: They might meet. The poor man might give away a cure for the rich man's disease.)* Read the story to find out if your prediction is correct. AL

L Literary Element

Cultural Allusions Say: Allusions might have different meanings in different cultures. What does a star represent in our culture? *(Possible response: A star represents hope. People wish on a star for things to happen.)* OL

Use the CheckPoint questions provided on Presentation Plus! to check for understanding of cultural allusions. These questions can be used with interactive response keypads for immediate student feedback.

Literature Online

Interactive Literary Elements Handbook Have students access the Web site to improve their understanding of cultural allusions.

Differentiated Instruction

Nature Journals Encourage students to look closely at the natural world around them. They do not need to go into a forest to observe nature. They can find insects in a schoolyard, birds in a parking lot, or people in a mall. Invite students to choose one spot from which to observe (human or animal) nature. Encourage them to visit that spot several times to record how nature changes at different times of the day or on different days of the week. Instruct students to record their observations in one of the following ways: by taking notes, drawing pictures, or tape-recording their impressions. Have them share their observations with the rest of the class. AS

Objectives

- Make predictions
- Make connections from text to self
- Identify literary elements: cultural allusions
- Understand dialogue

Teach

R Reading Skill

Predicting Ask: What are three details you learned about the story from looking at the title and skimming the first page? *(Possible responses: The story is about how everyone is connected; it tells about a rich man with an incurable eye disease and his search for a cure; it tells about a generous peddler who gives away so much candy he is always poor.)* What can you predict about the story based on those details? *(The generous peddler will have something to do with helping the rich man find a cure.)* OL AL

Readability Scores
Dale-Chall: 4.8
DRP: 51
Lexile: 750

READING WORKSHOP 3

We Are All One

by Laurence Yep

Long ago there was a rich man with a disease in his eyes. For many years, the pain was so great that he could not sleep at night. He saw every doctor he could, but none of them could help him.

"What good is all my money?" he groaned. Finally, he became so desperate that he sent criers[1] through the city offering a reward to anyone who could cure him.

Now in that city lived an old candy peddler. He would walk around with his baskets of candy, but he was so kind-hearted that he gave away as much as he sold, so he was always poor. 1

1. Before modern forms of communication, ***criers*** gave people the news. Some *criers* were public officials who announced important events; others were hired by individuals.

Practice the Skills

1 Key Reading Skill

R **Predicting** What do you expect this folktale will be about? What will happen to the rich man? What will the peddler do? Base your answers on the story's title and on the first three paragraphs. Write your predictions in your Learner's Notebook.

Additional Support

Leveled Reading An adapted version of this selection (4th grade readability) is available on page 186 of *Jamestown Literature: An Adapted Reader* for Grade 7.

English Language Coach

Retelling a Story with Dialogue
Every culture has stories that have been passed down from generation to generation. Some of those stories tell about respecting nature or being kind to people and animals. Ask small groups of students to share stories from their culture about kindness to people or animals or respecting nature. Then, have students choose one story and create a brief written retelling of it. Encourage students to use dialogue so that they can practice the correct placement of quotation marks and dialogue tags. EL

READING WORKSHOP 3

When the old peddler heard the announcement, he remembered something his mother had said. She had once told him about a magical herb that was good for the eyes. So he packed up his baskets and went back to the single tiny room in which his family lived. **R**

When he told his plan to his wife, she scolded him, "If you go off on this crazy hunt, how are we supposed to eat?" **2**

Usually the peddler gave in to his wife, but this time he was stubborn. "There are two baskets of candy," he said. "I'll be back before they're gone."

The next morning, as soon as the soldiers opened the gates, he was the first one to leave the city. He did not stop until he was deep inside the woods. As a boy, he had often wandered there. He had liked to pretend that the shadowy forest was a green sea and he was a fish slipping through the cool waters.

As he examined the ground, he noticed ants **scurrying** about. On their backs were larvae[2] like white grains of rice. A rock had fallen into a stream, so the water now spilled into the ant's nest. **3**

"We're all one," the kind-hearted peddler said. So he waded into the shallow stream and put the rock on the bank. Then with a sharp stick, he dug a shallow ditch that sent the rest of the water back into the stream. **L**

Without another thought about his good deed, he began to search through the forest. He looked everywhere; but as the day went on, he grew sleepy. "Ho-hum. I got up too early. I'll take just a short nap," he decided, and lay down in the shade of an old tree, where he fell right asleep.

In his dreams, the old peddler found himself standing in the middle of a great city. Tall buildings rose high overhead. He couldn't see the sky even when he tilted back his head. An escort of soldiers marched up to him with a loud clatter of their black lacquer armor. "Our queen wishes to see you," the captain said.

2. ***Larvae*** (LAR vee) is the plural form of *larva*. They're insects at a very young, wormlike stage of development.

Vocabulary

scurrying (SKUR ee ing) *v.* running or moving quickly or excitedly

Practice the Skills

2 English Language Coach

Dialogue One purpose of dialogue is to give information about characters. What can you tell about the candy seller's wife from what she says here?

3 Key Literary Element

Cultural Allusions In many cultures, ants stand for the positive values of hard work and determination. Anyone who has ever watched ants has seen how busy they seem. Why do you think the storyteller uses ants here? What message might they give to the peddler and to readers?

Teach

R Reading Skill

Review Inferring Ask: What does the peddler decide to do? *(He decides to look for an herbal cure for the rich man's eye disease.)* What can you infer about the peddler from his decision to look for a cure? *(Possible response: You can infer that he likes to help people.)* **OL AL**

L Literary Element

Review Character Say: You can tell a lot about a person's character from his or her actions. What can you tell about the peddler from his decision to help the ants? *(You can tell that he is kind and concerned with all life, not just with the life of the rich man.)* **AS**

Reading in the Real World

Citizenship The belief that animal life is as sacred as human life is important in many religions, including Buddhism, which is practiced in China, where this story is set. Have students research Buddhism, from its beginnings in India to its spread to Japan, China, and the United States. Suggest that they try to answer these questions: What are the main beliefs common to the different sects of Buddhism? How do Buddhists practice their religion? Students might interview a member of a local Buddhist temple to find out more about the religion. Have students present their findings in an oral report. **OL AL**

Objectives

- Make predictions
- Recognize and analyze cultural allusions
- Make inferences
- Read and understand dialogue
- Use quotation marks and dialogue tags
- Conduct research

READING WORKSHOP 3

Teach

R Reading Skill

Predicting Ask: How does the dream help you predict the outcome of the story? *(The queen says that if the peddler keeps looking, he will surely find the herb.)* OL

Viewing the Art

Ask: What does this picture show? *(It shows a man, probably the peddler, walking alone along a path.)* How does the picture help you understand the setting of the story? *(Possible response: It helps me understand that the peddler takes a long, lonely journey in a beautiful natural setting.)* BL OL

The frightened peddler could only obey and let the fierce soldiers lead him into a shining palace. There, a woman with a high crown sat upon a tall throne. Trembling, the old peddler fell to his knees and touched his forehead against the floor.

But the queen ordered him to stand. "Like the great Emperor Yü of long ago, you tamed the great flood. We are all one now. You have only to ask, and I or any of my people will come to your aid."

The old peddler cleared his throat. "I am looking for a certain herb. It will cure any disease of the eyes."

R The queen shook her head **regretfully**. "I have never heard of that herb. But you will surely find it if you keep looking for it."

And then the old peddler woke. Sitting up, he saw that in his wanderings he had come back to the ants' nest. It was there he had taken his nap. His dream city had been the ants' nest itself.

"This is a good **omen**," he said to himself, and he began searching even harder. He was so determined to find the herb that he did not notice how time had passed. He was surprised when he saw how the light was fading. He looked all around then. There was no sight of his city—only strange hills. He realized then that he had searched so far he had gotten lost. 4

Night was coming fast and with it the cold. He rubbed his arms and hunted for shelter. In the twilight, he thought he could see the green tiles of a roof.

He stumbled through the growing darkness until he reached a ruined temple. Weeds grew through cracks in the stones and most of the roof itself had fallen in. Still, the ruins would provide some protection.

Detail of Eight Views at the Confluence of the Hsiao and Hsiang Rivers. Zosan.

4 Key Reading Skill

Predicting Why does the peddler think that he will find the herb? Will he find his way home? Write your predictions in your Learner's Notebook.

Vocabulary

regretfully (rih GRET ful ee) *adv.* in a way that shows sorrow, distress, or disappointment

omen (OH mun) *n.* a sign or event thought to predict good or bad fortune

Additional Support

Literature Focus Lesson

Cultural Allusions The story alludes to the legend of the great emperor Yü and his taming of the great floods. According to the legend, about 4,000 years ago in ancient China, Yü built canals that led a river into the sea, preventing flooding that had previously caused great damage. Yü is believed to be the founder of China's oldest dynasty, called Hsia. **Ask:** Why might this cultural allusion have been included in the story? *(Possible response: It shows that the queen in the peddler's dream thinks he is doing something very important.)* OL

As he started inside, he saw a centipede with bright orange skin and red tufts of fur along its back. Yellow dots covered its sides like a dozen tiny eyes. It was also rushing into the temple as fast as it could, but there was a bird swooping down toward it. R1

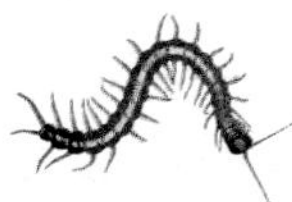

Visual Vocabulary
A ***centipede*** is a long, flat insect with many pairs of legs. The prefix *centi-* means either "hundred" or "hundredth part of." The root word *pede* comes from the Latin word for "foot."

The old peddler waved his arms and shouted, scaring the bird away. Then he put down his palm in front of the insect. "We are all one, you and I." The many feet tickled his skin as the centipede climbed onto his hand.

Inside the temple, he gathered dried leaves and found old sticks of wood and soon he had a fire going. The peddler even picked some fresh leaves for the centipede from a bush near the temple doorway. "I may have to go hungry, but you don't have to, friend."

Stretching out beside the fire, the old peddler pillowed his head on his arms. He was so tired that he soon fell asleep, but even in his sleep he dreamed he was still searching in the woods. Suddenly he thought he heard footsteps near his head. He woke instantly and looked about, but he only saw the brightly colored centipede.

"Was it you, friend?" The old peddler chuckled and, lying down, he closed his eyes again. "I must be getting nervous."

"We are one, you and I," a voice said faintly—as if from a long distance. "If you go south, you will find a pine tree with two trunks. By its roots, you will find a magic bead. A cousin of mine spat on it years ago. Dissolve that bead in wine and tell the rich man to drink it if he wants to heal his eyes." R2

The old peddler trembled when he heard the voice, because he realized that the centipede was magical. He wanted to run from the temple, but he couldn't even get up. It was as if he were glued to the floor. 5

But then the old peddler reasoned with himself: If the centipede had wanted to hurt me, it could have long ago. Instead, it seems to want to help me.

So the old peddler stayed where he was, but he did not dare open his eyes. When the first sunlight fell through the root, he raised one eyelid cautiously. There was no sign of the centipede. He sat up and looked around, but the magical

Practice the Skills

5 English Language Coach

Dialogue How can you tell that, this time, it is not the peddler who says "We are one, you and I"? Whose voice does the peddler hear? Why do you think this character begins by repeating what the peddler said earlier?

Teach

R1 Reading Skill

Predicting Ask: Knowing what you know about the peddler, what do you think he will do when he sees the bird swooping down toward the centipede? *(He will protect the centipede.)* What clues in the text helped you guess this? *(He says, "We are all one," and he has helped the ants.)* OL

R2 Reading Skill

Review Understanding Cause and Effect Ask: How is the peddler rewarded for helping the centipede? *(The centipede tells him how to find the herb.)* OL

Literature Focus Lesson

Plot Remind students that the plot is the series of events in a story that shows the characters in action, trying to resolve one or more than one conflict or problem. One way to determine a story's plot is to identify the problems. In "We Are All One," for example, the rich man's problem with his eyes sets the story's events in motion. Next, students should ask themselves: What characters are involved? What will happen next? What is the solution to the problem?

Have students answer this question about the plot of the story: Why does the peddler become involved with the rich man's problem? *(He wants to help him.)* OL

Objectives
- Make predictions
- Understand cause and effect
- Understand dialogue
- Understand cultural allusions
- Analyze art
- Analyze plot

READING WORKSHOP 3

Teach

V Vocabulary

Context Clues Ask: If you didn't know what the word *frustration* meant, what context clues could help you figure it out? *(Possible responses: "wept," "his old eyes were too weak")* AS

C Critical Thinking

Comprehension Say: The peddler is exhausted and feels as though he can't go on. What does he do next? *(He calls for the ants to help him.)* Why do you think the ants come? *(They come because he helped them.)* OL

Old Man Seated with a Servant Reading, 18th century. Artist unknown. Gouache on paper. Nottingham City Museums and Galleries, Great Britain.

centipede was gone.

He followed the centipede's instructions when he left the temple. Traveling south, he kept a sharp eye out for the pine tree with two trunks. He walked until late in the afternoon, but all he saw were normal pine trees. 6

Wearily he sat down and sighed. Even if he found the pine tree, he couldn't be sure that he would find the bead. Someone else might even have discovered it a long time ago. 7

But something made him look a little longer. Just when he was thinking about turning back, he saw the odd tree. Somehow his tired legs managed to carry him over to the tree, and he got down on his knees. But the ground was covered with pine needles and his old eyes were too weak. The old peddler could have wept with **frustration**, and then he remembered the ants. 8 V

He began to call, "Ants, ants, we are all one."

Almost immediately, thousands of ants came boiling out of nowhere. Delighted, the old man held up his fingers. "I'm looking for a bead. It might be very tiny." C

Then, careful not to crush any of his little helpers, the old man sat down to wait. In no time, the ants reappeared with a tiny bead. With trembling fingers, the old man took the bead

Vocabulary

frustration (frus TRAY shun) *n.* irritation at being kept from doing or achieving something

Practice the Skills

6 Key Literary Element

Cultural Allusions The pine tree is an allusion to eternal life and health because it stays green year round, even in the snow. How might the pine tree relate to the way the peddler feels?

7 Key Reading Skill

Predicting Does the peddler's conversation with the centipede make it seem more likely or less likely that he will find the herb? Why? Write your prediction in your Learner's Notebook.

8 Reviewing Skills

Comparing and Contrasting What part of the description of the peddler here reminds you of the rich man?

Additional Support

Differentiated Instruction

The Quest The quest—a search or pursuit to find some object or achieve some goal—is a theme in literature and popular drama. It can be found in works ranging from the ancient Greek myths to the contemporary *Lord of the Rings* trilogy and the *Star Wars* movies. Encourage advanced learners to determine the quest in "We Are All One." Then, have them conduct research to find out more about stories that are based on a quest. What elements do many of these stories have in common? Why might these types of stories have endured for so long? AL from them and examined it. It was colored orange and looked as if it had yellow eyes on the sides.

There was nothing very special about the bead, but the old peddler treated it like a fine jewel. Putting the bead into his pouch, the old peddler bowed his head. "I thank you and I thank your queen," the old man said. After the ants disappeared among the pine needles, he made his way out of the woods. C

The next day, he reached the house of the rich man. However, he was so poor and ragged that the gatekeeper only laughed at him. "How could an old beggar like you help my master?"

The old peddler tried to argue. "Beggar or rich man, we are all one."

But it so happened that the rich man was passing by the gates. He went over to the old peddler. "I said anyone could see me. But it'll mean a stick across your back if you're wasting my time."

The old peddler took out the pouch. "Dissolve this bead in some wine and drink it down." Then, turning the pouch upside down, he shook the tiny bead onto his palm and handed it to the rich man.

The rich man immediately called for a cup of wine. Dropping the bead into the wine, he waited a moment and then drank it down. Instantly the pain vanished. Shortly after that, his eyes healed.

The rich man was so happy and grateful that he doubled the reward. And the kindly old peddler and his family lived comfortably for the rest of their lives. 9 ○

Practice the Skills

9 BIG Question

BQ Why do you think Chinese parents shared this story from their homeland with their children who were born in America? What advice does the story offer? Write your answer on the "We Are All One" page of Foldable 6. Your response will help you complete the Unit Challenge later.

Teach

C Critical Thinking

Comprehension **Ask:** How does the peddler's conversation with the ants reflect his belief that "we are all one"? *(Possible response: His respectful treatment of the ants, bowing and thanking them, reflects his belief that all beings on earth are equal.)* AL

BQ 

To whom might you tell this story and why? *(Possible response: to someone who has treated another person unkindly, to show him or her that kind actions have good consequences.)* AS

Assess

Use the CheckPoint questions provided on Presentation Plus! to check for comprehension of the selection. These questions can be used with interactive response keypads for immediate student feedback.

Literature Focus Lesson

Theme Remind students that a story's theme is the message about life that the author conveys using characters, plot, dialogue, and other story elements. Have students consider what the old peddler does for the ants and the centipede and how they help him in return. What message about life does this convey? *(Possible response: We will be helped in life if we help others.)* Tell students that stories may have more than one theme. Encourage them to look for other themes in this story. BL OL

Objectives
- Make predictions
- Make inferences
- Understand dialogue
- Determine theme
- Recognize and understand cultural allusion

Assess

Resources for page 722

- Selection Quick Check
- Selection and Unit Assessment
- ExamView Assessment Suite
- Interactive Tutor: Self-Assessment

Students can respond to the *After You Read* items in their Learner's Notebook or on a separate sheet of paper.

Answering the BIG Question

1. Possible response: The philosophy that "we are all one" is important in Buddhism and the Chinese culture.
2. His first act of kindness is to save the ants' home.
3. He talks to his wife, the ant queen, the centipede, the ants as a group, the gatekeeper, and the rich man (and himself).

Critical Thinking

4. Possible response: The rich man's words make him seem cruel. He may be reacting to the pain he's feeling.
5. Possible response: I don't think the peddler will change. He is kind and money isn't important to him.
6. Possible response: The only character presented in enough depth to be lifelike is the peddler. The plot is interesting, and the resolution is very satisfying.

After You Read

We Are All One

Objectives (pp. 722–723)
Reading Make predictions • Make connections from text to self
Literature Identify literary elements: cultural allusions
Vocabulary Understand dialogue
Grammar Use punctuation: commas in complex sentences

Answering the BIG Question

1. Why do you think telling this story is a part of Chinese culture?
2. **Recall** What is the peddler's first act of kindness toward another creature?
   TIP Right There
3. **Scan** Glance quickly through the story to find each person and creature the peddler talks to throughout the story. Name each one.
   TIP Think and Search

Critical Thinking

4. **Infer** What do the rich man's first words to the peddler tell you about his personality? Do you think that the disease in his eyes is the reason for his bad behavior?
   TIP Think and Search
5. **Analyze** Do you think the peddler's behavior will change now that he is rich? Explain.
   TIP Author and Me
6. **Evaluate** Did the story present lifelike characters, an interesting plot, and a good ending? Why or why not?
   TIP Author and Me

Talk About Your Reading

Literature Groups The theme of much popular literature is a *quest,* a search for some object or an attempt to reach some goal. What is the quest in "We Are All One"? In other words, what is the peddler searching for or trying to achieve? With your group, share ideas about other stories you know that are based on a quest.

Write to Learn Think about the quest stories your group discussed. Besides the quest, what else do these stories have in common? Write your thoughts in a short paragraph.

Talk About Your Reading

Possible response:
The peddler is searching for a cure for the rich man. Students might mention other quest stories, such as *Star Wars, The Chronicles of Narnia* series, *The Hobbit,* and *The Matrix.*

Skills Review

Key Reading Skill: Predicting

7. You were asked to write down three predictions as you read the story. Which of your predictions turned out to be right? Which were wrong?

Key Literary Element: Cultural Allusions

8. In Chinese tradition, the pine tree stands for health and eternal life. Does it seem right that the peddler is looking for a pine tree? Explain your answer.

Reviewing Skills: Comparing and Contrasting

9. Compare and contrast the peddler's dream city to the ants' real city. What is the same about them? What is different about them?

Vocabulary Check

Answer each of the following questions.

10. Which is the best synonym for **scurrying**?
    - stomping
    - whizzing
    - running
11. Which of the following is supposed to be said **regretfully**?
    - an apology
    - an invitation
    - a joke
12. What do people think an **omen** can tell them about?
    - the present
    - the past
    - the future
13. Which of the following might a person do to show **frustration**?
    - clap wildly
    - throw something
    - shrug
14. **English Language Coach** Think back to the dialogue in the story. Did you ever have trouble figuring out who was talking? What helped you know?

Grammar Link: Commas in Complex Sentences

When a complex sentence begins with a dependent clause, put a comma after the clause.

- If you have questions, you can call me.

  dependent *independent*

Watch Out! Put a comma after the dependent clause, not after the subordinating conjunction.

Wrong: Although, I studied I did not get an "A."

Right: Although I studied, I did not get an "A."

When a complex sentence begins with an independent clause, the comma is usually omitted. Compare the following complex sentences:

Dependent first—comma: Because I am the oldest kid in my family, I often have to baby-sit.

Independent first—no comma: I often have to baby-sit because I am the oldest kid in my family.

Grammar Practice

On a separate piece of paper, copy the complex sentences below. Add or leave out a comma in any sentence that is punctuated wrong. (Not all sentences are punctuated wrong.)

15. Eduardo has loved cars, since he was a child.
16. When he was little he played with toy cars.
17. Eduardo would own a real car if he could.
18. When he is sixteen, he will go for his license.

Literature Online

Web Activities For eFlashcards, Selection Quick Checks, and other Web activities, go to www.glencoe.com.

READING WORKSHOP 3

Skills Review

Key Reading Skill: Predicting

7. Responses will vary.

Key Literary Element: Cultural Allusions

8. Possible response: It seems right that the peddler is looking for a pine tree because he is trying to find an herb to heal the rich man.

Reviewing Skills: Comparing and Contrasting

9. Possible response: The peddler's dream city has tall buildings and he can't see the sky. There are soldiers in the city. In the ants' real city, the trees and people all probably look like tall buildings to the ants. The queen's throne and the soldiers are in the peddler's city dream but not in the ants' city.

Vocabulary Check

10. running
11. an apology
12. the future
13. throw something
14. It was confusing when a voice spoke to the peddler in the temple. Then the peddler figures out it is the magic centipede speaking.

Grammar Link: Commas in Complex Sentences

Grammar Practice

15. Eduardo has loved cars since he was a child.
16. When he was little, he played with toy cars.
17. Correct as is.
18. Correct as is.

Close

Ask students to discuss why people might want to share this story.

Focus

BELLRINGER Options

Daily Language Practice Transparency

Focus Activity Say: Name one thing you'd like to change about your modern folktale.

Teach

W1 Writing

Revising Ask: Why might it be a good idea to put your writing aside before revising it? *(Possible response: You might not notice things immediately after writing.)* OL

W2 Writing

Point of View Ask: What clue will let you know if you have shifted to first-person point of view? *(Use of the word I by the narrator.)* BL

Resources for page 724

Use the Writing Workshop Graphic Organizer BLM in the Unit 6 Resource Booklet.

Use the Grammar and Writing Workshop Transparencies, Unit 6.

WRITING WORKSHOP PART 2

Modern Folktale

Revising, Editing, and Presenting

ASSIGNMENT Rewrite a folktale in the present

Purpose: To tell a story using all of the elements of a folktale

Audience: You, your teacher, and your classmates

Now it's time to make any changes you want to make to your folktale. That's right. You can change anything! You can even rewrite entire sections if you're not happy with them.

When you're finished revising, you'll prepare your folktale to share it with others. Also, you'll keep a copy of it in a writing portfolio so that you and your teacher can evaluate your writing progress over time.

Revising Rubric

Your revised folktale should have

- well-developed characters
- dialogue
- a theme
- a third-person point of view
- correct spelling, grammar, usage, and mechanics

Revising

Make It Better

W1 Parts of your story that seemed perfectly clear when you were writing your draft may sound confusing to you now. Don't worry. Now's your chance to experiment with changes.

1. Read the latest version of your draft. Write down any thoughts you have or changes you want to make in the margins of your paper. You can pause and make the changes as you read, or you can just make notes about what you want to change and go back later.

be more specific — "Where are you going?" asked Dan.

2. Check your draft against the Revising Rubric to make sure you have all of the elements that you need to have in your folktale. Ask yourself questions like these. Then make any necessary changes.

W2
- Is the third-person point of view consistent throughout the story?
- Will readers feel like they "know" my characters?
- Is the dialogue interesting and descriptive?
- Is the theme well-developed?

3. Don't bore your readers! Mix up the way you start your sentences and use different types of sentences. If most of your sentences start with the same word or words, try starting some of your sentences with an adjective or an adverb. If you use a lot of simple sentences, combine some sentences to make them compound or complex sentences.

Objectives
(pp. 724–729)
Writing Revise writing for key elements, style, and word choice
Grammar Write compound and complex sentences
Listening, Speaking, and Viewing Present folktale • Use appropriate expressions and gestures • Maintain effective eye contact and posture • Ask for feedback

Additional Support

English Language Coach

Varying Sentences Have students revise the following sentences as indicated. Then, have them choose one paragraph from their folktales and work with a partner to revise sentence beginnings to create variety in their writing.

Add an adjective or an adverb to the beginning of these sentences:

1. The hare begged the lion for lunch. *(Famished, the hare begged the lion for lunch.)*
2. The little girl skipped along the path. *(Happily, the little girl skipped along the path.)*

EL BL

Editing

Finish It Up

You've done a lot of work writing your folktale. Now clean up your writing so readers can focus on your story instead of your mistakes.

Literature Online

Writing Models For models and other writing activities, go to www.glencoe.com.

Guide Your Readers

Remember that a paragraph is a group of sentences that relate to one main idea. Your use of paragraphs should guide readers through your writing. When you write expository texts such as summaries and reports, you often have a topic sentence followed by supporting details. You start a new paragraph when you change topics.

Sometimes it's tricky to know where to start a new paragraph when you're writing a story. It can be hard to tell exactly when you're changing topics, and you often don't use a clear topic sentence and supporting details structure.

Here are some good reasons to start a new paragraph in a story.

The narrator switches to a new idea (such as from description to action or from description of one character to description of another).
The time or place changes.
The action switches from one character to another.
You are quoting dialogue and the speaker changes.*

*In truth, this last reason to start a new paragraph is not optional. When you are using dialogue, you *must* start a new paragraph every time the speaker changes.

W

Here's an example from "Brer Rabbit and Brer Lion," retold by Julius Lester.

> "What's your hurry, Brer Rabbit?"
>
> "Run, Brer Lion! There's a hurricane coming."
>
> Brer Lion got scared. "I'm too heavy to run, Brer Rabbit. What am I going to do?"
>
> "Lay down, Brer Lion. Lay down! Get close to the ground!"

The narrator may not always say who is talking, but readers can keep track by looking at the paragraphing. (In the dialogue above, readers can also figure out who is talking by looking at the direct address in the dialogue.)

Look over your draft and make sure that your paragraphing guides your readers through your story.

Writing Tip

Conventions Be sure to punctuate your dialogue correctly so readers know exactly what words the character says. If you need a reminder on how to punctuate dialogue, see page R36.

WRITING WORKSHOP PART 2

Teach

W Writing

Writing Paragraphs Ask: Why is it sometimes hard to know where to start a new paragraph when you're writing a story? *(Possible responses: It can be hard to know when you're changing topics. Also, narratives don't always use a clear topic sentence and supporting details structure.)* **BL** Look back at "The Boy and His Grandfather" on page 684. Tell why you think the author started a new paragraph at 1) "It so happened . . .," and 2) "My little one . . ." *(1. because he's beginning a new topic; 2. because there is dialogue)* **OL**

Literature Online

Writing Models Have students access the Web site for an additional and interactive Writing Workshop-based student model.

Differentiated Instruction

Using Transitions Have students write the following transitional words and phrases in their Learner's Notebook. Encourage students to use the words frequently to combine ideas and show shifts in time. Tell them to review their work and add transitional words where needed.

After/Afterwards
Before/Beforehand
In the morning/afternoon
Lastly
Later/Later that day/week/month
Next
Soon
Then

EL **BL** **OL**

Objectives

- Write stories to entertain
- Write using the writing process
- Edit writing for Standard English grammar, usage, and mechanics
- Correctly use paragraphing
- Write compound and complex sentences

Teach

W Writing

Presentation Ask: Why do you think readers will take your work more seriously if you present it neatly? *(Possible response: If I put more time into my presentation, it shows readers that I care about what I wrote.)* OL

Applying Good Writing Traits

Presentation

The way you present, or share, the final version of your writing makes a difference. Your ideas and writing could be fantastic, but if your presentation is poor, few people will want to read your writing.

What Is Presentation?

Presentation is the way words and design elements such as titles and illustrations look on a page. When you are making notes or jotting down ideas, it does not matter much what your writing looks like. It's just for you at that point. But when you are preparing any final assignment, you want to make it look polished and professional.

Why Is Presentation Important in My Writing?

W
- A neat, clean presentation makes your work more inviting.
- Readers will take your writing more seriously if it looks like you put time into the presentation.
- A thoughtful presentation makes your work easy to understand and is more likely to get your ideas across.

How Do I Do It?

- If you write your final folktale by hand, make sure to form the letters clearly and leave the same amount of space between words. If you type your folktale on a computer, make sure to choose a readable font and double-space the lines of text.
- Leave a big enough margin (space) around your writing so that the page does not look sloppy or cramped.
- Include a title and page numbers so that readers can follow your organization.
- If you enjoy drawing, you might include one or more illustrations. You could, instead, use illustrations from other sources. (Look at "We Are All One" and "Aunty Misery" for ideas if you want to illustrate your folktale.)

Write to Learn After you edit your writing, follow the guidelines above to make a clean, neat draft of your folktale.

Analyzing Cartoons
It only takes the guy on the left a quick look to see that his friend's report is better than usual. He knows that good presentation makes any written assignment more inviting.

Additional Support

English Language Coach

Fragments and Run-on Sentences
Remind students that a complete sentence has a subject and a predicate. Write the following sentences on the board and have students tell whether each of them is a complete sentence (S), a fragment (F), or a run-on (R).

1. The boy and his friends looking for wood. (F)
2. The little rabbit jumped high. (S)
3. The grandfather loved his son he loved his grandson, too. (R)

Remind students to use complete sentences in their narratives. BL EL OL

Editing Checklist

For your final copy, read your folktale aloud and use the Editing Checklist to help you spot errors. Use the proofreading symbols in the chart on page R74 to mark needed corrections.

- ☑ Sentences are complete. There are no fragments or run-ons.
- ☑ Compound and complex sentences are correctly punctuated.
- ☑ Spelling and capitalization are correct (Remember that the first word in each line of dialogue should be capitalized).
- ☑ Quotation marks and end punctuation are in the correct places.
- ☑ English conventions are broken only to create a specific effect.

W1

Writing Tip

Spelling Check your writing against a list of commonly confused or misused words. Common mistakes include *their/they're/there, its/it's,* and *your/you're.*

W2

Writing Tip

Punctuation Place a question mark or exclamation point inside quotation marks when it punctuates the quotation and outside when it punctuates the main sentence.

Presenting

Show It Off

You've probably made a lot of changes to your folktale, so now make a clean copy of it. If you're writing by hand, copy your folktale neatly in print or cursive on a separate piece of paper. If you're using a computer, make your changes and corrections and print a clean copy.

Writing Tip

Handwriting The slant of your writing should be consistent, whether you are printing or writing in cursive.

Follow these steps to make a class binder called *Folktales of Our Times.*

1. Make a cover for your story. On a clean sheet of paper, neatly write the name of your folktale in fancy lettering.
2. Add illustrations that represent the action or the theme of your story. You may also cut and paste images from magazines or images downloaded from your computer.
3. If you want, you can also decorate the pages of your story or add pages with designs and images.
4. Three-hole punch your papers and put them all in a binder. You may want to work with your classmates to design a cover for the binder, too.

Active Writing Model

The beginning of the folktale starts right away with the action of the story.

The writer develops Jack's character by showing that he has a wild imagination.

Writer's Model

Sir John J. Rabbit strolled across the park. He had just come from tea with the Queen and the other knights. Well, he hadn't actually been inside the palace. Or seen the Queen. Or drunk a single sip of tea. But, in his imagination, it had been a very nice tea party. He only imagined being a knight too. (To everyone else, he was Jack.) Being "Sir John" was just much more interesting.

Teach

W1 Writing

Editing Ask: What might be the benefit of using an editing checklist? *(It will remind you to look for all the different types of errors.)* OL

W2 Writing

Spelling Ask: What are some other spelling mistakes that may not show up on spell-check? *(Possible responses: hare/hair, hear/here, wear/where.)* Oftentimes, these homophones, which are words that sound the same but have different meanings, will not show up on spell-check. OL

Differentiated Instruction

Revising Dialogue Tell students that good writers know how to create dialogue that sounds like something a real person would say. Explain that we often do not speak how we write, so writing dialogue can be a challenge. How can students create good dialogue? They can read it aloud to themselves or to a friend and then revise anything that sounds "stiff" or out of character. Have students pay special attention to dialogue as they revise their work. OL

Objectives

- Write stories to entertain
- Write using the writing process
- Edit writing for Standard English grammar, usage, and mechanics
- Correctly use paragraphing
- Write compound and complex sentences

Teach

W Writing

Revising Say: Read the Writer's Model and evaluate it, using the following questions:

- Are the characters interesting and believable?
- Is the dialogue interesting?
- Does the story include a theme?
- Is the story told using third-person narration?
- What other details about the characters or plot would I like to know?

Use these questions to evaluate your own work. OL

WRITING WORKSHOP PART 2

Active Writing Model

Writer's Model

As he was about to cross the street, a few leaves blew into his face. "My word!" he said, brushing them away. "Was that a cyclone? How interesting!" Now, Jack had never seen or heard or been in a cyclone. He'd never even been anyplace where there'd ever been a cyclone. It was just such an interesting word.

The writer uses third-person point of view here and throughout the story. The words "me," "my," and "I" appear only in dialogue.

Suddenly, he bumped into someone. It was Duke Lion. (He wasn't a real duke. He had as much royal blood as a turnip has, and his name was Dan D. Lion.)

"Oh, my dear sir," said Jack, "forgive me. The cyclone, you see–"

This dialogue gives clues to Jack's character and lets readers "hear" how he speaks.

"Cyclone? Cyclone! Cyclone!" For such a big, strong beast, Dan tended to be rather nervous. "Where's the cyclone? What shall I do? Where can I hide? How–"

The writer plays with the conventions of writing to create a specific effect. Here and elsewhere, the writer uses an incomplete sentence to show that one character interrupted the other.

"Relax, dear fellow," said Jack. "You look as though you're going to faint. Lie down on the ground."

"The wind might blow me away!"

"Maybe if you held on to that tree..." Jack suggested.

"Are there ants?" asked Dan. "Ants make me jumpy."

Jack thought a bit longer. "Why don't I tie you to the Queen's water fountain?" Jack asked, as he pointed to a taxicab parked in the street.

The setting is vague, but the park, the street, and the taxi let readers know that the story takes place in a city.

Dan was confused, but he was running out of time so he let Jack tie him to the taxi. After being firmly tied to the taxi for a few minutes, however, he grew impatient. "Where's the cyclone? And," he went on, "what is a cyclone?"

Sir John J. Rabbit didn't hear the question. In fact, he barely noticed the now-distant roar of Dan D. Lion. The taxicab had driven away, and the knight was lost in thought. "I wonder when the Queen's enemies will strike next. We knights must protect her."

The theme is stated indirectly, through the events of the folktale.

Additional Support

Differentiated Instruction

Presenting the Stories Tell students there are many options for presenting their stories. Students might like to create a Modern Folktale Web site and post their stories to the site. A volunteer could use input from classmates to create the home page, and each student could design his or her own link. Another option would be for students to videotape themselves telling their stories aloud. The class could compile a videotape of stories to share with their family and friends. If students choose to tell their stories aloud for videotaping, they should be sure to use their voice, facial expressions, and body language to create interest. AS

Listening, Speaking, and Viewing

Storytelling

Storytelling is a very old tradition and a great way to share a tale.

What Is Storytelling?

Storytelling is just what it looks like–telling a story. The term *storyteller* refers to a person who passes down traditional stories or who creates and tells new stories.

Why Is Storytelling Important?

Stories are entertaining, but they can also teach you about yourself, others, and the world. They can help you figure out who you are and who you want to be. And you can learn about others' experiences through stories.

How Do I Tell a Story?

Whether you're spinning a tale you know by heart or telling a story you've written yourself, the following guidelines can help.

- Practice, practice, practice! Learn your story well enough so you don't have to read it word-for-word. Practice in front of a mirror or in front of a friend who can provide feedback.
- Stand or sit with good posture; it helps your voice to carry.
- Look at your listeners. When they return your gaze, you have their attention. Maintain eye contact as you speak. **LSV1**
- Change positions from time to time so that you don't get tense.
- Vary your volume and pacing to fit the story.
- Keep checking your listeners' responses. If they fidget, ask yourself why.
- Change your voice, posture, and gestures to fit your characters.
- Use silence. A well-timed pause is powerful. When your story's action peaks, pause for a beat. Let your listeners feel the suspense.

Share Your Story Tell your folktale to a small group of listeners. Practice your story enough so you can maintain eye contact with your audience. Use the guidelines above to really bring your audience into your story. **LSV2**

When you're finished, ask the listeners to comment, using these questions as guides:

- Which of my techniques were especially effective?
- What is one change that might improve my storytelling?

Analyzing Cartoons
Before TVs, CDs, DVDs, and video games, storytelling was what entertainment was all about. Today, storytelling links us to other places, people, and events–past and present, far and near. What? You've never heard a story–or told one?

Differentiated Instruction

Using Your Body to Tell a Story
Good oral storytellers use their bodies as well as their voices to tell a story. Have students practice telling their story in front of a mirror. Tell them to pay attention to whether their facial expressions and body language match the story. For example, they might leap out of their seat to show excitement or pace around the room to show nervousness. Students can also use expressions and gestures to differentiate between different characters. For example, they might depict a large animal by moving around slowly with their arms spread wide and a small animal by moving quickly. **AS**

Teach

LSV1 Speaking

Eye Contact Say: Why is it important to make eye contact with your audience while you're telling a story? *(Possible responses: You're making contact with them to keep them interested. Your story will be more interesting if your audience can see your facial expressions and sense your own interest in the story.)* If you look down at your paper while you read, you may not project your voice well enough, and your audience may not hear your story. Read your story to yourself several times until you can tell it mostly from memory. **OL**

LSV2 Speaking

Note Cards Say: If you have a hard time remembering all the details of your story, you can create 5" by 7" note cards. On each note card, write one or two main details to help you remember characters, plot, dialogue, and sequence of events. **AS**

Objectives
- Write stories to entertain
- Write using the writing process
- Edit writing for Standard English grammar, usage, and mechanics
- Correctly use paragraphing
- Write compound and complex sentences
- Show action with movement, gestures, and expressions
- Use effective eye contact and posture
- Ask for feedback from the audience

Skill Lesson: Analyzing

Objectives covered in this workshop:
- Analyze texts using various reasoning skills

Teaching Students to Analyzing

Why Is It Important?

- Analysis helps readers understand how text works, including authors' choices of words to create mood or settings, of how characters respond to other characters and events, etc.
- Analytic skills are essential to critical reading – to determining an author's purpose for writing and what the author hopes the reader will believe after reading the work.
- Analysis of texts can help make readers better writers

How to Help Students Get It

- By reminding students that stories can mean different things to different readers, teachers help them develop an interest in exploring different perspectives on the story and learn that there is no one "right" meaning to a text
- Emphasize that the author and reader work together to make meaning and that analyzing the author's choices increases appreciation of the writers' skills
- Encourage students to read a text from different perspectives to show how beliefs can influence the meaning of a text
- Remind students that it is crucial to consider who the author is and why they have written the text, and that this is especially important when reading information that has been unfiltered by anyone beyond the writer, such as blogs and other Internet sites.

Reading to Answer The Big Question

Voices-and Stories-from the Past

This informational article from TIME describes the remarkable Library of Congress collection of audio recordings of former slaves. These stories will help students learn more about life was like for enslaved people in America.

Aunty Misery

In this folktale, the neighborhood children harass Aunty Misery and steal fruit from her trees until a sorcerer grants her a wish. But when Death comes for a visit, Aunty Misery uses her wits to outsmart him too. Students will learn that this entertaining tale reveals that they can always count on two things in life: misery and death.

Workshop Resources

Pacing (Days) Standard	Block	Lesson	Student Materials	Teacher Resources
1		Key Skill Lesson: Analyzing	Key Reading Skills Practice English Language Coach	Bellringer Options Transparencies Read Aloud, Think Aloud Transparencies Presentation Plus!
2		"Voices- and Stories- from the Past"	Literary Analysis Transparencies Glencoe Online Selection Vocabulary Development Academic Vocabulary Development English Language Coach Active Reading Graphic Organizer Literary Analysis StudentWorks Plus Online Student Edition Literature Classics Selection and Unit Assessments	Literary and Text Analysis Transparencies Puzzlemaker Skill Level Up! BookLink 3 Assessment by Learning Objective (Diagnostic and Formative) Interactive Tutor Self-Assessment TeacherWorks Plus
2		Aunt Misery	Glencoe Online Selection Vocabulary Development Academic Vocabulary Development English Language Coach Active Reading Graphic Organizer Literary Analysis StudentWorks Plus Online Student Edition Literature Classics Selection and Unit Assessments	Literary and Text Analysis Transparencies Puzzlemaker Skill Level Up! BookLink 3 Assessment by Learning Objective (Diagnostic and Formative) Interactive Tutor Self-Assessment TeacherWorks Plus

Keys for Unit Resource

- Blackline Master
- Workbook
- Supplemental Text
- CD-ROM
- DVD
- Transparency
- Web-based
- Fast Files

Level Appropriate Code

AS = Activities for all students
AL = Activities for students working above grade level
OL = Activities for students working at grade level
BL = Activities for students working below grade level
EL = Activities for English language learners

Focus

BELLRINGER Options

- Selection Focus Transparency
- Daily Language Practice Transparency

Focus Activity Say: What might be some benefits of telling another person about painful experiences in your life? *(Possible answers: You might get sympathy; the other person might have experienced something similar; you won't be alone in your pain.)*

Teach

R Reading Skill

Analyzing Ask: What are some questions you might ask to analyze characters, plot, and an informational essay? *(Possible responses: **Characters:** Why did the character do that? What did the character say? **Plot:** What is the conflict? What happened first, second, third, etc.? How was the conflict resolved? **Informational essay:** What are the main ideas of this essay? What details support these main ideas?)* Write these questions in your Learner's Notebook and use them to help you analyze the stories in this workshop. AS

READING WORKSHOP 4

Skills Focus

You will practice using these skills when you read the following selections:

- "Voices—and Stories—from the Past," p. 734
- "Aunty Misery," p. 742

Reading

- Analyzing

Literature

- Recognizing and understanding dialect
- Understanding what dialect contributes to a nonfiction selection

Vocabulary

- Distinguishing between literal and metaphoric meanings
- Academic Vocabulary: *analyzing*

Writing/Grammar

- Identifying and correcting run-on sentences

Objectives (pp. 730–731)
Reading Analyze text

Skill Lesson

Analyzing

Learn It!

What Is It? Analyzing is looking at separate parts of a thing so that you can better understand the whole thing. When you read, you analyze the different parts of a selection in order to understand the whole selection. For example, to analyze

R
- characters, think about what they think, do, and say
- plot, think about the problem or conflict, the events, the climax, and the resolution
- an informational essay, think about main ideas and supporting details

Analyzing Art
This man looks deep in thought. He may be analyzing a problem. When you analyze something, you look at its separate parts to help you understand the entire thing.

Academic Vocabulary

analyzing (AN uh ly zing) *n.* the act of taking something apart to examine the separate pieces

Additional Support

Reading in the Real World

Citizenship Many police departments have a Victim Services department that may include a Crisis Response Team of professionals and volunteers who help people through difficult experiences. Invite a member of a Victim Services department to the classroom to talk about how he or she helps people through a crisis, such as a bad car accident. Have students focus on finding out how talking about a difficult situation can help people through a hard time. AS

Why Is It Important? Analyzing helps you look carefully at a piece of writing. When you analyze a selection, you'll learn the author's purpose for writing. You'll figure out what a character is really like. Analyzing can also help you understand characters' actions.

R1

How Do I Do It? Think about what the author says through characters, setting, and plot, particularly when analyzing fiction. Also look at the characters' values, and the author's style to figure out the story's theme. To analyze informational text, look at the main ideas and how the piece is organized.

R2

Literature Online

Study Central Visit www.glencoe.com and click on Study Central to review analyzing.

Below are points from a fictional story.

- Crystal, Sara, and May are sisters.
- They each have different interests and groups of friends. Crystal loves theater, Sara is a cheerleader, and May is in the National Honor Society.
- Crystal is falsely accused of cheating on a test. The PTA wants to make an example of her, although she did nothing wrong.
- Sara and May rally around their sister. Three very different groups of teenagers come together to protest unfair treatment.

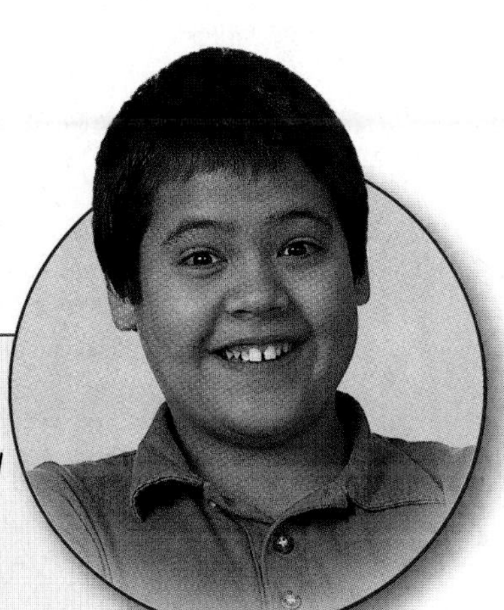

Three different sisters—what kind of girls are they? Crystal has to be smart to learn all those lines, so why would she cheat? At least her sisters believe her. They all must be pretty popular to be able to get all their friends to protest for Crystal. I guess the main thing is even though they're different, they're still sisters.

Practice It!

Look back at a story or article you have already read from this book. Choose a paragraph or two. Look at the characters' actions and what they say and do in certain situations. Decide what the author may want you to understand.

Use It!

As you read, remember how you examined parts of other selections in order to get a better understanding of the whole work.

Teach

Literature Online

Study Central Have students access the Web site to review analyzing and to complete a related activity.

R1 Reading Skill

Analyzing Ask: What are some benefits of analyzing a selection? *(Possible responses: It helps you look carefully at a selection; you learn the author's purpose; you learn about a character and his or her motivations; you learn about the plot and theme.)* **AS**

R2 Reading Skill

Analyzing Ask: According to the "How Do I Do It?" section, how do you analyze informational text? *(You look at the main ideas and how the piece is organized.)* **BL** Why might it be helpful to look at the main idea sentences when you're analyzing nonfiction? *(Possible response: You can find out the main points the author is trying to make.)* **OL**

Resources for page 731

- Use Reading Skills Transparency in *Read Aloud, Think Aloud,* Unit 6, to help students practice analyzing.

Reading Fluency

Reading Aloud Have students improve their reading fluency by taking turns reading aloud one or both of these selections with a partner. Encourage students to focus on reading smoothly, using punctuation and content as a guide for pausing or stopping. Suggest partners provide each other with constructive criticism on tone, pitch, volume, and pace. **EL** **BL**

Objectives

- Analyze text
- Improve fluency by reading aloud

Teach

More About the Author

Kathryn Satterfield loved English and history in school. She has used both of these subjects in her career as a writer, composing a biography of Ben Franklin and conducting interviews about history for *TIME for Kids.*

V Vocabulary

Sentences After students have written their sentences, tell them to rewrite the sentences, and, this time, insert a blank where each vocabulary word should be. Then have students read their sentences to the class and ask volunteers to fill in each blank with the correct vocabulary word. AS

Before You Read

Voices—and Stories—from the Past

Meet the Author

Kathryn Satterfield is the editor of *Time for Kids.* She shares stories because she likes "the idea of being able to reach out to a lot of people at once."

Literature Online

Author Search For more about Kathryn Satterfield, go to www.glencoe.com.

Objectives (pp. 732–737)
Reading Analyze text • Make connections from text to self
Literature Identify literary elements: dialect
Vocabulary Distinguish literal from metaphoric meanings

Vocabulary Preview

emancipation (ih man suh PAY shun) *n.* the act of freeing or being freed, as from slavery **(p. 734)** *Enslaved people dreamed of emancipation and a new life.*

contemporary (KUN tem puh rair ee) *adj.* living now; of the present time **(p. 736)** *The American Memory Web site is a great resource for contemporary Americans.*

illuminate (ih LOO muh nayt) *v.* to light up; make clear **(p. 736)** *The stories on the Web site illuminate the life of slavery.*

Write to Learn For each vocabulary word, write a sentence using the word correctly. V

English Language Coach

Literal and Metaphoric Word Meanings A **metaphor** is a way of describing something by saying it is something else. The two things are actually very different, but they are similar in some way. For example, "Rex is a bear of a man" is a metaphor. It uses the word *bear* to suggest that Rex is big and powerful.

Most words started out with just one meaning and gradually developed more. Originally, a *rat* was only an animal. It came to also have the meaning "one who is disloyal" because it was so often used metaphorically to mean this.

Here is a word you will read in "Voices—and Stories—from the Past."

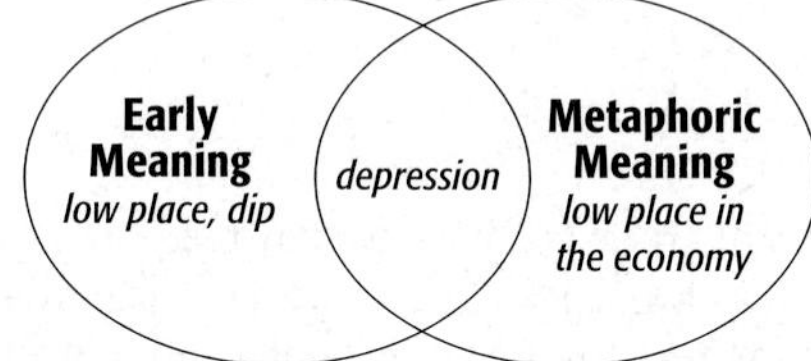

Partner Talk The underlined words below use meanings that developed metaphorically over time. Work with a partner to decide what each word probably means.

1. What he said was full of **poisonous** lies.
2. Her response to my question was **icy**.

Additional Support

Author Search To expand students' appreciation of Kathryn Satterfield, have them access the Web site for additional information and resources.

English Language Coach

Literal vs. Metaphoric Word Meanings Give students the following tips for telling the difference between literal and metaphoric meanings:

1. Use a dictionary to look for a word's literal meaning.
2. Use context clues to decide if the meaning is literal. Try replacing the word with its literal definition. Does the sentence still make sense?
3. If the meaning is not literal, look in the dictionary for a metaphoric meaning of the word.

Have students work with a partner to complete the Partner Talk exercise on page 732. EL

Skills Preview

Key Reading Skill: Analyzing

Before you read "Voices—and Stories—from the Past," think about the purpose of the parts of an informational article:

- What are the main ideas in the introduction, body, and conclusion?
- What information do the headings provide?

Write to Learn Use your Learner's Notebook to jot down what you already know about the parts of informational articles. Keep your ideas in mind as you read the selection.

Key Literary Element: Dialect

Dialect is the language spoken in one area or by one group of people. When we read dialect, it is different from words we usually see in print. Words are spelled differently—they are spelled according to how the speaker pronounces them. The grammar is usually in non-standard English. Some forms of dialect even have their own vocabulary. Some of the quotations you read in "Voices—and Stories—from the Past" are written in the dialects that they were spoken in. **L**

Use this tip to understand and appreciate dialect:

- Try to hear each speaker.
  How is the voice different from your own?

List-Group-Label Think of the different regions of the United States and try to list the dialects. Do you have cousins in the South? Do they sound different from you? What about a friend from the East Coast? As a class, share your examples. Group the examples and label them with the names of places or groups of speakers.

Interactive Literary Elements Handbook
To review or learn more about the literary elements, go to www.glencoe.com.

Get Ready to Read

Connect to the Reading

Reflect on things you have learned about slavery through books and television. History doesn't capture what slavery was *really* like—only those who were there can truly tell the story. How would you feel to be enslaved? How would it feel to taste freedom? **R**

List Ideas With a small group, predict what you may hear in the voices and words of former enslaved Americans.

Build Background

This article is about a remarkable collection of voices telling stories of what it was like to live in slavery.

- The Library of Congress is our national library. It contains the history of the United States in many forms of media.
- Finding the important pieces of African American history can sometimes be difficult. Often, museums and archives in the past did not think this history was important.
- The people who conducted these interviews tried to record the spoken dialect of the formerly enslaved people as closely as possible.

Set Purposes for Reading

BIG Question Read "Voices—and Stories—from the Past" to learn what life was like for some enslaved persons in America.

Set Your Own Purpose What would you like to learn from the selection to help you answer the Big Question? Write your own purpose on the "Voices—and Stories—from the Past" page of Foldable 6.

Keep Moving

Use these skills as you read the following selection.

Teach

L Literary Element

Dialect Ask: How might reading a new dialect aloud help you understand it? *(Possible response: Dialect is spelled as it is pronounced, so reading it aloud will help you guess what words mean.)* **AL**

R Reading Skill

Review Connecting Say: Imagine what it would be like to tell your story after years of enslavement. What benefits might you get from telling your story? *(Possible response: You could tell the bad things that happened in the hopes that they'd never happen to another person.)* **OL**

Literature Online

Interactive Literary Elements Handbook Have students access the Web site to improve their understanding of dialect.

CheckPoint

Use the CheckPoint questions provided on Presentation Plus! to check for analyzing skills and to build background. These questions can be used with interactive response keypads for immediate student feedback.

Literature Focus Lesson

Nonfiction Remind students that nonfiction selections usually include the following elements:

- Main ideas are supported by details.
- Facts, opinions, and anecdotes may be included.
- The author generally tries to present an unbiased view of his or her subject.
- The text uses chronological order, subject order, or order of importance to present the details.
- The writer might quote experts to support certain facts or opinions.

Have students determine which elements of nonfiction articles are included in "Voices—and Stories—from the Past." **OL**

Objectives

- Analyze text
- Make connections from text to self
- Identify literary elements: dialect
- Distinguish literal from metaphoric meanings

Teach

Viewing the Photo

Ask: What does this photograph show? *(It shows a woman from history, possibly a slave.)* **BL** Why is it an appropriate photo for this article? *(Possible response: Showing a woman from the time is appropriate for an article about real, everyday people who lived during hard times and told their stories afterwards.)* **AL**

R Reading Skill

Review Determining the Main Idea **Ask:** What are the main ideas expressed on this page? *(Possible response: The Civil War freed many slaves, who all had a story to tell. The Library of Congress has released the interviews of formerly enslaved African Americans. The stories are told 60 years after their freedom.)* **OL**

Readability Scores
Dale-Chall: 7.9
DRP: 59
Lexile: 1090

READING WORKSHOP 4

TIME

VOICES—and Stories—from the PAST

History, as told by the people who lived it

Library of Congress

SARAH ASHLEY was 93 when she recalled her days on a Texas plantation.

By KATHRYN SATTERFIELD

The American Civil War (1861–1865) freed some 4 million people from slavery. Every one of these people had a story to tell about their lives. Now, two Slave Narratives collections at the Library of Congress give people around the world a chance to hear and read some of those stories. **1**

In January 2004, the Library of Congress released a collection of audio recordings, *Voices from the Days of Slavery.* For the first time, 23 recordings of interviews with formerly enslaved African Americans—as told in their own voices—can be heard online at the Library of Congress's American Memory website. **R**

Speaking at least 60 years after their **emancipation**, the African American storytellers discuss their experiences as enslaved people. They also tell about their lives as free men and women. Written transcripts are provided to help listeners follow along.

Visitors to the site can hear people like Charlie Smith recall coming from Africa as an enslaved boy and working on a ranch in Texas.

1 Reviewing Skills

Predicting Quickly skim the headings in this article. What type of information do you predict you will read about the formerly enslaved people?

Vocabulary

emancipation (ih man suh PAY shun) *n.* the act of freeing or being freed, as from slavery

Additional Support

Differentiated Instruction

Reading Circle Have students form reading circles, and have each student read aloud one of the excerpts from the stories of the freed slaves. After reading each excerpt, have students stop to analyze it. Encourage students to tell

- what they learned about the person
- what difficulties the person suffered
- what examples of dialect the person used

Have students share their overall opinion of the stories with the group. How was it different to learn about slavery from these people than to learn about it from a regular history book? **EL** **OL**

READING WORKSHOP 4

Library of Congress

JAMES GREEN, shown here in 1937, told of being bought for $800.

The audio recordings on the website were made between 1932 and 1975. Language and folklore experts and others working to preserve American history conducted the interviews in nine southern states.

Isom Moseley was just a boy at the time of emancipation, but he recalls that things were slow to change. "It was a year before the folks knowed they was free," he says.

Michael Taft, the head of the library's archive[1] of folk culture, says the recordings help reveal something that written stories cannot. "The power of hearing someone speak is so much greater than reading something from the page," Taft says. "It's how something is said—the dialect, the low pitches, the pauses—that helps tell the story." 2 R1

The Narratives in Print

If you want to *read* stories of formerly enslaved African Americans, the Library of Congress's American Memory website also offers print versions of their stories. During the Great **Depression** of the 1930s, the federal government hired out-of-work writers to interview and record the experiences and opinions of everyday people. As part of this project, thousands of formerly enslaved people in 17 states were interviewed. 3 R2

One result of these oral history interviews is the *Born in Slavery* collection, a set of 2,300 autobiographical documents. The interviewers—most of whom were white—made an effort to capture in writing the speech patterns of the men and women with whom they spoke.

1. An ***archive*** (AR kyv) is a collection of items kept safe for the future in a special place.

2 Key Reading Skill

Analyzing Here, Taft analyzes the things that make hearing someone speak powerful. What advantages are there to reading someone's words instead of hearing them?

3 English Language Coach

Literal and Metaphoric Word Meanings Has the writer used the early meaning of **depression** here or the metaphoric meaning that developed over time? How do you know?

Library of Congress

JENNY PROCTOR began working in the cotton fields when she was 10. She was 87 when she shared her memories of slavery.

Teach

R1 Reading Skill

Review Summarizing Ask: According to Michael Taft, how are oral recordings better than written stories? *(They are more powerful because the dialect, pitches, and pauses all help tell the story.)* Do you agree with Taft? Why or why not? *(Possible response: I agree. I think that hearing people's voices would make them seem more real and their stories more vivid.)* **OL**

R2 Reading Skill

Analyzing Ask: What is the main idea of The Narratives in Print portion of the article? *(Thousands of formerly enslaved people were interviewed during the Great Depression. The* Born in Slavery *collection has 2,300 autobiographical documents that try to capture the speech patterns of the interviewees.)* **OL** What do you think the author's purpose was for including this information in the article? *(Possible response: To make more people interested in the oral history interviews.)* **AL**

Differentiated Instruction

Learning About a Life Have advanced learners visit the Library of Congress's Web site "Born in Slavery: Slave Narratives from the Federal Writer's Project" and choose one person to learn more about. Students should read the person's narrative and then write a synopsis of the person's life and experiences. Students can share what they learn in a written presentation, in an oral presentation, or on a poster. Encourage students to include a portion of the person's narrative and a photograph, if possible, in their presentation. **AL**

Objectives
- Make predictions
- Analyze nonfiction
- Analyze a photograph
- Summarize
- Read and understand dialect

Teach

Viewing the Photo

Ask: Do you think this photo was a good choice for this article? Explain your answer. *(Possible response: Yes, this photograph shows me a real person who was interviewed for the Slave Narratives.)* **AS**

L Literary Element

Dialect Say: Point out a sentence written in dialect on pages 736–737. *(Possible response: **Dialect:** "Dey say we git smarter den day was if we learn anything, but we slips around and gits hold of dat Webster's old blue-back speller, and we hides it 'til way in de night, and den we lights a little pine torch . . . and studies dat spellin' book.)* **OL** Then, restate the sentence in standard English. *(Possible response: **Standard English:** They said we would get smarter than they were if we learned anything, but we snuck around and got hold of the Webster's old blue-back speller, and we hid it until late at night, and then we lit a little pine torch . . . and studied that spelling book.)* **OL**

These interviews gave formerly enslaved African Americans a chance to share their memories of life in bondage. For **contemporary** Americans, the audio and print versions of the Slave Narratives provide historical accounts of what it was like to be enslaved in the United States. The narratives **reflect** the time and place at which they were created. They **illuminate** a world that is important for all Americans to explore. Following are excerpts from the Slave Narratives collections. **4**

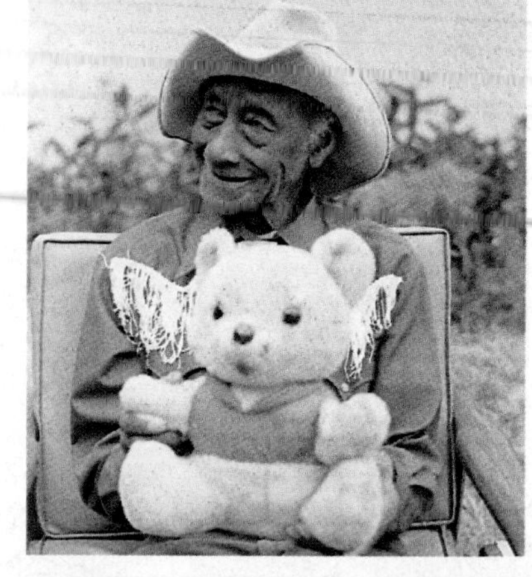

Courtesy Polk County Democrat

CHARLIE SMITH spoke to interviewers in 1975.

Masters, the Big House, and Learning

Enslaved people started working at a very early age: many began their labors in the master's house, where they served as playmates for white children. Despite this closeness, African American and white children could not attend school together. In fact, in most states it was against the law for enslaved people to be educated.

"My earliest recollection is the day my old boss presented me to his son, Joe, as his property. I was about 5 years old, and my new master was only 2. . . . No, sir, I never went into books. I used to handle a big dictionary three times a day, but it was only to put it on a chair so my young master could sit up higher at the table. I never went to school. I learned to talk pretty good by associating with my masters in their big house."

—**Martin Jackson, Texas**

"I remember quite well how those poor little children used to have to eat. They were fed in boxes and troughs, under the house. They were fed cornmeal mush and beans. When this was poured into their box they would gather around it the same as we see pigs, horses, and cattle gather around troughs today."

—**Octavia George, Oklahoma**

"None of us was 'lowed [allowed] to see a book or try to learn. Dey say we git smarter den dey was if we learn anything, but we slips around and gits hold of dat Webster's **L**

4 English Language Coach

Literal and Metaphoric Word Meanings Do you think **reflect** is being used with its earliest meaning, here, or one that developed metaphorically? Why?

Vocabulary

contemporary (KUN tem puh rair ee) *adj.* living now; of the present time

illuminate (ih LOO muh nayt) *v.* to light up; make clear

Additional Support

Literature Focus Lesson

Character Motivation You can tell a lot about a person's character from how he or she acts. A person's choices for acting are called his or her motivations. Have students reread the excerpt of the interview with Jenny Proctor from Texas (pp. 736–737). What can students infer about Jenny Proctor and her motivations from the story she tells? *(Possible responses: You can tell she was motivated by a desire to learn despite the fact that her owner didn't want her to. She was so determined that she sneaked a spelling book and studied it late at night.)* **OL**

old blue-back speller, and we hides it 'til way in de night, and den we lights a little pine torch . . . and studies dat spellin' book. We learn it too."

—**Jenny Proctor, Texas**

Work

By age 12, most children worked in the fields, where they grew crops like tobacco, rice, and cotton. Enslaved people generally worked six days a week, from sunrise to sunset.

"Bells and horn! Bells for dis, and horns for dat! All we knowed was go and come by de bells and horns! Old ram horn blow to send us all to de field. We all line up, about 75 field [workers], and go by de tool shed and git our hoes, or maybe go hitch up de mules to de plows."

—**Charley Williams, Arkansas**

"I used to have to pick cotton, and sometime I pick 300 pound and tote it a mile to de cotton house. Some pick 300 to 800 pound cotton and have to tote de bag de whole mile to de gin[2]. Iffen dey didn't do dey work, dey git whip till dey have blister on 'em. . . . I never git whip, 'cause I allus git my 300 pound." 5

—**Sarah Ashley, Texas**

5 Key Literary Element

L **Dialect** This page includes good examples of dialect. Which words are different from words you might write or say?

Slave Family Life

Approximately one in three enslaved families was split apart. One-fifth of all enslaved children were separated from their parents.

"I never knowed my age till after de war . . . and then marster gits out a big book, and it shows I's 25 year old. It shows I's 12 when I is bought and $800 is paid for me. . . . My mammy was owned by John Williams in Petersburg, in Virginia, and I come born to her on dat plantation. . . . Then, one day along come a Friday, and that a unlucky star day, and I playin' round de house, and Marster Williams come up and say, 'Delis will you 'low Jim walk down de street with me?' My mammy say, 'All right, Jim, you be a good boy,' and dat de las' time I ever heard her speak, or ever see her." 6

—**James Green, Texas**

—Updated 2005, from *TIME for Kids*, February 6, 2004

6 BIG Question

BQ Why is it important that the stories of formerly enslaved people be shared? Write your answer on the "Voices—and Stories—from the Past" page of Foldable 6. Your response will help you complete the Unit Challenge later.

2. The word ***gin*** (jin) refers to the cotton gin, a machine that removes sticky seeds from cotton. The invention of the cotton gin led to a great increase in the number of enslaved persons in America because cotton then became highly profitable.

L Literary Element

Dialect Ask: How might these stories have been different if the writers hadn't been so careful to capture the people's dialect? *(Possible response: The stories might not have been so powerful because they wouldn't have been told in the people's true voice.)* **AL**

Ask: What reason for telling stories did you learn from reading this selection? *(Possible response: I learned that stories can be told to keep the past alive and to help people understand a terrible part of our country's history so it is never repeated.)* **AS**

Assess

CheckPoint

Use the CheckPoint questions provided on Presentation Plus! to check for comprehension of the selection. These questions can be used with interactive response keypads for immediate student feedback.

Reading in the Real World

College Have students conduct online research to learn more about the Emancipation Proclamation. Students can use the following research questions as a guide:

- What did the Emancipation Proclamation do?
- Who issued it?
- How did it change life for enslaved people in this country?
- What were its limitations?

Have students present their findings to the class in a brief oral presentation. **OL**

Objectives
- Analyze nonfiction
- Describe character motivation
- Read and understand dialect
- Distinguish literal from metaphoric meanings

Assess

Resources for page 738

- Selection Quick Check
- Selection and Unit Assessment
- ExamView Assessment Suite
- Interactive Tutor: Self-Assessment

Students can respond to the *After You Read* items in their Learner's Notebook or on a separate sheet of paper.

Answering the BIG Question

1. Former slaves might have wanted to tell people how bad their lives were so that there would never be slavery again.
2. Interviewers who were working for the federal government collected these stories for the Library of Congress and its Web site.
3. The work was very hard and often done in the cotton fields, and children started working at about age 12. Many families were split up.

Critical Thinking

4. Possible response: *Voices from the Days of Slavery* is a set of audio recordings. *Born in Slavery* is a print collection. Both tell the stories of people who were enslaved.
5. Possible response: Many formerly enslaved people might have died already, so we couldn't hear their stories.

After You Read

Voices—and Stories—from the Past

Objectives (pp. 738–739)
Reading Analyze text
Literature Identify literary elements: dialect
Vocabulary Distinguish literal from metaphoric meanings
Writing Create a graphic organizer
Grammar Identify run-on sentences

Answering the BIG Question

1. Why do you think these people wanted to share their stories? Explain your answers with details from the article.
2. **Recall** Who conducted these interviews?
   TIP **Right There**
3. **Summarize** In two or three sentences, describe the work and family life of enslaved people. Base your summary on facts from this article.
   TIP **Author and Me**

Critical Thinking

4. **Compare and Contrast** The Library of Congress released two collections: *Voices from the Days of Slavery* and *Born in Slavery.* List three ways in which these two collections are alike and/or different.
   TIP **Think and Search**
5. **Evaluate** Slavery officially ended in 1863. What do you think would have happened if we had waited any longer to interview former slaves?
   TIP **On My Own**

Write About Your Reading

Make a cluster diagram, spider web, or other graphic organizer to show the main parts of this article and what you learned about slavery from reading the article.

Your organizer should show facts about how enslaved people lived. Include details about topics such as these:

- Plantation work
- Education
- Family life and life on the plantation

Share your work with a partner. Talk about the best ways to combine your work into one organizer that shows the most important ideas.

Write About Your Reading

Possible response:

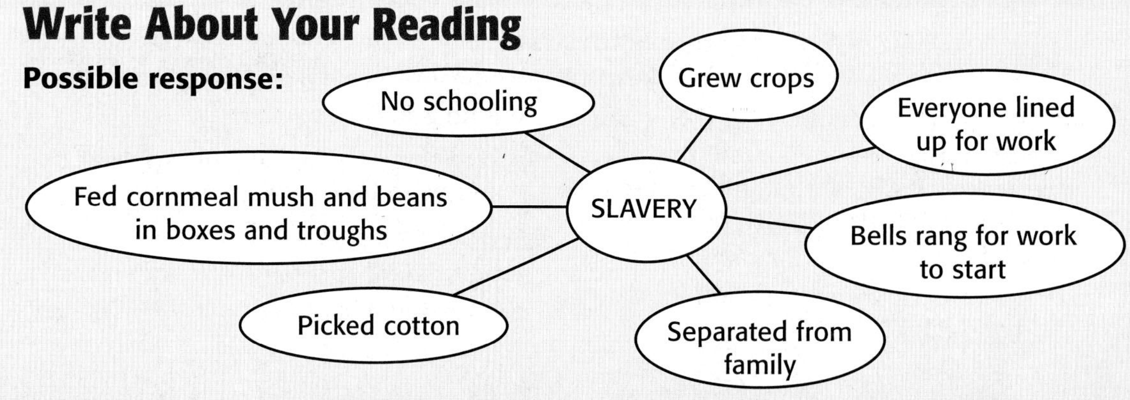

Skills Review

Key Reading Skill: Analyzing

6. You did some reading and thinking before you read "Voices—and Stories—from the Past." Decide how helpful each activity listed below was to you by rating it as *very helpful, helpful*, or *not helpful*. Explain why. Look back at page 733 if you need help recalling the activity.
   - Reviewing the parts of an informational article
   - Reading the facts in **Build Background**
   - Setting a purpose for your reading

Key Literary Element: Dialect

7. Write one example of dialect in this article.
8. How does dialect help you experience the voices from the past?

Reviewing Skills: Predicting

9. Explain what you were able to correctly predict about what you read in this selection by using the title, illustrations, or headings.

Vocabulary Check

For 10–12, copy the vocabulary words. After each word, add its correct meaning.

10. emancipation current or present
11. contemporary to shed light on
12. illuminate the act of granting freedom

13. **Academic Vocabulary** What do you think it was like for a person to eat from a feeding trough or not to be able to learn to read? Analyze and explain.
14. **English Language Coach** Charley Williams describes the bells and horns that sent workers to their plows. Given what you know about plows and the work involved in using them, what do you think *plow* means in this statement: "I can't go to bed until I **plow** through this homework"?

Grammar Link: Run-on Sentences

Do not run two or more sentences together. This mistake is called a run-on sentence.

Run-on: Randi plays her guitar it relaxes her.

It's also incorrect to separate sentences by putting just a comma between them.

Wrong: Randi plays her guitar, it relaxes her.

To fix a run-on sentence, separate the sentences with a period. Or put a comma and a coordinating conjunction between the run-together sentences.

Period: Randi plays her guitar. It relaxes her.

(,) and coordinating conjunction: Randi plays her guitar, and it relaxes her.

You can also fix a run-on sentence by adding a subordinating conjunction to one of the clauses.

Subordinating conjunction: Randi plays her guitar because it relaxes her.

Grammar Practice

On another piece of paper, copy and fix the following run-on sentence two different ways.

It takes practice to play well Randi doesn't mind.

Literature Online

Web Activities For eFlashcards, Selection Quick Checks, and other Web activities, go to www.glencoe.com.

Skills Review

Key Reading Skill: Analyzing

6. Responses will vary.
   - It was very helpful because it reminded me to look for main ideas.
   - It was helpful to read the facts before I read the article.
   - It was helpful to find out more about what it was like to be an enslaved person.

Key Literary Element: Dialect

7. Responses will vary.
8. Possible response: It helps the people seem more real because it's how they actually talked.

Reviewing Skills: Predicting

9. Possible response: I would hear stories about the past.

Vocabulary Check

10. the act of granting freedom
11. current or present
12. to shed light on
13. Possible response: It would have been a terrible way to be treated.
14. Possible response: until I finish all this difficult homework

Close

Have students explain what they learned from reading this story to help them answer the the Big Question.

Grammar Link: Run-on Sentences

Grammar Practice

Possible responses:

1. It takes practice to play well. Randi doesn't mind.
2. It takes practice to play well, but Randi doesn't mind.

Literature Online

Web Activities Have students access the Web site for interactive activities that will help them assess their understanding of the selection.

Teach

More About the Author

Judith Ortiz Cofer was deeply influenced by the women storytellers in her family. She describes how her mother, who had little formal education, could walk into a room, say "I have a story to tell," and gain the attention of everyone present. Cofer has said that "the women in my family were wonderful storytellers who infected me at a very early age with the desire to tell stories." Cofer's writing, such as her retelling of "Aunty Misery," a Puerto Rican tale, reflects the split between her two childhood homes, Puerto Rico and the United States.

EL Language Coach

Metaphoric Word Meanings Challenge students to find out how these words developed. They should find the original metaphor and how it was used. Have them share their findings with the class. AL

Before You Read Aunty Misery

Judith Ortiz Cofer

Meet the Author

Judith Ortiz Cofer was born in Puerto Rico in 1952. Today, she lives in Georgia, but her close ties to a Spanish-speaking culture show up in "Aunty Misery" and many of her other works. As she says, "I've just brought the island with me." See page R2 of the Author Files for more on Judith Ortiz Cofer.

Author Search For more about Judith Ortiz Cofer, go to www.glencoe.com.

Objectives (pp. 740–745)
Reading Analyze text • Make connections from text to self
Literature Identify literary elements: dialect
Vocabulary Distinguish literal from metaphoric meanings

Vocabulary Preview

sorcerer (SOR sur ur) *n.* a person who practices magic with the help of spirits **(p. 743)** *The sorcerer cast a spell to help Aunty Misery.*

taunt (tawnt) *v.* to make fun of in a mean way **(p. 744)** *Children often stopped to taunt Aunty Misery.*

gnarled (narld) *adj.* rough, twisted, and knotty, as a tree trunk or branches **(p. 744)** *That gnarled tree hadn't grown straight for many years.*

potions (POH shunz) *n.* drinks, especially drinks that are supposed to have magical powers **(p. 745)** *People stopped buying medicines and potions, believing they weren't necessary.*

Write to Learn For each vocabulary word, write a clue, such as "It can describe a tree trunk." Have a partner name the word.

English Language Coach

Literal and Metaphoric Word Meanings A **metaphor** is a comparison between two unlike things that says that one is the other. "The team's catcher was a tank" is a metaphor because the catcher isn't actually a tank; he's just big and strong and hard to overcome, like an army tank.

If a word is used metaphorically for long enough, its metaphoric meaning may become one of its **literal** meanings—an actual meaning found in a dictionary. So if you *plant* your feet, you just put them down firmly. A man with a heart of *gold* does not have metal in his chest. *Pearls* of wisdom are simply valuable bits of knowledge.

If you know one meaning of a word, such as *plant*, you can usually figure out a meaning that developed metaphorically. Or if a word is used metaphorically, such as *tank*, you can usually figure out what is being suggested by its use. As with many other vocabulary skills, you can use what you know to figure out what you don't know.

Partner Talk Each underlined word below has a meaning that developed metaphorically from its original meaning. Work with a partner to decide what is meant by each sentence. EL

1. Isn't that big car a gas **hog**?
2. Give me time to **digest** the idea.
3. The police officer chased the thief and **collared** him.
4. The workers were unhappy that their boss was such a **dinosaur**.

Additional Support

Author Search To expand students' appreciation of Judith Ortiz Cofer, have them access the Web site for additional information and resources.

Literature Focus Lesson

Fable A fable is a kind of folktale in which a brief story is used to teach a lesson about human nature. Some of the most famous fables were written by Aesop, who is thought to have been a slave in ancient Greece. The characters in fables are often animals who speak and act like people. Usually a fable, such as "Aunty Misery," for example, concludes with a clearly stated moral, or lesson. What is the moral, or stated lesson, of "Aunty Misery"? (People can always count on death and misery in the world.) OL

Skills Preview

Reading Skill: Analyzing

Analyzing a story involves looking at the different parts and the way they work together. As you read "Aunty Misery," think about these parts of the story:

- Character: Who is the main character and what kind of person is this character?
- Setting: What do you learn about the setting? Is it very clear and realistic? Is it simple, like a poster or a mural?
- Plot: Does the plot move logically from one event to the next?
- Theme: What seems to be the main message the author wants you to come away with?

Write to Learn Use your Learner's Notebook to jot down what you already know about analyzing stories. Keep your ideas in mind as you read the selection and use this skill.

Key Literary Element: Dialect

When you read a story, you expect all the words to be in English. Sometimes an author will use words from another language in the story, especially if the author is from another country or speaks another language.

Dialect can also be mixing words from two languages, which is something that a native speaker would not do. For example, *La Tia Misery*. *La Tia* is Spanish for "aunt." Native speakers would simply say *La Tia Miseria*, or Aunt Misery. **L**

Use these tips to help you figure out the effect of those words.

- Learn what the words mean.
- Ask yourself: Why does the author put these words and not other words in a different language?
- Relate the words to the characters, the plot, or the theme.
  What do the words tell you about the story?
- Decide what using the words adds to the story.
  How do these words make the story more interesting, true to life, wise, or funny?

Literature Online

Interactive Literary Elements Handbook To review or learn more about the literary elements, go to www.glencoe.com.

Get Ready to Read

Connect to the Reading

What good and bad things can everyone expect to find, or "run into," in life? As you read "Aunty Misery," think about how her problems are like and unlike those of everyone else.

Build Background

This folktale is set in a Spanish-speaking country in the distant past.

- A folktale is a story that has been handed down. This folktale has magical characters and presents some events that could never really happen.
- In folktales, Death is often presented as a character that comes to visit. Naturally, few characters are happy to see him.
- Folktales often include trickster characters. Their cleverness helps them overcome people or things who are stronger or more powerful.

C

Set Purposes for Reading

Read "Aunty Misery" to see how one culture tries to explain suffering and death.

Set Your Own Purpose

What would you like to learn from the selection to help you answer the Big Question? Write your own purpose on the "Aunty Misery" page of Foldable 6.

Keep Moving

Use these skills as you read the following selection.

Teach

L Literary Element

Dialect Ask: What definition of *dialect* is expressed here? *(Dialect is the mixing of words from two languages.)* **BL** Why might Cofer include this type of dialect in a story? *(Possible response: She is telling the story for American readers so she uses mostly English words, but she includes some Spanish words because the story was originally told in Spanish.)* **AL**

C Critical Thinking

Evaluation Say: As you read, take notes on the magical characters and events in the story. Note which events could really happen and which could not. **BL**

CheckPoint

Use the CheckPoint questions provided on Presentation Plus! to check for analyzing skills and to build background. These questions can be used with interactive response keypads for immediate student feedback.

Reading Fluency

Reading Silently Students can improve their fluency by reading along silently as you read the selection aloud. Be sure to vary your pitch to suit the meaning of each passage and to use punctuation to guide pausing. If you choose, you might stop after one or two paragraphs and ask a volunteer from the class to read a paragraph aloud. **EL** **BL**

Objectives

- Analyze text
- Make connections from text to self
- Identify literary elements: dialect
- Distinguish literal from metaphoric meanings

Teach

R Reading Skill

Analyzing **Ask:** Why is the old lady unhappy? *(because the children steal her fruit and yell insults at her)* OL Why might the neighborhood children call her "Aunty Misery"? *(Possible response: because she is unhappy; because she so old; because she is all alone)* AL

C Critical Thinking

Evaluation **Ask:** What events in the second paragraph could really take place? Which event could not? *(A traveler could really stop by and spend the night. He could not really grant a wish.)* BL

Readability Scores
Dale-Chall: 5.2
DRP: 57
Lexile: 1050

READING WORKSHOP 4

Aunty Misery

A Folktale from Puerto Rico

by Judith Ortiz Cofer

This is a story about an old, a very old woman who lived alone in her little hut with no other company than a beautiful pear tree that grew at her door. She spent all her time taking care of this tree. The neighborhood children drove the old woman crazy by stealing her fruit. They would climb her tree, shake its delicate limbs, and run away with armloads of golden pears, yelling insults at *la Tia Miseria*,[1] Aunty Misery, as they called her. 1

One day, a traveler stopped at the old woman's hut and asked her for permission to spend the night under her roof. Aunty Misery saw that he had an honest face and bid the pilgrim come in. She fed him and made a bed for him in front of her hearth. In the morning the stranger told her that he would show his gratitude for her hospitality by granting her one wish.

1. ***La Tia Miseria*** (luh TEE uh mih zuh REE uh)

Practice the Skills

1 Key Reading Skill

Analyzing Think about the main character. Does she have a family? How does she spend her time? Why does the tree mean so much to her? What problem does she have?

Additional Support

Leveled Reading An adapted version of this selection (4th grade readability) is available on page 176 of *Jamestown Literature: An Adapted Reader* for Grade 7.

Literature Focus Lesson

Personification Tell students that personification is a literary element in which an abstract quality, like happiness or hunger, is given human qualities. Personification is frequently used in poetry. Often, a personified quality is capitalized. As they read "Aunty Misery", ask students to name two qualities that are made into humans in this selection. *(misery and death)* OL

READING WORKSHOP 4

Still Life with Skull, 1895–1900, Paul Cezanne, oil on canvas, ©The Barnes Foundation, Merion, Pennsylvania, USA.

"There is only one thing that I desire," said Aunty Misery.

"Ask, and it shall be yours," replied the stranger, who was a sorcerer in disguise.

"I wish that anyone who climbs up my pear tree should not be able to come back down until I permit it." **R**

"Your wish is granted," said the stranger, touching the pear tree as he left Aunty Misery's house. **2**

Vocabulary

sorcerer (SOR cur ur) *n.* a person who practices magic with the help of spirits

Practice the Skills

2 Reviewing Skills

Understanding Cause and Effect What causes the stranger to grant Aunty Misery's wish?

Teach

Viewing the Art

Ask: What do you think the skull in this painting refers to? *(Death)* Do you think this is a good illustration for this story? Explain your answer. *(Possible response: Yes, the story is about misery and death.)* **AL**

R Reading Skill

Analyzing Ask: How does Aunty Misery solve the problem between her and the children? *(She asks the sorcerer to put a spell on the tree so that no one who climbs it can come down without her permission.)* **OL** What do you think of her plan? *(Possible response: It is a clever plan and the children will never bother her again.)* **AL**

Differentiated Instruction

Art This story is full of vivid imagery. Have students choose one image from the story and paint it. They might choose to show Aunty Misery watching the children climb the tree or the untrustworthy visitor at the door of Aunty Misery's house. Have students use different colors in their paintings to express the different characters; for example, they might use black for Death, bright colors for the children, and gray for Aunty Misery. Share students' artwork on a class bulletin board. **AS**

Objectives

- Make connections from self to text
- Analyze story elements
- Illustrate a story

READING WORKSHOP 4

Teach

L Literary Element

Review Character Ask: What does this paragraph tell you about Aunty Misery? *(Possible response: She's crafty, but she is also kind enough to let the children go.)* OL

R Reading Skill

Review Predicting Ask: Based on what you know about Aunty Misery, what do you think she will say or do to Death? *(Responses will vary. Students may predict that she will trick Death.)*

And so it happened that when the children came back to taunt the old woman and to steal her fruit, she stood at her window watching them. Several of them shimmied[2] up the trunk of the pear tree and immediately got **stuck** to it as if with glue. She let them cry and beg her for a long time before she gave the tree permission to let them go on the condition that they never again steal her fruit, or bother her. 3

Time passed and both Aunty Misery and her tree grew bent and gnarled with age. One day another traveler stopped at her door. This one looked untrustworthy to her, so before letting him into her home the old woman asked him what he was doing in her village. He answered her in a voice that was dry and hoarse, as if he had swallowed a desert: "I am Death, and I have come to take you with me."

2. ***Shimmied*** means climbed by using the hands, arms, feet, and legs to pull and push oneself up.

Vocabulary

taunt (tawnt) *v.* to make fun of in a mean way

gnarled (narld) *adj.* rough, twisted, and knotty, as a tree trunk or branches

Practice the Skills

3 English Language Coach

Literal and Metaphoric Word Meanings The original meaning of **stuck** is "fastened to something with a sharp object." How do you suppose the later meanings "unable to move" and "unable to go forward" developed from this?

Additional Support

Reading in the Real World

College Have students work alone, in pairs, or in groups to study the culture of Puerto Rico. Have each student research one of the following:

- the history of the people
- the geography of their homeland
- their religion (and their beliefs about death)
- their art and music
- their food
- their festivals and other celebrations

Have students combine what they have learned and plan a group presentation that includes maps, pictures, and music. EL OL

Thinking fast Aunty Misery said, "All right, but before I go I would like to pluck some pears from my beloved tree to remember how much pleasure it brought me in this life. But I am a very old woman and cannot climb to the tallest branches where the best fruit is. Will you be so kind as to do it for me?"

With a heavy sigh like wind through a tomb, Señor[3] Death climbed the pear tree. Immediately he became stuck to it as if with glue. And no matter how much he cursed and threatened, Aunty Misery would not allow the tree to release Death.

Many years passed and there were no deaths in the world. The people who make their living from death began to protest loudly. The doctors claimed no one bothered to come in for examinations or treatments anymore, because they did not fear dying; the pharmacists' business suffered too because medicines are, like magic **potions**, bought to prevent or postpone the inevitable; priests and undertakers were unhappy with the situation also, for obvious reasons. There were also many old folks tired of life who wanted to pass on to the next world to rest from miseries of this one. **4**

La Tia Miseria was blamed by these people for their troubles, of course. Not wishing to be unfair, the old woman made a deal with her prisoner, Death: if he promised not ever to come for her again, she would give him his freedom. He agreed. And that is why there are two things you can always count on running into in this world: Misery and Death: La miseria y la muerte.[4] **5** **BQ** **L** ❍

3. ***Señor*** (sen YOR) is Spanish for "Mister."
4. ***Y la muerte*** (ee luh MWAIR tay)

Vocabulary

potions (POH shunz) *n.* drinks, especially drinks that are supposed to have magical powers

Practice the Skills

4 Key Literary Element

Dialect If foreign words appear often in a story, that may indicate that it is written in a dialect. A few foreign words can also give the story a foreign feeling. Which do you think is the case here?

5 BIG Question

Death has always been a fear and a fascination for people. Why do you think people have shared this folktale again and again? Write your answer on the "Aunty Misery" page of Foldable 6. Your response will help you complete the Unit Challenge later.

Teach

L Literary Element

Dialect Ask: Why might the writer have chosen to present the message of this story in both Spanish and English? *(Possible response: The story is originally from Puerto Rico, so she might have been honoring its history by using Spanish to present its message.)* **AL**

BQ 

Ask: When might you tell a folktale such as this one? *(Possible response: You might tell it around a campfire. When someone complains about life's misery, you might tell it to show that suffering is inevitable.)* **AL**

Assess

Use the CheckPoint questions provided on Presentation Plus! to check for comprehension of the selection. These questions can be used with interactive response keypads for immediate student feedback.

Differentiated Instruction

Comparing and Contrasting Have students discuss how Death and Aunty Misery are alike and different. Encourage students to use a Venn diagram to compare and contrast these two characters from the story. When students have completed the comparison, have them compare their response with a partner. **AS**

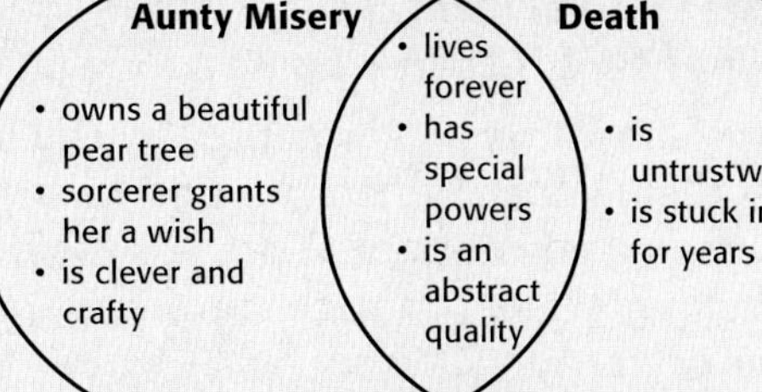

Objectives
- Analyze a story
- Distinguish literal from metaphoric meanings
- Read and understand dialect

Assess

Resources for page 746

- Selection Quick Check
- Selection and Unit Assessment
- ExamView Assessment Suite
- Interactive Tutor: Self-Assessment

Students can respond to the *After You Read* items in their Learner's Notebook or on a separate sheet of paper.

Answering the BIG Question

1. Responses will vary. Students may say they would share it because it is interesting and easy to remember.
2. By means of her wish, she makes them get stuck in the tree, unable to come down until she lets them.
3. The first stranger grants Aunty Misery one wish in return for her kindness to him.

Critical Thinking

4. Students may say that Aunty Misery solves the problem of the children stealing her fruit. She solves the problem of Death's first visit.
5. Possible response: No one is able to die. She makes a deal because she does not want to be unfair.
6. Responses will vary. Students may say the ending is excellent. Aunty Misery escapes death, and that is why there is always misery in life.

After You Read | Aunty Misery

Answering the BIG Question

1. Would you share this story with someone else? Why or why not?
2. **Recall** How does Aunty Misery punish the children who steal her pears?
   TIP **Right There**
3. **Summarize** What happens when the first stranger visits Aunty Misery?
   TIP **Think and Search**

Critical Thinking

4. **Analyze** Aunty Misery is a problem solver. Support this statement with two events from the story.
   TIP **Author and Me**
5. **Infer** What causes Aunty Misery to finally make a deal with death?
   TIP **Author and Me**
6. **Evaluate** Do you think this story has a good ending? Explain.
   TIP **On My Own**

Talk About Your Reading

Literature Groups Folktales like "Aunty Misery" are brief, but they usually have all the elements of a short story. With your group, identify these elements of "Aunty Misery."

- characters—the people in the story
- setting—the time and place
- plot—the events of the story
- moral—a lesson about right and wrong

Write to Learn Think about a fable you might write. On a separate sheet of paper, make notes on the characters, setting, plot, and moral of your own fable.

Objectives (pp. 746–747)
Reading Analyze text
Literature Identify literary elements: dialect
Vocabulary Distinguish literal from metaphoric meanings
Writing Write a fable
Grammar Correct run-on sentences

Talk About Your Reading

Possible response:

- **Characters:** Aunty Misery, the children, the sorcerer, Death
- **Setting:** Aunty Misery's home a long time ago
- **Plot:** Aunty Misery is tormented by children who steal from her pear tree. A sorcerer stays the night and offers her one wish. She wishes that anyone who climbs her tree should get stuck until she lets them go. The children get stuck and they don't bother her again. Then she convinces Death to climb the tree, and no one dies for many years. Aunty Misery finally agrees to let Death go if she can live forever.
- **Moral:** Misery and death are part of life.

Skills Review

Key Reading Skill: Analyzing

7. The story described the problems that occurred when people could not die. In your opinion, what good things would happen if people could not die?

Key Literary Element: Dialect

8. Which Spanish words appear in this story and what do they mean?

Reviewing Skills: Understanding Cause and Effect

9. Explain what causes Señor Death to get stuck in Aunty Misery's tree.

Vocabulary Check

Complete each group with the correct word from the list.

sorcerer taunt gnarled potion

10. drink, beverage, ___
11. twisted, knotty, ___
12. tease, insult, ___
13. wizard, magician, ___

English Language Coach Each of the underlined words is used with an easy meaning in "Aunty Misery." Use that meaning to figure out the related meaning used in the question.

14. Which of the following is one of a person's limbs?
    - a backbone
    - an ear
    - an arm
15. A fruitful effort is one that
    - has good results.
    - bad results.
    - no results.
16. If stories touch you, they
    - bore you.
    - confuse you.
    - affect your feelings.

Grammar Link: Run-on Sentences

Run-on: I like baseball I like football even more.
Run-on: I like baseball, I like football even more.

Review the three ways to fix a run-on sentence:

A. Separate the sentences with a period.
- I like baseball. I like football even more.

B. Put a comma and a coordinating conjunction between the sentences.
- I like baseball, but I like football even more.

C. Add a subordinating conjunction to one of the clauses.
- Though I like baseball, I like football even more.

Grammar Practice

17. Copy the following paragraph on another piece of paper. Then find and fix the two run-on sentences. Use any of the three ways shown above to make your corrections.

Last summer my family and I went to New York City. I had never been in a big-city cab before, it was quite an experience. At first the traffic was heavy we just crawled along. When we got out of the traffic, the driver started speeding. He was going so fast that I thought we were going to crash. I was relieved to reach our hotel.

Literature Online

Web Activities For eFlashcards, Selection Quick Checks, and other Web activities, go to www.glencoe.com.

Skills Review

Key Reading Skill: Analyzing

7. Possible responses: People wouldn't miss their loved ones; people would become wiser and wiser as they lived.

Key Literary Element: Dialect

8. *La Tia Miseria* means "Aunty Misery"; *la miseria y la muerte* mean misery and death.

Reviewing Skills: Understanding Cause and Effect

9. Possible response: He gets stuck because Aunty Misery thinks fast and convinces him to climb the tree. Once he is up there, he cannot get down. The sorcerer has granted Aunty Misery's wish to have anyone who climbs the tree get stuck in it until she lets them go.

Vocabulary Check

10. potion
11. gnarled
12. taunt
13. sorcerer
14. an arm
15. has good results.
16. affect your feelings.

Close

Ask students to tell whether they think this story has a good or a bad ending and why. Ask them to discuss why someone would want to share this story.

Grammar Link: Run-on Sentences

Grammar Practice

17. Possible response: Last summer my family and I went to New York City. I had never been in a big-city cab before. It was quite an experience. At first the traffic was heavy, so we just crawled along. When we got out of the traffic, the driver started speeding. He was going so fast that I thought we were going to crash. I was relieved to reach our hotel.

Literature Online

Web Activities Have students access the Web site for interactive activities that will help them assess their understanding of the selection.

Comparing Cultural Context

UNIT 6

Objectives covered in this workshop:
- Analyze literature from various cultures
- Analyze texts using various reasoning skills

Teaching Students to Compare Cultural Context

Why Is It Important?

- Comparing and contrasting selections enhances comprehension because students are prompted to pay attention to certain aspects of literature
- Comparing cultural context can make students aware of cultural allusions, settings, experiences, and other details important to understanding texts
- Comparing cultural context can also help students become more appreciative of diverse cultures

How to Help Students Get It

- Encourage students to notice and question anything that they are unfamiliar with
- Encourage students to remain sensitive to other cultures while asking questions
- Tell students to substitute something from their culture that may have similar significance or meaning

Aunt Sue's Stories

This poem by Langston Hughes describes a young child listening to his aunt's stories about slave life. Students will find out the power and importance of telling these stories.

I Ask My Mother to Sing

In this poem, the speaker listens to his mother and grandmother sing a song about life in China. Although the speaker has never been to the places described in the song, he feels similar emotions because of the women's singing.

Workshop Resources

Pacing (Days) Standard	Block	Lesson	Student Materials	Teacher Resources
1		Key Skill Lesson: Comparing Cultural Context	Key Reading Skills Practice English Language Coach	Bellringer Options Transparencies Read Aloud, Think Aloud Transparencies Presentation Plus!
2		"Aunt Sue's Stories"	Literary Analysis Transparencies Glencoe Online Selection Vocabulary Development Academic Vocabulary Development English Language Coach Active Reading Graphic Organizer Literary Analysis StudentWorks Plus Online Student Edition Literature Classics Selection and Unit Assessments	Literary and Text Analysis Transparencies Puzzlemaker Skill Level Up! BookLink 3 Assessment by Learning Objective (Diagnostic and Formative) Interactive Tutor Self-Assessment TeacherWorks Plus
2		"I Ask My Mother to Sing"	Glencoe Online Selection Vocabulary Development Academic Vocabulary Development English Language Coach Active Reading Graphic Organizer Literary Analysis StudentWorks Plus Online Student Edition Literature Classics Selection and Unit Assessments	Literary and Text Analysis Transparencies Puzzlemaker Skill Level Up! BookLink 3 Assessment by Learning Objective (Diagnostic and Formative) Interactive Tutor Self-Assessment TeacherWorks Plus

Keys for Unit Resource

- Blackline Master
- Workbook
- Supplemental Text
- CD-ROM
- DVD
- Transparency
- Web-based
- Fast Files

Level Appropriate Code

AS = Activities for all students
AL = Activities for students working above grade level
OL = Activities for students working at grade level
BL = Activities for students working below grade level
EL = Activities for English language learners

Focus

BELLRINGER Options

Daily Language Practice Transparency

Focus Activity Ask: Have you ever heard adults telling stories about the past, perhaps about before you were born? What was it like to listen to these stories? *(Responses will vary.)*

Teach

L Literary Element

Cultural Context Say: Think of some of the different cultures in this country. *(Possible responses: Hispanic American, Chinese American, African American, Jewish American)* Tell one custom of your own culture. OL How might this be similar to or different from the customs of other cultures? *(Responses will vary.)* AL

COMPARING LITERATURE WORKSHOP

Aunt Sue's Stories

by Langston Hughes

&

I Ask My Mother to Sing

by Li-Young Lee

Skills Focus

You will use these skills as you read and compare the following selections:

- "Aunt Sue's Stories," p. 751
- "I Ask My Mother to Sing," p. 753

Reading

- Comparing and contrasting

Literature

- Recognizing and analyzing cultural context

Writing

- Writing a compare and contrast essay

Objectives (pp. 748–749)
Reading Compare and contrast: cultural context

If you compare groups or singers, you probably think—among other things—about the songs they perform, the way you feel when you hear them, and the images that go through your mind when you listen to them. When you compare two poems, you also think about these things. Poems can also make you feel a certain way and imagine certain images.

How to Compare Literature: Cultural Context

Before you can compare anything, you need to know what points, or characteristics, you'll use for your comparison. When you read and compare "I Ask My Mother to Sing" and "Aunt Sue's Stories," you'll be looking especially at the cultural context of each poem.

L Cultural context involves the values, beliefs, goals, and customs of a particular group of people or of a community. The two poets you'll look at in this workshop are both Americans, but they have links to very different cultures. As you read their poems, look for details that give you information about the cultural context. Consider these things:

- setting
- places mentioned
- feelings expressed
- what people in the poem value
- references to past events
- experiences, shared or otherwise

Additional Support

Literature Focus Lesson

Speaker Tell students that in poetry, the narrator is called the speaker. The speaker of a poem might be the poet or a fictional or real character. The speaker's words communicate a particular tone or attitude toward the subject of the poem.

As students read "Aunt Sue's Stories" and "I Ask My Mother to Sing" have them tell who they think is the speaker of each poem. Then ask them to describe each speaker's attitude towards the subject. OL

Get Ready to Compare

As you read, keep track of the cultural details in a chart like the one below. Copy it into your Learner's Notebook and take notes as you read the poems.

Categories	"Aunt Sue's Stories"	"I Ask My Mother to Sing"
Setting		
Places Mentioned		
Feelings Expressed		
References To Past Events		
What People in the Poem Value		
Experiences–Shared or Otherwise		
Other Details		

L

Use Your Comparison

After you read the selections, think about the influence of cultural context and its power over what happens. For example, in "I Ask My Mother to Sing," the poet says that both his mother and grandmother are crying. Use the steps to think about how important culture is to that moment:

1. Both are singing and thinking about another place, another time.
2. What they are thinking about is something they can no longer experience.
3. The speaker may share the emotion, but he describes his mother and grandmother crying.
4. What the speaker feels may be different from what the two women feel.
5. Therefore, cultural context seems to be key to what people in the poem are feeling.

When you make your comparison later, you will use these steps to figure out how important cultural context is in these two poems.

Teach

L Literary Element

Cultural Context Say: Pay careful attention to the background information you learn about each poet. Ask yourself, "What culture does each poet come from?" and "How might this culture affect the poet's message?" **AL**

Assess/Close

Say: According to "Use Your Comparison," what should you do after you read the selections? *(Possible response: You should think about the influence of cultural context and its power over what happens.)* **AS**

Resources for page 749

Use the Comparing Literature Graphic Organizer BLM in the Unit 6 Resource Booklet.

Reading Fluency

Reading Poetry Tell students that reading poetry can be challenging because poets often choose to break up sentences into several lines. This doesn't mean, however, that students should stop at the end of a line when they're reading. Instead, they should let punctuation and sense tell them when to pause or stop reading. Have students take turns reading the poems aloud, being sure to use punctuation and not line breaks to guide them in when to stop reading. Tell students to pause briefly after a comma and slightly longer at the end of a sentence. **BL** **EL**

Objectives

- Compare and contrast works of literature
- Understand the influence of cultural context
- Identify the speaker in a poem
- Read poetry with fluency

Teach

More About the Author

Langston Hughes spent much of his childhood traveling from place to place as his mother and stepfather looked for work. He lived with his parents, his grandmother, and other adults in many different cities. Hughes's grandmother, Mary Langston, was a great influence on him. According to Hughes, she used to sit him on her lap, like Aunt Sue in the poem, and tell him "long, beautiful stories about people who wanted to make the Negroes free."

R Reading Skill

Review Connecting **Say:** Tell what you know about slavery in this country. *(Possible responses: African Americans were forced to work on Southern plantations. Many slaves were treated brutally; all were denied basic freedoms.)* **OL** Why might African Americans want to tell stories about slavery? *(Possible response: To tell younger people about the strength and sorrow of enslaved people.)* **AL**

Before You Read Aunt Sue's Stories

Meet the Author

Langston Hughes was born in Joplin, Missouri. He attended Columbia University in New York and quickly became a major figure in the Harlem Renaissance of the 1920s. Controversial for his references to race, Hughes was both praised and attacked. He lived in many places throughout the world and died in New York in 1967. See page R4 of the Author Files for more on Langston Hughes.

Author Search For more about Langston Hughes, go to www.glencoe.com.

Objectives (pp. 750–751)
Reading Compare and contrast: cultural context
Vocabulary Interpret metaphorical meanings

Get Ready to Read

English Language Coach

Double Meanings in Poetry When a word has both literal and metaphorical meanings, writers can never completely ignore either one. When you read, you will often think of both meanings, whether you realize it or not. In fact, poets count on you to "get" the different meanings.

In "Aunt Sue's Stories," Langston Hughes uses the phrase "the flow of old Aunt Sue's voice." Aunt Sue is talking smoothly and without stopping. That's all it really means. But Hughes talks about black people mingling in that flow. He expects you to think about and feel Aunt Sue's voice as a river.

As you read this poem, look for words that carry a lot of meaning. Say the words of the poem out loud and feel the meanings those words have for you.

Connect to the Reading

R This poem is about people whose culture is rooted in America, though they came from another land originally. African slaves were brought from Africa, and the culture of slavery left a deep mark on the entire country.

Think back to what you know about slavery. If you didn't grow up in this country and never studied that subject, don't worry. Classmates may be able to help you out. As you read, try to get a sense of how the people in the poem feel about their experiences and how alive the past is for them.

Set Purposes for Reading

BIG Question Read to find out how the speaker in the poem thinks about the stories his aunt has to tell.

Set Your Own Purpose

What would you like to learn about the experiences and stories of the people in the poem? Write your own purpose on the Comparing Literature page of Foldable 6.

Additional Support

Author Search To expand students' appreciation of Langston Hughes, have them access the Web site for additional information and resources.

English Language Coach

Literal and Figurative Use of Words
Tell students that poets use metaphors and similes to describe something or someone in a new and different way. Have students identify whether the following are similes or metaphors, what two things are being compared in each, and why.

1. Her love was a prickly thorn. *(Metaphor: compares love to a thorn to show how painful it can be.)*
2. The oven was as hot as the sun. *(Simile: compares an oven to the sun to show how hot it is.)* **EL** **BL**

Aunt Sue's Stories

by Langston Hughes

Under the Midnight Blues, 2003. Oil on board. Colin Bootman. Private Collection.

Aunt Sue has a head full of stories.
Aunt Sue has a whole heart full of stories. 1
Summer nights on the front porch
Aunt Sue cuddles a brown-faced child to her bosom
And tells him stories.

Black slaves
Working in the hot sun,
And black slaves
Walking in the dewy night,*
And black slaves
EL Singing sorrow songs* on the banks of a mighty river 2
Mingle themselves softly
In the flow of old Aunt Sue's voice,
Mingle themselves softly
In the dark shadows that cross and recross
Aunt Sue's stories.

And the dark-faced child, listening,
Knows that Aunt Sue's stories are real stories.
He knows that Aunt Sue never got her stories
L Out of any book at all,
But that they came
Right out of her own life.

The dark-faced child is quiet
Of a summer night
Listening to Aunt Sue's stories. 3 ❍

9. ***Dewy*** (DOO ee) means "covered with dew," the moisture that settles on plants and grass during the night or early morning.

11. ***Sorrow songs*** refers to music like the blues, spirituals, and other traditional African American songs.

Practice the Skills

1 English Language Coach

Double Meanings in Poetry Is a "whole heart full" any different from "a heart full"? Do you think you're supposed to think of more than one meaning for *heart*?

2 Comparing Literature

Cultural Context Two rivers have strong associations with slavery. The Ohio River divided slave states from free states. Many slaves worked plantations near the Mississippi River and in its ports.

3 BIG Question

BQ Why does Aunt Sue tell her stories? Write your answer on the Comparing Literature page of Foldable 6.

COMPARING LITERATURE

Teach

EL Language Coach

Double Meanings **Say:** The words *dark shadows* are being used figuratively here to represent something else. Darkness often represents something negative. What might the dark shadows of Aunt Sue's stories be? *(Possible response: the sadness and terrible pain suffered by the black slaves)* EL

L Literary Element

Cultural Context **Ask:** What lines tell you that Aunt Sue's stories are part of her cultural heritage? *("But that they came/ Right out of her own life.")* OL How do you think the poem would be different if Aunt Sue were telling the boy stories she'd read in a book? *(Possible response: The poem would be less powerful. It is meaningful because Aunt Sue's stories are real.)* AL

BQ

Ask: Why might Aunt Sue tell her stories to the child? *(Possible response: She might tell them so that he will know about his family's past.)* OL

Literature Focus Lesson

Alliteration Tell students that alliteration is the repetition of initial consonant sounds, such as the repetition of *r* in the sentence, "I remember the red ribbon on the rocking horse." Writers and poets use alliteration to give their writing a musical or rhythmical air. Have students write a sentence that uses alliteration and share it with the class. Then, have them look for examples of alliteration in "Aunt Sue's Stories." *(Possible response: slaves/Singing sorrow songs)* AS

Objectives

- Compare and contrast: cultural context
- Interpret metaphorical meanings

Teach

More About the Author

A year after Li-Young Lee was born, his father spent more than a year as a political prisoner in Indonesia because of his nationality and his interest in Western culture and ideas. Lee's family's exile and his cultural background are the subject of many of his poems.

R Reading Skill

Review Connecting **Say:** At the beginning of the workshop, you talked about your experience of listening to adults telling stories about the past. Think about your experience as you read "I Ask My Mother to Sing." How would you feel if you heard the song the speaker's mother and grandmother sing? *(Possible response: I might feel sorrow because they probably miss their homeland, but I may also feel wonder and awe hearing about places I've never been.)* OL

Before You Read

I Ask My Mother to Sing

Li-Young Lee

Meet the Author

Li-Young Lee was born in 1957 in Indonesia of Chinese parents. His family left Indonesia because of anti-Chinese attitudes there. They came to the United States in 1964. Lee currently lives in Chicago with his wife and children. Asked how he creates poetry, Lee replied, "I am on the job twenty-four hours a day. I'm absorbing it. I just absorb it." See page R4 of the Author Files for more on Li-Young Lee.

Author Search For more about Li-Young Lee, go to www.glencoe.com.

Objectives (pp. 752–753)
Reading Compare and contrast: cultural context

Get Ready to Read

Connect to the Reading

R You're going to read a poem about people whose cultural heritage is from China. You may already know a lot about China, and this could help you with the reading. Don't worry, though, if you've never heard of the places the poem mentions. What's important is to imagine the scene the poem paints. Try to connect the poem to your own experience.

Build Background

- Li-Young Lee spent his early childhood in Asia but never lived in China. He was educated in the United States.
- Lee's father read to him in both Chinese (poems) and English (the King James Bible).
- Peking is an old name for Beijing (bay JING), the capital of the Republic of China. The Summer Palace was one of several beautiful palaces in Beijing built by the Chinese emperors.
- The Stone Boat is an amazing work of art at the Summer Palace. Not a real boat, it's made of marble and has colored glass windows.
- According to an old Chinese saying, "water can carry the boat as well as overturn it." It means that water (symbolizing the people) can keep the royal boat (the country's leader or government) floating but can also make it sink.

Set Purposes for Reading

BIG Question Read to find out how the speaker relates to his mother's song and how he feels about it.

Set Your Own Purpose

What would you like to learn about the experiences and stories of the people in the poem? Write your own purpose on the Comparing Literature page of Foldable 6.

Additional Support

Literature Online

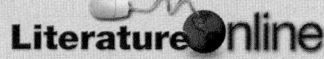

Author Search To expand students' appreciation of Li-Young Lee, have them access the Web site for additional information and resources.

Reading in the Real World

College Have students search online for information about the places mentioned in the poem.

- Where is Peking?
- What does the Summer Palace look like?
- What is a Stone Boat?

Students should download images and create presentations with illustrations to introduce the class to these places. Interested students might write poems describing some of the places. Tell students to use figurative language, such as metaphors or similes, in their poems. AL

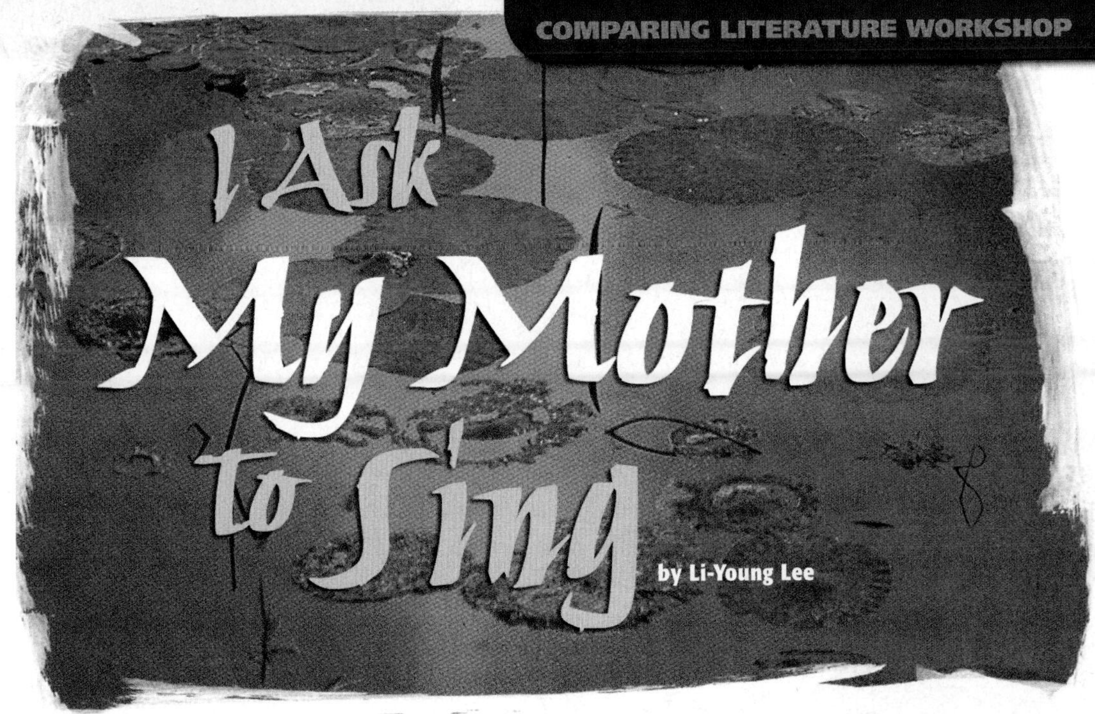

She begins, and my grandmother joins her.
Mother and daughter sing like young girls.
C If my father were alive, he would play
his accordion and sway like a boat.
I've never been in Peking, or the Summer Palace,
nor stood on the great Stone Boat to watch
the rain begin on Kuen Ming Lake, the picnickers
running away in the grass. **1**

But I love to hear it sung;
how the waterlilies fill with rain*
until they overturn, spilling water into water,
then rock back, and fill with more.

BQ Both women have begun to cry.
But neither stops her song. **2** ❍

10. ***Waterlilies*** have large, showy flowers and big, flat leaves that float on the water.

Practice the Skills

1 Comparing Literature

Cultural Context What details help you imagine the scene that the poem describes? List them on your Comparison Chart.

2 BIG Question

The speaker's mother sings a song about life in another country. The song makes the speaker think about memories of the past. What does the song seem to mean to the speaker?

Teach

C Critical Thinking

Comprehension Ask: What two things are being compared in the phrase "sway like a boat"? *(The father's swaying is compared to a boat's movement to show what his father's movement would look like.)* **AS**

BQ 

Ask: Why might the grandmother and the mother cry as they sing their song? *(Possible response: They might cry because they miss their homeland.)* **OL**

Differentiated Instruction

Illustration Visual students might appreciate and understand the poems more by drawing an illustration depicting the scene of each one. Have students read the poems carefully to look for clues about the setting and the characters.

- What is the setting of each poem?
- Who are the characters in each poem?
- What are the characters doing?

Have students answer these questions before they begin their illustrations. Have students share their illustrations with the class. **EL** **OL**

Objectives
- Compare and contrast: cultural context

Assess

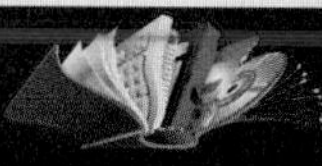

Resources for page 754

- Selection Quick Check
- Comparing Literature Assessment

Reading/Critical Thinking

Aunt Sue's Stories

1. Possible response: Line 1: Aunt Sue knows stories. Line 2: Aunt Sue has many feelings about her stories.
2. Possible response: He means that the stories are true stories from Aunt Sue's life, not other people's stories.
3. Possible response: "I Ask My Mother to Sing" uses a simile. "Aunt Sue's Stories" uses words figuratively but doesn't include similes or metaphors.

I Ask My Mother to Sing

4. Possible response: The speaker is not as attached to Chinese culture. He likes hearing the song, but he doesn't cry because he's never been to the places.
5. Possible response: They want to tell the speaker about China. They want to remember their past.

After You Read

Aunt Sue's Stories & I Ask My Mother to Sing

Objectives (pp. 754–755)
Reading Compare and contrast: cultural context
Writing Create a chart to compare and contrast texts

Reading/Critical Thinking

Aunt Sue's Stories

1. **Infer** The first two lines of "Aunt Sue's Stories" are:

   Aunt Sue has a head full of stories.
   Aunt Sue has a whole heart full of stories.

   What is the difference in meaning between the two lines?

   TIP **Think and Search**
2. **Infer** What does the speaker mean when he says that "Aunt Sue never got her stories / Out of any book at all"?

   TIP **Author and Me**
3. **Analyze** How do the two poems differ in their use of figurative language?

   TIP **Think and Search**

I Ask My Mother to Sing

4. **Interpret** How does the speaker's attachment to the culture of China compare with that of his mother and grandmother?

   TIP **Author and Me**
5. **Infer** At the end of the poem, why do the women continue to sing, even though they are crying?

   TIP **Author and Me**

Writing: Compare the Literature

Use Your Notes (Continued on page 755)

Similarities	Differences
Both poems express strong feelings about the past.	Setting is not specified in "I Ask My Mother to Sing." Setting is on a porch in summer in "Aunt Sue's Stories."
The people in both poems value history and family.	Specific places are mentioned only in "I Ask My Mother to Sing."

Writing: Compare the Literature

Use Your Notes

Follow these steps to use the notes on your Comparison Chart to compare the cultural context in "I Ask My Mother to Sing" and "Aunt Sue's Stories."

Step 1: Look over the chart you completed. Underline the details that are similar for both selections. Circle the details that are different.

Step 2: On a separate sheet of paper, make a list of those details that are similar and those that are different.

Step 3: Look at the new list you've made. For example, both poems bring out feelings of sorrow about the past. Think about whether that means the people in both poems feel sorry that the past is behind them or whether they have quite different feelings about the past.

Step 4: Notice which cultural points are important in both poems and which are important in just one of the poems. You will use this information to back up your statements in the assignment. Put a check beside the details that are most important to the speaker.

Get It on Paper

To show what you think about the importance of cultural context in "I Ask My Mother to Sing" and "Aunt Sue's Stories," copy and complete these statements on a separate sheet of paper.

1. In "I Ask My Mother to Sing," references to place are important because (add your ideas).
2. The most important aspect of culture in "I Ask My Mother to Sing" is (add your ideas) because (add your reasons).
3. In "Aunt Sue's Stories," cultural context is important because (add your ideas).
4. The most important aspect of culture in "Aunt Sue's Stories" is (add your ideas) because (add your reasons using details from the Comparison Chart).

5. In both poems, the cultural context of the past was something that the speaker and his family (choose: grieved for or wanted to return to or felt completely differently about) as shown in the stories that they tell.

Literature Online

Web Activities For eFlashcards, Selection Quick Checks, and other Web activities, go to www.glencoe.com.

6. (Continued from page 754)

Similarities	Differences
The people in both poems have experienced sorrow.	The people in "I Ask My Mother to Sing" miss their country. Aunt Sue does not miss the past.

COMPARING LITERATURE

Get It on Paper

1. Possible response: In "I Ask My Mother to Sing," references to places are important because the mother and grandmother are remembering the places of their past.
2. Possible response: The most important aspect of culture in "I Ask My Mother to Sing" is setting because the memory of places in China makes the mother and grandmother cry and gives the speaker joy.
3. Possible response: In "Aunt Sue's Stories," cultural context is important because Sue's people have suffered greatly due to slavery, which is the topic of her stories.
4. Possible response: The most important aspect of culture in "Aunt Sue's Stories" is references to past events because these events shaped Sue's life and her stories.

BIG Question

5. Possible response: In both poems, the cultural context of the past is something that the speaker and his family felt completely differently about as shown in the stories they tell.

Close

Hold a class discussion based on students' responses to question 5 on this page. Encourage students to explain their responses.

The Unit Challenge

Focus

BELLRINGER Options

- Selection Focus Transparency
- Daily Language Practice Transparency

Focus Activity Ask: If you had to choose one story from this unit to share with a friend, which one would it be and why?
This discussion will remind students of the selections they've read, which will help them begin the group activity or the solo activity.

Teach

Group Activity: Sharing-Stories Reading List

- Be sure students complete the assignment in order. Tell them not to start their list of selections until they've reviewed the different reasons for telling stories.
- Each group member should contribute at least one selection to the list of stories that illustrate the answer to the Big Question.
- If possible, for a final draft, have one group member create the final list on a computer. Have students choose a different font and color for each story.

UNIT 6 WRAP-UP

Answering The BIG Question Why Do We Share Our Stories?

You've just read folktales, stories, and poems that help you think about why we share our stories. Now use what you've learned to do the Unit Challenge.

The Unit Challenge

Choose Activity A or Activity B and follow the directions for that activity.

A. Group Activity: Sharing-Stories Reading List

Best-of-the-best lists are always popular. There are lists of the best movies, songs, and music videos. Now it's your turn to make a list.

- You and four other students will share your favorite stories by listing what you think are the ten best stories for kids your age.

1. Discuss the Assignment

- Choose one group member to be the note-taker for the discussion.
- Use your Unit 6 Foldable to review your notes about why we share our stories.
- Recall funny stories like "Charles" as well as serious stories like "The Boy and His Grandfather." Are these the kinds of stories that kids will like?

2. Brainstorm a List

- Brainstorm a list of stories that illustrate the answer to the Big Question.
- For example, if one of your reasons for sharing stories is to have fun, then you would include stories that are funny, scary, or entertaining. They might be stories in this unit or earlier units in this textbook. Or they might be stories you've read on your own. (It's okay to list books, too.) If you want, make your list look like this one.

SHARING-STORIES READING LIST
Best Stories to Read for Fun
1.
2.
3.
4.

3. Select the Best of the Best As a group, decide which stories best illustrate each reason. Answer the following questions:

- Would most of my friends enjoy reading this story? Why or why not? (If not, think about crossing the title off your list.)
- Is there anything about this story that parents or teachers might object to? (If so, cross the title off your list.)
- Does this story clearly demonstrate one of our reasons for sharing stories? (If not, cross the title off your list.)

4. Present Your List

- Check to make sure all the titles on your list are correctly spelled.
- Make sure you have listed at least ten stories.
- Read your list aloud to the class or post it on a bulletin board in your classroom or school library.

Assess/Close

Group Activity

Ask: What reasons for telling stories did you learn in this unit? Were any of the reasons surprising? Explain.

B. Solo Activity: "Two Thumbs Up, Two Thumbs Down!"

Sometimes it's easy to get into a story. The characters seem real. Their problems interest you. Then, when you read the ending, you think, Aha! Perfect! That's exactly the way this story should end! Other times, you can hardly wait to put a story down. In Activity B, you'll write a short review telling why you think a story of your choice is—or is not—worth sharing with other kids your age.

1. Decide on a Story

- Choose a story that you strongly like or dislike. The story might be from Unit 6 or earlier units in this textbook. Or the story might be one you've read on your own.
- Review the notes you made on your Unit 6 Foldable. Then ask yourself these questions:
- Which selection in Unit 6 did I enjoy the most?
- Why do I think this story should be shared with other kids my age?
- Which selection did I enjoy the least?
- What are some reasons that I think this story isn't worth sharing?

2. Analyze the Story

- Look at the separate parts of the story.
- Think about whether each part is good or bad and why. That will help you figure out why you like (or dislike) the story as a whole.
- Jot down your ideas on a chart like the one pictured.

3. Start Writing

- Begin by stating your opinion of the story. (Be sure to include the title of the story and the name of the author.) Then give a few short reasons for your opinion. Your opening might be as simple as this:
- "The Boy and His Grandfather," by Rudolfo A. Anaya, is definitely worth sharing with other students. I think they'll like this story for many reasons. (Then list the reasons.)

4. Present Your Story Review

- When you have finished writing, reread your review.
- Correct any misspellings or errors in grammar.
- Present your review to your classmates.

Big Question Link to Web resources to further explore the Big Question at www.glencoe.com.

Teach

Solo Activity: "Two Thumbs Up, Two Thumbs Down!"

- Students having a hard time selecting a story might look over this book's Table of Contents to remind them of what they've read.
- When students create their web diagram, they should write details about the plot, characters, problems, and ending that make the story worth or not worth reading.
- Tell students their reviews should be one or two paragraphs long. They should start by telling the name of the story, whether or not it is worth sharing, and why.
- Have students use examples from the selection to support their reasons.
- Students can present their reviews orally or by posting them on a class bulletin board.

Assess/Close

Solo Activity

Have students share the reasons for telling stories they learned in this unit. Which of those reasons might they use for telling the story they reviewed?

Objectives
- Create a list
- Evaluate fiction
- Write a review

Vocabulary Preview
List the following words on the board:

- cordially
- barren
- fanciful
- sensation
- colossal

Review their definitions before students begin reading.

Build Background
Stories about the legendary giant Paul Bunyan were first published in Minnesota in 1910, but they were told years earlier in lumber camps around the country. As the stories were passed on, Paul's deeds grew more and more incredible until the stories developed into the type of folklore called tall tales.

Teach

C Critical Thinking
Analysis Ask: What details do you learn about Paul Bunyan in the storyteller's note that make this selection a "tall tale"? *(He is taller than a redwood tree, stronger than fifty grizzly bears, and smarter than a library full of books.)* OL

Readability Scores
Dale-Chall: 7.1
DRP: 58
Lexile: 1100

UNIT 6

Your Turn: Read and Apply Skills

Audrey Wood

Meet the Author
Storytelling and art have always been part of Audrey Wood's life. When she was very young, her mother told her fantasy stories about amazing people. Wood's father was an artist for Ringling Bros. Circus. A little later in life, Wood carried on the family storytelling tradition by making up stories to entertain her little sisters. Today Wood is a well-known author and illustrator of children's books.

Author Search For more about Audrey Wood, go to www.glencoe.com.

by Audrey Wood

C ***Storyteller's Note*** *Now I suppose that you have heard about the mighty logger Paul Bunyan and his great blue ox named Babe. In the early days of our country, Paul and Babe cleared the land for the settlers, so farms and cities could spring up. And you probably know that Paul was taller than a redwood tree, stronger than fifty grizzly bears, and smarter than a library full of books. But you may not know that Paul was married and had two fine children.*

One day when Paul Bunyan was out clearing a road through the forests of Kentucky, a great pounding began to shake the earth. Looking around, Paul discovered an enormous hole in the side of a hill. The lumberjack pulled up an acre of dry cane and fashioned a torch to light his way.

Paul climbed inside the hole and followed the sound underground for miles, until he came to a large cavern glistening with crystals. By the flickering light of his torch, he saw a gigantic woman banging a behemoth[1] pickax against a wall.

It was love at first sight.

"I'm Carrie McIntie," the gigantic woman said. "I was sitting on the hill when my lucky wishbone fell down a crack into the earth. I've been digging all day trying to find it."

With a grin on his face as wide as the Missouri River, Paul reached into his shirt pocket. "I've got one too," he said,

1. A ***behemoth*** (bih HEE muth) object is really, really big.

Additional Support

Author Search To expand students' appreciation of Audrey Wood, have them access the Web site for additional information and resources.

Literature Focus Lesson
Summary "The Bunyans" is a modern retelling of the tall tale about how the famous giant woodsman Paul Bunyan and his family create some of the natural wonders of North America. Bunyan marries a woman as gigantic as he is, and they have two children who are equally strong and large. Bunyan creates Niagara falls, his son Little Jean creates Bryce Canyon, the Great Sand Dunes of Colorado, and Big Sur. Together, the family creates the Rocky Mountains. Ma creates Old Faithful in Yellowstone National Park. Teeny becomes a fashion designer and makes skirts from air balloons and blouses from ship sails. Little Jean studies astronomy and goes to Mars.

The Bunyans, illustration by David Shannon from THE BUNYANS by Audrey Wood. Published by the BLUE SKY PRESS. Illustrations © 1996 by David Shannon. Reprinted by permission of Scholastic Inc. THE BLUE SKY PRESS is a registered trademark of Scholastic Inc.

pulling out *his* lucky wishbone. "Marry me, Carrie, and we'll share mine."

Carrie agreed, and their wedding invitations were mailed out right away.

The invitations were so large, only one needed to be sent to each state. Everyone could read them for miles!

The invitations said: *You are cordially invited to the mammoth*[2] *wedding of Paul Bunyan and Carrie McIntie.* The couple were married in the enormous crystal chamber that Carrie had carved, and after the ceremony, folks began to call it "Mammoth Cave." The giantess had dug more than two hundred miles, making it the longest cave in the world, so the name fit perfectly. **R**

Paul and Carrie settled down on a farm in Maine, and soon there were two new Bunyans. While Pa Bunyan traveled with his logging crew, Ma Bunyan worked the farm and cared for their jumbo boy, named Little Jean, and their gigantic girl, named Teeny. **C**

One morning when Pa Bunyan was home between jobs, Ma Bunyan cooked up a hearty breakfast of pancakes and syrup. Teeny was wrestling with her big purple puma named Slink and accidentally dumped a silo of syrup on her head. Teeny's hair was so sweet, bears crawled into it and burrowed deep in her curls. Try as they might, Pa and Ma Bunyan couldn't wash them out.

Visual Vocabulary
The ***puma*** (PYOO muh) is a large, yellowish, wild cat. It's also called *cougar* and *mountain lion.*

2. ***Cordially*** means "in a genuinely warm and friendly way." ***Mammoth*** means "really big; huge."

Teach

Viewing the Painting

Ask: How does the artist show how enormous Bunyan and Babe are? *(The artist puts trees, another person, and rocks in the painting to show how big Bunyan and Babe are compared to them.)* **OL**

R Reading Skill

Review Predicting Say: Bunyan's wife-to-be, Carrie, creates Mammoth Cave. What do you predict the family might do once the children get older? *(Possible response: They might create other enormous structures.)* **AL**

C Critical Thinking

Comprehension Ask: What is humorous about the names of the Bunyans' children? *(They are called "Little" and "Teeny" even though they are both enormous.)* **OL**

Literature Focus Lesson

Tall Tales Tall tales are wildly imaginative stories, usually passed down orally, about fantastic adventures or amazing feats of folk heroes in realistic local settings. They are a specific type of American folktale that often describes one aspect of frontier life, such as logging or cattle ranching. Many tall tales explain the creation of mountains, lakes, and canyons. Some tall tales are based on the deeds of people who actually lived, for example, Annie Oakley and Davy Crockett. In tall tales, the characters, their physical attributes, and their deeds are grossly exaggerated for humorous effect. As students read "The Bunyans" have them look for these elements of the tall tale. **OL**

Objectives
- Read and analyze the elements of tall tales
- Analyze a painting
- Make predictions
- Analyze humor
- Learn new vocabulary

Teach

C Critical Thinking

Comprehension **Ask:** What are the exaggerated details in the story up to this point? *(Possible responses: Paul digs up an acre of cane, Carrie digs Mammoth Cove, the wedding invitations are enormous, Teeny wrestles with a puma, bears burrow in Teeny's curls, and Paul digs a hole in the riverbed to create Niagara Falls.)* **OL**

EL Language Coach

Idioms **Say:** The term "tongue-tied" is an idiomatic expression. Paul Bunyan mixes up his words and says "brice nanyon, coy" instead of "nice canyon, boy." Considering this, what do you think it means if you are tongue-tied? *(It means you get your words muddled up and don't say them correctly.)* **EL**

"We'll need a forceful shower of water to get rid of those varmints!"[3] Ma Bunyan declared.

Pa Bunyan had an idea. He placed his daughter on Babe, and he led them to the Niagara River in Canada. The gargantuan[4] father scooped out a huge hole in the middle of the riverbed. As the great river roared down into the deep hole, Teeny cried out in delight, "Niagara falls!" Teeny showered in the waterfall, and the pesky bears were washed downstream. **C**

When Little Jean was five, he wanted to work too, so he followed his pa out to his logging camp in Montana. Thinking his son was too young to do much of anything, Paul set Little Jean down in a barren canyon in Utah to play for the day. When the lumberjack went to fetch him, he couldn't believe his eyes. Little Jean had carved the canyon into a wonderland of fanciful[5] shapes.

Pa Bunyan got tongue-tied and said, "That's a mighty *brice* nanyon, coy, I mean, a mighty nice canyon, boy!" Somehow part of the mix-up stuck. **EL**

To this day the canyon is known as Bryce Canyon.

After all that sculpting, Little Jean's shoes were full of sand. Pa knew Ma Bunyan wouldn't want her clean floors dirtied up, so he told Little Jean to sit down and empty out his shoes.

The sand from Little Jean's shoes blew away on the eastern wind and settled down a state away. It covered a valley ten miles long, making sand dunes eight hundred feet high. Everyone knows that's how the Great Sand Dunes of Colorado came to be.

One summer, Little Jean and Teeny wanted to go to the beach. Ma Bunyan told them to follow a river to the ocean. But all the rivers flowed west back then, so they missed the Atlantic Ocean and ended up on the other side of the country instead.

Ma Bunyan tracked them out to the Pacific Ocean, where she found Teeny riding on the backs of two blue whales and Little Jean carving out fifty *zigzag* miles of the California coast.

When Ma Bunyan saw what her son had done, she exclaimed, "What's the big idea, sir!?" From that time on, the scenic area was known as Big Sur.

Ma Bunyan knew she had to put up a barrier to remind her children not to wander off too far. So, on the way home, everyone pitched in and built the Rocky Mountains. Teeny gathered up and sorted out all the rivers, letting some flow east and others west. After that, the children had no trouble following the eastern rivers down to the Atlantic Ocean. And when they wanted to go out exploring, Ma Bunyan would call out, "Now don't cross the Continental Divide, children!"

The best thing about camping is sleeping outdoors, and the worst thing is not having enough hot water. That's why the Bunyans always camped in Wyoming. By the time their camping years were over, Ma Bunyan had poked more than three hundred holes in the ground with her pickax and released tons of hot water from geysers.[6] But Ma got

3. Here, the ***varmints*** are pesky animals.
4. The word ***gargantuan*** comes from the name of a fictional giant, and it's another word that means "really big; huge."
5. A ***barren*** place has little or no plant life. Anything that is ***fanciful*** shows imagination in design or construction.
6. A ***geyser*** (GY zur) is an underground spring heated by hot lava under the earth's surface.

Additional Support

Differentiated Instruction

Less-Proficient Readers To help students monitor their comprehension while reading the story, you may wish to provide them with some clues to connect each play on words with an actual landmark in the United States. As students read the story, have them complete a chart with the other stories of landmark creations. **BL**

Bunyan Action	Landmark Connection
Carrie McIntie was looking for her wishbone and dug an enormous crystal chamber on the side of a hill.	Mammoth Cave

tired of poking so many holes, so she made a geyser that blew every hour on the hour. After that, there was a steady supply of hot water to keep the giants' clothes and dishes sparkling clean. **R**

Teeny named the geyser Old Faithful, and to this day, Old Faithful still blows its top every hour in Yellowstone National Park.

As our great country grew up, so did the Bunyan children. When the kids left home, Ma and Pa Bunyan retired to a wilderness area, where they still live happily.

Teeny hitched a ride on a whale over to England and became a famous fashion designer. Her colorful skirts made from air balloons and her breezy blouses cut from ship sails were a sensation[7] at the first World's Fair in London. **L**

Little Jean traveled to Venice, Italy, where he studied astronomy and art. Every day, the gondoliers would take their passengers down the Grand Canal[8] to watch the giant artist chiseling his marble sculptures.

Visual Vocabulary
A ***gondolier*** (gon duh LEER) operates a gondola—a long, narrow, flat-bottomed boat with high peaks at the ends.

After graduation, Little Jean decided to explore new lands, as his parents had done. So he took two great jumps and one flying leap and bounded up into outer space.

The Bunyans, illustration by David Shannon from THE BUNYANS by Audrey Wood. Published by the BLUE SKY PRESS. Illustrations © 1996 by David Shannon. Reprinted by permission of Scholastic Inc. THE BLUE SKY PRESS is a registered trademark of Scholastic Inc.

In 1976, the year of our country's bicentennial, a spacecraft sent by the National Aeronautics and Space Administration was on a mission to study Mars. The spacecraft was named *Viking I,* and it took many photographs of the surface of the planet. One mysterious photo looked like a face carved out of colossal rock. **C**

Some say the photograph is not a face, but an illusion caused by light and shadows on the rock. Others think the famous "Martian face" is just the spitting image of Little Jean Bunyan. If that's so, who knows what he's up to on the other planets.

Only time will tell! ○

7. Here, ***sensation*** means "a cause of excitement of great interest; a wonder."
8. The city of ***Venice*** (VEN is) has canals for streets, and the ***Grand Canal*** is its main street.

Teach

R Reading Skill

Review Understanding Cause and Effect **Ask:** Why does Ma create Old Faithful? *(to create a steady supply of hot water for cleaning)* **BL**

L Literary Element

Review Character **Ask:** In what way are Teeny and Little Jean just like other kids? *(They grow up, move away from home, and find careers of their own.)* **OL**

C Critical Thinking

Analysis **Ask:** How does the author modernize this American frontier tall tale? *(The author has Little Jean Bunyan go into outer space where he seems to have left a colossal carving of his face on Mars.)* **OL**

Differentiated Instruction

Telling Tall Tales "The Bunyans" is a wildly imaginative story about the adventures of the Bunyan family. This American tall tale has been passed down orally, each generation adding a little more to it. Have students work alone or in pairs to create their own tall tales. They can be about any subject or personality they choose, but the narrators must speak directly to the listeners. Encourage students to have the characters use authentic dialect or idioms to make the presentations more intriguing. When their stories are ready, the students may present them orally to the class. **AL**

Objectives
- Read and analyze the elements of tall tales
- Analyze humor
- Write and tell tall tales
- Learn new vocabulary

Tips for Independent Reading

Tell students to let their interests guide them in selecting books for independent reading. Have students look over the descriptions of the books shown here to see if any of them catch their attention.

Fiction

Remind students that one reason to tell stories is to share information about a culture, a person, or an event. Explain that reading fiction can provide information about real people, places, and events because authors often include these in their stories. Have students tell what they might learn about the experiences of enslaved people by reading the folktales they told.

Ask students to share an example of a fictional story they've read before that has given them insight into a real person, event, or culture.

UNIT 6

Reading on Your Own

To read more about the Big Question, choose one of these books from your school or local library. Work on your reading skills by choosing books that are challenging to you.

Fiction

The People Could Fly: American Black Folktales
retold by Virginia Hamilton

This collection contains twenty-four folktales told by enslaved people and formerly enslaved people. Included are animal tales, tall tales, supernatural tales, and tales of freedom. If you like folktales, *The People Could Fly* is a must-read.

On Her Way: Stories & Poems about Growing Up Girl
edited by Sandy Asher

Whether traveling west in a wagon train or overcoming terrible illness, the girls in this collection face life's challenges with strength and courage. Read this collection to discover what's great about "growing up girl."

Where Angels Glide at Dawn: New Stories from Latin America
edited by Lori M. Carlson and Cynthia L. Ventura

Homes and families provide the background for several of these ten stories from Latin America. The stories display a variety of cultures and writing styles.

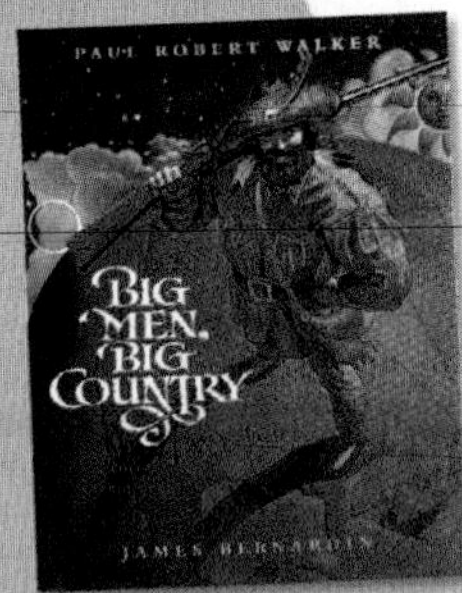

Big Men, Big Country: A Collection of American Tall Tales
by Paul Robert Walker

The stories in this collection portray nine American tall-tale heroes, including Paul Bunyan, Pecos Bill, Sluefoot Sue, and Davy Crockett.

Additional Support

Differentiated Instruction

GLENCOE BOOKLINK Use the Glencoe BookLink CD-ROM to create customized reading lists to help students answer the Big Questions. Suggestions for Unit 6:
Grade 4: *All Stories Are Anansi's* by Harold Courlander
Grade 5: *Elizabeth Blackwell: The First Woman Doctor* by Francene Sabin
Grade 6: *The Enchanted Raisin* by Jacqueline Balcells
Grade 7: *Space Challenger: The Story of Guion Bluford* by Jim Haskins and Kathleen Bensen
Grade 8: *Once Upon A Time* by Alan Trussell-Cullen

Nonfiction

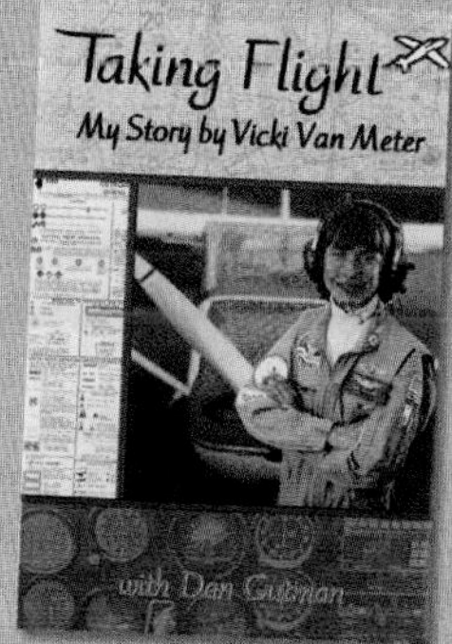

Taking Flight: My Story by Vicki Van Meter
by Vicki Van Meter;
with Dan Gutman

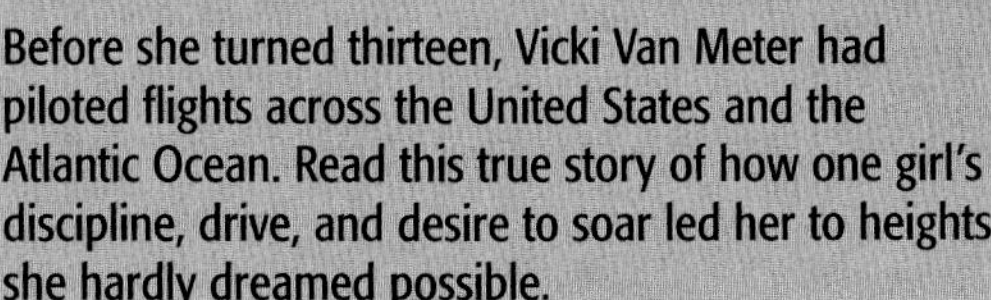

Before she turned thirteen, Vicki Van Meter had piloted flights across the United States and the Atlantic Ocean. Read this true story of how one girl's discipline, drive, and desire to soar led her to heights she hardly dreamed possible.

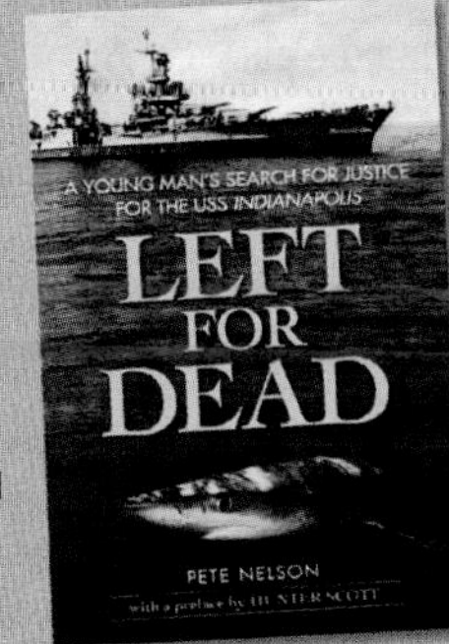

Left for Dead: A Young Man's Search for Justice for the USS *Indianapolis*
by Pete Nelson;
with a preface by Hunter Scott

When Japanese torpedoes sank the USS *Indianapolis* in July 1945, survivors were stranded in cold Pacific waters for four days before help arrived. Fifty years later, eleven-year-old Hunter Scott's research on the subject brought new facts to light about what happened, and why, that harrowing week in July.

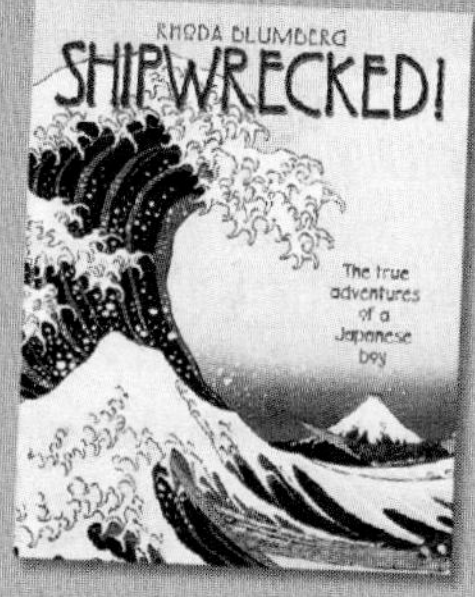

Shipwrecked! The True Adventures of a Japanese Boy
by Rhoda Blumberg

Shipwrecked on an island and rescued by whalers, Manjiro goes on to experience a life of adventures that takes him around the globe and back again. From the high seas to the samurai sword, Manjiro's story will thrill and inspire the adventurer in you.

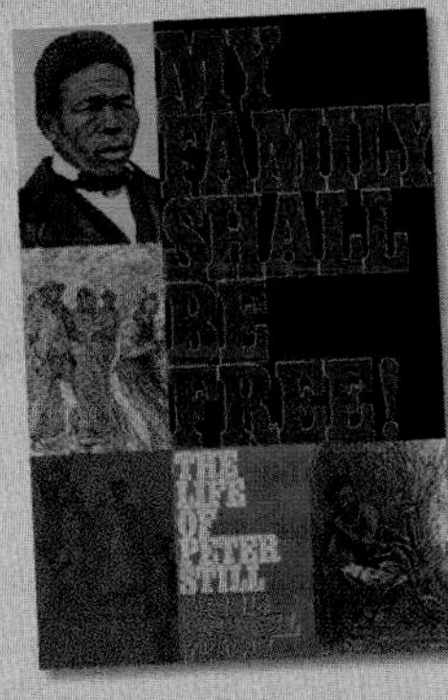

My Family Shall Be Free! The Life of Peter Still
by Dennis Brindell Fradin

Born a slave on a plantation around 1800, Peter Still was over forty years old when he bought his freedom and, amazingly, reunited with the mother and siblings he thought he'd lost forever.

READING ON YOUR OWN

Nonfiction

Share with students that the books on this page all tell the true stories of extraordinary people.

Biography and Autobiography

Ask: Which two stories on this page are biographies? *(*Shipwrecked! *and* My Family Shall Be Free!*)* How can you tell? *(They are stories about a real person's life told by another person.)* **OL** What kind of nonfiction story is *Taking Flight: My Story by Vicki Van Meter? (It is an autobiography because it is a story about a real person told by that person.)* **OL**

About the Subjects

Have students share information they have about the subjects on this page. You might point out that many slaves were separated from their loved ones during the time of slavery. What other details about slavery might students learn by reading *My Family Shall Be Free!*? *(Students may say they might learn how it felt to work hard for no reward or what it was like to become free after so many years as a slave.)*

Objectives

- Read fiction and nonfiction independently
- Understand the differences between biography, autobiography, and other works of nonfiction

Test-Taking Tips

FAQ Students may find it helpful to look over the questions before they begin reading. Tell students not to spend too much time doing this; they should skim and not read the questions.

TIP If students are asked to determine the theme, they should begin by asking themselves, "What message about life is the author trying to convey?" Once students have answered this question, they can select from the possible answer choices.

Test Practice

Part 1: Literary Elements

Read the passage. Then write the numbers 1 through 4 on a separate sheet of paper. For the first three questions, write the letter of the right answer next to the number for that question. Write your answer to the final question next to number 4.

from "Blues Ain't No Mockin Bird," by Toni Cade Bambara

"Go tell that man we ain't a bunch of trees."

"Ma'am?"

"I said to tell that man to get away from here with that camera." Me and Cathy look over toward the meadow where the men with the station wagon'd been roamin around all mornin. The tall man with a huge camera lassoed to his shoulder was buzzin our way.

"They're makin movie pictures," yelled Tyrone . . . .

"They're makin movie pictures," sang out Terry.

"That boy don't never have anything original to say," say Cathy grown-up.

By the time the man with the camera had cut across our neighbor's yard, the twins were out of the trees swingin low and Granny was onto the steps, the screen door bammin soft and scratchy against her palms. "We thought we'd get a shot or two of the house and everything and then—"

"Good mornin," Granny cut him off. And smiled that smile.

"Good mornin," he said, head all the way down the way Bingo does when you yell at him about the bones on the kitchen floor. "Nice place you got here, aunty. We thought we'd take a—"

"Did you?" said Granny with her eyebrows. Cathy pulled up her socks and giggled.

"Nice things here," said the man, buzzin his camera over the yard. The pecan barrels, the sled, me and Cathy, the flowers, the printed stones along the driveway, the trees, the twins, the toolshed.

"I don't know about the thing, the it, and the stuff," said Granny, still talkin with her eyebrows. "Just people here is what I tend to consider."

Camera man stopped buzzin. Cathy giggled into her collar.

"Mornin', ladies," a new man said. He had come up behind us when we weren't lookin. "And gents," discoverin the twins givin him a nasty look. "We're filmin for the county," he said with a smile. "Mind if we shoot a bit around here?"

"I do indeed," said Granny with no smile. Smilin man was smilin up a storm. So was Cathy. But he didn't seem to have

Objectives
Literature Identify literary elements: theme, character, dialect, cultural context

another word to say, so he and the camera man backed on out the yard, but you could hear the camera buzzin still. "Suppose you just shut that machine off," said Granny real low through her teeth, and took a step down off the porch and then another.

"Now, aunty," Camera said, pointin the thing straight at her.

"Your mama and I are not related."

Smilin man got his notebook out and a chewed-up pencil. "Listen," he said movin back into our yard, "we'd like to have a statement from you . . . for the film. We're filmin for the county, see. Part of the food stamp campaign. You know about the food stamps?"

Granny said nuthin.

---

1. Which of the following sentences from the passage is written in dialect?

A. Cathy giggled into her collar.

B. "I said to tell that man to get away from here with that camera."

C. "That boy don't never have anything original to say," say Cathy grown-up.

D. "We thought we'd get a shot or two of the house and everything and then–"

2. Granny's statements and actions suggest that she is

A. quiet and shy

B. confident and firm

C. selfish and uncaring

D. friendly and cooperative

3. What does this passage suggest a theme of the story will be?

A. Making movies can be difficult.

B. It's peaceful and pretty in the country.

C. We should make visitors feel welcome.

D. People's privacy and dignity should be respected.

4. What makes Granny treat the camera men the way she does? Use details from the passage to support your answer.

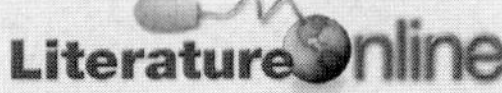

Unit Assessment To prepare for the Unit test, go to www.glencoe.com.

Test Practice

Part 1: Literary Elements

1. C
2. B
3. D
4. The cultural context could be modern rural African American. Details such as the dialect spoken by the narrator and her family, the description of the setting, and the mention of a movie camera and food stamps support this conclusion.
5. Sample response: Granny treats the camera men the way she does because she thinks they are nosy and disrespectful. To her, the men care more about things than people. Granny cares more about people than things. This becomes clear when she says, "I don't know about the thing, the it, and the stuff . . . . Just people here is what I tend to consider."

Resources for pages 764–769

Use these resources to review, assess, or reteach the Unit: Active Learning and Note-Taking Guide, Selection and Unit Assessment, ExamView Assessment Suite, and Differentiated Instruction Tool Software.

Unit Assessment Have students access the Web site to prepare for the Unit 6 test.

Test-Taking Tips

TIP Students might find it helpful when reading nonfiction pieces on a test to start by reading the first and last sentence of every paragraph to get an overview of the main ideas of the passage.

TIP If students come across a question they find difficult, have them read over each possible answer choice. Tell students to eliminate any choices that are obviously wrong and then make an educated guess based on the choices left.

Part 2: Reading Skills

Read the passage. Then write the numbers 1 through 5 on a separate sheet of paper. For the first four questions, write the letter of the right answer next to the number for that question. Write your answer to the final question next to number 5.

Global Warming

1 It's getting warmer here on Earth. Scientists say our planet's surface temperature has gone up one degree F over the last century. And there's reason to believe the temperature will keep on rising in the future. This trend is known as global warming. Many scientists think that global warming is a serious problem. They believe that even small rises in temperature could cause big changes on Earth. Here are some of those possible changes:

2 **Rise in Sea Level** A warmer climate might cause the world's glaciers to melt. (These huge, thick slabs of ice are found mainly in Antarctica, Greenland, and other cold places.) When glaciers melt and form water, some of the water goes into the sea. More water in the sea means a higher sea level. The level could also rise for another reason. Water expands, or takes up more space, as it becomes warmer. So if global warming raises the temperature of sea waters, the warmer water will expand and the sea level will rise.

3 **Flooding and Damage to Plants and Animals** A rise in sea level could cause huge floods to occur. Land along seacoasts could end up under water or could be washed away. Salt from seawater could get into the soil, harming plant and animal life.

4 **Drought and Smaller Food Supply** Global warming might also cause less rain to fall in some areas of the Earth. Droughts—long periods without rain—could harm crops in these areas. And smaller crops could lead to food shortages.

5 **Health Problems** Some scientists believe that global warming may also cause an increase in malaria rates. Malaria is a serious disease that is spread by a certain kind of mosquito. Like all mosquitoes, the malaria mosquito breeds in hot weather. Warmer temperatures might also cause an increase in the number of heart attacks that people suffer. That's because very warm weather can be a strain on the human heart.

6 Clearly, the possible effects of global warming are serious. Can we stop them from happening? Some scientists believe that we can. But in order to do so, we

Objectives
Reading Make predictions • Ask questions • Understand cause and effect • Analyze text

will have to change our ways. Our use of fossil fuels may be the number one cause of global warming. Here's why. When fossil fuels are burned, they give off a gas called carbon dioxide. This gas absorbs heat from the sun. Then it reflects the heat back into the Earth's lower atmosphere (the gases near the surface of the Earth). When too much heat is reflected back, the temperature of the Earth rises.

7 We release carbon dioxide into the atmosphere whenever we drive cars powered by a fossil fuel such as gas. And because much of our electricity is made by burning coal, another fossil fuel, our use of electricity also adds to the carbon dioxide level. The solution to the global warming problem lies with us. To cut down on the amount of carbon dioxide in the atmosphere, we must cut back on our use of fossil-fuel energy. Here are some ways to do that:

- *Drive less* Walk, ride your bike, take public transportation, or carpool. Do what you can to cut down on the amount of time your family spends driving the car.
- *Use less electricity* Turn out the lights when you leave a room. Turn off your computer and your TV when you're not using them.
- *Support the use of solar power* Solar power—power created by the heat of the sun—is clean, natural, and renewable. That means that as long as there's a sun, there will be solar energy. Let people know the pluses of solar power. And use solar power yourself. For example, dry your clothes on a clothesline outdoors instead of in a dryer.

---

1. Which of the following is a cause of global warming?

A. the addition of sea salt to the soil
B. the melting of glaciers in Antarctica
C. a decrease in rainfall in farming country
D. an increase in the level of carbon dioxide in the atmosphere

2. Which of the following would most likely occur if everyone switched from fossil fuels to solar power?

A. Air pollution would increase.
B. Global warming would decrease.
C. The supply of solar energy would decrease.
D. The level of carbon dioxide in the air would increase.

3. The answer to which of the following questions would help readers understand paragraph 6?

A. What are fossil fuels?
B. Why does the sun give off heat?
C. Who discovered global warming?
D. Where is the upper atmosphere located?

4. Which of the following is the best analysis of how the passage is organized?

A. time order
B. comparison and contrast
C. problem, cause, and solution
D. most important idea to least important idea

5. Name and explain three possible effects of global warming. Use details from the passage to support your explanations.

Test Practice

Part 2: Reading Skills

1. D
2. B
3. A
4. C
5. Students should include three of the following effects: (1) Glaciers might melt, and the resulting water could cause the level of the sea to rise. (2) Water in the ocean might expand as it is heated, which could also cause the sea level to rise. (3) A rise in sea level could cause floods to occur in coastal regions. (4) Salt from seawater could damage plants and animals that live in coastal regions. (5) Droughts could occur. (6) Food shortages might occur in drought areas. (7) There might be more cases of malaria because the mosquito that carries the disease breeds in hot weather. (8) There might be an increase in the heart attack rate because hot weather can put a strain on the human heart.

Test Practice

Part 3: Vocabulary Acquisition and English Language Skills

1. C
2. D
3. B
4. D
5. A
6. C
7. B
8. A
9. C
10. D

Part 3: Vocabulary Acquisition and English Language Skills

On a separate sheet of paper, write the numbers 1 through 10. Next to each number, write the letter of the right answer for that question.

Write the letter of the word that means about the same as the underlined word.

1. to taunt someone

A. hit
B. teach
C. tease
D. praise

2. gnarled fingers

A. long
B. smooth
C. crossed
D. twisted

3. solemnly made a promise

A. falsely
B. seriously
C. carelessly
D. needlessly

4. regretfully saying no

A. angrily
B. secretly
C. repeatedly
D. sadly

5. contemporary fads

A. present-day
B. short-lived
C. high-risk
D. old-fashioned

Objectives
Vocabulary Understand idioms • Understand slang • Distinguish literal from metaphoric meanings
Grammar Identify direct objects • Identify indirect objects • Use compound and complex sentences • Combine sentences • Identify and correct run-on sentences • Correct errors in writing conventions

Choose the correct answer for each question.

6. Which phrase contains slang?

A. a cool breeze
B. cool the soup
C. a cool song
D. such cool weather

7. What does the underlined idiom mean in the following sentence? This is hard; would you lend a hand?

A. clap
B. help me
C. watch me
D. write it down

8. Read the following dialogue. What does the underlined dialect mean?

"I'm right peckish, mate," Algie complained.
"Okay. We'll get something to eat in a few minutes," Ben replied.

A. "I'm very hungry, friend."
B. "I'm eager to work, sailor."
C. "I'm right and you're wrong, wife."
D. "I'm in an awfully good mood, buddy."

9. Use what you know about the word *pull* to figure out what pull means in the following sentence. I wish I had some pull where I work.

A. time
B. supplies
C. influence
D. vacation time

10. In which sentence is the phrase "in hot water" used figuratively?

A. Wash the dishes in hot water.
B. We poached the eggs in hot water.
C. She burned her finger in hot water.
D. If you lie to Dad, you'll be in hot water.

Part 4: Grammar and Writing Skills

Write the numbers 1–8 on a separate sheet of paper. Then write the letter of the right answer next to the number for that question.

1. Which of the following sentences contains a direct object?

A. The trees bent in the storm.
B. Jeff returned at four o'clock.
C. Jaguars run as fast as the wind.
D. Casey loves cereal for breakfast.

2. What is the indirect object in the sentence below?

Maurice showed the doctor his swollen ankle.

A. Maurice
B. doctor
C. swollen
D. ankle

3. Which of the following is a run-on sentence?

A. I'll help you with math I'm good at it.
B. We could study together at my house or yours.
C. Call me if you don't understand the story problems.
D. At first they seem hard, but they get easier with practice.

4. Which of the following is correctly punctuated?

A. The game was great our team won by three points.
B. I thought we would lose, our star player was injured.
C. We will probably be in the playoffs, but there are no guarantees.
D. We can't lose any more players, or any more games in our division.

Read the paragraph. Then answer the questions that follow.

[1]I didn't want to go to school I was feeling sick. [2]"I wonder just how sick you are" my mom said. [3]"I guess your much too sick to go to the mall and look at new radios and cell phones tonight." [4]I had forgotten that we were suppose to go shopping for my birthday presents.

5. Which correction should be made to sentence 1?

A. Insert a comma after "school."
B. Insert "and" after "school."
C. Insert "because" after "school."
D. Insert a comma and "but" after "school."

6. Which correction should be made to sentence 2?

A. Change "I" to "i."
B. Insert a comma after "are."
C. Insert a question mark after "are."
D. Change "mom" to "Mom."

7. Which correction should be made to sentence 3?

A. Change "your" to "you're."
B. Change "too" to "to."
C. Change "mall" to "Mall."
D. Change "radios" to "radioes."

8. Which correction should be made to sentence 4?

A. Change "had forgotten" to "have forgot."
B. Insert a period after "forgotten" and capitalize "that."
C. Change "suppose" to "supposed."
D. Change "presents" to "presence."

Test Practice

Part 4: Grammar and Writing Skills

1. D
2. B
3. A
4. C
5. C
6. B
7. A
8. C

UNIT 7

Skills Scope and Sequence

Readability Scores Key
Dale-Chall/DRP/Lexile

PACING (DAYS) STANDARD	BLOCK	INSTRUCTIONAL SEGMENT LITERATURE	READING SKILLS	LITERARY ELEMENTS
1	1	**Unit Warm-Up, pp. 772–775** Genre Focus: "One" by James Berry SE p. 775	Evaluating, SE p. 774 Interpreting, SE p. 774 Monitoring comprehension, SE p. 774 Connecting, SE p. 774 Fluency, TWE p. 771	Sound Devices, SE p. 774, TWE p. 775 Symbolism, SE p. 774 Rhyme, Rhythm, and Meter, SE p. 774 Figurative Language, SE p. 774 Repetition, TWE p. 774
3	2	**Reading Workshop 1, pp. 776–793** "Annabel Lee" by Edgar Allan Poe SE p. 780 "Names/Nombres" by Julia Alvarez **6.9/59/1130**, SE p. 786	Evaluating, SE pp. 776, 777, 779, 781, 783, 785, 787, 788, 793 Connecting, pp. 787, 793 Fluency, TWE p. 780	Sound Devices, SE pp. 779, 780, 783, TWE p. 778 Figurative Language, SE pp. 785, 786, 789, 793, TWE p. 784 Word Choice, TWE p. 779 Theme, TWE p. 791
1		**Writing Workshop, Part 1, pp. 794–797** Writing Product: Poem		
3	1	**Reading Workshop 2, pp. 798–813** "Diondra Jordan" by Nikki Grimes **5.2/49/760**, SE p. 802 "if" by Diondra Jordan, SE p. 805 "Face It" by Janet S. Wong, SE p. 810 "Almost Ready" by Arnold Adoff, SE p. 811	Interpreting, SE pp. 798, 799, 801, 802, 803, 805, 807, 809, 810, 813 Connecting, SE pp. 804, 807 Evaluating, SE p. 813 Fluency, TWE p. 811	Symbolism, SE pp. 801, 804, 805, 807, 809, 810, 813 Sound Devices, SE p. 14 Poetic Elements, TWE p. 808

Unit 7 Big Question

The question, "What Makes You Tick?" is designed to help students analyze their thoughts and feelings and better understand their motivations. In this unit, students will read about a variety of motives and ideals that make people tick.

Unit 2 Genre

Through the words of poetry in this unit, students will be exposed to different aspects of who they are and examine the things that inspire them. The poems and other selections will also help students answer the Big Question.

CRITICAL THINKING	VOCABULARY	WRITING AND GRAMMAR	LISTENING, SPEAKING, AND VIEWING
	Indefinite Pronouns, TWE p. 775		Viewing the Photo, TWE p. 770
	Latin Roots, SE pp. 790, 791, TWE pp. 790, 791 Academic vocabulary, SE p. 776 Vocabulary Preview, SE pp. 778, 784 Vocabulary Check, SE p. 783 Visual Vocabulary, SE p. 789 Contractions, TWE p. 788	Write About Your Reading, SE p. 792 Finding Subjects and Verbs, SE p. 783 Tricky Subjects and Verbs, SE p. 793	Talk About Your Reading, SE p. 782 Viewing the Painting, TWE p. 786
	Slang, TWE p. 796	Writing a Poem, SE p. 792 Subject-Verb Agreement, SE p. 797	
Evaluate, SE pp. 806, 812 Draw Conclusions, SE p. 806 Interpret, SE p. 806 Infer, SE p. 812	Latin Roots, SE pp. 800, 803 Vocabulary Preview, SE pp. 800, 808 Vocabulary Check, SE p. 807 Symbolism, TWE p. 799 Academic Vocabulary, SE p. 807 Anglo-Saxon Origins, SE pp. 808, 810, 811, TWE pp. 809, 811 Build Background, TWE pp. 800, 803	Write About Your Reading, SE p. 806 Making *To Be* Agree, SE p. 807 Agreement in Inverted Sentences, SE p. 813	Talk About Your Reading, SE p. 812

Skills Scope and Sequence *continued*

Readability Scores Key
Dale-Chall/DRP/Lexile

PACING (DAYS) STANDARD	BLOCK	INSTRUCTIONAL SEGMENT LITERATURE	READING SKILLS	LITERARY ELEMENTS
3	cont'd. ↓	**Reading Workshop 3, pp. 814–829** "Miracles" by Walt Whitman, SE p. 818 "The Pasture" by Robert Frost, SE p. 819 Reading, Writing, Rapping by Elizabeth Wellington **7.3/60/1060**, SE p. 824	Monitoring Comprehension, SE pp. 814, 815, 817, 818, 819, 821, 823, 825, 826, 829 Fluency, TWE p. 818	Rhyme, Rhythm, and Meter, SE pp. 817, 819, 821, 823, 827, 829
1		**Writing Workshop, Part 2, pp. 830–833** Writing Product: Poem		
2	1	**Reading Workshop 4, pp. 834–851** "Growing Pains" by Jean Little p. 838 "What Makes Teens Tick?" by Claudia Wallis **6.5/62/1020**, SE p. 844	Understanding sequence, SE pp. 204, 207, 212, 213, 215, 217, 221 Connecting, SE pp. 834, 835, 837, 839, 841, 846 Interpreting, SE pp. 839, 841	Sensory Details, SE pp. 207, 209, 215, 217, 218, 221; TWE pp. 207, 216 Figurative Language, pp. 837, 838, 841, 844, 846, 847, Speaker, TWE p. 836
2	2	**Comparing Literature Workshop** "The Women's 400 Meters" by Lillian Morrison, SE p. 852 "To James" by Frank Horne, SE p. 856 "Slam, Dunk, and Hook" by Usef Komunyakaa, SE p. 858	Fluency, TWE p. 857	Symbols, TWE p. 859 How to Compare Literature: Figurative Language, SE pp. 852, 853 Figurative Language, SE pp. 855, 856, 857, 858, 859, 860, TWE p. 853 Sensory Language, TWE p. 852
2	1	**Unit Wrap-Up, pp. 862–875** The Giggle Prescription by Tracy Eberhart and Robert A. Barnett **5.4/65/1130**, SE p. 864	Reading Independently, SE pp. 864, 867, 868, 869 Standardized Test Practice, SE pp. 870–875 Fluency, TWE p. 866	Summary, TWE p. 864

UNIT 7

Professional Development Center

Kathleen Hinchman

From Your Authors:

Preparing Students to Read Poetry

Tap into students' knowledge of the genre. To gain an understanding of what students already know about the genre, teachers can ask students to brainstorm what they already know about poetry, perhaps drawing a web of students' ideas as they speak. Students may remember that sometimes poetry rhymes or has rhythm, that it's a way of expressing feelings, that wording matters, and that there are different types of poetry. The teacher's web can show relationships between students' ideas about form, function, and word selection. Students can be invited to bring in favorite bits of poetry, such as lyrics to favorite songs, raps, or jump rope rhymes as they engage in the reading and writing required in this unit.

Make personal connections. Generations of young people have ended up disliking poetry because they could not figure out why teachers identified only some poetry interpretations or themes as correct. Instead of being the teacher who perpetuates such antipathy, ask students to share their interpretations first, building small group, and, then, whole class discussions from their ideas. To do this, teachers may find it helpful to invite a group of students to listen to or read from the same poem and to write about the poem—anything they wanted—for a few minutes after the reading. Invite students to tell one another something about what they wrote, choosing whether or not they actually want to share their quick write. This can be followed with a discussion of similarities and differences in students' responses, which can, in turn, lead into a discussion of interpretations—perhaps comparing students' responses to interpretations published in literary criticisms. Seeing how classmates bring prior knowledge to their interpretations of poetry can help students learn to discern themes with increasing acumen.

Gerald Romero
Pojoaque Middle School – NM

Teacher to Teacher

Unit 7: What makes you tick?

Our school is located within a tri-lingual district composed of Anglo, Hispanic American, and Native American students. So, when opening the unit "What makes you tick?" I use each student's native culture as a starting point. We discuss who we are and what makes us who we are from a cultural standpoint, and students write an essay on this topic from the perspective of their own cultural backgrounds. They share their essays in class, and we talk about cultural differences. Then students create a pictorial autobiography using pictures of themselves growing up. They put these pictures on a poster or some other background; list all their hobbies, interests, and activities; and describe their likes and dislikes. They include information about various personal attitudes and use adjectives to describe their qualities.

Literature Launchers

Set the scene with Glencoe's Literature Launchers, engaging video segments that introduce each unit's genre focus. Each video brings the genre to life, relating it to your students' worlds.

Insert the Glencoe Literature Launchers Prereading DVD into your DVD player. Select the Unit 7 Launcher from the menu to introduce the genre and Big Question for this unit.

Online Essay Grader

Use Glencoe's Online Essay Grading to score your students' writing and to provide individualized feedback to each student automatically.

You and your students can visit www.glencoe.com to link to the essay grader. *Students* can enter their essays and receive feedback on demand. *You* can manage demographic data, assign tests and generate individual student and aggregated reports. The essay grader can help you

- Save time with automatic scoring and individualized feedback.
- Supplement in-class writing instruction using guided writing practice.
- Get reports for individual students or for special populations.
- Track student improvement over time.

REAL Success: Reading Excellence at All Levels

Glencoe now provides all of your students with the tools they need to become better, more enthusiastic readers. The REAL Success suite of reading and language arts products encourages reading excellence by meeting the needs of students at all levels. Glencoe products that can be used in conjunction with Unit 7 include the following:

- Jamestown Literature: An Adapted Reader
- Jamestown *Reading Fluency*
- Jamestown *Critical Reading Series, In the Line of Duty*
- *Vocabulary Builder*
- *The Glencoe Reader, Course 2*

To order these products, call Glencoe at 1-800-USA-READ.

Teacher Wraparound Edition Key

Level Appropriate Code

AS = Activities for all students

AL = Activities for students working above grade level

OL = Activities for students working at grade level

BL = Activities for students working below grade level

EL = Activities for English language learners

Teacher Wraparound Prompts

R **Reading Skill** These activities help you teach reading skills and vocabulary.

V **Vocabulary** These activities help students comprehend words and incorporate into reading.

C **Critical Thinking** These strategies help students apply and extend what they have learned.

BQ **BIG Question** These activities and questions prompt students to prepare to answer the Big Question.

W **Writing** These activities provide writing opportunities to help students practice writing and comprehend text.

L **Literary Element** These activities and questions help students comprehend selections and learn more about each genre.

E **Text Element** These activities help students comprehend text elements.

LSV **Listening, Speaking, Viewing** These activities help students practice listening, speaking, and viewing skills.

EL **English Language Coach** These skills help English language learners as well as students who need additional reading support.

Additional Glencoe Resources

FOLDABLES™ Study Organizer

Dinah Zike's Foldables

Foldables are three-dimensional, interactive graphic organizers that help students practice basic writing skills, review key vocabulary terms, and answer Big Questions. Every unit contains a foldable activity. You can find the pattern and directions for the Unit 7 Foldable in the Unit 7 Resources Fast Files booklet. You can use the foldables as they are presented or modify them to suit the needs of your students. More information about foldables for Unit 7 can be found on page R8.

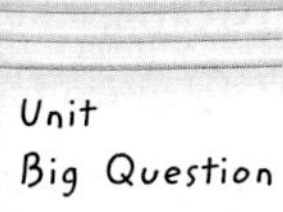

Glencoe Literature Library

The collection of hardcover books include full-length novels, novellas, plays and works of nonfiction. Each volume consists of at least one complete extended-length reading accompanied by several related readings from a broad range of genres. A separate Study Guide for each Glencoe Literature Library book provides teaching notes and reproducible activity pages for students.

Glencoe Literature Library titles that complement this unit include:

The Call of the Wild by Jack London
High elk's Treasure by Virginia Driving Hawk Sneve
I, Juan de Pareja by Elizabeth Borton de Treviño
Journey to Jo'burg: A South African Story by Beverley Naidoo

For a wealth of online resources that support the instruction in Unit 7 of *Glencoe Literature: Reading with Purpose,* students and teachers can visit our Web site at www.glencoe.com. Students will find additional learning, practice, and assessment opportunities such as these, which are noted in the student text:

- **Big Question Overview**
- **Study Central**
- **Author Search**
- **Writing Models**
- **Interactive Literary Elements Handbook**
- **Web Activities**

Teachers will find planning and instructional tools that include the following:

- **Book Lesson Plans**
- **Teacher Forum**
- **Professional Development**
- **Web Activities Lesson Plans (with answers to student activities)**

Go to www.glencoe.com to see the entire selection of Reading with Purpose online resources.

GLENCOE BOOKLINK

Use the Glencoe BookLink 3 CD-ROM, a database of more than 26,700 titles, to *create customized reading lists* for your students.

- Search for award-winning titles, (e.g., Newbery Award winners, Coretta Scott King Award winners, and Caldecott Medal winners) and for books on several state-recommended reading lists.
- Find Degrees of Reading Power™ (DRP) and Lexile™ readability scores for all selections.
- Organize reading lists by students' reading level, author, genre, theme, or area of interest.
- Get a brief summary of each selection.

You can find recommended leveled readings for this unit with Reading on Your Own (see page 120)

Glencoe's **Presentation Plus!**, a multimedia teaching tool, lets you present dynamic lessons that will engage your students. Using Microsoft PowerPoint,® you can customize the presentations to create your own personalized lessons. Use **CheckPoint** questions with interactive response keypads to get immediate student feedback during lessons, to increase student participation, and to assess student comprehension.

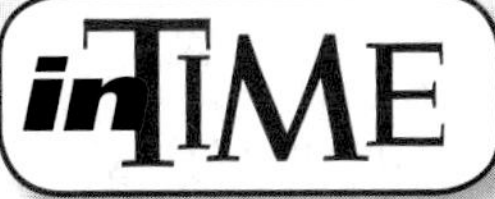

A lively collection of articles drawn from issues of the TIME family of magazines helps students develop the skills they need to interact with informational text in a meaningful way. Each of the news stories, feature articles, reviews, profiles, and essays in the magazine connect to an author, work, or theme in *Glencoe Literature: Reading with Purpose.* Articles for Unit 7 are found in Volume A. See the *inTIME* Teacher's Guide for specific connections to each unit and for reproducible student worksheets designed to develop students' reading and critical thinking skills.

Additional Instructional Support

WRITING, GRAMMAR, AND SPELLING

- Real Success in Writing: Research and Reports
- Writing Constructed Responses Sourcebook
- Spelling Power eWorkbook
- Grammar & Composition Handbook
- Grammar and Language Workbook
- Revising with Style eWorkbook

READING AND LITERATURE

- Active Learning and Note Taking Guide
- inTime Magazines
- Backpack Reader Volume 1
- Literature Library
- Literature Launchers Pre-Reading Videos DVD
- Literature Classics

TRANSPARENCIES

- Read Aloud, Think Aloud
- Literary and Text Analysis Transparencies
- Bellringer Options Transparencies
- Grammar and Writing Workshop Transparencies
- Fine Arts Transparencies

TECHNOLOGY

- TeacherWorks Plus
- StudentWorks Plus
- BookLink 3
- Skill Level Up!
- ExamView Assessment Suite
- Interactive Tutor Self-Assessment
- Listening Library CD
- Spanish Listening Library CD
- Literature Classics
- Literature Launchers Pre-Reading Videos DVD
- Literature Library ExamView Assessment Suite
- Vocabulary Puzzlemaker
- Literature Library Vocabulary Puzzlemaker
- glencoe.com
- Online Student Edition
- Presentation Plus!
- Glencoe Online Essay Grading

ENGLISH LANGUAGE LEARNER

- English Language Coach
- Fluency Practice and Assessment
- inTime Magazines (Spanish)
- Spanish Listening Library CD

PROFESSIONAL DEVELOPMENT

- Professional Development Package

UNIT 7

Unit Resources

Reading with Purpose offers a comprehensive package of tools to optimize student learning and the teaching experience. Each resource has been designed to assist students in specific areas and to offer instructional support for teachers. While all of these areas are covered in the core textbook, some students may need extra practice or additional help in specific areas. The resource package is designed so that you, the teacher, can choose which items will best assist your students. You may also use these resources as homework assignments and for assessment purposes. The following are resources recommended for use with Unit 7.

Keys for Unit Resources

- Blackline Master
- Workbook
- Supplemental Text
- CD-ROM
- DVD
- Transparency
- Web-based
- Fast Files

Essential Instructional Support

FAST FILE UNIT 7 RESOURCES

Reading and Literature

- Academic Vocabulary Development
- Big Question: School to Home Connection
- The Big Question Foldable
- Genre Study
- Unit Challenge: Planner and Rubrics
- Comparing Literature Graphic Organizer
- Key Reading Skills Practice
- Active Reading Graphic Organizers
- Literary Analysis
- Selection Vocabulary Development

Writing, Grammar, and Spelling

- Spelling and Handwriting Practice
- Grammar Practice
- Writing Workshop Graphic Organizer

Listening, Speaking, and Viewing

- Viewing and Representing Activities
- Listening and Speaking Activities

English Language Learners

- English Language Coach

DIFFERENTIATED INSTRUCTION

- Leveled Vocabulary Development
- Skills Level Up!
- Listening Library CD
- BookLink 3
- Literature Library Vocabulary Puzzlemaker
- Vocabulary Puzzlemaker

ASSESSMENT

- Selection and Unit Assessments
- Selection Quick Checks
- Assessment by Learning Objectives
- Rubrics for Assessing Student Writing, Listening, and Speaking
- Glencoe Online Essay Grading
- Interactive Tutor Self-Assessment
- ExamView Assessment Suite
- Literature Library ExamView Assessment Suite

CRITICAL THINKING	VOCABULARY	WRITING AND GRAMMAR	LISTENING, SPEAKING, AND VIEWING
Synthesize, SE p. 820 Infer, SE pp. 820, 828 Interpret, SE pp. 820, 828	Vocabulary Preview, SE pp. 822, 816, 822 Vocabulary Check, SE pp. 821, 829 Greek Roots, SE pp. 822, 824 Idioms, TWE p. 824 Future Tense, TWE p. 819 Build Background, TWE p. 814	Agreement with Compounds, SE p. 821 Write About Your Reading, SE p. 820 Subjects Separated from Verbs, SE p. 829	Viewing the Photo, TWE p. 825
			Poetry Reading or Poetry Slam!, p. 833 Say-Back, TWE p. 833
Infer, SE p. 840 Evaluate, SE p. 840 Connect, SE p. 850 Analysis, TWE p. 844 Comprehension, TWE p. 847 Application, TWE p. 849	Vocabulary Preview, SE p. 842 Vocabulary Check, SE pp. 841, 851 Word Origins, SE p. 839 Lanuage Growth, SE pp. 845, 846, TWE pp. 842, 845 Content-Area Vocabulary, TWE p. 844	Write About Your Reading, SE pp. 840, 850 Agreement with Indefinite Pronouns, SE p. 841 Writing Application, SE p. 841 Agreement with Collective Nouns, SE p. 851	View the Painting, TWE p. 838
Analysis, TWE p. 858 Evaluate, SE p. 861, TWE p. 857 Interpret, SE p. 861 Connect, SE p. 861	Descriptive Verbs, TWE p. 855 Vocabulary Preview, SE p. 854 Roots, SE pp. 854, 857, 859, TWE p. 857 Vocabulary Check, SE p. 860	Writing: Compare the Literature, SE p. 862	Viewing the Photo, TWE p. 856
	Humorous Writing, TWE p. 867 Fiction, TWE p. 868 Nonfiction, TWE p. 869		Group Activity: Character Study, SE p. 862 Solo Activity: Personal Reflection

Teacher Chat Room

Reading and Writing Poetry

Before you begin this unit or at some time during the unit, talk with other teachers about ways they have taught poetry. Have a lunchtime discussion group or an after-school hour for professional development and discuss the following questions and answers from our authors:

How can I make poetry interesting to middle school students?

Middle grade students will like poetry more when they discover that their favorite lyrics or nursery rhymes are a kind of poetry, that their own first response is grounding for poetic interpretation, and, most importantly, that poetry represents a unique, intense way of representing important insights. To help students immerse themselves in different kinds of poetry,

- Bring stacks of a wide range of poetry to your classroom. Include poems ranging from the Shel Silverstein poetry students will remember from their elementary school reading to the Robert Frost poems appreciated by older readers.
- Invite students to work in inquiry groups, reading poetry to themselves and each other and finding poetry to share with the rest of the class in a daily "read aloud" that ends each day's inquiry.
- Students can bring in examples of poetry they find at home, in song lyrics, and on the Internet in youth poetry collections.
- Maintain an ongoing discussion, noting the reasons individuals find particular poems engaging. Tie this discussion to the study of poetry throughout history, noting variations in use and form represented by Homer, Chaucer, Shakespeare, and more contemporary poets.

How can I help students to understand poetry from different historical periods?

Invite students to team up and engage in brief inquiry about particular time periods during which poetry was written, noting historical events or issues of gender, race, or class that might have affected the ways in which individuals chose to represent ideas. Students can then read bits of poetry to see what they can discern of its meaning or historical content, comparing their responses to various published literary explanations, and sharing their findings with the class.

What language and structures do poetry writers use, and how can writers use these elements in their own writing?

Teachers should explain that authors use poetic devices to come up with the concise representations that make poetry what it is. Students can learn that authors use such poetic devices to tell the stories in narrative poems or to make points in lyric poems.

Teach figurative language and sound devices as they are needed to interpret particular poems, one or two at a time. Post these on a bulletin board or work wall for later reference. Conduct brief mini lessons during the writers workshop that refer back to examples in poetry that has been read. Invite students to draft bits of poetry using devices taught in these mini lessons.

Key Unit Objectives

- Answer the Big Question
- Identify, understand, and apply strategies for reading poetry
- Analyze the literary elements of poetry
- Write poetry

BIG Question

Why Is It Important?

Addressing this Big Question helps students analyze their thoughts and feelings and better understand their motivations.

Viewing the Photo

Say: Michael Jordan is considered one of the most talented athletes of all time. Do you agree with him that you have to expect things of yourself before you can do them? *(Possible response: Yes, I agree. If you don't expect yourself to succeed, you probably won't.)* **OL** What do you think the woman in the photo expected of herself? *(Possible response: She expected herself to work hard to become an athletic, limber dancer.)* **AS**

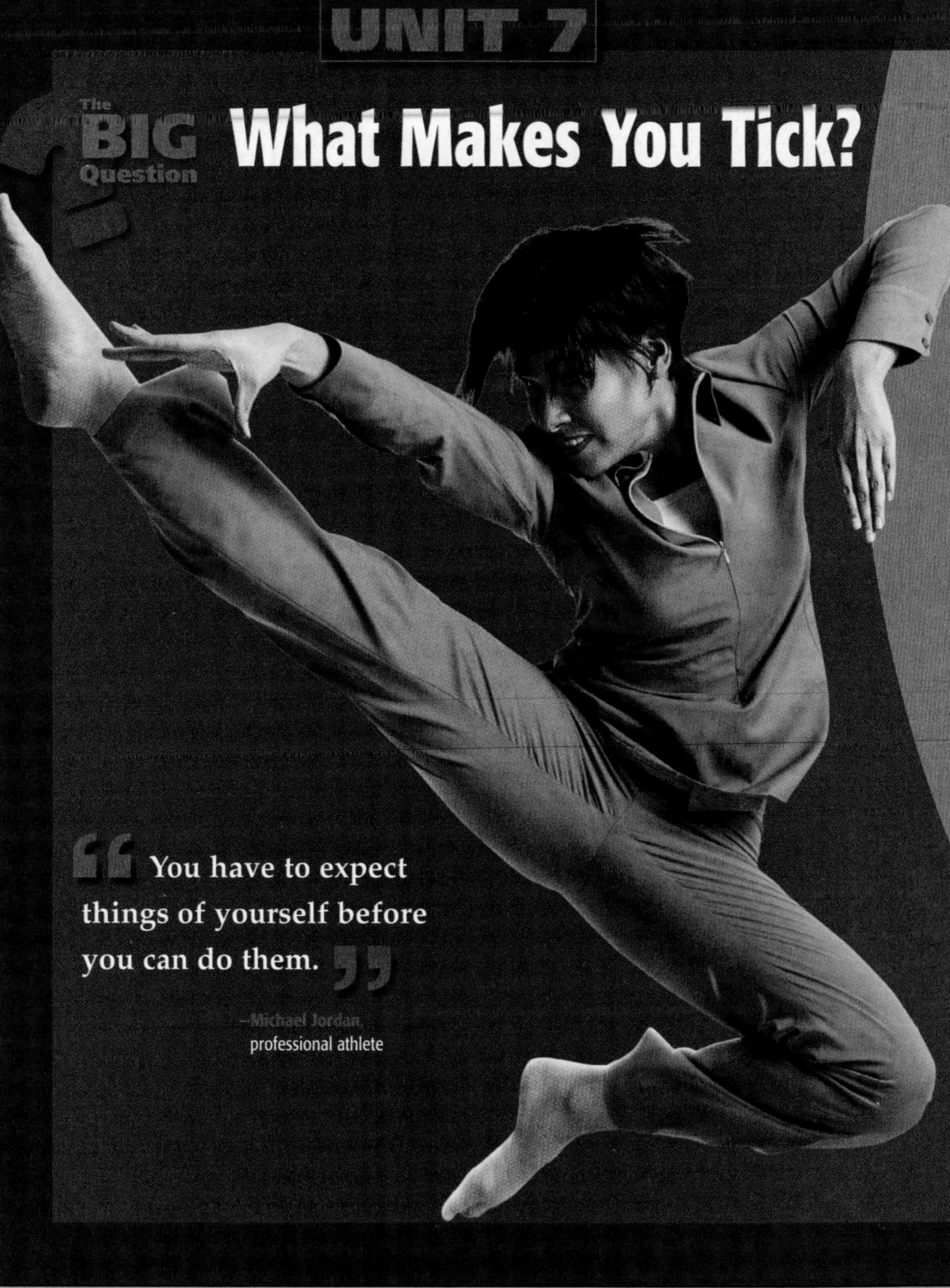
UNIT 7
The BIG Question
What Makes You Tick?
"You have to expect things of yourself before you can do them."
—Michael Jordan, professional athlete

Unit Skills

The BIG Question: What Makes You Tick?
Genre Focus: Poetry

Reading Skills
- Evaluating, p. 776
- Interpreting, p. 798
- Monitoring comprehension, p. 814
- Connecting, p. 834

Vocabulary
- Latin roots, p. 784
- Anglo-Saxon origins, p. 808
- Greek roots, p. 822
- Word origins, p. 836

Literary Elements
- Sound devices, p. 779
- Symbolism, p. 801
- Rhyme, rhythm, and meter, p. 817
- Figurative language, p. 837

Writing Skills/Grammar
- Poetry, pp. 794, 830
- Subject and verb agreement, pp. 783, 807, 813, 821, 829, 841, 851

LOOKING AHEAD

The skill lessons and readings in this unit will help you develop your own answer to the Big Question.

About the Reading

Each selection in this unit provides insights that can help students address the question, "What makes you tick?" Students consider different aspects of who they are and examine the things that inspire them.

About the Skills

The skills taught in this unit have been selected because they are particularly helpful when reading the featured genre—poetry. Each reading selection provides students with opportunities to practice and develop these skills.

No Child Left Behind

As part of NCLB, the U.S. Department of Education has developed research-based texts on a variety of topics. *Put Reading First* observes that students learn vocabulary through both direct learning (memorizing words, learning word structure) and indirect learning (speaking to others, reading on their own, and listening to an adult read). Help students expand their vocabulary using both direct and indirect vocabulary instruction while teaching Unit 7.

Reading Fluency

Reading Poetry Tell students that paying attention to rhythm is especially important when reading poetry. Poems, like songs, have their own beat. Model for students how to read poetry by reading aloud one of the poems in the unit. Use the tone, pitch, and volume of your voice to create meaning, and show students how to use punctuation, rather than line endings, to tell them when to pause. **BL**

Have students take turns reading aloud the same poem you chose. Encourage them to use their voices creatively as they read. Then have students tell whether it was easy or difficult to find the "beat" of the poem. **OL**

Focus

BELLRINGER Options

- **Literature Launcher: Prereading DVD**
- **Daily Language Practice Transparency**

Focus Activity Write on the board: Ask students to complete the statement: My special talent, belief, or way of seeing the world is ______. *(Responses will vary.)*

Teach

R Reading Skill

Connecting Ask students to write several sentences in their Learner's Notebook to answer the following questions:

- What are some things or ideas you value?
- What qualities do you admire in your family or friends?
- What inspires you to keep going when things are rough? OL

BQ BIG Question

- Have students read the profiles and look at the pictures of Jenny and Micah.
- Have students discuss the advice they would give to Micah. Then have them discuss the types of things that can motivate people. OL

Connecting to The BIG Question

What Makes You Tick?

R What gets you going? What makes you want to do your best? When you figure this out, you'll know what makes you "tick." It may be a talent, a value, a belief, a person, or something else. It may be many things. In this unit, you'll read what makes other people tick. You'll see how learning about themselves has affected their decisions and relationships.

Real Kids and the Big Question

Jenny had a tough writing assignment from her teacher. Jenny didn't really care about writing; but now she has a new teacher, and she wants to do her best work. She spent days writing, proofing, and rewriting her paper. Nervously, she turned it in. Finally, when she got her paper back, she received a note from her teacher praising her hard work. Why might the teacher's praise motivate Jenny to do more writing?

BQ **Micah** really likes hanging out with her friends. She also likes helping out at her little sister's day-care center. She thinks this is important, because someday she would like to be a teacher. When her friends give her a hard time about it, she laughs it off. But Micah would like them to respect her decision and stop giving her a hard time. If you were Micah, what would you tell your friends?

Warm-Up Activity

In a small group, share ideas about what you think Jenny and Micah might do. Then write a letter to Jenny or Micah, telling what you think. Share your letter with the class.

Additional Support

Reading in the Real World

Career As Micah explores her interest in teaching, she will find that future job opportunities for teachers are expected to be good. In fact, job opportunities for teachers are expected to remain good to excellent as a large number of teachers retire in the next decade. Micah will find that the teaching field includes many areas of specialization and that mathematics, science, bilingual education, and foreign language teachers are in very high demand. Most states require general education teachers to obtain a bachelor's degree and complete a teacher training program. Teachers may complete additional training and move into positions such as guidance counselors or administrators. OL

You and the Big Question

Reading about what makes others tick will help you think about and define what makes you tick. Using the reading selections in this unit, you'll be better able to answer the Big Question.

BQ

Big Question Link to Web resources to further explore the Big Question at www.glencoe.com.

Plan for the Unit Challenge

At the end of the unit, you'll use notes from all of your reading to complete the Unit Challenge.

You will choose one of the following activities:

A. Character Study Work with classmates to conduct an interview with a character in this unit and draw conclusions about what makes him or her tick.

B. Personal Reflection Make a collage showing things that make you tick.

- Start thinking about which activity you'd like to do so that you can narrow your focus as you read each selection.
- In your Learner's Notebook, write your thoughts about the activities. Which sounds like fun? Which will help you answer the Big Question?
- As you read, note what makes each character or speaker tick and why.
- List the kinds of things that make you tick—music, poetry, books, friends, and so on.

Keep Track of Your Ideas

FOLDABLES™ Study Organizer

As you read, you'll make notes about the Big Question. Later, you'll use these notes to complete the Unit Challenge. See page R9 for help with making Foldable 7. This diagram shows how it should look.

1. Make one Foldable page for each selection. At the end of the unit, you'll staple the pages together into one Foldable.
2. Label the front of the fold-over page with the selection title. (See page 771 for the titles.)
3. Below the title, write the label **My Purpose for Reading.**
4. Open the Foldable. Label the inside page **The Big Question.**

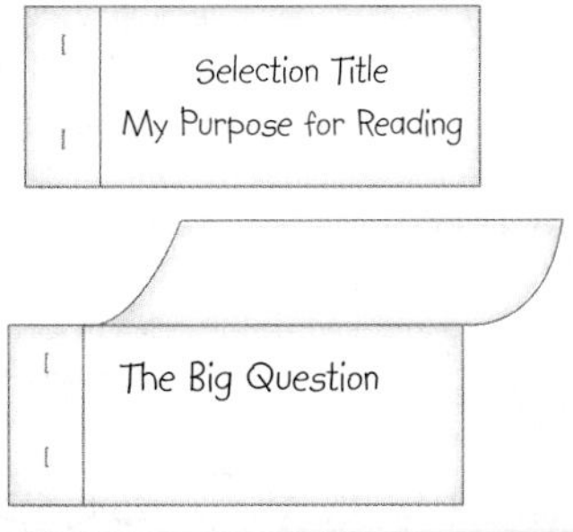

Teach

BQ

Have students write their initial response to what makes them tick in their Learner's Notebook. AS

Literature Online

Big Question Have students access the Web site for English and Spanish summaries and annotated links to related Web resources.

FOLDABLES™ Study Organizer

For each selection they read, students will enter notes about how that selection applies to the Big Question. For details about using Dinah Zike's Foldables, see p. R9.

Assess/Close

Ask students to share their thoughts about what makes them tick.

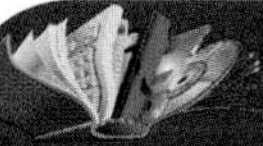

Resources for page 773

- Use the Unit Challenge Planner BLM in the Unit 7 Resource Booklet.
- Use the Foldable BLM in the Unit 7 Resource Booklet.

Differentiated Instruction

Exploring Vocations Encourage students to look through newspapers and magazines to find three pictures of people doing jobs that look interesting, such as taking care of animals, sculpting a statue, or cooking a meal. After students have located their pictures, have them write a caption under each one, explaining why they chose the picture and what qualities they think a person would need to do the job well. When students have finished annotating their pictures, lead a discussion about what makes people tick and what qualities can help them in the work they do every day. AS

Objectives
- Connect prior knowledge and experiences to literature
- Understand qualities needed to perform different kinds of work

Focus

BELLRINGER Options

- **Selection Focus Transparency**
- **Daily Language Practice Transparency**

Focus Activity Say: Songs and chants are a type of poetry. Think of a playground game that includes a rhythmic chant, such as a verse that kids recite when skipping rope. Why are these playground poems fun to say? *(Possible responses: The chants have rhythm and rhyme; they often have funny and clever word plays.)*

Teach

R Reading Skill

How to Read Poetry Say: Look at the reading skills on this page and tell how you might use them as you read poetry. *(Possible response: **Evaluating:** You will have an opinion about whether you like a particular poem. **Interpreting:** Some poems are like puzzles, and you have to look for clues to figure out a poem's meaning. **Monitoring comprehension:** Poems often have literary elements that take more than one reading to figure out. **Connecting:** You might have experience with a poem's subject or emotions.)* OL

UNIT 7 GENRE FOCUS: POETRY

Skills Focus
- Key skills for reading lyric and narrative poetry
- Key literary elements of lyric and narrative poetry

Skills Model

You will see how to use the key reading skills and literary elements as you read
- **"One,"** by James Berry, p. 775

Poetry looks different from stories and other kinds of literature. Poetry is written in **verse**–that is, in lines instead of in running text. Poetry may be a bigger part of your life than you realize. The songs you enjoy are poems. There are two main types of poetry:
- **Narrative poetry** tells a story.
- **Lyric poetry** tells about the poet's feelings or emotions.

Why Read Poetry?

Reading poetry is a special experience. When you read a poem, you'll learn
- to appreciate the use of rhyme, rhythm, and meter
- to understand sensory language
- to see what makes a poet tick

How to Read Poetry

Key Reading Skills

These key reading skills are especially useful tools for reading and understanding poetry. The skills are modeled in the Active Reading Model on page 775; you'll learn more about them later in this unit.

- **Evaluating** You make judgments or form opinions about what you read. (See Reading Workshop 1.)
- **Interpreting** You use your own understanding to decide what the events or ideas in a selection mean. (See Reading Workshop 2.)
- **Monitoring comprehension** You read a passage again to fully understand what a writer means. (See Reading Workshop 3.)
- **Connecting** You recognize part of yourself in what you read. Connecting makes reading more meaningful and will help you understand and remember what you read. (See Reading Workshop 4.)

R

Key Literary Elements

Recognizing and thinking about the following literary elements will help you understand more fully what the author is telling you.

- **Sound devices:** techniques that create patterns and emphasize words and ideas, such as alliteration and assonance. (See "Annabel Lee.")
- **Symbolism:** the use of people, things, and experiences to stand for more than they really are. (See "Diondra Jordan.")
- **Rhyme, rhythm, and meter:** the repetition of sounds, usually at the ends of lines, and the pattern of beats and stresses within lines. (See "The Pasture.")
- **Figurative language:** imaginative language used for descriptive effect. (See "What Makes Teens Tick?")

Objectives (pp. 774–775)
Reading Evaluate text • Interpret text • Monitor comprehension: rereading • Make connections from text to self
Literature Identify literary devices: sound, symbolism, rhyme, rhythm, meter, figurative language

Additional Support

Literature Focus Lesson

Repetition Explain to students that repetition is a sound device that can be used to add emphasis in poetry. The repetition of words and phrases can add structure and organization to a poem and emphasize key points. A poem will sometimes repeat key words and phrases with a slight change, playing with readers' expectations and surprising readers with an unexpected idea.

Ask students to think of favorite songs that repeat words or phrases. Have students explain why the songwriter might have chosen to repeat these words or phrases. OL

As students read "One," have them note which words and phrases are repeated. BL

One

by James Berry

The notes in the side columns model how to use the skills and elements you read about on page 774.

Poetry

ACTIVE READING MODEL

Only one of me [1]
and nobody can get a second one
from a photocopy machine.

Nobody has the fingerprints I have.
Nobody can cry my tears, or laugh my laugh
or have my expectancy* when I wait. [2]

But anybody can mimic* my dance with my dog.
Anybody can howl how I sing out of tune. [3]
And mirrors can show me multiplied
many times, say, dressed up in red
or dressed up in grey. [4]

Nobody can get into my clothes for me
or feel my fall for me, or do my running.
Nobody hears my music for me, either.

I am just this one.
Nobody else makes the words
I shape with sound, when I talk.

But anybody can act how I stutter in a rage.
Anybody can copy echoes I make.
And mirrors can show me multiplied
many times, say, dressed up in green
or dressed up in blue. [5] [6] ○

6 ***Expectancy*** is the feeling one has while looking forward to something.

7 To ***mimic*** is to copy or imitate.

[1] Key Reading Skill
R **Connecting** *I can relate. There's only one of me, too.*

[2] Key Literary Element
L1 **Symbolism** *The fingerprints could be a symbol for identity—the qualities that make a person unique.*

[3] Key Literary Element
L2 **Sound Devices** *I like that the ow sound is repeated.*

[4] Key Reading Skill
Monitoring Comprehension, Interpreting *After rereading, I get it. A mirror shows how you look, not who you are.*

[5] Key Reading Skill
Evaluating *I think the speaker feels unique because there is only one of him or her.*

[6] Key Literary Element
Rhyme, Rhythm, Meter *I can't see any rhyme or set rhythm. This must be "free verse," because it has no fixed pattern.*

Write to Learn The speaker reveals a lot in a few lines. Write down what you think makes the speaker tick.

Literature Online **Study Central** Visit www.glencoe.com and click on Study Central to review poetry.

English Language Coach

Indefinite Pronouns Illustrate the difference between the two indefinite pronouns *(nobody, anybody)* repeated in the poem. First, have the entire class stand up. Then read the poem aloud. When you read statements that include *nobody,* have the class sit. When you read statements that include *anybody,* have the class stand and read the statements with you.

When the class has finished reading, have them discuss the difference between the pronouns. Ask them why they think the writer uses these word choices to describe "only one of me." **EL**

UNIT 7 GENRE FOCUS

Teach

R Reading Skill

Connecting Say: What is it about you that makes you feel there is "only one of you"? *(Responses will vary.)* **OL** Why is it important to recognize the ways in which we are unique? *(Possible response: It helps us build self-esteem.)* **AL**

L1 Literary Element

Symbolism Ask: What might mirrors and the photocopy machine symbolize? *(Possible response: reproduction, or copying, rather than originality)* **AL**

L2 Literary Element

Sound Devices Ask: What is the effect of repetition in the poem? *(Possible response: It draws the reader's attention to important ideas.)* **OL**

Resources for page 775

Use the Genre Study BLM in the Unit 7 Resource Booklet.

Literature Online

Study Central Have students access the Web site to review poetry and to complete a related activity.

Objectives
- Evaluate text
- Interpret text
- Monitor comprehension: rereading
- Make connections from text to self
- Identify literary devices: sound, symbolism, rhyme, rhythm, meter, figurative language

Evaluating

UNIT 7

Objectives covered in this workshop:

- Evaluate poétic styles
- Evaluate texts

Teaching Students to Evaluate

Why Is It Important?

- Evaluating is making a judgment or forming an opinion about a text. Students will learn that they can evaluate a character, the author's craft, or the value of the information in a text.
- Evaluating helps students become wise readers. For example, they can judge whether an author is qualified to speak about a topic or whether the author's points make sense. They can also avoid being misled by what they read.
- Evaluating will also help them make good decisions about situations in their daily lives, such as what to listen to or watch next.

How to Help Students Get It

As students read, they should ask themselves questions such as the following:

- Is this character realistic and believable? Are the feelings and events in the story or poem realistic and believable?
- Does the author use language, tone, and style that keep you interested in the characters and plot?
- Is this author qualified to write about this subject? Is this author biased? Does this author present opinions as facts?

Reading to Answer the Big Question

Annabel Lee

In this tragic poem by Edgar Allan Poe, the speaker laments the loss of his beloved wife, Annabel Lee. Students will find out that despite her death, she is still the most important thing in the speaker's life.

Names/Nombres

In this short autobiographical work, Julia Alvarez discusses the many names – family names, nicknames, school names, American names, and Spanish names – she has had and how her feelings about her names changed at different periods in her life.

Workshop Resources

Pacing (Days) Standard	Block	Lesson	Student Materials	Teacher Resources
1		Key Skill Lesson: Evaluating	Key Reading Skills Practice English Language Coach	Bellringer Options Transparencies Read Aloud, Think Aloud Transparencies Presentation Plus!
2		"Annabel Lee"	Literary Analysis Transparencies Glencoe Online Selection Vocabulary Development Academic Vocabulary Development English Language Coach Active Reading Graphic Organizer Literary Analysis StudentWorks Plus Online Student Edition Literature Classics Selection and Unit Assessments	Literary and Text Analysis Transparencies Puzzlemaker Skill Level Up! BookLink 3 Assessment by Learning Objective (Diagnostic and Formative) Interactive Tutor Self-Assessment TeacherWorks Plus
2		"Names/ Nombres"	Glencoe Online Selection Vocabulary Development Academic Vocabulary Development English Language Coach Active Reading Graphic Organizer Literary Analysis StudentWorks Plus Online Student Edition Literature Classics Selection and Unit Assessments	Literary and Text Analysis Transparencies Puzzlemaker Skill Level Up! BookLink 3 Assessment by Learning Objective (Diagnostic and Formative) Interactive Tutor Self-Assessment TeacherWorks Plus

Keys for Unit Resource

- Blackline Master
- Workbook
- Supplemental Text
- CD-ROM
- DVD
- Transparency
- Web-based
- Fast Files

Level Appropriate Code

AS = Activities for all students
AL = Activities for students working above grade level
OL = Activities for students working at grade level
BL = Activities for students working below grade level
EL = Activities for English language learners

Focus

BELLRINGER Options

- Selection Focus Transparencies
- Daily Language Practice Transparency

Focus Activity Say: You evaluate all the time. Think about when you go shopping for clothing. How do you decide what you like? *(Possible responses: I look at different things, such as size, fit, color, and style, and choose what I like best.)*

Teach

R Reading Skill

Evaluating Ask: What words or phrases that show value or judgment might you use in evaluating a song? *(Possible responses: good lyrics, catchy tune, boring, meaningful)* What words might you use to evaluate a book? *(Possible responses: flat characters, interesting plot, complex story, captivating)* OL

V Vocabulary

Academic Vocabulary Say: Look at the definition at the bottom of page 776. What are some synonyms for *evaluating? (judging, grading, ranking)* OL

Skills Focus

You will practice using these skills when you read the following selections:

- "Annabel Lee," p. 780
- "Names/Nombres," p. 786

Reading

- Evaluating poetry through an understanding of genre and literary elements

Literature

- Identifying and explaining the effects of sound devices such as alliteration and assonance

Vocabulary

- Using structural analysis to understand word meanings
- Academic Vocabulary: *evaluating*

Writing/Grammar

- Identifying subjects and verbs

Skill Lesson

Evaluating

Learn It!

What Is It? When you make a judgment or form an opinion about something that you're reading, you're **evaluating**. You ask yourself these questions:

- Is the author's message clearly expressed?
- R Does the author use literary elements such as tone and style to interest you in the characters and the plot?
- Is the narrator's voice believable? Are the feelings and events in the poem or story realistic?

Analyzing Cartoons
The kids evaluate plot and character development to judge whether something is worth watching. While reading, you can evaluate these and other literary elements.

Objectives (pp. 776–777)
Reading Evaluate text

Academic Vocabulary

V **evaluating** (ee VAL yoo ayt ing) *v.* finding value; judging or determining worth

Additional Support

Reading in the Real World

Career Ask students whether a movie review has ever influenced their decision to see a particular movie. Tell students that critics review not only movies but also books, plays, music, dance, and art exhibits. Have students find a review of a book, movie, or performance they have just read or seen. Tell them to decide whether they agree or disagree with the reviewer's evaluation. Then, have students share their opinions in a small group or class discussion. Encourage them to use details from the book, movie, or performance to support their opinion. OL AL

Why Is It Important? You evaluate songs and movies when you discuss what you like and don't like about them with your friends. Evaluating helps you make good decisions about what you will listen to or watch next. Evaluating what you read helps make you a smart reader. R1

Study Central Visit www.glencoe.com and click on Study Central to review evaluating.

How Do I Do It? Below is an excerpt from the poem "One," by James Berry. In this stanza, the voice that the poet created—the speaker of the poem—talks about being unique. Read how one student evaluated the text. R2

Only one of me
And nobody can get a second one
From a photocopy machine.

The speaker is saying that there's no one else like him or her in the world. A photocopy machine can't make another person like him or her because it can make only copies of things. The speaker is saying that every person is an original. Using the image of a photocopier is a good way for the poet to get his point across.

Practice It!

What do you know about evaluating a poem or a short story? In your Learner's Notebook, write questions you can ask yourself to help you evaluate

- how well the poet or author expresses ideas.
- the speaker's or narrator's voice.
- the language used in the poem or story.

Use It!

As you read "Annabel Lee" and "Names/Nombres," ask yourself the questions you thought of. Write your answers in your Learner's Notebook.

Teach

Literature Online

Study Central Have students access the Web site to review evaluating and to complete a related activity.

R1 Reading Skill

Review Connecting Ask: Do you find it helpful when friends suggest that you check out—or ignore—a new movie, book, or music CD? Why or why not? *(Possible response: I find it helpful because it helps me avoid items that I probably wouldn't like.)* **BL** Do evaluations vary, depending on who is making them? Explain. *(Possible response: Tastes differ, so people's evaluations will not always be the same.)* **OL**

R2 Reading Skill

Evaluating Say: Reread "One." Then finish this sentence: "Using the image of a photocopier is a good way for the poet to get his point across because ___." *(Possible response: a photocopier reproduces an original item)* **OL**

Resources for page 777

Use Reading Skills Transparency in *Read Aloud, Think Aloud,* Unit 7, to help students practice evaluating.

Differentiated Instruction

Evaluation Charts Have the class create an evaluation chart to help them evaluate the selections they will read in this unit. Tell them to consider what elements are important in each. Have students add to column 1 as they learn about new elements. Collect their completed charts at the end of the unit. **AS**

Evaluating a Poem		
Element	**Rating**	**Reason for Rating**
Use of sound devices	Excellent	Poet uses lots of alliteration

Objectives

- Evaluate text by using criteria related to genre and purpose
- Use textual evidence to support opinions

Teach

More About the Author

People have suggested that "Annabel Lee" reflects Edgar Allan Poe's sorrow over the loss of his young wife, Virginia Eliza Clemm. Poe married her when she was just 13 years old, and the two of them were thought to be very much in love. Unfortunately, like many other loved ones in Poe's life, Virginia died early. She developed tuberculosis at age 19 and died at age 25.

V Vocabulary

Writing Sentences Point out that most of Poe's poems have a dark and gloomy mood. Challenge students to write sentences that reflect this mood. *(Responses will vary.)* **AS**

Before You Read Annabel Lee

Meet the Author

Edgar Allan Poe was born in 1809. The topic of death played a large part in Poe's writing. He is best known for his mystery stories and his tales of horror and madness. However, he wanted to be remembered for his poetry. Poe said, "With me poetry has not been a purpose but a passion." "Annabel Lee" was published two days after his untimely death in 1849. See page R6 of the Author Files for more on Edgar Allan Poe.

Literature Online

Author Search For more about Edgar Allan Poe, go to www.glencoe.com.

Objectives (pp. 778–781)
Reading Evaluate text • Make connections from text to self
Literature Identify literary devices: alliteration, assonance
Vocabulary Use prior knowledge

Vocabulary Preview

coveted (KUV it id) *v.* wanted what another person had **(p. 780)** *Rita coveted her sister's bracelet so much that she decided to buy one exactly like it for herself.*

tomb (toom) *n.* vault, chamber, or grave for the dead **(p. 781)** *In ancient China, an emperor was buried in an underground tomb, along with thousands of clay soldiers and horses.*

V **Write to Learn** For each vocabulary word, write a sentence using that word in your Learner's Notebook. Find a partner and check each other's sentences to make sure that you used the words correctly.

English Language Coach

Using What You Know Later in this unit, you'll learn about particular roots that will help you unlock the meanings of unfamiliar words. In the meantime (and all the time), you should realize that you know more than you think you do, and you should *use that knowledge.* Look at this example from "One":

"Nobody can . . . have my <u>expectancy</u> when I wait."

A footnote defined *expectancy* for you. Did you really need that help? Maybe not!

Word	expectancy
What You Know About It	It must be a noun ("my expectancy"). It looks like it contains *expect.* It has something to do with waiting.
What It Might Mean	Whatever *expect* means when it's made into a noun—maybe "way of expecting" or "feeling of expecting."

The "what it might mean" idea makes sense in the poem. This is a good clue that what the word *might* mean is likely to be what it *does* mean. (If you want to be absolutely sure of what a word means, use a dictionary.)

Individual Activity In your Learner's Notebook, make a chart like the one shown above. Write one of the underlined words from these sentences. Then fill in the chart.

Our Friday quizzes were <u>inescapable</u>.

The guests wore <u>finery</u>.

<u>Familiarize</u> yourself with the rules.

Additional Support

Literature Online

Author Search To expand students' appreciation of Edgar Allan Poe, have them access the Web site for additional information and resources.

Literature Focus Lesson

Sound Devices One of Edgar Allan Poe's poems, "The Bells," uses repetition and onomatopoeia: repeated refrains that imitate the ringing of bells. Read aloud the following stanza from "The Bells," and discuss with students the ways Poe uses words to capture the various sounds of bells.

Keeping time, time, time,
In a sort of Runic rhyme,
To the tintinnabulation that so musically wells
From the bells, bells, bells, bells,
Bells, bells, bells—
From the jingling and the tinkling of the bells.

OL

Skills Preview

Key Reading Skill: Evaluating

Evaluating is making a judgment or forming an opinion about what you are reading.

Write to Learn In your Learner's Notebook, write the questions below. As you read the following poem, use the questions to help you evaluate.

- Does the poet's writing style make his or her ideas clear?
- Does the poet succeed in making you understand the speaker's feelings? Why or why not?

Key Literary Element: Sound Devices

Sometimes authors repeat consonant sounds at the beginnings of words in a text. This technique is called **alliteration.** Authors use alliteration to stress certain words. Read aloud the following sentence: "As we left the beach, the seagull soared into the clouds." When you hear the *s* sound twice in a row, your attention is drawn to the words *seagull* and *soared.* L

Authors may also repeat vowel sounds. This is called **assonance.** In "Annabel Lee," Poe repeats the vowel sound "u" in the line "To shut her up in a sepulchre…" When you read this line aloud, you can hear how Poe wants to emphasize those words with the vowel sound.

Use these tips to help you recognize alliteration and assonance.

- Read the poem aloud, exaggerating the pronunciation of words.
  Do you hear any repeated consonant sounds?
- Read the poem again slowly.
  Do you hear any repeated vowel sounds?
- How does the alliteration and assonance affect the way the poem flows?

LiteratureOnline

Interactive Literary Elements Handbook
To review or learn more about the literary elements, go to www.glencoe.com.

Get Ready to Read

Connect to the Reading

Think about how it might feel to lose someone who is close to you. That's how the speaker of the poem feels after his beloved Annabel Lee dies. There are many ways of "losing" those we love. Friends move away. Brothers and sisters grow up and leave home. Families split up. All of these things can bring grief and a sense of great loss. R

Partner Talk With a partner, discuss how you felt when you lost someone who was important to you. How did losing this person change your life?

Build Background

Edgar Allan Poe lived a life as tragic as the lives he describes in some of his famous horror tales. The one shining light in his life was his love for his young wife, Virginia.

- Many people believe that Poe wrote "Annabel Lee" after his wife died of tuberculosis, a disease of the lungs.
- Tuberculosis was the same illness that caused Poe's mother's death when he was two years old.

Set Purposes for Reading

BIG Question Read "Annabel Lee" to find out who is important to the speaker—who helps make him tick.

Set Your Own Purpose What would you like to learn from the poem to help you answer the Big Question? Write your own purpose on the "Annabel Lee" page of Foldable 7.

Keep Moving

Use these skills as you read the following selection.

READING WORKSHOP 1

Teach

L Literary Element

Sound Devices Say: Listen to this example of alliteration: "A minor melody captured my mood." What sound is repeated? *(the* m *sound)* **BL** What is the effect of repeated sounds in this example? *(Possible response: The repeated* m *sound emphasizes important words.)* **AL**

R Reading Skill

Review Connecting
Say: The speaker in "Annabel Lee" vividly recalls his dead beloved. What special qualities do you remember about friends or family members when they are away? *(Responses will vary.)* **OL** Why do you think so many poets write about grief and loss? *(Possible response: Grief and loss are universal feelings. Writing about loss can help people cope with their grief.)* **AL**

CheckPoint

Use the CheckPoint questions provided on Presentation Plus! to check students' understanding of evaluating and to build background. These questions can be used with interactive response keypads for immediate student feedback.

Literature Focus Lesson

Word Choice Point out that poets must choose their words carefully. Have students listen to the following examples and identify which synonym works better in each sentence to create intensity, alliteration, or assonance.

1. He was a **sad** man.
   He was a **heartbroken** man.
2. The wind **whistled** in the willows.
   The wind **blew** in the willows.
3. People **walked** through the zoo in search of the pandas.
   People **paraded** through the zoo in search of the pandas.

Encourage students to think about Poe's word choice as they read "Annabel Lee." **OL**

Objectives
- Evaluate text
- Make connections from text to self
- Identify literary devices: alliteration, assonance
- Use prior knowledge

READING WORKSHOP 1

Teach

L1 Literary Element

Sound Devices Say: Find all of the words that begin with the consonant *l* in the first stanza. How does alliteration emphasize a particular idea in this section? *(Possible response: Alliteration ties together the words* lived, Lee, love, *and* loved. *Alliteration emphasizes the speaker's main idea: the love between him and his bride, Annabel Lee.)* **OL** How would you describe the effect of the repeated *"l"* sound? Is it startling or soothing? *(Possible response: The "l" sound has a soothing effect, similar to a lullaby.)* **AL**

L2 Literary Element

Sound Devices Say: Say the following line to yourself: *"She* was a child and *I* was a child." What vowel sound do you hear most frequently in this line? *(long i)* What words does this vowel sound connect? *(*child *and* I*)* **OL**

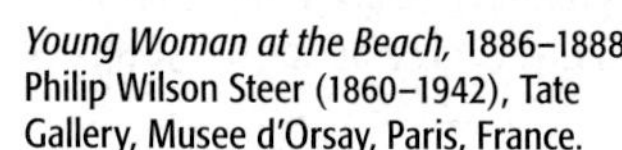
Young Woman at the Beach, 1886–1888. Philip Wilson Steer (1860–1942), Tate Gallery, Musee d'Orsay, Paris, France.

by Edgar Allan Poe

It was many and many a year ago,
  In a kingdom by the sea,
That a maiden there lived whom you may know
  By the name of Annabel Lee;—
And this maiden she lived with no other thought
  Than to love and be loved by me. **1**

She was a child and *I* was a child,
  In this kingdom by the sea,
But we loved with a love that was more than love—
  I and my Annabel Lee—
With a love that the wingéd seraphs* of heaven
  Coveted her and me. **2**

---

11 ***Seraphs*** (SAIR ufs) are high-ranking angels who are said to burn with love for God.

Vocabulary

coveted (KUV it id) *v.* wanted what another person had

Practice the Skills

1 Key Literary Element

L1 **Sound Devices** In lines 5 and 6, Poe uses alliteration by repeating the consonant *l.* Why do you think he draws attention to these words?

2 Key Literary Element

L2 **Sound Devices** Remember that assonance is the repetition of vowel sounds. Identify an example of assonance in line 7.

Additional Support

Reading Fluency

Focusing on Alliteration Have student partners read aloud the first two stanzas of the poem, focusing on the alliteration. Have partners take turns reading and listening. Encourage the listening partner to close his or her eyes to focus closely on the poem's sound and meaning. After each stanza, have partners tell what they noticed about the sounds in the poem. Students should practice reading the stanzas until they can read the alliterative elements comfortably and expressively. **OL**

And this was the reason that, long ago,
In this kingdom by the sea,
A wind blew out of a cloud by night
Chilling my Annabel Lee;
So that her high-born **kinsmen** came
And bore her away from me,
To shut her up in a sepulchre*
In this kingdom by the sea. **3**

The angels, not half so happy in Heaven,
Went envying her and me:—
Yes! that was the reason (as all men know,
In this kingdom by the sea)
That the wind came out of the cloud, chilling
And killing my Annabel Lee.

R1 But our love it was stronger by far than the love
Of those who were older than we—
Of many far wiser than we—
And neither the angels in Heaven above,
Nor the demons down under the sea,
Can ever dissever* my soul from the soul
Of the beautiful Annabel Lee:— **4**

For the moon never beams without bringing me dreams
Of the beautiful Annabel Lee;
And the stars never rise but I see the bright eyes
Of the beautiful Annabel Lee;
And so, all the night-tide, I lie down by the side
Of my darling, my darling, my life and my bride,
In her sepulchre there by the sea—
In her **tomb** by the side of the sea. **5** ❍

19 A ***sepulchre*** (SEP ul kur) is a burial place.

32 To ***dissever*** (di SEV ur) is to separate or split apart.

Vocabulary

tomb (toom) *n.* vault, chamber, or grave for the dead

Practice the Skills

3 English Language Coach

Using What You Know You know that *kin* means "relatives." What is the most likely meaning of **kinsmen?**

4 Key Reading Skill

R2 **Evaluating** Does Poe succeed in showing you how deeply the speaker loves Annabel Lee? Explain your answer.

5 BIG Question

BQ What gives the speaker's life meaning? Record your answers on the "Annabel Lee" page of Foldable 7. Your response will help you complete the Unit Challenge.

READING WORKSHOP 1

Teach

R1 Reading Skill

Evaluating Ask: What does the fifth stanza say about the couple's youth and wisdom? *(Possible response: They were deeply in love even though they were young and unwise.)* **OL** Does this description convince you of their love? Explain. *(Responses will vary.)* **AL**

R2 Reading Skill

Evaluating Say: Poe repeats *ever* to stress the idea that nothing can truly separate him and his love. Do you think this repetition is effective? Explain. *(Possible response: It makes the idea stand out.)* **OL**

BQ

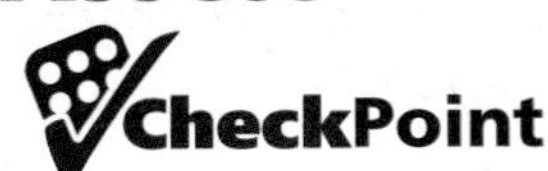

Ask: What advice would you give the speaker? *(Possible response: I'd tell him to remember his wife but to also look for other ways to be happy.)* **BL**

Assess

CheckPoint

Use the CheckPoint questions provided on Presentation Plus! to check for comprehension of the selection. These questions can be used with interactive response keypads for immediate student feedback.

Differentiated Instruction

Illustrating Ask students to close their eyes, and read aloud to them the last four stanzas of "Annabel Lee." Before you read, ask students to think about the following questions as they listen:

- What do you think Annabel Lee's funeral looked like?
- What is the setting of Annabel Lee's final resting place?
- How does the speaker describe Annabel Lee's appearance?

Then tell students to draw an illustration for the poem. Encourage students to match their illustrations to the speaker's point of view and descriptions. **OL**

Objectives

- Evaluate, analyze, and interpret what you read
- Identify and evaluate the effectiveness of alliteration and assonance

Assess

Resources for page 782

- Selection Quick Check
- Selection and Unit Assessment
- ExamView Assessment Suite
- Interactive Tutor: Self-Assessment

Students can respond to the *After You Read* items in their Learner's Notebook or on a separate sheet of paper.

Answering the

1. Possible responses include answers in which students acknowledge the importance of friends and family members in their lives.
2. Annabel Lee is the speaker's wife; the two were in love.
3. Possible response: The speaker says that a chill wind, sent by jealous angels, killed Annabel Lee.

Critical Thinking

4. Possible response: Annabel Lee has been the most important part of the speaker's life. After her death, his grief is overwhelming.
5. Possible response: The speaker claims that Annabel Lee had "no other thought" than the couple's love.
6. Possible responses may note that the intensity of the couple's love seems true. The killing wind from heaven does not seem realistic.

After You Read

Annabel Lee

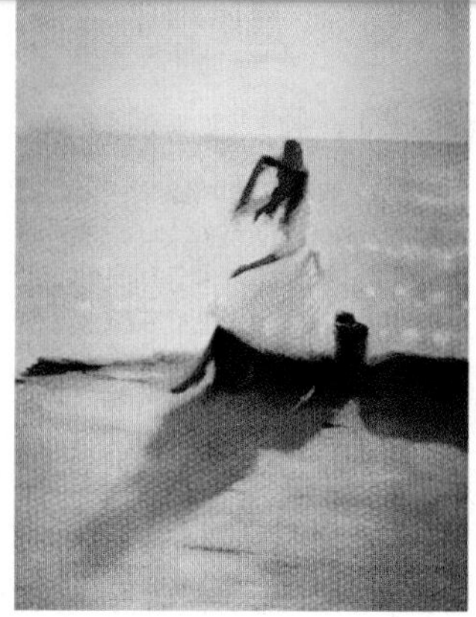

Answering the BIG Question

1. How has reading this poem made you think about who is important to you and what makes you tick?
2. **Recall** What is the relationship between the speaker and Annabel Lee?
   TIP **Right There**
3. **Recall** According to the speaker, why did Annabel Lee die?
   TIP **Right There**

Critical Thinking

4. **Analyze** How important is Annabel Lee to the speaker? Explain.
   TIP **Author and Me**
5. **Infer** How did Annabel Lee feel about the speaker?
   TIP **Author and Me**
6. **Evaluate** Does this poem seem realistic to you? Explain.
   TIP **Author and Me**

Talk About Your Reading

Literature Groups Have you ever heard the expression, "It is better to have loved and lost than never to have loved at all"? In your group, discuss the expression and how it relates to the poem.

- What does the expression mean?
- Do you agree or disagree with the expression?
- How do you think the speaker in "Annabel Lee" would feel about the expression?

Write to Learn After your group discusses this expression, write your own thoughts on a separate sheet of paper.

Objectives (pp. 782–783)
Reading Evaluate text • Make connections from text to self
Literature Identify literary devices: alliteration, assonance
Vocabulary Identify word structure: suffixes, roots
Grammar Identify subjects and verbs

Talk About Your Reading

Write to Learn

Sample response:

The expression, "It is better to have loved and lost than never to have loved at all" means that loving someone is worth the risk of losing him or her. I agree with this expression. It would be horrible to go through life without ever deeply loving anyone. I think the grieving speaker in "Annabel Lee" would agree with the expression as well. He is not sad that he loved Annabel Lee. He is sad that she has died.

Skills Review

Key Reading Skill: Evaluating

7. Did the poet do a good job of keeping you interested in the poem while you were reading? Which parts of the poem grabbed your interest? Explain.
8. What is your opinion of the speaker of the poem? Do you think you can trust what the speaker tells readers about Annabel Lee? Explain.

Key Literary Element: Sound Devices

For each line below, write whether Poe is using alliteration, assonance, or both. Then copy the words in which the sound device appears. Remember, alliteration is the repetition of consonant sounds, and assonance is the repetition of vowel sounds.

9. So that her high-born kinsmen came
10. Yes! that was the reason (as all men know,
11. Of those who were older than we– / Of many far wiser than we–
12. But we loved with a love that was more than a love

Vocabulary Check

Answer *true* or *false* to each statement.

13. Saying you **coveted** something means that you stole or borrowed it.
14. The Great Pyramid of Egypt is a **tomb.**
15. **Academic Vocabulary** What do you look for when you **evaluate** a poem?
16. **English Language Coach** Considering what you know about the word *covet* and what you know about suffixes, what do you think a *covetous* look might be?

Grammar Link: Finding Subjects and Verbs

Sometimes it's hard to tell what verb form to use. To get the right form, you must first find the subject and verb in a sentence. Here's a quick review of how to find subjects and verbs.

- The subject tells who or what the sentence is about. The verb tells what the subject does, is, or has.

  Natalie brings her lunch to school.

  (Who or what is the sentence about? *Natalie.* What does Natalie do? She *brings.*)
- A verb can be one word or a whole phrase. The most important word in the phrase is the main verb. The other verbs are helping verbs.

  I could have done better on that test.

  (*I* is the subject. *Done* is the main verb; *could have* are helping verbs.)
- Subjects and verbs can be compound.

  Al and I jumped and shouted for joy.

  (*Al and I* is a compound subject. *Jumped and shouted* is a compound verb.)

Grammar Practice

On a separate piece of paper, copy each sentence. Underline the subject once and the verb twice.

17. Elms grow tall and give shade.
18. We will be planting more trees this spring.
19. Maples and elms have beautiful leaves.

Web Activities For eFlashcards, Selection Quick Checks, and other Web activities, go to www.glencoe.com.

Skills Review

Key Reading Skill: Evaluating

7. Possible responses: I was interested in the mysterious events. I also enjoyed the way the poet makes use of sound devices, such as alliteration.
8. Possible response: The speaker expresses his personal feelings, so his descriptions of Annabel Lee reflect his emotions, not necessarily the truth.

Key Literary Element: Sound Devices

9. alliteration: *her, high-born* (*h* sound) and *kinsmen, came* (*k* sound)
10. alliteration: *that, the* (*th* sound)
11. assonance: *those, older* (*o* sound); alliteration: *were, wiser, we* (*w* sound)
12. alliteration and assonance: *loved, love* (*l* and *o* sounds); alliteration: *that, than* (*th* sound)

Vocabulary Check

13. false
14. true
15. Possible response: I look for an interesting rhythm and rhyme pattern and interesting word choices.
16. A *covetous* look is a look that is prompted by desire.

Grammar Link: Finding Subjects and Verbs

Grammar Practice

17. Elms grow tall and give shade.
18. We will be planting more trees this spring.
19. Maples and elms have beautiful leaves.

Close

Ask students to think of people who contribute to the way students "tick." Encourage students to think about the notable qualities or traits that they try to copy from these important people.

Literature Online

Web Activities Have students access the Web site for interactive activities that will help them assess their understanding of the selection.

Teach

More About the Author

Julia Alvarez was raised in the Dominican Republic. When she was ten years old, her family had to flee the country for political reasons. In unfamiliar New York City, she felt out of place until, she says, "magic happened in my life" in the form of a writing assignment. "I realized that I had lost the island we had come from, but with the words and encouragement of my teacher, I had discovered an even better world: the one words can create in a story or poem."

V Vocabulary

Word Roots Say: When you are given new vocabulary words, look carefully at each word to see whether you recognize the word's root. Note any words whose roots you recognize from this unit. Look up the definition of any word that you do not recognize, and try to identify word parts that can help you understand the meaning of other vocabulary words. EL BL OL

Before You Read

Names/Nombres

Julia Alvarez

Meet the Author

Asked where she finds the ideas for her richly detailed stories, Julia Alvarez says, "I think when I write, I write out of who I am and the questions I need to figure out. A lot of what I have worked through has to do with coming to this country and losing a homeland and a culture, as a way of making sense." See page R1 of the Author Files for more on Julia Alvarez.

Author Search For more about Julia Alvarez, go to www.glencoe.com.

Objectives (pp. 784–791)
Reading Evaluate text • Make connections from text to self
Literature Identify literary devices: figurative language
Vocabulary Identify Latin roots

Vocabulary Preview

ironically (eye RAW nik lee) *adv.* in a way that is different from what is expected **(p. 787)** *It rained every day except Friday. Ironically, that's the only day I brought my umbrella.*

initial (ih NISH ul) *adj.* at the beginning; first **(p. 789)** *Our initial idea was to have the pep rally on the football field.*

merge (murj) *v.* to join together so as to become one; unite **(p. 789)** *When the two classes merge, there won't be enough seats for everyone.*

vaguely (VAYG lee) *adv.* in a way that is not clear, exact, or definite **(p. 789)** *Elise wasn't sure who had come to the picnic. She vaguely remembered that her cousin had been there.*

specified (SPES uh fyd) *v.* explained or described in detail **(p. 789)** *At the box office, we specified that we wanted front-row seats.*

exotic (eg ZAW tik) *adj.* strangely attractive; foreign **(p. 789)** *Michael has never been to Puerto Rico and thinks it is an exotic place.*

chaotic (kay AW tik) *adj.* confused, disorganized **(p. 789)** *On the day of the clearance sale, the scene at the mall was chaotic.*

Write to Learn With a partner, choose three vocabulary words. Write one paragraph that uses all three words.

English Language Coach

Latin Roots In "Names/Nombres," the narrator tells someone where she's from without specifying, or naming exactly, the island where her family had lived. *Specify* has the Latin root *spec,* meaning "to observe or look at." Some English words that have *spec* as a root are more clearly connected to the Latin meaning. For example, *inspect* and *spectator* have to do with observing.

V Even though Latin is no longer spoken anywhere, it is one of the main sources of English words. This chart shows another common Latin root.

Root	Meaning	Examples
dict	say, speak	predict, dictionary, verdict, dictator, contradict

Partner Talk With a partner, discuss how the Latin root is involved in the meaning of each of the example words.

Additional Support

Author Search To expand students' appreciation of Julia Alvarez, have them access the Web site for additional information and resources.

Literature Focus Lesson

Figurative Language Similes and metaphors can make comparisons vivid, striking, and memorable. For example, Alvarez uses a metaphor when she calls her name "an orchestra of sound." Discuss this metaphor with students, asking them what they think it means. Have students brainstorm other names or items that produce this "orchestra of sound." Ask students to think of similes that could express the same idea as this metaphor. With students, discuss the role of figurative language in writing. Ask students to explain why devices such as similes and metaphors are effective tools for description. OL AL

Skills Preview

Key Reading Skill: Evaluating

Sometimes when you evaluate a short story, you form an opinion about how well an author tells the story.

- Is the story meaningful? Why or why not?
- Is the story believable and realistic? Why or why not?

Write to Learn As you read the story, think of other questions that help you evaluate. Write three questions and answers in your Learner's Notebook.

Key Literary Element: Figurative Language

- A **simile** is an expression that uses *like* or *as* to compare two unlike things. The phrase "a person who runs like the wind" is a simile that says a person runs fast.
- A **metaphor** is an expression that compares two unlike things and describes one thing as if it were another. In the sentence "Seth is a cheetah on the racetrack," the author says Seth is a cheetah to show that Seth runs fast.

As you read, use these tips to help you identify and understand similes and metaphors:

- Look for comparisons.
  What two things does the author compare?
- Think about what the two things have in common.
  What is the author saying is alike about these two things?
- Think about why the author wants you to compare these two things.
  How does the comparison help the author explain his or her idea?

L

Interactive Literary Elements Handbook
To review or learn more about the literary elements, go to www.glencoe.com.

Get Ready to Read

Connect to the Reading

In "Names/Nombres," Julia Alvarez talks about the names she's used throughout her life. Her different names say different things about her. As you read, think about your names or nicknames.

- Do they represent different things about who you are? Explain.
- Which name or nickname do you like best? Why?

R

Partner Talk Discuss with a partner what your name means to you and to your family and friends. Take notes. These will help you with the Unit Challenge.

Build Background

This selection is set in the early 1960s in New York City.

- Julia Alvarez was born in New York, but she lived in the Dominican Republic until she was ten.
- The Dominican Republic is located on the island of Hispaniola in the Caribbean.
- *Nombres* is Spanish for "names."

Set Purposes for Reading

BIG Question Read the selection "Names/Nombres" to find out why names are important to Julia Alvarez. How do they help her get through life?

Set Your Own Purpose What would you like to learn from the story to help you answer the Big Question? Write your own purpose on the "Names/Nombres" page of Foldable 7.

Keep Moving

Use these skills as you read the following selection.

Teach

L Literary Element

Figurative Language Ask: Why do you think a writer would want to use a comparison rather than a regular description? *(Possible response: to create a memorable image)* **OL** What are some effects of figurative language? *(Possible response: Comparisons that exaggerate certain qualities may add humor.)* **AL**

R Reading Skill

Review Connecting Ask: If you moved to another country, would you be okay with people changing your name? Why or why not? *(Students may say that they'd be okay with people changing the pronunciation but wouldn't be okay with a new name.)* **AS**

CheckPoint

Use the CheckPoint questions provided on Presentation Plus! to check students' understanding of evaluating and to build background. These questions can be used with interactive response keypads for immediate student feedback.

Literature Online

Interactive Literary Elements Handbook Have students access the Web site to improve their understanding of figurative language.

Objectives

- Evaluate text
- Make connections from text to self
- Identify literary devices: figurative language
- Identify Latin roots

Reading in the Real World

Citizenship In the selection, the author tells the significance or meaning of each name she mentions. Encourage students to think about the origins and importance of their own names. Have students interview family members and people in their neighborhood. Tell students to ask these people what their names mean and about the significance of their names. Invite students to share their findings with the class. Discuss any trends, such as especially popular names or common ethnic backgrounds, which appear in students' findings. **OL** **EL**

Teach

Viewing the Painting

Ask: How would you describe the young girl in the portrait? *(Possible response: She looks Hispanic and is posed very formally. She seems slightly nervous or sad.)* **OL** How does this illustration relate to the text? *(Possible response: The subject of the text is a young Hispanic girl like the one in the painting. At one point, Julia is nervous about whether she and her family will be let into the United States.)* **AL**

R Reading Skill

Evaluating Say: The narrator begins her story by comparing the immigration officer's pronunciation of her last name with her own pronunciation of it. Do you think she does a good job of setting up the problem in the story? Why or why not? *(Possible response: She does a good job of showing how people mispronounce her name. By showing how she says her name, she is able to illustrate how others butcher it.)* **AL**

Readability Scores
Dale-Chall: 6.9
DRP: 59
Lexile: 1130

READING WORKSHOP 1

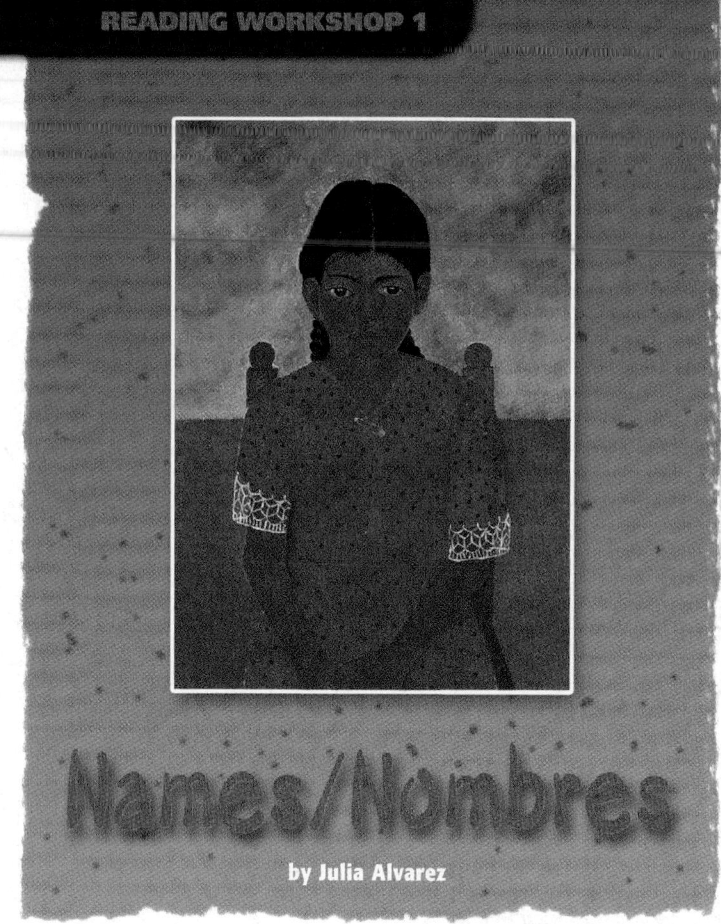

Names/Nombres

by Julia Alvarez

Portrait of Virginia, 1929. Frida Kahlo. Fundacion Dolores Olmedo, Mexico City, D.F., Mexico.

When we arrived in New York City, our names changed almost immediately. At Immigration, the officer asked my father, *Mister Elbures,* if he had anything to declare. My father shook his head, "No," and we were waved through. I was too afraid we wouldn't be let in if I corrected the man's pronunciation, but I said our name to myself, opening my mouth wide for the organ blast of the a, trilling my tongue for the drumroll of the *r, All-vah-rrr-es!* How could anyone get *Elbures* out of that orchestra of sound? **1**

At the hotel my mother was *Missus Alburest,* and I was *little girl,* as in, "Hey, little girl, stop riding the elevator up and down. It's *not* a toy!"

When we moved into our new apartment building, the super called my father *Mister Alberase,* and the neighbors who

Practice the Skills

1 Key Literary Element

Figurative Language Alvarez uses figurative language to compare an organ blast to how she makes the *a* sound. This would be a metaphor if she said, "My *a* is an organ blast." Find a similar figurative expression in this paragraph.

Additional Support

Leveled Reading An adapted version of this selection (5th and 6th grade readability) is available on page 240 of *Jamestown Literature: An Adapted Reader* for Grade 7.

Differentiated Instruction

Building Background The Alvarez family arrived in New York around 1960, when Julia Alvarez was ten years old. The family immigrated to the United States from the Dominican Republic to escape the dictatorship of Rafael Trujillo. Trujillo ruled the Dominican Republic from 1930 to 1961. During this time, Dominicans enjoyed some prosperity, but they lost much of their personal and political freedom. Trujillo remained leader of the country by controlling its army and assassinating his opponents. Trujillo was killed by his political foes in 1961. Share this information with students, and ask students what it might be like to leave a country to find political freedom. **OL**

became mother's friends pronounced her name *Jew-lee-ah* instead of *Hoo-lee-ah.* I, her namesake, was known as *Hoo-lee-tah* at home. But at school, I was *Judy* or *Judith,* and once an English teacher mistook me for *Juliet.* **2**

It took awhile to get used to my new names. I wondered if I shouldn't correct my teachers and new friends. But my mother argued that it didn't matter. "You know what your friend Shakespeare said, *'A rose by any other name would smell as sweet.'*"[1] My family had gotten into the habit of calling any literary figure "my friend" because I had begun to write poems and stories in English class.

By the time I was in high school, I was a popular kid, and it showed in my name. Friends called me *Jules* or *Hey Jude,* and once a group of troublemaking friends my mother forbid me to hang out with called me *Alcatraz.*[2] I was *Hoo-lee-tah* only to Mami and Papi and uncles and aunts who came over to eat *sancocho*[3] on Sunday afternoons—old world folk whom I just as soon would go back to where they came from and leave me to pursue whatever mischief I wanted to in America. *JUDY ALCATRAZ:* the name on the Wanted Poster would read. Who would ever trace her to me? **3**

My older sister had the hardest time getting an American name for herself because Mauricia did not translate into English. **Ironically**, although she had the most foreign-sounding name, she and I were the Americans in the family. We had been born in New York City when our parents had first tried immigration and then gone back "home," too homesick to stay. My mother often told the story of how she had almost changed my sister's name in the hospital.

After the delivery, Mami and some other new mothers were cooing over their new baby sons and daughters and exchanging names and weights and delivery stories. My mother was embarrassed among the Sallys and Janes and Georges and

1. This line is from William Shakespeare's play *Romeo and Juliet.*
2. ***Alcatraz*** (AL kuh traz) is an island in San Francisco Bay that once was the home of a tough federal prison.
3. ***Sancocho*** (san KOH choh) is a meat stew.

Vocabulary

ironically (eye RAW nik lee) *adv.* in a way that is different from what is expected

Practice the Skills

2 Reviewing Skills

R1 **Connecting** Has anyone ever mispronounced your name or called you by the wrong name? If so, how did you feel?

3 Key Reading Skill

R2 **Evaluating** Do you think the author really liked having more than one name? Why or why not?

Reading in the Real World

Citizenship The immigration officer asks Señor Alvarez whether he has "anything to declare" to make sure that he is entering the United States legally. Immigrants face further questions when applying for United States citizenship. Direct students to use library or Internet resources to find information from the Immigration and Naturalization Service about these questions. Direct student pairs to role-play for the class the question-and-answer session that an immigrant might face. Encourage students to find the Oath of Allegiance and to learn what the United States citizenship ceremony involves. AL

Teach

R1 Reading Skill

Review Connecting Say: What names have you encountered that were difficult to pronounce correctly at first? *(Responses will vary.)* BL What can you do to pronounce a foreign name correctly? *(Possible response: You can find a foreign language dictionary to see the rules of pronunciation. If you know the person, you can ask politely how to pronounce his or her name.)* EL OL

R2 Reading Skill

Evaluating Say: The kids at school refer to the author by different nicknames. How can you tell whether she likes these nicknames? *(She playfully imagines herself as wanted criminal "Judy Alcatraz," indicating that she is not bothered by their nicknames for her.)* OL Why do you think Julia's friends call her "Alcatraz"? *(Possible response: Troublemaking friends give Julia this nickname. Alcatraz and Alvarez sound similar, and the nickname shows that the author's troublemaking friends think that she is one of them.)* AL

Objectives
- Evaluate text
- Connect to the text
- Conduct research
- Analyze artwork

Teach

R1 Reading Skill

Review Identifying Author's Purpose and Perspective **Ask:** What adjectives does Alvarez use to describe the name Mauricia? *(rich and noisy)* BL What do these words tell you about Alvarez's opinion of the name? *(Possible response: They suggest she likes it.)* OL

EL Language Coach

Contractions **Ask:** What two words make up the contraction *why'd*? *(why did)* What are the main verb and helping verb in the question? *(Did is the helping verb. The main verb is give.)* EL

R2 Reading Skill

Evaluating **Ask:** How does the author convey the mispronunciation of her sister's name? *(The author spells people's attempts to say her sister's name the way they say them.)* Do you think this is an effective way to convey the pronunciations? *(Possible response: The phonetic spellings are effective because they help readers hear the way the characters are speaking.)* OL

Johns to reveal the rich, noisy name of *Mauricia,* so when her turn came to brag, she gave her baby's name as *Maureen.*

"Why'd ya give her an Irish name with so many pretty Spanish names to choose from?" one of the women asked her.

My mother blushed and admitted her baby's real name to the group. Her mother-in-law had recently died, she apologized, and her husband had insisted that the first daughter be named after his mother, *Mauran.* My mother thought it the ugliest name she had ever heard, and she talked my father into what she believed was an improvement, a combination of *Mauran* and her own mother's name *Felicia.*

"Her name is *Mao-ree-chee-ah,*" my mother said to the group.

"Why that's a beautiful name," the new mothers cried. "*Moor-ee-sha, Moor-ee-sha,*" they cooed into the pink blanket.

Moor-ee-sha it was when we returned to the States eleven years later. Sometimes, American tongues found even that mispronunciation tough to say and called her *Maria* or *Marsha* or *Maudy* from her nickname *Maury.* I pitied her. What an awful name to have to transport across borders! 4

My little sister, Ana, had the easiest time of all. She was plain *Anne*—that is, only her name was plain, for she turned out to be the pale, blond "American beauty" in the family. The only Hispanic-seeming thing about her was the affectionate nickname her boyfriends sometimes gave her, *Anita,* or as one goofy guy used to sing to her to the tune of the Chiquita Banana advertisement, *Anita Banana.*

Later, during her college years in the late '60s, there was a push to pronounce Third World[4] names correctly. I remember calling her long distance at her group house and a roommate answering.

"Can I speak to Ana?" I asked, pronouncing her name the American way.

"Ana?" The man's voice hesitated. "Oh! you mean *Ah-nah!*"

Our first few years in the States, though, ethnicity[5] was not yet "in." Those were the blond, blue-eyed, bobby socks years of junior high and high school before the '60s ushered in peasant

4. ***Third World*** refers to poorer, less developed countries, mainly in Latin America, Africa, and Asia.

5. ***Ethnicity*** (eth NIS uh tee) is a word for certain traits that a group of people share, such as culture, history, race, and national origin. U.S. citizens come from many ethnic backgrounds.

Practice the Skills

4 Key Reading Skill

Evaluating Evaluate the ideas in this paragraph. Is Alvarez complaining that Americans are lazy with foreign names? Is she complaining about parents who give their children difficult names?

Additional Support

Differentiated Instruction

Making Graphic Organizers Have students make three word webs to show the different names each child in the Alvarez family is called. Write each child's actual name in a center circle. Then, write the child's nicknames and other names she is called in outer circles. BL

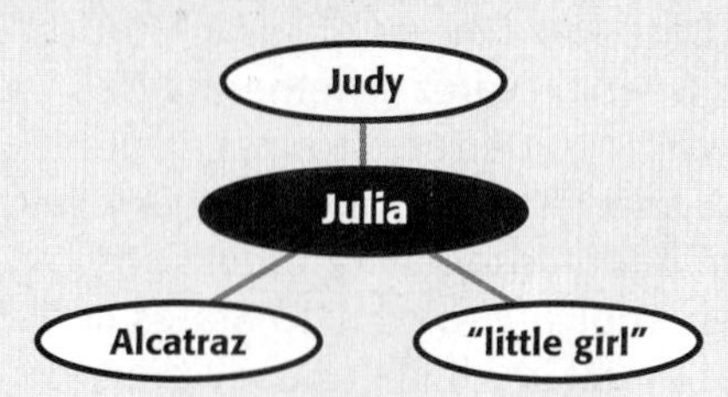

READING WORKSHOP 1

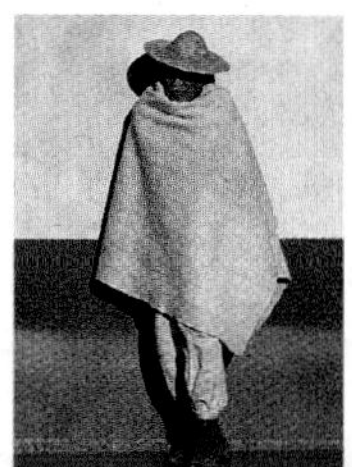

Visual Vocabulary
A ***serape*** (suh RAW pay) is a blanketlike outer garment similar to a shawl and is worn chiefly by men in Latin American countries. Some serapes are brightly colored and boldly patterned.

blouses, hoop earrings, serapes. My **initial** desire to be known by my correct Dominican name faded.

I just wanted to be Judy and **merge** with the Sallys and Janes in my class. But inevitably,[6] my accent and coloring gave me away. "So where are you from, Judy?"

"New York," I told my classmates. After all, I had been born blocks away at Columbia Presbyterian Hospital.

"I mean, *originally.*"

"From the Caribbean," I answered **vaguely**, for if I **specified**, no one was quite sure what continent our island was on.

R1 "Really? I've been to Bermuda. We went last April for spring vacation. I got the worst sunburn! So, are you from Portoriko?"

"No," I shook my head. "From the Dominican Republic."

"Where's that?"

"South of Bermuda."

They were just being curious, I knew, but I burned with shame whenever they singled me out as a "foreigner," a rare, **exotic** friend.

"Say your name in Spanish, oh please say it!" I had made mouths drop one day by rattling off my full name, which according to Dominican custom, included my middle names, mother's and father's surnames for four generations back.

R2 "Julia Altagracia Maria Teresa Alvarez Tavares Perello Espaillat Julia Pérez Rochet González," I pronounced it slowly, a name as **chaotic** with sounds as a Middle Eastern bazaar or market day in a South American village. 5

6. ***Inevitably*** means "in a way that cannot be avoided."

Vocabulary

initial (ih NISH ul) *adj.* at the beginning; first

merge (murj) *v.* to join together so as to become one; unite

vaguely (VAYG lee) *adv.* in a way that is not clear, exact, or definite

specified (SPES uh fyd) *v.* explained or described in detail

exotic (eg ZAW tik) *adj.* strangely attractive; foreign

chaotic (kay AW tik) *adj.* confused, disorganized

Practice the Skills

5 Key Literary Element

Figurative Language What two things does Alvarez compare here? Does she use a simile or a metaphor? How can you tell?

Teach

R1 Reading Skill

Review Identifying Author's Purpose and Perspective **Ask:** To what Caribbean Island does Alvarez refer when she mentions "Portoriko"? *(She refers to Puerto Rico.)* BL Why does Alvarez use a phonetic spelling? *(Possible response: Alvarez uses a phonetic spelling to emphasize that people in the United States do not pronounce Spanish words as she does.)* OL

R2 Reading Skill

Evaluating **Ask:** Do you think Alvarez's comparison of the sound of her name to the sounds of a Middle Eastern bazaar or a South American market day is effective? Explain. *(Responses will vary. Students may say that the comparison is effective because it emphasizes how different Alvarez feels from her friends and gives a sense of how exotic her name seems to her classmates.)* OL

Differentiated Instruction

Building Background In Hispanic culture, a person's name includes information about both the mother's and the father's family. A person's first name is called the *nombre de pila,* or baptismal name. A "middle name" is called a *secundo nombre.* It is placed directly after the *nombre de pila.* The father's family name, or *apellido paterno,* follows this name. The *apellido materno,* or mother's family name, is placed next. A woman typically adds her husband's family name to the end of her own name, with the prefix *de,* or "of." Ask students how their names would be different if they followed these traditions. OL

Objectives
- Evaluate text
- Identify and explain the effects of figurative language
- Create graphic organizers to understand text

Teach

Viewing the Painting

Say: Artist Fernando Botero is Colombian. What elements of the painting depict Hispanic culture? *(Possible responses may include the painting's use of color, the style of the woman's long skirt, or the brightly colored bird under the chair.)* **AL** How does the artwork add to your understanding of the story? *(Possible responses: The men wear fedora hats, as do Alvarez's uncles. The theme of music in the picture suggests Julia's descriptions of names and fast-paced English.)* **OL**

EL Language Coach

Latin Roots Say: The word root *flor* is also found in *Florida*, the name of a southeastern state. Why is *Florida* a good name for this state? *(Possible response: Florida has a warm, humid climate that supports plentiful plant growth, so it is appropriate that the state name includes the word root meaning "flower.")* **EL**

READING WORKSHOP 1

The Musicians, 1979. Fernando Botero. Oil on canvas, 85 3/4 x 74 /34 in. Private collection.

I suffered most whenever my extended family attended school occasions. For my graduation, they all came, the whole noisy, foreign-looking lot of old, fat aunts in their dark mourning dresses and hair nets, uncles with full, droopy mustaches and baby-blue or salmon-colored suits and white pointy shoes and fedora[7] hats, the many little cousins who snuck in without tickets. They sat in the first row in order to better understand the Americans' fast-spoken English. But how could they listen when they were constantly speaking among themselves in **florid**-sounding phrases, rococo[8] consonants, rich, rhyming vowels. Their loud voices carried . . . **6**

How could I introduce them to my friends? These relatives had such complicated names and there were so many of them, and their relationships to myself were so convoluted.[9] There was my Tía Josefina, who was not really an aunt but a much older cousin. And her daughter, Aída Margarita,

7. A ***fedora*** (fuh DOR uh) is a soft, felt hat with a curved brim and a crease along the top. See *The Musicians* at the top of this page.
8. ***Florid*** and ***rococo*** (ruh KOH koh) both mean "very showy or flowery."
9. Something that is ***convoluted*** is twisted and wound around. The rest of this paragraph identifies some of the writer's convoluted family relationships.

Practice the Skills

6 English Language Coach

EL **Latin Roots** Can you think of another word that has the root *flor?* (Hint: It has to do with flowers, just as **florid** does.)

Additional Support

Differentiated Instruction

Illustrating the Alvarez Family The author provides many details in describing her relatives. With students, generate a list of the details that describe the appearance of Alvarez's family members. Ask students to draw family portraits depicting the author and her family at the graduation. Remind students that this family portrait should include aunts, uncles, and other members of the author's extended family. **EL BL OL**

READING WORKSHOP 1

who was adopted, *una hija de crianza.* My uncle of affection, Tío José, brought my *madrina* Tía Amelia and her *comadre* Tía Pilar. My friends rarely had more than their nuclear family[10] to introduce.

After the commencement[11] ceremony my family waited outside in the parking lot while my friends and I signed yearbooks with nicknames which recalled our high school good times: "Beans" and "Pepperoni" and "Alcatraz." We hugged and cried and promised to keep in touch.

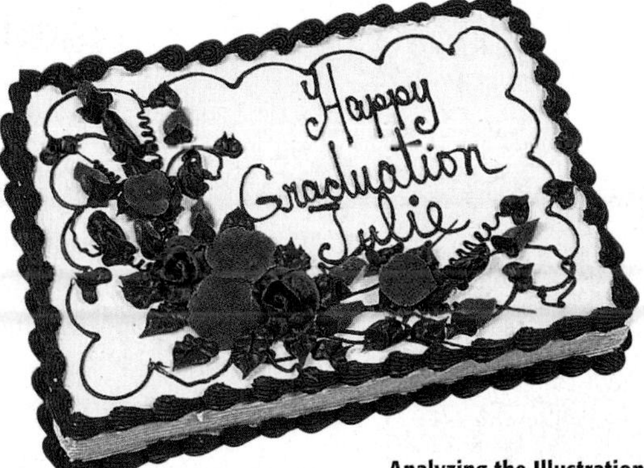

Analyzing the Illustration Imagine that this traditional American cake was for a boy named Jules. At his graduation party, how should Jules deal with the cake decorator's mistake?

Our good-byes went on too long. I heard my father's voice calling out across the parking lot, *"Hoo-lee-tah! Vámonos!"*[12]

Back home, my *tíos* and *tías* and *primas,* Mami and Papi, and *mis hermanas* had a party for me with *sancocho* and a storebought *pudín,*[13] inscribed with *Happy Graduation, Julie.* **BQ** There were many gifts—that was a plus to a large family! I got several wallets and a suitcase with my initials and a graduation charm from my godmother and money from my uncles. The biggest gift was a **portable** typewriter from my parents for writing my stories and poems. **7** **EL**

Someday, the family predicted, my name would be well-known throughout the United States. I laughed to myself, wondering which one I would go by. **8** ❍

Practice the Skills

7 **English Language Coach**

Latin Roots The root of **portable** is *port.* Think about what one is *able* to do with something portable. Can you guess what *port* means?

8 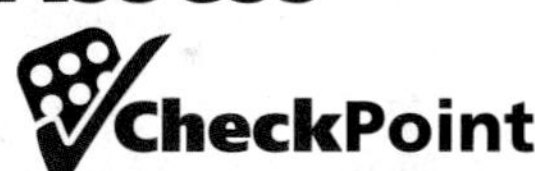

What do names mean to the author, and how do they help make her who she is? Explain your answers on the "Names/Nombres" page of Foldable 7. Your response will help you complete the Unit Challenge later.

---

10. Parents and their children make up what is called a ***nuclear family.*** An ***extended family*** includes other close relatives, such as grandparents, aunts, uncles, and cousins.

11. A ***commencement*** is a graduation ceremony.

12. ***Vámonos*** (VAW moh nohs) means "Let's go."

13. A ***pudín*** (poo DEEN) is a pudding.

Teach

EL Language Coach

Latin Roots Say: The Latin root *port* appears in the words *transport* and *import.* How are these words similar in meaning? *(When you* transport *something, you move it. When you* import *something, you bring it in. Both words are related to movement.)* What do you think the root *port* means? *(to move or carry)* **EL**

BQ BIG Question

Ask: After reading about the author's commencement party, what do you think motivates her? *(Possible responses: the love and support of her large family; her desire to write stories)* **OL**

Assess

CheckPoint

Use the CheckPoint questions provided on Presentation Plus! to check for comprehension of the selection. These questions can be used with interactive response keypads for immediate feedback.

Literature Focus Lesson

Theme Remind students that sometimes a piece of writing has a stated theme—one that is expressed directly. More often, a piece of writing has an implied theme, which is revealed gradually as the piece unfolds. Ask students these questions related to theme:

- What is the theme of "Names/Nombres"? *(Possible theme: What we are called relates to how we see ourselves.)*
- Is the theme stated directly or implied? *(implied)*
- How does the title of the story relate to the theme? *(Possible response: It represents Julia's conflicting feelings about her names.)* **OL** **AL**

Objectives

- Make inferences
- Identify and explain the effects of figurative language
- Identify and analyze the theme of a work
- Use word roots to determine meaning
- View and analyze artwork

Assess

Resources for page 792

- Selection Quick Check
- Selection and Unit Assessment
- ExamView Assessment Suite
- Interactive Tutor: Self-Assessment

Students can respond to the *After You Read* items in their Learner's Notebook or on a separate sheet of paper.

Answering the BIG Question

1. Students may describe ways that their family and ethnic culture shape their values.
2. The Alvarez family's name is mispronounced.
3. The name *Mauricia* does not translate into English.

Critical Thinking

4. Possible response: The author shows affection for her family and seems proud of it. Nevertheless, she sometimes finds her large, noisy family embarrassing.
5. Possible response: Blending in is important to Alvarez when she first arrives in New York. As she grows older, she is more comfortable with cultural differences.
6. Possible response: The author may realize that her name shows her cultural background.

After You Read

Names/Nombres

Answering the BIG Question

1. After reading "Names/Nombres," what ideas do you have about what makes you tick? Is your ethnic heritage a part of who you are? Explain.
2. **Recall** What happens almost immediately when Alvarez's family arrives in New York?
   TIP Right There
3. **Recall** Why does Alvarez's sister Mauricia have a hard time getting an American name?
   TIP Right There

Critical Thinking

4. **Analyze** How does Alvarez feel about her family and her family's culture as she grows older?
   TIP Author and Me
5. **Infer** How does Alvarez's attitude about blending in with her classmates change as she grows older?
   TIP Think and Search
6. **Interpret** Why do you think the author chooses to write under the name of Julia Alvarez?
   TIP Author and Me

Write About Your Reading

Write a letter to Julia Alvarez that compares her experiences to your experiences. Include details about your family and friends. Think about these questions to get started:

- When you were young, did someone ever mispronounce your first or last name? How did you feel?
- Did you ever wish you had a different name? If so, what is it? Why do you like it?
- Do your friends call you nicknames? What are they?
- Does your family call you a different name than your friends call you? Which name do you like better? Why?

Objectives (pp. 792–793)
Reading Evaluate text • Make connections from text to self
Literature Identify literary devices: figurative language
Vocabulary Identify synonyms
Grammar Identify subjects and verbs

Write About Your Reading

Possible response:

Dear Julia Alvarez,

My family calls me by a pet name that used to embarrass me. My older sister couldn't say my name properly when I was born, so everyone in the family called me "Kappy," the baby-talk name she made up. Now that I am in junior high, I want to be called "Kathleen" because I want to be taken seriously, and I want to hear my beautiful, grown-up name. I'm still glad, though, when I hear the name "Kappy," because the person who says it has known and loved me for a long time.

—Kathleen "Kappy" McGee

Skills Review

Key Reading Skill: Evaluating

7. Would you recommend this story to anyone? Why or why not? Think about how you evaluate the story.

Key Literary Element: Figurative Language

8. Write down the word or words in this example that make the phrase a simile:

   a name as chaotic with sounds as a Middle Eastern bazaar

9. Is this an example of simile, metaphor, or neither?

   they singled me out as a "foreigner"

Reviewing Skills: Connecting

10. Alvarez does not want to be a "rare, exotic friend." How would you feel if people only talked to you about your name and where you were from? Why?

Vocabulary Check

For each word in bold, choose the word that means most nearly the same thing.

11. ironically	surprisingly	warmly	happily
12. initial	last	first	time
13. merge	combine	destroy	elevate
14. vaguely	uncertainly	largely	jumpy
15. specified	used	explained	wondered
16. exotic	boring	foreign	excited
17. chaotic	neat	cute	messy

Grammar Link: Tricky Subjects and Verbs

Usually the subject comes before the verb in a sentence. There are two main exceptions.

- **Questions** In many questions, all or part of the verb comes before the subject.

  Do you and your friends have plans?

  helping verb / subject / main verb

  To make it less tricky to find the subject and verb, turn the question into a statement.

  You and your friends do have plans.

- **Here/There** The words *here* and *there* cannot be subjects. To find the subject of a sentence that begins with *here* or *there,* omit the word. Find the verb; then ask yourself, who or what ___?

  Example: There is a big party on Saturday.

  Omit *there*; then find the verb.

  ~~There~~ is a big party on Saturday.

  Ask, who or what is? *Party* is.

  There is a big party on Saturday.
  verb subject

Grammar Practice

On a separate piece of paper, copy each sentence. Underline the subject once and the verb twice.

18. Is my brother at baseball practice?
19. Here is his baseball jersey.
20. Are you and Bill going to the game?

Writing Application Review your letter to Julia Alvarez. Look for questions and for sentences that begin with *here* or *there.* Underline the subject once and the verb twice in these sentences.

Web Activities For eFlashcards, Selection Quick Checks, and other Web activities, go to www.glencoe.com.

Skills Review

Key Reading Skill: Evaluating

7. Possible responses: I would recommend this story because it is both tender and funny. It is a story about fitting in to a new place, a situation that people must often cope with.

Key Literary Element: Figurative Language

8. as...as
9. neither

Reviewing Skills: Connecting

10. Responses will vary, but students may say that they would not like to be singled out for such attention. They may say that they would prefer that people be interested in *who* they are, not just their name and home country.

Vocabulary Check

11. surprisingly
12. first
13. combine
14. uncertainly
15. explained
16. foreign
17. messy

Literature Online

Web Activities Have students access the Web site for interactive activities that will help them assess their understanding of the selection.

Grammar Link: Tricky Subjects and Verbs

Grammar Practice

18. Is my brother at baseball practice?
19. Here is his baseball jersey.
20. Are you and Bill going to the game?

Close

Ask students to describe situations in which they might want to be called by courtesy titles such as *Dr. Sanchez* or *Professor Smith.* Have students think about the Big Question as they explain what people's names reveal about their relationships with others.

Poetry

UNIT 7

Teaching Students to Write a Poem

Why Is It Important?

- Poetry provides a unique opportunity to indulge in play with language.
- Figurative language plays a large role in every communication, written or spoken. Writing a poem will expand students' awareness of the plethora of metaphors in their own verbal lives.
- Students may find it easier to appreciate or analyze poetry after they have created some of their own.
- Revision, the "re-seeing," is especially important to this genre. If the student's poem is short, each word in it must contribute greatly to the whole.
- Poetry can be a place for self expression; academic, or purely personal.
- Students may find that revision of all written work becomes clearer after applying the practice to something personally meaningful, like a "what makes me tick" poem.

How to Help Students Get It

- Review the definitions of verse and stanza with students.
- Share a few of your own favorite "bite-size" poems with the class. You can read them aloud, have students read them, or even just post them in stations around the classroom.
- Consider transcribing the lyrics to some songs your students are familiar with. Seeing the terminology of poetry applied to familiar text may clarify the concepts, especially rhyme pattern and alliteration.
- Discuss some popular clichés and identify them as metaphors and similes. (Sleep like a baby, faster than a locomotive, etc.)
- Provide students with access to a thesaurus, in print or online.
- Bring in a short sample of your own favorite author and read aloud a section that exemplifies one of the literary concepts applicable to poetry.
- Review the definitions of mood and tone with students.

Writing Trait: Word Choice

Words are the building blocks of a written work; the author must choose wisely and assemble them well. Strong, active words generally provoke a more favorable response than overused or passive words. By selecting precise words that have the desired connotation, an author can control the effect of the completed text.

Objectives covered in this workshop:

- **Writing** Summarize to inform develop drafts; categorize information; main idea and supporting details
- **Grammar** Identify and correctly use verbs

Traits of Good Writing	
Ideas	the message or the theme and the details that develop it
Organization	the arrangement of main points and supporting details
Voice	a writer's unique way of using tone and style
 **Word Choice:** the vocabulary a writer uses to convey meaning	• Does the writer use lively verbs to show action? • Does the writer use vivid words to create word pictures in the readers' minds? • Does the writer use precise words to explain his or her ideas simply and clearly?
Sentence Fluency	the smooth rhythm and flow of sentences that vary in length and style
Convention	correct spelling, grammar, usage, and mechanics
Presentation	the way words and design elements look on a page

Workshop Resources

Pacing (days) Standard	Block	Lesson	Student Materials	Teacher Resources
1		Prewriting	Writing Workshop Graphic Organizer Grammar Practice Spelling and Handwriting Practice Spelling Power eWorkbook Interactive Grammar and Language Workbook Grammar and Composition Handbook	TeacherWorks Plus Presentation Plus! Rubrics for Assessing Student-Writing, Listening, and Speaking
2		Drafting	Real Success in Writing: Research and Reports Writing Constructed Responses Sourcebook	Grammar and Writing Workshop Transparency
1		Editing	Interactive Grammar and Language Workbook Grammar and Composition Handbook	Grammar and Writing Workshop Transparency
2		Revising	Real Success in Writing: Research and Reports Writing Constructed Responses Sourcebook	Interactive Grammar and Language Workbook
2		Presenting	Real Success in Writing: Research and Reports Writing Constructed Responses Sourcebook	Rubrics for Assessing Student Writing, Listening, and Speaking

Focus

BELLRINGER Options

Daily Language Practice Transparency

Focus Activity Ask: If you had to choose one object that best shows who you are, what would it be and why? *(Responses will vary.)*

Teach

L Literary Element

Sound Devices Write the following lines on the board:

I thoughtfully write on the paper with a pencil.
I pensively push the pencil across the page.

Say: The two lines mean the same thing, yet they are different. How? *(The second line includes alliteration.)* OL

Resources for page 794

- Use the Writing Workshop Graphic Organizer BLM in the Unit 7 Resource Booklet.
- Use the Grammar and Writing Workshop Transparencies, Unit 7.

WRITING WORKSHOP PART 1

Poem

Prewriting and Drafting

ASSIGNMENT Write a poem

Purpose: To write a poem about an object that shows what makes you tick

Audience: You, your teacher, and possibly some classmates

Writing Rubric

As you work through this assignment, you should

- follow poetic conventions of verse and stanza
- develop a rhyme pattern
- use figurative language and sensory details
- use word choice to set a tone

See page 832 in Part 2 for a model of a poem.

Objectives (pp. 794–797)
Writing Use the writing process: draft • Write a poem • Use literary elements: conventions of poetry, figurative language
Vocabulary Use synonyms
Grammar Use correct subject-verb agreement

Writing a poem will help you express your feelings about the Unit 7 Big Question: What makes you tick?

Poetry is probably a bigger part of your life than you realize. Think of songs that you enjoy. Songs are poems set to music. Poetry appeals to your emotions and senses in the same way that music does.

Prewriting

Get Ready to Write

L Writing a poem is like writing a song. Both the poet and the songwriter use rhythm and rhyme and express emotions and ideas. Writing a poem is also like painting a picture. An artist uses shape and color to put an image on canvas. A poet uses words to put an image in the reader's mind.

Gather Ideas

Pretend that you are about to paint a portrait. First, you have to decide what to paint. Some artists choose simple, everyday objects like pieces of fruit. Artists can paint an ordinary object in such detail that it becomes a work of art. You can do the same thing in poetry—using words instead of paint!

Choose a Topic

Choose an object to write about that you know well and can picture in your mind. Or select one object that you can place in front of you on your desk. Either way, you should choose something that shows what makes you tick. The object could be a piece of furniture, a favorite book, your shoe, a favorite toy from when you were a child, a pencil, a soda can, or almost any *thing.*

Write your object in your Learner's Notebook. Then answer these questions.

1. What color is it?
2. What shape is it?
3. Is it heavy or light?
4. Does it have a smell or a taste?
5. Does it remind you of a person?
6. What is your best memory of it?

Additional Support

Differentiated Instruction

Word Pictures To give students practice describing an object, bring in several objects, such as an old shoe, an apple with a bite taken out of it, and a sparkly necklace. Have each student choose one object and write

- one sentence using sensory words (words appealing to the five senses) to describe the object
- one sentence using a simile or metaphor to describe the object
- one sentence using alliteration or assonance to describe the object
- one sentence using personification to describe the object

Challenge members of the class to guess which image each writer describes. AS

Drafting

Start Writing!

There is no right or wrong way to start a poem. Just start writing about your object in any way you like.

Literature Online

Writing Models For models and other writing activities, go to www.glencoe.com.

Get It on Paper

- Read the notes in your Learner's Notebook.
- Use a favorite memory to start your poem.
- Include a sensory detail such as how the object smells or tastes.

Remember that poets write in verse—that is, in single lines of text—instead of in continuous text as the author of a story would do. Although poems may look different from what you are used to reading, they can still tell stories and express ideas. They also include figurative language. Gary Soto wrote a poem about a tortilla! Here's part of that poem.

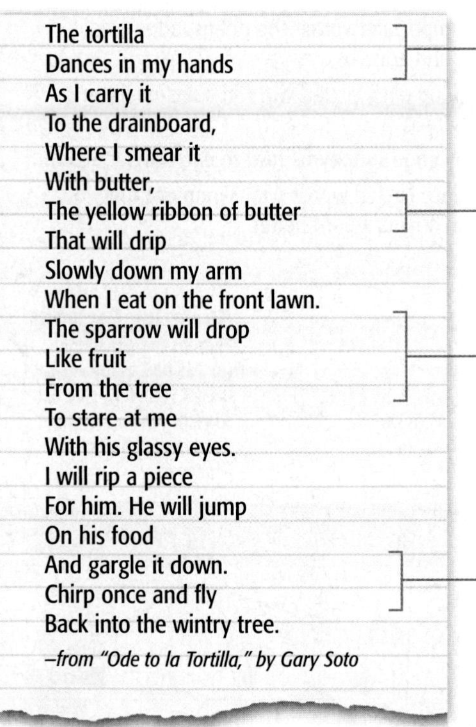

The tortilla
Dances in my hands
As I carry it
To the drainboard,
Where I smear it
With butter,
The yellow ribbon of butter
That will drip
Slowly down my arm
When I eat on the front lawn.
The sparrow will drop
Like fruit
From the tree
To stare at me
With his glassy eyes.
I will rip a piece
For him. He will jump
On his food
And gargle it down.
Chirp once and fly
Back into the wintry tree.
—from "Ode to la Tortilla," by Gary Soto

Personification Personification gives human characteristics to nonhuman objects. A tortilla can't dance, of course. Soto says this to describe carrying a tortilla that's fresh from the frying pan—it's hot! So his hand makes it dance.

Metaphor A metaphor compares two unlike things without using the word *like* or *as*. Here, Soto's metaphor compares a yellow ribbon and butter. It's an unusual way to describe butter, but it creates an effective image in the reader's mind.

Simile A simile uses the word *like* or *as* to compare two unlike things. It's a good, easy way to make the reader notice similarities between things. Soto compares the sparrow to fruit, or the way the sparrow will drop to the way fruit drops from a tree.

Sensory Detail Words and phrases that appeal to any of the five senses are a good way to add interesting detail. Soto's sparrow "gargles" and "chirps." These words appeal to the senses of taste and hearing.

W

WRITING WORKSHOP PART 1

Teach

Literature Online

Writing Models Have students access the Web site for an additional and interactive Writing Workshop-based student model.

W Writing

Figurative Language Ask students to identify whether the following are examples of personification, similes, metaphors, or sensory details.

1. She was as pretty as a blue sky on a sunny day. *(simile)*
2. Her tangled hair was a bat's nest. *(metaphor)*
3. The tree whispered in the wind. *(personification)*
4. The ice cream was cold and sweet. *(sensory details)*
5. The old man clung to his opinions like a spider to its web. *(simile)* **OL**

Differentiated Instruction

Poem Starters During the prewriting process, suggest that students complete the following sentences to help them brainstorm ideas for their poems.

Focus on Favorite Memory
- I remember seeing…
- I remember touching…
- I remember tasting…
- I remember hearing…
- I remember smelling…

Focus on Object
The object looks like ___ because…
The object feels like ___ because…
The object tastes like ___ because…
The object sounds like ___ because…
The object smells like ___ because…
OL

Objectives
- Use the writing process: draft a poem
- Use literary elements: conventions of poetry, figurative language
- Understand similes and metaphors

Teach

W Writing

Word Choice Say: The emotional atmosphere, or feeling, of a poem is called the mood. Writers choose words and details to create a mood or feeling that brings a scene to life. Reread the excerpt from "Ode to la Tortilla" on page 795. How does the poem make you feel? *(Responses will vary. Students may suggest that the poem makes them feel warm or comfortable.)* Which words or phrases in the poem create this feeling for you? *(Responses will vary. Students may suggest "yellow ribbon of butter.")* OL

Assess

Have each student exchange the first draft of his or her poem for a partner's first draft and critique the partner's work. For example, did the partner include precise words? Are there better synonyms that might replace some of the writer's words? After a few minutes, tell each student to assess his or her partner's feedback, make any needed revisions, and save the revised draft for later use.

Applying Good Writing Traits

Word Choice

Poems are usually short, yet they may express complicated ideas and feelings. So good poets choose their words very carefully.

What Is Word Choice?

Many words have synonyms—words that mean the same or nearly the same thing. But a writer can't use just any synonym in place of a word. For example:

- Two synonyms for *breeze* are *gust* and *draft.*
- A breeze is a gentle wind that continues to blow.
- A gust is a short, not-so-gentle burst of wind.
- W A draft is a strong flow of air—usually indoors.
- If you're describing a quiet, pleasant setting, *breeze* is the best word choice. But if you want to suggest something less pleasant, one of the other words could work better.

Why Is Word Choice Important?

Good word choices will help you express your thoughts and emotions more clearly, and they'll make your writing more interesting. This is important in all kinds of writing—poetry, fiction, and nonfiction. But word choice is especially important in poetry. Again, most poems are fairly short. That means every word in a poem has to do more work than the same word would do in a story.

How Do I Do It?

- Determine your purpose for writing. Do you want to entertain? Inform? Reflect? Persuade?
- Decide who your audience is.
- Choose words that are appropriate for your purpose and for your audience. A letter to your best friend should probably not sound the same as a report for your social studies class.
- Choose words that create the mood you want. *Dark, mysterious,* and *spooky* help to set one mood. *Sparkling, magical,* and *enchanting* describe a very different mood.

Write to Learn

When you have a draft of your poem, circle the more important words—the nouns, adjectives, verbs, and adverbs.

- Look up each circled word in a dictionary or thesaurus.
- Copy good synonyms next to each circled word.
- Replace circled words with synonyms that you think fit your poem better.

Analyzing Cartoons
Perhaps the girl should say "as bad as my vocabulary." Well, let's give her a break. Finding the right word can often be . . . whatever.

Additional Support

English Language Coach

Slang Explain the punch line of the comic strip to students who are learning English. The film *Valley Girls,* released in 1983, presents a suburban California girl who is part of a social group defined by its slang and superficial values. The slang, which is still used today, includes the words *like* and *whatever.*

- *Like* is used as a meaningless modifier, or a word that limits the meaning of another word or phrase.
- *Whatever* is used to refer to anything that leaves doubt.

Explain to students that the joke is that the girl criticizes her partner's vocabulary but is unable to come up with precise words herself. EL

Grammar Link

Subject-Verb Agreement

Do you ever use *was* when you should use *were* or *don't* when *doesn't* is correct? Learn the basics of subject-verb agreement to fix this problem.

What Is It?

Subject-verb agreement is picking the verb form that matches, or agrees with, the subject.

1. If the subject of a sentence is *he, she, it,* or its equal, the verb must end in *–s.*

- *He* wants a car. • *Al* wants a car.
  (*He* = one male. *Al* = one male. *Al* = *he.*)
- *She* drives a bus. • *Lu* drives a bus.
  (*She* = one female. *Lu* = one female. *Lu* = *she.*)
- *It* runs on gas. • The *bus* runs on gas.
  (*It* = one thing. A *bus* = one thing. *Bus* = *it.*)

2. If the subject of a sentence is *I, you, we, they,* or its equal, the verb does not end in *–s.*

- *I* want pizza. • *You* make good pizza.
- *We* like them. • *Ed and I* like them.
  (*We* = *I* + other people. *Ed and I* = *I* + other people. *Ed and I* = *we.*)
- *They* taste good. • The *pizzas* taste good.
  (*They* = two or more things. *Pizzas* = two or more things. *Pizzas* = *they.*)
- *They* use a recipe from Italy.
- *Gino and Marie* use a recipe from Italy.
  (*They* = two or more people. *Gino and Marie* = two or more people. *Gino and Marie* = *they.*)

Why Is It Important?

Good grammar and good writing go hand in hand. When your subjects and verbs agree, readers can focus on your ideas, not on your mistakes.

How Do I Do It?

Follow these steps to subject-verb agreement.

Step 1: Find the subject and verb in the sentence.

- She plays the tuba in the school band.

Step 2: Apply the subject-verb agreement rules.

- She plays the tuba in the school band.
  (The subject is *she,* so the *–s* on *plays* is correct.)

Grammar Practice

On a separate piece of paper, write the subject and the correct verb form for each sentence.

1. Colin always (give, gives) his all.
2. He never (do, does) anything halfway.
3. Colin and his sister (work, works) hard.

Writing Application Look again at your poem. Fix any mistakes in subject-verb agreement.

Looking Ahead

Part 2 of this Writing Workshop is coming up later. Save the writing you did so far; you'll need it later to finish your poem.

Differentiated Instruction

Additional Practice Provide students who need additional practice items with the following sentences. Have them identify the subject and the correct verb form for each sentence.

1. Gary Soto (write, writes) poems about important memories in his life. *(Gary Soto; writes)*
2. His book (contain, contains) twenty-one poems. *(book; contains)*
3. The poems (speak, speaks) about food, animals, people, possessions, and places. *(poems; speak)*
4. The end of the book (feature, features) a list of Spanish words and their English translations. *(end; features)* **EL** **BL**

WRITING WORKSHOP PART 1

Teach

Grammar Link
Subject-Verb Agreement

Say: This Grammar Link will help you understand subject-verb agreement. A subject is the part of a sentence that tells what the sentence is about. A verb expresses the action or state of being of the subject. What is the basic rule of subject-verb agreement? *(If the subject is* he, she, it, *or its equal, then the verb ends with the letter* s. *If the subject is* I, you, we, they, *or its equal, the verb does not end with the letter* s.*)* **OL**

Write the following sentences on the board:

- *She like ___ clocks.*
- *I like ___ clocks.*

Ask: The verb in which sentence needs the letter *s* added to it? Why? *(The verb in the first sentence needs the* s *because the subject of the sentence is* she.*)* **BL**

Grammar Practice

1. Colin; gives
2. He; does
3. Colin and his sister; work

Objectives

- Write poems
- Use the writing process
- Use appropriate word choice for audience and purpose
- Use word choice and figurative language to create meaning and set a tone
- Use correct subject-verb agreement
- Understand synonyms
- Use a thesaurus to determine shades of meaning

Interpreting

Objectives covered in this workshop:
- Interpret

Teaching Students to Interpret

Why Is It Important?

- Every reader constructs meaning on the basis of what he or she understands about the world. Students will learn how to use their own understanding of the world to decide what the events or ideas in a selection mean.
- Finding meanings as students read is all about interacting with the text. Interpreting text will allow students to become more active readers.
- Students will learn how to determine what an author is *really* saying in his or her work.

How to Help Students Get It

- Have students think about what they already know about themselves and the world, and how it relates to the topic of each selection.
- Tell students to ask themselves questions as they read such as, What is the author really trying to say here? What larger idea might these events be about?
- Remind students that interpreting is more than just remembering and understanding facts—it's creating meaning in text by using what they know about the world around them.

Reading to Answer the Big Question

Diondra Jordan

A young girl thinks about who she is and what is important to her as she works on her self-portrait in this short story. Students will find out how she overcomes people's assumptions about her abilities and how she stays true to herself.

Face It

In this poem the speaker describes that although she has the traits from two different cultures, her personal characteristics are what define her identity and make her tick.

Almost Ready

The poem describes a young boy who is struggling to get himself ready for a party. Students will identify with how the speaker is not yet comfortable with his true self.

READING WORKSHOP 2

Teach

L Literary Element

Review Author's Craft Ask: What do you notice about the types of sentences the author uses in the first paragraph? *(She uses complete and incomplete sentences.)* **OL** Why do you think the author includes incomplete sentences? *(Possible response: to capture the narrator's voice, which is friendly and reflects the narrator's age)* **AL**

R Reading Skill

Interpreting Ask: What does Raul do that impresses the narrator? *(He leaves his painting out on the teacher's desk, where anyone can see it.)* **BL** What does this action suggest about his personality? *(Possible response: It suggests he is confident and proud of his work.)* **OL** Why might other students, such as the speaker, be more careful about where they leave their art? *(Possible response: Other students might be more sensitive to criticism.)* **AL**

Readability Scores
Dale-Chall: 5.2
DRP: 49
Lexile: 760

Diondra Jordan

by Nikki Grimes

If only I was as bold as Raul. The other day, he left one of his paintings out on Mr. Ward's desk where anybody could see it. Which was the point. He sometimes works at Mr. Ward's desk during lunch. The wet paintbrushes sticking up out of the jar are always a sign that he's been at it again. So of course, anybody who glances over in that direction will be tempted to stop by and look. **1**

This particular painting was rough, but anyone could tell it was Raul. A **self-portrait**. He'll probably hang it in class

Vocabulary

self-portrait (self POR trut) *n.* a painting or photograph of an artist by that artist

Practice the Skills

1 Key Reading Skill

Interpreting Have you ever known someone like Raul? How did you feel about him or her? How do you think the narrator feels about Raul?

Additional Support

Differentiated Instruction

Comparing Self-Portraits to Photographs Tell students that a self-portrait can reveal a lot about how the artist sees himself or herself. Have students use Internet and library resources to find a self-portrait of Frida Kahlo, Pablo Picasso, Vincent van Gogh, or William H. Johnson. Then, have them find photograph(s) of the artist. Ask students to compare the self-portrait to the photograph(s).

- What features does the artist emphasize or change in the self-portrait?
- Does the self-portrait look like the artist? Why or why not? **OL**
- What do the mood and the colors used suggest about how the artist views himself or herself? **AL**

Skills Preview

Key Reading Skill: Interpreting

To interpret "Diondra Jordan," think about word choice and phrasing. Think about her view of the world. What do you already know about yourself and the world that helps you understand what the author is *really* saying?

Partner Talk As you read "Diondra Jordan," pick three lines from the story or poem and talk with a partner about what Diondra is *really* saying.

Key Literary Element: Symbolism

When a person, a place, an object, or an action represents something else it becomes a symbol. In literature, this is known as **symbolism.** Writers use symbolism in poems and stories to add meaning and to emphasize themes. L

- A tree may be a symbol for life.
- A mountain may be a symbol for strength.
- An island may be a symbol for loneliness.

Use these tips to help you recognize symbolism.

- Look for repeated words, images, or actions.
  What do they mean? Why are they important?
- When a character takes action, what are the reasons? Think about a time you made something for someone. Your action was a symbol of how you felt.
  How is the action a symbol of who he or she is or how he or she feels?
- Look for things or ideas that are important to the writer, speaker, or character.
  What does he or she care about? Why?

Partner Talk With a partner, match these symbols with their meanings.

Symbol	Possible Meaning
rose dove river	peace time love

Get Ready to Read

Connect to the Reading

If you created a self-portrait, how would you make yourself look? What would you use to make it—pencils, paints, ink? What would be in the background? What would you be doing? Would the self-portrait be in color? R

Write to Learn In your Learner's Notebook, write about something positive that you've always wanted to do but have been afraid to do. What holds you back?

Build Background

Writers and other artists often focus on identity. This story mentions the Harlem Renaissance and identity.

- In the 1920s, the Harlem neighborhood of New York experienced a creative movement of African American literature, art, and music; this became known as the Harlem Renaissance.
- African American writers gained a wide audience and received the praise of critics.
- The works of the Harlem Renaissance often centered around the question of identity.

Set Purposes for Reading

Read "Diondra Jordan" to find out what makes a student artist tick.

Set Your Own Purpose What would you like to learn from the story to help you answer the Big Question? Write your own purpose on the "Diondra Jordan" page of Foldable 7.

Literature Online

Interactive Literary Elements Handbook
To review or learn more about the literary elements, go to www.glencoe.com.

Keep Moving

Use these skills as you read the following selection.

Teach

L Literary Element

Symbolism Ask: What symbols might you see as you walk or ride to school? *(Possible responses: Red and green lights symbolize "stop" and "go.")* What symbols might you see in the cafeteria? *(Students might mention dollars and cents signs or symbols for cafeteria foods.)* OL

R Reading Skill

Review Connecting Ask: What would be the setting of your self-portrait? *(Responses will vary.)* BL What object might you include that could have a symbolic meaning? *(Responses will vary.)* OL

CheckPoint

Use the CheckPoint questions provided on Presentation Plus! to check for interpreting skills and to build background. These questions can be used with interactive response keypads for immediate student feedback.

Literature Online

Interactive Literary Elements Handbook Have students access the Web site to improve their understanding of symbolism.

Reading in the Real World

College Students who would like to study art may be interested to learn that self-portraits have existed for many thousands of years. A number of self-portraits in different media survive from the ancient world, and many early painters "signed" their work by incorporating small images of themselves into paintings. In modern times, self-portraits often depict an artist's more abstract and emotional concepts of self. Self-portraits also exist as poems and other works of literature. In the selection, students create self-portraits through both art and poetry. As a class, discuss the concept of the self-portrait. Brainstorm with students other ways they could create self-portraits that express who they are. OL

Objectives

- Interpret text
- Make connections from text to self
- Identify literary devices: symbolism
- Identify Anglo-Saxon roots

Teach

More About the Author

Nikki Grimes was born in Harlem, New York, in 1950. She says she has lived in every borough of New York City except Staten Island. Her writing draws on her urban childhood by portraying relationships between African American family members and within communities.

V Vocabulary

Connecting Words Say: When you are given a new set of vocabulary words, examining relationships between the words can help cement the words' meanings in your memory. For example, in this selection, the words *self-portrait* and *gallery* connect because a self-portrait is a type of art, and art is displayed in a gallery. Find a way to connect the words *tirade* and *identity* and the words *identity* and *self-portrait.* Explain the connections in your Learner's Notebook. OL

Before You Read Diondra Jordan

Nikki Grimes

Meet the Author

As a child, Nikki Grimes moved a lot. She constantly had to adjust to new homes, new friends, and new schools. She found comfort in reading. She says that "Books were my soul's delight. Even so, in one sense, the stories I read betrayed me. Too few gave me back my mirror image. . . . 'When I grow up,' I thought, 'I'll write books about children who look and feel like me.'"

Author Search For more about Nikki Grimes, go to www.glencoe.com.

Objectives (pp. 800–805)
Reading Interpret text • Make connections from text to self
Literature Identify literary devices: symbolism
Vocabulary Identify Latin roots

Vocabulary Preview

self-portrait (self POR trut) *n.* a painting or photograph of an artist by that artist **(p. 802)** *It was clear that Raul had been working on a self-portrait.*

gallery (GAL ur ee) *n.* a room used for a special purpose (such as showing pictures) **(p. 803)** *With pictures hung everywhere, the classroom became our gallery.*

identity (eye DEN tuh tee) *n.* the qualities and features that make one person different from another **(p. 803)** *Art class is a good place to explore identity.*

tirade (TY rayd) *n.* a long, angry speech **(p. 803)** *Max launched into an angry tirade when he was accused of cheating on the test.*

V

Write to Learn In your Learner's Notebook, answer these questions.

1. What would you focus on if you were going to make a self-portrait: your face, your personality, or both? Explain.
2. What kind of gallery would you want to hang your self-portrait in? What other kinds of art would be in there?
3. How would you show your identity in the self-portrait?
4. What makes you feel like going into a tirade?

English Language Coach

Latin Roots The common Latin root *vis* or *vid* is found in both simple and difficult words. If you learn to recognize it in simple words, you can use your knowledge of it when you run across it in difficult ones.

Root	Found In
vis *or* vid	vision, visual, video, visibile, visit
mem	remember, memory, memo, memorable
sent *or* sens	sensitive, sentimental, sensory

Partner Talk With a partner, use the examples above to figure out what the roots are likely to mean. Then, with your partner, find *vista, memoir,* and *sentimental* in a dictionary. See if these words are related to the meanings you guessed for *vis/vid, mem,* and *sent/sens.*

Additional Support

Author Search To expand students' appreciation of Nikki Grimes, have them access the Web site for additional information and resources.

English Language Coach

Build Background Nikki Grimes's story about self-expression draws on the Harlem Renaissance for inspiration. Tell students that this creative outpouring centered on an exploration of African American culture, experience, and pride. Have students choose one painter, poet, or fiction writer from the Harlem Renaissance and learn two interesting facts about the person. OL Students who are interested can do a more in-depth study about the life of one of the Harlem Renaissance artists and share their findings in a class discussion. AL

Why Is It Important? Every reader creates meaning by using what he or she understands about the world. Finding meaning as you read is all about getting the most out of a text.

How Do I Do It? Think about what you already know about yourself and the world. Ask yourself: What is the author really trying to say here? What larger ideas might these events be about? Here's how one student interprets a sentence from "Names/Nombres." **R**

Study Central Visit www.glencoe.com and click on Study Central to review interpreting.

I just wanted to be Judy and merge with the Sallys and Janes in my class.

The author wants to be Judy and merge with the Sallys and Janes. I know that merge means "to join together to be one." Sometimes it's easier to join in with the crowd if you're not different, but sometimes different is good. I think the author is different from the other girls in the class and is having a hard time fitting in.

Practice It!

In your Learner's Notebook, practice interpreting the bold-faced lines below from "Annabel Lee." Ask yourself these questions:

- What does the selection say about the topic?
- What do I know about myself and the world as it relates to this topic?
- What is the author *really* saying? Is there a larger picture?

She was a child and I was a child,
In this kingdom by the sea,
But we loved with a love that was more than love–
I and my Annabel Lee–

Use It!

As you read "Diondra Jordan," "Face It," and "Almost Ready," remember to use the questions above to help you interpret the texts. Write the questions in your Learner's Notebook ahead of time, and answer them whenever you need help interpreting.

Teach

Literature Online

Study Central Have students access the Web site to review interpreting and to complete a related activity.

R Reading Skill

Interpreting Ask: Why might one person's interpretation of a poem be different from another person's? *(Possible response: When you interpret a poem, you draw on personal knowledge and experience. Different people will have had different life experiences and so may have different interpretations of a poem.)* **AL**

Resources for page 799

Use Reading Skills Transparency in *Read Aloud, Think Aloud,* Unit 7, to help students practice interpreting.

English Language Coach

Symbolism Tell students that interpreting texts may include decoding symbols. Remind students that symbols are objects or images that stand for other objects, people, or ideas. Write the following list of words on the board, and ask students to identify what the images represent.

- eagle *(Possible responses: freedom, nature, the United States)*
- heart *(Possible responses: love, romance, Valentine's Day)*
- fox *(Possible responses: cleverness, mischief)*
- balanced scales *(Possible responses: justice, fairness)*
- shadows *(Possible responses: coming trouble, evil, despair)* **EL**

Objectives
- Interpret text
- Activate prior knowledge
- Identify symbols

Focus

BELLRINGER Options

- **Selection Focus Transparencies**
- **Daily Language Practice Transparency**

Focus Activity Say: Have you ever asked for permission to do something and been told, "Maybe"? You might have been able to interpret the person's facial expression, tone of voice, and responses to previous situations to tell whether that "maybe" actually meant "yes" or "no." Tell what happened. *(Responses will vary.)*

Teach

R Reading Skill

Interpreting Say: You interpret information all the time, even when you look at a box of cereal. How can you interpret information on a cereal box to tell if the cereal is healthful? *(Possible response: You might interpret information on the box about vitamins and fiber to find out whether the food is healthful.)* **OL**

READING WORKSHOP 2

Skills Focus

You will practice using these skills when you read the following selections:

- "Diondra Jordan," p. 802
- "Face It," p. 810
- "Almost Ready," p. 811

Reading

- Interpreting

Literature

- Identifying symbolism and explaining its effects

Vocabulary

- Using structural analysis to understand word meanings
- Academic Vocabulary: *interpret*

Writing/Grammar

- Using appropriate word choice
- Using correct subject-verb agreement

Objectives (pp. 798–799)
Reading Interpret text

Skill Lesson

Interpreting

Learn It!

What Is It? When you **interpret**, you use your own understanding of the world to decide what the events or ideas in a selection mean.

- Interpreting is more than just remembering and understanding the facts. **R**
- When you use what you've learned from your own experiences to understand what the author is *really* saying, you are interpreting.

Analyzing Cartoons
When you interpret what you read, you combine what's in the text with your own knowledge to figure out what the author is saying. But first you have to read the book.

Academic Vocabulary

interpret (in TUR prit) *v.* to explain the meaning of; to make understandable

Additional Support

Reading in the Real World

College Tell students that in high school and college they will be asked to write essays in which they interpret literary works. Point out that although interpretations will vary from person to person, students must support their interpretations with their own knowledge and with details from the text. **OL**

Have students draw a fourth frame for the cartoon in which the character on the left answers Holly's question about literature being open to interpretation. Use this example to reinforce Holly's failure to realize that interpretations must be supported both by textual evidence and by prior knowledge and experience. **AL**

Workshop Resources

Pacing (days) Standard	Block	Lesson	Student Materials	Teacher Resources
1		Key Skill Lesson: Interpreting	Key Reading Skills Practice English Language Coach	Bellringer Options Transparencies Read Aloud, Think Aloud Transparencies Presentation Plus!
2		"Face it"	Literary Analysis Transparencies Glencoe Online Selection Vocabulary Development Academic Vocabulary Development English Language Coach Active Reading Graphic Organizer Literary Analysis StudentWorks Plus Online Student Edition Literature Classics Selection and Unit Assessments	Literary and Text Analysis Transparencies Puzzlemaker Skill Level Up! BookLink 3 Assessment by Learning Objective (Diagnostic and Formative) Interactive Tutor Self-Assessment TeacherWorks Plus
2		"Almost Ready"	Glencoe Online Selection Vocabulary Development Academic Vocabulary Development English Language Coach Active Reading Graphic Organizer Literary Analysis StudentWorks Plus Online Student Edition Literature Classics Selection and Unit Assessments	Literary and Text Analysis Transparencies Puzzlemaker Skill Level Up! BookLink 3 Assessment by Learning Objective (Diagnostic and Formative) Interactive Tutor Self-Assessment TeacherWorks Plus

Keys for Unit Resource

- Blackline Master
- Workbook
- Supplemental Text
- CD-ROM
- DVD
- Transparency
- Web-based
- Fast Files

Level Appropriate Code

AS = Activities for all students
AL = Activities for students working above grade level
OL = Activities for students working at grade level
BL = Activities for students working below grade level
EL = Activities for English language learners

Back in September, Mr. Ward covered two of the classroom walls with black construction paper and then scattered paper frames up and down the walls, each one a different size and color. Now half the room looks sort of like an art **gallery**, which was the idea. We're supposed to use the paper frames for our work. Whether we put up poems or photographs or even paintings is up to us, so long as the work is ours and we can tie it in with our study of the Harlem Renaissance. I guess Raul's self-portrait fits, since we've been talking a lot about **identity**. He'll probably put it up next to his poem. You should have seen him hang that thing. You'd think he was handling a million-dollar masterpiece the way he took his time placing it just so. If you look close, you can see the smudges where he erased a word or two and rewrote it. Mr. Ward must be in shock. He can never get Raul to rewrite a lick of homework or anything else. And don't even talk to him about checking his spelling! He'll launch into a **tirade** on you in a minute. "What?" he'll snap. "You think Puerto Ricans can't spell?" Forget it. Anyway, I dare you to find one misspelled word in that poem of his! Maybe it's a **visual** thing. Maybe he wants his poem to look as good as his self-portrait. And it is good. 2 3

I've never tried doing a self-portrait, but why not? I could maybe do one in charcoal.[1] I like drawing faces in charcoal. I've been drawing since I can't remember when. Not that anyone here knows that, except Tanisha, and she found out by accident when she came to my house to study once and saw a couple of drawings

1. A stick of ***charcoal,*** or a charcoal pencil, can be used to make drawings in tones of black.

Vocabulary

gallery (GAL ur ee) *n.* a room used for a special purpose (such as showing pictures)

identity (eye DEN tuh tee) *n.* the qualities and features that make one person different from another

tirade (TY rayd) *n.* a long, angry speech

Practice the Skills

2 Key Reading Skill

R **Interpreting** The students have been talking a lot about identity. What does the word *identity* mean here? Why does Mr. Ward encourage the students to create poems, photographs, and paintings to express their identities?

3 English Language Coach

Latin Roots Diondra says "Maybe it's a visual thing." What is the root of **visual**? What does she mean by saying this?

Teach

R Reading Skill

Interpreting Say: Recall what you have learned about the Harlem Renaissance. How does this artistic movement relate to the theme of identity? *(Possible response: Artists of the Harlem Renaissance found new ways to express their identities. Much of the work they produced was about expressing identity.)* OL

Viewing the Painting

Say: Paintings can tell a lot about a person. Look at the painting on this page. What can you tell about the girl from her facial expression and the way she is standing? *(Possible response: Her posture and expression make her look shy and uncertain of herself.)* OL

English Language Coach

Art Words Students may not be familiar with all of the words used to describe paintings and art. Invite students to use dictionaries, encyclopedias, and other resources to familiarize themselves with these terms. Encourage students to find examples to illustrate the terms when possible.

- frame
- masterpiece
- charcoal
- watercolor
- easel
- pen and ink

EL

Objectives

- Interpret text
- Identify and analyze elements of author's craft
- Interpret visual art
- Learn content-area words
- Use root words to determine meaning

READING WORKSHOP 2

Teach

R Reading Skill

Review Connecting Say: Diondra's mother shows her pride in her daughter's artwork by hanging it in the living room. How do you show approval of someone in a nonverbal way? *(Possible responses: by smiling or waving; by sitting or standing near someone to show support)* BL

BQ 

Ask: What assumptions do people make about Diondra because of her appearance? *(Diondra is tall, so people assume that she must be an athlete rather than an artist.)* BL What can you learn from Diondra about judging people on the basis of their appearance? Can you always tell what makes them tick? *(Possible responses: People's looks don't always tell the whole story about what makes them tick. Not until we get to know a person do we have a good idea of what they think is important in life.)* OL

hanging in my room. Mom loves my watercolors[2] and she hung one in the living room, but it isn't signed. Nobody ever mentions it, especially not my father. He's not too wild about my art. Mostly, he's disappointed, first off that I wasn't born a boy, and second that I won't play ball like one. I'm six feet tall, almost as tall as he, and he figures the height is wasted on me since I don't share his dreams of me going to the WNBA.[3] I keep telling him not to hold his breath. **4**

I hate always being the tallest girl in school. Everybody expects me to play basketball, so they pick me for their team, throw me the ball, and wait for me to shoot. Big mistake. I fumble it every time. Then they have the nerve to get mad at me, like I did it on purpose! But basketball is not my game. I have no game. I'm an artist, like Raul. The difference is, I don't tell anybody. I refuse to give them new reasons to laugh at me. The Jolly Green Giant jokes are bad enough. **5**

Yeah, it's definitely time to try a self-portrait. I think I'll paint myself in front of an easel. With a basketball jersey sticking up out of the trash. Then I could hang it in Mr. Ward's class. See if anybody notices. **6**

R Practice the Skills

4 Reviewing Skills

Connecting Diondra thinks that her father is disappointed in her. Have you ever thought that a family member was disappointed in something you did? What happened, and how did you feel?

5 BIG Question

Think about what you've learned about Diondra so far. What makes her tick? Support your answer with details, and record it on the "Diondra Jordan" page of Foldable 7. Your response will help you complete the Unit Challenge later.

6 Key Literary Element

Symbolism A symbol is something that means more than just what it is. What do the self-portraits symbolize in this selection?

2. A ***watercolor*** is a type of painting made by mixing water and paint on the paper.
3. The ***WNBA*** is the Women's National Basketball Association, a professional basketball league for women.

Additional Support

Differentiated Instruction

Making Self-Portraits Diondra imagines creating a self-portrait that features herself as a painter and a basketball jersey symbolically sticking out of a trash can. Challenge students to create visual self-portraits that express their identities. Tell students that they should include a sketch, painting, or photograph of themselves that reveals something they truly treasure or enjoy doing. Ask students to include symbols that represent their likes and dislikes. Encourage students to think of a title for the self-portrait that indicates what makes them tick. EL BL

if

by Diondra Jordan

If I stood on tiptoe
reached up and sculpted
mountains from clouds
would you laugh out loud?

If I dipped my brush in starlight
painted a ribbon of night
on your windowsill
would you still laugh? L1

If I drew you adrift
in a pen and ink sea
in a raging storm
would you laugh at me?

If I planted watercolor roses
in your garden
would you laugh then?
Or would you breathe deep
to sample their scent?
I wonder. 7 8 ❍

Practice the Skills

7 Key Literary Element

L2 **Symbolism** A symbol is something that means more than just what it is. What might the *watercolor roses* in lines 13–18 symbolize? Think back to Diondra's story for help with this symbol.

8 Key Reading Skill

Interpreting What do you think Diondra is saying in her poem? Think about what you know about her, and think about your own experiences.

Reading in the Real World

Citizenship Read this quotation from the conclusion of Henry David Thoreau's *Walden,* and discuss its meaning with students. *"If a man does not keep pace with his companions, perhaps it is because he hears a different drummer. Let him step to the music which he hears, however measured or far away."*

Point out that Diondra is someone who "hears a different drummer." Ask students to tell what they think this means. OL Have them identify people in their community who may hear a different drummer. Encourage students to think about how marching to a different beat may lead or help people to do great things. AL

Teach

L1 Literary Element

Review Author's Craft Ask: What generalization can you make about the images that Diondra describes in the first three stanzas of her poem? *(The images are not realistic. Sculpted mountains and starlight paint are imaginary images.)* OL What effect do you think the author wants to create with these images? *(Possible response: The author describes heroic, superhuman feats that she thinks might change people's opinions of her.)* AL

L2 Literary Element

Symbolism Ask: What might Diondra mean when she says that she will plant watercolor roses? *(Possible response: She will paint roses.)* OL What might a person smelling Diondra's watercolor roses symbolize? *(Possible response: an acceptance of Diondra as an artist)* AL

Assess

Use the CheckPoint questions provided on Presentation Plus! to check for comprehension of the selection. These questions can be used with interactive response keypads for immediate student feedback.

Objectives

- Evaluate, interpret, and draw conclusions about text
- Identify symbols and explain their meanings
- Make connections between self and text

Assess

Resources for page 806

- Selection Quick Check
- Selection and Unit Assessment
- ExamView Assessment Suite
- Interactive Tutor: Self-Assessment

Students can respond to the *After You Read* items in their Learner's Notebook or on a separate sheet of paper.

Answering the BIG Question

1. Responses will vary. Students may say that they, too, are artists. They may observe that, like Diondra, they also hide a part of their identity.
2. Raul leaves a self-portrait on Mr. Ward's desk.
3. Diondra's father wishes that his daughter aspired to play in the WNBA.

Critical Thinking

4. Responses will vary. Like Diondra, some students may believe that school allows students to explore aspects of themselves that are not supported at home.
5. Possible response: Diondra feels self-conscious. She doesn't trust that her secret will be respected.
6. Possible response: Grimes includes the poem to let the reader know that Diondra chooses to make her inner self known to others.

After You Read | Diondra Jordan

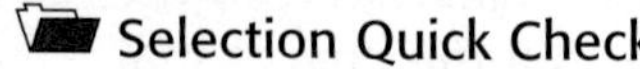

Answering the BIG Question

1. Compare what makes you tick with what makes Diondra Jordan tick. Explain how you are like Diondra and how you are different from her.
2. **Recall** What kind of painting does Raul leave on Mr. Ward's desk?
   TIP **Right There**
3. **Summarize** Why doesn't Diondra's father like her art?
   TIP **Think and Search**

Critical Thinking

4. **Evaluate** Is school a good place for students such as Diondra and Raul to discover who they are and what makes them tick? Explain your answer with details from the story and from your own experience.
   TIP **Author and Me**
5. **Draw Conclusions** Why is Diondra afraid to tell people that she is an artist?
   TIP **Author and Me**
6. **Interpret** Why does Nikki Grimes include Diondra Jordan's poem at the end of the story?
   TIP **Author and Me**

Write About Your Reading

Write a short self-portrait. Describe who you are. If you want to draw a picture with your written self-portrait, you can, but be sure to answer these questions in your writing:

- If you had to use three specific words to describe yourself, what would those words be?
- What kind of hobbies or interests do you have that others know you for (your athletic or art skills, or your ability to write well)? Do you have any hobbies that you would like to tell people about? What are they? What is it about the hobbies that you like?
- What makes you tick?

Objectives (pp. 806–807)
Reading Interpret text • Make connections from text to self
Literature Identify literary devices: symbolism
Vocabulary Identify Latin roots
Writing Respond to literature: self-portrait
Grammar Use correct subject-verb agreement: *be* verbs

Write About Your Reading

Sample response:
Friendly, energetic, musical: These three words describe me perfectly. My mom calls me a bundle of energy, and it's true. I always feel that I have to be moving or talking to someone or doing something. The only time I feel calm is when I'm playing the piano. I could sit for hours at a piano and never want to move more than my fingers on the keys and my feet on the pedals. I sometimes play for my friends, and they call me "Maestro" when I do!

Skills Review

Key Reading Skill: Interpreting

7. What personal experiences did you use to interpret this story? What larger ideas in the story did they make you think about?
8. Did using the reading skill of interpreting help you understand and enjoy the story? Explain.

Key Literary Element: Symbolism

9. The narrator says that she will paint a self-portrait and show a basketball jersey in the trash. What might the jersey in the trash symbolize?

Reviewing Skills: Connecting

10. If Diondra were a student in your class, how would students react to her poem? How would you react to her problems?

Vocabulary Check

Choose the vocabulary word that best complete each sentence.

identity self-portrait tirade gallery

11. Wow, your ___ really does look like you.
12. I sent the note without signing it so no one would know my ___.
13. There were many paintings and sculptures in the ___.
14. Don't launch into a ___ just because I forgot to return your art supplies.
15. **Academic Vocabulary** What can you **interpret** from a self-portrait?
16. **English Language Coach** Diondra's height is *evident.* Her interest in art is not. How does the meaning of the root *vid* connect to the meaning of *evident?*

Grammar Link: Making *To Be* Agree

The verb *to be* has a variety of forms in the present and past tenses.

Present Tense Forms of *To Be*

Singular	Plural
I **am**	We **are**
You **are**	You **are**
He, she, it **is**	They **are**

Past Tense Forms of *To Be*

Singular	Plural
I **was**	We **were**
You **were**	You **were**
He, she, it **was**	They **were**

Always use the form of *to be* that agrees with the subject of the sentence. For example, which past-tense form of *to be* is right for the sentence below?

- The players (was, were) late for the game.

  (The subject is *players. Players* is equal to *they.* The right past-tense form to go with *they* is *were.*)

Grammar Practice

On a separate piece of paper, write the correct form of *to be* for each sentence.

17. I (am, is, are) your friend.
18. You (was, were) with me from the start.
19. The other kids (wasn't, weren't) friendly.
20. You and I (was, were) meant to be friends.

Writing Application Look again at the Write About Your Reading assignment you completed. Fix any mistakes you made in your use of the verb *to be.*

Web Activities For eFlashcards, Selection Quick Checks, and other Web activities, go to www.glencoe.com

Skills Review

Key Reading Skill: Interpreting

7. Possible response: I thought of times when I was misunderstood or did not feel comfortable expressing myself. I thought about the larger issues of acceptance and individualism.
8. Possible response: Interpreting helped me because I was able to put myself in Diondra's position.

Key Literary Element: Symbolism

9. Possible response: It symbolizes her refusal to play basketball.

Reviewing Skills: Connecting

10. Possible response: Some students might compliment Diondra on her poem. I would try to be understanding of her problems.

Vocabulary Check

11. self-portrait
12. identity
13. gallery
14. tirade
15. Responses will vary.
16. Possible response: *Vid* is found in words that have something to do with being able to see something. *Evident* describes something you can easily see.

Grammar Link: Making *To Be* Agree

Grammar Practice

17. am
18. were
19. weren't
20. were

Close

Ask students to summarize what they learned about individuality and self-expression from Diondra's story.

Teach

More About the Authors

Janet Wong is both an attorney and a poet. She has compared poetry to shouting, saying, "Since you can't yell at the top of your lungs for a very long time, you have to decide what you really need to say, and say it quickly."

Arnold Adoff's poems often reflect the African American experience, and he enjoys writing poetry for young people. He once said, "By the time we reach adulthood, we are closed and set in our attitudes. The chances of a poet reaching us are very slim. But I can open a child's imagination, develop his appetite for poetry, and, most importantly, show him that poetry is a natural part of everyday life."

V Vocabulary

Word Roots **Say:** When you encounter unfamiliar words, use your knowledge of word roots to separate them into their word parts. EL OL

Before You Read

Face It *and* Almost Ready

Meet the Authors

Janet Wong's mother is Korean. Her father is Chinese. "Growing up, I never felt very Korean," Wong says."... for the first time I find myself craving Korean beef bone soup and kimchi, which I used to hate."

Janet Wong

An award-winning poet, teacher, and lecturer, Arnold Adoff believes that "writing a poem is making music with words and space."

Arnold Adoff

Literature Online

Author Search For more about Janet Wong and Arnold Adoff, go to www.glencoe.com.

Objectives (pp. 808–811)
Reading Interpret text • Make connections from text to self
Literature Identify literary devices: symbolism
Vocabulary Identify Anglo-Saxon roots

Vocabulary Preview

English Language Coach

Anglo-Saxon Origins Anglo-Saxon is the name of the language also known as Old English. It developed when the Angles and the Saxons conquered England in the fifth century.

- Anglo-Saxon, or Old English, was spoken and written in England for hundreds of years.
- Old English was gradually replaced by Middle English.
- Middle English was gradually replaced by Modern English.

During those many years, words came into English from other languages, too. We tend to study the roots of those words more than we study Old English roots because the words Old English gave us are so simple.

Some Words with Anglo-Saxon Roots	
come	forget
bread	hate
wife	friend
child	dinner
love	neighbor

Old English spelling was simple for the people who spoke it because words were spelled *exactly the way they sounded.* Over time, the pronunciations changed. Unfortunately, the spellings often did not!

sight was pronounced (sort of like) *sikt*
knight was pronounced (sort of like) *kih nikt*

Guess the Roots Guess which word in each pair is the one that came from Old English. Then check your guesses in a dictionary. (The history of a word is given inside [ ] marks at the beginning of the dictionary entry. "OE" means "Old English.")

1. chicken / poultry
2. construct / build
3. begin / initiate
4. break / fracture

Additional Support

Literature Online

Author Search To expand students' appreciation of these authors, have them access the Web site for additional information and resources.

Literature Focus Lesson

Poetic Elements Free verse has no set meter, line length, or rhyme pattern. The poems in this workshop are written in free verse. Have students recall the first few lines of several popular songs and determine whether those lines are written in free verse. OL

The poems in this workshop also use a device called **anaphora**, the repetition of initial words over successive phrases. Encourage students to use anaphora in short poems of their own. Provide students with stems to get them started. Write on the board:

I hope that ____.

Have students write four to six sentences, using this sentence opener. AL

Skills Preview

Key Reading Skill: Interpreting

Think about what you already know and what the author is really saying. Use these questions to interpret the poems.

- What does the selection say?
- What do you know about yourself and the world as it relates to this topic?
- What is the author *really* saying; is there a larger idea?

R

Write to Learn In your Learner's Notebook, answer these questions as you read the poem.

Key Literary Element: Symbolism

A symbol is something that represents something else. **Symbolism** means the use of symbols in a work of literature. For example, a rose can represent love. Writers use symbols to share ideas in a memorable way. As you read, use these tips to help you find symbolism. Look for

- Items that seem significant or important to the speaker
  What meaning does the item have for the speaker beyond what it seems to have for the reader? What is the item's relationship to the speaker?
- Objects, people, or images that might represent something else
  What traits or qualities does this item have that may make it a symbol?

Partner Talk With a partner, take turns reading "Face It" aloud to each other. As you read, talk about the symbols in the poem and what they mean.

Literature Online

Interactive Literary Elements Handbook
To review or learn more about the literary elements, go to www.glencoe.com.

Get Ready to Read

Connect to the Reading

What is the *real you* like? Think about your physical characteristics and your personality traits. Which are family traits? Which are unique to you?

Write to Learn In your Learner's Notebook, make a chart showing your personality traits and some physical characteristics. Label the ones you think are family traits and those that are unique to you.

Build Background

Our cultural and ethnic background is also part of what makes us tick. Janet S. Wong, the author of "Face It," writes: "Sometimes the first question a stranger will ask me, even before learning my name, is 'What are you?' or 'Where are you from?' These kinds of people usually stare hard at my face, as if they are testing themselves on how well they can tell the difference between Chinese, Korean, and Japanese."

- The speaker in the poem "Face It" is part Chinese and part French.
- The speaker has traits from both cultures, but the speaker's personal characteristics help her define her identity.

Set Purposes for Reading

BIG Question Read "Face It" and "Almost Ready" to find out what makes the speakers tick.

Set Your Own Purpose What would you like to learn from the poems to help you answer the Big Question? Write your own purpose on the "Face It" page of Foldable 7.

Keep Moving

Use these skills as you read the following selections.

Teach

R Reading Skill

Interpreting Say: When you interpret, you use what you know about the world to determine what a person is really saying. How would you paraphrase Shakespeare's famous quotation, "A rose / By any other name would smell as sweet"? *(Possible response: A rose will smell good no matter what it is called.)* **OL** What larger point about names was Shakespeare making? *(Possible response: The name of something isn't important. The essence of the thing is what matters.)* **AL**

CheckPoint

Use the CheckPoint questions provided on Presentation Plus! to check for interpreting skills and to build background. These questions can be used with interactive response keypads for immediate student feedback.

Literature Online

Interactive Literary Elements Handbook Have students access the Web site to improve their understanding of symbolism.

English Language Coach

Anglo-Saxon Origins Explain to students the difference between Latin and Old English roots. The word *Saxon* refers to Saxony, an area of northern Germany. The Anglo-Saxons had a language that sounded like modern German. As a result, modern English words of Anglo-Saxon origin are often spelled in a way that resembles German pronunciation. On the other hand, Latin was spoken by ancient Romans. That language spread throughout Europe as the Roman Empire grew, resulting in languages such as Italian, French, Spanish, and Portuguese. Consequently, modern English words with Latin roots are often spelled like words in French, Italian, Spanish, and Portuguese. **EL**

Objectives
- Ask questions
- Make connections from text to self
- Identify literary devices: symbolism
- Identify Anglo-Saxon roots

Teach

R1 Reading Skill

Interpreting **Say:** People sometimes say that something is "more than the sum of its parts." How does looking at a person's individual "parts" differ from looking at him or her as a whole? *(Possible response: When you look at a whole person, you're seeing more than just his or her cultural heritage or appearance. You're seeing the person's unique personality.)* **AL**

R2 Reading Skill

Review Inferring **Ask:** Do you think the speaker views her "big-talking mouth" as a positive or a negative trait? *(Possible response: The speaker seems to poke fun at being outspoken and probably is proud of this trait.)* **OL** What values might be important to a person with a "big-talking mouth?" *(Possible response: self-expression and communication)* **AL**

READING WORKSHOP 2

Face It

by Janet S. Wong

My nose belongs
to Guangdong, China—
short and round, a Jang family nose.

My eyes belong
to Alsace, France—
wide like Grandmother Hemmerling's. **1** **2**

But my mouth, my big-talking mouth, belongs **R2**
to me, alone. **3** ❍

Practice the Skills

1 Key Reading Skill

R1 **Interpreting** Why is the speaker talking about parts of the face? What does this say about the speaker?

2 Key Literary Element

Symbolism What do facial features inherited from relatives symbolize to the speaker?

3 English Language Coach

Anglo-Saxon Roots Because most of the poem's words, except for names, come from Old English, they are very simple. What is the effect of the poet's use of such simple words?

Additional Support

Reading in the Real World

Citizenship Have students conduct research about their family history, focusing on their ethnic origins. Encourage students to interview parents and grandparents in order to discover where family members were born and raised, what languages they spoke, and when they came to the United States. If students don't have access to this information, have them look online or at the library to find general information about their cultural heritage. Invite students to present their findings to the class. **OL** Encourage students to represent the class ethnicities graphically in a circle graph or bar graph. **AL**

READING WORKSHOP 2

ALMOST READY

by Arnold Adoff

I
am
going
to
her
birth-
day
party

as
this
cool
and
in-
control
young
dude:

as
soon
as
I
find
my
new
shirt, 4

as
soon
as
I
find
my
hip
shoes,

as
soon
as
I
find
my
deep
voice,

as
soon
as
I
find
my
right
mask. 5

Practice the Skills

4 English Language Coach

EL **Anglo-Saxon Roots** This word is from the Old English word *scyrte,* meaning "short garment." What other word do we get from *scyrte?* (Just pronounce the OE word!)

5 BIG Question

BQ For each of these poems, what makes the speaker tick? Record your answers in Foldable 7. Your responses will help you complete the Unit Challenge later.

Teach

EL Language Coach

Anglo-Saxon Roots Ask: Which word in the poem do you think comes from the Old English word *scōh* (pronounced skoh)? *(shoes)* OL

BQ BIG Question

Ask: What is the speaker in the poem concerned about? *(looking and sounding cool and in control)* OL What do you think the writer is saying motivates young people? Do you agree with his opinion? *(Possible response: He is saying young people are motivated by a desire to look and act cool. I think this is true of some young people but not all of them.)* AL

CheckPoint

Use the CheckPoint questions provided on Presentation Plus! to check for comprehension of the selections. These questions can be used with interactive response keypads for immediate student feedback.

Reading Fluency

Choral Reading Perform a choral reading of "Face It" with the entire class. Use a transparency or rewrite the poem on the board. Scan each word and underline words and syllables students think should be stressed. Put a mark next to places where students should pause. Have students vote in cases where they disagree about delivery. Keep the poem on the board or transparency with your markings so that students can remember the vocal cues they agreed on. Then have the class read the poem aloud together. OL

Objectives

- Interpret elements of poetry
- Make inferences
- Identify and explain the use of symbolism
- Use structural analysis to understand word meanings through knowledge of Anglo-Saxon roots and word parts

Assess

Resources for page 812

- Selection Quick Check
- Selection and Unit Assessment
- ExamView Assessment Suite
- Interactive Tutor: Self-Assessment

Students can respond to the *After You Read* items in their Learner's Notebook or on a separate sheet of paper.

Answering the BIG Question

1. Responses will vary. Students might note that their unique personality is what makes them tick.
2. The poem focuses on the speaker's clothes and "mask," or outward persona.
3. The third stanza has two lines instead of three. The speaker talks about something that belongs only to her and no one else: her big mouth.

Critical Thinking

4. Students may say that "Face It" is about being honest about what makes people tick, and "Almost Ready" is about growing up and having concerns about fitting in.
5. Students will probably agree that people are a combination of their genetic history and their own unique traits.
6. Students may say that they, too, focus on their appearance before going to a party.

After You Read

Face It *and* Almost Ready

Answering the BIG Question

1. Do you think that where your ancestors are from has anything to do with what makes you tick? Does your appearance make you tick?
2. **Recall** What images does the poem "Almost Ready" focus on?
   TIP **Right There**
3. **Compare and Contrast** How does the third stanza of "Face It" differ from the first two stanzas?
   TIP **Right There**

Critical Thinking

4. **Infer** How do the titles of these poems and the images presented in them relate to the Big Question?
   TIP **Author and Me**
5. **Evaluate** Do you agree with the speaker of "Face It" that people are a combination of their ancestors' characteristics and their own unique traits? Explain.
   TIP **On My Own**
6. **Connect** How do *you* prepare to go to a party? In what ways are you like the speaker of "Almost Ready"? In what ways are you different?
   TIP **Author and Me**

Talk About Your Reading

Literature Groups Both of these poems offer surprise endings. In your group, discuss these endings.

- In "Almost Ready," the speaker says "as soon as I find my right mask." What does this line mean? Do you agree or disagree that clothes and a "deep voice" can be masks?
- The poem "Face It" also ends with a surprise. When the speaker refers to her "big-talking mouth," what is she telling about herself?

Write to Learn If you had to write a poem about yourself, which of these two poems would you use as a model? Try writing a poem about yourself. Use either "Face It" or "Almost Ready" as your model. Share your poem with your group.

Objectives (pp. 812–813)
Reading Interpret text • Make connections from text to self
Literature Identify literary devices: symbolism
Vocabulary Identify Anglo-Saxon roots
Writing Respond to literature: poem
Grammar Use correct subject-verb agreement: inverted sentences

Talk About Your Reading

Literature Groups

Possible responses:
"As soon as I find my right mask" means "as soon as I find a way to present myself that others will find acceptable." Yes, your clothes and your voice can be masks, because you can use both to hide your real personality. The speaker in "Face It" is suggesting that she says what she believes, not what others tell her to say.

Skills Review

Key Reading Skill: Interpreting

7. Think about the words in the first poem's title. Think about those words in a statement like "Face it: We lost the game." How do you interpret the title, "Face It"?
8. How does the arrangement of lines in "Almost Ready" add to the poem's meaning? Explain.
9. "Almost Ready" suggests that young people often show an outside that looks "cool and in-control" even when they feel quite differently inside. Do you agree? Explain your answer.
10. What does the title "Almost Ready" suggest about the inner conflict the speaker is feeling?

Key Literary Element: Symbolism

11. In "Face It," what does the speaker's nose symbolize to the speaker?
12. In "Almost Ready," what do the shirt, "hip" shoes, and deep voice symbolize to the speaker?

Reviewing Skills: Evaluating

13. Did you find these poems humorous, serious, or both? Explain.

Reviewing Literary Elements: Sound Devices

14. Identify the sound device (or devices) used in the third stanza of "Face It."

Vocabulary Check

15. **English Language Coach** The speaker of "Face It" talks about being a combination of traits from different sources. How is English similar? Can you think of any words that we could say belong to American English alone? *Jazz* is one word that was first used in the United States. What might be another?

Grammar Link: Agreement in Inverted Sentences

Make sure the subjects and verbs in inverted sentences agree. In an inverted sentence, all or part of the verb comes before the subject. Two kinds of inverted sentences are questions and sentences that begin with *here* or *there.* (See the Grammar Link on page 793.)

- **Questions** To check subject-verb agreement in questions, change the questions into statements. That makes it easier to find the real subject.

  Question: Where is the keys?

  Statement: The keys is where.

  The subject is *keys. Keys* is plural, or equal to *they.* So the right verb form is *are,* not *is.*

  Agreement: Where **are** the **keys?**

- ***Here* and *there*** cannot be subjects. To find the subject of a sentence that begins with *here* or *there,* mentally omit the word. Find the verb; then ask yourself, who or what ___?

  There was two people in line.

  ~~There~~ was two people in line.

  The verb is *was.* Who or what was? *People* was. *People* is the subject. *People* is plural, or equal to *they.* So the right verb form is *were,* not *was.*

Grammar Practice

On a separate piece of paper, write the subject and the correct verb form for each sentence.

16. There (goes, go) Jermaine and Annie.
17. What (is, are) they wearing?
18. (Does, Do) the twins have to dress alike?
19. Here (is, are) their matching sweaters.

Web Activities For eFlashcards, Selection Quick Checks, and other Web activities, go to www.glencoe.com.

READING WORKSHOP 2

Skills Review

Key Reading Skill: Interpreting

7. Possible response: Literally, it refers to the speaker's face; figuratively, it means to own up to something.
8. Possible response: It calls attention to words that are repeated, as well as those that are different.
9. Responses will vary.
10. Possible response: The speaker is struggling with growing up and fitting in.

Key Literary Element: Symbolism

11. Possible response: her Chinese heritage
12. Students may suggest the image of a "cool" and "in-control" person.

Reviewing Skills: Evaluating

13. Possible response: The poems deal with serious topics in a humorous way.

Reviewing Literary Elements: Sound Devices

14. repetition (of "mouth") and alliteration ("my mouth")

Vocabulary Check

15. Students may note that English is also a combination of different languages, but slang words belong to American English.

Grammar Link: Agreement in Inverted Sentences

Grammar Practice

16. Jermaine and Annie; go
17. they; are
18. twins; Do
19. sweaters; are

Close

Have students think of times when a person's appearance might be a good indication of what makes him or her tick, as well as times when it might be misleading.

Monitoring Comprehension

Objectives covered in this workshop:

- Recognize and use a variety of comprehension strategies
- Monitor comprehension and make modifications

Teaching Students to Monitor Comprehension

Why Is It Important?

- When students don't understand a selection, they're not really reading it. The whole point of reading is to understand a piece of text.
- Students will learn to think about whether they understand what they're reading by monitoring their comprehension of the selection.
- Asking themselves questions as they read will help them build their overall reading skills as well.

How to Help Students Get It

- Tell students to keep asking themselves questions about main ideas, characters, and events as they read.
- Remind students that to *monitor* something is to pay attention to it and that *comprehension* is understanding.
- When they can't answer a question about what they've read, have them review, read more slowly, or ask someone to help them.

Reading to Answer the Big Question

Miracles

In this poem by Walt Whitman, everyday occurrences are described as "miracles." It's the small details in life that are enjoyable to the poet.

The Pasture

Robert Frost creates a vivid picture of the country in this poem. As students read, they will discover the connection Frost feels to nature and how it makes him tick.

Reading, Writing, and Rapping

This informational selection describes an innovative school program that helps students improve their academic skills by running a fictional record label. Students will identify with how these teens learn about themselves and the world around them through music.

Workshop Resources

Pacing (days) Standard	Block	Lesson	Student Materials	Teacher Resources
1		Key Skill Lesson: Comprehension	Key Reading Skills Practice English Language Coach	Bellringer Options Transparencies Read Aloud, Think Aloud Transparencies Presentation Plus!
2		"Miracles"	Literary Analysis Transparencies Glencoe Online Selection Vocabulary Development Academic Vocabulary Development English Language Coach Active Reading Graphic Organizer Literary Analysis StudentWorks Plus Online Student Edition Literature Classics Selection and Unit Assessments	Literary and Text Analysis Transparencies Puzzlemaker Skill Level Up! BookLink 3 Assessment by Learning Objective (Diagnostic and Formative) Interactive Tutor Self-Assessment TeacherWorks Plus
2		"The Pasture" "Reading, Writing, Rapping"	Glencoe Online Selection Vocabulary Development Academic Vocabulary Development English Language Coach Active Reading Graphic Organizer Literary Analysis StudentWorks Plus Online Student Edition Literature Classics Selection and Unit Assessments	Literary and Text Analysis Transparencies Puzzlemaker Skill Level Up! BookLink 3 Assessment by Learning Objective (Diagnostic and Formative) Interactive Tutor Self-Assessment TeacherWorks Plus

Keys for Unit Resource

- Blackline Master
- Workbook
- Supplemental Text
- CD-ROM
- DVD
- Transparency
- Web-based
- Fast Files

Level Appropriate Code

AS = Activities for all students
AL = Activities for students working above grade level
OL = Activities for students working at grade level
BL = Activities for students working below grade level
EL = Activities for English language learners

Focus

BELLRINGER Options

- **Selection Focus Transparencies**
- **Daily Language Practice Transparency**

Focus Activity Say: If someone were having trouble following the plot of a movie, what would you recommend that person do? *(Responses will vary. Students may suggest stopping the movie and replaying the confusing parts or talking with someone who has seen it.)*

Teach

R Reading Skill

Monitoring Comprehension

Ask: What are some ways to monitor your comprehension as you read poetry? *(Responses may include reading a poem aloud a few times, and to think about what the author is trying to convey.)* OL

V Vocabulary

Academic Vocabulary

Ask: What person or aspect of your daily life might you spend time monitoring? *(Responses will vary. Students may say a sibling or a part of their daily life such as feeding a pet.)* OL

READING WORKSHOP 3

Skills Focus

You will practice using these skills when you read the following selections:

- "Miracles," p. 818
- "The Pasture," p. 819
- "Reading, Writing, Rapping," p. 824

Reading

- Monitoring comprehension

Literature

- Identifying rhyme, rhythm, and meter in poetry
- Understanding the effects of rhyme, rhythm, and meter

Vocabulary

- Use structural analysis to understand word meanings
- Academic Vocabulary: *monitoring*

Writing/Grammar

- Using correct subject-verb agreement

Objectives (pp. 814–815)
Reading Monitor comprehension

Skill Lesson

Monitoring Comprehension

Learn It!

R **What Is It?** **Monitoring comprehension** means checking to make sure that you understand what you read. To monitor comprehension, you review, reread slowly, or ask someone to help you. For example, when you read the poem "Annabel Lee," you could have monitored your comprehension by stopping to ask yourself questions. If you couldn't answer a question, you would go back and reread.

- To *monitor* something is to pay attention to it.
- *Comprehension* is understanding, especially understanding a reading.
- *Monitoring comprehension* is paying attention to your understanding.

Analyzing Cartoons
Hobbes makes a good point. If you don't care about understanding a piece of writing, read it as fast as you can. If you *do* want to understand, rereading can help.

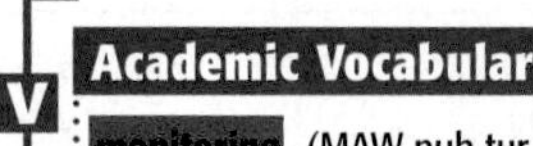

V **Academic Vocabulary**

monitoring (MAW nuh tur ing) *v.* paying attention to or keeping track of

Additional Support

English Language Coach

Build Background Explain to students that the comic strip *Calvin and Hobbes* pokes fun at many parts of daily life. One of the elements of the humor in this particular comic strip is that it reveals a truth about reading. If Calvin and others like him are not really interested in comprehending a text, they might as well quickly flip through the pages instead of reading them. But to fully enjoy a book or learn from it, you can't just flip through the pages. You have to read carefully and ask yourself questions to ensure you understand what you're reading. EL

Why Is It Important? How do you feel when you realize that you've read a whole page and have no idea what you just read? You might feel frustrated. When you monitor your comprehension, you check often to make sure that you understand what you're reading. When you start to drift off, you catch yourself.

R

How Do I Do It? To monitor your comprehension, ask yourself these questions:

- Do I understand all of the words?
- Do I see how this sentence fits in with what I've read so far?
- Do I know what the author is trying to say?

If you don't know the answers to these questions, rereading can help. Here's how one student used these questions to monitor comprehension while reading the poem "One":

But anybody can mimic my dance with my dog.
Anybody can howl how I sing out of tune.

At first I wasn't sure what mimic meant. I looked it up and saw that it means copy. I wasn't sure how this part of the poem fit with what I had read so far. Then I reread the first part of the poem. I noticed that it was about how no one could be a perfect copy of me. I guess this part of the poem shows another side. Someone might not be a perfect copy, but he or she could still copy me in some ways.

Study Central Visit www.glencoe.com and click on Study Central to review monitoring comprehension.

Practice It!

Did you understand everything on this page? Or did you find yourself going back to reread? In your Learner's Notebook, write about a spot on this page that confused you. How did rereading help you understand? If you didn't need to reread, write three things that you learned from what you read.

Use It!

As you read, stop often to ask yourself the following questions:

- Do I understand what I just read?
- Do I understand how this fits with the reading as a whole?

In your Learner's Notebook, keep track of your answers to the questions. Be sure to note times when you had to reread to answer the questions.

Teach

Literature Online

Study Central Have students access the Web site to review monitoring comprehension and to complete a related activity.

R Reading Skill

Monitoring Comprehension

Say: Reread the *Why Is It Important?* section. What are some reasons why you might not remember or understand what you've read? *(Responses will vary. Students may suggest the following reasons: they are thinking about something else; the book has really long sentences; the subject matter is unfamiliar; or there are many unfamiliar vocabulary words.)* **BL** What should you do when this happens? *(Possible responses: reread; look up difficult words; ask for help in understanding difficult ideas.)* **OL**

Resources for page 815

Use Reading Skills Transparency in *Read Aloud, Think Aloud,* Unit 7, to help students practice monitoring comprehension.

Reading in the Real World

College Tell students that monitoring comprehension and taking careful notes are essential skills for success in college because of the large amount of reading students must do. Suggest that students use the following graphic organizer to take notes as they read the selections in this workshop. **OL**

What I Read	How It Fits with the Whole	Reread
first stanza of "Miracles"	lists everyday events the speaker considers miracles	lines 3–13

Objectives

- Recognize and draw upon a variety of comprehension strategies
- Monitor comprehension and make modifications by rereading a portion aloud

Teach

More About the Authors

Walt Whitman spent many years writing poems for *Leaves of Grass.* "Song of Myself" is the most well-known selection of the collection, which was considered a new kind of poetry, very different from the sentimental rhyming poetry of the same time period. Like "Miracles," "Song of Myself" is a free-verse poem that celebrates life. Whitman wrote, "I celebrate myself, and sing myself."

Robert Frost became the first poet to read a poem at a presidential inauguration when John F. Kennedy took the presidential oath of office in 1961. Many of his poems are set in the New England countryside, and he uses the simple speech of the region in his poems about life there. Poetry, Frost said, "makes you remember what you didn't know you knew."

Before You Read | Miracles *and* The Pasture

Meet the Authors

Walt Whitman loved the people and places of America. *Leaves of Grass,* his famous collection of poetry, celebrates the variety and vastness of this country. See page R7 of the Author Files for more on Walt Whitman.

For much of his life, Robert Frost lived on farms in New England and wrote poems about the area. "Three things have followed me," he wrote, "writing, teaching, and a little farming." See page R3 of the Author Files for more on Robert Frost.

Author Search For more about Walt Whitman and Robert Frost, go to www.glencoe.com.

Objectives (pp. 816–819)
Reading Monitor comprehension
• Make connections from text to self
Literature Identify literary devices: rhyme, rhythm, meter
Vocabulary Use structural analysis: roots, prefixes, suffixes

Vocabulary Preview

English Language Coach

Using What You Know It's a good idea to memorize certain common word parts—roots, prefixes, and suffixes—especially those from Latin and Greek. They show up in many words, and their meanings can be a big help in figuring out the meanings of unfamiliar words.

However, using what you know works both ways. You can often figure out the meaning of an unfamiliar word by thinking about a familiar one that has some of the same parts.

The familiar words, below, appear in Walt Whitman's poem "Miracles."

Familiar	Unfamiliar
opposite	oppositional
quiet	quietude
curve	curvature
distinct	distinctive

Use What You Know Use what you know about the familiar words above to choose the correct unfamiliar word for each blank below.

1. Her shoulders were so slumped that she looked as if she had ___ of the spine.
2. I always recognize Antonio's voice on the phone because he has such a ___ accent.
3. You mom is relaxing for a few minutes, so try not to disturb her ___.
4. The soldiers were slowed by the ___ actions of the enemy.
5. Phew! How could you have failed to notice the ___ white stripe down that "black cat's" back?
6. For every action of mine, the mule responded with some ___ action of its own, and we got nowhere!
7. You can see a ship's sails on the horizon before you see the whole ship because of the ___ of the earth.
8. Paco enjoyed the soothing ___ of the meadow in which the only sound was the faint, distant song of a wren.

Additional Support

Author Search To expand students' appreciation of these authors, have them access the Web site for additional information and resources.

Differentiated Instruction

Poetry Bumper Stickers Provide students with a collection of other poems by Walt Whitman and Robert Frost. Suggest that each student find one quotable line that he or she especially likes. Tell students to design bumper stickers that feature their choices, including artwork and lettering. OL

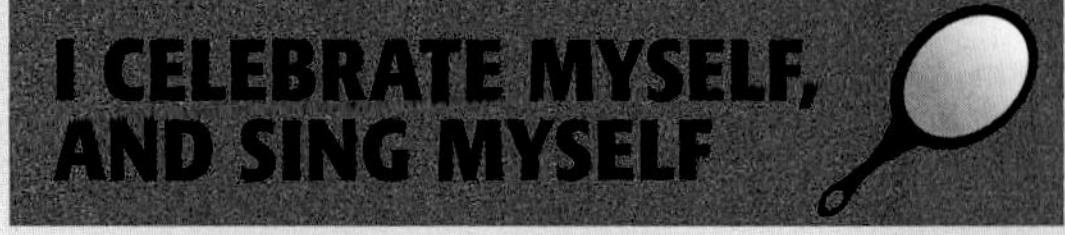

Skills Preview

Key Reading Skill: Monitoring Comprehension

Sometimes poetry is hard to understand. Stay on track by asking yourself questions as you read: **R**

- Do I know what these words mean?
- Can I explain this stanza in my own words?
- Do I understand how this stanza fits in with the rest of the poem?

Key Literary Element: Rhyme, Rhythm, and Meter

A **rhyme** is made up of two or more words that appear close to one another and whose sounds match: knew/dew, boast/toast. Rhymes form a pattern that connects the lines of poem. Rhymes may also show you which words the poet thinks are important.

- End rhyme is at the end of a poem's lines.
- Internal rhyme is within a single line.
- Slant rhyme is when the end sounds are similar but not identical.

Poems have **rhythm** just as songs do. Rhythm is the pattern of beats made by the parts that are stressed, or spoken with greater force, and the parts that are softer, or spoken with less force. Often all stanzas in a poem have the same rhythm. **L**

Some poems have a predictable rhythm, called **meter.** To find meter, look for a pattern of stressed and unstressed syllables.

As you read, use these tips to help you think about rhyme, rhythm, and meter.

- Look for rhyming words, especially at the end of a line.
  Are any rhyming words in the two poems?
- See whether the poem has rhythm.
  Is there a pattern of beats?
- Try to find meter in the poems.
  Is there a predictable pattern or rhythm?

Get Ready to Read

Connect to the Reading

What small things do you appreciate? The speakers in both poems talk about the small details or events that they enjoy.

Partner Talk Share with a partner your thoughts about what you appreciate. List three small things that you appreciate most about life.

Build Background

- Both Walt Whitman and Robert Frost worked at many different kinds of jobs and had widely varying experiences.
- Whitman lived during the time of the Civil War and helped take care of wounded soldiers.
- For ten years Frost lived on a farm, but he was not suited for farm life and eventually had to give it up.
- Although both men lived through difficult times and tragedies, their poems show an appreciation for the world around them.

Set Purposes for Reading

Read to find out how Whitman feels about the universe and Frost feels about nature.

Set Your Own Purpose What would you like to learn to help you answer the Big Question? Write your own purpose on the "Miracles" page of Foldable 7.

Literature Online

Interactive Literary Elements Handbook
To review or learn more about the literary elements, go to www.glencoe.com.

Keep Moving

Use these skills as you read the following selections.

Teach

R Reading Skill

Monitoring Comprehension
Ask: Why is it important that you be able to state a stanza's ideas in your own words? *(Possible response: This will show you understand what you've read.)* **OL**

L Literary Element

Rhyme, Rhythm, and Meter **Say:** One of the poems you read in this workshop will have a predictable rhythm, whereas the other will not. Read both poems and determine which style you prefer. Be sure to explain why. *(Responses will vary.)* **OL**

CheckPoint

Use the CheckPoint questions provided on Presentation Plus! to review monitoring comprehension. These questions can be used with interactive response keypads for immediate student feedback.

Literature Online

Interactive Literary Elements Handbook Have students access the Web site to improve their understanding of rhyme, rhythm, and meter.

Differentiated Instruction

Thinking about Miracles Ask students to suggest possible definitions for the word *miracle,* and record students' definitions on the board. Add a dictionary definition when students have finished. Then, tell students to select their favorite definitions and record them in their Learner's Notebook. Invite students to write about miracles in their own lives that fit the definitions they have selected. Encourage students to share their entries with the class. **OL** After students have read "Miracles," lead a discussion regarding the similarities and differences between students' definitions and entries and Whitman's poem. **AL**

Objectives

- Monitor comprehension
- Make connections from text to self
- Identify literary devices: rhyme, rhythm, meter
- Use structural analysis: roots, prefixes, suffixes

Teach

R Reading Skill

Monitoring Comprehension
Ask: What does the poet mean when he says, "As to me I know of nothing else but miracles"? *(Possible response: He means that to him, everything is a miracle.)* OL What, then, do you think is the main message of this poem? *(Possible response: Each small element or interaction of life is a miracle.)* AL

BQ 

Say: Think of all the specific items listed in this poem. What word or words might you use to describe all these items? *(Possible responses: life, the world)* With this idea in mind, what do you think makes Whitman tick? *(Possible response: Whitman's understanding that all the elements that make up life are miracles)* OL

Miracles

by Walt Whitman

R
Why, who makes much of a miracle?
As to me I know of nothing else but miracles,
Whether I walk the streets of Manhattan,
Or dart my sight over the roofs of houses **toward** the sky,
Or wade with naked feet along the beach just in the edge of
 the water,
Or stand under trees in the woods,
Or talk by day with any one I love . . .
Or sit at table at dinner with the rest,
Or look at strangers opposite me riding in the car.
Or watch honey-bees busy around the hive of a summer
 forenoon,
Or animals feeding in the fields,
Or birds, or the wonderfulness of the sundown, or of stars
 shining so quiet and bright,
Or the exquisite delicate thin curve of the new moon in
 spring;
These with the rest, one and all, are to me miracles,
The whole referring, yet each distinct and in its place.* 1

To me every hour of the light and dark is a miracle,
Every cubic inch of space is a miracle,
Every square yard of the surface of the earth is spread with
 the same,
Every foot of the interior swarms with the same. 2

To me the sea is a continual miracle,
The fishes that swim—the rocks—the motion of the waves—
 the ships with men in them,
What stranger miracles are there? 3 ○

15 This line suggests that all of these small, separate miracles are involved in, or refer to, some greater miracle.

Practice the Skills

1 English Language Coach

Using What You Know The meaning of the Old English suffix *-ward* is easy: "in the direction of." Here, it appears in the familiar word **toward**. What do *earthward* and *skyward* mean?

2 Key Reading Skill

Monitoring Comprehension In line 19, what does "the same" mean? (Reread the two lines before this one. Notice the word that ends each of them.)

3 BIG Question

BQ According to the poem, what is important to Whitman? What makes him tick? Write your answer on the "Miracles" page of Foldable 7. Your response will help you complete the Unit Challenge later.

Additional Support

Reading Fluency

Reading "Miracles" Although "Miracles" does not have a regular rhythm or meter, it does have its own unique beat. Give students a copy of the poem to mark. Then, have them read the poem silently, while putting a mark next to each word they stress. Have students form groups and take turns reading all or part of the poem aloud. Encourage them to try different ways to read the poem, finding the "music" in the language and expressing it to the group. OL Have students discuss how reading the poem and hearing it read aloud have helped them understand its meanings. AL

The Pasture

by Robert Frost

I'm going out to clean the pasture spring;
I'll only stop to rake the leaves away
(And wait to watch the water clear, I may):
I shan't be gone long.—You come too. 4 5

I'm going out to fetch the little calf
That's standing by the mother. It's so young,
It totters when she licks it with her tongue.
I shan't be gone long.—You come too. 6 ❍

Hay Meadows, 1938. Adolf Dehn, Watercolor on white wove paper, 14 1/4 X 21 3/8 in., Terra Foundation for American Art, Chicago.

Practice the Skills

4 Key Literary Element

L1 **Rhyme, Rhythm, and Meter** Frost creates rhythm in the poem by adding punctuation. Where should you pause when reading this poem aloud or to yourself?

5 Key Literary Element

L2 **Rhyme, Rhythm, and Meter** Each stanza repeats a pattern of rhyme. In the first stanza, lines 2 and 3 rhyme. Does the same rhyme pattern appear in the second stanza? What else is the same in the two stanzas?

6 Key Reading Skill

R **Monitoring Comprehension** What is this poem about? Reread it to make sure that you're right. Focus on the meaning of the word *spring.*

READING WORKSHOP 3

Teach

L1 Literary Element

Rhyme, Rhythm, and Meter Say: When reading poetry, remember to pause only when you reach a punctuation mark. How should the length of a pause after a comma differ from the length of a pause after a dash, semicolon, colon, or period? *(Commas require shorter pauses than dashes, semicolons, colons, and periods.)* AL

L2 Literary Element

Review Author's Craft
Ask: What words does the poet repeat in the poem? *(He repeats the words "I'm going out," "I shan't be gone long," and "You come too" in the two stanzas.)* BL What does this repetition emphasize? *(Possible response: It emphasizes that the speaker wants a friend to come with him.)* OL

R Reading Skill

Monitoring Comprehension
Ask: Besides a time of year, what could the word *spring* mean? *(Possible response: a source of water in the ground)* AL

English Language Coach

Future Tense Remind students that there are several ways to express the future tense in English: Use the helping verb *shall* or *will* with the base form. Use *going to* with the present tense of *be* and the base form of a verb. Use *about to* with the present tense of *be* and the base form of a verb. Use the present tense with an adverb that shows the future.

Tell students that Frost uses two of these ways in his poem. In one, he uses an old-fashioned contraction *(shan't).* Have students write the two sentences Frost uses that express the future tense. Then have them write their own sentences using each of the four different ways to form the future tense. EL

Objectives
- Monitor comprehension through a variety of comprehension strategies, including rereading
- Identify and explain the effects of literary devices
- Use structural analysis to understand word meanings through knowledge of roots and word parts

Assess

Resources for page 820

- Selection Quick Check
- Selection and Unit Assessment
- ExamView Assessment Suite
- Interactive Tutor: Self-Assessment

Students can respond to the *After You Read* items in their Learner's Notebook or on a separate sheet of paper.

Answering the BIG Question

1. Responses will vary. Students may say that Whitman loves the simple things in life, whereas Frost appreciates the seasons and the rituals that accompany them.
2. Possible response: walking the streets of Manhattan; looking at the sky; walking barefoot on the beach
3. The speaker plans to clean the spring and fetch the calf.

Critical Thinking

4. Possible response: planting a garden, writing in a journal, or doing laundry because these actions also are common, everyday "miracles"
5. Responses will vary. Some students may say that the repeated line emphasizes that the speaker wants someone to accompany him.
6. Responses will vary. Students may say that both poets view life and nature as meaningful.

After You Read

Miracles *and* The Pasture

Objectives (pp. 820–821)
Reading Monitor comprehension • Make connections from text to self
Literature Identify literary devices: rhyme, rhythm, meter
Vocabulary Use structural analysis: roots, prefixes, suffixes
Writing Respond to literature: poem
Grammar Use correct subject-verb agreement: compounds

Answering the BIG Question

1. What do you think Whitman and Frost love about life? Explain.
2. **Recall** The speaker in "Miracles" calls many events miracles. List three of these events.
   TIP **Right There**
3. **Recall** What two chores is the speaker of "The Pasture" planning to do?
   TIP **Right There**

Critical Thinking

4. **Synthesize** What other miracles could have been included in Whitman's list? Give at least three possibilities. Explain.
   TIP **Author and Me**
5. **Infer** Why do you think Frost ends both stanzas with the same line?
   TIP **Author and Me**
6. **Interpret** What attitude toward life and nature do the authors show in these poems?
   TIP **Author and Me**

Write About Your Reading

Pretend that Frost wanted to write a poem based on one of the events in Whitman's "Miracles." Use these questions to help you write a short poem or stanza in Frost's style.

Step 1: What event will you focus on from "Miracles"? Announce this event in your first line.

Step 2: Plan the next two lines of your poem. What can you say about this event? What two rhyming words will you use for the second and third lines?

Step 3: Write a line to end the poem.

Step 4: Write the poem in your Learner's Notebook. Use the format below. Don't forget to include end punctuation.

I'm going out to
I'll
(And
I shan't be gone long.—You come too.

Write About Your Reading

Possible response:

I'm going out to walk along the beach;
I'll only stop to touch some seaweed or a shell
(And wait, I may, to watch the tide swell):
I shan't be gone long.—You come too.

I'm going out to watch the setting of the sun
That's sinking into the ocean. It's so red,
It fills me with warmth as if I'm wrapped in the soft comfort of bed.
I shan't be gone long.—You come too.

Skills Review

Key Reading Skill: Monitoring Comprehension

7. Think about a place in one of the poems where you had to stop and reread. What confused you? Where did you find the answer that helped you go on reading?

Key Literary Element: Rhyme, Rhythm, and Meter

8. "Miracles" does not use meter, or a regular pattern of rhythm. Why do you think Whitman decided not to use meter in the poem?
9. The second stanza of "The Pasture" contains the rhyme *young/tongue.* What does the calf being young have to do with the mother licking it with her tongue?

Vocabulary Check

10. **Academic Vocabulary** If a doctor tells you to monitor what you eat, what is he or she telling you to do?

English Language Coach The word *forenoon* was not defined for you in "Miracles" because it's a familiar word for "morning."

- Given the meaning of *forenoon,* think of what the word part *fore-* means.

Now use your knowledge of *fore-* to come up with ideas about what the following words mean.

11. foretell
12. forefathers
13. forejudge
14. foreseeable
15. foregone (Hint: What do you think it would mean if someone said that winning tomorrow's game "is a foregone conclusion"?)

Grammar Link: Agreement with Compounds

A **compound subject** is two or more subjects joined by a conjunction.

The verb form that agrees with a compound subject depends on the conjunction that is used to join the subjects. Here are the rules.

- **Subjects joined by *and*:** When *and* joins subjects, use the plural verb form.

  The student president and principal are there.

  (student president + principal = they. Use *are.*)

  There were a discussion and a vote.

  (discussion + vote = they. Use *were.*)
- **Subjects joined by *or* or *nor*:** When *or* or *nor* joins compound subjects, the verb agrees with the subject that is closer to it.

  Cookies or cake is always served.

  (*Cake* is closer to the verb. Cake = *it.* Use *is.*)

Grammar Practice

On a separate piece of paper, write the subject and the correct verb form for each sentence.

16. Neither my sister nor I (am, is, are) going.
17. Here (comes, come) the teacher and principal.
18. When (does, do) you and your dad plan to go?
19. The kids or their sitter (has, have) ordered pizza.

Writing Application Look again at the Write About Your Reading assignment you completed. Fix any subject-verb mistakes you made.

Web Activities For eFlashcards, Selection Quick Checks, and other Web activities, go to www.glencoe.com.

Skills Review

Key Reading Skill: Monitoring Comprehension

7. Responses will vary.

Key Literary Element: Rhyme, Rhythm, and Meter

8. Responses will vary. Students may say that Whitman's message is that there is beauty in everything. A patterned structure could work against this message.
9. Possible response: Cows use their tongues to bathe their young.

Vocabulary Check

10. Possible response: to pay attention to what you eat
11. to determine something before it happens
12. ancestors, people who lived long ago
13. to judge before all of the information is available
14. something can be visualized before it actually happens
15. it has already happened or been accomplished

Close

Ask students to summarize what they have learned about what makes these two poets tick. Have them tell whether they agree with the poets' messages and why or why not.

Grammar Link: Agreement with Compounds

Grammar Practice

16. sister nor I; am
17. teacher and principal; come
18. you and your dad; do
19. kids or sitter; has

Literature Online

Web Activities Have students access the Web site for interactive activities that will help them assess their understanding of the selection.

Teach

More About the Author

Elizabeth Wellington writes about fashion and style for all sorts of people. She has written articles about products for bald people, natural African hairstyles, and the popularity of denim clothing and tennis shoes.

V Vocabulary

Greek Roots With the chart on this page as a starting point, have students create Greek root word cards. Working in pairs, students can write a Greek root on one side of a card and its meaning on the other side. Students can then challenge other members of the class to write as many examples of words containing that root as possible. **OL** Students having difficulty finding examples of words with Greek roots can use dictionaries. **BL** **EL**

Before You Read

Reading, Writing, Rapping

Meet the Author

Elizabeth Wellington worked as a fashion writer at *The News and Observer* in Raleigh, North Carolina. She has written about fashion for *The Philadelphia Inquirer* since 2002. Her fashion column appears every other Sunday, and her stories appear in the paper's Daily Magazine section.

Author Search For more about Elizabeth Wellington, go to www.glencoe.com.

Objectives (pp. 822–827)
Reading Monitor comprehension
• Make connections from text to self
Literature Identify literary devices: rhyme, rhythm, meter
Vocabulary Use structural analysis: roots, prefixes, suffixes

Vocabulary Preview

dissect (dih SEKT) *v.* to examine carefully and in close detail **(p. 825)** *We had to dissect the song before we could record it.*

obvious (AWB vee us) *adj.* easily seen or understood **(p. 825)** *Hip-hop has an obvious appeal for various school-age groups.*

shunning (SHUN ing) *v.* avoiding; keeping away from **(p. 825)** *Teachers who have been shunning hip-hop should take another look at it.*

era (AIR uh) *n.* a period in history **(p. 826)** *Hip-hop could only have developed in an era of high technology.*

Write to Learn For each vocabulary word, write a sentence using the word correctly.

English Language Coach

Greek Roots The students you'll read about in the next selection have a "microsociety class." In this class, the students make a model version of a recording studio. The word part *micro* comes from Greek and means "small." You have seen it in *microscope* (which allows one to see small things) and *microphone* (which allows small sounds to be heard).

The English language "borrowed" many roots, prefixes, and suffixes from Greek. Some are called "combining forms" because they are so often used with other Greek parts.

This chart shows six common Greek roots or combining forms.

V

Root	Meaning	Examples
auto	self	automatic, automobile
bio	life	biology, biography
cycle	circle	bicycle, recycle
geo	Earth	geography, geology
graph	write / draw	autograph, graphics
log / logy	word / study / speech	dialogue, biology

Partner Talk With a partner, discuss how the Greek root or combining form is involved in the meaning of each of the example words for that root. (Several of the words involve *two* Greek roots or combining forms.)

Additional Support

Author Search To expand students' appreciation of Elizabeth Wellington, have them access the Web site for additional information and resources.

Differentiated Instruction

Building Background Suggest that students research the contributions of one of the following pioneers of rap music. Students can find information on the Internet or interview older students, family members, or neighbors who are familiar with this musical genre.

- Afrika Bambaataa
- Beastie Boys
- DJ Grand Wizard Theodore
- DJ Hollywood and/or Kool Herc
- Fatback Band
- Grandmaster Flash
- Grandmaster Melle Mel
- Run-DMC
- Salt-N-Pepa
- Sugarhill Gang

OL

Skills Preview

Key Reading Skill: Monitoring Comprehension

You can catch yourself when you're not following a reading. Perhaps you get distracted by something going on around you or realize that you have "blanked out" and don't know what you've read. Many people show some signs that their attention is wandering. What signs tell you that your attention is wandering?

Write to Learn In your Learner's Notebook, list two ways that you can tell you've lost track of a reading. Watch for these signs as you read this selection.

Key Literary Element: Rhyme, Rhythm, and Meter

Rhyme and **rhythm** are important in hip-hop. Think about your favorite song. Does it contain rhymes? Does it have a good beat? A singer or MC creates vocal patterns by stressing certain words, and the music usually reinforces that rhythm. Some songs have a **meter,** or predictable rhythm; some don't.

As you read, keep these points in mind:

- Rhyme and rhythm are "hooks" that pull the reader or listener along.

  How do the rhymes and rhythms help to keep you in the song and understand the message?
- Meter is often used to reflect the message.

  Is there a predictable rhythm? Is the message straightforward or more complicated?

Partner Talk Read "The Pasture" (p. 819) aloud, as if it were the lyrics to a rap song. Get a good feel of the rhyme, rhythm, and meter.

Interactive Literary Elements Handbook
To review or learn more about the literary elements, go to www.glencoe.com.

Get Ready to Read

Connect to the Reading

The classes described in "Reading, Writing, Rapping" are using song lyrics to help them learn. What line from a song has made you really think about an idea or issue?

Partner Talk With a partner, talk about different ideas that you've thought about after listening to music. How did listening to a particular song make you interested in an idea or issue?

Build Background

"Reading, Writing, Rapping" talks about hip-hop music in the classroom. You've probably heard some hip-hop or rap, which is rhythmic, rhyming speech on top of music.

Rap first gained importance with the release of "Rapper's Delight" in 1979 by New York's Sugarhill Gang.

Set Purposes for Reading

BIG Question Read "Reading, Writing, Rapping" to find out how some teens learn about themselves and the world from music.

Set Your Own Purpose What would you like to learn to help you answer the Big Question? Write your own purpose on the "Reading, Writing, Rapping" page of Foldable 7.

Keep Moving

Use these skills as you read the following selection.

Teach

R Reading Skill

Monitoring Comprehension
Ask: What techniques do you use to refocus your attention when you find your mind wandering? *(Responses will vary. Students may suggest taking a break or engaging in a brief physical activity.)* OL

L Literary Element

Rhyme **Ask:** Why might songwriters use rhyme? *(Possible responses: for a musical effect; to tie lyrics together; to help them remember lyrics)* OL

CheckPoint

Use the CheckPoint questions provided on Presentation Plus! to review monitoring comprehension. These questions can be used with interactive response keypads for immediate student feedback.

Literature Online

Interactive Literary Elements Handbook Have students access the Web site to improve their understanding of rhyme, rhythm, and meter.

Differentiated Instruction

Influence of Rap Share with students the following information about rap.

By the late 1980s, rap music took on social and political agendas. Rapper Chuck D. called rap the "black CNN." Supporters of rap have suggested that rap music is about improving self-esteem and introducing black history into mainstream culture.

Invite students to discuss their response to this information. Do they agree that rap music is about improving self-esteem? Why or why not? What important information might rappers convey in the "black CNN"? AL

Objectives

- Monitor comprehension
- Make connections from text to self
- Identify literary devices: rhyme, rhythm, meter
- Use structural analysis: roots, prefixes, suffixes

Teach

R1 Reading Skill

Review Inferring **Ask:** How might students at Talley Middle School benefit from studying microsociety? *(Responses will vary. Students may suggest that such a program will prepare students for jobs in the real world.)* OL

R2 Reading Skill

Monitoring Comprehension
Ask: What have you learned on the first page about the students in Ms. Bishop's class? *(Possible response: They are in the eighth grade; they are in a school program where they learn school subjects by running a make-believe record label; they write rap songs; and they feel challenged.)* OL

Readability Scores
Dale-Chall: 7.3
DRP: 60
Lexile: 1060

READING WORKSHOP 3

INFORMATIONAL TEXT
WEB SITE
philly.com

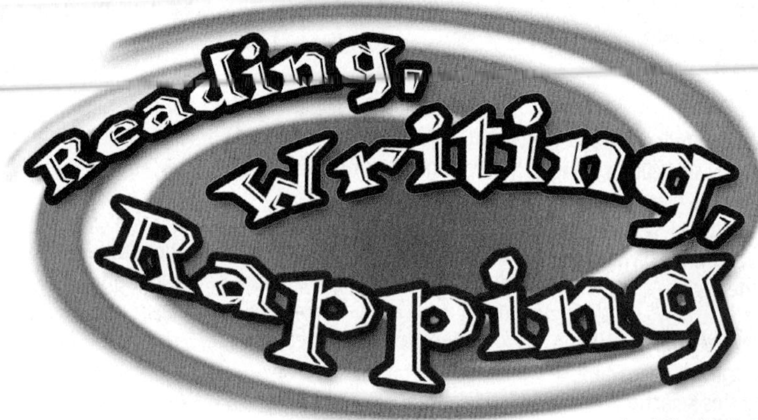

by Elizabeth Wellington

Hip-hop's going from the top of the charts to the head of the class. Teachers are using hip-hop as a learning tool—sometimes on the sly.

The beats seeping out of Room 214 suck Talley Middle School students down the hallway. It's first period: microsociety[1] class. R1

The Delaware eighth graders' assignment: to compose a rap around the theme "Achievement Matters." They shake their heads as they write. This is right up their alley. Here, they practice reading, writing, and math skills by running a make-believe record label. Their rhymes are written in stanzas; they learn about budgets and use high-tech music equipment to earn grades. Students say they love Jennifer Bishop's class. R2

"I think it's better than all the other classes I'm taking," said Michael Hurtt, 13, whose rap name is Miraculous. "It challenges me. It's helping me . . . use similes and **metaphors**. Bigger words. You learn how not to include just the basic words when you talk." 1

Such enthusiasm is why teachers are using hip-hop to teach students. Teachers are taking hip-hop's best—the catchy beats, clever use of words, and social messages—to encourage students to learn.

1. ***Microsociety*** is a school program that has students construct a model version of a real-world institution, such as a museum or a recording studio.

Practice the Skills

1 English Language Coach

Greek Roots Our word **metaphor** comes from the Greek *metaphora,* meaning "a transfer." *Meta* means "over or across." *Phor* comes from a word meaning "to carry." How does a metaphor "transfer" something or "carry something across"?

Additional Support

English Language Coach

Idioms Point out the phrase *right up their alley* on this page. Have students use clues in the passage to determine its meaning *(suited to people's tastes or abilities).* Also, show students the phrase *off the bat* on page 825, which means "immediately."

Assign to pairs of students some other common English idioms that involve transportation or sports references. Instruct students to learn their idioms' meanings by looking up the main words in the dictionary or online. EL

- have a ball
- play ball
- get the ball rolling
- round the bend
- rock the boat
- out of bounds
- burn your bridges
- steer clear of

Some high school teachers are pulling lyrics from popular artists to help students build reading-comprehension skills. The idea is that a 14-year-old would rather **dissect** the meaning of Jay-Z's "Excuse Me, Miss" than Shakespeare's *A Midsummer Night's Dream.* R1

"Hip-hop is a vehicle through which school concepts can make sense," said Shuaib Meacham, an assistant professor at the University of Delaware, who shows teachers in the state how to blend hip-hop into their curriculums.

"Without engagement, you can't connect students to skills so that they want to learn," Meacham said. "Hip-hop grabs them off the bat." 2

A lot of things are behind hip-hop's move into the classroom. The **obvious** reason is that elements of the genre—its slang, fashion, and message—are a part of pop culture, from television to political campaigns.

But it's also because hip-hop's earliest fans are slipping into teaching, administration, and even political offices that decide how children learn. Detroit Mayor Kwame Kilpatrick, 31, virtually ran on a hip-hop platform. And last month, Kilpatrick held the country's largest hip-hop summit to date, during which rap mogul Russell Simmons[2] suggested that teachers use hip-hop instead of **shunning** it.

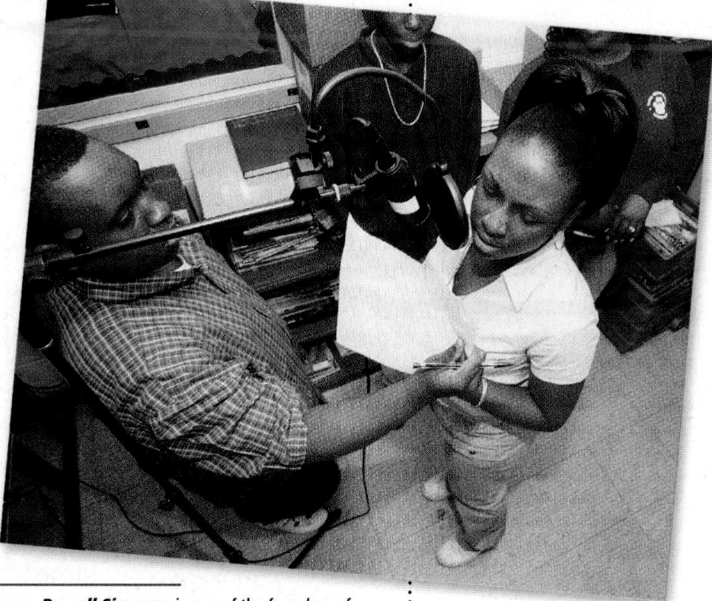

2. A ***mogul*** (MOH gul) is a rich, powerful person. ***Russell Simmons*** is one of the founders of Def Jam Records, which has released many popular rap albums.

Vocabulary

dissect (dih SEKT) *v.* to examine carefully and in close detail

obvious (AWB vee us) *adj.* easily seen or understood

shunning (SHUN ing) *v.* avoiding; keeping away from

Practice the Skills

2 Key Reading Skill

Monitoring Comprehension
Check your understanding by asking yourself questions as you read. What does Shuaib Meacham think about hip-hop in the classroom? If you don't remember, reread to find out. R2

READING WORKSHOP 3

Teach

Viewing the Photo

Say: Photos help provide readers with additional information as they read. What information does this photo provide? *(Possible response: It illustrates how students in Ms. Bishop's class work together when recording their music.)* BL

R1 Reading Skill

Review Evaluating

Ask: What do hip-hop and Shakespeare's poetry have in common? *(Hip-hop, like Shakespeare's verse, relies on rhyme, rhythm, and meter.)* OL Do you think a work of Jay-Z is an acceptable substitute for one of Shakespeare's works in the classroom? Why or why not? *(Responses will vary. Some students may say that if the works of both artists help them understand rhyme, rhythm, and meter, then it doesn't matter whether they study Jay-Z's work or Shakespeare's.)* AL

R2 Reading Skill

Monitoring Comprehension

Ask: What questions will help you monitor your comprehension of this article? *(Possible responses: Why is hip-hop useful in the classroom? Who supports using hip-hop in the classroom?)* OL

Differentiated Instruction

Slang Dictionary Tell students that *slang* is the words and phrases groups of people come up with to communicate with one another. One of the attributes of the hip-hop culture is its slang. The following terms entered the English language via hip-hop:

chill *v.* check one's enthusiasm

def *adj.* excellent; first-rate

dis *v.* show disrespect for

fly *adj.* fashionable; stylish; attractive

Have students use a standard dictionary entry as a model for creating their own slang dictionaries. Encourage students to give definitions for the slang words they use with their friends. AS

Objectives

- Make inferences and evaluate text
- Recognize and draw upon a variety of comprehension strategies, such as rereading
- Use structural analysis to understand word meanings through knowledge of Greek roots and word parts

Teach

R1 Reading Skill

Review Inferring Ask: Why might school boards not approve of hip-hop in the classroom? *(Responses will vary. Students may suggest that hip-hop is too controversial or that hip-hop is viewed as pop culture rather than as a subject worthy of academic study.)* **OL**

R2 Reading Skill

Monitoring Comprehension Ask: What are some ways to remember important people, such as Kelly Quintero, who are mentioned in an article? *(Possible responses: underline important names and pieces of information; take notes on a separate sheet of paper)* **BL**

READING WORKSHOP 3

But not everyone is quick to welcome hip-hop in the classroom. "We found that teachers are using pieces of the [hip-hop] lifestyle in the classroom in their own way. But they are not letting their school boards know because they are afraid their superiors won't approve," said Kelly Quintero, coauthor of "Shades of Literacy: Hip-Hop as Authentic Poetry," published by the National Association of English Teachers. **R1**

Still, there are a few classrooms across the United States and locally where hip-hop has made appearances, said Dennis Creedon, who works in the Philadelphia school system's Office of Creative and Performing Arts. **3**

At a Northeast Philadelphia school, a teacher taught his students a rap to help them with the **era** from the Revolutionary War to the Civil War, Creedon said. And a music teacher turned Mozart's The Magic Flute,[3] into a hip-hopera.

Practice the Skills

3 Key Reading Skill

R2 **Monitoring Comprehension** Who are Kelly Quintero and Dennis Creedon? You may need to reread to find the answer.

3. ***The Magic Flute*** is an opera by the composer Wolfgang Amadeus Mozart (1756–91).

Vocabulary

era (AIR uh) *v.* a period in history

Additional Support

Reading in the Real World

Career Invite students to brainstorm careers that Jennifer Bishop's students might be interested in after being in her class. Suggest that students consult career Web sites as well as career handbooks for help. Tell students to pick one job and record its title, job description, and a brief explanation of how the job relates to the experiences of Bishop's students. Then have students tell whether they'd be interested in the job themselves. **AS**

READING WORKSHOP 3

"Children understand this culture, and this gets their attention," Creedon said. "Still, we have to be aware what kind of music they are listening to, because music enters our consciousness on a deeper level." R

Bishop's class started working on its rap label in September. Since then, she said, she has seen her students' writing skills improve. They can master music equipment, and most important, they are excited about learning.

At the end of the school year, the class will produce a six-song CD that includes tunes the students wrote about writer's block, poverty, and the struggles of being a middle-schooler.

Within minutes of getting their assignment Monday morning, the first group comes up with an Ashanti-style[4] hook:

You can achieve it. . . .
All you got to do is believe it.

Kevin Barnes, 15, isn't having the same kind of luck with lyrics. While his friends are tapping their feet to the beat as they write, Kevin is stuck.

"I really got writer's block," he said, shaking his head. "I just can't make this happen. I got so much stuff in my head. I can't put it on paper."

He walks to the stairwell. Within 15 minutes, his notebook is filled with tiny handwriting. He grabs the mike, and just like Brooklyn-born rapper Notorious B.I.G., he starts to flow.

It's KO the kid. Achievement's the bid
Never ever lost a battle. Cause I'm in it to win
Cuz I step to the plate. With the bat as my mate.
And the other teams say. That fat boy's in shape.
Cuz I'm achieving. Coke and drugs I'm leaving.
In the car, I'm speeding
And I'm still achieving. 4 5

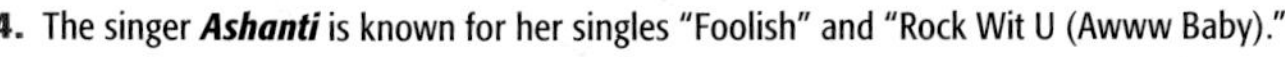

4. The singer ***Ashanti*** is known for her singles "Foolish" and "Rock Wit U (Awww Baby)."

Practice the Skills

4 Key Literary Element

Rhyme, Rhythm, and Meter What words does Kevin Barnes rhyme? Do his lyrics create rhythm? Is there a regular meter?

5 BIG Question

BQ What do you think makes these students tick? Write your answer on the "Reading, Writing, Rapping" page of Foldable 7. Your response will help you complete the Unit Challenge later.

Teach

R Reading Skill

Monitoring Comprehension

Ask: What concern does Creedon have about exposing children to rap music? *(He is worried that music enters our consciousness on a deeper level. He thinks people need to be aware of the kind of music they are listening to.)* OL Do you agree with his concern? Why or why not? *(Possible response: I do agree. Listening to negative, explicit lyrics makes me feel uncomfortable and depressed.)* AL

BQ BIG Question

Ask: Other than rap music, what would you say makes the students in Jennifer Bishop's class tick? *(Responses will vary. Students may suggest that self-expression makes Bishop's students tick.)* AS

CheckPoint

Use the CheckPoint questions provided on Presentation Plus! to check for comprehension of the selection. These questions can be used with interactive response keypads for immediate student feedback.

Differentiated Instruction

What's in a Name? Rappers have rap names. Point out that Bishop's student Michael Hurtt christened himself Miraculous. Jay-Z and Notorious B.I.G. are also mentioned in the article. Discuss with students why rappers might adopt rap names. Then ask students to give themselves rap names and explain in prose or verse their reasons for selecting their names. Invite students to share their names and explanations with the class. If possible, have students speak into a microphone. OL

Objectives
- Evaluate text
- Recognize and draw upon a variety of comprehension strategies, such as rereading
- Identify and explain the effects of literary devices, including rhyme, rhythm, and meter

Assess

Resources for page 828

- Selection Quick Check
- Selection and Unit Assessment
- ExamView Assessment Suite
- Interactive Tutor: Self-Assessment

Students can respond to the *After You Read* items in their Learner's Notebook or on a separate sheet of paper.

Answering the BIG Question

1. Responses will vary. Students may say that music makes them tick because it expresses how they feel.
2. Social studies and music classes have been taught using hip-hop.
3. Possible response: Students and teachers support the use of hip-hop in the classroom because students are familiar with and interested in the subculture.

Critical Thinking

4. Possible response: Walking helps Kevin Barnes free his thoughts.
5. Possible response: A hip-hopera is an opera done in hip-hop style.
6. Responses will vary. Students may suggest peer pressure or parental relationships.

After You Read

Reading, Writing, Rapping

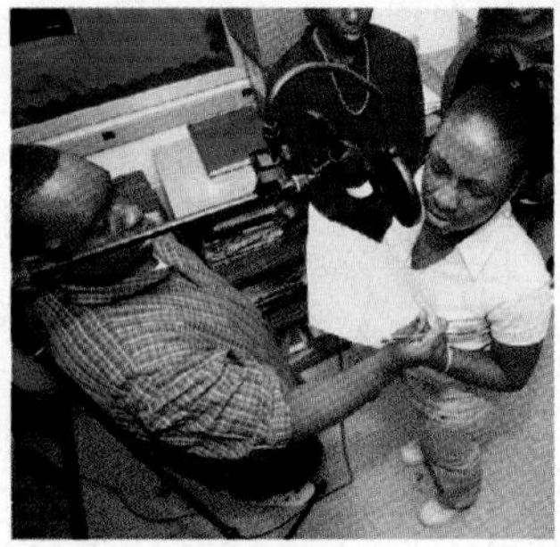

Objectives (pp. 828–829)
Reading Monitor comprehension • Make connections from text to self
Literature Identify literary devices: rhyme, rhythm, meter
Vocabulary Use structural analysis: roots, prefixes, suffixes
Writing Respond to literature: rap song
Grammar Use correct subject-verb agreement

Answering the BIG Question

1. Does music make you tick they way it makes the students in the article tick? Why or why not?
2. **Recall** Give two examples of school subjects that have been taught using hip-hop.
   TIP **Right There**
3. **Summarize** Why do students and teachers support using hip-hop in the classroom?
   TIP **Think and Search**

Critical Thinking

4. **Infer** What do you think helped Kevin Barnes solve his writer's block? Explain.
   TIP **Author and Me**
5. **Interpret** What is a hip-hopera?
   TIP **Author and Me**
6. **Connect** Jennifer Bishop's class wrote songs about the struggles of being a middle-schooler. What issue might one of these songs address?
   TIP **On My Own**

Write About Your Reading

Write the lyrics to a short rap song about a specific event in your life. You can follow the pattern of the song by Kevin Barnes. Use the following steps to get started.

Step 1: What event are you going to write about? Jot down three or four details about the event. Include details that use at least two senses, such as sight and hearing.

Step 2: How did you feel about this event? What particular details made you feel this way?

Step 3: What are three rhymes that you can use in your rap song? Where will you put them?

Write About Your Reading

Possible response:
It's the b-ball kid. Here's my bid:
Amy pushed me in the key.
Left the court so I wouldn't kick her in the knee.
Had to apologize, say I was sorry, to the team.
Didn't think I'd walk that beam.
But, I gotta play ball,
No reason to stall.

Teach

R Reading Skill

Monitoring Comprehension
Ask: How many stanzas does the writer use? *(three)* **BL** When do the stanza breaks occur? *(The first break occurs when there is a time change. The second break occurs when there is a shift in ideas.)* **OL**

L1 Literary Element

Author's Craft Ask: What is the tone of the poem? *(The speaker is annoyed with time.)* **OL** How does the writer achieve this tone? *(The writer repeatedly uses the word* ticktock *to intrude on the speaker's activity.)* **AL**

L2 Literary Element

Author's Craft Ask: What is the mood of the poem? *(The mood is rushed.)* **OL** How does the writer achieve this mood? *(The writer uses personification to suggest that the sandman and the speaker are in a race.)* **AL**

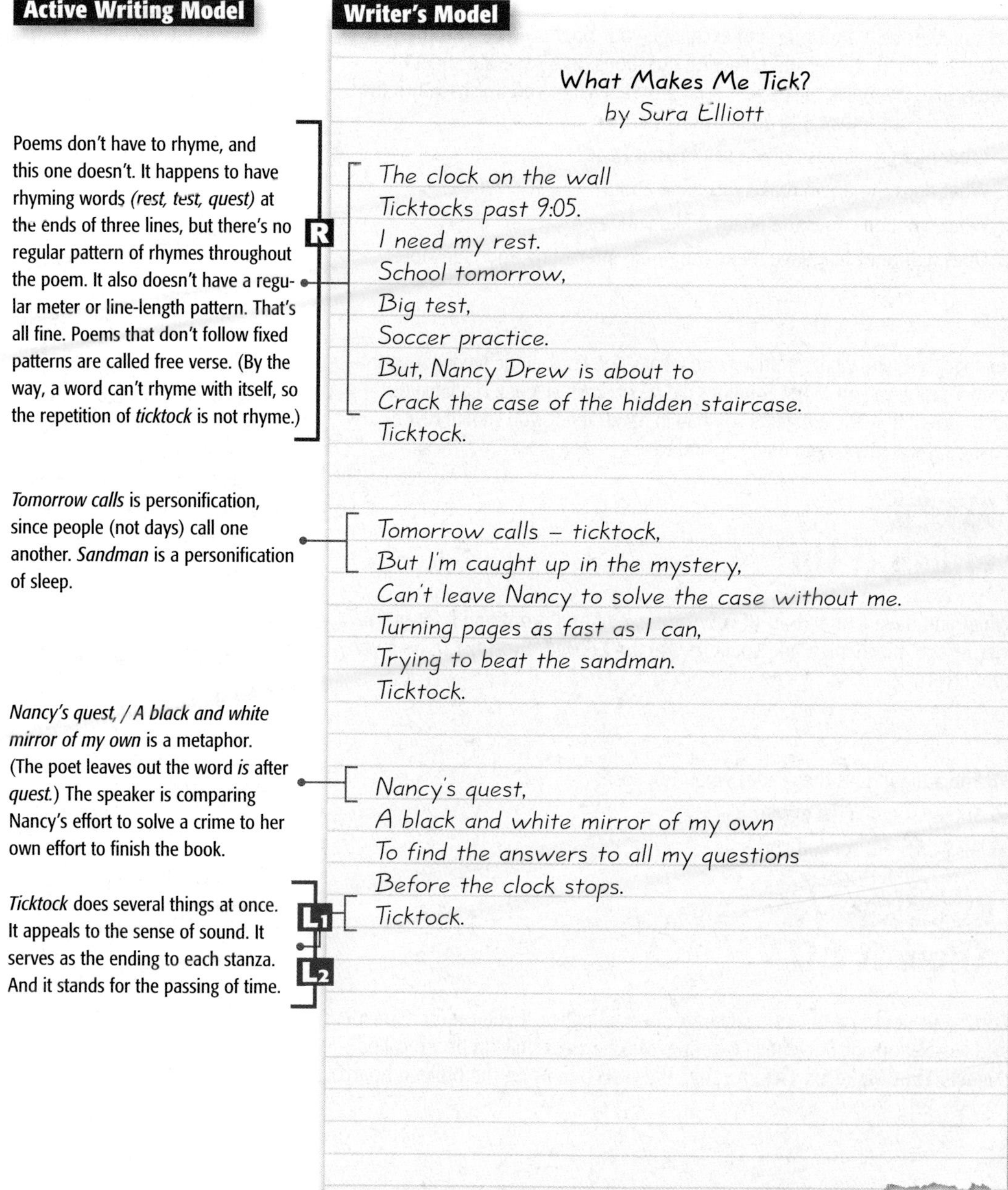

WRITING WORKSHOP PART 2

Active Writing Model

Poems don't have to rhyme, and this one doesn't. It happens to have rhyming words *(rest, test, quest)* at the ends of three lines, but there's no regular pattern of rhymes throughout the poem. It also doesn't have a regular meter or line-length pattern. That's all fine. Poems that don't follow fixed patterns are called free verse. (By the way, a word can't rhyme with itself, so the repetition of *ticktock* is not rhyme.) **R**

Tomorrow calls is personification, since people (not days) call one another. *Sandman* is a personification of sleep.

Nancy's quest, / A black and white mirror of my own is a metaphor. (The poet leaves out the word *is* after *quest.*) The speaker is comparing Nancy's effort to solve a crime to her own effort to finish the book.

Ticktock does several things at once. It appeals to the sense of sound. It serves as the ending to each stanza. And it stands for the passing of time. **L1** **L2**

Writer's Model

What Makes Me Tick?
by Sura Elliott

The clock on the wall
Ticktocks past 9:05.
I need my rest.
School tomorrow,
Big test,
Soccer practice.
But, Nancy Drew is about to
Crack the case of the hidden staircase.
Ticktock.

Tomorrow calls – ticktock,
But I'm caught up in the mystery,
Can't leave Nancy to solve the case without me.
Turning pages as fast as I can,
Trying to beat the sandman.
Ticktock.

Nancy's quest,
A black and white mirror of my own
To find the answers to all my questions
Before the clock stops.
Ticktock.

832 UNIT 7 What Makes You Tick?

Additional Support

Reading in the Real World

Citizenship Encourage interested students to start a creative writing club. Have students determine a time and meeting place, such as the school cafeteria after hours or a nearby coffee shop or teen center. Students might pick different topics to write about each week, or they might just write about topics that interest them. Encourage students to use what they've learned about writing, revising, and providing positive feedback. After students have met several times, they might organize a reading night, when they read their work aloud to an invited audience. Have students describe the experience for the class. **AL**

Partner Talk

Get together with a partner and exchange your poems. Read your partner's poem, and then answer the following questions on a separate sheet of paper. Give examples to support each answer. When you finish, return the poem and your answers to your writing partner.

1. What mental images do you see in your head?
2. What does the poem make you think about?
3. What emotions does the poem make you feel?
4. Does figurative language make the poem interesting and enjoyable?

R

Literature Online

Writing Models For models and other writing activities, go to www.glencoe.com.

Use Feedback to Revise

Feedback tells you what's working and what's not. Look at the feedback your partner just gave you. What emotions did he or she feel when reading your poem? Were they the emotions you had in mind? If not, you should revise, paying special attention to meaning and tone.

W

Writing Tip

Revising Think about how your poem looks on the page. If you're writing about an object that has a definite shape, consider writing the poem in that shape.

Editing

Finish It Up

When you have a final draft of your poem, edit and proofread it for grammar, usage, mechanics, and spelling. Use the **Editing Checklist** to help you spot errors.

Editing Checklist

- ☑ Punctuation tells the reader when to pause.
- ☑ Subjects and verbs agree.
- ☑ All words are spelled correctly.

Writing Tip

Subject-Verb Agreement If a prepositional phrase separates a subject from its verb, ignore the phrase, and revise the verb so that it agrees with the subject.

Writing Tip

Spelling Remember that some nouns have the same singular and plural forms. Examples: *deer/deer, species/species, sheep/sheep.* Use a dictionary to check the singular and plural forms of any nouns that you're not sure about.

Presenting

Show It Off

Copy your poem neatly on a separate sheet of paper. If you prefer, type it. Add illustrations or decorative lettering. Make a class bulletin board called **Objects That Make Us Tick.** Arrange the class poems on the bulletin board.

Differentiated Instruction

The Shape of Poetry Tell students that poets communicate meaning through word arrangement. Help students notice the way poets arrange the words on the page, use space or indentations, create open space, and so on. Share with students some of the poetry of e.e. cummings and others to illustrate this point.

If students are interested in shaping their poems, suggest they create outlines for their shapes on sheets of paper. Tell students to write their poems so that their words fill the shapes. Students can cut the pattern lines away from their poems and then mount the poems on sheets of construction paper. OL

WRITING WORKSHOP PART 2

Teach

R Reading Skill

Monitoring Comprehension
Say: Before answering questions about your partner's poem, read it three times. How did your understanding of the poem change with each rereading? *(Responses will vary. Students may say that they understood the use of figurative language better with each reading.)* OL

W Writing

Partner Feedback Help students practice phrasing feedback in positive ways. Read aloud the writer's model on page 832. Then share and discuss two possible responses to question 3 under Partner Talk:

Response 1: *The poem bores me.*
Response 2: *The repetition of "ticktock" makes me feel rushed.*
Say: The first response hurts the writer's feelings and provides no useful feedback. The second response provides the writer with a genuine reaction from the reader. It is better to select and comment on a quotation so that the writer can assess the effectiveness of his or her writing. OL

Literature Online

Writing Models Have students access the Web site for an additional and interactive Writing Workshop-based student model.

Objectives

- Write poems
- Use the writing process
- Use literary elements and devices
- Revise drafts for word choice
- Edit writing for correct subject-verb agreement

Focus

BELLRINGER Options

Daily Language Practice Transparency

Focus Activity Ask: What does poetry allow you to do that other forms of writing do not? *(Responses will vary.)*

Teach

W Writing

Connecting Ask: How do you want readers to connect with your poem? Explain. *(Responses will vary.)* OL What poetic devices have you used to help readers understand your message? *(Responses will vary. Students may say that they have included similes or metaphors or that they have used word choice to create a familiar mood.)* AL

Resources for page 830

- Use the Writing Workshop Graphic Organizer BLM in the Unit 7 Resource Booklet.
- Use the Grammar and Writing Workshop Transparencies, Unit 7.

WRITING WORKSHOP PART 2

Poem

Revising, Editing, and Presenting

ASSIGNMENT Write a poem

Purpose: To write a poem about an object that shows what makes you tick

Audience: You, your teacher, and possibly some classmates

In Writing Workshop Part 1, you learned about verse, figurative language, and word choice. In Part 2, you'll experiment with words as you work toward a finished poem. Also, you'll keep a copy of it in a writing portfolio so that you and your teacher can evaluate your writing progress over time.

Revising

Make It Better

The revision process allows you to think about how your ideas are organized and expressed in your poem. It also gives you a chance to look over each word that you've chosen. Use the chart below to help you revise your poem.

Do you . . .	*Hints for Revising*
follow poetic conventions of verse and stanza?	Write in verse–single lines of text–and stanzas–sets of lines. Start a new stanza to show a change in setting, tone, or mood. Like a paragraph in a story, a stanza is a set of lines that helps organize your ideas.
use sensory details?	Sensory details appeal to the senses of sight, smell, taste, touch, and sound. They help readers "tune in" to what you're saying.
use figurative language to create strong images?	Create stronger images by using figurative language: • simile *(the breeze is like a kiss)* • metaphor *(the breeze is a kiss)* and • personification *(the breeze kisses me)*
use vocabulary to express a tone and to set a mood?	Tone is your attitude toward the subject, ideas, theme, or characters in your poem. Mood is the atmosphere you want your readers to feel. Careful word choices are important in establishing both tone and mood.

W

Revising Rubric

Your revised poem should have

- vivid, concise words that tell readers exactly what you are thinking
- subjects and verbs that agree
- words and images that express your message
- mood and tone that reflect your feelings

Objectives (pp. 830–833)
Writing Revise your writing for key elements, style, and word choice
Grammar Use correct subject-verb agreement
Listening, Speaking, and Viewing Present poem • Use appropriate expressions and gestures • Listen for elements of poetry

Additional Support

Differentiated Instruction

More Hints for Revision Provide students with the following additional hints for revising to help them with sound devices and tone.

- Create sound patterns. For example, if you're writing about sleep, you might choose to end every other line with a word that ends with the *z* sound.
  I wake to the alarm clock buzz,
  Bury my head and snooze.
- Use word choice to create a tone. A poet's tone may be witty or serious, sad or upbeat, scholarly or sarcastic, or admiring or angry.
  I choose clocks that remind me of myself—loud and persistent. OL

Skills Review

Key Reading Skill: Monitoring Comprehension

7. As you read "Reading, Writing, Rapping," what parts were easy to understand? What parts gave you trouble? Rank the following three parts of the selection according to how easily you understood them, with 1 being the easiest and 3 the hardest. Explain your rankings.
   - Description of Jennifer Bishop's class (p. 824)
   - Quotation from Shuaib Meacham (p. 825)
   - Rap lyrics by Kevin Barnes (p. 827)
8. How did rereading help you understand the most difficult part of the selection?

Key Literary Element: Rhyme, Rhythm, and Meter

9. One group of students rhymed "achieve it" with "believe it." What could they have rhymed with "it's right"?
10. Why is rhythm important in hip-hop?

Vocabulary Check

Match each vocabulary word with the synonym that best fits it. You will use two words twice.

dissect obvious shunning era

11. time
12. avoiding
13. period
14. clear
15. analyze
16. plain
17. **English Language Coach** The students use "high-tech music equipment." *Tech* is a shortened version of *technology. Techn* is a Greek combining form that means "art, skill, or system." How is it related to today's meaning of *technology*?

Grammar Link: Subjects Separated from Verbs

Subject-verb agreement can be challenging when a prepositional phrase separates the subject from its verb. When the subject and verb are not next to each other, you may wonder what the real subject of the sentence is. For example, in the sentence below is the subject *One* or *children?*

One of the children (is, are) lost.

Here's a hint: **Subjects and predicates do not appear in prepositional phrases.** If you mentally leave out the prepositional phrase from the sentence, the real subject becomes easier to find.

One ~~of the children~~ (is, are) lost.
prepositional phrase

(Once the prepositional phrase is gone, it's easy to see that the subject is *One.* Since the subject is *One,* the right verb form is *is.*)

Grammar Practice

On a separate piece of paper, copy the sentences below. Cross out the prepositional phrase that separates the subject and verb in each sentence. Underline the subject once and the correct verb form twice.

18. The purpose of the quizzes (is, are) clear.
19. A few students in our class (is, are) behind.
20. Quizzes on reading assignments (keeps, keep) us on our toes.
21. The student with the best grades (wins, win) a prize.

Writing Application Look back at the Write About Your Reading assignment you completed. Check to make sure all the subjects and verbs agree. Fix any mistakes.

Web Activities For eFlashcards, Selection Quick Checks, and other Web activities, go to www.glencoe.com.

Skills Review

Key Reading Skill: Monitoring Comprehension

7. Responses will vary. Students should explain their rankings thoroughly.
8. Responses will vary. Students may note that it was easier to understand the second time around.

Key Literary Element: Rhyme, Rhythm, and Meter

9. Responses will vary. Students may suggest *its might* or *it's tight.*
10. Possible response: Rhythm is important because sound, movement, and dance are important parts of hip-hop.

Vocabulary Check

11. era
12. shunning
13. era
14. obvious
15. dissect
16. obvious
17. Responses will vary. Some students may say that technology is about sharp-ening skills and developin advanced systems.

Close

Have students explain whethe teachers should include hip-h in the classroom.

Grammar Link: Subjects Separated from Verbs

Grammar Practice

18. The purpose ~~of the quizzes~~ is clear.
19. A few students ~~in our class~~ are behind.
20. Quizzes ~~on reading assignments~~ keep us on our toes.
21. The student ~~with the best grades~~ wins a prize.

WRITING WORKSHOP PART 2

Listening, Speaking, and Viewing

Poetry Reading or Poetry Slam!

Three thousand years ago, some Greek guy stood up and read his poem aloud. He had invented the public poetry reading. And poets haven't stopped talking ever since.

Analyzing Cartoons
How does reading aloud help Calvin appreciate the poem? (And what effect does listening have on Hobbes?)

What Is It?

In modern times, as far as most people were concerned, there were two kinds of poetry readings. There were stuffy poets reading stuffy poems in stuffy university lecture halls. And there were weird hippie-poets reading weird poems in weird bookstores.

Then along came slams! At a poetry slam, poets recite–and shout, cry, scream, laugh, chant, and whisper–their works. Audiences listen attentively–and cheer, boo, clap, hiss, and stomp–and then give the poets and poems scores.

The important thing is that, whether it's a traditional reading or a slam, poetry is read out loud to an audience that wants to listen.

Why Is It Important?

Reading a poem silently is okay. You can enjoy it. But there's something missing. Poetry, like music, is *meant* to be heard. In fact, poetry and music share many qualities–beat, tone, mood, and even melody.

How Do I Do It?

To read poetry aloud, pay attention to these hints:

- Pause at the end of a sentence (a complete thought). Don't pause at the end of a line just because it's the end of the line.
- Decide ahead of time which important words to emphasize with your voice.
- Vary the speed, volume, and pitch of your voice so that your poem comes alive for your listeners.
- Speak loudly and clearly enough so that everyone in your audience can hear and understand you.
- Practice reading the poem aloud in private before you read in front of anyone else.

To be a good listener, follow these hints:

- Pay attention to each word the reader says, as well as to his or her voice and gestures.
- Listen for figurative language, rhyme, rhythm, and other poetry "tricks."
- Try to connect to the poem's theme and message.

LSV

Talk It Out In a small group, plan either a poetry reading or a poetry slam. In either case, you'll need a day, a time, a place, and an audience. You'll have to figure out how to get the audience (invitations and posters, for example).

You should also decide how many poets will read, in what order, and how many poems each will read. If you do a poetry slam, you also need to establish rules and a scoring system.

Teach

LSV Listening, Speaking, and Viewing

Say-Back Say: One strategy to use in active listening is called "say-back." That is, you say back to the speaker what you have just heard. In a conversation, you would paraphrase to show your understanding. At a poetry slam, you can literally say back a word or a phrase. This technique creates a call-and-response rhythm for the slam. For example, if Sara Elliott were to read "What Makes Me Tick" at the slam, audience members might start saying back the line "ticktock." If they do so quietly and rapidly while Elliot reads, the audience becomes part of the poem. OL

Close

Have students recall hints for becoming a good listener. Ask them if they can think of other techniques to help them become better listeners.

Reading Fluency

Reading and Speaking Fluent readers read at an appropriate speed; identify words quickly; and use proper pitch, stress, and phrasing. After students have practiced reading their poems aloud, have students who have difficulty with fluency read their poems privately to you. Use this opportunity to assess each student's fluency. If a student does not read at an appropriate pace, what seems to be slowing him or her down? Does the student have problems with word recognition? Does the student fail to read phrases accurately? To help students with fluency, read their poems to them line by line, having the students repeat your pitch, stress, phrasing, and speed. EL

Objectives

- Read poetry aloud for appreciation and understanding of literary elements
- Listen to a proficient model of oral reading
- Appreciate and analyze literary elements in the spoken word

Connecting

Objectives covered in this workshop:
- Make connections in literary texts

Teaching Students to Connect

Why Is It Important?

- Students will learn how to link what they read to events in their own lives or to other selections they've already read.
- Connecting will help students get more involved in their reading.
- Connecting will also help students recall information and ideas in a selection better as they link events, emotions, and characters to their own lives.

How to Help Students Get It

- List some of the topics that will be covered in a reading selection and have students make a connection to each one.
- Have students ask themselves questions as they read such as, Do I know someone like this? Have I ever felt this way? What else have I read that is like this selection?
- Remind students that making connections while they read makes the selection more meaningful.

Reading to Answer the Big Question

Growing Pains

In "Growing Pains," a situation in which a mother and child get angry with each other is described. This poem illustrates the struggle that adolescents face in growing both physically and emotionally.

What Makes Teens Tick?

This TIME magazine article details scientific studies of how changes in people's brains affect how they think and act. Students will learn that some scientists think that chemical changes in teenager's brains are what cause them to engage in risky behavior around their friends.

Workshop Resources

Pacing (Days) Standard	Block	Lesson	Student Materials	Teacher Resources
1		Key Skill Lesson: Connecting	Key Reading Skills Practice English Language Coach	Bellringer Options Transparencies Read Aloud, Think Aloud Transparencies Presentation Plus!
2		"Growing Pains"	Literary Analysis Transparencies Glencoe Online Selection Vocabulary Development Academic Vocabulary Development English Language Coach Active Reading Graphic Organizer Literary Analysis StudentWorks Plus Online Student Edition Literature Classics Selection and Unit Assessments	Literary and Text Analysis Transparencies Puzzlemaker Skill Level Up! BookLink 3 Assessment by Learning Objective (Diagnostic and Formative) Interactive Tutor Self-Assessment TeacherWorks Plus
2		"What Makes Teens Tick"	Glencoe Online Selection Vocabulary Development Academic Vocabulary Development English Language Coach Active Reading Graphic Organizer Literary Analysis StudentWorks Plus Online Student Edition Literature Classics Selection and Unit Assessments	Literary and Text Analysis Transparencies Puzzlemaker Skill Level Up! BookLink 3 Assessment by Learning Objective (Diagnostic and Formative) Interactive Tutor Self-Assessment TeacherWorks Plus

Keys for Unit Resource

- Blackline Master
- Workbook
- Supplemental Text
- CD-ROM
- DVD
- Transparency
- Web-based
- Fast Files

Level Appropriate Code

AS = Activities for all students
AL = Activities for students working above grade level
OL = Activities for students working at grade level
BL = Activities for students working below grade level
EL = Activities for English language learners

Focus

BELLRINGER Options

- **Selection Focus Transparency**
- **Daily Language Practice Transparency**

Focus Activity Ask: Which story or poem you've read this year have you connected with most? For example, you might have identified with a character, an event, or a setting in a particular selection. *(Responses will vary. Students should be able to draw comparisons between the selection and their personal experiences.)*

Teach

R Reading Skill

Connecting Ask: How does thinking about your connections with a selection make it more meaningful? *(Responses will vary. Students may say that a selection is more meaningful if they can identify with and understand where the characters are coming from.)* OL

Skills Focus

You will practice using these skills when you read the following selections:

- "Growing Pains," p. 838
- "What Makes Teens Tick?" p. 844

Reading

- Connecting

Literature

- Understanding the use of figurative language
- Identifying and explaining the effects of figurative language such as simile, metaphor, and imagery

Vocabulary

- Understanding English as a changing language
- Understanding historical influences on English

Writing/Grammar

- Using correct subject-verb agreement with indefinite pronouns

Skill Lesson

Connecting

Learn It!

R **What Is It?** When you get involved in what you are reading, you usually identify with the characters, situations, or events in the selection. **Connecting** is linking what you read to your own experiences or to other selections you've already read. You may remember a time when you, a family member, or a friend had to go through a similar situation. Or maybe the selection makes you think about a character from another story that you've read. Thinking about these connections while you read makes the selection more meaningful.

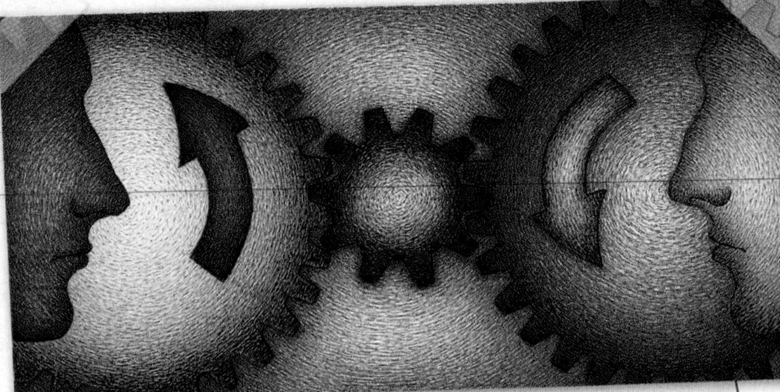

Analyzing Art
Link what you know to what you read. Think about people you know and situations you've experienced. Then connect them to characters and situations in your reading.

Objectives (pp. 834–835)
Reading Make connections with text

Additional Support

Differentiated Instruction

Connecting with Art Help students analyze the images in the art on this page. Discuss what the circles might mean in reference to the term *connecting,* particularly since they are displayed here as wheels. Ask students to explain the significance of the arrows and help them see that the arrows might signify continuous movement, showing that we are continuously affected by each other. Discuss with them how the picture illustrates the idea that connecting with someone else and with what they read is an ongoing process. OL

Focus

BELLRINGER Options

- **Selection Focus Transparency**
- **Daily Language Practice Transparency**

Focus Activity Ask: Which story or poem you've read this year have you connected with most? For example, you might have identified with a character, an event, or a setting in a particular selection. *(Responses will vary. Students should be able to draw comparisons between the selection and their personal experiences.)*

Teach

R Reading Skill

Connecting Ask: How does thinking about your connections with a selection make it more meaningful? *(Responses will vary. Students may say that a selection is more meaningful if they can identify with and understand where the characters are coming from.)* OL

READING WORKSHOP 4

Skills Focus

You will practice using these skills when you read the following selections:

- "Growing Pains," p. 838
- "What Makes Teens Tick?" p. 844

Reading

- Connecting

Literature

- Understanding the use of figurative language
- Identifying and explaining the effects of figurative language such as simile, metaphor, and imagery

Vocabulary

- Understanding English as a changing language
- Understanding historical influences on English

Writing/Grammar

- Using correct subject-verb agreement with indefinite pronouns

Objectives (pp. 834–835)
Reading Make connections with text

Skill Lesson

Connecting

Learn It!

What Is It? When you get involved in what you are reading, you usually identify with the characters, situations, or events in the selection. **Connecting** is linking what you read to your own experiences or to other selections you've already read. You may remember a time when you, a family member, or a friend had to go through a similar situation. Or maybe the selection makes you think about a character from another story that you've read. Thinking about these connections while you read makes the selection more meaningful.

Analyzing Art
Link what you know to what you read. Think about people you know and situations you've experienced. Then connect them to characters and situations in your reading.

Additional Support

Differentiated Instruction

Connecting with Art Help students analyze the images in the art on this page. Discuss what the circles might mean in reference to the term *connecting,* particularly since they are displayed here as wheels. Ask students to explain the significance of the arrows and help them see that the arrows might signify continuous movement, showing that we are continuously affected by each other. Discuss with them how the picture illustrates the idea that connecting with someone else and with what they read is an ongoing process. OL

Workshop Resources

Pacing (Days) Standard	Block	Lesson	Student Materials	Teacher Resources
1		Key Skill Lesson: Connecting	Key Reading Skills Practice English Language Coach	Bellringer Options Transparencies Read Aloud, Think Aloud Transparencies Presentation Plus!
2		"Growing Pains"	Literary Analysis Transparencies Glencoe Online Selection Vocabulary Development Academic Vocabulary Development English Language Coach Active Reading Graphic Organizer Literary Analysis StudentWorks Plus Online Student Edition Literature Classics Selection and Unit Assessments	Literary and Text Analysis Transparencies Puzzlemaker Skill Level Up! BookLink 3 Assessment by Learning Objective (Diagnostic and Formative) Interactive Tutor Self-Assessment TeacherWorks Plus
2		"What Makes Teens Tick"	Glencoe Online Selection Vocabulary Development Academic Vocabulary Development English Language Coach Active Reading Graphic Organizer Literary Analysis StudentWorks Plus Online Student Edition Literature Classics Selection and Unit Assessments	Literary and Text Analysis Transparencies Puzzlemaker Skill Level Up! BookLink 3 Assessment by Learning Objective (Diagnostic and Formative) Interactive Tutor Self-Assessment TeacherWorks Plus

Keys for Unit Resource

- Blackline Master
- Workbook
- Supplemental Text
- CD-ROM
- DVD
- Transparency
- Web-based
- Fast Files

Level Appropriate Code

AS = Activities for all students
AL = Activities for students working above grade level
OL = Activities for students working at grade level
BL = Activities for students working below grade level
EL = Activities for English language learners

Why Is It Important? Connecting your personal experiences to the events, characters, or ideas in a selection helps you better understand what you read. Connections make reading much more interesting and help you recall information and ideas. For example, if you've performed in front of people before, you may understand why a character feels nervous before going on stage for the first time.

Literature Online

R **Study Central** Visit www.glencoe.com and click on Study Central to review connecting.

How Do I Do It? As you read a selection, ask yourself connecting questions such as these: *Do I know someone like this character? Have I ever felt the way this character feels? What opinions do I already have about this topic? What else have I read that reminds me of this situation?*

Here's how one student connected this stanza from the poem "One," by James Berry, to his own experiences:z

Nobody can get into my clothes for me
or feel my fall for me, or do my running.
Nobody hears my music for me, either.

This reminds me of the time when I fell during the soccer game. The rest of the game went on around me. No one seemed to notice, but it was a big deal to me. I think that's what the poem is about: what it's like to have my own experiences in life.

Practice It!

Here are some topics that you'll find in the reading selections in this workshop. Make a connection to each one. Think about things you've read, events in your life, or even people in the news that link to these topics. In your Learner's Notebook, write a connection to each topic.

- Family disagreements
- Growing up
- The brain
- Taking chances

Use It!

As you read, think about other reading selections you've read in this book that might help you connect with the new selections. Write your new connections and ideas in your Learner's Notebook.

Teach

Literature Online

Study Central Have students access the Web site to review connecting and to complete a related activity.

R Reading Skill

Connecting Ask: What are the benefits of connecting to reading? *(Possible response: Benefits include understanding the reading, making the reading more interesting, and helping to recall information and ideas.)* OL Why would almost everyone have some connection to the topics listed in the *Practice It!* section? *(These are universal topics or experiences with which almost everyone is familiar.)* AL

Resources for page 835

Use Reading Skills Transparency in *Read Aloud, Think Aloud,* Unit 7, to help students practice connecting.

Reading in the Real World

Career Explain to students that connecting is more than just a reading skill; some people use it as the basis for their jobs. School guidance counselors, for example, must connect with students to help advise them about college, career choices, and other life decisions. Guidance counselors must use their experience to identify with the problems students face and help them make good choices. Many states require counselors to have a master's degree, a state counseling license, and teaching experience. Have students who are interested in this career interview a guidance counselor to find out more. OL

Objectives

- Make connections with texts
- Use artwork to connect to liter text

Teach

More About the Author

Jean Little is a lover of animals and of people. She lives in a large, pink house with her sister, her grandniece and nephew, four dogs, two cats, two parrots, and two turtles. The chaos of Little's household inspires her writing. She tells readers, "Always remember that the best place for your nose is inside a book."

V Vocabulary

Word Origins **Say:** One way to learn and remember vocabulary words is to understand their changing meanings. Next to the chart in your Learner's Notebook, write how the old meaning and today's meaning of each word might connect. For example, *mail* used to mean something that is small and carried around, like a bag or wallet. **EL** **OL**

Before You Read Growing Pains

Jean Little

Meet the Author

Jean Little was born in 1932 with poor eyesight. As she grew older, her sight improved enough so that she could learn to read on her own. When she was eighteen, a magazine published two of her poems. She remembers her father reading them aloud. "I listened," she says, "and [when] his voice broke, I knew why I wanted to be a writer." See page R4 of the Author Files for more on Jean Little.

Literature Online

Author Search For more about Jean Little, go to www.glencoe.com.

Objectives (pp. 836–839)
Reading Make connections with text
Literature Identify literary devices: figurative language
Vocabulary Explore word origins

Vocabulary Preview

English Language Coach

Word Origins The meanings of words often change over time, sometimes quite a bit. In the poem you are about to read, someone apologizes. *Apology* is an example of a word that has gone through an important change in meaning.

- *Apology* comes from the Greek *apologia,* which means "a speech made in defense."
- Today, *apology* means "an expression of regret for having done something wrong."

These two meanings have a certain similarity, but they are quite different. Today, a person who "apologized" by defending what he or she had done would be missing the whole point of making an apology!

The meanings of words also grow. A noun may be created by a word that started out as a verb, or the other way around. Sometimes new phrases are created, and they become a permanent part of the language. In the poem you are about to read, a child is bawled out.

- *Bawl* has been used in English for 600 years. It originally meant "to make a sound like a cow." Today it has still has a very similar meaning: "to yell, bellow, or cry loudly."
- To *bawl out,* meaning "to scold loudly" was born right here in the United States in the early part of the 20th century.

On Your Own Copy the chart shown below in your Learner's Notebook. Then fill in the "Old Meaning" and "Today's Meaning" for the two remaining words. (The oldest meaning for a word is usually the *first* one given in a dictionary entry.)

Word	Old Meaning	Today's Meaning
mail *(n.)*	a bag or wallet	something sent through the postal service
meat *(n.)*		
awful *(adj.)*		

Additional Support

Literature Online

Author Search To expand students' appreciation of Jean Little, have them access the Web site for additional information and resources.

Literature Focus Lesson

Speaker Explain to students that the *speaker* in a poem is the person speaking the words in the poem. The speaker of a poem is similar to the narrator of a story. He or she is not necessarily the poet or author. Discuss with students the distinction between the speaker and the poet. Ask if any of them have ever read a poem in which it was important to understand who the speaker of the poem was in order to understand the meaning of the poem. Have students tell who the speaker is in Little's poem "Growing Pains." How is the speaker different from the poet? **OL**

Skills Preview

Key Reading Skill: Connecting

The title of the poem "Growing Pains" refers to growing up. As you read the poem, connect the events in the poem to

- things that have happened that made you realize you were growing up.
- other poems and stories about growing up.

R

Write to Learn In your Learner's Notebook, write about three or four events that made you realize you were growing up. Refer to your examples as you read the poem to help you connect to it.

Key Literary Element: Figurative Language

Figurative language is imaginative language used by writers for descriptive effect. Descriptive language makes the reading selection more interesting and colorful.

Some examples of figurative language are simile and metaphor. A **simile** uses the words *like* or *as* to compare unlike things. "When my brother gets angry, he's as loud as thunder" is a simile.

A **metaphor** also compares two unlike things, but it does not use *like* or *as*. In a metaphor, one thing is described as if it *were* another. "That science test was a piece of cake" is a metaphor.

L

Use these tips to help you identify and understand similes and metaphors.

- Look for comparisons.
  How are the two things similar? How are they different?
- Think about why the author would make the comparison.
  How does the comparison help the author explain his or her idea?
- Look for sensory details.
  To which of the five senses do the details appeal?

Write It Down Use figurative language to write a sentence about growing up. Be sure to use the tips above to create a simile or metaphor.

Get Ready to Read

Connect to the Reading

"Growing Pains" describes a situation in which a mother and child get angry with each other. Think about how you feel when you are angry or when someone is angry with you.

Partner Talk With a partner, talk about how you felt when you and a close relative or friend were angry with each other. Talk about how you responded.

Build Background

The poem you are about to read is "Growing Pains."

- The term "growing pains" has more than one meaning. Some children feel physical pain in their legs, perhaps because the bones grow longer and stretch the muscles. And some children feel emotional pain or stress as they get older and accept more responsibilities.
- The poem's speaker is probably your age. The poet, Jean Little, was that age in the 1940s. It seems that disagreements between kids and parents have been part of growing up for a long time.

Set Purposes for Reading

Read the poem "Growing Pains" to find out how the speaker feels about growing up.

Set Your Own Purpose What would you like to learn from the poem to help you answer the Big Question? Write your own purpose on the "Growing Pains" page of Foldable 7.

Literature Online

Interactive Literary Elements Handbook
To review or learn more about the literary elements, go to www.glencoe.com.

Keep Moving

Use these skills as you read the following selection.

READING WORKSHOP 4

Teach

R Reading Skill

Connecting **Ask:** What thoughts, feelings, or experiences help you recognize that you are growing up? *(Students may suggest understanding the consequences of their actions.)* **OL**

L Literary Element

Figurative Language **Say:** There are many common similes and metaphors related to physical growth:

- She's growing like a weed.
- He's a giant!

Explain the meaning of each. *(Responses will vary.)* **OL**

Literature Online

Interactive Literary Elements Handbook Have students access the Web site to improve their understanding of figurative language.

CheckPoint

Use the CheckPoint questions provided on Presentation Plus! to review connecting and to build background. These questions can be used with interactive response keypads for immediate student feedback.

Reading in the Real World

Citizenship To reinforce the point that tension between parents and children is a universal topic, invite students to speak with an adult in their lives about parent-child relationships. Provide students with the following interview questions:

- When you were growing up, with whom did you live? How would you describe your relationship?
- Did you ever argue? What about? How did those arguments make you feel? How do you feel about those arguments now?

Have students share the results of their interviews with the class. **AS**

Objectives

- Make connections with text
- Identify literary devices: figurative language
- Explore word origins

READING WORKSHOP 4

Teach

Viewing the Painting

Ask: What emotions does the girl in the painting seem to be feeling? *(Possible responses: sadness, hurt)* **BL** How can the photo help you connect with the feelings of the speaker in this poem? *(Possible response: The girl in the picture appears to be sad like the girl in the poem.)* **OL**

L Literary Element

Figurative Language

Ask: When the speaker's mother compares the speaker's room to a pigsty, what is she saying about the room? *(The speaker's room is dirty and messy.)* **OL**

Painting of a Young Girl, 1993. Alan Byrne. Oil on canvas, 53.3 x 43.2 cm. Private Collection.

Growing Pains

by Jean Little

Mother got mad at me tonight and bawled me out.
She said I was lazy and self-centered.
She said my room was a pigsty.
She said she was sick and tired of forever nagging but
  I gave her no choice. **1**

Practice the Skills

1 Key Literary Element

L **Figurative Language** A metaphor describes one thing as if it were another. Find the metaphor in these five lines.

Additional Support

Reading in the Real World

Citizenship Share the following tips for conflict management with students:

- Know how you feel about the problem and share these feelings calmly.
- Be an active listener.
- Recommend solutions to the problem.

Invite students to analyze the conflict management style of the speaker and her mother, using these questions:

- Which techniques do the characters each practice? Which do they ignore?
- How does each character feel at the end of the conflict?
- What techniques might leave both of them feeling more satisfied? **AL**

She went on and on until I began to cry. 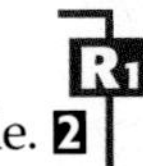
I hate crying in front of people. It was horrible. **2**

I got away, though, and went to bed and it was over.
I knew things would be okay in the morning;
Stiff with being sorry, too **polite**, but okay.
I was glad to be by myself. **3**

Then she came to my room and apologized.
She explained, too.
Things had gone wrong all day at the store.
She hadn't had a letter from my sister and she was worried.
Dad had also done something to hurt her.
She even told me about that.
Then *she* cried.
I kept saying, "It's all right. Don't worry."
And wishing she'd stop.

I'm just a kid.
I can forgive her getting mad at me. That's easy.
But her sadness . . .
I don't know what to do with her sadness. **R2**
I yell at her often, "You don't understand me!"
But I don't want to have to understand her.
That's expecting too much. **4** **5** ❍

Practice the Skills

2 **Key Reading Skill**

Connecting How do you feel when someone is angry with you? How do you make yourself feel better?

3 **English Language Coach**

Word Origins Originally, **polite** meant "polished," as a stone might be. Later it came to mean "elegant and sophisticated." Now it means "having good manners." What connection do you see between one meaning and the next?

4 **Reviewing Skills**

Interpreting What line shows the speaker's sympathy toward her mother? Which line expresses the speaker's helplessness?

5 **BIG Question**

BQ Do you think the speaker is ready to take on adult responsibilities? Write your answer on the "Growing Pains" page of Foldable 7. Your response will help you complete the Unit Challenge later.

READING WORKSHOP 4

Teach

R1 Reading Skill

Connecting Ask: What kinds of things cause you to cry? *(Responses will vary.)* **BL** **Ask:** Why does the speaker cry? *(Students may say because her mother criticizes her.)* **OL**

R2 Reading Skill

Review Interpreting Ask: How do the speaker's feelings change? *(Possible response: At first, she feels bad because her mother criticizes her. Then, she feels bad that her mother is sad, but thinks it isn't fair of her mother to ask for understanding.)* **OL**

BQ BIG Question

Ask: Why does the speaker think it's too much for her to have to understand her mother? *(The speaker says that she's just a kid.)* **OL** Is this a valid reason? Explain. *(Responses will vary.)* **AL**

Assess

Use the CheckPoint questions provided on Presentation Plus! to check for comprehension of the selection. These questions can be used with interactive response keypads for immediate student feedback.

Differentiated Instruction

Short Play The speaker describes an argument and conversation with her mother. Invite pairs of students to compose dialogue for a short play about the argument and reconciliation. Tell students that they cannot contradict any information in the poem, but they can invent information that is not directly stated. When students complete their short play, have them practice reading it aloud several times, using voice and body language to convey their feelings. Then, invite student pairs to perform their plays for the class. **OL**

Objectives

- Make connections with text
- Identify figurative language in poetry
- Use artwork to connect to te

Assess

Resources for page 840

- Selection Quick Check
- Selection and Unit Assessment
- ExamView Assessment Suite
- Interactive Tutor: Self-Assessment

Students can respond to the *After You Read* items in their Learner's Notebook or on a separate sheet of paper.

Answering the BIG Question

1. Responses will vary. Students might note that they feel either more or less grown-up than the girl in the poem.
2. The speaker feels so bad that she starts crying.
3. Students may say sadness, hurt, or anger.
4. Events include the mom getting upset at the speaker, the speaker crying in response, and the mom later explaining that she had been angry for many reasons. Feelings include sadness, frustration, anger, guilt, and hurt.

Critical Thinking

5. Possible response: The mother yells at the speaker because the mother is upset about other things.
6. Possible response: that she's supposed to understand her mother
7. Responses will vary. Students should explain their response.

After You Read | Growing Pains

Answering the BIG Question

1. After reading the poem, what are your thoughts about your relationships and growing up?
2. **Recall** How does the speaker feel just after her mother yells at her?
   TIP **Right There**
3. **Recall** What are the feelings the speaker experiences?
   TIP **Think and Search**
4. **Summarize** What events and feelings would you include in a short summary of this poem?
   TIP **Think and Search**

Critical Thinking

5. **Infer** What does the speaker suggest actually caused her mother to yell at her?
   TIP **Author and Me**
6. **Infer** The speaker says that she's upset about her mother's sadness. What else does the speaker suggest is upsetting to her?
   TIP **Author and Me**
7. **Evaluate** The poem's speaker says that she does not want to have to understand her mother's feelings. What do you think about this statement? Explain your answer.
   TIP **On My Own**

Write About Your Reading

Has a younger brother or sister or a good friend ever asked you for advice? Do you enjoy giving people words of wisdom?

Imagine that the speaker of this poem has sent the poem to your school advice column, and you are the person who gives the advice. What advice would you give to the speaker of the poem?

Write a three paragraph response to the speaker. Try to give her advice related to each stanza of the poem.

Objectives (pp. 840–841)
Reading Make connections with text
Literature Identify literary devices: figurative language
Vocabulary Explore word origins
Grammar Use correct subject-verb agreement: indefinite pronouns

Write About Your Reading

Possible response:
I can see why you are having a tough time. It sounds like your mom made you upset. It is okay to show your emotion by crying.

Sometimes when we feel angry or hurt, we need to get away and think about the situation. But these feelings will often still be there later, and it may be helpful to talk about them.

It sounds as though your mom had a hard day and took it out on you. I think you should tell her it is hard to hear about her problems. Ask her to act more like your mother than your friend.

Skills Review

Key Reading Skill: Connecting

8. What connections did you make while reading "Growing Pains"? Give an example of one of the following:
   - a connection to an event in your own life
   - a connection to another story or poem
   - a connection to a historical or current event

Key Literary Element: Figurative Language

9. What forms of figurative language do you see in "Growing Pains"? Give one example and explain what it means.
10. Why do poets use figurative language?
11. How do you think the author's use of figurative language affects your interpretation of the poem?

Reviewing Skills: Interpreting

12. Does the speaker in the poem think that she deserved to be "bawled out"? How can you tell?

Vocabulary Check

English Language Coach The dictionary, *any* dictionary, is nothing more than a record of how people spell and pronounce words, and what they use them to mean. So dictionaries change as language changes. Words enter the language; words drop out of the language; words get new meanings.

13. What meaning of *mad* did the speaker use in lines 1 and 21? What does a dictionary record as the word's original meaning? How might the word have developed its newer meaning?
14. What meaning of *kid* did the speaker use in line 20? What does a dictionary record as the word's original meaning? How might the word have developed its newer meaning?
15. The word *okay* didn't exist at all before 1839. What can you find out about the history of this word by looking in a dictionary?

Grammar Link: Agreement with Indefinite Pronouns

Indefinite pronouns do not refer to a particular person, place, or thing. Certain indefinite pronouns are always singular, or equal to *he, she,* or *it.*

anybody	every	nobody
anyone	everybody	no one
anything	everyone	nothing
each	everything	somebody
either	neither	someone

See if you can make the subject and verb agree in the sentences below. (Use the chart for help.)

Everybody (was, were) cold.

(*Everybody* is singular, or equal to *he, she,* or *it.* So the right verb form is *was.*)

Each of the students (has, have) a book.

(Subjects and predicates cannot be in prepositional phrases. Omit the phrase.)

Each ~~of the students~~ (has, have) a book.

(The subject is *each,* so the right verb form is *has.*)

Grammar Practice

On a separate piece of paper, copy each sentence below. Underline the subject of each sentence once and the correct verb form twice.

16. (Is, Are) somebody able to lend us money?
17. Everything in those stores (is, are) expensive.
18. Neither of us (has, have) money for clothes.

Writing Application Look again at the Write About Your Reading assignment you completed. Fix any subject-verb mistakes you made.

Web Activities For eFlashcards, Selection Quick Checks, and other Web activities, go to www.glencoe.com.

Skills Review

Key Reading Skill: Connecting

8. Responses will vary.

Key Literary Element: Figurative Language

9. Possible response: The mother makes a metaphor comparing the daughter's room to a pigsty.
10. Responses will vary.
11. Responses will vary.

Reviewing Skills: Interpreting

12. Possible response: She does not feel she deserved to be bawled out. She gets so upset she cries.

Vocabulary Check

13. Students may say that *mad* means "angry" in both lines and that the original meaning is "insane." Responses about development will vary.
14. Students may say that *kid* means "child" and that the original meaning of *kid* is "a young goat." Responses about development will vary.
15. Possible response: *Okay* was coined in America, originally written as O.K. to represent the slang "oll korrect," or "all correct."

Grammar Link: Agreement with Indefinite Pronouns

Grammar Practice

16. Is somebody able to lend us money?
17. Everything in those stores is expensive.
18. Neither of us has money for clothes.

Literature Online

Web Activities Have students access the Web site for interactive activities that will help them assess their understanding of the selection.

Close

Ask students to tell what makes the speaker of this poem tick.

Teach

More About the Author

Claudia Wallis made *TIME* magazine history in 1987, when she was named senior editor. Wallis was only the third woman to earn this title. As the managing editor of *TIME for Kids* (1995–2003), she played a lead role in the creation of separate editions for different age groups, as well as a related magazine titled *Go Places with TFK*. Wallis is now editor-at-large at *TIME*.

V Vocabulary

Quick Check Ask the following questions:

1. Is a bland dinner tasteless or flavorful? *(tasteless)*
2. If you peer at something, do you glance at it or study it carefully? *(study it carefully)*
3. If you have a craving for candy, do you want some or are you sick of it? *(want some)*
4. Is an abnormality common or uncommon? *(uncommon)*
5. If you're in adolescence, are you more likely to be in middle school or college? *(middle school)* OL

Before You Read What Makes Teens Tick?

Meet the Author

Claudia Wallis wanted to become a scientist or a doctor when she was a kid. Instead, she became a writer and editor at *TIME* magazine. As a reporter, she covered medicine and science for *TIME*. Then she became the managing editor of *TIME for Kids*. Wallis says that the best thing about her job is that she loves "constantly learning new things, seeing fantastic pictures from all over the world—and universe."

Author Search For more about Claudia Wallis, go to www.glencoe.com.

Objectives (pp. 842–849)
Reading Make connections with text
Literature Identify literary devices: figurative language
Vocabulary Explore language growth

Vocabulary Preview

V

bland (bland) *adj.* dull; unexciting **(p. 844)** *The walls were a bland white.*

adolescence (ad uh LES uns) *n.* the period between childhood and adulthood **(p. 844)** *Scientists used to believe that the brain was fully developed before adolescence.*

peer (peer) *v.* to look closely **(p. 845)** *Modern technology allows scientists to peer inside the brain.*

abnormality (ab nor MAL uh tee) *n.* anything that is not normal or usual **(p. 845)** *The doctor said there was no abnormality in the boy's brain.*

craving (KRAY ving) *n.* a strong desire or longing **(p. 848)** *A craving for adventure can cause a teenager to take risks.*

Group Activity Take turns using each word correctly in sentences.

English Language Coach

Language Changes and Growth There are many ways in which the meanings of words change and grow. A few ways follow.

- **Widening or Narrowing:** A meaning may get "wider" and begin to include more than it did originally. Or a meaning may get more narrow.
- **Figurative Use:** Many words keep their original meaning while also developing a figurative meaning. If the figurative meaning is used often enough, it becomes one of the dictionary definitions of the word.
- **Association:** A word may develop such a strong connotation that it comes to actually *mean* what it was once associated with.

Word	Old Meaning	New/Additonal Meaning	Type of Change
fever	a high temperature from illness	a state of nervous excitement	widening
girl	any young person	a young female person	narrowing
crane	a large, wading bird with a long neck	a machine with a long moveable arm	figurative use
beads	prayers	small objects that can be strung together	association (due to use of prayer beads)

On Your Own What do you think is a most likely explanation for how or why the following meanings developed?

from *ear* "what one uses to hear" to *ear* of corn
from *fishy* (like a fish) to *fishy* (suspicious)

Additional Support

Author Search To expand students' appreciation of Claudia Wallis, have them access the Web site for additional information and resources.

English Language Coach

Language Changes and Growth
Discuss with students the various ways the English language grows and changes. Suggest that they think about the appliances and products they find in their homes. Over time, many products, such as tissues and vacuum cleaners, come to be known by their most common brand names. In addition, point out that the English language has adopted and changed many words from other languages. Ask students if they can think of words from their native language that are similar to English words. Have them check to see if the English language adopted these words. EL

Skills Preview

Key Reading Skill: Connecting

"What Makes Teens Tick?" suggests that some of the changes in the way teenagers act are related to physical changes. Have you noticed any changes in the way you think or act?

Write to Learn In your Learner's Notebook, write about a teenager that you know or have read about who went through many changes when he or she became a teenager. How did this person act? How did the people who knew the teenager react to his or her changes?

Key Literary Element: Figurative Language

Prose writers and poets use similes and metaphors to compare things in fresh ways. A simile compares by using the words *like* or *as.* A *metaphor,* on the other hand, compares two things without using *like* or *as.*

The sheets were as cold *as* ice cubes.

Sheila's room is a disaster zone.

Use these tips to help you find and understand similes and metaphors.

- Look for comparisons that use *like* or *as.*
  Think about why the writer makes the comparison. Does it make the description more interesting?
- Look for descriptions or comparisons that aren't exactly true.
  If the comparison isn't actually true, it's probably a metaphor or simile.
- Ask yourself what the items being compared have in common.

L

Interactive Literary Elements Handbook
To review or learn more about the literary elements, go to www.glencoe.com.

Get Ready to Read

Connect to the Reading

Scientists are studying how changes in people's brains affect how they think and act. Some scientists think that chemical changes in teenagers' brains might make them more likely to take risks around their friends. Do you ever take risks around your friends that you wouldn't take if you were alone?

R

Partner Talk With a partner, talk about why teenagers are more likely to take risks than younger or older people.

Build Background

In "What Makes Teens Tick?" you'll learn about how your brain changes as you get older.

- The brain has several regions. Two of the most important are the cerebral cortex, where thought takes place, and the cerebellum, which controls movement and balance.
- The brain is made of cells called neurons. Neurons carry messages.
- Neurons connect to one another at meeting points called synapses. Chemical and electrical reactions at the synapses pass messages from one neuron to another.

Set Purposes for Reading

BIG Question Read "What Makes Teens Tick?" to find out how processes in the developing brain make young people act different ways.

Set Your Own Purpose What would you like to learn from the article to help you answer the Big Question? Then write your own purpose for reading on the "What Makes Teens Tick" page of Foldable 7.

Keep Moving

Use these skills as you read the following selection.

Teach

R Reading Skill

Connecting Say: Have you ever taken a risk you shouldn't have? *(Responses will vary.)* What are some reasons young people take risks around their friends? *(Possible responses: Kids want to fit in with their friends and look cool; Kids don't think about consequences sometimes; Kids believe they won't ever get hurt.)* OL

L Literary Element

Figurative Language Say: In your Learner's Notebook, create one simile and one metaphor to describe a teenager. *(Responses will vary.)* OL

CheckPoint

Use the CheckPoint questions provided on Presentation Plus! to review connecting and to build background. These questions can be used with interactive response keypads for immediate student feedback.

Interactive Literary Elements Handbook Have students access the Web site to improve their understanding of figurative language.

Reading in the Real World

Citizenship Have students speak with teenagers and adults about the correlation between age and risk-taking behavior. Provide students with these survey questions. Have students make generalizations based on the results of the survey.

Age ___________ Gender ___________

Write "A" if you agree with these statements:

_____ I would like to go bungee jumping.

_____ I would like to drive a race car.

_____ I do not use crosswalks.

_____ I am more likely to take risks when my friends are around. OL

Objectives

- Make connections with text
- Identify literary devices: figurativ language
- Explore language growth

Teach

L Literary Element

Figurative Language
Say: Notice Wallis's sensory language in the first paragraph. To which senses does she appeal? *(Responses will vary. Students may note the following: sound= buzz; sight=drape, spreading, bland)* OL

C Critical Thinking

Analysis Ask: Other than money, why might the Mann brothers have agreed to participate in the study? *(Responses will vary. Students may say that the study will help them learn more about themselves and their own behaviors.)* OL

Readability Scores
Dale-Chall: 6.5
DRP: 62
Lexile: 1020

TIME

What Makes Teens Tick?

"Making mistakes is part of how the brain grows."

Developing brains and hormones help shape teen behavior

By CLAUDIA WALLIS

Five young men in sneakers and jeans troop into a waiting room at the National Institutes of Health (NIH)[1] in Bethesda, Maryland. They drape themselves all over the chairs, spreading out backpacks, a DVD player, and a laptop loaded with computer games. Their presence adds a buzz to the **bland** hospital setting. Twins Corey and Skyler Mann, 16, and their big brothers Anthony and Brandon, 18, who are also twins, plus oldest brother Christopher, 22, are here to have their heads examined. Literally. The five brothers from Orem, Utah, are volunteers for a major study that's been going on since 1991. Its goal: to determine how the brain develops from childhood into **adolescence** and on into early adulthood. 1

1. The ***National Institutes of Health*** is a U.S. government agency in charge of carrying out and supporting medical research.

Vocabulary

bland (bland) *adj.* dull; unexciting

adolescence (ad uh LES uns) *n.* the period between childhood and adulthood

1 Key Literary Element

Figurative Language The writer very helpfully tells us she's using a figurative expression "literally." What would be the common *figurative* meaning of "have their heads examined"?

Additional Support

English Language Coach

Content-Area Vocabulary This selection includes science terminology that may be new to students. Help students determine the meaning of any of the following words that may be unfamiliar:

- brain
- develop/development
- researchers
- subjects (as in research subjects)
- environment
- genetic codes (genes)
- brain cells/nerve cells
- hormones

Encourage students to use context clues and dictionaries to determine the meaning of any unfamiliar words. EL

This project is the brainchild of Jay Giedd *(Geed),* a doctor at the National Institute of Mental Health. Giedd has spent many years using magnetic resonance imaging[2] (MRI) to take pictures of brains to **peer** inside the heads of thousands of kids and teenagers. For each volunteer, he creates a unique photo album. Giedd takes images of each volunteer's brain every two years. Each photo album is a record of the brain's changes and growth. R1

Before Giedd's studies, most scientists believed that the brain was fully developed by age 12. However, Giedd has proved that the brain continues to change well past age 12. In fact, it doesn't fully develop until age 25. Researchers now are looking at how these later changes might help explain some teen behaviors such as excitability, risk taking, and rule breaking.

In recent years, Giedd has shifted his focus to twins, which is why the Manns are such exciting subjects. Most brain development seems to be genetic. Other, smaller changes in the brain, however, are influenced by experience and the environment. Twins start out with identical or similar genetic codes. But then experiences take them along different paths. 2 By studying twins, Giedd hopes to separate the influences of genes and experiences in the development of the teen brain. Eventually, he hopes to find, for instance, that Anthony's plan to become a pilot and Brandon's plan to study law will cause brain differences that can be seen on future MRIs. R2

Throughout the afternoon, the Mann brothers take turns completing various brain tests. Then they head downstairs to get their MRIs. Anthony stretches out on the examining table and slides his head into the MRI machine's giant magnetic ring.

The brain of each brother is scanned three times. The first scan is a quick survey that lasts one minute. The second scan lasts two minutes and shows any damage or **abnormality**.

2. A ***brainchild*** is a product of one's creative imagination. ***Magnetic resonance imaging*** uses magnets to produce high-quality computer images of the body's internal organs.

Vocabulary

peer (peer) *v.* to look closely

abnormality (ab nor MAL uh tee) *n.* anything that is not normal or usual

2 English Language Coach

Language Growth Twins, says the article, take different **paths.** Does one go off on a bicycle path while the other takes a footpath? Or can this statement be explained by a growth in the original meaning of *path* as "a narrow trail"? EL

Teach

R1 Reading Skill

Review Monitoring Comprehension Ask: What does Giedd do in his study? *(He takes pictures of the brains of kids and teenagers every two years to record growth.)* BL How has Giedd's experiment proven most scientists wrong? *(Possible response: By taking pictures of people's brains every two years, Giedd has proven the brain doesn't fully develop until age 25.)* OL

EL Language Coach

Language Growth Say: Look up the word *path* in the dictionary. What other meaning beside "narrow trail" do you see? *(course, direction)* How does experience lead twins to take different directions in their lives? *(Possible response: They have different life experiences.)* EL OL

R2 Reading Skill

Review Understanding Cause and Effect Ask: Why are twins an exciting subject for Giedd? *(Possible response: Because twins' brains begin almost identical genetically, Giedd can study how two similar brains develop differently because of different experiences and environments.)* OL

Objectives

- Draw conclusions from text
- Understand figurative language in prose
- Identify sensory details
- Understand cause and effect
- Monitor comprehension
- Analyze words that have change[d] meaning over time

Reading in the Real World

Citizenship Students may enjoy conducting their own research about identical twins. If there are identical twins in your school, ask them whether they would be willing to talk with students about their experiences. If not, encourage students who have twins in their family or neighborhood to talk with them. Before their interviews, students should prepare a list of questions similar to the ones below.

- What was it like as a child to be a twin? What funny experiences did you have?
- What is the best thing about being a twin? What is the worst thing? OL

Teach

L Literary Element

Figurative Language
Ask: What simile does the author use to explain the fatty layer covering branches of nerve cells in the brain? *(Possible response: She compares the thickening of fatty coverings to tree rings.)* OL

R1 Reading Skill

Connecting **Say:** The article says that during the second stage of development, cells and connections that are used the most survive and thrive. Think about the activities and hobbies that you engage in most often. What parts of your brain will grow the most? *(Responses will vary, but students who play a lot of sports may say that the nerve cells in the part of the brain that controls movement will grow.)* OL

R2 Reading Skill

Review Understanding Cause and Effect **Ask:** Why would the nerve cells in the branches that control the fingers thicken in a piano player's brain? *(Possible response: The cells and connections that are used the most survive and thicken.)* OL

READING WORKSHOP 4

The third scan is 10 minutes long and shows the greatest detail. Giedd watches as Anthony's brain appears on a computer screen. The machine scans 124 slices of the brain, each slice as thin as a dime. It takes twenty hours of computer time to process the images. 3

Under Construction

Before birth, nerve cells in the brain undergo a phase in which they multiply and grow rapidly. Then the brain gets rid of cells that aren't needed. Giedd's studies show that brain cells undergo a second phase of change that starts in childhood and lasts until the early twenties. Unlike the earlier phase, which changes the number of nerve cells, the second one changes the number of connections between the nerve cells.

When a child is between 6 and 12 years old, nerve cells become bushier. Each nerve cell **branches** out to other nerve cells. These branches carry signals between the cells. This process peaks when girls are about 11 and boys are about 12½. Then some of the branches are slowly thinned out over several years. 4

At the same time, a fatty layer covers branches of the nerve cells that remain. With each passing year, the fatty coverings thicken, much like tree rings. During this time, a person's brain has fewer but faster connections. It's a trade-off. The brain becomes more efficient but is probably losing its potential for learning and its ability to recover from trauma.[3]

Most scientists believe that genes as well as experience cause changes in the brain during this second phase of brain development. One scientist, Gerald Edelman, describes the process as survival of connections that are most used. The cells and connections that are used the most survive and thrive, while those that aren't used shrink and die. So how you spend your time during this phase *may* be very important. Research shows, for instance, that practicing piano quickly thickens the branches of nerve cells in parts of the brain that control the fingers. 5

3. A ***trauma*** is a serious injury or shock.

3 Key Literary Element

Figurative Language The comparison "each slice as thin as a dime" is literal, not figurative. This is not a simile because each slice *really is* as thin as a dime.

4 English Language Coach

Language Growth The original meaning of **branch** is "a limb of a tree." Why do you suppose this word came to be used as a verb meaning "to grow out in different directions"?

5 Key Reading Skill

Connecting Think about a person who is good at a particular activity—an athlete or a musician, for example. In your Learner's Notebook, describe how this person performs. Given what you've read, what do you think this person might have done during the second phase of brain development?

Additional Support

Reading in the Real World

Career Psychologists study the human mind and human behavior. Research psychologists study how physical, emotional, and environmental factors affect mood and behavior. They might use questionnaires, interviews, surveys, and other methods to find out how and why people behave, think, and feel in certain ways. Many psychologists have a PhD, although some have only a master's degree. Psychiatrists, on the other hand, have medical degrees, and often focus on the use of medications as treatment for mental illnesses. Have students interested in the field of mental health learn more about one of these careers. AL

READING WORKSHOP 4

Giedd's research suggests that the cerebellum, a part of the brain that controls both physical and mental activities, reacts to experience. Giedd hopes his studies of twins will provide more information about the second phase that occurs in the teen brain. "We're looking at what [teens] eat, how they spend their time—is it video games or sports? Now the fun begins," **C** says Giedd.

Brain Development and Behavior

Is there a link between the changing brain structure of teens, hormones, and teen behavior? About the time that the teen brain goes through the second phase of change, the body is also dealing with an attack of hormones. Hormones are chemicals that speed up or slow down cell processes. Some hormones that are very active in the brain affect mood and excitability. 6

"The parts of the brain responsible for things like thrill seeking are getting turned on in big ways around [this

6 **Key Literary Element**

L **Figurative Language** The writer uses a metaphor—"an attack of hormones"—to describe the release of hormones in teens' bodies. What does this metaphor tell you about the release of hormones?

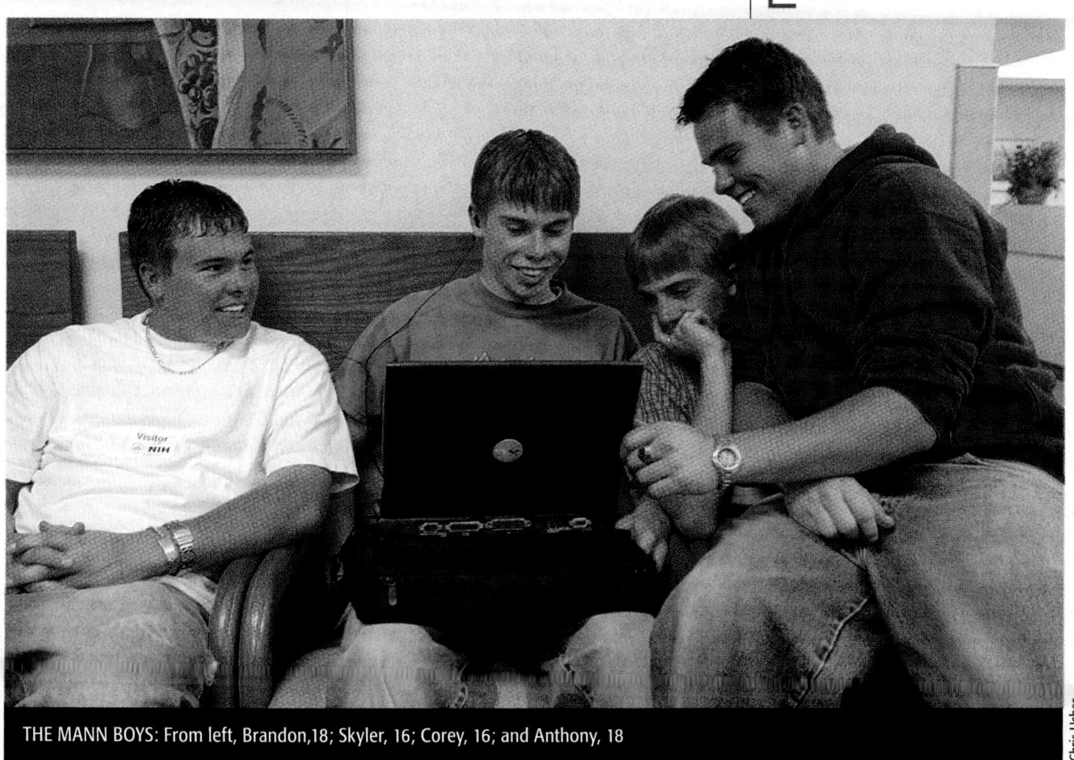

THE MANN BOYS: From left, Brandon,18; Skyler, 16; Corey, 16; and Anthony, 18

Chris Usher

Teach

C Critical Thinking

Comprehension Ask: Why does Giedd say, "Now the fun begins?" *(Possible response: Now that Giedd understands the physical workings of the brain, he looks forward to studying the effects of environmental and experiential variables.)* **OL**

L Literary Element

Figurative Language Ask: What does the word *attack* make you think of? *(Responses will vary. Students may say* battles *or* invasions.*)* **BL** How does this help you figure out the literal meaning of "an attack of hormones"? *(Possible response: Hormones take over teens' lives and cause them to do things they didn't do previously.)* **OL**

Reading in the Real World

Citizenship Share the following information with students:

As nighttime approaches, a gland at the base of the brain releases a hormone called melatonin. This hormone tells the body to start shutting down for sleep. Studies show that it takes longer for melatonin levels to rise in teenagers than in children and adults. So teens may be wide awake late at night and have a difficult time getting up for school the next morning.

Have students discuss how this may affect their performances in school. Invite them to write an editorial about their findings. **AL**

Objectives
- Make connections with text
- Comprehend text
- Understand cause and effect
- Understand figurative language in prose

READING WORKSHOP 4

Teach

R Reading Skill

Connecting Ask: Would you agree to participate in a scientific study such as this one? Explain. *(Responses will vary. Students may say that they'd like to be a part of scientific research that might help adults better understand teenagers.)* **OL**

BQ 

Ask: What factors other than brain development might affect teen behavior? *(Responses will vary. Students may suggest experiences, feelings, and peer pressure.)* **OL** How might Giedd's study be useful to parents, teachers, and teenagers? *(Responses will vary. Students may say that understanding teen behavior would help parents and teachers communicate better with teens. Teens themselves might gain a degree of self-understanding that would help them make better decisions.)* **AL**

time]," says Temple University psychologist Laurence Steinberg. A **craving** for adventure often brings about the need for exploration. Teens might feel a sense of excitement about leaving home and finding their own way in the world. But these urges can also place teens at risk because the parts of the brain responsible for making good decisions are still developing. But Steinberg thinks the proof isn't there yet. "In all likelihood, [teen] behavior is changing because the brain is changing," he says. More and more psychologists, however, are trying to get that proof.

Steinberg, for example, has been studying why people take risks. In an experiment using a driving-simulation game, he studied teens and adults as they decided whether to run a yellow light. Both teens and adults made safe choices when playing alone. But teens started to take more risks in the presence of their friends, whereas adults over age 20 didn't show much change in their behavior. **R**

Other studies of the teen brain and behavior are ongoing. It's nice to know, however, that teen behavior is not just a matter of strong will. "There's a debate over how much conscious[4] control kids have," Giedd says. "Making mistakes is part of how the brain grows." But don't be surprised when adults offer advice. They're trying only to make up for what the teen brain still lacks. **7**

—**Updated 2005 from TIME, May 10, 2004**

7 BIG Question

BQ What does this article suggest about the relationship between brain development and teen behavior? Do you think this article tells the whole story? Discuss with a partner, and write your answer on the "What Makes Teens Tick" page of Foldable 7. Your response will help you complete the Unit Challenge later.

4. ***Conscious*** behavior is behavior that a person is aware of and has control over.

Vocabulary

craving (KRAY ving) *n.* a strong desire or longing

Additional Support

Differentiated Instruction

Writing a Summary This article contains some complicated information about the brain and human development. Have students imagine they've been asked to present the information to a younger audience. Have them skim the article, looking for the main ideas and supporting details, and then write a brief summary of the important points in the article. Have each student swap summaries with a partner and compare which details each person thought were important. Then have students make sure they have simplified the language so that a younger audience can understand the basic ideas. **OL**

READING WORKSHOP 4

Inside the Adolescent Brain

Corpus Callosum

This is thought to be involved in problem solving and creativity. It is a bundle of nerve fibers that connects the left and right sides of the brain. During the teen years, these nerve fibers thicken and handle information more and more efficiently.

Basal Ganglia

These four parts help the brain prioritize information. They are connected to the prefrontal cortex and active in small and large motor movements. While they are growing, preteens may benefit from exposure to music and sports.

Prefrontal Cortex

Located just behind the forehead, this part of the brain is the center of decision making and judgment. It grows during the preteen years. Then it shrinks as nerve connections are thinned out during the teen years. This is the last part of the brain to develop.

Amygdala

This is the emotional center of the brain. In dealing with emotional information, teens tend to rely heavily on the amygdala. Adults depend on the sensible prefrontal cortex, which is underdeveloped in teens. This may explain why some teens react more impulsively than adults.

Cerebellum

This area plays a role in physical coordination and may also regulate some thought processes. It supports activities of higher learning like mathematics and music. New research shows that it changes a lot during the teen years, increasing the number of nerve cells and their connections.

Teach

C Critical Thinking

Application Ask: Which part of the brain processes emotional information? *(The amygdala processes emotional information.)* **OL** Which part of the brain probably has the most influence on risk-taking behaviors? *(The prefrontal cortex probably has the most influence on risk-taking behaviors because it controls judgment.)* **AL**

R Reading Skill

Review Evaluating Ask: Does this graphic help you understand the different parts of the brain? Why or why not? *(Possible response: Yes, the graphic helps me understand different parts of the brain. I can see clearly where each part is located in the boy's skull, and I can read what each part does.)* **BL**

Assess

Use the CheckPoint questions provided on Presentation Plus! to check for comprehension of the selection. These questions can be used with interactive response keypads for immediate student feedback.

Reading in the Real World

College Point out to students that a diagram can be an excellent tool for understanding and recalling information. Suggest that they photocopy it or make a sketch of it in their notes. Then, students could add information to the diagram, such as what each area of the brain controls, along with a few examples. Reviewing diagrams in preparation for a study group or a test is a quick and easy practice. **OL** Suggest that students work with partners to practice this strategy by reviewing the diagram on this page and adding some of the information they learn from it to their Learner's Notebook. **BL**

Objectives
- Make connections with text
- Evaluate text features
- Paraphrase or summarize nonfiction texts
- Understand figurative language in prose

Assess

Resources for page 850

- Selection Quick Check
- Selection and Unit Assessment
- ExamView Assessment Suite
- Interactive Tutor: Self-Assessment

Students can respond to the *After You Read* items in their Learner's Notebook or on a separate sheet of paper.

Answering the

1. Responses will vary. Students may say that this information helps explain why they sometimes act unreasonably.
2. around age six
3. Giedd studies twins because their brains begin as almost genetic copies. He can then note changes to the brains based on varying experiences and environment.

Critical Thinking

4. Possible response: The nerve cells in the visual area of the brain would probably thicken because of use.
5. Possible response: A teenager is more likely to behave badly when with friends because friends increase the sense of excitement associated with bad behavior.
6. Possible response: Giedd's study may inspire young people to learn skills while they are young.

After You Read

What Makes Teens Tick?

Chris Usher

Objectives (pp. 850–851)
Reading Make connections with text
Literature Identify literary devices: figurative language
Vocabulary Explore language growth
Grammar Use correct subject-verb agreement: collective nouns

Answering the BIG Question

1. After reading this article, what new thoughts and ideas do you have about what makes you behave the way you do?
2. **Recall** When does the second phase of brain development begin?
   TIP **Right There**
3. **Recall** Why does Dr. Giedd study twins?
   TIP **Right There**

Critical Thinking

4. **Infer** Suppose that someone studied painting and drawing during his or her teen years. What do you expect would happen to the branches of nerve cells in the visual area of this person's brain?
   TIP **Think and Search**
5. **Infer** After reading the article, do you think that a teenager is more likely to behave badly when alone or with friends? Explain.
   TIP **Think and Search**
6. **Connect** Giedd's studies show that brain development continues through teenage and young adult years. How could Giedd's research affect when and how you plan to learn those skills?
   TIP **Author and Me**

Write About Your Reading

Design a cover for the issue of *Time* that contains "What Makes Teens Tick?" The cover should have a full-page illustration or picture, as well as text (one or two sentences) to catch people's attention.

Step 1: Decide what the important ideas in the story are. What ideas connect the sections of the story? List three or four main topics.

Step 2: Identify a visual image that could represent each topic you listed. Does your image make it clear what the article is about?

Step 3: Choose the two most striking images. Is it possible to combine them into a single cover illustration?

Write to Learn Use your notes to draw a cover illustration. Write one or two sentences that tell what the article is about. Make sure that your sentences capture your reader's interest.

Write About Your Reading

Possible response:
I would show a cartoon picture of a teenager with her brain exposed, running a yellow light. I'd label the prefrontal cortex of her brain, and place an "Under Construction" sign over it. The text for the story would read "Do teenagers' brains make them behave badly? Researchers have discovered a link between brain development and behavior."

Skills Review

Key Reading Lesson Skill: Connecting

7. Giedd's studies show that hormones turn on parts of the brain responsible for thrill-seeking behavior in teenagers. But the parts of the brain responsible for good decision-making aren't fully developed yet. Does your experience with teenagers support or oppose this idea? Explain.

Key Literary Element: Figurative Language

8. The article says about the twins, "Their presence adds a buzz to the bland hospital setting." What type of figurative language does the author use in this sentence?
9. In the sentence quoted above, what is the writer comparing the twins to?

Vocabulary Check

Choose the best word from the list to complete each sentence below. Rewrite each sentence with the correct word in place.

peer adolescence bland abnormality craving

10. The decorations were too ___ to catch the kids' attention.
11. The doctor was concerned about the ___ he found in his tests.
12. Once he reached ___, he knew he would become an adult soon.
13. I get a ___ for cranberries every fall.
14. Ryan used a telescope to ___ at the strange man on the street.
15. **English Language Coach** Look at the following words from the article:

    sneakers jeans laptop pilot

    Guess which two words had different meanings in 1850 than their most common meanings today. Guess which two words didn't even exist then.

Grammar Link: Agreement with Collective Nouns

A **collective noun** names a group.

- audience
- faculty
- jury
- class

A collective noun is considered to be singular when it names a group that acts as a unit. A collective noun is considered to be plural when it refers to the members of a group acting as individuals.

- **Singular Collective:** The class is taking a test.

  (Everyone in the class is doing the same thing. Since the group is acting as one unit, the collective noun *class* is singular.)
- **Plural collective:** The jury do not agree.

  (The members of the jury are acting as individuals. Since the group is not acting as one unit, the collective noun *jury* is plural.)

Grammar Practice

On a separate piece of paper, copy each sentence below. Underline the subject of each sentence once and the correct verb form twice.

16. The committee (is, are) arguing about the issue.
17. The faculty (meets, meet) every Wednesday.
18. The orchestra (is, are) beginning the first song.

Writing Application As you write the text for your magazine cover, be sure that your subjects and verbs agree.

Literature Online

Web Activities For eFlashcards, Selection Quick Checks, and other Web activities, go to www.glencoe.com.

Skills Review

Key Reading Skill: Connecting

7. Responses will vary. Students may say that they know teenagers who make bad decisions.

Key Literary Element: Figurative Language

8. The writer uses a metaphor.
9. The writer compares the twins to bees. The energy that the twins bring to the hospital is like that of the activity in a beehive.

Vocabulary Check

10. bland
11. abnormality
12. adolescence
13. craving
14. peer
15. *Sneakers* and *pilot* have different meanings today. *Laptops* and *jeans* didn't exist in 1850.

Close

Ask students whether they've changed their minds about what makes them tick after reading this article.

Literature Online

Web Activities Have students access the Web site for interactive activities that will help them assess their understanding of the selection.

Grammar Link: Agreement with Collective Nouns

Grammar Practice

16. The committee are arguing about the issue.
17. The faculty meets every Wednesday.
18. The orchestra is beginning the first song.

Comparing Figurative Language

UNIT 7

Objectives covered in this workshop:
- Connect, compare, and contrast figurative language across texts
- Find similarities and differences across texts

Teaching Students to Compare Figurative Language

Why Is It Important?

- Comparing figurative language helps students generate a better picture of the characters and events in a selection.
- Comparing figurative language also helps students pay more attention to specific details.
- Looking at the figurative language from two different types of genres helps students make connections from text to text.

How to Help Students Get It

- Have students keep track of the figurative language as they read. You may choose to have them create a chart for each selection.
- Tell students to think about how the figurative language helps them better understand the similarities and differences between the characters, settings, and events in each selection.
- Remind students to look for the language that includes similes, metaphors, and sensory images in the selections.

Reading to Answer the Big Question

The Women's 400 Meters

This poem describes a group of runners at the start of a race. Using figurative language, it shows how the drive to win is what makes these athletes tick.

To James

The speaker in this poem encourages a boy to succeed in his efforts to win a race.

Slam, Dunk, & Hook

This poem describes how the fast-pace rhythm of basketball is what makes a group of young men tick.

Workshop Resources

Pacing (Days) Standard	Pacing (Days) Block	Lesson	Student Materials	Teacher Resources
1		Comparing Literature: Comparing Figurative Language	Key Reading Skills Practice English Language Coach	Bellringer Options Transparencies Read Aloud, Think Aloud Transparencies Presentation Plus!
2		"Slam, Dunk & Hook"	Literary Analysis Transparencies Glencoe Online Selection Vocabulary Development Academic Vocabulary Development English Language Coach Active Reading Graphic Organizer Literary Analysis StudentWorks Plus Online Student Edition Literature Classics Selection and Unit Assessments	Literary and Text Analysis Transparencies Puzzlemaker Skill Level Up! BookLink 3 Assessment by Learning Objective (Diagnostic and Formative) Interactive Tutor Self-Assessment TeacherWorks Plus
2		"The Women's 400 Meters" "To James"	Glencoe Online Selection Vocabulary Development Academic Vocabulary Development English Language Coach Active Reading Graphic Organizer Literary Analysis StudentWorks Plus Online Student Edition Literature Classics Selection and Unit Assessments	Literary and Text Analysis Transparencies Puzzlemaker Skill Level Up! BookLink 3 Assessment by Learning Objective (Diagnostic and Formative) Interactive Tutor Self-Assessment TeacherWorks Plus

Keys for Unit Resource

- Blackline Master
- Workbook
- Supplemental Text
- CD-ROM
- DVD
- Transparency
- Web-based
- Fast Files

Level Appropriate Code

AS = Activities for all students
AL = Activities for students working above grade level
OL = Activities for students working at grade level
BL = Activities for students working below grade level
EL = Activities for English language learners

Focus

BELLRINGER Options

- Selection Focus Transparencies
- Daily Language Practice Transparency

Focus Activity Say: In this workshop, you'll compare the figurative language in three poems. Think about your pet or a pet you know. Then write one simile and one metaphor about the pet. Share your figurative language with the class. *(Possible responses: My cat is as fluffy as a soft, white cotton ball; my friend's watchdog is a rock.)*

Teach

L Literary Element

Figurative Language Ask: What is the name of language that helps readers see, hear, feel, smell, or taste what the writer describes? *(sensory language)* **OL** Revise your pet similes and metaphors to include sensory language. *(Possible response: In the hushed silence of the warm house, my cat sleeps, curled up in his bed, fluffy and soft as a white cotton ball.)* **AL**

COMPARING LITERATURE WORKSHOP

The Women's 400 Meters

by Lillian Morrison

& To James

by Frank Horne

& Slam, Dunk, & Hook

by Yusef Komunyakaa

Skills Focus

You'll use these skills as you read and compare the following selections:

- "The Women's 400 Meters," p. 855
- "To James," p. 856
- "Slam, Dunk, & Hook," p. 858

Reading

- Making connections across texts
- Comparing/contrasting figurative language in different texts

Literature

- Identifying and explaining the effects of figurative language in poetry

Writing

- Write using comparison and contrast

Objectives (pp. 852–853)
Reading Compare and contrast: figurative language

You compare things by thinking about how they're alike and different. For example, you know that dogs and cats are alike and different. Both are pets. Both come in different colors. But you wouldn't take your cat for a run in the park, and you wouldn't expect your dog to purr.

In literature you make comparisons too. You look at important elements, such as language and theme. Thinking about similarities and differences helps you understand how different works of literature are connected.

How to Compare Literature: Figurative Language

When you read the three poems in this workshop, you'll compare the way each poem uses figurative language.

Remember that figurative language is imaginative language that writers use to make descriptions more meaningful. Keep an eye out for figures of speech, or expressions, such as similes and metaphors.

- A simile uses the words *like* or *as* to compare two unlike things. **L**

  Tom slid into the room like a snake.

- A metaphor compares two unlike things but doesn't use *like* or *as.* It describes one thing as if it were another.

  Tom's a snake!

Also look for other language that helps the reader see, hear, feel, smell, or taste what the writer describes.

Additional Support

Literature Focus Lesson

Sensory Language Remind students that sensory language helps a writer clarify ideas. Sensory language intensifies the reader's interaction with the text, allowing him or her to experience events and emotions in a more meaningful way. For example, a reader can imagine only so much with the sentence, "The food was not very good." Have students compare this sentence to "The stew solidified into an oval pool of muddy, brown fat." Students should see that the second sentence provides much more description and allows them to "see" the unappetizing meal. Have students note sensory details and describe their effects. **AS**

Get Ready to Compare

As you read, keep track of figurative language using a web like the one below. Copy this web into your Learner's Notebook, and use it to take notes as you read. Make a separate web for each poem. In the center circle, write the title of the poem. In each outer circle, write an example of figurative language from the poem. Later, you'll use your notes to write your comparison.

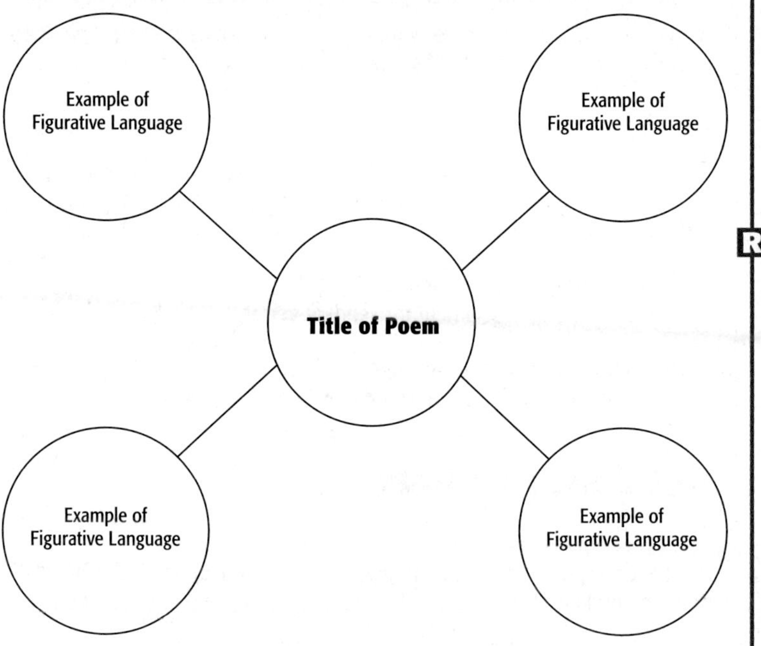

R

Use Your Comparison

Even if you don't realize it, you come across figurative language all the time. One place you'll find it is in advertising. An ad for a brand of shampoo may tell you that your hair will smell like a spring garden when you use the product.

Think about the advertisements that you have seen recently—in print or on radio or TV. Choose one that contains figurative language. Discuss your chosen ad with a partner. What effect is the figurative language meant to have on a reader or viewer? Summarize your ideas in your Learner's Notebook.

L

COMPARING LITERATURE

Teach

R Reading Skill

Review Taking Notes Tell students to draw their webs large enough to fill a page in their notebooks. Ask them how a web like this might help them organize their notes. *(Possible response: I will be able to see each example of figurative language clearly and to easily note how many examples of figurative language each poem has.)* OL

L Literary Element

Figurative Language Ask: What does the figurative language in the ad you chose make you think about? Were all of your associations positive? *(Responses will vary.)* OL

Assess/Close

Tell students to write a one- to two-sentence ad containing figurative language. Have them share their ads with the class and discuss their use of figurative language. OL AL

Resources for page 853

Use the Comparing Literature Graphic Organizer BLM in the Unit 7 Resource Booklet.

English Language Coach

Recognizing Types of Figurative Language For additional practice identifying figurative language, write the following three sentences on the board, and ask students to identify the simile, the metaphor, and the sensory language. Remind students that similes contain the words like or as but metaphors do not.

- The toothpaste, minty sweet, tingled against my bare teeth, finally free from braces. (*sensory language*)
- Your eyes are like the sun. (*simile*)
- You are my sunshine. (*metaphor*)

Suggest to students that they continue to look for figurative language as they read the poems. EL BL

Objectives

- Find similarities and differences across texts
- Connect, compare, and contrast figurative language across texts
- Identify and explain literary devices
- Use graphic organizers to understand texts

Teach

More About the Authors

Lillian Morrison has said of her love of poetry and sports: "I love rhythms, the body movement implicit in poetry, explicit in sports . . . I am drawn to athletes, dancers, drummers, jazz musicians . . . who symbolize for us something joyous, ordered, and possible in life."

Dr. Frank Horne, an optometrist, was a politically active poet who participated in President Roosevelt's Black Cabinet, a group of presidential advisers who discussed social problems and solutions.

Yusef Komunyakaa's poetry combines his varied childhood experiences, his affection for jazz and blues, and his time in Vietnam into unified works. His poems demonstrate that many different experiences can be collected in a single, beautiful work.

Before You Read

The Women's 400 Meters, To James, *and* Slam, Dunk, & Hook

Meet the Authors

Full-time author and poet Lillian Morrison is a sports fan who has written collections of poems about sports. See page R5 of the Author Files for more on Lillian Morrison.

Frank Horne once coached a high school track team. At the beginning of his writing career, he told other African American poets, "Your task is definite, grand, and fine."

Yusef Komunyakaa uses his Louisiana childhood and experiences in Vietnam as resources for his poetry. A winner of the Pulitzer Prize for Poetry in 1994, he writes poems on many subjects. See page R4 of the Author Files for more on Yusef Komunyakaa.

Literature Online

Author Search For more about Lillian Morrison, Frank Horne, and Yusef Komunyakaa, go to www.glencoe.com.

Objectives (pp. 854–859)
Reading Compare and contrast: figurative language
Vocabulary Use structural analysis: roots

Vocabulary Preview

insignia (in SIG nee uh) *n.* a mark or sign that indicates rank, authority, or honor **(p. 858)** *The insignia showed that Mercury was the gods' messenger.*

feint (faynt) *v.* to move in a way that's meant to trick an opponent **(p. 859)** *The player's attempt to feint to the outside didn't fool anyone.*

English Language Coach

Roots A root is the main part of a word that carries the main meaning. Other pieces can be attached to a root to change its meaning, or a root can stand alone.

The root ***phon*** means "sound" or "voice."
A *telephone* is an instrument for sending voices.

The root ***align*** means "to arrange in a line."
Align is a root word that can stand alone.

Get Ready to Read

Connect to the Reading

Is there one sport that you like to play more than anything else? What is it? Why do you like it? How do you feel before, during, and after you play?

Build Background

The poems in this workshop are about track and basketball.

- Track-and-field events are the oldest organized sports. In races like the 400-meter dash, runners begin in a crouch. When the race begins, the runners leap into a full stride and run at top speeds to the finish line.
- James Naismith invented basketball in 1891. He hung two peach baskets on opposite sides of a gym and used a soccer ball. The rules he made up form the basis of the game today.

Set Purposes for Reading

BIG Question Read these poems to find out why athletes love to play.

Set Your Own Purpose What would you like to learn from the poems to help you answer the Big Question? Write your own purpose on the Comparing Literature page of Foldable 7.

Additional Support

Author Search To expand students' appreciation of these authors, have them access the Web site for additional information and resources.

Reading in the Real World

Citizenship Invite students to talk with an adult about his or her favorite pastime as a child and/or teenager. Provide these questions:

- What was your favorite pastime? How did you feel while engaging in it?
- Do you engage in this pastime now? Why or why not? If so, does the pastime create the same feelings in you? Explain.
- If you could, would you return to the days of being a young person engaged in this pastime? Why or why not?

Have students discuss their interviews and the transition from childhood to adulthood. OL

The Women's 400 Meters

by Lillian Morrison

Skittish,*
they flex knees, drum heels and
shiver at the starting line

waiting the gun
to pour them over the stretch
like a breaking wave. **1**

Bang! they're off
careening* down the lanes,
each chased by her own bright tiger. **2** ❍

1 Someone who is ***skittish*** is restlessly active or nervous.

8 Someone who is ***careening*** is rushing and swerving as if out of control.

Practice the Skills

1 Comparing Literature

L **Figurative Language** What is the simile in this stanza? Look for the word *like.* What two things is the poet comparing?

2 BIG Question

BQ What does the bright tiger symbolize? Write your answer in Foldable 7.

English Language Coach

Descriptive Verbs Point out that the verbs the poet uses provide information about the runners. On the board, list the following verbs. Provide students with dictionaries, and have students work together to define each verb in the context of the poem. Record the definitions on the board.

- flex
- drum
- shiver
- wait
- pour
- break
- careen
- chase

Lead students in a discussion about how the poet's verb choices affect the reader's image of the runners. **EL**

Teach

L Literary Element

Figurative Language
Ask: What is the poet comparing in the second stanza? *(running a race and a breaking wave)* **OL** How is running a race like a breaking wave? *(Possible response: A breaking wave moves quickly, powerfully, and continuously. To win a race, the athlete must move in the same way.)* **AL**

BQ BIG Question

Ask: What does a bright tiger make you think of? *(Responses will vary. Students may suggest power, speed, or grace.)* **OL** Why do you think the poet describes each runner as being "chased by her own bright tiger"? *(Responses will vary. Students may say that the tiger represents the goals and competitive spirit of each runner.)* **AL**

Objectives

- Compare and contrast: figurative language
- Use structural analysis

Teach

Viewing the Photo

Say: Look closely at this photograph. What words describe the runners? *(Possible responses: powerful, energized, fast, determined)* **BL** As you read the poem "To James," find descriptive words in the poem that match the picture. *(Possible responses: flung, catapulted, lurched, sinews tightened)* **OL**

C Critical Thinking

Analysis Ask: Who do you think is the speaker of this poem? What clues tell you this? *(Possible response: The speaker might be James's coach, parent, or friend. Lines 12–14 suggest that the speaker is close to James because he or she "lurched with" him, indicating he or she might have helped James practice running and watched him race before.)* **AL**

by Frank Horne

Do you remember
how you won
that last race . . . ?
how you flung your body
at the start . . . **3**
how your spikes
ripped the cinders
in the stretch . . .
how you catapulted*
through the tape . . .
do you remember . . . ?
Don't you think
C I lurched* with you
out of those starting holes . . . ?

9 To ***catapult*** is to leap or hurl oneself, as if from a giant slingshot.

13 To ***lurch*** is to move forward suddenly in a jerky manner; stagger.

Practice the Skills

3 Comparing Literature

Figurative Language
Descriptive words help you visualize the runner. When he *flung* his body, he threw it forcefully. What other words on this page help you visualize the runner running?

Additional Support

Differentiated Instruction

Are They Heroes? Many people look up to sports stars as heroes or role models. Hold a class discussion in which you ask students whether they believe sports stars should be considered heroes or role models. If students have differing opinions, have volunteers from each side prepare a two-minute presentation on their side of the issue. Encourage students to list as many reasons as possible why sports stars should or should not be considered heroes or role models. Have students consider other members of society who might be considered heroes. **BL** **OL** **AL**

Don't you think
my sinews* tightened
at those first
few strides . . .
and when you flew into the stretch
was not all my thrill
of a thousand races
in your blood . . . ?
At your final drive
through the finish line
did not my shout
tell of the
triumphant ecstasy*
of victory . . . ? **4**

Live
as I have taught you
to run, Boy—
it's a short dash. **5** **6**
Dig your starting holes
deep and firm
lurch out of them
into the straightaway
with all the power
that is in you
look straight ahead
to the finish line **C**
think only of the goal
run straight
run high
run hard
save nothing
and finish
with an ecstatic burst
that carries you
hurtling*
through the tape
to victory . . . **7** ○

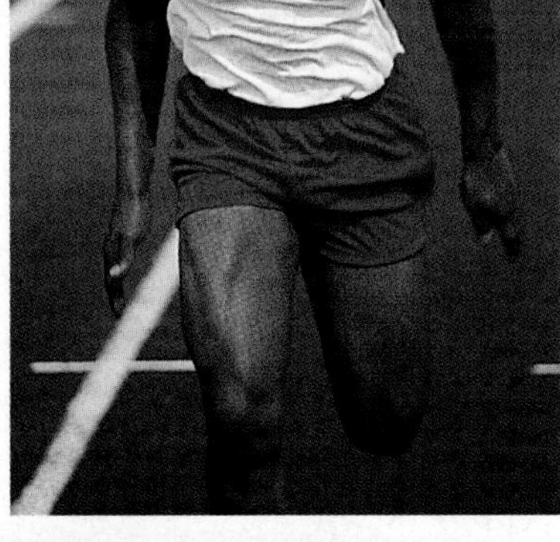

16 ***Sinews*** (also called tendons) are cords of tissue that connect muscles to bones.

27 ***Triumphant ecstasy*** is a state of overwhelming joy or delight as a result of success or winning.

49 If you are ***hurtling***, you are moving quickly or forcefully.

Practice the Skills

4 **English Language Coach**

EL **Roots** The Latin root *vict* means "to conquer." Which word in the first stanza contains the root *vict?* What does the word mean?

5 **Comparing Literature**

Figurative Language How does the speaker tell the boy to live? Does the poet use a simile or metaphor? How can you tell?

6 **Comparing Literature**

Figurative Language The metaphor in line 32 compares *it* to a *short dash.* What two things is the poet talking about?

7  BIG Question

DQ In the last stanza, what advice does the speaker give the boy about how to achieve his goals? Write your answer in Foldable 7.

Teach

EL Language Coach

Roots Say: Use your knowledge of the root vict to define victory. Check your explanation against the dictionary definition, and revise your work if necessary. *(The word victory means success in any contest or struggle with an opponent.)* **EL**

C Critical Thinking

Evaluation Say: In the third stanza of the poem, the speaker is no longer discussing an actual race. Instead, the speaker compares life to a short dash and gives James advice about life. Do you agree with the speaker's advice to James to "look straight ahead" and "think only of the goal"? Why or why not? *(Some students may agree with this advice, saying that it is important to be goal-oriented in life. Others may note the importance of stopping to enjoy the fun things in life.)* **AL**

BQ BIG Question

Ask: Is being the best—in sports, at school, in art—something that makes you tick? Why or why not? *(Responses will vary. Some students may say that striving to be the best is what motivates and defines them, whereas others may say that they feel more inclined to try all types of experiences.)* **AS**

Reading Fluency

Reading Aloud Have pairs take turns reading Horne's poem aloud. Point out that this poem has particularly short lines. Remind students to let punctuation, not line endings, tell them when to pause. Invite students to raise their voice when appropriate, such as in the lines, "did not my shout/tell of the/triumphant ecstasy/of victory . . . ?" Have students practice reading aloud several times, noting any difficult words they might ask for help pronouncing. Then have volunteers read the poem aloud to the class. Encourage them to use their voice and body language to emphasize the speaker's points. **EL** **BL**

Objectives

- Compare and contrast information in different texts
- Identify and explain the effects of literary devices, including similes
- Understand roots and root-based words

Teach

L Literary Element

Figurative Language
Ask: How does a basketball sound when it goes through the net? *(Possible response: The ball swishes through the net, sounding like wind through a tunnel.)* BL To what does "a hot/Swish of strings like silk" refer? *(Possible response: a basketball going through the hoop; the strings are the hoop; the poet compares them to silk)* OL

C Critical Thinking

Analysis Say: Notice the references to Mercury, angels, a labyrinth, and storybook sea monsters. What do these images suggest about how the speaker remembers feeling during these basketball games? *(Possible response: The speaker remembers feeling like a god or like a character in a fantastical story.)* OL

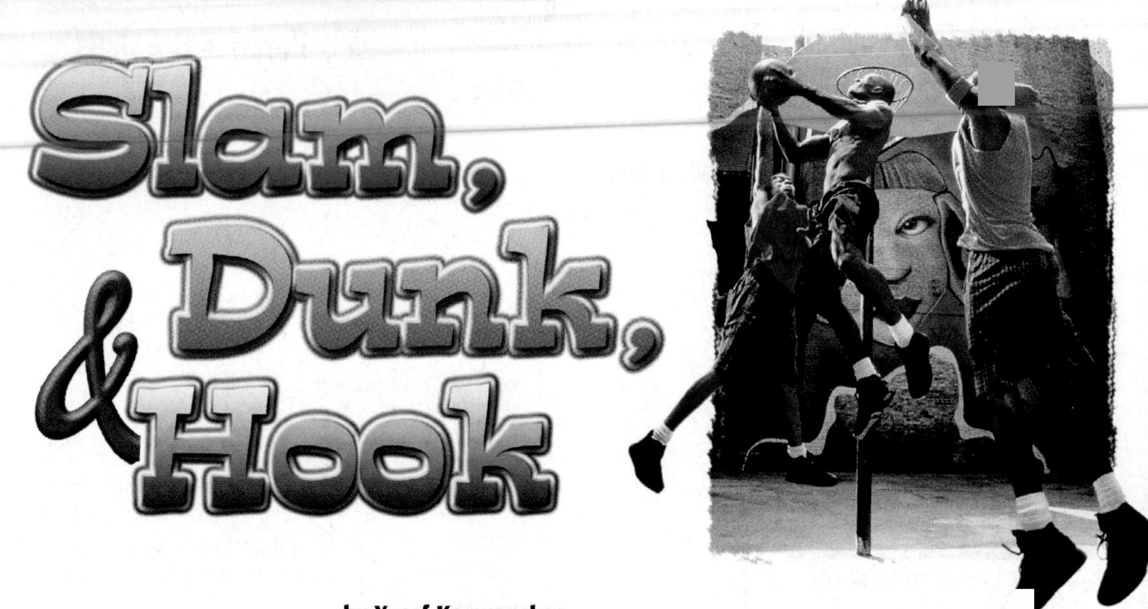

Slam, Dunk, & Hook

by Yusef Komunyakaa

C

Fast breaks. Lay ups. With Mercury's*
Insignia on our sneakers,
We outmaneuvered* the footwork
Of bad angels. Nothing but a hot
Swish of strings like silk 8
Ten feet out. In the roundhouse
Labyrinth* our bodies
Created, we could almost
Last forever, poised in midair
Like storybook sea monsters.
A high note hung there

1 In Roman mythology, ***Mercury*** was the messenger of the gods. He wore sandals that had small wings on them.

3 If you ***outmaneuvered*** (owt muh NOO vurd) someone, you used clever movements to defeat that person.

7 Here, ***roundhouse*** refers to wide, swinging arm movements, and a ***labyrinth*** is a confusing, complicated arrangement.

Vocabulary

insignia (in SIG nee uh) *n.* a mark or sign that indicates rank, authority, or honor

Practice the Skills

8 Comparing Literature

L **Figurative Language** There's a simile in this line. What two things does the poet compare?

Additional Support

Differentiated Instruction

The Music of Movement
Komunyakaa's work is influenced by his love of jazz and blues. Have students locate musical references in the poem. (hot swish of strings; a high note hung there a long second; sprung rhythm; jibed; lyric) OL One of the characteristics of jazz is improvisation, or the act of composing and performing simultaneously. If possible, play several examples of jazz for students. Invite students to identify times when the musicians sound as though they're improvising. Then, ask students to describe how improvisation is also an element of playing basketball. AL

A long second. Off
The rim. We'd corkscrew
Up & dunk balls that exploded
The skullcap of hope & good
Intention. Bug-eyed, lanky, **9**
All hands & feet . . . sprung rhythm.
We were metaphysical* when girls
Cheered on the sidelines.
Tangled up in a falling,
Muscles were a bright motor
Double-flashing to the metal hoop
Nailed to our oak. **10**
When Sonny Boy's mama died
He played nonstop all day, so hard
Our backboard splintered.
Glistening with sweat, we jibed*
& rolled the ball off our
Fingertips. Trouble
Was there slapping a blackjack*
Against an open palm.
Dribble, drive to the inside, **feint**,
& glide like a sparrow hawk. **11**
Lay ups. Fast breaks.
We had moves we didn't know
We had. Our bodies spun
On swivels of bone & faith,
Through a lyric slipknot
Of joy, & we knew we were
Beautiful & dangerous. **12** ❍

18 Here, ***metaphysical*** means beyond the limits of the physical world.
27 To ***jibe*** is to be in harmony with one another.
30 A ***blackjack*** is a flexible, leather-covered weapon used to hit an opponent.

Vocabulary

feint (faynt) *v.* to move in a way that's meant to trick an opponent

Practice the Skills

9 English Language Coach

Roots The root *tend* means "to stretch toward." **Intention** is from this root. It means "an expected goal" or "something that one plans to do."

10 Comparing Literature

L1 **Figurative Language** What does the metaphor in line 21 compare muscles to?

11 Comparing Literature

L2 **Figurative Language** A player is compared to a sparrow hawk, a bird that flies at high speeds and changes directions quickly. How does this simile help you visualize the player's movements?

12 BIG Question

BQ This poem suggests different reasons that people play basketball. Describe two of these reasons. Write your answer in Foldable 7. Your response will help you complete the Unit Challenge.

Teach

L1 Literary Element

Figurative Language Ask: How are muscles like a motor? *(Possible response: Groups of muscles work together to power the body, just as a motor works with other machine parts to power it.)* **AL**

L2 Literary Element

Figurative Language
Ask: Why did the poet choose a sparrow hawk for the simile, instead of a turkey or a chicken, for example? *(Possible response: The simile suggests that each player is quick and agile, like a sparrow hawk. Turkeys and chickens are generally tame and slow, unlike the players.)* **OL**

BQ BIG Question

Ask: Why does Sonny Boy play basketball nonstop when his mother dies? *(Possible response: Sonny Boy uses basketball as a way of dealing with his grief over the loss of his mother.)* **OL**

Literature Focus Lesson

Symbols Remind students that symbols are things or ideas that represent other things or ideas. Ask students what sports symbolize in the three poems.

- "The Women's 400 Meters": What do the bright tigers symbolize? (*Possible response: the women's will to win*)
- "To James": What does the race symbolize for the speaker? (*Possible response: being successful in life*)
- "Slam, Dunk, & Hook": What does playing basketball symbolize? (*Possible response: power and confidence*)

Have students discuss other ideas sports might symbolize. **OL** **AL**

Objectives
- Compare and contrast information in different texts
- Identify and explain the effects of literary devices, including similes
- Understand roots and root-based words

Assess

Resources for page 860

 Selection Quick Check

 Comparing Literature Assessment

Vocabulary Check

1. feint
2. insignia
3. Possible responses: *memo:* a short note written as a reminder; *memorial:* a day or monument intended to celebrate a person or an event; *remember:* to recall

Comparing Literature

4. No
5. metaphor
6. simile
7. No
8. simile
9. simile
10. metaphor

After You Read

The Women's 400 Meters & To James & Slam, Dunk, & Hook

Vocabulary Check

Write the correct word for each definition.

insignia feint

1. ___ to move in a way that's meant to trick an opponent
2. ___ a mark or sign that indicates rank, authority, or honor
3. **English Language Coach** The word *memory* comes from the Latin root *mem,* meaning "to bring to mind." Name another word that comes from the root *mem.* What does that word mean?

Comparing Literature

Figurative Language

The following sentences may contain figurative language. Some sentences do not. If a sentence contains a figure of speech, identify it as a *simile* or a *metaphor.* Write *No* if the sentence doesn't contain a figure of speech.

4. They forgot their troubles as they played.
5. That test was a piece of cake.
6. She jumped up and down, flapping her arms like a chicken.
7. James felt so worried that he was unable to sleep.
8. The two front-runners were as confident as gold medalists.
9. Sweat poured down his face like a rushing river.
10. She was a doll for watching my cat.

Objectives (pp. 860–861)
Reading Compare and contrast: figurative language
Writing Respond to literature: write about figurative language

Writing: Compare the Literature

15. Have students use their webs to create a two-column chart like the one below. To save space, students can write the page number rather than the poem's title.

Metaphors	Similes
"each chased by her own bright tiger" (p. 855)	"like a breaking wave" (p. 855)
"it's a short dash" (p. 857)	"a hot swish of strings like silk" (p. 858)
"Muscles were a bright motor" (p. 859)	"poised in midair like storybook sea monsters" (p. 858)

Reading/Critical Thinking

Answer the following questions.

The Women's 400 Meters & To James

11. Evaluate Explain the second stanza of "The Women's 400 Meters." How effective is the poet's description?

TIP **Author and Me**

12. Interpret How does the speaker in "To James" feel about the runner? How can you tell?

TIP **Author and Me**

Slam, Dunk, & Hook

13. Connect What experience of your own does this poem remind you of? Explain.

TIP **Author and Me**

14. Evaluate Is "Slam, Dunk, & Hook" a good title for this poem? Explain.

TIP **Author and Me**

Writing: Compare the Literature

Use Your Notes

15. Use the notes on your webs to compare figurative language in "Slam, Dunk, & Hook," "To James," and "The Women's 400 Meters."

Step 1: Look over the webs that you have completed. Underline any metaphors. Circle the similes.

Step 2: On a separate sheet of paper, make a two-column chart of the figurative language you found. Write the metaphors in the first column and the similes in the second column.

Step 3: Look at your chart. In a short paragraph, explain how the figurative language adds to or doesn't add to the meanings of the poems.

Step 4: Look at what kinds of figurative language appear in all of the poems and what kinds appear in only one or two poems. You will use this information to back up what you write.

Get It on Paper

Compare the way that the three poems use figurative language by copying and answering these questions.

16. What is the best example of figurative language in "The Women's 400 Meters"? Why?

17. What is the best example of figurative language in "To James"? Why?

18. What is the best example of figurative language in "Slam, Dunk, & Hook"?

19. In which poem does figurative language play the biggest role? Why? In which poem does it play the smallest role? Why?

BIG Question

20. In each of the selections, you read about what makes athletes tick. Answer these questions in your Learner's Notebook:

- How are the ideas about what makes athletes tick in the three selections alike?
- How are they different?

Reading/Critical Thinking

11. Responses will vary. Students may say the runners wait for the sound of the starting gun to propel them through the race in the same way that the current causes waves to break.

12. Possible response: The speaker is emotionally connected to James because the speaker experiences James's movements and feelings in his or her own body.

13. Responses will vary. Students may say it reminds them of how they feel when they are playing basketball or another team sport.

14. Responses will vary. Students may say that the title contains active verbs and that the poem itself is active.

Close

Have students state which of the three poems is their favorite and why.

16. Possible response: The best example is the line "chased by her own bright tiger" because it appeals to the reader's senses of touch and sight.

17. Possible response: The best example is "save nothing…" because in a race, as in life, there is no reward for holding back.

18. Possible response: The best example is "Our bodies spun / On swivels of bone & faith, / Through a lyric slipknot / Of joy" because the poet invites the reader to bask in the glory of youth with him.

19. Possible response: Greatest role: in "Slam, Dunk, & Hook." The poet's message relies on images from mythology, music, and sports. Smallest role: "The Women's 400 Meters." This poem captures only a brief moment of action.

20. Responses will vary.

Focus

BELLRINGER Options

Daily Language Practice Transparency

Focus Activity Ask: From the poems and stories we've read in this unit, how do you think people figure out what makes them tick? Explain.

The discussion will remind students of the selections they have read, which will help them begin the group activity or the solo activity.

Teach

Group Activity: Character Study

- Remind students to think about characters' actions, not just their statements.
- Help groups determine how to classify answers that cannot easily be categorized.
- Make sure that students complete their charts with adequate time remaining.
- To help students draw conclusions, have them complete the following statement: Because of the way the character ___________, I conclude that ___________ makes him/her tick.

Assess/Close

Group Activity

Ask: How can you use what you have learned from the characters in this unit to increase your understanding of what brings out the best in you? *(Suggest that students write their answers in their Learner's Notebook.)*

UNIT 7 WRAP-UP

Answering The BIG Question: What Makes You Tick?

You've just read other people's responses to the Big Question: What makes you tick? Now use what you've learned to do the Unit Challenge.

The Unit Challenge

Choose Activity A or Activity B, and follow the directions for the activity you've chosen.

A. Group Activity: Character Study

The editor of *Tick* magazine wants to know what brings out the best in the characters and speakers in this unit. Your group has been asked to interview the characters and speakers.

1. **"Talk" to the Characters** Each group member identifies one character or speaker and tells how that person would answer these questions:
   - Who or what is most important to you?
   - Why?

   If other group members have different ideas, they can add answers. Have one or two group members record all of the answers.

2. **Study the Answers** Look for similarities among the answers so that you can organize them into categories:
   - **People** (friends, family)
   - **Feelings** (love, friendship, happiness)
   - **Things** (possessions, money)
   - **Ideas and Goals** (fame, peace, success)

   Some answers may fit into two or more categories. Make a chart with a column for each category, and write the responses in the appropriate spaces.

People	Feelings	Things	Ideas and Goals

3. **Draw Conclusions** As a group, check to see which categories have the most entries. What general statements can you make about individual characters and speakers? What conclusions can you form about what makes people tick?

4. **Present Your Findings** Choose one or two people to present the group's work to the class. How do all the groups' conclusions add to your understanding of what brings out the best in people?

B. Solo Activity: Personal Reflection

The characters and speakers in this unit share their private thoughts and feelings about their own identities. Now it's your turn to share some of the things that you like and that make you tick. Follow these steps to make a self-portrait collage.

1. **Plan Your Collage** Review the information you wrote about yourself in your Learner's Notebook. Create a web diagram like the one below and include the most important things that make you who you are.

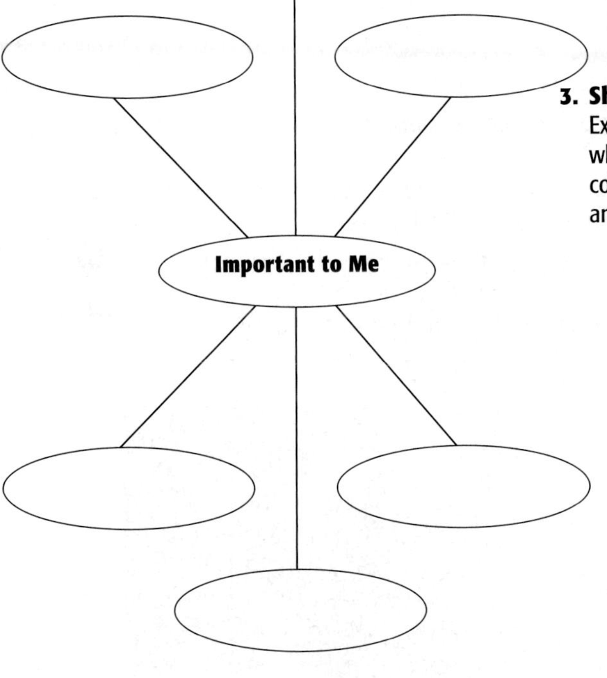

2. **Put It Together** Using what you identified as being important to you, begin to gather images and words for your collage.
   - Search through old magazines or catalogs for pictures and words that represent what's important to you. (Make sure that no one else wants the magazines or catalogs before you start cutting.)
   - Find photos and create your own drawings.
   - Decide how you want to arrange things before you glue them down. Try different arrangements. Throw out images that don't work. Add more images as needed.
   - When you're happy with your collage, glue the pictures onto a sheet of heavy paper or poster board.

3. **Show It** Present your collage to your class. Explain why you chose certain images and what they represent to you. Compare collages with classmates. Discuss similarities and differences.

Big Question Link to Web resources to further explore the Big Question at www.glencoe.com.

Teach

Solo Activity: Personal Reflection

- If students need help completing their webs, have them brainstorm answers to the following questions: *What do I go out of my way to do? What is something I would spend extra time to accomplish? Whom do I especially want to please? Whose opinion do I most value?*
- Remind students to include only information they do not mind sharing with the class. Tell them that they will discuss their collages with classmates.
- Discuss with students how pictures in their collages can be symbols of things that are important to them. Tell them that they can include captions that explain the symbolism of the pictures.
- If students cannot find a picture to represent a particular idea, encourage them to draw it themselves or create it using a computer graphics program.

Assess/Close

Solo Activity

Encourage students to study their webs and write what they learned about themselves and what brings out the best in them. Invite students to share their reflections with the class.

Objectives
- Create a character study
- Organize information graphically

Focus

Vocabulary Preview
List the following words on the board:

- tension
- withstand
- digestive
- contagious
- immune system

Review their definitions before students begin reading.

Build Background
- Cholesterol is a waxy substance that can build up in blood vessels and restrict blood flow. A heart attack occurs when blocked arteries cut off blood to the heart.
- To prevent heart disease, doctors recommend that people control their weight, avoid smoking, eat right, and exercise.

Teach

R Reading Skill
Review Connecting **Ask:** Why might laughter be important for a healthy life? *(Students may say that relieving stress through laughter might make people healthier.)* OL

Readability Scores
Dale-Chall: 5.4
DRP: 65
Lexile: 1130

Your Turn: Read and Apply Skills

TIME

The Giggle Prescription

Laughter is the best medicine

By TRACY EBERHART and ROBERT A. BARNETT

Go ahead, grin. Or better yet, laugh out loud. Laughter is an important part of a healthy life, according to Lee Berk, assistant professor of family medicine at the University of California. R "Just thinking about a silly video you are going to watch

Arni Katz/Index Stock

Additional Support

Literature Focus Lesson

Summary In "The Giggle Prescription," the authors discuss medical studies that reveal how laughter reduces stress and may improve overall health. Studies have documented that laughter can improve circulation, boost the immune system, and reduce the risk of heart attack. For these reasons, some hospitals and nursing homes are incorporating programs that encourage their patients to laugh. The authors recommend that people incorporate humor into their lives.

"The Carcajou and the Kincajou" and "The Termite," two poems by Ogden Nash, create humorous effects through rhyme, meter, and wordplay. OL

...THE DAM IS JUST PHASE ONE. WE'LL BE ADDING A CLUBHOUSE BY THE LAKE AND AN 18-HOLE CHAMPIONSHIP GOLF COURSE!...
3/1 WILLIS & OHMAN
www.comicspage.com
Tribune Media Services

can reduce feelings of tension, anger, and sadness," says Berk.

Berk and other researchers have done studies to confirm that laughing spells keep your body and mind healthy. In fact, Berk says, "Laughter is an instant vacation."

Laughing for a few seconds may give you the same workout as a minute of aerobic exercise by increasing the activity of the heart and stimulating circulation.[1] A good case of the giggles massages not only the heart but also the lungs, muscles, and digestive system. This increased physical activity, coupled with the feel-good mental benefits of having a good laugh, may have lifesaving effects.

According to studies done by doctors at the University of Maryland Medical Center in Baltimore, people with heart disease were 40% less likely to laugh in a variety of situations compared with people of the same age without heart disease. This may mean, researchers say, that laughing can have something to do with helping to keep your heart healthy. Doctors are not sure exactly how laughter helps prevent heart disease, but they do know that mental stress causes physical changes that damage the lining of blood vessels, which can cause them to swell. At these sites of swelling, fat and cholesterol often build up, which can cause heart attacks. And because laughter can reduce mental stress, it may actually protect you against a heart attack!

Laughing prevents disease and eases pain

Part of laughter's benefit is its positive effect on the immune system, which is the system that helps the body fight disease. Laughter helps your body stop the release of a hormone that weakens the immune system. Laughter also boosts your body's production of certain cells and proteins that fight infection and disease.

Hospitals and nursing facilities have learned to utilize[2] another of laughter's great benefits. Doctors have learned that, if a patient is in pain, a good laugh can help. Fits of laughter boost chemicals in the brain

1. ***Stimulating circulation*** is encouraging the movement of blood through the body.

2. To ***utilize*** (YOO tih lyz) is to make use of.

Teach

Viewing the Cartoon

Ask: Why is the beaver's statement humorous? *(Possible responses: The cartoon plays on the idea that beavers are hard workers; the beavers in the strip are building elaborate projects for leisure purposes.)* **AL**

L Literary Element

Review Figurative Language Ask: What do you think Lee Berk means when he says that laughter is "an instant vacation"? *(Possible response: Laughter "takes you away" or gives you a break from your usual activities in that it is both relaxing and entertaining.)* **OL** Why do you think a vacation could be healthful? *(Possible response: It could give you a chance to rest; it could be a break from tension or stress.)* **BL**

Differentiated Instruction

Historical Humor Encourage students to participate in stress reduction by learning more about classic comedians and comedy teams such as Charlie Chaplin, Stan Laurel and Oliver Hardy, or Lucille Ball. Ask students to find information about each comedian's style of humor and have students share a joke or anecdote with the class. **OL** If possible, show brief films or clips from television shows such as *The Ed Sullivan Show* or Sid Caesar's *Your Show of Shows*. Establish a short "laugh medicine" time when students can share something humorous and appropriate with the class. **BL**

Objectives
- Make connections from text to self
- Understand figurative language
- Use text features

Teach

R1 Reading Skill

Review Evaluating Ask: Based on the information you've read, would you include a laughter program if you were an administrator at a hospital? Why or why not? What might prevent you from doing so? *(Possible response: I would institute a laughter program because there is evidence it may help patients heal. Cost may be a factor, but you could probably get volunteers to help.)* **OL**

R2 Reading Skill

Review Connecting Ask: Does laughter ever help you avoid worrying about little problems? *(Responses will vary.)* **BL** Think of people you know who enjoy laughing and sharing funny stories. In what way does laughter have a positive effect on their lives? *(Responses will vary. Students may observe that laughter can bring people together or that it can help them overcome tension.)* **OL**

that control pain. Your ability to withstand pain is raised during laughter and for a short time after you laugh. For this reason, many hospitals use laughter programs, including clowns and other performing artists, as part of their patients' treatment. R1

R2 But maybe kids already know that laughing makes them feel good. Studies show that young people laugh many more times a day than older people. Just try to keep your ability to laugh as you get older. And remember to be silly. It's good for you!

For a long and healthful life, eat right, get plenty of sleep, and laugh as often as you can. Don't just wait for funny things to happen. Plan for humor in your life.

- Watch funny movies (with other people if possible). Laughing is contagious.
- Create a humor journal. Record some of the funny things that happen to you. When you talk about your day with family or friends, find the humorous moments in it.
- Observe young children. They do and say a lot of funny things.
- Collect funny cartoons. Post some around your room.
- Read joke books or funny stories.
- Visit a zoo and watch the monkeys.
- Spend time with people who have a good sense of humor.
- Play charades, using only funny titles.

—Updated 2005, from *Parenting*, May 2003 and Fall 2000

Additional Support

Reading Fluency

Comedy Act Find examples of humorous stories or jokes and distribute them to students. Have students work with partners to read the material and discuss what elements, such as wordplay, make an item funny. Answer any questions that students have about pronunciation or meaning. Demonstrate the importance of timing in comedy by reading aloud a piece such as Abbott and Costello's "Who's on First?" routine. Then provide students with time to practice reading their stories or jokes until they can present them smoothly. Encourage students to vary their delivery, and discuss the effects as a class. **OL**

Meet the Author

Ogden Nash was one of America's best-loved poets. Born in 1902, he produced more than thirty volumes of poems. In the 1950s and 1960s, he began writing poetry for children. Nash said, "The main thing I find in writing for children is to absolutely avoid the tendency to write down to them." See page R6 of the Author Files for more on Ogden Nash.

LiteratureOnline

Author Search For more about Ogden Nash, go to www.glencoe.com.

The Carcajou and the Kincajou

by Ogden Nash

They tell me of a distant zoo
Where a carcajou met a kincajou.
Full soon to savage blows they came
From laughing at each other's name
The agile[1] ajous fought till dark
And carc slew kinc and kinc slew carc,
And beside the conquered kincajou
Lay the carcass[2] of the carcajou. ❍

L

The Termite

by Ogden Nash

Some primal[3] termite knocked on wood
And tasted it, and found it good,
And that is why your Cousin May
Fell through the parlor floor today. ❍

R

1 Something that's ***agile*** (AJ ul) is able to move quickly.
2 A ***carcass*** is a dead body.
3 Here, ***primal*** means "from the earliest time; original."

Teach

L Literary Element

Review Rhyme, Rhythm, and Meter **Ask:** What is the rhyming pattern of "The Carcajou and the Kincajou"? *(The last word in each line is part of a rhyming pair: zoo/kincajou, came/name, dark/carc, kincajou/carcajou.)* **BL**
What is the effect of rhyme on the poem? *(Possible responses: It adds humor to the poem; it ties together each pair of lines.)* **OL** What patterns in meter do you hear? *(alternating unstressed and stressed syllables)* What is the effect of the meter on the poem? *(Possible responses: The meter makes the poem sound like a fairy tale; the words seem to be skipping along.)* **AL**

R Reading Skill

Review Monitoring Comprehension **Ask:** What do termites eat in "The Termite"? *(wood)* **BL** Why does Cousin May fall through the floor? *(The floor has been eaten by termites.)* **OL**

English Language Coach

Humorous Writing Write the following words on the board: savage, slew, conquered, carcass. Discuss with students the literal meaning of the words and ask why these words seem unusual in the context of a silly poem. Explain that humorous writing often involves a contrast between style and content. **EL**

Have students write in the style of Nash's poems by choosing a silly subject and treating it with great importance. Discuss possible topics and titles, giving examples such as "The Battle of the Recycling Bin" or "The Curious Fate of the Algebra Assignment." Ask volunteers to share their poems with the class. **OL** **AL**

Objectives

- Identify and explain the effects of sound devices such as rhyme, rhythm, and meter
- Interpret text
- Connect prior knowledge and experience to characters, themes, and events
- Evaluate text

Tips for Independent Reading

Encourage students to find a quiet place to read where they will be free of outside distractions, such as other people talking, the radio, or the television. Tell students they should also avoid inner distractions, such as worrying about a test or an unresolved issue. Tell students they should allow reading to help them focus their mind on one thing at a time, which is an important life skill.

Fiction

Tell students that reading fiction exposes them to the interests of others, which may inspire them to broaden their views or try new things.

Ask students to share an example of a fictional story they've read that helped explain what made a person or group of people tick. Encourage students to talk about how reading the story has influenced their attitudes or interests.

UNIT 7

Reading on Your Own

To read more about the Big Question, choose one of these books from your school or local library. Work on your reading skills by choosing books that are challenging to you.

Fiction

Come Sing, Jimmy Jo
by Katherine Paterson

This novel tells the story of young James Johnson, who is discovered by a country music agent and thrust into a life on the road with his musical family.

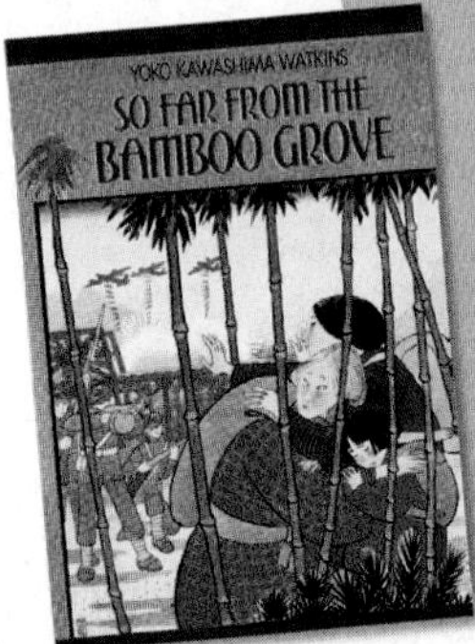

So Far from the Bamboo Grove
by Yoko Kawashima Watkins

In this novel based on the author's experience, Yoko and her family must leave their home in North Korea and go through many hardships to get to Japan.

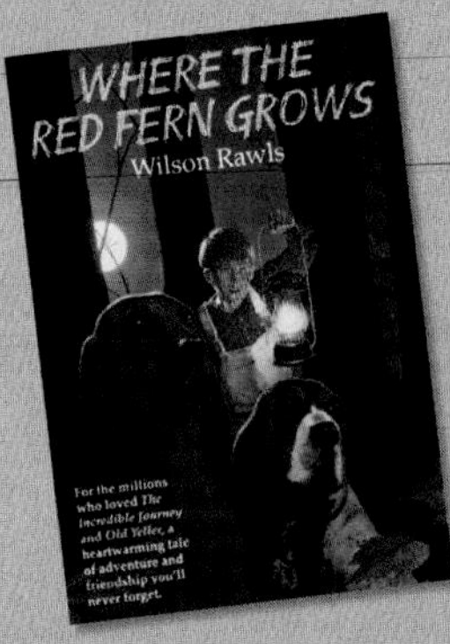

Where the Red Fern Grows
by Wilson Rawls

In this well-loved classic, a yound boy and the pair of hunting dogs he trains learn about hunting and life in the Oklahoma Ozarks. This story has become a favorite among young readers.

Letters from Vinnie
by Maureen Stack Sappéy

Based on a true story, this novel is told through the letters that young Vinnie Ream writes to her friend Regina. Vinnie describes Washington, D.C., during the Civil War; her loyalty to Abraham Lincoln; and her passion for capturing Lincoln's character in sculpture.

Additional Support

Differentiated Instruction

GLENCOE BOOKLINK Use the Glencoe BookLink CD-ROM to create customized reading lists to help students answer the Big Question. Suggestions for Unit 7:

Grade 4: *Alphabet City Ballet* by Erika Tamar
Grade 5: *The Jazz Man* by Mary Hays Weik
Grade 6: *The Horsecatcher* by Mari Sandoz
Grade 7: *Jim Thorpe: 20th-Century Jock* by Robert Lipsyte
Grade 8: *The Longitude Prize* by Joan Dash

Nonfiction

Talkin' About Bessie: The Story of Aviator Elizabeth Coleman
by Nikki Grimes
Illustrated by E. B. Lewis

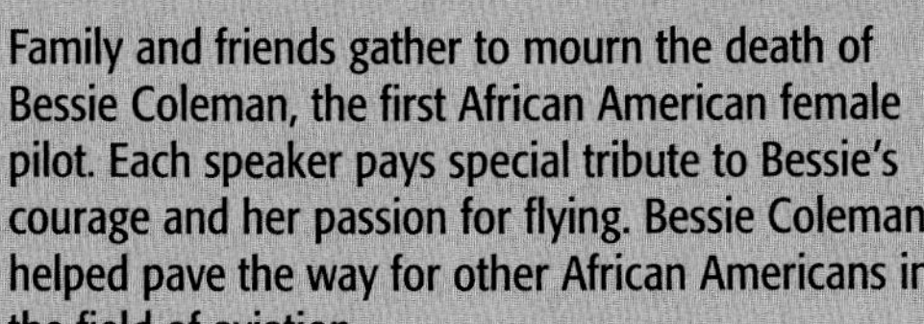

Family and friends gather to mourn the death of Bessie Coleman, the first African American female pilot. Each speaker pays special tribute to Bessie's courage and her passion for flying. Bessie Coleman helped pave the way for other African Americans in the field of aviation.

Vaqueros: America's First Cowmen
by Martin W. Sandler

The author looks at the history of vaqueros, or Hispanic cowmen, and their influence on cowboy folklore. The book retells legends of the vaqueros, including their courage, loyalty, and heroism, and what makes the vaqueros tick.

Guts: The True Stories Behind *Hatchet* and the Brian Books
by Gary Paulsen

In a collection of wilderness survival and hunting essays, Paulsen compares his own life to the fictional adventures of Brian Robeson in *Hatchet* and its sequels.

Andy Warhol, Prince of Pop
by Jan Greenberg and Sandra Jordan

The authors describe how Warhol, the man who said everyone would have 15 minutes of fame, made his art. Warhol took everyday images like soup cans and elevated them to art. He became the symbol of the 1960s American art movement known as Pop.

READING ON YOUR OWN

Nonfiction

Tell students that all of the books on this page are works of nonfiction. Remind them that such books give factual information about people and events.

Life Stories

Tell students that writers may choose to tell a person's life story in a number of ways. If the subject is still alive, writers may conduct an interview with him or her. Writers may also choose to contact family members and friends of the subject. In other cases, writers may read other books or articles about the person and combine information from different sources. Encourage students to consider how the author of each book might have researched his or her subject.

About the Subjects

Invite students to share what they know about the subjects on this page. Students who liked Nikki Grimes's style in "Diondra Jordan" might enjoy reading *Talkin' About Bessie,* which tells the story of the first African American female pilot, Bessie Coleman. Students interested in learning about cowboys might like *Vaqueros,* which provides information about Hispanic cowhands and their impact on folklore. Fans of Gary Paulsen's fiction can learn about his real life in *Guts: The True Stories Behind* Hatchet *and the Brian Books.* Art fans might want to read about pop art in *Andy Warhol, Prince of Pop*.

Test-Taking Tips

TIP Point out that students can use the process of elimination to guess the answer to difficult multiple-choice questions. Have students read the question, and then read each possible answer to see if it could be correct. Tell students to eliminate any answers that are obviously incorrect. If students are left with two possible choices, tell them to make an educated guess.

TIP Tell students they should read the poem, read the questions, and then read the poem again before they answer the questions. Because poems are generally shorter than prose pieces, they should have time to read a poem several times during a test. Each time, they will likely see a new element they did not notice before.

Test Practice

Part 1: Literary Elements

1. A

2. C

Resources for pages 870–875

Use these resources to review, assess, or reteach the Unit: Active Learning and Note-Taking Guide, Selection and Unit Assessment, ExamView Assessment Suite, and Differentiated Instruction Tool Software.

Test Practice

Part 1: Literary Elements

Read the first poem. On a separate sheet of paper, write the numbers 1–7. Next to numbers 1 and 2, write the letter of the correct answer.

The Eagle

by Alfred Lord Tennyson

He clasps the crag with crooked hands;
Close to the sun in lonely lands,
Ringed with the azure[1] world, he stands.

The wrinkled sea beneath him crawls;
He watches from his mountain walls,
And like a thunderbolt[2] he falls.

1. sky blue
2. a single flash of lightning with its accompanying thunder

1. Which of the following lines contains alliteration?
- **A.** 1
- **B.** 3
- **C.** 4
- **D.** 6

2. The main way in which the eagle is "like a thunderbolt" is in
- **A.** its beauty
- **B.** the noise it makes
- **C.** the speed of its fall
- **D.** the shape of its fall

Read the following poem. On your paper, write the letter of each correct answer for questions 3–6. Next to number seven, write your answer to the final question.

Objectives (pp. 870–871)
Literature Identify literary devices: symbolism, sound, rhythm, metaphor

Your World

by Georgia Douglas Johnson

Your world is as big as you make it.
I know, for I used to abide[1]
In the narrowest nest in a corner,
My wings pressing close to my side.

But I sighted the distant horizon
Where the sky line encircled the sea
And I throbbed with a burning desire
To travel this immensity.[2]

I battered the cordons[3] around me
And cradled my wings on the breeze
Then soared to the uttermost reaches
With rapture,[4] with power, with ease!

1. Here, *abide* means either "live" or "remain."
2. Anything huge, in size or distance, is an *immensity.*
3. *Cordons* are barriers or, sometimes, guards that prevent getting into or out of an area.
4. *Rapture* is intense joy.

---

3. Which of the following lines of the poem rhyme?

A. 1 and 3
B. 2 and 4
C. 5 and 6
D. 9 and 11

4. Which pair of words from the poem provides an example of assonance?

A. *I, abide*
B. *wings, side*
C. *encircled, sea*
D. *cradled, breeze*

5. What does the nest seem to symbolize in this poem?

A. a small world with no room for growth
B. a danger from which the speaker must escape
C. a childhood home to which the speaker longs to return
D. the controls that are put on the young to keep them safe

6. Think about which words in the last two lines are emphasized by the meter. This use of rhythm helps to communicate the idea that

A. anything is possible
B. life is full of surprises
C. we must not give up when life is hard
D. small changes should come before large ones

7. To what is the speaker compared throughout this poem? Do you think this metaphor is effective? Explain.

Unit Assessment To prepare for the Unit test, go to www.glencoe.com.

Test-Taking Tip

TIP Advise students to note, when reading poetry, any words or images that stand out. A poet may use these words as signals to draw the reader's attention to the meaning or message of a poem. If students are allowed to write on test selections, tell them to consider underlining significant words or images as they read.

Test Practice

Part 1: Literary Elements *(continued)*

3. B
4. A
5. A
6. A
7. The speaker is compared to a bird. Students' responses about the effectiveness of the metaphor will vary. Some students may feel it is very effective because it shows the vast difference between being in a tiny world in the corner of a nest and being able to fly around the whole world.

Literature Online

Unit Assessment Have students access the Web site to prepare for the Unit 7 test.

Test-Taking Tip

TIP Point out that if students cannot answer one or more of the questions, they should proceed with the rest of the test. They can return to more difficult questions when they have completed all of the questions that they can answer easily.

Part 2: Reading Skills

Read the poems. Then, on a separate sheet of paper, write the numbers 1–4. For the first three questions, write the letter of the right answer next to the number for that question. Then, next to number four, write your answer to the final question.

Primer Lesson

by Carl Sandburg

Look out how you use proud words.
When you let proud words go, it is
not easy to call them back.
They wear long boots, hard boots; they
walk off proud; they can't hear you
calling—
Look out how you use proud words.

Flint

by Christina Rossetti

An emerald is as green as grass;
A ruby red as blood;
A sapphire shines as blue as heaven;
A flint[1] lies in the mud.

A diamond is a brilliant stone,
To catch the world's desire;
An opal holds a fiery spark;
But a flint holds fire.

1. A *flint* is a stone that produces a spark when struck by steel.

Objectives
Reading Evaluate text • Interpret text • Make connections from text to self

1. Which of the following might be said by someone who is making connections while reading "Primer Lesson"?
   A. "I remember when I regretted a remark."
   B. "I wonder why Sandburg didn't use rhyme."
   C. "This is an interesting way of giving a warning."
   D. "This poem gives human traits to proud words."

2. The speaker of "Primer Lesson" describes proud words as wearing "hard boots" to suggest that such words
   A. have practical uses
   B. can hurt other people
   C. are heavy and awkward
   D. protect the person who says them

3. What does "Primer Lesson" offer as the main reason that you should "look out how you use proud words"?
   A. People do not understand them.
   B. They reach people's ears quickly.
   C. It's difficult to use them correctly.
   D. Once said, they can't be taken back.

4. The words of "Flint" describe jewels and flint. Interpreting those words and how they are used in the poem suggests that jewels and flint represent
   A. wealth and poverty
   B. nature and technology
   C. imagination and reality
   D. beauty and inner qualities

5. What is the most reasonable interpretation of the last line of "Flint"?
   A. Flint can be dangerous.
   B. Flint can do only ordinary things.
   C. Flint has a value not found in other stones.
   D. The ability to do something is less important than actually doing it.

6. Choose one of the two poems to evaluate. That is, tell whether you think the poem is good and explain your reasoning.

UNIT 7 ASSESSMENT

Test Practice

Part 2: Reading Skills

1. A
2. B
3. D
4. D
5. C
6. Responses will vary. Students should use specific details from the poem to evaluate it.

Test Practice

Part 3: Vocabulary Skills and Acquisition

1. C
2. A
3. C
4. B
5. D
6. C
7. A
8. B
9. D
10. C

Part 3: Vocabulary Skills and Acquisition

On a separate sheet of paper, write the numbers 1–10. Next to each number, write the letter of the right answer for that question.

For questions 1–5 write the letter of the word or phrase that means about the same as the underlined word.

1. if roads <u>merge</u>

A. end **B.** need repair **C.** come together **D.** become dangerous

2. her <u>initial</u> comment

A. first **B.** quiet **C.** shortened **D.** most important

3. to express his <u>identity</u>

A. ability **B.** feelings **C.** individuality **D.** hopes and goals

4. to be <u>virtually</u> impossible

A. totally **B.** practically **C.** proven to be **D.** the opposite of

5. to <u>master</u> long division

A. teach **B.** enjoy **C.** begin to learn **D.** become skilled in

6. The Greek prefix *hyper-* means "overly, too much." What is a synonym for <u>hypersensitive</u>?

A. kind **B.** cruel **C.** touchy **D.** difficult

7. The Latin root *ject* means "to throw," and the prefix *pro-* means "forward." Who would need to <u>project</u> (pro JEKT) his or her voice?

A. a singer on stage **B.** a person with a secret **C.** a tourist in a foreign country **D.** someone who has a sore throat

8. The Greek root *path* means "feeling," and the prefix *a-* means "without." What would someone do to show <u>apathy</u>?

A. nod **B.** shrug **C.** frown **D.** applaud

9. The Greek root *phon* means "sound." What would the <u>phonetic</u> spelling of "pharmacy" be?

A. phar **B.** frmcy **C.** pharmacy **D.** farmuhsee

10. The Anglo-Saxon root *flot* means "to hold up by air or water." Which of the following is used for <u>flotation</u>?

A. a rocket **B.** a television **C.** a life preserver **D.** a sink or bathtub

Objectives
Vocabulary Use structural analysis • Use context clues

Part 4: Writing Skills

Read each sentence, and decide which forms of the verbs in parentheses are correct. On a separate sheet of paper, write the numbers 1–8. Next to each number, write the letter of the correct verb forms for that sentence.

1. The news (is, are) bad today, as everyone who (reads, read) the paper can tell.

A. is, reads **C.** are, reads
B. is, read **D.** are, read

2. Both of my aunts or my cousin Nita (comes, come) by every day, and no one (is, are) happier about that than I am.

A. comes, is **C.** come, is
B. comes, are **D.** come, are

3. How (does, do) Chip and Rocky feel when guests from out of town (shows, show) up?

A. does, shows **C.** do, shows
B. does, show **D.** do, show

4. He and she (is, are) sure that one of our team's fastest runners (is, are) going to win the track meet today.

A. is, is **C.** are, is
B. is, are **D.** are, are

5. Outside the walls (was, were) a forest, but only one of the trees (was, were) big enough to use for lumber.

A. was, was **C.** were, was
B. was, were **D.** were, were

6. (Has, Have) you ever noticed that the most colorful birds in the jungle (is, are) as beautiful as jewels?

A. Has, is **C.** Have, is
B. Has, are **D.** Have, are

7. There (goes, go) my best friend, and here (is, are) the books she left for me.

A. goes, is **C.** go, is
B. goes, are **D.** go, are

8. The owner of those five dogs (is, are) always busy walking them, but he (don't, doesn't) seem to mind.

A. is, don't **C.** are, don't
B. is, doesn't **D.** are, doesn't

Objectives
Grammar Use correct subject-verb agreement

Test Practice

Part 4: Writing Skills

1. A
2. Accept A or C
3. D
4. C
5. A
6. D
7. B
8. B

TIP Encourage students to use any remaining time they have for completing a test to review their answers. Tell them to make sure that each answer is marked clearly and that all written responses are legible.

UNIT 8

Skills Scope and Sequence

Readability Scores Key
Dale-Chall/DRP/Lexile

PACING (DAYS) STANDARD	BLOCK	INSTRUCTIONAL SEGMENT LITERATURE	READING SKILLS	LITERARY ELEMENTS
1	1	**Unit Warm-Up, pp. 878–883** Genre Focus: It Was Not My Finest Hour" by Linda Meyers Donelson **5.2/57/850**, SE p. 881	Visualizing, SE p. 880 Skimming and Scanning, SE p. 880 Clarifying, SE p. 880 Predicting, SE p. 880 Fluency, TWE p. 877	Imagery, SE p. 880 Organization, SE p. 880 Figurative language, SE p. 880 Teleplay, SE p. 880 Imagery, TWE p. 880 Author's Purpose, TWE p. 882
3	2	**Reading Workshop 1, pp. 884–907** "Kingdoms of Gold and Salt" Collected by Basil Davidson **5.3/57/1010**, SE p. 886 "Antaeus" by Borden Deal **5.1/52/1000**, SE p. 892	Visualizing, SE pp. 884–885, 887, 888, 891, 893, 894, 896, 898, 900, 907 Inferring, SE pp. 897, 900, 903, 907 Fluency, TWE p. 893	Imagery, SE pp. 887, 889, 891, 893, 895, 899, 901, 902, 905, 907 Nonfiction, TWE p. 886 Narrator, TWE p. 892 Plot, TWE p. 895 Sensory Imagery, TWE p. 899 Short Story, TWE p. 903
1		**Writing Workshop, Part 1, pp. 908–911** Writing Product: A Word Picture	Fluency, TWE p. 911	Word picture, SE pp. 908–909 Combining Sensory Details, TWE p. 910
3	1	**Reading Workshop 2, pp. 912–929** Getting There, SE p. 914 "Letters from Home" by Graeme Davis **4.8/63/1070**, SE p. 920	Skimming and Scanning, SE pp. 912–913, 915, 917, 919, 921, 922, 924, 925, 929 Fluency, TWE p. 925	Organization, SE pp. 915, 917, 918, 921, 924, 929 Author's Purpose, TWE p. 916 Informational Text, TWE p. 920 Drama, TWE p. 926
3	1	**Reading Workshop 3, pp. 930–947** "Ah, Wilderness!" by Amanda Hinnant, updated from *Real Simple* **7.1/61/1190**, SE p. 932 Photographing History **4.6/56/770**, SE p. 940	Clarifying, SE pp. 930-931, 933, 935, 939, 941, 942, 945, 947 Fluency, TWE p. 934	Figurative Language, SE pp. 933, 936, 939, 941, 943, 944, 947 Internet Information, TWE p. 940

Unit 8 Big Question

The question, **"What is a community?"** is designed to help students think critically about what defines a community, how a community helps define themselves, and how they in turn help define the community. In this unit, students will learn about communities from different times and places around the world.

Unit 8 Genre

Many of the stories in this unit are historical documents, which include a wide range of written materials from nonfiction articles to journal entries. These selections will also help students answer the big question: What is a community? Use these historical documents to help students understand the wide variety of communities in their world.

CRITICAL THINKING	VOCABULARY	WRITING AND GRAMMAR	LISTENING, SPEAKING, AND VIEWING
	Identifying and Understanding Compound words, TWE p. 881		Group Discussion, SE p. 878 Viewing the Photo, TWE p. 876
Infer, SE pp. 890, 906 Evaluate, SE pp. 890, 906 Comprehension, TWE p. 895 Analysis, TWE p. 896	Compound words, SE pp. 886, 889, 891, 892, 895, 898, TWE pp. 886, 892, 898 Dialect and Regionalism, TWE p. 896 Word Parts, TWE p. 901 Historical Influences, TWE p. 902 Adjectives, TWE p. 905	Write to Learn, SE pp. 887, 892 Write About Your Reading, SE p. 890 Hyphens, SE pp. 891, 907	Partner Talk, SE pp. 886, 893 Viewing the Art, TWE pp. 888, 898 Viewing the Photo, TWE pp. 889, 894, 896, 897
Evaluate, TWE p. 909	Describing the Topic, TWE p. 908	Descriptive Writing: A Word Picture—prewriting and drafting, SE pp. 908–911 Purpose, SE p. 909 Organization, SE p. 909 Sentence Fluency, SE p. 910 Apostrophes, SE p. 911	
Infer, SE pp. 918, 928 Evaluate, SE pp. 918, 928, TWE pp. 923, 927 Use Text Features, SE p. 928 Analysis, TWE p. 925 Synthesis, TWE p. 927	Acronyms and Abbreviations, SE pp. 914, 916, 919, 920, 923, 929, TWE pp. 914, 923 ELC: Skim, Scan, or Study, TWE p. 912 ELC: Primary Sources, TWE p. 923 Compound Words, TWE p. 926 Plurals, TWE p. 925	Write About Your Reading, SE pp. 918, 928 Colons, SE pp. 919, 929 On Your Own: Writing Acronyms and Abbreviations, SE p. 920 Make a List, SE p. 921	Partner Talk, SE pp. 914, 915, 921 Viewing the Graphic Art, TWE pp. 916, 917 Viewing the Art, TWE pp. 922, 923, 924, 925 Viewing the Photo, TWE p. 926
Analyze, SE pp. 938, 946, TWE p. 945 Evaluate, SE p. 946, TWE pp. 936, 943 Synthesis, TWE p. 936	Borrowed Words, SE pp. 932, 934, 947, TWE p. 930 Historical Influences on English, SE pp. 940, 942, TWE pp. 942, 945 Figurative Language, TWE p. 933 Compound Words, TWE p. 935	Write to Learn, SE p. 933 Write About Your Reading, SE pp. 938, 946 Semicolons, SE pp. 939, 947	Partner Talk, SE pp. 932, 933, 940, 941 Viewing the Photo, TWE pp. 935, 936, 937, 942, 944 Viewing the Art, TWE p. 943

Skills Scope and Sequence *continued*

Readability Scores Key
Dale-Chall/DRP/Lexile

PACING (DAYS) STANDARD	BLOCK	INSTRUCTIONAL SEGMENT LITERATURE	READING SKILLS	LITERARY ELEMENTS
1	cont'd. ↓	**Writing Workshop, Part 2, pp. 948–951** Writing Product: A Word Picture	Fluency, TWE p. 951	Descriptive Images, TWE p. 949
2	1	**Reading Workshop 4, pp. 952–981** The Monsters Are Due On Maple Street by Rod Serling: Act I SE p. 954 The Monsters Are Due On Maple Street by Rod Serling: Act II SE p. 969	Predicting, SE pp. 952–953, 955, 957, 960, 963, 964, 966, 968, 969, 971, 973, 974, 976, 981 Drawing Conclusions, SE p. 961 Inferring, SE pp. 976, 981 Fluency, TWE pp. 956, 963, 978	Teleplay, SE pp. 955, 956, 959, 962, 963, 964, 965, 968, 969, 970, 972, 977, 981, TWE pp. 952, 969 Science Fiction, TWE p. 961 Creating Suspense, TWE p. 962 Protagonist and Antagonist, TWE p. 972 Dramatic Action, TWE p. 974 Element of Drama, TWE p. 975
2	2	**Reading Across Texts Workshop, pp. 982-995** Teacher Hero: Erin Gruwell by Jerrilyn Jacobs **5.4/64/1070**, SE p. 984 from *Zlata's Diary* by Zlata Filipovic **5.1/49/680**, SE p. 988	How to Read Across Texts, SE pp. 982-983, 986, 987, 989, 990, 992 Predicting, SE p. 985 Understanding Cause and Effect, SE p. 986 Visualizing, SE p. 991 Fluency, TWE p. 993	Imagery, SE p. 990 Visualizing, SE p. 991 Organization, SE p. 993 Text Structure, TWE p. 982 Journal Entry, TWE p. 988 Narrative, TWE p. 992
2	1	**Unit Wrap-Up, pp. 996–1007** There Is No Word for Goodbye by Mary TallMountain SE p. 998	Reading independently, SE pp. 998–999 Assessment, SE pp. 1003-1004	Assessment, SE p. 1002 Summary, TWE p. 998 Fiction, TWE p. 1000 Nonfiction, TWE p. 1001

CRITICAL THINKING	VOCABULARY	WRITING AND GRAMMAR	LISTENING, SPEAKING, AND VIEWING
Comparing, TWE p. 950 Analyze, TWE p. 951		Descriptive Writing: a Word Picture Revising, Editing, and Presenting, SE pp. 948–949 Writing Tip: Using Technology, SE p. 949 Writing Tip: Spelling, SE p. 949 Active Writing Model, SE p. 950	Visuals, SE p. 951
Infer, SE pp. 968, 980 Interpret, SE p. 980 Analyze, SE pp. 971, 977, 980 Evaluation, TWE pp. 957, 965, 967 Comprehension, TWE pp. 963, 967 Synthesis, TWE p. 972	English as a Changing Language, SE pp. 954, 958, 959, 968, 969, 970, 978, 981, TWE pp. 955, 958, 959, 964, 966, 971 Vocabulary Preview, SE pp. 954, 969 Vocabulary Check, SE pp. 968, 981 Multiple-Meaning Words, TWE pp. 960, 979 Word Origins, TWE p. 965 Figurative Language, TWE p. 972	Write to Learn, SE pp. 954, 955, 980 On Your Own: Chart, SE p. 954 Write About Your Reading, SE p. 968 Quotation Marks, SE p. 981	Partner Talk, SE p. 955 Class Discussion, SE p. 969 Talk About Your Reading, SE p. 980 Viewing the Art, TWE pp. 958, 975 Viewing the Photo, TWE p. 962
Interpret, SE p. 995 Infer, SE p. 995 Evaluate, SE p. 995, TWE p. 986 Analyze, TWE p. 986, 991	Academic Vocabulary, SE pp. 982, 994 Historical Influences on English, SE pp. 984, 986, 988, 992, 994, TWE pp. 983, 984, 992 Vocabulary Preview, SE pp. 984, 988 Vocabulary Check, SE p. 994 Connotation, TWE p. 985 Borrowed Words, TWE p. 990	Comparison chart, SE p. 983 Write About Your Reading, SE p. 995	Viewing the Photo, TWE pp. 985, 989, 991
	Assessment, SE p. 1005	Writing a Community Newsletter, SE p. 997 Assessment, SE pp. 1006–1007	Community Mural, SE p. 996 Viewing the Photo, TWE p. 999

UNIT 8

Unit Resources

Reading with Purpose offers a comprehensive package of tools to optimize student learning and the teaching experience. Each resource has been designed to assist students in specific areas and to offer instructional support for teachers. While all of these areas are covered in the core textbook, some students may need extra practice or additional help in specific areas. The resource package is designed so that you, the teacher, can choose which items will best assist your students. You may also use these resources as homework assignments and for assessment purposes. The following are resources recommended for use with Unit 8.

Keys for Unit Resources

- Blackline Master
- Workbook
- Supplemental Text
- CD-ROM
- DVD
- Transparency
- Web-based
- Fast Files

Essential Instructional Support

FAST FILE UNIT 8 RESOURCES

Reading and Literature

- Academic Vocabulary Development
- Big Question: School to Home Connection
- The Big Question Foldable
- Genre Study
- Unit Challenge: Planner and Rubrics
- Comparing Literature Graphic Organizer
- Key Reading Skills Practice
- Active Reading Graphic Organizers
- Literary Analysis
- Selection Vocabulary Development

Writing, Grammar, and Spelling

- Spelling and Handwriting Practice
- Grammar Practice
- Writing Workshop Graphic Organizer

Listening, Speaking, and Viewing

- Viewing and Representing Activities
- Listening and Speaking Activities

English Language Learners

- English Language Coach

DIFFERENTIATED INSTRUCTION

- Leveled Vocabulary Development
- Skills Level Up!
- Listening Library CD
- BookLink 3
- Literature Library Vocabulary Puzzlemaker
- Vocabulary Puzzlemaker

ASSESSMENT

- Selection and Unit Assessments
- Selection Quick Checks
- Assessment by Learning Objectives
- Rubrics for Assessing Student Writing, Listening, and Speaking
- Glencoe Online Essay Grading
- Interactive Tutor Self-Assessment
- ExamView Assessment Suite
- Literature Library ExamView Assessment Suite

UNIT 8

Unit Resources

Reading with Purpose offers a comprehensive package of tools to optimize student learning and the teaching experience. Each resource has been designed to assist students in specific areas and to offer instructional support for teachers. While all of these areas are covered in the core textbook, some students may need extra practice or additional help in specific areas. The resource package is designed so that you, the teacher, can choose which items will best assist your students. You may also use these resources as homework assignments and for assessment purposes. The following are resources recommended for use with Unit 8.

Keys for Unit Resources

- Blackline Master
- Workbook
- Supplemental Text
- CD-ROM
- DVD
- Transparency
- Web-based
- Fast Files

Essential Instructional Support

FAST FILE UNIT 8 RESOURCES

Reading and Literature

- Academic Vocabulary Development
- Big Question: School to Home Connection
- The Big Question Foldable
- Genre Study
- Unit Challenge: Planner and Rubrics
- Comparing Literature Graphic Organizer
- Key Reading Skills Practice
- Active Reading Graphic Organizers
- Literary Analysis
- Selection Vocabulary Development

Writing, Grammar, and Spelling

- Spelling and Handwriting Practice
- Grammar Practice
- Writing Workshop Graphic Organizer

Listening, Speaking, and Viewing

- Viewing and Representing Activities
- Listening and Speaking Activities

English Language Learners

- English Language Coach

DIFFERENTIATED INSTRUCTION

- Leveled Vocabulary Development
- Skills Level Up!
- Listening Library CD
- BookLink 3
- Literature Library Vocabulary Puzzlemaker
- Vocabulary Puzzlemaker

ASSESSMENT

- Selection and Unit Assessments
- Selection Quick Checks
- Assessment by Learning Objectives
- Rubrics for Assessing Student Writing, Listening, and Speaking
- Glencoe Online Essay Grading
- Interactive Tutor Self-Assessment
- ExamView Assessment Suite
- Literature Library ExamView Assessment Suite

CRITICAL THINKING	VOCABULARY	WRITING AND GRAMMAR	LISTENING, SPEAKING, AND VIEWING
Comparing, TWE p. 950 Analyze, TWE p. 951		Descriptive Writing: a Word Picture Revising, Editing, and Presenting, SE pp. 948–949 Writing Tip: Using Technology, SE p. 949 Writing Tip: Spelling, SE p. 949 Active Writing Model, SE p. 950	Visuals, SE p. 951
Infer, SE pp. 968, 980 Interpret, SE p. 980 Analyze, SE pp. 971, 977, 980 Evaluation, TWE pp. 957, 965, 967 Comprehension, TWE pp. 963, 967 Synthesis, TWE p. 972	English as a Changing Language, SE pp. 954, 958, 959, 968, 969, 970, 978, 981, TWE pp. 955, 958, 959, 964, 966, 971 Vocabulary Preview, SE pp. 954, 969 Vocabulary Check, SE pp. 968, 981 Multiple-Meaning Words, TWE pp. 960, 979 Word Origins, TWE p. 965 Figurative Language, TWE p. 972	Write to Learn, SE pp. 954, 955, 980 On Your Own: Chart, SE p. 954 Write About Your Reading, SE p. 968 Quotation Marks, SE p. 981	Partner Talk, SE p. 955 Class Discussion, SE p. 969 Talk About Your Reading, SE p. 980 Viewing the Art, TWE pp. 958, 975 Viewing the Photo, TWE p. 962
Interpret, SE p. 995 Infer, SE p. 995 Evaluate, SE p. 995, TWE p. 986 Analyze, TWE p. 986, 991	Academic Vocabulary, SE pp. 982, 994 Historical Influences on English, SE pp. 984, 986, 988, 992, 994, TWE pp. 983, 984, 992 Vocabulary Preview, SE pp. 984, 988 Vocabulary Check, SE p. 994 Connotation, TWE p. 985 Borrowed Words, TWE p. 990	Comparison chart, SE p. 983 Write About Your Reading, SE p. 995	Viewing the Photo, TWE pp. 985, 989, 991
	Assessment, SE p. 1005	Writing a Community Newsletter, SE p. 997 Assessment, SE pp. 1006–1007	Community Mural, SE p. 996 Viewing the Photo, TWE p. 999

Additional Instructional Support

WRITING, GRAMMAR, AND SPELLING

- Real Success in Writing: Research and Reports
- Writing Constructed Responses Sourcebook
- Spelling Power eWorkbook
- Grammar & Composition Handbook
- Grammar and Language Workbook
- Revising with Style eWorkbook

READING AND LITERATURE

- Active Learning and Note Taking Guide
- inTime Magazines
- Backpack Reader Volume 1
- Literature Library
- Literature Launchers Pre-Reading Videos DVD
- Literature Classics

TRANSPARENCIES

- Read Aloud, Think Aloud
- Literary and Text Analysis Transparencies
- Bellringer Options Transparencies
- Grammar and Writing Workshop Transparencies
- Fine Arts Transparencies

ENGLISH LANGUAGE LEARNER

- English Language Coach
- Fluency Practice and Assessment
- inTime Magazines (Spanish)
- Spanish Listening Library CD

PROFESSIONAL DEVELOPMENT

- Professional Development Package

TECHNOLOGY

- TeacherWorks Plus
- StudentWorks Plus
- BookLink 3
- Skill Level Up!
- ExamView Assessment Suite
- Interactive Tutor Self-Assessment
- Listening Library CD
- Spanish Listening Library CD
- Literature Classics
- Literature Launchers Pre-Reading Videos DVD
- Literature Library ExamView Assessment Suite
- Vocabulary Puzzlemaker
- Literature Library Vocabulary Puzzlemaker
- glencoe.com
- Online Student Edition
- Presentation Plus!
- Glencoe Online Essay Grading

Additional Glencoe Resources

FOLDABLES™ Study Organizer — Dinah Zike's Foldables

Foldables are three-dimensional, interactive graphic organizers that help students practice basic writing skills, review key vocabulary terms, and answer Big Questions. Every unit contains a foldable activity. You can find the pattern and directions for the Unit 8 Foldable in the Unit 8 Resources Fast Files booklet. You can use the foldables as they are presented or modify them to suit the needs of your students. More information about foldables for Unit 8 can be found on page R8.

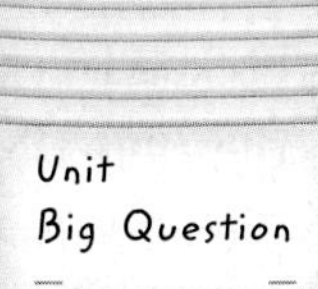

Glencoe Literature Library

The collection of hardcover books include full-length novels, novellas, plays and works of nonfiction. Each volume consists of at least one complete extended-length reading accompanied by several related readings from a broad range of genres. A separate Study Guide for each Glencoe Literature Library book provides teaching notes and reproducible activity pages for students.

Glencoe Literature Library titles that complement this unit include:

Across Five Aprils by Irene Hunt
Blizzard! by Jim Murphy
Flight #116 Is Down by Caroline Cooney

Literature Online

For a wealth of online resources that support the instruction in Unit 8 of *Glencoe Literature: Reading with Purpose,* students and teachers can visit our Web site at www.glencoe.com. Students will find additional learning, practice, and assessment opportunities such as these, which are noted in the student text:

- **Big Question Overview**
- **Study Central**
- **Author Search**
- **Writing Models**
- **Interactive Literary Elements Handbook**
- **Web Activities**

Teachers will find planning and instructional tools that include the following:

- **Book Lesson Plans**
- **Teacher Forum**
- **Professional Development**
- **Web Activities Lesson Plans (with answers to student activities)**

Go to www.glencoe.com to see the entire selection of Reading with Purpose online resources.

GLENCOE BOOKLINK

Use the Glencoe BookLink 3 CD-ROM, a database of more than 26,700 titles, to *create customized reading lists* for your students.

- Search for award-winning titles, (e.g., Newbery Award winners, Coretta Scott King Award winners, and Caldecott Medal winners) and for books on several state-recommended reading lists.
- Find Degrees of Reading Power™ (DRP) and Lexile™ readability scores for all selections.
- Organize reading lists by students' reading level, author, genre, theme, or area of interest.
- Get a brief summary of each selection.

You can find recommended leveled readings for this unit with Reading on Your Own (see page 120).

Glencoe's **Presentation Plus!**, a multimedia teaching tool, lets you present dynamic lessons that will engage your students. Using Microsoft PowerPoint,® you can customize the presentations to create your own personalized lessons. Use **CheckPoint** questions with interactive response keypads to get immediate student feedback during lessons, to increase student participation, and to assess student comprehension.

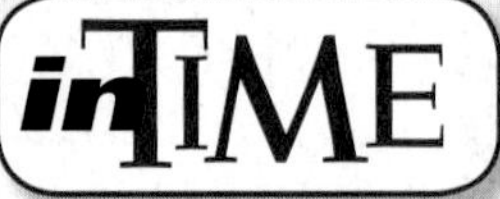

A lively collection of articles drawn from issues of the TIME family of magazines helps students develop the skills they need to interact with informational text in a meaningful way. Each of the news stories, feature articles, reviews, profiles, and essays in the magazine connect to an author, work, or theme in *Glencoe Literature: Reading with Purpose.* Articles for Unit 8 are found in Volume A. See the *inTIME* Teacher's Guide for specific connections to each unit and for reproducible student worksheets designed to develop students' reading and critical thinking skills.

Additional Glencoe Resources

FOLDABLES™ Study Organizer — Dinah Zike's Foldables

Foldables are three-dimensional, interactive graphic organizers that help students practice basic writing skills, review key vocabulary terms, and answer Big Questions. Every unit contains a foldable activity. You can find the pattern and directions for the Unit 8 Foldable in the Unit 8 Resources Fast Files booklet. You can use the foldables as they are presented or modify them to suit the needs of your students. More information about foldables for Unit 8 can be found on page R8.

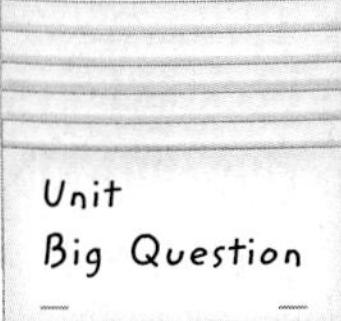

Glencoe Literature Library

The collection of hardcover books include full-length novels, novellas, plays and works of nonfiction. Each volume consists of at least one complete extended-length reading accompanied by several related readings from a broad range of genres. A separate Study Guide for each Glencoe Literature Library book provides teaching notes and reproducible activity pages for students.

Glencoe Literature Library titles that complement this unit include:

Across Five Aprils by Irene Hunt
Blizzard! by Jim Murphy
Flight #116 Is Down by Caroline Cooney

Literature Online

For a wealth of online resources that support the instruction in Unit 8 of *Glencoe Literature: Reading with Purpose,* students and teachers can visit our Web site at www.glencoe.com. Students will find additional learning, practice, and assessment opportunities such as these, which are noted in the student text:

- **Big Question Overview**
- **Study Central**
- **Author Search**
- **Writing Models**
- **Interactive Literary Elements Handbook**
- **Web Activities**

Teachers will find planning and instructional tools that include the following:

- **Book Lesson Plans**
- **Teacher Forum**
- **Professional Development**
- **Web Activities Lesson Plans (with answers to student activities)**

Go to www.glencoe.com to see the entire selection of Reading with Purpose online resources.

Glencoe BookLink

Use the Glencoe BookLink 3 CD-ROM, a database of more than 26,700 titles, to *create customized reading lists* for your students.

- Search for award-winning titles, (e.g., Newbery Award winners, Coretta Scott King Award winners, and Caldecott Medal winners) and for books on several state-recommended reading lists.
- Find Degrees of Reading Power™ (DRP) and Lexile™ readability scores for all selections.
- Organize reading lists by students' reading level, author, genre, theme, or area of interest.
- Get a brief summary of each selection.

You can find recommended leveled readings for this unit with Reading on Your Own (see page 120).

Presentation Plus! / CheckPoint

Glencoe's **Presentation Plus!**, a multimedia teaching tool, lets you present dynamic lessons that will engage your students. Using Microsoft PowerPoint,® you can customize the presentations to create your own personalized lessons. Use **CheckPoint** questions with interactive response keypads to get immediate student feedback during lessons, to increase student participation, and to assess student comprehension.

inTIME

A lively collection of articles drawn from issues of the TIME family of magazines helps students develop the skills they need to interact with informational text in a meaningful way. Each of the news stories, feature articles, reviews, profiles, and essays in the magazine connect to an author, work, or theme in *Glencoe Literature: Reading with Purpose.* Articles for Unit 8 are found in Volume A. See the *inTIME* Teacher's Guide for specific connections to each unit and for reproducible student worksheets designed to develop students' reading and critical thinking skills.

Additional Instructional Support

WRITING, GRAMMAR, AND SPELLING

- Real Success in Writing: Research and Reports
- Writing Constructed Responses Sourcebook
- Spelling Power eWorkbook
- Grammar & Composition Handbook
- Grammar and Language Workbook
- Revising with Style eWorkbook

READING AND LITERATURE

- Active Learning and Note Taking Guide
- inTime Magazines
- Backpack Reader Volume 1
- Literature Library
- Literature Launchers Pre-Reading Videos DVD
- Literature Classics

TRANSPARENCIES

- Read Aloud, Think Aloud
- Literary and Text Analysis Transparencies
- Bellringer Options Transparencies
- Grammar and Writing Workshop Transparencies
- Fine Arts Transparencies

TECHNOLOGY

- TeacherWorks Plus
- StudentWorks Plus
- BookLink 3
- Skill Level Up!
- ExamView Assessment Suite
- Interactive Tutor Self-Assessment
- Listening Library CD
- Spanish Listening Library CD
- Literature Classics
- Literature Launchers Pre-Reading Videos DVD
- Literature Library ExamView Assessment Suite
- Vocabulary Puzzlemaker
- Literature Library Vocabulary Puzzlemaker
- glencoe.com
- Online Student Edition
- Presentation Plus!
- Glencoe Online Essay Grading

ENGLISH LANGUAGE LEARNER

- English Language Coach
- Fluency Practice and Assessment
- inTime Magazines (Spanish)
- Spanish Listening Library CD

PROFESSIONAL DEVELOPMENT

- Professional Development Package

Literature Launchers

Set the scene with Glencoe's Literature Launchers, engaging video segments that introduce each unit's genre focus. Each video brings the genre to life, relating it to your students' worlds.

Insert the Glencoe Literature Launchers Pre-Reading Videos DVD into your DVD player. Select the Unit 8 Launcher from the menu to introduce the genre and Big Question for this unit.

Online Essay Grader

Use Glencoe's Online Essay Grading to score your students' writing and to provide individualized feedback to each student automatically.

You and your students can visit www.glencoe.com to link to the essay grader. *Students* can enter their essays and receive feedback on demand. *You* can manage demographic data, assign tests and generate individual student and aggregated reports. The essay grader can help you

- Save time with automatic scoring and individualized feedback.
- Supplement in-class writing instruction using guided writing practice.
- Get reports for individual students or for special populations.
- Track student improvement over time.

REAL Success: Reading Excellence at All Levels

Glencoe now provides all of your students with the tools they need to become better, more enthusiastic readers. The REAL Success suite of reading and language arts products encourages reading excellence by meeting the needs of students at all levels. Glencoe products that can be used in conjunction with Unit 8 include the following:

- Jamestown Literature: An Adapted Reader
- Jamestown *Reading Fluency*
- Jamestown *Critical Reading Series, In the Line of Duty*
- *Vocabulary Builder*
- *The Glencoe Reader, Course 2*

To order these products, call Glencoe at 1-800-USA-READ.

Teacher Wraparound Edition Key

Level Appropriate Code

AS = Activities for all students

AL = Activities for students working above grade level

OL = Activities for students working at grade level

BL = Activities for students working below grade level

EL = Activities for English language learners

Teacher Wraparound Prompts

R **Reading Skill** These activities help you teach reading skills and vocabulary.

V **Vocabulary** These activities help students comprehend words and incorporate into reading.

C **Critical Thinking** These strategies help students apply and extend what they have learned.

BQ BIG Question These activities and questions prompt students to prepare to answer the Big Question.

W **Writing** These activities provide writing opportunities to help students practice writing and comprehend text.

L **Literary Element** These activities and questions help students comprehend selections and learn more about each genre.

E **Text Element** These activities help students comprehend text elements.

LSV **Listening, Speaking, Viewing** These activities help students practice listening, speaking, and viewing skills.

EL **English Language Coach** These skills help English language learners as well as students who need additional reading support.

UNIT 8

Professional Development Center

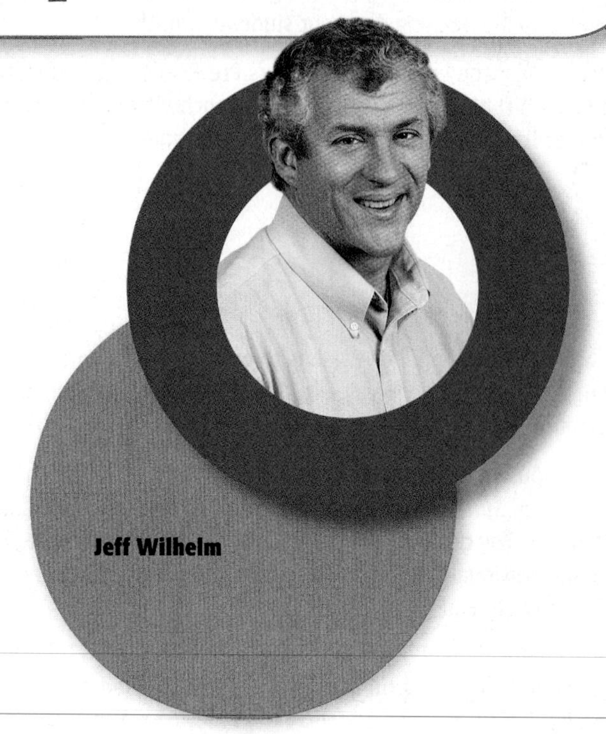
Jeff Wilhelm

From An Author:

Preparing Students to Read Historical Documents

Community and Kids As you introduce the Big Question "What Is a Community," help students understand that a community is a group of people with some commonality. They can be members of a family, member of a neighborhood, members of the same cultural background, members of the same school, etc. Before you introduce the importance of historical documents, make sure students have a good grasp on the concept of community.

Historical Documents Help students understand what kind of documents they are currently making within their communities. Do they send emails or letters? Do they keep diaries or journals? Have they ever clipped a photo or article from a newspaper or magazine? Explain how these items can become historical documents. Have students bring in one of these items and have them predict how a teenager in year 2050 would respond to the content of some of their historical documents.

Once you think students have a clear understanding of these documents, you may proceed to share how you will study historical documents in this unit. Tell them they will read letters, a train schedule, a website, and a diary entry—all of which can be considered historical documents. They will also read other genres that are centered around the Big Question of community.

Vallye Blanton
Lake Park Elementary
Lake Park, GA

Teacher to Teacher

What Is a Community?

To introduce this theme, I make a four column chart on a large roll of paper, labeling each column with one of the words *No Place Like Home.* Then I read a poem to the students that reflects the theme. After reading, we discuss what home means to them, other stories they have read about home, and what home may mean to other people. From the discussion, students add words to the four original columns, plus they add new columns. They may add columns such as *country, neighborhood, family.* Students then choose one of the columns and write a story about the ideas presented in it. I provide an "author's chair" for students to read their stories to the class.

Teacher Chat Room

Using Historical Documents

Before you begin this unit or at some time during the unit, talk with other teachers about ways they have used historical documents. Have a lunchtime discussion group or an after-school hour for professional development and discuss the following questions and answers from our authors:

How do I make historical documents interesting to students?

One key way to make students interested in historical documents is to point out to them the historical documents they are creating today. When students realize that historical documents were at one time functional documents that helped people live day to day or helped them communicate with others, students are less likely to think of the documents as "boring." Relating a document to a modern-day form of communication will help students understand its significance.

How do I help students learn from reading historical documents?

Help students see "beyond" the information so they can grasp the meaning behind the text. Have students ask themselves: wWhy is this important? Why would someone write this in a letter or a journal entry? What is going on in the world or local community that could provoke the writer to respond in such a way? Why would someone need to use this document? How would it help a user.? Help students develop critical thinking skills while examining these documents.

Encourage students to read "historical" documents they create or use. Perhaps they can find a letter, report card, or other documentation that is at least one year old. Have them review the document and analyze its content. What was going on at the time? Why was the document created? What conclusions would someone reading this document in 50 years be able to make?
Discuss the reasons why historical documents survive. Why do people or governments preserve them? Why is it important for us to know what life was like decades or hundreds of years ago? Remind students that in addition to telling us details about the everyday life of people who lived in a certain time period, historical documents can teach us about their ideas and values.

UNIT 8

The BIG Question

What Is a Community?

"It takes a village to raise a child."

—Nigerian proverb

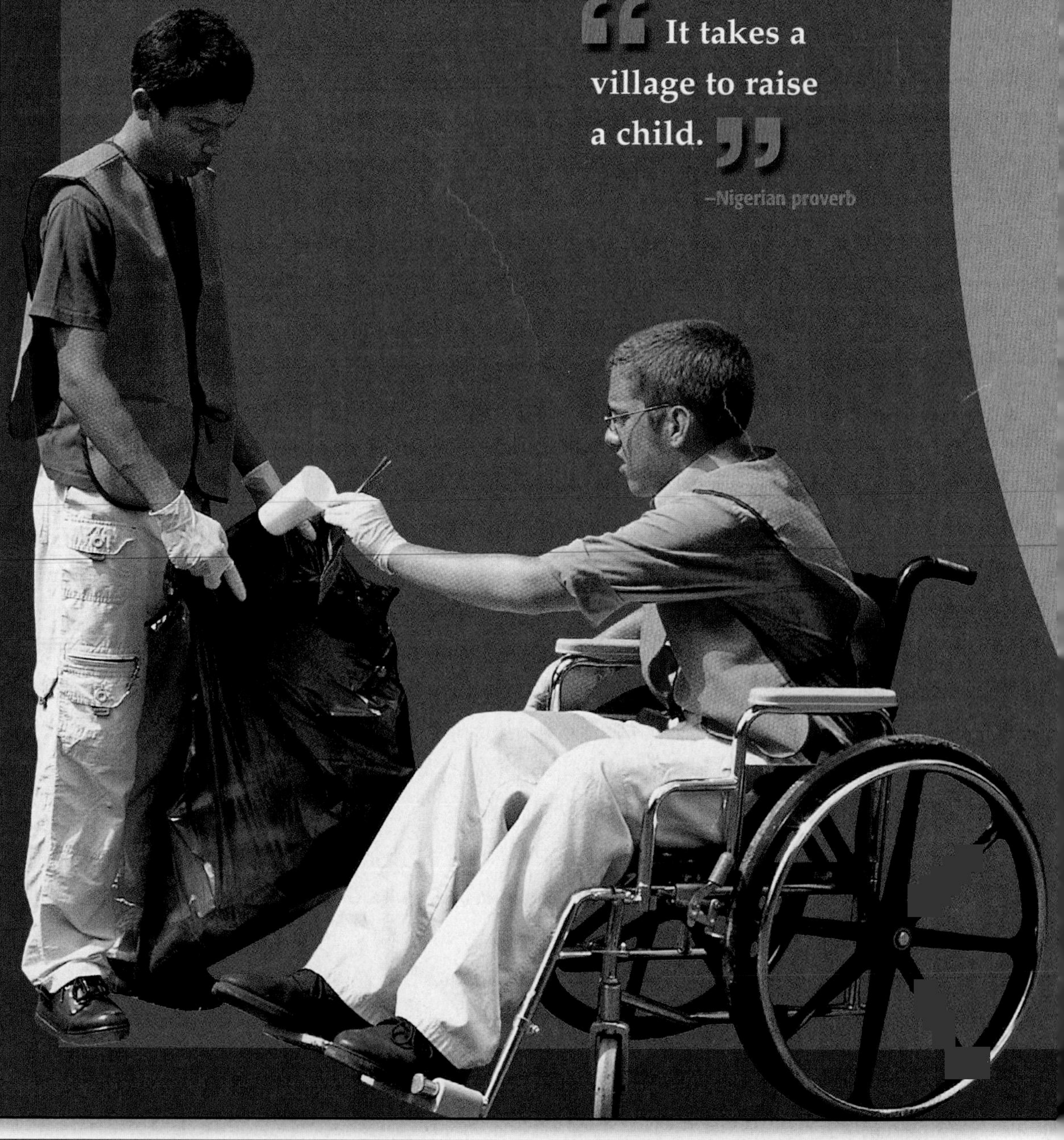

Key Unit Objectives

- Answer the Big Question
- Apply strategies for reading historical documents
- Analyze the literary elements of historical documents
- Write a word picture

Why Is It Important?

Addressing this Big Question helps students understand how people and communities shape each other.

Viewing the Photo

Ask: If you could "step into" this photograph and ask these boys why they are picking up trash, how might their answers reflect what they think about their community? *(Responses will vary; students should note that these boys probably want to keep their community clean.)*

Unit Skills

BIG Question **What Is a Community?**

Genre Focus: Historical Documents

Reading Skills

- Visualizing, p. 884
- Skimming and scanning, p. 912
- Clarifying, p. 930
- Predicting, p. 952

Vocabulary

- Compound words, p. 886

Literary Elements

- Imagery, p. 887
- Organization, p. 915
- Figurative language, p. 933
- Teleplay, p. 955

Writing Skills/Grammar

Descriptive writing, pp. 908, 948

LOOKING AHEAD

The skill lessons and readings in this unit will help you develop your own answer to the Big Question.

About the Reading

Each selection in this unit helps students answer the question, "What is a community?" Through the selections, students visit communities in different places as well as in different times. The selections show how people and communities shape each other.

About the Skills

The skills in this unit have been selected to help students read and understand the featured genre—historical documents. Each reading selection gives students opportunities to practice and develop skills needed to read and understand different kinds of historical documents.

No Child Left Behind

NCLB places great emphasis on improving English fluency. Teaching the skills targeted in this unit will help students achieve greater English fluency.

Reading Fluency

Reading Historical Documents In order for students to become fluent in reading historical documents, students need to hear and analyze good examples of the genre written at appropriate reading levels. To help students who are new to the genre, you might read some selections aloud, showing how each document may call for a different kind of fluency. Students will benefit from hearing the difference between how you read "Letters from Home" and how you read "The Monsters Are Due on Maple Street." BL EL

Focus

BELLRINGER Options

- Literature Launcher: Prereading DVD
- Daily Language Practice Transparency

Focus Activity Say: What makes a community? People do! People who live in the same place form one kind of community. People who share interests or beliefs make another type. What kinds of communities do you belong to? *(Responses will vary.)*

Teach

BQ 

- Ask students to read the profiles of Martin and Tasha.
- Have students form groups to talk about the differences between Martin's and Tasha's situations.
- Have students discuss what advice they would give both Martin and Tasha. **OL**

Literature Online

Big Question Have students access the Web site for English and Spanish summaries and annotated links to related Web resources.

Connecting to  What Is a Community?

No matter who you are or where you live, you're part of a community. Your community helps define you, and you help define it. But what *is* a community? In one sense, it's a group of people living in a particular town or area. In another sense, it's people sharing similar interests, goals, or beliefs. In this unit, you'll read about communities from different times and from places all around the world.

Real Kids and the Big Question

MARTIN was born in a small country outside the United States. There, he knew everyone and everyone knew him. Then his family moved to a big city in the United States, and Martin began to feel a little lost. He doesn't think he will ever adjust to all the streets and people. What advice would you give him?

BQ

TASHA has seen her community go through a lot of changes. Now, new businesses and people are coming in. On the one hand, this means more jobs and opportunities. On the other hand, Tasha feels that her neighbors, who have been around a long time, are being pushed aside. What can she do?

Group Discussion

In a small group, discuss ways that people in a community can help newcomers feel more at home. Then think of people who have lived in your community for a long time. Make a list of questions you would like to ask them about the history of your community.

Additional Support

Reading in the Real World

Career Tasha's concern for her community might lead her to choose a career as a community organizer. Community organizers work to make positive changes on the local level. Sometimes this is called "grass roots" work. Community organizers might lead meetings and events and even raise money. Ask students to research the role of community organizers and to list the skills they need to be effective. **AS**

You and the Big Question

Reading about communities both in historical times and in modern times will help you think about your own community. You'll see how people and communities shape one another—and how they both shape history.

Big Question Link to Web resources to further explore the Big Question at www.glencoe.com.

Plan for the Unit Challenge

At the end of the unit, you'll use notes from all your reading to complete the Unit Challenge, which will explore your answer to the Big Question.

You will choose one of the following activities:

A. Community Mural You'll work with a group to make a mural about the people and communities that you'll read about in this unit's selections.

B. Community Newsletter You'll describe your community and what it has to offer.

- Start thinking about which activity you'd like to do so that you can focus your thinking as you read each selection.
- In your Learner's Notebook, write your thoughts about which activity you'd like to do.
- Brainstorm people or organizations from your community that have made a difference in your life, or in the lives of people you know. How did they help? What did they do? Jot down some ideas.

Keep Track of Your Ideas

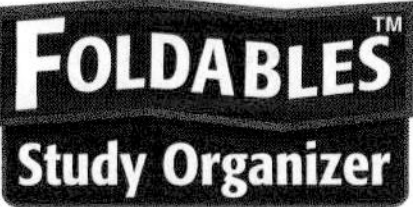

As you read, you'll make notes about the Big Question. Later, you'll use these notes to complete the Unit Challenge. See pages R9-R10 for help with making Foldable 8. This diagram shows how it should look.

1. Make one page for each selection. At the end of the unit, you'll staple the pages together into one Foldable.
2. Label the front of the fold-over page with the selection title. (See page 877 for the titles.)
3. Open the fold-over page. On the right side, write the label **My Purpose for Reading.**
4. Open the Foldable all the way. At the top center, write the label **The Big Question.**

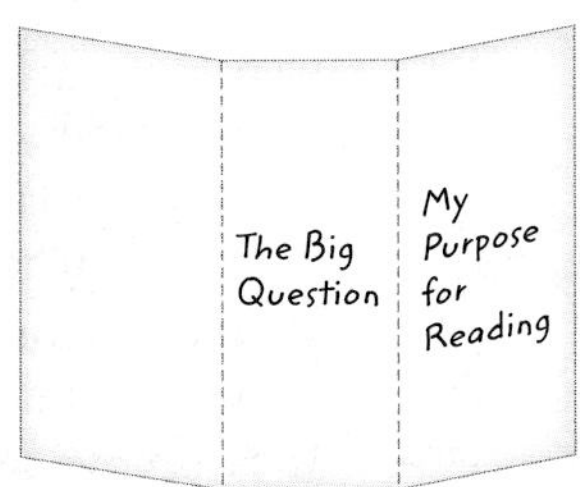

Differentiated Instruction

Visual Clues Draw students' attention to the photographs of Martin and Tasha on page 878. Discuss how the photographs illustrate or complement the text. Ask students to think about the visual clues provided by the pictures. These clues can provide a context that helps clarify the meanings of the paragraphs. AS

Encourage students to cut and paste photographs from magazines into their Learner's Notebook to illustrate their ideas when they make entries about the Big Question. BL EL

UNIT 8 WARM-UP

Teach

Say: Think about one of the communities you are a part of. Write a short description of this community, and show why it is important to you. *(Responses will vary.)* AS

FOLDABLES™ Study Organizer

For each selection they read, students will enter notes about how that selection applies to the Big Question. For details about using Dinah Zike's Foldables, see page R8.

Assess/Close

Ask students to share why knowing what a community is might be important in their own lives.

Resources for page 879

- Use the Unit Challenge Planner BLM in the Unit 8 Resource Booklet.
- Use the Foldable BLM in the Unit 8 Resource Booklet.

Objectives
- Recognize how people and communities shape one another
- Research careers
- Use photographs to interpret text

FOCUS

BELLRINGER Options

Daily Language Practice Transparency

Focus Activity Say: What do you think of when I say "historical document"? A letter, a cartoon and even a shopping list can all be historical documents. So, what makes a document historical? *(Responses will vary.)*

Teach

R Reading Skill

How to Read Historical Documents Ask: How might each reading skill help you read historical documents? *(Possible responses: **visualizing** helps you understand what the author is describing; **skimming and scanning** helps you find the main idea; **clarifying** helps you understand difficult or confusing words or ideas as you read; **predicting** helps you connect what you know with what is going on in the text.)* OL

UNIT 8 GENRE FOCUS: HISTORICAL DOCUMENTS

Skills Focus

- Key skills for reading historical documents
- Key elements of historical documents

Skills Model

You will see how to use the key reading skills and elements as you read

- "It Was Not My Finest Hour," p. 881

Don't run away! **Historical documents** are not what you think. A historical document can be anything from the U.S. Constitution to a shopping list. It can be a letter to a Roman emperor, a magazine article about hula hoops, or a holy book. It can, in fact, be almost anything that's written—about anything, by anyone.

Why Read Historical Documents?

Historians look for broken clay tablets, dusty newspapers, moldy menus, and other writings. Why? Because these things tell about people and communities in past times. No one plans to write a historical document. (Okay, maybe Thomas Jefferson did.) Most people write because they have something to say, and we can learn from their writings, even if they didn't have us in mind.

How to Read Historical Documents

Key Reading Skills

These reading skills are especially useful tools for reading and understanding historical documents. The skills are modeled in the Active Reading Model on pages 881–883; you'll learn more about them later.

R

- **Visualizing** Picture in your mind what the writer is describing. (See Reading Workshop 1.)
- **Skimming and scanning** Get an idea of what a selection is about by skimming—running your eyes over the page. Scanning is reading quickly to find specific information. (See Reading Workshop 2.)
- **Clarifying** Clear up (clarify) what you don't understand as you read. (See Reading Workshop 3.)
- **Predicting** Make guesses about what will happen; then read on to see if your predictions are correct. (See Reading Workshop 4.)

Key Literary Elements

Recognizing and thinking about the following elements will help you understand more fully what the writers are saying.

- **Imagery:** language that helps the reader see, hear, feel, smell, and taste what the writer is describing (See "Kingdoms of Gold and Salt.")
- **Organization:** the way ideas in a selection are structured (See "Getting There.")
- **Figurative language:** language used for a descriptive effect (See "Photographing History.")
- **Teleplay:** a play written or adapted for television (See "The Monsters Are Due on Maple Street.")

Objectives (pp. 880-883)
Reading Visualize • Skim and scan text • Clarify ideas and text • Make predictions
Literature Identify literary devices: imagery, figurative language • Identify literary elements: organization, teleplay

Additional Support

Literature Focus Lesson

Imagery Tell students that an author uses imagery to help readers picture what they read. Imagery is language that helps the reader see, hear, feel, smell, and even taste what the writer is describing. To create imagery, writers use colorful and rich words and phrases to provide details about people, places, things, and scenes. Vivid imagery makes writing come to life and draws the reader into the story. Ask students to describe details of an object in the classroom and then have classmates guess what the object is. BL OL

INFORMATIONAL TEXT
HISTORICAL DOCUMENT

It Was Not My Finest Hour

by Linda Meyers Donelson

East Cameroon
February, 1966

Dear Mom, 1

EL I'm making Valentines as the sun goes down. I've drawn a picture of myself in a cannibal's stewpot, waving an American flag. I'm working by candlelight. I broke the mantle of my kerosene[1] lantern again with too much vigorous pumping. R

The sun is setting over a small cornfield below my house—built for the *Directeur* of our school who found the house too small. From the *ecole secondaire*[2] you can see the town of M'Balmayo across the valley. After dark, charcoal fires spring up along the main road, and you can hear drums. Now that the students have left for the day, the nearest human being is a quarter of a mile away from me.

One of my students died over the weekend, of malaria.[3] I'm twenty-one years old, and this is the first time someone close to me has died. 2

It's four months since I began teaching with almost no experience. Thankfully, I'm not struggling so much now with classroom discipline. I think I've found my sense of humor, which helps.

My French is improving, but speaking to the students is still humiliating. I babysat with the *Directeur's* three-year-old daughter last night, who corrected my French as I read her a story.... 3

1. ***Kerosene*** is a fuel made from oil.
2. ***Directeur*** is the French word for a school principal, and ***ecole secondaire*** is a secondary school, or high school. This part of Africa was colonized by France.
3. ***Malaria*** is a disease that causes long, high fevers; it's found mostly in hot, humid climates.

The notes in the side columns model how to use the skills and elements you read about on page 880.

Historical Documents

ACTIVE READING MODEL

1 Key Reading Skill
Skimming and Scanning *This is a letter from Linda in East Cameroon. I think that's in Africa.*

2 Key Reading Skill
Predicting *My guess is she'll mention other bad times but nothing bad enough to really scare her mom.*

3 Key Literary Elements
Organization, Teleplay *It's organized the way most personal letters are, jumping from idea to idea as Linda thinks of things. It's definitely not a teleplay, but it might make a good TV show.*

Teach

EL Language Coach

Compound Words **Say:** What two words combine to make the word *stewpot*? (stew *and* pot) Use the meanings of these words to find the meaning of the compound word. *(a pot that is used to cook stew)* OL EL

R Reading Skill

Visualizing **Say:** Visualizing is a great way to remember information in fiction and nonfiction. When you visualize, you picture in your mind's eye what the writer is describing. Close your eyes as I read the first paragraph aloud. What do you "see"? *(Responses will vary.)* OL

Resources for page 881

Use the Genre Study BLM in the Unit 8 Resource Booklet.

Readability Scores
Dale-Chall: 5.2
DRP: 57
Lexile: 850

English Language Coach

Identifying and Understanding Compound Words Remind students that compound words are formed by putting two words together. A compound word derives its meaning from the definitions of the individual words. Give two examples of compound words ("ice cream" and "shoelace"). Ask students to use the meaning of each word part to define the compound word. Then ask the class to come up with other examples and explain why their examples are compound words. OL EL

Objectives
- Visualize text
- Skim and scan text
- Make predictions
- Identify literary elements: organization, teleplay
- Understand compound words

Teach

L Literary Element

Figurative Language Say: The writer wants to give her readers a clear picture of what her life in Cameroon is like. Writers can help readers "see" a story by using more than just descriptive words. Well-chosen verbs also help the story come to life. What words does the writer use in paragraph 2 to tell how she feels about the roaches? *(Possible response: She's* terrified *they will land on her while she sleeps, and she can hear them* skitter *under the toilet seat.)* OL

R Reading Skill

Skimming and Scanning Ask: If you take a quick look at this piece of writing, can you tell what kind of writing it is? *(a letter)* BL **Ask:** If you run your eyes over the page, what is the general idea of the letter? *(Possible response: to describe what life is like in this faraway place)* OL

UNIT 8 GENRE FOCUS

ACTIVE READING MODEL

I bought some steak today. The butcher works in a covered area in the center of the outdoor market, with carcasses hanging from the ceiling. You point to the part you want, and he slices it off with his *panga* and wraps it for you in a banana leaf. You should see the black vultures lined up along the roof of the shelter, waiting for the day's leavings![4]... 4 5 R

My kerosene refrigerator went out again; there's something wrong with the wick. I don't like to go in the kitchen after dark because the cockroaches are as big as mice! Some of the grounds workers put up a mosquito net around my bed. There are no mosquitoes, but I've been terrified of flying roaches landing on me during the night. Anytime you sit down on the toilet, you hear them skitter under the seat. 6 L

I'm teaching some English classes now at the forestry school. This is to give me more to do, since there isn't enough work for me. I was sent here because the President of the country comes from this area, but they don't really need another English teacher.

This afternoon I met a young man walking on the path near my house. His name is Albert. He was reading a textbook as he strolled. He offered to teach me some

4 Key Reading Skill
Visualizing *This description helps me see the butcher's part of the market pretty well.*

5 Key Literary Element
Organization *This paragraph is well organized, starting with a general idea and then adding details.*

6 Key Literary Element
Figurative Language *This extreme exaggeration emphasizes how big the cockroaches are.*

4. ***Carcasses*** are the bodies of dead animals. A ***panga*** is a knife. ***Vultures*** are large birds that feed on dead animals and, here, the scraps of meat (***leavings***) the butcher throws out.

Additional Support

Literature Focus Lesson

Author's Purpose Remind students that author's purpose is the reason something is written. A writer may have more than one purpose. Lead a discussion on what reasons an author might have for writing. Discuss how an author might write to teach or instruct. Discuss why some authors might want to entertain. Be sure to talk about the purpose a writer might have for writing a letter. Have students work alone, in pairs, or in small groups to read this letter. Ask them to decide what the author's purpose is for writing this letter. How does using imagery help her accomplish this purpose? OL

ACTIVE READING MODEL

pigeon English (which is spoken in West Cameroon). This should be fun and will make the evenings less lonely.

I learned my lesson about not keeping pets in Africa. I've finished my series of fourteen rabies shots in the stomach. I never should have accepted a puppy from the students, even though they were just trying to keep me from being lonely.

I haven't had as much trouble with back pains this week, but now I have a dry cough that won't stop. There is a kind of worm that moves through your lungs, climbs over your windpipe and falls into your stomach. I hope I don't have it!

I can hear an owl now and some shrieking from the forest behind the house—probably the tree hyrax. I don't walk outside after dark because of snakes in the grass. A mamba actually got into the privy of one of the Volunteers, but fortunately it didn't hurt her.[5] 7

7 Key Literary Element
Imagery *This makes me see and hear and feel things that I really don't want to!*

Gail's house in Obala opens right onto the main street. A few weeks ago I came inside, put my purse on the table, and someone reached right in and took it! When I went to the embassy to get a new passport, a stern official asked, "Do you know what American passports sell for in Cairo?"

Thanks for the news about the draftees from my high school class. I sent President Johnson a letter, telling him to stop sending troops to Vietnam! Hundreds have been killed on both sides; to me, it's like murdering them. (I hope this letter isn't intercepted! A Peace Corps Volunteer was sent home recently for writing a postcard that criticized U.S. foreign policy.) 8

8 Key Reading Skill
R **Clarifying** *I don't know much about Vietnam or President Johnson. I'll have to look them up.*

For the Easter holiday we're attending a conference in West Cameroon, where there are lots of Peace Corps Volunteers. The hotel in Buea serves spumoni ice cream. Technically, we are Cameroon VI, but our group is the first ever in East Cameroon. The fifteen of us will never forget each other. I'm sending Valentines to all of them! L

Love, Linda ○

5. A ***tree hyrax*** is a small mammal that looks like a woodchuck but is more closely related to animals with hoofs. A ***mamba*** is a snake. A ***privy*** is an outhouse, or outdoor toilet.

Teach

R Reading Skill

Clarifying Say: Sometimes selections have difficult or confusing ideas or words, but you can use strategies to clarify something you don't understand. Follow these steps to clarify something in this letter that you do not understand.

- Reread the word or section.
- Ask questions about what you don't understand.
- Look up words you don't know. **OL**

L Literary Element

Organization Ask students what they noticed about how the letter is organized. *(It jumps around.)* **Ask:** Does it bother you that the letter jumps from idea to idea? Why? *(Possible response: No, because the events are interesting. The style makes the letter seem realistic and natural.)* **Ask:** Why do you think the author ended her letter by telling that she is sending valentines to the others in her group? *(Possible response: This reinforces to Linda's mother how important these people are to Linda.)* **OL**

Reading in the Real World

Citizenship Ask students what it means to be a citizen of the world. In what way is helping in another country being a world citizen? How did going to Cameroon help the letter writer? With students, make a list of different ways someone can be a citizen of the world. What are some faraway places students might want to visit? What would they like to do there? You might also ask students to write their own letters about an experience they would like to have as a "citizen of the world." **AS**

Objectives
- Visualize text
- Clarify ideas and text
- Skim and scan text
- Identify literary elements and devices: organization, imagery, figurative language

Visualizing

Objectives covered in this workshop:

- Describe mental images that text descriptions evoke

Teaching Students to Visualize

What Is It?

- Visualizing is picturing a writer's ideas or descriptions
- Visualizing helps students better understand what the author saying
- Visualizing helps students remember what they have read

How to Help Students Get It

- Remind students to pay attention to each detail the writer uses to describe a character, the setting, etc.
- Tell students to constantly ask themselves as they read: What would this look like? How would this work?
- Some students may benefit from actually drawing their visualizations. Encourage students to keep unlined paper near by when they are reading selections in this unit. When they feel the need to see a description more vividly, invite them to draw what they visualize.

Reading to Answer The Big Question

Kingdoms of Gold and Salt

This informational text includes three short pieces about ancient African empires written by Arab writers who visited the empires at different times. As students read the selection, they will find out details about life and government in communities of ancient Africa.

Antaeus

In this short story, a boy from rural Alabama moves to a northern city where he makes friends with a group of boys who like to hang out on a factory roof. He successfully convinces the group to try growing a garden on the rooftop. This selection will allow students to think about what it's like to try to fit into a new community and how communities help define and make them who they are.

Workshop Resources

Pacing (Days) Standard	Block	Lesson	Student Materials	Teacher Resources
1		Key Skill Lesson: Visualizing	Key Reading Skills Practice English Language Coach	Bellringer Options Transparencies Read Aloud, Think Aloud Transparencies Presentation Plus!
2		"The Monsters Are Due on Maple Street: Act 1"	Literary Analysis Transparencies Glencoe Online Selection Vocabulary Development Academic Vocabulary Development English Language Coach Active Reading Graphic Organizer Literary Analysis StudentWorks Plus Online Student Edition Literature Classics Selection and Unit Assessments	Literary and Text Analysis Transparencies Puzzlemaker Skill Level Up! BookLink 3 Assessment by Learning Objective (Diagnostic and Formative) Interactive Tutor Self-Assessment TeacherWorks Plus
2		"The Monsters Are Due on Maple Street: Act 2"	Glencoe Online Selection Vocabulary Development Academic Vocabulary Development English Language Coach Active Reading Graphic Organizer Literary Analysis StudentWorks Plus Online Student Edition Literature Classics Selection and Unit Assessments	Literary and Text Analysis Transparencies Puzzlemaker Skill Level Up! BookLink 3 Assessment by Learning Objective (Diagnostic and Formative) Interactive Tutor Self-Assessment TeacherWorks Plus

Keys for Unit Resource

- Blackline Master
- Workbook
- Supplemental Text
- CD-ROM
- DVD
- Transparency
- Web-based
- Fast Files

Level Appropriate Code

AS = Activities for all students
AL = Activities for students working above grade level
OL = Activities for students working at grade level
BL = Activities for students working below grade level
EL = Activities for English language learners

Focus

BELLRINGER Options

- **Selection Focus Transparency**
- **Daily Language Practice Transparency**

Focus Activity Say: Visualizing is a little like setting up a movie theater in your head. Describe the last time you had to visualize something based on what someone told you or what you read. *(Responses will vary.)*

Teach

R Reading Skill

Visualizing Say: Visualizing is a skill you may use without even noticing it. You automatically visualize a villain in a mystery book or you picture the steps in a science experiment. Write a description or draw a picture of a character in a well-known book or story; then compare what you wrote or drew with a partner. AS

V Vocabulary

Academic Vocabulary
Ask: Look at the word at the bottom of the page. What are some other words that mean the same thing? *(Possible responses: picture, imagine, think about, envision)* EL BL

READING WORKSHOP 1

Skills Focus

You will practice using these skills when you read the following selections:

- "Kingdoms of Gold and Salt," p. 886
- "Antaeus," p. 892

Reading

- Visualizing

Literature

- Identifying imagery
- Using imagery to connect with texts

Vocabulary

- Identifying and understanding compound words
- Academic Vocabulary: *visualize*

Writing/Grammar

- Using hyphens

Skill Lesson

Visualizing

Learn It!

What Is It? When you **visualize**, you create pictures in your mind. As you read nonfiction, you may picture the steps of a process or a place the writer is describing. As you read fiction, you may picture what a character or setting looks like.

- Visualizing helps you "see" settings, characters, and actions.
- Visualizing is using your imagination to picture information from the text

Analyzing Cartoons
Each family member visualizes his or her own idea of the perfect tree. Visualize while you read to get a better understanding of the text.

Objectives (pp. 884–885)
Reading Visualize

Academic Vocabulary

visualize (VIZH oo uh lyz) *v.* to form a mental picture of; call to mind

Additional Support

English Language Coach

Analyzing Cartoons Cartoons are a good way to help students visualize text. Besides being funny, they pack a lot of meaning into a picture. In this cartoon, each person is visualizing what he or she thinks is a perfect tree. Ask students why they think each person's visualization is different. Discuss how each person has a different idea of a perfect tree. Explain to students that when they visualize what they read, they too will have different "pictures" in their minds than their classmates have. EL BL

Why Is It Important? Visualizing makes a selection more vivid—it helps you "see" people, places, and things. If you visualize while you read the selections, you will remember them better later.

Study Central Visit www.glencoe.com, and click on Study Central to review visualizing.

How Do I Do It? As you read, imagine what the characters look like. Picture the setting—a city street, the desert, or the surface of the moon. If you are reading nonfiction, picture the steps of a process or the details that a writer describes. Take notes or make sketches of what you "see" in your mind. Here's what one student wrote after reading the following passage from "It Was Not My Finest Hour":

R

> I bought some steak today. The butcher works in a covered area in the center of the outdoor market, with carcasses hanging from the ceiling. You point to the part you want, and he slices it off...and wraps it for you in a banana leaf. You should see the black vultures lined up along the roof of the shelter, waiting for the day's leavings!

I can imagine the reddish color of the raw meat hanging from the ceiling, and I can see the butcher slicing off a chunk of steak and wrapping it in a green banana leaf. I bet the vultures on the roof of the shelter look vicious.

Practice It!

Below are some topics that are related to the selections in this workshop. In your Learner's Notebook, write or sketch what you "see" in your mind when you think about

- deserts
- kings
- a rooftop garden

Use It!

As you read, remember the notes you jotted down or the sketches you made to practice visualizing. When you find a person, place, or thing that you can visualize really well, add notes or sketches to your Learner's Notebook.

Reading in the Real World

Citizenship After reading a letter from Cameroon, students may be more aware of things they notice and care about in their own neighborhoods or communities. Ask students to write a letter to themselves in their Learner's Notebook about what they'd like to do to make their neighborhood a better (cleaner or safer or friendlier) place. Suggest that they keep the letter, as they may want to add to it or change it later in the unit. AS

Teach

LiteratureOnline

Study Central Have students access the Web site to review visualizing and to complete a related activity.

R Reading Skill

Visualizing Ask: What are some ways that the letter writer makes the setting of the butcher shop vivid? *(Possible responses: She uses words and phrases like "carcasses," "wraps it for you in a banana leaf," and "black vultures lined up along the roof.")* Why do vivid words help you remember what you read? *(Possible response: They paint a more detailed picture.)* OL

Resources for page 885

Use Reading Skills Transparency in *Read Aloud, Think Aloud,* Unit 8, to help students practice visualizing.

Objectives

- Describe mental images that text descriptions evoke
- Depict characters or scenes from stories, using a variety of artistic media

Teach

More About the Author

Basil Davidson, the historian who found these documents, first became fascinated with African history during World War II. He took the time to become an expert on Africa's past and present. He is praised for using sound archaeological and historical evidence and for being the first to popularize African history.

EL Language Coach

Compound Words Say: You can often get clues to the meaning of a compound word by looking at each word separately and then putting the words together. If you put the word *surf* together with the word *board*, you have something to ride a wave on. *(a surfboard)* **Ask:** What does it mean when you put *easy* and *going* together? *(relaxed, unhurried)* Have students think of other compound words they know. EL BL

Before You Read
Kingdoms of Gold and Salt

Meet the Author

The three parts of this selection were written by Muslim historians more than 500 years ago. In the twentieth century, Basil Davidson found their descriptions among old texts and included them in his own histories of Africa. Davidson has written more than twenty books about Africa.

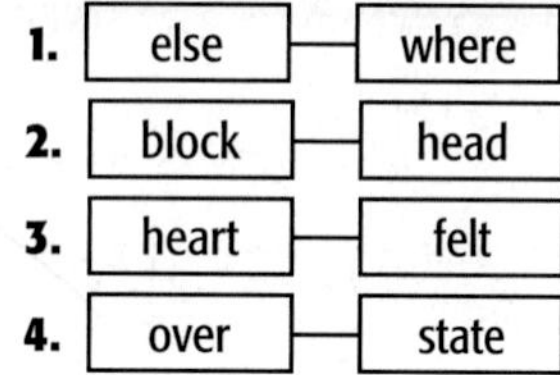

Author Search For more about Basil Davidson, go to www.glencoe.com.

Objectives (pp. 886–889)
Reading Visualize • Make connections from text to self
Literature Identify literary devices: imagery
Vocabulary Identify compound words

Vocabulary Preview

English Language Coach

Compound Words Compound words are formed by putting two words together. The meaning of the compound word combines the meanings of the individual words in some way. If you see an unfamiliar word that is made from words you know, think about the meanings of the individual words.

Words that form compounds can be spelled

- closed (birthday).
- hyphenated (worn-out).
- or open (high school).

EL

Below are examples of compound words and their definitions.

Compound Word	Definition
moonlight	the light of the moon
baseball	a game played with a bat, ball, and four bases
rowboat	a small boat designed to be rowed
aftereffect	a later result

Partner Talk With a partner, talk about the individual words that form the compound words below. Then match each compound word with its definition below.

1. else — where
2. block — head
3. heart — felt
4. over — state

a. to exaggerate
b. sincere
c. in or to another place
d. a foolish person

Additional Support

Author Search To expand students' appreciation of Basil Davidson, have them access the Web site for additional information and resources.

Literature Focus Lesson

Nonfiction Remind students that nonfiction is writing that tells about real people, places, events, and ideas. Writers want to make this writing interesting for people to read, so they use good descriptive skills. If possible, show students an example of nonfiction writing without vivid imagery and one with vivid imagery. Have students discuss which piece of nonfiction writing is more appealing to them. AS

Skills Preview

Key Reading Skill: Visualizing

Before you read the selection, visualize

- what Africa's land looks like
- what ancient kings wore
- ancient weapons

Write to Learn In your Learner's Notebook, jot down a few notes about the pictures that came to mind when you thought about the topics above. After you read, check to see if what you visualized from the text matches your notes.

Key Literary Element: Imagery

Imagery is language that helps readers see, hear, feel, smell, and taste the scenes described in a piece of writing. Writers use words and phrases that help readers visualize people, places, and things.

As you read nonfiction, use these tips to help you understand imagery.

- Look for details about the place the writer is describing.
  What do the details help you see in your mind?
- Look for details about the people discussed in the selection.
  How does the writer describe people's physical features, clothing, and body language?
- Look for items that the writer describes.
  What details help you see the item in your mind? What does the item feel, smell, or taste like?

Interactive Literary Elements Handbook
To review or learn more about the literary elements, go to www.glencoe.com.

Get Ready to Read

Connect to the Reading

During the Middle Ages (1000–1600 A.D.), the kings of Europe lived in castles, and knights on horseback protected them. What do you know about the rich and powerful kings of Africa during this time?

Whole Class Discussion As a class, make a list of what you know about kings and knights of the Middle Ages. Think about how kings dressed, what weapons they had, who they ruled, and where their riches came from. Make a separate list of things you would like to learn about ancient African kings.

Build Background

L

You're going to read three short pieces about ancient African empires. The pieces were written by three Arab writers who visited the empires at different times.

- Ancient Ghana covered much of what is now Mali. Ghana became wealthy and powerful by controlling trade in gold, ivory, and salt. (The modern nation of Ghana is farther south and was not part of the ancient kingdom.)
- "The King of Ghana" describes a visit to the royal court during the eleventh century.
- By the mid-1200s, Ghana had become part of the new empire of Mali. "The Sultan of Mali" describes the king at that time. (*Sultan* means "king.")
- In "White Gold," a third writer describes an amazing city in Mali in 1352.

Set Purposes for Reading

BIG Question Read the selection to find out about kings and communities of ancient Africa.

Set Your Own Purpose What would you like to learn from the selection to help you answer the Big Question? Write your own purpose on the "Kingdoms of Gold" page of Foldable 8.

Keep Moving

Use these skills as you read the following selection.

Teach

L Literary Element

Imagery Say: When you're trying to identify imagery, look at the details. The details are often adjectives (such as *slimy* toads), adverbs (such as spoke *nervously*), or verbs (such as "He *quivered* before the king").

Write the following sentences on the board and have students add adjectives, adverbs, or verbs to help others visualize the imagery.

- Mike ate a sandwich for lunch.
- Jonita sang a song.
- Larry ran to catch up with his dad. OL

Use the CheckPoint questions provided on Presentation Plus! to check students' understanding of visualizing and to build background. These questions can be used with interactive response keypads for immediate student feedback.

Literature Online

Interactive Literary Elements Handbook Have students access the Web site to improve their understanding of imagery.

Differentiated Instruction

Using Graphics Before students begin reading about ancient Africa, suggest that they meet in groups and talk about Africa. Use the KWL chart as a model to draw on the board for the groups to copy. Discuss as a class what students already know and then prompt the groups to continue sharing as they fill out the "K" and "W" columns and later complete the "L" column. EL OL

K: What I Know About Africa	W: What I Want to Know About Africa	L: What I Learned About Africa

Objectives

- Visualize
- Make connections from text to self
- Identify literary devices: imagery
- Identify compound words

Teach

R Reading Skill

Visualizing **Say:** Which words help you visualize the king's court? *(Possible responses include* pavilion, ten pages, shields, gold-mounted swords, sons of the princes, gate, guarded, dogs, *etc.)* BL

Viewing the Art

Ask: How does the illustration of the king compare to your visual image of the king's court? *(Responses will vary.)* AS

Readability Scores
Dale-Chall: 5.3
DRP: 57
Lexile: 1010

READING WORKSHOP 1

INFORMATIONAL TEXT
HISTORICAL DOCUMENT

Kingdoms of Gold and Salt

collected by Basil Davidson

The King of Ghana

When the king gives audience to his people, to listen to their complaints and to set them to rights, he sits in a pavilion around which stand ten pages[1] holding shields and gold-mounted swords. On his right hand are the sons of the princes of his empire, splendidly clad and with gold plaited[2] in their hair. The governor of the city is seated on the ground in front of the king, and all around him are his counselors in the same position. The gate of the chamber is guarded by dogs of an excellent breed. These dogs never leave their place of duty. They wear collars of gold and silver, ornamented with metals. The beginning of a royal audience is announced by the beating of a kind of drum they call *deba*. This drum is made of a long piece of hollowed wood. The people gather when they hear its sound. 1

—Abu Ubayd al-Bakri

Practice the Skills

1 Key Reading Skill

R **Visualizing** Can you imagine, or visualize, the scene in the king's court? Who stands and sits around him? Draw a picture of the scene that shows the king and his people.

The Sultan of Mali

The sultan of this kingdom presides in his palace on a great balcony called *bembe* where he

1. A ***pavilion*** is a large tent. A ***page*** is an attendant.
2. ***Clad*** means "clothed" or "dressed." ***Plaited*** means "woven" or "braided."

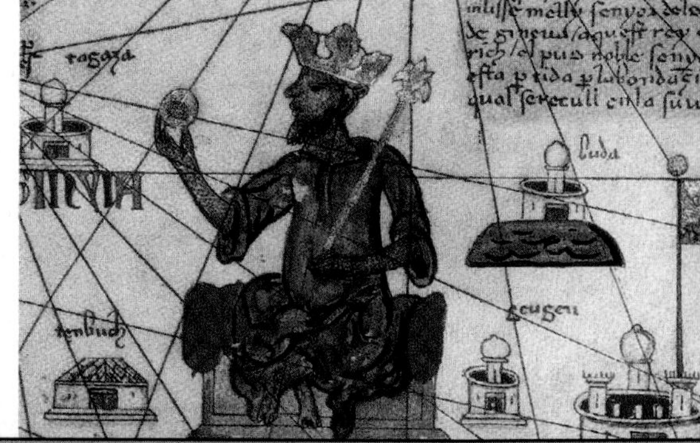

A map of ancient Mali in the 14th century shows King Mansa Musa on his throne.

Additional Support

Reading in the Real World

Career Students with strong visual skills may be interested in careers in art. Careers in art often involve different media—from films and graphic arts to simple line drawing. People find jobs in galleries, folk and history museums, and in illustration departments of publishing companies. Ask students to observe the artwork they see in one day and keep a log of it in their Learner's Notebook. Have students review their logs in class and use them to compile a class list of career options for artists. Then have them consider the roles that artists play in a community. AS

READING WORKSHOP 1

has a seat of ebony[3] that is like a throne fit for a large and tall person: on either side it is flanked by elephant tusks turned towards each other. His arms stand near him, being all of gold, saber, lance, quiver,[4] bow and arrows. He wears wide trousers made of about twenty pieces [of stuff] of a kind which he alone may wear. . . . His officers are seated in a circle about him, in two rows, one to the right and one to the left; beyond them sit the chief commanders of his cavalry[5]. . . .

The officers of this king, his soldiers and his guard receive gifts of land and presents. Some among the greatest of them receive as much as fifty thousand *mitqals*[6] of gold each year, besides which the king provides them with horses and clothing. **2**

—**Ibn Fadl Allah al Omari**

White Gold

Its houses and mosques[7]. . . are built of blocks of salt, roofed with camel skins. There are no trees there, nothing but sand. In the sand is a salt mine; they dig for the salt, and find it in thick slabs . . . [They] use salt as a medium of exchange . . . they cut it up into pieces and buy and sell with it. The business done at Taghaza . . . amounts to an enormous figure in terms of <u>hundredweights</u> of gold-dust. **3** **4** ❍ **C**

—**Ibn Battuta**

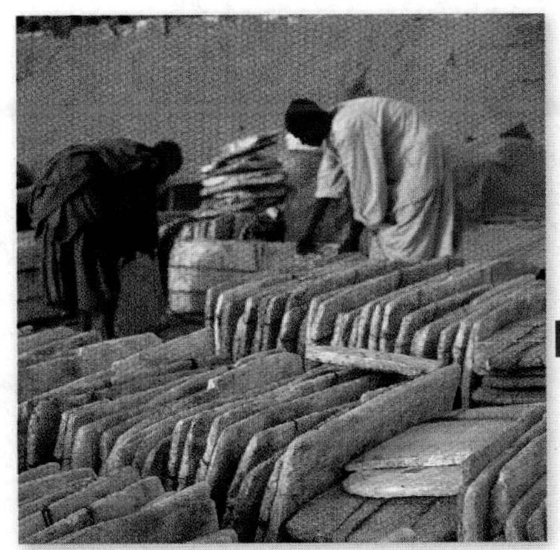

Slabs of rock salt are for sale in a market in Mopti, Mali.

3. ***Ebony*** is a hard, heavy wood.
4. The king's ***arms*** refer to his weapons made of gold, including a ***saber*** (a kind of sword), a ***lance*** (a pole), and a ***quiver*** (a basket that holds bows and arrows).
5. Troops of soldiers mounted on horseback are called ***cavalry***.
6. ***Mitqals*** are an ancient unit of measure.
7. A ***mosque*** is a Muslim place of worship.

Practice the Skills

2 **BIG Question**

The king and the sultan surround themselves with people, jewels, and weapons. What does this say about their communities? Write your answer on the "Kingdoms of Gold" page of Foldable 8. Your response will help you complete the Unit Challenge later.

3 **Key Literary Element**

Imagery What words or phrases help you understand how it would feel to be in Taghaza? If you were digging with the people, what might your skin and mouth feel like?

4 **English Language Coach**

Compound Words
<u>**Hundredweights**</u> is a compound word. It means units of weight equal to 100 pounds. What two words make up this compound word?

Teach

E Text Element

Review Titles and Heads
Ask: What is the title of this collection of documents? *(Kingdoms of Gold and Salt)*
Ask: Do you think this title is appropriate? Explain your answer. *(Possible response: Yes, the documents show how parts of Africa were filled with gold and salt.)* **OL**

C Critical Thinking

Analysis **Ask:** How did the salt mines influence the structure, or makeup, of the Taghazan community? *(Possible response: The activity of the community centered on the salt mines, which provided jobs, income, trade, and building materials.)* **AL**

Assess

CheckPoint

Use the CheckPoint questions provided on Presentation Plus! to check for comprehension of the selection. These questions can be used with interactive response keypads for immediate student feedback.

Differentiated Instruction

Salt Research Students who like to solve problems by reasoning or logic might like to find out more about how people built houses out of salt and used salt for money. Suggest that interested students research how big the blocks of salt were that were mined for building. Were they the same ones used for the medium of exchange? What kind of tool did people use to cut hard blocks of salt? How was gold-dust weighed? Was salt weighed the same way? Encourage students to present their findings to the class. **AL**

Objectives
- Describe mental images that text descriptions evoke
- Identify imagery that appeals to the senses
- Identify compound words

Assess

Resources for page 890

- Selection Quick Check
- Selection and Unit Assessment
- ExamView Assessment Suite
- Interactive Tutor: Self-Assessment

Students can respond to the *After You Read* items in their Learner's Notebook or on a separate sheet of paper.

Answering the BIG Question

1. Responses will vary but may include the idea that a strong ruler, a natural resource, or an industry may form the base of a community.
2. The King and the Sultan presented themselves in a grand manner, surrounded by their counselors, soldiers, and princes.
3. Salt and gold made the kingdoms rich. Some of the greatest officers of the Sultan of Mali received as much as fifty thousand mitqals of gold every year.

Critical Thinking

4. Possible responses may include the idea that the king bought the loyalty of his subjects by rewarding them with gifts.
5. Responses will vary. Students should use examples to support their evaluation.

After You Read

Kingdoms of Gold and Salt

Answering the BIG Question

1. After reading "Kingdoms of Gold and Salt," what are your thoughts about what makes a community?
2. **Recall** When the King of Ghana or the Sultan of Mali appeared in public, how did they present themselves?

   TIP **Think and Search**

3. **Recall** What made the ancient kingdoms of Africa rich? Use details from the texts to support your answer.

   TIP **Think and Search**

Critical Thinking

4. **Infer** Why do you think the Sultan of Mali gave his soldiers and guards gifts of land, gold, horses, and clothing?

   TIP **Author and Me**

5. **Evaluate** How well did the writers communicate their ideas to you? Did they do a good job describing the scenes?

   TIP **Author and Me**

Write About Your Reading

Use the RAFT system to write about "Kingdoms of Gold and Salt."

Role: A new member of the court of the Sultan of Mali or the King of Ghana

Audience: A friend who lives in a different part of Africa

Format: A letter

Topic: Explain your role in the community. Describe

- your position (or job) at the court
- whether you like what you do
- the king
- your relationship with him
- what you think of him and his court
- how he treats you

Objectives (pp. 890–891)
Reading Visualize • Make connections from text to self
Literature Identify literary devices: imagery
Vocabulary Identify compound words
Grammar Use punctuation: hyphens

Write About Your Reading

Possible response:

Dear Olodu,

You were right, my friend, to encourage me to come along with the horse exchange from Yoruba to Oyo. I have become a guard here at the palace because this king wanted someone who knew how to work with iron tools. I am using all the tools I used to plant yams and plantains on your father's farm. Most of all, I like this king, for he honors people's artwork. He has asked me to make a casting in iron of his third son. Will you come visit me at the next horse exchange?

Your friend,

Amaka

Skills Review

Key Reading Skill: Visualizing

6. How did the Before You Read activities on pages 886–887 help you visualize as you read?
7. Which of the three descriptions in this selection best helped you visualize the scene? Explain your answer with details and examples from the selection.
8. How did visualizing help you understand what life was like in ancient Africa?

Key Literary Element: Imagery

9. Did the imagery in the selections most appeal to your sense of sight, hearing, touch, smell, or taste? Give examples.
10. Which of your senses—sight, hearing, touch, smell, or taste—did the selections not appeal to?
11. Look back at the three selections. Choose your favorite example of imagery and explain why you like it.

Vocabulary Check

12. **Academic Vocabulary** What does it mean to **visualize** as you read?

English Language Coach Combine each word in the first column with a word in the second column. Each new word should be a compound word.

13. grand light
14. touch board
15. blue ache
16. card mother
17. row berry
18. moon plane
19. tooth down
20. air boat

Grammar Link: Hyphens in Compounds

A hyphen (-) is a punctuation mark that is used to show that words or parts of word belong together.

This is a well-written story for children.
(It's not a *well* story or just a *written* story; it's a *well-written* story. The hyphen shows that the words go together as a compound adjective.)

Theo wrote the story for his six-year-old.
(The hyphens show that the words *six, year,* and *old* go together as a compound noun.)

- Hyphenate compound adjectives when they come *before* the word they describe but not when they come *after*.

Compound Before: a multiple-choice test

Compound After: a test that is multiple choice

- Do not hyphenate compound adjectives that follow this pattern: *-ly* word + adjective.

Wrong: They are a happily-married couple.

Right: They are a happily married couple.

- Most compound nouns are not hyphenated. When you don't know whether to hyphenate a compound noun, check a dictionary.

Grammar Practice

Copy the sentences below. Add a hyphen to each underlined word pair that needs one.

21. Janelle is a fun loving person.
22. She is also a truly loyal friend.
23. That is why she is so well liked.

Writing Application Circle any hyphens you used in the Write About Your Reading assignment you completed. Fix any mistakes you made.

Web Activities For eFlashcards, Selection Quick Checks, and other Web activities, go to www.glencoe.com.

READING WORKSHOP 1

Skills Review

Key Reading Skill: Visualizing

6. Responses will vary.
7. Responses will vary, but students should cite examples and details.
8. Responses will vary, but students should cite details to show how visualizing helped them.

Key Literary Element: Imagery

9. Responses will vary but should indicate that the images most appealed to the sense of sight.
10. Possible response: There were no images that appealed to the sense of smell.
11. Responses will vary but should include details from the text.

Vocabulary Check

12. Possible response: to picture in your mind what you are reading about
13. grandmother
14. touchdown
15. blueberry
16. cardboard
17. rowboat
18. moonlight
19. toothache
20. airplane

Grammar Link: Hyphens in Compounds

Grammar Practice

21. Janelle is a fun-loving person.
22. She is also a truly loyal friend.
23. That is why she is so well liked.

Literature Online

Web Activities Have students access the Web site for interactive activities that will help them assess their understanding of the selection.

Close

Ask students to discuss what they learned from the documents to help them answer the Big Question.

Teach

More About the Author

Borden Deal has said that he wanted his books to be "a panorama of the New South." He was energized at seeing people build highways and run for public office in the South. He heralded its rise from a losing war. And, always, he wanted to show his characters preserving their beloved land.

EL Language Coach

Compound Words Review with students the simple rule for spelling compound words: Keep the original spelling of both words, no matter how they begin or end. Give these examples to your students to spell as compound words:
day + time = daytime
day + light = daylight
man + eating = man-eating
EL BL

Before You Read Antaeus

Meet the Author

Borden Deal often wrote about the world he knew best–the South and African American culture. Born in Mississippi into a farming family, Deal wrote about people and their relationship to the land. He once said that his characters "live and work in real time, in real places. . . ." See page R2 of the Author Files for more on Borden Deal.

Author Search For more about Borden Deal, go to www.glencoe.com.

Objectives (pp. 892–905)
Reading Visualize • Make connections from text to self
Literature Identify literary devices: imagery
Vocabulary Identify compound words

Vocabulary Preview

robust (roh BUST) *adj.* strong and full of energy. **(p. 895)** *Robust and ready, he had no trouble lifting the boxes.*

resolute (REZ uh loot) *adj.* determined; stubborn **(p. 895)** *She was resolute and insisted on finishing the test.*

obscure (ub SKYOOR) *adj.* difficult to understand **(p. 896)** *That's an obscure text; no one can figure out what it means.*

awe (aw) *n.* wonder combined with respect **(p. 898)** *Jana and I were amazed and in awe of Lisa's abilities.*

bravado (bruh VAW doh) *n.* a false show of bravery **(p. 901)** *Juan's bravado disappeared when he realized his opponent might win the fight.*

flourishing (FLUR uh shing) *adj.* growing or developing successfully; doing very well **(p. 902)** *Thanks to our careful attention, we had a flourishing lawn.*

nurtured (NUR churd) *v.* cared for and helped grow; form of the verb *nurture* **(p. 904)** *He nurtured the garden and watered it while I was away.*

Small Group Work Form a group of three people. Have each person choose two vocabulary words. For each vocabulary word, write a sentence using that word. Share your sentences with one another and write them in your Learner's Notebook.

English Language Coach

Compound Words Some compound words require hyphens; some don't. There isn't any simple rule about when hyphens are needed. If you aren't sure, check a dictionary. There *is* a simple rule for *spelling* compound words. Keep the original spelling of both words, no matter how the words begin or end.

EL

surf + board = surfboard
side + walk = sidewalk
night + time = nighttime

Write to Learn Find the misspelled compound word in each sentence below. Write its correct spelling.

1. Mrs. Hart's grandaughter plays the violin.
2. My dad is a bookeeper at a small company.

Additional Support

Author Search To expand students' appreciation of Borden Deal, have them access the Web site for additional information and resources.

Literature Focus Lesson

Narrator Start by telling a brief story from a particular point of view. After telling the story, ask students to tell you if the story was told from the first- or third-person point of view.

Ask students to get into groups of three and allow time for each group to tell a story about their community from the point of view they know better. Afterwards, suggest that they reverse and tell a short part of the tale from the other point of view. Discuss how point of view changes the story. AS

Skills Preview

Key Reading Skill: Visualizing

R

Before you read the selection, think about what you know about

- rural and farming life in southern states such as Alabama
- kids who belong to gangs in cities
- how to grow a garden

Partner Talk Write a list of words that describe the above topics. Compare your list with your partner's list. Can you visualize what you both have come up with?

Key Literary Element: Imagery

Imagery is an important part of fiction. Authors use imagery to help readers imagine the people, places, and things in a story or poem. Descriptive words or phrases can bring you into the story and help you see and feel what is happening.

As you read fiction, use these tips to help you understand imagery.

- Look at how the author describes the characters.
  What do they look like? What do their actions or facial expressions tell you about them?
- Look at the words that describe the setting.
  Can you imagine this place in your mind? What does it look, smell, or feel like?
- Pay attention to how the author describes objects.
  What objects are important in the story? How does the narrator or character describe them?

Interactive Literary Elements Handbook
To review or learn more about the literary elements, go to www.glencoe.com.

Get Ready to Read

Connect to the Reading

BQ

Have you ever felt like you didn't belong? Did your family, or a family you know, ever leave the place they came from and go somewhere completely new? As you read "Antaeus," think about how it feels to move to an unfamiliar place.

Small Group Work In a small group, discuss what it feels like to be a stranger in a new place. How would you feel about your old community? What would you do to fit into the new community?

Build Background

The following selection is about a boy who moves from a farm in Alabama to a city.

- In the 1940s, when this story takes place, kids who lived on farms were often responsible for raising their own crops.
- In a Greek myth, Antaeus (an TAY us) is a super-hero, a man so strong he can beat anyone—as long as he keeps his feet on the ground.
- Heracles (HEH ruh kleez), another Greek hero, defeats Antaeus by lifting him off the ground.
- Antaeus loses all his strength when his contact with the ground is broken.

Set Purposes for Reading

BIG Question Read the selection to find out how our communities help define us and make us who we are.

Set Your Own Purpose What would you like to learn from the story to help you answer the Big Question? Write your own purpose on the "Antaeus" page of Foldable 8.

Keep Moving

Use these skills as you read the following selection.

Reading Fluency

Build Fluency Students who have difficulty reading nonstandard English or passages with regionalisms may benefit from listening to a good reader. Ask volunteers to read the story to a small group, as the others follow along, or make a tape of this story for students to follow. BL EL Ask students to share their thoughts on how hearing dialogue read aloud can help them understand what's going on more quickly than just reading it to themselves. AS

Teach

R Reading Skill

Visualizing **Say:** Discuss what you and your partner have described about rural life in Alabama, kids in gangs, and growing a garden. What words or imagery would you use to help others visualize what you have discussed? *(Responses will vary.)* AS

BQ 

Say: In "Antaeus," the narrator brings the main character, T. J., into his group of friends, his community. What has happened to you when you brought someone new into your home to meet your family or into your neighborhood to meet your friends? *(Responses will vary.)* AS

CheckPoint

Use the CheckPoint questions provided on Presentation Plus! to check students' understanding of visualizing the writer's descriptions. These questions can be used with interactive response keypads for immediate student feedback.

Literature Online

Interactive Literary Elements Handbook Have students access the Web site to improve their understanding of imagery.

Objectives

- Use imagery to visualize and understand descriptions
- Identify and understand compound words

Teach

Viewing the Photo

Ask: How does the picture of the parapet help you make predictions about the setting of the story? About the community in the story? *(Responses will vary but should include the idea that the setting will be a rooftop and the story will be about an urban community.)* **AS**

L Literary Element

Review Symbolism Say: Notice the title and think about the information you learned in the Build Background section. What might Antaeus symbolize? *(Possible response: Antaeus might symbolize strength because the name refers to a Greek mythological giant who had superhuman strength.)* Antaeus drew his strength from the earth. Think about this symbolism as you continue to read the story. **OL**

Readability Scores
Dale-Chall: 5.1
DRP: 52
Lexile: 1000

READING WORKSHOP 1

L

Antaeus

by Borden Deal

This was during the wartime, when lots of people were coming North for jobs in factories and war industries,[1] when people moved around a lot more than they do now, and sometimes kids were thrown into new groups and new lives that were completely different from anything they had ever known before. I remember this one kid, T. J. his name was, from somewhere down South, whose family moved into our building during that time. They'd come North with everything they owned piled into the back seat of an old-model sedan that you wouldn't expect could make the trip, with T. J. and his three younger sisters riding shakily on top of the load of junk. **1**

Our building was just like all the others there, with families crowded into a few rooms, and I guess there were twenty-five or thirty kids about my age in that one building. Of course, there were a few of us who formed a gang and ran together all the time after school, and I was the one who brought T. J. in and started the whole thing.

Visual Vocabulary
A ***parapet*** is a low, protective wall along the edge of a roof or balcony.

The building right next door to us was a factory where they made walking dolls. It was a low building with a flat, tarred roof that had a parapet all around it about head-high, and we'd found out a long time before that no one, not even the watchman, paid any attention to the roof because it was higher than any of the other buildings around. So my gang used the roof as a

1. During World War II (1939-1945), many U.S. industries switched from making consumer goods to producing weapons and equipment for the military.

Practice the Skills

1 Key Reading Skill

Visualizing Reread the last sentence of this paragraph. Then close your eyes. Can you picture T. J. and his sisters riding in the car on top of their belongings?

Additional Support

Differentiated Instruction

Spatial or Visual Cues Some students make good use of any graphic feature supplied with a text. Suggest that these students skim the story and notice photos or special type treatment. Have them write in their Learner's Notebook any quick impressions they have before reading the story. (For instance, they might ask: *Why is there grass under the title? Does the lettering of the title mean anything?*) Then, as they read and gain information about the setting and characters, have them add this information to their notes. **OL**

READING WORKSHOP 1

headquarters. We could get up there by crossing over to the fire escape from our own roof on a plank and then going on up. It was a secret place for us, where nobody else could go without our permission. **2**

I remember the day I first took T. J. up there to meet the gang. He was a stocky, **robust** kid with a shock of white hair, nothing sissy about him except his voice; he talked in this slow, gentle voice like you never heard before. He talked different from any of us and you noticed it right away. But I liked him anyway, so I told him to come on up. **3** **R**

We climbed up over the parapet and dropped down on the roof. The rest of the gang were already there.

"Hi," I said. I jerked my thumb at T. J. "He just moved into the building yesterday."

He just stood there, not scared or anything, just looking, like the first time you see somebody you're not sure you're going to like.

"Hi," Blackie said. "Where are you from?"

"Marion County," T. J. said.

We laughed. "Marion County?" I said. "Where's that?"

He looked at me for a moment like I was a stranger, too. "It's in Alabama," he said, like I ought to know where it was.

"What's your name?" Charley said.

"T. J.," he said, looking back at him. He had pale blue eyes that looked washed-out, but he looked directly at Charley, waiting for his reaction. He'll be all right, I thought. No sissy in him, except that voice. Who ever talked like that?

"T. J.," Blackie said. "That's just initials. What's your real name? Nobody in the world has just initials."

"I do," he said. "And they're T. J. That's all the name I got." **C**

His voice was **resolute** with the knowledge of his rightness, and for a moment no one had anything to say. T. J. looked around at the rooftop and down at the black tar under his feet. "Down yonder where I come from," he said, "we played out in the woods. Don't you-all have no woods around here?" |

"Naw," Blackie said. "There's the park a few blocks over, but it's full of kids and cops and old women. You can't do a thing."

Vocabulary

robust (roh BUST) *adj.* strong and full of energy

resolute (REH zuh loot) *adj.* determined; stubborn

Practice the Skills

2 English Language Coach

Compound Words
Headquarters is a compound word that means "the place where a group meets and performs activities." Find another compound word in this paragraph. What does it mean?

3 Key Literary Element

Imagery Reread the description of T. J. What words help you see what he looks like and hear what he sounds like?

Teach

R Reading Skill

Visualizing Say: Given the imagery thus far in this story, how would you describe T. J.? *(Responses may include: stocky kid, white hair, gentle voice)* **BL**

C Critical Thinking

Comprehension Ask: When Blackie told T. J. that no one had just initials, explain why you think T. J. simply said, "I do." What can you conclude about T. J. from his answer? *(Possible responses: He does not question his name because it is what he has always been known as. He is not easily shaken by other people's questions.)* **OL**

Literature Focus Lesson

Plot To understand a story, it helps to see what its plan is. Students can enhance their comprehension by making a story map as they read. Copy the sequence of events chart to help students start making their own maps. This can be a simple map, or it can be elaborate if students want to extend subplots off the main sequence. **OL**

Objectives
- Monitor comprehension as you read
- Use imagery to visualize and understand descriptions
- Identify and understand compound words
- Identify literary elements: plot

Teach

Viewing the Photo

Say: Look at the photo on this page. What do you think it refers to: T. J.'s hometown or T. J.'s new setting? Explain your answer. *(Responses will vary; students may think the photo reflects the city because there are no fields in it.)* **AS**

C Critical Thinking

Analysis Say: From what you've read so far, infer why the other boys were angry at first when T. J. said he had planted his own corn and cotton. *(Responses will vary. Students may say that the other boys resented T. J. for feeling a sense of pride in activities that they had no understanding of.)* **Ask:** Why are the boys puzzled by T. J.'s responses? *(Responses will vary but should indicate that the boys come from different worlds.)* **OL** How do the boys' different communities affect their ability to understand each other? *(Possible responses: Having been raised in a rural community, T. J. cannot imagine that anyone would not understand farming. Having been raised in a city, the boys may have never seen a farm or a farm animal.)* **AL**

Practice the Skills

T. J. kept looking at the tar under his feet. "You mean you ain't got no fields to raise nothing in? . . . no watermelons or nothing?"

"Naw," I said scornfully. "What do you want to grow something for? The folks can buy everything they need at the store."

He looked at me again with that strange, unknowing look. "In Marion County," he said, "I had my own acre of cotton and my own acre of corn. It was mine to plant and make ever' year."

He sounded like it was something to be proud of, and in some **obscure** way it made the rest of us angry. Blackie said, "Who'd want to have their own acre of cotton and corn? That's just work. What can you do with an acre of cotton and corn?" **C**

T. J. looked at him. "Well, you get part of the bale offen[2] your acre," he said seriously. "And I fed my acre of corn to my calf." **4**

We didn't really know what he was talking about, so we were more puzzled than angry; otherwise, I guess, we'd have chased him off the roof and wouldn't let him be part of our gang. But he was strange and different, and we were all attracted by his stolid[3] sense of rightness and belonging, maybe by the strange softness of his voice contrasting our own tones of speech into harshness.

4 Key Reading Skill

Visualizing Pay attention to the dialogue between T. J. and the gang. How do you visualize the different expressions on the boys' faces?

2. ***Offen*** is an informal way of saying *off of.* T. J. is describing a sharecropper, who farms land owned by someone else and shares the crop or the profit from its sale with the landowner.
3. ***Stolid*** means "firm and unemotional."

Vocabulary

obscure (ub SKYUR) *adj.* difficult to understand

Additional Support

English Language Coach

Dialect and Regionalism Some students may have some difficulty understanding the way T. J. speaks. Explain that T. J.'s dialect differs a little from the standard form. His dialect comes from a specific region and time. (Dialect example: *"You get part of the bale offen your acre."*) T. J.'s language is also an example of regionalism in the way that it focuses on ways of planting in the South. (Regionalism example: *"I had my own acre of cotton..."*) Ask students to find another example of dialect and another of regionalism on this page. **OL** **EL**

He moved his foot against the black tar. "We could make our own field right here," he said softly, thoughtfully. "Come spring we could raise us what we want to—watermelons and garden truck[4] and no telling what all."

"You'd have to be a good farmer to make these tar roofs grow any watermelons," I said. We all laughed.

But T. J. looked serious. "We could haul us some dirt up here," he said. "And spread it out even and water it, and before you know it, we'd have us a crop in here." He looked at us intently. "Wouldn't that be fun?" **5**

"They wouldn't let us," Blackie said quickly.

"I thought you said this was you-all's roof," T. J. said to me. "That you-all could do anything you wanted to up here."

"They've never bothered us," I said. I felt the idea beginning to catch fire in me. It was a big idea, and it took a while for it to sink in; but the more I thought about it, the better I liked it. "Say," I said to the gang. "He might have something there. Just make us a regular roof garden, with flowers and grass and trees and everything. And all ours, too," I said. "We wouldn't let anybody up here except the ones we wanted to." **L**

"It'd take a while to grow trees," T. J. said quickly, but we weren't paying any attention to him. They were all talking about it suddenly, all excited with the idea after I'd put it in a way they could catch hold of it. Only rich people had roof gardens, we knew, and the idea of our own private domain[5] excited them. **R**

"We could bring it up in sacks and boxes," Blackie said. "We'd have to do it while the folks weren't paying any attention to us, for we'd have to come up to the roof of our building and then cross over with it."

"Where could we get the dirt?" somebody said worriedly.

"Out of those vacant lots over close to school," Blackie said. "Nobody'd notice if we scraped it up."

I slapped T. J. on the shoulder. "Man, you had a

4. Here, ***truck*** refers to vegetables, especially those driven by truck from farms to markets.
5. A ***domain*** is the area under the rule or control of a person or group.

Practice the Skills

5 **Reviewing Skills**

Inferring Why does T. J. want to plant a garden? Think about what he has told the boys about his old home.

Reading in the Real World

Citizenship Many students are interested and involved in environmental efforts to preserve Earth. Ask interested students to go to the library and find out the value of having gardens of grass, vegetables, and flowers in a neighborhood. Encourage them to find out the specific benefits people share when they live by growing things. **OL** Ask your student researchers to present their findings on "How gardens improve quality of life." **AL**

READING WORKSHOP 1

Teach

L Literary Element

Imagery Talk about what T. J. is imagining when he wants to plant watermelons. Then talk about how the narrator begins to buy into the idea. **Ask:** What imagery does the author use to help you know the narrator is excited about T. J.'s idea? *(Possible response: The narrator starts imagining flowers and grass and trees and making the garden a private place.)* **OL**

R Reading Skill

Visualizing **Say:** Describe what all the boys are doing as they talk about how to start the garden up on the roof. *(Possible response: They are all imagining how to get dirt up to the roof.)* **BL**

Viewing the Photo

Say: Describe this field of cotton, using as many images as you can that appeal to your sense of touch. *(Possible responses: soft, marshmallow, fluffy)* **BL** Compare the photo on this page to the one on page 896. **Ask:** What type of community does each photo symbolize? *(Possible response: The photo on page 896 symbolizes an urban community, whereas the photo on page 897 symbolizes a rural community.)* **AL**

Objectives
- Describe mental images that text descriptions evoke
- Use imagery to visualize and understand descriptions

Teach

Viewing the Art

Say: Suppose you are standing at this window right after you've put the vase of flowers on the sill. As you look out on the city, what do you think your flowers add to this scene? *(Possible response: They add a beauty and softness to the sharp-angled buildings.)* OL

EL Language Coach

Compound Words Ask students to say the rule for spelling compound words. *(Spell each word in its original form.)* Tell students that words such as *afternoon* and *watermelon* are examples of closed spellings, in which there is no space or hyphen between the two words. Have students give you examples of hyphenated and open compound words. *(Possible responses: merry-go-round, tree house)* OL EL

R Reading Skill

Visualizing Say: Draw what you see in your mind as you read the narrator's description of how T. J. hauls earth to the roof. *(Responses will vary.)* OL

READING WORKSHOP 1

wonderful idea," I said, and everybody grinned at him, remembering that he had started it. "Our own private roof garden."

He grinned back. "It'll be ourn," he said. "All ourn." Then he looked thoughtful again. "Maybe I can lay my hands on some cotton seed, too. You think we could raise us some cotton?"

We'd started big projects before at one time or another, like any gang of kids, but they'd always petered out for lack of organization and direction. But this one didn't; somehow or other T. J. kept it going all through the winter months. He kept talking about the watermelons and the cotton we'd raise, come spring, and when even that wouldn't work, he'd switch around to my idea of flowers and grass and trees, though he was always honest enough to add that it'd take a while to get any trees started. He always had it on his mind, and he'd mention it in school, getting them lined up to carry dirt that **afternoon**, saying in a casual way that he reckoned a few more weeks ought to see the job through. 6

Our little area of private earth grew slowly. T. J. was smart enough to start in one corner of the building, heaping up the carried earth two or three feet thick so that we had an immediate result to look at, to contemplate with **awe**. Some of the evenings T. J. alone was carrying earth up to the building, the rest of the gang distracted by other enterprises[6] or interests, but T. J. kept plugging along on his own, and eventually we'd all come back to him again, and then our own little acre would grow more rapidly. 7

He was careful about the kind of dirt he'd let us carry up there, and more than once he dumped a sandy load over the parapet into the areaway below because it wasn't good enough. He found out the kinds of earth in all the vacant lots for blocks around. He'd pick it up and feel it and smell it,

6. Here, ***enterprises*** mean "projects or activities."

Vocabulary

awe (aw) *n.* wonder combined with respect

Early New York Evening, 1954. Jane Freilicher. Oil on canvas, 51 ½ x 31 ¾ in. Private collection. Courtesy Tibor de Nagy Gallery, New York.

Analyzing the painting How does putting a few flowers on a window sill compare with T. J.'s need for plant life?

Practice the Skills

6 English Language Coach

EL **Compound Words** Look at the two words that form **afternoon**. Write a definition of the compound word. Do you see any other compound words in this paragraph?

7 Key Reading Skill

R **Visualizing** The roof looks different than it did in the beginning of the story. How do you visualize it now?

Additional Support

Differentiated Instruction

Sequencing Some students may find it helpful to put the garden preparation steps on these two pages into chronological order. Suggest that students make a graphic organizer like the one below to put the steps in order. They can draw their boxes large enough to write each step in a box. BL

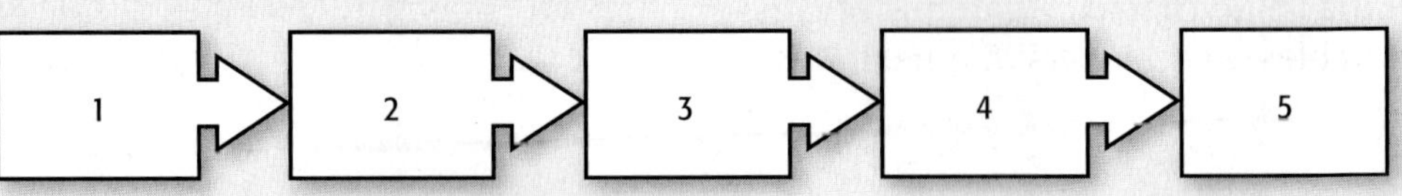

frozen though it was sometimes, and then he'd say it was good growing soil or it wasn't worth anything, and we'd have to go on somewhere else.

Thinking about it now, I don't see how he kept us at it. It was hard work, lugging paper sacks and boxes of dirt all the way up the stairs of our own building, keeping out of the way of the grown-ups so they wouldn't catch on to what we were doing. They probably wouldn't have cared, for they didn't pay much attention to us, but we wanted to keep it secret anyway. Then we had to go through the trap door to our roof, teeter over a plank to the fire escape, then climb two or three stories to the parapet, and drop them down onto the roof. All that for a small pile of earth that sometimes didn't seem worth the effort. But T. J. kept the vision bright within us, his words shrewd and calculated[7] toward the fulfillment of his dream; and he worked harder than any of us. He seemed driven toward a goal that we couldn't see, a particular point in time that would be definitely marked by signs and wonders that only he could see. **BQ**

The laborious earth just lay there during the cold months, inert[8] and lifeless, the clods lumpy and cold under our feet when we walked over it. But one day it rained, and afterward there was a softness in the air, and the earth was live and giving again with moisture and warmth. **8**

That evening T. J. smelled the air, his nostrils dilating with the odor of the earth under his feet. "It's spring," he said, and there was a gladness rising in his voice that filled us all with the same feeling. "It's mighty late for it, but it's spring. I'd just about decided it wasn't never gonna get here at all."

We were all sniffing at the air, too, trying to smell it the way that T. J. did, and I can still remember the sweet odor of the earth under our feet. It was the first time in my life that spring and spring earth had meant anything to me. I looked at T. J. then, knowing in a faint way the hunger within him through the toilsome[9] winter months, knowing the dream that lay behind his plan. He was a new Antaeus, preparing his own bed of strength.

7. T.J.'s words are clever and practical (***shrewd***) and reasoned out beforehand (***calculated***).

8. The earth is ***laborious*** because getting it to the roof was such labor, or work. Something that's ***inert*** has no power to move or act.

9. The months are ***toilsome*** in that they are difficult and tiring.

Practice the Skills

8 Key Literary Element

L **Imagery** What words describe how the earth looks during the winter months? What words help you feel the earth? Could you imagine how the earth looks and feels if the author wrote, "The earth just lay there during the winter months"? Why or why not?

Literature Focus Lesson

Sensory Imagery Language that appeals to the senses is often used in poetry. It is also effectively used in short stories like *Antaeus*. Suggest that any poets in your class reread the last two full paragraphs and write down some of the sensory words or ideas in one column. In the matching column, ask them to write a sensory image of their own that expresses a similar idea of the seasons. **OL**

READING WORKSHOP 1

Teach

BQ BIG Question

Ask: What did T. J.'s organization of dirt hauling do to the group of friends? How did the work make the group more of a community? *(Possible responses: He looked as if he knew what he was doing, and he did a lot of the hard work himself. When everyone helped, it gave them a feeling that they were part of a group that was making something valuable.)* **OL**

L Literary Element

Imagery **Ask:** How did the author describe the earth? Discuss the students' responses and write them on the board, organizing their images into seasons. How did T. J. know it was spring? *(He could smell it.)* **BL**

Objectives
- Describe mental images that text descriptions evoke
- Use imagery to visualize and understand descriptions
- Identify and understand compound words

READING WORKSHOP 1

Teach

R1 Reading Skill

Review Inferring Before students read the narrator's comments, ask them to make inferences about why T. J. agrees to plant grass. *(Possible response: He is a good negotiator.)* OL

R2 Reading Skill

Review Predicting **Say:** The boys have planted grass and have agreed to plant watermelons on the roof. What do you think will happen next? *(Possible responses: They will plant more stuff. Someone will find out and make them leave the roof.)* OL

"Planting time," he said. "We'll have to find us some seed."

"What do we do?" Blackie said. "How do we do it?"

"First we'll have to break up the clods," T. J. said. "That won't be hard to do. Then we plant the seed, and after a while they come up. Then you got you a crop." He frowned. "But you ain't got it raised yet. You got to tend it and hoe it and take care of it, and all the time it's growing and growing, while you're awake and while you're asleep. Then you lay it by when it's growed and let it ripen, and then you got you a crop."

"There's these wholesale seed houses over on Sixth," I said. "We could probably swipe some grass seed over there."

T. J. looked at the earth. "You-all seem mighty set on raising some grass," he said. "I ain't never put no effort into that. I spent all my life trying not to raise grass."

"But it's pretty," Blackie said. "We could play on it and take sunbaths on it. Like having our own lawn. Lots of people got lawns."

"Well," T. J. said. He looked at the rest of us, hesitant for the first time. He kept on looking at us for a moment. "I did have it in mind to raise some corn and vegetables. But we'll plant grass." 9

He was smart. He knew where to give in. And I don't suppose it made any difference to him, really. He just wanted to grow something, even if it was grass. R1

"Of course," he said. "I do think we ought to plant a row of watermelons. They'd be mighty nice to eat while we was a-laying on that grass."

We all laughed. "All right," I said. "We'll plant us a row of watermelons."

Things went very quickly then. Perhaps half the roof was covered with the earth, the half that wasn't broken by ventilators, and we swiped pocketfuls of grass seed from the open bins in the wholesale seed house, mingling among the buyers on Saturdays and during the school lunch hour. T. J. showed us how to prepare the earth, breaking up the clods and smoothing it and sowing the grass seed. It looked rich and black now with moisture, receiving of the seed, and it seemed that the grass sprang up overnight, pale green in the early spring. 10 R2

We couldn't keep from looking at it, unable to believe that

Practice the Skills

9 Reviewing Skills

Inferring Remember that the boys live in the city. Why do you think they are only interested in growing grass?

10 Key Reading Skill

Visualizing Picture in your mind what the garden looks like.

Additional Support

Reading in the Real World

Citizenship Ask students to imagine they live in a building where kids were making a rooftop garden and they knew that the roof was not a safe place for it. How would they go about communicating with the kids?

Encourage students to get into groups and research peer mediation and how its techniques help students to deal with peers in polite and effective ways. Ask students to envision how the narrator's group might react to another kid explaining that the roof is not a safe place to plant grass. OL Have a volunteer group role play such a scene, using some peer mediation skills. AL we had created this delicate growth. We looked at T. J. with understanding now, knowing the fulfillment of the plan he had carried alone within his mind. We had worked without full understanding of the task, but he had known all the time.

We found that we couldn't walk or play on the delicate blades, as we had expected to, but we didn't mind. It was enough just to look at it, to realize that it was the work of our own hands, and each evening, the whole gang was there, trying to measure the growth that had been achieved that day.

One time a foot was placed on the plot of ground, one time only, Blackie stepping onto it with sudden **bravado**. Then he looked at the crushed blades and there was shame in his face. He did not do it again. This was his grass, too, and not to be desecrated.[10] No one said anything, for it was not necessary. EL L

T. J. had reserved a small section for watermelons, and he was still trying to find some seed for it. The wholesale house didn't have any watermelon seed, and we didn't know where we could lay our hands on them. T. J. shaped the earth into mounds, ready to receive them, three mounds lying in a straight line along the edge of the grass plot.

We had just about decided that we'd have to buy the seed if we were to get them. It was a violation of our principles, but we were anxious to get the watermelons started. Somewhere or other, T. J. got his hands on a seed catalog and brought it one evening to our roof garden.

"We can order them now," he said, showing us the catalog. "Look!"

We all crowded around, looking at the fat, green watermelons pictured in full color on the pages. Some of them were split open, showing the red, tempting meat, making our mouths water. **11**

"Now we got to scrape up some seed money," T. J. said, looking at us. "I got a quarter. How much you-all got?"

10. If you treated something holy with disrespect, you *desecrated* it.

Vocabulary

bravado (bruh VAW doh) *n.* a false show of bravery

Practice the Skills

11 Key Literary Element

Imagery Does the description of the watermelon appeal to your sense of sight, hearing, touch, smell, or taste? Why?

Teach

EL Language Coach

Historical Influences Ask students if they know how we got the word *bravado.* Ask volunteers to look up *brave* in a dictionary that includes word histories and report on it to the class. *(Possible responses: a Middle English word with Latin (barbarus) and Greek (barbaros) origins.)* EL BL Discuss how these words could lead to our modern-day meaning of *bravado.* AL

L Literary Element

Imagery Ask two volunteers to pantomime what happens to Blackie when he steps on the grass in the second full paragraph on page 901. Remind students to let the writer's imagery guide them in their actions. AL

English Language Coach

Word Parts Students who look up *bravado* will see that it is divided into word parts. Help students to understand that knowing the word parts helps them to sound out the word and figure out the word's meaning.

Root. The base part of a word is its *root*—example: *dear,* which means beloved.

Prefix. This is added at the beginning of the word—example: *en*dear, which means to *make* beloved.

Suffix. This is added at the end of the word—endear*ing*, which means inspiring a feeling of charm. EL OL

Objectives
- Describe mental images that text descriptions evoke
- Use imagery to visualize and understand descriptions
- Identify the impact of historical influence on English

READING WORKSHOP 1

Teach

EL Language Coach

Historical Influences Say: Look at the word *esoteric*. Then, look at the bottom of the page to find out what it means. Ask a volunteer to look up the word to see what its origin is. *(*Esoteric *is from the Greek* eso, *meaning "within.")* EL BL **Ask: How is the word's origin similar to its meaning today?** *(Possible response:* Esoteric *refers to something known just within a certain group, or beyond the understanding of most people.)* AL

We made up a couple of dollars among us and T. J. nodded his head. "That'll be more than enough. Now we got to decide what kind to get. I think them Kleckley Sweets. What do you-all think?"

He was going into esoteric[11] matters beyond our reach. We hadn't even known there were different kinds of melons. So we just nodded our heads and agreed that yes, we thought the Kleckley Sweets too. EL

"I'll order them tonight," T. J. said. "We ought to have them in a few days."

"What are you boys doing up here?" an adult voice said behind us.

It startled us, for no one had ever come up here before, in all the time we had been using the roof of the factory. We jerked around and saw three men standing near the trap door at the other end of the roof. They weren't policemen, or night watchmen, but three men in plump business suits, looking at us. They walked toward us.

"What are you boys doing up here?" the one in the middle said again.

We stood still, guilt heavy among us, levied[12] by the tone of voice, and looked at the three strangers.

The men stared at the grass **flourishing** behind us. "What's this?" the man said. "How did this get up here?"

"Sure is growing good, ain't it?" T. J. said conversationally. "We planted it."

The men kept looking at the grass as if they didn't believe it. It was a thick carpet over the earth now, a patch of deep greenness startling in the sterile[13] industrial surroundings. 12

"Yes, sir," T. J. said proudly. "We toted that earth up here and planted that grass." He fluttered the seed catalog. "And we're just fixing to plant us some watermelon."

The man looked at him then, his eyes strange and faraway. "What do you mean, putting this on the roof of my

11. ***Esoteric*** (es uh TAIR ik) means beyond the understanding or knowledge of most people.
12. Here, ***levied*** means "enforced."
13. Most often, ***sterile*** (STAIR ul) is used to mean free from bacteria—like a surgeon's instruments. Here, the meaning is "having little or no plant life."

Vocabulary

flourishing (FLUR uh shing) *adj.* growing or developing successfully; doing very well

Practice the Skills

12 Key Literary Element

Imagery A metaphor compares two things that are seemingly unalike. What is the metaphor in this paragraph? Explain how the details help you see and feel the grass.

Additional Support

Differentiated Instruction

Interpersonal Skills Have students analyze the way T. J. talks to his friends and the conversation he makes with the adults. In groups, students could also skim the previous pages of the selection to find other examples of how T. J. handles people with his words. Have them discuss how he gets what he wants through being able to converse with people. Then ask each group to role play how they would handle a conversation with the adults in this scene. OL

READING WORKSHOP 1

building?" he said. "Do you want to go to jail?"

T. J. looked shaken. The rest of us were silent, frightened by the authority of his voice. We had grown up aware of adult authority, of policemen and night watchmen and teachers, and this man sounded like all the others. But it was a new thing to T. J.

"Well, you wasn't using the roof," T. J. said. He paused a moment and added shrewdly, "So we just thought to pretty it up a little bit."

"And sag it so I'd have to rebuild it," the man said sharply. He started turning away, saying to another man beside him, "See that all that junk is shoveled off by tomorrow."

"Yes, sir," the man said.

T. J. started forward. "You can't do that," he said. "We toted it up here, and it's our earth. We planted it and raised it and toted it up here."

The man stared at him coldly. "But it's my building," he said. "It's to be shoveled off tomorrow."

"It's our earth," T. J. said desperately. "You ain't got no right!"

The men walked on without listening and descended clumsily through the trap door. T. J. stood looking after them, his body tense with anger, until they had disappeared. They wouldn't even argue with him, wouldn't let him defend his earth rights. **L**

He turned to us. "We won't let 'em do it," he said fiercely. "We'll stay up here all day tomorrow and the day after that, and we won't let 'em do it."

We just looked at him. We knew that there was no stopping it.

He saw it in our faces, and his face wavered for a moment before he gripped it into determination. "They ain't got no right," he said. "It's our earth. It's our land. Can't nobody touch a man's own land." **13** **R**

We kept looking at him, listening to the words but

Practice the Skills

13 **Reviewing Skills**

Inferring Why do you think T. J. is the only boy upset? Why is he the only one who says, "Can't nobody touch a man's own land"?

Teach

L Literary Element

Review Plot Say: Remember that most works of fiction are about some kind of conflict. That is what a plot does—it creates conflict. What is the conflict at this point in the story? *(Possible responses: The conflict is about property: who has the right to use the roof, and who has the right to say what the roof is used for. The conflict is between the boys and the owner of the building, between kids and the adult world.)* **OL**

R Reading Skill

Review Activating Prior Knowledge Ask: What do you know about T. J. that helps you understand his perspective when he says, "Can't nobody touch a man's own land"? *(Possible response: T. J. is from an Alabama farming community, where a person's land is treated with great respect, so he feels the men are violating his property.)*

Literature Focus Lesson

Literary Elements of the Short Story To map out a story, and figure out how everything weaves together, use a graphic organizer that contains the elements of a story. Copy a chart like this and ask students to fill in each box with an element from *Antaeus*. **OL**

Characters are the actors of the story.

Point of View is who tells the story.

Setting is the story's time and place.

Plot is the story line of events.

Theme is the story's main message.

Objectives
- Describe mental images that text descriptions evoke
- Use imagery to visualize and understand descriptions
- Identify the impact of historical influence on English
- Identify conflict in the story

Teach

V Vocabulary

Word Choice **Ask:** Why do you think the author chose to use the word *nurtured* instead of *cared for* or *helped to grow*? Do you think this choice helps the story? Explain. *(Possible response:* Nurtured *implies a more loving attitude and gives a better picture of how the boys felt about growing the grass.)* **OL**

L Literary Element

Imagery **Ask:** After reading about how T. J. looked and how the dirt looked as it was thrown over the parapet, how would you describe T. J.'s anger? *(Possible response: It was wild and full of righteousness and defeat all at once.)* **OL**

knowing that it was no use. The adult world had descended on us even in our richest dream, and we knew there was no calculating the adult world, no fighting it, no winning against it.

We started moving slowly toward the parapet and the fire escape, avoiding a last look at the green beauty of the earth that T. J. had planted for us, had planted deeply in our minds as well as in our experience. We filed slowly over the edge and down the steps to the plank, T. J. coming last, and all of us could feel the weight of his grief behind us.

"Wait a minute," he said suddenly, his voice harsh with the effort of calling.

We stopped and turned, held by the tone of his voice, and looked up at him standing above us on the fire escape.

"We can't stop them?" he said, looking down at us, his face strange in the dusky light. "There ain't no way to stop 'em?"

"No," Blackie said with finality.[14] "They own the building."

We stood still for a moment, looking up at T. J., caught into inaction by the decision working in his face. He stared back at us, and his face was pale and mean in the poor light, with a bald nakedness in his skin like cripples have sometimes. **14**

"They ain't gonna touch my earth," he said fiercely. "They ain't gonna lay a hand on it! Come on."

He turned around and started up the fire escape again, almost running against the effort of climbing. We followed more slowly, not knowing what he intended to do. By the time we reached him, he had seized a board and thrust it into the soil, scooping it up and flinging it over the parapet into the areaway below. He straightened and looked at us.

"They can't touch it," he said. "I won't let 'em lay a dirty hand on it!"

We saw it then. He stooped to his labor again, and we followed, the gusts of his anger moving in frenzied labor among us as we scattered along the edge of earth, scooping it and throwing it over the parapet, destroying with anger the growth we had **nurtured** with such tender care. The soil carried so laboriously upward to the light and the sun **V** **L**

14. Blackie speaks with decisiveness (***finality***); the issue is settled.

Vocabulary

nurtured (NUR churd) *v.* cared for and helped grow

Practice the Skills

14 Key Reading Skill

Visualizing Picture T.J.'s face. How does this help you understand his feelings?

Additional Support

Reading in the Real World

Career The turn of events in the story may make some students empathize with what T. J. is going through. Empathy is an important quality for counselors to have. One particular qualification for work in this field is listening skills. Counselors listen to clients talk about their concerns and then respond thoughtfully. Their responses involve nonverbal communication as well as speech. A successful counselor knows how to build a relationship based on trust.

Have students research more qualifications of a good counselor and imagine how a counselor might help T. J. deal with his anger. **AL** cascaded swiftly into the dark areaway, the green blades of grass crumpled and twisted in the falling. **15**

It took less time than you would think; the task of destruction is infinitely easier than that of creation. We stopped at the end, leaving only a scattering of loose soil, and when it was finally over, a stillness stood among the group and over the factory building. We looked down at the bare sterility of black tar, felt the harsh texture of it under the soles of our shoes, and the anger had gone out of us, leaving only a sore aching in our minds, like overstretched muscles.

T. J. stood for a moment, his breathing slowing from anger and effort, caught into the same contemplation of destruction as all of us. He stooped slowly, finally, and picked up a lonely blade of grass left trampled under our feet and put it between his teeth, tasting it, sucking the greenness out of it into his mouth. Then he started walking toward the fire escape, moving before any of us were ready to move, and disappeared over the edge.

We followed him, but he was already halfway down to the ground, going on past the board where we crossed over, climbing down into the areaway. We saw the last section swing down with his weight, and then he stood on the concrete below us, looking at the small pile of anonymous[15] earth scattered by our throwing. Then he walked across the place where we could see him and disappeared toward the street without glancing back, without looking up to see us watching him.

They did not find him for two weeks.

Then the Nashville police caught him just outside the Nashville freight yards. He was walking along the railroad track, still heading South, still heading home. **16**

As for us, who had no remembered home to call us, none of us ever again climbed the escapeway to the roof. ❍

15. The word ***anonymous*** has two meanings: "of unknown authorship or origin" and "lacking personality or special features."

Practice the Skills

15 **Key Literary Element**

Imagery Look for one description that shows how T. J. and the boys look and feel as they shovel the earth. Look for another description that shows how the earth looks as they throw it over the parapet. Write these descriptions in your Learner's Notebook.

16 **BIG Question**

BQ What do you think T. J. would say about the city? What do you think the narrator would say about T. J. fitting into a city community? Write your answer on the "Antaeus" page of Foldable 8. Your response will help you complete the Unit Challenge later.

English Language Coach

Adjectives Remind students that most adjectives come before the nouns they modify. Write the following sentence from page 905 of the selection on the board:

We looked down at the bare sterility of the black tar, felt the harsh texture of it under the soles of our shoes, and the anger had gone out of us, leaving only a sore aching in our minds, like overstretched muscles.

Have students copy the sentence and work alone or in pairs to correctly underline the adjectives. (Responses: bare; black; harsh; sore; overstretched) **EL** **BL**

READING WORKSHOP 1

Teach

R Reading Skill

Review Drawing Conclusions Discuss with students how the narrator or Blackie would be accepted in T. J.'s community in the South. **Ask:** Do you think T. J. tried to be part of a community while he was in the North? *(Possible response: He tried to be part of the group of boys.)* **AS** **Ask:** From the ending, what conclusion would you draw about why T. J. was heading back to the South? *(Possible response: He could feel at home only where he could be close to the earth again.)* **OL**

BQ **BIG Question**

Discuss with students what they think about different types of communities. **Ask:** How would T. J. define community? *(Possible responses: T. J. might think of a community as a group of people who work the land.)*

Assess

Use the CheckPoint questions provided on Presentation Plus! to check for comprehension of the selection. These questions can be used with interactive response keypads for immediate student feedback.

Objectives
- Describe mental images that text descriptions evoke
- Use imagery to visualize and understand descriptions
- Identify the impact of historical influence on English

Assess

Resources for page 906

- Selection Quick Check
- Selection and Unit Assessment
- ExamView Assessment Suite
- Interactive Tutor: Self-Assessment

Students can respond to the *After You Read* items in their Learner's Notebook or on a separate sheet of paper.

Answering the BIG Question

1. Responses will vary.
2. At first, the boys react to T. J. with curiosity and confusion.
3. The other boys get interested in T. J.'s idea, so he becomes a kind of leader.

Critical Thinking

4. Possible response: The boys grow from not caring about growing things to loving the sight of grass and having a sense of pride.
5. Possible response: because it would stir painful memories
6. Possible response: Yes. The description of the boys' activity, from hauling the dirt to planting the grass seed to finally destroying their rooftop garden, seems believable.
7. Possible responses: He showed them an example of being a person of principle.

After You Read

Antaeus

Answering the BIG Question

1. How does the story "Antaeus" help you think about the Big Question: What is a community?
2. **Recall** How do the boys in the gang react to T. J. in the beginning of the story?
   TIP **Right There**
3. **Summarize** What happens after T. J. joins the gang?
   TIP **Think and Search**

Critical Thinking

4. **Infer** How do the boys in the gang change by the end of the story?
   TIP **Author and Me**
5. **Infer** Why do you think the boys never again go up to the roof?
   TIP **Author and Me**
6. **Evaluate** Do you think this story is believable? Why or why not? Give examples to support your answers.
   TIP **Author and Me**
7. **Evaluate** What do you think was the most important thing that T. J. taught the members of the gang? Explain.
   TIP **Author and Me**

Talk About Your Reading

Literature Groups With your group, discuss T. J.'s connection to nature.

- What does the earth mean to him?
- Why does he need to plant a garden in the city?
- Do you think T. J. could ever be happy living in a city?

Debate the question: Can country people and city people be happy trading places? Support your ideas with examples from the story.

Objectives (pp. 906–907)
Reading Visualize • Make connections from text to self
Literature Identify literary devices: imagery
Vocabulary Use context clues
Grammar Use punctuation: hyphens

Talk About Your Reading

Possible response:

- T. J. feels that the earth is life. It provides everything a human being needs to survive.
- The earth is so important to T. J. that he knows he can't live or breathe without something growing. So he plants the garden.
- T. J. could probably not be happy in the city as a youngster and maybe not as a young adult. It's possible that he could change as an adult.
- I think T. J. shows that he can survive in the city, because he does for awhile. He is able to adapt his ideas about planting crops to creating a rooftop garden.

Skills Review

Key Reading Skill: Visualizing

8. Choose one scene in the story that you visualized. What details helped you visualize the scene?

9. How did visualizing the scenes in the story help you understand or connect to it? In your answer, give examples or details from the story.

Key Literary Element: Imagery

10. Pick out an example of imagery from the story. Does the imagery describe a person, place, or thing? How does it help you see, hear, feel, smell, or taste what you read about?

Reviewing Skills: Inferring

11. After he destroys the roof garden, why does T. J. head for his old home?

Vocabulary Check

Match the vocabulary word from the list below to the word that means its opposite.

robust resolute obscure awe nurtured

12. clear
13. neglected
14. scorn
15. undecided
16. sickly

Complete each sentence with the best vocabulary word from the list below.

resolute obscure awe bravado flourishing

17. Her directions were often ___ because she either said too much or too little.

18. After several weeks of good food and exercise, the children were ___.

19. Jed was ___ about keeping his job and wouldn't quit, no matter how hard it became.

20. Lucky's loud barking at other dogs is all ___; he'd hide if he weren't safe behind a fence.

21. We watched with ___ as the ball Tiffany hit sailed out of the park.

Grammar Link: Hyphens

Use a hyphen (-) to show that you have divided a word that won't fit at the end of a line.

To finish on time, we must hit the ground running.

- Always divide a word between its syllables. If you aren't sure how a word should be divided, check a dictionary. Syllable breaks are shown with bullets.

  an • i • ma • tion

- Words are divided in ways that will help a reader pronounce the word as it is read. This sometimes makes the word look wrong. If *knowledge* were divided know-ledge, a reader might pronounce it *NO ledj* as he or she was reading along.

  knowl-edge *not* know-ledge

- Never divide a word that is only one syllable.

  Wrong: There stood Mardi, the most beautiful h-
  orse I had ever seen.

- Many words that look as if they have two syllables really have only one. This happens when there's a silent *e* in what looks like the second syllable. Do not divide these words.

  looked *not* look-ed

- There must be more than one letter in any divided part.

  again *not* a-gain
  odor *not* o-dor

Grammar Practice

Copy each word below, showing one correct way of dividing it at the end of a line.

22. brittle
23. caravan
24. enormous
25. popular

Web Activities For eFlashcards, Selection Quick Checks, and other Web activities, go to www.glencoe.com.

Skills Review

Key Reading Skill: Visualizing

8. Responses will vary, but they should include examples like the one on page 898 in which T. J. and the other boys are beginning the task of setting up "our little area of private earth."

9. Possible responses: Visualizing the scenes made me see how hard T. J. worked. The serious look on his face showed how much the garden meant to him.

Key Literary Element: Imagery

10. Possible response: In the scene at the end, T. J. asks the other boys if they can stop the adults. I can feel how hurt he is.

Reviewing Skills: Inferring

11. Possible response: T. J. misses being part of a community that respects nature.

Vocabulary Check

12. obscure
13. nurtured
14. awe
15. resolute
16. robust
17. obscure
18. flourishing
19. resolute
20. bravado
21. awe

Grammar Link: Hyphens

Grammar Practice

Possible responses:

22. brit tle
23. car avan
24. enor mous
25. pop ular

Close

Ask students to summarize what T. J. did to try to be part of his friends' city community.

Descriptive Writing: A Word Picture

UNIT 8

Objectives covered in this workshop:

- **Writing** Summarize to inform develop drafts; categorize information; main idea and supporting details
- **Grammar** Identify and correctly use verbs

Teaching Students to Write a Word Picture

Why Is It Important?

- Descriptive writing can make a person, place, or thing come to life.
- Descriptive writing is one of the four major modes of writing.
- Writing about a specific place in the community will help students think about what defines the community.
- Practicing descriptive writing will also help students practice reading actively and visualizing.
- Thinking about the way their special place is a part of the community enhances student's ability to connect while reading and writing.
- By choosing a place that is personally meaningful, students can come to understand the importance of community.

How to Help Students Get It

- Encourage students to place themselves in the setting as they write.
- Ask students to keep all five senses in mind, not concentrating entirely on sight or sound.
- Students may want to start by identifying what makes their place special and incorporating that into the physical features of the place.
- Remind students that whichever order they choose to organize their description in, an introduction will orient the reader and set a purpose for the piece.
- Visual learners may benefit from drawing a map of their place as part of the prewriting process.
- Read aloud only the first sentence from several different stories or poems to help students understand the importance of a good opening sentence.
- Kinesthetic learners may want to write about the physical sensation of being in their special place, and auditory learners may focus on what it sounds like in their chosen place.
- To improve sentence fluency, have students write each sentence on a new line. This will help them see the patterns in their sentences more easily than in paragraph form, and decide which sentences to lengthen or shorten.
- Have students compare their first and last paragraphs, and ask if the writing stayed on topic throughout, or 'drifted' off subject from beginning to end.

Traits of Good Writing	Student Checklist
Ideas	the message or the theme and the details that develop it
Organization	the arrangement of main points and supporting details
Voice	a writer's unique way of using tone and style
Word Choice	the vocabulary a writer uses to convey meaning
Sentence Fluency: he smooth rhythm and flow of sentences that vary in length and style	• Do sentences vary in length and structure? • Do transition words and phrases show connections between ideas and sentences? • Does parallelism help balance and unify related ideas?
Conventions	correct spelling, grammar, usage, and mechanics
Presentation	the way words and design elements look on a page

Workshop Resources

Pacing (days) Standard	Block	Lesson	Student Materials	Teacher Resources
1		Prewriting	Writing Workshop Graphic Organizer Grammar Practice Spelling and Handwriting Practice Spelling Power eWorkbook Interactive Grammar and Language Workbook Grammar and Composition Handbook	TeacherWorks Plus Presentation Plus! Rubrics for Assessing Student-Writing, Listening, and Speaking
2		Drafting	Real Success in Writing: Research and Reports Writing Constructed Responses Sourcebook	Grammar and Writing Workshop Transparency
1		Editing	Interactive Grammar and Language Workbook Grammar and Composition Handbook	Grammar and Writing Workshop Transparency
2		Revising	Real Success in Writing: Research and Reports Writing Constructed Responses Sourcebook	Interactive Grammar and Language Workbook
2		Presenting	Real Success in Writing: Research and Reports Writing Constructed Responses Sourcebook	Rubrics for Assessing Student Writing, Listening, and Speaking

Focus

BELLRINGER Options

Daily Language Practice Transparency

Focus Activity Ask: If you had to describe a special place in your community, what interesting and vivid details would you include? *(Responses will vary.)* **Say:** In this Writing Workshop, you will create a word picture of a special place in your community.

Teach

 **Writing**

Figurative Language Ask: Why might you use vivid images when creating a word picture? *(Possible response: to help your readers get a full impression of what you want to describe)* OL

Resources for page 908

- Use the Writing Workshop Graphic Organizer BLM in the Unit 8 Resource Booklet.
- Use the Grammar and Writing Workshop Transparencies, Unit 8.

WRITING WORKSHOP PART 1

Descriptive Writing: A Word Picture

Prewriting and Drafting

ASSIGNMENT Write a description of a special place

Purpose: To vividly describe a place in your community

Audience: Your teacher, your classmates, and possibly others in your community

Writing Rubric

As you work through this writing assignment, you should

- write a descriptive essay about a special place
- use vivid images and support those images with sensory details
- arrange details in spatial order or order of importance
- write a conclusion that tells why the place is special
- develop sentence fluency

See page 950 in Part 2 for a model of descriptive writing.

Objectives (pages 908–911)
Writing Use the writing process: draft • Write a description • Use literary elements: imagery, sensory details • Write with fluency and clarity
Grammar Use punctuation: apostrophes

W Individual places help to make a community what it is. Think of places in your community—a beautiful building, a store that's been there for fifty years, a set of train tracks, a quiet park. In this Writing Workshop, you'll create a word picture of a place. Describing it can help you answer the Unit 8 Big Question: What Is a Community? As you write your description, refer to the **Writing Handbook** (pp. R65-R78).

Prewriting

Get Ready to Write

Draw from your experiences and knowledge of places near where you live to choose a topic and collect details.

Find a Topic

These steps will help you think of possible topics and choose a topic.

1. Brainstorm a list of places in your community. It might help you to think of all the places you go in a day, a week, or maybe even a month.
2. Circle the places on your list that you think are interesting or special.
3. Choose one circled place. You'll gather details about this place.

Gather Ideas and Choose a Topic

W Visualize the place and write down as many details as you can.

1. Make a cluster diagram to help you recall the details. First identify your place and draw an oval around the words. Add ovals for sensory details as well as for details about how you feel when you're there.

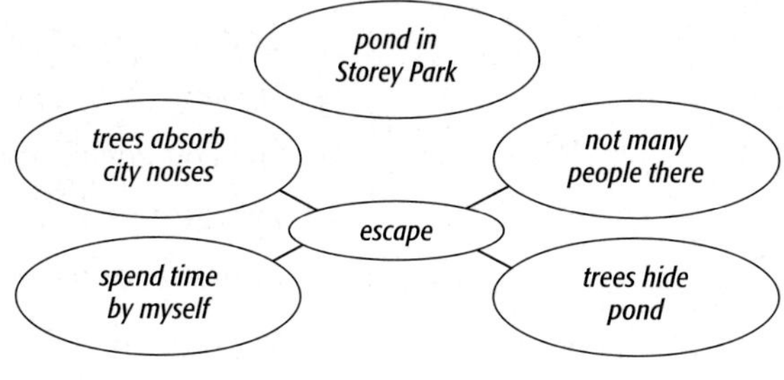

Additional Support

English Language Coach

Describing the Topic You may wish to have English language learners draw pictures of the places they have chosen to describe. First ask students to work in small groups to discuss their topics. Then have students create illustrations of their topics, encouraging them to draw with as much detail as possible. They can then use their drawings to find descriptive words and phrases in preparation for writing. Using both the illustration and the cluster diagram, students can then proceed to the next step in the Writing Workshop process. EL BL

2. Freewrite about the place for five minutes. Write descriptions, experiences, feelings—whatever comes to mind. Then read what you wrote. Is your word picture coming into focus? If not, add more details.
3. Choose one main impression, or general feeling, to focus your description. Write that main idea as a phrase or sentence.

The pond in Storey Park is an escape from the city.

4. Decide whether to organize your description by **spatial order** or **order of importance.** Then use a graphic like this one to organize your details. (It uses spatial order, but you can adapt it for order of importance.)

Closest		**entrance to the park**
➡	**Details**	golden color tickle of grass hard, dry ground
Ahead		**cluster of trees**
➡	**Details**	hide the pond from view absorb the sounds of the city make the pond a private place
Farthest		**the pond itself**
	Details	crunchy, brightly colored leaves peaceful water the sounds of animals

Drafting

Start Writing!

Gather all of the prewriting you've done. Your graphic organizer and your notes will help you as you start writing.

Get It on Paper

Use these tips as you write your draft.

- Begin with a single image of the place. Then give your main impression near the end of the first paragraph.
- Support your main impression and any general statements with sensory details.
- Try ending your description by explaining why you think the place is special or how it affects the community.

Writing Tip

Purpose Decide whether you want your readers to laugh, understand, or wonder about the place you describe. Your description of the place should match your writing purpose.

Writing Tip

W C

Organization For spatial order, choose a spot to start from. Then describe things from right to left, closest to farthest, or top to bottom. For order of importance, start with the most important details and work to the least important. (Or go from least to most important.)

Writing Tip

Drafting If you think of a new idea or detail, go ahead and write about it. You can decide whether or not to include the new detail when you revise.

Writing Models For models and other writing activities, go to www.glencoe.com.

Teach

W Writing

Organization Read the following passage to students.

It was a low building with a flat, tarred roof that had a parapet all around it about head-high, and we'd found out a long time before that no one paid any attention to the roof because it was higher than any of the other buildings around. So my gang used the roof as a headquarters.
—Borden Deal, *Antaeus*

Ask: What do you notice about the organization in this passage? *(Possible response: The passage starts by describing the building's height, then its unusual aspects, and finally its use.)* **BL** **Ask:** What kind of organization does this passage use? *(Students may say that it describes things by order of importance.)* **OL**

C Critical Thinking

Evaluation Ask: Why is it important to organize a descriptive text? *(Possible response: Organization helps make the description clear.)* **OL**

Literature Online

Writing Models Have students access the Web site for an additional and interactive Writing Workshop-based student model.

Differentiated Instruction

Visual Representation Students who enjoy drawing, designing, and building may wish to complement their descriptive passages with something visual. Discuss the ways in which a place could be represented visually. The ways might include drawing, sculpting, building, or painting. Give students an opportunity to create artwork of their own for the places they have chosen to describe. Set up an exhibition of their paintings, sculptures, blueprints, and models alongside the descriptive passages they have written. Invite other classes to come and see the exhibit. **AS**

Objectives
- Write descriptions using the writing process
- Support statements with images and sensory details
- Organize details effectively

Teach

W Writing

Sentence Fluency **Say:** Sometimes you can make your sentences flow better by making them longer. Matching the rhythm and flow of your words to what's happening is a technique that you can use to control your sentences.

Read the following passage to the class. Have students explain how the picture builds within the second, longer sentence.

Our little area of private earth grew slowly. T. J. was smart enough to start in one corner of the building, heaping up the carried earth two or three feet thick so that we had an immediate result to look at, to contemplate with awe.
—Borden Deal, *Antaeus*

(Possible responses: The second, longer sentence flows because it is not chopped up into smaller phrases. The length of the second sentence helps to build the action, heaping words as the boys heap the earth.) OL

WRITING WORKSHOP PART 1

Applying Good Writing Traits

Sentence Fluency

Sentences can be long or short, simple or complicated. When you talk with friends, you use a mixture of simple, compound, and complex sentences. Writers do the same thing.

Analyzing Cartoons Jeremy's thoughts show strong sentence fluency—they have rhythm and flow. If only his spoken words showed the same fluency!

What Is Sentence Fluency?

Sentence fluency is the smooth flow of varying sentence length and style. Writing that has strong sentence fluency sounds natural and is easy to read aloud.

Sentence fluency includes many aspects of your writing.

- word choice
- rhythm of the words and sentences
- sentence beginnings
- sentence lengths
- sentence structures
- sentence fragments

Why Is Sentence Fluency Important?

You might not realize it, but sentence fluency is an important part of your writing style and voice.

In addition, strong sentence fluency

- strengthens the message of your writing
- helps keep your readers interested
- makes your writing easier to understand

How Do I Do It?

The best way to check for sentence fluency is to read your writing aloud. You may want to read it several times and focus on a different element of sentence fluency each time.

- Listen to the rhythm of your sentences, even if you haven't edited your grammar and punctuation yet. Does your writing flow smoothly from one sentence to the next? Do your sentences follow different sentence patterns? If not, you may want to combine or break up some sentences to improve the flow.
- Listen to the beginnings of your sentences. "We went to the arcade. We walked. We saw our friends." These sentences are boring! To improve fluency, combine some of the sentences and think of new sentence beginnings: "We wandered over to the arcade and stood in the doorway. Almost immediately, Jackie and Maurice popped out of nowhere."
- Try to match the rhythm and flow of the words to the mood and content of your writing. Long and flowing sentences often work well for descriptions. Short sentences emphasize the importance of a point. W

Write to Learn In Writing Workshop Part 2, you'll revise your draft to improve your sentence fluency. But you can practice right now. Select three sentences from your draft. Experiment with sentence fluency by rewriting the ideas from those sentences in two or three different ways.

Additional Support

Literature Focus Lesson

Combining Sensory Details Divide students into groups of four or five. Give each group a picture that has a lot of details in it. Ask all the group members to look carefully at the details of the picture for two to three minutes. Then have each student write three details that describe the scene. Remind students to base each of the details on one of the five senses. Then tell each group to combine all the sensory details into one description and present it to the whole class. BL OL

Grammar Link

Apostrophes

Though the apostrophe (') is a small mark of punctuation, it can raise big questions for writers. This Grammar Link will help you answer questions about apostrophe use.

What Are Apostrophes?

Apostrophes are punctuation marks that have two main uses: (1) to show that letters have been left out of contractions (2) to show that something belongs to someone.

W

Why Are Apostrophes Important?

Like all punctuation marks, apostrophes can help you express your ideas more clearly when you write. If you use apostrophes correctly, you will help your readers understand what you mean.

How Do I Use Apostrophes in My Writing?

1. Use an apostrophe to show that letters have been left out of a shortened word or phrase.
   - doesn't (short for *does not*)

     (The apostrophe signals that the letter *o* is missing.)
2. Use an apostrophe along with the letter *s* to show ownership, or possession.
   - Dad'**s** car

     (The **'s** signals that the car belongs to Dad.)

Here are the rules of possession in more detail:

a. To form the possessive of a singular noun, add an apostrophe and an –*s* ('s).

- that student'**s** essay
- James'**s** hat

b. To form the possessive of a regular plural noun, add an apostrophe after the final –*s*.

- two cit**ies'** mayors
- the Jones**es'** house

c. To form the possessive of an irregular plural noun, add an apostrophe and an –*s* ('s).

- children'**s** games
- women'**s** sports

Look out! Do not use apostrophes in possessive pronouns (*yours, his, hers, its, ours, theirs*).

Wrong: Is that book your'**s**?
Right: Is that book **yours**?

Wrong: The dog chased **it's** tail.
Right: The dog chased **its** tail.

Grammar Practice

Each sentence below has a misused apostrophe. On a separate piece of paper, correct each mistake in apostrophe use and explain your correction.

1. Many people went to the Smith's yard sale.
2. They sold two pairs of mens' boots at their sale.
3. They also sold their youngest childs' old bike.
4. Though some sales fail, their's was a success!

Writing Application Look at your draft again. Fix any mistakes in the use of apostrophes.

Looking Ahead

Keep the writing you did here. In Part 2, you'll learn how to turn your draft into a really great word picture.

Reading Fluency

Listening and Editing Some students may benefit from reading aloud one paragraph of their papers in small groups. Have the other students listen and tell what phrases or sentences do not sound clear. Reading aloud can help students *hear* important errors that need to be corrected. Remind students that reading their writing aloud to themselves can also help them to correct awkward-sounding phrases and to make their descriptions smooth. EL OL

WRITING WORKSHOP PART 1

Teach

W Writing

Using Apostrophes Explain that a contraction is a word made by combining two words and leaving out one or more than one letter. An apostrophe replaces the missing letter or letters.

Have students work in pairs to put the apostrophe where it belongs in each word.

- you + are = youre *(you're)*
- we + have = weve *(we've)*
- they + would = theyd *(they'd)*

BL OL

Grammar Practice

1. Smiths'; add an apostrophe after the final –*s* of a regular plural noun.
2. men's; add an apostrophe and an –*s* to an irregular plural noun.
3. child's; add an apostrophe and an –*s* to a singular noun.
4. theirs; do not use an apostrophe with a possessive pronoun.

Assess/Close

Have students check the three sentences they worked on from their drafts for the proper use of apostrophes and make needed revisions.

Objectives
- Write descriptions using the writing process
- Support statements with images and sensory details
- Organize details effectively
- Combine sentences for fluency and coherence
- Use varied word choices
- Use apostrophes correctly

Skimming and Scanning

Objectives covered in this workshop:
- Skim and scan

Teaching Students to Skim and Scan

Why Is It Important?

- Skimming and scanning are very useful tools when readers need to find information quickly
- Skimming includes reviewing the selection to get an idea of what it is about.
- Skimming is best used when students need to find out how helpful a document will be; they will not need to read it all if it does not contain the information they are searching for.
- Scanning is glancing over a selection to find specific information, such as the time a bus leaves from a certain station.

How to Help Students Get It

- Tell students that they already use these skills
- While skimming, students should read headlines, headings, captions and part of the first paragraph to get an idea of what the piece is about.
- While scanning, students should look for key words that would help them
- Before skimming and scanning, make sure students know what they are looking for.

Reading to Answer The Big Question

The Greentown Arena and **Getting There**
This selection includes both a train schedule and a Web page for an event arena. Students will learn how to use these tools as a way to get around a community—both real and virtual—and also get an idea of special and everyday activities within a community.

Letters from Home
Artifacts and first-hand accounts are included in this informational text about an ancient Roman fort. Students will learn that even in ancient times, people who were far from home stayed in touch with their families, friends, and other members of their communities.

Workshop Resources

Pacing (Days) Standard	Pacing (Days) Block	Lesson	Student Materials	Teacher Resources
1		Key Skill Lesson: Skimming and Scanning	Key Reading Skills Practice English Language Coach	Bellringer Options Transparencies Read Aloud, Think Aloud Transparencies Presentation Plus!
2		"The Greentown Arena" "Getting There"	Literary Analysis Transparencies Glencoe Online Selection Vocabulary Development Academic Vocabulary Development English Language Coach Active Reading Graphic Organizer Literary Analysis StudentWorks Plus Online Student Edition Literature Classics Selection and Unit Assessments	Literary and Text Analysis Transparencies Puzzlemaker Skill Level Up! BookLink 3 Assessment by Learning Objective (Diagnostic and Formative) Interactive Tutor Self-Assessment TeacherWorks Plus
2		"Letters from Home"	Glencoe Online Selection Vocabulary Development Academic Vocabulary Development English Language Coach Active Reading Graphic Organizer Literary Analysis StudentWorks Plus Online Student Edition Literature Classics Selection and Unit Assessments	Literary and Text Analysis Transparencies Puzzlemaker Skill Level Up! BookLink 3 Assessment by Learning Objective (Diagnostic and Formative) Interactive Tutor Self-Assessment TeacherWorks Plus

Keys for Unit Resource

- Blackline Master
- Workbook
- Supplemental Text
- CD-ROM
- DVD
- Transparency
- Web-based
- Fast Files

Level Appropriate Code

AS = Activities for all students
AL = Activities for students working above grade level
OL = Activities for students working at grade level
BL = Activities for students working below grade level
EL = Activities for English language learners

Focus

BELLRINGER Options

Daily Language Practice Transparency

Focus Activity Say: How does learning to navigate, or move around, your community help you feel more a part of it? *(Possible responses: It makes me feel like I belong when I know my way around and I know other people.)* AS

Teach

R Reading Skill

Skimming and Scanning
Ask: How do you think skimming and scanning can help you? *(Possible response: Skimming can give me a general idea about the text, and scanning can help me pinpoint specific information.)* OL

V Vocabulary

Academic Vocabulary Say: Read the definition of the word *relevant*. Name two synonyms and two antonyms for *relevant*. *(Possible response: synonyms—important, related; antonyms—unimportant, unnecessary)* OL

READING WORKSHOP 2

Skills Focus

You will practice using these skills when you read the following selections:

- "Getting There," p. 916
- "The Greentown Arena," p. 917
- "Letters from Home," p. 922

Reading

- Skimming and scanning

Literature

- Using organization to understand texts

Vocabulary

- Recognizing and using shortened forms of words (acronyms and abbreviations)
- Academic Vocabulary: *relevant*

Writing/Grammar

- Using colons and semicolons

Objectives (pp. 912–913)
Reading Skim and scan text

Skill Lesson

Skimming and Scanning

Learn It!

What Are They? Skimming and scanning are strategies you can use to improve your reading skills. Both strategies involve taking a fast look at text before doing a more careful reading.

- Skimming is quickly looking over a selection to see what it's about.
- Scanning is quickly searching through a selection to find specific information or details.
- Scanning is most useful when you're looking for key words or phrases that are **relevant** to the topic for which you need information.

Analyzing Cartoons
Skimming the Cliffs Notes won't help this boy pass his test, but it will give him an idea of the topics covered in the books.

Academic Vocabulary

relevant (REH leh vint) *adj.* relating to what is being discussed or considered

Additional Support

English Language Coach

Skim, Scan, or Study Remind students that they read for different purposes. Their purpose determines whether they skim, scan, or study a text. Use a graphic organizer like the one here to help students learn how to use these strategies correctly. EL OL

Read	Skim	Scan	Study
Purpose	Find main ideas	Find details	Understand information
How	Read first paragraph; titles and subtitles	Look for organization; key words	Read slowly; possibly reread

Why Are They Important? Skimming and scanning are time savers. They help you "read smart" by letting you plan *how* to read a selection. More specifically, skimming tells you what a selection is about, how easy or hard it will be to read, and how quickly or slowly you'll need to read. Scanning helps you find a fact or detail.

Literature Online

Study Central Visit www.glencoe.com and click on Study Central to review skimming and scanning.

How Do I Do Them? To skim, read the title of the selection. Quickly read the first paragraph or two and look for a main idea. Then look for important details by reading subheads and boldfaced words. To scan, look for key words as you quickly move your eyes over lines of text. Here's how one student skimmed and scanned an article while doing research. **R**

Sprains: Healing and Preventing

A sprain is a stretch or tear in the thick bands of tissue that connect bones. Experts recommend that simple sprains be treated with the RICE technique (Rest, Ice, Compression, Elevation).

Step 1: Rest

For my speech, I plan to explain how to treat a sprained ankle. From skimming the title and first paragraph, I can see this article has information I need. But I'm not sure what compression is. I'll scan the subheads to find "Compression," and look for key words to find the answer.

Practice It!

Skim the list below. Then, in your Learner's Notebook, jot down one question you'd like to answer by reading about each topic.

- a train schedule
- a seating map for a sports arena
- ordinary people's lives during the Roman Empire

Use It!

Skim the selections before you read them. Then scan each selection to see whether it answers your Learner's Notebook questions.

Reading in the Real World

Career Suggest a project in which interested students can find out more about a career they want to pursue. Have students skim and scan at least five documents (Internet articles, job listings, college catalogs, etc.) to find answers to the following questions:

- What type of education or training is needed for this career?
- What skills does one need to be successful in this career?
- What is the salary range for a position in this career? **OL**

Teach

Literature Online

Study Central Have students access the Web site to review skimming and scanning and to complete a related activity.

R Reading Skill

Skimming and Scanning

Say: You use skimming and scanning strategies all the time, so you should learn how to use them well.

Skimming Make sure students understand that skimming should be done when they have a lot to read and their time is limited. Have students tell you how they skim. *(Responses will vary.)*

Scanning Make sure students understand that scanning involves moving the eyes quickly down the page, searching for specific words or ideas. Ask students what types of aids help them to scan. *(Possible responses: boldfaced or italic items; different fonts or sizes; ideas in margins; the use of organizing words like* first, next, *and* last.*)* **BL** **OL**

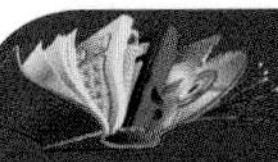

Resources for page 913

- Use Reading Skills Transparency in *Read Aloud, Think Aloud,* Unit 8, to help students practice skimming and scanning.

Objectives

- Skim and scan text for main idea and details
- Use synonyms and antonyms

Teach

More About the Authors

Technical writers write about all areas of information—from train scheduling to communicating expert knowledge. Technical writers can't forget their audience. They need to deliver information to readers who may have no technical background. Most technical writers become "translators," for they turn technical vocabulary into words that nontechnical people can understand.

EL Language Coach

Acronyms and Abbreviations Invite students into a conversation about all the things they read on their way to school. Ask them if they read any abbreviations or acronyms. Make a list of words the students bring up and add them to the lists students make in Partner Talk. *(Responses will vary.)* EL OL

Before You Read Getting There

Meet the Authors

Very few technical writers are famous. You rarely see their names in print. Yet we all read the work of these specialized writers. They are the behind-the-scenes people who write—and sometimes design—maps, schedules, instructions, manuals, and other important materials.

Author Search For more about technical writers, go to www.glencoe.com.

Objectives (pp. 914–917)
Reading Skim and scan text
Literature Identify literary elements: organization
Vocabulary Identify acronyms and abbreviations

Vocabulary Preview

accommodations (uh kaw muh DAY shunz) *n.* a place to stay or sleep, often where food is served **(p. 917)** *Before we left on our trip, we booked accommodations at a hotel for two nights.*

configurations (kun fig yur AY shunz) *n.* the arrangements of parts **(p. 917)** *Look at the seating configurations on the stadium's Web site to find out where we will be sitting at the game.*

Write to Learn In your Learner's Notebook, answer each of the questions about the vocabulary words.

1. **Accommodations** Where would you want to stay if you had to go on a trip and pick your own accommodations? What would the accommodations be like?
2. **Configurations** What do you like best about the configurations of your school? What, if anything, would you change?

English Language Coach

Acronyms and Abbreviations When you see the letters USA, you know what they stand for: the *U*nited *S*tates of *A*merica. USA is a kind of abbreviation, or shortened way of writing the name of the nation. This kind of abbreviation is called an **acronym.**

- An acronym is a word formed from the beginning letters of a name.
- Acronyms are sometimes formed by combining beginning letters, or parts of a series of words.
- Abbreviations are shortened forms of words. Two common abbreviations are Mr. for Mister and Mrs. for Missus. We use abbreviations every day—in conversations, to text messages over the phone, or to chat online.

EL

Partner Talk Copy the chart below and work with a partner to come up with three more acronyms. Add them to the chart.

Acronym	Stands For
CD	**C**ompact **D**isc
DVD	**D**igital **V**ideo **D**isc
NBA	**N**ational **B**asketball **A**ssociation

Additional Support

Differentiated Instruction

Innovative Learners The selections in this part of the workshop are written to be useful. Many students need to see the usefulness in what they learn. Set up a cooperative learning situation in which a group takes an issue—for example, finding new ways to divide the school field and/or blacktop for different kinds of sports. The students should brainstorm their topic and write up a plan to submit to the proper school authorities. AL

Skills Preview

Key Reading Skill: Skimming and Scanning

Before you read, skim the schedule on page 917 and the map on page 916. Get an idea of what they are about. Look for the following elements:

- titles
- subheads
- words in bold type

Key Literary Element: Organization

Organization is the order in which information is presented. One pattern of organization is **general to specific.** In this pattern, a general, or "big," idea is followed by specific, or "small," details. The title and first few paragraphs give you the "big picture" of what the selection is about. Then the sections and paragraphs that follow give you the "little" details that make up the big picture.

The information in maps, charts, and Web sites may also be organized from general to specific. For example, a Web page usually begins with a title (general) that is followed by subtitles (more specific). When you click on a subtitle, you get additional facts and details (even more specific).

Partner Talk With a partner, choose one of the general topics below. List specific details you might use to describe the general topic.

- a friend or family member's personality
- a favorite book, movie, or TV program
- a music group
- a sports team
- a store, restaurant, or other place in your town

Literature Online

Interactive Literary Elements Handbook
To review or learn more about the literary elements, go to www.glencoe.com.

Get Ready to Read

Connect to the Reading

R No matter where you live, you need to know your way around your community. That's why you need to know how to read maps and other graphics. And if you use a computer, you may also need to find your way around a virtual community—one that's on the Internet rather than in the real world. As you read the selections, think about how reading visuals can help you find your way around both kinds of communities.

Write to Learn In your Learner's Notebook, write about a map or a schedule that you use. What information does it give you?

Build Background

L The selections you are about to read are from a train schedule and a Web site.

- A train schedule is a kind of chart. Information in charts is organized in vertical (up-and-down) columns and horizontal (left-to-right) rows. To find specific information on a chart, you must look in the correct column and row.
- Most Web sites begin with a menu, or a list of topics to choose from. By clicking on a topic, you get further information about it.

Set Purposes for Reading

BIG Question Read "Getting There" to get an idea of special and everyday activities in a community.

Set Your Own Purpose What else would you like to learn from the selection to help you answer the Big Question? Write your own purpose on the "Getting There" page of Foldable 8.

Keep Moving

Use these skills as you read the following selection.

Teach

L Literary Element

Organization Say: Go to any Web site and you will probably find the big picture first, and then the links will lead you to the details of that picture. OL

R Reading Skill

Skimming and Scanning
Ask: How do you use the skimming strategy when you first open the home page of a Web site? *(Possible response: by looking over the main items on the site)* When would you use scanning? *(Possible response: when I want to see if specific information is included)* OL

CheckPoint

Use the CheckPoint questions provided on Presentation Plus! to check for skill with the strategies of skimming and scanning. These questions can be used with interactive response keypads for immediate student feedback.

Literature Online

Interactive Literary Elements Handbook Have students access the Web site to improve their understanding of organization.

Reading in the Real World

Citizenship Students interested in maps and compasses may want to make a map for students in the lower grades to show them important places around the community. These students may want to look at some maps in the library to see different ways of drawing neighborhood maps. Have students suggest some of the areas they think are important for the younger students to know about. The maps may include: fire station, post office, school, library, busy streets, bridges, and parks. OL

Objectives

- Skim and scan text
- Identify literary elements: organization
- Identify acronyms and abbreviations

Teach

Viewing the Graphic Art

Ask: How can something as ordinary and everyday as a train schedule require important reading skills? *(Possible response: You need to know how to read the schedule to get where you want to go.)* **BL**

R Reading Skill

Skimming and Scanning

Say: Sometimes the train schedule is the most important thing you may read all day. Why? *(You wouldn't get anywhere without it.)* You don't want to look at all the train schedules available at a station. Skimming and scanning train schedules helps you to narrow your focus. Describe how you would do this. *(Responses will vary, but should describe going from the general to the specific.)* **OL**

Schedules and Web sites help you locate information quickly. You can use them to find your way around, plan ahead, and participate in fun events.

Getting There

Train Schedule 1

#317 Oakwood - Greentown Line

Sunday

Stations		AM	AM	AM	PM	PM	PM	PM
• Oakwood	LV:	7:05	9:05	10:05	2:05	5:05	7:05	10:05
• Rose Park		7:13	9:13	10:13	2:13	5:13	7:13	10:13
• Denfield		7:17	9:17	10:17	2:17	5:17	7:17	10:17
• Glenmoor		7:21	9:21	10:21	2:21	5:21	7:21	10:21
• River Grove		7:24	9:24	10:24	2:24	5:24	7:24	10:24
University Park		7:27	9:27	10:27	2:27	5:27	7:27	10:27
• Norwood		7:31	9:31	10:31	2:31	5:31	7:31	10:31
• Branston		7:35	9:35	10:35	2:35	5:35	7:35	10:35
• Fox Ridge		7:39	9:39	10:39	2:39	5:39	7:39	10:39
Lincoln Heights		7:42	9:42	10:42	2:42	5:42	7:42	10:42
• Lincoln		7:45	9:45	10:45	2:45	5:45	7:45	10:45
• Maple Crest		↓	9:47	10:47	↓	↓	↓	↓
• Evansville		↓	9:50	10:50	↓	↓	↓	↓
• Marion		7:50	9:54	10:54	2:50	5:50	7:50	10:50
Kingston		7:53	9:58	10:58	2:53	5:53	7:53	10:53
• Greentown	AR:	8:09	10:13	11:13	3:09	6:09	8:09	11:09

2

Practice the Skills

1 English Language Coach

Abbreviations Scan the first few rows of the schedule to find the abbreviation LV. It stands for "leave"—the time that the train leaves each station. What do you think the abbreviation AR stands for at the bottom of the schedule? Why do you think the writer used abbreviations?

2 BIG Question

How important do you think public transportation is in creating good, healthy communities?

Additional Support

Literature Focus Lesson

Author's Purpose Most students need help presenting information clearly and with their audience in mind. Have students form pairs and analyze the thinking process the writer of this train schedule may have gone through to present the information this way. Some points for students to discuss:

- What words and numbers are most important?
- How should they be presented so that they can be understood at a glance?
- What graphic aids support the information? **OL**

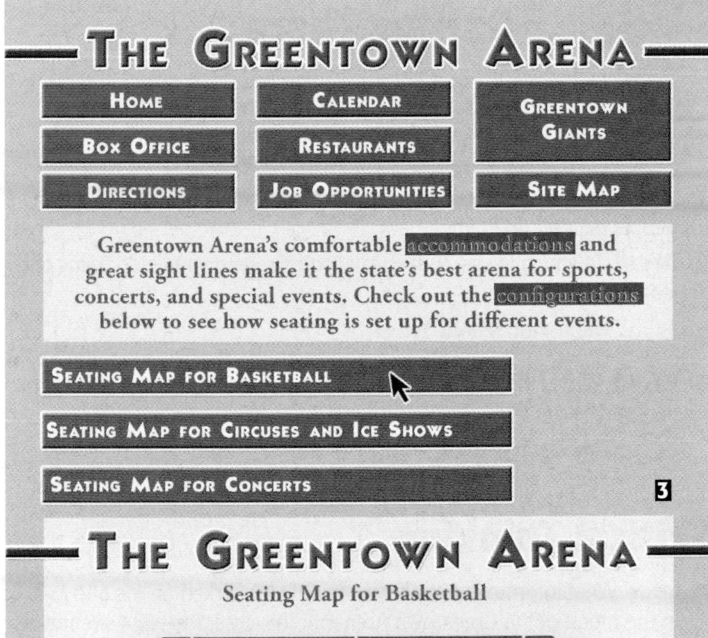

THE GREENTOWN ARENA
HOME
CALENDAR
GREENTOWN GIANTS
BOX OFFICE
RESTAURANTS
DIRECTIONS
JOB OPPORTUNITIES
SITE MAP
Greentown Arena's comfortable accommodations and great sight lines make it the state's best arena for sports, concerts, and special events. Check out the configurations below to see how seating is set up for different events.
SEATING MAP FOR BASKETBALL
SEATING MAP FOR CIRCUSES AND ICE SHOWS
SEATING MAP FOR CONCERTS

3

THE GREENTOWN ARENA

Seating Map for Basketball

CLICK ON SECTION TO PURCHASE TICKETS

4 5

Vocabulary

accommodations (uh kaw muh DAY shunz) *n.* a place to stay or sleep, often where food is served

configurations (kun fig yur AY shunz) *n.* the arrangements of parts

Practice the Skills

3 Key Reading Skill

Skimming and Scanning Skim the title at the top of the page and the subtitles in the boxes below the title. Then skim the paragraph below the boxes. What is this Web site about?

4 Key Literary Element

L **Organization** The general idea of the second visual is stated in the subtitle, "Seating Map for Basketball." What are the specific parts of the map?

5 BIG Question

What do public places such as sports arenas add to communities? Write your answer on the "Getting There" page of Foldable 8. Your response will help you complete the Unit Challenge later.

Teach

Viewing the Graphic Art

Ask: What are the two parts of this graphic presentation? *(Possible response: The top part gives information about Greentown Arena, and the bottom part is a map of a seating plan.)* BL

L Literary Element

Organization Say: Describe how you would surf this Web site to find the following:

- tickets for an event *(click on Box Office)*
- a summer job *(click on Job Opportunities)*
- a seating map for a circus *(click on Seating Map for Circuses and Ice Shows)*
- tickets for seats on the east side of the basketball court *(click on Seating Map for Basketball, then click on section 30)* OL

CheckPoint

Use the CheckPoint questions provided on Presentation Plus! to check for comprehension of the selections. These questions can be used with Interactive response keypads for immediate student feedback.

Reading in the Real World

Citizenship Ask students to think of places in their communities, such as sports arenas, that bring people together. Make a list of these places. Assign each student a place to research and have the student share information about the place with the class. AS

If the place has a seating chart, have the student print it out and create questions about it that are like the questions in this workshop. Have the student present his or her questions to the class with a copy of the seating chart so students can practice skimming and scanning. AL

Objectives

- Skim and scan
- Use text organization to find and understand main ideas and supporting details
- Recognize and understand clipped or shortened words and acronyms to identify whole words and their meanings

Assess

Resources for page 918

- Selection Quick Check
- Selection and Unit Assessment
- ExamView Assessment Suite
- Interactive Tutor: Self-Assessment

Students can respond to the *After You Read* items in their Learner's Notebook or on a separate sheet of paper.

Answering the

1. Responses will vary.
2. Maple Crest and Evansville
3. The events are basketball games, circuses, ice shows, and concerts. There are seating charts for these events.

Critical Thinking

4. Possible response: I'd find a complete menu of all the different kinds of information I could access on the Web site.
5. Possible response: This information is probably reliable because this is the official Web site for this arena.

After You Read

Getting There

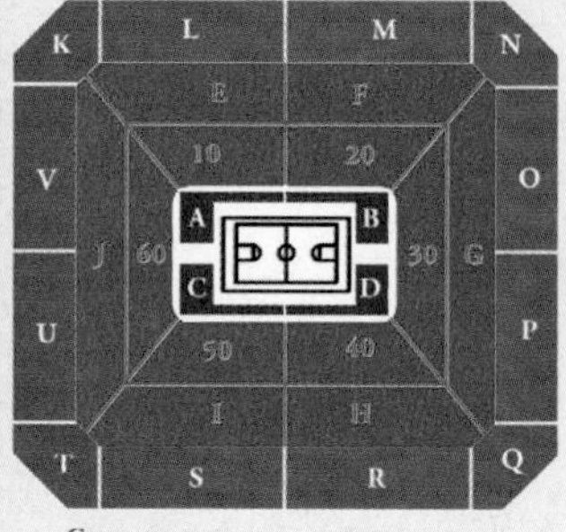

Objectives (pp. 918–919)
Reading Skim and scan text
Literature Identify literary elements: organization
Vocabulary Identify acronyms and abbreviations
Writing Write a monologue
Grammar Use punctuation: colons

Answering the

1. List two places that are important in your community and explain why people depend on them.
2. **Recall** In which towns on the Oakwood-Greentown line do trains only stop two times a day?
   TIP Think and Search
3. **Recall** What kinds of events take place in the Greentown Arena? How do you know?
   TIP Think and Search

Critical Thinking

4. **Infer** What information might you find if you clicked on the Site Map in the menu of the Greentown Arena? In this case, the word *site* means "Web site."
   TIP Author and Me
5. **Evaluate** Should you trust the information you get from Web sites like the Greentown Arena? Why or why not?
   TIP Author and Me

Write About Your Reading

Pretend you are a Greentown tour guide with a bus full of out-of-town tourists. Write a monologue (a brief speech) about what you will say to the tourists. You'll want to point out the most interesting places to go and tell them how to get there.

- Use your imagination to think of three interesting or fun places for the tourists to visit.
- Explain how to use the Greentown Arena Web site and the train schedule to find and get to exciting events.
- Think about the names of stops on the train schedule. For example, University Park may stop by a university. Where might the other stops lead to?

Write About Your Reading

Possible response:

Welcome aboard the Greentown Line. My name is Kristi Martin, and I will tell you some of the best sites in Greentown, so you can get on and off this train at any stop—all for one low fare. To learn more about this area, be sure to visit www.greentown.org. And don't forget to pick up a train schedule!

Take care of the kids first. Let them play in either of our two parks: University Park has lots of swings and Rose Park dazzles you with its rolling hills and gardens. In Norwood and Denfield, you'll find nature preserves. You'll have birds feeding out of your hand. For a gourmet snack, try The Plaza Cafe in Kingston. Enjoy your day!

Skills Review

Key Lesson Skill: Skimming and Scanning

6. How did skimming and scanning before you read help you to understand the information in "Getting There"?

Key Literary Element: Organization

7. What is the purpose of the line map at the bottom of the train schedule?
8. What are the general headings on the Greentown Arena Web site? What specific information do these headings provide?

Vocabulary Check

Answer *true* or *false* to each statement

9. An **arena** is a place to eat and sleep overnight.
10. **Accommodations** hold sporting events.
11. A building's map of **configurations** will include the west wing.
12. **Academic Vocabulary** If you need information about Greentown's history, which source would you go to for **relevant** information: a book about the early settlers of Greentown, a magazine article about famous hip-hop artists of Greentown, or a Web site about upcoming events in the Greentown Arena? Why?
13. **English Language Coach** Use the first letters of each word in the following names to figure out the acronyms for these organizations:
    - Bay Area Rapid Transit
    - Iowa Department of Transportation
    - Los Angeles Police Department
    - Columbia Broadcasting Services
    - United Nations International Children's Emergency Fund

Grammar Link: Colons

A colon (:) is a punctuation mark that is used to signal a list or series of items at the end of a sentence. Often (but not always), the list or series is introduced by *the following* or *as follows.*

- Bring the following items: a pen, a notebook, and your textbook.
- Many people are going: Bo, Lou, and Elyn, among others.

Look out! Do not separate a verb from its object or complement with a colon.

Wrong: The kids in my group are: Erin, Jim, and Andre.
Right: The kids in my group are Erin, Jim, and Andre.

Grammar Practice

Rewrite the following sentences. Then insert a colon in each sentence that needs one. (Some sentences do not need a colon.)

14. My favorite foods include eggs, ham, and beets.
15. Recycle only these materials glass, paper, and plastic.
16. Nadia, my friend from sixth grade, is tall, smart, and pretty.
17. The following students must report to the principal Diane Larson, Manny Greene, and Scott Freeman.

Writing Application Circle any colons you used in your Write About Your Reading assignment. If you didn't use any colons, rewrite two of your sentences to include colons.

Web Activities For eFlashcards, Selection Quick Checks, and other Web activities, go to www.glencoe.com.

Skills Review

Key Lesson Skill: Skimming and Scanning

6. Possible response: Skimming and scanning helped me get an idea of what was on the schedule and the Web site.

Key Literary Element: Organization

7. Possible response: The line map shows the positions of the stations and the distances between them.
8. General headings are the eight areas at the top—Home, Box Office, etc. The headings are links on the Web site to more detailed information.

Vocabulary Check

9. False
10. False
11. True
12. A book on early settlers
13. BART, IDOT, LAPD, CBS, UNICEF

Grammar Link: Colons

Grammar Practice

14. My favorite foods include eggs, ham, and beets.
15. Recycle only these materials: glass, paper, and plastic.
16. Nadia, my friend from sixth grade, is tall, smart, and pretty.
17. The following students must report to the principal: Diane Larson, Manny Greene, and Scott Freeman.

Close

Ask students to write a paragraph describing how they would research to learn more about their community.

Literature Online

Web Activities Have students access the Web site for interactive activities that will help them assess their understanding of the selection.

Teach

More About the Author

Graeme Davis has long been curious about the past and what it leaves in its path. At age five, he boasted about creating his first museum—mostly stones. His degree, naturally, was in archaeology. He's recently been involved in turning historical settings into interactive games for children.

V Vocabulary

Ask students to use both vocabulary words in one sentence. Review their sentences. AS

Before You Read | Letters from Home

Meet the Author

Graeme Davis says, "I started writing stories at the age of about five, and by the age of seven I was winning prizes for research and writing projects at school." He's been writing ever since, on subjects ranging from *Dungeons and Dragons* to the mysteries of ancient Egypt.

Author Search For more about Graeme Davis, go to www.glencoe.com.

Objectives (pp. 920–927)
Reading Skim and scan text • Make connections from text to self
Literature Identify literary elements: organization
Vocabulary Identify acronyms and abbreviations

Vocabulary Preview

V

sufficiently (suh FISH unt lee) *adv.* enough to meet the needs of the situation **(p. 922)** *The cookies were sufficiently baked, but some were a bit soft on the inside.*

policy (PAW luh see) *n.* a regular or usual way of handling things **(p. 923)** *Their school policy is to call home if you miss class for three days in a row—it's even in the handbook.*

Write to Learn Study the definition of the word *policy*. Then make up a policy of your own. It might be a belief you have on how to be a good friend or how to deal with conflict. Write a few sentences in your Learner's Notebook explaining your policy.

English Language Coach

Acronyms and Abbreviations What can you do if you don't know what an abbreviation or an acronym stands for? Look in a dictionary, of course! Many standard abbreviations and acronyms—those used by a lot of people—are defined in the dictionary. Look up an abbreviation or acronym the same way you look up a word. Here's a sample entry (*abbr* stands for "abbreviation"):

SPCA *abbr* Society for the Prevention of Cruelty to Animals

If the acronym or abbreviation is not in the regular dictionary, try looking in a specialized dictionary. Many public libraries have dictionaries of abbreviations and acronyms in their reference sections. The Internet also has specialized dictionaries.

On Your Own Use a dictionary to look up the acronyms and abbreviations below. In your Learner's Notebook, jot down what they stand for.

MBA **NWS** **IAAF**

Then see if you can create the acronyms for these popular Internet terms.

- frequently asked questions
- as soon as possible
- be right back
- by the way
- know what I mean?
- thanks in advance

Additional Support

Author Search To expand students' appreciation of Graeme Davis, have them access the Web site for additional information and resources.

Literature Focus Lesson

Informational Text Explain that a 2,000-year-old letter or report may be as interesting as a good story. Sometimes it's what you know *about* the document that creates intrigue. Ask students to gather in groups and brainstorm this question: *What makes information interesting?* Some things to consider in the discussion:

- the age of the documents
- the details in the documents
- how time and place contribute to reading about a birthday invitation, being out of cash, or what's new OL

Skills Preview

Key Reading Skill: Skimming and Scanning

Before you read the selection, skim it to get a general idea of what it is about. Look for subtitles and headings, key words, captions, and other text features. Next, scan the article to find out:

- Where the letters in the selection are from
- Who found the letters
- What kinds of subjects the letters are about

Partner Talk With a partner, read aloud the subtitles, headings, and captions in the selection. Also, point out any patterns you notice in the text. Which parts of the text are written by author Graeme Davis, and which parts are letters?

Key Literary Element: Organization

You have seen visuals that are organized in the general-to-specific pattern. The selection that you are about to read is organized the same way—except that it is a print selection, rather than a visual one. As you read the selection, think about how the general introduction prepares you for the specific letters that follow.

General-to-Specific Organization

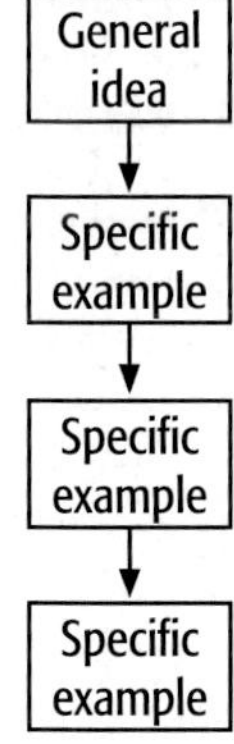

Interactive Literary Elements Handbook
To review or learn more about the literary elements, go to www.glencoe.com.

Get Ready to Read

Connect to the Reading

If you have ever been away from home, you know how good it feels to get a letter from a friend or family member.

- As you read the selection, notice what's on the minds of the people writing to each other long ago.
- R Think about how their lives were different from our lives today—and yet how they were also similar.

Make a List If one of your family members were far away from home, what would you want to tell him or her in a letter? Make a list of your ideas.

Build Background

The selection you are about to read includes ancient letters from the ruins of an old Roman fort.

- The Roman Empire was based in Rome, which is the modern capital of Italy.
- At the height of its power, the Roman Empire stretched as far north as Great Britain.
- The Romans built military posts wherever they went to try to keep order.
- One Roman emperor, Hadrian (HAY dree in), built a wall to protect his troops from the local people who were not under Roman control. This wall was seventy-five miles long and about eight feet thick. L

Set Purposes for Reading

BIG Question Read the selection to find out how, in ancient times, soldiers and other people far from home stayed in touch with their families, friends, and other members of their communities.

Set Your Own Purpose What else would you like to learn from the selection to help you answer the Big Question? Write your own purpose on the "Letters from Home" page of Foldable 8.

Keep Moving

Use these skills as you read the following selection.

Differentiated Instruction

Connecting to Music Explain that a community can be made up of people interested in a type of music. Ask students who enjoy expressing themselves musically to show the class how they connect to the history of what they perform. Have students select the genre of music they are most interested in.

- Have students bring in their instruments and sheet music.
- Ask them to demonstrate how what they already know about music helps them to learn new music.
- Finally, have students show how they connect modern life with the genre of music they selected by giving a performance. AL

Teach

L Literary Element

Organization Say: There are many ways to organize information in any kind of text. How would you organize steps in a recipe? *(Responses should include some idea of chronological order.)* How is chronological order different from spatial order? *(spatial: from near to far or from high to low; chronological: in time sequence)* OL

R Reading Skill

Review Connecting Ask: How does it feel to get a letter from a friend or family member? Or how did a character you read about feel after getting a letter from a friend? *(Responses will vary.)* BL

CheckPoint

Use the CheckPoint questions provided on Presentation Plus! to review skimming and scanning skills. These questions can be used with interactive response keypads for immediate student feedback.

Literature Online

Interactive Literary Elements Handbook Have students access the Web site to improve their understanding of organization.

Objectives
- Skim and scan text
- Make connections from text to self
- Identify literary elements: organization
- Identify acronyms and abbreviations

Teach

Viewing the Art

Ask: What time in history does this art make you think of? *(Possible response: Roman soldiers early in the A.D. era.)* OL

R Reading Skill

Skimming and Scanning

Say: You know how to skim and scan now, so describe how you would get an idea of the difficulty level of this selection. *(Possible response: Skim this page to find unfamiliar words, scan the footnotes and vocabulary at the bottom of the page, and make a note in my Learner's Notebook.)* OL

Readability Scores
Dale-Chall: 4.8
DRP: 63
Lexile: 1070

INFORMATIONAL TEXT
MAGAZINE
from *Dig*

Letters from Home 1

by Graeme Davis

Vindolanda was first built as a garrison at the extreme edge of the Roman world. Yet it was not as isolated as it might seem, since Vindolanda was part of a series of forts built to protect the northern boundary of Rome's province of Britannia.[1] Lying just to the south of the Wall, it continued to be used as a fort after Hadrian's Wall was built.

The soldiers at Vindolanda, like military personnel everywhere, must have looked forward to receiving letters from home. In 1973, archaeologists[2] found some letters dating to the end of the first century and early second century A.D., just a few years before Hadrian's Wall was built. They were **sufficiently** well-preserved to be readable. To date, more than

1. ***Garrison*** is another word for "fort." A ***province*** is a region of a country or, in this case, of an empire. ***Britannia*** is an old name for what is now Great Britain.
2. ***Archaeologists*** (ar kee AWL uh jists) study ancient cultures by examining their tools, pottery, buildings, and so on.

Vocabulary

sufficiently (suh FISH unt lee) *adv.* enough to meet the needs of the situation

Practice the Skills

1 Key Reading Skill

Skimming and Scanning R
Before you read, skim and scan the selection to get an idea of how difficult it is. Do you see words that you don't know? Do some parts look easier or harder than others? Start to read the selection. Read faster in places you understand easily, and slow down in places where it is more difficult to understand.

Additional Support

Reading in the Real World

Citizenship Students may find it helpful to research how the Romans were responsible for some of the ways in which cities are built today. Take these students to the library and ask them to focus on how the Roman achievements in building cities promoted a sense of community. Give them the tip that "roads" might be a good topic to start with, as they are a major way of linking people in communities. AS

READING WORKSHOP 2

An engraving of Roman soldiers building a fort. Taken from Trajan's Column, a monument built in the early 2nd century to honor the emperor Trajan.

1,100 documents have come to light, offering a unique insight into what life was like in the area. 2

It was Roman **policy** to station units far away from the provinces in which they had been recruited. The Romans favored this practice because they believed the soldiers would then have no ties to the people they might be fighting and would not become caught up in local politics or independence movements. The troops stationed at Hadrian's Wall came from every part of the empire except Britain. At one time, units of Syrian archers[3] were stationed there—the cold and damp of northern Britain must have come as a shock! C EL

3 ***Archers*** were soldiers armed with bows and arrows.

Vocabulary

policy (PAW luh see) *n.* a regular or usual way of handling things

Practice the Skills

2 English Language Coach

Acronyms and Abbreviations A.D. is an abbreviation for the Latin words *Anno Domini*, meaning "in the year of our Lord." The abbreviation is used to show dates since the birth of Jesus. Use your dictionary to find out what these abbreviations stand for: B.C., C.E., B.C.E.

Teach

Viewing the Art

Ask: What activity is shown in this picture? What people seem to be in charge? *(Possible response: It looks like the men are building a wall and soldiers are the ones in charge.)* OL

EL Language Coach

Acronyms and Abbreviations **Ask:** Why do you think C.E. was added as a way to identify dates? *(Students may say that "Common Era" is more respectful of people's religious beliefs, and Christians can still use C.E. to stand for Christian Era.)* AL

C Critical Thinking

Evaluation **Say:** The Romans' policy was to keep soldiers out of local politics by placing them far from their home provinces. How well do you think that policy worked? *(Responses will vary but may indicate that the policy might not have worked well because of people's attachment to their home communities.)* AS

English Language Coach

Primary Sources Some English language learners may have difficulty with the antiquated writing of these kinds of primary sources. If possible, have on hand modern examples of primary sources as well (e.g., Maya Angelou's *I Know Why the Caged Bird Sings*). Show students how modern and ancient writings can both be primary sources, for they are first-hand accounts of an event that is witnessed by the person describing it. Ask students to look up the meaning of secondary source and give some examples of it. EL OL

Objectives

- Adjust reading rate based on purpose for reading and on the difficulty, form, and style of text
- Skim and scan to preview text
- Recognize and understand acronyms and abbreviations to identify whole words and their meanings
- Use text features to interpret text

READING WORKSHOP 2

Teach

Viewing the Art

Ask: What kinds of items are shown in this photo? How do you think they were used by the soldiers? *(Responses will vary.)* BL

R Reading Skill

Skimming and Scanning

Say: After you skim and scan the selection, predict what the letters are about. **Ask:** What text features and words helped you decide what these letters are about? *(Responses will vary but should note that the heads help decipher the letters.)* After students have read the letters, have them discuss how accurate their predictions were. OL

Reading the Letters 3

Two types of document have been uncovered at Vindolanda. The first type was written in ink directly on thin slips of wood. The second consists of wooden tablets with a recessed center filled with black wax in which letters were incised with a metal stilus.[4] The wax could then be smoothed over so that the tablet could be used again. Although in almost every case the wax has long since disappeared, scratches made by the writer's stilus remain visible in the wooden backing. In fact, the scratches are similar to the impression a pen makes in the next sheet of paper if you press too hard when writing on a pad.

Because the pieces of wood had spent centuries in garbage pits, they were discolored. However, with the aid of infrared photography,[5] archaeologists are able to make out what was written on some of them. Research continues, and more documents are constantly being interpreted. On the next four pages are excerpts from several Vindolanda letters. 4

A Birthday Invitation from a Lady

Claudia Severa to her Lepitlina, greetings. On 11 September, sister, for the celebration of my birthday, I give you a warm invitation to make sure that you come to us.

A Readiness Report

18 May, net number of the First Cohort of Tungrians, commanded by Julius Verecundus the prefect: 752, including 6 centurions.[6]

Of whom there are absent: guards of the governor, 46; at the office of Ferox at Coria, 337, including 2 centurions; at London, 1 centurion [writing becomes fragmentary] Total

Pottery from Stonea Grange in Roman Britain, 2nd Century. British Museum, London, Great Britain.

4. To ***incise*** means to cut into or carve. A ***stilus*** is a hard-pointed instrument used for writing or making marks in something hard.
5. ***Infrared photography*** can take pictures of things that are not visible to the human eye.
6. This letter writer is simply reporting the number of soldiers available for fighting and other duties. The ***First Cohort of Tungrians*** was a group of soldiers from Tungria, which is present-day Belgium and Holland. A ***prefect*** was a high Roman official, and ***centurions*** were officers, each in command of 100 soldiers.

Practice the Skills

3 Key Literary Element

Organization Skim the first paragraph on this page. How does the first sentence help you understand what the paragraph is generally about? What are two specific details that you expect to find in the paragraph?

4 Key Reading Skill

R **Skimming and Scanning** Skim this page. What do you think these first two letters are about?

Additional Support

Reading in the Real World

Career Have students who are interested in infrared photography do research for the class. Use the following questions as focusing points:

- How is infrared photography different from other kinds of photography? What equipment is used?
- Why does it require special skill?
- When and how did infrared techniques begin?
- Who uses infrared photography and why?
- How does infrared photography help us understand ancient communities? AL

READING WORKSHOP 2

absentees: 456, including 5 centurions.

Remainder present: 296, including 1 centurion.

From these: sick, 15; wounded, 6; suffering from inflammation of the eyes; 10. Total of these: 31.

Remainder, fit for active service: 265, including 1 centurion.

Send Money! 5

Several times I have written to you that I have bought about five thousand *modii* of grain, on account of which I need cash. Unless you send me some cash, at least 500 *denarii*,[7] I shall lose the deposit I put down of around 300 *denarii* [for a shipment of grain], and I shall be embarrassed. So, I ask you, send me some cash as soon as possible."

A portrait of the emperor Hadrian is engraved on this bronze coin from the 2nd century. British Museum, London, Great Britain.

Shipment of Parts

Metto to Advectus, very many greetings.

I have sent you wooden materials through the agency of Saco: 34 wheel hubs, 38 axles for carts including one axle turned on the lathe, 300 spokes, 26 bed boards, 8 seats, [writing becomes fragmentary] 6 benches, and 6 goat-skins. I pray that you are in good health, brother.[8] C

A Care Package from Home

I have sent you . . . [word missing] . . . pairs of socks from Sattua, two pairs of sandals and two pairs of underpants . . .

This shoe probably belonged to a child in the 1st or 2nd century. It was found in what is now London. British Museum, London, Great Britain.

7. ***Modii*** (MOH dee) is the plural form of *modius*, a Roman unit of measure. ***Denarii*** (duh NAR ee) is the plural of *denarius*, a Roman coin.

8. Advectus may have been related. It's more likely, however, that he uses the word ***brother*** as a sign of friendship, just as men do today.

Practice the Skills

5 Key Reading Skill

Skimming and Scanning

What does the letter writer need money for? Scan the paragraph to find out.

Teach

Viewing the Art

Ask: What type of person was most likely engraved on ancient coins? *(Responses will vary.)* **OL**

C Critical Thinking

Analysis Ask: Why do you think the phrases "writing becomes fragmentary" and "word missing" are in brackets? *(Possible response: They are not part of the original text but are added to let the reader know that words are missing.)* **OL**

R Reading Skill

Review Connecting

Say: The Roman community described in these letters may remind you of your community in some ways. In other ways, it may seem very different. Name two similarities and two differences. *(Possible responses: Similar—birthday celebrations and care packages; Different—forms of communication and transportation)* **AS**

Reading Fluency

Mood Suggest that students get into small groups and take turns reading aloud each of the ancient writings. Suggest that they help each other get in the mood of each piece by imagining the person who is writing and the setting. For example, maybe the writer who sent the care package is the mother or wife of a soldier. If students can get into the time and place of a text, it can help their fluency. **EL** **BL**

Objectives

- Adjust reading rate based on purpose for reading and on the difficulty, form, and style of text
- Skim and scan to preview text
- Use organization of text to locate relevant information on a topic
- Use text features to interpret text
- Research career information

READING WORKSHOP 2

Teach

Viewing the Photo
Ask: If you were an archaeologist and you were approaching this place for the first time, what would you want to know about it? *(Responses will vary.)* OL

EL Language Coach

Compound Words Say: Look at the footnote for *messmate.* What was a mess? *(the room where soldiers ate)* Name two more compound words you can make with *mates. (Possible responses: classmates, teammates)* Based on the words you came up with, what do you think the word *mates* means? *(Possible response: companions, people who are with you)* BL EL

L Literary Element

Review Tone Ask: In general, what is the tone of the letters in this selection? *(Possible response: somewhat formal)* OL

The ruins of a commander's residence in Vindolanda.

What's New?

Chrauttius to Veldeius his brother and old messmate,[9] very many greetings. And I ask you, brother Veldeius—I am surprised that you have written nothing back to me for such a long time—whether you have heard anything from our elders, or about . . . [name missing] . . . in which unit he is; and greet him from me, and Virilis the veterinary doctor. Ask Virilis whether you may send through one of our friends the pair of shears[10] that he promised me in exchange for money. And I ask you, brother Virilis, to greet from me our sister Thuttena. Write back to me how Velbuteius is. I hope you enjoy the best of fortune. Farewell.

An Appeal to the Governor

As befits an honest man, I implore your lordship not to allow me, an innocent man, to have been beaten with rods and, my lord, since I was unable to complain to the prefect because he

Practice the Skills

9. These men may have been real brothers and were once soldiers together. The soldiers' dining room was called the "mess," and their ***messmates*** were those they ate with.
10. ***Shears*** are large scissors.

EL

Additional Support

Literature Focus Lesson

Drama Some students may enjoy turning "An Appeal to the Governor" into a scene for a play. As a class, brainstorm the dramatic elements needed:

- Plot—what's the basic event that happens? *(imprisoned man seeks justice)*
- Setting—Where does the plot take place? *(letter writer's prison cell; Governor's office)*
- Characters—who is involved in the plot? *(letter writer, Governor, prefect, beneficiarius, other centurions)*
- Dialogue—what words will show the characters' personalities?

(activity continued on page 927)

was detained[11] by ill-health, I have complained in vain to the *beneficiarius* [another official] and the rest of the centurions of his unit. Accordingly, I implore your mercifulness not to allow me, a man from overseas and an innocent one, about whose good faith you may [ask anyone], to have been bloodied by rods as if I had committed some crime. 6 ○

Practice the Skills

6 BIG Question

What do members of a community count on one another for? Write your answer on the "Letters from Home" page of Foldable 8. You may also want to make some sketches to show how you picture the people mentioned in these letters. Your response will help you answer the Unit Challenge later.

C1 BQ C2

11. To ***implore*** is to beg. ***Detained*** means "held up" or "stopped from going."

Teach

C1 Critical Thinking

Synthesis Ask: If you look back over the kinds of letters that remain from the past, what would you say to summarize how these people lived? *(Possible responses should include some sense of the ordinary needs these soldiers had, of their reliance on families, other soldiers, and even on their superiors.)* OL

C2 Critical Thinking

Evaluation Ask: How is the struggle to form helpful communities the same today as it was in the time of the Roman Empire? *(Responses will vary.)* OL

BQ BIG Question

Ask: Why did the letter writer believe the Governor would help him? *(Possible response: The governor is the top government official.)* OL

Assess

Use the CheckPoint questions provided on Presentation Plus! to check for comprehension of the selection. These questions can be used with interactive response keypads for immediate student feedback.

(continued from page 926)

Once the class decides on a basic idea for each element, assign groups to complete each of these tasks:

- Write the scene.
- Create a setting.
- Choose characters or have auditions.
- Practice the dialogue and match actions to it. Remember, the theme of the play is one man's struggle against a foreign community. OL

Objectives

- Use text features to interpret text
- Summarize and evaluate text
- Recognize compound words

Assess

Resources for page 928

- Selection Quick Check
- Selection and Unit Assessment
- ExamView Assessment Suite
- Interactive Tutor: Self-Assessment

Students can respond to the *After You Read* items in their Learner's Notebook or on a separate sheet of paper.

Answering the

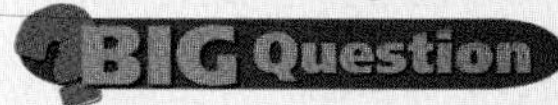

1. Responses will vary.
2. in modern day Britain
3. members of the soldiers' families, military officers, the soldiers themselves, the Governor
4. daily life

Critical Thinking

5. Responses will vary. Students may say people far from home find it hard to make ties with strangers.
6. Possible response: The pits are often full of things that ancient people used. Archaeologists learn about cultures from the objects.
7. Responses will vary but will probably indicate that the selection is about ancient ruins and pieces of writing.
8. Responses will vary. Students may say that these letters represent the lives of only a few people.

After You Read

Letters from Home

Objectives (pp. 928–929)
Reading Skim and scan text
Literature Identify literary elements: organization
Vocabulary Identify acronyms and abbreviations
Grammar Use punctuation: colons

Answering the

1. How does the selection "Letters from Home" help you think about the Big Question: What Is a Community?
2. **Recall** Where are the ancient Roman ruins of Vindolanda located?
   TIP **Right There**
3. **Recall** Who received these "letters from home"?
   TIP **Right There**
4. **Summarize** What were the letters mostly about?
   TIP **Think and Search**

Critical Thinking

5. **Evaluate** The purpose of the Roman policy–to station soldiers far from their own homes–was to keep the soldiers from having ties with the people they were fighting. Do you think this policy made sense? Explain your answer.
   TIP **Author and Me**
6. **Infer** Why are garbage pits of great importance to archaeologists? Give details from the text in your answer.
   TIP **Author and Me**
7. **Use Text Features** What quick information do you get from the text features when you skim and scan the selection?
   TIP **Author and Me**
8. **Evaluate** Do you think these letters are reliable sources to help you learn about life in the days of the Roman Empire? Why or why not?
   TIP **Author and Me**

Write About Your Reading

Use the RAFT system to write about "Letters from Home."

Role: a friend

Audience: a soldier stationed far from home

Format: letter

Topic: Write a letter to a soldier stationed far away. Tell about news from home (your community) and how you hope he or she can return soon.

Write About Your Reading

Possible response:

Dear Cyrus,

Are you still hard at work rebuilding the wall that you spoke to us about last time? Papa has all of us carrying stones to the wall around our home, too. Remember how the stones were loose and we used to build small forts from the rubble? Even four-year-old Claudia must carry stones and help. She cries for you at night.

When does your prefect say you can come home? Please try to come before the winter solstice.

Your loyal brother,

Basil

Skills Review

Key Reading Skill: Skimming and Scanning

9. Name one thing you learned about the selection by skimming and one thing you learned by scanning.
Which skill–skimming or scanning–most helped you understand the selection?

Key Literary Element: Organization

10. Look at the subhead "Reading the Letters" on page 924 of the selection. How does this general subhead sum up the information in the section?

11. What are two specific details that explain the subhead "Reading the Letters"?

12. Do you think the selection would have been easier or harder to understand if the general introduction to the article had been left out? Explain your answer.

Vocabulary Check

For each word in dark type, choose the word or phrase below it that means most nearly the same thing.

13. sufficiently
well done
quickly
honestly

14. policy
law
guiding idea
benefit

15. English Language Coach Explain the difference between the abbreviations B.C. and A.D. How do historians use these abbreviations to talk about time?

Grammar Link: Colons

Use a colon to separate hours and minutes in expressions of time.

- 1:15 P.M.

Also use a colon after the salutation in a business letter.

- Dear Sir:
- Dear Sir or Madam:
- Dear Mr. Yamaguchi:

Grammar Practice

Rewrite the following sentences. Add a colon where needed in each.

16. Dear Ms. Kowalski

17. School starts at 735 A.M.

18. Our flight leaves at 630.

Writing Application Add two colons correctly to the Write About Your Reading assignment you completed.

Web Activities For eFlashcards, Selection Quick Checks, and other Web activities, go to www.glencoe.com.

Skills Review

Key Reading Skill: Skimming and Scanning

9. Responses may include skimming examples such as learning that soldiers celebrated birthdays and wrote home for money. Scanning examples may include that the military people tallied how many soldiers they had at different posts.

Key Literary Element: Organization

10. Responses will vary.

11. Possible response: One type of letter was written with ink on a slip of wood. The other type of letter could still be seen because of how deeply the writer's stilus scratched into the wax and left an impression on the pad beneath.

12. Possible response: The general introduction made reading easier because it sets the scene of Vindolanda's forts, which gives the reader a picture of soldiers far from home.

Close

Ask students to discuss what they've learned from these selections to help them answer the Big Question.

Vocabulary Check

13. well done

14. guiding idea

15. B.C. refers to "Before Christ," and A.D. means "Anno Domino," in the year of Our Lord. These abbreviations help historians make general or specific references to time.

Grammar Link: Colons

Grammar Practice

16. Dear Ms. Kowalski:

17. School starts at 7:35 A.M.

18. Our flight leaves at 6:30.

Clarifying

UNIT 8

Objectives covered in this workshop:

- Clarify understanding of difficult or confusing text

How to Help Students Clarify

Why Is It Important?

- Clarifying helps students clear up difficult portions of text
- Often times students need to clarify one idea before they can grasp another idea in a selection
- When students gain clarifying skills, they become better readers and have more confidence in reading new passages

How to Help Students Get It

- Tell students to reread sections that are not clear.
- They should stop to clarify ideas before they get too far into a text.
- Encourage students to use dictionaries to look up unfamiliar words and to keep the definitions in their Learner's Notebook so they can refer to it often.
- Emphasize the importance of context clues. What else is being said in the paragraph? Can this information help clarify the confusing part?
- Encourage students to practice several of the other reading strategies they have learned to clarify information. Questioning, responding, connecting, and activating prior knowledge can be particularly helpful when clarifying.

Reading to Answer The Big Question

Ah, Wilderness!

The Bailis family has learned to live comfortably in the austere mountain environment outside of Telluride, Colorado, by generating their own power with solar panels and wind energy. Students will discover how the environment can shape a family community in this informational article from TIME.

Photographing History

This short biography describes the accomplishments of America's first famous photographer, Matthew Brady, who gained fame taking pictures of notable Americans and of the brutality of the Civil War. Students will discover how both the events of the time and his community affected Brady's life.

Teach

More About the Author

Amanda Hinnant is a versatile writer. As a contributing author for the book *Real Simple Solutions,* Hinnant wrote an article that helps grocery shoppers by explaining how shelves are organized by brands. She also cowrote a paper that discusses the Internet skills of young adults.

V Vocabulary

Word Origins Say: Latin is considered a dead language; that is, people rarely speak Latin in everyday life. Yet, many of our words come from Latin words. In Latin, the word *solus* means *alone.* Which vocabulary word comes from this Latin word? *(solitary)* **OL** What other English words come from this Latin word? *(Possible responses: solo, solitaire, solitude)* **AL**

Before You Read

Ah, Wilderness!

Meet the Author

Amanda Hinnant started writing in high school and never stopped. She has written for magazines including *Glamour* and *Time.* She got the idea for this article when she was stuck in an elevator on the 41st floor of a building in New York. The idea of being able to create your own power seemed very appealing to her.

Author Search For more about Amanda Hinnant, go to www.glencoe.com.

Objectives (pp. 932–937)
Reading Clarify ideas and text • Make connections from text to self
Literature Identify literary devices: figurative language
Vocabulary Identify borrowed words

Vocabulary Preview

V

plunges (PLUN jiz) *v.* dips or moves downward suddenly; form of the verb *plunge* **(p. 934)** *As one boy plunges into a snowdrift, another secretly makes snowballs!*

solitary (SAWL uh tair ee) *adj.* all alone **(p. 934)** *The family lives a solitary life at home.*

generate (JEN uh rayt) *v.* to produce or create **(p. 935)** *The family uses two methods to generate energy.*

rationing (RASH un ing) *n.* the controlled use of something **(p. 935)** *Everyone in the family makes rationing energy a way of life.*

trek (trek) *n.* a slow or difficult journey **(p. 936)** *Nobody seemed to mind the trek from home to town.*

English Language Coach

Borrowed Words As immigrants come to an English-speaking country, they bring words from their own languages. Sometimes these words become part of their new country's language, too.

Word	Source	Original meaning
admiral	Arabic	commander
cookie	Dutch	small cake

Partner Talk With a partner, use a dictionary to look up each word below. From what language did English borrow each word?

- **sauna**
- **robot**
- **chocolate**
- **banana**
- **bandana**
- **loot**
- **zebra**
- **caravan**
- **pajamas**
- **boss**

Additional Support

Author Search To expand students' appreciation of Amanda Hinnant, have them access the Web site for additional information and resources.

Differentiated Instruction

Research Reporting Nonfiction writers often research by visiting a location or person that can provide information on their topics. They take careful notes to be sure that their research reports are factual and accurate. You may wish to take students to a nearby recycling center, alternative energy provider, or other location where they can obtain information on "earth-friendly" lifestyles. Have them take notes and work in groups to create a poster or drawing to convey the primary message of the center. **OL**

Why Is It Important? Getting a clear picture of what you read helps you understand and use information. Authors often build ideas on one another. If you don't clear up a confusing part, you may not understand main ideas or information that comes later. For example, if you don't understand the set-up directions for your new sound system, it's unlikely that you'll be listening to your new CD anytime soon!

Literature Online

Study Central Visit www.glencoe.com, and click on Study Central to review clarifying.

How Do I Do It? Try one or more of these techniques:

- Slowly reread the hard parts.
- Put ideas in your own words.
- Ask questions.
- Look up unfamiliar words.

R

Here's how one student clarified a passage from a historical document. Read the passage, which is from an oath pledged by ancient Greek soldiers.

"I will not bring dishonor upon my weapons nor desert the comrade by my side. I will strive to hand on my fatherland greater than I found it."

I don't get that last sentence. What does "strive to hand on my fatherland" mean? Who's handing what to whom? I'll slow down and reread the sentence. Oh, now I see. "Hand on" is like "hand down." The soldiers will hand down their country to the next generation in better shape than they found it.

Practice It!

Read the passage below. Use one or more of the clarifying techniques to clarify any parts you find hard. Then, in your Learner's Notebook, put the passage in your own words.

"We Spartans have many reasons to expect success in battle—first, superiority in numbers and military experience, and second, general and unvarying obedience in the execution of orders."

Use It!

Clarify passages you find hard or confusing as you read the selections.

Teach

Literature Online

Study Central Have students access the Web site to review clarifying and to complete a related activity.

R Reading Skill

Clarifying **Ask:** How would you clarify what the writer means by: "I will strive to hand on my fatherland greater than I found it"? OL *(Possible response: Carefully reread the sentence, then look up the meaning of* Fatherland *or any other unfamiliar word, and try to put the sentence in your own words.)*

Resources for page 931

- Use Reading Skills Transparency in *Read Aloud, Think Aloud,* Unit 8, to help students practice clarifying.

Reading in the Real World

Citizenship World languages—both past and present—have influenced the English language. This is especially true of Greek. Many English words come directly from Greek or are made of two or more Greek words. Have students work in pairs to find the etymology, or origin, of the following words in an unabridged dictionary: chaos, crisis, oxygen, copper, government, nuclear, catastrophe, hypodermic, hydrogen, philosophy, paleontology. Then ask them to find two additional words with Greek origins. OL

Objectives

- Clarify ideas and text
- Explore word origins to understand historical influences on English word meanings and usage

Focus

BELLRINGER Options

Daily Language Practice Transparency

Focus Activity Ask: What is your idea of a community? *(Possible response: A community is a group of people who live together and support one another.)* OL

Teach

R Reading Skill

Clarifying Ask: When might you want to clarify what someone says to you? *(Possible response: If the doctor gave me instructions about medicine, I'd want to be sure they were clear.)* OL

V Vocabulary

Academic Vocabulary Say: Read the definition of *clarify* in the first bulleted point of the *What Is It?* section. From the definition, can you figure out the base word of *clarify?* *(clear)* AL

READING WORKSHOP 3

Skills Focus

You will practice using these skills when you read the following selections:

- "Ah, Wilderness!" p. 934
- "Photographing History," p. 942

Reading

- Clarifying difficult or confusing text

Literature

- Understanding figurative language

Vocabulary

- Understanding historical influences on the English language
- Academic Vocabulary: *clarify*

Writing/Grammar

- Using semicolons correctly

Skill Lesson

Clarifying

Learn It!

R **What Is It?** Sometimes selections contain difficult or confusing ideas or words. Sometimes a word, a sentence, an idea, or even a whole section of text can be confusing. When you don't understand something you're reading, you need to **clarify** it.

- V Clarify means to make something clear so you or anyone else can understand it.
- When you clarify, you look at difficult sections of a text in order to clear up what is confusing.

Analyzing Cartoons

Why does the kid ask his mom to clarify what she wants? When something in a text isn't clear to you, you can reread it, look in a dictionary, or ask for help.

Objectives (pp. 930–931)
Reading Clarify ideas and text

Academic Vocabulary

clarify (KLAIR uh fy) *v.* to make understandable

Additional Support

English Language Coach

Borrowed Words Science and technology have added many words to the English language, especially in the 20th century. Words that many people use today were unknown to their great-grandparents! Write these word pairs on the board: microchip and byte; vaccine and chemotherapy; solar panel and hydroelectricity. Ask students from what areas of study we received these words. Then ask them to name other science and technology words that they know. EL AL

Workshop Resources

Pacing (Days) Standard	Block	Lesson	Student Materials	Teacher Resources
1		Key Skill Lesson: Clarifying	Key Reading Skills Practice English Language Coach	Bellringer Options Transparencies Read Aloud, Think Aloud Transparencies Presentation Plus!
2		"Ah, Wilderness"	Literary Analysis Transparencies Glencoe Online Selection Vocabulary Development Academic Vocabulary Development English Language Coach Active Reading Graphic Organizer Literary Analysis StudentWorks Plus Online Student Edition Literature Classics Selection and Unit Assessments	Literary and Text Analysis Transparencies Puzzlemaker Skill Level Up! BookLink 3 Assessment by Learning Objective (Diagnostic and Formative) Interactive Tutor Self-Assessment TeacherWorks Plus
2		"Photographing History"	Glencoe Online Selection Vocabulary Development Academic Vocabulary Development English Language Coach Active Reading Graphic Organizer Literary Analysis StudentWorks Plus Online Student Edition Literature Classics Selection and Unit Assessments	Literary and Text Analysis Transparencies Puzzlemaker Skill Level Up! BookLink 3 Assessment by Learning Objective (Diagnostic and Formative) Interactive Tutor Self-Assessment TeacherWorks Plus

Keys for Unit Resource

- Blackline Master
- Workbook
- Supplemental Text
- CD-ROM
- DVD
- Transparency
- Web-based
- Fast Files

Level Appropriate Code

AS = Activities for all students
AL = Activities for students working above grade level
OL = Activities for students working at grade level
BL = Activities for students working below grade level
EL = Activities for English language learners

Skills Preview

Key Reading Skill: Clarifying

Skim "Ah, Wilderness!" before you read it. Look to see whether there are any words you don't know. List them in your Learner's Notebook. Then try to clarify their meanings by looking for context clues. R

Write to Learn Jot down definitions for the words on your list. As you read, see if your definitions make sense.

Key Literary Element: Figurative Language

Figurative language is language that is used for descriptive effect, but is not meant to be taken literally, or at face value. Suppose, for example, that you say to your friends at lunch, "I'm so hungry I could eat a horse." None of your friends is likely to think you're going to dine on roast pony. They understand that you're using figurative language to say that you're unusually hungry.

Two common kinds of figurative language are similes and metaphors. Both are comparisons between very different things that are similar in some important way. Similes are signaled by the words *like, as,* or *than.* Metaphors are more direct. They do not contain signal words.

Partner Talk Fire up your imagination. With a partner, create your own similes by filling in the blanks below. Be original. Try not to use similes that you've heard before.

- That man is taller than ___.
- That girl is as beautiful as ___.
- The sunshine is like ___.

Interactive Literary Elements Handbook To review or learn more about the literary elements, go to www.glencoe.com.

Get Ready to Read

Connect to the Reading

Have you ever wished you didn't have to depend on other people? The people in this selection live so far from other people that they have to generate their own electricity. As you read this selection, think about how your life would change if you lived like this family.

Partner Talk With a partner, list things you do or use everyday that require electricity.

Build Background

The Bailis family uses two natural sources of energy: wind and the sun.

- Sol is another name for the sun. Solar means "related to the sun."
- Wind is actually a form of solar energy. The sun heats Earth's air unevenly and causes it to move. Wind is the result.
- *Solar collectors* are devices that get heated by the sunshine. They store the heat they collect, so it can be used later to heat a home.
- The use of solar energy became popular when oil prices rose in 1973–1974. Now the government gives people tax help if they use solar energy instead of gas, oil, or coal.

Set Purposes for Reading

BIG Question Read "Ah, Wilderness!" to discover how the Bailises' environment shapes their family community. 

Set Your Own Purpose What else would you like to learn from the article to help you answer the Big Question? Write your own purpose on the "Ah, Wilderness!" page of Foldable 8.

Keep Moving

Use these skills as you read the following selection.

Teach

R Reading Skill

Review Predicting **Ask:** Based on your skimming of "Ah, Wilderness!" what do you predict you will learn? *(Possible response: I'm going to learn about a family that enjoys living in the wilderness.)* AS

BQ 

Ask: To what community could children who live far away from a city or town belong? *(Possible responses: family, school, church)* AS

CheckPoint

Use the CheckPoint questions provided on Presentation Plus! to check for prior knowledge of clarifying skills. These questions can be used with interactive response keypads for immediate student feedback.

Literature Online

Interactive Literary Elements Handbook Have students access the Web site to improve their understanding of figurative language.

English Language Coach

Figurative Language Students who need help identifying what is being compared in similes and metaphors might find the following "equation" helpful. Because two things are compared or similar, students can think of them as "equal." Have students use the equation formula for any similes or metaphors they come across. EL BL

My love (x) is like (=) a red, red rose (y). *(Simile)*

My brother (x) is a (=) thorn (y) in my side. *(Metaphor)*

Objectives

- Clarify ideas and text
- Make connections from text to self
- Identify literary devices: figurative language
- Identify borrowed words

Teach

R1 Reading Skill

Clarifying **Ask:** How does the writer clarify the meaning of the word *mesa? (She puts a definition right after the word.)* OL

R2 Reading Skill

Review Visualizing **Ask:** Which vocabulary word helps you visualize how quickly the setting changes when the sun sets? *(plunges)* OL

Readability Scores
Dale-Chall: 7.1
DRP: 61
Lexile: 1190

READING WORKSHOP 3

TIME

Ah, WILDERNESS!

Living in the middle of nowhere with solar panels and a few snowmobiles is not a choice many would make. But the Bailis family did—and they've never looked back

By AMANDA HINNANT

On this sunny day, the Bailis home has a breathtaking view of aspen forests and majestic, snow-capped mountains. The Bailises live on a **mesa**, a raised area of land with a flat top and steep cliffs on all sides, about twenty miles outside of Telluride, Colorado. R1 Later, as twilight approaches, shadows outline the black trees and the San Juan Mountains[1]. Then, with surprising quickness, the sun sets, and the mesa **plunges** into a deep, silent, **solitary** darkness. R2 1

In contrast to the dark, hushed outdoors, the Bailis living room is bathed in light and positively hums with activity. Light from the fireplace, the center of the family's house, casts a warm, buttery glow over Ray and Beth Bailis and their boys, Max, 8, and Finn, 3. Beth and Max are working at the

1. The ***San Juan Mountains*** in Colorado are some of the highest and most rugged mountains in the United States.

1 English Language Coach

Borrowed Words English borrowed the word *mesa* from a Spanish word for "table." In what way is a *mesa* like a table? Reread the definition of *mesa* in the first paragraph.

Vocabulary

plunges (PLUN jiz) *v.* dips or moves downward suddenly

solitary (SAWL uh tar ee) *adj.* all alone

Additional Support

Reading Fluency

Reading Along Students who have difficulty reading and visualizing selections with a great deal of descriptions might benefit from reading along silently with a tape. Ask students to pause the tape periodically to take notes or sketch a scene that has just been described. They can also ask themselves questions about the selection to test their understanding of what they have read and heard. EL BL

READING WORKSHOP 3

computer while Ray and Finn are happily playing a board game.

Besides living in the middle of nowhere, the Bailis family lives "off the grid," which means that they **generate** their own energy instead of relying on the area's power company. But being independent of the power company doesn't mean that it's the Dark Ages at the Bailis residence. Their home has all the modern conveniences that any 21st-century family could hope to have: microwave, Internet, washer and dryer, television. A big difference, however, is that the Bailises must plan the use of these appliances carefully. They know exactly how much or how little energy they can use. Running too many appliances at once will shut down the inverter[2], which is roughly the same as blowing a fuse in your home. **2**

For this family, **rationing** energy has practically become second nature and is also a way to be closer to nature. Solar panels on the roof soak up the sun's energy, and a wind generator uses the wind to generate most of the house's power. For sunless days with little wind, when neither solar panels nor a wind generator can do any good, there's a propane generator in the back.

Most of the time, Beth says, remote living makes you feel like you can do anything. And the Bailises know from experience that they can handle just about anything. When they moved into their house, it was heated by a woodstove that needed to be fed at 3 a.m., the propane generator didn't work very well, the roof didn't have any solar panels, and the old windows let the cold air leak in. Life in this remote spot was a lot like camping indoors. They burned lots and lots of **EL**

Thayer Allyson Gowdy

The Bailises' Colorado home in the San Juan Mountains generates its own power—day *and* night.

2 Key Reading Skill

Clarify "Dark Ages" refers to the Middle Ages (about 476 to 1000 A.D.). When the writer says the family is not living in the Dark Ages, she means the family is not backward, or out of step with modern times. But she also means something else. In what other way is the family not living in the dark?

2. An ***inverter*** is a **device** that converts electricity into a form that can be used in a home.

Vocabulary

generate (JEN uh rayt) v. to produce or create

rationing (RASH un ing) *n.* the controlled use of something

Teach

Viewing the Photo

Ask: Why might someone who views the photo be surprised to learn that the Bailises generate their own power? *(Possible response: The house is brightly and completely lit, despite the darkness of the evening.)* **OL**

EL Language Coach

Compound Words Say: Remember that compound words get their meanings from the definitions of the individual words that make them up. What compound word names the device the Bailises used to heat their home when they first moved in? *(woodstove)* **BL** From its name, what can you tell about how it operates? *(It burns wood.)* **OL**

Reading in the Real World

Citizenship Solar energy is one form of renewable energy. The selection discusses the inconvenience of the woodstove, which uses an energy source that would disappear if trees weren't replanted. Ask students to work in groups to do research and create comparison charts that show five sources of energy. **OL** Have students discuss the impact these sources have on communities and what responsibility citizens have to use energy wisely. **AL**

Objectives

- Clarify difficult or confusing text
- Identify and understand the meanings of compound words
- Analyze photos

Teach

Viewing the Photo

Ask: After looking at their facial expressions, how do you think the Bailises feel about their lifestyle? *(Possible response: happy, satisfied, content)* **AS**

C1 Critical Thinking

Evaluation Ask: Based on what you know about the Bailises' lifestyle, do you think you would enjoy living as they do? Why or why not? *(Responses will vary.)* **AS**

C2 Critical Thinking

Synthesis Ask: Why do you think Beth wants her sons to be connected with nature? What are some of the benefits of being close to nature? *(Possible responses: Beth likes the freedom and safety of being connected with nature. Living close to nature is probably cleaner, healthier, more peaceful, less stressful, etc.)* **OL**

READING WORKSHOP 3

candles and learned how to survive on very little energy without letting it affect them too much.

Today snow is landing all around the house, swirling past the windows as if in a just-shaken snow globe. The snow determines how the Bailises dress as well as how they drive. Early on this snowy morning, the family members bundle into snow clothes. Each individual has two sets of gloves, goggles, and scarves (because one set is always wet). There aren't any snowplows rumbling by to clear the road so, from about November to May each year, the Bailis family must ride on snowmobiles from their house to their cars, parked 2½ miles away on the main road. Everything they carry, including briefcases, groceries, mail, and garbage, has to fit onto their snowmobiles or the sleds behind them. Beth and Ray commute to Telluride, where she is a landscape designer and he is in sales, and the boys make the **trek** into town to go to school. 3

3 Key Literary Element

Figurative Language What does the writer compare the swirling snow to? (Hint: look for the signal words *as if.*) In what way are the two things in the comparison similar? How are they different?

The chilly weather doesn't daunt[3] Max and Finn, who love the snow. "My boys are true polar bears," Beth says. When they are not busy with schoolwork or chores, they enjoy romping around outside. The boys may have inherited their love of the outdoors from their mother, who grew up on a large cattle ranch in Missouri and spent most of her childhood outside. "I was a child of nature," Beth says. "I would leave the house in the morning and not come back until the afternoon. Fishing, walking the creek—I never felt afraid."

Beth hopes her boys will be connected with nature in the same way. Already she sees evidence of this connection dawning. She loves how Max, in all his self-portraits and family sketches, includes the mountain range behind their house. "He really has a sense of where he is from and who he is," she says.

Thayer Allyson Gowdy

The family gathers for an early Sunday dinner.

3. To ***daunt*** someone is to scare.

Vocabulary

trek (trek) *n.* a slow or difficult journey

Additional Support

Reading in the Real World

Career Students who are interested in energy conservation and environment-friendly lifestyles might want to research an environmental science career. Take students to the library to gather information on careers in waste or water management, pollution control, or alternate energy production. Ask students to create a pamphlet, poster, and presentation on their career for a classroom "job fair." Make sure they include information about the impact people in these fields have on their communities. **OL**

She expects that her boys' upbringing will help them feel unique[4], the way she felt when she left the ranch and went to college. "It just gives them an identity," she explains. 4

Home Off the Range

The Bailises are just like any other American family—except . . .

- "Traffic" sounds they sometimes hear outside the house often come from a "bugling" herd of elk.
- Beth celebrates a sunny, windy day by running the vacuum cleaner and the dishwasher at the same time.
- The family snowmobiles have names: the Pig, Phazer, Wildcat, and Kitty Cat (the child-size one).
- They know the exact longitude and latitude of their house in case they have to be rescued by helicopter.
- The family is so accustomed to the 9,900-foot altitude that, when they visit Ray's sisters in California, they get giddy from the higher level of oxygen.
- Beth worries about mountain lions when the boys play out back.

—Updated 2005, from *Real Simple*, March 2004

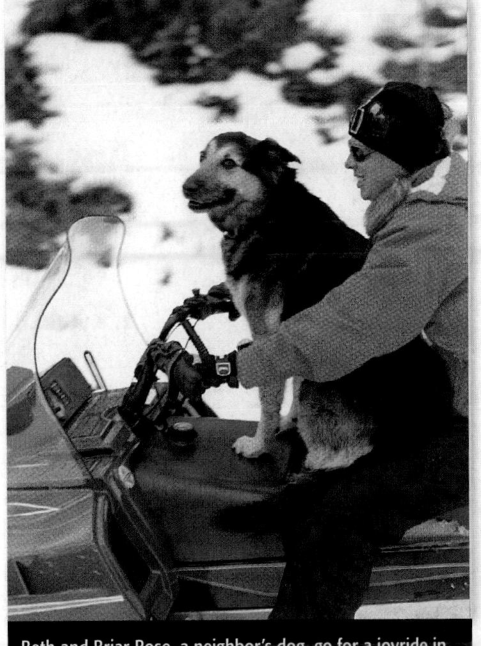

Thayer Allyson Gowdy

Beth and Briar Rose, a neighbor's dog, go for a joyride in early winter.

4 BIG Question

BQ How do you think growing up on a cattle ranch affected Beth's decision to raise her family in the wilderness? Write your answer on your "Ah, Wilderness!" FOLDABLE. Your response will help you answer the Unit Challenge later.

4. A ***unique*** (yoo NEEK) person is one of a kind, special because he or she is different from others.

READING WORKSHOP 3

Teach

Viewing the Photo

Ask: Why might people such as the Bailises' neighbor have a pet like Briar Rose? *(Possible response: Because they live far away from others, they need a pet for company and possibly for security.)* OL

BQ 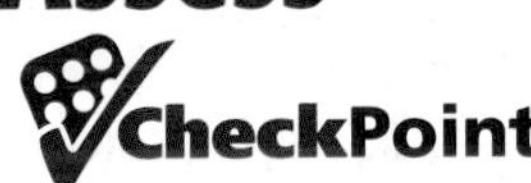

Ask: To what communities do Ray and Beth Bailis belong? *(Possible response: They have a work community and a family. They belong to a community of parents from their children's school.)* OL

Assess

CheckPoint

Use the CheckPoint questions provided on Presentation Plus! to check for comprehension of the selection. These questions can be used with interactive response keypads for immediate student feedback.

Differentiated Instruction

Compare and Contrast Students who need help with comparison and contrast may find a comparison/contrast T-chart like the one here helpful. Ask them to create a T-chart of the information provided in the "Home Off the Range" section on page 937. EL BL

Bailises	Your Family

Objectives
- Make evaluations based on text
- Analyze photos
- Make connections from text to self

Assess

Resources for page 938

- Selection Quick Check
- Selection and Unit Assessment
- ExamView Assessment Suite
- Interactive Tutor: Self-Assessment

Students can respond to the *After You Read* items in their Learner's Notebook or on a separate sheet of paper

Answering the BIG Question

1. Responses will vary.
2. During the winter, the family uses snowmobiles to reach their cars, which are parked 2.5 miles from their house.
3. At first, the house was heated by a woodstove. Its propane generator didn't work well, and the windows allowed cold air to leak in.

Critical Thinking

4. Possible response: The writer points out that the Bailis family has all of the modern conveniences of most other homes: washer, dryer, microwave, TV, and the Internet.
5. Possible response: As a child, Mrs. Bailis lived on a cattle ranch and spent a lot of time outside. Now, her lifestyle allows her to interact with nature on the land that surrounds her home.
6. Responses will vary.

After You Read | Ah, Wilderness!

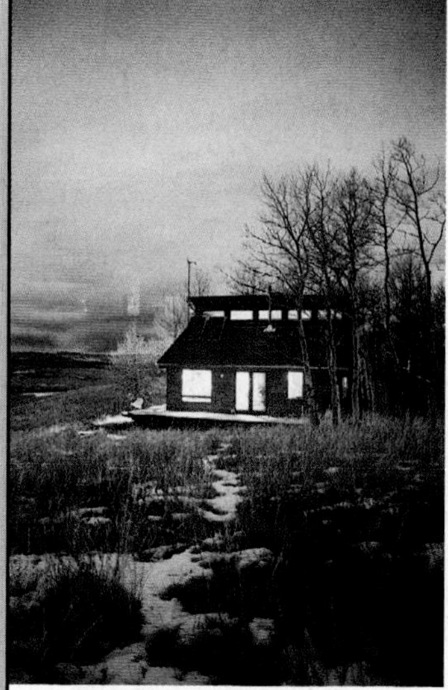

Answering the BIG Question

1. After reading "Ah, Wilderness," what new ideas do you have about what makes a community?
   TIP On My Own
2. **Recall** How do the Bailises get to work and school during the winter?
   TIP Right There
3. **Summarize** What was the Bailis house like when they first moved in?
   TIP Right There

Critical Thinking

4. **Analyze** How does the writer show that the Bailis family doesn't live as differently from other people as one might think?
   TIP Think and Search
5. **Compare** In what way is Mrs. Bailis's life now similar to that of her childhood?
   TIP Author and Me
6. **Predict** Based on the environment in which they were raised, predict how the Bailis boys will live as adults.
   TIP Author and Me

Objectives (pp. 938–939)
Reading Clarify ideas and text • Make connections from text to self
Literature Identify literary devices: figurative language
Vocabulary Identify synonyms
Grammar Use punctuation: semicolons

Write About Your Reading

Imagine that you are going to do a television interview with the Bailis family. Make a list of at least four questions that you would ask Mr. and Mrs. Bailis or the boys.

- Assume the viewers of your program have already read "Ah, Wilderness!"
- Don't ask questions that were already answered by the article, unless you want to get additional details.
- Avoid asking questions that could be answered "yes" or "no."
- Try to ask questions that require detailed answers. Sometimes you might have to explain what you're looking for before you ask a question.
  I'd like to know more about your wind generator. Can you explain how it works?

Write About Your Reading

Possible response:
Question 1: How would you compare the cost of your lifestyle, including the purchase of items such as snowmobiles and solar panels, with that of other Americans?
Question 2: Do you get a lot of visitors?
Question 3: What did your families say when they learned where you would be living?
Question 4: What have you done or would you do in a medical emergency?
Question 5: Have you ever regretted your choice of lifestyle? When and why? Were you able to resolve the problem?

Skills Review

Key Reading Skill: Clarifying

7. Writers use different techniques to clarify ideas. In paragraph 4, the writer compares the early days in the Bailis home to camping indoors. Explain how this comparison gives you a clearer picture of how the family had to live at first.

Key Literary Element: Figurative Language

8. On page 936, Beth uses a metaphor when she says, "My boys are true polar bears." Think about the comparison. In what way or ways are the boys like polar bears?

Vocabulary Check

9. Choose the word in this list that is closest in meaning to the word **solitary.**

   alone happy disappointed

10. Choose the word in the list that is closest in meaning to the word **plunges.**

    runs flies falls

11. Choose the word in the list that is closest in meaning to the word **generate.**

    apply create find

12. Choose the word in the list that is closest in meaning to the word **trek.**

    ship problem journey

13. Choose the word or phrase in the list that is closest in meaning to the word **rationing.**

    running out of destroying using carefully

14. **Academic Vocabulary** What are some ways to **clarify** information as you read?

Grammar Link: Semicolons

A semicolon (;) is used to join main clauses in a compound sentence when the clauses are not joined by a coordinating conjunction. (The coordinating conjunctions are *and, but, or, nor, for, so.*) Compare the sentences below.

I play drums; my brother plays guitar.

(The semicolon joins the main clause *I play drums* to the main clause *my brother plays guitar.*)

I play drums, and my brother plays guitar.

Semicolons are a good way to fix run-on sentences when the sentences in the run-on are short and closely related.

Run-on: I'll bring soft drinks, you bring chips.

(The sentence is a run-on because a comma alone is not strong enough to join main clauses.)

Revision: I'll bring soft drinks; you bring chips.

Grammar Practice

Rewrite the sentences below. Use a semicolon to fix each run-on.

15. We all want to go to the movies, we just can't agree on what to see.
16. I want to see a comedy horror movies are so violent.
17. Going to the movies is good renting videos is even better.

Writing Application Rewrite two of your questions from your Write About Your Reading assignment and use semicolons.

Web Activities For eFlashcards, Selection Quick Checks, and other Web activities, go to www.glencoe.com.

Skills Review

Key Reading Skill: Clarifying

7. Responses will vary but may include students' reflections on camping trips they have taken.

Key Literary Element: Figurative Language

8. Possible responses may include the idea that the boys enjoy playing outdoors despite the cold and snow.

Vocabulary Check

9. alone
10. falls
11. create
12. journey
13. using carefully
14. Possible responses: looking up unknown words in the dictionary, asking others about the selection, reading further in the text, rereading, restating ideas

Close

Ask students to write a paragraph about their family community.

Literature Online

Web Activities Have students access the Web site for interactive activities that will help them assess their understanding of the selection.

Grammar Link: Semicolons

Grammar Practice

15. We all want to go to the movies; we just can't agree on what to see.
16. I want to see a comedy; horror movies are so violent.
17. Going to the movies is good; renting videos is even better.

Teach

More About the Author

To create textbooks, writers need certain skills. They must first understand what is being taught. Many textbook writers have college degrees in science, math, English, and social sciences. The knowledge they gained in college helps them understand concepts and communicate them to students. Some textbook writers must also understand kids. They should know what kids like and understand; they should write in language that communicates to kids.

BQ 

Say: How might your community change during your lifetime? *(Possible response: As I grow up, I may leave my parents and start my own family. I may move to a new area and make friends or work with new people.)* **OL**

Before You Read | Photographing History

Meet the Author

This selection was written for a school textbook. (Textbook writers are not credited as "authors" of the books and lessons they write.) Textbook writers try to make difficult subjects easier to understand. Text features, like the photographs in this selection, are important tools that help both the writer and the reader.

Objectives (pp. 940–945)
Reading Clarify ideas and text • Make connections from text to self
Literature Identify literary devices: figurative language
Vocabulary Identify historical influences on English

Vocabulary Preview

English Language Coach

BQ **Historical Influences on English** The history of a language and its people go hand in hand. English, for example, contains many words that come from Latin because the ancient Roman Empire extended to Great Britain. When the Romans lived in Great Britain, they brought Latin, their language, with them. Because the Romans had been influenced by the ancient Greeks, they brought words that had been shaped by Greek as well.

Word	Source	Original Meaning
script	Latin: *scriptum*	something written
autograph	Greek: *auto* + *graph*	self + write

Partner Talk Together, use a dictionary to look up each word below. From what language did each word come?

- **hydrant**
- **aquarium**
- **gymnasium**
- **biology**
- **phonograph**
- **telescope**
- **psychology**
- **meter**
- **incredible**
- **sergeant**
- **table**

Additional Support

Literature Focus Lesson

Internet Information Nonfiction writers use all types of sources to get information for their work: magazines, books, pamphlets, newspapers, journals, and the Internet. While it is important for writers to evaluate all sources, it's especially important to evaluate Internet sources. Are they reliable? Is the information accurate? Is the information biased? As a class, create a checklist that will help students evaluate Internet information. **OL**

Skills Preview

Key Reading Skill: Clarifying

Before you read, copy the chart below into your Learner's Notebook.

Words	Reread	Questions

As you read the selection, list any words you don't know in the **Words** column.

Note the page and paragraph numbers of any confusing sections you might need to reread under the **Reread** column.

Write questions about anything you don't understand in the **Questions** column.

Key Literary Element: Figurative Language

Recall that figurative language is not meant to be taken literally. Instead, it is used for descriptive effect. By showing how two very different things are similar in some way, authors help readers understand everyday things in fresh new ways.

Interactive Literary Elements Handbook To review or learn more about the literary elements, go to www.glencoe.com.

Get Ready to Read

Connect to the Reading

Think about old family pictures that you've seen. What interesting stories have you learned by looking through the photos with family members?

Partner Talk Cameras are not always available and, of course, there was a time when they didn't exist. What pictures of people in your family or community do you wish you had? Why?

Build Background

In this selection, you will read about one of the first famous photographers in America. His name was Mathew Brady and he took pictures during the Civil War. Brady devoted his time and money to creating a photographic history of this tragic time.

- A civil war is one in which citizens of the same country fight each other. The U.S. Civil War, a battle between northern and southern states, lasted four years.
- Nearly one million people were wounded or died in the Civil War.
- Mathew Brady was the first photographer to show the world photos taken of actual events in the war. His photographs of dead soldiers brought the reality of war to the nation.

Set Purposes for Reading

BQ BIG Question Read "Photographing History" to discover how the community and the events of the time shaped Mathew Brady.

Set Your Own Purpose What else would you like to learn from the story to help you answer the Big Question? Write your own purpose on the "Photographing History" page of Foldable 8.

Keep Moving

Use these skills as you read the following selection.

Teach

R Reading Skill

Clarifying Say: Some selections take place in the past and refer to events that occurred long before readers were born. How might readers clarify terms and events they don't recognize? *(Possible response: They could use reference books, such as dictionaries and encyclopedias, to get information that will help them understand the selection.)* BL EL

BQ 

Say: In what ways do your communities give you support and encouragement to succeed? *(Responses will vary.)* OL

CheckPoint

Use the CheckPoint questions provided on Presentation Plus! to check for clarifying skills and to build background. These questions can be used with interactive response keypads for immediate student feedback.

Literature Online

Interactive Literary Elements Handbook Have students access the Web site to improve their understanding of figurative language.

Differentiated Instruction

Clarifying Remind students of writing techniques that help readers clarify information.

- Examples help readers picture an idea in everyday life.
- Word definitions within the same sentence (or shortly afterward) clear up confusion.
- Explanations later in the text give more information and a clearer understanding.

Students should make a note in their Learner's Notebook when these techniques are used in this selection and tell whether or not the techniques helped them clarify information. EL BL

Objectives
- Clarify ideas and text
- Make connections from text to self
- Identify literary devices: figurative language
- Identify historical influences on English

Teach

Viewing the Photo
Ask: How does the picture help you predict that the selection will be about a person or event from the past? *(Possible response: The hairstyle and clothing of the man in the picture are not from current times.)* **AS**

EL Language Coach
Historical Influences on English Say: The word *camera* comes from the Latin language. It means *room* or *chamber.* How might this definition connect to the present-day definition of *camera? (Possible response: The camera can be considered a small, enclosed chamber in which a picture is captured.)* **OL AL**

Readability Scores
Dale-Chall: 4.6
DRP: 56
Lexile: 770

INFORMATIONAL TEXT
TEXTBOOK
from *The Contemporary Reader*

Photographing History

Look at a book of **photographs** from the time of the Civil War. One photo shows the sad face of Abraham Lincoln[1] staring back at you. In another photo, an army general leans against a tree. Still another shows a field littered with the bodies of soldiers. Each photo looks as if it could have come from today's newspapers. Yet these people and events are from a time almost 150 years ago. Who is responsible for these photos from so long ago? A man named Mathew Brady made it his life's work to create and collect pictures of his time. **1**

Mathew Brady was born in 1823 in Warren County, New York. His parents had come to this country from Ireland. When Mathew was 16 years old, he left home to live in New York City. First he worked as a clerk in a store, but soon he started his own business. He made and sold jewelry cases. In his spare time, he studied photography under Samuel B. Morse. At that time, photography was very new. Not many people knew how to use a camera, so Brady was lucky to find someone to teach him. His teacher was a man of many talents. Besides teaching photography classes, Morse was a noted painter and a teacher of painting. In addition, he was the inventor of the telegraph.[2] Brady quickly learned all that Morse could teach him and, in 1844, opened his own photography studio. **2**

1. ***Abraham Lincoln*** was the president during the Civil War; he was assassinated shortly after it ended.
2. The ***telegraph*** allowed people to send messages through electrical wires.

Practice the Skills

1 English Language Coach
EL **Historical Influences on English** The word **photograph** comes from the Greek word *photo,* meaning "light," and the Greek word *graph,* meaning "write."

2 Key Reading Skill
Clarifying The author talks about Samuel Morse, who was a photographer, painter, teacher, and inventor. Why is he important to an article about Mathew Brady?

Additional Support

English Language Coach

Building Background To understand Brady's community and how its lack of acceptance of Brady's civil war pictures affected him, students may wish to research the causes and issues of the American Civil War. **EL OL** Students can write letters to Mr. Brady as if they were living in post–Civil War United States, explaining how they felt about his war pictures. **AL**

Assess

Resources for page 946

- Selection Quick Check
- Selection and Unit Assessment
- ExamView Assessment Suite
- Interactive Tutor: Self-Assessment

Students can respond to the *After You Read* items in their Learner's Notebook or on a separate sheet of paper.

Answering the BIG Question

1. Responses will vary.
2. Possible responses include Abraham Lincoln and Prince, later King, Edward.
3. Morse invented the telegraph and taught photography and painting. Morse taught Brady photography.
4. Brady took charge of makeup and lighting and told people where to sit or stand.

Critical Thinking

5. Responses will vary, but they should show that Brady's posed portraits were popular, but the community rejected his war photos.
6. Possible response: An individual's contributions are not always evident during the person's lifetime.
7. Responses will vary.
8. Responses will vary.
9. Responses will vary.

After You Read

Photographing History

Answering the BIG Question

1. What are your thoughts about how community makes you who you are after reading "Photographing History"?
2. **Recall** What important people and events did Mathew Brady photograph?
   TIP Right There
3. **Recall** Who was Samuel B. Morse? How was he important to Brady's life?
   TIP Right There
4. **Summarize** In what ways did Brady act as a movie director?
   TIP Think and Search

Critical Thinking

5. **Infer** How did the world in which Brady lived affect his life and career?
   TIP Author and Me
6. **Analyze** What was the main point the author wanted to make?
   TIP Author and Me
7. **Connect** If you were a photographer, what events would you be most interested in photographing? Explain why.
   TIP On My Own
8. **Evaluate** Do you agree that it was understandable for people in Brady's day to ignore his collection of war photos?
   TIP Author and Me
9. **Respond** How did you respond to the events near the end of Brady's life? Were you surprised? Were you saddened? Explain.
   TIP On My Own

Objectives (pp. 946–947)
Reading Clarify ideas and text • Make connections from text to self
Literature Identify literary devices: figurative language
Vocabulary Identify word structure: Greek and Latin roots
Writing Respond to literature: journal
Grammar Use punctuation: semicolons

Write About Your Reading

Write a journal entry as if you were one of Mathew Brady's photographers taking pictures on the battlefield.

- Describe what you see and how you feel.
- Think about the challenges you would face in regard to your health, safety, travel, and living and working conditions.
- Also consider how you would react to seeing people suffering and dying.

Write About Your Reading

Possible response:
Today I saw sights I never again want to see. Boys younger than I lay on the ground, screaming in pain and calling for their mothers. Some of them have been there for hours, waiting their turns to be picked up and taken to the surgical tent for care. Some people are too far gone, and soldiers carrying stretchers walk right past them. The smell is awful, a mixture of blood and gunpowder. What am I doing here? When might a stray bullet hit me? This war should never have been. As soon as I can, I will go back home. I hope I can forget the sights I've seen.

Photographers also took pictures of fields after the battles—fields covered with dead soldiers. Many people at that time imagined war to be a glorious adventure, so these photos shocked them. The pictures showed the true horrors of war.

When photos from Brady's collection were printed in magazines, they were always labeled "Photograph by Brady." However, these photos were really the work of many different people. C

It did not matter to Brady that he might not have even been present when the photos were taken. Some people quit working for Brady because he refused to give them credit for their pictures. 4

A Brady photo of Native Americans who toured with P. T. Barnum's American Museum in March, 1863.

After the War

Brady's collection of pictures grew and grew until, by the end of the war, he had over 3,500 photos. Brady thought that many people would want to buy his photos. However, this did not happen. People were eager to put the war behind them.[5] They didn't want to see pictures that reminded them of the past. Besides, most people did not have extra money to spend on photos. 5 R

Brady had spent his entire fortune of $100,000 on his Civil War project. He could not make this money back. At last, in 1875, Congress purchased his entire collection for only $25,000. After Brady paid back everyone he owed, he didn't have enough money to run his own studio. He went to work for other photographers. In 1887 his wife died and he was alone. When he died in 1896, he was penniless.

The Importance of Mathew Brady

Brady did not get rich from his Civil War pictures, but he and his work have made our lives richer. He changed photography forever. He showed that the camera could be used not just for making portraits but also for recording history. The pictures Brady took or collected give us a remarkable glimpse at the important people and events of the 19th century. ❍

5. When people wanted to ***put the war behind them,*** they were trying to forget it and move on with their lives.

Practice the Skills

4 **Key Reading Skill**

Clarifying The photographers who worked for Brady did not get credit for their work. What information does the author give to help you understand why Brady took credit for their photographs?

5 **BIG Question**

How did the community react to Brady's Civil War project after the war ended? Why? Write your answer on the "Photographing History" page of Foldable 8. Your response will help you complete the Unit Challenge later.

READING WORKSHOP 3

Teach

C Critical Thinking

Analysis Ask: Do you think it was okay for Brady to put his name on all of the war photos, even though he didn't personally take all of them? Explain your answer. *(Responses will vary.)* How did this affect Brady's reputation in the community of photographers? *(Possible responses: Some photographers who worked for Brady were angry and quit. Others may not have been willing to work for him.)* **OL**

R Reading Skill

Review Skimming and Scanning Ask: What features in this selection make skimming and scanning for information easier? *(Possible response: section headings)* **AS**

Assess

CheckPoint

Use the CheckPoint questions provided on Presentation Plus! to check for comprehension of the selection. These questions can be used with interactive response keypads for immediate student feedback.

English Language Coach

Historical Influences on English

The English language grew with vocabulary from the American Civil War. While some expressions still have their original meanings, others have completely different meanings today. List the following words and phrases on the board: chief cook and bottle washer, bread basket, horse sense, hunkey dorey, housewife, bummer. Have students work in groups to find these terms' original meanings and their current definitions. **OL** **AL**

Objectives

- Analyze photos
- Read to clarify information
- Skim and scan to preview text

READING WORKSHOP 3

Teach

Viewing the Photos

Ask: How might a photo of soldiers or generals today be different from these Brady photos? Why? *(Possible response: Because cameras are smaller and easier to use, many photos today are not posed.)* **OL** **AL**

R Reading Skill

Clarifying Ask: How did the writer clarify Brady's use of other photographers to take war pictures? *(Possible response: The writer explains that taking pictures of the war was a huge job, and "Brady soon saw that he couldn't do it alone.")* **OL**

C Critical Thinking

Analysis Say: In a larger sense, our country is a community. What happened to that community during the Civil War? *(Possible response: The country became divided into two opposing communities.)* **OL**

King Edward VII of England. While visiting New York, the prince came to Brady's studio to have his picture taken.

The Civil War Years

The following year, civil war broke out in the United States. Brady decided to take pictures of the war. His friends worried that he would not be safe, but Brady wouldn't change his mind. Brady later said, "A spirit in my feet said, 'Go,' and I went." **3**

Taking pictures of the war was a huge job. Brady soon saw that he couldn't do it alone. Instead, he became the manager of the project. He set up teams of photographers and provided them with the equipment they needed. These photographers followed the troops across the country. Back in New York, Brady saved and protected their negatives. A negative is the plate from which a photo is made. Once Brady had the negatives from his teams of photographers, he could make copies of their photos. In addition, Brady also bought photos from other photographers. **R**

At that time, cameras were large and bulky. It took photographers a long time to set up their equipment. Also, it took 15 to 30 seconds to take a picture. If anyone moved, the picture would be blurry. For these reasons, the photographers did not take pictures of battles. They preferred to take photos of soldiers in camp or generals posing. Often, the people in the photo are leaning against trees or tent poles to help them stand still.

Practice the Skills

3 Key Literary Element

Figurative Language Brady's feet did not literally contain spirit. What does Brady's figure of speech mean?

Brady's photos of (left to right) Abraham Lincoln, Union Civil War soldiers, southern Senator Hiram Revels, and Walt Whitman.

Additional Support

Reading in the Real World

Career Students who are interested in photography may wish to learn more about this career. Arrange for a local photographer to visit the classroom. Have students write interview questions before the visit, focusing on different aspects of photography as a career. If the photographer has agreed, invite interested students to bring in photos they have taken for the photographer's evaluation and suggestions. **AS**

Practice the Skills

Mathew Brady's gallery in New York City.

Brady's Studio

Brady worked hard to make his studio the best in the city. He spent a great deal of money on the finest furniture, backgrounds, and cameras. He hired the best staff he could find. Brady did not always take the pictures himself. Often he behaved like the director of a movie. He took charge of makeup and lighting, and he told people where they should sit or stand. Later, after the pictures were taken and developed, he sometimes painted the photos to make the people look better. **3**

In 1845 Brady started collecting portraits of famous Americans. A portrait is a picture of a person, especially the face. In his lifetime, Brady took portraits of 16 presidents. Not all of these men were photographed while they were in office. For example, John Quincy Adams[3] was an old man when Brady took his picture. Brady photographed Abraham Lincoln several times. One of his best-known portraits of Lincoln was used as a model for the image on the U.S. penny. **L**

In 1849 Brady went to Washington, D.C. There, he met and married Juliet Handy. Soon after, he put together a book titled *Gallery of Illustrious*[4] *Americans*. It was a collection of photos he had taken of famous people from all over the United States. In 1851 Mr. and Mrs. Brady traveled to Europe. At a photography contest in London, Brady impressed everyone with his book of portraits. He won a gold medal. **C**

Brady's New York studio became very popular—and not only with New Yorkers. In 1860 an important Englishman became a customer. It was Prince Edward, who later became

3 Key Literary Element

Figurative Language A simile is a kind of figurative language that uses *like* or *as* to compare two unlike things. Find the simile in this paragraph. To what is Brady being compared? How does this simile help you understand Brady?

3. ***John Quincy Adams*** was the sixth president of the United States (1825–1829).
4. ***Illustrious*** (ih LUS tree us) people are famous for their outstanding accomplishments.

READING WORKSHOP 3

Teach

Viewing the Art

Ask: How does this work of art help to illustrate the selection? *(Possible response: It shows people of the time period in a portrait gallery.)*

L Literary Element

Figurative Language Say: Remember that a metaphor compares two people or things by stating that one *is* another. Complete this metaphor by filling in the name of a currently famous person in the field of entertainment, sports, or art. *Brady was the _______ of the photography world. (Responses will vary.)* **AS**

C Critical Thinking

Evaluation Ask: Why might Brady have put together his book *Gallery of Illustrious Americans? (Possible response: People could see his work in the book and decide to hire him to photograph them.)* **OL**

Differentiated Instruction

Visual Learners Some students may enjoy putting together their own version of the *Gallery of Illustrious Americans.* Have students work alone or in pairs to choose 15 to 20 Americans living today who are famous for their outstanding accomplishments. Then have students search for portraits of the individuals on the Internet or in the library and gather them into a binder. You may want to have students include a brief biography about each individual next to their portrait. Then have students display their books in the classroom for other students to view. **OL**

Objectives
- Analyzing photos and artwork
- Identifying word origins and how they contribute to contemporary meanings
- Understanding figurative language

Skills Review

Key Reading Skill: Clarifying

10. Authors can often predict what their reading audience may already know and what might be new information.

To clear up new, confusing, or difficult sections or words, authors sometimes give examples or definitions within the same sentence or paragraph.

How does the author of "Photographing History" define the word *negative*? What are some other words or terms the author defines for you?

11. Review the Words-Reread-Questions chart you made (p. 941). Did using this chart help you

- clarify unfamiliar words?
- clarify confusing sections of text?
- answer questions you had?

Explain your answers.

Key Literary Element: Figurative Language

12. On page 945, the author says, "Brady did not get rich from his Civil War pictures, but he and his work have made our lives richer." Explain the two meanings of the word "rich" in the quotation.

Vocabulary Check

13. English Language Coach Remember that many English words come from other languages. Scan "Photographing History" to find words with the following Greek or Latin word parts. If you don't know what a word means, look it up in the dictionary.

- graph
- tele
- photo
- pict

Grammar Link: Semicolons with Conjunctive Adverbs

When you join two main clauses with a conjunctive adverb, put a semicolon before the conjunctive adverb and a comma after it. Here is a short list of conjunctive adverbs.

What is it?	What does it express?
therefore	cause and effect, conclusion
consequently	cause and effect, result
however	contrast
otherwise	an alternative

- Mei got every question right on her test; therefore, she deserves an A.
- Liu turned her paper in late; however, she did a really good job on it.
- Jorge needs to show up to class; otherwise, he won't be able to catch up.

Grammar Practice

Rewrite each sentence and insert a semicolon and the appropriate conjunctive adverb in the blank.

14. The teacher gave us material from Chapter 4 on the test ___ it wasn't covered in class.

15. Tan's history class is very difficult ___ his grades are good.

16. A student who finds a subject hard has to study more ___ the student has less free time.

Writing Application Circle all the semicolons and conjunctive adverbs in your Write About Your Reading assignment. Fix any mistakes you made.

Literature Online

Web Activities For eFlashcards, Selection Quick Checks, and other Web activities, go to www.glencoe.com.

Skills Review

Key Reading Skill: Clarifying

10. A negative is a plate from which a photo is made. Other examples will vary.

11. Responses will vary.

Key Literary Element: Figurative Language

12. Possible response: Although Brady did not become *wealthy* (rich), he and his work made our lives *more complete and satisfying* (richer).

Vocabulary Check

13. *Graph* comes from the Greek *graphos,* which means *written. Tele* means *distant* or *far off. Photo* means *light. Pict* comes from *picti,* meaning *painted.* Examples of words from the selection that include these word parts are *picture, photograph,* and *telegraph.*

Literature Online

Web Activities Have students access the Web site for interactive activities that will help them assess their understanding of the selection.

Close

Ask students to write a paragraph about how communities contribute to people's successes or failures.

Grammar Link: Semicolons with Conjunctive Adverbs

Grammar Practice

14. The teacher gave us material from Chapter 4 on the test; however, it wasn't covered in class.

15. Tan's history class is very difficult; however, his grades are good.

16. A student who finds a subject hard has to study more; consequently, the student has less free time. (therefore may also be used)

Focus

BELLRINGER Options

Daily Language Practice Transparency

Focus Activity Say: Read the draft of your word picture. Do any sentences sound awkward?

Teach

W1 Writing

Organization Ask: Why is it important to review the organization of your word picture? *(Possible response: It affects how the reader identifies with my word picture.)* OL

W2 Writing

Word Picture Ask: Why do sensory details help make your word picture vivid? *(Possible response: The details help readers see the word picture.)* OL

Resources for page 948

- Use the Writing Workshop Graphic Organizer BLM in the Unit 8 Resource Booklet.
- Use the Grammar and Writing Workshop Transparencies, Unit 8.

WRITING WORKSHOP PART 2

Descriptive Writing: A Word Picture
Revising, Editing, and Presenting

ASSIGNMENT Write a description of a special place

Purpose: To vividly describe a place in your community

Audience: Your teacher, your classmates, and possibly others in your community

Revising Rubric

Your revised description should have

- vivid images supported with sensory details
- a clear organization
- a satisfying conclusion
- strong sentence fluency

See page 950 for a model of descriptive writing.

Objectives (pages 948–951)
Writing Revise your writing for key elements, style, and word choice
Listening, Speaking, and Viewing Use visuals in presentation • Use appropriate expressions and gestures

In Writing Workshop Part 1, you drafted a word picture. Now you will revise and edit your description to turn it into a final product. Also, you'll keep a copy of it in a writing portfolio so that you and your teacher can evaluate your writing progress over time.

Revising

Make It Better

The point of revising is to improve your writing. Adding details, deleting parts that don't work, rewording sentences, reorganizing paragraphs—all of these actions are part of revising.

Take a Fresh Look

Reread your draft. As you read, ask yourself questions like the ones below. You can make changes now or write notes to yourself so you can go back and make the changes later.

- W1 Does my word picture follow a clear pattern of organization?
- W2 Do sensory details support and develop my main impression of the place?
- Do I include any details that are unrelated to the impression?
- Does my conclusion bring the description to a satisfying end?

Focus on the Opener

Read the following sentence.

My favorite place is a pond in Storey Park.

Would you be excited to read the rest of the description after an opening like that? Probably not. It's important to grab your readers' attention right away so they *want* to read the rest of what you have to say.

As I reached down to pick up the baseball my brother had thrown into the woods, I saw something sparkle through the trees.

Additional Support

Differentiated Instruction

Reorganize Visually Say: To track the order of their work, students may want to use a simple sequence graphic organizer like the sample one here. BL OL

1. Introduce the pond: *I remember the first day I saw Storey Park pond.* Maybe I should lead up to my discovery by telling about how I "found" it while playing catch.
2. Why I like the pond: *There are lots of trees around, so many people don't know it's there.* I should liven it up and make readers want to go there!
3. What might happen to the pond: *Someday I might move away, but I'll always remember the pond.* I need to make sure I bring my description to a clear end.

Focus

BELLRINGER Options

Daily Language Practice Transparency

Focus Activity Say: Read the draft of your word picture. Do any sentences sound awkward?

Teach

W1 Writing

Organization Ask: Why is it important to review the organization of your word picture? *(Possible response: It affects how the reader identifies with my word picture.)* OL

W2 Writing

Word Picture Ask: Why do sensory details help make your word picture vivid? *(Possible response: The details help readers see the word picture.)* OL

Resources for page 948

- Use the Writing Workshop Graphic Organizer BLM in the Unit 8 Resource Booklet.
- Use the Grammar and Writing Workshop Transparencies, Unit 8.

WRITING WORKSHOP PART 2

Descriptive Writing:

A Word Picture

Revising, Editing, and Presenting

ASSIGNMENT Write a description of a special place

Purpose: To vividly describe a place in your community

Audience: Your teacher, your classmates, and possibly others in your community

Revising Rubric

Your revised description should have

- vivid images supported with sensory details
- a clear organization
- a satisfying conclusion
- strong sentence fluency

See page 950 for a model of descriptive writing.

Objectives (pages 948–951)
Writing Revise your writing for key elements, style, and word choice
Listening, Speaking, and Viewing Use visuals in presentation Use appropriate expressions and gestures

In Writing Workshop Part 1, you drafted a word picture. Now you will revise and edit your description to turn it into a final product. Also, you'll keep a copy of it in a writing portfolio so that you and your teacher can evaluate your writing progress over time.

Revising

Make It Better

The point of revising is to improve your writing. Adding details, deleting parts that don't work, rewording sentences, reorganizing paragraphs—all of these actions are part of revising.

Take a Fresh Look

Reread your draft. As you read, ask yourself questions like the ones below. You can make changes now or write notes to yourself so you can go back and make the changes later.

- W1 Does my word picture follow a clear pattern of organization?
- W2 Do sensory details support and develop my main impression of the place?
- Do I include any details that are unrelated to the impression?
- Does my conclusion bring the description to a satisfying end?

Focus on the Opener

Read the following sentence.

My favorite place is a pond in Storey Park.

Would you be excited to read the rest of the description after an opening like that? Probably not. It's important to grab your readers' attention right away so they *want* to read the rest of what you have to say.

As I reached down to pick up the baseball my brother had thrown into the woods, I saw something sparkle through the trees.

Additional Support

Differentiated Instruction

Reorganize Visually Say: To track the order of their work, students may want to use a simple sequence graphic organizer like the sample one here. BL OL

1. Introduce the pond: *I remember the first day I saw Storey Park pond.* Maybe I should lead up to my discovery by telling about how I "found" it while playing catch.

2. Why I like the pond: *There are lots of trees around, so many people don't know it's there.* I should liven it up and make readers want to go there!

3. What might happen to the pond: *Someday I might move away, but I'll always remember the pond.* I need to make sure I bring my description to a clear end.

Skills Review

Key Reading Skill: Clarifying

10. Authors can often predict what their reading audience may already know and what might be new information.

To clear up new, confusing, or difficult sections or words, authors sometimes give examples or definitions within the same sentence or paragraph.

How does the author of "Photographing History" define the word *negative*? What are some other words or terms the author defines for you?

11. Review the Words-Reread-Questions chart you made (p. 941). Did using this chart help you
- clarify unfamiliar words?
- clarify confusing sections of text?
- answer questions you had?

Explain your answers.

Key Literary Element: Figurative Language

12. On page 945, the author says, "Brady did not get rich from his Civil War pictures, but he and his work have made our lives richer." Explain the two meanings of the word "rich" in the quotation.

Vocabulary Check

13. English Language Coach Remember that many English words come from other languages. Scan "Photographing History" to find words with the following Greek or Latin word parts. If you don't know what a word means, look it up in the dictionary.
- graph
- tele
- photo
- pict

Grammar Link: Semicolons with Conjunctive Adverbs

When you join two main clauses with a conjunctive adverb, put a semicolon before the conjunctive adverb and a comma after it. Here is a short list of conjunctive adverbs.

What is it?	What does it express?
therefore	cause and effect, conclusion
consequently	cause and effect, result
however	contrast
otherwise	an alternative

- Mei got every question right on her test; therefore, she deserves an A.
- Liu turned her paper in late; however, she did a really good job on it.
- Jorge needs to show up to class; otherwise, he won't be able to catch up.

Grammar Practice

Rewrite each sentence and insert a semicolon and the appropriate conjunctive adverb in the blank.

14. The teacher gave us material from Chapter 4 on the test ___ it wasn't covered in class.

15. Tan's history class is very difficult ___ his grades are good.

16. A student who finds a subject hard has to study more ___ the student has less free time.

Writing Application Circle all the semicolons and conjunctive adverbs in your Write About Your Reading assignment. Fix any mistakes you made.

Literature Online

Web Activities For eFlashcards, Selection Quick Checks, and other Web activities, go to www.glencoe.com.

Skills Review

Key Reading Skill: Clarifying

10. A negative is a plate from which a photo is made. Other examples will vary.

11. Responses will vary.

Key Literary Element: Figurative Language

12. Possible response: Although Brady did not become *wealthy* (rich), he and his work made our lives *more complete and satisfying* (richer).

Vocabulary Check

13. *Graph* comes from the Greek *graphos,* which means *written. Tele* means *distant* or *far off. Photo* means *light. Pict* comes from *picti,* meaning *painted.* Examples of words from the selection that include these word parts are *picture, photograph,* and *telegraph.*

Literature Online

Web Activities Have students access the Web site for interactive activities that will help them assess their understanding of the selection.

Close

Ask students to write a paragraph about how communities contribute to people's successes or failures.

Grammar Link: Semicolons with Conjunctive Adverbs

Grammar Practice

14. The teacher gave us material from Chapter 4 on the test; however, it wasn't covered in class.

15. Tan's history class is very difficult; however, his grades are good.

16. A student who finds a subject hard has to study more; consequently, the student has less free time. (therefore may also be used)

Practice the Skills

Mathew Brady's gallery in New York City.

Brady's Studio

Brady worked hard to make his studio the best in the city. He spent a great deal of money on the finest furniture, backgrounds, and cameras. He hired the best staff he could find. Brady did not always take the pictures himself. Often he behaved like the director of a movie. He took charge of makeup and lighting, and he told people where they should sit or stand. Later, after the pictures were taken and developed, he sometimes painted the photos to make the people look better. **3**

In 1845 Brady started collecting portraits of famous Americans. A portrait is a picture of a person, especially the face. In his lifetime, Brady took portraits of 16 presidents. Not all of these men were photographed while they were in office. For example, John Quincy Adams[3] was an old man when Brady took his picture. Brady photographed Abraham Lincoln several times. One of his best-known portraits of Lincoln was used as a model for the image on the U.S. penny.

In 1849 Brady went to Washington, D.C. There, he met and married Juliet Handy. Soon after, he put together a book titled *Gallery of Illustrious*[4] *Americans.* It was a collection of photos he had taken of famous people from all over the United States. In 1851 Mr. and Mrs. Brady traveled to Europe. At a photography contest in London, Brady impressed everyone with his book of portraits. He won a gold medal. **C**

Brady's New York studio became very popular—and not only with New Yorkers. In 1860 an important Englishman became a customer. It was Prince Edward, who later became

3 **Key Literary Element**

L **Figurative Language** A simile is a kind of figurative language that uses *like* or *as* to compare two unlike things. Find the simile in this paragraph. To what is Brady being compared? How does this simile help you understand Brady?

3. ***John Quincy Adams*** was the sixth president of the United States (1825–1829).
4. ***Illustrious*** (ih LUS tree us) people are famous for their outstanding accomplishments.

Teach

Viewing the Art

Ask: How does this work of art help to illustrate the selection? *(Possible response: It shows people of the time period in a portrait gallery.)*

L Literary Element

Figurative Language Say: Remember that a metaphor compares two people or things by stating that one *is* another. Complete this metaphor by filling in the name of a currently famous person in the field of entertainment, sports, or art. *Brady was the _______ of the photography world. (Responses will vary.)* **AS**

C Critical Thinking

Evaluation Ask: Why might Brady have put together his book *Gallery of Illustrious Americans? (Possible response: People could see his work in the book and decide to hire him to photograph them.)* **OL**

Differentiated Instruction

Visual Learners Some students may enjoy putting together their own version of the *Gallery of Illustrious Americans.* Have students work alone or in pairs to choose 15 to 20 Americans living today who are famous for their outstanding accomplishments. Then have students search for portraits of the individuals on the Internet or in the library and gather them into a binder. You may want to have students include a brief biography about each individual next to their portrait. Then have students display their books in the classroom for other students to view. **OL**

Objectives
- Analyzing photos and artwork
- Identifying word origins and how they contribute to contemporary meanings
- Understanding figurative language

Teach

Viewing the Photos

Ask: How might a photo of soldiers or generals today be different from these Brady photos? Why? *(Possible response: Because cameras are smaller and easier to use, many photos today are not posed.)* OL AL

R Reading Skill

Clarifying Ask: How did the writer clarify Brady's use of other photographers to take war pictures? *(Possible response: The writer explains that taking pictures of the war was a huge job, and "Brady soon saw that he couldn't do it alone.")* OL

C Critical Thinking

Analysis Say: In a larger sense, our country is a community. What happened to that community during the Civil War? *(Possible response: The country became divided into two opposing communities.)* OL

King Edward VII of England. While visiting New York, the prince came to Brady's studio to have his picture taken.

The Civil War Years

The following year, civil war broke out in the United States. Brady decided to take pictures of the war. His friends worried that he would not be safe, but Brady wouldn't change his mind. Brady later said, "A spirit in my feet said, 'Go,' and I went." 3

Taking pictures of the war was a huge job. Brady soon saw that he couldn't do it alone. Instead, he became the manager of the project. He set up teams of photographers and provided them with the equipment they needed. These photographers followed the troops across the country. Back in New York, Brady saved and protected their negatives. A negative is the plate from which a photo is made. Once Brady had the negatives from his teams of photographers, he could make copies of their photos. In addition, Brady also bought photos from other photographers. R

At that time, cameras were large and bulky. It took photographers a long time to set up their equipment. Also, it took 15 to 30 seconds to take a picture. If anyone moved, the picture would be blurry. For these reasons, the photographers did not take pictures of battles. They preferred to take photos of soldiers in camp or generals posing. Often, the people in the photo are leaning against trees or tent poles to help them stand still.

Practice the Skills

3 Key Literary Element

Figurative Language Brady's feet did not literally contain spirit. What does Brady's figure of speech mean?

Brady's photos of (left to right) Abraham Lincoln, Union Civil War soldiers, southern Senator Hiram Revels, and Walt Whitman.

Additional Support

Reading in the Real World

Career Students who are interested in photography may wish to learn more about this career. Arrange for a local photographer to visit the classroom. Have students write interview questions before the visit, focusing on different aspects of photography as a career. If the photographer has agreed, invite interested students to bring in photos they have taken for the photographer's evaluation and suggestions. AS

That's better! If the first sentence you write down isn't a good opener, write a new one. One trick is to steal a good sentence from later in your description and turn it into your opening sentence.

Improve Your Sentence Fluency

Read your description aloud to yourself or to a partner. Does your writing sound natural? Is it easy to read, or do you stumble on awkward sentences?

- If many of your sentences have the same rhythm, try varying the sentence structures. Combine some sentences and break up others.
- If many of your sentences start with the same words, rewrite some of them. Try starting sentences with adjectives or adverbs or changing the order of some of the words in the sentence.
- Match the flow of the sentences to your message. Remember, long and flowing sentences often work well for descriptions. Short sentences help to emphasize a point.

W

Writing Tip

Using Technology If you are writing on a computer, copy your draft before you revise. By saving the original, you are free to experiment. If an experiment doesn't turn out well, you can return to your original draft and try it again.

Writing Tip

Spelling If you're not absolutely sure you spelled a word correctly, check the spelling in a dictionary. Misspelled words can distract readers' attention from your ideas.

Editing

Finish It Up

Read your word picture one sentence at a time and use the **Editing Checklist** to help you spot errors. Use the proofreading symbols in the chart on page R74 to mark needed corrections.

Editing Checklist

- ☑ Verbs and subjects agree and all verb tenses are correct.
- ☑ Pronouns refer clearly to their antecedents and agree with them in person, number, and gender.
- ☑ All sentences are complete (except for fragments used for effect).
- ☑ Punctuation is correct. (Double-check apostrophes.)
- ☑ Capitalization and spelling are correct.

Writing Models For models and other writing activities, go to www.glencoe.com.

Presenting

Show It Off

After you're finished making changes, make a fresh copy of your word picture. Print or write neatly and form your letters carefully.

You may want to submit your description to a magazine that publishes young people's writing. Search the Internet to find Web sites and magazines that might publish your word picture. Once you gather a few titles, search further to find contact information for the Web sites and magazines. You may even want to look for guidelines for submitting your writing.

Literature Focus Lesson

Descriptive Images When revising and refining their passages, students may benefit from hearing which of their descriptions and images classmates enjoy most. To provide this benefit, set up small writing workshop groups around the classroom. Then give students time to read their passages aloud to their groups. Ask listeners to write down notes about the descriptions, images, or impressions they liked best. When a student has finished reading, the other writers in the workshop group can let him or her know which details made an impression on them. BL OL

Teach

W Writing

Sentence Fluency Say: To keep readers interested, you should write sentences of different lengths and different types. Practice sentence fluency by combining the four sentences of each group into one interesting topic sentence.

1. a. Bicycling is fun.
   b. It is a healthy form of exercise.
   c. You also get to see the countryside.
   d. You can travel with friends.
   (Possible response: Bicycling is a fun and healthy form of exercise in which you get to travel with friends and see the countryside.)
2. a. Kyle paints portraits.
   b. Kyle is my cousin.
   c. He has many portraits in his studio.
   d. His work is well known and respected.
   (Possible response: My cousin Kyle, a well-known and respected portrait painter, has many portraits in his studio.) OL AL

Objectives

- Revise writing for key elements, style, and word choice
- Support statements with images and sensory details
- Revise writing to improve organization and sentence fluency

Teach

R Reading Skill

Review Visualizing Read the passage aloud. **Ask:** What images did you visualize? *(Students may say that they imagined the woods; the pond; the concrete; the grass; the reflections on the water; the squirrels and geese.)* BL OL

W Writing

Revising Ask: How does the writer vary the structure of the third sentence in the paragraph to keep the flow of language interesting? *(Possible response: The sentence starts out with a phrase.)* BL How does this help make the writing more engaging? *(Students might say that varying the sentence structure adds dimension to the paragraph and makes it more vivid.)* OL

C Critical Thinking

Comprehension Ask: Why do you think the writer compares the feeling of hard concrete under his feet with the sea of grass? *(Possible response: The park offers such a big change from the hard realities of the city.)* What does the change in atmosphere do to his mind? *(It quiets him and makes him peaceful.)* AL

Active Writing Model

The opening sentences draw readers into the description.

The writer clearly states the main impression before giving descriptive details.

The writer uses varied sentence structures and sentence beginnings to keep the language interesting and flowing.

Here and elsewhere, the writer uses transition phrases to guide the reader and make the spatial organization clear.

Sensory details help readers imagine the pond and the trees. The details also support and explain the writer's main impression of the pond.

The writer brings the description to a clear end by reflecting on the pond and the future.

Writer's Model

When I close my eyes, I can relive the moment when I saw the pond for the first time. My brother and I were playing catch in Storey Park, and he had thrown the ball over my head and into a thick patch of trees. I trudged back into the woods, and as I reached down to pick up the ball, I saw something sparkle through the trees. Then I spotted the pond. I felt like I was in a dream! My brother and I had been playing in the park for years and had never known it was there. Over the past two years, that pond has become my own private escape.

Fall is the best season to visit the pond. After school, I rush home to our apartment and drop my backpack in the kitchen. Yelling out to my mother, I dash back out. I don't need to tell my mother where I'm going because she already knows.

I sprint the two blocks to the park, feeling the hard, cold concrete under my feet. But the minute I enter the park, I find myself in a sea of grass. In the distance, I can see the clump of trees that hide the pond from sight. As I get closer, the trees get bigger and bigger, and I start to hear the rustling of the brightly colored leaves.

The reflection of the trees and the sky dancing on the water greets me as I make my way to the pond. Squirrels chase each other, chattering loudly. And sometimes geese stop by the pond and add their calls to the other sounds. But the trees absorb the noises of the city, and the few people I've seen there remain quiet, as I do.

It seems as if nothing can go wrong here at the quiet and peaceful pond. The natural scene is an escape from the buildings, people, and cars of the city. Often I'm the only person there, and the pond feels like it's mine.

Someday I'll probably move away from here or the pond will become crowded with people, but for now, I enjoy my peaceful escape. And no matter what happens, I'll always have the memory of the first time I saw the pond.

Additional Support

Differentiated Instruction

Students who like to draw or paint can accompany a word picture with art. Students can use their own word pictures, or a classmate's, and try to express in art exactly what the writer is describing. Have students set up a rubric for themselves that may include some of the following points:

- interpret the writer's mood or tone
- focus on one main idea from the word picture
- include the details that seem most important in the word picture
- check with the writer for an evaluation of accuracy or valid representation AS

Listening, Speaking, and Viewing

Visuals

You've probably heard the expression "a picture is worth a thousand words." Writing vivid descriptions is an important skill, but sometimes nothing but a visual will do.

Analyzing Cartoons The girls obviously know how to get information from visuals. . . . It's their ability to *visualize* that they need to improve.

What Are Visuals?

Visuals are pieces of art or information that require you to use your sense of sight. Visuals include maps, graphs, charts, timelines, illustrations, and photographs, to name a few.

Why Are Visuals Important?

There are two main reasons. One reason is that people learn in different ways. To understand information, some people need to read it. Others need to see it. And still others need to touch it or hear it. When you include visuals in your writing, you make it easier for readers to understand and remember the information.

Another reason is that some things are difficult or impossible to explain using words. A visual can show an idea that would take hundreds of words to explain.

How Do I Use Visuals in My Writing?

C Visuals aren't always needed, but almost any kind of writing can benefit from a visual. Some writing topics lend themselves to certain kinds of visuals naturally.

- Maps show features of places and where they are in relation to other places.
- Graphs and charts can help readers understand statistics. Both kinds of visuals can clearly show how statistics compare or how a statistic changes over time.
- Timelines help readers see when events happened.
- Illustrations show an artist's idea of what a character or place looks like. They work especially well with fiction writing because the characters and places are imaginary.
- Photographs show what people, places, and objects actually look like. They work especially well with nonfiction writing because the people, places, and objects are real.

Visual Practice Sometimes visuals capture a thought or feeling found in the text. Find or create a visual that captures the same feeling as your main impression of the place you described. For example, if your main impression is one of peace, create a visual that you think represents peace. The point is to visually represent the feeling in a new way, so don't limit yourself to images of the place you described. Be creative! Search for images in magazines and on the Internet, or draw or paint an image.

Reading Fluency

Reading and Listening Take some of the word pictures the students created in this unit and give them to groups comprised of two pairs each. The students will perform a variation of "echo reading" by reading aloud in pairs. Each pair will take a natural division of text (every other paragraph) and practice their parts. Then they will speak aloud their assigned parts and listen to the other pair. OL

Teach

C Critical Thinking

Analysis Present these text situations and ask students for the best visual to fit each text.

- biography of a World War II hero
- a description of the parts of a flower
- a Web site for a local high school basketball team's play-off games
- a son's letter to his parents, giving them directions for getting to his camp for a visit
- a poem about too many chairs at the dinner table EL BL OL
- a research report on the abolitionist movement
- a Web site evaluating the number of highway accidents in every state in the U.S. AL

(Responses will vary but should indicate an understanding of when various visuals, such as photos, maps, charts, etc., are used.)

Assess/Close

Partner Activity

Choose one of the text examples listed above, find a similar text, and make the appropriate visual. Or, make a list of steps for creating an appropriate visual. AS

Objectives
- Write descriptions using the writing process
- Support statements with images and sensory details
- Revise writing to improve organization and sentence fluency
- Select and produce visuals to improve and develop meanings
- Create a visual message

Predicting

UNIT 8

Objectives covered in this workshop:
- Make predictions

Teaching Students to Predict

Why Is It Important?

- Predicting helps readers monitor comprehension when they compare what they had expected to what they have actually read.
- Predicting engages students more actively with the texts they are reading.
- Predicting is a familiar strategy that can serve as a way into discussions of how using strategies enhance their comprehension.

How to Help Students Get It

- Point out that reading is an interactive process involving both the reader and the author.
- Emphasize that using background knowledge (including what they have already read in the text) to make a prediction is one way to become more engaged with what they are reading
- Predicting is one way to make inferences since to make a prediction, readers have to think about what is already read, what they know about the kinds of events or information they are reading about, and construct an idea of what will happen next.

Reading to Answer The Big Question

The Monsters Are Due on Maple Street

Everything seems normal on a typical suburban street until a mysterious flash of light seems to cause the power in all homes and cars to go out. The tension increases as more unexplainable activities occur until those whom were once friendly neighbors turn against each another in panic and fear. The terrifying possibilities when a community starts to fall apart are dramatized in this classic teleplay from the Twilight Zone TV series.

Workshop Resources

Pacing (Days) Standard	Pacing (Days) Block	Lesson	Student Materials	Teacher Resources
1		Key Skill Lesson: Predicting	Key Reading Skills Practice English Language Coach	Bellringer Options Transparencies Read Aloud, Think Aloud Transparencies Presentation Plus!
2		"The Monsters Are Due on Maple Street: Act 1"	Literary Analysis Transparencies Glencoe Online Selection Vocabulary Development Academic Vocabulary Development English Language Coach Active Reading Graphic Organizer Literary Analysis StudentWorks Plus Online Student Edition Literature Classics Selection and Unit Assessments	Literary and Text Analysis Transparencies Puzzlemaker Skill Level Up! BookLink 3 Assessment by Learning Objective (Diagnostic and Formative) Interactive Tutor Self-Assessment TeacherWorks Plus
2		"The Monsters Are Due on Maple Street: Act 2"	Glencoe Online Selection Vocabulary Development Academic Vocabulary Development English Language Coach Active Reading Graphic Organizer Literary Analysis StudentWorks Plus Online Student Edition Literature Classics Selection and Unit Assessments	Literary and Text Analysis Transparencies Puzzlemaker Skill Level Up! BookLink 3 Assessment by Learning Objective (Diagnostic and Formative) Interactive Tutor Self-Assessment TeacherWorks Plus

Keys for Unit Resource

- Blackline Master
- Workbook
- Supplemental Text
- CD-ROM
- DVD
- Transparency
- Web-based
- Fast Files

Level Appropriate Code

AS = Activities for all students
AL = Activities for students working above grade level
OL = Activities for students working at grade level
BL = Activities for students working below grade level
EL = Activities for English language learners

Focus

BELLRINGER Options

- **Selection Focus Transparencies**
- **Daily Language Practice Transparency**

Focus Activity Ask: What would happen if people in a community suddenly turned against each other? List some words that describe how people in that situation might feel. *(Possible responses: suspicious, fearful, paranoid, distrustful)* OL

Teach

R Reading Skill

Predicting Say: Predicting is something you probably do all the time without even thinking about it. For example, when you watch a scary movie, what kinds of things do you predict? *(Possible responses: who the next victim will be; how the hero will defeat the monster or bad guy)* BL OL

READING WORKSHOP 4

Skills Focus

You will practice using these skills when you read the following selections:

- The Monsters Are Due on Maple Street, Act I, p. 956
- The Monsters Are Due on Maple Street, Act II, p. 970

Reading

- Predicting

Literature

- Identifying and understanding the elements of a teleplay

Vocabulary

- Learning about English as a changing language

Writing/Grammar

- Using quotation marks correctly

Objectives (pp. 952–953)
Reading Make predictions • Make connections from text to self
Literature Identify literary elements: teleplay
Vocabulary Identify English language changes

Skill Lesson

Predicting

Learn It!

What Is It? Predicting is saying what will happen before it happens, and there's a whole lot of predicting going on. For starters:

- Weather forecasters predict that tomorrow will be sunny and dry (or cold and rainy).
- Sports writers predict that the home team will win (or lose) Tuesday's game.
- Financial experts predict that prices will go up this week.
- Candidates predict that they'll be elected in November. (Do they ever predict that they'll lose?)

R

Then there are the "psychic" hotlines, the daily horoscopes, and the people who tell your future by reading your palm—for ten bucks.

Predictions fascinate us, especially when they turn out right. (When they don't, we forget them.) And we all make predictions, right or wrong, often without thinking much about it.

Predicting what will happen next in a movie or story is part of the fun.

Analyzing Cartoons
The student's mom uses prior knowledge to make a prediction. What do you predict will happen when you take your report card home?

Additional Support

Literature Focus Lesson

Elements of a Teleplay Explain that a teleplay is a play written especially for television. The author describes the scenes and characters, which helps you, the reader, visualize them. When you watch a movie on TV, you see how the director visualized the author's words. Ask students to think of a scene from a recent TV show or movie, and have them write a description of that scene. Then have them read their descriptions aloud while the rest of the class listens carefully. Ask students to comment on how each description helped them visualize the scene. BL OL

Why Is It Important? As you become interested in a story, you'll want to find out what happens next. Predicting gives you a reason to read.

How Do I Do It? While you read, pause to ask yourself, "What might happen next?" Take notes as you read to help you make a guess that's based on what you've already read. Here's what one student predicted while reading a story called "The Sweet Deal."

> Jamal carefully unrolled three hundred-dollar bills that he'd kept in his back pocket all week. His father wanted him to save money for college. But Mike and Jamal had a deal worked out. . . .
>
> Now Mike smiled as he took the money from Jamal. "Yeah, you're a good kid. That's why I'm selling you this baby so cheap.
>
> "Thanks," Jamal replied. "I can't wait to drive it." His eyes shone with excitement.
>
> "It's all yours," said Mike, not quite meeting Jamal's eyes. "Uh, I have to go now—see you around!" With that, the older boy disappeared around the corner.

There's something sneaky about Mike. He didn't look right at Jamal while they were talking and he left quickly. I predict that Mike's old car won't run.

Literature Online

Study Central Visit www.glencoe.com and click on Study Central to review predicting.

Practice It!

Below are two events in "The Monsters Are Due on Maple Street." Talk with a partner about what could happen next in each situation. Remember that you can think of more than one prediction. **R**

- The lights on a whole block go out.
- A mysterious figure approaches a crowd.

Use It!

As you read "The Monsters Are Due on Maple Street," remember the predictions you made. If you make other predictions, add them to your notes.

Teach

Literature Online

Study Central Have students access the Web site to review predicting and to complete a related activity.

R Reading Skill

Predicting Read aloud the title of the selection, "The Monsters Are Due on Maple Street." **Ask:** What kind of predictions can you make, based on the title? *(Possible response: The people who live on Maple Street are expecting monsters to arrive.)* **BL** **Ask:** How did you make your predictions for the Practice It! activity? What did you base them on? *(Responses will vary. Students may say that they used prior knowledge to make their predictions and that they based their predictions on things that happened to them or people they know.)* **OL**

Resources for page 953

- Use Reading Skills Transparency in *Read Aloud, Think Aloud,* Unit 8, to help students practice predicting.

Differentiated Instruction

Predicting After students read the excerpt from "The Sweet Deal," have them think of a time when they made a prediction, correctly or incorrectly, about a real-life situation. Tell students to complete one of the following activities to evaluate the importance of predicting as a real-life skill:

- write about their predicting experience
- act out their experience with one or more than one partner
- create a questionnaire about using predicting in real life and distribute it to other students

Have students share their work with the class. **AS**

Objectives

- Make predictions
- Understand literary elements: teleplay

Teach

More About the Author

"You're traveling through another dimension, a dimension not only of sight and sound but of mind; a journey into a wondrous land whose boundaries are that of imagination—next stop, the Twilight Zone!" With these words, Rod Serling introduced his hit series to millions of television viewers each week. *The Twilight Zone* ran from 1959 to 1964, and Serling himself wrote many of the teleplays for the show. His writing became known for surprising twist endings and thought-provoking commentary on social themes.

V Vocabulary

Definitions Say: Look at the three vocabulary words for this selection. What do you notice is similar about all three? *(Response: They are all adjectives.)* **BL** Have students use each word in a sentence in their Learner's Notebook. **OL**

Before You Read

The Monsters Are Due on Maple Street, Act I

Rod Serling

Meet the Author

Rod Serling (1924–1975) was one of the most popular writers in television broadcasting. His "The Monsters Are Due on Maple Street" is from the hit series *The Twilight Zone.* Serling once said, "...the moment we clasp hands with our neighbor, we build the first span to bridge the gap between the young and the old." See page R6 of the Author Files for more on Rod Serling.

Literature Online

Author Search For more about Rod Serling, go to www.glencoe.com.

Objectives (pp. 954–967)
Reading Make predictions • Make connections from text to self
Literature Identify literary elements: teleplay
Vocabulary Identify English language changes

Vocabulary Preview

V

reflective (rih FLEK tiv) *adj.* showing serious and careful thinking; thoughtful **(p. 958)** *He was reflective and calm when he decided not to fight.*

intimidated (in TIM uh day tid) *adj.* frightened or threatened **(p. 961)** *He was intimidated by the crowd, but he continued to speak.*

defiant (dih FY unt) *adj.* showing bold resistance to authority or an opponent **(p. 963)** *He was defiant and refused to cooperate.*

Write to Learn Choose the word that means the opposite of each vocabulary word.

reflective	serious	patient	thoughtless
defiant	meek	courageous	bold
intimidated	scared	confident	helpless

English Language Coach

English as a Changing Language As you learned in Unit 7, new words enter the English language all the time, and the meanings of old words change. The word *e-mail,* which didn't even exist in the 1950s, is now both a noun and a verb. Or think of *cool,* which once referred only to temperature.

The play you're about to read includes many words that are fairly recent additions to the language or that have changed in meaning. The first few pages of Act 1 include *engine,* which used to mean "any machine," and *oddball,* which wasn't a word until 1948.

One way that words enter the language is by being shortened, or "clipped." Here are two clipped words used in Act 1:

Clipped Word	Original Word
gas	gasoline
phone	telephone

On Your Own Copy a blank version of the chart shown above into your Learner's Notebook. Write the following clipped words in the left column, and then provide the original word for each in the right column. (Some you may already know; others you may need to look up in a dictionary.)

exam	pants	van	zoo
memo	fan	math	stereo

Additional Support

Author Search To expand students' appreciation of Rod Serling, have them access the Web site for additional information and resources.

Reading in the Real World

Career Some students may be interested in careers as script writers for television or movies. Tell them about the Scriptwriters Network and its annual High School Fellowship Program. This program is held in conjunction with the Los Angeles Public Library Young Adult Services. The program mentors young writers and helps them develop their work from conception to finished script, culminating in the production of live performances by professional directors and actors. Students who are interested can find more information on the Web or look for organizations that mentor young scriptwriters in their area. **OL** **AL**

Skills Preview

Key Reading Skill: Predicting

Predictions don't come out of nowhere. They're based on the predictor's knowledge and experience. Wrong predictions result from incorrect or incomplete information.

To predict while you're reading a story, use what the story tells you as well as what you know from your own experience. Before you read "The Monsters Are Due on Maple Street," think about

- how people deal with their fears
- what causes people to turn against one another

R

Write to Learn Predict what might happen in each situation above. Make a list of your predictions.

Key Literary Element: Teleplay

A **teleplay,** a play written for television, must deliver all its ideas through dialogue and stage directions. The TV audience will hear the dialogue, but stage directions are written for a second audience-the actors, directors, and crew members who bring the teleplay to life. In stage directions, the writer can

- describe the characters, settings, costumes, mood, and atmosphere needed for the story.
- express thoughts that help the cast and crew understand what they need to know.
- tell the actors, camera operators, and other crew members what to do.

When a teleplay is published, the stage directions help readers to visualize characters and events.

Partner Talk With a partner, think of examples of stage directions. What might stage directions tell an actor to do? What might they tell a camera operator to do?

Interactive Literary Elements Handbook
To review or learn more about the literary elements, go to www.glencoe.com.

Get Ready to Read

Connect to the Reading

How would you and your neighbors react if the power suddenly went out and cars wouldn't start? That's what happens one evening on Maple Street, USA, in the selection. What do you think would cause this to happen?

Write to Learn Write for five minutes about a time you didn't believe a friend. What did he or she tell you? How did you react?

Build Background

"The Monsters Are Due on Maple Street" teleplay first aired on TV in 1960. The stage directions for a teleplay include special terms that involve camera angles and movements. Knowing the most important terms can help you visualize the action.

- *Pan* means to turn the camera to follow or scan a person or object.
- *Cut* means to switch the camera from one scene to another.
- A *close-up* is when the camera moves close to a subject, such as a person's face.
- A *long shot* is when the camera films a subject from a long distance away.

Set Purposes for Reading

BQ

BIG Question Read Act I of "The Monsters Are Due on Maple Street" to discover what happens to relationships in a friendly community when mysterious things happen.

Set Your Own Purpose What else would you like to learn from the selection to help you answer the Big Question? Write your own purpose on the "Monsters Are Due" page of Foldable 8.

Keep Moving

Use these skills as you read the following selection.

READING WORKSHOP 4

Teach

R Reading Skill

Predicting Ask: How do people react in the face of things they don't understand? *(Possible response: with fear, confusion, and distrust)* OL

BQ

Ask: What are some ways the members of a community might react to a shared crisis? *(Possible responses: They might stand together in solidarity. They might break apart and feel like it's every person for him or herself.)* OL

CheckPoint

Use the CheckPoint questions provided on Presentation Plus! to check for predicting skills and to build background. These questions can be used with interactive response keypads for immediate student feedback.

Interactive Literary Elements Handbook Have students access the Web site to improve their understanding of teleplay.

English Language Coach

English as a Changing Language

Write the following words on the board: *cell phone, e-mail, DVD.* Tell students that if you had said these words 100, 50, or even 20 years ago, no one would have known what you were talking about. Discuss the role that television has played in adding new words to the English language, such as *teleplay.* Have students brainstorm other words from the television industry. Then ask students to think of other developments in technology that have led to new words and expressions. EL BL OL

Objectives
- Make predictions
- Make connections from text to self
- Identify literary elements: teleplay
- Identify English language changes

Teach

L Literary Element

Teleplay Say: Read the list of characters. What do you notice? *(Possible responses: There is a narrator. Some characters have names and some don't. Many of the characters are residents of one street.)* BL Scan the first two pages. How do you know when each character is speaking? *(Each speaker's name is set in capital letters and followed by a period.)* OL

R Reading Skill

Review Visualizing

Ask: Can you visualize the opening shots described in the stage directions? In your own words, explain the movement of the camera that is described on the first page. *(Responses will vary. Students may say the camera starts with a clear shot of bright planets and stars in the sky, then moves, or pans, across the sky and down towards Earth, focusing on a street sign, and then showing us an entire street.)* BL OL

Readability Scores
Dale-Chall: 4.9
DRP: N/A
Lexile: N/A

READING WORKSHOP 4

THE MONSTERS Are Due on Maple Street

by Rod Serling

CHARACTERS

Narrator	Figure One	Figure Two
Residents of Maple Street:		
Steve Brand	Charlie's Wife	Mrs. Goodman
Mrs. Brand	Tommy	Woman
Don Martin	Sally, Tommy's Mother	Man One
Pete Van Horn	Les Goodman	Man Two
Charlie		

L

Act I

[Fade in on a shot of the night sky. The various nebulae[1] *and planet bodies stand out in sharp, sparkling relief, and the camera begins a slow pan across the Heavens.]* 1

NARRATOR'S VOICE. There is a fifth dimension beyond that which is known to man. It is a dimension as vast as space, and as timeless as infinity. It is the middle ground between light and shadow—between science and superstition. And it lies between the pit of man's fears and the summit of his knowledge. This is the dimension of imagination. It is an area which we call The Twilight Zone.

R *[The camera has begun to pan down until it passes the horizon and is on a sign which reads "Maple Street." Pan down until we are shooting down at an angle toward the street below. It's a tree-lined, quiet residential American street, very typical of the small*

1. The word ***nebulae*** (NEB yuh lee) refers to bright, cloudlike masses of dust and gases that are visible in the night sky.

Practice the Skills

1 Key Literary Element

Teleplay This text is in italics and is surrounded by brackets. What part of the teleplay is this?

Additional Support

Leveled Reading An adapted version of this selection (3rd grade readability) is available on page 142 of *Jamestown Literature: An Adapted Reader* for Grade 7.

Reading Fluency

Read Along Students who have difficulty reading and visualizing selections with stage directions and dialogue might benefit from reading along silently with a taped version of the selection. Ask students to pause the tape periodically to take notes or sketch a scene that has just been described. They can also ask themselves questions about the selection to test their understanding of what they have read and heard. EL BL

READING WORKSHOP 4

town. The houses have front porches on which people sit and swing on gliders, conversing across from house to house. STEVE BRAND *polishes his car parked in front of his house. His neighbor,* DON MARTIN, *leans against the fender watching him. A Good Humor man rides a bicycle and is just in the process of stopping to sell some ice cream to a couple of kids. Two women gossip on the front lawn. Another man waters his lawn.*]

R

NARRATOR'S VOICE. Maple Street, U.S.A., late summer. A tree-lined little world of front porch gliders, hop scotch, the laughter of children, and the bell of an ice cream vendor.

C

[*There is a pause and the camera moves over to a shot of the Good Humor man and two small boys who are standing alongside, just buying ice cream.*]

L

NARRATOR'S VOICE. At the sound of the roar and the flash of light it will be precisely 6:43 P.M. on Maple Street.

[*At this moment one of the little boys,* TOMMY, *looks up to listen to a sound of a tremendous screeching roar from overhead. A flash of light plays on both their faces and then it moves down the street past lawns and porches and rooftops and then disappears. Various people leave their porches and stop what they're doing to stare up at the sky.* STEVE BRAND, *the man who's been polishing his car, now stands there transfixed,*[2] *staring upwards. He looks at* DON MARTIN, *his neighbor from across the street.*]

STEVE. What was that? A meteor?

DON. [*Nods.*] That's what it looked like. I didn't hear any crash though, did you?

STEVE. [*Shakes his head.*] Nope. I didn't hear anything except a roar.

MRS. BRAND. [*From her porch.*] Steve? What was that?

STEVE. [*Raising his voice and looking toward porch.*] Guess it was a meteor, honey. Came awful close, didn't it? **2**

MRS. BRAND. Too close for my money! Much too close.

[*The camera pans across the various porches to people who stand there watching and talking in low tones.*]

2. To be ***transfixed*** is to be made motionless, as from wonder or fear.

Practice the Skills

2 Key Reading Skill

Predicting Don and Steve think the roar and flash of light was a meteor. What do you think it was? Write your answer in your Learner's Notebook.

Teach

C Critical Thinking

Evaluation Ask: What kind of neighborhood or community are we introduced to in the beginning of the teleplay? *(Possible response: a typical American, suburban, small-town neighborhood on a typical summer evening)* **OL** Why do you think this setting was chosen? *(Possible response: It seems like such a "normal" place—the kind of place where nothing too unusual ever happens—so the characters' response to the unusual situation that is unfolding might be very dramatic.)* **AL**

L Literary Element

Teleplay Say: On this page, notice that we hear the narrator's voice but do not see him or her. Instead we see images of the street. This technique is called a voice-over. What effect does the use of a voice-over have on you? *(Possible responses: It has a slightly creepy effect, as if the narrator knows more than we do and more than the characters do. It makes you feel as if you were looking at creatures in a laboratory on whom an experiment is about to be conducted.)* **OL AL**

Differentiated Instruction

Reading Aloud To make this opening scene come alive, assign students parts and have them read the first two pages aloud. You can assign more than one student to read the stage directions and the part of the narrator. Have students reading the same part sit together. Explain that other students will get a chance to read aloud from the teleplay as you continue reading in the selection. Assign the smaller parts to English Language Learners or students who are reading below grade level. **EL BL OL**

Objectives
- Make predictions
- Identify and understand elements of a teleplay
- Evaluate a teleplay
- Visualize text

READING WORKSHOP 4

Teach

Viewing the Art

Say: Look at the painting. Notice the title, date, and painter's name. Edward Hopper is known for his paintings of small town and big city life in America in the 1950s. Rod Serling also began his career as a writer in the 1950s. How is the painting similar to the scene you imagined of Maple Street? How is it different? *(Possible responses: Similar—small-town feeling, peaceful; different—gas station, not residential)* **BL** **OL**

R Reading Skill

Review Skimming and Scanning **Say:** Notice that the narrator's voice appears again at the top of this page. Now, skim and scan the rest of the selection. Does the narrator's voice appear again in this Act? *(No)* **BL** Why do you think this is so? *(Possible response: so that the focus of the story can shift to the characters' actions)* **OL** **AL**

Portrait of Orleans, 1950. Edward Hopper, Oil on canvas, 26 X 40 in. Fine Arts Museum of San Francisco.

R NARRATOR'S VOICE. Maple Street. Six-forty-four P.M. on a late September evening. [*A pause.*] Maple Street in the last calm and **reflective** moment . . . before the monsters came!

[*The camera slowly pans across the porches again. We see a man screwing a light bulb on a front porch, then getting down off the stool to* **flick** *the switch and finding that nothing happens.* **3** *Another man is working on an electric power mower. He plugs in the plug, flicks on the switch of the power mower, off and on, with nothing happening.*

Through the window of a front porch, we see a woman pushing her finger back and forth on the dial hook. Her voice is indistinct and distant, but intelligible and repetitive.]

WOMAN. Operator, operator, something's wrong on the phone, operator!

[*MRS. BRAND comes out on the porch and calls to STEVE.*]

Vocabulary

reflective (rih FLEK tiv) *adj.* showing serious and careful thinking; thoughtful

Practice the Skills

3 English Language Coach

English as a Changing Language The verb **flick** came into English in 1816 and means "to move with a light, quick stroke." One of the noun meanings of *flick* is a clipped form of *flicker,* which is what people used to call a movie.

Additional Support

English Language Coach

English as a Changing Language
This teleplay was written before cell phone and digital technology were invented. A telephone once had a *dial hook.* To make a call, you *dialed a number.* On the board, draw an old-fashioned phone dial and demonstrate with your finger how it worked. The expressions *dial hook* and *dial a number* have almost passed out of the English language. Ask students to list expressions related to new telephone technology. **EL** **BL**

READING WORKSHOP 4

MRS. BRAND. [*Calling.*] Steve, the power's off. I had the soup on the stove and the stove just stopped working.

WOMAN. Same thing over here. I can't get anybody on the phone either. The phone seems to be dead.

[*We look down on the street as we hear the voices creep up from below, small, mildly disturbed voices highlighting these kinds of phrases:*]

VOICES.
Electricity's off.
Phone won't work.
Can't get a thing on the **radio**.
My power mower won't move, won't work at all.
Radio's gone dead! 4

[*PETE VAN HORN, a tall, thin man, is seen standing in front of his house.*]

VAN HORN. I'll cut through the back yard . . . See if the power's still on on Floral Street. I'll be right back!

[*He walks past the side of his house and disappears into the back yard. The camera pans down slowly until we're looking at ten or eleven people standing around the street and overflowing to the curb and sidewalk. In the background is STEVE BRAND's car.*] 5

STEVE. Doesn't make sense. Why should the power go off all of a sudden, and the phone line?

DON. Maybe some sort of an electrical storm or something.

CHARLIE. That don't seem likely. Sky's just as blue as anything. Not a cloud. No lightning. No thunder. No nothing. How could it be a storm?

WOMAN. I can't get a thing on the radio. Not even the portable.

[*The people again murmur softly in wonderment and question.*]

CHARLIE. Well, why don't you go downtown and check with the police, though they'll probably think we're crazy or something. A little power failure and right away we get all flustered[3] and everything.

3. To be ***flustered*** is to be embarrassed, nervous, or confused.

Practice the Skills

L R

4 English Language Coach

English as a Changing Language The word **radio** entered the English language around 100 years ago as a noun. Within ten years, people began using *radio* as a verb.

5 Literary Element

Teleplay What do the stage directions on this page tell you that the dialogue doesn't tell you? What do the stage directions help you visualize, or see in your mind? Give examples.

Teach

L Literary Element

Review Point of View

Say: Describe how the point of view suddenly shifts and then shifts back again. *(Possible response: The point of view goes from the main characters on the street to the voices of unnamed characters, then back to the main characters again.)* BL OL

R Reading Skill

Review Understanding Sequence

Suggest that students use the following graphic organizer to track the sequence of events as they unfold. Students can go back and fill in events from the beginning and continue as they read the selection. OL

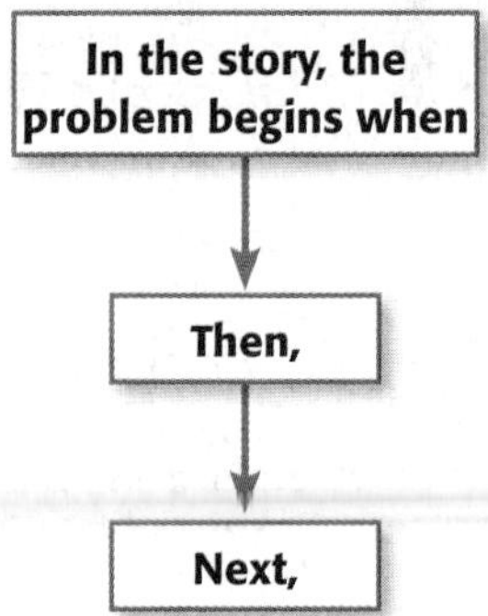

English Language Coach

English as a Changing Language

Point out the word *portable*. Ask students to name technological devices that can be carried around with us. Point out that today, since so many devices are portable, we don't bother to call them portable anymore. OL Also point out that *portable* comes from the Latin word *portare*, "to carry." Ask English Language Learners if they recognize a word with the same root in their first languages. *(French: porter, Spanish: portar)* Ask students to explain the meanings of these words. *(to carry)* EL

Objectives

- Identify and understand elements of a teleplay
- Identify components of the etymology of language, including word origins and how they contribute to contemporary meanings
- Use text features to interpret a selection
- Skim and scan text

Teach

R Reading Skill

Review Connecting Ask: Have you ever been in a situation where something went wrong and you didn't know the cause? How did that situation compare to the one in the teleplay? *(Responses will vary.)* How would you start to feel in this situation? Would you start to feel frightened? Why or why not? *(Responses will vary. Students may say that the mounting tension would make them start to feel uneasy.)* AS

EL Language Coach

Multiple-Meaning Words
Say: The stage directions describe Tommy as a "serious-faced fourteen-year-old in spectacles . . . ." One definition for spectacles is a pair of glasses. Another is a disturbing or unusual event. What is the correct definition for the word as it is used here? *(glasses)* EL BL

STEVE. It isn't just the power failure, Charlie. If it was, we'd still be able to get a broadcast on the portable. 6

[*There's a murmur of reaction to this.* STEVE *looks from face to face and then over to his car.*]

STEVE. I'll run downtown. We'll get this all straightened out.

[*He walks over to the car, gets in it, turns the key. Looking through the open car door, we see the crowd watching him from the other side.* STEVE *starts the engine. It turns over sluggishly and then just stops dead. He tries it again and this time he can't get it to turn over. Then, very slowly and reflectively, he turns the key back to "off" and slowly gets out of the car.*
The people stare at STEVE. *He stands for a moment by the car, then walks toward the group.*]

STEVE. I don't understand it. It was working fine before . . .

DON. Out of gas?

STEVE. [*Shakes his head.*] I just had it filled up.

WOMAN. What's it mean?

CHARLIE. It's just as if . . . as if everything had stopped. [*Then he turns toward* STEVE.] We'd better walk downtown. [*Another murmur of assent*[4] *at this.*]

STEVE. The two of us can go, Charlie. [*He turns to look back at the car.*] It couldn't be the meteor. A meteor couldn't do *this.*

R

[*He and* CHARLIE *exchange a look, then they start to walk away from the group.*
We see TOMMY, *a serious-faced fourteen-year-old in spectacles who stands a few feet away from the group. He is halfway between them and the two men, who start to walk down the sidewalk.*]

EL

TOMMY. Mr. Brand . . . you better not!

STEVE. Why not?

TOMMY. They don't want you to.

4. An expression of agreement is ***assent.***

Practice the Skills

6 **Key Reading Skill**

Predicting Do *you* think it's "just a power failure"? If not, what else could it be? What will happen next?

Additional Support

Differentiated Instruction

Word Origins Tell students that the word *spectacle* comes from the Latin root *spectare,* "to watch" or "to see." Have students brainstorm a list of words that come from the same root. *(spectator, spectacular, inspect, inspection, respect)* OL AL Invite English Language Learners to share words that are from the same root in their first languages. EL

[STEVE and CHARLIE exchange a grin, and STEVE looks back toward the boy.]

STEVE. Who doesn't want us to?

TOMMY. *[Jerks his head in the general direction of the distant horizon.]* Them!

STEVE. Them?

CHARLIE. Who are them?

TOMMY. *[Very intently.]* Whoever was in that thing that came by overhead.

[STEVE knits his brows for a moment, cocking his head questioningly. His voice is intense.]

STEVE. What?

TOMMY. Whoever was in that thing that came over. I don't think they want us to leave here.

[STEVE leaves CHARLIE and walks over to the boy. He kneels down in front of him. He forces his voice to remain gentle. He reaches out and holds the boy.]

R

STEVE. What do you mean? What are you talking about?

TOMMY. They don't want us to leave. That's why they shut everything off.

STEVE. What makes you say that? Whatever gave you that idea?

WOMAN. *[From the crowd.]* Now isn't that the craziest thing you ever heard?

TOMMY. *[Persistently but a little* **intimidated** *by the crowd.]* It's always that way, in every story I ever read about a ship landing from outer space. 7

WOMAN. *[To the boy's mother, SALLY, who stands on the fringe of the crowd.]* From outer space, yet! Sally, you better get that boy

Vocabulary

intimidated (in TIM uh day tid) *adj.* frightened or threatened

Practice the Skills

7 Reviewing Skills

Drawing Conclusions Tommy's ideas are based on science fiction stories he has read. It seems reasonable for a young boy to draw these conclusions. Considering what you've read so far, what conclusions do you draw? Who are "they," and what do "they" want?

Teach

R Reading Skill

Predicting **Say:** What idea does Tommy introduce that changes the situation? *(that aliens are responsible for what is happening)* BL Do you think his idea will affect the mood of the people? What effect might it have? *(Possible response: Yes, the idea will feed their imaginations, and they will start to get very uneasy and paranoid.)* OL

Literature Focus Lesson

Science Fiction Invite students to talk about whether stories about space ships are popular. Ask students to tell why they think such stories are or are not popular, and encourage them to discuss science fiction books they've read or movies they've seen. Talk about the fact that people are fascinated with the idea of life on other planets. Also discuss how in most movies with space ships, the aliens' purpose for coming to Earth is to conquer the planet. Have them discuss why that might be so. OL

Objectives

- Make predictions
- Identify and understand elements of a teleplay
- Identify components of the etymology of language, including word origins and how they contribute to contemporary meanings

Teach

Viewing the Photo

Ask: What mood does the photo create? *(Responses will vary. Students may say that the photo combines the light in the window with the darkness outside to create a mysterious and isolated mood.)* **OL** How does the author create a similar mood? *(Possible response: The author creates a similar effect by combining the "normal" setting of a typical residential street with the unexplainable and strange events that are occurring.)* **AL**

V Vocabulary

Synonyms and Antonyms **Say:** Read the definition of optimism. Now name one synonym and one antonym for optimism. *(Possible response: hopefulness, pessimism)* **AS**

of yours up to bed. He's been reading too many comic books or seeing too many movies or something.

SALLY. Tommy, come over here and stop that kind of talk.

STEVE. Go ahead, Tommy. We'll be right back. And you'll see. That wasn't any ship or anything like it. That was just a . . . a meteor or something. Likely as not—[*He turns to the group, now trying to weight his words with an optimism*[5] *he obviously doesn't feel but is desperately trying to instill*[6] *in himself as well as the others.*] No doubt it did have something to do with all this power failure and the rest of it. Meteors can do some crazy things. Like sunspots.

DON. [*Picking up the cue.*] Sure. That's the kind of thing—like sunspots. They raise Cain[7] with radio reception all over the world. And this thing being so close—why, there's no telling the sort of stuff it can do. [*He wets his lips, smiles nervously.*] Go ahead, Charlie. You and Steve go into town and see if that isn't what's causing it all.

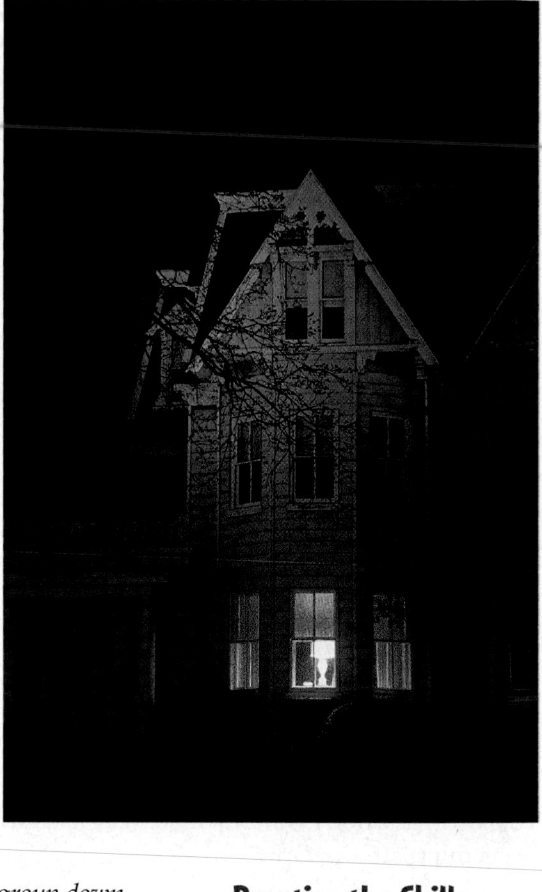

[*STEVE and CHARLIE again walk away from the group down the sidewalk. The people watch silently. TOMMY stares at them, biting his lips, and finally calling out again.*] 8

TOMMY. Mr. Brand!

[*The two men stop again. TOMMY takes a step toward them.*]

TOMMY. Mr. Brand . . . please don't leave here.

[*STEVE and CHARLIE stop once again and turn toward the boy. There's a murmur in the crowd, a murmur of irritation and*

5. ***Optimism*** means "a hopeful or cheerful view of things." 
6. To ***instill*** is to gradually cause to feel or have.
7. ***(raise Cain)*** This expression means "cause trouble."

Practice the Skills

8 Key Literary Element

Teleplay Would you be able to visualize Tommy and his actions without the stage directions? Why or why not?

Additional Support

Literature Focus Lesson

Creating Suspense Discuss the word *suspense* with students. Have them review the sequence of events in the story that have led to this point. Then have them identify the points where the suspense increases, such as the flash overhead, the electricity going off, and Tommy's speech. Then discuss how the author increases the suspense on this page by having Tommy call out to the men again after they have dismissed his idea and started to walk away. Explain that suspense is a very important technique in the screenwriter's toolbox. **BL** **OL**

concern as if the boy were bringing up fears that shouldn't be brought up; words which carried with them a strange kind of validity[8] *that came without logic but nonetheless registered and had meaning and effect. Again we hear a murmur of reaction from the crowd.* TOMMY *is partly frightened and partly* ***defiant*** *as well.*] **9**

TOMMY. You might not even be able to get to town. It was that way in the story. Nobody could leave. Nobody except—

STEVE. Except who?

TOMMY. Except the people they'd sent down ahead of them. They looked just like humans. And it wasn't until the ship landed that—

[*The boy suddenly stops again, conscious of the parents staring at them and of the sudden hush of the crowd.*]

SALLY. [*In a whisper, sensing the antagonism*[9] *of the crowd.*] Tommy, please son . . . honey, don't talk that way—

MAN ONE. That kid shouldn't talk that way . . . and we shouldn't stand here listening to him. Why this is the craziest thing I ever heard of. The kid tells us a comic book plot and here we stand listening—

[STEVE *walks toward the camera, stops by the boy.*]

STEVE. Go ahead, Tommy. What kind of story was this? What about the people that they sent out ahead?

TOMMY. That was the way they prepared things for the landing. They sent four people. A mother and a father and two kids who looked just like humans . . . but they weren't. **10**

[*There's another silence as* STEVE *looks toward the crowd and then toward* TOMMY. *He wears a tight grin.*]

BQ

STEVE. Well, I guess what we'd better do then is to run a check on the neighborhood and see which ones of us are really human.

8. Something that's true is *valid* and has ***validity***.
9. The ***antagonism*** (an TAG uh niz um) of a crowd is their unfriendly feelings and behavior.

Vocabulary

defiant (dih FY unt) *adj.* showing bold resistance to authority or an opponent

Practice the Skills

9 Key Literary Element

C **Teleplay** What do these stage directions tell you about the crowd? Give details.

10 Key Reading Skill

Predicting How do you predict the neighbors will react to Tommy and his story? Will they believe him or not?

Reading Fluency

Build Fluency To build fluency, have students read aloud in a small group. Group members can take turns reading the parts. Encourage students to notice when speakers break off in the middle of a sentence. Encourage other students to jump in and pick up the thread of the dialogue. Have students practice this technique until they can read with fluency, approximating the sound of a real-life dialogue. **EL** **BL**

Teach

C Critical Thinking

Comprehension Ask: Does the role of the crowd gradually become more important? Explain your answer. *(Possible response: Yes, in the stage directions the individuals of the community are now described as one, as a crowd, reacting and feeling together.)* **OL**

BQ 

Ask: What effect do Tommy's words have on the community? *(Possible response: His words make people feel uncomfortable. These words begin to plant seeds of doubt in the neighbors about one another and cause them to start to suspect that someone among them is responsible for the strange occurrences.)* **OL** **AL**

Objectives
- Make predictions
- Identify and understand elements of a teleplay
- Use text features to interpret text

Teach

R Reading Skill

Predicting Ask: Why do you think Pete Van Horn has not returned yet? *(Responses will vary. Students may say that maybe something terrible happened to him, like Tommy predicted might happen if anyone left. Some may say that it is a clue about something that will happen later in the story.)* AS

L Literary Element

Teleplay Ask: Why do you think some characters have no names? What role do they play in the story? *(Responses will vary. Students may say they are just other neighbors. Some may say that they play a role by asking questions or saying things that everyone is just thinking.)* AS

[There's laughter at this, but it's a laughter that comes from a desperate attempt to lighten the atmosphere. It's a release kind of laugh. The people look at one another in the middle of their laughter.]

CHARLIE. There must be somethin' better to do than stand around makin' bum jokes about it. [*Rubs his jaw nervously.*] I wonder if Floral Street's got the same deal we got. [*He looks past the houses.*] Where is Pete Van Horn anyway? Didn't he get back yet? R

[Suddenly there's the sound of a car's engine starting to turn over. We look across the street toward the driveway of LES GOODMAN*'s house. He's at the wheel trying to start the car.]*

SALLY. Can you get it started, Les?

[He gets out of the car, shaking his head.]

GOODMAN. No dice.

[He walks toward the group. He stops suddenly as behind him, inexplicably[10] *and with a noise that inserts itself into the silence, the car engine starts up all by itself.* GOODMAN *whirls around to stare toward it.*
The car idles roughly, smoke coming from the exhaust, the frame shaking gently.
GOODMAN*'s eyes go wide, and he runs over to his car.*
The people stare toward the car.] 11

MAN ONE. He got the car started somehow. He got his car started!

[The camera pans along the faces of the people as they stare, somehow caught up by this revelation and somehow, illogically, wildly, frightened.] 12

WOMAN. How come his car just up and started like that? L

SALLY. All by itself. He wasn't anywheres near it. It started all by itself.

*[*DON *approaches the group, stops a few feet away to look toward* GOODMAN*'s car and then back toward the group.]*

---

10. Something that happens ***inexplicably*** (in eks PLIK uh blee) is impossible to understand or explain.

Practice the Skills

11 Key Reading Skill

Predicting What will the group think about Goodman's car starting by itself?

12 Key Literary Element

Teleplay When a camera pans, it follows or scans something. Why do you think the writer chose to pan the faces of the people in the crowd?

Additional Support

English Language Coach

English as a Changing Language

The expression *no dice* comes from the 1920s, when gambling with dice was a popular pastime. The expression means "impossible" or "no way." Have students discuss expressions we have today for "impossible" or "no way." Talk about where these expressions come from and explain their meanings. Also have English Language Learners share expressions they know from other languages that mean "no way." AS

DON. And he never did come out to look at that thing that flew overhead. He wasn't even interested. [*He turns to the faces in the group, his face taut and serious.*] Why? Why didn't he come out with the rest of us to look?

CHARLIE. He always was an oddball. Him and his whole family. Real oddball.

DON. What do you say we ask him?

Visual Vocabulary
A ***metamorphosis*** is a complete change, as when a caterpillar becomes a butterfly.

C [*The group suddenly starts toward the house. In this brief fraction of a moment they take the first step toward performing a* metamorphosis *that changes people from a group into a mob. They begin to head purposefully across the street toward the house at the end. Steve stands in front of them. For a moment their fear almost turns their walk into a wild stampede, but Steve's voice, loud, incisive,*[11] *and commanding, makes them stop.*] 13 EL

STEVE. Wait a minute . . . wait a minute! Let's not be a mob!

[*The people stop as a group, seem to pause for a moment, and then much more quietly and slowly start to walk across the street.* GOODMAN *stands alone facing the people.*]

GOODMAN. I just don't understand it. I tried to start it and it wouldn't start. You saw me. All of you saw me.

[*And now, just as suddenly as the engine started, it stops and there's a long silence that is gradually intruded upon by the frightened murmuring of the people.*]

GOODMAN. I don't understand. I swear . . . I don't understand. What's happening?

DON. Maybe you better tell us. Nothing's working on this street. Nothing. No lights, no power, no radio. [*And then meaningfully*] Nothing except one car—yours! R

[*The people pick this up and now their murmuring becomes a loud chant filling the air with accusations and demands for action.*]

11. Steve's ***incisive*** voice is sharp and forceful.

Practice the Skills

13 Key Literary Element

Teleplay Reread the details in the stage direction. How would you act if you were an actor in this crowd? What kind of body language and facial expressions would you use?

READING WORKSHOP 4

Teach

C Critical Thinking

Evaluation Ask: What is the difference between a *crowd* and a *mob? (Possible response: A crowd is a group of people; a mob is a group of people with one single intention.)* **OL**

EL Language Coach

Word Origins The word *mob* comes from the Latin word *mobile* meaning "fickle," or "crowd." Have students look up the word *fickle* and say what it means *(changeable; unstable, particularly when it comes to emotions or feelings)* **BL** Ask students how the etymology of the word helps them understand the meaning of *mob* and the meaning of the related word *mobile. (Possible response: A* mob *is a crowd of people with unstable, changeable emotions, while* mobile *means movable or capable of moving.* **OL**

R Reading Skill

Predicting Ask: What action do you think the mob might take? *(Responses will vary. Students may mention that the crowd might try to take their frustrations out on Les Goodman.)* **AS**

Differentiated Instruction

Word Origins Encourage students to use etymology to help them define words. Have students look up the etymology of the word *metamorphosis. (Latin, from Greek: meta "beside or after" + morph "form")* Ask students to explain how the etymology of the word helps them understand the word's meaning. *(A metamorphosis is a transformation, a process that takes something from one form to another.)* **OL AL**

Objectives
- Make predictions
- Identify components of the etymology of language, including word origins and how they contribute to contemporary meanings
- Identify and understand elements of a teleplay

Teach

R Reading Skill

Review Evaluating Say: When Les Goodman's car starts up by itself and the light on his porch goes out, the crowd's suspicions start to fall on him. Why do you think the writer gave this character the name *Goodman?* *(Responses will vary. Some may say it means literally that he is a "good man," although the crowd is beginning to become suspicious of him.)* **OL**

C Critical Thinking

Analysis Say: In "Photographing History," you read about the Civil War period, a time when our country was torn apart because of different beliefs in the North and the South. What tears the neighborhood community apart in "The Monsters Are Due on Maple Street"? *(Possible responses: disloyalty, fear)* **OL**

Two of the men pass DON *and head toward* GOODMAN, *who backs away, backing into his car and now at bay.*][12]

GOODMAN. Wait a minute now. You keep your distance—all of you.

So I've got a car that starts by itself—well, that's a freak thing, I admit it. But does that make me some kind of a criminal or something? I don't know why the car works—it just does!

[*This stops the crowd momentarily and now* GOODMAN, *still backing away, goes toward his front porch. He goes up the steps and then stops to stand facing the mob.*
We see a long shot of STEVE *as he comes through the crowd.*]

STEVE. [*Quietly.*] We're all on a monster kick, Les. Seems that the general impression holds that maybe one family isn't what we think they are. Monsters from outer space or something. Different than us. Fifth columnists[13] from the vast beyond. [*He chuckles.*] You know anybody that might fit that description around here on Maple Street? **14**

GOODMAN. What is this, a gag or something? This a practical joke or something?

[*We see a close-up of the porch light as it suddenly goes out. There's a murmur from the group.*]

GOODMAN. Now I suppose that's supposed to incriminate me! The light goes on and off. That really does it, doesn't it? **R**

[*He looks around the faces of the people.*]

I just don't understand this— [*He wets his lips, looking from face to face.*] Look, you all know me. We've lived here five years. Right in this house. We're no different from any of the rest of you! We're no different at all. Really . . . this whole thing is just . . . just weird—

WOMAN. Well, if that's the case, Les Goodman, explain why— [*She stops suddenly, clamping her mouth shut.*]

GOODMAN. [*Softly.*] Explain what?

12. ***(at bay)*** This describes the position of a cornered animal that is forced to turn and face its pursuers.
13. ***Fifth columnists*** are traitors.

Practice the Skills

14 Key Reading Skill

Predicting Look back at the prediction you made about the crowd responding to Tommy's story (p. 963). Was your prediction correct?

Additional Support

English Language Coach

English as a Changing Language
Expressions originate or start in different fields, such as medicine, law, and technology. The expression *fifth columnists* comes to us from military history. The expression was first used in 1936 when Spain was in the middle of a civil war. Four columns, or units, of rebel troops were attacking Madrid. Inside the city, many citizens were sympathetic to the rebels. They became known as the "fifth column." Ask students if they can think of any other expressions that have become part of the English language that come to us from military terminology. *(Some examples: flak, flak jacket, camouflage, four-gun salute)* **AL**

STEVE. [*Interjecting.*] Look, let's forget this—

CHARLIE. [*Overlapping him.*] Go ahead, let her talk. What about it? Explain what?

WOMAN. [*A little reluctantly.*] Well . . . sometimes I go to bed late at night. A couple of times . . . a couple of times I'd come out on the porch and I'd see Mr. Goodman here in the wee hours of the morning standing out in front of his house . . . looking up at the sky. [*She looks around the circle of faces.*] That's right, looking up at the sky as if . . . as if he were waiting for something. [*A pause.*] As if he were looking for something.

[*There's a murmur of reaction from the crowd again. We cut suddenly to a group shot. As* GOODMAN *starts toward them, they back away frightened.*] C1

GOODMAN. You know really . . . this is for laughs. You know what I'm guilty of? [*He laughs.*] I'm guilty of insomnia.[14] Now what's the penalty for insomnia? [*At this point the laugh, the humor, leaves his voice.*] Did you hear what I said? I said it was insomnia. [*A pause as he looks around, then shouts.*] I said it was insomnia! You fools. You scared, frightened rabbits, you. You're sick people, do you know that? You're sick people—all of you! And you don't even know what you're starting because let me tell you . . . let me tell you—this thing you're starting—that should frighten you. As God is my witness . . . you're letting something begin here that's a nightmare! 15 C2

14. ***Insomnia*** is restless sleep or the inability to fall asleep.

Practice the Skills

15 **BIG Question**

What do you think the author is saying about the relationships between members of a community? Should you trust your neighbors? Why or why not? Write your answers on the "Monsters Are Due" page of Foldable 8. Your response will help you answer the Unit Challenge later.

Teach

C1 Critical Thinking

Comprehension Ask: Why does the crowd back away from Mr. Goodman after the woman tells how she saw Mr. Goodman looking up at the sky late at night? *(Possible response: They are suddenly afraid that maybe he really is not one of them.)* OL

C2 Critical Thinking

Comprehension Say: Les Goodman tells the crowd that they are sick and that they should be frightened of what they're starting. What does he mean? *(Possible responses: They are sick because they are allowing their fears to turn them into a mob, looking for someone to blame. They should be frightened of what they're starting—looking for a scapegoat, someone to sacrifice to give them the sense that they are taking action and are still in control.)* OL

CheckPoint

Use the CheckPoint questions provided on Presentation Plus! to check for comprehension of the selection. These questions can be used with interactive response keypads for immediate student feedback.

Differentiated Instruction

Etymology Have students look up the etymology of the word *insomnia.* Explain that it comes from a combination of the Latin prefix *in-* meaning "not" + *somnus* meaning "sleep." Explain that many words are made up of a prefix plus a root word. AS Ask English Language Learners if they can think of words from their first language that are related to or come from the root word *somnia.* Have them explain to the class what these words mean. EL

Objectives
- Make predictions
- Identify components of the etymology of language, including word origins and how they contribute to contemporary meanings

Assess

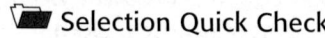

Resources for page 968

- Selection Quick Check
- Selection and Unit Assessment
- ExamView Assessment Suite
- Interactive Tutor: Self-Assessment

Students can respond to the *After You Read* items in their Learner's Notebook or on a separate sheet of paper.

Answering the

1. Responses will vary.

Critical Thinking

2. Students may note that the crowd is reacting out of fear and losing control.

Skills Review

Key Reading Skill: Predicting

3. Responses will vary. Students should mention specific clues from the selection.

Key Literary Element: Teleplay

4. Responses will vary. Students should show understanding of the differences between stage directions and dialogue.

Vocabulary Check

5. intimidated
6. defiant
7. reflective
8. *gasoline, examination,* and *pantaloons*

After You Read

The Monsters Are Due on Maple Street, Act I

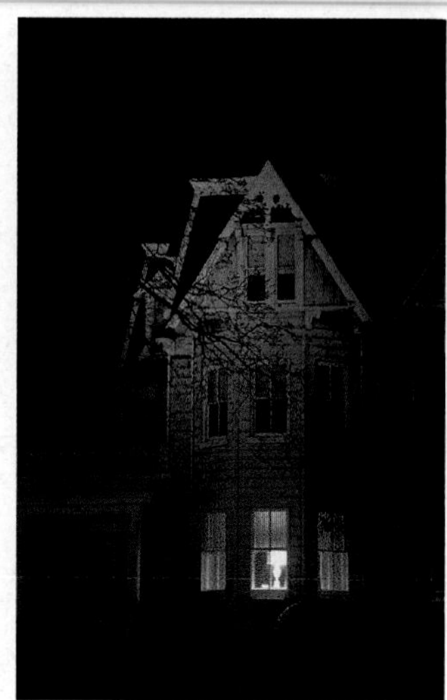

Answering the

1. After reading Act I of the selection, what do you think a community is? What should a community be like?

Critical Thinking

2. **Infer** What kind of "nightmare" is Goodman talking about at the end of Act I?

Tip **Author and Me**

Write About Your Reading

Pretend you are a person who lives on Maple Street. You have been watching and listening to the events. Write a journal entry that describes your feelings about the events and the people on your street.

Skills Review

Key Reading Skill: Predicting

3. Review the predictions you made as you read. Which predictions were correct? What clues in the selection helped you make good predictions?

Key Literary Element: Teleplay

4. Which part of the teleplay—the dialogue or the stage directions—has most helped you understand the characters so far? Why?

Vocabulary Check

Write the vocabulary word that each clue describes.

reflective **intimidated** **defiant**

5. This is how bullies want their victims to feel.
6. This is how people feel when they fight back.
7. This is being quiet and thoughtful.
8. **English Language Coach** What are the original, longer forms of the clipped words *gas, exam,* and *pants*?

Objectives (pp. 968–979)
Reading Make predictions • Make connections from text to self
Literature Identify literary elements: teleplay
Vocabulary Identify English language changes

Write About Your Reading

Possible response:
This evening something very strange happened. Many of us were outside on the street when a bright flash passed across the sky. After that, all kinds of strange things started to happen. All the lights on our block went out, and people's cars wouldn't start. It just didn't seem to make any sense. We were all looking for rational explanations when Sally's kid, Tommy, started talking about space ships and aliens and whatnot. Everybody started getting really creeped out. I just don't know where this is going to end, but if there isn't some reasonable explanation soon, I'm afraid people are going to take things into their own hands.

Before You Read

The Monsters Are Due on Maple Street, Act II

Vocabulary Preview

V

legitimate (lih JIT uh mit) *adj.* following the rules; lawful; allowed **(p. 970)** *Kicking the ball past that line isn't legitimate.*

explicit (eks PLIS it) *adj.* clearly expressed **(p. 979)** *She told us exactly what to do. Her directions were explicit.*

prejudices (PREJ uh dis us) *n.* unfavorable opinions or judgments formed unfairly **(p. 979)** *Malik has prejudices against green beans and broccoli but has never eaten them.*

English Language Coach

English as a Changing Language In many cases, a dictionary will tell you when a word entered the English language. The year will appear in parentheses just before the definition.

tele·play (tel ə plā) *n* (1952): a play written for television

Skills Preview

Key Reading Skill: Predicting

Before you read Act II, consider what you know about

- mob or group behavior
- the causes of violence

Key Literary Element: Teleplay

As you read, pay attention to how the stage directions help you understand actions, learn about characters, and visualize the scene.

Get Ready to Read

Class Discussion Discuss why people might behave differently in a group than when they are alone. Think about how people act on teams or in groups.

Keep Moving

Use these skills as you read the following selection.

Teach

V Vocabulary

Prefixes, Suffixes, and Root Words Say: One way to learn and remember the vocabulary words is to break them down into their smaller parts: prefixes, suffixes, and root words. What ideas do you have about the meaning of the word parts that make up these vocabulary words? Find the meaning of the root words in a dictionary. *(Possible response:* legit *is related to the root word meaning "legal";* ex + plicit *means "unfold";* pre + judice *means "judge before")* **AL**

CheckPoint

Use the CheckPoint questions provided on Presentation Plus! to check for predicting skills to the text and to build background. These questions can be used with interactive response keypads for immediate student feedback.

Literature Focus Lesson

Teleplay In a teleplay, as in a movie or a book, the story can jump around in time. A *flashback* is the term for a jump backwards in time. Writers use flashbacks to give us information about things that happened before the present moment. At other times, the story can jump forward in time, or *flash-forward.* It is up to the viewer to follow these jumps in time and to keep track of the sequence of events.

Tell students to continue adding to their sequence of events graphic organizer as they read Act II of this selection. Remind them that they can add boxes onto the organizer as necessary. **AS**

Objectives

- Use elements of teleplay to understand a selection
- Identify components of the etymology of language, including word origins and how they contribute to contemporary meanings

Teach

R1 Reading Skill

Review Clarifying **Ask:** How much time has passed between the end of Act I and the beginning of Act II? How do you know? *(Possible response: About a few hours have passed. Act I begins at 6:43 p.m. in late summer, so it was probably still fairly light outside. Act II begins with Mrs. Goodman lighting a candle in the entry hall at night, so now it must be dark outside, and therefore a few hours later.)* OL AL

R2 Reading Skill

Review Comparing and Contrasting **Say:** Compare the beginning of Act I to the beginning of Act II. How are things the same? How have things changed? *(Possible response: The activity takes place on the same street, on the same night, and with the same people. But now it's full night, homes are lit by candles, and people are talking in small clusters, hushed and frightened, as two people suspiciously watch the Goodmans' house.)* AS

Act II

R1 *[We see a medium shot of the goodman entry hall at night. On the side table rests an unlit candle. mrs. goodman walks into the scene, a glass of milk in hand. She sets the milk down on the table, lights the candle with a match from a box on the table, picks up the glass of milk, and starts out of scene. mrs. goodman comes through her porch door, glass of milk in hand. The entry hall, with table and lit candle, can be seen behind her.*

R2 *Outside, the camera slowly* ***pans*** *down the sidewalk, taking in little knots of people who stand around talking in low voices. At the end of each conversation they look toward les goodman's house. From the various houses we can see candlelight but no electricity, and there's an all-pervading quiet that blankets the whole area, disturbed only by the almost whispered voices of the people as they stand around. The camera pans over to one group where charlie stands. He stares across at goodman's house.*

We see a long shot of the house. Two men stand across the street in almost sentry-like poses. Then we see a medium shot of a group of people.] 1 2

SALLY. *[A little timorously.]*[1] It just doesn't seem right, though, keeping watch on them. Why . . . he was right when he said he was one of our neighbors. Why, I've known Ethel Goodman ever since they moved in. We've been good friends—

CHARLIE. That don't prove a thing. Any guy who'd spend his time lookin' up at the sky early in the morning—well, there's something wrong with that kind of person. There's something that ain't **legitimate**. Maybe under normal circumstances we could let it go by, but these aren't normal circumstances. Why, look at this street! Nothin' but candles. Why, it's like goin' back into the dark ages or somethin'!

1. ***Timorously*** means "lacking courage or self-confidence; timidly."

Vocabulary

legitimate (lih JIT uh mit) *adj.* following the rules; lawful; allowed

Practice the Skills

1 Key Literary Element

Teleplay How do the camera directions help you understand what the neighbors are thinking and talking about?

2 English Language Coach

English as a Changing Language You've learned that **pan** means "to follow or scan something" by rotating the camera. Look up the word in the dictionary. What year did *pan* take on this meaning?

Additional Support

Differentiated Instruction

Timeline Some readers may find it helpful to use a timeline to follow the sequence of events. As students read Act II, help them use a timeline to track key moments in the story and to follow the leap forward in time that occurs between the Acts.

- Help students to think about how much time elapses between different events and to mark their timelines accordingly.
- Students may wish to label their timelines with character names and their actions or with pictures that describe events. BL

READING WORKSHOP 4

[*STEVE WALKS DOWN THE STEPS OF HIS PORCH, WALKS DOWN THE STREET OVER TO* LES GOODMAN'S *HOUSE, AND THEN STOPS AT THE FOOT OF THE STEPS.* GOODMAN *STANDS THERE, HIS WIFE BEHIND HIM, VERY FRIGHTENED.*]

GOODMAN. Just stay right where you are, Steve. We don't want any trouble, but this time if anybody sets foot on my porch, that's what they're going to get—trouble!

STEVE. Look, Les—

GOODMAN. I've already explained to you people. I don't sleep very well at night sometimes. I get up and I take a walk and I look up at the sky. I look at the stars!

MRS. GOODMAN. That's exactly what he does. Why this whole thing, it's . . . it's some kind of madness or something.

STEVE. [*Nods grimly.*] That's exactly what it is—some kind of madness.

CHARLIE'S VOICE. [*Shrill, from across the street.*] You best watch who you're seen with, Steve! Until we get this all straightened out, you ain't exactly above suspicion yourself.

STEVE. [*Whirling around toward him.*] Or you, Charlie. Or any of us, it seems. From age eight on up.

WOMAN. What I'd like to know is—what are we gonna do? Just stand around here all night? **C**

CHARLIE. There's nothin' else we can do! [*He turns back looking toward* STEVE *and* GOODMAN *again.*] One of 'em'll tip their hand. They got to. **3**

STEVE. [*Raising his voice.*] There's something you can do, Charlie. You could go home and keep your mouth shut. You could quit strutting around like a self-appointed hanging judge and just climb into bed and forget it.

CHARLIE. You sound real anxious to have that happen, Steve. I think we better keep our eye on you too!

DON. [*As if he were taking the bit in his teeth, takes a hesitant step to the front.*] I think everything might as well come out now. [*He turns toward* STEVE.] Your wife's done plenty of talking,

Practice the Skills

3 Key Reading Skill

Predicting Charlie predicts that those responsible for the mysterious events on Maple Street will accidentally reveal themselves. Do you agree? What do you think will happen next?

Teach

C Critical Thinking

Analysis Ask: What makes Steve different from his neighbors? *(He tries to prevent his neighbors from getting carried away.)* **OL** Do you think this difference was clear before this night? Why or why not? Explain your response. *(Responses will vary. Students may say that since Steve seems to be the only one who isn't quick to make accusations, maybe he was always more clearheaded than his neighbors.)* **AL**

English Language Coach

English as a Changing Language

Some expressions in English remain in our usage though they came from earlier historical periods. Tell students that three expressions on this page relate to the days when Americans were still settling the West. The expression *tip their hand* refers to card players when they show their hand of cards. A *hanging judge* is a judge who is prone to finding people guilty and sending them to be hanged. The expression *taking the bit in his teeth* refers to the practice of putting a bit, or steel fitting, in a horse's mouth. The bit is the part of the harness that goes over a horse's head and makes it possible for a rider to steer the horse. **EL OL**

Objectives

- Make predictions
- Clarify text
- Draw inferences
- Use elements of teleplay to understand a selection
- Identify components of the etymology of language, including word origins and how they contribute to contemporary meanings

Teach

L Literary Element

Review Figurative Language Say: The expression *kangaroo court* refers to a court that "jumps" to invalid or incorrect conclusions. How are the people of Maple Street acting like a kangaroo court? *(Possible response: They are jumping to conclusions and making accusations without doing any investigation or using rational thought.)* OL AL

C Critical Thinking

Synthesis Say: You have seen that Steve is emerging as a character with a distinct point of view—that everyone should cool off. Which character seems to be emerging as his main opponent? *(Charlie)* BL What is this character's point of view? *(Possible response: He wants to find a culprit or scapegoat and take some action against him or her.)* OL

Steve, about how odd you are!

CHARLIE. [*Picking this up, his eyes widening.*] Go ahead, tell us what she's said. 4

[*We see a long shot of* STEVE *as he walks toward them from across the street.*]

STEVE. Go ahead, what's my wife said? Let's get it all out. Let's pick out every idiosyncrasy of every single man, woman, and child on the street. And then we might as well set up some kind of kangaroo court.[2] How about a firing squad at dawn, Charlie, so we can get rid of all the suspects? Narrow them down. Make it easier for you. L

DON. There's no need gettin' so upset, Steve. It's just that . . . well . . . Myra's talked about how there's been plenty of nights you spent hours down in your basement workin' on some kind of radio or something. Well, none of us have ever seen that radio—

[*By this time* STEVE *has reached the group. He stands there defiantly close to them.*]

CHARLIE. Go ahead, Steve. What kind of "radio set" you workin' on? I never seen it. Neither has anyone else. Who you talk to on that radio set? And who talks to you? C

STEVE. I'm surprised at you, Charlie. How come you're so dense all of a sudden? [*A pause.*] Who do I talk to? I talk to monsters from outer space. I talk to three-headed green men who fly over here in what look like meteors.

[*STEVE'S WIFE STEPS DOWN FROM THE PORCH, BITES HER LIP, CALLS OUT.*]

MRS. BRAND. Steve! Steve, please. [*Then looking around, frightened, she walks toward the group.*] It's just a ham radio[3] set, that's all. I bought him a book on it myself. It's just a ham radio set. A lot of people have them. I can show it to you. It's right down in the basement.

STEVE. [*Whirls around toward her.*] Show them nothing! If they

---

2. An ***idiosyncracy*** (id ee uh SINK ruh see) is an odd little habit, gesture, or way of acting. A ***kangaroo court*** is an unofficial trial in which fair legal procedures are ignored.
3. ***Ham radio*** is a hobby in which a person operates his or her own radio station, sending messages by voice or Morse code.

Practice the Skills

4 Key Literary Element

Teleplay What do the stage directions tell you about Charlie? What is he eager to do?

Additional Support

Literature Focus Lesson

Protagonist and Antagonist Tell students that in drama and in novels, writers often set two characters in opposition to each other. Often these two characters represent two sides of a conflict. Explain that the *protagonist* is the name for the main character. The *antagonist* is the name for the character that stands up *against* the protagonist. Both these terms, *protagonist* and *antagonist,* come from Greek: *proto* meaning "first" + *agonistes* meaning "actor" or "combatant"; *ant* meaning "against or opposite" + *agonistes.* The Greeks invented many elements of theater that we still draw on. Have students research other elements of Greek theater that are still used today. AL want to look inside our house—let them get a search warrant.

CHARLIE. Look, buddy, you can't afford to—

STEVE. [*Interrupting.*] Charlie, don't tell me what I can afford! And stop telling me who's dangerous and who isn't and who's safe and who's a menace. [*He turns to the group and shouts.*] And you're with him, too—all of you! You're standing here all set to crucify—all set to find a scapegoat[4]—all desperate to point some kind of a finger at a neighbor! Well now look, friends, the only thing that's gonna happen is that we'll eat each other up alive— 5

[*He stops abruptly as Charlie suddenly grabs his arm.*]

CHARLIE. [*In a hushed voice.*] That's not the only thing that can happen to us.

[*Cut to a long shot looking down the street. A figure has suddenly materialized in the gloom and in the silence we can hear the clickety-clack of slow, measured footsteps on concrete as the figure walks slowly toward them. One of the women lets out a stifled cry. The young mother grabs her boy as do a couple of others.*] 6 L

TOMMY. [*Shouting, frightened.*] It's the monster! It's the monster!

[*Another woman lets out a wail and the people fall back in a group, staring toward the darkness and the approaching figure. We see a medium group shot of the people as they stand in the shadows watching.* DON MARTIN *joins them, carrying a shotgun. He holds it up.*]

DON. We may need this.

STEVE. A shotgun? [*He pulls it out of* DON'S *hand.*] Good Lord—will anybody think a thought around here? Will you people wise up? What good would a shotgun do against—

[*Now* CHARLIE *pulls the gun from* STEVE'S *hand.*]

CHARLIE. No more talk, Steve. You're going to talk us into a grave! You'd let whatever's out there walk right over us, wouldn't yuh? Well, some of us won't!

[*He swings the gun around to point it toward the sidewalk.*]

4. A ***scapegoat*** is someone who is made to take the blame and suffer for the mistakes or misfortunes of another person or a group.

Practice the Skills

5 **BIG Question**

What is Steve saying about his community? How do you think the neighbors treated one another before this evening? Write your answers on your Foldable. Your response will help you answer the Unit Challenge later.

6 **Key Reading Skill**

R **Predicting** Who is the dark figure down the street? How do you think the group will respond as it comes closer?

Teach

L Literary Element

Teleplay Ask: How does the writer increase the suspense just as Steve is about to talk some sense into the crowd? *(He introduces yet another frightening element: the dark figure.)* Have students add the event to their sequence charts or timelines. AS

R Reading Skill

Predicting Review students' predictions. Ask them to explain their answers and use information from the text to support their predictions. AS

Differentiated Instruction

Visualizing Students who are interested in painting or drawing may wish to draw the scene of the dark figure in the gloom that walks towards the frightened crowd. Challenge students to consider the camera angle described in the stage directions (*long shot looking down the street*). Some students may wish to write journal entries describing the moment from the point of view of someone in the crowd and tell the person's thoughts and feelings at that moment. AS

Objectives
- Make predictions and draw inferences, using evidence from a text
- Use elements of teleplay to understand a selection
- Identify components of the etymology of language, including word origins and how they contribute to contemporary meanings

Teach

L Literary Element

Teleplay Say: Up until this point in the story, the tension has been slowly building and building. The climax of a play or story is the moment when the tension reaches its highest point—and something happens. What moment would you say is the climax of Act II? *(when Charlie shoots Pete Van Horn)* **OL**

R Reading Skill

Predicting Say: Go back and check your prediction from the previous page. Did you predict that the figure in the gloom would be Pete Van Horn? Why or why not? *(Responses will vary. Students should say what led them to make their prediction.)* **BL** How do you predict Charlie will react once he realizes whom he has shot? *(Responses will vary. Students may say that he'll probably continue to act in an unreasonable and out of control way, and not take full responsibility for his action.)* **OL**

The dark figure continues to walk toward them.

The group stands there, fearful, apprehensive, mothers clutching children, men standing in front of wives. CHARLIE *slowly raises the gun. As the figure gets closer and closer he suddenly pulls the trigger. The sound of it explodes in the stillness. There is a long angle shot looking down at the figure, who suddenly lets out a small cry, stumbles forward onto his knees and then falls forward on his face.* DON, CHARLIE, *and* STEVE *race forward over to him.* STEVE *is there first and turns the man over. Now the crowd gathers around them.*] **L**

STEVE. [*Slowly looks up.*] It's Pete Van Horn.

DON. [*In a hushed voice.*] Pete Van Horn! He was just gonna go over to the next block to see if the power was on—

WOMAN. You killed him, Charlie. You shot him dead! **R**

CHARLIE. [*Looks around at the circle of faces, his eyes frightened, his face contorted.*] But . . . but I didn't know who he was. I certainly didn't know who he was. He comes walkin' out of the darkness—how am I supposed to know who he was? [*He grabs* STEVE.] Steve—you know why I shot! How was I supposed to know he wasn't a monster or something? [*He grabs* DON *now.*] We're all scared of the same thing, I was just tryin' to . . . tryin' to protect my home, that's all! Look, all of you, that's all I was tryin' to do. [*He looks down wildly at the body.*] I didn't know it was somebody we knew! I didn't know—

[*There's a sudden hush and then an intake of breath. We see a medium shot of the living room window of* CHARLIE's *house. The window is not lit, but suddenly the house lights come on behind it.*] **7**

WOMAN. [*In a very hushed voice.*] Charlie . . . Charlie . . . the lights just went on in your house. Why did the lights just go on?

DON. What about it, Charlie? How come you're the only one with lights now?

GOODMAN. That's what I'd like to know.

[*A pause as they all stare toward* CHARLIE.]

Practice the Skills

7 Key Reading Skill

Predicting Think about how the neighbors have acted all night. How do you think they'll respond to Charlie now?

Additional Support

Literature Focus Lesson

Dramatic Action Write the terms below on the board and explain that they can be used to chart the dramatic action in a piece of literature.

- **exposition**–the explanation of the basic conflict
- **rising action**–the series of events that lead up to the climax
- **climax**–the moment when the conflict reaches its height
- **falling action**–the series of events that follow the climax
- **resolution**–the final outcome

Invite students to copy the terms in their Learner's Notebook and use them to chart the rest of the story. **AS**

READING WORKSHOP 4

Looking Back, 1984. Evelyn Williams, (charcoal on paper), Private Collection.

Viewing the Art: How would you describe the facial expressons of the people in this drawing? Do you think the characters in the teleplay have similar looks on their faces? Explain your answer.

GOODMAN. You were so quick to kill, Charlie and you were so quick to tell us who we had to be careful of. Well, maybe you had to kill. Maybe Peter there was trying to tell us something. Maybe he'd found out something and came back to tell us who there was amongst us we should watch out for—

[*CHARLIE BACKS AWAY FROM THE GROUP, HIS EYES WIDE WITH FRIGHT.*]

Teach

Viewing the Art

Ask: How does the image on this page make you feel, and why? *(Responses will vary. Students may say that the image is unsettling or disturbing and that it makes them feel uneasy and uncomfortable because it's as if the figures in the picture are looking right at them, the viewers.)* **BL** How does the picture relate to this moment in the story? *(Possible response: It captures the mood of the moment in the story when the crowd sees the lights come on in Charlie's house. They are already horrified about the shooting, and now they are all more rattled, scared, and accusing than before.)* **OL**

Literature Focus Lesson

Elements of Drama Explain to students that the chorus was one of the most important elements of ancient Greek theater. The chorus was a group of people who spoke together, as a choir. This group usually represented the citizens of a city. The chorus commented on the action and warned the main characters about the possible consequences of their actions. Divide the class into small groups. Tell each group to choose a passage from the teleplay and learn to speak it together. Encourage each group to review its passage, making sure everyone understands and can pronounce all the words. Then have each group practice speaking together slowly and clearly. **EL** **BL** **OL**

Objectives

- Make predictions and draw inferences, using evidence from a text
- Use elements of teleplay to understand a selection
- Use text features to interpret text

READING WORKSHOP 4

Teach

 **Reading Skill**

Predicting **Ask:** Can you predict whom Charlie will name? *(Responses will vary. Students may predict that he'll name someone in the cast who hasn't been accused yet, or that, because he is so cowardly, he'll pick on someone who is more defenseless than he is.)* OL

BQ 

Ask: What has happened to the community at this point? *(It has completely surrendered to a mob mentality.)* AS

CHARLIE. No . . . no . . . it's nothing of the sort! I don't know why the lights are on, I swear I don't. Somebody's pulling a gag or something. 8

[*He bumps against* steve, *who grabs him and whirls him around.*]

STEVE. A *gag*? A gag? Charlie, there's a dead man on the sidewalk and you killed him. Does this thing look like a gag to you?

[CHARLIE BREAKS AWAY AND SCREAMS AS HE RUNS TOWARD HIS HOUSE.]

CHARLIE. No! No! Please!

[*A man breaks away from the crowd to chase* charlie. *We see a long angle shot looking down as the man tackles* charlie *and lands on top of him. The other people start to run toward them.* charlie *is up on his feet, breaks away from the other man's grasp, lands a couple of desperate punches that push the man aside. Then he forces his way, fighting, through the crowd to once again break free, jumps up on his front porch. A rock thrown from the group smashes a window alongside of him, the broken glass flying past him. A couple of pieces cut him. He stands there perspiring, rumpled, blood running down from a cut on the cheek. His wife breaks away from the group to throw herself into his arms. He buries his face against her. We can see the crowd converging on the porch now.*] 9 BQ

VOICES.
It must have been him.
He's the one.
We got to get Charlie.

[*Another rock lands on the porch. Now* charlie *pushes his wife behind him, facing the group.*]

CHARLIE. Look, look I swear to you . . . it isn't me . . . but I do know who it is . . . I swear to you, I do know who it is. I know who the monster is here. I know who it is that doesn't belong. I swear to you I know.

GOODMAN. [*Shouting.*] What are you waiting for?

Practice the Skills

8 Reviewing Skills

Inferring Why does Charlie now say that someone is pulling a gag, or joke?

9 Key Reading Skill

R **Predicting** Think about how Charlie has acted toward his neighbors. How do you predict Charlie will defend himself and his wife from the crowd?

Additional Support

Differentiated Instruction

Finding Images In a teleplay or movie, the camera can pick out details of a scene by presenting a series of quick close-ups and images. Have students list the images that the camera picks up to depict the violence that erupts. *(Possible responses: rock smashing a window; flying broken glass; cuts on Charlie's face and blood running down his face)* Then have them look for other uses of this technique on the next pages and explain how they paint a picture of violence. OL

WOMAN. [*Shouting.*] Come on, Charlie, come on.

MAN ONE. [*Shouting.*] Who is it, Charlie, tell us!

DON. [*Pushing his way to the front of the crowd*] All right, Charlie, let's hear it!

[*CHARLIE'S EYES DART AROUND WILDLY.*]

CHARLIE. It's . . . it's . . .

MAN TWO. [*Screaming.*] Go ahead, Charlie, tell us.

CHARLIE. It's . . . it's the kid. It's Tommy. He's the one.

[*There's a gasp from the crowd as we cut to a shot of sally holding her son tommy. The boy at first doesn't understand and then, realizing the eyes are all on him, buries his face against his mother.*]

SALLY. [*Backs away.*] That's crazy! That's crazy! He's a little boy.

WOMAN. But he knew! He was the only one who knew! He told us all about it. Well, how did he know? How could he have known?

[*The various people take this up and repeat the question aloud.*]

VOICES.
How could he know?
Who told him?
Make the kid answer.

DON. It was Charlie who killed old man Van Horn.

WOMAN. But it was the kid here who knew what was going to happen all the time. He was the one who knew!

C

[*We see a close-up of steve.*]

STEVE. Are you all gone crazy? [*Pause as he looks about.*] Stop.

[*A fist crashes at steve's face, staggering him back out of the frame of the picture.*
There are several close camera shots suggesting the coming of violence. A hand fires a rifle. A fist clenches. A hand grabs the hammer from van horn's body, etc. Meanwhile, we hear the following lines.] **10**

Practice the Skills

10 Key Literary Element

L

Teleplay Reread the stage directions. Pretend you are watching the action on TV. Visualize what the people and actions look like.

Teach

C Critical Thinking

Analysis Ask: Is it true that Tommy knew all along what would happen? *(Responses will vary. Students may say that he may not have known that this particular situation would ever develop, but that the way the events unfolded actually mirrored the stories from his books. So, in a way, he did know.)* **AL**

L Literary Element

Teleplay Have students share their visualizations. Some students may want to sketch their visualizations and present them to the class. Have students discuss the differences and similarities of their visualizations. **AS**

Literature Focus Lesson

Foreshadowing Another technique that writers of fiction often use is called *foreshadowing.* Foreshadowing is a way of suggesting, or dropping a hint about, what will happen. Talk about what Tommy says in Act 1 on page 963. According to him, the space creatures in the stories he's read prepare for their landing by sending out creatures who look like humans, but who are actually one of them. Ask students to explain whether or not Tommy's prediction came true. *(Possible response: Yes, in a way, it has, because people who look like ordinary, reasonable human beings have turned into monsters, attacking and killing one another for no good reason.)* **OL**

Objectives
- Make predictions and draw inferences, using evidence from a text
- Use elements of teleplay to understand a selection
- Understand elements of literature, including foreshadowing

Teach

L Literary Element

Teleplay Say: Once the climax is reached in a story, it is followed by the falling action. How would you describe the events from the shooting of Pete Van Horn up to this point? *(Possible response: The community falls apart completely, until finally all the people are just running around from one house to another, accusing first this person, then that one, as if they have all completely lost their minds.)* AS

R Reading Skill

Predicting Ask: Who or what do you think is really responsible for the lights going on and off on Maple Street? *(Responses will vary. Students may suspect that someone or something is observing the events as they unfold on Maple Street and is contributing to the chaos from outside of the situation.)* OL AL

READING WORKSHOP 4

DON. Charlie has to be the one—Where's my rifle—

WOMAN. Les Goodman's the one. His car started! Let's wreck it.

MRS. GOODMAN. What about Steve's radio—He's the one that called them—

MR. GOODMAN. Smash the radio. Get me a hammer. Get me something.

STEVE. Stop—Stop—

CHARLIE. Where's that kid—Let's get him.

MAN ONE. Get Steve—Get Charlie—They're working together. L

[The crowd starts to converge around the mother, who grabs the child and starts to run with him. The crowd starts to follow, at first walking fast, and then running after him.
We see a full shot of the street as suddenly CHARLIE'S *lights go off and the lights in another house go on. They stay on for a moment, then from across the street other lights go on and then off again.]*

MAN ONE. [*Shouting.*] It isn't the kid . . . it's Bob Weaver's house.

WOMAN. It isn't Bob Weaver's house, it's Don Martin's place.

CHARLIE. I tell you it's the kid.

DON. It's Charlie. He's the one.

[We move into a series of close-ups of various people as they shout, accuse, scream, interspersing these shots with shots of houses as the lights go on and off, and then slowly in the middle of this nightmarish morass[5] *of sight and sound the camera starts to pull away, until once again we've reached the opening shot looking at the Maple Street sign from high above.* R
The camera continues to move away until we ***dissolve*** *to a shot looking toward the metal side of a space craft, which sits shrouded in darkness. An open door throws out a beam of light from the illuminated interior.* 11

5. ***Interspersing*** means "scattering or mixing in over brief periods." A ***morass*** (muh RAS) is any difficult or confused condition or situation.

Practice the Skills

11 English Language Coach

English as a Changing Language Dissolve is a word that describes a camera effect, where one scene slowly fades and another scene appears. This is a newer meaning of the word. What is an older meaning of the word *dissolve?*

Additional Support

Reading Fluency

Echo Reading Have students practice echo reading this page of the teleplay. Assign each part to a pair of students or a small team. Encourage students to feel the rhythm of the text, with one person interrupting and speaking over another, until they can read the page fluently. Remind them that on this page, the characters are frightened, upset, and confused. EL BL

Two figures silhouetted against the bright lights appear. We get only a vague feeling of form, but nothing more **explicit** *than that.*]

FIGURE ONE. Understand the procedure now? Just stop a few of their machines and radios and telephones and lawn mowers . . . Throw them into darkness for a few hours, and then you just sit back and watch the pattern.

FIGURE TWO. And this pattern is always the same?

FIGURE ONE. With few variations. They pick the most dangerous enemy they can find . . . and it's themselves. And all we need do is sit back . . . and watch. **R**

FIGURE TWO. Then I take it this place . . . this Maple Street . . . is not unique.

FIGURE ONE. [*Shaking his head.*] By no means. Their world is full of Maple Streets. And we'll go from one to the other and let them destroy themselves. One to the other . . . one to the other . . . one to the other—

[*Now the camera pans up for a shot of the starry sky and over this we hear the narrator's voice.*]

NARRATOR'S VOICE. The tools of conquest do not necessarily come with bombs and explosions and fallout.[6] There are weapons that are simply thoughts, attitudes, prejudices—to be found only in the minds of men. For the record, **prejudices** can kill and suspicion can destroy and a thoughtless frightened search for a scapegoat has a fallout all its own for the children . . . and the children yet unborn. [*A pause.*] And the pity of it is . . . that these things cannot be confined to . . . The Twilight Zone! **12** ○ **EL**

6. ***Fallout*** is the radioactive dust particles that result from a nuclear explosion.

Vocabulary

explicit (eks PLIS it) *adj.* clearly expressed

prejudices (PREJ uh dis us) *n.* unfavorable opinions or judgments formed unfairly

Practice the Skills

12 **BIG Question**

What does the narrator say can harm communities? Write your answer on the "Monsters Are Due" page of Foldable 8. Your response will help you answer the Unit Challenge later.

Teach

R Reading Skill

Predicting Say: Review the predictions you made throughout the story. How many of them were correct? What did you predict incorrectly? *(Responses will vary.)* **AS**

EL Language Coach

English as a Changing Language Say: The word *fallout* is a relative newcomer to the English language. *Fallout* was a term coined to describe how radioactive particles fall back to Earth after a nuclear explosion. Another meaning of the word is "adverse, unwanted side effects." Compare the two uses of the word in the narrator's final speech. What is suggested? *(Possible response: That there can be psychological fallout as dangerous as nuclear fallout when a community turns on itself.)* **OL** **AL**

Assess

Use the CheckPoint questions provided on Presentation Plus! to check for comprehension of the selection. These questions can be used with interactive response keypads for immediate student feedback.

Reading in the Real World

Citizenship It takes courage for an individual to resist a mob mentality. Remind students that when Rod Serling was writing his teleplays, the nightmarish memories of World War II were still fresh in people's minds. Nazi Germany, an entire country, was overrun by a mob mentality—with murderous consequences for millions of people. Invite students to discuss what it takes for an individual to resist a mob mentality. Guide them to think of examples from their own lives, when they were pressured by peers to "act cool" or do things they felt weren't right. How did they react? What did they do? **AS**

Objectives
- Make predictions and draw inferences, using evidence from a text
- Use elements of teleplay to understand a selection
- Identify components of the etymology of language, including word origins and how they contribute to contemporary meanings

Assess

Resources for page 980

- Selection Quick Check
- Selection and Unit Assessment
- ExamView Assessment Suite
- Interactive Tutor: Self-Assessment

Students can respond to the *After You Read* items in their Learner's Notebook or on a separate sheet of paper.

Answering the

1. Responses will vary. Students may mention that it's best to look for rational explanations.
2. He shoots him.
3. Possible responses: fear of the dark; fear of the unknown

Critical Thinking

4. Responses will vary. Students may say that Steve probably does think they are intelligent and reasonable people, because when they start to fall apart, he appeals to their intelligence and their reason.
5. Possible response: At the beginning, the mood is pleasant, lazy, and everyday. The flash in the sky causes everything to change.
6. Responses will vary, but students could say that the author wants us to think about what responsibility individuals have to their communities.

After You Read

The Monsters Are Due on Maple Street, Act II

Answering the

1. How might the people of Maple Street have solved their problems differently? What are some good ways for communities to solve their problems?
2. **Recall** When Charlie thinks the strange figure is an enemy, what does he do?
   TIP **Right There**
3. **Summarize** What makes the people of Maple Street act so angry and scared?
   TIP **Think and Search**

Critical Thinking

4. **Infer** Before the trouble begins on Maple Street, does Steve think that his neighbors are intelligent and reasonable people? Why or why not?
   TIP **Author and Me**
5. **Interpret** At the beginning of the teleplay, what is the mood on Maple Street? What causes the mood to change?
   TIP **Author and Me**
6. **Analyze** What does the author want us to think about at the ending?
   TIP **Author and Me**

Talk About Your Reading

Literature Groups "The Monsters Are Due on Maple Street" describes a neighborhood changed by fear. In your group, talk about the main questions in this teleplay:

- Who are the real monsters on Maple Street?
- How does fear change people?

Support your ideas with examples from the play.

Write to Learn Imagine that you are one of the aliens on the spacecraft. Describe what you and your fellow aliens did and what happened as a result. Explain how you were able to get the "Earthlings" to accomplish your goals.

Objectives (pp. 980–981)
Reading Make predictions • Make connections from text to self
Literature Identify literary elements: teleplay
Vocabulary Identify English language changes
Grammar Use punctuation: quotation marks

Talk About Your Reading

Write to Learn

Possible response:

It took only a few hours to accomplish our goal, that is, to plant the seed of doubt and confusion among a community of otherwise intelligent, reasonable Earthlings. After disabling their primitive electrical systems and their cars, we were able to sit back and watch while the Earthlings went from a stage of confusion to fear, until finally they transformed into a murderous mob. I had no idea it would be this easy to bring out the violent side of these seemingly peaceful Earthlings. But this training session completely convinced me that conquest of Earth will be a cinch.

Skills Review

Key Reading Skill: Predicting

7. Did you predict that aliens were causing the problems on Maple Street? If yes, why did you think so? If no, why didn't you think so?
8. Did predicting as you read help you to understand and get interested in the story? Explain.

Key Literary Element: Teleplay

9. Find where Act II begins. Why do you think Serling divided the teleplay at this particular part?

Reviewing Skills: Inferring

10. Why do the people of Maple Street turn into a dangerous mob?

Vocabulary Check

Answer each statement *true* or *false*.

11. **Explicit** directions are difficult to follow.
12. A person with **prejudices** has an open mind.
13. If you have a **legitimate** case, you may win in court.
14. **English Language Coach** Look up the term "twilight zone." Is this an old term or a new term? Today, what might you use the term to describe?

Grammar Link: Quotation Marks

The major use of quotation marks is to set off direct quotations. These are statements that tell exactly, word-for-word, what someone said.

- Use a comma to separate a phrase such as "she said" from the quotation itself. If this phrase is used at the end of the quote, the comma goes inside the closing quotation marks.
  Jo said, "I don't know the answer. Ask Jamal."
  "I don't know the answer. Ask Jamal," said Jo.
- Use quotation marks with both parts of a divided quote.
  "I don't know the answer," said Jo. "Ask Jamal."
- Exclamation points and question marks go inside the quotation marks if they are part of the quote.
  "Does Jamal know the answer?" asked Tito.
  Amy said, "Don't ask me again!"
- Exclamation points and question marks go outside the quotation marks if they aren't part of the quote.
  Did Jamal say, "I won't tell you"?
  Rob actually said, "I don't know, either"!

Look out! Don't use quotation marks with indirect quotations. These are statements that do not report word-for-word what someone said.

Wrong: John said "he was going on vacation."

Right: John said he was going on vacation.

Another use of quotation marks is to identify the title of a story, essay, poem, song, or book chapter.

My story is called "One Lucky Day."

He sang "The Farmer in the Dell" to the baby.

Look out! Don't use quotation marks for long works, such as novels, plays, or movies. These titles are italicized (or, in handwriting, underlined).

The movie *Apollo 13* was made from a book named *Lost Moon*.

The movie Apollo 13 was made from a book named Lost Moon.

Grammar Practice

Copy these sentences, adding quotation marks and other punctuation where needed.

1. Where were you asked Mel I've been calling you
2. We saw Romeo and Juliet at a new theater
3. Did Marva really say That's my new bike
4. Chiyo said that I should mind my own business
5. When are you leaving asked Randy

Literature Online

Web Activities For eFlashcards, Selection Quick Checks, and other Web activities, go to www.glencoe.com.

Skills Review

Key Reading Skill: Predicting

7. Responses will vary.
8. Responses will vary.

Key Literary Element: Teleplay

9. Responses will vary. Students may say that he ends Act I with a warning about what lies ahead unless people get a grip on themselves, and that Act II starts after some time has passed, and people seem to have calmed down.

Reviewing Skills: Inferring

10. Students may note that people couldn't explain why things wouldn't work, so they began to blame one another.

Vocabulary Check

11. false
12. false
13. true
14. Possible response: Today it might describe the area of cyberspace where IRC (Internet Relay Chat) operators "live."

Close

Ask students to write about how individuals can resist developing a mob mentality.

Grammar Link: Quotation Marks

Grammar Practice

15. "Where were you?" asked Mel. "I've been calling you."
16. We saw *Romeo and Juliet* at a new theater.
17. Did Marva really say, "That's my new bike"?
18. Chiyo said that I should mind my own business.
19. "When are you leaving?" asked Randy.

Reading Across Texts: Author's Credibility

Objectives covered in this workshop:

- Find similarities and differences across texts
- Connect, compare, and contrast author's credibility across texts

How to Help Students Read for Author's Credibility

Why Is It Important?

- Students need to be able to differentiate between credible statements and information and questionable information.
- Knowing when an author is credible will help students choose helpful sources when creating their own documents

How to Help Students Get It

- Have students look for author's bias
- Have students look at the writer's sources—those cited and implied.
- Have students think about the author's background and why would this writer be writing about the particular subject.

Reading Across Texts

Teacher Hero: Erin Gruwell

A teacher in a tough inner-city school uses an innovative approach to get her students interested in reading and writing. Students will learn how people adversely affected by one type of community can find something positive in another.

from *Zlata's Diary*

A young Bosnian girl writes first-hand accounts in her diary of the war in Sarajevo. Readers will see how the war changed Zlata's community.

Reading Across Texts Workshop Resources

Pacing (Days) Standard	Block	Lesson	Student Materials	Teacher Resources
1		Reading Across Texts: Reading for Author's Credibility	Key Reading Skills Practice English Language Coach	Bellringer Options Transparencies Read Aloud, Think Aloud Transparencies Presentation Plus!
2		"Teacher Hero"	Literary Analysis Transparencies Glencoe Online Selection Vocabulary Development Academic Vocabulary Development English Language Coach Active Reading Graphic Organizer Literary Analysis StudentWorks Plus Online Student Edition Literature Classics Selection and Unit Assessments	Literary and Text Analysis Transparencies Puzzlemaker Skill Level Up! BookLink 3 Assessment by Learning Objective (Diagnostic and Formative) Interactive Tutor Self-Assessment TeacherWorks Plus
2		From *Zlata's Diary*	Glencoe Online Selection Vocabulary Development Academic Vocabulary Development English Language Coach Active Reading Graphic Organizer Literary Analysis StudentWorks Plus Online Student Edition Literature Classics Selection and Unit Assessments	Literary and Text Analysis Transparencies Puzzlemaker Skill Level Up! BookLink 3 Assessment by Learning Objective (Diagnostic and Formative) Interactive Tutor Self-Assessment TeacherWorks Plus

Keys for Unit Resource

- Blackline Master
- Workbook
- Supplemental Text
- CD-ROM
- DVD
- Transparency
- Web-based
- Fast Files

Level Appropriate Code

AS = Activities for all students
AL = Activities for students working above grade level
OL = Activities for students working at grade level
BL = Activities for students working below grade level
EL = Activities for English language learners

Focus

BELLRINGER Options

Daily Language Practice Transparency

Focus Activity Write the following question and chart on the board: How would you go about comparing two difficult experiences? You might start thinking about the comparison with a chart like this one, which shows the different experiences of two students:

	Jacinta	Liam
Experience	Best friend moves far away	Fails math class
Response		
Solution		

Teach

R Reading Skill

Review Identifying Author's Purpose Say: When you read these selections, you'll first want to decide on the author's purpose. Before reading, ask yourself:

- Who is the author?
- What connection does the author have to the topic?
- Where did the author find information about the topic? *(Responses will vary.)* OL

Teacher Hero: Erin Gruwell

by Jerrilyn Jacobs

& Zlata's Diary

by Zlata Filipović

Skills Focus

You will use these skills as you read and compare the following selections:

- "Teacher Hero: Erin Gruwell," p. 985
- from *Zlata's Diary*, p. 989

Reading

- Read and understand informational text representing a wide variety of authors, subjects, and genres
- Clarify understanding of texts by creating graphic organizers
- Analyze author's credibility

Objectives
(pp. 982–983)
Reading Compare and contrast: author's credibility across texts

You've seen one of those popular crime shows on TV. A crime was committed, and a detective has to figure out who did it. Witnesses tell what they saw, but their stories don't match. Which witnesses are believable? Who can a good detective trust?

How to Read Across Texts: Author's Credibility

R

When you compare two pieces of nonfiction, you have to think like a detective. To help decide whether a witness is credible, a detective would consider questions like these:

- Who is this person?
- Where did he or she get this information?
- Does this person have personal feelings and opinions that might influence what he or she says?

As a reader, you need to consider the same sorts of questions about writers:

- What are the writer's **qualifications?** Does he or she know about this topic because of formal education, research, or personal experiences?
- What are the writer's **sources?** Was the writer a witness to events? If not, does he or she identify where the information came from? Are those sources credible?
- Does the author show **bias** for or against the subject?

Academic Vocabulary

bias (BY us) *n.* an opinion based on personal preferences or unfair judgments

Additional Support

Literature Focus Lesson

Comprehension Strategy: Text Structure The way students read can influence how they will judge the author's credibility. Here are four tips to remember:

- Preview the selection by skimming and scanning to identify the author's tone. Do you expect to laugh or cry?
- Clarify by asking yourself if the writer makes the ideas and events clear. Can you understand the main idea?
- Ask questions as you read so that you understand how the details fit in and enhance the essay.
- Evaluate as you read. Are the ideas presented logically? Do you agree with the author's opinion? OL

Get Ready to Compare

As you read, keep track of these details on a chart like the one below. Copy it into your Learner's Notebook, and take notes as you read. After you read, you'll use your notes to write your comparison.

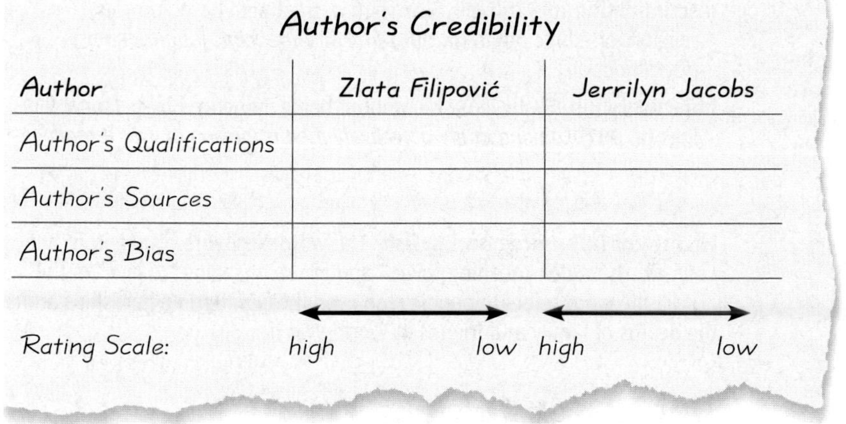

Author's Credibility

Author	Zlata Filipović	Jerrilyn Jacobs
Author's Qualifications		
Author's Sources		
Author's Bias		
Rating Scale:	high ↔ low	high ↔ low

R

Use Your Comparison

Comparing two pieces of nonfiction writing isn't going to mean much unless you, the reader, get tough. Don't be a pushover. Don't buy everything the writers say. Ask yourself whether a writer has a bias. It's up to you to decide.

Suppose you had to read research papers about cars of the future written by two classmates. Use these steps to help you make your comparison.

1. Ask yourself what you know about each student's background and qualifications?

   Well, I know David's crazy about cars. He's always reading some car magazine. I know Janet rides a bike to school and thinks that cars are bad for the environment.

2. Think about the facts you listed, and ask yourself if each writer has a bias for or against the subject.

   Their biases are clear and they don't make a big secret out of it. David is biased in favor of cars, and Janet is biased against them.

3. Now think about the sources each student used. Do these sources seem credible, or believable?

   Both David and Janet include a bibliography. But David listed a Web site that sounded a little strange. I checked and found out that it doesn't exist. David just made it up. Janet's sources are all solid environmental organizations.

4. Finally, add up the evidence—the writer's background and qualifications, the reliability of the writer's sources, and the writer's bias (if any). Then you can decide whether to trust what the writer says.

Teach

R Reading Skill

Review Comparing and Contrasting Say: Look at the chart on this page and decide if it will fit your purposes. As you read, you may alter it to fit the way you want to take notes. Remember that you are not just choosing which essay you *like* the best. You want to be able to explain your choice by comparing how two writers present their material. So think about how you will find:

- the authors' qualifications
- the sources the authors used
- how the authors show bias **AS**

Assess/Close

Say: Imagine that Jacinta and Liam from page 982 are both writing about their difficult experiences. How might each writer use sources? *(Possible response: Liam may quote his teacher in his response.)* What might give each writer credibility? *(Both have experienced these situations personally.)* **OL**

Resources for page 983

Use the Comparing Literature Graphic Organizer BLM in the Unit 8 Resource Booklet.

English Language Coach

Historical Influences on English The first selection deals with a *hero*, a word that has its origins in ancient mythology. For thousands of years this word has meant a man of great courage, often godlike, who has risked his life for others. It's not clear when *heroine* came into the language, but the word *hero* is now considered not to be gender-specific. It can be used to refer to both men and women. Suggest that students use a good dictionary or the Internet to find all the derivations of the base word *hero.* **EL** **OL**

Objectives

- Find similarities and differences across texts
- Compare and contrast authors' credibility across texts
- Understand historical influences on English word meanings and usage

Teach

More About the Author

Jerrilyn Jacobs has written many biographical essays about heroes—often about persons whom she's discovered are doing heroic things in the face of extremely difficult circumstances. She has written about a 12-year-old peacemaker named Craig Kielburger who helps free kids in Afghanistan. She's done a piece on 8-year-old Brandon Keefe who found a way to start a library for kids in a region without one. Jacobs allows students to write about their heroes and post their essays on the "My Hero" Web site.

EL Language Coach

Historical Influences on English **Ask:** What image comes to mind when I say *survivor*? What does the word mean to you? *(Possible responses: A survivor is someone who can stay alive through great difficulties.)* **BL** **OL**

Before You Read

Teacher Hero: Erin Gruwell

Meet the Author

Jerrilyn Jacobs has worked on the sets of film and television projects and in advertising. For her full-time job, she teaches Media Studies at the Taft High School in Los Angeles. On her website, she says, "In our information rich world, knowing how to ask the right question is where it all begins!"

Author Search For more about Jerrilyn Jacobs, go to www.glencoe.com.

Objectives (pp. 984–987)
Reading Compare and contrast: author's credibility across texts
• Make connections from text to self
Vocabulary Identify historical influences on English

Vocabulary Preview

tolerance (TAWL ur uns) *n.* sympathy for people, beliefs, or ideas that are different from one's own **(p. 985)** *Her class urged people to replace their prejudices with tolerance.*

discrimination (dis krih mih NAY shin) *n.* treatment based on class, religion, or ethnic origin **(p. 986)** *African Americans fought against discrimination.*

objectively (ub JEK tiv lee) *adv.* without being influenced by personal feelings **(p. 987)** *Looking at life objectively means looking at it as it really is.*

English Language Coach

EL **Historical Influences on English** The word **survivors** comes from two Latin words—*super,* meaning "over," and *vivere,* meaning "to live." In this article, the word refers to people who lived through terrible hardships and the deaths of family and friends in World War II.

Get Ready to Read

Connect to the Reading

What makes someone a hero? Who are your heroes? Exchange thoughts with a partner about what makes someone a hero to you.

Build Background

- In Holland during World War II, a woman named Miep Gies helped Anne Frank's family hide from the Nazis. They were eventually found and sent to concentration camps, where most of the family died. Anne's diary was published after the war.
- In the United States during the 1960s, civil rights workers called Freedom Riders helped African Americans in the South register to vote.

Set Purposes for Reading

BIG Question Read to find out how real-life heroes changed the lives of students in a real-life class.

Set Your Own Purpose What would you like to learn from this article? Write your own purpose on the "Teacher Hero" page of Foldable 8.

Additional Support

Author Search To expand students' appreciation of Jerrilyn Jacobs, have them access the Web site for additional information and resources.

Reading in the Real World

Citizenship Most cities, towns, or neighborhoods are home to citizens who have escaped war or persecution. Take students to the library to investigate the lives of these survivors. First talk about:

- Why it helps a community to learn about its survivors
- Why it may help survivors to know others care about what happened to them.

If students know any survivors personally, encourage them to tell these survivors' stories to the class. **OL**
Suggest that students try to find a resource describing the experiences of a little-known survivor. **AL**

Dear Diary,

. . . the only heroes I ever read about ran around in tight, colorful underwear and threw buildings at each other for fun. But today, that all changed. A true hero leaped off the pages of a book to pay my class a special visit. Her name is Miep Gies and she is the lady Anne Frank wrote about in her diary. I can't believe that the woman responsible for keeping Anne Frank alive in the attic came to speak to us in person!

—Diary 42, *The Freedom Writers Diary*

INFORMATIONAL TEXT

WEB SITE

myhero.com

Teacher Hero: Erin Gruwell

by Jerrilyn Jacobs

For Erin Gruwell, walking into her first teaching job was like entering a war zone. Gruwell was given a class of "sure-to-drop-outs," students no other teacher wanted, students who weren't expected to succeed. The school was tough, racially divided, and gang-infested. Fights and even murders were part of the students' experience. Some of the kids were homeless. Others came from broken or abusive homes. They saw people they knew using drugs every day. There were few places to go to be safe and few people they could count on. **1**

Gruwell was white, wore suits to class and looked like the well-educated product of a safe suburban life. The administrators expected her to quit as soon as she came up against violence and hatred in her classroom. Instead she threw out the curriculum[1] and dedicated her class to learning about peace and **tolerance**. Her first weapon was *The Diary of* **EL**

1 A *curriculum* is the plan of study for a class.

Vocabulary

tolerance (TAWL ur uns) *n.* sympathy for people, beliefs, or ideas that are different from one's own

Practice the Skills

1 Reviewing Skills

Predicting What do you predict will happen to Erin Gruwell in this class? On what do you base your prediction?

Teach

Viewing the Photo

Ask: How do you think this teacher feels about teaching? *(Possible response: She probably enjoys teaching because she looks like she likes kids and they look like they like her.)* **BL**

EL Language Coach

Connotation Say: The author uses the word *weapon* when she describes the teacher giving her students *The Diary of Anne Frank* to read. What connotation of *weapon* is she using here? *(Possible response: Here, weapon means something that can be used to get the upper hand in a situation, not something that is deadly or harmful.)* **OL** Why do you think the writer uses the word *weapon* here? *(Possible responses: The writer is describing a classroom environment in which the teacher may have needed something with which to defeat the negative attitudes in the classroom. The book can be seen as a tool that the students can use to help them deal with their own difficult situations.)* **AL**

Readability Scores

Dale-Chall: 5.4

DRP: 64

Lexile: 1070

Reading in the Real World

Citizenship *Tolerance* is the ability to show respect and recognition for the practices of other people. Tolerance is a large concept that is explored in museums and in many films. Suggest that students start a classroom museum for tolerance. Volunteers can bring in symbols of things they believe in or practice. Have students discuss the range of different objects brought in by class members and how it sometimes takes understanding to have *tolerance* for one another's ways. **AS**

Objectives

- Compare and contrast: author's credibility across texts
- Make connections from text to self
- Identify historical influences on English

Teach

C1 Critical Thinking

Analysis Ask: Why did Ms. Gruwell's students decide to call themselves the Freedom Writers? *(Possible responses: They were influenced by reading about the Freedom Riders. By choosing this name, they showed that they wanted to follow in their footsteps, but as writers.* Writers *is a play on the word* riders.*)* **OL** **AL**

C2 Critical Thinking

Evaluation Ask: Why was it effective for Ms. Gruwell to have her students read *Zlata's Diary*? *(Possible responses: It had become known as an important survival story. Zlata was a preteen when she wrote the diary and the kids could relate to her.)* **OL**

Anne Frank and lessons about the Holocaust.[2] She thought her students might relate to Anne's situation.

> *"Just like [Anne], I knew the feeling of* **discrimination** *and to be looked down upon . . . like her, 'I sometimes feel like a bird in a cage and just want to fly away.' The first thing that came to my mind was that Ms. G was right. I did find myself within the pages of the book, like she said I would."*
>
> —Diary 36, *The Freedom Writers Diary* **2**

Gruwell brought in Holocaust **survivors** as guest speakers. She worked a second job on weekends so she could take the students to movies and on field trips. **3**

Inspired by their readings and field trips, Gruwell's students started keeping diaries in which they wrote about their daily battles and experiences. For some of them, Gruwell's class was the only place where anyone wanted to hear their stories. For others, it was the first safe place to share them. **4**

Gruwell's class became like a family. They made a life-altering "Toast for Change," where they all agreed to give themselves a chance to start life over. Inspired by the stories of the original Freedom Riders who fought segregation and prejudice, they called themselves *The Freedom Writers*. All the time they continued writing in their diaries. **5** **C1**

Gruwell's class then read *Zlata's Diary* which was written by a teenaged girl about her experience of the war in Bosnia. Once again, the students found similarities between their situation and hers. They admired the author's courage and her determination to work for peace. **C2**

Gruwell wanted her students to know that if they worked together they could accomplish important things. They raised money to bring Zlata Filipovic from Ireland (where she has been living) to visit their school and share what she had learned from living through a war. Zlata encouraged the students in

2. The ***Holocaust*** is the name given to the Nazis' murder of about six million Jews during World War II.

Vocabulary

discrimination (dis krih mih NAY shin) *n.* treatment based on class, religion, or ethnic origin

Practice the Skills

2 Reading Across Texts

Author's Sources Why do you think Jacobs includes excerpts from Freedom Writers' diaries? Do you think these are reliable sources? Why or why not? As you read, look for other sources of information that Jacobs includes.

3 English Language Coach

Historical Influences on English One meaning of **survivors** is "those who outlived others."

4 Reviewing Skills

Understanding Cause and Effect What caused Gruwell's students to start keeping diaries of their own? How did their reading and field trips affect them?

5 Reading Across Texts

Author's Bias Do you think Jacobs has a bias about her subject? What would you say her bias is?

Additional Support

Differentiated Instruction

Intrapersonal The students in this selection must have felt connected to Zlata Filipovic's diary in a personal way. It affected them enough to act. Invite students to come up with a community service project that they think they can do. A small group should spearhead the project and assign tasks such as promotion and fund-raising activities. **AS**

their efforts to fight stereotypes[3] and racial prejudices in their own lives. She became their friend and role model.

> *"Writing about the things that happen to us allows us to look* **objectively** *at what's going on around us and turn a negative experience into something positive and useful. This process requires a lot of work, effort and greatness, but it is possible, and the Freedom Writers have proved it—they've chosen a difficult, but powerful, path."*
>
> —Zlata Filipović, from the foreword to *The Freedom Writers Diary*

Gruwell also brought Miep Gies to visit the students and share her experiences. Miep Gies was deeply moved by the students' concern and commitment to change, calling them "the real heroes." **R**

Eventually the Freedom Writers' stories gained media attention. They began traveling around the country, presenting their ideas on education to the Secretary of Education in Washington, D.C., accepting awards, and giving television and newspaper interviews. They even testified before Congress, where they received standing ovations.[4]

Their diary entries and more exciting details of their adventures have been collected in *The Freedom Writers Diary: How a Teacher and 150 Teens Used Writing to Change Themselves and the World Around Them.*

These kids, once written off as dropouts, graduated high school and went to college thanks to The Tolerance Education Foundation, an organization Erin Gruwell helped set up to help pay their tuition.[5] Their successes continued to grow, and as they traveled the country, visiting prisons and reform schools they became ambassadors for tolerance and peace. **BQ**

Gruwell became a hero to her students. Through her continued work she is a hero for all of us concerned with educating our children for peace. 6 7 ❍

3. A ***stereotype*** is an oversimplified or biased idea about a group of people.
4. Gruwell's students ***testified,*** or presented evidence, to Congress about their work as Freedom Writers. A ***standing ovation*** is when an audience stands up and claps.
5. ***Tuition*** is the charge made for instruction at a college or private school.

Vocabulary

objectively (ub JEK tiv lee) *adv.* without being influenced by personal feelings

Practice the Skills

6 BIG Question

Think about how Erin Gruwell helped change her students' lives. Is it possible for one person to make a difference in a community? Explain your answer on the "Teacher Hero" page of Foldable 8.

7 **Reading Across Texts**

Author's Credibility

Fill in the "Teacher Hero: Erin Gruwell" part of your chart, and use the chart to begin comparing the two texts.

Teach

R Reading Skill

Review Clarifying

Ask: When Miep Gies visited the students, who did the author say was very moved? *(Miep Gies)* **BL** Why does that seem unexpected? *(Possible response: Even after the hardships she experienced herself, she felt that the students' dedication to their cause was heroic.)* **OL**

BQ 

Ask: How did the survivors' stories make a difference to a community of students? *(Responses will vary. Students may say that the stories of other people's hardships inspired them to make changes in their own communities.)* **OL**

CheckPoint

Use the CheckPoint questions provided on Presentation Plus! to check for students' comprehension. These questions can be used with interactive response keypads for immediate student feedback.

Reading in the Real World

Citizenship Discuss how to write an article about what happened to Ms. Gruwell's students and how to get it published in your neighborhood or local newspaper. Here are some places to start:

- Have students read *The Freedom Writers Diary.*
- Find The Tolerance Education Foundation on the Web.
- Look in the Congressional Record for a summary of the students' testimonial before Congress.

Then have students work in small groups to decide on the purpose of their article and to write a draft. **OL**

Objectives

- Find similarities and differences across texts
- Understand historical influences on English word meanings and usage
- Evaluate text
- Analyze text

Teach

More About the Author

Once Zlata Filipović was sent safely to Paris in 1993, she began to live the ordinary life of a student again, studying at the International School. Her diary has accomplished what she wanted: to keep the plight of the children of Sarajevo alive. She has taken a world tour with her parents to promote peace and was awarded the "Special Child of Courage Award" by the Simon Wiesenthal Centre.

V Vocabulary

Antonyms Check students' comprehension of the vocabulary words by having them choose the antonym for each word from the lists below.

cope	**aggressor**
submit	invader
manage	attacker
survive	defender
handle	opponent OL AL

Before You Read from *Zlata's Diary*

Zlata Filipović

Meet the Author

When Zlata Filipović started to write a diary, she was almost eleven years old. She lived with her parents in the city of Sarajevo, in Bosnia, part of the old Yugoslavia. Her life was very ordinary; she went to school, did her homework, and hung out with her friends. All that changed in 1992 when war broke out. For Zlata, "That was the day that time stood still." In her diary, she recorded the horrors of war that she and her friends and family experienced.

Literature Online

Author Search For more about Zlata Filipović, go to www.glencoe.com.

Objectives (pp. 988–993)
Reading Compare and contrast: author's credibility across texts
• Make connections from text to self
Vocabulary Reading Visualize • Skim and scan text • Clarify ideas and text
• Make predictions

Vocabulary Preview

cope (cohp) *v.* to struggle or deal with in the hope of being successful **(p. 989)** *Zlata's mother had to cope with bombs and a fear of mice.*

V **agressor** (uh GRES ur) *n.* a person, group, or nation that causes a conflict or war **(p. 993)** *In a civil war, it can be difficult to determine the aggressor.*

English Language Coach

Historical Influences on English In her diary, Zlata uses the word **politics** to refer to the ways in which people try to hold control of the government. The word comes from a Greek word meaning "citizen," which came from another Greek word meaning "city."

The English word *politicians* refers to elected officials and candidates, as well as to private citizens who are influential in a political party's affairs.

Get Ready to Read

Connect to the Reading

How would it feel to watch your city or community turn into a war zone?

Build Background

- As this selection begins, war has broken out in the city of Sarajevo, which is the capital of Bosnia, then part of the country of Yugoslavia.
- Zlata began her diary before the war and continued during the war. In 1993, she was airlifted to safety in Paris, and her diary was published.
- Today, *Zlata's Diary* has been published in more than twenty languages. Zlata has traveled around the world with her parents, speaking up for children in war zones and promoting peace.

Set Purposes for Reading

BIG Question Read to see how war changed Zlata's community.

Set Your Own Purpose What else would you like to learn from Zlata's experiences? Write your own purpose on the "Zlata's Diary" page of Foldable 8.

Additional Support

Author Search To expand students' appreciation of Zlata Filipović, have them access the Web site for additional information and resources.

Literature Focus Lesson

Journal Entry Remind students that a diary, or journal, is a day-to-day account of events, experiences, or ideas that is usually kept for personal use. When journals or diaries become public, it is usually because the entries included events that went beyond the individual's interests. When such a diary is published, the diary is unique in the way it combines ordinary, day-to-day living and historic events. Ask students to choose a major event, such as 9/11/01, and create a journal entry about what they were doing that day. Remind them to make a personal connection between the big event and their everyday lives. OL

from Zlata's Diary

by Zlata Filipović

Saturday, May 2, 1992

Dear Mimmy,[1]
Today was truly, absolutely the worst day ever in Sarajevo. The shooting started around noon. Mommy and I moved into the hall. Daddy was in his office, under our apartment, at the time. We told him on the intercom to run quickly to the downstairs lobby where we'd meet him. We brought Cicko [Zlata's canary] with us. The gunfire was getting worse, and we couldn't get over the wall to the Bobars',[2] so we ran down to our own cellar. **1**

The cellar is ugly, dark, smelly. Mommy, who's terrified of mice, had two fears to **cope** with. The three of us were in the same corner as the other day. We listened to the pounding shells,[3] the shooting, the thundering noise overhead. We even **L**

1. Zlata decided on ***Mimmy*** as her diary's name, knowing that Anne Frank had called hers Kitty.
2. The ***Bobars*** are close, neighbors and family friends of the Filipovićs
3. ***Shells*** are explosives fired from a gun or cannon.

Vocabulary

cope (cohp) *v.* to struggle or deal with in the hope of being successful

Practice the Skills

1 Reading Across Texts

Author's Qualifications
How does Zlata know about the fighting—from education, research, or personal experience? Do you think she's a credible writer? Why or why not?

Teach

Viewing the Photo

Say: Look at the photograph on this page. What does it tell you about the topic of this selection? *(Possible response: It indicates that the selection will be about a very traumatic and devastating event in the author's life.)* **OL**

L Literary Element

Review Sensory Imagery
Ask: What skill does Zlata Filipović use to make the events she describes come alive for the reader? *(Possible response: She uses sensory language to describe what she experiences, such as the sound of the shooting and the ugliness and smells of the musty cellar.)* **OL**

Readability Scores
Dale-Chall: 5.1
DRP: 49
Lexile: 680

Reading in the Real World

Citizenship Tell students to gather in groups to discuss the following issue: Why should citizens in one country or region care about the well-being of citizens in other countries? Allow students time to give their first impressions of the issue. Have resource materials on hand, such as those from Educators for Social Responsibility **http://www.esrnational.org/guide.htm**, or take students to the library so that they can further investigate the topic. Then have students come up with ways to present their ideas to the whole class. **OL**

Objectives
- Compare and contrast: author's credibility across texts
- Make connections from text to self
- Visualize
- Skim and scan text
- Clarify ideas and text
- Make predictions

Teach

L1 Literary Element

Review Organization Ask: In the longest paragraph on this page, how does the writer organize all the things she has observed? *(Possible response: by time, as if moving through the day; also by events in sequence, through watching TV and finding out terrible news, through coming out of the cellar and seeing the destruction, and ending with the hope that she'll never again have such an awful day.)* **OL**

L2 Literary Element

Review Imagery Ask: What effect does the writer create by saying that a neighborhood is *knee-deep* in glass? *(Possible response: She shows there is a lot of shattered glass and makes the situation sound destructive and dangerous.)* **OL**

heard planes. At one moment I realized that this awful cellar was the only place that could save our lives. Suddenly, it started to look almost warm and nice. It was the only way we could defend ourselves against all this terrible shooting. We heard glass shattering in our street. Horrible. I put fingers in my ears to block out the terrible sounds. I was worried about Cicko. We had left him behind in the lobby. Would he catch cold there? Would something hit him? I was terribly hungry and thirsty. We had left our half-cooked lunch in the kitchen. **2**

When the shooting died down a bit, Daddy ran over to our apartment and brought us back some sandwiches. He said he could smell something burning and that the phones weren't working. He brought our TV set down to the cellar. That's when we learned that the main post office (near us) was on fire and that they had kidnapped our President. At around 8:00 we went back up to our apartment. Almost every window in our street was broken. Ours were all right, thank God. I saw the post office in flames. A terrible sight. The fire-fighters battled with the raging fire. Daddy took a few photos of the post office being devoured by the flames. He said they wouldn't come out because I had been fiddling with something on the camera. I was sorry. The whole apartment smelled of the burning fire. God, and I used to pass by there every day. It had just been done up. It was huge and beautiful, and now it was being swallowed up by the flames. It was disappearing. That's what this neighborhood of mine looks like, my Mimmy. I wonder what it's like in other parts of town? I heard on the radio that it was awful around the Eternal Flame. The place is knee-deep in glass. We're worried about Grandma and Granddad. They live there. Tomorrow, if we can go out, we'll see how they are. A terrible day. This has been the worst, most awful day in my eleven-year-old life. I hope it will be the only one. Mommy and Daddy are very edgy. I have to go to bed. **3**

Ciao![4]

Zlata

4. The Italian word ***ciao*** (chow) is an expression said when greeting or leaving. So it can mean both "hello" and "goodbye."

Practice the Skills

2 Reviewing Elements

Imagery What words help you see, hear, and smell the cellar and the fighting outside?

3 Reading Across Texts

Author's Sources From where does Zlata get information about her neighborhood and town? Do her sources seem reliable? Explain.

Additional Support

English Language Coach

Borrowed Words If students are not familiar with the word *ciao*, explain that it means "hello" and "goodbye" in Italian, but that it is used in many other countries too. Ask students for words in other languages that mean both hello and goodbye, or both please and thank you. Then have students make a list of the borrowed words they know and use.

Some suggestions may be:

mañana voilà
hors d'oeuvre café
nuance solo

Ask English Language Learners to tell what English words they use when speaking with people in their first language. **EL** **OL**

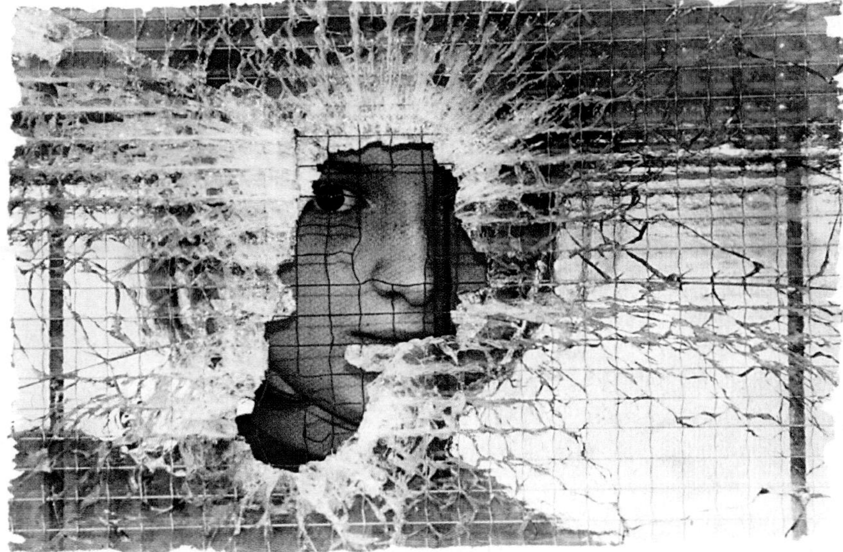

Ten-year old Medina Suman looks out from the bullet-shattered window of her home in Sarajevo.

Analyzing the photo: How does this image help you understand what it felt like to live in Bosnia during wartime?

Sunday, May 3, 1992

Dear Mimmy,
Daddy managed to run across the bridge over the Miljacka and get to Grandma and Granddad. He came running back, all upset, sweating with fear and sadness. They're all right, thank God. Tito Street looks awful. The heavy shelling has destroyed shop windows, cars, apartments, the fronts and roofs of buildings. Luckily, not too many people were hurt because they managed to take shelter. Neda (Mommy's girlfriend) rushed over to see how we were and to tell us that they were OK and hadn't had any damage. But it was terrible. **4**

We talked through the window with Auntie Bodia and Bojana just now. They were in the street yesterday when that heavy shooting broke out. They managed to get to Stela's cellar.
Zlata

Tuesday, May 5, 1992

Dear Mimmy,
The shooting seems to be dying down. I guess they've caused enough misery, although I don't know why. It has something

Practice the Skills

4 Reviewing Skills

Visualizing Imagine what Tito Street looks like. What details help you visualize it?

Teach

Viewing the Photo

Say: Describe the girl's expression. *(Possible responses: fearful; anxious; worried)* **BL** What does her expression suggest about her feelings at this moment? *(Responses will vary. Students may say that she is very afraid and concerned about what is happening to her and her family and community.)* **OL**

C Critical Thinking

Analysis Ask: Why do you think the writer's father was "all upset, and sweating with fear" when he said that the grandparents were all right? *(Possible response: Even though they survived, he was still worried about their safety in the future.)* **OL**

Differentiated Instruction

Spatial Students who tend to see things through drawing or in other visual ways may want to describe what they are reading through a work of art. Encourage students to study the photograph on this page, as well as those on other pages, to inspire them. They should make their artwork express their own representation of the photographs and the writer's words. **EL** **BL** **OL**

Objectives
- Find similarities and differences across texts
- Understand influences on the English language
- Understand organization and imagery in literature
- Use text features to interpret text

Teach

EL Language Coach

Historical Influences on English Ask students for their definition of the concept of *politics*. Ask for examples of how students use politics in school, in their communities, and in family interactions. *(Responses will vary.)* OL AL

R Reading Skill

Review Understanding Persuasive Techniques

Ask: At the top of the page, how is Zlata trying to influence "Mimmy" by the way she describes her hopes for peace? *(Responses will vary but should make note of her wish to "live and breathe as human beings again.")* How does her age influence her persuasive tone? *(Responses will vary. Students may say that Zlata is so young and has been through war, lending credibility to her position that adults use bad politics to solve their problems.)* OL

to do with **politics**. I just hope the "kids"[5] come to some agreement. Oh, if only they would, so we could live and breathe as human beings again. The things that have happened here these past few days are terrible. I want it to stop forever. PEACE! PEACE! 5 6

I didn't tell you, Mimmy, that we've rearranged things in the apartment. My room and Mommy and Daddy's are too dangerous to be in. They face the hills, which is where they're shooting from. If only you knew how scared I am to go near the windows and into those rooms. So, we turned a safe corner of the sitting room into a "bedroom." We sleep on mattresses on the floor. It's strange and awful. But, it's safer that way. We've turned everything around for safety. We put Cicko in the kitchen. He's safe there, although once the shooting starts there's nowhere safe except the cellar. I suppose all this will stop and we'll all go back to our usual places.

Ciao!

Zlata

Thursday, May 7, 1992

Dear Mimmy,

I was almost positive the war would stop, but today . . . Today a shell fell on the park in front of my house, the park where I used to play and sit with my girlfriends. A lot of people were hurt. From what I hear Jaca, Jaca's mother, Selma, Nina, our neighbor Dado and who knows how many other people who happened to be there were wounded. Dado, Jaca, and her mother have come home from the hospital, Selma lost a kidney but I don't know how she is, because she's still in the hospital AND NINA IS DEAD. A piece of shrapnel lodged[6] in her brain and she died. She was such a sweet, nice little girl. We went to kindergarten together, and we used to play

5. Zlata and her friends refer to the leaders on both sides of the war as the ***kids.***

6. ***Shrapnel*** is a large shell loaded with metal fragments or pellets, which are also sometimes called *shrapnel.* The shell is meant to explode in the air over a target, spreading its contents across a wide area. Here, ***lodged*** means "stuck."

Practice the Skills

5 English Language Coach

Historical Influences on English One definition of **politics** (the original one) is simply the "art or science of government."

6 Reading Across Texts

Author's Bias Zlata calls leaders of the warring sides the "kids." Do you think she's showing bias? (Check the definition on page 982.)

A playground in Bosnia in spring 1996. The war officially ended in September 1995.

Additional Support

Literature Focus Lesson

Narrative Every narrative tells a story that has a main idea, details, characters, and a setting. Most importantly, a narrative has a plot. The event at the bottom of this page turns the diary from a young girl's observation of physical destruction in war to a story of the very serious consequences of that destruction. When Zlata's friend Nina is killed, the war and all the destruction become a lot more vivid. Ask students to tell other stories they know about real people who have been through a difficult ordeal. Suggest that telling these stories often helps people get through the frustration and grief of those experiences. AS

together in the park. Is it possible I'll never see Nina again? Nina, an innocent eleven-year-old little girl—the victim of a stupid war. I feel sad. I cry and wonder why? She didn't do anything. A disgusting war has destroyed a young child's life. Nina, I'll always remember you as a wonderful little girl. **7**
Love, Mimmy,
Zlata

Wednesday, May 13, 1992

Dear Mimmy,
Life goes on. The past is cruel, and that's exactly why we should forget it.

The present is cruel, too, and I can't forget it. There's no joking with war. My present reality is the cellar, fear, shells, fire.

Terrible shooting broke out the night before last. We were afraid that we might be hit by shrapnel or a bullet, so we ran over to the Bobars'. We spent all of that night, the next day, and the next night in the cellar and in Nedo's apartment. (Nedo is a refugee from Grbavica. He left his parents and came here to his sister's empty apartment.) We saw terrible scenes on TV. The town in ruins, burning, people and children being killed. It's unbelievable.

The phones aren't working; we haven't been able to find out anything about Grandma and Granddad, Melica, how people in other parts of town are doing. On TV we saw the place where Mommy works, Vodoprivreda, all in flames. It's on the aggressor's side of town (Grbavica).[7] Mommy cried. She's depressed. All her years of work and effort up in flames. It's really horrible. All around Vodoprivreda there were cars burning, people dying, and nobody could help them. God, why is this happening? **8**

I'M SO MAD I WANT TO SCREAM AND BREAK EVERYTHING!
Your Zlata

7. ***Grbavica*** is a suburb of Sarajevo on the edge of a large area controlled by the Serb nationalists.

Vocabulary

aggressor (uh GRES ur) *n.* a person, group, or nation that causes a conflict or war.

Practice the Skills

7 Reviewing Elements

Organization Zlata organizes this entry from general to specific. What is the general idea? What specific details support the general idea?

8 BIG Question

BQ How does the war change the communities of Sarajevo? What do you think Zlata would say is the most important part of her community? Write your answers on the "Zlata's Diary" page of Foldable 8. Your response will help you complete the Unit Challenge later.

Teach

BQ 

As students discuss and take notes on how the war changed Zlata Filipović's community of Sarajevo, ask them to think about how the past, present, and future affect any community. Discuss how the past stays with a community and how building a future that is better can help people to heal from even the worst events. Point out Zlata's suggestion that they should forget the cruel past. **Ask:** What do you think she might do in order to heal and go on with life? How do you think her community will rebuild? *(Responses will vary. Students may suggest that the community will begin by clearing the debris and rebuilding the city.)* **OL**

Reading Fluency

Build Fluency Have students who need extra help with their reading find a quiet place to practice reading the passage aloud. Have them reread the passage several times until they can smoothly read all the sentences with expression and understanding. Remind them to try to make their reading sound like natural speech. It may also be helpful to write out phonetic pronunciations of the names of people and places so students can say them naturally as well. **EL** **BL**

Objectives

- Find similarities and differences across texts
- Understand historical influences on English word meanings and usage
- Understand the use of narrative in literature

Assess

Resources for page 994

 Selection Quick Check

 Comparing Literature Assessment

Vocabulary Check

Teacher Hero: Erin Gruwell

1. Discrimination
2. objectively
3. tolerance

from *Zlata's Diary*

4. cope
5. aggressor
6. Possible response: on prejudices and opinions
7. *Metro* comes from the Greek word for "mother." *Metropolis* means "a major city."
8. Responses will vary. Students should demonstrate a clear understanding of the definition.

After You Read

Teacher Hero: Erin Gruwell & Zlata's Diary

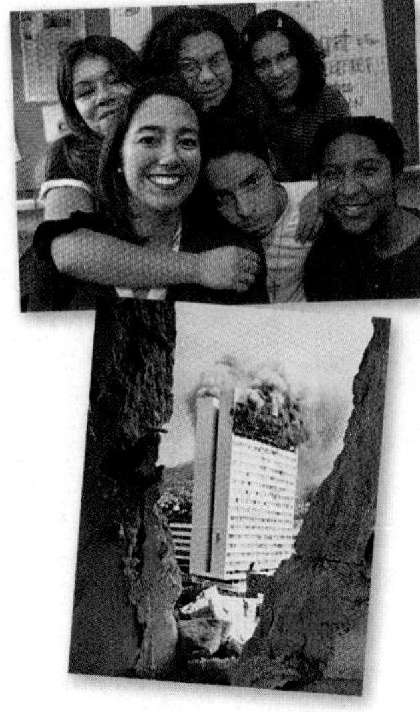

Objectives (pp. 994–995)
Reading Compare and contrast across texts
Vocabulary Identify historical influences on English
Writing Write to compare and contrast: author's credibility

Vocabulary Check

Teacher Hero: Erin Gruwell

On a separate sheet of paper, copy each sentence, filling in the blank with the best word from the list below.

tolerance discrimination objectively

1. ___ is acting differently toward someone because of his or her race, religion, or ethnic background.
2. Writers who express ideas ___ do not show or discuss their personal feelings.
3. When you show understanding and sympathy for other people, you show ___.

from Zlata's Diary

On a separate sheet of paper, write the vocabulary word that relates to each statement.

cope aggressor

4. The people in Zlata's community had to deal with the effects of war.
5. For Zlata, this word identifies the side that killed her neighbors and destroyed her community.

Academic Vocabulary

6. When you show **bias,** on what do you base your opinion?

English Language Coach

7. In a dictionary, look up the word *metropolis*. Write down the origin and meaning of *metro* and the first meaning of *metropolis*.
8. The word **survivor** comes from Latin words meaning "over" and "to live." Using the Latin definitions, write a definition in your own words for the word *survivor*.

Reading/Critical Thinking

On a separate sheet of paper, answer the following questions. The Tip after each question gives hints about where to find the information you need.

Teacher Hero: Erin Gruwell

9. **Interpret** Why do you think Miep Gies called Erin Gruwell's students "the real heroes" after visiting their class?

   TIP Think and Search

10. **Evaluate** How did the school stereotype Erin Gruwell and her students at the beginning of the article, and how did Gruwell and her students break those stereotypes?

    TIP Right There

from *Zlata's Diary*

11. **Infer** Zlata writes, "The past is cruel, and that's exactly why we should forget it." Do you think she will forget the past as she goes on in life?

    TIP Author and Me

12. **Evaluate** What do you think about the events that Zlata describes?

    TIP Author and Me

Web Activities For eFlashcards, Selection Quick Checks, and other Web activities, go to www.glencoe.com.

Write About Your Reading

Use Your Notes

13. Follow these steps and use the notes on your chart to compare the authors' credibility in these two selections.

    Step 1: Look over your chart. Consider each author's credentials (qualifications for writing about her subject), her sources of information (how reliable you think they are), and the author's bias.

    Step 2: Rate each author's credibility, using the High-Low rating scale at the bottom of the chart. Place a vertical line at the point between high and low where you rate her credibility.

Get It On Paper

To show how you compare the credibility of authors Zlata Filipović and Jerrilyn Jacobs, copy and complete these statements on a separate piece of paper.

14. On a scale of 10 (high) to 1 (low), I rate Zlata Filipović's credibility as ___.
15. I think Zlata Filipović's credibility as a writer is (very high, high, not very high, low) because (add your reasons, using details from the Author's Credibility chart).
16. On a 10 (high) to 1 (low) scale, I rate Jerrilyn Jacobs's credibility as ___.
17. I think Jerrilyn Jacobs's credibility as a writer is (very high, high, not very high, low) because (add your reasons, using details from the Author's Credibility chart).

BIG Question

18. What happens in a community when people do *not* have faith and trust in each other? What can happen when they *do* believe in each other?

Reading/Critical Thinking

Teacher Hero: Erin Gruwell

9. Responses will vary. Students may say that she was impressed with their dedication and wanted to inspire them to continue with their efforts.
10. Possible response: The school assumed that the students would never be achievers and that Gruwell would quit pretty quickly; Gruwell did not quit, and the students went on to become high achievers.

from *Zlata's Diary*

11. Responses will vary. Students may say that she might be able to put it behind her, but her diary will always be there to keep the memory alive.
12. Responses will vary. Students may say that it's inspiring that Zlata made it through such a horrific experience alive and well.

Write About Your Reading

Use Your Notes

13. Responses will vary. Students should use their charts to respond.

Get It On Paper

14. Responses will vary.
15. Responses will vary.
16. Responses will vary.
17. Responses will vary.

BIG Question

18. Responses will vary. Students may say that lack of faith and trust causes a breakdown in a community, while extraordinary things can happen when people do believe in each other.

The Unit Challenge

Focus

BELLRINGER Options

Daily Language Practice Transparency

Focus Activity Ask: Of the selections you read in this unit, which do you think best describes what a community is? Why?
The discussion will remind students of the selections they've read, which will help them begin the group or the solo activity.

Teach

Group Activity: Community Mural

- Ask one group member to volunteer to be note-keeper.
- Make sure each group completes step 2 by the middle of the class period so there will be enough time for them to make their murals.
- Have the groups first try out several layouts and then choose the one all the group members like best.
- If there is text or graphics on the mural, all group members should proofread it for errors.

Assess/Close

Group Activity

Ask: In what ways does your mural answer the question, "What is a community?" *(Suggest that students write responses in their Learner's Notebook.)*

UNIT 8 WRAP-UP

Answering the Big Question: What Is a Community?

You've just read selections about communities. You've read what people wrote hundreds of years ago about their communities. You've seen how useful a train schedule can be to a community today. Now use what you've learned to complete the Unit Challenge.

The Unit Challenge

Choose Activity A or Activity B and follow the directions for that activity.

A. Group Activity: Community Mural

You and a group of classmates will create a mural about the idea of "community." The overall theme is the Nigerian saying, "It takes a village to raise a child." (If you like, you can choose a different theme.) Of course, you won't actually paint your mural on a wall, but you'll make a model on poster board.

1. Discuss the Assignment

- First, brainstorm with your group what you think the saying means. Who in a community "helps raise a child?" Choose a note-taker to jot down a list of organizations and people who serve this purpose in a community. Review the information that you wrote on the Foldable. Organize information into categories such as these:
- **People** (parents, grandparents, teachers, crossing guards)
- **Organizations/Places** (school, church, home, stores, boys and girls clubs, Boy Scouts, Girl Scouts)
- Think about the selections you read about different kinds of communities. Think about who and what made up each community.

2. Prepare and Plan

- Before you begin, create a sketch (a rough idea) of what your mural will look like.
- Gather all the art materials you'll need (poster board, paint and paintbrushes, markers, magazine pictures, scissors, etc.). When you all agree on an idea, divide the work among group members.

3. Create Your Mural

- Work together to create a mural that shows off your community and who or what helps to make it what it is.
- Use your rough sketches, your Foldable notes, and ideas you got from reading the selections in this unit.
- Clean up after yourselves. That's an important part of life in a community.

4. Present Your Mural

- Find a good place in your classroom or school to hang your community mural.
- Offer your class mural to the Chamber of Commerce as a way to advertise your community.

B. Solo Activity: Community Newsletter

One of the characters in the selections is moving to your community. Write a community newsletter that tells what your community has to offer, such as schools, libraries, shops, and playgrounds.

1. Getting Started

- Decide what kind of information you want to include in your newsletter. You'll want to include the name of the community, location, and some facts about it.
- You may have to go to the library or resource center at school to gather any new facts.

In your Learner's Notebook, organize the information in an outline. The outline below may give you ideas about the kinds of information to look for.

I. Community
  A. Name
  B. Location
II. Features
  A. Parks and playgrounds
  B. Other recreational facilities
  C. Natural features
III. Stores, businesses, and industries
IV. Other institutions and services
  A. Schools
  B. Houses of worship
  C. Charitable organizations
  D. Family shelters and food pantries
  E. Government services

Big Question Link to Web resources to further explore the Big Question at www.glencoe.com.

2. Write It

- From your outline, choose three or four interesting places, services, or other topics to write about as features of your community.
- Brainstorm key words and phrases about the places or services. Use them as subheads.
- Write one or two paragraphs that explain each topic, telling why each one is important.
- Reserve one section of the newsletter for a community guide. Here you can provide lists that might be helpful to new (or current) residents, such as population statistics and schools.
- Review your newsletter to see that it's clear and makes sense. Check your spelling, grammar, and punctuation.

3. Present It

Present your newsletter to the class. If possible, photocopy it for each classmate, or make a couple of copies that students can "check out."

Teach

Solo Activity: Community Newsletter

- Have students choose the character who is moving to their community.
- Ask students to think about what kind of information and resources the character would want or need to know about a new community.
- Encourage students to use the sample outline to create their own outlines in their Learner's Notebook.
- Have students use their outlines to choose three or four interesting places, services, or other topics to write about as important features of their community.
- Help students find sources of statistical information about their community and the addresses of local schools, community organizations, and businesses.
- Tell students they may photocopy their newsletter and distribute it to classmates.

Assess/Close

Solo Activity

Ask students to identify which character they chose. Then have them explain why the character would be interested in the features that they focused on in their newsletters.

Objectives

- Create a work of art for the community
- Write a newsletter about the community

Focus

Vocabulary Preview

List the following words on the board and review their definitions:

- rippled
- wind-tanned

Build Background

When Mary TallMountain's mother died, she was adopted by a non-Native American couple and taken away from her village. At first, she was traumatized by the loss of her family and homeland, and by the unfamiliarity of mainstream American culture. She used her writing as a way to reclaim her heritage, her family, and her own voice.

Teach

R1 Reading Skill

Review Skimming and Scanning Ask: What do you see in this selection that tells you about the genre? *(Possible response: It is written in short stanzas. It is a poem.)* BL OL

R2 Reading Skill

Review Predicting Ask: How do you predict Sokoya will respond to the question? *(She will probably say there isn't a word for goodbye.)* OL

Your Turn: Read and Apply Skills

Mary TallMountain

Meet the Author

Mary TallMountain was born in 1918 in Alaska near the Yukon River. After her mother died, Mary dealt with her feelings by writing stories and poems. She also wrote about the new community she lived in and loved, San Francisco. There, she started TallMountain Circle, an organization that gives awards to writers and artists who help make their communities better. See page R7 of the Author Files for more on Mary TallMountain.

Author Search For more about Mary TallMountain, go to www.glencoe.com.

There Is No Word For Goodbye

by Mary TallMountain

Sokoya,* I said, looking through
the net of wrinkles into
wise black pools
of her eyes.

What do you say in Athabaskan*
when you leave each other?
What is the word
for goodbye? R2

A shade of feeling rippled
the wind-tanned skin.
Ah, nothing, she said,
watching the river flash. R1

She looked at me close.
We just say, Tlaa. That means,
See you.
We never leave each other.
When does your mouth
say goodbye to your heart?

1 ***Sokoya*** means "aunt."

5 ***Athabaskan*** is a language, or group of languages, spoken by American Indians mainly in western Canada, Alaska, and the U.S. Southwest.

Additional Support

Literature Online

Author Search To expand students' appreciation of Mary TallMountain, have them access the Web site for additional information and resources.

Literature Focus Lesson

Summary In this poem, a child asks an older female family member what is the American Indian word for goodbye. The aunt responds by telling the child that there is no word for goodbye, and she mentions an image that reminds us of the interconnectedness of all things. AS

She touched me light
as a bluebell.
You forget when you leave us,
You're so small then.
We don't use that word.

We always think you're coming back,
but if you don't,
we'll see you some place else.
You understand.
There is no word for goodbye. ❍

Teach

Viewing the Photo

Say: In your own words, describe the photo. What information does it convey? *(Possible response: The old woman looks like she's wearing traditional Native American beads, which shows us her heritage. She is not smiling, and her deeply lined face and white hair suggest that she has lived a long and possibly difficult life.)* **BL** **OL**

Differentiated Instruction

Understanding Imagery

Mary TallMountain uses imagery in her poem. Have students copy the following chart and fill it in. Help them identify imagery in the poem and describe what it means to them. **OL**

The Imagery	What It Means
"When does your mouth/say goodbye to your heart?"	*This image really makes it clear that we never really say goodbye–we are always part of each other.*

Objectives

- Make predictions and draw inferences using evidence from a text
- Describe mental images that text descriptions evoke
- Use text features to interpret text
- Scan to preview text

Tips for Independent Reading

Stress the importance of reading a variety of selections that present different types of communities. Suggest books, such as those listed here, related to the Big Question.

Fiction

Explain to students how reading about characters who are a part of different types of communities, whether social, school, work, home, or geographic, helps them better understand the communities in their own lives.

Ask students to relate a story or a book they've already encountered that showed what makes a community. They may name fictional stories from this unit.

UNIT 8

Reading on Your Own

To read more about the Big Question, choose one of these books from your school or local library. Work on your reading skills by choosing books that are challenging to you.

Fiction

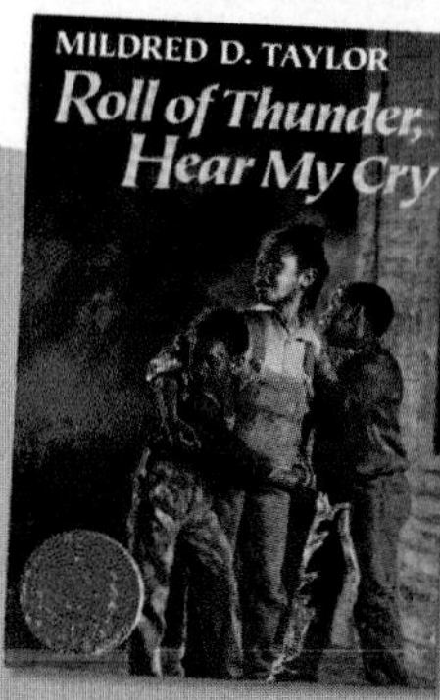

Roll of Thunder, Hear My Cry
by Mildred D. Taylor

This story of an African American family is set in rural Mississippi during the 1930s. Cassie and her family are determined to hang on to their land and remain where they belong.

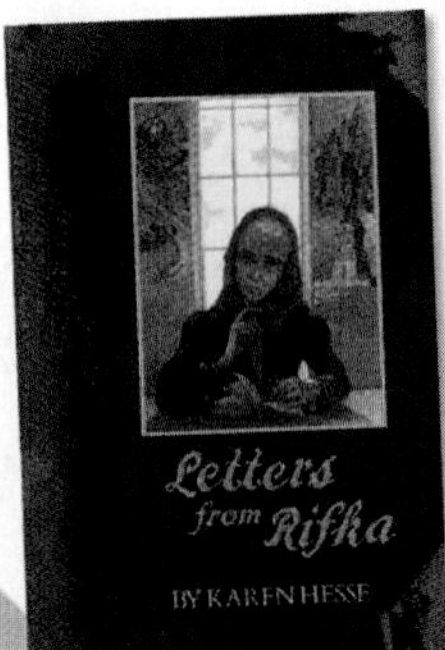

Letters from Rifka
by Karen Hesse

Letters tell the story of a Russian girl's journey to the United States in 1919.

When Thunders Spoke
by Virginia Driving Hawk Sneve

Norman Two Bull lives on a Dakota reservation and is not interested in the "old ways" of the Sioux. But when he finds an ancient relic and strange things begin to happen, he learns about the power of his people.

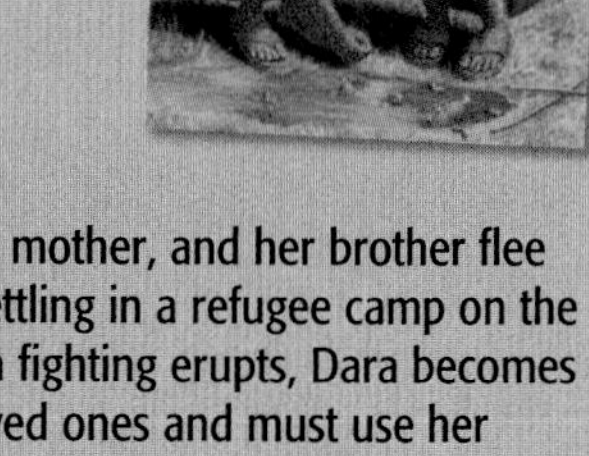

The Clay Marble
by Minfong Ho

In the 1970s, Dara, her mother, and her brother flee war-torn Cambodia, settling in a refugee camp on the Thailand border. When fighting erupts, Dara becomes separated from her loved ones and must use her courage to find her family.

Additional Support

Differentiated Instruction

GLENCOE BOOKLINK Use the Glencoe Booklink CD-ROM to create customized reading lists to help students answer the Big Question. Suggestions for Unit 8:

Grade 4: *The Circuit* by Francisco Jimenez
Grade 5: *In the Year of the Boar and Jackie Robinson* by Betty Bao Lord
Grade 6: *Thank You in Arabic* by Naomi Shihab Nye
Grade 7: *The Lost Garden* by Laurence Yep
Grade 8: *Americans All* by Michael Dorris

Nonfiction

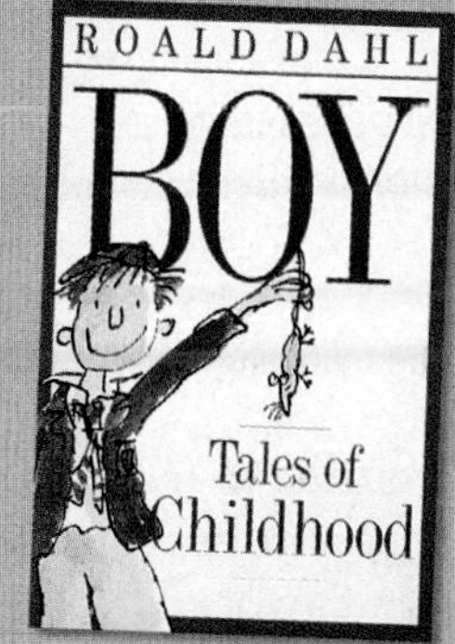

Boy: Tales of Childhood
by Roald Dahl

The popular novelist shares funny and sometimes sad stories of his childhood. Included are descriptions of his misadventures in boarding school and tales of his summer vacations on a remote island in Norway.

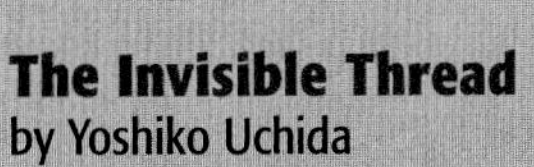

The Invisible Thread
by Yoshiko Uchida

The popular author describes growing up in Berkeley, California, as a Japanese American. During World War II, thousands of Asian Americans, including Uchida's family, were forced from their homes and sent to an isolated concentration camp in Nevada.

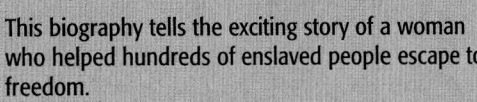

The Endless Steppe: Growing Up in Siberia
by Esther Hautzig

The author describes her family's capture by the Russian army in 1941. Sent to a forced-labor camp in Siberia, they struggle to stay together, keep hope, and make a new life.

Harriet Tubman: Conductor on the Underground Railroad
by Ann Petry

This biography tells the exciting story of a woman who helped hundreds of enslaved people escape to freedom.

READING ON YOUR OWN

Nonfiction

Explain to students that the books featured on this page are all nonfiction. In them, the authors tell about their lives or the lives and experiences of other real people in different kinds of communities.

About the Subjects

Fictional characters Cassie and Dara learn that family is an important kind of community as they struggle to survive in hard times. A young Native American boy recognizes how cultural traditions create special communities. Authors Esther Hautzig and Roald Dahl give real accounts of their lives in funny, and not so funny, situations within their communities. Real-life people Harriet Tubman and Rifka face journeys that define what community means to them.

Ask: How might reading the books on these pages help you learn about different kinds of communities? *(Possible response: The books, about both real and fictional people, show that families, schoolmates, ethnic and racial groups, and geographic locations can all represent communities for people.)* **OL**

Test-Taking Tips

TIP Remind students to read each question carefully and to make sure they understand what the question is asking before looking for the answer.

TIP Remind students that a primary source is an original document or piece of writing that is either an eyewitness account of a past event or written at the time that the event occurred.

TIP Remind students that sometimes the main idea of a passage is not explicitly stated. Sometimes the reader must infer the main idea from the passage.

Test Practice

Part 1: Literary Elements

1. A
2. Accept B or C
3. C
4. Responses will vary.

Unit Assessment Have students access the Web site to prepare for the Unit 8 test.

Test Practice

Part 1: Literary Elements

On a separate sheet of paper, write the numbers 1–4. For the first three questions, write the letter of the right answer next to the number for that question. Then, next to number 4, write your answer to the final question.

1. If you were doing research on the American Civil War, which of the following would be an example of a primary source?

A. A letter written by a Union soldier
B. A biography of Gen. Robert E. Lee
C. A history text written for young children
D. A historian's description of the first battle

2. Which of the following is the main use of text features?

A. To predict outcomes
B. To locate information
C. To clarify difficult text
D. To understand the author's purpose

Read the following paragraph. Then answer questions 3 and 4.

According to recent news reports, there is a new service available to meet a serious modern-day need: the need for sleep. The demands of jobs or school and family, along with desires for a social life, leave most people without enough time to sleep. Now a new firm, PowerNap, has the answer. It is building "Sleep Centers," where, for a fee, people can lie down and catch some shut-eye. That's right. For about 70 cents a minute, shoppers in malls and airports will be able to use small rooms with beds and piped-in music to catch up on their nap needs.

3. Which of the following is the main idea of this passage?

A. People no longer get enough sleep.
B. It can be expensive to use a Sleep Center.
C. A new service provides nap spaces for a fee.
D. People in malls and airports need a place to nap.

4. Do you predict success or failure for PowerNap Sleep Centers? What is one piece of evidence from the passage that supports your prediction?

Objectives
Reading Skim and scan text • Clarify ideas and text • Make predictions
Literature Identify literary elements: organization

Unit Assessment To prepare for the Unit test, go to www.glencoe.com.

Part 2: Reading Skills

Read the passage. Then, write the numbers 1–5 on a separate sheet of paper. For the first four questions, write the letter of the right answer next to the number for that question. Then, next to number five, write your answer to the final question.

Where the Deer and the Cheetahs and the Elephants and the Buffalo Roam

1 Can you imagine driving across the United States, and seeing signs telling you that there are lions, cheetahs, elephants, and camels up ahead? One day, these animals will roam freely in parts of North America, if a group of scientists have their way.

"Re-wilding" the Environment

2 Scientists at Cornell University recently announced a plan to help both endangered African animals and our own environment by bringing animals in danger of extinction to the Southwest. There, on our plains and grasslands, those animals would live and graze and hunt. The scientists call this idea "Pleistocene re-wilding."

3 The Pleistocene era began about 1.8 million years ago and lasted until after humans arrived in North America, perhaps about 13,000 years ago. During that era, many long-extinct animals lived in North America, such as the cheetah, a kind of camel, and at least five relatives of today's elephants. These animals disappeared as humans arrived on the continent.

4 Now, an article in *Nature* magazine reports that scientists want to bring these animals' closest surviving relatives—and others—back to America. But the plan isn't just simply to let wild animals loose on the North American plains; the idea involves placing the animals on large pieces of private land.

Healthy Ecosystems, Greater Biodiversity

5 Researchers say they believe large wild animals could help to create healthier ecosystems by increasing biodiversity, which is the variety of different plants and animals in an environment. It is well known that every plant and animal serves a purpose in its environment. Often, large animals hunt smaller animals. If a large animal becomes extinct, smaller animals may take over an environment and, for example, eat all the grasses. Such a change can threaten an entire ecosystem, turning grasslands into deserts.

UNIT 8 ASSESSMENT

TIP Remind students that readers take notice of text features when they skim to preview a selection. Text features might include photos, graphs, charts, captions, subheads, and words in boldface.

TIP Remind students to refer back to the passage to find evidence for their answers when they begin to answer the questions. Students need only to refer back to the passage to find clues in the text to help them with their responses.

Resources for pages 1002–1007

Use these resources to review, assess, or reteach the Unit: Active Learning and Note-Taking Guide, Selection and Unit Assessment, ExamView Assessment Suite, and Differentiated Instruction Tool Software.

Test Practice

Part 2: Reading Skills

1. B
2. D
3. B
4. A
5. Responses will vary.

Public Acceptance Is the Key

6 "Gaining public acceptance is going to be a huge issue," Donlan says, "especially when you talk about reintroducing predators [animals that hunt]." But, he says, there are many benefits to the idea of re-wilding. It would help to protect the species that remain on earth and restore natural environments. In addition, according to Cornell's researchers, the plan would create new jobs in eco-tourism and land management. This could be a great advantage for people living in the struggling economies of the Great Plains and Southwest.

---

1. If you were not sure what the term "Re-wilding" meant in the first subhead, which paragraph contains information that could help you clarify the term?

A. Paragraph 1
B. Paragraph 2
C. Paragraph 4
D. Paragraph 5

2. Which prediction is best supported by the article?

A. No one will support the plan to "re-wild" North America.
B. People in the Southwest will begin moving to coastal areas.
C. Lions and elephants will be roaming the Great Plains quite soon.
D. Scientists will try to gain public support for the "re-wilding" idea.

3. Which fact can a reader learn by only skimming the passage?

A. "Re-wilding" may have economic benefits in the Southwest.
B. There were once several varieties of elephants in North America.
C. The first humans arrived in North America during the Pleistocene Era.
D. Successful "re-wilding" will depend on convincing the public to accept it.

4. Scan the selection to find the answer to this question: Which paragraph first mentions Cornell University?

A. Paragraph 2
B. Paragraph 3
C. Paragraph 5
D. Paragraph 6

5. Write a short paragraph that describes what a person carefully reading the selection might visualize.

Objectives
Reading Visualize • Skim and scan text • Clarify ideas and text • Make predictions
Vocabulary Identify synonyms • Identify historical influences on English • Identify borrowed words

Part 3: Vocabulary Skills

On a separate sheet of paper, write the numbers 1–10. Next to each number, write the letter of the right answer for that question.

For questions 1–5, write the letter of the word or phrase that means about the same as the underlined word.

1. poorly clad
- **A.** fed
- **B.** dressed
- **C.** taught
- **D.** housed

2. to be resolute
- **A.** happy
- **B.** unsure
- **C.** frightened
- **D.** determined

3. to generate energy
- **A.** use
- **B.** save
- **C.** create
- **D.** waste

4. a feeling of awe
- **A.** wonder
- **B.** delight
- **C.** jealousy
- **D.** deep fear

5. to be defiant
- **A.** strong
- **B.** intelligent
- **C.** disobedient
- **D.** hidden from view

6. Which of the following is an acronym?
- **A.** ATM
- **B.** Tues.
- **C.** Xmas
- **D.** Mister

7. The "etymology" of a word is its
- **A.** use
- **B.** history
- **C.** spelling
- **D.** pronunciation

8. A "borrowed" word is a word from a foreign language that
- **A.** becomes part of another language
- **B.** is translated into another language
- **C.** takes on a new meaning in a new language
- **D.** is spelled the same as a word in another language

9. Which of the following is a "clipped" word?
- **A.** tip
- **B.** home
- **C.** exam
- **D.** glass

10. Which of the following words is most likely to be the latest addition to the English Language?
- **A.** barn
- **B.** throne
- **C.** theater
- **D.** videotape

Test Practice

Part 3: Vocabulary Skills

1. B
2. D
3. C
4. A
5. C
6. A
7. B
8. A
9. C
10. D

Test Practice

Part 4: Writing Skills

1. A
2. B
3. D
4. A
5. B
6. D
7. C

Part 4: Writing Skills

On a separate sheet of paper, write the numbers 1–14. Next to each number, write the letter of the right answer for that question.

1. Which of the following words could be divided with a hyphen if it appeared at the end of a line?

A. into
B. least
C. branch
D. through

2. Which of the following underlined words is written correctly?

A. It was an <u>allday</u> meeting.
B. They lived in <u>prehistoric</u> times.
C. Several <u>expresidents</u> agreed to meet.
D. Her behavior shows her <u>selfconfidence</u>.

3. Which of the following sentences is written correctly?

A. Exactly twenty two minutes later, at 7 18, the siren went off.
B. Exactly twenty-two minutes later, at 7 18, the siren went off.
C. Exactly twenty two minutes later, at 7:18, the siren went off.
D. Exactly twenty-two minutes later, at 7:18, the siren went off.

4. A colon is often useful punctuation when a writer needs to

A. introduce a list
B. provide an example
C. emphasize words that follow
D. show that words are being repeated

5. Which of the following sentences is written correctly?

A. Its too bad the bird hurt its wing.
B. It's too bad the bird hurt its wing.
C. Its too bad the bird hurt it's wing.
D. It's too bad the bird hurt it's wing.

6. In the sentence below, which word should go in the blank?

I fell off when the ___ saddle slipped sideways.

A. horse
B. horses
C. horses'
D. horse's

7. Which of the following sentences is written correctly?

A. I dont think thats theirs.
B. I don't think thats theirs.
C. I don't think that's theirs.
D. I don't think that's their's.

Objectives
Grammar Use punctuation: apostrophes, colons, semicolons, hyphens, quotation marks
Writing Establish a writing plan
• Gather and organize information

8. Which of the following sentences is written correctly?

A. Shawan arrived at four; Cheryl got there earlier.

B. Shawan arrived at four, Cheryl got there earlier.

C. Shawan arrived at four; and Cheryl got there earlier.

D. Shawan arrived at four, however, Cheryl got there earlier.

9. What change should be made to the sentence below?

Marvin said "that he'd like to be included."

A. Capitalize *that*.

B. Insert a comma after *said*.

C. Remove the quotation marks.

D. Begin the quotation after *that*.

10. What change should be made to the sentence below?

Sonia yelled, "There is nothing wrong with me"!

A. Change *There* to *there*.

B. Remove the comma after *yelled*.

C. Begin the quotation before *Sonia*.

D. Put the exclamation mark inside the quotation marks.

11. While working on a research paper, which of the following should you do *first*?

A. take notes

B. choose a topic

C. prepare an outline

D. write a thesis statement

12. The details that a writer should be *most* careful to include in a research paper are those that

A. the writer finds most interesting

B. can be put inside quotation marks

C. best support the paper's thesis statement

D. appear most often on the writer's note cards

13. Note cards for a research report should be organized according to

A. the ideas they contain

B. the order in which you took them

C. the kind of source they came from

D. whether they contain quotes or not

14. What is the purpose of using citations in a research report?

A. to prove that various experts agree with each other

B. to show that, if the facts are wrong, it's not your fault

C. to show where you got the information you are including

D. to serve as a substitute for quotation marks around a quote

Part 4: Writing Skills *(continued)*

8. A

9. C

10. D

11. C

12. B

REFERENCE SECTION

AUTHOR FILES

Joan Aiken (1924–2004)

- was the daughter of a Canadian writer and an American Pulitzer prize-winning poet
- decided to be a writer when she was only five years old; bought herself a notebook with birthday money, started writing, and never stopped
- was homeschooled until she was twelve at which time she was sent to a boarding school

Probably best known for her children's novel *The Wolves of Willoughby Chase*

Julia Alvarez (1950–)

- was born in New York City, but lived in the Dominican Republic until she was ten, then returned to New York to stay
- decided to be a writer while in high school
- has written many award-winning books
- is now a professor at Middlebury College

Quote: *"I am a Dominican, hyphen, American. . . . As a fiction writer, I find that the most exciting things happen . . . where two worlds collide or blend together."*

Rudolfo A. Anaya (1937–)

- was the son of a *vaquero* or horseman
- said he was changed forever at the age of sixteen after a diving accident that almost killed him and left him temporarily paralyzed
- taught junior high and high school while he developed his writing skills
- is Professor Emeritus of English at the University of New Mexico

Quote: *"It's good to be a Chicano!"*

Maya Angelou (1928–)

- was originally named Marguerite Johnson; Maya is the name her brother called her as a child
- at the age of three, was sent to live with her grandmother who ran the only black-owned general store in the town of Stamps, Arkansas
- has been a professor at Wake Forest University for more than twenty years
- speaks French, Spanish, Italian, Arabic, and Fanti (a language of southern Ghana) fluently

Isaac Asimov (1920–1992)

- was born in Russia; immigrated to U.S. with family at age three; grew up in Brooklyn, NY
- earned a Ph.D. in chemistry at Columbia University; taught at Boston University
- is the author of about 500 books: science fiction, mystery, nonfiction science, history, and more
- wrote about space travel, but feared flying; flew only twice in his lifetime

Best known for his robot stories–*I, Robot* and *The Rest of the Robots,* and his Foundation series

Toni Cade Bambara (1939–1995)

- changed her name from Miltona Mirkin Cade to Toni Cade Bambara in 1970, after she found *Bambara* in a sketchbook in a family trunk
- studied acting and mime in Italy and France
- worked as an investigator for the New York State Department of Welfare for two years
- was encouraged by her mother to be creative

Quote: *"She gave me permission to wonder, to dawdle, to daydream."*

Ray Bradbury (1920–)

- does not like technology even though he writes about it; he doesn't drive a car, use a computer, or fly in airplanes
- feels that much of his work is too fantastic to be considered science fiction which he said he felt had to be based on possibilities for the future
- has written more than 30 books and 600 short stories

Quote: *"The great fun in my life has been getting up every morning and rushing to the typewriter…"*

Gwendolyn Brooks (1917–2000)

- born in Topeka, Kansas, but lived most of her life in Chicago
- in 1950 became the first African American woman to be awarded a Pulitzer Prize
- followed Carl Sandburg as poet laureate of Illinois in 1968; served until her death in 2000

Quote: *"I felt that I had to write. Even if I had never been published, I knew that I would go on writing, enjoying it, and experiencing the challenge."*

Joseph Bruchac (1942–)

- lives in the Adirondack Mountain foothills with his wife in the same house where he was raised
- established workshops and taught creative writing classes in prisons throughout the country
- is a professional storyteller
- believes that the best stories tell people how to act toward the earth and each other and believes that they can "help guide a young person along a trail on which his or her feet have never been"

Judith Ortiz Cofer (1952–)

- grew up speaking Spanish at home, but learned English well enough to become a writer and college professor
- lives in Georgia on a farm that has been in her husband's family for generations
- believes that immigrants do not have to choose one identity over another and says she uses her art "as a bridge between my cultures… traveling back and forth without fear and confusion"

Margaret Danner (1915–1984)

- wrote her first prize-winning poem, "The Violin," when she in eighth grade; violin imagery appears in many later poems
- got to know other young American poets while working as editor for *Poetry* magazine
- established Boone House, an arts center for children, while serving as poet in residence at Wayne State University in Detroit
- African trip in 1966 influenced her later poetry

Borden Deal (1922–1985)

- was given the name Loyse Youth Deal at birth
- was a Mississippi native, son of a farming family
- wrote about the South and African-American culture from his personal experience
- wrote mostly about people's attachment to the land on which they live
- enjoyed fishing, golf, and playing the guitar
- wanted his books to be a "panorama of the New South"

Gregory Djanikian (1949–)

- was born in Alexandria, Egypt, but immigrated to the United States when he was eight years old
- grew up in New York and Pennsylvania
- started writing when he was in college
- writes about life in America and problems in Armenia (his family is Armenian)
- lives near Philadelphia with his wife and children
- directs a creative writing program at a university

Quote: *"Djanikian is masterful in his control of where a poem is going–and the reader with it."*

Michael Dorris (1945–1997)

- is considered one of the most recognized Native American writers of both fiction and non-fiction
- was the first single father in America to adopt a child; eventually adopted two boys and a girl
- researched fetal alcohol syndrome and wrote an award-winning book on it when his first adopted son was found to have the disorder
- married Louise Erdrich; they had three girls
- wrote two books with Erdrich, who was also an award-winning author

Rita Dove (1952–)

- grew up in a home full of books and enjoyed writing and putting on plays
- in high school, with her brother, created a comic book featuring superheroes Jet Boy and Jet Girl
- was the youngest person and first African American appointed poet laureate of the U. S.
- won many other awards for her poetry, including the famous Pulitzer Prize

Quote: *"I see poetry as the root of all writing."*

Robert Frost (1874–1963)

- lived during times of great change; was born less than ten years after the Civil War and died less than ten years before a man walked on the moon
- decided to be a poet when he was sixteen
- married Elinor White and had six children; Elinor and four of the children died during his lifetime
- was very shy, but developed a style of reading poetry that made him one of the most popular performers in America and overseas

Nicholas Gage (1939–)

- spent his first nine years in a remote Greek village where there were no lights, cars, or radios
- was separated from his father because of wars and did not get to meet him until he was nine
- lost his mother when she was executed for arranging his escape from guerilla soldiers
- wrote a best-selling book about his mother's life
- lives with his wife in Massachusetts, where they work together on writing projects

Ernesto Galarza (1905–1984)

- was born in a small Indian village in Mexico
- came to the U.S. with his mother and uncles when he was six years old as part of huge group fleeing the violence of a revolution in Mexico
- learned English quickly and won a college scholarship; also earned a doctorate degree
- fought against abuse of farmworkers, especially poor wages and bad living conditions

Quote: *"He was an inspiration."*

O. Henry (1862–1910)
- was raised by his grandmother when his mother died; his father spent all his time on an invention
- became a registered pharmacist
- fled to Honduras after being accused of stealing; came back home to Texas because his wife was dying
- published a newspaper called *Rolling Stone*
- wrote nearly 300 stories, 80 of them Westerns
- had millions of his books sold all over the world
- died poor and in debt

Langston Hughes (1902–1967)
- was elected class poet in the eighth and twelfth grades
- had lived in Missouri, New York, Ohio, Mexico, Kansas, Colorado, and Illinois by the age of twenty
- had been a truck farmer, cook, waiter, sailor, doorman, and traveled extensively before the first of his books was published
- experimented with jazz and blues rhythms in his poetry; many of his poems have been set to music
- A critic said that Hughes's poems were meant "to be read aloud, crooned, shouted, and sung."

Shirley Jackson (1919–1965)
- was born to a well-off San Francisco, CA, family
- began writing poems, stories, notes, journals as a child
- eventually wrote 1,000 words every day, working at home
- received a record-breaking amount of mail from readers after the *New Yorker* published "The Lottery" in 1948, "a memorable and terrifying masterpiece"
- wrote novels and stories that are still in print–try: "Charles," "One Ordinary Day, with Peanuts"

Yusef Komunyakaa (1947–)
- was awarded the Bronze Star while serving as an army correspondent in Viet Nam
- taught elementary school in New Orleans and creative writing at several universities
- married Mandy Sayer, an Australian writer
- has won many important awards for his poetry
- is determined to explore the history of his African American ancestors and his own personal history
- lives in New York City and is a professor at Princeton University

Li-Young Lee (1957–)
- is the great-grandson of China's first president
- family from Indonesia to Pittsburgh, PA after his father had been jailed for political reasons
- is inspired by the Bible, Tang dynasty poetry, and poems by Robert Louis Stevenson
- lives in Chicago with his wife and their two sons

Quote: *"Each poem presents its own demands, its own requirements, and its own pleasures. Every encounter with the page is new. I proceed by unknowing."*

Jean Little (1932–)
- was born and lived in Taiwan until age seven
- had very poor eyesight
- was a teacher for children with disabilities
- has written 31 books; many award-winning
- has two dogs, two cats, a dwarf rabbit, and two African Gray parrots
- prefers to read children's books because she says they "communicate a sense of growth and hope and love."

Eve Merriam (1916–1992)

- started writing poetry as a young child
- wrote advertisements, articles, picture books, biographies, and plays, as well as poetry
- felt that it is important to address social issues such as war, pollution, racism, and addiction to watching television when writing for young people
- was married to Oscar-winning screenwriter Waldo Salt

Quote: *"No one learns to love poetry without hearing it read out loud."*

Edna St. Vincent Millay (1916–1992)

- was encouraged by her mother to be ambitious and to appreciate music and literature
- entered a poetry contest that helped her win a scholarship to Vassar College
- used modern ideas with traditional poetry styles
- was a very popular poet during her lifetime

Quote by author Thomas Hardy: *"America has two great attractions: the skyscraper and the poetry of Edna St. Vincent Millay."*

Lillian Morrison (1917–)

- grew up in a city in New Jersey
- has made books her life's work
- believes that the best way to introduce young people to poetry is to find topics that interest them
- has put together collections and written her own books of poems on different subjects such as sports, science fiction, and women's history
- says that for her, poetry involves body movement; she is inspired by athletes, dancers, drummers, and jazz musicians

Walter Dean Myers (1937–)

- went to live with foster parents in Harlem after his mother died when he was two
- had a speech impediment and at the suggestion of a teacher, began to write down his thoughts
- thought he could never go to college, but always kept writing, and after serving in the army was able to pay for tuition with money from the G.I. Bill of Rights
- gets up every day by 5 A.M., walks 5 miles, and writes 10 pages before stopping
- says rewriting is more fun for him than writing

Lensey Namioka (1929–)

- says she is the only person in the world named Lensey; her father made up the name
- is the daughter of a linguist (an expert in languages) and a doctor/writer
- was encouraged by her parents to love music which became a subject for many of her books
- is from China and her husband is from Japan, so she is interested in writing about both places
- has been writing books for more than thirty years and has won numerous awards

Ogden Nash (1902–1971)

- had a relative who was a Revolutionary War general after whom Nashville, TN, was named
- went to a boarding school when he was fifteen
- started out writing for an advertising agency
- wrote plays and screenplays for movies
- used puns, creative misspellings, invented words, surprise rhymes, and irregular line lengths

Quote: *"I'm very fond of the English language. I tease it, and you only tease the things you love."*

Alfred Noyes (1880–1958)

- was born in England, but lived in the United States and Canada during World War II.
- had his first book, *The Loom of Years,* published when he was only twenty-one
- was the most popular poet of his time by the age of thirty, but after more modern poetry came in style, many critics called his poems old-fashioned
- slowly went blind during last ten years of life
- retired and died on the Isle of Wight, England

Rosa Parks (1913–2005)

- went to a school that closed three extra months a year for African American children to go to work
- traveled around the country to encourage voting
- was awarded the Congressional Gold Medal
- is called "Mother of the Civil Rights Movement"
- after her death, was the first woman to lie in state in the Capitol

Quote: *"When you led, you had no way of knowing if anyone would follow."*

Edgar Allan Poe (1809–1849)

- lost his parents, who were professional actors, when he was three years old
- struggled with poverty all of his life
- started writing poetry when he was a teenager
- joined the army and attended West Point
- worked as an editor of magazines
- helped develop murder mystery, science fiction, treasure mystery, and horror story formats
- was a major influence on American writers

Rod Serling (1924–1975)

- was encouraged to be creative from an early age
- received a Purple Heart medal for wounds while serving as a paratrooper during WW II
- worked at a radio station after college graduation
- wrote very controversial dramas and frequently battled with censors about revisions
- won six Emmy Awards for his scriptwriting
- cowrote the screenplay for the original *Planet of the Apes*

Quote: *"You're traveling through another dimension . . . next stop, the Twilight Zone!"*

Robert Service (1874–1958)

- lived and traveled in many different countries
- was an instant success after his first book was published
- worked as a correspondent, an ambulance driver, and an intelligence officer during WW I
- had several of his books made into movies
- has three schools named after him in Alaska and Canada and was honored on a Canadian stamp
- was the most popular poet in America, but called himself "only a 'rhymer' and an 'inkslinger.'"

Gary Soto (1952–)

- is a third-generation Mexican American
- has edited story collections; written poetry, essays, novels, young adult and children's books; and has made movies
- taught English and Chicano Studies at the University of California, Berkeley
- enjoys theater, tennis, basketball, traveling, and occasionally working in the garden

Quote: *"I discovered that reading builds a life inside the mind."*

Mary TallMountain (1918–1994)

- was born in Nulato, Alaska, on the Yukon River, one hundred miles south of the Artic Circle
- lost her mother, brother, and step parents at an early age and moved away with adoptive family
- found writing about the Yukon River area a way to reclaim her family and homeland

Quote: *"Her spirit and her ability to connect the different worlds of her experience teach us much about how to live our lives properly."*

Piri Thomas (1928–)

- grew up in El Barrio, a poor district in New York, during the Great Depression
- wrote a book which made the term *el barrio*, meaning "the neighborhood," familiar to many
- had to rewrite his first book after the only copy of the manuscript was accidentally destroyed
- says his focus in life is to inspire youth

Quote: *"You have to be careful how you use words because they can be bullets or butterflies."*

Walt Whitman (1819–1892)

- worked as a printer, an editor, a newspaper reporter, and at other jobs while writing forgettable poems and novels before 1855
- published nine different editions of *Leaves of Grass* between 1855 and 1892, revising and adding new poems with each edition
- worked as a volunteer aide in hospitals, caring for sick and wounded soldiers during Civil War
- became a strong influence on many later poets who imitated his usually rhymeless free verse

Jane Yolen (1928–)

- is the daughter of two authors; her father also popularized kite flying, and her mother created crossword puzzles for magazines
- studied music and ballet
- has written more than 250 books which have been translated into twenty-two languages
- ran a workshop for new authors for twenty years

Quote: *"My advice for young people interested in writing: read and write. Read and read and read."*

Laurence Yep (1948–)

- grew up in San Francisco in an African American neighborhood, but went to school in Chinatown
- began reading science fiction in high school; sold his first story to a science fiction magazine at age eighteen
- spent six years researching Chinese American history to prepare for writing *Dragonwings*
- said he enjoys writing for young readers "because you can get back to old-fashioned storytelling."

Paul Zindel (1936–2003)

- had a troubled childhood—said in an interview, "I felt worthless as a kid, and dared to speak and act my feelings only in fantasy and secret"
- wrote stories that involve the gap between teens and the adults who don't understand them
- wrote a memoir, *The Pigman and Me*, and the novel, *The Pigman*, which were key works

Quote: *"I know it's a continuing battle to get through the years between twelve and twenty . . . so I write always from their point of view."*

FOLDABLES™

by Dinah Zike, M.Ed., Creator of Foldables™

Reading and Thinking with Foldables™

As you read the selections in each unit, the following Foldables will help you keep track of your ideas about the Big Questions. Follow these directions to make your Foldable, and then use the directions in the Unit Warm Up for labeling your unit Foldable.

Foldable 1 and Foldable 8—For Units 1 and 8

Step 1 Place a sheet of paper in front of you with the long side at the top. Fold the right side of the paper over twice, making sure to leave at least a half-inch uncovered margin at the left side.

Step 2 Label the front of the folded paper with the title of the first selection in Reading Workshop 1.

Step 3 Unfold the paper once. On the right side, at the top, write the label **My Purpose for Reading**.

Step 4 Open the Foldable all the way. Across the top, write the label **The Big Question**.

Step 5 Repeat the above directions for each remaining selection in the four Reading Workshops and the Comparing Literature or Reading Across Texts Workshop.

At the end of the unit, you use the half-inch margin space at the left to staple all of the fold-over pages together.

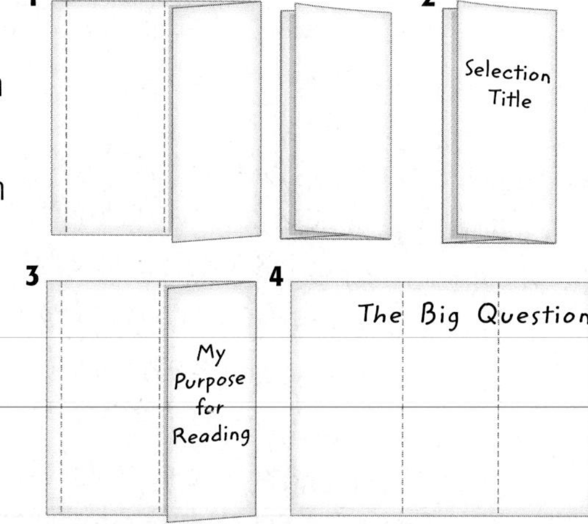

Foldable 2 and Foldable 6—For Units 2 and 6

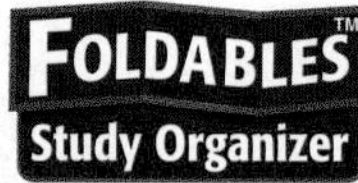

Step 1 Stack three sheets of paper with their top edges about a half-inch apart. These top edges will be tabs, so be sure to keep them straight.

Step 2 Fold up the bottom edges of the papers to form six tabs. Align the edges so that all of the layers or tabs are the same distance apart. Crease the bottom tightly.

Step 3 Follow steps 1 and 2 again to make a second set of tabbed pages. Then place the two sets of tabbed pages back-to-back and staple them together at the bottom.

Step 4 On the top page of one side of the tabbed pages, write the unit number and the big question. Then, working your way up, label the

1

2

3

Unit
Big Question

Continued on page R9

Continued from page R8

tabs in order with the titles of the reading selections in the Reading Workshops and the Comparing Literature Workshop. Use both tabbed sides.

Step 5 Below each title, write **My Purpose for Reading**. A third of the way down from that, write the label **The Big Question**.

Foldable 3 and Foldable 5—For Units 3 and 5

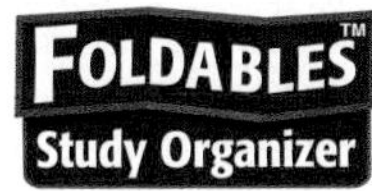

Step 1 With the long side at the top, fold a sheet of paper into thirds.

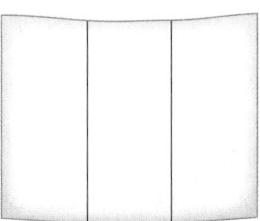

Step 2 Open the Foldable. Fold the bottom edge up two inches and crease well. Glue the outer edges of the tab to create three pockets. Staple both sides of the middle pocket. Use these pockets to hold notes you will take on index cards.

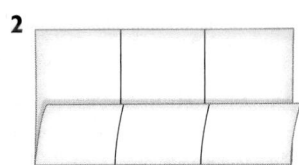

Step 3 Label the left pocket **My Purpose for Reading.**
Label the center pocket **The Big Question.**
Label the right pocket **My Thoughts.**

Step 4 On the front of the Foldable, list all the selections in the Reading Workshops and the Comparing Literature Workshop (in Unit 3) or Reading Across Texts Workshop (in Unit 5).

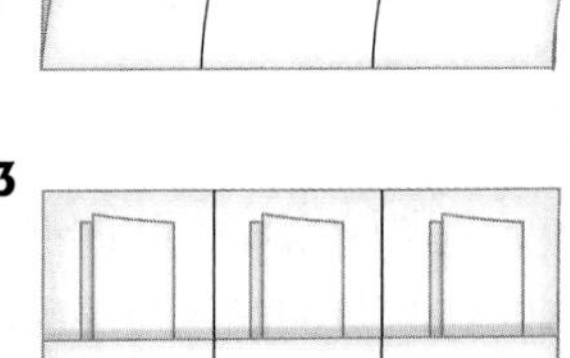

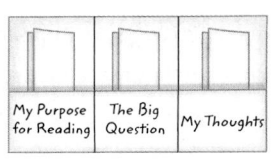

Foldable 4 and Foldable 7—For Units 4 and 7

Step 1 With the long side of the pages at the top, fold twelve (for Unit 4) or thirteen (for Unit 7) sheets of paper in half from top to bottom.

Step 2 Separate the sheets. On each folded sheet, make a cut through only the top half, 1 inch from the left side of the top flap. Cut to the fold line.

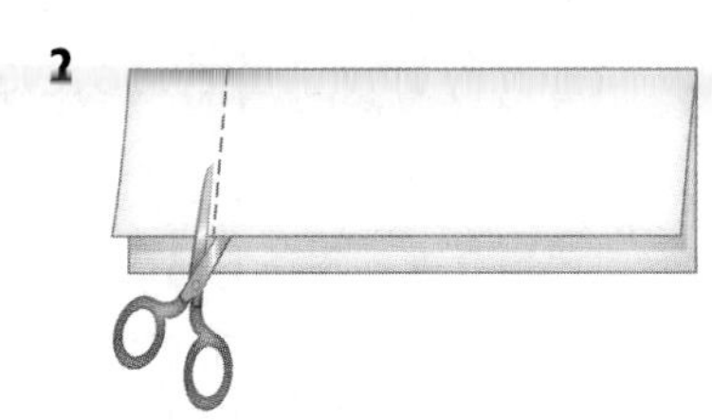

Step 3 Place the folded sheets one on top of the other. On the left side, staple the sections together.

Step 4 Label the front of each fold-over page with the selection title. Below the title, write the label **My Purpose for Reading.**

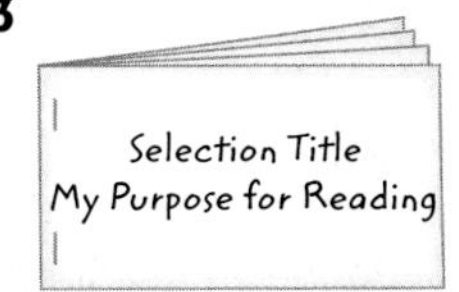

Step 5 Open the Foldable. Label the top of the inside page **The Big Question.**

You'll use this Foldable for each Reading Workshop and the Reading Across Texts Workshop (in Unit 4) or Comparing Literature Workshop (in Unit 7).

LITERARY TERMS HANDBOOK

A

Act A major unit of a drama. A play may be subdivided into several acts. Many modern plays have two or three acts. A short play can be composed of one or more scenes but only one act.

See also SCENE.

Alliteration The repitition of consonant sounds, usually at the beginnings of words or syllables. Alliteration gives emphasis to words. For example,

Over the cobbles he clattered and clashed

See page 779.

Allusion A reference in a work of literature to a well-known character, place, or situation in history, politics, or science or from another work of literature, music, or art.

See page 705.

Analogy A comparison between two things, based on one or more elements that they share. Analogies can help the reader visualize an idea. In informational text, analogies are often used to explain something unfamiliar in terms of something known. For example, a science book might compare the flow of electricity to water moving through a hose. In literature, most analogies are expressed in metaphors or similes.

See also METAPHOR, SIMILE.

Anecdote A brief, entertaining story based on a single interesting or humorous incident or event. Anecdotes are frequently biographical and reveal some aspect of a person's character.

Antagonist A person or force that opposes the protagonist, or central character, in a story or a drama. The reader is generally meant not to sympathize with the antagonist.

See also CONFLICT, PROTAGONIST.

Anthropomorphism Representing animals as if they had human emotions and intelligence. Fables and fairy tales often contain anthropomorphism.

Aside In a play, a comment made by a character that is heard by the audience but not by the other characters onstage. The speaker turns to one side, or "aside," away from the other characters onstage. Asides are common in older plays–you will find many in Shakespeare's plays–but are infrequent in modern drama.

Assonance The repetition of vowel sounds, especially in a line of poetry.

See page 779. See also RHYME, SOUND DEVICES.

Author's purpose The intention of the writer. For example, the purpose of a story may be to entertain, to describe, to explain, to persuade, or a combination of these purposes.

Autobiography The story of a person's life written by that person. *Rosa Parks: My Story,* by Rosa Parks with Jim Haskins, is an example of autobiography.

See also BIOGRAPHY, MEMOIR.

B

Ballad A short musical narrative song or poem. Folk ballads, which usually tell of an exciting or dramatic episode, were passed on by word of mouth for generations before being written down. Literary ballads are written in imitation of folk ballads.

See also NARRATIVE POETRY.

Biography The account of a person's life written by someone other than the subject. Biographies can be short or book-length.

See page 132. See also AUTOBIOGRAPHY, MEMOIR.

C

Character A person in a literary work. (If a character is an animal, it displays human traits.) Characters who show varied and sometimes contradictory traits are called **round.** Characters who reveal only one personality trait are called **flat.** A **stereotype** is a flat character of a familiar and often-repeated type. A **dynamic** character changes during the story. A **static** character remains primarily the same throughout the story.

See page 323.

Characterization The methods a writer uses to develop the personality of the character. In **direct characterization,** the writer makes direct statements about a character's personality. In **indirect characterization,** the writer reveals a character's personality through the character's words and actions and through what other characters think and say about the character. These techniques are frequently blended, as in the characterization of the two boxers in Piri Thomas's story "Amigo Brothers."

See page 683.

Climax The point of greatest emotional intensity, interest, or suspense in a narrative. Usually the climax comes at the turning point in a story or drama, the point at which the resolution of the conflict becomes clear. The climax in O. Henry's "After Twenty Years" occurs when Bob discovers that the man he thinks is Jimmy Wells is actually someone else.

Comedy A type of drama that is humorous and has a happy ending. A heroic comedy focuses on the exploits of a larger-than-life hero. In American popular culture, comedy can take the form of a scripted performance involving one or more performers—either as a skit that is part of a variety show, as in vaudeville, or as a stand-up monologue.

See also HUMOR.

Conflict The central struggle between opposing forces in a story or drama. An **external conflict** exists when a character struggles against some outside force, such as nature, society, fate, or another person. An **internal conflict** exists within the mind of a character who is torn between opposing feelings or goals.

See page 277. See also ANTAGONIST, PLOT, PROTAGONIST.

Consonance A pleasing combination of sounds, especially in poetry. Consonance usually refers to the repetition of consonant sounds in stressed syllables.

See also SOUND DEVICES.

D

Description Writing that seeks to convey the impression of a setting, a person, an animal, an object, or an event by appealing to the senses. Almost all writing, fiction and nonfiction, contains elements of description.

See page 605.

Details Particular features of things used to make descriptions more accurate and vivid. Authors use details to help readers imagine the characters, scenes, and actions they describe.

Dialect A variation of language spoken by a particular group, often within a particular region. Dialects differ from standard language because they may contain different pronunciations, forms, and meanings.

See page 733.

Dialogue Conversation between characters in a literary work.

See page 301. See also MONOLOGUE.

Drama A story intended to be performed by actors on a stage or before movie or TV cameras. Most dramas before the modern period can be divided into two basic types: tragedy and comedy. The script of a drama includes dialogue (the words the actors speak) and stage directions (descriptions of the action and scenery).

See also COMEDY, TRAGEDY.

E

Essay A short piece of nonfiction writing on a single topic. The purpose of the essay is to communicate an idea or opinion. A **formal essay** is serious and impersonal. A **informal essay** entertains while it informs, usually in a light conversational style.

Exposition The part of the plot of a short story, novel, novella, or play in which the characters, setting, and situation are introduced.

Extended metaphor An implied comparison that continues through an entire poem.

See also METAPHOR.

F

Fable A short, simple tale that teaches a moral. The characters in a fable are often animals who speak and act like people. The moral, or lesson, of the fable is usually stated outright.

Falling action In a play or story, the action that follows the climax.

See also PLOT.

Fantasy A form of literature that explores unreal worlds of the past, the present, or the future.

Fiction A prose narrative in which situations and characters are invented by the writer. Some aspects of a fictional work may be based on fact or experience. Fiction includes short stories, novellas, and novels.

See also NOVEL, NOVELLA, SHORT STORY.

Figurative language Language used for descriptive effect, often to imply ideas indirectly. Expressions of figurative language are not literally true but express some truth beyond the literal level. Although it appears in all kinds of writing, figurative language is especially prominent in poetry.

See page 785. See also ANALOGY, FIGURE OF SPEECH, METAPHOR, PERSONIFICATION, SIMILE, SYMBOL.

Figure of speech Figurative language of a specific kind, such as **analogy, metaphor, simile,** or **personification.**

First-person narrative. *See POINT OF VIEW.*

Flashback An interruption in a chronological narrative that tells about something that happened before that point in the story or before the story began. A flashback gives readers information that helps to explain the main events of the story.

Folklore The traditional beliefs, customs, stories, songs, and dances of the ordinary people (the "folk") of a culture. Folklore is passed on by word of mouth and performance rather than in writing.

See also FOLKTALE, LEGEND, MYTH, ORAL TRADITION.

Folktale A traditional story passed down orally long before being written down. Generally the author of a folktale is anonymous. Folktales include animal stories, trickster stories, fairy tales, myths, legends, and tall tales.

See page 652. See also LEGEND, MYTH, ORAL TRADITION, TALL TALE.

Foreshadowing The use of clues by an author to prepare readers for events that will happen in a story.

Free verse Poetry that has no fixed pattern of meter, rhyme, line length, or stanza arrangement.

See also RHYTHM.

G

Genre A literary or artistic category. The main literary genres are prose, poetry, and drama. Each of these is divided into smaller genres. For example: **Prose** includes fiction (such as novels, novellas, short stories, and folktales) and nonfiction (such as biography, autobiography, and essays). **Poetry** includes lyric poetry, dramatic poetry, and narrative poetry. **Drama** includes tragedy, comedy, historical drama, melodrama, and farce.

H

Haiku Originally a Japanese form of poetry that has three lines and seventeen syllables. The first and third lines have five syllables each; the middle line has seven syllables.

Hero A literary work's main character, usually one with admirable qualities. Although the word *hero* is applied only to males in traditional usage (the female form is *heroine*), the term now applies to both sexes.

See also LEGEND, MYTH, PROTAGONIST, TALL TALE.

Historical fiction A novel, novella, play, short story, or narrative poem that sets fictional characters against a historical backdrop and contains many details about the period in which it is set.

See also GENRE.

Humor The quality of a literary work that makes the characters and their situations seem funny, amusing, or ludicrous. Humorous writing can be as effective in nonfiction as in fiction.

See also COMEDY.

I

Idiom A figure of speech that belongs to a particular language, people, or region and whose meaning cannot be obtained, and might even appear ridiculous, by joining the meanings of the words composing it. You would be using an idiom if you said you *caught* a cold.

Imagery Language that emphasizes sensory impressions to help the reader of a literary work see, hear, feel, smell, and taste the scenes described in the work.

See page 887. See also FIGURATIVE LANGUAGE.

Informational text One kind of nonfiction. This kind of writing conveys facts and information without introducing personal opinion.

See page 4.

Irony A form of expression in which the intended meaning of the words used is the opposite of their literal meaning. *Verbal irony* occurs when a person says one thing and means another—for example, saying "Nice guy!" about someone you dislike. *Situational irony* occurs when the outcome of a situation is the opposite of what was expected.

L

Legend A traditional story, based on history or an actual hero, that is passed down orally. A legend is usually exaggerated and gains elements of fantasy over the years. Stories about Daniel Boone and Davy Crockett are American legends.

Limerick A light humorous poem with a regular metrical scheme and a rhyme scheme of *aabba.*

See also HUMOR, RHYME SCHEME.

Local color The fictional portrayal of a region's features or peculiarities and its inhabitants' distinctive ways of talking and behaving, usually as a way of adding a realistic flavor to a story.

Lyric The words of a song, usually with a regular rhyme scheme.

See also RHYME SCHEME.

Lyric poetry Poems, usually short, that express strong personal feelings about a subject or an event.

M

Main idea The most important idea expressed in a paragraph or an essay. It may or may not be directly stated.

Memoir A biographical or autobiographical narrative emphasizing the narrator's personal experience during a period or at an event.

See also AUTOBIOGRAPHY, BIOGRAPHY.

Metaphor A figure of speech that compares or equates seemingly unlike things. In contrast to a simile, a metaphor implies the comparison instead of stating it directly; hence, there is no use of connectives such as *like* or *as.*

See page 785. See also FIGURE OF SPEECH, IMAGERY, SIMILE.

Meter A regular pattern of stressed and unstressed syllables that gives a line of poetry a predictable rhythm. For example, the meter is marked in the following lines from "The Courage That My Mother Had," by Edna St. Vincent Millay:

> **Thĕ góldĕn broóch mȳ móthĕr wóre**
> **Shĕ léft bĕhínd fŏr mé tŏ weár. . . .**

See page 817. See also RHYTHM

Monologue A long speech by a single character in a play or a solo performance.

Mood The emotional quality or atmosphere of a story or poem.

See also SETTING.

Myth A traditional story of unknown authorship, often involving goddesses, gods, and heroes, that attempts to explain a natural phenomenon, a historic event, or the origin of a belief or custom.

N

Narration Writing or speech that tells a story. Narration is used in prose fiction and narrative poetry. Narration can also be an important element in biographies, autobiographies, and essays.

Narrative poetry Verse that tells a story.

Narrator The person who tells a story. In some cases the narrator is a character in the story.

See page 139. See also POINT OF VIEW.

Nonfiction Factual prose writing. Nonfiction deals with real people and experiences. Among the categories of nonfiction are biographies, autobiographies, and essays.

See page 333. See also AUTOBIOGRAPHY, BIOGRAPHY, ESSAY, FICTION.

Novel A book-length fictional prose narrative. The novel has more scope than a short story in its presentation of plot, character, setting, and theme. Because novels are not subject to any limits in their presentation of these elements, they encompass a wide range of narratives.

See also FICTION.

Novella A work of fiction shorter than a novel but longer than a short story. A novella usually has more characters, settings, and events and a more complex plot than a short story.

O

Onomatopoeia The use of a word or a phrase that actually imitates or suggests the sound of what it describes.

See also SOUND DEVICES.

Oral tradition Stories, knowledge, customs, and beliefs passed by word of mouth from one generation to the next.

See also FOLKLORE, FOLKTALE, LEGEND, MYTH.

P

Parallelism The use of a series of words, phrases, or sentences that have similar grammatical form. Parallelism emphasizes the items that are arranged in the similar structures.

See also REPETITION.

Personification A figure of speech in which an animal, object, or idea is given human form or characteristics.

See page 795. See also FIGURATIVE LANGUAGE, FIGURE OF SPEECH, METAPHOR.

Plot The sequence of events in a story, novel, or play. The plot begins with **exposition,** which introduces the story's characters, setting, and situation. The plot catches the reader's attention with a **narrative hook.** The **rising action** adds complications to the story's conflict, or problem, leading to the **climax,** or point of highest emotional pitch. The **falling action** is the logical result of the climax, and the **resolution** presents the final outcome.

See page 349.

Plot twist An unexpected turn of events in a plot. A surprise ending is an example of a plot twist.

Poetry A form of literary expression that differs from prose in emphasizing the line as the unit of composition. Many other traditional characteristics of poetry—emotional, imaginative language; use of metaphor and simile; division into stanzas; rhyme; regular pattern of stress, or meter—apply to some poems.

See page 774.

Point of view The relationship of the narrator, or storyteller, to the story. In a story with **first-person point of view,** the story is told by one of the characters, referred to as "I." The reader generally sees everything through that character's eyes. In a story with a **limited third-person point of view,** the narrator reveals the thoughts of only one character, but refers to that character as "he" or "she." In a story with an **omniscient point of view,** the narrator reveals the thoughts of several characters.

See page 65.

Props Theater slang (a shortened form of *properties*) for objects and elements of the scenery of a stage play or movie set.

Propaganda Speech, writing, or other attempts to influence ideas or opinions, often through the use of stereotypes, faulty generalizations, logical fallacies, and/or emotional language.

Prose Writing that is similar to everyday speech and language, as opposed to poetry. Its form is based on sentences and paragraphs without the patterns of rhyme, controlled line length, or meter found in much poetry. Fiction and nonfiction are the major categories of prose. Most modern drama is also written in prose.

See also DRAMA, ESSAY, FICTION, NONFICTION.

Protagonist The central character in a story, drama, or dramatic poem. Usually the action revolves around the protagonist, who is involved in the main conflict.

See ANTAGONIST, CONFLICT.

Pun A humorous play on two or more meanings of the same word or on two words with the same sound. Today puns often appear in advertising headlines and slogans—for example, "Our hotel rooms give you suite feelings."

See also HUMOR.

R

Refrain A line or lines repeated regularly, usually in a poem or song.

Repetition The recurrence of sounds, words, phrases, lines, or stanzas in a speech or piece of writing. Repetition increases the feeling of unity in a work. When a line or stanza is repeated in a poem or song, it is called a refrain.

See also PARALLELISM, REFRAIN.

Resolution The part of a plot that concludes the falling action by revealing or suggesting the outcome of the conflict.

Rhyme The repetition of sounds at the ends of words that appear close to each other in a poem. **End rhyme** occurs at the ends of lines. **Internal rhyme** occurs within a single line. **Slant rhyme** occurs when words include sounds that are similar but not identical. Slant rhyme usually involves some variation of **consonance** (the repetition of consonant sounds) or **assonance** (the repetition of vowel sounds).

See page 823.

Rhyme scheme The pattern of rhyme formed by the end rhyme in a poem. The rhyme scheme is designated by the assignment of a different letter of the alphabet to each new rhyme. For example, one common rhyme scheme is *ababcb.*

Rhythm The pattern created by the arrangement of stressed and unstressed syllables, especially in poetry. Rhythm gives poetry a musical quality that helps convey its meaning. Rhythm can be regular (with a predictable pattern or meter) or irregular, (as in free verse).

See page 817. See also METER.

Rising action The part of a plot that adds complications to the problems in the story and increases reader interest.

See also FALLING ACTION, PLOT.

S

Scene A subdivision of an act in a play. Each scene takes place in a specific setting and time. An act may have one or more scenes.

See also ACT.

Science fiction Fiction dealing with the impact of real science or imaginary superscience on human or alien societies of the past, present, or future. Although science fiction is mainly a product of the twentieth century, nineteenth-century authors such as Mary Shelley, Jules Verne, and Robert Louis Stevenson were pioneers of the genre.

Screenplay The script of a film, usually containing detailed instructions about camera shots and angles in addition to dialogue and stage directions. A screenplay for an original television show is called a teleplay.

See also DRAMA.

Sensory imagery Language that appeals to a reader's five senses: hearing, sight, touch, taste, and smell.

See page 207. See also VISUAL IMAGERY.

Sequence of events The order in which the events in a story take place.

Setting The time and place in which the events of a short story, novel, novella, or play occur. The setting often helps create the atmosphere or mood of the story.

See page 179.

Short story A brief fictional narrative in prose. Elements of the short story include **plot, character, setting, point of view, theme,** and sometimes symbol and irony.

See page 254.

Simile A figure of speech using like or as to compare seemingly unlike things.

See page 785. See also FIGURATIVE LANGUAGE, FIGURE OF SPEECH.

Sound devices Techniques used to create a sense of rhythm or to emphasize particular sounds in writing. For example, sound can be controlled through the use of **onomatopoeia, alliteration, consonance, assonance,** and **rhyme.**

See page 779. See also RHYTHM.

Speaker The voice of a poem—sometimes that of the poet, sometimes that of a fictional person or even a thing. The speaker's words communicate a particular tone or attitude toward the subject of the poem.

Stage directions Instructions written by the dramatist to describe the appearance and actions of characters, as well as sets, costumes, and lighting.

Stanza A group of lines forming a unit in a poem. Stanzas are, in effect, the paragraphs of a poem.

Stereotype A character who is not developed as an individual but as a collection of traits and mannerisms supposedly shared by all members of a group.

Style The author's choice and arrangement of words and sentences in a literary work. Style can reveal an author's purpose in writing and attitude toward his or her subject and audience.

See page 441.

Suspense A feeling of curiosity, uncertainty, or even dread about what is going to happen next. Writers increase the level of suspense in a story by giving readers clues to what may happen.

See also FORESHADOWING, RISING ACTION.

Symbol Any object, person, place, or experience that means more than what it is. **Symbolism** is the use of images to represent internal realities.

See page 801.

T

Tall tale A wildly imaginative story, usually passed down orally, about the fantastic adventures or amazing feats of folk heroes in realistic local settings.

See page 757. See also FOLKLORE, ORAL TRADITION.

Teleplay A play written or adapted for television.

See page 955.

Theme The main idea of a story, poem, novel, or play, usually expressed as a general statement. Some works have a **stated theme,** which is expressed directly. More frequently works have an **implied theme,** which is revealed gradually through other elements such as plot, character, setting, point of view, symbol, and irony.

See page 591.

Third-person narrative. *See POINT OF VIEW.*

Title The name of a literary work.

See page 41.

Tone The attitude of the narrator toward the subject, ideas, theme, or characters. A factual article would most likely have an objective tone, while an editorial on the same topic could be argumentative or satiric.

See page 419.

Tragedy A play in which the main character suffers a downfall. That character often is a person of dignified or heroic stature. The downfall may result from outside forces or from a weakness within the character, which is known as a tragic flaw.

V

Visual imagery Details that appeal to the sense of sight.

Voice An author's distinctive style or the particular speech patterns of a character in a story.

See also STYLE, TONE.

The Writing Process

The writing process consists of five stages: prewriting, drafting, revising, editing/proofreading, and publishing/presenting. By following the stages in order, you can turn your ideas into polished pieces of writing. Most writers take their writing through all five stages, and repeat stages when necessary.

The Writing Process

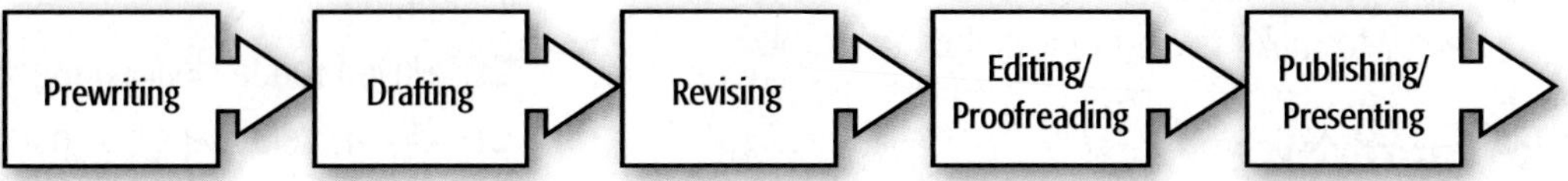

Prewriting

Prewriting is the process of gathering and organizing your ideas. It begins whenever you start to consider what you will write about or what will interest your readers. Try keeping a small notebook with you for several days and using it to jot down possible topics. Consult the chart below for tips on using the prewriting techniques known as listing, questioning, and clustering.

Listing, Questioning, and Clustering
LISTING List as many ideas as you can–whatever comes into your head on a particular subject. This is called brainstorming. Then go back over the list and circle the ideas you like best. Eventually you'll hit on an idea you can use.
QUESTIONING If your audience is your classmates, ask yourself questions such as the following: • *What do my friends like to learn about?* • *What do my friends like to read about?* • *What have I done that my friends might like to hear about?*
CLUSTERING Write your topic in the middle of a piece of paper. Organize related ideas around the topic in a cluster of circles, with lines showing how the ideas are related. Clustering can help you decide which part of a topic to write about.

When you have selected your topic, organize your ideas around the topic. Identify your main ideas and supporting ideas. Each main idea needs examples or facts to support it. Then write a plan for what you want to say. The plan might be an organized list or outline. It does not have to use complete sentences.

Drafting

Drafting is the stage that turns your list into sentences and paragraphs. Use your prewriting notes to remember what you want to say. Begin by writing an introduction that gets the reader's attention. Move ahead through the topic, paragraph by paragraph. Let your words flow. This is the time to express yourself or try out a new idea. Don't worry about mistakes in spelling and grammar; you can correct them later. If you get stuck, try one of the tricks below.

Tips for drafting

- Work on the easiest part first. You don't have to begin at the beginning.
- Make a diagram, sketch, or drawing of the topic.
- Focus on just one sentence or paragraph at a time.
- Freewrite your thoughts and images. You can organize them later.
- Pretend that you are writing to a friend.
- Ask more questions about your topic.
- Speak your ideas into a tape recorder.
- Take a break. Take a walk or listen to music. Return to your writing later.

Revising

The goal of revising is to make your writing clearer and more interesting. When you revise, look at the whole piece of writing. Ask whether the parts go together smoothly and whether anything should be added or

deleted. You may decide to organize the draft in a different way. Some writers make several revisions before they are satisfied. Ask yourself these questions:

- ☑ Did I stick to my topic?
- ☑ Did I accomplish my purpose?
- ☑ Did I keep my audience in mind?
- ☑ Does my main idea come across clearly?
- ☑ Do all the details support the main idea?
- ☑ Did I give enough information? too much?
- ☑ Did I use transition words such as *first, then* and *next* to make my sentences flow smoothly?

Tips for revising

- Step back. If you have the time, set your draft aside for a while. When you look at it again, you may see it from a new point of view. You may notice that some information is missing or that part of the paper is disorganized.
- Read your paper aloud. Listen carefully as you read your paper aloud. How does it sound?
- Have a writing conference with a peer reviewer, one of your friends or classmates. A second opinion helps. Your reader can offer a fresh point of view.

Peer review

You can direct peer responses in one or more of the following ways.

- Ask readers to tell you what they have read in their own words. If you do not hear your ideas restated, revise your writing for clarity.
- Ask readers to tell you the part they liked best and why. You may want to expand those parts.
- Repeat what the readers have told you in your own words. Ask the readers if you have understood their suggestions.
- Discuss your writing with your readers. Listen to their suggestions carefully.

As you confer, make notes of your reviewers' comments. Then revise your draft, using your own judgment and including what is helpful from your reviewers' comments.

Editing/Proofreading

When you are satisfied with the changes you've made, edit your revised draft. Replace dull, vague words with lively verbs and precise adjectives. Vary the length of your sentences. Take time to correct errors in spelling, grammar, capitalization, and punctuation. Refer to the Proofreading Checklist on page R67 and on the inside back cover of this book.

Editing for style

Use the following checklist:

- ☑ Have I avoided clichés?
- ☑ Have I avoided wordiness?
- ☑ Is the tone of my writing appropriate to my purpose?
- ☑ Have I made clear connections between ideas?
- ☑ Do my sentences and paragraphs flow smoothly?

Publishing/Presenting

Now your writing is ready for an audience. Make a clean, neat copy, and add your name and date. Check that the paper has a title. If you wish, enclose the paper in a folder or binder to give it a professional look. Hand it in to your teacher, or share it in one of the ways described below. When the paper is returned, keep it in your writing portfolio.

Ideas for presenting

- **Illustrations** A photograph, diagram, or drawing can convey helpful information.
- **Oral presentation** Almost any writing can be shared aloud. Try including music, slides, or a group oral reading.
- **Class book** A collection of class writing is a nice contribution to the school library.
- **Newspaper** Some schools have a school newspaper. Local newspapers often publish student writing, especially if it is about local people and events.
- **Literary magazine** Magazines such as *Cricket* and *MidLink* publish student writing. Some schools have a literary magazine that publishes student writing once or twice a year.
- **Bulletin board** A rotating display of student writing is an effective way to see what your classmates have written. Illustrations and photographs add interest.

Some writing, such as journal writing, is private and not intended for an audience. However, even if you don't share your paper, don't throw it away. It might contain ideas that you can use later.

Proofreading Help

Use this proofreading checklist to help you check for errors in your writing, and use the proofreading symbols in the chart below to mark places that need corrections.

- ☑ Have I avoided run-on sentences and sentence fragments and punctuated sentences correctly?
- ☑ Have I used every word correctly, including plurals, possessives, and frequently confused words?
- ☑ Do verbs and subjects agree? Are verb tenses correct?
- ☑ Do pronouns refer clearly to their antecedents and agree with them in person, number, and gender?
- ☑ Have I used adverb and adjective forms and modifying phrases correctly?
- ☑ Have I spelled every word correctly, and checked the unfamiliar ones in a dictionary?

Proofreading Symbols		
⊙	Lieut Brown	Insert a period.
∧	No one came the party.	Insert a letter or a word.
≡	I enjoyed paris.	Capitalize a letter.
/	The Class ran a bake sale.	Make a capital letter lowercase.
⁀ ‿	The campers are home sick.	Close up a space.
(sp)	They visited N.Y.	Spell out.
∧ ∧	Sue please come I need your help.	Insert a comma or a semicolon.
∿	He enjoyed feild day.	Transpose the position of letters or words.
#	alltogether	Insert a space.
ϑ	We went to to Boston.	Delete letters or words.
∨ ∨ ∨	She asked, Whos coming?	Insert quotation marks or an apostrophe.
/ = /	mid January	Insert a hyphen.
¶	"Where?" asked Karl. "Over there," said Ray.	Begin a new paragraph.

WRITING HANDBOOK

Writing Modes

There are four main types, or modes, of writing—expository, descriptive, narrative, and persuasive. Each mode has its own purpose and characteristics.

Expository Writing

Expository writing communicates knowledge. It provides and explains information; it may also give general directions or step-by-step instructions for an activity.

Use this checklist as you write.

- ☑ Is the opening paragraph interesting?
- ☑ Are my explanations accurate and complete? Is information clear and easy to read?
- ☑ Is information presented in a logical order?
- ☑ Does each paragraph have a main idea? Does all the information support the main idea?
- ☑ Does my essay have an introduction, a body, and a conclusion?
- ☑ Have I defined any unfamiliar terms?
- ☑ Are my comparisons clear and logical?

Kinds of expository writing

Expository writing covers a wide range of styles. The chart below describes some of the possibilities.

Descriptive Writing

Descriptive writing can make a person, place, or thing come to life. The scene described may be as unfamiliar and far away as the bottom of the sea or as familiar and close as the gym locker room. By presenting details that awaken the reader's senses, descriptive writing can help your readers see the world more clearly.

Use this checklist to help you revise your description.

- ☑ Does my introduction identify the person or place that will be described?
- ☑ Are my details vivid? Are nouns and adjectives precise?
- ☑ Do all the details contribute to the same impression?
- ☑ Is it clear why this place or person is special?
- ☑ Are transitions clear? Do the paragraphs follow a logical order?
- ☑ Does each paragraph contain a main idea?
- ☑ Have I communicated a definite impression or mood?

Kinds of Expository Writing	Examples
Instructional writing	Explain how to train for a cross-country race, how to arrange a surprise party, or how to avoid cleaning up your room.
Compare-and-contrast essay	Compare two athletes or two sports, two fictional characters, two books or movies, two places, or two kinds of vacations.
Step-by-step directions	Give directions for building a model plane, making apple pie, or drawing on a computer screen.
Information and explanation	Explain what causes sunspots, how plants grow in the desert, or why camels have a hump.
Report or essay	Write a book report, a report on the Buddhist religion, or a report on a new wildlife center.

Narrative Writing

Narrative writing tells a story, either real or fictional. It answers the question *What happened?*

A well-written narrative holds the reader's attention by presenting interesting characters in a carefully ordered series of events.

This checklist will help you improve your narrative.

- ☑ Does my first sentence get the reader's attention?
- ☑ Are the characters and setting introduced with enough detail?
- ☑ Do the characters speak and behave realistically?
- ☑ Are the events narrated in an order clear enough for the reader to follow?
- ☑ Are there places where dialogue should be added?
- ☑ Is my ending satisfying to the reader?

Persuasive Writing

Persuasive writing presents an opinion. Its goal is to make readers feel or think a certain way about a situation or an idea. The writer includes facts and opinions often designed to urge readers to take action. Good persuasive writing can sometimes be hard to resist.

As you revise your persuasive writing, use this checklist as a guide.

- ☑ Is my main idea expressed in a clear statement?
- ☑ Have I presented good reasons to support my point of view?
- ☑ Have I supported my reasons with facts and opinions?
- ☑ Have I taken account of the opposing points of view?
- ☑ Have I addressed the interests of my audience?
- ☑ Have I ended with a strong closing statement?

Research Report Writing

When you write a research report, you explore a topic by gathering factual information from several different resources. Through your research, you develop a point of view or draw a conclusion. This point of view or conclusion becomes the main idea, or thesis, of your report.

Select a Topic

Because a research report usually takes time to prepare and write, your choice of topic is especially important. Follow these guidelines.

- Brainstorm a list of questions about a subject you would like to explore. Choose one that is neither too narrow nor too broad for the length of paper you will write. Use that question as your topic.
- Select a topic that genuinely interests you.
- Be sure you can find information on your topic from several different sources.

Do Research

Start by looking up your topic in an encyclopedia to find general information. Then find specific information in books, magazines, and newspapers, on CD-ROMs and the Internet, and from personal interviews when this seems appropriate. Use the computerized or card catalog in the library to locate books on your topic. Then search for up-to-date information in periodicals (magazines) or newspapers and from electronic sources, such as CD-ROMs or the Internet. If you need help in finding or using any of these resources, ask the librarian.

As you gather information, make sure each source you use relates closely to your topic. Also be sure that your source is reliable. Be extra careful if you are using information from the Internet. If you are not sure about the reliability of a source, consult the librarian or your teacher.

Make Source Cards

In a research report, you must document the source of your information. To keep track of your sources, write the author, title, publication information, and location of each source on a separate index card. Give each source card a number and write it in the upper right-hand corner. These cards will be useful for preparing a bibliography.

Sample Source Card

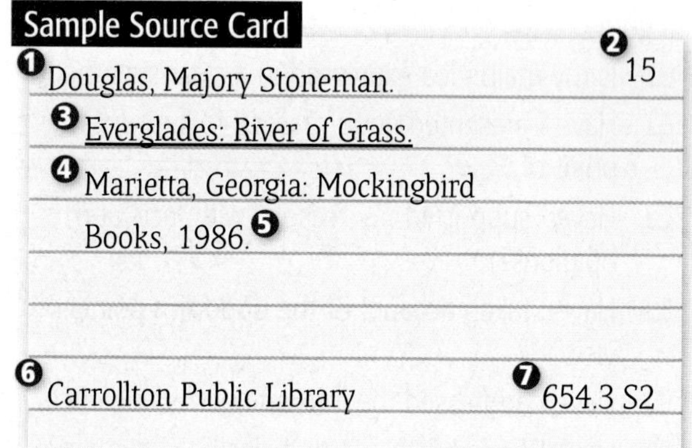
❶ Douglas, Majory Stoneman. ❷ 15

❸ Everglades: River of Grass.

❹ Marietta, Georgia: Mockingbird Books, 1986. ❺

❻ Carrollton Public Library ❼ 654.3 S2

❶ Author
❷ Source number
❸ Title
❹ City of publication/Publisher
❺ Date of publication
❻ Location of source
❼ Library call number

Take Notes

As you read, you encounter many new facts and ideas. Taking notes will help you keep track of information and focus on the topic. Here are some helpful suggestions:

- Use a new card for each important piece of information. Separate cards will help you to organize your notes.
- At the top of each card, write a key word or phrase that tells you about the information. Also, write the number of the source you used.
- Write only details and ideas that relate to your topic.
- Summarize information in your own words.
- Write down a phrase or a quote only when the words are especially interesting or come from an important source. Enclose all quotes in quotation marks to make clear that the ideas belong to someone else.

This sample note card shows information to include.

Sample Note Card

❶ Functions of Wetlands ❷ 15

Besides furnishing a home for a variety of wildlife, the wet, spongy soil of wetlands maintains the level of the water table.

p. 79 ❸

❶ Write a key word or phrase that tells you what the information is about.
❷ Write the source number from your source card.
❸ Write the number of the page or pages on which you found the information.

Develop Your Thesis

As you begin researching and learning about your topic, think about the overall point you want to make. Write one sentence, your *thesis statement,* that says exactly what you plan to report on.

Sample Thesis Statement

Everglades National Park is a beautiful but endangered animal habitat.

Keep your thesis in mind as you continue to do research and think about your topic. The thesis will help you determine what information is important. However, be prepared to change your thesis if the information you find does not support it.

Write an Outline

When you finish taking notes, organize the information in an outline. Write down the main ideas that you want to cover. Write your thesis statement at the beginning of your outline. Then list the supporting details. Follow an outline form like the one on the next page.

(1) Everglades National Park is a beautiful but endangered animal habitat.

I. Special aspects of the Everglades
    A. Characteristics of wetlands
    (2) B. Endangered birds and animals
II. Pressures on the Everglades
    A. Florida agriculture
    B. Carelessness of visitors
III. How to protect the Everglades
    A. Change agricultural practices
    B. Educate park visitors
        1. Mandatory video on safety for individuals and environment (3)
        2. Instructional reminders posted throughout the park

(1) The thesis statement identifies your topic and the overall point you will make.

(2) If you have subtopics under a main topic, there must be at least two. They must relate directly to your main topic.

(3) If you wish to divide a subtopic, you must have at least two divisions. Each must relate to the subtopic above it.

Document Your Information

You must document, or credit, the sources of all the information you use in your report. There are two common ways to document information.

Footnotes

To document with footnotes, place a number at the end of the information you are documenting. Number your notes consecutively, beginning with number 1. These numbers should be slightly raised and should come after any punctuation. The documentation information itself goes at the bottom of the page, with a matching number.

In-text number for note:

The Declaration of Independence was read in public for the first time on July 6, 1776.[3]

Footnote at bottom of page:

[3] John Smith, The Declaration of Independence (New York: DI, 2001) 221.

Parenthetical Documentation

In this method, you give the source for your information in parentheses at the end of the sentence where the information appears. You do not need to give all the details of the source. Just provide enough information for your readers to identify it. Here are the basic rules to follow.

- Usually it is enough to give the author's last name and the number of the page where you found the information.

  The declaration was first read in public by militia colonel John Nixon (Smith 222).

- If you mention the author's name in the sentence, you do not need to repeat it in the parentheses.

  According to Smith, the reading was greeted with wild applause (224).

- If your source does not identify a particular author, as in a newspaper or encyclopedia article, give the first word or two of the title of the piece.

  The anniversary of the reading was commemorated by a parade and fireworks ("Reading Celebrated").

Full information on your sources goes in a list at the end of your paper.

Bibliography or Works Cited

At the end of your paper, list all the sources of information that you used in preparing your report. Arrange them alphabetically by the author's last name (or by the first word in the title if no author is mentioned) as shown below. Title this list *Works Cited.* (Use the term *bibliography* if all your sources are printed media, such as books, magazines, or newspapers.)

Works Cited ❶

❷ Bertram, Jeffrey. "African Bees: Fact or Myth?" *Orlando Sentinel* 18 Aug. 1999: D2.

❸ Gore, Rick. "Neanderthals." National Geographic. January 1996: 2–35. ❽

❹ Gould, Stephen J. The Panda's Thumb. New York: W. W. Norton & Co., 1982.

❺ "Governor Chiles Vetoes Anti-Everglades ❾ Bills–5/13/98." Friends of the Everglades. May 1998. 26 Aug 1998 <http://www.everglades.org/pressrel_may28.htm>.

❻ "Neanderthal man." The Columbia Encyclopedia. 5th Edition. New York: Columbia University Press, 1993.

❼ Pabst, Laura (Curator of Natural History Museum), Interview. March 11, 1998.

❶ Indent all but the first line of each item.

❷ Newspaper article

❸ Magazine article

❹ Book with one author

❺ On-line article

❻ Encyclopedia

❼ Interview

❽ Include page numbers for a magazine article but not for a book, unless the book is a collection of essays by different authors.

❾ Include database (underlined), publication medium (online), computer service, and date of access.

Business Writing

Two standard formats for business letters are block style and modified block style. In block style all the parts of the letter begin at the left-hand margin.

Business Letter

The following business letter uses modified block style

❶ 10 Pullman Lane
Cromwell, CT 06416
January 16, 2006

❷ Mr. Philip Fornaro
Principal
Cromwell School
179 West Maple St.
Cromwell, CT 06416

❸ Dear Mr. Fornaro:

❹ My friends and I in the seventh grade at Brimmer Middle School feel that there is not enough to do in Cromwell during the winter vacation week. Some students can afford to go away for vacation. Many families, however, cannot afford to go away, or the parents have to work.

❺ I would like to suggest that you keep the Brimmer Middle School gym open during the vacation week. If the gym were open, the basketball teams could practice. The fencing club could meet. We could meet our friends there instead of going to the mall.

❻ Thanks for listening to my request. I hope you will think it over.

❼ Sincerely,
Kim Goodwin
Kim Goodwin

❶ In the heading, write your address and the date on separate lines.

❷ In the inside address, write the name and address of the person to whom you are sending the letter.

❸ Use a colon after the greeting.

❹ In your introduction, say who you are and why you are writing.

❺ In the body of your letter, provide details concerning your request.

❻ Conclude by restating your purpose and thanking the person you are writing to.

❼ In the closing, use *Sincerely, Sincerely yours,* or *Yours truly* followed by a comma. Include both your signature and your printed or typed name.

General guidelines

Follow these guidelines when writing a business letter.

- Use correct business-letter form. Whether you write by hand, or use a computer, use 81/2-by-11-inch white or off-white paper. Be sure your letter is neat and clean.
- Use Standard English. Check your spelling carefully.
- Be polite, even if you are making a complaint or expressing a negative opinion.
- Be brief and to the point. State your reason for writing within the first two or three sentences.
- Include all necessary information.
- If you are making a request, be specific. Make sure what you are asking is reasonable. Express your appreciation at the end of the letter.
- Be considerate. Request only information you cannot get another way.
- When expressing an opinion or a complaint, state your reasons clearly and logically. Avoid emotional language.
- When requesting an interview, make it easy for the interviewee to meet with you. Suggest a few dates.

Writing a Memo

A memo, or memorandum, is a brief, efficient way of communicating information to another person or group of people. It begins with a header that provides basic information. A memo does not have a formal closing.

TO: *Brimmer Banner* newspaper staff
FROM: Terry Glinski
SUBJECT: Winter issue
DATE: January 18, 2006

Articles for the winter issue of the *Brimmer Banner* are due by February 1. Please see Terry about your assignment as soon as possible! The following articles or features have not yet been assigned:

Cafeteria Mess: Who Is Responsible?
Teacher Profile: Mr. Jinks, Ms. Magee
Sports roundup

Using a Computer for Writing

Using a computer offers advantages at every stage of the writing process.

Prewriting

A computer can help you gather and organize ideas and information.

Brainstorming

While brainstorming for topics or details, you can dim the computer screen and do "invisible writing." Some writers find that this technique allows their ideas to flow more freely.

Researching

Use the Internet or a CD-ROM encyclopedia to find not only text and pictures, but also sound, animated cartoons or graphics, and live-action video clips.

Outlining

Some word-processing programs offer an outlining feature that automatically indents headings and uses different type styles for main headings and subheadings.

Drafting/Revising

Most word-processing programs make it easy to do the following.

- *insert* new text at any point in your document
- *delete* or *copy* text
- *move* text from one position to another
- *undo* a change you just made
- *save* each draft or revision of your document
- *print* copies of your work-in-progress for others to read

Editing/Proofreading

You can edit and proofread directly on the computer, or you can mark your changes on a printout, or hard copy, and then input the changes on screen. The following word-processing features are helpful.

- **Grammar checker** The computer finds possible errors in grammar and suggests revisions.
- **Spelling checker** The computer finds misspellings and suggests corrections.
- **Thesaurus** If you want to replace an inappropriate or overused word, you can highlight the word and the computer will suggest synonyms.
- **Search and replace** If you want to change or correct something that occurs several times in your document, the computer can quickly make the change throughout the document.

TIP

The grammar checker, spelling checker, and thesaurus cannot replace your own careful reading and judgment. Because English grammar is so complex, the suggestions that the grammar checker makes may not be appropriate. Also, the spelling checker will not tell you that you have typed *brake* when you meant *break,* for example, because both are valid words. The thesaurus may offer you several synonyms for a word, but you need to consider the connotations of each before deciding which, if any, fits your context.

Presenting

The computer allows you to enhance the readability, attractiveness, and visual interest of your document in many ways.

Formatting your text

The computer gives you a variety of options for the layout and appearance of your text. You can easily add or change the following elements.

- margin width
- number of columns
- type size and style
- page numbering
- header or footer (information such as a title that appears at the top or bottom of every page)

Visual aids

Some word-processing programs have graphic functions that allow you to create graphs, charts, and diagrams. Collections of *clip art,* pictures you can copy and paste into your document, are also available.

Troubleshooter

Use the Troubleshooter to recognize and correct common writing errors.

Sentence Fragment

A sentence fragment does not express a complete thought. It may lack a subject or verb or both.

- **Problem: Fragment that lacks a subject**

The lion paced the floor of the cage. Looked hungry. *frag*

Solution: Add a subject to the fragment to make a complete sentence.

The lion paced the floor of the cage. He looked hungry.

- **Problem: Fragment that lacks a predicate**

I'm painting my room. The walls yellow. *frag*

Solution: Add a predicate to make the sentence complete.

I'm painting my room. The walls are going to be yellow.

- **Problem: Fragment that lacks both a subject and a predicate**

We walked around the reservoir. Near the parkway. *frag*

Solution: Combine the fragment with another sentence.

We walked around the reservoir near the parkway.

TIP

You can use fragments when talking with friends or writing personal letters. Some writers use fragments to produce a special effect. Use complete sentences, however, for school or business writing.

Run-on Sentence

A run-on sentence is two or more sentences written incorrectly as one sentence.

- **Problem: Two main clauses separated only by a comma**

Roller coasters make me dizzy, I don't enjoy them. *run-on*

Solution A: Replace the comma with a period or other end mark. Start the second sentence with a capital letter.

Roller coasters make me dizzy. I don't enjoy them.

Solution B: Replace the comma with a semicolon.

Roller coasters make me dizzy; I don't enjoy them.

- **Problem: Two main clauses with no punctuation between them**

Acid rain is a worldwide problem there are no solutions in sight. *run-on*

Solution A: Separate the main clauses with a period or other end mark. Begin the second sentence with a capital letter.

Acid rain is a worldwide problem. There are no solutions in sight.

Solution B: Add a comma and a coordinating conjunction between the main clauses.

Acid rain is a worldwide problem, but there are no solutions in sight.

- **Problem: Two main clauses with no comma before the coordinating conjunction**

Our chorus has been practicing all month but we still need another rehearsal. *run-on*

Solution: Add a comma before the coordinating conjunction.

Our chorus has been practicing all month, but we still need another rehearsal.

Lack of Subject-Verb Agreement

A singular subject calls for a singular form of the verb. A plural subject calls for a plural form of the verb.

- **Problem: A subject that is separated from the verb by an intervening prepositional phrase**

The two policemen at the construction site looks bored. *agr*

The members of my baby-sitting club is saving money. *agr*

Solution: Make sure that the verb agrees with the subject of the sentence, not with the object of the preposition. The object of a preposition is never the subject.

The two policemen at the construction site look bored.

The members of my baby-sitting club are saving money.

TIP

When subject and verb are separated by a prepositional phrase, check for agreement by reading the sentence without the prepositional phrase.

- **Problem: A sentence that begins with *here* or *there***

Here come the last bus to Pelham Heights. *agr*

There is my aunt and uncle. *agr*

Solution: In sentences that begin with *here* or *there*, look for the subject after the verb. Make sure that the verb agrees with the subject.

Here comes the last bus to Pelham Heights.

There are my aunt and uncle.

- **Problem: An indefinite pronoun as the subject**

Each of the candidates are qualified. *agr*

All of the problems on the test was hard. *agr*

Solution: Some indefinite pronouns are singular; some are plural; and some can be either singular or plural, depending on the noun they refer to. Determine whether the indefinite pronoun is singular or plural, and make sure the verb agrees with it.

Each of the candidates is qualified.

All of the problems on the test were hard.

- **Problem: A compound subject that is joined by *and***

Fishing tackle and a life jacket was stowed in the boat. *agr*

Peanut butter and jelly are delicious. *agr*

Solution A: If the compound subjects refer to different people or things, use a plural verb.

Fishing tackle and a life jacket were stowed in the boat.

Solution B: If the parts of a compound subject name one unit or if they refer to the same person or thing, use a singular verb.

Peanut butter and jelly is delicious.

- **Problem: A compound subject that is joined by *or* or *nor***

Either my aunt or my parents plans to attend parents' night. *agr*

Neither onions nor pepper improve the taste of this meatloaf. *agr*

Solution: Make the verb agree with the subject that is closer to it.

Either my aunt or my parents plan to attend parents' night.

Neither onions nor pepper improves the taste of this meatloaf.

Incorrect Verb Tense or Form

Verbs have different tenses to show when the action takes place.

- **Problem: An incorrect or missing verb ending**

  The Parks Department install a new water fountain last week.

  They have also plant flowers in all the flower beds.

  Solution: To form the past tense and the part participle, add *-ed* to a regular verb.

  The Parks Department installed a new water fountain last week.

  They have also planted flowers in all the flower beds.

- **Problem: An improperly formed irregular verb**

  Wendell has standed in line for two hours.

  I catched the fly ball and throwed it to first base.

  Solution: Irregular verbs vary in their past and past participle forms. Look up the ones you are not sure of.

  Wendell has stood in line for two hours.

  I caught the fly ball and threw it to first base.

- **Problem: Confusion between the past form and the past participle**

  The cast for *The Music Man* has began rehearsals.

  Solution: Use the past participle form of an irregular verb, not its past form, when you use the auxiliary verb *have*.

  The cast for *The Music Man* has begun rehearsals.

- **Problem: Improper use of the past participle**

  Our seventh grade drawn a mural for the wall of the cafeteria.

  Solution: Add the auxiliary verb *have* to the past participle of an irregular verb to form a complete verb.

  Our seventh grade has drawn a mural for the wall of the cafeteria.

TIP

Because irregular verbs vary, it is useful to memorize the verbs that you use most often.

Incorrect Use of Pronouns

The noun that a pronoun refers to is called its antecedent. A pronoun must refer to its **antecedent** clearly. Subject pronouns refer to subjects in a sentence. Object pronouns refer to objects in a sentence.

- **Problem: A pronoun that could refer to more than one antecedent**

  Gary and Mike are coming, but he doesn't know the other kids.

  Solution: Substitute a noun for the pronoun to make your sentence clearer.

  Gary and Mike are coming, but Gary doesn't know the other kids.

- **Problem: Personal pronouns as subjects**

  Him and John were freezing after skating for three hours.

  Lori and me decided not to audition for the musical.

  Solution: Use a subject pronoun as the subject part of a sentence.

  He and John were freezing after skating for three hours.

  Lori and I decided not to audition for the musical.

- **Problem: Personal pronouns as objects**

  Ms. Wang asked Reggie and I to enter the science fair

  Ms. Wang helped he and I with the project.

  Solution: Use an object pronoun as the object of a verb or a preposition.

  Ms. Wang asked Reggie and me to enter the science fair.

  Ms. Wang helped him and me with the project.

Incorrect Use of Adjectives

Some adjectives have irregular forms: comparative forms for comparing two things and superlative forms for comparing more than two things.

Problem: Incorrect use of *good, better, best*

Their team is more good at softball than ours. *adj*

They have more better equipment too. *adj*

Solution: The comparative and superlative forms of *good* are *better* and *best*. Do not use *more* or *most* before irregular forms of comparative and superlative adjectives.

Their team is better at softball than ours.

They have better equipment too.

Problem: Incorrect use of *bad, worse, worst*

The flooding on East Street was the baddest I've seen. *adj*

Mike's basement was in badder shape than his garage. *adj*

Solution: The comparative and superlative forms of *bad* are *worse* and *worst*. Do not use *more* or *most* or the endings *-er* or *-est* with *bad*.

The flooding on East Street was the worst I've seen.

Mike's basement was in worse shape than his garage.

Problem: Incorrect use of comparative and superlative adjectives

The Appalachian Mountains are more older than the Rockies. *adj*

Mount Washington is the most highest of the Appalachians. *adj*

Solution: Do not use both *-er* and *more* or *-est* and *most* at the same time.

The Appalachian Mountains are older than the Rockies.

Mount Washington is the highest of the Appalachians.

Incorrect Use of Commas

Commas signal a pause between parts of a sentence and help to clarify meaning.

Problem: Missing commas in a series of three or more items

Sergio put mustard catsup and bean sprouts on his hot dog. *com*

Solution: If there are three or more items in a series, use a comma after each one, including the item preceding the conjunction.

Sergio put mustard, catsup, and bean sprouts on his hot dog.

Problem: Missing commas with direct quotations

"A little cold water" the swim coach said "won't hurt you." *com*

Solution: The first part of an interrupted quotation ends with a comma followed by quotation marks. The interrupting words are also followed by a comma.

"A little cold water," the swim coach said, "won't hurt you."

Problem: Missing commas with nonessential appositives

My sneakers a new pair are covered with mud. *com*

Solution: Determine whether the appositive is important to the meaning of the sentence. If it is not essential, set off the appositive with commas.

My sneakers, a new pair, are covered with mud.

Incorrect Use of Apostrophes

An apostrophe shows possession. It can also indicate missing letters in a contraction.

Problem: Singular possessive nouns

A parrots toes are used for gripping. *poss*

The bus color was bright yellow. *poss*

Solution: Use an apostrophe and an *s* to form the possessive of a singular noun, even one that ends in *s*.

A parrot's toes are used for gripping.

The bus's color was bright yellow.

Problem: Plural possessive nouns ending in *-s*

The visitors center closes at five o'clock. *poss*

The guide put several tourists luggage in one compartment. *poss*

Solution: Use an apostrophe alone to form the possessive of a plural noun that ends in *s*.

The visitors' center closes at five o'clock.

The guide put several tourists' luggage in one compartment.

Problem: Plural possessive nouns not ending in *-s*

The peoples applause gave courage to the young gymnast. *poss*

Solution: Use an apostrophe and an *s* to form the possessive of a plural noun that does not end in *s*.

The people's applause gave courage to the young gymnast.

Problem: Possessive personal pronouns

Jenny found the locker that was her's; she waited while her friends found their's. *poss*

Solution: Do not use apostrophes with possessive personal pronouns.

Jenny found the locker that was hers; she waited while her friends found theirs.

Incorrect Capitalization

Proper nouns, proper adjectives, and the first words of sentences always begin with a capital letter.

Problem: Words referring to ethnic groups, nationalities, and languages

Many canadians in the province of quebec speak french. *cap*

Solution: Capitalize proper nouns and adjectives that refer to ethnic groups, nationalities, and languages.

Many Canadians in the province of Quebec speak French.

Problem: Words that refer to a family member

Yesterday aunt Doreen asked me to baby-sit. *cap*

Don't forget to give dad a call. *cap*

Solution: Capitalize words that are used as part of or in place of a family member's name.

Yesterday Aunt Doreen asked me to baby-sit.

Don't forget to give Dad a call.

TIP

Do not capitalize a word that identifies a family member when it is preceded by a possessive adjective: *My father bought a new car.*

Problem: The first word of a direct quotation

The judge declared, "the court is now in session." *cap*

Solution: Capitalize the first word in a direct quotation.

The judge declared, "The court is now in session."

TIP

If you have difficulty with a rule of usage, try rewriting the rule in your own words. Check with your teacher to be sure you understand the rule.

Troublesome Words

This section will help you choose between words and expressions that are often confusing or misused.

accept, except

Accept means "to receive." *Except* means "other than."

Phillip walked proudly to the stage to accept the award.

Everything fits in my suitcase except my sleeping bag.

affect, effect

Affect is a verb meaning "to cause a change in" or "to influence." *Effect* as a verb means "to bring about or accomplish." As a noun, *effect* means "result."

Bad weather will affect our plans for the weekend.

The new medicine effected an improvement in the patient's condition.

The gloomy weather had a bad effect on my mood.

ain't

Ain't is never used in formal speaking or writing unless you are quoting the exact words of a character or a real person. Instead of using *ain't,* say or write *am not, is not, are not;* or use contractions such as *I'm not, she isn't.*

The pizza is not going to arrive for another half hour.

The pizza isn't going to arrive for another half hour.

a lot

The expression *a lot* means "much" or "many" and should always be written as two words. Some authorities discourage its use in formal writing.

A lot of my friends are learning Spanish.

Many of my friends are learning Spanish.

all ready, already

All ready, written as two words, is a phrase that means "completely ready." *Already,* written as one word, is an adverb that means "before" or "by this time."

By the time the fireworks display was all ready, we had already arrived.

all right, alright

The expression *all right* should be written as two words. Some dictionaries do list the single word *alright* but usually not as a preferred spelling.

Tom hurt his ankle, but he will be all right.

all together, altogether

All together means "in a group." *Altogether* means "completely."

The Minutemen stood all together at the end of Lexington Green.

The rebel farmers were not altogether sure that they could fight the British soldiers.

among, between

Use *among* for three or more people, things, or groups. Use *between* for two people, things, or groups.

Mr. Kendall divided the jobs for the car wash among the team members.

Our soccer field lies between the gym and Main Street.

amount, number

Use *amount* with nouns that cannot be counted. Use *number* with nouns that can be counted.

This recipe calls for an unusual amount of pepper.

A record number of students attended last Saturday's book fair.

bad, badly

Bad is an adjective; it modifies a noun.
Badly is an adverb; it modifies a verb, an adjective, or another adverb.

The badly burnt cookies left a bad smell in the kitchen.

Joseph badly wants to be on the track team.

beside, besides
Beside means "next to." *Besides* means "in addition to."

The zebra is grazing beside a wildebeest.

Besides the zoo, I like to visit the aquarium.

bring, take
Bring means "to carry from a distant place to a closer one." *Take* means "to carry from a nearby place to a more distant one."

Please bring a bag lunch and subway money to school tomorrow.

Don't forget to take your art projects home this afternoon.

can, may
Can implies the ability to do something. *May* implies permission to do something.

You may take a later bus home if you can remember which bus to get on.

TIP

Although *can* is sometimes used in place of *may* in informal speech, a distinction should be made when speaking and writing formally.

choose, chose
Choose means "to select." *Chose,* the past tense of *choose,* means "selected."

Dad helped me choose a birthday card for my grandmother.

Dad chose a card with a funny joke inside.

doesn't, don't
The subject of the contraction **doesn't** *(does not)* is the third-person singular (*he* or *she*). The subject of the contraction **don't** *(do not)* is *I, you, we,* or *they.*

Tanya doesn't have any tickets for the concert.

We don't need tickets if we stand in the back row.

farther, further
Farther refers to physical distance. *Further* refers to time or degree.

Our new apartment is farther away from the school.

I will not continue this argument further.

fewer, less
Fewer is used to refer to things or qualities that can be counted. *Less* is used to refer to things or qualities that cannot be counted. In addition, *less* is used with figures that are regarded as single amounts.

Fewer people were waiting in line after lunch.

There is less fat in this kind of peanut butter.

Try to spend less than ten dollars on a present. [The money is treated as a single sum, not as individual dollars.]

good, well
Good is often used as an adjective meaning "pleasing" or "able." *Well* may be used as an adverb of manner telling how ably something is done or as an adjective meaning "in good health."

That is a good haircut.

Marco writes well.

Because Ms. Rodriguez had a headache, she was not well enough to correct our tests.

in, into
In means "inside." *Into* indicates a movement from outside toward the inside.

Refreshments will be sold in the lobby of the auditorium.

The doors opened, and the eager crowd rushed into the auditorium.

it's, its
Use an apostrophe to form the contraction of *it is.* The possessive of the personal pronoun *it* does not take an apostrophe.

It's hard to keep up with computer technology.

The computer industry seems to change its products daily.

lay, lie

Lay means "to place." *Lie* means "to recline."

I will lay my beach towel here on the warm sand.

Help! I don't want to lie next to a hill of red ants!

learn, teach

Learn means "to gain knowledge." *Teach* means "to give knowledge."

I don't learn very quickly.

My uncle is teaching me how to juggle.

leave, let

Leave means "to go away." *Let* means "to allow." With the word *alone,* you may use either *let* or *leave.*

Huang has to leave at eight o'clock.

Mr. Davio lets the band practice in his basement.

Leave me alone. Let me alone.

like, as

Use *like,* a preposition, to introduce a prepositional phrase. Use *as,* a subordinating conjunction, to introduce a subordinate clause. Many authorities believe that *like* should not be used before a clause in formal English.

Andy sometimes acts like a clown.

The detective looked carefully at the empty suitcase as she examined the room.

TIP

As can be a preposition in cases like the following: *Jack went to the costume party as a giant pumpkin.*

loose, lose

Loose means "not firmly attached." *Lose* means "to misplace" or "to fail to win."

If you keep wiggling that loose tooth, you might lose it.

raise, rise

Raise means to "cause to move up." *Rise* means "to move upward."

Farmers in this part of Florida raise sugarcane.

The hot air balloon began to rise slowly in the morning sky.

set, sit

Set means "to place" or "to put." *Sit* means "to place oneself in a seated position."

I set the tips of my running shoes against the starting line.

After running the fifty-yard dash, I had to sit down and catch my breath.

than, then

Than introduces the second part of a comparison. *Then* means "at that time" or "after that."

I'd rather go to Disney World in the winter than in the summer.

The park is too crowded and hot then.

their, they're

Their is the possessive form of they. *They're* is the contraction of *they are.*

They're visiting Plymouth Plantation during their vacation.

to, too, two

To means "in the direction of." *Too* means "also" or "to an excessive degree." *Two* is the number after one.

I bought two tickets to the concert.

The music was too loud.

It's my favorite group too.

who, whom

Who is a subject pronoun. *Whom* is an object pronoun.

Who has finished the test already?

Mr. Russo is the man to whom we owe our thanks.

who's, whose

Who's is the contraction of *who is. Whose* is the possessive form of *who.*

Who's going to wake me up in the morning?

The policeman discovered whose car alarm was making so much noise.

Mechanics

This section will help you use correct capitalization, punctuation, and abbreviations in your writing.

Capitalization

Capitalizing Sentences, Quotations, and Salutations

Rule: A capital letter appears at the beginning of a sentence.

Example: **A**nother gust of wind shook the house.

Rule: A capital letter marks the beginning of a direct quotation that is a complete sentence.

Example: Sabrina said, "**T**he lights might go out."

Rule: When a quoted sentence is interrupted by explanatory words, such as she said, do not begin the second part of the sentence with a capital letter.

Example: "There's a rainbow," exclaimed Jeffrey, "**o**ver the whole beach."

Rule: When the second part of a quotation is a new sentence, put a period after the explanatory words; begin the new part with a capital letter.

Example: "Please come inside," Justin said. "**W**ipe your feet."

Rule: Do not capitalize an indirect quotation.

Example: Jo said that **t**he storm was getting worse.

Rule: Capitalize the first word in the salutation and closing of a letter. Capitalize the title and name of the person addressed.

Example: **D**ear **D**r. **M**enino
Dear **E**ditor
Sincerely

Capitalizing Names and Titles of People

Rule: Capitalize the names of people and the initials that stand for their names.

Example: **M**alcolm **X** **J. F. K.**
Robert **E. L**ee **Q**ueen **E**lizabeth I

Rule: Capitalize a title or an abbreviation of a title when it comes before a person's name or when it is used in direct address.

Example: **D**r. **S**alinas
"Your patient, **D**octor, is waiting."

Rule: Do not capitalize a title that follows or is a substitute for a person's name.

Example: Marcia Salinas is a good **d**octor.
He asked to speak to the **d**octor.

Rule: Capitalize the names and abbreviations of academic degrees that follow a person's name. Capitalize Jr. and Sr.

Example: Marcia Salinas, **M.D.**
Raoul Tobias, **A**ttorney
Donald Bruns **S**r.
Ann Lee, **P**h.**D.**

Rule: Capitalize words that show family relationships when used as titles or as substitutes for a person's name.

Example: We saw **U**ncle Carlos.
She read a book about **M**other **T**eresa.

Rule: Do not capitalize words that show family relationships when they follow a possessive noun or pronoun.

Example: Your **b**rother will give us a ride.
I forgot my **m**other's phone number.

Rule: Always capitalize the pronoun I.

Example: After **I** clean my room, **I**'m going swimming.

Capitalizing Names of Places

TIP

Do not capitalize articles and prepositions in proper nouns: *the Rock of Gibraltar, the Statue of Liberty.*

Rule: Capitalize the names of cities, counties, states, countries, and continents.

Example: **S**t. **L**ouis, **M**issouri
Marin **C**ounty
Australia
South **A**merica

Rule: Capitalize the names of bodies of water and other geographical features.

Example: the **G**reat **L**akes **C**ape **C**od
the **D**ust **B**owl

Rule: Capitalize the names of sections of a country and regions of the world.

Example: **E**ast **A**sia
New **E**ngland
the **P**acific **R**im
the **M**idwest

Rule: Capitalize compass points when they refer to a specific section of a country.

Example: the **N**orthwest the **S**outh

Rule: Do not capitalize compass points when they indicate direction.

Example: Canada is **n**orth of the United States.

Rule: Do not capitalize adjectives indicating direction.

Example: **w**estern Utah

Rule: Capitalize the names of streets and highways.

Example: **D**orchester **A**venue **R**oute 22

Rule: Capitalize the names of buildings, bridges, monuments, and other structures.

Example: **L**incoln **M**emorial
Chesapeake **B**ay **B**ridge

Capitalizing Other Proper Nouns and Adjectives

Rule: Capitalize the names of clubs, organizations, businesses, institutions, and political parties.

Example: **H**ouston **O**ilers
the **F**ood and **D**rug **A**dministration
Boys and **G**irls **C**lub

Rule: Capitalize brand names but not the nouns following them.

Example: **Z**ippo brand energy bar

Rule: Capitalize the names of days of the week, months, and holidays.

Example: **S**aturday **J**une
Thanksgiving **D**ay

Rule: Do not capitalize the names of seasons.

Example: **w**inter, **s**pring, **s**ummer, **f**all

Rule: Capitalize the first word, the last word, and all important words in the title of a book, play, short story, poem, essay, article, film, television series, song, magazine, newspaper, and chapter of a book.

Example: ***N**ot **W**ithout **L**aughter*
***W**orld **B**ook **E**ncyclopedia*
"**J**ingle **B**ells"
Star **W**ars
Chapter 12

Rule: Capitalize the names of ethnic groups, nationalities, and languages.

Example: **L**atino **J**apanese
European **S**panish

Rule: Capitalize proper adjectives that are formed from the names of ethnic groups and nationalities.

Example: **S**hetland pony
Jewish holiday

LANGUAGE HANDBOOK

Punctuation

Using the Period and Other End Marks

Rule: Use a period at the end of a declarative sentence.

My great-grandfather fought in the Mexican Revolution.

Rule: Use a period at the end of an imperative sentence that does not express strong feeling.

Please set the table.

Rule: Use a question mark at the end of an interrogative sentence.

How did your sneakers get so muddy?

Rule: Use an exclamation point at the end of an exclamatory sentence or a strong imperative.

How exciting the play was!

Watch out!

Using Commas

Rule: Use commas to separate three or more items in a series.

The canary eats bird seed, fruit, and suet.

Rule: Use commas to show a pause after an introductory word and to set off names used in direct address.

Yes, I offered to take care of her canary this weekend.

Please, Stella, can I borrow your nail polish?

Rule: Use a comma after two or more introductory prepositional phrases or when the comma is needed to make the meaning clear. A comma is not needed after a single short prepositional phrase, but it is acceptable to use one.

From the back of the balcony, we had a lousy view of the stage.

After the movie we walked home. (no comma needed)

Rule: Use a comma after an introductory participle and an introductory participial phrase.

Whistling and moaning, the wind shook the little house.

Rule: Use commas to set off words that interrupt the flow of thought in a sentence.

Tomorrow, I think, our projects are due.

Rule: Use a comma after conjunctive adverbs such as *however, moreover, furthermore, nevertheless,* and *therefore.*

The skating rink is crowded on Saturday; however, it's the only time I can go.

Rule: Use commas to set off an appositive if it is not essential to the meaning of a sentence.

Ben Wagner, a resident of Pittsfield, won the first round in the golf tournament.

Rule: Use a comma before a conjunction (*and, or, but, nor, so, yet*) that joins main clauses.

We can buy our tickets now, or we can take a chance on buying them just before the show.

Rule: Use a comma after an introductory adverb clause.

Because I stayed up so late, I'm sleepy this morning.

Rule: In most cases, do not use a comma with an adverb clause that comes at the end of a sentence.

The picnic will be canceled unless the weather clears.

Rule: Use a comma or a pair of commas to set off an adjective clause that is not essential to the meaning of a sentence.

Tracy, who just moved here from Florida, has never seen snow before.

Rule: Do not use a comma or pair of commas to set off an essential clause from the rest of the sentence.

Anyone who signs up this month will get a discount.

Rule: Use commas before and after the year when it is used with both the month and the day. If only the month and the year are given, do not use a comma.

On January 2, 1985, my parents moved to Dallas, Texas.

I was born in May 1985.

Rule: Use commas before and after the name of a state or a country when it is used with the name of a city. Do not use a comma after the state if it is used with a ZIP code.

The area code for Concord, New Hampshire, is 603.

Please forward my mail to 6 Madison Lane, Topsham, ME 04086

Rule: Use commas or a pair of commas to set off an abbreviated title or degree following a person's name.

The infirmary was founded by Elizabeth Blackwell, M.D., the first woman in the United States to earn a medical degree.

Rule: Use a comma or commas to set off *too* when *too* means "also."

We, too, bought groceries, from the new online supermarket.

Rule: Use a comma or commas to set off a direct quotation.

"My nose," exclaimed Pinocchio, "is growing longer!"

Rule: Use a comma after the salutation of a friendly letter and after the closing of both a friendly letter and a business letter.

Dear Gary,

Sincerely,

Best regards,

Rule: Use a comma when necessary to prevent misreading of a sentence.

In math, solutions always elude me.

Using Semicolons and Colons

Rule: Use a semicolon to join the parts of a compound sentence when a coordinating conjunction, such as *and, or, nor,* or *but,* is not used.

Don't be late for the dress rehearsal; it begins at 7 o'clock sharp.

Rule: Use a semicolon to join parts of a compound sentence when the main clauses are long and are subdivided by commas. Use a semicolon even if these clauses are already joined by a coordinating conjunction.

In the gray light of early morning, on a remote airstrip in the desert, two pilots prepared to fly on a dangerous mission; but accompanying them were a television camera crew, three newspaper reporters, and a congressman from their home state of Nebraska.

Rule: Use a semicolon to separate main clauses joined by a conjunctive adverb. Be sure to use a comma after the conjunctive adverb.

We've been climbing all morning; therefore, we need a rest.

Rule: Use a colon to introduce a list of items that ends a sentence. Use words such as *these, the following,* or *as follows* to signal that a list is coming.

Remember to bring the following items: a backpack, a bag lunch, sunscreen, and insect repellent.

Rule: Do not use a colon to introduce a list preceded by a verb or preposition.

Remember to bring a backpack, a bag lunch, sunscreen, and insect repellent. (No colon is used after *bring.*)

Rule: Use a colon to separate the hour and the minutes when you write the time of day.

My Spanish class starts at 9:15.

Rule: Use a colon after the salutation of a business letter.

Dear Dr. Coulombe:
Director of the Personnel Dept.:

Using Quotation Marks and Italics

Rule: Use quotation marks before and after a direct quotation.

"Curiouser and curiouser," said Alice.

Rule: Use quotation marks with both parts of a divided quotation.

"This gymnastics trick," explained Amanda, "took me three months to learn."

Rule: Use a comma or commas to separate a phrase such as *she said* from the quotation itself. Place the comma that precedes the phrase inside the closing quotation marks.

"I will be late," said the cable technician, "for my appointment."

Rule: Place a period that ends a quotation inside the closing quotation marks.

Scott said, "Thanks for letting me borrow your camping tent."

Rule: Place a question mark or an exclamation point inside the quotation marks when it is part of the quotation.

"Why is the door of your snake's cage open?" asked my mother.

Rule: Place a question mark or an exclamation point outside the quotation marks when it is part of the entire sentence.

How I love "The Pit and the Pendulum"!

Rule: Use quotation marks for the title of a short story, essay, poem, song, magazine or newspaper article, or book chapter.

short story: "The Necklace"
poem: "The Fish"
article: "Fifty Things to Make from Bottlecaps"

Rule: Use italics or underlining for the title of a book, play, film, television series, magazine, newspaper, or work of art.

book: *To Kill a Mockingbird*
magazine: *The New Republic*
painting: *Sunflowers*

Rule: Use italics or underlining for the names of ships, trains, airplanes, and spacecraft.

ship: *Mayflower*
airplane: *Air Force One*

Using Apostrophes

Rule: Use an apostrophe and an *s ('s)* to form the possessive of a singular noun.

my brother's rock collection
Chris's hat

Rule: Use an apostrophe and an *s ('s)* to form the possessive of a plural noun that does not end in *s.*

the geese's feathers
the oxen's domestication

TIP

If a thing is owned jointly by two or more individuals, only the last name should show possession: *Mom and Dad's car.* If the ownership is not joint, each name should show possession: *Mom and Dad's parents are coming for Thanksgiving.*

Rule: Use an apostrophe alone to form the possessive of a plural noun that ends in *s.*

the animals' habitat
the instruments' sound

Rule: Use an apostrophe and an *s ('s)* to form the possessive of an indefinite pronoun.

everyone's homework
someone's homework

Rule: Do not use an apostrophe in a possessive pronoun.

The dog knocked over its dish.
Yours is the best entry in the contest.
One of these drawings must be hers.

Rule: Use an apostrophe to replace letters that have been omitted in a contraction.

it + is = it's
can + not = can't
I + have = I've

Rule: Use an apostrophe to form the plural of a letter, a figure, or a word that is used as itself.

Write three 7's.
The word is spelled with two m's.
The sentence contains three and's.

Rule: Use an apostrophe to show missing numbers in a year.

the class of '02

Using Hyphens, Dashes, and Parentheses

Rule: Use a hyphen to show the division of a word at the end of a line. Always divide the word between its syllables.

With the new recycling program, more residents are recycling
their trash.

TIP

One-letter divisions (for example, *e-lectric*) are not permissible. Avoid dividing personal names, if possible.

Rule: Use a hyphen in a number written as a compound word.

He sold forty-six ice creams in one hour.

Rule: Use a hyphen in a fraction.

We won the vote by a two-thirds majority.

Two-thirds of the votes have been counted.

Rule: Use a hyphen or hyphens in certain compound nouns.

great-grandmother

merry-go-round

Rule: Hyphenate a compound modifier only when it precedes the word it modifies.

A well-known musician visited our school.

The story was well written.

Rule: Use a hyphen after the prefixes *all-*, *ex-*, and *self-* when they are joined to any noun or adjective.

all-star

ex-president

self-conscious

Rule: Use a hyphen to separate any prefix from a word that begins with a capital letter.

un-American

mid-January

Rule: Use a dash or dashes to show a sudden break or change in thought or speech.

Daniel—he's kind of a pest—is my youngest cousin.

Rule: Use parentheses to set off words that define or helpfully explain a word in the sentence.

The transverse flute (*transverse* means "sideways") is a wind instrument.

Abbreviations

Rule: Abbreviate the titles *Mr., Mrs., Ms.,* and *Dr.* before a person's name. Also abbreviate any professional or academic degree that follows a name. The titles *Jr.* and *Sr.* are *not* preceded by a comma.

Dr. Stanley Livingston (doctor)

Luisa Mendez, M.A. (Master of Arts)

Martin Luther King Jr.

Rule: Use capital letters and no periods with abbreviations that are pronounced letter by letter or as words. Exceptions are *U.S.* and *Washington, D.C.,* which do use periods.

NAACP	National Association for the Advancement of Colored People
UFO	unidentified flying object
MADD	Mothers Against Driving Drunk

Rule: With exact times use A.M. (*ante meridiem,* "before noon") and P.M. (*post meridiem,* "after noon"). For years use B.C. (before Christ) and, sometimes, A.D. (*anno Domini,* "in the year of the lord," after Christ).

8:15 A.M.	6:55 P.M.
5000 B.C.	A.D. 235

Rule: Abbreviate days and months only in charts and lists.

School will be closed on

Mon., Sept. 3

Wed., Nov. 11

Thurs., Nov. 27

Rule: In scientific writing abbreviate units of measure. Use periods with English units but not with metric units.

inch(es) in.	yard(s) yd.
meter(s) m	milliliter(s) ml

LANGUAGE HANDBOOK

Rule: On envelopes only, abbreviate street names and state names. In general text, spell out street names and state names.

Ms. Karen Holmes

347 Grandville St.

Tilton, NH 03276

Karen lives on Grandville Street in Tilton, New Hampshire.

Writing Numbers

Rule: In charts and tables, always write numbers as numerals. Other rules apply to numbers not in charts or tables.

Student Test Scores

Student	Test 1	Test 2	Test 3
Lai, W.	82	89	94
Ostos, A.	78	90	86

Rule: Spell out a number that is expressed in one or two words.

We carried enough supplies for twenty-three days.

Rule: Use a numeral for a number of more than two words.

The tallest mountain in Mexico rises 17,520 feet.

Rule: Spell out a number that begins a sentence, or reword the sentence so that it does not begin with a number.

One hundred forty-three days later the baby elephant was born.

The baby elephant was born 143 days later.

Rule: Write a very large number as a numeral followed by the word *million* or *billion.*

There are 15 million people living in or near Mexico City.

Rule: Related numbers should be written in the same way. If one number must be written as a numeral, use numerals for all the numbers.

There are 365 days in the year, but only 52 weekends.

Rule: Spell out an ordinal number (*first, second*).

Welcome to our fifteenth annual convention.

Rule: Use words to express the time of day unless you are writing the exact time or using the abbreviation A.M. or P.M.

My guitar lesson is at five o'clock. It ends by 5:45 P.M.

Rule: Use numerals to express dates, house and street numbers, apartment and room numbers, telephone numbers, page numbers, amounts of money of more than two words, and percentages. Write out the word *percent.*

August 5, 1999

9 Davio Dr.

Apartment 9F

24 percent

Spelling

The following rules, examples, and exceptions can help you master the spelling of many words.

Spelling *ie* and *ei*

Put *i* before *e* except when both letters follow *c* or when both letters are pronounced together as an **a** sound.

believe	sieve	weight
receive	relieve	neighborhood

It is helpful to memorize exceptions to this rule. Exceptions include the following words: *species, science, weird, either, seize, leisure,* and *protein*.

Spelling unstressed vowels

Notice the vowel sound in the second syllable of the word *won-d_r-ful*. This is the unstressed vowel sound; dictionary respellings use the schwa symbol (ə) to indicate it. Because any of several vowels can be used to spell this sound, you might find yourself uncertain about which vowel to use. To spell words with unstressed vowels, try thinking of a related word in which the syllable containing the vowel sound is stressed.

Unknown Spelling	Related Word	Word Spelled Correctly
wond_rful	wonder	wonderful
fort_fications	fortify	fortifications
res_dent	reside	resident

Suffixes and the silent *e*

For most words with silent *e*, keep the e when adding a suffix. When you add the suffix *-ly* to a word that ends in *l* plus silent *e*, drop the *-le*. Also drop the silent *e* when you add a suffix beginning with a vowel or a *y*.

wise + ly = wisely
peaceful + ly = peacefully
skate + ing = skating
gentle + ly = gently

There are exceptions to the rule, including the following:

awe + ful = awful
judge + ment = judgment
true + ly = truly
noise + y = noisy
dye + ing = dyeing
mile + age = mileage

Suffixes and the final *y*

When you are adding a suffix to words ending with a vowel + *y*, keep the *y*. For words ending with a consonant + *y*, change the *y* to *i* unless the suffix begins with *i*. To avoid having two *i*'s together, keep the *y*.

enjoy + ment = enjoyment
merry + ment = merriment
display + ed = displayed
lazy + ness = laziness
play + ful = playful
worry + ing = worrying

Note: For some words, there are alternate spellings:

sly + er = slyer or slier
shy + est = shyest or shiest

Adding prefixes

When you add a prefix to a word, do not change the spelling of the word.

un + done = undone
re + schedule = reschedule
il + legible = illegible
semi + sweet = semisweet

Doubling the final consonant

Double the final consonant when a word ends with a single consonant following one vowel and the word is one syllable, or when the last syllable of the word is accented both before and after adding the suffix.

sit + ing = sitting
rub + ing = rubbing
commit + ed = committed
confer + ed = conferred

Do not double the final consonant if the suffix begins with a consonant, if the accent is not on the last syllable, or if the accent moves when the suffix is added.

cancel + ing = canceling
commit + ment = commitment
travel + ed = traveled
defer + ence = deference

Do not double the final consonant if the word ends in two consonants or if the suffix begins with a consonant.

climb + er = climber
nervous + ness = nervousness
import + ance = importance
star + dom = stardom

When adding *-ly* to a word that ends in *ll*, drop one *l*.

hill + ly = hilly full + ly = fully

Forming compound words

When forming compound words, keep the original spelling of both words.

home + work = homework
scare + crow = scarecrow
pea + nut = peanut

Forming Plurals

General Rules for Plurals		
If the noun ends in	**Rule**	**Example**
s, ch, sh, x, or *z*	add *-es*	loss➛losses, latch➛latches, box➛boxes, bush➛bushes, quiz➛quizzes
a consonant + *y*	change *y* to *i* and add *-es*	ferry➛ferries, baby➛babies, worry➛worries
a vowel + *y*	add *-s*	chimney➛chimneys, monkey➛monkeys, toy➛toys
a vowel + *o*	add *-s*	cameo➛cameos, radio➛radios, rodeo➛rodeos
a consonant + *o*	add *-es* but sometimes add *-s*	potato➛potatoes, echo➛echoes photo➛photos, solo➛solos
f or *ff*	add *-s* but sometimes change *f* to *v* and add *-es*	proof➛proofs, bluff➛bluffs sheaf➛sheaves, thief➛thieves, hoof➛hooves
lf	change *f* to *v* and add *-es*	calf➛calves, half➛halves, loaf➛loaves
fe	change *f* to *v* and add *-s*	knife➛knives, life➛lives

Special Rules for Plurals	
Rule	**Example**
To form the plural of most proper names and one-word compound nouns, follow the general rules for plurals.	Jones➛Joneses, Thomas➛Thomases, Hatch➛Hatches
To form the plural of hyphenated compound nouns or compound nouns of more than one word, make the most important word plural.	credit card➛credit cards mother-in-law➛mothers-in-law district attorney➛district attorneys
Some nouns have irregular plural forms and do not follow any rules.	man➛men, foot➛feet, tooth➛teeth
Some nouns have the same singular and plural forms	deer➛deer, species➛species, sheep➛sheep

LISTENING, SPEAKING, AND VIEWING HANDBOOK

Listening Effectively

A large part of the school day is spent either listening or speaking to others. By becoming a better listener and speaker, you will know more about what is expected of you and understand more about your audience.

Listening to instructions in class

Some of the most important listening in the school day involves listening to instructions. Use the following tips to help you.

- First, make sure you understand what you are listening for. Are you receiving instructions for homework or for a test? What you listen for depends upon the type of instructions being given.
- Think about what you are hearing, and keep your eyes on the speaker. This will help you stay focused on the important points.
- Listen for keywords, or word clues. Examples of word clues are phrases such as *above all, most important,* or *the three basic parts.* These clues help you identify important points that you should remember.
- Take notes on what you hear. Write down only the most important parts of the instructions.
- If you don't understand something, ask questions. Then if you're still unsure about the instructions, repeat them aloud to your teacher to receive correction on any key points that you may have missed.

Interpreting nonverbal clues

Understanding nonverbal clues is part of effective listening. Nonverbal clues are everything you notice about a speaker *except* what the speaker says. As you listen, ask yourself these questions:

- Where and how is the speaker standing?
- Are some words spoken more loudly than others?
- Does the speaker make eye contact?
- Does he or she smile or look angry?
- What message is sent by the speaker's gestures and facial expression?

PRACTICE

Work with a partner to practice listening to instructions. Each of you should find a set of directions for using a simple device–for example, a mechanical tool, a telephone answering machine, or a VCR. Study the instructions carefully. If you can bring the device to class, ask your partner to try to use it by following your step-by-step instructions. If you cannot have the device in class, ask your partner to explain the directions back to you. Then change roles and listen as your partner gives you a set of directions.

Speaking Effectively

- Speak slowly, clearly, and in a normal tone of voice. Raise your voice a bit, or use gestures to stress important points.
- Pause a few seconds after making an important point.
- Use words that help your audience picture what you're talking about. Visual aids such as pictures, graphs, charts, and maps can also help make your information clear.
- Stay in contact with your audience. Make sure your eyes move from person to person in the group you're addressing.

Speaking informally

Most oral communication is informal. When you speak casually with your friends, family, and neighbors, you use informal speech. Human relationships depend on this form of communication.

- Be courteous. Listen until the other person has finished speaking.
- Speak in a relaxed and spontaneous manner.
- Make eye contact with your listeners.
- Do not monopolize a conversation.
- When telling a story, show enthusiasm.
- When giving an announcement or directions, speak clearly and slowly. Check that your listeners understand the information.

Presenting an oral report

The steps in preparing an oral report are similar to the steps in the writing process. Complete each step carefully and you can be confident of presenting an effective oral report.

Steps in Preparing an Oral Report	
Prewriting	Determine your purpose and audience. Decide on a topic and narrow it.
Drafting	Make an outline. Fill in the supporting details. Write the report.
Revising and editing	Review your draft. Check the organization of ideas and details. Reword unclear statements.
Practicing	Practice the report aloud in front of a family member. Time the report. Ask for and accept advice.
Presenting	Relax in front of your audience. Make eye contact with your audience. Speak slowly and clearly.

PRACTICE

Pretend that you have been invited to give an oral report to a group of fifth graders. Your report will tell them what to expect and how to adjust to new conditions when they enter middle school. As you plan your report, keep your purpose and your audience in mind. Include lively descriptions and examples to back up your suggestions and hold your audience's attention. As you practice giving your report, be sure to give attention to your body language as well as your vocal projection. Ask a partner to listen to your report to give you feedback on how to improve your performance. Do the same for your partner after listening to his or her report.

Viewing Effectively

Critical viewing means thinking about what you see while watching a TV program, newscast, film, or video. It requires paying attention to what you hear and see and deciding whether information is true, false, or exaggerated. If the information seems to be true, try to determine whether it is based on a fact or an opinion.

Fact versus opinion

A **fact** is something that can be proved. An opinion is what someone believes is true. **Opinions** are based on feelings and experiences and cannot be proved.

Television commercials, political speeches, and even the evening news contain both facts and opinions. They use emotional words and actions to persuade the viewer to agree with a particular point of view. They may also use faulty reasoning, such as linking an effect with the wrong cause. Think through what is being said. The speaker may seem sincere, but do his or her reasons make sense? Are the reasons based on facts or on unfair generalizations?

Commercials contain both obvious and hidden messages. Just as you need to discover the author's purpose when you read a writer's words, you must be aware of the purpose of nonverbal attempts to persuade you. What does the message sender want, and how is the sender trying to influence you?

For example, a magazine or TV ad picturing a group of happy teenagers playing volleyball on a sunny beach expresses a positive feeling. The advertiser hopes viewers will transfer that positive feeling to the product being advertised—perhaps a soft drink or a brand of beachwear. This technique, called **transfer,** is one of several propaganda techniques regularly used by advertisers to influence consumers.

Following are a few other common techniques.

Testimonial—Famous and admired people recommend or praise a product, a policy, or a course of action even though they probably have no professional knowledge or expertise to back up their opinion.

Bandwagon—People are urged to follow the crowd ("get on the bandwagon") by buying a product, voting for a candidate, or whatever else the advertiser wants them to do.

Glittering generalities—The advertiser uses positive, good-sounding words (for example, *all-American* or *medically proven*) to impress people.

PRACTICE

Think of a television commercial that you have seen often or watch a new one and take notes as you watch it. Then analyze the commercial.

- What is the purpose behind the ad?
- What is expressed in written or spoken words?
- What is expressed nonverbally (in music or sound effects as well as in pictures and actions)?
- What methods does the advertiser use to persuade viewers?
- What questions would you ask the advertiser if you could?
- How effective is the commercial? Why?

Working in Groups

Working in a group is an opportunity to learn from others. Whether you are planning a group project (such as a class trip) or solving a math problem, each person in a group brings specific strengths and interests to the task. When a task is large, such as planting a garden, a group provides the necessary energy and talent to get the job done.

Small groups vary in size according to the nature of the task. Three to five students is a good size for most small-group tasks. Your teacher may assign you to a group, or you may be asked to form your own group. Don't work with your best friend if you are likely to chat too much. Successful groups often have a mix of student abilities and interests.

Individual role assignments give everyone in a group something to do. One student, the group recorder, may take notes. Another may lead the discussion, and another report the results to the rest of the class.

Roles for a Small Group	
Reviewer	Reads or reviews the assignment and makes sure everyone understands it
Recorder 1 (of the process)	Takes notes on the discussion
Recorder 2 (of the results)	Takes notes on the final results
Reporter	Reports results to the rest of the class
Discussion leader	Asks questions to get the discussion going; keeps the group focused
Facilitator	Helps the group resolve disagreements and reach a compromise

For a small group of three or four students, some of these roles can be combined. Your teacher may assign a role to each student in your group. Or you may be asked to choose your own role.

Tips for working in groups

- Review the group assignment and goal. Be sure that everyone in the group understands the assignment.
- Review the amount of time allotted for the task. Decide how your group will organize its time.
- Check that all the group members understand their roles in the group.
- When a question arises, try to solve it as a group before asking a teacher for help.
- Listen to other points of view. Take turns during a discussion.
- When it is your turn to talk, address the subject and help the project move forward.

STUDY AND TEST-TAKING SKILLS HANDBOOK

Study Skills

Studying for school and doing your homework are like any other tasks—if you understand your assignment, set a goal, and make a plan, you'll save time and do great work. The tips that follow will teach you the skills you need to make schoolwork easier and more enjoyable.

Get Organized

- Keep an assignment notebook. Keep it up to date.
- Keep your notes for each course together in one place.
- Find a good place to study. Choose a place that has as few distractions as possible. Try to study in the same place each day.
- Try to study at the same time each day.
- Don't study one subject too long. If you haven't finished after thirty minutes, switch to another subject.
- Take notes on your reading. Keep your notes in one place.

Understand Your Purpose

The purpose is the reason you have been given a particular assignment. If you understand the purpose, you should be able to set a goal to work toward. With schoolwork, this means making sure you understand your assignment and you know how long you have to do it.

Set goals

These steps will help you set study goals for an assignment.

1. Listen as the teacher explains the assignment. Find out everything you need to do to finish the assignment.
2. Understand the quality of work your teacher expects from you. Are you supposed to turn in a finished paper or a rough draft?
3. Find out how much time you have. Ask: Is everything due on the same day, or are some parts due earlier?
4. In your assignment notebook, write down the assignment details and the dates when your work is due.

Homework Checklist

Goal: To understand and finish my homework assignment.

Plan: Follow these steps to reach my goal:

- ☑ Bring home the all the materials I need, including this textbook, and my notebook.
- ☑ Find a quiet space where I can concentrate. Also, make sure I have a table or other hard, flat surface to write on.
- ☑ Keep my notebook out and take notes as I read.
- ☑ Write down questions about the parts of the assignment that I don't understand. Ask my teacher or an adult at home to help me understand.
- ☑ Check this plan from time to time to make sure I stay on task.
- ☑ Take my completed homework back to school and hand it in.

Make a Plan

Making a plan is the best way to reach your goals. Try to make plans that include the work you have finish and the time you have until the assignment is due. Think about how you study best, when you might need help, and what gets in your way.

You can use a **task, obstacle, and solution chart** to show

1. what you need to do (task)
2. what might get in your way (obstacle)
3. how you can get around an obstacle (solution)

Karen's goal is to read a chapter of science before school tomorrow. Check out the chart she made, which includes **task, obstacle, and solution.**

1. (task)	I have to…	read chapter 4 tonight
2. (obstacle)	But…	after dinner I have basketball practice
3. (solution)	So I need to…	read before practice

Try it! In your **Learner's Notebook,** make your own **task, obstacle, and solution chart** for an assignment from this book. You can use Karen's plan as a model.

Take Notes

Writing notes about what you read or what you hear in a presentation will help you remember information you're expected to learn. The Cornell Note-Taking System is a way to organize the notes you take in class or the notes you take as you read. Use this system to organize your note-taking and make sense of the notes you take.

Cornell Notes

Divide the pages that you're using for notes into two sections or columns as shown below. As you read or listen, write notes in Section B. In Section A, write the highlights (main ideas and vocabulary) from Section B.

Section A [highlights]	Section B [notes]
Use this section SECOND. Review the notes you took in Section B and write in this section: • Vocabulary words to remember • Main idea statements • Questions and other hints that will help you remember the information	Use this section FIRST. As you read or listen, take notes in this section: • When you're taking notes on your reading, write down the subtitles that break the text into different section. In most cases, subtitles form an outline of the information in a chapter. • Write down the most important information: main ideas and concepts. Don't write every word or take time to write complete sentences. (Hint: if the teacher writes something on the board, it's probably important.) • Use abbreviations and shortened word forms to get the ideas on paper quickly. (For example, POV is a good abbreviation for Point of View.) • Define new terms and concepts in your own words so that you'll be able to understand them later.

Model These are some notes one student made as she read about biographies and autobiographies.

A.	*B. Looking at the Genre: Biography*
biography	*What is it?* *real people, real life*
autobiography	*Autobiography is about yourself* *Why is it important?* *many reasons (interest, learn, entertain, etc.)* *What are the important elements?*
Major elements of biography	*Narrator: who tells the story* *Point of view: from who's telling the story* *Setting: time and place of a story*

Try It! Divide a sheet of paper into two columns as shown above. Practice taking notes using the Cornell system as you read your homework assignment.

Test-Taking Skills

How well you perform on a test is not a matter of chance. Some specific strategies can help you answer test questions. This section of the handbook will show how to improve your test-taking skills.

Tips for preparing for tests

Here are some useful suggestions for preparing to take a test.

- Gather information about the test. When will it be given? How long will it take? Exactly what material will it cover?
- Review material from your textbook, class notes, homework, quizzes, and handouts. Review the study questions at the end of each section of a textbook. Try to define terms in boldface type.
- Make up some sample questions and answer them. As you skim selections, try to predict what may be asked.
- Draw charts and cluster or Venn diagrams to help you remember information and to picture how one piece of information relates to another.
- Give yourself plenty of time to study. Avoid cramming for a test. Several short review sessions are more effective than one long one.
- In addition to studying alone, study with a partner or small group. Quiz one another on topics you think the test will cover.

Plan your strategy

Try following these steps:

- Read all directions carefully. Understanding the directions can prevent mistakes.
- Ask for help if you have a question.
- Answer the easier items first. By skipping the hard items, you will have time to answer all the easy ones.
- In the time that is left, return to the items you skipped. Answer them as best you can. If you won't be penalized for doing so, guess at an answer.
- If possible, save some time at the end to check your answers.

Objective Tests

An objective test is a test of factual information. The questions are usually either right or wrong; there is no difference of opinion. On an objective test, you are asked to recall information, not to present your ideas. Objective test questions include true-or-false items, multiple-choice items, fill-in-the-blanks statements, short-answer items, and matching items. At the beginning of an objective test, scan the number of items. Then budget your time.

Multiple-choice items Multiple-choice questions ask you to answer a question or complete a sentence. They are the kind of question you will encounter most often on objective tests. Read all the choices before answering. Pick the best response.

What is a peninsula?

(a) a range of mountains

(b) a circle around the moon

(c) a body of land surrounded by water on three sides

Correct answer: (c)

- Read the question carefully. Be sure that you understand it.
- Read all the answers before selecting one. Reading all of the responses is especially important when one of the choices is "all of the above" or "none of the above."
- Eliminate responses that are clearly incorrect. Focus on the responses that might be correct.
- Look for absolute words, such as *never, always, all, none.* Most generalizations have exceptions. Absolute statements are often incorrect. (Note: This tip applies to true/false items also.)

Answering essay questions

Essay questions ask you to think about what you have learned and to write about it in one or more paragraphs. Some tests present a choice of essay questions. If a test has both an objective part and an essay part, answer the objective questions first, but leave yourself enough time to work on the essay.

Read the essay question carefully. What does it ask you to do? Discuss? Explain? Define? Summarize? Compare and contrast? These key words tell what kind of information you must give in your answer.

Key Verbs in Essay Questions	
Argue	Give your opinion and supporting reasons.
Compare and contrast	Discuss likenesses and differences.
Define	Give details that show exactly what something is like.
Demonstrate	Give examples to support a point.
Describe	Present a picture with words.
Discuss	Show detailed information on a particular subject.
Explain	Give reasons.
Identify	Give specific characteristics.
List (also outline, trace)	Give details, give steps in order, give a time sequence.
Summarize	Give a short overview of the most important ideas or events.

Tips for answering essay questions

You might wish to consider the following suggestions:

- Read the question or questions carefully. Determine the kind of information required by the question.
- Plan your time. Do not spend too much time on one part of the essay.
- Make a list of what you want to cover.
- If you have time, make revisions and proofreading corrections.

Taking standardized tests

Standardized tests are taken by students all over the country. Your performance on the test is compared with the performance of other students at your grade level. There are many different kinds of standardized tests. Some measure your progress in such subjects as English, math, and science, while others measure how well you think. Standardized tests can show how you learn and what you do best.

Preparing for standardized tests

There is no way to know exactly what information will be on a standardized test, or even what topics will be covered. The best preparation is to do the best you can in your daily schoolwork. However, you can learn the *kinds* of questions that will appear on a standardized test. Some general tips will also help.

Tips for taking standardized tests

You might find the following suggestions helpful.

- Get enough sleep the night before the test. Eat a healthful breakfast.
- Arrive early for the test. Try to relax.
- Listen carefully to all test directions. Ask questions if you don't understand the directions.
- Complete easy questions first. Leave harder items for the end.
- Be sure your answers are in the right place on the answer sheet.
- If points are not subtracted for wrong answers, guess at questions that you aren't sure of.

Analogies Analogy items test your understanding of the relationships between things or ideas. On standardized tests, analogies are written in an abbreviated format, as shown below.

man : woman :: buck : doe

The symbol : means "is to"; the symbol :: means "as."

This chart shows some word relationships you might find in analogy tests.

Relationship	Definition	Example
Synonyms	Two words have a similar meaning.	huge : gigantic :: scared : afraid
Antonyms	Two words have opposite meanings.	bright : dull :: far : near
Use	Words name a user and something used.	farmer : tractor :: writer : computer
Cause-Effect	Words name a cause and its effect.	tickle : laugh :: polish : shine
Category	Words name a category and an item in it.	fish : tuna :: building : house
Description	Words name an item and a characteristic of it.	knife : sharp :: joke : funny

GLOSSARY/GLOSARIO
Academic and Selection Vocabulary

English	Español
A	
abnormality (ab nor MAL uh tee) *n.* anything that is not normal or usual **(p. 842)**	**anomalía** *s.* algo que no es lo normal o usual
accommodations (uh kaw muh DAY shuns) *n.* a place to stay or sleep, often one where food is served **(p. 910)**	**alojamiento** *s.* lugar donde estar o dormir, a menudo donde se sirve comida
accomplish (uh KAWM plish) *v.* to finish; complete **(p. 67)**	**realizar** *v.* terminar; acabar
accumulate (uh KYOO myuh layt) *v.* to increase gradually in quantity or number **(p. 660)**	**acumular** *v.* aumentar gradualmente en cantidad o número
adolescence (ad uh LES uns) *n.* the period between childhood and adulthood **(p. 842)**	**adolescencia** *s.* periodo entre la niñez y la edad adulta
aggressor (uh GRES ur) *n.* a person, group, or nation that causes a conflict or war **(p. 987)**	**agresor(a)** *s.* persona, grupo o nación que causa un conflicto armado o una guerra
aggrieved (uh GREEVD) *adj.* feeling insulted or unfairly treated **(p. 380)**	**injuriado(a)** *adj.* sentirse insultado o tratado injustamente
agitated (AJ uh tayt ud) *adj.* excited, nervous, or disturbed; stirred up **(p. 382)**	**agitado(a)** *adj.* emocionado, nervioso; incitado
analyzing (AN uh ly zing) *n.* the act of taking apart to examine the separate pieces **(p. 730)**	**análisis** *s.* separación de las partes de un todo para examinarlo
angling (ANG ling) *v.* trying to get; form of the verb *angle* **(p. 352)**	**{ir} a la caza de** *col.* procurar obtenerlo; expresión coloquial de *caza*
aromas (uh ROH muz) *n.* pleasing smells or scents **(p. 189)**	**aromas** *s.* olores o perfumes agradables
assess (uh SES) *v.* to determine the meaning or importance of; analyze **(p. 183)**	**evaluar** *v.* determinar la importancia de algo; analizar
assurance (uh SHUR uns) *n.* confidence; certainty **(p. 479)**	**garantía** *s.* seguridad; certeza
atrocious (uh TROH shus) *adj.* very bad; terrible; horrible **(p. 547)**	**atroz** *adj.* grave; terrible; horrible
authoritarian (uh thor ih TAIR ee un) *adj.* having or expecting complete obedience **(p. 484)**	**autoritario(a)** *adj.* que impone su autoridad
avidly (AV id lee) *adv.* eagerly; enthusiastically **(p. 489)**	**ávidamente** *adv.* ansiosamente; con un deseo intenso
awe (aw) *n.* wonder combined with respect **(p. 886)**	**admiración** *s.* sorpresa combinada con respeto
B	
banished (BAN ishd) *adj.* sent away; form of the verb *banish* **(p. 232)**	**desterrado(a)** *adj.* que fue enviado a un lugar lejano; forma del verbo *desterrar*
barren (BAIR un) *adj.* plain, empty, dull, not interesting **(p. 431)**	**insulso(a)** *adj.* simple, sin gracia, aburrido, falto de interés

bias (BY us) *n.* an opinion based on personal preferences or unfair judgments **(p. 982)**

parcialidad *s.* opinión falta de neutralidad basada en preferencias personales o prejuicios

bland (bland) *adj.* dull; unexciting **(p. 842)**

insulso(a) *adj.* apagado; sin gracia

bold (bohld) *adj.* confident; daring **(p. 363)**

audaz *adj.* resuelto; atrevido

boutique (boo TEEK) *n.* a small, fashionable store **(p. 592)**

boutique *s.* tienda pequeña de ropa de moda

bravado (bruh VAW doh) *n.* a false show of bravery **(p. 890)**

bravuconada *s.* que parece valiente pero no lo es

brooch (brohch) *n.* a piece of jewelry pinned to one's clothing **(p. 458)**

broche *s.* joya que se lleva prendida a la ropa

browsed (browzd) *v.* looked through in a casual way; form of the verb *browse* **(p. 106)**

curioseó *v.* miró superficialmente; echó un vistazo; forma del verbo *curiosear*

C

campus (KAM pus) *n.* the land and buildings of a school **(p. 29)**

campus *s.* terrenos y edificios de una universidad

category (KAT uh gor ee) *n.* a type or group **(p. 105)**

categoría *s.* división, tipo o grupo para clasificar una lista o sistema

cease-fire (SEES fyr) *n.* a stop, or ending, to acts of war **(p. 421)**

alto el fuego *s.* suspensión o detención de actos bélicos

chaotic (kay AW tik) *adj.* confused; disorganized **(p. 784)**

caótico(a) *adj.* confuso; desordenado

charred (chard) *adj.* burned **(p. 566)**

chamuscado(a) *adj.* quemar superficialmente

clarify (KLAIR uh fy) *v.* to make understandable **(p. 926)**

clarificar *v.* aclarar, explicar

cliques (cleeks *or* kliks) *n.* groups of people who leave others out **(p. 172)**

camarillas *s.* grupos exclusivos de personas que discriminan a otros

compassion (kum PASH un) *n.* deep concern for the troubles of others, mixed with a desire to help; sympathy **(p. 451)**

compasión *s.* conmiseración por los problemas ajenos; lástima, piedad

complied (kum PLYD) *v.* did what was asked or ordered; went along with; form of the verb *comply* **(p. 141)**

acataron *v.* cumplieron con un pedido u orden; estuvieron de acuerdo con; forma del verbo *acatar*

conceded (kun SEE dud) *v.* accepted as true; form of the verb *concede* **(p. 180)**

admitió *v.* aceptar que sea cierto o correcto, forma del verbo *admitir*

concentration (kawn sen TRAY shun) *n.* the ability to focus one's attention **(p. 190)**

concentración *s.* capacidad de mantener la atención fija en algo

concept (KAWN sept) *n.* an idea or thought **(p. 559)**

concepto *s.* una idea

conclusions (kun KLOO shunz) *n.* opinions or judgments arrived at through careful analysis **(p. 266)**

conclusiones *s.* opiniones o afirmaciones que resultan de un cuidadoso análisis

condition (con DISH un) *n.* state of being **(p. 42)**

condición *s.* estado, situación de una persona o cosa

configuration (kun fig yuh RAY shun) *n.* the arrangement of a thing's parts **(p. 910)**

configuración *s.* disposición de las partes de una cosa

consciously (KAWN shus lee) *adv.* knowingly, on purpose **(p. 106)**

deliberadamente *adv.* voluntariamente, hecho a propósito

consecutive (kun SEK yuh tiv) *adj.* following one after the other in order **(p. 587)**

consecutivo(a) *adj.* que sigue inmediatamente a otro elemento

conspicuous (kun SPIK yoo us) *adj.* quite noticeable **(p. 662)**

llamativo(a) *adj.* evidente o notorio

consumption (kun SUMP shun) *n.* the act of using up, spending, or wasting **(p. 560)**

consumo *s.* acción de usar, gastar o consumir

contemplate (KON tem playt) *v.* to think about slowly and carefully **(p. 210)**

contemplar *v.* considerar con atención y cuidado

contemporary (KUN tem puh rair ee) *adj.* living now **(p. 736)**

contemporáneo(a) *adj.* en la época en que se vive

cope (kohp) *v.* to deal with and try to overcome problems; often used with the word *with* **(p. 618)**

sobrellevar *v.* soportar dificultades y tratar de hacer frente a los problemas

corporate (KOR pur ut) *adj.* belonging to or having to do with a company **(p. 586)**

corporativo(a) *adj.* perteneciente o relativo a una compañía

corresponded (kor uh SPAWN did) *v.* wrote letters to each other; form of the verb *correspond* **(p. 314)**

se correspondían *v.* se escribían cartas entre sí; forma del verbo *corresponder(se)*

coveted (KUV it id) *v.* wanted what another person had; form of the verb *covet* **(p. 778)**

codiciaba *v.* deseaba con ansia la riqueza ajena; forma del verbo *codiciar*

craving (KRAY ving) *n.* a strong desire or longing **(p. 842)**

ansia *s.* deseo vivo o vehemente

criticize (KRIT uh syz) *v.* to point out what is wrong or bad about someone or something **(p. 143)**

criticar *v.* indicar lo desfavorable o lo que está mal acerca de alguien o de algo

cultures (KUL churz) *n.* groups of people who share a history and way of life **(p. 171)**

culturas *s.* grupos de personas que comparten historia y modos de vida comunes

cynically (SIN uh kul ee) *adv.* in a way that shows doubt or disbelief; doubtfully **(p. 671)**

escépticamente *adv.* que muestra duda y descreimiento; con desconfianza

D

debate (dih BAYT) *n.* a discussion that involves contrasting opinions **(p. 607)**

debate *s.* intercambio de ideas y opiniones

decipher (dih SY fur) *v.* to figure out the meaning of **(p. 546)**

descifrar *v.* interpretar el significado de algo

defiant (dih FY unt) *adj.* showing resistance to authority or an opponent **(p. 952)**

desafiante *adj.* que contradice la autoridad o a un oponente

dejected (dee JEK tud) *adj.* sad or depressed **(p. 354)**

abatido(a) *adj.* desanimado o deprimido

depressed (dee PRESD) *adj.* very sad; deeply unhappy **(p. 161)**

deprimido(a) *adj.* muy triste; desdichado

desperate (DES pur ut) *adj.* so needy as to be willing to try anything **(p. 219)**

desesperado(a) *adj.* que está tan necesitado que recurre a cualquier solución

destination (des tuh NAY shun) *n.* the place one plans or hopes to reach at the end of a journey **(p. 537)**

destino *s.* punto de llegada al que se planea o desea llegar al final de un viaje

destiny (DES tuh nee) *n.* what the future holds for a person **(p. 313)**

destino *s.* lo que el futuro le depara a una persona

determined (dih TUR mund) *adj.* having firmly decided; unwilling to change one's mind **(p. 57)**

decidido(a) *adj.* firme; que no vacila

devastating (DEV uh stayt ing) *adj.* causing a lot of pain or damage **(p. 279)**

devastador(a) *adj.* que destruye o causa mucho dolor

diagnosis (dy ug NOH sus) *n.* a doctor's identification of a patient's illness; any expert's finding of the nature of a problem **(p. 688)**

diagnóstico *s.* cuando el médico identifica la enfermedad de un paciente; reconocimiento de la naturaleza de un problema

dignity (DIG nuh tee) *n.* a sense of self-respect; a calm outward appearance **(p. 51)**

dignidad *s.* sentido de respeto; que muestra decoro

diploma (dih PLOH muh) *n.* a piece of paper saying that a person has graduated from a school **(p. 163)**

diploma *s.* documento académico que acredita que una persona se ha graduado

disadvantaged (dis ad VAN tijd) *adj.* lacking in basic needs; poor **(p. 148)**

necesitado(a) *adj.* que carece de lo necesario para vivir; pobre

discarding (dis KARD ing) *n.* the act of throwing out or getting rid of **(p. 625)**

desechar *s.* acción de arrojar o deshacerse de algo

discipline (DIH suh plin) *n.* control of behavior, especially self-control **(p. 219)**

disciplina *s.* control del comportamiento, especialmente del propio

discrimination (dis krim ih NAY shin) *n.* treatment based on class, religion, or ethnic origin rather than on worth **(p. 986)**

discriminación *s.* actitud por la que se considera inferior a una persona o colectividad por su clase social, religión o raza

dismally (DIZ muh lee) *adv.* in a sad or gloomy way **(p. 315)**

sombríamente *adv.* triste o melancólico

disruptions (dis RUP shuns) *n.* unwanted breaks or interruptions **(p. 709)**

interrupciones *s.* cortes o intromisiones no deseados

dissect (dih SEKT) *v.* to examine carefully and in close detail **(p. 822)**

diseccionar *v.* examinar cuidadosa y detalladamente

dominated (DAH muh nay tid) *v.* was the main thing; form of the verb *dominate* **(p. 303)**

dominaban *v.* era la cosa predominante; forma del verbo *dominar*

drenched (drencht) *v.* soaked or covered with liquid; form of the verb *drench* **(p. 16)**

empapó *v.* mojado del todo o cubierto de líquido; forma del verbo *empapar*

E

ecstatic (ek STAT ik) *adj.* filled with great joy **(p. 488)**

extasiado(a) *adj.* lleno de placer

elaborate (ih LAB ur uht) *adj.* planned or carried out carefully **(p. 325)**

elaborado(a) *adj.* hecho o realizado con cuidado

emancipation (ih man suh PAY shun) *n.* the act of freeing or being freed, as from slavery **(p. 734)**

emancipación *s.* acción de liberarse o de ser liberado, por ej. de la esclavitud

emerged (ih MURJD) *v.* came out; form of the verb *emerge* **(p. 566)**

apareció *v.* salió; forma del verbo *aparecer*

empathize (EM puh thyz) *v.* to understand another person's feelings **(p. 271)**

identificarse *v.* tener los mismos sentimientos que otra persona

encounter (in KOWN tur) *n.* an unexpected meeting **(p. 107)**

encuentro casual *s.* coincidencia inesperada de dos o más personas

endurance (en DUR uns) *n.* the ability to handle stress **(p. 443)**

resistencia *s.* capacidad de resistir o aguantar

energized (EN ur jyzd) *adj.* active or lively **(p. 465)**

vigorizado(a) *adj.* activo o con vigor

enhance (en HANS) *v.* to improve; make better or bigger **(p. 465)**

mejorar *v.* perfeccionar; hacer mejoras o agrandar

ensure (en SHUR) *v.* to guarantee or make certain **(p. 478)**

asegurar *v.* garantizar o dejar certeza de algo

entice (en TYS) *v.* to attract by making (something) seem desirable; tempt **(p. 498)**

atraer *v.* ganar la atención haciendo que algo parezca deseable; tentar

entitled (in TY tuld) *adj.* having a right to do something **(p. 71)**

autorizado(a) *adj.* tener el derecho de hacer algo

era (AIR uh) *n.* a period in history **(p. 822)**

era *s.* periodo histórico

evading (ih VAY ding) *v.* keeping away or avoiding; form of the verb *evade* **(p. 288)**

evadiendo *v.* esquivando o evitando un daño; forma del verbo *evadir*

evaluating (ee VAL yoo ayt ing) *v.* finding value; judging or determining worth; form of the verb *evaluate* **(p. 776)**

evaluando *v.* señalando el valor; estimar o calcular el valor de algo; forma del verbo *evaluar*

eventually (eh VEN choo ul lee) *adv.* in the end; finally **(p. 29)**

inevitablemente *adv.* tarde o temprano; finalmente

evidence (EV ih dens) *n.* information, facts, or objects that help prove something **(p. 306)**

pruebas *s.* información, hechos u objetos que demuestran algo

exemplary (eg ZEMP luh ree) *adj.* so good that it can serve as an example to others **(p. 208)**

ejemplar *adj.* que es tan bueno que sirve de modelo a los demás

exotic (eg ZAW tik) *adj.* strangely attractive; foreign **(p. 784)**

exótico(a) *adj.* extravagante; extranjero

explicit (eks PLIS it) *adj.* clearly expressed **(p. 968)**

explícito(a) *adj.* que expresa con claridad

extinction (ek STING shun) *n.* the act of wiping out of existence or having been wiped out of existence **(p. 618)**

extinción *s.* acción de acabar del todo algo o de hacerlo desaparecer gradualmente

F

fantastic (fan TAS tik) *adj.* not real; imaginary; amazing **(p. 533)**

fantástico(a) *adj.* que no es real; que es imaginario; que es de fantasía

features (FEE churz) *n.* special qualities, parts, or sections **(p. 556)**

características *s.* cualidades, piezas o secciones especiales

feint (faynt) *v.* to move in a way that's meant to trick an opponent **(p. 859)**

amagar *v.* hacer un movimiento o finta para engañar al oponente

flailed (flayld) *v.* swung wildly; form of the verb *flail* **(p. 288)**

se agitaban *v.* mover violentamente de un lado al otro; forma del verbo *agitarse*

flawless (FLAW les) *adj.* perfect; without mistakes **(p. 362)**

impecable *adj.* perfecto; sin fallas

flourishing (FLUR uh shing) *adj.* growing or developing successfully; doing very well **(p. 890)**

floreciente *adj.* que está en pleno desarrollo; próspero

focus (FOH kus) *v.* to keep one's mind on something; concentrate **(p. 442)**

concentrar(se) *v.* enfocar los pensamiento en algo; centrar(se)

formidable (for MID uh bul) *adj.* causing fear or wonder because of size, strength, or power **(p. 226)**

formidable *adj.* que impone respeto y temor por su tamaño, fuerza o poder

frail (frayl) *adj.* lacking in strength; weak **(p. 427)**

frágil *adj.* poco resistente; débil

frenzy (FREN zee) *n.* unusual mental excitement leading to wild activity **(p. 566)**

frenesí *s.* exaltación violenta del ánimo o de un sentimiento

frequently (FREE kwunt lee) *adv.* often **(p. 682)**

frecuentemente *adv.* a menudo

frustration (frus TRAY shun) *n.* irritation at being kept from doing or achieving something **(p. 720)**

frustración *s.* fracaso por la imposibilidad de realizar o lograr algo

fuming (FYOO ming) *adj.* angry **(p. 353)**

{echar} humo *col.* enfadado; expresión coloquial de *humo*

funding (FUN ding) *n.* money given for a special reason or purpose **(p. 149)**

fondos *s.* recursos monetarios destinados a un propósito o razón determinados

G

gallery (GAL ur ee) *n.* a room used for a special purpose (such as showing pictures) **(p. 800)**

gallería *s.* habitación usada para pasear por ella o para exhibir cuadros

generate (JEN uh rayt) *v.* to produce or create **(p. 928)**

generar *v.* producir o crear

gestured (JES churd) *v.* showed (something) by a motion of the hand or other part of the body; form of the verb *gesture* **(p. 106)**

gesticuló *v.* indicó (algo) haciendo gestos con las manos o partes del cuerpo; forma del verbo *gesticular*

glimpse (glimps) *n.* a quick look **(p. 29)**

vistazo fugaz *s.* vistazo breve

global (GLOH bul) *adj.* related to or happening throughout the whole world **(p. 421)**

mundial *adj.* relativo a todo el mundo o que sucede en todo el planeta

gnarled (narld) *adj.* rough, twisted, and knotty, as a tree trunk or branches **(p. 744)**

retorcido(a) *adj.* rugoso, torcido y nudoso como el tronco y las ramas de un árbol

H

habitat (HAB uh tat) *n.* the place where a plant or animal naturally lives and grows; home **(p. 618)**

hábitat *s.* lugar donde una especie de plantas o animales vive y se desarrolla naturalmente; hogar

habitual (huh BI chuh ul) *adj.* regular; usual; done out of habit **(p. 312)**

habitual *adj.* regular; usual; que se hace por hábito

haggard (HAG urd) *adj.* looking worn out from grief, worry, or illness **(p. 381)**

demacrado(a) *adj.* delgado y de mal aspecto causado por sufrimiento, preocupación o enfermedad

hurtle (HUR tul) *v.* to move fast with a lot of force **(p. 378)**

precipitar *v.* movimiento acelerado y con fuerza

I

identity (eye DEN tuh tee) *n.* the qualities and features that make one person different from another **(p. 800)**

identidad *s.* cualidades y rasgos de una persona que la diferencian de las demás

ignorant (IG nur unt) *adj.* without an education or knowledge of something **(p. 164)**

analfabeto(a) *adj.* que no tiene educación o que desconoce algo

illegal (ih LEE gul) *adj.* against the law **(p. 59)**

ilegal *adj.* que es contra la ley

illuminate (ih LOO muh nayt) *v.* to light up; make clear **(p. 736)**

clarificar *v.* ilustrar; explicar

immigrated (IM uh gray tud) *v.* moved into a new country; form of the verb *immigrate* **(p. 532)**

inmigró *v.* se mudó a otro país; forma del verbo *inmigrar*

implied (im PLYD) *v.* suggested; hinted; form of the verb *imply* **(p. 451)**

insinuó *v.* sugirió; dio a entender; forma del verbo *insinuar*

impoverished (im PAW vur ishd) *adj.* reduced to poverty; made very poor **(p. 486)**

empobrecido(a) *adj.* reducido a la pobreza; hacerse pobre

impress (im PRES) *v.* to have a strong effect on **(p. 30)**

impresionar *v.* producir un profundo efecto sobre

inconvenience (in kun VEEN yuns) *n.* something that causes difficulty, discomfort, or bother **(p. 566)**

inconveniente *s.* dificultad, impedimento, obstáculo

ingenious (in JEEN yus) *adj.* clever; imaginative **(p. 96)**
ingenioso(a) *adj.* inteligente; creativo

initial (ih NISH ul) *adj.* at the beginning; first **(p. 784)**
inicial *adj.* al principio; primero

insignia (in SIG nee uh) *n.* a mark or sign that indicates rank, authority, or honor **(p. 858)**
insignia *s.* señal o emblema que indica rango, autoridad u honor

insistent (in SIS tuhnt) *adj.* not giving up; demanding attention **(p. 325)**
insistente *adj.* que se mantiene firme; que solicita atención

insolently (IN suh lunt lee) *adv.* in a boldly rude manner **(p. 668)**
insolentemente *adv.* con atrevimiento y descaro

inspired (in SPY urd) *v.* made someone want to do; form of the verb *inspire* **(p. 59)**
inspiró *v.* motivar a alguien a hacer algo; forma del verbo *inspirar*

interference (in tur FEER uns) *n.* the act of getting in the way and slowing normal progress or development **(p. 609)**
interferencia *s.* acción de interponerse en el camino de algo y de aminorar su progreso o desarrollo

interpret (in TUR prit) *v.* to explain the meaning of; to make understandable **(p. 798)**
interpretar *v.* explicar el significado de algo; hacer comprensible

intimidated (in TIM uh day tid) *adj.* frightened or threatened **(p. 952)**
acobardado(a) *adj.* temeroso o amedrentado

invaluable (in VAL yoo uh bul) *adj.* so valuable that a price can't be estimated; extremely desirable or important **(p. 585)**
invaluable *adj.* tiene tanto valor que no se puede estimar su precio; que es extremadamente importante o deseado

ironically (eye RAW nik lee) *adv.* in a way that is different from what one would expect **(p. 784)**
irónicamente *adv.* que es de un modo ilógico o inesperado

J

jest (jest) *n.* a joke, prank, or amusing remark **(p. 389)**
chanza *s.* chiste, broma u ocurrencia graciosa

L

legitimate (lih JIT uh mit) *adj.* following the rules; lawful; allowed **(p. 968)**
legítimo(a) *adj.* conforme a las reglas; lícito; permitido

looms (loomz) *v.* appears as a threat or danger; form of the verb *loom* **(p. 607)**
amenaza *v.* que presenta una amenaza o peligro inminente; forma del verbo *amenazar*

M

margin (MAR jin) *n.* the blank space around the printed area on a page **(p. 42)**
margen *s.* espacio en blanco que se deja en una página entre sus bordes y la parte escrita

menace (MEN us) *n.* a threat or danger **(p. 226)**
amenaza *s.* intimidación o peligro

merge (murj) *v.* to join together to become one; unite **(p. 784)**
fundir *v.* unir para formar una sola cosa; unificar

meticulously (muh TIK yuh lus lee) *adv.* carefully and correctly **(p. 181)**
meticulosamente *adv.* con cuidado y detalle

modestly (MAW dist lee) *adv.* in a shy way; not confidently **(p. 327)**
modestamente *adv.* con vergüenza; tímidamente

monitor (MAW nuh tur) *v.* to watch over or check on **(p. 546)**
supervisar *v.* vigilar o verificar

mortified (MOR tih fyd) *adj.* greatly embarrassed **(p. 488)**

avergonzado(a) *adj.* muy abochornado

motives (MOH tivz) *n.* the needs or desires that cause a person to take action **(p. 177)**

motivos *s.* necesidades o deseos que provocan la acción de una persona

N

neglected (nih GLEK tud) *v.* ignored; not cared for; form of the verb *neglect* **(p. 682)**

abandonado(a) *adj.* ignorado; descuidado

nimble (NIM bul) *adj.* light and quick in movement **(p. 285)**

ágil *adj.* de movimientos ligeros y rápidos

notions (NOH shunz) *n.* ideas, beliefs, or opinions **(p. 232)**

nociones *s.* ideas, creencias u opiniones

nurtured (NUR churd) *v.* cared for and helped grow; form of the verb *nurture* **(p. 890)**

cultivó *v.* cuidar y ayudar al desarrollo; forma del verbo *cultivar*

O

objectively (ub JEK tiv lee) *adv.* without being influenced by personal feelings **(p. 987)**

objetivamente *adv.* que no está influenciado por sentimientos personales

obligation (awb luh GAY shun) *n.* a duty; a promise to perform an act **(p. 631)**

obligación *s.* un deber; algo que se tiene que hacer

oblivious (uh BLIV ee us) *adj.* not noticing; not aware of **(p. 566)**

ajeno(a) *adj.* distante; que no tiene conocimiento o no está prevenido de algo

obnoxious (ub NAWK shus) *adj.* annoying and disagreeable **(p. 227)**

detestable *adj.* muy malo y desagradable

obscure (ub SKOOR) *adj.* difficult to understand **(p. 890)**

oscuro(a) *adj.* difícil de comprender

obvious (AWB vee us) *adj.* easily seen or understood **(p. 822)**

obvio(a) *adj.* que es evidente y comprensible

omen (OH mun) *n.* a sign or event thought to predict good or bad fortune **(p. 718)**

augurio *s.* señal o indicio que se cree que predice la buena o mala suerte

ominous (AW muh nus) *adj.* threatening harm or evil **(p. 183)**

ominoso(a) *adj.* de mal agüero, peligroso

optimistic (awp tuh MIS tik) *adj.* taking the view that things will turn out well; hopeful **(p. 173)**

optimista *adj.* que ve el aspecto favorable de las cosas; que tiene esperanza

P

paradise (PAIR uh dys) *n.* a beautiful, wonderful, happy place; heaven **(p. 592)**

paraíso *s.* un lugar bello, maravilloso y feliz; el cielo

peer (peer) *v.* to look closely **(p. 842)**

atisbar *v.* observar con cuidado

permanent (PUR muh nunt) *adj.* lasting **(p. 88)**

permanente *adj.* duradero

persistently (pur SIS tunt lee) *adv.* over and over again; repeatedly **(p. 228)**

continuamente *adv.* una y otra vez; repetidamente

perspective (pur SPEK tiv) *n.* a belief or set of beliefs; opinion; way of looking at or thinking about something **(p. 454)**

perspectiva *s.* visión o creencias; opinión; punto de vista

persuasive (pur SWAY siv) *adj.* able to convince someone to do something **(p. 272)**

persuasivo(a) *adj.* capaz de convencer a alguien de hacer algo

physical (FIZ ih kul) *adj.* having to do with the body **(p. 444)**

físico(a) *adj.* relativo al cuerpo humano

plunges (PLUN juz) *v.* dips or moves downward suddenly; form of the verb *plunge* **(p. 928)**

baja {en picada} *v.* bajar o moverse hacia abajo y a gran velocidad; frase verbal con la palabra *picada*

poised (poyzd) *adj.* in a position of being ready **(p. 548)**

preparado(a) *adj.* estar listo para hacer algo

policy (PAW luh see) *n.* a regular or usual way of handling things **(p. 916)**

política *s.* normas o directrices que rigen el manejo de algo

possessive (puh ZES iv) *adj.* wanting to keep something for oneself **(p. 335)**

posesivo(a) *adj.* persona absorbente en su trato con los demás

possibilities (paw suh BIL uh teez) *n.* things that could or might happen **(p. 535)**

potencialidades *s.* cosas que pueden suceder o existir

potentially (puh TEN shuh lee) *adv.* possibly **(p. 19)**

potencialmente *adv.* posiblemente

potions (POH shunz) *n.* drinks, especially drinks that are supposed to have magical powers **(p. 745)**

pociones *s.* bebida preparada que supuestamente tiene propiedades mágicas

pranks (praynks) *n.* playful jokes or tricks **(p. 336)**

bromas *s.* bullas y travesuras de niños

precisely (prih SYS lee) *adv.* exactly **(p. 43)**

exactamente *adv.* precisamente

prejudices (PREJ uh dis us) *n.* unfavorable opinions or judgments formed unfairly **(p. 968)**

prejuicios *s.* opinión o juicio desfavorable formado con datos inadecuados

previewing (PREE vyoo ing) *v.* seeing beforehand; form of the verb *preview* **(p. 38)**

ver con anterioridad *v.* ver de antemano

principle (PRIN suh pul) *n.* a basic idea or concept **(p. 478)**

principio *s.* norma o idea fundamental

prior (PRY ur) *adj.* earlier; coming before **(p. 136)**

previo *adj.* anterior; que viene primero

process (PRAW ses) *n.* a series of actions or steps to follow in doing or making something **(p. 78)**

proceso *s.* conjunto de acciones o pasos sucesivos para hacer algo

prohibiting (proh HIB it ing) *adj.* preventing or forbidding **(p. 626)**

prohibitorio(a) *adj.* que impide o veda

prominent (PRAW mih nunt) *adj.* easy to see; standing out **(p. 498)**

prominente *adj.* destacado; que sobresale

propelled (proh PELD) *v.* pushed or moved forward by a force or *as if* by one; form of the verb *propel* **(p. 27)**

propulsó *v.* empujar o mover hacia delante; forma del verbo *propulsar*

prosperity (praw SPAIR uh tee) *n.* the condition of being successful or having good fortune **(p. 626)**

prosperidad *s.* tener éxito o buena suerte

psychology (sy KAW luh jee) *n.* the study of human thought and behavior **(p. 148)**

psicología *s.* ciencia que estudia la conducta y los procesos mentales

Q

quarried (KWAIR eed) *adj.* cut or blasted from the earth for use in construction **(p. 458)**

extraído(a) {de cantera} *adj.* cortado o cavado del suelo para usarlo en la construcción

R

rationing (RASH un ing) *n.* the controlled or limited use of **(p. 928)**
racionamiento *s.* distribución controlada o limitada

raucous (RAW kus) *adj.* loud and rough sounding **(p. 668)**
estentóreo(a) *adj.* de voz fuerte y ruidosa

receptive (rih SEP tiv) *adj.* open to ideas and requests **(p. 67)**
receptivo(a) *adj.* que está abierto a recibir estímulos

reclining (rih KLYN ing) *v.* lying down; form of the verb *recline* **(p. 43)**
recostado *v.* echado; forma del verbo *recostar*

recovered (ree KUHV urd) *v.* found something that was lost or stolen; form of the verb *recover* **(p. 307)**
recobró *v.* recuperó algo que se había perdido o robado; forma del verbo *recobrar*

reduce (rih DOOS) *v.* to use less of; make less of **(p. 560)**
reducir *v.* disminuir el uso de algo; producir menos

reflective (rih FLEK tiv) *adj.* showing serious and careful thinking; thoughtful **(p. 952)**
meditabundo(a) *adj.* que piensa con seriedad y cuidado; pensativo

reformation (reh fur MAY shun) *n.* a change for the better; improvement **(p. 671)**
reforma *s.* cambio para bien; mejora

refugee (REF yoo jee) *n.* a person who flees for safety, especially because of war or natural disaster **(p. 82)**
refugiado(a) *s.* persona que huye buscando seguridad, generalmente de una guerra o de un desastre natural

regretfully (rih GRET ful ee) *adv.* in a way that shows sorrow, distress, or disappointment **(p. 718)**
apenado(a) *adj.* que muestra pena, aflicción o desilusión

relevant (REH luh vunt) *adj.* having a connection to **(p. 478)**
vigente *adj.* válido o que está en vigor

requirement (rih KWY ur munt) *n.* a demand or condition **(p. 479)**
requisito *s.* exigencia o condición necesarias

reserve (rih ZURV) *n.* land set aside for a special purpose **(p. 16)**
reserva *s.* tierra destinada para un propósito especial

resists (rih ZISTS) *v.* holds off the force or effect of; form of the verb *resist* **(p. 582)**
resiste *v.* que se opone a la fuerza o al efecto de otra cosa; forma del verbo *resistir*

resolute (REZ uh loot) *adj.* determined; stubborn **(p. 890)**
resuelto(a) *adj.* demasiado determinado; perseverante

resources (REE sor suz) *n.* supplies that can be used as needed **(p. 560)**
recursos *s.* bienes disponibles para resolver necesidades

respond (rih SPOND) *v.* to react **(p. 298)**
responder *v.* reaccionar

restore (rih STOR) *v.* to bring back into existence or to an original condition; renew **(p. 607)**
recuperar *v.* volver a poner como estaba o devolver a su estado; renovar

ritual (RICH oo ul) *n.* a set routine **(p. 356)**
ritual *s.* una rutina establecida

robust (roh BUST) *adj.* strong and full of energy **(p. 890)**
robusto(a) *adj.* fuerte y vigoroso

rotate (ROH tayt) *v.* to turn around **(p. 98)**
rotar *v.* dar vueltas

S

sacrifices (SAK ruh fy siz) *n.* important things that a person gives up to help others **(p. 271)**
sacrificios *s.* cosas importantes a las que alguien renuncia para ayudar a los demás

scurrying (SKUR ee ing) *v.* running or moving quickly or excitedly; form of the verb *scurry* **(p. 717)**
corriendo *v.* yendo de prisa o moviéndose con rapidez; forma del verbo *correr*

secretive (SEE krih tiv) *adj.* seeming to keep secrets; holding back information **(p. 378)**

hermético(a) *adj.* impenetrable o reservado

selfless (SELF lus) *adj.* having no concern for oneself; thinking of others first **(p. 51)**

desinteresado(a) *adj.* que no lo mueve el interés por un beneficio personal; que piensa primero en los demás

self-portrait (self POR trut) *n.* a painting or photograph of an artist by that artist **(p. 800)**

autoretrato *s.* retrato o fotografía que un artista plástico hace de sí mismo

sequence (SEE kwens) *n.* the order of events; the arrangement of things in time, space, or importance **(p. 204)**

secuencia *n.* orden de sucesos; sucesión de cosas en tiempo, espacio o grado de importancia

setback (SET bak) *n.* an unexpected difficulty or stop in progress **(p. 688)**

contratiempo *s.* revés inoportuno o que impide el progreso

shriveled (SHRIV uld) *adj.* shrunken and wrinkled **(p. 566)**

consumido(a) *adj.* encogido y arrugado

shunning (SHUN ing) *v.* avoiding; keeping away from; form of the verb *shun* **(p. 822)**

eludiendo *v.* evitando; manteniéndose a distancia; forma del verbo *eludir*

simultaneously (sy mul TAY nee us lee) *adv.* at the same time **(p. 670)**

simultáneamente *adv.* al mismo tiempo

sincerity (sin SAIR uh tee) *n.* the quality of meaning what one says and does **(p. 336)**

sinceridad *s.* veracidad, honestidad

skeptics (SKEP tiks) *n.* people who doubt or don't believe something **(p. 325)**

escépticos *s.* personas que dudan o no creen en algo

slung (slung) *adj.* hung or thrown loosely **(p. 426)**

colgado(a) *adj.* que pende o que está echado por encima de algo

solemnly (SAH lum lee) *adv.* very seriously **(p. 212)**

solemnemente *adv.* con mucha seriedad

solitary (SAWL uh tair ee) *adj.* all alone **(p. 928)**

solitario(a) *adj.* solo, sin compañía

solitude (SAWL uh tood) *n.* the state of being alone **(p. 660)**

soledad *s.* falta de compañía, estar solo

sorcerer (SOR sur ur) *n.* a person who practices magic with the help of spirits **(p. 743)**

hechicero(a) *s.* persona que practica la magia para obtener ayuda de espíritus

specified (SPES ih fyd) *v.* explained or described in detail; form of the verb *specify* **(p. 784)**

especificamos *v.* explicamos o describimos detalladamente; forma del verbo *especificar*

stationary (STAY shun air ee) *adj.* not moving; staying still **(p. 98)**

fijo(a) *adj.* inmóvil; que se mantiene en el lugar

sternly (STURN lee) *adv.* in a strict or firm way **(p. 304)**

severamente *adv.* con severidad y firmeza

stifling (STY fling) *v.* holding back or stopping; form of the verb *stifle* **(p. 302)**

reprimiendo *v.* conteniendo o deteniendo; forma del verbo *reprimir*

stranded (STRAN dud) *adj.* left somewhere and not able to leave **(p. 357)**

varado(a) *adj.* quedarse detenido en un lugar con dificultades para continuar

structure (STRUK shur) *n.* the arrangement of parts; the way in which a thing is put together **(p. 474)**

estructura *s.* distribución de las partes; orden en el cual se arma algo

stunned (stund) *adj.* shocked; surprised; amazed **(p. 365)**

atónito(a) *adj.* pasmado; sorprendido; anonadado

subjected (sub JEK tid) *adj.* exposed (to); forced to hear or see; form of the verb *subject (to)* **(p. 170)**

sometido(a) *adj.* estar expuesto (a); ser forzado a escuchar o ver algo; forma del verbo *someter* **(a)**

succeeded (suk SEED ud) *v.* followed; happened after; form of the verb *succeed* **(p. 381)**

transcurrieron *v.* {las horas} pasaron, corrieron; forma del verbo *transcurrir*

sufficiently (suh FISH unt lee) *adv.* in a way that is enough to meet the needs **(p. 916)**

suficientemente *adv.* de modo que es bastante para lo que se necesita

summarize (SUM ur yz) *v.* to tell the main points briefly **(p. 528)**

resumir *v.* exponer de forma breve y esencial

swarmed (swormd) *v.* moved in a large group; form of the verb *swarm* **(p. 82)**

aglomeró *v.* amontonar y agrupar desordenadamente; forma del verbo *aglomerar*

synthesizing (SIN thuh sy zing) *n.* combining ideas in order to form a new idea **(p. 320)**

síntesis *s.* combinación de ideas para formar un resumen

T

tact (takt) *n.* the ability to handle people or situations without causing bad feelings **(p. 488)**

tacto *s.* habilidad para tratar con personas o asuntos delicados sin herir sentimientos

tantalizing (TAN tuh ly zing) *adj.* desirable but just out of reach **(p. 208)**

tentador(a) *adj.* deseable; apetecible

taunt (tawnt) *v.* to make fun of in a mean way **(p. 744)**

mofar(se) *v.* burlarse de alguien con malicia

tendency (TEN dun see) *n.* the way something is likely to be or behave; likelihood **(p. 96)**

tendencia *s.* propensión a seguir un fin o a que algo suceda; inclinación

theme (theem) *n.* the main idea of a story, poem, or play **(p. 102)**

tema *s.* idea principal de un cuento, poema u obra de teatro

thrive (thryv) *v.* to grow with good force and energy **(p. 606)**

desarrollar(se) *v.* crecer con fuerza y energía

tirade (TY rayd) *n.* a long, angry speech **(p. 800)**

diatriba *s.* discurso largo y ofensivo

tolerance (TAWL ur uns) *n.* sympathy for people, beliefs, or ideas that are different from one's own **(p. 986)**

tolerancia *s.* respeto o consideración por las personas, creencias o ideas que son diferentes

tomb (toom) *n.* a vault, chamber, or grave for the dead **(p. 778)**

tumba *s.* bóveda, cámara o sepultura para enterrar un cadáver

torrent (TOR unt) *n.* a strong rush of anything (usually water) flowing swiftly and wildly **(p. 386)**

torrente *s.* abundancia de cosas que fluyen rápida e impetuosamente

transforming (trans FORM ing) *v.* changing; form of the verb *transform* **(p. 631)**

transformando *v.* cambiando; forma del verbo *transformar*

trek (trek) *n.* a slow or difficult journey **(p. 928)**

viaje {arduo} *s.* desplazamiento lento y difícil

triumphant (try UM funt) *adj.* joyful in victory; successful **(p. 67)**

triunfal *adj.* victorioso; que tiene éxito

U

ultimately (UL tuh mit lee) *adv.* in the end; finally **(p. 485)**

finalmente *adv.* en última instancia; a la larga

unique (yoo NEEK) *adj.* unlike anything else **(p. 17)**

incomparable *adj.* que no tiene comparación

V

vaguely (VAYG lee) *adv.* in a way that is not clear, exact, or definite **(p. 784)**

vagamente *adv.* de un modo poco claro, impreciso, o indefinido

vaults (vawltz) *n.* locked rooms or boxes for keeping money and valuables **(p. 363)**

bóvedas de seguridad *s.* cámaras blindadas que sirven para guardar dinero y objetos de valor

vicinity (vuh SIN ih tee) *n.* the area around a certain place **(p. 312)**

alrededores *s.* territorio que rodea a cierto lugar

visible (VIZ uh bul) *adj.* able to be seen **(p. 324)**

visible *adj.* que se puede ver

visualize (VIZH oo uh lyz) *v.* to form a mental picture of; call to mind **(p. 884)**

visualizar *v.* formar en la mente; recordar

visually (VIZH oo uh lee) *adv.* using or appealing to the sense of sight **(p. 416)**

visualmente *adv.* que usa imágenes que se perciben con la vista

vividly (VIV ud lee) *adv.* clearly **(p. 107)**

vívidamente *adv.* con claridad

volunteer (vol un TEER) *n.* one who offers to do something by choice, without being forced **(p. 50)**

voluntario(a) *s.* persona que se ofrece a hacer algo por propia voluntad, y no por fuerza

W

warrant (WAR unt) *n.* a document, or piece of paper, that gives a police officer the right to do something, such as arrest a person **(p. 143)**

orden de detención *s.* documento que autoriza a un oficial de la policía a realizar un arresto

wary (WAIR ee) *adj.* careful, alert **(p. 282)**

cauteloso(a) *adj.* cuidadoso, con precaución

whims (wimz) *n.* sudden urges, desires, or ideas **(p. 566)**

antojos *s.* deseo vivo, intenso y pasajero de algo

whimsical (WIM zih kul) *adj.* light and natural; not serious **(p. 706)**

fantasioso(a) *adj.* imaginativo y poco serio

wholeheartedly (hohl HAR tid lee) *adv.* sincerely and enthusiastically **(p. 226)**

de todo corazón *fr. adv.* con sinceridad y entusiasmo; frase adverbial

worthwhile (wurth whyl) *adj.* having value or goodness; deserving one's efforts or attention **(p. 688)**

{vale} la pena *col.* que tiene aprecio y estimación; que merece el esfuerzo y la atención; frase con la palabra *pena*

writhed (rythd) *v.* twisted and turned, as from suffering; form of the verb *writhe* **(p. 389)**

retorció *v.* torció dando vueltas, esp. de dolor; forma del verbo *retorcer(se)*

INDEX OF SKILLS

References beginning with R *refer to Handbook pages.*

References beginning with RH *refer to the Reading Handbook.*

Literary and Text Elements

Reading and Thinking

Grammar and Language

Vocabulary

Writing

Listening, Speaking, and Viewing Skills

Research and Study Skills

INDEX OF AUTHORS AND TITLES

A

B

C

D

E

F

G

H

I

J

INDEX OF ART AND ARTISTS

ACKNOWLEDGMENTS

Unit 1

"Flash Flood" by William M. Hendryx, reprinted with permission from the November 2004 Reader's Digest. Copyright © 2004 by the Reader's Digest Assn., Inc.

"Paddling Dicey Waters" by Lew Freedman. From *Chicago Tribune,* July 1, 2002. Copyright © 2005 by Chicago Tribune Company.

From "Seventh Grade" from *Baseball in April and Other Stories*, copyright © 1990 by Gary Soto. Reprinted by permission of Harcourt, Inc.

"Where You Are" from *The Invention of New Jersey* by Jack Anderson, © 1969. Reprinted by permission of the University of Pittsburgh Press.

"Message of Hope" by Ericka Sóuter and Dietlind Lerner. From *People,* February 7, 2005.

"Teaching Nepalis to Read, Plant, and Vote" by Lesley Reed. *Faces: People, Places, and Cultures,* April 2005.

"May I Have Your Autograph?" by Marjorie Sharmat, copyright © 1984, from *Sixteen: Short Stories by Outstanding Writers for Young Adults,* ed. by Donald R. Gallo.

"Suzy and Leah" by Jane Yolen. Copyright © 1993 by Jane Yolen. Originally published by *American Girl Magazine*. Reprinted by permission of Curtis Brown, Ltd.

From *How Things Work* by the Editors of Consumer Guide.® Copyright © 1990 by Publications International, Ltd.

"Summer Reading" by Michael Dorris. *Detroit News,* May 1991.

"The First Book," from *On the Bus With Rosa Parks,* W.W. Norton & Co. © 1999 by Rita Dove. Reprinted with permission of the author.

"The Day It Rained Cockroaches" from *The Pigman & Me* by Paul Zindel. Copyright © 1991 by Paul Zindel.

Unit 2

"Tony Hawk: Chairman of the Board" by Steve Pittman. From SPORTS ILLUSTRATED FOR KIDS Books. Copyright © 2001 by Time Inc.

From *Rosa Parks: My Story* by Rosa Parks with Jim Haskins, copyright © 1992 by Rosa Parks. Used by permission of Dial Books for Young Readers, A Division of Penguin Young Readers Group, A Member of Penguin Group (USA) Inc., 345 Hudson Street, New York, NY 10014. All rights reserved.

Excerpted from *The Kid's Guide to Social Action: How to Solve the Social Problems You Choose–and Turn Creative Thinking into Positive Action (Revised, Expanded, Updated Edition)* by Barbara A. Lewis © 1998. Used with permission from Free Spirit Publishing Inc., Minneapolis, MN; 1-866-703-7322; www.freespirit.com. All rights reserved.

"An Hour with Abuelo" from *An Island Like You: Stories of the Barrio* by Judith Ortiz Cofer. Published by Orchard Books/Scholastic Inc. Copyright © 1995 by Judith Ortiz Cofer. Reprinted by permission.

"Toward a Rainbow Nation" by Lavendhri Pillay. From *No More Strangers Now: Young Voices from a New South Africa,* interviews by Tim McKee. Copyright © 1998 by Timothy Saunders McKee.

"New Directions" from *Wouldn't Take Nothing For My Journey Now* by Maya Angelou, copyright © 1993 by Maya Angelou. Used by permission of Random House, Inc.

"The War of the Wall," from *Deep Sightings and Rescue Missions* by Toni Cade Bambara. Copyright © 1996 by The Estate of Toni Cade Bambara.

"The Liberation Army Dancer" from *Red Scarf Girl: A Memoir of the Cultural Revolution*, by Ji Li Jiang. Copyright © 1997 by Ji Li Jiang. Forward copyright © 1997 by HarperCollins Publishers. Used by permission of HarperCollins Publishers.

"Miracle Hands" by Christina Cheakalos and Matt Birkbeck, updated 2007 from. © Time Inc.

From *Barrio Boy* by Ernesto Galarza. Copyright © 1971 by the University of Notre Dame Press: Notre Dame, Indiana.

"How I Learned English" by Gregory Djanikian. Reprinted by permission of the author.

"Graduation Address" by Robert Fontaine, from *The Big Book of Skits,* © 1996 and *Plays, the Drama Magazine for Young People* © May 2001, reprinted with the permission of the publishers *Plays*/Sterling Partners, Inc., PO Box 600160, Newton, MA 02460

Unit 3

"Broken Chain" from *Baseball in April and Other Stories,* copyright © 1990 by Gary Soto. Reprinted by permission of Harcourt, Inc.

"Friendships and Peer Pressure" from *Teen Health,* copyright © 2005 by Glencoe/McGraw-Hill.

"Amigo Brothers" by Piri Thomas. Reprinted by permission of the author.

"Framed" from *Six-Minute Mysteries* by Don Wulffson. Copyright © 1994 by RGA Publishing Group, Inc.

"Loser" from *The Girl in the Flammable Skirt* by Aimee Bender. Copyright © 1998 by Aimee Bender.

"Friends Forever" by Sari Locker. Updated 2005 from *Teen People,* May 19, 1998.

"The Good Samaritan" from *Finding Our Way* by René Saldaña, Jr. Copyright © 2003 by René Saldaña, Jr.

"The Brink's Robbery" from *The Wild Side: Crime and Punishment.* Copyright © 2001 by NTC/Contemporary Publishing Group, Inc.

"Lob's Girl" from *A Whisper in the Night* by Joan Aiken. Delacorte Press. Copyright © 1984 by Joan Aiken Enterprises, Ltd. Used by permission of Brandt & Hochman Literary Agents, Inc.

"Home" from *Maud Martha* by Gwendolyn Brooks. Copyright © 1991 by Gwendolyn Brooks Blakely. Reprinted by consent of Brooks Permission.

Unit 4

Excerpted from "Ban Hockey Thug for Life," an editorial in *The Denver Post*, March 11, 2004. Reprinted by permission of *The Denver Post*.

"Thank You Ma'am" by Langston Hughes. Copyright © 1958 by Langston Hughes. Copyright renewed 1986 by George Houston Bass.

"What Exercise Can Do for You" by Sheila Globus. *Current Health*, 1997. Reprinted by permission of WRC Media, Inc.

"Oprah Winfrey" by Sidney Poitier. from *TIME,* April 26, 2004.

"The Courage That My Mother had" by Edna St. Vincent Millay. From *Collected Poems,* HarperCollins. Copyright © 1954, 1982 by Norma Millay Ellis. All rights reserved.

"Two People I Want to Be Like" from *If Only I Could Tell You,* by Eve Merriam. Copyright © 1983 by Eve Merriam. Reprinted by permission of Marian Reiner.

From "Should Naturalized Citizens be President?" by John Yinger and Matthew Spalding. Published in *The New York Times Upfront,* February 14, 2005. Copyright © 2005 by Scholastic, Inc. Reprinted by permission.

"The Teacher Who Changed My Life" by Nicholas Gage. Reprinted by permission of the author.

"Take the Junk Out of Marketing Food to Kids" from *Detroit Free Press (via Knight-Ridder/Tribune News Service),* January 19, 2005. Copyright © 2005 by Detroit Free Press.

Unit 5

From *The Story of Music, Volume 6: From Rock and Pop to Hip-Hop*. Copyright © The Brown Reference Group plc. Originally published in the US by Grolier. Reprinted by permission of The Brown Reference Group.

"Lafff" by Lensey Namioka, copyright © 1993, from *Within Reach,* ed. by Donald R. Gallo. Reprinted by permission of Lensey Namioka. All rights are reserved by the Author.

"Cyber Chitchat" by Cindy Kauffman, from *Chocolate for a Teen's Dreams,* Copyright © 2003, ed. by Kay Allenbaugh.

"Conserving Resources" from *Glencoe Science,* copyright © 2006 by Glencoe/McGraw-Hill.

"There Will Come Soft Rains," by Ray Bradbury. Reprinted by permission of Don Congdon Associates, Inc. Copyright © 1950 by Crowell Collier Publishing Company, 1977 by Ray Bradbury.

"The Next Big Thing" by Maryanne Murray Buechner and Mitch Frank, updated 2007 from *TIME,* September 8, 2003. © Time Inc.

"Big Yellow Taxi," by Joni Mitchell. Copyright © 1970 Siquomb Publishing Corp. All rights administered by Song/ATV Music Publishing, 8 Music Square West, Nashville, TN 37203. All rights reserved. Used by permission.

"Fireproofing the Forests" by J. Madeleine Nash, updated 2005, from *TIME,* August 18, 2003. © Time Inc.

From "Missing: The Frog Population in Costa Rica is Declining. Scientists Search for Answers" by Claire Miller. Published in *Scholastic Superscience Red,* April 2005. Copyright © 2005 by Scholastic Inc. Reprinted by permission.

"Birdfoot's Grampa" from *Entering Onondaga,* copyright © 1975 by Joseph Bruchac. Reprinted by permission of Barbara S. Kouts.

"America the Not-so-Beautiful" from *Not That You Asked . . .* by Andrew A. Rooney. Copyright © 1989 by Random House.

"A Glimpse of Home" by Kathryn Sullivan. Copyright © 2002. Reprinted with permission.

"Key Item" by Isaac Asimov. Published by permission of the Estate of Isaac Asimov, c/o Ralph M. Vicinanza, Ltd.

Unit 6

"Brer Rabbit and Brer Lion" from *The Tales of Uncle Remus* by Julius Lester. Copyright © 1987 by Julius Lester, text. Used by permission of Dial Books for Young Readers, A Division of Penguin Young Readers Group, A Member of Penguin Group (USA) Inc., 345 Hudson Street, New York, NY 10014. All rights reserved.

"The Lion, the Hare and the Hyena" from *Nelson Mandela's Favorite African Folktales,* edited by Nelson Mandela. Copyright © 2002 in this selection by Tafelberg Publishers Ltd. Used by permission of W.W. Norton & Company, Inc.

"Charles" from *The Lottery* by Shirley Jackson. Copyright © 1948, 1949 by Shirley Jackson, and copyright renewed © 1976 by Laurence Hyman, Barry Hyman, Mrs. Sarah Webster and Mrs. Joanne Schnurer.

"The Boy and His Grandfather" by Rudolfo Anaya, from *Cuentos: Tales from the Hispanic Southwest.* Copyright © 1980 by the Museum of New Mexico Press. Reprinted by permission.

"Jeremiah's Song" by Walter Dean Myers. Reprinted by permission of Miriam Altshuler Literary Agency, on behalf of Walter Dean Myers. Copyright © 1987 by Walter Dean Myers.

"We Are All One" from *The Rainbow People* by Laurence Yep. Copyright © 1989 by Laurence Yep.

"Voices–and Stories–from the Past" by Kathryn Satterfield, updated 2006 from *TIME for Kids,* February 6, 2004.

"Aunty Misery" by Judith Ortiz Cofer. Reprinted by permission of the author.

"Aunt Sue's Stories," from *The Collected Poems of Langston Hughes* by Langston Hughes, copyright © 1994 by The Estate of Langston Hughes. Used by permission of Alfred A. Knopf, a division of Random House, Inc.

"I Ask My Mother to Sing," from *Rose* by Li-Young Lee. Copyright © 1986 by Li-Young Lee. BOA Editions. Reprinted by permission of The Permissions Company.

The Bunyans by Audrey Wood, illustrated by David Shannon. Text copyright © 1996 by Audrey Wood, illustrations copyright © 1996 by David Shannon. All rights reserved.

Unit 7

"One" from *When I Dance,* copyright © 1991, 1988 by James Berry.

"Names/Nombres" by Julia Alvarez. First published in *Nuestro,* March 1985. Reprinted by permission of Susan Bergholz Literary Services, New York. All rights reserved.

"Diondra Jordan" from *Bronx Masquerade* by Nikki Grimes. Copyright © 2002 by Nikki Grimes. Used by permission of Dial Books for Young Readers, a Division of Penguin Young Readers Group, a Member of Penguin Group (USA), 345 Hudson Street, New York, NY 10014. All rights reserved.

"Ode to la Tortilla" from *Neighborhood Odes*, copyright © 1992 by Gary Soto. Reprinted by permission of Harcourt, Inc.

"Face It," reprinted with the permission of Margaret K. McElderry Books, an imprint of Simon & Schuster Children's Publishing Division, from *A Suitcase of Seaweed and Other Poems*, by Janet S. Wong. Copyright © 1996 Janet S. Wong.

"Almost Ready" from *Slow Dance Heartbreak Blues* by Arnold Adoff. Copyright © 1995 by Arnold Adoff.

"Reading, Writing, Rapping" by Elizabeth Wellington. From *The Philadelphia Inquirer.* Copyright © 2003 by The Philadelphia Inquirer.

"Growing Pains" from *Hey World, Here I Am!* Copyright © 1986 by Jean Little.

"What Makes Teens Tick?" by Claudia Wallis, updated 2007 from. © Time Inc.

"The Women's 400 Meters," from *The Sidewalk Racer and Other Poems of Sports and Motion* by Lillian Morrison. Copyright © 1965, 1967, 1968, 1977 by Lillian Morrison. Used by permission of Marian Reiner for the author.

Yusef Komunyakaa, "Slam, Dunk and Hook" from *Magic City,* © 1992 by Yusef Komunyakaa and reprinted by permission of Wesleyan University Press.

"The Giggle Prescription" by Tracy Eberhart and Robert A. Barrnett, updated 2007 from. © Time Inc.

"The Carcajou and the Kincajou" and "The Termite" from *Candy is Dandy: The Best of Ogden Nash.*

Unit 8

"It Was Not My Finest Hour" by Linda Meyers Donelson.

"Kingdoms of Gold and Salt" from *Discovering Our Past: Medieval and Early Modern Times,* copyright © 2006 by Glencoe/McGraw-Hill.

"Letters from Home" by Graeme Davis. *dig,* May/June 2005.

"Ah, Wilderness!" by Amanda Hinnant, updated 2006 from *Real Simple,* March 2004. Copyright © TIME Inc.

"Photographing History" from *The Contemporary Reader,* copyright © 2003 by Glencoe/McGraw-Hill.

"The Monsters Are Due On Maple Street" by Rod Serling. All rights reserved. © 1960 Rod Serling; © 1988 by Carolyn Serling, Jodi Serling and Anne Serling.

"Teacher Hero: Erin Gruwell" by Jerrilyn Jacobs from *The My Hero Project* www.myhero.com.

"Saturday, May 2, 1992," "Sunday, May 3, 1992," "Tuesday, May 5, 1992," "Thursday, May 7, 1992," "Wednesday, May 13, 1992," from *Zlata's Diary* by Zlata Filipovic. Copyright © 1994 Editions Robert Laffont/Fixot. Used by permission of Viking Penguin, A Division of Penguin Group (USA) Inc.

"There Is No Word for Goodbye" by Mary Tallmountain. Reprinted by permission of Tallmountain Circle.

Illustrations

Annette Lasker
Anthology, Inc.
Mazer Corporation
Moonlight Studios
Morgan-Cain & Associates

Photography

Abbreviation key: AH=Aaron Haupt Photography; AR=Art Resource, New York; BAL=Bridgeman Art Library, London/New York; CB=Corbis/Bettmann; CI=Christie's Images; LPBC/AH=book provided by Little Professor Book Company. Photo by AH; LOC=Library of Congress; PR=Photo Researchers; SIS=Stock Illustration Source; SS=SuperStock; TSI=Tony Stone Images; TSM=The Stock Market.

Cover (t)Allan Davey/Masterfile, (b)John Foster/Masterfile; viii CORBIS; x AFP/Getty Images; xii Gilles Mingasson/Getty Images; xiv Bruce Fleming/Masterfile; xvi NASA; xviii Randy Faris/CORBIS; xx Rubberball/SS; xxii Laura Sifferlin; xxiv (l)Getty Images, (r)Getty Images; xxv (t)Getty Images, (tc)Clay Bennett/The Christian Science Monitor, (b)Getty Images, (bc)Getty Images; xxvi Getty Images; xxvii (l)Getty Images, (r)Getty Images; xxx Geoff Butler; xxxvi Dinah Mite Activities; xxxvii (t)Getty Images, (b)Getty Images; RH Getty Images; RH19 (l)Greg Kuchik/Getty Images, (r)Mel Curtis/Getty Images; ii CORBIS; 2 (l)Ariel Skelley/CORBIS, (r)CORBIS; 5 Tim Davis/Stone/Getty Images; 8 Tom Spitz; 10 Tom Spitz; 12 UNIVERSAL PRESS SYNDICATE; 13 John Evans; 14 Lew Freedman/Chicago Tribune; 16 David Freeman; 18 Michael & Patricia Fogden/Minden Pictures; 20 David Freeman; 21 David Freeman; 22 David Freeman; 24 Courtesy Gary Soto; 26 Mark Gervase/Getty Images; 29 Alamy Images; 30 Rob Lewine/CORBIS; 32 Mark Gervase/Getty Images; 35 CORBIS; 38 Universal Press Syndicate; 39 Richard Hutchings/PR; 40 Jack Anderson; 43 Images.com/CORBIS; 44 Images.com/CORBIS; 48 Louise Gubb; 49 Louise Gubb; 50 (t)Louise Gubb, (b)Louise Gubb; 51 Louise Gubb; 52 Louise Gubb; 54 Universal Press Syndicate; 55 Laura Sifferlin; 56 Courtesy Lesley Reed; 58 Alison Wright/CORBIS; 59 Dinesh Dhungel; 60 (t)Dinesh Dhungel, (b)Dinesh Dhungel; 62 Alison Wright/CORBIS; 64 Andrew Sharmat; 66 (t)James L. Amos/CORBIS, (b)Alamy Images; 68 Karen Beard/Getty Images; 70 Patrik Giardino/CORBIS; 77 Universal Press Syndicate; 78 Universal Press Syndicate; 79 John Evans; 80 Jason Stemple; 82 Getty Images; 84 CORBIS; 86 Bettmann/CORBIS; 89 Bettmann/CORBIS; 92 Getty Images; 97 Stefano Bianchetti/CORBIS; 99 Mark Burnett; 100 Stefano Bianchetti/CORBIS; 104 Hulton Archive/Getty Images; 105 BAL; 106 BAL; 108 Tim Wright/CORBIS; 109 Art Resource; 110 (t)BAL, (b)Art Resource; 114 (l)David Zindel, (r)V. Brockhaus/Zefa/CORBIS; 115 CORBIS; 117 Alexandra Day/CORBIS; 118 BAL/Getty Images; 120 (tl)Eclipse Studios, (tr)Eclipse Studios, (tr)Eclipse Studios, (bl)Eclipse Studios, (br) Eclipse Studios; 121 (tl)Eclipse Studios, (bl)Eclipse Studios, (br)Eclipse Studios; 124 Gabe Palmer/Zefa/CORBIS; 128 AFP/Getty Images; 130 (l)Ariel Skelley/CORBIS, (r)Lawrence Manning/CORBIS; 133 J. Grant Brittain; 136 Randy Glasbergen; 137 Laura Sifferlin; 138 Bob Fitch/Black Star; 140 Bettmann/CORBIS; 141 The publisher wishes to thank The National Association for the Advancement of Colored People for authorizing the use of this photograph.; 142 AP/Wide World Photos; 144 Bettmann/CORBIS; 146 Courtesy of Barbara A. Lewis; 148 Dalie Jimenez; 150 Dalie Jimenez; 156 Universal Press Syndicate; 157 Matt Meadows; 158 Miriam Berkley; 160 (inset)Getty Images, Images.com/CORBIS; 162 Erich Lessing/AR; 163 AR; 165 Zurbaran Galleria/SS; 166 Images.com/CORBIS; 168 Anna C. Blackshaw; 170 Anna C. Blackshaw; 171 Anna C. Blackshaw; 173 Anna C. Blackshaw; 174 Anna C. Blackshaw; 176 Universal Press Syndicate; 177 Laura Sifferlin; 178 Thomas Lau/CORBIS; 180 William Manning/CORBIS; 181 CORBIS; 182 (t)Russell Lee/CORBIS, (b)Mark Burnett; 183 Becky Luigart-Stayner/CORBIS; 186 Bill Gaskins; 188 Zoran Milch/Masterfile; 191 Lee Snider/Photo Images/CORBIS; 193 Brenda Tharp/CORBIS; 196 Lee Snider/Photo Images/CORBIS; 199 Universal Press Syndicate; 203 King Features Syndicate; 204 CORBIS; 205 John Evans; 206 Ji-li Jiang; 209 Snark/AR; 210 Dennis Cox/Alamy; 211 Giry Daniel/Sygma/CORBIS; 212 Hulton Archive/Getty Images; 214 Hulton Archive/Getty Images; 218 Courtesy John Chung; 219 Andrew Kist; 220 Andrew Kist; 224 Courtesy Stanford University News Service; 225 Hulton-Deutsch/CORBIS; 226 Getty Images; 227 CORBIS; 228 (l)City of Sacramento Archives and Museum Collection, (r)CORBIS; 229 CORBIS; 230 CORBIS; 231 Tommy Leonardi; 232 H. Armstrong Roberts; 233 Image.com/CORBIS; 234 (t)Hulton-Deutsch/CORBIS, (b)H. Armstrong Roberts; 239 Pete Gardner/Getty Images; 240 Images.com/CORBIS; 241 Images.com/CORBIS; 242 (tl)Eclipse Studios, (tr)Eclipse Studios, (bl)file photo, (br)Eclipse Studios; 243 (tl)Eclipse Studios, (tr)Eclipse Studios, (bl)Eclipse Studios, (br)Eclipse Studios; 250 Gilles Mingasson/Getty Images; 252 (l)Ariel Skelley/CORBIS, (r)Julie Houck/CORBIS; 255 Richard Smith/CORBIS; 258 Alan & Sandy Carey/PR; 261 Richard Laird/FPG; 263 Mark Steinmetz; 266 King Features Syndicate; 267 Getty Images; 270 Roy Morsch/Zefa/CORBIS; 271 Joseph Sohm/ChromoSohm/CORBIS; 273 Ed Kashi/CORBIS; 274 Roy Morsch/Zefa/CORBIS; 276 Courtesy Piri Thomas; 278 Joe McBride/CORBIS; 280 Getty Images; 283 Bill Angresano; 286 Shawn Frederick/CORBIS; 288 Bettmann/CORBIS; 290 Joe McBride/CORBIS; 294 King Features Syndicate; 298 Universal Press Syndicate; 299 Getty Images; 300 Pam

Wulffson; 302 CORBIS; 305 BAL; 308 CORBIS; 310 Bettmann/CORBIS; 312 AR; 314 Underwood & Underwood/CORBIS; 316 San Diego Museum of Art, Gift of Anne R. and Amy Putnam; 318 AR; 320 Universal Press Syndicate; 321 John Evans; 322 Jerry Bauer; 324 G. Moon/Photex/Zefa/CORBIS; 326 Images.com/CORBIS; 328 Images.com/CORBIS; 330 G. Moon/Photex/Zefa/CORBIS; 334 Robin Bowman; 335 Janie Airey/Digital Vision/Getty Images; 337 Photodisc/Getty Images; 338 Robin Bowman; 345 King Features Syndicate; 346 Universal Press Syndicate; 347 Getty Images; 348 Rene Saldana; 350 Louis K. Meisel Gallery/CORBIS; 352 Images.com/CORBIS; 354 Joson/Zefa/CORBIS; 355 Alamy Images; 356 Tom Merton/Getty Images; 358 Louis K. Meisel Gallery/CORBIS; 362 (t)Bettman/CORBIS, (b)Time Life Pictures/Getty Images; 363 Bettman/CORBIS; 364 Carl Iwasaki/Time & Life Pictures/Getty Images; 366 Bettman/CORBIS; 370 Rod Delroy; 371 Joel Sartore/Getty Images; 372 Franz Gorski/Peter Arnold, Inc.; 374 BAL; 377 CI; 378 Onne Van Der Wal; 381 Peter Henschel/FPG; 385 AP/Wide World Photos; 387 Fine Art Photographic Library/CORBIS; 390 James Wyeth; 392 (t)Joel Sartore/Getty Images, (b)Fine Art Photographic Library/CORBIS; 396 (t)UPI/Bettmann/CORBIS, (b)Courtesy Pinkie Gardner; 397 Christian Pierre/SS; 398 AR; 399 Elizabeth Barakah Hodges/SS; 400 (tl)Eclipse Studios, (tr)file photo, (bl)file photo, (br)file photo; 401 (tl)Eclipse Studios, (tr)Eclipse Studios, (bl)Eclipse Studios, (br) Eclipse Studios; 408 Bruce Fleming/Masterfile; 410 (l)Gabe Palmer/CORBIS, (r)CORBIS; 415 Andy Clark/CORBIS; 416 Universal Press Syndicate; 417 John Evans; 418 Clay Bennett; 420 Clay Bennett/The Christian Science Monitor; 421 (t)Clay Bennett/The Christian Science Monitor, (b)Clay Bennett/The Christian Science Monitor; 422 Clay Bennett/The Christian Science Monitor; 424 Schomburg Center for Research in Black Culture, The New York Public Library - Astor, Lenox and Tilden Foundation; 427 Doug Martin; 428 AR; 429 Hampton University Museum, Hampton, VA.; 430 Photograph courtesy of Gwendolyn Knight Lawrence/AR; 432 Hampton University Museum, Hampton, VA.; 438 King Features Syndicate; 439 John Evans; 440 Courtesy of Sheila Globus; 442 Warrren Morgan/CORBIS; 445 Joseph Sohm/ChromoSohm/CORBIS; 446 Joseph Sohm/ChromoSohm/CORBIS; 450 Dave Allocca/DMI/Time Life Pictures/Getty Images; 452 Dave Allocca/DMI/Time Life Pictures/Getty Images; 454 Universal Press Syndicate.; 455 Laura Sifferlin; 456 (t)LOC/CORBIS, (b)Bachrach/Printed by permission of Marian Reiner; 458 SS; 459 Images.com/CORBIS; 460 (t)SS, (b)Images.com/CORBIS; 469 Universal Press Syndicate; 473 Universal Press Syndicate; 474 Universal Press Syndicate; 475 John Evans; 476 (t)Syracuse University Photographer Stephen Sartori, (b)Andrew Blasko/ Heritage Foundation; 478 Ted Soqui/CORBIS; 482 Allen/Gamma-Liaison Agency; 485 Eddie Adams; 487 Courtesy Nicholas Gage; 488 Courtesy Nicholas Gage; 490 J. Noelker/The Image Works; 492 Eddie Adams; 497 Images.com/CORBIS; 500 (t)JupiterImages, (b)Troy Wayrynen/Columbian/NewSport/CORBIS; 502 Images.com/CORBIS, Ted Soqui/CORBIS; 506 UPI/Bettmann/CORBIS; 507 Iconica/Getty Images; 509 Bob Krist/CORBIS; 510 Paul Nicklen/National Geographic/Getty Images; 512 (tl)Eclipse Studios, (tr)Eclipse Studios, (bl)Eclipse Studios, (br)Eclipse Studios; 513 (tl)Eclipse Studios, (tr)Eclipse Studios, (bl)Eclipse Studios, (br)Eclipse Studios; 516 KLEIN/Peter Arnold, Inc.; 520 NASA; 522 (l)Daniel Erickson, (r)Rob Lewine/Zefa/CORBIS; 525 Duane Rieder/Getty Images; 526 S.I.N./CORBIS; 527 Burke/Triolo/Getty Images; 528 UNIVERSAL PRESS SYNDICATE; 529 John Evans; 530 Courtesy Lensey Namioka, photo by Don Perkins; 532 Detlev Van Ravenswaay/Science Photo Library; 533 Everett Collection; 535 Erik Von Weber/Getty Images; 536 LWA-Dann Tardif/CORBIS; 540 CORBIS; 542 Detlev Van Ravenswaay/Science Photo Library; 544 Courtesy Cindy Kauffman; 548 Stewart Cohen/Getty Images; 550 Stewart Cohen/Getty Images; 556 Getty Images; 557 Laura Sifferlin; 560 CORBIS; 563 Bisson Bernard/Sygma/CORBIS; 564 CORBIS; 566 Satelight/Gamma Liaison; 568 Brad Wrobleski/Masterfile; 569 Lois Ellen Frank/CORBIS; 570 Garry Black/Masterfile; 573 Vera Storman/Getty Images; 575 Jim Zuckerman/CORBIS; 576 Garry Black/Masterfile; 578 King Features Syndicate; 579 John Evans; 583 Bettmann/CORBIS; 584 Friday Associates; 585 Jack W. Aeby; 586 (t)Courtesy Motorola, (b)IBM; 588 Bettmann/CORBIS; 590 Henry Diltz/CORBIS; 593 Patti Mollica/SS; 594 Patti Mollica/SS; 597 King Features Syndicate; 601 Universal Press Syndicate; 602 King Features Syndicate; 603 John Evans; 607 AP Wide World; 608 William F. Cambell; 610 William F. Cambell; 612 AP Wide World; 614 courtesy Joseph Bruchac; 616 Michael Fogden/ Animals Animals-Earth Scenes; 617 Michael Fogden/Animals Animals-Earth Scenes; 618 Michael and Patricia Fogden/CORBIS; 619 James L. Amos/CORBIS; 620 (t)Michael Fogden/ Animals Animals-Earth Scenes, (b)James L. Amos/CORBIS; 624 Keith Bedford/Stinger/Getty Images; 625 Stephen Ferry/Getty Images; 627 Jeff Sherman/Getty Images; 628 Getty Images; 629 COSI; 630 NASA; 631 (t)NASA, (b)NASA; 632 (t)Jeff Sherman/Getty Images, (b)NASA; 635 Tom Stewart/CORBIS; 636 (l)Peter C. Jones/Alex Gotfryd/Bettmann/CORBIS, (r)PHOTO MEDIA/Retrofile; 638 PHOTO MEDIA/Retrofile; 640 (tl)Eclipse Studios, (tr)Eclipse Studios, (bl)Eclipse Studios, (br)Eclipse Studios; 641 (tl)Eclipse Studios, (tr)Eclipse Studios, (bl)Eclipse Studios, (br)Eclipse Studios; 648 Randy Faris/CORBIS; 650 (l)Think Stock/Getty Images, (r)CORBIS; 655 Christian Pierre/SS; 656 Universal Press Syndicate; 657 Getty Images; 662 Siede Preis/Getty Images; 666 Lawrence J. Hyman/courtesy Bantam Books; 668 Matt Meadows; 670 Simon Watson/Getty Images; 672 BAL; 674 Matt Meadows; 680 King Features Syndicate; 681 John Evans; 682 Miriam Berkley; 684 (inset)Kevin Fleming/CORBIS, (frame)Getty Images; 685 AR; 686 Kevin Fleming/CORBIS; 688 Constance Myers; 691 BAL; 692 Jim Erickson/CORBIS; 695 Maurice Faulk/SS; 698 Will & Deni McIntyre/Getty Images; 700 Jim Erickson/CORBIS; 702 King Features Syndicate; 703 John Evans; 704 Mary Moylan; 706 Written and Illustrated by Mark Crilley. Used with Permission. AKIKO is a trademark of Sirius Entertainment; 707 Written and Illustrated by Mark Crilley. Used with Permission. AKIKO is a trademark of Sirius Entertainment; 708 Written and Illustrated by Mark Crilley. Used with Permission. AKIKO is a trademark of Sirius Entertainment; 709 Written and Illustrated by Mark Crilley. Used with Permission. AKIKO is a trademark of Sirius Entertainment; 710 Written and Illustrated by Mark Crilley. Used with Permission. AKIKO is a trademark of Sirius Entertainment; 711 Written and Illustrated by Mark Crilley. Used with Permission. AKIKO is a trademark of Sirius Entertainment; 714 Courtesy Scholastic Books; 716 BAL; 718 CORBIS; 719 C. Allan Morgan/Peter Arnold, Inc.; 720 BAL; 722 CORBIS; 726 Randy Glasbergen; 729 Universal Press Syndicate; 730 Images.com/CORBIS; 731 John Evans; 734 LOC; 735 (l)LOC, (r)LOC; 736 Courtesy Polk County Democrat; 738 LOC; 740 Miriam Berkley; 743 BAL; 744 Stapleton Collection/CORBIS; 746 BAL; 750 Schomburg Center for Research in Black Culture, The New York Public Library - Astor, Lenox and Tilden Foundation; 751 Colin Bootman/BAL; 752 Dorothy Alexander; 753 Keren Su/CORBIS; 754 (t)Colin Bootman/BAL, (b)Keren Su/CORBIS; 758 Courtesy Audrey Wood; 759 (t)Reprinted by permission of Scholastic., (b)Daniel J. Cox/CORBIS; 761 (l)Dennis Degnan/CORBIS, (r)Reprinted by permission of Scholastic.; 762 (tl)Eclipse Studios, (tr)Eclipse Studios, (bl)Eclipse Studios, (br)Eclipse Studios; 763 (tl)Eclipse Studios, (tr)Eclipse Studios, (bl)Eclipse Studios, (br)Eclipse Studios; 770 Rubberball/SS; 772 (l)Laurence Dutton/Getty Images, (r)Syracuse Newspapers/Randi Anglin/The Image Works; 776 Universal Press Syndicate; 777 Getty Images; 778 FPG; 780 AR; 782 AR; 784 Theo Westernberger/Gamma-Liaison Network; 786 Schalkwijk/AR; 789 Robert Van Der Hilst/Stone; 790 CI; 791 Mark Burnett; 792 Schalkwijk/AR; 796 Universal Press Syndicate; 798 Universal Press Syndicate; 799 Getty Images; 800 Steve Elliot; 802 Getty Images; 803 David Nicholls/CORBIS; 805 Francisco Cruz/SS; 806 Getty Images; 808 (t)Courtesy Simon & Schuster, (b)Virginia Hamilton Adoff; 810 Roy Morsch/Zefa/CORBIS; 811 SS; 812 Roy Morsch/Zefa/CORBIS; 814 Universal Press Syndicate; 815 Getty Images; 816 (t)FPG, (b)E.O. Hoppe/CORBIS; 819 Terra Foundation for American Art, Chicago/AR; 820 Terra Foundation for American Art, Chicago/AR; 825 David Swanson/The Philadelphia Inquirer; 826 David Swanson/The Philadelphia Inquirer; 827 David Swanson/The Philadelphia Enquirer; 828 David Swanson/The Philadelphia Inquirer; 833 Universal Press Syndicate; 834 Images.com/CORBIS; 835 Getty Images; 836 Courtesy Penguin Books, Toronto; 838 BAL; 840 BAL; 847 Chris Usher; 849 Diagram: Joe Lertola Photo: Trujillo-Paumier/The Image Bank/Getty Images; 850 Chris Usher; 855 BONGARTS/SportsChrome; 856 Spencer Rowell/FPG; 857 Blair Seitz/PR;

858 Carl Schneider/Gamma-Liaison International; 860 (t)BONGARTS/SportsChrome, (b)Carl Schneider/Gamma-Liaison International; 864 Arni Katz/Index Stock; 865 Tribune Media Services; 867 Hulton-Deutsch Collection/CORBIS; 868 (tl)Eclipse Studios, (tr)Eclipse Studios, (bl)Eclipse Studios, (br)Eclipse Studios; 869 (tl)Eclipse Studios, (tr)Eclipse Studios, (bl)Eclipse Studios, (br)Eclipse Studios; 876 Laura Sifferlin; 878 (l)Arthur Tilley/Getty Images, (r)Jim West/The Image Works; 881 Dennis Stock/Magnum Photos; 882 Bettmann/CORBIS; 883 Ian Berry/Magnum Photos; 884 Universal Press Syndicate; 885 John Evans; 888 (t)Yann Arthus-Bertrand/CORBIS, (b)The British Library / HIP / The Image Works; 889 Nik Wheeler/CORBIS; 890 Yann Arthus-Bertrand/CORBIS; 892 Babs H. Deal/AP/Wide World Photos; 894 SS; 896 William Whitehurst/CORBIS; 897 Richard Hamilton/CORBIS; 898 Tibor de Nagy Gallery, New York; 903 CORBIS; 906 William Whitehurst/CORBIS; 910 King Features Syndicate; 912 Universal Press Syndicate; 913 John Evans; 920 Graeme Davis; 922 The British Museum/HIP/The Image Works; 923 Ancient Art & Architecture Collection; 924 The Image Works; 925 (t)The British Museum/HIP/The Image Works, (b)HIP / Art Resource; 926 David Lyons / Alamy; 928 Ancient Art & Architecture Collection; 930 Universal Press Syndicate; 931 Laura Sifferlin; 935 Thayer Allyson Gowdy; 936 Thayer Allyson Gowdy; 937 Thayer Allyson Gowdy; 938 Thayer Allyson Gowdy; 942 HUlton-Deutsch/CORBIS; 943 Picture HIstory; 944 (l)Picture History, (cl)LOC, (cr)CORBIS, (r)National Portrait Gallery/Smithsonian Institution/AR; 945 Picture History; 946 HUlton-Deutsch/CORBIS; 951 Universal Press Syndicate; 952 Universal Press Syndicate; 953 John Evans; 954 Bettman/CORBIS; 958 Fine Arts Museums of San Francisco; 962 K. Carpentar/RobertStock; 965 ET Archive, London/SS; 968 K. Carpentar/RobertStock; 970 Images.com/CORBIS; 975 BAL; 980 BAL; 985 Courtesy Erin Gruwell Education Project and the Freedom Writers @ www.gruwellproject.org; 988 Les Stone/CORBIS; 989 Reuters/CORBIS; 991 Reuters/CORBIS; 992 Rikard Larma/Getty Images; 994 Courtesy Erin Gruwell Education Project and the Freedom Writers @ www.gruwellproject.org; 998 University of Fairbanks, AK; 999 Michio Hoshino/Minden Picures.; 1000 (tl)Eclipse Studios, (tr)Eclipse Studios, (bl)Eclipse Studios, (br)Eclipse Studios; 1001 (tl)Eclipse Studios, (tr)LPBC/AH, (bl)Eclipse Studios, (br)Eclipse Studios.